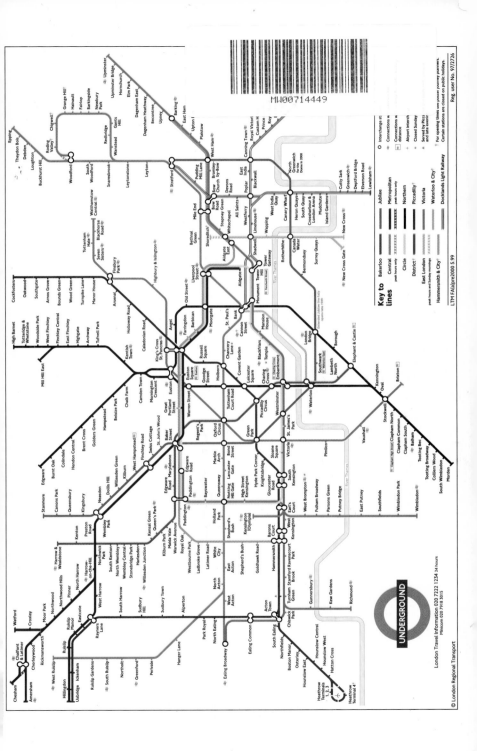

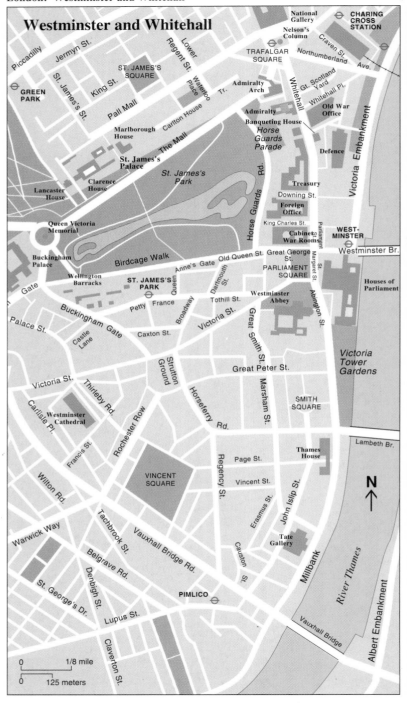

Westminster and Whitehall

Soho and Covent Garden

N

1/8 mile
125 meters
Southampton Row

Lincoln's Inn Fields
HOLBORN
Kingsway
BLOOMSBURY SQUARE
Holborn
High
Bloomsbury Way
Bloomsbury St.
Great Russell St.
Newton St.
Parker St.
Great Queen St.
Russell St.
Drury Lane
Bow St.
Shorts Gardens
Endell St.
Neal St.
Earlham St.
Langley St.
Shelton St.
Monmouth St.

Aldwych
ALDWYCH
Waterloo Br.
Lancaster Pl.
Wellington St.
Catherine St.
Savoy St.
Savoy Hotel
Cleopatra's Needle
Victoria Embankment
Charing Cross Station
Charing Cross
Chandos Pl.
William IV St.
St. Martin-in-the-Fields
St.Martins La.
New Row
Bedfordbury
St.Martins
Maiden La.
Henrietta St.
Southampton
King St.
St. Paul's Covent Garden
Floral Pl.
Royal Opera
COVENT GARDEN
Floral Hall
Theatre Museum
London Transport Museum
COVENT GARDEN
The Strand
Garrick St.
National Gallery
Leicester Sq.
Irving St.
Orange St.
St. Martin's St.
LEICESTER SQUARE
Whitcomb St.
Haymarket
Coventry St.
Lisle St.
Cranbourne St.
CHINATOWN
Gerrard St.
Shaftesbury Ave.
PICCADILLY CIRCUS
Glasshouse St.
Regent St.
Piccadilly
Jermyn St.
Albemarle St.
Dover St.
Royal Academy
Burlington Gardens
Old Bond St.
Savile Row
Clifford St.
St. George St.
New Bond St.
BERKELEY SQUARE
Berkeley St.
Long Acre
National Jazz Center
LEICESTER SQUARE
CAMBRIDGE CIRCUS
Shaftesbury Ave.
Charing Cross Rd.
Greek St.
Frith St.
Dean St.
Wardour St.
Berwick St.
Old Compton St.
St. Anne's
Windmill St.
Brewer St.
Lexington St.
GOLDEN SQUARE
Beak St.
SOHO
Poland St.
Marshall St.
Carnaby St.
Broadwick St.
Great Marlborough St.
Regent St.
Argyll St.
OXFORD CIRCUS
Oxford St.
Noel St.
Great Chapel St.
Bateman St.
Carlisle St.
Meard St.
Frith St.
SOHO SQUARE
Charles II Statue
St. Barnabas in Soho
Sutton Row
St. Giles St.
High St.
New Oxford St.
TOTTENHAM COURT RD.
Tottenham Court Rd.
Rathbone Pl.
Newman St.
Berners St.
Eastcastle St.
Margaret St.
CAVENDISH SQUARE
HANOVER SQUARE
New Bond St.

Buckingham Palace and Mayfair

Henrietta Pl.

Oxford St.

OXFORD CIRCUS

Great Marlborough St.

Wigmore St.

Orchard St.

BOND ST

S. Molton St.

HANOVER SQUARE

Oxford St.

Marble Arch

North Row

N. Audley St.

Duke St.

Davies St.

New Bond St.

St. George St.

Conduit St.

Regent St.

Broadwick St.

Green St.

Brook St.

Clifford St.

Lee's Pl.

Grosvenor St.

Woods Mews

Upper Brook St.

U.S. Embassy

GROSVENOR SQUARE

Grosvenor Mews

Bruton St.

Burlington Gdns.

Museum of Mankind

Culross St.

Park St.

S. Audley St.

Grosvenor Chapel

Farm St.

Hill St.

Hay's Mews

BERKELEY SQUARE

Old Bond St.

Burlington Arcade

Royal Academy

Chesterfield Hill

Queen St.

Berkeley St.

Clarges St.

Piccadilly

Duke St.

Jermyn St.

Charles St.

Curzon St.

Half Moon

GREEN PARK

St. James's St.

HYDE PARK

Park Lane

Hertford St.

Old Park La.

Piccadilly

GREEN PARK

St. James's Palace

Wellington Museum

HYDE PARK CORNER

Wellington Arch

Constitution Hill

The Mall

Knights bridge

Wilton Pl.

Grosvenor Cr.

Grosvenor Pl.

Buckingham Palace Gardens

Buckingham Palace

Birdcage Walk

Wilton Crescent

Halkin St.

Chapel St.

Upper Belgrave St.

The Royal Mews

Buckingham Gate

Palace St.

Sloane St.

BELGRAVE SQUARE

Lower Grosvenor Pl.

Bressenden Pl.

Pont St.

Belgrave Pl.

Lower Belgrave St.

Grosvenor Gdns.

Cadogan Pl.

Chesham St.

Lyall St.

Eaton Pl.

EATON SQUARE

Eccleston St.

Buckingham Palace Rd.

Victoria Station

Victoria St.

Vauxhall Br.

Wilton Rd.

Sloane St.

Elizabeth St.

CHESTER SQUARE

Ebury St.

King's Rd.

S. Eaton Pl.

Eaton Terr.

Chester Row

SLOANE SQUARE

Hugh St.

Belgrave Rd.

Warwick Way

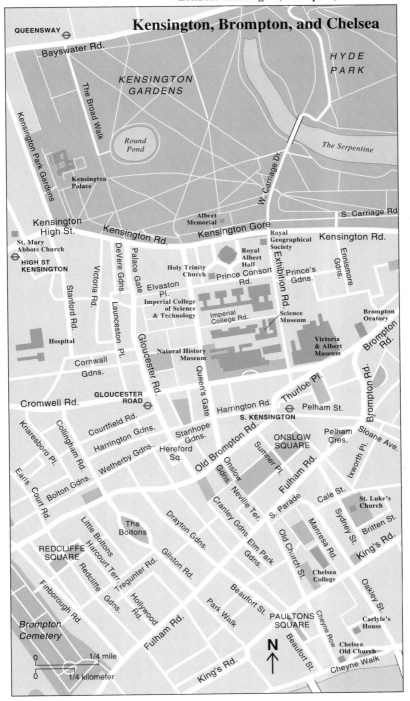

Kensington, Brompton, and Chelsea

QUEENSWAY

Bayswater Rd.

KENSINGTON GARDENS

The Broad Walk

HYDE PARK

Kensington Park Gardens

Round Pond

The Serpentine

W. Carriage Dr.

Kensington Palace

Albert Memorial

S. Carriage Rd.

Kensington High St.

Kensington Rd.

Kensington Gore

Kensington Rd.

St. Mary Abbots Church

HIGH ST KENSINGTON

DeVere Gdns.

Palace Gate

Holy Trinity Church

Royal Albert Hall

Prince Consort Rd.

Royal Geographical Society

Exhibition Rd.

Prince's Gdns.

Ennismore Gdns.

Victoria Rd.

Launceston Pl.

Elvaston Pl.

Imperial College of Science & Technology

Imperial College Rd.

Science Museum

Brompton Oratory

Stanford Rd.

Hospital

Cornwall Gdns.

Gloucester Rd.

Natural History Museum

Queen's Gate

Victoria & Albert Museum

Brompton Rd.

Cromwell Rd.

GLOUCESTER ROAD

Thurloe Pl.

Harrington Rd.

S. KENSINGTON

Pelham St.

Brompton Rd.

Knaresboro Pl.

Collingham Rd.

Courtfield Rd.

Harrington Gdns.

Stanhope Gdns.

Old Brompton Rd.

ONSLOW SQUARE

Pelham Cres.

Sloane Ave.

Wetherby Gdns.

Hereford Sq.

Onslow Gdns.

Sumner Pl.

Fulham Rd.

Ixworth Pl.

Earl's Court Rd.

Bolton Gdns.

Neville Ter.

S. Parade

Cale St.

Sydney St.

St. Luke's Church

Drayton Gdns.

Cranley Gdns.

Elm Park Gdns.

Old Church St.

Manresa Rd.

Britten St.

King's Rd.

REDCLIFFE SQUARE

The Boltons

Little Boltons

Harcourt Terr.

Tregunter Rd.

Gilston Rd.

Chelsea College

Oakley St.

Finborough Rd.

Redcliffe Gdns.

Hollywood Rd.

Beaufort St.

Park Walk

PAULTONS SQUARE

Cheyne Row

Carlyle's House

Brompton Cemetery

Fulham Rd.

King's Rd.

Beaufort St.

Chelsea Old Church

Cheyne Walk

0   1/4 mile
0   1/4 kilometer

N

The City

Leman St.

Commercial St.

Mansell St.

Middlesex St.

ALDGATE EAST

Widegate St.

Houndsditch

Minories

Royal Mint St.

E. Smithfield

St. Katharine's Way

Tower Br. Approach

Tower Br.

ALDGATE

Aldgate

Liverpool St. Station

Bishopsgate

Old Broad St.

St. Mary Axe

Fenchurch St.

Fenchurch St. Station

Pepys St.

TOWER HILL

TRINITY SQUARE

Tower Hill

The Tower

Tower Pier

Seething La.

St. Olave's

Mark La.

Mincing La.

All Hallows

Lloyd's

Leadenhall St.

Lime St.

Leadenhall Market

Gt. Tower St.

St. Dunstan's

Lower Thames St.

HMS Belfast

Sun St.

South Pl.

London Wall

London Stock Exchange

Throgmorton Ave.

Throgmorton St.

Gracechurch St.

Cornhill

St. Mary at Hill

Billingsgate Market

FINSBURY CIRCUS

MOORGATE

Moorfields

Threadneedle St.

St. Margaret's

Bank of England

BANK

Lombard St.

King William St.

Eastcheap

Monument St.

The Monument

MONUMENT

St. Mary Abchurch

St. Magnus Martyr

London Br.

Chiswell St.

Ropemaker St.

Silk St.

Fore St.

Moorgate

Coleman St.

Bassinghall Ave.

Basinghall St.

Lothbury St.

Princes St.

Poultry

Mansion House

St. Stephen Walbrook

Walbrook

Temple of Mithras

Cloak La.

CANNON

Cannon St.

Queen St.

Cannon St. Station

Southwark Br.

Beech St.

Barbican Centre

St. Giles without Cripplegate

Museum of London

London Wall

Wood St.

Guildhall

King St.

Gresham St.

Milk St.

Cheapside

St. Mary le Bow

Watling St.

Bread St.

St. Mary Aldermary

MANSION HOUSE

River Thames

Aldersgate St.

St. Bartholomew the Great

Little Britain

St. Martin's-Le-Grand

New Change

ST. PAUL'S

St. Paul's Cathedral

St. Andrew-by-the-Wardrobe

St. Benet's

Puddle Dock

Blackfriars Station

Upper Thames St.

BARBICAN

Long La.

West Smithfield

Gilspur St.

Newgate St.

Old Bailey

Warwick La.

Ludgate Hill

Cannon St.

Queen Victoria St.

St. John St.

Cowcross St.

Smithfield Market

Snow Hill

Holborn Viaduct Station

Holborn Viaduct

Old Bailey

Fleet La.

LUDGATE CIRCUS

New Bridge St.

Blackfriars Br.

BLACKFRIARS

FARRINGDON

Farringdon Rd.

Ely Pl.

Hatton Garden

Greville St.

Clerkenwell Rd.

New Fetter La.

Fetter La.

Shoe Lane

GOUGH SQ.

St. Bride St.

Fleet St.

Tudor St.

Temple Ave.

The Temple

Blackfriars

Victoria Embankment

N

Temple Church

Middle Temple La.

1/4 mile

1/4 km

Rome: Vatican City

Vatican City

1 Basilica San Pietro
2 Sacristia
3 Piazza San Pietro
4 Sistine Chapel
5 Vatican Museums
6 Vatican Museum entrance
7 Castel Sant'Angelo

CITTÀ DEL VATICANO

Tiber River

GIANICOLO

Campi Sportivi

440 yards

400 meters

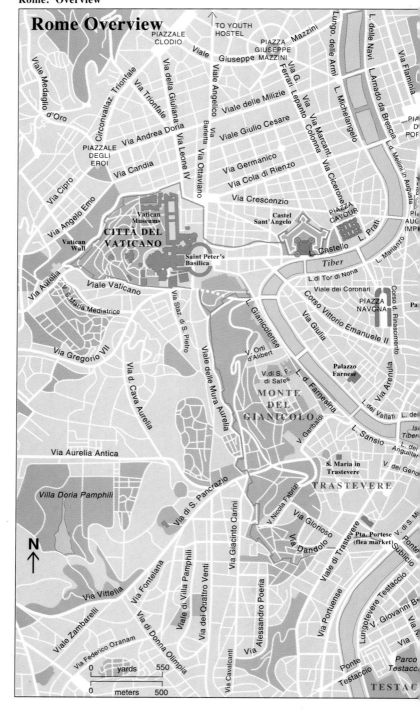

Rome Overview

Rome: Transportation

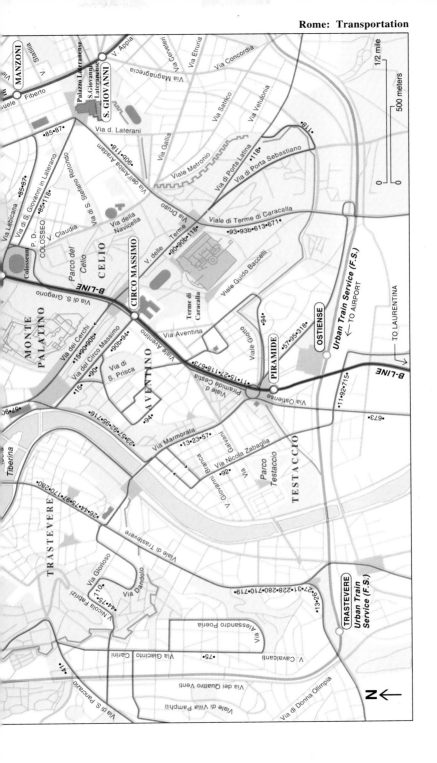

Rome: Transportation

Central Rome

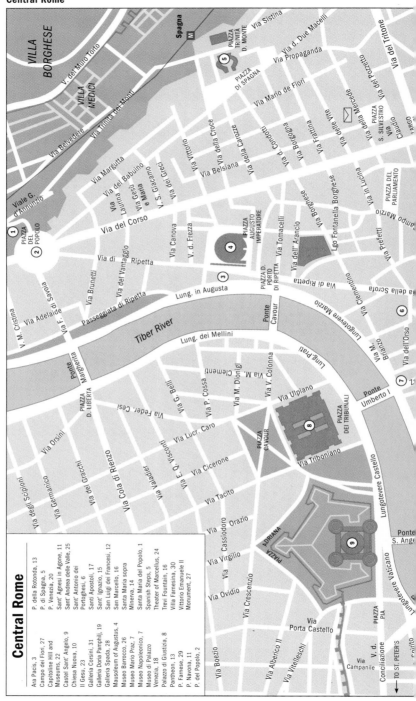

Central Rome

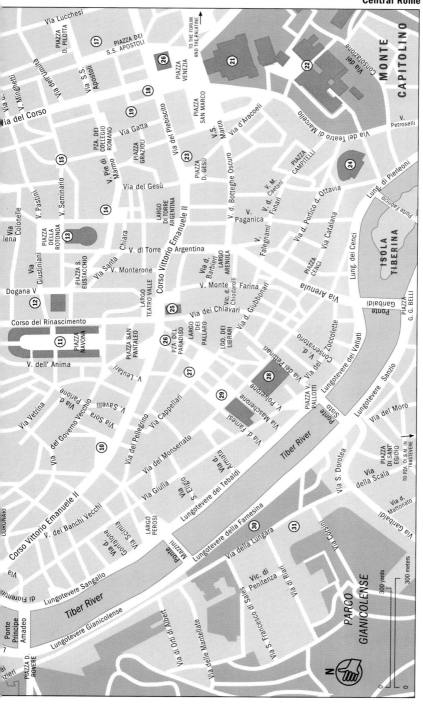

Rome: Villa Borghese

Villa Borghese

V. Puglia
V. Romagna
Via Quintina
Via Boncompagni
V. Giovannelli
Via di S. Teresa
Via d'Italia
Corso d'Italia
Via Sardegna
Via Sicilia
Via Piemonte
Giovanni Paisiello
PIAZZALE DEI RAIMUNDI
PIAZZA E. SIENKIEWICZ
Via Toscana
Via S. Mercadante
V. P. Raimondi
Via dei Dain
Museo Borghese
Via Marche
Via dell'Uccelleria
Viale Museo Borghese
Via Pinciana
Via Vittorio Veneto
Via Emilia
Viale dei Cavalli Marini
V. Puazzi
Pineta
Via Liguria
Via Ludovisi
Viale del Giardino
PIAZZA DI SIENA
Viale Casina di Raffaello
V. d. Goethe
Via Aurora
GIARDINO ZOOLOGICO
Via Ulisse Aldrovandi
Viale P. Canonica
V. di S. Paolo del Brasile
PIAZZALE BRASILE
Via Porta Pinciana
VILLA BORGHESE
Viale d. Aranciera
PIAZZALE DI CANESTRE
Viale Galoppatoio
V. del Muro Torto
Via del Babuino
Spagna
M A LINE
Galleria Nazionale d'Arte Moderne
Via Bernadotte
V. d. V. F. Laguardia
PIAZZALE DEL FIOCCO
D. Magnolie
Viale del Belvedere
VILLA MEDICI
Viale Trinità dei Monti
PIAZZALE PAOLA BORGHESE
Viale delle Belle Arti
Viale Madama
V. Washington
PIAZZALE DEI MARTIRI
Viale Valadier
Via del Babuino
Museo di Villa Giulia
VILLA STROHL FERN
VILLA RUFFO
Via del Corso
Via del Vantaggio
PIAZZA AUGUSTO IMPERATORE
V. di S. Eugenio
Flaminio
M
PIAZZA DEL POPOLO
Via A. Canova
Via della Croce
Via di Villa Giulia
Via Flaminia
Via Brunetti
Via Vittoria
Via Flaminia
PIAZZALE FLAMINIO
Via Ripetta
PIAZZA DELLA MARINA
V. G. Pisanelli
V. Romanosi
V. Disavoia
V. Savoia
Lungotevere in Augusta
V. D. A. Azuni
Lungotevere Arnaldo da Brescia
Via Brescia
Ponte Margherita
Lungotevere delle Navi
Lungotevere d. Mellini
Ponte d. Risorg.
Ponte G. Matteotti
Fiume Tevere
Ponte Nenni
Via Fed. Cesi
D. LIBERTA
Via G. Belli
PIAZZA MONTE GRAPPA
Lungotevere delle Armi
Lungotevere Michelangelo
Via dei Gracchi
Via Valadier
Via E. Q. Visconte
Via Giuseppe Mazzini
PIAZZA DELLE CINQUE GIORNATE
Via Giulio Cesare
A LINE
Via degli Scipioni
Via Pompeo Magno
PIAZZA COLA DI RIENZO
Via Boezio
Via G. Nicotera
Via della Milizie
Lepanto
M
Via Marc. Colonna
Via Settembrini
Via Ezio

N

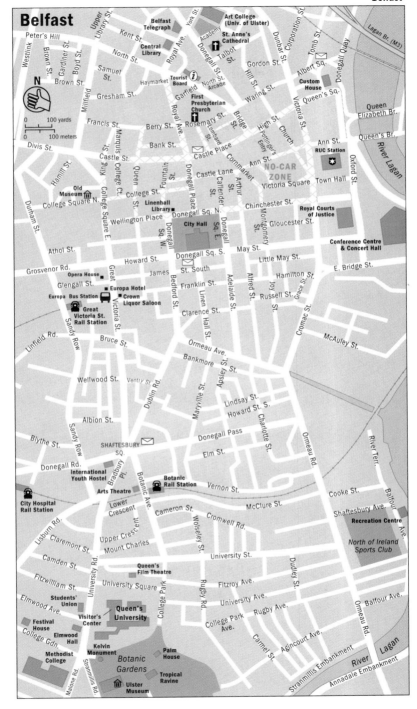

Belfast

Peter's Hill

Upper Library St.
Kent St.
North St.

Central Library
Belfast Telegraph
Art College (Univ. of Ulster)
St. Anne's Cathedral

York St.
Academy St.
Talbot St.
Gordon St.
Dunbar St.
Corporation St.
Tomb St.
Albert Sq.
Lagan Br. (M3)
Donegall Quay

Brown St.
Gardiner St.
Boyd St.
Samuel St.
Brown St.
Gresham St.

Westlink
Millfield
Haymarket
Tourist Board
Garfield
North St. Arcade

Royal Ave.
Donegall St.

Hill St.
Waring St.
Victoria St.

Custom House
Queen's Sq.
Queen Elizabeth Br.

N

0   100 yards
0   100 meters

Francis St.
First Presbyterian Church
Berry St.
Royal Ave.
Rosemary St.
Lombard St.
Bridge St.
High St.
Church
Ann St.
Queen's Br.

Bank St.
Castle Place
Cornmarket
Ann St.
Pottinger's Entry
RUC Station
River Lagan
Queen's Br.

Divis St.
Hamill St.
Castle St.
Queen
College Ct.
Fountain St.
Castle Lane
Arthur St.
Callender St.
Victoria Square
Town Hall
Oxford St.

Old Museum
College Square N.
College St.
Linenhall Library
Donegall Place
Donegall Sq. N.
Chinchester St.
Royal Courts of Justice

NO-CAR ZONE

Durham St.
College Square E.
Wellington Place
Donegall Sq. W.
City Hall
Donegall Sq. E.
Montgomery St.
Gloucester St.
Conference Centre & Concert Hall

Athol St.
Howard St.
Donegall Sq. S.
May St.
Little May St.
E. Bridge St.

Grosvenor Rd.
Opera House
Great Victoria St.
James St. South
Franklin St.
Adelaide St.
Alfred St.
Joy St.
Russell St.
Hamilton St.
Grace St.
Cromac St.

Glengall St.
Europa Hotel
Crown Liquor Saloon
Europa Bus Station
Great Victoria St. Rail Station

Linfield Rd.
Sandy Row
Bruce St.
Linen Hall St.
Clarence St.
Ormeau Ave.
McAuley St.

Wellwood St.
Ventry St.
Bankmore St.
Apsley St.

Albion St.
Dublin Rd.
Maryville St.
Lindsay St.
Howard St. S.
Charlotte St.
Donegall Pass
Ormeau Rd.

Blythe St.
Sandy Row
SHAFTESBURY SQ.
Elm St.
River Terr.

Donegall Rd.
International Youth Hostel
Bradbury Pl.
Botanic Ave.
Vernon St.

Arts Theatre
Botanic Rail Station
Cooke St.
Shaftesbury Ave.

City Hospital Rail Station
Lower Crescent
Cameron St.
McClure St.
Recreation Centre
Balfour Ave.

Lisburn Rd.
Claremont St.
Upper Cres.
Ave.
Cromwell Rd.
North of Ireland Sports Club

Camden St.
Mount Charles
Woolsley St.
University St.
Dudley St.

Fitzwilliam St.
University Rd.
Queen's Film Theatre
Fitzroy Ave.
Balfour Ave.

Students' Union
University Square
College Park
University Ave.
Rugby Ave.

Elmwood Ave.
Visitor's Center
Queen's University
College Park
Rugby Rd.
College Park Ave.
Agincourt Ave.
Ormeau Rd.

Festival House
Elmwood Hall
Kelvin Monument
Palm House
Carmel St.

Methodist College
Botanic Gardens
Tropical Ravine
Stranmillis Embankment
River Lagan

College Gdn.
Malone Rd.
Stranmillis Rd.
Ulster Museum
Annadale Embankment

Dublin

N

0   200 yards
0   200 meters

North Circular Rd.
Drumalee Rd.
Prussia St.
Grangegorman Uppe
Grangegorman Tower
Phibsborough Rd.
Royal Canal Bank
Auburn Rd.
Wells
Fonte
Western
Dominic

Aughrim St.
Ross St.
Oxmantown Rd.
Ben Eder Rd.
Manor St.
Halliday Rd.
Harold Rd.
Kirwan St.
Prebend St.
Constitution Hill
King's Inns

O'Devaney Gdns.
Ivar St.
Manor Pl.
Mt. Temple Rd.
Stirrup Rd.
Stoney Batter

Linenhall Ter.
Lisburn St.

Arbour Hill
Brunswick St. N
King St. N
Church St. Upper
King St. N.
Halston St.
Anna St. N.
Cuckoo Ln.
Beresford St.

Montpelier Hill
Blackhall Pl.
Queen St.
Smithfield St.
Ceol
Old Jameson Distillery
Bow St.
Mary's Ln.
Greek St.
Markets

Benburb St.
St. Michan's

Wolfe Tone Quay
Church St.
Chancery St.

Heuston Station
Victoria Quay
Ellis Quay
Arran Quay
Inns Quay
Merchants' Qua
The Fourcourts
O'Donova
Rossa Bri
Wood Qu

Guinness Brewery
Watling S
Bonham S
Island St.
Bridgefoot St.
Usher's Quay
St. Augustine St.
Bridge St.
Wine
tavern St.
City Offices

Steevens La.
Oliver Bond St.
Cook St.
High St.
Back Ln.
St. Audoens
Christ Churc Cathedral

James's St.
Thomas St.
Cornmarket
John Dillon St.
Nicholas St.
Basin St. Lwr.
Guinness Hopstore
Francis St.
Ross Rd
Bridge Rd

Portland St. W
Rainsford St.
Hanbury Ln.
Bull Alle

Basin St. Upper
Bellevue St.
Thomas Ct.
Earl St.
Swift's Alley
Meath St.
Patrick St.

Bond St.
Meath Pl.
Carman's Hall
St. Patri Cathe

Newport St.
Pim St.
Marrowbone Ln.
Summer St.
Pimlico
Ardee St.
The Coombe
Dean St.
Kevin S

Grand Canal Bank
Our Lady's Rd.
Lourdes Rd.
Cork St.
St. Thomas Rd.
Chamber St.
Newmarket St.
Ward's Hill
New Rd.
New St. S

Rosary Rd.
Brickfield Ln. S
Mill St.
Fumbally Ln.
Lon

Reuben Ave.
Reuben St.
Cork St.
Cameron St.
Donore Ave.
Brown St. S.
O'Curry Rd.
St. Thomas Rd.
Clarence Man
Blackpits
Malpas St. Lwt.
Clanbrassil St. Lwr.

St. Theresa Gds.
Donore Rd.
Susan Ter.
O'Donovan
Marty Pl.
Vern

TO ✈ ↗

🏛 St. George's

Temple St. N.

sington St.

ton St. Lr.
Pl.

Mountjoy
Sq.

North

Charles St. Great

Rutland
St. Upr.

Summer St.

N. Circular Rd

William St. N

Dunne St.

Gardiner Pl.

East

Portland Row

Buckingham St. Upr

Empress Pl.

Killarney St.

Amiens St.

gh Lane
Gallery 🏛

Dublin Writers
Museum 🏛 🏛 Abbey
Presbyterian

Denmark St. Great

St. George's

Hill St.

Gardiner St.
Middle

Gardiner Ln.

Summerhill Rd.

R utland St. Lwr.

Buckingham St. Lwr.

Wax
seum 🏛

Parnell St. E.

Garden of
Remembrance

James Joyce
Center

✝

Sean Mac Dermott St.

Connolly
Station 🚉

Dominick Pl.

Parnell Sq. W.

Parnell
Sq.

🏛 Gate Theatre

Marlborough St.

Gardiner St. Lower

Railway St.

Foley St.

Sheriff St. Lwr.

ck St. Lower

Parnell Sq. S.

O'Connell St. Upper

Corporation St.

Inner Dock

Commons St.

ell St.

Rotunda
Hospital ✚

Moore Ln.

Tyrone
House

Talbot St.

Store St.

Store St.

Financial Services
Center

Moore St.

Henry St.

Moore St. Market ■

Earl St. N.

✝

Busaras 🚌

George's
Dock

rvis St.

Mary St.

General
Post Office ✉

Prince's St. N

O'Connell St. Lower

Abbey St. Lower

Liberty
Hall

Beresford St.

Custom
House

Custom House Quay

North Wall

St. Mary's
Church ✝

Abbey St. Middle

Global
Internet
Cafe

Memorial Rd.

Amiens St.

Talbot Ln.

Liffey St. Upr.

■ Hot Press

Lotts Row

Eden Quay

y St. Upper

Liffey St. Lwr.

Strand St. Great

Bachelors Walk

O'Connell
Bridge

Burgh Quay

George's Quay

City Quay

Ormond Quay

Ha'Penny
Footbridge

Aston Quay

Poolbeg

Tara St.
Station 🚉

River Liffey

Gloucester St.

Lombard St. E.

Creighton St.

Wellington Quay

Fleet St.

D'Olier St.

Tara St.

Luke St.

Moss St.

Townsend St.

Princes St.

ssex St. E.

Temple Bar

Temple Ln.

Stock Exchange ■

Bank of
Ireland ■

Eustace St.

Cope St.

Anglesea St.

College Gre

Westmoreland St.

Pearse St.

Lombard St. E.

Sandwith St. Lwr.

Town
Hall

Sycamore St.

S. Great Georges St.

Dame St.

College St.

Suffolk St.

✝

Pearse
Station 🚉

✝

Boyne St.

Sandwith St. Upr.

in
stle

ⓘ

Wicklow St.

Nassau St.

Trinity
College

Westland Row

Lincoln Pl.

American
Express ■

Central
Cybercafé ■

Grafton St.

Fenian St.

Denzille Ln.

Drury St.

Clarendon St.

William St. S.

Chatham St.

Anne St. S.

Duke St.

Frederick St.

Frederick Ln.

Molesworth St.

National
Library 🏛

National
Gallery 🏛

Holles St.

Planet
yber Cafe ■
ongford St. Gt.

Stephen St. Lwr.

Mercer St. Upr.

Mercer St. Lwr.

Dawson St.

Kildare St.

Mansion
House

Leinster
House 🏛

National
Museums 🏛

Merrion
Sq.

North

Mount St.
Lwr.

elaide
spital

Aungier St.

York St.

Government
Buildings

Merrion Row

South

eter
Row

St. Stephen's Green N

St. Stephen's Green E

Hume St.

Baggot St. Lower

Fitzwilliam La.

Mount St. Upr

Wexford St.

St. Stephen's
Green

St. Stephen's Green W

Mercer St.

Harcourt St.

Camden St.

wr.

ants St.

University College
Dublin

National
Concert Hall

St. Stephen's Green S

Earlsfort Ter.

Leeson St. Lwr.

Pembroke St. Lwr.

Quinn's Ln.

Fitzwilliam
Sq.

Pembroke St. Upr.

Fitzwilliam St. Upr.

Leeson Ln.

Number
29 ■

James's St. E.

Fitzwilliam St. Lwr.

Lad Ln.

Bank of
Ireland

Cork and Galway

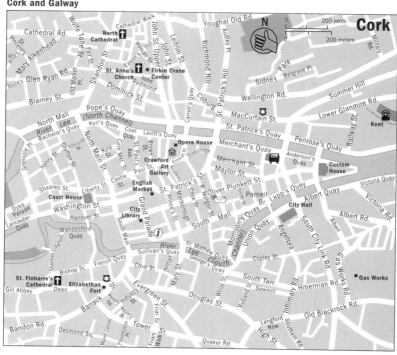

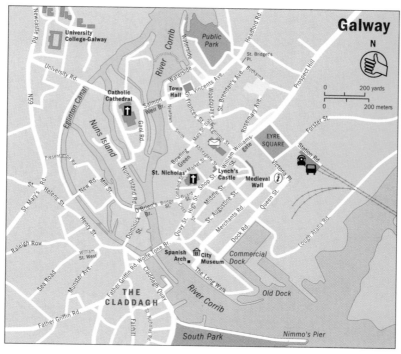

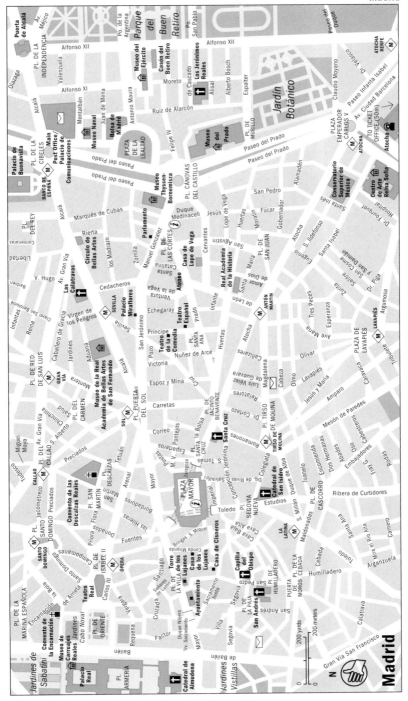

Madrid

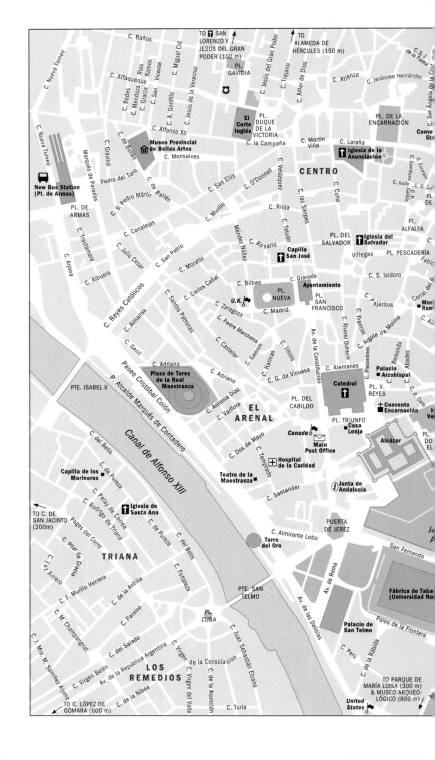

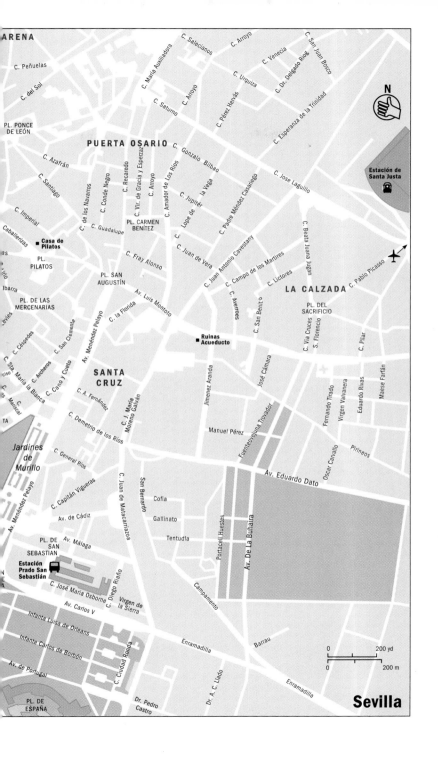

Sevilla

Madrid Metro

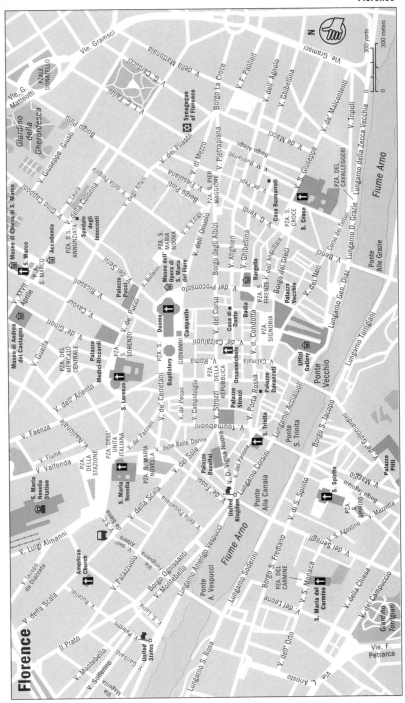

Florence

Florence

N

0 300 yards
0 300 meters

Il Prato

V. Montebello
Via Magenta
V. Solferino

V. della Scala
V. Rucellai
V. Palestro

American Church

V. Jacopo da Diacceto

United States

V. S. Lucia

V. S. Caterina da Siena

V. Luigi Almanni

S. Maria Novella Station

V. Faenza

V. Fiume
V. Valfonda

V. Nazionale

PZA. DELLA STAZIONE

PZA. DELL' UNITA ITALIANA

V. del Melarancio

S. Maria Novella

PZA. S. MARIA NOVELLA

V. della Scala

V. de' Tornabuoni

V. della Porcellana

Palazzo Rucellai

V. N. D. Vigna Nuova

V. del Parione

Lungarno Corsini

Ponte Alla Carraia

United Kingdom

V. del Sole

V. delle Belle Donne

V. dei Banchi

V. de' Panzani

PZA. S. Giovanni

PZA. DEL MERCATO CENTRALE

PZA. S. LORENZO

S. Lorenzo

Palazzo Medici-Riccardi

V. de' Ginori

V. Guelfa

V. dell' Ariento

V. XXVII Aprile

Museo di Andrea del Castagno

Museo di Chiesa di S. Marco

S. Marco

PZA. S. MARCO

Accademia

V. Ricasoli

V. Cavour

V. de' Pucci

Palazzo Pucci

PZA. SS. ANNUNZIATA

Spedale degli Innocenti

V. della Colonna

V. Laura

V. degli Alfani

V. della Pergola

Borgo Pinti

Giardino della Gherardesca

Vle. G. Matteotti

PZALE. DONATELLO

V. G. Carducci

Vle. Gramsci

V. G. Giusti

Borgo Pinti

V. Giuseppe Giusti

V. C. Ferni

V. Gino Capponi

V. S. Sebastiano

V. del Servi

Duomo

Campanile

Baptistery

V. de' Cerretani

V. de' Pecori

V. Campidoglio

V. Strozzi

V. della Spada

Palazzo Strozzi

Palazzo Davanzati

V. Porta Rossa

V. Tournabuoni

V. Calimala

V. Calimaruzza

Orsanmichele

PZA. DELLA REPUBBLICA

V. Roma

V. de' Calzaiuoli

V. del Corso

Casa di Dante

Badia

Bargello

Museo dell' Opera di S. Maria del Fiore

Museo dell' Opera di S. Maria del Fiore

PZA. S. MARIA NUOVA

V. dell' Oriuolo

V. S. Egidio

Borgo degli Albizi

V. del Proconsolo

V. Pandolfini

V. Ghibellina

V. Alighieri

PZA. S. PIER MAGGIORE

V. Pietrapiana

V. de' Pilastri

V. di Mezzo

V. Fiesolana

Synagogue of Florence

V. della Mattonaia

Borgo La Croce

V. F. Paolieri

V. dell' Agnolo

V. Ghibellina

V. de' Macci

Casa Buonarroti

V. M. Buonarroti

Borgo Allegri

V. de' Pepi

V. G. Verdi

PZA. S. CROCE

S. Croce

PZA. DEL CAVALLEGGERI

V. de' Malcontenti

V. Tripoli

V. S. Giuseppe

Lungarno della Zecca Vecchia

Fiume Arno

Lungarno delle Grazie

Corso dei Tintori

Ponte Alle Grazie

V. de' Benci

Borgo dei Greci

Borgo Santa Croce

V. dell' Anguillara

PZA. S. FIRENZE

Palazzo Vecchio

PZA. SIGNORIA

V. d. Condotta

Uffizi Gallery

Ponte Vecchio

Lungarno Acciaiuoli

Lungarno Gen. Diaz

Lungarno Torrigiani

V. de' Neri

V. de' Greci

Ponte S. Trinita

Borgo S. Jacopo

S. Trinita

Ponte S. Trinita

V. de Guicciardini

Palazzo Pitti

V. Maggio

V. Mazzetta

PZA. S. SPIRITO

S. Spirito

V. di S. Spirito

V. S. Agostino

V. del Serragli

Borgo Tegolaio

Borgo S. Frediano

PZA. DEL CARMINE

S. Maria del Carmine

V. del Leone

V. S. Monaca

V. dell' Orto

Vle. L. Ariosto

Lungarno S. Rosa

Lungarno Amerigo Vespucci

Fiume Arno

Ponte A. Vespucci

Borgo Ognissanti

V. Palazzuolo

V. il Prato

Lungarno Soderini

Lungarno Amerigo Vespucci

V. della Chiesa

V. del Campuccio

Giardino Torrigiani

Vle. F. Petrarca

Venice

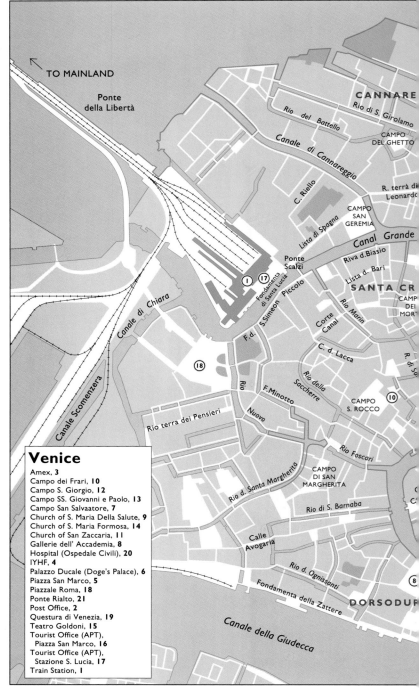

TO MAINLAND

Ponte della Libertà

CANNARE

Rio del Battello

Rio di S. Girolamo

CAMPO DEL GHETTO

Canale di Cannareggio

C. Riello

R. terrà di Leonardo

CAMPO SAN GEREMIA

Lista di Spogna

Canal Grande

Ponte Scalzi

Riva d.Biasio

Lista d. Bari

SANTA CR

Canale di Chiara

Fondamenta di Santa Lucia

F.d. S.Simeon Piccolo

Rio Marin

CAMP DEI MORT

Corte Canal

C. d. Lacca

R. di Sp

F.d. S.Simeon

Canale Scomenzera

Rio

F.Minotto

Rio della Saccherre

Nuovo

CAMPO S. ROCCO

Rio terra dei Pensieri

Rio Foscari

CAMPO DI SAN MARGHERITA

Rio d. Santa Margherita

Rio di S. Barnaba

Calle Avogaria

C

Rio d. Ognissonti

DORSODUF

Fondamenta della Zattere

Canale della Giudecca

Venice

Amex, **3**
Campo dei Frari, **10**
Campo S. Giorgio, **12**
Campo SS. Giovanni e Paolo, **13**
Campo San Salvaatore, **7**
Church of S. Maria Della Salute, **9**
Church of S. Maria Formosa, **14**
Church of San Zaccaria, **11**
Gallerie dell' Accademia, **8**
Hospital (Ospedale Civili), **20**
IYHF, **4**
Palazzo Ducale (Doge's Palace), **6**
Piazza San Marco, **5**
Piazzale Roma, **18**
Ponte Rialto, **21**
Post Office, **2**
Questura di Venezia, **19**
Teatro Goldoni, **15**
Tourist Office (APT),
  Piazza San Marco, **16**
Tourist Office (APT),
  Stazione S. Lucia, **17**
Train Station, **1**

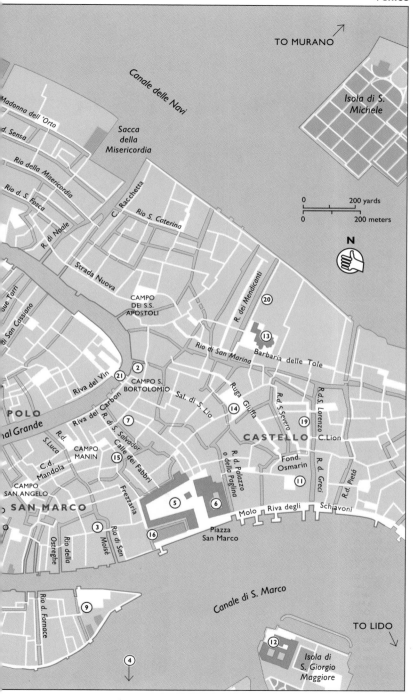

TO MURANO

Isola di S. Michele

Canale delle Navi

Madonna dell'Orto

d. Sensa

Rio della Misericordia

Rio d. S. Fosca

R. di Noale

Sacca della Misericordia

C. Racchetta

Rio S. Caterina

Strada Nuova

Due Torri

di San Cassiano

CAMPO DEI S.S. APOSTOLI

R. dei Mendicanti

20

13

Rio di San Marina

Barbaria delle Tole

0   200 yards
0   200 meters

N

2

Riva del Vin

21

CAMPO S. BORTOLOMIO

Sal. di S. Lio

Ruga Giuffa

14

R.d. s.Severo

R.d.S. Lorenzo

POLO

al Grande

R. d.

Riva del Carbon

R. d. S. Salvador

7

Calle dei Fabbri

19

CASTELLO

C.Lion

S.Luca

CAMPO MANIN

15

R. d. Palazzo o della Paglina

Fond. Osmarin

R. d. Greci

R.d. Pietà

C. d. Mandola

CAMPO SAN ANGELO

Frezzaria

11

SAN MARCO

O

3

Rio di San

Moisé

5

6

Molo

Riva degli

Schiavoni

16

Piazza San Marco

Ostreghe

Rio della

Rio d. Fornace

9

Canale di S. Marco

TO LIDO

4

12

Isola di S. Giorgio Maggiore

Milan

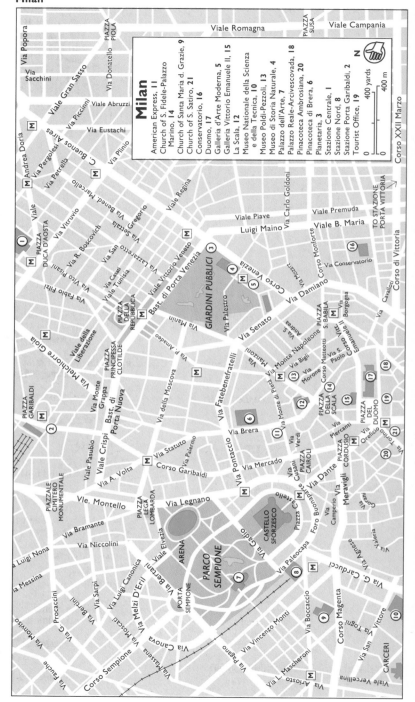

Milan

American Express, 11
Church of S. Fidele-Palazzo
  Marino, 14
Church of Santa Maria d. Grazie, 9
Church of S. Satiro, 21
Conservatorio, 16
Duomo, 17
Galleria d'Arte Moderna, 5
Galleria Vittorio Emanuele II, 15
La Scala, 12
Museo Nazionale della Scienza
  e della Tecnica, 10
Museo Poldi-Pezzoli, 13
Museo di Storia Naturale, 4
Palazzo dell'Arte, 7
Palazzo Reale-Arcivescovada, 18
Pinacoteca Ambrosiana, 20
Pinacoteca di Brera, 6
Planetaria, 3
Stazione Centrale, 1
Stazione Nord, 8
Stazione Porta Garibaldi, 2
Tourist Office, 19

0   400 yards
0   400 m

▨ Let's Go writers travel on your budget.

"Guides that penetrate the veneer of the holiday brochures and mine the grit of real life."

—*The Economist*

"The writers seem to have experienced every rooster-packed bus and lunar-surfaced mattress about which they write."

—*The New York Times*

"All the dirt, dirt cheap."

—*People*

▨ Great for independent travelers.

"The guides are aimed not only at young budget travelers but at the independent traveler; a sort of streetwise cookbook for traveling alone."

—*The New York Times*

"A guide should tell you what to expect from a destination. Here *Let's Go* shines."

—*The Chicago Tribune*

"An indispensible resource, *Let's Go*'s practical information can be used by every traveler."

—*The Chattanooga Free Press*

▨ Let's Go is completely revised each year.

"A publishing phenomenon...the only major guidebook series updated annually. *Let's Go* is the big kahuna."

—*The Boston Globe*

"Unbeatable: good sight-seeing advice; up-to-date info on restaurants, hotels, and inns; a commitment to money-saving travel; and a wry style that brightens nearly every page."

—*The Washington Post*

▨ All the important information you need.

"*Let's Go* authors provide a comedic element while still providing concise information and thorough coverage of the country. Anything you need to know about budget traveling is detailed in this book."

—*The Chicago Sun-Times*

"*Let's Go* guidebooks take night life seriously."

—*The Chicago Tribune*

Let's Go Publications

Let's Go: Alaska & the Pacific Northwest 2002
Let's Go: Amsterdam 2002 **New Title!**
Let's Go: Australia 2002
Let's Go: Austria & Switzerland 2002
Let's Go: Barcelona 2002 **New Title!**
Let's Go: Boston 2002
Let's Go: Britain & Ireland 2002
Let's Go: California 2002
Let's Go: Central America 2002
Let's Go: China 2002
Let's Go: Eastern Europe 2002
Let's Go: Egypt 2002 **New Title!**
Let's Go: Europe 2002
Let's Go: France 2002
Let's Go: Germany 2002
Let's Go: Greece 2002
Let's Go: India & Nepal 2002
Let's Go: Ireland 2002
Let's Go: Israel 2002
Let's Go: Italy 2002
Let's Go: London 2002
Let's Go: Mexico 2002
Let's Go: Middle East 2002
Let's Go: New York City 2002
Let's Go: New Zealand 2002
Let's Go: Paris 2002
Let's Go: Peru, Ecuador & Bolivia 2002
Let's Go: Rome 2002
Let's Go: San Francisco 2002
Let's Go: South Africa with Southern Africa 2002
Let's Go: Southeast Asia 2002
Let's Go: Southwest USA 2002 **New Title!**
Let's Go: Spain & Portugal 2002
Let's Go: Turkey 2002
Let's Go: USA 2002
Let's Go: Washington, D.C. 2002
Let's Go: Western Europe 2002

Let's Go **Map Guides**

Amsterdam	New Orleans
Berlin	New York City
Boston	Paris
Chicago	Prague
Dublin	Rome
Florence	San Francisco
Hong Kong	Seattle
London	Sydney
Los Angeles	Venice
Madrid	Washington, D.C.

Let's Go
WESTERN
EUROPE
2002

Marianne Cook editor

Anna Byrne associate editor
James Crawford associate editor
Harriett Green associate editor
Celeste Ng associate editor

Roxanna Curto researcher-writer

Noah Askin map editor

Brady R. Dewar managing editor

St. Martin's Press ≋ New York

HELPING LET'S GO If you want to share your discoveries, suggestions, or corrections, please drop us a line. We read every piece of correspondence, whether a postcard, a 10-page email, or a coconut. Please note that mail received after May 2002 may be too late for the 2003 book, but will be kept for future editions. **Address mail to:**

> **Let's Go: Western Europe**
> **67 Mount Auburn Street**
> **Cambridge, MA 02138**
> **USA**

Visit Let's Go at **http://www.letsgo.com**, or send email to:

> **feedback@letsgo.com**
> **Subject: "Let's Go: Western Europe"**

In addition to the invaluable travel advice our readers share with us, many are kind enough to offer their services as researchers or editors. Unfortunately, our charter enables us to employ only currently enrolled Harvard students.

Maps by David Lindroth copyright © 2002, 2001, 2000, 1999, 1998, 1997, 1996, 1995, 1994, 1993, 1992, 1991, 1990, 1989, 1988 by St. Martin's Press.

Distributed outside the USA and Canada by Macmillan.

Let's Go: Western Europe Copyright © 2002 by Let's Go, Inc. All rights reserved. Printed in the United States of America. No part of this book may be used or reproduced in any manner whatsoever without written permission except in the case of brief quotations embodied in critical articles or reviews. Let's Go is available for purchase in bulk by institutions and authorized resellers. For information, address St. Martin's Press, 175 Fifth Avenue, New York, NY 10010, USA.

ISBN: 0-312-27068-2

First edition
10 9 8 7 6 5 4 3 2 1

Let's Go: Western Europe is written by Let's Go Publications, 67 Mount Auburn Street, Cambridge, MA 02138, USA.

Let's Go® and the thumb logo are trademarks of Let's Go, Inc. Printed in the USA on recycled paper with biodegradable soy ink.

ADVERTISING DISCLAIMER All advertisements appearing in Let's Go publications are sold by an independent agency not affiliated with the editorial production of the guides. Advertisers are never given preferential treatment, and the guides are researched, written, and published independent of advertising. Advertisements do not imply endorsement of products or services by Let's Go, and Let's Go does not vouch for the accuracy of information provided in advertisements.

If you are interested in purchasing advertising space in a Let's Go publication, contact: Let's Go Advertising Sales, 67 Mount Auburn St., Cambridge, MA 02138, USA.

ABOUT LET'S GO

FORTY-TWO YEARS OF WISDOM

For over four decades, travelers crisscrossing the continents have relied on *Let's Go* for inside information on the hippest backstreet cafes, the most pristine secluded beaches, and the best routes from border to border. *Let's Go: Europe*, now in its 42nd edition and translated into seven languages, reigns as the world's bestselling international travel guide. In the last 20 years, our rugged researchers have stretched the frontiers of backpacking and expanded our coverage into the Americas, Australia, Asia, and Africa (including the new *Let's Go: Egypt* and the more comprehensive, multi-country jaunt through *Let's Go: South Africa & Southern Africa*). Our new-and-improved City Guide series continues to grow with new guides to perennial European favorites Amsterdam and Barcelona. This year we are also unveiling *Let's Go: Southwest USA*, the flagship of our new outdoor Adventure Guide series, which is complete with special roadtripping tips and itineraries, more coverage of adventure activities like hiking and mountain biking, and first-person accounts of life on the road.

It all started in 1960 when a handful of well-traveled students at Harvard University handed out a 20-page mimeographed pamphlet offering a collection of their tips on budget travel to passengers on student charter flights to Europe. The following year, in response to the instant popularity of the first volume, students traveling to Europe researched the first full-fledged edition of *Let's Go: Europe*. Throughout the 60s and 70s, our guides reflected the times—in 1969, for example, we taught you how to get from Paris to Prague on "no dollars a day" by singing in the street. In the 90s we focused in on the world's most exciting urban areas to produce in-depth, fold-out map guides, now with 20 titles (from Hong Kong to Chicago) and counting. Our new guides bring the total number of titles to 57, each infused with the spirit of adventure and voice of opinion that travelers around the world have come to count on. But some things never change: our guides are still researched, written, and produced entirely by students who know first-hand how to see the world on the cheap.

HOW WE DO IT

Each guide is completely revised and thoroughly updated every year by a well-traveled set of nearly 300 students. Every spring, we recruit over 200 researchers and 90 editors to overhaul every book. After several months of training, researcher-writers hit the road for seven weeks of exploration, from Anchorage to Adelaide, Estonia to El Salvador, Iceland to Indonesia. Hired for their rare combination of budget travel sense, writing ability, stamina, and courage, these adventurous travelers know that train strikes, stolen luggage, food poisoning, and marriage proposals are all part of a day's work. Back at our offices, editors work from spring to fall, massaging copy written on Himalayan bus rides into witty, informative prose. A student staff of typesetters, cartographers, publicists, and managers keeps our lively team together. In September, the collected efforts of the summer are delivered to our printer, who turns them into books in record time, so that you have the most up-to-date information available for your vacation. Even as you read this, work on next year's editions is well underway.

WHY WE DO IT

We don't think of budget travel as the last recourse of the destitute; we believe that it's the only way to travel. Our books will ease your anxieties and answer your questions about the basics—so you can get off the beaten track and explore. Once you learn the ropes, we encourage you to put *Let's Go* down and strike out on your own. You know as well as we that the best discoveries are often those you make yourself. When you find something worth sharing, please drop us a line. We're Let's Go Publications, 67 Mount Auburn St., Cambridge, MA 02138, USA (feedback@letsgo.com). For more info, visit our website, www.letsgo.com.

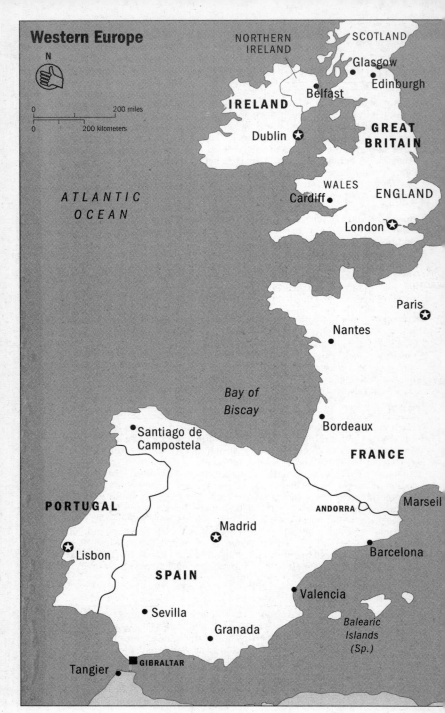

Western Europe

N

0   1   200 miles
0   200 kilometers

ATLANTIC OCEAN

SCOTLAND

Glasgow
Edinburgh

NORTHERN IRELAND

Belfast

IRELAND

Dublin ✪

GREAT BRITAIN

WALES   ENGLAND

Cardiff ●

Dublin

London ✪

Paris ✪

Nantes ●

Bay of Biscay

Bordeaux ●

FRANCE

Santiago de Campostela ●

PORTUGAL

ANDORRA

Marseil

Madrid ✪

Lisbon ✪

SPAIN

Barcelona ●

Valencia ●

Sevilla ●

Granada ●

Balearic Islands (Sp.)

Tangier ●   ■ GIBRALTAR

VI

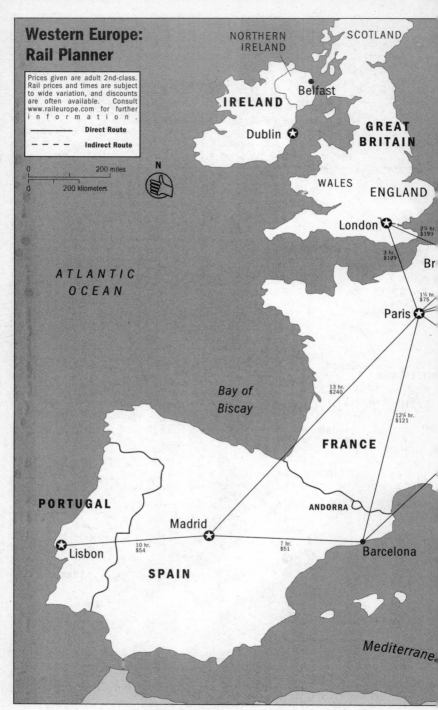

Western Europe: Rail Planner

Prices given are adult 2nd-class. Rail prices and times are subject to wide variation, and discounts are often available. Consult www.raileurope.com for further information.

——————— **Direct Route**

— — — — **Indirect Route**

0   200 miles

0   200 kilometers

N

SCOTLAND

NORTHERN IRELAND

Belfast

IRELAND

Dublin

GREAT BRITAIN

WALES

ENGLAND

London

2¾ hr.
$199

3 hr.
$199

Br

ATLANTIC OCEAN

1½ hr.
$75

Paris

Bay of Biscay

13 hr.
$240

12¼ hr.
$121

FRANCE

PORTUGAL

ANDORRA

Madrid

Lisbon

10 hr.
$54

7 hr.
$51

Barcelona

SPAIN

Mediterrane

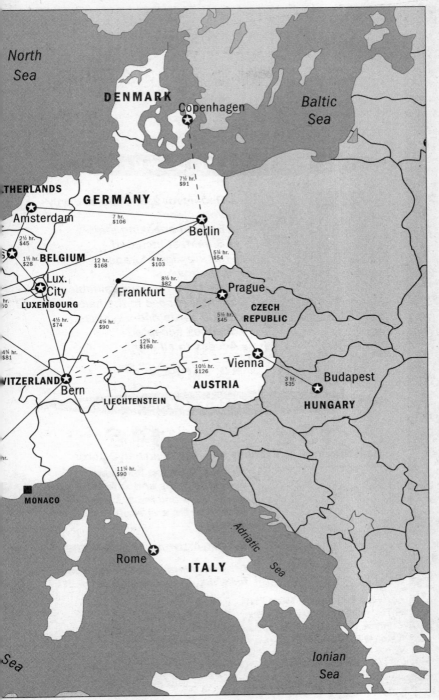

PARIS

Auberge Internationale des Jeunes

THE BEST VALUE DOWNTOWN

- Rooms for 2, 3, 4 persons only
- Very clean
- English speaking staff
- Breakfast included
- Free luggage storage
- Free showers
- Free safes for your valuables
- Internet access in the hall
- Credit cards and travellers' cheques accepted
- Access to all sights

NO CURFEW

HOSTEL IN THE CITY CENTRE OF PARIS

13€
from November to February

14€
from March to October

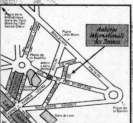

An ideal location for young people, a lively and safe area with many cafés and pubs. Laundromats, boulangeries and supermarkets nearby.

INTERNATIONAL ATMOSPHERE

Other Hostels might be less comfortable, and more expensive...!!

10, rue Trousseau - 75011 Paris - France
Tel.: (+33) 01 47 00 62 00 - Fax : (+33) 01 47 00 33 16
Internet : http://www.aijparis.com - E-mail : aij@aijparis.com
Métro : LEDRU-ROLLIN - Line 8 (Next to Bastille station)

BOOKINGS ARE POSSIBLE BY FAX OR E-MAIL

H O S T E L   I N   P A R I S

CONTENTS

MAPS

✚ Hospital	✈ Airport	🏛 Museum	▲ Mountain	
✪ Police	🚌 Bus Station	♦ Hotel/Hostel		
✉ Post Office	🚆 Train Station	⛺ Camping	Park	
ⓘ Tourist Office	M METRO STATION	☕ Food & Drink		
$ Bank	⚓ Ferry Landing	🛍 Shopping	Beach	
Embassy/Consulate	🕆 Church	♪ Arts & Entertainment		
■ Site or Point of Interest	✡ Synagogue	Nightlife	Water	
☎ Telephone Office	Mosque	📺 Internet Café		
Theater	Castle	········ Pedestrian Zone	The Let's Go thumb always points NORTH.	

RESEARCHER-WRITERS

Roxanna Curto *Belgium, Denmark, Luxembourg*
With her easygoing manner and her beautiful French, Roxanna gained admirers both at *Let's Go* and abroad. Accompanied by Jude Law and Snuffleupagus, she immersed herself in hostel culture, critiqued contemporary art, and navigated her way through hordes of British schoolchildren—and no matter how demanding the itinerary, she always managed to enjoy herself. We wish her the best of luck at grad school next year.

Regional Editors And Researcher-writers

AMSTERDAM
Karen Kiang	*Editor*
Monica Noelle Sullivan	*Associate Editor*
David Fagundes	*Amsterdam, Arnhem, Haarlem, The Hague, Scheveningen, Wadden Is.*
Rebecca Shapiro	*Amsterdam, Apeldoorn, Groningen, Hoge Veluwe, Hoorn, Maastricht, Utrecht*
Meredith Schweig	*Amsterdam, Delft, Edam, Gouda, Noordwijk, Rotterdam, Zaanse Schans*

AUSTRIA AND SWITZERLAND
David Huyssen	*Editor*
Abigail Burger	*Associate Editor*
Matthew R. Cordell	*Graubünden, Jungfrau, Swiss National Park, Ticino*
Mattias Frey	*Lower Austria, Upper Austria, Vienna*
Kalen Ingram	*Bern, Lac Léman, Neuchâtel, Northwestern Switzerland, Zurich*
Chris Townsend	*Hohe Tauern, Liechtenstein, Salzburg, Tyrol*
Eugénie Suter	*Salzburger Land, Styria, Upper Austria*

BARCELONA
Sarah Thérèse Kenney	*Editor*
Monica Noelle Sullivan	*Associate Editor*
Emily Gann	*Researcher-Writer*
Tom Malone	*Researcher-Writer*
Meredith Petrin	*Researcher-Writer*

BRITAIN
Matthew B. Sussman	*Editor*
Kate D. Nesin	*Associate Editor*
Matthew D. Firestone	*Central and Southern Scotland, Northeast and Northwest England*
Nathaniel D. Myers	*Midlands, Northwest England, Wales*
Jennifer O'Brien	*East Anglia, Heart of England, Midlands, Northeast and South England*
A. Morgan Rodman	*Heart of England, Midlands, Northern and Southwest England*
Robert Willison	*Central Scotland, Glasgow, Highlands and Islands*

EASTERN EUROPE
Katharine M. Holt	*Editor*
Martha Deery, Eliot I. Hodges, Avi Steinberg	*Associate Editors*
Eli Bard Richlin	*Czech Republic*
Ben Wasserstein	*Hungary*

FRANCE
Emily Jane Griffin	*Editor*
Sarah E. Eno, Sarah Y. Resnick	*Associate Editors*
Rebecca Bienstock	*The Alps, Côte d'Azur, Corsica*
Tamar Katz	*Berry-Limousin, The Loire Valley, Périgord, Poitou-Charentes*
Catherine Koss	*Brittany, Western Normandy*
Annalise Nelson	*Alsace, Champagne, Eastern Normandy, Flanders, Franche-Comté, Lorraine*
Angela Peluse	*Burgundy, Lyon, Provence*
Nathaniel L. Schwartz	*Aquitaine, Gascony, Languedoc-Roussillon, Pays Basque, Périgord*

GERMANY
Emily Harrison	*Editor*
Andrea Deeker	*Associate Editor*
Jesse Andrews	*Berlin, Brandenburg, Saxony-Anhalt*
Caryn Davies	*Bavaria*
Daniel C. Fehder	*Bremen, Hesse, Lower Saxony, North Rhine-Westphalia*
E. Rebecca Gantt	*Hesse, Saxony, Thuringia*
Aaron Parsons	*Baden-Württemberg, Lower Saxony, Rhineland-Palatinate, Saxony-Anhalt*
Marah Stith	*Hamburg, Mecklenburg-Western Pomerania, Schleswig-Holstein*
Eugénie E. Suter	*Baden-Württemberg*

GREECE

Erzulie D. Coquillon	Editor
John Mazza	Associate Editor
Alaina Aguanno	Athens, The Cyclades
Helen Dimos	The Dodecanese
Kate Greer	Ionian Islands, Peloponnese
Andrew Kleimeyer	Central and Northern Greece
Helen Stevens	Crete, The Cyclades
Jonathan Wood	Central Greece, Northeastern Aegean Islands, Saronic Gulf, The Sporades

IRELAND

Daniel L. Wagner	Editor
Sonja Nikkila	Associate Editor
Sheila A. Baynes	Southwest
Melissa Johnson	Dublin, East, Midlands, Southeast
Michael Liam O'Byrne	Co. Antrim, Connemara, Derry, Donegal
Jacob Rubin	Co. Clare, Galway, Sligo, Westport

ITALY

Shannon F. Ringvelski	Editor
David James Bright, Sarah Y. Resnick	Associate Editors
Jeffrey Barnes	Tuscany and Umbria
Eric Graves Brown	Friuli-Venezia Giulia, Trentino-Alto Adige, Valle d'Aosta, The Veneto
Dennis Feehan	Liguria, Sardinia
Celeste Fine	Apulia, Campania
David Justin Hodge	Emiglia-Romagna, Lombardy, The Piedmont
Megan E. Low	Sicily

LONDON

D. Jonathan Dawid	Researcher-Writer and Editor

PARIS

Anne Jump	Editor
Valérie de Charette	Researcher-Writer
John Hulsey	Researcher-Writer
Heidi Morrison	Researcher-Writer

ROME

Carla Mastraccio	Editor
Charles DeSimone	Researcher-Writer
Amber Lavicka	Researcher-Writer
Christina Rosenberger	Researcher-Writer

SPAIN AND PORTUGAL

George B. R. de Brigard	Editor
M. Sofía Vélez, Sarah C. Jessop	Associate Editors
Melissa L. Gibson	Asturias, Castilla y León, Galicia
Marla Kaplan	Islas Baleares, Valencia
Aaron Litvin	Portugal
Rianna Stefanakis	Madrid
Heidi T. Wasson	Extremadura, Pyrenees
Christian Westra	Algarve, Andalucía

Let's Go

Publishing Director
Sarah P. Rotman
Editor-in-Chief
Ankur N. Ghosh
Production Manager
Jen Taylor
Cartography Manager
Dan Barnes
Design & Photo Manager
Vanessa Bertozzi
Editorial Managers
Amélie Cherlin, Naz F. Firoz,
Matthew Gibson, Sharmi
Surianarain, Brian R. Walsh
Financial Manager
Rebecca L. Schoff
Marketing & Publicity Managers
Brady R. Dewar, Katharine
Douglas, Marly Ohlsson
New Media Manager
Kevin H. Yip
Online Manager
Alex Lloyd
Personnel Manager
Nathaniel Popper
Production Associates
Steven Aponte, Chris Clayton,
Caleb S. Epps, Eduardo Montoya,
Melissa Rudolph
Some Design
Melissa Rudolph
Office Coordinators
Efrat Kussell, Peter Richards

Director of Advertising Sales
Adam M. Grant
Senior Advertising Associates
Ariel Shwayder, Kennedy Thorwarth
Advertising Associate
Jennie Timoney
Advertising Artwork Editor
Peter Henderson

President
Cindy L. Rodriguez
General Manager
Robert B. Rombauer
Assistant General Manager
Anne E. Chisholm

ACKNOWLEDGMENTS

In memory of Haley Surti.

WEUR THANKS: EEUR and Financial for amusing us, encouraging us, and tolerating us. Noah, Dan B., and Mapland for fabulous maps, and for accommodating all our requests. Caleb, Jen, and Melissa for computer genius and crisis control. Europe regional and city editors for valued advice and crunched copy. The 3rd floor for yummy snacks and funny pranks. Brady for reminding us to stay calm. All the Western Europe RWs for wonderful copy and countless tips. Ankur and Sarah for supporting and counseling us. Kate D. for WEUR 01. Super proofers. The Princes. Time to Recenter.

MARE THANKS: Amy (my BF) for special nicknames, secret meetings, and creative translations... You'll find your prince some day. Anna for booty slaps and country tunes; James for Canadian cultural hegemony and literary witticisms; Harriett for The Heartland and pop music singalongs; and Celeste for Dim Sum and candy/cookie breaks. Jascha and EEUR for The Avulator and other avant-gardisms. Natalie and Ben for luuuuuuuuuuuuv and The Fly Garden. The Eliot crew for beach trips, bbqs, and barhopping. Wayland people for lunch/dinner dates. RCS for making me smile. Holdenites for late-night munchies. Leila for advice, notes, and love schemes. Katherine for movie nights. Adam, Moumy, and (surtout) Jair for the splendid vacation. Mom, Dad, and Matt for love and support. Genève 107fm and Princess Mette-Marit for inspiration.

ANNA THANKS: Mare, the guiding light of the WEUR bookteam; Harriett, for her sensitivity towards Bourbon Chicken; Celeste, for her infinite computer wisdom and Swedish fish; James, for his love of America, especially Texas; and Jascha, for his humor. To the SPAM folks—George, Sophia, and Sarah, for their infinite knowledge of, well, SPAM. Justin, for being a great, enthusiastic RW. And who could forget the fam, Mom, Dad, Em, Rach, Matt for being so interesting and loving; Melissa, Meggie, Cait, Megha, Ryan, Paul, the Big Green Egg, the Wrap, Ginger, my SA skanks, and high UV indexes.

JAMES THANKS: SuperMareAmy, the editing behemoth, for infinite wisdom and guidance; Celeste, because she tuned into the obscure wavelength; Harriett, for tolerating Canuck absurdity; Anna, because she didn't beat me too much; and Jascha, since he showed me Cassandra. To B&I, GRE, and IRE for superlative copy. To the roommate triumfourate, for innumerable laughs and teaching me so very much; the Purple Flower; Mum, Dad, and Si for support long distance; to Nikki, Netties, and Sonja for kicking me in the ass, compassionate ears, and expanding my mind, Gros Bisous.

HARRIETT THANKS: Princesses and pop-queens Mare and Amy (someday your princes will come!); Anna, who knows what it means to love the Heartland and Tim McGraw; Celeste, for the talks and abundance of food; Jascha, for opening new and awesome musical doors; and James, for truly appreciating the wisdom of the Muppets. FRA and ITA for their editorial support. Jenny for friendship, insights, and lovable wackiness; Mom, Dad, Heather, Hillary, and Harrison for your endless love and support through everything this year; and God for blessing me with this opportunity.

CELESTE THANKS: The whole ▨(W)EUR team: Mare for being a lovable Swiss miss; Amy, for the chocolate-covered strawberries; James for being on my wavelength (most of the time); Harriett for all the lunchtime chats; Jascha for keeping it funky; and Anna for all the loooooooove. Avi for all the light housework; Emily, Andrea, David, Abi, and the GER/A&S folks for all their hard work. Annie for making me laugh for more than a decade (even ☎ long distance); Mom, Dad, & Sis for raising me, teaching me, loving me, and humoring me. And ▨ Matt, for keeping me sane, understanding me, and loving me.

Western Europe Editor
Marianne Cook
Europe Editor
Amy Cain
Associate Editors
Anna Byrne, James Crawford, Harriett Green, Jascha Hoffman (Eastern Europe), Celeste Ng
Managing Editor
Brady R. Dewar
Map Editor
Noah Askin

HOW TO USE THIS BOOK

Our little book, our first, is all grown up, and ready to go on her first date. We've watched in awe as the child we called *Let's Go: Western Europe 2002* slowly matured into the sophisticated individual she is today. We've watched her move from painting caves in kindergarten, to storming castles in her rebellious years, to writing sonnets for her first big crush. So before you take her out, as tender and loving parents we have a few simple words of advice—treat her well; we have a shotgun and a shovel.

Let's Go: Western Europe 2002 is far more than a foxy lady in a cute blue-and-yellow outfit. She is one of your best friends and closest travel companions. She can tell you where to stay in Rome and how to find the best hiking trails in Switzerland, but she isn't the jealous type. She's confident—you can leave her alone and just go. We promise that she'll always be there for you when you need her.

ORGANIZATION OF THIS BOOK

FIRST DATE. Straighten that tie, buy those flowers, it's time to take this book out on the town (or hiking trail, or beach, or mountain village, for that matter). Begin by getting to know a little bit of everything about Western Europe. The first chapter, **Discover Western Europe,** provides you with an overview of travel in the region, including general **Suggested Itineraries** that give you an idea of what you shouldn't miss, and how long it will take to see it. For more specific itineraries, look in the individual country chapters. The chapter **Western Europe: The Grand Tour** shows you some of the highlights of the history of Western Europe, and should be used along with the cultural and historical introductions at the beginning of each chapter. The **Essentials** section outlines the practical information you will need to prepare for and execute your trip.

GOING STEADY. Well, you've gone through the ritual of the first date, and now you're ready to move on to a more, shall we say, intimate relationship with this book. Get up-close and personal with the real text—countless artistic masterpieces, myriad castles, and some smutty jokes thrown in for kicks. Each chapter contains historical background, suggested itineraries, and a country-specific essentials section, followed by the regional coverage. *Let's Go: Western Europe 2002* is organized alphabetically by country for quicker access. The **Heading East** chapter at the very end of the book provides information on travel to Prague and Budapest, gateway cities to Eastern Europe.

LANGUAGE OF LOVE. Communication is the key to any good relationship. The appendix contains a **phrasebook** of handy phrases in Czech, Danish, Dutch, English, French, German, Greek, Hungarian, Italian, Portuguese, and Spanish, and as well as pronunciation tips. A **glossary** of foreign and technical (e.g. architectural) words is also included.

A FEW NOTES ABOUT LET'S GO FORMAT

RANKING ESTABLISHMENTS. In each section (accommodations, food, etc.), we list establishments in order from best to worst. Our absolute favorites are so denoted by the highest honor given out by *Let's Go*, the *Let's Go* thumbs-up (🖐).

PHONE CODES AND TELEPHONE NUMBERS. The **phone code** for each region, city, or town appears opposite the name of that region, city, or town, and is denoted by the ☎ icon. **Phone numbers** in text are also preceded by the ☎ icon.

GRAYBOXES AND WHITEBOXES. Grayboxes at times provide wonderful cultural insight, at times simply crude humor. In any case, they're usually amusing, so enjoy. **Whiteboxes,** on the other hand, provide important practical information, such as warnings (🖐) or helpful hints and further resources (🖐).

A NOTE TO OUR READERS The information for this book was gathered by *Let's Go* researchers from May through August of 2001. Each listing is based on one researcher's opinion, formed during his or her visit at a particular time. Those traveling at other times may have different experiences since prices, dates, hours, and conditions are always subject to change. You are urged to check the facts presented in this book beforehand to avoid inconvenience and surprises.

DISCOVER WESTERN EUROPE

If Western Europe were in high school, she'd be the girl that all the other students love to hate. She has a voice crafted by the likes of Verdi and Mozart. When she opens her mouth in class, pearls of wisdom from Dante, Sartre, and Kierkegaard drop forth. She was a classic before the word had meaning, and the rest of the class hurries frantically to copy her style. She wore a toga in the court of Caesar, and now adorns herself in the more terrestrial chic of Chanel and Armani. She moves from sipping ambrosia to champagne with seamless grace but isn't above tossing back a few pints of Guinness, or screaming herself hoarse at a football match. Why waste the time envying a creation this divine when Western Europe is there for the taking, an inexhaustible supply of art, music, and natural beauty? This is one Homecoming queen who is far from unapproachable. So ask her out. Go.

FIGURES AND FACTS

POPULATION: 371,100,000.

LAND MASS: 2.5 million sq. km, almost equal to the Sahara Desert.

HIGHEST POINT: Mont Blanc, France (4,807m above sea level).

LOWEST POINTS: Lemmefjord, Denmark and Prins Alexander Polder, The Netherlands (7m below sea level).

FACT: Every year the average Western European drinks 82L of beer and 17L of wine and consumes 19kg of cheese.

FACT: If a colony of honeybees has an average wing length of larger than 9.5mm, it is known as a European colony.

FACT: The world's largest pair of jeans (23m long) was created by Lee Jeans Europe and displayed at the Atomium in Brussels, Belgium in 1992.

WHEN TO GO

The Renaissance masterpieces of Italy, the ancient ruins of Greece, and the medieval castles of England know no season—they are timeless. However, more pragmatic concerns emerge regarding the most opportune time to visit Western Europe. Summer is the high-season for travel in Western Europe. Throngs of tourists fill hostels and crowd museums, particularly during the months of July and August; you may find June or September a better time to travel. Additionally, climate can serve as a very good guide for the best time to travel in certain areas.

Avg. Temp. & Rainfall	January			April			July			October		
	°C	°F	in	°C	°F	in	°C	°F	in	°C	°F	in
Amsterdam	3	38	3.1	8	47	1.5	17	62	2.9	11	51	4.1
Athens	10	50	1.9	15	59	0.9	27	81	0.2	19	67	2.1
Berlin	-1	31	1.6	8	46	1.6	18	65	2	9	49	1.0
Copenhagen	1	33	1.7	6	43	1.6	17	62	2.6	9	49	2.1
Dublin	6	42	2.5	8	47	1.9	16	60	2.6	11	51	2.9
London	4	39	3.1	8	46	2.1	17	62	1.8	11	51	2.9
Madrid	6	42	1.8	12	53	1.8	24	76	0.4	14	58	1.8
Paris	4	39	0.2	10	50	0.2	19	67	0.2	12	53	0.2
Prague	-2	29	0.8	7	45	1.4	17	63	2.6	8	47	1.2
Rome	8	47	3.2	13	55	2.6	75	75	.6	18	64	4.5
Vienna	0	32	1.5	9	49	2	20	68	2.9	11	51	1.9

THINGS TO DO

Western Europe can be as overwhelming as it is exciting. In this section, and
throughout the rest of the book, we humbly suggest ways to approach your trip.
For more specific regional attractions, see the **Suggested Itineraries** section at the
beginning of each chapter. There are more **monuments, castles, beaches, museums, mountains,** and **nightclubs** than you can visit in two lifetimes. You will bear
witness to the ghosts of saints and conquerors (not to mention a few of their preserved body parts) and revel in the legacies of once-proud empires. However,
your greatest memories will likely be unexpected and intangible, like languorous
late evenings spent walking through a tiny coastal town whose name you hadn't
known before you arrived. If traveling is analogous to a love affair, then Western
Europe is that first whirlwind fling, consuming and unforgettable. Don't fight
it—let the streets of Paris, the mountains of Switzerland, and the clubs of Madrid
work their magic.

THE CULTURAL TAPESTRY

Western Europe has enough "culture" to keep you busy for a lifetime. But there's
not nearly enough time to see every ornate church and crumbling Roman amphitheater in all of Europe—they've been building monuments for centuries, and
you've been only traveling for... much shorter than that. You want the highlights,
the must-sees of art and architecture, and you want them now. **London** (p. 154) is
one of Europe's finest museum cities: peruse the Rosetta Stone, the Elgin Marbles, and other imperialist booty at the **British Museum;** saunter through the histories of art, design, and style at the **Victoria and Albert Museum;** and don't miss
the staggering converted power plant housing the **Tate Modern Gallery.** Royals do
the waving thing around **Buckingham Palace** while choirboys croon at **Westminster Abbey** and **St. Paul's Cathedral.** Venture away from the city to ponder the mysteries of **Stonehenge** and scale the towers of magnificent **Warwick Castle. West
Belfast** (p. 589) is a maze of murals and color, with political quotes and symbols
adorning street walls.

On the other side of the Channel, **Paris** (p. 288) contains a string of absolute
gems—the *Venus de Milo* and *Mona Lisa* at the **Louvre** will halt you in your
tracks; the **Musée d'Orsay** will impress and leave an impression with all that is
Impressionist; and the pipes and modern art of the **Centre National d'Art et de Culture Georges-Pompidou** will wriggle their way into your heart. Stroll the streets of
Paris, soaking in the city's various architectural styles, especially the breathtaking **Cathédrale de Nôtre-Dame.** Outside of Paris, the *châteaux* of the **Loire Valley**
(p. 329) and Normandy's fortified abbey **Mont-St Michel** (p. 324) are also must-
sees, as is the staggering royal grandeur of palatial **Versailles** (p. 317)

From France, swing over to Spain to witness the shimmering **Museo Guggenheim** in Bilbao (p. 887) before continuing on to the museums of **Madrid** (p. 797):
the **Prado** shelters the world's largest collection of paintings; the **Museo Thyssen-
Bornemizsa** surveys major artistic trends in painting from the 14th to 20th centuries; and the **Museo Nacional Centro de Arte Reina Sofía** holds Picasso's *Guernica.*
From there, head south to Muslim-infused Andalucía to view the **mosque** in **Córdoba** (p. 837) and the **Alhambra** in **Granada** (p. 845). Before leaving Spain, delight
in **Barcelona**'s fanciful *Modernista* buildings and its museums devoted to Picasso and Miró (p. 854).

A quick train ride along the Riviera will bring you to Italy. First stop: **Venice** (p.
651), from the Venetian art at the **Accademia** to the modern art in the **Collezione
Guggenheim.** Next up: **Florence** (p. 668), home of the Renaissance; you could
lounge for an entire day at the splendid **Uffizi,** then drool for another at the image
of human perfection, Michelangelo's *David,* in the **Accademia. Rome** (p. 606)
almost invented architecture as we know it; can we say **Pantheon, Colosseum,** and
Forum? Michelangelo's *Pietà* in **St. Peter's Basilica,** not to mention the **Sistine
Chapel** in the **Vatican Museums,** astound. Dive off the heel of the boot into Greece,

where the crumbling **Acropolis,** the foundation of Western civilization, still towers above **Athens** (p. 507). After visiting one of the foremost collections of classical art at Athens's **National Archaeological Museum,** journey to the ancient world's navel to learn your fate from the **oracle** at **Delphi** (p. 516) or visit the **temple of Apollo** on **Delos** (p. 532).

Back on the continent, **Vienna** (p. 85) hosts the renowned **Kunsthistoriches Museum** and the Klimt-rich **Austrian Gallery.** Cross the German border and peruse the **Neue** and **Alte Pinakothek** in **Munich** (p. 479) before heading north to **Weimar** (p. 436), birthplace of the **Bauhaus** architectural movement. Continue on to **Berlin** (p. 401), one of the world's great museum cities, with collections encompassing all subjects and eras. The biggest sin you could commit in **Amsterdam** (p. 725) would be to miss the famed **Rijksmuseum** and **van Gogh Museum.**

LET'S GO HEDONISM

All work and no play makes Jack (or Jane) a very dull budget traveler. In the bacchanalian tradition of early pleasure-seekers such as Nero and Oscar Wilde, we are proud to present the essential stops for any Debauchery Grand Tour. Begin your descent into immodesty in **Spain,** on the wild isle of **Ibiza** (p. 891), where substance takes a back seat to style, style, and more style, and the outrageous clubs sport diversions ranging from foam and cream parties to live sex shows. Move on to France, where the **Cote d'Azur** (p. 353) sparkles with sun-drenched beaches. Shed your inhibitions and your swimsuit to join the naked throngs on the shores of **Les Pissarelles** in **Cap D'Ail** (p. 361). Head to the famous **Monte Carlo Casino** (p. 361) for a game of highstakes roulette with some of the beautiful people and rid yourself of those weighty traveler's checks while sipping champagne. If wild gyrations under the hot sun have left you drained, crawl to **The Netherlands** for a visit to that bastion of high culture, the **Sex Museum** (p. 738) in **Amsterdam,** and peruse various objects of erotic art. Walk that special someone through the city's famous **Red Light District** (p. 737), where any fantasy can become reality—for a price. No good scout can earn his hedonism merit badge without a trip to Germany for Berlin's famous **Love Parade** (p. 423), where 1.5 million participants engage in a 54hr. orgiastic parade of techno music, ecstasy dropping, and libidinous satisfaction. On to **Italy,** to rage in the clubs of **Milan** (p. 629), and break the hearts of a few dozen supermodels. Satisfy your need for cultural enlightenment with a visit to **Amalfi** to gaze at the **Fontana di Sant'Andrea** (p. 694), a marble nude who squeezes her breasts as water pours forth from her nipples.

OH, WINE AND DINE ME

You can work up quite an appetite trekking through the museums, mountain ranges, and marketplaces of Western Europe. Fortunately, the region has more specialized dishes than you could safely sample. Fuel up for the big trip in **Lesvos,** Greece (p. 540), with a hearty meal of *souvlaki*—cap the meal with a taste of *ouzo,* a local licorice-flavored alcoholic treasure. After you ferry to Italy, work your way north: **Naples** (p. 688) invented *pizza* and first boiled *spaghetti,* while **Florence** (p. 668) claims to be the birthplace of the most sumptuous, creamy *gelato* on the continent. Those without a sweet tooth can sip a hot, strong cup of *espresso* in the cafes that line the canals of **Venice** (p. 651). From northern Italy, wind your way along the Mediterranean coast, hit **Provence** (p. 344) to quench your thirst with a glass of *pastis,* and head into **Valencia** (p. 852), where tangy juicy oranges complement the world-famous *paella.* The center of the sherry triangle is at **Jerez de la Frontera,** (p. 836) but the port from **Porto** (p. 782) will draw you to the northwest of the Iberian peninsula, also home to *vinho verde,* a sparkling wine grown only between Porto and the Spanish border. Don't miss the marzipan in **Toledo** (p. 816).

A trip through Germany, Austria, Switzerland, Belgium, and France is no less delicious. Chug a *Maß* of beer, while tasting a *Weißwurst* in a *Biergarten* in

Munich (p. 479), and then stop in **Lübeck** (p. 448) for some sweet marzipan. Vegetarians should keep their eyes open for *Spätzle* in **Vienna** (p. 85); meat-eaters and herbivores alike could pass up main courses for *Sacher Torte* or *Linzer Torte* at any *Konditorei* in **Salzburg** (p. 99). Hit up **Neuchâtel** (p. 911) for world-famous pastries and make a stop at the Lindt and Sprügli Chocolate Factory in **Zurich** (p. 913). Devour a stack of delectable chocolate-topped waffles in **Brussels** (p. 125). After stopping in **Strasbourg** (p. 378) for the wines of Alsace-Lorraine, head to **Lyon** (p. 370), one of the strongest contenders for the title of gastronomic capital of Western Europe. There you'll find *andouillettes*, sausages made of cow intestines, *cocons*, chocolates wrapped in marzipan, and even *palets d'or*, recognized as the best chocolates in France, and not just because they are dipped in gold powder.

THE GREAT OUTDOORS

When the whirlwind cosmopolitan lifestyle gets too dizzying, escape to the strikingly diverse European outdoors. Britain brims with national parks; the **Lake District National Park** (p. 221) is often considered the most beautiful. For starker natural beauty, head north to the **Scottish Highlands:** The **Isle of Skye** (p. 247) and the **Outer Hebrides** (p. 247) are particularly breathtaking. Ireland's **Ring of Kerry** holds wee Irish towns (p. 574), while **Killarney National Park** (p. 573) features spectacular mountains. Back on the continent in the French Alps, **Chamonix** (p. 368) tempts skiers with some of the world's steepest slopes, while the remote **Crozon Peninsula** (p. 328) is a hiker's paradise. Spain's **Parque Nacional de Ordesa** (p. 876) is set amongst the breath-taking Pyrenees. In Italy, the five sparkling villages of **Cinque Terre** (p. 641) are a pleasant day's hike, while the soaring **Dolomites** (p. 649) and its surrounding **Lakes** (p. 647) accommodate a wide range of activities. Across the Mediterranean, just north of Sicily, the **Aeolian Islands** (p. 701) boast pristine beaches, bursting volcanoes, and bubbling thermal springs. Drop down to Greece and take a two-day hike to the summit of **Mt. Olympus** (p. 526), where the reclining gods sipped ambrosia. Head to Crete to get in touch with your inner mountain goat with a trek down the **Samaria Gorge** (p. 538). For some fresh Swiss Alpine air, head to the glaciers of **Grindelwald** (p. 925), make the pilgrimage to the **Matterhorn,** near **Zermatt** (p. 926), or dive into the adventure sports of **Interlaken** (p. 923). From there, explore **Berchetsgaden** (p. 494) in Germany's Bavarian Alps and take to the hiking trails of the **Black Forest** (p. 476). Austria's **Kitzbühel** (p. 110) and **Innsbruck** (p. 112) will satisfy any remaining desire for hiking and skiing.

OFF THE BEATEN PATH...

Sticking to a Eurailpass itinerary will barely skim over the treasure trove of sights hidden in Europe's coffers. So stray away from the well traveled! Ireland's west coast boasts a gorgeous collection of natural wonders: bike or hike through the jagged moonscape of **The Burren** (p. 577); admire the soaring 214m spires of **Cliffs of Moher** (p. 577); or explore the **Inishowen Peninsula** (p. 583), an untouristed mosaic of mountains and white sand beaches. To the south, white houses and ruins in **Arcos de la Frontera** (p. 837) and stomach-churning gorges of **Ronda** (p. 837) arrest travelers' eyes. Squeezed into the Pyrenees between Spain and France, a visit to the ski slopes of tiny **Andorra** (p. 73) is truly memorable. In France, small and charming **Annecy** (p. 369), in the Alps borders Europe's purest lake. Bypass the more popular Riviera towns for the refreshing villages in the **Corniches** (p. 360). Take a ferry over to the gorgeous beaches and quaint towns of **Corsica** (p. 362) and the mountainous terrain of neighboring **Sardinia** (p. 703). In Italy, **Trieste** (p. 666) is a fascinating combination of Slovenian and Italian culture. The **Amalfi Coast** (p. 694) is an extreme mixture of rugged cliffs and serene coastal towns. **Stromboli**'s active volcano belches lava and rocks nightly (p. 703). In the Greek Peloponnese lie the tiny, relaxing towns of **Dimitsana** and **Stemnitsa** (p. 518). On the mainland stands the exquisite, Byzantine **Osios Loukas** (p. 527), the most beautiful of Greece's monasteries; the mythical **Oracle of Dodoni** (p. 528) is Greece's oldest.

ON THE BEACH

It would be a shame if you spent your entire time in Western Europe on its velvety beaches; but if you must, we will indulge. Even England hosts a tempting beach culture when it's not raining: The old artists' enclave of **St-Ives** (p. 195) offers sparkling beaches and incredibly blue water, while **Newquay** (p. 196) is a surfing hotspot. **Malin Head** (p. 583), at Ireland's northernmost point on the **Inishowen Peninsula**, is covered with semi-precious stones. France's **La Rochelle** (p. 333) abounds with sun-drenched beaches, while the untouristed beaches of **St-Jean-Cap-Ferrat** (p. 361), near Nice in the **Corniches**, give it the nickname "Peninsula of Dreams." Skip down to Portugal, to party all night and sun all day along the **Algarve**, particularly in **Lagos** (p. 776). Along Spain's **Costa del Sol**, the beaches in **Marbella** (p. 850) shine with 320 days of sun per year, while **Tossa del Mar** along the jagged **Costa Brava** (p. 874) is framed by red cliffs. Spain's islands overwhelm with sunburned debauchery: the **Balearic Islands** are a must for party kids: **Ibiza** (p. 891) is manic by night. Move along to the Italian Riviera for **Finale Ligure** (p. 639) and **Camogli** (p. 640), before traveling to Tuscany and the enchanting island of **Elba** (p. 684). Explore the rugged beauty of the **Amalfi Coast** (p. 694) and ferry over to the island paradise of **Capri** (p. 696). Next, sail over to the Greek islands: **Corfu** harbors the beautiful beach of **Agios Gordios** (p. 528), while whitewashed towns balancing on plunging cliffs, burning black-sand beaches, and deeply scarred hills comprise **Santorini's** (p. 536) dramatic landscape.

▨ LET'S GO PICKS

BEST INDULGENCES: Nibbling **gold-dusted chocolate** in Lyon (p. 370), sampling **all things herbal** in Amsterdam (p. 725), spooning delectable **gelato** in Florence (p. 668), and sipping **high tea** in London (p. 154).

BEST OF THE MACABRE: Cappuchin friars propped 8000 bodies against the walls of the **Cappuchin Catacombs** in Palermo (p. 699); the **Basilica of the Holy Blood** in Bruges (p. 131) has a relic that allegedly holds Christ's blood; and the **Cattedrale di San Giovanni** in Turin (p. 666) houses a shroud supposedly worn by Christ at his crucifixion. The interior of **Igreja Real de São Francisco** in Évora (p. 775) is made entirely out of skeleton pieces.

BEST PLACES TO MOOCH: Sample free whiskey at the **Old Jameson Distillery** in Dublin (p. 563), taste free brew at the **Heineken Brewery** in Amsterdam (p. 737), and sip free champagne at **Moët & Chandon** in Epernay (p. 385). Then you can camp at **Odysseus's landing point** in Ithaka (p. 530), munch at the **Lindt and Sprügli Chocolate Factory** in Zurich (p. 913), and gawk at the **Mercedes-Benz Museum** in Stuttgart (p. 475), all for free.

BEST PLACES TO SMOOCH: Beside the **Trevi Fountain** in Rome (p. 606), atop the **Eiffel Tower** in Paris (p. 306), on a **gondola tour** of Venice (p. 651), at the **Temple to Aphrodite** in Corinth (p. 522), in the middle of the **Via del Amore** in Cinque Terre (p. 641), or on the desert plateau of Sagres (p. 778), once thought to be the **edge of the world.**

BEST FESTIVALS: Bareback horse races take **Siena** by storm during **Il Palio** (July 2 and Aug. 16; p. 682) and the bulls run for **San Fermines** in Pamplona (July 6-14; p. 877). "Yes" is the magic word during **Love Parade** in Berlin, (July 12; p. 423); the **Ediburgh Fringe Festival** (Aug. 6-28; p. 233) entertains with all things artsy; and merry **Oktoberfest** revelers in Munich consume of 1.2 million gallons of beer (Sept. 21-Oct. 6; p. 479).

DISCOVER

SUGGESTED ITINERARIES

There is no formula for the perfect itinerary in Western Europe. Here we humbly suggest a few routes—just to give you an idea of what is possible. **The Basics** below outlines our skeletal suggestions for the best of Europe. We've also included some regional itineraries to help you plan a few extra forays. These other itineraries can be thought of as **Building Blocks** to tack onto a basic route. For more in-depth suggestions, see the **Suggested Itineraries** sections in individual country chapters.

THE BASICS

THE GRAND TOUR: BEST OF WESTERN EUROPE IN 1 MONTH . Start out in **London**, spinning from theaters to museums to pubs (4 days, p. 154). Chunnel to the world-class galleries and chic shops of **Paris** (4 days, p. 288), and slip south to daring and colorful **Barcelona** (2 days, p. 854). Return to France for an all-night party in **Nice** (1 day, p. 356); recover in the blissful **Cinque Terre** on the Italian Riviera (1 day, p. 641). Prop up the leaning tower of **Pisa** (1 day, p. 683), be enchanted by Renaissance art in **Florence** (2 days, p. 668), and don your toga in **Rome** (3 days, p. 606). Float down the canals of **Venice** by gondola (2 days, p. 651) on your way to the opera in **Vienna** (2 days, p. 85). Sip absinthe in starlet **Prague** (2 days, p. 931) and sample the frothy brew in **Munich** (2 days, p. 479) before heading up to funky **Berlin** (2 days, p. 401), and then relax with a day in the EU capital, **Brussels** (p. 125).

THE BEST OF WESTERN EUROPE IN 9 WEEKS . From **London** (4 days, p. 154), meander the halls of **Cambridge** (1 day, p. 207) or **Oxford** (1 day, p. 196), then

catch a play in Shakespeare's **Stratford-Upon-Avon** (1 day, p. 203), before heading to **Dublin,** home to Joyce and Guinness (2 days, p. 553). Chunnel from London to **Paris** (4 days, p. 288) and then gape at **Versailles** (1 day, p. 317). From the castle-dotted **Loire Valley** (1 day, p. 329), go test your taste buds in the vineyards of **Bordeaux** (1 day, p. 336). Proceed to the Iberian peninsula to rage in the clubs of **Madrid** (2 days, p. 797), and bask on the beaches of **Lisbon** (2 days, p. 762). After heading back east to **Barcelona** (3 days, p. 854), spend a day each in festive **Avignon** (p. 345), **Aix-en-Provence** (p. 348), and **Nice** (p. 356). Next replenish in the **Cinque Terre** (2 days, p. 641), send postcards from **Pisa** (1 day, p. 683), and continue on to **Florence** (2 days, p. 668). Stop at the stunning *duomo* in **Siena** (1 day, p. 682) en route to **Rome** (3 days, p. 606). Glide through **Venice** (2 days, p. 651) on your way to posh **Milan** (1 day, p. 629). Grapple the Matterhorn from **Zermatt** (1 day, p. 926), and conquer the Swiss Alps around **Interlaken** (1 day, p. 923). Be a diplomat for a day in **Geneva** (1 day, p. 903), and stock up on chocolate in **Zurich** (1 day, p. 913). Satiate your urge for *The Sound of Music* in **Salzburg** (1 day, p. 99) and waltz your way through **Vienna** (2 days, p. 85), then kick back for 2 days in either the baths of **Budapest** (p. 942) or the bars of **Prague** (p. 931). From

DISCOVER

Munich, take a sobering daytrip to **Dachau** (3 days, p. 489). Move up the pastoral **Romantic Road** (2 days, p. 491), then cruise down the spectacular **Rhine River** (1 day, p. 467). From **Berlin** (2 days, p. 401) and reckless **Hamburg** (1 day, p. 439), head north to cosmopolitan **Copenhagen** (2 days, p. 256) and continue on to **Amsterdam** (3 days, p. 725). Spend a day each in **Brussels** (p. 125) and **Bruges** (p. 131) before heading home.

360) before hitting the world-famous casinos of **Monte-Carlo** (1 day, p. 361). Take a breather by relaxing in the placid waters of **Finale Ligure** (1 day, p. 639) and hiking through the colorful villages of Italy's **Cinque Terre** (1 day, p. 641). Admire the architecture of **Genoa** (1 day, p. 638) before oohing and aahing over **Florence**'s magnificent art collection (3 days, p. 668). Check out the two-toned *duomo* of **Siena** (2 days, p. 682) and indulge your gladiatorial fantasies in capital city **Rome** (4 days, p. 606).

THE BEST OF THE MEDITERRANEAN IN 6 WEEKS. Begin in the flower-filled *terrazas* of **Sevilla** (2 days, p. 827) before basking on the soft-sand beaches of **Cádiz** (2 days, p. 836). Stand on the imposing Rock of **Gibraltar** (1 day, p. 844) en route to partying with the beautiful people in the Costa del Sol resort town of **Marbella** (1 day, p. 850). Skip inland to **Granada** (2 days, p. 845), and wind your way through Moorish fortresses. From **Valencia** (2 days, p. 852), hop around the **Balearic Islands** between **Ibiza**'s foam parties and **Menorca**'s raw beaches (3 days, p. 892). Ferry to vibrant **Barcelona** (3 days, p. 854), before hitting the **Costa Brava** and the Dalí museum in **Figueres** (2 days, p. 874). Head to France's *provençal* **Nimes** (1 day, p. 345) and follow van Gogh's traces through **Arles** (1 day, p. 346). More fun awaits in **Avignon** (1 day, p. 345), before you revel in **Aix-en-Provence** (1 day, p. 348). Taste the *bouillabaisse* in **Marseilles** (1 day, p. 349), and move on to all that glitters on the Côte d'Azur: **Cannes** (2 days, p. 354) is the star-studded diamond, and **Nice** (2 days, p. 356) is the party haven. Explore the gorgeous clifftop villages of the **Corniches** (1 day, p.

BUILDING BLOCKS

THE BEST OF SOUTHERN ITALY AND GREECE IN 4 WEEKS. View the rubble of the toga-clad empire, the cathedrals of high Christianity, and the art of the Renaissance in **Rome** (5 days, p. 606). From **Naples** (2 days, p. 688), home to the world's best pizza and pickpockets, daytrip to **Pompeii** (1 day, p. 693) and check out lifelike Roman remains buried in AD 79. Then escape to the sensuous paradise of **Capri** (2 days, p. 696). Hop off the boot from **Bari** (p. 697) or **Brindisi** (p. 698), for which overnight ferries go to Greece (1 day). Get off at **Corfu** (1 day, p. 528), beloved by literary luminary Oscar Wilde and partiers alike, or continue on to **Patras** (1 day, p. 517). Wrestle in **Olympia** (1 day, p. 518) before beginning your Peloponnesian adventure with a survey of the ancient ruins in **Napflion, Mycenae,** and **Epidavros** (3 days, p. 521). Get initiated in the "mysteries of love" in equally ruinous **Corinth** (1 day, p. 522). On to chaotic **Athens,** a jumble of things ancient and modern (2 days, p. 507). Succumb to your longing in the Cyclades: party all

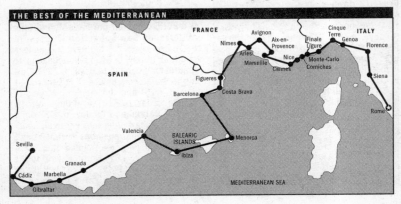

THE BEST OF THE MEDITERRANEAN

FRANCE — Avignon — Aix-en-Provence — Finale Ligure — Cinque Terre — Genoa — ITALY
Nimes — Arles — Nice — Monte-Carlo — Florence
Marseille — Cannes — Corniches
SPAIN — Figueres — Siena
Barcelona — Costa Brava — Rome
Valencia — BALEARIC ISLANDS — Menorca
Sevilla — Granada — Ibiza
Cádiz — Marbella
Gibraltar
MEDITERRANEAN SEA

DISCOVER

BEST OF SOUTHERN ITALY AND GREECE

night long on **Mykonos** (1 day, p. 532) and repent the morning after at the Temple of Apollo in **Delos** (1 day, p. 532), before continuing on to the earthly paradise of **Santorini** (2 days, p. 536). Catch the ferry to **Crete**, where chic **Iraklion** and **Knossos,** home to the Minotaur, await (2 days, p. 537). Base yourself in **Rethymno** or **Hania** and hike the **Samaria Gorge** (2 days, p. 538).

THE BEST OF BRITAIN AND IRELAND IN 3 WEEKS. From **London** (4 days, p. 154), get studious in **Cambridge** (1 day, p. 207) and **Oxford** (1 day, p. 196), then take to the

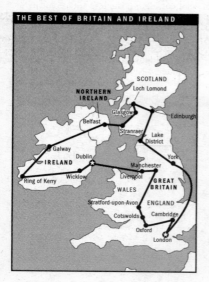

THE BEST OF BRITAIN AND IRELAND

Cotswolds (1 day, p. 202). Love all things Shakespeare in **Stratford-Upon-Avon** (1 day, p. 203), and move on to party in **Manchester** (1 day, p. 213). Trip down Penny Lane in **Liverpool** (1 day, p. 214), home of the Beatles. Cross the Irish Sea to **Dublin** (3 days, p. 553), the latest international favorite, and daytrip to the **Wicklow Mountains** (1 day, p. 566). Run the **Ring of Kerry** (2 days, p. 574) circuit before listening to *craic* in **Galway** (2 days, p. 578), the culture capital. Take in the murals at **Belfast** (2 days, p. 584) and from there it's back across the Irish Sea to **Stranraer,** energetic **Glasgow** (1 day, p. 240), and nearby **Loch Lomond.** Then jump over to historic and exuberant **Edinburgh** (3 days, p. 233). The **Lake District** (2 days, p. 221) offers scenic diversions, and historic **York** (1 day, p. 216) completes the journey. Return to London to kick back with a West End play and a glass of Tetley's bitter.

THE BEST OF SPAIN AND PORTUGAL IN 5 WEEKS . Hop off the Paris-Madrid train at gorgeous **San Sebastián** (2 days, p. 882), and check out the new Guggenheim in **Bilbao** (1 day, p. 887) before heading to **Madrid** for urban fun (4 days, p. 797). Daytrip to the austere palace of **El Escorial** (1 day, p. 815) and the medieval streets of **Toledo** (1 day, p. 816). Visit the university town of **Salamanca** (1 day, p. 823) and then cross the border into Portugal, heading up to the unpretentious **Porto** (2 days, p. 782). Marvel at the painted tiles in **Lisbon** (3 days, p. 762) with a daytrip to the town of **Sintra** (1 day, p. 771). Bake in the sun along the Algarve in **Lagos** (3

THE BEST OF SPAIN AND PORTUGAL

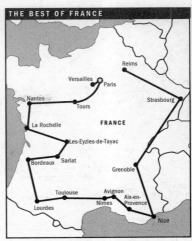

THE BEST OF FRANCE

days, p. 776), where hordes of visitors dance the night away. Sleep off your hangover on the 7hr. express bus from Lagos to **Sevilla** (2 days, p. 827) and prepare for a romantic stroll along the Guadalquivir River. Delve deeper into Arab-influenced Andalucía—don't miss the Mezquita in **Córdoba** (2 days, p. 837) and the Alhambra in **Granada** (2 days, p. 845). From Granada head up the Mediterranean Coast to stop in **Valencia** (1 day, p. 852) for the *paella* and oranges. Move on to northeastern Spain and hit sunny **Costa Brava** (2 days, p. 874), artsy **Figueres** (1 day, p. 874), and medieval **Girona** (1 day, p. 873). Finish up your journey in colorful **Barcelona** (4 days, p. 854).

THE BEST OF FRANCE IN 3 WEEKS.

You'll need at least four days to see the sights and shops of **Paris** (p. 288)—make time for a daytrip to **Versailles** (p. 317). Then travel to **Tours** (2 days, p. 330) in the Loire Valley to explore beautiful châteaux. Next, head down to **Nantes** (1 day, p. 328) for medieval sights and modern nightlife, before soaking up the sun in beach-blessed **La Rochelle** (2 days, p. 333). For a change of pace, visit the 17,000-year-old cave paintings of **Les-Eyzies-de-Tayac** (1 day, p. 334) and stroll through the golden streets of **Sarlat** (1 day, p. 334). Sniff, swirl, and spit in **Bordeaux** (2 days, p. 336) before following the pilgrims to miraculous **Lourdes** (1 day, p. 339). Zip southward for some Franco-Spanish flavor in **Toulouse** (1 day, p. 340). Head east to reach the magnificent Roman ruins of **Nîmes** (1 day, p. 345), the birthplace of denim. The stunning Gothic fortifications of the Palais des Papes cast shadows over festive **Avignon** (1 day, p. 345). Students have been partying in elegant **Aix-en-Provence** (1 day, p. 348) for 600 years, but for non-stop action go to **Nice** (2 days, p. 356), undisputed capital of the Riviera. For a change of scenery, climb into the Alps to reach dynamic **Grenoble** (2 days, p. 367). **Strasbourg** (1 day, p. 378) offers a pleasant blend of French and German culture. Finish off in style with a tasting at one of the many champagne *caves* in **Reims** (1 day, p. 384).

THE BEST OF GERMANY, AUSTRIA, AND SWITZERLAND IN 5 WEEKS.

Spend five days raging in **Berlin**'s chaotic nightclubs and recovering in the capital's museums and cafes (4 days, p. 401). Move north, where **Hamburg** fuses port town burliness with cosmopolitan flair (2 days, p. 439), before admiring Germany's greatest cathedral in **Cologne** (1 day, p. 455). Meander through **Bonn** (1 day, p. 461) and explore Germany's oldest university in **Heidelburg** (1 day, p. 471). Drool over Porsches and Mercedes-Benzes in ultramodern **Stuttgart** (1 day, p. 475), then relive your favorite Grimms' fairy tales in the **Black Forest** (1 day, p. 476). Cross into Switzerland and enjoy medieval sights in **Basel** (1 day, p. 911) before stopping for pastries in **Neuchâtel** (1 day, p. 911). Play world leader in **Geneva** (2 days, p. 903), shimmy over to capital city **Bern** (1 day, p. 920), and listen to jazz in **Mon-**

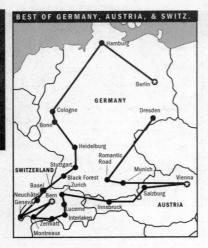

BEST OF GERMANY, AUSTRIA, & SWITZ.

treaux (1 day, p. 910). Ogle the Matterhorn from **Zermatt** (1 day, p. 926), and explore the Alps from **Interlaken** (2 days, p. 923). Take a train to the fairytale hamlet of **Lucerne** (1 day, p. 919) before tasting the nightlife in **Zurich** (1 day, p. 913). Skip over to Austria for skiing in **Innsbruck** (1 day, p. 112). Follow Mozart's footsteps in **Salzburg** (2 days, p. 99), then take in the enormous charm of **Vienna** (3 days, p. 85). Head back into Germany to **Munich** (1 day, p. 479) for boisterous beer halls and a daytrip to mad King Ludwig's Castles (1 day, p. 493). Admire the scenery along the **Romantic Road** (2 days, p. 491), but save the last dance for **Dresden** (1 day, p. 427).

WESTERN EUROPE: THE GRAND TOUR

Ah, Western Europe. It arrests our adjective pool—ostentatious and elegant, tumultuous and serene. Underneath this multitude lies enough history to keep you busy for a lifetime and then some. During your travels, each country's political and cultural histories will emerge everywhere—from architecture to landscapes to the people. Below is a very brief primer on the major intellectual and political movements that forged four millennia of Western European identity. Use this abridged history along with the historical and cultural introductions at the beginning of each country chapter to truly partake in the delights of Western Europe.

IN THE BEGINNING...(2000 BC-AD 565)

From the din and tundra of the Paleolithic and Neolithic periods, some restless Indo-Europeans from the East migrated westward during the 18th and 17th centuries BC to the Aegean Sea. Inter-marriage with the natives gave rise to the **Greeks** and created the cornerstone of Western European civilization. Siege-happy, they overthrew the **Minoans** in the 15th century BC, and sacked Troy in the **Trojan War** (1500 BC). Between 337 and 323 BC, **Alexander the Great** expanded the Greek Empire across Europe, and autonomous **city-states** grew in size, power, and cultural influence with **Athens** (p. 507) and **Sparta** (p. 520) as the two dominant cities. At the height of **Classical Greece** (500-400 BC), Athens produced the art, literature, and philosophy that have been the keystone of Western culture ever since. Unable to withstand the military might of the **Romans,** by 133 BC Greece had all but fallen to the Roman empire. Rome expanded its empire over most of Western Europe through the **Punic Wars,** ruling the continent with its distinctive government and adopting (plagiarizing) Greek culture. Although there were no distinct nations, transportation arteries sprung up between cities and the empire kept general peace, **pax romana** style. **Diocletian** tried in AD 293 to strengthen his control over the empire by dividing East and West between himself and a co-emperor. Yet Emperor **Constantine the Great** revoked this agreement and reunited the Roman Empire between 306-337, moving its capital to Byzantium (a.k.a. Constantinople a.k.a. Istanbul) and declaring Christianity the new state religion.

EARLY MIDDLE AGES (AD 476-1000)

There's nothing like 200 years of **Huns, Visigoths,** and **Vandals** to spoil a perfectly good empire. In 476, the last Roman emperor was forced into retirement and the Germanic barbarians began a 150-year political renovation of the Roman Empire, reverting cities to tribal kingdoms. As life became increasingly localized, Western Europe tumbled into the poorly-lit **Dark Ages** (AD 500 to 1200). In 800AD, the Pope crowned Frankish king **Charlemagne** Holy Roman Emperor and united the divided East and West of Christian Europe. Following the death of Charlemagne's son, **Louis the Pious,** the Carolingian Empire was divided among his three sons, thus decentralizing power and leading to the rise of local lords. Europe was now divided into three parts: the **Byzantine Empire** (the East and parts of Italy), **Islamic Europe** (Spain and Portugal), and **Latin Christendom** (France, Belgium, Germany, Britain, and parts of Italy).

HIGH MIDDLE AGES (1000-1300)

When the milliennial apocalypse didn't arrive in AD 1000, the first order of business was to establish a stable political system. Carolingian rulers established **feudalism,** a system of local government without a state that subjected agrarian **vassals** to the dictates of their **lords.** Above this political hierarchy, however, reigned the Church, an extremely wealthy and powerful institution that dictated law. Pope **Innocent III** financed and advised regional kings to advance his goal of Christian unification to the point that they viewed him as a feudal lord. The High Middle Ages were marked by costly and occasionally successful attempts to extend Christianity.

From 1095 to 1291, Western Europeans launched the **Holy War,** or the seven **Crusades,** against the Islamic East, although the most successful crusades attacked heathens within Europe itself. In the 13th century, Christianity claimed Spain, Italy, Prussia, and the Baltic regions. Overall, the wars both strengthened and demonstrated the might of Christian Europe.

THE RENAISSANCE (1350-1550)

In a fit of nostalgia for the Corinthian columns and toga parties of yore, 14th-century Italy helped Classicism stage a comeback with the **Renaissance** (literally, "rebirth"). Poets **Dante, Petrarch,** and **Boccaccio,** and the artist **Giotto,** set the stage during the 12th and 13th centuries with poetry and art that celebrated the inherent dignity and beauty of humankind. In the 14th century, sculptors and artists **Donatello, Michelangelo,** and **Da Vinci** provided the artistic apotheosis of **Humanism,** an outlook that treated rhetoric and the Classics as a celebration of human self-respect and preparation for a life of virtue. However, the **Black Death** (bubonic and pneumonic plague) devastated the continent, wiping out 25 million Europeans from 1347 to 1352.

The Renaissance also fostered the **Age of Exploration** that began in the 1490s, with the expansion of Spain's and Portugal's colonial empires. The period featured England's oddly-named **Hundred Years War** with France, which lasted from 1337 to 1453 but saw only 44 years of actual fighting. Although the English won early battles, they were eventually expelled from France. Squabbles within the Roman Catholic Church escalated into **The Great Schism,** during which multiple popes bickered over church power from 1378 to 1417. The election of an Italian Cardinal during the **Council of Constance** ended the schism, but papal authority remained weak.

PROTESTANT REFORMATION (1517-1555)

In 1517, **Martin Luther's** *95 Theses* sparked the Protestant Reformation in Germany. The shocking treatise resulted in Luther's 1521 excommunication, and before the decade ended, the Holy Roman Empire was divided by the issue of reformation. **Henry VIII's** divorce from **Catherine of Aragon** in 1534 to wed **Anne Boleyn** broke England from the Roman Catholic Church and caused a rift over which heads would (literally) roll for years. With the **Act of Supremacy** in 1534, Henry declared himself head of not only state, but of the new Protestant church as well, instigating the **English Reformation.** Later in the 16th century, **John Calvin** led the **Genevan Reformation** in Switzerland to establish too-late-you're-already-going-to-hell **Calvinism** as the dominant Protestant force in Europe.

Yet the movement toward Reformation did not go unchecked. The **Council of Trent** (1545-1563), the 19th ecumenical council of the Roman Catholic Church, formed the keystone of the **Counter-Reformation** argument. While the council refuted all criticism from Protestants, it also made sweeping reforms to correct the many abuses within the Church. Most importantly, the council halted the sale of **indulgences,** which forgave neglected penances or unrepented sins. In 1555, however, with the **Peace of Augsburg, Charles V** of the Holy Roman Empire granted the princes of Germany the right to establish the religion of their own people, whether that was Catholicism or Protestantism.

REVOLUTION IN THOUGHT (1555-1648)

Unwilling to witness the fracturing of his empire, Charles V abdicated all his titles in 1555. His brilliant solution to the lack of unity was to further divide power; his brother **Ferdinand I** gained control of the Austrian Habsburg lands, while his son **Philip II** ruled Spain and The Netherlands. Workaholic Philip II obsessed over the necessity for Catholic reform while propelling Spain into its Golden Age, **siglo de oro,** as the greatest power in Europe. Spanish troops and gold supported the Catholic cause in Western Europe, aiding rebellions against England's Protestant **Queen Elizabeth** and removing French Protestant **Huguenots** from power. The Spaniards were driven out of The Netherlands by **William of Orange** in the first phase of the **Eighty Years' War** (1568-1648). From 1618-1648, the **Thirty Years' War** made Germany a battlefield doormat as Protestant forces asserted their independence from the Roman Catholic Church and the Holy Roman Empire. The **Treaty of Westphalia** in 1648 reinforced the Peace of Augsburg's principle of *cuius regio eius religio* (whose region, his religion) and set European political geography for the next century. Calvinism was added to the list of (barely) tolerable religions, thus ensuring the safety of Calvinism in The Netherlands. In the aftermath, the Holy Roman Empire was severely weakened—Spain fell from her diva spotlight as Philip II's Catholic crusade crashed in flames, Queen Elizabeth restored the Protestant church, and a Huguenot sat on the throne in France.

The late 17th century exploded with political and intellectual revolutions. England plunged into civil war, and France, under the beaming "Sun King" **Louis XIV,** became the greatest power in Western Europe. The **Scientific Revolution** of the 17th century broke out of the medieval box to challenge traditional thought. **Galileo, Descartes, Newton,** and **Hobbes** were among the many whose works marked the revolution, each contributing to the belief in harmony, logic, and human abilities. The popularization of scientific thought and method and their increasing pertinence to everyday life, medicine, and politics formed the basis for the ideas of the **Age of Enlightenment**.

AGE OF ENLIGHTENMENT (1688-1789)

During the Enlightenment, thinkers such as **Voltaire, Charles-Louis Montesquieu, John Locke, Thomas Hobbes,** and **Jean-Jacques Rousseau** made the radical proposition that reason and science, rather than a mysterious God, could reveal the truth of life. By reasoning out the universal laws of nature, they claimed, one could achieve freedom and happiness. This age's questioning spirit also affected the conception of the state—**Frederick II** of Prussia, **Catherine the Great** of Russia, and **Joseph II** of the Habsburg empire were monarchs known as the **enlightened despots,** who combined liberal reforms with measures to maintain control over peasants.

Unfortunately, these utopian ideals didn't halt sparring monarchies. In the **War of the Spanish Succession** (1701-1714), Austria and Britain went to war to keep Louis XIV's son, Philip V, from the Spanish throne. This was settled by the **Treaty of Utrecht,** which allowed Philip to take the throne but forbade him from merging the empire with France. The **Seven Years' War** (1756-1763) saw Austria and France ally to fight Prussia and Britain over colonies. War eventually spread to North America, the Caribbean, and India, hinting at the impending wave of imperialism.

FRENCH REVOLUTION AND NAPOLEON (1789-1814)

Louis XIV's full ascension to the French throne in 1661 ushered in an era of dictatorial, aristocratic **absolutism** and excess, perhaps best exemplified by the 14,000-room palace of **Versailles** (hey, everyone needs a little place in the country; see p. 317). Prompted by a financial crisis and a disgruntled population, **Louis XVI** called the first (and last) assembly of the **Estates General** in over 175 years, consisting of representatives from the three classes: nobility, clergy, and the common people. From this organization, the populace broke away, declaring itself the **National Assembly**. After chaos erupted, the radical **Jacobin** faction took control, abolished the monarchy, and declared France a Republic, symbolized by the storming of the **Bastille** on July 14, 1789 (see p. 307). The Revolution entered a more radical phase, dubbed the **Terror,** when counter-revolutionaries were weeded out and justice summarily dispensed by "Madame" Guillotine. The **Directory,** a second try at representative government, was established in 1794, but lasted only five years when a little man with a big ego, **Napoleon Bonaparte,** after waging victorious military campaigns in Italy and in Egypt, deposed the Directory and declared himself Emperor and "consul for life" in 1804. The **Napoleonic Code,** a direct result of the Age of Enlightenment ideals, defined property rights, declared all people equal before the law, and affirmed religious freedoms. Seeking to expand his control, he abolished the Holy Roman Empire and dismembered Prussia—by 1810, most of Europe was either annexed by or allied to France. After wars with Britain and Spain, Napoleon's **Grand Army** was disastrously defeated in Russia in 1812, after which he abdicated and was sent into luxurious exile on **Elba** to think up witty palindromes. Bourbon rule was restored in France in 1814 under Louis XVIII, but the **Congress of Vienna** in 1814 left France without Napoleon's land acquisitions.

INDUSTRIAL REVOLUTION (1760-1848)

With the invention of the steam engine, spinning mill, and **Spinning Jenny** (cotton spinning machine) in the 18th century, the Industrial Revolution was off to a running start, but still confined largely to Britain. From 1800 to 1850 it spread rapidly throughout Europe, bringing with it **urbanization** and greater life expectancy. **Factories,** especially for textiles and iron, were the Industrial Age's most visible symbol, but the period also saw heightened international trade and the birth of socialist ideology (**St. Simon, Marx,** and **Engels**). Heightened urbanization provided mobility for the peasant class, although conditions in slums remained deplorable, with rampant overcrowding and primitive sanitation tainting upper-class tennis matches and tea parties.

Industrial changes were harbingers of other social revolutions, as liberal revolts broke out in Spain, Italy, Portugal, Germany, Russia, and Poland from 1815 to 1848. The 19th century also brought new independence for several countries, as Belgium wrested autonomy from The Netherlands in 1830 and the Turks recognized Greek independence in 1832. An 18-year-old **Queen Victoria** ascended the British throne in 1837, giving rise to the era of her name.

NATIONAL UNIFICATION (1851-1867)

During the mid-19th century, European nations, inspired by the "survival of the fittest" ideology of **Social Darwinism,** consolidated land and power. Taking the lead from his dear old uncle, President Louis Napoleon dissolved the National Assembly and declared himself **Emperor Napoleon III.** In Italy, the efforts of **Victor Emmanuel II** and **General Giuseppe Garibaldi** from 1859 to 1870 managed to unify Italy despite long-standing regional tensions. Meanwhile, back in Prussia, newly appointed Prime Minister **Otto von Bismarck** unified the German Empire, including the new lands Prussia had garnered as spoils during the **Austro-Prussian** and **Franco-Prussian Wars** (1866 and 1870-71, respectively). As massive monarchal alliances became trendy, the **Dual Monarchy** of Austria-Hungary was created in 1867, the same year that the **British Reform Bill** doubled the number of English voters by granting suffrage to all household heads.

INVENTION AND IMPERIALISM (1870-1911)

Continuing innovation brought rapid industrialization to Europe with the spread of electricity and the invention of the sewing machine, telephone, and automobile. Railways surged across the continent, standards of living skyrocketed, and the service industry provided many women of the new and expanding middle class gainful employment. Chancellor Bismarck gave the **industrial bourgeoisie** something to cheer about as he enacted the world's first unemployment insurance in 1883. European powers, led by Germany and Britain, extended their long arms to Africa and Asia, establishing dominance during the **Age of Imperialism.** Explorers and missionaries were the first to introduce Europe to Africa, desiring to socialize an otherwise "primitive" continent. **King Leopold II** of Belgium was especially attracted to the potential wealth of Africa, while the British and French also ventured into the "dark continent" to secure political clout and plunder diamonds. The Dutch, British, and Russian imperialists also began to occupy parts of Asia, creating powerful empires while suppressing the revolts of native inhabitants.

WORLD WAR I (1914-1918)

The assassination of the Austro-Hungarian **Archduke Francis Ferdinand** in Serbia in 1914 was the straw that broke Europe's back. Through Bismarck's masterful diplomacy, the continent had become a mess of opposing alliances: Britain and France ended centuries of conflict in 1904 by forming the **Entente Cordiale,** an alliance which Russia later joined to create the **Triple Entente.** The assassination prompted Austria-Hungary to issue a military ultimatum to Serbia, backed by Germany's recently unified state and Turkey (forming an alliance of their own, the **Central Powers**). The standoff brought Russia into the conflict, prompting Germany to declare war against her. Germany, seeking to destroy the allied Franco-British threat, advanced quickly through Belgium and France before stalling at the **Battle of the Marne** in 1914, starting four long years of **trench** warfare. The United States was drawn into the war when Germany's practice of **unrestricted submarine warfare** became intolerable, and the American entry in 1917 was followed in short order by the Allied victory on November 11, 1918. In 1919, the **Big Four** (Orlando of Italy, Lloyd George of Britain, Clemenceau of France, and Wilson of the US) forced Germany to accept full responsibility for the Great War in the **Treaty of Versailles**—in the **war guilt clause,** the weak new **Weimar Republic** in Germany was forced to assume the financial burden of the war. The treaty also paved way for the **League of Nations.**

INTERWAR YEARS (1919-1938)

For Germany, the Treaty of Versailles was in many ways disastrous: the Allies demanded enormous reparations, apportioned significant German territory, stole all bratwurst, and limited the size of its standing military. This humiliation, combined with hyperinflation of the 1920s, the **Great Depression,** and alienating urbanization, set the stage for Austrian **Adolph Hitler**'s rise to power. As the leader of the **National Socialist German Workers' Party (NSDAP),** also known as the **Nazis,** Hitler pushed a program of Aryan supremacy (based on anti-Semitism and German racial purity), playing on the post-war insecurities of the Germans. By the 1930s, many European countries were dictatorships, most prominently fascist Italy under **Benito Mussolini,** autarchic Spain, commanded by **General Francisco Franco,** and of course, the newly-created Union of Soviet Socialist Republics, led by **Joseph Stalin.** By 1933, Hitler had been appointed chancellor of Germany; he banned all other parties and created a totalitarian state. The **Kristallnacht** (Night of Broken Glass), on November 9, 1938, saw the destruction of Jewish stores and homes throughout Germany, as well as attacks against and the imprisonment of thousands of Jews.

WORLD WAR II (1939-1945)

Continuing German expansion, Hitler, facilitated by British Prime Minister **Neville Chamberlain**'s naïve appeasement policy, moved into Czechoslovakia and then Poland, initiating WWII on September 1, 1939. Britain and France, bound by treaty to help Poland, declared war on Germany. As Germany overran Denmark, Norway, Luxembourg, Belgium, The Netherlands, and France with its **Blitzkrieg** (Lightning-War) offensives, Chamberlain resigned and **Winston Churchill** assumed the British helm. France, despite the elaborate fortifications of the **Maginot Line,** fell to the German offensive, leading to Nazi occupation and the formation of the puppet **Vichy** regime. Russia stayed neutral because of a secret non-aggression pact signed with Hitler. This short-lived treaty only lasted until the Nazis invaded the Soviet Union in 1941; however, German forces were unable to break through during the Russian winter. In the same year, the US, prompted by the Japanese bombing of Pearl Harbor, entered the fray. The Allied landings at **Normandy** (p. 320) on June 6, 1944 **(D-Day),** turned the war's tide and marked the beginning of a bloody, arduous advance across Western Europe. Paris was liberated by Allied forces in September 1944, and Berlin was captured by the Red Army in April 1945. Hitler's **Third Reich,** which he had boasted would last for a thousand years, was dissolved after just twelve. The **Holocaust,** Hitler's "final solution to the Jewish problem," involved establishing mass concentration camps, the most infamous being **Auschwitz-Birkenau.** German forces ultimately killed at least six million Jews and countless other "undesirables," including homosexuals, mentally disabled people, Gypsies, Slavs, and political dissidents.

COLD WAR (1946-1989)

In 1945, the US, Britain, and the USSR met at **Yalta** to lay the foundation of the **United Nations,** plan the occupation of Nazi Germany, and determine spheres of influence in post-war Europe. Three **occupation zones** were set up in Germany, with Berlin under joint control. Berlin became the symbol of mounting tension between the Western capitalist world, led by the US, and the communist sphere, controlled by the USSR. East Germany, under the USSR, became known as the **German Democratic Republic. Julius** and **Ethel Rosenberg** brought the secrets of the atomic bomb to Russia, paving way to a 50-year American nuclear **arms race** with the USSR. In 1949, the American, British, and French zones became the **German Federal Republic.** Berlin itself was divided between the two opposing spheres, a division later marked by the construction of the **Berlin Wall** in 1961 (see p. 401). The **North Atlantic Treaty Organization (NATO)** was formed in 1949, by a band of 12 nations; it was countered by the Soviet alliance formed by the **Warsaw Pact** (1955). While the US was stricken with McCarthyism and anti-communist fervor, in Western Europe, the foundations for the now vibrant European Union (EU) were laid with the **European Economic Community** (EEC) in 1957—a tariff-free trading zone involving France, Belgium, The Netherlands, Luxembourg, Italy, and West Germany. Britain, Denmark, and Ireland joined in 1973, followed by Greece, Spain, Portugal, Eastern Germany, Austria, Sweden, and Finland over the next 20 years.

WESTERN EUROPE TODAY: EUROPEAN UNION

The fall of the Berlin Wall in November 1989 symbolized the fall of communism and the Cold War in the Western world. Focus then turned toward the European Community and the creation of one market with no borders. At the **Treaty of Maastricht** in 1991, the **European Union** was created from the European Economic Community, eliminating national barriers for the movement of goods, services, workers, and capital. Twelve EU members—Austria, Belgium, Germany, Greece, Finland, France, Ireland, Italy, Luxembourg, The Netherlands, Portugal, and Spain—will adopt the **Euro (€)** as legal tender on January 1, 2002, with domestic currencies phased out entirely by July 1, 2002 (see p. 23). Thirteen Eastern European countries are currently undergoing the application processes to join the EU, signifying the general European movement toward integration.

ESSENTIALS

So you want to conquer Western Europe, the world's seat of culture and civilization. The first and most important step to any adventure is organization. The time and effort you put into taking care of details and formalities, from the procurement of passports and visas to the purchase of the proper camping accessories, can save you tons of stress and ensure more time in your favorite European cafes and clubs.

DOCUMENTS AND FORMALITIES

Information on European **consular services** at home, as well as foreign consular services in Europe, is located in individual country chapters.

ENTRANCE REQUIREMENTS.

Passport (p. 17). Required for all citizens visiting Western Europe.

Visa (p. 18). Most Western European countries require visas for citizens of South Africa, but not for citizens of Australia, Canada, Ireland, New Zealand, the UK, or the US. They are required for stays longer than three months.

Inoculations (p. 29). Travelers to Western Europe should be up to date on vaccines for measles, mumps, rubella, diptheria, tetanus, pertussis, polio, haemophilus influenza B, hepatitis B, and hepatitis A.

Work Permit (p. 18). Required for all foreigners planning to work in Western Europe, except for citizens of EU member countries.

Driving Permit (p. 60). An International Driving Permit is recommended for all those planning to drive.

PASSPORTS

REQUIREMENTS. Citizens of Australia, Canada, Ireland, New Zealand, South Africa, the UK, and the US need valid passports to enter Western European countries, and to re-enter their home countries. Austria, Denmark, Italy, Spain and Switzerland deny entrance if the holder's passport expires in under three months; all other countries deny entrance if the holder's passport expires in under six months. Returning home with an expired passport is illegal, and may result in a fine.

PHOTOCOPIES. Be sure to photocopy the page of your passport with your photo, passport number, and other identifying information, as well as any visas, travel insurance policies, plane tickets, or traveler's check serial numbers. Carry one set of copies in a safe place, apart from the originals, and leave another set at home. Consulates also recommend that you carry an expired passport or an official copy of your birth certificate in a part of your baggage separate from other documents.

LOST PASSPORTS. If you lose your passport, immediately notify the local police and the nearest embassy or consulate of your home government. To expedite its replacement, you will need to know all information previously recorded and show ID and proof of citizenship. In some cases, a replacement may take weeks to process, and it may be valid only for a limited time. Any visas stamped in your old passport will be irretrievably lost. In an emergency, ask for immediate temporary traveling papers that will permit you to re-enter your home country. Due to relative diplomatic stability of Western Europe, travelers should have less trouble in receiving a emergency traveling certificate or replacement passport expediently. Your passport is a public document belonging to your nation's government. You may have to surrender it to a foreign government official, but if you don't get it back in a reasonable amount of time, inform the nearest mission of your home country.

NEW PASSPORTS. Citizens of Australia, Canada, Ireland, New Zealand, the UK, and the US can apply for a passport at the nearest post office, passport office, or court of law. Citizens of South Africa can apply for a passport at the nearest Office of Foreign Affairs. Any new passport or renewal applications must be filed well in advance of the departure date, although most passport offices offer rush services for a very steep fee. Citizens living abroad who need a passport or renewal services should contact the nearest consular service of their home country.

Australia: (☎ 13 12 32; www.dfat.gov.au/passports). Apply for a passport at a post office, passport office (all state capitals and Newcastle), or overseas embassies and diplomatic missions. Passports $132 (32-page) or $198 (64-page); valid for 10 years. Children $66 (32-page) or $99 (64-page); valid for 5 years.

Canada: The Passport Office, Department of Foreign Affairs and International Trade, Ottawa, ON K1A OG3 (☎800-567-6868 or 613-994-3500; www.dfait-maeci.gc.ca/passport). Applications available at passport offices, Canadian missions, and post offices. Standard processing time is 5 days if you drop off your application in person, 10 days by mail. Passports CDN$60; valid for 5 years.

Ireland: Pick up an application at a *Garda* station or post office, or request one from a passport office. Then apply by mail to the Passport Office, Setanta Centre, Molesworth St., Dublin 2 (☎01 671 1633; fax 671 1092; www.irlgov.ie/iveagh), or the Passport Office, Irish Life Building, 1A South Mall, Cork (☎021 27 25 25 or 021 27 69 64). Passports IR£45/€57.15 (32-page) or £55/€69.85 (48-page); valid for 10 years. Under 16 or over 65 £10/€12.70; valid for 3 years.

New Zealand: Send applications to the Passport Office, Department of Internal Affairs, P.O. Box 10526, Wellington (☎0800 22 50 50 or 04 474 8100; fax 04 474 8010; www.passports.govt.nz). Standard processing time is 10 working days. Passports NZ$80; valid for 10 years. Children NZ$40; valid for 5 years. 3-day "urgent service" NZ$160; children NZ $120.

South Africa: Passports are issued only in South Africa, but all applications must still be submitted or forwarded to the nearest South African consulate. Processing time is 3 to 6 months. Passports ZAR192; valid for 10 years. Children 136; valid for 5 years. For more information and to download the required forms in pdf format, check out http://usaembassy.southafrica.net/VisaForms/Passport/Passport2000.html.

UK: (Info ☎0870 521 0410; www.open.gov.uk/ukpass/ukpass.htm). Get an application from a passport office, main post office, travel agent, or online (for UK residents only) at www.ukpa.gov.uk/forms/f_app_pack.htm to order an application packet, or complete the application online at www.passport-application.gov.uk/. Then apply by mail or in person at a passport office or through a High Street Partner (highly recommended). Passports UK£28; valid for 10 years. Under-15 £14.80; valid for 5 years. The process takes about 4 weeks; applying through a High Street Partner is an additional £4; faster service is an additional £12 at the passport office.

US: (☎900-225-5674 ($0.35/minute) or 888-362-8668 ($4.95/call); www.travel.state.gov/passport_services.html). Apply at any federal or state courthouse, authorized post office, or US Passport Agency (in most major cities); see the Government/State Department section of the telephone book or a post office for addresses. Processing takes 3-4 weeks. New passports $60; valid for 10 years. Under 16 $40; valid for 5 years. Passports may be renewed by mail or in person for $40. Add $35 for 3-day expedited service.

VISAS AND WORK PERMITS

VISAS. Some countries require a visa—a stamp, sticker, or insert in your passport specifying the purpose of your travel and the permitted duration of your stay—in addition to a valid passport for entrance. Most standard visas cost US$10-70, are valid for one to three months, and must be validated within six months to a year from the date of issue. The countries covered by *Let's Go: Western Europe* do not require visas for citizens of Australia, Canada, Ireland,

ONE EUROPE. The idea of European unity has come a long way since 1958, when the European Economic Community (EEC) was created in order to promote solidarity and cooperation between its six founding states. Since then, the EEC has become the European Union (EU), with political, legal, and economic institutions spanning 15 member states: Austria, Belgium, Denmark, Finland, France, Germany, Greece, Ireland, Italy, Luxembourg, The Netherlands, Portugal, Spain, Sweden, and the UK.

What does this have to do with the average non-EU tourist? In 1999 the EU established **freedom of movement** across 14 European countries—the entire EU minus Denmark, Ireland, and the UK, with the addition of Iceland and Norway. This means that border controls between participating countries have been abolished, and visa policies harmonized. While you're still required to carry a passport (or government-issued ID card for EU citizens) when crossing an internal border, you're free to travel between all participating states. Britain and Ireland have also formed a **common travel area,** abolishing passport controls between the UK and the Republic of Ireland. This means that the only times you'll see a border guard within the EU are traveling between the British Isles and the Continent and in and out of Denmark.

For more important consequences of the EU for travelers, see **The Euro** (p. 23) and **Customs in the EU** (p. 21).

New Zealand, the UK, or the US for stays shorter than three months. Under the 1995 Schengen agreement, travelers from these countries are also allowed to travel freely for up to 90 days between the Schengen countries of Austria, Belgium, Denmark, Finland, France, Germany, Greece, Iceland, Italy, Luxembourg, The Netherlands, Norway, Portugal, Spain and Sweden. All European countries, except for the UK, Ireland, and Switzerland, require visas for South African citizens. Travelers to Andorra should contact a French or Spanish embassy for more information, while those going to Liechtenstein should contact a Swiss embassy. In any case, check with the nearest embassy or consulate of your desired destination for up-to-date information. US citizens can consult www.travel.state.gov/foreignentryreqs.html. US citizens can also take advantage of the **Center for International Business and Travel** (☎ 800-925-2428), which secures visas for travel to almost all countries for a variable service charge.

The visa requirements above only apply to stays shorter than three months. If you plan to stay longer than 90 days, or if you plan to work or study abroad, your requirements will differ (see **Alternatives to Tourism,** p. 67).

IDENTIFICATION

In Western Europe, personal identification is absolutely essential. When you travel, always carry two or more forms of identification on your person, including at least one photo ID; a passport with a driver's license or birth certificate is usually adequate. Many establishments, especially banks, may require several IDs in order to cash traveler's checks. Never carry all your forms of ID together; split them up in case of theft or loss.

For more information on all the forms of identification listed below, contact the organization that provides the service, the **International Student Travel Confederation (ISTC),** Herengracht 479, 1017 BS Amsterdam, The Netherlands (☎ 31 20 421 28 00; fax 421 28 10; www.istc.org).

TEACHER & STUDENT IDENTIFICATION. The **International Student Identity Card (ISIC),** the most widely accepted form of student ID, provides discounts on sights, accommodations, food, and transport. In the countries covered by *Let's Go: Western Europe,* you can get anything from 50% off a room in an Athens hotel to a free 50 liters of gas at certain Irish stations. The ISIC is preferable to an institution-spe-

ESSENTIALS

cific card (such as a university ID) because it is more likely to be recognized (and honored) abroad. All cardholders have access to a 24hr. emergency helpline for medical, legal, and financial emergencies (in North America call 877-370-ISIC, elsewhere call US collect +1 715-345-0505, UK collect +44 20 8762 8110, or France collect +33 155 633 144), and holders of US-issued cards are also eligible for insurance benefits (see **Insurance,** p. 33). Many student travel agencies issue ISICs, including STA Travel in Australia and New Zealand; Travel CUTS in Canada; usit World in Ireland and Northern Ireland; SASTS in South Africa; Campus Travel and STA Travel in the UK; Council Travel (www.counciltravel.com/idcards/default.asp) and STA Travel in the US (see p. 45).

The card is valid from September of one year to December of the following year and costs US$22. Applicants must be degree-seeking students of a secondary or post-secondary school and must be of at least 12 years of age. Because of the proliferation of fake ISICs, some services (particularly airlines) require additional proof of student identity, such as a school ID or a letter attesting to your student status, signed by your registrar and stamped with your school seal. The **International Teacher Identity Card (ITIC)** offers the same insurance coverage as well as similar but limited discounts. The fee is AUS$13, UK£5, or US$22.

YOUTH IDENTIFICATION. The International Student Travel Confederation also issues a discount card to travelers who are 26 years old or under, but are not students. This one-year **International Youth Travel Card** (**IYTC**; formerly the **GO 25** Card) offers many of the same benefits as the ISIC. Most organizations that sell the ISIC also sell the IYTC (US$22).

ISICONNECT SERVICE. If you are an ISIC card carrier and want to avoid buying individual calling cards or wish to consolidate all your means of communication during your trip, you can activate your ISIC's ISIConnect service, a new integrated communications service (powered by eKit.com). With ISIConnect, one toll-free access number in each country (http://www.isiconnect.ekit.com/ekit/Info/Access-numbers) gives you access to several different methods of keeping in touch via the phone and Internet, including: a reduced-rate international calling plan that treats your ISIC card as a universal **calling card;** a personalized **voicemail** box accessible from payphones anywhere in the world or for free over the Internet; **faxmail** service for sending and receiving faxes via email, fax machines, or pay phones; various **email** capabilities, including a service that reads your email to you over the phone; an online **"travel safe"** for storing (and faxing) important documents and numbers; and a 24hr. emergency **help line** (via phone or email at ISIConnect@ekit.com) offering assistance and medical and legal referrals. To activate your ISIConnect account, visit the service's comprehensive website (www.isiconnect.ekit.com) or call the customer service number of your home country (which is also your home country's access number): in Australia 800 114 478; in Canada 877-635-3575; in Ireland 800 555 180 or 800 577 980; in New Zealand 0800 114 478; in the UK 0800 376 2366 or 0800 169 8646; in the US 800-706-1333; and in South Africa 0800 992 921 or 0800 997 285.

CUSTOMS

Upon entering a country, you must declare certain items from abroad and pay a duty if the items' total value exceeds the allowance established by that country's customs service. Upon returning home, you must declare all articles acquired abroad and pay a duty on the value of articles in excess of your home country's allowance. Note that goods and gifts purchased at **duty-free** shops abroad are not exempt from duty or sales tax at your point of return and thus must be declared as well; "duty-free" merely means that you need not pay a tax in the country of purchase. Duty-free allowances were abolished for travel between EU member states, but still exist for those arriving from outside the EU. Also be sure to keep receipts for all goods acquired abroad.

TAXES. The European Union imposes a **value-added tax (VAT)** on goods and services purchased within the EU (usually included in the sticker price). Non-EU citizens may obtain a **refund** only for taxes paid on retail goods. As the VAT in Europe ranges from 15 to 25%, you may find it worth the hassle of filing for a refund. There are several ways to getting back your refund: the easiest and most common method is to use a refund service. Every time you make a purchase, request for a "tax-free shopping cheque" and then save the receipts from all of the purchases for which you want a refund. Upon leaving the last EU country on your itinerary, present your (unused) goods, invoices, and passport to Customs for validation and have them stamp your tax-free shopping cheques. Then take the stamped cheques to the refund service's airport office for an immediate cash refund, drop the cheques in a special box, have a check sent to a chosen address, or have the refund credited to your credit card in your own currency. Note that stores use different refund services, and you must go to each refund service to receive your refunds. Global Refund and CashBack are the largest refund services found in Europe. Another way is to get a refund directly from the store if they are willing to process refunds—ask for a VAT refund form, have it stamped by the Customs official and mail it back to the store. This option is worthwhile for large purchases or if the merchant will credit the refund to your credit card. The last and least viable way is to ask for two charge slips when making purchases with a credit card—one slip with the amount of sale after deducting the VAT and the other with the amount of VAT. After they receive your mailed Customs-stamped VAT form, the store merchant will destroy the slip with the VAT amount without submitting it. Keep in mind that goods must be taken out of the country within three months of the end of the month of purchase, and that some stores require minimum purchase amounts to become eligible for refund. For more information on tax-free shopping, see www.globalrefund.com.

 CUSTOMS IN THE EU. As well as freedom of movement of people within the EU (p. 19), travelers in the countries that are members of the EU (Austria, Belgium, Denmark, Finland, France, Germany, Greece, Ireland, Italy, Luxembourg, The Netherlands, Portugal, Spain, Sweden, and the UK) can also take advantage of the freedom of movement of goods. This means that there are no customs controls at internal EU borders (i.e., you can take the blue customs channel at the airport), and travelers are free to transport whatever legal substances they like as long as it is for their own personal (non-commercial) use—up to 800 cigarettes, 10L of spirits, 90L of wine (60L of sparkling wine), and 110L of beer. You should also be aware that duty-free was abolished on June 30, 1999 for travel between EU member states; however, travelers between the EU and the rest of the world still get a duty-free allowance when passing through customs.

FURTHER RESOURCES

Australia: Australian Customs National Information Line (in Australia ☎1300 363 263, from elsewhere call 61 2 6275 6666; www.customs.gov.au).

Canada: Canadian Customs, 2265 St. Laurent Blvd., Ottawa, ON K1G 4K3 (☎800-461-9999 (24hr.) or 506-636-5064; http://www.ccra-adrc.gc.ca/customs/individuals/canadians-e.html).

Ireland: Customs Information Office, Irish Life Centre, Lower Abbey St., Dublin 1 (☎01 878 8811; fax 878 0836; www.revenue.ie/customs.htm; custserv@revenue.ie).

New Zealand: The Customhouse, 17-21 Whitmore St., Box 2218, Wellington (☎04 473 6099; fax 473 7370; www.customs.govt.nz).

South Africa: Commissioner for Customs and Excise, Privat Bag X47, Pretoria 0001 (☎012 314 9911; fax 012 328 6478; www.gov.za).

UK: Her Majesty's Customs and Excise, Dorset House, Stamford Street, London SE1 9PY (☎084 5010 9000; fax 084 8910 3933; www.hmce.gov.uk).

US: US Customs Service, 1300 Pennsylvania Ave. NW, Washington, D.C. 20229 (☎202 354-1000; fax 354-1010; www.customs.gov).

ESSENTIALS

Money From Home In Minutes.

If you're stuck for cash on your travels, don't panic. Millions of people trust Western Union to transfer money in minutes to over 185 countries and over 95,000 locations worldwide. Our record of safety and reliability is second to none. You can even send money by phone without leaving home by using a credit card. For more information, call Western Union: USA 1-800-325-6000, Canada 1-800-235-0000.

www.westernunion.com

WESTERN UNION | **MONEY TRANSFER**

The fastest way to send money worldwide.

©2001 Western Union Holdings, Inc. All Rights Reserved.

MONEY

CURRENCY AND EXCHANGE

As a general rule, it's cheaper to convert money in Europe than at home. However, you should bring enough foreign currency to last for the first 24 to 72 hours of a trip to avoid being penniless should you arrive after bank hours or on a holiday. Travelers from the US can get foreign currency from the comfort of home: **International Currency Express** (☎ 888-278-6628) delivers foreign currency or traveler's checks 2nd-day (US$12) at competitive exchange rates.

When changing money abroad, try to go only to banks or bureaux de change that have at most a 5% margin between their buy and sell prices. Since you lose money with every transaction, **convert large sums** (unless the currency is depreciating rapidly), **but no more than you'll need.**

If you use traveler's checks or bills, carry some in small denominations (the equivalent of US$50 or less) for times when you are forced to exchange money at disadvantageous rates, but bring a range of denominations since charges may be levied per check cashed. Store your money in a variety of forms; ideally, you will at any given time be carrying some cash, some traveler's checks, and an ATM and/or credit card. All travelers should also consider carrying some US dollars (about $50), which are often preferred by local tellers.

THE EURO. Since January 2001, the official currency of 12 members of the European Union—Austria, Belgium, Finland, France, Germany, Greece, Ireland, Italy, Luxembourg, The Netherlands, Portugal, and Spain—has been the euro. Actual euro banknotes and coins will be available beginning on January 1, 2002; but don't throw out your francs, pesetas, and Deutschmarks just yet. The old national currencies remain legal tender through July 1, 2002, after which it's all euros all the time. *Let's Go: Western Europe* lists prices in both denominations, euros (€) and national currency based on actual figures or fixed conversion rates. The currency has some important—and positive—consequences for travelers hitting more than one euro-zone country. For one thing, money-changers across the euro-zone are obliged to exchange money at the official, fixed rate (see below), and at no commission (though they may still charge a small service fee). So now you can change your guilders into escudos and your escudos into lire without losing fistfuls of money on every transaction. Second, euro-denominated travelers checks allow you to pay for goods and services across the euro-zone, again at the official rate and commission-free.

The exchange rate between euro-zone currencies was permanently fixed on January 1, 1999 at 1 EUR = 40.3399 BEF (Belgian francs) = 1.95583 DM (German marks) = 166.386 ESP (Spanish pesetas) = 6.55957 FRF (French francs) = 0.787564 IER (Irish pounds) = 1936.27 ITL (Italian lire) = 40.3399 LUF (Luxembourg francs) = 2.20371 NLG (Dutch guilders) = 13.7603 ATS (Austrian schillings) = 200.482 PTE (Portuguese escudos) = 5.94573 FIM (Finnish markka). For more info, see www.europa.eu.int.

For **currency exchange information** please see the opening page of each country chapter. Check a large newspaper or the web (e.g. www.letsgo.com, http://finance.yahoo.com, or www.bloomberg.com) for the latest exchange rates.

TRAVELER'S CHECKS

Traveler's checks (American Express and Visa are the most recognized) are one of the safest and least troublesome means of carrying funds. Several agencies and banks sell them for a small commission. Each agency provides refunds if checks

ESSENTIALS

are lost or stolen, and many provide additional services, such as toll-free refund hotlines abroad, emergency message services, and stolen credit card assistance. Traveler's checks are widely accepted throughout Western Europe, preferably in US currency, and can be exchanged into the local currency's cash upon arrival.

While traveling, keep check receipts and a record of which checks you've cashed separate from the checks themselves. Also leave a list of check numbers with someone at home. Never countersign checks until you're ready to cash them, and always bring your passport with you to cash them. If your checks are lost or stolen, immediately contact a refund center (of the company that issued your checks) to be reimbursed; they may require a police report verifying the loss or theft. Less-touristed countries may not have refund centers at all, in which case you might have to wait to be reimbursed. Ask about toll-free refund hotlines and the location of refund centers when purchasing checks, and always carry emergency cash.

American Express: Call 1800 251 902 in Australia; in New Zealand 0800 441 068; in the UK 0800 521 313; in the US and Canada 800-221-7282. Elsewhere call US collect 801-964-6665; www.americanexpress.com. Traveler's checks are available in 11 currencies at 1-4% commission at banks and AmEx offices, commission-free at AAA offices for AAA members. *Cheques for Two* can be signed by either of 2 traveling partners.

Citicorp: In the US and Canada call 800-645-6556 (24 hr.); elsewhere call US collect 813-623-1709. Traveler's checks (available only in US dollars, British pounds, and German marks) at 1-2% commission.

Thomas Cook MasterCard: In the US and Canada call 800-223-7373; in the UK call 0800 622 101; elsewhere call UK collect 44 17 3331 8950. Checks available in 13 currencies at 2% commission. Thomas Cook offices cash checks commission-free.

Visa: In the US call 800-227-6811; in the UK call 0800 895 078; elsewhere call UK collect + 44 20 7937 8091; www.visa.com. Checks available in most popular currencies.

CREDIT CARDS

Where they are accepted, credit cards often offer superior exchange rates—up to 5% better than the retail rate used by banks and other currency exchange establishments. Credit card companies may also offer services such as insurance or emergency help, and credit cards are sometimes required to reserve hotel rooms or rental cars. **MasterCard** (a.k.a. Eurocard or Access) and **Visa** (a.k.a. Carte Bleue or Barclaycard) are the most welcomed; **American Express** cards work at some ATMs and at AmEx offices and major airports. However, budget travelers may find that some of the establishments they frequent do not accept credit cards.

Credit cards are also useful for **cash advances,** which allow you to withdraw local currency from associated banks and ATMs throughout Western Europe instantly. However, transaction fees for all credit card advances (up to US$10 per advance, plus 2-3% extra on foreign transactions after conversion) tend to make credit cards a more costly way of withdrawing cash than ATMs or traveler's checks. In an emergency, however, the transaction fee may prove worth the cost. To be eligible for an advance, you'll need to get a **Personal Identification Number (PIN)** from your credit card company (see **Cash Cards (ATM Cards),** below). Be sure to check with your credit card company before you leave home, though; in certain circumstances companies have started to charge a foreign transaction fee.

CREDIT CARD COMPANIES. Visa (US ☎ 800-336-8472) and **MasterCard** (US ☎ 800-307-7309) are issued in cooperation with banks and other organizations. Many **American Express** (US ☎ 800-843-2273) cards have annual fees of up to US$55. AmEx cardholders may cash personal checks at AmEx offices abroad, access emergency medical and legal assistance (24hr.; in North America call 800-554-2639, elsewhere call US collect 715-343-7977), and enjoy American Express Travel Service benefits (including plane, hotel, and car rental reservations; baggage loss and flight insurance; mailgram and international cable services; and held mail). The **Discover Card** (in US call 800-347-2683, elsewhere call US collect 801-902-3100) offers cashback bonuses on most purchases, but it may not be readily accepted.

CASH CARDS (ATM CARDS)

Cash cards—popularly called ATM cards—are widespread in Western Europe. Depending on the system that your home bank uses, you can most likely access your personal bank account from abroad. ATMs get the same wholesale exchange rate as credit cards, but there is often a limit on the amount of money you can withdraw per day (around US$500), and computer networks sometimes fail. There is typically also a surcharge of US$1-5 per withdrawal. Be sure to memorize your PIN code in numeric form since machines elsewhere often don't have letters on their keys. Also, if your PIN is longer than four digits, ask your bank whether you need a new number. For more information, see the **Pin Numbers and ATMs** box below.

The two major international money networks are **Cirrus** (US ☎ 800-424-7787) and **PLUS** (US ☎ 800-843-7587). To locate ATMs around the world, call the above numbers, or consult www.visa.com/pd/atm or www.mastercard.com/atm. Major banks that feature Cirrus or Plus ATMs include France's **Carte Bleue Groupe**, Italy's **Banca Monte dei Paschi Di**, Spain's **Banco Santander** and Germany's **Sparkasse**. Most ATMs charge a transaction fee that is paid to the bank that owns the ATM.

Visa TravelMoney allows you to access money from any ATM that accepts Visa cards. (For local customer assistance in Europe, go to www.visa.com/pd/trav to find the specific toll-free number for the country you're in, or call the international Toll-Free AT&T Direct Access Code for your country (www.att.com/traveler). You deposit an amount before you travel (plus a small administration fee), and you can withdraw up to that sum. The cards, which give you the same favorable exchange rate for withdrawals as a regular Visa, are especially useful if you plan to travel through many countries. Obtain a card by either visiting a nearby Thomas Cook or Citicorp office, by calling toll-free in the US ☎ 877-394-2247, or checking with your local bank to see if it issues TravelMoney cards. **Road Cash** (US ☎ 877-762-3227; www.roadcash.com) issues cards in the US with a minimum US$300 deposit.

PIN NUMBERS & ATMS. To use a cash or credit card to withdraw money from a cash machine (ATM) in Europe, you must have a four-digit **Personal Identification Number (PIN)**. If your PIN is longer than four digits, ask your bank whether you can just use the first four, or whether you'll need a new one. **Credit cards** don't usually come with PINs, so if you intend to hit up ATMs in Europe with a credit card to get cash advances, call your credit card company before leaving to request one.

People with alphabetic, rather than numeric, PINs may also be thrown off by the lack of letters on European cash machines. The following chart gives the corresponding numbers to use: 1=QZ; 2=ABC; 3=DEF; 4=GHI; 5=JKL; 6=MNO; 7=PRS; 8=TUV; and 9=WXY. Note that generally if you mistakenly punch the wrong code into the machine three times, it will swallow your card, and getting it back from the bank may prove challenging.

GETTING MONEY FROM HOME

AMERICAN EXPRESS. Cardholders can withdraw cash from their checking accounts at any of AmEx's major offices and many representative offices (up to US$1000 every 21 days; no service charge, no interest). AmEx "Express Cash" withdrawals from any AmEx ATM in Western Europe are automatically deducted from the cardholder's checking account or line of credit. Cardholders may withdraw up to US$1000 in any seven-day period (2% transaction fee for cash, 1% for traveler's checks; minimum US$2.50, maximum US$20). To enroll in the Express Cash program or to locate the nearest Express Cash machine, cardmembers may call 800-227-4669 in the US. Elsewhere call US collect 801 964-6665.

WESTERN UNION. Travelers from the US, Canada, and the UK can wire money abroad through Western Union's money transfer services. In the US call 800-325-

6000; in Canada 800-235-0000; in the UK 0800 833 833. To wire money, track your money, or locate the nearest office, consult www.westernunion.com.

FEDERAL EXPRESS. Some people choose to send cash via FedEx to avoid transmission fees and taxes. While FedEx is reasonably reliable, note that this method is **illegal**. In the US and Canada, FedEx can be reached by calling 800-463-3339; in the UK 0800 123 800; in Ireland 800 535 800; in Australia 13 26 10; in New Zealand 0800 733 339; and in South Africa 011 923 8000.

US STATE DEPARTMENT (US CITIZENS ONLY). In dire emergencies only, the US State Department will forward money within hours to the nearest consular office, which will then disburse it according to instructions for a US$15 fee. If you wish to use this service, you must contact the Overseas Citizens Service division of the US State Department (☎202-647-5225; nights, Sundays, and holidays 202-647-4000).

COSTS

The cost of your trip will vary considerably, depending on where you go, how you travel, and where you stay. The single biggest cost of your trip will probably be your round-trip **airfare** to Europe (see p. 45); a **railpass** would be another major predeparture expense (see p. 55). Before you go, spend some time calculating a reasonable per-day **budget** that will meet your needs.

STAYING ON A BUDGET. To give you a general idea, a bare-bones day in Western Europe (camping or sleeping in hostels, buying food at supermarkets) would cost about US$25-35, excluding the cost of a plane ticket and railpass; a slightly more comfortable day (sleeping in hostels and the occasional budget hotel, eating one meal a day at a restaurant, going out at night) would run US$35-50; and for a luxurious day, the sky's the limit. Countries such as Britain, France, and Switzerland tend to be more costly for tourists, while Spain and Greece are relatively inexpensive alternatives. Also, don't forget to factor in emergency reserve funds (at least US$200) when planning how much money you'll need.

TIPS FOR SAVING MONEY. Considering that saving just a few dollars a day over the course of your trip might pay for days or weeks of additional travel, the art of penny-pinching is well worth learning. Learn to take advantage of freebies: for example, museums will typically be free once a week or once a month, and cities often host free open-air concerts and cultural events (especially in the summer). Bring a sleepsack (see p. 34) to save on sheet charges in European hostels, and do your laundry in the sink (unless you're explicitly prohibited from doing so). You can split accommodations costs (in hotels and some hostels) with trustworthy fellow travelers; multi-bed rooms almost always work out cheaper per person than singles. The same principle will also work for cutting down on the cost of restaurant meals. You can also buy food in supermarkets instead of eating out; you'd be surprised how tasty (and cheap) simple bread can be with cheese or spread.

With that said, **don't go overboard with your budget obsession.** Though staying within your budget is important, don't do so at the expense of your sanity or health. Going to Munich without hitting a beer garden or visiting London without seeing a play simply because it's "out of your budget" defeats the purpose of your visit.

TIPPING AND BARGAINING

In most Western European countries, the 5-10% gratuity is already included in the food service bill, but an additional 5-10% tip for very good service is often also polite. Note that in Germany, the tip is handed directly to the server instead of being left on the table. For other services such as taxis or hairdressers, a 10-15% tip is recommended. Also, watch and learn from other customers to gauge what are the appropriate actions. Bargaining is an essential skill for shopping in Greece; otherwise, bargaining will be a very limited factor in your European shopping and will probably only be useful at places like outdoor markets in Italy, Britain, and Ireland.

SAFETY AND SECURITY

PERSONAL SAFETY

EXPLORING. To avoid unwanted attention, try to blend in as much as possible. Respecting local customs (in many cases, dressing more conservatively) may placate would-be hecklers. Familiarize yourself with your surroundings before setting out, and carry yourself with confidence; if you must check a map on the street, duck into a shop. If you are traveling alone, be sure someone at home knows your itinerary, and never admit that you're traveling alone.

When walking at night, stick to busy, well-lit streets and avoid dark alleyways. Do not attempt to cross through parks, parking lots, or other large, deserted areas. Look for children playing, women walking in the open, and other signs of an active community. If you feel uncomfortable, leave as quickly and directly as you can, but don't allow fear of the unknown to turn you into a hermit. Careful, persistent exploration will build confidence and make your stay even more rewarding.

SELF DEFENSE. There is no sure-fire way to avoid all the threatening situations you might encounter when you travel, but a good self-defense course will give you concrete ways to react to unwanted advances. **Impact, Prepare, and Model Mugging** can refer you to local self-defense courses in the US (☎ 800-345-5425; info@impact-safety.org; www.impactsafety.org). Visit the website at www.impactsafety.org/chapters.htm for a list of nearby chapters. Workshops (2-3hr.) start at US$75; full courses run US$340-500.

TRANSPORTATION. If you are using a **car,** learn local driving signals and wear a seatbelt. Children under 40 lbs. should ride only in a specially designed carseat, available for a small fee from most car rental agencies. Study route maps before you hit the road, and if you plan on spending a lot of time on the road, you may want to bring spare parts. If your car breaks down, wait for the police to assist you. For long drives in desolate areas, invest in a cellular phone and a roadside assistance program. Be sure to park your vehicle in a garage or well traveled area, and use a steering wheel locking device in larger cities. **Sleeping in your car** is one of the most dangerous (and often illegal) ways to get your rest.

For info on the perils of **hitchhiking,** see p. 53.

TERRORISM AND CIVIL UNREST. Risks tend to be localized and rarely directed toward tourists; when in doubt, ask locals. Still, certain areas occasionally have moments of unrest: **Corsica** in Italy and the **Pays Basque** in France have well-established separatist movements, and the **November 17** group in Greece are well known for their anti-Western and anti-NATO acts, but they do not target tourists. Though the peace process in **Northern Ireland** is progressing, tension and violence tend to surround the July "marching season," when Protestants hold celebratory parades that provoke the Catholics. For more information on terrorism and civil unrest, contact the travel advisories listed in the box below.

FINANCIAL SECURITY

PROTECTING YOUR VALUABLES. There are a few steps you can take to minimize the financial risk associated with traveling. First, **bring as little with you as possible.** Leave expensive personal belongings (watches, jewelry, electronic equipment) at home; chances are you'd break them, lose them, or get sick of lugging them around anyway. Second, buy a few combination **padlocks** to secure your belongings either in your pack—which you should **never leave unattended**—or in a hostel or train station locker. Third, **carry as little cash as possible;** instead, carry traveler's checks and ATM/credit cards in a **money belt**—not a "fanny pack"—along with your passport and ID cards. Fourth, **keep a small cash reserve separate from your primary stash.**

TRAVEL ADVISORIES. The following government offices provide travel information and advisories by telephone, by fax, or via the web:

Australian Department of Foreign Affairs and Trade: ☎02 6261 1111; www.dfat.gov.au.

Canadian Department of Foreign Affairs and International Trade (DFAIT): In Canada call 800-267-8316, elsewhere call 613-944-4000; http://voyage.dfait-maeci.gc.ca. Call for their free booklet, *Bon Voyage...But.*

New Zealand Ministry of Foreign Affairs: ☎04 494 8500; fax 494 8506; www.mft.govt.nz/trav.html.

United Kingdom Foreign and Commonwealth Office: ☎020 7008 0232; fax 7008 0155; www.fco.gov.uk.

US Department of State: ☎202-647-5225, automatic faxback 202-647-3000; http://travel.state.gov. For *A Safe Trip Abroad,* call 202-512-1800.

About US$50 (US$ is best) should be sewn into or stored in the depths of your pack, along with your traveler's check numbers and important photocopies.

CON ARTISTS & PICKPOCKETS. Among the more colorful aspects of large cities are **con artists.** They often work in groups, and children are among the most effective. They possess an innumerable range of ruses. Beware of certain classics: sob stories that require money, rolls of bills "found" on the street, or mustard spilled (or saliva spit) onto your shoulder to distract you while they snatch your bag. Don't ever hand over your passport to someone whose authority you question (ask to accompany them to a police station if they insist), and **don't ever let your passport out of your sight.** Similarly, don't let your bag out of sight; never trust a "station-porter" who insists on carrying your bag or stowing it in the baggage compartment or a "new friend" who offers to guard your bag while you buy a train ticket or use the restroom. Beware of **pickpockets** in city crowds, especially on public transportation. Also, be alert in public telephone booths. If you must say your calling card number, do so very quietly; if you punch it in, make sure no one can look over your shoulder.

ACCOMMODATIONS & TRANSPORTATION. Never leave your belongings unattended; crime occurs in even the most demure-looking hostel or hotel. Bring your own **padlock** for hostel lockers, and don't ever store valuables in any locker.

Be particularly careful on **buses** and **trains;** horror stories abound about determined thieves who wait for travelers to fall asleep. Carry your backpack in front of you where you can see it. When traveling with others, sleep in alternate shifts. When alone, use good judgment in selecting a train compartment: never stay in an empty one, and use a lock to secure your pack to the luggage rack. Try to sleep on top bunks with your luggage stored above you (if not in bed with you), and keep important documents and other valuables on your person.

If traveling by **car,** don't leave valuables (such as radios or luggage) in it while you are away. If your tape deck or radio is removable, hide it in the trunk or take it with you. Similarly, hide baggage in the trunk—although savvy thieves can still tell if a car is heavily loaded by the way it sits on its tires.

DRUGS AND ALCOHOL

Drug and alcohol laws vary widely throughout Europe: for example, in The Netherlands you can buy soft drugs on the open market, while in Austria you can find yourself in deep trouble with a drop of alcohol in your blood while driving. You're subject to the laws of the country in which you travel when you're abroad, so familiarize yourself with those laws before leaving. If you carry **prescription drugs,** it is vital to have both a copy of the prescriptions themselves and a note from a doctor, especially at border crossings. **Avoid public drunkenness;** it is culturally unacceptable and against the law in many countries, and can also jeopardize your safety.

TROUBLE WITH THE LAW. Travelers who run into trouble with the law, both accidentally and knowingly, do not carry over the rights of their home country; instead, they have the same rights as a citizen of the country they are in. Law mandates that police notify the embassy of a person's home country if they are arrested. Once in custody, a traveler is entitled to a visit from a consular officer. These officers can provide lists of local law firms, information on the local legal system, and can contact friends and family. They cannot, however, demand the release of citizens abroad. Being mindful of a country's laws before setting out to travel is the best way to avoid trouble with the law. US citizens should check out the Department of State's website (www.state.gov) for more information.

HEALTH

Common sense is the simplest prescription for good health while you travel. Drink lots of fluids to prevent dehydration and constipation. Wear sturdy, broken-in shoes and clean socks, and use talcum powder to keep your feet dry.

BEFORE YOU GO

Preparation can help minimize the likelihood of contracting a disease and maximize the chances of receiving effective health care in the event of an emergency. For tips on packing a basic **first-aid kit** and other health essentials, see p. 35.

In your **passport,** write the names of any people whom you wish to be contacted in case of a medical emergency, and also list any allergies or medical conditions of which you would want doctors to be aware. Matching a prescription to a foreign equivalent is not always easy, safe, or possible. Carry up-to-date, legible prescriptions or a statement from your doctor stating the medication's trade name, manufacturer, chemical name, and dosage. While traveling, be sure to keep all medication with you in your carry-on luggage.

Many of the drugs commonly available in the US, Canada, Australia, Britain, Ireland, and South Africa are available throughout Western Europe as well, along with several others that may not be available in your home country.

IMMUNIZATIONS AND PRECAUTIONS

Travelers over two years old should be sure that the following vaccines are up to date: MMR (for measles, mumps, and rubella); DTaP or Td (for diptheria, tetanus, and pertussis), OPV (for polio), HbCV (for haemophilus influenza B), and HBV (for hepatitis B), and the varicella vaccine (for those who have never had the chicken pox; pregnant women should NOT get this vaccine). Other highly recommended vaccines are the influenza and pneumococcal vaccines. Hepatitis A vaccine and/or immune globulin (IG) is recommended for travelers going to Eastern or Southern Europe. While yellow fever is only endemic to parts of South America and sub-Saharan Africa, many countries may deny entrance to travelers arriving from these zones without a certificate of vaccination. For more **region-specific information** on vaccination requirements, as well as recommendations on immunizations and prophylaxis, consult the CDC (see below) in the US or the equivalent in your home country, and check with a doctor for guidance.

USEFUL ORGANIZATIONS & PUBLICATIONS

The **US Centers for Disease Control and Prevention (CDC; ☎**877-FYI-TRIP; www.cdc.gov/travel) maintains an international fax information service and an international traveler hotline (☎404-332-4559). The CDC's comprehensive booklet *Health Information for International Travel*, an annual rundown of disease, immunization, and general health advice, is free online or US$25 via the Public Health Foundation (☎877-252-1200). Consult the appropriate government agency of your home country for consular information sheets on health, entry requirements, and other issues for various countries (see the listings in the box on **Travel Advisories,** p. 28). For quick information on health and other travel warnings, call the **Overseas Citizens Services** (☎ 202-647-5225; after-hours 202-647-4000), or contact a passport agency, embassy, or consulate abroad. US citizens can send a self-addressed, stamped envelope to the Overseas Citizens Services, Bureau of Consular Affairs #4811, US Department of State, Washington, D.C. 20520. For information on medical evacuation services and travel insurance firms, see the US government's website at http://travel.state.gov/medical.html or the **British Foreign and Commonwealth Office** website at www.fco.gov.uk.

For detailed information on travel health, including a country-by-country overview of diseases, try the *International Travel Health Guide*, by Stuart Rose (Travel Medicine, US$24.95; www.travmed.com). For general health information, contact the American Red Cross (☎ 800-564-1234).

MEDICAL ASSISTANCE ON THE ROAD

The health care systems in the countries covered by *Let's Go: Western Europe* are of excellent quality overall and medical services are widely available in just about every town and city. Large cities and many smaller towns will have English-speaking doctors. Public hospitals are much more common and are usually comparable to the quality of those in any other major Western industrialized country, but private clinics are especially recommended in Greece. All EU citizens can receive free first-aid and emergency services with the presentation of an E11 form. Make sure to have adequate health insurance that covers various emergency situations while traveling abroad (p. 33).

If you are concerned about being able to access medical support while traveling, there are special support services you may employ. The *MedPass* from **GlobalCare, Inc.,** 2001 Westside Pkwy. #120, Alpharetta, GA 30004, USA (☎ 800-860-1111; fax 770-475-0058; www.globalems.com), provides 24hr. international medical assistance, support, and medical evacuation resources. The **International Association for Medical Assistance to Travelers** (IAMAT; US ☎ 716-754-4883, Canada ☎ 416-652-0137, New Zealand ☎ 03 352 20 53; www.sentex.net/~iamat) has free membership, lists English-speaking doctors worldwide, and offers detailed info on immunization requirements and sanitation. If your regular **insurance** policy does not cover travel abroad, you may wish to purchase additional coverage (see p. 33).

Those with medical conditions (diabetes, allergies to antibiotics, epilepsy, heart conditions) may want to obtain a stainless-steel **Medic Alert** ID tag (first year US$35, annually thereafter $20) that identifies the condition and gives a 24hr. collect-call number. Contact the Medic Alert Foundation, 2323 Colorado Ave, Turlock, CA 95382, USA (☎ 888-633-4298; www.medicalert.org). The **American Diabetes Association**, 1660 Duke St., Alexandria, VA 22314 (☎ 800 232 34 72; www.diabetes.org), offers copies of the article "Travel and Diabetes" and multilingual diabetic ID card.

ONCE IN WESTERN EUROPE

ENVIRONMENTAL HAZARDS

Heat exhaustion and dehydration: Heat exhaustion can quickly overcome you while hiking around coastal and Mediterranean countries such as southern France, Spain, Portugal, Greece, and Italy, where temperatures easily soar over 90 degrees Fahrenheit (30 degrees Celsius). Heat exhaustion, characterized by dehydration and salt deficiency, can lead to fatigue, headaches, and wooziness. Avoid it by drinking plenty of fluids, eating salty foods (e.g. crackers), and avoiding dehydrating beverages (e.g. alcohol, coffee, tea, and caffeinated soda). Continuous heat stress can eventually lead to heatstroke, characterized by a rising temperature, severe headache, and cessation of sweating. Victims should be cooled off with wet towels and taken to a doctor.

Hypothermia and frostbite: Europe also has plentiful wintry attractions, and the Alps will have definite risks for cold weather health hazards. A rapid drop in body temperature is the clearest sign of overexposure to cold. Victims may also shiver, feel exhausted, have poor coordination or slurred speech, hallucinate, or suffer from amnesia. **Do not let hypothermia victims fall asleep,** or their body temperature will continue to drop and they may die. To avoid hypothermia, keep dry, wear layers, and stay out of the wind. When the temperature is below freezing, watch out for frostbite. If the skin turns white, waxy, and cold, do not rub the area. Drink warm beverages, get dry, and slowly warm the area with dry fabric or steady body contact until a doctor can be found.

High altitude: When hiking through mountainous areas like the Pyrenees or the Alps, allow your body a couple of days to adjust to the thin air before exerting yourself. Note that alcohol is more potent and UV rays are stronger at high elevations.

Sunburn: If you're prone to sunburn, bring sunscreen with you (it's often more expensive abroad), and apply it liberally and often to avoid burns and risk of skin cancer. If you are planning on spending time near water, in the desert, or in the snow, you are at greater risk of getting burned, even through clouds. If you are sunburned, drink more fluids than usual and apply an aloe-based lotion.

INSECT-BORNE DISEASES

Many diseases are transmitted by insects—mainly mosquitoes, fleas, ticks, and lice. Be aware of insects in wet or forested areas, especially while hiking and camping. Mosquitoes are most active from dusk to dawn. Wear long pants and long sleeves, tuck your pants into your socks, and buy a mosquito net. Use insect repellents, such as DEET, and soak or spray your gear with permethrin (licensed in the US for use on clothing). Consider natural repellents like vitamin B-12 or garlic pills. To stop the itch after being bitten, try Calamine lotion or topical cortisones (like Cortaid), or take a bath with a half-cup of baking soda or oatmeal. Ticks—responsible for Lyme and other diseases—can be particularly dangerous in rural and forested regions throughout Western Europe. Pause periodically while walking to brush off ticks using a fine-toothed comb on your neck and scalp. Do not try to remove ticks by burning them or coating them with nail polish remover or petroleum jelly. If you find a tick attached to your skin, grasp the head with tweezers as close to your skin as possible and apply slow, steady traction.

Leishmaniasis: A parasite transmitted by sand flies and humans, leishmaniasis has been reported in Switzerland, Italy, Spain, and southern France. Common symptoms are fever, fatigue and weakness, and swelling of the spleen. Leishmania infection can cause the skin disease cutaneous leishmaniasis, skin lesions, and can affect the mucous membranes, producing ulcers. There is a treatment, but currently no vaccine.

Lyme disease: A bacterial infection carried by very tiny deer ticks and marked by a circular bull's-eye rash of 2 in. or greater diameter. Later symptoms include fever, headache, fatigue, and aches and pains. Antibiotics are effective if administered early. Left untreated, Lyme can cause problems in joints, the heart, and the nervous system. Removing a tick within 24 hours greatly reduces the risk of infection.

Tick-borne encephalitis: A viral infection of the central nervous system transmitted during the summer by tick bites (primarily in wooded areas) or by consumption of unpasteurized dairy products. Symptoms range from nothing to headaches and flu-like symptoms to swelling of the brain (encephalitis). While a vaccine is available in Europe, the immunization schedule is impractical, and the risk of contracting the disease is relatively low, especially if precautions are taken against tick bites. This disease occurs in wooded areas of Western Europe, particularly in Austria, Germany, and Switzerland.

FOOD- & WATER-BORNE DISEASES

Prevention is the best cure: be sure that your food is properly cooked and the water you drink is clean. Peel fruits and veggies and try to avoid tap water (including ice cubes and anything washed in tap water, like salad). Watch out for food from markets or street vendors that may have been cooked in unhygienic conditions. Other culprits are raw shellfish, unpasteurized milk, and sauces containing raw eggs. Buy bottled water, or purify your own water by bringing it to a rolling boil or treating it with **iodine tablets;** note however that some parasites such as *giardia* have exteriors that resist iodine treatment, making boiling a more reliable treatment for water.

Always wash your hands before eating or bring a quick-drying purifying liquid hand cleaner. Your bowels will thank you.

Mad Cow Disease: Bovine spongiform encephalopathy (BSE), better known as Mad Cow Disease, is a chronic degenerative disease affecting the central nervous system of cattle. The disease broke out in alarming numbers of cattle in Western Europe in 2001. The human variant is called Cruetzfeldt-Jakob disease (nvCJD), and both forms of the disease involve invariably fatal brain diseases. Information on nvCJD is not conclusive, but the disease is supposedly caused by consuming infected beef; however, the risk is very small (around 1 case per 10 billion servings of meat). It is believed that consuming milk and milk products does not pose a risk.

Parasites: Microbes, tapeworms, etc. that hide in unsafe water and food. **Giardiasis,** for example, is acquired by drinking untreated water from streams or lakes all over the world (including Western Europe). Symptoms include swollen glands or lymph nodes, fever, rashes or itchiness, digestive problems, eye problems, and anemia. Boil water, wear shoes, avoid bugs, and eat only cooked food.

Traveler's diarrhea: Results from drinking untreated water or eating uncooked foods; a temporary (and fairly common) reaction to the bacteria in new food ingredients. Symptoms include nausea, bloating, urgency, and malaise. Try quick-energy, non-sugary foods with protein and carbohydrates to keep your strength up. Over-the-counter anti-diarrheals (e.g. Immodium) may counteract the problems, but can complicate serious infections. The most dangerous side effect is dehydration; drink 8 oz. of water with ½ tsp. of sugar or honey and a pinch of salt, try uncaffeinated soft drinks, or munch on salted crackers. If you develop a fever or your symptoms don't go away after 4-5 days, consult a doctor. Consult a doctor for treatment of diarrhea in children.

OTHER INFECTIOUS DISEASES

Foot and Mouth Disease (FMD): Foot and Mouth Disease experienced one of its worst outbreaks in 2001, largely in the United Kingdom and other countries in Western Europe. FMD is easily transmissible between cloven-hooved animals (cows, pigs, sheep, goats and deer), but does not pose a health threat to humans, causing few or mild symptoms. Western European countries have not, as of publication, restricted travel to infested countries, but do limit excursions to farms and other rural areas. FMD is believed to be killed by heat, making cooked meats apparently safe for consumption; fish, poultry, fruits, and vegetables pose no FMD risk.

Hepatitis B: A viral infection of the liver transmitted via bodily fluids or needle-sharing. Symptoms may not surface until years after infection. Vaccinations are recommended for health-care workers, sexually active travelers, and anyone planning to seek medical treatment abroad. The 3-shot vaccination series must begin 6 months before traveling.

Hepatitis C: Like Hep B, but the mode of transmission differs. IV drug users, those with occupational exposure to blood, hemodialysis patients, and recipients of blood transfusions are at the highest risk, but the disease can also be spread through sexual contact or sharing items like razors and toothbrushes that may have traces of blood on them.

Rabies: Transmitted through the saliva of infected animals; fatal if untreated. By the time symptoms appear (thirst and muscle spasms), the disease is in its terminal stage. If you are bitten, wash the wound thoroughly, seek immediate medical care, and try to have the animal located. A rabies vaccine, which consists of 3 shots given over a 21-day period, is available but is only semi-effective.

AIDS, HIV, AND STDS

For detailed information on **Acquired Immune Deficiency Syndrome (AIDS)** in Western Europe, call the **US Centers for Disease Control**'s 24hr. hotline at ☎ 800-342-2437, or contact the **Joint United Nations Programme on HIV/AIDS (UNAIDS)**, 20, av. Appia, CH-1211 Geneva 27, Switzerland (☎ 41 22 791 36 66; fax 22 791 41 87). The Council on International Educational Exchange's pamphlet, *Travel Safe: AIDS and International Travel*, is posted on their website (www.ciee.org/Isp/safety/travelsafe.htm), along with links to other online and phone resources. Note that many Western European countries screen incoming travelers for AIDS, primarily those planning extended visits for work or study, and some deny entrance to those who test HIV-positive. Contact the consulate of the country you will be going to for up-to-date information.

Sexually transmitted diseases (STDs) such as gonorrhea, chlamydia, genital warts, syphilis, and herpes are easier to catch than HIV and can be just as deadly. **Hepatitis B and C** are also serious STDs (see the listings above for these diseases). Though condoms may protect you from some STDs, oral or even tactile contact can lead to transmission. Warning signs include swelling, sores, bumps, or blisters on sex organs, the rectum, or the mouth; burning and pain during urination and bowel movements; itching around sex organs; swelling or redness of the throat; and flu-like symptoms. If these symptoms develop, see a doctor immediately.

WOMEN'S HEALTH

Women traveling in unsanitary conditions are vulnerable to **urinary tract** and **bladder infections,** common and very uncomfortable bacterial conditions that cause a burning sensation and painful (sometimes frequent) urination. To try to avoid these infections, drink plenty of vitamin-C-rich juice and clean water, and urinate frequently, especially right after intercourse. Untreated, these infections can lead to kidney infections, sterility, and even death. If symptoms persist, see a doctor.

Vaginal yeast infections may flare up in hot and humid climates. Wearing loosely fitting trousers or a skirt and cotton underwear will help, as will over-the-counter remedies like Monistat or Gynelotrimin. Bring supplies from home if you are prone to infection, as they may be difficult to find on the road. In a pinch, some travelers use a natural alternative such as eating plain yogurt.

Since **tampons, pads,** and reliable **contraceptive devices** are sometimes hard to find abroad and your preferred brand will not always be available, bring supplies with you. If you're on the **pill,** bring enough pills to allow for loss or extended stays. If you need an **abortion** while abroad, in the UK contact Marie Stopes International, (☎0171 574 7400, fax 574 7417, services@stopes.org.uk, www.mariestopes.org.uk). Elsewhere in Europe, see www.ippf.org/regions/europe for country profiles and organizations to contact. In some countries, especially in eastern and southern Europe, it may be necessary to leave the country to find safe abortion services.

INSURANCE

Travel insurance generally covers four basic areas: medical/health problems, property loss, trip cancellation/interruption, and emergency evacuation. Although your regular insurance policies may well extend to travel-related accidents, you may consider purchasing separate travel insurance if the cost of potential trip cancellation/interruption is greater than you can absorb. Prices for travel insurance purchased separately generally run about US$50 per week for full coverage, while trip cancellation/interruption may be purchased separately at a rate of about $5.50 per $100 of coverage.

Medical insurance (especially university policies) often covers costs incurred abroad; check with your provider. **US Medicare** does not cover foreign travel. **Canadians** are protected by their home province's health insurance plan for up to 90 days after leaving the country; check with the provincial Ministry of Health or Health Plan Headquarters for details. **Australians** traveling in the UK, The Netherlands, or Italy are entitled to many of the services provided at home as part of the Reciprocal Health Care Agreement. **Homeowners' insurance** (or your family's coverage) often covers theft during travel and loss of travel documents (passport, plane ticket, rail-pass, etc.) up to US$500. Again, check with your insurance provider.

ISIC and **ITIC** (see p. 19) provide basic insurance benefits, including US$100 per day of in-hospital sickness for up to 60 days, $3000 of accident-related medical reimbursement, and $25,000 for emergency medical transport. Cardholders have access to a toll-free 24hr. helpline (run by the insurance provider TravelGuard) for medical, legal, and financial emergencies overseas (US and Canada ☎ 877-370-4742, elsewhere call US collect 715-345-0505). **American Express** (US ☎ 800-528-4800) grants most cardholders automatic car rental insurance (collision and theft, but not liability) and ground travel accident coverage of $100,000 on flight purchases made with the card.

INSURANCE PROVIDERS. Council and **STA** (see p. 45) offer a range of plans that can supplement your basic coverage. Other private insurance providers in the US and Canada include: **Access America** (☎ 800-284-8300); **Berkely Group/Carefree Travel Insurance** (☎ 800-645-2424; www.berkely.com); **Globalcare Travel Insurance** (☎ 800-821-2488; www.globalcare-cocco.com); and **Travel Assistance International** (☎ 800-821-2828; www.worldwide-assistance.com). Providers in the **UK** include **Campus Travel** (☎ 018 6525 8000) and **Columbus Travel Insurance** (☎ 020 7375 0011). In **Australia**, try **CIC Insurance** (☎ 9202 8000).

PACKING

Pack lightly. Lay out only what you absolutely need, then take half the clothes and twice the money. The less you have, the less you have to lose (or store, or carry on your back). Any extra space left will be useful for any souvenirs or items you might pick up along the way. If you plan to do a lot of hiking, also see **Camping & the Outdoors,** p. 38. Europe's varied climes provide a wealth of options for packing, so review the major stops on your itinerary. While shorts, swim gear, and sandals may be the rule of thumb for warm Mediterranean countries like Spain, Greece, or Italy, sturdy shoes and a jacket will be necessary for outdoor adventures in Switzerland and Germany.

LUGGAGE. If you plan to hike your way through Western Europe and cover most of your itinerary by foot, a sturdy **frame backpack** is unbeatable. (For the basics on buying a pack, see p. 39.) Toting a **suitcase** or **trunk** is fine if you plan to live in one or two major cities, like Rome, London, or Paris, and explore from there, but a very bad idea if you're going to be moving around a lot. In addition to your main piece of luggage, a **daypack** (a small backpack or courier bag) is a must.

CLOTHING. No matter when you're traveling, it's always a good idea to bring a **warm jacket,** fleece pullover or wool sweater, a **rain jacket** (Gore-Tex® is both waterproof and breathable), sturdy shoes or **hiking boots,** and **thick socks. Flip-flops** or waterproof sandals are must-haves for grubby hostel showers. You may also want to add one outfit beyond the jeans and T-shirt uniform, and maybe a nicer pair of shoes if you have the room. If you plan to visit any religious or cultural sites, such as Vatican City, remember that you'll need something besides tank tops and shorts to be respectful.

SLEEPSACK. Some hostels require that you either provide your own linen or rent sheets from them. Save cash by making your own sleepsack: fold a full-size sheet in half the long way, then sew it closed along the long side and one of the short sides.

CONVERTERS & ADAPTERS. In Western Europe, electricity is 220 volts AC and 240V in Britain and Ireland—enough to fry any 110V North American appliance. (220/240V electrical appliances don't like 110V current, either.) **Americans** and **Canadians** should buy an **adapter** (which changes the shape of the plug) and a **converter** (which changes the voltage; US$20). Don't make the mistake of using only an adapter (unless appliance instructions explicitly state otherwise). **New Zealanders** and **South Africans** (who both use 220V at home) as well as **Australians** (who use 240/250V) won't need a converter, but will need a set of adapters to use electronics.

TOILETRIES. Toothbrushes, towels, cold-water soap, talcum powder (to keep feet dry), deodorant, razors, tampons, and condoms are often available, but may be difficult to find, so bring extras along. **Contact lenses,** on the other hand, may be expensive and difficult to find, so bring enough extra pairs and solution for your entire trip. Also bring your glasses and a copy of your prescription in case you need emergency replacements. If you use heat-disinfection, either switch temporarily to a chemical disinfection system (check first to make sure it's safe with your brand of lenses), or buy a converter to 220/240V.

FIRST-AID KIT. For a basic first-aid kit, pack: bandages, pain reliever, antibiotic cream, a thermometer, a Swiss Army knife, tweezers, moleskin, decongestant, motion-sickness remedy, diarrhea or upset-stomach medication (Pepto Bismol or Imodium), an antihistamine, sunscreen, insect repellent, burn ointment, and a syringe for emergencies (get an explanatory letter from your doctor).

FILM. Film and developing in Western Europe are expensive, so consider bringing enough film for your entire trip and developing it at home. Less serious photographers may want to bring a **disposable camera** or two rather than an expensive permanent one. Despite disclaimers, airport security X-rays *can* fog film, so buy a lead-lined pouch at a camera store or ask security to hand-inspect it. Always pack film in your carry-on luggage, since higher-intensity X-rays are used on checked luggage.

OTHER USEFUL ITEMS. For safety purposes, you should bring a **money belt** and small **padlock.** Basic **outdoors equipment** (plastic water bottle, compass, waterproof matches, pocketknife, sunglasses, sunscreen, hat) may also prove useful. **Quick repairs** of torn garments can be done on the road with a needle and thread; also consider bringing electrical tape for patching tears. Doing your **laundry** by hand (where it is allowed) is both cheaper and more convenient than doing it at a laundromat—bring detergent, a small rubber ball to stop up the sink, and string for a makeshift clothes line. **Other things** you're liable to forget: an umbrella; sealable **plastic bags** (for damp clothes, soap, food, shampoo, and other spillables); an **alarm clock;** safety pins; rubber bands; a flashlight; earplugs; garbage bags; and a small **calculator.**

IMPORTANT DOCUMENTS. Don't forget your passport, traveler's checks, ATM and/or credit cards, and adequate ID (see p. 19). Also check that you have any of the following that might apply to you: a hosteling membership card (see p. 36); driver's license (see p. 19); travel insurance form (see p. 33); or a rail or bus pass (see p. 43).

ACCOMMODATIONS

HOSTELS

Western Europe in the summer is overrun by young budget travelers. Hostels are the hub of this subculture, providing opportunities for young people from all over the world to meet, find travel partners, and learn about places to visit. At US$10-25 per night, only camping is cheaper. Guests tend to be in their teens and 20s, but most hostels welcome travelers of all ages, though some German hostels are only open to those under 26. In northern Europe, especially in Germany and Denmark, many hostels have special family rooms. In the average hostel, however, you and anywhere from one to 50 roommates will sleep on bunk beds in a gender-segregated room, with common bathrooms and a lounge down the hall. The hostel warden may be a laid-back student, a hippie dropout, or a crotchety disciplinarian. Hostels sometimes have kitchens for your use, bike or moped rentals, storage areas, and/or laundry facilities.

Some hostels close during certain daytime lockout hours (from morning to mid-afternoon), have a curfew (a distinct cramp in your style if you plan to rage in town), don't accept reservations, or impose a maximum stay. Conditions are generally spartan and crowded, and you may run into screaming pre-teen tour groups. Quality varies dramatically: some hostels are set in gorgeous castles, others in run-down barracks. Most hostels prohibit sleeping bags: you can typically rent sheets from them, or you can avoid the charge by making a sleepsack (see p. 34).

ESSENTIALS

HOSTELS.net
Home of Hostels of Europe

[1 Use your Hostels of Europe Card

In Europe's
300 Top
Independent
Hostels in 25
countries
(for 5 to 15% discounts on beds and tours)

[2 Use Hostels.net to reserve ahead

Fast & Secure Online Reservations
at the the Hostels of Europe.

Purchase online at www.hostels.net

HOSTELLING INTERNATIONAL

A hostel membership allows you to stay at hostels throughout Western Europe at unbeatable prices, and you usually not need be a youth to benefit. Joining the youth hostel association in your own country (listed below) automatically grants you membership privileges in **Hostelling International (HI)**, a federation of national hosteling associations. HI hostels are scattered throughout Western Europe and are typically less expensive than private hostels—affiliates comply with given standards and regulations, and normally display the blue HI triangle. *Hostelling International Guide to Europe* (UK£8 or US$11) lists every HI-affiliated hostel in Europe and details the **International Booking Network** (Australia ☎ 029 261 1111; Canada ☎ 800-663-5777; England and Wales ☎ 162 958 1418; Northern Ireland ☎ 123 232 4733; Republic of Ireland ☎ 01 830 1766; NZ ☎ 03 379 9808; Scotland ☎ 870 155 3255; US ☎ 800-909-4776; www.hostelbooking.com). HI's umbrella organization's web page (www.iyhf.org) lists the web addresses and phone numbers of all national associations and is a great place to research hostelling of specific regions. Other hostelling websites include www.hostels.com and www.hostelplanet.com.

Most HI hostels also honor **guest memberships**—you'll get a blank card with space for six validation stamps. Each night you'll pay a nonmember supplement (one-sixth the membership fee) and earn one guest stamp; get six stamps, and you're a member. This system works well in most of Western Europe, but you may occasionally need to remind the hostel reception. Most student travel agencies (see p. 45) sell HI cards, as do all of the national hosteling organizations listed below. All prices listed below are valid for **one-year memberships** unless otherwise noted.

A HOSTELER'S BILL OF RIGHTS. Unless we state otherwise, you can assume that every hostel we list has certain standard features: no lockout, no curfew, free hot showers, secure luggage storage, and no key deposit.

An Óige (Irish Youth Hostel Association), 61 Mountjoy St., Dublin 7 (☎01 830 4555; fax 830 5808; anoige@iol.ie; www.irelandyha.org). IR£10/€12.70, under 18 IR£4/€5.10.

Australian Youth Hostels Association (AYHA), Level 3, 10 Mallett St., Camperdown NSW 2050 (☎02 9565 1699; fax 9565 1325; www.yha.org.au). AUS$52, under 18 AUS$16.

Hostelling International-American Youth Hostels (HI-AYH), 733 15th St. NW #840, Washington, D.C. 20005 (☎202-783-6161; fax 783-6171; www.hiayh.org). US$25, under 18 free.

Hostelling International-Canada (HI-C), 400-205 Catherine St., Ottawa, ON K2P 1C3 (☎800-663-5777 or 613-237-7884; fax 237-7868; www.hostellingintl.ca). CDN$35, under 18 free.

Hostelling International Northern Ireland (HINI), 22-32 Donegall Rd., Belfast BT12 5JN, Northern Ireland (☎028 9031 5435; fax 02890 43 96 99; www.hini.org.uk). UK£10, under 18 £6.

Hostels Association of South Africa, 3rd fl. 73 St. George's St. Mall, P.O. Box 4402, Cape Town 8000 (☎021 424 2511; fax 424 4119; www.hisa.org.za). ZAR45.

Scottish Youth Hostels Association (SYHA), 7 Glebe Crescent, Stirling FK8 2JA (☎017 8689 1400; fax 017 8689 1333; www.syha.org.uk). UK£6.

Youth Hostels Association (England and Wales) Ltd., Trevelyan House, 8 St. Stephen's Hill, St. Albans, Hertfordshire AL1 2DY, UK (☎0870 870 8808; fax 017 2784 4126; www.yha.org.uk). UK£12.50, under 18 £6.25, families £25.

Youth Hostels Association of New Zealand (YHANZ), P.O. Box 436, 193 Cashel St., 3rd Floor Union House, Christchurch 1 (☎03 379 9970; fax 03 365 4476; www.yha.org.nz). NZ$40, under 17 free.

OTHER TYPES OF ACCOMMODATIONS

YMCAS AND YWCAS

Young Men's Christian Association (YMCA) lodgings are usually cheaper than a hotel but more expensive than a hostel. Not all YMCA locations offer lodging; those that do are often located in urban downtowns. Many YMCAs accept women and families; some will not lodge those under 18 without parental permission.

World Alliance of YMCAs, 12 Clos Belmont, 1208 Geneva, Switzerland (☎41 22 849 5100, fax 849 5110; www.ymca.int).

Y's Way International, 224 E. 47th St., New York, NY 10017 (☎212-308-2899; fax 308-3161). For a small fee ($3 in North America, $5 elsewhere), this "booking service" makes reservations for YMCAs throughout Western Europe.

HOTELS, GUESTHOUSES, AND PENSIONS

Hotels are relatively expensive in Austria, Britain, Switzerland, and northern Europe, where rock bottom for one or two people is US$25 each. Elsewhere, couples and larger groups can usually get by fairly well. You'll typically share a hall bathroom; a private bathroom will cost extra, as may hot showers. In Britain and Ireland, a large breakfast is often included; elsewhere a continental breakfast consisting of a roll, jam, coffee or tea, is served. Some hotels offer "full pension" (all meals) and "half pension" (no lunch). Smaller **guesthouses** and **pensions** are often cheaper than hotels. If you make **reservations** in writing, indicate your night of arrival and the number of nights you plan to stay. The hotel will send you a confirmation and may request payment for the first night. Not all hotels take reservations, and few accept checks in foreign currency. Enclosing two **International Reply Coupons** will ensure a prompt reply (each US$1.05; available at any post office).

BED & BREAKFASTS (B&Bs)

For a cozy alternative to impersonal hotel rooms, B&Bs (private homes with rooms available to travelers) range from the acceptable to the sublime. Hosts will sometimes go out of their way to be accommodating by accepting travelers with pets, giving personalized tours, or offering home-cooked meals—the British and Irish versions are generally extra heavy on bacon and eggs. On the other hand, many B&Bs do not provide phones, TVs, or private bathrooms. For more info on B&Bs, see **InnFinder**, 6200 Gisholt Dr. #105, Madison, WI 53713 (☎608-285-6600; fax 285-6601; www.inncrawler.com), or **InnSite** (www.innsite.com).

UNIVERSITY DORMS

Many **colleges and universities** open their residence halls to travelers when school is not in session; some do so even during term-time. These dorms are often close to student areas—good sources for information on things to do—and are usually very clean. Getting a room may take a couple of phone calls and require advanced planning, but rates tend to be low, and many offer free local calls. For instance, the University of London opens its residential halls to visiting students during vacation periods with single rooms from UK£18.50-£25 including breakfast and dinner. For more information, contact the **University of London Intercollegiate Halls of Residence** vacation list (www.lon.ac.uk/accom/site3/Vacation.htm).

HOME EXCHANGES AND HOME RENTALS

Home exchange offers the traveler various types of homes (houses, apartments, condominiums, villas, even castles), plus the opportunity to live like a native and to cut down on accommodation fees. For more information, contact **HomeExchange.Com** (☎805-898-9660; www.homeexchange.com), **Intervac International Home Exchange** (www.intervac.com), or **The Invented City: International Home Exchange** (US ☎800-788-CITY, elsewhere US collect ☎415-252-1141; www.invented-city.com). **Home rentals** are more expensive than exchanges, but they can be cheaper than comparably-serviced hotels. Both home exchanges and rentals are ideal for families with children, or travelers with special dietary needs; you often get your own kitchen, maid service, TV, and telephones.

CAMPING AND THE OUTDOORS

Organized campgrounds exist just outside most Western European cities, and are accessible by foot, car, and/or public transportation. Showers, bathrooms, and a small restaurant or store are common; some have more elaborate facilities. Prices are low (US$5-15 per person), with additional charges for tents and cars. **Free camping** is less common, but allows you to camp in parks or public land for free. Campers heading to Western Europe should consider buying an **International Camping Carnet**—an ID card similar to a hostel membership card, it is required at a few organized campgrounds and provides discounts at many. It is available in North America from the **Family Campers and RVers Association** and in the UK from **The Caravan Club** (see below). For information about camping, hiking, and biking, write or call the publishers and organizations listed below to receive a free catalog.

USEFUL PUBLICATIONS AND RESOURCES

Automobile Association, A.A. Publishing. Orders and enquiries to TBS Frating Distribution Centre, Colchester, Essex, CO7 7DW, UK (☎012 0625 5678; www.theaa.co.uk). Publishes *Camping and Caravanning: Europe* (UK£9) and *Britain & Ireland* (UK£9), as well as *Big Road Atlases* for Europe, Germany, and Britain.

The Caravan Club, East Grinstead House, East Grinstead, West Sussex, RH19 1UA, UK (☎01342 32 69 44; www.caravanclub.co.uk). For UK£27.50, members receive equipment discounts, a 700pp directory and handbook, and a monthly magazine.

The European Federation of Campingsite Organisations, EFCO Secretariat, 6 Pullman Court, Great Western Road, Gloucester, GL 1 3 ND (UK ☎145 252 6911; efco@bhhpa.org.uk; www.campingeurope.com). The website has a comprehensive list of links to camping sites in most Western European countries.

Family Campers and RVers/National Campers and Hikers Association, Inc., 4804 Transit Rd. #2, Depew, NY 14043, USA (☎800-245-9755; fax 716-668-6242; www.fcrv.org). Membership fee (US$25) includes their publication *Camping Today*.

The Mountaineers Books, 1001 SW Klickitat Way #201, Seattle, WA 98134, USA (☎800-553-4453 or 206-223-6303; www.mountaineersbooks.org). Over 400 titles on hiking, biking, mountaineering, natural history, and conservation.

Sierra Club Books, 85 2nd St., 2nd fl., San Francisco, CA 94105, USA (☎415-977-5500; www.sierraclub.org/books). Publishes general resource books on camping and women traveling in the outdoors, as well as *Adventuring in the Alps*, which features detailed information on hiking in France, Austria, Switzerland Germany, Liechtenstein and Italy (US$15).

WILDERNESS SAFETY

THE GREAT OUTDOORS

Stay warm, stay dry, and stay hydrated. The vast majority of life-threatening wilderness situations can be avoided by following this simple advice. Prepare yourself for an emergency, however, by always packing raingear, a hat and mittens, a first-aid kit, a reflector, a whistle, high energy food, and extra water for any hike. Dress in wool or warm layers of synthetic materials designed for the outdoors; never rely on cotton for warmth, as it is useless when wet.

Check **weather forecasts** and pay attention to the skies when hiking, as weather patterns can suddenly change. Let someone know when and where you are going hiking—either a friend, your hostel, a park ranger, or a local hiking organization. Do not attempt a hike beyond your ability—you may be endangering your life. For information about outdoor ailments, see p. 29.

CAMPING AND HIKING EQUIPMENT

WHAT TO BUY...

Good camping equipment is both sturdy and light. Camping equipment in Australia, New Zealand, and the UK is generally more expensive than in North America.

Sleeping Bag: Most sleeping bags are rated by season ("summer" means 30-40°F at night; "four-season" or "winter" often means below 0°F). They are made either of **down** (warmer and lighter, but more expensive, and miserable when wet) or of **synthetic** material (heavier, more durable, and warmer when wet). Prices range US$80-210 for a summer synthetic to 250-300 for a good down winter bag. **Sleeping bag pads** include foam pads ($10-20), air mattresses ($15-50), and Therm-A-Rest self-inflating pads ($45-80). Bring a **stuff sack** to store your bag and keep it dry.

Tent: The best tents are free-standing (with their own frames and suspension systems), set up quickly, and only require staking in high winds. Low-profile dome tents are the best all-around. Good tents start at US$90 for a 2-person model, $300 for a 4-person model. Seal the seams of your tent with waterproofer, and make sure it has a rain fly. Other tent accessories include **battery-operated lanterns, plastic groundcloths,** and nylon **tarps.**

Backpack: Internal-frame packs mold better to your back, have a lower center of gravity, and flex adequately to allow you to hike difficult trails. **External-frame packs** are more comfortable for long hikes over even terrain, as they keep weight higher and distribute it more evenly. Make sure your pack has a strong, padded hip-belt to transfer weight to your legs. Any serious backpacking requires a pack of at least 4000 in^3, plus 500 in^3 for sleeping bags in internal-frame packs. Sturdy backpacks cost anywhere from US$125-420—this is one area in which it doesn't pay to economize. Fill up any pack with something heavy and walk around the store with it to get a sense of how it distributes weight before buying it. Either buy a **waterproof backpack cover,** or store all of your belongings in plastic bags inside your pack.

Boots: Be sure to wear hiking boots with good **ankle support.** They should fit snugly and comfortably over 1-2 pairs of wool socks and thin liner socks. Break in boots over several weeks first in order to spare yourself painful and debilitating blisters.

Other Necessities: Synthetic layers, like those made of polypropylene, and a **pile jacket** will keep you warm even when wet. A **"space blanket"** will help you to retain your body

ENVIRONMENTALLY RESPONSIBLE TOURISM. The idea behind responsible tourism is to leave no trace of human presence behind. A campstove is safer and more efficient than vegetation for cooking, but if you must make a fire, keep it small and use only dead branches or brush rather than cutting vegetation. Make sure your campsite is at least 150 ft. (50m) from water supplies or bodies of water. If there are no toilet facilities, bury human waste (but not paper) at least four inches (10cm) deep and above the high-water line, and 150 ft. or more from any water supplies and campsites. Always pack your trash in a plastic bag and carry it with you until you reach the next trash receptacle. For more information on these issues, contact one of the organizations listed below.

Earthwatch, 3 Clock Tower Place #100, Box 75, Maynard, MA 01754, USA (☎800-776-0188; www.earthwatch.org).

Ecotourism Society, P.O. Box 668, Burlington, VT 05402, USA (☎802-651-9818; www.ecotourism.org).

National Audubon Society, Nature Odysseys, 700 Broadway, New York, NY 10003, USA (☎212-979-3066; www.audubon.org).

Tourism Concern, Stapleton House, 277-281 Holloway Rd., London N7 8HN, UK (☎020 7753 3330; www.tourismconcern.org.uk).

heat and doubles as a groundcloth (US$5-15). Plastic **water bottles** are virtually shatter- and leak-proof. Bring **water-purification tablets** for when you can't boil water. Although most campgrounds provide campfire sites, you may want to bring a small **metal grate** or **grill** of your own. For those places that forbid fires or the gathering of firewood (this includes virtually every organized campground in Europe), you'll need a **camp stove** (the classic Coleman starts at $40) and a propane-filled **fuel bottle** to operate it. Also don't forget a **first-aid kit, pocketknife, insect repellent, calamine lotion,** and **waterproof matches** or a **lighter.**

...AND WHERE TO BUY IT

The mail-order/online companies listed below offer lower prices than many retail stores, but a visit to a local camping or outdoors store will give you a good sense of the look and weight of certain items.

Campmor, 28 Parkway, P.O. Box 700, Upper Saddle River, NJ 07458, USA (☎888-226-7667; www.campmor.com).

Discount Camping, 880 Main North Rd., Pooraka, South Australia 5095, Australia (☎08 8262 3399; www.discountcamping.com.au).

Eastern Mountain Sports (EMS), 327 Jaffrey Rd., Peterborough, NH 03458, USA (☎888-463-6367 or 603-924-7231; www.shopems.com)

L.L. Bean, Freeport, ME 04033, USA (☎800-441-5713, UK ☎0800 891 297; www.llbean.com).

Mountain Designs, P.O. Box 1472, Fortitude Valley, Queensland 4006, Australia (☎073 252 8894; www.mountaindesign.com.au).

Recreational Equipment, Inc. (REI), Sumner, WA 98352, USA (☎800-426-4840; www.rei.com).

YHA Adventure Shop, 14 Southampton St., London, WC2E 7HA, UK (☎020 7836 8541). The main branch of one of Britain's largest outdoor equipment suppliers.

CAMPERS AND RVS

Renting an RV will always be more expensive than tenting or hosteling, but it's cheaper than staying in hotels and renting a car (see **Rental Cars,** p. 60), and the convenience of bringing along your own bedroom, bathroom, and kitchen makes it an attractive option, especially for older travelers and families with children.

Rates vary widely by region, season (July and August are the most expensive months), and type of RV. It always pays to contact several different companies to compare vehicles and prices.

Auto Europe (US ☎888-223-5555, UK ☎0800 899 893; www.autoeurope.com) rents RVs in London, Paris, Lyon, Nice, Marseilles, Dusseldorf, Frankfurt, Hamburg, Munich, Barcelona, and Madrid.

FURTHER RESOURCES

Camping Your Way through Europe, Carol Mickelsen. Twin Peaks Press (US$15).

Europe by Van and Motorhome, David Shore and Patty Campbell (US$14; ☎/fax 800-659-5222; shorecam@aol.com; http://members.aol.com/europevan).

Great Outdoor Recreation Pages (www.gorp.com).

ORGANIZED ADVENTURE TRIPS

Organized adventure tours offer another way of exploring the wild. Activities include hiking, biking, skiing, canoeing, kayaking, rafting, climbing, photo safaris, and archaeological digs. Tourism bureaus can often suggest parks, trails, and outfitters; other good sources for info are stores and organizations that specialize in camping and outdoor equipment like REI and EMS (see above).

Specialty Travel Index, 305 San Anselmo Ave. #313, San Anselmo, CA 94960, USA (☎800-442-4922; www.specialtytravel.com). Tours worldwide.

KEEPING IN TOUCH

BY MAIL

SENDING MAIL HOME

Airmail is the best way to send mail home from Western European countries. Average travel time for a letter to North America is seven days, although times are more unpredictable from smaller towns. **Aerogrammes,** printed sheets that fold into envelopes and travel via airmail, are available at post offices. It helps to write "airmail" on the front (or, *por avión, mit Luftpost, via aerea*, etc.), but *par avion* is generally understood. Most post offices will charge exorbitant fees or simply refuse to send aerogrammes with enclosures. For exact postage for postcards and letters sent from Western Europe, see individual country introductions.

Surface mail is by far the cheapest and slowest way to send mail. It takes one to three months to cross the Atlantic and two to four to cross the Pacific—good for items you won't need to see for a while, such as souvenirs or other articles you've acquired along the way that are weighing down your pack.

SENDING MAIL TO WESTERN EUROPE

Mark envelopes "air mail" and "par avion," or your letter or postcard will never arrive. In addition to the standard postage system whose rates are listed below, **Federal Express** (Australia ☎13 26 10, US and Canada ☎800-247-4747, New Zealand ☎0800 733 339, UK ☎0800 123 800) handles express mail services from most countries to Western Europe; for example, they can get a letter from New York to Berlin in 3 business days for US$27.50.

Australia: Allow 5-7 days for regular **airmail** to Western Europe. Postcards and letters up to 20g cost AUS$1; packages up to 0.5kg $13, up to 2kg $46. **EMS International Courier** can get a letter there in 2-3 days for $32. www.auspost.com.au/pac.

Canada: Allow 4-7 days for regular **airmail** to Western Europe. Postcards and letters up to 20g cost CDN$1.05; packages up to 0.5kg $10.20, up to 2kg $34.00. www.canada-post.ca/CPC2/common/rates/ratesgen.html#international.

Ireland: Allow 2-3 days for regular airmail to the UK, and 4-6 days to continental Europe. Postcards and letters up to 25g cost IR£0.30/€0.40 to the UK, £0.32/€0.45 to the continent. International Swiftpost zips letters to some major European countries for an additional £26/€33.05 on top of priority postage. www.letterpost.ie.

New Zealand: Allow 6-12 days for regular airmail to Western Europe. Postcards NZ$1.50. Letters up to 200g cost $2-5; small parcels up to 0.5kg $16.50, up to 2kg $52.61. www.nzpost.net.nz/nzpost/control/ratefinder.

UK: Allow 2-3 days for airmail to Western Europe. Letters up to 20g cost UK£0.36; packages up to 0.5kg £2.67, up to 2kg £9.42. UK Swiftair delivers letters a day faster for an extra £2.85. http://www.royalmail.com/International/calculator/.

US: Allow 4-7 days for regular **airmail** to Western Europe. Postcards/aerogrammes cost US$0.70; letters under 1 oz. $0.80. Packages under 1 lb. cost $14; larger packages up to 5 lb. cost $22.75). **Global Express Mail** takes 2-3 days and costs $20/24.75 (0.5-1 lb.). **US Global Priority Mail** delivers small/large flat-rate envelopes to Western Europe in 3-5 days for $5/$9. http://ircalc.usps.gov.

RECEIVING MAIL IN WESTERN EUROPE

There are several ways to arrange pick-up of letters sent to you by friends and relatives while you are abroad. Mail can be sent via **Poste Restante** (French for General Delivery; *Lista de Correos* in Spanish, *Fermo Posta* in Italian, and *Postlagernde Breife* in German) to almost any city or town in Western Europe with a post office. Address mail to be held in the following way: Steven SMITH, Poste Restante, London SW1. The mail will go to a special desk in the central post office, unless you specify a post office by street address or postal code. It's best to use the largest post office, since mail may be sent there regardless. It is usually safer and quicker, though more expensive, to send mail express or registered. Bring your passport (or other photo ID) for pick-up; there may occasionally be a small fee. If the clerks say there is nothing for you, have them check under your first name as well. *Let's Go* lists post offices in the **Practical Information** section for each city and most towns.

American Express's travel offices throughout the world offer a free **Client Letter Service** (mail held up to 30 days and forwarded upon request) for cardholders who contact them in advance. Address the letter in the same way shown above. Some offices will offer these services to non-cardholders (especially AmEx Traveler's Cheque holders), but call ahead to make sure. *Let's Go* lists AmEx office locations for most large cities in **Practical Information** sections; for a complete, free list, call AmEx (US ☎800-528-4800).

BY TELEPHONE

CALLING HOME FROM WESTERN EUROPE

A **calling card** is probably your cheapest bet. Calls are billed collect or to your account. You can frequently call collect without even possessing a company's calling card just by calling their access number and following the instructions. **To obtain a calling card** from your national telecommunications service before leaving home, contact the appropriate company listed below:

AT&T (US)	800-222-0300
British Telecom	800 345 144
Canada Direct	800-668-6878
Ireland Direct	800 400 000
MCI (US)	800-444-3333
Sprint (US)	800-877-4646
Telecom New Zealand	0800 000 000
Telkom South Africa	10 219
Telstra Australia	13 22 00

To call home with a calling card, contact the operator for your service provider in the appropriate country by dialing the toll-free access number provided in the Essentials chapter for each country under **Communications.** You can usually make **direct international calls** from pay phones, but if you aren't using a calling card, you may need to drop your coins as quickly as your words. Where available, prepaid phone cards (see below) and occasionally major credit cards can be used for direct international calls, but they are still less cost-efficient. Placing a **collect call** through an international operator is a more expensive alternative. You can typically place collect calls through the service providers listed above, even if you don't possess one of their phone cards.

CALLING WITHIN WESTERN EUROPE

For **local calls,** the simplest way to call within a country in Western Europe may be to use a coin-operated phone. However, much of Western Europe has switched to a **prepaid phone card** system, and, in some countries, you may have a hard time finding any coin-operated phones at all. Phone cards (usually available at newspaper kiosks and tobacco stores) carry a certain amount of phone time, measured in units. Investing in a phone card usually saves time and money in the long run; just use any leftover time on a call home before leaving the country. The computerized phone will tell you how much time, in units, you have left on your card. Another kind of prepaid telephone card comes with a Personal Identification Number (PIN) and a toll-free access number. Instead of inserting the card into the phone, you call the access number and follow the directions on the card. Cards can be used to make international as well as domestic calls. **Phone rates** are highest in the morning, lower in the evening, and lowest on Sundays and late at night.

TIME DIFFERENCES

Greenwich Mean Time (GMT) is five hours ahead of New York time, eight hours ahead of Vancouver and San Francisco time, two hours behind Johannesburg time, 10 hours behind Sydney time, and 12 hours behind Auckland time. Great Britain and Portugal both operate on GMT, while Greece is two hours ahead. All other countries listed in *Let's Go: Western Europe* are one hour ahead of GMT.

BY EMAIL AND INTERNET

Email has become the joy of backpackers worldwide, from Kathmandu to Cairo, so it's no surprise that it now a popular and easily accessible option in Western Europe as well. Though in some places it's possible to forge a remote link with your home server, using telnet or some other protocol, in most cases this is a much slower (and more expensive) option than taking advantage of free **web-based email accounts** (e.g., www.hotmail.com, www.yahoo.com, www.youpy.fr, http://mail.voila.fr, http://mail.wordwalla.com). Travelers with laptops can call an internet service provider via a **modem.** Long-distance phone cards specifically intended for such calls can defray normally high phone charges; check with your long-distance phone provider to see if it offers this option. **Internet cafes** and the occasional free internet terminal at a public library or university are listed in the **Orientation** and **Practical Information** sections of major cities. For lists of additional cybercafes in Western Europe, check out http://cybercaptive.com or www.cyberiacafe.net/cyberia/guide/ccafe.htm.

GETTING TO WESTERN EUROPE

BY PLANE

When it comes to airfare, a little effort can save you a bundle. Courier fares are the cheapest if your plans are flexible enough to deal with the restrictions on available dates. Tickets bought from consolidators and standby seating are also good deals, but last-minute specials, airfare wars, and charter flights often beat these fares. The key is to hunt around, to be flexible, and to ask persistently about discounts. Students, seniors, and those under 26 should never pay full price for a ticket.

Take advantage of the specialty and high-speed trains of Europe!

FREE Thomas Cook timetable with railpass orders over $1,000   We offer most European railpasses

The search for the perfect railpass and backpack has ended

The Backpack Traveler offers expert advice and service on railpasses, backpacks, youth hostels and travel gear

Our goal is to make your trip safe, comfortable and easy while saving you money.

With your Eurail/Europass you'll receive the lowest price available plus the following special offers:

- **Free** 2nd day shipping
- **Free** Eurail video
- **Free** timetable
- **Free** rail map
- **Free** 500 page rail guide
- **Free** Thomas Cook Timetable on rail orders over $1,000

That's not all. We carry a great selection of backpacks and over a hundred travel products including sleep sacks, money belts and laundry gear.

- When you buy a Eurail or Europass, you'll receive $20 off any Jansport backpack
- Youth hostel memberships and ISE Student Discount Cards are available
- Our entire catalog is now online at: www.europebytrain.com

We specialize in Eurail, Europass, Britrail, Eurostar and most country passes

Call today for a FREE catalog and railpass brochure

1-800-688-9577

The Backpack Traveler

PO Box 1386, San Juan Capistrano, CA 92693

Catalog and rail brochure   **www.europebytrain.com**

ESSENTIALS

AIRFARES

Timing: Airfares to Western Europe peak between mid-June and early Sept.; holidays are also expensive. The cheapest times to travel are Nov. to mid-Dec. and early Jan. to Mar. Midweek (M-Th morning) round-trip flights run US$40-50 cheaper than weekend flights, but they are generally more crowded and less likely to permit frequent-flier upgrades. An "open return" ticket can be pricier than fixing a return date and paying later to change it.

Route: Round-trip flights are by far the cheapest; "open-jaw" (arriving in and departing from different cities, e.g. New York-Paris and Rome-New York) tickets tend to be pricier. Patching one-way flights together is the most expensive way to travel.

Round the World (RTW): If Western Europe is only one stop on a more extensive globe-hop, consider a round-the-world (RTW) ticket. Tickets usually include at least 5 stops and are valid for about a year; prices range US$1200-5000. Try **Northwest Airlines/ KLM** (US ☎800-447-4747; www.nwa.com) or **Star Alliance**, a consortium of 22 airlines including United Airlines (US ☎800-241-6522; www.star-alliance.com).

Gateway Cities: Flights between capitals or regional hubs will offer the cheapest fares. The cheapest gateway cities to Western Europe are typically London, Paris, Amsterdam, and Frankfurt.

Boarding: Confirm international flights by phone within 72hr. of departure. Most airlines require that passengers arrive at the airport at least 2hr. before departure. One carry-on item and 2 checked bags is the norm for non-courier flights.

BUDGET AND STUDENT TRAVEL AGENCIES

While knowledgeable agents specializing in flights to Western Europe can make your life easy and help you save, they may not spend the time to find you the lowest possible fare—they get paid on commission. Travelers holding **ISIC and IYTC cards** (see p. 19) qualify for big discounts from student travel agencies. Most flights from budget agencies are on major airlines, but in peak season some may sell seats on less reliable chartered aircrafts.

Council Travel (www.counciltravel.com). Countless US offices, including branches in Atlanta, Boston, Chicago, L.A., New York, San Francisco, Seattle, and Washington, D.C. Check the website or call 800-2-COUNCIL (226-8624) for the office nearest you.

CTS Travel, 44 Goodge St., **London** W1T 2AD (☎0207 636 0031; fax 0207 637 5328; ctsinfo@ctstravel.co.uk).

STA Travel, 7890 S. Hardy Dr. Ste. 110, Tempe AZ 85284 (24hr. reservations and info ☎800-777-0112; fax 480-592-0876; www.statravel.com). A student and youth travel organization with countless branches worldwide (check their website for a listing of all their offices), including US offices in Boston, Chicago, L.A., New York, San Francisco, Seattle, and Washington, D.C. Ticket booking, travel insurance, railpasses, and more. In the UK, 11 Goodge St., **London** W1T 2PF or call 0870 160 6070. In New Zealand, 10 High St., **Auckland** (☎09 309 0458). In Australia, 366 Lygon St., **Melbourne** Vic 3053 (☎039 349 4344).

StudentUniverse, 545 5th Ave., Suite 640, New York, NY 10017 (toll-free customer service ☎800-272-9676, outside the US 212-986-8420; help@studentuniverse.com; www.studentuniverse.com). An online student travel service offering discount ticket booking, travel insurance, railpasses, destination guides, and much more. Customer service line open M-F 9am-8pm and Sa noon-5pm EST.

Travel CUTS (Canadian Universities Travel Services Limited), 187 College St., **Toronto,** ON M5T 1P7 (☎416-979-2406; fax 979-8167; www.travelcuts.com). 60 offices across Canada. Also in the UK, 295-A Regent St., **London** W1R 7YA (☎0207-255-1944).

usit World (www.usitworld.com). Over 50 usit campus branches in the UK (www.usitcampus.co.uk), including 52 Grosvenor Gardens, **London** SW1W 0AG (☎0870 240 1010), **Manchester** (☎0161 273 1880), and **Edinburgh** (☎0131 668 3303). Nearly 20 usit NOW offices in Ireland, including 19-21 Aston Quay, O'Connell Bridge, **Dublin** 2 (☎01 602 1600; www.usitnow.ie), and **Belfast** (☎02 890 327 111; www.usitnow.com). Offices also in Athens, Auckland, Brussels, Frankfurt, Johannesburg, Lisbon, Luxembourg, Madrid, Paris, Sofia, and Warsaw.

ESSENTIALS

ESSENTIALS

DISCOVER • EXPLORE • EXPERIENCE

council travel

America's Leader In Student Travel

CALL 1-800-2COUNCIL
CLICK www.counciltravel.com
VISIT one of our 75 retail locations

Wasteels, Skoubogade 6, 1158 Copenhagen K., (☎3314-4633; fax 7630-0865; www.wasteels.dk/uk). A huge chain with 165 locations across Europe. Sells tickets at 30-45% discount and 2nd-class international point-to-point train tickets with unlimited stopovers for those under 26 (sold only in Europe).

COMMERCIAL AIRLINES

The commercial airlines' lowest regular offer is the APEX (Advance Purchase Excursion) fare, which provides confirmed reservations and allows "open-jaw" tickets. Generally, reservations must be made seven to 21 days ahead of departure, with seven- to 14-day minimum-stay and up-to-90-day maximum-stay restrictions. These fares carry hefty cancellation and change penalties (fees rise in summer). Book peak-season APEX fares early; by May you will have a hard time getting your desired departure date. Use Microsoft Expedia (msn.expedia.com) or Travelocity (www.travelocity.com) to get an idea of the lowest published fares, then use the resources outlined here to try to beat those fares. Low-season fares should be notably cheaper than the high-season (mid-June to Aug.) ones listed here.

TRAVELING FROM NORTH AMERICA

Basic round-trip fares to Europe range from roughly US$200-750: to Frankfurt, $300-750; London, $200-600; Paris, $250-800. Standard commercial carriers like **American** (☎800-433-7300; www.aa.com) and **United** (☎800-241-6522; www.ual.com) will probably offer the most convenient flights, but they may not be the cheapest, unless you manage to grab a special promotion. Flying one of the following airlines might be a better deal if any of their limited departure points is convenient for you.

Icelandair: ☎800-223-5500; www.icelandair.com. Stopovers in Iceland for no extra cost on most transatlantic flights. New York to Frankfurt May-Sept. US$500-730; Oct.-May $390-$450. For last-minute offers, subscribe to their email.

Finnair: ☎800-950-5000; www.us.finnair.com. Cheap round-trips from San Francisco, New York, and Toronto to Helsinki; connections throughout Europe.

Martinair: ☎800-627-8462; www.martinairusa.com. Fly from California or Florida to Amsterdam mid-June to mid-Aug. US$880; mid-Aug. to mid-June $730.

TRAVELING FROM THE UK & IRELAND

Because of the myriad carriers flying from the British Isles to the continent, we only include discount airlines or those with cheap specials here. The **Air Travel Advisory Bureau** in London (☎020 7636 5000; www.atab.co.uk) provides referrals to travel agencies and consolidators that offer discounted airfares out of the UK.

Aer Lingus: Ireland ☎01 886 8888; www.flyaerlingus.com. Return tickets from Belfast, Dublin, Cork, Galway, Kerry, and Shannon to Amsterdam, Brussels, Düsseldorf, Frankfurt, Madrid, Milan, Munich, Paris, Rome, Stockholm, and Zürich (IR£102-244/€129.55-309.85).

British Midland Airways: UK ☎0870 607 0555; www.britishmidland.com. Departures from throughout the UK. London to Brussels (UK£83), Madrid (£194), Milan (£108), and Paris (£87).

buzz: UK ☎0870 240 7070; www.buzzaway.com. A subsidiary of KLM. From London to Berlin, Frankfurt, Helsinki, Milan, Montpellier, Paris, and Vienna (UK£30-70). Tickets can not be changed or refunded.

easyJet: UK ☎0870 600 0000; www.easyjet.com. London to Amsterdam, Athens, Barcelona, Geneva, Madrid, Nice, Palma, and Zurich (UK£47-136). Online tickets.

Go-Fly Limited: UK ☎0845 605 4321, elsewhere call UK +44 1279 66 63 88; www.go-fly.com. A subsidiary of British Airways. From London to Barcelona, Copenhagen, Edinburgh, Naples, Prague, Rome, and Venice (return UK£53-180).

KLM: UK ☎0870 507 4074; www.klmuk.com. Cheap return tickets from London and elsewhere direct to Amsterdam, Brussels, Frankfurt, and Zurich; via Amsterdam Schiphol Airport to Düsseldorf, Milan, Paris, Rome, and other popular destinations.

Ryanair: Ireland ☎01 812 1212, UK 0870 156 9569; www.ryanair.ie. From Dublin, London, and Glasgow to destinations in France, Germany, Ireland, Italy, Scandinavia, and elsewhere. Deals from as low as UK£9 on limited weekend specials.

ESSENTIALS

Sheep Tickets.

Visit **StudentUniverse.com** for real deals on student travel anywhere.

 StudentUniverse.com   **Real Travel Deals**

800.272.9676

ESSENTIALS

TRAVELING FROM AUSTRALIA & NEW ZEALAND

Air New Zealand: New Zealand ☎0800 352 266; www.airnz.co.nz. Auckland to London and Frankfurt.

Qantas Air: Australia ☎13 13 13, New Zealand ☎0800 808 767; www.qantas.com.au. Flights from Australia and New Zealand to London for around AUS$2400-3000 depending on the season.

Singapore Air: Australia ☎13 10 11, New Zealand ☎0800 808 909; www.singaporeair.com. Flies from Auckland, Sydney, Melbourne, and Perth to Amsterdam, Brussels, Frankfurt, London, Manila, and more.

Thai Airways: Australia ☎1300 651 960, New Zealand ☎09 377 3886; www.thaiair.com. Auckland, Sydney, and Melbourne to Amsterdam, Frankfurt, and London.

TRAVELING FROM SOUTH AFRICA

Air France: ☎011 880 8040; www.airfrance.com. Johannesburg to Paris; connections throughout Europe.

British Airways: ☎086 001 1747; www.british-airways.com/regional/sa. Johannesburg to London direct, and connections to the rest of Western Europe from ZAR3400.

Lufthansa: ☎011 484 4711; www.lufthansa.co.za. From Cape Town and Johannesburg to Germany with connections throughout Western Europe.

Virgin Atlantic: ☎011 340 3400; www.virgin-atlantic.co.za. Flies to London from both Cape Town and Johannesburg.

AIR COURIER FLIGHTS

Those who travel light should consider courier flights. Couriers help transport cargo on international flights by using their checked luggage space for freight. Generally, couriers must travel with carry-ons only and must deal with complex flight restrictions. Most flights are round-trip only, with short fixed-length stays (usually one week) and a limit of a one ticket per issue. Most of these flights also operate only out of major gateway cities, mostly in North America. Generally, you must be over 21 (in some cases 18). In summer, the most popular destinations usually require an advance reservation of about two weeks (you can usually book up to two months ahead). Super-discounted fares are common for "last-minute" flights (three to 14 days ahead).

TRAVELING FROM NORTH AMERICA

Round-trip courier fares from the US to Western Europe run about US$200-500. Most flights leave from New York, Los Angeles, San Francisco, or Miami in the US; and from Montreal, Toronto, or Vancouver in Canada. The organizations below provide their members with lists of opportunities and courier brokers worldwide for an annual fee (typically US$50-60). Alternatively, you can contact a courier broker (such as the last three listings) directly; most charge registration fees, but a few don't. Prices quoted below are round-trip.

Air Courier Association, 15000 W. 6th Ave. #203, Golden, CO 80401 (☎800-282-1202, www.aircourier.org). Ten departure cities throughout the US and Canada to London, Madrid, Paris, Rome, and throughout Western Europe (high-season US$150-360). One-year $49.

Global Courier Travel, P.O. Box 3051, Nederland, CO 80466 (www.globalcouriertravel.com). Searchable online database. Six departure points in the US and Canada to Amsterdam, Athens, Brussels, Copenhagen, Frankfurt, London, Madrid, Milan, Paris, and Rome. One-year US$40, 2 people $55.

International Association of Air Travel Couriers (IAATC), 220 South Dixie Highway #3, P.O. Box 1349, Lake Worth, FL 33460 (☎561-582-8320; fax 582-1581; www.courier.org). From 9 North American cities to Western European cities, including London, Madrid, Paris, and Rome. One-year US$45-50.

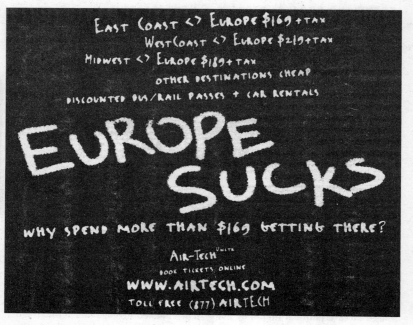

EAST COAST <> EUROPE $169 +TAX
WEST COAST <> EUROPE $219 +TAX
MIDWEST <> EUROPE $189 +TAX
OTHER DESTINATIONS CHEAP
DISCOUNTED BUS/RAIL PASSES + CAR RENTALS

EUROPE SUCKS

WHY SPEND MORE THAN $169 GETTING THERE?

Air-Tech UNLTD
BOOK TICKETS ONLINE
WWW.AIRTECH.COM
TOLL FREE (877) AIRTECH

NOW Voyager, 74 Varick St. #307, New York, NY 10013 (☎212-431-1616; fax 219-1753; www.nowvoyagertravel.com). To Amsterdam, Brussels, Copenhagen, Dublin, London, Madrid, Milan, Paris, and Rome (US$499-699). Usually one-week max. stay. One-year $50. Non-courier discount fares also available.

Worldwide Courier Association (☎800-780-4359, ext. 441; www.massiveweb.com). From New York, San Francisco, Los Angeles, and Chicago to Western Europe, including London, Milan, Paris, and Rome (US$259-299). One-year $58.

FROM THE UK, IRELAND, AUSTRALIA, & NEW ZEALAND

Although the courier industry is most developed from North America, there are limited courier flights in other areas. The minimum age for couriers from the **UK** is usually 18. **Brave New World Enterprises,** P.O. Box 22212, London SE5 8WB (guideinfo@nry.co.uk; www.nry.co.uk/bnw) publishes a directory of all the companies offering courier flights in the UK (UK£10, in electronic form £8). The **International Association of Air Travel Couriers** (see above) often offers courier flights from London to Budapest. **Global Courier Travel** (see above) also offer flights from London and Dublin to continental Europe. **British Airways Travel Shop** (☎0870 606 1133; www.batravelshops.com) arranges some flights from London to destinations in continental Europe (specials may be as low as £60; no registration fee). From **Australia** and **New Zealand, Global Courier Travel** (see above) often has listings from Sydney to London and Auckland to London or Frankfurt.

STANDBY FLIGHTS

Traveling standby requires considerable flexibility in arrival and departure dates and cities. Companies dealing in standby flights sell vouchers rather than tickets, along with the promise to get to your destination (or near your destination) within a certain window of time (typically 1-5 days). You call in before your specific window of time to hear your flight options and the probability that you will be able to board each flight. You can then decide which flights you want to try to make, show up at the appropriate airport at the appropriate time, present your voucher, and board if space is available. Vouchers can usually be bought for both one-way and round-trip travel. You may receive a monetary refund only if every available flight within your date range is full; if you opt not to take an available (but perhaps less convenient) flight, you can only get credit toward future travel. Carefully read agreements with any company offering standby flights as tricky fine print can leave you in a lurch. To check on a company's service record in the US, call the **Better Business Bureau** (☎ 212-533-6200). It is difficult to receive refunds, and clients' vouchers will not be honored when an airline fails to receive payment in time. One established standby company in the US is **Whole Earth Travel Inc.**, 325 W. 38th St., New York, NY 10018 (☎ 800-326-2009; fax 212-864-5489; www.4standby.com), which offers one-way flights to groups of European cities from the Northeast (US$169), West Coast and Northwest ($249), and the Midwest ($219). Another location is at 13470 Washington Blvd. Suite 205, Marina Del Rey, CA 90292 (☎ 800-397-1098).

TICKET CONSOLIDATORS

Ticket consolidators, or **"bucket shops,"** buy unsold tickets in bulk from commercial airlines and sell them at discounted rates. The best place to look is in the Sunday travel section of any major newspaper (such as *The New York Times*), where many bucket shops place tiny ads. Call quickly, as availability is typically extremely limited. Not all bucket shops are reliable, so insist on a receipt that gives full details of restrictions, refunds, and tickets, and pay by credit card (in spite of the 2-5% fee) so you can stop payment if you never receive your tickets. For more info, see www.travel-library.com/air-travel/consolidators.html.

TRAVELING FROM THE US & CANADA

Travel Avenue (☎ 800-333-3335; www.travelavenue.com) searches for best available published fares and then uses several consolidators to attempt to beat that fare. **NOW Voyager,** 74 Varick St. Ste. 307, New York, NY 10013 (☎ 212-431-1616; fax 219-1793; www.nowvoyagertravel.com), arranges discounted flights, mostly from New York, to Barcelona, London, Madrid, Milan, Paris, and Rome. Other consolidators worth trying are **Interworld** (☎ 305-443-4929; fax 443-0351); **Pennsylvania Travel** (☎ 800-331-0947); **Rebel** (☎ 800-227-3235; travel@rebeltours.com; www.rebeltours.com); **Cheap Tickets** (☎ 800-377-1000; www.cheaptickets.com); and **Travac** (☎ 800-872-8800; fax 212-714-9063; www.travac.com). Yet more consolidators on the web include the **Internet Travel Network** (www.itn.com); **Travel Information Services** (www.tiss.com); **TravelHUB** (www.travelhub.com); and **The Travel Site** (www.thetravelsite.com). Keep in mind that these are just suggestions to get you started in your research; *Let's Go* does not endorse any of these agencies. As always, be cautious, and research companies before you hand over your credit card number.

TRAVELING FROM THE UK, AUSTRALIA, & NEW ZEALAND

In London, the **Air Travel Advisory Bureau** (☎ 020 7636 5000; www.atab.co.uk) can provide names of reliable consolidators and discount flight specialists. From Australia and New Zealand, look for consolidator ads in the travel section of the *Sydney Morning Herald* and other papers.

CHARTER FLIGHTS

Charters are flights that a tour operator contracts with an airline to fly extra loads of passengers during peak season. Charter flights fly less frequently than major airlines, make refunds particularly difficult, and are almost always fully booked. Schedules and itineraries may also change or be cancelled at the last moment (as late as 48 hours before the trip, and without a full refund), and check-in, boarding, and baggage claim are often much slower. However, they can also be cheaper.

Discount clubs and **fare brokers** offer members savings on last-minute charter and tour deals. Study contracts closely; you don't want to end up with an unwanted overnight layover. **Travelers Advantage,** Trumbull, CT, USA (☎ 203-365-2000; www.travelersadvantage.com; US$70 annual fee) specializes in European travel and tour packages.

BY CHUNNEL FROM THE UK

Traversing 43km under the sea, the Chunnel is undoubtedly the fastest, most convenient, and least scenic route from England to France.

BY TRAIN. Eurostar, Eurostar House, Waterloo Station, **London** SE1 8SE (UK ☎ 0990 186 186; US ☎ 800-387-6782; elsewhere call UK 123 361 7575; www.eurostar.com, www.raileurope.com) runs a frequent train service between London and the continent. Ten to twenty-eight trains per day run to Paris (3hr., US$75-159, 2nd class), and Brussels (3hr., 50min., $75-159, 2nd class). Routes include stops at Ashford in England and Calais and Lille in France. Book at major rail stations in the UK by phone or on the web.

BY BUS. Both **Eurolines** and **Eurobus** provide bus-ferry combinations (see p. 59).

BY CAR. If you're traveling by car, **Eurotunnel** (UK ☎ 0800 96 99 92; www.eurotunnel.co.uk) shuttles cars and passengers between Kent and Nord-Pas-de-Calais. Return fares for vehicle and all passengers range from UK£219-299 with car, £259-598 with campervan, and £119-299 for a trailer/caravan supplement. Same-day return costs £110-150, five-day return £139-195. Book online or via phone. Travelers with cars can also look into sea crossings by ferry (see below).

BY BOAT FROM THE UK AND IRELAND

The following fares are **one-way** for **adult foot passengers** unless otherwise noted. Though standard return fares are in most cases simply twice the one-way fare, **fixed-period returns** (usually within five days) are almost invariably cheaper. Ferries run **year-round** unless otherwise noted. **Bikes** are usually free, although you may have to pay up to UK£10 in high-season. For a **camper/trailer** supplement, you will have to add anywhere from £20-140 to the "with car" fare. If more than one price is quoted, the quote in UK£ is valid for departures from the UK. A directory of ferries in this region can be found at www.seaview.co.uk/ferries.html.

Brittany Ferries: UK ☎ 087 0901 2400, France ☎ 08 25 82 88 28; www.brittany-ferries.com. **Plymouth** to **Roscoff,** France (6hr.; in summer 1-3 per day, off-season 1 per week; UK£20-58 or 140-300F/€21.35-45.70) and **Santander,** Spain (24-30hr., 1-2 per week, return £80-145). **Portsmouth** to **St-Malo** (8¾hr., 1-2 per day, 150-320F/€22.90-48.80) and **Caen** (6hr, 1-3 per day, 140-290F/€21.35-44.25), France. **Poole** to **Cherbourg** (4¼hr., 1-2 per day, 140-290F/€21.35-44.25). **Cork** to **Roscoff** (13½hr., Apr.-Sept. 1 per week, 340-650F/€51.85-99.10).

DFDS Seaways: UK ☎ 087 0533 3000; www.scansea.com. **Harwich** to **Hamburg** (20hr.) and **Esbjerg,** Denmark (19hr.). **Newcastle** to **Amsterdam** (14hr.); **Kristiansand,** Norway (19hr.); and **Gothenburg,** Sweden (22hr.).

Fjord Line: www.fjordline.no. Norway ☎ 55 54 88 00; UK ☎ 019 1296 1313. **Newcastle, England** to **Stavanger** (19hr.) and **Bergen** (26hr.), Norway. Also between **Bergen** and **Egersund,** Norway, and **Hanstholm,** Denmark.

Hoverspeed: UK ☎ 087 0240 8070, France ☎ 03 21 46 14 54; www.hoverspeed.co.uk. **Dover** to **Calais** (35-55min., every hr., UK£24) and **Ostend,** Belgium (2hr., 5-7 per day, £28). **Folkestone** to **Boulogne,** France (1hr., 3-4 per day, £24). **Newhaven** to **Dieppe,** France (2¼-4¼hr., 1-3 per day, £28).

Irish Ferries: France ☎ 01 44 94 2040, Ireland ☎ 1890 31 31 31, UK ☎ 08705 17 17 17; www.irishferries.ie. **Rosslare** to **Cherbourg** (18hr., IR£57-82/€72.40); **Roscoff** (17hr., Apr.-Sept. 1-9 per week, 470-680F/€71.65-103.70); and **Pembroke,** England (3¾hr.). **Holyhead,** England to **Dublin** (2-3hr., return £20-60/€25.40-78.20).

P&O North Sea Ferries: UK ☎ 0870 129 6002; www.ponsf.com. Daily ferries from **Hull** to **Rotterdam,** The Netherlands (13½hr.) and **Zeebrugge,** Belgium (14hr.). Both UK£38-48, students £24-31, cars £63-78. Online bookings.

P&O Stena Line: UK ☎ 087 0600 0611, from Europe 13 04 86 40 03; www.posl.com. **Dover** to **Calais** (1¼hr., 30 per day, UK£24).

SeaFrance: UK ☎087 0571 1711, France ☎03 21 46 80 00; www.seafrance.co.uk.
Dover to **Calais** (1½hr., 15 per day, UK£15).
Stena Line: UK ☎1233 64 68 26; www.stenaline.co.uk. **Harwich,** England to **Hook of Holland** (5hr., UK£25). **Fishguard** to **Rosslare** (1-3½hr., £22-30). **Holyhead** to **Dublin** (4hr., £18-20) and **Dún Laoghaire** (1-3½hr., £20-28). **Stranraer** to **Belfast** (1¾-3¼hr., Mar.-Jan., £18-24).

GETTING AROUND WESTERN EUROPE

Fares on all modes of transportation are either single (one-way) or return (round-trip). "Period returns" require you to return within a specific number of days; "day return" means you must return on the same day. Unless stated otherwise, *Let's Go* always lists single fares. round-trip fares on trains and buses in Western Europe are generally double the one-way fare.

BY PLANE

Though flying is almost invariably more expensive than traveling by train, if you are short on time (or flush with cash) you might consider it. Student travel agencies sell cheap tickets, and budget fares are frequently available in the spring and summer on high-volume routes between northern Europe and resort areas in Italy, Greece, and Spain; consult budget travel agents and local newspapers. For info on cheap flights from Britain to Western Europe, see **Traveling from the UK,** p. 47.

In addition, a number of European airlines offer discount coupon packets. Most are only available as tack-ons for transatlantic passengers, but some are stand-alone offers. Most must be purchased before departure, so research in advance.

Alitalia: US ☎800-223-5730; www.alitaliausa.com. "Europlus" allows you to tack on 3 or more flights to 30 airports in Europe and North Africa. Must be purchased in conjunction with an Alitalia transatlantic flight; the first ticket must be booked to a specific city, but the remaining trips can be determined as you go. US$299 for 3; each additional ticket $100.

Austrian Airlines: US ☎800-843-0002; www.austrianair.com/greatdeals/europe_airpass.html. "European Airpass," good to cities served by AA and partner airlines, is available in the US to Austrian Airlines transatlantic passengers (min. 3 tickets, max. 10). Price based on mileage between destinations.

Europe by Air: US ☎888-321-4737; www.europebyair.com. Coupons good on 30 partner airlines to 150 European cities in 30 countries. Must be purchased prior to departure. US$99 each, excluding airport tax. Also offers 15- and 21- day unlimited passes, $699-$899.

Iberia: US ☎800-772 46 42; http://194.224.55.25/ibusa/ofertas/index.html. "Euro-Pass" allows Iberia passengers flying from the US to Spain to tack on additional destinations in Europe (min. 2). Most US$125 each; some $155 each.

KLM/Northwest: US ☎800-800-1504. "Passport to Europe," available to transatlantic passengers on either airline, connects 90 European cities; min. 3, max. 12. US$100 each.

Lufthansa: US ☎800-399-5838; www.lufthansa.com. "Discover Europe" is available to US travelers booked on a transatlantic Lufthansa flight (min. 3, max. 9). US$119 each.

SAS: US☎800-221-2350; www.flysas.com/airpass.html. One-way coupons for travel within Europe. US$65-225, 8 max. Most are available only to transatlantic SAS passengers, but some United and Lufthansa passengers also qualify.

BY TRAIN

Trains in Western Europe are generally comfortable, convenient, and reasonably swift. Second-class travel is pleasant, and compartments, which seat two to six, are great places to meet fellow travelers. All prices listed below are second-class fares.

ESSENTIALS

LETS GO SPECIAL!

Buy a Rail Pass

And Get ALL this FREE

Eurotrip Discount Guide
Save hundreds of dollars at thousands of European shops, restaurants, museums and more.

One FREE night at The Pink Palace
Includes breakfast and dinner at the world famous youth resort in Corfu, Greece.

Expert Advice and Service
We have helped thousands of people travel Europe by rail over the last 10 years. We'll help

Passes issued on the spot
Your pass is delivered to your door within 1-2 days. RUSH ORDERS are our specialty.

FREE Eurail timetable and map ➤ with every order

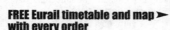

PLUS
NO handling fees · NO busy signals · NO lines · NO hassles

GUARANTEED BEST PRICES

ORDER ONLINE and SAVE on Pass Protection

www.LETSRAIL.com

Powered by

**or Call 1-888-RAIL-PASS
(1-888-724-5727)**

Visit these helpful sites when planning your trip
www.EUROTRIP.com and www.RAILSAVER.com

Trains, however, are not always safe; for **safety tips,** see p. 28. For long trips, make sure you are on the correct car, as trains sometimes split at crossroads. Towns listed in parentheses about European train schedules require a train switch at the town listed immediately before the parenthesis.

You can either buy a **railpass,** which allows unlimited travel within a particular region for a given period of time, or rely on buying individual **point-to-point** tickets as you go. Almost all countries give students or youths (usually defined as anyone under 26) direct discounts on regular domestic rail tickets, and many also sell a student or youth card that provides 20-50% off all fares for up to a year.

RESERVATIONS. While seat reservations are required only for selected trains (usually on major lines), you are never guaranteed a seat without one (usually US$3-10 extra). Reservations are available on major trains as much as two months in advance, and Europeans often reserve far ahead of time; you should strongly consider reserving during peak holiday and tourist seasons (at the very latest a few hours ahead). It will be necessary to purchase a **supplement** ($10-50) or special fare for high- speed or high-quality trains such as the Cisalpino, Spain's AVE, Finland's Pendolino S220, Italy's ETR500 and Pendolino, Germany's ICE, and certain French TGVs. InterRail holders must also purchase supplements ($10-25) for trains like EuroCity, InterCity, Sweden's X2000, and many French TGVs; these supplements are unnecessary for Eurailpass and Europass holders.

OVERNIGHT TRAINS. Night trains have their advantages: you won't waste valuable daylight hours traveling, and you will be able to forego the hassle and considerable expense of securing a night's accommodation. However, night travel has its drawbacks as well: discomfort and sleepless nights are the most obvious; the scenery probably won't look as enticing in pitch black, either. **Sleeping accommodations** on trains differ from country to country, but typically you can either sleep upright in your seat (for free) or pay for a separate space. **Couchettes** (berths) typically have four to six seats per compartment (about US$20 per person); **sleepers** (beds) in private sleeping cars offer more privacy and comfort, but are considerably more expensive ($40-150). If you are using a railpass valid only for a restricted number of days, inspect train schedules to maximize the use of your pass: an overnight train or boat journey uses up only one of your travel days if it departs after 7pm (you need only write-in the next day's date on your pass).

SHOULD YOU BUY A RAILPASS? Railpasses were conceived to allow you to jump on any train in Europe, go wherever you want whenever you want, and change your plans at will. In practice, it's not so simple. You still must stand in line to validate your pass, pay for supplements, and fork over cash for seat and couchette reservations. More importantly, railpasses don't always pay off. Consult our **railplanner** (p. 958) to estimate the point-to-point cost of each leg of your journey; add them up and compare the total with the cost of a railpass. If you are planning to spend extensive time on trains, hopping between big cities, a railpass would probably be worth it. But in many cases, especially if you are under 26, point-to-point tickets may prove cheaper.

You may find it tough to make your railpass pay for itself in Belgium, Greece, Ireland, Italy, Luxembourg, The Netherlands, Portugal, or Spain, where train fares are reasonable, distances short, or buses preferable. If, however, the total cost of your trips nears the price of the pass, the convenience of avoiding ticket lines may be worth the difference.

MULTINATIONAL RAILPASSES

EURAILPASS. Eurail is valid in most of Western and Northern Europe: Austria, Belgium, Denmark, Finland, France, Germany, Greece, Hungary, Italy, Luxembourg, The Netherlands, Norway, Portugal, the Republic of Ireland, Spain, Sweden, and Switzerland. It is not valid in the UK. Standard **Eurailpasses,** valid for a consecutive number of days, are most suitable for those planning on spending extensive time on trains every few days. **Flexipasses**, valid for any 10 or 15 (not necessarily consecutive) days in a two-month period, are more cost-effective for those traveling longer distances less frequently. **Saverpasses** provide first-class travel for travelers in groups of two to five (prices are per person). **Youthpasses** and **Youth Flexipasses** provide parallel second-class perks for those under 26. All prices below are in US dollars, unless otherwise noted.

EURAILPASSES	15 DAYS	21 DAYS	1 MONTH	2 MONTHS	3 MONTHS
1st class Eurailpass	$554	$718	$890	$1260	$1558
Eurail Saverpass	$470	$610	$756	$1072	$1324
Eurail Youthpass	$388	$499	$623	$882	$1089

EURAIL FLEXIPASSES	10 DAYS IN 2 MONTHS	15 DAYS IN 2 MONTHS
1st class Eurail Flexipass	$654	$862
Eurail Saver Flexipass	$556	$732
Eurail Youth Flexipass	$458	$599

Passholders receive a timetable for major routes and a map with details on possible ferry, steamer, bus, car rental, hotel, and Eurostar (see p. 52) discounts. They often also receive reduced fares or free passage on many bus and boat lines. **Eurail freebies** (excepting surcharges such as reservation fees and port taxes) include: ferries between **Ireland** (Rosslare/Cork) and **France** (Cherbourg/Le Havre); sightseeing cruises on the Rhine (Cologne-Mainz) and Mosel (Koblenz-Cochem), as well as Europabus rides down the Romantic Road (Frankfurt-Füssen; 75% off) and Castle Road (Mannheim-Heidelberg-Nuremberg), in **Germany;** ferries between **Italy** and **Sardinia** (Civitavecchia-Golfo Aranci), **Sicily** (Villa S. Giovanni-Messina), and **Greece** (Brindisi-Patras); and boat trips between **Sweden** and **Denmark** (Helsingborg-Helsingør), **Germany** (Trelleborg-Sassnitz), and **Finland** (Ümea/Sundsvall-Vaasa).

EUROPASS. The Europass is a slimmed-down version of the Eurailpass: it allows five to 15 days of unlimited travel in any two-month period within France, Germany, Italy, Spain, and Switzerland. **First-Class Europasses** (for individuals) and **Saverpasses** (for people traveling in groups of 2-5) range from $348/296 per person (5 days) to $688/586 (15 days). **Second-Class Youthpasses** for those ages 12-25 cost $244-482. For a fee, you can add **additional zones** (Austria/Hungary; Belgium/Luxembourg/The Netherlands; Greece Plus, including the ADN/HML ferry between Italy and Greece; and/or Portugal): $60 for one associated country, $100 for two. You are entitled to the same **freebies** afforded by the Eurailpass (see above), but only when they are within or between countries that you have purchased. Plan your itinerary before buying a Europass: it will save you money if your travels are confined to three to five adjacent Western European countries, or if you only want to go to large cities, but would be a waste if you plan to make lots of side-trips. If you're tempted to add many rail days and associate countries, consider a Eurailpass.

SHOPPING AROUND FOR A EURAIL- OR EUROPASS. Eurailpasses and Europasses are designed by the EU itself, and are purchasable only by non-Europeans almost exclusively from non-European distributors. These passes must be sold at uniform prices determined by the EU. However, some travel agents tack on a $10 handling fee, and others offer certain bonuses with purchase, so shop around. Also, keep in mind that pass prices usually go up each year, so if you're planning to travel early in the year, you can save cash by purchasing before January 1 (you have three months from the purchase date to validate your pass in Europe).

It is best to buy your pass before leaving; only a few places in major European cities sell them, and at a marked-up price. Once in Europe, you'd probably have to use a credit card to buy over the phone from a railpass agent in a non-EU country (one on the North American East Coast would be closest) who could send the pass to you by express mail. Eurailpasses are non-refundable once validated; if your pass is completely unused and invalidated and you have the original purchase documents, you can get an 85% refund from the place of purchase. You can get a replacement for a lost pass only if you have purchased insurance on it under the Pass Protection Plan ($10). Eurailpasses are available through travel agents, student travel agencies like STA and Council (see p. 45), and **Rail Europe,** 500 Mamaroneck Ave., Harrison, NY 10528 (US ☎ 888-382-7245, fax 800-432-1329; Canada ☎ 800-361-7245, fax 905-602-4198; UK ☎ 0990 84 88 48; www.raileurope.com) or **DER Travel Services,** 9501 W. Devon Ave. #301, Rosemont, IL 60018 (US ☎ 888-337-7350; fax 800-282-7474; www.dertravel.com).

INTERRAIL PASS. If you have lived for at least six months in one of the European countries where InterRail Passes are valid, they prove an economical option. There are eight InterRail zones: A (Great Britain, Northern Ireland, and the Republic of Ireland), B (Norway, Sweden, and Finland), C (Germany, Austria, Denmark, and Switzerland), D (Croatia, Czech Republic, Hungary, Poland, and Slovakia), E (France, Belgium, The Netherlands, and Luxembourg), F (Spain, Portugal, and Morocco), G (Greece, Italy, Slovenia, and Turkey, including a Greece-Italy ferry), and H (Bulgaria, Romania, Yugoslavia, and Macedonia). The **Under 26 InterRail Card** allows either 22 days or one month of unlimited travel within one, two, three, or all of the eight zones; the cost is determined by the number of zones the pass covers (UK£129-229). If you buy a ticket including the zone in which you have claimed residence, you must still pay 50% fare for tickets inside your own country. The **Over 26 InterRail Card** provides the same services as the Under 26 InterRail Card, but at higher prices: £185-319.

Passholders receive **discounts** on rail travel, Eurostar journeys, and most ferries to Ireland, Scandinavia, and the rest of Europe. Most exclude **supplements** for high-speed trains. For info and ticket sales in Europe, contact **Student Travel Center,** 24 Rupert St., 1st fl., London W1V 7FN (☎ 020 74 37 81 01; fax 020 77 34 38 36; www.student-travel-centre.com). Tickets are also available from travel agents or main train stations throughout Europe.

OTHER MULTINATIONAL PASSES. If your travels will be limited to one area, regional passes are often good values. The **ScanRail Pass,** which gives you unlimited rail travel in Denmark, Finland, Norway, and Sweden, is available both in the UK and the US (standard/under 26 passes for 5 out of 15 days of 2nd-class travel $204/153, 10 days out of 2 months $310/233, 21 consecutive days $360/270). The **Benelux Tourrail Pass** for Belgium, The Netherlands, and Luxembourg is available in the UK, in the US (5 days in 1 month 2nd-class $155, under 26 $104; 50% discount for companion traveler), and at train stations in Belgium and Luxembourg (but not The Netherlands). The **Balkan Flexipass** is valid for travel in Bulgaria, Greece, the Former Yugoslav Republic of Macedonia, Montenegro, Romania, Serbia, and Turkey (5 days in 1 month $152, under 26 $90). The **European East Pass** covers Austria, the Czech Republic, Hungary, Poland, and Slovakia (5 days in 1 month $210).

DOMESTIC RAILPASSES

If you are planning to spend a significant amount of time within one country or region, a national pass—valid on all rail lines of a country's rail company—would probably be more cost-effective than a multinational pass. But consider the cons as well: many national passes are limited, and don't provide the free or discounted travel on many private railways and ferries that Eurail does. However, several national and regional passes offer companion fares, allowing two adults traveling together to save about 50% on the price of the second pass. Some of these passes can be bought only in Europe, some only outside of Europe; check with a railpass agent or with national tourist offices.

NATIONAL RAILPASSES. The domestic analogs of the Eurailpass, national railpasses are valid either for a number of consecutive days or for a specific number of days within a given time period. Usually, they must be purchased before you leave. Though they will usually save frequent travelers some money, in some cases (particularly in Eastern Europe) you may find that they are actually a more expensive alternative to point-to-point tickets. Examples include the **Britrail Pass, BritIreland**

E
S
S
E
N
T
I
A
L
S

FURTHER READING & RESOURCES ON TRAIN TRAVEL.

Point-to-point fares and schedules: www.raileurope.com/us/rail/fares_schedules/index.htm. Allows you to calculate whether buying a railpass would save you money. For a more convenient resource, see our **railplanner** (p. 958).

European Railway Servers: mercurio.iet.unipi.it/home.html. Links to rail servers throughout Europe.

Info on rail travel and railpasses: www.eurorail.com, www.raileuro.com.

Eurail and Train Travel Guide to Europe. Houghton Mifflin (US$15).

Europe By Eurail 2000, Laverne Ferguson-Kosinski. Globe Pequot Press ($17).

Guide to European Railpasses, Rick Steves. Available online and by mail. (US ☎425-771-8303; fax 425-671-0833; www.ricksteves.com). Free; delivery $8.

On the Rails Around Europe: A Comprehensive Guide to Travel by Train, Melissa Shales. Thomas Cook Ldt. ($19).

Thomas Cook European Timetable, updated monthly, covers all major and most minor train routes in Europe. In the US, order it from Forsyth Travel Library ($28; ☎800-367-7984; www.forsyth.com). In Europe, find it at any Thomas Cook Money Exchange Center. Alternatively, buy directly from Thomas Cook (www.thomascook.com).

Flexipass, Freedom of Scotland Travelpass, Irish Explorer, Ireland's **Emerald Isle Card** and **Irish Rover, France Flexipass, German Flexipass, Austrian Flexipass, Greek Flexipass, Italian Railpass** and **Flexipass, Swiss Railpass** and **Flexipass, Holland Flexipass, Norway Flexipass, Sweden Railpass, Finnrail Flexipass, Iberic Flexipass, Spain Flexipass, Portuguese Flexipass, Bulgarian Flexipass, Polrail Pass, Czech Flexipass, Hungarian Flexipass,** and **Romanian Flexipass.** For more info, contact Rail Europe (see p. 56).

EURO DOMINO. Like the Interrail Pass, the Euro Domino pass is available to anyone who has lived in Europe for at least six months; it differs in that it is only valid in one country (which you designate upon buying the pass). It is available for 29 European countries including Morocco. Reservations must still be paid for separately. The Euro Domino pass is available for 1st- and 2nd-class travel (with a special rate for under 26ers), for three to eight days of unlimited travel within a one-month period. Euro Domino is not valid on Eurostar or Thalys trains. **Supplements** for many high-speed trains are included (Spanish AVE is not), though you must still pay for **reservations** where they are compulsory (e.g., about 20F/€3.05 on the TGV). The pass must be bought within your country of residence (except for the Euro Domino Plus pass in The Netherlands, which also includes all bus, tram, and metro rides and can be bought in The Netherlands); each country has its own price for the pass. Inquire with your national rail company for more info.

REGIONAL PASSES. Another type of regional pass covers a specific area within a country or a round-trip from any border to a particular destination and back; these are useful as supplements when your main pass isn't valid. The **Prague Excursion Pass** is a common purchase for Eurailers, whose passes are not valid in the Czech Republic; it covers travel from any Czech border to Prague and back out of the country (round-trips must be completed within 7 days; 2nd-class $35, under 26 $30). The **Copenhagen Pass** is valid for Europass or German railpass holders from any German or Danish border to Copenhagen and back, while the **BritRail Southeast Pass** permits unlimited travel in southeast England (3 out of 8 days US$73).

RAIL-AND-DRIVE PASSES. In addition to simple railpasses, many countries (as well as Europass and Eurail) offer rail-and-drive passes, which combine car rental with rail travel—a good option for travelers who wish both to visit cities accessible by rail and to make side trips into the surrounding areas. Contact a budget travel agency for more information (see p. 45).

DISCOUNTED TICKETS

For travelers under 26, **BIJ** tickets (Billets Internationals de Jeunesse, a.k.a. **Wasteels, Eurotrain**, and **Route 26**) are a great alternative to railpasses. Available for international trips within Europe and for travel within France as well as most ferry services, they knock 20-40% off regular 2nd-class fares. Tickets are good for 60 days after purchase and allow a number of stopovers along the normal direct route of the train journey. Issued for a specific international route between two points, they must be used in the direction and order of the designated route and must be bought in Europe. The equivalent for those over 26, **BIGT** tickets provide a 20-30% discount on 1st- and 2nd-class international tickets for business travelers, temporary residents of Europe, and their families. Both types of tickets are available from European travel agents, at Wasteels or Eurotrain offices (usually in or near train stations), or directly at the ticket counter in some nations. For more info, contact **Wasteels**, Victoria Station, London SW1V 1JT (☎ 0171 630 7627).

BY BUS

Though European trains and railpasses are extremely popular, in some cases buses prove a better option. In Spain and Hungary, the bus and train systems are on par; in Britain, Greece, Ireland, Portugal, and Turkey, bus networks are more extensive, efficient, and often more comfortable; and in Iceland and parts of northern Scandinavia, bus service is the only ground transportation available. In the rest of Europe, bus travel is more of a crapshoot; scattered offerings from private companies are often cheap, but sometimes unreliable. Amsterdam, Athens, Istanbul, London, Munich, and Oslo are centers for lines that offer long-distance rides across Europe. Often cheaper than railpasses, **international bus passes** typically allow unlimited travel on a hop-on, hop-off basis between major European cities. These services in general tend to be more popular among non-American backpackers. Note that **Eurobus,** a UK-based bus service, is no longer in operation.

Busabout, 258 Vauxhall Bridge Rd., London SW1V 1BS (☎ 171 950 1661; fax 950 1662; www.busabout.com). Offers 5 interconnecting bus circuits covering 60 cities and towns in Europe. Consecutive Day Passes and FlexiPasses both available. Consecutive day standard/student passes are valid for 15 days ($US229/207), 21 days ($324/295), 1 month ($428/384), 2 months ($666/592), 3 months ($740/894), or for the season ($977/873).

Eurolines, 52 Grosvenor Gardens, London SW1 (☎ 1582 400 694; www.eurolines.co.uk or www.eurolines.com). The largest operator of Europe-wide coach services. Unlimited 30-day (UK£229, under 26 and over 60 £199) or 60-day (£279/249) travel between 30 major European cities in 16 countries.

BY CAR

Cars offer speed, freedom, access to the countryside, and an escape from the town-to-town mentality of trains. Unfortunately, they also insulate you from the *esprit de corps* of rail travel. Although a single traveler won't save by renting a car, four usually will. If you can't decide between train and car travel, you may benefit from a combination of the two; RailEurope and other railpass vendors offer rail-and-drive packages for both individual countries and all of Europe. Fly-and-drive packages are also often available from travel agents or airline/rental agency partnerships.

Before setting off, know the laws of the countries in which you'll be driving (e.g., keep left in Ireland and the UK). Roads in Western Europe are generally excellent, but keep in mind that each area has its own hazards. Even in areas with official speed limits, Europeans tend to drive *fast*, and roads are often curvy, particularly in mountainous areas. Road conditions fluctuate with the seasons; for instance, winter weather will make driving difficult in some countries, while summer weather causes flooding in others. For an informal primer on European road signs and conventions, check out www.travlang.com/signs. Additionally, the **Association for Safe International Road Travel (ASIRT),** 11769 Gainsborough Rd., Potomac, MD

20854, USA (☎301-983-5252; fax 983-3663; www.asirt.org), can provide more specific information about road conditions. ASIRT considers road travel (by car or bus) to be relatively **safe** in Denmark, Ireland, The Netherlands, Switzerland, and the UK. Western Europeans use unleaded **gas** almost exclusively. Carry emergency equipment with you and know what to do in case of a breakdown.

DRIVING PERMITS AND CAR INSURANCE

INTERNATIONAL DRIVING PERMIT (IDP). If you plan to drive a car while abroad, you must be over 18 and have an **International Driving Permit (IDP),** though certain countries allow travelers to drive with a valid American or Canadian license for a limited number of months. It may be a good idea to get one anyway, in case you're in a situation (e.g. an accident or stranded in a small town) where the police do not know English. Information on the IDP is printed in ten languages, including Spanish, French, Italian, Portuguese, and German.

Your IDP, valid for one year, must be issued in your own country before you depart. An application for an IDP usually needs to include one or two photos, a current local license, an additional form of identification, and a fee. To apply, contact the national or local branch of your home country's automobile association.

CAR INSURANCE. Most credit cards cover standard insurance. If you rent, lease, or borrow a car, you will need a **International Insurance Certificate** to certify that you have liability insurance and that it applies abroad. Certificates can be obtained at car rental agencies, car dealers (for those leasing cars), some travel agents, and some border crossings. Rental agencies may require you to purchase theft insurance in countries that they consider to have a high risk of auto theft.

RENTING A CAR

You can rent a car from a US-based firm (Alamo, Avis, Budget, or Hertz) with European offices, from a European-based company with local representatives (Europcar), or from a tour operator (Auto Europe, Europe By Car, or Kemwel Holiday Autos) that will arrange a rental for you from a European company at its own rates. Multinationals offer greater flexibility, but tour operators often strike better deals. Picking up your car in Belgium, Germany, or The Netherlands is usually cheaper than renting in Paris. Expect to pay US$80-400 per week, plus tax (5-25%), for a teensy car. Reserve ahead and pay in advance if at all possible. It is always significantly less expensive to reserve a car from the US than from Europe. Always check if prices quoted include tax and collision insurance; some credit card companies cover the deductible on collision insurance, allowing their customers to decline the collision damage waiver. Ask about discounts and check the terms of insurance, particularly the size of the deductible. Rates are generally lowest in Belgium, Germany, The Netherlands, and the UK, and highest in Scandinavia and Eastern Europe. Ask airlines about special fly-and-drive packages; you may get up to a week of free or discounted rental. Minimum age varies by country, but is usually 21 to 25. At most agencies, all that's needed to rent a car is a license from home and proof that you've had it for a year. Car rental in Europe is available through the following agencies:

Auto Europe, 39 Commercial St, P.O. Box 7006, Portland, ME 04112, USA (☎888-223-5555; fax 207-842-2222; www.autoeurope.com).

Avis (US ☎800-230-4898, Canada ☎800-272-5871, UK ☎0870 606 01 00, Australia ☎13 63 33; www.avis.com).

Budget, 4225 Naperville Rd., Lisle, IL 60532, USA (☎800-527-0000 or 630-955-1900; www.budget.com).

Europe by Car (US ☎800-223-1516 or 212-581-3040; www.europebycar.com)

Europcar, 3, av. du Centre, 78 881 Saint Quentin en Yvelines Cedex, France (☎331 30 44 90 00), US ☎678-461-9880; www.europcar.com).

Hertz 225 Brae Blvd., Park Ridge, NJ 07656, USA (☎800-654-3131, Canada ☎800-263-0600, UK ☎0870 844 8844, Australia ☎613 96 98 25 55; www.hertz.com).

Kemwel Holiday Autos (US ☎800-576-1590 or ☎914-825-3000; www.kemwel.com).

LEASING A CAR

For longer than 17 days, leasing can be cheaper than renting; it is often the only option for those ages 18 to 21. The cheapest leases are agreements to buy the car and then sell it back to the manufacturer at a prearranged price. As far as you're concerned, though, it's a lease and doesn't entail enormous financial transactions. Leases generally include insurance coverage and are not taxed. The most affordable ones usually originate in Belgium, France, or Germany. Expect to pay around US$1100-1800 (depending on size of car) for 60 days. Contact **Auto Europe, Europe by Car,** or **Kemwel Holiday Autos** (see above) before you go.

BUYING A CAR

If you're brave and know what you're doing, **buying** a used car or van in Western Europe and selling it just before you leave can provide the cheapest wheels for longer trips. Check with consulates for import-export laws concerning used vehicles, registration, and safety and emissions standards. Camper-vans and motor homes give the advantages of a car without the hassle and expense of finding lodgings. Most of these vehicles are diesel-powered and deliver roughly 24 to 30 miles per gallon of diesel fuel, which is cheaper than regular gas.

BY BOAT

Most European ferries are quite comfortable; the cheapest ticket typically still includes a reclining chair or couchette. Fares jump sharply in July and August. Ask for **discounts**; ISIC holders can often get student fares, and Eurailpass holders get many reductions and free trips (for examples of popular freebies, also see p. 55). You'll occasionally have to pay a port tax (under US$10). For more info, consult the *Official Steamship Guide International* (available at travel agents) or www.youra.com/ferry.

ENGLISH CHANNEL AND IRISH SEA FERRIES

Ferries are frequent and dependable. The main route from England to France is Dover-Calais. The main ferry port on the southern coast of England is Portsmouth, with connections to France and Spain. Ferries also cross the Irish Sea, connecting Northern Ireland with Scotland and England and the Republic of Ireland with Wales.

NORTH AND BALTIC SEA FERRIES

Ferries in the **North Sea** are reliable and go everywhere. Those content with deck passage rarely need to book ahead. For ferries heading to and from the UK, see p. 52. **Baltic Sea** ferries service routes between Poland and Scandinavia.

Color Line: Norway ☎ 46 22 94 44 00; www.colorline.com. Offers ferries between Norway and Denmark, and Sweden and Germany.

Polferries: Sweden ☎ 46 40 97 61 80; www.polferries.se. Ystad, Sweden, to Świnoujście (7hr.), Poland, and Oxelösund-Stockholm, Sweden, to Gdańsk, Poland (17hr.).

Silja Line: US sales ☎ 800-323-7436, Finland ☎ 358 09 18041; www.silja.com. Helsinki to Stockholm (16hr., June-Dec.); Tallinn, Estonia (3hr., June to mid-Sept.); and Rostock, Germany (23-25hr., June to mid-Sept.). Also Turku, Finland, to Stockholm (12hr.).

MEDITERRANEAN AND AEGEAN FERRIES

Mediterranean ferries may be the most glamorous, but they can also be the most rocky. Ferries run from Spain to Morocco, from Italy to Tunisia, and from France to Morocco and Tunisia. Reservations are recommended, especially in July and August. **Bring toilet paper.** Ferries run on erratic schedules, with similar routes and varying prices. Shop around, and beware of dinky, unreliable companies that don't take reservations. Ferries float across the **Adriatic** from Ancona and Bari, Italy to Split and Dubrovnik, respectively, in Croatia.

Ferries also run across the **Aegean,** from Ancona, Italy, to Patras, Greece (19hr.), and from Bari, Italy, to Igoumenitsa (9hr.) and Patras (15hr.), Greece. **Eurail** is valid on certain ferries between Brindisi, Italy, and Corfu (8hr.), Igoumenitsa, and Patras, Greece. Countless ferry companies operate these routes simultaneously; see specific country chapters for more information.

ESSENTIALS

BY BICYCLE

Today, biking is one of the key elements of the classic budget Eurovoyage. With the proliferation of mountain bikes, you can do some serious natural sightseeing. Many airlines will count your bike as your second free piece of luggage; a few charge extra (US$60-110 one-way). Bikes must be packed in a cardboard box with the pedals and front wheel detached; many airlines sell bike boxes at the airport ($10). Most ferries let you take your bike for free or for a nominal fee, and you can always just ship your bike on trains. Renting a bike beats bringing your own if you plan to bike in one or two regions. Some youth hostels rent bicycles for low prices. In Switzerland, train stations rent bikes and often allow you to drop them off elsewhere; check other countries for similar deals. In addition to **panniers** in which you can pack your luggage, you'll need a good **helmet** ($25-50) and a U-shaped **Citadel** or **Kryptonite lock** (from $30). For equipment, **Bike Nashbar**, 6103 State Rte. 446, Canfield, OH 44406 (☎800-627 42 27; www.nashbar.com), ships anywhere in the US or Canada. For more country-specific books on biking through France, Germany, Ireland, or the UK, or to purchase the more general *Europe by Bike*, by Karen and Terry Whitehall ($15), try **Mountaineers Books**, 1001 S.W. Klickitat Way #201, Seattle, WA 98134 (☎800-553-4453; www.mountaineersbooks.org).

If you are nervous about striking out on your own, **Blue Marble Travel** (Canada ☎519-624-2494, France ☎01 42 36 02 34, US ☎973-326-9533; www.bluemarble.org) offers bike tours for small groups for ages 20-50 through the Alps, Austria, France, Germany, Italy, Portugal, Scandinavia, and Spain. **CBT Tours**, 2506 N. Clark St. #150, Chicago, IL 60614, USA (☎800-736-2453; www.cbttours.com), offers full-package 7- to 12-day biking, mountain biking, and hiking tours (around $100 per day) to Belgium, the Czech Republic, England, France, Germany, The Netherlands, Italy, Ireland, Scotland, and Switzerland.

BY MOPED AND MOTORCYCLE

Motorized bikes don't use much gas, can be put on trains and ferries, and are a good compromise between costly car travel and the limited range of bicycles. However, they're uncomfortable for long distances, dangerous in the rain, and unpredictable on rough roads. Always wear a helmet, and never ride with a backpack. If you've never ridden a moped before, a twisting Alpine road is not the place to start. Expect to pay about US$20-35 per day; try auto repair shops, and remember to bargain. Motorcycles are more expensive and normally require a license, but are better for long distances. Before renting, ask if the price includes tax and insurance, or you may be hit with an unexpected fee. Avoid handing your passport over as a deposit; if you have an accident or mechanical failure you may not get it back until you cover all repairs. Pay ahead of time instead. For more information, try *Motorcycle Journeys through the Alps and Corsica* by John Hermann or *Motorcycle Touring and Travel* by Bill Stermer (both Whitehorse Press, $20).

BY FOOT

Europe's grandest scenery can often be seen only by foot. *Let's Go* describes many daytrips for those who want to hoof it, but native inhabitants (Europeans are fervent hikers), hostel proprietors, and fellow travelers are the best source of tips. Many European countries have hiking and mountaineering organizations; alpine clubs in Germany, Austria, Switzerland, and Italy, as well as tourist organizations in Scandinavia, provide simple accommodations in splendid settings.

BY THUMB

No one should hitch without careful consideration of the risks involved. Hitching means entrusting your life to a random person who happens to stop beside you on the road and risking theft, assault, sexual harassment, and unsafe driving. In spite

Let's Go strongly urges you to consider the risks before you choose to hitch. We do not recommend hitching as a safe means of transportation, and none of the information presented here is intended to do so.

of this, there are advantages to hitching when it is safe: it allows you to meet local people and get where you're going, especially in northern Europe and Ireland, where public transportation is sketchy. The choice, however, remains yours.

Britain and Ireland are probably the easiest places in Western Europe to get a lift. Hitching in Scandinavia is slow but steady. Long-distance hitching in the developed countries of Europe demands close attention to expressway junctions, rest stop locations, and often a destination sign. Hitching in southern Europe is generally mediocre. France is the worst place to hitchhike. In some central and eastern European countries, the line between hitching and taking a taxi is quite thin.

Safety-minded hitchers avoid getting in the back of a two-door car (or any car they wouldn't be able to get out of in a hurry) and never let go of their backpacks. If they ever feel threatened, they insist on being let off immediately. Acting as if they are going to open the car door or vomit on the upholstery will usually get a driver to stop. Hitchhiking at night can be particularly dangerous; experienced hitchers stand in well-lit places, and expect drivers to be leery of nocturnal thumbers.

For women traveling alone, hitching is just too dangerous. A man and a woman are a safer combination, two men will have a harder time, and three will go nowhere. Where one stands is vital. Experienced hitchers pick a spot outside of built-up areas, where drivers can stop and return to the road without causing an accident, and where they have time to look over potential passengers as they approach. Hitching (or even standing) on super-highways is usually illegal: one may only thumb at rest stops or at the entrance ramps to highways. In the **Practical Information** section of many cities, *Let's Go* lists the tram or bus lines that take travelers to strategic hitching points. Finally, success will depend on appearance. Successful hitchers travel light and stack their belongings in a compact but visible cluster. Most Europeans signal with an open hand rather than a thumb; many write their destination on a sign in large, bold letters and draw a smiley-face under it. Drivers prefer hitchers who are neat and wholesome. No one stops for anyone wearing sunglasses.

Most Western European countries offer a ride service (listed in the **Practical Information** for major cities), a cross between hitchhiking and the ride boards common at many universities, which pairs drivers with riders; the fee varies according to destination. **Eurostop International** (**Verband der Deutschen Mitfahrzentralen** in Germany and **Allostop** in France) is one of the largest in Europe. Riders and drivers can enter their names on the internet through the **Taxistop** website (www.taxistop.be).

SPECIFIC CONCERNS

WOMEN TRAVELERS

Women exploring on their own inevitably face some additional safety concerns, but it's easy to be adventurous without taking undue risks. If you are concerned, consider staying in hostels which offer single rooms that lock from the inside or in religious organizations with rooms for women only. Communal showers in some hostels are safer than others; check them before settling in. Stick to centrally located accommodations and avoid solitary late-night treks or metro rides.

Always carry extra money for a phone call, bus, or taxi. **Hitchhiking** is never safe for lone women, or even for two women traveling together. Choose train compartments occupied by women or couples; ask the conductor to put together a women-only compartment if there isn't one. Look as if you know where you're going and approach older women or couples for directions if you're lost or uncomfortable.

ESSENTIALS

Generally, the less you look like a tourist, the better off you'll be. Dress conservatively, especially in rural areas. Trying to fit in can be effective, but dressing to the style of an obviously different culture may cause you to be ill at ease and a conspicuous target. Wearing a conspicuous **wedding band** may help prevent unwanted overtures. Some travelers report that carrying pictures of a "husband" or "children" is extremely useful to help prove marriage status. Even a mention of a husband waiting back at the hotel may be enough in some places to discount your potentially vulnerable, unattached appearance.

FURTHER READING: WOMEN TRAVELERS.

Active Women Vacation Guide, Evelyn Kaye. Blue Panda Publications (US$18).

A Foxy Old Woman's Guide to Traveling Alone: Around Town and Around the World, Jay Ben-Lesser. Crossing Press ($11).

A Journey of One's Own: Uncommon Advice for the Independent Woman Traveler, Thalia Zepatos. Eighth Mountain Press ($17).

Safety and Security for Women Who Travel, Sheila Swan. Travelers' Tales Guides, Inc. ($13).

Your best answer to verbal harassment is no answer at all; feigning deafness, sitting motionless, and staring straight ahead at nothing in particular will do a world of good that reactions usually don't achieve. The extremely persistent can sometimes be dissuaded by a firm, loud, and very public "Go away!" in the appropriate language. Don't hesitate to seek out a police officer or a passerby if you are being harassed. Memorize the emergency numbers in places you visit, and consider carrying a whistle or airhorn on your keychain. A self-defense course will not only prepare you for a potential attack, but will also raise your level of awareness of your surroundings as well as your confidence (see **Self Defense**, p. 27). Also be sure you are aware of the health concerns that women face when traveling (see p. 33).

For general information, contact the National Organization for Women (NOW), 733 15th St. NW, Fl. 2, Washington, DC 20005 (☎202-628-8669; www.now.org), which has branches across the US that can refer women travelers to rape crisis centers and counseling services. In addition, *Journeywoman* (www.journeywoman.com) posts an online newsletter and other resources providing female-specific travel tips. *Women Traveling Together* (www.women-traveling.com) places women in small groups to explore the world together.

TRAVELING ALONE

There are many benefits to traveling alone, including independence and greater interaction with locals. On the other hand, any solo traveler is a more vulnerable target of harassment and street theft. Lone travelers need to be well-organized and look confident at all times. Try not to stand out as a tourist, and be especially careful in deserted or very crowded areas. If questioned, never admit that you are traveling alone. Maintain regular contact with someone at home who knows your itinerary. For more tips, pick up *Traveling Solo* by Eleanor Berman (Globe Pequot Press, US$17), or *Travel Alone & Love It: A Flight Attendant's Guide to Solo Travel* by Sharon B. Wingler (Chicago Spectrum Press, $15). You can also subscribe to **Connecting: Solo Travel Network,** 689 Park Road, Unit 6, Gibsons, BC V0N 1V7, Canada (☎604-886-9099; www.cstn.org; membership $28).

Alternatively, several services link solo travelers with companions who have similar travel habits and interests; for a bimonthly newsletter for single travelers seeking a travel partner, contact the **Travel Companion Exchange,** P.O. Box 833, Amityville, NY 11701 (☎800-392-1256; www.whytravelalone.com; $48). For group tours in Western Europe that join single people together, try **O Solo Mio**, 636 Los Altos Rancho, Los Altos, CA 94024 (☎800-959-8568 or 650-917-0817; fax 650-941-5334; www.osolomio.com).

OLDER TRAVELERS

Senior citizens are eligible for a wide range of discounts on transportation, museums, movies, theaters, concerts, restaurants, and accommodations. If you don't see a senior citizen price listed, ask, and you may be delightfully surprised. However, keep in mind that some hostels do not allow guests over age 26. The books *No Problem! Worldwise Tips for Mature Adventurers*, by Janice Kenyon (Orca Book Publishers, US$16) and *Unbelievably Good Deals and Great Adventures That You Absolutely Can't Get Unless You're Over 50*, by Joan Rattner Heilman (NTC/Contemporary Publishing, $13) are both excellent resources. For more information, contact one of the following organizations:

ElderTreks, 597 Markham St., Toronto, ON M6G 2L7, Canada (☎800-741-7956; www.eldertreks.com). Adventure travel programs for the 50+ traveler.

Elderhostel, 11 Ave. de Lafayette, Boston, MA 02111, USA (☎877-426-8056; www.elderhostel.org). Organizes 1- to 4-week "educational adventures" throughout Western Europe on varied subjects for those 55+.

The Mature Traveler, P.O. Box 15791, Sacramento, CA 95852, USA (☎800-460-6676). Deals, discounts, and travel packages for the 50+ traveler. Subscription $30.

Walking the World, P.O. Box 1186, Fort Collins, CO 80522, USA (☎800-340-9255; www.walkingtheworld.com), organizes trips for 50+ travelers in many Western European countries.

BISEXUAL, GAY, & LESBIAN TRAVELERS

Attitudes toward bisexual, gay, and lesbian travelers are particular to each region in Western Europe. Consult the **Further Reading** box below for books that include individual country information. Acceptance is generally highest in large cities. Listed below are contact organizations, mail-order bookstores, and publishers that offer materials addressing some specific concerns. **Out and About** (www.planetout.com) offers a biweekly newsletter addressing travel concerns and a comprehensive site addressing gay travel issues.

Gay's the Word, 66 Marchmont St., London WC1N 1AB, UK (☎44 20 7278 7654; www.gaystheword.co.uk). The largest gay and lesbian bookshop in the UK, with both fiction and non-fiction titles. Mail-order service available.

Giovanni's Room, 1145 Pine St., Philadelphia, PA 19107, USA (☎215-923-2960; www.queerbooks.com). An international lesbian/feminist and gay bookstore with mail-order service (carries many of the publications listed below).

International Gay and Lesbian Travel Association, International Lesbian and Gay Association (ILGA), 81 r. Marché-au-Charbon, B-1000 Brussels, Belgium (☎32 2 502 2471; www.ilga.org). Provides political information, such as homosexuality laws of individual countries.

> **FURTHER READING: BISEXUAL, GAY, & LESBIAN.**
> *Damron Men's Travel Guide, Damron Women's Traveller, Damron's Accommodations,* and *Damron Amsterdam Guide.* Damron Travel Guides (US$10-19). For more info, call 800-462-6654 or visit www.damron.com.
> *Ferrari Guides' Gay Travel A to Z, Ferrari Guides' Men's Travel in Your Pocket,* and *Ferrari Guides' Inn Places.* Ferrari Publications ($16-20). Purchase the guides online at www.ferrariguides.com.
> *The Gay Vacation Guide: The Best Trips and How to Plan Them,* Mark Chesnut. Citadel Press ($15).
> *Odysseus International Gay Travel Planner,* Eli Angelo and Joseph Bain. Odysseus Enterprises. ($31).
> *Spartacus International Gay Guide 2001-2002,* Bruno Gmunder Verlag (US$33).

ESSENTIALS

TRAVELERS WITH DISABILITIES

Countries vary in accessibility to travelers with disabilities. Some national and regional tourist boards provide directories on the accessibility of various accommodations and transportation services. If these services are not available, contact institutions directly. Those with disabilities should inform airlines and hotels of their disabilities when making reservations; some time may be needed to prepare special accommodations. Call ahead to restaurants, museums, and other facilities to find out about the existence of ramps, the widths of doors, the dimensions of elevators, etc. The **Green Book** (http://members.nbci.com/thegreenbook/home.html) has a partial listing of disabled-access accommodations and sights throughout Western Europe. **Guide dog owners** should inquire as to the quarantine policies of each destination country. At the very least, they will need to provide a certificate of immunization against rabies.

Rail is probably the most convenient form of travel for disabled travelers in Europe: many stations have ramps, and some trains have wheelchair lifts, special seating areas, and specially equipped toilets. Greece and Spain's rail systems have limited resources for wheelchair accessibility. For those who wish to rent cars, some major **car rental** agencies (Hertz, Avis, and National) offer hand-controlled vehicles.

FURTHER READING: TRAVELERS WITH DISABILITIES.
Access in London, Gordon Couch. Cimino Publishing Group (US$12).
Around the World Resource Guide, Patricia Smither. Access for Disabled American Publishing ($15).
Resource Directory for the Disabled, Richard Neil Shrout. Facts on File ($45).
Wheelchair Around the World, Patrick D. Simpson. Pentland Press. ($25).
Wheelchair Through Europe, Annie Mackin. Graphic Language Press ($13).

USEFUL ORGANIZATIONS

Mobility International USA (MIUSA), P.O. Box 10767, Eugene, OR 97440, USA (voice and TDD ☎541-343-1284; www.miusa.org). Sells *A World of Options: A Guide to International Educational Exchange, Community Service, and Travel for Persons with Disabilities* (US$35).

Moss Rehab ResourceNet (www.mossresourcenet.org). An internet information resource center on international travel accessibility and concerns for those with disabilities.

Society for the Advancement of Travel for the Handicapped (SATH), 347 5th Ave., #610, New York, NY 10016, USA (☎212-447-7284; www.sath.org). An advocacy group that publishes free online travel info and the travel magazine *OPEN WORLD* (US$18, free for members). Annual membership $45, students and seniors $30.

TOUR AGENCIES

Directions Unlimited, 123 Green Ln., Bedford Hills, NY 10507, USA (☎800-533-5343). Books individual and group vacations for the physically disabled; not an info service.

The Guided Tour Inc., 7900 Old York Rd., #114B, Elkins Park, PA 19027, USA (☎800-783-5841; www.guidedtour.com). Organizes travel programs for persons with developmental and physical challenges in Ireland and Paris.

MINORITY TRAVELERS

In general, minority travelers will find a high level of tolerance in large cities; the small towns and the countryside are more unpredictable. *Romany* (Gypsies) encounter the most hostility throughout Eastern Europe, and travelers with darker skin might be mistaken for them and face unpleasant consequences. Other minority travelers, especially those of African or Asian descent, will usually meet with more curiosity than hostility; travelers of Arab ethnicity may be treated more suspiciously. Skinheads are on the rise in Europe, and minority travelers, especially Jews and blacks, should regard them with caution. Anti-Semitism is still a problem in many countries; it is generally best to be discreet about your religion. Still, attitudes will vary; travelers should use common sense—consult **Safety and Security** (see p. 27) for tips on how to avoid unwanted attention.

TRAVELERS WITH CHILDREN

Family vacations often require that you slow your pace and always require that you plan ahead. When deciding where to stay, remember the special needs of young children; if you pick a B&B or a small hotel, call ahead and make sure it's child-friendly. If you rent a car, make sure the rental company provides a car seat for younger children. **Be sure that your child carries some sort of ID** in case of an emergency or in case he or she gets lost. Museums, tourist attractions, accommodations, and restaurants often offer discounts for children. Children under two generally fly for 10% of the adult airfare on international flights (this does not necessarily include a seat). International fares are usually discounted 25% for children from two to 11. For more info, consult one of the following books:

Backpacking with Babies and Small Children, Goldie Silverman. Wilderness Press (US$10).

Take Your Kids to Europe, Cynthia W. Harriman. Cardogan Books ($18).

How to take Great Trips with Your Kids, Sanford and Jane Portnoy. Harvard Common Press ($10).

Have Kid, Will Travel: 101 Survival Strategies for Vacationing With Babies and Young Children, Claire and Lucille Tristram. Andrews McMeel Publishing ($9).

Adventuring with Children: An Inspirational Guide to World Travel and the Outdoors, Nan Jeffrey. Avalon House Publishing (U$15).

Trouble Free Travel with Children, Vicki Lansky. Book Peddlers ($9).

DIETARY CONCERNS

Vegetarians should have no problem finding suitable cuisine in most of Western Europe. Particularly in city listings, *Let's Go* notes many restaurants that cater to vegetarians or that offer good vegetarian selections. The North American Vegetarian Society, P.O. Box 72, Dolgeville, NY 13329, USA (☎518-568-7970; www.navs-online.org), publishes information about vegetarian travel, including *Transformative Adventures, Vacations and Retreats* (US$15). For more information, visit your local bookstore, health food store, or library, and consult *The Vegetarian Traveler: Where to Stay if You're Vegetarian,* by Jed and Susan Civic (Larson Publications, $16) and *Europe on 10 Salads a Day,* by Greg and Mary Jane Edwards (Mustang Publishing, $10).

Travelers who keep **kosher** should contact synagogues in larger cities for information on kosher restaurants. Your own synagogue or college Hillel should have access to lists of Jewish institutions across the nation. If you are strict in your observance, you may have to prepare your own food on the road. Two good resources are the *Jewish Travel Guide,* by Michael Zaidner (Vallentine Mitchell, $17) and *A Travel Guide to Jewish Europe,* by Ben G. Frank (Pelican Publishing, $23).

ALTERNATIVES TO TOURISM

For an extensive listing of "off-the-beaten-track" and specialty travel opportunities, try the **Specialty Travel Index,** 305 San Anselmo Ave. #313, San Anselmo, CA 94960, USA (☎800-442-4922; www.specialtytravel.com; US$10). **Transitions Abroad** (www.transabroad.com) publishes a bimonthly online newsletter for work, study, and specialized travel abroad.

STUDYING ABROAD

The opportunities for studying in Western Europe are plenty: whether you seek a college semester abroad, a summer of foreign-language immersion, or a top-notch cooking school, you are almost sure to find a program tailored to your needs. Most American undergraduates enroll in programs sponsored by US universities. Those with adequate language skills may find it cheaper to enroll directly in a European university (though getting credit may be more difficult). Direct enrollment usually involves passing a language-proficiency test.

Studying abroad in Western Europe, particularly enrolling as a full-time student, generally requires applying for a special study **visa**, issued for a duration longer than a tourist visa. Applying for such a visa usually requires proof of admission to an appropriate university or program. In some countries, student status will affect your right to work. Info on visa and other requirements should be available from foreign embassies at home. For further info, including links to many study abroad organizations, check out **We Study Abroad** (www.westudyabroad.com).

UNIVERSITY PROGRAMS

American Institute for Foreign Study, College Division, River Plaza, 9 West Broad St., Stamford, CT 06902, USA (☎800-727-2437, ext. 5163; www.aifsabroad.com). Organizes programs for high school and college study in universities in Austria, Czech Republic, England, France, The Netherlands, Ireland, Italy, and Spain.

Arcadia University for Education Abroad, 450 S. Easton Rd., Glenside, PA 19038, USA (☎866-927-2234; www.arcadia.edu/cea). Operates programs in Britain, Greece, Ireland, Italy, Scotland, Spain, and Wales. Costs range from US$2400 (summer) to $20,000 (full-year).

Central College Abroad, Office of International Education, 812 University, Pella, IA 50219, USA (☎800-831-3629 or 641-628-5284; studyabroad.com/central). Offers semester- and year-long programs in Austria, Britain, France, The Netherlands, and Spain. $25 application fee.

Council on International Educational Exchange (CIEE), 633 3rd Ave., 20th Fl., New York, NY 10017-6706 USA (☎888-268-6245; www.ciee.org/isp) sponsors work, volunteer, academic, and internship programs throughout Western Europe.

Institute for Study Abroad, Butler University (ISA), 1100 W. 42nd Street, Suite 305, Indianapolis, IN 46208-3345 USA (☎800-858-0229 or 317-940-9336; fax 940-9704; www.isabutler.org). A semester abroad program affiliated with the major universities of Australia. Programs in Britain and Ireland. The ISA program takes care of university applications, student visas, and housing, and provides personal guidance while abroad. $40 application fee.

International Association for the Exchange of Students for Technical Experience (IAESTE), 10400 Little Patuxent Pkwy. #250, Columbia, MD 21044-3510, USA (☎410-997-2200; www.aipt.org). 8- to 12-week programs in many Western European countries for college students who have completed 2 years of technical study. $25 application fee.

School for International Training, College Semester Abroad, Admissions, Kipling Rd., P.O. Box 676, Brattleboro, VT 05302, USA (☎800-336-1616; www.sit.edu). Semester- and year-long programs throughout Western Europe run $10,600-13,700. Also runs the **Experiment in International Living** (☎800-345-2929; fax 802-258-3428; eil@worldlearning.org), 3- to 5-week summer programs that offer high-school students cross-cultural homestays, community service, ecological adventure, and language training in Britain, France, Ireland, Italy, Spain and Switzerland, and cost $1900-5000.

LANGUAGE SCHOOLS

Eurocentres, 101 N. Union St. #300, Alexandria, VA 22314, USA (☎703-684-1494; fax 684-1495; www.eurocentres.com) or in Europe, Head Office, Seestr. 247, CH-8038 Zurich, Switzerland (☎41 1 485 50 40; fax 41 481 61 24; info@eurocentres.com). Language programs for beginning to advanced students with homestays in Britain, France, Germany, Italy, and Spain.

ESSENTIALS

Language Immersion Institute, 75 South Manheim Blvd., SUNY-New Paltz, New Paltz, NY 12561, USA (☎914-257-3500; www.newpaltz.edu/lii). 2-week summer language courses and overseas courses in France, Italy, and Spain. Program fees are about US$295 for a weekend or $750 per 2 weeks.

LanguagesPLUS, 317 Adelaide St. W., Suite 900, Toronto, Ontario M5V-1P9 (US ☎888-526-4758 or 416-925-7117; fax 925-5990; www.languagesplus.com), runs 1- to 36-week programs in Britain, France, Spain, Italy, and Germany that include tuition, accommodations with host families or apartments, and activities. Must be 18+.

World Exchange, Ltd., White Birch Rd., Putnam Valley, NY 10579 (US ☎800-444-3924; 845-526-2505; fax 845-528-9187; www.worldexchange.org), offers 1- to 4-week language-based homestay programs in France and Spain.

FURTHER READING & RESOURCES: STUDYING ABROAD.
StudyAbroad.Com Program Search (www.studyabroad.com)
Academic Year Abroad 2001-2002. Institute of International Education Books (US$47).
Peterson's Study Abroad 2001. Peterson's ($30).
Peterson's Summer Study Abroad 2001. Peterson's ($30).
Vacation Study Abroad 2000-2001. Institute of International Education Books ($43).

WORKING ABROAD

There's no better way to submerge yourself in a foreign culture than to become part of its economy. **European Union citizens** can work in any EU country, and if your parents were born in an EU country, you may be able to claim the right to a work permit. Friends and family in Western Europe can often help expedite work permits or arrange work-for-accommodations swaps. In general, **non-EU citizens** can officially hold a job in Western Europe only with a **work permit,** obtained by your employer, usually demonstrating that you have skills that locals lack. Reportedly, many permit-less agricultural workers go untroubled. Contact the consulate or embassy of your destination country for more information.

For US college students, recent graduates, and young adults, the simplest way to get legal work permission to work abroad is through **Council on International Exchange Work Abroad Programs** (see p. 45). Fees range from US$300-425. Council can help you obtain a three- to six- month work permit and visa and also provides assistance finding jobs and housing.

FURTHER READING: WORKING ABROAD.
Directory of Jobs and Careers Abroad. Vacation Work Publications (US$17).
How to Get a Job in Europe, Robert Sanborn and Cheryl Matherly. Surrey Books ($22).
International Jobs: Where they Are, How to Get Them, Eric Kocher and Nina Segal. Perseus Books ($17).
International Directory of Voluntary Work. Vacation Work ($16).
Overseas Summer Jobs 2001, David Woodworth. Vacation Work ($17).
Teaching English Abroad, Susan Griffith and Victoria Pybus. Vacation Work ($18).
Work Abroad: The Complete Guide to Finding a Job Overseas, Clayton Hubbs. Transitions Abroad ($16).
Work Your Way Around the World, Susan Griffith. Vacation Work ($18).

AU PAIR ORGANIZATIONS

Accord Cultural Exchange, 750 La Playa, San Francisco, CA 94121, USA (☎415-386-6203; www.cognitext.com/accord). US$40 program fee.

Childcare International, Ltd., Trafalgar House, Grenville Pl., London NW7 3SA, UK (☎44 020 8906 3116; fax 8906 3461; www.childint.co.uk). UK£100 application fee.

InterExchange, 161 6th Ave., New York, NY 10013, USA (☎212-924-0446; fax 924-0575; info@interexchange.org, www.interexchange.org).

ESSENTIALS

ESSENTIALS

TEACHING ENGLISH

International Schools Services, Educational Staffing Program, P.O. Box 5910, Princeton, NJ 08543, USA (☎609-452-0990; www.iss.edu). Recruits teachers and administrators for American and English schools throughout Western Europe. US$150 program fee.

Office of Overseas Schools, US Department of State, Room H328, SA-1, Washington, D.C. 20522, USA (☎202-261-8200; fax 261-8224; www.state.gov/www/about_state/ schools). Keeps a comprehensive list of schools abroad and agencies that arrange placement for Americans to teach abroad.

ARCHAEOLOGICAL DIGS

Archaeological Institute of America, 656 Beacon St., Boston, MA 02215, USA (☎617-353-9361; www.archaeological.org). The *Archaeological Fieldwork Opportunities Bulletin* (US$20 for non-members) lists field sites throughout Western Europe. Purchase the bulletin from Kendall/Hunt Publishing, 4050 Westmark Dr., Dubuque, Iowa 52002, USA (☎800-228-0810).

VOLUNTEERING ABROAD

Volunteer jobs are readily available, and many provide room and board in exchange for labor. You can sometimes avoid high application fees by contacting the individual workcamps directly.

Earthwatch, 3 Clocktower Pl., P.O. Box 75, Maynard, MA 01754, USA (☎800-776-0188; www.earthwatch.org). Arranges 1- to 3-week programs in all over Western Europe to promote conservation of natural resources. Programs average US$1600.

Habitat for Humanity International, 121 Habitat St., Americus, GA 31709, USA (☎800-422-4828; www.habitat.org). Offers opportunities in Germany, Britain, The Netherlands, and Portugal, to live and build houses in a host community. $1200-3500.

Service Civil International Voluntary Service (SCI-IVS), 814 NE 40th St., Seattle, WA 98105, USA (☎/fax 206-545-6585; www.sci-ivs.org). Arranges placement in workcamps in Denmark, Belgium, and The Netherlands for those 18+. Registration $65-150.

Volunteers for Peace, 1034 Tiffany Rd., Belmont, VT 05730, USA (☎802-259-2759; www.vfp.org). Arranges placement in workcamps in Western Europe. Annual *International Workcamp Directory* $20. Registration fee $200. Free newsletter.

OTHER RESOURCES

Let's Go tries to cover all aspects of budget travel, but we can't put *everything* in our guides. Listed below are books and websites that can serve as jumping off points for your own research.

TRAVEL PUBLISHERS AND BOOKSTORES

Adventurous Traveler Bookstore, 245 S. Champlain St., Burlington, VT 05401, USA (☎800-282-3963; www.adventuroustraveler.com), offers information and gear for outdoor and adventure travel.

Bon Voyage!, 2069 W. Bullard Ave., Fresno, CA 93711, USA (☎800-995-9716, elsewhere call US 559-447-8441; fax 447 84 56; www.bon-voyage-travel.com), specializes in Europe and sells videos, travel gear, books, maps, and railpasses. Free newsletter.

Hippocrene Books, Inc., 171 Madison Ave., New York, NY 10016, USA (☎718-454-2366; ww.hippocrenebooks.com). Publishes travel guides, as well as foreign language dictionaries and learning guides; free catalog.

Hunter Publishing, 130 Campus Dr., Edison, NJ 08818, USA (☎800-255-0343; www.hunterpublishing.com). Has an extensive catalog of travel guides and diving and adventure travel books.

Rand McNally, 8255 N. Central Park Ave., Skokie, IL 60076, USA (☎800-275-7263; international 847-329-6656; fax 329-6659; www.randmcnally.com), publishes a number of comprehensive road atlases (from US$10).

Travel Books & Language Center, Inc., 4437 Wisconsin Ave. NW, Washington, D.C. 20016, USA (☎800-220-2665; www.bookweb.org/bookstore/travelbks). Sells travel aids, language cassettes, dictionaries, travel books, atlases, and maps. No web orders, but ships worldwide.

WORLD WIDE WEB

Almost every aspect of budget travel is accessible via the web. Within 10 minutes at the keyboard, you can make a reservation at a hostel, get advice on travel hotspots from other travelers who have just returned from Western Europe, or find out exactly how much a train from Paris to Munich costs.

Listed here are some budget travel sites to start off your surfing; other relevant web sites are listed throughout the book. Because website turnover is high, use search engines (such as www.google.com) to strike out on your own.

THE ART OF BUDGET TRAVEL

Backpacker's Ultimate Guide: www.bugeurope.com. Tips on packing, transportation, and where to go. Also tons of country-specific travel information.

Backpack Europe: www.backpackeurope.com. Helpful tips, a bulletin board, and links.

How to See the World: www.artoftravel.com. A compendium of great travel tips, from cheap flights to self-defense to interacting with local culture.

Rec. Travel Library: www.travel-library.com. A fantastic set of links for general information and personal travelogues.

TripSpot: www.tripspot.com/europefeature.htm. An outline of links to help plan trips, transportation, sleeping accommodations, and packing.

INFORMATION ON WESTERN EUROPE

Atevo Travel: www.atevo.com/guides/destinations. Detailed introductions, travel tips, and suggested itineraries.

CIA World Factbook: www.odci.gov/cia/publications/factbook/index.html. Tons of vital statistics on Western European geography, government, economy, and people.

Foreign Language for Travelers: www.travlang.com. Provides free online translating dictionaries and lists of phrases in many Western European languages.

Geographia: www.geographia.com. Highlights, culture, and people of Western Europe.

Lycos: http://travel.lycos.com. General introductions to cities and regions throughout Western Europe, accompanied by links to histories, news, and local tourism sites.

MyTravelGuide: www.mytravelguide.com. Country overviews, with everything from history to transportation to live web cam coverage.

PlanetRider: www.planetrider.com. A subjective list of links to the "best" websites covering the culture and tourist attractions of Western Europe.

TravelPage: www.travelpage.com. Links to official tourist office sites in Western Europe.

Virtual Tourist: www.virtualtourist.com. Countless travel tips and tools, plus links to transportation and accommodation sites.

World Travel Guide: www.travel-guides.com/navigate/world.asp. Helpful practical info.

FURTHER READING: SURFING THE WEB.
Internet Travel Planner, Michael Shapiro. Globe Pequot Press (US$19)
Travel Planning Online for Dummies, Noah Vadnai. IDG Books ($25).
Ten Minute Guide to Travel Planning on the Net, Thomas Pack. QUE. ($15).
300 Incredible Things for Travelers on the Internet, Ken Leebow. 300Incredible.com ($9).

AND OUR PERSONAL FAVORITE...

Let's Go: www.letsgo.com. Our constantly expanding website features photos and streaming video, online ordering of all our titles, info about our books, a travel forum buzzing with stories and tips, and links that will help you find everything you ever wanted to know about Western Europe.

ESSENTIALS

Mooooore Room.

Real American Airlines deals
for students and faculty,
online at StudentUniverse.
Earn AAdvantage miles and
enjoy *more room throughout
Coach only on American*.

 StudentUniverse.com

featuring
AmericanAirlines

800.272.9676

RESTRICTIONS: A portion of or all travel may be on American Eagle, American's regional airline affiliate. American Airlines, American Eagle and AAdvantage are marks of American Airlines, Inc. American Airlines reserves the right to change AAdvantage program rules, regulations, travel awards and special offers at any time without notice, and to end the AAdvantage program with six months notice. American Airlines is not responsible for products or services by other participating companies. *Only American has removed rows of seats throughout Coach to provide more room for more Coach passengers than any other airline. Now available on all two-class, three-class aircraft; reconfiguration in progress; not available on American Eagle.

ANDORRA

PHONE CODES | Country code: 376. International dialing prefix: N/A.

Squint carefully at a map of Western Europe, and between France and Spain you'll find Andorra (pop. 65,000; 468 sq. km). This tiny nation is known primarily for its mix of stunning vistas and **duty-free shopping.** The neon-lit streets may seem a striking contrast to the peaceful landscapes, but then Andorra has a long-standing tradition of cultural juxtaposition. Known formally as **Principat d'Andorra**, it is governed by **two co-princes,** but it is the **Consell General** that possesses the bulk of the political power and represents the seven parishes of the nation. The story goes that **Charlemagne** gave Andorra its freedom in AD 803, after wresting it from the Moors, as a reward for the inhabitants' aid in the battle. Over the next dozen centuries, Andorra was the rope in a large-scale game of tug-of-war between the Spanish and the French. Only in 1990 did Andorra create a commission to draft a **democratic constitution,** which it adopted on March 14, 1993.

Andorra today is somewhat less progressive than other Western European nations. In the 1993 election, only the 10,000 native Andorrans (out of 65,000 total inhabitants) were granted the vote; women have had suffrage only since 1970. The citizenry is comfortably **trilingual,** but the official language, Catalan, is still spoken with pride. Andorra has no **currency** of its own. All establishments are required to accept both *pesetas* and *francs*, although *pesetas* are more prevalent. In fact, currency seems to flow like water, as the **absence of sales tax** draws consumers from all over Europe. With Andorran towns spaced mere minutes apart and an extensive local bus system, a single day can include wading through aisles of duty-free perfume, hiking through a pine-scented valley, eating *formatge de tupi* (cheese fermented with garlic and brandy in an earthenware container), and relaxing in a luxury spa. **Phones** require an STA *teletarjeta* (telecard) available at the tourist office, post office, or any kiosk (500ptas/€3). You cannot make collect calls, and AT&T does not have an international access code. **Directory assistance:** ☎111.

SUGGESTED ITINERARIES

THE BEST OF (OKAY, ALL OF) ANDORRA IN THREE DAYS Three days in Andorra should be spent enjoying the outdoor activities that this tiny nation has to offer. First, spend, spend, spend in the duty-free shops of **Andorra la Vella** (1 day, p. 74). Then hike Andorra's mountains, including its tallest peak, **Pic Alt de la Coma Pedrosa** (2946m) in nearby (and what isn't?) **La Massana** (2 days, p. 75). In the winter, these same mountains offer unparalleled skiing—swoosh down the slopes until you collapse.

⌐ TRANSPORTATION
The only way to get to Andorra is by **car** or **bus,** as the country has no airport or train station. Visitors are required to show a valid passport or an EU identity card to enter the country. All traffic from France must enter through the town of **Pas de la Casa;** the Spanish gateway town is **La Seu d'Urgell. Andor-Inter/Samar buses** (Madrid ☎914 68 41 90, Toulouse ☎05 61 58 14 53, Andorra ☎82 62 89) connect Andorra la Vella to **Madrid** (9hr.; departs Tu, F, and Sa-Su at 11am; W-Th and Su at 10pm; 5200ptas/€31.25), while **Alsina Graells** (in Andorra ☎82 65 67) and **Eurolines**

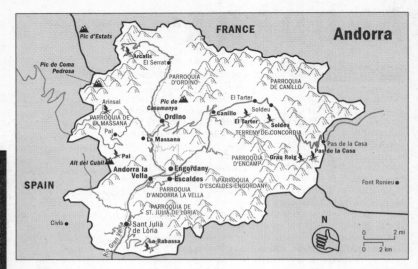

run to **Barcelona** (3-4hr., 4 per day, 2855-2975ptas/€17-18). All buses arrive at and depart from **Estació d'Autobusos,** on C. Bonaventura Riberaygua. To get to the station from Pla. Princep Benlloch, follow Av. Meritxell, turn right after crossing the river, and then take the first left; take the fourth right and go straight for four and a half blocks (20min.). To go anywhere else in Spain, take a **La Hispano-Andorra bus** (☎82 13 72) from Andorra la Vella to La Seu d'Urgell (30min.; 6-8 per day, M-Sa 7:45am-8pm, Su 8:45am-8pm; 400ptas/€2.40) and change an Alsina Graells bus.

Driving in Andorra la Vella is a nightmare. The main road turns into a parking lot, and drivers will find a map totally useless—it's best to follow signs and desert the car as soon as possible in one of the city's parking lots. Efficient **intercity buses** (100-300ptas/€1.80) connect the villages. All buses stop in Andorra la Vella, so don't worry about finding the right bus—look at the direction sign in the front window.

ANDORRA LA VELLA

Andorra la Vella (pop. 20,000), the country's capital, is little more than a narrow, cluttered road flanked by shop after duty-free shop. All buses terminate at the **Estació d'Autobusos,** on C. Bonaventura Riberaygua. To get to the **tourist office** on Avinguda Meritxell from the **barri antic** (old quarter), follow the main road past Pyrénées, the department store, and the office is on the left-hand side. (Open July-Aug. daily 9am-9pm; Sept.-June reduced hours.) Send **email** from **@Centre,** C. Maria Pla., 8. (☎86 09 30. Open M-Sa 7am-3am. 125ptas/€0.75 per min., 500ptas/€3 per hr. MC/V.) Dream of duty-free cheese at **Hotel Viena,** C. de la Vall, 3. (singles 4000ptas/€24; doubles 5000ptas/€30.) Drool at the chocolate bars at the **supermarket** in **Grans Magatzems Pyrénées,** Av. Meritxell, 11. (Open Sept.-July M-F 9:30am-8pm, Sa 9:30am-9pm, Su 9:30am-7pm; Aug. M-Sa 9:30am-9pm, Su 9:30am-7pm.)

ELSEWHERE IN ANDORRA

"Elsewhere" is where to go in Andorra. The **Caldea-Spa,** in nearby **Escaldes-Engordany,** is the largest in all of Europe, with luxurious treatments and prices to match. (☎80 09 95. Open daily 10am-11pm. 3000ptas/€18 for 3hr., which includes the baths and relaxing light treatments.) **Ordino** (pop. 2219) is convenient for hiking and skiing adventures; an easy 4hr. hike from town tours the lakes of **Tristaina.** In Andorra, "bigger is better," unless, of course, you're talking about Ordino's megasmall ⬛**Microminiature Museum,** Edifici Coma. (☎83 83 38. Open Tu-Sa 9:30am-1:30pm and 3:30-7pm, Su 9:30am-1:30pm. 300ptas/€1.80.) The tiny town of **Canillo**

(pop. 952), in the center of the country, suffers from the same architectural bland-
ness as the rest of Andorra, but is surrounded by fine scenery and great **skiing. Sol-
deu-El Tarter** (☎89 05 00) occupies 840 hectares of skiable area between Andorra la
Vella and Pas de la Casa, France; **free buses** transport skiers from hotels in Canillo.

OUTDOOR ACTIVITES

An extensive network of **hiking** trails traverses the country. The free and multilingual tourist office brochure *Sports Activities* includes suggested itineraries,
potential routes, and bike rental locations, and is helpful for planning excursions.
La Massana is home to Andorra's tallest peak, **Pic Alt de la Coma Pedrosa** (2946m).
For organized hiking trips, try the **La Rabassa Sports and Nature Center** (☎32 38 68
or 32 62 22), in the parish of Sant Juliàde Lòria, in the southwest corner of
Andorra. In addition to *refugio*-style accommodations, the center has mountain
biking, guided hikes, horseback riding, archery, and other field sports. In the winter, Andorra offers **skiing** opportunities galore. The four outstanding resorts within
its boundaries all rent equipment and attract the masses. **Pal** (☎73 70 00) is very
popular. For more info inquire at **SKI Andorra** (☎86 43 89; www.skiandorra.ad) or
the tourist offices.

ANDORRA

AUSTRIA
(ÖSTERREICH)

AUSTRIAN SHILLING

US$1 = 16.15AS	10AS = US$0.62
CDN$1 = 10.58AS	10AS = CDN$0.95
UK£1 = 22.71AS	10AS = UK£0.44
IR£1 = 17.47AS	10AS = IR£0.57
AUS$1 = 8.14AS	10AS = AUS$1.23
NZ$1 = 6.53AS	10AS = NZ$1.53
ZAR1 = 1.95AS	10AS = ZAR5.13
EUR€1 = 13.76AS	10AS = EUR€0.73

PHONE CODE	**Country Code:** 43. **International dialing prefix:** 00 (900 in Vienna)

The mighty Austro-Hungarian Empire may have crumbled after World War I, but Austria (pop. 8.1 million; 83,858 sq. km) remains a complex, multi-ethnic country with a fascinating history. Drawing on centuries of Habsburg political maneuvering, Austria has become a skillful mediator between Eastern and Western Europe. But Austria is renowned not so much for its strategic political situation as for its brilliant artists, writers, and musicians. From Gustav Klimt's colorful patterned paintings to Arthur Schnitzler's dark insights into imperial decadence to Beethoven's thundering symphonies, Austria has had an indelible impact on Western art and literature. Austria owes its contemporary fame and fortune to a combination of its rich history and its overpowering Alpine landscape. A mention of Austria evokes images of onion-domed churches, snow-capped Alpine peaks, lush meadows of wildflowers, thick and dark forests, and mighty castles—*The Sound of Music* in a nutshell. For extensive and entertaining information on Austria's attractions, pick up a copy of *Let's Go: Austria & Switzerland 2002*.

SUGGESTED ITINERARIES

THREE DAYS Spend all three days in **Vienna** (p. 85), the imperial headquarters of romance. From the stately **Staatsoper** to the glittering **Musikverein,** the majestic **Hofburg** to the simple **Kirche am Steinhof,** Vienna's attractions will leave you with enough sensory stimulation to last until your next vacation.

ONE WEEK Begin in the Western Austrian mountain town of **Kitzbühel** (1 day, p. 110) for an array of hiking and skiing opportunities. Stop in **Salzburg** (1 day, p. 99) to see the home of the *Sound of Music* and Mozart. Move on to the Salzkammergut region to hike in the **Echental Valley** (1 day, p. 108) and wonder at the **Dachstein Ice Caves** (1 day, p. 108). End by basking in the glory of **Vienna** (3 days, p. 85).

BEST OF AUSTRIA, TWO WEEKS Start in **Bregenz** for sublime views (1 day, p. 116). Take the train to **Innsbruck** to see museums and mountains (1 day, p. 112), then swing by **Kitzbühel** for hiking and skiing (2 days, p. 110). Next, tour **Hallstatt,** famous for stunning hikes and nearby ice caves (2 days, p. 107). Overdose on Maria von Trapp and Mozart in **Salzburg** (2 days, p. 99). To see rural Austria with no pretension, take a bus to **Grünau** (1 day, p. 108). Head to **Graz** (1 day, p. 116) for its Mediterranean feel and throbbing nightlife, then make your way to **Vienna** for a grand finale of romance and waltzes (4 days, p. 85).

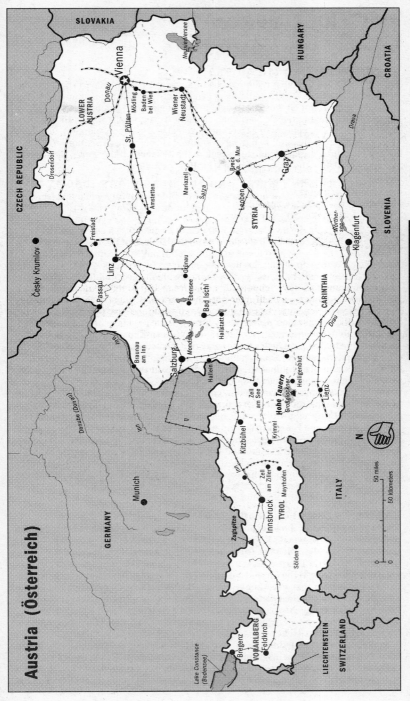

Austria (Österreich)

AUSTRIA

LIFE AND TIMES

HISTORY AND POLITICS

IN THE BEGINNING (TO AD 950)

By 6000 BC, even the most remote areas of Austria had become part of a vigorous commercial network that linked mining centers and agricultural communities. The **Romans** conquered their Austrian neighbors to secure the Danube frontier against marauding Germanic tribes. Germanic raids, however, finally forced the Romans to retreat in the 5th century AD. Over the next 300 years, various peoples, including the Huns, Ostrogoths, and Langobards romped through the Austrian territories. Eventually, three groups divided the region: the **Alemanni** in the south, the **Slavs** in the southwest, and the **Bavarians** in the north.

THE HOLY ROMAN EMPIRE AND THE HABSBURGS (950-1740)

Austria had its first taste of imperialism in the mid-9th century when **Charlemagne,** founder of the Holy Roman Empire, expanded his kingdom eastward. When he died, the kingdom collapsed and the eastern regions were overrun by pillaging tribes. After driving the invaders out, **Holy Roman Emperor Otto II** entrusted Margrave Liutpoldus (a.k.a. **Leopold of Babenberg**) with the defense of the eastern territories. The Babenberg dynasty concentrated on stabilizing the frontiers but also extending its protectorate by shrewdness and strategic marriages.

Unfortunately for the dynasty, the last Babenberg died childless, leaving the country fragmented. Through a bloody conflict, **Rudolf of Habsburg** emerged with the crown, beginning six centuries of Habsburg rule in Austria. Gradually, they accumulated the various regions that make up modern Austria and then some. Friedrich III, for instance, strategically arranged the marriage of his son, **Maximilian I,** to gain Habsburg control of much of Western Europe. Another politically motivated marriage put **Charles V** in charge of a vast empire encompassing Austria, The Netherlands, several Spanish holdings—proving that all you need is land, not love. As if this weren't enough, Charles was elected **Holy Roman Emperor** in 1519, gaining nominal control of Germany as well.

Despite their massive possessions and imperial veneer, the Habsburg ship hit rough waters in the 16th and 17th centuries as a result of Martin Luther's **Protestant Reformation.** Early victories over Protestant forces during the **Thirty Years' War** (1618-1648) restored Habsburg control of Bohemia, where they promptly (and forcibly) converted most of the peasants back to Catholicism. Soon after, though, the Ottoman Turks besieged Vienna until **Prince Eugene of Savoy** drove them out. After the death of the last Spanish Habsburg, the plucky Eugene came through again when he led the Habsburg troops to victory over the French in the **War of Spanish Succession,** which ended with a treaty giving Spain to France, while the Habsburgs gained Belgium, the fishy Sardinia, and parts of Italy.

CASTLES CRUMBLE (1740-1914)

Like a house of cards, the Habsburg empire teetered as it grew. When **Maria Theresa** ascended the throne in 1740, her neighbors were eager to see Habsburg power diminished. King **Friedrich the Great** of Prussia snatched a prosperous Habsburg province that Maria Theresa was never able to re-claim. The marriage of her daughter **Marie Antoinette** to the future King **Louis XVI** was a tragic attempt to forge an alliance with France that was quickly negated by the **French Revolution.** After the Revolution, **Napoleon Bonaparte,** making up for his shortcomings, secured French possession of many Austrian territories. French troops even invaded Vienna, where Napoleon took up residence in Maria Theresa's favorite palace, Schönbrunn (see p. 96), and married her granddaughter.

Napoleon's success led to the official establishment of the Austrian empire. In 1804, Franz II renounced his claim to the now-defunct Holy Roman crown and proclaimed himself **Franz I,** Emperor of Austria. During the Congress of Vienna, which redrew the map of Europe after Napoleon's defeat, Austrian Chancellor **Clemens**

It's Your World...

www.mci.com/worldphone

© 2001, WorldCom, Inc. All Rights Reserved.

WorldPhone. Worldwide

MCI[SM] gives you the freedom of worldwide communications whenever you're away from home. It's easy to call to and from over 70 countries with your MCI Calling Card:

1. Dial the WorldPhone* access number of the country you're calling from.
2. Dial or give the operator your MCI Calling Card number.
3. Dial or give the number you're calling.

• Austria	0800-200-235	• Luxembourg	8002-0112
• Belgium	0800-10012	• Netherlands	0800-022-91-22
• Denmark	8001-0022	• Spain	900-99-0014
• France	0-800-99-0019	• Switzerland	0800-89-0222
• Germany	0800-888-8000	• United Kingdon	0800-89-0222 BT
• Italy	172-1022		0500-89-0222 CWC
• Liechtenstein	809-8000		

Sign up today!

Ask your local operator to place a collect call
(reverse charge) to MCI in the U.S. at:

1-712-943-6839

For additional access codes or to sign up, visit us at www.mci.com/worldphone

www.mci.com/worldphone

© 2001, WorldCom, Inc. All Rights Reserved.

A ROSE BY ANOTHER NAME? Medieval history celebrates Austria's two major ruling families: the Babenbergs (976-1246) and the Habsburgs (1278-1918). Unfortunately for the history books, the Babenbergs were actually named Poppon; furthermore, their family seat was not the Castle Babenberch in Bamberg, Germany, but a nameless castle somewhere in German Swabia. The name Babenberg was an invention of the 12th-century historian Otto von Freising, himself a Poppon, who found the name of his ancestor Poppon von Grabfeld ("from the graveyard") unsuitable and casually renamed the dynasty "Babenberg." This relatively harmless deception quickly became an integral part of Austrian history, with the result that historians today still refer to the "Babenbergs" without a second thought.

Wenzel Lothar von Metternich tried to restore the old order while orchestrating the re-consolidation of Austrian power. He managed to usher in a long peace of commerce and industry. In the spring of 1848, the French philosophy of **middle-class revolution** reached Austria. Students and workers revolted and took control of the imperial palace, demanding a written constitution and freedom of the press. The movement was divided, and the rebellion was promptly quashed. Nevertheless, the epileptic emperor Ferdinand I was eventually pressured to abdicate in favor of his nephew, **Franz Josef I,** whose 68-year reign was one of Austria's longest.

Austria's status in Europe continued to shift throughout Franz Josef's life. Prussia, under **Otto von Bismarck,** dominated European politics, defeating Austria in 1866 and establishing the **dual Austro-Hungarian monarchy**. Unfortunately, burgeoning nationalist sentiments led to severe divisions within the new multinational. Tired and disheartened after 50 years on the throne, poor Joseph was saddened by the suicide of his only son and the murder of his wife. He wanted to maintain Austrian *Ruhe und Ordnung* (peace and order), but he couldn't stop the tide of modernity.

CURRENTS OF MODERNITY (1914-1945)

Brimming with ethnic tension and locked into a rigid system of alliances from 19th-century wars, the Austro-Hungarian Empire was a disaster waiting to happen. The necessary spark was the assassination of Austrian archduke and heir **Franz Ferdinand** in June 1914 by a Serbian nationalist in Sarajevo. Austria's declaration of war against Serbia set off a chain reaction that pulled most of Europe into the conflict, marking the beginning of **World War I.** Franz Josef died in 1916, leaving the throne to his reluctant grandnephew **Karl I,** who struggled in vain to preserve the Habsburg empire. Despite his valiant efforts and those of the army, the people's declarations of democratic independence ensured the demise of the monarchy. On November 11, 1918, Karl finally made peace, but only after the first **Republic of Austria** was established, ending the 640-year-old Habsburg dynasty.

Between 1918 and 1938, Austria had its first, bitter taste of parliamentary democracy, the **First Republic.** The Republic suffered massive inflation, unemployment, and near economic collapse, but was stabilized by the mid-1920s. In 1933, the weak coalition government gave way when **Engelbert Dollfuss** declared martial law in order to protect Austria from Hitler. Two years later Dollfuss was assassinated by Austrian Nazis. The well-known conclusion to the tale of the First Republic is the Nazi **annexation** of Austria. In 1938, the new Hitler-appointed Nazi chancellor invited German troops into Austria. While **World War II** raged, tens of thousands of Jews, political dissidents, disabled and mentally disabled people, Gypsies, and homosexuals were forced by the **Nazis** to emigrate or sent to concentration camps.

After Soviet troops brutally liberated Vienna in 1945, Austria was divided into four zones of occupation by Allied troops. As a Nazi victim, however, Austria still enjoyed some political rights. During the occupation, the Soviets tried to make Austria a Communist state, but having failed, they finally settled for stripping their sector of any moveable infrastructure. Despite Russian plundering and severe famines in the late 1940s, the American **Marshall Plan** helped to jump-start the Austrian economy, laying the foundation for Austria's present prosperity.

AUSTRIA

The **Federal Constitution** (1945) and the **State Treaty** (1955, establishing Austrian independence and sovereignty) formed the basis for the current Austrian nation, which is frequently referred to as the **Second Republic.** These documents provided for a president (head of state) who is elected for six-year terms; a chancellor (head of government), usually the leader of the strongest party; a bicameral parliamentary legislature; and strong provincial governments. Until very recently the government has been dominated by two parties, the **Social Democratic Party** (SPÖ) and the **People's Party** (ÖVP). The two parties have built up one of the world's most successful industrial economies with enviably low unemployment and inflation rates. Today, Austria has emerged as a progressive model of the social democratic welfare state. During the 1990s the country moved toward closer European unification. In 1994 **Thomas Klestil,** the current President, was elected on a European integration platform. In 1995 the country joined the **European Union** (EU), the people having accepted membership through a national referendum. Along with 11 other EU members, Austria will adopt the **Euro** on January 1, 2002, and will phase out its shillings by July of the same year.

HAIDER AND THE FREEDOM PARTY

In the past few years international attention has turned to Austria because of the political gains made by the far-right **Freedom Party.** This party is infamous primarily for its leader **Jörg Haider,** who entered the public eye for his anti-immigrant stance and his many remarks that have been seen as Nazi-sympathetic. Haider euphemistically referred to the Nazi camps as "punishment camps" rather than concentration camps, and called for Austrian military members who fought for the Nazis to have pride in their work. In the November 1999 elections, Haider's party claimed 27% of the vote (second among all parties), effectively breaking up the traditional two-party lock that the SPÖ and ÖVP held on the country's politics since WWII. (The SPÖ came in first in these elections with 33% of the vote, but refused to form a coalition with Haider's party.) Though Haider did not have a post in the new federal government—he remains governor of the province of Carinthia—the new government was met by fierce protests both domestically and internationally. In Vienna, 100,000 protestors turned out on the day that members of the Freedom Party were sworn in, and the **European Union** levied unprecedented political sanctions against Austria. (The sanctions were lifted in September 2000.)

While Haider's rise may seem scary, consider the actual circumstances before avoiding Austria. The primary reasons for the swing toward Haider's party are independent of Haider's racist views, and the Freedom Party's success in 1999 should not be seen the Austrian people's endorsement of Haider: the election had the lowest voter turnout in Austria's post-war history. In the 2001 elections the party slipped 8 percent, which analysts see as the result of public disapproval of its policies. For an interesting form of protest, see **Austrian Graffiti, XXX**.

THE ARTS

VISUAL ART AND ARCHITECTURE

Landlocked in the middle of Europe and rolling with cash, the Habsburgs married into power and bought into art. Truly Austrian art emerged in the works of **Gustav Klimt** (see p. 97) and his followers, who founded the **Secession movement.** Secessionists sought to create space and appreciation for symbolism, Impressionism, and other new artistic styles. This can be seen in Klimt's later paintings, such as *The Kiss* (1907-08), which combines naturalistic portraits with abstractly patterned backgrounds. **Oskar Kokoschka** and **Egon Schiele** revolted against "art *qua* art," seeking to present the energy formerly concealed behind the Secession's aesthetic surface. Schiele, like the young Kokoschka, painted with a feverish intensity in line and color. His paintings are controversial even today for their depictions of tortured figures seemingly destroyed by their own bodies or by debilitating sexuality. His *The Self Seer* (1911) and *Embrace* (1917) show his emphasis on expression.

In 1897, the new artists split from the old as proponents of modernism took issue with the Viennese Academy's conservatism. This gave rise to the **Jugendstil** (a.k.a. **Art Nouveau**) movement, which aimed to formulate a new way of seeing the world. The new way turned out to be the ethic of function over form, which was embraced by Vienna's artistic elite and most notably by the guru of architectural modernism, **Otto Wagner**. These ideals later influenced the **Bauhaus** of Weimar Germany and paved the way for **Adolf Loos** who proclaimed: "Ornamentation is criminal."

The emergence of architecture in Austria began with the extravagance of the **Baroque** style. With fluidly ornate forms orchestrated into a succession of grand entrances, dreamy vistas, and overwrought, cupid-covered façades, the Baroque invokes what was then the most popular art form in Europe, music. This style is exhibited exquisitely in the Schönbrunn (see p. 96) and Hofburg (see p. 95) palaces. Austria's 19th-century conservative modernism is showcased by the Ringstraße (see p. 86), the broad boulevard that encircles Vienna; this historicist taste came to be known as the **Ringstraße Style.** In the 1920s and early 1930s, the Social Democratic administration built thousands of apartments in large **municipal projects,** their style reflecting the newfound assertiveness of the workers' movement and the ideals of **urban socialism.** The most outstanding project of the era is the **Karl-Marx-Hof** in Vienna. The huge structure, completed in 1930, extends over 1km and consists of 1,600 apartments clustered around several courtyards. **Hans Hollein** contributed to Viennese **postmodern** architecture in the **Haas House.**

LITERATURE

Many of Austria's great writers were immigrés, but native Austrians have made important contributions to the literary scene as well. The *Song of the Nibelungs* (c. 1200), of unknown authorship, is one of the most impressive heroic epics in German. In the 19th century, **Johann Nestroy** wrote biting comedies and satires, such as *The Talisman* (1840), that lampooned social follies. **Adalbert Stifter,** often called Austria's greatest novelist, wrote with classical themes and strongly metaphysical descriptions of nature. His short stories and novels, such as *The Condor* (1840) and *Indian Summer* (1857), represent the height of Austria's classical style. A classicist with a more lyrical style, **Franz Grillparzer** penned pieces about the conflict between a life of thought and a life of action in such plays as *The Waves of the Sea and Love* (1831).

Around 1890, Austrian literature rapidly transformed in the heat of the "merry apocalypse" atmosphere that permeated society at the turn of the century. The literature dating from this second heyday of Austrian culture, known as **fin de siècle,** is legendary. **Karl Kraus** implacably unmasked the crisis, **Arthur Schnitzler** dramatized it, **Hugo von Hofmannsthal** ventured a cautious eulogy, and **Georg Trakl** commented on the collapse in feverish verse. The cafe provided the backdrop for the fin de siècle literary landscape. Meanwhile, the world's most famous psychoanalyst, **Sigmund Freud,** developed his theories of sexual repression and the subconscious— and no young man has looked at his mother in the same way ever since.

Many of Austria's literary titans, such as **Marie von Ebner-Eschenbach** and **Franz Kafka,** lived within the Habsburg protectorate of Bohemia. Ebner-Eschenbach is often called the greatest female Austrian writer, known for her vivid individual portraits and her defense of women's rights, while Kafka showed he was master of the surreal in *The Metamorphosis* (1915), a bizarre tale that presents the idea of waking up and *really* not feeling like yourself. Austrian literature today is still affected and informed by its literary tradition, but there is plenty of innovation as well. **Ingeborg Bachman** has sensitively examined the complexities of womanhood, while **Thomas Bernhard** has provided mature and insightful critiques of Austrian society.

MUSIC

The first major musician of Viennese classicism was **Josef Haydn,** whose oratorio *The Creation* (1798) is a choral standard, but the work of **Wolfgang Amadeus Mozart** (see p. 104) represents the pinnacle of the time period. A child prodigy and brilliant composer, he produced such well-known pieces as *A Little Night Music* (1787) and *The Requiem* (unfinished). His work has been proclaimed to be "the culmination of all beauty in music." Although German-born, **Ludwig van Beethoven** lived in Vienna for much of his life and composed some of his most famous works there. In the 19th century, **Johannes Brahms** straddled musical traditions to become the grand old man of the Viennese music scene, and **Anton Bruckner** created complicated orchestrations that earned him recognition as one of the world's greatest symphonic masters. Between **Johann Strauss the Elder** and his son, **Johann Strauss the Younger**, the Strauss family kept Vienna on its toes for much of the century by creating exhilarating **waltzes** that broke free from older, more formal dances. In the modern era, **Arnold Schönberg** rejected tonal keys in favor of atonality, which produced a highly abstracted sound. **Anton von Webern** and **Alban Berg** were both students of Schönberg and suffered under Nazi occupation for their "degenerate art."

FOOD AND DRINK

Loaded with fat, salt, and cholesterol, traditional Austrian cuisine is a cardiologist's nightmare but the palate's delight. Staple foods include pork, veal, sausage, eggs, cheese, bread, and potatoes. Austria's best known dish, *Wienerschnitzel,* is a breaded meat cutlet (usually veal or pork) fried in butter. Vegetarians should look for Spätzle (noodles), *Eierschwammerl* (tiny yellow mushrooms), or anything with the word "Vegi" in it. The best discount supermarkets are **Billa** and **Hofer,** where you can buy cheap rolls, fruits, and veggies. Natives nurse their sweet tooths with *Kaffee und Kuchen* (coffee and cake). Try *Sacher Torte,* a rich chocolate cake layered with marmalade; *Linzer Torte,* a light yellow cake with currant jam; *Apfelstrudel;* or just about any pastry. Austrian **beers** are outstanding—try *Stiegl Bier,* a Salzburg brew; *Zipfer Bier* from upper Austria; and *Gösser Bier* from Styria.

ESSENTIALS

DOCUMENTS AND FORMALITIES

Citizens of Australia, Canada, New Zealand, South Africa, and the US need valid passports to enter Austria and can stay three months without a visa.

> **Austrian Embassies at Home: Australia,** 12 Talbot St., Forrest, Canberra ACT 2603 (☎(02) 62 95 15 33; fax 62 39 67 51). **Canada,** 445 Wilbrod St., Ottawa, ON KIN 6M7 (☎613-789-1444; fax 789-3431). **Ireland,** 15 Ailesbury Court Apts., 93 Ailesbury Rd., Dublin 4 (☎(01) 269 45 77 or 269 14 51; fax 283 08 60). **New Zealand,** Level 2, Willbank House, 57 Willis St., Wellington (☎(04) 499 63 93; fax 499 63 92). **South Africa,** 1109 Duncan St., Momentum Office Park, Brooklyn, Pretoria 0011 (☎(012) 46 33 61; fax 46 11 51). **UK,** 118 Belgrave Mews West, London SW1 X 8HU (☎(020) 72 35 37 31; fax 344 02 92). **US,** 33524 International Ct. NW, Washington, D.C. 20008-3035 (☎202-895-6700; fax 895-6750).
>
> **Foreign Embassies in Austria:** All foreign embassies are in **Vienna** (p. 89).

TRANSPORTATION

BY PLANE. The only major international airport is Schwechat Flughafen in **Vienna.** European flights also land in Graz, Innsbruck, and Salzburg. From the UK, **buzz** (☎(0870) 240 70 70; www.buzzaway.com), a subsidiary of KLM, flies to Vienna.

BY TRAIN. The **Österreichische Bundesbahn (ÖBB),** Austria's federal railroad, operates an efficient 5760km of tracks accommodating frequent, fast, and comfortable trains. The ÖBB publishes the yearly *Fahrpläne Kursbuch Bahn-Inland*, a compilation of all transportation schedules in Austria. **Eurail, InterRail,** and **Europe East** passes are valid in Austria. The **Austrian Railpass** allows three days of travel within any 15-day period on all rail lines; it also entitles holders to 40% off on bike rentals at train stations (2nd-class US$107, each additional day US$15).

BY BUS AND CAR. The efficient Austrian bus system consists mainly of orange **BundesBuses,** which cover areas inaccessible by train. They usually cost about as much as trains, and railpasses are not valid. A **Mehrfahrtenkarte** gives you six tickets for the price of five. For **bus info,** dial (0222) 711 01 within Austria, 7am-8pm. Driving is a convenient way to see the more isolated parts of Austria, but many small towns prohibit cars. Roads are generally very good and well-marked, and Austrian drivers are quite careful. Renting a car is usually cheaper in Germany.

BY BIKE AND BY THUMB. Bicycling is a great way to get around Austria; the roads are generally level and safe and many private companies and train stations rent bikes. If you get a bike at a train station, you can return it to any participating station. Consult tourist offices for bike routes and maps. *Let's Go* does not recommend hitchhiking. A safer option are the **Mitfahrzentrale** (ride-sharing services) in larger cities, which pair drivers with riders. The fee varies by destination.

TOURIST SERVICES AND MONEY

EMERGENCY	Police, ☎ 133. Ambulance, ☎ 144. Fire, ☎ 122.

TOURIST OFFICES. Virtually every town in Austria has a **tourist office,** most marked by a green "i" sign. You may run into language difficulties in the small-town offices, but most brochures are available in English. The web site for Austrian tourism is www.experienceaustria.com.

CURRENCY AND EXCHANGE. The unit of currency in Austria is the **Schilling,** (AS, ÖS, or S). Each *Schilling* is subdivided into 100 *Groschen* (g). Coins come in 2, 5, 10, and 50g and 1, 5, 10, and 20AS denominations. Bills come in 20, 50, 100, 500, 1000, and 5000AS amounts. Austria has accepted the **Euro** (€) as legal tender, and Schillings will be phased out by July 1, 2002. For more information, see p. 23.

Prices: If you stay in hostels and prepare most of your own food, expect to spend anywhere from 400-850AS/€29-€62, or US$30-65, per person per day. Accommodations start at about 150AS/€10.90, or US$10, while a basic sit-down meal usually costs around 170AS/€13, or US$12.

Tipping and bargaining: In Austria, menus will say whether service is included (*Preise inclusive* or *Bedienung inclusiv*); if it is, you don't have to tip. If it's not, leave a tip up to 10%. Austrian restaurants expect you to seat yourself, and servers will not bring the bill until you ask them to do so. Say *Zahlen bitte* (TSAHL-en BIT-uh) to settle your accounts, and don't leave tips on the table. Be aware that some restaurants charge for each piece of bread that you eat during your meal. Don't expect to bargain in shops or markets in Austria, except at the Naschmarkt in Vienna and flea markets.

Taxes: Austria has a 20-34% **value-added tax (VAT),** which is applied to all purchases of books, clothing, souvenir items, art items, jewelry, perfume, alcohol, cigarettes, etc. You can get it refunded if the total is at least 1000AS (US$95) at one store.

ACCOMMODATIONS AND CAMPING

Always ask if your lodging provides a **guest card** (*Gästekarte*), which grants discounts on local activities, town museums, and public transportation. In Austria, the 10AS/€0.75 tax that most accommodations add to your bill funds these discounts—take advantage of them to get your money's worth.

HOSTELS. In Austria, the *Österreicher Jugendherbergsverband-Hauptverband* (OJH) runs the over 80 hostels in the country. Because of the rigorous standards of the national organizations, hostels are usually as clean as any hotel. While the clientele of the hostels varies, HI hostels tend to be oriented toward families and school groups. Most hostels charge 179-300AS/€13-22 a night for dorms. Non-HI members can stay in all of these hostels but are usually charged a surcharge.

AUSTRIA

HOTELS. Hotels are expensive (singles 200-350AS/€15-26; doubles 400-800AS/€30-59). The cheapest hotel-style accommodations have **Gasthof, Gästehaus,** or **Pension-Garni** in the name. Breakfast *(Frühstück)* is almost always included.

PRIVATE ROOMS AND PENSIONS. Renting a *Privatzimmer* (room in a family home) is an inexpensive and friendly way to house yourself. Such rooms generally include a sink and use of a toilet and shower. Many places rent private rooms only for longer stays or levy a surcharge (10-20%) for stays less than three nights. Rooms run 250-400AS/€18.15-29 a night. Slightly more expensive, *Pensionen* (pensions) are similar to American and British bed-and-breakfasts. In both cases, breakfast is *de rigeur.* Contact the local tourist office for a list of private rooms.

CAMPING. Camping in Austria is less about getting out into nature and more about having a cheap place to sleep; most sites are large plots with many vans and cars. Campsites are usually open in the summer only. Prices run 50-70AS/€3.65-5 per person and 25-60AS/€1.85-€4.50 per tent (plus 8-9.50AS/€0.60-0.70 tax if over age 15), so camping is seldom much cheaper than hostelling.

HIKING AND SKIING

Nearly every town and city has a series of **hiking** trails in its vicinity; consult the local tourist office. Trails are usually marked with either a red-white-red marker—meaning only sturdy boots and hiking poles are necessary—or a blue-white-blue marker, which means mountaineering equipment is needed. Most mountain hiking trails and mountain huts are only open from late June to early September because of snow in the higher passes. Western Austria is one of the world's best **skiing** regions; the areas around Innsbruck and Kitzbühel are saturated with lifts and runs. High season normally runs from mid-December to mid-January and from February to March. Tourist offices provide information on regional skiing and can suggest budget travel agencies that offer ski packages.

COMMUNICATION

MAIL. Letters take 1-2 days within Austria. **Airmail** to North America takes 5-7 days, but up to 2 weeks to Australia and New Zealand. Mark all letters and packages "mit Flugpost" or "par avion." Address mail to be held in this format: FirstName SUR-NAME, Postlagernde Briefe, A-1010 Vienna, Austria.

TELEPHONES. You can usually make international calls from a coin-operated pay phone, but it's better to buy **phone cards** *(Wertkarten)* at post offices, train stations, and *Tabak/Trafik* (50-100AS/€3.65-7.30). Direct dial access numbers include: **AT&T,** ☎(0800) 20 02 88; **British Telecom,** ☎(0800) 20 02 09; **Canada Direct,** ☎(0800) 20 02 17; **Ireland Direct,** ☎(0229) 03 03 53; **MCI,** ☎(0800) 20 02 35; **Sprint,** ☎(0800) 20 02 36; **Telecom New Zealand,** ☎(0800) 20 02 22; **Telkom South Africa,** ☎(0800) 20 02 30.

INTERNET ACCESS. Most towns in Austria have Internet cafes. Rates are usually about 50-100AS/€3.65-7.30 per hr.

LANGUAGE. German is the first language. English is the most common second language in Austria, but outside of cities and among older residents, English is less common. *Grüss Gott* is the typical greeting. For phrases, see p. 953.

LOCAL FACTS

Time: Austria is 1hr. ahead of Greenwich Mean Time (GMT).

When to Go: Warm sweaters are the rule from Sept.-May, while summer is rainy and humid. July is usually the hottest month at up to 38°C (100°F), while Feb. is the coldest, with temperatures down to -10°C (5°F). Mountainous areas get cooler and wetter the higher you go. Snow cover lasts from late Dec. to Mar. in the valleys.

Holidays: New Year's Day (Jan. 1-2); Epiphany (Jan. 6); Good Friday (Mar. 29); Easter Monday (Apr. 1); Labor Day (May 1); Ascension (May 9); Whitmonday (May 20); Corpus Christi (May 30); Assumption Day (Aug. 15); Austrian National Day (Oct. 26); All Saints' Day (Nov. 1); Immaculate Conception (Dec. 8); Christmas (Dec. 25-26). **Festivals:** Just about everything closes down on public holidays, so plan accordingly. Austrians celebrate **Fasching** (Carnaval) during the 1st 2 weeks of Feb. Austria's most famous summer **music festivals** are the **Wiener Festwochen** (mid-May to mid-June) and the **Salzburger Festspiele** (late-July to late-Aug.).

VIENNA (WIEN) ☎0222

From its humble origins as a Roman camp along the Danube, Vienna became the cultural heart of Europe for centuries, the setting for fledgling musicians, writers, artists, philosophers, and politicians to achieve greatness—or infamy. Viennese satirist Karl Kraus once dubbed the city—the birthplace of psychoanalysis, atonal music, functionalist architecture, Zionism, and Nazism—a "laboratory for world destruction." At the height of its artistic ferment at the turn of the century, during the smoky days of its great cafe culture, the Viennese were already self-mockingly referring to their city as the "merry apocalypse": its smooth veneer of waltzes and *Gemütlichkeit* (good nature) concealed a darker side expressed in Freud's theories, Kafka's dark fantasies, and Mahler's deathly beautiful music. Vienna has a reputation for living absent-mindedly in this grand past, but as the last fringes of the Iron Curtain have been drawn back, Vienna has tried to revitalize its political, cultural, and economic life to re-establish itself as the gateway to Eastern Europe and as a place where experimentalism thrives.

✈ INTERCITY TRANSPORTATION

BY PLANE. The **Wien-Schwechat Flughafen** (☎700 72 22 31, departure info ☎700 72 21 84) is home to **Austrian Airlines.** (☎517 89; www.aua.com. Open M-F 7am-10pm, Sa-Su 8am-8pm.) Daily flights to and from **New York** and frequent flights to **Berlin, London, Rome,** and other major cities are available.

The **airport** is far from the city center (18km); the cheapest way to reach the city is S7 "Flughafen/Wolfsthal," which stops at **Wien Mitte** (30min., every 30min. 5am-9:30pm, 38AS/€2.80; Eurail not valid). The heart of the city, **Stephansplatz,** is a short metro ride from Wien Mitte on the U3 line. It's more convenient (but also more expensive) to take the **Vienna Airport Lines Shuttle Bus,** which runs between

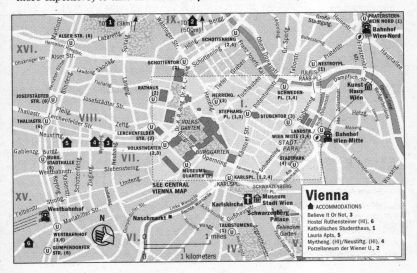

AUSTRIA

the airport and the City Air Terminal, at the Hilton opposite Wien Mitte. (Every 20min. 6:30am-11:10pm, every 30min. midnight-6am; 70AS/€5.10.) **Buses** connect the airport to the **Südbahnhof** and **Westbahnhof** (see below) every 30min. from 8:55am-7:25pm and every hr. from 8:20pm-8:25am.

BY TRAIN. Vienna has two main train stations with international connections. For general train information, dial 17 17 (24hr.) or check www.bahn.at.

Westbahnhof, XV, Mariahilferstr. 132. Most trains from this station head **west,** but a few go east and north. To: **Amsterdam** (14½hr., 7:17pm, 2280AS/€165.70); **Berlin Zoo** (11hr., 9:19pm, 1682AS/€122.25); **Bregenz** (8hr., 5 per day 5am-10:15pm, 790AS/ €57.45); **Budapest** (3-4hr., 6 per day 8:25am-6pm, 428AS/€31.10); **Hamburg** (9½hr., 10:17am and 7:45pm, 2410AS/€175.15); **Innsbruck** (5-6hr., every 2hr. 5am-11:25pm, 660AS/€48); **Munich** (4½hr., 5 per day 5:45am-3:45pm, 824AS/€60); **Paris** (14hr., 8:47am and 8:21pm, 2140AS/€155.55); **Salzburg** (3½hr., every hr., 460AS/€33.45); **Zurich** (9¼hr., 3 per day 7:15am-9:15pm, 1104AS/€80.25). The **information counter** is open daily 7:30am-8:40pm.

Südbahnhof, X, Wiedner Gürtel 1a. On the D tram. To get to the city take the tram (dir.: Nußdorf) to "Opera/Karlspl." Trains leave for destinations **south** and **east.** To: **Berlin Ostbahnhof** (9¼hr., 10:55am, 1160AS/€84.30); **Graz** (2¾hr., every hr. 6am-10:30pm, 310AS/€22.55); **Krakow** (7-8hr., 9:25am and 9:25pm, 496AS/€36.05); **Prague** (4½hr., 3 per day 6:55am-2:55pm, 524AS/€38.10); **Rome** (14hr., 7:34am and 7:36pm, 1352AS/€98.30); **Venice** (9-10hr., 3 per day 7:30am-10:30pm, 880AS/€64). The **information counter** is open daily 6:30am-9:20pm.

BY BUS AND BOAT. Travel by bus in Austria is seldom cheaper than travel by train; compare prices before buying a ticket. **City bus terminals** are located at Wien Mitte/Landstr., Hütteldorf, Heiligenstadt, Floridsdorf, Kagran, Erdberg, and Reumannpl. Domestic **BundesBuses** run from these stations to local and international destinations. (Ticket counter open M-F 6am-5:50pm, Sa-Su 6am-3:50pm.) Many international bus lines also have agencies in the stations, each with different hours. For bus information, call BundesBus (☎711 01; 7am-7pm).

HITCHHIKING AND RIDE SHARING. While *Let's Go* does not recommend hitching, **hitchhikers** headed for Salzburg have been seen taking U4 to "Hütteldorf"; the highway leading to the Autobahn is 10km farther. Hitchers traveling south often ride tram #67 to the last stop and wait at the rotary near Laaerberg. A safer alternative is ride sharing; **Mitfahrzentrale Wien,** VIII, Daung. 1a, off Laudong., pairs drivers and riders. Call to see which rides are available, then, to meet your ride, take tram #43 to "Skodag." and walk down Skodag. to Daung. (☎408 22 10. Open M-F 8am-noon and 2-7pm, Sa-Su 1-3pm.) A ride to **Salzburg** costs 210AS/€15.30, to **Prague** 450AS/€32.70. Reservations two days in advance are recommended.

✈ ORIENTATION

Vienna is divided into 23 **districts** *(Bezirke).* The first is the *Innenstadt* (city center), defined by the **Ringstraße** on three sides and the Danube Canal on the fourth. The Ringstraße (or "Ring") consists of many different segments, each with its own name: Opernring, Kärntner Ring, Dr.-Karl-Lueger-Ring, etc. Many of Vienna's major attractions are in District I and immediately around the Ringstraße. Districts II-IX spread out from the city center following the clockwise, one-way traffic of the Ring. The remaining districts expand from yet another ring, the **Gürtel** ("belt"). Like the Ring, this major two-way thoroughfare has numerous segments, including Margaretengürtel, Währinger Gürtel, and Neubaugürtel. Street signs indicate the district number in Roman or Arabic numerals *before* the street and number, and postal codes correspond to the district number: 1010 for the first district, 1020 for the second, 1110 for the eleventh, etc. **Let's Go includes district numbers for establishments in Roman numerals before the street address.**

Central Vienna

▲ ACCOMMODATIONS
Studenten Wohnheim
der Hochschule für Musik, 8

● FOOD
Brezel'wölb, 1
Café Central, 3
Kleines Café, 7
La Crêperie, 6
Margaritaville, 4
Maschu Maschu, 2
Rosenberger Markt, 9
Trzesniewski, 5

AUSTRIA

LITTLE PIECES OF REVOLUTION Travelers may be perplexed by the little paper strips taped around columns in train stations, subway stops, and crowded streets. The slips, known as *Pflücktexte* (from *pflücken*, to pluck), contain short poems with vaguely anti-establishment messages and are meant to be "plucked" from the columns, whereupon they are mysteriously replaced. *Let's Go* sleuths have determined that the poems are composed by one Helmut Seethaler, Wasnerg. 43/8, 1200 Wien, who offers more insurgent poems via mail "for a small bill."

▐ LOCAL TRANSPORTATION

Public transportation in Vienna is extensive and dependable; call 580 00 for general info. The **subway** (U-Bahn), **tram** (Straßenbahn), **elevated train** (S-Bahn), and **bus** systems operate under one ticket system. A **single fare** (22AS/€1.60 if purchased on a bus, 19AS/€1.40 if purchased in advance from a machine in a station, ticket office, or tobacco shop), lets you travel to any single destination in the city and switch from bus to U-Bahn to tram to S-Bahn, as long as your travel is uninterrupted. To **validate a ticket,** punch it in the machine immediately upon entering the first vehicle, but don't stamp it again when you switch trains. A ticket stamped twice or not stamped at all is invalid, and plainclothes inspectors may fine you 560AS/€40.70 plus the ticket price. Other ticket options (available at the same places as pre-purchased single tickets) are a **24hr. pass** (60AS/€4.40), a **3-day "rover" ticket** (150AS/€10.90), a **7-day pass** (155AS/€11.30; valid M 9am to M 9am), or an **8-day pass** (300AS/€21.80; valid any 8 days, not necessarily consecutive; valid also for several people traveling together). The **Vienna Card** (210AS/€15.30) offers free travel for 72hr. as well as discounts at museums, sights, and events.

Regular trams and subway cars stop running between 12:30am and 5am. **Nightbuses** run every 30min. along most tram, subway, and major bus routes. "N" signs with yellow cat eyes designate night bus stops. (15AS/€1.10 or 4 for 45AS/€3.30; day transport passes not valid.) A complete night bus schedule is available at bus info counters in U-Bahn stations.

The **public transportation information line** has live operators that give public transportation directions to any point in the city. (☎790 91 05. Open M-W, F 8am-3pm, Th 8am-5:30pm.) **Information stands** (marked with an "i") in many stations help with purchasing tickets and have an indispensable free pocket map of the U- and S-Bahn systems. Stands in the U-Bahn at Karlspl., Stephanspl., and the Westbahnhof are the most likely to have information in English. (Open M-F 6:30am-6:30pm, Sa-Su and holidays 8:30am-4pm.)

Taxis: (☎313 00, 401 00, 601 60, or 814 00). Stands at Westbahnhof, Südbahnhof, Karlspl. in the city center, and by the Bermuda Dreiecke for late-night revelers. Accredited taxis have yellow and black signs on the roof. Rates generally 27AS/€2 plus 14AS/€1.05 per km. 27AS/€2 extra Su, holidays, and nights (11pm-6am).

Car Rental: Avis, I, Opernring 3-5 (☎587 62 41). Open M-F 7am-8pm, Sa 8am-2pm, Su 8am-1pm. **Hertz** (☎70 07 26 61), at the airport. Open M-F 7:15am-11pm, Sa 8am-8pm, Su 8am-11pm.

Bike Rental: At Wien Nord and Westbahnhof. 150AS/€10.90 per day, 90AS/€6.55 with train ticket from day of arrival. **Pedal Power,** II, Ausstellungsstr. 3 (☎729 72 34), rents bikes (60AS/€4.40 per hr., 395AS/€28.75 for 24hr. with delivery) and offers bike tours of the city (180-280AS/€13.10-20.35). Discounts for students and Vienna Card holders. Open May-Sept. 8am-8pm. Pick up *Vienna By Bike* at the tourist office for details on the bicycle scene.

⁊ PRACTICAL INFORMATION

TOURIST AND FINANCIAL SERVICES

Main Tourist Office: I, Albertinapl. (www.info.wien.at). Follow Operng. up 1 block from the Opera House. The staff dispenses a free map of the city and the pamphlet *Youth Scene,* and books rooms for a 40AS/€2.95 fee plus 1-night deposit. Open 9am-7pm. **Branch Offices: Westbahnhof,** open daily 7:30am-8:40pm; **Vienna International Airport,** in arrival hall, open 8:30am-9pm.

Jugend-Info Wien (Vienna Youth Information Service): I, Bellaria-Passage (☎17 99), in the underground passage. Enter at the "Dr.-Karl-Renner-Ring/Bellaria" stop (trams #1, 2, 46, 49, D, or J) or at the "Volkstheater" U-Bahn station. Hip staff has the free *Jugend in Wien* brochure, information on cultural events and housing, and discount concert and theater tickets. Open M-Sa noon-7pm.

Embassies and Consulates: Australia: IV, Mattiellistr. 2 (☎(01) 512 85 80). **Canada,** I, Laurenzerberg 2 (☎(01) 531 38 30 00; fax 531 38 33 21). **Ireland,** I, Rotenturmstr. 16-18, 5th fl. (☎(01) 71 54 24 60). **New Zealand,** The New Zealand Embassy in Berlin, Germany, has responsibility for Austria. Friedrichstr. 60, 10117 Berlin (☎(030) 20 62 10; fax 20 62 11 14). **Consulate, Vienna,** XIX, Springsiedelg. 28 (☎318 85 05). **South Africa,** XIX, Sandg. 33 (☎(01) 320 64 93; fax 320 64 93 51). **UK,** III, Jauresg. 12 (☎(01) 716 13 51 51; fax 716 1359 00). **US,** IX, Boltzmanng. 16 (☎(01) 313 39; fax 406 52 60).

Currency Exchange: ATMs are your best bet. **Banks** and **airport exchanges** use the same official rates. Minimum commission 65AS/€4.75 for traveler's checks, 10AS/€0.75 for cash. Most open M-W and F 8am-12:30pm and 1:30-3pm, Th 8am-12:30pm and 1:30-5:30pm. The 24hr. exchange at the **main post office** has excellent rates and an 80AS/€5.85 fee to change up to US$1100 in traveler's checks.

American Express: I, Kärntnerstr. 21-23, P.O. Box 28, A-1015 (☎515 40), down the street from Stephanspl. Cashes AmEx and Thomas Cook (3% commission) checks, sells theater, concert, and other tickets, and holds mail for 4 weeks. Open M-F 9am-5:30pm, Sa 9am-noon.

LOCAL SERVICES

Luggage Storage: Lockers are 30-50AS/€.2.20-3.65 per 24hr. at all train stations. Adequate for sizable backpacks. **Luggage watch** 30AS/€2.20. Open 4am-1:15am.

Bi-Gay-Lesbian Organizations: The bisexual, gay, and lesbian community in Vienna is more integrated than in other Austrian cities. Pick up either the monthly magazine (in German) called *Extra Connect;* the free monthly publication *Bussi* at any gay bar, cafe, or club; or consult the straight *Falter* newspaper, which also lists gay events. **Rosa Lila Villa,** VI, Linke Wienzeile 102 (☎586 81 50), is a favored resource and social center for homosexual Viennese and visitors alike. Friendly staff speaks English and provides information, a library, and nightclub listings. Open M-F 5-8pm.

Laundromat: Schnell und Sauber, VII, Westbahnhofstr. 60; U6 to "Burgg. Stadthalle." Wash 60AS/€4.40, dry 10AS/€0.75 per 15min. Soap included. Open 24hr.

Public Showers and Toilets: At Westbahnhof, in **Friseursalon Navratil** downstairs from subway passage. Well maintained. 30min. shower 54AS/€3.95, with soap and towel 66AS/€4.80 (10AS/€0.75 extra on Su). Showers also available at **Jörgerbad,** XVII, Jörgerstr. 42-44, and at the airport. There are cheap pay toilets in most U-bahn stations and a special *Jugendstil* toilet in Graben (9am-7pm, requires 1AS or 5AS coin).

 CRIME IN THE CITY. Vienna is a metropolis with crime like any other; use common sense, especially after dark. Karlspl. is home to many pushers and junkies. Avoid areas in districts V, X and XIV, as well as **Landstraßer Hauptstraße** and **Prater Park,** after dark. The Red Light District covers sections of the Gürtel.

EMERGENCY AND COMMUNICATION

Emergencies: Police, ☎ 133. **Ambulance,** ☎ 144. **Fire,** ☎ 122.

Crisis Hotlines: All have English speakers. **Rape Crisis Hotline:** ☎ 523 22 22. M 10am-6pm, Tu 2-6pm, W 10am-2pm, Th 5-9pm. **24hr. immediate help:** ☎ 717 19.

Medical Assistance: Allgemeines Krankenhaus (hospital), IX, Währinger Gürtel 18-20 (☎ 404 00 19 64). **Emergency care,** ☎ 141. **24hr. pharmacy,** ☎ 15 50. Consulates have lists of English-speaking doctors, or call **Fachärzte Zugeck** (☎ 512 18 18; 24hr.).

Internet Access: bigNET.Internet.cafe I, Kärntnerstr. 61 (☎ 503 98 44), I, Hoher markt 8-9 (☎ 533 29 39), and the recently opened, largest Internet cafe in Austria, Mariahilferstr. 27. 50AS/€3.65 per 30min. and hip English-speaking "crew." **Libro,** XXII, Donauzentrum (☎ 202 52 55), provides free access at 6 terminals. Open M-F 7am-7pm, Sa 9am-5pm. **Jugend-Info des Bundesministeriums,** I, Franz-Josefs-Kai 51 (☎ 533 70 30), has free access at 2 PCs. Open M-F 11am-6pm.

Post Offices: Hauptpostamt, I, Fleischmarkt 19. Open 24hr. Address mail to be held: SURNAME, FirstName; Postlagernde Briefe; Hauptpostamt; Fleischmarkt 19; A-1010 Wien. Branches throughout the city and at the train stations; look for the yellow signs with the trumpet logo. **Postal Codes:** A-1XX0, where XX is the number of the district in Arabic numerals (ex.: District I: A-1010, District II: A-1020, District 17: A-1170.)

ΓΛ ACCOMMODATIONS AND CAMPING

One of the few unpleasant aspects of visiting Vienna is the hunt for cheap rooms during peak tourist season (June-Sept.). Write or call for reservations at least five days in advance, or plan to call from the train station between 6 and 9am to put your name down for a reservation. If your choice is full, ask to be put on a waiting list, or ask for suggestions. Those unable to find a hostel bed should consider a *Pension.* The summer crunch for budget rooms is slightly alleviated in July, when university dorms convert into makeshift hostels. If you're staying for a longer period of time, try **Odyssee Reisen und Mitwohnzentrale,** VIII, Laudong. 7, which arranges for you to housesit or sublet apartments. Bring your passport to register. (☎ 402 60 61. Open M-F 10am-2pm and 3-6pm.) **Arwag** offers similar services via the web (www.arwag.at) or its 24hr. hotline (☎ 79 70 01 18).

HOSTELS

▩ **Wombats City Hostel,** XIV, Grang. 6 (☎ 897 23 36). Exit Westbahnhof at the main exit and turn right onto Mariahilferstr., turn right onto Rosinag. and continue until Grang. (2nd left). While right next to the train tracks and near a number of auto-body shops, this superb modern hostel compensates with a pub and various other perks. Breakfast 35AS/€2.55. Shower included. Laundry 50AS/€3.65. **Internet** 1AS/€0.10 per min. **Bike** or **in-line skate** rental 100AS/€7.30 per day. 2-, 4-, and 6-bed dorms 190-245AS/€13.85-17.85 per person.

▩ **Hostel Ruthensteiner (HI),** XV, Robert-Hamerlingg. 24 (☎ 893 42 02). Exit Westbahnhof at the main entrance, turn right, and head to Mariahilferstr.; turn right onto Mariahilferstr. and continue until Haidmannsg. Turn left, then take the 1st right on Robert-Hammerlingg. This top-notch hostel has an extremely knowledgeable, English-speaking staff, spotless rooms, and a snack bar. Breakfast 29AS/€2.15. Showers and sheets (except for 10-bed rooms) included. Lockers and kitchen available. **Internet** from 20AS/€1.45. 4-night max. stay. Reception 24hr. Reservations recommended, but owners often hold beds for spontaneous travelers. "The Outback" summer dorm 135AS/€9.85; 4- to 10-bed dorms 135-159AS/€9.85-11.60; 3- to 5-bed dorms 169-179AS/€12.30-13; doubles 470-518AS/€34.20-37.65. AmEx/MC/V.

▩ **Believe It Or Not,** VII, Myrtheng. 10, Apt. #14 (☎ 526 46 58). From Westbahnhof, take U6 (dir.: Heiligenstadt) to "Burgg./Stadthalle," then bus #48A (dir.: Ring) to "Neubaug." Walk back on Burgg. 1 block and take the 1st right on Myrtheng. Ring the bell. A converted apartment, this sociable hostel has a kitchen and 2 co-ed bedrooms full of bunks. Reception 8am until early afternoon—call early. Lockout 10:30am-12:30pm. Dorms 160AS/€11.65; Nov.-Easter 110AS/€8.

Myrthengasse (HI), VII, Myltheng. 7, across the street from Believe It or Not (above), and **Neustiftgasse (HI)**, VII, Neustiftg. 85 (☎ 523 63 16). These simple, modern hostels, under the same management, are 20min. from the *Innenstadt*. Breakfast and sheets included. Laundry 50AS/€3.65. **Internet** 60AS/€4.40 for 30min. Reception at Myrtheng. 24hr. Lockout 9am-2pm. Single-sex rooms. Curfew 1am. Reservations recommended. 5-day max. stay. Jan. 7-Mar. 10 and Nov. 4-Dec. 23 4- to 6-bed dorms with shower 185AS/€13.45; 2-bed dorms with shower 245AS/€17.85. Mar. 11-Nov. 3 and Dec. 24-Jan. 6 200AS/€14.55, 260AS/€18.90. Nonmembers add 40AS/€2.95. AmEx/MC/V.

Hostel Zöhrer, IX, Skodag. 26 (☎ 406 07 30). From Westbahnhof take tram #5 to "Laudongaße," backtrack, take the 2nd right at Daung. and walk 1 block to Skodag. Breakfast, kitchen, and shower included. Lockout 11am-2pm. Reservations recommended. 6- to 8- bed dorms 180AS/€13.10; doubles 480AS/€34.90; triples 690AS/€50.15.

Schloßherberge am Wilhelminenberg (HI), XVI, Savoyenstr. 2 (☎ 485 85 03, ext. 700). Take U6 to "Thaliastr.," then tram #46 (dir.: Joachimsthalerpl.) to "Maroltingerg." or tram #44 from Schottentor to "Wilhelminenstr." Then (in either case) take bus #146B or #46B to "Schloß Wilhelminenberg." Enter the palace gates and follow the signs. Exceptional hostel with views of Vienna, but beware that nightlife will be difficult from here—the last bus is at 12:15am. Breakfast, showers, and sheets included. Laundry 65AS/€4.75. Reception 7am-11pm. Lockout 9am-2pm. Reserve at least 2 days in advance. 4-bed dorms 245AS/€17.85; 3-bed dorms 295AS/€21.45; singles 560AS/€40.70; doubles 390AS/€28.35. AmEx/MC/V.

Turmherberge Don Bosco, III, Lechnerstr. 12 (☎ 713 14 94). Take U3 to "Kardinal-Nagl-Pl.," take the Kardinal-Nagl-Pl. exit facing the park, walk through the park, and turn right onto Erdbergstr.; Lechnerstr. is the 2nd left. The cheapest beds in town, in a bare former bell tower that gets hot in summer—though sex-segregated quarters help keep things cool. Lockout 9:30am-5pm. Curfew 11:45pm. Open Mar.-Nov. 80AS/€5.80; under 19 78AS/€5.70.

HOTELS AND PENSIONS

The prices are higher here, but you pay for convenient reception hours, no curfews, and no lockouts.

Lauria Apartments, VII, Kaiserstr. 77, Apt. #8 (☎ 522 25 55). From Westbahnhof, take tram #5 to "Burgg." Fully equipped kitchens. Sheets and TV included. Reception 8am-noon. 2-night min. Dorms 160AS/€11.65; singles and student-bunk twins 450AS/€32.70; doubles 550AS/€40, with shower 750AS/€54.50; student-bunk triples 600AS/€43.60; triples 750AS/€54.50, 900AS/€65.40; quads 900AS/€65.40, 1050AS/€76.30. AmEx/MC/V, except for dorm beds.

Pension Wild, VIII, Langeg. 10 (☎ 406 51 74; fax 402 21 68). Take U2 to "Lerchenfelderstr.," and take the 1st right onto Langeg. Friendly, English-speaking staff and bright decorations. Kitchen access. Breakfast and shower included. Reception 6am-10pm. Reservations by fax recommended. Singles 490-890AS/€35.65-64.70; doubles 590-1140AS/€42.90-82.85; triples 1050-1380AS/€76.35-100.30. AmEx/MC/V.

Pension Reimer, IV, Kircheng. 18 (☎ 523 61 62), is centrally located and has huge, comfortable, and clean rooms. Breakfast included. Singles 510AS/€37, in winter 470AS/€34.20. Doubles 660-760AS/€48-55.25, with bath 880AS/€64; in winter 680AS/€49.50, 810AS/€59. MC/V for long stays only.

Pension Falstaff, IX, Müllnerg. 5 (☎ 317 91 27). Take U4 to "Roßauer Lände," cross Roßauer Lände, head down Grünentorg., and take the 3rd left onto Müllnerg. Breakfast included. Reception 7:30am-9pm. Singles 450AS/€32.70, with shower 550AS/€40; doubles 690-890AS/€50.15-64.70. 10% discount for stays of 1 week or more in off season; 15% for 2 weeks, 30% for more than 1 month. 100AS/€7.30 reduction Nov. 1-Mar. 30 (excluding Christmas and Jan.). MC/V.

UNIVERSITY DORMITORIES

From July through September, many university dorms become hotels, usually with singles, doubles, and a few triples and quads. These rooms don't have much in the way of character, but showers and sheets are standard, and their cleanliness and relatively low cost suffice for most budget travelers, particularly for longer stays.

Porzellaneum der Wiener Universität, IX, Porzellang. 30 (☎31 77 28 20). From Südbahnhof, take tram D (dir.: Nußdorf) to "Fürsteng." From Westbahnhof, take tram #5 to "Franz-Josefs Bahnhof," then tram D (dir.: Südbahnhof) to "Fürsteng." Great location in the student district. Sheets included. Reception 24hr. Call ahead. Singles 210AS/ €15.25; doubles 420AS/€30.50; quads 840AS/€61.

Katholisches Studentenhaus, XIX, Peter-Jordanstr. 29 (☎34 74 73 12). From Westbahnhof, take U6 (dir.: Heiligenstadt) to "Nußdorferstr.," then bus #35A or tram #38 to "Hardtg." and turn left. From Südbahnhof, take tram D to "Schottentor," then tram #38 to "Hardtg." Reception until 10pm. Call ahead. Singles 250AS/€18.20; doubles 400AS/€29.

Studentenwohnheim der Hochschule für Musik, I, Johannesg. 8 (☎514 84 48). Walk 3 blocks down Kärnterstr. away from Stephansdom and turn left onto Johannesg. Unbeatable location and cheap meals. Breakfast and showers included. Reception 24hr. Reserve well in advance. Singles 440AS/€32; doubles 780AS/€56.70; triples 840AS/€61; quads 1000AS/€72.70; quints 1250AS/€91. All rooms 390AS/€28.35 per person, 500AS/€36.35 per person for single occupancy.

CAMPING

Wien-West, Hüttelbergstr. 80 (☎914 23 14). Take U4 to "Hütteldorf," then bus #14B or 152 (dir.: Campingpl.) to "Wien West." This campground, 8km from the city center, is crowded but grassy and pleasant. Laundry, grocery stores, wheelchair access, and cooking facilities. Reception 7:30am-9:30pm. Closed Feb. July-Aug. 75AS/€5.45 per person, 68AS/€4.95 rest of the year; 45AS/€3.30 per tent. Electricity 40AS/€2.95.

Aktiv Camping Neue Donau, XXII, Am Kleehäufel 119 (☎202 40 10), is 4km from the city center and adjacent to Neue Donau beaches. Take U1 to "Kaisermühlen" and bus #91a to "Kleehäufel." Laundry, supermarket, and kitchen. Open May 14-Sept. 10. July-Aug. 75AS/€5.45 per person, 45AS/€3.30 per tent. May, June, and Sept. 48AS/ €3.50 per person, 40AS/€2.95 per tent. Electricity 40AS/€2.95. Showers included.

◘ FOOD

Vienna's restaurants are as varied as its cuisine. The restaurants near **Kärntnerstraße** are generally expensive—a better bet is the neighborhood north of the university and near the *Votivkirche* (take U2 to "Schottentor"), where **Universitätsstraße** and **Währingerstraße** meet. Cafes with cheap meals also line **Burggasse** in District VI. The area radiating from the **Rechte** and **Linke Wienzeile** near Naschmarkt (take U4 to "Kettenbrückeg.") houses a range of cheap restaurants, and the **Naschmarkt** itself contains open-air stands where you can purchase bread and a variety of ethnic foods. Almost all year long, **Rathausplatz** hosts food stands tied into the current festival. The open-air **Brunnenmarkt** (take U6 to "Josefstädterstr." then walk up Veronikag. 1 block and turn right) is cheap and cheerful.

As always, supermarkets provide building blocks for cheap, solid meals. The lowest prices are on the shelves of **Billa**, **Hofer**, and **Spar**. Kosher groceries are available at the **Kosher Supermarket**, II, Hollandstr. 10 (☎216 96 75).

RESTAURANTS

INSIDE THE RING

▨ **Margaritaville**, I, Bartensteing. 3. Take U2 to "Lerchenfelderstr.," exit onto Museumstr., and cut across the triangular green to Bartensteing. Offers authentic Tex-Mex food among Spanish-speakers. Open M-F 4pm-midnight, Sa-Su 11am-midnight. MC/V.

Maschu Maschu, I, Rabensteig 8. In the Bermuda Dreiecke; serves filling and super-cheap Israeli *falafel* (41AS/€3) and *schwarma*. Open 11:30am-late.

La Crêperie, I, Grünangerg. 10, off Singerstr. near Stephanspl. Scrumptious crêpes, both sweet and savory (48-250AS/€3.50-18.20). Open 11:30am-midnight. AmEx/MC/V.

Trzesniewski, I, Dorotheerg. 1, 3 blocks down the Graben from the Stephansdom. This unpronounceable but famous establishment has been serving petite open-faced sand-wiches for over 80 years. A filling lunch–6 slices and a mini-beer–costs 69AS/€5. This was Kafka's favorite place to eat. Open M-F 8:30am-7:30pm, Sa 9am-5pm.

Rosenberger Markt, I, Mayserderg. 2, off Kärntnerstr. This chaotic subterranean buffet offers a gargantuan selection of decent food at reasonable prices. You pay by the size of your plate, not by weight, so pile high. Salads 33-74AS/€2.40-5.40, vegetable dishes 24-69AS/€1.75-5. Open 10:30am-11pm. AmEx/MC/V.

Brezelg'wölb, I, Lederhof 9, near Am Hof, off Drahtg. Hearty Viennese cuisine in a quiet setting. Open daily 11:30am-1am; hot food served until midnight. AmEx/MC/V.

OUTSIDE THE RING

OH Pot, OH Pot, IX, Währingerstr. 22. Take U2 to "Schottentor." This adorable joint serves filling "pots" (88-125AS/€6.40-€9.10), stew-like veggie or meat concoctions. Open M-F 7:30am-11pm, Sa-Su 6pm-late. MC/V.

Tunnel, VIII, Florianig. 39. Take U2 to "Rathaus," then, with your back to the *Rathaus*, head right on Landesgerichtstr. and left on Florianig. Pronounced "Too-nehl," this stu-dent crowd paradise is prized for its dilapidated hipness and live nightly music. Daily lunch *Menüs* 55AS/€4. Italian, Austrian, and Middle Eastern dishes, with many vege-tarian options (48-82AS/€3.50-6). Open daily 9am-2am.

Blue Box, VII, Richterg. 8. Take U3 to "Neubaug.," turn onto Neubaug., and take the 1st left onto Richterg. Blue Box is a restaurant by day and a club by night. Dishes are fresh and original, and DJs spin the latest trance and trip-hop. Open M 6pm-2am, Tu-Th and Su 10am-2am, F-Sa 10am-4am. V.

Zum Mogulhof, VII, Burgg. 12. Ample portions of delicious Indian food—both vegetarian and meat—served by candlelight amid crimson carpets and velvet wallpaper. Open daily 11:30am-2:30pm and 6-11:30pm. MC/V.

Elsäßer Bistro, IX, Währingerstr. 32. U2 to "Schottentor." In the palace that houses the French Cultural Institute—walk in the garden and follow your nose for an extravagant meal. Wonderful food, with prices hovering around 120AS/€8.75, and beautiful French wines. Open M-F 11am-3pm and 6-11pm.

Fischerbräu, XIX, Billrothstr. 17. Take U6 to "Nußdorfer Str.," follow exit sign to Döblinger Hauptstr., turn left onto it, then left on Billrothstr. Popular spot for young locals with music, home-brewed beer (large 41AS/€3), and delicious veal sausage (64AS/€4.65). Open M-F 4pm-1am, Sa-Su 11am-1am.

University Mensa, IX, Universitätsstr. 7, on the 7th fl. of the university building, between U2 stops "Rathaus" and "Schottentor." Ride the old-fashioned *Pater Noster* elevator (which has no doors and never stops, so jump in and out and say your prayers) to the 6th fl. and head up 1 flight of stairs. Not much atmosphere, but the food is cheap. Typ-ical cafeteria meals 40-60AS/€2.90-4.40. Open M-F 11am-2pm. Closed July-Aug. but snack bar still open 8am-3pm.

◨ COFFEEHOUSES

There is an unwritten rule for the Vienna coffeehouse: the coffee matters, but the atmosphere matters more. The 19th-century coffeehouse was a haven for artists, writers, and thinkers who flocked there and stayed long into the night composing operettas, writing books, and cutting into each other's work. The bourgeoisie fol-lowed suit, and the coffeehouse became the living room of the city. The original lit-erary cafes were **Café Griensteidl, Café Central,** and **Café Herrenhof**. Cafes still exist under all these names, but only Café Central looks like it used to. Delectable pastries round out the experience. To see a menu, ask for a *Karte*. Most cafes also serve hot food, but ordering anything but pastries with coffee just isn't done. The most serious dictate of coffeehouse etiquette is that you linger. The waiter (known as *Herr Ober*) will serve you as soon as you sit down, then leave you to sip, read, and brood. Newspapers and magazines, many in English, are neatly racked for patrons. When you are ready to leave, just ask to pay: *"Zahlen bitte!"* Vienna has dozens of coffeehouses; the best are below.

Kleines Café, I, Franziskanerpl. 3. Turn off Kärtnerstr. onto Weihburg. and follow it to the Franziskanerkirche. This tiny, cozy cafe features tables spilling out into the courtyard and salads that are minor works of art. Open M-Sa 10am-2am, Su 1pm-2am.

Café Central, I, at the corner of Herreng. and Strauchg. inside Palais Fers. Café Central has unfortunately surrendered to tourists because of its fame, but this mecca of the cafe world is definitely worth a visit. Open M-Sa 8am-8pm, Su 10am-6pm. AmEx/MC/V.

Hotel Sacher, I, Philharmonikerstr. 4. Behind the opera house. This historic sight has served world-famous *Sacher Torte* (50AS/€3.65) in red velvet opulence for years. Cafe open daily 11am-11:30pm; bakery open 9am-11:30pm. AmEx/MC/V.

Café Sperl, VI, Gumpendorferstr. 11. Take U2 to "Museumsquartier," exit to Mariahilferstr., walk 1 block on Getreidemarkt, and turn right on Gumpendorferstr. Built in 1880, Sperl is one of Vienna's oldest and most beautiful cafes. Open M-Sa 7am-11pm, Su 3-11pm; July-Aug. closed Su.

⊙ SIGHTS

Vienna's streets are by turns startling, cozy, scuzzy, and grandiose; expect contrasts around every corner. To wander on your own, grab the brochure *Vienna from A to Z* (with Vienna Card 50AS/€3.65; available at the tourist office). The range of available **tours** is overwhelming—there are 42 themed walking tours alone, detailed in the brochure *Walks in Vienna* from the tourist office. Contact **Vienna-Bike**, IX, Wasag. (☎319 12 58), for **bike rental** (60AS/€4.40) or a 2-3hr. **cycling tour** (280AS/€20.35). **Bus tours** are given by **Vienna Sight-seeing Tours**, III, Stelzhamerg. 4/11 (☎712 46 83), and **Cityrama**, I, Börgeg. 1 (☎534 13). Tours start at 400AS/€29. The sights below are arranged for a do-it-yourself walking tour.

INSIDE THE RING

District I is Vienna's social and geographical epicenter as well as a gallery of the history of aesthetics, from Romanesque to *Jugendstil* (Art Nouveau).

STEPHANSPLATZ. *(Take U1 or U3 to "Stephansplatz.")* Right at the heart of Vienna, this square is home to the massive **Stephansdom** (St. Stephen's Cathedral), Vienna's most treasured symbol. The North Tower was originally intended to match the South Tower, but construction ceased after a spooky tragedy (see **A Bad Pact with the Devil,** below). The elevator in the North Tower *(open Apr.-June and Sept.-Oct. 9am-6pm; July-Aug. 9am-6:30pm; Nov.-Mar. 8:30am-5pm; 50AS/€3.65)* leads to a view of the city; the 343 steps of the South Tower climb to a 360-degree view *(open 9am-5:30pm;*

A BAD PACT WITH THE DEVIL

In the 16th century, during the construction of the North Tower of the Stephansdom, a young builder named Hans Puchsbaum wished to marry his master's daughter. The master promised his consent if Hans finished the entire North Tower, alone, within a year. Faced with this impossible task, Hans despaired until a stranger offered to help him—on condition that Hans not speak the name of God or any other holy name. The tower grew by leaps and bounds until the young mason spotted his love one day and called out her name, "Maria!" Unfortunately, Maria was also the name of the Blessed Virgin. The scaffolding collapsed and Hans plummeted to his death. Rumors of a satanic pact spread, and work on the tower ceased, leaving it in its present condition.

35AS/€2.55). Downstairs in the **catacombs,** the skeletons of thousands of plague victims line the walls. The **Gruft** (vault) stores all of the Habsburg innards. *(Cathedral tours M-Sa 10:30am and 3pm, Su and holidays 3pm; in English at 3:45pm. 45AS/€3.30.)*

GRABEN AND PETERSPLATZ. *(From Stephanspl., follow Graben.)* Now closed to any traffic except feet and hooves, this boulevard was once a moat surrounding the Roman camp that became Vienna. The landscape of Graben is full of *Jugendstil* architecture, including the **Ankerhaus** (#10), the red marble **Grabenhof** by Otto Wagner, and the underground public toilet complex, designed by Adolf Loos. Two blocks down in **Petersplatz** stands the 1663 **Pestsäule** (Plague Column), which was built to commemorate the passing of the Black Death.

HOHER MARKT. *(Take Milchg. out of Peterspl., turn right, and go 3 blocks on Tuchlauben; Hoher Markt is on the right.)* Once both market and execution site, **Hoher Markt** was the heart of the Roman encampment, Vindobona. **Roman ruins** lie beneath the shopping arcade on its south side. *(Open Tu-Su 9am-12:15pm and 1-4:40pm. 25AS/€1.85, students 10AS/€0.75.)* The biggest draw is the 1914 *Jugendstil* **Ankeruhr** (clock). Twelve 3m historical figures—from Marcus Aurelius to Maria Theresa to Joseph Haydn—rotate past the old Viennese coat of arms accompanied by music of their time period. *(1 figure per hr. At noon all figures appear in succession.)*

STADTTEMPEL. *(Follow Judeng. from Hoher Markt to Ruprechtspl.)* Almost hidden away in Ruprechtspl. at Seitenstetteng. 2-4 is the 1826 **Stadttempel** (City Temple), the only synagogue in Vienna to escape Nazi destruction during *Kristallnacht* because it was concealed from the street. *(Bring your passport. Open Su-F. Free.)*

ALTES RATHAUS. *(Backtrack to Hoher Markt and follow Wipplingerstr.)* The **Altes Rathaus** (Old Town Hall), Wipplingerstr. 8, was the government seat from 1316 to 1885. It's also home to the **Austrian Resistance Museum,** chronicling anti-Nazi activity during World War II and temporary exhibits. (Open M, W, Th 9am-5pm. Free.)

AM HOF AND FREYUNG. *(From Judenpl., take Drahtg., which runs into Am Hof.)* The grand courtyard **Am Hof,** which was once a medieval jousting square, now houses the **Kirche am Hof** (Church of the Nine Choirs of Angels; built 1386-1662). In the middle of the square looms the black **Mariensäule** (Column to Mary), erected by Emperor Ferdinand III to thank the Virgin Mary for her protection during the Thirty Years' War. Just west of Am Hof, the **Austriabrunnen** (Austria fountain) sits in the center of an uneven square called **Freyungasse.** Freyung ("sanctuary") got its name from the **Schottenstift** (Monastery of the Scots) just behind the fountain. The square was once used for public executions, but the annual **Christkindl markt** (Christ Child market) held here in December blots out such unpleasant memories.

MICHAELERKIRCHE. *(From Freyung, follow Herreng. to Michaelerpl.)* **Michaelerplatz** is named for the **Michaelerkirche** occupying the block between Kohlmarkt and Habsburgerg. The church's foundation dates back to the early 13th century, but construction continued until 1792. *(Open May-Oct. M-F 11am-5pm. 25AS/€1.85, students 10AS/€0.75.)*

HOFBURG. *(Head through the half-moon-shaped Michaelertor in Michaelerpl.)* The sprawling **Hofburg** was the winter residence of the Habsburgs emperors. Construction began in 1279, and hodge-podge additions and renovations continued until the end of the family's reign in 1918. The Hofburg is divided into several sections:

> **In der Burg.** When you come through the Michaelertor, you'll first enter the courtyard called In der Burg ("within the fortress"). On your left is the red-and-black-striped **Schweizertor** (Swiss Gate), erected in 1552. On the right side of the Michaelertor is the entrance to the **Kaiserappartements** (Imperial Apartments). They were once the private quarters of Emperor Franz Josef and Empress Elisabeth, but neither of them spent much time here (or with each other, for that matter), so the rooms are disappointingly lifeless. The **Hofsilber und Tafelkammer** (Court Silver and Porcelain Collection), on the ground floor opposite the ticket office, displays examples of the ornate Imperial cutlery. *(Both open 9am-4:30pm. Combined admission 95AS/€6.90, students 75AS/€5.45.)*

AUSTRIA

Alte Burg. Behind the Schweizertor lies the **Schweizerhof,** the inner courtyard of the Alte Burg (Old Fortress), which stands on the same site as the original 13th-century palace. The stairs to the right of the Schweiztor lead to the Gothic **Burgkapelle** (chapel), where the members of the **Wiener Sängerknaben (Vienna Boys' Choir)** raise their heavenly voices every Su. Beneath the stairs is the entrance to the **Weltliche und Geistliche Schatzkammer** (Worldy and Spiritual Treasury), containing Habsburg jewels, the crowns of the Holy Roman and Austrian Empires, the "horn of a unicorn" (really a narwhale's horn), and a tooth allegedly from the mouth of John the Baptist. *(Open W-M 10am-6pm. 100AS/€7.30, students 70AS/€5.10. Free audio guide available in English.)* Attached to the northeast side of the Alte Burg is the **Stallburg,** the home of the **Royal Lipizzaner stallions.** The cheapest way to get a glimpse of the famous steeds is to watch them train. *(Mid-Feb. to June and late Aug. to early Nov. Tu-F 10am-noon. Tickets at the door at Josefspl., Gate 2, from about 8:30am. 160AS/€11.65.)*

Neue Burg. Built between 1881 and 1926, the Neue Burg (New Fortress) is the youngest wing of the palace. The double-headed golden eagle crowning the roof symbolizes the double empire of Austria-Hungary. Today, the Neue Burg houses Austria's largest library, the **Österreichische Nationalbibliothek** (Austrian National Library). The buff statues allegedly inspired the 11-year-old Arnold Schwarzenegger, then on his 1st visit to Vienna, to pump up. *(Open Oct.-June M-F 9am-7pm, Sa 9am-12:45pm; July-Aug. and Sept. 23-30 M-F 9am-3:45pm, Sa 9am-12:45pm; closed Sept. 1-22.)* The Neue Burg is also home to the fantastic **Völkerkunde Museum** (see Museums, p. 97).

Augustinerkirche. High masses are still held in the 14th-century **Augustinerkirche** (St. Augustine's Church). The hearts of the Habsburgs are stored in the **Herzgrüftel** (Little Heart Crypt). (Open M-Sa 10am-6pm, Su 11am-6pm. Mass 11am. Free.)

NEUER MARKT. *(From Albertina in the Hofburg, walk down Tegetthoffstr.)* The spectacular Neuer Markt is centered around the **Donnerbrunnen,** a graceful fountain representing the Danube and her four tributaries. Inside the **Kapuzinerkirche** (Church of the Capuchin Friars), on the southwest corner of the Neuer Markt, is the **Kaisergruft** (Imperial Vault), which holds the remains of all Habsburg rulers since 1633, minus heart and entrails. *(Open 9:30am-4pm. 50AS/€3.65, students 40AS/€2.90.)*

OUTSIDE THE RING

As the city expands beyond the Ring in all directions, the distance between notable sights also expands. But what the area outside the Ring gives up in accessibility, it makes up for in its varied attractions.

KARLSPLATZ AND NASCHMARKT. *(Take U1, U2, or U4 to "Karlspl." Or, from Neuer Markt, follow Kärntnerstr. to Karlspl., on the left.)* Karlspl. is home to Vienna's most beautiful Baroque church, the **Karlskirche,** an eclectic masterpiece combining a Neoclassical portico with a Baroque dome and towers on either side. *(Open M-F 7:30am-7pm, Sa 8:30am-7pm, Su 9am-7pm. Free.)* West of Karlspl., along Linke Wienzeile, is the **Naschmarkt,** a colorful, multi-ethnic food bazaar. On Saturdays, the Naschmarkt becomes a massive flea market. *(Open M-F 7am-6pm, Sa 7am-1pm.)*

SCHLOß BELVEDERE. *(Take tram #71 or tram D one stop past "Schwarzenbergpl." Or, from Karlspl., face the Künstlerhaus and turn right on Friedrichstr., follow it to Schwarzenbergpl., and head southeast, away from the city center.)* **Schloß Belvedere** (Belvedere Castle) was originally the summer residence of Prince Eugène of Savoy, Austria's greatest military hero, and Archduke Franz Ferdinand lived here until his 1914 assassination. The grounds stretch from the Schwarzenberg Palace to the Südbahnhof and contain three spectacular gardens and several excellent museums (see p. 97).

SCHLOß SCHÖNBRUNN. *(Take U4 to "Schönbrunn.")* From its humble beginnings as a hunting lodge, **Schönbrunn** ("beautiful brook") was Maria Theresa's favorite residence. Tours of some of the palace's 1500 rooms reveal the elaborate taste of her era. Both the Grand (44 rooms) and the Imperial (22 rooms) tours give you access to the **Great Gallery,** where the Congress of Vienna met, and the **Hall of Mirrors,** where six-year-old Mozart played. *(Palace open Apr.-June and Sept.-Oct. daily 8:30am-*

AUSTRIAN GRAFFITI Scratched into the stones near the entrance of the Stephansdom is the mysterious abbreviation "O5." It's not a sign of hoodlums up to no good, but rather a reminder of a different kind of subversive activity. During WWII, "O5" was the secret symbol of Austria's resistance movement against the Nazis. The capital letter "O" and the number "5," for the fifth letter of the alphabet, form the first two letters of "Oesterreich"—meaning Austria. Recently the monogram has received new life. Every time alleged Nazi collaborator and ex-president of Austria Kurt Waldheim attends mass, the symbol is highlighted in chalk. Throughout the city, "O5"s have also been appearing on buildings and flyers in protest against the anti-immigrant policies of Jörg Haider and the Freedom Party.

5pm; Nov.-Mar. 8:30am-4:30pm; July-Aug. 8:30am-7pm. Imperial Tour 105AS/€7.65, students 95AS/€6.90. Grand Tour 135AS/€9.85, students 110AS/€8. Audio guides included. Guided tour 170AS/€13.35, students 145AS/€10.55.) Even more impressive than the palace are the classical **gardens** behind it, which contain a hodgepodge of attractions, including the **Schmetterlinghaus** (Butterfly House) and the **Gloriette**, an ornamental temple with a beautiful view. (Park open 6am-dusk. Free.)

ZENTRALFRIEDHOF. The **Zentralfriedhof** (Central Cemetery) is the place to pay respects to your favorite (de)composer. Behind **Tor II** (2nd gate) are Beethoven, Strauss, and an honorary monument to Mozart, whose true resting place is an unmarked paupers' grave in the **Cemetery of St. Mark,** III, Leberstr. 6-8. **Tor I** leads to the **Jewish Cemetery,** which mirrors the fate of Vienna's Jewish population—many of the headstones are cracked, broken, or neglected because the families of most of the dead are gone from Austria. **Tor III** leads to the Protestant section and the new Jewish cemetery. (Main entrance at XI, Simmeringer Hauptstr. 234. Take tram #71 from Schwarzenbergpl. or tram #72 from Schlachthaus; the tram stops 3 times, at each of the gates. You can also take S-7 to "Zentralfriedhof," which stops along the southwest wall of the cemetery. Open May-Aug. daily 7am-7pm; Mar.-Apr. and Sept.-Oct. 7am-6pm; Nov.-Feb. 8am-5pm.)

🏛 MUSEUMS

Vienna owes its vast selection of masterpieces to the acquisitive Habsburgs and to the city's own crop of art schools and world-class artists. An exhaustive list is impossible to include here, but the tourist office's free *Museums* brochure lists all opening hours and admission prices. All museums run by the city of Vienna are **free on Friday** before noon (except on public holidays). If you're going to be in town for a while, invest in the **Museum Card** (ask at any museum ticket window).

▨ **Österreichische Galerie** (Austrian Gallery), III, Prinz-Eugen-Str. 27, in the Belvedere Palace behind Schwarzenbergpl. (see p. 96). Walk up from the Südbahnhof, take tram D to "Schloß Belvedere", or tram #71 to "Unteres Belvedere." The collection is split into 2 parts. The **Upper Belvedere** houses Austrian Art and other European art of the 19th and 20th centuries, including Klimt's *The Kiss*. The **Lower Belvedere** contains the **Baroque Museum**'s extensive collection of sculptures, David's portrait of Napoleon on horseback, and the **Museum of Medieval Austrian Art.** Both Belvederes open Tu-Su 10am-6pm, Upper Belvedere open until 9pm on Th. 100AS/€7.30, students 70AS/€5.10.

▨ **Kunsthistorisches Museum** (Museum of Fine Arts). Take U2 to "Museumsquartier," U2/U3 to "Volkstheater" or tram #1, 2, D, or J. Across from the Burgring and Heldenpl. on Maria Theresa's right. The KHM houses the world's 4th-largest art collection, including Venetian and Flemish paintings, classical art, and an Egyptian burial chamber. Open Tu-Su 10am-6pm. In summer English guided tours at 3pm (30AS/€2.20). 120AS/€8.75, students 80AS/€5.85.

▨ **Museum für Völkerkunde** (Ethnology Museum), I, in the Neue Burg on Heldenpl. (see p. 96). Take U2, U3, or tram #1, 2, D, or J to "Volkstheater." Collected here are Benin bronzes, Chinese paper kites, West African Dan heads, and a Japanese Doll Festival.

AUSTRIA

The focal point, however, is undoubtedly the crown of Montezuma, still drawing a crowd of protesters wishing its return to Mexico. Open Apr.-Dec. W-M 10am-6pm. 100AS/ €7.30, students 70AS/€5.10; free entry on May 16, Oct. 26, and Dec. 10 and 24.

Museumsquartier. Take U2 to "Museumsquartier", or U2, U3, tram 1#, 2, D, or J to "Volkstheater." A 60,000 sq. m conglomeration of museums, including: Kunsthalle Wien, which features thematic exhibitions of international contemporary artists (open daily 10am-7pm, Th until 10pm; Exhibition Hall 1 80AS/€5.85, students 60AS/€4.40; Exhibition Hall 2 60AS/€4.40, students 40AS/€3; both 100AS/€7.30, students 80AS/€5.85) and Museum Moderner Kunst (Museum of Modern Art), which holds Central Europe's largest collection of modern and contemporary art in a brand-new building (open Tu-Su 10am-6pm, until 9pm on Th; 90AS/€6.50, students 70AS/€5).

Kunst Haus Wien, III, Untere Weißgerberstr. 13. Take U1 or U4 to "Schwedenpl.," then tram N to "Radetzkypl." This museum, built by artist and environmental activist Friedenreich Hundertwasser, displays much of his work. The building notably lacks straight lines, which Hundertwasser called "the Devil's work"; even the floor bends and swells. The Kunst Haus also hosts exhibits of contemporary art from around the world. Open daily 10am-7pm. 95AS/€6.90, students 70AS/€5.10; M half-price.

Historisches Museum der Stadt Wien (Historical Museum of the City of Vienna), IV, Karlspl., to the left of the Karlskirche (see p. 96). This amazing collection of historical artifacts and paintings documents Vienna's evolution from a Roman encampment, through the Turkish siege of Vienna, to the subsequent 640 years of Habsburg rule. Open Tu-Su 9am-6pm. 50AS/€3.65, students 20AS/€1.45.

Sigmund Freud Haus, IX, Bergg. 19. Take U2 to "Schottentor," then walk up Währingerstr. to Bergg or take tram D to "Schlickg." Sorry folks, the famed couch is not here, but this former Freud home provides lots of photos and documents, including the young Freud's report cards and circumcision certificate. Open July-Sept. 9am-6pm; Oct.-June 9am-4pm. 70AS/€5.10, students 45AS/€3.30.

Lipizzaner Museum, I, Reitschulg. 2. If you ever liked horses, this is the place for you. What used to be the imperial pharmacy is now a museum dedicated to the imperial horses, featuring paintings, harnesses, video clips, and a small viewing window to the stables. Open daily 9am-6pm. 70AS/€5.10, students 50AS/€3.65.

🎵 ENTERTAINMENT

While Vienna offers all the standard entertainments in the way of theater, film, and festivals, the heart of the city beats to music. All but a few of classical music's marquee names lived, composed, and performed in Vienna. Mozart, Beethoven, and Haydn wrote their greatest masterpieces in Vienna, creating the **First Viennese School;** a century later, Schönberg, Webern, and Berg teamed up to form the **Second Viennese School.** Every Austrian child must learn to play an instrument during schooling, and the Vienna **Konservatorium** and **Hochschule** are world-renowned conservatories. All year, Vienna has performances ranging from the above-average to the sublime, with many accessible to the budget traveler. Note that the venues below have **no performances in July and August.**

Staatsoper, Opernring 2 (www.wiener-staatsoper.at), is Vienna's premier opera, performing nearly every night Sept.-June. To get tickets: **Standing-room tickets** are the cheapest; 500 are available for every performance, but they can only be bought 1 per person right before the performance (30-50AS/€2.20-3.65). Formal dress not necessary, but no shorts. **Box office tickets in advance**: purchase through the official ticket offices by fax, phone, or in person. The main office is the Bundestheaterkasse, I, Hanuschg. 3, around the corner from the opera. (☎514 44 78 80; fax 514 44 29 69. Open M-F 8am-6pm, Sa-Su 9am-noon, 1st Sa of each month 9am-5pm.) There is also a ticket office inside the Staatsoper, open during the same hours. Tickets (140-3500AS/€10-255) may be purchased 1 month before performance. **Web site:** www.bundestheater.at, allows you to purchase tickets in advance; 20% commission.

Wiener Philharmoniker (Vienna Philharmonic Orchestra) plays in the **Musikverein,** Austria's—perhaps the world's—premier concert hall. Ways to get tickets: Contact the **box office** of the Musikverein; **standing room tickets** must also be bought in advance. Write or visit Gesellschaft der Musikfreunde, Bösendorferstr. 12, A-1010 Wien. Stop by the **Bundestheaterkasse** (see Staatsoper, above, for hours and information). **Web site:** www.wienerphilharmoniker.at. Note that it charges a hefty commission.

Wiener Sängerknaben (Viennese Boys' Choir) sings during mass every Su at 9:15am (mid-Sept. to May only) in the **Hofburgkapelle** (U3 "Herreng."). For more information, contact hofmusikkapelle@asn-wien.ac.at.

FESTIVALS

Vienna hosts an array of important annual festivals, mostly musical. The **Vienna Festival** (mid-May to mid-June) has a diverse program of exhibitions, plays, and concerts. (☎58 92 20; www.festwochen.or.at.) The Staatsoper and Volkstheater host the annual **Jazzfest Wien** during the first weeks of July, featuring many famous acts. (☎503 5647; www.viennajazz.org.) From mid-July to mid-August, the **Im-Puls Dance Festival** (☎523 55 58; www.impuls-tanz.com) attracts some of the world's great dance troupes and offers seminars to enthusiasts. In mid-October, the annual city-wide international film festival, the **Viennale,** kicks off.

■ NIGHTLIFE

With one of the highest bar-to-cobblestone ratios in the world, Vienna is a great place to party, whether you're looking for a quiet evening with a glass of wine or a wild night in a disco full of black-clad Euro musclemen and drag queens. Take U1 or U4 to "Schwedenplatz," which will drop you within blocks of the **Bermuda Dreiecke** (Triangle), an area packed with lively, crowded clubs. If your vision isn't foggy yet, head down **Rotenturmstraße** toward Stephansdom or walk around the areas bounded by the Jewish synagogue and Ruprechtskirche. Slightly outside the Ring, the streets off **Burggasse** and **Stiftgasse** in the 7th district and the **university quarter** (Districts XIII and IX) have tables in outdoor courtyards and loud, hip bars.

Viennese nightlife starts late, often after 11pm. For the scoop, pick up a copy of the indispensable **Falter** (28AS/€2), which prints listings of everything from opera and theater to punk concerts and updates on the gay/lesbian scene.

- **Objektiv,** VII, Kirchbergg. 26. Take U2 or U3 to "Volkstheater," walk down Burgg. 2 blocks, and turn right on Kirchbergg. to find one of the most eclectic bars in Vienna. A mellow atmosphere, lively local crowd, and cheap drinks top things off. Happy Hour daily 11pm-1am. Open daily 6pm-2am.

- **U-4,** XII, Schönbrunnerstr. 222. Take U4 to "Meidling Hauptstr." In the late 80s, U-4 hosted Nirvana, Mudhoney, and Hole before they were famous. 2 dance areas, multiple bars. Check in advance to catch the theme night for you. Th Heaven Gay Night. Cover 100AS/€7.30. Open daily 10pm-5am.

Café MAK, I, Stubenring 3-5, inside the Museum für Angewandte Kunst. This cafe is a rowdy bar by night with techno-rave parties on Sa in July. Open Tu-Su 10pm-2am.

SALZBURG ☎ 0662

From its position as the ecclesiastical center of Austria, Salzburg offers both spectacular sights and a rich musical culture. Whether it's enthusiastic tourists singing songs, street musicians playing medieval ballads, or a famed soprano bringing the house down, Salzburg's streets really do resonate with music. The city's passion for homegrown genius Wolfgang Amadeus Mozart in particular and the arts in general reaches a dizzying climax every summer during the **Salzburger Festspiele** (see p. 105), a five-week music festival featuring hundreds of operas, concerts, plays, and open-air performances.

AUSTRIA

⌐ TRANSPORTATION

Trains: Hauptbahnhof (☎ 05 17 17 for information) in Südtirolerpl. To: **Graz** (4hr., every 2hr. 5:20am-5:10pm, 460AS/€33.45); **Innsbruck** (2hr., every 2hr. 12:35am-9:15pm, 380AS/€27.65); **Klagenfurt** (3hr., 7 per day, 360AS/€26.20); **Munich** (2hr., 27 per day 4:00am-11:30pm, 298AS/€21.70); **Vienna** (3½hr., 29 per day 2:15am-9:30pm, 460AS/€33.50); **Zurich** (6hr., 3 per day 12:35am-12:30pm, 884AS/€64.25). Reservations ☎ 051717, daily 7am-10pm. Ticket office open 24hr.

Public Transportation: Lokalbahnhof (☎ 44 80 61 66), next to the train station. Single tickets (20AS/€1.45) are available at automatic machines or from the bus drivers. Books of 5 tickets (90AS/€6.55), daypasses (40AS/€2.95), and week passes (125AS/€9.10) are available at *Tabak* shops (newsstand/tobacco shops) and at the ticket office. Punch your ticket when you board in order to validate it. Buses usually make their last run at 10:30-11:30pm, but **BusTaxi** fills in when the public buses stop. Get on at Hanuschpl. or Theaterg. and tell the driver where you need to go. (Every 30min. nightly 11:30pm-1:30am. 35AS/€2.55 for any distance within the city limits.)

✦ 🛈 ORIENTATION AND PRACTICAL INFORMATION

Just a few kilometers from the German border, Salzburg covers both banks of the **Salzach River.** Two hills loom up in the skyline: the **Monchsberg** over the *Altstadt* (old city) on the south side and the **Kapuzinerberg** by the *Neustadt* (new city) on the north side. The *Hauptbahnhof* is on the northern side of town beyond the *Neustadt;* buses #1, 5, 6, 51, and 55 connect it to downtown. From the bus, disembark at "Mirabellplatz" in the *Neustadt;* on foot, turn left out of the station onto Rainerstr. and follow it all the way (under the tunnel) to Mirabellpl.

Tourist Office, Mozartpl. 5 (☎ 88 98 73 30; www.salzburginfo.or.at), in the *Altstadt.* From the train station, take bus #5, 6, 51, or 55 to "Mozartsteg," cross the river, then curve around the building into Mozartpl. The office gives free hotel maps (exactly the same as the 10AS/€0.75 city map), offers guided tours of the city (daily 12:15 pm, 100AS/€7.30), and sells the **Salzburg Card,** which grants admission to all museums and sights and unlimited use of public transportation (24hr. card 230AS/€16.75, 48hr. 320AS/€23.25, 72hr. 410AS/€29.80). The staff will also reserve rooms for a 30AS/€2.20 fee. Open July-Aug. M-Sa 9am-7pm; Sept.-June M-Sa 9am-6pm.

Consulates: South Africa, Buchenweg 14 (☎ 62 20 35). Open M-F 8am-1pm and 2-5pm. **UK,** Alter Markt 4 (☎ 84 81 33). Open M-F 9am-noon. **US,** Alter Markt 1/3 (☎ 84 87 76), in the *Altstadt.* Open M, W, and F 9am-noon.

Currency Exchange: Rieger Bank, at Alter Markt 15, has extended currency exchange hours. Open July-Aug. M-F 9am-8pm, Sa 9am-6:30pm, Su 9:30am-5pm; Sept.-June M-F 9am-6pm, Sa 9am-3pm, Su 10am-5pm.

American Express: Mozartpl. 5, A-5020 (☎ 80 80), near the tourist office. Provides all banking services; no commission on AmEx checks. Holds mail, books tours, and reserves *Festspiele* tickets. Open M-F 9am-5:30pm, Sa 9am-noon.

Luggage Storage: At the train station. Lockers 30-50AS/€2.20-3.65 for 24hr. Luggage check 30AS/€2.20 per piece per calendar day. Open 6am-10pm.

Bi-Gay-Lesbian Organizations: Homosexual Initiative of Salzburg (HOSI), Müllner Hauptstr. 11 (☎ 43 59 27), hosts regular workshops and meetings, including a **Café-bar** open F from 9pm and Sa from 8pm.

Laundromat: Norge Exquisit Textil Reinigung, Paris-Lodronstr. 16 (☎ 87 63 81). Self-serve wash and dry 125AS/€9.10. Open M-F 7:30am-4pm, Sa 8-10am. Full-serve 185AS/€13.50; pick it up the next day. Open M-F 7:30am-6pm, Sa 8am-noon.

Emergencies: Police, ☎ 133. **Ambulance,** ☎ 144. **Fire,** ☎ 122.

Pharmacies: Elisabeth-Apotheke, Elisabethstr. 1a (☎ 87 14 84). Most pharmacies open M-F 8am-6pm, Sa 8am-noon. There are always three pharmacies open for emergencies; check the list on the door of any closed pharmacy.

Medical Assistance: Call the **hospital,** Dr. Franz-Rebirl-Pl. 5 (☎ 658 00).

AUSTRIA

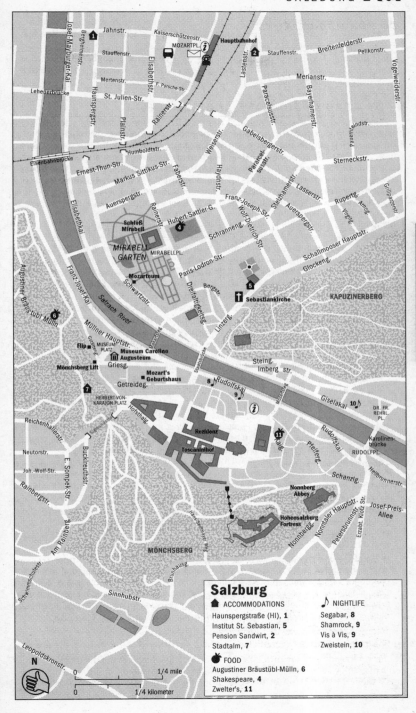

AUSTRIA

Salzburg

🏠 ACCOMMODATIONS

Haunspergstraße (HI), 1
Institut St. Sebastian, 5
Pension Sandwirt, 2
Stadtalm, 7

🍎 FOOD

Augustiner Bräustübl-Mülln, 6
Shakespeare, 4
Zwelter's, 11

♪ NIGHTLIFE

Segabar, 8
Shamrock, 9
Vis à Vis, 9
Zweistein, 10

Internet Access: Cybar, Gstätteng. 3 (☎84 48 23), and **Internet Café,** Mozartpl. 5 (☎84 48 22), Both 2AS/€0.15 per min., minimum 20AS/€1.45. Both open Nov.-May daily 10am-11pm; June-Oct. daily 10am-midnight.

Post Office: At the *Hauptbahnhof* (☎88 30 30), with **currency exchange.** Address mail to be held: FirstName SURNAME, *Postlagernde Briefe*, Bahnhofspostamt, **A-5020** Salzburg. Open M-F 6:30am-9:30pm, Sa 8am-8pm, Su 1-6pm.

■ ■ ACCOMMODATIONS AND CAMPING

Salzburg has no shortage of hostels—but then, it has no shortage of tourists either. Housing in Salzburg is expensive; most affordable options lie on the outskirts of town. Be wary of hotel hustlers at the station—they are up to no good. Instead, ask for the tourist office's list of **private rooms** or consult the *Hotel Plan* (which has info on hostels). From mid-May to mid-September, hostels fill by mid-afternoon, so call ahead, and be sure to make reservations during the *Festspiele* (see p. 105).

IN SALZBURG

Stadtalm, Mönchsberg 19c (☎84 17 29). Take bus #1 (dir.: Maxglan) to "Mönchsbergaufzug," then go down the street and through the stone arch on the left to the Mönchsberglift (elevator) and ride up (9am-11pm, round-trip 27AS/€2). At the top, turn right, climb the steps, and follow signs for "Stadtalm." Breakfast included. Showers 10AS/€0.75 per 4min. Reception 9am-8pm. Curfew 1am. Reservations recommended. Open May-Sept. Dorms 170AS/€12.40. AmEx/DC/MC/V.

Institut St. Sebastian, Linzerg. 41 (☎87 13 86). From the station, take bus #1, 5, 6, 51, or 55 to Mirabellpl. Continue in same direction as the bus, turn left onto Bergstr., and then left onto Linzerg; the hostel is through the arch on the left. Rooftop terrace with postcard views of the city. Kitchen facilities. Free lockers. Sheets 30AS/€2.20. Laundry free of charge, but sign up ahead of time. Reception 8am-noon and 4-9pm. No curfew. Dorms 190AS/€13.80; singles 360AS/€26.20, with shower 420AS/€30.55; doubles 530AS/€38.55, 720AS/€53.25; triples 675AS/€49, 930AS/€67.60; quads 956AS/€69.50, 1120AS/€81.40.

International Youth Hotel (YoHo), Paracelsusstr. 9 (☎87 96 49 or 834 60). Exit the train station to the left down Rainerstr., turn left onto Gabelsbergerstr. through the tunnel, and take the 2nd right onto Paracelsusstr. Filled with beer-sipping postcard writers and a frat-party atmosphere in the evening, this hostel is a bare-bones place to crash. There are no room keys. Breakfast 35-50AS/€2.50-3.65. Showers 10AS/€0.75 per 6min. 24hr. lockers 10AS/€0.75. Linens 100AS/€7.30 deposit. Reception 24 hr. Front door locks at 1am; ring the bell to get in at any time. 6-8 person dorms 170AS/€12.40; 4-person dorms 190/€13.80; 2-person dorms 220AS/€16; all rooms 20AS/€1.45 cheaper after the 1st night.

Jugendherberge Haunspergstraße (HI), Haunspergstr. 27 (☎87 50 30), near the train station. Walk straight out Kaiserschützenstr., which becomes Jahnstr, then take the 3rd left onto Haunspergstr. Breakfast (7am-8:30am), shower, and sheets included. Key deposit 100AS/€7.30. Reception 7am-2pm and 5pm-midnight. Checkout 9am. No curfew. Open July-Aug. 3- or 4-person dorms 200AS/€14.55; singles 260AS/€18.90.

Pension Sandwirt, Lastenstr. 6a (☎fax 87 43 51). Exit the main train station from the platform #13 staircase, cross the footbridge, turn right onto Lastenstr., and go behind the building with the Post sign. The down-to-earth hosts of this bed-and-breakfast speak excellent English and will let you use their washing machine for free. Breakfast included. Singles 300AS/€21.80; doubles 480AS/€34.90, with shower 580AS/€42.15; triples 720AS/€52.35; quads 920AS/€66.90.

IN KASERN BERG

Rooms on **Kasern Berg** are officially out of Salzburg, which means the tourist office can't officially recommend them, but the personable hosts and bargain prices make these *Privatzimmer* a terrific housing option. All northbound regional trains run to Kasern Berg (generally 4min.; every 30min. 6:15am-11:15pm; 20AS/€1.45, Eurail valid). Get off at the first stop, "Salzburg-Maria Plain," and take the only road uphill. All the Kasern Berg pensions are along this road.

⧈ Haus Christine, Panoramaweg 3 (☎45 67 73; haus.christine@gmx.at). Haus Christine has spacious rooms with a friendly family atmosphere. Breakfast included. Laundry free. Make sure to sign the guest book. 180-200AS/€13-14.50 per person. MC/V.

⧈ Haus Lindner, Panoramaweg 5 (☎45 66 81). Right next to Haus Christine, Matilda (Christine's sister) offers homey rooms, some with mountain views. Breakfast included. Call for pickup from the station. 170-200AS/€12.35-14.50 per person.

Germana Kapeller, Kasern Bergstr. 64 (☎45 66 71). Lively hostess Germana speaks good English and maintains trim rooms, some with hand-carved furniture and balconies. Breakfast and showers included. 200AS/€14.50 per person.

Haus Moser, Turnerbühel 1 (☎45 66 76). Climb up the hidden stairs (very steep) on the right side of Kasern Berg road across from Germana Kapeller or use the driveway entrance at beginning of Kasern Berg road. Charming, elderly couple offers comfortable rooms in this dark-timbered home. Free drinks, all-you-can-eat breakfast, and shower included. Laundry free. 170-200AS/€12.35-14.50.

CAMPING

Panorama Camping Stadtblick, Rauchenbichlerstr. 21 (☎45 06 52; fax 45 80 18, panorama.camping@utanet.com). Take bus #51 to "Itzling-Pflanzmann," turn around and walk back 50m, then turn right onto Rauchenbichlerstr., cross the footbridge, and continue along the gravel path. On-site store. Laundry 70AS/€5.10. Open Mar. 2 to Oct. 31. 75AS/€5.45, *Let's Go* readers 70AS/€5.10; tent 20AS/€1.45; bed in a tent 100AS/€7.27.

⧆ FOOD

With countless beer gardens and pastry-shop patios, Salzburg is a great place to eat outdoors. Local specialties include *Salzburger Nockerl* (egg whites, sugar, and raspberry filling baked into three mounds that represent the three hills of Salzburg), *Knoblauchsuppe* (a rich cream soup loaded with croutons and pungent garlic), and the world-famous **Mozartkugeln** (hazelnut coated in marzipan, nougat, and chocolate). **Supermarkets** cluster on the Mirabellpl. side of the river (open M-F 6am-7pm, Sa 6am-1pm, and **open-air markets** are held on Universitätpl.

Zweitler's, Kaig. 3 (☎84 00 44), in the *Altstadt*. From the tourist office, head to the back left corner of Mozartpl. In the evening, the cozy wooden interior turns into a lively bar. Try the *Spinatnockerl* (spinach baked with cheese and parsley; 88AS/€6.40). Open daily 4pm-1am, during the *Festspiele* 11am-1am. AmEx/MC/V.

Café Tomaselli, Alter Markt 9 (☎84 44 88), has been a favorite haunt for wealthier Salzburger clientele since 1705. Try the hot chocolate with rum (55AS/€4), guaranteed to warm your belly. English language newspapers available for leisurely perusal. Open M-Sa 7am-9pm, Su 8am-9pm.

Shakespeare, Hubert-Sattlerg. 3 (☎87 91 06), off Mirabellpl. This artsy, eclectic spot serves a variety of different foods, from surprisingly good Chinese dishes to Italian and Austrian ones. Large, spicy platter of Szechaun chicken 116AS/€8.45. Open M-F 9am-1am, Sa-Su 4pm-1am. DC/MC/V.

Zum Fidelen Affen, Priesterhausg. 8 (☎87 73 61), off Linzerg. This popular restaurant serves hearty, honest Austrian food that keeps everyone coming back "To the Jolly Monkey." Meals 95-155AS/€6.90-11.25. Open M-Sa 5pm-11pm.

Augustiner Bräustübl-Mülln, Augustinerg. 4 (☎43 12 46). From the *Altstadt*, follow the footpath from Hanuschpl. along the river, curving to the left; Augustinerg. will be on your left. Serving home-brewed beer since 1621, this gigantic complex seats 2800 in the outdoor *Biergarten* and 4 gigantic indoor halls. The stands outside sell snacks to soak up the suds. Open M-F 3pm-11pm, Sa-Su 2:30pm-11pm. No credit cards.

👁 SIGHTS

Salzburg is a relatively small town with a disproportionate number of *Sehenswür-digkeiten* (things worth seeing). Whether you're into decadent floral gardens or stoic fortresses, Salzburg's got something for you.

THE NEUSTADT

MIRABELL PALACE AND GARDENS. Mirabellplatz holds the marvelous **Schloß Mirabell,** which the supposedly celibate Archbishop Wolf Dietrich built for his mistress Salome Alt and their 10 children in 1606. Behind the palace, the delicately cultivated **Mirabellgarten** is a maze of seasonal flower beds and groomed shrubs. From one of the hedge-enclosed clearings in the Mirabellgarten, you can see a tiny wooden, moss-covered shack called the **Zauberflötenhäuschen,** allegedly where Wolfgang Amadeus composed *The Magic Flute* in just five months. It was transplanted from Vienna as a gift to the **Mozarteum,** Salzburg's music school.

MOZARTS WOHNHAUS. Just down the street from the Mozarteum stands the house in which the composer lived from 1773 to 1780. See some Mozart memorabilia, and hear lots of excerpts from his music, but be prepared to get frustrated by the museum's audio guides. (*Makartpl. 8. Open Sept.-June daily 9am-6pm, July-Aug. until 7pm. 65AS/€4.75, students 50AS/€3.65.*)

SEBASTIANSKIRCHE AND MAUSOLEUM. A little way down Linzerg. from the river stands the 18th-century **Sebastianskirche,** with a graveyard containing the gaudy **mausoleum** of Prince Archbishop Wolf Dietrich. Ornate gravestones and frescoes line the walls. The tombs of Mozart's wife (Constanze) and father (Leopold) are along the main path. (*Linzerg. 41. Open Apr.-Oct. 9am-7pm, Nov.-Mar. 9am-4pm.*)

THE ALTSTADT

In the shadow of the hill-top fortress, arcade passages lead to the tourist-jammed **Getreidegasse.** The buildings in this area are some of the oldest in the city; many of the shops have wrought-iron signs dating from the Middle Ages, when the illiterate needed pictorial aids to understand which store sold what.

MOZARTS GEBURTSHAUS. Mozart's *Geburtshaus* (birthplace), on the 2nd floor of Getreideg. 9, holds an impressive collection of the child genius's belongings: his first violin, a pair of keyboardish instruments, and a lock of hair purportedly from his noggin. Come before 11am to avoid the crowd. (☎84 43 13. *Open July-Aug. 9am-6:30pm; Sept.-June 9am-5:30pm. 70AS/€5.10, students and seniors 55AS/€4.*)

TOSCANINIHOF, CATACOMBS, AND THE DOM. Steps lead from **Toscaninihof,** the courtyard of **St. Peter's Monastery,** up the Mönchesberg cliffs. Adjacent to Toscaninihof, **Stiftskirche St. Peter** features a marble portal from 1244. In the 18th century, the building was remodeled in Rococo style. (*Open daily 9am-12:15pm and 2:30-6:30pm.*) Near the far end of the cemetery, against the Mönchsberg, is the entrance to the **Catacombs,** where the old stone passageways will make you feel like a monk from centuries past. In the lower room (St. Gertrude's Chapel), a fresco commemorates the martyrdom of Thomas á Beckett. (☎784 74 35. *Open May-Sept. Tu–Su 10:30am-5pm; Oct.-Apr. W-F 10:30am-4pm, Sa-Su 10:30am-4pm. 12AS/€0.90, students 8AS/€0.60.*) The exit at the other end of the cemetery from the Stiftskirche leads to the immense Baroque **Dom** (cathedral), where Mozart was christened in 1756 and later worked as *Konzertmeister* and court organist. The cathedral boasts five organs which, when all played at once, create a phenomenal surround-sound experience. The square leading out of the cathedral, **Domplatz,** features a statue of the Virgin Mary and figures representing Wisdom, Faith, the Church, and the Devil. Be prepared to give a donation on the way out.

RESIDENZ. Salzburg's ecclesiastical elite have resided in the magnificent Residenz for the last 700 years. Stunning Baroque **Prunkräume** (state rooms) house gigantic ceiling frescoes (including a three-dimensional one by Rottmayr), gilded furniture, Flemish tapestries from the 1600s, and ornate stucco work. A **gallery** exhibits 16th-to 19th-century art. *(☎804 22 69. Residenz open 10am-5pm. 100AS/€7.30, students 76AS/€5.50. Audio-guide included.)*

FESTUNG HOHENSALZBURG. Built between 1077 and 1681, **Festung Hohensalzburg (Hohensalzburg Fortress),** which looms over Salzburg from atop Mönchesberg, is the largest completely preserved castle in Europe—probably because it was never successfully attacked. *(Take the trail (20min.) or the Festungsbahn (funicular, every 10min.) up to the fortress from the Festungsg. May-Sept. 9am-9pm; Oct.-Apr. 9am-5pm. Ascent 76AS/ €5.50, round-trip 87/€6.35; includes entrance to fortress.)* The castle contains a "torture" chamber (which was never used), formidable Gothic state rooms, the fortress organ (nicknamed the "Bull of Salzburg" for its off-key snorting), the archbishop's medieval indoor toilet (a technological marvel in its day), and an impregnable watchtower with an unmatched view of the city and surrounding mountains. The **Burgmuseum** inside the fortress displays medieval instruments of torture and has side-by-side histories of Salzburg, the Festung, and the world. *(☎842 430. Grounds open mid-June to mid-Sept. 8:30am-8pm; mid-Sept. to mid-Mar. 9:30am-5pm; mid-Mar. to mid-June 9am-6pm. Interior open mid-June to mid-Sept. 9:30am-5pm; mid-Sept. to mid-Mar. 9am-5pm; mid-Mar. to mid-June 9:30am-5:30pm. If you walk up, entrance to fortress is 49AS/€3.60; combo ticket including fortress, castle interiors, and museum 98AS/€7.15.)*

🏛 MUSEUMS

Salzburg's small, specialized museums often get lost in the shadow of the *Festung, The Sound of Music,* and the *Festspiele.* There are also private galleries on **Sigmund-Haffnergasse** that allow budget art viewing.

ART MUSEUMS. The **Museum Carolino Augusteum** houses local Roman and Celtic artifacts on its ground floor, including mosaics and burial remains, naturally preserved thanks to the region's salt. *(Museumpl. 1. ☎84 11 34. Open F-W 9am-5pm, Th until 8pm. 40AS/€2.95, students 15AS/€1.10.)*

OTHER MUSEUMS. The **Haus der Natur,** opposite the Carolino Augusteum, is an 80-room behemoth with an eclectic collection, from live alligators and giant snakes to huge rock crystals. *(Museumpl. 5. ☎84 26 53 or 84 23 22. Open daily 9am-5pm. 60AS/€4.40, students 35AS/€2.55.)* Just inside the main entrance to the *Dom,* the **Dom Museum** houses an unusual collection called the **Kunst- und Wunderkammer** (Art and Curiosity Cabinet) that includes old door locks, a big globe with men and beasts dancing across it, and a giant lobster claw, all collected by the archbishop to impress distinguished visitors. In the main museum, the gigantic Rupertskreuz (Cross of Rupert) stands guard over the back room *(☎84 41 89. Open mid-May to mid-Oct. M-Sa 10am-5pm, Su 1pm-6pm. 62AS/€4.50, students 20AS/€1.45. Guided tours Sa 10:30am. 20AS/€1.45.)* Down the stairs between Residenzpl. and Dompl., the **Domgrabungsmuseum** displays excavations of the Roman ruins under the cathedral, some of which date back as far as the 2nd century. *(☎84 52 95. Open May-Oct. W-Su 9am-5pm. 25AS/€1.85, students 10AS/€0.75.)*

🎵 ENTERTAINMENT AND MUSIC

Max Reinhardt, Richard Strauss, and Hugo von Hofmannsthal founded the renowned **Salzburger *Festspiele*** (Festivals) in 1920. Ever since, Salzburg has been a musical mecca from late July to the end of August. On the eve of the festival's opening, over 100 dancers don regional costumes, accessorize with torches, and perform a *Fackeltanz* (torchdance) on Residenzpl. During the festivities themselves, operas, plays, films, concerts, and tourists overrun every available public space. Information and tickets for *Festspiele* events are available through the **Festspiele Kartenbüro** (ticket office) and **Tageskasse** (daily box office) in Karajanpl., against the mountain and next to the tunnel. (Open M-F 9:30am-3pm; July 1 to July 22 M-Sa 9:30am-5pm; July 23 through the end of the festival daily 9:30am-6:30pm.)

Even when the *Festspiele* are not on, many other concerts and events occur around the city. The **Salzburg Academy of Music and Performing Arts** performs a number of concerts on a rotating schedule in the **Mozarteum**, and the **Dom** also has a concert program in July and August (Th and F 11:15am. 120AS/€8.75, students 100AS/€7.30). In addition, from May through August there are **outdoor performances,** including concerts, folk-singing, and dancing, around the Mirabellgarten. The tourist office has leaflets on scheduled events, but an evening stroll through the park might prove just as enlightening. Mozartpl. and Kapitelpl. are also popular stops for talented street musicians and touring school bands.

⬛ NIGHTLIFE

Munich may be known as the world's beer capital, but a lot of that liquid gold flows south to Austria's **Biergärten** (beer gardens). These lager oases cluster in the city center by the Salzach River. Altstadt nightclubs (especially along Gstätteng. and near Chiemseeg.) attract younger types and tourists.; the other side of the river has a less juvenile atmosphere. Settle into an armchair at **Vis à Vis,** Rudolfskai 24. (Open 8pm-4am.) **Shamrock,** Rudolfskai 24, has plenty of room and nightly live music. (Open daily 3pm-4am.) **Zweistein,** Giselakai 9, is *the* place to come for Salzburg's gay and lesbian scene. (Open Su-W 8pm-4am, Th-Sa 8pm-5am.) Sip cocktails (most 78AS/€5.70) under the sloping stone roof at **Flip,** Gstatteng. 17. (Open 8pm-4am.) **Segabar,** Rudolfskai 18, has a party scene popular with the younger crowd. (Cover 40AS/€2.95. Open F-Sa 8pm-4am, Su-Th 8pm-2am.)

⬛ DAYTRIPS FROM SALZBURG

LUSTSCHLOß HELLBRUNN

Take bus #55 (dir.: Anif) to "Hellbrunn" from the train station, Mirabellpl., or Mozartsteg.

Just south of Salzburg lies the unforgettable **Lustschloß Hellbrunn,** a sprawling estate with a large palace, fish ponds, flower gardens, and tree-lined footpaths through grassy fields. Tours of the castle last 15-30min. and give a brief overview of the rooms. Archbishop Markus amused himself with the **Wasserspiele** (literally "water games"), elaborate water-powered figurines and a booby-trapped table that could spout water on his drunken guests. Prepare yourself for an afternoon of wet surprises; pictures of you getting sprayed are available at the end of the tour. (☎820 00 30. Open July-Aug. 9am-10pm; May-June and Sept. 9am-5:30pm; Apr. and Oct. 9am-4:30pm. Mandatory castle tour 40AS/€2.95, students 30AS/€2.20. Wasserspiele tour 80AS/€5.85, students 60AS/€4.40. Combined tour 100AS/€7.30, students 80AS/€5.85.)

UNTERSBERG PEAK

Take bus #55 past Hellbrunn to "St. Leonhard."

Charlemagne supposedly rests deep beneath the ground at luscious **Untersberg Peak,** prepared to return and reign over Europe when he is needed. A **cable car** glides over the rocky cliffs to the summit, and from there **hikes** lead off into the distance. The quick hike over the alpine ridge out to the next (somewhat higher) peak, the Salzburger Hochthron, lasts about 30min. On top is a memorial cross and some unbelievable mountain scenery. Don't leave your camera behind on this trip. (☎(06246) 87 12 17 or 724 77. July-Sept. Su-Tu and Th-Sa 8:30am-5:30pm; Mar.-June and Oct. 9am-5pm; Dec.-Feb. 10am-4pm. Ascent 135AS/€9.85, descent 120AS/€8.75, round-trip 225AS/€16.35; students 105AS/€7.65, 80AS/€5.85, 155AS/€11.30.)

THE SALZKAMMERGUT

Every summer, bands of Austrian schoolchildren, tour groups of elderly Europeans, and tourists in-the-know come to the smooth lakes and furrowed mountains of the Salzkammergut. The region takes its name from the salt mines that, in their glory days, underwrote Salzburg's architectural treasures; today, the white gold of the Salzkammergut is no longer salt, but pure sunshine on sparkling water in summer and tons of fresh snow in winter. The area is easily navigable, with 2000km of footpaths, 12 cable cars and chairlifts, and dozens of hostels. The mountainous area is barren of rail tracks; **buses** are the best way to travel into and through the region.

HALLSTATT ☎ 06134

Teetering on the banks of the Hallstättersee at the southern tip of the Salzkammergut, tiny Hallstatt seems to defy gravity by clinging to the face of a stony slope. Hallstatt is easily the most beautiful lakeside village in the Salzkammergut, if not in all of Austria. Back when Rome was still a village, the "white gold" from the salt mines made Hallstatt a world-famous settlement. The 2500-year-old **Salzbergwerke** are the oldest saltworks in the world; zip down a wooden mining slide on a burlap sack to an eerie lake deep inside the mountain on a fascinating guided tour (1hr., in English and German). Be sure to ask for a salt rock as a souvenir, and pick up the photo taken when you zoomed down the slide. (☎ 06132 200 2400. Open May-Sept. daily 9:30am-4:30pm; Oct. 9:30am-3pm. 140AS/€10.20; guest card holders, students, and seniors 126AS/€9.20.) In the 19th century, Hallstatt was also the site of an immense, incredibly well-preserved Iron Age archaeological find; the **Prähistorisches Museum,** across from the tourist office, and the smaller **Heimatmuseum,** around the corner, exhibit some of the treasures. The museums are being combined, with the new complex slated to open in May 2002, so hours and prices may change. (www.museum-hallstatt.at. Open Apr. daily 10am-4pm; May-Sept. 10am-6pm; Oct. 10am-4pm. 82.60AS/€6; English texts 25AS/€1.85.) From the ferry dock, follow the signs marked "K.Kirche" to the fascinating **charnel house** next to St. Michael's Chapel, a bizarre repository filled with the remains of over 610 villagers dating from the 16th century on; the latest were added in 1995. The dead were previously buried in the mountains, but villagers soon ran out of space and transferred older bones to the charnel house to make room for more corpses. Today, the skulls of the dead are neatly stacked on a shelf supported by femurs, tibiae, and fibulae. (Open May-Oct. daily 10am-4pm. 10AS/€0.75, students 5AS/€0.40.)

Buses are the cheapest way to get to Hallstatt from Salzburg (130AS/€9.45) but require layovers in both Bad Ischl and Gosaumühle.The **train station** is on the other side of the lake; however, there is no staffed office to help travelers. All trains come from Attnang-Puchheim in the north or Stainach-Irdning in the south. **Trains** run hourly to Bad Ischl (30min., 38AS/€2.75) and Salzburg via Attnang-Puchheim (210AS/€15.25). A **ferry** shuttles passengers between the town and the station (10min., 7am-6:40pm, 25AS/€1.85). The **tourist office,** Seestr. 169, finds rooms and offers help with the town's fairly random system of street numbers. (☎ 82 08; www.tiscover.com/hallstatt. Open July-Aug. M-F 9am-5pm, Sa 10am-4pm, Su 10am-2pm; Sept.-June M-F 9am-noon and 2-5pm.) To reach **Gästehaus Zur Mühle,** Kirchenweg 36, from the tourist office, walk uphill, heading for a short tunnel at the upper right corner of the square; it's right at the end of the tunnel, by the waterfall. (☎ 83 18. Breakfast 40AS/€2.95. Showers included. Sheets 40AS/€2.95. Reception 10am-2pm and 4-10pm. Closed Nov. Dorms 120AS/€8.75.) **Jugendherberge Lahn,** Salzbergstr. 50, has sunny dorms and a laid-back, familiar atmosphere. From the bus station, take Malerweg across the stream and then follow the main road; the hostel is the pink and white building on the right. (☎ 82 12 or (0664) 792 03 15. Breakfast 34.40AS/€2.50. Showers included. Sheets 45.40AS/€3.30. Open May to mid-Oct. Dorms 110AS/€8. Call ahead.) To get to **Camping Klausner-Höll,** Lahnstr. 201, turn right out of the tourist office and follow Seestr. for 10min. (☎ 832 24. Breakfast 70-110AS/€5.10-8. Showers included. Laundry service 100AS/€7.30. Gate closed daily noon-3pm and 10pm-7:30am. Open mid-Apr. to mid-Oct. 67AS/€4.86; tent 45AS/€3.27; electricity 35AS/€2.54.) The cheapest eats are at the **Konsum supermarket** across from the bus stop (open M-Tu and Th-F 7:30am-12:30pm and 3-6pm, W 7:30am-12:30pm, Sa 7:30am-noon); the butcher's counter prepares sandwiches on request. **Postal code:** A-4830.

AUSTRIA

▶ DAYTRIPS FROM HALLSTATT

HIKING IN ECHENTAL

Hallstatt offers some of the most spectacular day hikes in the Salzkammergut. The tourist office offers an excellent Dachstein **hiking guide** (80AS/€5.90; in English), which details 38 hikes in the area, as well as **bike** (148AS/€10.75) and **mountain bike** (98AS/€7.15) **trail maps.** The **Salzbergwerk (salt mine) hike** is a simple gravel hike leading to the salt-mine tour; walk to the Salzbergbahn and take the road to the right upward, turning at the black and yellow "Salzwelten" sign. The **Waldbackstrub Waterfalll hike** is a light, 1¾hr. walk along a tumbling crystal-clear stream and up to a spellbinding waterfall. From the bus station, follow the brown sign reading "Malerweg" near the supermarket and continue to follow the "Malerweg" signs until the "Waldbachstrub" sign appears (about 40min.). The waterfall is in the **Echental,** a valley carved out millennia ago by glaciers and now blazed with trails leading deep into the valley. The **Gangsteig,** a slippery, primitive stairway, is carved into the side of a cliff, but is for experienced hikers only; don't go without a professional guide. Those with less gumption can visit the **Glacier Gardens** in the valley.

DACHSTEIN ICE CAVES

From Hallstatt, walk to the Lahn bus station by heading down Seestr. with the lake to your left, and catch the bus to Obertraun (10min., every hr. 8:30am-4:45pm, 27AS/€2). Stop at the "Dachstein" cable car station, then ride up to "Schönbergalm" for the ice and mammoth caves. (Every 15 min. 8:40am-5:30pm, 170AS/€12.40 round-trip.) The cave temperatures are near freezing, so wear good footwear and something warm.

In **Obertraum,** at the other end of the lake, the magnificent **Dachstein Ice Caves** are proof of the region's geological hyperactivity. The eerie light of the caves casts fascinating shadows on the immense but intricate rock and ice formations. Tours are required and offered in English and German; you'll be assigned to a group at the Schönbergalm station. (☎ (06134) 84 00. Open May to mid-Oct. daily 9am-5pm. Admission to each cave 100AS/€7.30; guest card holders and students 90AS/€6.60.)

GRÜNAU   ☎07616

Grünau is a tiny community with an incredible backyard ideal for almost any kind of outdoor activity. The real reason to visit is ◪**The Treehouse,** Schindlbachstr. 525, a backpacker's dream resort. The incredibly friendly staff will organize adventure tours, including **canyoning** (690AS/€50.15), **rafting** (500AS/€36.35 per half-day), **bungee jumping** (1,000AS/€72.70, only on weekends), a **flight** over the surrounding mountains (440AS/€32 per person, 4 person minimum), and **horseback riding** (120AS/€8.75 per hr.). To strike out on your own, rent a **mountain bike** (80AS/€5.85 per day) or ask the staff about **hiking** trails. For winter visitors, the ski lift is a 5min. walk from the front door, and snow gear (jackets, snowsuits, gloves, etc.) is provided free of charge. Day ski-lift passes are 260AS/€18.90, and **skis** and **snowboards** are available for rent (120AS/€8.75 and 150AS/€10.90).

Regular **trains** service Grünau from Wels, on the Vienna-Salzburg rail line (1hr., 6:45am-8:45pm, 84AS/€6.10). Call ahead to the hostel, and one of the staff will pick you up at the station free of charge. Rooms feature private showers and goosedown blankets, and resort amenities include a TV room with hundreds of English-language movies, book-exchange library, sauna, basketball and tennis courts, **Internet** (25AS/€1.85 for 15 min.), and two in-house bars for nighttime revelry. (☎84 99; treehousehotel@hotmail.com; www.hostels.com/treehouse. Breakfast buffet included. 3-course dinners 90AS/€6.55. 6-bed dorms 170AS/€12.35; doubles 480AS/€34.90; triples 460AS/€33.45; quads 440AS/€32. AmEx/MC/V.)

BAD ISCHL   ☎ 06132

Bad Ischl was a salt-mining town for centuries until a certain Dr. Franz Wirer arrived in 1821 to study the curative properties of the heated brine baths in the area. Today the bath facilities are mostly in the posh **Kaiser Therme**, Bahnhofstr. 1, a resort across from the tourist office. Splash around in the heated salt baths with whirlpool (9am-10pm, 117AS/€8.50) or relax in the spacious sauna (daily 1:30-10pm, Tu men only, Th women only; 166 AS/€12.10 for 3hr.). Other than the salt baths, Bad Ischl's main attraction is the **Kaiservilla,** the summer palace of former Austro-Hungarian emperor Franz Josef. Inside is an eclectic collection of relics, including the desk where he signed the 1914 declaration of war against Serbia that led to WWI, and his extensive collection of mounted animal horns. Entrance is allowed only through a guided tour in German, with English text available. (☎ 232 41. Open May to mid-Oct. 9-11:45am and 1-4:45pm. 130AS/€9.45.) Bad Ischl offers incredible **hiking** too; pick up a free trail map at the tourist office.

Only one **train** comes through the station, running between **Attnang-Puchheim** in the north (1hr., 4:30am-8:45pm, 89AS/€6.50) and **Hallstatt** (30min., 6:15am-6:15pm, 89AS/€6.50). **Buses** leave for Salzburg every hour (1½hr., 5am-7:15pm). To reach the **tourist office,** Bahnhofstr. 6, turn left onto Bahnhofstr. from the station and walk for 2min. (☎ 277 57. Open June-Sept. M-F 8am-6pm, Sa 9am-3pm, Su 10am-1pm; Oct-May M-F 8:30am-noon and 1:30-5pm, Sa 9am-noon.) Every guest who stays the night in Bad Ischl must pay a **Kurtax** (June to mid-Sept. 25-30AS/€1.85-€2.20 per person per night depending on proximity to the city center; mid-Sept. to May 13-15AS/€0.95-1.10), which entitles you to a **guest card** good for discounts. To reach the **Jugendgästehaus (HI),** Am Rechenstag 5, turn left on Bahnhofstr. from the tourist office, turn right on Kaiser-Franz-Josef-Str., and keep going until you see the sign on the left. The hostel offers newly renovated four-bed rooms, each with its own bath. (☎ 265 77. Breakfast included. Reception 10am-1pm and 5-7pm. Check-out 9am. No curfew, but quiet hour 10pm. Reservations recommended. Dorms 220AS/€16; singles 320AS/€23.25; doubles 540AS/€39.25. **HI membership required.**) Stop for a kebab (40AS/€2.90) at the nearby **Bistro Oriental,** Kreuzplatz 13—it's tiny but modern and very clean. (Open daily 10am-10pm.) The **Konditorei Zauner,** Pfarrg. 7 (☎ 235 22), has an international reputation for heavenly sweets and tortes (30-100AS/€2.20-€7.30). **Postal code:** A-4820.

HOHE TAUERN NATIONAL PARK

The enormous **Hohe Tauern** range, part of the Austrian Central Alps, boasts 246 glaciers and 304 mountains over a 3000m expanse. One of the park's goals is preservation, so there are no large campgrounds or recreation areas. With the exception of the park's mountainous core, many of the meadows and valleys are used for agriculture and forestry. The center of the park is **Franz-Josefs-Höhe** and the **Pasterze glacier,** which sits right above the town of Heiligenblut. Aside from skiing and hiking, the main tourist attractions are the **Krimml Waterfalls,** in the northwestern corner near Zell am See, and the **Großglocknerstraße** (Bundesstr. 107), a spectacular high mountain road that runs north/south from Zell am See through Franz-Josef-Höhe. The best way to explore this rare preserve is to **hike** one of the park's numerous trails, ranging from pleasant ambles to difficult mountain ascents. *An Experience in Nature,* available at park offices and area tourist offices, gives descriptions and maps of 84 different hikes.

▇ TRANSPORTATION. Trains arrive in Zell am See from: Innsbruck (1½-2hr., 2am-11:30pm, 270AS/€19.65); Kitzbühel (45min., 12:45am-8:30pm, 112AS/€8.15); Salzburg (1½hr., 22 per day 3am-10pm, 150AS/€10.90). From Zell am see, a **rail** line runs west along the northern border of the park, terminating in Krimml (1½hr., 19 per day 6am-10:55pm, 93AS/€6.75); a **bus** also runs directly to the Höhe (2hr.; June 14-Sept. 30 daily 9:20am, July 7-Sept. 30 also daily 12:20pm; July 7-Sept. 8 also daily

10:45am; 107AS/€7.80). The park itself is criss-crossed by **buses** that all stop at the Höhe but operate on very complicated timetables; be sure to ask for specific connections at local tourist offices.

FRANZ-JOSEFS-HÖHE. This large observation and tourist center offers an amazing view of the Großglockner (3797m). The Höhe has its own park office and information center near the beginning of the parking area. (Open mid-May to mid-Oct. daily 10am-4pm; July-Aug. 9am-6pm.) The elevator next to the information center leads to the **Swarovski Observation Center,** a crystal-shaped building with binoculars for viewing the surrounding terrain. (Open daily 10am-4pm. Free.) Some of the larger souvenir shops sell inexpensive sandwiches for 19-29AS/€1.40-2.10.

HEILIGENBLUT. The most convenient base for exploring the Hohe Tauern region, Heiligenblut got its name ("holy blood") from a legend about a Byzantine general who perished nearby in a snowstorm while carrying a vial of Christ's blood, which is now housed in the town church. Heiligenblut can be reached by **bus** from **Franz-Josefs-Höhe** (runs May-Oct., 30min.; July-Sept. 9:30am-4:30pm; 40AS/€2.90.) and **Zell am See** (2½hr., 3 per day 9:20am-12:20pm, 147AS/ €10.70; connection in Franz-Josefs-Höhe). The **tourist office,** Hof 4, up the street from the bus stop, has information about accommodations and hiking. (☎200 121. Open Sept.-June M-F 8:30am-noon and 2:30-6pm, Sa 9am-noon and 4-6pm; July-Aug. M-F 8:30am-6pm, Sa 9am-noon and 4-6pm.)

KRIMML. Over 400,000 visitors per year come to see the extraordinary **Krimml Waterfalls**—a set of three cascades spanning 380m. (8am-6pm 20AS/€1.45; free after 6pm.) These waterfalls are usually enjoyed as a daytrip from Zell am See; **buses** run from Zell am See (1½ hr., 11 per day 6am-8:55pm, 103AS/€7.50) to "Maustelle Ort," the start of the path to the falls. For the **tourist office,** Oberkrimml 37, follow the road from the "Krimml Ort" bus stop and turn right in front of the church. (☎72 39. Open M-F 8am-noon and 2:30-5:30pm, Sa 8:30-10:30am.)

TYROL (TIROL)

Tyrol's mountains overwhelm the average mortal with their superhuman scale and beauty. This topography has made it impossible for Tyrol to avoid becoming one of the primary mountain playgrounds for the world. But Tyrol has more to offer than just inclines. The urbane city of Innsbruck shows why it was a Habsburg favorite with a seamless blend of gilded houses and snowy mountains.

KITZBÜHEL
☎05356

Kitzbühel welcomes tourists with glitzy casinos and countless pubs, yet few visitors remain at ground level long enough to enjoy them. The mountains surrounding the city invite wealthy vacationers and ski bums alike. The Kitzbühel **ski area,** the "Ski Circus," is regarded as one of the best in the world. A one-day **ski pass** (400-450AS/€29.10-32.70) or a 3- or 6-day summer **vacation pass** (3-day 450AS/€32.70, 6-day 595AS/€43.25) grants passage on all lifts and the shuttle buses that connect them; purchase either at any lift or the **Aquarena,** which offers free pool access with admission and sauna and solarium access for a fee. (☎643 85. Open daily 9am-8pm. 90AS/€6.55, with guest card 80AS/€5.85; free entry in winter with ski passes of 2 days or more, in summer with either vacation pass.) For summer visitors, more than 70 **hiking trails** snake up the mountains surrounding Kitzbühel, providing a variety of pleasurable day hikes and a wide range of difficulty levels. To avoid getting lost, pick up a *Hiking Trail Map* free of charge at the tourist office. **Mountain bike trails** abound; rent a bike from **Stanger Radsport,** Josef-Pirchlstr. 42. (☎625 49. Open M-F 8am-noon and 1:15-6pm, Sa 9am-noon. 250AS/€18.20 per day.) If you'd rather relax than hike, the **Kitzbüheler Hornbahn lift** (190AS/€13.85, with guest card 170AS/€12.35) ascends to the **Alpenblumengarten,** where more than 120 different types of flowers blossom each spring. (Open late-May to mid-Oct.

8:30am-5pm.) The **Schwarzsee,** near Camping Schwarzsee, is famed for its healing **mud baths.** (☎623 81. Open daily 8am-6pm. 40AS/€2.90, after noon 30AS/€2.20, after 4pm 15AS/€1.10; 11% discount with guest card.) They also rent electric boats (150AS/€10.90 per hr.) and rowboats (45-85AS/€3.30-6.20 per hr.).

   Trains leave from the **Hauptbahnhof,** Bahnhofpl. 1 (☎640 55 13 85), to: Innsbruck (1hr., every other hour, 184AS/€13.40); Salzburg (2½hr., 9 per day, 260AS/€18.90); Vienna (6hr., 6:25am-12:45am, 570AS/€41.45). Buses depart regularly from the Hauptbahnhof and take you just about anywhere. To reach the **Fußgängerzone** (pedestrian zone) from the Hauptbahnhof, head straight down Bahnhofstr. and turn left at the main road. The **tourist office,** Hinterstadt 18, is near the Rathaus (city hall) in the Fußgängerzone. (☎62 15 50; www.kitzbuehel.com. Open July-Aug. and Christmas to mid-Mar. M-F 8:30am-6:30pm, Sa 8:30am-noon and 4-6pm, Su 10am-noon and 4-6pm; Nov. to Christmas and mid-Mar. to June M-F 8:30am-12:30pm and 2:30-6pm, Sa 8:30am-noon.) Make sure to pick up a free **guest card,** which provides discounts, free **guided hikes** (Jun.-Oct. M-F 8:45 am), and free **informative tours** (M 10am) from the tourist office. For **Internet** access, try **Cafe Hölzl,** 4 Jochbergstr. (☎632 37. Open daily 9-1am. 10AS/€0.75 per 5min.) From the Hauptbahnhof, turn left after at the end of the street and look left for the clean and fuss-free **Pension Hörl,** Josef-Pirchlstr. 60. (☎631 44. Breakfast included. Reception 7am-9pm. In summer 200-260AS/€14.55-18.90, with bath 230-290AS/€16.75-21.10; in winter add 20AS/€1.45.) For **Camping Schwarzsee,** Reitherstr. 24, take the train to Schwarzsee and follow the tracks past the bathing areas around the back of the lake; it's behind the Bruggerhof Hotel (15min.). (☎62 80 60. Reception 8am-5pm. 90-108AS/€6.55-7.85 plus 9-11AS/€0.65-0.80 recycling fee per person, depending on season.) Although many of Kitzbühel's restaurants prepare gourmet delights at astronomical prices, cheaper locales pepper the area surrounding the Fußgängerzone. **SPAR** supermarket, Bichlstr. 22, is at the intersection with Ehrenbachg. (Open M-F 8am-7pm, Sa 7:30am-1pm.) **Postal code:** A-6370.

ZILLER VALLEY (ZILLERTAL)

Extending from the Tuxer Alps, through the Zillertaler Alps, and to the Kitzbüheler Alps in the north, the Ziller Valley (*Zillertal*) provides spectacular, affordable, and easily accessible **hiking** and **skiing** away from crowds. The towns in the narrow valley offer some of the best hiking in western Austria, with more footpaths than roads and more trail guides than police officers.

⌨ TRANSPORTATION. The valley runs south from Jenbach through Zell am Ziller and Mayrhofen. Everyone entering the valley must go through Jenbach; you can get there easily from Innsbruck (20min., 72AS/€5.25, Eurail valid). From Jenbach, the **Zillertalbahn (Z-bahn),** an efficient network of private buses and trains, connects the towns. The Z-bahn has two types of trains, the **Dampfzug** (a more expensive, slower, touristy steam train) and the **Triebwagen,** which leaves daily every hour from 6am to 9pm. Note that travel on the Z-bahn is not covered by rail passes.

ZELL AM ZILLER. Zell am Ziller, 20km south of Jenbach, was founded by monks in the 8th century—"Zell" means "chapel"— but became a materialistic gold-mining town in the 1600s. Today, it offers skiing and hiking without resort-town hype. **Ski passes** are available at cable car stations. (1-day 380AS/€27.65; 2-day 710AS/€51.60; 3-day 1015AS/€73.80.) Two ski lifts also take you into the alps for **hiking:** the **Kreuzjochbahn** (open 8:40am-12:10pm and 1-5:10pm; round-trip 182AS/€13.25) and the **Gerlossteinbahn** (open 8:30am-12:15pm and 1-5pm; round-trip 120AS/€8.75). For look at Zell's history, take a tour of the nearby **gold mine,** which includes a scenic 45min. hike to the mine entrance. (2hr. tours May-Sept. daily, every hr. on the hr. 9am-6pm. 130AS/€9.45.) The **tourist office,** Dorfpl. 3a, has maps and information on skiing and accommodations. From the rail station, head right along Bahnhofstr. and turn right at the end. (☎(05282) 228 10. Open M-F 8:30am-12:30pm and 2:30-6pm, Sa 9am-noon and 4-6pm; July-Oct. also Su 9am-noon and 4-6pm.)

AUSTRIA

MAYRHOFEN. Mayrhofen provides endless opportunities for hiking and skiing. The **Penkenbahn**, a lift system of gondolas right above the town, runs to the top of the 1850m Penkenberg and several easy paths. (May 24-Oct. 7 9am-5pm; 165AS/€12.) The **Ahornbahn** lift ascends to a variety of both easy and difficult hikes. (June 16-Oct. 14, every 30min. 8:30am-noon and 12:30-5pm; 165AS/€12.) In winter, **skiers** and **snowboarders** flock to the Ahorn, Penken, and Horberg ski areas above town, all of which are covered by the **Ski Mayrhofen pass** (1-day 370AS/€27; 3-day 1000AS/€72.70). Mayrhofen is easily accessible via Z-Bahn from **Jenbach** (1hr., 24 per day 6am-9pm, 73AS/€5.30) and **Zell am Ziller** (15min., 24 per day 6:35am-9:50pm, 24AS/€1.75). The **tourist office,** Dursterstr. 225, has information on outdoor activities and accommodations and leads free **guided hikes and tours,** varying from short walks around town to 5hr. mountain hikes. (☎67 60. Hikes/tours mid-May to mid-Oct. M-F, call ahead for times. Tourist office open M-F 8am-6pm, Sa 9am-noon, Su 10am-noon; July-Aug. also Sa 2-6pm.)

INNSBRUCK   ☎0512

The 1964 and 1976 winter Olympics were held in Innsbruck, bringing international recognition to this beautiful mountain city. The nearby Tyrolean Alps await skiers and hikers, while back in town, the tiny Altstadt's cobblestoned streets are peppered with fancy façades and remnants of the Habsburgs Empire.

⌨ ⚡ TRANSPORTATION AND PRACTICAL INFORMATION

Trains: Hauptbahnhof, Südtirolerpl. (☎05 17 17). At least 1 ticket counter open 24hr. Trains to: **Munich** (2hr., 13 per day 4:30am-8:30pm, 416AS/€30.25); **Salzburg** (2-2½hr., 13 per day 2:35am-11:30pm, 380AS/€27.60); **Vienna Westbahnhof** (5½-7hr., 10 per day 2:30am-12:30am, 660AS/€48); **Zurich** (4hr., 4 per day 2:35am-12:40pm, 600AS/€43.60).

Public Transportation: For schedules and information on transportation in Innsbruck, head to the **IVB** Office, Stainerstr. 2, near Maria-Theresien-Str. (☎530 17 99. Open M-F 7:30am-6pm.) The main bus station is in front of the main entrance to the train station. Single-ride 22AS€1.60, 24hr. ticket 44AS/€3.20. Most buses stop running around 10:30 or 11:30pm; 3 *Nachtbus* lines run after hours.

Tourist Office: Innsbruck Tourist Office, Burggraben 3 (☎588 50), off the end of Museumstr., up 2 flights of stairs. The helpful staff sells maps (10AS/€0.75) and the **Innsbruck Card,** which provides free access to many attractions and unlimited public transportation. (24hr. 260AS/€19, 48hr. 330AS/€24, 72hr. 400AS/€29.) Open M-F 8am-6pm, Sa 8am-noon.

Laundromat: Bubblepoint Waschsalon, Brixnerstr. 1, or at Andreas-Hofer-Str. at the corner of Franz-Fischer-Str. Wash 55AS/€4, dry 10AS/€0.75 per 10min. **Internet** 20AS/€1.45 per 20min. Open M-F 8am-10pm, Sa-Su 8am-8pm.

Emergencies: Police, ☎133. **Ambulance,** ☎144 or 142. **Fire,** ☎122.

Internet Access: International Telephone Discount, Bruneckstr. 12 (☎59 42 72 61). Turn right from the train station; it's on the left just past the end of Südtirolerpl. 1.50AS/€0.10 per min. Open daily 9am-11pm.

Post Office: Maximilianstr. 2 (☎500 79 00). Open M-F 7am-11pm, Sa 7am-9pm, Su 8am-9pm. Address mail to be held: Postlagernde Briefe für FirstName SURNAME, Hauptpostamt, Maximilianstr. 2, A-6020 Innsbruck. **Postal Code:** A-6020.

⌂ ACCOMMODATIONS

Inexpensive accommodations are scarce in June when only two hostels are open: **Jugendherberge Innsbruck** and **Jugendherberge St. Niklaus.** The opening of student dorms to backpackers in July and August somewhat alleviates the crush. Visitors should join the free **Club Innsbruck** by registering at any Innsbruck accommodation. Membership gives discounts on skiing, bike tours, and the club's hiking program.

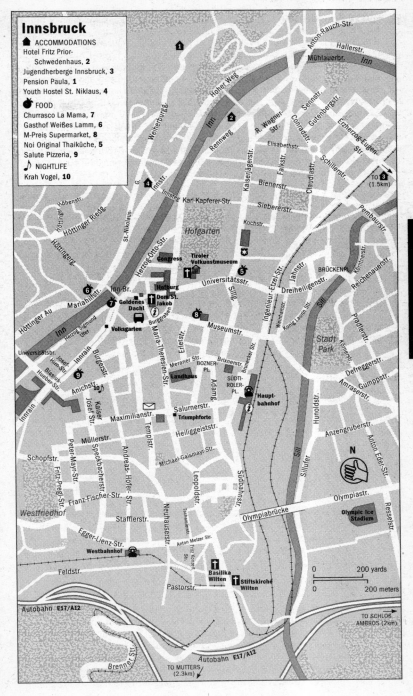

Innsbruck

ACCOMMODATIONS
Hotel Fritz Prior-
 Schwedenhaus, **2**
Jugendherberge Innsbruck, **3**
Pension Paula, **1**
Youth Hostel St. Niklaus, **4**

FOOD
Churrasco La Mama, **7**
Gasthof Weißes Lamm, **6**
M-Preis Supermarket, **8**
Noi Original Thaiküche, **5**
Salute Pizzeria, **9**

NIGHTLIFE
Krah Vogel, **10**

AUSTRIA

Haus Wolf, Dorfstr. 48 (☎54 86 73). Exit the train station through the main exit (under the neon clock); at the 3rd traffic island, take the Stubaitalbahn to "Mutters," walk toward the church, and turn right on Dorfstr. This suburban house is run by the gregarious Titti Wolf. Breakfast and shower included. 170-180AS/€12.35-13 per person.

Hostel Fritz Prior-Schwedenhaus (HI), Rennweg 17b (☎58 58 14). From the station, take bus A or tram 4 to "Handelsakademie," continue to the end and straight across Rennweg to the river. Spacious, clean rooms with private shower and bathroom. No door locks, but closet keys available. Breakfast (7-8am), 45AS/€3.30. Sheets 20AS/€1.45. Laundry 75AS/€5.45. Reception 7-9:30am and 5-10:30pm. Lockout 9:30am-5pm. Curfew 10:30pm; keys with ID deposit. Open July 1-Aug. 31 and Dec. 27-Jan. 5. Dorms 125AS/€9.10; doubles 370AS/€26.90; triples 495AS/€36.

Jugendherberge Innsbruck (HI), Reichenauer Str. 147 (☎34 61 79). From the train station, take tram #3 to "Sillpark" and bus O to "Jugendherberge." **Internet** 1AS/€0.10 per min.; after 9pm 1AS/€0.10 per 2min. Breakfast, hall showers, and sheets included. Laundry until 10pm, 45AS/€3.30. Reception daily 5-10pm, July-Aug. also 3-5pm. Lockout 10am-5pm. Curfew 11pm; key available. Quiet time from 10pm. 6-bed dorms 155AS/€11.25 1st night, then 125AS/€9.10; 4-bed dorms 190AS/€13.85, 160AS/€11.65; doubles with shower 260AS/€18.90; singles with shower 360AS/€26.20; non-HI add 40AS/€2.90.

Pension Paula, Weiherburgg. 15 (☎29 22 62). Take bus D to "Schmelzerg." and head uphill. Large, well-furnished rooms, many with balconies. Breakfast included. Reservations recommended in summer. Singles 350AS/€25.45, with shower 450AS/€32.70; doubles 580AS/€42.15, 700AS/€50.90; triples 770AS/€56, 930AS/€67.60.

Youth Hostel St. Niklaus (HI), Innstr. 95 (☎286 515). From the train station take bus D to "Schmelzerg." (22AS/€1.60) and cross the street. Breakfast and showers included. **Internet** 2A/€0.20 per min. Reception 8am-2pm and 5-10pm. Lockout 10am-5pm. Curfew 11pm; key available with 200AS/€14.55 or passport deposit. 6- to 8-bed dorms 190AS/€13.80 1st night, then 180AS/€13.10; 4-bed dorms 205AS/€14.90; doubles 500AS/€36.35, with shower and toilet 600AS/€43.60.

🍴 FOOD

From the Altstadt, cross the river to Innstr. for ethnic restaurants and cheap pizzerias. There are **M-Preis Supermarkets** at Museumstr. 34 and across from the train station on the corner of Salurnerstr. and Sterzingerstr. Hours are generally M-F 7:30am-6:30pm, Sa 7:30am-5pm.

Salute Pizzeria, Innrain 35. A popular student hangout near the university. Walk up to the counter to order, but make sure to grab a seat; Salute is never empty for long. Pizza from 40AS/€2.90, pasta from 60AS/€4.40. Open daily 11am-midnight.

Noi Original Thaiküche, Kaiserjägerstr. 1, cooks up Thai soups and deliciously spiced dishes. Open M-F 11:30am-3pm and 5-11pm, Sa 5-11pm.

Churrasco la Mamma, Innrain 2, next to the bridge. Outdoor seating, good pasta (from 85AS/€6.20) and pizza (from 79AS/€5.75). Open daily 9am-midnight. AmEx/MC/V.

Gasthof Weißes Lamm, Mariahilfstr. 12, on the 2nd fl. Serves honest Austrian fare, catering mostly to a local crowd. Daily *Tagesempfehlungen* (soup, entree, and salad) from 85AS/€6.20. Open F-W noon-2pm and 6pm-midnight. MC/V.

👁 SIGHTS

Inside the **Goldenes Dachl** (Golden Roof) on Herzog-Friedrich-Str., the tiny **Maximilianeum** commemorates emperor Maximilian I and provides a solid introduction to Innsbruck's history and culture. (Open May-Sept. 10am-6pm; Oct.-Apr. Tu-Su 10am-12:30pm and 2-5pm. 50AS/€3.65, students 20AS/€1.45.) A block behind the Goldenes Dachl rise the twin towers of the **Dom St. Jakob,** which display *trompe l'oeil* ceiling murals and an altar painting by Cranach the Elder. (Open Apr.-Sept. daily 8am-7:30pm; Oct.-Mar. 8am-6:30pm. Free.) Behind the Dom and to the right is the entrance to the grand **Hofburg,** remodeled by Empress Maria Theresa to include imposing furniture, large portraits (including Marie Antoinette, head intact) and elaborate chandeliers. (☎58 71 86. Open daily 9am-5pm. 70AS/€5.10, students 45AS/€3.30.) Across Rennweg sits the **Hofkirche** (Imperial Church), with 28 larger-than-life bronze statues of Habsburg saints and Roman emperors, some by Dürer. (Open daily 9am-5pm. 30AS/€2.20, students 20AS/€1.45.) The **Tiroler Volkskunstmuseum** (Tyrolean Folk Art Museum), in the same building, details the everyday life of the Tyrolean people. (Open M-Sa 9am-5pm, Su 9am-noon. 60AS/€4.40, students 35AS/€2.55.) Up Rennweg past the Dom, the **Hofgarten** (Imperial Garden) is a beautifully manicured park, complete with pond, flower beds, a concert pavilion, and an outdoor chess set with huge pieces.

HIKING AND SKIING

A **Club Innsbruck** membership (available at accommodations) grants access to a **hiking** program with guides, transportation, and equipment (including boots) at no additional cost. Participants assemble in front of the Congress Center (June-Sept. daily at 9am) and return by mid-afternoon. To hike on your own, take the #6 tram to Igls (35min., every hr. on the hr. 8am-7am, 22AS/€1.60). Once there, head out of the station toward town and follow the signs to "Patscherkofel Seilbahnen," a lift that takes you up to moderate hikes (round-trip 190AS/€13.85). For Club-Innsbruck-led **ski excursions,** just take the complimentary ski shuttle (schedules at the tourist office) to any suburban cable car. The **Innsbruck Gletscher Ski Pass** (available at all cable cars and at Innsbruck-Information offices) is valid for all 59 lifts in the region. (With Club Innsbruck card 3-day 1101AS/€80, 6-day 1941AS/€141). The tourist office also rents **ski equipment** (160- 270AS/€11.65-19.65 per day) and offers summer ski packages (640AS/€46.55 including bus, lift, and rental).

NIGHTLIFE

Nightlife revolves around the area between the university quarter and the Altstadt. The **Viaduktbogen** is a stretch of themed bars huddled beneath the arches of the railway along Ingenieur-Etzel-Str. For the very latest club and rave events, stop by Treibhaus (see below) and pick up one of the fliers on the grand piano. The **▧Hofgarten Café,** inside the Hofgarten park, is *the* place to be on summer nights. (Open daily 10am-4am.) At **Krah Vogel,** Anichstr. 12, off Maria-Theresien-Str., a hip, student-age crowd fills up the tables and small garden patio in the back. (Open daily 10am-2am.) **Die Alte Piccolo Bar,** Seilerg. 2, attracts a primarily gay male crowd, though women are welcome. Take the 2nd left after entering the Altstadt from Maria-Theresien-Str. (Open Th-Tu 10pm-4am.)

DAYTRIP FROM INNSBRUCK

SCHLOß AMBRAS

The castle stands in a park to the southeast of Innsbruck and is accessible by tram #6 (dir.: Igls) to "Tummelplatz/Schloß Ambras" (22AS/€1.60, 20min.). Follow the signs from the stop. Alternatively, take the shuttle that leaves every hr. from Maria-Theresien-Str., just opposite McDonald's. (Apr.-Oct every hr. 10am-5pm; round-trip 30AS/€2.20.)

In the late 16th century, Archduke Ferdinand II transformed a royal hunting lodge into one of Austria's most beautiful castles, **Schloß Ambras,** and filled it with vast collections of art, armor, weapons, and trinkets, all of which are now on display. Across the grounds in the Hochschloß is the famous **Spanischer Saal** (Spanish Room), where light streams in from the windows onto portraits of the Habsburg rulers. Upstairs is the impressive three-floor **Portrait Gallery** (open only in summer). The **gardens** outside, which vary from manicured shrubs with modern sculptures to shady, forested hillsides, provide relief from the opulence, but keep an eye out

AUSTRIA

for the **peacocks.** (Schloßstr. 20. ☎ 34 84 46. Dec.-Mar. open daily 2-5pm except Tu; 60AS/€4.40, students 40AS/€2.90. Apr.-Oct. open daily 10am-5pm; 100AS/€7.30, students 70AS/€5.10. Tours in either season 30AS/€2.20 extra.)

BREGENZ   ☎ 05574

The wooden **Martinturm** rules the *Oberstadt* ("high city") with Europe's largest onion dome. Next door is the **Martinskirche,** filled with 14th-century frescoes. Hike up Schloßbergstr. to the **St. Gallus Pfarrkirche,** a white stucco sanctuary that glows under lavish gold ornaments and a detailed painted ceiling. From the tourist office, walk down the *Fußgängerzone* (pedestrian zone) to reach the fantastically bizarre ◪**Kunsthaus Bregenz,** which features outlandish modern art and installations. (Open Tu-W and F-Su 10am-6pm, Th 10am-9pm. 65AS/€4.75; students 45AS/€3.30.) Stretch your legs along the **Strandweg** and **Seepromenade,** which follow the Bodensee from one end of town to the other. All along the waterfront, rose gardens and ice cream stands surround playgrounds and mini-golf courses. The concrete monstrosity on the edge of the lake is not a ski ramp gone awry but rather Europe's largest **floating stage** and the centerpiece for the annual **Bregenzer Festspiele,** held from mid-July to mid-August. In 2002, Puccini's *La Bohème* will run from July 18-Aug. 18. Tickets go on sale in October (300-1600AS/€21.80-116.28). For more info, call 40 76 or visit www.bregenzerfestspiele.com.

Trains go to: Feldkirch (30-45min., 2-4 per hr. 5:15am-12:01am, 58AS/€4.25); Innsbruck (2¼hr., 8 per day 5am-9:40pm, 320AS/€23.25); St. Gallen (45min., 4 per day 10:40am-8:40pm, 130AS/€9.45); **Zurich** (1¾hr., 4 per day 10:40am-8:40pm, 368AS/€26.75). To reach the **tourist office,** Bahnhofstr. 14, from the train station, face away from the tracks and turn left; it will be on the right. The staff makes hotel reservations (30AS/€2.20) and has *Privatzimmer* lists, hiking and city maps, and a free **Internet** terminal. (☎ 495 90. Open M-F 9am-noon and 1-5pm, Sa 9am-noon; during the *Festspiele* M-Sa 9am-7pm, Su 4-7pm.) At the **Jugendgästehaus (HI),** Mehrerauerstr. 3-5, all rooms have bathrooms and showers. From the station, cross the bridge over the tracks, walk left through the parking lot, and look for the yellow brick building on your left. (☎ 428 67. **Internet** 40AS/€23.25 per hr. Sheets, towels, and breakfast included. Laundry 60AS/€4.40. Reception 7am-10pm. Lockout 10pm; key with deposit. Check-out 10am. Dorms Apr.-Sept. 234AS/€17 per person, Oct.-Mar. 207AS/€15; singles 331AS/€24, 304AS/€22; doubles 606AS/€44, 552AS/€40. For stays less than 3 nights, add 42AS/€3. MC/V.) To reach **Pension Sonne,** Kaiserstr. 8, go right from the station up Bahnhofstr. into the city, then turn right on Kaiserstr. (Breakfast included. Reception 7:30am-10pm. Singles 370-460AS/€26.90-33.45; doubles 340-420AS/€24.75-30.55; triples 300-370AS/€21.80-26.90; quads 280AS/€20.35 (none with shower). During the *Festspiele*, add 90AS/€6.55. MC/V.) ◪**Zum Goldnen Hirschen,** Kirchstr. 8, serves great local cuisine. (Open 10am-midnight. AmEx/MC/V.) **SB Restaurant,** on the first floor of the "GWL" mall building in the *Fußgängerzone,* has self-serve salad bars (10AS/€5.85 per 100g) and cafeteria-style entrees. (Open M-F 8:30am-5:30pm, Sa 8:30am-3pm.) Below the restaurant is a **SPAR Supermarkt.** (Open M-Th 8am-7pm, F 8am-7:30pm, Sa 8am-5pm.) **Postal Code:** A-6900.

STYRIA (STEIERMARK)

Styria, promoted by tourist offices as "the Green Heart of Austria," is Austria's second-largest province (in terms of geography, not population). The mountainous region preserves many of Austria's ancient forests and folk traditions, including a gamey local cuisine and a dialect that few outsiders can understand.

GRAZ   ☎ 0316

Wonderfully under-touristed, Graz's *Altstadt* rewards the traveler with its unhurried, Mediterranean feel as the sun sets on the red-tiled roofs and Baroque domes. The second-largest of Austria's cities, it keeps a sweaty and energetic nightlife thanks to the 45,000 students at Karl-Franzens-Universität. In July and August, Graz's renowned music venues attract a multitude of festivals.

⛿ TRANSPORTATION. Flights arrive at **Flughafen Graz,** 9km from the city center; take bus #631 from the airport into town (20min., ever hr. 6:10am-11:30pm, 20AS/ €1.45). Trains run from the **Hauptbahnhof,** Europapl. (☎05 17 17 12; open 7am-8:45pm), to: Innsbruck (6hr., 4 per day 8:20am-10pm, 570AS/€41.45); Munich (via Salzburg, 808AS/€58.75); Salzburg (4¼hr., 4 per day 6:30am-8:20pm, 460AS/ €33.45); Vienna Südbahnhof (2½hr., 9 per day 5:30am-9:20pm, 340AS/€24.75); Zurich (8½hr., 10pm, 1002AS/€80.10). The **Graz-Köflach Bus** (GKB), Köflacherg. 35-41 (☎5987), runs daily 24hr.

⛃ PRACTICAL INFORMATION. From the train station, go down Annenstr. and cross the Hauptbrücke (bridge) to reach **Hauptplatz,** the center of town. Five minutes away is **Jakominiplatz,** the hub of the public transportation system, and **Herrengasse,** a pedestrian street lined with cafes and boutiques, connects the two. The **tourist office,** Herreng. 16, has free city maps and a guide to walking the city. The staff offers English-language **tours** of the *Altstadt* (2hr.; Apr.-Oct. Tu-Su 4pm, Nov.-Mar. Sa 2:30pm; 75AS/€5.45) and makes free room reservations. (☎807 50. Open June-Sept. M-F 9am-7pm, Sa 9am-6pm, Su 10am-4pm, holidays 10am-3pm; Oct.-May M-F 9am-6pm, Sa 9am-3pm, Su 10am-3pm.) **Café Zentral,** Andreas-Hofer-Pl. 9, has **Internet access.** (☎832 468. 60AS/€4.40 per hr. Open M-F 6am-midnight, Sa 6am-noon.) **Postal code:** A-8010.

⛿⛃ ACCOMMODATIONS AND FOOD.
In Graz, most budget hotels, guest houses, and pensions are pricey, and many are out in the boondocks. Luckily, the web of local transport provides a reliable and easy commute to and from the city center. To reach **Jugendgästehaus Graz (HI),** Idlhofg. 74, from the train station, cross the street, head right on Eggenberger Gürtel, turn left on Josef-Huber-G., then take the first right; the hostel is through the parking lot. Buses #31 and 32 run here from Jakominipl. The hostel also offers **Internet** (20AS/€1.50 for 20min.). (☎71 48 76. Breakfast included. Laundry 20AS/€1.50. Key deposit 300AS/€21.90. Reception 7am-10pm. From 10pm-2am, doors open every 30min. 4-bed dorms 230AS/€16.75; singles 325AS/€23.65; doubles 550AS/€40; all rooms with bath. 30AS/€2.20 surcharge for stays of less than 3 nights. If the hostel is full, you can stay in the "Notlager," basement rooms with hall bath, for 190AS/ €13.80. V/ MC.) For **Camping Central,** Martinhofstr. 3. Take bus #32 from Jakominipl. to "Bad Straßgang" (10min.) and follow the signs, turning right at the Mondo supermarket. This small, clean campground includes admission to the luxurious swimming pool. (☎0676 378 51 02. Shower included. Laundry 60AS/€4.40. Reception 7am-10pm. Open Apr.-Oct. 155AS/€11.30 per person, includes tent site; each additional adult 80AS/€5.85.)

Find an inexpensive meal on **Hauptplatz,** where concession stands sell sandwiches and *Wurst* (20-40AS/€1.45-2.95), ice cream, and other fast food. There are also **markets** along Rösselmühlg., an extension of Josef-Huber-G., and on Jakoministr., directly off Jakominipl. Cheap student hangouts line **Zinzendorfgasse** near the university, and a supermarket, **Sparmarkt,** is just a few blocks from the hostel on Prankerg. (Open M-Th 8am-7pm, F 7:30am-7:30pm, Sa 7:30am-5pm). **China Restaurant Mond,** Harrachg. 12a (☎356979), serves an all-you-can-eat lunch buffet (M-F 11:30am-2:30pm) for a skinny 69AS/€5.10, or try the daily menu (11:30am-3pm, 49AS/€3.60). No wonder it's often packed with locals. **Da Vinci,** Jakominipl. 19, keeps customers happy and waiters busy with cheap, delicious pizzas (66-89AS/€4.80-6.50) and pasta (65-85AS/€4.75-6.20). (☎818 171. Open daily 11am-11pm.)

⛿⛃ SIGHTS AND ENTERTAINMENT. North of Hauptpl., the wooded **Schloßberg** (literally "Castle Mountain") rises 123m above Graz. The hill is named for the castle which stood there from 1125 until 1809, when it was destroyed by Napoleon's

AUSTRIA

troops. Though the castle is mostly gone, the Schloßberg remains a beautiful city park. Climb the zigzagging stone steps of the **Schloßbergstiege,** built by Russian prisoners during WWI, for sweeping views of the vast Styrian plain. The **Landhaus,** which houses the tourist office, is a sight itself; the building was remodeled by architect Domenico dell'Allio in 1557 in Lombard style. The **Landeszeughaus** (Provincial Arsenal), Herreng. 16, details the history of Ottoman attacks on the arsenal and has enough spears, muskets, and armor to outfit 28,000 burly mercenaries. (☎01 798 10. Open Mar.-Oct. Tu-Su 9am-5pm, Nov.- Dec. Tu-Su 10am-3pm. 20AS/€1.50.) At the solemn 17th-century Habsburg **Mausoleum,** the elaborate domed tomb holds the remains of Ferdinand II in an underground chamber. (Open M-Sa 11am-noon and 2-3pm. 10AS/€0.75, guide text 3AS/€0.25.)

The hub of after-hours activity is the so-called **Bermuda Triangle,** an area of the old city behind Hauptpl. and bordered by Mehlpl., Färberg., and Prokopig. At **Kulturhauskeller,** Elisabethstr. 30, a young crowd demands ever louder and more throbbing dance music, but the partying doesn't get started until 11pm on weekends. (Weißbier 38AS/€2.80. No sports or military clothing. 19+. Obligatory coat check and security fee 25AS/€1.85. Open Tu-Sa from 10pm.) Have a chat over your beer at **Triangel,** Burgg. 15, a low-key bar with vaulted brick ceilings, mirrored arches, and a clientele of trendy twenty-somethings. (Occasional bands. No cover. Open Tu-Sa 9:30pm-4am.)

CARINTHIA (KÄRNTEN)

The province of Carinthia covers the southernmost part of Austria. Natives consider Carinthia a vacation paradise, thanks to its scenic vistas, relaxing lakesides, and beautiful abbeys and castles. If you'll be in Carinthia for a while, consider a **Kärnten Card,** good for up to three weeks of unlimited local transportation, free admission to area sights and museums, and many discounts. The card, available at area tourist offices, is a great deal at 395AS/€25.75.

KLAGENFURT   ☎0463

Situated on the eastern edge of the idyllic Wörthersee, Klagenfurt (pop. 90,000) is a major summertime destination for Austrians. The Wörthersee is the warmest alpine lake in Europe and serves as Europe's largest skating arena in winter. Klagenfurt is home to no fewer than 23 castles and mansions; pick up the tourist office's free brochures *From Castle to Castle* and *A Walk Round Klagenfurt's Old Town* to help you explore. At the edge of Alterpl. stands the 16th-century **Landhaus,** originally an arsenal and later the seat of the provincial diet. Inside, 665 brilliant coats of arms blanket the walls; artist Johann Ferdinand Fromiller took nearly 20 years to complete these pieces. *(Open Apr.-Sept. M-F 9am-1pm and 2-5pm. 15AS/€1.10, students 5AS/€0.40.)* The **Landesmuseum** (Historical Museum), one of Klagenfurt's largest, houses the *Lindwurmschädel,* the alleged skull of the legendary Lindwurm (see below). *(Museumg. 2. Open Tu-Sa 9am-4pm, Su 10am-1pm. 40AS/€2.95, students 20AS/€1.50.)*

Trains leave the **Hauptbahnhof,** at the intersection of Südbahngürtel and Bahnhofstr., to: Graz (3hr., 16 per day 4:15am-8:30pm, 360AS/€26.20); Salzburg (3½hr., 10 per day 5:20am-7:50pm, 360AS/€26.20); Vienna (4hr., 17 per day 1:45am-8:30pm, 480AS/€34.90). The **tourist office** is on the 1st floor of the Rathaus in Neuer Pl.; from the station, go down Bahnhofstr. and left on Paradeiserg., which opens into Neuer Pl. (☎53 72 23. Open May-Sept. M-F 8am-8pm, Sa-Su 10am-5pm; Oct.-Apr. M-F 8am-5pm.) To get to **Jugendherberge Klagenfurt,** Neckheimg. 6, at Universitätstr., take bus #40, 41, or 42 from the train station to "Heiligengeistpl.," then bus #10 or 11 to "Neckheimg." from stand #2. (Breakfast and sheets included. Reception 7am-noon and 5-10pm. No curfew. Singles 315AS/€22.90; doubles 480AS/€34.90; nonmembers 40AS/€2.95 extra.) **Jugendgästehaus Kolping,** Enzenbergstr. 26, is a student dorm during the school year. From the train station, head right down Bahnhofstr., then turn right on Viktringer Ring, left on Völkermarkter Ring, right at Feldmarschall-Conrad-Pl., and right on Enzenbergstr. (Breakfast included July and Aug.

DRAGON'S TALE Once upon a time, the settlement of Klagenfurt was harassed by a most unwelcome winged lizard—the *Lindwurm* (Dragon). This virgin-consuming monster terrorized the area until Hercules dispatched the beast and saved the village. Centuries later, the "skull" of the slain beast was found, proving many an old wives' tale about the heroic founding of the town. The overjoyed townspeople commissioned the statue of the *Lindwurm* on Neuer Platz, which became the town's symbol even though, in 1840, scientists proved the "skull" belonged not to the beast of legend but to a pre-historic rhino. Klagenfurt's collective heart broke in 1945 when an Allied soldier climbed onto the sensitive *Lindwurm's* tail, snapping it in two, but the beast has since recovered and terrorizes Klagenfurt once more.

Reception open 24hr. during July and Aug., otherwise closed from Sa 5pm to Su 5pm. Open early July to early Sept. 260AS/€18.90 per person with HI card; 40AS/€2.95 extra for single-night stay; non-HI members and non-students add 20AS/€1.45.) **Neuer Platz, Kardinalplatz** and **Burggasse** have cheap places to eat, but almost all restaurants (except a few by the beaches and the train station) are closed on Sundays. The tourist office prints *Sonntagsbraten*, a pamphlet listing the addresses and operating hours of cafes, restaurants, clubs, and bars that are open on Sundays. There is a **SPAR supermarket** on the corner of Bahnhofstr. and Miesstalerstr. (Open M-F 7:30am-6:30pm, Sa 7:30am-5pm.) **Postal Code:** A-9020.

AUSTRIA

BELGIUM
(BELGIQUE, BELGIË)

BELGIAN FRANCS

US$1 = 44.03BF	10BF = US$0.23
CDN$1 = 28.55BF	10BF = CDN$0.35
UK£1 = 63.74BF	10BF = UK£0.16
IR£1 = 51.23BF	10BF = IR£0.20
AUS$1 = 23.60BF	10BF = AUS$0.42
NZ$1 = 19.36BF	10BF = NZ$0.52
ZAR1 = 5.32BF	10BF = ZAR1.88
EUR€1 = 40.34BF	10BF = EUR€0.25

PHONE CODE | Country Code: 32. **International dialing prefix:** 00.

Situated between France and Germany, little Belgium (pop. 10.2 million; 30,510 sq. km) rubs shoulders with some of Western Europe's most powerful cultural and intellectual traditions. Travelers too often mistake Belgium's subtlety for dullness, but its cities offer some of Europe's finest art and architecture, and its castle-dotted countryside provides a beautiful escape for hikers and bikers. Brussels, the capital and home to NATO and the European Union, buzzes with international decision-makers. Regional tension persists within Belgium's borders between Flemish-speaking Flanders and French-speaking Wallonie. But some things transcend politics: from the deep caves of the Ardennes to the white sands of the North Sea coast, Belgium's diverse beauty is even richer than its chocolate.

SUGGESTED ITINERARIES

THREE DAYS Jump into the heart of **Brussels** (p. 125), the **Grand-Place,** declared by Victor Hugo to be "the most beautiful square in the world." Witness Brussels's most giggled-at sight, the **Mannekin Pis,** a statue of a cherubic boy continuously urinating. Visit the **Belgian Comic Strip Centre** and pick up the requisite **Tintin** paraphernalia. Check out the **Musées Royaux des Beaux Arts** and take a trip up to the **Atomium.**

ONE WEEK After three days in **Brussels,** head to **Antwerp** and stroll along the Meir for tasty beer and fine chocolates (1 day, p. 135). Move on to beautiful **Bruges** to climb the 366 steps of the Belfort (2 days, p. 131). Lay out on the beaches of the **North Sea coast,** parking your pack in **Zeebrugge** or **Ostend** (1 day, p. 135).

BEST OF BELGIUM IN 10 DAYS After your week in **Brussels, Bruges,** and **Antwerp,** visit **Ypres** to remember victims of the Great War (1 day, p. 137). Next, get chills in the medieval torture chamber of Gravensteen in **Ghent** (1 day, p. 136). Head south to explore the castle-dotted **Wallonie** region, where you can hike, bike, kayak, and spelunk (1 day, p. 138). Don't miss the glittering gold treasury in the cathedral of **Tournai** (1 day, p. 138).

BELGIUM

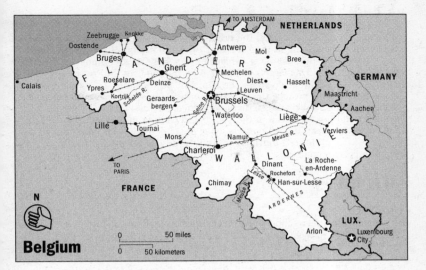

Belgium

LIFE AND TIMES

HISTORY AND POLITICS

Belgium's strategic location between several European powers has long been coveted by military and political leaders, including **Julius Caesar** and **Charlemagne.** The 14th century witnessed a golden period of prosperity in the Belgian region, with a boom in the cloth industry. In the next several centuries, the territory passed through the hands of the Spanish, the Austrians, the French, and finally the Dutch. Only in 1830 did Belgium gain independence by popular **revolution** from the Kingdom of The Netherlands. The newly freed Belgians established a constitutional monarchy, selecting **Leopold I** of Saxe-Coburg as their first king. In 1839, the European powers declared Belgium a perpetually neutral state. Belgium was a pioneer in European industrialization; coal production boosted the first national railway program in Europe during the 1930s. Other major projects in the 19th century included **colonial expansion** in Africa, most notably in the present-day **Congo.** Despite these international successes, Belgium experienced internal discontent due to poor labor conditions, prompting major social reforms under **King Leopold II.**

THE WORLD WARS (1914-1945)

The Germans invaded in the 20th century, flagrantly violating Belgium's neutral status during both World Wars. The **Treaty of Versailles,** the settlement of WWI, granted Belgium monetary and territorial reparations as recompense for the widespread devastation produced by German occupation. In WWII, **King Leopold III's** rapid **surrender** shocked not only the Belgians, but the British and the French as well, as they were suddenly faced with the advancing German army. Belgium's post-war economic recovery was impressively swift, for its second wartime destruction was relatively limited. Of greater concern was the political disorganization upon the return of **King Leopold** from Austria in 1945, where he had been sent during Nazi rule. Popular disapproval of his alleged defeatism led to his abdication in 1951.

BELGIUM TODAY

With the exception of the brief period after the Treaty of Versailles when Belgium was allied with France, the country has maintained a neutral political stance while remaining at the forefront of international affairs. Most significantly, Belgium is the seat of the **European Union.** Belgian government in the 19th and 20th centuries was largely dominated by the minority of French speakers, despite cries of injustice from the Flemish population. To ease tensions between these two groups, the constitution was revised in 1980 to grant more autonomy to each of the three distinctive linguistic and cultural communities: **Flemish** in the north, **French** in the south, and **German** in the east. The Belgian king, currently **Albert II,** is the official head of state, but he is accountable to the democratically elected **parliament.** Day-to-day government is run by his appointed prime minister.

THE ARTS

PAINTING

Despite representing a school of painting known as the Flemish Primitives, **Jan van Eyck** in fact refined techniques of oil painting, working with layers of glaze to produce pieces of amazing detail. His most well-known painting is the *Adoration of the Mystic Lamb* (1432), the altarpiece of **St. Bavo's Cathedral** in **Ghent** (see p. 136). **Pieter Bruegel the Elder** shifted artistic focus from the sacred to the profane, choosing to depict commonplace scenes over legendary themes. **Peter Paul Rubens** was **Antwerp**'s most famous artistic son; his paintings are distinctive for their religious symbolism, reflecting the turbulent climate of the **Counter-Reformation,** and for their fluid incorporation of the Italian Renaissance style. Ruben's assistant **Anthony van Dyck** was also a prominent member of the Flemish school of painting. Van Dyck's elegant portraits of the aristocracy gained him widespread renown and influenced **portraiture** style across the continent. In the 20th century, the leader of the **Surrealists** was **René Magritte,** who attempted to bring new and unusual meaning to ordinary household objects such as pipes, apples, instruments, and chairs. His most famous icon is probably the bowler-hatted man.

MUSIC

César Franck, the influential **Romantic** musician and organist, is Belgium's best-known composer. His symphonies and sonatas combined technical expertise with emotional energy. **Adolphe Sax,** born in **Dinant** (see p. 139), a musical instrument inventor, introduced the **saxophone** to the world. **Jacques Brel** was the voice of the nation; his most famous ballad, *Ne me quitte pas* (1959), has been covered by, among countless other musicians, **Sting.**

COMIC-STRIPS AND MYSTERIES

In the 20th century, Belgian talent made its presence known in the world of **comic-strips** and **detective novels.** In Brussels, museums are dedicated to the history of cartooning, where tribute is paid to the work of **Georges Remi,** better-known as **Hergé,** creator of **Tintin** (see p. 129), and to **Peyo,** father of the **Smurfs.** The cunning **Commissaire Maigret** was another famous Belgian creation of the past century, conceived by the enigmatic **Georges Simenon,** who authored a 76-novel mystery series. **Henri Michaux** stretched the bounds by even Surrealist standards. His poetry explored the inner self and blurred the boundary between fantasy and reality.

FOOD AND DRINK

Belgian cuisine, a combination of French and German traditions, is praised throughout Western Europe, but a native meal may cost as much as a night in a decent hotel. *Moules* (steamed mussels), regarded as the national dish, are usually tasty and reasonably affordable (around 430BF/€10.70 per pot). Belgians claim

BELGIUM

that they invented **frites** (potato fries), which they drown in mayonnaise and consume in abundance. Belgian **beer** is both a national pride and a national pastime; more varieties—over 300, ranging from ordinary **Pilsners** to religiously brewed **Trappist** ales—are produced here than in any other country. Regular or quirky blonde goes for as little as 40BF/€1, and dark beers cost about 60-90BF/€1.50-2.25 per bottle. Leave room for Belgian **waffles** (*gaufres*)—soft, warm, glazed ones on the street (50BF/€1.25) and bigger, crispier ones piled high with toppings at cafes (80-200BF/€2-5)—and for the famous delectable Godiva **chocolates**.

ESSENTIALS

DOCUMENTS AND FORMALITIES

Visas are generally not required for tourist stays under three months; South African citizens are the exception.

Belgian Embassies at Home: Australia, 19 Arkana St, Yarralumla, Canberra, ACT 2600 (☎(02) 62 73 25 01; fax 62 73 33 92). **Canada,** 80 Elgin St., 4th fl., Ottawa, ON K1P 1B7 (☎613-236-7267; fax 236-7882. **Ireland,** 2 Shrewsbury Road, Ballsbridge, Dublin 4 (☎(353) 269 20 82; fax 283 84 88). **New Zealand,** Axon House, Willeston St. 1-3, 12th fl., PB 3379, Wellington (☎(04) 472 95 58; fax 471 27 64). **South Africa,** 625 Leyds St., Muckleneuk, Pretoria 0002 (☎(2712) 44 32 01; fax 44 32 16). **UK,** 103-105 Eaton Sq, London SW1W 9AB (☎(020) 7470 37 00; fax 7259 62 13; www.belgium-embassy.co.uk). **US,** 3330 Garfield St NW, Washington, D.C. 20008 (☎202-333-6900; fax 333-3079; www.diplobel.org/usa).

Foreign Embassies in Belgium: All foreign embassies are in **Brussels** (see p. 125).

TRANSPORTATION

BY PLANE. Several major airlines fly into **Brussels** from Europe, North America, and Africa; many offer cheap deals. **Sabena** (Belgium ☎(02) 723 62 19; US ☎800-955-2000; www.sabena.com) serves many locations, including Australia, Ireland, North America, South Africa, and the United Kingdom.

BY TRAIN AND BUS. The extensive and reliable **Belgian Rail** (www.sncb.be) network traverses the country in 4hr. **Eurail** is valid in Belgium (in the US, call 877-456-RAIL; in Canada 800-361-RAIL). The **Benelux Tourrail Pass** covers five days of travel in Belgium, The Netherlands, and Luxembourg in any one-month period (4680BF/€116, under 26 3510BF/€87). The best deal for travelers under 26 may be the **Go Pass,** which allows 10 trips over six months in Belgium and may be used by more than one person (1550BF/€38.45). For travelers over 26, the **Rail Pass** allows 10 trips in Belgium after 9am (2280BF/€56.55). Because the train network is so extensive, **buses** are used primarily for municipal transport (40-50BF/€1-1.25).

BY FERRY. P&O European Ferries (UK ☎(01482) 795141, Belgium ☎(050) 54 34 30; www.ponsf.com) cross the Channel from **Zeebrugge,** north of Bruges, to **Hull, England** (14hr.; departures at 6:15pm; £38-48, under 26 £24-31). **Ostend Lines** also crosses from Ostend to **Ramsgate, England,** 2hr. from London's Victoria Station (☎(059) 55 99 55; 6 per day, 1600BF/€39.70 round-trip). For info on Ostend, Zeebrugge, and Knokke, see p. 135.

BY CAR, BIKE, AND THUMB. Belgium honors most foreign driver's licenses, including those from Australia, Canada, the EU, and the US. **Speed limits** are 120kph on motorways, 90kph on main roads, and 50kph elsewhere. **Fuel** costs about 40BF/€1 per liter. **Biking** is popular, and many roads have bike lanes (which you are required to use). **Hitchhiking** is not popular in Belgium and is not recommended as a safe means of transport, but hitchers still report a fair amount of success in some areas. *Let's Go* does not recommend hitchhiking.

BELGIUM

TOURIST SERVICES AND MONEY

EMERGENCY	Police, ☎101. Ambulance, ☎105. Fire, ☎100.

TOURIST OFFICES. Bureaux de Tourisme, marked by green-and-white signs labelled "i," are supplemented by **Infor-Jeunes/Info-Jeugd,** a service that helps young people secure accommodations. For info, contact the main office of the **Belgian Tourist Board,** 63 r. de Marché aux Herbes, B-1000 Brussels. (☎ (02) 504 03 90; fax 504 02 70; www.tourism-belgium.net. Open 9am-6pm.) The weekly English-language *Bulletin* (85BF/€2.15 at newsstands) lists everything from movies to job openings.

Tourist Offices at Home: Canada, P.O. Box 760, Succursale NDG, Montréal, Quebec H4A 3S2 (☎514-484-3594; fax 489-8965) or 43, r. de Buade, Bureau 525, Quebec Ville, Quebec, G1R 4A2 (Wallonie office; ☎(418) 692-4939; fax 692-4974). **UK,** 225 Marsh Wall, London E14 9FW (Brussels and Ardennes office; ☎(0906) 302 0245; fax (020) 7531 0393) or 31 Pepper St., London E14 9RW (Flanders office; ☎(09001) 887799; fax (020) 7458 0045); both http://antor.com/Belgium. **US,** 780 3rd Ave., Ste. 1501, New York, NY 10017 (☎212-758-8130; fax 355-7675; www.visitbelgium.com).

CURRENCY AND EXCHANGE. The unit of currency is the **Belgian franc;** bills come in 100, 200, 500, 1000, 2000, 5000, and 10,000 denominations; coins in 1, 5, 20 and 50. 100 *centimes* make up one *franc.* Belgium has accepted the **Euro (€)** as legal tender, and *francs* will be phased out by July 1, 2002. For more information, see p. 23.

Prices: Expect to pay 800-1200BF/€19.85-29.75 for a room; 380-550BF/€9.45-13.65 for a hostel bed; 200-500BF/€5-12.40 for a cheap restaurant meal; and 250-500BF/€6.20-12.40 for a day's groceries. A bare-bones day in Belgium might cost US$15-30; a slightly more comfortable day might cost US$30-40.

Tipping and Bargaining: Restaurants and taxis usualy include service charges in the price, but tip for exceptional service. Give bathroom attendants 10-20BF/€0.25-0.50.

Taxes: Belgium's **value-added tax (VAT)** (generally 21%) is always included in price; refunds (usually 17% of purchase price) are available for a min. purchase of 5000BF/€123.95 per invoice.

ACCOMMODATIONS AND CAMPING

Hotels in Belgium are fairly expensive, with "trench-bottom" singles from 800BF/€19.85 and doubles at 1000-1100BF/€24.80-27.30. Belgium's 31 **HI youth hostels,** which charge about 405BF/€10.05 per night, are generally modern and many boast cheap bars, but **private hostels** often cost the same and are much nicer. Pick up a free copy of *Camping* at any tourist office for complete listings of hostels and campsites. **Campgrounds** charge about 130BF/€3.25 per night. An **international camping card** is not required in Belgium.

COMMUNICATION

MAIL. A postcard or letter (up to 20g) sent to a destination within the European Union costs 21BF/€0.55, and to the rest of the world costs 34BF/€0.84. Most post offices open M-F 9am to 4 or 6pm (sometimes with a midday break) and sometimes Sa 9 or 10am to noon or 1pm.

TELEPHONES. Most phones require a 200BF/€5 phone card, available at PTT offices and magazine stands. Rarer coin-operated phones are more expensive and require either 5BF or 20BF coins. Calls are cheapest from 6:30pm to 8am and Sa-Su. For **operator assistance** within Benelux, dial 13 07; for **international assistance,** 13 04 (10BF/€0.25). **International direct dial** numbers include: **AT&T,** ☎0800 100 10; **British Telecom,** ☎0800 89 0032; **Canada Direct,** ☎0800 100 19 or 0800 700 19; **Ireland Direct,** ☎0800 10 353; **MCI,** ☎0800 100 12; **Sprint,** ☎0800 100 14; **Telecom New Zealand,** ☎0800 100 64; **Telkom South Africa,** ☎0800 100 27; **Telstra Australia,** ☎0800 100 61.

BELGIUM

INTERNET ACCESS. There are cybercafes in the larger towns and cities in Belgium. For access to the web, expect to pay 100-130BF/€2.50-3.25 per 30min.

LANGUAGES. Flemish (a variety of Dutch, spoken in Flanders), French (spoken in Wallonie), and German. Most people, especially in Flanders, speak English. In Brussels, both Flemish and French are used. For the basics, see p. 953.

LOCAL FACTS

Time: Belgium is 1hr. ahead of Greenwich Mean Time (GMT).

When to Go: Belgium, temperate and rainy, is best visited May to Sept., when temperatures average 13-21°C (54-72°F). Winter temperatures average 0-5°C (32-43°F). Bring a sweater and umbrella whenever you go.

Hours: Banks are generally open M-F 9am to 3:30pm or 4pm, sometimes with a lunch break. **Stores** are open M-Sa 10am-6pm. Most **sights** open Su but close M except in Bruges and Tournai, where museums are closed Tu or W. Most stores close on holidays; museums stay open during all except for Christmas, New Year's, and Armistice Day.

Holidays: New Year's Day (Jan. 1); Easter (Mar. 31); Easter Monday (Apr. 1); Labor Day (May 1); Ascension Day (June 9); Whit Sunday (May 19); Whit Monday (May 20); Independence Day (July 21); Assumption Day (Aug. 15); All Saints Day (Nov. 1); Armistice Day (Nov. 11); Christmas (Dec. 25).

Festivals: Ghent hosts the **Gentse Feesten,** also know as 10 Days Off (July 20-29). Wallonie hosts a slew of quirky and creative carnival-like festivals, including the **Festival of Fairground Arts** (late May), **Les Jeux Nautiques** (early Aug.), the **International French-language Film Festival** (early Sept.) in Namur, and the **International Bathtub Regatta** (mid-Aug.) in Dinant.

BRUSSELS (BRUXELLES, BRUSSEL) ☎02

Despite the city's instant association with NATO and the European Union, the diplomats in suits have always been outshone by the two boy heroes that Brussels loves best: Tintin and the Mannekin Pis. In the late 1920s, cartoonist Hergé created a comic strip hero, Tintin, who, followed by his faithful white dog Snowy, righted international wrongs long before Brussels became the capital of the EU. The cherubic Mannekin Pis perpetually pees three blocks from the Grand-Place, ruining any semblance of formality that could be caused by international politics. The museums of Brussels are rich with collections of Flemish masters, modern art, and antique sculptures, but you don't need to go inside for a visual feast—restaurants, lounges, and movie theaters that keep the town abuzz are built in the style of Art Nouveau architect Victor Horta.

▐ TRANSPORTATION

Flights: Brussels International Airport (info ☎ 753 42 21; www.BrusselsAirport.be) has flights to major international destinations (see p. 123, for Sabena Belgian World Airlines information). Trains run to the airport, 14km from the city, from Gare du Midi (25min., every 20min., 90BF/€2.25); all stop at Gare Centrale and Gare du Nord.

Trains: Info ☎ 555 25 55. All international trains stop at **Gare du Midi/Zuid;** most also stop at **Gare Centrale** (near the Grand-Place) or **Gare du Nord** (near the Botanical Gardens). To: **Amsterdam** (2½hr., 1310BF/€32.50, under 26 640BF/€15.90); **Antwerp** (30min., 200BF/€4.96); **Bruges** (45min., 390BF/€9.70); **Cologne** (2¾hr.; 1260BF/€31.25, under 26 900BF/€22.35); **Luxembourg City** (1¾hr., 930BF/€23.05); **Paris** (1½hr.; 2180BF/€54.05, under 26 1000BF/€24.80). **Eurostar** goes to **London** (2¾hr.; from 6200BF/€153.70, under 26 2100BF/€52.10).

Buses: Société des Transports Intercommunaux Bruxellois (STIB), Gare du Midi. Open M-F 7:30am-5pm, 1st and last Su of each month 8am-2pm. Also at the Porte de Namur and Rogier Métro stops. Open M-F 8:30am-5:15pm. Schedule info ☎ 515 20 00.

Public Transportation: Runs daily 6am-midnight. 1hr. tickets (55BF/€1.40) valid on **buses,** the **Métro (M),** and **trams.** Day pass 145BF/€3.60, 5-trip pass 240BF/€5.95, 10-trip pass 360BF/€8.95.

Hitchhiking: *Let's Go* does not recommend hitchhiking. Hitchers headed to **Antwerp** and **Amsterdam** take tram #52 or 92 from Gare du Midi or Gare du Nord to Heysel; **Ghent** and **Bruges,** bus #85 from the Bourse to the stop before the terminus, then follow E40 signs; **Paris,** tram #52, 55, or 91 to r. de Stalle, then walk toward the E19.

✴🛈 ORIENTATION AND PRACTICAL INFORMATION

Most major attractions are clustered between the **Bourse** (Stock Market) to the west, the **Parc de Bruxelles** to the east, and the **Grand-Place.** Two **Métro** lines circle the city, and efficient trams run north to south. A **tourist passport** (*Carte d'un Jour;* 300BF/€7.45 at the TIB and bookshops) includes two days of public transit, a map, and reduced museum prices.

Tourist Offices: National, 63 r. du Marché aux Herbes (☎504 03 90; fax 504 02 70), 1 block from the Grand-Place. Books rooms all over Belgium and offers the free weekly *What's On.* Open M-F 9am-6pm, Su 10am-2pm. **TIB (Tourist Information Brussels;** ☎513 89 40), on the Grand-Place, in the Town Hall, offers walking tours (3hr.; 800BF/ €19.90, students 720BF/€17.90). Open July-Aug. M-F 9am-6pm; May-June and Sept.-Oct. M-F 9am-6pm, Sa-Su 9am-1pm and 2-6pm; Nov.-Apr. Su only 10am-2pm.

Budget Travel: Infor-Jeunes, 9A r. du St. Catherine (☎514 41 11; bruxelles@inforjeunes.be). Budget travel info for young travelers. Open M-F 10am-5pm.

Embassies: Australia, 6-8 r. Guimard, 1040 (☎231 05 00; fax 230 68 02). **Canada,** 2 av. Tervueren, 1040 (☎741 06 11; fax 448 00 00). **Ireland,** 89/93 r. Froissart, 1040 (☎230 53 37; fax 230 53 12). **New Zealand,** 47 bd. du Régent, 1000 (☎513 48 56). **South Africa,** 26 r. de la Loi (☎285 44 02). Generally open M-F 9am-5pm. **UK,** 85 r. Arlon (☎287 62 11; fax 287 63 55). **US,** 27 bd. du Régent, 1000 (☎508 21 11; fax 511 96 52; www.usinfo.be). Open M-F 9am-noon.

Currency Exchange: Many exchange booths near the Grand-Place stay open until 11pm. Most banks and booths charge 100-150BF/€2.50-3.75 commission to cash checks. **CBC-Automatic Change,** 7 Grand-Place (☎547 11 29). Open 24hr.

Gay and Lesbian Services: Call 733 10 24 for info on local events. Staffed Tu 8-10pm, W 8-11pm, F 8-11pm.

Laundromat: Salon Lavoir, 62 r. Blaes, around the corner from the Jeugdherberg Bruegel. M: Gare Centrale. Wash and dry 240BF/€5.95. Open daily 7am-10pm.

Emergencies: Ambulance or **first aid,** ☎100. **Police,** ☎101.

Pharmacies: Neos-Bourse Pharmacie (☎218 06 40), bd. Anspach at r. du Marché-aux-Polets. M: Bourse. Open M-F 8:30am-6:30pm, Sa 9am-6:30pm.

Medical Assistance: Free Clinic, 154a chaussée de Wavre (☎512 13 14). Misleading name—you'll have to pay. Open M-F 9am-6pm. **Medical Services,** 24hr. ☎479 18 18.

Internet Access: easyEverything, 9-13 de Brouckère. Approx. 50BF/€1.25 per 66min.

Post Office: (info ☎226 23 10 or 226 23 11), pl. de la Monnaie, Centre Monnaie, 2nd fl. M: de Brouckère. Open M-F 8am-7pm, Sa 9:30am-3pm. Address mail to be held: First Name SURNAME, Poste Restante, pl. de la Monnaie, **1000** Bruxelles, Belgium.

🛏 ACCOMMODATIONS

Accommodations in Brussels can be difficult to find, especially on weekends in June and July. In general, hotels and hostels are well-kept and centrally located. Staffs will call each other if prospective guests arrive and they are booked.

Hôtel Pacific, 57 r. Antoine Dansaert (☎511 84 59). M: Bourse; follow the street directly in front of the Bourse, which becomes Dansaert after the intersection; it's on the right. Excellent location and basic rooms. Breakfast and showers included. Reception 7am-midnight. Curfew midnight. Singles 1200BF/€29.75; doubles 2000BF/€49.60.

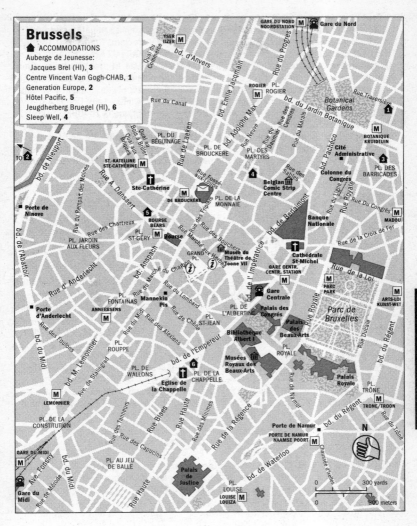

Brussels

▲ ACCOMMODATIONS

Auberge de Jeunesse:
  Jacques Brel (HI), **3**
Centre Vincent Van Gogh-CHAB, **1**
Generation Europe, **2**
Hôtel Pacific, **5**
Jeugdherberg Bruegel (HI), **6**
Sleep Well, **4**

Sleep Well, 23 r. du Damier (☎218 50 50; info@sleepwell.be), near Gare du Nord. M: Rogier; exit onto r. Jardin Botanique, face the pyramid and go right; take the 1st right on r. des Cendres, then at the intersection go slightly to the right and continue onto r. de Damier. Breakfast included. **Internet** access. Curfew 3am. Lockout 10am-4pm. Dorms 490-655BF/€16.25; singles 950BF/€23.55; doubles 1450BF/€35.95.

Auberge de Jeunesse "Jacques Brel" (HI), 30 r. de la Sablonnière (☎218 01 87), on pl. des Barricades. M: Botanique. From the Métro, walk down Rue Royale away from the domed building at the end of the street, with the botanical gardens to your right, and take the 1st right onto Sablonnière. Spacious rooms. Breakfast included. Dinner 295BF/€7.35. Sheets 130BF/€3.25. Reception 8am-1am. Dorms 430BF/€10.70; singles 820BF/€20.35; doubles 1200BF/€29.75; triples 1530BF/€37.95.

Centre Vincent Van Gogh-CHAB, 8 r. Traversière (☎217 01 58). M: Botanique; exit on r. Royale, head right (facing the Jardin Botanique), and turn right again. **Internet** 50BF/€1.25 per 15min. Laundry 180BF/€4.50. Reception 7am-2am. Dorms 340-480BF/€8.45-11.90; singles 700BF/€17.35; doubles 1120-1160BF/€27.80-28.75.

Jeugdherberg Bruegel (HI), 2 r. de Saint Esprit (☎511 04 36; jeugdherberg.bruegel@ping.be). From the back exit of Gare Centrale, go right on bd. de l'Empereur, past Palais de Congrès on your left, and take the 2nd left after pl. de la Justice. Sheets 130BF/€3.25. Reception 7am-1am. Lockout 10am-2pm. Curfew 1am. Dorms 430BF/€10.70; singles 820BF/€20.35; doubles 1200BF/€29.75; quads 2040BF/€50.60.

Generation Europe (HI), 4 r. de l'Eléphant (☎410 38 58; gener.europe@infonie.be; www.laj.be). M: Comte de Flandre; take the "Maison Communale" exit and follow the yellow signs. Be careful walking there at night. Private bathrooms. Reception 7:30am-1am. Lockout 11am-3pm. Sheets and breakfast included. Laundry 200BF/€5. Dorms 505BF/€12.50; singles 908BF/€22.50; doubles 1412BF/€35.

◖ FOOD

Cheap restaurants cluster around the **Grand-Place.** Shellfish and speciality *paella* are served up on **rue des Bouchers,** just north of Grand-Place. The small restaurants on **quai aux Briques,** in the Ste-Catherine area behind pl. St-Gery, serve cheaper seafood to a local clientele. Just south of Grand-Place, the **rue du Marché-aux-Fromages** has Greek eateries. **Belgaufras** is everywhere and has hot waffles (50-80BF/€1.25-2).

Léon, r. des Bouchers 18 (☎511 14 15). Famed seafood popular with locals and tourists alike. Mussels and chips 600F/€14.90 (enough for 2). Open daily noon-11pm.

Sole d'Italia, r. Grétry 67. Offers huge servings of spaghetti with bread for only 195BF/€4.85. Open daily noon-3pm and 6-11pm.

Zebra, St-Gèry 33-35. This chic cafe is centrally located and serves light, tasty sandwiches and pastas (around 250BF/€6.20). Open daily 10am-1am.

Hemispheres, r. de l'Ecuver 65 (☎513 93 70). Libyan, Turkish, Chinese, and Indian cuisine convene at this summit of great Eastern platters. Vegetarian meals 280-400BF/€6.95-9.95. Open M-F noon-3pm and 6:30-10:30pm, Sa 6:30pm-midnight.

Ultième Hallutinatie, Rue Royale 316. Bring your camera to this splendid stained glass Art Nouveau house and garden. Salads, pastas, and omelettes in the **Tavern** from 250BF/€6.20. Open M-F noon-2:30pm and 6pm-midnight, Sa until 1am, Su closed.

◉ SIGHTS

GRAND-PLACE AND ENVIRONS. One look and you'll understand why Victor Hugo called the gold-trimmed **Grand-Place** "the most beautiful square in the world." A daily flower market and feverish tourist activity add color. At night 800 multi-colored floodlights illuminate the **Town Hall** on the Grand Place, accompanied by loud classical music. *(Apr.-Aug. and Dec. daily around 10 or 11pm.)* Three blocks behind the Town Hall on the corner of r. de l'Etuve and r. du Chêne is Brussels' most giggled-at sight, the **Mannekin Pis,** a statue of an impudent boy (with an apparently gargantuan bladder) steadily urinating. One story goes that a 17th-century mayor promised to build a statue in the position that his lost son was found; another says it commemorates a boy who ingeniously defused a bomb. Locals have created hundreds of outfits for him, competitively dressing him with the ritual coats of their organization or region, each with a little hole for his you-know-what. *(Free. He's always peeing.)*

ART MUSEUMS. The ▧**Musées Royaux des Beaux Arts** houses the **Musée d'Art Ancien,** the **Musée d'Art Moderne,** a sculpture gallery, and temporary exhibitions. The *blue* and *brown* sections of the museum make up the Musee d'Art Ancien, which houses a huge collection by the Flemish masters. The 15th- to 16th-century *blue* section features Bruegel the Elder's *Landscape with the Fall of Icarus;* the 17th- to 18th-century *brown* section showcases the impressive Salle de Rubens, one of the museum's primary attractions. Across the main entrance hall, the *yellow* and *green* sections make up the Musée d'Art Moderne. The 19th-century *yellow* section shows Dutch and Flemish Impressionists alongside paintings by Seurat and Gauguin, portraits by Van Gogh and Gericault, a large Ensor collection, and works by Neoclassicists Ingres, Delacroix, and David, including David's *Death of Marat*. Finally, the 20th-century *green* section, located deep in the basement, offers works by Miró, Picasso, Brussels-based Magritte, and a collection of the latest, cutting-edge works. The panoramic view of Brussels' cityscape from the 4th floor of the 19th-century wing alone is worth the admission fee. *(R. de la Régence 3. M: Parc or port de Namur, a block south of the Parc. ☎508 33 33. Open Tu-Su 10am-5pm. 15th- to 16th- and 19th-century rooms and the Gallery of Sculptures close noon-1pm; 17th- to 18th- and 20th-century rooms close 1-2pm. 150BF/€3.75, students 100BF/€2.50. 1st W of each month free 1-5pm.)* The enormous **Musée du Cinquantenaire (Musées Royaux d'Art et d'Histoire)** covers a wide variety of periods and parts—Roman torsos without heads, Syrian heads without torsos, and Egyptian caskets with feet. The eerily illuminated "Salle au Tresor" is one the museum's main attractions. *(10 parc du Cinquantenaire. M: Mérode. ☎741 72 11. From the station, walk straight through the arch, turn left, go past the doors that appear to be the entrance, and turn left again for the real entrance. Open Tu-Su 10am-5pm. 150BF/€3.75, students 100F/€2.50.)* 20th-century master Baron Victor Horta's graceful home, today the **Musée Horta**, is a skillful application of his Art Nouveau style to a domestic setting. *(25 r. Américaine. M: Louise; walk down av. Louise, bear right on r. Charleroi, and turn left on r. Américaine (15-20min.). ☎543 04 90. Open Tu-Su 2-5:30pm. 200BF/€5.)*

BELGIAN COMIC STRIP CENTRE. This museum in the "Comic Strip Capital of the World" pays homage to *les bandes dessineés* with hundreds of Belgian comics. The **museum library,** in a renovated Art Noveau textile warehouse, features a reproduction of Tintin's rocket ship and works by over 700 artists. For Tintin souvenirs, check out the museum store or the Tintin Boutique near the Grand-Place. *(20 r. des Sables. M: Rogier. ☎219 19 80. From Gare Centrale, take bd. de l'Impératrice until it becomes bd. de Berlaimont, and turn left onto r. des Sables. Open Tu-Su 10am-6pm. 200BF/€5.)*

ATOMIUM AND BRUPARCK. The **Atomium,** a shining 102m monument of aluminum and steel built for the 1958 World's Fair, represents an iron crystal structure magnified 165 billion times. Inside is a **science museum** featuring fauna and minerals from around the world. The Atomium towers over the **Bruparck entertainment complex,** home of the **Kinepolis cinema** and **IMAX,** the largest movie theater in Europe, as well as **Mini-Europe** (a collection of European landmarks in miniature) and the **Oceade** water park. *(Bd. du Centenaire. M: Huysel. ☎474 89 77. Atomium open daily Apr.-Aug. 9am-7:30pm; Sept.-Mar. 10am-5:30pm. 220BF/€5.45. Movies 250BF/€6.20. Mini-Europe open daily Mar.-June 9:30am-5pm; July-Aug. 9:30am-7pm. 380BF/€9.45. Oceade open Apr.-June Tu-F 10am-6pm, Sa-Su 10am-10pm; Sept.-Mar. W-F 10am-6pm, Sa-Su 10am-10pm. 490BF/€12.15)*

OTHER SIGHTS. In the glorious **Galerie St. Hubert,** one block behind the Grand-Place, you can window-shop for everything from square umbrellas to marzipan frogs. Built over six centuries, the magnificent **Cathédral Saint Michel** is an excellent example of the Gothic style and mixes in a little Romanesque and modern architecture for good measure. *(Pl. St-Gudule, just north of Gare Centrale. Open M-F 7am-7pm, Sa-Su 8:30am-7pm. Free.)* The charming hills of **Sablon** are home to antique markets, art gal-

BELGIUM

INTERNATIONAL MAN OF MYSTERY Tintin (pronounced "tan-tan") is the greatest comic-strip hero in the French-speaking world. From Nice to Quebec City, the journalist remains perpetually young to fans who play the hardest of hardball at auctions for Tintin memorabilia. His creator, Georges Rémi (whose pen-name "Hergé," are his initials pronounced backwards) sent him to the Kremlin, Shanghai, the Congo, outer space, and the wilderness of... Chicago. Countless dissertations and novels have been written about Tintin's possible androgyny; many also say that Indiana Jones was Tintin made into a man. But Tintin is more than your average cartoon joe: when former French president Charles de Gaulle was asked whom he feared the most, he replied, "Tintin is my only international competitor."

leries, and cafes. Around **Place au Jeu de Balle,** you can practice the fine art of bargaining at the morning **flea market.** The **European Parliament** has been called Caprice des Dieux—"Whim of the Gods"—perhaps because of its exorbitant cost. *(43 r. Wiertz. M: Schuman. ☎ 284 34 53. Visits M-Th 10am and 5pm, F 10am. Apr. 14-Oct.13 also open Sa 10, 11:30am, and 2:30pm.)* The gorgeous **Botanical Gardens** on Rue Royale sit next to a 12th-century château. *(Open in summer daily 10am-5:30pm; in winter 10am-4pm.)*

🎵 ENTERTAINMENT AND NIGHTLIFE

For info on events, check *What's On,* available from the tourist office. The flagship of Brussels' theater network is the beautiful **Théâtre Royal de la Monnaie,** on pl. de la Monnaie. (M: de Brouckère. Info ☎ (070) 233 939; www.lamonnaie.be. 300-3000BF/ €7.45-74.40). Renowned throughout the world for its opera and ballet, the theater's performance of the opera *Muette de Portici* in August 1830 inspired the audience to take to the streets and begin the revolt that led to Belgium's independence. Experience a distinctly Belgian art form at the **Musée du Théâtre Toone VII,** 21 r. des Bouchers, a 170-year-old puppet theater that stages marionette performances. (☎ 513 54 86. Shows in French; in German, Flemish, or English upon request. Usually Tu-Sa 8:30pm. 400BF/€9.95, students 250BF/€6.20.) In summer, **concerts** are held on the **Grand-Place,** the **Place de la Monnaie,** and in the **Parc de Bruxelles.**

On summer nights, the **Grand-Place** and the **Bourse** come to life with street performers and live concerts. The nightlife in Brussels ranges from catching a drink on a cobblestone street at the Grand-Place to dancing the night away at a raging disco near the Bourse. Today the 19th-century puppet theater **Poechenellekelder,** r. de Chêne 5, across from the Mannekin Pis, is filled with lavishly costumed marionettes and a nice selection of Belgian beers. (Beers from 50BF/€1.25. Open Su-Th noon-midnight, F-Sa noon to 1 or 2am.) **À La Bécasse,** r. de Tabora 11, two of Brussels' oldest and best-known cafes, specialize in the local wheat beer. (Beer 50-90BF/€1.25-2.25. Open daily 10am-midnight.) **L'Archiduc,** 6 r. Dansaert, is a pricey but still casual Art Deco lounge-turned-jazz-bar. (Open daily 4pm-late.) **Le Fuse,** 208 r. Blaes, one of Belgium's trendiest clubs, pays homage to the gods of techno and rave. (Open daily 10pm-late.) Gay men socialize in a mellow atmosphere at **L'Incognito,** 36 r. des Pierres, off r. de Midi. (☎ 513 37 88. Open daily 4pm-dawn.)

📷 DAYTRIPS FROM BRUSSELS

WATERLOO

Bus W leaves pl. Rouppe near Brussels' Gare Midi (every 51min., 105BF/€2.60) and stops at Waterloo Church, across the street from Musée Wellington, at a gas station near Lion's Mound, and at the train station in Braine L'Alleud. Belgian Railways offers a B-excursion ticket, which gives round-trip transit between Brussels Midi (also available from Brussels Nord) and Braine L'Alleud, a bus pass from Braine L'Alleud to Waterloo, and entrance to all sights (710BF/€17.60, students 660BF/€16.40).

At Waterloo, site of the famous Napoleonic battle, war buffs and fans of the diminutive dictator shell out for a glimpse of the town's slice of history. **The Lion's Mound,** 5km outside of town, is a huge hill overlooking the battlefield; nearby, the **Visitors Center** houses a panoramic painting of the battle and a brief movie about Waterloo. (Open Apr.-Sept. daily 9:30am-6:30pm; Oct. 9:30am-5:30pm; Nov.-Feb. 10:30am-4pm; Mar. 10:30am-5pm. Lion's Mound 40BF/€1; with movie and panorama 305BF/ €7.60, students 250BF/€6.20.) In the center of Waterloo, **Musée Wellington,** Chaussée de Bruxelles 147, was the British general's headquarters and has battle artifacts. (Open Apr.-Oct. daily 9:30am-6:30pm; Nov.-Mar. 10:30am-5pm. 100BF/ €2.50, students 80BF/€2.) Next door is the **tourist office,** Chaussée de Bruxelles 149. (☎ 354 99 10. Open Apr. to mid-Nov. daily 9:30am-6:30pm; mid-Nov. to Mar. 10:30am-5pm.) Cheap restaurants cluster around the Lion's Mound.

MECHELEN (MALINES)

Trains arrive from Brussels and Antwerp (both 15min., 120BF/€3).

Historically the ecclesiastical capital of Belgium, Mechelen is best known today for its treasure-filled churches and its grim role in the Holocaust. Down Consciencestr. from the station, the stately **St. Rumbold's Cathedral** features gorgeous stained-glass windows and **St. Rumbold's Tower,** which rises 97m over **Grote Markt** and contains two carillons (sets of 49 bells) that chime out the town's daily rhythm. You can climb the tower with a guide. (M 2:15pm and 7:15pm. 100BF/€2.50.) Early Renaissance buildings, including the **Stadhuis** (city hall), line the Grote Markt. (Open M-Sa 8:30am-5:30pm, Su 2-5:30pm.) The 15th-century **Church of St. John** boasts Rubens's magnificent triptych *The Adoration of the Magi* (1619). The ▨**Jewish Museum of Deportation and Resistance,** 153 Goswin de Stassartstr., is housed in the 18th-century military barracks used as a temporary camp for Jews en route to Auschwitz-Birkenau during the Holocaust. From the Grote Markt, follow Wollemarkt, which becomes Goswin de Stassartstr. (☎(015) 29 06 60. Open Su-Th 10am-5pm, F 10am-1pm. Free.) On your way back to the station, stop by the **botanical gardens** along the canal for a picnic. The **tourist office** in the Stadhuis finds rooms for free. (☎(015) 29 76 55. Open Easter-Oct. M-F 8am-6pm, Sa-Su 9:30am-12:30pm and 1:30-5pm; June-Sept. M until 7pm; Nov.-Easter reduced hours.) **Postal Code:** 2800.

FLANDERS (VLAANDEREN)

Boogie the night away in Antwerp, relax in beautiful Bruges, and sate your castle-cravings at Ghent's Gravensteen in Flanders, the Flemish-speaking part of Belgium. Historically, the delta of the river Schelde at Antwerp provided the region with a major port, and the production and trade of linen, wool, and diamonds created great prosperity. Flanders' Golden Age was during the 16th century, when its commercial centers were among the largest cities in Europe and its innovative artists motivated the Northern Renaissance. Today, the well-preserved Gothic cities of Flanders, rich in art and friendly people, hold Belgium's strongest attractions.

BRUGES (BRUGGE) ☎050

The capital of Flanders is one of the most beautiful cities in Europe, and tourists know it: famed for its lace and native Jan van Eyck, Bruges is the largest tourist attraction in the country. Canals carve their way through rows of stone houses and lead to the breathtaking Gothic Markt. The city remains one of the best-preserved examples of Northern Renaissance architecture. Its beauty belies the destruction sustained in World War I; eight decades after the war, farmers still uncover 200 tons of artillery every year as they plough their fields. In 2002, Bruges will be honored as the "Cultural Capital of Europe" and will host a major celebration of the arts throughout the year (☎44 20 02; info@brugge2002.be; www.brugge2002.be).

⬕ TRANSPORTATION

Trains: Leave from **Stationsplein** (☎38 23 82. Open daily 7am-9pm), 15min. south of the city, for: **Brussels** (1hr., 380BF/€9.45); **Antwerp** (1hr., 395BF/€9.80); **Ghent** (25min., 175BF/€4.35); **Ostend** (17min., 110BF/€2.75); **Zeebrugge** (10min., 80F/€2).

Bike Rental: At the train station (☎30 23 29); 325BF/€8.10 per day, 500BF/€12.40 deposit. **'t Koffieboontje,** Hallestr. 4 (☎33 80 27), off the Markt by the belfry. 325BF/€8.10 per day, 225BF/€5.60 per half-day; student discount. Open daily 9am-10pm. Many hostels and hotels also rent bikes for about 300BF/€7.45 per day. Pick up *5x by bike around Bruges* (50BF/€1.25) at the tourist office for routes and tours.

Hitchhiking: Those hitching to Brussels reportedly take bus #7 to St. Michiels or pick up the highway behind the train station. *Let's Go* does not recommend hitchhiking.

⬧ 🛈 ORIENTATION AND PRACTICAL INFORMATION

Bruges is enclosed by a circular canal, with the train station just beyond its southern extreme. Its historic district is entirely accessible on foot; the other main form of transportation is the local bus system. The dizzying Belfort (belfry) towers high at the center of town, presiding over the handsome square of the Markt.

Tourist Office: Burg 11 (☎44 86 86; toerisme@brugge.be; www.brugge.be), in Burg Square. Head left from the station to 't Zand square, right on Zuidzandstr., and right on Breidelstr. through the Markt (15min.). Books rooms (400BF/€9.95 deposit) and sells maps (25BF/€0.65). Open Apr.-Sept. M-F 9:30am-6:30pm, Sa-Su 10am-noon and 2-6:30pm; Oct.-Mar. M-F 9:30am-5pm, Sa-Su 9:30am-1pm and 2-5:30pm. Office at the train station open 10:30am-1:15pm and 2-5:30pm.

Tours: Quasimodo Tours (☎37 04 70; www.quasimodo.be), leads excellent 30km countryside bike and bus tours to windmills, castles, and WWII bunkers. Bike tours depart mid-Mar. to Sept. daily from the tourist office at the Burg. 650BF/€16.15, under 26 550BF/€13.65. The Triple Treat trip on M, W, F visits medieval castles, with chocolate and beer stops along the way. 1500BF/€37.20, under 26 1200BF/€29.75.

Currency Exchange: Currency exchanges fill the streets around the Markt, but there is no place to change money at the train station.

Luggage Storage: At the train station; 55-130BF/€1.40-3.25. **Lockers** at the tourist office; 50BF/€1.25.

Laundromat: Belfort, Ezelstr. 51, next to Snuffel's Sleep-In (see p. 133). Wash 100-140BF/€2.50-3.50, dry 200-300BF/€5-7.45. Open daily 7am-10pm.

Emergencies: ☎100. **Police,** ☎101. Police station at Hauwerstr. 7 (☎44 88 44).

Internet Access: The Coffee Link, Mariastraat 38 (☎34 99 73), in the Oud Sint-Jon Historic Hospital. 50BF/€1.25 for 15min. Open M-Sa 10am-9:30pm, Su 10am-7:30pm.

Post Office: Hoedenmakerstr. 2. Open M-F 9am-5pm, Tu 9am-7pm. Address mail to be held: FirstName SURNAME, Poste Restante, Hoedenmakerstr. 2, Brugge **8000.**

⌂ ACCOMMODATIONS

Reasonable accommodations are available just a few blocks away from the center, but can be hard to come by on weekends when tourists flock to Bruges.

The Passage, Dweersstr. 26 (☎34 02 32). From the station, cross the street and go left along the path; at the end, bear left on 't Zand, take a right on Zuidzanstr., and take the 1st left onto Dweersstr. Recently remodeled and ideally located. Breakfast 100BF/€2.50. Reception 8:30am-midnight. Closed mid-Jan. for renovations. Dorms 450BF/€11.20; singles 900BF/€22.35; doubles 1400BF/€37.70.

Hotel Lybeer, Korte Vuldersstr. 31 (☎33 43 55; hotel.lybeer@pandora.be). From the station bear left to the traffic lights, cross the street in front, and go left along the path. At the end of the path bear left onto 't Zand then turn right onto Zuidanstr. Take the 1st right onto Hoogste van Brugge, followed by an immediate left. Ideal location. Old-fashioned charm with modern comforts. Backpacker-friendly. Free **Internet.** Breakfast included. Reception 8am-10:30pm. Singles 900BF/€22.50; doubles 1600BF/€39.70; triples 2175BF/€53.95; quads 2800BF/€69.45.

't Keizershof, Oostmeers 126 (☎33 87 28; hotel.keizershof@12move.be). From the station, walk to the traffic lights on the left, cross the street, and follow signs pointing to the Memling Museum and Oud St. Jan. The hotel is 80m up on your left. Pretty, comfortable rooms on a quiet street. Breakfast included. Laundry 300BF/€7.45. Singles 988BF/€24.5; doubles 1452BF/€36; triples 2178BF/€54; quads 2602BF/€64.5.

Charlie Rockets, Hoogstr. 19 (☎33 06 60; info@charlierockets.com). From Markt follow Breidelstr., which becomes Hoogstr. Central location. Packed restaurant-bar. Breakfast 100BF/€2.50. Reception 8am-4am. Dorms 1980BF/€49.10-2790BF/€69.20; doubles 1500BF/€37.20 with breakfast included.

Bauhaus International Youth Hotel, Langestr. 133-137 (☎34 10 93; info@bauhaus.be). Take bus #6 or 16 to "Gerechtshof" and go right about 50m.; it's on your left.

Cybercafe and popular bar. Nearby laundromat. Breakfast 80BF/€2. Reception 8am-2am. Dorms 380BF/€9.45; singles 550-900BF/€13.65-22.35; doubles 1000-1400BF/€24.80-34.70; triples 1350-1950BF/€33.50-48.35.

Snuffel's Sleep-In, Ezelstr. 49 (☎33 31 33). From Markt, follow St-Jakobsstr. (bearing right at Moerstr.), which becomes Ezelstr. (10min.). Or take bus #3 or 13 from the station to "Normaalschool." **Internet**. Breakfast 80BF/€2. Sheets 80BF/€2. Reception 8am-6am. Snug dorms 350-390BF/€8.70-9.70; quads 1960BF/€48.60.

Europa International Youth Hostel (HI), Baron Ruzettelaan 143 (☎35 26 79; brugge@vjh.be). Quiet, away from the Markt and the nightlife. Turn right from the station and follow Buiten Katelijnevest to Baron Ruzettelaan (15min.). Or take bus #2 to "Wantestraat." Breakfast included. Sheets 125BF/€3.10. Key deposit 100BF/€2.50. Reception 7:30-10am and 1-11pm. 430BF/€10.70; nonmembers 530BF/€13.15.

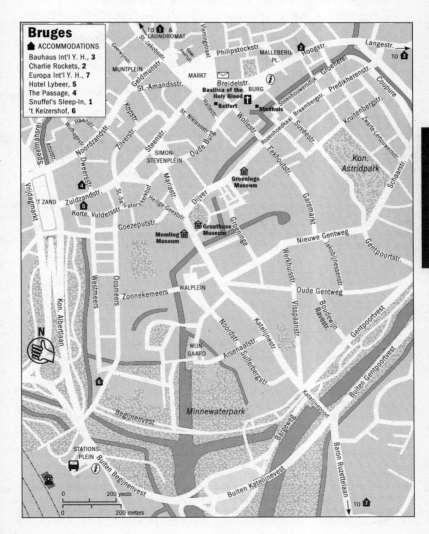

Bruges

⌂ ACCOMMODATIONS
Bauhaus Int'l Y. H., **3**
Charlie Rockets, **2**
Europa Int'l Y. H., **7**
Hotel Lybeer, **5**
The Passage, **4**
Snuffel's Sleep-In, **1**
't Keizershof, **6**

BELGIUM

Camping: St-Michiel, Tillegemstr. 55 (☎38 08 19). From the station, take bus #7 to "Jagerstr." Go left on Jagerstr., bear left at the 1st intersection, staying on Jagerstr., and go around the rotary to Tillegemstr. 115BF/€2.85 per person, 135BF/€3.35 per tent.

🍴 FOOD

Splurge on Belgium's famous *mosselen* (mussels), which at 450-500BF/€11.20-12.40 often include appetizers and dessert, even in the Markt. From the Burg, cross the river and turn left to buy fresh seafood at the **Vismarkt.** For cheaper fare, head to **Nopri Supermarket,** Noordzandstr. 4, just off 't Zand. (Open M-Sa 9:30am-6:30pm.)

Ganzespel, Ganzestr. 37, serves up hearty portions of simple food. From Burg, turn up Hoogstr. and take the 2nd right after the river. Meals 245-530BF/€6.10-13.15. Quiche 230BF/€5.70. Open W-F noon-2:30pm and 6-10pm, Su noon-10pm.

The Gran Kaffee de Passage, Dweerstraat 26-28, prepares traditional Belgian cuisine (180-450BF/€4.50-11.20). Open daily 5pm-late.

Café Craenenburg, Markt 16. Grab a quick snack on the terrace (390-495BF/€9.70-12.30) and watch the passersby. Open daily 7am-1am.

Het Brood, Philipstockstraat 21. Organic yogurts, sandwiches, and salads. Open M and W-Sa 7am-6pm, Su 8am-6pm.

De Belegde Boterham, Kleine St. Amandstr 5, off Steenstr. Salads 195-395BF/€4.85-9.80, sandwiches 195-295BF/€4.85-7.35. Open M-Sa noon-5pm.

👁 SIGHTS

Small enough to be thoroughly explored by short walks and lined with gorgeous canals, Bruges is best seen on foot. The tourist office leads **walking tours** (July-Aug. daily 3pm; 150BF/€3.75). **Boat tours** also ply Bruges' canals (every 30min., 190BF/€4.70); ask at the tourist office or pick up tickets at the booth on the bridge between Wollestr. and Dijver. The **museum combination ticket** covers the Gruuthuse, the Groeninge Museum, the Arentshuis, and the Stadhuis (400BF/€9.95).

MARKT AND BURG. Over the **Markt** looms the 88m medieval bell tower of the **Belfort.** Climb its dizzying 366 steps during the day for a great view; return at night when the tower serves as the city's torch. *(Open daily 9:30am-5pm. Tickets sold until 4:15pm. Bell concerts M, W, Sa 9pm; Su 2:15pm. 100BF/€2.50, students 80BF/€2.)* Behind the Markt, the **Burg** square is dominated by the flamboyant Gothic façade of the medieval **Stadhuis** (City Hall), filled with paintings and wood carvings. Upstairs is a gilded hall where many Bruges residents still get married. *(Open daily 9:30am-5pm. 150BF/€3.75.)* Hidden in the corner of the Burg next to the Stadhuis, the **Basilica of the Holy Blood** houses a relic that allegedly holds the blood of Christ. *(Open daily Apr.-Sept. 9:30am-noon and 2-6pm; Oct.-Mar. 10am-noon and 2-4pm; closed W afternoon. Free. Worship of relic F 8:30-10am (ground floor), 10-11am and 3-4pm (upstairs). 40BF/€1.)*

MUSEUMS. From the Burg, follow Wollestr. left and head right on Dijver to reach the **Groeninge Museum** for a comprehensive collection of Belgian and Dutch paintings from the last six centuries, featuring works by Bruges-based Jan Van Eyck, Bruges-born Hans Memling, and the master of medieval macabre himself, Hieronymous Bosch. *(Dijver 12. Open daily 9:30am-5pm. In winter closed Tu. Last tickets sold at 4:30pm. 250BF/€6.20, students 200BF/€5.)* Next door, the **Gruuthuse Museum** houses an amazing collection of weapons, tapestries, musical instruments, and coins that date back to the 6th century. The spare room in back is perhaps the biggest treasure in the museum—you can sneak a peek into the Church of Our Lady (see below) next door. *(Dijver 17. Open Apr.-Sept. daily 9:30am-5pm; Oct.-Mar. closed Tu. 130BF/€3.25, students 100BF/€2.50.)* Continue as Dijver becomes Gruuthusestr. and walk under the stone archway to enter the **Memling Museum,** housed in **St. John's Hospital,** one of the oldest surviving medieval hospitals in Europe. *(Mariastr. 38. Open Apr.-Sept. daily 9:30am-5pm; Oct.-Mar. Th-Tu 9:30am-12:30pm and 2-5pm. 80BF/€2, students 50BF/€1.25.)*

BELGIUM

OTHER SIGHTS. The 13th- to 16th-century **Church of Our Lady,** at Mariastr. and Gruuthusestr. near the Groeninge Museum, contains Michelangelo's *Madonna and Child* as well as medieval frescoed tomb fragments and the 16th-century mausoleums of Mary of Burgundy and Charles the Bold. *(Open daily 10am-noon and 2-5pm. Church free; tomb fragment viewing 70BF/€1.75, students 35BF/€0.90.)* From the Church, turn left, follow Mariastr., and turn right onto Stoofstr., where you will come to Walplein. Cross the footbridge to enter the Beguinage, a grassy cove encircled by the picturesque residences of medieval cloistered women, inhabited today by Benedictine nuns. *(Open Mar.-Nov. daily 10am-noon and 1:45-5pm; in summer until 6pm. Gate closes at sunset. 60BF/€1.50.)* The 230-year-old windmill **Sint-Janshuismolen,** is still used to grind flour. From the Burg, follow Hoogstr., which becomes Langestr., and turn left at the end on Kruisvest. *(Open May-Sept. daily 9:30am-12:30pm and 1:30-5pm. 40BF/€1, students 20BF/€0.50.)* The **Minnewater** (Lake of Love), on the southern end of the city, has a less-than-romantic history as the site of ammunition dump, but you'd never know it from the picnickers lounging happily in the beautiful park.

🎵 ENTERTAINMENT

The best nighttime entertainment is wandering through the city's romantic streets and over its cobblestoned bridges, but if that isn't enough, take your pick from the 300 varieties of beer at **'t Brugs Beertje,** Kemelstr. 5, off Steenstr. (☎33 96 16. Open M 4pm-1am, F-Sa 4pm-2am, Su 4pm-1am.) Next door, the **Dreipelhuisje** serves tantalizingly fruity *jenever*, a flavored Dutch gin; beware that the flavors mask a very high alcohol content. (Open M-F 6pm-midnight, Sa-Su 6pm-2am.) **Rica Rokk,** 't Zand 6, is popular with local twenty-somethings. (Beers from 50BF/€1.25. No cover. Open daily 8am-5am.) Next door, **The Break,** 't Zand 9, has pulsing music and glammed up faces. (Beer from 55BF/€1.40. No cover. Open M-Sa 10am-late, Su 1pm-late.)

🎯 DAYTRIPS FROM BRUGES

ZEEBRUGGE AND OSTEND

For info on ferries from Ostend to the UK, see p. 52. Get ferry tickets from travel agents, at ports, or in the Ostend train station. Trains run to Zeebrugge (15min., 3 per hr., 150BF/€3.75) and Ostend (15min., 3 per hr., 110BF/€2.75).

The towns along the North Sea coast of Belgium make a lovely excursion. Zeebrugge boasts an international port, a large fish market, and a promenade that extends far into the sea. Ostend has a popular beach lined with restaurants and bars. To get from the Ostend train station to the **De Ploate Youth Hostel (HI),** Langestr. 82, cross the bridge directly in front of the station, turn right on Visserkaai, follow the Promenade for 10min., and turn left on Langestr. (☎(059) 80 52 97; deploate@travel.to; http://travel.to/deploate. Reception 7:30am-midnight. Curfew midnight. Dorms 510BF/€12.65, nonmembers 610BF/€15.15.)

ANTWERP (ANTWERPEN, ANVERS)   ☎03

Antwerp is distinctly cosmopolitan. Its main street, the **Meir,** features windows showcasing trendy clothing, diamond jewelry, and delectable chocolate; in the pubs at the end of the Meir, beer flows so cheaply that crowds pass another round in lieu of breakfast. Take a stroll down the promenade by the **Schelde River** to see the 13th-century **Steen Castle,** which houses the National Maritime Museum (open Tu-Su 10am-5pm; 150BF/€4), or walk along the **Cogels Osylei** past fanciful Art Nouveau mansions. In the city's historic center, the cathedral bells chime in harmony with the accordion music of the street performers. The **Cathedral of Our Lady,** Groenpl. 21, boasts a magnificent Gothic tower and Rubens's *Descent from the Cross.* (Open M-F 10am-5pm, Sa 10am-3pm, Su 1-4pm. 80BF/€2.) Nearby, the dignified Renaissance **Stadhuis** (City Hall) stands in Grote Markt. (Call 203 95 33 for tour times. 30BF/€30.75.) The **Mayer van den Bergh Museum,** Lange Gasthuisstr. 19, fea-

BELGIUM

tures a formerly private collection and showcases Bruegel's *Mad Meg.* (Open Tu-Su 10am-5pm. 150BF/€3. F free.) The **Rubens Huis,** Wapper 9-11, off Meir, was built by Antwerp's favorite son and is filled with his works. (Open Tu-Su 10am-5pm. 200BF/€5. F free.) The **Royal Museum of Fine Arts,** Leopold De Waelpl. 1-9, has one of the world's finest collections of Old Flemish Master paintings. (Open Tu-Su 10am-5pm. 150BF/€3.75, students 120BF/€3; F free.) Pick up *Play* at the tourist office for information on Antwerp's 300 bars and nightclubs. The streets behind the cathedral stay crowded; **Bierland,** Korte Nieuwstr. 28, is a popular student hang-out. (Open Su-Th 9am-noon, F-Sa 8am-2am.) Next to the cathedral, over 600 Flemish religious figurines hang out with drinkers at **Elfde Gebod,** Torfburg 10. (Beer 70-120BF/€1.75-3. Open daily noon-1am, Sa-Su until 2am.) Sample local *elixir d'Anvers* in the candle-lit, 15th-century **Pelgrom,** Pelgrimstr. 15. (Open daily noon-late.) Gay nightlife clusters on **Van Schoonhovenstr.,** just north of Centraal Station.

Trains go from Berchem Station to: Amsterdam (2hr., 970BF/€24); Brussels (45-53min., 200BF/€5); Rotterdam (1½hr., 700BF/€17.35). To get from the station to the **tourist office,** Grote Markt 15, take tram #8 to "Groenplaats." (☎232 01 03. Open M-Sa 9am-6pm, Su 9am-5pm). The **New International Youth Hotel,** Provinciestr. 256, is centrally located. To get there, take tram #2, 11, or 15 to "Plantin," go under the bridge onto Baron Joostensstr., take a right onto Van Den Nestlei, and then take a left onto Kruikstr. followed by an immediate right onto Provinciestr. (☎230 05 22. Breakfast and sheets included. Reception 8am-11pm. No lockout. 8-bed dorms 3760BF/€93.25; singles 1020BF/€25.30; doubles 1560BF/€38.70; quads 2560BF/€63.50.) To reach the modern **Jeugdherberg Op-Sinjoorke (HI),** Eric Sasselaan 2, take tram #8 or 11 to "Groenplaats," then take tram #2 (dir.: "Hoboken") to "Bouwcentrum." From the tram stop, walk toward the fountain, take a left and follow the yellow signs. (☎238 02 73. Breakfast included. Sheets 135BF/€3.35. Lockout 10am-4pm. Dorms 430BF/€10.70, nonmembers 530BF/€13.15; doubles 585BF/€14.50.) To get to **Scoutel,** Stoomstr. 3, from the station, turn left on Pelikaanstr., left on Langekievitstr., and right on Stoomstr.; the entrance faces the bridge. (☎226 46 06. Breakfast included. Reception 8am-7pm. Singles 1050F/€26, under 26 950BF/€23.55; doubles 1610BF/€39.95, 1410BF/€34.95; triples 1995BF/€49.95, 1755BF/€43.55.) Near the Jeugdherberg Op-Sinjoorke, there is **camping** at **Sted. Kamp Vogelzangan.** Follow the directions to the hotel; when you get off the tram, face the Bouwventrum, turn right, walk away from the fountain, cross the street to take the first left, and the campground will be on your left after the gates. (Open Apr.-Sept. 65BF/€1.65 per person, 35BF/€0.90 per car, 35BF/€0.90 per tent, 85BF/€2.15 per tent with electricity.) **Ultimatum,** on the Grote Markt at Suikerrui, has outdoor seating and dishes from Norway, Russia, and Morocco. (Open daily 11am-late. Kitchen closes at 11pm.) Middle Eastern veggies are at **Mama's Garden,** Oude Korenmarkt 41. (Open Su-Th noon-5am, F-Sa noon-7am.) After a night of partying, head to the **Kiekekot,** Grote Markt 35, for chicken at 4am. (Open M, W, Th 6pm-4am; F 6pm-6am; Su 12:30pm-4am; closed Tu and Sa.) **Postal Code:** 2000.

GHENT (GENT)   ☎09

At the heart of the Flemish textile industry, Ghent prospered throughout the Middle Ages. Today, many of its grand buildings and monuments stand in proud testament to its former grandeur. During the "10 Days Off" celebration, also known as the **Gentse Feesten** (Ghent festivities; July 20-29, 2002; ☎269 09 45), which commemorates the first vacation granted to sweatshop workers in 1860, the streets fill with performers, live music, carnival rides, and great food and beer; the festivities also bring 11 nights of international DJs. The **Leie canal** runs through the center of the city and wraps around the **Gravensteen,** St-Veerlepl. 11, a sprawling medieval fortress whose shadowy halls and spiral staircases will give you chills before you even reach the crypt, dungeon, and torture chamber. (Open daily Apr.-Aug. 9am-6pm; Sept.-Mar. 9am-5pm. 200BF/€5, students 100BF/€2.50.) The castle is near the historic **Parter-shol** quarter, a network of well-preserved 16th- to 18th-century houses. Wind your way up the towering **Belfort** to experience some major vertigo. (Open mid-Mar. to mid-Nov. daily 10am-12:30pm and 2-5:30pm. 100BF/€2.50.) The **Stadhuis** (Town

Hall) is a mix of Gothic and Renaissance architecture. A block away on Limburg-str., the 14th- to 16th-century **Saint Bavo's Cathedral** boasts van Eyck's *Adoration of the Mystic Lamb* and Rubens's *The entry of St. Bavo into the monastery.* (Cathedral open Apr.-Oct. daily 8:30am-6pm; Nov.-Mar. M-Sa 8:30am-5pm, Su 2-7pm. Free. Crypt and *Mystic Lamb* open M-Sa 9:30am-5pm, Su 1-5pm. 100BF/ €2.50, audio tour included; children 50BF/€1.25, audio tour excluded.) Head to Citadel Park, near the center, to see the 14th- to 16th-century Flemish school collection at the **Museum voor Schone Kunsten** (Museum of Fine Arts). (Open Tu-Su 9:30am-5pm. 100BF/€2.50, students 50BF/€1.25.) Also located in Citadel Park is the **SMAK,** the **Stedelijk Museum voor Actuele Kunst** (Municipal Museum for Contemporary Art. Open Tu-Su 10am-6pm; 200BF/€5, students 150BF/€3.75). **Vooruit,** a huge Art Deco bar on St-Pietersnieuwstr., was once the meeting place of the Socialist Party and was later occupied by Nazis in WWII. (Open daily 11:30am-10pm.) Beer lovers flock to **Dulle Grief,** on the Vrijdagmarkt, for the 1.2L "Max" for 350BF/ €8.70. (Open M 4:30pm-12:30am, Tu-Sa noon-12:30am, Su noon-7:30pm.)

   Trains run from Sint-Pietersstation (accessible by tram #1 or 12) to Brussels (40min., 245BF/€6.10) and Bruges (20min., 175BF/€4.35). The **tourist office** is in the crypt of the belfry, Botermarkt 17a. (☎266 52 32. Open Apr.-Oct. daily 9:30am-6:30pm; Nov.-Mar. 9:30am-4:30pm.) **De Draeke (HI),** St-Widostr. 11, in the shadow of a castle, blends into downtown Ghent despite its modernity. From the station, take tram #1, 10, or 11 to "Gravensteen" (15min.). Facing the castle, head left, then head right on Gewad and right again on St-Widostr. (☎233 70 50. Breakfast included. Sheets 125BF/€3.15. Reception daily 7:30am-11pm. Dorms 510BF/€12.65; singles 820BF/€20.40; doubles 1200BF/€29.75; nonmembers add 100BF/€2.50.) **The Hotel Flandria,** Barrestr. 3, offers big breakfasts. (☎223 06 26. Reception 7am-9pm. Singles 1600BF/€39.70; doubles 1800-1900BF/€44.70-47.10.) To get to **Camping Blaarmeersen,** Zuiderlaan 12, take bus #9 from Sint-Pietersstation and ask the driver to connect you to bus #38 to Blaarmeersen. When you get off, take the first street on your left to the end. (☎221 53 99. Open Mar. to mid-Oct. 130BF/€3.25 per person, 140BF/€3.50 per tent.) Good meals run about 250BF/€6.20; try around **Korenmarkt,** in front of the post office; **Vrijdagmarkt,** a few blocks from the town hall; and **St-Pietersnieuwstr.,** down by the university. Students meet up at **Magazyne,** Bredestraat 159, for cheap, hearty fare in the historic district. (Lunch served from 12-2pm, dinner from 6-10pm.) The **Fritz Tearoom,** Korte Dagsteeg Walpoortstr., has hot sandwiches, pasta, and great waffles. (Open daily 8am-6:30pm.) **Postal Code:** 9000.

YPRES (IEPER)   ☎57

"We are the dead. Short days ago/We lived, felt dawn, saw sunset glow/Loved and were loved, and now we lie/In Flanders fields." Canadian soldier John McCrae wrote these famous words during WWI at the Battle of Ypres Salient. Ypres, once a medieval textile center, was completely destroyed by the long combat; reconstruction took more than 40 years. Today the town is surrounded by British cemeteries and filled with memorial sites, drawing victims' families as well as British tourist and school groups. In **Flanders Field Museum,** Grote Markt 34, documents and films attempt to convey the triumphs and the tribulations of the Great War. (Open daily Apr.-Sept. 10am-6pm; Oct.-Mar. until 5pm. 250BF/€6.20.) The museum is housed in the **Cloth Hall,** a grand medieval Gothic building—formerly used for textile production—that presides over **Grote Markt,** the town center. Next door stands **St. Martin's Cathedral,** another splendid example of the Gothic style. Cross the street in front of St. Martin's and head right to reach the Anglican **St. George's Memorial Church,** Elverdingsestr. 1, constructed in 1928-1929 in tribute to war victims; each brass plaque and kneeling pillow commemorates a specific individual or unit. (Both churches free and open to the public except during services.) Diagonally across Grote Markt from St. Martin's is the somber **Menin Gate,** on Menenstr., upon which are inscribed the names of 54,896 British soldiers who were lost in the trenches and did not receive burial. At 8pm each evening, the **Last Post** bugle ceremony honors those who defended Ypres during the historic battle. Around Ypres there are over 150 **Brit-**

ish cemeteries. From Menin Gate, take the **Rose Coombs Walk** to visit the nearby **Ramparts Cemetery,** where row upon row of white crosses face the river.

Trains run from the train station to: Bruges via Courtrai (2hr., 340BF/€8.45) and Ghent (1hr., 305BF/€7.60). The **Visitors Center,** housed in the Cloth Hall in Grote Markt, provides information on surrounding cemeteries and memorials. To get there from the train station, head straight down Stationsstr., turn left onto Tempelstr., and then right onto Boterstr. (☎22 85 84. Open Apr.-Sept. M-Sa 9am-6pm, Su 10am-6pm; Oct.-Mar. M-Sa 9am-5pm, Su 10am-5pm.) The **Old Tom** hotel, Grote Markt 8, has charming but pricey rooms in an ideal location. (☎20 15 41. Singles 1950BF/€48.40; doubles 2300BF/€57; triples 3150BF/€78.) Many inexpensive restaurants line the Grote Markt.

WALLONIE

The towns in the **Ardennes** offer a relaxing hideaway, with hiking trails that lead through deep forests to impressive citadels and cool caves. The most exceptional portion of the Belgian Ardennes lies in the southeast corner, where gorgeous trainrides sweep through peaceful farmland. Although nature lovers will probably want to spend a night in this part of the Wallonie wilderness, urban addicts pressed for time can always enjoy the scenery on their way to Brussels, Paris, or Luxembourg.

TOURNAI   ☎069

The first city liberated by Allied forces, Tournai's medieval old town escaped major damage in WWII. Once a Roman trading post and the original capital of France, Tournai is a peaceful town less touristed than its Flemish counterparts. The city's most spectacular sight is its Romanesque and Gothic **cathedral,** with a **treasure room** that houses medieval goldware and some of St. Thomas à Becket's threads. (Open Apr.-Oct. daily 9am-noon and 2-6pm; off-season until 4pm. Treasure room 30BF/€0.75.) The stunning Art Nouveau building of the **Museum of Fine Arts,** Enclos St-Martin, houses a fine collection of Flemish paintings. (Open daily 10am-noon and 2-5:30pm. 120BF/€3, students 80BF/€2.)

Trains run from the station at pl. Cromberg (☎88 62 23) to Brussels-Midi (1hr., 350BF/€8.70). To get to the **tourist office,** 14 Vieux Marché Aux Poteries, exit the station, walk straight to the city center (15min.), and go around the left side of the cathedral. (☎22 20 45. Open M-F 9am-6pm, Sa 10am-1pm and 3-6pm, Su 10am-noon and 2-6pm.) To get to the **Auberge de Tournai,** r. St-Martin, continue straight up the hill from the tourist office or take bus #7 or 88 (40BF/€1) from the station. (☎21 61 36. Sheets 130BF/€3.25. Reception 9am-noon and 5-10pm. Dorms 430BF/€10.70, nonmembers 530BF/€13.15.) The area around **Grand-Place** has cheap eats.

NAMUR   ☎081

The quiet city of **Namur,** in the heart of Wallonie, is the last sizable outpost before the wilderness of the Ardennes. The nearby **hiking, biking, caving,** and **kayaking** options make it the best base for exploring the area. The foreboding **citadel,** on top of a rocky hill to the south, was built by the Spanish in the Middle Ages, expanded by the Dutch in the 19th century, the site of a bloody battle in WWI, and occupied until 1978. Climb up or take a **mini-bus** from the tourist office at Sq. Leopold and r. de Grognon (every hr., 40BF/€1); the bus will let you off at the Citadel, where you can pick up a **tour** of the fortress. (Open daily 11am-5pm. 210BF/€5.25.)

Trains link Namur to Brussels (1hr., 245BF/€6.10). Two **tourist offices,** one a few blocks left of the train station at place de la Gare, facing r. Godefroid, and the other in the **Hôtel de Ville,** help plan excursions. (Train station ☎22 28 49, Hôtel de Ville ☎24 64 44; www.ville.namur.be. Both open daily 9:30am-6pm.) To reach the friendly **Auberge Félicien Rops (HI),** 8 av. Félicien Rops, take bus #3 directly to the door, or take bus #4 and ask the driver to let you off. (☎22 36 88; namur@laj.be. **Bikes** 500BF/€12.40 per day. Breakfast included. Sheets 110BF/€2.75. Laundry 260BF/€6.45. Reception 7:30am-1am. Lockout 11am-3pm. Dorms 440BF/€10.95; singles 820BF/€20.35; doubles 1210BF/€30; nonmembers add 100BF/€2.50.) To

BELGIUM

camp at **Les Trieux,** 99 r. des Tris, 6km away in Malonne, take bus #6. (☎ 44 55 83. Open Apr.-Oct. 85BF/€2.15 per person or per tent.) If you're in the mood for Italian, step into the 15th-century cellar of **La Cava,** r. de la Monnaie 20. (Main dishes 220-380BF/€5.45-9.45. Open daily noon-11pm.) Try the regional Ardennes ham (from 70F/€1.75) at one of the sandwich stands throughout the city.

DINANT   ☎ 082

The tiny town of Dinant boasts wonders out of proportion to its size. The imposing **citadel** towers over the Meuse river. Ride the cable car up over the forest or brave the steep steps along the fortress. (☎ 22 36 70. Citadel 19F/€0.50. Open daily 10am-6pm. Mandatory tours in French and Dutch every 20min.) Bring a sweater to the tour of the chilly, cascade-filled caves of **La Grotte Merveilleuse,** route de Phillippe-ville 142. To reach the Grotte from the citadel, cross the bridge and take the second left onto rte. de Phillippeville. (Open Apr.-Oct. daily 10am-6pm; Mar. and Nov. 11am-5pm. 190BF/€4.75. Mandatory tours in French, Dutch, and English every hr., on the hr.) Dinant is also a good base for climbing and kayaking excursions. **Dakota Raid Adventure,** r. Saint Roch 17, leads rock-climbing daytrips in the area. (☎ 22 32 43. Open daily 10am-5pm.) Dinant is accessible by **train** from Brussels (1½hr., 360BF/€8.95) or by **bike** from Namur; on summer weekends, take a one-way river cruise from Namur (3½hr.). The **tourist office,** Quai Cadoux 8, helps plan outdoor activities (including kayaking trips) and books rooms. (☎ 22 28 70.) With your back to the train station, turn right, take the first left, and the next left will land you there.

▶ **DAYTRIPS FROM NAMUR: HAN-SUR-LESSE AND ROCHEFORT. Han-sur-Lesse**'s most famous treasures are its caves, particularly the **Grotte de Han,** and its wild animal reserve. The caves, known as **grottoes,** boast large caverns with ancient rock formations. They can be seen on the combined tram-foot-boat trip sold at the **Domain of the Grottoes** office, 2 r. J. Lamote. (☎ (084) 37 72 13. 395BF/€9.80. Small tip expected for tours given in English.) Safari-cars voyage through the **Wild Animal Reserve** of a local Han estate, where you can see cross-bred version of extinct animals, once typical in the Northern Ardennes and resurrected with a little help from the international animal gene pool, producing extremely hairy mules, small horses, and lots of wild pigs. (290BF/€7.20; purchase at tourist office.) Buses and safari-cars pick you up outside the Domain for the respective expeditions. (Apr. every hr. 10am-noon and 1:30-4:30pm; May-June every 30min. 10am-noon and 1:30-4:30pm; July-Aug. every 15min. or 30min. 10-11:30am and 1-5:30pm.)

Across the street from the Domain, the **tourist office,** 1 Place Theo Lannoy, sells maps of Han's five **hiking trails** for 100BF/€2.50. All trails are manageable for able walkers, although two involve steep peaks. (☎ (084) 37 75 96. Open daily 9:30am-4pm. Closed weekends in Jan.) Han has neither train station nor bank machine. To get to Han, take the **train** from Namur to Jemelle (40min., every 40min., 250BF/€6.20) and then **bus** #29 from the Jemelle train station (every hr., 63BF/€1.60).

Nearby **Rochefort** features the impressive ruins of a château as well as some spectacular caves. This little town is very French, so you'll likely have to dust off that pocket dictionary of yours. Hike up to the crumbled **Château Comtal** for a breathtaking view of the Northern Ardennes, and then visit the archeological museum perched alongside. (☎ (084) 21 44 09; malagne@skynet.be. Site open daily 10am-6pm. 60BF/€1.50.) The **Grotte de Lorette** is the most famous cave in town. (☎ (084) 21 20 80. Tours June-Aug. every 30-45min. 10am-5pm; Feb.-Apr. and Sept.-Nov. every 1½hr. 10am-4:30pm.) The **tourist office,** 5 r. de Behogne, provides more information on Rochefort's attractions. (☎ (084) 34 51 72; rochefort.tourisme@skynet.be.) To reach Rochefort, take the **train** from Namur to Jemelle (40min., every 40min., 250BF/€6.20), and then **bus** #29 from Jemelle (43BF/€1.10).

BELGIUM

BRITAIN

BRITISH POUNDS

US$1 = UK£0.69	UK£1 = US$1.44
CDN$1 = UK£0.45	UK£1 = CDN$2.23
IR£1 = UK£0.80	UK£1 = IR£1.25
AUS$1 = UK£0.37	UK£1 = AUS$2.71
NZ$1 = UK£0.30	UK£1 = NZ$3.30
ZAR1 = UK£0.08	UK£1 = ZAR11.99
EUR€1 = UK£0.63	UK£1 = EUR€1.58

PHONE CODE   Country Code: 44. International dialing prefix: 00.

Take pity on "this earth of majesty, this seat of Mars." After Britain (pop 57.9 million; 230,681 sq. km) founded modern democracy, led the Industrial Revolution, spread colonies across the globe, and helped stave off Nazi Europe in World War II, a former colony displaced it as the world's economic power. Indeed, the last century has not been kind to the Empire, especially now that her once proud dominions of Northern Ireland and Scotland have gained fledgling autonomy. Travelers should be aware that names hold political force. "Great Britain" refers to England, Scotland, and Wales; it's neither accurate nor polite to call a Scot or Welshman "English." The political term "United Kingdom" refers to these nations as well as Northern Ireland; *Let's Go* uses the term "Britain" to refer to England, Scotland, and Wales because of legal, geographical, and currency distinctions. At first glance, Britain may not seem exotic enough for more than a cursory visit, but allow time for medieval castles, rugged coasts, sweeping greenery, and eerie prehistoric monuments that hearken back to another era. For more detailed coverage of Britain and London, pore over *Let's Go: Britain and Ireland 2002* or *Let's Go: London 2002.*

SUGGESTED ITINERARIES

THREE DAYS Spend it all in **London** (p. 154), the city of tea, royalty, and James Bond. After a stroll through **Hyde Park,** head to **Buckingham Palace** for the changing of the guard. View the renowned collections of the **British Museum** and the **National Gallery.** Spend a night at the **Royal National Theatre** and pub it in the **East End.**

ONE WEEK Begin in **Oxford** (1 day, p. 196) and travel north to Scotland for one day in **Glasgow** (p. 240). Then head over for two days in lively **Edinburgh** (p. 233) before chugging back to **London** (3 days).

BEST OF BRITAIN, THREE WEEKS Start in **London** (4 days), where you'll spin from museums to theatres to clubs all in a day. Take in the mysterious pillars at **Stonehenge** (1 day, p. 191) and move on to **Oxford** (1 day) to tour the colleges

that have housed prime ministers, authors, and famous scientists. Then stop by **Cheltenham** and amble through the rolling hills of the **Cotswolds** (1 day, p. 202). Head to Shakespeare's home town of **Stratford-upon-Avon** (1 day, p. 203), and then on to **Conwy** and **Caernarfon** (2 days, p. 231) for their castles. Spend some time wandering the streets of the Beatles' home town, **Liverpool** (2 days, p. 214), before heading to **Manchester** for its nightlife (1 day, p. 213). Move on to **Glasgow** (1 day) and nearby **Loch Lomond** (1 day, p. 245). Swing by the **Isle of Arran** (1 day, p. 244) for rural diversions; you'll need the rest before exuberant **Edinburgh** (3 days). Head to the **Lake District** (2 days, p. 221), historic **York** (1 day, p. 216), and walk the halls of **Cambridge** (1 day, p. 207).

BRITAIN

LIFE AND TIMES

HISTORY AND POLITICS

EARLY INVADERS (3100 BC-AD 597)

The stone circles at **Stonehenge** and **Avebury** (see p. 192) bear mute witness to the isle's earliest inhabitants, whose peace was shattered by various Celtic and Roman invasions. The Romans under Julius Caesar proved victorious when he invaded in 55 BC and occupied southern Britain until AD 410, establishing **Londinium** as the Roman Empire's farthest outpost. The fierce resistance of the Pictish tribes in the north inspired the Romans to construct **Hadrian's Wall** (c. AD 122)—an edifice 112km long and 3.6m high—in an effort to limit the northern threat. The 4th century AD brought the decline of the Roman Empire, leaving Britain vulnerable to raids from still more foreigners. The Germanic Angles, Saxons, and Jutes established settlements and kingdoms alongside those of the resilient Celts.

CHRISTIANITY AND THE NORMANS (597-1154)

Roman Christianity officially arrived in 597 when the eager missionary **St. Augustine** successfully converted King Æthelbert of Kent and founded England's first church, in Canterbury (see p. 187). Its spread was immortalized by the **Venerable Bede** in 731 with his *Ecclesiastical History of the English People*, in which he became the first to systematically employ the Anno Domini (AD) system of dating. Relative peace ensued until 1066, when William I (better known as **William the Conqueror**) of Normandy invaded England, winning the pivotal **Battle of Hastings**, and succeeded as King of England. William promptly set about cataloguing his new English acquisitions in the epic sheepskin **Domesday Book,** completed in 1088. This compilation of all landholders and their possessions served as the starting point of the written history of most English towns and introduced the island to **feudalism**.

PLANTAGENETS AND TUDORS (1154-1547)

Henry Plantaganet (later **Henry II**), William's distant cousin, ascended to the throne in 1154 and initiated the conquest of Ireland. His son, **Richard the Lionheart,** taxed nobles to finance the **Third Crusade** to Jerusalem, where he won access to the Holy Shrines. Soon after that expansion of power, noblemen, tired of royal abuses of authority, forced his brother King John to sign the **Magna Carta** in 1215 (see p. 191). The document has been credited with laying the groundwork for modern democracy—the first **Parliament** convened 50 years later in 1265. While Britain's territory expanded, the population suffered a serious blow under the **Black Death** (plague) which ravaged more than one-third of all Britons between 1348 and 1361.

While **King Richard II** was on a trip to Ireland in 1399, his cousin **Henry Bolingbroke** invaded Britain and snatched the throne. This move put the Lancasters in control, and gave Shakespeare great dramatic material. More Shakespearian subject matter was created when **Henry V** defeated the French in the **Battle of Agincourt** (1415), a legendary victory for the British underdogs. But his son, **Henry VI** (despite being crowned King of France in 1431) dropped the gauntlet, lost all English land in France, was diagnosed as mad in 1453, and was eventually executed in the Tower of London. Henry VI was replaced by **Richard, Duke of York,** and eventually by Richard's son Edward IV, who led the Yorkists against the House of Lancaster in the **Wars of the Roses** (1455-1485). Boy-king Edward V ascended to the throne in 1483 at the tender age of 12, but was soon beheaded by his loving uncle Richard III.

After the turmoil of the Wars of the Roses, the Lancasters emerged victorious and inaugurated the rule of the **House of Tudor** under Henry VII, a dynasty that survived until 1603. His successor, **Henry VIII,** reinforced England's imperial control over the Irish, proclaiming himself their king in 1542. In his infamous battle with the Pope over multiple marriages, Henry converted Britain from Roman Catholicism to Protestantism, establishing the Anglican Church and placing himself at its head (ironic, since most of his wives lost theirs) in the **Act of Supremacy** of 1534.

BRITAIN

Britain

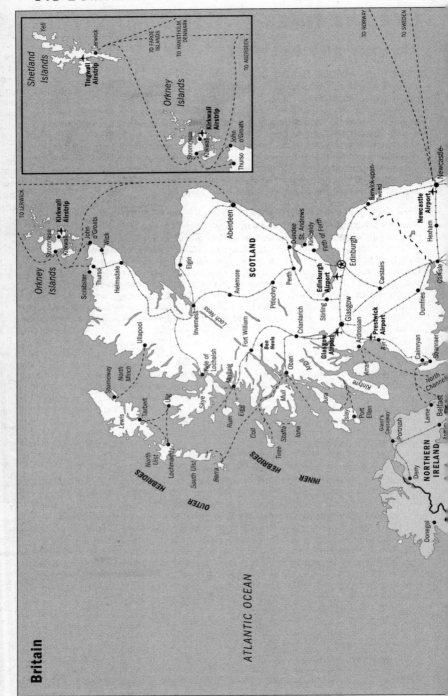

REPUBLICANISM AND RESTORATION (1547-1688)

Despite Henry VIII's attempts to solidify the Protestant stronghold, his sudden death in 1547 did not help the cause. Instead, it gave rise to the staunch Catholic **Bloody Mary,** so named for her vicious persecution of Protestants. In a nice spate of sibling rivalry, **Elizabeth I** reversed the religious convictions imposed by her sister and cemented the success of the Reformation—under her reign the British defeated the **Spanish Armada** in 1588 to become Europe's leading power.

Tensions erupted in the **English Civil Wars** (1642-1651). The monarchy was abolished when Parliament saw to it that Charles I and his head parted company, and the first **British Commonwealth** was founded in 1649. **Oliver Cromwell** emerged as a rebellious and adept military leader whose massacre of nearly half of the Irish earned him eternal bitterness from Britain's neighbor. Cromwell's son Richard succeeded him as Lord Protector, but he lacked the leadership to retain the republic. Much to the relief of the masses, Charles II was brought back to power unconditionally in 1660. But the **Restoration** did not signal the end of the troubles: intense debate over the right of Charles II's fervently Catholic brother, James II to ascend to the throne during the **Exclusion Crisis** established two political parties, the Whigs (who were firmly Protestant) and the Tories (more Catholic).

PARLIAMENT AND THE CROWN (1688-1800)

The relatively bloodless **Glorious Revolution** erupted in 1688 to prevent James II from establishing a Catholic dynasty; Dutch Protestant **William of Orange** and his wife Mary were crowned when they agreed to the **Bill of Rights.** The ascension of **William and Mary** marked the end of a century of violent upheaval. The Bill of Rights quietly revolutionized the relationship between the Crown and Parliament, bringing a triumphant Parliamentary leadership to the fore. Over the course of the 18th century, the office of **Prime Minister** gradually eclipsed the monarchy as the seat of power in British government under the authority of the master negotiator **Robert Walpole** and the astute politician **William Pitt the Younger.**

EMPIRE AND INDUSTRY (EARLY 19TH CENTURY)

During the 18th and 19th centuries, Britain came to rule more than a quarter of the world's population and two-fifths of its land. To begin, the **Cape of Good Hope** was captured by the British in order to secure shipping routes to the Far East. Parliament soon realized they were on to a good thing, acquiring all of Australia and New Zealand by 1840, and throwing in the Western Pacific Islands for good measure in 1877. Recognizing the wealth of India in 1857, Parliament requested that the East India Trading Company cede control of the sub-continent to the Crown, making governmental control of the Empire complete. By the mid-1800s, it could be rightfully said that "The sun never sets on the British Empire."

The **Industrial Revolution** allowed Britain to attain the military and economic power necessary for colonization. In one of the greatest social changes in British history, massive portions of the rural populace migrated to towns, lured by growing opportunities in industrial employment. British entrepreneurs grew wealthy, as did the British government, giving both groups the means to enlarge the Empire. But world domination did not last long—the American colonies declared freedom in 1776, and as early as 1839 some Asian colonies began to accrue limited **self-determination.** Nationalistic movements accelerated greatly after World War I, and the majority of the British Empire dissolved during the 20th century. Since the 1997 transfer of **Hong Kong** back to China, Britain's biggest colony is Bermuda.

THE VICTORIAN ERA (19TH CENTURY)

The stable rule of **Queen Victoria** dominated the 19th century in foreign and domestic politics, social changes, and even stylistic mores. She oversaw the beginnings of domestic industrial regulation, spurred by conflict among the social classes and often frightening workplace conditions. The **Reform Act** of 1832 provided sweeping changes in working conditions while the **Chartist Movement** of the mid-19th century pressed for universal male suffrage. The 1840s brought the **Irish Potato Famine,** which killed over a million people and caused twice that many to emigrate. Increasing troubles with Ireland plagued the nation and Prime Minister **William Gladstone**'s 1880 attempt to introduce a Home Rule Bill for Ireland splintered the Labour Party. Despite this, the government still faced the possibility of civil war in Ireland—a threat interrupted by the explosion of **World War I**.

THE WORLD WARS (1914-1945)
World War I, The Great War, brought British military action back to the European stage, but scarred the British spirit as it devastated a large part of the younger male generations. The technological explosion of the 19th century was evident in the new weapons and trench warfare introduced during the war. The gas attacks and the tanks caused unprecedented casualties on both sides. With the end of World War I, hope for a new beginning within England was generally lost even though women gained suffrage at this time. The 1930s brought depression and mass unemployment; during this period famed social economist **John Maynard Keynes** came to the fore. In December 1936, King Edward VIII shocked the world with the announcement of his abdication. Meanwhile, tensions in Europe were once again escalating with the German reoccupation of the Rhineland.

Despite **Neville Chamberlain**'s attempts at **appeasement** with Hitler, peace could only last so long. In response to the German invasion of Poland, Britain declared war on Germany on September 3, 1939, thus precipitating the outbreak of **World War II**. The British were forced to face German air attacks as early as the summer of 1940, when the prolonged air-war, the **Battle of Britain** began. London, Coventry, and other British cities were demolished by the bombings of the early 40s. The fall of France in 1940 precipitated the end of the Chamberlain government and the creation of a war cabinet led by the determined and eloquent **Winston Churchill**. American forces in Europe augmented the Allied effort in the June 6, 1944 **D-Day Invasion** of Normandy; the invasion reversed the tide of the war and eventually brought peace to Europe in May 1945.

THE POST-WAR YEARS (1945-1979)
The growing affluence and diversity of the postwar era propelled Britain to the center of popular culture. The extension of the welfare state with the creation of the **National Health Service** in 1946 guaranteed government-funded medical care to all Brits. Later, Harold Wilson's Labour government relaxed divorce and homosexuality laws and abolished capital punishment. **Edward Heath** finally succumbed to the pressures of the continent and Britain joined the European Economic Community (now the **European Union**) in 1971, which has received a rocky welcome from some British citizens and Parliament members.

Increasing economic problems in the 1970s stemmed from Britain's colonial retreat. Conservative and Labour governments alike floundered in attempts to curtail unemployment while maintaining a base level of social welfare benefits. Government after government wrangled with labor unions, culminating in a series of public-service strikes in early 1979, called the **Winter of Discontent,** which literally left piles of garbage lying in the streets.

THE THATCHER YEARS AND BEYOND (1980-1997)
It was against this backdrop that Britain grasped for change, electing the Tory **Margaret Thatcher** as Prime Minister, putting faith in her nationalism and Victorian values. Thatcher's term was hexed by economic recession, but by 1983 British victory against Argentina in the territorial dispute for the **Falkland Islands** and the embarrassing disarray of the Labour Party clinched her second term. Thatcher turned from the war in the islands to "the enemy within," referring to the labor unions, while denationalizing and dismantling the welfare state with legislation— she once quipped, "There is no such thing as society."

Thatcher's policies brought dramatic prosperity to many, but heightened the divide between rich and poor. Thatcher's undoing came with her refusal to let go of the unpopular **poll tax** and her resistance to the EEC. Though still divided on

Europe, the Tory Party conducted a vote of no-confidence that led to Thatcher's 1990 resignation and the intra-party selection of **John Major** as prime minister. As the Labour party was unable to shed its image of ineffectiveness gained in the 70s, Mayor led the Tories to another victory in the 1992 elections. However, Major's popularity dwindled during the severe economic recession of the 90s. Meanwhile, the Labour Party, under the leadership of charismatic **Tony Blair,** cut ties with the labor unions, refashioned itself into an alternative for discontented voters, and finally began to rise in the popularity.

BRITAIN TODAY

Despite tense relations with unions, the "new" Labour Party claimed a clear victory under Blair in the May 1997 elections, garnering the biggest Labour majority in history. In 1998, Blair nurtured closer relations with the EU, maintained a moderate economic and social position, and was named one of *People Magazine's* 50 Most Beautiful People. All in all, not a bad year for Tony. 1999 was more turbulent, with Blair gaining the title of "little Bill Clinton" for his blind following of American foreign policy in the Kosovo crisis. Under Blair, Britain has held fast to its refusal to adopt the **Euro** (the unified European currency), but his rhetoric and actions give conflicting indicators for the unified currency's future in the UK. Blair closely repeated his 1997 electoral performance with another landslide victory in the June 2001 election amidst the lowest voter turnout in British political history.

National sovereignty has become a key issue on the domestic front as well. In a September 1997 referendum, Scotland voted for **Scottish devolution,** providing the Scots with their own Parliament and the possibility of independence. Not one to be left behind for long, the **Welsh** also demanded more political autonomy while still retaining 40 representatives in Parliament.

ROYALTY TODAY. It's not easy being Queen Elizabeth II. There has been no end of unabashedly publicized disaster. In 1992 over a hundred rooms in **Windsor Palace** burned, and in 1993 the Queen began to pay income tax. The sad spectacle of royal life took a tragic turn in 1997 as **Princess Diana** was killed in a car crash in a Paris tunnel. The outpouring of grief from a considerable portion of Brits was likened to the public reaction to the death of Prime Minister Winston Churchill.

Most recently, royal-watchers are hoping that the marriage of the youngest royal brother, **Edward,** who tied the knot in the summer of 1999 to public relations specialist **Sophie Rhys-Jones,** will fare better than those of his three divorced siblings. However, it is clearly the young **Prince William** on whom the spotlight shines brightest, as he continues his studies at **St. Andrew's University** in Scotland.

THE ARTS

LITERATURE

OLD ENGLISH AND THE MIDDLE AGES. Perhaps the finest piece of Old English poetry for which record does exist is **Beowulf.** Dated tenuously at the first half of the 7th century, the rhythmic religious poem details the prince Beowulf's struggle against the monster Grendel. **Geoffrey Chaucer,** writing centuries later, tapped into the spirited side of Middle English; his *Canterbury Tales* (c. 1387) remain some of the funniest—and sauciest—stories in the English canon. The need to adapt religious material into a form understood by the masses led **John Wycliffe** and his followers to make the first translation of the **Bible** into English in the 1380s, an act which gave the English language credibility. In the mid-16th century King James sent 47 translators to bring forth a Word of God the Protestant King could tolerate. The resulting **King James Version** of the Bible, completed in 1611, rumbles with magnificent pace and rhetoric, and remains a literary monument to this day.

THE ENGLISH RENAISSANCE. Advances in education and printing technology allowed writers to reach a large market of readers, which caused a flourishing of English literature under Elizabeth I. **John Donne,** the pastor of London's St. Paul's

Cathedral (see p. 169) and the English language's first urban poet, wrote introspective metaphysical and devotional poetry while penning erotic verse on the side. The era's greatest contributions to English literature came in drama, with the appearance of the first professional playwrights. **Christopher Marlowe** guided *Tamburlaine* (c. 1587) and *Dr. Faustus* (c. 1588) into the English conscience. But the English literary figure par excellence is still **William Shakespeare,** who mixed high and low art to create some of the finest comedies, histories, and tragedies ever to grace the world. An entire town bustles year-round in tribute to the man (see **Stratford-upon-Avon,** p. 203) who coined a staggering number of words, including "scuffle," "arouse," and "bump." However, his plays, especially *Hamlet* (1600), *King Lear* (1605) and *The Tempest* (1611) remain the truest monuments to his genius.

SHAKESPEARE MADE EASY

I'm dying for a drink.	I would give all my fame for a pot of ale. *(Henry V III, ii)*
I love you.	Doubt thou the stars are fire; Doubt that the sun doth move; Doubt truth to be a liar; But never doubt I love. *(Hamlet II, ii)*
I hate you.	Thou art a boil, a plague-sore, or embossed carbuncle, in my corrupted blood. *(King Lear II, iv)*
It's not the size, it's how you use it.	He does it with a better grace, but I do it more natural. *(Twelfth Night II, iii)*

GODS AND MEN. The British Puritans of the late 16th and early 17th centuries produced a huge volume of obsessive and beautiful literature. In *Paradise Lost* (1667), the epic poem to end all epic poems, blind **John Milton** gave Satan, Adam, and Eve a complexity the Bible did not grant them. Another Puritan vision came from **John Bunyan,** whose *Pilgrim's Progress* (1678) charts the Christian's quest for redemption in a world awaiting the apocalypse. The major literary figure and critic of the late 18th century was **Samuel Johnson,** whose greatest achievement was spending nine years writing the first definitive English **dictionary.**

THE ENGLISH NOVEL COMES INTO ITS OWN. In 1719, **Daniel Defoe** inaugurated the era of the English novel with his popular island-bound *Robinson Crusoe*. **Jane Austen** brought the novel to new heights, slyly criticizing self-importance in *Pride and Prejudice* (1813) and *Emma* (1815). The harsh industrialization of the Victorian period spawned numerous classic novels—**Charles Dickens**'s often biting, sometimes sentimental works, like *A Christmas Carol* (1843) draw on the bleakness of his childhood in Portsmouth (see p. 190). From their Haworth home, the **Brontë sisters** composed works of great intensity: Emily's *Wuthering Heights* (1847) and Charlotte's *Jane Eyre* (1846) are outstanding examples. **Thomas Hardy** closed out the Victorian age on a dark note in the fate-ridden Wessex landscapes of *Jude the Obscure* (1895) and *Tess of the d'Urbervilles* (1891). Like Hardy, **George Eliot** (her real name was Mary Ann Evans) was drawn to the security of traditional village life. Her *Middlemarch* (1871) details the lives of an entire town.

Partly in reaction to the rationalism of the preceding century, the early 19th century saw the rise of the **Romantic** literary movement. The beginning of Romanticism in Britain is generally considered to have come with the joint publication of *Lyrical Ballads* in 1798 by **William Wordsworth** and **Samuel Taylor Coleridge.** Their colleagues **John Keats** and **Percy Bysshe Shelley** authored passionate and sensual poems in their tragically short lifetimes—both died before age 30. Meanwhile, the poetry of the Victorian age struggled with the impact of societal changes. **Alfred Lord Tennyson** spun gorgeous verse about faith and doubt for over a half-century, while **Matthew Arnold** rebelled against the industrialization of literature.

BRITAIN

THE MODERN AGE. After World War I, London became the home of artistic movements like the **Bloomsbury Group,** pulling the world's intellects into its midst. **Virginia Woolf,** a key group member, explored the private yearnings of the mind in *To the Lighthouse* (1927). **T.S. Eliot**'s *The Waste Land* (1922), one of this century's most important poems, is a picture of a fragmented, motionless world waiting for the end. Although he spoke only a few words of English when he arrived in the country from Poland at age 21, **Joseph Conrad** proceeded to masterfully employ the language to examine evil in *Heart of Darkness* (1902).

LATE 20TH CENTURY LITERATURE. In 1949, **George Orwell**'s *1984* depicted a ravenous totalitarian state striving to strip the world of memory and words of meaning. Later, the end of British Empire and rising affluence splintered British literature in a thousand directions. Nostalgia pervades the poems of **Philip Larkin** and **John Betjeman,** which search for beauty amidst knowledge of mortality, in contrast to the vigorous poems of the Yorkshire-raised **Ted Hughes** and **Tony Harrison.** Postcolonial voices have also become an important literary force in an increasingly multicultural country. Hong Kong native **Timothy Mo** examines British rule in East Asia in *An Insular Possession* (1986), while India-born **Salman Rushdie**'s spellbinding *Midnight's Children* (1981) is a glorious amalgam of Indian myth and modern culture. British playwrights, as always, continue to innovate. **Tom Stoppard** challenged everything you knew about theater in grim yet hysterical plays like *Rosencrantz and Guildenstern are Dead* (1967).

VISUAL ARTS

British art has long been dominated by continental influences; however, in the 18th century English artists came into their own. **Sir Joshua Reynolds** (1723-92) was one of the most prominent portraitists of the 18th century and in 1768 he helped found the **Royal Academy of Art,** now located in Piccadilly (see p. 165). In the 19th century, **J.M.W. Turner** glorified the English countryside with his light-filled oil landscape paintings. The art of illustration flourished in this period, typified by the output of mystic artist and lyric poet **William Blake.** The 20th century has seen revolutionary ideas shaking traditional artistic concepts. The disturbing meat-filled portraits of **Francis Bacon** have transformed British portraiture, while **Henry Moore** has set major trends in 20th century sculpture.

ARCHITECTURE

British architecture has traditionally been based on the ecclesiastical model of cloisters and courtyard. Oxford's colleges (see p. 196), especially **New College** and **Balliol College,** are structured in this manner, are as London's many other official buildings, and the law offices and residences in **Inns of Court, Houses of Parliament** (see p. 173). **Inigo Jones** added an Italian flare to the Covent Garden piazza (see p. 165). The **Great Fire of London** in 1666 destroyed more than 13,000 houses in the center of the city and halted the use of wood and straw as building materials. The fire also gave **Sir Christopher Wren** an opportunity to work his magic rebuilding **St. Paul's Cathedral** (see p. 169). Centuries later, the destruction of the centers of London and Coventry in World War II let British architects think outside traditional patterns. London's industrial docklands were replaced with **Canary Wharf** and one of the few skyscrapers in London, while parts of Coventry's bombed cathedral can be seen interwoven with the striking new one. Other post-war buildings include the **Barbican Arts Complex** (p. 176), which uses modern styling around traditional courtyards. The original Londinium has also seen some considerable renovation in recent years—Richard Rodgers' **Lloyd's Building** (see p. 170) juxtaposes futuristic metal design with Victorian chimneys. Travelers using Stansted Airport will get to see **Sir Norman Foster**'s brilliant use of glass and metal tree-like forms.

MUSIC

CLASSIC. Britain was long called "a land without music." While this isn't entirely true, recognized British masterpieces are few and far between. The late 19th century did, however, see **Gilbert and Sullivan** pen opperettas filled with social satire and farce, such as *H.M.S. Pinafore* (1878) and *The Mikado* (1885). Serious music in Britain began a late 19th century renaissance under **Edward Elgar**, whose pomp is outweighed by circumstances of eloquence, like his *Enigma Variations* (1896).

THE BRITISH ARE COMING. Britain has continually been the source of much innovation in popular music. After World War II, imported American rock and blues inspired the first wave of **British Invasion** rock groups. From Liverpool (see p. 214), **The Beatles** stood at the fore of every musical and cultural trend, weaving the classic songs that have become part of the international cultural vocabulary. Their Satanic Majesties **The Rolling Stones** emerged as London's harder-edged answer to the Fab Four. **The Who** began as Kinks-like popsters, then expanded into "rock operas" like *Tommy* (1975) and *Quadrophenia* (1979)—the latter chronicling fights between the "rockers" (who liked leather jackets and America) and the "mods" (who liked speed, androgeny, and The Who). The **Yardbirds** spun off guitar heroes **Eric Clapton** and **Jimmy Page,** who went on to dominate mass markets in the 70s through their bands (**Cream** and **Led Zeppelin** respectively). The same period also saw the rise of "progressive-rock" groups like **Yes, Genesis,** and **Pink Floyd.**

ANARCHY IN THE UK. The theatrical excess of **Queen** and **Elton John** characterized mid-70s rock. "Pub rock" groups tried to return rock to the people, leading to the punk movement. The **Sex Pistols** kicked it off and indelibly marked music and culture while **The Clash** made political punk with an idealistic leftist slant. Perhaps the most popular of punk's first-wave bands among the British was **The Jam.** Long before Girl Power sloganeering, the all-female **Slits** mixed their punk with reggae. Inspired by punk's DIY ethos, but adding synthesizers, **The Cure** shook teens everywhere. From the same anti-establishment impulses as punk came the metal of **Ozzy Osbourne** and **Iron Maiden,** which was much less acclaimed but still attracted a cult following. Sheffield's **Def Leppard** took the hard-rock-big-hair ethic through the 80s.

SYNTH-POP, INDIE, AND DANCE. Alas, punk died an angry death with **Sid Vicious,** leaving the music scene increasingly receptive to the burgeoning field of electronic music. **Duran Duran** and the **Eurythmics** may have more successfully crossed the Atlantic to dominate American charts, but **Depeche Mode** and the ever-witty **The Pet Shop Boys** refined the synth-pop message and kept the home crowds dancing through the night. The producing machine of **Stock, Aitken, and Waterman** churned out a string of embarrassingly catchy hits, while **Wham!** managed to be equally shameful on their own. Fortunately, Manchester took on the role of center of musical development throughout the 80s. This, in turn, evolved in the mid-90s into the sounds of a diverse range of indie bands held together under the "Britpop" label, including the Beatles-esque **Oasis,** the glam **Suede,** and the wry **Blur.** Rising above the mess is **Radiohead** whose subtle atmospherics and complex, densely-layered arena rock never cease to amaze.

The pop charts have also been subject to the musical stylings of the **Spice Girls** and the extremely successful **Robbie Williams.** The music of other cultures, including the sitar-tinged Indian sounds of **Cornershop,** continues to influence the direction of British pop, keeping it fresh. The rave scene (and the synthetic drugs that accompanied it) exploded in Britain in the late 80s, while the Big Beat dance-rock sound of **The Chemical Brothers** and **Fatboy Slim** continue to draw the punters into the clubs. Britain in the new millenium continues to stake its long-standing claim on musical innovation with the "in the house music" of **Basement Jaxx** and the drum 'n' bass of **Roni Size** and **Reprazent.**

FILM

The British film industry experienced its first major success with **Sir Laurence Olivier**'s intellectual *Henry V* (1944). Master of suspense **Alfred Hitchcock** snared (and scared) audiences with numerous films including *Dial M for Murder* (1954) and *Psycho* (1960). **David Lean** employed the brilliant **Sir Alec Guinness** in *Lawrence of Arabia* (1962) and in *Dr. Zhivago* (1965). Also a master comedian in films like

BRITAIN

Barnacle Bill (1957), Sir Guinness then became most famous as the original *Obi-Wan Kenobi* in the original *Star Wars* (1977). The 60s phenomenon of "swingin' London" created momentum for the British film industry and jump-started international interest in British culture. Scot **Sean Connery** drank the first of many martinis, shaken not stirred, as **James Bond** in *Dr. No* (1962). Adopted Brit **Stanley Kubrick** went beyond the infinite without leaving England in *2001: A Space Odyssey* (1968) and descended into mayhem in *A Clockwork Orange* (1971).

Elaborate period dramas and offbeat, independent films have come to represent contemporary British film. The heroic sagas of **Hugh Hudson's** *Chariots of Fire* (1981) and **Richard Attenborough's** *Gandhi* (1982) swept the Oscars in successive years. The comedy group **Monty Python** created two instant cult favorites in *Monty Python and the Holy Grail* (1974) and *Monty Python's Life of Brian* (1979). The British Tourist Authority produces a "Movie Map" that lists more than 200 movie locations across the country (www.visitbritain.com/moviemap).

FOOD AND DRINK

British cuisine's deservedly lackluster reputation redeems itself in a few areas. Britain is largely a nation of carnivores; the best native dishes are the **roasts**—beef, lamb, and Wiltshire hams. And meat isn't just for dinner; the British like their famed breakfasts meaty and cholesterol-filled. Before you leave the country, you must try any of the sweet, glorious British **puddings.** The "ploughman's lunch" consists of cheese, bread, and salt. Caffs are the British equivalent of US dinners. To escape English food, try Chinese, Greek, or especially **Indian** cuisine. British **tea** refers both to a drink and a social ritual. The drink is served strong and milky; if you want it any other way, say so. Afternoon **high tea**, the event, is served around 4pm and includes salad, sandwiches, and pastries. Cream tea, a specialty of Cornwall and Devon, includes toast, crumpets, scones, jam, and clotted cream.

The British **pub** is truly a social institution. Drinks (**mostly beer**) are generally served from 11am to 11pm, Sundays noon to 10:30pm. British beer is usually served room temperature, though lager (the European equivalent of American beer) is served colder. **Real ales** are beers naturally carbonated by an ongoing fermentation process. Traditional **cider**, a fermented apple juice, is a potent and tasty alternative to beer. Pub grub is fast, filling, and generally cheap.

FLAKES AND SMARTIES British food has character (of one sort or another), and the traditional menu is a mad hodgepodge of candy, crisps, yeasts, and squashes. Britain has a greater variety of **candy** for sale than most countries. Candy to watch out for includes Cadbury Flake, Crunchies (made out of honeycombed magic), and the ever-popular Smarties. Watch out for the orange ones—they're made of orange chocolate. Potato chips, or **crisps** as they are known in England, are not just salted, but come in a range of flavors, including Prawn Cocktail, Beef, Chicken, Fruit 'n' Spice, and the more traditional Salt & Vinegar. All this sugar and salt can be washed down with the pineapple-and-grapefruit-flavored soda Lilt or a can of Ribena, a red currant syrup which has to be diluted with water. This latter beverage belongs to a family of drinks known as **squash**, all of which are diluted before consumption. But the food that expatriate Britons miss most is **Marmite**, a yeast extract spread on toast. If you weren't fed Marmite as a baby, you'll never appreciate it; most babies don't either.

ESSENTIALS

DOCUMENTS AND FORMALITIES

EU citizens do not need a visa to enter Britain or Ireland. For visits of less than six months, citizens of Australia, Canada, New Zealand, South Africa, and the US do not need a visa to enter.

British Embassies and High Comissions at Home: **Australia**, British High Commission, Commonwealth Ave., Yarralumla, Canberra, ACT 2600 (☎(02) 6270 6666; www.uk.emb.gov.au). **Canada**, British High Commission, 80 Elgin St., Ottawa, K1P 5K7 (☎613-237-1530; www.britain-in-canada.org). **Ireland**, British Embassy, 29 Merrion Rd., Ballsbridge, Dublin 4 (☎(01) 205 3700; www.britishembassy.ie). **New Zealand**, British High Commission, 44 Hill St., Thorndon, Wellington 1 (☎(04) 472 6049; www.britain.org.nz). **South Africa**, British High Commission, 91 Parliament St., Cape Town 8001 (☎(021) 461 7220). **US**, British Embassy, 3100 Massachusetts Ave. NW, Washington, D.C. 20008 (☎202-588-6500; www.britainusa.com).

Foreign Embassies in Britain: All foreign embassies are in **London** (p. 154).

TRANSPORTATION

BY PLANE. Most flights into Britain that originate outside Europe land at **London's Heathrow** and **Gatwick** airports. Flights from Europe also hit **Luton** and **Stansted**, near London, as well as **Cardiff, Liverpool, Manchester, Edinburgh**, and **Glasgow**.

BY TRAIN. There is no longer a single national rail company, although the various companies are often still referred to under the umbrella of "British Rail." Prices and schedules often change: find up-to-date information from **National Rail Inquiries** (☎(08457) 484950), or online at **Railtrack** (www.railtrack.co.uk; no price information). Despite multiple providers, rail service in Britain is extensive (and expensive). The **BritRail Pass**, available to non-British travelers outside Britain, allows unlimited travel in England, Wales, and Scotland (8-day US$265, under 26 US$215; 22-day US$499, US$355), but must be **bought before traveling to Britain.** The one-year **Young Person's Railcard** (£18), which grants 33% off most fares in addition to discounts on some ferries, is available to those ages 16 to 25, and to full-time students at British universities over age 25, at major British Rail Travel Centres in the UK. **Eurailpasses** are **not valid** in Britain.

BY BUS. Long-distance coach travel in Britain is more extensive than in most European countries, and is the cheapest travel option. **National Express** (☎(08705) 808080; www.gobycoach.co.uk) is the principal long-distance coach service operator in Britain, although **Scottish Citylink** (☎(08705) 505050) has coverage in Scotland. **Discount Coachcards,** available for seniors (over 50), students, and young persons (ages 16-25) for £9, reduce fares on National Express by about 30%. For those planning a lot of coach travel, the **Tourist Trail Pass** offers unlimited travel for a number of days within a given period (2 days out of 3 £49; students, seniors, and children £39, 5 out of 10 £85/£69; 7 out of 21 £120/£94; 14 out of 30 £187/£143).

BY FERRY. Numerous ferry lines ply the route across the English Channel; the most popular crossing is from **Dover** to **Calais, France.** Ask for **discounts; ISIC** holders can sometimes get student fares, and **Eurailpass-holders** can get many reductions and free trips. Book ahead June through August. Other routes between the Continent and England include **Bergen, Norway** to **Lerwick** or **Newcastle; Esbjerg, Denmark** to **Harwich; Göteborg, Sweden** to **Harwich** or **Newcastle; Hamburg** to **Harwich** or **Newcastle; Ostend, Belgium** to **Ramsgate; Hook of Holland** to **Harwich.** For info on boats from **Wales** to **Dublin** and **Rosslare, Ireland,** see p. 223; from **Scotland** to **Belfast,** see p. 232; from **England** to the **Continent,** see p. 187.

BY CAR. You must be 17 and have a license to drive in Britain. The country is covered by a high-speed system of **motorways** ("M-roads") that connect London with major cities around the country. Remember you may not be used to **driving on the left,** or driving a **manual transmission** (far more common than automatic transmissions in cheap rental cars); give way to the right at roundabouts. **Roads** are generally well maintained, but parking in London is impossible and traffic is slow.

BY BIKE AND BY THUMB. Much of Britain's countryside is well suited for **biking.** Many cities and villages have bike rental shops and maps of local cycle routes; ask

BRITAIN

at the Tourist Information Centre. Large-scale Ordnance Survey maps detail the extensive system of long-distance **hiking** paths. TICs and National Park Information Centres can provide extra information about routes. *Let's Go* does not recommend **hitchhiking**; it is illegal on **M motorways** and always risky.

TOURIST SERVICES AND MONEY

EMERGENCY Police, ☎999. Ambulance, ☎999. Fire, ☎999.

TOURIST OFFICES. The **British Tourist Authority** (BTA; www.visitbritain.com) is an umbrella organization coordinating the activities of the four separate UK tourist boards outside the UK.

Tourist Boards at Home: Australia, Level 16, Gateway, 1 Macquarie Pl., Circular Quay, Sydney NSW 2000 (☎(02) 9377 4400; www.visitbritain.com/au). **Canada,** Air Transit Bldg., 5915 Airport Rd., Ste. 120, Mississauga, ON L4V 1T1 (☎888-847-4885; www.visitbritain.com/ca). **New Zealand,** 151 Queen St., 17th fl., Auckland 1 (☎(09) 303 1446). **South Africa,** Lancaster Gate, Hyde Park Ln., Hyde Park, Sandton 2196 (☎(011) 325 0343). **US,** 551 5th Ave. #701, New York, NY 10176 (☎800-462-2748 or 212-986-2200; www.btausa/BTA-USA.htm).

CURRENCY AND EXCHANGE. The **Pound Sterling** is the main unit of currency in the United Kingdom. It is divided into 100 *pence*, issued in standard denominations of 1p, 2p, 5p, 10p, 20p, 50p, and £1 in coins, and £5, £10, £20, and £50 in notes. (Scotland uses a £1 note, and you may see the discontinued £2 coin.) Scotland has its own bank notes, which can be used interchangeably with English currency, though you may have difficulty using Scottish £1 notes outside Scotland.

Prices: Britain is expensive. Expect to spend anywhere from £15-30 per person per day, depending on where you choose to visit. Accommodations start at about £6 a night for a bed in a hostel in rural areas, or £14-15 per night in a B&B, while a basic sit-down meal at a pub costs about £5. London in particular is a budget-buster, with £25-35 a day being the bare minimum for accommodations, food, and transport.

Tipping and bargaining: Tips in restaurants are usually included in the bill (sometimes as a "service charge"); if gratuity is not included then you should tip 10-15%. Tipping the barman in pubs is not at all expected, though a waiter or waitress should be tipped. Taxi drivers should receive a 10% tip, and bellhops and chambermaids usually expect somewhere between £1 and £3. Aside from open-air markets, don't expect to barter anywhere else, including hostels, taxis, and tour guides.

Taxes: Britain has a 17.5% **value-added tax (VAT),** a sales tax applied to everything except food, books, medicine, and children's clothing. The tax is included within the price indicated—no extra expenses should be added at the register. Visitors to Britain may get a VAT refund on goods (but not services) purchased in Britain.

ACCOMMODATIONS AND CAMPING

Youth hostels in Britain are run by the **Youth Hostels Association (YHA) of England and Wales** (☎(0870) 870 8808; www.yha.org.uk) and the **Scottish Youth Hostels Association (SYHA)** (☎(1786) 891 400; www.syha.org.uk); usually, you must be a member of an HI-affiliated association to stay in any of their hostels. Most HI hostels also honor **guest memberships**—you'll get a blank card with space for six validation stamps. Each night you'll pay a nonmember supplement (one-sixth the membership fee) and earn one guest stamp; get six stamps, and you're a member. Unless noted as "self-catering," the YHA hostels listed in *Let's Go* (not including SYHA) offer cooked meals at standard rates—breakfast £3.20, small/ standard packed lunch £2.80/3.65, evening meal £4.15 (£4.80 for a 3-course meal in some hostels), and children's meals (breakfast £1.75, lunch or dinner £2.70). In Britain, a bed in a hostel will cost around £6 in rural areas, £12 in larger cities, and £13-20 in London.

For a cozier alternative to impersonal hotel rooms, **B&Bs** and guest houses (often private homes with rooms available to travelers) range from the acceptable to the sublime. You can book B&Bs by calling directly, or by asking the local **Tourist Information Centre (TIC)** to help you find accommodations; most can also book B&Bs in other towns. TICs usually charge a 10% deposit on the first night's or the entire stay's price, deductible from the amount you pay the B&B proprietor; often a flat fee of £1-3 is added on. **Campsites** tend to be privately owned, with basic ones costing £3 per person, and posh ones costing up to £10 per person. **It is illegal to camp in national parks,** since much of their land is privately owned.

COMMUNICATION

MAIL. To send a **postcard** to another European country costs £0.36; to send one to other international destinations via airmail is £0.40. To send a **letter** within Britain costs £0.27. To send one airmail to a European country (including the Republic of Ireland) is £0.37 (up to 20g), and to non-European international destinations cost £0.45 for letters up to 10g, and UK£0.65 for letters weighing 10-20g. Address *Poste Restante* to the post office, highlighting the last name (FirstName SURNAME, *Poste Restante*, New Bond St. Post Office, Bath BA1 1A5, United Kingdom).

TELEPHONES. Public pay phones in Britain are mostly run by **British Telecom (BT).** The BT phonecard, available in denominations from £2-20, is probably a useful purchase, since BT phones tend to be omnipresent. Public phones charge a minimum of 10p for calls. For **directory inquiries,** which are free from payphones, call 192 in Britain. **International direct dial numbers** include: **AT&T,** ☎ 0800 013 0011; **British Telecom (Ireland),** ☎ 0800 550144; **Canada Direct,** ☎ 0800 890016; **Ireland,** ☎ 0800 890353; **MCI,** ☎ 0800 890222; **Telecom New Zealand,** ☎ 0800 890064; **Sprint,** ☎ 0800 890877; **Telkom South Africa,** ☎ 0800 890027; **Telstra Australia,** ☎ 0800 890061.

INTERNET ACCESS. Britain is one of the world's most online countries, and cybercafes can usually be found in larger cities. They cost £4-6 an hour, but often you can pay only for time used, not for the whole hour. Online guides to cybercafes in Britain and Ireland that are updated daily include **The Cybercafe Search Engine** (http://cybercaptive.com) and **Cybercafes.com** (www.cybercafes.com).

LANGUAGE. The official languages are English and Welsh. Scottish Gaelic, though unofficial, is spoken in some parts of Scotland along with English.

LOCAL FACTS

Time: Britain is often on Greenwich Mean Time (GMT), but "British Summer Time" (late-Mar. to late-Oct.) is 1hr. ahead of GMT.

When to Go: In summer, temperatures average 12-21°C (55-70°F); in winter, 2-7°C (36-41°F). The mild temperatures are often accompanied by rain. Spring is a good time to visit the countryside.

Holidays: New Year's Day (Jan. 1); Good Friday (Apr. 13); Easter Sunday and Monday (Apr. 15 and 16); May Day (May 6); Bank holiday (May 27); and Christmas (Dec. 25-26). Scotland also kicks back on Jan. 2 and Aug. 5 (both bank holidays).

Festivals: The largest festival in the world is the **Edinburgh International Festival** (Aug. 11-31); also highly recommended is the **Fringe Festival** (Aug. 4-26). Manchester's Gay Village hosts **Mardi Gras** (late Aug.). Muddy fun abounds at the **Glastonbury Festival.** **Highland Games** offer caber-tossing goodness in Edinburgh (mid-July).

BRITAIN

ENGLAND

In a land where the staid and stately once prevailed, where "public" schools mean "private," and where royalty have indelibly left their mark on almost every nook, England's 20th-century image of England as the aging seat of a dying empire has been turned on its ear in recent years. Conservatism has been given the boot in two successive elections, a wild profusion of the avant-garde has emerged from hallowed academic halls, and—shock! horror! dismay!—even the Queen must pay taxes on her vast holdings. More than ever, England is embracing its sizable immigrant communities and allowing the venerable class boat to be rocked; the country that once determined the meaning of "civilised" for many people now takes a page, culinarily and otherwise, from former fledgling colonies. The vanguard of art, music, film, and eclecticism, England is a young, hip nation looking forward. But traditionalists can rest easy; for all the moving and shaking in large metropolises, around the corner there are handfuls of quaint towns, dozens of picturesque castles, and scores of comforting cups of tea.

LONDON ☎020

The crown jewel of Britain's sceptered isle, London lives to a beat all its own, where all partake of the hybrid fruits of a thousand cultural cross-fertilizations. Here is where Jinnah and Gandhi studied; where the Mayflower set sail and Thomas Paine wrote *The Rights of Man;* where Voltaire, Marx, and Freud sought refuge from persecution; where thousands arrive each day to seek a better future. The world's first industrial city, London turned postmodern when her rivals were still modernizing: distinctions between past and future, east and west are meaningless in a place where tradition fuses with innovation and a resident is as likely to hail from Asia as Essex. To the visitor, London offers a bewildering array of choices: tea at the Ritz or chilling in the Fridge; Leonardo at the National or Damian at the Tate Modern; Rossini at the Royal Opera or Les Miz at the Palace; Bond Street couture or Covent Garden cutting-edge. Such a city truly deserves an entire book to itself—*Let's Go: London 2002* is just the ticket.

✈ INTERCITY TRANSPORTATION

Flights: Heathrow (☎(0870) 000 0123) is London's main airport; **Underground** (Piccadilly Line) heads to central London (40-60min.; every 4-5min.; £3.50, under 16 £1.50); the **Heathrow Express** train shuttles to Paddington station (☎(0845) 600 1515; 15min.; every 15min.; £12, round-trip £22). From **Gatwick Airport** (☎(0870) 000 2468), the **Gatwick Express** heads to Victoria (☎(0870) 0002 468; 30-35min.; every 15min.; hourly 5am-midnight; £10.50, round-trip £20), as do cheaper **Connex** commuter trains (☎(0870) 603 0405; 37-42min; £8.20, round-trip £16.40).

Trains: London has 8 major stations: **Charing Cross** (serves south England); **Euston** (the north and northwest); **King's Cross** (the north and northeast); **Liverpool St.** (East Anglia); **Paddington** (the west); **St. Pancras** (Midlands and northwest); **Victoria** (the south); **Waterloo** (the south, southwest, and the Continent). All stations are linked by Underground. Get info at station ticket office or from **National Rail Inquiries Line** (☎(08457) 484950; www.britrail.com).

Buses: Long-distance buses (known as **coaches** in the UK) arrive in London at **Victoria Coach Station,** 164 Buckingham Palace Rd. (Tube: Victoria); some services stop at nearby **Eccleston Bridge,** behind Victoria train station.

✦ ORIENTATION

The heart of London is the vaguely defined **West End,** which stretches east from Park Lane to Kingsway and south from Oxford St. to the River Thames; within this area you'll find the shopping streets around **Oxford Circus,** aristocratic **Mayfair,** the bars and clubs of **Soho,** the street performers and boutiques of **Covent Garden,** and the grandeur of **Trafalgar Square.** East of the West End, you pass legalist **Holborn** before hitting the ancient **City of London** (a.k.a. "the City"), site of the original Roman settlement and home to St. Paul's Cathedral and the Tower of London. The City's eastern border jostles the ethnically diverse, working-class **East End.**

Westminster extends south of Trafalgar Sq. along the Thames; this is the heart of royal and political London, with the Houses of Parliament, Buckingham Palace, and

Westminster Abbey; farther west lies artsy, prosperous **Chelsea.** Across the river from Westminster and the West End, the **South Bank** has an incredible variety of entertainment and museums, from Shakespeare's Globe to the Tate Modern. The enormous space of **Hyde Park** lies to the west of the West End; along its southern border crowd chi-chi **Knightsbridge,** home to Harrods and Harvey Nicks, and posh **Kensington.** North of Hyde Park are media-infested **Notting Hill** and B&B-filled **Bayswater.** Bayswater, Mayfair, and **Marylebone** meet at Marble Arch, on Hyde Park's northeast corner; from here, Marylebone stretches west to meet bookish **Bloomsbury,** north of Soho and Holborn. Farther from the center, **Camden Town, Islington, Hampstead,** and **Highgate** lie to the north of Bloomsbury and the City.

London is an enormous city with barely a straight street to its name; a good street atlas is essential for efficient navigation. The best is *London A to Z*, available at all bookstores and many newsagents and souvenir stores.

⊏ LOCAL TRANSPORTATION

Public Transportation: Run by Transport for London (TfL; 24hr. info and assistance ☎ 7222 1234; www.transportforlondon.gov.uk). Pick up free maps at tube stations. Pick up free maps and guides at TfL **Information Centres** (look for the lower-case "i" logo on signs) at the following Tube stations: Euston, James's Park, King's Cross, Liverpool St., Oxford Circus, Piccadilly St., Victoria, and Heathrow Terminals 1, 2, 3.

Underground: The Underground (a.k.a. Tube) network is divided into 6 concentric zones; fares depend on the number of zones crossed. Buy your ticket before you board and pass it through automatic gates at both ends of your journey. A one-way trip in Zone 1 costs £1.50. The Tube runs approx. 5:30am-12:30am, depending on the line.

Buses: Divided into 4 zones; zones 1-3 are identical to the Tube zones. Fares are £0.70-1 depending on the zones. Regular buses run 6am-midnight or so, after which a limited network of **Night Buses** (prefixed by "N") takes over; fares for Night Buses are £1.50 for Zone 1, elsewhere £1.

Passes: The **Travelcard** is valid for travel on all TfL services; available in daily, weekend, weekly, monthly, and annual periods. 1-Day travelcard from £4 (Zones 1-2). All passes expire at 4:30am the morning after the printed expiry date (so a 1-day pass works for a post-clubbing bus home).

Licensed Taxicabs: An illuminated "taxi" sign on the roof signals availability. Expensive, but drivers know their stuff; tip 10%. For pick-up, call Computer Cabs (☎ 7286 0286), £1.20 extra charge.

Minicabs: Service offered by drivers in private cars. Cheaper than black cabs, but less reliable—stick to a reputable company. Teksi (☎ 8455 9999) offers 24hr. pickup anywhere in London.

⁊ PRACTICAL INFORMATION

TOURIST, FINANCIAL, AND LOCAL SERVICES

Tourist Offices: Britain Visitor Centre (www.visitbritain.com), 1 Regent St. Tube: Oxford Circus. Ideal for travelers headed beyond London. Open M 9:30am-6:30pm, Tu-F 9am-6:30pm, Sa-Su 10am-4pm. **London Visitor Centres** (www.londontouristboard.com) are run by the London Tourist Board. Books accommodations for £5; call 7932 2020. Locations include: **Heathrow Terminals 1,2,3,** in the Tube station; open Oct- Aug. daily 8am-6pm; Sept. M-Sa 9am-7pm and Su 8am-6pm; **Liverpool Street,** in the Tube station; open June-Sept. M-Sa 8am-7pm, Su 8am-6pm; Oct.-May daily 8am-6pm; **Victoria Station,** station forecourt; open Easter-Sept. M-Sa 8am-8pm, Su 8am-6pm; Oct.-Easter daily 8am-6pm; **Waterloo International,** arrivals hall; open daily 8:30am-10:30pm.

Embassies: Australia, Australia House, Strand (☎ 7379 4334). Tube: Temple. Open 9:30am-3:30pm. **Canada,** MacDonald House, 1 Grosvenor Sq. (☎ 7258 6600). Tube: Bond St. Open daily 8:30am-5pm. **Ireland,** 17 Grosvenor Pl. (☎ 7235 2171). Tube: Hyde Park Corner. Open M-F 9:30am-4:30pm. **New Zealand,** New Zealand House, 80 Haymarket (☎ 7930 8422). Tube: Leicester Sq. Open M-F 10am-noon and 2-4pm. **South Africa,** South Africa House, Trafalgar Sq. (☎ 7451 7299). Tube: Charing Cross. Open M-F 8:45am-12:45pm. **United States,** 24 Grosvenor Sq. (☎ 7499 9900). Tube: Bond St. Open M-F 8:30am-12:30pm and 2-5pm. Phones answered 24hr.

BRITAIN

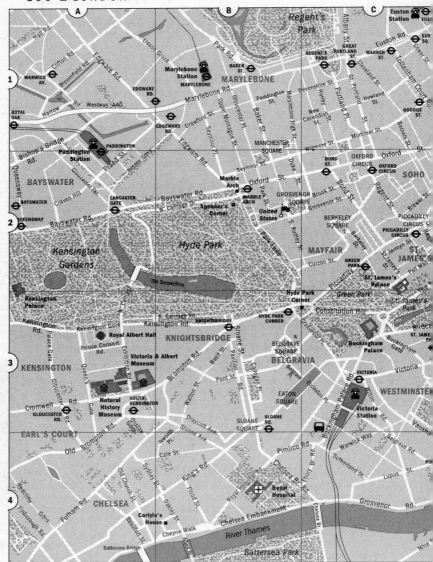

Central London: Major Street Finder

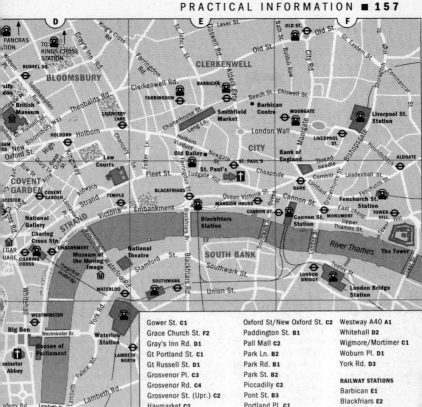

Currency Exchange: The best rates are found at banks, such as **Barclays, HSBC, Lloyd's, National Westminster** (NatWest), and **Royal Bank of Scotland.** Most banks open M-F 9:30am-4:30pm.

American Express: Offices throughout London; ☎(0800) 521313 for the nearest one.

Gay and Lesbian Services: London Lesbian and Gay Switchboard (☎7837 7324). 24hr. advice and support service.

EMERGENCY AND COMMUNICATIONS

Emergency (Medical, Police, and Fire): ☎999; no coins required.

Hospitals: For non-life threatening injuries, you can be treated at no charge in the Accidents and Emergency (A&E) ward of a hospital. The following have 24hr. walk-in A&E (also known as casualty) departments: **Royal London Hospital,** Whitechapel Rd. (☎7377 7000. Tube: Whitechapel); **Royal Free,** Pond St. (☎7794 0500. Tube: Belsize Park or Rail: Hampstead Heath); **St. Mary's,** Praed St. (☎7725 6666. Tube: Paddington); **St. Thomas's,** Lambeth Palace Rd. (☎7928 9292. Tube: Waterloo); **University College Hospital,** Grafton Way (☎7387 9300; Tube: Warren St.)

Chemists (Pharmacies): Most chemists keep standard store hours (approx. M-Sa 9:30am-5:30pm). Late-night chemists are rare; 2 are given below. **Zafash Pharmacy,** 233 Old Brompton Rd. (☎7373 2798. Tube: Earls Court), is open 24hr. **Bliss Chemists,** 5-6 Marble Arch (☎7723 6116. Tube: Marble Arch), opens daily 9am-midnight

Police: London is covered by 2 police forces: the **City of London Police** (☎7601 2222) for the City of London, and the **Metropolitan Police** (☎7230 1212) for the rest. The main central-London station is **West End Central:** 27 Savile Row (☎7437 1212). Tube: Oxford Circus or Piccadilly Circus. Open 24hr.

Internet Access: Cybercafes punctuate London. ■ **easyEverything** (☎7907 7800; www.easyeverything.com) cybercafes are open 24hr., with prices from £1 per hr. Locations include 9-13 Wilson Rd, directly opposite Victoria Station.

Post Office: Post offices are everywhere; call (08457) 740740 for locations. When sending mail to London, be sure to include the full post code, since London has 7 King's Roads, 8 Queen's Roads, and 2 Mandela Streets. The largest office is the **Trafalgar Square Post Office,** 24-28 William IV St., WC2N 4DL (☎7484 9304; Tube: Charing Cross). All mail sent *Poste Restante* or general delivery to unspecified post offices ends up here. Open M-Th and Sa 8am-8pm, F 8:30am-8pm.

▐ ACCOMMODATIONS

No matter where you plan to stay, it is essential to **plan ahead,** especially in summer; London accommodations are almost always booked solid. Be sure to check the cancellation policy before handing over the deposit; some are non-refundable.

ACCOMMODATION DISTRICTS

Budget accommodations lie all over London, but most are concentrated in a few areas; if you land without a reservation, these are the best places to start hunting.

WESTMINSTER. Quiet **Pimlico,** south of Victoria station, is full of budget hotels; the highest concentration is along **Belgrave Road.** Places tend to be nicer the farther you go from the station. Though fairly close to major sights such as Parliament and Buckingham Palace, there's little in the way of restaurants and nightlife.

EARL'S COURT. West of Kensington, this area feeds on budget tourism, spewing forth souvenir shops and bureaux de change. Some streets seem populated solely by B&Bs and hostels. The area has a vibrant gay and lesbian population and is also tremendously popular with Aussie travelers cooling their heels in London (in the 1970s, it earned the nickname "Kangaroo Valley"). Be careful at night and beware of guides trying to lead you from the station to a hostel. Some B&Bs conceal grimy rooms behind fancy lobbies and well-dressed staff; always ask to see a room.

BAYSWATER. The streets between **Queensway** and **Paddington Station** house London's highest concentration of cheap sleeps, with countless hostels, B&Bs, and budget hotels. Fairly central, with plenty of nearby restaurants, but accommodations vary in quality—be sure to see a room first.

BLOOMSBURY. Bloomsbury is the best-located accommodation district for nightlife, with dozens of B&Bs and student halls within striking distance of Soho and the British Museum. Plenty of cheap restaurants add to the allure of this quiet, academic neighborhood. Many B&Bs are on busy roads, so be wary of noise levels; also, the neighborhood becomes seedy toward King's Cross.

YHA/HI HOSTELS

London hostels are not always able to accommodate every written request for reservations, much less on-the-spot inquiries, but they frequently hold a few beds available—it's always worth checking. To secure a place, show up as early as possible, or call in advance and book with a credit card. In order to stay at YHA hostels, you usually must be a member; see **Accommodations and Camping,** p. 152. **Linens** are included at all London hostels, but **towels** are not; rent one from reception ($3.50). All hostels have well-equipped kitchens, laundry facilities, and luggage storage in addition to in-room **lockers** (padlock required); most have a **cafeteria** for cheap evening meals ($5). YHA hostels also sell discount tickets to theaters and major attractions. None have **lockouts** or **curfews.**

■ **YHA Hampstead Heath,** 4 Wellgarth Rd., NW11 (☎8458 9054). From Golders Green Tube (Zone 3), turn left onto North End Rd.; Wellgarth Rd. is a 10min. walk up on the left. Out-of-the-way location is main disadvantage of this manorial hostel with a large garden. **Internet.** Currency exchange. Breakfast included. 24hr. reception. 4- to 6-bed dorms £19.90; doubles £46, family (at least 1 child under 18) £36; triples £67, £53; quads £82, £51; quints £101, £88; 6-person rooms £121, £102. AmEx/MC/V.

YHA City of London, 36 Carter Ln., EC4 (☎7236 4965). Tube: St. Paul's. In the frescoed former buildings of St. Paul's Choir School, within spitting distance of the cathedral. Single-sex dorms have interlocking bunks and sinks. **Internet.** Secure luggage storage. Currency exchange. English breakfast included. Reception 7am-11pm. Dorms £21.15-24.70, under 18 £18.90-21; private rooms £23.70-£138, families £41-123. MC/V.

YHA Earl's Court, 38 Bolton Gdns., SW5 (☎7373 7083). Tube: Earl's Court. Rambling Victorian townhouse, more casual than most YHAs. Ongoing refurbishment is replacing interlocking triple-deckers with bunks and adding more bathrooms. All dorms single-sex. Reserve 1 month ahead. Prepacked continental breakfast £3.30. Dorms £18.50, under 18 £16.50; twins (breakfast included) £51. AmEx/MC/V.

YHA Holland House, Holland Walk, W8 (☎7937 0748). Tube: High St. Kensington. On the edge of Holland Park, accommodation is split between a 17th-century mansion and a 1970s unit; dorms in both are similar, with 12-20 bunks. Book 1 month ahead in summer. Breakfast included. £20.50, under 18 £18.50. AmEx/MC/V.

YHA Oxford Street, 14-18 Noel St., W1 (☎7734 1618). Tube: Oxford Circus. Small, spare hostel, with limited facilities but an unbeatable location for Soho nightlife. Reserve at least 1 month ahead. Prepacked continental breakfast £3.30. 3- to 4-bed dorms £21.50, under 18 £17.50; 2-bed dorms £23.50.

PRIVATE HOSTELS

Private hostels don't require a YHA/HI membership, serve a more youthful clientele, and are generally much cheaper. On the other hand, standards vary widely; generally, private hostels are less well-maintained than YHA hostels, and occasionally don't have single-sex rooms. Pricing schemes are similar to YHA hostels.

■ **The Generator,** Compton Pl. (off 37 Tavistock Pl.), WC1 (☎7388 7666). Tube: Russel Square. In a former police station, this hostel is straight out of *Blade Runner*, with cell-like units housing metal bunks. Basement dorms have lockers and military-style bathrooms. Bar and cafeteria. **Internet.** Rules enforced (no noise after 9pm). Reserve ahead for weekends. Dorms £15-22.50; twins £46-53; singles £36.50-41. MC/V.

BRITAIN

■ **Hyde Park Hostel,** 2-6 Inverness Terr., W2 (☎ 7229 5101). Tube: Queensway or Bayswater. Space-filling configurations of bunks in women's and mixed dorms leave little room, but smaller rooms are more spacious and bathrooms a cut above average. **Internet,** bar, cafeteria, kitchen, laundry, lounge, luggage room. Continental breakfast included. Ages 16-35 only. Reserve 2 weeks ahead. Dorms £10-17.50; twins £40-45. MC/V.

■ **Indian YMCA,** 41 Fitzroy Sq., W1 (☎ 7387 0411). Tube: Warren St. Great location by a Georgian square. Standard rooms, with desk and phone, and institutional shared bathrooms, but price includes continental breakfast and Indian dinner. Reservations essential. Dorms £20; singles £33; doubles £46, with bath £52. AmEx/MC/V.

Hyde Park Inn, 48-50 Inverness Terr., W2 (☎ 7229 0000). Very cheap and fairly cheerful. Smaller dorms are more spacious. **Internet.** Kitchen, laundry, lockers (£1 per day), luggage store (£1.50 per bag per day). Continental breakfast included. £10 key/linen deposit. Dorms £9-19; singles £29-32; double/twins £18-21. MC/V (2.5% surcharge).

International Student House, 229 Great Portland St., W1 (☎ 7631 8300). Tube: Great Portland St. A thriving international metropolis. **Internet,** bar, cafeteria, fitness center, laundry. Continental breakfast included (for dorms £2). £10 key deposit. Reception M-F 7:45am-10:30pm, Sa-Su 8:30am-10:30pm. Reserve at least 1 month ahead. Dorms £10; singles £31, with bath £33; twins £45, £51; triples £60; quads £70. MC/V.

STUDENT RESIDENCE HALLS

The best accommodation deals in town are in university residence halls, which often rent out rooms over the summer and (less frequently) Easter vacations—you can often get a single for little more (and sometimes less) than the price of a hostel bed. Don't expect luxury—student dorms are the same the world over—but rooms are generally clean and well equipped, and the halls often have extra facilities such as bars, games rooms, and sports facilities.

■ **High Holborn Residence,** 178 High Holborn, WC1 (☎ 7379 5589). Tube: Holborn. Comfortable modern student residence. Flats of 4-5 rooms, with phone, shared kitchen and bathroom. Continental breakfast included. Laundry. Open mid-June to late Sept. Singles £28-35; twins £47-57, with bath £57-67; triples with bath £67-77. MC/V.

Carr-Saunders Hall, 18-24 Fitzroy St., W1 (☎ 7580 6338). Tube: Warren St. Rooms larger than most most student halls and have sink and phone. Breakfast included, served on the panoramic roof terrace. Reserve 8 weeks ahead for July-Aug. Open Easter and mid-June to mid-Sept. Singles £23.50-27; twins £37-45, with bath £42-50. MC/V.

Commonwealth Hall, 1-11 Cartwright Gardens, WC1 (☎ 7685 3500). Tube: Russell Sq. Post-war block with 400 basic, student singles; unbeatable value. English breakfast included. Open Easter and mid-June to mid-Sept. Reserve 2 months ahead July-Aug.; no walk-ins. Singles £22, with dinner £26; students £19 (dinner included). MC/V.

Rosebery Hall, 90 Rosebery Ave., EC1 (☎ 7278 3251). Tube: Angel. Exit left from the Tube, cross the road, and take the 2nd right into Roseberry Ave. (10min.). Modern student residence arranged around a sunken garden. Open Easter and mid-June to mid-Sept. Reserve 6 weeks ahead for July; £10 cancellation fee. English breakfast included. Singles £26-31; twins £46, economy £36, with bath £57; triples £55. MC/V.

BED AND BREAKFASTS

WESTMINSTER

■ **Luna Simone Hotel,** 47/49 Belgrave Rd., SW1 (☎ 7834 5897). Tube: Victoria. Stuccoed Victorian facade conceals ultra-modern rooms with TV, phone, kettle, and hairdryer. English breakfast. Singles £35-40, with bath £35-45; doubles £50-65, £60-80; triples with bath £80-100. Discount for long stays in low season. MC/V.

■ **Morgan House,** 120 Ebury St., SW1 (☎ 7730 2384). Tube: Victoria. 11 beautifully kept rooms, with TVs, kettles, phones, and some fireplaces. English breakfast. Singles £42, with bath £65; doubles £62, £80; quads with bath £120. MC/V.

Georgian House Hotel, 35 St. George's Drive, SW1 (☎ 7834 1438). Tube: Victoria. Rooms are large and well-equipped, with TV, phone, hairdryer, kettle, and matching furniture. English breakfast. Singles £36; doubles £42; triples £69; quads with bath £90; quints with bath £96. MC/V.

Melbourne House, 79 Belgrave Rd., SW1 (☎ 7828 3516). Tube: Pimlico. Extraordinarily clean and well-kept. Non-smoking rooms have TV, phone, and kettle. Continental breakfast. Singles £30, with bath £55; doubles with bath £75; triples with bath £95; quads with bath £110. MC/V (payment on arrival; cash preferred).

KENSINGTON AND EARL'S COURT

■ **Vicarage Private Hotel,** 10 Vicarage Gate, W8 (☎ 7229 4030). Tube: High St. Kensington. Beautifully kept house with ornate hallways, TV lounge, and superb rooms: cast-iron beds, solid wood furnishings, lovely drapes, kettle and hairdryer. English breakfast. Singles £45; doubles £74, with bath £98; triples £90; quads £98. No credit cards.

Abbey House Hotel, 11 Vicarage Gate, W8 (☎ 7727 2594). Tube: High St. Kensington. Spacious pastel rooms with TV, desk, and sink. Very helpful staff. English breakfast. Singles £45; doubles £74; triples £90; quads £100. No credit cards.

Beaver Hotel, 57-59 Philbeach Gdns., W14 (☎ 7373 4553). Tube: Earl's Court. Displays unusual attention to detail. Spotless bathrooms, many with bathtub. English breakfast. Singles £40, with bath £60; doubles with bath £85; triples with bath £99. AmEx/MC/V.

BAYSWATER

■ **Admiral Hotel,** 143 Sussex Gdns., W2 (☎ 7723 7309). Tube: Paddington. Beautifully kept B&B. 19 summery, non-smoking rooms with bathroom, TV, and kettle. Singles £40-48; doubles £55-70; triples £75-90; quads £88-100; quints £92-115. MC/V.

■ **Hyde Park Rooms Hotel,** 137 Sussex Gdns. W2 (☎ 7723 0225). Tube: Paddington. White rooms with fluorescent-colored bedspreads all have sink and TV. Reserve 2 weeks ahead in summer. Singles £30, with bath £40; doubles £40-45, £50-55; triples £60, £72; quads £80, £96. AmEx/MC/V (5% surcharge).

Barry House Hotel, 12 Sussex Pl., W2 (☎ 7723 7340). Tube: Paddington. Very bright if slightly tight rooms with phone, TV, kettle, and hairdryer; most with en suite bathrooms. Singles £32-38, with bath £48-50; doubles £78, £65; triples £92, £75; quads £114, £99; quints £125, £109. AmEx/MC/V (3% surcharge).

Cardiff Hotel, 5-9 Norfolk Sq., W2 (☎ 7723 9068). Tube: Paddington. All rooms have cream fleur-de-lys wallpaper, TV, kettle, and phone; most with new wood furnishings. English breakfast. Singles with shower £45, with bath £55-69; doubles with bath £79; triples with bath £90; quads with bath £99; quints with bath £120. MC/V.

Garden Court Hotel, 30-31 Kensington Gdns. Sq., W2 (☎ 7229 2553). Tube: Bayswater. The snazzy reception feels like a 3-star Tuscan resort, but rooms are solidly English B&B. English breakfast. Singles £39, with bath £58; doubles £58, £88; triples £72, £99; family quads (2 double beds) £82, £120. MC/V.

BLOOMSBURY

■ **Crescent Hotel,** 49-50 Cartwright Gdns., WC1 (☎ 7387 1515). Tube: Russell Sq. A real family-run atmosphere, with artistic rooms. All rooms have TV, kettle, and phone. Singles £43, with shower £48, with bath £70; doubles with bath £82; triples with bath £93; quads with bath £105. More for one-night stays; discounts for over a week. MC/V.

■ **Arosfa Hotel,** 83 Gower St., WC1 (☎ 7636 2115). Tube: Warren St. The Iberian owners ensure that this small, non-smoking B&B lives up to its Welsh name (meaning "place to rest"). Guests have access to rear garden. English breakfast. Singles £37; doubles £50, with bath £66; triples £68, £79; quads with bath £92. MC/V (2% surcharge).

George Hotel, 58-60 Cartwright Gdns., WC1 (☎ 7387 8777). Tube: Russell Sq. Meticulous rooms with TV, kettle, phone, and sink. Forward-facing 1st-floor rooms are best, with high ceilings and tall windows. **Internet.** Singles £50, with shower £65, with shower and WC £75; doubles £69.50, £77, £90; triples £83, £91.50, £105; quads £95. 10% discount for stays over 7 days (Nov.-June only). MC/V.

Hotel Ibis Euston, 3 Cardington St., NW1 (☎ 7304 7712). Tube: Euston. Predominantly French staff preside over the 350 spacious, modern rooms of this European hotel chain. Cable TV, A/C, phone, desk, and bathroom. 24hr. snack bar. Restaurant serves 2-course dinner (£8) 6-10:30pm. Breakfast £4.50. Doubles and twins £70. MC/V.

BRITAIN

Langland Hotel, 29-31 Gower St., WC1 (☎7636 5801). Tube: Goodge St. Family atmosphere, wood-framed beds, solid furniture, and plenty of spacious, sparkling bathrooms help this B&B stand out. All rooms with TV, kettle, and fan. Singles £40, with bath £55; doubles £50, £75; triples £70, £90; quads £90, £110; quints £100. AmEx/MC/V.

Ruskin Hotel, 23-24 Montague St., WC1 (☎7636 7388). Tube: Holborn. Overlooking the east wing of the British Museum, the Ruskin lives up to its location with artsy decor including a replica Greek frieze above the staircase and a original scene of Camden Town circa 1801. All rooms have phone, kettle, and hairdryer. English breakfast. Singles £47; doubles £67, with bath £84; triples £82, £92. AmEx/MC/V.

🔅 FOOD AND PUBS

Forget stale food stereotypes: in terms of quality and choice, London's restaurants offer a gastronomic experience as diverse, stylish, and satisfying as you'll find anywhere on the planet—until you see the bill. Any restaurant charging under £10 for a main course is regarded as "cheap"; add drinks and service and you're nudging £15. That said, it *is* possible to eat cheaply—and well—in London. The trick, as always, is knowing where and (just as importantly) when to eat. Lunchtime and early-evening **special offers** make it possible to dine in style and stay on budget, while **pub grub,** as elsewhere in Britain, offers hearty, if not always wholesome, food for lunch and occasionally dinner. Many of the best budget meals are found in the amazing variety of **ethnic restaurants.** For the best and cheapest ethnic food, head to the source: Whitechapel for Bengali *baltis*, Islington for Turkish *meze*, Marylebone for Lebanese *shwarma*, and Soho for Cantonese *dim sum*.

AFTERNOON TEA

Afternoon tea is perhaps the high point of English cuisine. A social ritual as much as a meal, at its best it involves a long afternoon of sandwiches, scones, pastries, tinkling china, and restrained conversation. The inherent qualities of "tiffin" notwithstanding, the main attraction of afternoon tea today is the chance to lounge in sumptuous surroundings that at any other time would be beyond all but a Sultan's budget. Note that you'll often need to book in advance, especially for weekends, and many hotels have a strict dress code.

The Lanesborough, Hyde Park Corner (☎7259 5599). Tube: Hyde Park Corner. For sheer opulence, the Regency's interior out-ritzes the Ritz. No official dress code. Set tea £22.50, champagne tea £26.50; à la carte includes scones with jam and clotted cream, £6.50. Min. charge £9.50 per person.

The Orangery, Kensington Palace (☎7938 1406). Tube: High St. Kensington. Built for Queen Anne's dinner parties, this airy building is now a popular setting for light lunches (£7-8) and afternoon teas (from £8). Open daily 10am-6pm. MC/V.

The Ritz, Piccadilly (☎7493 8181). Tube: Green Park. The world's most famous tea. Reserve at least 1 month ahead for the weekday sittings, 3 months for weekends; alternatively, skip lunch and arrive at noon for an early tea. No jeans or trainers; jacket and tie preferred for men. Sittings daily at 3:30 and 5pm. Set tea £27. AmEx/MC/V.

RESTAURANTS AND PUBS BY NEIGHBORHOOD

THE WEST END

🍽 **busaba eathai,** 106-110 Wardour St. (☎7255 8686). Tube: Tottenham Court Rd. Wildly popular Thai eatery from the founder of Wagamama. Get in line for great food (£5-8) at shared square tables in a cozy, wood-paneled room. Open M-Th noon-11pm, F-Sa noon-11:30pm, Su noon-10pm. AmEx/MC/V.

Bar Italia, 22 Frith St. (☎7437 4520). Tube: Tottenham Court Rd. A fixture of the late-night Soho scene. You won't find anything stronger than an espresso here (£1.60), but it's still *the* place for a post-club panini (£3.50-5). Open 24hr. except M 3-7am.

Lamb and Flag, 33 Rose St. (☎7497 9504). Tube: Leicester Sq. Traditional dark-wood interior. Food daily noon-3pm. Live jazz upstairs Su 7:30pm. Open M-Th 11am-11pm, F-Sa 11am-10:45pm, Su noon-10:30pm.

Neal's Yard Bakery & Tearoom, 6 Neal's Yard (☎ 7836 5199). Tube: Covent Garden. Open-air counter sells fresh bread made from organic flour (from £0.90) and vegan faves like beanburgers (£2.85 eat-in, £2.20 take-away). Open M-Sa 10:30am-4:30pm.

Wong Kei, 41-43 Wardour St. (☎ 7437 3071). Tube: Piccadilly Circus. Renovations have removed much of this Chinatown stalwart's kitschy charm, but little else has changed: the waiters remain as famously curt as ever, and prices are rock-bottom. Won-ton noodle soup £2.50, roast duck and rice £3.50. Open daily noon-11:30pm. Cash only.

HOLBORN AND CLERKENWELL

▨ **Bleeding Heart Tavern,** corner of Greville St. and Bleeding Heart Yard (☎ 7404 0333). Tube: Farringdon. This establishment is split between the light, laid-back upstairs pub and the cosy restaurant below, whose thick tablecloths, fresh roses, and candles make a romantic backdrop to hearty English fayre, such as spit-roasted pork with crackling (£8). Get 2 courses for £10 5-7:30pm. Tavern open M-F 11am-11pm. AmEx/MC/V.

▨ **Ye Olde Cheshire Cheese,** Wine Office Ct. by 145 Fleet St. (☎ 7353 6170). Tube: Blackfriars. Dark labyrinth of oak-panelled rooms on 3 floors, dating from 1667; a onetime haunt of Johnson, Dickens, Mark Twain, and Theodore Roosevelt. Multiple bars and restaurants dish out traditional English food at every price range. Open M-F 11:30am-11pm, Sa 11:30am-3pm and 5:30-11pm, Su noon-3pm. Food M-F noon-9:30pm, Sa noon-2:30pm and 6-9:30pm, Su noon-2:30pm. AmEx/MC/V.

Tinseltown 24-Hour Diner, 44-46 St. John St. (☎ 7689 2424). Tube: Farringdon. Cavernous underground haven for pre- and post-clubbers. Food ranges from burgers (£5.50) to full-on shakes with added chocolate bar (£3.50). Open 24hr.

THE CITY OF LONDON

▨ **Futures,** 8 Botolph Alley, off Botolph Ln. (☎ 7623 4529). Tube: Monument. Suits besiege this tiny take-away for a changing variety of vegetarian dishes (£2-4). Open M-F 7:30-10am and 11:30am-3pm. **Branch** in Exchange Sq. (behind Liverpool St).

The Place Below, St. Mary-le-Bow. (☎ 7329 0789). Tube: St. Paul's. In the 11th-century crypt of St. Mary-le-Bow church, vegetarian dishes provide salvation for the weary traveler. Salads and hot dishes £6.50-7.50, sandwiches £5; take-away £1-2 less (plenty of benches in the churchyard). Open M-F 7:30am-4pm, lunch 11:30am-2:30pm. MC/V.

Simpson's, Ball Court, off 38½ Cornhill (☎ 7626 9985). Tube: Bank. "Established 1757" says the sign on the alley leading to this pub; indeed, it remains so traditional that a man stands in the door to greet you. Different rooms divide the classes: drinkers populate the basement wine bar (sandwiches £2-4) and ground-floor bar, diners the ground-floor and upstairs restaurants (main dishes £6-7). Open M-F 11:30am-3pm.

SOUTH BANK

▨ **Tas,** 72 Borough High St. (☎ 7403 7200; Tube: London Bridge) and 33 The Cut (☎ 7928 2111; Tube: Waterloo). Stylish and affordable Turkish food. Stews and baked dishes—many vegetarian—outshine the kebabs. Main courses £6-8. Live music from 7:30pm. Reservations essential. Open M-Sa 12:30-11:30pm, Su 12:30-10:30pm. AmEx/MC/V.

Gourmet Pizza Co., Gabriel's Wharf, 56 Upper Ground (☎ 7928 3188). Tube: Southwark. On the embankment, this adventurous pizzeria offers the best-value riverside dining in town. Pizzas £6-9. Open M-Sa noon-11pm. AmEx/MC/V.

WESTMINSTER

▨ **Jenny Lo's Teahouse,** 14 Eccleston St. (☎ 7259 0399). Tube: Victoria. Stripped-down Chinese fare at communal tables. *Cha shao* (pork noodle soup) £5. Teas (from £0.85), blended in-house, are served in hand-turned stoneware. Open M-F 11:30am-3pm and 6-10pm, Sa noon-3pm and 6-10pm. £5 min. Cash only.

Red Lion, 48 Parliament St. (☎ 7930 5826). Tube: Westminster. *The* MPs' hangout, where the Chancellor's press secretary was infamously overhead leaking information in 1998. A "division bell" alerts MPs to drink up when a vote is about to be taken. Dishes £3-6. Open M-Sa 11am-11pm, Su noon-7pm; food served daily noon-3pm. MC/V.

BRITAIN

KNIGHTSBRIDGE AND BELGRAVIA

▧ **Stockpot,** 6 Basil St. (☎ 7589 8627). Tube: Knightsbridge. Many worse restaurants get away with charging twice the prices of this supercheap stalwart. No-frills pinewood interior is the setting for bargains like beef stroganoff (£3.65) and grilled lamb cutlets (£4.30). 2-course set menu £3.90. Open M-Sa 7:30am-11pm, Su noon-10:30pm.

KENSINGTON AND EARL'S COURT

▧ **The Troubadour,** 265 Old Brompton Rd. (☎ 7370 1434). Tube: Earl's Court. Cosy old-fashioned interior festooned with curios and a shady rear garden. Sandwich platters £4-5, hot specials £5-10. Poetry and folk-music nights. Open daily 9am-midnight. MC/V.

Raison d'Être, 18 Bute St. (☎ 7584 5008). Tube: South Kensington. Catering to the local French community with a bewildering range of filled *baguettes* (£2.20-5) and *salades* (£3.50-4.70). Open M-F 8am-6pm, Sa 9:30am-4pm. Cash only.

NOTTING HILL AND BAYSWATER

▧ **George's Portobello Fish Bar,** 329 Portobello Rd. (☎ 8969 7895). Tube: Ladbroke Grove. Choose your piece from the recently-fried fillets on display or ask them to rustle up a new one (£4-5), add a generous helping of chunky chips (£1), and wolf it down outside (no inside seating). Open Su-F 11am-midnight, Sa 11am-9pm. Cash only.

▧ **Royal China,** 13 Queensway (☎ 7221 2535). Tube: Bayswater. Renowned for London's best *dim sum* (£2-3 per dish; count on 3-4 dishes each), served M-Sa noon-5pm, Su 11am-5pm; on weekends, arrive early or expect to wait 30-45min. Open M-Th noon-11pm, F-Sa noon-11:30pm, Su 11am-10pm. AmEx/MC/V.

Books for Cooks, 4 Blenheim Crescent (☎ 7221 1992). Tube: Ladbroke Grove. Eric and his crew of culinary pros "test" recipes from new titles. You can rely on the cakes (£2). Food served M-Sa 10am-2:30pm or so. Bookstore open M-Sa 10am-6pm. AmEx/MC/V.

MARYLEBONE AND BLOOMSBURY

▧ **Diwana Bhel Poori House,** 121-123 Drummond St. (☎ 7387 5556). Tube: Warren St. No frills or frippery here—just great, cheap south-Indian vegetarian food. Fill yourself for £5. Open daily noon-11:30pm. AmEx/MC/V.

ECCo (Express Coffee Co.), 46 Goodge St. (☎ 7580 9250). Eleven-inch thin-crust pizzas, made to order, cost an incredible £3; sandwiches and baguettes from £1, rolls from £0.50. Buy any hot drink before noon and get a fresh-baked croissant for free. Pizzas available from noon on. Open daily 7am-11pm. Cash only.

The Lamb, 94 Lamb's Conduit St. (☎ 7405 0713). Tube: Russell Sq. This old-fashioned pub is an actors' hangout—regulars include Peter O'Toole—and fading daguerreotypes of past thespian tipplers line the walls. The "snob screens" around the bar once provided privacy for "respectable" men meeting ladies of ill-repute. Open M-Sa 11am-11pm, Su noon-10:30pm. Food served M-Sa noon-2:30pm and 6-9pm, Su noon-2:30pm. MC/V.

Zizzi, 34 Paddington St. (☎ 7224 1450). Tube: Baker St. Take a hint from the show-off chefs using a wood-fired oven and try hand-thrown pizzas (£5-7.50). *Al frecso* dining in summer. Reserve F-Sa. Open Su-Th 11am-11pm, F-Sa 11am-11:30pm. AmEx/MC/V.

👁 SIGHTS

ORGANIZED TOURS

The classic London **bus tour** is on an open-top double-decker—and in good weather, it's undoubtedly the best way to get a good overview of the city. Tickets for the **Big Bus Company,** 48 Buckingham Palace Rd., are valid for 24hr. on three hop-on, hop-off routes, with 1hr. walking tours and a short Thames cruise included. (☎ 7233 9533; www.bigbus.co.uk. £15, kids £7.) For a more in-depth account, you can't beat a **walking tour** led by a knowledgeable guide. **Original London Walks** is the biggest walking-tour company, running 12-16 walks per day, from "Magical Mystery Tour" to nighttime "Jack the Ripper's Haunts" and guided visits to larger museums. Most walks last 2hr., starting from a convenient Tube station. (☎ 7624 9255; www.walks.com. £5, students and seniors £4, under 16 free.)

BRITAIN

THE WEST END

MAYFAIR AND ST. JAMES'S

Home to Prince Charles, the Ritz, and exclusive gentlemen's clubs, this is London's aristocratic quarter; on **Jermyn Street,** one block south of Piccadilly, stores cater to traditional English squires with hand-cut suits and hunting gear.

BURLINGTON HOUSE. The only one of Piccadilly's aristocratic mansions to survive, Burlington House was built in 1665. Today, it houses numerous regal societies, including the **Royal Academy,** heart of the British artistic establishment and home to some excellent exhibitions (see p. 180).

ST. JAMES'S PALACE. Built in 1536, St. James's is London's only remaining purpose-built palace (Buckingham Palace was a rough-and-ready conversion job). Prince Charles lives here now, while the Queen Mum bunks next door at Clarence House. The only part of the Palace you're likely to get into is the **Chapel Royal,** open for Sunday services from October to Easter at 8:30 and 11am. From Easter to September, services are held in the Inigo Jones-designed **Queen's Chapel,** across Marlborough Rd. from the Palace. *(Between the Mall and Pall Mall. Tube: Green Park.)*

SOHO

Soho has a history of welcoming all colors and creeds to its streets. Early settlers included French Huguenots fleeing religious persecution in the 17th century, but these days Soho is less gay Paris, more plain gay: a concentration of gay-owned restaurants and bars has turned **Old Compton Street** into the heart of gay London.

PICCADILLY CIRCUS. In the glow of its lurid neon signs, five of the West End's major arteries merge and swirl round the **statue of Eros,** dedicated to the Victorian philanthropist, Lord Shaftesbury. Eros originally pointed down Shaftesbury Ave., but recent restoration work has put his aim significantly off. *(Tube: Piccadilly Circus.)*

LEICESTER SQUARE. Amusements at this entertainment nexus range from London's largest cinemas to the **Swiss Centre** glockenspiel, whose atonal renditions of Beethoven's *Moonlight Sonata* are enough to make even the tone-deaf weep. *(Rings M-F at noon, 6, 7, and 8pm; Sa-Su noon, 2, 4, 5, 6, 7, and 8pm.)* Be true to your inner tourist by having your name engraved on a grain of rice, getting a henna tattoo, and sitting for a caricature. *(Tube: Leicester Sq. or Piccadilly Circus.)*

CHINATOWN. Pedestrianized, tourist-ridden **Gerrard Street,** with scroll-worked dragon gates and pagoda-capped phone booths, is the contrasted heart of this tiny slice of Canton, but gritty **Lisle Street,** one block to the south, has a more authentic feel. Chinatown is most vibrant during the raucous Chinese New Year in February. *(Between Leicester Sq., Shaftesbury Ave., and Charing Cross Rd.)*

COVENT GARDEN

Covent Garden piazza—first laid out by Inigo Jones in the 17th century—is one of the few parts of London popular with locals and tourists alike. On the very spot where Samuel Pepys saw England's first Punch and Judy show, street performers still entertain the thousands who flock here year round. *(Tube: Covent Garden.)*

THE ROYAL OPERA HOUSE. The Royal Opera House reopened in 2000 after a major expansion. After wandering the ornate lobby of the original 1858 theater, head up to the enormous **Floral Hall.** From here, take the escalator to reach the **terrace,** with great views of London. *(Bow St. Open daily 10am-3:30pm. 1¼hr. backstage tours M-Sa 10:30am, 12:30, and 2:30pm; reservations essential. £7, students £6.)*

THEATRE ROYAL DRURY LANE. Founded in 1663, this is the oldest of London's surviving theaters; David Garrick ruled the roost here in the 18th century. The theater even has a ghost—a corpse and dagger were found bricked up in the wall in the 19th century. This and other pieces of Drury Ln. lore are brought back to life in the actor-led backstage tours. *(Entrance on Catherine St. ☎ 7240 5357. Tours Su-Tu and Th-F 3 per day; W and Sa 2 per day. £7.50, children £5.50.)*

BRITAIN

National Film Theatre

National Theatre

7

SOUTH BANK

Sumne

Southwark St.

Festival Hall

Hayward Gallery

8

Upper Ground

Stamford St.

Cornwall Rd.

Hatfields

Blackfriars Rd.

In the shell of a former power station, **Tate Modern** is the world's largest modern art museum.

Mepham St.

WATERLOO

SOUTHWARK

6

9

Jubilee Gardens

Belvedere Rd.

York Rd.

Created by a non-profit community developer, **Gabriel's Wharf** is a flower-strewn haven of crafts, boutiques, and pavement cafes.

finish

LAMBETH

LAMBETH NORTH

Westminster

Bridge Rd.

Waterloo Rd.

Lancaster St. Rd.

Borough St. Rd.

London Rd.

Newington

The concrete megalith of the **South Bank Centre** harbors one of Europe's premier cultural centres.

th Palace Rd.

Lambeth Palace Gardens

When it comes to views, nothing compares with a spin on the **London Eye**.

Lambeth Rd.

Geraldine Mary Harmsworth Park

St. George's Rd.

Kennington Rd.

Brook Drive

Finish off your day in a state of composure upon **Westminster Bridge**.

Newington Butts

← If you're not exhausted by now, continue over the river for Parliament, Big Ben, Westminster Abbey, and Buckingham Palace.

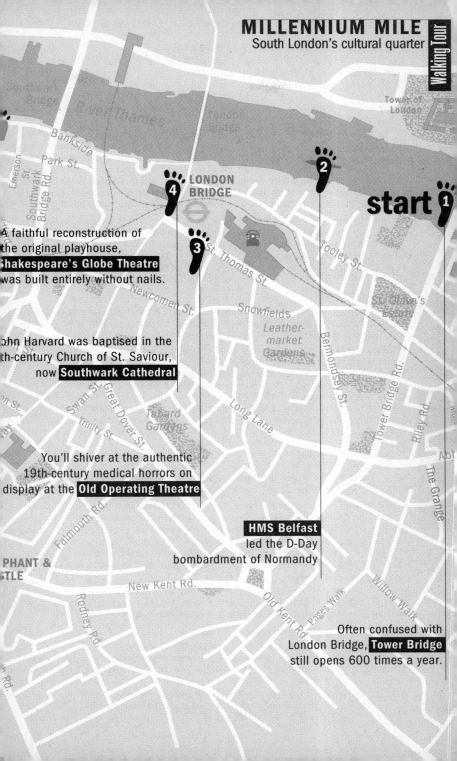

MILLENNIUM MILE
South London's cultural quarter

Walking Tour

Tower of London

River Thames

Southwark Bridge

Bankside

Park St.

Emerson St.

Southwark Bridge Rd.

London Bridge

4 LONDON BRIDGE

2

start **1**

3

A faithful reconstruction of the original playhouse, **Shakespeare's Globe Theatre** was built entirely without nails.

Tooley St.

St. Olave's Estate

St. Thomas St.

Newcomen St.

Snowfields

Leather-market Gardens

John Harvard was baptised in the 12th-century Church of St. Saviour, now **Southwark Cathedral**

Bermondsey St.

Tower Bridge Rd.

Riley Rd.

Swan St.

Great Dover St.

Trinity St.

Tabard Gardens

Long Lane

The Grange

You'll shiver at the authentic 19th-century medical horrors on display at the **Old Operating Theatre**

Falmouth Rd.

HMS Belfast led the D-Day bombardment of Normandy

Willow Walk

ELEPHANT & CASTLE

New Kent Rd.

Rodney Rd.

Old Kent Rd.

Pages Walk

Often confused with London Bridge, **Tower Bridge** still opens 600 times a year.

TRAFALGAR SQUARE AND THE STRAND

John Nash first suggested laying out **Trafalgar Square** in 1820, but it took almost 50 years for London's largest traffic roundabout to take on its current appearance: Nelson on his granite pillar only arrived in 1843, and the bronze lions in 1867. The square commemorates Nelson's victory over Napoleon's navy at the Battle of Trafalgar in 1805; the reliefs at the column's base are cast from captured French and Spanish cannons. Every December the square hosts a giant **Christmas Tree,** donated by Norway to thank the British for assistance against the Nazis. *(Tube: Charing Cross.)*

ST. MARTIN-IN-THE-FIELDS. James Gibbs's 1720s creation was the model for countless Georgian churches in Britain and America. It's still the Queen's parish church; look for the royal box to the left of the altar. Downstairs the **crypt** has a life all of its own, home to a **cafe,** bookshop, art gallery, and the **London Brass Rubbing Centre.** *(St. Martin's Lane, in the northeast corner of Trafalgar Sq. Tube: Leicester Sq. ☎ 7766 1100. Brass Rubbing Centre open M-Sa 10am-6pm, Su noon-6pm. Brass rubbing £5-8.)*

SOMERSET HOUSE. A magnificent Palladian structure completed in 1790, Somerset House was London's first purpose-built office block. Originally home to the Royal Academy and the Royal Society, the building now harbors the magnificent ▓**Courtauld Institute** (see p. 179). From mid-December to mid-January, the central **Fountain Courtyard** is iced over to make an open-air rink. *(On the Strand. Tube: Charing Cross. ☎ 7845 4600. Tours Tu, Th, Sa 2 per day £2.75. Courtyard open daily 7:30am-11pm.)*

HOLBORN

Squeezed between the unfettered capitalism of the City and the rampant commercialism of the West End, Holborn is historically the London home of two of the world's least-loved professions—lawyers and journalists.

INNS OF COURT. These venerable institutions provide apprenticeships for law students and house the chambers of practising barristers. Most were founded in the 13th century when a royal decree barred the clergy from the courts, giving rise to a class of professional advocates. Most impressive of the four Inns are those of the Middle and Inner **Temple,** south of Fleet St. *(Between Fleet St., Essex St., Victoria Embankment, and Temple Ave./Bouvier St.; numerous passages lead from these streets into the Temple. Tube: Temple.)* The 12th-century **Temple Church** is the finest surviving round church in England. *(☎ 7353 3470. Open W-Th 11am-4pm, Sa 9:30am-1:30pm, Su 12:45-4pm. Free.)* Shakespeare performed the premier of *Twelfth Night* in front of Elizabeth I in **Middle Temple Hall**—the large wooden dining table is made from the hatch of Sir Francis Drake's *Golden Hinde.* According to Shakespeare's *Henry VI,* the red and white flowers of the War of the Roses were plucked in **Middle Temple Garden,** south of the hall. *(Middle Temple Garden open May-Sept. M-F noon-3pm. Free.)*

FLEET STREET. Named for the river (now underground) that flows from Hampstead to the Thames, Fleet Street has an association with publishing going back to the days when Wyken de Worde relocated from Westminster to the precincts of **St. Bride's** church, since then known as "the printer's cathedral." Christopher Wren's odd steeple was the inspiration for the tiered wedding cake, invented by a local baker. *(St. Bride's Ave., just off Fleet St. Tube: Temple. Open daily 8am-4:45pm. Free.)*

ROYAL COURTS OF JUSTICE. This elaborate neo-Gothic structure—easily mistaken for a cathedral—straddles the official division between Westminster and the City of London; the courtrooms are open to the public during cases. *(Where the Strand becomes Fleet St. ☎ 7936 6000. Tube: Temple. Open M-F 9am-6pm. Cases start 10am.)*

THE CITY OF LONDON

*The **City of London Information Centre,** St. Paul's Churchyard (☎ 7332 1456; Tube: St. Paul's) offers acres of leaflets and maps, sells tickets to sights and shows, and gives info on a host of traditional municipal events. Open Apr.-Sept. daily 9:30am-5pm; Oct.-Mar. M-F 9:30am-5pm, Sa 9:30am-12:30pm.*

Until the 18th century, the City *was* London, the rest being merely outlying villages. Its appearance belies its 2000-year history; what few buildings survived the Great Fire of 1666 and the Blitz of 1940-43 are now overshadowed by giant temples of

BRITAIN

commerce. Yet the 20th century had a more profound effect on the City than the cosmetic rearrangement of the Blitz: as its power in the world of international finance grew, so the City's relevance to ordinary Londoners diminished. Nowadays, of the 300,000 who work here, only 8000 people call the City home.

ST. PAUL'S CATHEDRAL

St. Paul's Churchyard. Tube: St. Paul's. ☎ 7246 8348. Audioguides £3.50, students £3. 1½hr. tours M-F 4 per day. £2.50, students £2. Open M-Sa 8:30am-4pm; open for worship daily 7:15am-6pm. £5, students £4; worshippers free.

Sir Christopher Wren's masterpiece is the fifth cathedral to occupy the site; the original was built in AD 604. Wren's succeeded "Old St. Paul's," begun in 1087 and with a steeple one-third as high again as the current 111m dome. By 1666, when the Great Fire swept away it away, Old St. Paul's was ripe for replacement, having been used as a marketplace and barracks during the Civil War. After having three designs rejected by the bishops, Wren, with Charles II's support, just started building—sneakily, he had persuaded the king to let him make "necessary alterations" as work progressed, and the building that emerged from the scaffolding in 1708 bore little resemblance to the "Warrant Model" Charles had approved.

With space to seat 2500 worshippers, the **nave** is festooned with monuments to great Britons; unlike at Westminster Abbey however, no one is buried in the cathedral floor—the tombs, including those of Nelson, Wellington, and Florence Nightingale, are all downstairs, in the **crypt.** Surrounded by Blake, Turner, and Henry Moore, Christopher Wren lies beneath the epitaph *Lector, si monumentum requiris circumspice* ("Reader, if you seek his monument, look around"). For a different perspective on the second-tallest freestanding **dome** in Europe (after St. Peter's in the Vatican), climb the 259 steps to the **Whispering Gallery** on its inner surface. The gallery is a perfect resonating chamber: whisper into the wall, and your friend on the opposite side should be able to hear you. From here 119 more steps reach to **Stone Gallery,** on the outer base of the dome, and another 152 to the vertiginous **Golden Gallery** at the summit. Back inside, the marble **High Altar** is overlooked by the mosaic of *Christ Seated in Majesty.* The north quire aisle holds Henry Moore's *Mother and Child.* Soon after the sculpture's arrival, guides insisted a plaque be affixed because no one knew what it was. The statue of **John Donne** in the south quire aisle is one of the few monuments to survive from Old St. Paul's.

THE TOWER OF LONDON

Tower Hill. Tube: Tower Hill. ☎ 7709 0765. Audioguides £3. Free 1hr. tours, M-Sa 9:30am-3:30pm, Su 10am-3:30pm. Open Mar.-Oct. M-Sa 9am-5:30pm, Su 10am-5:30pm; Nov.-Feb. closes 4:30pm. £11.30, students £8.50. Tickets also sold at Tube stations; buy them in advance since lines at the door are horrendous.

The Tower of London, palace and prison of English monarchs for over 900 years, is steeped in blood and history. Conceived by William the Conqueror more to provide protection from than to his new subjects, the wooden palisade of 1067 was replaced in 1078 by a stone structure that over the next 20 years would grow into the White Tower. Colorfully dressed Yeomen Warders, or "Beefeaters"—a reference to their daily allowance of meat in former times—double as guards and tourist guides; to be eligible for Beefeaterhood, candidates must have 20 years distinguished service in the armed forces, and an appetite for flash photography.

From **Middle Tower,** you pass over the moat (now a garden) and enter the **Outer Ward** though **Byward Tower.** Just beyond Byward Tower, the **Bell Tower** dates from 1190; the curfew bell has been rung nightly for over 500 years. The stretch of the Outer Ward along the Thames is **Water Lane,** which until the 16th century was adjacent to the river. **Traitor's Gate** was built by Edward I for his personal use, but is now associated with the prisoners who passed through it on their way to execution at **Tower Green.** Some of the victims are buried in the **Chapel Royal of St. Peter ad Vincula,** including Henry VIII's wives Catherine Howard and Anne Boleyn, and Catholic martyr Sir Thomas More. The green abuts the **White Tower,** the castle's original fortification, now home to a fearsome display of arms and armor from the Royal Armory; one look at Henry VIII's "generous" suit will show why he never had any

BRITAIN

trouble remarrying. Across the green, **Bloody Tower** is so named because here Richard III imprisoned and then murdered his nephews, the rightful Edward V (aged 12) and his brother, before usurping the throne in 1483.

The most famous of the sights in the Tower are the **Crown Jewels;** moving walkways ensure no awestruck gazers hold up the queue. While the eye is naturally drawn to the **Imperial State Crown,** home to the Stuart Sapphire along with 16 others, 2876 diamonds, 273 pearls, 11 emeralds, and a mere five rubies, don't miss the **Sceptre with the Cross,** topped with First Star of Africa, the largest quality-cut diamond in the world. This was hewn from an even larger monster, the 3106-carat Cullinan diamond (the largest ever found); Scotland Yard mailed the stone third-class from South Africa in an unmarked brown parcel. Other famous gems include the **Koh-i-Noor,** set into the **Queen Mother's Crown;** legend claims the stone will only bring luck to women. A fascinating history of the jewels with numerous retired crowns is displayed in the **Martin Tower,** at the end of **Wall Walk.**

OTHER CITY OF LONDON SIGHTS

GUILDHALL. In this vast Gothic hall, the representatives of the City's 102 guilds, from the Fletchers (arrow-makers) to the Information Technologists, meet the third Thursday of every month at the **Court of Common Council,** under the Lord Mayor and followed by a sword-wielding entourage. *(Off Gresham St. Tube: St. Paul's.* ☎ *7606 3030. Open May-Sept. M-F 10am-5pm; Sa-Su 10am-4pm; Oct.-Apr. closed Su. Free.)*

BANK OF ENGLAND AND ENVIRONS. Government financial difficulties led to the founding of the "Old Lady of Threadneedle St." in 1694—the bank's creditors supplied £1.2 million, and the national debt was born. Other hallowed institutions stand on the streets nearby: the **Stock Exchange,** on Throgmorton St.; the **Royal Exchange,** between Cornhill and Threadneedle St., founded in 1566; and the 18th-century **Mansion House,** on Walbrook, the official residence of the Lord Mayor. The most famous modern structure in the City is **Lloyd's of London,** on Leadenhall, designed by Richard Rogers. With metal ducts, lifts, and chutes on the outside, it wears its heart (or at least its internal organs) on its sleeve. *(Tube: Bank.)*

MONUMENT. Raised in 1677, Christopher Wren's 60m-tall column stands exactly that distance from the bakery on Pudding Lane where the Great Fire started in 1666. Bring stern resolution to climb its 311 steps. *(Monument St. Tube: Monument.* ☎ *7276 2717. Open daily 10am-6pm. £1.50; joint ticket with Tower Bridge Experience £6.75.)*

TOWER BRIDGE. This iconic symbol of London is often mistaken for its plain upriver sibling, London Bridge—the story goes that when an Arizonan millionaire bought the previous London Bridge and shifted it stone-by-stone to the US, he thought he was getting Tower Bridge. The **Tower Bridge Experience** offers a cutesy introduction to the history and technology of the unique lifting mechanism, although the view isn't all it's cracked up to be. *(Tube: Tower Hill. Open Apr.-Oct. daily 10am-6:30pm; Nov.-Mar. 9:30am-6pm. £6.25, students £4.25.)*

WREN CHURCHES. Aside from St. Paul's Cathedral, the City's greatest architectural treasures are the 22 surviving churches designed by Christopher Wren to replace those lost in the Great Fire of 1666. The most famous is **St. Mary-le-Bow;** tradition holds that cockneys are those born within range of its bells. For the past 800 years, the Archbishop of Canterbury has sworn in bishops in the 11th-century crypt, whose "bows" (arches) gave the church its epithet. *(Cheapside, by Bow Ln.* ☎ *7246 5139. Tube: St. Paul's. Open M-F 6:30am-6pm. Free.)* **St. Stephen Walbrook** (built 1672-9) was Wren's personal favorite. The plain exterior gives no inkling of the wide dome that floats above Henry Moore's mysterious free-form altar (1985). *(39 Walbrook. Tube: Bank. Open M-Th 9am-4pm, F 9am-3pm. Free.)*

SOUTH BANK

From the Middle Ages until Cromwell spoiled the party, the South Bank was London's entertainment quarter; banished from the strictly-regulated City, all manner of illicit attractions sprouted in "the Borough," at the southern end of London

BRITAIN

Bridge. Today, the South Bank is once again at the heart of London entertainment, with some of the city's top concert halls, theaters, cinemas, and galleries.

LONDON EYE. Also known as the Millennium Wheel, at 135m the London Eye is the world's biggest observational wheel. The ellipsoid glass "pods" give uninterrupted views at the top of each 30min. revolution: on clear days Windsor is visible in the west. *(Jubilee Gardens, between County Hall and the Festival Hall. Tube: Waterloo.* ☎*(0870) 500 0600. Open late May to early Sept. daily 9:30am-10pm; Apr. to late May and late Sept. 10:30am-8pm; Jan.-Mar. and Oct.-Dec. 10:30am-7pm. Ticket office opens 30min. earlier. Ticket office in corner of County Hall; advance booking advised. July-Sept. £9.50; Oct.-June £9.)*

THE SOUTH BANK CENTRE. Sprawling on either side of Waterloo Bridge along the Thames, this symphony of concrete is Britain's premier cultural center. Its nucleus is the **Royal Festival Hall**, a classic piece of white 1950s architecture. Close by the Festival Hall, the **Purcell Room** and **Queen Elizabeth Hall** cater for smaller concerts, while just behind, the spiky ceiling of the **Hayward Gallery** shelters excellent shows of modern art. On the embankment beneath Waterloo Bridge, the **National Film Theatre** offers London's most varied cinematic fare, while past the bridge looms the **National Theatre** (see p. 181). To find out how one of the world's largest, most modern theaters operates, join a backstage tour. *(On the riverbank between Hungerford and Waterloo Bridges. Tube: Waterloo. Tours M-Sa 10:15am, 12:15, and 5:15pm. £5.)*

TATE MODERN AND THE MILLENNIUM BRIDGE. Squarely opposite each other on Bankside are the biggest success and most abject failure of London's millennial celebrations. **Tate Modern** (see p. 178), created from the shell of the Bankside power station, is as visually arresting as its contents are thought-provoking. Built to link the Tate to the City, the **Millennium Bridge** was completed six months too late for the Y2K festivities, and, following a literally shaky debut, quickly closed down. It should reopen sometime in 2002. *(Queen's Walk, Bankside. Tube: Southwark.)*

SHAKESPEARE'S GLOBE THEATRE. In the shadow of Tate Modern, the half-timbered Globe (opened 1997) rises just 200m from where the original burned down in 1613. Try to arrive in time for a tour of the theater itself, given mornings only during the performance season. *(Bankside. Tube: Southwark.* ☎*7902 1500. Open May-Sept. daily 9am-noon and 1-4pm (exhibition only); Oct.-Apr. 10am-5pm. £7.50, students £6. See also p. 181.)* Nearby lie the ruins of the 1587 **Rose Theatre,** Bankside's first, where both Shakespeare and Marlowe performed. The site was rediscovered in 1989; not much is left, though the outline is clearly visible. *(56 Park St.* ☎*7593 0026. Open daily 11am-5pm. £4, students £3; £1 less with Globe exhibition ticket.)*

OTHER SOUTH BANK SIGHTS. The giant **HMS Belfast** aided the bombardment of Normandy during D-Day and supported UN forces in Korea before graciously retiring in 1965. Kids will love clambering over the decks and aiming the anti-aircraft guns at dive-bombing seagulls. Dozens of narrow passages, steep staircases, and ladders make exploring the boat a physical challenge in itself. *(At the end of Morgans Ln. off Tooley St. Tube: London Bridge.* ☎*7940 6300. Open Mar.-Oct. daily 10am-6pm; Nov.-Feb. 10am-5pm. £5.40, students £4.)* The giant curved façade of **County Hall,** almost opposite the Houses of Parliament, houses two of London's most-advertised and least-impressive sights, the **London Aquarium** and **Dalí Universe.** *(Westminster Bridge Rd. Tube: Westminster. Aquarium* ☎*7967 8000. Open daily 10am-6pm, last admission 5pm. £8.50. Dalí* ☎*7620 2720. Open daily 10am-5:30pm. £8.50, students £6.)* **Vinopolis** is a Dionysian Disneyland offering patrons an interactive (yes, that means samples) tour of the world's wine regions. *(1 Bank End. Tube: London Bridge.* ☎*(0870) 4444 777 (24hr.); Open Tu-F and Su 11am-6pm, M 11am-8pm, Sa 11am-9pm. £11.50, seniors £10.50.)* The **London Dungeon** is always mobbed with thousands of kids waiting to revel in tasteful displays about Jack the Ripper, the Fire of London, and anything else remotely connected to horror in Britain. *(28-34 Tooley St. Tube: London Bridge.* ☎*(0870) 846 0666. Open mid-July to Aug. daily 10:30am-8pm; Apr. to mid-July and Sept.-Oct. 10:30am-5:30pm; Nov.-Mar. 10:30am-5pm. £10.95, students £9.50.)*

BRITAIN

WESTMINSTER

The City of Westminster, now a borough of London, has been the seat of English, and then British, power for over a thousand years. William the Conqueror was crowned in Westminster Abbey on Christmas Day, 1066, and his successors built the Palace of Westminster that would one day house Parliament.

BUCKINGHAM PALACE

The Mall; entrance to State Rooms on Buckingham Palace Rd. Tube: Victoria, Green Park, or St. James's Park. ☎ 7839 1377. State Rooms open early Aug.-Sept. daily 9:30am-4:30pm. Tickets ☎ 7321 2233 or (from late July) the Ticket Office, Green Park. £11.

Originally built for the Dukes of Buckingham, Buckingham House was acquired by George III in 1762, and converted into a full-scale palace by George IV. Even so, the palace was found to be too small for Victoria's growing brood; a solution was found by closing off the three-sided courtyard, concealing the best architecture with Edward Blore's uninspiring façade. During the summer opening of the **State Rooms,** visitors have access to the **Throne Room,** the **Galleries** (with pictures by Rubens, Rembrandt, and Van Dyck), and the **Music Room,** where Mendelssohn, among others, played for Queen Victoria. In the opulent **White Room,** the large mirror fireplace conceals a door used by the Royal Family at formal dinners. Since 2001, Liz has also allowed a brief excursion into the **gardens**—keep off the grass!

CHANGING OF THE GUARD. The Palace is protected by a detachment of Foot Guards in full dress uniform. Accompanied by a band, the "New Guard" starts marching down Birdcage Walk from Wellington Barracks around 10:30am, while the "Old Guard" leaves St. James's Palace around 11:10am. When they meet at the gates of the palace, the officers touch hands, symbolically exchanging keys, *et voilà*, the guard is changed. Show up well before 11:30am and stand directly in front of the palace; for a less-crowded close-up of the marching guards, stand along the Mall between the Victoria Memorial and St. James's Palace or along Birdcage Walk. *(Apr.-Oct. daily; Nov.-Mar. every other day, provided the Queen is in residence, it's not raining too hard, and there are no pressing state functions. Free.)*

OTHER PALACE SIGHTS. A working carriage house, the **Royal Mews**'s main attraction is the collection of coaches, from the "glass coach" used to carry Diana to her wedding to the four-ton Gold State Coach and the carriage horses. *(Buckingham Palace Rd. Tube: St. James's Park or Victoria. ☎ 7839 1377. Open M-Th noon-4pm. £4.)* In a new extension to the Palace, the **Queen's Gallery** will open in spring 2002, displaying artworks from the richly endowed Royal Collection. *(Buckingham Palace Rd. Tube: St. James's Park. For hours and prices, call Buckingham Palace, ☎ 7839 1377.)*

WESTMINSTER ABBEY

Parliament Sq.; access Old Monastery, Cloister, and Garden from Dean's Yard, behind the Abbey. Tube: Westminster. Abbey ☎ 7222 7110, Old Monastery ☎ 7222 5897. Abbey open M-F 9am-4:45pm, Sa 9am-2:45pm, Su for services only. £6, students £3; entry to services is free. Old Monastery £2.50; joint entry with Abbey £1 extra on Abbey prices. Pyx Chamber and Museum open daily 10:30am-4pm. Chapter House open Apr.-Oct. daily 10am-5:30pm; Nov.-Mar. 10am-4pm. Cloisters open daily 8am-6pm. Garden open Apr.-Sept. Tu-Th 10am-6pm; Oct.-Mar. Tu-Th 10am-4pm. Cloisters and Garden free.

On December 28, 1065, Edward the Confessor, last Saxon King of England, was buried in the church of the West Monastery; almost exactly a year later, the Abbey saw the coronation of William the Conqueror. Thus even before it was completed, the Abbey's twin traditions as the figurative birthplace and literal resting place of royalty had been established. It was this royal connection that allowed Westminster, uniquely of the great monasteries of England, to escape wholesale destruction during Henry VIII's campaign against the Pope.

The **north transept** contains memorials to Victorian statesmen, including Prime Ministers Disraeli and Gladstone. Early English kings lie arrayed around the Confessor's tomb in the **Shrine of St. Edward,** behind which the **Coronation Chair** stands at the entry to the Tudor **Lady Chapel.** Henry VII and his wife Elizabeth lie at the end of the chapel. Queen Elizabeth I and the cousin she had beheaded, Mary Queen of Scots, are buried on opposite sides of the chapel. **Poet's Corner** begins with Geoffrey Chaucer, buried in 1400; plaques at his feet commemorate both poets and prose writers, as does the stained-glass window above. At the center of the Abbey, the **Sanctuary** holds the altar; this is where coronations and royal weddings are held. After a detour through the Cloisters, visitors re-enter into the nave. At the western end is the **Tomb of the Unknown Warrior,** with an epitaph poured from molten bullets; just beyond is the simple grave of **Winston Churchill.** The north aisle holds **Scientists Corners,** with physicists and biologists arrayed around Isaac Newton and Charles Darwin, respectively. The **Old Monastery** sights include the **Great Cloister,** festooned with monuments and plaques, from whence passages lead to the **Chapter House,** the original meeting place of Parliament; the **Pyx Chamber,** formerly the Abbey treasury; and the **Abbey Museum,** with an array of royal funeral effigies. The pleasant **Gardens** are also reached from the cloisters; concerts are occasionally held here in summer.

THE HOUSES OF PARLIAMENT

Parliament Sq. Tube: Westminster. ☎ 7219 4272. Debates: Open to all while Parliament is in session (Oct.-July.). Advance tickets required for Prime Minister's Question Time (W 3-3:30pm). M-Th after 6pm and F are least busy. Lords usually sits M-W from 2:30pm, Th 3pm, occasionally F 11:30am; closing times vary. Commons sits M-W 2:30-10:30pm, Th 11:30am-7:30pm, F 9:30am-3pm. Free. Tours Aug.-Sept. M-Sa 9:15am-4:30pm; reserve at Ticketmaster (☎ 7344 9966); in person from mid-July. £3.50.

The Palace of Westminster, as the building in which Parliament sits is officially known, has been at the heart of English governance since the 11th century, when Edward the Confessor established his court here. William the Conqueror found the site to his liking, and under the Normans the palace was greatly extended. Westminster Hall aside, what little of the Norman palace to remain was entirely destroyed in the massive conflagration of October 16, 1834; the rebuilding started in 1835 under the joint command of Charles Barry and Augustus Pugin.

OUTSIDE THE HOUSES. At the midpoint of the complex, a statue of Oliver Cromwell stands in front of **Westminster Hall,** the sole survivor of the 1834 fire. Unremarkable from the outside, the Hall's chief feature is a magnificent hammerbeam roof, constructed in 1394 and considered the finest timber roof ever made. During its centuries as a law court, famous defendants here included Thomas More and Charles I. These days, it sees use for public ceremonies and occasional exhibitions. The **Clock Tower** is mistakenly known as **Big Ben,** a name which strictly refers only to the bell within—it's named after the robustly proportioned Sir Benjamin Hall, who served as Commissioner of Works when the bell was cast in 1858

DEBATING CHAMBERS. Visitors to the debating chambers first pass through **St. Stephen's Hall.** Formerly the king's private chapel, in 1550 St. Stephen's became the meeting place of the House of Commons. MPs have since moved down the corridor, but four brass markers mark where the Speaker's Chair used to stand. At the end of the hall, the **Central Lobby** marks the separation of the two houses, with the Commons to the north and the Lords to the south. The ostentatious **House of Lords** is dominated by the Throne of State under a gilt canopy. The Lord Chancellor presides over the Peers from the giant red **Woolsack.** In contrast is the restrained **House of Commons,** with simple green-backed benches under a plain wooden roof. This is not entirely due to the difference in class—the Commons was bombed in 1941, and rebuilding took place during a time of post-war austerity. The **Speaker** sits at the rear of the chamber, with government MPs to his right and the opposition to his left. With room for only 437 out of 635 MPs, its hectic when all attend.

OTHER WESTMINSTER SIGHTS

WHITEHALL. A street synonymous with the British civil service, Whitehall was the main royal palace from 1532 until a fire in 1698. All that remains is Inigo Jones's **Banqueting House,** with magnificent ceiling paintings by Rubens. Charles I was executed on a scaffold outside the house in 1649. *(Whitehall. Tube: Westminster. ☎ 7930*

4179. Open M-Sa 10am-5pm; last admission 4:30pm. £3.90, students £3.10, children £2.30.) Opposite Banqueting house, tourists line up to be photographed with the burnished cuirassiers of the Household Cavalry at **Horseguards** (the guard is changed M-F 11am, Sa 10am). Just off Whitehall, King James St. leads to the **Cabinet War Rooms,** where Churchill, his ministers, generals, and support staff lived and worked underground from 1939 to 1945. Highlights include the small room containing the top-secret transatlantic hotline—the official story was that it was Churchill's personal loo. (Clive Steps. Tube: Westminster. ☎ 7930 6961. Open Apr.-Sept. daily 9:30am-6pm; Oct.-Mar. daily 10am-6pm. £5.40, students £3.90.) Current Prime Minister Tony Blair has an easier time on **Downing Street,** separated from Whitehall by steel gates. Traditionally the Prime Minister lives at no. 10, but Tony's family is too big, so he has swapped with the Chancellor, Gordon Brown, at no. 11.

WESTMINSTER CATHEDRAL. London's first Catholic cathedral since Henry VIII espoused Protestantism was started in 1887; in 1903, money ran out, leaving the interior only partially completed. The blackened brick domes contrast dramatically with the swirling marble of the lower walls and the magnificence of the side chapels. A lift carries visitors up the striped 83m **bell tower.** (Cathedral Piazza, off Victoria St. Tube: Victoria. ☎ 7798 9055. Cathedral open daily 7am-7pm. Free; suggested donation £2. Bell Tower open Apr.-Nov. daily 9am-5pm; Dec.-Mar. Th-Su 9am-5pm. £2, students £1.)

KENSINGTON AND KNIGHTSBRIDGE

Nobody took much notice of **Kensington** before 1689, when the newly crowned William III and Mary II moved into Kensington Palace. The next significant date was in 1851, when the Great Exhibition brought in enough money to finance the museums and colleges of South Kensington. Now home to London's most expensive stores, including Harrods and Harvey Nichols, it's hard to imagine that in the 18th century **Knightsbridge** was a racy district known for its taverns and its highwaymen.

KENSINGTON PALACE. Remodelled by Wren for William III and Mary II in 1689, parts are still in use as a royal residence—Princess Diana was the most famous recent inhabitant. Inside, the **Royal Ceremonial Dress Collection** displays 19th-century court costumes along with the Queen's demure evening gowns and some of Diana's more provocative numbers. Hanoverian economy is evident in the *trompe l'oeil* decoration in the **State Apartment,** carried out by William Kent for George I. (Eastern edge of Kensington Gardens; enter through the park. Tube: High St. Kensington. ☎ 7937 9561. Open Mar.-Oct. daily 10am-5pm, Nov.-Feb. 10am-4pm. £8.80.)

HYDE PARK AND KENSINGTON GARDENS. Surrounded by London's wealthiest neighborhoods, giant Hyde Park has served as the model for city parks around the world, including Central Park in New York and Paris's Bois de Boulogne. **Kensington Gardens,** to the west, is contiguous with Hyde Park. The 16 hectare **Serpentine** was created in 1730; innumerable people pay to row and swim here. At the northeastern corner of the park, near Marble Arch, proselytizers, politicos, and flat-out crazies dispense their knowledge to bemused tourists at **Speaker's Corner** on Su. (Tube: Queensway, Lancaster Gate, Marble Arch, Hyde Park Corner, High St. Kensington. ☎ 7298 2100. Hyde Park open daily 5am-midnight; Kensington Gdns. open daily dawn-dusk. Free.)

APSLEY HOUSE AND WELLINGTON ARCH. Apsley House, revelling in the address "No. 1, London," was bought in 1817 by the Duke of Wellington. On display is Wellington's outstanding collection of art, much of it given in gratitude by the crowned heads of Europe following the battle of Waterloo. The majority of paintings hang in the **Waterloo Gallery,** where the Duke would hold his annual banquet. (Hyde Park Corner. Tube: Hyde Park Corner. ☎ 7499 5676. Open Tu-Su 11am-5pm. £4.50, students £3.) Across from Apsley House, the **Wellington Arch** was built in 1825. In 1838 it was dedicated to the Duke of Wellington, and later encumbered by a gigantic statue, much to the horror of its architect, Decimus Burton. Inside the arch, the viewing platforms delight. (Hyde Park Corner. Tube: Hyde Park Corner. ☎ 7930 2726. Open Apr.-Sept. W-Su 10am-6pm; Oct. 10am-5pm; Nov.-Mar. 10am-4pm. £2.50, students £1.90.)

MARYLEBONE AND BLOOMSBURY

Marylebone's most famous resident (and address) never existed; 221b Baker Street was the fictional lodging house of Sherlock Holmes. 221 Baker St. is actually the headquarters of the Abbey National bank (there was never a 221b). A little further down the street, the **Sherlock Holmes Museum** (see p. 180) gives its address out as 221b, although a little sleuthing will reveal that it in fact stands at no. 239. East of Marylebone, Bloomsbury's intellectual reputation was bolstered in the early 20th century as Gordon Sq. resounded with the philosophizing and womanizing of the **Bloomsbury Group,** an early 20th-century coterie of intellectuals including Virginia Woolf, John Maynard Keynes, Lytton Strachey, and Bertrand Russell.

■ **BRITISH LIBRARY.** Since its 1998 opening the new British Library has won plaudits from visitors and users alike. Underground, 325km of shelving can hold up to 12 million books. The brick building is home to a dramatic glass cube containing the 65,000 volumes of George III's King's Library, the reading rooms, and a stunning display of books, manuscripts, and artifacts, from the second-century *Unknown Gospel* to Joyce's handwritten draft of *Finnegan's Wake*. (96 Euston Rd. ☎ 7412 7332. Tube: King's Cross. Tours M, W, F 3pm; Sa 10:30am and 3pm; £5, students £3.50. Tours including reading rooms Tu 6:30pm, Su 11:30am and 3pm; £6, £4.50. Reservations recommended for all tours. Open M and W-F 9:30am-6pm, Tu 9:30am-8pm, Sa 9:30am-5pm, Su 11am-5pm. Free.)

ACADEMIA. The strip of land along **Gower Street** and immediately to its west is London's academic heartland. Established in 1828, **University College London** was the first in Britain to admit Catholics, Jews, and women. The embalmed body of founder **Jeremy Bentham** has occupied the South Cloister since 1850. (Main entrance on Gower St. South Cloister entrance through the courtyard. Tube: Warren St.) Now the administrative HQ of the University of London, **Senate House** was the model for the Ministry of Truth in *1984*—George Orwell worked there as part of the BBC propaganda unit in WWII. (At the southern end of Malet St. Tube: Goodge St.)

NORTH LONDON

CAMDEN TOWN

An island of good, honest tawdriness in an increasingly affluent sea, Camden Town has effortlessly thrown off attempts at gentrification thanks to the ever-growing **Camden Market** (see p. 184). Now London's fourth-most popular tourist attraction, on weekends the market presents a variety of life unmatched even by **London Zoo,** a serene jaunt up the **Regent's Canal** from the market's nerve-center in Camden Lock.

LONDON ZOO. Thousands of little critters from around the world run around freely, their guardians trying frantically to keep up, as the animals look on with indifference from their enclosures. Penguin feeding (2:30pm daily) is always popular, as is the elephant washing (3:30pm); for other activities, check the *Daily Events* leaflet. (Main gate on Outer Circle, Regent's Park. ☎ 7449 6552. Tube: Camden Town plus 12min. walk or short jaunt on bus #274. Open daily 10am-5:30pm. £10, students £8.50.) If you don't want to walk, the **London Waterbus Company** runs to the zoo from Camden Lock. (Camden Lock. Tube: Camden Town. ☎ 7482 2550. Apr.-Oct. every hr. 10am-5pm; Nov.-Mar. Sa-Su every hr. 11am-4pm. Trip to the Zoo, including admission, £10.50.)

HAMPSTEAD

Hampstead first caught the attention of well-heeled Londoners in the 17th century. In the 1930s, Hampstead found itself at the forefront of a European avant-garde in flight from fascism. Residents such as Aldous Huxley, Piet Mondrian, Barbara Hepworth, and Sigmund Freud lent the area a cachet that grows to this day.

HAMPSTEAD HEATH. Hampstead Heath is one of the last remaining commons in England, open to all since at least 1312. **Parliament Hill** is the highest open space in London, with excellent views across the city. Further north, ■**Kenwood** is a picture-perfect 18th-century country estate, designed by Robert Adams for the including works by Rembrandt, Vermeer, and Botticelli. (Tube: Hampstead or Rail: Hampstead Heath. Heath open 24hr. Kenwood open Apr.-Sept. daily 8am-8pm; Oct.-Mar. 8am-4pm.)

BRITAIN

WEST LONDON

ROYAL BOTANICAL GARDENS, KEW. No ordinary park, Kew is a living collection of thousands of flowers, fruits, trees, and vegetables from across the globe. The three great **conservatories**, housing a staggering variety of plants ill-suited to the English climate, are the highlight of the gardens. Most famous is the steamy **Palm House,** home to "The Oldest Pot Plant In The World," which is not at all what it sounds like but interesting nonetheless. The **Temperate House** is the largest ornamental glasshouse in the world, although the **Princess of Wales Conservatory** has a larger area. The interior is divided into 10 different climate zones, including one entirely devoted to orchids. *(Main entrance at Victoria Gate. Tube: Kew Gardens. ☎ 8940 5622. Open Apr.-Aug. M-F 9:30am-6:30pm, Sa-Su 9:30-7:30pm; Sept.-Oct. daily 9:30am-6pm; Nov.-Mar. daily 9:30am-4:15pm. Glasshouses close Apr.-Oct. 5:30pm; Nov.-Mar. 3:45pm. Students £4.50, £6.50. "Late entry" (45min. before close) £4.50.)*

■ **HAMPTON COURT PALACE.** Although a monarch hasn't lived here for 250 years, Hampton Court still exudes regal charm. Cardinal Wolsey built the first palace here in 1514, showing the young Henry VIII how to act the part of a splendid and powerful ruler. In 1689, William III and Mary II employed Christopher Wren to bring Hampton Court up to date. In addition to touring the sumptuous rooms of the palace, including **Henry VIII's State Apartments** and William's **King's Apartments,** be sure to leave time for the vast gardens, including the devilishly difficult **maze.** *(Take the train from Waterloo (32min., every 30min., day return £4) or a boat from Westminster Pier (4hr.; 4 per day; £10, round-trip £14); to leave time to see the palace, take the boat one way and return by train. ☎ (020) 8781 9500. Open mid-Mar. to late Oct. M 10:15am-6pm, Tu-Su 9:30am-6pm; late Oct. to mid-Mar. closes 4:30pm. Palace and gardens £10.80, students £8.30. Maze only £2.90. Gardens (excl. south gardens) free.)*

EAST LONDON

THE EAST END AND DOCKLANDS

The boundary between the East End and City of London is as sharp today as it was when Aldgate and Bishopsgate were real gateways in the wall separating the rich and powerful City from the poorer quarters to the east. The oldest part of the East End, **Whitechapel** thronged with Jewish refugees from Eastern Europe in the 19th century; today it's the heart of London's Bangladeshi community, centered around the restaurants, spice shops, and markets of **Brick Lane.** The most recent wave of immigrants is made up of artists; the former **Truman Brewery,** at no. 91 and 150, is now occupied by media consultancies and a cafe-bar-club trio that together form one of London's hottest nightspots. *(Tube: Aldgate East or Liverpool St.)* An island of Anglicanism amid a spectrum of other traditions, **Christ Church** is Nicholas Hawksmoor's largest church, and considered by many to be his masterpiece; only now is it slowly being restored to its former glory. *(Commercial St., opposite Spitalfields market. ☎ 7247 7202. Tube: Liverpool St.)* Where it touches the river, the East End becomes **Docklands.** This man-made archipelago of docks and wharves was for centuries the commercial heart of the British Empire. In 1981, the Thatcher government decided to redevelop this vast area as a showpiece of unrestrained entrepreneurial development. The main attraction of the regeneration is **Canary Wharf,** with Britain's highest skyscraper, the 240m, pyramid-topped **One Canada Square.** Under the tower, the vast **Canada Place** and **Cabot Square** malls suck in shoppers from all over London, while the dockside plaza is lined with pricey corporate drinking and eating haunts. *(Tube: Canary Wharf.)*

GREENWICH

*All sights are closest to Docklands Light Railway: Cutty Sark. The **Greenwich TIC,** Pepys House, 2 Cutty Sark Gdns. (☎ (0870) 608 2000), sells the Greenwich Passport Ticket, giving entry to the National Maritime Museum, the Royal Observatory, and the Cutty Sark. £12, students £9.60. Open daily 10am-5pm.*

Greenwich's position as the "home of time" is intimately connected to its maritime heritage—the Royal Observatory, site of the Prime Meridian, was founded to pro-

BRITAIN

duce star charts once essential to navigation. If you're planning on spending a day or so sightseeing here, consider buying the Greenwich Passport (see above).

RIVER TRIPS. The most pleasant way of getting to Greenwich is via the 1hr. boat trip from Westminster. TfL Travelcard holders get 33% off riverboat fares. **Westminster Passenger Association** boats head from Westminster Pier for Greenwich. "Sail&Rail" tickets combine a one-way boat trip with unlimited all-day travel on the DLR. *(☎ 7930 4097. Apr. to early Oct. daily every 3min. 10:30am-5pm, last departure from Greenwich 6pm. £6, round-trip £7.50, Sail&Rail £8.30.)*

ROYAL OBSERVATORY. Charles II founded the Royal Observatory in 1675 to find a way of calculating longitude at sea; the **Prime Meridian** (which marks 0° longitude) started out as the axis along which the astronomers' telescopes swung. Next to the meridian, Wren's **Flamstead House** retains its original interior in **Octagon Room,** with long windows designed to accommodate telescopes. Next to the Meridian Building's telescope display, climb the **Observatory Dome** to see the 71cm telescope constructed in 1893. It hasn't been used since 1954, but you can still get a peak at the stars at the **Planetarium** in the South Building. *(Greenwich Park. ☎ 8312 6565. Open daily 10am-5pm. £6, students £4.80; with National Maritime Museum and Queen's House £10.50, students £8.40. Planetarium £2 extra.)*

ROYAL NAVAL COLLEGE. On the site of Henry VIII's Palace of Placentia, the Royal Naval College was founded by William III in 1694 as the Royal Hospital for Seamen. In 1998, Greenwich's naval association ended when the University of Greenwich blew in. Buy a ticket to see the **Painted Hall** and the simple **Chapel,** with Benjamin West's painting of a shipwrecked St. Paul. *(King William Walk. ☎ 8269 4744. Open M-Sa noon-5pm, Su 12:30-5pm. £3.)*

CUTTY SARK. Last of the great tea clippers, even landlubbers will appreciate the Cutty Sark's thoroughbred lines—launched in 1869, she was the fastest ship of her time, making the round-trip from China in only 120 days. *(King William Walk, by Greenwich Pier. ☎ 8858 3445. Open daily 10am-5pm, last entry 4:30pm. £3.50, students £2.50.)*

🏛 MUSEUMS

Centuries as the capital of an empire upon which the sun never set, together with a decidedly English penchant for collecting, have endowed London with a spectacular set of museums. Art lovers, history buffs, and amateur ethnologists won't know which way to turn when they arrive. And there's even better news for museum lovers. Once some of the capital's most expensive attractions, the government now plans to return all major collections to free admission.

BRITAIN

🏛 BRITISH MUSEUM

Great Russell St., Bloomsbury. Rear entrance on Montague St. Tube: Tottenham Court Rd. ☎ 7323 8000. Audioguides £2.50. Highlights Tour (1½hr.) M-Sa 10:30am and 1pm; Su 11am, 12:30, 1:30, 2:30, and 4pm. £7, students £4. Great Court open M 9am-6pm, Tu-W and Su 9am-9pm, Th-Sa 9am-11pm; galleries open Sa-W 10am-5:30pm, Th-F 10am-8:30pm. Free; £2 suggested donation. Temporary exhibitions around £7, students £3.50.

The funny thing about the British Museum is that there's almost nothing British in it. In 1824 work started on the current Neoclassical building, which took another 30 years to construct. The opening of the **Great Court**—the largest covered square in Europe—in Dec. 2000 finally restored to the museum its focal point. For the past 150 years used as the book stacks of the British Library (now transferred to St. Pancras; see p. 175), the courtyard remains dominated by the enormous rotunda of the **Reading Room,** whose desks have shouldered the weight of research by Marx, Lenin, Trotsky, and almost every major British writer and intellectual.

The most famous items in the collection are found in the **Western Galleries;** here Room 4 harbors Egyptian sculpture, including the **Rosetta Stone,** and Room 18 is entirely devoted to the Athenian **Elgin Marbles.** Other highlights include giant **Assyrian** and **Babylonian** reliefs, the Roman **Portland Vase,** and bits and bobs from two

Wonders of the Ancient World, the **Temple of Artemis** at Ephesus and the **Mausoleum of Halikarnassos.** Just when you thought you'd nailed antiquity, the **Northern Galleries** strike back with eight galleries of **mummies** and **sarcophagi** and nine of artifacts from the ancient Near East, including the **Oxus Treasure** from Iran. Also in the northern wing are the excellent **African** and **Islamic** galleries, the giant **Asian** collections, and the frankly pathetic **Americas** collection. The upper level of the **South** and **East Galleries** is dedicated to ancient and medieval **Europe,** and some of the pieces are actually British. Famous remains include the preserved body of **Lindow Man,** an Iron Age Celt apparently sacrificed in a gruesome ritual (Room 50), and treasures excavated from the **Sutton Hoo Burial Ship** (Room 41). Room 42 has the enigmatic **Lewis Chessmen,** an 800-year-old chess set mysteriously abandoned in Scotland.

◪ NATIONAL GALLERY

Main entrance on north side of Trafalgar Sq. Tube: Charing Cross or Leicester Sq. ☎ 7747 2885. Audioguides free; £4 suggested donation. 1hr. gallery tours daily 11:30am and 2:30pm, W also 6:30pm; free. Open Th-Tu 10am-6pm; W 10am-9pm, Sainsbury Wing exhibitions to 10pm. Free; some temporary exhibitions £6-7, students £3.

The National Gallery was founded by an Act of Parliament in 1824, with 38 pictures displayed in a townhouse; it grew so rapidly in size and popularity that a purpose-built gallery was constructed in 1838. The new **Sainsbury Wing** houses the oldest, most fragile paintings, including the 14th-century English *Wilton Diptych*, Botticelli's *Venus and Mars*, and the *Leonardo Cartoon*, a detailed preparatory drawing by Leonardo da Vinci for a never-executed painting. With paintings from 1510 to 1600, the **West Wing** is dominated by the Italian **High Renaissance** and **early Flemish** art. In Room 8, the artistic forces of Rome and Florence fight it out, with versions of the *Madonna and Child* by Raphael and Michelangelo. Continuing our chronological journey, the **North Wing** spans the **17th century,** with an exceptional array of Flemish work. Room 23 boasts no fewer than 17 Rembrandts; the famous *Self Portrait at 63* gazes knowingly at his *Self Portrait at 34*. The **East Wing,** home to paintings from **1700-1900,** is the most popular in the gallery, thanks to the array of Impressionists including Van Gogh's *Sunflowers* and Cézanne's *Bathers* in Room 45, and two of Monet's *Waterlilies* (Room 43). A reminder that of art on this side of the Channel, Room 34 flies the flag with six luminous Turners.

TATE BRITAIN

Millbank, near Vauxhall Bridge, in Westminster. Wheelchair access via Clore Wing. Tube: Pimlico. ☎ 7887 8008; www.tate.org.uk. Audioguides £1. Highlights Tour: M-F 2:30, 3:30pm, Sa 3pm; free. Open daily 10am-5pm. Free; special exhibitions £3-5.

The original Tate opened in 1897 as a showcase for modern British art. Before long, the remit had expanded to include contemporary art from all over the world, as well as British art from the Middle Ages on. Despite many expansions, it was clear that the dual role was too much for one building; the problem was resolved in 1999 with the relocation of almost all the contemporary art to the new Tate Modern at Bankside (see below). At the same time, the original Tate was rechristened and rededicated to British art. The **Clore Gallery** continues to display the Turner Bequest of 282 oils and 19,000 watercolors; other painters to feature heavily are William Blake, John Constable, Joshua Reynolds, Dante Gabriel Rossetti, Lucien Freud, and David Hockney. Despite the Tate Modern's popular explosion, the annual **Turner Prize** for contemporary art is still held here. After a decade that saw Damien Hirst, Chris Ofili, and Rachel Whiteread take the prize, an apparent backlash started in 1999 when Tracey Emin's unmade bed famously failed to win. The shortlisted works show from early November to mid-January every year.

TATE MODERN

Bankside, the South Bank; main entrance on Holland St. Tube: Blackfriar's. ☎ 7887 8888; www.tate.org.uk. Audioguides: £1. Tours meet on the gallery concourses; free. History/ Memory/Society 10:30am, level 3; Nude/Body/Action 11:30am, level 3; Landscape/ Matter/Environment 2:30pm, level 5; Still Life/Object/Real Life 3:30pm, level 5. Open Su-Th 10am-6pm, F-Sa 10am-10pm. Free; special exhibitions £5-7, students £1 off.

Since opening in May 2000, Tate Modern has been credited with single-handedly reversing the long-term decline in museum-going numbers in Britain. The largest modern art museum in the world, its most striking aspect is the building, formerly the Bankside power station. A conversion by Swiss firm Herzog and de Meuron has added a seventh floor with wraparound views of north and south London, and turned the old **Turbine Hall** into an immense atrium that often overpowers the installations commissioned for it. For all its popularity, the Tate has been criticized for its controversial curatorial method, which groups works according to themes rather than period or artist: the four overarching divisions are **Still Life/Object/Real Life** and **Landscape/Matter/Environment** on level 3, and **Nude/Action/Body** and **History/Memory/Society** on level 5. Even skeptics admit that this arrangement throws up some interesting contrasts, such as the nascent geometry of Cézanne's *Still Life with Water Jug* overlooking the checkerboard tiles of Carl André's *Steel Zinc Plain* and the juxtaposition of Monet's *Waterlilies* with Richard Long's energetic *Waterfall Line*. On the other hand, the "Inner Worlds" array of works by Dalí, Miró, Magritte, Ernst, and de Chirico proves only that Surrealism by any other name is no less bizarre. The achievement of the thematic display is that it forces visitors into contact with an exceptionally wide range of art. It's now impossible to see the Tate's more famous pieces, which include Marcel Duchamp's *Large Glass* and Picasso's *Weeping Woman*, without also confronting challenging and invigorating works by little-known contemporary artists.

VICTORIA AND ALBERT

Main entrance on Cromwell Rd., in Kensington. Tube: South Kensington. ☎ 7942 2000. Introductory tours daily 10:30, 11:30am, 1:30, and 2:30pm; W also 4:30pm. Gallery talks daily 1pm; free. Talks, tours, and live music W from 6:30pm; last F of month also fashion shows, debates, and DJs. Open Th-Tu 10am-5:45pm, W and last F of month 10am-10pm. Free; additional charge for some exhibitions.

Founded in 1852 to encourage excellence in art and design, the V&A is the largest museum of the decorative (and not so decorative) arts in the world—as befits an institution dedicated to displaying "the fine and applied arts of all countries, all styles, all periods." The subject of a £31 million refit, the vast **British Galleries** hold a series of recreated rooms from every period between 1500 and 1900, mirrored by the vast **Dress Collection,** a dazzling array of the finest *haute couture* through the ages. The ground-floor **European** collection range from fourth-century tapestry to Alfonse Mucha posters; if you only see one thing in the museum, make it the **Raphael Gallery,** hung with paintings commissioned by Leo X in 1515. The **Sculpture Gallery,** home to Canova's *Three Graces* (1814-17), is not to be confused with the **Cast Courts,** a plaster-cast collection of the world's sculptural greatest hits, from Trajan's Column to Michelangelo's *David*. The V&A's **Asian** collections are particularly formidable—if the choice of objects occasionally seems to rely on national clichés (Indian carvings, Persian carpets, Chinese porcelain, Japanese ceramics), it says more about how the V&A has formed opinion than followed it. In contrast to the geographically laid-out ground floor, the **upper levels** are mostly arranged in specialist galleries devoted to everything from jewelry to musical instruments to stained glass. An exception to the materially themed arrangements is the large **20th-century** collections, featuring design classics from Salvador Dalí's 1936 "Mae West" sofa lips to a pair of 1990s rubber hotpants. The 6-level **Henry Cole** wing is home to the V&A's collection of **British paintings,** including some 350 works by Constable and numerous Turners. Also here is a display of **Rodin** bronzes, donated by the artist, and the "world's greatest collection" of **miniature portraits,** including Holbein's *Anne of Cleves*. The **Frank Lloyd Wright** gallery contains a full-size recreation of the office commissioned by Edgar Kauffmann for his department store in 1935.

OTHER MUSEUMS AND GALLERIES

▨ **Courtauld Institute,** Somerset House, Strand (☎ 7848 2549). Tube: Charing Cross. The small, outstanding collection ranges from 14th- to the 20th-century abstractions, focusing on Impressionism, including Manet's *A Bar at the Follies Bergères*, van Gogh's *Self Portrait with Bandaged Ear*, and Cézanne's *The Card Players*. Open M-Sa 10am-6pm, Su noon-6pm. £4; free M 10am-2pm.

BRITAIN

■ **Imperial War Museum,** Lambeth Rd. (☎ 7416 5320). Tube: Lambeth North. The commendably un-jingoistic exhibits follow every aspect of war from 1914, covering conflicts large and small. Most heart-rending is the Holocaust Exhibition, a 2-fl. exposition of Nazi atrocities against not only Jews, but also gays, gypsies, and the disabled. Open daily 10am-6pm. £6.50, students £5.50; free after 4:30pm.

■ **Institute of Contemporary Arts (ICA),** Nash House, the Mall (☎ 7930 3647). Tube: Charing Cross. Down the road from Buckingham Palace, Britain's center for contemporary arts is nicely located for attacking the establishment. Open M noon-11pm, Tu-Sa noon-1am, Su noon-10:30pm; galleries close 7:30pm. M-F £1.50, Sa-Su £2.50.

■ **London's Transport Museum,** Covent Garden Piazza (☎ 7565 7299). Tube: Covent Garden or Charing Cross. Informative *and* fun. Kids and adults will find themselves engrossed in the history of London's public transportation system. Open Sa-Th 10am-6pm, F 11am-6pm. £6, students £4, under 16 free with adult.

■ **Museum of London,** London Wall; enter through the Barbican. (☎ 7600 3699). Tube: Barbican. This engrossing collection traces the history of London from its foundations to the present day. Open M-Sa 10am-5:50pm, Su noon-5:50pm. £5, students £3.

■ **National Maritime Museum,** Trafalgar Rd., Greenwich (☎ 8858 4422). Dockland's Light Railway: Cutty Sark. Broad-ranging, child-friendly displays cover almost every aspect of seafaring history. The naval portraits in the neighboring Queen's House take 2nd place to Inigo Jones's architecture. Open daily June to early Sept. 10am-6pm, early Sept. to May 10am-5pm. £7.50; students £6. Combined ticket with Queen's House and Royal Observatory £10.50, students £8.40. For Greenwich Passport ticket, see p. 176.

■ **Natural History Museum,** Cromwell Rd. (☎ 7942 5000). Tube: South Kensington. This cathedral-like building is home to an array of animals and minerals, though remarkably few vegetables. Highlights include a frighteningly realistic T-Rex, and the engrossing interactive *Human Biology* gallery. Open M-Sa 10am-5:50pm, Su 11am-5:50pm. Free.

Royal Academy, Burlington House, Piccadilly (☎ 7300 8000). Tube: Piccadilly Circus. Founded in 1768 as both an art school and meeting place for Britain's foremost artists, the Academy holds outstanding exhibitions on all manner of art. Open Sa-Th 10am-6pm, F 10am-10pm. Around £7; students £1-4 less.

Saatchi Gallery, 98a Boundary Rd. (☎ 7624 8299). From St. John's Wood Tube, head down Grove End Rd., turn right into Abbey Rd.; Boundary Rd. is a 12min. up on the left. Works from Charles Saatchi's vast collection of contemporary British art. The only permanent piece on display is Richard Wilson's 1987 installation *20:50*, a whole room filled with used oil. Open Sept.-July Th-Su noon-6pm. £5, students £3.

Sir John Soane's Museum, 13 Lincoln's Inn Fields. Tube: Holborn. Architect John Soane let his imagination run free when designing this intriguing museum for his own collection of art. Open Tu-Sa 10am-5pm, 1st Tu of month also 6-9pm. Free; £1 donation.

Wallace Collection, Manchester Sq. (☎ 7563 9500). Tube: Bond St. Palatial Hertford House holds a stunning array of porcelain, medieval armor, and the largest weaponry collection outside the Tower of London. Open M-Sa 10am-5pm, Su noon-5pm. Free.

National Portrait Gallery, St. Martin's Pl. (☎ 7312 2463). Tube: Leicester Sq. This artistic *Who's Who* in Britain began in 1856 as "the fulfillment of a patriotic and moral ideal." Open M-W and Sa-Su 10am-6pm, Th-F 10am-9pm. Free; exhibitions up to £5.

Sherlock Holmes Museum, 239 Baker St. (marked 221b; ☎ 7935 8866). Tube: Baker St. It takes a master sleuth to deduce that this meticulously recreated home-from-Holmes is entirely fictional. Or is it? Open daily 9:30am-6:30pm. £6, ages 7-16 £4.

♫ ENTERTAINMENT

On any given day or night in London, you can choose from the widest range of entertainment a city can offer. The West End is perhaps the world's theater capital, supplemented by an adventurous "fringe" and a justly famous National Theatre, while new bands spring eternal from the fountain of London's many music venues. Dance, film, comedy, sports, and countless more happenings will leave you amazed at the variety of listings. Whatever you're planning to do, *Time Out* magazine's weekly listings will be indispensable. ($2.20, every W.)

THEATER

The stage for a national dramatic tradition over 500 years old, London theaters maintain unrivaled breadth of choice. At a **West End** theater (a term referring to all the major stages, whether or not they're actually in the West End), you can expect a professional, if mainstream production, top-quality performers, and (usually) comfortable seats. **Off-West End** theaters usually present more challenging work, while remaining as professional as their West End brethren. The **Fringe** refers to the scores of smaller, less commercial theaters, often just a room in a pub basement with a few benches and a team of dedicated amateurs.

The **Leicester Square Half-Price Ticket Booth** is run by the theaters themselves and releases (genuine!) half-price tickets on the day of the show. The catch is that you have to buy them in person, in cash, with no choice in seating (most expensive tickets sold first) and no way of knowing in advance what shows will have tickets available that day. Come early and be prepared to wait, especially Sa. (South side of Leicester Sq.—look for the long lines. Tube: Leicester Sq. £2 booking fee per ticket. Max. 4 tickets per person. Open M-Sa 10am-7pm, Su noon-2:30pm.)

Barbican Theatre, Barbican; main entrance on Silk St. (☎ 7638 8891). Tube: Barbican. A futuristic auditorium seating 1166 in steeply raked, forward-leaning balconies. In May 2002, the **Royal Shakespeare Company** will give its last performances in residence at the Barbican. Tickets £6-30, cheapest M-F evening and Sa matinee. Student standbys from 9am day of performance. In the same complex, **The Pit** is an intimate 200-seater theater used primarily for new and experimental productions. Tickets £10-15.

National Theatre, just downriver of Waterloo bridge (info ☎ 7452 3400, box office ☎ 7452 3000). Tube: Waterloo. Since opening in 1963, the National has been at the forefront of British theater. The **Olivier** stage seats 1160 in a fan-shaped open-stage layout; the **Lyttelton** is a proscenium theater with 890 seats; and the 300-seat **Cottesloe** offers flexible staging for experimental dramas. Box office open M-Sa 10am-8pm. Horrendously complex pricing scheme; basically £10-30, day seats (from 10am) £10-13, standby (2hr. before curtain) £15; students £8-15.

Royal Court Theatre, Sloane Sq. (☎ 7565 5000). Called "the most important theater in Europe" by the *New York Times;* dedicated to challenging new writing and innovative interpretations of classics. Experimental work runs in the intimate Upstairs auditorium. Main stage £5-25; students £9 in advance, £5 day of performance; standing places £0.10 1hr. before curtain. Upstairs £5-15, students £9. M all seats £5.

Shakespeare's Globe Theatre, 21 New Globe Walk (☎ 7401 9919). Tube: London Bridge. This may be a faithful reproduction of the original 16th-century playhouse where Shakespeare himself performed. Choose between the backless wooden benches or stand through a performance as a "groundling." For tours of the Globe, see **Sights,** p. 171. Performances mid-May to late Sept. Tu-Sa 7:30pm, Su 6:30pm; from June also Tu-Sa 2pm, Su 1pm. Box office open M-Sa 10am-6pm, until 8pm on performance days. Seats £11-27, students £9-23; yard (i.e. standing) £5.

CINEMA

London's film scene offers everything. The degenerate heart of the celluloid monster is **Leicester Square** (p. 165), where the latest releases premiere a day before hitting the chains. The dominant mainstream chain is **Odeon** (☎ 0870 5050 00), and **The Empire** (☎ (0870) 010 2030) is the most famous first-run theater. Tickets to West End cinemas are £8-10; weekday screenings before 5pm are usually cheaper.

BFI London IMAX Cinema (☎ 7902 1234), at the south end of Waterloo bridge, accessed via underground walkways. Tube: Waterloo. Stunning glass drum houses the UK's biggest screen. £6.95, students and seniors £5.95, kids £4.95; extra film £4.20.

National Film Theatre (NFT), on the south bank, right underneath Waterloo Bridge (☎ 7928 3232). Tube: Waterloo, Embankment, or Temple. One of the world's leading cinemas, with a mind-boggling array of films. 6 different movies hit the 3 screens every evening, starting around 6pm. All films £6.85, students £5.25.

BRITAIN

The Prince Charles, Leicester Pl. (☎ 7957 4009). Tube: Leicester Sq. Features *Sing-a-long-a-Sound-of-Music*, where Von Trappists dress as everything from nuns to "Ray, a drop of golden sun" (F 7:30pm, Su 2pm; £12.50), and the live-troupe-accompanied *Rocky Horror Picture Show* (F 11:45pm; £6, students £3). Otherwise it screens 2nd-run Hollywood and recent independent. £3.50, M-F before 5pm £1.75, M evenings £2.

MUSIC

ROCK AND POP

Birthplace of the Rolling Stones, the Sex Pistols, and the Chemical Brothers, home to Madonna and Paul McCartney, London is a town steeped in rock 'n' roll history.

Borderline, Orange Yard, off Manette St. (☎ 7734 2095). Tube: Tottenham Court Rd. Basement space still trading off its secret REM gig years ago, now used for lesser-known groups. Music M-Sa from 8pm. Box office open M-F 1-7:30pm. £5-10 in advance.

The Water Rats, 328 Grays Inn Rd. (☎ 7837 7269). Tube: King's Cross/St. Pancras. A pub-café by day, a stomping venue for top new talent by night. Oasis were signed here after performing their 1st London gig. Open for coffee M-F 8am-noon, surprisingly good lunches (£4-6) M-F noon-2pm, and music M-Sa 8pm-midnight (cover £5, students £4).

CLASSICAL

Home to four world-class orchestras, three major concert halls, two opera houses, two ballet companies, and scores of chamber ensembles, London is ground zero for serious music. To hear some of the world's top choirs for free, head to Westminster Abbey (p. 172) or St. Paul's Cathedral (p. 169) for Evensong.

Barbican Hall, details as for Barbican Theatre (p. 181). Tube: Barbican. One of Europe's leading concert halls. The resident **London Symphony Orchestra** plays throughout year; the hall also hosts international orchestras, jazz, and world musicians. Tickets £6-35.

English National Opera, at the Coliseum, St. Martin's Lane (☎ 7632 8300). Tube: Charing Cross or Leicester Sq. All the classics, plus contemporary and avant-garde work, sung in English. £6-60; under 18 half-price with adult. Day seats for the dress-circle (£29) and balcony (£3) released M-F 10am (12:30pm by phone). Standbys from 3hr. before curtain; students £12.50, seniors £18.

The Proms (www.bbc.co.uk/proms/), at the Royal Albert Hall, Kensington Gore. Tube: Knightsbridge. Summer season of classical music, with concerts every night from mid-July to mid-Sept. "Promenade" refers to the tradition of selling dirt-cheap standing tickets; lines often start forming mid-afternoon. Tickets go on sale in mid-May (£5-30); standing places sold from 1½hr. before the concert (£3).

Royal Opera House, Bow St. (☎ 7304 4000). Tube: Covent Garden. Also home to the **Royal Ballet.** Productions tend to be conservative but lavish, like the wealthy patrons. Standing room and restricted-view seating in the upper balconies is under £5. Standby 4hr. before curtain £12.50-15. Day seats £10-40 from 10am on performance day.

Royal Festival Hall, on the south bank of the Thames between Hungerford and Waterloo bridges (☎ 7960 4242). Tube: Waterloo or Embankment. 2500-seat concert hall with the best acoustics in London. The 2 resident orchestras, the **Philharmonia** and the **London Philharmonic,** predominate, but big-name jazz, latin, and world-music groups also visit. Classical concerts £6-30; others around £10-30.

JAZZ, FOLK, AND WORLD

London's **jazz** scene is small but serious; top clubs pull in big-name performers from across the world. **Folk** and **world** music keep an even lower profile, mostly restricted to pubs and community centers.

Ronnie Scott's, 47 Frith St. (☎ 7439 0747). Tube: Tottenham Court Rd. London's oldest and most famous jazz club. Music starts M-Sa 9:30pm-3am, Su 8:30-11:30pm. Reservations recommended—if it's sold out, try coming back at midnight to catch the 2nd set. Cover M-Th £15, F-Sa £20, Su £8-12; students £9 M-W. AmEx/MC/V.

Spitz, 109 Commercial St. (☎ 7392 9032). Tube: Shoreditch. Hosts an eclectic range of live music, from jazz and world music to indie pop and rap. All profits go to help Bosnian and Kosovar children. Music Tu-Sa 8pm; cover £5-8.

BRITAIN

SPECTATOR SPORTS

FOOTBALL. During the season (late August to May), over half a million people attend professional football matches every Saturday, dressed with fierce loyalty in team colors. Though violence at stadiums has dogged the game for years, the atmosphere has become much tamer now. The big three London teams are **Arsenal,** Highbury Stadium, Avenell Rd. (☎7704 4000; Tube: Arsenal), **Chelsea,** Stamford Bridge, Fulham Rd. (☎7386 7799; Tube: Fulham Broadway), and ⬛**Tottenham Hotspur,** White Hart Lane (☎8365 5000; BR: White Hart Lane).

RUGBY. Rugby was allegedly created when a confused Rugby School student picked up a regular football and ran it into the goal. The most significant contests, including the springtime **Six Nations Championship** (England, Scotland, Wales, Ireland, France, and Italy) are played at **Twickenham** (☎8831 6666; Rail: Twickenham).

CRICKET. London's two grounds stage both county and international contests. **Lord's,** St. John's Wood Rd. (☎7432 1033; Tube: St. John's Wood) is the home turf of the **Marleybone Cricket Club (MCC),** the established governing body at cricket. The **Oval,** Kennington (☎7582 7764; Tube: Oval) also fields test matches. Every summer a touring nation plays England in a series of matches around the country, including a customary thrashing every four years at the hands of the ⬛**Australian Cricket Team.**

TENNIS. Every year, for two weeks in late June and early July, tennis buffs all over the world focus their attention on **Wimbledon.** Reserve months ahead or arrive by 6am (gates open 10:30am) to secure one of the 500 Centre and no. 1 court tickets sold every morning; otherwise, settle for a "grounds" tickets to the outer courts. (All England Lawn Tennis Club. Tube: Southfields or Rail: Wimbledon. ☎8971 2473. Grounds £7-12, after 5pm £5-7; show courts £17-50.)

🔲 SHOPPING

From its earliest days, London has been a trading city, its wealth and power built upon almost two millennia of commerce. Today even more so than at the Empire's height, London's economy is truly international—and thanks to the outward-looking and fundamentally eclectic nature of Londoners' diverse tastes, the range of goods is unmatched anywhere. From Harrods' proud boast to supply "all things to all people," to African crafts on sale in Brixton market, you could shop for lifetime.

DEPARTMENT STORES

Fortnum & Mason, 181 Piccadilly (☎7734 8040). Tube: Green Park. Founded in 1707, and famed for a sumptuous food hall with chandeliers, fountains, and liveried clerks; London's snootiest department store. Open M-Sa 10am-6:30pm. AmEx/MC/V.

Harrods, 87-135 Old Brompton Rd. (☎7730 1234). Tube: Knightsbridge. The only thing bigger than the store itself is the price mark-up. No wonder only tourists and oil sheikhs actually shop here. Bewildering. Open M-Sa 10am-7pm. AmEx/MC/V/Your Soul.

Harvey Nichols, 109-125 Knightsbridge (☎7235 5000). Tube: Knightsbridge. Imagine Bond St., Rue St. Honore, and Fifth Avenue all rolled up and translated into 5 floors of fashion, from the biggest names to the hippest contemporary unknowns. Open M-Tu and Sa 10am-7pm, W-F 10am-8pm, Su noon-6pm. AmEx/MC/V.

Selfridges, 400 Oxford St. (☎7629 1234). Tube: Bond St. The total department store. With 14 cafes and restaurants, a hair salon, and a hotel, shopaholics need never leave. Open M-W 10am-7pm, Th-F 10am-8pm, Sa 9:30am-7pm, Su noon-6pm. AmEx/MC/V.

CLOTHING AND FOOTWEAR

⬛ **Cyberdog/Cybercity,** Stables Market (☎7482 2842). Tube: Camden Town. Unbelievable club clothes for superior lifeforms. Alien goddesses will want to try on steel corsets with rubber breast hoses. Open M-F 11am-6pm, Sa-Su 10am-7pm. AmEx/MC/V.

Miss Sixty, 39 Neal St. (☎7836 3789). Tube: Covent Garden. The newest clothing craze. Bright, patterned, and skin-hugging female fashions in a laid-back and sexy style. Open M-W and F-Sa 10am-6:30pm, Th 10am-7:30pm, Su noon-6pm. AmEx/MC/V.

BRITAIN

Dr. Marten's Dept. Store, 1-4 King St. (☎7497 1460). Tube: Covent Garden. Tourist-packed 5-tiered megastore, with baby docs, papa docs, and the classic yellow-stitched boots. Open M-W and F-Sa 10am-7pm, Th 10:30am-8pm, Su noon-6pm. AmEx/MC/V.

Dolly Diamond, 51 Pembridge Rd. (☎7792 2479). Tube: Notting Hill Gate. Jackie Onassis or Audrey Hepburn? Choose your look from the great selection of classic 50s-70s clothes, along with some elegant 20s-40s evening gowns. Open M-F 10:30am-6:30pm, Sa 9:30am-6:30pm, Su 11am-5pm. "Cash preferred."

BOOKSTORES

In London, even the chain bookstores are wonders. An exhaustive selection of bookshops lines Charing Cross Rd. between Tottenham Court Rd. and Leicester Sq.; many vend secondhand paperbacks. Establishments along Great Russell St., by the British Museum, and Cecil Court, near Leicester Sq., stock esoteric and specialized books on any subject from Adorno to the Zohar.

Foyles, 113-119 Charing Cross Rd. (☎7437 5660). Tube: Tottenham Ct. Rd. The bookshop of last resort. Has absolutely every book you'll ever want, while doing its best to ensure you never find it. Open M-Sa 9:30am-7:30pm, Su noon-6pm. AmEx/MC/V

Sotheran's of Sackville Street, 2-5 Sackville St. (☎7439 6151). Tube: Piccadilly Circus. While hushed atmosphere gives an impression of exclusivity, affordable books abound, and the staff charms. Open M-F 9:30am-6pm, Sa 10am-4pm. AmEx/MC/V

Waterstone's, 203-206 Piccadilly (☎7851 2400). Tube: Piccadilly Circus. Europe's largest bookshop, on 8 floors, with cafe, **Internet** station, and posh basement restaurant. Open M-Sa 10am-11pm, Su noon-6pm. AmEx/MC/V.

RECORD STORES

London crawls with music junkies, and the city has a record collection to match. Don't expect any bargains; remember, when it comes to records, "import" means "rip-off." Megastores carry vinyl versions of most major-label releases, but to get those rare promos, white labels, or collectibles, go to an independent record store.

Black Market, 25 D'Arblay St. (☎7437 0478). Tube: Oxford Circus. All-vinyl dance haven; house and garage, great drum 'n' bass section below. Open M-Sa 11am-7pm.

HMV, 150 Oxford St., W1 (☎7631 3423). Tube: Oxford Circus. 3 massive floors, with an exceptional range of new vinyl on the ground floor, especially dance music. Open M-Sa 9am-8pm, Su noon-6pm. AmEx/DC/MC/V.

Rough Trade, 130 Talbot Rd. (☎7229 8541). Tube: Ladbroke Grove. Branch at 16 Neal's Yard (☎7240 0105; Tube: Covent Garden). Birthplace of the legendary independent label. Open M-Sa 10am-6:30pm, Su 1-5pm. AmEx/MC/V.

Uptown Records, 3 D'Arblay St. (☎7434 3639). Tube: Oxford Circus. Ever wondered what DJs do in the daytime? You'll find lots of them working in this small all-vinyl store. Open M-W and F-Sa 10:30am-7pm, Th 10:30am-8pm. AmEx/MC/V.

STREET MARKETS

Camden Markets, off Camden High St. and Chalk Farm Rd. Tube: Camden Town. Now London's 4th-biggest tourist attraction, the market fills all available space on Sundays with hordes on the lookout for the latest mainstream, vintage, and offbeat fashions.

Camden Lock Market, from the railway bridge to the canal. Arranged around a food-filled courtyard on the Regent's Canal, mostly indoor shops sell pricier items such as carpets and household goods. Most stalls operate F or Sa-Su only.

Camden Canal Market, down the tunnel opposite Camden Lock, starts out promisingly with jewelry and watches, then degenerates rapidly into sub-par club clothes and tourist trinkets. The canalside location makes it a good spot for a bite to eat, though. Open F-Su.

Brick Lane Market. Tube: Shoreditch or Aldgate East. Famous weekly market with a South Asian flair (food, rugs, spices, bolts of fabric, strains of sitar). Open Su 8am-2pm.

Petticoat Lane Market. Tube: Liverpool St., Aldgate, or Aldgate East. Block after block of cheap clothing, with lots of leather jackets around Aldgate East. The real action begins at about 9:30am. Open Su 9am-2pm; starts shutting down around noon.

OTHER SPECIALTY STORES

Lush (☎(01202) 668 545). 5 locations, including 123 King's Rd. (Tube: Sloane Sq.); Covent Garden Piazza (Tube: Covent Garden) and 40 Carnaby St. (Tube: Oxford Circus). All-natural cosmetics that look good enough to eat. Vegan cosmetics with a green dot.

Hamley's, 188 Regent St. (☎7734 3161). Tube: Oxford Circus. Seven floors filled with every possible toy and game. Open M-F 10am-8pm, Sa 9:30am-8pm, Su noon-6pm.

NIGHTLIFE

The West End, and in particular **Soho,** is the scene of most of London's after-dark action, from the glitzy (and best avoided) Leicester Sq. tourist traps such as the Hippodrome and Equinox to semi-secret underground clubs. The other major axis of London nightlife is the East's **Shoreditch** and **Hoxton** (known as Shoho).

BARS

In London these days, drinking is the new dancing. An explosion of club-bars has invaded the previously forgotten zone between pubs and clubs, with stylish surroundings, top-flight DJs, and plentiful lounging space. Usually, club-bars are open from noon or early evening to 1 or 2am; skip the cover charge by arriving early and staying put as the scene shifts around you. And remember—don't tip the barman!

Soshomatch, 2 Tabernacle St. (☎7920 0701). Tube: Moorgate. A 2-floor bar/restaurant that converts into a stylish club Th-Sa; DJ-driven atmosphere with comfy leather couches. Open M-W 11am-midnight, Th-Sa 11am-2pm. Cover F-Sa £5. AmEx/MC/V.

AKA, 18 West Central St. (☎7419 9199). Tube: Tottenham Ct. Rd. There's nowhere like the candlelit island lounge for people-watching. Cocktails £6-7. "Members only"; you may join at the door. Dress nicely! Open Su-F 6pm-3am, food to 1am. Cover Free-£5.

Dogstar, 389 Coldharbour Ln. (☎7733 7515). Tube: Brixton. At 9pm, the tables are cleared from the dance floor and the projectors turned on. House, hiphop, and dance music. Open Su-Th noon-2am, F-Sa noon-4am. Cover Su-Th free; F £5, 10-11pm £4, free before 10pm; Sa £7, 10-11pm £5, free before 10pm.

Freud, 198 Shaftesbury Ave. (☎7240 9933). Invigorate your psyche in this offbeat underground hipster hangout. Sand-blasted walls occasionally echo to live music. Cheap cocktails (from £3.40) beat an hour on the couch. Light meals 11am-4:30pm (£3.50-6). Open M-Sa 11am-11pm, Su noon-10:30pm. No cover. MC/V.

Shoreditch Electricity Showrooms, 39a Hoxton Sq. (☎7739 6934). Tube: Old St. If you wanted to know where the super-cool go, this is the answer. Bottled beer £2.70-3. Food served 1-3:45pm, e.g. crispy squid (£5). Open Tu-W noon-11pm, Th noon-midnight, F-Sa noon-1am, Su noon-10:30pm. No cover. AmEx/MC/V.

Vibe Bar, 91-95 Brick Ln. (☎7247 3479). Tube: Aldgate East. Young, fun, clubby bar, with an interior straight out of a style mag; DJs M-F from 7:30pm and Sa-Su 6pm; in summer, the fun extends outside with a 2nd DJ working the shady courtyard. Tends toward soul/jazz/funk. Open Su-Th noon-11pm, F-Sa noon-1am. Cover Free-£2.

NIGHTCLUBS

Every major DJ in the world either lives in London or makes frequent visits to the city. Such is the variety and fast-changing nature of London nightlife that even weekly publications have trouble keeping up; use the listings below as a guide, but check *Time Out* or call the club before heading out to prevent any surprises. As with bars, arrive earlier for cheaper cover charges.

Fabric, 77a Charterhouse St. (☎7336 8898). Tube: Farringdon. Bigger than a B52 and 100 times as loud. When they power-up the underfoot subwoofer, lights dim across London. 3 dance floors, chill-out beds, multiple bars, and unisex toilets crammed with up to 2500 dance-crazed Londoners. Yow. Various monthlies F 9:30pm-5am, Sa mega dance fest *Fabric Live* 9:30pm-7am. Cover £10-15.

BRITAIN

🖼 **Scala,** 275 Pentonville Rd. (☎ 7833 2022, tickets 7771 2000). Tube: Kings Cross. Huge main floor embraces its cinematic past: DJs spin from the projectionist's box, ramped balconies provide multiple levels, and a giant screen pulsates with visuals as 3m pyramids of speakers detonate the bass. F gay/mixed eclectica 10pm-5am; Sa was in flux at press time but tends to be house-dominated; every other Su *Latin 8* has salsa 8pm-2am, with a free dance workshop 8:30-9:30pm. Dress up. Cover £8-10.

93 Feet East, 150 Brick Lane (☎ 7247 3293). Tube: Aldgate East. One of the hottest new clubs in East London. Barn-like main dance floor and sofa-strewn upstairs room. W salsa with a live Latin band 7-11pm; Th world-dance mixes 9pm-3am; F techno and house (9pm-3am); Sa anything from house to ska 9pm-2am. Cover £3-10.

Cargo, Kingsland Viaduct, 83 Rivington St. (☎ 7739 3440). Tube: Old Street. Despite the superclub trimmings—2 enormous arched rooms, fab acoustics, movie projectors, and an intimate candle-lit lounge—Cargo is crippled by a 1am license. On the plus side, the place is kicking by 9:30pm. Strong Latin lineup with mixing DJs and live music. Open M-F noon-1am, Sa 6pm-1am, Su noon-midnight. Cover £3-7.

The Fridge, Town Hall Parade, Brixton Hill (☎ 7326 5100). Tube: Brixton. Turn left from the station and bear right at the fork onto Brixton Hill. Gant split-level dance floor. F total trance glo-stick madness 10pm-6am; Sa usually gay nights 10am-6pm. Cover £9-13. After parties start Sa-Su mornings 5:30am at the neighboring Fridge Bar (£6).

Ministry of Sound, 103 Gaunt St. (☎ 7378 6528). Tube: Elephant and Castle. Take the exit for South Bank University. The granddaddy of all serious clubbing—arrive early or queue all night. Dress code generally casual, but famously unsmiling doorstaff make it sensible to err on the side of smartness (*no* sports shoes!). F garage and R&B 10:30pm-6am; Sa US and vocal house midnight-9am. Cover £12-15.

Sound, 10 Wardour St. (☎ 7287 1010). Tube: Leicester Sq. A real labyrinth, with rooms spread over 4 floors. Th R&B, soul, and UK garage 10pm-3am; F R&B 10pm-4am; Sa 🖼 *Carwash* 1970s retro fest—funky dress a must 10pm-4:30am. Cover £5-12.

Velvet Room, 143 Charing Cross Rd. (☎ 7734 4687). Tube: Tottenham Court Rd. Small, showing its age, and packed even midweek—come here for the music, not the posing scene. M gay night, with R&B and hiphop 10pm-3am; Tu garage 10:30pm-3am; W 🖼 *Swerve* with Brazilian-flavored drum 'n' bass 10pm-2:30am; Th funky techno 10pm-3am, F trance 10pm-4:30am; Sa house 10pm-4am. Cover £4-10.

GAY AND LESBIAN NIGHTLIFE

London has a very visible gay scene, ranging from flamboyant to mainstream. *Time Out* devotes a section to gay listings, and gay newspapers include *Capital Gay*, *Pink Paper*, and *Shebang* (for women). *Boyz* magazine (free from gay bars) and the *Ginger Beer* web site (www.gingerbeer.co.uk) track the gay and lesbian nightlife scenes respectively. Soho (especially **Old Compton Street**) is the heart of gay London, with smaller scenes in Islington, Earl's Court, and Brixton.

The Box, 32-34 Monmouth St. (☎ 7240 5828). Recently renovated, this spacious gay/mixed bar-brasserie is popular with a stylish media/fashion crowd. Daily changing food specials (main courses around £9). They're very proud of their Ally McBeal-style unisex toilets. Also sells club tix. Open M-Sa 11am-11pm, Su 7-10:30pm. MC/V.

Candy Bar, 23-24 Bateman St. (☎ 7437 1977). Tube: Tottenham Ct. Rd. The UK's 1st full-time lesbian den. Groovy bar and basement dance floor. DJs W-Su. Open M-Tu 5pm-1am, W-F 5pm-3am, Sa 3pm-3am, Su 5-11pm. Cover F-Sa £5 after 9pm.

Comptons of Soho, 53 Old Compton St. (☎ 7479 7461). Tube: Leicester Sq. Soho's "official" gay pub is always busy. Horseshoe bar encourages the exchange of meaningful glances, while upstairs (opens 6pm) offers a more mellow scene with pool table. Open M-Sa 11am-11pm, Su noon-10:30pm. MC/V.

G-A-Y (☎ (0906) 100 0160). M and Th at the Mean Fiddler, 165 Charing Cross Rd., F-Sa at the London Astoria, 157 Charing Cross Rd. Tube: Tottenham Court Rd. London's biggest gay and lesbian scene, 4 nights a week. M *Pink Pounder* 90s classics with 70s-80s faves in the bar; F *Camp Attack* attitude-free 70s and 80s cheese; Sa *G-A-Y* big night out, rocking the capacity crowd with commercial-dance DJs, and live pop performances. Open M, Th, F until 4am, Sa until 5am. Cover free-£10.

BRITAIN

Vespa Lounge, St. Giles Circus (☎ 7836 8956). Tube: Tottenham Court Rd. Relaxed lesbian lounge bar with comfy seats, pool table. Thai food from downstairs Conservatory restaurant. "Laughing Cows" comedy night 1st Su of month (£5-8), plus occasional theme nights. Gay men welcome as guests. Open M-Sa 6-11pm, Su 6-10:30pm.

DAYTRIPS FROM LONDON

OXFORD. The university town bustles with activity and overflows with grandeur. Enjoy the punting and the festivals (see p. 196).

STRATFORD-UPON-AVON. Stratford crawls with everything Shakespeare. Enjoy a show or explore the Bard's birthplace and various residences (see p. 203).

STONEHENGE. The incredible 7m-high monoliths of Stonehenge, which date from 1500 BC, lie near Salisbury, under 2hr. by train from London (see p. 191).

SOUTHERN ENGLAND

Sprawling toward the continent, the landscape of southern England simultaneously asserts Britain's island heritage and reveals a continental link deeper than the Chunnel. Early Britons settled the counties of Kent, Sussex, and Hampshire from across the English Channel, and William the Conqueror left his mark upon the downsland in the form of awe-inspiring cathedrals. But Geoffrey Chaucer, Jane Austen, Charles Dickens, E.M. Forster, and Virginia Woolf also all drew inspiration from these lands. To the west, the counties of Somerset, Avon, and Wiltshire boast Salisbury's medieval cathedral, the Roman Baths at Bath, and the forever-mysterious Stonehenge. Even farther west, a mist of legends shrouds the counties of Dorset, Somerset, Devon, and Cornwall in England's West Country, home to Bronze Age barrows and King Arthur.

FERRIES AND TRAINS TO FRANCE, SPAIN, AND BELGIUM

Ferries run from **Dover** (see p. 188) to **Calais, France** (see p. 387) and **Ostend, Belgium** (see p. 135). Ferries also chug from **Portsmouth** (see p. 190) to **St-Malo** (see p. 326) and **Caen, France** (see p. 321); from **Plymouth** (see p. 194) to **Roscoff, France** and **Santander, Spain;** from **Folkestone** to **Boulogne, France** (see p. 387); from **Newhaven** to **Dieppe, France** (see p. 321). Travelers with cars can head through the **Chunnel** (from Kent to Nord-Pas-de-Calais) on **Eurotunnel.** For detailed info on over-and- underwater transport options to the continent, see p. 52.

CANTERBURY ☎ 01227

Six hundred years ago, in his famed *Canterbury Tales*, Chaucer captured the irony of tourists visiting England's most famous execution site. His sometimes lewd, sometimes irreverent tales speak of the pilgrims of the Middle Ages who flocked from London to the **Canterbury Cathedral.** Archbishop Thomas à Becket was beheaded there in 1170 after an irate Henry II asked, "Will no one rid me of this troublesome priest?" (☎ 762862. Cathedral open Easter-Sept. M-Sa 9am-6:30pm, Su 12:30-2:30pm and 4:30-5:30pm; Oct.-Easter M-Sa 9am-5pm, Su 12:30-2:30pm and 4:30-5:30pm. Evensong services M-F 5:30pm, Sa 3:15pm, Su 6:30pm. £3.50, students £2.50. Audio tour £2.50.) **The Canterbury Tales,** on St. Margaret's St., is a museum that simulates the journey of Chaucer's pilgrims; the gap-toothed Wife of Bath and her waxen companions will entertain you with an abbreviated, Modern English version of the *Tales.* (☎479227. Open July-Aug. daily 9am-5.30pm; Mar.-June and Sept.-Oct. 9:30am-5:30pm; Nov.-Feb. Su-F 10am-4:30pm, Sa 9:30am-5:30pm. £5.90, students £4.90.) On Stour St., the **Canterbury Heritage Museum** tells the history of Canterbury from medieval times to WWII. (☎452747. Open June-Oct. M-Sa 10:30am-5pm, Su 1:30-5pm; Nov.-May M-Sa 10:30am-5pm. £1.90, students £1.20.) To see two of South

BRITAIN

England's most storied castles, head 20km southeast to **Deal.** Here you'll find **Deal Castle,** which was designed by Henry VIII as a coastal fortification, as well as **Walmer Castle,** which has been converted from a military bastion to an elegant country estate. **Trains** leave regularly from Canterbury (£3).

For those who can't travel to Canterbury on horseback with a group of verbally gifted pilgrims, **trains** from London's Victoria Station arrive at Canterbury's **East Station** (1½hr., every 30min., £15.70), while trains from London's Charing Cross and Waterloo Stations arrive at **West Station** (1½hr., every hr., £15.70). **National Express buses** (☎ (08705) 808080) arrive from London at St. George's Ln. (2hr., 1 per hr., £6-8). The **TIC,** 34 St. Margaret's St., stocks free mini-guides to Canterbury. (☎780063. Open M-Sa 9:30am-5:30pm, Su 10am-4pm.) Check email at **I2M Internet Cafe,** corner of St. Dunstan's St. and Station Rd. West. (☎478778; www.i2m.co.uk. Open M-Sa 10am-6pm, Su noon-5pm. £3 per hr.) **B&Bs** cluster near both train stations; around the intersections of London Rd. and Whitstable Rd., and High St. and New Dover Rd. **The Tudor House,** 6 Best Ln., is off High St. in the town center. Eat breakfast in front of a Tudor fireplace in this flowery 16th-century house. Try to get a front room for a gorgeous view of the Cathedral. (☎765650. Singles £18; doubles £36, with bath, £44.) The **Hampton House,** 40 New Dover Rd. (☎464912), offers quiet, luxurious rooms for £20-25, and the wonderfully named **Let's Stay,** 26 New Dover Rd (☎463628), has beds for £11 and vegetarian breakfasts on request. **The Camping and Caravaning Club Site,** on Bekesbourne Ln., has good facilities. (☎463216. £4.75 pitch fee; £5.30 per person.) **High Street** is crowded with pubs, and restaurants. For **groceries,** head to **Safeway supermarket,** on St. George's Pl. (Open M-F 8am-8pm, Su 10am-4pm.) **Marlowe's,** 55 St. Peter's St., prides itself on an eclectic mix of vegetarian and beefy English, American, and Mexican styles. (☎462194. Open daily 11:30am-10:30pm.) **C'est la Vie,** 17b Burgate, attracts locals and students who take away inventive sandwiches on freshly baked bread. (☎457525. Open daily 9am-6pm.) **Postal code:** CT1 2BA.

DOVER   ☎ 01304

The puttering of ferries, the constant hum of hovercrafts, and the chatter of French families *en vacance* coming through the Channel Tunnel drown out the roar of the English Channel at Dover, Britain's most vital port. The magnificent **Dover Castle** reigns supreme over the famous **White Cliffs;** even a brief visit reminds why it is famed both for its setting and impregnability. (Buses from the town center run every hr. daily Apr.-Sept., fare £0.55. Castle and complex open Apr.-Sept. daily 10am-6pm; Oct. 10am-5pm; Nov.-Mar. 10am-4pm. £7, concessions £5.30, children £3.50, families £17.50.*) **Trains** chug to Dover's **Priory Station** from London's Victoria, Waterloo East, London Bridge, and Charing Cross stations (2hr., every 45min., £17.50). National Express **buses** run regularly from London's Victoria Coach Station to the bus station on Pencester Rd. and then on to the **Eastern Docks** (2¾hr., 23 per day, £10), where P&O Stena Line and Hoverspeed depart from the Prince of Wales Pier for Calais (foot passengers £27). Buses also make trips to **Canterbury** (45min., £4). The **TIC,** on Townwall St., has lodgings info and ferry and Hovercraft tickets. (☎ (01304) 205108; fax 245409. Open daily 9am-6pm.) The **YHA Charlton House Youth Hostel,** 306 London Rd., is 800m from the train station; turn left onto Folkestone Rd., then left again at the roundabout onto High St., which becomes London Rd. The hostel is farther from the center of Dover than the private B&Bs: expect more barren and unfriendly streets. (☎ (01304) 201314. Kitchen. Lockout 10am-1pm. Curfew 11pm. Dorms £11, under 18 £7.80.) The **Gladstone Guest House,** 3 Laureston Pl., offers wonderful views and tastefully decorated rooms with hand-crafted furniture. (☎208457. Singles £25-28; doubles £44-48.) **Harthorn Farm,** at Martin Mill Station off the A258, offers **camping.** (June to mid-Sept. Two people with car and tent June to mid-Sept. £11; Mar.-May and mid-Sept. to Oct. £9. £3 per extra person.) Cheap food is available from dawn to dusk in the fish and chip shops on **London Road** and **Biggin Street,** and a decent pub lunch can be had anywhere in the city center. **Postal code:** CT16 1PB.

BRIGHTON
☎ 01273

According to legend, the future King George IV scuttled into Brighton (pop. 250,000) for some decidedly un-regal hanky-panky around 1784. Today, Brighton is still the unrivaled home of the "dirty weekend"—it sparkles with a tawdry luster all its own. Before indulging, check out England's longtime obsession with the Far East at the excessively ornate **Royal Pavilion**, on Pavilion Parade, next to Old Steine. (☎ 290900. Open June-Sept. daily 10am-6pm; Oct.-May 10am-5pm, £5.20, concessions £3.75. Guided tours at 11:30am and 2:30pm, £1.25. Audio tour £1.) Around the corner on Church St. stands the **Brighton Museum and Art Gallery,** with paintings, English pottery, and a wild collection of Art Deco and Art Nouveau pieces—leer at Salvador Dalí's sexy red sofa, *Mae West's Lips.* (☎ 290900. Open M-Tu and Th-Sa 10am-5pm, Su 2-5pm. Free.) Before heading out to the rocky **beach,** stroll the **Lanes,** a jumble of 17th-century streets forming the heart of Old Brighton. Brighton brims with nightlife options; pick up *The Punter* or *What's On* (at music stores, news agents, and pubs).

Take a drink to the beach and watch the sunset at **Fortune of War,** 157 King's Rd. Arches. (Open M-Sa 10:30am-11pm, Su 11am-10:30pm) or sup at a former parish house, now a rock n' roll shrine, **The Font and Firkin,** 7 Union St., The Lanes. (☎ 747727. Open M-Sa noon-11pm, Su noon-10:30pm.) **Paradox** and **Event II,** on West St., are the most popular clubs. **The Beach,** 171-181 King's Rd. Arches, produces some of the beachfront's phattest beats, while **Casablanca,** on Middle St., plays live jazz to a student crowd. Converted WWII tunnels of **Zap Club,** on King's Rd., provide space for dirty dancing. (Most clubs in Brighton are open M-Sa 10pm-2am.) Brighton is also *the* gay nightlife spot in Britain outside London; pick up *Gay Times* (£2.75) or *Capital Gay* (free) at newsstands. **Queen's Arms,** 8 George St. (☎ 696873), packs an vibrant gay and lesbian crowd into its Saturday night cabaret.

Trains (☎ (0345) 484950) roll to London (1¼hr., 6 per hr., £10.50) and Portsmouth (1½hr., every hr., round-trip £12.30). National Express **buses** (☎ 383744) head to London (2hr., 15 per day, round-trip £8). The **TIC** is at 10 Bartholomew Sq. (☎ (09067) 112255. Open M-Tu and Th-F 9am-5pm, W and Sa 10am-5pm; Mar.-Oct. also Su 10am-4pm.) The rowdy **Brighton Backpackers Hostel,** 75-76 Middle St., is the best place for meeting other backpackers. (☎ 777717; fax 887788; stay@brighton-backpackers.com. **Internet** £1.50 per 30min. Dorms £10-11; doubles £25.) **Baggies Backpackers,** 33 Oriental Pl., has mellow vibes, exquisite murals, and a mosaic floor. Head west of West Pier along King's Rd., and Oriental Pl. is on the right. (☎ 73 37 40; www.cisweb.co.uk/baggies. Dorms £10; doubles £27.) To get to the **YHA youth hostel,** on Patcham Pl., 6km away, take Patcham bus #5 or 5A from Old Steine in front of the Royal Pavilion to the Black Lion Hotel. (☎ 556196. Curfew 11pm. Dorms £11, under 18 £7.) For cheap eats, try the fish and chip shops along the beach and north of the Lanes, or head to **Safeway supermarket,** 6 St. James's St. (☎ 570363. Open M-Sa 8am-9pm, Su 11am-5pm.) **Postal code:** BN1 1BA.

CHICHESTER
☎ 01243

The remains of Roman walls and an imposing Norman cathedral provide the backdrop for Chichester's (pop. 30,000) superb theater, arts festivals, and gallery exhibits. The **cathedral,** built in 1091, houses a glorious stained glass window by Marc Chagall. (Open daily 7:30am-7pm; off-season 7:30am-5pm. £2 donation encouraged.) The remarkably well-preserved **Roman Palace** in nearby **Fishbourne,** dating from AD 80, is the largest Roman residence ever excavated in Britain. From the Ave de Chartres roundabout in Chichester, head west on Westgate, which becomes Fishbourne Rd. (A259) for 2½km; or take bus #11, 56, or 700 from the center of town and then walk 5min. to the palace. (Open Aug. daily 10am-6pm; Mar.-July and Sept.-Oct. 10am-5pm; Feb. and Nov.-Dec. 10am-4pm; Jan. Sa-Su 10am-4pm. £4.50, students £3.90.) Should your tastes drift to the romantic, head to the gorgeous fairytale **castle,** one of the best in Britain, in nearby **Arundel.** (☎ 882173. Open Apr.-Oct. Su-F noon-5pm. £7.50, children £5, family £21.) To reach wonderful flights of fancy, take a train from Chichester (20min., 2 per hr., £3.40).

BRITAIN

Trains (☎ (08457) 484950) run to: Brighton (50min., 2-3 per hr., round-trip £8.10); London's Victoria Station (1½hr., 3 per hr., round-trip £17.20); Portsmouth (40min., 2-3 per hr., round-trip £4.90). **Buses** (☎ (01903) 237661) depart from opposite the train station on Southgate. National Express runs to London (1 per day, round-trip £9); Coastline serves Brighton (#702; 3hr., 2 per hr., £4.60) and Portsmouth (#700 and 701; 1hr., 2 per hr., £3.90). To get to the **TIC,** 29a South St., turn left as you exit the station onto Southgate, which becomes South St. (☎ 775888. Open M-Sa 9:15am-5:15pm; July-Aug. also Su 10am-4pm.) **Hedgehogs,** 45 Whyke Ln., has cozy rooms near the town center. (☎ 780022. Singles £23-24; doubles £36-38.) Camp at **Southern Leisure Centre,** on Vinnetrow Rd., a 15min. walk out of town. (☎ 787715. Open Apr.-Oct. £3 per person, £8-10 per tent.) **Postal code:** PO19 1AB.

PORTSMOUTH   ☎ 023

Set Victorian prudery against prostitutes, drunkards, and a lot of cursing sailors, and there you have a basic 900-year history of Portsmouth (pop. 190,500). On the **seafront,** visitors relive D-Day, explore warships, and learn of the days when Britannia truly ruled the waves. War buffs and historians will want to plunge head first into the unparalleled **Naval Heritage Centre,** in the Naval Base, which houses a virtual armada of Britain's most storied ships. The center includes England's first attempt at a warship, Henry VIII's Mary Rose. Although Henry was particularly fond of her, she—like many women with whom Henry associated—passed on before her time, sinking soon after setting sail from Portsmouth in July 1545. Napoleon must be rolling in his little coffin to know that the HMS Victory, which clinched Britain's reputation as king of the high seas when it defeated him at the Battle of Trafalgar in 1805, is still afloat, next to the ironically christened HMS Warrior (she never saw even a shot of battle). The five galleries of the **Royal Naval Museum** fill in the historical gaps between the three ships. The entrance is next to the TIC on The Hard—follow the signs to "Portsmouth Historic Ships." (Ships open Mar.-Oct. daily 10am-5:30pm; Nov.-Feb. 10am-5pm. Individual site tickets £6. All-inclusive Passport ticket £17.50, seniors £15.50, children £12.50.)

For information on **ferries** to France, see p. 52. **Trains** (☎ (0345) 484950) run to Southsea Station, on Commercial Rd., from: Chichester (40min., 2 per hr., £5); London's Waterloo Station (1½hr., 3 per hr., £19); Salisbury (2hr., every hr., £8.25). National Express **buses** (☎ (08705) 808080) rumble from London (2½hr., 1 per hr., £10.50) and Salisbury (2hr., 1 per day, £8.25). The **TIC** is on The Hard. (☎ 9282 6722. Open daily 9:30am-5:45pm.) Moderately priced **B&Bs** (around £20) clutter **Southsea,** 2½km east of The Hard along the coast. Take any Southsea bus and get off at The Strand to reach the energetic and lively ◼ **Portsmouth and Southsea Backpackers Lodge,** 4 Florence Rd. (☎ 9283 2495. Dorms £10; doubles £22.) **Birchwood Guest House,** 44 Waverly Rd., offers bright, spacious ensuite rooms and ample breakfasts. (☎ 9281 1337. Singles £18; doubles £36.) Take any bus to Cosham (including #1, 3, and 40) to the police station and follow the signs to get to the **YHA Portsmouth** at Wymering Manor, on Old Wymering Ln., Medina Rd., in Cosham. (☎ 9237 5661. Lockout 10am-5pm. Curfew 11pm. Open Feb.-Aug. daily; Sept.-Nov. F-Sa. Dorms £9.15, under 18 £6.20.) The **Tesco supermarket,** on Craswell St., is just off the town center. (☎ 839222. Open M 7am through Sa 10pm, Su 10am-4pm.) **Pubs** near The Hard provide weary sailors with galley fare and jars of gin. **Postal code:** PO1 1AA.

WINCHESTER   ☎ 01962

The glory of Winchester (pop. 32,000) stretches back to Roman times. William the Conqueror deemed it the center of his kingdom, and years later, Jane Austen and John Keats both lived and wrote in town. Duck under the archway, pass through the square, and behold the 900-year-old **Winchester Cathedral,** 5 The Close. Famed for the small stone figure in its nave, the 169m long cathedral is the longest medieval building in Europe; the interior holds magnificent tiles and Jane Austen's tomb—while staring at her memorial plaque, don't walk past (or over) Jane herself. The **Norman crypt,** supposedly the oldest in England, can only be viewed in the summer by guided tour. The 12th-century Winchester Bible resides in the library. (Open daily 7:15am-5:30pm; East End closes 5pm. Free tours 10am-3pm. Suggested donation £3.50, students £2.30.) About 25km north of Winchester is the meek village of **Chawton**, where Jane Austen lived. It was in her **cottage** that she penned *Pride and Prejudice, Emma, Northanger Abbey*, and *Persuasion*, among others—some of her manuscripts are on display. Take Hampshire **bus** #X64 (M-Sa 11 per day, round-trip £4.50), or the London and Country bus #65 on Sun., from the bus station; ask to be let off at the Chawton roundabout and follow the signs. (☎ (01420) 83262. Open Mar.-Dec. daily 11am-4:30pm; Jan.-Feb. Sa-Su 11am-4:30pm. £3.50.) **Royal Oak,** on Royal Oak Passage, next to Godbegot House off High St., is yet another pub touting itself as the UK's oldest. (Open daily 11am-11pm.)

Trains (☎ (0345) 484950) arrive at Winchester's Station Hill, at City Rd. and Sussex St., from London's Waterloo Station (1hr., 2 per hr., £16.60) and Portsmouth (1hr., every hr., £7). National Express **buses** (☎ (08705) 808080) go to London (1½hr., 7 per day, £12); Hampshire Stagecoach (☎ (01256) 464501) goes to Salisbury (#68; 45min., 7 per day, round-trip £4.45) and Portsmouth (#69; 1½hr., 12 per day, round-trip £4.45). The **TIC,** The Guildhall, Broadway, is across from the bus station. (☎840500; fax 850348. Open June-Sept. M-Sa 10am-6pm, Su 11am-2pm; Oct.-May M-Sa 10am-5pm.) The lovely home of **Mrs. P. Patton,** 12 Christchurch Rd., between St. James Ln. and Beaufort Rd., is near the cathedral. (☎854272. Singles £25-28; doubles £33-40.) Go past the Alfred statue, across the bridge, and left before Cricketers Pub to reach the **YHA youth hostel,** 1 Water Ln. (☎853723. Lockout 10am-5pm. Curfew 11pm. Open July-Aug. daily; mid-Feb. to June and Sept.-Oct. M-Sa. £9.25.) A **Sainsbury's** supermarket is on Middle Brook St., off High St. (Open M-Th 8am-6:30pm, F 8am-9pm, Sa 7:30am-6pm.) **Postal code:** SO23 8WA.

SALISBURY   ☎ 01722

Salisbury (pop. 36,890) revolves around ▊**Salisbury Cathedral** and its spire that rises an astounding 123m. The bases of the pillars literally bend inward under the strain of 6400 tons of limestone; if a pillar rings when you knock on it, you should probably move away. (☎555120. Open June-Aug. M-Sa 7:15am-8:15pm, Su 7:15am-6:15pm; Sept.-May daily 7:15am-6:15pm. Free tours May-Oct. M-Sa 9:30am-4:45pm; Nov.-Feb. M-Sa 10am-4pm; May-Sept. Su 4-6:15pm. 1½hr. Roof and tower tours; May-Sept. M-Sa 11am, 2, 3pm, Su 4:30pm; June-Aug. M-Sa also 6:30pm; winter hours vary. £3, concessions £2. Call ahead. Evensong M-Sa 5:30pm, Su 3pm. Donation £3.50, students and seniors £2.50.) One of four surviving copies of the **Magna Carta** rests in the **Chapter House.** (Open June-Aug. M-Sa 9:30am-7:45pm, Su 9:30am-5:30pm; M-Sa Sept.-May 9:30am-5:30pm, Su 1-3:15pm. Free.)

Trains arrive on South Western Rd from London (1½hr., every hr., £22-30) and Winchester (1½hr., every hr., £10.60). National Express **buses** (☎ (08705) 808080) pull into 8 Endless St. from London's Victoria Station (2¾hr., 4 per day, £11.50); Wilts & Dorset buses (☎336855) arrive from Bath (#X4; 2hr., 6 per day, £3). The **TIC** is on Fish Row in the Guildhall; turn left on South Western Rd., bear right on Fisherton St., continue on Bridge St., cross the bridge onto High St., and walk straight down Silver St., which becomes Butcher Row and Fish Row (10-15min.). From the bus station, head left on Endless St., which (shockingly) ends and becomes Queen St. Turn right at the first old building on the right to enter Fish Row, to reach the TIC. (☎334956. Open June-Sept. M-Sa 9:30am-6pm, Su 10:30am-4:30pm; Oct.-Apr. M-Sa 9:30am-5pm; May M-Sa 9:30am-5pm, Su 10:30am-4:30pm.) From the TIC, head left on Fish Row, right on Queen St., left on Milford St., and under the overpass to find the **YHA youth hostel,** in Milford Hill House, on Milford Hill. (☎327572. Lockout 10am-1pm. Curfew 11:30pm. Dorms £11. **Camping** £7 per person.) **Matt and Tiggy's,** 51 Salt Ln., a welcoming 450-year-old house with warped floors and exposed ceiling beams, is just up from the bus station. (☎327443. Dorms £11-12). At ▊**Harper's "Upstairs Restaurant,"** 6/7 Ox Rd., inventive international and English dishes (£6-10) make hearty meals, and the "8B48" (2 courses for £8 before 8pm) buys a heap of food. (☎333118. Open M-F noon-2pm and 6-9:30pm, Sa noon-2pm and 6-10pm, Su 6-9pm.) **Sainsbury's supermarket** is at The Maltings. (Open M-Th 8am-8pm, F 8am-9pm, Sa 7:30am-7pm, Su 10am-4pm.) **Postal code:** SP1 1AB.

BRITAIN

🛡 DAYTRIPS FROM SALISBURY

STONEHENGE

*Wilts & Dorset **buses** (☎336855) connect from Salisbury's center and train station (40min., round-trip £5.25). (Open June-Aug. daily 9am-7pm; mid-Mar. to May and Sept. to mid-Oct. 9:30am-6pm; mid-Oct. to mid-Mar. 9:30am-4pm. £4.20, students £3.20.)*

Perhaps the gentle giants on Salisbury's windswept plain will remain fascinating for millennia to come, both for their mystery and staggering longevity. A sunken colossus amid swaying grass and indifferent sheep, Stonehenge stands unperturbed by 80km/h whipping winds and legions of people who have visited for over 5000 years. The monument's present shape—once a complete circle of 7m high stones weighing up to 45 tons—dates from about 1500 BC. The most famous Stonehenge legend holds that the circle was built of Irish stones magically transported by Merlin. Other tales attribute the monument to giants, Phoenicians, Mycenaean Greeks, Druids, Smurfs, Romans, Danes, and aliens. In any case, the laborers' technological capabilities were more advanced than we can imagine; their unknown methods continue to elude archaeologists. For centuries, religious devotees have come for its mystical karmic energies, building temples and leaving us to marvel at the awe-inspiring nature of the site. Pagans use the stone circle to celebrate the Summer Solstice. You may admire Stonehenge for free from nearby Amesbury Hill, 2½km up A303, or pay admission at the site.

AVEBURY

*Take **bus** #5 or 6 from Salisbury to Avebury (1½hr., 6 per day, £3.90).*

Avebury sprouts from within a **stone circle** that is the third largest of its kind in Europe. Avebury's sprawling titans were constructed over 500 years before Stonehenge. Just outside the circle is **Silbury Hill,** built in 2660 BC; the curious man-made mound represents another archaeological mystery. The **TIC** is near the car park close to the stone circle. (☎(01672) 539425. Open W-Sa 10am-5pm, Su 10am-4pm.)

BRISTOL   ☎0117

The southwest's largest city, Bristol (pop. 401,000) hums along as a working business center by day and jumps into energetic revelry by night. **John Wesley's Chapel,** the oldest Methodist building in the world, sits incongruously opposite The Galleries, Bristol's shopping shrine. (Open M-Sa 10am-4pm. Free.) Remnants of Saxon and Norman architecture linger in **Bristol Cathedral,** proudly overlooking the College Green. (Open daily 8am-6pm. Evensong 5:15pm. Donation £2.) Elizabeth I termed the medieval church of **St. Mary Redcliffe,** 10 Redcliffe Parade West, the "fairest, goodliest, and most famous Parish Church in England." (Open in summer M-Sa 8am-8pm, Su 7:30am-8pm; in winter M-Sa 8am-5.30pm, Su 7:30am-8pm.) Bristol's newest attraction, **Explore@Bristol,** Explore Lane, educates all ages with interactive exhibits, live wildlife, and multimedia presentations. (☎915 5000. Explore open daily 10am-6pm. £6.50.) The ▨**Clifton Suspension Bridge,** Brunel's architectural masterpiece spanning the Avon Gorge, is at the end of a pleasant walk through Clifton. Nearby on Sion Pl., the **Bridge House Visitors Centre** documents the history of the bridge and gives a course in bridge engineering. (☎974 4664. Open Apr.-Sept. daily 10am-5pm; Oct.-Mar. M-F 11am-4pm, Sa-Su 11am-5pm. £1.50.)

Trains (☎(08457) 484950) come to Bristol Temple Meads Station from: Bath (20min., 3 per hr., £4.60); Cardiff (50min., 2 per hr., £8.90); London Paddington station (1½hr., 2per hr., £36). National Express **buses** (☎(08705) 808080) trundle into the Marlborough St. Station from Cardiff (1¼hr., 11 per day, £4.50) and London (2½hr., 21 per day, £10). The **TIC,** The Annex, Wildscreen Walk, Harbourside, is adjacent to Explore@Bristol. (☎926 0767. Open July-Aug. M-W and Sa-Su 10am-6pm, Th-F 10am-8pm; Sept.-July daily 10am-6pm.) ▨**Bristol Backpackers,** 17 St. Stephen's St., a new independent hostel in an old newspaper building, is making headlines. (☎925 7900. Dorms £12.50.) The local **YHA Youth Hostel,** Hayman House,

BRITAIN

is at 14 Narrow Quay. (☎922 1659. Dorms £12.15, under 18 £8.35.) **Boston Tea Party,**
75 Park St., keeps Bristol buzzing with its exquisite selection of coffees and sandwiches for £3-5. (☎929 8601. Open M 7am-6pm, Tu-Sa 7am-10pm, Su 9am-7pm.)

EXETER   ☎ 01392

Besieged by William the Conqueror in 1068 and flattened by German bombs in 1942,
Exeter (pop. 110,000), has undergone frantic rebuilding resulting in an odd mixture
of the venerable and the banal: Roman and Norman ruins poke out from parking
lots, and the cash registers of a bustling department store rest on a medieval catacomb. **Exeter Cathedral** was heavily damaged in WWII but retains exquisite detail.
The cathedral library's **Exeter Book** is the richest treasury of early Anglo-Saxon
poetry in the world. (☎255573. Cathedral open daily 7am-6:30pm. Library open M-F
2-5pm. Evensong M-F 5:30pm, Sa-Su 3pm. Free tours Apr.-Oct. M-F 11:30am and
2:30pm, Sa 11am. Donation £2.50.) Six-hundred-year-old **underground passages** are
accessible from Romangate Passage on High St. (☎265887. Open July-Sept. M-Sa
10am-5:30pm; Oct.-June Tu-F 2-5pm, Sa 10am-5pm. Tours £3.75, students £2.75.
Book tickets in person by noon during July and Aug.)

   Trains arrive in Exeter from Bristol (1½hr., every hr., £13.60) and London's Paddington Station (2½hr., 2 per hr., £39). National Express **buses** (☎(08705) 808080)
pull into Paris St., off High St. just outside the city walls, from London's Victoria
Coach Station (4hr., every 1½hr., round-trip £16) and Bath (2¾hr., 3 per day, £13);
walk through the arcade to Sidwell St. and turn left to reach High St. The **TIC**, at the
Civic Centre, in the City Council Building on Paris St., is opposite the rear of the bus
station. (☎265700. Open M-Sa 9am-5pm; summer also Su 10am-4pm.) To reach the
YHA youth hostel, 47 Countess Wear Rd., 3km from the city center off Topsham Rd.,
take minibus K or T from High St. to the Countess Wear Post Office (£0.97), follow
Exe Vale Rd. to the end and turn left. (☎873329. Reception 8-10am and 5-10pm.
Dorms £11, under 18 £7.75. **Camping** half-price.) Pack a picnic at **Sainsbury's super-
market,** in the Guildhall Shopping Centre off High St. (Open M-W and F 8am-6:30pm,
Th 8am-7pm, Sa 7:30am-6pm, Su 10:30am-4:30pm.) **Postal code:** EX1 1AA.

DARTMOOR NATIONAL PARK

Dartmoor is strewn with remnants of the past, from oddly balanced granite *tors* to
Neolithic rock formations. Ramblers across the park will find the skeleton of a mining industry and the heavily guarded **Princetown prison.** Due to rough terrain and a
harsh climate, Dartmoor has remained largely untouched except by sheep and wild
ponies. Today, many spirits linger in Dartmoor's mystical bleakness, the most famous
being the canine immortalized by Sir Arthur Conan Doyle's *Hound of the Basker-
villes.* The last castle to be built in England isn't Norman or Tudor—it's **Castle Drogo,**
built by tea baron Julius Drewe. (Open Apr.-Oct. Sa-Th 11am-5:30pm. £5.40, grounds
only £2.60.) **National Park Information Centres** are found in **Ivybridge** (☎(01752) 897035.
Open July-Aug. M-F 9am-5pm, Sa 10am-4pm, Su 10am-2pm; Sept.-June M-Sa 9am-
5pm.); **Princetown** High Moorland Visitor Centre, in the former Duchy Hotel.
(☎(01822) 890414. Open in summer daily 10am-5pm; in winter 10am-4pm); **Tavistock,**
Town Hall, Bedford Sq. (☎(01822) 612938. Open Easter-Oct. M-Sa 10am-5pm; Nov.-
Easter M-Tu and F-Sa 10am-4pm.) Visitors should not underestimate Dartmoor's
moody weather or treacherous terrain. The Ministry of Defense uses the moor for **target practice,** and the boundaries of dangerous areas change yearly; consult your map
and check weekly firing times at TICs. An *Ordnance Survey Outdoor Leisure 28*
map (£6.50), a compass, and waterproof garb are essential. Stick to the marked paths.
Dartmoor Visitor, free at TICs, provides maps and information on accommodations
and food. TICs offer detailed guides to walks, some with map supplements (£0.50-9).
The official **Dartmoor Rescue Group** is on call through the police (**emergency** ☎999).

   Buses are infrequent; plan well ahead, using the bus schedules available at every **TIC**
in and around Dartmoor. The best day to travel to Dartmoor by bus is Sunday, when
frequencies increase and the **Sunday Rover** allows unlimited bus travel (£5, students
£4.50). The **Transmoor Link** (Stagecoach Devon bus #82; late May to Sept.; M-Sa 3 per

BRITAIN

day, Su 5 per day; £5) cuts through the middle of the park on its southwest-northeast route between Plymouth and Exeter. **Plymouth Buses** run to: Ivybridge (#X80, 30min., 3 per hr.); Okehampton (#86; M-F 9 per day, Su 2 per day); Tavistock (#83, 84, or 86; 1hr.; 4 per hr.). For more info, contact the **Devon County Council's Public Transportation Helpline.** (☎ (01392) 382800. Open M-F 8:30am-5pm.) The invaluable *Dartmoor Public Transportation Guide* is available in any nearby bus station or TIC. Spend the night at **Bellever (YHA),** 1½km southeast of Postbridge village on bus #82 from Plymouth or Exeter to Postbridge. (☎ (01822) 880227. Open July-Aug. daily; Apr.-June M-Sa; Sept.-Oct. Tu-Sa. Dorms £10, under 18 £6.90.) **Okehampton (YHA),** Klondyke Rd., offers occasional rock climbing outings in addition to rooms. (☎ (01837) 53916. Open Feb.-Nov. Dorms £11, under 18 £7.50.) Although official campsites exist, many travelers **camp** on the open moor. Dartmoor land is privately owned, so ask permission before crossing or camping on land. Backpack camping is permitted on the non-enclosed moor land more than 100m away from the road or out of sight of inhabited areas. Campers may only stay for one night in a single spot. Don't build fires in the moors unless posted signs say you may do so. To camp at an official site, try **Ashburton Caravan Park,** Waterleat, Ashburton (☎ (01364) 652552. July-Aug. £10 per 2-person tent.; Easter-June and Sept.-Oct. £7.50), or **Higher Longford Farm,** Moorshop, Tavistock. (☎ (01822) 613360. £7.50 for 1st adult, £2 per additional adult.)

PLYMOUTH ☎ 01752

Plymouth is a famed port—the English fleet sailed from here to defeat the Spanish Armada in 1588, and Sir Francis Drake, Captain Cook, the Pilgrims, Lord Nelson, and millions of emigrants to the United States and New Zealand earned Plymouth a spot in the history books in their haste to escape it. Heed their age-old message. **Trains** (☎ (0345) 484950) run from Plymouth Station, on North Rd, to London Paddington Station (4hr., 17 per day, £60) and Penzance (2hr., 21 per day, £10.30); take Western National bus #14, 16b, 72, 83, or 84 to the city center at Royal Parade; it's a long walk—take the bus. **Buses** leave from Bretonside Station, near St. Andrew's Cross at the east end of Royal Parade; National Express (☎ (08705) 808080) goes to London (4½hr., £20), and Stagecoach Devon runs to Exeter (#X38, 1¼hr., £4.85). For **ferries** (☎ (0990) 360360) departing from the Millbay Docks (take bus #33 or 34 to the docks; 15min.) for France and Spain, see p. 187. The **TIC** is in Island House, 9 The Barbican. (☎ 304849. Open M-Sa 9am-5pm, Su 10am-4pm.) Take bus #15 or 81 from the train station or Royal Parade to Stoke to find the **YHA youth hostel,** Belmont House, on Belmont Pl. (☎ 562189. Lockout 10am-5pm. Curfew 11pm but a code allows later access. Reserve ahead. Dorms £10.15.) **Plymouth Backpackers Hotel,** 172 Citadel Rd., is two blocks from the west end of the Hoe. (☎ 225158. Laundry. Dorms £8.50; singles £10; triples £27.) A **Sainsbury's** is in the Armada Shopping Centre. (Open M-Sa 8am-8pm, Su 10am-4pm.) **Postal Code:** PL1 1AB.

THE CORNISH COAST

With lush cliffsides stretching out into the Atlantic, Cornwall's terrain doesn't feel quite like England. Indeed, Cornwall's isolation made it a favored place for Celtic migration in the face of Saxon conquest, and though the Cornish language is no longer spoken, the area remains protective of its distinctive past. England's southwest tip has some of the broadest, sandiest beaches in northern Europe, and the surf is up year-round whether or not the sun decides to break through.

▗ TRANSPORTATION

By far the best location for exploring the region is Penzance, the southwestern terminus of Britain's **trains** (☎ (08457) 484950). The main rail line from **Plymouth** to **Penzance** bypasses the coastal towns, but there is connecting rail service to **Newquay, Falmouth,** and **St. Ives. Rail Rover** tickets make it even easier (3 days unlimited travel within a 7-day span £25.50, 8 out of 15 days £40). The **Western National bus** network is similarly thorough, although the interior is not served as well as the coast. Buses run frequently from **Penzance** to **Land's End** and **St. Ives,** as well as from **St. Ives** to **Newquay,** stopping in the smaller towns along these routes. Many buses don't run on Sundays, and many run only May-Sept.; call Western National (☎ (01209) 719988) to check.

PENZANCE. Penzance is the very model of an ancient English pirate town: water-logged, stealthy, and unabashed. A Benedictine monastery was built on the spot where St. Michael dropped by in AD 495, and today **St. Michael's Mount** sits off-shore. The interior is unspectacular, but the grounds are more textured, and the 30-story views are captivating. (Open Apr.-Oct. M-F 10:30am-5:30pm; in summer also most weekends; Nov.-Mar. in good weather. £4.40.) A causeway links the mount to the island; or take ferry bus #2 or 2A to Marazion (M-Sa 3 per hr., round-trip £0.80) and catch a ferry during high tide (round-trip £1). **Trains** (☎ (08457) 484950) go to: Exeter (3hr., every hr., £18.60); London (5½hr., every hr., £54); Plymouth (2hr., every hr., £10). National Express (☎ (08705) 808080) **buses** run to London (8hr., 8 per day, £27) and Plymouth (3hr., 2 per hr., £6). Between the two stations is the **TIC,** on Station Rd. (☎ (01736) 362207. Open in summer M-F 9am-5pm, Sa 9am-4pm, Su 10am-1pm; in winter M-F 9am-5pm, Sa 10am-1pm.) **Penzance Backpackers,** Blue Dolphin, Alexandra Rd., is a relaxed, eclectic place to take a load off. (☎ (01736) 363836. Dorms £8-9; doubles £18-22.) **The Turk's Head** pub, 49 Chapel St., was built in the 13th century and sacked by Spanish pirates in 1595.

ST. IVES. St. Ives perches 15km north of Penzance, on a spit of land lined by pas-tel beaches and azure waters. Virginia Woolf was bewitched by the energy of the Atlantic at St. Ives: her masterpiece *To the Lighthouse* is thought to refer to the Godrevy Lighthouse in the distance. Whether seeking the perfect subject or the per-fect strip of sand, St. Ives has it, if hidden beneath a veneer of postcards and ice cream cones. Some **trains** (☎ (08457) 484950) go directly to Penzance (3-6 per day), but most connect via St. Erth (10min., 2 per hr., £3). Western National **buses** go to Penzance (3 per hr., off-season M-Sa only, £2.50) and Newquay (#57). National Express (☎ (08705) 808080) stops in St. Ives between Plymouth and Penzance (6 per day). The **TIC** is in the Guildhall on Street-an-Pol. From the stations, walk down to the foot of Tregenna Hill and turn right. (☎ (01736) 796297. Open M-Sa 9:30am-6pm, Su 10am-1pm; closed Sa-Su in winter.) **St. Ives International Backpackers,** The Stenmack, fills a 19th-century Methodist church. (☎ (01736) 799444. Dorms £8-12.) Places to camp abound in nearby **Hayle;** try **Trevalgan Camping Park** (☎796433). **Fore Street** is packed with small bakeries; many places also sell Cornish cream teas.

FALMOUTH. Seven rivers flow into the historic port of Falmouth (pop. 18,300), which is guarded by two spectacular castles. **Pendennis Castle,** built by Henry VIII to keep French frigates out of Falmouth, now features a walk-through diorama. (Open July-Aug. daily 9am-6pm; Apr.-June and Sept. 10am-6pm; Oct. 10am-5pm; Nov.-Mar. 10am-4pm. £3.80, students £2.90.) Across the channel lies another Henry VIII cre-ation, the magnificently preserved **St. Mawes Castle.** (Open Apr.-Sept. daily 10am-6pm; Oct. 10am-5pm; Nov.-Mar. F-Tu 10am-1pm and 2-4pm. 1hr. audio tour included. £2.50, students £1.90.) An occasionally wet ferry from the Town Pier and The Quay (20min., 2 per hr., round-trip £3.50) shuttles to St. Mawes. To taste the surf, head to one of Falmouth's three **beaches. Trains** (☎ (0345) 484950) arrive in town from: Exeter (3½hr., 6 per day, £24); London Paddington (5½hr., every hr., £64); Plymouth (2hr., 9-17 per day, £9.70). National Express (☎ (08705) 808080) **buses** roll in from London (6½hr., 2 per day, £34.50). To get to the **tourist information,** 28 Killigrew St., The Moor, follow signs to Killigrew St. or Kimberley Park Rd., then go downhill toward the river. (☎ (08700) 110018. Open Apr.-Sept. M-Sa 9:30am-5:30pm; July-Aug. also Su 10am-2pm; Oct.-Mar. M-F 9am-5:30pm.) None of the **train stations** sell tickets; get 'em at **Newell's Travel Agency,** 26 Killigrew St., on The Moor, next to the TIC. (☎ (01326) 315066. Open M-F 9am-5:30pm, Sa 9am-4pm.) Find com-fortable accommodations in **Castleton Guest House,** 68 Killigrew St., in a 200-year-old house. (☎ (01326) 311072. From £18 per person.) You won't escape Falmouth without picking up a classic Cornish pasty; the local **W.C. Rowe** and **Pengenna** baker-ies vie for the title of best in the city. **Postal code:** TR11 3RB.

BRITAIN

NEWQUAY. An outpost of surfer subculture, Newquay lures the bald, the bleached-blond, and even the blue-haired, to its surf and pubs. Winds descend on **Fistral Beach** with a vengeance, creating what some consider the best surfing conditions in all of Europe, and the enticing **Lusty Glaze Beach** beckons from the bay side. The party beast stirs around 9pm and reigns into the wee hours. Drink up at **The Red Lion,** on North Quay Hill, at Tower Rd., then ride the wave down Fore St. to **Sailors.** (Cover £4-10.) Go on and shake what your momma gave you at **Bertie's,** on East St. (Open until 1am.) From the train station, off Cliff Rd., **trains** go to Penzance (2hr., every hr., £10.30) and Plymouth (2hr., every hr., £8.10). From the **bus station,** 1 East St., Western National runs to St. Ives (2hr., June-Sept. 1 per day, £5). National Express (☎(08705) 808080) runs to London (5¾hr., 3 per day, £26.50). Facing the street from the train station, go four blocks left to reach the **TIC,** on Marcus Hill. (☎(01637) 854022. Open M-Sa 9am-6pm, Su 9am-4pm; reduced hours in winter.) **Newquay Backpackers International,** 69-73 Tower Rd., offers free shuttle service to its sister hostel in St. Ives. (☎(01637) 879366. **Internet.** Dorms £10.)

EAST ANGLIA AND THE MIDLANDS

The plush green farmlands and watery fens of **East Anglia** stretch northeast from London, cloaking the counties of Cambridgeshire, Norfolk, and Suffolk. Although industry is modernizing the economies of Cambridge and Peterborough, the area in between is still characterized by its sheer flatness; much of the rustic beauty that inspired the landscape paintings of natives Constable and Gainsborough remains. To the west lie the **Midlands**—the term evokes images of industrial cities, thanks to the "dark satanic mills" foreseen by William Blake that overran the area during the Industrial Revolution. But the heart of England contains its fair share of England's must-sees; Manchester and Liverpool are home to innovative music, art, and nightlife scenes, while Lincoln and Chester tell many of their tales in Latin.

OXFORD ☎01865

Almost a millennium of scholarship lies within Oxford—22 British Prime Ministers were educated here, and the alumni registry reads like a who's who of British history, literature and philosophy. Henry II founded the university, Britain's first, in 1167. Although today, trucks rumble, bus brakes screech, and bicycles scrape past pedestrians packing the streets, the university and the town still maintain an air of nobility. Oxford has an irrepressible grandeur, and there are pockets of respite to charm and edify the academic pilgrim: the basement room of **Blackwell's Bookstore,** the impeccable galleries of the **Ashmolean,** and the studiously maintained quadrangles of Oxford's 29 colleges.

▐ TRANSPORTATION

Trains: Botley Road (☎794422), down Park End, west of Carfax. Ticket office open M-F 6am-8pm, Sa 6:45am-8pm, Su 7:45am-8pm. **Thames trains** (☎08457) run from London Paddington Station (1hr., 2-4 per hr., round-trip £14.80).

Buses: Bus station, Gloucester Green. **Oxford CityLink** (☎785400). Open daily 6:30am-6:30pm. Connects from: **London Victoria** (1¾hr.; 1-4 per hr.; round-trip £7.50, students £6.50); **Gatwick airport** (2hr.; every hr. daytime, every 2 hr. at night; round-trip £19); **Heathrow airport** (2 per hr., round-trip £12). **National Express** (☎(08705) 808080) offers national routes.

Public Transportation: The **Oxford Bus Company** (☎785400) and **Stagecoach** (☎772250). Local services board on streets around Carfax. Fares are low (most 70p).

BRITAIN

BRITAIN

Oxford

◯ **COLLEGES**

All Souls College, 12
Balliol College, 21
Brasenose College, 13
Christ Church, 2
Corpus Christi College, 3
Exeter College, 16
Hertford College, 17
Jesus College, 15
Keble College, 24

Lincoln College, 14
Magdalen College, 7
Harris Manchester
  College, 18
Mansfield College, 23
Merton College, 4
New College, 11
Nuffild College, 28
Oriel College, 5
Pembroke College, 1
The Queen's College, 10

Regent's Park College, 26
Somerville College, 25
St. Catherine's College, 9
St. Hilda's College, 8
St. John's College, 22
St. Peter's College, 29
Trinity College, 20
University College, 6
Wadham College, 19
Worcester College, 27

▲ **ACCOMMODATIONS**

Falcon Private Hotel, D
Heather House, G
Newton House, E
Old Mitre Rooms, C
Oxford Backpackers
  Hostel, B
Oxford Camping and
  Caravaning, F
YHA Oxford, A

Mesopotamia
River Cherwell
Addison's Walk
The Plain
TO Cowley Rd.
(.5 mi.)
Iffley Rd.
St. Clement's Rd.
Path Along River Cherwell
Cricket Ground
Holywell Mill Stream
Manor Rd.
Magdalen Grove Park
Botanic Gardens
Merton Field
St. Cross Rd.
Longwall St.
Rose Ln.
St. Cross Rd.
Mansfield Rd.
Jowett Walk
Holywell St.
Holywell Music Room
Queens Ln.
High St.
Logic Ln.
Merton
Dead Man's Walk
Savile Rd.
New College Ln.
St. Mary's
Magpie Ln.
Christ Church Cathedral
Love Ln.
South Parks Rd.
Parks Rd.
Bodleian Library
Catte St.
Radcliffe Camera
Radcliffe Sq.
Oriel St.
King Edward St.
Sheldonian Theatre
Museum of the History of Science
Turl St.
Alfred St.
Blue Boar St.
Broad St.
Oxford Story
Blackwells
Ship St.
Cornmarket St.
Market St.
Town Hall
Museum of Oxford
Painted Room
Pharmacy
Brewer St.
Pembroke St.
Blackhall St.
Museum Rd.
Magdalen St.
Friars Entry
St. Michael's St.
George St.
New Inn Hall St.
Carfax Tower
Queen St.
St. Ebbe's St.
Littlegate St.
Museum of Modern Art
Westgate Shopping Centre
TO D, E, F (600m), LONDON, AND M4
St. Giles St.
Pusey St.
Beaumont
Gloucester
Ashmolean Museum
St. John's St.
Alfred Ln.
TAXI
New Rd.
Banbury Rd.
TO A423
Woodstock Rd.
TO BLENHEIM PALACE, STRATFORD-UPON-AVON, A34, AND A44
Gloucester Green
Walton St.
Worcester St.
Richmond Rd.
Nelson St.
Walton Crescent St.
Oxford University Press
Great Clarendon St.
Hart St.
Botley Rd.
Park End
Hythe Bridge St.
Worcester St.
Castle Mill Stream
Oxford Canal
N
200 yards
200 meters
0

▶ ⏻ ORIENTATION AND PRACTICAL INFORMATION

The easiest way to orient yourself in Oxford is to locate the colossal Carfax Tower. **Queen, High, St. Aldate's,** and **Cornmarket** streets intersect at **Carfax,** the town center. The colleges are all within 1½km of one another, mainly to the east of Carfax along **High Street** and **Broad Street** The **bus station** and the **TIC** lie to the northwest on Gloucester Green—from Carfax, follow Cornmarket St. to George St. and turn right onto Gloucester. Take Queen St. (which changes names to New Rd. and then Park End) to get to the **train station.**

Tourist Office: TIC, The Old School, Gloucester Green (☎726871; fax 240261). Beside the bus station. Books rooms for a £2.50 fee and a 10% deposit. Accommodations list £0.60. Map £1. **Walking tours** depart 2-5 times per day (10:30am-2pm; £5). Open Oct.-Easter M-Sa 9:30am-5pm; Easter-Oct. M-Sa 9:30am-5pm and Su 10am-3:30pm.

American Express: 4 Queen St. (☎207101) Open M-Tu and Th-F 9am-5:30pm, W 9:30am-5:30pm, Sa 9am-5pm, call for Su hours.

Luggage storage: Pensioners' Club (☎242237), in Gloucester Green. By the bus station. Storage for up to a few weeks. £1-2 donation requested. Open M-Sa 9am-4:45pm.

Gay and Lesbian Services: Gay Switchboard, Oxford Friend (☎726893)

Emergency: ☎999.

Police: Stations on St. Aldates and Speedwell St. (☎266000)

Crisis Line: Samaritans 123 Iffley Rd. (☎722122) Hotline 24hr; drop-in daily 8am-10pm.

Pharmacy: Boots 6 Cornmarket St. (☎247461) Open M-Sa 8:45am-6pm, Su 11am-5pm.

Internet Access: Mr. Pickwick Papers, 90,The Gallery, Gloucester Green, (☎793149) Located next to the bus station. £1 per 30min. Open M-Sa 5am-6:30pm, Su 7am-6pm.

Post Office: 102-104 St. Aldates St. (☎202863) Open M-F 9am-5:30pm, Sa 9am-6pm. **Postal code:** OX1.

⌂ ACCOMMODATIONS

In summer, book at least a week ahead. **B&Bs** line the main roads out of town and are accessible by Cityline buses or a 15-45min. walk. More B&Bs are located in the 300s on **Banbury Road** (take buses #2A, 2C, or 2D). Cheaper ones are in the 200s and 300s on **Iffley Road** (bus #4), between 250 and 350 on **Cowley Road** (buses #51 or 52), and on **Abingdon Road** in South Oxford (bus #16). Expect to pay £20-25.

Oxford Backpacker's Hotel, 9a Hythe Bridge St. (☎721761). Between the bus and train stations, a short walk away from most sights. Lively atmosphere with an inexpensive bar, a pool table, and constant music. Guests must show passport. **Internet** access £1.50 per 15min. Laundry £2.50. Dorms £11-12.

YHA Oxford, 2a Botley Rd. (☎762997). An immediate right from the train station onto Botley Rd. Superb location and bright surroundings. Generous rooms and facilities include kitchen, laundry, supplies store, and lockers. Most rooms have 4-6 bunks. Breakfast included. Dorms £18, under 18 £13.50. £1 discount for students.

Heather House, 192 Iffley Rd. (☎249757). Take the bus marked "Rose Hill" from the bus station, train station, or Carfax Tower (70p). Sparkling, modern rooms. Singles £30, for 1 night, £27; doubles with bath £58/54.

Falcon Private Hotel, 88-90 Abingdon Rd. (☎511122; reservations@thefalconhotel.freeserve.co.uk; www.oxfordcity.co.uk/hotels/falcon). Provides a great base to nest while exploring Oxford. Singles £36; doubles £58-68.

Old Mitre Rooms, 4b Turl St. (☎279821; fax 279963). Lincoln College dorms. Open July to early Sept. Singles with bath £32; doubles with bath £53; triples with bath £63.50.

Newton House, 82-84 Abingdon Rd. (☎240561), 800m from town; take any Abingdon bus across Folly Bridge. Dark wardrobes await Narnia fans. Singles £48; doubles £54-64, with bath £58; price varies with season.

Camping: Oxford Camping and Caravaning, 426 Abingdon Rd. (☎244088). Behind the Touchwoods camping store. 84 sites. Toilet and laundry facilities. Showers free. 2-night max. stay for nonmembers. £4.90-6.25 per tent.

BRITAIN

🔲 FOOD

Oxford students bored with cafeteria food sustain a market for budget eats in town. After hours, **kebab vans** roam around **Broad Street, High Street, Queen Street,** and **St. Aldates Street** If you're staying across Magdalen Bridge, try restaurants along the first four blocks of **Cowley Road.** The **Covered Market** between Market St. and Carfax has produce, deli goods, and breads. (Open M-Sa 8am-5:30pm.) Pick up **groceries** at **J. Sainsbury** in the Westgate Centre mall on Queen St. (Open M-F 8am-8pm, Sa 7:30am-7pm, Su 11am-5pm.) Across Magdalen Bridge is the vegan-friendly **Uhuru Wholefoods,** 48 Cowley Rd. (Open M-F 10am-6pm, Sa 9:30am-5:30pm.)

🔲 **The Nosebag,** 6-8 St. Michael's St. (☎721033). Unique gourmet-grade menu served casual style in quaint 15th-century building. Lunch under £6.50, dinner under £8. Open M 9:30am-5:30pm, Tu-Th until 10pm, F-Sa until 10:30pm, Su until 9pm.

Café CoCo, 23 Cowley Rd. (☎200232). Lively atmosphere and great Mediterranean menu. Main dishes £5.95-8.50. Open daily 10am-11pm.

Chiang Mai, 130a High St. (☎202233), tucked down an alley. Popular Thai restaurant with plenty of veggie options. Try the jungle curry with wild rabbit (£6.95). Main dishes £5.50-9. Open M-Sa noon-2:30pm and 6-11pm, Su noon-3pm and 6-10pm. Reserve for dinner in advance or go for lunch to beat the crowds.

Harvey's of Oxford, 58 High St. (☎723152), near Magdalen College. Eat and run at 1 of Oxford's better take-aways. Cherry-apple flapjacks 85p, mighty sandwiches £1.60-2.90 and a great variety of coffee. Open M-F 8am-7pm, Sa 8am-6pm, Su 8:30am-6pm.

Heroes, 8 Ship St. (☎723459). Filled with students dining on sandwiches, freshly-baked breads, and a variety of meat and cheese fillings (£1.90-3.65). Popular for takeout, but has a small eat-in area. Open M-F 8am-7pm, Sa 8:30am-5pm, Su 10am-5pm.

👁 SIGHTS

Oxford first earned its name as a place where oxen could ford the Thames, and three of **Oxford University**'s favorite sons—Lewis Carroll, C.S. Lewis, and J.R.R. Tolkien—sat near the stone-bridged waters of the Isis (as the Thames is known here) dreaming of crossings through mirrors, wardrobes, or mountain passes. The TIC's *Welcome to Oxford* guide (£2) lists the colleges' public visiting hours. The university has also been a breeding ground for England's leaders. Christ Church College alone has produced 13 prime ministers, while St. John's College was home to collegiate rocker Tony Blair.

CARFAX AND SOUTH OF CARFAX. For a fantastic view of the city, hike up the 99 spiral stairs of **Carfax Tower,** at the corner of Queen St. and Cornmarket St. (☎792653. Open Apr.-Oct. daily 10am-5:30pm; Nov.-Mar. 10am-3:30pm. £1.20.) Down St. Aldate's St. from Carfax, **Christ Church College** has Oxford's grandest quad and its most socially distinguished students. The **Christ Church Chapel** is also Oxford's cathedral. The Reverend Charles Dodgson (better known as Lewis Carroll) was friendly with Dean Liddell of Christ Church. The Cheshire Cat first grinned and vanished from the largest tree in the garden and the White Rabbit can be spotted fretting in the hall's stained glass. (☎276492. Open M-Sa 9:30am-5:30pm, Su 11:30am-5:30pm. Services Su 8, 10, 11:15am, 6pm; weekdays 7:30am, 6pm. £2.50.) Behind Christ Church Chapel, up on Merton Rd., is **Merton College,** where J.R.R. Tolkien lectured while inventing Elvish tales in his spare time. Nearby **St. Alban's Quad** has some of the university's best gargoyles. (☎276310. Open M-F 2-4pm, Sa-Su 10am-4pm. Free.) Walk back up to High St. and head east for the **Botanic Garden.** A sumptuous array of plants have flourished here for three centuries. The path connecting the Botanic Garden to the Christ Church Meadow provides a beautiful view of the Thames as well as the cricket and tennis on the opposite bank. (Open Apr.-Sept. daily 9am-5pm; Oct.-Mar. 9am-4:30pm. Greenhouses open daily 2-4pm. Late June to early Sept. £2; free the rest of the year.)

BRITAIN

NORTH OF CARFAX. From Carfax, head up Cornmarket St., which becomes Magdalen St., and turn left onto Beaumont St. for the imposing **Ashmolean Museum**. It houses works by Leonardo, Monet, Manet, van Gogh, Michelangelo, Rodin, and Matisse, while the **Cast Gallery,** behind the museum, exhibits over 250 casts of Greek sculptures—the finest Classical collection outside London. (☎278000. Open Tu-Sa 10am-5pm, Su 2-5pm. Free.) The **Bodleian Library,** at Catte St., is Oxford's principal reading and research library, with over five million books. Take High St. and turn left on Catte. As a copyright library, it receives a free copy of every book printed in Great Britain. No one has ever been permitted to take out a book, not even Cromwell. (☎277224. Open M-F 9am-6pm, Sa 9am-1pm. £3.50.) The **Sheldonian Theatre,** Broad St., beside the Bodleian, is a Roman-style jewel of an auditorium designed by Christopher Wren where graduation ceremonies are conducted in Latin. The cupola of the theater affords an inspiring view of the spires of Oxford. (☎277299. Open M-Sa 10am-12:30pm and 2-4:30pm. £1.50, children £1.) On Broad St. you could browse for days at **Blackwell's Bookstore,** which according to the *Guinness Book of Records* is the largest room devoted to bookselling in the world. (☎792792. Open M and W-Sa 9am-6pm, Tu 9:30am-6pm, Su 11am-5pm.) **New College,** New College Ln., named because it was founded by William of Wykeham "only" in 1379, has become one of Oxford's most prestigious colleges. From Carfax, head down High St. and turn onto Catte St.; New College Ln. is to the right. The bell tower has gargoyles representing the Seven Deadly Sins on one side, and the Seven Virtues on the other, all equally grotesque. Use the Holywell St. Gate. (☎279555. Open Easter-Oct. daily 11am-5pm; Nov.-Easter 2-4pm. £1.50 in the summer.) Oscar Wilde attended **Magdalen** (MAUD-lin) **College,** considered by many to be Oxford's most handsome college. (☎276000. Open July-Sept. M-F noon-6pm, Sa-Su 2-6pm; Oct.-June 2-5pm. Apr.-Sept. £2, students £1; Oct.-Mar. free.)

🎵🎭 ENTERTAINMENT AND NIGHTLIFE

PUNTING

A traditional pastime in Oxford is punting on the river Thames (known in Oxford as the Isis) or on the River Cherwell (CHAR-wul). Punters receive a tall pole, a small oar, and an travel advisory before venturing out in boats that resemble shallow gondolas. Don't try swimming in any of the canals; you could wind up with a tetanus shot and stitches—be mindful that it is very easy to fall in. Also, don't be surprised if you suddenly come across **Parson's Pleasure,** a small riverside area where men sometimes sunbathe nude. **Magdalen Bridge Boat Co.,** Magdalen Bridge, east of Carfax along High St., rents from Mar. to Nov. (☎202643. Open daily 10am-9pm. M-F £9 per hr., Sa-Su £10 per hr. Deposit £20 plus ID.)

CONCERTS AND THEATER

Music and drama at Oxford are cherished arts. Attend a concert or Evensong service at one of the colleges—the **New College Choir** is one of the best boy choirs around—or a performance at the **Holywell Music Rooms,** on Holywell St., the oldest in the country. The **Oxford Playhouse,** 11-12 Beaumont St, is a venue for bands, dance troupes, and the Oxford Stage Company. (☎798600. Tickets from £6, standby tickets available for seniors and students.) The **Oxford Union,** St. Michael's St., puts up solid theater productions (£8, students £5). The **City of Oxford Orchestra,** the professional orchestra, plays a summer subscription series in the Sheldonian Theatre. (☎744457. Tickets £10-15, 25% student discount.)

PUBS AND NIGHTLIFE

Pubs far outnumber colleges in Oxford; many even consider them the city's prime attraction. The popular student bar **Turf Tavern,** on 4 Bath Pl., off Holywell St., is a sprawling 13th-century pub tucked away in an alleyway. (Open M-Sa 11am-11pm, Su noon-10:30pm. Kitchen open noon-8pm.) **The Eagle and Child,** 49 St. Giles, quenched the thirsts of C.S. Lewis and J.R.R. Tolkien for a quarter-century; *The*

Chronicles of Narnia and *The Hobbit* were first read aloud here. (Open M-Sa 11am-11pm, Su 11am-10:30pm.) **The Kings Arms,** Holywell St., draws in a huge young crowd. The coffee room at the front of the bar lets quieter folks avoid the merry masses. (Open M-Sa 10:30am-11pm, Su 10:30am-10:30pm.) **The Bear,** Alfred St., established in 1242, is covered with over 5000 ties from Oxford students and visiting celebrities. (Open M-Sa noon-11pm, Su 6-10:30pm.)

Although pubs in Oxford tend to close down by 11pm, nightlife can last until 3am; grab *This Month in Oxford* at the TIC. For starters, check out **Freud's,** 119 Walton St., in former St. Paul's Parish Church, a cafe by day and hot dance club by night. (Open M-Tu until 11pm, W-Th until 1am, F-Sa until 2am, Su until 10:30 pm.) **Walton Street** and **Cowley Road** host late-night clubs, as well as a jumble of ethnic restaurants, used bookstores, and alternative shops.

FESTIVALS

The university celebrates **Eights Week** at the end of May, when all the colleges enter crews in the bumping races while others nibble strawberries and sip champagne on the banks. In early September, **St. Giles Fair** invades Oxford's main streets with an old-fashioned carnival, complete with Victorian roundabout and whirligigs.

⬛ DAYTRIP FROM OXFORD

BLENHEIM PALACE

*Stagecoach Express **buses** (☎ (01865) 772250) run to Blenheim Palace from Gloucester Green station in Oxford (20min., round-trip £3.50); the same bus also goes to Stratford and Birmingham. Blenheim lies in Woodstock, 13km north of Oxford on the A44.*

The largest private home in England and one of the loveliest, **Blenheim** (BLEN-em) **Palace** features sprawling grounds, a lake, and a fantastic garden. While attending a party here, Winston Churchill's mother gave birth to the future Prime Minister in a closet; his grave rests appropriately nearby in the village churchyard of **Bladon.** The Duke of Marlborough's rent is a single French franc, paid each year to the Crown— not a bad deal for a palace with 187 furnished rooms. Blenheim's full glory (and fake snow) is displayed in Kenneth Branagh's 4hr. film *Hamlet.* (☎ (01993) 811091. Open mid-Mar. to Oct daily 10:30am-5:30pm; grounds open year-round 9am-9pm. £9, students and seniors £7, children £4.50.)

WINDSOR   ☎ 01753

The town of Windsor and the attached village of Eton are completely overshadowed by their two bastions of the British class system, Windsor Castle and Eton College. Windsor itself was built up around the castle during the Middle Ages, and is now filled with specialty shops, tea houses, and pubs. Within the ancient stone walls of **Windsor Castle** lie some of the most sumptuous rooms in Europe and some of the rarest artwork in the Western world. Built by William the Conqueror as a fortress rather than as a residence, it has grown over nine centuries into the world's largest inhabited castle. When the Queen is home, the Royal Standard flies in place of the Union Jack—be prepared for (and call ahead to find out about) unexpected closings of large portions of the castle. The **Changing of the Guard** takes place in front of the Guard Room at 11am on most days; see them before and after the ceremony marching through the streets of Windsor proper. Passing through the Norman Tower and Gate (built by Edward III from 1359-60), you will come upon the **upper ward.** Many of its rooms are open to the public, and are richly decorated with art from the massive Royal Collection, including works by Holbein, Rubens, Rembrandt, and van Dyck. The **middle ward** is dominated by the **Round Tower** and its surrounding moat and rose garden. A stroll from the lower ward reveals **St. George's Chapel,** where 10 sovereigns rest eternally, including George V, Queen Mary, Edward IV, Charles I, and Henry VI. Henry VIII lies below a remarkably humble stone. (☎ 868286, 24hr. info ☎ 831118. Open Apr.-Oct. daily 10am-5:30pm, last entry 4pm; Nov.-Mar. 10am-4pm, last entry 3pm. £11, over 60 £9, under 17 £5.50, families

BRITAIN

£27.50.) **Eton College,** founded by Henry VI in 1440, is still England's preeminent public (which is to say, private) school, but has educated notable dissidents like Aldous Huxley and George Orwell. Wander around the schoolyard, a central quad complete with a statue of Henry VI. (10min. down Thames St. from the town center, across the river. ☎671177. Tours depart daily 2:15 and 3:15pm. Tours £3.60, under 16 £3. Open July-Aug. and late Mar. to mid-Apr. daily 10:30am-4:30pm; other times 2-4:30pm. £3, under 16 £2.25.)

Windsor is probably best seen as a daytrip from London. Two train stations are near Windsor Castle; follow the signs. **Trains** (☎(08457) 484950) pull into Windsor and Eton Central from London Victoria and London Paddington via Slough (50min., 2 per hr., round-trip £6.90). Trains come in at Windsor and Eton Riverside from London Waterloo (50min., 2 per hr., round-trip £6.90). Green Line (☎8668 7261) **buses** #700 and 702 make the trip from London, leaving from Eccleston Bridge, behind Victoria station (1-1½hr., round-trip £5.50-6.70). If you intend to spend the night, the **YHA Windsor** is located at Edgeworth House, Mill Ln. (☎861710. Dorms £10.85, under 18 £7.40.) **The Waterman's Arms,** a traditional pub (c. 1542), is just over the bridge into Eton and to the left at Brocas St., next to the Eton College Boat House. It's still a local favorite with delicious cod, chips, and salad for £4.50. (☎861001. Open M-Sa noon-2:30pm and 6-11pm, Su noon-3pm and 7-10pm.)

THE COTSWOLDS

Stretching across western England—bounded by Banbury in the northeast, Bradford-upon-Avon in the southwest, Cheltenham in the north, and Malmesbury in the south—the Cotswolds' verdant, vivid hills enfold tiny towns barely touched by modern life. These old Roman settlements and tiny Saxon villages, hewn from the famed Cotswold stone, demand a place on any itinerary, although their relative inaccessibility via public transportation will necessitate extra effort to get there.

◱ TRANSPORTATION. Useful gateway cities are Cheltenham, Oxford, and Bath. **Trains** (☎(08457) 484950) to Cheltenham arrive from: Bath (1½hr., every hr., £11.10); Exeter (2hr., every 2hr., £28.50); London (2½hr., every hr., £31.50). National Express **buses** (☎(08705) 808080) also roll in from: Exeter (3½hr., every 2hr., £18); London (3hr., every hr., £10.50); Stratford-Upon-Avon (2¼hr., 2 per day, £7.50). For connections to Oxford, see p. 196; connections to Bath, see p. 205.

From Oxford, **trains** zip to Charlbury (20min., every hr., £3.80) and Moreton-in-Marsh (30min., every hr., £7.50)—the only villages in the Cotswolds with train stations. Several **bus** companies cover the Cotswolds, but most routes are very infrequent (1-2 per week). Two unusually regular services run from Cheltenham: **Pulham's Coaches** (☎(01451) 820369) run to Moreton via Bourton-on-the-Water and Stow-on-the-Wold (50min., M-Sa 7 per day, £1.50); **Castleway's Coaches** (☎(01242) 602949) depart for Broadway via Winchcombe (50min., M-Sa 4 per day, £1.80). Snag the *Connection* timetable from any bus station or **TIC,** and the Cheltenham TIC's *Getting There from Cheltenham.*

Local roads are perfect for biking; the closely spaced villages make ideal watering holes. **Country Lanes Cycle Centre** rents bikes at the Moreton-on-the-Marsh train station. (☎(01608) 650065. £14 per day. Call ahead. Open daily 9:30am-5:30pm.) Experience the Cotswolds as the English have for centuries by treading well-worn footpaths from village to village. **Cotswold Way,** spanning 160km from Bath to Chipping Camden, gives hikers glorious vistas of hills and dales. The *Cotswold Way Handbook* (£2) lists **B&Bs** along the Cotswold Way.

CHELTENHAM. The spa town of Cheltenham (pop. 107,000) is a pleasant break from the heavily touristed Bath and Stratford. A useful launching pad into the rest of the Cotswolds, this city also has a large student population that brings the pubs and clubs to life at night. Enjoy the diuretic and laxative effects of the waters at the **Town Hall.** Sip, don't gulp. (Open M-F 9:30am-5:30pm. Water tasting free.) Manicured gardens adorn shops and houses around town, but for a real floral fix, sunbathe at the exquisite **Imperial Gardens,** just past **The Promenade** away from the center of

BRITAIN

town. **Trains** run into town at the station on Queen's Rd. The **TIC,** 77 The Promenade, one block east of the bus station, posts vacancies after-hours. (☎ (01242) 522878. Open M-Sa 9:30am-5:15pm.) The well-situated **YMCA,** on Vittoria Walk, accepts both men and women. At Town Hall, turn left off Promenade and walk three blocks—Vittoria Walk is on the right. (☎524024. Breakfast included. Reception 24hr. Singles £15.) **Cross Ways,** 57 Bath Rd., features home-sewn bedding and curtains, and a tasty breakfast with veggie options. (☎527683; crossways@btinternet.com. £20-22 per person.) **Benton's Guest House,** 71 Bath Rd., has an exuberant garden and breakfasts that barely fit on the plates. (☎517412. £25-35.) Fruit stands and bakeries dot **High Street.** Down the road, **Tesco** has **groceries.** (Open M-Tu and Sa 7:30am-7pm, W-F 7:30am-8pm.) **Postal code:** GL50 1AA.

STOW-ON-THE-WOLD, WINCHCOMBE, AND CIRENCESTER. Stow-on-the-Wold is a sleepy town with fine views, cold winds, and authentic prisoner's stocks. The **TIC** is in Hollis House on The Square. (☎(01451) 831082. Open Easter-Oct. M-Sa 9:30am-5:30pm, Su 10:30am-4pm; Nov.-Easter M-Sa 9:30am-4:30pm.) The **YHA youth hostel** stands just a few yards from the stocks. (☎(01451) 830497. Open Apr.-Oct. £10.85, students £9.85.)

   West of Stow-on-the-Wold and 10km north of Cheltenham on A46, **Sudeley Castle,** once the manor of King Ethelred the Unready, enserfs the town of Winchcombe. (Open Apr.-Oct. daily 10:30am-5pm. £6.20) Just 2½km southwest of Sudeley Castle lies **Belas Knap,** a 4000-year-old burial mound, evidence that the area was inhabited in pre-historic times. The **TIC** is in Town Hall. (☎(01242) 602925. Open Apr.-Oct. M-Sa 10am-1pm and 2-5pm, Su 10am-1:30pm and 2-5pm.)

   Sometimes regarded as the capital of the region, Cirencester is the site of Corinium, a Roman town founded in AD 49, second in importance only to Londinium. Its **Corinium Museum,** on Park St., houses a formidable collection of Roman paraphernalia. (Open Apr.-Oct. M-Sa 10am-5pm, Su 2-5pm; Nov.-Mar. Tu-Sa 10am-5pm, Su 2-5pm. £2.50, students £1.) The **Cirencester Parish Church** is Gloucestershire's largest parish church. The money to build it was endowed by wealthy local wool merchants. (Open daily 10am-5pm.) On Fridays, the town turns into a mad **antique marketplace.** The **TIC** is in Corn Hall, on Market Pl. (☎(01285) 65 41 80. Open Apr.-Oct. M 9:45am-5:30pm, Tu-Sa 9:30am-5:30pm; Nov.-Mar. daily 9:30am-5pm.) Cirencester and the ruins are best seen as a daytrip from Cheltenham.

STRATFORD-UPON-AVON   ☎01789

Former native William Shakespeare is now the area's industry; you'll find even the most vague of connections to the Bard exploited here to their full potential. Of course, all the perfumes of Arabia will not sweeten the exhaust from tour buses, but beyond the "Will Power" t-shirts, the essence of Shakespeare does lurk in Stratford: in the groves of the once-Forest of Arden and in the Fpin-drop silence before a soliloquy in the Royal Shakespeare Theatre.

▤ JOURNEY'S END. Thames **trains** roll in from: London's Paddington Station (2¼hr., 7-10 per day, round-trip £22.50); Birmingham (1hr., £3.60); Warwick (25min., £2.60). National Express runs **buses** from London's Victoria Station (3hr., 4 per day, round-trip £4); Stagecoach buses come from Oxford (round-trip £5.25).

▨ HERE CEASE MORE QUESTIONS. The **TIC,** Bridgefoot, across Warwick Rd. at Bridge St. toward the waterside park, sells maps and offers a free accommodations guide. (☎293127. Open Apr.-Oct. M-Sa 9am-6pm, Su 11am-5pm; Nov.-Mar. M-Sa 9am-5pm.) Romeo and Juliet would have lived happily ever after if they had email; surf the **Internet** at **Java Café,** 28 Greenhill St. (£3 per 30min., £5 per hr.; students £2.50, £4.) **Postal code:** CV37 6PU.

▥ TO SLEEP, PERCHANCE TO DREAM. To B&B or not to B&B? This hamlet has tons of them (£15-26), but 'tis nobler in summer to make advance reservations. The nearest hostel is more than 3km away, and the cost is comparable to many B&Bs after adding in round-trip bus fare. Keep an eye out for B&Bs on **Grove Road,**

BRITAIN

Evesham Place, and **Evesham Road.** In a recently redecorated Tudor-style home, **Brad-bourne Guest House,** 44 Shipston Rd., is an 8min. walk away from the town center. (☎204178. Singles £25-30; doubles £44-48.) Warm and attentive proprietors consider **The Hollies,** 16 Evesham Pl., their labor of love. (☎266857. Doubles £35, with bath £45.) The **Stratford Backpackers Hotel,** 33 Greenhill St., is conveniently located just across the bridge from the train station and has clean rooms, a common room, and a kitchen. (☎263838. Dorms £12.) The **YHA youth hostel,** Hemmingford House, on Wellesbourne Rd., Alveston, has large, attractive grounds; take bus #X18 from Bridge St.; it which runs every hour for £1.70. (☎29 70 93. Breakfast included. Reception 7am-midnight. Dorms £15.50, under 18 £11.55.) **Riverside Caravan Park,** Tiddington Rd., 1½km east of Stratford on B4086, provides beautiful, but sometimes crowded, sunset views of the Avon. (☎292312. Open Easter-Oct. Tent and 2 people £7, each additional person £1.) Await what dreams may come.

🞕 **FOOD OF LOVE. Hussain's Indian Cuisine,** 6a Chapel St., has fantastic chicken *tikka masala;* keep an eye out for regular Ben Kingsley. (Lunch £6, main dishes from £6.50. Open daily 5pm-midnight, also Th-Su 12:30-2:30pm.) Drink deep ere you depart at the 🞕**Dirty Duck Pub,** on Waterside, a destination of the theater crowd and the actors themselves. (Traditional pub lunch £3-9, dinner £6-18. Open M-Sa 11am-11pm, Su noon-10:30pm.) To get to the **Safeway supermarket** on Alcester Rd., take the Avon shuttle from the town center, or just cross the bridge past the rail station. (Open M-Th and Sa 8am-9pm, F 8am-10pm, Su 10am-4pm.)

🞕 **THE GILDED MONUMENTS.** Bardolatry peaks around 2pm, so try to hit any Will-centered sights before 11am or after 4pm. Die-hard fans can buy the **combination ticket** (£12, students £11) for admission to five official Shakespeare properties: Shakespeare's Birthplace, Anne Hathaway's cottage (1½km away), Mary Arden's House and Countryside Museum (6½km away), New Place and Nash's House, and Hall's Croft. For a little less of the Bard, buy a **Shakespeare's Town Heritage Trail ticket** (£8.50, students £7.50), which covers only the sights in town—the Birthplace, Hall's Croft, and New Place. **Shakespeare's Birthplace,** Henley St., is equal parts period re-creation and Shakespeare's life-and-works exhibition. (Open Mar. 20-Oct. 19 M-Sa 9am-5pm, Su 9:30am-5pm; Oct. 20-Mar. 19 M-Sa 9:30am-4pm, Su 10am-4pm. £6.) **New Place,** on High St., was Stratford's hippest address when Shakespeare bought it in 1597. Only the foundation remains—it can be viewed from **Nash's House,** which belonged to the husband of Shakespeare's granddaughter. **Hall's Croft** and **Mary Arden's House** also capitalize on tenuous connections to Shakespeare's extended family, but provide exhibits of what life was like in Elizabethan times. For dramatic cohesiveness, pay homage to Shakespeare's grave—his little, little grave—in the **Holy Trinity Church,** on Trinity St. (£0.60.)

🞕 **THE PLAY'S THE THING.** Get thee to a performance at the world-famous **Royal Shakespeare Company;** recent sons include Kenneth Branagh and Ralph Fiennes. Tickets (£5-40) for all three theaters—the Royal Shakespeare Theatre, the Swan Theatre, and The Other Place—are sold through the box office in the foyer of the Royal Shakespeare Theatre, on Waterside. (Reservations from 9am ☎403403, 24hr. recording ☎403404. Open M-Sa 9am-8pm; arrive at least 20min. before opening for same-day sales. Student standbys for £8-12 exist in principle.)

🞕 **EXCURSION FROM STRATFORD: WARWICK CASTLE.** One of England's finest medieval castles, Warwick Castle makes an excellent daytrip from Stratford. Climb the 530 steps to the top of the towers of Warwick and see the countryside unfold like a fairy tale kingdom of hobbits and elves. The dungeons are filled with life-size wax figures of people preparing for battle, while "knights" and "craftsmen" talk about their trades. (Open Apr.-Oct. daily 10am-6pm; Nov.-Mar. 10am-5pm. Mid-May to early-Sept. £11.50, students £8.60; Mar. to early May and early Sept. to mid-Feb. £10.25, students £7.80.) **Trains** arrive from Stratford (20min., round-trip £4) and Birmingham (40min., round-trip £4.70).

BRITAIN

BIRMINGHAM ☎ 0121

Birmingham, industrial heart of the Midlands, is resolutely modern in its style, packing its city center with convention-goers, cell phones, and three-piece suits. Twelve minutes south of town by rail lies ◙Cadbury World, an unabashed celebration of the delectables from the chocolate company. Take a train from New St. to Bournville, or buses #83, 84, or 85 from the city center. (☎451 4180. Open daily 10am-3pm; closed certain days Nov.-Feb. £8, students and seniors £6.50, children £6. Includes about 3 free bars of chocolate.) The **Barber Institute of Fine Arts,** in the University of Birmingham on Edgbaston Park Rd., displays works by artists as diverse as Rubens, Gainsborough, and Magritte. Take bus #61, 62, or 63 from the city center. (☎414 7333. Open M-Sa 10am-5pm, Su 2-5pm. Free.) Weekends bustle with waves of students, locals, and clubbers. Pick up a copy of the bimonthly *What's On* or the monthly *Leap* to discover the latest hot-spots. **Broad Street** holds trendy cafe-bars and clubs, while the area around **Essex Street** offers a gay-friendly scene. **Stoodibakers,** 192 Broad St., draws a trendy flock. (☎643 5100. Cover £4 after 9:30pm F-Sa. Open until 4am.) The **City of Birmingham Symphony Orchestra** plays in the the acoustically superb Symphony Hall at the Convention Centre on Broad St. (☎780 3333. Box office open M-F 10am-8pm, Sa 10am-10pm; Su hours depend on showtimes. Tickets £5-32; student standbys £7.50 after 1pm on concert days.) The **Birmingham Jazz Festival** (☎454 7020) brings over 200 jazz singers and instrumentalists to town during the first two weeks of July; book through the TIC.

Birmingham is the center of a web of train and bus lines between London, central Wales, southwest England, and all points north. **Trains** arrive in New St. Station (☎(08457) 484950), Britain's busiest station, from: Liverpool Lime St. (1½hr., 1-2 per hr., £18.50); London Euston (2hr., 2 per hr., £22.50); Manchester Piccadilly (2½hr., every hr., £14.20); Nottingham (1¼hr., 2-4 per hr., £8.20) and Oxford (1¼hr., 1-2 per hr., £14.20). Some trains pull into Moor St. and Snow Hill stations. National Express **buses** (☎(08705) 808080) arrive in Digbeth Station from: Cardiff (2¼hr., 4 per day, round-trip £18.75); Liverpool (2½hr., 15 per day, round-trip £11); London (3¼hr., every hr., round-trip £15); Manchester (2½hr., every 2hr., round-trip £12.50). The **TIC,** at 2 City Arcade, makes room reservations. (☎643 2514; fax 616 1038. Open M-Sa 9:30am-5:30pm.) Access the **Internet** at **NetAdventure Cyber Café,** 68-70 Dalton St. (☎693 6655. £3 per hr., £1 minimum.) Despite its size, Birmingham has no hostels, and inexpensive B&Bs are rare; **Hagley Road** is your best bet for B&Bs. To reach **Grasmere Guest House,** 37 Serpentine Rd., take bus #22, 23, or 103 from Colmore Row to the Duke of York pub, and turn right off Harborne Rd. onto Serpentine Rd. (☎/fax 427 4546. £15 per person, with bath £25.) Take bus #128 or 129 from Colmore Row in the city center (10min.), to reach **Woodville House,** 39 Portland Rd., which is comfortable, affordable, and well-located. (☎454 0274. Singles £18; doubles £30, with bath £35.) Birmingham's eateries conjure up expensive delights, as well as the requisite cheap cod and kebabs. **Al Frash,** 186 Ladypool Rd., has tasty, generous portions of Balti chicken for £3.90. (☎753 3120. Open daily 5pm-1am.) **Postal code:** B2 4AA.

BATH ☎ 01225

A visit to the elegant Georgian city of Bath (pop. 83,000) remains *de rigueur*, even if today it's more of a museum (or a museum gift shop) than a resort. But expensive trinkets can't conceal the fact that Bath, immortalized by Austen and Dickens, once stood second only to London as the social capital of England.

◪◪◪ **PRACTICAL INFO, ACCOMMODATIONS, AND FOOD. Trains** head frequently to: Bristol (15min., 3 per hr., £4.60); Exeter (1¼hr., every hr., £21.50); London's Paddington Station (1½hr., 2 per hr., £34). National Express **buses** (☎(08705) 808080) run to London's Victoria Station (3hr., 9 per day, £11.50) and Oxford (2hr., 6 per day, £12). Both arrive near the southern end of Manvers St.; walk up Manvers to the Terrace Walk roundabout and turn left on York St. to reach the **TIC,** in Abbey Chambers. (☎477101. Open May-Sept. M-Sa 9:30am-6pm, Su 10am-4pm; Oct.-Apr. M-Sa 9:30am-5pm, Su 10am-4pm.)

B&Bs (from £18) cluster on **Pulteney Road, Pulteney** and **Crescent Gardens,** and **Widcombe Hill. The YHA youth hostel,** on Bathwick Hill, is in a secluded mansion 20 steep minutes above the city; catch Badgerline bus #18 (dir.: University) from the bus station or the Orange Grove rotary. (☎465674. Laundry. Dorms £11, under 18 £7.75.) The **International Backpackers Hostel,** 13 Pierrepont St., is up the street from the stations and is just three blocks from the baths. (☎446787. **Internet.** Breakfast £1. Laundry £3. Dorms £12.) To get to **Toad Hall Guest House,** 6 Lime Grove, go across Pulteney Bridge and through Pulteney Gardens. (☎423254. £20-26 per person.) To reach **Newton Mill Camping,** 4km west on Newton Rd., take bus #5 from the bus station (round-trip £1.60) to Twerton and ask to be let off at the campsite. (☎333909. Reserve ahead. 2 people, tent, and car £11.95.) **Guildhall Market** is between High St. and Grand Parade. (Open M-Sa 8am-5:30pm.) Try ◙**Tilleys Bistro,** 3 North Parade Passage, for French or English fare. (Open M-Sa noon-2:30pm and 6:30-11pm, Su 6:30-10:30pm.) **The Pump Room,** in Abbey Courtyard, holds a monopoly on Bath Spa mineral water (£0.50). **Postal code:** BA1 1A5.

◙◙ **SIGHTS AND ENTERTAINMENT.** Once the spot for naughty sightings, the **Roman Baths** are now a must-see for all. Most of the visible complex is not actually Roman, but rather reflects Georgian dreams of what Romans might have built. The ◙**Roman Baths Museum** underneath reveals genuine Roman Baths and highlights the complexity of Roman engineering, which included central heating and internal plumbing. Its recovered artifacts, scale models, and hot springs bring back to life the Roman spa city Aquae Salis—first unearthed in 1880 by sewer diggers. (Open Apr.-July and Sept. daily 9am-6pm; Aug. 9am-6pm and 8pm-10pm; Oct.-Mar. 9:30am-5pm; last admission 30min. before closing. £6.70.) Penny-pinchers can view one bath for free by entering through the **Pump Room** in Abbey Churchyard. Next to the baths, the towering and tombstoned 15th-century **Bath Abbey** has a whimsical west façade with several angels climbing ladders up to heaven—and, curiously enough, two climbing down. (Open M-Sa 9am-4:30pm, Su 1pm-2:30pm and 4:30-5:30pm. £1.50.) Head north up Stall St., turn left on Westgate St., and turn right on Saw Close to reach Queen Sq., where Jane Austen lived at #13. Continue up Gay St. to **The Circus,** where Thomas Gainsborough, William Pitt, and David Livingstone once lived. To the left down Brock St. is the **Royal Crescent,** a half-moon of Gregorian townhouses bordering **Royal Victoria Park.** The **botanical gardens** within nurture 5000 species of plants. (Open M-Sa 9am-dusk, Su 10am-dusk. Free.) Backtrack down Brock St. and bear left at the Circus (or take a right at The Circus from Gay St.) to reach Bennett St. and the dazzling **Museum of Costume,** which will satisfy any fashion fetish. (Open daily 10am-5pm. £3.90; joint ticket with Roman Baths £7.50.) **The Garrick's Head,** St. John's Pl., is a scoping ground for the stage door of the Theatre Royal, while the **The Pig and Fiddle** pub, on the corner of Saracen St. and Broad St., packs in a rowdy young crowd.

GLASTONBURY ☎ 01458

The reputed birthplace of Christianity in England and the seat of Arthurian myth, Glastonbury (pop. 6900) has evolved into an intersection of mysticism and religion. Present-day pagan pilgrimage site **Glastonbury Tor** is supposedly the site of the mystical Isle of Avalon, where the Messiah is slated to return. To make the trek up to the Tor, turn right at the top of High St., continue up to Chilkwell St., turn left onto Wellhouse Ln., and take the first right up the hill (buses in summer £0.50). On your way down, visit the **Chalice Well,** on the corner of Welhouse Ln., the supposed resting place of the Holy Grail. (Open daily Easter-Oct. 10am-6pm; Nov.-Feb. 1-4pm. £1.50.) Back in town, the ruins of **Glastonbury Abbey,** England's oldest Christian foundation, stands behind the archway on Magdalene St. (Open daily June-Aug. 9am-6pm; Sept.-May 9:30am-6pm. £3, students £2.50.) No trains serve Glastonbury, but Baker's Dolphin **buses** (☎(01934) 616000) run from London (3¼hr., 1 per day, round-trip £5), while Badgerline buses (☎(01225) 464446) run from Bath (£4; change at Wells). From the bus stop, turn right on High St. to reach the **TIC,** The Tribunal, 9 High St. (☎832954. Open Apr.-Sept. Su-Th 10am-5pm, F-Sa 10am-5:30pm;

BRITAIN

Oct.-Mar. S-Th 10am-4pm, F-Sa 10am-4:30pm.) **Glastonbury Backpackers,** in the Crown Hotel on Market Pl., contributes its own splashes of color to the city's tie-dye. (☎833353. **Internet.** Dorms £10; doubles £26-30.) Sleep in comfort at **Blake House,** 3 Bove Town. (☎831680. £19 per person.) **Postal code:** BA6 9HG.

CAMBRIDGE
☎01223

The university began a mere 792 years ago when rebels defected from nearby Oxford to this settlement on the River Cam. Today, in contrast to its sister institution, Cambridge (pop. 105,000) is steadfastly determined to remain a city under its academic robes—the TIC "manages," rather than encourages, visitors. Most colleges close to visitors during official quiet periods in May and early June, but when exams end, cobblestoned Cambridge explodes in gin-soaked glee. ▧**May Week** (in mid-June, naturally) hosts a dizzying schedule of cocktail parties.

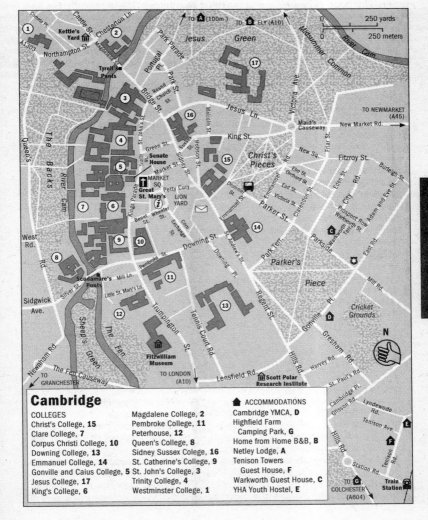

BRITAIN

Cambridge

COLLEGES
Christ's College, **15**
Clare College, **7**
Corpus Christi College, **10**
Downing College, **13**
Emmanuel College, **14**
Gonville and Caius College, **5**
Jesus College, **17**
King's College, **6**

Magdalene College, **2**
Pembroke College, **11**
Peterhouse, **12**
Queen's College, **8**
Sidney Sussex Colege, **16**
St. Catherine's College, **9**
St. John's College, **3**
Trinity College, **4**
Westminster College, **1**

♠ ACCOMMODATIONS
Cambridge YMCA, **D**
Highfield Farm
   Camping Park, **G**
Home from Home B&B, **B**
Netley Lodge, **A**
Tenison Towers
   Guest House, **F**
Warkworth Guest House, **C**
YHA Youth Hostel, **E**

▐▀ TRANSPORTATION

Trains: (☎(0345) 484950), Station Rd. Tickets sold daily 5am-11pm. To: **London's King's Cross Station** and **London's Liverpool Street Station** (1¼hr., 2 per hr., £14.50).

Buses: Drummer St. **National Express** (☎(01604) 620077) arrives from **London's Victoria Station** (2hr., 17 per day, from £8). National Express and **Stagecoach** buses go to **Oxford** (2¾hr., 10 per day, £7). **Cambus** (☎423554) runs local routes (£0.85-1.60).

Bike Rental: Mike's Bikes, 28 Mill Rd. (☎312591). £8 per day, £10 per week. Open M-Sa 9am-6pm, Su 10am-4pm.

✳❼ ORIENTATION AND PRACTICAL INFORMATION

Cambridge, about 95km north of London, is an old city; streets twist haphazardly. The city has two main avenues, both of which suffer from multiple personality disorder. The main shopping street starts at **Magdalene** (MAUD-lin) **Bridge** and becomes **Bridge Street, Sidney Street, St. Andrew's Street, Regent Street,** and finally **Hills Road.** The other—alternately **St. John's Street, Trinity Street, King's Parade, Trumpington Street,** and **Trumpington Road**—is the academic thoroughfare, with several colleges lying between it and the River Cam. The two streets merge at **St. John's College.** From the bus station at **Drummer Street,** a quick walk down **Emmanuel Street** will land you right in the shopping district near the TIC. To get to the heart of things from the train station on **Station Road,** turn right onto Hills Rd., and continue straight ahead.

TIC: (☎322640.), Wheeler St., just south of the marketplace. Books rooms for £3 fee plus a 10% deposit. Mini-guide £0.40, maps £0.20. Offers **walking tours** of the city and some colleges (£7). Open Apr.-Oct. M-F 10am-5:30pm, Sa 10am-5pm, Su 11am-4pm; Nov.-Mar. M-F 10am-5:30pm, Sa 10am-5pm. Info on city events is available at **Cambridge Corn Exchange** (☎357851), Corn Exchange St., across from the TIC.

American Express: 25 Sidney St. (☎(08706) 001060). Open M-F 9am-5:30pm, W 9:30am-5:30pm, Sa 9am-5pm.

Laundromat: Clean Machine, 22 Burleigh St. (☎578009). Open daily 8am-8pm.

Emergency: Dial 999; no coins required. **Police** (☎358966). The central police station is on Parkside at the corner of East Rd.

Medical Assistance: Addenbrookes Hospital, (☎245151) Hill Rd. Catch Cambus #4, 5 or 5a from Emmanuel St. (£1), and get off where Hill Rd. intersects Long Rd.

Internet Access: CB1, 32 Mill Rd. (☎576306), near the youth hostel. £0.05 per min. Open daily 10am-8pm.

Post Office: 9-11 St. Andrew's St. (☎323325). Open M-Sa 9am-5:30pm. Address mail to be held to FirstName SURNAME, *Poste Restante,* 9-11 St. Andrews St. Post Office, Cambridge, England. **CB2 3AA.**

▐▙ ACCOMMODATIONS

This university town teaches travelers to book ahead. Many of the **B&Bs** around **Portugal Street** and **Tenison Road** are open only in July and August. Check the list at the TIC, or pick up their guide to accommodations (£0.50).

YHA Youth Hostel, 97 Tenison Rd. (☎354601). Relaxed, welcoming atmosphere. Well-equipped kitchen, laundry, TV lounge, and a great cafeteria. In the summer, call *several* weeks ahead. Dorms £15.10, under 18 £11.40.

Cambridge YMCA, Gonville Pl. (☎356998). The other backpacker hotspot in a thriving college town. Large, clean rooms, if a slightly industrial feel. Breakfast included. Singles £23, shared room (usually doubles) £37.

Tenison Towers Guest House, 148 Tenison Rd. (☎566511). 2 blocks from the train station. Fresh flowers grace an impeccable house. Singles £20-25; doubles £40-50.

Home from Home B&B, 39 Milton Rd. (☎323555). A 20min. walk from the city center. Pricey but worthwhile, thanks to sparkling, spotless rooms and a pleasant hostess. Full

English breakfast included. Call ahead with a credit card for reservations. Singles from £35; doubles from £48; discounts for longer stays.

Netley Lodge, 112 Chesterton Rd. (☎363845). Plush red carpets and a conservatory lush with greenery welcome you to sunny rooms. Roses inside and out—hostess Mrs. Mikolajczyk is a study in elegance. Singles £22-24; doubles £40.

Warkworth Guest House, Warkworth Terr. (☎363682). Sunny rooms near the bus station; the spot for those seeking more privacy than the nearby hostels, but it'll cost you. Packed lunch on request. Singles £30, with bath £35; doubles £55, £60.

Highfield Farm Camping Park, Long Rd., Comberton (☎262308). Take Cambus #118 from the Drummer St. bus station. (every 45min.) Open Apr.-Oct. Call ahead. £7 per tent, with car £8.75; off season £6.25, £7.25.

🍴 FOOD

Cantabrigians are too busy learning Latin to flavor their food, so try the bright pyramids of fruit and vegetables at **Market Square** (Open M-Sa 9:30am-4:30pm.) Students buy their gin and cornflakes at **Sainsbury's,** 44 Sidney St., the only grocery store in the middle of town. (Open M-F 8am-9pm, Sa 7:30am-9pm, Su 11am-5pm.) The alcohol-serving curry houses on **Castle Hill** are also popular.

▨ Nadia's, 11 St. John's St. (☎460961). An uncommonly good bakery with reasonable prices. Wonderful pancakes and quiches (£0.80-1.25). Open daily 8:30am-5pm. Also at 16 Silver St. and 20 King's Parade.

Hobbs' Pavillion, Parker's Piece (☎367480), off Park Terr. Renowned for imaginative, thin, rectangular pancakes and a Mars Bar and ice cream pancakes for £3.95—you won't need to eat again for 2 weeks. Open Tu-Sa noon-2:15pm and 6-9:45pm.

Rainbow's Vegetarian Bistro, 9a King's Parade (☎321551). A tiny, creative burrow featuring delicious international vegan and vegetarian fare. Open M-Sa 11am-11pm.

Clown's, 54 King St. (☎355711). Everything from cakes to toasties to lasagna £1.20-5.95, plus some of the best coffee in Cambridge. Open daily 7:30am-midnight.

The Little Tea Room, 1 All Saints' Passage (☎366033), off Trinity St. Hopelessly pretentious, yet the place to go for afternoon tea. "Traditional English cream tea" £3.95 (pot of tea, scone, clotted cream, jam). Open M-Sa 10am-5:30pm, Su 1-5:30pm.

Tatties, 11 Sussex St. (☎323399). Dedicated to 1 of the most popular dishes in England, Tatties' jacket potatoes. Fillings range from butter (£1.95) to Philly cheese and smoked salmon (£5.75). Open M-Sa 8:30am-7pm, Su 10am-5pm.

👁 SIGHTS

Cambridge is an architect's fantasia—it packs some of the most breathtaking examples of English architecture into less than 1 sq km. If you are pressed for time, visit at least one chapel (preferably King's), one garden (try Christ's), one library (Trinity's is the most interesting), and one dining hall (you'll have to adopt a convincing student disguise to get in). The familiar **Bridge of Sighs** at **St. John's College** is another particularly exquisite sight if you can squeeze it in. Cambridge is most exciting during the university's three eight-week terms: Michaelmas (Oct.-Dec.), Lent (Jan.-Mar.), and Easter (Apr.-June). Most of the colleges are open daily from 9am to 5:30pm, but hours vary often. A few are closed to sightseers during the Easter term, and virtually all are closed during exams (mid-May to mid-June).

TRINITY COLLEGE. Founded in 1546 by Henry VIII, the college is the wealthiest at Cambridge, for which it has become legendary—rumors say it was once possible to walk from Cambridge to Oxford without stepping off Trinity land. Sir Isaac Newton, who lived in E-entry for 30 years, originally measured the speed of sound by stamping his foot in the cloister along the north side of the **Great Court**—the largest courtyard in Cambridge. The college also houses the stunning **Wren Library,** which keeps such notable treasures as A.A. Milne's handwritten manuscript of *Winnie the Pooh* and less momentous achievements by Milton, Byron, Tennyson, and

BRITAIN

Thackeray, many of whom are alums of the college. *(Trinity St. ☎ 338400. Chapel and courtyard open daily 10am-5pm. Library open M-F noon-2pm, Sa 10:30am-12:30pm. Both closed during exams. Entry Easter-Oct. £1.75, otherwise free.)*

KING'S COLLEGE. E.M. Forster's alma mater dominates King's Parade St. from street level to skyline. Founded in 1441 by Henry VI, the college houses **King's College Chapel,** a spectacular Gothic monument with elaborately carved interiors. The interior of the chapel consists of one huge chamber cleft by a carved wooden choir screen. Heralding angels crown the screen and flit about against the backdrop of the world's largest fan-vaulted ceiling. Tudor roses, symbols of Henry VIII's reign, abound. Rubens's magnificent *Adoration of the Magi* hangs behind the altar. ▓**Evensong** is held most evenings in the Chapel at 5:30pm and is breathtaking to behold. *(King's Parade. ☎ 331100. College open M-F 9:30am-4:30pm, Su 9:30am-2:30pm. Tours arranged through the TIC. Entry £3.50, students £2.50, under 12 free.)*

ST. JOHN'S COLLEGE. Established in 1511 by Lady Margaret Beaufort, mother of Henry VIII, St. John's is one of seven Cambridge colleges founded by women (but *for* men). A copy of Venice's **Bridge of Sighs** connects the older part of the college to the neo-Gothic extravagance of New Court. The **School of Pythagoras,** a 12th-century pile of wood and stone, supposedly the oldest complete building in Cambridge, hides in St. John's Gardens. *(St. John's St. ☎ 338600. Chapel and grounds open daily 10am-4:45pm. Evensong 6:30pm most nights. Entry £2, students £1.20, families £4.)*

QUEENS' COLLEGE. Queen's has the only unaltered Tudor courtyard in Cambridge. The **Mathematical Bridge,** just past Cloister Court, was built in 1749 without a single bolt or nail, instead relying on mathematical principles. A meddling Victorian took apart the bridge to see how it worked and the inevitable occurred—he couldn't put it back together without using steel rivets every two inches. *(Silver St. ☎ 335511. College open Mar.-Oct. daily 10am-4:30pm. Closed during exams. Entry £1.)*

CHRIST'S COLLEGE. Founded as "God's house" in 1448, Christ's has won fame for gorgeous gardens and its association with John Milton. Charles Darwin dilly-dallied through Christ's before dealing a blow to its religious origins. *(St. Andrews St. ☎ 334900. Gardens open summer M-F 9:30am-noon; term-time M-F 9am-4:30pm. Entry Free.)*

FITZWILLIAM MUSEUM. A welcome break from the academia of the colleges, the Fitzwilliam Museum dwells within an immense Roman-style building. The museum stocks a hoard of Egyptian, Chinese, Japanese, and Greek treasures that only the Brits could have assembled, as well as an intimate collection of French Impressionist works. *(Trumpington St. ☎ 332900. Open Tu-Sa 10am-5pm, Su 2:15-5pm. Guided tours Sa 2:30pm. Free, but suggested donation £3. Tours £3.)*

▓**KETTLE'S YARD.** Created as a refuge of light and of the visual arts and music, the museum houses beautifully displayed early 20th-century artworks. *(☎ 352124. House open Apr.-Sept. Tu-Sa 1:30-4:30pm, Su 2-4:30pm; Oct.-Mar. Tu-Su 2-4pm; gallery open year-round Tu-Su 11:30am-5pm. Free.)*

🎵 ENTERTAINMENT

The best source of info on student activities is the student newspaper *Varsity;* the TIC's free *Cambridge Nightlife Guide* is also helpful. **Punts** (gondola-like boats) are a favored form of entertainment in Cambridge. Beware that punt-bombing—jumping from bridges into the river alongside a punt, thereby tipping its occupants into the Cam—has evolved into an art form. **Tyrell's** (☎ 352847), Magdalene Bridge, rents boats for £8 per hr. plus a £40 deposit. Even more traditional than punting is **pub-crawling;** Cambridge hangouts offer good pub-crawling year-round, though they lose some of their character in the summer. Live music of all kinds rollicks nightly at the **Boat Race,** 170 East Rd. **The Eagle,** Benet St., is the oldest pub in Cambridge. Nobel laureates Watson and Crick once rushed into the Eagle breathless to announce their discovery of the DNA double helix—unimpressed, the barmaid insisted they settle their four-shilling tab before she'd serve them a toast. (Open 11am-11pm, Su noon-10:30pm.) **The Mill,** Mill Ln. off Silver St. Bridge, claims the riv-

BRITAIN

erside park as its own on spring nights for punt and people-watching. (Open M-Sa noon-11pm, Su noon-10:30pm.) **Bar Coast,** Quayside, has frequent dance nights, from disco to "uplifting house and garage." The gay crowd downs ale at **The Town and Gown,** on Poundhill off Northhampton. Students drink at the **Anchor,** Silver St., and a visit to **The Rattle and Hum,** 4 King St., is mandatory before hitting clubs.

⚡ DAYTRIP FROM CAMBRIDGE

GRANTCHESTER

To reach Grantchester Meadows from Cambridge, take the path that follows the River Granta (about 45min.). Grantchester itself lies about 1½km from the meadows; ask the way at 1 of the neighborhood shops. Alternatley, hop on Stagecoach Cambus #118 and hop off at the town's bus stand (9-11 per day from Drummer St., round-trip £1.20)

Weary travelers searching for rejuvenation after the bustle of the college town head to the idyllic setting of Grantchester, once a stomping ground for Cambridge literati including Virginia Woolf, Robert Brooke, E.M. Forster, and Ludwig Wittgenstein. Wander past the town to the idyllic **Orchard Tea Gardens** on Mill Way, where these same luminaries gathered and raised a cuppa. The weathered 14th-century **Parish Church of St. Andrew and St. Mary,** on Millway, is beautifully intimate.

NORWICH ☎ 01603

One of England's largest and most populous cities before the Norman invasion, Norwich (rhymes with "porridge;" pop. 120,700) today conceals its medieval heritage behind a modern façade. The 11th-century **Norwich Cathedral** and the 12th-century **Norwich Castle,** where King John signed the Magna Carta in 1215, reign over puzzling, winding streets. (Cathedral open mid-May to mid-Sept. daily 7am-7pm; mid-Sept. to mid-May 7am-6pm. £3 suggested donation.) **Trains** (☎ (08457) 484950) arrive frequently at the corner of Riverside and Thorpe Rd. from Cambridge (1½hr., 12 per day, £10.90-11.40) and London's Liverpool St. Station (2hr., M-Sa 30 per day, £31). National Express **buses** (☎(08705) 808080) travel from Surrey St. to Cambridge (2hr., 1 per day, round-trip £10) and London (3hr., 7 per day, £14.20). The **TIC,** in The Forum at Millenium Plain on Bethel Street, has an essential city guide map (£0.30). Head right from the train station, take a left on Prince of Wales Rd., and cross the bridge to the castle. From the bus station, head left on Surrey St. and then right on St. Stephen's St. to the castle. (☎666071. Open June-Sept. M-Sa 9:30am-5pm; Oct.-May M-F 9:30am-4:30pm, Sa 9:30am-1pm and 1:30-4:30pm.) The **Earlham Guest House,** 147 Earlham Rd., offers cheerful rooms and a refreshing garden. (☎459469. Singles £21; doubles £42-48.) In the heart of the city is one of England's largest and oldest open-air **markets** (open M-Sa 8:30am-4:30pm) as well as a trove of excellent restaurants. **Postal code:** NR1 3DD.

NOTTINGHAM ☎ 0115

Nottingham's (pop. 261,500) age-old tradition of taking from the rich and giving to the poor lives on as modern-day Robin Hoods lure visitors to Nottingham with a tourist industry that boasts little substance but plenty of thrill. ⚑ **The Galleries of Justice,** High Pavement, is an interactive museum that puts presumably innocent tourists on trial, throws them behind bars, and lets them see the English prison system through the eyes of the convicted. (Open Tu-Su 10am-5pm. £6.95, students £5.95.) Originally constructed in 1068 by William the Conqueror, the remains of **Nottingham Castle,** atop a sandstone rise in the south of the city, now house the **Castle Museum.** (Open Mar.-Oct. daily 10am-5pm; Nov.-Feb. Sa-Th 10am-5pm. M-Th free; Sa-Su £2, students £1.) From the museum entrance, enter **Mortimer's Hole,** a 100m long underground passageway from the castle to the base of the cliff. (£2, students £1.) **Trains** (☎ (08457) 484950) arrive on Carrington St. from Lincoln (1hr., 7-32 per day, £7) and London (2hr., 1 per hr., £37). National Express **buses** (☎(08705) 808080) pull in between Collin and Canal St. from London (3hr., 7 per day, £15). The **TIC,** 1-4 Smithy Row, is just off Old Market Sq. (☎(0115) 915 5330. Open M-F 9am-5:30pm, Sa 9am-

BRITAIN

5pm; Aug.-Sept. also Su 10am-3pm.) To sleep at **Igloo,** 110 Mansfield Rd., take bus #90 from the train station to Mansfield Rd. (☎ (0115) 947 5250. Dorms £12.) **Ye Olde Trip to Jerusalem,** 1 Brewhouse Yard, the "Oldest Inn in England," poured its first drink in 1189. **Postal code:** NG1 2BN.

LINCOLN   ☎ 01522

Medieval streets, half-timbered Tudor houses, and a 12th-century cathedral are all relative newcomers to Lincoln (pop. 77,000), originally built as a town for retired Roman legionnaires. The king of the hill is undoubtedly the magnificent ▪Lincoln Cathedral. (Open June-Aug. M-Sa 7:15am-8pm, Su 7:15am-6pm; Sept.-May. M-Sa 7:15am-6pm, Su 7:15am-5pm. £3.50.) **Lincoln Castle** houses one of the four surviving copies of the Magna Carta. (Open Apr.-Oct. M-Sa 9:30am-5:30pm, Su 11am-5:30pm; Nov.-Mar. M-Sa 9:30am-4pm, Su 11am-4pm. £2.50.) The station on St. Mary's St. receives frequent **trains** (☎ (08457) 484950) from London's King's Cross Station (2½hr.; M-Sa 1 per hr., Su every 2hr.; round-trip £40.50) and Nottingham (1hr.; M-Sa 2 per hr., Su 7 per day; round-trip £5.85). Opposite the train station, National Express **buses** (☎ (08705) 808080) pull in from London (5hr., 2 per day, £18). From either station, walk up High St., which becomes The Strait and then Steep Hill Rd., to reach the **TIC,** 9 Castle Hill. (☎ (01522) 529828. Open M-Th 9:30am-5:30pm, F 9:30am-5pm, Sa-Su 10am-5pm.) **B&Bs** (£17-20) line Carline and Yarborough Rd., west of the castle. To get to the lovely **YHA Lincoln,** 77 South Park Ave., veer right from the train station, turn right on Pelham Bridge, which becomes Canwick Rd., and turn right on South Park Ave. (☎ (01522) 522076. Lockout 10am-5pm. Curfew 11pm. Open Feb.-Oct. Dorms £11, under 18 £7.40.) **Postal code:** LN5 7XX.

PEAK DISTRICT NATIONAL PARK

A green cushion between England's industrial giants of Manchester, Sheffield, and Nottingham, Britain's first national park sprawls across 1400 sq. km of rolling hills and windswept moors, offering a playground for its 22 million urban neighbors. In the northern Dark Peak area, deep *groughs* (gullies) gouge the hard peat moorland against a backdrop of gloomy cliffs, and well-marked footpaths lead over mildly rocky hillsides to village clusters. Abandoned milestones, derelict lead mines, and country homes are scattered throughout the southern White Peak.

Contact **Peak District National Park Office,** Aldern House, Barlow Rd., Bakewell DE4 5AE (☎ (01629) 816200), for more info. The **National Park Information Centres** at **Bakewell** (see below), **Castleton** (☎ (01433) 620679), and **Edale** (☎ (01433) 670207) offer walking guides; you can also ask questions at **TICs** in **Buxton** (☎ (01298) 25106) and **Matlock Bath** (☎ (01629) 55082). **YHA youth hostels** in the park cost £7.50-13.75 and can be found in **Bakewell** (see below), **Buxton** (☎ (01298) 22287), **Castleton** (see below), **Edale** (see below), and **Matlock** (☎ (01629) 582983). There are 13 **YHA Camping Barns** (£3.60 per night) throughout the park; book ahead at the **Camping Barns Reservation Office,** 6 King St., Clitheroe, Lancashire BB7 2EP (☎ (01200) 420102). The park authority operates six **Cycle Hire Centres** (£10 per day); call **Ashbourne** (☎/fax (01335) 343156) or **Hayfield** (☎ (01663) 746222) for info.

▐ **TRANSPORTATION.** The invaluable *Peak District Timetable* (£0.60; available in all Peak TICs) has transport routes and a map. Two **rail** lines originate in **Manchester** and enter the park from the west: one stops at **Buxton** near the park's edge (1hr., every hr., £5.30), and the other crosses the park via **Edale, Hope** (near Castleton), and **Hathersage** (1½hr.; 9-17 per day; Manchester to Sheffield £10.40, Manchester to Edale £6.30) on its way to **Sheffield.** From the south, a train heads from **Nottingham** to **Matlock,** on the park's southeastern edge. Trent **bus** TP (Transpeak; ☎ (01298) 230 98) serves the southern half of the park, stopping at **Buxton, Bakewell, Matlock,** and **Derby** between Manchester and Nottingham. A one-day **Wayfarer** pass (£7) covers unlimited train and bus travel within Greater Manchester, including most of the Peak District.

BAKEWELL, EDALE, AND CASTLETON. The Southern Peak is better served by public transportation than its northern counterpart, and is consequently more trampled. Fifty kilometers southeast of Manchester, **Bakewell** is the best spot for exploration. Located near several scenic walks through the White Peaks, the town is known for its Bakewell pudding, created when a flustered cook inadvertently erred while making a tart. Bakewell's **National Park Information Centre** (☎ (01629) 813227), is in Old Market Halland Bridge St. The small and cozy **YHA youth hostel,** Fly Hill, is 5min. from the town center. (☎ (01629) 812313. Open mid-July to Aug. daily; Sept.-Oct. and Easter to mid-July F-Sa. Dorms £8.50.) **Postal code:** DE45 1EF.

The northern Dark Peak area contains some of the wildest and most rugged hill country in England. **Edale** offers little in the way of civilization other than a church, cafe, pub, school, and nearby **YHA youth hostel.** (☎ (01433) 67 03 02. Dorms £11.) Its environs, however, are arguably the most spectacular in northern England. The National Park Authority's *8 Walks Around Edale* (£1.20) details nearby **hiking** trails. Stay at the hostel (see above) or **camp** at **Fieldhead,** behind the TIC. (☎ 670386. £3.40 per person, £1.20 per car. Showers £0.50.) From Edale, the 5½km hike to **Castleton** affords a breathtaking view of the dark gritstone Edale Valley (Dark Peak) and the lighter limestone Hope Valley (White Peak) to the south. Castleton's river-carved limestone engulfs several famous caverns; **Treak Cliff Cavern** holds breathtaking stalagtite chambers and massive seams of the unique Blue John Stone. (☎ 620571. Mandatory 40min. tours, every 15-30min. £5.50, seniors £5, students and YHA members £4.50, children £3.) Stay at the excellent **YHA youth hostel** (☎ (01433) 620235; open Feb. to late Dec.; dorms £13.75) or **Cryer House,** across from the TIC (☎ (01433) 620244; doubles with bath £44).

MANCHESTER   ☎ 0161

The Industrial Revolution transformed the once unremarkable village of Manchester into a northern hub, now Britain's second-largest urban conglomeration. With few comely corners and fewer budget accommodations in the city center, Manchester proves that you don't have to be pretty to be popular, attracting thousands with its pulsing nightlife and vibrant arts scene. The exception to Manchester's unspectacular buildings is the neo-Gothic **Manchester Town Hall,** in St. Peter's Sq. behind the TIC. Nearby, the domed **Central Library,** one of the largest municipal libraries in Europe, includes the UK's second-largest Judaica collection. (☎ 234 1900. Open M-Th 10am-8pm, F-Sa 10am-5pm.) In the **Museum of Science and Industry,** on Liverpool Rd. in Castlefield, working steam engines provide a dramatic vision of Britain's industrialization. (☎ 832 1830. Open daily 10am-5pm. £6.50, students £3.50.) At the **Manchester United Museum and Tour Centre,** on Sir Matt Busby Way, at the Old Trafford football stadium, you can learn all about Manchester United, England's best-known football team. Follow the signs up Warwick Rd. from the Old Trafford Metrolink stop. (Open daily 9am-5pm. Tours run every 10min., 9:40am-4:30pm. Museum £5.50, seniors and children £3.75. Tour £3, seniors and children £2.) One of Manchester's biggest draws is its artistic community, most notably its theater and music scenes; the **Royal Exchange Theatre,** on St. Ann's Sq., regularly puts on Shakespeare and original works. (☎ 833 98 33. Box office open M-Sa 9:30am-7:30pm. M-Th and Sa tickets £7-23. Student discounts available.) Come nightfall, try the lively pub ◼**The Lass O'Gowrie,** 36 Charles St., for good food at even better prices. (Food served 9am-7pm. Open M-Sa 11am-11pm, Su 11:30am-10:30pm.) A sleek player in Manchester's trendsetting club scene is **Infinity,** on Peter St., which plays a hypnotizing mix of house and trance. (Dress smart. Cover M-Th £2-4, F-Sa £6-8. Open M-W 9am-2pm, Th-Sa 9pm-3am. Northeast of Princess St., the **Gay Village** rings merrily at night; drink at bars lining **Canal Street,** the in the village. **Manto's,** at #46, fills with all ages, genders, and orientations for the Sa night/Su morning "Breakfast Club." (Cover £6. Open daily 2-6am.)

Trains leave **Piccadilly Station,** on London Rd., and **Victoria Station,** on Victoria St., for: Birmingham (1¾hr., 2 per hr., £14.20); Chester (1hr., 1 per hr., £8.50); Edinburgh (4hr., 12 per day, £41.60-51.50); Liverpool (50min., 2 per hr., £6.95); London Euston (2½hr., 1 per hr., £84.50); York (40min., 2 per hr., £15.80). **Piccadilly Gardens**

BRITAIN

is home to about 50 bus stops; pick up a free route map at the TIC. National Express **buses** (☎ (08705) 80 80 80) go from Chorlton St. to Liverpool (50min.; 1 per hr.; £4, round-trip £6.50) and London (4-5hr.; 7 per day; £15, round-trip £24). The **Manchester Visitor Centre,** in the Town Hall Extension on Lloyd St., has helpful maps and books accommodations for £2.50. (☎ 234 31 57; info (0891) 71 55 33. Open M-Sa 10am-5:30pm, Su 11am-4pm.) Check **email** at **interc@fe,** Piccadilly Square on the 1st floor of Debenhams. (☎ 832 86 66. £1.50 per 30min. Open M and W-F 9:30am-5:30pm, Tu 10am-5:30pm, Sa 9am-5:30pm, Su 11am-4:30pm.) Take bus #33 from Piccadilly Gardens toward Wigan to reach the swanky **YHA Manchester,** Potato Wharf, Castle-field. (☎ 839 99 60; manchester@yha.org.uk. **Internet.** Lockers £1-2. Laundry £1.50. Reception 7am-11:30pm. Dorms £18, under 18 £13.10.) To get to the friendly **Wood-ies Backpackers Hostel,** 19 Blossom St., Ancoats, walk 5min. up Newton St. from Pic-cadilly Gardens and cross Great Ancoats St.; it's just past the Duke of Edinburgh pub. (☎ 228 34 56; backpackers@woodiesuk.freeserve.co.uk. Laundry. Dorms £12, £60 per week.) **Cornerhouse Café,** 70 Oxford St., is part of the trendy Cornerhouse Arts Centre. (☎ 228 76 21. Main dishes from £3.50. Open daily 11am-8:30pm; kitchen open noon-2:30pm and 5-7pm; bar open M-Sa noon-11pm, Su noon-10:30pm.) **On the 8th Day,** 107 Oxford Rd., serves up vegetarian and vegan fare for under £4. (☎ 273 1850. Open M-F 9am-7pm, Sa 10am-4:30pm.) **Tesco supermarket** is on Market St. (Open M-Sa 8am-8pm, Su 11am-5pm.) **Postal code:** M2 2AA.

CHESTER
☎ 01244

With fashionable shops in faux-medieval houses, tour guides in full Roman armor, a town crier in Georgian uniform, and a Barclays bank occupying a wing of the cathe-dral, Chester at times resembles an American theme-park collage of Ye Olde English Towne. Originally built by frontier-forging Romans, the crowded but lovely town now maintains a pace to match the races that circle its internationally cele-brated **Roodee** racetrack. The famous **city walls** completely encircle the town. Just outside Newgate lies the base of the largest Roman **amphitheater** in Britain. (Always open. Free.) Its lions, tigers, and playfully gladitorial orangutans have all relocated to the **Chester Zoo.** Take bus #8 or 8X from the bus exchange behind the town hall. (☎ 380280. Open 10am-5:30pm; Open until 7pm in high season. £10.) Fight your way through the throngs for a visit to the brilliant stained-glass windows and cloisters of the awe-inspiring **cathedral.** (Open 8am-6pm. Free tours May-Oct. Suggested dona-tion £3.) Pubs line **Lower Bridge Street** and **Watergate Street.**

Trains arrive from: Holyhead, Wales (1½hr., every hr., £16.70); London (2½hr., every 1-2 hr., £48.40); Manchester Piccadilly (1hr., every 1-2 hr., £8.80). Merseyrail arrives from Liverpool (1½hr., every 1-2hr., £3.20). National Express **buses** arrive on Delamere St. from London (5½hr., 5-6 per day, £16.50) and Manchester (1¼hr., 3 per day, £4.50). From Foregate St., enter the city walls onto Eastgate St. and turn right on Northgate St. to reach the **TIC,** in the Town Hall, Northgate St.; from the bus sta-tion, turn left on Upper Northgate St. and head through Northgate. (☎ 402111. Open May-Oct. M-Sa 9am-6pm, Su 10am-4pm; Nov.-Apr. M-Sa 9am-5:30pm.) **B&Bs** (from £15) cluster on **Hoole Road,** 5min. from the train station; turn right from the exit, climb the steps to Hoole Rd., and turn right over the railroad tracks. To get to the **YHA youth hostel,** Hough Green House, 40 Hough Green, take bus #7 or 16 for 2½km. (☎ 680056. **Internet.** Laundry. Reception 7am-10:30pm. Open mid-Jan. to mid-Dec. Dorms £14.50, under 18 £11.25) **Philpotts,** 2 Goss St., off Watergate St., stuffs great ingredients, such as tuna with sweet corn and Somerset brie, into baguettes for £1.60-2.30. (Open M-Sa 8am-2:30pm.)

LIVERPOOL
☎ 0151

On the banks of the Mersey, much of Liverpool's (pop. 520,000) history is rooted in its docks. A transformed Albert Dock studded with restaurants and museums, two enormous cathedrals, a dynamic arts scene, and wild nightlife, make Liverpool a great destination for travelers. Oh yeah—and the Beatles.

BRITAIN

TICKET TO RIDE. Trains (☎ (08457) 484950) connect Liverpool's Lime St. Station to: Birmingham (1¾hr., 2-5 per day, £18.50); Edinburgh (4 hr., every 2hr., £42); Glasgow (4½ hr., every hr., £39); London Euston (3hr., every hr., £48.40) and Manchester Piccadilly (1½hr., 2 per hr., £7.20). National Express **buses** (☎ (08705) 808080) depart from the Norton St. Coach Station for: London (4½hr., 5 per day, £16.50); Birmingham (2½hr., 5 per day, £7.50); Manchester (1hr., 1-2 per hr., £4.50). The Isle of Man Steam Packet Company (☎ (08705) 523523) runs **ferries** to the Isle of Man (2½ hr.; Apr.-Oct. 1-3 per day, less frequently in winter; foot passengers £26-29) and Dublin (4hr., Mar.-Oct.1 per day, £17-26).

HELP! The main **TIC**, in the Queen Square Centre in Queen Sq., sells the handy *Visitor Guide to Liverpool and Merseyside* (£1.50) and books beds for a 10% deposit. (☎ (0906) 680 6886, £0.25 per min. Open M and W-Sa 9am-5:30pm, Tu 10am-5:30pm, Su 10:30am-4:30pm.) **Phil Hughes** runs an excellent Beatles tour in an 8-seater bus. (☎ 236 9091. £11.50.) Check **email** for free at the **Central Library**, William Brown St., at rows upon rows of computer terminals. (☎ 233 5835. Open M-Sa 9am-5pm, Su noon-5pm.) **Postal code:** L1 1AA.

HARD DAY'S NIGHT. Cheap hotels are mostly on **Lord Nelson Street**, adjacent to the train station, and **Mount Pleasant**, one block from Brownlow Hill—it's best to check all establishments at the TIC first. **Embassie Youth Hostel**, 1 Falkner Sq., 15-20min. from the bus or train station at the end of Canning St., feels like a laid-back student's flat, with laundry, TV, pool table, kitchen, and all the toast and jam you can eat. (☎ 707 1089. Dorms £13.50.) The **YHA Liverpool**, 24 Tabley St., The Wapping, is in an ideal location. From the train station, follow the signs to Albert Dock, turn left on Strand St., and it's on the left. (☎ 709 8888; Laundry. Breakfast included. Dorms £18, under 18 £13.50.) **Selal Housing Group**, 1 Rodney St., just off Mt. Pleasant, is a former YWCA that accepts both men and women. (☎ 709 7791. £12.) **Belvedere Hotel**, 83 Mount Pleasant, is one of the few family-run guest houses in the city center. (☎ 709 2356. Breakfast included. £20.) For camping, go to **Abbey Farm**, Dark Ln., Ormskirk, on the northern rail line from Lime St. station. (☎ (01695) 572686. £5 per 1-person tent, £6.50 for 2-person tent. Electricity £1.50.)

STRAWBERRY FIELDS FOREVER. Trendy vegetarian cafes and reasonably-priced Indian restaurants line **Bold Street**, while cheap takeouts cluster on **Hardnon Street** and **Berry Street.** Self-caterers should try **St. John's Market**, sprawled across the top of St. John's shopping mall, for fresh produce and local color. **Tavern Co.**, Queen Sq., serves great Mexican food in wine-bar ambience. Hearty burritos and creative taco salads go for £5-7. (Open M-Sa noon-11pm, Su noon-10:30pm; food served M-Th and Su until 10pm, F-Sa until 11pm.) The book-lined walls of **The Beehive** pub, 7 Paradise St., offer an escape from the masses. (Open M-Sa 11am-11pm, Su noon-10:30pm; food served M-Sa 11am-11pm, Su noon-3pm. Light streams in through the windows of the two floors of **Hole in the Wall**, School Ln. The sweets and sandwiches are particularly scrumptious at £3-4.50. (Open daily noon-6pm.)

MAGICAL MYSTERY TOUR. At Albert Dock, **The Beatles Story** pays tribute to the group's work with John Lennon's white piano, a recreation of the Cavern Club, and, of course, a yellow submarine. (Open Apr.-Oct. daily 10am-6pm; Nov.-Mar. 10am-5pm; £7, students £5.) The TIC's **Beatles Map** (£2.50) leads through Beatles-themed sights, including Strawberry Fields and Penny Lane. The **Beatles Shop**, 31 Matthew St., is loaded with souvenirs and memorabilia. (Open M-Sa 9:30am-5:30pm, Su 11am-4pm.) Liverpool's heyday as a major port has passed, but the six floors of the **Merseyside Maritime Museum**, at Albert Dock, impressively recreate something of the slave trade and the Battle of Britain. (Open daily 10am-5pm. Free.) **Albert Dock**, at the western end of Hanover St., is a series of Victorian warehouses transformed into a complex of restaurants and museums; don't miss the impressive, though intimate, modern art collection at a branch of London's **Tate Gallery.** (Open Tu-Su 10am-6pm. Free; some special exhibits £3.) **The Museum of Liverpool**

BRITAIN

Life traces Liverpool's history of stormy labor struggles, race relations, and the city's sporting heritage. (Open daily 10am-5pm. Free.) Begun in 1904, the Anglican **Liverpool Cathedral** on Upper Duke St. boasts the highest Gothic arches ever built, the largest vault and organ, and the highest and heaviest bells in the world. Climb to the top of the 100m tower for a view stretching to North Wales. (Cathedral open daily 9am-6pm; tower open daily 11am-4pm. Suggested donation ₤2.50. Tower admission ₤2.) In contrast, the **Metropolitan Cathedral of Christ the King,** Mt. Pleasant, with gorgeous neon-blue stained glass, looks more like an inverted rocket launcher than a house of worship. (Open in summer M-F 8am-6pm, Sa-Su 8:30am-6pm; in winter M-F 8am-6pm, Sa 8:30am-6pm, Su 8:30am-5pm. Free.) If not here for the Beatles, tourists usually arrive for the football. **Liverpool** and **Everton football clubs**—intense rivals—both offer tours of their grounds (Anfield and Goodison Park respectively). Locals favor Everton; Liverpool's supporters tend to be from outside the city. (Bus #26 from the city center travels to both stadiums. Everton tour ₤5.50. Liverpool tour ₤8.50, book for both tours in advance).

▉▉ PLEASE PLEASE ME. Pubs teem in almost every street in Liverpool; **Slater Street** in particular brims with ₤1 pints. Try *Ink*, or the *Liverpool Echo* for up-to-date arts and nightlife info. John Lennon once said that the worst thing about being famous was "not being able to get a quiet pint at the Phil"; the rest of us can sip in solitude at **The Philharmonic,** 36 Hope St. (Draughts ₤1.70 and up. Open M-Sa noon-11pm, Su 12-10:30pm.) **The Jacaranda,** Slater St., site of the first paid Beatles gig, has live bands and a small dance floor. (Open M-Sa noon-2am, Su noon-10:30pm.) **The Caledonia Laundromatic Super Pub** is on corner of Catherine St. and Caledonia St. Half-launderette, half-pub, this funky multi-tasker *hasn't* been visited by the Beatles—boy did they miss out. (DJs nightly. Open M-Sa noon-11pm, Su noon-10:30pm.) **Baa Bar,** 43 Fleet St., is a far-from-sheepish gay-friendly bar with cappuccino during the day and cheap beer at night. (Open M-Sa 10am-2am.) ▉**Cream,** in Wolstonholme Sq. off Parr St., is Liverpool's world-renowned superclub. (Open Sa and last F of every month. Cover ₤11.) **The Cavern Club,** 10 Mathew St., is on the site where the Fab Four gained prominence; today it plays regular club music (M and F-Sa 9pm-2am; free before 10pm) and showcases live music. At the end of August, a **Beatles Convention** draws fans from around the world.

NORTHERN ENGLAND

Cradled between the Pennines rising to the west and the North Sea spreading to the east, the northeastern vistas span between calm coastal corners and rich national parkland; the isolation of the dales and villages bears testament to the region's primarily agricultural bent. Extensive path systems lace the gray and purple moors that captured the Brontës' imagination shimmer in iridescent splendor as do the emerald dales that figure so prominently in James Herriot's loving tales. Northeast England still has a rugged feel in its wilderness and sense of humor.

YORK ☎ 01904

More organized than the Roman with his long spear, more ruthless than the Viking with his broad sword, more thorough than the Norman with his strong bow, the Tourist vanquishes all with her zoom camera. Unlike those before her, she invades neither for wealth nor power. She comes for history: medieval thoroughfares, Georgian townhouses, and the largest Gothic cathedral in Britain.

▉ TRANSPORTATION

Trains: York Station, Station Rd. Ticket office open M-Sa 5:45am-10:15pm, Su 7:30am-10:10pm. Trains (☎(08457) 484950) from: **Edinburgh** (2-3hr., 2 per hr., £49); **London King's Cross** (2hr., 2 per hr., £61); **Manchester Piccadilly** (1½hr., 2 per hr., £16.10); **Newcastle** (1hr., 2 per hr., £14.60).

BRITAIN

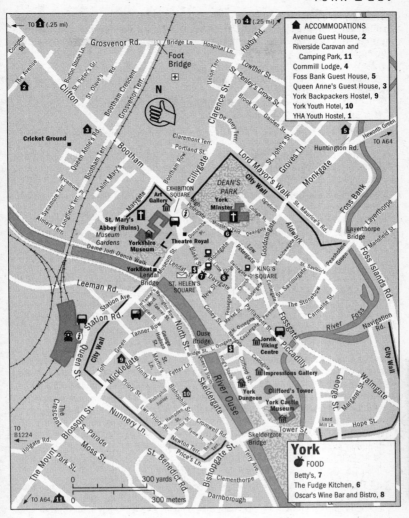

ACCOMMODATIONS
Avenue Guest House, **2**
Riverside Caravan and
Camping Park, **11**
Cornmill Lodge, **4**
Foss Bank Guest House, **5**
Queen Anne's Guest House, **3**
York Backpackers Hostel, **9**
York Youth Hotel, **10**
YHA Youth Hostel, **1**

York
FOOD
Betty's, **7**
The Fudge Kitchen, **6**
Oscar's Wine Bar and Bistro, **8**

Buses: (☎ 551400), **bus stations** at Rougier St., Exhibition Sq., the train station, and on Piccadilly. **National Express** (☎(08705) 808080) from: **Edinburgh** (5hr., 2 per day, £22); **London** (4½hr., 6 per day, £17); **Manchester** (3hr., 6 per day, £8).

Local Transportation: Call **First York** (☎622992, bus times 551400) for info. Ticket office open M-Sa 8:30am-4:30pm. **Yorkshire Coastliner** (☎(0113) 244 8976 or (01653) 692556) runs buses from the train station to Castle Howard (see p. 220).

Bike Rental: Bob Trotter, 13 Lord Mayor's Walk (☎622868). From £8 per day plus £50 deposit. Open M-Sa 9am-5:30pm, Su 10am-4pm.

ORIENTATION AND PRACTICAL INFORMATION

York's streets are generally winding, short, and rarely labeled, while the longer ones change names every block or so. Fortunately, most attractions lie within the city walls, so you can't get too lost, and the **Minster** (cathedral), visible from seemingly every point, provides an easy marker. The **River Ouse** (OOZE) cuts through the city, curving from west to south. The city center lies between the Ouse and the Minster; **Coney Street, Parliament Street,** and **Stonegate** are the main thoroughfares.

TIC: De Grey Rooms, Exhibition Sq. (☎621756). Books rooms for £3 plus a 10% deposit. The *York Visitor Guide* (£0.50) includes a detailed map. *Snickelways of York* (£5) is an offbeat self-tour guide. Open June-Oct. daily 9am-6pm; Nov.-May 9am-5pm. A **branch** is in the train station. Open June-Oct. M-Sa 9am-8pm, Su 9am-5pm; Nov.-May daily 9am-5pm. Stocks the *York Cycle Route Map.*

American Express: 6 Stonegate (☎670030). Open M-F 9am-5:30pm, Sa 9am-5pm; in summer currency exchange also open Su 10:30am-4:30pm.

Laundromat: Haxby Road Washeteria, 124 Haxby Rd. (☎623379). Open M-F 8am-6pm, Sa 8am-5:30pm, Su 8am-4:30pm. Last wash 2hr. before close.

Police: (☎631321), Fulford Rd.

Hospital: York District Hospital (☎631313), off Wigginton Rd. Take bus #1, 2, 3, or 18 from Exhibition Sq. and ask for the hospital stop.

Internet Access: The **Cafe of the Evil Eye,** 42 Stonegate (☎640002). £1 per hr.

Post Office: 22 Lendal (☎617285). **Bureau de change.** Open M-Tu 8:30am-5:30pm, W-Sa 9am-5:30pm. **Postal Code:** YO1 2DA.

☞ ACCOMMODATIONS

Competition for inexpensive B&Bs (from £18) is fierce during summer. The TICs can offer assistance. B&Bs are concentrated on the side streets along **Bootham** and **Clifton,** in the **Mount** area down Blossom St., and on **Bishopsthorpe Road,** due south of town. Book weeks ahead in summer, especially for hostels and campsites.

■ **Avenue Guest House,** 6 The Avenue (☎620575), off Clifton on a quiet, residential side street. Enthusiastic hosts provide immaculate rooms with soft beds. Some family rooms with baths. All rooms with TVs. Singles £15-17; doubles £28-32, with bath £30-40.

■ **York Backpackers Hostel,** 88-90 Micklegate (☎627720). Fun atmosphere in a stately, 18th-century urban mansion. Kitchen and laundry facilities. "Dungeon Bar" open 3 nights per week, long after the pubs close. Dorms £9-12; doubles £30.

YHA York (☎653147), Water End, Clifton. From Exhibition Sq., walk about 1km on Bootham and take a left at Water End. Excellent (but pricey) facilities. Reception open 7am-10:30pm. Bedroom lockout 10am-1pm. Open mid-Jan. to mid-Dec. Dorms £16, under 18 £12; singles £18.50; doubles £37; family rooms £52 or £78.

York Youth Hotel, 11-15 Bishophill Senior (☎625904). An excellent place to meet fellow travelers. Breakfast £2-3. Sheets £1. Laundry facilities. Key deposit £5. 24hr. reception. Bar open 9pm-1am. Dorms £9-11; singles £13-14; twins £24-33.

Foss Bank Guest House, 16 Huntington Rd. (☎635548). Walk or take bus #B5 or B6 from the train station. Comfortable beds and wooden desks in clean rooms. All rooms have showers and sinks. Some with bathtubs or TVs. Singles £17-19; doubles £37-44.

Queen Anne's Guest House, 24 Queen Anne's Rd. (☎629389), a short walk out Bootham from Exhibition Sq. Spotless single and double rooms with TVs; some doubles with baths. Large breakfasts fit for a queen. Singles from £16; doubles from £32.

Cornmill Lodge, 120 Haxby Rd. (☎620566). From Exhibition Sq. go up Gillygate to Clarence St. and then Haxby Rd. Purify body and soul in this vegetarian B&B; clean, convivial rooms with TV. Singles from £20; doubles from £40.

Camping: Riverside Caravan and Camping Park (☎705812), York Marine Services, Ferry Ln., Bishopthorpe, 3km south of York off the A64. Take bus #23 from the bus station and ask the driver to let you off at the campsite (every 30min., return £1.30). Pleasant riverside site. July-Aug. £8 for tent and 2 people; Sept.-June £7.

BRITAIN

⚫ FOOD

Expensive tea rooms, medium-range bistros, and cheap eateries rub elbows in York. Greengrocers peddle at **Newgate market** between Parliament St. and Shambles. (Open M-Sa 9am-5pm; Apr.-Dec. also Su 9am-4:30pm.) ◼**The Fudge Kitchen,** High Petergate, displays over 20 scrumptious flavors of homemade fudge sold by the slice for £2.50-3. (Open M-Sa 10am-5:30pm.) **Oscar's Wine Bar and Bistro,** 8 Little Stonegate, stuffs patrons with massive portions of hearty pub grub for £6-8. (Open daily 11am-11pm.) **Betty's,** 6-8 Saint Helen Sq., embodies the quintessential tea room experience, established in 1919 and serving the full range of teas, sweets, and main dishes for £3-8. (Open daily 9am-9pm.)

👁 🎵 SIGHTS AND ENTERTAINMENT

The best introduction to York is the 4km walk along its **medieval walls.** Beware of the tourist stampede, which slows only in the early morning and just before the walls and gates close at dusk. At the TIC, ask for the useful *York Visitors Guide,* and then hit the cobblestone streets. A free **walking tour** is offered daily by the **Association of Voluntary Guides** (☎630284) leaving from the York City Art Gallery, across from the TIC. Everyone and everything converges at the enormous ◼**York Minster,** built between 1220 and 1470. Half of all the medieval stained glass in England glitters here; the **Great East Window** depicts the beginning and end of the world in over 100 scenes. Climb 275 steps to the top of the **Central Tower** for a view over York's roof-tops. Evensong is a particularly magical introduction to the cathedral. (Cathedral open summer daily 7am-8:30pm; winter 7am-6pm. Evensong M-F 5pm, Sa-Su 4pm. Tours 9:30am-3:30pm. Tower open June-Sept. daily 9:30am-6:30pm; Mar. and Nov. 10am-4:30pm; Apr. and Oct. 10am-5:30pm; May 10am-6pm. £3.)

The ◼**York Castle Museum,** at the Eye of York, housed in a former debtor's prison, lives up to its billing as Britain's premier museum dedicated to everyday life. It contains **Kirkgate,** an intricately reconstructed Victorian shopping street complete with carriage, and **Half Moon Court,** its Edwardian counterpart. (Open Apr.-Oct. daily 9:30am-5pm; Nov.-Mar. 9:30am-4:30pm. £5.75, concessions £3.50.) The **Jorvik Museum Centre (the Viking Centre),** Coppergate, is one of the busiest places in York; visit early or late to avoid lines, or book at least 24hr. in advance. Visitors wander through the York of AD 948, with authentic artifacts and painfully accurate smells, to discover Norse truths. No, the Vikings did not wear horns. (☎643211. M-F 9am-5pm; Open Apr.-Oct. daily 9am-5:30pm; Nov.-Dec. 10am-4:30pm; Jan.-Mar. Su-F 9am-3:30pm, Sa 9am-4:30pm. £6.95, concessions £5.95.)

Hidden within the four gorgeous hectares of the **Museum Gardens,** the **Yorkshire Museum** presents Roman, Anglo-Saxon, and Viking artifacts, as well as the £2.5 million **Middleham Jewel** (c. 1450). In the museum gardens, peacocks strut among the haunting ruins of **St. Mary's Abbey,** once the most influential Benedictine monastery in northern England. Visit the basement of the museum to get the lowdown on abbey life. (Enter from Museum St. or Marygate. ☎551800. Open daily 10am-5pm. £3.95, concessions £2.95, families £11.50. Gardens, pigeons, and abbey ruins free.)

The weekly *What's On* and *Artscene* guides, available at the TIC, have listings on live music, theater, cinema, exhibitions, and more. In **King's Square** and on **Stonegate,** barbershop quartets share the pavement with jugglers, magicians, and politicians. There are more **pubs** in the center of York than there are gargoyles on the east wall of the Minster. York's dressy new club, **The Gallery,** 12 Clifford St., has two dance floors and six bars. (Cover varies. Open F-W 9:30pm-2am, Th 10pm-2am.) The excellent **Toff's,** 3-5 Toft Green, plays mainly house and dance music. (No running shoes. Cover £3.50. Open M-Sa 9pm-2am.) **Fibber's,** Stonebow House, the Stonebow, doesn't lie about the quality of live music playing nightly at 8pm.

BRITAIN

◥ DAYTRIP FROM YORK

◪ CASTLE HOWARD

24km northeast of York. Yorkshire Coastliner bus #842 runs half-day excursions to the castle (5 per day, return £4.50); your bus ticket gets you reduced admission. ☎(01653) 648333. Open mid-Mar. to Nov. daily 11am-4:30pm; gardens mid-Mar. to Nov. daily 10am-6:30pm. £7.50, concessions £6.75. Gardens only £4.50.

The breathtakingly baroque Castle Howard presides over 4 sq. km of stunning grounds that teem with gardens, fountains, lakes, and brazen roaming peacocks. The **long gallery** provides a dazzling and dwarfing promenade between enormous windows and shelves stuffed with books. Head to the **chapel** for the kaleidoscopic stained glass. Be sure to see the white and gold domed **Temple of the Four Winds**, with a hilltop perch that offers views of rolling hills, still waters, and lazy cows.

DURHAM CITY   ☎ 0191

Spiralling medieval streets, footbridges, and restricted vehicle access make clifftop Durham pedestrian-friendly. Durham's only claim to being a "city" is the magnificent **Durham Cathedral**, England's finest of the Norman era; it houses the tomb of the **Venerable Bede,** author of *The Ecclesiastical History of the English People.* The view from the **tower** easily compensates for the 325-step climb. (Cathedral open May-Sept. daily 7:30am-8pm; Oct.-Apr. 7:30am-6pm. Tower open mid-Apr. to Sept. 9:30am-4pm; Oct. to mid-Apr. M-Sa 10am-3pm. Suggested donation £2.50.) Across the cathedral green, **Durham Castle** was once a key defensive fortress. Wander along the **River Wear** for tranquil shade, ambling waters, and views of the cathedral and castle; or rent a rowboat from **Brown's Boathouse Centres,** on Elvet Bridge (£2.50 per hr.). Starting around 11pm, head to the intersection of **Crossgate** and **North Road**, just across Framwellgate Bridge, where pubs and clubs await with open doors. Other major town events include the **Durham Regatta** in the middle of June, and Britain's second-largest **beer festival** in early September.

    Trains (☎(08457) 484950) run to: London (3hr., every hr., £75); Newcastle (20min., 2 per hr., £5); York (1hr., 2 per hr., £20). **Buses** leave North Rd. for London, Edinburgh, and Newcastle. To reach the **TIC**, Market Pl., from the station, descend the hill on the paved Station Approach and take the left stairs down to the Millburngate Bridge roundabout; cross the bridge and turn right at the first intersection to reach Market Pl. (☎384 3720; fax 386 3015; tic@durhamtic.demon.co.uk. Open July-Aug. M-Sa 10am-5:30pm, Su 11am-4pm; June and Sept. M-Sa 10am-5:30pm; Oct.-May M-Sa 10am-5pm.) Cruise the **Internet** at **Reality-X Durham,** 1 Framwellgate Bridge. (☎384 5700. £3 per 30min. Open daily 10am-8pm.) A large supply of cheap **dormitory rooms** surround the cathedral. (☎374 3454. Open July-Sept. and around Easter and Christmas.) **University College** in Durham Castle has rooms (☎374 3863; singles £20.50), and **Mrs. Koltai** runs a comfy **B&B**, 10 Gilesgate (☎386 2026; singles £20). The **Indoor Market,** off Market Pl., features produce, butchers and bakers. (Open M-Sa 9am-5pm.) **Postal code:** DH1 3RE.

NEWCASTLE-UPON-TYNE   ☎ 0191

Hardworking Newcastle is legendary for its pub and club scene. While you can still see straight, explore the masterful **Tyne Bridge**, neighboring **Castle Keep**, the elegant **Cathedral Church of St. Nicholas**, the highly interactive **International Centre for Life**, and the avant-garde ◪**Laing Art Gallery.** (Castle open Apr.-Sept. Tu-Su 9:30am-5:30pm; Oct.-Mar. daily 9:30am-4:30pm. £1.50, concessions £0.50. Church open M-F 7am-6pm, Sa 8am-4pm, Su 7am-noon and 4-7pm. Free. Centre open daily 10am-6pm. £6.95, seniors and students £5.50, children £4.50, families £19.95. Gallery open M-Sa 10am-5pm, Su 2-5pm. Free.) At night, the rowdy area of **Bigg Market** features the highest concentration of pubs in England, while **Quayside** (KEY-side) is slightly more relaxed and attracts local students. To partake in the pub experience, try flashy **Chase**, 10-15 Sandhill, or beachy **Offshore 44**, 40 Sandhill. (Both open M-Sa

BRITAIN

11am-11pm and Su noon-6am). Revelers sway even before they've imbibed at **The Tuxedo Princess,** a boat/dance club under the Tyne Bridge. (Open M and W-Sa 7:30pm-2am.) Gays and lesbians flock to Waterloo St. to drink and dance at **Rockshots 2** (Open M-Sa 7pm-2am) and **The Powerhouse** (Open M and Th 10pm-2am, Tu-W 11pm-1am, F-Sa 10pm-3am.)

Trains (☎ (08457) 484950) leave for London (3hr., every hr., ₤75) and Edinburgh (1½hr.; M-Sa 23 per day, Su 9 per day; ₤33). National Express **buses** (☎ 08705 808080) leave Percy St. for London (6hr., 6 per day, round-trip ₤32) and Edinburgh (3hr., 3 per day, round-trip ₤21). The **TIC,** 132 Granger St., facing Grey's Monument, has essential maps. (☎ 277 8000. Open M-W and F-Sa 9:30am-5:30pm, Th 9:30am-7:30pm; June-Sept. also Su 10am-4pm.) To get to the lively **YHA youth hostel,** 107 Jesmond Rd., take the metro to "Jesmond," turn left on Jesmond Rd., and walk past the traffic lights (☎ 281 2570. Lockout 10am-5pm. Curfew 11pm, or ask for the code. Open Feb.-Dec. Dorms ₤10.85, under 18 ₤7.15.) The **University of Northumbria,** Coach Ln., offers centrally located dorm rooms. (☎ 227 4024. Breakfast included. Open late Mar. to mid-Apr. and June to mid-Sept. Singles ₤18.75; doubles ₤35.) **Don Vito's,** 82 Pilgrim St., stands out among the many Italian eateries. (☎ 232 8923. Open M-F 11:45am-2pm and 5-10pm, Sa 11:45am-10:30pm.) **Postal code:** NE1 7AB.

LAKE DISTRICT NATIONAL PARK

In the Lake District, quite possibly the most beautiful place in England, mountainsides plummet down to shores gently embraced by lapping waves, and water winds its way in every direction. The area's jagged peaks and windswept fells stand in desolate splendor, except in July and August, when outdoor enthusiasts outnumber water molecules. Use **Windermere, Ambleside, Grasmere,** and **Keswick** as bases from which to ascend into the hills—the farther west you go from the **A591** connecting these towns, the more countryside you'll have to yourself.

The **National Park Visitor Centre** is in **Brockhole,** halfway between Windermere and Ambleside. (☎ (015394) 46601. Open Easter-Oct. daily 10am-5pm; Oct.-Easter Sa-Su 10am-5pm.) **National Park Information Centres** book accommodations and dispense info on the camping-barn network. While **B&Bs** line every street in every town (₤15-20) and the region has the highest concentration of youth hostels in the world, lodgings do fill up in July and Aug.; book ahead.

◼ TRANSPORTATION. Two rail lines (☎ (08457) 484950) flank the park: the south-north **Preston-Lancaster-Carlisle** line skirts the park's eastern edge, while the **Barrow-Carlisle** line serves the western coast. On the former, **Oxenholme,** on the southeastern edge of the Lake District, and **Penrith,** to the northeast, are accessible from: Manchester Piccadilly Station (2hr., 5-7 per day, ₤12.70); Edinburgh (2½-3hr., 6 per day, ₤30.80); London Euston Station (4-5hr., 11-16 per day, ₤59.60). From Oxenholme, a short branch line covers the 16km to Windermere (20min., every hr., ₤3.50). National Express **buses** (☎ (08705) 808080) go directly to Windermere from London (7½hr., 1 per day, ₤26), and continue north through Ambleside and Grasmere to Keswick. **Stagecoach Cumberland buses** (☎ (01946) 63222) serve over 25 towns and villages within the district; pick up the essential *Lakeland Explorer* at any TIC. An **Explorer ticket** offers unlimited all-day travel on all area Stagecoach buses (₤6.50) or buy the highly recommended unlimited 4-day travel ticket (₤15). The Ambleside YHA Youth Hostel offers a convenient **minibus service** (☎ (015394) 323 04. ₤2.50) between hostels as well as free service from the Windermere train station to the Windermere and Ambleside hostels. Cyclists can get **bike rental** info at TICs; *Ordnance Survey Cycle Tours* (₤10) has route maps.

WINDERMERE AND BOWNESS. Windermere and sidekick **Bowness-on-Windermere** fill to the gills with vacationers in summer, when sailboats and waterskiers swarm over Lake Windermere. **Windermere Lake Cruises** runs the **Lake Information Centre** (☎ (015394) 43360), at the north end of Bowness Pier, which provides maps, rents rowboats and motorboats, and books lake cruises. From Easter to October, boats sail north to Waterhead Pier in Ambleside (30min., 2 per hr.,

BRITAIN

round-trip £5.70) and south to Lakeside (40min., every hr., round-trip £6). The

---

BEFORE THERE WERE POWERBARS... About the only thing more common in Lakeland than tourists and outdoor shops is the hiking essential known by locals as mint cake. Although there are multiple varieties of mint cake for sale, the original recipe dates back to 1913 when James Wilson of Kendal boiled down sugar, peppermint oil and a touch of salt in an open copper pan to create a delicious and nourishing energy food. Since then, Kendal Mint Cakes have accompanied backpackers to the top of Mt. Everest and deep into the Sahara Desert. Before setting out on your expedition to the nearby fells, be sure to bring along a few mint cakes (for an extra energy boost, try the chocolate-covered variety). Beware: at 95 grams of sugar per serving, you'd better save room in your rucksack for a toothbrush!

---

train station sends Lakeland Experience **buses** to Bowness (#599; 3 per hr., £1). The **TIC** is next door. (☎(015394) 46499. Open July-Aug. daily 9am-7:30pm; Easter-June and Sept.-Oct. 9am-6pm; Nov.-Easter 9am-5pm.) The local **National Park Information Centre**, on Glebe Rd., is beside Bowness Pier. (☎(015394) 42895. Open July-Aug. daily 9:30am-6pm; Apr.-June and Sept.-Oct. 9am-5:30pm; Nov.-Mar. F-Su 10am-4:30pm.) To get to the spacious **YHA youth hostel**, on High Cross, Bridge Ln., Troutbeck, 1½km north of Windermere off A591, take the Ambleside bus to Troutbeck Bridge and walk 1.25km uphill, or catch the YHA shuttle from the train station. (☎(015394) 43543. Bike rental. Open mid-Feb. to Oct. £11.) To reach the social **Lake District Backpackers Hostel**, on High St., look for the sign on the right as you descend the hill from the train station (2min.) or call for free pick-up. (☎(015394) 46374. Reception 9am-1pm and 5-9pm. £11) **Camp at Limefitt Park**, 7.25km north of the pier on A592, below the Kirkstone path. (☎(015394) 32300. £3 per person; 2 people with tent and car £12). **Postal Code:** LA23 1AA.

AMBLESIDE. About a couple kilometers north of Lake Windermere, Ambleside has adapted to the tourist influx without selling its soul. You can't go wrong **hiking** in any direction near Ambleside; however, hidden trail markings, steep slopes, and weather-sensitive visibility all necessitate a good map and compass. Excellent guided **walks** leave from National Park and TICs. The top of **Loughrigg**, 4km from Ambleside (5.75km circuit descent), provides a view of higher surrounding fells. For gentler, shorter hikes, *Ambleside Walks in the Countryside* (£0.30) lists three easy walks from the town center. Lakeslink **bus** #555 (☎(015394) 32231; every hr.) rolls into Kelsick Rd. from Windermere, Grasmere, and Keswick. The **TIC** is located at Central Buildings, Market Place (☎(015394) 31576. Open daily 9am-5:30pm.) To reach the **National Park Information Centre**, Waterside, walk south on Lake or Borrans Rd. from town to the pier. (☎(015394) 32729. Open daily Easter-Oct. 9:30am-6pm.) Bus #555 also stops in front of the superb ◨**Ambleside YHA Youth Hostel**, 1½km south of Ambleside and 5km north of Windermere, on the northern shore of Windermere Lake. (☎(015394) 32304; ambleside@yha.org.uk. Bike rental. Nov.-Feb. curfew midnight. £11.15.) **Postal Code:** LA22 9BU.

GRASMERE. The peace that Wordsworth enjoyed in the village of Grasmere is still apparent on quiet mornings. The 17th-century ◨**Dove Cottage**, 10min. from the center of town, was Wordsworth's home from 1799 to 1808, and remains almost exactly as he left it; next door is the outstanding **Wordsworth Museum**. (Both open mid-Feb. to mid-Jan. daily 9:30am-5pm. £5, students £4.20.) The **Wordsworth Walk** (9.75km) circumnavigates the two lakes of the Rothay River, passing his onetime residence Dove Cottage, Wordsworth's grave, and ◨**Rydal Mount**, where he lived until his death. (Open Mar.-Oct. daily 9:30am-5pm; Nov.-Feb. W-M 10am-4pm. £3.75, students £3.25.) **Bus** #555 stops in Grasmere every hour on its way south to Ambleside or north to Keswick; bus #599 between Boweness and Grasmere stops every 20min. The combined **TIC** and **National Park Information Centre** lies on Redbank Rd. (☎(015394) 35245. Open Easter-Oct. daily 9:30am-

5:30pm; Nov.-Easter F-Su 10am-4pm.) **Grasmere YHA** (☎(015394) 35316) is split into two buildings: **Butterlip How (YHA)** and **Thorney How (YHA).** To reach **Butterlip How,** on Easedale Rd., follow the road to Easedale and turn right down the signposted drive. (Open Apr.-Oct. daily; Nov.-Jan. F-Sa; Feb.-Mar Tu-Sa. £12.50.) To reach **Thorney How,** follow Easedale Rd. 0.75km out of town, turn right at the fork, and look for it down on the left. (Open Apr.-Sept. daily; mid-Feb. to Mar. and Oct.-Dec. Th-M. £10) Sarah Nelson's famed Grasmere Gingerbread, a staple since 1854, is a steal at £0.22 in **Church Cottage,** outside St. Oswald's Church. (Open Easter-Nov. M-Sa 9:15am-5:30pm, Su 12:30-5:30pm; Dec.-Easter M-Sa 9:15am-5pm, Su 12:30-5pm.) **Postal Code:** LA22

KESWICK. Between towering Skiddaw peak and the north edge of Lake Derwentwater, Keswick (KEZ-ick) rivals Windermere as the Lake District's tourist capital but surpasses it in charm. A popular day hike that starts from the town center visits the lake shore and two popular viewpoints nearby. Leave Keswick Market Place by Borrowdale Rd. and soon after turn right into Lake Road, which passes the boathouses and jetties by the lakeshore. A footpath continues on from the road that leads to **Friar's Crag** (praised by Ruskin, Wordsworth, and *Let's Go*), a rocky and wooded promontory with views down Derwentwater to the **Jaws of Borrowdale,** where the valley narrows between steep, tooth-like hills. After conquering the fells, retrace the path back to the boat landings, and take the path on the right just before the public toilets into **Cockshott Wood.** Continue on this path into **Castlehead Wood,** and then follow the rocky trail up to the top of **Castle Head.** To return to Keswick, continue through the woods and then follow the path to Springs Road. Follow the road to the end and turn left onto Ambleside road, which returns you to the marketplace. The **National Park Information Centre,** in Moot Hall, is behind the clock tower in Market Sq. (☎(017687) 72645. Open daily Aug. 9:30am-6pm; Sept.-July 9:30am-5:30pm.) From the TIC, bear left down Station Rd. and follow the signs to the stellar **Keswick YHA Youth Hostel.** (☎(017687) 72484. Kitchen. Curfew 11:30pm. Open mid-Feb. to late Dec. £11.) It's worth the 3.25km ride south on B5289 (bus #79; every hr.) to Seatoller to stay at the ▓**Derwentwater YHA Youth Hostel,** in Barrow House, Borrowdale, where you can relax by its waterfall. (☎(017687) 77246. Open Jan.-Oct. £11.) **Camp** at **Castlerigg Hall,** southeast of Keswick on A591. (☎(017687) 72437. Showers £0.50. Open Apr.-Nov. £2.70-3.20 per person, £1 per car.) **Postal Code:** CA12

WALES

Wales borders England, but if many of the 2.9 million Welsh people had their way, it would be floating oceans away. Since England solidified its control over the country with the murder of Prince Llywelyn ap Gruffydd in 1282, relations between the two have been marked by a powerful unease. Wales clings steadfastly to its Celtic heritage, continuing a centuries-old struggle for independence. Travelers come for sandy beaches, grassy cliffs, and dramatic mountains that typify the rich landscape of this corner of Britain, or to scan the numerous castles that dot the towns—remnants of centuries of warfare with England. Enjoy the unique landscapes and cultures, and avoid calling the Welsh "English" at all costs.

⛴ FERRIES TO IRELAND

Irish Ferries (☎(1890) 313131; www.irishferries.ie) run to **Dublin** from **Holyhead** (2hr., round-trip £28-60) and to **Rosslare** from **Pembroke** (4hr., round-trip £28-35). **Stena Line** (☎(08705) 707070; www.stenaline.co.uk), runs from **Holyhead** to **Dublin** (4hr., £18-20) and **Dún Laoghaire** (1-3½hr., UK£20-28). **Swansea Cork Ferries** (☎(01792) 456116) run from King's Dock, **Swansea** to **Cork** (10hr., £24-34).

BRITAIN

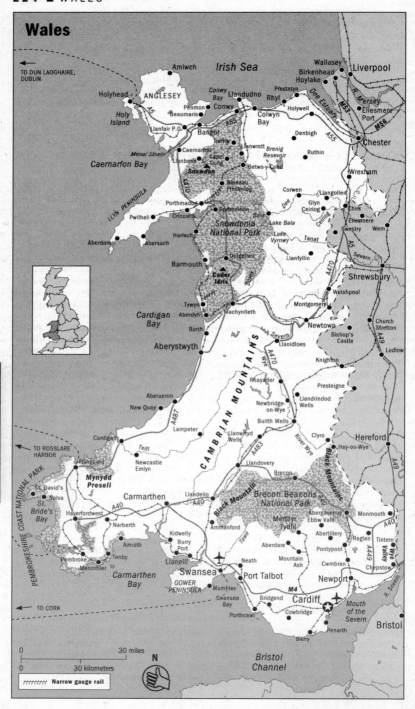

Wales

TO DUN LAOGHAIRE,
DUBLIN

Irish Sea

Amlwch

Holyhead
ANGLESEY
Holy
Island
Penmon
Beaumaris
Llanfair P.G.

Conwy
Bay
Llandudno
Conwy
Colwyn
Bay

Prestatyn
Rhyl
Holywell

Wallasey
Birkenhead
Hoylake

Liverpool
R. Mersey
Ellesmere
Port
M56

Chester

Denbigh
Ruthin

Wrexham

M53

Bangor
Trefriw
Llanrwst
Betws-y-Coed
Capel
Curig
Llanberis
Caernarfon
Menai Strait
Caernarfon Bay

Snowdon

Brenig
Resevoir

Corwen
Llangollen
Glyn
Ceiriog
Chirk
Ellesmere
Swestry
Wem

Blaenau
Ffestiniog

Porthmadog
Portmeirion
Criccieth
Bala
Lake Bala
Dee

LLYN PENINSULA
Pwllheli

*Snowdonia
National Park*

Lake
Vyrnwy

Llanfyllin

Tanat

A5

Aberdaron
Abersoch

Harlech

Barmouth

Dulgellau

*Cader
Idris*

Severn
Welshpool
Montgomery

Shrewsbury

Tywyn
Aberdyfi
Machynlleth

*Cardigan
Bay*

Borth

Newtown

Bishop's
Castle

Church
Stretton

Ludlow

A49

Aberystwyth

Severn
Llanidloes

Wye

Rhayader

Knighton

Presteigne

A470

Newbridge-
on-Wye

Llandrindod
Wells

Aberaeron

New Quay

Lampeter

Llanwrtyd
Wells

Builth Wells

Clyro
Hay-on-Wye

Hereford

A49

C A M B R I A N   M O U N T A I N S

A487
A483

River Wye

Cardigan

Teifi

Newcastle
Emlyn

Llandovery

Brecon

Black Mountains

Mynydd
Preseli

Fishguard

TO ROSSLARE
HARBOR

St. David's
Solva
St.
Bride's
Bay

Haverfordwest
Narberth

Carmarthen

Llandeilo
A40

Black Mountain

*Brecon Beacons
National Park*

Abergavenny
Monmouth
A40

PEMBROKESHIRE COAST NATIONAL PARK

Amroth

Kidwelly
Burry
Port

Ammanford

Merthyr
Tydfil
Ebbw Vale

Abertillery

Raglan
Tintern
Valley

Pembroke
Manorbier
Tenby

Llanelli

Aberdare
Mountain
Ash

Pontypool

Cwmbran

Chepstow

Neath
Tawe

TO CORK

*Carmarthen
Bay*

Swansea

Port Talbot

M4

Newport

Mumbles

*GOWER
PENINSULA*
*Swansea
Bay*

Bridgend

Cowbridge

Cardiff

R. Severn

*Mouth
of the
Severn*

Bristol

Porthcawl

Barry

Penarth

0   30 miles
0   30 kilometers

N

*Bristol
Channel*

//////// **Narrow gauge rail**

BRITAIN

CARDIFF (CAERDYDD)   ☎029

Formerly a sleepy provincial town, Cardiff (pop. 340,000) burst onto the scene in the late 19th century as the main shipping port of Welsh coal; at its height, it was the world's busiest seaport. Today, in Wales' buzzing capital, theaters and clubs mingle with remnants of its past. Climb the Norman keep of the flamboyant **Cardiff Castle** for a sweeping view of the city and tour its mock-medieval interior, where each room is decorated according to a different theme. (Open Mar.-Oct. daily 9:30am-6pm; Nov.-Feb. 9:30am-4:30pm. £5.25, children £4.20, family £14.75.) The **National Museum and Gallery of Wales,** in the Civic Centre across North Rd. from the castle, houses an impressive collection of Western European art and an audio-visual exhibit on the "Evolution of Wales." (☎2039 7951. Open Tu-Su 10am-5pm. Free.) Recently renovated from the elegant old Cardiff theater, **The Prince of Wales,** at the corner of St. Mary's St. and Wood St., is a sprawling pub that puts out a fantastic performance. Grab a pint (£1.29 and up) or try the mixed grill (£4.99). (☎2064 4449. Open M-Sa 11am-11pm, Su noon-10:30pm.) Cardiff's specialty, **Brains S.A.** (Special Ale), known by locals as "Brains Skull Attack," is proudly served in many local pubs. Head to the **Clwb Ifor Bach** (the Welsh Club), 11 Womanby St., for dancing and the local music scene. (Cover £2-8. Open M-Th until 2am, F-Sa until 3am.) The mighty **Zeus,** Greyfriars Rd., is a cavernous club where the party pulses until the wee hours. (☎2037 7014. Enforced smart-casual dress code. Cover £2.50-5, free before 10:30pm with flier. Open Tu-Th 9pm-2:30am, F-Sa 9pm-3:30am.)

Trains (☎(08457) 484950) stop in Cardiff from London's Paddington Station (2hr., 1 per hr., £37); Bath (1-1½hr., 3 per hr., £11.90); Edinburgh (7hr., 7 per day, £100.80). National Express **buses** (☎(0990) 808080) roll to Cardiff from London's Victoria Station (3½hr., 12 per day, £14) and Manchester (6hr., 11 per day, £25). Schedules for **local buses** are available at the Wood St. bus station. (Open M and F 8am-5:30pm, Tu-Th and Sa 8:30am-5:30pm. Fares £0.55-1.40.) The **TIC,** at 16 Wood St. across from the bus station, books B&Bs and stocks maps. (☎2022 7281. Open Jul.-Aug. M-Sa 9am-6pm, Su 10am-4pm; Sept.-June M-Sa 9am-5pm, Su 10am-4pm.) **Internet Exchange** is located at 8 Church St., by St. John's Church. (☎2023 6048. £2 per hr., 1hr. minimum. Open M-Sa 9am-9pm, Su 10am-7pm.) The best **B&Bs** are off Cathedral Rd. (take bus #32 or walk 15min. from the castle). To get to the colorful **Cardiff International Backpacker,** 98 Neville St., from the train station, go down Wood St., cross the river, turn right on Fitzham Embankment, and turn left at the end of the road onto Despenser St. (☎2034 5577; fax 2023 0404. Toast and tea included. Dorms £14; doubles £36; triples £42.) **Anned Lon,** 157-159 Cathedral Rd., has comfortably elegant interiors and all rooms have a color TV and sinks. (☎2022 3349. Singles £18-20; doubles £36-40.) For quick food and a wide variety of options, head to the Victorian **Central Market,** in the arcade between St. Mary St. and Trinity St. (Open M-Sa 8am-5pm.) ◨**Celtic Cauldron Wholefoods,** 47-49 Castle Arcade, serves traditional Welsh food, including rarebit and laverbread. (☎2038 7185. Meals £3.50-9.50. Open June-Aug. M-Sa 8:30am-9pm, Su 10am-4pm; Sept.-May M-Sa 8:30am-6pm, Su 11am-4pm.) **Postal code:** CF10 2SJ.

⚡ DAYTRIP FROM CARDIFF: CAERPHILLY CASTLE. Thirteen kilometers north of Cardiff, Caerphilly Castle floats above its moats and mossy grove. Begun in 1268 by Norman warlord Gilbert de Clare, its water systems, concentric stone walls, catapults, and pivoting drawbridges made it the most technologically advanced fortification of its time. Today its main tower leans a precarious 10 degrees from the vertical, presiding over the ducks and kingfishers that besiege the grounds. Take the **train** (20min., M-Sa 2 per hr., £2.50) or hourly buses #26, 71, or 72 from Central Station stand B3. (☎2088 3143. Open June-Sept. daily 9:30am-6pm; Apr.-May and Oct. 9:30am-5pm; Nov.-Mar. M-Sa 9:30am-4pm, Su 11am-4pm. £2.50, children £2, families £7.) Lying 6½km west of Cardiff, the open air **Museum of Welsh Life** is home to more than 40 authentic buildings from all corners of Wales, reassembled into an interactive telling of Welsh history. The ironworkers' cottages, old Victorian schoolhouse, mills, saddlery, and other sites

BRITAIN

arranged across the 41 green hectares of St. Fagan's Park are busily tended by traditionally garbed craftspeople. Quieter **St. Fagan's Castle** also marks the grounds with its gardens highlighted by a reflecting pool, and is haunted by Sarah, the Welsh-singing ghost who is said to wander the place. (☎ 2057 3500. Open June-Sept. daily 10am-5pm. Free.) The hourly **bus** #32 runs to the museum from Central Station stand B4.

WYE VALLEY

Stitching back and forth across the southern Welsh-English border, the Wye River has carved a valley sought out for its fertile tranquility; Wordsworth once came to the Wye Valley (Afon Gwy) to escape the "fever of the world." Today visitors hike, peddle, and paddle through lands unsullied by tourism. With legendary castles, abbeys, and trails tracing the Wye from its spring in central Wales to its confluence with the Severn near Chepstow, the valley merits inclusion in any itinerary.

▛ TRANSPORTATION. The valley is best entered from the south, at Chepstow. **Trains** chug to Chepstow from Cardiff and Newport (40min.; M-Sa 8 per day, Su 7 per day; £5.20) and Hereford (1hr., every hr., £11.70), the nearest station to Hay-on-Wye. National Express **buses** (☎ (08705) 808080) also drive from London (2¼hr., 10 per day, £16.50) and Cardiff (50min., 5 per day, £3.25). Be aware that bus service in the region is rare on Sundays. Pick up *Discover the Wye Valley on Foot and by Bus* in area TICs for schedules. Stagecoach Red and White local bus #69 loops between Chepstow, Tintern, and Monmouth (4-8 per day). One-day **Network Rider passes** (£4.50) and week-long **Primerider** passes (£16), available from Stagecoach drivers, will save frequent bus travelers money.

Hiking grants the most stunning vistas of the valley. The **Wye Valley Walk** treks north from Chepstow, passing Tintern Abbey, and the nesting peregrines on the way to Prestatyn. **Offa's Dyke Path** clears 285km of hiking and biking paths along the length of the Welsh-English border. All trails have walks of varying length and difficulty; consult the **Offa's Dyke Association** (☎ (01547) 528753) and the *Walking Wales* guide, free at TICs, for guidance.

CHEPSTOW AND TINTERN. Chepstow's strategic position at the mouth of the river and the base of the English border made it an important fortification and commerce center in Norman times. **Chepstow Castle,** Britain's oldest stone castle, grows seamlessly from the cliff it stands on and yields awesome views of the Wye River. (Open Apr.-May daily 9:30am-4pm; June-Sept. 9:30am-6pm; Oct.-Mar. M-Sa 9:30am-4pm, Su 11am-4pm. £3; students, seniors, and children £2; families £18.) **Trains** arrive on Station Rd.; **buses** stop in front of the Somerfield supermarket. Purchase tickets at **The Travel House,** 9 Moor St. (☎ (01291) 623031. Open M-Sa 9am-5:30pm.) The **TIC** is in the castle parking lot. (☎ (01291) 623772; www.chepstow.co.uk. Open Apr.-Sept. daily 10am-5:35pm; Oct.-Mar. 10am-4:30pm.) For lodging, take bus #69 to the **YHA Youth Hostel** near Tintern (see below) or be welcomed at **Lower Hardwick House,** 350m up Mt. Pleasant from the bus station. (☎ (01291) 622162. Singles £18; doubles £30-36; camping £5 per tent.) **Postal code:** NP16 5DA.

Eight kilometers north of Chepstow on A466, the haunting arches of ◪**Tintern Abbey** shade crowds of tourists in the summer and "connect the landscape with the quiet of the sky"—a phrase from Wordsworth's famous poem, written just a few kilometers away. (☎ (01219) 689251. Open June-Sept. daily 9:30am-6pm; Apr.-May and Oct. 9:30am-5pm; Nov.-Mar. M-Sa 9:30am-4pm, Su 11am-4pm. £2.50; students, seniors, and children £2; families £7.) Near the iron footbridge, marked footpaths lead to **Offa's Dyke** (45min.) and to **Devil's Pulpit** (1½hr.), from which Satan is said to have tempted the monks as they worked in the fields. A couple kilometers to the north on the A466, the **TIC** is housed in a train at the **Old Station.** (☎/fax (01291) 689566. Open Apr.-Oct. daily 10:30am-5:30pm.) The **YHA Youth Hostel,** 6½km northeast of Tintern across the English Border, occupies the 13th-century

St. Briavel's Castle castle. From the A466 or Offa's Dyke, follow signs for 3.25km from Bigsweir Bridge to St. Briavel's. (☎ (01594) 530272. Dorms £10.85, under 18 £7.40.) The **Wye Barn Bed and Breakfast** is 180m north of the abbey. (☎ (01291) 689456. Singles £22.50.) **Postal code:** NP6 6SB.

HEREFORD. Ideal for excursions into Wales, **Hereford, England** (pop. 60,000) also draws its own visitors with the 11th-century **cathedral** and the 13th-century **Mappa Mundi** within—a map of the world drawn on animal skin circa 1290. (Cathedral open Th-Tu until evensong at 6pm, W all day. Mappa Mundi shown May-Sept. M-Sa 10am-4:15pm, Su 11am-3:15pm; Oct.-Apr. M-Sa 11am-3:15pm. £4, students £3.50.) The **TIC**, 1 King St, in front of the cathedral, books beds for a 10% deposit. (☎ (01432) 268430. Open May-Sept. M-Sa 9am-5pm, Su 10am-4pm; Oct.-Apr. M-Sa 9am-5pm.) The T-junction at the end of **Bodenham Road** hosts many of the cheaper B&Bs in town (around £20 per night). Also try **Bourvrie House,** 26 Victoria St., a mere 5min. from downtown. (☎ 266265. TVs. Singles £20; doubles £18.50 per person; family room £23 per person.) **Postal code:** HR4 9HQ.

HAY-ON-WYE. If not for bookseller Richard Booth, Hay-on-Wye might still be just a pretty freckle on the scenic toes of the Black Mountains. Instead, Booth transformed it into the world-renowned Town of Books, where 40 secondhand and antiquarian bookstores attract browsers from all corners of the globe to the busy stone alleyways. The ode to books climaxes every summer in a literary festival where notables such as P.D. James and Toni Morrison give readings. The **TIC**, on Oxford Rd., books beds for £2. (☎ (01497) 820144; www.hay-on-wye.co.uk. Open Apr.-Oct. daily 10am-1pm and 2-5pm; Nov.-Mar. 11am-1pm and 2-4pm.) **The Bear,** Bear St., has cozy rooms and warm hospitality. (☎ (01497) 821302; fax 820506. Call ahead. Singles from £24.) **Postal code:** HR3 5AE.

BRECON BEACONS NATIONAL PARK

The *Parc Cenedlaethol Bannau Brycheiniog* encompasses 1344 dramatic square kilometers of barren peaks, well-watered forests, and windswept moors. The park is divided into four regions: the rugged country around the remote western **Black Mountain; Fforest Fawr,** containing the spectacular waterfalls of Ystradfellte; the eastern **Black Mountains** (different from Black Mountain); and the **Beacon** peaks, where King Arthur's mountain fortress is thought to have once stood.

⌁ TRANSPORTATION. The market towns on the fringe of the park, particularly **Brecon,** on its northern edge, make pleasant touring bases. **Trains** (☎ (08457) 484950) run from London's Paddington station to Abergavenny at the park's southeastern corner and to Merthyr Tydfil on the southern edge. National Express (☎ (08705) 808080) **bus** #509 runs once a day to Brecon, on the northern side of the park, from London and Cardiff. Stagecoach Red and White (☎ (01633) 266336) crosses the park en route to Brecon from: Cardiff via Merthyr Tydfil (#43 changing to #X4; 1½hr., M-Sa 5 per day, £5-7); Abergavenny (#20 and 21; 1hr., M-Sa 5 per day; or bus #29, Su 2 per day; £3-4.10); Hereford as well as Hay-on-Wye (#39, 45min., M-Sa 5 per day; Yeomans bus #40, Su 2 per day. £2.80-4.10).

BRECON (ADERHONDDU). Just north of the mountains, Brecon is the best hiking base. This quiet market town takes on a temporary vibrancy with an exceptional **jazz festival** during the second weekend in August, attracting such luminaries as Branford Marsalis and Keb' Mo'. **Buses** arrive at the **Bulwark,** the central square. The **TIC** is in the parking lot; walk through Bethel Square on Lion St. (☎ (01497) 623156. Open daily 10am-6pm; in winter 9:30am-5:30pm.) The **Brecon Beacons National Park Information Centre** is in the same building (☎ (01497) 623156). B&Bs tile **The Watton,** 3min. from the town center (£17-20). Only 2min. from the TIC lies **Bikes and Hikes,** the Struet, a hostel that offers not only what its name suggests but also comfortable rooms, a pool table, a lounge, a kitchen, and friendly hospitality.

(☎610071. £12.50. Call in advance.) Camp at **Brynich Caravan Park,** 2½km east of town on the A40, signposted from the A40-A470 roundabout. (☎(01874) 623325. Showers and laundry. Open Mar.-Oct. £6.50-£7.50, £4 per walk-in.)

THE WATERFALL DISTRICT. Forest rivers tumble through rapids, gorges, and spectacular falls near Ystradfellte, about 11km southwest of the Beacons. The **YHA Ystradfellte** is a perfect launching point. (☎(01639) 720301. Open Apr. to mid-Jul. and Sept.-Oct. F-Tu; mid-Jul. to Aug. daily. Dorms £8.10, under 18 £5.65.) 5min. away at **Porth-yr-Ogof** the River Mellte ducks into a cliff cave and re-emerges as an icy pool. Follow marked paths from Gwann Hepste and stand on the cliff face behind the **Sgwdyr Eira** waterfall. To the west near **Abercrave,** the **Dan-yr-Ogof Show-caves** impress with enormous stalagmites. From YHA Ystradfellte, 16km of trails pass **Fforest Fawr,** the headlands of the Waterfall District, on their way to the caves. (☎(01639) 730284, 24hr. information line 730801. Tours every 20min. Open Apr.-Oct. 10:30am-3pm, slightly later in summer. Tours £7.50, children £4, under 3 free.) **Stagecoach Red and White** bus #63 (1½hr.; M-Sa 3 per day, Su 4 per day; £3.66) pauses at the hostel, caves, and country park en route from Brecon.

THE BLACK MOUNTAINS. Located in the easternmost section of the park, the Black Mountains are a group of long, lofty ridges offering 130 sq. km of solitude, linked by unsurpassed ridge-walks. Invest in the Ordnance Survey Outdoor Leisure map 13 (£6.50). Begin forays from **Crickhowell,** or travel the eastern boundary along **Offa's Dyke Path,** which is dotted with a handful of impressive ruins, notably the Llanthony Priory. There is almost no public transportation along valley routes, but Stagecoach Red and White #39 does descend the north side of the Black Mountains. The **YHA Capel-y-ffin** (kap-EL-uh-fin), along Offa's Dyke Path, is 13km from Hay-on-Wye. Take Stagecoach Red and White bus #39 from Hereford to Brecon, stop before Hay, and walk uphill. (☎(01873) 890650. Lockout 10am-5pm. Open July-Sept. daily; Oct. F-Tu; Nov. and Mar.-June Sa-Su. Dorms £7.35, students £6.35.) **Camping** is allowed if hostel is full. (£3.67 per person.)

THE BRECON BEACONS. At the center of the park, these peaks lure hikers with pastoral slopes and barren peaks. Since many paths are not marked, Landranger Ordnance Survey maps 12 and 13 (£6.50 each) are essential to navigate the park. A 1hr. walk from the Mountain Centre past daredevil sheep and panoramic views ends at the scant remains of an **Iron-Age fort.** The most convenient route to the top of **Pen-y-Fan** (pen-uh-van; 886m) begins at **Storey Arms,** a large parking lot and bus stop 8km south of Libanus on the A470. Unfortunately, frequent use has led to erosion of this trail. A more pleasant hiking route starts in **Llanfaes,** Brecon's western suburb, and passes **Llyn Cwm Llwch** (HLIN koom hlooch), a 600m-deep glacial pool. Walk 5km from Llanfaes down Ffrwdgrech Rd. to the car park (take the middle fork after the first bridge) where the trail begins.

▶ **DAYTRIP FROM BRECON BEACONS NATIONAL PARK.** The **Big Pit Natonal Mining Museum,** amid the silent hillsides of Blaenavon, recalls the industrial age that shaped and transformed Wales. Ex-miners lead visitors down a 90m shaft to a 19th-century coal mine that operated until 1980, telling stories as grim as the mine itself. Dress warmly and wear sensible shoes. (☎(01495) 790311. Open Mar.-Nov. daily 9:30am-5pm. Last guided tour at 3:30pm. Free.) From Abergavenny, take **bus** #X4 to Bryn Mawr (13 per day, £3.32), then #30 to Blaenavon (1 every 2hr.).

ABERYSTWYTH ☎01970

Halfway down the sweeping Cardigan Bay coastline, the university town of Aberstwyth offers easy access to all of Wales and plenty of raucous pubs as you wait for your connection. The **National Library of Wales,** off Penglais Rd., houses the earliest surviving manuscript of *The Canterbury Tales* and almost every book written in Welsh pertaining to Wales. (Open M-F 9:30am-6pm, Sa 9:30am-5pm. Free.) Aberystwyth's beachfront and promenade remain as they were in Victorian times and can be viewed from the top of **Constitution Hill.** The ▨**Electric Cliff Railway** ascends the 131m at an angle usually reserved for rollercoasters; at the top, the *Camera Obsucra* allows you to spy on Aberyswythians. (☎617642. Open July-Aug. daily 10am-6pm; mid-Mar. to June and Sept.-Oct. 10am-5pm. Trains 6 per hr.; return ₤2.25, students and seniors ₤1.75, children ₤1, under 5 free, families ₤5.80-6.75. Camera obscura free.) With a spare half-day, don't miss the steam engine ride on the **Vale of Rheidol Railway,** which travels through the mountains, waterfalls, and gorges of the **Devil's Bridge** area. (☎625819. Call for schedule. Rides ₤11, Accompanied children ₤2.) The **train station,** on Alexandria Rd., is at the receiving end of the main rail line from England into central Wales. For destinations on the scenic Cambrian Coast to the north, ride to **Machynlleth** (30min., 4-7 per day, ₤4) for connections. National Express (☎(08705) 808080) **bus** #420 runs to London (7hr., 1 per day via Birmingham, ₤19.25). A single TrawsCambria bus #701 runs daily from Cardiff (4hr., 2 per day, ₤10.90). **Arriva Cymru** (☎(08706) 082608) covers buses in the region; call for schedules. The **TIC,** in Lisburne House on Terrace Rd., has information on B&Bs. (☎612125. Open July-Aug. daily 9am-6pm; Sept.-June M-Sa 10am-5pm.) **Mrs. E. V. Williams,** 28 Bridge St. (☎612550), offers large rooms with exceptionally comfortable beds. ₤15 per person. Eat and drink at **The Academy,** St. James Sq., a chapel converted into a lively student pub. (Open M-Sa 11am-11pm, Su 11am-10:30pm.) **Postal code:** SY23 1DE.

LLYN PENINSULA   ☎01766

The Llyn has been a hotbed of tourism since the Middle Ages, when crowds of religious pilgrims tramped through on their way to Bardsey Island, just off the wild western tip of the peninsula. Now eager apostles to the cult of the sun make the pilgrimage to the endless beaches that line the southern coast, putting their faith in the region's unusually good weather. **Porthmadog,** on the southeastern part of the peninsula, is the main gateway. This travel hub's principal attraction is the jolly puffing **Ffestiniog Railway,** which runs from Harbour Station on High St into the hills of Snowdonia (☎516000; mid-Feb. to Nov. 1hr., 2-10 per day, ₤13.80). **Portmeirion,** 3.25km east of Porthmadog, proves an eccentric landmark of Italy-fixation, with Mediterranean courtyards, pastel houses, palm trees, and exotic statues constituting an otherworldly diversion from the standard Welsh castles and cottages. (Open daily 9:30am. Shops close at 5:30, but it's possible to stay later. ₤5, students ₤4; reduced Nov.-Mar.) **Bus** #98 runs from Porthmadog to Minffordd, a scenic 2½km from Portmeirion. Minffordd is an easy and scenic 30min. walk from Portmeirion; just follow the signs. Minffordd is also a stop on the Cambrian Coaster **train** line (M-Sa 6-7 times per day), while other trains arrive through the adjacent Snowdonia National Park. A Cambrian Coaster Day Ranger (₤6.60) is a sound investment for a day's worth of train travel. The **TIC** is at the opposite end of High St. (☎512981. Open Easter-Oct. daily 10am-6pm; Nov.-Easter 9:30am-5pm.) Sleep comfortably in Lawrence of Arabia's first home at **Snowdon Backpackers,** 10min. from the train station down Church St., and take advantage of its lovely TV lounge. (☎515354. Apr.-Oct. ₤12.50 per person; Nov.-Mar. ₤11.50 per person.)

SNOWDONIA NATIONAL PARK

Rough and handsome, misty purple and mossy green, the highest mountains of England and Wales dominate horizons across the 2175 sheep-dotted sq. km from forested Machynlleth to sand-strewn Conwy. The Welsh call it *Eryri*, Place of Eagles, and Snowdonia's misty crags, lonely and barren at the peaks, are as dramatic and powerfully graceful as this most royal of Welsh symbols. Although these lands lie largely in private hands, endless public footpaths accommodate droves of visitors with untrammeled corners and quiet hikes. The **Snowdonia National Park Information Headquarters,** Penrhyndeudraeth, Gwynedd, Wales (☎(01766) 770274), stocks walk leaflets and Ordnance Survey Maps (₤5.25-6.50). They an best direct you to the nearest of the eight quality **YHAs** in the park and the region's other **TICs.** Check out www.gwynedd.gov.uk for information on bus schedules and tourist information for the region.

BRITAIN

▐ TRANSPORTATION

Trains (☎ (08457) 484950) stop at several large towns on the park's outskirts, including **Bangor** (see p. 231) and **Conwy** (see p. 231). The **Conwy Valley Line** runs through the park from **Llandudno** through **Betws-y-Coed** to **Blaenau Ffestiniog** (1hr., 2-7 per day, round-trip £14.20). Buses run to the interior from these towns and others near the edge of the park, such as **Caernarfon** (see p. 231). At Blaneau Ffestiniog the Conwy Valley Line connects with the narrow-gauge **Ffestiniog Railway** (☎ (01766) 516000), which runs through the mountains to Porthmadog, meeting the Cambrian Coaster to **Llanberis** and **Aberystwyth.** Consult the *Gwynedd Public Transport Maps and Timetables*, available in all regional TICs.

▐ HIKING

Mount Snowdon (*Yr Wyddfa*, "the burial place") is the highest peak in England and Wales, measuring 1085m, and the park's most popular destination. Six principal paths of varying difficulties wind their way up Snowdon; TICs and National Park Information Centres provide guides on these ascents. Experienced climbers go beyond Snowdon's tended paths, carting pick-axes and ropes to the **Ogwen Valley.** There, climbs to **Devil's Kitchen** *(Twll Du)*, the **Glyders** *(Glyder Fawr* and *Glyder Fach)*, and **Tryfan** all begin from **Llyn Ogwen.** Those attempting the climbs should pick up both the appropriate Ordnance Survey maps and the *Walk About Guides*, which give directions, map references, and severity ratings for the climbs.

Weather on Snowdonia's exposed mountains shifts quickly and unpredictably. No matter how beautiful the weather is below, it will be cold and wet in the high mountains. Arm yourself with wet-weather gear, gloves, a hat, and wool sweater. Peel off the layers on the descent. Pick up the Ordnance Survey Maps Landranger 115: *Snowdon and Surrounding Area* (scale 1:50,000; £5.25) and Outdoor Leisure 17: *Snowdonia, Snowdon, and Conwy Valley Areas* (scale 1:25,000; £6.50), as well as individual path guides. Maps are available at Park Information Centres and most bookstores. Contact **Mountaincall Snowdonia** (☎ (0891) 500449; £0.36-0.48 per min.) for the local forecast, ground conditions, or a three- to five-day forecast. Weather forecasts are also tacked outside Park Information Centres. Park rangers lead day-walks; ask at the Centres. Land in Snowdonia is privately owned—stick to public pathways or ask the owner's consent to hike through.

LLANBERIS ☎ 01286

One of the few small Welsh villages lively even on Sundays, lovely Llanberis owes its outdoorsy bustle to the popularity of Mt. Snowdon, whose ridges and peaks unfold just south of town. **Parc Padarn** holds a host of attractions, from hikes the lovely lake **Llyn Padarn** to tours of the **Welsh Slate Museum.** (☎ 870630. Open Easter-Oct. daily 10am-5pm; Nov.-Easter Su-F 10am-4pm. Free.) To view the plummeting **Ceunant Mawr,** an angled waterfall, follow the well-marked 1km footpath on Victoria Terr. by the Victoria Hotel. The long and gentle Llanberis path up Snowdon commences by the **Snowdon Mountain Railway,** which travels to the summit if you don't fancy a climb. (☎ 870223. £16.90 round-trip, children £11.90.) Catch **KMP** (☎ 870880) **bus #88** from **Caernarfon** (25min., 1-2 per hr., £1.60); or **Arriva** bus **#77** from **Bangor** (40min.; M-Sa 1 per hr., Su 8 per day; £1.55). The **TIC,** 41a High St., doles out tips on hikes and books accommodations. (☎ (01766) 870765. Open Easter-Oct. daily 10am-6pm; Nov.-Easter W and F-Su 11am-4pm.) Plenty of sheep keep hostelers company at the **YHA Llanberis.** (☎ 870280. Open Apr.-Aug. daily; Sept.-Oct. Tu-Sa.; Nov.-Mar. F-Sa. Dorms £10, under 18 £6.90.)

HARLECH ☎ 01766

This tiny coastal town just south of the Llyn Peninsula commands panoramic views of sea, sand, and Snowdonian summits. Its position on the Cambrian Coaster rail line makes it easily accessible. High above the rail, sea, and brown sugar sand dunes, **Harlech Castle** crowns a 60m-high rock and rides high on the chain of Edward I's impressive Welsh castles. (☎780552. Open Apr.-May and Oct. daily 9:30am-5pm; June-Sept. daily 9:30am-6pm; Nov.-Mar. M-Sa 9:30am-4pm, Su 11am-4pm. £3, students £2.) The TIC, Gwyddfor House, Stryd Fawr, doubles as a **Snowdonia National Park Information Centre.** (☎780658. Open Easter-June and Sept.-Oct. daily 10am-1pm and 2-6pm; July-Aug 10am-6pm.) Revel in spacious rooms and what may be the best view in Harlech at **Arundel,** Stryd Fawr. Walk past the TIC on Stryd Fawr and take a right before the Yr Ogof Bistro. Energetic Mrs. Stein (pronounced Steen) will come pick you up if the climb from the train station does not appeal. (☎780637. £15 per person.) **Yr Ogof Bistro,** left of the castle on Stryd Fawr, offers some of the best cuisine around. (Open daily 7-9:30pm.)

NORTHERN COAST

CAERNARFON   ☎01286

Majestic and fervently Welsh, the walled city of Caernarfon (car-NAR-von) sails on the shifting tides of the Menai Strait with the mountains in its wake and a world-famous castle at the helm. Built by Edward I beginning in 1283, the **Caernarfon Castle** was left unfinished when Eddie ran out of money and became distracted by unruly Scots. (☎677617. Open June-Sept. daily 9:30am-6pm; Apr.-May and Oct. daily 9:30am-5pm; Nov.-Mar. M-Sa 9:30am-4pm, Su 11am-4pm. £4.20, concessions £3.20.) Arriva Cymru (☎(08706) 082608) **bus** #5, 5a, 5b, or 5x arrives from Bangor (25min., M-Sa every 10-20min., Su 1 per hr., £1.55) and Conwy (1¼hr., 1-2 per hr., £2.85). TrawsCambria bus #701 arrives daily from Cardiff (7½hr.) and Holyhead (1½hr). National Express (☎(08705) 808080) bus #545 arrives daily from London via Chester (8hr., 1 per day, £21). The **TIC,** on Castle St., is opposite the castle gate. (☎672232. Open Apr.-Oct. daily 10am-6pm; Nov.-Mar. Th-Tu 9:30am-4:30pm.) Stay in comfortable bunks at **Totter's Hostel,** 2 High St. (☎672963. Dorms £11.) The **Floating Restaurant,** in the waters of Slate Quay, has views to port, starboard, and aft that complement good eats. (☎672896. Open Easter to mid-Sept. 10:30am-7:30pm.) Join the town and down a pint at **Anglesey Arms** on the Promenade below the castle. (Open M-Sa 11am-11pm, Su noon-10:30pm.)

BANGOR   ☎02148

This Victorian port and university town is a convenient locale for exploring the nearby Isle of Anglesey. The wildly opulent **Penrhyn Castle** stands testament to the staggering wealth accumulated by Welsh slate barons over a century ago. To get there, walk up High St. toward the pier, turn right on the A5122, and head 1½km north. (Open July-Aug. W-M grounds 10am-5:30pm, castle 11am-4:30pm; late Mar. to June and Sept.-Oct. W-M 11am-5pm, noon-4:30pm. Castle and grounds £6, grounds only £3.) **Trains** arrive on Holyhead Rd., at the end of Deiniol Rd., from Chester (1hr., 1-2 per hr., £11.90) and Holyhead (30min., 1-2 per hr., £5). **Buses** roll in on Garth Rd., down the hill from the town clock; Arriva Cymru arrives from Holyhead (#4; 1¼hr., M-Sa 2 per hr., round-trip £3.90). Arriva comes from Caernarfon (#5, 5a, 5b, 5c, and 5x; 25min., every 10min.-1hr., round-trip £2.35) and Conwy (#5 and 5X; 40min.; 1-2 per hr.; £2.35). TrawsCambria bus #701 follows the coast from Cardiff (7¾hr., 1 per day, £19.80). National Express arrives from London (8½hr., 1 per day, £21). The **TIC,** in the Town Hall, is on Deiniol Rd. opposite Theatre Gwynedd. (☎352786. Open Easter-Sept. daily 10am-1pm and 2-6pm; Oct.-Easter F-Sa 10am-1pm and 2-6pm.) To reach the **YHA Bangor,** in Tan-y-Bryn, 800m from the town center, follow High St. to the water and turn right at the end on A5122 (Beach Rd.), and turn right at the sign. (☎353516. Reception 7am-11pm. Open Jan.-Nov. Dorms £11, under 18 £7.50.) High St. has many fruit shops, cafes, and a **Kwik Save** supermarket. (Open M-Sa 8am-10pm, Su 10am-4pm.)

CONWY. The central attraction of this modern tourist mecca is the 13th-century **Conwy Castle,** built as yet another link in Edward I's chain of impressive North Wales fortresses. (Open June-Sept. daily 9:30am-6pm; Apr.-May and Oct. 9:30am-

BRITAIN

5pm; Nov.-Mar. M-Sa 9:30am-4pm, Su 11am-4pm. Tours £1. £3.60, students £2.60.) **Arriva Cymru** (☎(08706) 082608) buses #5 and 5X frequently arrive from Caernarfon and Bangor (£3). **National Express** buses (☎(08705) 808080) arrive from: Liverpool (2¾hr., 1 per day); Manchester (4hr., 1 per day, £10.75); Newcastle (10hr., 1 per day). Find bus timetables at the **TIC**, at the castle entrance. (☎592248. Open Easter-Oct. daily 9:30am-6pm; Nov.-Mar. Th-Sa 10am-4pm.) **Swan Cottage**, 18 Berry St., is one of the few B&Bs within the city walls, featuring cozy rooms with timber ceilings. The loft room charms with a view of the estuary. (☎596840. £16 per person.)

ISLE OF ANGLESEY

The isle's old name is *Mona mam Cymru* (Mona the mother of Wales), and attracts visitors to the pre-historic ruins and eerie Celtic burial mounds set in its flat landscape. **Bryn Celli Ddu** (bryn kay-HLEE thee), "The Mound in the Dark Grove," is a burial chamber dating from the late Neolithic period and the most famous of Anglesey's remains. Take Bangor-Holyhead bus #4 (M-Sa 9 per day) and walk 1½km from the staion, or walk there from Llanfair P.G.; ask at the TIC. Less pre-historic is ▓**Beaumaris Castle**, Beaumaris, the last of Edward I's Welsh fortresses and now a World Heritage Site. (☎810361. Open June-Sept. daily 9:30am-6pm; Apr.-May and Oct. 9:30am-5pm; Nov.-Mar. M-Sa 9:30am-4pm, Su 11am-4pm. £2.50, students £2.) Across the Britannia Bridge from Bangor sits the longest-named village in the world, **Llanfairpwllgwyngyllgogerychwyrndrobwllllantysiliogogogoch** (Llanfair P.G.), although there's little to see apart from the sign at the train station. Llanfair P.G. holds Anglesey's sole **TIC**. (☎(01248) 713177. Open Apr.-Oct. M-Sa 9:30am-5:30pm, Su 10am-5pm; Nov.-Mar. M-F 9:30am-1pm and 1:30-5pm, Su 10am-5pm.) **Ferries** run to Dublin, Ireland from Holyhead. Get to Holyhead via hourly **trains** (☎(08457) 484950) from: Bangor (30min., £5.05); Chester (1½hr., £16.15); London (4½-6hr., £57.30) Arriva Cymru **bus** #4 (☎(01248) 750444) travels from Bangor via Llanfair P.G. (1¼hr., 2 per hr., £3.90).

SCOTLAND

At its best, Scotland is a world apart, a defiantly distinct nation within the United Kingdom with a culture and view all its own. Exuberant Glasgow boasts a mind-bending nightlife, Aberdeen features grand, regal architecture, and Edinburgh is the festive epicenter of Scottish culture. A little over half the land size of England but with a tenth of its population, Scotland possesses open spaces and natural splendor its southern neighbor cannot rival. The heather-covered mountains and glassy lochs (narrow lakes) of the west coast and luminescent mists of the Hebrides demand worship; the farmlands to the south and the rolling river valleys of the east coast display a gentler beauty; and the frayed northwestern coast, cut by sea lochs and girded by islands, remains the most beautiful region in Scotland and one of the last stretches of true wilderness in Western Europe.

▐ TRANSPORTATION

National Express buses (☎(08705) 808080) connecting England with **Glasgow** and **Edinburgh** (10hr., 5 per day, £28) are much cheaper than **ScotRail trains** (☎(0141) 332 9811 or (08547) 484950; 5hr., round-trip £80-90). **British Airways** (☎(08457) 773 3377) sells a limited number of APEX return tickets from £70. **British Midland** (☎(08706) 070555) offers a Saver fare from **London** to **Glasgow** (from £70 round-trip). Reserve far, far ahead (at least 2 weeks) for the cheapest fare. Scotland is also linked by **ferry** to **Northern Ireland**. From **Stranraer**, **Stena Line** (☎(1233) 646826) ferries skim the water to **Belfast** (1¾-3¼hr., 10 per day, £29-31).

Frequent trains and buses run throughout the **Lowlands** (south of Stirling and north of the Borders). In the **Highlands,** trains snake slowly on a few restricted routes, bypassing almost the entire Northwest region. Bus service is reduced in the Northwest Highlands and it grinds to a standstill on Sundays. In general, **buses** are more frequent, more extensive, and always cheaper than trains. **Citylink** (☎ (08705) 505050) operates most intercity service buses. The **Freedom of Scotland Travelpass** (any 4 in 8 days £79; any 8 in 15 days £109) allows unlimited train travel and transportation on certain ferry lines. Purchase the pass at almost any train station or order through Rail Europe (see p. 55). **Hop-on, hop-off bus tours** are often a good way to reach more inaccessible areas: try **Haggis,** or **MacBackpackers** (p. 238).

EDINBURGH   ☎ 0131

Framed by rolling hills and the blue Firth of Forth, Edinburgh (ED-din-bur-ra; pop. 500,000) is the jewel of Scotland. The country's capital since the 12th century, seeds of Reformation were sown here in the 16th century when John Knox became the minister of the High Kirk of St. Giles. An outpouring of talent later made the city a capital of the Enlightenment; the philosopher David Hume presided over a republic of letters that fostered both Adam Smith's invisible hand and Sir Walter Scott's literary wanderings. Today, Edinburgh Castle watches over a litany of literary ghosts, exuberant festivals, and the omnipresent pint of dark ale.

▐ TRANSPORTATION

Flights: Edinburgh International Airport, 11.25km west of the city center (☎ 333 1000). **LRT's Airlink 100** (☎ 555 6363; £3.30) and the **Edinburgh Airbus Express** (☎ 556 2244; £3.60) shuttle to the airport (25min.); both depart from Waverley Bridge.

Trains: Waverley Station (☎ (0345) 484950), near the center of town between North and Waverley Bridges. To: **Glasgow** (1hr., 2 per hr., £7.30); **Aberdeen** (2½hr., every hr., £28); **London**'s King's Cross (5hr., every 30min., £80-90).

Buses: The **south side of St. Andrew Square** (☎ (08705) 505950), 3 blocks from the east end of Princes St., functions as the temporary **St. Andrew Square Bus Station** until early 2002. **Scottish Citylink** buses (☎ (0990) 505050) serve: **Aberdeen** (every hr., £14.50) **Glasgow** (4 per hr., £3); **Inverness** (every hr., £14). **National Express** goes to **London** twice daily (£28).

Public Transportation: Although your feet will suffice, and are often faster, Edinburgh does have an efficient, comprehensive bus system. **Lothian Regional Transport (LRT)** (☎ 555 6363), with a fleet of maroon double-deckers, provides the best service. Be sure to carry coins; drivers do not carry much change for the £0.80-1 fares. Buy 1-day **Day-Saver Ticket** (£2.40, children £1.50), and longer-term passes from any driver or from the main office, 1-4 Shrub Pl., on the Old Town side of Waverley Bridge.

Bike Rental: Edinburgh Rent-a-Bike, 29 Blackfriars St. (☎ 556 5560), off High St. Bikes £5-15 per day. City tours and Highland safaris also available. Open July-Sept. 9am-9pm; Oct.-June 10am-6pm.

Hitchhiking: *Let's Go* does not recommend hitching. Those who choose to hitch to Newcastle, York, or Durham often take bus #15, 26, or 43 to get to the Musselburgh and A1; to other points south, take bus #4 or 15 to Fairmilehead and A702 to Biggar. To points north, take bus #18 or 40 to Barnton and the Forth Rd. Bridge.

✴ ▐ ORIENTATION AND PRACTICAL INFORMATION

Edinburgh's short distances, quiet streets, and abundance of shops make it a glorious city for walking—just remember that because it is a city on a hill, you'll be hiking up as well as down. **Princes Street** is the main thoroughfare in **New Town,** the northern section of Edinburgh. **The Royal Mile** (Lawnmarket, High St., and Canongate) is the major road in the Old Town—the southern half of the city—and connects **Edinburgh Castle** and **Holyrood Palace. North Bridge, Waverley Bridge,** and **The Mound** connect the Old and New Towns. **Waverley** train station lies between North Bridge and Waverley Bridge, in what used to be a loch. The **St. Andrew Square** bus station, re-opening in early 2002, is three blocks from the east end of Princes St.

BRITAIN

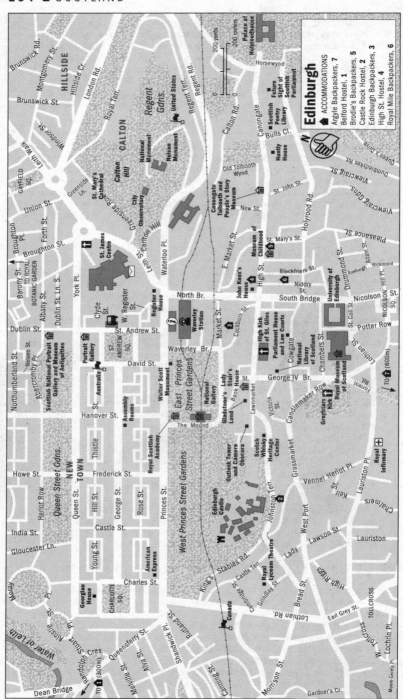

Edinburgh

↑ ACCOMMODATIONS
Argyle Backpackers, 7
Belford Hostel, 1
Brodie's Backpackers, 5
Castle Rock Hostel, 2
Edinburgh Backpackers, 3
High St. Hostel, 4
Royal Mile Backpackers, 6

Tourist Office: Edinburgh and Scotland Information Centre, Waverley Market, 3 Princes St. (☎473 3800), next to Waverley Station. Books rooms for a £3 fee with a 10% deposit. Sells bus, tour, and theater tickets. Open July-Aug. M-Sa 9am-8pm, Su 10am-8pm; May-June and Sept. closes at 7pm; Oct.-Apr. closes at 6pm.

Budget Travel Services: Radical Travel Centre, 60 High St. (☎557 9393), is geared toward backpackers, and can help get you the best rates on car rentals and other travel-related services. Open daily 8am-7pm. **Edinburgh Travel Centre,** in Potterow Union, Bristo Sq. (☎668 2221). Also at 92 South Clerk St. (☎667 9488). Both open M-W and F 9am-5:30pm, Th 10am-5:30pm, Sa 10am-1pm.

American Express: 139 Princes St. (☎718 2503), 5 long blocks west of Waverley Station. Mail held. Open M-F 9am-5:30pm, Sa 9am-4pm.

Gay and Lesbian Services: Gay and Lesbian Switchboard (☎556 4049). Pick up *Gay Information* at the TIC or *Gay Scotland* at bookstores.

Emergency: Dial 999; no coins required. **Police,** 5 Fettes Ave. (☎311 3131).

Crisis Lines: Rape Crisis Centre, (☎556 9437). Staffed M-W and F 7-9pm, Th 1-3pm, Sa 9:30-11am.

Hospital: Royal Infirmary of Edinburgh, 1 Lauriston Pl. (☎536 1000 or 536 4040 for emergencies). From The Mound, take bus #23 or 27.

Internet Access: easyEverything, 58 Rose St. (☎220 3577), is the undisputed champion of cheap Internet access. Rates fluctuate, but £1 can often get you as many as 3hr. of emailing. Open 24hr.

Post Office: Main office at 8-10 St. James Centre (☎556 9546). Address mail to be held: FirstName SURNAME, *Poste Restante,* GPO, 8-10 St. James Centre, Edinburgh **EH1 3SR,** Scotland, UK. Open M 9am-5:30pm, Tu-F 8:30am-5:30pm, Sa 8:30am-6pm.

ACCOMMODATIONS

Edinburgh is packed with backpacker hostels, but in Festival season (late July-early Sept.), there are few available rooms. Book ahead. The TIC has free hostel lists and finds rooms ($3 with 10% deposit). Most of Edinburgh's countless **B&Bs** are clustered in three areas: **Bruntsfield** to the southwest, **Newington** in the southeast, and **Leith** in the northeast.

Brodies Backpackers, 12 High St. (☎/fax 556 6770), at St. Mark's St. Friendly, relaxed, and delightfully cozy, but with only 57 beds; book ahead. Some bunk beds are named after characters from *Trainspotting,* Scottish Islands, and brands of Whisky. Reception open 7am-midnight. Dorms M-Th £11.90, F-Su £13.50. Prices higher in Aug.

Edinburgh Backpackers, 65 Cockburn St. (☎220 1717, reservations ☎221 0022.) From North Bridge, turn right onto High St. and right again onto Cockburn St. "Legendary" guided pub crawls Tu in summer. Pool table, ping-pong, TV, and **Internet access.** Reception 24hr. Check-out 10am. Dorms £12, £15 during Festival season.

Scotland's Top Hostels (www.scotlands-top-hostels.com). This chain has a triple presence in Edinburgh with the following three well located hostels. Reception open 24hr. For all, dorms are single-sex, *from* £10.50-13. £0.30 credit card surcharge.

Castle Rock Hostel, 15 Johnston Terr. (☎225 9666). Walking toward the castle on the Royal Mile, turn left onto Johnston Terr. Gigantic, with regal views of the castle. **Internet access.** Breakfast £1.60. Laundry service. Book ahead (*months* ahead for Aug.).

Royal Mile Backpackers, 105 High St. (☎557 6120). Walk down High St. from Cockburn St.; the hostel is directly opposite the red Telecom Centre. Fosters a great communal feeling due to its comfortable size. Laundry £2.50.

High St. Hostel, 8 Blackfriars St. (☎557 3984). Spacious accommodations and vibrant youthful energy. Pool table and TV. Continental breakfast £1.60.

Belford Hostel, 6-8 Douglas Gdns. (☎225 6209, reservations ☎221 0022). Take bus #2, 26, 31 or 36, 85, or 86 from Princes St. Get off at Haymarket Station, cross the road, and head back towards Princes St. Take the 2nd left onto Palmerston Pl., and go to the end. Dorms £11-13.50; doubles £37.50-42.50.

BRITAIN

Argyle Backpackers, 14 Argyle Pl. (☎667 9991), south of the Meadows and the Royal Mile. Take bus #40 or 41 from The Mound to Melville Dr. 2 cozy, renovated townhouses with a relaxing back patio. Some rooms with TV. Check-out 10:30am. Dorms £10; doubles £30. £5 more in Aug.

Camping: Edinburgh Caravans, Marine Dr. (☎312 6874), by the Forth. Take bus #28A from Frederick St. off Princes St. (£0.90). Toilets, electricity, showers, hot water, and laundry machines. Arrive before 8pm. Open Apr.-Oct. £4 per person, £1.50 per car.

▐ FOOD

You can get haggis cheap in many pubs. South Clerk St. and Lothian Rd. have plenty of shops offering reasonably priced Chinese or Indian takeout. For groceries, try **Sainsbury's Central** on South Saint David St., just north of the Scott monument. (Open M-Sa 7am-9pm, Su 9am-8pm.)

▓ The Basement, 10a-12a Broughton St (☎557 0097). The menu changes daily, with plenty of vegetarian options and Thai and Mexican specialties. A lively mix of students and musicians in its candle-lit, cavernous environment. Kitchen open daily noon-10pm.

The Black Medicine Coffee Co., 2 Nicolson St. (☎622 7209). Native American interior designs draw a sophisticated student crowd. Many sandwiches and smoothies (£1-3). Live music (mainly acoustic guitar) Th and Su afternoons. Open daily 8am-8pm.

The Last Drop, 72-74 Grassmarket. "Haggis, tatties, and neeps" (haggis, potatoes, and turnips) in omnivorous and veggie versions. The whole menu (save the steak) is £3 for students and hostelers until 7:30 pm. A packed pub at night. Open daily 10am-2am.

Ndebele, 57 Home St (☎221 1141). Named after a southern African tribe, it serves copious amounts of exotic grub for under £5. Daily African specials and a huge array of African and South American coffees and juices. Open daily 10am-10pm.

Kebab Mahal, 7 Nicolson Sq (☎667 5214). An Indian restaurant where chicken *tikka masala* is the specialty (£5.25) but the kebabs (£2.25-4.50) are tasty too. Open Su-Th noon-midnight, F-Sa noon-2am; closed F for lunch.

The City Cafe, 19 Blair St. (☎220 0125). Right off the Royal Mile, this Edinburgh institution serves venison burgers (£4-6) and incredible shakes, immortalized in the movie *Trainspotting.* Dance club downstairs. Open daily 11am-1am. Food served until 10pm.

▣ SIGHTS

With museums, gardens, and castles in abundance, Edinburgh is a marvel of sights. Experience the heritage of this Scottish capital city from the traditional to the contemporary on a tour from Edinburgh Castle to the new Scottish Parliament, with stops at the Royal Museum and Holyrood Park between.

THE OLD TOWN AND THE ROYAL MILE

The Royal Mile (Lawnmarket, High St., Canongate) defines the length of the Old Town. Defended by Edinburgh Castle at the top of the hill and the Palace of Holyroodhouse at the bottom, the Old Town once packed thousands of inhabitants into a few square kilometers—still visible in the narrow shop fronts and thirteen-story slum buildings—but today the street is more the domain of tourists.

▓ EDINBURGH CASTLE. Crowning the Royal Mile, the castle contains structures that were rebuilt in recent centuries. Inside, **St. Margaret's Chapel,** a 12th-century Norman church, is believed to be Edinburgh's oldest edifice. The castle displays the 15th-century Scottish Crown Jewels and the legendary **Stone of Scone.** *(The top of the Royal Mile. Open Apr.-Sept. daily 9:30am-6pm; Oct.-Mar. 9:30am-5pm. £7.)*

ALONG THE ROYAL MILE. Near the Castle, through Milne's Close, the new **Scottish Parliament** convenes in the temporary **Debating Chamber.** Watch the MPs debate. *(Sept.-June, W 2:30-5:30pm, Th 9:30am-12:30pm and 2:30-5:30pm. Free.)* You can also get reserved tickets (bookings ☎348 5411) in the nearby Visitor Centre, at the corner of the Royal Mile and the George IV Bridge. *(☎348 5000. Open Sept.-June M and F 10am-5pm, Tu-Th 9am-5pm; July-Aug. M-F 10am-5pm. Last admission 15min. before closing. Free.)*

BRITAIN

HAGGIS: WHAT'S IN THERE? Although restaurants throughout Scotland produce steamin' plates o' haggis for eager tourists, we at *Let's Go* believe all should know what's inside that strange-looking bundle before taking the plunge. An age-old recipe calls for the following ingredients: the large stomach bag of a sheep, the small (knight's hood) bag, the pluck (including lungs, liver, and heart), beef, suet, oatmeal, onions, pepper, and salt. Today's haggis is available conveniently canned and includes: lamb, lamb offal, oatmeal, wheat flour, beef, suet, onions, salt, spices, stock, and liquor (1%). Restaurants will probably serve it to you in non-traditional forms as well: unbagged (like a sloppy joe), vegetarian, and deep-fried in batter and 15cm of grease.

Nearby, **Lady Stair's House,** a 17th-century townhouse, contains the **Writer's Museum,** with memorabilia and manuscripts belonging to three of Scotland's greatest literary figures: Robert Burns, Sir Walter Scott, and Robert Louis Stevenson. *(Through the passage at 477 Lawnmarket St. Open M-Sa 10am-5pm; during Festival also Su 2-5pm. Free.)* The **High Kirk of St. Giles** (St. Giles Cathedral), Scotland's principal church, once stood at the center of the country's turbulent religious history. Here, John Knox delivered the fiery Presbyterian sermons that drove Mary, Queen of Scots, into exile. Now it offers free concerts year-round. *(Where Lawnmarket becomes High St., opposite Parliament. Open Easter to mid-Sept. M-F 9am-7pm, Sa 9am-5pm, Su 1-5pm; mid-Sept. to Easter M-Sa 9am-5pm, Su 1-5pm. Suggested donation £1.)* The 17th-century chapel **Canongate Kirk** is the resting place of Adam Smith; royals also worship here when in residence. Canongate, the steep hill at the end of the Mile, has **two museums** and an excellent **Scottish Poetry Library,** all of them free. *(Museums open M-Sa 10am-5pm; during Festival also Su 2-5pm. Library open M-F noon-6pm, Sa noon-4pm.)*

PALACE OF HOLYROODHOUSE. Once the home of Mary, Queen of Scots, this spectacular Stewart palace, which dates from the 16th and 17th centuries, is now Queen Elizabeth II's official residence in Scotland. Behind the palace lies the 12th-century abbey ransacked during the Reformation. *(At the eastern end of the Royal Mile. Open Apr.-Oct. daily 9:30am-5:15pm; Nov.-Mar. M-Sa 9:30am-3:45pm; closed during official residences in late May and late June to early July. £6.)*

OTHER SIGHTS IN THE OLD TOWN. On Chambers St., just south of the George IV Bridge, the new **Museum of Scotland** and the connected **Royal Museum** are not to be missed. The former houses a definitive collection of Scottish artifacts in a stunning contemporary building; the latter contains a varied mix of art and natural history, plus the new **Millenium Clock,** which chimes every hour. *(Open M and W-Sa 10am-5pm, Tu 10am-8pm, Su noon-5pm. Admission includes both museums; £3, students £1.50. Free Tu 4:30-8pm.)* Just across the street stands the statue of Greyfriar's loyal pooch, Bobby, marking the entrance to **Greyfriar's Kirk,** built in 1620 in a beautiful and supposedly haunted churchyard. *(Gaelic services Su 12:30pm, English 11am. Kirk open Easter-Oct. M-F 10:30am-4:30pm, Sa until 2:30pm. Free.)* Be sure to explore the nearby streets: **Candlemaker's Row, Victoria Street,** and the **Grassmarket,** where Edinburgh's criminals once hung from the gallows.

THE NEW TOWN

Edinburgh's New Town is a masterpiece of Georgian planning. James Craig, a 23-year-old architect, won the city planning contest in 1767 with the design you see today: the three main parallel streets (Queen, George, and Princes) form a rectangular, symmetrical gridiron linking two large squares (Charlotte and St. Andrew). The design was chosen to reflect the Scottish Enlightenment's belief in order. One compelling stop in the New Town the elegant **Georgian House,** a restored townhouse. *(7 Charlotte Sq. From Princes St., turn right on Charlotte St. and take your 2nd left. Open Apr.-Oct. M-Sa 10am-5pm, Su 2-5pm. £5, students £3.50.)* The **Walter Scott Monument** is a grotesque Gothic "steeple without a church" containing statues of Scott and his dog. Climb the 287-step staircase for an eagle's-eye view of Princes St. Gardens, the castle, and Old Town's Market St. *(On Princes St., between The Mound and Waverley Bridge. Open Apr.-Sept. M-Sa 9am-6pm; Oct.-Mar. M-Sa 9am-3pm. £2.50.)*

BRITAIN

THE NATIONAL GALLERIES. Today you can enlighten yourself by viewing the premier works of art in the elegant New Town buildings of the **National Galleries of Scotland.** There are four galleries, and all are free (sometimes a charge for special exhibits) and top-rate. A free shuttle bus runs between them every hour. *(All open M-Sa 10am-5pm, Su noon-5pm.)* The flagship of these four is the **National Gallery of Scotland,** on the Mound, which houses a superb collection of works by Renaissance, Romantic, and Impressionist masters and a fine spread of Scottish art. *(This gallery also open during Festival M-Sa 10am-6pm, Su 11am-6pm.)* The **Scottish National Portrait Gallery,** 1 Queen St., north of St. Andrew Sq, mounts the mugs of famous Scots. West of town, across the street from each other, lie the **Scottish National Gallery of Modern Art,** 75 Belford Rd., and the new **Dean Gallery,** 73 Belford Rd., specializing in Surrealist and Dadaist art, accessible by Bus #13 from Princes St. or a 15min. walk down Queensferry Rd., then Beford Rd. For information on Edinburgh's other (mostly free) museums, pick up the *Edinburgh Gallery Guide* at the TIC.

GARDENS AND PARKS. You're depriving yourself of quite an experience if you don't at least try to climb **Arthur's Seat,** the extinct volcano at the east end of the city and Edinburgh's sample of the Highlands. Along with the **Salisbury Crags,** it rises from the vast **Holyrood Park,** at the east end of the Royal Mile; a relatively easy 45min. walk up the mountain culminates with a stunning view of the city. For more great views, try the even easier **Calton Hill,** just past the east end of Princes St., which also boasts the towering **Nelson Monument** and an ersatz Parthenon. A little more manicured are the lovely **Royal Botanic Gardens,** north of the city center. Keep walking north along Hanover St. from Princes St. or take buses #23 or 27. *(☎552 71 71. Open daily Apr.-Aug. 9:30am-7pm; Mar. and Sept. until 6pm; Feb. and Oct. until 5pm; Nov.-Jan. until 4pm. Free.)*

🎭🎟 ENTERTAINMENT AND NIGHTLIFE

The summer season overflows with music in the gardens and a multitude of theater and film events around town. For details on pubs and clubs, pick up *The List* (£1.95). Perhaps the most omnipresent form of tourist entertainment are the countless **walking tours** available around the city. The most worthwhile is the McEwan's Edinburgh Literary Pub Tour (☎226 6665), a 2hr. alcohol-friendly crash course in Scottish literature, led by professional actors. (£7, children and students £5.) If you're not epileptic, squeamish, prone to motion sickness, or possibly pregnant, consider a one-on-one encounter with the MacKenzie Poltergeist of Greyfriar's Cemetery on the **City of the Dead Tour**.

HIKING. If you have limited time in Scotland, there is a thriving industry of backpacker tour companies eager to whisk you away into the Highlands. The two main companies, **MacBackpackers,** 105 High St. (☎558 9900; www.macbackpackers.com. Day trips £15, 3 to 7 day tours £39-129, Jump on-Jump off £55), and **HAGGIS,** 60 High St. (☎557 9393; www.radicaltravel.com. Day trips £19, 3 to 6 day tours £79-139, Flexitour from £85), both offer a number of tours of the Highlands that depart from Edinburgh. Especially good are their hop-on, hop-off tours which let you travel Scotland at your own pace, but with the convenience of their transportation and company. An alternative is **Celtic Connection,** which covers both Scotland and Ireland in a variety of 3 to 7 day tours, with one-way, round-trip, or hop-on, hop-off options. Book ahead. Prices do not include lodging. (☎225 3330; www.thecelticconnection.co.uk. Tours £85-149.)

THEATER, MUSIC AND FILM. The **Festival Theatre,** 13-29 Nicholson St., stages ballet and opera, while the affiliated **King's Theatre,** 2 Leven St., promotes serious and comedic fare, musicals, and opera. Same-day seats (£5.50) for the Festival Theatre go on sale daily at 10am. (☎529 6000. Box office open daily 11am-6pm.) Scottish bands and country dancing abound at the **Ross Open-Air Theatre.** (☎228 8616. From 7pm.) The **Filmhouse,** 88 Lothian Rd., offers quality cinema—European, art house, and Hollywood. (☎228 2688. Tickets £1.20-5.20.)

FESTIVALS. For a few weeks in August, Edinburgh hosts the spectacular ◀**Edinburgh International Festival** (Aug 11 - Aug 31 in 2002), featuring a kaleidoscopic program of music, drama, dance, and art. Tickets ($5-50) are sold beginning in April, but you can usually get tickets at the door; look for half-price tickets after 1pm on performance days. For tickets and a schedule, contact **The HUB,** Edinburgh's Festival Centre, Castlehill, Edinburgh EH1 2NE. It's the church-like structure just downhill from the Castle. (Info ☎ 473 2001; www.edinburghfestivals.co.uk). Around the festival has grown a more spontaneous ◀**Festival Fringe** (Aug. 4-26 in 2002), which now includes over 500 amateur and professional companies presenting theater, comedy, children's shows, folk and classical music, poetry, dance, and opera events that budget travelers may find more suitable for their wallets (usually free-$5). Contact the **Fringe Festival Office,** 180 High St., Edinburgh EH1 1QS. (☎ 226 5257, bookings ☎ 226 5138; www.edfringe.com. Box office open July M-F 10am-6pm; daily in Aug.) Another August festival is the **Military Tattoo**—a spectacle of military bands, bagpipes, and drums—considered by some to be the highlight of the month. For tickets ($9-21), contact the **Tattoo Ticket Sale Office,** 33-34 Market St. (☎ 225 1188; fax 225 8627. Open M-F 10am-4:30pm or until the show. Shows M-Sa night.) And finally, don't forget the excellent **International Film Festival** (Aug. in at The Filmhouse; ☎ 228 4051; tickets on sale at end of July) and **International Jazz and Blues Festival** (late-July to early-Aug.; ☎ 467 5200, tickets $5-30 go on sale in May).

NIGHTLIFE. If you can't find a pub in Edinburgh, you're not looking hard enough. Edinburgh claims to have the highest density of pubs anywhere in Europe, and we don't doubt it. Any news agent can provide you with an indispensable guide to the hippest of these pubs and clubs: *The List* ($1.95) is life. Pubs directly on the **Royal Mile** usually attract an older crowd, while students tend to loiter in the **Old Town** pubs clustered around the university. ◀**The Tron,** 9 Hunter Sq., off the High St. is smashingly popular with smashingly drunk youths, who benefit from its many student/hostelee deals. There's frequent live music on its three hopping floors. (☎ 226 0931. Open daily 11:30am-1am.) Just across the street is **The City Cafe,** 19 Blair St., with its smoky bar and pool tables upstairs and dance club below. More of the young and tightly-clad frequent **The Three Sisters,** 139 Cowgate, a packed indoors/outdoors pub and meat market. (Open daily 9am-1am.) ◀**The Globe,** 3a Merchant Street, across from Greyfriar's Cemetery, deservedly bills itself as Edinburgh's true backpacker destination. If you're feeling particularly adventurous, absinthe shots direct from the Czech Republic are only $4. (Open M-Sa 11am-11pm, Su 12:30-11pm.) The new **Espionage Bar and Club Complex,** Victoria St., has five floors of trendy partying in exotic settings. (No cover. Open daily 5pm-3am, until 4am on weekends.) If it's 1am and you're still not ready to stop pounding back rounds, make **Subway** on Cowgate your next destination. (Su-Th drinks are only a quid. Open 7pm-3am.) The Broughton St. area of the New Town (better known as the **Broughton Triangle**) is the center of the lesbian, gay, and bisexual community of Edinburgh. **C.C. Bloom's,** 23-24 Greenside Pl. on Leith St., is a super-friendly, super-fun gay club with no cover. (Open daily 6pm-3am; until 5am during the Festival.) **Planet Out,** 6 Baxter's Pl., is a mellow gay bar with fluffy couches; ideal to prepare for a wild, unsavory night on the town. (Open M-F 4pm-1am and S-Su 2pm-1am.)

◢ DAYTRIP FROM EDINBURGH

ST. ANDREWS

Stagecoach Express Fife buses (☎ 474238) pull in from Edinburgh (bus #X59 or X60; 2hr.; 2 per hr. until 6:45pm, fewer on Su; £5.70, students £3.60) and Glasgow (#X24, change at Glenrothes to #X59; 2½hr.; M-Sa Every hr., fewer on Su; £5.50). Trains (☎ (0345) 550033) from Edinburgh stop 11km away at Leuchars (1hr., every hr., £8.10), where buses #93, 94, 95, and 96 (£1.45) depart for St. Andrews.

The "tyrannising game" of golf overruns the small city of St. Andrews; the rules of the sport were formally established here. The **Old Course,** a frequent site of the Brit-

BRITAIN

ish Open, is a golf pilgrim's Canterbury. (☎(01334) 466666 for reservations; or enter the on-the-spot lottery for starting times. £80 per round.) The **Balgove Course** is a much cheaper alternative, offering nine holes for £7. If you're more interested in watching than playing, the **British Golf Museum,** next to the Old Course, details the ancient origins of golf. (Open Easter-Oct. daily 9:30am-5:30pm; Nov.-Easter Th-M 11am-3pm. £3.75, students £2.75.) Despite the onslaught of pastel and polyester, one need not worship the wedge to love this city; its medieval streets and castle ruins transcend even golf. Though today it's only a shell, in the Middle Ages pilgrims journeyed to **St. Andrews Cathedral** to pray at the Saint's Shrine. Nearby, **St. Andrews Castle** maintains secret tunnels, bottle-shaped dungeons, and high stone walls to keep rebellious heretics in or out. (Cathedral and castle open Apr.-Sept. daily 9:30am-6:30pm; Oct.-Mar. 9:30am-4:30pm. Joint ticket £3.75.) Scotland's oldest university, **St. Andrews,** founded in the 15th century, lies west of the castle, between North St. and The Scores; ▧Prince William is a currently a student.

To get to the **TIC,** 70 Market St., from the bus station, turn right on City Rd. and take the first left. (☎(01334) 472021. Open July-Aug. M-Sa 9:30am-7pm, Su 11am-6pm; May-June and Sept. M-Sa 9:30am-6pm, Su 11am-5pm; Apr. daily 9:30am-5pm; Oct.-Mar. M-Sa 9:30am-5pm.) Just across the street, hop on the **Internet** at **Costa Coffee,** 83 Market St. (£1.50 per 15min., students £0.75. Open M-Sa 8am-8pm, Su 10am-8pm.) The TIC has **B&B** lists (many B&Bs line **Murray Pl.** and **Murray Park** near the bus station). **Brownlees,** 7 Murray Pl., offers elegant housing only a few blocks from the Old Course. (☎(01334) 473868. £18-25 per person.)

GLASGOW ☎0141

Although it has traditionally suffered a reputation for industrial lackluster, Scotland's largest city, Glasgow (pop. 675,000), thrives with a renewed energy. Today's Glasgow is an architectural wonder, from the stately Victorian beauty of the City Chambers in George Square, to the dazzling curves of its brand new £100 million Science Centre. The millions of pounds the city has poured into the arts are reflected in its free museums, extensive galleries, and first-rate theaters; the West End oozes with trendy, vibrant creativity. While it rivals Edinburgh, its sister to the east, in cultural attractions, Glasgow also remains much less touristy, infused with a flourishing economy, a passion for football, and the energy of spirited locals.

▣ TRANSPORTATION

Flights: Glasgow Airport (☎887 1111), 15km west in Abbotsinch. Citylink buses connect to **Buchanan Station** (20min., 2 per hr., £3).

Trains: 2 main stations. **Central Station,** on Gordon St. U: St. Enoch. To: **London-King's Cross** (5-6hr., 5-20 per day, £50) and **Stranraer** (2½hr., 3-8 per day, £15.30). **Queen St. Station,** on George Sq. U: Buchanan St. To: **Aberdeen** (2½hr., 11-24 per day, £36.40); **Edinburgh** (50min., 2 per hr., £7.30); **Inverness** (3¼hr., 5 per day, £29.90). Bus #398 runs between the 2 stations (4 per hr., £0.50).

Buses: Buchanan Station (☎(0870) 608 2608), on North Hanover St., 2 blocks north of the Queen St. Station. **Scottish Citylink** (☎(08705) 505050) to: **Aberdeen** (4hr., 1 per hr., £14.50); **Edinburgh** (1hr., 2-4 per hr., £3); **Inverness** (3½-4½hr., 1 per hr., £12.80); **Oban** (3hr., 2-3 per day, £10.70). **National Express** (☎(08705) 80 80 80) buses arrive daily from **London** (8hr.; 1 per hr.; £22, round-trip £31).

Public Transportation: The circular **Underground (U)** subway line, a.k.a. the "Clockwork Orange" runs M-Sa 6:30am-10:45pm, Su 11am-6pm. Single fare £0.80. Wave to stop **buses,** and carry exact change. Single fare £0.45-0.95.

✳▣ ORIENTATION AND PRACTICAL INFORMATION

George Square is the physical center of town. Sections of **Sauchiehall Street, Argyle Street,** and **Buchanan Street** are pedestrian areas. **Charing Cross,** in the northwest, where Bath St. crosses M8, is used as a reference landmark. The vibrant **West End**

BRITAIN

BRITAIN

Glasgow

ACCOMMODATIONS
Alamo Guest House, 7
Glasgow Backpackers, 4
Bunkum Backpackers, 2
McLay's Guest House, 9
Seton Guest House, 15
SYHA Glasgow, 5

MUSIC AND CLUBS
Archaos, 12
Sub Club, 13

FOOD
Bay Tree Vegetarian Cafe, 1
Grosvenor Cafe, 8
Insomnia Cafe, 6
Willow Tea Rooms, 10

PUBS
Babbity Bowster, 14
Horseshoe Bar, 11
Uisge Beatha, 3

500 yards
500 meters
N

TO NECROPOLIS (100 yd)
St. Mungo Museum
Provand's Lordship (100 yd)
Royal Infirmary
Glasgow Cathedral
CATHEDRAL SQ.
John Knox St.
Castle St.
Duke St.
High St. Station
TO PEOPLE'S PALACE
Gallowgate

Broomhill Park
Pinkston Rd.
Baird St.
Lister St.
St. James's Rd.
N. Wallace St.
Kyle St.
Cathedral St.
St. Mungo Ave.
North Hanover St.
Taylor St.
George St.
Strathclyde University
Campus Village
High St.
Blackfriars St.
Albion St.
Tontine
Tron Steeple, Tron Theatre
Osborne St.
Bridgegate

Dobbie's Loan
Buchanan Bus Station
Killermont St.
Royal Concert Hall
Queen St. Station
City Chambers
GEORGE SQ.
Stirling's Library
Gallery of Modern Art
Ingram St.
Wilson St.
Hutcheson St.
Glassford St.
Stockwell St.
Trongate

Port Dundas
Renton
Milton St.
Stewart St.
Cowcaddens Rd.
Parliamentary Rd.
Cambridge St.
Rose St.
COWCADDENS
Theatre Royal
Glasgow Film Theater
McLellan Galleries
Sauchiehall St.
Buchanan St.
BUCHANAN ST.
NELSON MANDELA PL.
Buchanan Galleries
W. Nile St.
Nile St.
Renfield St.
W. George St.
Union St.
Gordon St.
Central Station
Princes Sq.
Argyle
St. Enoch Shopping Centre
ST. ENOCH SQ.
Argyle St.
Howard St.
Jamaica St.
Clyde St.

Con St.
TO QUEEN'S CROSS
W. Graham St.
Buccleuch St.
Dalhousie St.
ST. GEORGE'S CROSS
Great Western Rd.
Renfrew St.
Scott St.
Hill St.
Garnet St.
Glasgow School of Art
Bath St.
Dalhousie St.
W. Regent St.
Pitt St.
Holland St.
W. George St.
Blythswood St.
Douglas St.
Campbell St.
Wellington St.
Hope St.
Oswald St.
Robertson St.
York St.
James Watt St.
Brown St.
McAlpine St.
Washington St.
Anderston Cross Bus Station
Cadogan St.
Waterloo St.
Argyle St.
Broomielaw
River Clyde

Elmbank St.
Newton St.
W. Princes St.
Grant St.
St. George's Rd.
Woodlands Rd.
Granville St.
North St.
Cleveland St.
Beltane St.
St. Vincent St.
Bothwell St.
Anderston Station
Hydepark St.
Anderston Quay
M8
Springfield Quay
TO GLASGOW SCIENCE CENTRE

Mitchell Library
Elderslie
Berkeley St.
Woodside Pl.
Newton Pl.
Sandyford Pl.
Elderslie St.
Kent Rd.
Claremont St.
Finnieston St.
Houldsworth St.
Minerva St.
Greenhill St.

TO 2 (800 m) AND 3 (100 yd)
Park Quad.
Park Circus
Park Terr.
Lynedoch Pl.
Woodlands Rd.
Woodlands Terr.
KELVINGROVE PARK
Royal Terr.
Kelvin Way
River Kelvin
Hunterian Museum and Art Gallery
Glasgow University
Kelvingrove Art Gallery and Museum
Museum of Transport
Kelvin Hall
TO BYRES RD., BOTANIC GARDEN, AND 8
Argyle St.
Kelvinhaugh St.
St. Vincent Crescent
Minerva Way
Clydeside Expwy.

BURRELL COLLECTION, POLLOCK PARK, GREENOCK & GLASGOW AIRPORTS

City Hall/Ticket Centre
Strathclyde University
George St.
Montrose St.
John St.
Cochrane St.
Virginia St.
Princes Sq.
Buchanan St.
Argyle Arcade
M8

revolves around **Byres Road** and **Glasgow University,** 1½km northwest of the city center. To reach the **TIC** from **Central Station,** exit on **Union Street,** turn left, walk two blocks, turn right on **St. Vincent Street,** and it's 3½ blocks up on your right. From **Queen Street Station,** exit onto **George Street,** and cross George Sq. From the **Buchanan Bus Station,** exit on **North Hanover Street** and follow it right to George Sq.

Tourist Office: 11 George Sq. (☎204 4400; fax 221 3524). U: Buchanan St. Books rooms for £2 fee plus 10% deposit. **Walking tours** depart M-Sa 6pm, Su 10:30am (1½hr.; £5, students £4). Open July-Aug. M-Sa 9am-8pm, Su 10am-6pm; June and Sept. M-Sa 9am-7pm, Su 10am-6pm; Oct.-May M-Sa 9am-6pm.

American Express: 115 Hope St. (☎(08706) 001060). Open July-Aug. M-F 8:30am-5:30pm, Sa 9am-5pm; Sept.-June M-F 8:30am-5:30pm, Sa 9am-noon.

Laundromat: Coin-Op Laundromat, 39/41 Bank St. (☎339 8953). U: Kelvin Bridge. Open M-F 9am-7:30pm, Sa-Su 9am-5pm.

Emergency: ☎999; no coins required. **Police** (☎532 3000), on Stewart St.

Hospital: Glasgow Royal Infirmary, 84-106 Castle St. (☎211 4000).

Internet Access: Best deal in town is **easyEverything** 57-61 St. Vincent Street (☎222 2365). £1 buys 40-75min. Open 24hr. **The Internet Café,** 569 Sauchiehall St. (☎564 1052.) serves the West End. £3 per 30min. Open M-Th 9am-11pm, F-Su 9am-7pm.

Post Office: 47 St. Vincent St. Address mail for holding: FirstName SURNAME, *Poste Restante,* 47 St. Vincent St., **G2 5QX** Glasgow, UK. Open M-Sa 8:30am-5:30pm.

▛ ACCOMMODATIONS

Reserve B&Bs and hostels in advance, especially in August. Last-minute planners should call **SYHA Loch Lomond** (see p. 249). Most B&Bs cluster on **Great Western Road,** in the university area, or near **Westercraigs Road,** east of the Necropolis.

Bunkum Backpackers, 26 Hillhead St. (☎581 4481). Though located away from the city center, Bunkum is minutes away from the vibrant West End. Spacious dorms with comfy beds. Lockers. Laundry (£1.50 wash). Dorms £9, £45 per week.

Glasgow Backpackers Hostel, 17 Park Terr. (☎332 9099). U: St. George's Cross. Clean, friendly, and social hostel close to the West End party scene. **Internet.** Laundry (£2.50 for wash, dry, and fold). Open July-Sept. Dorms £10.50; twins £24.

SYHA Glasgow, 7-8 Park Terr. (☎332 3004). U: St. George's Cross. From Central Station, take bus #44 from Hope St., ask for the 1st stop on Woodlands Rd., then follow the signs. This hostel maintains an air of luxury. All rooms with bath. TV and game rooms. Breakfast included. Laundry. Dorms July-Aug. £11.50, under 18 £9.50; Sept.-Oct. £11, £9.50; Nov.-Feb. £10, £8.50; Apr.-June £11, £9.50.

McLay's Guest House, 268 Renfrew St. (☎332 4796). Excellent central location near the Glasgow School of Art and Sauchiehall St. With satellite TV and phones in each of the 62 rooms and 3 dining rooms, it looks and feels more like a hotel than a B&B. Singles £22, with bath £27; doubles £38, £46.

Alamo Guest House, 46 Gray St. (☎339 2395), opposite the Kelvingrove Museum. Gracious proprietors and spacious, quiet rooms. Singles £20-22; doubles from £34.

Seton Guest House, 6 Seton Terr. (☎556 7654), 20min. east of George Sq. Hop on bus #6, 6A, or 41A. Kindly hosts keep large immaculate rooms with ornate chandeliers. Out of the way, but all the quieter for it. Singles £17; doubles £32.

▛ FOOD

The area bordered by **Otago Street** in the west, **St. George's Road** in the east, and along **Great Western Road Woodlands Road,** and **Eldon Street** brims with cheap kebab 'n' curry joints. **Byres Road** and **Ashton Lane,** a tiny cobblestoned alley parallel to Byres Rd, thrive with cheap, trendy cafes. **Woodlands Grocers,** 110 Woodlands Rd., is open 24hr.; a **Safeway** is at 373 Byres Rd. (Open M-Sa 8am-8pm, Su 9am-7pm.)

BRITAIN

Grosvenor Café, 31-35 Ashton Ln. (☎339 1848). Stuff yourself silly from the endless menu, but beware of the long lines. Desserts and stuffed rolls £0.95-£1.20, bigger dishes £3-4. A more elaborate dinner menu (main courses £5.25-8.45) is available Tu-Sa 7-11pm. Open M 9am-7pm, Tu-Sa 9am-11pm, Su 10:30am-5:30pm.

Insomnia Café, 38/40 Woodlands Rd., near the hostels, is the hip place to gorge, day or night. Cafe and adjoining deli open 24hr.

Bay Tree Vegetarian Café, 403 Great Western Rd., at Park Rd., also near the hostels (cut through Kelvingrove Park). Pitas with hummus and salad for £3.50-4.50. Open M-Sa 9am-9pm, Su 9am-8pm.

The Willow Tea Room, 217 Sauchiehall St. (☎332 05 21), upstairs from Henderson the Jewellers. A Glasgow landmark. Sip 1 of 28 kinds of tea. £1.20-1.45 per pot. High tea £7.75. Open M-Sa 9:30am-4:30pm, Su noon-4:15pm.

👁 SIGHTS

The red-paved **George Square** marks the busiest part of the city. The **City Chambers,** on the east side of the square, conceal an ornate marble interior in the Italian Renaissance style. (☎287 4017. Tours M-F 10:30am and 2:30pm.) Follow George St. from the square and take a left on High St., which turns into Castle St., to reach the Gothic **Glasgow Cathedral,** the only full-scale cathedral spared the fury of the 16th-century Scottish Reformation. (Open Apr.-Sept. M-Sa 9:30am-6pm, Su 2-5pm; Oct.-Mar. M-Sa 9:30am-4pm, Su 2-4pm. Free.) On the same street is the **St. Mungo Museum of Religious Life and Art,** 2 Castle St., which surveys every religion from Hindu to Yoruba. (Open M-Sa 10am-5pm, Su 11am-5pm. Free.) Behind the cathedral is the spectacular **Necropolis,** a terrifying hilltop cemetery filled with broken tombstones. (Free.) In the West End, the large, wooded **Kelvingrove Park** lies on the banks of the River Kelvin. In the southwest corner of the park, at Argyle and Sauchiehall Sts., sits the magnificent, spired **Kelvingrove Art Gallery and Museum,** which shelters works by van Gogh, Monet, and Rembrandt. (U: Kelvin Hall. Open M-Th and Sa 10am-5pm, F and Su 11am-5pm. Free.) Farther west rises the Gothic edifices of the **University of Glasgow.** The main building is on University Ave., which runs into Byres Rd. While walking through campus, which has churned out 57 Nobel laureates, stop by the **Hunterian Museum** or the **Hunterian Art Gallery,** across the street. (U: Hillhead. Open M-Sa 9:30am-5pm. Free.) Several buildings designed by Charles Rennie Mackintosh, Scotland's most famous architect, are open to the public; the **Glasgow School of Art,** 167 Renfrew St., south of the river, reflects a uniquely Glaswegian Modernist style. (Tours M-F 11am and 2pm, Sa 10:30am. £5, students £3.) If you're tired of all that culture, (window) shop till you drop at **Princes Square,** 48 Buchanan St., a gorgeous high-end shopping mall. If your wallet has any life left, hit **Sauchiehall Street,** which hosts shops and art galleries as well.

🎵📷 ENTERTAINMENT AND NIGHTLIFE

Glaswegians have a reputation for partying hard. *The List* (£1.95 from newsagents) lets you know which club is best each night. The infamous **Byers Road** pub crawl slithers past the University of Glasgow area, starting at Tennant's Bar and heading toward the River Clyde. ▧**Uisge Beatha,** 232 Woodlands Rd., serves over 100 kinds of malt whisky. (☎564 1596. £1.85-£35 for each. Open M-Th 11am-11pm, F-Sa 11am-midnight, Su 12:30-11pm.) Go to ▧**Babbity Bowster,** 16-18 Blackfriar St. for friendliness, good drink, and football talk. Remember; when you step into the bar, you're a Glasgow Celtic fan. (☎552 5055 M-Sa 8am-midnight, Su 8am-midnight.) **Russell Bar-Café,** 77 Byres Rd., is a log cabin with live DJs and meal deals. (☎334 4973. Open Su-Th 11am-11pm, F-Sa 11am-midnight.) Fifteen bartenders staff the largest continuous bar in the UK at **Horseshoe Bar,** 17-21 Drury St. (☎204 4056. Open M-Sa 8am-midnight, Su 12:30pm-midnight.) Look for skeletons hanging outside the windows of club **Archaos,** 25 Queen St. (☎204

3189. Cover £3-9. Open Th-Su until 3am, Sa until 3:30am.) All types grind at sweaty **Sub Club,** 22 Jamaica St. (☎ 248 4600. Cover £3-6, Sa £8. Open Th-F and Su 11pm-3am, Sa 11pm-3:30am.)

STRANRAER ☎01776

On the westernmost peninsula of Dumfries and Galloway, Stranraer's primary draw is that it provides ferry access to Northern Ireland. **Stena Line** (☎ (0990) 707070; www.stenaline.co.uk) sails to Belfast (1¾hr.; 5 per day; £18-24, students and seniors £14-17, children £9-12). **Trains** (☎ (0345) 484950) arrive from Glasgow (2½hr., 2-7 per day, £16), as do Citylink **buses** (#923; ☎ (08705) 505050; 2½hr., 2 per day, £8.50). National Express buses (☎ (08705) 808080) roll in from London (9hr., 2 per day, £33) and Manchester (5½hr., 1 per day, £26). The **TIC** is on Harbour St. (☎ 702595. Open June-Sept. M-Sa 9:30am-5:30pm, Su 10am-4:30pm; Apr.-May and Oct. M-Sa 10am-5pm; Nov.-Mar. M-Sa 11am-4pm.) If you're marooned, try the **Jan Da Mar Guest House,** 1 Ivy Pl., on London Rd. (☎ 706194. Singles £18; doubles £32.) The **Tesco supermarket** is on Charlotte St. at Port Rodie near the terminal. (Open M-F 8:30am-8pm, Sa 8am-6pm, Su 10am-5pm.)

STIRLING ☎01786

The third point of a strategic triangle completed by Glasgow and Edinburgh, Stirling has historically presided over north-south movement in the region; it was once said that "he who controlled Stirling controlled Scotland." At the 1297 Battle of Stirling Bridge, **William Wallace** (of *Braveheart* fame) outwitted and overpowered the English army, enabling Robert the Bruce to finally overthrow the English in 1314 at **Bannockburn,** 3.25km south of town, and lead Scotland to a 400-year-long stretch of independence. The ■**Stirling Castle** possesses prim gardens and superb views of the Forth Valley that belie its militant and murderous past. (Open Apr.-Oct. daily 9:30am-6pm; Nov.-Mar. 9:30am-5pm. £6, seniors £4.50, children £1.50.) The castle also contains the fascinating **Regimental Museum of the Argyll and Sutherland Highlanders.** (Open Easter-Sept. M-Sa 10am-5:45pm, Su 11am-4:45pm; Oct.-Easter daily 10am-4:15pm. Free.) The 19th-century **Wallace Monument Tower,** on Hillfouts Rd., 2½km from town, features incredible wind-whipped views. Check out Wallace's 1.5m sword on display; the handle is rumored to be made of the flayed skin of his wife's murderer. (Open July-Aug. daily 9:30am-6:30pm; June and Sept. 10am-6pm; Mar.-May and Oct. 10am-5pm; Nov.-Feb. 10am-4pm. £3.30.)

Trains run from Goosecroft Rd. (☎ (08457) 484950) to: Aberdeen (2hr.; M-Sa every hr., Su 6 per day; £28); Edinburgh (50min., 2 per hr., £5.10); Glasgow (30min., 1-3 per hr., £4.30); Inverness (3hr., 4 per day, £32). National Express **buses** also run from Goosecroft Rd. to Glasgow (2-3 per hr., £3.60) and Inverness (every hr., £11.40). The **Stirling Visitor Centre** is next to the castle. (☎ (01786) 46 25 17. Open daily July-Aug. 9am-6:30pm; Apr.-June and Sept.-Oct. 9:30am-6pm; Nov.-Mar. 9:30am-5pm.) In town, the **TIC** awaits at 41 Dumbarton Rd. (☎ 47 50 19. Open July-Aug. M-Sa 9am-1:30pm, Su 9:30am-6:30pm; June and Sept. M-Sa 9am-6pm, Su 10am-4pm; off-season M-Sa 10am-5pm.) The **SYHA Stirling,** on St. John St., halfway up the hill to the castle, occupies the shell of the first Separatist Church in Stirling. In summer, overflow singles in the **Union Street Annexe,** known in cooler months as University of Stirling dorms, are the same prices as the hostel. (☎ 47 34 42. Reception 7am-11:30pm. Curfew 2am. Dorms £10.) The **Willy Wallace Hostel,** 77 Murray Pl., holds clean rooms in a social environment, near to both the bus and train stations. (☎ 44 67 73. Dorms £10; doubles £26.) **Postal code:** FK8 2BP.

ISLE OF ARRAN

With both gentle lowland hills and majestic Highland peaks, the glorious Isle of Arran (AH-ren) justifiably bills itself as "Scotland in Miniature." In the north, the gray, craggy peaks of Goatfell and the Caisteal range surge above the pine-filled foothills. Prehistoric stone circles and lone standing stones rise suddenly out of the mist in the west, while the eastern coastline winds south past meadows and white beaches. Arran is a popular destination for both **hikers** and **bikers.** Biking on the hilly island is a rewarding challenge; the full circuit takes about 9hr. Pick up a free copy of the SYHA's *Cycling on Arran.* The best walks on the island are well marked, while more demanding hikes are detailed in *Seventy Walks in Arran* (£2.50) and *My Walks of Arran* (£2.25), both available at the TIC in Brodick. To reach Arran, take a **train** to **Ardrossan** from **Glasgow Central** (☎ (08457) 484950. 45min., 4-5 per day, £4.50). From Ardrossan, the **Caledonian-MacIntyre** ferry makes the crossing to **Brodick** on Arran in sync with the train schedule (☎ 30 21 66; 1hr., 4-5 per day, £4.40). On the island, the best **bus** pass is the **Rural Day Card** which grants a full day of travel on Arran's buses (available on the bus; £3, children £1.50). The **Stagecoach Western** office is at Brodick pier. (☎ (01770) 302000. Open daily 8am-5pm.) Their **full-day tour** from Brodick Pier travels the perimeter of the island, stopping in Lochranza, Blackwaterfoot, and Whiting Bay. (Departs daily June-Sept. 11am, returns 4:20pm; £7, children £5.)

BRODICK ☎ 01770

In addition to its major transportation connections, Arran's main town (pop. 2000) holds a glorious castle against a backdrop of rugged mountains and a peaceful bay. The center of Brodick is along Shore Rd., to the right as you disembark from the ferry. Shore Rd. becomes Low Glencoy Rd., which reaches the absolutely fabulous ▒**Brodick Castle.** The edifice surveys the harbor from above fantastic wild and walled gardens; the wooded **country park** around the castle has marked trails for self-guided walks. Built on the site of an old Viking fort, the castle contains a fine porcelain collection, paintings, and scores of dead beasties—the former inhabitants, the Dukes of Hamilton, supposedly shot everything winged or hooved. Otherwise, experience the castle vicariously, on the back of a Royal Bank of Scotland £20 note. (☎ 302202. Open Apr.-June and Oct. daily 11am-4:30pm; July-Aug. daily 11am-5pm. Castle and gardens £6; students £4. Gardens only £2.50.) The **Arran Heritage Museum,** features a working forge and a cottage stuffed with 19th-century household and farming tools. (☎ 302636. Open Apr.-Oct. daily 10:30am-4:30pm. £2.25, seniors £1.50, children £1.) The well-marked path up popular **Goatfell** (874m), Arran's highest peak, begins on the road between the Arran Heritage Museum and Brodick Castle; the hike averages 4-5hr.

Arran's **TIC** is located at the base of the pier. (☎ 302140; fax 302395. Open June-Sept. M-Sa 9am-7:30pm, Su 10am-5pm; Oct.-May M-F 9am-5pm, Sa 10am-5pm.) Expansive yet inexpensive rooms abound at the **Arran Hotel,** on Shore Rd. across from the ferry port. (☎ 302265. Singles £20.) To reach the rooms of Mrs. Macmillan, at **Glenard House,** Manse Rd., head away from the pier on Shore Rd. and turn left just after the Heathfield Hotel; it's the fourth house on the left. (☎ 302318. Open Apr.-Oct. Singles £18; doubles £36.) **Camp** at the **Glen Rosa Farm,** 3.25km north of Brodick on the coastal road B880 to Corrie. (☎ 302380. Toilets and cold water. £2.50 per person.) The shores of Whiting Bay, 13km south of Brodick, house a stone **SYHA Hostel** amid rolling hills. (☎ 700339. Lockout 10:30am-5pm. Curfew 11:45pm. Dorms £8.25, under 18 £7.) You can stock up on groceries at the **Co-op,** across from the ferry terminal. (☎ 302515. Open M-Sa 8am-10pm, Su 9am-7pm.)

LOCH LOMOND ☎ 01389

With Britain's largest inland freshwater body as its base, the landscape of Loch Lomond is filled with lush bays, thickly wooded islands, and bare hills. Hikers on the northeastern edge of Loch Lomond are rewarded with stunning views, quiet splendor, and small beaches. The **West Highland Way** snakes along the entire eastern side of the Loch, stretching 155km from Milngavie north to Fort William.

BALLOCH

Balloch, at the southern tip of Loch Lomond, is the major town in the area. Across the River Leven, the **Balloch Castle Country Park** provides 80ha of gorgeous grounds, as well as a 19th-century castle housing a **Visitors Centre.** Look for the pixies in **Fairy**

BRITAIN

Glen. (Park open daily dawn-dusk. Visitors Centre open Easter-Oct. daily 10am-6pm. Free.) **Sweeney's Cruises** boat tour departs from the TIC side of the River Leven. (☎ (01389) 752376; 1hr., every hr., £4.80.)

Trains arrive on Balloch Rd., opposite the TIC, from Glasgow's Queen St. Station (45min., 2 per hr., £3.20). Citylink **buses** (☎ (08705) 808080) #926, 975, and 976 arrive from Glasgow (3-5 per day, £3.60). First Midland (☎ (01324) 613777) travels from Stirling (1½hr., 3 per day, £4.60). Buses arrive down Balloch Rd., across the bridge to the left of the **TIC,** in Old Station Building. (☎ (01389) 753533. Open July-Aug. daily 9:30am-7pm; June 9:30am-6pm; Sept. 9:30am-7pm; Apr.-May and Oct. 10am-5pm.) **B&Bs** congregate on **Balloch Road.** ◪**SYHA Loch Lomond,** 3.25km north of town, is one of Scotland's largest hostels in a stunning 19th-century castle-like building. (☎ (01389) 850226. Call ahead. Dorms £11.75.) To reach the **SYHA Rowardennan,** the first hostel along the West Highland Way, take the Inverberg ferry across the Loch to Rowardennan (☎ (01301) 702 356. May-Sept. 3 per day, £4). Huge windows at the hostel put the Loch in your lap. (☎ (01360) 870259. Curfew 11:30pm. Open Mar.-Oct. Dorms £9.) The **Tullichewan Caravan and Camping Site,** on Old Luss Rd., is up Balloch Rd. from the TIC. (☎ (01389) 759475. Reception 8:30am-10pm. Tent and 2 people £6.50-9, with car £8.50-12.50.)

TROSSACHS

The gentle mountains and lochs of the Trossachs form the northern boundary of central Scotland. A road for walkers and cyclists traces the Loch's shoreline; most tourists' stamina give out after a kilometer, leaving the Loch's joys to more hardy travelers. The **Steamship Sir Walter Scott** runs between Loch Katrine's Trossachs Pier and Stronachlachar. (☎ (01877) 376316. Apr.-Oct. 2-3 per day, £4.60-6.) Only a few buses each day link to the area's two main towns, **Aberfoyle** and **Callander.** Citylink **bus** #974 runs through Edinburgh and Stirling to Fort William, stopping in Callander (2hr., 2 per day, £7). The Trossachs Trundler is a 1950s-style bus that creaks to Callander, Aberfoyle, and Trossachs Pier in time for the sailing of the *Sir Walter Scott* (July-Sept. Su-F 4 per day, £8). Bus #59 from Stirling connects with the Trundler in Callander. Call the **Stirling Council Public Transport Helpline** (☎ (01786) 442707) for info. **Trossachs Cycle Hire,** on the pier, rents bikes. (☎ (01877) 382614. Open Apr.-Oct. daily 8:30am-5:30pm. £12 per day.)

FORT WILLIAM AND BEN NEVIS

With a slew of beautiful lochs and valleys, **Fort William** makes an excellent base camp for mountain excursions to **Ben Nevis** (1342m), the highest peak in Britain. To ascend the well-beaten trail from Fort William to the summit, go 800m north on A82 and follow signs (5-6hr. round-trip). Buses and trains leave from the northern end of High St. **Trains** arrive in Fort William from Glasgow's Queen St. Station (3¾ hr., 2-4 per day, £18) and London's Euston Station (12hr., 3 per day, £70-96.50). Scottish Citylink (☎ (08705) 505050) goes to Edinburgh (6hr., 2 per day, £15.20), Glasgow (3hr., 4 per day, £11.90); Inverness (2hr., 5-6 per day, £7.20). The nearby **TIC** provides info on the West Highlands. (☎ 703781. Open mid-June to mid-July M-Sa 9am-7pm, Su 10am-6pm; mid-July to Aug. M-Sa 9am-8:30pm, Su 9am-6pm; Sept.-Oct. M-Sa 9am-6pm, Su 10am-5:30pm; Nov.-Mar. M-Sa 9am-5pm, Su 10am-4pm; Mar.-June M-Sa 9am-6pm, Su 10am-4pm.) By far the best place to stay within striking distance of Ben Nevis is the comfy ◪**Farr Cottage Accommodation and Activity Centre** in Corpach. Owner Stuart Nicol Stuart puts on his kilt almost every night and gives Scottish history lessons and whisky talks and samples). (☎ (01397) 772315. **Internet.** Laundry. Dorms £11.) To get there, take the train two stops north of Fort William or ride the bus from the car park on Middle St.; located behind the post office (10min., M-Sa 1-3 per hr., £0.80). The **Fort William Backpackers Guesthouse,** on Alma Rd., is 5min. from the Fort William train station. (☎ (01397) 700711. Curfew 2am. Dorms £10-11.) The **Glen Nevis Caravan & Camping Park** is 5½km east of town on Glen Nevis Rd. (☎ (01397) 702191. Showers included. Open mid-Mar. to Oct. Tent and 2 people £7.10, with car £12.)

THE INNER HEBRIDES

ISLE OF SKYE

Often described as the shining jewel in the Hebridean crown, Skye radiates unparalleled splendor from the serrated peaks of the Cuillin Hills to the rugged northern tip of the Trotternish Peninsula. Touring Skye takes effort; pick up *Public Transport Guide to Skye and the Western Isles* (£1) at a TIC. **Buses** on the island are infrequent; **biking** and **hiking** are better options. **MacBackpackers** in Kyleakin (☎ (01599) 534510) offers **minibus day tours** (£15) and the 🌿**Skye Trekker Tour,** a two-day hike with camping equipment provided (£45).

KYLE OF LOCHALSH AND KYLEAKIN. The **Skye Bridge** links Kyle of Lochalsh, the last stop on the mainland before the Isle, with Kyleakin, on Skye's southeastern tail. On the mainland side perches the made-for-postcard **Eilean Donan Castle,** which struck a pose for the movie *Highlander.* (Open Apr.-Oct. daily 10am-5:30pm; Mar. and Nov. 10am-3pm. £3.95, students £3.20; families £9.50.) Take a Scottish Citylink bus and get off at Dornie. **Trains** (☎ (08457) 484950) arrive in Kyle from Inverness (2½hr.; 2-4 per day, £15). The train station (☎ (01599) 534205) is near the pier and the **TIC** is on the hill right above. The staff books beds on either side of the channel for £3. (☎ (01599) 534276. Open Apr.-Oct. M-Sa 9am-5:30pm; July-Sept. Su 10am-4pm.) **Skye-Ways** (☎ (01599) 534328), in conjunction with **Scottish Citylink,** runs **buses** through Kyle of Lochalsh on their way to Kyleakin from: Fort William (2hr., 3 per day, £11); Glasgow (5½hr., 3 per day, £18); Inverness (2½hr., 2 per day, £10). **Cúchulainn's Backpackers Hostel,** in Kyle of Lochalsh, has especially cozy beds. (☎ (01599) 534492. Sheets £0.50. Dorms £9.)

When you're ready to skip the mainland and dive into Skye, traverse the 2½km footpath or take the **shuttle bus** (2 per hr., £0.70) across the Skye Bridge. Across the water, quiet Kyleakin harbor is resplendent at sunset. A climb up memorial hill leads to the small ruins of **Castle Moil;** cross the bridge behind the SYHA hostel, turn left, follow the road to the pier, and take the gravel path. Lodgings cluster along the park a few hundred yards from the pier. The best place to stay is the fun and comfortable 🌿**Dun Caan Hostel.** (☎ (01599) 534087. Book ahead. Dorms £10.)

SLIGACHAN. West of Kyleakin, the smooth, conical Red Cuillin and the rough, craggy Black Cuillin Hills meet in Sligachan, where paths wind their way up the mountains. If you plan to scale some peaks, stay at the **SYHA Glenbrittle** in Glenbrittle near the southwest coast, where expert mountaineers can give you advice on exploring the area. (☎ (01478) 640278. Dorms £8.50.) For camping, head to the excellent **Glenbrittle Campsite.** (☎ (01478) 640404. Open Mar.-Oct. £3.50 per person.) Take bus #360 from Portree and Sligachan to Glenbrittle (M-Sa 2 per day).

PORTREE. In northern Skye is the island's capital, **Portree** (pop. 2500), with busy shops and an attractive harbor. Buses run from Portree to **Dunvegan Castle,** the seat of the clan MacLeod. The castle holds the **Fairy Flag,** made of silk originally dated from the 4th-7th centuries and swathed in clan legend. (☎ (01478) 521206. Open late-Mar. to Oct. daily 10am-5:30pm; Nov.-Mar. 11am-4pm. £5.50, students £5. Gardens only £3.80.) **Buses** stop at Somerled Sq. The busy **TIC** is on Bayfield Rd., a block from the harbor. (☎ (01478) 612137. Open July-Aug. M-Sa 9am-8pm, Su 10am-6pm; Sept.-Oct. and Apr.-June M-F 9am-5:30pm, Su 10am-5pm; Nov.-Apr. M-F 9am-5pm, Sa 10am-4pm.) The **Portree Independent Hostel** is right off Somerled Sq. (☎ (01478) 613737. Dorms £9.50; doubles £21.)

THE OUTER HEBRIDES (WESTERN ISLES)

The magical Outer Hebridean archipelago is not just extraordinarily beautiful, but also astoundingly ancient. Much of its exposed rock has existed for about three billion years, more than half as long as the planet, and inhabitants of the island in the distant past have left behind a rich sediment of tombs, standing stones (including

BRITAIN

the remarkable stone circle at Callanish on Lewis), and Neolithic antiquities. The vehemently Calvinist islands of Lewis and Harris observe the Sabbath strictly: all shops, restaurants, and public transportation **close on Sundays.** Television and tourism are diluting some local customs, but the islands are remote enough to retain much of their charm, and Gaelic is still heard on the streets.

▐ TRANSPORTATION. Three Caledonian MacBrayne **ferries** (☎(01475) 650100) serve the Western Isles from **Oban** to **Barra,** from **Skye** to **Harris,** and from **Ullapool** to **Lewis.** Ferries and infrequent **buses** connect the islands; **hitchers** and **cyclists** enjoy success except during frequent rain storms (*Let's Go* does not recommend hitchhiking). Save for bilingual Stornoway and Benbecula, all road signs are only in Gaelic. TICs often carry translation keys, and *Let's Go* lists Gaelic equivalents after English place names where necessary. For transport information, consult the *Skye and Western Isles Public Transport Travel Guide* (£1 at TICs).

LEWIS AND HARRIS. The island of **Lewis** (Leodhas) is famous for its atmosphere: drifting mists off the Atlantic Ocean shroud the untouched stretches of moorland and small lochs in quiet luminescence. The unearthly setting is ideal for exploring the island's many archaeological sites, most notably the **Callanish Stones,** an extraordinary (and isolated) Bronze Age circle. Buses on the W2 route from Stornoway run past the stones at Calanais (M-Sa 5 per day). Caledonian MacBrayne **ferries** from Ullapool on the mainland serve **Stornoway** (Steornobhaigh; pop. 8000), the largest town in northwestern Scotland (M-Sa 2-3 per day; £13, 5-day return £22.35). To get from the ferry terminal to the **TIC,** 26 Cromwell St., turn left from the pier, then hang a right on Cromwell St. (☎(01851) 703088. Open Mar.-Sept. M-Sa 9am-6pm and to meet late ferries; Oct.-Feb. M-Sa 9am-5pm.) For a place to lay your head and wax your surf board, head to the new **▧Fair Haven Hostel,** at the intersection of Francis and Keith St. (☎(01851) 705862. Dorms £10, with cooked breakfast £12.50, with full board £20.) Go ahead and take in dinner here—their freshly cooked meals are better than anything at a comparable price in town.

Although **Harris** (Na Hearadh) is technically part of the same island as Lewis, it is an entirely different world. Lewis is mainly flat and watery, while Harris is more rugged and spectacular, with steely mountains ranged against each other. Toward the west coast, the **Forest of Harris** (a treeless mountain range) descends to brilliant crescents of yellow beaches bordered by indigo waters and *machair*—meadows of soft green grass and summertime flowers. **Ferries** serve **Tarbert** (An Tairbeart), the biggest town on Harris, from Uig on Skye (M-Sa 1-2 per day; £8.50, round-trip £14.55). Pick up essential *Ordnance Survey* hiking maps at the **TIC,** on Pier Rd. (☎(01859) 502011. Open early-Apr. to mid-Oct. M-Sa 9am-5pm and for late ferry arrivals.) Walk up the hill behind the TIC and turn left at the grocery store to reach the comfy **Rockview Bunkhouse,** Main St. (☎(01859) 502211. Dorms £9.)

BARRA. Little Barra, the southern outpost of the Outer Isles, is an unspeakably beautiful composite of moor, *machair*, and beach. On sunny days, the island's colors are unforgettable: white sand dunes crown turquoise waters against a backdrop of green mountain slopes. **Kisimul Castle,** bastion of the old Clan MacNeil, floats in stately solitude in the middle of Castlebay Harbor. (☎(01871) 810313 for pickup at the pier. £3, students £2.30). The west coast is flanked on one side by the idyllic **beach** of **Halaman Bay,** and on the other by misty mountains speckled with **standing stones and ruins.** Caledonian MacBrayne **ferries** (☎(01475) 650100) stop at **Castlebay** (Bagh A Chaisteil), Barra's primary town, on their way from Oban on the mainland (5hr., 4 per week, £18.75). You can see almost all of Barra in a day; inquire at the TIC about the **postbus,** or rent a bike from **Castlebay Cycle Hire** (☎(01871) 810284. £11 per day. Open daily 10am-1pm) and follow A888, which circles 22km around the island. The Castlebay **TIC** is around the bend to the right from the pier. (☎(01871) 810336. Open mid-Mar. to mid-Oct. M-Sa 9am-5pm, Su 10-11am; also for late ferry arrivals.) Barra is home to a new hostel, the excellent **aki Hostel,** a 5min. walk from the pier. (☎(01871) 810443. £10. Camping £7.)

ABERDEEN
☎01224

The din of the student party scene, the hum of a vibrant arts community, and the swish of Britain's North Sea oil industry offset the perennial grayness of Aberdeen's skies. **Old Aberdeen** and **Aberdeen University** are a short bus ride (#1-4 or 15), or a long walk along King St. from the city center. The **King's College Visitor Centre,** just off High St., greets you at the other end with an exhibit on how students used to live. (☎273702. Open M-Sa 10am-5pm, Su noon-5pm. Free.) Peaceful **King's College Chapel** dates from the 16th century. (Open daily 9am-4:30pm. Tours July-Aug. Su 2-5pm.) The twin-spired **St. Machar's Cathedral,** with a heraldic ceiling and stained glass, was built in the 14th century. (Open daily 9am-5pm, Su services 11am and 6pm.) The 🖼**Lemon Tree Café and Theatre,** 5 West North St. (☎642230), near Queen St., presents folk, jazz, drama, and dance. Excellent free museums abound, including the **Aberdeen Art Gallery,** on Schoolhill (Open M-Sa 10am-5pm, Su 2-5pm), the **Aberdeen Maritime Museum,** Shiprow (Open M-Sa 10am-5pm, Su noon-3pm), and the Gothic **Marischal Museum** (Open M-F 10am-5pm, Su 2-5pm).

 Trains and **buses** arrive on Guild St. Scotrail (☎(0345) 550033) from Edinburgh (2½hr., every hr., £21); Glasgow (2hr., every hr., £28); Inverness (2¼hr., 10 every 90min., £18.20). Scottish Citylink buses (☎(08705) 505050) roll in from Edinburgh (4hr., every hr., £14.50) and Glasgow (3½ hr., every hr., £14.50); Citylink and Bluebird buses (☎212266) come from Inverness (3½hr., every hr., £9). Turn right on Guild St., left on Market St., and make the first right onto Shiprow to get to the **TIC,** in Provost Ross's House, Shiprow. (☎288828. Open July-Aug. M-Sa 9:30am-7pm, Su 10-4; Sept.-June M-Sa 9:30am-5pm.) Take bus #14 or 15 from Union St. to Queen's Rd. to reach the **SYHA King George VI Memorial Hostel,** 8 Queen's Rd. (☎646988. Breakfast included. Laundry. Check-out 9:30am. Lockout 9:30am-1:30pm. Curfew 2am. Dorms £10.25-13.25.) Don't miss out on 🖼**The Ashvale,** 42-48 Great Western Rd. Three-time winner of Scotland's Fish and Chip Shop of the year award and a frequent winner of the UK Fish and Chip of the Year Award, The Ashvale is nothing less than an Aberdeen institution. Don't miss the delicious haddock supper (£3.50). Takeaway around back. (☎596981. Open daily 11:45am-1am.) A Tesco **supermarket** is in front of the St. Nicholas Centre on Union St. (Open M-W and Sa 7:30am-7pm, Th 7:30am-8:30pm, F 7:30am-7:30pm, Su 10am-5pm.)

INVERNESS AND LOCH NESS
☎01463

The charms of Inverness, like the Loch Ness monster herself, are somewhat elusive, but still satisfying. Disillusionment awaits those who remember Inverness as the home of Shakespeare's *Macbeth*. Nothing of the "Auld Castlehill" remains; the present reconstructed **castle** looks like it was made out of pink Legos this very morning. (Tours Easter-Nov. M-Sa 10:30am-5:30pm. £3, students and seniors £2.70.) The **Tourist Trail Day Rover bus** (summer only; £6, students £4) allows unlimited travel to most sights near Inverness. The Jacobite cause died in 1746 on **Culloden Battlefield,** east of Inverness; take **Highland county bus** #12 from the post office at Queensgate (£2 round-trip). Just 2½km south of Culloden, the stone circles and chambered cairns (mounds of rough stones) of the **Cairns of Clava** recall civilizations of the Bronze Age. Bus #12 will also take you to the **Cawdor Castle;** the home of the Cawdors since the 15th century; don't miss the maze. (Open May-Sept. daily 10am-5:30pm. £5.50, students and seniors £4.50, children £2.80.) And, of course, no trip to Inverness would be complete without taking in the deep and mysterious **Loch Ness,** which guards its secrets 7½km south of Inverness. In AD 565, St. Columba repelled a savage sea beast as it attacked a monk; whether a prehistoric leftover, giant seasnake, or cosmic wanderer, the monster has captivated the world's imagination ever since. Tour agencies are the most convenient ways to see the loch; **Guide Friday** offers a 3hr. bus and boat tour. (☎224000. May-Sept. daily 10:30am and 2:30pm. £14.50, students and seniors £11.50, children £6.50.) Or, let **Kenny's Tours** take you around the entire loch and back to Inverness on a minibus. (☎252411. Tours 10:30am-5pm. £12.50, students £9.50.) Even if you don't see the real monster, vendors are all too happy to sell you a cute stuffed one.

BRITAIN

Trains (☎(08457) 484950) run from Academy St., in Station Sq., to: Aberdeen (2¼hr., 7-10 per day, £18.20); Edinburgh (3½-4hr., 1-2 per hr., £30.60); Glasgow (3½hr., 5-7 per day, £30.60); London (8hr., 1 per day, £27-98). Scottish Citylink **buses** (☎(08705) 505050) run from Farraline Park, off Academy St to Edinburgh (4½hr., 8-10 per day, £14) and Glasgow (4½hr., 10-12 per day, £14). To reach the **TIC**, Castle Wynd, from the stations, turn left on Academy St. then right onto Union St. (☎234353 Open roughly mid-June to Aug. M-Sa 9am-7pm, Su 9:30am-5pm; Sept. to mid-June M-Sa 9am-5pm, Su 10am-4pm.) ◪**Mr. and Mrs. Lyall**, 20 Argyll St., with its friendly atmosphere and ample living space, is probably the best value B&B in the Highlands. (☎710267. Continental breakfast included. £10.) To reach the **Inverness Student Hotel**, 8 Culduthel Rd., face the TIC, go left on Bridge St. then right on Castle St. to Culduthel Rd. (☎236556. Reception 6:30am-2:30am. Check-out 10:30am. Dorms July-Sept. £11; Oct.-June £10.)

GLENCOE ☎01855

Stunning in any weather, Glencoe is perhaps best seen in the rain, when a slowly drifting web of mist over the valley laces the innumerable rifts and crags of the steep slopes, and silvery waterfalls cascade into the River Coe. Glencoe is infamous as the site of the 1692 **Massacre of Glencoe,** when the Clan MacDonald unkowingly welcomed a company of Campbell soldiers, henchmen of William III, into their chieftain's home. After enjoying the MacDonalds' hospitality for over a week, the soldiers proceeded to slaughter their hosts. Today, walkers stroll the floor of the cup-shaped valley, rockclimbers head for the cliffs, and winter ice-climbers hack their way up frozen waterfalls. Well-equipped and sure-footed hikers can scramble up the 1147m **Bidean nam Bian** or try the 6½km traverse of the **Aonach Eagach** ridge on the north side of the glen. Saner walkers can find the **Hidden Valley,** where the MacDonalds once hid their pilfered cattle. The trail follows the stream on the south side of the glen, just west of the Coe Gorge (3hr. round-trip). Or avoid the 305m climb by taking the **Glencoe Ski Centre Chairlift,** located off the A82 in the middle of Glencoe. (☎851226. Open June-Aug. daily 9:30am-4:30pm. £4.) On a rainy day, head for the thatched-roof **Glencoe Folk Museum** in Glencoe village. (☎811664. Open Easter-Oct. M-Sa 10am-5:30pm. £1.)

Glencoe Village, essentially one street, rests at the edge of Loch Leven, at the western end of Glencoe. The A82 runs the length of the valley. Scottish Citylink (☎(08705) 505050) **buses** arrive in Glencoe village from Edinburgh (2 per day, £14) and Glasgow (3hr., 4 per day, £10). Post buses putter daily but at irregular times around the area; get the schedule from the TIC. The **Glencoe Visitors Centre** is 5km southeast of Glencoe Village on the A82. (☎811307. Open mid-May to Aug. daily 9:30am-5:30pm; Apr. to mid-May and Sept.-Oct. 10am-5pm.) The **TIC,** is in Ballachulish, 1½km west of the village. (☎811296. Open July-Aug. M-Sa 9am-6:30pm, Su 10am-5pm; Apr.-June M-Sa 10am-5pm, Su 10am-5pm; Sept.-Oct. M-Sa 9am-5pm.) For bike rental, try **Mountain Bike Hire,** at the Clachaig Inn, across the river from the Visitors Centre. (☎811252. £12 per day.) The **SYHA Glencoe** is 3.25km southeast of Glencoe Village. (☎811219. **Internet.** Reception 7am-midnight. Curfew midnight. Dorms £8.50.) The **Leacantium Farm Bunkhouse** is 450m away from the hostel and has three bunkhouses. (☎811256. £7.50.) The farm's **Red Squirrel Camp Site** pitches tents next door (£4.50 per person; showers £0.50.)

BRITAIN

DENMARK
(DANMARK)

DANISH KRONER

US$1 = 8.31KR	10KR = US$1.20
CDN$1 = 5.45KR	10KR = CDN$1.84
UK£1 = 11.85KR	10KR = UK£0.84
IR£1 = 9.46KR	10KR = IR£1.06
AUS$1 = 4.30KR	10KR = AUS$2.33
NZ$1 = 3.56KR	10KR = NZ$2.81
ZAR1 = 0.99KR	10KR = ZAR10.07
EUR€1 = 7.45KR	10KR = EUR€1.34

PHONE CODE | **Country Code: 45. International dialing prefix:** 00.

Like Thumbelina, the heroine of native son Hans Christian Andersen's fairy tales, Denmark (pop. 5.3 million; 43,094 sq. km) has a tremendous personality crammed into a tiny body. Danes delight in their eccentric traditions, such as burning witches in effigy on Midsummer's Eve and eating pickled herring on New Year's Day. Although the Danes are justifiably proud of their fertile farmlands and pristine beaches, their sense of self-criticism is reflected in the Danish literary canon: the more famous voices are Andersen, Søren Kierkegaard, and Isak Dinesen. Wedged between Sweden and Germany, the country is the geographic and cultural bridge between Scandinavia and continental Europe. With its Viking past behind it, Denmark now has one of the most comprehensive social welfare structures in the world, and liberal immigration policies have diversified the erstwhile homogeneous population. Today, Denmark has a progressive youth culture that beckons travelers to the hip pub scene in Copenhagen. Contrary to the suggestion of a certain English playwright, very little seems to be rotten in the state of Denmark.

SUGGESTED ITINERARIES

THREE DAYS Explore chic and progressive **Copenhagen**. Get your kicks in the **Tivoli** amusement park and delight in the **Little Mermaid** statue.

BEST OF DENMARK, 9 DAYS Start in wonderful **Copenhagen** (3 days, p. 256). For the best beaches in Denmark, take a ferry to **Bornholm** island (1 day, p. 265). Shoot south to rockin' **Roskilde** (1 day, p. 263). Move west to catch some more rays on **Funen** island. Don't miss **Odense** (1 day, p. 265), the hometown of Hans Christian Andersen. Then hop a ferry to the idyllic **Ærø** (1 day, p. 267), a throwback to the Denmark of several centuries ago. Cross the Lillebælt to **Jutland** to chill with laid-back students in **Århus** and play with blocks at **Legoland** (1 day, p. 268). On your way south, stop in **Ribe**, a well-preserved medieval town (1 day, p. 272).

DENMARK

LIFE AND TIMES

HISTORY AND POLITICS

The former home base of raiding Vikings, Denmark has done its share of pillaging. Danes evolved from nomadic hunters to farmers during the Stone Age, and from the 8th to 11th centuries AD they proceeded to sack and rob the English coast as Vikings. Denmark, then called **Jutland**, was Christianized in the 10th century under **King Harald the Bluetooth.** Under the rule of Harald's descendents, Denmark gained dynastic control over Norway, Iceland, and Sweden. However, various disputes plagued the Danish throne, and in 1282 regal power was ultimately made accountable to the **Danehof**, a council composed of high nobles and church leaders. In the 16th century, the **Protestant Reformation** swept through Denmark, and **Lutheranism** was established as the state denomination. The next several centuries were overall a disastrous period for Denmark; its involvement in the **Thirty Years War** (1618-1648), the **Napoleonic Wars** (1799-1815), and the **War of 1864,** as well as a prolonged squabble with Sweden, resulted in severe financial and territorial losses. Denmark's neutrality during **World War I** proved fiscally beneficial, as Denmark profited by trade with the warring nations. **World War II** saw the country occupied by Nazis, but Denmark refused to comply with pressure to persecute Jewish citizens. After World War II, Denmark took its place on the international stage, becoming a founding member of **NATO** (1949) and joining the **European Union** (1972).

DENMARK TODAY. Denmark's support for the European Union has been lukewarm; the country has declined to accept common defense and single currency, among other EU policies. 20th-century Denmark has been plagued by periodic economic setbacks and a high budget deficit. However, its **social welfare system** is recognized as one of the world's best, as all citizens receive a wide range of free benefits. The government is a **constitutional monarchy** in which the monarch, **Queen Margrethe II,** is the nominal head of state, while major decision-making power is vested in the unicameral legislature, led by Prime Minister **Poul Rasmussen.**

THE ARTS

The relatively small population of Denmark has scarcely precluded the development of a rich cultural life. On the literary front, the fairy tales of **Hans Christian Andersen**—from the Little Mermaid to the Ugly Duckling—have delighted children throughout the world for generations. Philosopher and theologian **Søren Kierkegaard** developed the "leap of faith," the idea that religious belief is beyond the bounds of human reason. **Karen Blixen** gained fame under the name **Isak Dinesen,** detailing her life experiences in the book *Out of Africa* (1937). Denmark's most famous musician, **Carl Nielsen,** composed six symphonies with unusual tonal progressions that won him international recognition (see p. 265). Director **Carl Dreyer** explored complex religious themes in his films; the most well-known is *The Passion of Joan of Arc* (1928).

FOOD AND DRINK

A "Danish" in Denmark is a *wienerbrød* ("Viennese bread"), found in bakeries alongside other flaky treats. For more substantial fare, Danes favor open-faced sandwiches called *smørrebrød*. For cheap eats, look for **lunch specials** *(dagens ret)* and all-you-can-eat buffets (*spis alt du kan* or *tag selv buffet*). National beers are Carlsberg and Tuborg; bottled brew tends to be cheaper. A popular alcohol alternative is *snaps* (or *aquavit*), a clear distilled liquor flavored with fiery spices, usually served chilled and unmixed. Many **vegetarian** *(vegetarret)* options are the result of Indian and Mediterranean influences, but salads and veggies *(grøntsaker)* can be found on most menus. For more on being veggie in Denmark, contact **Dansk Vegetarforening,** Borups Allé 131, 2000 Frederiksberg (☎38 34 24 48).

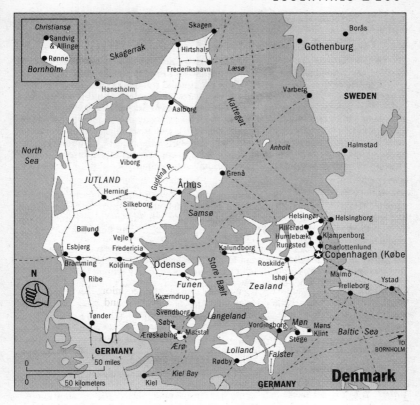

Denmark

ESSENTIALS

DOCUMENTS AND FORMALITIES

Visas are generally not required for tourist stays under three months; South African citizens are the exception.

Danish Embassies at Home: Australia, 15 Hunter St., Yarralumla, ACT 2600 (☎(02) 62 73 21 95; fax 62 73 38 64). **Canada,** 47 Clarence St., Ste. 450, Ottawa, ON K1N 9K1 (☎613-562-1811; fax 562-1812; www.tradecomm.com/danish). **Ireland,** 121 St. Stephen's Green, Dublin 2 (☎(01) 475 64 04; fax 478 45 36; www.denmark.ie). **New Zealand** (consulate), Level 7, 45 Johnston St., Wellington, P. O. Box 10-874 (☎(04) 471 05 20; fax 471 05 21). **South Africa,** 8th fl., Sanlam Centre, corner of Pretorius and Andries St., P.O. Box 2942, Pretoria 0001 (☎(012) 322 05 95; fax 322 05 96). **UK,** 55 Sloane St., London SW1X 9SR (☎(020) 73 33 02 00 or 72 35 12 55; fax 73 33 02 70; www.denmark.org.uk). **US,** 3200 Whitehaven St. NW, Washington, D.C. 20008-3683 (☎202-234-4300; fax 328-1470; www.denmarkemb.org).

Foreign Embassies in Denmark: All foreign embassies are in **Copenhagen** (see p. 256).

TRANSPORTATION

BY PLANE. The airport in **Copenhagen** (see p. 256) handles international flights from cities around the world, mostly by SAS, Delta, United, British Airways, Air France, KLM, Lufthansa, and Swissair. **Billund Airport** (☎76 50 50 50; www.billund-

DENMARK

airport.dk) in Jutland handles flights to other European cities. SAS (Scandinavian Airlines; US ☎ 800-437-5804; www.scandinavian.net), the national airline company, offers youth, spouse, and senior discounts to some destinations.

BY TRAIN AND BY BUS. Eurail is valid on all state-run **DSB** routes. The *buy-in-Scandinavia* **Scanrail Pass** allows five days within 15 (1540kr, under 26 1155kr) or 21 consecutive days (2390kr, 1795kr) of unlimited rail travel through Denmark, Norway, Sweden, and Finland, as well as many 25-50% discounted ferry and bus rides. This differs from the *buy-outside-Scandinavia* **Scanrail Pass,** which allows five days within two months (US$204, under 26 $153), 10 days within two months ($310, $233), or 21 consecutive days ($360, $270). Visit www.scanrail.com for more info. Remote towns are typically served by **buses** from the nearest train station. The national **bus** network is also reliable and fairly cheap. You can take buses or trains over the new **Østersund bridge** from Copenhagen to Malmö, Sweden.

BY FERRY. Railpasses earn discounts or free rides on many Scandinavian ferries. The free *Vi Rejser* newspaper, at tourist offices, can help you sort out the dozens of smaller ferries that serve Denmark's outlying islands. For info on ferries from **Copenhagen** to **Norway, Sweden,** and **Poland,** see p. 256. For more on connections from **Jutland** to **England, Sweden,** and **Norway,** see p. 267; from **Bornholm** to **Sweden** and **Germany,** see p. 265.

BY CAR. Roads are **toll-free,** except for the **Storebæltsbro** (Great Belt Bridge; 210kr) and the **Øresund bridge** (around 300kr). **Car rental** is generally around US$75 per day, plus insurance and a per-kilometer fee; to rent a car, you must be at least 20 years old (in some cases even 25). Speed limits are 50kph (30mph) in urban areas, 80kph (50mph) on highways, and 110kph (68mph) on motorways. **Service centers** for motorists, called Info-terias, are spaced along Danish highways. **Gas** averages 6.50kr per liter. Watch out for bikes, which have the right-of-way. For more info on driving in Denmark, contact the **Forenede Danske Motorejere (FDM),** Firskovvej 32, Box 500, DK-2800 Lyngby (☎ 70 13 30 40; fax 45 27 09 33; www.fdm.dk).

BY BIKE AND BY THUMB. Flat terrain, well-marked bike routes, bike paths in the countryside, and bike lanes in towns and cities make Denmark a cyclist's dream. You can **rent bikes** (40-55kr per day) from some tourist offices, rental shops, and a few train stations. The **Dansk Cyklist Førbund** (Danish Cycle Federation), Rømersg. 7, 1362 Copenhagen K (☎ 33 32 31 21; fax 33 32 76 83; www.dcf.dk), can hook you up with longer-term rentals. For info on bringing your bike on a train (which costs 50kr or less), pick up *Bikes and Trains* at any train station. **Hitchhiking** is legal in Denmark, but *Let's Go* does not recommend hitchhiking.

TOURIST SERVICES AND MONEY

EMERGENCY	**Police,** ☎ 112. **Ambulance,** ☎ 112. **Fire,** ☎ 112.

TOURIST OFFICES. Contact the main tourist board in Denmark at Vesterbrog. 6D, 1620 Copenhagen V (☎ 33 11 14 15; dt@dt.dk; www.visitdenmark.dt.dk).

Tourist Boards at Home: UK, 55 Sloane St., London SW1X 9SY (☎ (171) 259 5958). **US,** 18th fl., 655 3rd Ave., New York, NY 10017 (☎ 212-885-9700).

CURRENCY AND EXCHANGE. The Danish unit of currency is the **kroner** (kr), divided into 100 *øre.* The easiest way to get cash is from **ATMs: Cirrus** and **PLUS** cash cards are widely accepted, and many machines give advances on credit cards.

Prices: Denmark has a high cost of living; expect to spend from US$30 (hostels and supermarkets) to $60 (cheap hotels and restaurants) per day.

Tipping: There are no hard and fast rules, but it's always polite to round up to the nearest 10kr in restaurants and for taxis. In general, service at restaurants is included in the bill. Tipping up to 15% is becoming common in Copenhagen.

Taxes: Denmark's **value-added tax (VAT)** is one of the highest in Europe, a flat 25% on just about everything except food. You can get a VAT refund upon leaving the country if you have spent at least US$95 in one store.

ACCOMMODATIONS AND CAMPING

While Denmark's **hotels** are generally expensive (300-850kr per night), the country's 101 **HI youth hostels** *(vandrerhjem)* are cheap (dorms less than 100kr per night; nonmembers add 25kr), well-run, and have no age limit. Sheets cost about 45-50kr. Breakfasts usually run 45kr. Reception desks normally close for the day around 8 or 9pm. Reservations are required in winter and highly recommended in summer, especially near beaches. Make sure to arrive before check-in to confirm your reservation. For more info, contact the **Danish Youth Hostel Association** (☎31 31 36 12; ldv@danhostel.dk; www.danhostel.dk) or grab a *Danhostel* booklet at any tourist office. Many tourist offices book rooms in private homes (125-175kr).

Denmark's 525 official **campgrounds** (about 60kr per person) rank from one-star (toilets and drinking water) to three-star (showers and laundry) to five-star (swimming, restaurants, and stoves). You'll need either a **Camping Card Scandinavia,** available at campgrounds (1-year 75kr), or a **Camping Card International.** If you only plan to camp for a night, you can buy a 24hr. pass (20kr). The **Danish Camping Council** (*Campingradet;* ☎39 27 80 44) sells the campground handbook, *Camping Denmark,* and passes. Sleeping in train stations, parks, or on public property is illegal.

COMMUNICATION

MAIL. Mailing a postcard/letter to Australia, Canada, New Zealand, the US, or South Africa costs 5.50kr; to elsewhere in Europe, 4.50kr. Domestic mail costs 4kr.

TELEPHONES. There are no separate city codes; include all digits for local *and* international calls. Buy phone cards at post offices or kiosks (30 units 30kr; 53 units 50kr; 110 units 100kr). For **domestic directory info,** call 118; **international info,** 113; collect calls, ☎141. International direct dial numbers include: **AT&T,** ☎80 01 00 10; **British Telecom,** ☎0800 89 00 45; **Canada Direct,** ☎80 01 00 11; **Ireland Direct,** ☎80 01 03 53; **MCI,** ☎80 01 00 22; **Sprint,** ☎80 01 08 77; **Telecom New Zealand,** ☎80 01 00 64; **Telkom South Africa,** ☎80 01 00 27; **Telstra Australia,** ☎80 01 00 61.

LANGUAGE. Danish. The Danish add *æ* (like the "e" in "egg"), *ø* (like the "i" in "first"), and å (sometimes written as *aa;* like the "o" in "lord") to the end of the alphabet; thus Århus would follow Viborg in an alphabetical listing of cities. Knowing *ikke* ("not") will help you figure out such signs as "No smoking" *(ikke-ryger);* *aben/lukket* (O-ben/loock-eh) means open/closed. Nearly all Danes speak flawless English, but a few Danish words might help break the ice: try *skal* (skoal), or "cheers." Danish has a distinctive glottal stop known as a *stød.*

LOCAL FACTS

Time: Denmark is 1hr. ahead of Greenwich Mean Time (GMT).

When to Go: Denmark's climate is more solar than polar and more dry than wet. The four seasons are distinct and winters relatively mild.

Hours: Shop hours are normally M-Th from about 9 or 10am to 6pm and F until 7 or 8pm; they are also usually open Sa mornings (Copenhagen shops stay open all day Sa). Regular **banking** hours are M-W and F 9:30am-4pm, Th 9:30am-6pm.

Holidays: Easter (Mar. 31); Common Prayer Day (Apr. 26); Ascension Day (May 9); Whit Sunday and Monday (May 19-20); Constitution Day (June 5); Christmas (Dec. 24-26); and New Year's Eve (Dec. 31).

Festivals: Danes celebrate **Fastelavn** (Carneval) in Feb. and Mar. In May, the **Copenhagen Jazz Festival** features a week of concerts, many free. The **Roskilde Festival** is an immense open-air music festival held in Roskilde in June.

DENMARK

COPENHAGEN (KØBENHAVN)

Despite the swan ponds and cobblestone clichés that Hans Christian Andersen's fairy-tale imagery brings to mind, Denmark's capital is a fast-paced modern city that offers cafes, nightlife, and style to rival those of the great European cities. But if you are still craving Andersen's Copenhagen, the *Lille Havfrue* (Little Mermaid), Tivoli, and Nyhavn's Hanseatic gingerbread houses are also yours to discover.

▐ TRANSPORTATION

Flights: Kastrup Airport (☎32 47 47 47). S-trains connect the airport to Hovedbanegården (12min., every 20min., 18kr).

Trains: Trains stop at **Hovedbanegården** (Central Station). Domestic travel ☎70 13 14 15; international ☎70 13 14 16. To: **Berlin** (9hr.; 1 per day; 895kr, under 26 580kr); **Hamburg** (4½hr.; 5 per day; 485kr, under 26 320kr); **Oslo** (9hr.; 3 per day; 740kr, 530kr); **Stockholm** (5½hr.; 4-5 per day; 700kr, 540kr). **Reservations mandatory** (20kr). For cheaper travel to **Gothenburg, Stockholm, Oslo, Norway,** and **Östersund, Sweden,** buy a **Scanrabat** ticket a week ahead; you must reserve.

Ferries: Scandinavian Seaways (☎33 42 33 42) departs daily at 5pm for **Oslo** (16hr.; 480-735kr, under 26 315-570kr; Eurail and Scanrail 50% off). Trains to **Sweden** cross over on the **Helsingør-Helsingborg** ferry at no extra charge. Hourly **hydrofoils** (☎33 12 80 88) to **Malmö** go from Havneg., at the end of Nyhavn (40min., 19-49kr). Both **Flyvebådene** and **Pilen** run hourly hydrofoils to Malmö from 9am-11pm (45min., 50kr). **Polferries** (☎33 11 46 45) set out from Nordre Toldbod, 12A (off Esplanaden) Su, M, W 8am; Th-F 7:30pm to **Świnoujście, Poland** (10hr.; 340kr, with ISIC 285kr).

Public Transportation: Bus info ☎36 13 14 15 (daily 7am-9:30pm); **train** info ☎33 14 17 01 (daily 7am-9pm). **Buses** and **S-trains** (subways and suburban trains; M-Sa 5am-12:30am, Su 6am-12:30am) operate on a zone system; 2-zone **tickets** run 13kr; add 6kr per additional zone. The cheaper **rabatkort** (rebate card), available from kiosks and bus drivers, gets you 10 "clips," each good for 1 journey within a specified number of zones. The blue 2-zone *rabatkort* (80kr) can be clipped more than once for longer trips. Tickets and clips allow 1hr. of transfers. The **24hr. pass** grants unlimited bus and train transport in greater Copenhagen (70kr); buy at the Tivoli tourist office or any train station. **Railpasses,** including **Eurail,** are good on S-trains but not buses. **Night buses** run on limited routes during the remaining hours and charge double fare. The **Copenhagen Card,** sold in hotels, tourist offices, and train stations, grants unlimited travel in North Zealand, discounts on ferries to Sweden, and admission to most sights (24hr. 175kr, 48hr. 295kr, 72hr. 395kr), but isn't always worth it unless you plan to ride the bus frequently and see several museums per day. Copenhagen will open a newly renovated **metro** system in 2002, so public transportation should become even more efficient.

Taxis: ☎35 35 35 35, 38 77 77 77, or 38 10 10 10. Base fare 22kr; add 8kr per km 7am-4pm, 10kr per km 4pm-7am. Hovedbanegården to airport 150kr.

Bike Rental: City Bike lends bikes for free. Deposit 20kr at any of 150 bike racks citywide and retrieve the coin upon return at any rack. **Københavns Cykler,** Reventlowsg. 11 in Hovedbanegården (☎33 33 86 13), rents for 50kr per day, 90kr per 2 days, 125kr per 3 days; 300kr deposit. Open July-Aug. M-F 8am-5:30pm, Sa 9am-1pm, Su 10am-1pm; Sept.-June closed Su.

Hitchhiking: Use It has ride boards (see **Tourist Office,** below). *Let's Go* does not recommend hitchhiking.

✳▐ ORIENTATION AND PRACTICAL INFORMATION

Copenhagen lies on the east coast of the island of **Zealand** (Sjælland), across the sound (Øresund) from Malmö, Sweden. The new 28km **Øresund bridge and tunnel,** which opened July 1, 2000, established the first "fixed link" between the two countries. Copenhagen's **Hovedbanegården** (Central Station) lies near the city's heart. North of the station, **Vesterbrogade** passes **Tivoli** and **Rådhuspladsen** (the central

DENMARK

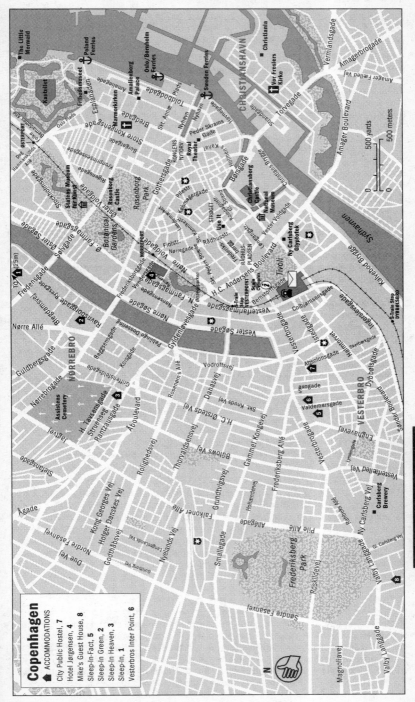

Copenhagen

⚓ ACCOMMODATIONS

City Public Hostel, 7
Hotel Jørgensen, 4
Mike's Guest House, 8
Sleep-In-Fact, 5
Sleep-In Green, 2
Sleep-In Heaven, 3
Sleep-In, 1
Vesterbros Inter Point, 6

DENMARK

square and terminus of most bus lines), then cuts through the city center as **Strøget** (STROY-yet), the world's longest pedestrian thoroughfare. The main pedestrian areas are **Orstedsparken, Botanisk Have,** and **Rosenborg Have.**

TOURIST, FINANCIAL, AND LOCAL SERVICES

Tourist Offices: Wonderful Copenhagen, Bernstorffsg. 1 (☎70 22 24 42; www.visit-copenhagen.dk). Head out the main exit of Hovedbanegården and go left past the back entrance to Tivoli. Open Jan.-Apr., early and late Oct., and Nov. Tu-F 10am-4pm, Sa 10am-1pm; May-June, Sept., mid-Oct., and Dec. M-F 10am-4pm, Sa 10am-1pm; July-Aug. M-F 10am-6pm, Sa 10am-2pm; consult web site for separate accommodations service and info-line hours. **Use It**, Rådhusstr. 13 (☎33 73 06 20; www.useit.dk). From the station, follow Vesterbrog., cross Rådhuspladsen onto Frederiksbergg. and turn right on Rådhusstr. Indispensable and geared toward budget travelers. Pick up a copy of *Play Time*, a comprehensive budget guide to the city. Provides daytime luggage storage, finds lodgings, and holds mail. Open mid-June to mid-Sept. daily 9am-7pm; mid-Sept. to mid-June M-W 11am-4pm, Th 11am-6pm, F 11am-2pm.

Budget Travel: Wasteels Rejser, Skoubog. 6 (☎33 14 46 33). Open M-F 9am-7pm, Sa 10am-3pm. **Kilroy Travels,** Skinderg. 28 (☎33 11 00 44). Open M-F 10am-5:30pm, Sa 10am-2pm.

Embassies: Australia (consulate), Strand Boulevarden 122, 5th fl. (☎39 29 20 77; fax 39 29 60 77). **Canada,** Kristen Bernikowsg. 1 (☎33 48 32 00; fax 33 48 32 21). **Ireland,** Østerbaneg. 21 (☎35 42 32 33; fax 35 43 18 58). New Zealanders should contact the **New Zealand** embassy in Brussels (see p. 125). **South Africa,** Gammel Vartovvej 8 (☎39 18 01 55; fax 39 18 40 06). **UK,** Kastelsvej 36-40 (☎35 44 52 00; fax 35 44 52 93). **US,** Dag Hammarskjölds Allé 24 (☎35 55 31 44; fax 35 43 02 23).

Currency Exchange: Forex, in Hovedbanegården. 25kr commission on cash, 15kr per traveler's check. Open daily 8am-9pm.

Luggage Storage: Free at **Use It** tourist office and most hostels. At **Hovedbanegården,** 25-35kr per 24hr. Open M-Sa 5:30am-1am, Su 6am-1am.

Laundromats: Look for **Vascomat** and **Møntvask** chains. At Borgerg. 2, Nansensg. 39, and Istedg. 45. Wash and dry 40-50kr. Most open daily 7am-9pm.

Gay and Lesbian Services: National Association for Gay Men and Women, Teglgårdsstr. 13 (☎33 13 19 48). Open M-F 5-7pm. The monthly *Gay and Lesbian Guide to Copenhagen* lists clubs, cafes, and organizations, and is available at several gay clubs (see p. 262). Also check out www.copenhagen-gay-life.dk, www.gayonline.dk., or www.panbladet.dk.

EMERGENCY AND COMMUNICATIONS

Emergencies: ☎112. **Police** (☎33 14 14 48), headquarters are at Polititorvet.

Pharmacy: Steno Apotek, Vesterbrog. 6c (☎33 14 82 66). Open 24hr.; ring the bell.

Medical Assistance: Doctors on Call (☎33 93 63 00). Open M-F 8am-4pm; after hrs., call 38 88 60 41. Visits 120-350kr. Emergency rooms at **Sundby Hospital,** Kastrup 63 (☎32 34 32 34), and **Bispebjerg Hospital,** Bispebjerg Bakke 23 (☎35 31 35 31).

Internet Access: Free at **Use It** and at **Copenhagen Hovedbibliotek** (Central Library), Krystalg. 15 (☎33 73 60 60; open M-F 10am-7pm, Sa 10am-2pm).

Post Office: In Hovedbanegården. Address mail to be held: FirstName SURNAME, Post Denmark, Hovedbangardens Posthus, Hovedbanegarden, **1570** Kobenhavn V. Mail also held at **Use It;** address mail to: FirstName SURNAME, *Poste Restante,* Use It, 13 Rådhusstræde, **1466** Copenhagen K, DENMARK.

ACCOMMODATIONS AND CAMPING

Comfortable and inexpensive accommodations can be hard to find in the city center, where most hostels are like enormous warehouses packed with 50 or more beds. On the upside, many hostels feature a lively social scene. For better accommodations try the Danhostels outside the city center or stay at the five-star hostel in nearby Ishoj (see p. 262). During holidays (such as the national vacation in early

August) and the largest festivals—especially Karneval (mid-May), Roskilde (late June), and Copenhagen Jazz (late July)—reserve rooms well in advance.

■ **Sleep-In-Fact,** Valdemarsg. 14 (☎33 79 67 79; info@sleep-in-fact.dk). Go out the back exit of Hovedbanegården, turn left onto Vesterbrog., then left again onto Valdemarstr. Clean, comfortable rooms in a brand new factory-turned-hostel. Bikes 40kr per day. Breakfast 30kr. Free lockers. Sheets 30kr. Reception 24hr. Lockout 10am-4pm. Open June 11-Sept. Dorms 110kr.

Hotel Jørgensen, Rømersg. 11 (☎33 13 81 86). 25min. from Hovedbanegården, 5min. from Strøget, on a quiet street. S-train: Nørreport; go right along Vendersg.; it's on the 2nd corner on the left. Central and friendly. Breakfast included. Sheets 30kr. Reception 24hr. Lockout 11am-3pm. No dorm reservations. Dorms 120kr; singles 400kr; doubles from 500kr; quads 640kr.

Vesterbros Interpoint, Vesterbros KFUM (YMCA), Valdemarsg. 15 (☎33 31 15 74). From Central Station, walk west on Vesterbrog. and turn left. Super-friendly staff; homey atmosphere. Breakfast 25kr. Sheets 15kr. Reception 8:30-11:30am, 3:30-5:30pm, and 8pm-12:30am. Curfew 12:30am. Open late June to early Aug. Dorms 85kr.

City Public Hostel, Absalonsg. 8 (☎33 31 20 70), in the Vesterbro Youth Center. From the station, walk away from the Rådhuspladsen on Vesterbrog. and turn left on Absalonsg. Prime location. Happening lounge and BBQ. Kitchen. Sheets 30kr. Reception 24hr. Open early May to late Aug. Dorms 120kr; with breakfast 140kr.

Sleep-In Heaven, Struenseg. 7 (☎35 35 46 48; sleepinheaven@get2net.dk), in Nørrebro. Take bus #8 (dir.: Tingbjerg) 5 stops to "Rantzausg."; continue in the same direction as the bus, then turn right on Kapelvej, left on Tavsensg., and left on (poorly marked) Struense. Lively social atmosphere. Close to hip Skt. Hans Torv nightlife. **Internet** 20kr per 30min. Reception 24hr. Dorms 100kr; doubles 400kr.

Sleep-In, Blegdamsvej 132 (☎35 26 50 59). Bus #1, 6, or 14: Trianglen. S-train: Østerport; facing the station, go left, walk 10min. up Hammerskjölds (across the square from the 7-11). Near the city center and Østerbro nightlife. Quantity over privacy at this popular (and noisy) warehouse of a hostel. **Internet.** Sheets 30kr. Reception 24hr. Lockout noon-4pm. Open July 28-Aug. No reservations. Dorms 90kr.

Sleep-In Green, Ravnsborgg. 18, Baghuset (☎35 37 77 77). Take bus #16 from the station to Nørrebrog, and then walk down Ravnsborgg. Cozy, eco-friendly dorms outside the city center. Organic breakfast 30kr. Sheets 30kr. Reception 24hr. Check-out noon. Lockout noon-4pm. Open mid-May to mid-Oct. Dorms 95kr.

Mike's Guest House, Kirkevænget 13 (☎36 45 65 40), 10min. by bus or train from Hovedbanegården. Call ahead. Clean, spacious rooms—some with private balconies—in Mike's own home. Quiet neighborhood. Singles 200kr; doubles 290kr; triples 400kr.

Ajax, Bavnehøj Allé 30 (☎33 21 24 56). S-train A: Sydhavn; walk north on Enghavevej (with the Netto on the left and train tracks on the right), turn left on Bavnehøj Allé, and look for signs on the right. Or bus #10 (dir.: Vigerslev), walk up Bavnehoj Allé. Kitchen and TV. Breakfast 20kr. Sheets 20kr. Reception 8am-midnight. Open July-Aug. Dorms 60kr; doubles 200kr; triples 225kr. Hostel tent 55kr; camping with your own tent 50kr.

København Vandrerhjem Bellahøj (HI), Herbergvejen 8 (☎38 28 97 15; bellahoj@danhostel.dk), in Bellahøj. Take bus #11 (dir.: Bellahoj/Bronshoj Torv) from the station to "Primulavej." Large, modern hostel far from the city center. Breakfast included. Sheets 35kr. Wash 25kr, dry 10kr. Reception 24hr. Open Mar. to mid-Jan. Dorms 95kr; doubles 250kr.

København Vandrerhjem Amager (HI), Vejlandsallé 200 (☎32 52 29 08). Take bus #46 (M-F 6am-5pm; night bus #96N) from Hovedbanegården; or catch the S-train to Valby, then take bus #100S (dir.: Svanemollen St.). Far from civilization in a huge nature reserve. Kitchen. Sheets 35kr. Laundry 25kr. Reception 24hr. Check-in 1-5pm. Open mid-Jan. to Nov. Dorms 90kr; nonmembers 110kr.

Bellahøj Camping, Hvidkildevej 66 (☎38 10 11 50), 5km from the city center. Take bus #11 to "Bellahøj." Shower included. Kitchen. Cafe and market. Reception 24hr. Open June-Aug. 57kr per person; tents available for extra charge.

DENMARK

Absalon Camping, Korsdalsvej 132, Rødovre (**☎**36 41 06 00), 9km from the city center. From Central Station, take bus #550S to "Korsdalsvej/Roskildevej" and tell the
driver to let you off at the campsite. Kitchen, laundry, and store. 58kr per person, 20kr
per tent; cabins 195kr plus 54kr per person.

FOOD

The Vikings once slobbered down mutton and salted fish in Copenhagen; today you
can seek out more refined offerings. Around **Kongens Nytorv,** elegant cafes serve
sandwiches *(smørrebrød)* for around 35kr. All-you-can-eat buffets (40-70kr) are
popular, especially at Turkish, Indian, and Italian restaurants. **Fakta** and **Netto supermarkets** are budget fantasies; there are several around the Nørreport area (S-Train:
Norreport). Open-air **markets** provide fresh fruits and veggies; try the one at **Israels
Plads** near Nørreport Station. (Open M-Th 9am-5:30pm, F 9am-6:30pm, Sa 9am-
3pm.) **Fruit stalls** line Strøget and the side streets to the north.

Nyhavns Færgekro, Nyhavn 5. Upscale fisherman's cottage atmosphere along the canal.
Lunch on 10 varieties of all-you-can-eat herring (89kr). Open daily 9:30am-11:30pm.

Café Norden, Østerg. 61, on Strøget and Nicolaj Plads, in sight of the fountain. A French-
style cafe with the best vantage point on Strøget. Crepes 59-62kr; sandwiches 59-64kr;
pastries 15-40kr. Open daily 9am-midnight.

Café Europa, Amagertorv 1, on Nicolaj Plads opposite Café Norden. If Norden is the
place to see, trendy Europa is the place to be seen. Sandwiches 23-44kr. Beer 45kr per
pint. Great coffee. Open M-W 9am-midnight, F-Sa 9am-1am, and Su 10am-7pm.

Kafe Kys, Læderstr. 7, on a quiet street running south of and parallel to Strøget. Sandwiches and salads 48-75kr. Beer 35kr. Open M-Th 11am-1am, F-Sa 11am-2am, Su
noon-10pm. Kitchen closes daily at 10pm.

Den Grønne Kælder, Pilestr. 48. Popular, classy vegetarian and vegan dining. Hummus
35-45kr. Veggie burgers 35kr. Meals 35-80kr. Open M-Sa 11am-10pm.

◎ SIGHTS

Compact Copenhagen is best seen by foot or bike; pick up a free **city bike** (see p.
256) to survey its stunning architecture. Various **tours** are detailed in Use It's *Play
Time* and tourist office brochures. The squares along the lively pedestrian **Strøget,**
which divides the city center, are **Nytorv, Nicolaj Plads,** and **Kungens Nytorv.** Opposite
Kungens Nytorv is **Nyhavn,** the "new port" where Hans Christian Andersen wrote his
first fairy tale, lined with Hanseatic houses and sailing boats. There are several
canal tours, but **Netto Boats** offers the best value (late Apr. to mid-Sept. every 20min.
10am-5pm; 20kr). **Bus #6** travels through Vesterbro, Rådhuspladsen, alongside
Strøget, and on to Østerbro, acting as a sight-seeing guide to the city.

CITY CENTER. The first sight you'll see as you exit the train station is **Tivoli,** the
famed 19th-century amusement park with botanical gardens, marching toy soldiers,
and rides. Wednesday and weekend nights culminate with music and fireworks. An
increasingly popular Christmas market is open mid-November through mid-December. *(Vesterbrog. 3. Open late Apr. to mid-Sept. Su-Th 11am-midnight, F-Sa 11am-1am. Children's rides open, others 11:30am. Admission 50kr; ride tickets 10kr, 1-5 tickets per ride.
Tour pass (full day, unlimited rides) 180kr.)* From Hovedbanegården, turn right on Bernstorffsg. and left on Tietgensg. to partake of the ancient and Impressionist art and
sculpture at the beautiful ▓**Ny Carlsberg Glyptoket.** *(Dantes Plads 7. Open Tu-Su 10am-
4pm. 30kr; free W and Su or with ISIC.)* Continue along Tietgensg., which becomes
Stormg., to dive into Denmark's Viking treasures and other tidbits of cultural history at the **National Museum.** *(Ny Vesterg. 10. ☎33 13 44 11. Open Tu-Su 10am-5pm. 40kr,
students 30kr; W free.)* **Christiansborg Castle,** Prins Jørgens Gård, features subterranean ruins, royal reception rooms, and the *Folketing* (Parliament) chambers. To
get there, continue down Tietgensg. from the city center and cross the canal. *(☎33
92 64 94. Tours May-Sept. daily 11am, 3pm; June-Aug. 11am, 1, and 3pm; Oct.-Apr. Tu-Th and
Sa-Su 11am and 3pm; 40kr. 20kr, students 15kr. Ask for free Parliament tours.)*

DENMARK

CHRISTIANSHAVN. In the southern section of Christianshavn, the "free city" of **Christiania,** founded in 1971 by youthful squatters in abandoned military barracks, is inhabited by a thriving group of artists and alterna-thinkers carrying 70s activism and free love into the new millennium. At Christmas, there is a fabulous market with curiosities from all over the world. Exercise caution in the **Pusher St.** area, aptly named as the site of *many* hash and marijuana sales. Possession of even small amounts can get you arrested. Always ask before taking pictures, **never** take pictures on Pusher St. itself, and exercise caution in the area at night. Climb the golden spire of **Vor Frelsers Kirke** (Our Savior's Church) for a great view. *(Sankt Annæg. 29. Turn left off Prinsesseg. Church open Mar.-Nov. daily 9am-4:30pm; Dec.-Feb. 10am-2pm. Free. Tower open Mar.-Nov. 9am-4:30pm. 20kr.)* The area is accessible from Hoved-banegården by bus #8; it stops right at the church.

FREDERIKSTADEN. Edvard Eriksen's **den Lille Havfrue (The Little Mermaid),** the tiny but touristed statue at the opening of the harbor, honors favorite son Hans Christian Andersen. *(S-train: Østerport; turn left out of the station, left on Folke Bernadottes Allé, go right and follow the path bordering the canal, go left up the stairs and then right along the street. Open daily 6am-dusk.)* Head back along the path bordering the canal and turn left to cross the moat to **Kastellet,** a 17th-century fortress-turned-park. Cross through Kastellet to the **Frihedsmuseet** (Museum of Danish Resistance), a fascinating museum that documents Denmark's efforts to rescue its Jews during the Nazi occupation from 1940 to 1945, as well as its period of acceptance of German "protection," when the Danish government arrested anti-Nazi saboteurs. *(At Churchillparken.* ☎ *33 13 77 14. Open May to mid-Sept. Tu-Sa 10am-4pm, Su 10am-5pm; mid-Sept. to Apr. Tu-Sa 11am-3pm, Su 11am-4pm. 30kr; W free.)* From the museum, walk south down Amalieng. to reach the lovely ■ **Amalienborg Palace,** residence of Queen Margarethe II and the royal family; most of the interior is closed to the public, but you can see the apartments of Christian VII. The changing of the palace guard takes place at noon on the brick plaza. *(*☎ *33 12 21 86. Open June-Aug. daily 10am-4pm; May-Oct. 10am-4pm; Nov.-Apr. Tu-Su 11am-4pm. 40kr, students 25kr.)* The 19th-century **Marmokirken** (Marble Church), opposite the palace, features an ornate interior and Europe's third-largest dome. *(Open M-Tu and Th-Sa 10:30am-4:30pm, W 10:30am-6:30pm, Su noon-4:30pm. Free. Dome 20kr.)* A few blocks north, **Statens Museum for Kunst** (State Museum of Fine Arts) displays an eclectic collection in a beautifully designed building. From the church, head away from Amalienborg, go left on Store Kongensg., turn right on Dronningens Tværg., and take an immediate right and then left onto Sølvg. *(Sølvg. 48-50.* ☎ *33 15 32 86. S-train: Nørreport; walk up Østervolg. Open Tu and Th-Su 10am-5pm, W 10am-8pm. 40kr; W Free.)* Opposite the museum, **Rosenborg Slot** (Rosenborg Palace and Gardens) hoards royal treasures, including the ■ **crown jewels.** *(Østervolg. 4A.* ☎ *33 74 84 94. S-train: Nørreport; walk up Østervolg. and it's on the left past the intersection. Open May-Sept. daily 10am-4pm; Oct. 11am-3pm; Nov.-Apr. Tu-Su 11am-2pm. 50kr, students 30kr.)*

OTHER SIGHTS. A trip to the **Carlsberg Brewery** will reward you with a wealth of ale-related knowledge and, more importantly, free samples. *(Ny Carlsbergvej 140.* ☎ *33 27 13 14. Take bus #6 west from Rådhuspladsen to Valby Langg. Open Tu-Su. 10am-4pm. Free.)* If the breweries haven't confused your senses enough, go play at the hands-on **Experimentarium** (Danish Science Center). *(Tuborg Havnevej 7. in Hellerup.* ☎ *39 27 33 33. Take bus #6 north from Rådhuspladsen. Open late June to mid-Aug. daily 10am-5pm; late Aug. to early June M and W-F 9am-5pm, Tu 9am-9pm, Sa-Su 11am-5pm. 85kr.)*

♫ ENTERTAINMENT

For events, consult *Copenhagen This Week* (free at hostels and tourist offices), or pick up *Use It News* from Use It. The **Royal Theater** is home to the world-famous Royal Danish Ballet; the box office is located at Tordenskjoldsg. 7. (Open M-Sa 10am-6pm.) For same-day half-price tickets, head to the **Tivoli ticket office,** Vesterbrog. 3. (☎33 15 10 12. Open mid-Apr. to mid-Sept. daily 9am-9pm; mid-Sept. to mid-Apr. 9am-7pm. Royal theater tickets available at 4 or 5pm, others at noon.) Call **Arte,** Hvidkildevej 64 (☎38 88 22 22), to ask about student discounts. The relaxed **Kul-Kaf-**

DENMARK

éen, Teglgårdsstr. 5, is a great place to see live performers and get info on music, dance, and theater. (Open M-Sa 11am-midnight.) During the world-class **Copenhagen Jazz Festival** (mid-July; ☎33 93 20 13; www.cjf.dk), the city teems with free outdoor concerts complementing the more refined venues. In anticipation of the summer blowout, the **Swingin' Copenhagen** festival sets the city grooving to traditional jazz (www.swingin-copenhagen.dk), and **Copenhagen Autumn Jazz** in early November keeps the city bopping long after summer is gone.

▌ NIGHTLIFE

Copenhagen's weekends often begin on Wednesday, and nights rock until 5am; "morning pubs" that open when the clubs close let you party around the clock. On Thursday, most bars and clubs have reduced covers and cheap drinks. The central pedestrian district reverberates with crowded bars and discos; **Kongens Nytorv** has fancier joints. Many buy beer at a supermarket and head to the boats and cafes of **Nyhavn** for its salty charisma. The **Scala** complex, opposite Tivoli, has many bars and restaurants; students enliven the cheaper bars in the **Nørrebro** area. Copenhagen's gay and lesbian scene is one of Europe's best.

■ **Park,** Østerbrog. 79, in Østerbro. Lose your inhibitions and your friends in this enormous club with 2 packed dance floors, live music hall, and rooftop patio. Pints 40kr. Cover F-Sa 50kr. Open Su-W 10am-2am, Th 10am-4am, F-Sa 10am-5am.

Rust, Guldbergsg. 8, in the Nørrebro. 20-somethings pack this disco with an underground feel. Long lines by 1am. Cover 50kr; free before 11pm. Open Tu-Su 10pm-5am.

Café Pavillionen, Borgmester Jensens Allé 45, in Fælleaparken. This summer-only outdoor cafe has local bands 8-10pm, plus a disco W-Sa 10pm-5am. On M, enjoy a concert 2:30-5pm, then tango lessons and dancing until midnight.

Enzo, Nørreg. 41. Doll yourself up and dance with a young stylish crowd. Dress code. 21+. Cover 60kr. Open F-Sa 9pm-5:30am.

IN Bar, Nørreg. 1. Drink cheap and then dance on the speakers. F-Sa cover 150kr, includes open bar. Th-Sa 20+. Open Su-Th 10pm-5am, F-Sa 10pm-10am.

JazzHouse, Niels Hemmingsens G. 10 (www.jazzhouse.dk). Turn left off Strøget from Gammeltorv (closer to Råhuspladsen) and Nytorv. Copenhagen's premier jazz venue makes for a sophisticated and potentially expensive evening. Check the calendar for prices. Concerts Su-Th 8:30pm, F-Sa 9:30pm. Club open midnight-5am.

PAN Club and Café, Knabrostr. 3. Gay cafe, bar, and disco. Homoguide available. Cover W 30kr, F-Sa 50kr; Th no cover. Cafe opens daily 8pm, disco 11pm. Both open late.

Sebastian Bar and Disco, Hyskenstr. 10, off Strøget. The city's best-known gay and lesbian bar. Homoguide available. Happy Hour 5-9pm. Open daily noon-2am.

▌ DAYTRIPS FROM COPENHAGEN

Stunning castles and white sand beaches hide in North, Central, and South Zealand. A northern train route (every 20min.) offers easy access to many attractive daytrips that lie within an hour of Copenhagen.

ISHØJ
Accessible by the S-train, lines A and E, from Copenhagen.

The small harbor town of Ishøj, just south of Copenhagen, is home to the **Arken Museum of Modern Art,** Skovvej 100, which features temporary exhibitions by notable contemporary artists; Edward Munch and Gerhard Richter were both recently featured. (☎43 54 02 22. Open Tu and Th-Su 10am-5pm, W 10am-9pm. 40kr, students 20kr; extra for some special exhibitions.) To get to the museum, take bus #128 from Ishøj Station (every hr., 13kr) or follow the signs from the station (45min. walk). To stay at the **Ishøj Strand Vandrerhjem,** Ishøj Strandvej 13, follow the signs from the station. (☎45 43 53 50 15. Breakfast 40kr. Sheets 40kr. Reception 8am-noon and 4-8pm. Dorms 100kr; singles 290-325kr; doubles 315-350kr.)

RUNGSTED AND HUMLEBÆK

Both Rungsted (30min., 40kr or 4 clips on the blue rabatkort) and Humlebæk (45min., 38.50kr or 4 clips) are on the Copenhagen-Helsingør northern line.

In North Zealand, the quiet harbor town of **Rungsted,** where Karen Blixen (pseudonym Isak Dinesen) wrote *Out of Africa,* houses the author's abode, personal belongings, and grave at the **Karen Blixen Museum,** Rungsted Strandvej 111. Follow the street leading out of the train station and turn right on Rungstedvej, then right again on Rungsted Strandvej.; or take bus #388 (2 per hr.) and tell the driver your destination. (☎45 57 10 57. Open May-Sept. daily 10am-5pm; Oct.-Apr. W-F 1-4pm, Sa-Su 11am-4pm. 35kr.) **Humlebæk,** farther up the coast, distinguishes itself with the spectacular **Louisiana Museum of Modern Art,** 13 Gl. Strandvej, named for the three wives (all named Louisa) of the estate's original owner. The museum contains works by Picasso, Warhol, Lichtenstein, Calder, and other 20th-century masters; the building and its sculpture-studded grounds overlooking the sea are themselves worth the trip. Follow signs 1½km north from the Humlebæk station or snag bus #388. (☎45 49 19 07 19. Open Th-Tu 10am-5pm, W 10am-10pm. 60kr, students 52kr.)

HILLERØD AND FREDENSBORG

Hillerød is at the end of S-train lines A and E via Lyngby (40min., 42kr). Frendensborg is on the Lille Nord rail line connecting Hillerød and Helsingør.

Hillerød is home of the moated ▧**Frederiksborg Slot,** arguably the most impressive of North Zealand's castles with exquisite Baroque gardens and brick ramparts. Free concerts are given Thursdays at 1:30pm on the famous 1610 **Esaias Compenius organ** in the chapel. To get there from the station, cross the street onto Vibekeg. and follow the signs. (Open Apr.-Oct. daily 10am-5pm; Nov.-Mar. 11am-3pm. 40kr, students 10kr.) A final stop on the northern castle tour is **Fredensborg Palace.** Built in 1722, the castle still serves as the spring and fall royal residence. (☎45 33 40 31 87. Palace open July 7-Aug. 5; mandatory tours every 15-30min. 1-4:30pm; call ahead about tours in English (2 per day). 30kr. Gardens open July 7-Aug. 5. 9am-5pm; free.) Sleep near the royals and enjoy a fantastic palace gardens view at **Fredensborg Youth Hostel (HI),** Østrupvej 3, 1km from the station. (☎48 48 03 15. Sheets 45kr. Reception 7am-9pm. Dorms 95kr; singles 185-210kr; doubles 260-325kr; triples 335-400kr.)

ROSKILDE

Accessible by train from Copenhagen (25-30min., 38.50kr or 4 clips).

In Central Zealand, Roskilde served as Denmark's first capital when King Harald Bluetooth built the country's first Christian church here in 980. Several Danish monarchs lie in the ornate sarcophagi of ▧**Roskilde Domkirke** in Dorkirkepladsen. (☎46 35 27 00. Open Apr.-Sept. M-F 9am-4:45pm, Sa 9am-noon, Su 12:30-4:45pm; Oct.-Mar. M-F 10am-3:45pm, Sa 11:30am-3:45pm, Su 12:30-3:45pm. Concerts June-Aug. Th 8pm. 15kr, students 10kr.) The **Viking Ship Museum,** Vindeboder 12, near Strandengen along the harbor, houses remnants of five trade ships and warships sunk circa 1060 and salvaged in the late 1960s. From the tourist office, walk to the cathedral and downhill through the park or take bus #605 (dir.: Boserup). In summer, book a ride on a Viking longboat, but be prepared to take an oar—Viking conquest is no spectator sport. (☎46 30 02 00. Museum open May-Sept. daily 9am-5pm; Oct.-Apr. 10am-4pm. May-Sept. 54kr; Oct.-Apr. 50kr. Boat trip 40kr; book ahead.) Roskilde hosts one of Europe's largest **music festivals** (June 27-30, 2002; ☎46 36 66 13; www.roskilde-festival.dk), drawing over 90,000 fans with bands such as REM, U2, Radiohead, Smashing Pumpkins, and Metallica. The **tourist office,** Gullandsstr. 15, sells festival tickets and books rooms for a 25kr fee. From the train station, turn left on Jernbaneg., right on Allehelgansg., left again on Barchog., and look to the left. (☎46 35 27 00. Open Apr.-June M-F 9am-5pm, Sa 10am-1pm; July-Aug. M-F 9am-6pm, Sa 10am-2pm; Sept.-Mar. M-Th 9am-5pm, F 9am-4pm, Sa 10am-1pm.) The **HI youth hostel,** Vindeboder 7, is on the harbor next to the Viking Museum shipyard. The gorgeous, modern facility is always booked during the festival. (☎46 35 21 84. Reception 9am-noon and 4-8pm. Open Feb.-Dec. Dorms 90kr; nonmembers 115kr.)

DENMARK

To camp by the beach at **Roskilde Camping,** Baunehøjvej 7, 4km north of town, take bus #603 toward Veddelev to "Baunehojvej." (☎46 75 79 96. Reception 8am-10pm. Open Apr. to mid-Sept. 60kr per person.)

KLAMPENBORG AND CHARLOTTENLUND
Both are at the end of S-train line C.

Klampenborg and Charlottenlund, on the coastal line, feature **topless beaches.** Although less ornate than Tivoli, **Bakken,** in Dyrehaven, Klampenborg, the world's oldest amusement park, delivers more thrills. From the Klampenborg train station, turn left, cross the overpass, and head through the park. (☎39 63 73 00. Open June to early Sept. daily noon-midnight; mid-Sept. to Apr. M-F 2pm-midnight, Sa 1pm-midnight, Su noon-midnight. Rides start at 2pm; 30-35kr each.) Bakken borders the **Jægersborg Deer Park,** the royal family's former hunting grounds, still home to their **Eremitage** summer chateau, many wooded paths, and over 2000 red deer.

MØN
Take the train from Copenhagen to Vordingborg, then bus #62 or 64 to Stege (20kr).

To see what Andersen called one of the most beautiful spots in Denmark, head south of Copenhagen to the isle of Møn's white cliffs. Locals travel to Møn to explore the gorgeous chalk cliffs and the pastoral landscape. **Liselund Slot,** the only thatched castle in the world, is surrounded by a lush green park with many hiking trails. To get there from Stege, take bus #632. Stay lakeside at the **youth hostel (HI),** Langebjergvej 1. (☎55 81 20 30. Breakfast 45kr. Sheets 30-45kr. Reception 8am-noon and 4-8pm. Dorms 95kr; singles 200kr; doubles 260kr.) Bus #632 runs directly to the campsite. For the hostel, take bus #632 to the campsite stop, backtrack, then take the first road on the right. During off-season (Sept. to mid-July), take bus #62 to "Magleby" and walk 2.5km down the road. The **Møns Turistbureau,** Storeg. 2, is at the bus stop in Stege. (☎55 86 04 10. Open June 15-Aug. M-F 10am-5pm, Sa 9am-6pm, Su 11am-1pm; Sept.-June 14 M-F 10am-5pm, Sa 9am-noon.)

HELSINGØR
Helsingør is at the end of the northern line (1hr.). Bus #340 and the train outside the station run from Helsingør to Hornbæk (20min., 20kr).

Helsingør is evidence of the Danish monarchy's fondness for lavish architecture. In a region famous for castles, the most famous is the 15th-century **Kronborg Slot** in Helsingør, also known as **Elsinore,** the setting for Shakespeare's *Hamlet* (although neither the historical "Amled" nor the Bard ever visited Kronborg). Viking chief Holger Danske is buried in the castle's spooky dungeon; legend has it that he still rises to face any threat to Denmark's safety. The castle also houses the **Danish Maritime Museum,** which contains the world's oldest sea biscuit, from 1853. From the train station, turn left and follow the signs on the waterfront to the castle. (☎45 49 21 30 78. Open May-Sept. daily 10:30am-5pm; Apr. and Oct. Tu-Su 11am-4pm; Nov.-Mar. Tu-Su 11am-3pm. 60kr.) The **tourist office,** Havnepladsen 3, is in the **Kulturhuset,** the large gray building across the street to the left of the station; the entrance is around the corner. (☎49 21 13 33. Open mid-June to Aug. M-Th 9am-5pm, F-Sa 10am-6pm, Su 10am-3pm; Sept. to mid-June M-F 9am-4pm, Sa 10am-1pm.) To reach the gorgeous beachfront ▓**Helsingør Vandrerhjem Hostel (HI),** Ndr. Strandvej 24, take bus #340 to "Hojstrup Trinbrat" and walk back along the street in the opposite direction of the bus route. Or take the train toward Hornbaek, get off at "Hojstrup," follow the path across the park, and it's on the other side of the street. (☎45 49 21 16 40; helsingor@danhostel.dk. Breakfast 45k. Sheets 45kr. Reception 8am-noon and 3-9pm. Open Feb.-Nov. Dorms 95kr; singles 225-300kr; doubles 250-325kr.) Camp by the coast at **Helsingør Camping,** Strandalleen 2; take the train toward Hornbæk and get off at "Campingvej." (☎49 28 12 12. 50kr per person, 35kr per tent.) **Hornbæk,** a small fishing town near Helsingør, offers beautiful beaches for relaxation. There's a wild **harbor festival** on the fourth weekend in July.

DENMARK

BORNHOLM

Ideal for avid bikers and nature-lovers, Bornholm's red-roofed cliffside villas may seem southern European, but the flowers and half-timbered houses are undeniably Danish. The unique **round churches** were both places of worship and fortresses for waiting out pirate attacks. The sandiest and longest **beaches** are at **Dueodde,** on the island's southern tip. For more info, check out www.bornholminfo.dk.

E TRANSPORTATION. Trains from Copenhagen to **Ystad, Sweden** are timed to meet the ferry to **Rønne,** Bornholm's capital (train ☎70 13 14 15; 1¾hr., 5-6 per day; ferry 1½hr.; total trip 190kr.) **Bornholmstrafikken** (Rønne ☎56 95 18 66, M-F 9am-5pm; Copenhagen ☎33 13 18 66; Ystad ☎+46 (411) 558 700; www.bornholmferries.dk) offers this combo train/ferry route and also operates ferries from **Fährhafen Sassnitz** in **Germany** (☎+49 38392 35226; 3½hr., 1-2 per day, 80-110kr.) Bornholm has an efficient local BAT **bus** service. (☎56 95 21 21; 35kr to Gudhjem or Sandvig-Allinge, 40kr to Svaneke; 24hr. pass 100kr.) There are numerous cycling paths between all the major towns; pick up a guide at the tourist office in Rønne.

RØNNE. Amid cafes and cobblestoned streets, tiny but charming Rønne, on the southwest coast, is Bornholm's principal port of entry. The town serves mainly as an outpost to biking trips through surrounding fields, forests, and beaches. Rent a **bike** from **Bornholms Cykeludlejning,** Ndr. Kystvej 5. (☎56 95 13 59. Reserve ahead. 65kr per day. Open May-Sept. daily 7am-4pm and 8:30-9pm.) The **tourist office,** Nordre Kystvej 3, a mirrored-glass building behind the gas station by the Bornholmstrafikken terminal, books private rooms for a 140kr fee. (☎70 23 20 76. Open mid-June to mid-Aug. M-Sa 10am-6pm, Su 10am-4pm; mid-Aug. to mid-June M-F 9am-4pm, Sa 10am-1pm.) The **HI youth hostel,** Arsenalvej 12, is in a quiet, wooded area near the coastline. From the ferry terminal, take the bus directly or walk 15min. along Munch Petersens Vej; when the road forks go left up the hill, then turn left onto Zahrtmannsvej, right at the roundabout onto Søndre Allé, right onto Arsenalvej, and follow the signs. (☎56 95 13 40. Reception Su-F 9am-8pm, Sa 8am-8pm. Dorms 100kr.) **Galløkken Camping** is centrally located at Strandvejen 4. (☎56 95 23 20. Open mid-May to Aug. 52kr per person.) Get **groceries** at **Kvickly,** in the Snellemark Centret opposite the tourist office. (Open mid-June to late Aug. daily 9am-8pm; Sept. to early June M-F 9am-8pm, Sa 8am-5pm, Su 10am-4pm.)

SANDVIG AND ALLINGE. On the tip of the spectacular northern coast, the white-sand beaches in these little towns attract bikers and bathers. A few kilometers from central Allinge down Hammershusvej, **Hammershus** is northern Europe's largest castle ruin. Near Sandvig is the fortified round church, **Østerlars Rundkirke;** take bus #3 or 9 to **Østerlars.** The **Nordbornholms Turistbureau,** Kirkeg. 4, is in Allinge. (☎56 48 00 01. Open June-Aug. M-F 10am-5pm, Sa 10am-3pm; Sept.-May closes Sa noon.) Just outside Sandvig is the **Sandvig Vandrerhjem (HI),** Hammershusvej 94. (☎56 48 03 62. Breakfast 45kr. Sheets 60kr. Reception 9-11am and 4-6pm. **HI members only;** sells HI cards. Open Apr.-Oct. Dorms 100kr; singles 250kr; doubles 350kr.) **Sandvig Familie Camping,** Sandlinien 5, has sites on the sea. (☎56 48 04 47. Rents **bikes.** Reception 8am-noon and 2-9pm. Open Apr.-Oct. 50kr per person, 15kr per tent.)

FUNEN (FYN)

Situated between Zealand to the east and the Jutland Peninsula to the west, the island of Funen is Denmark's garden. This remote breadbasket is no longer isolated from the rest of Denmark—a bridge and tunnel now connect it to Zealand. Pick up maps of the **bike paths** covering the island at Funen tourist offices (75kr).

ODENSE

A visit to this hometown of Hans Christian Andersen may explain why he once said "To travel is to live!": Odense (OH-n-sa) warrants only a short visit. At **H.C. Andersens Hus,** Hans Jensens Stræde 37-45, you can learn about the author's eccentricities

DENMARK

and see free performances of his work. From the tourist office, walk right on Vesterg. to Torveg., turn left, and turn right on Hans Jensens Str. (☎66 14 88 14. Performances June 19-July 30 11am, 1, 3pm. Museum open mid-June to Aug. daily 9am-7pm; Sept. to mid-June Tu-Su 10am-4pm. 30kr.) A few scraps of Andersen's own ugly-duckling childhood are on display at **H.C. Andersens Barndomshjem** (Childhood Home), Munkemøllestr. 3-5. (☎66 14 88 14. Open mid-June to Aug. daily 10am-4pm; Sept. to mid-June Tu-Su 11am-3pm. 10kr.) Next to the main H. C. Andersens Hus, don headphones and listen to the work of another Great Dane at the **Carl Nielsen Museum,** Claus Bergs G. 11. (☎66 14 88 14. Open July-Aug. Tu-Su noon-4pm; Sept.-May Th-Su noon-4pm. 15kr.) Walk back to the tourist office and all the way down Vesterg. to the outstanding ▓**Brandts Klædefabrik,** Brandts Passage 37 and 43. (☎66 13 78 97), which houses a modern art gallery, the **Museum of Photographic Art,** and the **Danish Press/Graphic Arts Museum.** (All open July-Aug. daily 10am-5pm; Sept.-June closed M. 30kr, 25kr, and 25kr, respectively; joint ticket 50kr.) The **Fyns Kunstmuseum** (Funen Art Gallery), Jernbaneg. 13, features Danish art. (☎66 14 88 14, ext. 4601. Open Tu-Su 10am-4pm. 25kr.)

Trains arrive from Copenhagen via Fredericia (2¼hr.) and from Svendborg via Kværndrup (1¼hr.). **Buses** depart behind the train station (13kr). The **tourist office,** on Rådhuspladsen, books rooms for a 25kr fee and sells the **Odense Adventure Pass,** good for museum admission, discounts on plays, and unlimited public transport (24hr. 85kr, 48hr. 125kr). From the train station, take Nørreg., which becomes Asylg., turn left at the end on Vesterg., and it'll be on the right. (☎66 12 75 20. Open June 15-Aug. M-Sa 9am-7pm, Su 10am-5pm; Sept.-June 14 M-F 9:30am-4:30pm, Sa 10am-1pm.) The **library** in the station has free **Internet.** (Open May-Sept. M-Th 10am-7pm, F 10am-4pm, Sa 10am-2pm; Oct.-Apr. M-Th 10am-7pm, Sa-Su 10am-4pm.) The brand-new **Danhostel Odense City (HI)** is attached to the station. (☎63 11 04 25. Reception open daily 8am-noon and 4-8pm. Call ahead. Dorms 145kr; singles 335kr; doubles 410kr; triples 495kr.) To camp next to the Fruens Boge park at **DCU Camping,** Odensevej 102, take bus #41 or 81. (☎66 11 47 02. Pool. Reception 7am-10pm. Open late Mar. to Sept. 50kr per person.) Get **groceries** at **Aktiv Super,** at Nørreg. and Skulkenborgg. (Open M-F 9am-7pm, Sa 8:30am-4pm, Su noon-4pm.)

🖪 **DAYTRIP FROM ODENSE: KVÆRNDUP.** Just a 30min. train ride south of Odense on the Svendborg rail line is the town of **Kværndup** and ▓**Egeskov Slot,** a stunning 16th-century castle that appears to float on the surrounding lake (it's actually supported by 12,000 oak piles). Spend at least 2hr. in the magnificent Renaissance interior and the equally splendid grounds, which include a large bamboo labyrinth. On summer Sundays at 5pm, classical concerts resound in the **Knight Hall.** (Open May-June and Aug.-Sept. daily 10am-5pm; July 10am-6pm. 55kr. Grounds open May and Sept. daily 10am-5pm; June and Aug. 10am-6pm; July 10am-8pm. 60kr. Ticket window closes 1hr. before castle.) To get here, exit the Svendborg-bound train at Kværndrup; go right from the station until you reach Bøjdenvej, the main road. Wait for bus #920 (every hr., 13kr), or turn right and walk 2km through wheat fields to the castle. The **tourist office,** Egeskovg. 1, is up the street from the castle ticket window and books rooms for a 30kr fee. (☎62 27 10 46. Open Sept. and Apr.-May daily noon-5pm; June noon-6pm; July noon-8pm; Aug. noon-6pm.)

SVENDBORG

On Funen's south coast, an hour from Odense by train, **Svendborg** is a beautiful harbor town and a departure point for ferries to the south Funen islands. Near Svendborg on an adjacent island, Tåsinge, the regal 17th-century estate of **Valdemars Slot,** built by Christian IV for his son, holds a new **yachting museum** and a **beach.** (☎62 22 61 06. Open year-round daily 10am-5pm. Castle 50kr, museum 25kr; joint ticket 65kr.) Cruise there on the antique passenger steamer **M/S Helge,** which leaves from Jensens Mole, behind the train station (45min., 4 per day, round-trip 55kr).

Ferries to Ærø (see below) leave behind the train station. The **tourist office,** on the Centrum Pladsen, books ferries and accommodations. From the train station, go left on Jernbaneg. and right onto Brog., which turns into Gerritsg., and right onto

Kyseborgstr., The office is on the right in the plaza. (☎62 21 09 80. Open late June to Aug. M-F 9am-6pm, Sa 9am-3pm; Sept. to mid-June M-F 9:30am-5:30pm, Sa 9:30am-1pm.) To get from the station to the five-star **HI youth hostel**, Vesterg. 45, turn left on Jernbaneg. and walk with the coast to your left, then go right onto Valdemarsg. which becomes Vesterg. (☎62 21 66 99; dk@danhostel-svenborg.dk. Bikes 50kr per day. Breakfast, sheets, and laundry 45kr each. Reception M-F 8am-6pm, Su 8am-noon and 4-6pm. Check-out 9:30am. Dorms 100kr; overflow mattresses on the floor 50kr.) To get to **Carlsberg Camping**, Sundbrovej 19, across the sound on Tåsinge, take bus #800, 801, or 910 from the ferry terminal to "Bregninge Tåsinge" and walk up the street. (☎62 22 53 84. Reception 8am-10pm. Open May-Oct. 51kr per person.) **Jette's Diner,** at Kullingg. 1 between the train station and the docks, puts a Danish spin on diner fare. (☎62 22 16 97. Open daily noon-9:30pm.) **Postal code:** 5700.

ÆRØ

The wheat fields, harbors, and cobblestone hamlets of Ærø (EH-ruh), a small island off the south coast of Funen, quietly preserve an earlier era in Danish history. Here cows, rather than real estate developers, lay claim to the beautiful land.

⚡ TRANSPORTATION. Several **trains** from Odense to **Svendborg** are timed to meet the **ferry** (☎62 52 40 00) from Svendborg to **Ærøskøbing** (1¼hr.; 6 per day; 75kr, round-trip 125kr; buy tickets on board). From **Mommark**, on Jutland, **Ærø-Als** (☎62 58 17 17) sails to **Søby** (☎62 58 17 17; 1hr.; Apr.-Sept. 2-5 per day, Oct.-Mar. Sa-Su only; 60kr), on Ærø's northwestern shore. **Bus** #990 travels between Ærøskøbing, Marstal, and Søby (16kr), but Ærø is best seen by **bike**.

ÆRØSKØBING. Thanks to economic stagnation followed by conservation efforts, the town of Ærøskøbing appears today almost as it did 200 years ago. Rosebushes and half-timbered houses attract tourists from Sweden and Germany as well as vacationing Danes. The **tourist office,** Vesterg. 1, opposite the ferry landing, arranges rooms (170kr) in private homes. (☎62 52 13 00. Open June-Aug. M-F 9am-5pm, Sa 9am-2pm, Su 10am-noon; Sept.-May M-F 9am-4pm, Sa 8:45-11:45am.) To get from the landing to the **HI youth hostel**, Smedevejen 15, walk left on Smedeg., which becomes Nørreg., Østerg., and finally Smedevejen. (☎62 52 10 44. Breakfast 40kr. Sheets 35kr. Reception 8am-noon and 4-8pm. Check-in by 5pm or call ahead. Reserve far in advance. Open Apr. to mid-Oct. Dorms 90kr; nonmembers 115kr.) **Ærøskøbing Camping,** Sygehusvejen 40b, is 10min. to the right along Sygehusvejen, of Vestre Allé as you leave the ferry. (☎62 52 18 54. Reception 8am-1pm and 3-9pm. Open May-Sept. 50kr per person, 20kr per tent.) **Emerko supermarket** is at Statene 3; walking uphill from the ferry on Vesterg., turn right on Sluttergyden, which becomes Statene. (Open M-Th 9am-5pm, F 9am-6pm, Sa 9am-4pm, Su 10am-4pm.)

JUTLAND (JYLLAND)

Homeland of the Jutes who joined the Anglos and Saxons in the conquest of England, the Jutland peninsula is Denmark's largest landmass. Beaches and camp-grounds mark the peninsula as prime summer vacation territory, while rolling hills, marshland, and sparse forests add color and variety. Jutland may be a bit out of the way, but you can take a weekend beach fling there without denting your budget.

⛴ FERRIES TO ENGLAND, NORWAY, AND SWEDEN

From **Esbjerg** (see p. 272), on Jutland's west coast, **DFDS** sails to Harwich, England (18hr., 3-4 per week). From **Frederikshavn** (see p. 270), on the northern tip of Jutland, **Stena Line** ferries (☎96 20 02 00; www.stenaline.com) leave for Gothenburg, Sweden (2-3¼hr.; 155kr; 50% off with Scanrail) and Oslo (8½hr.; 180kr; 50% off with Scanrail). **SeaCat** (☎96 20 32 00; www.silja.com), a subsidiary of Silja Line offers cheaper service to Gothenburg (2hr., 3 per day, 110-130kr). **Color Line** (☎99 56 20 00;

www.colorline.dk) sails to Larvik, Norway (6¼hr., 160-340kr; college students and seniors 50% off). Color Line boats also go from Hirtshals, on the northern tip of Jutland, to Oslo (8-8½hr., 160-350kr) and Kristiansand, Norway (2½-4½hr., 160-350kr).

ÅRHUS

Århus (ORE-hoos), Denmark's second-largest city and a Danish favorite, bills itself as "the world's smallest big city." Studded with impressive museums and architectural gems from prehistoric to modern times, the city is a visual treat. Many travelers to this manageably sized and laid-back student and cultural center find themselves agreeing that size doesn't matter.

TRANSPORTATION. Trains run to Århus from: Aalborg (1¾hr.); Copenhagen (3hr.); Fredericia (2hr.); Frederikshavn (2½hr.). Trains runs every 1-2hr. from Frederikshavn to Århus. Most public buses leave from the train station or outside the tourist office. **Tourist passes** (see below) include unlimited bus transportation.

PRACTICAL INFORMATION. The **tourist office,** in the town hall, books **private rooms** (125-175kr; no fee) and sells the **Århus Passport,** which includes unlimited public transit and admission to most museums and sights (1-day 88kr, 2-day 110kr). If you're only interested in one or two museums, consider the **Tourist Punch Ticket** (45kr), which provides unlimited bus transportation (24hr.). To find the office, go left across Banegardspladsen as you exit the train station, and take the first right on Park Allé. (☎89 40 67 00. Open late June to early Sept. M-F 9:30am-6pm, Sa 9:30am-5pm, Su 9:30am-1pm; early Sept. to Apr. M-F 9:30am-4:30pm, Sa 10am-1pm; May to mid-June M-F 9:30am-5pm, Sa 10am-1pm.) The main **library,** whose entrance is on Vesterg. 55 in Mølleparken, has free **Internet** access. From the center, walk away from the entrance to the cathedral on Store Torv, which becomes Vesterg. (Open May-Aug. M-Th 10am-7pm, F 10am-6pm, Sa 10am-2pm; Sept.-Apr. M 10am-10pm, Tu-Th 10am-8pm, F 10am-6pm, Sa 10am-3pm.) After-hours, try **Net House,** Norre Allé 66a, in the city center. (☎87 30 00 96. Open daily noon-midnight. 20kr per hr.) The **post office,** Banegardspladsen 1A, is right next to the main entrance to the train station. (☎89 35 80 00. Open M-F 9:30am-6pm, Sa 10am-1pm.) **Postal Code:** 8100.

ACCOMMODATIONS AND FOOD. The hip backpacker hang-out, **Århus City Sleep-In,** Havneg. 20, is 10min. from the train station in the middle of the city's nightlife. From the train station, follow Ryesg. (off of Banegardspladsen), which becomes Sønderg., all the way to the canal. Take the steps or elevator down to Aboulevarden, cross the canal and go right, walk to the end of the canal, go left on Mindebrog., crossing Skoleg., then left again on Havneg. (☎86 19 20 55; sleep-in@citysleep-in.dk. Kitchen. **Internet. Bikes** 50kr per day; deposit 200kr. Breakfast 35kr. Sheets 35kr; deposit 30kr. Laundry 25kr. Key deposit 50kr. Reception 24hr. Check-out noon. Dorms 95kr; doubles 240-280kr.) **Pavillonen (HI),** Marienlundsvej 10, is in the Risskov forest, 3km from the city center and 5min. from the beach. Take bus #1, 6, 9, 16, or 56 to Marienlund, then walk 300m into the park. (☎86 16 72 98; danhostel.aarhus@get2net.dk. Breakfast 45kr. Sheets 30kr. Laundry. Reception 7:30-10am and 4-11pm. Dorms 90kr, nonmembers 110kr; singles, doubles, and triples 270-400kr.) **Blommehavenn Camping,** Ørneredevej 35, in the Marselisborg forest, is by a beach and the royal family's summer residence. In summer, take bus #19 from the station to the grounds; in winter, take bus #6 to Hørhavevej. (☎86 27 02 07; info@blommehaven.dk. Reception Apr.-July 7:30am-10pm; Aug.-Mar. 8am-9pm. In summer 55kr per person.) **Den Grønne Hjørne,** Frederiksg. 60, has an all-you-can-eat Danish buffet (noon-10pm, 99kr). From the tourist office, turn left on Radhuspl., and then take an immediate right. (☎86 13 52 47. Open daily 11am-10pm.) Get **groceries** at **Fakta,** Østerg. 8-12. (Open M-F 9am-7pm, Sa 9am-4pm.)

SIGHTS AND ENTERTAINMENT. In the town center, the 13th-century **Århus Domkirke** (cathedral) dominates Bispetorv and the pedestrian streets. (☎86 12 38 45. Open May-Sept. M-Sa 9:30am-4pm; Oct.-Apr. 10am-3pm. Free.) Next door, reclaim herstory at the **Women's Museum,** Domkirkeplads 5, where provocative exhibits chronicle women throughout time. (☎86 13 61 44. Open June-Aug. daily 10am-5pm; Sept.-May Tu-Su 10am-4pm. 25kr.) Just west of the town center lies **Den Gamle By,** Viborgvej 2, an open-air museum displaying a collection of Danish buildings from the Renaissance through the 20th century. From the center, take bus #3, 14, 15, 25, or 51. (☎86 12 31 88. Open June-Aug. daily 9am-6pm; Apr.-May and Sept.-Oct. 10am-5pm; Nov.-Dec. 10am-4pm; Jan. 11am-3pm; Feb.-Mar. 10am-4pm. 60kr; Jan.-Mar. 45kr. Grounds free after-hours.) The **Århus Kunstmuseum,** on Vennelystparken, has a fine collection of Danish Golden Age paintings. (☎86 13 52 55. Open Tu-Su 10am-5pm, W to 8pm. 40kr.) Just outside town is the spectacular **Moesgård Museum of Prehistory,** Moesgård Allé 20, which chronicles Århus's history from 4000 BC through the Viking age. Two millennia ago, the casualties of infighting were entombed in a nearby bog and mummified by its acidity. Today you can visit the **▨Grauballe Man,** the only perfectly preserved bog person. Take bus #6 from the train station to the end. (Open Apr.-Sept. daily 10am-5pm; Oct.-Mar. Tu-Su 10am-4pm. 35kr, students 25kr.) Save time for the **Prehistoric Trail,** which leads from behind the museum to a sandy **beach** (3km). In summer, bus #19 (last bus 10:18pm) returns from the beach to the Århus station. The exquisite rose garden of **Marselisborg Slot,** Kongevejen 100, Queen Margarethe II's summer getaway, is open to the public. From the train station, take bus #1, 18, or 19. (Palace closed in July and whenever the Queen is in residence. Changing of the guard daily at noon.)

Åboulevarden, lined with trendy cafes, is the heart of the town. Århus hosts an acclaimed jazz festival in late July (www.jazzfest.dk). The **Århus Festuge** (☎89 31 82 70; www.aarhusfestuge.dk) is a rollicking celebration of theater, dance, and music. You can visit a smaller version of Tivoli, the **Tivoli Friheden,** Skovbrynet 1. Take bus #1, 4, 6, 8, 18, or 19. (☎86 14 73 00. Open June 19-Aug. 8 daily 2-11pm; Apr. 19-June 18 and Aug. 9-15 2-10pm. 35kr.) At night, chill at the jazz club **Bent J,** Nørre Allé 66 (☎86 12 04 92), which jams Monday evenings and occasionally on other weekdays. **Valdemar,** Store Torv 4, is a popular disco in the city center. (☎86 12 04 92. No cover. 23+. Open Th 11pm-5am, F-Sa 10pm-5am.) The **Pan Club,** Jægergårdsg. 42, has a cafe, bar, and mainly gay and lesbian dance club. (☎86 13 43 80. Cafe open M-Th 6pm-6am, F-Su 8pm-5am. Club cover F-Sa 50kr. Open W-Sa 11pm-5am.) **Åboulevarden** rocks at night, too; many bars offer live music and drink specials.

BILLUND

Billund is renowned as the home of **▨Legoland,** an amusement park built of 40 million Lego pieces. "Lego" is an abbreviation of *leg godt* (have fun playing). Don't skip the impressive indoor exhibitions. Unfortunately, private buses make Legoland a bit expensive. To get there, take the train from Århus to **Vejle** (45min., every hr.), then bus #912 or #244 (dir.: Grindsted). A ticket to the park includes access to all rides and costs 150kr for one day, 215kr for two days. (☎75 33 13 33; www.legoland.dk. Open July daily 10am-9pm; Mar.-June and Sept.-Oct. 10am-6pm; rides close 2hr. earlier.) **Billund airport** is the terminus for many **European flights** to Denmark; see p. 253 for more information. The Billund **tourist office,** by the entrance to Legoland, has information on accommodations and bus schedules (☎76 50 00 55; info@bgt.dk; www.billund.dk.) Bus #244 goes to the site shared by the high-quality **Billund Vandrerhjem (HI)** and **Billund Camping,** Ellehammers Allé 2; tell the bus-driver your destination. To stay at the hostel in summer, book in advance. (☎75 33 2777; billund@danhostel.dk; www.sima.dk/billund. Breakfast 45kr. Sheets 50kr. Reception 8am-9pm. Dorms 100kr; singles 360-400kr; doubles 380-400kr.)

AALBORG

Aalborg (OLE-borg) is the site of the earliest known Viking settlement. Check out these rowdy precursors at **Lindholm Høje,** Vendilavej 11, which has 700 graves and a museum of Viking life; take bus #6 or 25 (13kr) from outside the tourist office. (☎96 31 04 28. Site open daily dawn-dusk. Museum open Apr. to mid-Oct. daily 10am-5pm; late Oct. to mid-Mar. Tu and Su 10am-4pm. 20kr.) The frescoed 15th-century **Monastery of the Holy Ghost,** on C.W. Obelsplads, is Denmark's oldest social institu-

DENMARK

tion. From the tourist office, cross the street and head down Adelg.; the monastery is on the right. (English tours late June to mid-Aug. Tu and Th-F 1:30pm. 40kr.) The **Budolfi Church**, on Algade, has a brilliantly colored interior. From the tourist office, turn left onto Østeråg. and right on Algade. (Open May-Sept. M-F 9am-4pm, Sa 9am-2pm; Oct.-Apr. M-F 9am-3pm, Sa 9am-noon.) At the corner of Algade and Mollegad, in front of the Sallig department store, an elevator goes down to the medieval ruins of the **Franciscan Friary**. (Open Tu-Su 10am-5pm. 20kr; buy your ticket from the machine.) For serious rollercoasters, visit **Tivoliland**, on Karolinelundsvej. From the tourist office, turn left on Østeråg., turn right on Nytorv, and follow it until you see the rides. (Open Apr.-Sept. daily noon to 8pm. 40kr per ride; full-day 160kr.)

Trains arrive from Århus (1¾hr.) and Copenhagen. From the station, cross J.F.K. Plads, then turn left on Boulevarden, which becomes Østeråg., to find the **tourist office,** Østeråg. 8. (☎98 12 60 22. Open mid-June to mid-Aug. M-F 9am-6pm, Sa 10am-5pm; mid-Aug. to mid-June M-F 9am-4:30pm, Sa 9am-1pm.) The public library has free **Internet** access. (☎99 31 44 00. Open June-Aug. M-F 10am-7pm, Sa 10am-2pm; Sept.-May Sa until 3pm.) **Aalborg Vandrerhjem and Camping (HI),** Skydebanevej 50, has cabins with modern facilities next to a fjord. Take bus #2, 8, or 9 (dir.: Fjordparken) to the end. (☎98 11 60 44. Laundry. Reception late-June to mid-Aug. 7:30am-11pm; late-Jan. to mid-June and early-Aug. to mid-Dec. 8am-noon and 4-9pm. Dorms 85-100kr; singles 250-398kr; doubles 325-398kr. Camping 49kr.) Bars and restaurants line **Jomfru Ane Gade;** from the tourist office, turn right on Østeråg. and left onto Bispensg. Jomfru Ane Gade will be on your right. **Postal code:** 9000.

VIBORG

Sights cluster around the cobblestoned center of this well-preserved provincial town. In the mid-19th-century **Viborg Cathedral,** Sct. Mogensg. 4, enormous chalk reliefs depict Bible scenes. (Open June-Aug. M-Sa 10am-5pm, Su noon-5pm; Apr.-May and Sept. M-Sa 11am-4pm, Su noon-4pm; Oct.-Mar. M-Sa 11am-3pm, Su noon-3pm.) Next door, the **Skovgaard Museum,** Domkirkestr. 2-4, houses an impressive collection of paintings by the Danish Golden Age artist. (Open May-Sept. daily 10am-12:30pm and 1:30-5pm; Oct.-Apr. 1:30-5pm.) The **Stifts Museum,** Hjultorvet 9, presents the history of the town and region. (Open June-Aug. daily 11am-5pm; Sept.-May Tu-F 2-5pm, Sa-Su 11am-5pm.) Just outside of Viborg lie the limestone mines and subterranean rivers of ▧**Monsted Kalkgruber,** Kalkvaerksvej 8; take the train (dir.: Stuer) to nearby Stoholm. (Open mid-May to Oct. 10am-5pm. 30kr.)

Viborg lies on the Århus-Struer railway line; **trains** run to Århus (1½hr., every hr.). To get to the **tourist office,** Nytorv 9, from the station, go straight across the roundabout and onto Jernebaneg., go right onto Sct. Mathiasg., cross the plaza (Hjultorvet) and go left; it's in the main square. (☎86 61 16 66. Open mid-May to mid-June M-F 9am-5pm, Sa 9:30am-12:30pm; mid-June to Aug. M-F 9am-5pm, Sa 9am-3pm; Jan.-May and Sept.-Dec. M-F 9am-4pm, Sa 9:30am-12:30pm.) Across the river from the center lie the **youth hostel,** Vinkelvej 36 (☎86 67 17 81; viborg@danhostel.dk; reception daily 7:30am-noon and 2-10pm), and **Viborg So Camping,** Vinkelvej 36B (☎86 67 13 11; viborg@dcu.dk; same reception hours as hostel). To get to either one, take bus #707 from the station to Vinkelvej. Viborg's charm is best experienced by sitting outside and having a drink with the locals in the **Hjultorvet** area, in front of the Stifts Museum. For groceries, stop by the **Netto** on Vesterbrog. (☎43 56 88 11. Open M-F 9am-8pm, Sa 8am-5pm.)

FREDERIKSHAVN

Despite noble efforts to showcase its endearing streets and hospitality, Frederikshavn is best known and used for its **ferry** links (see p. 267). The **tourist office,** Skandia Torv, 1, inside the Stena Line terminal south of the rail station, reserves rooms for a 25kr fee. (☎98 42 32 66; fax 98 42 12 99; www.frederikshavn.dk. Open mid-June to mid-Aug. M-Sa 8:15am-7pm, Su 11am-7pm; mid-Aug. to mid-June M-Sa 9am-4pm.) From the tourist office, walk left 10min. to reach the bus and train stations. To get from the train and bus station to the **HI youth hostel,** Buhlsvej 6, walk right on Skipperg. for 10min., then turn left onto Norreg.; follow the signs. (☎98 42 14 75.

DENMARK

Reception in summer 8am-noon and 4-9pm. Always call ahead. Open Feb.-Dec. Dorms 53kr; singles 150-200kr; doubles 210-270kr.) **Nordstrand Camping** is at Apholmenvej 40. (☎98 42 93 50. Open Apr. to mid-Sept. 52kr per person, 30kr per tent.) **Postal code:** 9900.

SKAGEN

Perched on Denmark's northernmost tip, sunny Skagen (SKAY-en) is a beautiful summer retreat amid long stretches of sea and white-sand dunes. The houses are all painted in deep "Skagen yellow" and the roofs are covered in red tiles with white edges—supposedly decorated to welcome local fishers home from sea. The powerful currents of the North and Baltic Seas collide at **Grenen**. Don't try to swim in these **dangerous waters;** every year some hapless soul is carried out to sea. To get to Grenen, take bus #99 or 79 from the Skagen station to **Gammel** (11kr) or walk 3km down Fyrvej; turn left out of the train station and bear left when the road forks. In summer, you can climb the lighthouse tower for an amazing view of the rough seas at Grenen (5kr). The spectacular **Råberg Mile** sand dunes, formed by a 16th-century storm, migrate 15m east each year. From here, you can swim along 60km of **beaches,** where the endless summer light attracted Denmark's most famous late-19th-century painters. Their works are displayed in the wonderful **Skagen Museum,** Brøndumsvej 4. (☎98 44 64 44. Open June-Aug. daily 10am-6pm; Nov.-Mar. W-F 1-4pm, Sa 11am-4pm, Su 11am-3pm; Apr. and Oct. Tu-Su 11am-4pm; May and Sept. 10am-5pm. 50kr.) You can also tour the artists' homes at **Michael og Anna Archers Hus,** Markvej 2-4 (☎98 44 30 09; open mid-June to mid-Aug. daily 10am-6pm; May to mid-June and mid-Aug. to Sept. 10am-5pm; Apr. and Oct. 11am-3pm; Nov.-Mar. 11am-3pm; 40kr) and **Holger Drachmanns Hus,** Hans Baghsvej 21. (☎98 44 51 88. Open July daily 10am-5pm; June and Aug. to mid-Sept. 11am-3pm; mid-Sept. to mid-Oct. and May Sa-Su 11am-3pm. 20kr.) Skagen has a large annual **Dixieland music festival** in late June (up to 150kr); contact the tourist office for more info.

Nordjyllands Trafikselskab (☎98 44 21 33) runs **buses** and **trains** from Frederikshavn to Skagen (1hr.; 36kr, with Scanrail 50% off). Rent **bikes** at **Skagen CykelUdlejning,** Banegardspladsen, right next to the bus station. (☎98 44 10 70.) The **tourist office** is in the train station. (☎98 44 13 77; fax 98 45 02 94; www.skagen.dk. Open June-Aug. M-Sa 9am-7pm, Su 10am-2pm; Sept.-May reduced hrs.) The **Skagen Ny Vandrerhjem,** Rolighedsvej. 2, is wildly popular among vacationing Danish families. From the station, turn right on Chr. X's Vej, which turns into Frederikshshavnvej, and left on Rolighedsvej. (☎98 44 22 00. Reception 9am-noon and 4-6pm. Open Mar.-Nov. Dorms 100kr; singles 250-400kr; doubles 300-500kr.) **Campgrounds** abound in the area; most are open early May to early September (55kr per person). Bus #79 passes by several sites. Try **Grenen,** Fyrvej 16 (☎98 44 25 46), or **Øster Klit,** Flagbakkevej 53 (☎98 44 31 23), both near the city center.

FREDERICIA

Known primarily as a major railway junction, Fredericia is characterized by excessive military order, with perfectly straight streets set at right angles. The triangular center is bordered by coastlines on two sides and cannon-strewn **ramparts** on the third. Built in 1650 by King Frederik III, the moated ramparts were the sight of the famed Battle of Fredericia in 1849. The most impressive parts lie on Vester Voldg., near the tourist office. For a great view of the ramparts, the city, and its coastlines, climb the **White Water Tower** across the street from the tourist office. (Open May to mid-June daily 11am-4pm; mid-June to mid-Aug. 10am-5pm; mid-Aug. to Sept. 11am-4pm.) Military buffs will also want to visit the **Fredericia Museum,** Jernbaneg. 10, which chronicles the history of the ramparts. From the train station, go right and follow Jernbaneg. (☎72 10 69 80. Open daily 10am-4pm. 20kr.) At the **Air Raid Shelter Museum,** Norre Voldg., you can climb into a real concrete World War II shelter. From the tourist office, head right and walk along Norre Voldg. with the ramparts to your left. (☎72 10 69 80. Open mid-June to Aug. W and Sa-Su noon-4pm.)

Fredericia is located on the Esbjerg-Århus rail-line; **trains** arrive from: Århus (1¾hr.); Copenhagen (2hr.); Esbjerg (1hr.); Hamburg (3hr.). To get to the **tourist**

office, Danmarksg. 2A, from the station, go left across the plaza, and then turn right on Vesterbrog. At the roundabout, go right on Danmarksport. (☎75 92 13 77; www.fredericia.dk. Open June-Aug. M-F 9am-6pm, Sa 9am-2pm; Sept.-May M-F 9:30am-5pm, Sa 10am-1pm.) The lakeside **Fredericia Vandrerhjem and Kursuscenter (HI),** Vestre Ringvej 98, is a vacation spot in itself. From the station go left across the plaza, left on Vejlevej, pass under the bridge, go right on the first road past the lake, and follow the path. (☎75 92 12 87; fredericia@danhostel.dk. Breakfast 45kr. Sheets 45kr. Reception 8am-noon and 4-9pm. Dorms 100kr; doubles 350-400kr.) To camp by the coast, take bus #6 to **Trelde-Naes Camping,** Trelde Naesvej 297. (☎75 95 71 83. Reception 8am-10:30pm. 60kr per person.)

ESBJERG

In a little over 100 years Esbjerg has grown from a tiny port town to the bustling cultural, industrial, and commercial capital of West Jutland. The **Esbjerg Museum,** Torveg. 45, gives visitors a sense of the drastic changes that took place during this time of growth. The building also houses an exhibition on amber, the "Danish gold." From the tourist office, go right on Torveg. (☎75 12 78 11. Open June-Aug. daily 10am-4pm; Sept.-May closed M. 30kr, students 25kr.) For a glimpse of the latest in contemporary art, cross the square from the tourist office and follow Torvet to the end to reach the mirrored walls of the **Esbjerg Kunstmuseum,** Havneg. 20, designed by Jan and Jorn Utzon. (☎75 13 02 11. Open daily 10am-4pm. 30kr, students 25kr.) Next to the museum stands the city's symbol, a **water tower,** Havneg. 22, modeled on medieval German architecture. Check out the great harbor view. (Open June to mid-Sept. 10am-4pm; mid-Sept. to Oct. Sa-Su 10am-4pm. 15kr.)

   Trains run to: Århus (2hr., every 2hr.); Copenhagen (2½hr., every 2hr.); Fredericia (1hr., every hr.). For more info, call 75 12 33 77. **Ferries** head to Harwich, England (☎75 13 02 11; see p. 267). The **tourist office,** Skoleg. 33, is in the Old Courthouse in Market Square. From the station go left on Jernbaneg. and right on Skoleg. (☎75 12 55 99; www.esbjerg.dk. Open M-F 9am-5pm, Sa 10am-1pm; in summer Sa until 5pm.) The **Esbjerg Vandrerhjem (HI),** Gl. Vardevej 80, lies well outside the city center. Take bus #4 from the station. (☎75 12 42 58; esbjerg@danhostel.dk. Breakfast 45kr. Sheets 48kr. Reception 8am-noon and 4-8pm. Dorms 100kr; singles 250kr; doubles 300-350kr.)

RIBE

Well aware of their town's historic value, the town government of Ribe forged preservation laws forcing residents to maintain the character of their houses and to live in them year-round. The result is a magnificently preserved medieval town, situated beautifully on the salt plains near Jutland's west coast. Ribe is particularly proud of the arrival of migratory storks who always roost on the roof of the town hall. For a great view of the birds and the surrounding landscape, climb the 248 steps through the clockwork and huge bells of the 12th-century **cathedral** tower. (☎75 42 06 19. Open Apr.-Oct. M-Sa 10am-6pm, Su noon-6pm; May and Sept. M-Sa 10am-5pm, Su noon-6pm; Apr. and Oct. daily 11am-4pm; Nov.-Mar. M-Su 11am-3pm. 12kr.) Next to the **Det Gamle Rådhus** (Old Town Hall), Von Støckens Plads, a nameless former debtor's prison houses a small museum on medieval torture. (☎76 88 11 22. Open June-Aug. daily 1-3pm; May and Sept. M-F 1-3pm. 15kr.) Follow the **night watchman** on his rounds for an English or Danish tour of town beginning in Torvet, the main square. (35min. June-Aug. 8 and 10pm; May and Sept. 10pm. Free.) Across from the train station, **Museet Ribes Vikinger,** Odin Plads 1, houses artifacts recovered from an excavation of the town, once an important Viking trading post. To get the full story on the Vikings, sit through the hourly film, in English, Danish, and German. (☎76 88 11 22. Open Apr.-June and Sept.-Oct. daily 10am-4pm; July-Aug. 10am-6pm, W until 9pm; Nov.-Mar. Tu-Su 10am-4pm. 50kr.) Next door, the **Ribe Kunst Museum,** Sct. Nikolaig. 10, presents Danish paintings from the Golden Age to the present in a house built in the Dutch Renaissance style. (☎75 42 03 62. Open mid-June to Aug. daily 11am-5pm; Sept.-June Tu-Sa 1-4pm, Su 11am-4pm.) South of town, the open-air **Ribe Vikingcenter,** Lustrupvej 4, re-creates a Viking town, complete with farm and marketplace. (☎75 41 16 11. Open July-Aug. daily 11am-4:30pm; May-June and Sept. M-F 11am-4pm. 50kr.) The **Vadehavscentret** (Wadden Sea Center), Okholmvej 5 in Vestervedsted, does tours of the local marshes. Take the Mandobus (☎75 44 51 07; 50kr) from the station. (☎75 44 61 61. Open Apr.-Oct. daily 10am-5pm; Feb.-Mar. and Nov. 10am-4pm. 45kr. Combo bus and center 80kr.)

Trains to Ribe run from nearby Bramming (25min., 4-5 per day, 28kr) and Esbjerg (40min., every hr., 46kr). The **tourist office**, Torvet 3, has free maps and arranges accommodations for a 20kr fee. From the train station, walk down Dagmarsg., to the left of the Viking museum, and it'll be on your right in the main square. (☎75 42 15 030; www.ribe.dk. Open July-Aug. M-F 9:30am-5:30pm, Sa 10am-5pm; Apr.-June and Sept.-Oct. M-F 9am-5pm, Sa 10am-1pm; Nov.-Mar. M-F 9am-4:30pm, Sa 10am-1pm.) Access the **Internet** at **Gamer's Gateway**, Saltg. 20. (☎76 88 03 37. Open daily noon-midnight. 25kr per hr.) The central **Ribe Vandrerhjem (HI),** Sct. Pedersg. 16, offers **bike** rental (50kr per day) and a gorgeous view of the flatlands. From the station, cross the Viking Museum parking lot, bear right, walk down Sct. Nicolajg. to the end, turn right on Saltg., and immediately left on Sct. Petersg. (☎75 42 06 20. Breakfast 45kr. Sheets 38kr. Reception 8am-noon and 4-8pm; longer hours May-Sept. Open Feb.-Nov. Dorms 80-100kr; singles 250kr; doubles 295kr.) **Ribe Camping,** Farupvej 2, is 1½km from the town center. From the station, turn to face the Vikings Museum and go right on Rosen Allé until it becomes Norremarksvej. After the traffic light, go left along the bike path (Gronnestien) and cross onto Farupvej; it's on the second street on the right. Or grab bus #715 (every 1½hr.) from the station to "Gredstedbro." (☎75 41 07 77. 50kr per person; 2-person cabins 175kr.) **Supermarkets** are around the town center and near the hostel; most are open M-F 10am-6pm, Sa 10am-4pm.

FRANCE

FRENCH FRANCS

US$1 = 7.15F	1F = US$0.14
CDN$1 = 4.64F	1F = CDN$0.22
UK£1 = 10.35F	1F = UK£0.10
IR£1 = 8.33F	1F = IR£0.12
AUS$1 = 3.83F	1F = AUS$0.26
NZ$1 = 3.15F	1F = NZ$0.32
ZAR1 = 0.86F	1F = ZAR1.15
EUR€1 = 6.56F	1F = EUR€0.15

PHONE CODE — **Country Code:** 33. **International dialing prefix:** 00. France has no city codes.

Given the vast cultural and geographic diversity of their homeland, the French have long celebrated the senses like no one else: the vineyards of Bordeaux, the sandy expanses of the Riviera, and the crisp Alpine air all combine for an exhilarating experience. Superimposed on this reckless ride of sensation is the rationalism that has dominated French intellectual life for over 400 years. Sensuality and reason still meet in neighborhood brasseries and cafes, where lively conversation is enjoyed no less than the *plat du jour*. While France (pop. 59.3 million; 544,030 sq. km) no longer single-handedly controls the course of world events, it has secured a spot as one of the most influential forces in the course of Western history. As Napoleon once quipped, "'Impossible?' The word is not French." Pick up a copy of *Let's Go: France 2002* or *Let's Go: Paris 2002* for more fact- and flavor-filled coverage.

SUGGESTED ITINERARIES

THREE DAYS Don't even think of leaving **Paris**, the City of Light (p. 288). Explore the shops and cafés of the **Latin Quarter**, then cross the **Seine** to reach **Ile de la Cité** to admire **Sainte Chapelle.** Visit the wacky **Centre National d'Art et de Culture Georges Pompidou** before seeing a hotspot of 1789, the **Bastille.** Then swing through **Marais** for food and fun. The next day, stroll down the **Champs-Elysées,** starting at the **Arc de Triomphe,** meander through the **Jardin des Tuileries,** and over the Seine to the **Musée d'Orsay.** Peruse part of the **Louvre** the next morning, then head out for an afternoon at **Versailles.**

ONE WEEK After three days in **Paris,** chug to **Tours** (2 days; p. 331) and explore the **castles** of the **Loire Valley** (p. 329). Bike or bus to **Chenonceau** (p. 331), **Chambord** (p. 330), and **Saumur**

(p. 332). Then make your way to the fishy waters of **La Rochelle** (2 days; p. 333), via **Poitiers** (p. 334).

BEST OF FRANCE, THREE WEEKS Whirl through the **Loire Valley** (3 days; p. 329), before taking the train to the wine country of **Bordeaux** (2 days; p. 336). Check out **ee** (2 days; p. 340) before sailing through **Avignon** (p. 345), **Aix-en-Provence** (p. 348), and **Nimes** (p. 345) in sunny **Provence** (3 days; p. 344). Let loose your wild side in **Marseilles** and **Nice** (3 days; p. 356) on the **French Riviera** (p. 353). Show off your tan in the **Alps** (p. 366): scale the peaks near **Chamonix** (p. 368) and **Annecy** (2 days; p. 369). Party in **Lyon** (2 days; p. 370); and eat your fill in **Dijon** (1 day; p. 376). Return to Paris via the **Champagne** region (p. 384), visiting the *caves* of **Reims** (p. 384) and **Troyes** (2 days; p. 385).

FRANCE

LIFE AND TIMES

HISTORY AND POLITICS

FROM THE BEGINNING: 27,000 BC-AD 400

France has been a place of social sanctuary for more than just the past century—the rock shelter of **Cro-Magnon man** in the Dordogne Valley (see p. 335) houses skulls dating from approximately 27,000 years ago. By 4500 BC, **Neolithic** peoples carved out their place in history with giant stone monuments. These otherwise meaningless rocks were an impressive greeting for the Celtic **Gauls,** who arrived from the east around 600 BC. At the same time the Greeks founded the first beach resort, which eventually became Marseilles. Centuries later, in 125 BC, the **Romans** quickly established control of southern France and left their mark everywhere, from the well-preserved monuments of Provence to the French language itself. Under the Roman Empire, the Gauls had their regular dose of Germanic invasions until falling to the **Franks** and **Visigoths** in AD 260-276.

THE EARLY MIDDLE AGES: 400-843

During the early Middle Ages, the power of government fell increasingly to palace mayors (stewards of the king). This allowed **Pepin the Elder,** himself a palace mayor, to crown himself first monarch of the new **Carolingian** dynasty, which proceeded to crush the Muslim advance from Spain and thereby prevent the spread of Islam into Latin Europe. By 800, the Carolingians ruled most of Western Europe. On Christmas Day that year, their most famous son, **Charlemagne** (742-814), was crowned Holy Roman Emperor by Pope Leo III. Charlemagne expanded his territory and renewed interest in the art and literature of the ancients, initiating what is now known as the **Carolingian Renaissance.**

OF CAPETIANS AND THE HUNDRED YEARS WAR 843-1572

After the **Treaty of Verdun** in 843, which divided Europe into its modern boundaries, the Carolingian kings were little more than feeble figureheads. After the last one kicked the bucket in 987, the nobles elected **Hugh Capet** as king, whose only real power was over Paris and the tiny Ile-de-France. The Capetians soon faced the wrath of **William, Duke of Normandy,** who invaded England in 1066 and began centuries of Anglo-French warfare. The French throne was thrown into question in 1328 on the death of **Charles IV,** last of the Capetians. Charles had only daughters, and the traditional French law forced the nobles to give the throne to a family relative, **Philippe de Valois.** But when he stepped on English Aquitaine toes, Charles IV's nephew, **Edward III** of England, claimed the throne, starting the **Hundred Years' War** between the French and English. Salvation for the French came in 1429, when 17-year old **Joan of Arc** claimed divine inspiration and led the French army to a string of victories before her betrayal and capture by Burgundians, allies of the English. She was convicted of witchcraft and burned at the stake in Rouen in 1430. But the tide of war had turned—by 1453 only Calais was left in English hands.

RELIGIOUS WARS: 1572-1610

Catherine de Médici, regent for her son **Charles IX,** king of France, tried to reconcile the Huguenots (French Protestants) with the Catholics. Nevertheless, civil war followed the **St. Bartholomew's Day Massacre** in 1572, initiated by the Duc de Guise, who accepted nothing less than papal supremacy. Over 3000 Huguenots, who had gathered in Paris to celebrate the wedding of **Henri III**'s sister to their leader, Henri of Navarre, were killed. Henri III retaliated, ordering the duke's murder in 1588, but was assassinated himself a year later. Ascending the throne, **Henri IV** (formerly of Navarre) declared "Paris is well worth a mass," referring to his recent conversion to Catholicism. He did not abandon his Huguenot friends, and in 1598 the **Edict of Nantes** guaranteed their religious and political rights.

FRANCE

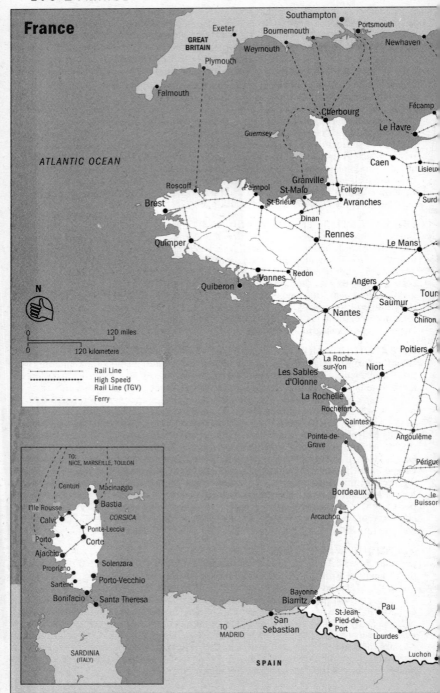

France

GREAT BRITAIN

Exeter
Southampton
Bournemouth
Portsmouth
Newhaven
Plymouth
Weymouth
Falmouth

Fécamp
Cherbourg
Le Havre
Guernsey
Caen
Lisieux

ATLANTIC OCEAN

Roscoff
Paimpol
Granville
Foligny
Surd
Brest
St-Malo
St-Brieuc
Avranches
Dinan
Quimper
Rennes
Le Mans

Vannes
Redon
Angers
Tour
Quiberon
Saumur
Chinon
Nantes

N

Poitiers

0   120 miles
0   120 kilometers

La Roche-sur-Yon
Niort
Les Sables d'Olonne
La Rochelle
Rochefort
Saintes
Angoulême

	Rail Line
	High Speed Rail Line (TGV)
	Ferry

Pointe-de-Grave

Périgue

TO: NICE, MARSEILLE, TOULON

Bordeaux
le Buissor

Centuri
Macinaggio
I'lle Rousse
Bastia
Calvi
CORSICA
Porto
Ponte-Leccia
Corte
Ajaccio
Propriano
Solenzara
Sartène
Porto-Vecchio
Bonifacio
Santa Theresa

Arcachon

SARDINIA (ITALY)

Bayonne
Biarritz
Pau
St-Jean-Pied-de-Port
TO MADRID
San Sebastian
Lourdes
Luchon

SPAIN

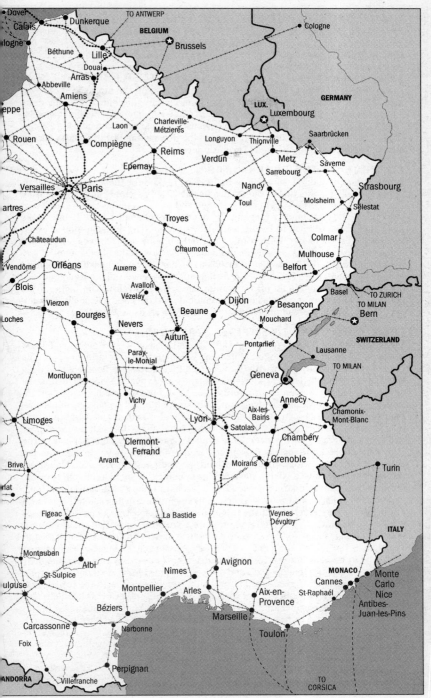

THE KINGDOM OF THE SUN: 1610-1789

First of the Bourbon family line, Henri IV succumbed to an assassin's dagger in 1610 and was succeeded by **Louis XIII.** Louis' ruthless and not-so-holy minister, **Cardinal Richelieu,** consolidated political power for the monarchy, creating a centralized bureaucracy. They were succeeded by another king-and-cardinal combo, **Louis XIV** and **Cardinal Mazarin.** The slippery Mazarin took charge until 1661, when Louis turned 24. Louis adopted the image of the Sun King and the motto *"L'état, c'est moi"* ("I am the state") to create a despotic monarchy that didn't take any crap. After moving the government to his new 14,000-room behemoth called **Versailles** (see p. 317), he revoked the Edict of Nantes in 1685, causing thousands of Protestants to flee from persecution, and initiated the devastating **War of Spanish Succession** (1701-1713) among the great European powers.

BOURBON ON THE ROCKS: 1789

While peasants blamed the soon-to-be-*ancien* regime for their mounting debts, Louis XVI called a meeting of the **Estates General.** This assembly of delegates from the three social classes—aristocrats, clergy, and well, everyone else—hadn't met since 1614, and after much wrangling, the bourgeois-dominated Third Estate broke away and declared itself to be the National Assembly. The Parisian mob stormed the **Bastille** prison (see p. 307) on July 14th, and a bloody orgy of revenge exploded across the nation. The Assembly responded in August with the abolishment of feudal privileges and the **Declaration of the Rights of Man.** When the petrified king tried to flee the country in 1791, he was arrested and imprisoned. As the Revolutionary armies miraculously fought off foreign invasion, the radical **Jacobin** faction took control of the Assembly, abolished the monarchy, and declared a **Republic.** In January 1793, the king was guillotined; the *ancien régime* was now passé.

FROM GUILLOTINE TO EMPIRE: 1789-1850

When the Church refused to bow to the National Assembly, it was abolished and replaced by the oxymoronic **Cult of Reason.** As the counter-revolutionary paranoia of the **Terror** set in, power lay with the "incorruptible" **Maximilien Robespierre** and his Committee of Public Safety. The slightest suspicion of royalist sympathy led to the chopping block, and even Dr. Guillotine himself did not escape his fearful invention. Robespierre ordered the execution of his revolutionary rivals, before his enemies commanded his own execution in 1794. Power was then entrusted to a five-man **Directory.** Meanwhile, a young Corsican general swept through northern Italy and forced the Austrians to surrender to France. Fearful of his rising popularity, the Directory jumped at **Napoleon Bonaparte**'s idea of invading Egypt to threaten the British colonies in India. After an ultimately unsuccessful mission, Napoleon returned with a focused goal to push forward politically. Napoleon kicked out the despised Directory, declaring himself First Consul in 1799, Consul for Life in 1802, and ultimately **Emperor** in 1804. Napoleon's most enduring achievement is his autocratic **legal code;** elements of it are still incorporated into French law. After crushing the Austrians, the Prussians, and the Russians, only Britain remained undefeated, safe in her island refuge following the destruction of the French fleet at Trafalgar in 1805. Napoleon's military demise came during the Russian campaign of 1812. The Russians withdrew before the advancing *Grande Armée*, ravaging their own land to deny the enemy food and shelter. In return for abdicating in 1814, he was given the Mediterranean island of Elba on which to chill with the turtles, and the monarchy was reinstated under **Louis XVIII,** younger brother of his headless predecessor. In what became known as the **Hundred Days,** Napoleon marched northward on March 26, 1815, to a rapturous reception as the king fled back to England. His fling ended three months later with the triumph of the Duke of Wellington on the field of Waterloo in Flanders. Napoleon was banished once again, this time to the remote St. Helena in the south Atlantic, where he died in 1821 of stomach cancer. Today, thousands still flock to pay their respects at his tomb at **Les Invalides** in Paris (see p. 306).

REVOLUTION AND EMPIRE, PART TWO: 1850-1904

In 1850, playing on the strength of his name, the former emperor's nephew **Louis Napoleon** was elected president. The constitution barred the popular ruler from seeking a second term, so he seized power in a coup in 1851, and then had a referendum which declared him **Emperor Napoleon III**. During his 18-year reign, France's grandeur was restored: **Baron Haussmann** rebuilt Paris, replacing medieval streets with grand boulevards along which troops could be deployed. Intent on reclaiming the territories of Alsace and Lorraine, Germany's **Bismarck** surprised and swiftly overran France; the emperor was captured and as German armies advanced, the **Third Republic** was declared in 1871. While the revolutionary **Léon Gambetta** successfully fought off Germans at Coulomiers, Paris held out for four months, with the residents reduced at the end to eating rats. When the government admitted defeat, the Parisian mob revolted and declared the **Commune,** crushed only after 4000 *communards* died in street battles and 25,000 Parisians were summarily executed in the name of order.

The Third Republic was further undermined by the **Dreyfus affair**. In 1894, Jewish army captain **Alfred Dreyfus** was convicted and exiled on trumped-up charges of treason. When the army did not reconsider even after Dreyfus's innocence was evident, France became polarized between those for and against Dreyfus. After **Emile Zola** condemned the army, government, and society for its anti-Semitic prejudice in his dramatic diatribe, *J'accuse*, the momentum became unstoppable. Dreyfus was finally pardoned in 1904.

WAR AND PEACE: 1904-1945

The 1871 unification of Germany had fundamentally changed the balance of power in Europe. After centuries of conflict, the **Entente Cordiale** brought Britain and France into cooperation in 1904. Along with czarist Russia the pair formed the **Triple Entente** to face the **Central Powers** of Germany and the Austro-Hungarian Empire. When **World War I** erupted in 1914, German armies rapidly advanced into France, but a stalemate soon emerged as the opposing armies dug into trenches along the length of the country. The withdrawal of newly revolutionary Russia in 1917 was balanced by the entry of the USA, and victory for the West came in 1918. Devastated by four years of fighting, and with 1.3 million dead, France pushed for crippling reparations from Germany in the **Treaty of Versailles;** these and accompanying humiliations were often invoked by **Hitler** in his rise to power.

During the **Great Depression** of the 1930s, France was politically paralyzed and incapable and unwilling to deal with the rising threat of Nazi Germany. **World War II** began with the German invasion of Poland in 1939. France declared war on Germany in response, and in May 1940 the Germans swept through Belgium into France, bypassing the **Maginot Line,** a string of fortresses along the German border that formed France's main defense. Allied defenses collapsed, and France surrendered in June. The Germans divided France, with the north under German occupation, and a puppet state in the south ruled from **Vichy** by WWI hero **Maréchal Pétain**. Though growing evidence indicates that many French people willingly collaborated with the Germans, today France prefers to commemorate the brave men and women of the **Resistance;** their headquarters in Lyon have now been made into a museum (see p. 370). Under the leadership of **Charles de Gaulle,** head of the French government-in-exile, French troops liberated Paris on August 25th, 1944.

AFTER THE WAR, A NEW HOPE FOR EUROPE: 1945-1962

The **Fourth Republic,** officially proclaimed in 1946, lacked a strong executive to keep the country running when the legislature stalemated, and over the next 14 years France saw 25 governments. Despite these problems, the economy was still steady, and when the constitution was reformed in 1958, the **Fifth Republic,** under the renewed leadership of the still-revered de Gaulle, inherited a sound industrial base. Fiercely nationalist, his foreign policy delicately played the US against the USSR to France's advantage, but his domestic conservatism was problematic. In **May 1968,** what started as a student protest against the university system rapidly grew into a full-scale revolt as workers struck in support of social reform. The aging general had lost his magic touch, and he resigned after a referendum defeat in 1969. During his reign, France's international relations changed significantly. Defeat in Indochina (now Vietnam) in 1954 and Algerian independence in 1962 (following eight years of civil war between native Arabs and French settlers) ended France's role as a colonial power. France joined the new era of European cooperation, designed to end the disastrous cycle of war that had pillaged the continent.

FRANCE TODAY

After de Gaulle resigned in 1969, the tone of the Fifth Republic changed fundamentally. His successor, the *Gaulliste* **Georges Pompidou,** combined a laissez-faire position toward business with less assertive foreign policy. While **François Mitterrand** began his presidential term in 1981 with widespread nationalization, the international climate could not support this socialist economy. By 1986, the right had control of parliament, and Mitterrand had to appoint the ruthless conservative **Jacques Chirac** as Prime Minister. The **far right** also flourished under the leadership of **Jean-Marie Le Pen,** who formed the **Front National** upon an anti-immigration platform. The healthy post-war economy had led to the development of a new working class from North Africa, and Le Pen was able to capitalize on racism against these immigrants. A transport strike and widespread terrorism damaged the right, allowing Mitterrand to win a second term in 1988. The French were more concerned with scandals involving Mitterrand's ministers than his grandiose architectural projects, and the left suffered crushing parliamentary defeats in the early 90s. Mitterrand further lost prestige when the 1991 referendum on the **Maastricht Treaty,** which would transform the European Community into the more closely integrated **European Union** (EU), scraped through with just 51% approval despite massive government support.

In the mid-90s, Mitterrand made two startling confessions: he had collaborated with the Vichy government before joining the Resistance in 1943, and he was seriously ill with cancer. His death in January 1996 came shortly after his arch-rival Chirac won the presidency. The ascendancy of the right was short-lived; in 1997, elections returned a socialist parliament, and Chirac was forced to accept his one-time presidential rival **Lionel Jospin** as prime minister. Recent allegations of corruption against Chirac during his mayoral term in Paris (1977-1995) have several parliamentary members calling for impeachment.

THE ARTS

FINE ARTS AND ARCHITECTURE

EARLY DAYS: FROM PREHISTORY TO AD 1300. The 17,000-year-old paintings of the **caves of Lascaux** (see p. 335) and **Les Eyzies de Tayac** (see p. 335) have been christened "the Sistine Chapel of pre-history." Under Charlemagne in the 8th and 9th centuries, French architects combined classical elements with northern-Barbarian tradition to create the **Romanesque** art form. This style was characterized by round arches and barrel-vaulting, projecting a simple grandeur exemplified by churches including the 11th-century church of the **Madeleine** at Vézelay (see p. 377). Gothic architecture evolved at the end of the 12th century, using a system of arches and flying buttresses (where they flew no one knows), with thin walls and jewel-like stained glass. The **Cathédrale Notre-Dame de Paris** (p. 303), built in 1163, is France's famous example of this intimidating style.

RENAISSANCE: 1300-1600. Exposed to the Renaissance during his Italian campaigns, François I invited the greatest living artists from Italy to work in France, including **Leonardo da Vinci** and **Il Rosso.** The result was one of subtle eroticism, focusing on scenes of court life and classical mythology.

GOING FOR BAROQUE: 1600-1700. **Baroque** architecture, characterized by elaborate ornamentation, reached its peak with the château of **Vaux-le-Vicomte,** which brought architect Louis **Le Vau,** artist Charles **Le Brun,** and landscaper Louis **Le Nôtre** together for the first time. Louis XIV was so impressed with their work that he gave

FRANCE

them the slightly bigger project of **Versailles** (see p. 317). The palace housed such Baroque sculptures as **Giradon**'s outdoor *Apollo Tended by the Nymphs* (1666) and Antoine **Coysevox**'s busts, reflected in the Hall of Mirrors. **Nicolas Poussin** led the Baroque painting movement and is also credited with developing the **Academic** style espoused by the *Académie Royale* after its foundation in 1648. The **Rococo** style, developed in the early 18th century, was all about decadence to the hilt.

ROMANCE IN THE AIR: 1800-1830. The most famous work from the 19th century is **Jacques-Louis David**'s *Coronation* (1807), depicting the moment Napoleon crowned himself emperor. In the decorative arts, the **Empire style** went on a Pharaonic frenzy inspired by Napoleon's Egyptian exploits. The Neoclassical agenda found its place in the two architectural monuments dedicated to the glory of the Grande Armée: the **Eglise de la Madeleine** (see p. 308) and the **Arc de Triomphe** (see p. 307) in Paris. While French architecture didn't think much of Romanticism, the visual arts thought differently. Even though **Jean-Auguste-Dominique Ingres** took up the neo-classical mantle, his interest in medieval and religious themes betrayed the Romantic taste for Gothic. His most celebrated work, the sensuous reclining nude of *Grande Odalisque* (1814; see p. 309), prefigures the oriental fascination of his younger contemporary **Eugène Delacroix**, whose bold brushwork, seen in *Liberty Leading the People* (1830; see p. 309), would prepare the way for Impressionism.

GET REALIST: 1830-1860. In the 1830s a group of painters settled near Fontainebleau to paint nature "unplugged." Led by **Théodore Rousseau** and **Jean-François Millet**, the artists of the **Ecole de Barbizon** had their own artistic organic movement. In the 1850s, this grew into the **Realist** movement under **Gustave Courbet**, with his controversial treatment of everyday subjects on a grand scale. In architecture, Neoclassicism continued to reign thanks to the dominant **Ecole des Beaux Arts**, and can be found in **Charles Garnier**'s Paris opera house (see p. 307).

IMPRESSIONS OF THE LATE 19TH CENTURY. In the 1860s, the young **Edouard Manet** moved away from Realism as he discovered that 3-D reproduction wasn't all it was cracked up to be. The small group of artists who jumped on his bandwagon were more concerned with the impressions the subject left, rather than the art technique used, and for this reason they became known as **Impressionists.** The sunny landscapes of **Claude Monet**, the rosy-cheeked faces of **Auguste Renoir**, and the peasant scenes of **Camille Pissarro** all injected everyday subjects with a sense of new freshness. In the 1880s and 1890s, the **Post-Impressionists** swung the other ways in their search of solidity and permanence. **Georges Seurat** and **Paul Signac** developed **Pointillism,** which uses tiny dots of colors to create a final image—Seurat's *A Sunday Afternoon on the Island of La Grande Jatte* (1884-86) is the most famous example. **Paul Cézanne,** often considered the father of modern art, created solidity and mass on his canvases through the use of geometric forms. Ex-stockbroker **Paul Gauguin** created his masterpieces in Tahiti; influenced by folk art, he developed a style involving broad expanses of color to create a spiritual effect.

EIFFEL AND HIS TOWER: 1876-1889. It took engineers to put new life into French architecture. In 1876, **Gustave Eiffel**, together with architect **Louis-Auguste Boileau,** designed a new building for *Le Bon Marché*, creating large skylit display cases. Nicknamed the "magician of iron," Eiffel is most famous for his tower namesake (see p. 306), the star exhibit of the Universal Exhibition of 1889. A century later, it stands as the best-loved landmark in France. Across the ocean, Eiffel also designed the internal structure of the Statue of Liberty.

WHEN ANIMALS ATTACK: 1877-1932. **Auguste Rodin** only achieved recognition at the age of 35, when critics found his nude *The Age of Bronze* (1877) a little too lifelike. However, his greatest influence on sculpture was his radical move away from realism with the towering *Balzac* (1898), which paved the way for abstraction. The Spaniard **Pablo Picasso,** the most prolific artist of the 20th century, developed many diverse styles during his 80-year career that was spent in France. He shot to notoriety in 1907 with *Les Demoiselles d'Avignon*, shocking both for its

FRANCE

illicit subject and for the angular treatment of the figures. This style foreshadowed **Cubism,** which presents the subject from many different angles at once to capture three dimensions on a flat plane. Meanwhile, Picasso's buddy **Henri Matisse** abandoned the technicality of Pointillism; heck, he abandoned the whole schbang and squeezed paint directly onto the canvas. Shocked Parisian critics called the artists associated with this raw new style **Fauves** (wild animals), and the name stuck. While **Fauvism** made only a brief splash on the canvas of time, Matisse's art remained a vibrant celebration of life as seen in works like *The Dance* (1909; see p. 311).

DADAISM AND SURREALISM: 1914-1939. After the First World War, a generation of young artists turned their backs on a world descending into chaos and formed an anti-art movement known as **Dada.** Already in 1913 **Marcel Duchamp** had exhibited *Bicycle Wheel* (now lost), a bicycle wheel on a stool. This was the first of his "ready mades," and by exhibiting such commonplace, mass-produced objects Duchamp started off the whole "But is it art?" question (oooh...). In 1924, **André Breton** published the *Surrealist Manifesto,* preaching the artistic supremacy of the subconscious. **Surrealism** rejected all traditional notions of art, but essentially pushed artists to reach into the depths of their creativity.

LITERATURE

EARLY READINGS. Epic poetry was represented by the *chansons de geste*, of which the most famous is the *The Song of Roland* (ca. 1000), the story of Charlemagne's nephew and his doomed struggle against the Moors. The publication of **François Rabelais'** novel *Pantagruel* in 1532 delighted many with its unusual combination of bodily functions and progressive ideas on education. **Michel de Montaigne,** prompted by the wars of religion, mused on the frailty of truth in his *Essays* (1580). His successor in the realm of philosophy was **René Descartes,** who proved his own existence with the irrefutable deduction "I think, therefore I am." Also influential was the equally diverse genius of **Blaise Pascal.** After a youth misspent inventing the mechanical calculator and the science of probabilities, he became a devotee of **Jansenism,** an influential Catholic reform movement that sought salvation through inner peace and contemplation. Retiring from public life, Pascal expounded the virtues of solitude in his best-known work, the *Thoughts* (1658). Another important Jansenist was the classically oriented tragedian **Jean Racine,** whose *Phèdre* (1677) is considered by many to be the greatest play in the French literary canon. His comic counterpart, **Molière,** satirized the social pretensions of his age by combining classical structures with hilarious farce. He and his actors formed the **Comédie Française,** now the world's oldest national theater company, which still produces the definitive versions of French classics at its theatre in Paris (see p. 311). Molière died in 1673, ironically during a performance of his satire on hypochondria, *The Imaginary Invalid.*

THE ENLIGHTENMENT. Social tensions created under Louis XIV prompted a period of intense philosophical activity in the years leading up to the Revolution. This **Enlightenment** was dominated by three intellectuals: **Charles-Louis de Montesquieu, Voltaire** (pseudonym of François-Marie Arouet), and **Jean-Jacques Rousseau.** In the influential *The Spirit of the Laws* (1750), Montesquieu examined the influence of non-political circumstances on government. Voltaire made his mark with his insistence on liberty and tolerance. His reputation as a writer rests on his short stories, such as *Candide* (1758). Rousseau thought that society needed to be entirely reshaped. In his *Social Contract* (1762), he made the statement that "man was born free, but he is everywhere in chains." Voltaire and Rousseau were both members of the *philosophes* (philosophers), a diverse group of thinkers bent upon social reform. They were led by **Denis Diderot,** who oversaw the landmark *Encyclopédie* (1765), which aimed to encompass the entire body of human knowledge.

THE EARLY 19TH CENTURY: INCURABLE ROMANTICS. The expressive ideals of **Romanticism** first appeared in Britain and Germany rather than analytically-minded France. However, once the French were bitten by Romanticism, the results were spectacular. The melancholy **Charles Baudelaire**'s *The Flowers of Evil* (1857) became one of the most influential collection of poems published in the 19th century. The great writers **Stendhal** and **Balzac** made the novel an influential literary medium. **Victor Hugo** dominated the Romantic age, with his novels *The Hunchback of Notre-Dame* (1831) and *Les Misérables* (1862) reaching near-mythical status. Aurore Dudevant, who took the pen-name **George Sand,** started a successful career as a novelist, speaking out against the social conventions restricting women in novels such as *Valentine* (1832).

MODERN LITERATURE. It took **Marcel Proust** seven volumes to vent about the elitism of his era in *Remembrance of Things Past* (1913-1927). Revolutionary in technique, this autobiographical portrait of upper-class society during the *Belle Epoque* inspires a fanaticism that puts *Star Wars* to shame. The rising threat of Nazi Germany also spurred a call to arms by writers, led by the indomitable **André Malraux.** His experience in the Chinese civil war supplied the subject for his masterpiece, *The Human Condition* (1933). Another adventurer, **Antoine de Saint-Exupéry,** used his experiences as an early aviation pioneer to create the beloved *The Little Prince* (1943). The post-war period was intellectually dominated by **existentialism,** which questioned the point of existence. An era of theater of the absurd followed: in **Jean-Paul Sartre**'s *No Exit* (1946), four people in a small room discover they are there for eternity, and come to the all-too-true conclusion that "hell is other people." Sartre's companion, **Simone de Beauvoir,** was mainly a novelist, but is best known for *The Second Sex* (1949), an essay attacking the myth of femininity. Though **Albert Camus** is often classed with Sartre, he could hardly be more different. He achieved fame with his debut novel *The Outsider* (1942), which tells the story of a dispassionate social misfit condemned to death for an unrepented murder.

CONTEMPORARY CINEMA

François Truffaut's filmmaking techniques paved the way for the New Wave movement that dominated French cinema though the 1970s. His landmark films include *The 400 Blows* (1959) and *Jules and Jim* (1961). Recently, the *Three Colors* trilogy (1993-94), *Manon of the Spring* (1987), and *Goodbye Children* (1987) have moved movie-goers around the world. Actor **Gérard Depardieu** (*Cyrano de Bergerac,* 1990, *My Father the Hero,* 1993) is renowned for roles both serious and comic, but **Jean Reno** has had more luck making the transition into Hollywood following the success of **Luc Besson**'s *The Professional* (1994), *Fifth Element* (1997), and *Taxi* (1998). On the opposite end of the spectrum from the *belle de jour* fare is the recent spate of **cinéma beur,** second-generation North Africans' brutally honest documentation of life in the HLMs (municipal housing) of suburban Paris. These inexpensive, grafitti-decor films, such as **Mathieu Kassovitz**'s *The Hatred* (1995), confront the traumas of urban racism. **Claire Denis**'s *Chocolate* (1988) gives a voice to France's tumultuous history of colonialism. Art cinema continues to prosper under **Marcel Hanoun** (*Noise of Love and War,* 1997) and **Jacques Doillon** (*Ponette,* 1997), while the French flock to hilarious low-budget comedies like **Jean-Marie Poiré**'s *The Visitors* (1992). Most recently, the 1999 film *The Taste of Others* has made waves on both sides of the Atlantic, winning a César (French Oscar), several film festival awards and a nomination for a 2000 Best Foreign Film Oscar.

FOOD AND DRINK

French chefs cook for the most finicky clients in the world—Charles de Gaulle once griped that no nation with 400 types of cheese could ever be united. The French **breakfast** *(le petit déjeuner)* is usually light, consisting of bread or sometimes croissants or *brioches* (pastry-like buttery breads), and espresso with hot milk *(café au lait)*. A full French **dinner** includes an **apéritif** (pre-dinner drink), an *entrée* (appetizer), *plat* (main course), salad, cheese, dessert, fruit, coffee, and a *digestif* (after-dinner drink). Most restaurants offer *un menu à prix fixe* (fixed-price meal) that costs less than ordering *à la carte.* The menu may include an *entrée* (appetizer), a main course *(plat),* cheese *(fromage),* and dessert, and start at around 60F/€9.15.

FRANCE

Odd-hour cravings can be satisfied at **brasseries,** the middle ground between cafes and the restaurants. The French take **wine** with virtually every meal. Heed the tale of the famous director who dared to order a Coke with his 1500F/€228.70 meal; he was promptly kicked out of the restaurant. Of him it was said, *"Il manque de savoir vivre"*—he doesn't know how to live. A warning to **vegetarians:** Trust no one. The concept of meatless life is foreign to most waiters and chefs; even a salad may have ham. You'll have more luck at **crêperies,** ethnic restaurants, and places catering to a younger crowd.

Cafes in France, haunts of intellectuals from Hemingway to Sartre, figure pleasantly in the daily routine. Prices are cheaper at the counter *(comptoir)* than in the seating area *(salle)*; outdoor seating *(la terrasse)* may be even more expensive. Coffee, beer, and (in the south) the anise-flavored *pastis* are staple cafe drinks. If you order *café*, you'll get espresso; for coffee with milk, ask for a *café crème*. *Bière à la pression*, or draught beer, is either pale *(blonde)* or dark *(brune)*. A glass of red is the cheapest wine in a cafe (starting at 4-6F/€0.65-0.95).

ESSENTIALS

DOCUMENTS AND FORMALITIES

For stays shorter than 90 days, only citizens of South Africa need a short-stay visa *(court séjour;* 30-day visas ZAR174.50; 90-day ZAR209.35-244.25). For stays longer than 90 days, all non-EU citizens need a long-stay visa (650F/€99.10). Non-EU nationals cannot work in France without a **work permit,** which requires a job offer; nor can they **study** without a **student visa,** which requires proofs of admission to a French university, financial independence, and medical insurance. For **au pair** and **teaching assistant** jobs, special rules apply; check with your local consulate.

French Embassies at Home: Australia, Consulate General, Level 26, St. Martins Tower, 31 Market St., Sydney NSW 2000 (☎(02) 92 61 57 79; fax 92 83 12 10; www.france.net.au/consulat/index.htm). **Canada,** Consulate General, 1 pl. Ville Marie, 26th fl., Montréal, QC H3B 4SE (☎514-878-4385; fax 878-3981; www.consulfrance-montreal.org); Consulat Général à Toronto, 130 Bloor St. West, Ste. #400, Toronto, ON M5S 1N5 (☎416-925-8041; fax 925-3076; www.consulfrance-toronto.org); **Ireland,** French Embassy, Consulate Section, 36 Ailesbury Rd., Ballsbridge, Dublin 4 (☎(01) 260 16 66; fax 283 01 78; www.ambafrance.ie). **New Zealand,** New Zealand Embassy and Consulate, 34-42 Manners St., P.O. Box 11-343, Wellington (☎(04) 384 25 55; fax 384 25 77; www.ambafrance.net.nz). **South Africa,** Consulate General at Johannesburg, 191 Smuts Ave., Rosebank; mailing address P.O. Box 1027, Parklands 2121 (☎(011) 778 5600; visas 778 5605; fax 778 5601; www.consulfrance.co.za); **UK,** Consulate General, P.O. Box 520, 21 Cromwell Rd., London SW7 2EN (☎(020) 7838 2000; fax 7838 2001; www.ambafrance.org.uk). **US,** Consulate General, 4101 Reservoir Rd. NW, Washington, D.C. 20007 (☎202-944-6000; fax 994-6148; www.consulfrance-washington.org; check out www.info-france-usa.org/america/consulat/consulat.htm for more information on other US consulates).

Foreign Embassies in France: All embassies are in **Paris** (see p. 292). There are **UK** consulates in Paris, Bordeaux, Lille, and Marseilles, and **US** consulates in Paris, Bordeaux, Lyon, Marseilles, Nice, Rennes, Strasbourg, and Toulouse.

TRANSPORTATION

BY PLANE. Airfares to France peak between June and September. The two major international airports in Paris are **Charles de Gaulle** and **Orly.** For info on cheap flights from the UK, see p. 47.

BY TRAIN. The French national railway company, **SNCF** *(Société Nationale de Chemins de Fer;* ☎08 36 35 35 35; www.sncf.fr), manages one of the most efficient transportation systems around. **TGV** *(train à grande vitesse,* or high-speed train), the fastest in the world, runs from Paris to major cities in France, as well as to Geneva and Lausanne, Switzerland. **Rapide** trains are slower, and local trains are the slowest of all, but are oddly called **Express** or **TER** *(Train Express Regional)*. The **Eurostar** provides rapid connections to London and Brussels (see p. 52). SNCF offers a wide range of discounted round-trip tickets called **tarifs découvertes**—you should rarely have to pay full price. Get a calendar from a train station detailing **période bleue** (blue period), **période blanche** (white period), and **période rouge** (red period) times and days; blue gets the most discounts, while red gets none. Those under age 25 have two great options: the **Découverte 12-25** (270F/€41.20) gives a 25% discount for any blue-period travel; and the **Carte 12-25** (270F/€41.20), valid for a year, is good for 25-50% off all TGV trains, 50% off all other trips that started during a blue period, and 25% off those starting in a white period. Tickets must be validated in the orange machine at the entrance to the platforms at the *gare* (train station) and re-validated at any connections in your trip. Seat **reservations**, recommended for international trips, are mandatory on EuroCity (EC), InterCity (IC), and TGV trains. All three require a ticket supplement (travelers under 26 with ID are entitled to a discount) and reservation fee.

The **Eurailpass** is valid in France. The SNCF's **France Railpass** grants three days of unlimited rail travel in France in any 30-day period (US$175; companion travelers $141 each; add up to 6 extra days for $30 each); the parallel **Youthpass** provides those under 26 with four days of unlimited travel within a two-month period ($130; up to 6 extra days $20 each). The **France Rail 'n Drive pass** combines three days of rail travel with two days of Avis car rental excluding insurance (US$240; companion travelers $170 each; extra rail days $30 each, extra car days $49).

BY BUS. Within France, long-distance buses are a secondary transportation choice; service is very infrequent compared to most other European countries. However, in some regions, buses can be indispensable for reaching out-of-the-way towns and sights. Bus services operated by the SNCF accept railpasses. Bus schedules usually indicate whether they run during *"période scolaire"* (school year), *"période de vacances"* (vacations), or both.

BY FERRY. Ferries across the English Channel *(La Manche)* link France to England and Ireland. The shortest and most popular route is between **Dover** (see p. 188) and **Calais** (see p. 387), and is run by **P&O Stena Line, SeaFrance,** and **Hoverspeed** (see p. 52). Hoverspeed also travels from **Dieppe** (see p. 321) to **Newhaven, England.** **Brittany Ferries** (☎ 08 03 82 88 28; www.brittanyferries.co.uk) travels from **Cherbourg** (see p. 323) to **Poole;** from **Caen** (see p. 321) to **Portsmouth;** from **St-Malo** (see p. 326) to **Portsmouth. Irish Ferries** (☎ 01 44 94 20 40; www.irishferries.ie) has overnight ferries from **Cherbourg** and **Roscoff** to **Rosslare Harbour, Ireland** (see p. 567). **Eurailpass** is valid on boats to Ireland (excluding 30F/€4.60 port tax). On Brittany Ferries, students receive a 10% discount. For schedules and prices on English Channel ferries, see p. 52. For info on ferries from **Nice** and **Marseilles** to **Corsica,** see p. 362.

BY CHUNNEL FROM THE UK. Traversing 43½km under the sea, the Chunnel is undoubtedly the fastest, most convenient, and least scenic route from England to France. **Eurostar** runs a frequent high-speed train service from London to Paris (3hr., 2nd class US$75-159) and Brussels (3hr., every hr., 2nd class US$75-159), with stops at Ashford in England and Calais and Lille in France. Book reservations in the UK, by phone, or over the web. (UK ☎ 0990 18 61 86, US 800-387-6782; elsewhere +44 1233 61 75 75; www.eurostar.com; www.raileurope.com.) Eurostar tickets can also be bought at most major travel agents. **Eurotunnel** shuttles cars and passengers between Kent and Nord-Pas-de-Calais (UK ☎ 0800 96 99 92, France ☎ 03 21 00 61 00; www.eurotunnel.co.uk).

BY CAR. Unless you are traveling in a group of three or more, you won't save money traveling long distance by car rather than train—thanks to highway tolls, high gasoline cost, and rental charges. If you can't decide between train and car travel, get a Rail 'n Drive pass from railpass vendors (see above). The French drive

FRANCE

on the right-hand side of the road; France maintains its roads well, but the landscape itself often makes the roads a menace, especially in twisting Corsica.

BY BIKE AND BY THUMB. Renting a bike beats bringing your own if your touring will be of one or two regions. Some youth hostels rent bicycles for low prices. **Mopeds** are a good compromise between the high cost of car travel and the limited range of bicycles. Expect to pay about 100-150F/€15.25-22.90 per day.

Many consider France the hardest country in Europe to get a lift. *Let's Go* does not recommend hitchhiking. In major cities there are ride-sharing organizations that pair drivers and riders. Contact **Eurostop International** (**Allostop** in France; www.ecritel.fr/allostop). Not all of these organizations screen drivers and riders.

TOURIST SERVICES AND MONEY

EMERGENCY	Police, ☎ 122. Ambulance, ☎ 123. Fire, ☎ 124.

TOURIST OFFICES. The extensive French tourism support network revolves around **syndicats d'initiative** and **offices de tourisme** (in the smallest towns, the **Mairie,** the mayor's office, deals with tourist concerns), all of which *Let's Go* labels "tourist office." All three distribute maps and pamphlets, help you find accommodations, and suggest excursions to the countryside. For up-to-date events and regional info, try www.francetourism.com.

CURRENCY AND EXCHANGE. The national currency of France is the **franc français** or French Franc (FF or F). Each franc is divided into 100 *centimes*. The franc is available in 20F, 50F, 100F, 200F, and 500F notes; two-tone 10F and 20F coins; silvery 1F, 2F, and 5F; and pale copper 5, 10, 20, and 50 *centimes* pieces. France has accepted the **Euro (€)** as legal tender, and francs will be phased out by July 1, 2002. For more information, see p. 23.

> **Prices:** If you stay in hostels and prepare your own food, expect to spend about 100-140F/€15.25-21.35 per person per day. **Accommodations** start at about 130F/€19.85 per night for a double, and a basic sit-down meal with wine costs 65F/€9.95.
>
> **Tipping and bargaining:** By law, service must be included at all restaurants, bars, and cafes in France. It is not unheard of to leave extra change at a cafe or bar, maybe a franc or two per drink; exceptionally good service may be rewarded with a 5-10% tip. Otherwise, tipping is only expected for **taxis** and **hairdressers;** 10-15% is the norm. **Bargaining** is appropriate at flea markets (*marchés aux puces*).
>
> **Taxes:** Most purchases in France include a 20.6% **value-added tax (VAT;** TVA is the French acronym). Non-EU residents (including EU citizens who reside outside the EU) in France for less than six months can reclaim 17.1% of the total price on purchases over 1200F/€182.95 made in one store. Only certain stores participate in this **vente en détaxe** refund process; ask before you buy.

ACCOMMODATIONS AND CAMPING

Hostels generally offer dormitory accommodations in large single-sex rooms with 4-10 beds, though some have as many as 60. A bed in a French hostel will average around 50-100F/€7.65-15.25. In France, the **Hostelling International (HI)** (see p. 36) affiliate is the **Fédération Unie des Auberges de Jeunesse (FUAJ)** and it operates 178 hostels within France. Some hostels accept reservations through the **International Booking Network** (see p. 35). Two or more people traveling together will often save money by staying in cheap **hotels** rather than hostels. The French government employs a four-star hotel ratings system depending on the facilities they provide; Most of the hotels *Let's Go* lists have zero to two stars, with a few three stars. *Let's Go* chooses hotels according to qualities such as convenience and money value. **Gîtes d'étapes** are rural accommodations for cyclists, hikers, and other ramblers. They are located in less populated areas, normally along popular trails; expect *gîtes* to provide beds, a kitchen, and resident caretaker. In many towns, **universities** open their dorms to travelers when out of session and sometimes also during term-time.

After 3000 years of settled history, true wilderness in France is hard to find. It's **illegal to camp** in most public spaces, including and especially national parks. Instead, look forward to organized *campings* (campsites), where you'll share your splendid isolation with vacationing families. Most campsites have toilets, showers, and electrical outlets, though you may have to pay extra for such luxuries (10-40F/€1.55-6.10); you'll often need to pay a supplement for your car, too (20-50F/€3.05-7.65). Otherwise, expect to pay 50-90F/€7.65-13.75 per site.

COMMUNICATION

MAIL. Airmail letters under 1 oz. between the US and France take 4-7 days and cost US$0.80. Letters from Canada cost CDN$1.05 for 20g. Allow at least 5 working days from Australia (postage AUS$1 for up to 20g) and 3 days from Britain (postage UK£0.30 for up to 20g). Envelopes should be marked *"par avion"* (airmail) to avoid having letters sent by sea. Mail can be held for pick-up through **Poste Restante** (General Delivery) to almost any city or town with a post office. Address letters to: SURNAME, FirstName; *Poste Restante: Recette Principale;* [5-digit postal code] TOWN; FRANCE; mark the envelope HOLD.

TELEPHONES. When calling from abroad, drop the leading zero of the local number. French pay phones only accept stylish microchip-toting phone cards called **Télécartes;** some pay phones in Paris also take credit cards. *Télécartes* are available in 50-unit (49F/€7.50) and 120-unit (98F/€14.95) denominations at train stations, post offices, and *tabacs*. *Décrochez* means pick up; you'll then be asked to *patientez* (wait) to insert your card; at *numérotez* or *composez* you can dial. Use only public **France Télécom** pay phones as privately owned ones charge more. An expensive alternative is calling collect *(faire un appel en PCV);* an English-speaking operator can be reached by dialing the appropriate service provider below. Directory assistance is ☎12. **International operator** ☎00 33 11. The international direct dial numbers are: **AT&T,** ☎0 800 99 00 11; **British Telecom,** ☎0 800 99 02 44; **Canada Direct,** ☎0 800 99 00 16 or 99 02 16; **Ireland Direct,** ☎0 800 99 03 53; **MCI,** ☎0 800 99 00 19; **Sprint,** ☎0 800 99 00 87; **Telecom New Zealand,** ☎0 800 99 00 64; **Telkom South Africa,** ☎0 800 99 00 27; **Telstra Australia,** ☎0 800 99 00 61.

INTERNET ACCESS. Most major **post offices** now offer Internet access; 50F/€7.65 buys 50min. of access, stored on a rechargeable card available at the office itself. Most large towns in France have a cyber cafe. Rates and speed of connection vary widely; occasionally there are free terminals in technologically themed museums or exhibition spaces. **Cybercafé Guide** (www.cyberiacafe.net/cyberia/guide/ccafe.htm#working_france) lists cyber cafes in France.

LANGUAGE. Contrary to popular opinion, even flailing efforts to speak French will be appreciated, especially in the countryside. Be lavish with your *Monsieurs, Madames,* and *Mademoiselles,* and greet people with a friendly *bonjour (bonsoir* in the evening). For basic French vocabulary and pronunciation, see p. 953.

LOCAL FACTS

Time: France is 1hr. ahead of Greenwich Mean Time (GMT).

When to Go: In summer, the temperature in Paris ranges 13-24°C (55-75°F); it's cooler in the North and Alps, while southern France has scorching heat. Winters are usually mild on the coasts, with frequent rains; the Alps and central France have snow and frost.

Hours: Just about everything opens at 9am, snoozes noon-2pm, and is closed Su; many provincial areas also shut down M. **Banks** tend to close around 4pm. Most **shops** generally stay open until 6:30pm. **Museums** close at least 1 day a week, usually M or Tu. Sights run by the local government tend to close M.

Holidays: New Year (Jan. 1); Easter Monday (April 5); Labor Day (May 1); Liberation Day (May 8); Ascension Day (June 1); Whitmonday (June 12); Bastille Day (July 14); Feast of the Assumption (Aug. 15); All Saints' Day (Nov. 1); Armistice Day (Nov. 11); and Christmas (Dec. 25).

Festivals: Most festivals, like **fête du cinema** and **fête de la musique** (late June, when musicians rule the streets), are in summer. The **Cannes Film Festival** (May; www.festival-cannes.com) is mostly for directors and stars, but provides good people watching. The **Festival d'Avignon** (July-Aug.; www.festival-avignon.com/gbindex3.html) is famous for its theater. **Bastille Day** (July 14) is marked by military parades, *bals des pompiers* (firemen's dances) and fireworks nationwide. Although you may not be competing in the **Tour de France** (3rd or 4th Su in July; www.letour.fr), you'll enjoy all the hype. Nice's **Vineyard Festival** (Sept.; www.nice-coteazur.org/americain/tourisme/vigne/index.html) celebrates the grape harvest with music, parades, and wine tastings. Nice and Nantes celebrate **Carnaval** in the last week or two before Ash Wednesday (culminating with Mardi Gras celebrations).

PARIS

City of light, of majestic panoramas and showy store windows, of the dark, and of the invisible—Paris somehow manages to be it all. From the twisting alleys that shelter the world's best bistros to broad avenues flaunting the latest in *haute couture*, from the ancient gargoyles of Notre Dame to the vibrant and wacky Centre Centre Georges-Pompidou, Paris is both a guardian of tradition and a leader of the cutting edge. You can't conquer Paris, but you can get acquainted in a few days, and after a little longer, you may have made a comfortable friend. For more dazzling detail of Paris and its environs, check out *Let Go: Paris 2002.*

✈ INTERCITY TRANSPORTATION

Flights: Aéroport Roissy-Charles de Gaulle (☎01 48 62 22 80; www.parisairports.com), 23km northeast of Paris, services most transatlantic flights. For flight info, call the 24hr. English-speaking information center. **Aéroport d'Orly** (English recording ☎01 49 75 15 15), 18km south of Paris, is used by charters and many continental flights. The cheapest and fastest ways to get into the city are by **RER** or **bus.**

Transportation to and from Roissy-CDG: By RER train, take the free shuttle bus (*navette*) from Terminal 2 to the Roissy train station. From there, commuter rail line RER B will transport you to central Paris. To transfer to the Métro, get off at Gare du Nord, Châtelet-Les-Halles, or St-Michel. To go to Roissy-CDG from Paris, take the RER B (30-35min., every 15min. 5am-12:30am, 49F/€7.50) to "Roissy," at the end of the line. Then change to the free shuttle bus (every 10min.). **Roissybus** (☎01 49 25 61 87) leaves from the corner of r. Scribe and r. Auber, near M: Opéra, and stops at all terminals. Buy tickets on bus (45min.; every 15min. 6am-8pm, every 20min. 8-11pm; 48F/€7.35). **Air France buses** (English recording ☎01 41 56 89 00) run often into the city. Buy tickets on bus (30-35min., 65-130F/€9.95-19.85).

Transportation to and from Orly: From Orly Sud gate H or gate I, platform 1, or Orly Ouest level 0, gate F, take the **Orly-Rail** shuttle bus (every 15min. 5:40am-11:15pm, 12F/€1.85) to "Pont de Rungis/Aéroport d'Orly," where you can board the **RER C2** for several destinations in Paris. (English information ☎08 36 68 41 14. 25min., every 15min. 6am-11pm, 35F/€5.35.) The RATP **Orlybus** (☎01 40 02 32 94) runs to the airport from M: Denfert-Rochereau. Board at Orly Sud, gate H, platform 4 or Orly Ouest level 1 (30min., every 15-20min. 6am-11:30pm, 35F/€5.35). **Air France Buses** run between Orly and **Gare Montparnasse** (30min.; every 12min. 6am-11pm; 50F/€7.65 1-way, 85F/€13 round-trip).

Trains: There are 6 train stations in Paris, each part of the Métro system and servicing a different geographic region.

Gare du Nord: M: Gare du Nord. Serves Belgium, Britain, northern France, northern Germany, The Netherlands, and Scandinavia. To: **Amsterdam** (4-5hr., 503F/€76.70); **Brussels** (2hr., 324F/€49.40); **Cologne** (4-5hr., 466F/€71.05). The **Eurostar** departs from here for **London** (2hr., up to 1700F/€259.20).

Gare de l'Est: M: Gare de l'Est. To Austria, eastern France, southern Germany, Luxembourg, and northern Switzerland. To: **Munich** (8-10hr., 683F/€104.15); **Vienna** (14hr., 1052F/€160.40); **Zürich** (6-7hr., 432F/€65.90).

Gare de Lyon: M: Gare de Lyon. To southeastern France, Greece, Italy, and parts of Switzerland. To: **Geneva** (3½-4hr., 420F/€64.05) and **Rome** (13hr., 828F/€126.25).

FRANCE

Gare d'Austerlitz: M: Gare d'Austerlitz. Serves southwestern France, the Loire Valley, Portugal, and Spain. To: **Barcelona** (9hr., 558F/€85.10) and **Madrid** (12-13hr., 713F/€108.70).

Gare St-Lazare: M: Gare St-Lazare. Serves Normandy. To: **Rouen** (1-2hr., 105F/€16).

Gare de Montparnasse: M: Montparnasse-Bienvenüe. Serves Brittany; also the departure point for **TGVs** to southwestern France.

Buses: Gare Routière Internationale du Paris-Gallieni, 28, av. du Général de Gaulle, just outside Paris in Bagnolet. M: Gallieni. **Eurolines** (☎08 36 69 52 52; www.eurolines.fr) sells tickets to most destinations in France and neighboring countries.

⚜ ORIENTATION

The **Ile de la Cité** and **Ile St-Louis** sit at the geographical center of the city, while the **Seine,** flowing east to west, splits Paris into two large expanses: the **Rive Gauche (Left Bank)** to the south and the **Rive Droite (Right Bank)** to the north. The Left Bank, with its older architecture and narrow streets, has traditionally been considered bohemian and intellectual, while the Right Bank, with its grand avenues and designer shops, is more chi-chi. Administratively, Paris is divided into 20 **arrondissements** (districts; e.g. 1er, 6ème) that spiral clockwise around the Louvre. Areas of interest are compact and central, and sketchier neighborhoods tend to lie on the outskirts of town. Refer also to this book's **color maps** of the city.

RIVE GAUCHE (LEFT BANK). The **Latin Quarter,** encompassing the 5ème and parts of the 6ème around the **Sorbonne** and the **Ecole des Beaux-Arts** (School of Fine Arts), has been home to students for centuries; the animated **Boulevard St-Michel** is the boundary between the two *arrondissements*. The area around east-west **Boulevard St-Germain,** which crosses bd. St-Michel just south of pl. St-Michel in the 6ème, is known as **St-Germain des Prés.** To the west, the gold-domed **Invalides** and the stern Neoclassical **Ecole Militaire,** which faces the **Eiffel Tower** across the **Champ-de-Mars,** recall the military past of the 7ème and northern 15ème, now full of traveling businesspeople. South of the Latin Quarter, **Montparnasse,** in the 14ème, eastern 15ème, and southwestern 6ème, lolls in the shadow of its tower. The glamorous **Boulevard du Montparnasse** belies the more residential districts around it. The eastern Left Bank, comprising the 13ème, is the city's newest hotspot, centered on the **Place d'Italie.**

RIVE DROITE (RIGHT BANK). The **Louvre** and **Rue de Rivoli** occupy the sight- and tourist-packed 1er and the more business-oriented 2ème. The crooked streets of the **Marais,** in the 3ème and 4ème, escaped Baron Haussmann's redesign of Paris and now support many diverse communities. From **Place de la Concorde,** at the western end of the 1er, **Avenue des Champs-Elysées** bisects the 8ème as it sweeps up toward the **Arc de Triomphe** at **Charles de Gaulle-Etoile.** South of the Etoile, old and new money fills the exclusive 16ème, bordered to the west by the **Bois de Boulogne** park and to the east by the Seine and the **Trocadéro,** which faces the Eiffel Tower across the river. Back toward central Paris, the 9ème, just north of the 2ème, is defined by the sumptuous **Opéra.** East of the 9ème, the 10ème hosts cheap lodgings and the **Gare du Nord** and **Gare de l'Est.** The 10ème, 3ème, and the happening 11ème, which peaks with the nightlife of **Bastille,** meet at **Place de la République.** South of Bastille, the 12ème surrounds the **Gare de Lyon,** petering out at the **Bois de Vincennes.** East of Bastille, the party atmosphere gives way to the quieter, more residential 20ème and 19ème, while the 18ème is home to **Montmartre,** capped by the **Sacré-Cœur.** To the east, the 17ème begins in the red-light district of **Pigalle** and bd. de Clichy, and grows more elegant toward the Etoile, the **Opéra Garnier,** and the 16ème. Continuing west along the *grande axe* defined by the Champs-Elysées, the skyscrapers of **La Défense,** Paris's newest quarter, are across the Seine from the Bois de Boulogne.

▤ LOCAL TRANSPORTATION

Public Transportation: The efficient **Métropolitain,** or **Métro (M),** runs 5:30am-12:30am. Lines are numbered and are generally referred to by their number and final destinations; connections are called *correspondances*. **Single-fare tickets** within the

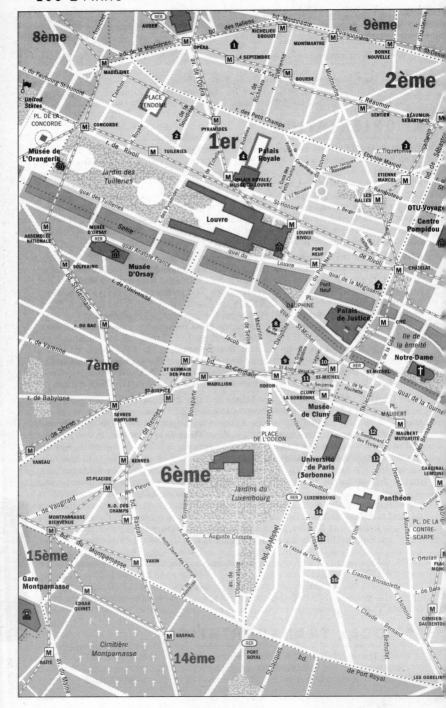

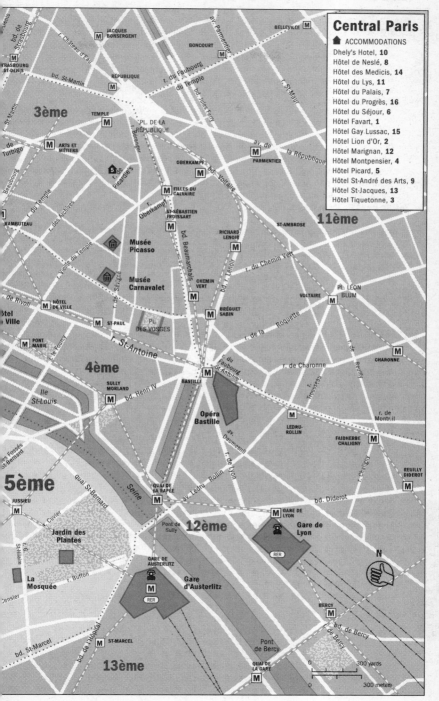

Central Paris

⌂ ACCOMMODATIONS

Dhely's Hotel, **10**
Hôtel de Neslé, **8**
Hôtel des Medicis, **14**
Hôtel du Lys, **11**
Hôtel du Palais, **7**
Hôtel du Progrès, **16**
Hôtel du Séjour, **6**
Hôtel Favart, **1**
Hôtel Gay Lussac, **15**
Hôtel Lion d'Or, **2**
Hôtel Marignan, **12**
Hôtel Montpensier, **4**
Hôtel Picard, **5**
Hôtel St-André des Arts, **9**
Hôtel St-Jacques, **13**
Hôtel Tiquetonne, **3**

city 8.50F/€1.30; **carnet** (packet) of 10 61F/€9.30. Buy extras for when ticket booths are closed (after 10pm) and hold on to your ticket until you exit. The **RER** *(Réseau Express Régional)*, the commuter train to the suburbs, serves as an express subway within central Paris; changing to and getting off the RER requires sticking your validated ticket into a turnstile. Watch the signboards next to the RER tracks and check that your stop is lit up before riding. **Buses** use the same 8.50F/€1.30 tickets (bought on the bus; validate in the machine by the driver), but transfer requires a new ticket. Buses run 6:30am-8:30pm, *Autobus du Soir* until 1am, and *Noctambus* (3-4 tickets) every hr. 1:30-5:30am at stops marked with the bug-eyed moon between the Châtelet stop and the *portes* (city exits). The **Mobilis** pass covers the Métro, RER, and buses only (1-day 33F/€5.05). To qualify for a weekly pass *(hebdomadaire)*, which expires every Su (87F/€13.30), bring a photo ID to the ticket counter to get the necessary **Carte Orange.** Refer to this book's **color maps** of Paris's transit network.

Taxis: Alpha Taxis (☎01 45 85 85 85); **Taxis 7000** (☎01 42 70 00 42). Cabs are expensive and only take 3 passengers. The meter starts running when you phone. Cab stands are near train stations and major bus stops.

Car Rental: Rent-a-Car, 79, r. de Bercy, 12ème (☎01 43 45 98 99). Open M-Sa 8:30am-7pm.

Bike Rental: Paris à velo, c'est sympa! 37, bd. Bourdon, 4ème (☎01 48 87 60 01; www.parisvelosympa.com). M: Bastille. Rentals available with a 2000F/€305 or credit card deposit. 24hr. rental 150F/€22.90; 9am-7pm 80F/€12.20; half day 60F/€9.15.

Hitchhiking: *Let's Go* does not recommend hitchhiking. Don't waste time at the *portes* of the city, as traffic there is too heavy for cars to stop.

🛂 PRACTICAL INFORMATION

TOURIST AND FINANCIAL SERVICES

Tourist Offices: Bureau d'Accueil Central, 127, av. des Champs-Elysées, 8ème (☎08 36 68 31 12; www.paris-touristoffice.com). M: Georges V. English-speaking and mobbed. Open daily 9am-8pm; low season Su 11am-6pm. **Branches** at Gare de Lyon (open M-Sa 8am-8pm) and the Eiffel Tower (open May-Sept. daily 11am-6pm).

Budget Travel: Office de Tourisme Universitaire (OTU), 119, r. St-Martin, 4ème (☎01 40 29 12 22; www.otu.fr). M: Centre Georges Pompidou. Sells ISICs and plane, train, and bus tickets at student discounts. Open M-F 10am-6:30pm, Sa 10am-5pm. Also at 39, av. G Bernanos, 5ème (☎01 44 41 38 50; M: Palais du Luxembourg), and 1, pl. de Lattre de Tassigny (☎01 44 05 49 85; M: Porte Dauphine). **Council Exchange,** 1, pl. Odéon, 6ème (☎01 44 41 89 80; www.councilexchange.org). M: Odéon. Sells ISICs and plane and train tickets. Open M-F 9:30am-6:30pm, Sa 10am-5pm.

Embassies: Australia, 4, r. Jean-Rey, 15ème (☎01 40 59 33 00; www.austgov.fr). M: Bir-Hakeim. Open M-F 9:15am-noon and 2-4:30pm. **Canada,** 35, av. Montaigne, 8ème (☎01 44 43 29 00). M: Franklin-Roosevelt or Alma-Marceau. Open M-F 9am-noon and 2-5pm. **Ireland,** 12, av. Foch, 16ème (☎01 44 17 67 48). M: Argentine. Open M-F 9:30am-noon. **New Zealand,** 7ter, r. Léonard de Vinci, 16ème (☎01 45 00 24 11). M: Victor-Hugo. Open M-F 9am-1pm and 2-5:30pm. **South Africa,** 59, quai d'Orsay, 7ème (☎01 53 59 23 23). M: Invalides. Open M-F 8:30am-12:30pm and 1:30-5:15pm. **UK,** 35, r. du Faubourg-St-Honoré, 8ème (☎01 44 51 31 00). M: Concorde. Open M-F 9:30am-12:30pm and 2:30-5pm. **US,** 2, av. Gabriel, 8ème (☎01 43 12 22 22). M: Concorde. Open M-F 9am-6pm.

Currency Exchange: Hotels, train stations, and airports offer poor rates but have extended hours; Gare de Lyon, Gare du Nord, and both airports have booths open 6:30am-10:30pm. Most **ATMs** accept **Visa** ("CB/VISA") and **MasterCard** ("EC"). Crédit Lyonnais ATMs take **AmEx;** Crédit Mutuel and Crédit Agricole ATMs are on the **Cirrus** network; and most Visa ATMs accept **PLUS**-network cards.

American Express: 11, r. Scribe, 9ème (☎01 47 14 50 00), opposite rear of the Opéra. M: Opéra or Auber. Mail held for cardholders and AmEx Travelers Cheques holders. Open M-F 9am-6:30pm, Sa 10am-5:30pm. Exchange counters open Su 10am-5pm.

FRANCE

LOCAL SERVICES

English-Language Bookstore: Shakespeare and Co., 37, r. de la Bûcherie, 5ème, across the Seine from Notre-Dame. M: St-Michel. Quirky, wide-ranging selection of new and used books. Open daily noon-midnight.

Gay and Lesbian Services: Centre Gai et Lesbien, 3, r. Keller, 11ème (☎01 43 57 21 47). M: Ledru Rollin. Info hub of all gay services and associations in Paris. English spoken. Open M-Sa 2-8pm, Su 2-7pm. **Les Mots à la Bouche**, 6, r. Ste-Croix de la Bretonnerie (☎01 42 78 88 30; www.motalabouche.com), is Paris's largest gay and lesbian bookstore and serves as an unofficial information center for queer life. M: Hôtel-de-Ville. Open M-Sa 11am-11pm, Su 2-8pm.

Laundromats: Laundromats are everywhere, especially in the 5ème and 6ème. **Arc en Ciel**, 62, r. Arbre Sec, 1er (☎01 42 41 39 39), offers **dry cleaning.** M: Louvre. Open M-F 8am-1:15pm and 2:30-7pm, Sa 8:30am-1:15pm.

EMERGENCY AND COMMUNICATIONS

Emergencies: Ambulance, ☎15. **Fire,** ☎18. **Police,** ☎17. For non-emergencies, head to the local *gendarmerie* (police force) in each *arrondissement*.

Crisis Lines: Rape, SOS Viol (☎0 800 05 95 95). Call free anywhere in France for counseling (medical and legal). Open M-F 10am-7pm. **SOS Help!** (☎01 47 23 80 80). Anonymous, confidential English crisis hotline. Open daily 3-11pm.

Pharmacies: Every *arrondissement* should have a **pharmacie de garde** open 24hr. in case of emergencies. The locations change, but the name of the nearest one is posted on each pharmacy's door. **British & American Pharmacy**, 1, r. Auber, 9ème (☎01 42 65 88 29). M: Auber or Opéra. Open M-F 8:30am-8pm, Sa 10am-8pm.

Medical Assistance: Hôpital Américain de Paris, 84, bd. Saussaye, Neuilly (☎01 46 41 25 25). M: Port Maillot, then bus #82 to the end of the line. A private hospital. **Hôpital Franco-Britannique de Paris**, 3, r. Barbès (☎01 46 39 22 22), in the suburb of Levallois-Perret. M: Anatole-France. Some English spoken. **Hôpital Bichat**, 46, r. Henri Buchard, 18ème (☎01 40 25 80 80). M: Port St-Ouen. Emergency services.

Telephones: To use the phones, you'll need to buy a **phone card** (*télécarte*), available at post offices, Métro stations, and *tabacs*. For **directory info,** call ☎12.

Internet Access: 📧 Easy Everything, 37, bd. Sébastopol, 1er (☎01 40 41 09 10). M: Châtelet-Les-Halles. Purchase a User ID for any amount. Min. 20F/€3.05 and recharge the ID with 10F/€1.55 or more. Number of minutes depends on the time of day and how busy the store is. Open 24hr. **Le Jardin de l'Internet,** 79, bd. St-Michel, 5ème (☎01 44 07 22 20). RER: Luxembourg. 15min. minimum. 1F/€0.15 per min., 40F/€6.10 per hr., 190F/€29 for 5hr. Open daily 9am-11pm. **WebBar,** 32, r. de Picardie, 3ème (☎01 42 72 66 55). M: République. 20F/€3.05 per hr. Open daily 8:30am-2am.

Post Office: Poste du Louvre, 52, r. du Louvre, 1er (info ☎01 40 28 20 40). M: Louvre. Open 24hr. Address mail to be held: SURNAME, FirstName *Poste Restante,* 52, r. du Louvre, 75001 Paris, France. **Postal Code:** 750xx, where "xx" is the *arrondissement* (e.g., 75003 for any address in the 3ème).

🏠 ACCOMMODATIONS

High season in Paris falls around Easter and from May to October, peaking in July and August. Paris's hostels skip many standard restrictions (sleep sheets, curfews, etc.) and they tend to have flexible maximum stays. The city's six HI hostels are **for members only.** The rest of Paris's dorm-style beds are either private hostels or quieter *foyers* (student dorms). Hotels may be the most practical accommodations for the majority of travelers. Expect to pay at least 150F/€22.90 for a single or 200-400F/€30.50-61 for a double *in the cheapest, luckiest of circumstances*. In cheaper hotels, few rooms have private baths; hall showers can cost 15-25F/€2.30-3.85 per use. Rooms fill quickly after morning check-out (10am-noon), so arrive early or reserve ahead. Many hotels accept reservations with a one-night credit card deposit. Most hostels and *foyers* include the **taxe de séjour** (1-5F/€0.15-0.80 per

FRANCE

person per day) in listed prices, but some do not. If you haven't reserved ahead, tourist offices (see p. 292) and other organizations (see below) can book rooms.

ACCOMMODATIONS SERVICES

La Centrale de Réservations (FUAJ-HI), 60, r. Vitruve, 20ème (☎01 55 25 35 20; fax 01 43 56 36 32). M: Port de Bagnolet or Maraichers. Open M-F 8:30am-5:30pm.

OTU-Voyage (Office du Tourisme Universitaire), 119, r. St-Martin, 4ème (☎08 20 817 817). 10F/€1.55 service fee. Full price due with reservation. English spoken. Open M-F 9:30am-7pm, Sa 10am-noon and 1:30-5pm.

1ER AND 2ÈME: LOUVRE-PALAIS ROYAL

Central to the **Louvre,** the **Tuileries,** the **Seine,** and the ritzy **Place Vendôme,** this area still has some budget hotels. In general, avoid r. St-Denis.

■ **Hôtel Montpensier,** 12, r. de Richelieu (☎01 42 96 28 50; fax 01 42 86 02 70). M: Palais-Royal. Walk around left side of the Palais-Royal to r. de Richelieu. Clean rooms and English-speaking staff. Breakfast 40F/€6.10. Shower 25F/€3.85. Reserve ahead. Singles with toilet 300F/€45.75; doubles 340F/€51.85. Rooms with bath 455F/€69.40; with bath and sink 535F/€81.60. Extra bed 80F/€12.20. AmEx/MC/V.

■ **Hôtel Tiquetonne,** 6, r. Tiquetonne (☎01 42 36 94 58; fax 01 42 36 02 94). M: Etienne-Marcel. Walk against traffic on r. de Turbigo; turn left on r. Tiquetonne. Near Marché Montorgueil and rowdy bars by Etienne-Marcel. Elevator. Breakfast 30F/€4.60. Showers 30F/€4.60. Closed Aug. and 1 week at Christmas. Singles 153-233F/€23.35-35.55; doubles 266F/€40.60. AmEx/MC/V.

Hôtel du Palais, 2, quai de la Mégisserie (☎01 42 36 98 25; fax 01 42 21 41 67). M: Châtelet-Les-Halles. Most rooms have views of the Seine and Left Bank. Breakfast 35F/€5.35. Reserve ahead. Singles 293F/€44.70, with bath 363F/€55.35; doubles 336F/€51.25, 366-396F/€55.80-60.40; triples 462F/€70.45; quad 562F/€85.70; quint 662F/€100.95; 6-person 772F/€117.70. Extra bed 70F/€10.70. AmEx/MC/V.

Hôtel Favart, 5, r. Marivaux (☎01 42 97 59 83; fax 01 40 15 95 58). M: Richelieu Drouot. Large rooms with bath. Breakfast included. Prices with *Let's Go:* singles 550F/€83.90; doubles 695F/€106; extra bed 100F/€15.25. AmEx/MC/V.

Centre International de Paris (BVJ)/Paris Louvre, 20, r. J.-J. Rousseau (☎01 53 00 90 90; fax 01 53 00 90 91). M: Louvre or Palais-Royal. From M: Louvre, take r. du Louvre away from the river, turn left on r. St-Honoré, and right on r. J.-J. Rousseau. Bright, dorm-style rooms. Breakfast and showers included. Reception 24hr. Phone reservations up to 1 week in advance. Rooms held for only 10min. after expected check-in time; call if you'll be late. 2- to 10-bed dorms 145F/€22.15 per person.

Hôtel Vivienne, 40, r. Vivienne (☎01 42 33 13 26; fax 01 40 41 98 19), off bd. Montmartre. M: Grands Boulevards. Singles 310F/€47.30, with toilet 480F/€73.20; doubles 400F/€61, 480F/€73.20. MC/V.

Hôtel Lion d'Or, 5, r. de la Sourdière (☎01 42 60 79 04; fax 01 42 60 09 14; www.hotelduliondor.com). M: Tuileries. Walk down r. du 29 Juillet away from the park, turn right on r. St-Honoré, and then left on r. de la Sourdière. Clean and carpeted rooms. Breakfast 35F/€5.35. Reserve 1 month ahead in high season. Singles with shower 380F/€57.95, with bath 480F/€73.20; doubles 480-560F/€73.20-85.40; triples 680F/€103.70, 750F/€114.35. Extra bed 60F/€9.15. AmEx/MC/V.

Hôtel des Boulevards, 10, r. de la Ville Neuve (☎01 42 36 02 29; fax 01 42 36 15 39). M: Bonne Nouvelle. Walk against traffic on av. Poissonnière and go right on r. de la Ville Neuve. Simple rooms with TVs and new carpets. Breakfast included. Reserve 2 weeks ahead and confirm with credit card deposit. 10% *Let's Go* discount. Singles and doubles 256F/€39, with bath 327-360F/€49-55; extra bed 66F/€10. AmEx/MC/V.

Hôtel Louvre-Richelieu, 51, r. de Richelieu (☎01 42 97 46 20; fax 01 47 03 94 13; www.perso.club-Internet.fr/joelgill). M: Palais-Royal. See directions for Hôtel Montpensier. 14 comfortable and clean rooms. English spoken. Breakfast 40F/€6.10. Reserve 3 weeks ahead in summer. Singles 260F/€39.65, with shower 360F/€54.90. Doubles 330F/€50.35, 460F/€70.15; triples 560F/€85.40. Extra bed 50F/€7.65. MC/V.

FRANCE

Hôtel La Marmotte, 6, r. Léopold Bellan (☎01 40 26 26 51; fax 01 42 42 96 20). M: Sentier. From the Métro, take r. Petit Carreaux and then turn right at r. Léopold Bellan. Quiet rooms with free safe-boxes. Breakfast 25F/€3.85. Shower 15F/€2.30. Reserve 1 month in advance. Singles and doubles 180-220F/€27.45-33.55, with shower 270-340F/€41.20-51.85; 2-bed doubles 380F/€57.95. Extra bed 80F/€12.20.

3ÈME AND 4ÈME: THE MARAIS

The Marais' 17th-century mansions now house budget hotels close to the **Centre Pompidou,** the **Ile St-Louis,** and bars. The area is convenient for sampling nightlife further away, as Paris's night buses converge in the 4ème at M: Châtelet.

▨ **Hôtel des Jeunes (MIJE)** (☎01 42 74 23 45; fax 01 40 27 81 64; www.mije.com) books beds in Le Fourcy, Le Fauconnier, and Maubuisson (see below), 3 small hostels located in old Marais residences. No smoking. English spoken. Breakfast, shower, and sheets included. Ages 18-30 only. 7-day max. stay. Reception 7am-1am. Curfew 1am. Arrive before noon (call ahead if late). Reserve 1 month in advance. 4- to 6-bed dorms 145F/€22.15; singles 240F/€36.60; doubles 175F/€26.70; triples 155F/€23.65.

Le Fourcy, 6, r. de Fourcy. M: St-Paul. Walk opposite the traffic down r. François-Miron and turn left on r. de Fourcy. Hostel surrounds a social courtyard.

Le Fauconnier, 11, r. du Fauconnier. M: St-Paul. Take r. du Prevôt, turn left on r. Charlemagne, and turn right on r. du Fauconnier. Steps away from the Seine and Ile St-Louis.

Maubuisson, 12, r. des Barres. M: Pont Marie. Walk opposite traffic on r. de l'Hôtel de Ville and turn right on r. des Barres, a silent street by the St-Gervais monastery. Elevator.

▨ **Hôtel du Séjour,** 36, r. du Grenier St-Lazare (☎/fax 01 48 87 40 36). M: Etienne-Marcel. A block from Les Halles and the Centre Pompidou. Clean, bright rooms. Reserve ahead. Showers 20F/€3.05. Reception 7am-10:30pm. Singles 200F/€30.50; doubles 275F/€42, with bath 355F/€54; extra person 150F/€22.90.

Hôtel Picard, 26, r. de Picardie (☎01 48 87 53 82; fax 01 48 87 02 56). M: Temple. Walk down r. du Temple, turn left on r. du Petit Thouars, and turn right at the end of the street. Simple pastel rooms. Breakfast 30F/€4.60. Showers 20F/€3.05. Reserve 2 weeks ahead. 5% *Let's Go* discount. Singles 210F/€32.05, with bath 260F/€39.65; doubles 250-270F/€38.15-41.20, 330F/€50.35; triples 520F/€79.30. MC/V.

Hôtel Bellevue et du Chariot d'Or, 39, r. de Turbigo (☎01 48 87 45 60; fax 01 48 87 95 04). M: Etienne-Marcel. Walk against traffic on r. de Turbigo. 59 clean and modern rooms. Breakfast 35F/€5.35. Reserve 2 weeks ahead. Singles 330F/€50.35; doubles 376F/€57.40; triples 480F/€73; quads 590F/€90. AmEx/MC/V.

Hôtel de Bretagne, 87, r. des Archives (☎01 48 87 83 14). M: Temple. Walk up r. du Temple, turn left onto r. de Bretagne; it's on the right. Friendly reception and well-kept rooms. Reserve a week ahead. Singles 170-350F/€25.95-53.40; doubles 210-230F/€32.05-35.10, with bath 390F/€59.50; triples 300F/€45.75, 500F/€76.25.

Castex Hôtel, 5, r. Castex (☎01 42 72 31 52; fax 01 42 72 57 91). M: Bastille or Sully-Morland. Modern stucco decor and peaceful rooms. Most rooms have full bath. Breakfast 35F/€5.35. Check-in 1pm. Reserve at least 1 month ahead by fax with a credit card number. Singles 260-310F/€39.65-47.30; doubles 340-380F/€51.85-57.95; triples 480F/€73.20. Extra bed 70F/€10.70. AmEx/MC/V.

Hôtel Andréa, 3, r. St-Bon (☎01 42 78 43 93; fax 01 44 61 28 36). M: Hôtel-de-Ville. On a quiet street 2 blocks from Châtelet. Renovated rooms with lots of conveniences. Reserve 1 month ahead with credit card number. Singles 360-380F/€54.90-57.95; doubles 470-580F/€71.70-88.45; triples 570-680F/€86.95-103.70. MC/V.

Hôtel de la Herse d'Or, 20, r. St-Antoine (☎01 48 87 84 09; fax 01 48 87 94 01). M: Bastille. Small and a bit dark, but clean rooms. Breakfast 25F/€3.85. Singles and doubles 190F/€29, with bath 230-320F/€35.10-48.80. AmEx/MC/V.

Hôtel de Roubaix, 6, r. Greneta (☎01 42 72 89 91; fax 01 42 72 58 79). M: Réaumur-Sébastopol or Arts et Métiers. From the Métro, walk up bd. de Sébastopol and turn left on r. Greneta. Friendly staff and clean rooms. Breakfast included. Reserve a week ahead. Singles 310-350F/€47.30-53.40; doubles 380-410F/€57.95-62.55; triples 450-500F/€68.65-76.25; quads 540F/€82.35; quints 570F/€86.95. MC/V.

FRANCE

5ÈME AND 6ÈME: THE LATIN QUARTER AND ST-GERMAIN-DES-PRES

The lively *quartier latin* and St-Germain-des-Prés offer proximity to the **Notre-Dame,** the **Panthéon,** the **Jardin du Luxembourg,** and the bustling student cafe-culture.

▨ **Hôtel Marignan,** 13, r. du Sommerard (☎01 43 54 63 81; fax 01 43 25 16 69). M: Maubert-Mutualité. From the Métro, turn left on r. des Carmes, then turn right on r. du Sommerard. Charismatic staff. Breakfast included. Free laundry. Reserve 2 months ahead with credit card or check deposit. Singles 290F/€44.25; doubles 400F/€61, with bath 460-590F/€70.15-89.95; triples 620-720F/€94.55-109.80; quads 650-790F/€99.10-120.45; quints 750-950F/€114.35-144.85.

▨ **Young and Happy (Y&H) Hostel,** 80, r. Mouffetard (☎01 45 35 09 53; fax 01 47 07 22 24). M: Monge. Cross r. Gracieuse and take r. Ortolan to r. Mouffetard. Clean rooms and commission-free currency exchange. Breakfast included. Sheets 15F/€2.30. Curfew 2am. Dorms 137-157F/€20.90-23.95. Jan.-Mar. 10F/€1.55 lower per night.

▨ **Hôtel St-Jacques,** 35, r. des Ecoles (☎01 44 07 45 45; fax 01 43 25 65 50). M: Maubert-Mutualité. Turn left on r. des Carmes, and then left on r. des Ecoles. Elegant rooms at reasonable rates. Singles 270F/€41.20, with bath 415F/€63.30; doubles 470F/€71.70, 630F/€96.05; triples 700F/€106.75. Daily tax 5F/€0.80. AmEx/MC/V.

Hôtel de Nesle, 7, r. du Nesle (☎01 43 54 62 41). M: Odéon. Walk up r. Mazarine, turn right onto r. Dauphine, and then turn left on r. du Nesle. Fantastic and absolutely sparkling. No reservations accepted; come at 10am. Singles 328F/€50, with bath 380-452F/€58-69; doubles 453F/€69, 650F/€99. Extra bed 79F/€12. AmEx/MC/V.

Hôtel du Lys, 23, r. Serpente (☎01 43 26 97 57; fax 01 44 07 34 90), off r. Danton. M: Odéon or St-Michel. French country feel. Reserve 1 month ahead. Singles 430-580F/€65.60-88.45; doubles 630F/€96.10; triples 680F/€103.70. MC/V.

Dhely's Hôtel, 22, r. de l'Hirondelle (☎01 43 26 58 25; fax 01 43 26 51 06). M: St-Michel. Modern facilities and quiet location. Reserve 2 weeks ahead with deposit. Singles 258-378F/€39.35-57.65, with shower 428-478F/€65.30-72.90; doubles 376-416F/€57.35-63.45, 466-516F/€71.10-78.70; triples 516-606F/€78.70-92.45, 606-752F/€92.45-114.70. Extra bed 100F/€15.25. MC/V.

Hôtel des Argonauts, 12, r. de la Huchette (☎01 43 54 09 82; fax 01 44 07 18 84). M: St-Michel. Take the 1st left off bd. St-Michel onto r. de la Huchette. Cheerful rooms. Reserve 3-4 weeks ahead. Singles 285F/€43.45, with bath 405F/€61.75; doubles 320F/€48.80, 460F/€70.15; triples 465F/€70.90 (request ahead). AmEx/MC/V.

Hôtel St-André des Arts, 66, r. St-André-des-Arts (☎01 43 26 96 16; fax 01 43 29 73 34). M: Odéon. Walk 1 block down r. de l'Ancienne Comédie, and turn right on r. St-André-des-Arts. Breakfast included. Reserve ahead. Singles 400F/€61; doubles 500-540F/€76.25-82.35; triples 610F/€93.05; quads 680F/€103.70. MC/V.

Hôtel du Progrès, 50, r. Gay-Lussac (☎01 43 54 53 18). M: Luxembourg. Walk away from Jardin du Luxembourg on r. Gay-Lussac. Cheap rooms with no frills (bring your own soap!). Reservation with deposit; call 2-3 weeks in advance. Singles 170-250F/€25.95-38.15, with bath 350F/€53.40; doubles 270-295F/€41.20-45, 360F/€54.90; triples 375F/€57.20. Cash or traveler's checks only.

Hôtel Gay-Lussac, 29 r. Gay-Lussac (☎01 43 54 23 96; fax 01 40 51 79 49). M: Luxembourg. Stately old rooms. Reserve by fax 1 month ahead. Singles 200F/€30.50, with bath 310-390F/€47.30-59.50; doubles 340F/€51.85, 420F/€64.05; triples 350F/€53.40, 370-480F/€56.45-73.20; quads 620F/€94.55.

Hôtel des Médicis, 214, r. St-Jacques (☎01 43 54 14 66). M: Luxembourg. Turn right on r. Gay-Lussac and then left on r. St-Jacques. Jim Morrison slummed here (room #4). Reception 9am-11pm. Arrive early in the morning and hope for a vacancy. Singles 100-200F/€15.25-30.50; doubles 200F/€30.50; triples 300F/€45.75.

Centre International de Paris (BVJ): Paris Quartier Latin, 44, r. des Bernardins (☎01 43 29 34 80; fax 01 53 00 90 91). M: Maubert-Mutualité. Walk down bd. St-Germain and turn right on r. des Bernardins. Boisterous and only slightly dingy hostel. Breakfast included. Reception 24hr. Reserve at least a week ahead and confirm, or arrive at 9am to check for rooms. 138 beds. 5- and 6-person dorms 145F/€22.15 per person; singles 175F/€26.70; doubles and triples 155F/€23.60 per person.

Hôtel le Central, 6, r. Descartes (☎01 46 33 57 93). M: Maubert-Mutualité. From the Métro, walk up r. de la Montaigne Ste-Geneviève. Near r. Mouffetard and Panthéon. Singles 163-213F/€24.85-32.50; doubles and triples 236-266F/€36-40.60. Cash only.

7ÈME: EIFFEL TOWER AND LES INVALIDES

This *arrondissement* boasts sights like the **Musée d'Orsay** and the **Eiffel Tower,** but it's not the best bet for a cheap room.

▨ **Hôtel du Champs de Mars,** 7, r. du Champ de Mars (☎01 45 51 52 30; fax 01 45 51 64 36). M: Ecole-Militaire. Reserve 1 month ahead; confirm by fax with credit card number. Singles 400F/€61; doubles 440F/€67.10; triples 560F/€85.40. MC/V.

Hôtel Eiffel Rive Gauche, 6, r. du Gros Caillou (☎01 45 51 24 56; fax 01 45 51 11 77; eiffel@easynet.fr). M: Ecole-Militaire. Walk up av. de la Bourdonnais, turn right on r. de la Grenelle, and then turn left on Gros-Caillou. A favorite of Anglophones. Breakfast 45F/€6.90. Singles 345-445F/€52.65-67.90; doubles 385-495F/€58.75-75.50, with twin beds 505F/€77.05; triples 495-595F/€75.50-90.75. Extra bed 90F/€13.75. MC/V.

Hôtel Amélie, 5, r. Amélie (☎01 45 51 74 75; fax 01 45 56 93 55; www.123france.com). M: Latour-Maubourg. Walk up bd. de la Tour Maubourg, turn left on r. de Grenelle, and turn right onto r. Amélie. Tiny yet charming. Breakfast 40F/€6.10. Reserve 2 weeks ahead. Singles 460F/€70.15; doubles 580F/€88.45. AmEx/MC/V.

Hôtel de la Paix, 19, r. du Gros-Caillou (☎01 45 51 86 17; fax 01 45 55 93 28). M: Ecole Militaire. Across from Hôtel Eiffel Rive Gauche. Clean and friendly. Breakfast 32F/€4.90. Reserve 1 week ahead. Singles 180F/€27.45, with shower 320F/€48.80; doubles 350-385F/€53.40-58.75; triple 480F/€73.20. Extra bed 100F/€15.25.

8ÈME: CHAMPS-ELYSÉES

Full of expensive shops and restaurants, grand boulevards, and grandiose monuments, the *8ème* is decidedly Paris's most glamorous *arrondissement*.

▨ **Hôtel Europe-Liège,** 8, r. de Moscou (☎01 42 94 01 51; fax 01 43 87 42 18). M: Liège. Walk down r. d'Amsterdam and turn left on r. de Moscou. Quiet and reasonably priced. 2 wheelchair-accessible rooms. Breakfast 37F/€5.65. Reserve 15 days ahead. Singles 390F/€59.50; doubles 500F/€76.25. AmEx/MC/V.

Hôtel d'Artois, 94, r. La Boétie (☎01 43 59 84 12 or 42 25 76 65; fax 01 43 59 50 70). M: St-Philippe de Roule. Near the Champs-Elysées. Spacious bathrooms and bedrooms. Showers 25F/€3.85. Reserve 2 weeks in advance Mar.-June. Singles 300F/€45.75, with bath 445F/€67.90; doubles 340F/€51.85, 490F/€74.75. MC/V.

Hôtel Madeleine Haussmann, 10, r. Pasquier (☎01 42 65 90 11; fax 01 42 68 07 93; www.3hotels.com). M: Madeleine. A bit expensive, but has excellent central location. 2 small wheelchair-accessible rooms. Breakfast 40F/€6.10. Reserve 1 month in advance. Singles 630F/€96.10; doubles 680F/€103.70; triples 790F/€120.50.

9ÈME AND 10ÈME: OPÉRA AND GARE DE NORD

There are plenty of hotels in the *9ème*, but many to the north are used for prostitution. Nicer but not-so-cheap hotels are available near the respectable and central bd. des Italiens and bd. Montmartre. A flock of inexpensive hotels roosts near the stations in the *10ème*, but the area is far from the action and rather unsafe.

▨ **Perfect Hôtel,** 39, r. Rodier (☎01 42 81 18 86 or 01 42 81 26 19; fax 01 42 85 01 38). M:Anvers or Gare du Nord. From M: Anvers, walk up on pl. Anvers, turn right on av. Trudaine, and then turn left on r. Rodier. From Gare du Nord, turn right on r. de Dunkerque; at pl. de Roubaix, veer left on r. de Maubeuge, veer right on r. Condorcet, and turn left on r. Rodier. The hotel comes close to perfection with recent renovations. English spoken. Breakfast free for *Let's Go* readers. Singles 190F/€29, with bath 295F/€45; doubles 190-223F/€29-34, 295F/€45; triples 295F/€45, 374F/€57. MC/V.

FRANCE

Hôtel Chopin, 10, bd. Montmartre, or 46, passage Jouffroy (☎01 47 70 58 10; fax 01 42 47 00 70). M: Grands Boulevards. Walk west on bd. Montmartre and turn right onto passage Jouffroy. Very clean, new rooms. Breakfast 40F/€6.10. Singles 355-495F/€54.14-69.40; doubles 450-520F/€68.65-79.30; triples 595F/€90.75. AmEx/MC/V.

Hôtel Palace, 9, r. Bouchardon (☎01 40 40 09 46; fax 01 42 06 16 90). M: Strasbourg/St-Denis. Walk up bd. St-Denis until the small arch; follow r. René Boulanger on the left, then turn left on r. Bouchardon. Breakfast 22F/€3.40. Reserve 2 weeks ahead. Singles 133F/€20.30, with shower 203F/€31; doubles 160-170F/€24.40-25.95, 236F/€36; triples 310F/€47.30; quads 380F/€57.95; quints 450F/€68.65. MC/V.

Hôtel Moderne du Temple, 3, r. d'Aix (☎01 42 08 09 04; fax 01 42 41 72 17). M: Goncourt. Walk with traffic on r. du Faubourg du Temple and then turn right on r. d'Aix. Simple, immaculate rooms. Breakfast 23F/€3.55. Singles 140-160F/€21.35-24.40, with bath 230/€35.10; doubles 190F/€29, 260F/€39.65. AmEx/MC/V.

11ÈME AND 12ÈME: BASTILLE AND RÉPUBLIQUE

A youthful and lively atmosphere pervades these *arrondissements*, but travelers should be cautious around pl. de la République and Gare de Lyon at night.

▨ **Hôtel de l'Aveyron,** 5, r. d'Austerlitz (☎01 43 07 86 86; fax 01 43 07 85 20). M: Gare de Lyon. Walk away from the train station on r. de Bercy and turn right on r. d'Austerlitz. Clean, unpretentious rooms. Reserve 1 month ahead. Singles and doubles 190F/€29, with shower 260F/€39.65; triples 250F/€38.15, 315F/€48.05. MC/V.

Centre International du Séjour de Paris: CISP "Ravel," 6, av. Maurice Ravel (☎01 44 75 60 00; fax 01 43 44 45 30). M: Porte de Vincennes. Walk east on cours de Vincennes, take the 1st right on bd. Soult, turn left on r. Jules Lemaître, and turn right on av. Maurice Ravel. Large, clean rooms, most with less than 4 beds. Breakfast included. Reception 6:30am-1:30am. Reserve ahead by phone. Dorms 126F/€19.25; singles 196F/€29.90; doubles 156F/€23.80. AmEx/MC/V.

Hôtel Moderne, 121, r. de Chemin-Vert (☎01 47 00 54 05; fax 01 47 00 08 31; www.modern-hotel.fr). M: Père Lachaise. A few blocks from the Métro. Newly renovated. Rooms are on the 6th fl.; no elevator. Breakfast 25F/€3.85. Singles 380F/€57.95; doubles 420F/€64.05; quads 510F/€77.80. Extra bed 110F/€16.80. MC/V.

Nièvre-Hôtel, 18, r. d'Austerlitz (☎01 43 43 81 51). M: Gare de Lyon or Quai de la Rapée. From Gare de Lyon, walk down r. de Bercy and take a right on r. d'Austerlitz. Recently renovated rooms with spotless bathrooms. Confirm reservations in writing. Singles 180F/€27.45; doubles 220-320F/€33.55-48.80. MC/V.

Auberge de Jeunesse "Jules Ferry" (HI), 8 bd. Jules Ferry (☎01 43 57 55 60; fax 01 43 14 82 09). M: République. Walk east on r. du Faubourg du Temple and turn right on the far side of bd. Jules Ferry. Clean rooms with 100 bunk beds and sinks. Party atmosphere. Breakfast and showers included. Lockers 10F/€1.55. Sheets included. Laundry 30F/€4.60. 7-night max. stay. **Internet** 1F/€0.15 per min. Reception 24hr. Lockout 10am-2pm. No reservations; arrive by 8am. Dorms 118-120F/€18-18.30. MC/V.

Mistral Hôtel, 3, r. Chaligny (☎01 46 28 10 20; fax 01 46 28 69 66). M: Reuilly-Diderot. Walk west on bd. Diderot and take a left onto r. Chaligny. A clean and reasonably priced hotel. Breakfast 35F/€5.35. Call 7am-midnight to reserve 2 weeks in advance and confirm in writing or by fax. Singles 205F/€31.25, with shower 253F/€38.60; doubles 281F/€42.85, with twin beds 306F/€46.65; triples 359F/€54.75; quads 412F/€62.85. Daily tax 3F/€0.50. MC/V.

Hôtel Notre-Dame, 51, r. de Malte (☎01 47 00 78 76; fax 01 43 55 32 31). M: République. Walk down av. de la République and go right on r. de Malte. Basic but upbeat rooms. Showers 22F/€3.40. Breakfast 35F/€5.35. Reserve 10 days ahead. Singles and doubles 210F/€32.05, with shower 255-390F/€38.90-59.50. AmEx/MC/V.

13ÈME AND 14ÈME: MONTPARNASSE

While the 13ème has few established hotels, there are some hostels with reasonable prices and easy access to the Métro. Just south of the Latin Quarter, Montparnasse mixes bohemian, intellectual charm with commercial centers and venerable cafes.

FRANCE

◾ **Ouest Hôtel**, 27, r. de Gergovie (☎01 45 42 64 99; fax 01 45 42 46 65). M: Pernety. Walk against traffic on r. Raymond Losserand and turn right on r. de Gergovie. Breakfast 20F/€3.05. Hall shower 20F/€3.05. Singles 120-160F/€18.30-24.40; doubles 160-200F/€24.40-30.50, with shower 220-230F/€33.55-35.10. MC/V.

Centre International du Séjour de Paris: CISP "Kellerman," 17, bd. Kellerman (☎01 44 16 37 38; fax 01 44 16 37 39; www.cisp.asso.fr). M: Porte d'Italie. This 396-bed hostel resembles a spaceship on stilts. Breakfast included. Reception 6:30am-1:30am. Wheelchair-accessible. Reserve 2-3 weeks in advance. 2- to 4-bed dorms 101-126F/€15.40-19.25; singles 196F/€29.90; doubles 156F/€23.80. AmEx/MC/V.

FIAP Jean-Monnet, 30, r. Cabanis (☎01 43 13 17 00, reservations 01 43 13 17 17; fax 01 45 81 63 91; www.fiap.asso.fr). M: Glacière. Walk down bd. Auguste-Blanqui, turn left on r. de la Santé, and right on r. Cabanis. 500-bed student center; spotless rooms. Breakfast included. Reserve 2-4 weeks in advance. Specifically request a dorm bed, or you will be booked a single. 50F/€7.65 deposit per person per night in check or credit card. Wheelchair-accessible. 5- to 8-bed dorms 139-194F/€21.35-29.60; singles 310F/€47.30; doubles 400F/€61; triples or quads 175F/€26.70 per person. MC/V.

15ÈME: INVALIDES AND ECOLE MILITAIRE

In the populous 15ème, hotels scramble for guests in the summer, and tourists can sometimes bargain for rates.

◾ **Hôtel Printemps**, 31, r. du Commerce (☎01 45 79 83 36; fax 01 45 79 84 88). M: La Motte-Picquet-Grenelle. Showers 15F/€2.30. Reserve 1 month ahead. Singles and doubles 176F/€26.85, with bath 216-256F/€32.95-39.05. MC/V.

Hôtel Camélia, 24, bd. Pasteur (☎01 47 83 76 35 or 01 47 83 69 91; fax 01 40 65 94 98). M: Pasteur. On a main boulevard by the Métro. Singles or doubles 220-400F/€33.55-61, with bath 320-400F/€48.80-61; extra bed 50F/€7.65. AmEx/MC/V.

17ÈME TO 20ÈME: PIGALLE AND MONTMARTRE

Around Montmartre, in the 18ème, hotel rates rise as you climb up to the Basilique Sacré-Coeur. At night, avoid M: Pigalle and M: Barbès-Rochechouart; use M: Abbesses instead, and be careful on deserted side streets. The 19ème and 20ème are not central; expect at least a 30min. Métro ride to the city's sights.

◾ **Hôtel Caulaincourt**, 2, sq. Caulaincourt, 18ème (☎01 46 06 46 06; fax 01 46 06 46 16; www.caulaincourt.com). M: Lamarck-Caulaincourt. Walk up the stairs to r. Caulaincourt and go right, between nos. 63 and 65. Simple rooms with views of Montmartre. Reserve 1 month ahead. Singles 175F/€26.68, with bath 235-320F/€35.85-48.80; doubles 230-250F/€35.06-38.11, 290-390F/€44.25-59.50; triples 340-360F/€51.85-54.90, 380-400F/€57.95-61. MC/V.

Village Hostel, 20 r. d'Orsel, 18ème (☎01 42 64 22 02; fax 01 42 64 22 04; www.villagehostel.fr). M: Anvers. Go up on r. Steinkerque and turn right on r. d'Orsel. New, clean, and cheap. Breakfast included. Reserve by fax or email; same-day phone reservations accepted. Dorms 137F/€20.90; doubles 314F/€47.90; triples 441F/€67.25.

◖ FOOD

For most Parisians, life is about eating. Scratch that. Life *is* eating. Establishments range from the famous repositories of *haute cuisine* to corner *brasseries*. Inexpensive bistros and *crêperies* offer the breads, cheeses, wines, pâtés, *pôtages*, and pastries central to French cuisine. *Gauche* or gourmet, French or foreign, you'll find it in Paris. **CROUS (Centre Regional des Oeuvres Universitaires et Scolaires)**, 39, av. Georges Bernanos, 5ème, has info on university restaurants. (☎01 40 51 37 10. M: Port-Royal. Open M-F 9am-5pm.) To assemble a picnic, visit the specialty shops of the **Marché Montorgueil**, 2ème, **rue Mouffetard**, 5ème, or the **Marché Bastille**, on bd. Richard-Lenoir (M: Bastille. Open Th and Su 7am-1:30pm).

FRANCE

ILE DE LA CITE AND ILE ST-LOUIS

■ **Le Caveau de Palais,** 19, pl. Dauphine (☎01 43 26 04 28). M: Cité. A chic, intimate restaurant. 2 *menus* (140F/€21.35 and 220F/€33.55) include appetizer, *plat*, and dessert. Reservations encouraged.

■ **Brasserie de l'Ile St-Louis,** 55, quai d Bourbon (☎01 43 54 02 59). M: Pont Marie. Cross the Pont Marie, turn right on r. St-Louis-en-l'Ile and walk to the end of the island. Old-fashioned brasserie is known for Alsatian specialities like *choucroute garnie* (95F/€14.50). Open M-Tu and F-Su noon-1am, Th 6pm-1am.

1ER AND 2ÈME: LOUVRE-PALAIS ROYAL

Cheap options surround **Les Halles,** 1er and 2ème. Near the **Louvre,** the small streets of the 2ème teem with traditional bistros.

■ **Jules,** 62, r. Jean-Jacques Rousseau (☎01 40 28 99 04). M: Les Halles. Subtle blend of modern and traditional French cooking. 4-course *menu* 130F/€19.85. Open M-F noon-2:30pm and 7-10:30pm.

■ **Le Fumoir,** 6, r. de l'Amiral Coligny (☎01 42 92 05 05). M: Louvre. Serves the best brunch in Paris (120F/€18.30). Coffee 15F/€2.30. Open daily 11am-2am.

Le Café Marly, 93, r. de Rivoli (☎01 49 26 06 60), in the Richelieu wing of the Louvre. M: Palais Royal. One of Paris's classiest cafes. Breakfast (80F/€12.20) served 8-11am. Main dishes from 100-130F/€15.25-19.85. Open daily 8am-2am.

Les Noces de Jeannette, 14, r. Favart, and 9, r. d'Amboise (☎01 42 96 36 89). M: Richelieu Drouot. *Menu du Bistro* (172F/€26.25) includes large salad entrees and grilled meat *plats*. Reserve ahead. Open daily noon-1:30pm and 7-9:30pm.

Le Dénicheur, 4, r. Tiquetonne (☎01 42 21 31 01). M: Etienne-Marcel. Diner turned disco/junkyard café. Dinner *menu* 98F/€14.95. Su brunch 85F/€13. Reservations recommended. Open Tu-Su noon-3:30pm and 7:30pm-1am.

La Victoire Suprême du Coeur, 41, r. des Bourdonnais (☎01 40 41 93 95). M: Châtelet. Run by the devotees of guru Sri Chinmoy. It's all vegetarian, and very tasty. All-day 3-course *menu* 95F/€14.50. Open M-F noon-3:30pm and 6-10pm, Sa noon-10pm.

3ÈME AND 4ÈME: THE MARAIS

The Marais offers chic bistros, kosher delis, and couple-friendly cafes.

■ **Piccolo Teatro,** 6, r. des Ecouffes (☎01 42 72 17 79). M: St-Paul. A romantic vegetarian hideout. Lunch *menus* 52-63F/€7.95-13. Open Tu-Sa noon-3pm and 7:15-11pm.

■ **Georges,** on the 6th fl. of the Centre Pompidou (☎01 44 78 47 99). M: Rambuteau. Ultra-sleek, zen-cool café, especially the terrace. Open W-M noon-2am.

Taxi Jaune, 13, r. Chapon (☎01 42 76 00 40). M: Arts et Métiers. The eclectic taxi-themed art may make a tourist or 2 look askance. Lunch *menu* 78F/€11.90 or 84F/€12.85. Open M-F noon-2:30pm and 7:30pm-2am; food served until 10:15pm.

Le Hangar, 12, impasse Berthaud (☎01 42 74 55 44). M: Rambuteau. Bright and intimate. Avocado gazpacho 52F/€7.95, fish and meat dishes 68-138F/€10.40-21.05. Open M 7:30pm-midnight, Tu-Sa noon-3pm and 7:30pm-midnight. Closed Aug.

Les Enfants Gâtés, 43, r. des Francs-Bourgeois (☎01 42 77 07 63). M: St-Paul. "Spoiled children" is a sexy spot to brood and linger. Coffee 15F/€2.30; brunch 95-135F/€14.50-20.60; food served until 4:30pm. Open daily 11am-8pm.

Café Beaubourg, 43, r. St-Merri (☎01 48 87 63 96), facing Centre Pompidou. M: Hôtel-de-Ville. This is *the* spot to see and be seen during the day. Coffee 17F/€2.60; breakfast 80F/€12.20; brunch 130F/€19.85. Open Su-Th 8am-1am, F-Sa 8am-2am.

Bofinger, 6, r. de la Bastille (☎01 42 72 05 23). M: Bastille. The lunch *menu* at 108F/€16.50 is a real steal. Go for the dressy atmosphere as much as the heavenly eats. Open daily noon-3pm and 7pm-midnight.

L'Apparement Café, 18, r. des Coutures St-Gervais (☎01 48 87 12 22). M: St-Paul. Next to the Picasso Museum. Coffee (12F/€1.85), make-your-own salads (45F/€6.90), Su brunch (95F/€14.50 or 125F/€19.05). Open M-Sa noon-2am, Su 11:30am-midnight.

FRANCE

5ÈME AND 6ÈME: THE LATIN QUARTER AND ST-GERMAIN-DES-PRÉS

La Truffière, 4, r. Blainville (☎01 46 33 29 82), near the r. Mouffetard. M: Place Monge. One serious restaurant. Lunch *menus* (90F/€13.75 and 120F/€18.30) feature south-western French cuisine. Reserve ahead. Open Tu-Su noon-2pm and 7-10:30pm.

Savannah Café, 27, r. Descartes (☎01 43 29 45 77). M: Cardinal Lemoine. Lebanese food. *Menu gastronomique* 142F/€21.65. Open M-Sa 7-11pm. Around the corner is **Comptoir Méditerranée,** 42, r. Cardinal Lemoine (☎01 43 25 29 08), with similar food, take-out, and lower prices (35-51F/€5.35-7.95). Open M-Sa 11am-10pm.

Aux Deux Magots, 6, pl. St-Germain-des-Prés (☎01 45 48 55 25), down from the Eglise St-Germain-des-Prés. M: St-Germain-des-Prés. Home to literati since 1885. Coffee 24F/€3.70, pastries 12-24F/€1.85-3.70. Open daily 7:30am-1:30am.

Le Petit Vatel, 5, r. Lobineau (☎01 43 54 28 49). M: Mabillon. Serves Mediterranean French specialties like *catalan pamboli* (bread with puréed tomatoes, ham, and cheese) for 60F/€9.15. Open Tu-Sa noon-2:40pm and 7-10:30pm.

Le Sélect, 99, bd. du Montparnasse (☎01 45 48 38 24), across the street from La Coupole. M: Vavin. Trotsky, Satie, Breton, Cocteau, and Picasso all frequented this huge Art Deco cafe. *Café* 7-12F/€1.10-1.85. Open daily 7am-3am.

La Palette, 43, r. de Seine (☎01 43 26 68 15). Truly the most authentic of the Left Bank's gallery cafes. Coffee 14F/€2.15, beer 25F/€3.85, wine 22-25F/€3.40-3.85, sandwiches 22-30F/€3.40-4.50. Open M-Sa 8am-2am.

La Crêpe Rit du Clown, 6, r. des Canettes (☎01 46 34 01 02). M: Mabillon. Don't let the clown deter you from the tasty, inexpensive crepes. Present *Let's Go* for a free *kir breton. Formule* 63F/€9.65, crêpes 35-42F/€5.35-6.45. Open M-Sa noon-11:30pm.

Café de Flore, 172, bd. St-Germain. M: St-Germain-des-Prés. Sartre composed *Being and Nothingness* here; Apollinaire, Picasso, Breton, and Thurber sipped brew. Espresso 25F/€3.85, pastries 38-65F/€5.80-9.95. Open daily 7am-1:30am.

7ÈME: EIFFEL TOWER AND LES INVALIDES

Café du Marché, 38, r. Cler (☎01 47 05 51 27). M: Ecole Militaire. Good, American-style food like a Caesar salad (50F/€7.65) or pastrami club sandwich (50F/€7.65). Open M-Sa 7am-1am (food served until 11pm), Su 7am-3pm.

Au Pied de Fouet, 45, r. de Babylone (☎01 47 05 12 27). M: Vaneau. Straightforward French home-cooking at bargain prices. Appetizers 13-20F/€2-3.05, main dishes 45-70F/€6.90-10.70. Open M-F noon-2:30pm and 7-9:30pm, Sa noon-2pm.

Le Lotus Blanc, 45, r. de Bourgogne (☎01 45 55 18 89). M: Varenne. Vietnamese specialties. Lunch and all-day *menus* (59-146F/€9.10-22.30). Reservations encouraged. Open M-Sa noon-2:30pm and 7-10:30pm. Closed Aug. 15-23.

8ÈME: CHAMPS-ELYSÉES

Antoine's: Les Sandwiches des 5 Continents, 31, r. de Ponthieu (☎01 42 89 44 20). M: Franklin D. Roosevelt. Bright, modern sandwich shop. 40F/€6.10 meal includes *panini,* yogurt, and a drink. Open M-F 8am-6pm.

Bangkok Café, 28, r. de Moscou (☎01 43 87 62 56). M: Rome. Talented Thai chef and French husband serve inventive salads (54-68F/€8.25-10.40) and meats (82-120F/€12.55-18.30). Open M-F noon-2:30pm and 7-11:30pm, Sa 7-11:30pm.

Fouquet's, 99, av. des Champs-Elysées (☎01 47 23 70 60). M: George V. Snobbery so "French" that it seems like a Disney caricature of itself. Main dishes 60-145F/€9.15-22.15. Food served all day in the cafe. Open daily 8am-2am.

9ÈME AND 10ÈME: OPÉRA AND GARE DU NORD

Haynes Restaurant Américain, 3, r. Clauzel (☎01 48 78 40 63). M: St-Georges. Head up on r. Nôtre Dame de Lorette, turn right on r. H. Monnier, and then right on r. Clauzel. A former hangout of Louis Armstrong, James Baldwin, and Richard Wright. Generous portions under 100F/€15.25. Open Tu-Sa 7pm-12:30am.

FRANCE

■ **Le Bistro de Gala,** 45, r. du Faubourg-Montmartre (☎01 40 22 90 50). M: Grands Boulevards. *Menu* is 170F/€25.95, but definitely worth it. Open M-F noon-2:30pm and 7-11:30pm, Sa 7-11:30pm. Reservations recommended.

■ **Cantine d'Antoine at Lili,** 95 quai de Valmy (☎01 40 37 34 86), on Canal St-Martin. M: Gare de l'Est. Too cute for words. Choose from a variety of flavored lemonades (15F/€2.30). Quiches 50F/€7.65. Open W-Sa 11am-1am, Su-Tu 11am-8pm.

11ÈME AND 12ÈME:BASTILLE AND RÉPUBLIQUE

■ **Chez Paul,** 13, r. de Charonne (☎01 47 00 34 57). M: Bastille. Worn exterior hides a kicking bistro. Peppercorn steak 78F/€11.90. Reservations a must. Open daily noon-2:30pm and 7pm-2am; food served until 12:30am. Closed for lunch Aug.1-15.

■ **Pause Café,** 41, r. de Charonne (☎01 48 06 80 33). M: Ledru-Rollin. Pause is all the cooler for having starred in the film *Chacun Cherche Son Chat.* Salads 40-50F/€6.10-7.63, beer 18F/€2.75. Open M-Sa 8am-2am, Su 8:30am-8pm.

13ÈME THROUGH 16ÈME: MONTPARNASSE

Scores of Asian restaurants cluster in Paris's **Chinatown**, south of pl. d'Italie on av. de Choisy. The 14ème is bordered at the top by the busy **boulevard du Montparnasse,** which is lined with a wide range of restaurants. R. du Montparnasse, which intersects with the boulevard, teems with reasonably priced *crêperies*. R. Daguerre is lined with vegetarian-friendly restaurants. Inexpensive restaurants cluster on r. Didot, r. du Commerce, r. de Vaugirard, bd. de Grenelle, and Gare Montparnasse.

■ **Café du Commerce,** 39, r. des Cinq Diamants (☎01 53 62 91 04). M: Pl. d'Italie. *Menus* 55-65F/€8.40-9.95, with options like steak with avocado and strawberries. Open daily noon-3pm and 7pm-2am. Reservations recommended.

■ **Chez Foong,** 32, r. Frémicourt (☎01 45 67 36 99). M: Cambronne. Superb Malaysian fare. 3-course *menus* 90F/€13.75 (M-F). Open M-Sa noon-2:30pm and 7-11pm.

La Coupole, 102, bd. du Montparnasse (☎01 43 20 14 20). M: Vavin. Its Art Deco chambers have hosted Lenin, Stravinsky, Hemingway, and Einstein. Coffee 11F/€1.70; *croque monsieur* 28F/€4.30. Open daily 7:30am-2am.

La Rotunde de la Muette, 12, Chaussée de la Muette (☎01 45 24 45 45), 2min. from the Métro. M: La Muette. Hip music and great outdoor seating. Open daily noon-11pm.

Chez Papa, 6, r. Gassendi (☎01 43 22 41 19). M: Denfert-Rochereau. Papa portraits and articles line the walls and special Papa dishes fill the menu. The best deal is the massive *salade boyarde* (40F/€6.10). *Menu* served until 9pm M-F (55F/€8.40). Also in the 8ème at 29, r. de l'Arcade (☎01 42 65 43 68); the 10ème at 206, r. Lafayette (☎01 42 09 53 87); and the 15ème at 101, r. de la Croix Nivert (☎01 48 28 31 88). Open daily 10am-1am. Reservations recommended.

17ÈME AND 18ÈME: MONTMARTRE

Bistros are around **Place du Tertre** and **Place St-Pierre.** Be cautious at night. Charming bistros and cafes line **Rue des Abbesses** and **Rue Lepic.**

■ **Le Soleil Gourmand,** 10, r. Ravignan (☎01 42 51 00 50). M: Abbesses. *Provençale* fare like 5-cheese *tartes* with salad (62F/€9.50) and house-baked cakes (30-44F/€4.60-6.75). Open daily 12:30-2:30pm and 8:30-11pm. Evening reservations a must.

■ **Chez Ginette,** 101, r. Caulaincourt (☎01 46 06 01 49), upstairs from the Métro. M: Lamarck-Caulaincourt. Monkfish with prawn sauce 100F/€15.25, specialty omelettes 40-55F/€6.10-8.40. Open M-Sa noon-2:30pm and 7:30pm-2am. Closed Aug.

👁 SIGHTS

In a few hours, you can walk from the heart of the Marais in the east to the Eiffel Tower in the west, passing most major monuments along the way. Try to reserve a day for wandering; you don't have a true sense of Paris until you know how close medieval Notre-Dame is to the modern Centre Pompidou, or the *Quartier*

FRANCE

Latin of students to the Louvre of kings. After dark, spotlights illuminate everything from the Panthéon to the Eiffel Tower, Notre Dame to the Obélisque.

ILE DE LA CITE AND ILE ST-LOUIS

CATHÉDRALE DE NOTRE DAME DE PARIS

M: St-Michel-Notre-Dame; exit on the island side. From the Left Bank, cross Pont au Double and turn right. Open M-F 8am-6:45pm, Sa-Su 8am-7:45pm. Towers open daily 9:30am-6pm; 35F/€15.35, under 25 23F/€3.55. Treasury open M-Sa 9:30-11:30am and 1-6pm; 15F/ €2.30, students 10F/€1.55. Crypt open daily 10am-6pm; 22F/€3.55, under 27 and over 60 free. Tours in English leave from the right of the entrance; W and Th noon, Sa 2:30pm; free.

This 12th- to 14th-century cathedral, begun under Bishop Maurice Sully, is one of the world's most famous and beautiful examples of medieval architecture. After the Revolution, the building fell into disrepair and was even used to shelter livestock until Victor Hugo's 1831 novel *Notre-Dame-de-Paris* (a.k.a. *The Hunchback of Notre Dame*) inspired citizens to lobby for restoration. Architect Eugène Viollet-le-Duc made subsequent modifications, including the addition of the spire and the gargoyles. The intricately carved, apocalyptic façade and soaring, apparently weightless walls, effects produced by brilliant Gothic engineering and optical illusions, are inspiring even for the most church-weary. The cathedral's biggest draws are its enormous stained-glass **rose windows** that dominate the north and south ends of the transept. At the center of the 21m north window is the Virgin, depicted as the descendant of the Old Testament kings and judges who surround her. The base of the south window shows Matthew, Mark, Luke, and John on the shoulders of Old Testament prophets, while in the central window, Christ is surrounded by the 12 apostles, virgins, and saints of the New Testament. A staircase inside the towers leads to a spectacular perch from which weatherworn gargoyles survey the city.

OTHER SIGHTS

ILE DE LA CITÉ. If any place could be called the heart of Paris, it is this island in the river. In the 3rd century BC, when it was inhabited by the *Parisii*, a Gallic tribe of hunters, sailors, and fishermen, the Ile de la Cité was all there was to Paris. Although the city has expanded in all directions, all distance-points in France are measured from *kilomètre zéro*, a sundial on the ground in front of Notre-Dame.

■ STE-CHAPELLE AND CONCIERGERIE. Within the courtyard of the **Palais de Justice,** which has housed Paris's district courts since the 13th century, the opulent, Gothic **Ste-Chapelle** was built by Saint Louis (Louis IX) to house his most precious possession, Christ's crown of thorns, now in Notre Dame. No mastery of the lower chapel's dim gilt can prepare the visitor for the **Upper Chapel,** where twin walls of stained glass glow and frescoes of saints and martyrs shine. *(4, bd. du Palais, within the structure Palais de la Cité. M: Cité. ☎01 53 73 58 51. Open Apr.-Sept. daily 9:30am-6:30pm; Oct.-Mar. 10am-5pm. 36F/€5.50, seniors and ages 18-25 23F/€3.55, under 18 free; joint ticket with Conciergerie 50F/€7.65.)* Around the corner is the **Conciergerie,** one of Paris's most famous prisons; Marie-Antoinette and Robespierre were imprisoned here during the Revolution. *(1, quai de l'Horloge. M: Cité. ☎01 53 73 78 50. Open Apr.-Sept. daily 9:30am-6:30pm; Oct.-Mar. 10am-5pm. 36F/€5.50, students 23F/€3.55; joint ticket with Ste-Chapelle 50F/€7.65. Includes French tour 11am and 3pm. For tours in English, call in advance.)*

ILE ST-LOUIS. The Ile St-Louis is home to some of Paris's most privileged elite, such as the Rothschilds and Pompidou's widow, and former home to other superfamous folks, including Voltaire, Baudelaire, and Marie Curie. At night, the island glows in the light of cast-iron lamps and candlelit bistros. Look for Paris's best ice cream at Ile St-Louis's ■**Berthillon,** 31, r. St-Louis-en-Ile. *(Walk across the Pont St-Louis from Notre-Dame; also across the Pont Marie from M: Pont Marie. Berthillon open Sept.to mid-July; take-out W-Su 10am-8pm; eat-in W-F 1-8pm, Sa-Su 2-8pm. Closed 2 weeks Feb. and Apr.)*

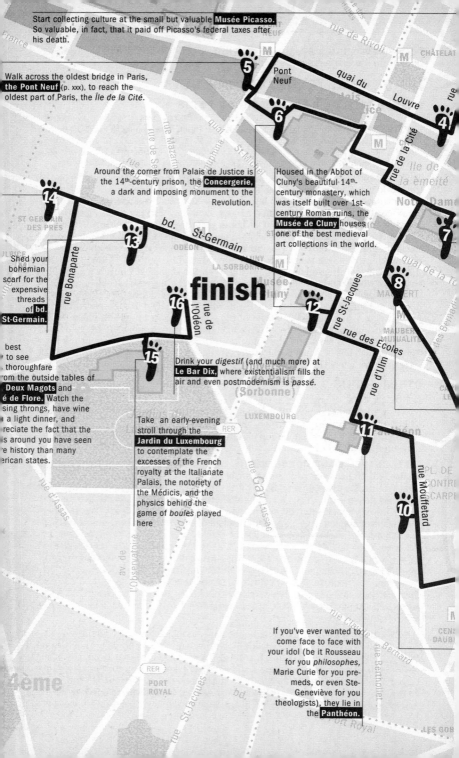

Start collecting culture at the small but valuable **Musée Picasso.** So valuable, in fact, that it paid off Picasso's federal taxes after his death.

Walk across the oldest bridge in Paris, **the Pont Neuf** (p. xxx), to reach the oldest part of Paris, the Île de la Cité.

Around the corner from Palais de Justice is the 14th-century prison, the **Concergerie,** a dark and imposing monument to the Revolution.

Housed in the Abbot of Cluny's beautiful 14th-century monastery, which was itself built over 1st-century Roman ruins, the **Musée de Cluny** houses one of the best medieval art collections in the world.

Shed your bohemian scarf for the expensive threads of **bd. St-Germain.**

best to see thoroughfare om the outside tables of **Deux Magots** and é de Flore. Watch the sing throngs, have wine a light dinner, and reciate the fact that the s around you have seen e history than many erican states.

finish

Drink your *digestif* (and much more) at **Le Bar Dix,** where existentialism fills the air and even postmodernism is *passé*.

Take an early-evening stroll through the **Jardin du Luxembourg** to contemplate the excesses of the French royalty at the Italianate Palais, the notoriety of the Médicis, and the physics behind the game of *boules* played here

If you've ever wanted to come face to face with your idol (be it Rousseau for you *philosophes*, Marie Curie for you pre-meds, or even Ste-Geneviève for you theologists), they lie in the **Panthéon.**

start

1 Find the trashy and philosophical, the art and anti-art at the *bouquinistes* along the **quai du Louvre.** These booths are here to browse in, their owners to bargain with.

3 The most recently-recognized form of art? Fashion. It's been around for a long time on **rue de Rivoli,** keeping les Parisiennes chic and *haute couture*-d.

2 Move on to the **Place des Vosges,** *the* cultural center of Paris during the 17th century. Salons, sipping, sarcasm, and sex went on in these beautiful *hôtels particuliers*. Stop in at the **Maison de Victor Hugo** to see a different side of this intellectual—his paintings.

The postcard-darling of Paris, **the Cathedral of Notre Dame** held Joan of Arc's heresy trial and saw the coronation of Napoleon. Abused throughout the last two centuries, however, it was only after the printing of Hugo's wildly popular *Hunchback of Notre Dame* that the government thought to restore it to its gothic glory.

Cross the Seine and enter the *Quartier Latin*, the academic center of Paris. First stop: **Shakespeare & Co.** Sylvia Beach no longer hosts Hemingway and Joyce, and Allen Ginsburg no longer rings up your purchases, but the selection is wonderful and you're sure to meet the latest crowds of ex-pats at Sunday tea.

The cool courtyards and ornate archways of the **Mosquée de Paris** provide a soothing setting for prayer, mint tea, or an afternoon in the *hammam*.

9 This *arrondissement* is for walking. Visit the small galleries that hide in every alley, buy your very own vintage accessory at Antiquités New-Puces at no. 45 (p. xxx), or grab a crêpe like a real starving student along **rue Mouffetard,** the neighborhood's main drag.

For students, poets, bohemians and *artistes*

Walkintour1

THE LATIN QUARTER AND ST-GERMAIN-DES-PRÉS

The autumn influx of Parisian students is the key to the *Quartier Latin*, so named because prestigious *lycées* and universities taught in Latin until 1798. Since the violent student riots in May 1968, many artists and intellectuals have migrated to the cheaper outer *arrondissements*, and the *haute bourgeoisie* have moved in. The 5ème still presents the most diverse array of bookstores, cinemas, bars, and jazz clubs in the city. Designer shops and galleries are near **St-Germain-des-Prés.**

CAFÉS. Cafes along bd. St-Germain have long been gathering places for literary and artistic notables. **Aux Deux Magots,** 6, pl. St-Germain-des-Prés, named for two porcelain figures that adorned a store selling Chinese silk and imports on the same spot in the 19th century, was a favorite hangout of Verlaine and Rimbaud, and later Breton, Artaud, and Picasso. The **Café de Flore,** 172, bd. St-Germain, established in 1890, was made famous in the 1940s and 50s by literati Sartre and Camus, who favored its wood-burning stoves over their cold apartments. *(M: St-Germain-des-Prés.)*

BOULEVARD ST-MICHEL AND ENVIRONS. At the center of the Latin Quarter, bd. St-Michel, which divides the 5ème and 6ème, is filled with cafes, restaurants, bookstores, and clothing boutiques. **Place St-Michel,** at its northern tip, is filled with students, often engaged in typically Parisian protests, and lots of tourists. *(M: St-Michel.)*

JARDIN DU LUXEMBOURG. South along bd. St-Michel, the formal French gardens of the Jardin du Luxembourg are fabulous for strolling, reading, and watching the famous *guignol* puppet theater. *(RER: Luxembourg; exit onto bd. St-Michel. The main entrance is on bd. St-Michel. Open Apr.-Oct. daily 7:30am-9:30pm; Nov.-Mar. 8:15am-5pm.)*

PANTHÉON. The **crypt** of the Panthéon, which occupies the highest point on the Left Bank, houses the tombs of Louis Braille, Victor Hugo, Jean Jaurès, Rousseau, Voltaire, and Emile Zola; you can spy each tomb from behind locked gates. The **dome** features uninspiring neoclassical frescoes. *(On pl. du Panthéon, east of the Jardin du Luxembourg. M: Cardinal Lemoine; follow r. du Cardinal Lemoine uphill and turn right on r. Clovis. Or, from RER: Luxembourg, head north on bd. St-Michel and turn right on r. Soufflot. Open in summer daily 9:30am-6:30pm; in winter 10am-6:15pm. 42F/€6.40, students 26F/€4.)*

EGLISE ST-GERMAIN-DES-PRÉS. Scarred by centuries of weather, revolution, and war, the Eglise St-Germain-des-Prés, which dates from 1163, is the oldest standing church in Paris. *(3, pl. St-Germain-des-Prés. M: St-Germain-des-Prés. Open daily 8am-7:45pm.)*

JARDIN DES PLANTES. Opened in 1640 to grow medicinal plants for King Louis XIII, the garden now features natural science museums and a **zoo,** which Parisians raided for food during the Prussian siege of 1871. *(On pl. Valhubert. M: Jussieu. Follow r. Jussieu southeast along the university building.)*

MOSQUÉE DE PARIS. The cool courtyards and ornate archways of this mosque provide a soothing setting for prayer, mint tea, or an afternoon in the *hammam. (Pl. du Puits de l'Ermite. M: Jussieu. From r. Linné, turn right on r. Lacépède, and left on r. de Quatrefages. Open June-Aug. Sa-Th 9am-noon and 2-6pm. Tours 15F/€2.30, students 10F/€1.55.)*

THE EIFFEL TOWER AND INVALIDES

EIFFEL TOWER. Built in 1889 as the centerpiece of the World's Fair, the *Tour Eiffel* has come to symbolize the city. Despite criticism, tacky souvenirs, and Gustave Eiffel's own sentiment that "France is the only country in the world with a 300m flagpole," the tower is unfailingly elegant and commands an excellent view of the city. At night, it will impress even the most jaded tourist. *(M: Bir Hakeim. Follow bd. de Grenelle to the Seine and turn right on quai Branly. Or, from RER: Champ de Mars-Tour Eiffel, follow quai Branly. Open June-Aug. daily 9am-midnight; Sept.-June. 9:30am-11pm. Lift to 1st fl. 24F/€3.70, 2nd fl. 45F/€6.90, 3rd fl. 65F/€9.95. Stairs to 1st and 2nd fl. 20F/€3.05.)*

INVALIDES. The tree-lined **Esplanade des Invalides** runs from the impressive **Pont Alexandre III** to the gold-leaf domed **Hôtel des Invalides.** The Hôtel, built for veterans under Louis XIV, now houses the **Musée de l'Armée** and **Napoleon's Tomb.** The **Musée Rodin** (see p. 310) is nearby on r. Varenne. *(M: Invalides, Latour Maubourg, or Varenne.)*

FRANCE

THE LOUVRE, OPERA, MARAIS, AND BASTILLE

■ **MARAIS.** This area, made up of the 3ème and 4ème *arrondissements*, became the most chic place to live with Henri IV's construction of the elegant **Place des Vosges** at the beginning of the 17th century; several remaining mansions now house museums. Today, the streets of the Marais house the city's Jewish and gay communities as well as fun, hip restaurants and shops. At the confluence of the 1er, 2ème, 3ème, and 4ème, the **Centre Pompidou** (see p. 310) looms like a colorful factory over the vast *place*, where artists, musicians, and pickpockets gather. Linger in the day, but be cautious at night. *(M: Rambuteau; take r. Rambuteau to pl. Georges Pompidou. Or, from M: Chatelet-Les Halles, take r. Rambuteau or r. Aubry le Boucher.)*

AROUND THE LOUVRE. World-famous art museum and former residence of kings, the **Louvre** (see p. 309) occupies about one-seventh of the 1er *arrondissement*. **Le Jardin des Tuileries,** at the western foot of the Louvre, was commissioned by Catherine de Médicis in 1564 and improved by André Le Nôtre (designer of the gardens at Versailles) in 1649. *(M: Tuileries. Open Apr.-Sept. daily 7am-9pm; Oct.-Mar. 7:30am-7:30pm. Free tours in English from the Arc de Triomphe du Carrousel.)* Three blocks north along r. de Castiglione, **Place Vendôme** hides 20th-century offices and luxury shops behind 17th-century façades. Look out for Napoleon on top of the column in the center of the *place*—he's the one in the toga. *(M: Tuileries or Concorde.)* The **Palais-Royal** was commissioned in 1632 by Cardinal Richelieu, who gave it to Louis XIII. In 1784, the elegant buildings enclosing the palace's formal garden became *galeries*, the prototype of a shopping mall. The revolutions of 1789, 1830, and 1848 all began with angry crowds in the same garden. *(M: Palais-Royal/Musée du Louvre or Louvre-Rivoli.)*

OPÉRA. North of the Louvre, Charles Garnier's grandiose **Opéra** was built under Napoleon III in the eclectic style of the Second Empire. Gobelin tapestries, gilded mosaics, a 1964 Marc Chagall ceiling, and a six-ton chandelier adorn the magnificent interior. *(M: Opéra. ☎ 08 36 69 78 68. Open in summer daily 10am-6pm; off-season 10am-5pm. 30F/€4.60, students 20F/€3.05. English tours in summer daily at noon; off-season varies; 60F/€9.15, students 45F/€6.90.)*

BASTILLE. Further east, Charles V built the Bastille prison to guard the eastern entrance to his capital. When it became a state prison under Louis XIII, it housed religious heretics and political undesirables. On July 14, 1789, revolutionaries stormed the Bastille, searching for gunpowder and political prisoners. By 1792, nothing was left of the prison but its outline on the *place*. On July 14, 1989, François Mitterrand inaugurated the glittering **Opéra Bastille** to celebrate the destruction of Charles's fortress. *(130, r. de Lyon. M: Bastille. ☎ 01 40 01 19 70. Daily tours usually at 1 or 5pm. 60F/€9.15, students 45F/€6.90.)*

CHAMPS-ELYSÉES, BOIS DE BOULOGNE, AND LA DÉFENSE

PLACE DE LA CONCORDE. Paris's most famous public square lies at the eastern end of the Champs-Elysées. Built between 1757 and 1777 for a monument to Louis X, the area soon became the *place de la Révolution*, site of the guillotine that severed 1343 necks from their blue-blooded bodies. After the Reign of Terror, the square was renamed (*concorde* means "peace"). The huge, rose-granite, 13th-century BC **Obélisque de Luxor** depicts the deeds of Egyptian pharaoh Ramses II. Given to Charles X by the Viceroy of Egypt, it is Paris's oldest monument. *(M: Concorde.)*

CHAMPS-ELYSÉES. Stretching west and anchored by the Arc de Triomphe on one end and the place de Concorde on the other, the **Avenue des Champs-Elysées** is lined with luxury shops, *haute couture* boutiques, cafes, and cinemas. The avenue is the work of Baron Haussmann, who was commissioned by Napoleon III to convert Paris into a grand capital with broad avenues, wide sidewalks, new parks, elegant housing, and sanitary sewers.

ARC DE TRIOMPHE. Napoleon commissioned the **Arc de Triomphe,** at the western terminus of the Champs-Elysées, in 1806 in honor of his Grande Armée. In 1940,

PARIS IS(N'T) BURNING As the Allied troops made their way to Paris after their successful landing on the beaches of Normandy, Hitler and the occupying Nazi forces in Paris prepared for a scorched-earth retreat. By August 23, 1944, following direct orders from Adolf Hitler, *Wehrmacht* engineers had placed mines at the base of every bridge in Paris. Despite Hitler's admiration of Napoleon's monumental tomb in the Invalides (see p. 306) during his smug visit in 1940, explosives were crammed into the basement of the Invalides, the Assemblée Nationale, and Notre Dame. The Opéra and Madeleine were to be destroyed, and the Eiffel Tower was rigged so that it would topple and prevent the approaching Allies from crossing the Seine. A brief order from German commander **Dietrich von Cholitz** would reduce every major monument in Paris—10 centuries of history—to heaps of rubble and twisted iron. Although in all other ways loyal to the Nazi party, von Cholitz simply couldn't oversee the destruction of a city such as Paris. Pestered by Hitler's incessant question, "Is Paris burning?" von Cholitz managed to stall until the Allies arrived. In 1968, he was awarded the French *Légion d'Honneur* for his bravery in the face of an irate Hitler.

Parisians were brought to tears as Nazis goose-stepped through the Arc; on August 26, 1944, British, American, and French troops liberating the city from Nazi occupation marched through to the roaring cheers of thousands. The terrace at the top has a fabulous view. (*On pl. Charles de Gaulle. M: Charles-de-Gaulle-Etoile. Open Apr.-Sept. daily 9:30am-11pm; Oct.-Mar. 10am-10:30pm. 42F/€6.45, under 26 26F/€4.*) The **Tomb of the Unknown Soldier** has been under the Arc since November 11, 1920. It bears the inscription, "Here lies a French soldier who died for his country, 1914-1918," but represents the 1,500,000 men who died during WWI.

THE MADELEINE. Mirrored by the Assemblée Nationale across the Seine, the Madeleine—formally called **Eglise Ste-Marie-Madeleine** (Mary Magdalene)—was begun in 1764 by Louis XV and modeled after a Greek temple. Construction was halted during the Revolution, when the Cult of Reason proposed transforming the building into a bank, a theater, or a courthouse. Characteristically, Napoleon decreed that it should become a temple to the greatness of his army, but Louis XVIII shouted, "It shall be a church!" Completed in 1842, the structure stands alone in the medley of Parisian churches, distinguished by four ceiling domes that light the interior, 52 exterior Corinthian columns, and a curious altarpiece. (*Pl. de la Madeleine. M: Madeleine. ☎ 01 44 51 69 00. Open daily 7:30am-7pm.*)

BOIS DE BOULOGNE. Avenue Foch, one of Haussmann's finest creations, runs from the Arc de Triomphe to the Bois de Boulogne. Though popular by day for picnics, the park is a risky choice at night—until recently it was home to many drug dealers and prostitutes. (*16ème. M: Porte Maillot, Sablons, Pont de Neuilly, or Porte Dauphine.*)

LA DÉFENSE. Outside the city limits, the skyscrapers and modern architecture of La Défense make up Paris's newest (unofficial) *arrondissement*, home to the headquarters of 14 of France's top 20 corporations. The **Grande Arche,** inaugurated in 1989, completes the *axe historique* running through the Louvre, pl. de la Concorde, and the Arc de Triomphe. There's yet another stunning view from the top. Trees, shops, and sculptures by Miró and Calder line the esplanade. (*M/RER: La Défense; M, zone 2; RER, zone 3. Arch open daily 10am-8pm. 46F/€7.05, students 35F/€5.35.*)

MONTMARTRE AND PERE-LACHAISE

BASILIQUE DU SACRE-COEUR. The Basilique du Sacré-Coeur crowns the **butte Montmartre** like an enormous white meringue. Its onion dome is visible from almost anywhere in the city, and its 112m bell tower is the highest point in Paris, offering a view that stretches up to 50km. (*35, r. du Chevalier de la Barre, 18ème. M: Château-Rouge, Abbesses, or Anvers. From Anvers, take r. de Steinkerque off bd. de Rochechouart and climb the steps. Open daily 7am-11pm; free. Dome and crypt open daily 9am-6pm; each 15F/€2.30, students 8F/€1.25.*) Nearby, **Place du Tertre** features outdoor cafés and sketch artists.

CIMETIÈRE PÈRE LACHAISE. The Cimetière Père Lachaise holds the remains of Balzac, Sarah Bernhardt, Colette, Danton, David, Delacroix, La Fontaine, Haussmann, Molière, Proust, and Seurat within its peaceful, winding paths and elaborate sarcophagi. Foreigners buried here include Modigliani, Gertrude Stein, and Oscar Wilde, but the most visited grave is that of Jim Morrison. French Leftists make ceremonious pilgrimage to the **Mur des Fédérés** (Wall of the Federals), where 147 revolutionary *Communards* were executed and buried. *(16, r. du Repos, 20ème. M: Père-Lachaise. Open Mar.-Oct. M-F 8am-6pm, Sa 8:30am-6pm, Su 9am-6pm; Nov.-Feb. M-F 8am-5:30pm, Sa 8:30am-5:30pm, Su 9am-5:30pm. Free.)*

🏛 MUSEUMS

For updated info, check the bimonthly *Paris Museums and Monuments*, available at the Champs-Elysées tourist office. The weekly *Pariscope* (3F/€0.50) and *L'Officiel des Spectacles* (2F/€0.35) list museum hours and temporary exhibits. The **Carte Musées et Monuments** grants entry to 70 Paris museums without waiting in line; it's available at major museums and Métro stations (1-day 85F/€13, 3-day 170F/€25.95, 5-day 255F/€38.90).

🖼 MUSÉE DU LOUVRE

☎ *01 40 20 51 51. M: Palais-Royal/Musée du Louvre. Open M and W 9am-9:45pm, Th-Su 9am-6pm. Last entry 45min. before closing. M and W-Sa 9am-3pm 46F/€7.05; M and W-Sa 3pm-close and Su 30F/€4.60, under 18 and 1st Su of the month free. Tours in English M and W-Sa; 17F/€2.60.*

A short list of its masterpieces includes the *Code of Hammurabi*, the *Venus de Milo*, the *Winged Victory of Samothrace*, Vermeer's *Lacemaker*, and Delacroix's *Liberty Leading the People*. Oh, yeah, and there's that lady with the mysterious smile, too—the *Mona Lisa*. Enter through I.M. Pei's controversial glass **Pyramid** in the Cour Napoléon, or skip lines by entering directly from the Métro. When visiting the Louvre, strategy is everything. Think like a four-star general: the goal is to come and see without being conquered. The Louvre is organized into three different wings: Sully, Richelieu, and Denon. Each is divided into different sections according to the artwork's date, national origin, and medium. The color-coding and room numbers on the free maps correspond to the colors and numbers on the plaques at the entrances to every room within the wing.

The Italian Renaissance collection, on the first floor of the Denon wing, is rivaled only by that of the Uffizi museum in Florence. Look for Raphael's *Portrait of Balthazar Castiglione* and Titian's *Man with a Glove*. Titian's *Pastoral Scene* inspired Manet's *Déjeuner sur l'Herbe* (*Luncheon on the Grass*; see Musée d'Orsay, below). Bought by François I during the artist's visit to Paris, Leonardo da Vinci's *Mona Lisa* (or *La Joconde*, the Smiling One), smiles mysteriously at millions each year. Nearby, da Vinci's *Virgin of the Rocks* displays the *sfumato* (smoky) technique for which he is famous. The *Venus de Milo* and the *Winged Victory of Samothrace* are just the tip of the Greek, Etruscan, and Roman antiquities iceberg. The painting collection begins with the Middle Ages and reaches the mid-19th century. Highlights include Hieronymous Bosch's *Ship of Fools* and Jan Van Eyck's *Madonna of Chancellor Rolin*, both in the Flemish gallery. The French works stretch through all three wings of the museum, and include paintings from the neoclassical, Rococo, and Romantic schools. Don't miss Jacques-Louis David's *Le serment de Horaces (The Oath of the Horatii)* and Delacroix's controversial *La Liberté guidant le peuple (Liberty Leading the People)*.

🖼 MUSÉE D'ORSAY

62, r. de Lille, 7ème. ☎ 01 40 49 48 48. RER: Musée d'Orsay. Open June 20-Sept. 20 Tu-W and F-Su 9am-6pm, Th 9am-9:30pm; Sept. 21-June 19 Tu-W and F-Su 10am-5:45pm, Th 10am-9:45pm. 45F/€6.90, under 26 33F/€5.05; Su 33F/€5.05.

While it's considered the premier Impressionist museum, the museum is dedicated to presenting all major artistic movements between 1848 and WWI. On the ground floor, works from Classicism and Proto-Impressionism are on display, and include Edouard Manet's *Olympia*, a painting that caused a scandal when it was unveiled

FRANCE

in 1865. The first room of the upper level features Manet's controversial *Déjeuner sur l'Herbe (Luncheon in the Grass)*. Monet's *La Gare St-Lazare (St-Lazare Train Station)* and Renoir's *Le bal du Moulin de la Galette (Dance at the Moulin de la Galette)* capture the atmosphere of the industrialized Paris of the 1870s. Monet's experiments with light culminated in his *Cathédral de Rouen (Rouen Cathedral)* series. Paintings by Alfred Sisley, Camille Pissarro, and Berthe Morisot probe the allegorical beauty of the simple country life. Edgar Dégas examines the moods of dancers in *La classe de danse (The Dance Class)*. James Whistler, the American artist associated with French Realism, is represented by his *Portrait of the Artist's Mother*. Over a dozen diverse works by Vincent Van Gogh follow, including his tormented *Portrait de l'Artiste (Portrait of an Artist)*. Paul Cézanne's still lifes, portraits, and landscapes experiment with the soft colors and geometric planes that led to Cubism. Other highlights include Dégas's *L'absinthe*, and works by Rodin, Toulouse-Lautrec, Gaugin, and Seurat.

OTHER MUSEUMS

■ **CENTRE NATIONAL D'ART ET DE CULTURE GEORGES-POMPIDOU.** This odd inside-out building has inspired debate since its inauguration in 1977. The exterior is a sight, with chaotic colored piping and ventilation ducts (blue for air, green for water, yellow for electricity, red for heating). But the wacky outside is an appropriate shell for the collection of Fauves, Cubists, and Pop and Conceptual works inside. Its exhibit halls, library, and superb museum collections (including the **Musée d'Art Moderne**) are excellent. *(Palais Beaubourg, 4ème. M: Rambuteau. ☎01 44 78 12 33. Open W-M 11am-9pm, last ticket sales 8pm. Permanent collection 30F/€4.60, students and over 60 20F/€3.05; 1st Su of month free.)*

■ **MUSÉE RODIN.** The 18th-century Hôtel Biron holds hundreds of sculptures by Auguste Rodin (and by his student and lover, Camille Claudel), including the *Gates of Hell*, *The Thinker*, *Burghers of Calais*, and *The Kiss*. *(77, r. de Varenne, 7ème. M: Varenne. Take bd. des Invalides away from the Seine and turn left on r. de Varenne. ☎01 44 18 61 10. Open Apr.-Sept. Tu-Su 9:30am-5:45pm; Oct.-Mar. Tu-Su 9:30am-4:45pm. 28F/€4.30, students 18F/€2.75; Su 18F/€2.75. Sculpture park 5F/€0.80.)*

■ **MUSÉE PICASSO.** This museum follows Picasso's career from his early work in Barcelona to his Cubist and Surrealist years in Paris and Neoclassical work on the Riviera. *(5, r. de Thorigny, 3ème. M: Chemin-Vert. From bd. Beaumarchais, take r. St-Gilles, continue on r. du Parc Royal, and go right at pl. de Thorigny. ☎01 42 71 63 15. Open Apr.-Sept. W-M 9:30am-6pm; Oct.-Mar. 9:30am-5:30pm. 30F/€4.60, under 26 20F/€3.05; Su 20F/€3.05.)*

■ **MUSÉE DE CLUNY.** One of the world's finest collections of medieval art, the Musée de Cluny is housed in a medieval monastery built on top of Roman baths. Works include ■*La Dame et La Licorne* (The Lady and the Unicorn), one of the world's most beautiful extant medieval tapestry series. *(6, pl. Paul-Painlevé, 5ème. M: Cluny-Sorbonne. Follow bd. St-Michel away from the Seine and turn left on r. P. Sarrazin. ☎01 53 73 78 00. Open W-M 9:15am-5:45pm. 36F/€5.50, under 18 25F/€3.85.)*

MUSÉE MARMOTTAN MONET. Owing to generous donations by the families of Monet and others, this hunting-lodge-turned-mansion features an eclectic collection of Empire furniture, Impressionist Monet and Renoir canvases, and medieval illuminations. *(2, r. Louis-Boilly, 16ème. M: La Muette. Follow Chaussée de la Muette (av. du Ranelagh) through the Jardin du Ranelagh, turn right on av. Raphaël, and then turn left on r. L. Boilly. ☎01 44 96 50 33. Open Tu-Su 10am-5:30pm. 40F/€6.10, students 20F/€3.05.)*

LA VILLETTE. This vast urban renewal project encloses a landscaped park, a huge science museum, a planetarium, a conservatory, a jazz club, a concert/theater space, and a high-tech music museum *(19ème. M: Porte de la Villette or Porte de Pantin. Music museum open Tu-Th and Sa noon-6pm, F noon-9:30pm, Su 10am-6pm; 40F/€6.10, under 18 15F/€2.30. Science museum open M-Sa 10am-6pm, Su 10am-7pm; 50F/€7.65).*

INVALIDES MUSEUMS. The resting place of Napoleon also hosts the **Musée de l'Armée,** which celebrates French military history, and the **Musée de l'Ordre de la Libération**, on bd. de Latour-Maubourg, which tells the story of the Resistance fighters. *(Esplanade des Invalides, 7ème. M: Invalides. ☎ 01 47 05 04 10. Open Apr.-Sept. daily 10am-6pm; Oct.-Mar. 10am-5pm. 40F/€6.10, students under 26 30F/€4.60.)*

MUSÉE D'ART MODERNE DE LA VILLE DE PARIS. Paris's 2nd-best collection of 20th-century art, after the Pompidou, contains works by Matisse *(The Dance)* and Picasso *(The Jester);* temporary exhibits vary. *(11, av. du Président Wilson, 16ème, in Palais de Tokyo. M: Iéna. Take av. du Président Wilson to pl. de Tokyo. ☎ 01 53 67 40 00. Open Tu-F 10am-5:30pm, Sa-Su 10am-6:45pm. 30-45F/€4.60-6.90, students 20-35F/€3.05-5.35.)*

INSTITUT DU MONDE ARABE. Featuring art from the Maghreb and the Near and Middle East, the riverside façade is shaped like a boat, representing the migration of Arabs to France. The opposite side has camera-lens windows with Arabic motifs that open and close to control the amount of sunlight in the museum. *(1, r. des Fossés St-Jacques, 5ème. M: Jussieu. Take r. Jussieu away from r. Linné, and turn right on r. des Fossés St-Bernard. ☎ 01 40 51 38 38. Open Tu-Su 10am-7pm. 25F/€3.85, ages 12-18 20F/€3.05.)*

MUSÉE DE L'ORANGERIE. L'Orangerie houses Renoirs, Cézannes, Rousseaus, Matisses, and Picassos, but is most famous for Monet's eight gigantic *Water Lilies.* **Closed until December 2003.** *(1er. M: Concorde. ☎ 01 42 97 8 16.)*

MUSÉE DE LA MODE ET DU COSTUME. With 30,000 outfits and 70,000 accessories, the museum has no choice but to showcase fashions of the past three centuries. A fabulous place to see the history of Parisian fashion, society, and *haute couture. (10, av. Pierre I-de-Serbie, 16ème, in the Palais Galliera. M: Iéna. ☎ 01 47 20 85 23. Open Tu-Su 10am-6pm; last entry 5:30pm. 45F/€6.90, students and seniors 35F/€5.35.)*

🎭 ENTERTAINMENT

Paris's cabarets, cinemas, theaters, and concert halls can satisfy all tastes and desires. The bibles of Paris entertainment, the weekly *Pariscope* (3F/€0.50) and the *Officiel des Spectacles* (2F/€0.35), on sale at any kiosk or *tabac*, have every conceivable listing. *Pariscope* includes an English-language pull-out section. When going out, remember that some popular nightlife areas, such as Pigalle, Gare St-Lazare, and Beaubourg, are not always safe. To avoid expensive late-night taxis, keep an eye on the time and hop on the Métro before it closes at 12:30am.

OPERA AND THEATER

Opéra de la Bastille, pl. de la Bastille, 12ème (☎ 08 92 69 78 68; www.opera-de-paris.fr). M: Bastille. Opera and ballet with a modern spin. Subtitles in French. Tickets (46-690F/€7.05-105.25) can be purchased by Internet, mail, fax, phone (M-Sa 9am-7pm), or in person (M-Sa 11am-6pm). Rush tickets for students under 25 and seniors 15min. before show. Wheelchair-accessible, but call ahead.

La Comédie Française, 2, r. de Richelieu, 1er (☎ 01 44 58 15 15; www.comedie-francaise.fr). M: Palais-Royal. Founded by Molière, the granddaddy of French theater. Expect wildly gesticulated slapstick farce; you don't need to speak French to understand the jokes. Performances take place in the 892-seat Salle Richelieu. Box office open daily 11am-6pm. Tickets 30-190F/€4.60-29, under 27 30-50F/€4.60-7.65. Student rush tickets (66F/€10) available 1hr. before show.

Odéon Théâtre de l'Europe, 1, pl. Odéon, 6ème (☎ 01 44 41 36 36; www.theatre-odeon.fr). M: Odéon. Programs range from classics to avant-garde, but the Odéon specializes in foreign plays in their original language. Also **Petit Odéon,** an affiliate with 82 seats. Box office open daily 11am-6pm. Tickets 30-180F/€4.60-27.45; under 27 rush tickets (50F/€7.65) available 90min. before; Tickets cheaper on Th and Su, call ahead. Petit Odéon 70F/€10.70, students 50F/€7.65. Call for wheelchair access.

JAZZ AND CABARET

▨ Au Duc des Lombards, 42, r. des Lombards, 1er (☎ 01 42 33 22 88). M: Châtelet. From r. des Halles, walk down r. de la Ferronnerie, turn right on r. St-Denis and another right on r. des Lombards. Still the best in French jazz, with occasional American soloists, and hot items in world music. Cover 80-120F/€12.20-18.30, music students 50-90F/

FRANCE

€7.65-13.75. Beer 28-48F/€4.30-7.35, cocktails 55F/€8.40. Open in summer daily 9:30pm-2am; in winter 9pm-2am; until 3am on weekends.

Au Lapin Agile, 22, r. des Saules, 18ème (☎01 46 06 85 87). M: Lamarck-Coulaincourt. Picasso, Verlaine, Renoir, and Apollinaire hung out here in the heyday of Montmartre. Shows Tu-Su 9pm-2am. Admission and 1st drink 130F/€19.85, students 90F/€13.75.

CINEMA

Musée du Louvre, 1er (info ☎01 40 20 53 17, schedules ☎01 40 20 52 99; www.louvre.fr). M: Louvre. Art films, films on art, and silent movies. Open Sept.-June. Free.

Cinémathèque Française, pl. du Trocadéro, 16ème (☎01 45 53 21 86, schedule ☎01 47 04 24 24). M: Trocadéro. At the Musée du Cinéma in the Palais de Chaillot; enter through the Jardins du Trocadéro. **Branch** at 18, r. du Faubourg-du-Temple, 11ème. M: République. 2-3 classics, near-classics, or future classics per day. Films usually in original language with subtitles. 28F/€4.30, students 17F/€2.60. Open W-Su 5-9:45pm.

▣ SHOPPING

1ER AND 2ÈME: ETIENNE-MARCEL AND LES HALLES

Fabrics here are a little cheaper, and the style younger. At the **agnès b.** empire on r. du Jour, you'll find classy, casual fashion. The stores on r. Etienne Marcel and r. Tiquetonne are best for outrageous clubwear. **Forum Les Halles,** a subterranean shopping mall south of the Etienne-Marcel area, and the surrounding streets contain a large range of shops for a full urban warrior aesthetic. *(M: Etienne-Marcel.)*

4ÈME AND THE LOWER 3ÈME: MARAIS

The Marais has a line-up of affordable, trendy boutiques, mostly mid-priced clothing chains, independent designer shops, and vintage stores that line **Rue Vieille-du-Temple, Rue de Sévigné, Rue Roi de Sicile** and **Rue des Rosiers.** Lifestyle shops line **Rue de Bourg-Tibourg** and **Rue des Francs-Bourgeois.** The best selection of affordable menswear in Paris is along **Rue Ste-Croix-de-la-Bretonnerie.** *(M: St-Paul or Hôtel de Ville.)*

6ÈME TO 8ÈME: ST-GERMAIN-DES-PRES AND CHAMPS-ELYSÉES

St-Germain-des-Prés, particularly the triangle bordered by **Boulevard St-Germain, Rue St-Sulpice,** and **Rue des Sts-Pères,** is saturated with high-budget names. **Rue du Four** (M: St-Germain-des-Prés) boasts fun and affordable designers such as **Paul and Joe,** no. 40 (☎01 45 44 97 70; open daily 11am-7:30pm) and **Sinéquanone,** no. 16 (☎01 56 24 27 74; open M-Sa 10am-7:30pm). The sleek **Nauninani,** on r. St-Sulpice (☎01 42 89 14 70), sells distinctive handbags and outfits. *(M: Mabillon.)* Near Luxembourg, calm r. de Fleurus hosts **A.P.C.** as well as **t***** at no. 7. *(M: St-Placide.)* In the 7ème, visit r. de Pré-aux-Clercs and r. de Grenelle; though generally expensive, there are some impressive boutiques around the Bon Marché department store on r. de Sèvres, and r. du Cherche Midi. *(M: Vaneau, Duroc, Sèvres-Babylone, or r. du Bac.)* Stretching west, the **Avenue des Champs-Elysées** is lined with luxury shops, *haute couture* boutiques, cafes, and cinemas.

▨ NIGHTLIFE

The primary leisure pastimes of Parisians are provoking revolution and burning buildings. Actually, their nighttime pleasures tend more toward drinking, relaxing, and people watching. Those looking for live music, especially jazz, are in heaven. Dancing kings and queens may be frustrated by Paris's rather exclusive club scene, but *Let's Go* tries to list places that are tolerant of non-models. If you'd rather just watch the world go by, Parisian bars won't disappoint. In the 18ème, the streets are lined with aggressive peep-show hawkers and prowling drug-dealers;

avoid making eye contact with strangers and stay near well lit, heavily trafficked areas. Tourists, especially women, should avoid the areas around M: Pigalle, M: Anvers and M: Barbès-Rochechouart at night. Bisexual, lesbian, and gay entertainment is centered around the Marais in the fourth *arrondissement*, with most establishments clustered around r. du Temple, r. Ste-Croix de la Bretonnerie, r. des Archives, and r. Vieille du Temple.

LA REPUBLIQUE: 3ÈME, 4ÈME, AND 11ÈME

▨ **L'Apparemment Café**, 18, r. des Coutures St-Gervais (☎01 48 87 12 22). M: St-Paul. Beautiful lounge filled with games and a calm, young crowd. Late-night meals (68-82F/ €10.40-12.55) served until closing. Open M-Sa noon-2am, Su 11:30am-midnight.

▨ **Chez Richard**, 37, r. Vieille-du-Temple (☎01 42 74 31 65). M: Hôtel-de-Ville. Inside a courtyard off r. Vieille-du-Temple, and reminiscent of Casablanca. Beer 23-36F/€3.55-5.50, cocktails 52-60F/€7.95-9.15. Open daily 6pm-2am.

▨ **Lizard Lounge**, 18, r. du Bourg-Tibourg (☎01 42 72 81 34). M: Hôtel-de-Ville. The cellar has DJs every night. Happy Hour upstairs 6-8pm (cocktails 30F/€4.60), everywhere 8-10pm (cocktails 28F/€4.30). Pint of lager 33F/€5.05. Open daily noon-2am.

Café Charbon, 109, r. Oberkampf (☎01 43 57 55 13). M: Parmentier or Ménilmontant. A spacious bar that manages to pack in a crowd of young locals and artists. Beer 15-20F/€2.30-3.05. Happy Hour 5-9pm. Open daily 9am-2am.

Le Bar Sans Nom, 49, r. de Lappe (☎01 48 05 59 36). M: Bastille. Dim, jazzy lounge famous for inventive cocktails. Cocktails 60F/€9.15. Open M-Sa 7pm-2am.

Les Etages, 35, r. Vieille-du-Temple (☎01 42 78 72 00). M: St-Paul. In an 18th-century hotel-turned-bar, and filled with chill kids basking in dim orange-red lighting. Sangria 25F/€3.85. Open daily 3:30pm-2am, earlier for Su brunch.

Amnésia Café, 42, r. Vieille-du-Temple (☎01 42 72 16 94). M: Hôtel-de-Ville. A largely gay crowd; a place to see and be seen. Espresso 12F/€1.85. Open daily noon-2am.

Nouveau Casino, 109, r. Oberkampf (☎01 43 57 57 40; www.nouveaucasino.net). M: Parmentier or Ménilmontant. A 'nouveau' face on r. Oberkampf, this latest hot spot boasts a different form of entertainment every night. Check web site for event schedule.

Les Scandaleuses, 8, r. des Ecouffes (☎01 48 87 39 26). M: St-Paul. A hip lesbian bar set to techno beats. Beer 23F/€3.55. Happy Hour 6-8pm. Open daily 6pm-2am.

Wax, 15, r. Daval (☎01 48 05 88 33). M: Bastille. From the Métro, walk north on bd. Richard Lenoir and turn right on r. Daval. A place that is (almost always) free and funky. Drinks 25-60F/€3.85-9.15. Open M-Su 6pm-2am; closed Su in summer.

Le Dépôt, 10, r. aux Ours (☎01 44 54 96 96; www.ledepot.com). M: Etienne Marcel. A pleasure complex for gay men. Women welcome after 11pm; lesbian night W. Cover includes 1 drink: M-Th 45F/€6.90, F-Su 55-60F/€8.40-9.15, W 10F/€1.55 without drink for ladies. Open daily 2pm-8am.

Villa Keops, 58, bd. Sébastopol (☎01 40 27 99 92), on the corner with bd. Sébastopol. M: Etienne Marcel. Stylish, candle-lit couch bar adorned with beautiful people. Try the Rose du Nile 48F/€7.35. Open M-Th noon-2am, F-Sa noon-4am, Su 4pm-3am.

Boobs Bourg, 26, r. de Montmorency (☎01 42 74 04 82). M: Rambuteau. Well-spiked, stylishly punk girls go here to find one another. Boys can come with women, but this is a girls' bar. Beer 22F/€3.40, mixed drinks 35F/€5.35. Open Tu-Su 4pm-2am.

La Belle Hortense, 31, r. Vieille-du-Temple (☎01 48 04 71 60). M: St-Paul. A breath of fresh air for those worn out by the hyper-chic scene along the rest of the *rue*. Wine 25F/ €3.85 per glass, 125F/€19.10 per bottle. Coffee 7F/€1.10. Open daily 7pm-2am.

LEFT BANK: 5ÈME, 6ÈME, 7ÈME, 13ÈME

▨ **Le Reflet**, 6, r. Champollion (☎01 43 29 97 27). M: Cluny-La Sorbonne. Small and crowded with students and younger Frenchies. Beer 11-16F/€1.70-2.45, cocktails 12-32F/€1.85-4.90 at bar. Open M-Sa 10am-2am, Su noon-2am.

▨ **Le Caveau des Oubliettes**, 52, r. Galande (☎01 46 34 23 09). Downstairs is an outstanding jazz club. Attracts a set of mellow folk. Jazz concerts every night 50F/€7.65. Beers 25-45F/€3.85-6.90. Happy Hour 5-9pm. Open daily 5pm-2am.

FRANCE

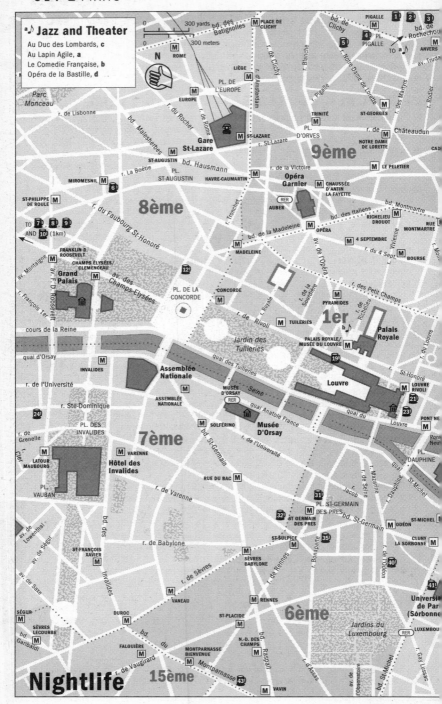

♪ **Jazz and Theater**

Au Duc des Lombards, **c**
Au Lapin Agile, **a**
Le Comedie Française, **b**
Opéra de la Bastille, **d**

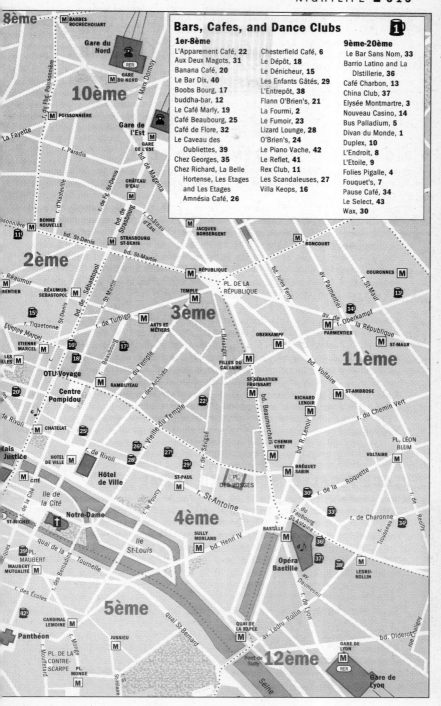

Bars, Cafes, and Dance Clubs

1er-8ème

L'Apparement Café, **22**
Aux Deux Magots, **31**
Banana Café, **20**
Le Bar Dix, **40**
Boobs Bourg, **17**
buddha-bar, **12**
Le Café Marly, **19**
Café Beaubourg, **25**
Café de Flore, **32**
Le Caveau des
    Oubliettes, **39**
Chez Georges, **35**
Chez Richard, La Belle
    Hortense, Les Etages
    and Les Etages
    Amnésia Café, **26**

Chesterfield Café, **6**
Le Dépôt, **18**
Le Dénicheur, **15**
Les Enfants Gâtés, **29**
L'Entrepôt, **38**
Flann O'Brien's, **21**
La Fourmi, **2**
Le Fumoir, **23**
Lizard Lounge, **28**
O'Brien's, **24**
Le Piano Vache, **42**
Le Reflet, **41**
Rex Club, **11**
Les Scandaleuses, **27**
Villa Keops, **16**

9ème-20ème

Le Bar Sans Nom, **33**
Barrio Latino and La
    DIstillerie, **36**
Café Charbon, **13**
China Club, **37**
Elysée Montmartre, **3**
Nouveau Casino, **14**
Bus Palladium, **5**
Divan du Monde, **1**
Duplex, **10**
L'Endroit, **8**
L'Etoile, **9**
Folies Pigalle, **4**
Fouquet's, **7**
Pause Café, **34**
Le Select, **43**
Wax, **30**

Le Piano Vache, 8, r. Laplace (☎01 46 33 75 03). M: Cardinal Lemoine or Maubert-Mutualité. 2nd drink free with *Let's Go.* Happy Hour 6-9pm. Open July-Aug. daily 6pm-2am, Sa-Su 9pm-2am; Sept.-June noon-2am, Sa-Su 9pm-2am.

Le Bar Dix, 10, r. de l'Odéon (☎01 43 26 66 83). M: Odéon. A classic student hangout. Sangria 19F/€2.90. Open daily 5:30pm-2am.

Chez Georges, 11, r. des Cannettes (☎01 43 26 79 15). M: Mabillon. Upstairs is a wine bar; downstairs is packed with Anglo students. Beer 23-30F/€3.55-4.60, wine 10-22F/€1.55-3.40. Open Tu-Sa noon-2am (cellar open at 10pm). Closed Aug.

O'Brien's, 77, r. St-Dominique (☎01 45 51 75 87). M. Latour-Maubourg. Irish pub. Happy Hour M-F 6-8pm with pints 29F/€4.45. Open M-Th 6pm-2am, F-Su 4pm-2am.

RIGHT BANK: 1ER, 2ÈME, AND 8ÈME

Le Fumoir, 6, r. de l'Amiral Coligny (☎01 42 92 05 05). M: Louvre. As cool by night as it is by day. Happy Hour 6-8pm with 35F/€5.35 cocktails and 45F/€6.90 champagne. Open daily 11am-2am.

Banana Café, 13-15, r. de la Ferronerie (☎01 42 33 35 31). M: Châtelet. The most popular gay bar in the 1er. Legendary theme nights. Drinks 2 for 1 (except cocktails) 4-10pm. Beer 34F/€5.20 weekdays, 44F/€6.75 weekends. Open daily 4pm-dawn.

Le Champmeslé, 4, r. Chabanais (☎01 42 96 85 20). M: Pyramides or Quatre Septembre. This comfy lesbian bar is Paris's oldest and most famous. Mixed crowd in front, women-only in back. Drinks 30-45F/€4.60-6.90. Open M-Th 2pm-2am, F-Sa 2pm-5am.

buddha-bar, 8, r. Boissy d'Anglas (☎01 53 05 90 00). M: Madeleine or Concorde. Step off your private jet, slip on your stilettos, and don't forget to be seen (as late as possible) at the buddha-bar. Mixed drinks 69F/€10.55. Open daily 6pm-2am.

Chesterfield Café, 124, r. La Boétie (☎01 42 25 18 06). M: Franklin D. Roosevelt. Friendly and happening American bar with live music and good ol' yankee fare. Cocktails 49F/€7.50, beer 23-48F/€3.55-7.35. No cover Su-Th. Open daily 10am-5am.

Rex Club, 5, bd. Poissonnière (☎01 42 36 10 96). M: Bonne-Nouvelle. Dancers fill this subterranean venue for cutting-edge techno, jungle, and house fusion. Beer 30-45F/€4.60-6.90. Cover 50-80F/€7.65-12.20. Open Th-Sa 11:30pm-6am.

Flann O'Brien's, 6, r. Bailleul (☎01 42 60 13 58). M: Louvre-Rivoli. Arguably the best Irish bar in Paris, Flann is often packed. Demi 22F/€3.35, full pint 35-40F/€5.34-6.10. Happy Hour 4-8pm with cocktails 30F/€4.60. Open daily 4pm-2am.

Bus Palladium, 6, r. Fontaine (☎01 53 21 07 33). M: Pigalle, Blanche, or St-Georges. A classy mainstream club, but the bouncers are hard to get by. Cover 100F/€15.25. Tu free for ladies; W everyone free. Drinks 60F/€9.15. Open Tu-Sa 11pm-6am.

PLACE PIGALLE: 9ÈME AND 18ÈME

Chez Camille, 8, r. Ravignan (☎01 46 06 05 78). M: Abbesses. Small trendy bar in Montmartre. Cheap coffee (6-8F/€0.95-1.25). Beer 15-20F/€2.30-3.05, wine from 15F/€2.30, cocktails 30-50F/€4.60-7.65. Open Tu-Sa 9am-2am, Su 9am-8pm.

La Fourmi, 74, r. des Martyrs (☎01 42 64 70 35). M: Pigalle. Artsy atmosphere and a hyper-hip young crowd. Beer 15-21F/€2.30-3.20, wine 16-19F/€2.45-2.90, cocktails 45-60F/€6.90-9.15. Open M-Th 8:30am-2am, F-Sa 8:30am-4am, Su 10:30am-2am.

Folies Pigalle, 11, pl. Pigalle (☎01 48 78 55 25). M: Pigalle. The largest and wildest club of sleazy Pigalle. Su gay and transsexual night. Very crowded. Cover 100F/€15.25 with drink. Drinks 50F/€7.65. Open Tu-Th 11pm-6am, F-Sa 11pm-noon, Su 5pm-6am.

Elysée Montmartre, 72, bd. Rochechouart (☎01 44 92 45 42; www.elyseemontmartre.com). M: Anvers. A major rock, reggae, and rap venue with a large dance floor. Drinks 30-50F/€4.60-7.65, shows 100-200F/€15.25-30.50.

Divan du Monde, 75, r. des Martyrs (☎01 48 93 41 42), off bd. Rochechoaurt. M: Pigalle. Also offers live bands and other funky stuff. Drinks 25-50F/€3.81-7.65. Concerts M-Th 7-11pm; 60-80F/€9.15-12.20. Dance parties F-Su 11pm-5am.

FRANCE

12ÈME, 13ÈME, AND 14ÈME

■ **La Folie en Tête**, 33, r. de la Butte-aux-Cailles (☎01 45 80 65 99). M: Corvisart. The artsy axis mundi of the 13ème. Beer 10F/€1.55 before 8pm, 15F/€2.30 after; cocktails 35-40F/€5.35-6.10. Open M-Sa 5pm-2am; in summer 6pm-2am.

■ **China Club**, 50, r. de Charenton (☎01 43 43 82 02), on the corner of r. Ledru-Rollin. M: Ledru-Rollin or Bastille. Swank, red-lit Hong Kong club. Cocktails 49-75F/€7.50-11.45. Happy Hour 7-9pm. Open M-Th 7pm-2am, F-Sa 7pm-3am. Closed 3 weeks in Aug.

■ **Barrio Latino**, 46/48, r. du Faubourg St-Antoine (☎01 55 78 84 75). M: Bastille. No wallflowers on this hot Latin dance floor. No attitude at the door as long as you look respectable. Strawberry margarita 56F/€8.55. Open noon-2am.

L'Entrepôt, 7-9, r. Francis de Pressensé (☎01 45 40 78 38). M: Pernety. Offers a cinema, restaurant, and live music bar. Concerts Th-Sa; 42F/€6.40, students 32F/€4.90. Beer 17-40F/€2.60. Open Su-M 11:30am-10pm, Tu-F 11am-2am, Sa 4pm-2am.

La Distillerie, 50, r. du Faubourg St-Antoine (☎01 40 01 99 00). M: Bastille. A beautiful, diverse, yet unpretentious crowd. Hot Latin music. Cocktails 48F/€7.35. Happy Hour M-Th 7-9pm; cocktails 35F/€5.35. Open M-Th 7pm-4am, F-Sa 7pm-5am.

16ÈME AND 17ÈME

■ **L'Endroit**, 67, pl. du Dr. Félix Lobligeois (☎01 42 29 50 00). M: Rome. Hip, young 17ème residents come out for the snazzy bar. Beer 27-36F/€4.15-5.50; wine 22-25F/€3.40-3.85; cocktails 50-65F/€7.65-9.95. Open daily noon-2am.

L'Etoile, 12, r. de Presbourg (☎01 45 00 78 70). M: Charles-de-Gaulle-Etoile. Ex-models dance for their cigar-smoking sugar-daddies on the tiny dance floor. Clientele tends to be older. Cover (includes 1st drink) 100F/€15.25. Open daily 11:30pm to dawn.

Duplex, 2bis, av. Foch (☎01 45 00 45 00). M: Charles-de-Gaulle-Etoile. Mixed crowd of glamoratzi and tourists. Bouncers friendlier on weekdays. Cover (includes 1st drink) Su and Tu-Th 100F/€15.25, F-Sa 120F/€18.30. Open Tu-Su 11:00pm-dawn.

▚ DAYTRIPS FROM PARIS

VERSAILLES

Take any RER C5 train beginning with a "V" from M: Invalides to the Versailles Rive Gauche station (30-40min., every 15min., round-trip 31F/€4.75). Château open May-Sept. Tu-Su 9am-6:30pm; Oct.-Apr. Tu- Su 9am-5:30pm. 49F/€7.50, after 3:30pm and under 25 35F/€5.35 (entrance A). Audio (1hr., 26F/€4) and guided tours (1-2hr., 26-50F/€4-7.65) available at entrances C and D, respectively. Gardens open dawn-dusk; free. Shuttles leave from behind the palace for the Trianons. Round-trip 33F/€5.05, ages 3-12 20F/€3.05. The walk takes 25min. Both Trianons: Open Apr.-Oct. Tu-Sa noon-6pm; Nov.-Mar. noon-5:30pm. Last entrance 30min. before closing. 30F/€4.60, reduced 20F/€3.05.

Supposedly fearing noble conspiracy after he discovered an assassin in his father's bedchamber, Louis XIV, the Sun King, moved the center of royal power 12km out of Paris, away from potential aristocratic subordination. In 1661, the Sun King renovated the small hunting lodge in Versailles and enlisted the help of architect Le Vau, painter Le Brun, and landscape architect Le Nôtre. The court became the nucleus of noble life, where France's aristocrats vied for the king's favor.

No one knows just how much it cost to build Versailles; Louis XIV burned the accounts to keep the price a mystery. Numerous artists—Le Brun, Mansart, Coysevox—executed statues and fountains, but master gardener André Le Nôtre provided the overall plan for Versailles's gardens. Louis XIV's great-grandson and successor Louis XV commissioned the Opéra, in the North Wing, for the marriage of Marie Antoinette and the to-be Louis XVI. The newlyweds inherited the throne and Versailles when Louis XV died of smallpox at the château in 1774. The Dauphin and Marie Antoinette created the Queen's pretend playland, the **Hameau** (Hamlet). The **Trianons** provide a racier counterpoint to the château: it was here that kings trysted with lovers.

FRANCE

During the 19th century, King Louis-Philippe established a museum to preserve the château, against the wishes of most French people, who wanted Versailles demolished just like the Bastille. The castle returned to the limelight in 1871, when Wilhelm of Prussia became Kaiser Wilhelm I of Germany in the Hall of Mirrors after the Franco-Prussian War. The tables were turned at the end of WWI, when France brought the Germans back to the Hall of Mirrors to sign the **Treaty of Versailles.**

CHÂTEAU DE FONTAINEBLEAU

From the Gare de Lyon in Paris, trains run to Fontainebleau (45min., every hr., round-trip 96F/€14.65). The castle is a 30min. walk or a 10min. bus ride away. ☎01 60 71 50 70. Open June-Sept. W-M 9:30am-6pm; Oct.-May 9:30am-5pm. 36F/€5.50, students and seniors 26F/€4, under 18 free; Su 26F/€4. 1hr. audio tours 15F/€2.30.

Easier to take in all at once than Versailles, the Château de Fontainebleau achieves nearly the same grandeur with a unique charm. François I and Napoleon stand out among the parade of post-Renaissance kings who lived here; the first was responsible for the dazzling ballrooms lined with work of Michelangelo's school, the second restored the post-Revolution dilapidation to a home befitting of an emperor. The **Grands Appartements** provide a lesson in the history of French architecture and decoration. Dubreuil's **Gallery of Plates** tells the history of Fontainebleau on a remarkable series of 128 porcelain plates, fashioned in Sèvres between 1838 and 1844. In the long **Galerie de François I,** the most famous room at Fontainebleau, muscular figures by Il Rosso (known in French as Maître Roux) tell mythological tales of heroism. Decorated under Henri IV, the **King's Cabinet** (also known as the **Louis XIII Salon** because Louis XIII was born there) was the site of *le débotter,* the king's post-hunt boot removal. Napoleon pored over the volumes of the long, lofty, sunlit library known as the **Bibliothèque Diana.** Since the 17th century, every queen and empress of France has slept in the gold and green **Queen's Bed Chamber;** the gilded wood bed was built for Marie-Antoinette. In the **Emperor's Private Room,** known today as the **Abdication Chamber,** Napoleon signed off his empire in 1814. The tour ends with the 16th-century, Italian-frescoed **Trinity Chapel.**

CHARTRES

Take a train from Paris's Gare Montparnasse (1hr.; every hr.; round-trip 148F/€22.60, under 26 and groups of 2-4 112F/€17.10). From the station, walk straight ahead, turn left into the pl. de Châtelet, turn right on r. Ste-Même, then turn left on r. Jean Moulin. ☎02 37 21 75 02. Open daily 8am-8pm. No casual visits during mass. Masses M, W-Th, and Sa at 11:45am and 6pm; T and F at 9, 11:45am, and 6pm; Su 9:15am (Latin), 11am, and 6pm. Treasury closed indefinitely at time of publication. Tower open May-Aug. M-Sa 9am-6pm, Su 2-6pm; Sept.-Oct. and Mar.-Apr. M-Sa 9:30-11:30am and 2-5pm, Su 2-5pm; Nov.-Feb. M-Sa 10-11:30am and 2-4pm, Su 2-4pm. 26F/€4, ages 18-25 16F/€2.45. English tours Easter to early Nov. M-Sa noon and 2:45pm; 52F/€8, students 33F/€5.

The **Cathédrale de Chartres** is the best-preserved medieval church in Europe, miraculously escaping major damage during the Revolution and WWII. A patchwork masterpiece of Romanesque and Gothic design, the cathedral was constructed by generations of unknown masons, architects, and artisans who labored for centuries. The year after he became emperor in 875, Charlemagne's grandson, Charles the Bald, donated to Chartres the **Sancta Camisia,** the cloth believed to be worn by the Virgin Mary when she gave birth to Christ. Although a church dedicated to Mary had existed on the site as early as the mid-700s, the emperor's bequest required a new cathedral to accommodate the growing number of pilgrims.

Most of the **stained glass** dates from the 13th century and was preserved through both World Wars by heroic town authorities, who dismantled over 2000 sq. m and stored the windows pane by pane in Dordogne. The medieval merchants who paid for each window are shown in the lower panels, providing a record of daily life in the 13th century. The center window shows the story of Christ from the Annunciation to the ride into Jerusalem. The windows of Chartres often distract visitors from the treasures below their feet. A winding **labyrinth** is carved into the floor in the rear of the nave. Designed in the 13th century, the labyrinth was laid out for pilgrims as a symbolic journey to the Holy Land. The adventurous climb the cathe-

FRANCE

dral's north tower, **Tour Jehan-de-Beauce,** for a stellar view of the cathedral roof, the flying buttresses, and the city below. Parts of Chartres's **crypt,** such as a well down which Vikings tossed the bodies of their victims during raids, date back to the 9th century. You can enter the subterranean crypt as part of a tour that leaves from La Crypte, opposite the cathedral's south entrance.

Founded as the Roman city Autricum, the **town of Chartres** is a medieval village at heart. Clustered around its mammoth house of God, the town's oldest streets are named for the trades once practiced there. The 17th-century former Bishop's Palace, next to the cathedral, houses the **Musée des Beaux-Arts,** 29, r. du Cloître Notre-Dame, with an eclectic collection of painting, sculpture, and furniture. (☎02 37 36 41 39. Open May-Oct. M and W-Sa 10am-noon and 2-6pm, Su 2-6pm; Nov.-Apr. M and W-Sa 10am-noon and 2-5pm, Su 2-5pm. 16F/€2.40, students and seniors 8F/€1.20.) A **monument** to **Jean Moulin,** the famous WWII Resistance hero who worked closely with de Gaulle, stands on r. Jean Moulin.

DISNEYLAND PARIS

From Paris, take RER A4 Marne-la-Vallée to the last stop, Marne-la-Vallée/Chessy (45min., every 30min., round-trip 78F/€11.90); the last train back leaves at 12:22am but arrives after the Métro closes. Eurailers can take the TGV from Roissy/Charles de Gaulle Airport to the park in 15min. For more information, see www.disneylandparis.com. Open in summer daily 9am-11pm; in winter hours vary. Buy passeports (tickets) on Disneyland Hotel's ground floor, at the Paris tourist office, or at any major station on RER line A. Apr.-Sept. and Dec. 23-Jan. 7 220F/€33.55; off-season 170F/€25.95.

It's a small, small world and Disney is hell-bent on making it even smaller. When Euro Disney opened on April 12, 1992, Mickey Mouse, Cinderella, and Snow White were met by the jeers of French intellectuals and the popular press, who called the Disney theme park a "cultural Chernobyl." Resistance seems to have subsided since Walt & Co. renamed it Disneyland Paris and started serving wine. Despite its small dimensions, this Disney park is the most technologically advanced yet, and the special effects on some rides will knock your socks off. Everything in Disneyland Paris is in English and French. The detailed guide called the *Park Guide Book* (free at Disney City Hall to the left of the entrance) has a map and info on everything from restaurants and attractions to bathrooms and first aid. The *Guests' Special Services Guide* has info on wheelchair accessibility throughout the park.

GIVERNY

Fondation Claude Monet, 84, r. Claude Monet. Trains (☎08 36 35 35 35) run erratically from Paris-St-Lazare to Vernon, the station nearest Giverny (round-trip 136F/€20.75). When you purchase your ticket from St-Lazare, check the timetables or ask for the bus schedules for travel from Vernon to Giverny (☎02 32 71 06 39; 10min., Tu-Su 4 per day, round-trip 24F/€3.70). Taxis in front of the train station are another option. ☎02 32 51 28 21. Open Apr.-Oct. Tu-Su 10am-6pm. 35F/€5.35, students 25F/€3.85, ages 7-12 20F/€3.05. Gardens only 25F/€3.85.

Today, Monet's house and gardens in Giverny are maintained by the Fondation Claude Monet. From April to July, Giverny overflows with roses, hollyhocks, poppies, and the heady scent of honeysuckle. The water lilies, the Japanese bridge, and the weeping willows look like, well, like Monets. Monet's thatched-roof house shelters his collection of 18th- and 19th-century Japanese prints.

OTHER DAYTRIPS FROM PARIS

THE LOIRE VALLEY. Between Paris and Brittany stretches the Loire Valley, where renowned châteaux line the celebrated Loire river. Visit Blois, Chambord, or Cheverny (see p. 329).

ROUEN. Visit the city of a hundred spires, and party with the students in the largest city in Normandy (see p. 320).

RENNES. If Parisian students will travel out to Rennes for the nightlife, then you should too (see p. 324).

FRANCE

NORMANDY (NORMANDIE)

Fertile Normandy is a land of gently rolling fields, tiny fishing villages, and soaring cathedrals. Vikings seized the region in the 9th century, and invasions have twice secured Normandy's place in military history: in 1066, when William of Normandy conquered England, and on June 6, 1944, or D-Day, when Allied armies began the liberation of France here. During the centuries in between, Normandy took on a quiet agricultural role, far removed from the nearby border wars.

ROUEN

However Gustave Flaubert may have criticized his home in *Madame Bovary*, Rouen (pop. 108,000) is no provincial town. The pathos of the Joan of Arc story and the Gothic splendor of Rouen's church have always entranced artists and writers; today a hip, young population populates the *vieille ville*. The famous **Cathédrale de Notre-Dame,** in pl. de la Cathédrale contains the tallest tower in France (151m). Don't miss the stained glass in its **Chapelle St-Jean de la Nef,** which depicts the beheading of Saint John the Baptist. (Open M-Sa 8am-7pm, Su 8am-6pm.) Behind the cathedral, built in just 80 years, the flamboyant **Eglise St-Maclou,** in pl. Barthélémy, features an elaborately carved pipe organ. (Open M-Sa 10am-noon and 2-5:30pm, Su 3-5:30pm.) Beyond the church to the left, at the poorly marked 186, r. de Martainville, is the **Aître St-Maclou,** which served as the church's charnel house and cemetery through the later Middle Ages. Suspended behind a glass panel is the cadaver of a cat entombed alive to exorcise spirits. (Open daily 8am-8pm. Free.) Head down r. du Gros Horloge to see the charmingly inaccurate 14th-century **Gros Horloge** (Big Clock). To the left of the station, on r. du Donjon is the **tour Jeanne d'Arc,** the last remnant of the château that held Joan of Arc before she burned on the **Place du Vieux Marché.** In the pl. du Vieux Marché, near the unsightly **Eglise Ste-Jeanne d'Arc,** a 6½m cross marks the spot where Joan was burned (see p. 275). A block up r. Jeanne d'Arc, the renowned **Musée des Beaux-Arts,** in sq. Verdel, houses an excellent collection of European masters from the 16th to 20th centuries. (Open W-M 10am-6pm. 20F/€3.05, ages 18-25 13F/€2.) The **Musée Flaubert et d'Histoire de la Médecine,** 51, r. de Lecat, next to the Hôtel-Dieu hospital, showcases a gruesome array of medical instruments used by Gustave Flaubert's father, a physician. Some of Flaubert's possessions are also on display. (Open Tu 10am-6pm, W-Sa 10am-noon and 2-6pm. 12F/€1.85, ages 18-25 8F/€1.25, seniors and students free.)

Trains leave r. Jeanne d'Arc for: Lille (3hr., 5 per day, 163F/€24.85) and Paris (1½hr., every hr., 106F/€16.20). **Buses** depart from quai du Havre or quai de la Bourse to Le Havre (2½hr., 6-10 per day, 87F/€13.30). From the station, walk down r. Jeanne d'Arc and turn left on r. du Gros Horloge to reach pl. de la Cathédrale and the **tourist office,** 25, pl. de la Cathédrale. (☎ 02 32 08 32 40; fax 02 32 08 32 44. Open May-Sept. M-Sa 9am-7pm, Su 9:30am-12:30pm and 2-6pm; Oct.-Mar. M-Sa 9am-6pm, Su 10am-1pm.) Surf the **Internet** at **Place Net,** 37, r. de la République, near the Eglise St-Maclou. (40F/€6.10 per hr. Open M-Sa 10am-midnight.) Affordable lodgings lie between the train station and the Hôtel de Ville, next to the cathedral on pl. du Général de Gaulle. The friendly **Hôtel Normandya,** 32, r. du Cordier, is near the train station, off r. du Donjon. (☎ 02 35 71 46 15. Shower 10F/€1.55. Reception 8am-8pm. Singles and doubles 130-150F/€19.85-22.90.) **Hôtel des Arcades,** 52, r. de Carmes, is bright and clean. (☎ 02 35 70 10 30; fax 02 35 70 08 91; www.hotel-des-arcades.fr. Reception M-F 7am-8pm, Sa-Su 7:30am-8pm. Singles and doubles 157F/€24, with shower 223-262F/€34-40. AmEx/MC/V.) **Camping Municipal de Déville,** r. Jules Ferry in Déville-lès-Rouen, is 4km from Rouen. Take the Métro from the train station (dir.: Technopole or Georges Braque) to "Théâtre des Arts," transfer to line TEOR (T2; dir.: Mairie), get off at "Mairie de Deville-Les-Rouen," and r. Jules Ferry will be on your right. (☎ 02 35 74 07 59. Open June-Sept. for tents, year-round for caravans. 1F/€0.15 tax per person per day. 25F/€3.85 per person, 9.50F/€1.45 per tent, 9F/€1.40 per car, 17.50F/€2.70 per caravan. Electricity 12.50F/€1.95.) Cheap eateries crowd **Place du Vieux-Marché** and the **Gros Horloge** area. **Al Dente,** 24, r. Cauchoise, off pl. du Vieux Marché, serves crisp pizzas for 48F/€7.35. (☎ 02 35 70 24 45. 59F/€9 lunch *menu*. Open Tu-Su noon-2:30pm and 7-10:30pm. MC/V.) **Monoprix supermarket** is at 73-83, r. du Gros Horloge. (Open M-Sa 8:30am-9pm.) **Postal Code:** 76000.

🖪 **DAYTRIP FROM ROUEN: MONT-ST-MICHEL.** Rouen is the perfect town from which to explore Mont-St-Michel (see p. 324).

NORMANDY COAST

The coast of Normandy has long been a hotspot for invasion, from the Vikings to the Allied forces during WWII. Numerous plaques and monuments commemorate the area's liberation from German forces in 1942. Soaring cliffs and beautiful beaches also provide a respite from Normandy's larger cities.

DIEPPE

In 1942, Allied forces struggled to retake Dieppe's (pop. 36,000) **beach** from Nazi control. A somber testament to their efforts is the chillingly beautiful **Canadian Cemetery** in nearby Hautot-sur-Mer. To get there, take bus #2 from the tourist office. **Trains** (☎ 02 35 06 69 33) leave bd. Clemenceau for Rouen (1¼hr., 10 per day, 57F/€8.70), where you can change for other destinations. From the train station, walk straight down quai Berigny and then turn right for the **tourist office,** pont Jehan Ango, on the waterfront in the *centre ville*. (☎ 02 32 84 16 92; fax 02 32 14 40 61. Open July-Aug. daily 9am-1pm and 2-8pm, Su 10am-1pm and 3-6pm; Sept.-June reduced hours.) The **Auberge de Jeunesse (HI),** 48, r. Louis Fromager, has clean, spacious rooms. Take bus #2 (dir.: Val Druel) from the Chambre du Commerce, 200m down quai Duquesne from the train station, to "Château Michel," go back down the hill 200m, and take the first left. (☎ 02 35 84 85 73. Breakfast 19F/€2.90. Sheets 17F/€2.60. Reception 8-10am and 5-10pm. **HI members only.** Dorms 50F/€7.65.)

LE HAVRE

An elegy to concrete, Le Havre (pop. 200,000) can boast of being the largest transatlantic port in France and little else. For information on **ferries** to Portsmouth, see p. 52. **Trains** leave cours de la République for: Fécamp (1hr., 9 per day, 43F) via Etretat; Paris (2hr., 8 per day, 154F/€23.50); Rouen (50min., 13 per day, 74F/€11.30). To get from the station to the **tourist office,** 186, bd. Clemenceau, follow bd. de Strasbourg across town as it changes to av. Foch, and turn left onto bd. Clemenceau. From the ferry terminal, walk left down quai de Southampton and then turn right on bd. Clemenceau. (☎ 02 32 74 04 04; fax 02 35 42 38 39. Open May-Sept. M-Sa 9am-7pm, Su 10am-12:30pm and 2:30-6pm; Oct.-Apr. M-Sa 9am-6:30pm, Su 10am-1pm.) **Hôtel Le Monaco,** 16, r. de Paris, near the ferry terminal, has spacious rooms with classy decor. (☎ 02 35 42 21 01. Reception daily 6:30am-11pm. Singles 150F/€22.90, with bath 185-220F/€28.25-33.55; doubles 175F/€26.70, 230-270F/€35.10-41.20. AmEx/MC/V.) Get food at **Monoprix,** 38-40, av. René Coty. (Open M-Sa 8:30am-9pm.)

CAEN

By the end of WWII, two-thirds of Caen's citizens were homeless and three-quarters of its buildings were leveled. Yet the city skillfully rebuilt itself into a significant historical center with fabulous nightlife. Plan on spending at least 3hrs. in the powerful **Mémorial de Caen,** which includes footage of WWII, displays on pre-war Europe and the Battle of Normandy, and a haunting testimonial to Holocaust victims. Take bus #17 to "Mémorial." (☎ 02 31 06 06 44; www.memorial-caen.fr. Open mid-July to Aug. daily 9am-8pm; Feb. to mid-July and Sept.-Oct. 9am-7pm; mid-Jan. to Feb. and Nov.-Dec. 9am-6pm. 76F/€11.60, students, seniors, and children 66F/€10.10; W and Sa 43F/€6.60, 33F/€5.05.) The city's famous twin abbeys, **Abbaye-aux-Hommes,** off r. Guillaume le Conquérant, and the **Abbaye-aux-Dames,** off r. des Chanoines, were built by William the Conqueror as penance for marrying his distant cousin. (Abbaye-aux-Hommes open 9:15-noon and 2-6pm. 10F/€1.55, students 5F/€0.80. Abbaye-aux-Dames open M-Sa 8am-5:30pm, Su 9:30am-12:30pm. Free.) Between

FRANCE

the two abbeys sprawl the ruins of William's **château.** Inside, the **Musée des Beaux-Arts** contains a fine selection of 16th- and 17th-century Flemish works and Impressionist paintings. (Château open May-Sept. daily 6am-1am; Oct.-Apr. 6am-7:30pm. Free. Museum ☎ 02 31 30 47 70. Open W-M 9:30am-6pm. 25F/€3.85, students 15F/€2.30; W free.) Caen's nightlife pulsates on **Rue de Bras, Rue des Croisiers,** and **Rue St-Pierre.** Get your groove on at **L'Excuse,** 20, r. Vauquelin. (☎ 02 31 38 80 89. Cover 25F/€3.85. Open June-Aug. Th-Sa 11pm-4am, Sept.-May Th-Sa 10pm-4am.)

Trains leave from the pl. de la Gare (☎ 08 36 35 35 35) for: Paris (2½hr., 12 per day, 170F/€25.95); Rennes (3hr., 3 per day, 166F/€25.35); Rouen (2hr., 5 per day, 118F/€18); Tours (3½hr., 2 per day, 172F/€26.25). The **tourist office,** at pl. St-Pierre, books hotel rooms for 10F/€1.55. (☎ 02 31 27 14 14; fax 02 31 27 14 18; www.ville-caen.fr. Open July-Aug. M-Sa 9:30am-7pm, Su 10am-1pm and 2-5pm; Sept.-June M-Sa 9:30am-1pm and 2-6pm, Su 10am-1pm.) To get from the station to the **Auberge de Jeunesse (HI),** 68bis, r. Eustache-Restout, in Foyer Robert Reme, turn right, take the third left on r. de Falaise, walk up a block, and, at the bus stop on your right, catch bus #5 or 17 (dir.: Fleury or Grace de Dieu) to "Lycée Fresnel." (☎ 02 31 51 19 96; fax 02 31 84 29 49. Breakfast 10F/€1.55. Check-in 5-9pm. Reception 5-10pm. Dorms 62F/€9.45.) For great rooms near the *centre ville,* try **Hôtel de la Paix,** 14, r. Neuve-St-Jean. (☎ 02 31 86 18 99; fax 02 31 38 20 74. Breakfast 30F/€4.60. Reception 24hr. Singles 150F/€22.90, with bath 170-190F/€25.95-29; doubles 170F/€25.95, 200-220F/€30.50-33.55; triples 240F/€36.60, 300F/€45.75; quads 320F/€48.80. MC/V.) **Terrain Municipal,** on rte. de Louvigny, has riverside **campsites.** Take bus #13 (dir.: Louvigny) to "Camping." (☎ 02 31 73 60 92. Reception 8am-1pm and 5-9pm. Gates closed 11pm-7am. Open June-Sept. 18F/€2.75 per person, 10.50F/€1.60 per tent, 10.50F/€1.60 per car.) Restaurants line the **quartier Vaugueux** as well as the streets between **Eglise St-Pierre** and **Eglise St-Jean.** Get your groceries at **Monoprix,** 45, bd. du Maréchal Leclerc. (Open Tu-Sa 9:15am-1pm and 3-11pm.) **Postal Code:** 14000.

BAYEUX

An ideal base for exploring the D-Day beaches, beautiful Bayeux (pop. 15,000) is also renowned for its 900-year-old **Tapisserie de Bayeux** that depicts the Norman conquest of England in 1066, in the **Centre Guillaume le Conquérant,** r. de Nesmond. (☎ 02 31 51 25 50. Open May-Aug. daily 9am-7pm; mid-Mar. to Apr. and Sept.to mid-Oct. 9am-6:30pm; mid-Oct. to mid-Mar. 9:30am-12:30pm and 2-6pm. 41F/€6.25, students 16F/€2.45.) Nearby is the 11th-century **Cathédrale Notre-Dame,** a fantastic mix of Gothic and Romanesque styles. (Open July-Aug. M-Sa 8am-7pm, Su 9am-7pm; Sept.-June M-Sa 8:30am-noon and 2:30-7pm, Su 9am-12:15pm and 2:30-7pm. Free.) The **Musée de la Bataille de Normandie,** on bd. Fabian Ware, recounts the summer of 1944 through old newspaper clippings, photographs, films, and uniforms. (☎ 02 31 92 93 41. Open May to mid-Sept. daily 9:30am-6:30pm; mid-Sept to Apr. 10am-12:30pm and 2-6pm. Closed last 2 weeks in Jan. 34F/€5.20, students 16F/€2.45.)

Trains leave pl. de la Gare for: Caen (20min., 15 per day, 32F/€4.90); Cherbourg (1hr., 12 per day, 82F/€12.50); Paris (2½hr., 12 per day, 174F/€26.55). To get from the station to the **tourist office,** pont St-Jean, turn left onto bd. Sadi-Carnot, then bear right at the roundabout, following the signs to the *centre ville.* Continue up r. Larcher, and turn right on r. St-Martin; the office will be on your left. (☎ 02 31 51 28 28; fax 02 31 51 28 29; www.bayeux-tourism.com. Open mid-June to mid-Sept. M-Sa 9am-7pm, Su 9:30am-12:30pm and 2:30-6:30pm; mid-Sept. to mid-June M-Sa 9am-noon and 2-6pm.) The **Family Home/Auberge de Jeunesse (HI),** 39, r. General de Dais is in the center of town. From the tourist office, turn right onto r. St-Martin, follow it through several name changes and turn left onto r. Général de Dais; it will be on the right. (☎ 02 31 92 15 22; fax 02 31 92 55 72. Breakfast included. Dorms 100F/€15.25; nonmembers 110F/€13.80.) Follow r. Genas Duhomme to the right off r. St-Martin, and walk down av. de la Vallée des Prés for **Camping Municipal,** on bd. d'Eindhoven. (☎ 02 31 92 08 43. Open May-Sept. 18.30F/€27.95 per person, 22.60F/€3.45 per tent and car.) Assuage your hunger at **La Table du Terroir,** 42, r. St-Jean, near the tourist office. (*Menus* 60-98F/€9.15-14.95. Open June-Sept. Tu-Sa noon-2:30pm and 7-10pm, Su noon-2:30pm; Oct.-May F-Sa 7-10pm.) **Postal Code:** 14400.

FRANCE

D-DAY BEACHES

In the pre-dawn hours of June 6, 1944, over one million Allied soldiers invaded the beaches of Normandy, code-named Utah and Omaha (American), Gold and Sword (British), and Juno (Canadian). Today, the battle's traces are visible in sobering monuments, remnants of German bunkers, and the pockmarked landscape.

📠 **TRANSPORTATION.** Most of the beaches and museums can be reached from Caen and Bayeux with **Bus Verts** (☎ 08 10 21 42 14); ask about the special **"D-Day" line** that runs from Arromanches to the Pointe du Hoc, stopping at the US Cemetery and Omaha Beach. Buy a day pass (100F/€15.25; 3-day pass 150F/€22.90) if you plan to make many stops. **Utah Beach** is only accessible by car or foot from **Ste-Mère-Eglise.** Take a **train** from Bayeux to Carentan (30min., 10 per day, 43F/€6.60) and then a **STN bus** from Caretan to Ste-Mère-Eglise (15min., 1 per day 12:50pm, return 6:35pm, 18.20F/€2.80). **Bus Fly,** r. des Cuisiners, runs tours with knowledgable English-speaking guides. (☎ 02 31 22 00 08; www.busfly.com. 4hr. tour 210F/€32.05, students 190F/€29; 8hr. tour 350F/€53.40, 320F/€48.80. Pick-up at 8:30am and 1pm from your hotel or hostel. Reservations required.)

BEACHES NEAR BAYEUX. The Americans spearheaded the western flank of the successful invasion at **Utah Beach.** Utah Beach's **Musée du Débarquement** contains displays of how 836,000 troops, 220,000 vehicles, and 725,000 tons of equipment landed. (☎ 02 33 71 53 35. Open June-Sept. daily 9:30am-7pm; Oct.-May reduced hours. 30F/€4.60.) Nearby **Ste-Mère-Eglise** was one of the most important targets of the invasion. The most difficult landing was that of the First US Infantry Division at **Pointe du Hoc.** Only 90 of the 225 specially trained US Rangers and 40 of the 2000 German prisoners stationed there survived. The grassy area beyond the cliffs is still marked by deep pits. Next to Colleville-sur-Mer and east of the Pointe du Hoc is **Omaha Beach,** often referred to as "bloody Omaha." Overlooking the beach are the 9387 American graves in the **American Cemetery.** (☎ 02 31 51 62 00; www.abmc.gov. Open mid-Apr. to Sept. daily 8am-6pm; Oct. to mid-Apr. 9am-5pm.) Ten kilometers north of Bayeux and just east of Omaha is **Arromanches,** a small town of prime strategic importance at the center of **Gold Beach,** where the British built **Port Winston** in a single day to provide shelter while the Allies unloaded their supplies. The excellent **Musée du Débarquement** on the beach uses detailed models to show how the port was put together under fire. (☎ 02 31 22 34 31; www.normandy1944.com. Open May-Aug. daily 9am-7pm; Sept. 9am-6pm; Oct.-May reduced hours. Closed Jan. 35F/€5.35, students 22F/€3.) The **Arromanches 360° Cinéma** combines images of modern Normandy with those of D-Day. (☎ 02 31 22 30 30. Open June-Aug. daily 9:40am-6:40pm; Sept.-May reduced hours. Closed Jan. 24F/€3.70.)

BEACHES NEAR CAEN. East of Arromanches lies **Juno Beach,** the landing site of the Canadian forces. The **Canadian Cemetery** is at **Bény-sur-Mer-Reviers.** The British anchored the easternmost flank of the invasion at **Sword Beach,** a successful mission accomplished with the quirky "Hobart's Funnies," tanks outlandishly fitted with construction equipment. The only French troops involved in the D-Day landings came ashore at **Ouistreham.** They and Normandy's resilient citizens are memorialized at the **No. 4 Commando Museum,** on pl. Alfred Thomas. (☎ 02 31 96 63 10. Open mid-Mar. to Oct. 10:30am-6pm. 25F/€3.85, students 15F/€2.30.)

CHERBOURG

Cherbourg (pop. 44,000) was the Allies' major supply port following the D-Day offensive of 1944. Today, the town's numerous ferry lines shuttle tourists from France to England and Ireland. **Ferries** leave from the *gare maritime,* northeast of the *centre ville,* along bd. Maritime, to Rosslare, Portsmouth, and Poole (see p. 52). Make sure to **reserve ahead** and check the most up-to-date ferry schedules. To reach the train station, go left at the roundabout onto av. A. Briand and follow it as it becomes av. Carnot. Turn right at the end of the canal onto av. Millet and it's ahead on the left (25min.). **Trains** go to: Bayeux (1hr., 8 per day, 82F/€12.50); Caen

F R A N C E

(1½hr., 10 per day, 100F/€15.25); Paris (3hr., 7 per day, 222F/€33.85); Rouen (4½hr., 4 per day, 186F/€28.40). Across from the station, STN (☎ 02 33 88 51 00) runs **buses** around the region. (Open M-F 8am-noon and 2-6pm.) For the **tourist office**, 2, quai Alexandre III, turn right from the ferry terminal onto bd. Felix Amiot. At the roundabout, go straight, continue around the bend to the left, and turn right at the first bridge to cross the canal; it's on your left. (☎ 02 33 93 52 02; fax 02 33 53 66 97; www.ot-cherbourg-cotentin.fr. Open June-Aug. M-Sa 9am-6:30pm, Su 10am-12:30pm; Sept.-May M-Sa 9am-12:30pm and 2-6pm.) To get from the tourist office to the new 100-bed **Auberge de Jeunesse (HI)**, 57, r. de l'Abbaye, walk onto quai de Caligny, left again on r. de Port, which becomes r. Tour Carrée and r. de la Paix, and bear left at the fork; it's on the left. (☎ 02 33 78 15 15; fax 02 33 78 15 16. Breakfast included. Reception 8am-noon and 6-11pm. Dorms 98F/€14.90 1st night, 80F/€12.20 afterwards.) Stock up for the ferry at the **Carrefour supermarket,** quai de l'Entrepôt, next to the station. (Open M-Sa 8:30am-9pm.) **Postal Code:** 50100.

MONT-ST-MICHEL

Rising like a vision from the sea, the fortified island of Mont-St-Michel (pop. 42) is a dazzling labyrinth of stone arches, spires, and stairways that climb up to the **abbey.** Adjacent to the abbey church, **La Merveille,** a 13th-century Gothic monastery, encloses a seemingly endless web of passageways and chambers. (Open mid-July to Aug. daily 9am-7pm; May to mid-July and Sept. 9am-5:30pm; Oct.-Apr. 9:30am-4:30pm. Admission 42F/€6.40, ages 18-25 26F/€4. 1hr. English tours free.) The Mont is most stunning at night, but plan carefully—there is no late-night public transport off the island. Mont-St-Michel is best visited as a daytrip via Courriers Bretons **bus** 104, r. Couesnon (☎ 02 33 60 11 43), in Pontorson, from Rennes (1½hr., 3-6 per day, 65F/€9.95) or St-Malo (1½hr., 2-4 per day, 57F/€8.70). STN buses also run from Pontorson (15min., 8 per day, 15F/€2.30). Hotels on Mont-St-Michel are expensive, starting at 300F/€45.75 a night. The **Pontorson tourist office,** pl. de l'Eglise, helps visitors find affordable accommodations (☎ 02 33 60 20 65; fax 02 33 60 85 67). The cheapest beds are at the **Centre Duguesclin (HI),** r. Général Patton. (☎/fax 02 33 60 18 65. Dorms 48F/€7.35, nonmembers 55F/€8.40.) **Postal Code:** 50116.

BRITTANY (BRETAGNE)

Lined with spectacular beaches, wild headlands, and cliffs gnawed by the sea into long crags and inlets, Brittany fiercely maintains its Celtic traditions despite Paris's age-old effort to Frenchify the province. Britons fled Anglo-Saxon invaders between the 5th and 7th centuries for this beautiful, wild peninsula and in the 800 years that followed, they defended their independence from Frankish, Norman, French, and English invaders. Breton traditions, dating from the Duchy's centuries of freedom, linger in the pristine islands off the Atlantic coast and lilting *Brezhoneg* (Breton) is heard at pubs and ports in the western part of the province.

RENNES

Rennes (pop. 210,000) tempers its Parisian sophistication with traditional Breton spirit. Its *vieille ville* of half-timbered medieval houses teems with hip cafes and bars so that by dusk, this youthful city—students comprise more than a quarter of its residents—invariably falls victim to the irresistible magnetism of its sizzling nightlife. A popular stopover between Paris and Mont-St.-Michel, Rennes also makes for a packed weekend excursion of its own.

▐ **TRANSPORTATION. Trains** leave from pl. de la Gare (☎ 02 99 29 11 92) for: Bordeaux (6¼hr., 30 per day, 420F/€64.05); Caen (3hr., 8 per day, 167F/€25.50); Marseilles (6hr., 13 per day, 560F/€85.40); Nantes (1¼-2hr., 7 per day, 114F/€17.40); Paris (2hr., every hr., 289-349F/€44.10-53.20); St-Malo (1hr., 15 per day, 70F/€10.70). **Buses** (☎ 02 99 30 87 80) leave the train station for: Angers (2½-3hr., 3-4 per day, 98-122F/€14.95-18.60) and Mont-St-Michel (2½hr., 1-2 per day, 64F/€9.75).

FRANCE

🛂 PRACTICAL INFORMATION. To get from the train station to the **tourist office,** 11, r. Saint-Yves, take av. Jean Janvier to quai Chateaubriand, turn left, walk along the river until you reach r. George Dottin, turn right and then right again on r. Saint-Yves. (☎ 02 99 67 11 11; fax 99 67 11 10. Open Apr.-Sept. M-Sa 9am-7pm, Su and holidays 11am-6pm. Closed Jan. 1, May 1, and Dec. 25.) Access the **Internet** via **Cybernet Online,** 22, r. St. Georges (☎ 02 99 36 37 41. 25F/€3.85 per 30min. Open M 2-8pm, Tu-Sa 10am-8pm; closed Aug. 1-20.) The **post office** is at 27, bd. du Colombier, one block left of the train station exit. (☎ 02 99 01 22 11.) **Postal Code:** 35032.

🛏🍴 ACCOMMODATIONS AND FOOD. The **Auberge de Jeunesse (HI),** 10-12 Canal St-Martin, provides cheap and decent lodging. From the train station, take av. Jean Janvier toward the canal (where it becomes r. Gambetta) for five blocks, turn left on r. des Fossés, take r. de la Visitation to pl. Ste-Anne, staying on the right; follow r. de St-Malo on your right until you cross the small canal; the hostel is on the right. (☎ 02 99 33 22 33; fax 02 99 59 06 21. Breakfast included. Reception 7am-11pm. 2- to 4-bed dorms 74F/€11.30; singles 129F/€19.70. MC/V.) **Hotel d'Angleterre,** 19, r. Marechal Joffre, can't be beat for location. From the train station's north entrance, proceed along av. Jean Janvier to bd. de la Liberte; after three blocks, take a right on r. Marechal Joffre, and it's on the right. (☎ 02 99 79 38 61; fax 02 99 79 43 85. Breakfast 31F/€4.75. Reception 7am-10:30pm. Singles 140F/€21.35; doubles 160F/€24.40, with bath 197-230F/€30-35.10; twin beds 195F/€29.75, 250-280F/€38.15-42.70. MC/V.) **Camping Municipal des Gayeulles,** deep within Parc les Gayeulles, is packed with activities. Take bus #3 (dir.: Gayeulles/St-Laurent) from pl. de la Mairie to the third stop after you reach the park ("camping"). Follow the paths and the signs to the campgrounds. (☎ 02 99 36 91 22. Reception mid-June to mid-Sept. 7:30am-1pm and 2-8pm; mid-Sept. to mid-June 9am-12:30pm and 4:30-8pm. Mid-June to mid-Sept. gates close at 11pm; mid-Sept. to mid-June 10pm. 20F/€3.05 per adult, 10F/€1.55 per car. Electricity 17F/€2.60. MC/V.) Look for food on **Rue St-Malo, Rue St-Georges,** or **Place St-Michel;** or, explore **Place des Lices** and its Saturday market. The upscale **Café Breton,** 14, r. Nantaise, serves Breton cuisine at reasonable prices. (☎ 02 99 30 74 95. Open M and Sa 9am-5:30pm, Tu-F 9am-11pm.)

🎭🎪 SIGHTS AND ENTERTAINMENT. Excellent examples of medieval architecture are near the tourist office on **Rue de la Psalette** and **Rue St-Guillaume.** At the end of St-Guillaume, turn left onto r. de la Monnaie to visit the imposing **Cathédrale St-Pierre,** which was begun in 1787. The center of attention is its carved and gilded altarpiece depicting the life of the Virgin. (Open daily 9:30am-noon and 3-6pm, closed Su 10:30am-11:30am for high mass.) Across the street from the cathedral, the **Portes Mordelaises,** down an alley bearing the same name, are the former entrance to the city and the last vestiges of the medieval city walls. The **Musée des Beaux-Arts,** 20, quai Emile Zola, houses a collection that includes Pharoic Egyptian pieces, works by de la Tour and Picasso, and contemporary works. (☎ 02 99 28 55 85 40. Open W-M 10am-noon and 2-6pm. 26F/€4, students 13F/€2, under 18 free.) Across the river and up r. Gambetta is the lush **Jardin du Thabor,** considered to be among the most beautiful gardens in France. (Open June-Sept. 7am-9:30pm.) Next door is the magnificent 11th- to 19th-century **Eglise Notre Dame** where you can gaze at the remnants of a 15th-century fresco depicting the Baptism of Christ.

With enough bars for a city twice its size and a collection of clubs that draws students from Paris and beyond, Rennes is a partier's mecca on weekend. Look for action in **Place Ste-Anne, Place St-Michel,** and the radiating streets. **Le Zing,** 5, pl. des Lices, packs the house with the young and beautiful. (☎ 02 99 79 64 60. Opens 2pm, active from midnight until 2am.) **L'Espace,** 45, bd. La Tour d'Auvergne, pounds all night with writhers of all sizes, styles, and sexual orientations. Upstairs, **L'Endroit** attracts a more relaxed mixed crowd. (☎ 02 99 30 21 95. Both open Th 11pm-4am, F-Sa 11pm-5am, Su-W midnight-4am. Cover 60F/€9.20, students 40F/€6.10.)

FRANCE

ST-MALO

St-Malo (pop. 52,000) is the ultimate oceanside getaway, combining miles of warm, sandy **beaches** and crystal blue waters with a historic *centre ville*. To the east of the city, the **Grand Plage** is the most popular beach. The best view of St-Malo is from its **ramparts**—enter the walled city through Porte St-Vincent and follow the stairs up on the right. **Trains** run from pl. de l'Hermine to: Dinan (1hr., 5 per day, 48F/€7.35); Paris (5hr., 3 per day, 321F/€48.95); Rennes (1hr., 8-12 per day, 69F/€10.55). As you exit the station, cross bd. de la République and follow esplanade St-Vincent to the **tourist office,** near the entrance to the old city. (☎ 02 99 56 64 48; fax 02 99 56 67 00; www.saint-malo-tourisme.com. Open July-Aug. M-Sa 8:30am-8pm, Su 10am-7pm; Sept.-June reduced hours.) The 247-bed **Auberge de Jeunesse (HI),** 37, av. du Révérend Père Umbricht, is near the beach. From the train station, take bus #5 (dir.: Parame or Davier) or bus #1 (dir.: Rotheneuf) to "Auberge de Jeunesse." (☎ 02 99 40 29 80; fax 02 99 40 29 02. Reception 24hr. Dorms 72-89F/€11-13.60.) **Hôtel Gambetta,** 40, bd. Gambetta, is off av. du Rev. Père Umbricht. (☎ 02 99 56 54 70. Showers 16F/€2.45. Singles 110-130F/€20-23; doubles 140-260F/€24-39.65; triples 300-350F/€45.70-53.40; quads 350-400F/€53.40-61. MC/V.) **Champion supermarket,** on av. Pasteur, is near the hostel. (Open M-F 8:30am-1pm and 3-7:30pm, Sa 8:30am-7:30pm, Su 9:30am-noon. Longer hours July-Aug.) **Postal Code:** 35400.

DINAN

Perhaps the best-preserved medieval town in Brittany, the cobblestone streets of Dinan (pop. 10,000) are lined with 15th-century houses inhabited by traditional artisans. On the ramparts, the 13th-century **Porte du Guichet** is the entrance to the **Château de Dinan,** also known as the Tour de la Duchesse Anne. Climb to the terrace to look over the town or inspect the galleries of the 15th-century **Tour de Coëtquen,** which houses a collection of funerary ornaments. (Open June-Sept. daily 10am-6:30pm; Oct.-May W-M reduced hrs. 25F/€3.85, students 10F/€1.55.) On the other side of the ramparts from the château is the **Jardin du Val Cocherel,** which holds bird cages and a checkerboard for life-sized chess pieces. (Open daily 8am-7:30pm.)

Trains run from the pl. du 11 novembre 1918 to Paris (3hr., 8 per day, 323F/€49.25) and Rennes (1hr., 8 per day, 72F/€11). To get from the station to the **tourist office,** r. du Château, bear left across pl. 11 novembre to r. Carnot, turn right on r. Thiers, turn left into the old city, and bear right onto r. du Marchix, which becomes r. de la Ferronnerie. Pass the large parking lots and it will be on your right. (☎ 02 96 87 69 76; fax 02 96 87 69 77; www.dinantourisme.com. Open mid-June to mid-Sept. M-Sa 9am-7pm, Su 10am-12:30pm and 2:30-6pm; mid-Sept. to mid-June M-Sa 9am-12:30pm and 2-6:15pm.) To walk to the **Auberge de Jeunesse (HI),** in Vallée de la Fontaine-des-Eaux, turn left as you exit the station, turn left across the tracks, turn right, and follow the tracks and signs downhill for 1km before turning right again; it will be on your right. (☎ 02 96 39 10 83; fax 02 96 39 10 62. Reception daily 8am-noon and 5-8pm. Curfew 11pm. 2- to 8-bed dorms 54F/€8.25.) **Hôtel du Théâtre,** 2, r. Ste-Claire, is in the heart of the *vieille ville.* (☎ 02 96 39 06 91. Singles 90F/€13.75; doubles 130-170F/€19.85-25.95; triples 225F/€34.30.) Get **groceries** at **Monoprix,** on r. de la Ferronnerie. (Open M-Sa 9am-7:30pm.) Inexpensive *brasseries* lie on **Rue de la Cordonnerie** and near **Rue de la Ferronnerie** and **Place des Merciers. Postal Code:** 22100.

ST-BRIEUC. Situated between the Côte d'Emeraude and the Côte de Granite Rose, St-Brieuc is a perfect base for daytrips to the scenic countryside. **Trains** arrive from Dinan (1hr., 2-3 per day, 84F/€12.85) and Rennes (1hr., 15 per day, 132F/€20.15). From the station, on bd. Charner, walk straight down r. de la Gare and bear right at the fork to reach pl. de la Résistance and the **tourist office,** 7, r. St-Gouéno. (☎ 02 96 33 32 50; fax 02 96 61 42 16; www.mairie-saint-brieuc.fr. Open July-Aug. M-Sa 9am-12:30pm and 2-7pm, Su 10am-1pm; Sept.-June M-Sa 9am-12:30pm and 2-6pm.) The **youth hostel** is in a 15th-century house 3km from town;

take bus #2 (dir.: Centre Commercial les Villages) and get off at the last stop. From the stop, turn right on bd. de l'Atlantique, take the 2nd left onto r. du Vau Meno, and turn right on r. de la Ville Guyomard; it will be on the left. (☎ 02 96 78 70 70. Breakfast included. Reception 8am-noon, 2-4pm and 8-10pm. Dorms 75F/€11.45. MC/V.)

CAP FRÉHEL. The rust-hued cliffs of **Cap Fréhel** mark the northern point of the Côte d'Emeraude. Catch a CAT **bus** from St-Brieuc (1½hr.; 3-4 per day; 45F/€6.90, students 36F/€5.50) and follow the red and white striped markers along the well-marked **GR34 trail** on the edge of the peninsula. There's also the scenic 90min. walk to **Fort La Latte,** a 13th-century castle complete with drawbridges. To reach the **Auberge de Jeunesse Cap Fréhel (HI),** in La Ville Hadrieux in Kerivet, get off the bus one stop after Cap Fréhel at "Auberge de Jeunesse," take the only road that branches from the stop, and follow the fir-tree hostel signs. (☎ 02 96 41 48 98; mid-Sept. to Apr. ☎ 02 98 78 70 70. Breakfast 19F/€2.90. Open May-Sept. Dorms 45F/€6.90.)

PAIMPOL. Paimpol (pop. 8200), northwest of St-Brieuc at the end of the Côte de Granite Rose, offers easy access to nearby islands, beaches, and hiking. The **train** (1hr., 4-5 per day, 70F/€10.70) and CAT buses (1¼hr.; 8 per day; 45F/€6.90, students 36F/€5.50) leave av. Général de Gaulle for St-Brieuc. From the station, walk down r. du 18 Juin and turn right on r. de l'Oise, which becomes r. St-Vincent, to reach the **tourist office,** pl. de la République. (☎ 02 96 20 83 16; fax 02 96 55 11 12. Open July-Aug. M-Sa 9am-7:30pm, Su 10am-1pm; Sept.-June Tu-Sa 10am-12:30pm and 2:30-6pm.) From the tourist office, walk toward the port, turn left after several blocks onto r. du Port, and look for the blue "H" on the **Hôtel Berthelot,** 1, r. du Port. (☎ 02 96 20 88 66. Singles and doubles 160F-240F/€24.40-36.60.)

BREST

Brest (pop. 156,217) slowly rose from the ashes of WWII to become a metropolis that blends the prosperity of a major port with the youthful energy of a university town. Brest's **château** was the only building in the town to survive WWII, and is now the world's oldest active military institution, as well as home to the **Musée de la Marine,** off r. de Château, which highlights the local maritime history. (Open Apr.-Sept. W-M 10am-6:30pm, Tu 2-6:30pm; Oct-Mar. Tu-Sa 10am-noon and 2-6pm. 29F/€4.60, students 20F/€3.05.) The newly renovated **Océanopolis Brest,** at port de Plaisance, has tropical, temperate, and polar pavilions and a coral reef accessible by a glass elevator. From the Liberty terminal, take bus #7 (dir.: Port de Plaisance; M-Sa every 30min. until 7:30pm, 6.50F/€1) to "Océanopolis." (☎ 02 98 34 40 40. Open Apr. to mid-Sept. daily 9am-7pm; mid-Sept. to May daily 9am-6pm. 90F/€13.75.)

Trains (☎ 02 98 31 51 72) leave pl. du 19ème Régiment d'Infanterie for: Nantes (4hr., 6 per day, 244F/€37.20) and Rennes (1½hr., 15 per day, 170F/€25.95). From the station, av. Georges Clemenceau leads to the intersection of r. de Siam and r. Jean Jaurès, and the **tourist office,** at pl. de la Liberté. (☎ 02 98 44 24 96. Open mid-June to mid-Sept. M-Sa 9:30am-12:30pm and 2-6:30pm, Su 2-4pm; mid-Sept. to mid-June M-Sa 10am-12:30pm and 2-6pm.) Get your **Internet** buzz at **Les Années Bleues,** 23, r. Bruat. (☎ 02 98 44 48 19. 30F/€4.60 for 30min., 50F/€7.65 for 1hr.; 1 drink included. Open Tu-Sa 10:30am-1am.) For the luxurious **Auberge de Jeunesse (HI),** 5, r. de Kerbriant, 4km away near Océanopolis, take bus #7 (dir.: Port de Plaisance) from opposite the station to its final stop (M-Sa until 7:30pm, Su until 6pm; 6.50F/€1); with your back to the bus stop, go left toward the beach, take an immediate left, and follow the signs to the hostel. (☎ 02 98 41 90 41. Breakfast included. Reception M-F 7-9am and 5-8pm, Sa-Su 7-10am and 5-8pm. Curfew July-Aug. midnight; Sept.-June 11pm; ask for a key. Dorms 74F/€11.30.) To reach **Camping du Goulet,** 7km from Brest, take bus #14 (dir.: Plouzane) to "Le Cosquer." (☎ 02 98 45 86 84. 22F/€3.35 per person, 25F/€3.85 per tent. Electricity 11-16F/€1.70-2.45. Shower included.) Try **L'Eurasie,** 48, r. Lyon (☎ 02 98 44 78 00) for low-priced East Asian cuisine with a French twist. (Open M noon-2pm, Tu-Sa noon-2pm and 7-11pm.) For **groceries,** try the **Monoprix,** 49, r. de Siam. (Open M-Sa 8:30am-7:30pm.) **Postal Code:** 29200.

FRANCE

CROZON PENINSULA

The virtually uninhabited *Presqu'île de Crozon* (Crozon Peninsula) tempts out-doorsmen of every persuasion: the rugged interior contains a dense web of trails, lined with *gîte d'étapes*, that are perfect for excellent hiking and cycling; and the coastline of sandy beaches and unusual rock formations accommodates activities such as scuba diving and kayaking. A 14km trail connects Morgat Port to the **Cap de la Chèvre** at the end of the peninsula, passing through pine forests and along ocean-side cliffs. Two of the peninsula's major towns are **Crozon** and **Morgat**. Most sights are in or near Morgat. From Brest, a **Vedettes Armoricaines** ferry (☎02 98 44 44 04) sails to **Le Fret** on the peninsula (4km from Crozon) and shuttles passengers to the major towns (45min.; Apr.-Oct. 3 per day; 50F/€7.65, with shuttle 57F/€8.70). **Effia Voyageurs buses** (☎02 98 93 06 98) connect Crozon to Brest (1½hr., 2-3 per day, 58F/€8.85). Buses also run to Crozon on their way to Quimper (4-6 per day, 11F/€1.70).

Only 2½km apart, **Crozon** and **Morgat** share multiple services and are often consid-ered as one town. The **Maison des Minéraux**, r. de la Cap de la Chèvre, about 4km from Morgat on D155, has the largest European collection of funky fluorescent min-erals. (☎02 98 27 19 73. Open July to mid-Sept. daily 10am-7pm; mid-Sept. to Apr. M-F 2-5:30pm; May-June 10am-noon and 2-5:30pm. 26F/€4, students 20F/€3.05.) The smooth **Plage de Morgat** spans ¼km of sand and shells. The **Plage du Porzic**, a quick swim or walk from the main beach, offers access to the smaller caves and a hiking trail that leads to the top of **Pointe des Menhirs**. Buses to Crozon stop at the **tourist office**. (☎02 98 27 07 92. Open July-Aug. M-Sa 9:30am-7pm, Su 10am-12:30pm; Sept.-June M-Sa 9:15am-noon and 2-6pm.) Take a left onto r. St-Yves, a right on r. Louis Pasteur, right on r. Alsace Lorraine and the second left on bd. de la France Libre, which will take you down to Morgat bd. de la Plage and the **tourist office** on the right. (☎02 98 27 29 49. Open July-Aug. M-Sa 10am-7pm; Sept.-June 10am-noon and 3-6pm.) Morgat has the only public **computer** at **Le Relais de Pecheur**, bd. de la Plage. (☎02 98 27 04 02. Open daily 10am-midnight. 1F/€0.15 per min., min. 10F/€1.55.) **Hôtel du Clos St-Yves**, 61, r. Alsace Lorraine, in Crozon, has decent rooms. (☎02 98 27 00 10. Doubles 150F/€22.90, with bath 250F/€38.15; triples 330F/€50.35. MC/V.) A few kilometers south of Morgat, in the village of St-Hernot, is the plush 20-bed **Gîte St-Hernot**, r. de la Cap de la Chèvre. (☎02 98 27 15 00. Breakfast 27F/€4.10. Doubles 55F/€8.40.) Get groceries at the central **Shoppi**. (Open July-Aug. M-Sa 8:30am-8pm, Su 9am-1pm; Sept.-June M-Sa 8:30am-12:30pm and 2:30-7:30pm, Su 9am-12:30pm.)

NANTES

Nantes (pop. 550,000) tastefully blends the distinct flavors of a modern high-tech industry, a classy pedestrian district, and historical sights reminiscent of its glori-ous, if gory, past. At the imposing **Château des Ducs de Bretagne,** Henri IV composed the **Edict of Nantes** (see p. 275), which granted considerable religious liberties to the Huguenots. The interim **Musée du Château des Ducs de Bretagne** hosts temporary exhibits. (☎02 40 41 56 56. Courtyard open for free visits July-Aug. daily 10am-7pm; Sept.-June 10am-6pm. Museum open July-Aug daily 10am-6pm; Sept.-June closed on Tu. 20F/€3.05, students 10F/€1.55.) Go inside the **Cathédrale St-Pierre** to gape at the soaring 38m Gothic vaults and the largest stained-glass window in the country. (Open daily 10am-7pm.) For fans of Captain Nemo, the **Musée Jules Verne**, 3, r. de L'Hermiage, on the opposite side of town, is a small museum with tons of informa-tion about the *Nantais* author and scientist. (☎02 40 69 72 52. Open M and W-Sa 10am-noon and 2-5pm, Su 2-5pm. 8F/€1.25, students 4F/€0.60; Su free.)

Trains run from 27, bd. de Stalingrad to: Bordeaux (4hr., 6-8 per day, 224F/€34.20); La Rochelle (2hr., 8-11 per day, 128F/€19.55); Paris (2-4hr., 20 per day, 299-372F/€45.60-56.75); Rennes (2hr., 3-10 per day, 114F/€17.40); Saumur (1¼hr., 7 per day, 100F/€15.25). To get from the train station to the **tourist office**, pl. du Com-merce, turn left out of the north entrance to the train station (*accés nord*), con-tinue straight along allée du Charcto, which becomes cours John Kennedy, and after the château, it will be up on your right in the FNAC building. (☎02 40 20 60 00; fax 02 40 89 11 99; www.reception.com/Nantes. Open M-Sa 10am-7pm.) Check your **email** at **Welcome Services Copy**, 70, r. Maréchal Joffre. (☎02 51 81 96 25. 35F/€5.35

per hr. Open M 2:30-7pm, Tu-F 9am-12:30pm and 2-7pm, Sa 10am-noon and 2:30-6pm.) To get from the train station to the 200-bed **Foyer des Jeunes Travailleurs, Beaulieu (HI),** 9, bd. Vincent Gâche, take the #10 bus (dir.: Francois Mitterrand) from opposite the south entrance to "Pl. du Commerce"; switch to the tramway #2 (dir.: Trocardinet) to "Vincent Gache," and bd. Vincent Gache is just ahead on the left. (☎02 40 12 24 00; fax 02 51 82 00 05. Breakfast 14F/€2.15. Reception 8am-9pm, call ahead for late night check-in. No curfew. 60F/€9.15, nonmembers 135F/€20.60.) The ◼**Hôtel St-Daniel,** 4, r. du Bouffay, is just off pl. du Bouffay. (☎02 40 47 41 25. Breakfast 25F/€3.85. Singles and doubles 160F/€24.40, with bath 180F/€27.45; triples and quads 230F/€35.10. AmEx/MC/V.) The biggest **market** in town is the **Marché de Talensac,** on r. de Bel-Air behind the post office. (Open Tu-Sa 9am-1pm.) **Monoprix** is at 2, r. de Calvaire, off cours de 50 Otages. (Open M-Sa 9am-9pm.) **Quartier St-Croix,** near pl. Bouffay, and **Rue Scribe** have cafes and bars. **Postal Code:** 44000.

LOIRE VALLEY (VAL DE LOIRE)

The Loire, France's longest and most celebrated river, meanders to the Atlantic through a valley overflowing with vineyards and majestic châteaux. The Loire also raised some of the brightest stars of French thought, including Rabelais, Descartes, and Balzac. Loire vineyards produce some of France's best wines, and the soil is among the country's most fertile. It is hardly surprising that a string of French (and English) kings chose to station themselves in opulent châteaux by these waters rather than in the dirt and noise of their capital cities.

▄ TRANSPORTATION

Faced with such widespread grandeur, many travelers plan over-ambitious itineraries—two châteaux a day is a good limit. Bikes are the best way to explore the region, since trains to châteaux are very infrequent. Tours is the region's best rail hub, although the châteaux Sully-sur-Loire, Chambord, and Cheverny aren't accessible by train. Many stations distribute the invaluable *Châteaux pour Train et Vélo* with train schedules and bike and car rental information.

ORLÉANS

A pleasant gateway from Paris into the Loire, Orléans (pop. 200,000) clings tightly to its historical claim to fame in Joan of Arc. Most of Orléans's historical and architectural highlights are near **Place Ste-Croix.** Joan of Arc triumphantly marched down nearby **Rue de Bourgogne,** the city's oldest street, in 1429; the scene is vividly captured in *Jeanne d'Arc*, at the **Musée des Beaux-Arts,** 1, r. Ferdinand Rabier. (☎02 38 79 21 55. Open Th-Sa 10am-6pm, Tu and Su 11am-6pm, W 10am-8pm. 20F/€3.05, students 10F/€1.55.) The **Eglise St-Paterne,** pl. Gambetta, is a massive showcase of modern stained glass. The stunning stained glass windows of **Cathédrale Ste-Croix,** pl. Ste-Croix, depict Joan's dramatic story. (Open July-Aug. daily 9:15am-noon and 2:15-7pm; Sept.-June reduced hrs. Free.) Forty-two kilometers from Orléans, the imposing 14th-century fortress **Sully-sur-Loire** dominates the southern bank of the Loire. Catch the bus at 2, r. Marcel Proust (1hr., 3 per day, 57F/€8.70).

Trains arrive at the Gare d'Orléans, on pl. Albert 1er, from: Blois (30min., 12 per day, 54F/€8.25); Paris (1¼hr., 3 per hr., 94F/€14.35); Tours (1hr., 12 per day, 91F/€13.90). To get from the station to the **tourist office,** 6, pl. Albert 1er, go left under the tunnel to pl. Jeanne d'Arc, and it's across the street on the right. (☎02 38 24 05 05; fax 02 38 54 49 84; www.tourismloiret.com. Open July-Aug. M-Sa 9am-7pm, Su 9:30am-12:30pm and 3-6:30pm; Apr.-June and Sept. M-Sa 9am-7pm, Su 10am-noon; Oct.-Mar. M-Sa 9am-6:30pm, Su 10am-noon.) To get to the **Auberge de Jeunesse (HI),** 1, bd. de la Motte Sanguin, take bus RS (dir.: Rosette) or SY (dir.: Concyr/La Bolière) from pl. d'Arc to "Pont Bourgogne"; follow bd. de la Motte and it's up on the right. (☎02 38 53 60 06. Reception daily 9am-noon and 5-10pm. 2- to 4-person dorms 61F/€9.30; singles 100F/€15.25.) Get **groceries** at **Carrefour,** in the mall at pl. d'Arc. (Open M-Sa 8:30am-9pm.) **Rue de Bourgogne** has eateries. **Postal Code:** 45000.

FRANCE

BLOIS

Blois (pop. 60,000) welcomes visitors to the Loire Valley with pastoral charm. Home to monarchs Louis XII and François I, Blois's **château** was the Versailles of the late 15th and early 16th centuries; today it is decorated with François I's painted and carved salamanders and displays the progression of French architecture from the 13th to the 17th century. Housed in the castle are excellent museums: the recently renovated **Musée de Beaux-Arts,** with a 16th-century portrait gallery; the **Musée d'Archéologie,** showcasing locally excavated glass and ceramics; and the **Musée Lapidaire,** preserving sculpted pieces from nearby châteaux. (☎02 54 78 06 62. Open July-Aug. daily 9am-7:30pm; Apr.-June and Sept. 9am-6pm; Jan.-Mar. Oct.-Dec. 9am-12:30pm and 2-5:30pm. 38F/€5.80, students 20F/€3.05.) At night, move from the cafes of **Place de la Résistance** to **Z 64**, 6, r. Maréchal de Tassigny, for cocktails, dancing, and karaoke. (☎02 54 74 27 76. Open Tu-Su 8:30am-4am.)

Trains leave the pl. de la Gare for: Orléans (30min., 14 per day, 54F/€8.25); Paris (1¾hr., 8 per day, 125F/€19.05) via Orléans; Tours (1hr., 10 per day, 57F/€8.70). **Transports Loir-et-Cher (TLC)** (☎02 54 58 55 44) sends buses from the station and pl. Victor Hugo to nearby châteaux (1¼hr., 4 per day, 35F/€5.35). Or rent a **bike** from **Cycles Leblond,** 44, levée des Tuileries, to take the hour-long ride to the valley. (☎02 54 74 30 13. 80F/€12.20 per day. Open daily 9am-9pm.) The **tourist office**, 3, av. Jean Laigret, can point the way. (☎02 54 90 41 41; fax 02 54 90 41 49; www.loiredeschâteaux.com. Open mid-Apr. to mid-Oct. Tu-Sa 9am-7pm, Su-M and holidays 10am-7pm; Jan.-Mar. and Oct.-Dec. M 10am-12:30pm and 2-6pm, Tu-Sa 9am-12:30pm and 2-6pm, Su 9:30am-12:30pm.) Five kilometers west is the **Auberge de Jeunesse (HI),** 18, r. de l'Hôtel Pasquier. To get there from the tourist office, follow r. Porte Côté, bear right along r. Denis Papin to the river, and take bus #4 (dir.: Les Grouets) to "Auberge de Jeunesse." (☎/fax 02 54 78 27 21. Reception 6:45-10am and 6-10:30pm. Lockout 10am-6pm. Curfew 10:30pm. Open Mar. to mid-Nov. Dorms 45F/€6.90.) **Le Pavillon,** 2, av. Wilson, has clean and bright rooms. (☎02 54 74 23 27; fax 02 54 74 03 36. Breakfast 35F/€5.35. Singles 120-240F/€18.30-36.60; doubles 240F/€36.60; quads 300F/€45.75. MC/V.) Fragrant *patisseries* entice from **Rue Denis Papin**, while **Rue Drussy, Rue St-Lubin,** and **Place Poids du Roi** have eateries. **Postal Code:** 41000.

▓ DAYTRIPS FROM BLOIS: CHAMBORD AND CHEVERNY. Built between 1519 and 1545 to satisfy François I's egomania, **Chambord** is the largest and most extravagant of the Loire châteaux. With 440 rooms, 365 fireplaces, and 83 staircases, the château rivals Versailles in grandiosity. To cement his claim, François stamped 700 of his trademark stone salamanders throughout this "hunting lodge" and built a spectacular double-helix staircase in the center of the castle. (☎02 54 50 40 00. Open July-Aug. daily 9am-6:45pm; Sept. and Apr.-June 9am-6:15pm; Oct.-Mar. 9am-5:15pm. 40F/€6.40, ages 18-25 26F/€4.) Take **TLC bus #2** from Blois (45min., 20F/€3.05); ride the TLC **Chambord-Cheverny bus circuit** from Blois (65F/€9.95, students 50F/€7.65, 25% discount off admission to châteaux with bus ticket); or **bike** from Blois. Take D956 south for 2 to 3km, and then go left on D33 (1hr.).

Cheverny and its manicured grounds are unique among the major châteaux. Its magnificent furnishings include elegant tapestries and delicate Delft vases. Fans of Hergé's *Tintin* books may recognize Cheverny's Renaissance façade as the inspiration for Marlinspike, Captain Haddock's mansion. The **kennels** hold 70 mixed English Poitevin hounds who stalk stags in hunting expeditions (Oct.-Mar. Tu and Sa). (☎02 54 79 96 29. Open Apr. to mid-Sept. daily 9:15am-6:15pm; July-Aug. 9:15am-6:45pm; Oct. and Mar. 9:30am-noon and 2:15-5:30pm; Nov.-Feb. 9:30am-noon and 2:15-5pm. 38F/€5.80, students 25F/€3.85.) Cheverny is accessible by **bus** (see above) or **bike** from Blois (take D956 south for 45min.).

AMBOISE

The battlements of the 15th-century **château** at Amboise (pop. 11,000) that six paranoid French kings called home, stretch protectively above the town. In the **Logis de Roi,** the main part of the château, intricate 16th-century Gothic chairs

FRANCE

stand over 2m high to prevent surprise attacks from behind. The jewel of the grounds is the 15th-century **Chapelle St-Hubert,** the final resting place of **Leonardo da Vinci.** (☎ 02 47 57 00 98. Open Apr.-June daily 9am-6:30pm; July-Aug. 9am-8pm; Sept.-Nov. 9am-6pm; Dec.-Jan. 9am-noon and 2-5pm; Feb.-Mar. 9am-noon and 2-5:30pm. 41F/€6.25, students 34F/€5.20.) Four hundred meters away is **Clos Lucé** manor, where Leonardo da Vinci spent the last four years of his life. Check out the collection of 40 unrealized inventions. (☎ 02 47 57 62 88. Open late Mar. to June daily 9am-7pm; July-Aug. daily 9am-8pm; Sept. to late Mar. reduced hours. 40F/€6.10, students 32F/€4.90.) **Trains** leave bd. Gambetta for: Blois (20min., 15 per day, 35F/€5.35); Orléans (1hr., 14 per day, 76F/€11.60); Paris (2¼hr., 5 per day, 147F/€22.45); Tours (20min., 14 per day, 28F/€4.30). The **Centre International de Séjour (HI) Charles Péguy,** on Ile d'Or, sits on an island in the middle of the Loire. (☎ 02 47 30 60 90; fax 02 47 30 60 91. Sheets 19F/€2.90. Reception M-F 3-7pm. Dorms 54F/€8.25.) **Postal Code:** 35400.

TOURS

Tours (pop. 250,000) is the bustling urban center of the Loire region, with a youthful student population filling its wide boulevards. The **Cathédrale St-Gatien,** on r. Jules Simon, is celebrated for its dazzling stained glass and a flamboyant Gothic cloister. (☎ 02 47 05 05 54. Cathedral open daily 9am-7pm. Free. Cloister open Easter-Sept. daily 9:30am-12:30pm and 2-6pm; Oct.-Mar. W-Su 9:30am-12:30pm and 2-5pm.) At the **Musée du Gemmail,** 7, r. du Murier, near pl. Plumereau, works of *gemmail* (a fusion of colored glass shards with enamel) by Picasso and Braque glow against dark velvet. (☎ 02 47 61 01 19. Open Apr. to mid-Nov. Tu-Su 10am-noon and 2-6:30pm; mid-Nov. to Mar. W-Su 10am-noon and 2-6:30pm. 30F/€4.60, students 20F/€3.05.) Stroll past the twin **Tours (towers) of Tours,** flanking r. des Halles, which are fragments of the huge 5th-century Romanesque Basilique St-Martin. **Place Plumereau** is the *place* to be: party with an older crowd at **Louis XIV,** or go upstairs to chill in the **Duke Ellington.** (Both open daily until 2am; Duke Ellington closed July-Aug.)

Trains leave from 3, r. Edouard Vaillant, at pl du Maréchal Leclerc, for: Bordeaux (2½hr., 6 per day, 229F/€34.95); Paris (2¼hr., 7 per day, 160F/€24.40); Poitiers (45min., 7 per day, 80F/€12.20). The **tourist office,** 78-82, r. Bernard Palissy, books rooms and arranges châteaux tours. (☎ 02 47 70 37 37; fax 02 47 61 14 22; www.ligeris.com. Open mid-Apr. to mid-Oct. daily 8:30am-7pm, Su 10am-12:30pm and 2:30-5pm; mid-Oct. to mid-Apr. M-Sa 9am-12:30pm and 1:30-6pm, Su 10am-1pm.) **Email** your friends and lovers from the **Cyber Gate,** 11, r. de Président Merville. (☎ 02 47 05 95 94. 5F/€0.80 per 15min. Open M 1pm-midnight, Tu-Sa 11am-midnight, Su 2-midnight.) Relax at the central ⚑**Foyer des Jeunes Travailleurs,** 24, r. Bernard Palissy. (☎ 02 47 60 51 51. Singles 100F/€15.25; doubles 160F/€24.40.) **Hôtel Regina,** 2, r. Pimbert, is a gem on a quiet street. (☎ 02 47 05 25 36; fax 02 47 66 08 72. Breakfast 27F/€4.15. Singles 130-180F/€19.85-27.45; doubles 140-240F/€21.35-36.60. MC/V.) **Place Plumereau** offers an amazingly diverse array of restaurants, cafes, and bars with menus from 70F/€10.70. **Le Charolais Chez Jean Michel,** 123, r. Colbert, serves local cuisine with regional wines. (62F/€9.45 and 74F/€11.30 3-course lunch *menus.* Open M 7:30-10:30pm, Tu-Sa noon-2pm and 7:30-10:30pm.) **Postal Code:** 37000.

▓ DAYTRIPS FROM TOURS

▓ CHENONCEAU

Trains from Tours roll into the station 2km away from the castle (45min., 3 per day, 36F/€5.50). Fil Vert buses also connect Tours with Chenonceau (25min., 2 per day, 13F/€2).

Perhaps the most exquisite château in France, Chenonceau arches gracefully over the Cher river. A series of women created the beauty that is the château: first Catherine, the wife of a royal tax collector; then Diane de Poitiers, the lover of Henri II; and then his widowed wife, Catherine de Médici. The part of the château bridging the Cher also marked the border between occupied and Vichy France during WWII. Chenonceau's beautiful setting makes it the most popular of all the Loire châteaux. (☎02 47 23 90 07; www.chenonceaux-sa.fr. Open mid-Mar. to mid-Sept. daily 9am-7pm; call for off-season hours. 50F/€7.65, students 40F/€6.10.)

LOCHES

Buses run from the Tours train station to Loches (50min., 4 per day, 49F/€7.50; pay on board). 9 trains also make the trip (1hr., 49F/€7.50).

Surrounded by a walled medieval town that merits a visit in itself, the château of **Loches** consists of two distinct structures at opposite ends of a hill. To the north, the 11th-century **keep** and watchtowers changed roles from keeping enemies out to keeping them in when Charles VII turned it into a state prison, complete with suspended cages. The **Logis Royal** honors the famous ladies who held court here, includes Agnès Sorel, the first Mistress of the King of France. (☎02 47 59 01 32. Open Apr.-Sept. daily 9am-7pm; Oct.-Mar. 9:30am-12:30pm and 2-5pm. Logis Royal or Donjon 24F/€3.65, students 17F/€2.60; both 32F/€4.90, students 22F/€3.35.)

SAUMUR

Saumur (pop. 30,000) is a refreshing break from the usual castle-heavy Loire fare, with many other attractions and an enchanting old quarter. The 14th-century **château** is best known for its cameo appearance in the famous medieval manuscript *Les très riches heures du duc de Berry;* it contains the **Musée des Arts Décoratifs,** with medieval and Renaissance works, and the horse-crazy **Musée du Cheval.** (☎02 41 40 24 40. Open July-Aug. daily 8:30am-10:30pm; June-Sept. 9:30am-6pm and 8:30-10:30pm; Oct.-May W-M 9:30am-noon and 2-5:30pm. 38F/€15.80, students 27F/€4.15; gardens 17F/€2.60.) **Gratien et Meyer,** on rte. de Montsoreau, gives tours of its wine *cave* and offers tastings. Take bus D from pl. Bilange to "Beaulieu." (☎02 41 83 13 32. Open mid-June to mid-Sept. daily 9am-6:30pm; mid-Sept. to May reduced hours. Tour 15F/€2.30; museum 25F/€3.85.) The **Musée de Champignon,** on rte. de Gennes in St-Hilaire-St-Florent, is a mushroom *cave* that traces the history of the mushroom in France, the world's third-largest mushroom producer. (☎02 41 50 31 55. Open Feb. 3-Nov. 11 daily 10am-7pm. 40F/€6.10, students 30F/€4.60.)

Trains leave av. David d'Angers for: Angers (30min., 23 per day, 43F/€6.55); Paris (1½hr., 8 per day, 248F/€37.85); Tours (45min., 21 per day, 57F/€8.70). The **tourist office,** pl. Bilange, next to pont Cessart, books beds (5F/€0.80 fee). Exit to the right of the station on av. David d'Angers, turn right onto pont des Cadets, and it will be on your left, at the corner of quai Lucien Gautier. Bus A will also go there from the train station. (☎02 41 40 20 60; fax 02 41 40 20 69. Open July-Aug M-Sa 9:15am-7pm, Su 10:30am-12:30pm and 2:30-5:30pm; Sept.-June M-Sa 9:15am-12:30pm and 2-6pm, Su 10:30am-5:30pm; mid-Oct. to mid-May Su open 10am-noon.) The modern **Centre International de Séjour,** r. de Verdun (*not* bd. de Verdun), is on Ile d'Offard. From the station, follow the directions above to pont des Cadets, turn left on r. Roi de Sicile after crossing the bridge, continue straight for 10min., and it's on the left. (☎02 41 40 30 00; fax 02 41 67 37 81. Reception 8am-8pm, until 9pm in summer. 2- to 8-bed dorms 85F/€12.95.) **Le Volney,** 1, r. Volney, is quiet. (☎02 41 51 25 41; fax 02 41 38 11 04. Singles and doubles 160-170F/€24.40-25.95, with shower 270F/€41.20. MC/V.) Get **groceries** at **Atac supermarket,** 6, r. Franklin D. Roosevelt, inside a shopping center. (Open M-Th 9am-7:30pm, F until 8pm, Sa until 7pm.) **Postal Code:** 49400.

⊠ DAYTRIP FROM SAUMUR: FONTEVRAUD ABBEY. Fourteen kilometers east of Saumur lies the **Abbaye de Fontevraud,** the largest existing monastic complex in Europe. The 12th-century abbey church serves as a Plantagenêt necropolis; **Eleanor of Aquitaine,** who lived out her days here after being repudiated by her second husband, **Henry II,** now lies next to him along with their son **Richard the Lionheart.** (☎02 41 51 71 41. Open June to mid-Sept. daily 9am-6:30pm; mid-Sept. to May 9:30am-12:30pm and 2-5:30pm. 36F/€5.50, students 23F/€3.50.) **Bus #16** leaves from Saumur's train station (25min., 3 per day, 14F/€2.15). The **tourist office** offers free maps of the town. (☎02 41 51 79 45. Open Apr. to mid-Oct. 10am-noon and 2:30-6:30pm.)

ANGERS

From behind the massive stone walls of their fortress in Angers (pop. 220,000), the **Château d'Angers,** on pl. Kennedy, the Dukes of Anjou ruled the surrounding area and a certain island across the Channel. The 13th-century château remains a well-preserved haven of medieval charm in a city filled with shops and sights. Inside the château is the 14th-century **Tapisserie de l'Apocalypse,** the world's largest tapestry. (Open June to mid-Sept. daily 9:30am-7pm; mid-Sept. to Oct. and mid-Mar. to May 10am-6pm; Nov. to mid-Mar. 10am-5pm. 36F/€5.50, students 23F/€3.55.) Angers's other woven masterpiece is the 1930 **Chant du Monde** ("Song of the World"), in the **Musée Jean Lurçat,** 4, bd. Arago. (☎02 41 24 18 45. Open mid-June to mid-Sept. daily 9am-6:30pm; mid-Sept. to mid-June Tu-Su 10am-noon and 2-6pm. 20F/€3.05.) In the *vieille ville* is the 12th-century **Cathédrale St-Maurice,** with its impressive collection of tapestries. A 28F/€4.30 ticket, sold at the tourist office, grants entry to five museums and the 50F/€7.65 *billet jumelé* includes château admission.

From r. de la Gare, **trains** leave for: Nantes (1hr., 5 per day, 84F/€12.85); Paris (2-4hr., 3 per day, 254-320F/€38.75-48.80); Tours (1hr., 7 per day, 86F/€13.15). **Buses** run from pl. de la République to Rennes (3hr., 2 per day, 97F/€14.80). To get from the station to the **tourist office,** at pl. du Président Kennedy, exit straight onto r. de la Gare, turn right at pl. de la Visitation on r. Talot, and turn left on bd. du Roi-René, and it's on the right, across from the château. (☎02 41 23 50 00; fax 02 41 23 50 09. Open June-Sept. M-Sa 9am-7pm, Su 10am-6pm; Oct.-May M-Sa 9am-6pm.) Access the **Internet** at **Cyber Espace,** 25, r. de la Roë. (☎02 41 24 92 71. 25F/€3.85 per hr. Open M-Th 10am-10pm, F-Sa 10am-midnight.) To get to the **Centre d'Accueil du Lac de Maine (HI),** 49, av. du Maine, take bus #6 or 16 to "Accueil Lac de Maine," turn around and cross the busy road, and follow the signs. (☎02 41 22 32 10; fax 02 41 22 32 11. Breakfast included. **HI members only.** Singles 177F/€27; doubles 120F/€18.30; quads 85F/€13.) Walk straight down r. de la Gare for the spacious **Royal Hôtel,** 8bis, pl. de la Visitation. (☎02 41 88 30 25; fax 02 41 81 05 75. Breakfast 30-32F/€4.60-4.90. Singles 110-138F/€16.80-21.05, with shower 200-260F/€30.50-39.65; doubles 260F/€39.65; quads 280F/€42.70. AmEx/MC/V.) Grab **groceries** in **Galeries Lafayette,** at r. d'Alsace and pl. du Ralliement. (Open M-Sa 9am-7pm.) **Postal Code:** 49052.

POITOU-CHARENTES

Poitou-Charentes, on the western shore of France, offers sun-drenched beaches, sedate canals, craggy cliffs, fertile plains, and a rich history. The *Côte d'Azur* may be tops in topless beaches, and the Loire Valley may be the king of châteaux, but no other region of France has so impressive a collection of both.

LA ROCHELLE

La Rochelle (pop. 100,000) has one great claim to fame—fish, and lots of it. As one of France's best-sheltered seaports, it was fought over by France and England during the Hundred Years' War. A magical world awaits in La Rochelle's popular **aquarium,** across from the Musée Maritime in Bassin des Grande Yacht. Hundreds of exotic fish, an octopus, and piranhas swim through realistic exhibits. (☎05 46 34 00 00. Open July-Aug. daily 9am-11pm; Apr.-June and Sept. 9am-8pm; Oct.-Mar. 9am-8pm. 65F/€9.95, students and children 45F/€6.90.) Climb up the fortifications of **Tour St-Nicolas** and **Tour de la Chaîne,** to the left as you face the harbor. (St-Nicolas ☎05 46 41 74 13; Chaîne 06 46 34 11 81. Open Apr.-Sept. daily 10am-7pm; Oct.-Mar. W-M 10am-12:30pm and 2-5:30pm. 26F/€4, ages 18-25 16F/€2.45, under 18 free.)

Trains leave bd. Maréchal Joffre for: Bordeaux (2hr., 5 per day, 136F/€20.75); Nantes (2hr., 5 per day, 128F/€19.55); Paris (5hr., 1 per day, 326F/€49.70; TGVs 3hr., 5 per day, 393F/€59.95); Poitiers (2hr., 8 per day, 120F/€18.30). The **tourist office,** pl. de la Petite Sirène, is in the quartier du Gabut. (☎05 46 41 14 68; fax 05 46 41 99 85; www.ville-larochelle.fr. Open July-Aug. M-Sa 9am-8pm, Su 11am-5pm; May-June and Sept. M-Sa 9am-7pm, Su 11am-5pm; Oct.-Apr. M-Sa 9am-noon and 2-6pm, Su 10am-noon.) Check **email** at **Centre Départemental d'Information Jeunesse**

FRANCE

(CDIJ), 2, r. des Gentilshommes. (☎ 05 46 41 16 36. 10F/€1.55 per hr. Open M 2-6pm, Tu-F 10am-12:30pm and 1:30-6pm.) Take bus #10 (dir.: Port des Minimes; every 20min. until 7:15pm, 8F/€1.25) from av. de Colmar, near the train station, to "Lycell Hotelier"; walk up to the rotary, veer left, walk down the road for 15min. and **Centre International de Séjour (HI)**, av. des Minimes, will be on the right. (☎ 05 46 44 43 11; fax 05 46 45 41 48. Breakfast included. Reception July-Aug. 8:30am-11pm; Sept.-June reduced hours. Dorms 75F/€11.45; singles 110F/€16.80.) **Postal Code:** 17000.

POITIERS

The renowned churches of Poitiers (pop. 83,000) were witness to the growth of Church power in the early Middle Ages. Façades in the 12th-century Romanesque ▓**Notre-Dame-la-Grande**, pl. de Gaulle, off Grand Rue, display the story of Christianity, while the massive **Cathédrale St-Pierre**, in pl. de la Cathédrale, off r. de la Cathédrale, contains an elaborate 18th-century Cliquot classical organ. Nearby is the 4th-century **Baptistère St-Jean**, on r. Jean Jaurès, the oldest Christian edifice in France. (Open July-Aug. daily 10am-12:30pm and 2:30-6pm; Apr.-June and Sept.-Oct. 10:30am-12:30pm and 3-6pm; Nov.-Mar. W-M 2:30-4:30pm. 4F/€0.60.)

Trains run from the station at bd. du Grand Cerf to: Bordeaux (2hr., 8 per day, 175F/€26.70); La Rochelle (1¾hr., 8 per day, 120F/€18.30); Paris (2½hr., 6 per day, 265-330F/€40.40-50.35); Tours (1hr., 5 per day, 98F/€14.95). The **tourist office,** 45, pl. Charles de Gaulle, is across from Notre Dame. (☎ 05 49 41 21 24; fax 05 49 88 65 84. Open mid-June to mid-Sept. M-Sa 9:30am-11pm, Su 10am-6pm; late Sept. to June M-Sa 10am-6pm.) For the **Auberge de Jeunesse (HI)**, 1, allée Tagault, catch bus #3 (dir.: Pierre Loti; every 30min., 8F/€1.25), by the traffic light ahead of the station, to "Cap Sud." (☎ 05 49 58 03 05. Breakfast 19F/€2.90. Reception daily 7am-noon and 4pm-midnight. **HI members only.** Beds 53F/€8.10.) **Postal Code:** 86000.

PÉRIGORD AND AQUITAINE

Périgord and Aquitaine present seductive images: green countryside splashed with yellow sunflowers, white chalk cliffs, golden white wine, plates of black truffles, and the smell of warm walnuts. First settled 150,000 years ago, the area around Les Eyzies-de-Tayac has produced more stone-age artifacts than anywhere on earth.

PÉRIGUEUX

The towering steeple and five massive cupolas of the **Cathédrale St-Front** dominate Périgueux (pop. 37,700) from above the Isle river. Nearly 1500 years of rebuilding, restoration, rethinking, and revision have produced the largest cathedral in southwestern France. (Open daily 8am-7:30pm.) West of the *vieille ville*, down r. de la Cité, the first-century **Tour de Vésone** towers as a better preserved remnant of Gallo-Roman Périgueux. (Open Apr.-Sept. daily 7:30am-9pm; Oct.-Mar. 7:30am-6:30pm.)

Trains leave r. Denis Papin for: Bordeaux (1½hr., 7 per day, 99F/€15.10); Paris (4-6hr., 12 per day, 277F/€42.25); Toulouse (4hr., 8 per day, 183F/€27.90). The **tourist office,** 26, pl. Francheville, has free maps. From the station, turn right on r. Denis Papin, bear left on r. des Mobiles-de-Coulmiers, which becomes r. du Président Wilson, take the next right after passing r. Guillier; it will be on the left. (☎ 05 53 53 10 63; fax 05 53 09 02 70. Open July-Aug. M-Sa 9am-7pm, Su 10am-6pm; Sept.-June M-Sa 9am-6pm.) Across from the train station, **Hôtel des Voyageurs**, 26, r. Denis Papin, has clean, bright rooms. (☎/fax 05 53 53 17 44. Breakfast 21F/€3.20. Singles 80F/€12.20; doubles 90F/€13.75, with shower 110F/€16.80.) **Monoprix supermarket** is on pl. de la République. (Open M-Sa 8:30am-8pm.) **Postal Code:** 24070.

SARLAT

The golden 14th- and 15th-century cobblestone streets of Sarlat (pop.10,700) draw both the tourist and movie cameras—*Cyrano de Bergerac* and *Manon des Sources* were filmed here. **Trains** leave from av. de la Gare for Bordeaux (2½hr., 4 per day, 119F/€18.15) and Périgueux (1½hr., 1 per day, 75F/€11.45). To reach the **tourist office,** on r. Tourny, follow av. de la Gare downhill to the left, turn right on av.

FRANCE

Thiers, which becomes av. Général Leclerc and later de la République; bear right on r. Lakanal, turn left onto r. de la Liberté and it will be in the Ancien Eveche. (☎ 05 53 31 45 45; fax 05 53 59 19 44. Open May-Sept. M-Sa 9am-7pm, Su 10am-noon and 2-6pm; Oct.-Apr. M-Sa 9am-noon and 2-7pm.) Rent **bikes** at **Peugeot Cycles,** 36, av. Thiers. (☎ 05 53 28 51 87. 70F/€10.70 for 24hr. Open Tu-Sa 9:30am-7pm. MC/V.) Sarlat's **Auberge de Jeunesse,** 77, av. de Selves, is only 10min. from the *vieille ville.* From the *vieille ville,* go straight along r. de la République, which becomes av. Gambetta, bear left at the fork onto av. de Selves, and it's on your right. (☎ 05 53 59 47 59; fax 05 53 30 21 27. Reception 6am-8:30pm. Open mid-Mar. to Nov. Reserve ahead. 60F/€9.15 1st night, 50F/€7.65 afterwards. **Camping** 35F/€5.35 per night.) For **Champion supermarket,** on rte. de Montignac; follow av. de Selves away from the *centre ville.* (Open M-Sa 9am-7:30pm, Su 9am-noon.) **Postal Code:** 24200.

🔁 DAYTRIPS FROM SARLAT AND PÉRIGUEUX

CAVE PAINTINGS

CFTA (☎ 05 55 86 07 07) runs buses to the caves of Lascaux, near the town of Montignac, from Périgueux (1½hr., 1 per day, 40F/€6.10). Buses also run every morning from Sarlat (20min., 3 per day, 30F/€4.60). Trains run to Les Eyzies-de-Tayac from Périgueux (30min., 4 per day, 40F/€6.10) and Sarlat (1hr., 3 per day, 47F/€7.20) via Le Buisson.

The most spectacular cave paintings ever discovered line the **caves of Lascaux,** near the town of **Montignac,** 25km north of Sarlat. They were discovered in 1940 by a couple teenagers, but were closed in 1963—the oohs and aahs of tourists fostered algae and micro-stalactites that ravaged the paintings. **Lascaux II** duplicates the original cave in the same pigments used 17,000 years ago. Although they may lack ancient awe and mystery, the new caves—filled with paintings of 5m tall bulls, horses, and bison—nevertheless manage to inspire a wonder all their own. The **ticket office** (☎ 05 53 35 50 10) shares a building with Montignac's **tourist office** (☎ 05 53 51 82 60), on pl. Bertram-de-Born. (Ticket office open 9am until tickets sell out.)

At the **Grotte de Font-de-Gaume,** 1km outside **Les Eyzies-de-Tayac** on D47, amazing 15,000-year-old paintings are still open for viewing. (☎ 05 53 06 86 00. Open Apr.-Sept. daily 9am-noon and 2-6pm; Mar. and Oct. 9:30am-noon and 2-5:30pm; Nov.-Feb. 10am-noon and 2-5pm. Reserve 1-2 weeks in advance for tickets. 36F/€5.50, ages 18-25 23F/€3.50, children free.) Get more information at the **Point Accueil Prehistoire,** across from the post office, on the main street (D47) through town. (☎ 06 86 66 54 43. Open daily 9:15am-1:30pm and 3-7pm.) The **tourist office** is located at pl. de la Mairie, before the Point Accueil. (☎ 05 53 06 97 05; fax 05 53 06 90 79. Open July-Aug. M-Sa 9am-8pm, Su 10am-noon and 2-6pm; Sept.-June reduced hours.)

THE DORDOGNE VALLEY

To get to and around the valley, you'll need to rent a car or be prepared for a good bike workout—the hills are steep but manageable. A Hertz car rental office is in front of the train station in Perigeux. To paddle down the Dordogne River, rent canoes from Cenac Canoes. (☎ 05 53 28 22 01. Half-day 150F/€22.90, whole day 240F/€36.60.)

Steep, craggy cliffs and poplar tree thickets overlook the slow-moving turquoise waters of the Dordogne River, 15km south of Sarlat. The town of **Castelnaud-La Chapelle,** 10km southwest of Sarlat, snoozes in the shadow of its pale yellow medieval stone château. (☎ 05 53 31 30 00. Open July-Aug. daily 9am-8pm; May-June and Sept. 10am-6pm; mid-Nov. to Feb. Su-F 2-5pm. 38F/€5.80.) **Domme** was built by King Philippe III (Philippe the Bold) in 1280 on a high dome of solid rock. Over 70 Templar Knights were imprisoned by King Philip IV in the **Porte des Tours.** The graffiti they scrawled upon the walls with their bare hands and teeth still remain. Consult the **tourist office,** on pl. de la Halle (☎ 05 53 31 71 00), for tours (1hr.; 1 per day; 25F/€3.85, children 18F/€2.75). You can also rent a **canoe** and paddle down the Dordogne to view the numerous châteaux on the hills. Ask at tourist offices for lists of *chambres d'hôtes,* which rent out cheap rooms.

FRANCE

BORDEAUX

Wrapped in emerald vineyards, Bordeaux (pop. 714,000) toasts the deep, violet wine that made it famous. A temple to wine connoisseurs, the city itself is also a trove of not-so-hidden delights. The Gothic cathedrals, public fountains, and historic mansions from the city's prosperous past blend with hot nightclubs, art galleries, and some of the best food in France for a unique and upbeat atmosphere.

🖥🔌 TRANSPORTATION AND PRACTICAL INFORMATION. Trains leave from the Gare Saint Jean, r. Charles Domercq (☎ 05 56 33 11 83), to: Paris (TGV: 3-4hr., 15-25 per day, 349F/€53.40); Nice (9-10hr., 5 per day, 436F/€66.50); Toulouse (2-3hr., 11 per day, 179F/€27.30). Follow the **Cours de la Marne** from the train station for a 30min. walk to **vieux Bordeaux,** the hub of the city. Take **bus** #7 or 8 (dir.: Grand Théâtre) from the station to pl. Gambetta and walk toward the Monument des Girondins to reach the **tourist office,** 12, cours du 30 Juillet, which arranges winery tours. (☎ 05 56 00 66 00; fax 05 56 00 66 01; www.bordeaux-tourisme.com. Open May-Oct. M-Sa 9am-7pm, Su 9:30am-6:30pm; Nov.-Apr. M-F 9am-6:30pm, Su 9:45am-4:30pm.) Another branch is at the train station. Surf the **Internet** at the central **Netzone,** 209, r. Sainte Catherine, near the pl. de la Victoire. (☎ 05 57 78 88 88. Open M-Sa 10am-8pm, Su 2-7pm. 35F/€5.35 per hr., students 30F/€4.60.) **Postal Code:** 33065.

🛏🍴 ACCOMMODATIONS AND FOOD. The newly renovated **Auberge de Jeunesse (HI),** 22, cours Barbey, still has a smaller branch at 208, cours de l'Argonne (☎ 05 56 94 51 66; fax 05 56 94 51 66), a 10min. walk from pl. de la Victoire. The main *auberge* is in a seedy area near the train station and 30min. from the *centre ville.* (☎ 05 56 33 00 70; fax ☎ 05 56 33 00 71. Breakfast 15F/€2.30. HI members 80F/€12.20; nonmembers extra 10F/€1.55 to stay 1 night.) For the **Hôtel Boulan,** 22, r. Boulan, take bus #7 or 8 from the station to the cours d'Albret; it's around the corner from the museum. (☎ 05 56 52 23 62; fax 05 56 44 91 65. Breakfast 20F/€3.05. Singles 110F/€16.80, with shower 130F/€19.85; doubles 130F/€19.85, 150F/€22.90. MC/V.) In the heart of *vieux Bordeaux* is the two-star **Hôtel Clemenceau,** 4, cours G. Clémenceau. (☎ 05 56 52 98 98; fax 05 56 81 24 91. Su-Th singles 170F/€25.95; doubles 200-230F/€30.50-35.10; F-Sa 150F/€22.90; 170F/€25.95.) **Camping les Gravières,** 35, av. Mirieu de Labarre, in Villeneuve d'Ornon, is far from any sights. Take bus B (dir.: Courrégean; 5-6 per day, 30min.) from pl. de la Victoire to the end. (☎ 05 56 87 00 36. 19F/€2.90 per person, 22F/€3.35 per tent, 30F/€4.60 for tent and car. MC/V.)

Living in the *région de bien manger et de bien vivre* (region of fine eating and living), *Bordelais* take their food as seriously as their wine. Hunt around **Rue St-Remi** and **Place St-Pierre** for splendid regional specialties, including oysters, beef braised in wine sauce, and the cake *canelé de Bordeaux.* **La Casuccia,** 49, r. Saint Rémi, is perfect for an intimate dinner or a casual outing. (☎ 05 56 51 17 70. Open 11:30am-midnight. MC/V.) Stock up at **Auchan supermarket,** at the Centre Meriadeck on r. Claude Bonnier. (☎ 05 56 99 59 00. Open M-Sa 8:30am-10pm.)

🎭🎷 SIGHTS AND ENTERTAINMENT. The best way to see the sights of Bourdeaux is to work your way into the center of town from the tourist office before heading down to the river. Start with the central monument of the city, the **Monument aux Girondins,** at the pl. de Quinconces, a few short blocks to your right as you exit the tourist office. The hundred-year-old monument, which commerates a group of revolutionary Girondins, and finely carved fountains, **Le Triomphe de la République** and **Le Triomphe de la Concorde,** are laden with symbolism, meaning, and pathos. The whole shebang is capped off with a stone **Lady Liberty,** "breaking the chains" of absolutist monarchical oppression. Retracing your steps, you can see the monumental **Grand Théâtre** on the other side of the tourist office, probably the most strictly classical opera house in the world. The colonnaded neoclassical façade conceals an even more impressive gilded interior. (Tours 30F/€4.60, students 20F/€3.05.) On pl. Pey-Berland is 900-year-old stunning **Cathédrale St-André,** Bordeaux's Gothic masterpiece. The bell-tower, the **Tour Pey-Berland,** juts 50m into the sky, a height capped by the grand statue of Notre-Dame d'Aquitaine. Climb all 229 spiraling steps to the

FRANCE

top for the view of your life. (Open Apr.-Oct. daily 7:30-11:30am and 2-6:30pm; Nov.-Mar. M-F 7:30-11:30am and 2-6:30pm. 25F/€3.85, under 25 and seniors 15F/€2.30.) From the cathedral, walk down cours Maréchal Joffre and turn right on r. Duffour Dubergier for the fascinating **Musée d'Aquitaine,** 20, cours Pasteur, which traces the history of Bordeaux and Aquitaine from pre-history to today. Then walk along quai Richelieu to **Place de la Bourse,** where the imposing pillars and pilasters, wrought iron façades, and fountain exemplify the 18th-century grandeur of Bordeaux.

Near the river, just off quai des Chartrons, is the **Vinorama de Bordeaux,** 12, cours du Medoc. Visitors carry around a tape recorder with the voice of "Bacchus" narrating the history of the wine-making process. Tour ends with brief wine-tasting session. (Open June-Sept. Tu-Sa 10:30am-12:30pm and 2:30pm-6:30pm, Su 2-6:30pm; Oct.-May Tu-F 2-6:30pm, Sa 10:30am-12:30pm and 2:30-6:30pm. 35F/€5.35.) The **Maison du Vin/CIVB,** 1, cours du 30 Juillet, opposite the tourist office, offers a 2hr. "Initiation to Wine Tasting" course that will leave you confident enough to waltz into any four-star restaurant. (☎ 05 56 00 22 66; www.vins-bordeaux.fr. Course offered twice weekly, 100F/€15.25. Open M-Th 8:30am-6pm, F 8:30am-5:30pm.) Locals buy wine at **Vinothèque,** 8, cours du 30 Juillet. (☎ 05 56 52 32 05. Open M-Sa 9:15am-7:30pm.)

▓ **DAYTRIP FROM BORDEAUX: ST-ÉMILION.** Just 35km northeast of Bordeaux, the viticulturists of St-Émilion have been refining their techniques since Roman times. Today, they gently crush hectares of grapes to produce 23 million liters of wine annually. Vineyards aside, the medieval-style village itself is a pleasure to visit, with its winding narrow streets and cafe-lined square. The **Eglise Monolithe** is the largest subterranean church is Europe. The **tourist office,** at pl. des Créneaux, near the church tower, rents **bikes** (90F/€13.75 per day) and offers guided tours to the local châteaux. (☎ 05 57 55 28 28. Open July-Aug. daily 9:30am-7pm; Sept.-June approx. 9:30am-12:30pm and 1:45-6pm.) **Trains** run from Bordeaux to St-Émilion (30min., 2 per day, 66F/€10.10; the only return train leaves at 6:30pm).

THE PAYS BASQUE AND GASCONY

South of Aquitaine, the forests recede and the mountains of Gascony begin, shielded from the Atlantic by the Basque Country. Long renowned as fierce fighters, the Basques continue to struggle today, striving to win independence for their long-suffering homeland. Unlike the separatist Basques, Gascons have long considered themselves French. Today, people come to Gascony to be healed: millions of believers descend on Lourdes hoping for miracle cures while thousands of others undergo scarcely more scientific treatments in the many *thermes* of the Pyrenees.

BAYONNE

Bayonne (pop. 43,000) is a city where the pace of life has not changed for centuries. Here the word for walk is *flaner*, meaning "to stroll," rather than *marcher* or even *se promener*. Towering above it all, the grand Gothic 13th-century **Cathédrale Ste-Marie** marks the leisurely passing of time with the tolling of its bells. (Open M-Sa 7am-noon and 3-7pm, Su 3:30-10pm. Free.) The **Musée Bonnat,** 5, r. Jacques Laffitte, in Petit-Bayonne, contains works by Degas, El Greco, and Goya. (Open Tu-Su 10am-6:15pm. 35F/€5.35, students 20F/€3.05.) The **Harmonie Bayonnaise** orchestra holds traditional Basque **concerts** in pl. de Gaulle. (July-Aug. Th at 9:30pm; Free.)

Trains depart from the station in pl. de la République, running to: Bordeaux (1½hr., 9 per day, 130-138F/€19.85-21.05); Toulouse (4hr., 5 per day, 200F/€30.50); San Sebastián, Spain (1½hr., with a change at Hendalye). Trains run between Bayonne and Biarritz (10min., 11 per day, 13F/€2), but the local bus network is more extensive and cheaper than regional transit. Local STAB **buses** depart from the **Hôtel de Ville** for Anglet and Biarritz (every 30-40min., last bus M-Sa 8pm, Su 7pm; 7.50F/€1.15). The **tourist office,** on pl. des Basques, finds rooms. From the train station, take the middle fork onto pl. de la République, veer right over pont St-Esprit, pass through pl. Réduit, cross pont Mayou, turn right on r. Bernède and turn left for a 15min. walk down pl. des Basques. (☎ 05 59 46 01 46; fax 05 59 59 37 55. Open July-

FRANCE

Aug. M-Sa 9am-7pm, Su 10am-1pm; Sept.-June M-F 9am-6:30pm, Sa 10am-6pm.) Decent lodgings are near the train station and pl. Paul Bert, but the closest hostel is in Anglet. The **Hôtel Paris-Madrid,** on pl. de la Gare, has cozy rooms. (☎05 59 55 13 98. Breakfast 25F/€3.85. Reception 6am-12:30am. Singles and doubles 95-180F/€14.50-27.45; triples and quads 235-250F/€35.85-38.10.) To get to **Camping de la Chêneraie,** take bus #1 from the station to the "Navarre" stop; the campground is a 1½km walk along the busy highway. (☎05 59 55 01 31. Reception open July-Aug. 8am-10pm; Easter-June and Sept. 8:30am-noon and 5-7:30pm. 26F/€3.90 per person, 58F/€8.85 per tent and car, 75F/€11.40 per caravan. Electricity 20F/€3.05.) Get groceries at **Monoprix supermarket,** 8, r. Orbe. (Open M-Sa 8:30am-7:30pm.)

🔁 **DAYTRIP FROM BAYONNE: ST-JEAN-PIED-DE-PORT.** The Pyrenean village of St-Jean-Pied-de-Port (pop. 1600) epitomizes the spicy splendor of the Basque interior. The narrow streets ascend through the *haute ville* to the dilapidated fortress, which hovers over the calm Nive. This medieval capital of Basse-Navarre still hosts a procession of pilgrims on their way to Santiago de Compostela, Spain, 900km away. **Trains** arrive from Bayonne (1hr., 5 per day, 47F/€7.20) at the station on av. Renaud. **Rent bikes** at **Garazi Cycles,** 1, pl. St-Laurent. (☎05 59 37 21 79. Passport deposit. 120F/€18.30 per day, 150F/€22.90 per weekend. Open M-Sa 8:30am-noon and 3-6pm.) From the station, turn right on av. Renaud, follow it up to av. de Gaulle, and turn right to reach the **tourist office,** 14, av. de Gaulle. (☎05 59 37 03 57; fax 05 59 37 34 91. Open July-Aug. M-Sa 9am-12:30pm and 2-7pm, Su 10:30am-12:30pm and 3-6pm; Sept.-June M-F 9am-noon and 2-7pm, Sa 9am-noon and 2-6pm.)

BIARRITZ

Biarritz (pop. 29,000) is not a budget traveler's dream, but its free **beaches** make a daytrip *de luxe.* Surfers and bathers fill the **Grande Plage,** while just to the north at the less-crowded **Plage Miramar,** bathers repose *au naturel.* A short **hike** to **Pointe St-Martin** affords a priceless view of the water. **BASC Subaquatique,** near Plateau de l'Atalaye (☎05 59 24 80 40), organizes **scuba** excursions in summer for 155F/€23.65.

Trains leave from **Biarritz-la-Négresse** (☎05 59 23 04 84), 3km from town, for Bordeaux (2hr., 7 per day, 133F/€20.30) and Paris (5hr., 5 TGVs per day, 442F/€67.40). STAB **bus** #1 or 2 to the central Hôtel de Ville (30min., 7.50F/€1.15). From there, the **tourist office,** 1, sq. d'Ixelles, is a brief walk up r. J. Petit, and helps with finding accommodations. (☎05 59 22 37 00. Open July-Aug. daily 8am-8pm; Sept.-June daily 9am-6pm.) The **Auberge de Jeunesse (HI),** 8, r. de Chiquito de Cambo, has a friendly staff and lakefront location. At the "Bois de Boulogne" stop on bus line #2. (☎05 59 41 76 00. Sheets 17F/€2.60. **HI members only.** 78F/€11.90 per person.) **Hôtel Barnetche,** 5bis, r. Charles-Floquet, in *centre ville.* (☎05 59 24 22 25. Breakfast included. In Aug., obligatory half-*pension* 100F/€15.25. Reception 7:30am-10:30pm, July-Aug. until 11pm. Open May-Sept. 12-bed dorm 110F/€16.80; doubles 380F/€57.95; triples and quads 160F/€24.40 per person.) **Shopi supermarket,** 2, r. du Centre, is just off r. Gambetta. (Open M-Sa 8:45am-12:25pm and 3-7:10pm.)

ANGLET

Anglet's *raison d'être* is its beaches, ranging from the perfect waves of the **Plage Les Cavaliers** to the topless **Plage des Sables d'Or.** Anglet hosts a number of professional surfing championships during the summer (free to spectators), including the **O'Neill Surf Challenge** and the **Europe Surfing Championship.** The **Rip Curl/Ecole Française de Surf,** av. des Dauphins, rents boards and arranges surfing lessons. (☎05 59 23 15 31. Boards half-day 60F/€9.15, 1 day 100F/€15.25; passport deposit. Lessons 220F/€33.55 for 1 person for 2hr. Open Apr.-Oct. daily 9:30am-7pm.) STAB **buses** connect Anglet to Bayonne and Biarritz (every 15min., 7.50F/€1.15). The **tourist office,** 1, av. de Chambre d'Amour, in pl. Leclerc, has information on surfing contests. (☎05 59 03 77 01. Open July-Sept. M-Sa 9am-7pm; Oct.-June M-F 9am-12:45pm and 1:45-6pm, Sa 9am-12:15pm.) The carefree **Auberge de Jeunesse (HI),** 19, rte. de Vignes, is just 600m uphill from the beach. From the Hôtel de Ville in Biarritz, take bus #4 (dir.: Bayonne Sainsontain) to "Auberge." From the train station in Bayonne,

FRANCE

take bus #4 to La Barre, then bus #9 or C to "Auberge." (☎ 05 59 58 70 00. Sheets 17F/€2.60. Reception 8:30am-10pm. Dorms 75F/€11.45.) The central **Camping Fontaine Laborde,** 17, allée Fontaine Laborde, caters to young surfers. Take bus #4 to Fontaine Laborde, down the road from the hostel. (☎ 05 59 03 48 16. 32F/€4.90 per person, 29F/€4.45 per site, 20F/€3.05 per car.) The strip behind the **Plage des Sables d'Or,** along **Avenue des Dauphins,** offers many eateries. **Postal Code:** 64600.

LOURDES

In 1858, 14-year-old Bernadette Soubirous saw the first of 18 visions of the Virgin Mary in the Massabielle grotto in Lourdes (pop. 16,300). Today five million rosary-toting faithful annually make the pilgrimage. For **Grotte de Massabielle (La Grotte)** and the three **basilicas,** follow av. de la Gare, turn left on bd. de la Grotte, and follow it to the right and across the river Gave. Processions depart daily from the grotto at 5pm and 8:45pm. (No shorts or tank tops. Grotto open daily 5am-midnight. Basilicas open Easter to Oct. daily 6am-7pm; Nov.-Easter 8am-6pm, excluding masses.)

Trains leave the station at 33, av. de la Gare, for: Bayonne (2hr., 5 per day, 108F/€16.50); Bordeaux (3hr., 7 per day, 176F/€26.85); Paris (7-9hr., 5 per day, 523F/€79.75); Toulouse (2½hr., 8 per day, 127F/€19.40). To get from the train station to the **tourist office,** on pl. Peyramale, turn right onto av. de la Gare, bear left onto av. Marasin, cross a bridge above bd. du Papacca, and climb uphill. The office is to the right. (☎ 05 62 42 77 40; fax 05 62 94 60 95. Open May-Oct M-Sa 9am-7pm; Nov. 1-15 M-Sa 9am-noon and 2-7pm; mid-Nov. to mid-Mar. M-Sa 9am-noon and 2-6pm; mid-Mar. to Apr. M-Sa 9am-noon and 2-7pm.) To find the clean and comfortable **Hôtel Saint-Sylve,** 9, r. de la Fontaine, follow av. Herlios away from the train station as it curves down the hill. Bear right and go under the bridge on bd. du Lapacca. Take the first left after the bridge uphill onto r. Basse and then the second right onto r. de la Fontaine. (☎/fax 05 62 94 63 48. Breakfast 25F/€4. Reception until 11:30pm. Open Apr.-Oct. Singles 80F/€13; doubles 180F/€28; triples 220F/€33.55.) **Camping de la Poste,** 26, r. de Langelle, is 2min. from the post office. (☎ 05 62 94 40 35. Open Easter to mid-Oct. 15F/€2.30 per person, 23F/€3.55 per site. Electricity 16F/€2.45. Showers 8F/€1.25.) Save money at **Prisunic supermarket,** 9, pl. du Champ-Commun. (Open M-Sa 8:30am-12:30pm and 2-7:30pm, Su 8am-noon.) **Postal Code:** 65100.

CAUTERETS

Nestled in a narrow, breathtaking valley on the edge of the **Parc National des Pyrenees Occidentales** is tiny, friendly Cauterets. Cauterets's hot sulfuric *thermes* have long been instruments of healing; for more information, contact **Thermes de Cesar,** av. Docteur Domer. (☎ 05 62 92 51 60. Open M-F 9am-12:30pm and 1:30-6pm, Sa 9am-12:30pm.) Today, most visitors come for the skiing and hiking. The **tourist office,** on pl. Foch, has free maps of ski trails. (☎ 05 62 92 50 27; www.cauterets.com. Open July-Aug. daily 9am-7pm; Sept.-June 9am-12:30pm and 2-6:30pm.) For more **hiking** information and advice, head to **Parc National des Pyrenees** (see below). **Skilys,** rte. de Pierrefitte, on pl. de la Gare, rents **bikes** and **skates.** (☎ 05 62 92 52 10. Bikes with guide 250-350F/€38.10-53.40 per day, without guide 100F/€15.25 per day; deposit 1500-2500F/€228.70-381.15. Open daily 9am-7pm; in winter 8am-7:30pm.)

SNCF **buses** run from pl. de la Gare to Lourdes (1hr.; 6 per day; 39F/€5.95, students 30F/€4.60). The **Hôtel Bigorre,** 15, r. de Belfort, has spacious rooms with views of the mountains. (☎ 05 65 92 52 81. Breakfast 30F/€4.60. Singles 100F/€15.25, with shower 150F/€22.90; doubles 150F/€22.90, 200F/€30.50; triples and quads 190-280F/€28.30-42.70.) The **Halles market,** on av. du Général Leclerc, has fresh produce. (Open daily 8:30am-12:30pm and 2:30-7:30pm.) **Postal Code:** 65110.

PARC NATIONAL DES PYRENEES

One of France's seven national parks, the **Parc National des Pyrenees** cradles endangered bears, lynxes, and marmots and 118 lakes in its mountains and valleys. The lush French and barren Spanish sides of the Pyrenees are a six- to seven-day round trip hike from Cauterets; but the trails in the park are designed for a range of aptitudes, from rugged outdoor enthusiasts to curious hikers. The **GR10** meanders

FRANCE

across the Pyrenees, connecting the Atlantic with the Mediterranean and looping through most major towns. For the major and minor hikes that run along it, pick up a purple map (58F/€9) at the Parc National Office. Many nearby **ski resorts** are accessible by SNCF **bus** from Cauterets or Lourdes. **Luz-Ardiden** offers downhill and cross-country skiing. (☎ 05 62 92 30 30. 135F/€20.60; student discounts available.)

The helpful staff at **Parc National Office,** Maison du Parc, pl. de la Gare, offers loads of free information on the park and the 15 different trails that begin and end in Cauterets, and also sells hiking and regional maps. (☎ 05 62 92 52 56; www.parc-pyrenees.com. Maps 42-58F/€6.40-8.85. Open daily June-Aug. 9:30am-noon and 3-7pm; Sept.-May M-Tu and F-Su 9:30am-12:30pm and 3-6pm, Th 3-6pm.) **Gîtes** are strategically placed in towns along the GR10. Reserve at least 48hr. ahead—the Parc National Office makes *gîte* reservations. (About 75F/€11.45 per night.)

LANGUEDOC-ROUSSILLON

A region called Occitania once stretched from the Rhône Valley to the foothills of the Pyrenees. It was eventually integrated into the French kingdom, but latent nationalism still lingers: many speak Catalán, a relative of the *langue d'oc;* the occitan banner, with its black cross against yellow and red stripes, is displayed throughout the region; and locals look to Barcelona, instead of Paris, for inspiration.

TOULOUSE

Just when French towns start blurring together, you discover Toulouse, or *la ville en rose* (the city in pink). The city's magnificent rose and white buildings give Toulouse (pop. 350,000) a worldly grandeur befitting the fourth-largest French city. Toulouse also has a rich history of independence—its powerful counts made life miserable for medieval French kings, and today its university pushes the frontiers of knowledge while the city prospers as capital of the French aerospace industry.

◨ TRANSPORTATION. Trains leave **Gare Matabiau,** 64, bd. Pierre Sémard, for: Bordeaux (2-3hr., 14 per day, 169F/€25.80); Lyon (6½hr., 3-4 per day, 310F/€47.30); Marseilles (4½hr., 8 per day, 246F/€37.55); Paris (8-9hr., 4 per day, 450F/€68.65). Next door to the train station, **buses** leave for Carcassonne (2¼hr., 63F/€9.65).

⊠ PRACTICAL INFORMATION. Toulouse sprawls on both sides of the Garonne; its center is a huge stone plaza known as the *Capitole.* Museums and sights are mostly within a small section east of the river, bounded by r. de Metz in the south, and by bd. Strasbourg and bd. Carnot to the north and east. To get from the train station to the **tourist office,** r. Lafayette, at Donjon du Capitôle in sq. Charles de Gaulle, turn left along the canal, turn right on the allée Jean Jaurès, bear right around pl. Wilson, turn right on r. Lafayette, and it's in a park near r. d'Alsace-Lorraine. (☎ 05 61 11 02 22; fax 05 61 22 03 63; www.mairie-toulouse.fr. Open May-Sept. M-Sa 9am-7pm, Su 10am-1pm and 2-6:30pm; Oct.-Apr. M-F 9am-6pm, Sa 9am-12:30pm and 2-6pm, Su 10am-12:30pm and 2-5pm.) Surf the **Internet** at **l'@fterbug,** 10, pl. St-Sernin, near the student quarter. (25F/€3.85 per hr. Open M-F noon-2am, Sa noon-5am, Su 2-10pm.) **Postal Code:** 31000.

◨◧ ACCOMMODATIONS AND FOOD. To reach the spacious and central **Hôtel des Arts,** 1bis, r. Cantegril, at r. des Arts near pl. St-Georges, take the Métro (dir.: Basso Cambo) to "Pl. Esquirol;" follow r. du Metz away from the river and r. des Arts is the third street on the left. (☎ 05 61 23 36 21; fax 05 61 12 22 37. Breakfast 25F/€3.85. Reserve ahead. Singles 95-135F/€14.50-20.60, with shower 145F/€22.15; doubles 160F/€24.40, 165F/€25.20. MC/V.) Bright **Hôtel Beauséjour,** 4, r. Caffarelli, just off allée Jean Jaurès, is near the train station. (☎/fax 05 61 62 77 59. Breakfast 23F/€3.55. Reception until 11pm. Singles and doubles 115F/€17.55, with bath 140-155F/€21.35-23.65. AmEx/MC/V.) **Camp** at **Pont de Rupé,** 21, chemin du Pont de Rupé, at av. des États-Unis (N20 north). Take bus #59 (dir.: Camping) to "Rupé."

FRANCE

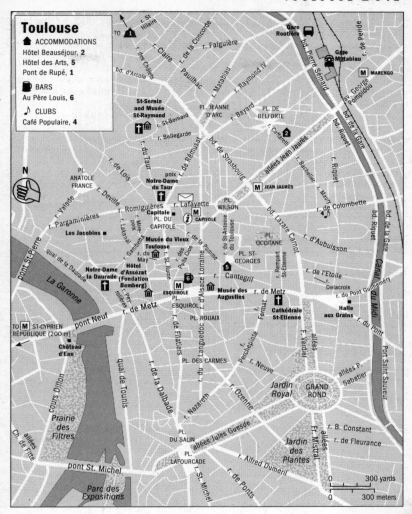

Toulouse

🏠 ACCOMMODATIONS
Hôtel Beauséjour, **2**
Hôtel des Arts, **5**
Pont de Rupé, **1**

🍺 BARS
Au Père Louis, **6**

♪ CLUBS
Café Populaire, **4**

(☎ 05 61 70 07 35; fax 05 61 70 00 71. 50F/€7.65 per person, 60F/€9.15 per 2 people; 17F/€2.60 per additional person.) Inexpensive eateries are in **Rue du Taur** in the student quarter; students can get hot meals at the 14 **Restaurants Universitaires** in Toulouse; inquire at **CROUS**, 58, r. du Taur, for more information. (☎ 05 61 12 54 00. Open M-F 8:30am-5:30pm; cafeterias open 11:30am-1:30pm and 6:30-8pm.)

🎭🎶 **SIGHTS AND ENTERTAINMENT.** The brick palace next door to the tourist office is the prominent **Capitole,** which has served as the seat of city government since the 11th century. The **Salle des Illustres** and **La Salle Henri Martin** upstairs are filled with sculpture and post-Impressionist *tableaux.* (Salles open M-F 8:30am-noon and 1:30-7pm, Sa-Su 10am-noon and 2-6pm. Free.) Just up r. du Taur from pl. du Capitole is the **Eglise Notre-Dame-du-Taur**, 12, r. du Taur, originally named St-Sernin-du-Taur after the priest Saturninus martyred in 250 after being tied to the tail of a wild bull by disgruntled pagans. (☎ 05 61 21 41 57. Open July-Sept. daily 9am-

FRANCE

6:30pm; Oct.-June 8am-noon and 2-6pm.) Continuing north on r. du Taur leads to the **Basilique St-Sernin**, the longest Romanesque structure in the world; its **crypt** houses a treasure trove of holy relics gathered from Charlemagne's time. (Church open July-Sept. M-Sa 9am-6:30pm, Su 9am-7:30pm; Oct.-June reduced hours. Free. Crypt open July-Sept. M-Sa 10am-6pm, Su 12:30-6pm; Oct.-June reduced hours. 10F/ €1.55.) Backtrack to the pl. du Capitole, take a right on r. Romiguières, and turn left on r. Lakanal to get to the 13th-century Southern Gothic **Refectoire des Jacobins,** which contains the ashes of St. Thomas Aquinas in an elevated underlit tomb. (Open daily 9am-7pm. Cloister 14F/€2.15.) Retracing your steps back down r. de Metz will take you to the newly restored **Hôtel d'Assézat**, at pl. d'Assézat. Its intricate, marble façade encloses the **Fondation Bemberg,** with a display of 28 Bonnards and some Dufys, Pisarros, and Gauguins. (☎ 05 61 12 06 89. *Fondation* ☎ 05 61 12 06 89. Open Tu and F-Su 10am-6pm, Th 10am-9pm. Groups 18F/€2.75, temporary exhibits 20F/€3.05.) Follow r. de Metz away from the river past pl. Esquirol to the **Musée des Augustins,** 21, r. de Metz, for an unsurpassed collection of Romanesque and Gothic sculptures. (☎ 05 61 22 21 82. Open Th-M 10am-6pm, W 10am-9pm. 14F/ €2.15, students free.) **La Cité de l'Espace** is devoted to Toulouse's space programs, complete with games and a planetarium. Take bus #19 to pl. de l'Indépendance and follow the signs. (☎ 05 62 71 64 80. Open mid-June to mid-Sept. Tu-Su 9:30am-7pm; mid-Sept. to mid-June 9:30am-6pm. 69F/€10.55. Planetarium 15F/€2.30.)

Toulouse has something to please almost any nocturnal whim, although nightlife is liveliest when students are in town, between October and May. Numerous cafes flank **Place St-Georges** and **Place du Capitole,** and late-night bars line **Rue St-Rome** and **Rue des Filatiers.** The venerable wine bar ◪**Au Père Louis**, 45, r. des Tourneurs, caters mostly to upscale crowds of locals. (☎ 05 61 21 33 45. Open M-Sa 8:30am-3pm and 5pm-10:30pm. Lunch is served noon-3pm.) **Cafe Populaire**, 9, r. de la Colombette, opens its welcoming walls and keeps itself lively by selling boxes of 13 beers for 120F/€18.30. (☎ 05 61 63 07 00. Open M-F 9pm-2am, Sa 3pm-6am.)

CARCASSONNE

When approaching breathtaking Carcassonne (pop. 45,000), you realize this is where Beauty may have fallen in love with the Beast. However, today the *cité*'s narrow streets are flooded with tourists. Built as a palace in the 12th century, the **Château Comtal,** 1, r. Viollet-le-Duc, became a citadel after a royal takeover in 1226. (☎ 04 68 25 01 66. Open June-Sept. daily 9am-7:30pm; Apr.-May and Oct. 9:30am-6pm; Nov.-Mar. 9:30am-5pm. 36F/€5.50, ages 18-25 23F/€3.55.) Turned into a fortress after the Black Prince destroyed Carcassonne in 1355, the Gothic **Cathédrale St-Michel,** r. Voltaire, in bastide St-Louis, still has fortifications on its southern side. (☎ 04 68 25 14 48. Open M-Sa 7am-noon and 2-7pm, Su 9:30am-noon.) Although nightlife is limited, several bars and cafes along **Boulevard Omer Sarraut** and **Place Verdun** are open until midnight. Locals dance all night at **La Bulle**, 115, r. Barbacane. (☎ 04 68 72 47 70. Cover 60F/€9.15 includes 1 drink. Open F-Sa until dawn.)

Trains (☎ 04 68 71 79 14) depart behind Jardin St-Chenier to: Marseilles (3hr., every 2hr., 205F/€31.30); Nice (6hr., 5 per day, 303F/€46.25); Nîmes (2½hr., 12 per day, 142F/€21.70); Toulouse (50min., 24 per day, 75F/€11.45). Shops, hotels, and the train station are in the **bastide St-Louis**, once known as the *basse ville.* From the station, walk down av. de Maréchal Joffre, which becomes r. Clemenceau; after pl. Carnot, turn left on r. Verdun, which leads to sq. Gambetta and the **tourist office,** 15, bd. Camille Pelletan, pl. Gambetta. (☎ 04 68 10 24 30; fax 04 68 10 24 38. Open July-Aug. daily 9am-7pm; Sept.-June 9am-12:15pm and 1:45-6:30pm.) The **Auberge de Jeunesse (HI),** r. de Vicomte Trencavel, is in the *cité.* (☎ 04 68 25 23 16; fax 04 68 71 14 84. Breakfast included. Sheets 17F/€2.60. **Internet** access 28F/€4.30 per hr. **HI members only.** Dorms 76F/€11.60. MC/V.) The **Hôtel St-Joseph,** 81, r. de la Liberté, has 37 rooms on a calm street 5min. from the train station. Take av. Maréchal Joffre across the canal, across bd. Omer Sarraut, and then continue for a block on r. G. Clemenceau before turning right. (☎ 04 68 71 96 89; fax 04 68 74 36 28. Breakfast 28F/€4.30. Singles 115F/€17.55, with shower 185F/€28.25; doubles 185F/€28.25; triples 245F/€37.35; quads 285-305F/

FRANCE

€43.50-46.55. MC/V.) **Camping de la Cité,** rte. de St-Hilaire, 2km from town across the Aude, has a pool and grocery store. A shuttle can take you there from the train station. (☎04 68 25 11 77. Reception 8am-9pm. Open Apr.-Sept. June-Sept. 95F/€14.50 per site and person, 28F/€4.30 per additional person; cheaper Apr.-May.) The regional speciality is *cassoulet* (a stew of white beans, herbs, and meat). Restaurants on **Rue du Plo** have 55-60F/€8.40-9.15 *menus*, but save room for dessert at one of the *crêperies* in **Place Marcou.** Eat like a king at **Les Fontaines du Soleil,** 32, r. du Plo. (☎04 68 47 87 06. Open mid-Feb. to mid-Nov. daily 11:30am-3pm and 7-10:30pm.) **Postal Code:** 11000.

FOIX

Il était une fois, as French fairy tales begin, that a town grew up at the base of a large castle. The fantastic **Château de Foix** towers over Foix's busy markets. (☎05 61 65 56 05. Open July-Aug. daily 9:45am-6:30pm; June and Sept. 9:45am-noon and 2-6pm; Oct.-May W-Su 10:30am-noon and 2-5:30pm. 25F/€3.85.) A one-hour boat ride winds through the caves on the **Labouiche,** the longest navigable underground river in Europe. There is no public transport to this sight—consider biking the 6km from Foix. (☎05 61 65 04 11. Open July-Aug. daily 9:30am-6pm; Sept.-June reduced hours. 46F/€7.05.) The **Grotte de Niaux,** 20km south of Foix, has 13,000-year-old paintings of leaping bison, deer, and horses. (☎05 61 05 88 37. Reservations only. Open Apr.-Oct. daily; Nov.-Mar. M only. 60F/€9.15, students 35F/€5.35.)

The **train station,** on av. Pierre Sémard, is north of the town, off the N20. (☎05 61 02 03 64. Open M-Sa 8:10am-12:20pm and 1:25-8:30pm, Su 8:15am-1:55pm and 2:15-10:20pm.) **Trains** go to Toulouse (1hr., 10 per day, 70F/€10.65). Salt Autocars **buses,** 8, allées de Villote (☎05 61 65 08 40), also runs to Toulouse (1¼hr., 2 per day, 50F/€7.65). **L.C.F. Motos,** 16, r. Labistour, rents bikes. (☎05 61 05 29 98. 95F/€14.50 per day. Open M 2-7pm, Tu-Sa 9am-noon and 2-7pm.) For the **tourist office,** 29, r. Théophile Delcassé, leave the train station and turn right; follow the street until you reach the main road (N20), continue to the second bridge, cross it, and follow cours G. Fauré for three blocks. The tourist office is on the corner. (☎05 61 65 12 12; fax 05 61 65 64 63. Open July-Aug. M-Sa 9am-7pm, Su 10am-12:30pm and 3-6:30pm; June and Sept. M-Sa 9am-noon and 2-6pm, Su 10am-12:30pm; Oct.-May M-Sa 9am-noon and 2-6pm.) To get to the **Foyer Léo Lagrange,** 16, r. Peyrevidal, turn right on cours Gabriel Fauré out of the tourist office and turn right again on r. Peyrevidal just after the Halle Aux Grains; it's on your right. (☎05 61 65 09 04; fax 05 61 02 63 87. Reception 8am-11pm. Dorms 90F/€13.75.) For food, head to **Casino** supermarket, r. Laffont. (Open M-Sa 9am-7pm.) **Postal Code:** 09000.

PERPIGNAN

Brilliant "blood and gold" flags line Perpignan's (pop. 130,000) bustling streets, testifying to its Catalan heritage. However, the city's best asset is its proximity to the beautiful towns of Collioure and Céret. Guarding the entrance to the *vieille ville,* **Le Castillet** holds the small **Casa Pairal,** a museum of Catalan history. (☎04 68 35 42 05. Open mid-June to mid-Sept. W-M 9:30am-7pm; mid-Sept to mid-June W-M 9am-6pm. 25F/€3.85, students 10F/€1.55.) At pl. Gambetta is the **Cathédrale St-Jean,** an impressive example of Gothic architecture. (☎04 68 51 33 72. Open daily 9am-noon and 3-7pm. Free.) The **Musée Hyacinthe Rigaud,** 16, r. de l'Ange, contains a small but impressive collection of 13th-century Spanish and Catalan paintings and works by Ingres, Picasso, Miró, and Dalí. (☎04 68 35 43 40. Open W-M noon-7pm. 25F/€3.85, 10F/€1.55.) An uphill walk across the *vieille ville* leads to the 15th-century Spanish **citadelle.** Traditional Catalonian dancing in front of Le Castillet makes for a colorful scene around pl. de Verdun, especially in summer (Tu, Th, Sa).

Trains leave the station on r. Courteline, off av. de Gaulle, from: Carcassonne (1½hr.; 2 per day, 70-80F/€10.70-12.20) via Narbonne; Nice (6hr., 3 per day, 299F/€45.60); Paris (6-10hr., 4 per day, 439-505F/€66.95-77); Toulouse (2½-3hr.; 15 per day, 143F/€21.80) via Narbonne. **Buses** leave 17, av. Général Leclerc for the beaches. The small *vieille ville,* just past the red **castillet** tower, makes a triangle bounded by the regional tourist office, **Place de la Victoire** (farther up the canal),

FRANCE

and the **Palais des Rois de Majorque.** To get from the train station to the **tourist office,** Palais de Congrès, pl. Armand Lanoux, follow av. du Gaulle to pl. de Catalogne, then take bd. Georges Clemenceau across the canal past Le Castillet as it becomes bd. Wilson. Follow the signs along the promenade des Platanes. (☎ 04 68 66 30 30; fax 04 68 66 30 26. Open June-Sept. M-Sa 9am-7pm, Su 10am-noon and 2-5pm; Oct.-May M-Sa 9am-noon and 2-6pm.) The central ◧ **Hôtel de l'Avenir,** 11, r. de l'Avenir, welcomes visitors with its cheery and colorful interior. (☎ 04 68 34 20 30; fax 04 68 34 15 63. Breakfast 25F/€3.85. Shower 15F/€2.30. Singles 90-190F/€13.75-29; doubles 120-190F/€18.30-29; quads 250F/€38.15. AmEx/MC/V.) A block from the train station, **Hôtel Express,** 3, av. de Gaulle, has clean functional rooms. (☎ 04 68 34 89 96. Breakfast 20F/€3.05. Shower 15F/€2.30. Reserve ahead. Singles and doubles 100-124F/€15.20-18.90; triples and quads 184-254F/€28.05-38.75. MC/V.) To get to **Camping Le Catalan** from the train station, take the bus (dir.: Bompas; 15min., 2 per day, 12F/€1.85) and ask to be let out at "camping Catalan." (☎ 04 68 63 16 92. July-Aug. 86F/€13.15 per 2 people; Mar.-June 63F/€9.60 per 2 people, additional person 16-24F/€2.45-3.65.) **Casino supermarket,** on bd. Félix Mercader, stocks food. (☎ 04 68 34 74 42. Open M-Sa 8:30am-8pm.) **Postal Code:** 66000 (66020 for *Poste Restante*).

▓ DAYTRIPS FROM PERPIGNAN

COLLIOURE

Trains (☎ 04 68 82 05 89) roll in to the station at the top of av. Aristide Maillol from Barcelona, Spain (3½hr., 5 per day, 79F/€12.05); Narbonne (1hr., 12 per day, 75F/€11.45); Perpignan (20min., 15 per day, 29F/€4.45).

Nestled where the Pyrenees tumble into the Mediterranean, tiny Collioure (pop. 2770) captured the fancy of Greeks and Phoenicians long before enrapturing Dalí, Picasso, and Matisse. The view of the harbor from the hulking stone **Château Royal,** stretching from pl. du 8 mai 1945 to the port, is worth the climb. (☎ 04 68 82 06 43. Open June-Sept. daily 10am-5:15pm; Oct.-May 9am-4:15pm. 20F/€3.05.) The **tourist office,** on pl. du 18 Juin, has info on **day hikes** and coastal bus routes. (☎ 04 68 82 15 47; fax 04 68 82 46 29. Open July-Aug. daily 9am-8pm; Sept.-June M-Sa 9am-noon and 2-6:30pm.) **Hôtel Triton,** 1, r. Jean Bart, is on the waterfront. (☎ 04 68 98 39 39; fax 04 68 82 11 32. Doubles 200F/€30.50, with toilet 280F/€42.70. AmEx/MC/V.)

CÉRET

Car Inter 66 (☎ 04 68 39 11 96, in Perpignan 04 68 35 29 02) runs buses from Perpignan (45min., 1 per hr., 35F/€5.35).

In the early 20th century, a series of artists that included Picasso, Chagall, Manolo, and Herbin discovered Céret (pop. 8000), in the foothills of the Pyrenees, and created a "Cubist Mecca." Some of their works are housed in the impressive **Musée d'Art Moderne,** 8, bd. Maréchal Joffre, up the hill and to the right of the tourist office. (☎ 04 68 87 27 76. Open mid-June to mid-Sept. daily 10am-7pm; May to mid-June and late Sept. W-M 10am-6pm; Oct-Apr. W-M 10am-6pm. July-Sept 45F/€6.90, students 30F/€4.60; Oct-June 35F/€5.35, students 20F/€3.05.) From the bus stop on av. George Clemenceau, the **tourist office,** 1, av. Clemenceau, is two blocks up the hill on the right. (☎ 04 68 87 00 53. Open July-Aug. M-Sa 9am-12:30pm and 2-7pm, Su 10am-12:30pm; Sept.-Oct. M-F 10am-noon and 2-5pm, Sa 10am-noon.)

PROVENCE

Carpets of olive groves and vineyards unroll along hills dusted with lavender, sunflowers, and mimosa, while the fierce winds of the *mistral* carry the scent of sage, rosemary, and thyme. Since Roman times, writers have rhapsodized about Provence's fragrant and varied landscape. From the Roman arena and cobblestone elegance of Arles to the lingering footsteps of Cézanne in Aix-en-Provence, life unfolds along Provence's shaded paths like a bottomless glass of *pastis*.

NÎMES

Southern France flocks to Nîmes (pop. 135,000) for the *férias*, celebrations featuring bullfights, flamenco dancing, and other hot-blooded fanfare. Yet Nîmes's star attractions are its incredible Roman structures. The magnificent **Les Arènes** is a well-preserved first-century Roman amphitheater, where bullfights and concerts are still held. (☎ 04 66 76 72 77. Open daily 9am-6:30pm; in winter 9am-5:30pm. 28F/€4.30, students 20F/€3.05.) North of the arena stands the exquisite **Maison Carrée**, a rectangular temple built in the first century BC. (☎ 04 66 36 26 76. Open daily 9am-noon and 2:30-7pm; in winter 9am-12:30pm and 2-6pm. Free.) Across the square, the **Carrée d'Art** houses an excellent collection of contemporary art. (☎ 04 66 76 35 70. Open Tu-Su 10am-6pm. 28F/€4.30, students 20F/€3.05.) To the left along the canals, off pl. Foch, the **Jardins de la Fontaine** hold the Roman ruins of the **Temple de Diane** and the **Tour Magne.** (Gardens open Apr. to mid-Sept. daily 7:30am-10pm; mid-Sept. to Nov. 7:30am-6:30pm; Nov.-Mar. 8am-7pm. Free. Tour Magne open July-Aug. daily 9am-7pm; Sept.-June 9am-5pm. 15F/€2.30, students 12F/€1.85.)

Trains chug from bd. Talabot to: Arles (30min., 10 per day, 48F/€7.35); Marseilles (1¼hr., 6 per day, 98F/€14.95); Toulouse (3hr., 10 per day, 187F/€28.55). **Buses** (☎ 04 66 29 52 00) depart from behind the train station for Avignon (1½hr., 2-8 per day, 44F/€6.75). The **tourist office** is at 6, r. Auguste, just off pl. Comédie and near the Maison Carrée. (☎ 04 66 67 29 11; fax 04 66 21 81 04. Open July-Sept. M-Sa 9:30am-12:30pm and 2-6pm, Su 9:30am-12:30pm and 1:30-3:30pm; Oct.-June M-F 9:30am-12:30pm and 2-6pm.) The newly renovated **Auberge de Jeunesse (HI)** is 4½km from quai de la Fontaine, at 257, chemin de l'Auberge de la Jeunesse, off chemin de la Cigale. Take bus #2 (dir.: Alès or Villeverte) to "Stade, Route d'Alès" and follow the signs uphill; after buses stop running, call for pick-up. (☎ 04 66 68 03 20; fax 04 66 68 03 21. Breakfast 21F/€3.20. Sheets 18F/€2.70 per week. Reception Mar.-Sept. 24hr. **HI members only.** 4- to 6-bed dorms 57F/€8.65. **Camping** 32.50F/€4.95. MC/V.) Stock up at **Marché U supermarket,** 19, r. d'Alès, downhill from the hostel. (Open M-Sa 8am-12:45pm and 3:30-8pm.) **Postal Codes:** 30000 and 30900.

▓ **DAYTRIP FROM NÎMES: PONT DU GARD.** In 19 BC, Augustus's close friend and advisor Agrippa built an aqueduct to channel water for 50km to Nîmes from the Eure springs near Uzès. The masterpiece of this 15-year project remains in the Pont du Gard, which bridges the gorge of the **Gardon River,** towering over sunbathers and swimmers. A great way to see the Pont du Gard is to start from **Collias,** 6km toward Uzès. Here **Kayak Vert** rents two-person canoes, solo kayaks, and bikes. (☎ 04 66 22 84 83. Trips to Pont du Gard 95F/€14.50; bikes 80F/€12.20 per half-day. Canoes and kayaks 35F/€5.35 per hr.) **STDG buses** (☎ 04 66 29 27 29) run to the Pont du Gard from Avignon (45min., 7 per day, 33F/€5.05) and Nîmes (30min., 2-5 per day, 31F/€4.75). **Camping le Barralet,** r. des Aires in Collias, offers a pool and hot showers. (☎ 04 66 22 84 52; fax 04 66 22 89 17. Open Mar.-Sept. 36-48F/€5.80-7.35 per person with car, 70-85F/€10.70-13 per 2 people, 85-105F/€13-16.05 per 3 people . MC/V.)

AVIGNON

Stendhal may have described Avignon (pop. 100,000) as "the city of pretty women," but it's chiefly known for the Festival d'Avignon, a huge theatrical celebration. The 14th-century golden ▨**Palais des Papes** launches gargoyles out over the city and the Rhône. Its walls are oddly cut with the tall, ecclesiastical windows of the **Grande Chapelle** and the dark cross of arrow-loops. In the **Grand Tinel,** a banquet hall 45m long, blue canvas flecked with gold stars deck the arched ceiling. (☎ 04 90 27 50 74. Open July-Sept. daily 9am-8pm; Apr.-June and Oct. 9am-7pm; Nov. to mid-Mar. 9:30am-5:45pm; mid-Mar to late Mar. 9:30am-6:30pm. 46F/€7.05.) Heading from the Palais des Papes towards the Rhône, the **Pont St-Bénézet** steps into the Rhône and stops partway with four arches. Housed on the second arch is

FRANCE

the **St-Nicolas Chapel,** dedicated to the patron saint of mariners. (Open Apr.-Nov. daily 9am-7pm; July-Sept. open until 8pm; Nov.-Mar. 9:30am-5:45pm.) The riotous **Festival d'Avignon,** also known as the **IN,** goes from early July to early August, as Gregorian chanters rub shoulders with *Odyssey*-readers and African dancers. (☎ 04 90 14 14 14. Tickets free-200F/€30.50. Reservations accepted from mid-June. Tickets available 45min. before shows; 50% student discount.) **Place des Corps Saints** has a few lively bars.

Trains (☎ 04 90 27 81 89) run from porte de la République to: Arles (30min., 10 per day, 36F/€5.50); Marseilles (1¼hr., 6 per day, 94F/€14.35); Nîmes (30min., 14 per day, 47F/€7.20); Paris (TGV 3½hr., 21 per day, 377-425F/€57.50-64.80). **Buses** leave from bd. St-Roch, to the right of the train station for: Arles (45min., M-Sa 5 per day, 49F/€7.50); Marseilles (2hr., 4 per day, 97F/€14.80); Nîmes (1-1½hr., 5 per day, 45F/€6.90). From the train station, walk through the porte de la République to the cours Jean Jaurès to reach the **tourist office,** 41, cours Jean Jaurès (☎ 04 32 74 32 74; fax 04 90 82 95 03. Open July M-Sa 10am-8pm, Su 10am-5pm; Apr.-June and Aug.-Sept. M-Sa 9am-6pm; Oct.-Mar. M-F 9am-6pm, Sa 9am-1pm and 2-5pm, Su 10am-noon.) The **post office** is on cours Président Kennedy, near the porte de la République. (☎ 04 90 27 54 00. Open M-F 8am-7pm, Sa 8am-noon.) Take an **Internet** break at **Parole d'Hommes,** 46, r. des Lices. (☎ 04 90 86 98 08. 35F/€5.35 per hr. Open M-Sa 10am-9:30pm.) Avignon's hotels and *foyers* usually have room outside of festival season. The **Foyer YMCA/UCJG,** 7bis, chemin de la Justice, is across the river in Villeneuve. From the station, turn left and follow the city wall, cross pont Daladier and Ile Barthelasse, walk straight ahead, and turn left on chemin de la Justice; it will be up the hill on your left. Or, from the post office, take bus #10 (dir.: Les Angles-Grand Angles) to "Général Leclerc" or bus #11 (dir.: Villeneuve-Grand Terme) to "Pont d'Avignon." (☎ 04 90 25 46 20; fax 04 90 25 30 64. Reception 9:30am-noon and 1:30-6pm. *Demi-pension* obligatory in July. Apr.-Oct. 170/ €25.95 per person; 110F/€16.80 per person for 2 people; 100F/€15.25 per person for 3 people. AmEx/MC/V.) The **Hôtel Splendid,** 17, r. Perdiguier, near the tourist office, lives up to its name. (☎ 04 90 82 71 55; fax 04 90 85 64 86. Breakfast 28F/ €4.30. Reception 7am-10:30pm. Singles 170-240F/€25.95-36.60; doubles 240-300F/ €36.60-45.75. MC/V.) **Camp** at **Pont d'Avignon,** 300, Ile de la Barthelasse, 10min. past Foyer Bagatelle. (☎ 04 90 80 63 50; fax 04 90 85 22 12. Reception daily 8:30am-8:30pm; July-Aug. until 10:45pm. Open Mar. 27-Oct. 28. 43-87.50F/€6.60-13.35 per person with tent or car, 60-125F/€9.15-19.10 per couple with tent or car.) **Rue des Teinturiers** hosts a few lively restaurants. A **Petit Casino** supermarket is on r. St-Agricol. (Open M-F 8:30am-1pm and 3-8pm, Su 8a m-2pm.) **Postal Code:** 84000 (for *Poste Restante* specify "Poste-Restante-Avignon").

◫ **DAYTRIP FROM AVIGNON: THE VAUCLUSE.** The Vaucluse is where all those perfect postcards of Provence come from. Tiny medieval villages perch on rocky escarpments, fields of lavender stretch as far as the eye can see, and ochre hills burn in the sunset. This mini-Eden has been home and inspiration to writers from Petrarch to the Marquis de Sade to Samuel Beckett. The region is most accessible by car; **Voyages Arnaud buses** (☎ 04 90 38 15 58) run from Avignon to Fontaine de Vaucluse (55min., 3 per day, 26F/€4).

ARLES

The passionate *corridas* (bullfights) lured Picasso to Arles (pop. 35,000), while van Gogh spent two years (and an ear) here. The great Roman arena **Les Arènes** binds together Arles's distant past and bustling present, and is still used for bullfights. (20F/€3.05, students 15F/€2.30. Bullfights from 90F/€13.75.) The city's Roman past is revived in the **Musée d'Arles Antique,** av. de la 1er D.F.L. (☎ 04 90 18 88 88. Open Mar.-Oct. daily 9am-7pm; Nov.-Feb. 10am-5pm. 35F/€5.35, students 25F/€3.85, children 5F/€0.80.) At the **Fondation Van Gogh,** 26, Rond-Point des Arènes, you'll only find tributes to the master by artists, poets, and composers. (☎ 04 90 49 94 04. Open Apr. to mid-Oct. daily 10am-7pm; mid-Oct. to Mar. Tu-Su 9:30am-noon and 2-5:30pm. 30F/€4.60, students 20F/€3.05.) The contemporary **Musée Réattu,** r. du

FRANCE

Avignon

♦ ACCOMMODATIONS
Foyer YMCA/UCJG, 2
Hôtel Splendid, 7
Pont d'Avignon Camping, 1

🏛 MUSEUMS
Musée du Petit Palais, 5
Musée Calvet, 4
Musée Louis Vouland, 3
Musée Lapidaire, 6
Maison Jean Vilar, 8

N

0   200 yards
0   200 meters

PORTE ST-LAZARE

Université

Shakespeare
Bookshop & Tearoom

St. Symphorien

Église
de la
Visitation

r. P. Sain

Palais de
Justice

Les
Halles

PORTE ST-
JOSEPH

PORTE DE
LA LIGNE

Notre Dame
des Doms

Rocher
des Doms

Palais
des
Papes

Pont St-Bénézet

Le Rhône

Ile de la Barthelasse

VILLENEUVE

Esplanade
St. Bénézet

PORTE DE
L'OULLE

PORTE ST-
DOMINIQUE

PORTE THIERS

PORTE
LIMBERT

PORTE
MAGNANEN

PORTE ST-
MICHEL

Parole
d'Hommes

Laundromat

PORTE DE LA
RÉPUBLIQUE

cours Jean Jaurès

cours JFK

PORTE
ST-CHARLES

PORTE
ST-ROCH

r. du Rempart St-Dominique

bd. Limbert

FRANCE

TO 2 (1.5km)
1 (1km)

Grand Prieuré, houses 57 drawings with which Picasso honored Arles in 1971. (Open Apr.-Sept. daily 10am-noon and 2-6:30pm; Oct.-Mar. reduced hours. 30F/€4.60, students 25F/€3.85.) Among Arles' many colorful *provençal* festivals is the **Fête d'Arles,** during the last weekend in June and first weekend in July, when bonfires blaze in the streets and the locals wear traditional costume.

Trains leave av. P. Talabot for: Avignon (30min., 15-19 per day, 36F/€5.50); Marseilles (1hr., 8 per day, 76F/€11.60); Montpellier (1hr., 6-7 per day, 76F/€11.60); Nîmes (30min., 7-15 per day, 42F/€6.40). To get to the **tourist office,** esplanade Charles de Gaulle, on bd. des Lices, turn left from the station, walk to pl. Lamartine, turn left and follow bd. Emile Courbes to the big intersection by the tower, and then turn right on bd. des Lices. (☎04 90 18 41 20; fax 04 90 18 41 29. Open Apr.-Sept. daily 9am-6:45pm; Oct.-Mar. M-Sa 9am-5:45pm, Su 10am-2:30pm.) To get from the tourist office to the **Auberge de Jeunesse (HI),** 20, av. Maréchal Foch, backtrack to bd. des Lices and cross it, continue down to av. des Alyscamps, and follow the signs. (☎04 90 96 18 25; fax 04 90 96 31 26. Sheets and breakfast included. Reception 7-10am and 5-11pm. Curfew 11pm; midnight in summer. Dorms 82F/€12.50 1st night, 70F/€11 thereafter.) The cheerful and warm **Hôtel Gauguin** is at 5, pl. Voltaire (☎04 90 96 14 35; fax 04 90 18 98 87. Doubles 180-210F/€27.45-32.05; 2 beds with bath 220F/€33.55; triples 260F/€39.65. MC/V.) **Monoprix supermarket,** on pl. Lamartine, is near the station. (Open M-Sa 8:30am-7:30pm.) Cafes in **Place du Forum** or **Place Voltaire,** pulse with music and lights. **Postal Code:** 13200.

▣ DAYTRIP FROM ARLES: THE CAMARGUE. Pink flamingos, black bulls, and the famous white Camargue horses roam freely across this protected wild marshland between Arles and the Mediterranean coast. Stop at the **Centre d'Information de Ginès,** along D570, for information. (☎04 90 97 86 32. Open Apr.-Sept. daily 10am-5:30pm; Oct.-Mar. Sa-Th 9:30am-5pm.) Stroll through the nearby **Parc Ornithologique de Pont de Gau** for views of birds and grazing bulls. (☎04 90 97 82 62. Open Apr.-Sept. daily 9am-dusk; Oct.-Mar. 10am-dusk. 36F/€5.50, children 18F/€2.75.) Call the **Association Camarguaise de Tourisme Equestre** (☎04 90 97 86 32) for information on horseback riding. Other options include jeep safaris (☎04 66 70 09 65; 2hr. trips 200F/€30.50, 4hr. trips 220F/€33.55) and boat trips (☎04 90 97 84 72; 1½hr., 3-4 per day, 60F/€9.15), which leave from Stes-Maries, Arles, or Aigues-Mortes. Bicycle trails may be difficult to ride. Trail maps are available from the **tourist office** in Stes-Maries-de-la-Mer at 5, av. Van Gogh. (☎04 90 97 82 55. Open daily July-Aug. 9am-8pm; Apr.-June reduced hours.) **Buses** (☎04 90 96 36 25) run from Arles to **Stes-Maries-de-la-Mer,** the Camargue's largest town (1hr., 4-6 per day, 39F/€5.95).

AIX-EN-PROVENCE

Famous for its festivals, fountains, and being the former home of Paul Cézanne and Victor Vasarely, Aix (pop. 150,000) panders to tourists without being spoiled by them. The **Chemin de Cézanne,** 9, av. Paul Cézanne, features a self-guided walking tour devoted to the artist, including his studio. (☎04 42 21 06 53. Open July-Aug. daily 10am-6:30pm; Apr.-May and Sept. 10am-noon and 2:30-6pm; Oct.-Mar. 10am-noon and 2-5pm. In summer 35F/€5.35; in winter 25F/€3.85; students, children, and seniors 10F/€1.55.) The **Fondation Vasarely,** av. Marcel-Pagnol, in Jas-de-Bouffan, designed by artist Victor Vasarely, is a must-see for modern art fans. (☎04 42 20 01 09. Open July-Sept. daily 10am-7pm; Oct.-May daily 10am-1pm and 2-6pm. 40F/€6.10, students 25F/€3.85.) **Cathédrale St-Sauveur,** r. Gaston de Saporta, on pl. de l'Université, is a dramatic mix of Romanesque, Gothic, and Baroque carvings and reliefs. (☎04 42 23 45 65. Open daily 8am-noon and 2-6pm.) Aix's **International Music Festival,** June through July, features operas and concerts. (☎04 42 17 34 34; www.aix-en-provence.com/festartlyrique. Tickets 100-350F/€15.25-53.40.) Aix also hosts a two-week **dance festival** (☎04 42 23 41 24; tickets 90-250F/€13.75-38.15, students 50-160F/€7.65-24.40). The **Office des Fêtes**

et de la Culture, Espace Forbin, 1, pl. John Rewald (☎ 04 42 63 06 75), has festival information. Bars and clubs line **Rue Verrerie.** House and club music pulsate at **Le Richelm,** 24, r. de la Verrerie. (☎ 04 42 23 49 29. Cover includes 1 drink: Tu-Th 60F/ €9.15, women free; F 80F/€12.20; Sa 100F/€15.25. Open Tu-Sa 11:30pm-dawn.) **Bistro Aixois,** 37, cours Sextius, off La Rotonde, packs in students. (☎ 04 42 27 50 10. Open daily 6:30pm-3 or 4am.)

Trains, at the end of av. Victor Hugo, off. r. Gustave Desplace, run almost exclusively from Marseilles (35min., 21 per day, 38F/€5.80). **Buses** (☎ 04 42 91 26 80), av. de l'Europe, run to Avignon (2hr., M-Sa 5 per day, 86F/€13.15) and Marseilles (30min., almost every 10min., 26F/€4). From the train station, follow av. Victor Hugo, bearing left at the fork, until it feeds into La Rotonde. On the left is the **tourist office,** 2, pl. du Général de Gaulle, which books rooms for free, sells a city museum pass (40-60F/€6.10-9.15), and stocks maps and guides. (☎ 04 42 16 11 61; fax 04 42 16 11 62. Open July-Aug. daily 8:30am-10pm; Sept.-June M-Sa 8:30am-10pm, Su 10am-6pm.) You can surf the **Internet** at **Millenium,** 6, r. Maz-arine, off cours Mirabeau. (☎ 04 42 27 39 11. 20F/€3.05 per hr. Open daily 10am-2am.) The excellent **Hôtel du Globe,** 74, cours Sextius, is 5min. from *centre ville.* (☎ 04 42 26 03 58; fax 04 42 26 13 68. Breakfast 49F/€8. Singles 180F/€27.45, with bath 200-298F/€30.50-45.55; doubles 298-335F/€45.55-51.10, 335-360F/€51.10-54.90; triples 389/€59.30, 399F/€60.85; quads 448F/€68.30.) **Hôtel des Arts,** 69, bd. Carnot, has compact modern rooms. (☎ 04 42 38 11 77; fax 04 42 26 77 31. Breakfast 28F/€4.30. Singles and doubles 149-205F/€22.75-31.25. MC/V.) To **camp** at **Arc-en-Ciel,** on rte. de Nice, take bus #3 from La Rotonde to "Trois Sautets" or "Val St-André." (☎ 04 42 26 14 28. 36F/€5.50 per person, 32F/€4.90 per tent site.) The roads north of **Cours Mirabeau** and **Rue Verrerie,** off Cordiliers, are packed with reasonable restaurants. Choose from three **Petit Casinos supermarkets** at 3, cours d'Orbitelle (open M-Sa 8am-1pm and 4-8pm); 16, r. Italie (open M-Sa 8am-1pm and 4:30pm-8pm, Su 8:30am-12:45pm); and 5, r. Sapora (open M and W-Sa 8:30am-7:30pm). **Postal Code:** 13100.

MARSEILLES (MARSEILLE)

France's third-largest city, Marseilles (pop. 900,000) is like the *bouillabaisse* dish for which it is famous: steaming hot and pungently spiced, with a little bit of every-thing mixed in. A mix of wild nightclubs, beaches, islands, gardens, and big-city adventure, Marseilles bites its thumb at the manicured nails of Monaco and struts a true, gritty urban intensity that can overwhelm the solo traveler.

▐ TRANSPORTATION

Flights: Aéroport Marseille-Provence (☎ 04 42 14 14 14). Flights to **Lyon** and **Paris.** Buses connect airport to Gare St-Charles (3 per hr., 5:30am-9:50pm, 50F/€7.65).

Trains: Gare St-Charles, pl. Victor Hugo (☎ 08 36 35 35 35). M: Gare St-Charles. To: **Lyon** (3½hr., 2-3 per day, 213F/€32.50); **Nice** (2¾hr., 13 per day, 152F/€23.20); **Paris** (4¾hr., 17 TGVs per day, 406-496F/€61.90-75.65).

Buses: Gare des Autocars, pl. Victor Hugo (☎ 04 91 08 16 40), half a block from the train station. M: Gare St-Charles. Open M-Sa 6:15am-7pm, Su 6-9am and 3-5:50pm. To: **Avignon** (2hr., 4 per day, 92F/€14.05); **Cannes** (2¼-3hr., 4 per day, 100F/ €15.25); **Nice** (2¾hr., 1 per day, 140F/€21.35).

Ferries: SNCM, 61, bd. des Dames (☎ 08 91 70 18 01). Ferries to **Corsica** (640-720F/ €97.60-109.80; 12% student discount) and **Sardinia** (750-850F/€114.35-129.60).

Local Transportation: RTM, 6-8, r. des Fabres (☎ 04 91 91 92 10). Tickets sold at bus and metro stations (Day pass 25F/€3.85; 7-14 voyages **Carte Liberté** 50-100F/ €7.65-15.25). **Metro** runs M-Th 5am-9pm and F-Su 5am-12:30am.

Taxis: (☎ 04 91 02 20 20). 24hr. 100-150F/€15.25-22.90 train station to hostels.

FRANCE

✦ ORIENTATION AND PRACTICAL INFORMATION

Although the city is divided into 16 *arrondissements*, Marseilles is understood by locals and visitors alike by neighborhood names and major streets. **La Canebière** divides the city into north and south, funneling into the **vieux port**, with its upscale restaurants and nightlife, to the east. North of the *vieux port*, working-class residents pile onto the hilltop neighborhood of **Le Panier**, east of which lies **Quartier Belsunce**, the hub of the city's Arab and African communities. While both the bus and train stations are near this dangerous quarter, atop bd. Athènes, staying on major streets can reduce risk of danger. The areas around the **Opéra** and r. Curiol are meeting grounds for prostitutes; be cautious after dark. A few blocks to the southeast, **Cours Julien** has a younger, countercultural feel to it. Both **metro** lines go to the train station; line #1 (blue) goes to the *vieux port*. The thorough **bus** system is essential to get to beaches, stretching along the coast southwest of the *vieux port*.

> ❗ Every woman who has traveled on the Riviera has a story to tell about men in the big beach towns. Unsolicited pick-up techniques range from subtle invitations to more, uh, bare displays of interest. Brush them off with a biting *"laissez-moi tranquille!"* ("leave me alone") or stony indifference, but don't be shy about enlisting the help of passersby or the police to fend off Mediterranean Don Juans. Don't venture far from the lively streets near the *Vieux Port* after dark. The areas around the quartier Belsunce and the bd. d'Athènes are also dangerous at night.

Tourist office: 4, La Canebière (☎ 04 91 13 89 00; fax 04 91 13 89 20). From the train station, descend the stairs and follow bd. Athènes, which becomes bd. Dugommier, and turn right on La Canebière. Open July-Aug. M-Sa 9am-8pm, Su 10am-6pm; Oct.-June M-Sa 9am-7pm, Su 10am-5pm. Annex (☎ 04 91 50 59 18) at the train station. Open daily 10am-6pm; weekends closed 3-4pm.

Currency exchange: La Bourse, 3, pl. Général de Gaulle (☎ 04 91 13 09 00). Good rates and no commission. Open M-F 8:30am-6:30pm, Sa 9am-5pm.

Police: 2, r. du Commissaire Becker (☎ 04 91 39 80 00). Also in the train station on esplanade St-Charles (☎ 04 91 14 29 97).

Internet: Info Café, 1, quai Rive Neuve (☎ 04 91 33 53 05). Open M-Sa 9am-10pm, Su 2:30-7:30pm. 25F/€3.85 per hr.

Post Office: 1, pl. Hôtel des Postes (☎ 04 91 15 47 20). Follow La Canebière toward the sea, and turn right onto r. Reine Elisabeth as it becomes pl. Hôtel des Postes. Address mail to be held: FirstName SURNAME, *Poste Restante*, 1, pl. Hotel des Postes, **13001** Marseille, France. **Postal Code:** 13001.

🏠 ACCOMMODATIONS

Marseilles has many cheap hotels but few reputable ones. Hotels listed here prioritize safety and location. Both hostels are far from the town center, but there is frequent, if time-consuming, bus service.

Auberge de Jeunesse Bonneveine (HI), impasse Bonfils (☎ 04 91 17 63 30; fax 04 91 73 97 23), off av. J. Vidal. Take Métro line #2 to "Rond-Point du Prado," and transfer to bus #44 to pl. Bonnefon. Then walk back toward the rotary, turn left at J. Vidal, and turn onto impasse Bonfils; it will be on the left. Breakfast included. 6-night max. stay. Reception daily 7am-1am. Reserve ahead. **HI members only.** Closed Dec. 22-Feb. Apr.-Aug. dorms 72-83F/€11-12.65; doubles 93-103F/€14.20-15.70; Sept.-Dec. and Feb.-Mar. dorms 67-78F/€10.25-11.90; doubles 93-98F/€14.20-14.95. MC/V.

Auberge de Jeunesse Chateau de Bois-Luzy (HI), allée des Primevères (☎/fax 04 91 49 06 18). By day, take bus #6 from cours J. Thierry at the top of La Canebière (away from the *port*) to "Marius Richard." Then turn right onto bd. de l'Amandiere and follow the road down to the right and around the soccer fields to reach the hostel. Night bus T also runs from "La Canebière" to "Marius Richard" at 9:10 and 9:50pm. Reception daily

Marseille

▲ ACCOMMODATIONS
Auberge de Jeunesse Bonneveine, 8
Auberge de Jeunesse Chateau de Bois-Luzy, 1
Hôtel Béarn, 7
Hôtel du Palais, 6
🍴 FOOD
Country Life, 5
O'Provençal Pizzeria, 2
♪ NIGHTCLUBS
Le Scandale, 4
Trolleybus, 3

bd. de la Blancarde
av. Marechal
CINQ AVENUES LONGCHAMP
To ↑ (4.5 km)
r. du Camas
r. Monte Cristo
bd. Chave
Palais Longchamp / Musée des Beaux-Arts
bd. Longchamp
bd. de la Libération
bd. Eugène Pierre
BAILLE
bd. National
bd. des Abeilles
r. St-Savournin
crs. St-Pierre
r. Château
r. de la Loublière Payan
r. de Lodi
av. Toulon
To 8 (5 km)
NOTRE DAME DU MONT-COURS JULIEN
PL. JEAN JAURÈS
bd. Baille
av. C. Canini
CANEBIÈRE REFORMES
SQ. STALINGRAD
crs. Gambetta
La Canebière
allées
r. de la liberté
bd. d'Athènes
bd. d' Athènes
Gare St-Charles
PL. DES MARSEILLAISES
bd. Voltaire
bd. Garibaldi
cours Lieutaud
cours Lieutaud
rue de Rome
av. du Prado
PL. CASTELLANE
CASTELLANE
Dr. Escat
PL. VICTOR HUGO ST-CHARLES
bd. M. Bourdet
r. d'Aix
r. des Dominicains
r. du Bois
C. Nédélec
bd. Dugommier
PL. DE ROME
r. Div. Flotte
r. Longue des Capucins
r. de Rome
r. d'Aubagne
r. St-Ferréol
Musée Cantini
ESTRANGIN PRÉFECTURE
r. Paradis
r. Breteuil
bd. Vauban
PL. JULES GUESDE
JULES GUESDE
COLBERT
PL. SADI CARNOT
Ste-barbe
barbusse
cours Belsunce
Pavillon
r. Grignan
r. du Dragon
r. Sylvabelle
r. de la Joliette
r. de la République
CORDERIE
H.
quai des Belges
PL. DU GAL DE GAULLE
cours J. Ballard
r. Fortia
crs. Pierre Puget
bd. Notre Dame
bd. André Aune
Basilique de Notre Dame de la Garde
JOLIETTE
bd. des Dames
R.J.F. Leca
r. du Panier
La Vieille Charité
r. de l'Evêché
VIEUX PORT-HÔTEL DE VILLE
r. de la Loge
r. Caisserie
r. Sainte
quai de Rive Neuve
PL. DE LA CORDERIE
bd. de la Corderie
r. de Breteuil
av. R. Schumann
M. Mazenod
quai de la Joliette
Cathédrale Nouvelle Major
SQ. PROTIS
quai de la Tourette
quai du Port
Vieux Port
Tunnel
Abbaye St-Victor
r. du Coteau
Bassin de la Grande Joliette
quai Jean Charcot
Jardin du Pharo
bd. Charles Livon
av. Pasteur
PL. DU 4 SEPTEMBRE
r. Chateaubriand
r. du Château Brun
ch. du Roucas Blanc
r. des Catalans
av. de la Corse
corniche Pres. J. F. Kennedy
Mediterranean Sea

500 yards
500 meters
N

FRANCE

7:30-noon and 5-10:30pm. Strict curfew May-Oct. 11pm; Nov.-Apr. 10:30pm. **HI members only.** Dorms 48F/€7.35; singles 70F/€10.70; doubles 55F/€8.40. Cash only.

Hôtel du Palais, 26, r. Breteuil (☎04 91 37 78 86; fax 04 91 37 91 19). Large air-conditioned and quiet rooms near the *vieux port.* Breakfast 30F/€4.60. Singles 195F/€29.75; doubles 230F/€35.10; triples 280F/€42.70, with bath 300F/€45.75. MC/V.

Hôtel Béarn, 63, r. Sylvabelle (☎04 91 37 75 83; fax 04 91 81 54 98), on a quiet sidestreet near from the port. Breakfast 25F/€3.85. Singles and doubles 110-140F/€16.80-21.35, with bath 210F/€32.05; triples 260F/€39.65. MC/V.

🍴 FOOD

For the city's famed seafood and North African fare, explore the *vieux port,* especially **Place Thiers** and **Cours d'Estienne d'Orves,** where one can eat *al fresco* for as little as 60F/€9.15. For a more artsy crowd and cheaper fare, head up to **Cours Julien,** northeast of the harbor. You can pick up groceries at **Monoprix supermarket,** on La Canebière, across from the AmEx office. (Open M-Sa 8:30am-8:30pm.)

O'Provençal Pizzeria, 7, r. de la Palud (☎04 91 54 03 10), off r. de Rome. Quickly serves up the best pizza in Marseilles. Open M-Sa 10am-3pm and 7pm-midnight.

Country Life, 14, r. Venture (☎04 96 11 28 00), off r. Paradis. All-you-can-eat vegan food. *Menu* 62F/€9.45, students 38F/€5.80. Open M-F 11:30am-2:30pm.

👁 SIGHTS

Marseilles in all its glory can be seen from the steps of the **Basilique de Notre Dame de la Garde.** Its golden statue of Madonna, affectionately known as *"la bonne mère,"* towers 230m above the city. From the tourist office, walk up r. Breteuil, turn left on r. Grignon as it becomes bd. de la Corderie, turn left on bd. Andre Aune, and climb up the stairs. (☎04 91 13 40 80. Open 7am-8pm, off-season 7am-7pm. Free.) The chilling catacombs of the fortified **Abbaye St-Victor,** on r. Sainte at the end of quai de Rive Neuve, contain an array of pagan and Christian relics including the remains of 3rd-century martyrs. (☎04 96 11 22 60. Open daily 8:30am-6:30pm. Crypts 10F/€1.55.) Take a boat out to the **Château D'If,** the sunblasted dungeon immortalized in Dumas' *Count of Monte Cristo,* or explore the windswept quarantine island of **Île Frioul.** (Boats ☎04 91 55 50 09. Depart from quai des Belges (20min., both islands 80F/€12.20). Château ☎04 91 59 02 30. Open Apr.-Sept. daily 9:30am-6:30pm; Oct.-Mar. Tu-Su 9:30am-5:30pm. 26F/€4, under 25 16F/€2.45.) The remains of the original port of Marseilles rest peacefully in the **Jardin des Vestiges.** Your ticket to the garden also admits you to the **Musée d'Histoire de Marseille.** (Gardens open Mar.-Nov. M-Sa noon-7pm; Dec.-Feb. noon-6pm. Entrance inside the Centre Bourse mall. Museum ☎04 91 90 42 22. 12F/€1.85, students 6F/€0.95.) Also worth a visit is **La Vieille Charite,** 2, r. de la Charite, an old poorhouse and orphanage that now shelters Egyptian, prehistoric, and classical collections. (☎04 91 14 58 80. Open June-Sept. W-M 11am-6pm; Oct.-May Tu-Su 10am-5pm. Temporary exhibits 18F/€2.75, permanent exhibits 12F/€1.85.) Bus #83 (dir.: Rond-Point du Prado) takes you from the *vieux port* to Marseilles's **public beaches.** Catch it on the waterfront side of the street and get off just after it rounds the statue of David (20-30min.). Both **Plage du Prado** and **Plage de la Corniche** offer wide beaches, clear water, and plenty of grass for impromptu soccer matches.

🔊 NIGHTLIFE

Despite Marseilles's reputation for seediness, you need only to be as cautious as in any major city, plus some. Try not to end up in the outer areas of the city since public transport closes at 9pm. People watching and nightlife center around **Place Thiers** and **Cours Julien.** Local and international DJs spin at **Trolleybus,** 24, quai de Rive Neuve, a mega-club in an 18th-century warehouse. (☎04 91 54 30 45. Beer

FRANCE

from 30F/€4.60, drinks 40F/€6.10. Sa cover 60F/€9.15 includes 1 drink. Open in summer W-Sa 11pm-7am; winter Th-Sa 11pm-7am.) The vibrant **Le Scandale,** 16, quai de Rive Neuve, is packed with locals and travelers. (☎04 91 54 46 85. Pints for 30F/€4.60. Happy Hour 6-10:30pm. Open daily 1pm-5am.) The friendly **L'Enigme,** 22, r. Beauvau, is one of the few gay/lesbian places around. (☎04 91 33 79 20. Before 10pm drinks 10F/€1.55; after 10pm 30F/€4.60. Open daily 7:30pm-2am.)

⚡ DAYTRIPS FROM MARSEILLES

CASSIS. Twenty-three kilometers from Marseilles is the charming resort town of Cassis. Follow the signs to the **Calanque de Port-Pin,** 1hr. east of town. From there it's a 30min. hike to the popular **En Vau** *calanque* and beach. A **bus** runs from Marseilles to Cassis (1hr.; 3 per day, in winter ask at bus station; 20F/€3.05). Two blocks down from the bus stop, turn right into the Jardin Public. The **tourist office** is on the left as you leave the park. (☎04 42 01 71 17; fax 04 42 01 28 31. Open July-Aug. daily 9am-7pm; Sept.-June reduced hours.) The **Auberge de Jeunesse de la Fontasse (HI),** 20km from Marseilles, off D559 near En Vau, is a sweaty 4km climb from the Cassis tourist office (1hr.). From Cassis's port, follow signs for the *calanques* and when the road ends at a fork, take the steep right path and look for signs engraved in rocks. (☎04 42 01 02 72. Reception daily 8-10am and 5-11pm. Closed Jan.-Feb. **HI members only.** Reserve ahead. Dorms 52F/€7.95.)

AIX-EN-PROVENCE. Just 35min. away is festive Aix-en-Provence, the cultural capital of Provence (see p. 348).

FRENCH RIVIERA. Mug for the camera at **Cannes** (see p. 354), toss some dice at the **Monte-Carlo casino** in **Monaco** (see p. 361), or just hit one of the beaches.

FRENCH RIVIERA (CÔTE D'AZUR)

Between Marseilles and the Italian border, sun-drenched beaches and warm waters of the Mediterranean form the backdrop for this fabled playground of the rich and famous—F. Scott Fitzgerald, Cole Porter, Picasso, Renoir, and Matisse all flocked to the coast in its heyday. The area today is crammed with as many budget tourists as high-flying millionaires, but the Riviera's seductive loveliness has been its undoing, as shrewd developers have turned the coast's beauty into big business.

ST-TROPEZ

Nowhere are the glitz and glamour of the Riviera more apparent than in the former fishing hamlet of St-Tropez. Though named after the Tuscan saint Saint Tropez, *St-Trop d'Aise* (Saint-Too-Much-Luxury) religiously devotes itself to the holy trinity of sun, sand, and big boats. For the ultimate Tropezian tan, visitors should head to the famed **Pampelonne** beachline (the "Capon-Pinet" stop on the free shuttle), where exclusive beach clubs alternate with public stretches of sand. Most beaches expect you to bask *au naturel*—tan lines mean you just arrived. The **chemin des Graniers** curves around the **citadel,** home to the **Musée Naval,** which chronicles the town's military history. (☎04 94 97 59 43. Open daily 10am-6pm; in winter 10am-noon and 1-5pm; closed Nov. Adults 25F/€3.85, students 15F/€2.30.) The path then leads to the small, uncrowded **Plage des Graniers,** the perfect picnic spot.

Sodetrav **buses** (☎04 94 97 88 51) head to St-Tropez from St-Raphaël (2hr., 8-14 per day, 55F/€8.40). The fastest, nicest, and (with a Fréjus hostel voucher) cheapest way to get St-Tropez is by **boat.** At the old port, Les Bateaux de St-Raphaël (☎04 94 95 17 46) sails in from St-Raphaël (1hr.; July-Aug. 2-5 per day; 60F/€9.15, round-trip 110F/€16.80). While the beaches make up much of St-Tropez's appeal, transportation logistics can be frustrating. A **free shuttle** *(navette municipale),* which leaves from the pl. des Lices, is the only source of public transportation to **Les Salins** and **Plage Tahiti** (4 per day). The **tourist office,** on quai Jean Jaurès, is on

FRANCE

the waterfront. (☎ 04 94 97 45 21; www.saint-tropez.st. Open July-Aug. daily 9:30am-1:30 pm and 3:30-10pm; May-June and Sept. 9:30am-1pm and 2-7pm; Oct.-Apr. 9am-noon and 2-6pm.) The closest youth hostel is in Fréjus (see below). A reasonable and convenient hotel in St-Tropez is **La Méditerranée**, 21, bd. Louis Blanc. From the dock or bus station, walk to av. Général Leclerc and turn left; it will be on your right. (☎ 04 94 97 00 44; fax 04 94 97 47 83. Breakfast 40F/€6.10. Closed mid-Nov. to mid-Mar. Singles 250F/€38.15; doubles 320F/€48.80, with bath 350-450F/€53.40-68.60; triples 500F/€76.25; quads 620F/€94.55. AmEx/MC/V.) **Camp** at **Les Prairies de la Mer** in Port Grimaud. (☎ 04 94 79 09 09; fax 04 94 79 09 10. Open Apr.-Oct. 82F/€12.50 per person and tent, 84F/€12.80 per couple, 115F/€17.55 per car.) Skip the swanky restaurants for the snack shops; try **Basilic Burger**, pl. des Remparts, for fresh salads and juicy hamburgers. (☎ 04 94 97 29 09. Open July-Aug. 9am-11:30pm; Sept.-June 9am-9pm. Cash only.) A **Prisunic supermarket** is at 7, av. du Général Leclerc. (Open M-Sa 8am-8pm, Su 9am-1pm.) The hippest bar for cosmopolitan youth is **Le Loft**, 9, r. des Remparts. (☎ 04 94 97 60 50. Open daily 9:30pm-3am.)

ST-RAPHAËL AND FRÉJUS

While Fréjus's fascinating Roman ruins have given it the nickname "Pompeii of Provence," its twin city of St-Raphaël is only good as a cheap base from which to visit St-Tropez. The Romans left their stamp with an **amphitheater**, in Fréjus on r. Henri Vadon. (Open Apr.-Oct. M and W-Sa 10am-1pm and 2:30-6:30pm; Nov.-Mar. M and W-F 10am-noon and 1:30-5:30pm, Sa 9:30am-12:30pm and 1:30-5:30pm.) St-Raphaël is a major stop on the coastal train line and gets most of the traffic. The city sends **trains** from the pl. de la Gare to Cannes (25min., 34F/€5.20) and Nice (1hr., 57F/€8.70). **Buses** leave from behind the train station in St-Raphaël for: Cannes (1¼hr., 8 per day, 35F/€5.35); Fréjus (30min., every 30min., 7F/€1.10); St-Tropez (1½hr., 10 per day, 55F/€8.40). The **tourist office** is opposite the train station. (☎ 04 94 19 52 52; www.saintraphael.com. Open July-Aug. daily 9am-8pm; Sept.-June M-Sa 9am-12:30pm and 2-6:30pm.) Take bus #6 from St-Raphaël to pl. Paul Vernet to get to the **tourist office** in **Fréjus**, 325, r. Jean Jaurès. (☎ 04 94 19 52 52; fax 04 94 83 85 40; www.ville-frejus.fr. Open daily 9am-7pm; Sept.-June M-Sa 9am-noon and 2-6pm.) From the station in St-Raphaël, exit onto bd. Felix Martin and take the second left onto av. Paul Doumer for the **Hôtel des Pyramides**, 77, av. Paul Doumer. (☎ 04 98 11 10 10; fax 04 98 11 10 20; www.saint-raphael.com/pyramides. Open mid-Mar. to mid-Nov. Singles 150F/€22.90; doubles 220-345F/€33.55-52.60; triples 340F/€51.85; quads 400F/€61. Extra bed 80F/€12.20. MC/V.) Take av. du 15ème Corps d'Armée from the tourist office in Fréjus, and turn left on chemin de Councillier after the next roundabout to reach the **Auberge de Jeunesse de St-Raphaël-Fréjus (HI)**, chemin du Counillier. (☎ 04 94 52 93 93; fax 04 94 53 25 86. Breakfast included. Curfew Sept.-June 10:30pm, July-Aug. midnight. 4- to 8-bed dorms 75F/€11.4. **Camping:** 40F/€6.10 per person with tent.) **Postal Codes:** St-Raphaël 83700; Fréjus 83600.

CANNES

With its renowned annual film festival in May, the **Festival International du Film**, Cannes (pop. 78,000) has more associations with stardom than any other place on the coast. None of the festival's 350 screenings are open to the public, but the sidewalk show is free. Yet for the other 11 months, Cannes is one of the most accessible of the Riviera's glam-towns. A palm-lined boardwalk, gorgeous sandy beaches, and innumerable boutiques ensure that anyone can sport the famous Cannes style. The best window-shopping along the Riviera lies along **Rue d'Antibes** and **Boulevard de la Croisette**. Farther west, the **Eglise de la Castre** and its courtyard stand on the hill on which *vieux Cannes* was built. Of Cannes's three **casinos**, the most accessible is **Le Casino Croisette**, 1, jetée Albert Edouard, next to the Palais des Festivals, with slots, blackjack, and roulette. (Gambling daily 7:30pm-4am; open for slots at 10am. No shorts, jeans, or t-shirts. 18+ with ID.) You can also lose your shirt dancing until dawn at Cannes's favorite discothèque, **Jane's**, at 38, r. des Serbes. (Cover Th 60F/€9.15, F-Su 100F/€15.25; includes 1st drink. Open Th-Su 11pm-dawn.) The centrally located **Cat Corner,** 22, r. Macé, is a magnet for Cannes' coolest. DJs spin house, R&B, and funk. (Cover 100F/€15.25. Open daily 11:30pm-5am.)

Coastal **trains** depart from 1, r. Jean-Jaurès, to: Antibes (15min., 14F/€2.15); Marseilles (2hr., 100F/€15.25); Monaco (1hr., 46F/€7.05); Nice (35min., 32F/€4.90); St-Raphaël (25min., 34F/€5.20). The **tourist office,** 1, bd. de la Croisette, helps find accommodations. (☎ 04 93 39 24 53; www.cannes-online.com. Open July-Aug. daily 9am-8pm; Sept.-June M-F 9am-6:30pm, Sa 9am-6:30pm, Su 10am-6pm.) **Branch** office at the train station. (Open M-F 9am-noon and 2-6pm.) Access the **Internet** at **Cyber Café Institut Riviera Langue,** 26, r. de Mimont. (35F/€5.35 per hr. Open daily 9am-10pm.) Hostels are 10-20min. farther from the beach than other lodgings, but are the cheapest options in town. The **Centre International de Séjour de Cannes (HI),** 35, av. de Vallauris, is only 10min. from the train station. To avoid the underground passageway, leave the station and turn left on bd. Jean-Jaurès, left on bd. de la République, and right on av. de Vallauris. (☎ 04 93 99 26 79; fax 04 93 99 26 79; www.perso.wanadoo.fr/hostelling-cannes. Reception 8am-12:30pm and 2:30-10:30pm. Curfew 2am. Dorms 70-80F/€10.70-12.20.) **Hotel Mimont,** 39, r. de Mimont, is two streets behind the train station, off bd. de la République. (☎ 04 93 39 51 64; fax 04 93 99 65 35. Singles 170-190F/€25.95-29; doubles 230-260F/€35.10-39.65; triples 325F/€49.55. AmEx/MC/V.) **Camp** at **Parc Bellevue,** 67, av. M. Chevalier, in La Bocca. Take the #9 bus to the La Boissière stop (30min.) and walk for 100m; it's on the right. (☎ 04 93 47 28 97. 60F/€9.15 per person and tent, 80-90F/€12.20-13.75 per couple with tent; 10F/€1.55 per car.) Save money at **Monoprix supermarket,** in Champion, 6, r. Meynadier. (Open M-Sa 9am-7:30pm.) Reasonably priced restaurants abound in the pedestrian zone around **Rue Meynadier. Postal Code:** 06400.

ANTIBES-JUAN-LES-PINS

Although officially joined under one name, Antibes-Juan-Les-Pins (pop. 75,000), Antibes and Juan-Les-Pins are 2km apart, with separate train stations and tourist offices. Blessed with beautiful beaches and a charming *vieille ville,* **Antibes** remains less touristy than Nice and more relaxed than St-Tropez. The **Musée Picasso,** in the Château Grimaldi, on pl. Mariejol, displays works by the master and his contemporaries. (☎ 04 92 90 54 20. Open June-Sept. Tu-Th and Sa-Su 10am-6pm, F 10am-10pm; Oct.-May Tu-Su 10am-noon and 2-6pm. 30F/€4.60, students 15F/€2.30.) **Musée Peynet,** pl. Nationale, has over 300 colorful *naïf* drawings by local artist Raymond Peynet. (☎ 04 92 90 54 30. Open June-Sept. daily 10am-6pm; Oct.-May 10am-noon and 2-6pm. 20F/€3.05, students 10F/€1.55.) **Trains** leave av. Robert Soleau for: Cannes (15min., every 30min., 14F/€2.15); Marseilles (2½hr., 15 per day, 139F/€21.20); Nice (30min., every 30min., 22F/€3.35). **Buses** (station open M-F 8am-noon and 2-6pm, Sa 9am-12:30pm and 2-5pm) leave from pl. de Gaulle for: Cannes (25min., every 30min., 15F/€2.30) and Nice (40min., every 20min., 26.50F/€4.05). Exit the station, turn right on av. Robert Soleau, and follow the "Maison du Tourisme" signs to the **tourist office** at 11, pl. de Gaulle. (☎ 04 92 90 53 00. Open July-Aug. M-Sa 8:45am-7:30pm, Su 9:30am-12:30pm; Sept.-June M-F 9am-12:30pm and 2-6:30pm, Sa 9am-noon and 2-6pm.) For the far-away but beautiful **Relais International de la Jeunesse (Caravelle 60),** at the intersection of bd. de la Groupe and av. l'Antiquité, from Juan-Les-Pins walk south on bd. Edouard Baudoin, which becomes bd. du M. Juin, cross the peninsula on chemin des Ondes, turn right on bd. Francis Meillard, turn left on bd. de la Garoupe, following the signs for Juan-Les-Pins Bord de Mer. Or, take bus #2A (every 40min., 7.5F/€1.15) from the bus station at pl. Guynemer in Antibes. (☎/fax 04 93 61 34 40. Reception daily 8-10am and 6-11pm. No curfew. Dorms 75F/€11.45.)

Come summer, the young and hip **Juan-Les-Pins** is synonymous with wild nightlife. Boutiques remain open until midnight, cafes until 2am, and nightclubs until past dawn. **Discothèques** are generally open from 11pm to 5am. (Cover approx. 100F/€15.25, usually includes 1st drink.) **Pulp,** at av. Gallice, fills with a hip crowd. (Cover 100F/€15.25. F ladies free. Open July-Sept. daily midnight-5am; Oct.-June F-Sa midnight 5am.) **La Fourmi Rouge,** at 5, bd. de la Pinede, is a mini *boîte* that spins techno. (Cover 40F/€6.10. Open mid-June to Aug. daily 11pm-5am; Sept. to mid-

FRANCE

June Th-Sa 11pm-5am.) **Trains** depart av. l'Esterel for: Antibes (5min., until 12:50am, 7F/€1.10); Cannes (10min., 13F/€2); Nice (30min., 24F/€3.70). From the station, walk striaght on av. du Maréchal Joffre and turn right onto av. Guy de Maupassant for the **tourist office,** 2min. away on the right, at the intersection of av. Admiral Courbet and av. Gillaumont at 51, bd. Guillaumont. To get from Antibes's pl. du Général de Gaulle to Juan-Les-Pins on foot, follow bd. Wilson, which runs right into the center of town (about 1½km). Rather than make the post-party trek back to Antibes, crash at **Hôtel Trianon,** 14, av. de L'Estérel. (☎/fax 04 93 61 18 11. Breakfast 25F/€3.85. Singles 180F/€27.45; doubles 215-260F/€32.80-39.65; triples 260-280F/€39.65-42.70.) **Postal Codes:** 06600 (Antibes) and 06160 (Juan-Les-Pins).

NICE

Sun-drenched and spicy, Nice (pop. 345,892) is the unofficial capital of the Riviera. Its pumping nightlife, top-notch museums, and bustling beaches are unerring tourist magnets. During the annual three-week **Carnaval,** in the second half of February, visitors and *Niçois* alike ring in the spring with wild revelry, grotesque costumes, and raucous song and dance. Prepare to have more fun than you'll remember.

▉ TRANSPORTATION

Flights: Aéroport Nice-Côte d'Azur (☎04 93 21 30 30). **Air France,** 10, av. Félix Faure (☎08 02 80 28 02), serves **Paris** (1427F/€217.60, under 25 424F/€64.65).

Trains: Gare SNCF Nice-Ville (☎04 92 14 81 62), on av. Thiers. Info office open M-Sa 8am-6:30pm, Su 8:30-11:15am and 2-6pm. To: **Cannes** (35min., every 15-45min., 32F/€4.90); **Marseilles** (2¾hr., every 30-90min., 152F/€23.20); **Monaco** (25min., every 10-30min., 20F/€3.05); **Paris** (7hr., 2-3 per day, 484F/€73.80).

Buses: 5, bd. Jean Jaurès (☎04 93 85 61 81), left at the end of bd. Jean Medecin. Office open M-Sa 8am-6:30pm. To: **Cannes** (1½hr., 3 per hr., 37.50F/€5.75) and **Monaco** (40min., 4 per hr., 20F/€3.05).

Ferries: SNCM, quai du Commerce (☎04 93 13 66 66). Take bus #1 or 2 (dir.: Port) from pl. Masséna. Take bus #1 or 2 from pl. Masséna. To **Corsica** (see p. 362). Reservations daily from 8am-noon and 2-5:45pm. Dock open M-F 6am-7pm.

Public Transportation: Sunbus, 10, av. Félix Faure (☎04 93 16 52 10), near pl. Leclerc and pl. Masséna. Long treks to museums, the beach, and hostels make the 25F/€3.85 day pass, 55F/€8.40 10-ticket *carnet,* 85F/€13 5-day pass, or 110F/€16.80 7-day pass well worth it. Individual tickets 8.50F/€1.30. Ask the tourist office for the **Sunplan** bus map and **Guide Infobus** for schedules and route info.

Bike and Scooter Rental: JML Location, 34, av. Auber (☎04 93 16 07 00), opposite the train station. Bikes 70F/€10.70 per day, 301F/€45.90 per week; credit card deposit required. Open June-Sept. daily 8am-6:30pm; Oct.-May M-F 8am-1pm and 2-6:30pm, Sa 8am-1pm, Su 9am-1pm and 4-6:30pm.

✳❷ ORIENTATION AND PRACTICAL INFORMATION

As you exit the train station, **Avenue Jean-Médecin,** on the left, and **Boulevard Gambetta,** on the right, run directly to the beach. **Place Masséna** is 10min. down av. Jean-Médecin. Along the coast, **Promenade des Anglais** is a people watching paradise. To the southeast, past av. Jean Médecin and toward the bus station, is **Vieux Nice.** Women should not walk alone after sundown, and everyone should **exercise caution** at night around the train station, in *Vieux Nice,* and on the Promenade des Anglais.

Tourist Office: Av. Thiers (☎04 93 87 07 07; fax 04 93 16 85 16; www.nicetourism.com; www.nice-coteazur.org), by the train station. Makes same-day hotel reservations; best chance of getting a room are between 9 and 11am. Ask for *Nice: A Practical Guide, Museums and Churches of Nice,* and a map. Open June-Sept. M-Sa 8am-8pm, Su 9am-7pm; Oct-May M-Sa 8am-7pm. Hotel reservation service June-Sept. only.

Nice

ACCOMMODATIONS

Hôtel Au Picardy, **7**
Hôtel Baccarat, **3**
Hôtel Belle Meunière, **4**
Hôtel des Flandres, **2**
Hôtel Les Orangiers, **5**
Hôtel Little Massena, **9**
Hôtel Notre Dame, **6**
Hôtel Petit Trianon, **10**
Les Mimosas, **8**
Relais International de la
Jeunesse "Clairvallon", **1**

N

0   400 yards
0   400 meters

FRANCE

Baie des Anges

Port

CHÂTEAU

VIEUX NICE

Musée d'Art Moderne et Contemporain

Cathédrale Ste-Réparate

Palais Lascaris

St-Jacques

Palais de Justice

Opéra

Hôtel de Ville

MASSENA

Musée Masséna

Basilique Notre-Dame

American Express

Gare Nice-Ville

Gare du Sud

Musée Chagall

Cathédrale Russe

Musée des Beaux-Arts (Jules Cheret)

Université

St-Martin

PL. ST-FRANÇOIS

PL. WILSON

PL. GNL. DE GAULLE

PL. FRANKLIN

PL. ARSON

PL. MAX BAREL

PL. GUYNEMER

PL. MASSENA

Promenade des Anglais

Quai des États-Unis

TO (3km) MUSÉE MATISSE (1.2km)

TO (4km)

American Express

Consulates: Canada, 10, r. Lamartine (☎04 93 92 93 22). Open M-F 9am-noon. **UK,** Le Palace, 8, r. Alphonse Karr (☎04 93 82 32 04). Open M, W, and F 9:30-11:30am. **US,** 7, av. Gustave V (☎04 93 88 89 55). Open M-F 9-11:30am and 1:30-4:30pm.

Currency Exchange: Cambio, 17, av. Thiers (☎04 93 88 56 80). Opposite the train station. No commission. Open daily 7am-10pm.

American Express: 11, promenade des Anglais (☎04 93 16 53 53). At r. des Congrès. Open daily 9am-8:30pm.

Laundromat: Laverie Niçoise, 7, r. d'Italie (☎04 93 87 56 50). Beside Basilique Notre-Dame. Open M-Sa 8:30am-12:30pm and 2:30-7:30pm.

Police: ☎04 93 17 22 22. At the opposite end of bd. M. Foch from bd. Jean Médecin.

Hospital: St-Roch, 5, r. Pierre Devoluy (☎04 92 03 33 75).

Internet Access: Organic CyberCafé, 16, r. Paganini. Mention *Let's Go* and pay 16F/€2.45 for 30min., 34F/€5.20 for 1hr. Open daily 9am-10pm. **Cyber Point,** 10, av. Félix Faure (☎04 93 92 70 63). 30F/€4.60 for 1hr. Open M-F 10:30am-1pm and 3-7pm, Sa-Su 11am-1pm and 3-7pm.

Post Office: 21, av. Thiers (☎04 93 82 65 22). Near the train station. Open M-F 8am-7pm, Sa 8am-noon. 24hr. **ATM.** Address mail to be held: FirstName SURNAME, *Poste Restante, Recette Principale,* Nice 06000, France. **Postal Code:** 06033 Nice Cedex 1.

■ ACCOMMODATIONS

To sleep easy, come to Nice with reservations. Affordable places surround the train station, but without reservations (made at least 2-3 weeks ahead in the summer), you'll be forced to risk a night on the beach or outside the train station. The city has two clusters of budget hotels: ones by the station are newer but badly located; those nearer to *vieux Nice* and the beach are convenient but less modern.

Relais International de la Jeunesse "Clairvallon," 26, av. Scudéri (☎04 93 81 27 63; fax 04 93 53 35 88), in Cimiez, 4km out of town. Take bus #15 (dir.: Rimiez; 20min., every 10min.) from the train station or pl. Masséna to Scudéri; then head uphill to the right and take your 1st left. In the luxurious villa with tennis courts and pool. Breakfast included. Check-in 5pm. Lockout 9:30am-5pm. Curfew 11pm. Dorms 82F/€12.50.

Hôtel Baccarat, 39, r. d'Angleterre (☎04 93 88 35 73), 2nd right off r. de Belgique. Large rooms in homey, secure atmosphere. 3- to 5-bed dorms 95F/€14.50; singles 187F/€28.55; doubles 230F/€35.10; triples 284F/€43.30. AmEx/MC/V.

Hôtel Little Masséna, 22, r. Masséna (☎04 93 87 72 34). Small but comfortable rooms. Singles and doubles 170F/€25.95, with bath 220-270F/€33.55-41.20. Extra person 30F/€4.60. Oct.-May prices 10-30F/€1.50-4.60 lower. MC/V.

Hôtel des Flandres, 6 r. de Belgique (☎04 93 88 78 94). Large rooms with high ceilings and private bathrooms. Breakfast 30F/€4.60. 5- to 6-person rooms 110F/€16.80 per person; singles 230F/€35.10; doubles 290-310F/€44.25-47.30; triples 370F/€56.45; quads 390-410F/€59.50-62.50. Extra bed 70F/€10.70. MC/V.

Hôtel Notre Dame, 22, r. de la Russie (☎04 93 88 70 44), 1 block west of av. Jean Médecin. Spotless, quiet rooms. Reception 24hr. Singles 200F/€30.50; doubles 250F/€38.15; triples 350F/€53.40; quads 400F/€61. Extra bed 60F/€9.15.

Hôtel Belle Meunière, 21, av. Durante (☎04 93 88 66 15), on a street facing the train station. Lively backpacker atmosphere in an elegant converted mansion. Breakfast included. Luggage storage 10F/€1.55. 4- to 5-bed co-ed dorms 80-115F/€12.20-17.55; doubles 290F/€44.25; triples 255F/€38.90, with shower 345F/€52.60.

Hôtel Les Orangiers, 10bis, av. Durante (☎04 93 87 51 41). Bright rooms, all with showers and fridges. Free luggage storage. Breakfast 20F/€4.60. Closed Nov. In summer dorms 85F/€13; singles 95-100F/€14.50-15.20; doubles 210-230F/€32.05-35.10; triples 270-300F/€41.20-45.70; quads 360F/€54.90. MC/V.

Les Mimosas, 26, r. de la Buffa (☎04 93 88 05 59). Close to the beach and r. Massena. Renovated homey rooms. Singles 170F/€25.95; doubles 200F/€30.50; triples 240F/€36.60; quads 310F/€47.30. Oct.-Apr. prices 30F/€4.60 lower. Cash only.

Hôtel Petit Trianon, 11, r. Paradis (☎04 93 87 50 46), off r. Massena. Humble but elegant rooms. Singles 100F/€15.25; doubles 200F/€30.50; triples 300F/€45.75. Extra bed 50F/€7.65.

Hôtel Au Picardy, 10, bd. Jean-Jaurès (☎04 93 85 75 51), across from the bus station. Near *Vieux Nice*. Breakfast 17.50F/€2.70. Singles 125-135F/€19.05-20.60, with shower 179F/€27.30; doubles 179F/€27.30, 209F/€31.90; triples 220-260F/€33.55-39.65; quads 260-299F/€33.65-45.60. Extra bed 45F/€6.90. Cash only.

◪ FOOD

Nice is a city of restaurants, outdoor terraces, and tiny holes-in-the-wall. *Vieux Nice* is crowded and touristy, but good eats are easy to find. Stock up at the **Prisunic supermarket**, 42, av. Jean Médecin. (☎04 93 62 38 90. Open M-Sa 8:30am-8:30pm.)

◪ **Lou Pilha Leva**, 13, r. du Collet (☎04 93 80 29 33). Get a lot of *niçois* food for little money. Pizza slices 10F/€1.55, *moules* (mussels) 37F/€5.65. Open daily 8am-11pm.

◪ **Speakeasy**, 7, r. Lamartine (☎04 93 85 59 50). Delectable and affordable vegetarian options. Open M-Sa for lunch 11:45am-2pm.

Acchiardo, 38, r. Droite (☎04 93 85 51 16), in *Vieux Nice*. Surprisingly reasonable pastas from 36F/€5.50. Open M-F noon-1:30pm and 7-9:30pm, Sa noon-1:30am.

◉ SIGHTS

Many visitors to Nice head straight for the beaches and don't retreat from the sun and water until the day is done. Whatever dreams you've had about Nice's beach, though, the hard reality is an endless stretch of rocks; bring a beach mat if you plan to soak up the sun in comfort. Contrary to popular opinion, there are things in Nice more worth doing than taking a long naked sunbath on a bunch of pebbles. Nice's **Promenade des Anglais,** named after the English expatriates who built it, is a sight in itself. At the **Négresco,** one of many luxury hotels lining the boulevard, the staff still don top-hats and 19th-century uniforms. If you follow the Promenade east of bd. Jean Jaurès, you'll stumble upon **Vieux Nice**, a medieval *quartier* whose twisting streets and sprawling terraces draw massive crowds. *Vieux Nice* hosts a number of lively morning markets, including a fish frenzy at **Place St-François.** The **Eglise St-Martin,** pl. Augustine, is the city's oldest church and site of Italian revolutionary Garibaldi's baptism. Further down the Promenade is **Le Château,** a hillside park crowned with the remains of an 11th-century cathedral. (Open daily 7am-8pm.)

Even burn-hard sunbathers will have a hard time passing by Nice's first-class museums. Walk 15min. north of the train station onto av. du Dr. Ménard to find the concrete and glass ◪**Musée National Message Biblique Marc Chagall,** which showcases his moving 17 *Message Biblique* paintings. You can also take bus #15 (dir.: Rimiez) to "Musée Chagall." (Open July-Sept. W-M 10am-6pm; Oct.-June 10am-5pm. 36F/€5.50, under 26 26F/€4.) Higher up the hill is the ◪**Musée Matisse,** 164, av. des Arènes de Cimiez, in a 17th-century Genoese villa. Take bus #15, 17, 20, or 22 to "Arènes." The museum's collection of paintings is disappointingly small, but the bronze reliefs and dozens of cut-and-paste *tableaux* are dazzling. (Open Apr.-Sept. W-M 10am-6pm; Oct.-Mar. 10am-5pm. 25F/€3.85, students 20F/€3.05.) Matisse, along with Raoul Dufy, is buried nearby in a cemetery beside the **Monastère Cimiez,** which contains a museum of Franciscan art and lovely gardens. (Museum open M-Sa 10am-noon and 3-6pm. Cemetery open daily 8am-6pm. Gardens open daily 8am-7pm, in winter 8am-7pm. Free.) Check out the onion-domed **Cathédrale Orthodoxe Russe St-Nicolas,** 17, bd. du Tzarevitch, west of bd. Gambetta near the train station, which was funded by Tsar Nicolas II. (Open June-Aug. daily 9am-noon and 2:30-6pm, Sept.-May daily 9:30am-noon and 2:30-5pm. 15F/€2.30, students 12F/€1.85.)

Closer to *Vieux Nice*, the **Musée d'Art Moderne et d'Art Contemporain,** on Promenade des Arts, on av. St-Jean Baptiste near pl. Garibaldi, features avant-

FRANCE

garde works by French and American provocateurs, including works by Lichtenstein, Warhol, and Klein. Take bus #5 (dir.: St-Charles) from the station to "Garibaldi." (Open W-M 10am-6pm. 20F/€3.05, students 10F/€1.55.) Traditionalists will enjoy the **Musée de Beaux Arts**, 33, av. Baumettes, off bd. Francois Grosso. The museum's collection of French academic painting is overshadowed by rooms devoted to Van Dongen and Raoul Dufy. From the train station, take bus #38 to "Chéret" or bus #12 to "Grosso." (Open Tu-Su 10am-noon and 2-6pm. 25F/€3.85, students 15F/€2.30.)

◘ NIGHTLIFE

FNAC, 24, av. Jean Médecin, in the Nice Etoile shopping center, sells tickets for performances around town. Nice's **Jazz Festival**, in mid-July at the Parc et Arènes de Cimiez near the Musée Matisse, attracts world-famous jazz and non-jazz musicians. (☎04 93 21 68 12; www.nicejazzfest.com. Tickets 50-250F/€7.60-38.10.) During **Carnaval**, in late February, Nice gives Rio a run for its money with two weeks of parades, outlandish costumes, fireworks, and parties. Here the party crowd swings long after the folks in St-Tropez and Antibes have called it a night. The bars and nightclubs around r. Masséna and *Vieux Nice* pulsate with dance, jazz, and rock. Local men have a reputation for hassling people on the Promenade; lone women and even those in groups should decide carefully where to walk at night. The dress code at all bars and clubs is simple: look good. Most pubs will turn you away if they catch you wearing shorts, sandals, or a baseball cap.

BARS

De Klomp, 6, r. Mascoinat (☎04 93 92 42 85). 40 types of whiskey (from 40F/€6.10) and 18 beers on tap (pint 45F/€6.90). A variety of live music from salsa to jazz every night. Happy Hour 5:30-9:30pm. Open M-Sa 5:30pm-2:30am, Su 8:30pm-2:30am.

Le Bar Des Deux Frères, 1, r. du Moulin (☎04 93 80 77 61). A young, funky crowd tosses back tequila (20F/€3.05) and beer (15F/€2.30). Open daily 9pm-3:30am; in winter closed M.

Wayne's, 15, r. de la Préfecture (☎04 93 13 46 99). Frat boys and their chicks dance the night away in this wild, crowded bar. Common denominators: young, Anglo, and on the prowl. Open Su-Th 11am-1am, F-Sa 11am-1:30am.

McMahon's, 50, bd. Jean Jaurès (☎04 93 71 16 23). Join the locals and expats who lap up Guinness at this low-key pub. Happy Hour daily 6-9pm. Open daily 6pm-2:30am.

Williams, 4, r. Centrale (☎04 93 62 99 63). When other bars close up, Williams keeps the kegs flowing. Karaoke nights M-Th. Live music F and Sa. Open M-Sa 11am-6am.

Nocy-Bé, 4-6, r. Jules Gilly (☎04 93 85 52 25). Take a time-out at this mellow Indian tea-room. Dozens of teas to choose from. Open W-M 4pm-12:30am.

CLUBS

Forum, 45-47, Promenade des Anglais (☎04 93 96 67 00). A tropical theme reigns in Nice's hottest club. Cover 100F/€15.25. Open F-Sa 11pm-6am.

La Suite, 2, r. Brea (☎04 93 92 92 91). This *petite boite* attracts a funky, well-dressed, moneyed crowd. Cover 80F/€12.20, W free. Open W-Su 11:30pm-2:30am.

Le Klub, 6, r. Halévy (☎06 60 55 26 61). Popular gay club caters to well-tanned crowd. Cover 70F/€10.70 Sa. Open July-Aug. daily 11:30pm-6am; Sept.-June closed M.

◘ DAYTRIPS FROM NICE

THE CORNICHES

*Trains and buses between Nice and Monaco serve most of the Corniche towns frequently. Hourly **trains** from Nice to Monaco stop at: Beaulieu-sur-Mer (10min., 12F/€1.85); Cap d'Ail (20min., 16F/€2.45); Eze-sur-Mer (16min., 13F/€2); Villefranche-sur-Mer (7min., 10F/€1.55). Also departing from the train station are numerous numbered **RCA buses***

(☎ 04 93 85 64 44), which run between Nice and Monaco, making different stops along the way. Bus #111 leaves Nice, stopping in Villefranche-sur-Mer (M-Sa 9 per day). 3 buses continue on to St-Jean-Cap-Ferrat. Bus #117 runs between Nice and Villefranche-sur-Mer (11 per day); Bus #112 travels from Nice to Monte-Carlo, stopping in Eze-le-Village (7 per day). RCA and Broch buses (☎ 04 93 31 10 52) run every hr. from Nice to: Beaulieu-sur-Mer (20min., 12F/€1.85); Cap d'Ail (30min., 17F/€2.60); Eze-le-Village (25min., 15F/€2.30); Monaco-Ville (40min., 20F/€3.05); Monte-Carlo (45min., 20F/€3.05); Villefranche-sur-Mer (10min., 8.50F/€1.30).

Rocky shores, pebble beaches, and luxurious villas glow along the Corniches, between hectic Nice and high-rolling Monaco. More relaxing than their glam-fab neighbors, these tiny towns have interesting museums, ancient finds, and breathtaking countryside. The train offers a glimpse of the coast up close, while bus rides on the high roads allow bird's-eye views of the steep cliffs and crashing sea below.

VILLEFRANCHE-SUR-MER. The town's narrow streets and pastel houses have enchanted Aldous Huxley, Katherine Mansfield, and many other artists. Strolling from the train station along quai Ponchardier, a sign to the *vieille ville* points to the spooky 13th-century **Rue Obscure,** the oldest street in Villefranche. At the end of the quai is the **Chapelle St-Pierre,** decorated by Jean Cocteau, former resident, filmmaker, and jack-of-all-arts. (☎ 04 93 76 90 70. Call ahead for hours. 12F/€1.85.) To get to the **tourist office** from the train station, exit on quai 1 and head inland on av. G. Clemenceau, continue straight when it becomes av. Sadi Carnot, and it will be at the end of the street. (☎ 04 93 01 73 68. Open July-Aug. daily 9am-noon and 2-6:30pm; mid-Sept. to June M-Sa 9am-noon and 2-6pm.)

ST-JEAN-CAP-FERRAT. A lovely town with an even lovelier beach, St-Jean-Cap-Ferrat is the trump card of the Riviera. The **Fondation Ephrussi di Rothschild,** just off av. D. Semeria, is a stunning Italian villa that houses the collections of the Baroness de Rothschild, including Monet canvases, Gobelins tapestries, and Chinese vases. The seven lush gardens reflect different parts of the world. (Open July-Aug. daily 10am-7pm; Sept.-Oct. and mid-Feb. to June daily 10am-6pm; Nov. to mid-Feb. M-F 2pm-6pm, Sa-Su 10am-6pm. 50F/€7.65, students 38F/€5.80.) The town's beautiful **beaches** merit the area's nickname *"presqu'île des rêves"* (peninsula of dreams).

EZE. Three-tiered Eze owes its fame to the pristine medieval town in the middle tier. It features the **Porte des Maures,** which served as a portal for a surprise attack by the Moors, and the **Eglise Paroissial,** containing sleek Phoencian crosses mixed with Catholic gilt. (Open daily 9am-noon and 2-6pm.) The best views are 40min. up the **Sentier Friedrich Nietzsche,** a windy trail where its namesake found inspiration; the path begins in **Eze Bord-du-Mer,** 100m east of the train station and tourist office, and ends near the base of the medieval city, by the **Fragonard parfumerie.**

CAP D'AIL. With 3km of cliff-framed foamy seashore, Cap d'Ail's **Les Pissarelles** draws hundreds of nudists, while **Plage Mala** is frequented by more modest folk. To get from the station to the **tourist office,** 87bis, av. de 3 Septembre, turn right at the village, continue on av. de la Gare, and turn left on r. du 4 Septembre. (☎ 04 93 78 02 33; fax 04 92 10 74 36. Open July-Aug. M-Sa 9am-12:30pm and 2:30-6:30pm, Su 9am-12:30pm; Sept.-June M-F 9am-12:30pm and 2-6pm, Sa 9am-12:30pm.) The **Relais International de la Jeunesse,** on bd. F. de May, has a waterfront location. (☎ 04 93 78 18 58; fax 04 93 53 35 88. Breakfast included. Open Apr.-Oct. 80F/€12.20.)

MONACO AND MONTE-CARLO

This tiny principality (pop. 5000) is, square centimeter for square centimeter, one of the wealthiest places in the world. At Monaco's spiritual heart is its famous casino in Monte-Carlo, a magnet for the wealthy and dissolute since 1885. The sheer spectacle of it all is definitely worth a daytrip from Nice.

PHONE CODE | **Country Code: 377. International Dialing Prefix: 00.**

FRANCE

📧 TRANSPORTATION. Trains (☎08 36 35 35 35) leave every 30min. for: Antibes (1hr., 38F/€5.80); Cannes (1hr., 46F/€7.05); Nice (25min., 20F/€3.05). **Bus** #4 links the train station to the casino in Monte-Carlo. (Tickets 8.50F/€1.30, 21.50F/€3.30 for a *carte* of 4. Buy tickets on board.)

🚩 PRACTICAL INFORMATION. Follow the signs in the train station for Le Rocher and Fontvieille to the **Avenue Prince Pierre** entrance; it's close to pl. d'Armes and the **La Condamine** quarter, Monaco's port and nightlife hub. To the right of La Condamine rises the *vieille ville*, **Monaco-Ville.** From the train station, bd. Princesse Charlotte or pl. St-Devote leads to **Monte-Carlo** and the casino. The **tourist office,** 2a, bd. des Moulins, near the casino, offers maps and reserves rooms. (☎92 16 61 16; fax 92 16 60 00. Open M-Sa 9am-7pm, Su 10am-noon.) Access the **Internet** at **Stars N' Bars,** at 6, quai Antoine 1er. (Open daily 10am-midnight. 40F/€6.10 for 30min.)

📧🍴 ACCOMMODATIONS AND FOOD. There's no need to stay in Monaco, since it is easily accessible from nearby coastal towns. Travelers between the ages of 16 and 31 can try the **Centre de Jeunesse Princesse Stéphanie,** 24, av. Prince Pierre, 100m uphill from the station. The hostel is strict and sterile. (☎93 50 83 20. Breakfast included. July-Aug 5-day max. stay, Sept.-June 7-day max. stay. Closed mid-Nov. to mid-Dec. Beds 100F/€15.25; July-Aug. 10- and 12-bed dorms 90F/€13.75. Cash only.) The **Hôtel Villa Boeri,** at 29, bd. du Général Leclerc, is in nearby Beausoleil, France. (☎04 93 41 78 10; fax 04 93 41 90 95. Breakfast 30F/€4.60. Singles 210-290F/€32.05-44.25; doubles 270-360F/€41.20-54.90; triples 335-420F/€51.10-64.05; quads 500F/€76.25. AmEx/MC/V.) At **L'Escale,** 17, bd. Albert 1er, pizzas and pastas start from 50F/€7.65. (☎93 39 13 44. Open daily noon-3 pm and 6-11 pm.)

📷🍴 SIGHTS AND ENTERTAINMENT. Monte-Carlo's wealth and allure revolve around the sumptuous **Monte-Carlo Casino,** at pl. du Casino, where Mata Hari shot a Russian spy. If you feel lucky, the slot machines open at 2pm, while blackjack and roulette open daily at noon (50F/€7.65 to enter). The exclusive *salons privés* require coat and ties and charge an extra 50F/€7.65 cover. A bit more relaxed, the **Café de Paris** next door opens at 10am and has no cover charge. All casinos have **dress codes** (no shorts, sneakers, sandals, or jeans). Guards are strict about the 21-year age minimum—bring a passport as proof. (☎92 16 20 00; www.casino-montecarlo.com.) After losing your shirt in Monte-Carlo, walk west to the cliffside palace of **Palais Princier,** the occasional home of Prince Rainier and his family. When the flag is down, the Prince is away and visitors can tour the lavish palace. (☎93 25 18 31. Open daily June-Sept. 9:30am-6pm; Oct. 10am-5pm. 30F/€4.60, students 15F/€2.30 before 5pm.) Next door, the stately **Cathédrale de Monaco,** at pl. St-Martin, is where former princes of Monaco are buried. Grace Kelly's tomb, behind the altar, is simply marked "Patritia Gracia." (☎93 30 87 70. Open Mar.-Oct. 7am-7pm, Nov.-Feb. 7am-6pm. Free.) Once run by Jacques Cousteau, the stunning **Musée Océanographique,** on av. St-Martin, houses thousands of marine animals. (☎93 15 36 00. Open daily July-Aug. 9am-8pm; Sept.-June reduced hours. 70F/€10.70, students and ages 6-18 35F/€5.35.) The **📷Private Collection of Antique Cars of H.S.H. Prince Rainier III,** on Terrasses de Fontvieille, features 105 of the sexiest and most stately cars ever made. (☎92 05 28 56. Open daily Dec.-Oct. 10am-6pm. 30F/€4.60, students 15F/€2.30.) Head up the port to **Café Grand Prix,** 1, quai Antoine 1er, where a mixed crowd dances late. (☎93 25 56 90. Open daily 10am-5am. No cover.)

CORSICA (LA CORSE)

Corsica's time bomb of a populace began the Corsican War of Independence, also known as the Forty Years War, with a series of rebellions in 1729. By 1755, the island had declared itself an autonomous state with its own constitution and university. Today, the *Front de Libération National de la Corse* (FLNC) continues

Monaco & Monte-Carlo

🏠 ACCOMMODATIONS

Centre de Jeunesse Princess Stéphanie, **3**
Hôtel Villa Boeri, **1**

🍎 FOOD

L'Escale, **2**

🍷 NIGHTLIFE

Café Grand Prix, **4**

bd. de Verdun

Musée National

Jardin Japonais

av. de Grande-Bretagne

av. de la République

bd. du Général Leclerc

bd. du Larvotto

av. de Princesse Grace

MONTE-CARLO

American Express

av. des Spélugues

Parc des Boulingrins

Café de Paris

PL. DU CASINO

Monte-Carlo Casino

Centre de Congrès Auditorium

BEAUSOLEIL

FRANCE

r. Bel Respiro

bd. Princesse Charlotte

av. des Beaux Arts

av. Princesse Alice

av. Henri Dunant

MONACO

bd. de Suisse

Palais de la Scala

av. de Monte-Carlo

Mediterranean Sea

av. de la Costa

av. d'Ostende

bd. des Moneghetti

av. du jardin Exotique

bd. Rainier III

train station tunnel entrances

Eglise Ste-Dévote

PL. STE-DÉVOTE

r. Grimaldi

Port de Monaco

Fort Antoine

bd. de Belgique

Supermarket

bd. Albert 1er

r. Suffren Reymond

r. Louis Notari

r. Princesse Caroline

Scruples Bookstore

Auto-Moto Garage

r. de Millo

LA CONDAMINE

quai Antoine 1er

av. de la Quarantaine
av. de la Porte Neuve

av. de la Turbie

av. Crovetto Frères

av. Prince Pierre

bd. de la Colle

PL. D'ARMES

av. du Port

MONACO-VILLE

St-Martin

Chemin des Pêcheurs

Compagnie Monégasque de Change

Parc Princesse Antoinette

Supermarket

bd. Charles III

PL. DU CANTON

Palais Princier

Palais de Justice

PL. DU PALAIS

r. Col. Bellando de Castro

Mairie (City Hall)

Musée Océanographique

Princesse Caroline's Villa

Cathédrale de Monaco

Jardins St-Martin

Jardin Exotique

bd. du Jardin Exotique

bd. Rainier III

av. Pasteur

bd. Charles III

The Private Collection of AntiqueCars of H.S.H. Prince Rainer III.

Port de Fontvieille

Quai de Sanbarbani

av. Prince Héréditaire Albert

Stade Louis II

FONTVIEILLE

Espace Fontvieille

CAP D'AIL

N

0   200 yards

0   200 meters

to try bombing its way to independence. However, these politics will have little effect on tourists, who are warmly received throughout the island, which offers a dazzling mixture of tiny villages and a wildly varied landscape.

⌐ TRANSPORTATION

Air France (Marseilles ☎04 91 00 33 83, Paris ☎08 20 82 08 20) and its subsidiary **Compagnie Corse Méditerranée (CCM)** fly to Ajaccio and Bastia from: Lyon (from 1114F/€170, students 924F/€141); Marseilles (912F/€139, students 839F/€128); Nice (912F/€139, students 839F/€128); Paris (from 1395F/€213, students 1094F/€167). There's also a direct flight from Lille to Bastia (from 1485F/€226.45, students 1360F/€207.35). In Ajaccio, the Air France/CCM office is at 3, bd. du Roi Jérôme (☎08 20 82 08 20). All fares listed here are without tax and round-trip. **Air Liberté** services Calvi and Porto Vecchio (Figari) from Marseilles and Nice. **Ferry** travel between the mainland and Corsica can be rough and sometimes not much cheaper than a flight. The **Société National Maritime Corse Méditerranée (SNCM)** (☎08 91 70 18 01; www.sncm.fr) sends ferries from Marseilles (265-300F/€40.40-45.70, under 25 230-265F/€35.10-40.40); Nice (225-255F/€34.30-38.90, under 25 195-225F/€29.75-34.30); Toulon (265-300F/€40.40-45.70, under 25 230-265F/€35.10-40.40) to Ajaccio, Bastia, Calvi, and Porto Vecchio. SNCM schedules and fees are listed in a booklet widely available at travel agencies or port offices. **All tickets must be reserved at least four days in advance. SAREMARE** (☎04 95 73 00 96) and **Moby Lines** (☎04 85 73 00 29; www.mobyline.de) run from Santa Teresa, in Sardinia, Italy to Bonifacio (4-10 per day, 50-75F/€7.60-11.40 per person and 140-280F/€21.35-42.70 per car). **Corsica Ferries** (☎08 03 09 50 95; www.corsicaferries.com) crosses from Livorno and Savona, Italy to Bastia (119-180F/€18.15-27.45). **Train** service in Corsica is slow and limited to the half of the island north of Ajaccio; **railpasses** are not valid. **Buses** aren't much better but provide more comprehensive service; call **Eurocorse Voyages** (☎04 95 21 06 30) for more info. **Hiking** is the best way to explore the island's mountainous interior. The **GR20** is an extremely difficult 14- to 15-day 200km trail that crosses the island. The popular **Mare e Monti** (10 days) and **Da Mare a Mare Sud** (4-6 days) trails are shorter and less challenging. The **Parc Naturel Régional de la Corse**, 2, Sargent Casalonga, in Ajaccio (☎04 95 51 79 10), publishes maps and a guide to *gîtes d'étapes*.

AJACCIO (AIACCIU)

Swinging Ajaccio (pop. 60,000) often trades in Corsican nationalism for the *français* flavor of life. Celebrating their diminutive native son is also a regular pastime, starting with the **Musée National de la Maison Bonaparte**, r. St-Charles, between r. Bonaparte and r. Roi-de-Rome. (☎04 95 21 43 89. Open Apr.-Sept. M 2-6pm, Tu-Su 9am-noon and 2-6pm; Oct.-Mar. M 2-4:45pm, Tu-Su 10am-noon and 2-4:45pm. 25F/€3.85, ages 18-25 17F/€2.60, under 18 free.) Inside the **Musée Fesch**, 50-52, r. Cardinal Fesch, you'll find an impressive collection of 14th- to 19th-century Italian paintings gathered by Napoleon's uncle Fesch. Also within the complex is the **Chapelle Impériale**, the final resting place of most of the Bonaparte family—but Napoleon himself is buried in a modest Parisian tomb. (☎04 95 21 48 17. Open July-Aug. M 1:30-6pm, Tu-Th 9am-6:30pm, F 9am-6:30pm and 9pm-midnight, Sa-Su 10:30am-6pm; Sept.-June reduced hours. Museum 35F/€5.35, students 25F/€3.85; chapel 10F/€1.55, students 5F/€0.75.) Southwest of Ajaccio, the striking black cliffs of **Îles Sanguinaires** loom over the sea. Nave Va **ferries**, at a kiosk on the port, run to the largest island. (☎04 95 51 31 31. Apr.-Oct. daily at 3:30pm. 120F/€18.30.)

Trains (☎04 95 23 11 03) leave pl. de la Gare, off bd. Sampiero, for Bastia (4hr., 4 per day, 143F/€21.85) and Calvi (4½hr., 2 per day, 166F/€25.35) via Ponte Leccia. Eurocorse Voyages **buses** (☎04 95 21 06 30) go to Bastia (3hr., 2 per day, 110F/€16.80) via Corte (1½hr., 65F/€9.95); Autocars SAIB (☎04 95 22 41 99) runs to Porto (2hr., 1-3 per day, 70F/€10.70); and Autocars Les Beaux Voyages (☎04 95 65 15 02) goes to Calvi (3½hr., M-Sa 1 per day, 135F/€20.60). The **tourist office** is at 3, bd. du roi Jérôme. (☎04 95 51 53 03; fax 04 95 51 53 01; www.tourisme.fr/

ajaccio. Open July-Sept. M-Sa 8am-8:30pm, Su 9am-1pm; Nov.-Feb. M-F 8am-6pm, Sa 8am-noon and 2-5pm; Mar.-June M-Sa 8am-7pm, Su 9am-1pm.) Get groceries at **Monoprix supermarket,** 31, cours Napoléon. (Open M-Sa 8:30am-7:15pm.) The serene **Hôtel Kallisté** is at 51, cours Napoléon. (☎ 04 95 51 34 45; fax 04 95 21 79 00; www.cyrnos.com. Oct.-June singles 260F/€39.65; doubles 290F/€44.25; triples 380F/€57.95; July and Sept.-Oct. rooms 290-460F/€44.25-70.15; Aug. 350-560F/€53.40-85.40. AmEx/MC/V.) **Hôtel le Dauphin,** 11, bd. Sampiero, is halfway between the station and port. (☎ 04 95 21 12 94; fax 04 95 21 88 69. July-Sept. Singles 280F/€42.70; doubles 350F/€53.40; triples 430F/€65.55; Oct.-June rooms 250-360F/€38.10-54.90. AmEx/MC/V.)

CALVI

"Corsica's Côte d'Azur," Calvi offers a lively port as well as gorgeous beaches, turquoise waters, and mountains. 6km of **public beaches** dotted by rocky coves wind around the coast. Visit the **citadel** and bask in the setting sun. **Trains** (☎ 04 95 65 00 61) leave pl. de la Gare, on av. de la République near Port de Plaisance, for Bastia (3hr., 2 per day, 108F/€16.50) and Corte (2½hr., 2 per day, 90F/€13.75). Les Beaux Voyages **buses** (☎ 04 95 65 15 02) leave pl. Porteuse d'Eau, by the taxi stand, for Ajaccio (4¾hr., 1 per day, 135F/€20.60) and Bastia (2¼hr., M-Sa 1 per day, 80F/€12.20). To reach the **tourist office,** Port de Plaisance, exit from the back of the train station (facing the beach), turn left, and follow the signs. (☎ 04 95 65 16 67; fax 04 95 65 14 09. Open May M-Sa 9am-6:30pm; June to mid-Sept. daily 9am-7pm; mid-Sept. to Apr. M-F 9am-5pm.) The central **BVJ Corsotel "Hôtel des Jeunes,"** on av. de la République, is opposite the train station. (☎ 04 95 65 14 15; fax 04 95 65 33 72. Breakfast 20F/€3.05. Open Apr.-Oct. Dorms 115F/€17.55; doubles 115-130F/€17.55-19.85.) The plush **Il Tramono,** rte. d'Ajaccio R.N. 199, is near the town center. (☎ 04 95 65 04 17; fax 04 95 65 02 40. Open Apr.-Oct. Doubles 180-320F/€27.50-48.80. Extra bed 80-100F/€12.20-15.25. MC/V.) **Camping International,** on RN 197, is 1km from town, past Super U. (☎ 04 95 65 01 75; fax 04 95 65 36 11. Open Apr.-Oct. July-Aug. 33F/€5.05 per person, 19F/€2.90 per tent, 10F/€1.55 per car; Apr.-June and Sept.-Oct. 22F/€3.35 per person, 15F/€2.30 per tent, 8F/€1.25 per car.)

BASTIA AND CAP CORSE

The transport hub of Bastia (pop. 40,000), Corsica's second-largest city, is a good base for a visit to the Cap Corse peninsula. At the northern end of town, the 14th-century **citadel,** also called Terra Nova, has beautiful views. The 18th-century **Eglise St-Jean Baptiste,** on pl. de l'Hôtel de Ville, is the stunning centerpiece of the photogenic port. **Trains** (☎ 04 95 32 80 61) depart from pl. de la Gare for Ajaccio (4hr., 4 per day, 143F/€21.80) and Calvi (3hr., 2 per day, 108F/€16.50). **Eurocorse buses** (☎ 04 95 21 06 30) leave r. du Nouveau Port for Ajaccio (3hr., 2 per day, 110F/€16.80). The **tourist office** is on pl. St-Nicholas. (☎ 04 95 54 20 40; fax 04 95 31 81 34. Open June-Sept. M-Sa 8am-8pm; Oct.-May M-Sa 8:30am-6pm.) The convenient **Hôtel Central,** 3, r. Miot has large, clean rooms. (☎ 04 95 31 71 12. Singles 230-300F/€35.10-45.70; doubles 250-400F/€38.10-61; triples 350-430F/€53.40-65.55; quads 490F/€74.70. AmEx/MC/V.) **Camp** at **Les Orangers,** is 4km north in Miomo. Take bus #4 from the tourist office to "Mioma Liciola" (every hr., 7.50F/€1.15) or follow bd. de Toga. (☎ 04 95 33 24 09. Open Apr. to mid-Oct. 25F/€3.85 per person, 13F/€2 per tent, 10F/€1.55 per car.) Delicious food is near the **citadel** and along **Quai des Martyrs de la Libération.**

The **Cap Corse** peninsula stretches north from Bastia, a string of former fishing villages connected by a narrow road of perilous curves and breathtaking views. Cap is a hiker's dream, with ancient Genoese towers and chapels hidden among forests and cliffs. **Transports Micheli,** in Ersa at the top of the peninsula, offers full-day tours of the Cap, departing from 1, r. de Nouveau Port in Bastia (☎ 04 95 34 64 02; July-Aug. Tu, Th, and Sa 9am; 150F/€22.90), but the cheapest and most convenient way to see Cap Corse is to take **bus #4** from pl. St-Nicolas in Bastia; politely ask the driver to drop you off wherever you feel the urge to explore (every 30min., 12-40F/€1.85-6.10). **Erbalunga** (20min., 12F/€1.85), with white pebble beaches and secluded flat rocks for sunbathing, is the most accessible of Cap Corse villages.

FRANCE

CORTE

"The heart of Corsica," Corte combines breathtaking natural scenery with an intellectual flair. Resting between sheer cliffs and snow-capped peaks, Corte houses the island's only university, whose students keep prices thankfully low. The town's *vieille ville*, with its steep streets and stone **citadel**, has always been a bastion of fierce Corsican patriotism. At the top of r. Scolisca, the **Musée de la Corse** displays a detailed history of Corsica. Entrance includes a visit to the only inland citadel. (☎ 04 95 45 25 45. Museum open June 20-Sept. 20 daily 10am-8pm; Sept. 21-Nov. Tu-Su 10am-6pm; Dec.-Mar. Tu-Sa 10am-6pm; Apr.-June 19 T-Su 10am-6pm. Citadel closes 1hr. earlier than museum. 35F/€5.35, students 20F/€3.05.)

Trains (☎ 04 95 46 00 97) leave from the rotary, where av. Jean Nicoli and the N193 meet, for: Ajaccio (2hr., 4 per day, 76F/€11.60); Bastia (1½hr., 4 per day, 67F/€10.25); Calvi (2½hr., 2 per day, 90F/€13.75) via Ponte-Lec cia. Eurocorse Voyages runs **buses** to Ajaccio (1¾hr., M-Sa 2 per day, 65F/€9.95) and Bastia (1¼hr., M-Sa 2 per day, 60F/€9.15). To reach the *centre ville* from the train station, turn right on D14 (av. Jean Nicoli), cross two bridges, and follow the road until it ends at **Cours Paoli**, Corte's main drag. A left turn leads to **Place Paoli**, the town center; at the *place*'s top right corner, climb the stairs of r. Scolisca for the citadel and the **tourist office**. (☎ 04 95 46 26 70; fax 04 95 46 34 05; www.corte-tourisme.com. Open July-Aug. daily 9am-8pm; May-June and Sept. M-Sa 9am-1pm and 2-7pm; Oct.-Apr. M-F 9am-noon and 2-6pm.) In the summer, students can stay in university housing for 100F/€15.25 per night; contact **CROUS**, 7, av. Jean Nicoli, before you arrive. (☎ 04 95 45 21 00; fax 04 95 61 01 57. Office open M-F 9am-noon and 2-3:30pm.) The youthful **Hôtel-Residence Porette (H-R)**, 6, allée du 9 Septembre, offers lots of amenities. Bear left from the train station to the stadium and follow it around for another 100m. (☎ 04 95 45 11 11; fax 04 95 61 02 85. Breakfast 34F/€5.20. Reception 24hr. Singles 135F/€21, with bath 199F/€30.35; doubles 145F/€22.15, 279-289F/€42.55; triples 329F/€50.20; quads 350F/€53.40.) The huge **Casino supermarket** is near the train station, on allée du 9 Septembre. (Open mid-June to Aug. daily 8:30am-7:30pm; Sept. to mid-June M-F 8:30am-12:30pm and 2-8pm, Sa 8:30am-7:30pm.) **Postal Code:** 20250.

PORTO VECCHIO

On an island full of memorable beaches, those on the Golfe de Porto Vecchio are still something to write home about. **Palombaggia** is about 2km long, and summer crowds thin out farther from the parking lot. Farther south, **Santa Giulia** is the most beautiful, a perfect circle of sand ringing a giant bay. Follow N198 for the stunning beaches north of Porto Vecchio. You'll reach **Punta di Benedettu** first, but it's worth the trek to continue on to **San Cipriano**, with anchored sailboats in its calm cove. From July to September, Trinitours **buses** (☎ 04 95 70 13 83) go to **Palombaggia** (1 per day, 25F/€3.85); updated schedules are posted on the tourist office wall. Eurocorse **buses** (☎ 04 95 70 13 83) stop in front of Trinitours on r. Pasteur, behind the tourist office, and run to Ajaccio (3hr., July-Sept. 3 per day, 125F/€19.05). **Autocars Rapides-Bleus** (☎ 04 95 31 03 79) leave 7, r. Jean Jaurès for Bastia (3hr., M-Sa 2 per day, 115F/€17.55). The **tourist office** is around the corner from pl. de la République. (☎ 04 95 70 09 58; fax 04 95 70 03 72; www.accueil-portovecchio.com. Open June-Sept. M-Sa 9am-8pm, Su 9am-1pm; Oct.-May M-F 9am-12:30pm and 2-6pm, Sa 9am-12:30pm.) **Le Modern**, 10, cours Napoleon, has prime location. (☎ 04 95 70 06 36; www.modernhotel.ifrance.com. Open Apr.-Sept. Reserve ahead. Doubles 250-480F/€38.10-73.20; triples 350-650F/€53.40-99.10.) **Postal Code:** 20137.

THE ALPS (LES ALPES)

The curves of the Chartreuse Valley rise to rugged Alpine crags in the Vercors range and ultimately crescendo into Europe's highest peak, Mont Blanc (4807m). Winter **skiers** enjoy some of the most challenging slopes in the world, and then in the summer, **hikers** take over the same mountains for endless vistas and clean air. Hiking trails are clearly marked but consider investing in a *Topo-Guide* (hiking map). Skiing arrangements should be made a couple months in advance; Chamonix and Val d'Isère are the easiest bases. **TGV trains** will whisk you from Paris to Grenoble and Annecy; from there, Alpine towns are serviced by scenic trains and slower **buses.**

GRENOBLE

Grenoble's (pop. 156,203) charming *vieille ville* hosts the eccentric cafes, dusty bookshops, and shaggy radicals found in any university town, but its snow-capped peaks and sapphire-blue lakes are cherished by athletes and aesthetes alike.

TRANSPORTATION AND PRACTICAL INFORMATION. Trains arrive at **Gare Europole,** pl. de la Gare, from: Annecy (2hr., 12 per day, 91F/€13.90); Lyon (1½hr., 18 per day, 99F/€15.10); Marseilles (2½-4½hr., 15 per day, 196-242F/€29.90-36.95); Nice (5-6½hr., 5 per day, 301F/€45.90); Paris (3hr., 6 per day, 378-474F/€57.65-72.30). **Buses** leave from the left of the station for Chamonix (3hr., F-M 1 per day, 168F/€25.65) and Geneva (3hr., 1 per day, 158F/€24.10). From the station, turn right on pl. de la Gare, take the 3rd left on av. Alsace-Lorraine, and follow the tram tracks on r. Félix Poulat and r. Blanchard, and the **tourist office,** 14, r. de la République will be on your left. (☎ 04 76 42 41 41; fax 04 76 00 18 98; www.grenoble-isere-tourisme.com. Open M-Sa 9am-6:30pm, Su 10am-1pm and 2-5pm.) **Cybernet Café,** 3, r. Bayard, is a funky **Internet** cafe and bar. (☎ 04 76 51 73 18. 40F/€6.10 per hr. Open M-Sa 10am-1am. Happy Hour 6-8:30pm.) **Postal Code:** 38000.

ACCOMMODATIONS AND FOOD. To get from the station to the **Auberge de Jeunesse (HI),** 10, av. du Grésivaudan, 4km away in Echirolles, follow the tram tracks down av. Alsace-Lorraine, turn right on cours Jean Jaurès, and take bus #1 (dir.: Pont Rouge) to "La Quinzaine"; it's behind the Casino supermarket. (☎ 04 76 09 33 52; fax 04 76 09 38 99. Breakfast included. Laundry. Reception M-Sa 7:30am-11pm, Su 7:30-10am and 5:30-11pm. Over 26 102F/€15.60; 4- to 6-bed dorms 72F/€11; singles 110F/€16.80; doubles 170F/€25.95. MC/V.) To reach **Le Foyer de l'Etudiante,** 4, r. Ste-Ursule, follow pl. Ste-Claire from the tourist office to pl. Notre-Dame, and take r. du Vieux Temple on the far right. (☎ 04 76 42 00 84; fax 04 76 44 96 67. 2-night min. stay. Reception 24hr. **Oct.-Apr. women only.** Dorms 60F/€9.15; singles 90F/€13.75; doubles 140F/€21.35.) **Hôtel de L'Europe,** 22, pl. Grenette, is in the *vieille ville.* (☎/fax 04 76 46 16 94. Reception 24hr. Singles 157F/€23.95, with bath 210-265F/€32.05-40.40; doubles 170F/€25.95, 230-289F/€35.10-44.10; triples 321F/€48.95; quads 400F/€61. AmEx/MC/V.) To reach **Camping Les 3 Pucelles,** 58, r. des Allobroges, in Seyssins, take tram A (dir.: Fontaine-La Poya) to "Louis Maisonnat," then take bus #51 (dir.: Les Nalettes) to "Mas des Iles"; it's down to the left. (☎ 04 76 96 45 73; fax 04 76 21 43 73. 48F/€7.35 per person, tent, and car.) Cafes and restaurants line **Place Notre-Dame** and **Place St-André** in the *vieille ville.* **La Galerie Rome,** 1, r. Trois-Cloîtres, serves Grenoble's trademark dish, *gratin dauphinois,* for 55F/€8.40. (Open M noon-2:30pm, Tu-Su noon-2:30pm and 7-10pm.) Stock up on **groceries** at **Monoprix,** opposite the tourist office. (Open M-Sa 8:30am-8pm.)

SIGHTS AND THE OUTDOORS. *Téléphériques* (lifts) depart from quai Stéphane-Jay every 10min. for the 16th-century **Bastille,** a fort that hovers above town. Descend via the **Parc Guy Pape,** which criss-crosses through the fortress and deposits you just across the river from the train station. (☎ 04 76 44 33 65. Open July-Aug. M 11am-12:15am, Tu-Su 9:15am-12:15am; Nov.-Feb. M 11am-6:30pm, Tu-Su 10:45am-6:30pm; low-season reduced hours.) Cross the Pont St-Laurent and go up Montée Chalemont for the futuristic **Musée Dauphinois,** 30, r. Maurice Gignoux. (☎ 04 76 85 19 01. Open June-Sept. W-M 10am-7pm; Oct.-May 10am-6pm. 21F/€3.20, students 10.50F/€1.60.) Grenoble's major attraction is its proximity to the slopes. The biggest and most developed **ski areas** are to the east in **Oisans;** the **Alpe d'Huez** boasts 220km of trails. (Tourist office ☎ 04 76 11 44 44. 213F/€32.50 per day, 1102F/€168.05 per week.) The **Belledonne** region, northeast of Grenoble, lacks the towering heights of the Oisans but is cheaper. (Tourist office ☎ 04 76 89 92 65.)

FRANCE

Chamrousse is its biggest and most popular ski area (lift tickets 144F/€22 per day, 564F/€86 per week), and has a **youth hostel** (☎ 04 76 89 91 31; fax 04 76 89 96 96). Only 30min. from Grenoble by **bus** (50F/€7.65), the resort also makes an ideal day-trip in summer. Favored among mountain climbers are the slopes of the **Vercors.** In traditional villages 40min. away, small ski resorts, such as **Gresse-en-Vercors,** have vertical drops of 1000m. (Tourist office ☎ 04 76 34 33 40. Lift tickets 80F/€12.20 per day, 473F/€73.15 per week.) Grenoble boasts plenty of funky cafes and bars; most nightspots are in the area between **Place St-André** and **Place Notre-Dame.**

CHAMONIX

The site of the first Winter Olympics in 1924, Chamonix (pop. 10,000) is the quintessential ski town. Its slopes are among the toughest in the world, and its mountains are a supreme challenge to scale. The town itself combines the natural majesty of Mont Blanc, the tallest mountain in Europe, with a lighthearted spirit. Be prepared to spend your days in the great outdoors and nights at raucous *après-ski* spots.

TRANSPORTATION. Trains (☎ 04 50 53 12 98) leave av. de la Gare for: Annecy (2½hr., 7 per day, 106F/€16.20); Geneva, Switzerland (2½hr., 6 per day, 135F/€20.60); Lyon (4-5hr., 6 per day, 190F/€29); Paris (6hr., 6 per day, 400-504F/€61-76.85). Société Alpes Transports **buses** (☎ 04 50 53 01 15) leave the train station for: Annecy (2¼hr., 1 per day, 95F/€14.50); Geneva, Switzerland (1½hr., 2 per day, 170-195F/€25.95-29.75); Grenoble (3hr., 1 per day, 161F/€24.55). Local **Chamonix Bus** buses connect with ski slopes and hiking trails (7.50F/€1.15).

PRACTICAL INFORMATION. From the station, follow av. Michel Croz, turn left on r. du Dr. Paccard, and take the first right to reach the pl. de l'Eglise and the **tourist office,** 85, pl. du Triangle de l'Amitié. (☎ 04 50 53 00 24; fax 04 50 53 58 90. Open July-Aug. daily 8:30am-7:30pm; Dec.-Feb. 8:30am-7pm; Mar.-June and Sept.-Nov. 9am-noon and 2-6pm.) The **Office de Haute-Montagne,** on the third floor of Maison de la Montagne, across from the tourist office, is a mountain information center. (☎ 04 50 53 22 08; www.ohm-chamonix.com. Open July-Aug. daily 9am-noon and 3-6pm; Sept.-June closed Su; Oct.-Nov. closed Sa.) **Postal Code:** 74400.

ACCOMMODATIONS AND FOOD. Chamonix has numerous cheap *gîtes* and dormitories, but they fill up fast, so call in advance. ◧**Red Mountain Lodge,** 435, r. Joseph Vallot, is more of a home than hostel. (☎ 04 50 53 94 97; fax 04 50 53 82 64; www.redmountainlodge.co.uk. Breakfast included. Dorms 100F/€15.25; doubles and triples 140F/€21.35 per person, with bath 160F/€24.40.) The **Auberge de Jeunesse (HI),** 127, montée Jacques Balmat, in Les Pélerins at the base of the Glacier de Bossons, offers all-inclusive winter **ski packages** (1550-3650F/€236.35-556.50 per week). Take the bus from the train station or pl. de l'Eglise (dir.: Les Houches) to "Pélerins Ecole" (4F/€0.60) and follow the signs uphill. By train, get off at "Les Pélerins" and follow the signs. (☎ 04 50 53 14 52; fax 04 50 55 92 34; www.aj-chamonix.fr.st. Breakfast included. Reception daily 8am-noon and 5-10pm. Dorms 85F/€12.95; singles and doubles 15F/€2.30 extra per person. MC/V.) The spacious **Hôtel le Stade,** 70, r. Whymper, is the 1st right after exiting straight from the train station. (☎ 04 50 53 05 44; fax 04 50 53 96 39. Singles 140F/€21.35; doubles 220F/€33.55, with bath 300F/€45.75; triples 315F/€48.05, 435F/€66.35.) Turn left from the base of the Aiguille du Midi *téléphérique,* continue past the main rotary, and look right to **camp** at **L'Ile des Barrats,** on rte. des Pélerins. (☎/fax 04 50 53 51 44. Reception July-Aug. daily 8am-10:30pm; May-June and Sept. 8am-noon and 4-7pm. Open May-Sept. 32F/€4.90 per person, 24F/€3.65 per tent, 13F/€2 per car.) A **Super U** is at 117, r. Joseph Vallot. (Open M-Sa 8:15am-7:30pm, Su 8:30am-noon.)

THE GREAT OUTDOORS. Whether you've come to climb up the mountains or to ski down them, you're in for a challenge. However, be cautious wherever you go—on average, one person per day dies on the mountains. Start with a trip to the **ice cave** that's carved afresh every year by **La Mer de Glace,** a glacier that slides 30m per year. Special trains (☎04 50 53 12 54) run from a small station next to the main one. (July-Aug. every 20min. daily 8am-6pm; May-June and Sept.1-15 every 30min. daily 8:30am-5pm; mid-Sept. to Apr. reduced service daily 10am-4pm. Round-trip 82F/€12.50.) The **Aiguille du Midi** *téléphérique* offers a pricey but knuckle-whitening ascent to the needle-point peak at the top. The first stop is only a starting point for hikes, but the final stop, **l'Aiguille du Midi,** reveals a fantastic panorama from 3842m. (☎04 50 53 30 80; 24hr. reservations ☎08 36 68 00 67. Round-trip 210F/€32.05.) Chamonix has hundreds of kilometers of hikes through forests and glaciers. The tourist office sells a hiking map (25F/€3.85) that has information on all the trails. If you plan to ski for a week, buy a **Cham'Ski** pass (1101.95/€168), available at the tourist office or major *téléphériques*, which gives unlimited access to the Chamonix Valley. To the south, **Le Tour-Col de Balme** (☎04 50 54 00 58), above the village of **Le Tour,** cuddles up to the Swiss border with intermediate slopes (day pass 153F/€23.35). On the other side of the valley, extreme skiers and snowboarders will enjoy **Les Grands Montets,** the *grande dame* of Chamonix's ski spots, with all advanced terrain and remodeled **snowboarding** facilities (day pass 200F/€30.50).

ANNECY

With narrow, cobblestone streets, winding canals, and a turreted castle, all bordering the purest lake in Europe, Annecy (pop. 55,000) is more like a fairytale than a modern city. The **Palais de l'Îsle** is a 13th-century castle once occupied by the counts of Geneva. The old prison section, where Resistance fighters were jailed, is more interesting than the museum. (☎04 50 33 87 31. Open June-Sept. daily 10am-6pm; Oct.-May W-M 10am-noon and 2-6pm. 20F/€3.05, students 5F/€0.80.) The elegant **Jardins de l'Europe** are Annecy's pride and joy. The **Pont des Amours** (Bridge of Love) connects the gardens with the grassy **Champ de Mars.** Dive into Annecy's crystalline **Lac d'Annecy** at the crowded **Plage des Marquisats,** to the south down r. des Marquisats. The 12th-century **château** is a short but steep climb from the *vieille ville*. (☎04 50 33 87 30. Open June-Sept. daily 10am-6pm; Oct.-May W-M 10am-noon and 2-6pm. 30F/€4.60, students 10F/€1.55; grounds free.) Annecy's Alpine forests boast excellent **hiking** and **biking** trails. The **Office National des Forêts** (04 50 23 84 10) distributes maps (20F/€3.05 at the tourist office or hostel) with several routes.

   Trains leave pl. de la Gare for: Chamonix (2½hr., 7 per day, 106F/€16.20); Grenoble (2hr., 12 per day, 91F/€13.90); Lyon (2hr., 7 per day, 117F/€17.85); Nice (6hr., 2 per day, 352F/€53.70); Paris (4hr., 9 per day, 370-465F/€56.45-70.90). Autocars Frossard **buses** (☎04 50 45 73 90) leave from next to the station for Geneva (1¼hr., 6 per day, 57F/€8.70) and Lyon (3½ hr., 2 per day, 102F/€15.55). To reach the **tourist office,** 1, r. Jean Jaurés, from the train station, take the underground passage to r. Sommeiller, walk straight to r. Vaugelas, turn left and walk left for four blocks, and enter the Bonlieu shopping mall in pl. de la Libération. (☎04 50 45 00 33; fax 04 50 51 87 20; www.lac-annecy.com. Open July-Aug. M-Sa 9am-6:30pm, Su 9am-12:30pm and 1:45-6:30pm; Sept.-June daily 9am-12:30pm and 1:45-6pm.) Feed your **Internet** cravings at **Syndrome Cyber-café,** near the train station. (40F/€6.10 per hr. Open M-Sa noon-10pm, Su 2-10pm.) In summer, you can reach the █Auberge de Jeunesse "La Grande Jeanne" (HI), rte. de Semnoz, via the *ligne d'été* (dir.: Semnoz) from the station (July-Aug. daily 6 per day, June and Sept. Sa-Su 6 per day; 6.50F/€1); at other times, take bus #1 (dir.: Marquisats) from the station to "Hôpital," turn right on av. du Tresum, and follow the signs for Semnoz. (☎04 50 45 33 19; fax 04 50 52 77 52. Breakfast included. Reception daily 8am-10pm. Dorms 74F/€11.30. AmEx/MC/V.) From the station, exit left, walk around to av. Berthollet, and turn left on av. de Cran to reach the **Hôtel Savoyard,** 41, av. de Cran. (☎04 50 57 08 08. Breakfast 20F/€3.05. Singles and doubles 124F/€18.90, with bath 154-224F/€23.50-34.15; triples 156F/€23.80, 226F/€34.45; quads 200F/€30.50, 266F/€40.55.) Camp at **Camping le Bélvèdere,** 8, rte. de Semnoz, near the youth hostel. (☎04 50 45 48 30. Reception daily 8am to 8 or 9pm. Open mid-Apr. to mid-Oct. 45F/€6.90 per person with tent, 65-85F/€9.95-12.95 per couple. AmEx/MC/V.) A **Monoprix supermarket** fills most of pl. de Notre-Dame. (Open M-Sa 8:30am-7:30pm.) **Postal Code:** 74000.

FRANCE

LYON

France's second-largest city is second in little else. With industrial and culinary *savoir faire*, Lyon (pop. 1.5 million) has established itself as a cultural and economical alternative to Paris. While the narrow twisting streets of *vieux Lyon* are lined with elegant 16th-century townhouses, Lyon is a modern city, with every urban comfort imaginable, from skyscrapers and cafes to speedy transport systems and lush parks to concert halls and *discothèques*.

▶ TRANSPORTATION

Flights: Aéroport Lyon-Saint-Exupéry (☎ 04 72 22 72 21), 25km east of Lyon. The TGV, which stops at the airport, is cheaper than the 50 daily flights to Paris. **Satobuses/ Navette Aéroport** (☎ 04 72 68 72 17) shuttle to Gare de Perrache, Gare de la Part-Dieu, and subway stops Jean Mace, Grange-Blanche, and Mermoz Pinel (every 20min. until 9pm, 52.50F/€8). **Air France** is at 17, r. Victor Hugo, 2ème (☎ 0 820 820 820).

Trains: Trains passing through Lyon stop only at **Gare de la Part-Dieu,** bd. Marius Vivier-Merle (M: Part-Dieu), in the business district on the east bank of the Rhône. Trains terminating at Lyon stop also at **Gare de Perrache,** pl. Carnot (M: Perrache). TGV trains to Paris stop at both. **SNCF info and reservation desk** at Part-Dieu open M-F 9am-7pm, Sa 9am-6:30pm; Perrache open M-F 9am-7pm, Sa 9am-6:30pm. To: **Dijon** (2hr., 13 per day, 137F/€20.90); **Geneva,** Switzerland (2hr., 6 per day, 118F/€18); **Grenoble** (1¼hr., 15 per day, 99F/€15.10); **Marseilles** (3hr., 13 per day, 221F/€33.70); **Nice** (6hr., 15 per day, 299F/€45.60); **Paris** (2hr., 20 TGVs per day, 324-410F/€49.40-62.50); **Strasbourg** (5½hr., 9 per day, 248F/€37.85).

Buses: On the lowest level of the Gare de Perrache (☎ 04 72 77 63 03), and also at Gare de Part-Dieu (**Allô Transports,** ☎ 04 72 61 72 61). Domestic companies include **Philibert** (☎ 04 78 98 56 00) and **Transport Verney** (☎ 04 78 70 21 01). **Eurolines** (☎ 04 72 56 95 30; fax 04 72 41 72 43) travels out of France. Ask about student prices. Station open M-Sa 8am-8:30pm.

Local Transportation: TCL (☎ 04 78 71 70 00), has info offices at both train stations and major *Métro* stops. Pocket maps are available from the tourist office or any TCL branch. Tickets are valid for all methods of mass transport, including the **Métro, buses, funiculars,** and **trams. Single-fare tickets,** valid for 1hr. in 1 direction, 8.50F/€1.30; **carnet of 10** 68.50F/€10.45, students 58.50F/€8.95. The *Ticket Liberté* day pass (24F/€3.75) allows unlimited use of all mass transit for the day. The efficient **Métro** runs 5am-midnight. **Buses** run 5am-9pm (a few until midnight).

Taxis: Taxi Radio de Lyon (☎ 04 72 10 86 86). To airport from either train station 7am-7pm 220-240F/€33.55-36.60, afterwards 300F/€45.75. 24hr.

✦ ▶ ORIENTATION AND PRACTICAL INFORMATION

Lyon is divided into nine *arrondissements* (districts). The 1er, 2ème, and 4ème lie on the **presqu'île** (peninsula), which juts south toward the confluence of the Saône and Rhône rivers. Starting south, the **2ème** *(centre ville)* includes the **Perrache** train station and **Place Bellecour.** In the **1er** is the nocturnal **Terraux** neighborhood with cafes and bars. Further north, is the **4ème** and the **Croix-Rousse.** The main pedestrian arteries of the *presqu'île* are **Rue de la République,** northeast of pl. Bellecour, and **Rue Victor Hugo,** to the south of pl. Bellecour. West of the Saône, is Vieux Lyon and **Fourvière Hill.** East of the Rhône (3ème and 6-8ème) lies the **Part-Dieu** train station, the commercial complex, and most of the city's population. Fourvière and its **Tour Metallique** are to the west, and the **Tour du Crédit Lyonnais** is to the east. Lyon's safe and simple **Métro** is the fastest way to reach the tourist office. From Perrache, take line A (dir.: Bonnevay); from Part-Dieu take B (dir.: Charpennes), and then take line A (dir.: Perrache); get off at "Bellecour" for the town center.

FRANCE

Amphithéâtre
des Trois Gaulles

r. des
Tables Claudiennes
M. des Carmelites
r. Burdeau
r. R. Leynaud
r. des Capucins
r. Romarin
r. Désirée
r. de l'Annonciade
r. du Sgt Blandan
r. Ste-Catherine
Hôtel
de Ville
PL. LOUIS
PRADEL
quai Jean Moulin
Sein
r. l'Arbre Sec
TO PARC DE LA TÊTE
D'OR (1km), CITÉ
INTERNATIONALE (1.5km)
AND CENTRE D'HISTOIRE
DE LA RESISTANCE ET
LA DEPORTATION

Rhône

PL. DE LA
COMEDIE
Opéra
M HÔTEL DE
VILLE

r. de la Martinière
r. d'Algère
PL. DES
TERREAUX
r. Paul Chenavard
Musée St-Pierre
d'Art Contemporain
du Président Edouard Herriot

quai St-Vincent
Musée
des Beaux-
Arts
r. de Constantine
r. Lanterne

1

quai de la Pêcherie
2
Longée
r. Neuve
r. de Brest
PL. DE
LA BOURSE
PL. DES CORDELIERS
r. Claudia
r. J. Serlin
r. Gentil

quai de Bondy
Saône
PL.
D'ALBON
quai St-Antoine
r. Grenette
r. Mercière
r. Tupin
r. Groiée
CORDELIERS

r. St-Paul
Gare St-Paul
Palais de la
Miniature
r. Fr. Vernay
PL. DU
CHANGE
quai Romain Rolland
r. Ferrandière
r. Thomassin
Pas de
l'Argue
r. de la
PL. DE LA
REPUBLIQUE
United
Kingdom
Stella
r. du Président Carnot
TO
GARE PART-DIEU
(1.5km)
quai Jules Courmont

M. des Carmes
M. St-Barthélemy
Musée
de la
Marionette
Pont
Alphonse Juin
r. de la Monnaie
r. J. de
Tournes
r. Childebert
PL. DES
JACOBINS
American
Express
République

M. Nicolas Lange
r. de la
Juiverie
r. du Bœuf
Palais de
Justice
P. du Palais
de Justice
quai des Célestins
r. de Savoie
r. Ch. Dullin
Emile
r. des Archers
Théâtre des Célestins
r. G. André
r. d'Amboise
Bellecordière
Hôpital
Hôtel
Dieu

Tour Métallique
M. des
Chazeaux
r. de la Bombarde
BELLECOUR
M

Chemin
du Rosaire
Basilique
Notre-Dame
de Fourvière
F FOURVIÈRE
M
Tour de
l'Observatoire
r. R. Radisson
r. Cléberg
PL.
ST-JEAN
Cathédrale
St-Jean
F M
VIEUX
LYON
ave A. Max
Pont
Bonaparte
r. de la Barre
PL.
BELLECOUR
i
TO INSTITUT
LUMIÈRE
(2.8km)
PL. ANTONIN
PONCET

Musée de
la Civilization
Gallo-Romaine
Montée du Chemin Neuf
3
ave. du Doyenné
quai Tilsitt
quai du Plat
r. A. Fochier
r. Fr. Dauphin
r. Ch. Bienner

Théâtres
Romains
r. de l'Antiquaille
F MINIMES
PL. DE LA
COMMANDERIE
r. Sala
r. Victor Hugo
r. J. A. Comte
r. de la Charité

Parc
Archéologique
P. St.
Georges
PL. ANTOINE
VOLLAN
r. Ste-Hélène
d'Auvergne
Musée Historique
des Tissus &
Musée Lyonnais
des Arts Décoratifs
r. Laurencin

ST-JUST
F
r. des Farges
0   200 yards
0   200 meters
quai Fulchiron
quai Tilsitt
r. Guynemer
r. Vaubecour
4
r. Jarente
AMPÈRE
VICTOR HUGO
M
r. des Remparts d'Ainay
PL.
AMPÈRE
r. Franklin

Saône
r. Bourgelat
Henri IV
PLACE
CARNOT
r. de Condé
r. Mazard
r. Duhamel

r. de Castries
r. d'Enghien
r. G. Plessier
PERRACHE
M
Gare de
Perrache
TO
(1.5km)
c. de Verdun

P. Kitchener
Marchand
autoroute A7
cours de Verdun
r. du Bélier

Lyon

⌂ ACCOMMODATIONS

Auberge de Jeunesse (HI), **3**
Hôtel St-Pierre Terreaux, **2**
Hôtel St-Vincent, **1**
Hôtel Vaubecour, **4**
Résidence B. Delessert, **5**

Funicular **F**
Métro **M**

FRANCE

Tourist Office: In the Tourist Pavilion, at pl. Bellecour, 2ème (☎04 72 77 69 69; fax 04 78 42 04 32). M: Bellecour. Indispensable **"Map and Guide"** (5F/€0.80), hotel reservation office, SNCF desk, and city tours (50-60F/€7.60-9.15, students 25-35F/€3.80-5.35). The **Lyon City Card** (90-200F/€13.75-30.50) authorizes unlimited public transport along with admission to the 14 biggest museums and various tours. Valid for 1, 2, or 3 days. Open May-Oct. M-Sa 9am-6pm; Nov.-Apr. daily 10am-6pm.

Consulates: Canada, 21, r. Bourgelat, 2ème (☎04 72 77 64 07). 1 block west of Ampere *Métro* stop. Open M-F 9am-noon. **Ireland,** 58, r. Victor Lagrange, 7ème (☎06 85 23 12 03). Open M-F 9am-noon. **UK,** 24, r. Childebert, 2ème (☎04 72 77 81 70). M: Bellecour. Open M-F 9am-12:30pm and 2-5:30pm. **US,** 16, r. de République, 2ème (☎04 78 38 33 03). In the World Trade Center. Open 9am-noon and 2-6pm.

Emergency: ☎17.

Police: 47, r. de la Charité (☎04 78 42 26 56).

Hospital/Medical Service: Hôpital Hôtel-Dieu, 1, pl. de l'Hôpital, 2ème (☎04 72 41 30 00), near quai du Rhône.

Internet Access: Station-Internet, 4, r. du President Carnot, 2ème. 40F/€6.10 per hr., students 30F/€4.60 per hr. Open M-Sa 10am-7pm. Also **Connectix Café,** 19, quai St-Antoine, 2ème. 50F/€7.65 per hr. Open M-Sa 11am-7pm.

Post Office: Pl. Antonin Poncet, 2ème (☎04 72 40 65 22), near pl. Bellecour. **Currency exchange.** Open M-F 8am-5pm, Su 8am-12:30pm. Address mail to be held: SURNAME, FirstName *Poste Restante,* pl. Antonin Poncet, **69002** Lyon, France. **Postal Codes:** 69001-69009; last digit indicates *arrondissement.*

▐ ACCOMMODATIONS

As a financial center, Lyon has few empty beds during the work week but openings on the weekends. Fall is actually the busiest season; it's easier and cheaper to find a place in the summer, but making reservations is still a good idea. Budget hotels cluster east of **Place Carnot,** near Perrache. Prices rise as you approach **Place Bellecour,** but there are less expensive options north of **Place des Terreaux.**

▨ **Hôtel St-Vincent,** 9, r. Pareille, 1er (☎04 78 27 22 56; fax 04 78 30 92 87). Just off the Quai St-Vincent, north of passerelle St-Vincent. Simple, elegant rooms. Breakfast 30F/€4.60. Reception 24hr. Reserve ahead. Singles with shower 180F/€27.45, with bath 230F/€35.10; doubles 230F/€35.10, 270F/€41.20. MC/V.

Auberge de Jeunesse (HI), 41-45, montée du Chemin Neuf, 5ème (☎04 78 15 05 50; fax 04 78 15 05 51). M: Vieux Lyon. From pl. Bellecour, walk toward the old city, cross pont Bonaparte, turn right through pl. St-Jean, turn left on r. de la Bombarde, take a hairpin left turn on montée du Chemin Neuf, and climb for 10min. Or, take the funicular from Vieux Lyon to "Minimes," walk down the stairs and go left down the hill. Breakfast included. Reception 24hr. **HI members only.** 4- to 8-bed dorms 75F/€11.45. V.

Résidence Benjamin Delessert, 145, av. Jean Jaurès, 7ème (☎04 78 61 41 41; fax 04 78 61 40 24). From Part-Dieu, take the Métro to "Jean Macé." From Perrache, take buses #11 or 39 to "Jean Macé," walk under the tracks, and look left after 3 blocks. Lively atmosphere. Reception 24hr. Singles 91F/€13.90, with shower 95F/€14.50.

Hôtel Vaubecour, 28, r. Vaubecour, 2ème (☎04 78 37 44 91; fax 04 78 42 90 17), on the east bank of the Saône. Elegantly furnished rooms. Breakfast 25F/€3.85. Reception 7am-midnight. Reserve ahead. Singles from 150F/€22.90; doubles from 170F/€25.95; triples and quads from 355F/€54.15. Extra bed 80F/€12.20. MC/V.

Hôtel St-Pierre des Terreaux, 8, r. Paul Chenavard (☎04 78 28 24 61; fax 04 72 00 21 07). M: Hotel de Ville. 5min. from Musée des Beaux Arts, the Opéra, and the bars. Breakfast 35F/€5.35. Reception 6:30am-midnight. Reserve well ahead. Singles 190-250F/€29-38.10; doubles 230-270F/€35.10-41.20. MC/V.

◖ FOOD

The galaxy of *Michelin* stars adorning Lyon's restaurants confirms the city's reputation as the culinary capital of the Western world. But if *haute cuisine* doesn't suit your wallet, try one of Lyon's many **bouchons,** cozy restaurants serving local

FRANCE

cuisine for low prices. *Bouchons* can be found in the **Terraux** district, along **Rue des Marronniers** and **Rue Mercière** (both in the 2*ème*), and on **Rue St-Jean** in Vieux Lyon. Ethnic restaurants are near **Rue de la République,** in the 2*ème*. A **Monoprix supermarket** is on r. de la République, at pl. des Cordeliers, 2*ème*. (Open M-Sa 8:30am-9:30pm.)

🎇 **Chez Mounier,** 3, r. des Marronniers, 2*ème* (☎04 78 37 79 26). This tiny place satisfies a discriminating local clientele with generous traditional specialties. 4-course *menus* 61-96F/€9.30-14.65. Open Tu-Sa noon-2pm and 7-10:30pm, Su noon-2pm.

Chabert et Fils, 11, r. des Marronniers, 2*ème* (☎04 78 37 01 94). One of the better-known *bouchons* in Lyon. For dessert, try the delicious *Guignol*. Lunch *menus* start at 50F/€7.65. Open daily noon-2pm and 7-11pm. MC/V.

Mister Patate, pl. St-Jean, 5*ème* (☎04 78 38 18 79). A fantastic vegetarian option with 44 potato specialties. Plates from 35-50F/€5.35-7.60. Open M-Sa 11:30am-3pm and 6-11:30pm, Su 11:30-3pm and 6-10pm.

PÂTISSERIE

Bernachon, 42, cours F. Roosevelt, 6*ème* (☎04 78 24 37 98). Lyon's grandest *pâtisserie* makes chocolate entirely from scratch. Locals take pride in the *cocons* (chocolates wrapped in marzipan). Open M-F 9am-7pm, Sa 8:30am-7pm.

👁 SIGHTS

VIEUX LYON. Nestled against the Saône at the bottom of Fourvière Hill, the narrow streets of *Vieux Lyon* wind between cafes, tree-lined squares, and magnificent medieval and Renaissance houses. The regal homes around **Rue St-Jean, Rue du Boeuf,** and **Rue Juiverie** have been the homes of Lyon's elite for over 400 years.

TRABOULES. The distinguishing feature of *Vieux Lyon* townhouses, these tunnels lead from the street through a maze of elaborate courtyards. At one time, *traboules* were used to transport silk safely from looms to storage rooms. During WWII, the passageways proved invaluable for information gathering and escape routes for the Resistance. Many are open to the public at specific hours; get a list of addresses from the tourist office or take a tour. *(Tours in the summer daily 2pm, irregular hours during rest of year; consult the tourist office. 60F/€9.15, students 30F/€4.60.)*

CATHÉDRALE ST-JEAN. The southern end of *Vieux Lyon* is dominated by the Cathédrale St-Jean, with soaring columns and delicate stained glass windows that look too fragile to have withstood eight centuries of religious turmoil. Henri IV met and married Maria de Médici here in 1600. Inside, automatons pop out of the 14th-century astronomical clock, every hour between noon and 4pm, in a re-enactment of the Annunciation. *(Open M-F 8am-noon and 2-7:30pm, Sa-Su 2-5pm. Free.)*

MUSÉE DE LA MARIONETTE. Down r. St-Jean, turn left at the pl. du Change for the **Hôtel de Gadagne** and its small museums. Inside is the **Musée de la Marionette,** displaying puppets from around the world, including models of **Guignol,** the famed local cynic, and his inebriated friend, Gnaffron. *(Pl. du Petit College, 5ème. M: Vieux Lyon. ☎04 78 42 03 61. Open W-M 10:45am-8pm. 25F/€3.85, students 13F/€2, 18 and under free.)*

FOURVIERE AND ROMAN LYON. From the corner of r. du Bœuf and r. de la Bombarde in *Vieux Lyon,* climb the stairs heading straight up to reach the **Fourvière Hill,** the nucleus of **Roman Lyon.** Continue up via the rose-lined **Chemin de la Rosaire,** and then through a garden to the **Esplanade Fourvière,** where a model of the cityscape points out local landmarks. *(Open daily 6:30am-9:30pm.)* Most prefer to take the less strenuous **funicular** *(la ficelle)* from the head of av. A. Max in Vieux Lyon, off pl. St-Jean, to the top of the hill. The **Tour de l'Observatoire** offers an incredible view—on a clear day, look for Mont Blanc, about 200km east. *(Open June-Sept. daily 10am-noon and 2-6pm; Oct.-May Sa-Su 1:30-5:30pm only. 10F/€1.55, students 5F/€0.75.)*

BASILIQUE NOTRE-DAME DE FOURVIÈRE. When the city was spared attack during the Franco-Prussian War, Lyon's archbishop made good on his promise to build a church. Inside the white, meringue-like exterior, the walls are decked with

FRANCE

gigantic, gilded mosaics depicting religious scenes, including Joan of Arc at Orléans and the naval battle of Lepante. *(Behind the Esplanade. Open daily 8am-7pm.)*

MUSÉE GALLO-ROMAIN. Almost invisible from the outside, circling deep into the historic hillside of Fourvière, the five levels of this brilliant museum hold a huge collection of arms, pottery, statues, and jewelry. Highlights include six brilliant mosaics and a bronze tablet inscribed with a speech by Lyon's native son, the Roman Emperor Claudius. *(17, r. Cléberg, 5ème. ☎ 04 72 38 81 90. Open Mar.-Oct. Tu-Su 10am-6pm; Nov.-Feb. Tu-Su 10am-5pm. 25F/€3.85, students 15F/€2.30.)*

LA PRESQU'ÎLE AND LES TERREAUX. Monumental squares, statues, and fountains highlight the Presqu'île, a lively area between the Rhône and the Saône. Its heart is **Place Bellecour,** an expanse of red gravel lined with shops and flower stalls. The pedestrian **Rue Victor Hugo** runs south from Bellecour, lined with boutiques and rollerbladers. To the north, the crowded **Rue de la République** is the urban aorta of Lyon. It runs through **Place de la République** and terminates at **Place Louis Pradel** in the 1er, at the tip of the chic and bustling Terreaux district. Nearby, at **Place Louis Pradel,** is the 17th-century **Hôtel de Ville.** The **Opéra,** pl. Louis Pradel, is a 19th-century neoclassical edifice supporting what looks like an airplane hangar.

▧ MUSÉE DES BEAUX-ARTS. Second only to the Louvre, the museum includes a comprehensive archeological wing, a distinguished collection of French paintings, works by Spanish and Dutch masters, a wing devoted to the Italian Renaissance, and a lovely sculpture garden. Even the more esoteric works are delightful. Be sure to visit Maillol's bronze *Venus*, whose classic composure is disrupted by a single displaced lock of hair. *(Pl. des Terreaux. ☎ 04 72 10 17 40. Open W-M 10:30am-6pm. 25F/€3.85, students 13F/€2.)*

CROIX-ROUSSE DISTRICT. Begun in the 15th century, Lyon's silk industry operated 28,000 looms by the 18th century, mainly in the Croix-Rousse district. Mass silk manufacturing is based elsewhere today, and Lyon's few remaining silk workers perform delicate handiwork of reconstructing and replicating rare patterns for museum and château displays.

MUSÉE HISTORIQUE DES TISSUS. It's not in the Croix-Rousse quarter, but textile and fashion fans—along with anyone else who's ever worn clothes—will have a field day here. This world-class collection includes wonderfully preserved examples of 18th-century elite garb and luminous silk wall hangings that look like stained glass windows. Included with admission is the neighboring **Musée des Arts Décoratifs,** housed in an 18th-century *hôtel*, with a comprehensive collection of period porcelain, furniture, and ornamental excess. *(34, r. de la Charité, 2ème. ☎ 04 78 38 42 00. Both museums open Tu-Su 10am-5:30pm. 30F/€4.60, students 15F/€2.30.)*

MODERN LYON. Lyon's newest train station and monstrous space-age mall form the core of the ultra-modern **Part-Dieu** district. Many see the place as an eyesore and consider its shops to be its greatest virtue—perhaps the only ones in France open between noon and 2pm. Locals call the **Tour du Crédit Lyonnais,** on the other end of the mall, *"Le Crayon"* (the pencil). Next to it, the shell-shaped **Auditorium Maurice Ravel** hosts major cultural events.

CENTRE D'HISTOIRE DE LA RESISTANCE ET DE LA DEPORTATION. The center is housed in a building in which Nazis tortured detainees during the Occupation. Here you'll find assembled documents, photos, and films of the Resistance, which was based in Lyon. The museum forces upon its visitors a haunting awareness of the context of genocide and resistance in France. *(14, av. Bertholet, 7ème. M: Jean Mace. ☎ 04 78 72 23 11. Open W-Su 9am-5:30pm. 25F/€3.85, students 13F/€2. Admission includes an audio guide in French, English, and German.)*

MUSÉE D'ART CONTEMPORAIN. In the super-modern **Cité International de Lyon** commercial complex, you'll find this extensive and entertaining mecca of modern art. All the museum's exhibits are temporary; the walls themselves are built anew each time. *(Quai Charles de Gaulle, , 6ème, next to Parc de la Tête d'Or. Bus #4 from M: Foch.* ☎ *04 72 69 17 18. Open Tu and Th-Su noon-7pm, W noon-10pm. 25F/€3.85, students 13F/€2.)*

PARC DE LA TÊTE D'OR. The massive park, one of the biggest in Europe, owes its name to a legend that a golden head of Jesus lies buried somewhere within its grounds. The park sprawls over 105 hectares, and you can rent paddle boats to explore its artificial lake and artificial island. Thousands of animals fill the zoo, and the 60,000-bush rose gardens are stunning in summer. *(☎ 04 78 89 02 03. Park open Apr.-Sept. daily 11am-7pm; Oct.-Mar. 6am-9pm.)*

⚡ NIGHTLIFE

At the end of June is the two-week **Festival du Jazz à Vienne,** which welcomes jazz masters to Vienne, a medieval town south of Lyon, accessible by bus or train. (☎ 04 74 85 00 05. Tickets 160F/€24.40, students 150F/€22.90.) **Les Nuits de Fourvière** is a two-month summer music festival held in the ancient Théâtre Romain and Odéon. (☎ 04 72 32 00 00. Tickets and info at the Théâtre Romain and the FNAC shop on r. de la Republique.) The biannual **Festival de Musique du Vieux Lyon,** 5, pl. du Petit Collège, 5ème, draws artists worldwide between mid-Nov. and mid-Dec. to perform in the churches of Vieux Lyon. (☎ 04 78 42 39 04. Tickets 90-230F/€13.75-35.05.)

Nightlife in Lyon is fast and furious. Students congregate in a series of bars on **Rue Ste-Catherine** (1er) until 1am before heading to the clubs. There's a whole row of semi-exclusive joints off the Saône, on **Quais Romain Rolland, de Bondy,** and **Pierre Scize** in Vieux Lyon (5ème). The city's best and most accessible late-night spots are a strip of riverboat dance clubs by the east bank of the Rhône.

▨ **Le Fish,** across from 21, quai Augagneur (☎ 04 72 87 98 98). Has theme nights with salsa, jungle, groove, hip-hop and disco. Cover 60-80F/€9.15-12.20, includes 1st drink, F-Sa free before 11pm. Open W-Sa 10pm-5am.

Le Chantier, 20, r. Ste-Catherine, 1er. Slip down the spiral slide to reach the dance floor downstairs. Open Tu-Sa 9pm-3am.

Ayers Rock Café, 2, r. Desiree (☎ 04 78 29 13 45) and the **Cosmopolitan** (☎ 04 72 07 09 80), next door. A hotspot for students, with lots of drinking (shooters 20F/€3.05) and fun bartenders. Open M-Sa 6pm-3am.

La Marquise (☎ 04 78 71 78 71), next to Le Fish. Draws big-name DJs for jungle and house. Cover 50F/€7.65. Open W-Sa 10pm-dawn.

L'United Café, impasse de la Pêcherie (☎ 04 78 29 93 18), in an alley off of quai de la Pêcherie. Plays American and Latino dance hits and the occasional slow song for a mixed gay-lesbian crowd. No cover; drinks from 35F/€5.35. Open daily 10pm-5am.

Le Village Club, 6, r. Violi (☎ 04 72 07 72 62), off r. Royale north of pl. Louis Pradel. Has fabulous drag queens nightly. Attracts a mostly mid-20s to mid-30s male crowd. Drinks 20-35F/€3.05-5.35. Open W-Th 9pm-3am, F-Sa 10pm-4am.

⚡ DAYTRIPS FROM LYON

ANNECY. A 2hr. train ride will take you into the fairytale city of Annecy, nestled in the French Alps (see p. 369).

BEAUJOLAIS

Guided bus tours in English are available from Lyon. ☎ 04 78 98 56 98. Apr.-Oct. Th-F and Su; tours leave at 1:15pm, return to Lyon at 7pm. 210F/€32.05.

The very mention of Beaujolais provokes a thirst for the cool, fruity wine that it exports. Beaujolais lies roughly between the Loire and the Saône, with Lyon and Mâcon on either end. The tourist offices dotting the countryside can provide suggested bike or car routes that wind through vineyards, sleepy villages, and medieval châteaux, with a few *dégustations* (tastings) thrown in for good measure.

FRANCE

BERRY-LIMOUSIN

Too often passed over for beaches and big cities, Berry-Limousin offers peaceful countryside, quaint villages, and fascinating towns. Bourges served as the capital of France and benefited from King Charles VII's financier, Jacques Cœur, who built a lavish string of châteaux. The region later became an artistic and literary breeding ground, home to Georges Sand, Auguste Renoir, and Jean Giraudoux.

BOURGES

In 1433, Jacques Coeur chose Bourges (pop. 80,000) as the site for one of his many châteaux. You'll see more of the unfurnished **Palais Jacques-Coeur** than he ever did, for he was imprisoned for embezzlement before its completion. (Open July-Aug. daily 9am-6pm; Apr.-June and Sept. 9am-noon and 2-6pm; Nov.-Mar. 9am-noon and 2-5pm. 36F/€5.50, ages 18-24 23F/€3.50, under 18 free.) The **Cathédrale St-Etienne,** has stunning 13th-century handiwork in the **tower** and **crypt,** a dramatic Gothic façade, and stained-glass windows. (Open Apr.-Sept. daily 8:30am-7:15pm; Oct.-Mar. 9am-5:45pm; closed Su 12:45-2pm. 36F/€5.50, students 23F/€3.50.) As you exit the cathedral, head right on r. des 3 Maillets and turn left on r. Molière for the **promenade des Remparts,** which offers a quiet stroll past ramparts and flowery gardens.

  Trains leave from the station at pl. Général Leclerc (☎02 48 51 00 00) for: Paris (2½hr., 5-8 per day, 156F/€23.80) and Tours (1½hr., 10 per day, 108F/€16.50). From the station, follow av. H. Laudier, which turns into av. Jean Jaurès, bear left onto r. du Commerce, and continue down r. Moyenne to reach the **tourist office,** 21, r. Victor Hugo. (☎02 48 23 02 60; fax 23 02 69. Open M-Sa 9am-7pm, Su 10am-7pm.) To get to the **Auberge de Jeunesse (HI),** 22, r. Henri Sellier, follow the above directions to r. du Commerce, bear right on r. des Arènes, which becomes r. Fernault, cross at the intersection to r. René Ménard, follow it to the right, and turn left at r. Henri Sellier. (☎02 48 24 58 09. Reception M-F 8am-noon and 2pm-1am, Sa-Su 8am-noon and 5-10pm. 3- to 8-bed dorms 50F/€7.65 per person.) For the **Centre International de Séjour, "La Charmille,"** 17, r. Félix-Chédin, cross the footbridge from the station over the tracks. (☎02 48 23 07 40. Singles 98F/€15; 2 or more people 72F/€11 per person. MC/V.) **Place Gordaine, Rue des Beaux-Arts, Rue Moyenne,** and **Rue Mirabeau** are lined with eateries. The **Leclerc supermarket** is on r. Prado off bd. Juraville. (Open M-F 9:15am-7:20pm, Sa 8:30am-7:20pm.) **Le Phénicien,** 13, r. Jean Girard, off pl. Gordaine, offers decent Middle Eastern cuisine. (Open M-Sa 11am-11pm.) **Postal Code:** 18000.

BURGUNDY (BOURGOGNE)

What the Loire Valley is to châteaux, Burgundy is to churches. During the Middle Ages, the duchy was the heart of the religious fever sweeping Europe: abbeys swelled in size and wealth, and towns eager for pilgrim traffic built magnificent cathedrals. Today, Burgundy's production of some of the world's finest wines and delectable dishes, like *coq au vin* and *bœuf bourguignon,* have made this region the homeland of Epicureans worldwide.

DIJON

Dijon (pop. 160,000) isn't just about the mustard. The capital of Burgundy is a charming city with gardens, a couple good museums, and fine wines. The diverse **Musée des Beaux-Arts** occupies the east wing of the colossal **Palais des Ducs de Bourgogne,** in pl. de la Libération at the center of the *vieille ville.* (☎03 80 74 52 70. Open W-M 10am-6pm. 22F/€3.35, students free, Su everyone free.) The **Horloge à Jacquemart,** ticking above the tower of **Eglise Notre-Dame,** in pl. Notre-Dame, is worth the maneuevering to see. The brightly tiled **Cathédrale St-Bénigne,** in pl. St-Bénigne, has a spooky circular crypt. (☎03 80 30 14 90. Open 9am-6:30pm. Crypt 7F/€1.10.) Next door, the **Musée Archéologique,** 5, r. Dr. Maret, features Gallo-Roman sculpture and Neolithic house wares. (☎03 80 30 88 54. Open June-Sept. Tu-Su 9am-6pm; Oct.-May Tu-Su 9am-noon and 2-6pm. 14F/€2.15, students free, Su everyone free.) Get your

FRANCE

Grey Poupon at the Maille Boutique, 32, r. de la Liberté, where *moutarde au vin* has been made since 1747. (☎ 03 80 30 41 02. Open M-Sa 9am-7pm.)

From the train station at cours de la Gare, at the end of av. Maréchal Foch, **trains** chug to: Lyon (2hr., 11 per day, 137F/€20.90); Nice (7-8hr. 9 per day, 386F/€58.85); Paris (1½hr., 14 TGVs per day, 213F/€32.50). The **tourist office,** on pl. Darcy, is a straight shot down av. Maréchal Foch from the station. (☎ 03 80 44 11 44. Open July-Aug. daily 9am-8pm; Sept.-June 9am-7pm.) To get to the huge **Auberge de Jeunesse (HI), Centre de Rencontres Internationales,** 1, av. Champollion, take bus #5 (or night bus A) from pl. Grangier to Epirey. (☎ 03 80 72 95 20; fax 03 80 70 00 61. Breakfast included. Dorms 72-78F/€11-11.90; singles 180F/€27.45; doubles and triples 90-155F/€13.75-23.65. MC/V.) **Hôtel Montchapet,** 26-28, r. Jacques Cellerier, north of av. Première Armée Française off pl. Darcy, is bright and comfortable. (☎ 03 80 53 95 00; fax 03 80 58 26 87. Breakfast 33F/€5.05. Reception 7am-10:30pm. Check-out 11am. Singles 155-250F/€23.65-38.10; doubles 230-296F/€35.10-45.15; triples and quads 347-378F/€52.90-57.65.) **Rues Berbisey** and **Monge** host a wide variety of low- to mid-priced restaurants. Fend for yourself at the **supermarket** in the **Galeries Lafayette,** 41, r. de la Liberté. (Open M-Sa 9am-7:15pm.) **Postal Code:** 21000.

◨ **DAYTRIP FROM DIJON: BEAUNE.** Wine has poured out of the well-touristed town of **Beaune,** just south of Dijon (25min., 28 trains per day, 38F/€5.80), for centuries. Surrounded by the famous Côte de Beaune vineyards, the town itself is packed with wineries offering free *dégustations* (tastings). The largest of the cellars belongs to **Patriarche Père et Fils,** 5-7, r. du Collège, a labyrinth of 5km of corridors packed with over four million bottles. (☎ 03 80 24 53 78. Open daily 9:30-11:30am and 2-5:30pm. 50F/€7.65.) The **tourist office,** 1, r. de l'Hôtel-Dieu, lists *caves* (cellars) in the region offering tours. (☎ 03 80 26 21 30; fax 03 80 26 21 39. Open mid-June to mid-Sept. M-Sa 9:30am-8pm, Su 9:30am-6pm; mid-Sept. to mid-June usually closes 1hr. earlier. **Wine Festival,** Nov. 16-18 9am-8pm.)

AVALLON AND VÉZELAY

High atop a hillside, the village of Vézelay (pop. 497) watches over dense forests and the misty gold of wheat. The houses, covered with red tile roofs and wild roses, seem lost in time. Vézelay lives up to its billing as one of the most beautiful villages in France. The town has been a major pilgrimage destination since the 11th century, thanks to the relics of Saint Mary Magdelene held within the **basilica.** The main attraction is the array of grotesque, lyrical carved capitals, which depict Biblical monsters and tales of violence. (Open daily 8am-7:30pm. 30F/€4.60 suggested donation.) **Avallon** (pop. 8560) is poor on museums and monuments but can be used as a base from which to explore nearby Vézelay.

Avallon has one of the region's few train stations. **SNCF trains** run to Dijon (2-3hr., 3 per day, 73F/€11.15) and Paris (2½-3hr. 1-4 per day, 155F/€23.65). On Saturdays, you can wait for the **bus** (☎ 03 86 33 35 95) which runs between Vézelay and Avallon. In summer, an **SNCF bus** leaves the train station at Avallon for Vézelay (22min., 23F/€3.50). The tiny **tourist office,** r. St-Pierre, just down the street from the church, offers free maps and a *guide pratique* with accommodations listings. (☎ 03 86 33 23 69. Open June-Oct. daily 10am-1pm and 2-6pm; Nov.-May closed Th.) The closest bank is in Avallon, but the **post office,** r. St-Etienne, has an **ATM.** (☎ 03 86 33 26 35. Open M-F 8:30am-12:30pm and 1:30-5pm, Sa 8:30-noon.) **Postal Code:** 89450.

ALSACE, LORRAINE, AND FRANCHE-COMTÉ

As first prize in the endless Franco-German border wars, France's northeastern frontier has long been a bloody battlefield. Given its ping-pong history, it's not surprising that the region's cuisine, architecture, and *patois* vary area to area. Germanic influences are most apparent in its cuisine, pairing *baguettes* and wine with sauerkraut and heavy German meats, adding heartiness to traditional delicacies.

STRASBOURG

Just a few kilometers from the Franco-German border, Strasbourg (pop. 260,000) has spent much of its history being annexed by one side or another. Today the city serves as a symbol of French-German *détente*, with as many *winstubs* as *pâtisseries* lining its squares. Strasbourg is also the joint center of the European Union, along with Brussels. This quaint and charming city makes a fantastic stopover.

⊑ TRANSPORTATION. Flights leave **Strasbourg-Entzheim** airport, 15km from Strasbourg. **Air France,** 15, r. des Francs-Bourgeois (☎ 03 88 55 29 09), flys frequently to: London (students from 595-1102F/€90.75-168.05); Lyon (students from 349-694F/€53.20-105.80); Paris (students from 263-522F/€40.10-79.60). **Shuttle buses** (☎ 03 88 77 70 70) run from the airport to Baggarsee and then to the tram that can be taken into town. (12min., 3-4 per hr. 5:30am-11pm, 27-49F/€4.15-7.50). Strasbourg is a major European rail hub. **Trains** (☎ 03 88 22 50 50) depart from pl. de la Gare to: Frankfurt (3hr., 18 per day, 240F/€36.60); Luxembourg (2½hr., 14 per day, 165F/€25.15); Paris (4hr., 16 per day, 226F/€34.45); Zürich (3hr., 3-4 per hr., 255F/€38.90). The **CTS tram line** provides frequent local service. (Tickets 7F/€1.10, carnet of 5 31F/€4.75, day pass 20F/€3.05. Available at *tabacs*.)

▉◪ ORIENTATION AND PRACTICAL INFORMATION. The *vieille ville* (old city) is an eye-shaped island in the center of the city, bounded on the north by a large canal and on the south by the river Ill. From the station, a right turn after crossing the bridge leads to **La Petite France,** a quaint old neighborhood with restaurants. The **tourist office,** 17, pl. de la Cathédrale, by the cathedral, offers free maps and makes hotel reservations for 10F/€1.55 plus deposit. (☎ 03 88 52 28 28. Open June-Sept. M-Sa 9am-7pm, Su 9am-6pm; Oct.-May daily 9am-6pm.) Surf the **Internet** at **Le Midi-Minuit,** 5, pl. de Corbeau. (30F/€4.60 per 30min. Open M-W 7am-7pm, Th-Sa 7am-10pm, Su 8am-7pm.) **Postal Code:** 67000 (67074 for *Poste Restante*).

▊▛ ACCOMMODATIONS AND FOOD. Make reservations or arrive early to find reasonable accommodations. **CIARUS (Centre International d'Accueil de Strasbourg),** 7, r. Finkmatt, has sparkling rooms and an international atmosphere. From the station, take r. du Maire-Kuss to the canal, turn left, and follow quais St-Jean, Kléber, and Finkmatt; turn left onto r. Finkmatt, and it's on the left. (☎ 03 88 15 27 88. **Internet** access available. Wheelchair-accessible. Breakfast included. Check-in 3:30pm. Check-out 9am. Curfew 1am. Dorms 94-126F/€14.35-19.25; singles 211F/€32.20. MC/V.) **Hôtel le Grillon,** 2, r. Thiergarten, is just one block from the station toward the center of Strasbourg. (☎ 03 88 32 71 88. Reception 6am-2am. Breakfast 32F/€4.90. Singles 180-240F/€27.45-36.60; doubles 230-280F/€35.10-42.70. MC/V.) **Hôtel de Bruxelles,** 13, r. Kuhn, is up the street from the train station. Ask to see your room in advance. (☎ 03 88 32 45 31. Breakfast 35F/€5.35. Singles and doubles 170-285F/€25.95-43.45; triples and quads 285-345F/€43.45-52.60. MC/V.) *Winstubs* are informal eateries traditionally affiliated with wineries that serve Alsatian specialties such as *choucroute garnie* (spiced sauerkraut with meats)—look in the **La Petite France** neighborhood, especially along **Rue des Dentelles** and **petite Rue des Dentelles.** Try **Place de la Cathédrale, Rue Mercière,** or **Rue du Vieil Hôpital** for restaurants, and **Place Marché Gayot,** off r. des Frères, for lively cafes. For **groceries,** stop by the **ATAC Supermarket,** 47, r. des Grandes Arcades, off pl. Kléber. (Open M-Sa 8:30am-8pm.)

◎◪ SIGHTS AND ENTERTAINMENT. The ornate, Gothic **Cathédrale de Strasbourg** thrusts 142m skyward. Inside, the **Horloge Astronomique** demonstrates the wizardry of 16th-century Swiss clockmakers. While you wait for the clock to strut its stuff—at 12:30pm, apostles troop out of the clock face while a cock crows to greet St. Peter—check out the **Pilier des Anges** (Angels' Pillar), a masterpiece of Gothic sculpture. You can climb the 330 steps of the **tower** in front of the clock to follow in the footsteps of young Goethe, who scaled it regularly to cure his fear of heights. (Cathedral open M-Sa 7-11:40am and 12:45-7pm, Su 12:45-6pm. Clock tickets 5F/€0.75. Tower open daily 9am-6:30pm; 20F/€3.05.) **Palais Rohan,** 2, pl.

FRANCE

Strasbourg

ACCOMMODATIONS

CIARUS, **1**
Hôtel de Bruxelles, **2**
Hôtel le Grillon, **3**

N

0   300 yards
0   300 meters

r. de Reims
PL. ARNOLD
r. L'Observatoire
av. General de Gaulle
al. de la Robertsau
r. Schwendi
quai Schwendi
quai Rouget de l'Isle
r. Goethe
av. de la Forêt Noire
Jardin Botanique
Musée Zoologique
r. de l'Université
PL. DE L'UNIVERSITÉ
Université
PL. D'ATHENES
r. du Rome
quai Zorn
av. d'Alsace
United States
quai du Maire Dietrich
bd. de la Victoire
r. du Maréchal Juin
r. de Jura
L'ILL
Contades Synagogue
Parc du Contades
av. de la Paix
r. du Maréchal Joffre
av. de la Marseillaise
r. de la Krutenau
PL. DE ZURICH
r. de Zurich
r. de Lucerne
r. du St-Gotthard
PL. DE LA RÉPUBLIQUE
r. d'Oberlin
Pont du Théâtre
quai Lezay-Marnésia
r. Brûlée
r. de l'Arc en Ciel
r. des Frères
r. des Juifs
Veaux
PL. DU MARCHE GAYOT
Palais Rohan
PL. DU CORBEAU
Musée Alsacien
PL. D'AUSTERLITZ
r. des Orphelins
TO COLMAR, E4, A5
av. des Vosges
quai J. Sturm
r. de la Fonderie
r. du Dôme
Cathédrale
PL. DE LA CATHÉDRALE
PL. BROGLIE
r. du Vieux Marché aux Poissons
quai St-Nicolas
r. de la 1ère Armée
PL. DE L'HOPITAL
r. Finkmatt
quai Finkmatt
r. Fosse des Treize
r. du Fbg. de Pierre
r. de la Nuée Bleue
PL. GUTENBERG
r. Gutenberg
Marché aux Poissons
r. de la Div. Leclerc
St-Thomas
quai St-Thomas
PL. KLEBER
r. Grands Arcades
r. aux F. Bourgeois
r. des Bonnes-Gens
r. du Travail
quai Kléber
quai de Sébastopol
bd. de Président Wilson
Les Halles
r. du Maras Vert
r. du Vieux Marché-aux-Vins
r. du 21 Novembre
Grand'Rue
r. des Dentelles
LA PETITE FRANCE
r. des Moulins
Ponts Couverts
quai de Turckheim
Hôpital Civil
quai Finkwiller
r. Humann
barrage Vauban
L'ILL
r. du Fbg de Saverne
r. Kageneck
r. Kuhn
quai St-Jean
quai de Paris
r. du Fbg National
ST-PIERRE LE VIEUX
r. Marie Kuss
r. Thiergarten
r. Désérte
r. de la Course
Ste-Marguerite
Musée d'Art Moderne et Contemporain
bd. de Metz
r. Rosheim
TO NANCY, METZ
bd. de Nancy
de Moïsheim
TO
bd. de Lyon

FRANCE

du Château, houses an excellent trio of small museums: the **Musée des Beaux-Arts, Musée des Arts Décoratifs,** and **Musée Archéologique.** (Open M and W-Sa 10am-noon and 1:30-6pm, Su 10am-5pm. 20F/€3.05 each; combined ticket for all 3 40F/€6.10, students 20F/€3.05.) Next door, **Maison de l'Oeuvre Notre-Dame,** 3, pl. du Château, houses some of the cathedral's statues and reconstructed stained glass. (Open Tu-Sa 10am-6pm, Su 10am-5pm. 20F/€3.05, students 10F/€1.55.) Across the canal from La Petite France, the collection of the new **Musée d'Art Moderne et Contemporain,** 1, pl. Hans Jean Arp, ranges from Impressionist to avant-garde. (Open Tu-W and F-Su 11am-7pm, Th noon-10pm. 30F/€4.60, students 20F/€3.05.) Take buses #23, 30, or 72 to L'Orangerie for **Parc L'Orangerie,** Strasbourg's spectacular park. There are free concerts in summer at the Pavillion Josephine (Th-Tu 8:30pm). On the northwest edge of L'Orangerie is the **Palais de l'Europe,** av. de l'Europe, the seat of the **Council of Europe;** the **European Parliament** is just opposite. During sessions (one week per month Sept.-July) you may register to sit in the visitor's gallery. (☎03 90 21 49 40. Bring your passport. 1hr. guided tours by advance request only.) For a little more fun, check out the free tour offered by the **Kronenbourg brewery,** 68, rte. d'Oberhausbergen. (☎03 88 27 41 59. Open M-Sa 9-10am and 2-3pm; in summer 9-11am and 2-5pm.) **Heineken,** 4-10, r. St-Charles, offers free tours for groups by advance reservation only. (☎03 88 19 59 53. Call to schedule; M-F 8am-noon, 1:30-4:30pm.) **Les 3 Brasseurs,** 22, r. des Veaux, offers more microbrewed suds. (Open daily 11:30am-1am.)

LA ROUTE DU VIN (WINE ROUTE)

The Romans were the first to ferment Alsatian grapes; today over 150 million bottles are sold yearly. The Alsatian vineyards flourish along a 170km corridor known as **La Route du Vin** (Wine Route), which stretches south along the foothills of the Vosges through 100 towns between **Strasbourg** (see p. 378) and **Mulhouse** (see p. 381). Hordes of tourists are drawn each year to explore the medieval villages and the numerous free *dégustations* (tastings) along the route. Accommodations tend to be expensive and transportation is infrequent in smaller towns; **Colmar** and **Sélestat** are excellent bases from which to explore the Route. Information can be found at the **Centre d'Information du Vin d'Alsace,** 12, av. de la Foire aux Vins (☎03 89 20 16 20), at the Maison du Vin d'Alsace in Colmar, and **tourist offices** in Strasbourg.

SÉLESTAT

Halfway between Colmar and Strasbourg, Sélestat (pop. 17,200) has managed to preserve its rich cultural heritage and avoid the touristed fate of larger Route du Vin towns. According to local legend, the town was founded by a giant named Sletto, whose massive thigh bone (which disbelievers claim to be a mammoth tusk) lies in the **Bibliothèque Humaniste,** 1, r. de la Bibliothèque. A storehouse for the products of Sélestat's 15th-century humanistic boom, the library contains a fascinating collection of ancient documents. (☎03 88 58 07 20. Open July-Aug. M and W-F 9am-noon and 2-6pm, Sa 9am-noon and 2-5pm, Su 2-5pm; Sept.-June closed Su. 20F/€3.05.)

Trains leave pl. de la Gare for Strasbourg (30min., 15 per day, 42F/€6.40). The **tourist office,** 10, bd. Gén. Leclerc, in the Commanderie St-Jean, rents **bikes.** (☎03 88 58 87 20. Open May-Sept. M-F 9am-12:30pm and 1:30-7pm, Sa 9am-noon and 2-5pm, Su 9am-3pm; Oct.-Apr. M-F 8:30am-noon and 1:30-6pm, Sa 9am-noon, Su closed except in Dec.) The ▓**Hôtel de l'Ill,** 13, r. des Bateliers, is off bd. des Thiers. (☎03 88 92 91 09. Breakfast 30F/€4.60. Reception daily 7am-3pm and 5-11pm. Singles 140-165F/€21.35-25.15; doubles 180-240F/€27.45-36.60; triples 400F/€70. MC/V.) **Camping Les Cigognes** is outside the ramparts, south of the *vieille ville.* (☎03 88 92 03 98. Reception July-Aug. 8am-noon and 3-10pm; May-June and Sept.-Oct. 8am-noon and 3-7pm. Open May-Oct. July-Aug. 50-60F/€7.65-9.15 per person, 70-80F/€10.70-12.20 per 2-3 people.) Try **Halte Pizzas,** 14, r. d'Iéna. (Open M-W 11am-2pm and 5-10pm, F-Sa 11am-2pm and 5-11:30pm, Su 5-10:30pm.) **Postal Code:** 67600.

FRANCE

COLMAR

Colmar's (pop. 65,000) pastel half-timbered houses, cobblestone walkways lined with flowers and bubbling fountains all give the town an innate intimate charm. The **quartier des Tanneurs** is filled with the city's quaintly restored Alsatian houses. Grünewald and Haguenauer's *Issenheim Altarpiece*, at the **Musée Unterlinden**, 1, r. d'Unterlinden, depicts the Crucifixion and other scenes in incredible detail. (Open Apr.-Oct. daily 9am-6pm; Nov.-Mar. W-M 10am-5pm. 35F/€5.35, students 25F/€3.85.) The **Eglise des Dominicains**, on pl. des Dominicains, houses Colmar's other major masterpiece, Schongauer's *Virgin in the Rose Bower*. (Open Apr.-Dec. 10am-1pm and 3-6pm. 8F/€1.25, students 6F/€0.95.) A great selection of local wines await at **Robert Karcher et Fils**, 11, r. de l'Ours, in the *vieille ville*. (☎03 89 41 14 42. Wine 26F/€4 and up. Open daily 8am-noon and 2-6pm. MC/V.)

Trains go to: Mulhouse (30min., 15 per day, 42F/€6.40); Paris (5hr., 10 per day, 255F/€38.90); Strasbourg (40min., 20 per day, 58F/€8.85). To get to the **tourist office**, 4, r. des Unterlinden, from the train station, turn left on av. de la République, follow it as it becomes r. Kléber, and walk through pl. du 18 Novembre to pl. Unter-linden. (☎03 89 20 68 92. Open July-Aug. M-Sa 9am-7pm, Su 9:30am-2pm; Apr.-June and Sept.-Oct. M-Sa 9am-6pm, Su 10am-2pm; Nov.-Mar. M-Sa 9am-noon and 2-6pm, Su 10am-2pm.) For the **Auberge de Jeunesse (HI)**, 2, r. Pasteur, take bus #4 (dir.: Logelbach) to "Pont Rouge." (☎03 89 80 57 39. Breakfast included. Sheets 20F/€3.05. Reception July-Aug. 7-10am and 5pm-midnight; Sept.-June 5-11pm. Curfew midnight. **HI members only.** Reserve in the summer. Closed mid-Dec. to mid-Jan. Dorms 71F/€10.85; singles 172F/€26.25; doubles 101F/€15.40. MC/V.) Take bus #1 (dir.: Horbourg-Wihr) to "Plage d'Ill" for **Camping de l'Ill**, overlooking the Vosges. (☎03 89 41 15 94. Reception July-Aug. daily 8am-10pm; Feb.-June and Sept.-Nov. 8am-8pm. Open Feb.-Nov. 18F/€2.75 per person, 10F/€1.55 per child, 10F/€1.55 per tent, 20F/€3.05 per site. Electricity 15F/€2.30.) Stock up at **Monoprix supermarket**, on pl. Unterlinden. (Open M-F 8am-8pm, Sa 8am-7:55pm.) **Tropic'ice**, pl. des Domin-icains, serves over 100 types of *galettes*, *crêpes*, and *coupes glacées*. (☎03 89 41 31 36. Open daily 11:30am-midnight.) **Postal Code:** 68000.

MULHOUSE

While this bustling town of 110,000 may not have Nancy's architecture or the gar-dens of Metz, Mulhouse boasts a plethora of fabulous museums on its periphery. Its historical district centers around the festive **Place de la Réunion**, which commemo-rates the "reunion" of Mulhouse with distant Paris in 1798 and 1918. Nearby is the **Temple de St-Etienne**, one of France's few Protestant Gothic cathedrals. (☎03 89 66 30 19. Open May-Sept. M and W-Su 10am-noon and 2-6pm.) The **Musée Français du Chemin de Fer**, 2, r. Alfred de Glehn, maintains a stunning collection of gleaming engines and railway cars. Take bus #17 (dir.: "Musées") from Porte Jeune Place. (☎03 89 42 25 67. Open Apr.-Sept. daily 9am-6pm, Oct.-Mar. 9am-5pm. 48F/€7.35, students 20F/€3.05.) Over 500 cars in mint condition are on display at the **Musée National de l'Automobile**, 192, av. de Colmar. Take buses #1, 4, 11, 13, or 17 north to "Musée Auto." (☎03 89 33 23 23. Open July-Aug. daily 9am-6:30pm; late Mar to June and Sept.-Oct. 9am-6pm; Nov. to late Mar. 10am-6pm. 65F/€9.95, students 46F/€7.05.) **Trains** run from bd. Général Leclerc to Paris (4½hr., 9 per day, 280F/€42.70) and Strasbourg (1hr., 14 per day, 87F/€13.30). The **tourist office**, 9, av. Foch, is two blocks up from the right end of the train station. (☎03 89 35 48 48; www.ot.ville-mulhouse.fr. Open July-Aug. M-Sa 9am-7pm, Su 10am-noon; Sept.-June M-F 9am-7pm, Sa 9am-5pm.) To get to the newly renovated **Auberge de Jeunesse (HI)**, 37, r. d'Ilberg, take bus #2 (bus S1 after 8:30pm; dir.: Loteaux) to "Salle des Sports." (☎03 89 42 63 28. **HI members only.** Breakfast 19F/€2.90. Sheets 17F/€2.60. Reception daily 8am-noon and 5-11pm, until midnight in the summer. 53F/€8.10. MC/V.) Hunt for food along **Rue de l'Arsenal**, or buy **groceries** at **Monoprix**, on the corner of r. du Sauvage and r. des Maréchaux. (Open M-F 8:15am-8pm, Sa 8:15am-7pm.) **Crampous Mad**, 14, impasse des Tondeurs, serves crepes (13-43F/€2-6.60) on a bright terrace. (Open M-F 11:30am-10pm, Sa 11:30am-11pm. MC/V.) **Postal Code:** 68100.

BESANÇON

Since Julius Caesar founded a military post here in 58 BC, Besançon (pop. 120,000) has intrigued military strategists because of its prime geographic location. Today Besançon boasts a smart, sexy student population and an impressive number of museums and discos. See the city's well-preserved Renaissance buildings from high up in the **citadel**, at the end of r. des Fusilles de la Résistance, designed by Louis XIV's architect, Vauban. Within the citadel, the **Musée de la Résistance et de la Déportation** (☎03 81 65 07 55) chronicles the Nazi rise to power and the German occupation of France. Other sights include a natural history museum, a zoo, an aquarium, and a folk arts museum. (☎03 81 65 07 50. Grounds open July-Aug. daily 9am-7pm; Apr.-June and Sept.-Oct. 9am-6pm; Nov.-Mar. 10am-5pm. Museums open Apr.-Oct. daily 9am-6pm; Nov.-Mar. 10am-5pm. 40F/€6.10, students 30F/€4.60.) The **Cathédrale St-Jean,** perched beneath the citadel, holds two treasures: the white marble **Rose de St-Jean** and the intricate 19th-century **Horloge Astronomique.** (Open W-M 9am-7pm. Free.) The **Musée des Beaux-Arts et d'Archéologie,** on pl. de la Révolution, houses an exceptional collection ranging from ancient Egyptian mummies to works by Matisse. (☎03 81 87 80 49. Open W-M 9:30am-6pm. 21F/€3.20, students free; Su and holidays free.) The area between **rues C. Pouillet** and **Pont Battant** buzzes with nightlife. **Madigan's,** pl. 8 Septembre, is packed every night with a young crowd. (Open M-Th 7am-1am, weekends until 2am.) Shoot pool at the surprisingly hip **Pop Hall,** 26, r. Proudhon. (Open M-Th 6pm-1am, Sa 3pm-2am, Su 6pm-2am.)

Trains pull up at the station on av. de la Paix (☎08 36 35 35 35), from: Paris Gare de Lyon (2½hr., 10 per day, 183F/€27.90); Dijon (1hr., 6 per day, 75F/€11.45); Strasbourg (3hr., 10 per day, 165F/€25.20). **Monts Jura buses,** 9, r. Proudhon (☎03 81 21 22 00), go to Pontarlier (1hr., 6 per day, 46.50F/€7.10). From the station, walk downhill and turn onto av. Maréchal Foch and continue to the left as it becomes av. de l'Helvétie, until you reach pl. de la Première Armée Française. The *vieille ville* is across the pont de la République; the **tourist office,** 2, pl. de la Première Armée Française, is in the park to the right. (☎03 81 80 92 55; www.besancon.com. Open Apr.-Sept. M 10am-7pm, Tu-Sa 9am-7pm; mid-June to mid-Sept. also open Su 10am-noon and 3-5pm; Oct.-Mar. M 10am-6pm, Tu-Sa 9am-6pm.) Surf the **Internet** at **Centre Information Jeunesse (CIJ),** 27, r. de la Republique. (Open M and Sa 1:30-6pm, Tu-F 10am-noon and 1:30-6pm. Free.) Check out the **Centre International de Séjour,** 19, r. Martin-du-Gard. Take bus #8 (dir.: Campus) from the "Foch" stop near the station, down in front of a gas station, to "Intermarché." (☎03 81 50 07 54. Reception 7am-1pm. 2-bed dorms 67F/€10.25, with bath 94F/€14.35; 3- and 4-bed dorms 53F/€8.10; singles 107F/€16.35, 163F/€24.85.) A variety of restaurants line **Rue Claude-Pouillet.** Buy groceries at **Monoprix,** 12, Grande Rue. (Open M-Sa 8:30am-9pm.) **La Boîte à Sandwiches,** 21, r. du Lycée, off r. Pasteur, serves sandwiches and salads. (Open M-Sa 11:30am-2:30pm and 6:30pm-midnight.) **Postal Code:** 25000.

▶ **DAYTRIP FROM BESANÇON: PONTARLIER AND THE JURA.** The sedate town of **Pontarlier** (840m), is a good base from which to explore the oft-overlooked Haut-Jura mountains. The Jura are best known for cross-country **skiing;** eight trails cover every skill level. (Day pass 30F/€4.60, under 17 20F/€3.05; available at the **Le Larmont** and **Le Malmaison** trails.) Le Larmont is the closest Alpine ski area (☎03 81 46 55 20). **Sport et Neige,** 4, r. de la République (☎03 81 39 04 69), rents skis (50F/€7.65 per day). In summer, **fishing, hiking,** and **mountain biking** are popular sports. Rent a **bike** from **Cycles Pernet,** 23, r. de la République. (☎03 81 46 48 00. 80F/€12.20 per day with passport deposit. Open Tu-Sa 9am-noon and 2-7pm.) **Monts Jura buses** (☎03 81 39 88 80) run to Besançon (1hr., 6 per day, 46.50F/€7.10). The **tourist office,** 14bis, r. de la Gare, has free regional guides and sells maps. (☎03 81 46 48 33; fax 03 81 46 83 32.) **L'Auberge de Pontarlier (HI),** 2, r. Jouffroy, is clean and central. (☎03 81 38 54 54. **HI members only.** Breakfast 19F/€2.90. Sheets 17F/€2.60. Reception 8am-noon and 5:30-10pm. Dorms 50F/€7.65; doubles 75F/€11.4.) **Postal Code:** 25300.

FRANCE

NANCY

Nancy (pop. 100,000) has always been passionate about beauty: the town that spawned the art-nouveau "Nancy school" is today the artistic and intellectual heart of modern Lorraine. The elaborate ◨**place Stanislas** houses three neoclassical pavilions separated by gilt iron fences, with *son-et-lumière* spectacles held nightly at 10pm in July and August. The collection in the **Musée des Beaux-Arts**, 3, pl. Stanislas, spans from the 14th century to today. (☎03 83 85 30 72. Open W-M 10am-6pm. 30F/ €4.60, students 15F/€2.30; W and 1st Su students free.) Pass through the five-arch **Arc de Triomphe** to the tree-lined **Place de la Carrière.** Portals of pink roses lead into the aromatic **Roseraie,** in the relaxing **Parc de la Pépinière,** just north of pl. de la Carrière. (Open May to mid-Sept. 6:30am-11:30pm; May and Sept. 1-14 closes at 10pm; Mar.-Apr. and mid-Sept. to Nov. closes at 9pm; Dec.-Feb. closes at 8pm. Free.)

Trains (☎03 83 22 12 46) depart from the station at pl. Thiers to: Metz (40min., 24 per day, 52F/€7.95); Paris (3hr., 14 per day, 213F/€32.50); Strasbourg (1hr., 19 per day, 112F/€17.10). Head left from the station and turn right on r. Raymond Poincaré, which leads straight to pl. Stanislas, the center of the city, and the **tourist office.** Ask for the invaluable *Le Fil d'Ariane* guide. (☎03 83 35 22 41; fax 03 83 35 90 10; www.ot-nancy.fr. Open Apr.-Sept. M-Sa 9am-7pm, Su 10am-5pm; Oct.-Mar. M-Sa 9am-6pm, Su 10am-1pm.) Access the **Internet** at **E-café**, on r. des Quatre Eglises. (☎03 83 35 47 34. 35F/€5.35 per hr. Open M-Sa 9am-9pm, Su 2-8pm.) **Centre d'Accueil de Remicourt (HI)**, 149, r. de Vandoeuvre, is in Villiers-lès-Nancy, 4km away. From the station, take bus #122 to "St-Fiacre" (dir.: Villiers Clairlieu; 2 per hr., last bus 8pm; confirm direction with the driver); head downhill from the stop, turn right on r. de la Grange des Moines, which turns into r. de Vandoeuvre. Look for signs pointing to Château de Remicourt. (☎03 83 27 73 67; fax 03 83 41 41 35. Breakfast included. Reception daily 9am-9pm. 3- to 4-bed dorms 82F/€12.50; doubles 97F/ €14.80. MC/V.) **Hôtel Le Jean Jaurès**, 14, bd. Jean-Jaurès, is elegant and clean. (☎03 83 27 74 14; fax 03 83 90 20 94. Reception 7am-11pm. Singles 230F/€35.06; doubles 260F/€39.65; triples 290F/€44.25. AmEx/MC/V.) Restaurants line **Rue des Maréchaux,** the nearby **Place Lafayette,** and **Place St-Epvre.** A SHOPI supermarket sits at 26, r. St-Georges. (Open M-F 8:30am-7:30pm, Sa 8:30am-7pm.) **Postal Code:** 54000.

METZ

Modern Metz (pop. 200,000) is a stroller's city, a place of classic fountains, sculptured gardens, and golden cobblestoned streets that reflect the town's mixed Franco-German heritage. The golden **Cathédrale St-Etienne**, pl. d'Armes, is the third-tallest nave in France. Marvel at its 6500m of stained-glass windows, including some by Marc Chagall. (Open M-Sa 9am-7pm, Su 1pm-7pm. Free.) At the other end of the r. des Clercs from pl. d'Armes lies the **Esplanade,** a broad formal garden accented by leisurely promenades. Down the steps from the Esplanade, shady paths wind through wooded parkland along the **Lac aux Cygnes.** Afterward, get down in the student-packed bars and cafes in **Place St-Jacques.**

Trains leave pl. du Général de Gaulle for: Luxembourg (45min., 12 per day, 68F/ €10.40); Nancy (40min., 31 per day, 52F/€7.95); Paris (3hr., 10 per day, 238F/€36.30); Strasbourg (1½hr., 7 per day, 116F/€17.70). To get from the station to the **tourist office,** on pl. d'Armes, turn right and then left onto r. des Augustins, and at pl. St-Simplice, turn left onto r. de la Tête d'Or, and right on r. Fabet. Or, take bus #11 (dir.: St-Eloy) or #9 (dir.: J. Bauchez) from pl. Charles de Gaulle to pl. d'Armes. (☎03 87 55 53 76. Open July-Aug. M-Sa 9am-9pm, Su 11am-5pm; Mar.-June and Sept.-Oct. M-Sa 9am-7pm, Su 11am-5pm; Nov.-Feb. M-Sa 9am-6:30pm, Su 11am-5pm.) Surf the **Internet** for free at the tourist office, or for free at **Espace Multimedia**, 6, r. Four de Cloitre, near the cathedral. (☎03 87 36 56 56. Open M and Th-Sa 9am-5pm, Tu-W 9am-8pm.) Take bus #3 (dir.: Metz-Nord) or 11 (dir.: St-Eloy) to "Pontiffroy" to reach the well-run **Auberge de Jeunesse (HI)**, 1, allée de Metz Plage. (☎03 87 30 44 02; fax 03 87 33 19 80. Breakfast included. Reception 7:30-10am and 5-10pm. 2- to 6-bed dorms 70F/€10.70 per person. Nonmembers 19F/€2.90 extra. MC/V.) Cheap eateries lie on **Rue du Pont des Morts,** in the **pedestrian district,** and toward the station on **Rue Coisin.** The ATAC supermarket is in the Centre St-Jacques, off pl. St-Jacques. (Open M-Sa 8:30am-7:30pm.) **Postal Code:** 57000.

FRANCE

VERDUN

Reminders of the Battle of Verdun, certainly the worst battle of World War I, are everywhere in the town, from the many war memorials to the pockmarked surface of the land. Despite Verdun's painstaking efforts to rebuild, this city's main draw will always be its tragic history. Built in 1200, the **Porte Chaussée**, on the quai de Londres, served as a prison and guard tower, and later as the entrance for troops during World War I. At the other end of the r. Frères Boulhaut, Rodin's bronze **Victory** guards the Port St-Paul. Marking the edge of the *haute ville*, the **Monument à la Victoire** rises above a flight of 72 granite steps. This tower stands atop the remains of the **Eglise de la Madeleine**, built in 1049 and bombed beyond recognition in 1916. (Open daily 9am-noon and 2-6pm.) The 4km of underground galleries in the massive **Citadelle Souterraine,** down r. de Rû, held supplies for the 10,000 soldiers sheltered there on their way to the front. (Open July-Aug. daily 9am-7pm; Apr.-June and Sept. 9am-6pm; Nov.-Mar. 9:30am-noon and 1-5pm. 35F/€5.35.)

Trains leave from pl. Maurice Genovoix for Metz (1½hr., 5 per day, 71F/€10.85). **Buses** run from pl. Vauban to Metz (2hr., 8 per day, 72F/€11). To get to the **tourist office,** pl. de la Nation, from the train station, take av. Garibaldi until you reach the bus station, turn left onto r. Frères Boulhaut, and continue until you reach the Port Chaussée. Turn left again, cross the bridge onto pl. de la Nation and the office will be on your right. (☎ 03 29 86 14 18; fax 03 29 84 22 42. Open July-Aug. M-Sa 8:30am-7:30pm, Su 9am-5pm; May-June and Sept. M-Sa 8:30am-6:30pm, Su 9am-5pm; Mar.-Apr. and Oct.-Feb. reduced hours.) The **Auberge de Jeunesse (HI),** pl. Monseigneur Ginisty, next to the cathedral at the Centre Mondial de la Paix, has simple, renovated rooms. From the train station, cross to the island with the Match supermarket in front of the station and turn right onto r. Louis Maury; continue up on r. de la Belle Vierge and the hostel is at the end of the cathedral. (☎ 03 29 86 28 28; fax 03 29 86 28 82. Sheets 17F/€2.60. Reception M-F 7:30am-11pm, Sa-Su 8-10am and 5-11pm. No curfew. Bunks 51F/€7.80, ages 4-10 27F/€4.15. Nonmembers 19F/€2.90 supplement for each of the 1st 6 nights. MC/V.) **Postal Code:** 55107.

CHAMPAGNE AND THE NORTH

John Maynard Keynes once remarked that his major regret in life was not having consumed enough champagne; a trip through the rolling vineyards and fertile plains of Champagne promises many opportunities to avoid his mistake. The term *champagne* is fiercely guarded; the name can only be applied to wines made from regional grapes and produced according to a rigorous, time-honored method. To the north, Flanders, the coastal Pas de Calais, and Picardy remain the final frontiers of tourist-free France. As you flee the ferry ports, don't overlook the intriguing Flemish culture of Arras and the world-class art collections of Lille.

REIMS

Reims (pop. 185,000) delights in the bubbly champagne of its famed *caves* and the beauty of its architectural masterpieces. The **Cathédrale de Notre-Dame,** built with golden limestone quarried in the Champagne *caves*, features sea-blue stained-glass windows by Marc Chagall. (☎ 03 26 77 45 25. Open daily 7:30am-7:30pm. Tours daily 2:30pm; less frequently in Oct. and late Mar. to mid-June. 35F/€5.35, ages 12-25 20F/€3.05.) Enter the adjacent **Palais du Tau,** at pl. du Cardinal Luçon, for dazzling 16th-century tapestries. (☎ 03 26 47 81 79. Open July-Aug. daily 9:30am-6:30pm; Sept. to mid-Nov and mid-Mar. to June daily 9:30am-12:30pm and 2-6pm; mid-Nov. to mid-Mar. M-F 10am-noon and 2-5pm, Sa-Su 10am-noon and 2-6pm. 26F/€4, students 21F/€3.20.) The firm of **Champagne Pommery,** 5, pl. du Général Gouraud, boasts the largest *tonneau* (vat) in the world. (☎ 03 26 61 62 56. Tours daily Apr.-Oct. 11am-7pm. 46F/€7.05, students 23F/€3.50.) For good deals on champagne, look for sales on local brands and check prices at Monoprix. Good bottles start at 60F/€9.15.

Trains (☎ 03 26 88 11 65) leave bd. Joffre for Paris (1½hr., 11 per day, 123F/€18.75). To get from the train station to the **tourist office,** 2, r. Guillaume de

Machault, follow the right-hand curve of the rotary to pl. Drouet d'Erlon, turn left onto r. de Vesle, turn right on r. du Tresor, and it's on the left before the cathedral. (☎03 26 77 45 25; fax 03 26 77 45 27. Open mid-Apr. to mid-Oct. M-Sa 9am-7pm, Su 10am-6pm; mid-Oct. to mid-Apr. M-Sa 9am-6pm, Su 10am-5pm.) Inexpensive hotels cluster west of pl. Drouet d'Erlon, above the cathedral, and near the *mairie*. The sunny and spotless **Au Bon Accueil**, 31, r. Thillois, is just off the central pl. d'Erlon. (☎03 26 88 55 74; fax 03 26 05 12 38. Breakfast 25F/€3.85. Reception 24hr. Reserve ahead. Singles 80-150F/€12.20-22.90; doubles 140-220F/€21.35-33.55. MC/V.) **Place Drouet d'Erlon** is crowded with cafes, restaurants, and bars. Relax at **Le Kraft**, 5, r. Salin, which includes restaurant, bar, and cocktail lounge. (☎03 26 05 29 29. Open M-F 11am-3am, Sa 6pm-3am.) **Monoprix supermarket** is at r. de Vesle and r. de Talley-rand. (Open M-Sa 8:30am-9pm.) **Postal Code:** 51100.

▶ DAYTRIP FROM REIMS: ÉPERNAY. Épernay (pop. 30,000), at the juncture of three wealthy grape-growing regions, is appropriately ritzy. **Avenue de Champagne** is distinguished by its palatial mansions, lush gardens, and swanky champagne firms. Both tours below offer a *petite dégustation* for those over 16. **Moët & Chandon**, 20, av. de Champagne, produces the king of all wines: **Dom Perignon**. (☎03 26 51 20 20. Open Apr. 1-Nov. 11 daily 9:30-11:30am and 2-4:30pm; Nov. 12-Mar. M-F only. 1hr. tour with one glass 40F/€6.10.) Ten minutes away is **Mercier**, 70, av. de Champagne, the self-proclaimed "most popular champagne in France," who gives tours in roller-coaster-like cars. (☎03 26 51 22 22. Open Mar.-Nov. M-F 9:30-11:30am and 2-4:30pm, Sa-Su 9:30-11:30am and 2-5pm; Dec. 1-19 and Jan. 13-Feb. Th-M only. 30min. tours 25F/€3.85.) **Trains** leave cour de la Gare for Paris (1¼hr., 18 per day, 109F/€16.65) and Reims (25min., 16 per day, 34F/€5.20). From the station, walk straight ahead through pl. Mendès France, go one block up r. Gambetta to the central **Place de la République**, and turn left on av. de Champagne to reach the **tourist office**, 7 av. de Champagne. (☎03 26 53 33 00. Open Easter-Oct. 15 M-Sa 9:30am-noon and 1:30-7pm, Su 11am-4pm; Oct. 16-Easter M-Sa 9:30am-12:30pm and 1:30-5:30pm.)

TROYES

While the city plan of Troyes resembles a champagne cork, this city shares little with its grape-crazy northern neighbors. Gothic churches, 16th-century mansions and an abundance of museums attest to the city's colorful role in French history, dating back to the Middle Ages. The **Musée de l'Art Moderne**, on pl. St-Pierre, has over 2000 modern works by French artists, including Rodin, Degas, and Seurat. (Open W-M 11am-6pm. 30F/€4.60, students 5F/€0.75; W free.) Cinemas and pool halls rub elbows with chic boutiques on **Rue Emile Zola**. On warm evenings, *Troyens* fill the cafes and taverns of **Rues Champeaux** and **Mole** near pl. Alexandre Israel.

Trains run from av. Maréchal Joffre to Paris (1½hr., 10 per day, 120F/€18.30) and Mulhouse (3hr., 6 per day, 205F/€31.25). The **tourist office** at 16, bd. Carnot, near the station, helps reserve rooms. (☎03 25 82 62 70; www.ot-troyes.fr. Open M-Sa 9am-12:30pm and 2-6:30pm.) Another branch is in the *vieille ville* on r. Mignard. (☎03 25 73 36 88. Open M-Sa 9am-12:30pm and 2-6:30pm, Su 10am-noon and 2-5pm.) Stay in large and airy rooms at **Les Comtes de Champagne**, 56, r. de la Monnaie. (☎03 25 73 11 70; fax 73 06 02. Reception 7am-11pm. Call ahead if possible. Singles 160-200F/€25-30.50; doubles 180-220F/€27.5-33.50; triples 290-360F/€44-55; quads 320-380F/€49-58. D/V.) **Camping Municipal**, 2km from Troyes, on N60, has showers and laundry. Take bus #1 (dir.: Pont St-Marie) and ask to be let off at the campground. (☎03 25 81 02 64. 25F/€3.85 per person, 30F/€4.60 per tent, 30F/€4.60 per car. Open Apr. to mid-Oct.) *Crêperies* and inexpensive eateries lie near **Rue Champeaux**, in *quartier* St-Jean, and on **Rue de la Cité**, near the cathedral. Stock up at **Monoprix supermarket**, 78, r. Emile Zola. (Open M-Sa 8:30am-8pm.) **Postal Code:** 10000.

▶ DAYTRIPS FROM TROYES: LES GRANDS LACS. About 30km from Troyes are the freshwater lakes of the **Forêt d'Orient. Lake Orient** welcome sunbathers, swimmers, and windsurfers, **Lake Temple** is reserved for fishing and bird-watching, and **Lake Amance** roars with speedboats from **Port Dierville**. The **Comité Départemental**

du Tourisme de l'Aube, 34, quai Dampierre, provides information on hotels and restaurants. (☎03 25 42 50 00; fax 03 25 42 50 88. Open M-F 8:45am-noon and 1:30-6pm.) The Troyes tourist office has bus schedules for routes to the Grands Lacs.

LILLE

A longtime international hub with a rich Flemish ancestry and exuberant nightlife, Lille (pop. 175,000) exudes big-city charm without the hassle. The impressive ▓Musée des Beaux-Arts, on pl. de la République (M: République), boasts a wide display of 15th- to 20th-century French and Flemish masters. (☎03 20 06 78 00. Open M 2-6pm, W-Th and Sa-Su 10am-6pm, F 10am-7pm. 30F/€4.60, students 20F/€3.05.) The Musée d'Art Moderne, 1, allée du Musée, in the suburb of Villeneuve d'Ascq, showcases Cubist and postmodern art, including works by Braque, Picasso, Léger, Miró, and Modigliani. Take the tram (dir.: 4 Cantons) to "Pont du Bois," then take bus #41 (dir.: Villeneuve d'Ascq) to "Parc Urbain-Musée." (☎03 20 19 68 68. Open W-M 10am-6pm; free 1st Su of every month 10am-2pm. 43F/€6.55, 2nd adult 24F/€3.65, students 10F/€1.55.) The Vieille Bourse (Old Stock Exchange), on pl. Général de Gaulle, epitomizing the Flemish Renaissance, houses flower and book markets. (Markets Tu-Su 9:30am-7:30pm.) Head down r. de Paris for the 14th- to 19th-century Eglise St-Maurice. (M: Rihour. Open M-F 7:15am-7pm, Sa 8am-7pm.) Pubs and bars line Rue Solférino and rue Masséna. The intimate Le Clave, 31, r. Massena, serves tropical drinks (from 25F/€3.85) and Afro-Cuban jazz. (☎03 20 30 09 61.)

Trains leave from Gare Lille Flandres, on pl. de la Gare (M: Gare Lille Flandres), for Brussels, Belgium (1½hr., 20 per day, 135F/€20.60) and Paris (1hr., 21 per day, 212-287F/€32.35-43.75). Gare Lille Europe, on r. Le Corbusier (M: Gare Lille Europe; ☎03 36 35 35 35), sends Eurostar trains to London, Brussels, and Paris and all TGVs to the south of France and Paris. From Gare Lille Flandres, walk straight down r. Faidherbe and turn left through pl. du Théâtre and pl. de Gaulle; behind the huge war monument is the castle housing the tourist office, pl. Rihour (M: Rihour), which offers free maps and currency exchange. (☎03 20 21 94 21; fax 03 20 21 94 20. Open M-Sa 9:30am-6:30pm, Su 10am-noon and 2-5pm.) A huge Carrefour supermarket is next to the Eurostar train station. (Open M-Sa 9am-10pm.) To reach the Auberge de Jeunesse (HI), 12, r. Malpart (M: Mairie de Lille), from Gare Lille Flandres, circle left around the station, turn right onto r. du Molinel, take the second left on r. de Paris, and take the 3rd right onto r. Malpart. (☎03 20 57 08 94; fax 03 20 63 98 93. Breakfast included. Sheets 18F/€2.75. Reception 7am-noon and 2pm-1am. Check-out 10:30am. Curfew 2am. Open Feb.-Dec. 17. 3- to 6-bed dorms 75F/€11.45; deposit of ID or 50F/€7.65 required.) The spotless Hôtel Faidherbe, 42, pl. de la Gare (M: Gare Lille Flandres), is noise-proof. (☎03 20 06 27 93; fax 03 20 55 95 38. Reception 24hr. Singles and doubles 170-260F/€25.95-39.65; extra person 50F/€7.65. Daily tax of 2F/€0.30 per person. 10% discount with *Let's Go*. AmEx/MC/V.) Restaurants and markets line Rues de Béthune and Léon Gambetta. Postal Code: 59000.

⧉ DAYTRIPS FROM LILLE: ARRAS AND VIMY. The town hall of Arras, housed in the gorgeous Hôtel de Ville, is built over the eerie Les Boves tunnels, which have sheltered both medieval chalk miners and British WWI soldiers (25F/€3.85, students 15F/€2.30). Bars and cafes line the lively Place des Héros. Trains leave pl. Maréchal Foch for Lille (45min., 21 per day, 54F/€8.25). From the train station, walk across pl. Foch to r. Gambetta, turn left on r. Desire Delansorne, turn left, and walk two blocks to reach the tourist office, on pl. des Héros, in the Hôtel de Ville. (☎03 21 51 26 95; fax 03 21 71 07 34; www.ot.arras.fr. Open May-Sept. M-Sa 9am-6:30pm, Su 10am-1pm and 2:30-6:30pm; Oct.-Apr. M-Sa 9am-noon and 2-6pm, Su 10am-12:30pm and 3-6:30pm.) Stay at the central Auberge de Jeunesse (HI), 59, Grand'Place. (☎03 21 22 70 02; fax 03 21 07 46 15. Reception 8am-noon and 5-11pm. Curfew 11pm. HI members only. Open Feb.-Nov. Dorms 50F/€7.65.)

The countryside surrounding Arras is dotted with war cemeteries and unmarked graves. The vast limestone Vimy Memorial, 12km from Arras, honors the more than 66,000 Canadians killed in WWI. The morbidly beautiful park, whose soil came from Canada, is dedicated to the crucial victory at Vimy Ridge in April 1917. The kiosk by the trenches is the starting point for an **underground tour** of the crumbling tunnels dug by British and Canadian soldiers. (☎ 03 21 59 19 34. Memorial open dawn-dusk. Free tunnel tours Apr. to mid-Nov. 10am-6pm.) The Vimy memorial is 2-3km from the town of **Vimy. Buses** run from Arras to Vimy (20min., M-Sa 7 per day, 14F/€2.15).

CALAIS

Calais (pop. 80,000) is the liveliest of the Channel ports, and with the Chunnel next door, English is spoken as often as French. Rodin's famous sculpture **The Burghers of Calais** stands in front of the **Hôtel de Ville**, at the juncture of bd. Jacquard and r. Royale. Follow r. Royale to the end of r. de Mer for Calais's wide, gorgeous **beaches.** For schedules and prices to **Dover, England,** see p. 52. During the day, free **buses** connect the ferry terminal and train station, **Gare Calais-Ville,** on bd. Jacquard, from which **trains** leave for: Boulogne (45min., 11 per day, 42F/€6.40); Lille (1¼hr., 12 per day, 86F/€13.15); Paris-Nord (3¼hr., 6 per day, 220-292F/€33.55-44.55). To reach the **tourist office,** 12, bd. Clemenceau, from the train station, turn left, cross the bridge, and it's on your right. (☎ 03 21 96 62 40; fax 03 21 96 01 92. Open M-Sa 9am-7pm, Su 10am-1pm.) **Morning markets** are held on pl. Crèvecoeur (Th and Sa) and on pl. d'Armes (W and Sa); or look for **Prisunic,** 17, bd. Jacquard. (Open M-Sa 8:30am-7:30pm, Su 10am-7pm.) The renovated **Centre Européen de Séjour/Auberge de Jeunesse (HI)**, av. Maréchal Delattre de Tassigny, is near the beach. (☎ 03 21 34 70 20; fax 03 21 96 87. Checkout 11am. Singles 126F/€19.25; doubles 94F/€14.35 per person 1st night, 80F/€12.20 per extra night. Nonmembers 10F/€1.55 extra.) The quiet **Hotel Bristol,** 13-15, r. du Duc de Guise, is off the main road. (☎/fax 03 21 34 53 24. Reception 24hr. Singles 150-200F/€22.90-30.50; doubles 160-250F/€24.40-38.15; 3- to 5-person rooms 270-380F/€41.20-57.95. MC/V.) **Postal Code:** 62100.

BOULOGNE-SUR-MER

With its refreshing sea breeze and lavish floral displays, Boulogne is by far the most attractive Channel port. The huge **Château-Musée,** r. de Bernet, houses an eclectic art collection that includes Napoleon's second-oldest hat. (☎ 03 21 10 02 20. Open M and W-Sa 10am-12:30pm and 2-5pm, Su 10am-12:30pm and 2:30-5:30pm. 20F/€3.05.) Just down r. de Lille, the 19th-century **Basilique de Notre-Dame** sits above 12th-century labyrinthine crypts. (Open Apr. to mid-Sept. daily 9am-noon and 2-6pm; mid-Sept. to Mar 10am-noon and 2-5pm. Crypt open M-Sa 2-5pm, Su 2:30-5pm. 10F/€1.55.) **Trains** leave **Gare Boulogne-Ville,** bd. Voltaire, for: Calais (30min., 18 per day, 42F/€6.40); Lille (2½hr., 11 per day, 108F/€16.50); Paris-Nord (2-3hr., 11 per day, 167-297F/€25.50-45.30). From the train station, turn right on bd. Voltaire, turn left on bd. Danou and follow it to pl. Angleterre; continue past pl. de France and pl. Frédéric Sauvage onto r. Gambetta and look right for the **tourist office,** 24, quai Gambetta. (☎ 03 21 10 88 10; fax 03 21 10 88 11. Open July-Aug. M-Sa 9am-7pm, Su 10am-1pm and 3-6pm; Sept.-June reduced hours.) The fantastic **Auberge de Jeunesse (HI)**, 56, pl. Rouget de Lisle, is across from the station. (☎ 03 21 99 15 30; fax 03 21 80 45 62. Breakfast included. **Internet** 30F/€4.60 per 30min. Reception 8am-1am; in winter until midnight. Curfew 1am. Bunks 85F/€13; nonmembers 19F/€2.90 extra per night up to 6 nights. MC/V.) **Champion supermarket,** on r. Daunou, is in the Centre Commercial de la Liane mall. (Open M-Sa 8:30am-8pm.) **Postal Code:** 62200.

GERMANY
(DEUTSCHLAND)

DEUTSCHMARKS

US$1 = DM2.18	1DM = US$0.46
CDN$1 = DM1.47	1DM = CDN$0.68
UK£1 = DM3.23	1DM = UK£0.31
IR£1 = DM2.48F	1DM = IR£0.40
AUS$1 = DM1.27	1DM = AUS$0.79
NZ$1 = DM0.97	1DM = NZ$1.04
ZAR1 = DM0.31	1DM = ZAR3.20
EUR€1 = DM1.96	1DM = EUR€0.51

PHONE CODE	Country Code: 49. International dialing prefix: 00.

Deutschland (pop. 82.8 million; 357,021 sq. km) is a nation saddled with an incredibly fractured duality. Steeped deeply in Beethoven's fiery orchestration and Goethe's Faustian whirlwind, modern Germany must also contend with the legacy of xenophobia and genocide left by Hitler and the Nazi Third Reich. Brahms, Wagner, and Liszt have since given way to Kraftwerk, Rammstein, and Hasselhof, but even now, more than a decade after the fall of the Berlin Wall, Germans are still fashioning a new identity for themselves. After centuries of war and fragmentation, Germany finds itself a wealthy nation at the forefront of both European and global politics. Its medieval castles, snow-covered mountains, and funky metropolises make Germany well worth a visit. For more comprehensive coverage, treat yourself to *Let's Go: Germany 2002.*

SUGGESTED ITINERARIES

THREE DAYS Enjoy two days in **Berlin** (p. 401): stroll along **Unter den Linden** and the **Ku'damm**, gawk at the **Brandenburger Tor** and the **Reichstag,** and explore the **Tiergarten.** Walk along the **East Side Gallery** and visit **Checkpoint Charlie** for a history of the Berlin Wall, then spend an afternoon at **Schloß Sans Soucci** (p. 425). Overnight to Bavarian **Munich** (p. 479) for a beer-filled last day.

ONE WEEK After scrambling through **Berlin** (3 days), head north to racy **Hamburg** (1 day; p. 439). Take in the splendor of **Cologne** (1 day; p. 455) before heading to the former West German capital **Bonn** (1 day; p. 461). End your trip in true Bavarian style with castles, churches, and beer in **Munich** (1 day).

BEST OF GERMANY, THREE WEEKS Start in **Berlin** (3 days). Party in **Hamburg** (2 days), stop by **Lübeck** for marzipan (1 day; p. 448), and zip to **Köln** (1 day). Peek at Charlemagne's remains in **Aachen** (1 day; p. 463) and explore **Bonn** (1 day). Spend a day in glitzy **Frankfurt** (p. 463), visit Germany's oldest university in **Heidelberg** (1 day; p. 471), then zoom to **Stuttgart** (2 days; p. 475). Get lost in a fairytale world by daytripping through the **Schwarzwald** (1 day; p. 476), listening to the Glockenspiel in **Munich** (1 day), and marvelling at **Neuschwanstein** (1 day; p. 493). Take in the view along the **Romantic Road** (2 days; p. 491) and in the **Saxon Switzerland** (1 day; p. 432) before ending your trip in **Dresden** (2 days; p. 427).

LIFE AND TIMES

HISTORY

EARLY HISTORY AND THE FIRST REICH (UNTIL 1400)

Early German history—actually, most of German history—can be summed up as alternating unification and fracture. The **Roman Empire** conquered and incorporated the independent tribes that had formerly occupied the area; Roman ruins can still be seen in **Trier** (see p. 470) and **Cologne** (see p. 455), for example. With the collapse of the Empire, the Germanic tribes separated again, only to be reunified in the 8th century by **Charlemagne** (Karl der Große to Germans) in an empire now known as the **First Reich,** or kingdom. Charlemagne established his capital at **Aachen** (see p. 463), where his earthly remains reside today. After Charlemagne's death, the empire was (surprise, surprise) split up, and without a strong leader, the former empire disintegrated into a decentralized **feudalism;** visit **Rothenburg** (see p. 492) for a glimpse into a medieval walled city typical of the time.

THE NORTHERN RENAISSANCE (1400-1517)

Inspired by the new philosophies of the Italian Renaissance, northern philosophers developed their own concept of **humanism,** focusing particularly on religious reform and a return to Classics (virtues and works). **Johannes Gutenberg** paved the way for widespread dissemination of ideas by inventing **moveable type** in Mainz (see p. 467); his Latin printing of the Bible is arguably the world's most seminal publication. This invention allowed rapid production of books, which increased literacy and put information (and inevitably, smut) in the hands of the people.

RELIGION AND REFORM (1517-1700)

On All Saints' Day, 1517, **Martin Luther** nailed his **95 Theses** to the door of Wittenberg's church (see p. 436), condemning the Catholic Church's extravagance and its practice of selling **indulgences**—certificates that promised to shorten the owner's stay in purgatory. Luther had initially been trained as a lawyer but had devoted his life to religion after seeing the light (literally) when he narrowly escaped being hit by lightning. His ideas sparked the **Protestant Reformation,** a period of intense religious debate. During this time, Luther translated the New Testament from Latin into German, standardizing the German language and allowing lay-people to read the Bible directly for the first time. Rising continent-wide tensions between Catholics and Protestants eventually led to the **Thirty Years' War** (1618-1648), a series of conflicts among the European powers. After the fighting, Germany emerged as a group of small, independent territories, each ruled by a local prince, ripe for conquering, separation, and re-conquering.

RISE OF BRANDENBURG-PRUSSIA (1700-1862)

Through a series of strategic marriages, the **Hohenzollern** family gained control over a large number of these territories. Their kingdom, Brandenburg-Prussia, became an absolutist state when **Frederick I** crowned himself king in 1701. His grandson, **Frederick the Great,** beautified the realm and dove into international politics, acquiring huge chunks of land and establishing Prussia as a major world power. When **Napoleon** began nibbling at its borders in the early 1800s, Prussia fractured again, remaining a loose and unstable confederation of states even after his defeat.

THE SECOND REICH (1862-1914)

In 1862, worldly aristocrat **Otto von Bismarck** was named chancellor. He believed that "blood and iron" (i.e., war and force) could create a strong and unified German nation. Bismarck consolidated Prussia into a powerful nation through a series of military movements. The culmination was the **Franco-Prussian War** in 1870: the technologically superior Prussian army swept through France, Bismarck gleefully besieged Paris, and the king of Prussia, **Wilhelm I,** was upgraded to **Kaiser of the German Reich** at the Palace of Versailles. Bismarck had presented Germany with an offer it couldn't refuse: unification in exchange for an authoritarian monarchy.

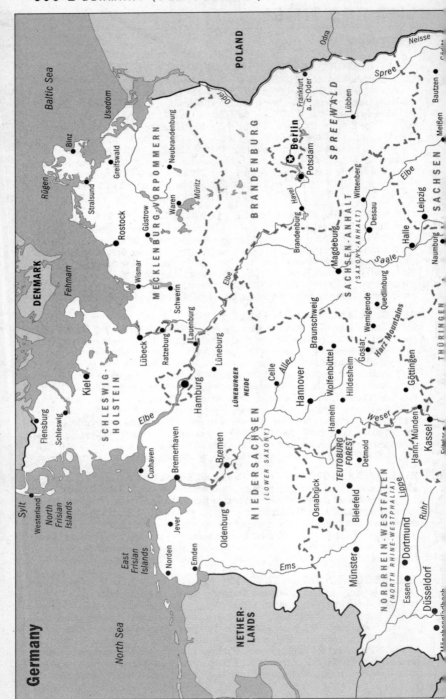

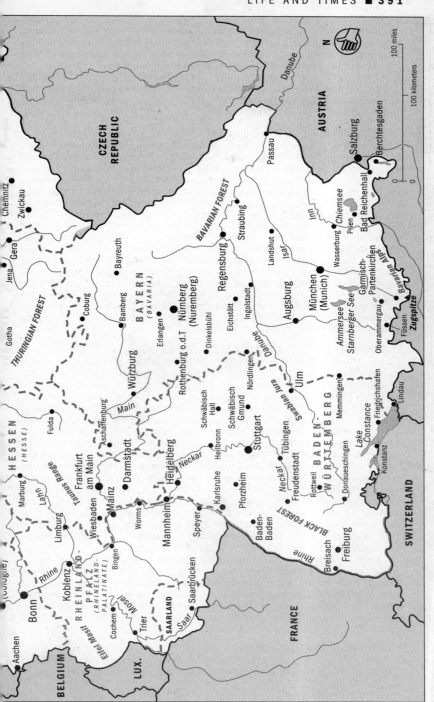

WORLD WAR I (1914-1918)

On the eve of **WWI,** Europe was entangled in a complex web of precarious alliances. In 1914, when a Serbian nationalist assassinated **Archduke Franz-Ferdinand,** the heir to the Austrian throne, Austria declared war on Serbia. Germany jumped in to help Austria, and the rest of Europe was soon drawn into full-blown war. After four agonizing years of trench warfare, Germany and its allies were defeated. Germany's aggressiveness in France, along with its policy of **unrestricted submarine warfare** on all ships entering European waters, allowed the victors to place responsibility for **The Great War** on Germany's shoulders.

THE WEIMAR REPUBLIC (1918-1933)

France insisted on a harsh peace in the **Treaty of Versailles,** which imposed staggering reparation payments, drastically reduced the German army, and officially ascribed the blame for the war to Germany. The defeated Germans had little choice but to accept the humiliating terms, and a new republic was set up in **Weimar** (see p. 436). Outstanding war debts and the burden of reparations produced staggering hyperinflation in 1922-23; paper money was worth more as fireplace fuel than currency. Already smarting from Versailles, the German people needed stability and relief from the post-war hardships, which a charismatic Austrian named **Adolf Hitler** seemed to promise. His party, the National Socialists (NSDAP, also known as the **Nazis**), was increasingly associated with German ultra-nationalist ideals.

Hitler's first attempt to seize power, the **Beer Hall Putsch** in Munich (1923), was unsuccessful, but as economic troubles worsened, more and more Germans were drawn to the Nazis and their promises of prosperity and community; party membership increased to more than a million by 1930. Hitler failed in a presidential bid against the nearly senile war-hero **Paul von Hindenburg** in 1932, but since elections made the Nazis the dominant party in the legislature, Hindenburg reluctantly appointed Hitler chancellor on January 30, 1933.

BEGINNING OF THE THIRD REICH (1933-39)

Hitler's platform, crystallized in the tome **Mein Kampf** *(My Struggle)*, provided a scapegoat for WWI losses—the Jews—and played on centuries-old feelings of anti-Semitism and German racial community. The new government quickly instituted a boycott of Jewish enterprises and expelled Jews from professional and civil service; rival parties that might have opposed the Nazis were outlawed or dissolved. In 1934, after Hindenburg's death, Hitler appropriated presidential powers for himself; that year, the first of the **Nürnberg Laws** were passed, depriving Jews of German citizenship and preventing intermarriage between Aryan and Jewish Germans—it was felt that the "debased" Jews would taint the pure and "superior" German blood. Nazis destroyed thousands of Jewish businesses, burned synagogues, and killed and deported thousands of Jews on **Kristallnacht** (Night of Broken Glass), November 9, 1938; only a few synagogues escaped (see p. 414). With the help of **Joseph Goebbels,** his minister of propaganda, Hitler consolidated his power by saturating mass culture—from art to literature to movies to music—with Nazi ideology: the Nazis burned books by Jewish and "subversive" authors at Bebelplatz in Berlin (see p. 413), banned American films and music, and destroyed "degenerate" art in favor of propagandist paintings and statues.

Hitler was also busy mounting a war effort. He first freed Germany from making reparations payments by abrogating the Treaty of Versailles. Next, he annexed Austria in an infamous attack known as the **Anschluß** (1938). Other nations, hoping that Hitler would be satisfied with these new acquisitions, followed a policy of **appeasement,** led by British Prime Minster **Neville Chamberlain,** and allowed Germany to take over the Sudetenland region (now in the Czech Republic). However, it soon became clear that Hitler was after more than small territorial gains.

WORLD WAR II (1939-1945)

On September 1, 1939, German tanks rolled into Poland. Britain and France, bound by treaty to defend Poland, immediately declared war on Germany, and the rest of

Europe was again dragged into global conflict. Germany's new tactic of mechanized **Blitzkrieg** (literally, "lightning war") quickly crushed Poland. Denmark, Norway, Belgium, The Netherlands, and France were soon overwhelmed as well.

The Nazis then began a two-front war, attacking westward in the aviary conflict of the **Battle of Britain** and eastward in the **invasion of the USSR.** However, daily air raids spurred the British to fight harder rather than submit; meanwhile, the *Blitzkrieg* faltered in the Russian winter and Hitler sacrificed thousands of German soldiers in his adamant refusal to retreat. The bloody **Battle of Stalingrad** (1942-43) marked a critical turning point in the East as the Soviets gained the upper hand. Soon Germany was retreating on all fronts. The Allied landing in Normandy on **D-Day** (June 6, 1944) preceded an arduous eastward advance across Europe; the Soviet Army rolled westward and took Berlin in April 1945. The Third Reich, which Hitler had boasted would endure for 1000 years, had lasted only 12.

THE HOLOCAUST. By the outbreak of WWII, Jews had lost virtually all rights and and were forced to identify themselves with a yellow Star of David patch. The Nazis portrayed Jews as the ultimate influence corrupting the German soul, and Hitler was fixated on his **Final Solution:** genocide. Seven death camps, including **Buchenwald** (see p. 437) and Auschwitz-Birkenau, were designed for morbidly efficient mass extermination; dozens of "labor" camps such as Bergen-Belsen and **Dachau** (see p. 489) were operating before war's end. Nearly six million Jews—two-thirds of Europe's Jewish population—mostly from Poland and the Soviet Union, were gassed, shot, starved, worked to death, or killed by exposure. Millions of other victims, including prisoners of war, Slavs, gypsies, homosexuals, the mentally disordered, and political opponents, also died in Nazi camps.

OCCUPATION AND DIVISION (1945-1949)

In July 1945, the United States, Great Britain, and the Soviet Union met at **Potsdam** to partition Germany into zones of occupation: the east under the Soviets, the west under the British and Americans, and Berlin under combined control. The Allied program for the **Occupation**—democratization, demilitarization, and de-Nazification—proceeded apace, but growing animosity between the Soviets and the Western Allies made joint control of Germany increasingly difficult. In 1947, the Allies merged their occupation zones into a single economic unit and began to rebuild a market economy with huge cash infusions under the American **Marshall Plan.** East and West Germany became increasingly distant, especially after the Western Allies introduced the **Deutschmark** into their zones.

THE FEDERAL REPUBLIC OF GERMANY (1949-1989)

The Federal Republic of Germany *(Bundesrepublik Deutschland)* was established as the provisional government of Western Germany on May 24, 1949. A **Basic Law** safeguarded individual rights and established a system of freely elected parliamentary assemblies. One of the most visionary paragraphs established a **Right of Asylum,** guaranteeing refuge to any person fleeing persecution.

As the only party untainted by the Third Reich, the Social Democratic Party seemed poised to dominate postwar German politics, but the **Christian Democratic Union (CDP)** provided some competition by uniting Germany's historically fragmented conservatives and centrists under a nondenominational platform. With former Cologne mayor **Konrad Adenauer** at the helm, the CDU won a small majority of seats in the Federal Republic's first general election. As chancellor, Adenauer unflaggingly pursued the integration of Germany into a unified Europe; West Germany was aligned with **NATO** (North Atlantic Treaty Organization) in 1955 and became one of the charter members of the European Economic Community (later the **European Union**) in 1957. The speedy fiscal recovery secured the future dominance of the CDU party. In 1982, Christian Democrat **Helmut Kohl** became chancellor and pursued a policy of welfare state cutbacks, tight monetary policy, and military cooperation with the US.

MEANWHILE... IN THE GERMAN DEMOCRATIC REPUBLIC

In spite of pledges to the contrary, the Soviets stopped holding free elections in their sector by 1949. On October 7, 1949, they declared the establishment of the **German Democratic Republic,** with the national capital in Berlin. Constitutional promises of civil liberties and democracy were empty: East Germany became unquestioningly subservient to the Soviet Union. The **Stasi,** or secret police, maintained a network of agents that strove to monitor every citizen from their headquarters in Berlin (see p. 417)—one in seven East Germans was a paid informant.

Many East Germans chose to escape such repression by emigrating to West Germany. By 1961, more than 3 million had illegally crossed the border, and the East German government decided to stop the exodus of young skilled workers. Overnight on August 12, the first barriers of the **Berlin Wall** were laid, and barbed wire and guns dissuaded further attempts to escape, making for a confusing and dangerous barrier between the two halves.

REUNIFICATION (1989)

When **Mikhail Gorbachev** took the helm of the USSR in 1985, liberalizing reform spread throughout the Eastern Bloc under his policy of *glasnost* (openness). East Germany, however, remained under tight control. *Die Wende* (the "turning" or "change," as the sudden toppling of the East is referred to in Germany) came in May 1989 when Hungary dismantled its barbed-wire border with Austria, giving East Germans an escape route to the West. In October, Gorbachev announced that the USSR would not interfere with East Germany's domestic affairs, and citizens began to demand free elections, freedom of press, and freedom of travel. The entire East German government resigned on November 8, and a day later, a Central Committee spokesperson announced the opening of all borders to the West.

The destruction of the Wall was the most symbolically significant turning point for Germans since the end of WWII. The signing of the **Four-Plus-Two Treaty** by the two Germanies and the four occupying powers on September 12, 1990, signaled the **end of a divided Germany.** On October 3, 1990, the Allies forfeited their occupation rights, East Germany ceased to exist, and Germany became one united sovereign nation for the first time in 45 years. However, East and West Germany did not come together on equal terms. The collapse of East Germany's inefficient industries and institutions led to massive unemployment and the Federal Republic's worst-ever recession. Many Westerners resented the inflation and taxes brought on by reunification, while Easterners missed the generous social benefits that communism had afforded them. Economic frustrations led to the scapegoating of foreigners, especially asylum-seekers from Eastern Europe and immigrant workers. Thankfully, violence has decreased greatly over the past few years.

GERMANY TODAY

After the dramatic fall of the Berlin Wall in 1989, Kohl and his CDU party seemed insurmountable. Carrying their momentum into the first all-German elections, the CDU scored a stunning victory. However, Kohl found it difficult to manage the reunification, and his popularity plummeted to the point where Easterners pelted him with rotten vegetables during one visit. In 1998, left-wing parties ousted the CDU, electing **Gerhard Schroeder** chancellor.

Germany's new place within Europe remains a great political question. The burden of the past makes everyone, including Germans themselves, nervous about Germany's participation in international military operations. In the summer of 2001, the government overwhelmingly voted to distribute 10 million DM ($4.3 million) among Nazi-era slave-laborers as belated compensation, signalling that Germany has come to grips, at least partially, with its Nazi past. Recently, Germany has begun to redefine its international role; in the **Kosovo** crisis, for example, Germany played a pivotal role in negotiating a peace accord, and German forces were present both at peacekeeping missions in Yugoslavia and flood relief operations in Africa. The persistent feeling among Germans now is that they should stay out of foreign policy, acting instead as a large, benign economic machine at the heart of the European Union, but such a neutral stance may not be possible for Europe's most populous and economically powerful nation.

THE ARTS

VISUAL ART

In the Renaissance, **Albrecht Dürer** emerged as a master of engraving and draftsmanship. His *Adam and Eve* still peppers advertisements today, and his *Self-Portrait at 20* (1500), was one of the first self-portraits in Europe. In the 19th century, **Caspar David Friedrich** painted dramatic mountain scenes and billowing landscapes that exemplify the Romantic style. However, it was in the 20th century that German art truly blossomed. The deliberate anti-realism of **German Expressionism** intensified color and object representation to project deeply personal emotions. A 1911 exhibition in Munich entitled **Der Blaue Reiter** (The Blue Rider), led by Russian emigré **Wassily Kandinsky,** displayed some of the first totally non-representational paintings in Western art. In the interwar period, artists became increasingly political in reaction to the rise of Fascism: **Max Beckmann** painted severely posed figures whose gestures and symbolism expressed a tortured view of man's condition, and **Max Ernst** started a **Dadaist** group in Cologne, conveying artistic nihilism through collage. During the Nazi era, almost all art was controlled by the state for propagandistic purposes, featuring idealized images of workers, soldiers, and citizens. Nevertheless, the German art scene bounced back after the war's end. **Anselm Kiefer** examines Germany's previously unapproachable past in his paintings, while **Josef Beuys**'s innovative art objects and performances challenge artistic conventions. The **Deichtorhallen Hamburg** (p. 446) showcases the city's contemporary art scene in rotating exhibits, while the **Kunst- und Ausstellungshalle der BRD** (in Bonn, see p. 461) features art so new you can smell the paint.

ARCHITECTURE AND DESIGN

Outstanding **Romanesque** cathedrals, featuring a clover-leaf floor plan, numerous towers, and a mitre-like steeple, can be found along the Rhine at **Trier** (see p. 470) and **Mainz** (see p. 467). The **Gothic** style, with its pointed spires and vaulted roofs, gradually replaced the Romanesque form between 1300 and 1500; stained glass windows fill otherwise gloomy interiors with divine light. The cathedral at **Cologne** (see p. 455) is one of the most famous German gothic structures. Secular architecture at the end of the Middle Ages was dominated by the **Fachwerk** (half-timbered) houses that can still be seen in the *Altstadt* ("old-town") sections of many German cities. In the 17th century, the **Baroque** style emerged with ostentatious decorations and sinuous contours; the **Zwinger** (see p. 430) in Dresden is a magnificent example. Baroque developed into the highly decorative **Rococo** style with ornately garnished buildings like **Schloß Sanssouci** (see p. 425). A simpler movement, **Neoclassicism,** arose in reaction to the frou-frou Rococo façades; the **Brandenburger Tor** (see p. 412) and the buildings along Unter den Linden in Berlin (see p. 412) use stylistic elements of Classical Greece and Rome. In 1919, Weimar saw the birth of the boxy **Bauhaus** style of architecture, which emphasized form based on function. The movement later moved to **Dessau**, where a school for design still flourishes.

LITERATURE

The first significant German novel, **Hans J. C. von Grimmelshausen**'s roguish series *Simplicissimus*, was written during the chaos of the Thirty Years' War, a period that saw little literary development due to political turmoil. By the 18th century, however, the German literary scene was flourishing. **Johann Wolfgang von Goethe** exemplified the Romantic era with emotional, dramatic masterpieces such as *Faust* (1832), while the **Brothers Grimm** transformed folk tales from an oral tradition into morbid, child-scaring (but classic) literature in the 19th century. A rush of real-

GERMANY

istic political literature emerged in the turbulent mid-19th century; **Heinrich Heine** was the one of the finest, writing witty satires as well as romantic poems. In the early 20th century, **Thomas Mann** carried the modern novel to a high point with *The Magic Mountain* (1924) and *Doctor Faustus* (1947), while **Hermann Hesse** experimented with Eastern motifs in the quasi-Buddhist novel *Siddhartha* (1922). **Rainer Maria Rilke,** living in Austria-Hungary, produced some of Germany's most enduring poems, and **Franz Kafka** examined the complications of modern existence (and the dilemma of *really* not feeling like yourself) in *The Metamorphosis* (1915).

Despite the disruption of WWI, the **Weimar era** was a period of active artistic production. **Erich Maria Remarque**'s *All Quiet on the Western Front* (1929), a blunt account of war's horrors, became an international bestseller. **Bertolt Brecht**'s dramas and poems presented humankind in all its grotesque absurdity (see p. 414). To nurse German literature back to health after the Nazi book-burning years, several writers, including **Günter Grass** and poet **Paul Celan,** joined to form **Gruppe 47,** named after the year of its founding. The group coined the term *Nullstunde* ("Zero Hour") to signify that after WWII, culture had to begin again. Much of the ensuing literature dealt with the problem of Germany's Nazi past; the novels of Grass and **Heinrich Böll** and the poetry of **Hans Magnus Enzensberger** turned a critical eye to post-war West Germany's repressive, overly organized tendencies.

PHILOSOPHY

Germany's philosophical tradition is one of the most respected in the world. Initially, philosophy dealt only with religion. In 1517, **Martin Luther**'s *95 Theses* denied papal infallibility, claiming that only scripture was holy and thus advocating a direct relationship with God; **Gottfried Wilhelm Leibnitz** thought of God as a watchmaker who set the individual's body and soul in motion like two synchronized clocks. In the **Enlightenment,** reason was the key word: **Immanuel Kant,** the foremost German thinker of the time, argued that ethics can be rationally deduced. **Georg W. F. Hegel** proposed that world history and the development of the individual consciousness could be understood as a thesis and antithesis, respectively, combining to form a new synthesis.

The 19th century brought several controversial but highly influential theories: the founder of modern socialism, **Karl Marx** (see p. 470) asserted that class conflict was the driving force of all history. **Friedrich Nietzsche** (see p. 436) developed the idea of the *Übermensch*, a super-man so wise and self-mastered that he could enjoy life even to the point of eternal repetition. **Max Weber** created the idea of the "Protestant Ethic," which related Protestantism to capitalism. In the interwar period, **Martin Heidegger** became one of the main exponents of Existentialism; his *Being and Time* (1927) examines the crisis of alienation in a world of technical development. After the fall of the Third Reich, thinkers **Theodor Adorno** and **Max Horkheimer** penned the classic *Dialectic of Enlightenment* (1947), which suggests that civilization ultimately culminates in fascism. More recently, **Jürgen Habermas** has criticized German reunification, citing the danger of joining two nations that have adopted very different cultures.

MUSIC

Johann Sebastian Bach was one of the first great German composers. His organ works are characterized by meticulous symmetries and regularities that reflect a careful spiritual order, while his orchestral works, such as the *Brandenburg Concerti* (c. 1721), explore the contrast between solo instruments and the chamber orchestra. Bach and his contemporary **Georg Friedrich Händel** composed during the Baroque period of the 17th century, which was known for its extravagant decoration and popularized the theme-and-variation pattern. Händel's *Messiah* (1741) is still widely performed today—Hallelujah!

The 19th century was an era of German musical hegemony. **Ludwig van Beethoven**'s symphonies and piano sonatas bridged Classicism and Romanticism with rhythmic drives and intense emotional expressionism; he is perhaps best known in popular culture for his dramatic *Fifth* and *Ninth Symphonies* (1808 and

1824, respectively). Meanwhile, **Felix Mendelssohn-Bartholdy** wrote more ethereal works, such as his musical interpretation of Shakespeare's *A Midsummer Night's Dream* (1826). The second generation of Romantic composers included **Johannes Brahms,** who imbued Classical forms with rich Romantic emotion. *Tristan and Isolde* (1859), *Lohengrin* (1850), and the other (interminably long) operas of **Richard Wagner** express the nationalist sentiments rising in the mid-19th century. His vision of **Gesamtkunstwerk** (total work of art) unified music, text, poetry, and philosophy as he glorified German legend.

Germany's postwar music scene is mostly transnational; Germans are more likely to listen to American pop than their own countrymen. Nevertheless, they have made important contributions to the field. Germany is best known internationally for pioneering **techno** with bands like ⦿Kraftwerk, to the delight of clubgoers worldwide. Rap and hip-hop have become quite popular since the rise of **Die fantastischen Vier,** the first German rap group.

FOOD AND DRINK

German cooking has a robust charm that is especially satisfying for meat-and-potato lovers. German delights include **Schnitzel** (a lightly fried veal cutlet), **Spätzle** (a southern noodle), and **Kartoffeln** (potatoes). The typical German **Frühstück** (breakfast) consists of coffee or tea with rolls, bread, cold sausage, eggs, and cheese. The main meal of the day, **Mittagessen** (lunch), includes soup, broiled sausage or roasted meat, potatoes or dumplings, and a salad or vegetable side dish. **Abendessen** or **Abendbrot** (dinner) is a reprise of breakfast, only beer replaces coffee and the selection of meats and cheese is wider. Many older Germans indulge in a daily ritual of **Kaffee und Kuchen** (coffee and cakes) at 3 or 4pm.

To eat on the cheap, stick to the daily *Tagesmenü* (fixed-price menu), buy food in supermarkets, or, if you have a student ID, head to a university **Mensa** (cafeteria). Fast-food *Imbiß* stands also provide inexpensive fare; try the delicious Turkish *Döner* (something like a gyro). In small towns, buy bread at a *Bäckerei* (bakery) and add sausage from a butcher (*Fleischerei* or *Metzgerei*).

German beer is maltier and more "bread-like" than other beers. One exception is **Pils,** or *Pilsner*, popular in the north; its clarity and bitter taste comes from extra hops. In the south, try **Weißbier,** a smooth refreshing wheat brew. Also sample the largely overlooked German **wines,** particularly the sweet (*lieblich* or *süß*) whites of the Rhine and Mosel valleys.

ESSENTIALS

DOCUMENTS AND FORMALITIES

Germany requires **visas** of South Africans, but not of nationals of Australia, Canada, the EU, New Zealand, or the US for stays of less than 90 days.

EMBASSIES AND CONSULATES

German Embassies at Home: Australia, 119 Empire Circuit, Yarralumla, Canberra, ACT 2600 (☎(02) 62 70 19 11; fax 62 70 19 51). **Canada,** 1 Waverly St., Ottawa, ON K2P OT8 (☎613-232-1101; fax 594-9330). **Ireland,** 31 Trimleston Ave., Booterstown, Blackrock, Co. Dublin (☎(01) 269 30 11; fax 269 39 46). **New Zealand,** 90-92 Hobson St., Thorndon, Wellington (☎(04) 473 60 63; fax 473 60 69). **South Africa,** 180 Blackwood St., Arcadia, Pretoria, 0083 (☎(012) 427 89 00; fax 343 94 01). **UK,** 23 Belgrave Sq., London SW1X 8PZ (☎(020) 78 24 13 00; fax 78 24 14 35). **US,** 4645 Reservoir Rd. NW, Washington, D.C. 20007-1998 (☎202-298-4393; fax 471-5558; www.germany-info.org).

Foreign Embassies in Germany: All embassies are in Berlin (see p. 407). For the latest information, call the **Auswärtiges Amt** in Berlin at ☎(030) 20 18 60.

GERMANY

TRANSPORTATION

BY PLANE. Most flights land in Frankfurt; Berlin, Munich, and Hamburg also have international airports. **Lufthansa,** the national airline, has the most flights in and out of the country, but they're not always the cheapest option. Flying within Germany is usually more expensive and less convenient than taking the train.

BY TRAIN. The **Deutsche Bahn (DB)** network (in Germany ☎(0180) 599 66 33; www.bahn.de) is Europe's best but also one of the most expensive. **RE** (Regional-Express) and the slightly slower **RB** (RegionalBahn) trains include a number of rail networks between neighboring cities. **IR** (InterRegio) trains, covering larger networks between cities, are speedy and comfortable. **D** trains are foreign trains that serve international routes. **EC** (EuroCity) and **IC** (InterCity) trains zoom along between major cities every hour 6am-10pm. The futuristic **ICE** (InterCityExpress) trains approach the luxury and kinetics of an airplane and run at speeds up to 280kph. On all trains, 2nd-class compartments are clean and comfortable. You must purchase a **Zuschlag** (supplement) to ride an IC or EC train. (DM7/€3.60 when bought in the station, DM9/€4.60 on the train.)

Designed for tourists, the German Railpass allows unlimited travel for four to 10 days within a four-week period. Non-Europeans can purchase German Railpasses in their home countries and—with a passport—in major German train stations (5-day DM418/€214, 10-day DM653/€334). The **German Rail Youth Pass** is for those under 26 (5-day DM333/€170, 9-day DM423/€216). The second-class **Twin Pass** is for two adults traveling together (5-day DM627/€320, 10-day DM978/€500). Travelers ages 12-25 can purchase **TwenTickets,** which knock 20% off fares between DM10-239/€5-123. A **Schönes-Wochenende-Ticket** (DM40/€20.45) gives up to five people unlimited travel on any of the slower trains (*not* ICE, IC, EC, D, or IR) from 12:01am Saturday until 3am Sunday, or 12:01am Sunday until 3am Monday. The **Guten-Abend-Ticket** is an excellent deal for long-distance night travel and allows travel anywhere (*not* on InterCityNight or CityNightLines) in Germany between 7pm (2pm Sa) and 3am. (2nd-class DM59/€30.20; F-Su DM15/€7.70 extra.) A great option for those making frequent and extensive use of German trains for more than one month, the **Bahncard** is valid for one year and gives a 50% discount on all trains. Passes are available at major train stations and require a passport-sized photo and mailing address in Germany. (2nd-class DM270/€138; age18-22, over 60, or students under 27 DM135/€69.)

Eurailpass is valid in Germany and provides free passage on urban S-Bahns and DB buses, but not on U-Bahns. **Public transit** is excellent in major cities and comes in four flavors: the **Straßenbahn** (streetcar), **S-Bahn** (surface rail), **U-Bahn** (underground subway), and regular **buses.** Consider buying a day card *(Tageskarte)* or multiple-ride ticket *(Mehrfahrkarte);* they usually pay for themselves quickly.

BY BUS. Bus service between cities and to outlying areas runs from the local **Zentralomnibusbahnhof (ZOB),** which is usually close to the main train station. Buses are often slightly more expensive than trains for comparable distances. Railpasses are not valid on any buses other than a few run by Deutsche Bahn.

BY CAR. German road conditions are generally excellent. It's true, there is no set speed limit on the **Autobahn,** only a recommendation of 130kph (81mph). Germans drive *fast.* Watch for signs indicating right-of-way (usually designated by a yellow triangle). The Autobahn is indicated by an intuitive "A" on signs; secondary highways, where the speed limit is usually 100kph, are accompanied by signs bearing a "B." Germans drive on the right side of the road. In cities and towns, **speed limits** hover around 30-60kph (18-38mph). Germans use unleaded **gas** almost exclusively; prices run around DM8.40/€4.30 per gal., or about DM2.15/€1.10 per L.

BY BIKE AND BY THUMB. Bikes are sight-seeing power tools; Germany makes it easy with its wealth of trails and bike tours. Cities and towns usually have designated bike lanes and biking maps. *Germany by Bike*, by Nadine Slavinski (Mountaineers Books, 1994, US$14.95), details 20 tours. *Let's Go* does not recommend **hitchhiking**. A better option are **Mitfahrzentralen,** agencies that pair up drivers and riders for a small fee; riders then negotiate payment for the trip with the driver. *Let's Go* lists these organizations in individual cites, where applicable.

TOURIST SERVICES AND MONEY

EMERGENCY Police, ☎ 110. Ambulance, ☎ 110. Fire, ☎ 112.

TOURIST OFFICES. Every city in Germany has a **tourist office,** usually located near the train station *(Hauptbahnhof)* or central square *(Marktplatz)*. All are marked by a thick lowercase **"i"** sign. The offices often book rooms for a small fee. The tourist information web site for Germany is www.germany-tourism.de.

MONEY. The **deutsche Mark** or **Deutschmark** (abbreviated DM) is the unit of currency in Germany. It is one of the most stable and respected currencies in the world; in most markets in Eastern Europe, "hard currency" means US dollars and Deutschmarks exclusively. One DM equals 100 *Pfennig* (Pf). Coins come in 1, 2, 5, 10, and 50Pf, and DM1, 2, and 5 amounts. Bills come in DM5, 10, 20, 50, 100, 200, 500, and 1000 denominations, though DM5 bills are now rare. Germany has accepted the **Euro (€)** as legal tender, and Deutschmarks will be phased out by July 1, 2002. For more information, see p. 23.

> **Prices:** If you stay in **hostels** and prepare your own food, expect to spend anywhere from DM40-80/€20-40 (US$19-38) per person per day.

> **Tipping and bargaining:** Most Germans just round up DM1-2/€0.50-1 in restaurants and bars, or when they receive a service, such as a taxi ride. Note that tips in Germany are not left lying on the table, but handed directly to the server when you pay. If you don't want any change, say *Das stimmt so* (das SHTIMMT zo). Germans rarely bargain except at flea markets.

> **Taxes:** Most goods and services bought in Germany will automatically include a **value-added tax (VAT)** of 15%. In German, this is called the *Mehrwertsteuer* **(MwSt).** Non-EU citizens can get the **VAT refunded** for large purchases of goods. At the point of purchase, ask for a Tax-Free Shopping Cheque, then have it stamped at customs upon leaving the country or at a customs authority. The goods must remain unused until you leave the country.

ACCOMMODATIONS AND CAMPING

HOSTELS. Germany currently has about **600 hostels**—more than any other nation on Earth. Hostelling in Germany is overseen by **Deutsches Jugendherbergswerk (DJH),** Bismarckstr. 8, D-32756 Detmold, Germany (☎ (05231) 740 10; fax 74 01 74; www.djh.de). DJH has recently initiated a growing number of **Jugendgästehäuser,** youth guest-houses that have more facilities and attract slightly older guests. DJH publishes *Jugendherbergen in Deutschland* (DM14.80/€7.50), a guide to all federated German hostels. Never leave your belongings unattended; crime can occur in even the most demure-looking hostel or hotel.

HOTELS. The cheapest hotel-style accommodations are places with Pension, Gasthof, Gästehaus, or Hotel-Garni in the name. Hotel rooms start at DM30/€15.35 for singles and DM40/€20.45 for doubles; in large cities, expect to pay nearly twice as much. Breakfast *(Frühstück)* is almost always available and often included.

PRIVATE ROOMS. The best bet for a cheap bed is often a *Privatzimmer* (a room in a family home). This option works best if you have a rudimentary knowledge of German. Prices generally run DM20-50/€10-25 per person. Travelers over 26 who would otherwise pay higher prices at youth hostels will find these rooms within budget range. Reservations are made through the local tourist office or through a private Zimmervermittlung (room-booking office) for free or a DM2-8/€1-4 fee.

GERMANY

CAMPING. Germans love camping; over 2,600 campsites dot the outskirts of even the most major cities. Facilities are well-maintained and usually provide showers, bathrooms, and a restaurant or store. Camping costs DM3-10/€1.50-5 per person, with additional charges for tents and vehicles. Blue signs with a black tent on a white background indicate official sites. **Deutscher Camping-Club (DCC)**, Mandlstr. 28, 80802 München (☎(089) 380 14 20), has more information, and the National Tourist Office distributes a free map, *Camping in Germany.*

COMMUNICATION

MAIL. Mail can be sent through **Poste Restante** *(Postlagernde Briefe)* to almost any German city or town with a post office. The mail will go to the main post office unless you specify a post office by street address or postal code.

TELEPHONES. Most public phones only accept **telephone cards.** You can pick up a **Telefonkarte** (phone card) in post offices, at a *Kiosk* (newsstand), or at selected Deutsche Bahn counters in major train stations. The cards come in DM12, 24, and 50 denominations. There is no standard length for city codes or phone numbers, but phone numbers usually have three to 10 digits; The smaller the city, the more digits in the city code. International direct dial numbers include: **AT&T**, ☎(800) 22 55 288; **British Telecom,** ☎(800) 89 00 49; **Canada Direct,** ☎(800) 888 00 14; **Ireland Direct,** ☎(08000) 800 353; **MCI,** ☎(800) 88 88 000; **Sprint,** ☎(800) 888 00 13; **Telecom New Zealand,** ☎(800) 080 00 64; **Telkom South Africa,** (800) 180 00 27; **Telstra Australia,** ☎(800) 08 00 061.

INTERNET ACCESS. Most German cities (as well as a surprising number of smaller towns) have at least one Internet cafe with web access for about DM3-7/€1.50-3.50 per 30min. Some German universities have banks of computers hooked up to the Internet in their libraries, although ostensibly for student use.

LANGUAGE. Many people in Western Germany speak English, but this is less common in the East. The letter ß is equivalent to a double *s*. For German tips, see p. 953.

Germany is no more dangerous than the rest of Western Europe, but violent crime does exist, particularly in big cities and economically depressed regions of the East. Many of Germany's neo-Nazis wear flight jackets over white short-sleeve shirts and tight jeans rolled to reveal high-cut combat boots. Skinheads tend to subscribe to a shoelace code, with white supremacists and neo-Nazis wearing white laces and anti-gay skinheads wearing pink laces. Left-wing anti-Nazi "S.H.A.R.P.s" (Skinheads Against Racial Prejudice) favor red laces.

LOCAL FACTS

Time: Germany is 1hr. ahead of Greenwich Mean Time (GMT); see back cover.

When to Go: Germany's climate is temperate, with rain year-round (especially in summer). Temperatures range between -1 to 2°C (30-36°F) in deep winter to 12-25°C (55-77°F) in July and Aug. The cloudy, temperate months of May, June, and Sept. are the best time to go, as there are fewer tourists and the weather is pleasant. Germans head to vacation spots *en masse* with the onset of school vacations in early July. Winter sports gear up Nov.-Apr.; high-season for skiing is mid-Dec. to Mar.

Holidays: Epiphany (Jan. 6); Ash Wednesday (Mar. 8); Good Friday (Apr. 21); Easter Sunday and Monday (Apr. 23-24); Labor Day (May 1); Ascension Day (June 1); Whit Sunday and Monday (June 11-12); Corpus Christi (June 22); Assumption Day (Aug. 15); Day of German Unity (Oct. 3); Reformation Day (Nov. 1); All Saint's Day (Nov. 1); and Christmas (Dec. 25-26). Expect reduced hours in establishments.

Festivals: Check out the **Fasching** in Munich (Jan. 7-Feb. 12), **Berlinale Film Festival** (Feb. 6-17), **Karneval** in Cologne (Feb. 7-11), **Christopher St. Day** in Berlin and other major cities (late June to early July), **Love Parade** in Berlin (mid-July), **Oktoberfest** in Munich (Sept. 21-Oct. 16), and **Christmas Market** in Nuremberg.

BERLIN
☎ 030

GERMANY

Don't wait any longer to see Berlin. The city is nearing the end of a massive transitional phase, developing from a newly reunited metropolis reeling in the aftermath of the Cold War to an epicenter of the European Union—and the Berlin of five or even two years into the future will be radically different from Berlin of today. Germany is the industrial leader of the continent, and when the Lehrter Stadtbahnhof (Europe's largest train station) opens in 2004, the capital city will essentially become the capital of Europe. However, in the wake of the Nazi regime and the Holocaust, Germans question their own ability—and right—to govern. The problem of *"Mauer im Kopf"* ("wall in the head;" the still-existing feelings of division between East and West) is more prevalent here than anywhere else. Indeed, the concept of a divided city is quite familiar to Berliners; Berlin is built not around a single center but around many colorfully varied neighborhoods. As a result, the atmosphere is the most diverse and tolerant of any of Germany's cities, with a world-famous gay and lesbian scene and an almost-non-existent racial crime rate. But the real reason to visit is the city's exquisite tension between past and future, conservation and modernization. No other city is currently poised to attain such geopolitical importance, and the air is taut with hope and foreboding.

✈ INTERCITY TRANSPORTATION

Berlin, in the northeastern corner of Germany, is rapidly becoming the hub of the national rail network, with rail and air connections to most other European capitals. Almost all European airlines have service to one of Berlin's three airports.

Flights: For information on all 3 airports, call (0180) 500 01 86. Currently, the city is condensing its airports, but for now, **Flughafen Tegel** remains Western Berlin's main airport. Express bus #X9 from "Bahnhof Zoo," bus #109 from "Jakob-Kaiser-Pl." on U7, or bus #128 from "Kurt-Schumacher-Pl." on U6. **Flughafen Tempelhof,** Berlin's smallest airport, has intra-German and intra-European flights. U6 to "Pl. der Luftbrücke." **Flughafen Schönefeld,** southeast of Berlin, has intercontinental flights. S45 or S9 to "Flughafen Berlin Schönefeld."

Train Stations: Trains to and from Berlin are serviced by **Zoologischer Garten** (almost always called **Bahnhof Zoo**) in the west and **Ostbahnhof** in the east. Most trains go to both stations, but some connections to East Germany only stop at Ostbahnhof. For **information** call (0180) 599 66 33 or visit www.bahn.de. Trains run to: **Dresden** (2¼hr., every 2hr., DM42/€22); **Frankfurt** (4hr., every hr., DM207/€106); **Hamburg** (2½hr., every hr., DM88/€45); **Cologne** (4¼hr., every hr., DM190/€98); **Leipzig** (2hr., every hr., DM65/€34 or 2¾hr., every hr., DM51/€26); **Munich** (6½-7hr., every hr., DM199/€102). **International connections** to most major European cities. Times and prices change frequently—check at the computers located in the train stations.

Buses: ZOB, the central bus station (☎302 53 61), is by the *Funkturm* near Kaiserdamm. U2 to "Kaiserdamm" or S4, S45, or S46 to "Witzleben." Check *Zitty* and *Tip* for deals on long-distance buses, or call **Gulliver's** travel agency, Hardenbergpl. 14 (☎311 02 11), at the opposite end of the bus parking lot from Bahnhof Zoo. Open daily 8am-8pm. To **Paris** (14hr., DM109/€56) and **Vienna** (10½hr., DM89/€46).

Mitfahrzentralen (Ride Sharing): City Netz, Joachimstaler Str. 17 (☎194 44) has a computerized ride-share database. U9 or U15 to "Kurfürstendamm." To **Hamburg** or **Hannover** DM30/€16; to **Frankfurt** or **Munich** DM35/€18. Open M-F 9am-8pm, Sa-Su 9am-7pm. **Mitfahrzentrale Zoo,** on the U2 platform (Pankow side) at "Bahnhof Zoo," is affiliated with Gulliver's (see **Buses,** above). Open M-F 9am-8pm, Sa-Su 10am-6pm. **Mitfahr2000,** Yorckstr. 52 (☎194 20 00; www.mitfahr.de), formerly the *Mitfahrtelefon für Schwule und Lesben* (Ride Sharing for Gays and Lesbians). Open daily, 8am-8pm.

Hitchhiking: *Let's Go* does not recommend hitchhiking as a safe mode of transportation. It is worth noting that hitchhiking across Europe, a beloved summer enterprise through the 80s, has become extremely dangerous in the past decade; also, remember that it is illegal to hitch at rest stops or anywhere along the highway.

GERMANY

✦ ORIENTATION

Berlin is an *immense* conglomeration of what were once two separate and unique cities. The former East contains most of Berlin's landmarks and historic sites, as well as many pre-fab concrete socialist architectural experiments. The former West functioned for decades as a small, isolated, Allied-occupied state and is still the commercial heart of united Berlin. The situation is rapidly changing, however, as businesses and embassies move their headquarters to Potsdamer Platz and Mitte in the East. The vast **Tiergarten,** Berlin's beloved park, lies in the center of the city; the grand, tree-lined **Straße des 17. Juni** runs through it from west to east and becomes **Unter den Linden** at the **Brandenburg Gate.** North of the Gate is the **Reichstag;** south of the Gate, **Ebertstraße** winds to glitzy **Potsdamer Platz.** Unter den Linden continues east through **Mitte,** an area filled with historical sites. The street change to **Karl-Liebknecht-Straße** before emptying into **Alexanderplatz,** home to Berlin's most visible landmark, the **Fernsehturm** (TV tower). At the east end of Mitte is **Museumsinsel** (Museum Island). Cafe- and shop-lined **Oranienburger Straße** cuts through the area of northeastern Mitte known as the **Scheunenviertel,** historically the center of Jewish life in Berlin.

The commercial district of Western Berlin lies at the southwest end of the Tiergarten and is centered around **Bahnhof Zoo** and the **Kurfürstendamm (Ku'damm** for short). To the east is **Breitscheidplatz,** marked by the bombed-out **Kaiser-Wilhelm-Gedächtniskirche** and the boxy **Europa-Center,** and **Savignyplatz,** one of many pleasant squares in **Charlottenburg.** Southeast of the Ku'damm, **Schöneberg** is a pleasant residential neighborhood renowned as the traditional nexus of the gay and lesbian community. Further south, **Dahlem** houses western Berlin's largest university complex. At the southeast periphery of Berlin lies **Kreuzberg,** a district home to an exciting mix of radical leftists, Turks, and homosexuals. Northeast of the city center, **Prenzlauer Berg** rumbles with a sublime cafe culture. East of Mitte, **Friedrichshain** is the center of Berlin's counterculture and nightlife.

If you're planning to stay more than a few days in Berlin, the blue-and-yellow **Falk Plan** (available at most kiosks and bookstores) is an indispensable city map that unfolds like a book and includes a street index (DM11/€6). Dozens of streets and subway stations in Eastern Berlin were named after Communist figures. Many, but not all, have been renamed in a process only recently completed; be sure that your map is up-to-date.

 SAFETY PRECAUTION! The media has sensationalized the new wave of Nazi extremism perhaps more than necessary; among major cities, Berlin has the fewest hate crimes per capita. There are only an estimated 750 neo-Nazi skinheads in Berlin. However, people of color as well as gays or lesbians should take precautions in the outlying areas of the eastern suburbs and perhaps avoid them altogether late at night. If you see dark-colored combat boots (especially with white laces) exercise caution, but do not panic.

⌐ LOCAL TRANSPORTATION

Public Transportation: It is impossible to tour Berlin on foot—fortunately, the extensive **bus, Straßenbahn** (streetcar), **U-Bahn** (subway), and **S-Bahn** (surface rail) systems will take you anywhere. Berlin is divided into 3 transit zones. **Zone A** encompasses central Berlin, including Tempelhof airport. Almost everything else falls into **Zone B,** while **Zone C** contains the outlying areas, including Potsdam and Oranienburg. An **AB ticket** is the best deal, as you can buy regional Bahn tickets for the outlying areas. A single ticket for the combined network (*Langstrecke* AB or BC, DM4.20/€2.30; or *Ganzstrecke* ABC, DM4.80/€2.45) is good for 2hr. after validation. However, since single tickets are pricey, it almost always makes sense to buy a pass: a **Tageskarte** (AB DM12.00/€6, ABC DM12.80/€6.50) is good from validation until 3am the next day; the **Welcome-**

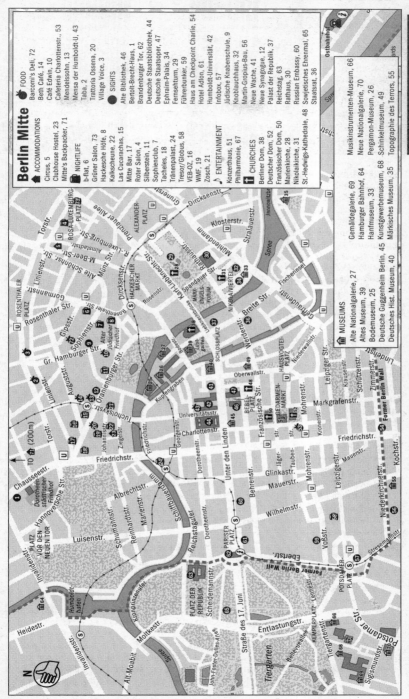

Berlin Mitte

⌂ ACCOMMODATIONS
Circus, 5
Clubhouse Hostel, 23
Mitte's Backpacker, 71

♪ NIGHTLIFE
b-flat, 6
Grüner Salon, 73
Hackesche Höfe, 8
Kalkscheune, 22
Las Cucarachas, 15
Mitte Bar, 17
Roter Salon, 4
Silberstein, 11
Sophienclub, 7
Tacheles, 18
Tränenpalast, 24
Tresor/Globus, 58
VEB-OZ, 16
WMF, 19
Zosch, 21

✦ FOOD
Barcomi's Deli, 72
Beth Café, 14
Café Edwin, 10
Cafeteria Charlottenstr., 53
Mendelssohn, 43
Mensa der Humboldt-U., 43
Taba, 2
Trattoria Ossena, 20
Village Voice, 3

● SIGHTS
Alte Bibliothek, 46
Bertolt-Brecht-Haus, 1
Brandenburger Tor, 62
Deutsche Staatsbibliothek, 44
Deutsche Staatsoper, 47
Ephraim-Palais, 34
Fernsehturm, 29
Führerbunker, 59
Haus am Checkpoint Charlie, 54
Hotel Adlon, 61
Humboldt-Universität, 42
Infobox, 57
Jüdische Knabenschule, 9
Knoblauchhaus, 32
Martin-Gropius-Bau, 56
Neue Wache, 41
Neue Synagoge, 12
Palast der Republik, 37
Reichstag, 63
Rathaus, 30
Russian Embassy, 60
Sowjetisches Ehrenmal, 65
Staatsrat, 36

♪ ENTERTAINMENT
Konzerthaus, 51
Philharmonie, 67

✝ CHURCHES
Berliner Dom, 38
Deutscher Dom, 52
Französischer Dom, 50
Marienkirche, 28
Nikolaikirche, 31
St.-Hedwigs-Kathedrale, 48

🏛 MUSEUMS
Alte Nationalgalerie, 27
Altes Museum, 39
Bodemuseum, 25
Deutsche Guggenheim Berlin, 45
Deutsches Hist. Museum, 40
Gemäldegalerie, 69
Hamburger Bahnhof, 64
Hanfmuseum, 33
Kunstgewerbemuseum, 68
Märkisches Museum, 35
Musikinstrumenten-Museum, 66
Neue Nationalgalerie, 70
Pergamon-Museum, 26
Schinkelmuseum, 49
Topographie des Terrors, 55

GERMANY

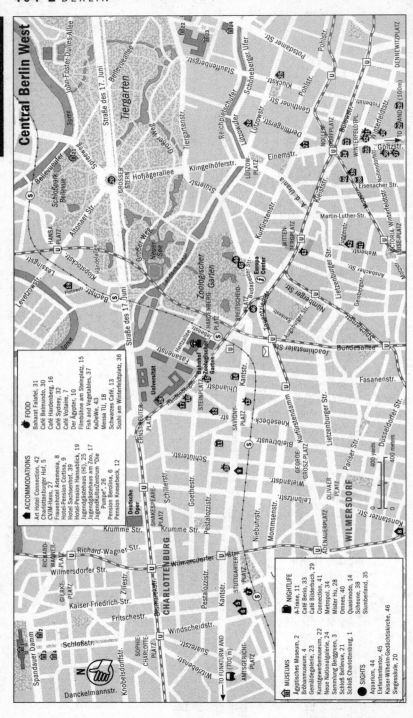

Central Berlin West

● FOOD

Baharat Falafel, 31
Café Belmundo, 30
Café Hardenberg, 16
Café Sydney, 32
Café Voltaire, 7
Der Ägypter, 10
FilmBühne am Steinplatz, 15
Fish and Vegetables, 37
KaDeWe, 43
Mensa TU, 18
Schwarzes Café, 13
Sushi am Winterfeldtplatz, 36

▲ ACCOMMODATIONS

Art Hotel Connection, 42
Charlottenburger Hof, 5
CVJM-Haus, 27
Frauenhotel Artemesia, 8
Hotel-Pension Cortina, 9
Hotel Sachsenhof, 39
Hotel-Pension Hansablick, 19
Jugendgästehaus (HI), 25
Jugendgästenhaus am Zoo, 17
JugendKulturZentrum "Die Pumpe", 26
Pension Berolina, 6
Pension Knesebeck, 12

♪ NIGHTLIFE

A-Trane, 11
Café Berio, 33
Café Bilderbuch, 29
Connection, 41
Metropol, 34
Mister Hu, 28
Omnes, 40
Quasimodo, 14
Scheune, 38
Slumberland, 35

▥ MUSEUMS

Ägyptisches Museum, 2
Bröhanmuseum, 4
Gemäldegalerie, 23
Kunstgewerbemuseum, 22
Neue Nationalgalerie, 24
Sammlung Berggruen, 3
Schloß Bellevue, 21
Schloß Charlottenburg, 1

● SIGHTS

Aquarium, 44
Elefantentor, 45
Kaiser-Wilhelm-Gedächtniskirche, 46
Siegessäule, 20

TO FUNKTURM AND (700 m)
TO ZOB AND (100 m)

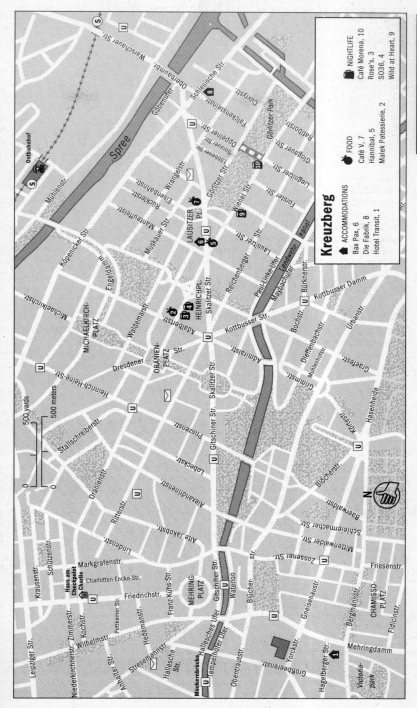

Kreuzberg

⌂ ACCOMMODATIONS
Bax Pax, 6
Die Fabrik, 8
Hotel Transit, 1

🍎 FOOD
Café V, 7
Hannibal, 5
Malek Patesslerie, 2

🍸 NIGHTLIFE
Café Morena, 10
Rose's, 3
SO36, 4
Wild at Heart, 9

N

Card (DM32/€17) is valid 72hr.; the **7-Tage-Karte** (AB DM44/€23, ABC DM55/€28) is good for 7 days; and the **Umweltkarte Standard** (AB DM105/€54, ABC DM130/€67) is valid for 1 calendar month. Within the validation period, tickets may be used on any S-Bahn, U-Bahn, bus, or streetcar. **Bikes** require an additional, reduced-fare ticket and are permitted on the U- and S-Bahn but not on buses and streetcars.

Purchasing and Validating Tickets: Buy tickets from *Automaten* (machines) or ticket windows in the U- and S-Bahn stations. When using an *Automat,* make your selection before inserting money; note that the machines will not give more than DM20/€10 change and that some machines do not take bills. *All tickets must be validated in the box marked "hier entwerfen" before boarding, or you may be slapped with a DM60/€30 fine.*

Night Transport: U- and S-Bahn lines generally don't run from 1-4am, although most S-Bahn lines run every hr. on weekend nights. The **U12** runs all night F and Sa, and the **U9** runs 24hr. all week long. A system of **night buses** (preceded by the letter N) centered on Bahnhof Zoo runs every 20-30min.; pick up the *Nachtliniennetz* map at a *Fahrscheine und Mehr* office.

Taxis: ☎26 10 26, 21 02 02, or 690 22. Call at least 15min. in advance. Women may request a female driver. Trips within the city can cost up to DM40/€21.

Car Rental: The **Mietwagenservice,** counter 21 in Bahnhof Zoo's *Reisezentrum*, represents Avis, Europcar, Hertz, and Sixt. Sixt open 24hr., Avis and Europcar open 7am-6:30pm, Hertz open 7am-8pm. Most companies also have offices in the Tegel Airport.

Bike Rental: The government's **bikecity** program rents bikes at Bahnhof Zoo (☎07 60 98 21 35 49), at the far end of Hardenbergpl. DM8/€4 per 3hr., DM15/€8 per 24hr.; students DM5/€3, DM8/€4. Open daily 10am-6pm.

▜ PRACTICAL INFORMATION

TOURIST AND FINANCIAL SERVICES

The monthly magazine *Berlin Programm* (DM3/€1.50) lists opera, theater, and classical music schedules. German-speakers should spring for *Tip* (DM4.30/€2.20) or *Zitty* (DM4.70/€2.40), which have the most comprehensive listings for film, theater, concerts, and clubs. For gays and lesbians, *Siegessäule, Sergej,* and *Gay-yellowpages* have entertainment listings and are offered in most tourist offices. For comprehensive information in English, check out www.berlin.de.

Tourist Offices:

EurAide (www.euraide.de), in Bahnhof Zoo, has excellent travel information, makes train and hotel reservations (DM7/€4 fee for hotels), and recommends hostels for free. Facing the Reisezentrum, go left and down the corridor on your right; it's on the left. Come early—the office gets packed, and like all Berlin tourist offices, they don't take phone calls. Open daily 8am-noon and 1-6pm.

Berlin Tourismus (☎25 00 25; fax 25 00 24 24) will send information and reserve rooms. Write in advance to: Berlin Tourismus Marketing GmbH, Am Karlsbad 11, 10785 Berlin. Other tourist offices do not give out phone numbers, so all telephone inquiries should be directed here. Open M-F 8am-7pm, Sa-Su 9am-6pm.

Europa-Center, on Budapester Str., has city maps (DM1/€0.51) and free transit maps. From Bahnhof Zoo, walk along Budapester Str. past the Kaiser-Wilhelm-Gedächtniskirche; the office is on the right after about 2 blocks (5min.). Open M-Sa 8:30am-8:30pm, Su 10am-6:30pm.

Tours:

Insider Tour (☎692 31 49) has superb and enthusiastic guides. Tours last 3½hr. and leave from the *McDonald's* by Bahnhof Zoo late Mar.-Nov. daily at 10am and 2:30pm (DM15/€8).

Berlin Walks (☎301 91 94; www.berlinwalks.com) offers a range of English-language walking tours, including Infamous Third Reich Sites, Jewish Life in Berlin, and Discover Potsdam. Their Discover Berlin Walk is one of the best ways to get acquainted with the city. Tours (2½-6hr.) daily 10am from the taxi stand in front of Bahnhof Zoo (Discover Potsdam meets 9am); in summer, the Discover Berlin Walk also meets 2:30pm. All tours DM18/€9, under 26 DM15/€8. Tickets available at EurAide.

Terry Brewer's Best of Berlin (☎70 13 16 56; www.brewersberlin.com) offers info-packed tours; guides Terry and Boris are legendary for their vast knowledge and engaging personalities. Tours (5-8 hours) daily 10:30am and 2:30pm from the Neue Synagoge on Oranienburger Str. (S-Bahn #1, 2, or 25 to "Oranienburger Str."). DM15/€8, under 14 free. No afternoon tour Nov.-Apr.

Budget Travel: STA, Goethestr. 73 (☎311 09 50). S3, S5, S7, S9, or S75 to "Savignypl." Open M-W and F 10am-6pm, Th 10am-8pm.

Embassies and Consulates: Berlin is building a new embassy complex, but the locations of the embassies and consulates remain in a state of flux. For the latest information, call the **Auswärtiges Amt Dienststelle Berlin** (☎20 18 60) or visit its office on the Werderscher Markt. U2 to "Hausvogteipl." **Australian Embassy,** Friedrichstr. 200 (☎880 08 80). U2 or U6 to "Stadtmitte." Open M-F 8am-1pm and 2-5pm; closes F at 4:15pm. Also Uhlandstr. 181-183 (☎880 08 80). U15 to "Uhlandstr." Open M-F 8:30am-1pm. **Canadian Embassy,** Friedrichstr. 95 (☎20 31 20), on the 12th fl. of the International Trade Center. S1, S2, S3, S5, S7, S9, S25 or S75 or U6 to "Friedrichstr." Open M-F 9am-noon, by appointment after 2pm. **Irish Embassy,** Friedrichstr. 200 (☎22 07 20). Open M-F 9:30am-noon and 2:30-4:45pm. **New Zealand Embassy,** Friedrichstr. 60 (☎20 62 10). Open M-F 9am-1pm and 2-5:30pm; closes F at 4:30pm. South **African Embassy,** Friedrichstr. 60 (☎22 07 30). **South African Consulate,** Douglasstr. 9 (☎82 50 11 or 825 27 11). S7 to "Grunewald." Open M-F 9am-noon. **UK Embassy,** Wilhelmstr. 70-71 (☎20 18 40). S1, S2, S3, S5, S7, S9, S25 or S75 or U6 to "Friedrichstr." Open M-F 9am-4pm. **US Citizens Service/US Consulate,** Clayallee 170 (☎832 92 33). U1 to "Oskar-Helene-Heim." Open M-F 8:30am-noon. Telephone advice M-F 2-4pm; after hours, call 830 50.

Currency Exchange: Geldwechsel, Joachimstaler Str. 7-9 (☎882 63 71), has decent rates and no commission. **ReiseBank,** at Bahnhof Zoo (☎881 71 17; open daily 7am-10pm) and Ostbahnhof (☎296 43 93; open M-F 7am-10pm, Sa 8am-8pm, Su 8am-noon, 12:30-4pm), is conveniently located but has worse rates.

American Express: Main Office, Bayreuther Str. 37 (☎21 49 83 63). U1, U2, or U15 to "Wittenbergpl." Holds mail, offers banking services, cashes AmEx traveler's checks with no commission. Expect long lines F and Sa. Open M-F 9am-6pm, Sa 10am-1pm. **Branch office,** Friedrichstr. 172 (☎20 17 40 12). U6 to "Französische Str." Offers the same services. Open M-F 9am-7pm, Sa 10am-1pm.

LOCAL SERVICES

Luggage Storage: In **Bahnhof Zoo.** Lockers DM2-6/€1-3 per day, depending on size. 72hr. max. M-F 7am-6pm, Sa-Su 9am-6pm. If all lockers are full, try **Gepäckaufbewahrung,** the next window over (DM4/€2 per piece per day). Open daily 6:15am-10:30pm. 24hr. lockers are available at **Ostbahnhof** and **Alexanderplatz.**

Bi-Gay-Lesbian Organizations: Lesbenberatung, Kulmer Str. 20a (☎215 20 00), offers counseling on lesbian issues. U7 to "Kleistpark." Open M-Tu and Th 4-7pm, F 2-5pm. **Mann-o-Meter,** Motzstr. 5 (☎216 80 08), off Nollendorfpl., has information on gay nightlife and accommodations. Open M-F 5-10pm, Sa-Su 4-10pm.

Laundromat: Waschcenter Schnell und Sauber at: Leibnizstr. 72 in **Charlottenburg** (S3, S5, S7, S9, or S75 to "Savignypl."); Wexstr. 34 in **Schöneberg** (U9 to "Bundespl."); Mehringdamm 32 in **Kreuzberg** (U6 or U7 to "Mehringdamm"); Torstr. 115 in **Mitte** (U8 to "Rosenthaler Pl."). Wash DM4-7/€2-4 per 6kg, dry DM1/€0.51 per 15min. Open daily 6am-11pm.

EMERGENCY AND COMMUNICATIONS

Emergency: Police, ☎110. **Ambulance and Fire,** ☎112.

Crisis Lines: English spoken at most crisis lines. **Sexual Assault Hotline** (☎251 28 28). Open Tu and Th 6-9pm, Su noon-2pm. **Schwules Überfall** (☎216 33 36), hotline and legal help for victims of gay bashing. Open daily 6-9pm. **Berliner Behindertenverband,** (☎20 43 847), information and advice for the handicapped. Open M-F 8am-4pm.

Pharmacies: Europa-Apotheke, Tauentzienstr. 9-12 (☎261 41 42), near the Europa- Center and Bahnhof Zoo. Open M-F 9am-8pm, Sa 9am-4pm. Closed pharmacies post signs directing you to the nearest open one.

Medical Assistance: The American and British embassies have a list of English-speaking doctors. **Emergency Doctor** (☎31 00 31); **Emergency Dentist** (☎011 41). Both 24hr.

Internet Access: easyEverything, the corner of Kurfürstendamm and Meineckestr. A DM5/€3 card gives about 1¼hr. of Internet access. Open 24hr. **Webtimes,** Chausseestr. 8 (☎280 49 890), in Mitte. U6 to "Oranienburger Tor." Open M-F 9am-midnight, Sa-Su 10am-midnight. DM7/€4 per hr. **Cyberb@r,** on the 2nd fl. of the Karstadt department store, Alexanderpl. DM3/€1.50 per 30min. M-F 10am-8pm, Sa 10am-4pm.

Post Offices: Joachimstaler Straße 7, down Joachimstaler Str. from Bahnhof Zoo, near the corner of Kantstr. Address mail to be held: Postlagernde briefe für FirstName SURNAME, Postamt in der Joachimstaler Str. 7, **10706** Berlin. Open M-Sa 8am-midnight, Su 10am-midnight. Branch office at **Tegel Airport** open daily 6:30am-9pm; branch office at **Ostbahnhof** open M-Sa 8am-8pm, Su 7am-6pm.

ACCOMMODATIONS AND CAMPING

Hostels in Berlin are either privately-owned or HI-affiliated and state-owned (*Jugendherbergen* and *Jugendgästehäuser*). **HI hostels** can be a great, cheap sleep, but they fill quickly, often impose a curfew, and are usually for **HI members only,** though you can usually get a nonmember's stamp (DM6/€3 extra) and spend the night. There are also over 4000 **private rooms** available in the city; ask at tourist offices for details, and be sure they know your language abilities (if any), since some host families may not speak English. For visits longer than four days, the various **Mitwohnzentralen** can arrange for you to housesit or sublet someone's apartment; for more information, contact **Home Company Mitwohnzentrale,** Joachimstaler Str. 17. (☎194 45; www.HomeCompany.de. U9 or U15 to "Kurfürstendamm." Open M-F 9am-6pm, Sa 11am-2pm.) For long stays or on weekends, reservations are essential. During the **Love Parade** (see p. 423), call at least two months ahead for a choice of rooms and at least two weeks ahead for any bed at all. Note that some hostels increase prices that weekend by up to DM20/€10 per night.

HOTELS, HOSTELS, AND PENSIONEN

MITTE

Mitte's Backpacker Hostel, Chausseestr. 102 (☎262 51 40). U6 to "Zinnowitzer Str." Friendly English-speaking staff, themed rooms, and a relaxed atmosphere. Bikes DM10/€5 per day. Kitchen and **Internet** access. Sheets DM4/€2. Laundry DM5/€3. Reception 24hr. No curfew. Dorms DM25/€13; 5- to 6-bed rooms DM27-29/€13-15; doubles DM76/€40; triples DM99/€51; quads DM124/€64.

Circus, Rosa-Luxemburg-Str. 39-41 (☎28 39 14 33). U2 to "Rosa-Luxemburg-Pl." Bike rental DM12/€6 per day. Sheets DM4/€2. 24hr. reception. No curfew. Reservations a must in summer; reconfirm 1 day before arrival. Apartment for 4 with kitchen and bath DM180/€92; 5- to 6-bed dorms DM25/€13; singles DM45/€23; doubles DM80/€42; triples DM105/€54; quads DM120/€64.

Clubhouse Hostel, Kalkscheunestr. 2 (☎28 09 79 79). S1, S2, or S25 to "Oranienburger Str." or U6 to "Oranienburger Tor." Enter from Johannisstr. 2 or Kalkscheunestr. **Internet** access DM1/€0.50 per 5min. Breakfast buffet DM7/€4. 24hr. reception and bar. No curfew. Call at least 2-3 days ahead. 5- to 7-bed dorms June-Sept. DM32/€17, Nov.-May. DM30/€16; 8- to 10-bed dorms DM27/€14, DM25/€13; singles DM60/€31, DM50/€26; doubles DM88/€46, DM80/€42.

Honigmond, Tieckstr. 12 (☎284 45 50). S1 or S2 to "Nordbahnhof" or U6 to "Zinnowitzer Str." This budget hotel has old-fashioned and well-furnished rooms. Reception 9am-6pm. Breakfast (DM7-16/€3-9) served M-F 9am-noon, Sa-Su 8:30am-2:30pm. Check-in 3pm-1am; if checking in after 8pm, call beforehand. Reservations recommended. Singles DM69-129/€35-66; doubles DM99-129/€50-66, with bath DM139-199/€71-102.

TIERGARTEN

Jugendgästehaus (HI), Kluckstr. 3 (☎261 10 97 or 261 10 98). From Bahnhof Zoo, take bus #129 (dir.: Hermannpl.) to "Gedenkstätte" or U1 to "Kurfürstenstr.," then walk up Potsdamer Str., turn left on Pohlstr., and right on Kluckstr. Bike rental DM15/€8 per day, students DM10/€5. Breakfast and sheets included. Key deposit DM10/€5. 24hr. reception. Lockout 9am-1pm. Curfew midnight; doors open every 30min. 12:30-6am. Reservations strongly recommended. 4- to 10-bed dorms DM34/€18, over 26 DM43/€22.

Hotel-Pension Hansablick, Flotowstr. 6 (☎390 48 00; fax 392 69 37; reserv@hotel-hansablick.de). S3, S5, S7, S9, or S75 to "Tiergarten." Slightly pricey, but all rooms have bath, hair dryer, phone, and cable TV. Call, write, or fax ahead for reservations. Discount rates available July-Aug. and mid-Nov. to Feb. Mention *Let's Go* for a 5% discount. 24hr. reception. Singles DM160/€82; doubles DM195-235/€99-121.

CHARLOTTENBURG

Jugendgästehaus am Zoo, Hardenbergstr. 9a (☎312 94 10), opposite the Technical University *Mensa.* Bus #145 to "Steinpl.," or walk from the back exit of Bahnhof Zoo straight down Hardenbergstr. Push hard on the front door. Reception 9am-midnight. Check-in 10am. Check-out 9am. Lockout 10am-2pm. No curfew. No reservations accepted. 4- to 8-bed dorms DM35/€18, over 26 DM40/€21; singles DM47/€24, DM52/€27; doubles DM85/€44, DM95/€49.

Hotel-Pension Cortina, Kantstr. 140 (☎313 90 59). S-Bahn #3, 5, 7, 9, or 75 to "Savignypl." High-ceilinged, bright rooms, friendly staff, and a great location within walking distance of Bahnhof Zoo. Large breakfast included. 24hr. reception. Reservations recommended. Dorms DM38-60/€19-31 depending on group size and season; singles DM60-90/€30-47; doubles DM90-150/€46-77.

Pension Knesebeck, Knesebeckstr. 86 (☎312 72 55; fax 313 95 07). S3, S5, S7, S9, or S75 to "Savignypl." Follow Knesebeckstr. to Kantstr., where it becomes Savignypl.; continue around the park semicircle. Breakfast included. Laundry DM8/€4. 24hr. reception. Phone reservations must be confirmed by fax, letter, or with a credit card. Singles DM75/€39, with shower DM85/€44; doubles DM120/€63, DM140/€72.

Pension Berolina, Stuttgarter Pl. 17 (☎32 70 90 72). S3, S5, S7, S9, or S75 to "Charlottenburg" or U7 to "Wilmersdorfer Str." Spartan rooms with linoleum floors, conveniently located near the S-Bahn. Shared bathrooms. TV DM4/€2 per day. Breakfast DM10/€5. Reservations recommended. Singles DM60/€30; doubles DM80/€41; triples DM90/€46; quads DM100/€51; quints DM110/€56.

SCHÖNEBERG AND WILMERSDORF

Studentenhotel Meininger 10, Meininger Str. 10 (☎78 71 74 14). U4, bus #146 or N46 to "Rathaus Schöneberg." Walk toward the Rathaus on Freiherr-vom-Stein-Str.; turn left onto Martin-Luther-Str. and right on Meininger Str. A bit cramped, but the atmosphere is lively and friendly. Breakfast and sheets included. Lockers DM10/€5 deposit. 24hr. reception. Co-ed dorms DM25/€13; singles DM66/€34; doubles DM88/€46; 3- to 6-bed rooms DM40/€21. 5% discount when you pull out your copy of *Let's Go.*

CVJM-Haus, Einemstr. 10 (☎264 91 00). U1, U2, U4, or U15 to "Nollendorfpl." Unlike most accommodations at this price, you will not sleep in a room with strangers. Conveniently located 1 block from Nollendorfpl.'s gay nightlife. Breakfast included. Sheets DM3/€1.50. Reception 8-11am and 4-9pm. Quiet time 10pm-7am and 1-3pm. Key available. Book in advance. DM40/€21 per person for singles, doubles, and dorms.

Jugendgästehaus Feurigstraße, Feurigstr. 63 (☎781 52 11). U7 to "Kleistpark," or bus #204 or 348 to "Kaiser-Wilhelm-Pl." Walk down Hauptstr., take the 2nd left onto Kollonenstr., then a right onto Feurigstr. Close to the Schöneberg bars; provides respite from the English-speaking hostel scene. Breakfast included. Sheets DM5/€3 if staying fewer than 3 nights, otherwise free. 24hr. reception, though staff is sometimes far from the desk; keep ringing. Call ahead. Dorms DM40/€21; singles DM55/€29; doubles DM100/€26.

JugendKulturZentrum "Die Pumpe," Lutzowstr. 42 (☎26 48 48 30). U1, U2, U4, or U15 to "Nollendorfpl." Take Einemstr. away from Nollendorfpl.; veer right onto Lützowpl., and turn right onto Lützowstr.; the "Pumpe" complex is 2 blocks down and includes a restaurant/cafe, day-care center, and dorm-style accommodations. Caters mostly to large groups. Breakfast available only for groups of 10 or more, DM6/€3. Door locked at 10pm. Key available. DM30/€16 per person; DM1.50/€0.80 more for kitchen access. Groups of 10 or more DM25/€13 per person.

Hotel Sachsenhof, Motzstr. 7 (☎216 20 74). U1, U2, U4, or U15 to "Nollendorfpl." Small, well-furnished rooms with phone and TV. Surrounded by Nollendorfpl.'s cafes and gay nightlife scene. Breakfast DM10/€5. 24hr. reception. Call for reservations 7am-11pm. Singles DM57/€29, with shower DM65/€34; doubles DM99/€51, DM126/€65; new double with shower DM146/€75, with full bath DM156/€80.

Art Hotel Connection, Fuggerstr. 33 (☎217 70 28; fax 217 70 30; info@arthotel-connection.de). U1, U2, or U15 to "Wittenbergpl.," on a side street off Martin-Luther-Str. **For gay and lesbian guests only.** All rooms have phone and TV. Breakfast included. Reservations for weekends required at least 1 month in advance. Singles DM110-160/€56-82; doubles 150-210/€76-108. Cheaper in winter.

Frauenhotel Artemisia, Brandenburgische Str. 18 (☎873 89 05). U7 to "Konstanzer Str." Pricey, but a rare bird—an immaculate, elegant hotel **for women only.** Breakfast included. Reception 7am-10pm. Singles DM109/€56, with shower DM148/€76; doubles DM170/€87, with bath DM198/€102. For stays of 5 nights or more in Jan., Feb., Aug., Nov., and Dec.: singles DM99-135/€50-69; doubles DM155-175/€80-90. Spend 3 or more nights and stay for free on your birthday.

KREUZBERG

Bax Pax, Skalitzer Str. 104 (☎69 51 83 22). U1 or U15 to "Görlitzer Bahnhof." Fuzzy blue carpets, a great location near Oranienstr., and a bed inside a VW Bug (really—ask for room 3!) add up to mellow good times. Kitchen open 24hr. Sheets DM4/€2. Reception 7am-10pm. No curfew. DM25-30/€12-16 per night.

Die Fabrik, Schlesische Str. 18 (☎611 71 16). U1 or U15 to "Schlesisches Tor" or bus #N65 to "Taborstr." This classy hostel in a former factory provides easy access to Kreuzberg nightlife. Breakfast DM5-15/€2-8. 24hr. reception. Call ahead. No curfew. 16-bed dorms DM30/€16; singles DM66/€34; doubles DM94/€48; triples DM120/€63; quads DM144/€76.

Hotel Transit, Hagelberger Str. 53-54 (☎789 04 70). U6, U7, or bus #N19 to "Mehringdamm." Sleek, modern rooms, with big-screen MTV lounge and well-stocked bar open 24hr. Breakfast included. 24hr. reception. Singles DM100/€52; doubles DM115/€60; triples DM150/€77; quads DM200/€103.

CAMPING

Deutscher Camping-Club runs the following campgrounds. Reservations are recommended; write to: Deutscher Camping-Club Berlin, Geisbergstr. 11, 10777 Berlin, or call 218 60 71 or 218 60 72. All Camping-Club sites DM9.90/€5 per person, DM7.40/€3.80 per tent.

Kohlhasenbrück, Neue Kreisstr. 36 (☎805 17 37). S7 to "Griebnitzsee," then turn right out of the station and follow Rudolf-Breitscheid-Str., which becomes Neue Kreisstr. A nature-intensive campground next to the Griebnitzsee and a protected wildlife area. Relatively easy access to the city. Open Mar.-Oct.

Kladow, Krampnitzer Weg 111-117 (☎365 27 97). U7 to "Rathaus Spandau," bus #135 (dir.: Alt-Kladow) to the end, and bus #234 to "Krampnitzer Weg/Selbitzerstr." Swimmable lake, store, and restaurant on premises. Open year-round.

🗘 FOOD

Berlin defies all expectations with both tasty home-grown options and terrific ethnic food from its Turkish, Indian, Italian, and Thai immigrants. Typical Berlin street food is Turkish; most *Imbiße* (fast-food snack stands) are open ridiculously late, some 24hr. The *Döner Kebap*, a sandwich of lamb or chicken and salad, has cornered the fast-food market, with *Falafel* running a close second; either makes a small meal for DM3-5/€1.50-3. Berlin's numerous relaxed cafes, restaurants, and *Kneipen* are also budget-friendly and usually offer meals of many sizes. **Aldi, Plus, Edeka,** and **Penny Markt** are the cheapest supermarket chains. Supermarkets are usually open Monday to Friday 9am-6pm and Saturday 9am-4pm. At Bahnhof Zoo, **Nimm's Mit** grocery store, near the Reisezentrum, is open 24hr. The best **open-air market** fires up Saturday mornings on Winterfeldtpl.

MITTE

Mensa der Humboldt-Universität, Unter den Linden 6, behind the university's main building. Meals DM2.50-6/€1.30-4. Student ID required. Open M-F 11:30am-2:30pm.

Café and Bistro Edwin, Große Hamburger Str. 15. Simple yet cheery, with outside seating. Su brunch buffet DM13.50/€7. Open M 1pm-late, Tu-Sa 11am-late, Su 10am-late.

Taba, Torstr. 164 (☎282 67 95). U8 to "Rosenthaler Pl." A popular Brazilian place. Buffet W-Th DM9/€5. Live music F-Su, disco Sa midnight-4am. Open W-Su from 7pm.

Beth Café, Tucholskystr. 40 (☎281 31 35), just off Auguststr. S1, S2, or S25 to "Oranienburger Str." Kosher restaurant in the heart of the Scheunenviertel. Open M-Th and Su 11am-10pm; F 11am-5pm, in winter 11am-3pm.

CHARLOTTENBURG

Mensa TU, Hardenbergstr. 34 (☎311 22 53). Bus #145 to "Steinpl.," or walk 10min. from Bahnhof Zoo. Meals (including good vegetarian dishes) DM4-5/€2-3 for students, others DM4-8/€2-4. Cafeteria downstairs has longer hours but slightly higher prices. *Mensa* open M-F 11:15am-2:30pm. Cafeteria open M-F 8am-7:45pm.

Filmbühne am Steinplatz, Hardenbergstr. 12 (☎312 65 89). This cafe at one of Berlin's independent theaters has an unhurried atmosphere and a vast menu. Dishes DM6-20/€3-11, drinks DM5/€3. Open M-Sa 9am-3am, Su 9am-2am. Films (usually subtitled) M DM8.50/€5, Tu-Su DM11/€6. Call 312 90 12 for film info.

Schwarzes Café, Kantstr. 148 (☎313 80 38). S3, S5, S7, S9, or S75 to "Savignypl." This cafe is *always* open, except Tu 3am-11am. Prices are a bit high (a milkshake is DM7/€3), but breakfast is served around the clock.

Website, Joachimstaler Str. 41 (☎88 67 96 30; www.vrcafe.de). Berlin's trendiest cybercafe, in a dark, digital-age lair with techno music and a glass floor that glows underfoot. Entrees are surprisingly tasty. Open daily 10am-2am. Kitchen open noon-10pm.

KaDeWe, Tauentzienstr. 21-24 (☎212 10). U1, U2, or U15 to "Wittenbergpl." The 6th-fl. food emporium of this tremendous department store features a wide range of dishes and an excitable Chinese cook. Open M-F 9:30am-8pm, Sa 9am-4pm.

SCHÖNEBERG

Baharat Falafel, Winterfeldtstr. 37 (☎216 83 01). U1, U2, U4, or U15 to "Nollendorfpl." This ain't no greasy *Döner* stand—it's all about falafel (DM6-7/€3-4). Open daily 11am-2am. Closed last week in July.

Fish and Vegetables, Goltzstr. 32 (☎215 74 55). U1, U2, U4, or U15 to "Nollendorfpl." A no-nonsense Thai restaurant. Dishes from DM6/€3. Open noon-midnight daily.

Café Belmundo, Winterfeldtstr. 36 (☎215 20 70), opposite Baharat Falafel. Truly spectacular baguettes from DM5.50/€3. Open daily 9am-1am. Kitchen open 11am-11pm.

Tim's Canadian Deli, Maaßenstr. 14 (☎217 56 960). U1, U2, U4, or U15 to "Nollendorfpl." Good bagels, outdoor seating, and veggie burgers—a rarity in Berlin. Open M-F 8am-1am, Sa-Su 9am-3am.

KREUZBERG

Hannibal, corner of Wienerstr. and Skalitzerstr (☎611 23 88). U1, U12 or U15, or bus N29 to "Görlitzer Bahnhof." Eclectic decor and massive Hannibal-burgers (DM11.50/€6). Open Su-Th 8am-4am, F-Sa 8am-5am.

Café V, Lausitzer Pl. 12 (☎612 45 05). U1 or U15 to "Görlitzer Bahnhof." Berlin's oldest vegetarian restaurant; vegan and fish entrees also available. Open daily 10am-1am.

Melek Pastanesi, Oranienstr. 28 (☎14 51 86). U1, U8, or U15 to "Kottbusser Tor." Delicious Turkish pastries sold around the clock for mere pocket change. A favorite stopping place for sugar-deprived late-night partygoers. 100g baklava DM1.40/€0.75.

PRENZLAUER BERG

Osswald, Göhrener Str. 5 (☎442 74 50). U2 to "Eberswalder Str." Popular with locals, this restaurant/bar serves simple but tasty German specialties. Open daily 9am-4am.

Malzcafe, Knaackstr. 99 (☎440 47 227). U2 to "Eberswalder Str." Off Danziger Str., this joint boasts funky decor, sandwiches from DM6.50/€4, a kitchen open until 1am, and garlic bread and nachos available until 3am. Open daily 10am-4am.

Sprelacart, Kollwitzstr. 18 (☎440 42 371). U2 to "Senefelderpl." This pleasant cafe has a variety of breakfast combos (DM11/€6), daily dinner specials from DM9/€5, and glowing fluorescent cows along the side of the building. Really. Open daily 10am-1am.

Café Restauration 1900, Husemannstr. 1 (☎442 24 94), at Kollwitzpl. U2 to "Senefelderpl." Serves gourmet eats to an older, fashionable, and *very* Prenzlauer Berg crowd. Open M-Sa 11am-2am, Su 10am-2am. Kitchen open until midnight.

◉ SIGHTS

Berlin's sights are spread out over an area eight times the size of Paris. For a guide to major neighborhoods, see **Orientation,** p. 402. Below, the sights are organized by *Bezirk* (district), beginning with Mitte and spiralling outward. Many of the sights lie along the route of **bus #100** from Bahnhof Zoo to Prenzlauer Berg; consider a transit pass (see p. 402), since it's impossible to see everything on foot.

MITTE

Formerly the heart of Imperial Berlin, Mitte contains some of Berlin's most magnificent sights and museums. Much of the neighborhood languished in disrepair during GDR (East German) days, but now that the government is back in town, the district is once again living up to its name (*Mitte* means center), as embassies and national institutes pour back into the area's rapidly-renovating streets.

UNTER DEN LINDEN

This area is best reached by taking S1, S2, or S25 to "Unter den Linden"; alternatively, bus #100 runs the length of the boulevard every 4-6min.

■ **BRANDENBURGER TOR AND PARISER PLATZ.** For decades a barricaded gateway to nowhere, the **Brandenburg Gate** is the most powerful emblem of reunited Germany and Berlin. Standing right in the center of the city, it was in no-man's land during the time of the wall; today it opens east onto **Pariser Platz** and Unter den Linden and west onto the Tiergarten and Str. des 17. Juni. All but a few of the venerable buildings near the gate have been destroyed, but a massive reconstruction effort has already revived such pre-war staples as the Hotel Adlon, once the premier address for all visiting dignitaries and celebrities.

RUSSIAN EMBASSY. Rebuilding the edifices of the rich and famous wasn't a huge priority in the workers' state, but one exception was this imposing *Palais*, Unter den Linden 55. The massive building, which takes up an entire block, reverted to an ordinary embassy at the end of the Cold War, and the huge bust of Lenin that once graced its red star-shaped topiary was quietly removed in 1994.

DEUTSCHE STAATSBIBILIOTHEK AND HUMBOLDT-UNIVERSITÄT. The library's shady, ivy-covered courtyard provides respite from the surrounding urban bustle. (*Unter den Linden 8.* ☎26 60. *Library open M-F 9am-9pm, Sa 9am-5pm. DM1/€0.50.*) Just beyond is the H-shaped main building of Humboldt University, Unter den Linden 6, whose alumni include Einstein, the Brothers Grimm, Bismarck, and Karl Marx. In the street, a triumphant **Friedrich the Great** stands guard on horseback.

NEUE WACHE. During the GDR era, the "New Guardhouse" was known as the "Monument to the Victims of Fascism and Militarism" and, ironically, was guarded by goose-stepping East German soldiers. After reunification, it was reopened in 1993 as a war memorial. The remains of an unknown soldier and an unknown concentration camp victim are buried inside with earth from Nazi concentration camps as well as the battlefields of Stalingrad, El Alamein, and Normandy. *(Unter den Linden 4. Open daily 10am-6pm.)*

BEBELPLATZ. On May 10, 1933, Nazi students burned nearly 20,000 books here by "subversive" authors such as Heinrich Heine and Sigmund Freud—both Jews. A plaque in the center of the square is engraved with Heine's eerily prescient 1820 quote: "Wherever books are burned, ultimately people are burned as well." The building with the curved facade is the **Alte Bibliothek,** which was once the royal library. On the other side of the square is the handsome **Deutsche Staatsoper** (opera house), fully rebuilt after the war from original sketches. The distinctive blue dome at the end of the square belongs to the **St.-Hedwigs-Kathedrale.** Built in 1773 as the first Catholic church erected in Berlin after the Reformation, it was burnt to a crisp by American bombers in 1943 and was rebuilt in the 1950s. *(Cathedral open M-Sa 10am-5pm, Su 1-5pm. Free.)*

■ POTSDAMER PLATZ. Built under Friedrich Wilhelm I with the primary purpose of moving troops quickly, Potsdamer Platz was chosen to become the new commercial center of Berlin after reunification. Completion is now in sight, and the cutting-edge, wildly ambitious architectural designs make for some spectacular sight-seeing. *(S-Bahn #1, 2, or 25 or U-Bahn #2 to "Potsdamer Pl.")*

FÜHRERBUNKER. Near Potsdamer Pl., unmarked and inconspicuous, lies the site of the bunker where Hitler married Eva Braun and then ended his life. Tourists looking for it often mistakenly head for the visible bunker at the southern edge of Potsdamer Platz; it's actually on the street In den Ministergärten, off Eberstr., behind a playground. Plans to restore the bunker were shelved amid fears that the site would become a shrine for the radical right.

GENDARMENMARKT

Several blocks south of Bebelplatz, **Gendarmentmarkt** is home to some of Berlin's most impressive 19th-century buildings. During the last week of June and the first week of July, the square transforms into an outdoor stage for classical concerts.

DEUTSCHER DOM. Gracing the southern end of the square, the Dom is not used as a church but instead houses **Fragen an die deutsche Geschichte** ("Questions asked of German History"), a government-sponsored exhibition on German political history. *(Gendarmenmarkt 5. Open Tu-Su 10am-6pm, June-Aug. until 7pm. Free.)*

FRANZÖSISCHER DOM. At the opposite end of the square from the Deutscher Dom, the Französischer Dom (French Cathedral) is now home to a restaurant and a small museum chronicling the French Huguenot diaspora. The tower offers a 360-degree panorama of the city. *(Gendarmenmarkt 5. Museum open Tu-Sa noon-5pm, Su 11am-5pm. DM3/€1.50, students DM2/€1. Restaurant open daily noon-1am. Tower open daily 9am-7pm. DM3/€1.50, students DM2/€1.)*

KONZERTHAUS AM GENDARMENMARKT. The Konzerthaus in between the two churches was badly damaged by World War II bombings. It reopened in 1984 as the most elegant concert venue in Berlin and hosts a variety of performances from chamber music to international orchestras. *(Gendarmenmarkt 2. ☎ 203 09 21 01.)*

MUSEUMSINSEL AND ALEXANDERPLATZ

After crossing over the Spree, Unter den Linden becomes Karl-Liebknecht-Str. and cuts through the **Museumsinsel** (Museum Island), home to five major museums and the **Berliner Dom.** Karl-Liebknecht-Str. continues into the monolithic **Alexanderplatz.** For information on the museums of Museumsinsel, see p. 418.

BERLINER DOM. This beautifully bulky, multiple-domed cathedral, one of Berlin's most recognizable landmarks, was built during the reign of Kaiser Wilhelm II and recently emerged from 20 years of restoration after being severely damaged by an air raid in 1944. *(Open daily 9am-7:30pm. Admission to Dom and crypt DM8/€4, students DM4/€2; admission to the Dom, crypt, tower, and galleries DM10/€5, students DM6/€3. Free organ recitals W-F at 3pm.)*

ALEXANDERPLATZ. Formerly the heart of Weimar Berlin, the plaza was transformed in East German times into an urban wasteland of fountains and pre-fab office buildings. In the 1970s, enormous neon signs like "Medical Instruments of the GDR—Distributed in All the World!" were added to satisfy the people's need for bright lights. Today the signs have vanished, and the square is filled with bourgeois German shoppers, tourists, and punks with dogs.

FERNSEHTURM. The TV tower, the tallest structure in Berlin at 368m, was originally intended to showcase East Germany's technological capabilities. It has acquired some colorful politically-infused nicknames, including "Walter Ulbricht's Last Erection," after an early German communist party leader. When the sun is out, the windows have a crucifix-shaped glint pattern known as the *Papsts Rache* ("pope's revenge"). *(Open Mar.-Oct. daily 9am-1am; Nov.-Feb. 10am-midnight. DM12/€6.)*

SCHEUNENVIERTEL AND ORANIENBURGER STRAße

Northwest of Alexanderpl., around Oranienburger Str. and Große Hamburger Str., lies the **Scheunenviertel,** once the center of Berlin's Orthodox Jewish community. Take S1, S2, or S25 to "Oranienburger Str." or U6 to "Oranienburger Tor." Today the Scheunenviertel is better known for its outdoor cafes than for its historical significance as Berlin's Jewish center, but the past few years have seen the opening of several Judaica-oriented bookstores and kosher restaurants.

NEUE SYNAGOGE. This huge synagogue was used for worship until 1940, when the Nazis occupied it and used it for storage. Amazingly, it survived *Kristallnacht*—the SS torched it, but a local police chief realized that the building was a historic monument and ordered the fire extinguished. The synagogue was later destroyed by bombing, but its restoration, largely financed by international Jewish organizations, was completed in 1995. The interior now houses an exhibit chronicling its history and temporary exhibits on the history of Berlin's Jews. *(Oranienburger Str. 30. Open May-Aug. Su-M 10am-8pm, Tu-Th 10am-6pm, F 10am-2pm. Museum DM9/€5, students DM6/€3. Permanent exhibit DM6/€3, students DM4/€2. Entry to the dome DM3/€1.50, students DM2/€1.)*

TIERGARTEN

Once a hunting ground for Prussian monarchs, the lush **Tiergarten** is now a vast landscaped park in the center of Berlin stretching from Bahnhof Zoo to the Brandenburg Gate. **Straße des 17. Juni** bisects the park from west to east, connecting Ernst-Reuter-Pl. to the Brandenburg Gate.

SIEGESSÄULE. In the heart of the Tiergarten, the slender 70m "victory column" commemorates Prussia's humiliating defeat of France in 1870. The gilded statue on top—Victoria, the goddess of victory—is made of melted-down French cannons. The 285 steps lead to a panoramic view of the city. *(Bus #100 or 187 to "Großer Stern." Open Apr.-Nov. M 1-6pm, Tu-Su 9am-6pm. DM2/€1, students DM1/€0.51.)*

■ **THE REICHSTAG.** Just north of the gate is the current home of Germany's governing body, the *Bundestag*. The glass dome on top is built around an upside-down solar cone that powers the building. A walkway spirals up the inside of the dome, leading visitors around a panoramic view to the top of the cone. *(☎22 62 9933 or 22 72 74 53. Open daily 8am-midnight; last entrance at 10pm. Free.)*

OTHER SIGHTS IN MITTE

BERTOLT-BRECHT-HAUS. If any single man personifies the political and aesthetic contradictions that is Berlin, it is **Bertolt Brecht,** who called the city home. Brecht lived and worked in this house from 1953 to 1956. *(Chausseestr. 125, near Schlegelstr. U6 to "Zinnowitzer Str." Mandatory German tours every 30min. Tu-F 10-11:30am, Th also 5-6:30pm; Sa 9:30am-1:30pm; every hr. Su 11am-6pm. DM6/€3, students DM3/€1.50.)*

DOROTHEENSTÄDTISCHER FRIEDHOF. Attached to Brecht's house is the cemetery where he and his wife are buried. *(Open daily from 8pm; Dec.-Jan. to 4pm, Feb. and Nov. to 5pm, Mar. and Oct. to 6pm, Apr. and Sept. to 7pm, May-Aug. to 8pm.)*

CHARLOTTENBURG

Charlottenburg, one of the wealthiest areas in Berlin, includes the area between the Ku'damm and the Spree river.

BAHNHOF ZOO

During the city's division, West Berlin centered around Bahnhof Zoo, the station which inspired U2's "Zoo TV" tour. (The U-Bahn line with the same name as the band runs through the station. Clever.) The area surrounding the station is a spectacular wasteland of department stores and peepshows intermingled with souvenir shops and G-rated attractions.

ZOOLOGISCHER GARTEN AND AQUARIUM. Across Bahnhof Zoo and through the corral of bus depots, the Zoo is one of the best in the world, with many animals displayed in open-air habitats instead of cages. The second entrance, across from Europa-Center, is the famous **Elefantentor,** Budapester Str. 34. *(Zoo open May-Sept. daily 9am-6:30pm; Oct.-Feb. 9am-5pm; Mar.-Apr. 9am-5:30pm. DM15/€8, students DM12/€6.)* Within the walls of the Zoo, but independently accessible, is the excellent Aquarium, which houses broad collections of insects and reptiles as well as endless tanks of rainbow-colored fish. Its pride and joy is the 450kg **Komodo dragon,** the world's largest reptile, a gift to Germany from Indonesia. *(Budapester Str. 32. Open daily 9am-6pm. Aquarium DM15/€8, students DM12/€6. Combination ticket to zoo and aquarium DM24/€13, students DM19/€10, children DM12/€6.)*

KAISER-WILHELM-GEDÄCHTNISKIRCHE. Nicknamed "the rotten tooth" by Berliners, the jagged edges of this shattered church stand as a reminder of the destruction caused by WWII. Built in 1852 in a Romanesque-Byzantine style, the church has an equally striking interior, with colorful mosaics covering the ceiling, floors, and walls. The ruins house an exhibit of shocking photos of the entire city in ruins just after the war. *(Exhibit open M-Sa 10am-4pm. Church open daily 9am-7pm.)*

SCHLOß CHARLOTTENBURG. The broad Baroque palace commissioned by Friedrich I for his second wife, Sophie-Charlotte, sprawls over a park on the northern edge of Charlottenburg. The Schloß's many buildings include the **Neringbau** (or **Altes Schloß**), the palace proper; the **Schinkel-Pavillon,** a museum dedicated to Prussian architect Karl Friedrich Schinkel; **Belvedere,** which houses the royal porcelain collection; and the **Mausoleum,** the final resting spot for most of the family. The **Schloßgarten** behind the main buildings is an elysium of small lakes, fountains, and carefully-planted rows of trees. *(Bus #145 from Bahnhof Zoo to "Luisenpl./Schloß Charlottenburg" or U7 to "Richard-Wagner-Pl." and walk about 15min. down Otto-Suhr-Allee. ☎ 32 09 11. **Altes Schloß** open Tu-F 9am-5pm, Sa-Su 10am-5pm; DM10/€5, students DM8/€4. **Schinkel-Pavillon** open Tu-Su 10am-5pm. DM4/€2, students DM3/€1.50. **Belvedere** open Apr.-Oct. Tu-Su 10am-5pm; Nov.-Mar. Tu-F noon-4pm, Sa-Su noon-5pm. DM4/€2, students DM3/€1.50. **Mausoleum** open Apr.-Oct. Tu-Su 10am-noon and 1-5pm. DM3/€1.50, students DM2/€1. **Schloßgarten** open Tu-Su 6am-9pm. Free. Ticket to entire complex DM14/€7, students DM10/€5.)*

OLYMPIA-STADION. At the western edge of Charlottenburg, the Olympic Stadium was erected for the 1936 Olympic Games, in which Jesse Owens, an African-American, triumphed over Nazi racial theories by winning four gold medals. Hitler refused to congratulate Owens because of his skin color, but there's now a Jesse-Owens-Allee to the south of the stadium. *(U2 to "Olympia-Stadion (Ost)" or S5 or S75 to "Olympiastadion." DM2/€1. Open daily in summer 8am-8pm, in winter 8am-3pm.)*

FUNKTURM. Erected in 1926 to herald the radio age, the Funkturm offers a stunning view of the city from its 125m observation deck. The world's first television transmission was made here in 1931. *(Take S45 or S46 to "Witzleben" or U2 to "Kaiserdamm." Panorama deck open daily 10am-11pm. DM6/€3.)*

GEDENKSTÄTTE PLÖTZENSEE. Housed in the terrifyingly well-preserved former execution chambers of the Third Reich, the memorial documents death sentences of "enemies of the people," including the officers who attempted to assassinate

Hitler in 1944. More than 2,500 people were murdered within this small, stark red brick complex. Still visible are the hooks from which victims were hanged. English literature is available. *(Hüttigpfad, off the main road where the bus stops, down Emmy-Zehden-Weg on Hüttigpfad. Take U9 to "Turmstr.," then bus #123 (dir.: Saatwinkler Damm) to "Gedenkstätte Plötzensee." Open Mar.-Oct. daily 9am-5pm; Nov.-Feb. 9am-4pm. Free.)*

SCHÖNEBERG AND WILMERSDORF

South of the Ku'damm, Schöneberg and Wilmersdorf are pleasant, middle-class residential districts noted for their shopping streets, lively cafes, and good restaurants. Schöneberg is also home to the more affluent segments of Berlin's gay and lesbian community (see **Gay and Lesbian Berlin**, p. 424).

RATHAUS SCHÖNEBERG. West Berlin's city government met here until the Wall fell in 1989. On June 26, 1963, exactly 15 years after the beginning of the Berlin Airlift, 1.5 million Berliners swarmed the streets beneath to hear John F. Kennedy reassure them of the Allies' commitment to the city in a speech that ended with the now-famous words *"Ich bin ein Berliner."* Today, the fortress with the little Berlin bear on top is home to Schöneberg's municipal government. *(John-F.-Kennedy-Pl. U4 to "Rathaus Schöneberg." Open daily 9am-6pm.)*

GRUNEWALD. This 300-hectare birch forest is home to the **Jagdschloß,** a restored royal hunting lodge containing a worthwhile collection of European paintings, including works by Rubens, van Dyck, and Cranach. The one-room hunting museum in the same building houses knives, guns, spears, crossbows, and racks of antlers and mounted wild boars. *(Am Grunewaldsee 29. U1 or U7 to "Fehrbelliner Pl.," then bus #115 (dir.: Neuruppiner Str.) to "Pücklerstr." Walk west 15min. on Pücklerstr. Open Tu-Su 10am-5pm. DM4/€2, students and seniors DM3/€1.50.)*

KREUZBERG

If you find the Ku'damm's consumerism nauseating, Kreuzberg provides the perfect dose of counter-culture relief as the indisputable center of Berlin's alternative *Szene*—it's filled with diverse ethnic groups, revolutionary graffiti, punks, and a large gay and lesbian community. Kreuzberg anti-government demonstrations are still frequent and intense. The most prominent is the annual May 1st parade, a series of chaotic riots focused mostly on venting steam against the Man.

⬛HAUS AM CHECKPOINT CHARLIE. A strange, fascinating exhibition —characterized by both earnest Eastern sincerity and glossy Western salesmanship—on the site of the famous border-crossing point, the Haus am Checkpoint Charlie is one of Berlin's most popular tourist attractions. The museum contains all types of devices used to get over, under, or through the wall as well as artwork, newspaper clippings, and photographs. *(Friedrichstr. 44. U6 to "Kochstr." ☎ 251 10 31. Open daily 9am-10pm. DM12/€6, students DM6/€3.)*

ORANIENSTRAßE. The area was the site of frequent riots in the 1980s, and the May Day parades always start at nearby Oranienpl. The rest of the year, revolution-minded radicals rub shoulders with tradition-oriented Turkish families while

---

WALKING MAN In east Berlin, you may notice that the crossing-light figures are thicker, bolder, and more eye-catching than those in west Berlin. The *Ampel-Männchen* ("little traffic-light guy") of east Berlin was drawn by cartoonist Karl Peglau during the days of the GDR. The *Ampel-Männchen*'s simple, cheerful design and easy visibility are supposed to appeal to children and the elderly, but he's beloved by just about everyone. When the city was reunified and the government planned to standardize the lights to the boring western design, east Berliners protested. Now, the *Ampel-Männchen* is a favorite figure for Berliners and tourists alike and has spawned his own line of t-shirts, mouse pads, key-chains, and strings of lights. Ah, capitalism.

an anarchist punk faction and a **boisterous gay and lesbian population** make things interesting after hours. Restaurants, clubs, and shops of all possible flavors make for interesting wandering. *(U1 or U15 to "Kottbusser Tor" or "Görlitzer Bahnhof.")*

EASTERN KREUZBERG. The tree-dotted strip of the canal near Kottbusser Damm, **Paul-Linke-Ufer,** may be the most graceful street in Berlin with its shady terraces and old façades. *(U8 to "Schönleinstr.")* This highly ethnic part of town is rich in Balkan and Turkish restaurants popular with radicals and students. The **Oberbaumbrücke** spanning the Spree was once a border crossing into East Berlin; it now leads to Friedrichshain's nightlife scene. *(U1 or U15 to "Schlesisches Tor.")*

FRIEDRICHSHAIN AND LICHTENBERG

◾**EAST SIDE GALLERY.** The longest remaining portion of the Wall, this 1.3km stretch of cement and asbestos slabs also serves as the world's largest open-air art gallery. The murals are the efforts of an international group of artists who gathered here in 1989 to celebrate the end of the city's division. In 1999, the same artists came together to repaint their work and cover the scrawlings of later tourists; however, would-be artists are rapidly defacing the wall once again. *(Along Mühlenstr. S3, S5, S6, S7, S9, or S75 or U1 or U15 to "Warschauer Str." and walk back toward the river.)*

KARL-MARX-ALLEE. The cornerstone of the East German national construction program, Karl-Marx-Allee became the showcase of the infant Communist government in the early 1950s, when it was known as Stalinallee. Billed as Germany's "first socialist road," the broad avenue ends at the "people's palaces" at Strausberger Pl. *(U5 to "Strausberger Pl.")*

FORSCHUNGS- UND GEDENKSTÄTTE NORMANNENSTRAßE. In the suburb of Lichtenberg stands perhaps the most hated and feared building of the GDR regime—the headquarters of the secret police, the **Staatssicherheit** or **Stasi.** The building once contained six million dossiers on citizens of the GDR, a country of only 16 million people. Since a 1991 law returned the records to their subjects, the "Horror-Files" have rocked Germany, exposing informants—and wrecking careers, marriages, and friendships—at all levels of society. Today, it displays tiny microphones and hidden cameras used for surveillance, Lenin busts, and countless other bits of bizarre memorabilia. Recall that this building is part of the history of many people still living; please be appropriately respectful. *(Ruschestr. 103, Haus 1. U5 to "Magdalenenstr." Walk up Ruschestr. and turn right on Normannenstr. ☎ 553 68 54. Open Tu-F 11am-6pm, Sa-Su 2-6pm. DM5/€3, students DM3/€1.50.)*

PRENZLAUER BERG

Northeast of Mitte lies Prenzlauer Berg, a former working-class district largely neglected by East Germany's reconstruction efforts. Many of the older buildings are crumbling at the edges, resulting in a charming state of age and graceful decay. Unlike the loud, raucous scene in Kreuzberg and Mitte, Prenzlauer Berg's streets are studded with trendy but casual cafes and bars.

KOLLWITZPLATZ. The heart of Prenzlauer Berg's cafe scene, Kollwitzpl., offers a little triangle of greenery centered around a statue of the square's namesake, visual artist **Käthe Kollwitz.** The monument has been painted a number of times—most notably with big pink polka-dots—in acts of affectionate rather than angry vandalism. *(U2 to "Senefelderpl.")*

JÜDISCHER FRIEDHOF. Prenzlauer Berg was one of the major centers of Jewish Berlin, especially during the 19th and early 20th centuries. The Jewish cemetery on Schönhauser Allee contains the graves of composer Giacomo Meyerbeer and painter Max Liebermann. *(Open M-Th 8am-4pm, F 8am-1pm. Men must cover their heads before entering the cemetery.)* Nearby stands the **Synagoge Rykestraße,** one of Berlin's loveliest synagogues, which was spared on *Kristallnacht* due to its inconspicuous location in a courtyard. *(Rykestr. 53.)*

🏛 MUSEUMS

Berlin is one of the world's great museum cities, with collections of art and artifacts encompassing all subjects and eras. The **Staatliche Museen zu Berlin (SMB)** runs over twenty museums, located in several major regions—**Museumsinsel, Kulturforum, Mitte/Tiergarten, Charlottenburg,** and **Dahlem.** Since these museums are government-run, their prices are standardized; a single admission costs DM4/€2, students DM2/€1. Admission is free the first Sunday of every month. A *Tageskarte* (DM8/€4, students DM4/€2) is valid for all SMB museums on the day of purchase; the *Drei-Tage-Karte* (DM16/€8, students DM8/€4) is valid for three consecutive days. Either can be bought at any SMB museum. Non-SMB-affiliated museums tend to be smaller and quirkier.

SMB MUSEUMS

MUSEUMSINSEL (MUSEUM ISLAND)

Museumsinsel contains five separate museums, although several are undergoing extensive renovation and both the **Neues Museum** and **Bodemuseum** remain closed until 2005. Take S3, S5, S7, S9 or S75 to "Hackescher Markt" or bus #100 to "Lustgarten." All museums offer free audio tours in English.

▨ Pergamonmuseum, Kupfergraben. One of the greatest ancient history museums, it's named for Pergamon, the city in Turkey from which the enormous **Altar of Zeus** (180 BC) in the main exhibit hall was taken. The museum features pieces of ancient Mediterranean and Near Eastern history, including the big blue **Ishtar Gate** of Babylon (575 BC) and the Roman **Market Gate of Miletus.** Open Tu-Su 10am-6pm. SMB prices.

Alte Nationalgalerie, Am Lustgarten. After extensive renovations, this renowned museum is once more open to the public. Caspar David Friedrich and Karl Friedrich Schinkel are but 2 names in an all-star cast. Open Tu-Su 10am-6pm. SMB prices.

Altes Museum, Am Lustgarten. The museum contains the *Antikensammlung,* an excellent permanent collection of Greco-Roman art. Open Tu-Su 10am-6pm. SMB prices.

KULTURFORUM

The **Tiergarten-Kulturforum** is a complex of museums at the eastern end of the Tiergarten, near the Staatsbibliothek and Potsdamer Pl. Take S1, S2, S25 or U2 to "Potsdamer Pl." and walk down Potsdamer Str.; the museums are on the right.

▨ Gemäldegalerie. One of Germany's most famous museums, and rightly so. It houses a stunning and enormous collection by Italian, German, Dutch, and Flemish masters, including works by Dürer, Rembrandt, Rubens, Vermeer, Raphael, Titian, and Botticelli. Open Tu-Fri 10am-6pm, Th until 10 pm; Sa-Su 10am-6pm. SMB prices.

Neue Nationalgalerie, Potsdamer Str. 50. This sleek building contains both interesting temporary exhibits and a formidable permanent collection, including works by Munch and Ernst. SMB prices for permanent collection; DM12/€6, students DM6/€3 for the whole museum. Open Tu-F 10am-6pm, Th until 10pm, and Sa-Su 11am-6pm.

MITTE AND TIERGARTEN

▨ Hamburger Bahnhof/Museum für Gegenwartkunst, Invalidenstr. 50-51. Berlin's foremost collection of contemporary art, housed in a converted train station, features works by Beuys, and Kiefer as well as in-your-face temporary exhibits. S3, S5, S7, S9, or S75 to "Lehrter Stadtbahnhof" or U6 to "Zinnowitzer Str." Open Tu, W, F 10am-6pm, Th 10am-10pm, Sa-Su 11am-6pm. DM10/€6, students DM5/€3. Tours Su 4pm.

CHARLOTTENBURG

The area surrounding **Schloß Charlottenburg** is home to a number of excellent museums. Take bus #145 to "Luisenpl./Schloß Charlottenburg" or U7 to "Richard-Wagner-Pl." and walk about 15min. down Otto-Suhr-Allee.

▨ **Ägyptisches Museum,** Schloßstr. 70. This stern Neoclassical building contains a famous collection of ancient Egyptian art: animal mummies, elaborately-painted coffins, a magnificent stone arch, papyrus scrolls, and the famous bust of **Queen Nefertiti** (1350 BC). Open Tu-Su 10am-6pm. DM8/€4, students DM4/€2.

Sammlung Berggruen, Schloßstr. 1, across from the Egyptian museum in an identical building. 3 floors offer a substantial collection of Picasso's life's work, including works that influenced him. The top floor exhibits Paul Klee paintings and Alberto Giacometti sculptures. Open Tu-F 10am-6pm, Sa-Su 11am-6pm. DM8/€4, students DM4/€2.

DAHLEM

This new complex of museums spans one enormous building in the center of Dahlem's university. Take U1 to "Dahlem-Dorf" and follow the "Museen" signs.

▨ **Ethnologisches Museum.** The Ethnological Museum dominates the main building, and it alone makes the trek to Dahlem worthwhile. The exhibits range from beautiful ancient Central American stonework to ivory African statuettes to enormous boats from the South Pacific. The **Museum für Indisches Kunst** (Museum for Indian Art) and the **Museum für Ostasiatisches Kunst** (Museum for East Asian Art), housed in the same building, are smaller but no less fascinating. Open Tu-F 10am-6pm, Sa-Su 11am-6pm. SMB prices.

INDEPENDENT (NON-SMB) MUSEUMS

EASTERN BERLIN

Deutsche Guggenheim Berlin, Unter den Linden 13-15. Located in a newly renovated building across the street from the Deutsche Staatsbibliothek, the museum features changing exhibits of contemporary avant-garde art. Open daily 11am-8pm, Th until 10pm. DM8/€4, students DM5/€3; M free.

Filmmuseum Berlin, 3rd and 4th floors of the Sony Center; Potsdamer Str. 2. S1, S2, S25 or U2 to "Potsdamer Pl." This brand-spanking-new museum shows the development of German film through history. The exhibits (with good captions in English) are fascinating, and the ultra-futuristic entrance is not to be missed. Open Tu-Su 10am-6pm, Th until 8pm. DM12/€6, students DM8/€4.

Deutsches Historisches Museum, Unter den Linden 1, in the Kronprinzenpalais. 3, S5, S7, S9, or S75 to "Hackescher Markt." Permanent exhibits trace German history from its beginnings until the Nazi era, while rotating exhibitions examine the last 50 years. Open Th-Tu 3-6pm. Free.

Hanfmuseum, Mühlendamm 5. U2 to "Klosterstr." Learn everything you wanted to know about marijuana, and maybe some things you didn't—did you know that hemp can serve as insulation? Open Tu-F 10am-8pm, Sa-Su noon-8pm. DM5/€3.

WESTERN BERLIN

Jüdisches Museum Berlin, Lindenstr. 9-14 (☎ 25 99 33). U6 to "Kochstr." Currently empty, this will eventually house Europe's largest Jewish museum. The zinc-plated, lighting-bolt-shaped building itself is a fascinating architectural experience: none of the walls are parallel, and the hallways take unnervingly strange turns. Entrance is through the older-looking building next door; call for exhibit times and prices.

Topographie des Terrors, behind the Martin-Gropius-Bau, at the corner of Niederkirchnerstr. and Wilhelmstr. S1, S2, or U2 to "Potsdamer Pl." This area was the site of the notorious Gestapo's headquarters. The comprehensive exhibit of photographs, documents, and German texts details the Nazi party's rise to power and the atrocities that occurred during the war. English guides are available, but you don't need to understand the captions to be moved by the photographs. Open Tu-Su 10am-6pm. Free.

♫ ENTERTAINMENT

Berlin has one of the most vibrant cultural scenes in the world: exhibitions, concerts, plays, and dance performances abound. Despite recent cutbacks, the city still has a generously subsidized art scene, and tickets are usually reasonable, especially with student discounts. Numerous festivals celebrating everything from Chinese film to West African music spice up the regular offerings; posters proclaiming special events festoon the city well in advance.

CONCERTS, OPERA, AND DANCE

Berlin reaches its musical zenith during the fabulous **Berliner Festwochen,** lasting almost all of September and drawing the world's best orchestras and soloists. The **Berliner Jazztage** in November, featuring top-notch jazz musicians, also brings in the crowds. For more information about either, call or write to Berliner Festspiele (☎25 48 92 50; www.berliner festspiele.de). In mid-July, the **Bachtage** offer an intense week of classical music, while every Saturday night in August, the **Sommer Festspiele** turns the Ku'damm into a concert hall with punk, steel-drum, and folk groups competing for attention. Look for concert listings in the monthly pamphlets *Konzerte und Theater in Berlin und Brandenburg* (free) and *Berlin Programm* (DM2.80/€1.40), as well as in the biweekly *Zitty* and *Tip* (all available at newsstands or tourist offices).

Berliner Philharmonisches Orchester, Matthäikirchstr. 1 (☎25 48 81 32; kartenbuero@philharmonic.sireco.de). Take S1, S2 or S25 or U2 to "Potsdamer Pl." and walk up Potsdamer Str. It may look bizarre, but this big yellow building was designed for acoustics—no matter where you sit, you'll hear the music perfectly. The *Berliner Philharmoniker* is one of the world's finest orchestras, but it's almost impossible to get a seat; check an hour before concert time or write at least 8 weeks in advance. Tickets start at DM14/€7 for standing room, DM26/€13 for seats. Box office open M-F 3:30-6pm, Sa-Su 11am-2pm. Closed from the end of June until the start of Sept.

Konzerthaus (Schauspielhaus am Gendarmenmarkt), Gendarmenmarkt 2 (☎203 09 21 01). U2 or U6 to "Stadtmitte." The opulent home of Berlin's symphony orchestra. Last-minute tickets are sometimes available. Box office open M-Sa noon-7pm, Su noon-4pm. The orchestra goes on vacation mid-July through Aug.

Deutsche Oper Berlin, Bismarckstr. 35 (☎341 02 49 for info, 343 84 01 for tickets; toll free ☎0 800 248 98 42). U2 to "Deutsche Oper." Berlin's best and youngest opera, featuring newly commissioned works as well as all the German and Italian classics. Tickets DM20-220/€10-110. 25% student discount available 1 week before performance. Box office open M-Sa 11am until 1hr. before performance, Su 10am-2pm. For program information, write to Deutsche Oper Berlin, Bismarckstr. 35, 10627 Berlin. Closed July-Aug.

Deutsche Staatsoper, Unter den Linden 7 (☎20 35 45 55; www.staatsoper-berlin.de). U6 to "Französische Str." Eastern Berlin's leading opera company, with sets and costumes on a big, bold scale. Tickets DM10-150/€5-77. 50% student discount on specified nights. Box office open M-F 10am-6pm, Sa-Su 2pm-6pm, and 1hr. before performance. Closed mid-July to Aug.

THEATER

Theater listings are available in the monthly pamphlets *Kultur!news* and *Berlin Programm*, as well as in *030*, *Zitty*, and *Tip* (all available at newsstands). In addition to the world's best German-language theater, Berlin has a lively English-language scene; look for listings that say *in englischer Sprache* ("in English").

Deutsches Theater, Schumannstr. 13a (☎28 44 12 25). U6, S1, S2, S3, S5, S7, S9, S25, or S75 to "Friedrichstr." or bus #147 to "Albrechtpl." Walk north on Friedrichstr., turn left on Reinhardtstr., and then right on Albrechtstr., which turns into Schumannstr. The best theater in the country, with innovative productions of the classics and newer works from Büchner to Mamet to Ibsen. Box office open M-Sa 11am-6:30pm, Su 3-6:30pm. Tickets DM12-60/€6-31, students DM16/€8.

Hebbel-Theater, Stresemannstr. 29 (☎25 90 04 27 or 25 90 04 49). U1, U6, or U15 to "Hallesches Tor." The most avant of the avant-garde theaters in Berlin, drawing cutting-edge talent from all over the world. Order tickets at the box office on Stresemannstr., by phone M-Su 4-7pm, or show up 1hr. before performance.

Berliner Ensemble, Bertolt-Brecht-Pl. 1 (☎282 31 60 or 28 40 81 55). U6 or S1, S2, S3, S5, S7, S9, S25, or S75 to "Friedrichstr." Hip repertoire, including Heiner Müller, young American playwrights, and Brecht. Tickets DM12-40/€6-21, students DM10/€5. Box office open M-Sa 8am-6pm, Su 11am-6pm, and 1hr. before performance.

FILM

Berlin is a movie-loving town; it hosts the international **Berlinale** film festival (Feb. 6-17, 2002), and on any night you can choose from over 150 different films, many in the original languages. *O.F.* next to a movie listing means original version (i.e., not dubbed); *O.m.U.* means original version with German subtitles. Check *Tip, Zitty,* or the ubiquitous blue *Kinoprogramm* posters plastered throughout the city.

Arsenal, in the Filmhaus at Potsdamer Pl. (☎26 95 51 00). U2, S1, S2, or S25 to "Potsdamer Pl." Showcases independent films as well as occasional classics.

Progress Studiokino Börse, Burgstr. 27 (☎24 00 3-500; www.kino-boerse.com). S3, S5, S7, S9, or S75 to "Hackescher Markt." Features a number of contemporary German films and frequent showings of the GDR-era cult classic "Die Legende von Paul und Paula." DM12/€6, students DM10/€5; Tu and Th DM8/€4.

Blow Up, Immanuelkirchstr. 14 (☎442 86 62). Tram #2, 3, or 4 to "Am Friedrichshain." Hard-hitting foreign films interspersed among classy indies and almost always something in English. DM11/€6; Tu-W (and always for students) DM8.50/€4.50.

Freiluftkino (open air cinema): Freiluftkino Hasenheide (☎62 70 58 85), at the Sputnik in Hasenheide park, screens everything from silent films to last year's blockbusters. U7 or U8 to "Hermannpl." **Freiluftkino Kreuzberg,** Mariannenpl. 2 (☎24 31 30 39), screens all flavors of foreign films. U1, U8, or U15 to "Kottbusser Tor." **Freiluftkino Friedrichshain,** in Volkspark Friedrichshain, shows contemporary offerings from Hollywood and German studios. U5 to "Straußberger Pl." DM10/€5 for all theaters; reduced admission M and W.

🗂 SHOPPING

The seven-story **KaDeWe department store** on Wittenbergpl. at Tauentzienstr. 21-24, is the largest department store in mainland Europe. The name is an abbreviation of *Kaufhaus des Westens* (Department Store of the West); for product-starved East Germans who flooded Berlin in the days following the opening of the Wall, KaDeWe *was* the West. (☎212 10. Open M-F 9:30am-8pm, Sa 9am-4pm.) The food department, on the 6th floor, has to be seen to be believed. The **Kurfürstendamm,** near Bahnhof Zoo, has almost every kind of shop imaginable. **Bleibtreustraße** has stores closer to the budget traveler's reach. On the other side of town, **Friedrichstraße,** especially south of Unter den Linden, also has a respectable shopping district. In addition, the new **Daimler-Benz** complex on **Potsdamer Platz** has more than 100 new shops and many restaurants, cafes, and pubs. There is a typical German *Fußgängerzone* (pedestrian zone) on **Wilmersdorfer Straße,** where bakeries, *Döner* joints, trendy clothing shops, and department stores abound (U7 to "Wilmersdorfer Str." or S3, S5, S7, S9, or S75 to "Charlottenburg.")

At Berlin's **flea markets,** you can occasionally find a fantastic bargain. The market on **Straße des 17. Juni** probably has the best selection of stuff, but the prices are higher. (S3, S5, S7, S9, or S75 to "Tiergarten." Sa-Su 10am-5pm.) The **Trödelmarkt** on Nostitzstr. 6-7 in Kreuzberg aims to help the homeless of Berlin. (U6 or U7 to "Mehringdamm." Tu 5-7pm, Th 11am-1pm and 3-6pm, Sa 11am-3pm.) Other markets are located near **Ostbahnhof** in Friedrichshain (by Erich-Steinfurth-Str.; S3, S5, S7, S9, or S75 to "Ostbahnhof;" Sa 9am-3pm, Su 10am-5pm) and on **Am Weidendamm** in Mitte (S1, S2, S3, S5, S7, S9, S25, S75, or U6 to "Friedrichstr."; Sa-Su 11am-5pm).

GERMANY

⚡ NIGHTLIFE

Berlin's nightlife is absolute madness. Bars typically open around 6pm and pack in around 10pm, just as the clubs are opening their doors. Bar scenes wind down between midnight and 6am, while club dance floors fill up around 1am and groove till dawn, when a variety of after-parties and 24hr. cafes keep up this seemingly perpetual motion. It's completely possible (if you can live without sleep) to party non-stop Friday night through Monday morning. The best sources of information about bands and dance venues are the bi-weekly magazines *Tip* (DM4.30/€2.20) and the superior *Zitty* (DM4.70/€2.40), available at all newsstands, or the free and highly comprehensive *030*, distributed in several hostels, cafes, and bars.

In west Berlin, **Savignyplatz,** near Zoologischer Garten, offers refined, laid-back cafes and jazz clubs. Gay life in Berlin centers around **Nollendorfplatz,** where the crowds are usually mixed and establishments range from the friendly to the crui-sey. **Gneisenaustraße,** on the western edge of Kreuzberg, offers a variety of ethnic restaurants and some good bars. Closer to the former Wall, a dizzying array of clubs and bars on and around **Oranienstraße** rage all night, every night with a superbly mixed crowd of partygoers both gay and hetero. In East Berlin, Kreuzberg's reputation as dance capital of Germany is challenged as clubs sprout up in **Mitte, Prenzlauer Berg,** and near **Potsdamer Platz.** Berlin's largest bar scene sprawls down **Oranienburger Straße** in Mitte; it's pricey, but never boring. **Prenzlauer Berg,** originally the edgy alternative to Mitte's trendier repertoire, has become a bit more classy and established, especially around **Kollwitzplatz.** South of it all, **Friedrichshain** has developed a reputation for lively, quirky nightlife, with a terrific group of bars along Simon-Dach-Str. and more on Gabriel-Max-Str.

If at all possible, try to hit (or, if you're prone to claustrophobia, avoid) Berlin during the **Love Parade,** usually held in the third weekend of July, when all of Berlin says "yes" to everything (see below). Prices hit astronomical heights during this weekend of hedonism and insanity, making it something of a rich kids' festival. It's also worth mentioning that Berlin has **de-criminalized marijuana possession** of up to eight grams, although the police can arrest you for any amount if they feel the need to, so exercise some discretion. Smoking in public is not officially accepted but is becoming more common in some clubs—you'll know which ones.

BARS AND CLUBS

MITTE

🎵 **Tresor,** Leipziger Str. 126a. U2, S1, S2, or S25 or bus #N5, N29 or N52 to "Potsdamer Pl." One of the most rocking techno venues in Berlin, Tresor provides a good mid-week option, as it's open W when many other clubs stay closed. Cover W DM5/€3, F DM10/€6, Sa DM15-20/€7-11. Open W and F-Sa 11pm-6am.

🎵 **VEB-OZ,** Auguststr. 92, at the corner of Oranienburger Str. S1, S2, or S25 to "Oranien-burger Str." The map of East Germany on the ceiling and the *Trabi* seat on the wall point to serious East Berlin attitude. Hours until at least 2-3am every night make a good weekday watering hole; most other area bars close by 1am. Open daily from 6pm.

Zosch, Tucholskystr. 30. U6 to "Oranienburger Tor." The bar on the ground floor is for relaxing, while the basement features great live music, fiction and poetry readings, and another bar. The performances (and crowds) vary wildly from day to day—W Dixieland jazz, other days vary. Open M-F from 4pm, Sa-Su from noon.

Hackesche Höfe, Rosenthaler Str. 40-41. S3, S5, S7, S9, or S75 to "Hackescher Markt." A series of interconnected courtyards containing restaurants, cafes, clubs, galleries, shops, and a movie theater. The low-key **Oxymoron** bar and restaurant offers a dance floor several nights a week. Restaurant open from noon, club open M and Th 7pm-late, Sa-Su 11pm-late. The **Sophienclub,** Sophienstr. 6, is a smaller club more focused on having fun than on being trendy, featuring soul, funk, house, and Britpop. Cover DM10/€5. Open Tu, Th-Sa from 10pm.

THE LOVE PARADE Every year during the third weekend in July, the Love Parade brings Berlin to its knees—its trains run late, its streets fill with litter, and its otherwise patriotic populace scrambles to the countryside in the wake of a wave of German teenagers dying their hair, dropping ecstasy, and getting down *en masse*. What started in 1988 as a DJ's birthday party has mutated into the world's only 1.5 million-person rave, dubbed *Die Größte Partei der Welt*, "the biggest party in the world." The city-wide party turns the Str. des 17. Juni into a riotous dance floor and the Tiergarten into a garden of iniquity. The BVG offers a "No-Limit-Ticket," useful for getting around from venue to venue during the weekend's **54 hours of nonstop partying** (DM10/€5, condom included). Club prices skyrocket for the event as the best DJs from Europe are imported for a frantic weekend of beat-thumping madness. It's an experience that you won't forget, unless of course, you party *too* hard. Then again, as far as the Love Parade goes, there's no such thing.

CHARLOTTENBURG (SAVIGNYPLATZ)

Quasimodo, Kantstr. 12a. U2, U12, S3, S5, S7, S9, or S75 to "Zoologischer Garten." A smoky basement jazz venue with a wide variety of artists and a lively crowd. Cover Tu and W DM5/€3; on weekends, cover depends on performance, ranging from free to DM45/€24. Concert tickets available from 5pm at the cafe upstairs or at Kant-Kasse ticket service (☎313 45 54). Open Tu, W, F, Sa from 9pm; occasionally open M and Su.

A-Trane, Bleibtreustr. 1. S3, S5, S7, S9, or S75 to "Savignypl." Known chiefly to a sizable crowd of jazz-loving locals, this club attracts very good musicians and showcases them in a mellow, intimate setting. Cover DM10-40/€5-21 (usually about DM20/€10 on weekends). Club open daily at 10pm; closes at 2am weekdays, later on weekends.

SCHÖNEBERG

☒ **Slumberland,** Winterfeldtpl. U1, 2, 4, 12, or 15 to "Nollendorfpl." An African-motifed cafe/bar complete with artwork, palm trees, and a sand floor. Plays contemporary R&B as well as Bob Marley. Open Su-Th 6pm-2am, F 6pm-5am, Sa 11am-5am.

Café Bilderbuch, Akazienstr. 28. U7 to "Eisenacher Str." A sophisticated, jazzy cafe with an over-30 crowd. Open M-F 9am-1am, Sa 9am-2am, Su 10am-2am.

KREUZBERG

☒ **SO36,** Oranienstr. 190. U1, U12, or U15 to "Görlitzer Bahnhof" or bus #N29 to "Heinrichpl." Berlin's only *truly* mixed club, with a clientele of hip heteros, gays, and lesbians grooving to a mish-mash of wild genres. Loud music and huge dance floor. M "Electric Ballroom," a techno party featuring Berlin's up-and-coming DJs. Th hip-hop, reggae, punk, ska, or concerts. Weekends run the gamut from techno to live concerts. Cover for parties DM8-15/€4-8, concerts DM15-35/€7-18. Open after 11pm.

Wild at Heart, Wiener Str. 20. This place is punk as f**k. Climb the stairs into this little cave of colored lights and red walls peppered with old show posters—and don't forget your leather jacket. Snarling guitars every night; if there's no live band, then a DJ or the jukebox will send your sinful soul straight to hell. Open daily from 8pm.

Café Morena, Wiener Str. 60. U1, U8, U12, or U15 to "Görlitzer Bahnhof." The crowd may be a little on the loud side, but that's what happens when you have Happy "Hour" every day from 7-8pm and midnight-2am. Trip-hop and trance pour out of the stereo like a smooth, frothy beer out of the tap. Open Su-Th 9am-4am, F-Sa 9am-5am.

FRIEDRICHSHAIN

☒ **Euphoria,** Grünbergerstr. 60 (☎29 00 46 83), on the corner of Simon-Dach Str. This orange hotspot serves possibly the best mixed drinks in Berlin. Happy Hour 6-8pm, all drinks half-price. Open Su-Th 10am-midnight, F-Sa 10am-1am.

Maria am Ostbahnhof, Str. der Pariser Kommune 8-10 (☎29 00 61 98). S3, S5, S7, S9, or S75 to "Ostbahnhof." Extremely popular. Concert nights bring clove smoke and hipsters that vary with the band. Concerts W and Th, DJs F and Sa. Cover DM5-20/€2-11. Open W-Th 10pm-late, F-Sa 11pm-late.

Dachkammer Bar (DK), Simon-Dach Str. 39. Bright, friendly, and super-popular with the Friedrichshain crowd, DK serves light entrees (from DM7.50/€4) and plenty of drinks to go around. Open M-F noon-late, Sa-Su 10am-late.

PRENZLAUER BERG

KulturBrauerei, Knaackstr. 97 (☎441 92 69). U2 to "Eberswalder Str." This enormous party space, located in a former East German brewery, houses everything from the highly popular clubs *Soda* and *Kesselhaus* to Russian theater, upscale cafes, and an art school. Because the venues include everything from disco to techno, reggae, and *Schlager,* it's best to call ahead. Cover varies wildly from venue to venue—DM3-30/€1.50-16 or more. Opening times vary from institution to institution as well.

Pfefferberg, Schönhauser Allee 176. U2 to "Senefelderpl." or bus #N58. Very popular with a slightly younger crowd. Techno, reggae, and world music are rotated weekly. Rooftop garden open in summer. Garden open M-F from 3pm, Sa-Su from midnight. Cover varies DM10-20/€5-11.

Manilo, Lychener Str. 19. U2 to "Eberswalder Str." *Kinderfreundliches* (kid-friendly) cafe by day, psychedelic chilling grounds by night. Open from 9am-late.

Knaack, Greifwalderstr. 224. Tram #2, 3, or 4 to "Am Friedrichshain." The Knaack is one of the few clubs for indie rock in Berlin. Tickets available on the billiard floor; cover varies. Check schedule for details.

GAY AND LESBIAN BERLIN

Berlin is one of the most gay-friendly cities on the Continent. During the Cold War, thousands of homosexuals flocked to Berlin for its left-wing activist scene. With the fall of the Wall, Berlin's *Szene* was once again revitalized by the emergence of east Berlin's heretofore heavily oppressed homosexual community, and many of the new clubs that have opened up in the past few years are situated in the eastern half of the city. All of **Nollendorfplatz** is a gay-friendly environment, but the main streets, including **Goltzstraße, Akazienstraße,** and **Winterfeldtstraße,** tend to contain mixed bars and cafes. The locally-dubbed **"Bermuda Triangle"** of Motzstr., Fuggerstr., and Eisenacherstr. is more purely gay. For up-to-date events listings, pick up a copy of the amazingly comprehensive *Siegessäule* (free in tourist offices).

SCHÖNEBERG

Metropol, Nollendorfpl. 5. U1, U2, U4, or U15 to "Nollendorfpl.," or buses #N5, N19, N26, N48, N52, or N75. The Metropol contains 3 dance venues: **Tanz Tempel, West-Side Club,** and **Love Lounge.** This club has only recently come out, and some of its parties are still mixed—every other F the Tanz Tempel and Love Lounge team up to host the heterosexual *Fisch Sucht Fahrrad* party. West-Side Club holds the infamous **"Fuck Naked Sex Party,"** as well as numerous other naked parties. The Love Lounge varies from mixed to completely gay, while Tanz Tempel is nearly always gay and open only on Sa. Hours vary—check *Siegessäule* or *Sergej* (available at tourist offices) for details.

Omnes, Motzstr. 8. U1, U2, U4, or U15 to "Nollendorfpl." A mainly male gay bar, Omnes planned its hours to accommodate revelers after a full night of partying. Open M-F from 8am, Sa-Su from 5am.

Anderes Ufer, Hauptstr. 157. U7 to "Kleistpark." A quieter, more relaxed *Kneipe* away from the club scene. Open Su-Th 11am-1am, F-Sa 11am-2am.

Scheune, Motzstr. 25. U1, U2, U4, or U15 to "Nollendorfpl." With fully covered windows and strong sound-proofing, Scheune increases the mystique by making you ring the bell to enter. Men only. Mostly techno. Cover varies. Open Su-Th 9pm-7am, F-Sa 9pm-9am.

KREUZBERG

Most bars and clubs here lie on and around Oranienstr. between Lausitzer Pl. and Oranienpl. Take U1, U8, U12, or U15 to "Kottbusser Tor" or U1, U12, or U15 to "Görlitzer Bahnhof." After hours, night bus #N29 runs the length of the strip.

■ **Rose's,** Oranienstr. 187 (☎ 615 65 70). Marked only by "Bar" over the door, it's Liberace meets Cupid meets Satan. A friendly, mixed gay and lesbian clientele packs this intense and claustrophobic party spot at all hours of night. Open daily 10pm-6am.

■ **SO36,** while usually a mixed club (see p. 423), sponsors 3 predominantly homosexual events. **Hungrige Herzen** (W after 10pm) is a jam-packed gay and (somewhat) lesbian trance and drum 'n bass party; delightful drag queens use super-soakers to cool off the flaming crowd. **Café Fatal** (Su) has a more relaxed atmosphere with ballroom dancing from 5pm. **Gayhane** (last Sa of each month) is a self-described "HomOrientaldancefloor" for a mixed-orientation crowd of Turks and Germans.

Flammende Herzen, Oranienstr. 170. Pleasant mixed-orientation cafe frequented by Kreuzberg's gay and lesbian community. People-watch outside or chill in the flaming orange interior among a never-boring crowd. Open daily from 11am.

FRIEDRICHSHAIN

Die Busche, Mühlenstr. 12. U1, U12, U15, S3, S5, S6, S7, S9, or S75 to "Warschauer Str." East Berlin's largest queer disco serves up an incongruous rotation of techno, top 40, and *Schlager.* Very cruisey. Open W and F-Su from 9:30pm. The party gets going around midnight. It *really* gets going around 3am. Cover DM6-10/€3-6.

◪ DAYTRIPS FROM BERLIN

KZ SACHSENHAUSEN

Take Berlin's S1 (dir.: Oranienburg) to the end (40min.). The camp is a 20min. walk from the station. Follow the signs from Stralsunderstr., turning right on Bernauer Str., left on Str. der Einheit, and right on Str. der Nationen.

The small town of Oranienburg, just north of Berlin, was home to the Nazi concentration camp Sachsenhausen, in which more than 100,000 Jews, communists, intellectuals, gypsies, and homosexuals were killed between 1936 and 1945. The Gedenkstätte Sachsenhausen was opened by the GDR in 1961. Parts of the camp have been preserved in their original forms, including sets of cramped barracks, but only the foundations of Station Z (where prisoners were methodically exterminated) remain. Barracks 38 and 39 feature displays on daily life in the camp during the Nazi period and on the lives of specific prisoners. The jail block contains a museum detailing its uses along with rotating exhibits on individual inmates. Broader exhibits on Sachsenhausen and the concentration camp experience reside in the museum buildings and *Industriehof.* The exhibits, however, aren't nearly as expressive of the desperation and despair of Sachsenhausen as the camp itself; its brutally blunt gray buildings, barbed-wire fencing, and vast, bleak spaces testify to the hopelessness that was life here. (*Str. der Nationen 22.* ☎ *(03301) 80 37 15. Open Apr.-Sept. Tu-Su 8:30am-6pm; Oct.-Mar. Tu-Su 8:30am-4:30pm. Last entry 30min. before closing. Free. Audio tour rental DM5/€3.*)

POTSDAM

Berlin's S7 runs from Bahnhof Zoo to Potsdam (30min., DM4.70/€2.40).

Visitors disappointed by Berlin's distinctly unroyal demeanor can get their Kaiserly fix in nearby Potsdam, the glittering city of Friedrich II (the Great). The 245-hectare **Park Sanssouci** is Friedrich's testament to the size of his treasury and the diversity of his aesthetic tastes. For information on the park, stop by the **Visitors Center** at the windmill. A **day ticket** (DM24/€12.27, students DM20/€10.25) gives access to all four of the park's castles. ■ **Schloß Sanssouci,** the park's main attraction, was built in 1747 to allow Friedrich to escape his wife. German tours are limited to 40 people and leave every 20min., but the final tour (5pm) usually sells out by 2pm, so come early. The tourist office leads English-language tours of the main Schloß only. (☎(0331) 969 41 90. *Open Apr.-Oct. Tu-Su 9am-5pm; Nov.-Mar. Tu-Su 9am-4pm. DM16/€8.20, students DM10/€5.15.*) The exotic gold-plated **Chinesisches Teehaus,** complete with a rooftop Buddha toting a parasol, contains 18th-century *chinoiserie* porcelain. (DM2/€1.05.) Next door is the **Bildergalerie,** whose collection of Caravaggio, van Dyck, and Rubens (some of them copies—but still impressive) recently opened after extensive restoration. (☎(0331) 969 41 81. *Open mid-May to mid-Oct. Tu-Su 10am-noon and 12:30-5pm. DM4/€2.05, DM6/€3.10 with tour; student discount DM1/€0.55.*) The nearby **Sizilianischer Garten** is perhaps the park's most stunningly beautiful garden. At the opposite end of the park is the largest of the castles, the 200-room **Neues Palais.** (☎(0331) 969 42 55. *Open Sa-Th Apr.-Oct. 9am-5pm; Nov.-Mar. 9am-4pm. DM10/€5.10, students DM8/€4.10; DM2/€1.05 extra in summer.*)

Potsdam's second park, Neuer Garten, contains several royal residences; to get there, take bus #692 to "Schloß Cecilienhof." At **Schloß Cecilienhof,** built in the style of an English Tudor manor, exhibits document the **Potsdam Treaty,** which was signed here in 1945. It was supposed to be the "Berlin Treaty," but the capital was too bombed-out to house the Allies' head honchos. (☎(0331) 969 42 44. *Open Tu-Su 9am-noon and 12:30-5pm. DM6/€3.10, DM8/€4.10 with tour; student discount DM2/€1.05.*) The garden also contains the **Marmorpalais,** a huge marble-intensive palace, as well as many other odd little buildings, including a replica of an Egyptian pyramid. (*Marmorpalais open Apr.-Oct. Tu-Su 10am-5pm; Nov.-Mar. Sa-Su 10am-4pm. DM4/€2.05, DM6/€3.10 with tour; student discount DM1/€0.55.*)

DRESDEN. Dresden hosts spectacular ruins, world-class museums, and gloriously reconstructed palaces and churches (see p. 427).

LEIPZIG. Two hours on a train take you to Leipzig, where people get their groove on in the depths of medieval tunnels (see p. 433).

EASTERN GERMANY

Saxony *(Sachsen)* is known primarily for Dresden and Leipzig, but the entire region offers a fascinating historical and cultural diversity that reveals a great deal about life in the former East. West of Saxony, Thuringia *(Thüringen)*, the "Green Heart of Germany," is a hilly and mostly pastoral land where Bach, Goethe, Schiller, Luther, and Wagner all left their mark. It's arguably the most beautiful landscape in Germany. North of Thuringia and Saxony, the endless grass plains of Saxony-Anhalt's *(Sachsen-Anhalt)* offer one of the region's more tranquil landscapes. Its high unemployment rate mirrors the economic woes of Eastern Germany as a whole, but many construction sites mushrooming across the *Land* point toward the future.

WITTENBERG ☎03491

The Protestant Reformation began here in 1517 when Martin Luther nailed his *95 Theses* to the door of the Schloßkirche, and Wittenberg has been nuts about its heretical son ever since—in 1938, they even renamed the town "Lutherstadt Wittenberg." All the major sights lie around **Collegienstraße**. The **Lutherhalle,** Collegienstr. 54, usually holds texts and art chronicling the Reformation, but while it's closed for renovations until October 2002, the exhibits are housed in the **Rathaus,** Markt 26. (*Open Apr.-Oct. daily 9am-6pm; Nov.-Mar. Tu-Su 10am-5pm. DM4/€2.05, students DM2/€1.05.*) Also on the Marktpl. is the **Stadtkirche St. Marien,** known for the dazzling altar painted by Lucas Cranach the Elder. (*Open M-F 9am-5pm, Su 11am-pm.*) The **Schloßkirche** on Schloßstr. holds a copy of Luther's *95 Theses* and (allegedly) Luther's body. The tower affords a sumptuous view of the surrounding countryside. (*Church open M-Sa 10am-5pm, Su 11:30am-5pm. Free. Tower open M-F 12-3:30pm, Sa-Su 10am-3:30pm. DM2/€1.05, students DM1/€0.55.*)

GERMANY

Trains leave the Hauptbahnhof for Berlin (1½hr., every 2hr., DM32/€16.40) and Leipzig (1hr., every 2hr., DM17/€8.70). From the station, follow the street as it curves right and continue until Collegienstr., the beginning of the **pedestrian zone.** The **tourist office,** Schloßpl. 2, at the end of the pedestrian zone, provides maps, leads tours (DM10/€5.15), and books rooms. (☎49 86 10. Open Mar.-Oct. M-F 9am-6pm, Sa 10am-3pm, Su 11am-4pm; Nov.-Feb. M-F 10am-4pm, Sa 10am-2pm, Su 11am-3pm.) The **Jugendherberge (HI)** is in the castle; cross the street from the tourist office and head into the castle's enclosure, then trek up the stairs to the right. (☎40 32 55. Breakfast included. Sheets DM6/€3.10. Key deposit DM10/€5.15. Reception 5-10pm. Lockout 10pm. Reservations recommended. Dorms DM22/€11.30, over 26 DM27/€13.85.) Cheap eats lie along the Collegienstr.-Schloßstr. strip, and there's a **City-Kauf supermarket,** Coswiger Str. 20, near the tourist office. (Open M-F 7am-6:30pm, Sa 8am-12:30pm.) **Creperie Lorette,** Collegienstr. 70, offers the best of both worlds: French food and German beer. (Open M-Sa from 11am, Su from 3pm.) **Postal Code:** 06886.

DRESDEN   ☎0351

The stunning buildings of Dresden's Altstadt look ancient, but most are newly reconstructed—the Allied bombings of February 1945 claimed over 50,000 lives and destroyed 75% of the city center. Today, Dresden pulses with a historical intensity yet feels fresh and vibrant, engaging visitors with world-class museums and partially reconstructed palaces and churches (reconstruction is scheduled for completion by 2006, the city's 800-year anniversary). However, Dresden is not all nostalgic appeals to the past; the city has entered the new millennium as a young, dynamic metropolis propelled by a history of cultural turbulence.

▐ TRANSPORTATION

Flights: Dresden's **airport** (☎881 33 60) is 9km from town; the S2 makes the 20min. trip from both train stations (2 per hr., 4am-midnight, DM5.80/€3).

Trains: From the **Dresden Hauptbahnhof,** in the Altstadt, and **Bahnhof Dresden Neustadt,** across the Elbe, travelers zoom to **Berlin** (2hr., every 2hr., DM52/€26.60); **Budapest** (10hr., 4 per day, DM125/€64); **Frankfurt** (7hr., 14 per day, DM136/€69.60); **Leipzig** (1½hr., 1-2 per hr., DM33/€16.90); **Munich** (7hr., 24 per day, DM148/€75.70); **Prague** (2½hr., 12 per day, DM38/€19.50); **Warsaw** (8hr., 8 per day, DM53/€27). Buy tickets from the automated machines in the main halls of both stations, or from the staff at the Reisezentrum desk.

Public Transportation: Dresden's **streetcars** are efficient and cover the whole city. **Single-ride** DM2.90/€1.50; 4 or fewer stops DM1.80/€0.95. **Day pass** DM8/€4.10; **weekly pass** DM25/€12.80. Most major lines run every hr. after midnight. Tickets are available from Fahrkarten dispensers at major stops, on the streetcars themselves, and from **Verkehrs-Info** stands in front of the Hauptbahnhof (M-F 7am-7pm). As you board, punch your ticket in the red contraptions at the bottom of the stairwells to each track.

⊁ ▐ ORIENTATION AND PRACTICAL INFORMATION

Dresden is bisected by the Elbe. The **Altstadt** lies on the same side as the Hauptbahnhof; **Neustadt,** to the north, escaped most of the bombing, paradoxically making it one of the oldest parts of the city. Many of Dresden's main attractions are centered between the **Altmarkt** and the **Elbe,** 5min. from the Neustadt.

TOURIST, FINANCIAL, AND LOCAL SERVICES

Tourist Office: 2 locations: **Prager Straße 3,** near the Hauptbahnhof (☎49 19 20; open M-F 9am-7pm, Sa 9am-4pm); **Theaterplatz** in the Schinkelwache, in front of the Semper-Oper (open M-F 10am-6pm, Sa 10am-4pm, Su 10am-1pm). Sells city maps (DM3/€1.55) and the **Dresden Card,** which includes 48hr. of public transit, free or reduced entry at many museums, and city tours (DM27/€13.80).

Currency Exchange: ReiseBank, in the Hauptbahnhof. 2.5-4.5% commission, depending on the amount; 1-1.5% for traveler's checks. Open M-F 7:30am-7:30pm, Sa 8am-noon and 12:30-4pm, Su 9am-1pm. A self-service machine is available after hours, but the rates are poor.

Luggage Storage: At both train stations. Lockers DM2-4/€1.05-2.05 for 24hr. storage.

Gay and Lesbian Organizations: Gerede-Dresdner Lesben, Schwule und alle Anderen, Prießnitzstr. 18 (☎802 22 51; 24hr. hotline ☎802 22 70). From Albertpl., walk up Bautzner Str. and turn left onto Prießnitzstr. Open Tu 10am-noon and 3-5pm, Th 3-5pm.

Laundromat: Groove Station, Katharinenstr. 11-13. Wash, dry, and cup of coffee DM8/€4.10; meanwhile, browse leather, tattoos, or piercings. Open M-Sa noon-late, Su 2pm-late.

EMERGENCY AND COMMUNICATIONS

Police: ☎110. **Ambulance and Fire:** ☎112.

Pharmacy: Apotheke Prager Straße, Prager Str. 3 (☎490 30 14). Open M-F 8:30am-7pm, Sa 8:30am-4pm. After hours, a sign indicates the nearest open pharmacies.

Internet Access: Mediacenter Internet Cafe, Schandauerstr. 64 (☎311 63 31). DM6/€3.10 per hr. Open M-W 2-9pm, Th 9am-midnight, F noon-midnight.

Post Office: Hauptpostamt, Königsbrücker Str. 21/29 (☎819 13 70), in Neustadt. Open M-F 8am-7pm, Sa 9am-1pm. Address mail to be held: *Postlagernde Briefe* für FirstName SURNAME, Hauptpostamt, **D-01099** Dresden, Germany.

◪ ◪ ACCOMMODATIONS AND CAMPING

If there's one thing that attests to Dresden's status as a city on the rise, it's the state of its accommodations. New hotels and hostels are constantly being planned, built, and opened, but on weekends it's hard to get a spot in anything with a good location—so call ahead.

▨ **Mondpalast Backpacker,** Katharinenstr. 11-13 (☎804 60 61). From Bahnhof Neustadt, walk down Antonstr. toward Albertpl., turn left onto Königsbrücker Str., and turn right on Katharinenstr.; the hostel is on the left. Located in the heart of the Neustadt scene, it's the hippest place in town. **Internet** access DM6-10/€3.10-5.15 per hr. Breakfast DM8/€4.10. Sheets DM5/€2.60. Key deposit DM10/€5.15. 24hr. reception. Call ahead. 8-bed rooms DM25/€12.80; 3- to 7-bed rooms DM28/€14.35; singles DM40/€20.50; doubles DM32/€16.40.

Hostel Die Boofe, Louisenstr. 20 (☎801 33 61). From the Neustadt, take the Schlesischerplz. exit, cross the parking lot, turn left on Dr. Friedrich Wolf Str., then hang a right on Lößnitz Str.; the hostel's on the right. A renovated apartment building set back in a small courtyard, this brand-new hostel offers immaculate rooms and cushy beds. Rents bikes (DM10/€5.15 per day) and scooters (DM15/€7.70 per day). **Internet** access DM10/€5.15 per hr. Breakfast DM8/€4.10. Sheets DM5/€2.60. 24hr. reception. Reservations recommended. Dorms DM26/€13.30; doubles DM79/€40.40 with sheets and breakfast.

Jugendherberge Dresden Rudi Arndt (HI), Hübnerstr. 11 (☎471 06 67). Take S8 (dir.: Südvorstadt) or S3 (dir.: Coschütz) to "Nürnberger Platz," follow Nürnberger Str., and turn right onto Hübnerstr. Or, from the Hauptbahnhof, turn left out of the Bayrischestr. exit, then take the 1st right (Fritz-Löffler-Str.); after 10min. turn right on Nürnbergerstr., then turn right on Hübnerstr. Breakfast included. Sheets DM5/€2.60 (required). Check-in 3pm-1am. Curfew 1am. Reservations recommended. Dorms DM26/€15.30, over 26 DM31/€15.85. **HI members only.**

Pension Raskolnikoff, Böhmische Str. 34 (☎804 57 06). Located right in the middle of the Neustadt, this 6-room pension is the perfect way to escape the hostel scene. Singles DM70/€35.80; doubles DM75/€38.35. Call ahead.

City-Herberge, Lignerallee 3 (☎485 99 00; fax 485 99 01). From the Hauptbahnhof, walk up St. Petersburger Str. and turn right at Lignerallee. Central location with access to public transportation. Bathrooms are shared but are still fairly private. Breakfast included. Reservations recommended. Apr.-June, Sept.-Oct., and Dec. singles DM70/

GERMANY

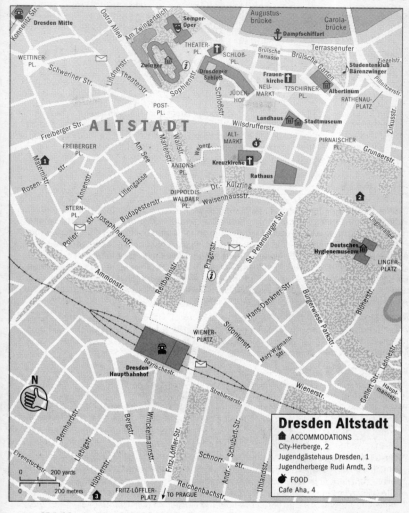

Dresden Altstadt

⌂ ACCOMMODATIONS
City-Herberge, 2
Jugendgästehaus Dresden, 1
Jugendherberge Rudi Arndt, 3

🍴 FOOD
Cafe Aha, 4

€35.80; doubles DM100/€51.15; July-Aug., Nov., and Jan.-Mar. singles DM60/ €30.70; doubles DM80/€40.90.

Campingplatz Mockritz, Boderitzerstr. 30 (☎ 47 15 250). Take bus #76 (dir.: Mockritz) to "Campingplatz Mockritz." This family-run camping spot lets you get away from the hustle and bustle of Dresden. Reception daily 8-11am and 4-9pm. DM8/€4.10 per person, DM4-6/€2.05-3.10 per tent.

🍴 FOOD

Unfortunately, the surge in Dresden tourism has raised food prices, particularly in the Altstadt. The cheapest eats in the Altstadt are at **supermarkets** or **Imbiß stands** along **Pragerstraße.** The **Neustadt,** between Albertpl. and Alaunpl., spawns a new bar every few weeks and rules the roost of quirky ethnic and student-friendly restaurants.

El Perro Borracho, Alaunstr. 70 (☎803 67 23). A tiny sparkle of sunny Spain. Try the tasty "mix & match" tapas. All main courses DM12/€6.15. Buffet breakfast Sa-Su 10am-3pm (DM14/€7.20). Open M-F 11:30am-1am, Sa-Su 10am-1am.

Raskolnikoff, Böhmische Str. 34 (☎804 57 06). Savory fare from all over the globe (DM6-24/€3.10-12.30) served to a local crowd. Open daily 10am-2am.

Blumenau, Louisenstr. 67 (☎802 65 02). One of the cheapest and most popular restaurants in the Neustadt. The menu changes unpredictably but most dishes run DM6-10/€3.10-5.15; breakfast (DM5-11/€2.60-5.65) until 4pm. Open daily 10am-3am.

Café Aha, Kreuzstr. 7 (☎492 33 79), across the street from the Kreuzkirche. A haven for environmentally conscious idealism, the restaurant serves healthy food produced by ecologically sound means and changes its menu monthly to introduce foods from countries that can't compete in the world market. Dishes DM8-20/€4.10-€10.25. Open daily 10am-midnight.

👁 SIGHTS

▨ ZWINGER. The extravagant art collection of Friedrich August I (the Strong), Prince Elector of Saxony and King of Poland, is housed in the magnificent **Zwinger** palace, a building championed as a triumph of Baroque design. The palace narrowly escaped destruction in the 1945 bombings; workers are busy restoring it to aesthetic perfection. In the Semper wing is the **Gemäldegalerie Alte Meister,** a world-class collection of paintings from 1400-1800. Across from the gallery is the **Rüstkammer,** a collection of courtly toys including silver- and gold-plated suits for both man and horse and a set of toddler-sized armor. (*☎491 46 19. Both open Tu-Su 10am-6pm. Joint admission DM7/€3.60, students DM4/€2.05. Tours F and Su at 4pm. DM1.*)

SEMPER-OPER. This famed opera house, one of Dresden's major attractions, reverberates with the same glorious luxury as the northern wing of the Zwinger. (*Theaterplatz 2. ☎491 14 96; fax 491 14 58. Check the main entrance for tour times, usually midday. DM9/€4.60, students DM6/€3.10.*)

KREUZKIRCHE. After being leveled four times (in 1669 by fire, in 1760 with the Seven Years War, again in 1897 by fire, and finally in February 1945 by Allied bombing), the interior remains in a damaged state as a powerful reminder of the war's destruction. The tower offers a bird's eye view of downtown Dresden. (*An der Kreuzkirche 6. ☎439 39 20. Open summer M-Tu and Th-F 10am-5:30pm, W and Sa 10am-4:30pm, Su noon-4:30pm; winter M-Sa 10am-3:30pm, Su noon-4:30pm. Free. Tower closes 30min. before the church. DM2/€1.05, children DM1/€0.55.*)

DRESDENER SCHLOß. Once the proud home of August the Strong, this palace was ruined in the Allied firebombing of 1945, but a good deal of its restoration is nearly complete. The 100m tall **▨ Hausmannsturm** hosts fascinating but sobering photographs and texts discussing the Allied bombings, and the top floor offers a 360-degree view of the city. (*Across from the Zwinger on Schloßpl. Open Apr.-Oct. Tu-Su 10am-6pm. DM5/€2.60, students and seniors DM3/€1.55.*) If you've been mistaking Friedrich the Earnest for Friedrich the Pugnacious, stop by the **Fürstenzug** (Procession of Electors) along Augustusstr., a 102m mural made of 24,000 tiles of Meißen china depicting the rulers of Saxony from 1123 to 1904.

NEUSTADT. Across the magnificent **Augustusbrücke,** Hauptstr. is home to the **Goldener Reiter,** a gold-plated statue of August the Strong atop a steed in pompous glory. August's nickname was reputedly a homage to his remarkable virility; legend has it he fathered 365 kids, though the official tally is 15. At the other end of Hauptstr., **Albertplatz** is the gateway to the Neustadt scene.

SCHLACHTHOFRINGE. The **Schlachthofringe** (Slaughterhouse Circle) is a 1910 housing complex in a more dismal part of Dresden, used during WWII as a P.O.W. camp. Its buildings have since been left to waste away. Novelist Kurt Vonnegut was imprisoned here during the bombing of Dresden, inspiring his masterpiece *Slaughterhouse Five.* (*Take bus #82 (dir.: Dresden Messe) to "Ostragehege."*)

Got ISIC?

SIC is your passport to the world.

Accepted at over 17,000 locations worldwide.
Great benefits at home and abroad!

apply for your International Student, Teacher or Youth Identity Card
CALL 1-800-2COUNCIL
CLICK www.counciltravel.com
VISIT your local Council Travel office

Bring this ad into your local Council Travel office and receive
a free Council Travel/ISIC t-shirt! *(while supplies last)*

FALL/WINTER 2001 • FREE

student **Travels**

WORK, STUDY, TRAVEL ABROAD

CZECH IT OUT!
Exploring Prague
and Other Pleasures
in the Czech Republic

BOSTON
Weekend Wandering
in Beantown

INSIDE
Your International
Student Identity Card
(ISIC) Application

PLUS
-Cuba
-Australia

Bedazzled
By**BRAZIL**

Boundless Attractions From Beautiful Beaches
to Spectacular Festivals to Lush Jungles

STOR
IN
FOR
YOUR
FREE
COPY
TODAY

STUDENT TRAVELS MAGAZINE
is now available at all Council Travel offices.

This FREE magazine is the student guide to getting
around the world - on a student's budget!

council
travel
America's Leader In Student Travel

Find your local office at
www.counciltravel.com

1-800-2COUNCIL

GERMANY

ALBERTINUM. The Albertinum holds the 🖼️**Gemäldegalerie der Neuen Meister,** which combines an ensemble of German and French Impressionists with a collection of Expressionists and Neue Sachlichkeit modernist works, including Otto Dix's renowned *War* triptych. *(☎ 491 47 14. Open F-W 10am-6pm. DM8/€4.10, students and seniors DM4.50/€2.30; includes admission to Grünes Gewölbe, a collection of Saxon figurines.)*

STADTMUSEUM. In the 18th-century Landhaus, the museum tells the story of the city since the 13th century. A colorful collection of 20th-century memorabilia completes the tale, from 1945 bomb shells to a collection of protest signs from the 1989 demonstrations. *(Wilsdrufferstr. 2, near Pirnaischer Platz. Open Sa-Th 10am-6pm; May-Sept. W until 8pm. DM4/€2, students DM2/€1.05.)*

DEUTSCHES HYGIENEMUSEUM. This ill-named museum long celebrated the health and cleanliness of East Germans. Now that the Party's over, the rather bizarre, interactive, and playful collection includes optical illusions, a hallway of condom propaganda, and a glass cow whose innards light up. *(Lingnerpl. 1. ☎ 48 46. Enter from Blüherstr. Open Tu and Th-F 9am-5pm, W 9am-8pm, Sa-Su 10am-6pm; May- June also M 9am-5pm. DM5/€2.60, students and seniors DM3/€1.55.)*

🎵 🎭 ENTERTAINMENT AND NIGHTLIFE

For centuries, Dresden has been a focal point for theater, opera, and music. The superb **Semper-Oper** (☎ 491 17 30) premiered many of Strauss and Wagner's greatest pieces, but tickets are hard to come by. Dresden's nightlife scene is young and dynamic; the **Neustadt,** roughly bounded by Königsbrückerstr., Bischofsweg, Kamenzerstr., and Albertpl., is its thudding heart. At last count, over 50 bars packed the area; *Kneipen Surfer* lists all of them.

DownTown, Katharinenstr. 11-13, below the Mondpalast hostel, keeps the beat going, fast and furious, as Dresden's young and energetic scene grooves to techno. Cover DM7/€3.60, students DM5/€2.60. Open 10pm-5am.

Scheune, Alaunstr. 36-40, is the granddaddy of the Neustadt scene; its eclectic dance floor specializes in world music. Cover varies. Club opens at 8pm. Bar open M-F 11am-2am, Sa-Su 10am-2am.

Flowerpower, Eschenstr. 11 (804 98 14). From Albertpl., walk up Konigsbrückerstr. and take a left on Eschenstr.; it's on the left. The club is packed with 20-somethings sitting around the colorful bar or getting down to popular tunes. M "student day" (beer and wine half-price). No cover. Open daily 8pm-5am.

Queens, Görlitzer Str. 3 (☎ 803 16 50). A popular gay bar with plenty of sparkle to go around. Drinks (DM4-12/€2.05-€6.15), music, and occasional special entertainment. F 70s/80s night. Open daily from 8pm.

🔁 DAYTRIP FROM DRESDEN

MEIßEN   ☎ 03521

Reach Meißen from Dresden by train (40min., DM8.70/€4.45).

Meißen, 30km from Dresden, is another testament to the frivolity of August the Strong. In 1710, the Saxon elector contracted severe *Porzellankrankheit* (the porcelain "bug," still afflicting tourists today) and turned the city's defunct castle into Europe's first porcelain factory. The building was once more tightly guarded than KGB headquarters to prevent competitors from learning its techniques; today anyone can tour the **Staatliche Porzellan-Manufaktur,** Talstr. 9 (☎ 468 208). Peruse finished products in the **Schauhalle** (DM9/€4.60, students DM7/€3.60), but the real fun lies in the high-tech tour of the *Schauwerkstatt* (show workshop), which demonstrates the manufacturing process. (Open daily 9am-6pm. DM5/€2.60. English headsets available.) Narrow, romantic alleyways lead up to the **Albrechtsburg** castle and cathedral. (Open Mar.-Oct. daily 10am-6pm; Nov.-Feb. 10am-5pm. Last entry 30min. before closing. DM7/€3.60, students DM5/€2.60.) From the train station, walk straight onto Bahnhofstr. and follow it over the Elbbrücke. Cross the bridge, continue straight to the Markt and turn right onto Burgstr. At the end of Burgstr., on Hohlweg, take the Schloßstufen (castle stairs) on your right, which lead up to Albrechtsburg. Next door looms the **Meißener Dom,** a Gothic cathedral which satisfies visitors with four 13th-century statues by the Naumburg Master, a triptych by Cranach the Elder, and the metal grave coverings of the Wettins. (Open Apr.-Oct. daily 9am-6pm; Nov.-Mar. 10am-4pm. DM4/€2.05, students DM3/€1.50.) The **tourist office,** Markt 3, is across from the church, and finds private rooms (DM30-50/€15.35-25.60) for a DM4/€2.05 fee. (☎419 40. Open Apr.-Oct. M-F 9am-6:30pm, Sa-Su 10am-4pm; Nov.-Mar. M-F 10am-5pm, Sa 10am-3pm.) **Postal Code:** 01662.

SAXON SWITZERLAND

Formerly one of East Germany's most beloved holiday destinations, Saxon Switzerland *(Sächsische Schweiz)*—so dubbed because of its stunning, Swiss-like landscape—is now one of unified Germany's favorite national parks. Its sandstone cliffs, sumptuous summits, and breathtaking hikes should be temptation enough to lure anyone off the path and into the hills for a few days.

TRANSPORTATION. Dresden's S1 (dir.: Schöna) runs from the Dresden Hauptbahnhof to Wehlen, Rathen, Königstein, and Bad Schandau. The S-Bahn stops just across the river from each of these towns; hop on a ferry to get to the sights (DM1.30/€0.70). Since *Wanderwege* (footpaths) crisscross the area, you can also easily hike from town to town if you're sick of being on the train. Wehlen is probably the ideal jumping-off point to explore other towns in Saxon Switzerland. From Bad Schandau at the end of the line, ride the S-Bahn back to Dresden (50min., every 30min., DM8.70/€4.45) or continue to Prague (2hr., every 2hr., DM30.80/€15.75).

RATHEN. Two beautiful hikes through the Bastei cliffs run from Wehlen to Rathen. One of the paths climbs up the cliffs and was a favorite of August the Strong; the other path—shorter and easier but much less impressive—is along the Elbe (45min., turn right after the ferry ramp). If you're not into hiking, take the Dresden S-Bahn to "Rathen" and cross from the station to the town by ferry (DM1.30/€0.70). Regardless of how you get there, Rathen makes a good starting point for hikes of any length because of its location on the edge of the **Sächsische Schweiz National Park.** The town also boasts the **Felsenbühne,** a beautiful open-air theater; its 2000 seats are carved into a cliff, and stone pillars loom over the stage. (Open 8am until 2hr. before rehearsal/event and 1hr. after rehearsal/event.) To get there, follow the signs from the ferry landing. Tickets and schedules are available from the **Theaterkasse,** on the way to the theater (☎77 70. DM6-39/€3-19.95).

The **tourist office** gives advice on hiking and finds rooms (DM22-35/€11.25-17.90) for free. From the ferry landing, take the main road, Zum Grünbar, for five minutes and it's on the left. (Open M-F 9am-noon and 1-6pm, Sa-Su 9am-2pm, closed weekends Nov. 1-Mar. 31.) For a knightly night, try **Burg Altrathen,** Am Grünbach 10 um 11, in a castle perched above the Elbe. Take a right up the narrow path to the left after the ferry landing, just past the Hotel Erbgericht. (☎76 00. Singles DM40-60/€20.45-30.70; doubles DM80-90/€40.90-46.) The purist will enjoy the sparse **Bergsteigerzimmer** ("mountain climber's room," mattress DM25/€12.80). For good eats and an even better view, hit the aptly-named **Pension Panoramo** (most meals DM12-18/€6.15-19.20), bright pink and up the right-hand slope. (Open M-F 5pm-11pm, Sa noon-11pm.) ☎035024.

HOHNSTEIN. The small village of Hohnstein ("high stone" in old Saxon) is linked to Rathen by two beautiful hikes through one of the national park's most stunning valleys. To get here, start at Rathen and follow the shorter (2hr.), more challenging red-striped path, or the longer (3hr.) green-striped path. On your way, be sure to stop at the **Hockstein,** an isolated outcropping with a spectacular view of the valley below. Alternatively, you can reach Hohnstein by taking the S-Bahn to "Pirna"(40min.) and then bus #236 or 237 from the Bahnhof (DM5.80/€3).

The **tourist office,** Rathausstr. 10, in the Rathaus, doles out info on trails and finds rooms for free. (☎194 33. Open M and W-F 9am-noon and 12:30-5pm, Tu 9am-noon and 12:30-6pm.) **Naturfreundehaus Burg Hohnstein,** Am Markt 1, is a hostel in a fortress that also includes a history and nature museum, lookout tower, and cafe-restaurant. (☎812 02. Breakfast and sheets included. Reception open daily 7am-8pm. The hostel offers singles, quads, and titanic 6- to 18-bed rooms for the same price per person, DM29.30/€15; nonmembers DM37.60/€19.25.) ☎035975.

KÖNIGSTEIN. Above the town looms the impressive fortress **Festung Königstein,** whose huge walls are built right into the same stone spires that made the Sächsische Schweiz famous. Replete with drawbridges and impenetrable stone walls, the fortress was later converted into a feared state prison. From the city, it's a 40-minute uphill struggle, but the view atop the fortress wall is worth sweating for; follow the signs to the well-worn path. (Open Easter-Sept. daily 9am-8pm; Oct. 9am-6pm; Nov.-Apr. 9am-5pm. DM7/€3.60, students and seniors DM5/€2.60.) The touristy **Festungs Express** is an option for those too tired to make the trek; rides leave from Reißigerplatz, just to the right down Bahnhofstr. from the S-Bahn station. (Runs Apr.-Oct., every half hr., 9am-6pm. One-way DM4/€2.05, round-trip DM6/€3.10.)

The **tourist office,** Schreiberberg 2, books rooms and houses the **post office.** It also has a list of available rooms, vacation houses, and *Pensionen;* prices are posted on a bulletin board outside when they're closed. From Reißigerpl., take Hainstr., turn left on Pirnaerstr., then right on Schreiberberg. (☎682 61. Open Apr.-Oct. M-F 9am-6pm, Sa 9am-noon; Nov.-Mar. M-F 9am-noon and 2-6pm; Sa 9-10:30am.) The **Naturfreundehaus,** Halbestadt 13, is an ideal place for families or groups, but a surcharge of DM10.75/€5.50 is added for single rooms. (☎035022 994 80. Breakfast included. Reception daily 6am-10pm.) **Schräger's Gasthaus,** on Kirchgasse, has antlers on the walls and hearty plates (DM8-20/€4.10-10.25) on the table. Thirsty? Toss one back at the **Biergarten and Speisehaus Amtshof,** 30 Pirnaerstr. Meals DM10-17/€5.15-8.70. (☎685 11. Open W-M 11am-3pm and 3:30-9:30pm.) ☎035021.

BAD SCHANDAU. The biggest town in the Sächsische Schweiz, Bad Schandau takes advantage of its location between the two halves of the national park by offering plenty of hiking opportunities. Take the *Kirnitzschtalbahn* trolley car (Mar.-Oct. every 30min. DM6/€3.10, DM8/€4.10 round-trip) to the Lichtenhain waterfall, a favorite starting point for three- and four-hour hikes on the Schrammsteine. Bad Schandau is more of a family vacation spot than any other town in the area, so hotels fill up quickly when the weather is good.

The S-Bahn runs to **Dresden** every 30min. (50min., DM8.70/€4.45). The **tourist office,** Markt 12, finds rooms (DM28-30/€14.35-15.35), suggests hikes, and offers city tours and trips to the Czech Republic. (☎900 30. Open Apr.-Oct. M-F 9am-7pm, Sa 9am-4pm, Su 1-5pm; Nov.-Mar. M-F 9am-6pm.) To rent a bike, try **Rund Um's Fahrradverleih,** Poststr. 14. (☎428 83. Open M-F 9am-noon and 2-6pm, Sa 9am-noon. DM15/€7.70 per day.) The **Jugendherberge Bad Schandau (HI),** Dorfstr. 14, is far from the center of town but convenient to several trailheads and a good starting point for day hikes. Walk 30min. down Rudolf-Sendig-Str., then go up in the elevator (DM2.50/€1.30) in the huge metal tower on your left; at the top take the paved path to the right and follow the signs. Or, take bus #255 to Ostauer Scheibe. (☎424 08. Breakfast included. Sheets DM6/€3.10. DM26/€13.30. **HI members only.**) In a town that shuts down before 11pm, **Sigl's,** Kirnitzschtalstr. 17, a bar-bistro, offers food and a wide selection of beers until 2am and doubles as a cheap hotel. (☎407 02. Singles DM55/€28.15; doubles DM70-90/€35.80-46.) ☎035022.

LEIPZIG   ☎0341

Leipzig may be small, but it's bursting with energy and style from museums, monuments to Bach, cafes, and a lively university culture. Unemployment still poses a problem, but Leipzig's fascinating role in historical change from the time of Napoleon to the fall of the Berlin Wall overshadows any current difficulties. Rushing resolutely yet cheerfully onward, Leipzig glows with a social and cultural scene full of innovation and confidence.

GERMANY

◧⃓ TRANSPORTATION AND PRACTICAL INFORMATION. Leipzig lies on the Berlin-Munich line, with regular InterCity service to Frankfurt. **Trains** run to: Berlin (2-3hr., 3 per hr., DM51/€26.10); Dresden (1½hr., every hr., DM33/€16.90); Frankfurt (5hr., 2 every 2hr., DM120/€61.40); Munich (6hr., every hr., DM133/€68). Leipzig's sights, nightlife, and university are all enclosed within a 1km ring. Cross Willy-Brandt-Pl. in front of the station and turn left at Richard-Wagner-Str. to reach the **tourist office**, Richard-Wagner-Str. 1, which has free city and transportation maps, sells the **Leipzig Card** (24hr. DM9.90/€5; 3-day DM21/€10.75), and books rooms for free. (Open M-F 9am-7pm, Sa 9am-4pm, Su 9am-2pm.) The **post office** is at Hauptpostamt 1, **04109** Leipzig. (Open M-F 8am-8pm, Sa 9am-4pm.)

◧⃔ ACCOMMODATIONS AND FOOD. To reach **Hostel Sleepy Lion,** Käthe-Kollwitz-Str. 3, cross both rings from the station and turn right onto Richard-Wagner-Str.; when it ends, cut left through the parking lot and the small park, cross the ring, and bear right onto Käthe-Kollwitz-Str. All rooms have shower and bathroom. (☎993 94 80. **Internet** DM4/€2 per hr. Breakfast DM6/€3. Sheets DM4/€2. Reception 24hr. 6- to 8-bed dorms DM28/€14; singles DM46/€23; doubles DM72/€36; quads DM120/€60.) **Jugendherberge Leipzig Centrum (HI),** Volksgartenstr. 24, is 15min. from the city; take streetcar #1 (dir.: Mockau Post) to "Löbauer Str.," walk right past the supermarket onto Löbauer Str., and take a right onto Volksgartenstr. (☎245 70 11. Breakfast included. Sheets DM6/€3.10. Reception 2:30-11pm. Curfew 1am. Dorms DM31/€15.85, under 26 DM26/€13.30.) For **Kosmos Hotel,** Gottschedstr. 1, follow the directions to Hostel Sleepy Lion; at the end of the park, keep left on Dittrichring and the hotel will be on the right. This hotel is part of a complex with a nightclub, theater, and restaurant. Be prepared: Gottschedstr. rocks until the wee hours. (☎233 44 20. Rooms have private bathrooms. Breakfast DM10/€5.10. Singles from DM50/25.60; doubles from DM70/€35.80.)

The *Innenstadt*, especially Grimmaischestr., has *Imbiß* stands, bistros, and bakeries. Outside the city center, **Karl-Liebknecht-Straße** (streetcar #1 or 10 to "Kochstr.") is packed with cheap *Döner* stands and cafes that double as bars. ◪**Avocado,** Karl-Liebknecht-Str. 79, has vegetarian and vegan options. (Open M-F 11:30am-1am, Sa 4pm-2am, Su 11am-1am.) **Zur Pleißenburg,** Schulstr. 2, just down Burgstr. from the Thomaskirche, is popular with locals and serves hearty fare. (Open daily 9am-5am.) **Ashoka,** Georgiring 8-9, serves respectable Indian food. (Open M-F noon-3pm and 5-11pm, Sa-Su noon-11pm.) Rub elbows with Leipzig University students at **Eck-Café,** in the courtyard of the university complex across from the Mensa. (Open Oct. to mid-July M-Th 9:30am-6:30pm, F 10am-3pm.) **Café le bit,** Kohlgartenstr. 2, is an **Internet** cafe with unusually good food. With your back to the station, turn left across Georgring onto Wintergartenstr., which becomes Rosa-Luxemburg-Str. and leads straight there. (**Internet** DM2.50/€1.30 per 30min. Open M-F 9am-3am, Sa-Su 10am-3am.) There's a **Plus supermarket** on the Brühl, near Sachsenpl. (Open M-F 8am-8pm, Sa 8am-4pm.)

◧⃔ SIGHTS AND ENTERTAINMENT. The heart of Leipzig is the **Marktplatz,** a colorful, cobblestoned square guarded by the slanted 16th-century **Altes Rathaus.** Head down Grimmaischestr. to the **Nikolaikirche,** where massive weekly demonstrations led to the fall of the GDR. (Open M-Sa 10am-6pm, Su after services. Free.) Backtrack to the *Rathaus* and follow Thomasg. to the **Thomaskirche;** Bach spent the last years of his life as cantor here, and his grave lies beneath the floor in front of the altar. (Open daily 9am-6pm. Free.) Just behind the church is the **Johann-Sebastian-Bach-Museum,** Thomaskirchhof 16. (Open daily 10am-5pm. DM6/€3.10, students DM4/€2.05. Free English cassette tours.) Head back to Thomasg., turn left, then turn right on Dittrichring to reach the ◪**Museum in der "Runden Ecke,"** Dittrichring 24, which displays stunningly blunt exhibits on the history, doctrine, and tools of the *Stasi* (secret police), including hidden cameras, telegram interceptors, and letter opening and re-sealing machines—1,500 letters a day were sent here for perusal. Ask for an English handout in the office. (Open daily 10am-6pm. Free.) Outside the city ring, the **Völkerschlachtdenkmal** memorializes the soldiers

GERMANY

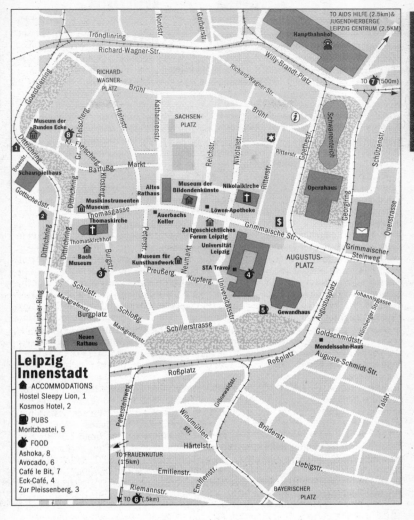

Leipzig Innenstadt

🛕 **ACCOMMODATIONS**
Hostel Sleepy Lion, 1
Kosmos Hotel, 2

🍺 **PUBS**
Moritzbastei, 5

🍴 **FOOD**
Ashoka, 8
Avocado, 6
Café le Bit, 7
Eck-Café, 4
Zur Pleissenberg, 3

who died in the 1813 Battle of Nations against Napoleon. Climb the 500 steps to the top for a fabulous view of Leipzig. (Streetcar #15 from the Hauptbahnhof to "Völkerschlachtdenkmal." Open Apr.-Oct. daily 10am-6pm; Nov.-Mar. 10am-5pm. Free. To ascend DM6/€3.10, students DM4/€2.05.)

Free magazines *Fritz* and *Blitz* and the superior *Kreuzer* (DM3/€1.55 at newsstands) fill you in on nightlife. **Barfußgäschen,** a street just off the Markt, serves as the see-and-be-seen bar venue for everyone from students to *Schicki-micki*s (yuppies). Just across Dittrichring on **Gottscheidstraße** and **Bosestraße** is a similar scene with a slightly younger crowd and slightly louder music. Leipzig University students spent eight years excavating this series of medieval tunnels so they could get their groove on in the ◪**Moritzbastei,** Universitätsstr. 9, which has multilevel dance floors and chill bars in fantastic cavernous rooms with vaulted brick ceilings. (☎ 702 59 13. Cover DM4-7/€2.05-3.60 for discos. Open M-F after 10am, Sa after 2pm.)

WEIMAR
☎ 03643

Weimar remains one of the most completely renovated cities in East Germany; intellectual energy resonates through the former home of Goethe, Schiller, and Herder. While countless German towns leap at any excuse to build memorials to Goethe (Goethe slept here, Goethe once asked for directions here, etc.), Weimar features the real thing: the **Goethehaus and Goethe-Nationalmuseum,** Frauenplan 1, present the poet's immaculately preserved private chambers. To get the most out of the largely unlabeled exhibits, pick up the handy English guide "Goethe's House on the Frauenplan at Weimar" (DM3/€1.55) at the desk. (Open mid-Mar. to mid-Oct. Tu-Su 9am-6pm; mid-Oct. to mid-Mar. Tu-Su 10am-4pm. Expect a wait of up to 2hr. in summer. DM10/€5.15, students and seniors DM8/€4.10.) Weimar's *other* pride and joy is the Bauhaus architectural movement, which began here; the **Bauhaus-Museum,** Theaterpl., showcases its history. (☎ 54 61 61. Open Apr.-Oct. Tu-Su 10am-6pm; Nov.-Mar. Tu-Su 10am-4:30pm. DM6/€3.10, students and seniors DM4/€2.05.) The **Neuesmuseum,** Weimarpl. 4, which opened in 2000, hosts fascinating rotating exhibits of modern art, including a clanking interactive "Terrororchestra," composed of knives, nails, and a hammer and sickle. (Open Tu-Su 10am-6pm. DM6/€3.10, students and children DM4/€2.05.) The sprawling **Park an der Ilm** was landscaped by Goethe. South of the town center in the **Historischer Friedhof,** Goethe and Schiller rest together in the basement of the **Fürstengruft** (Ducal Vault). Schiller, who died in an epidemic, was originally buried in a mass grave, but Goethe combed through the remains until he identified Schiller and had him interred in a tomb. Skeptics argued that Goethe was mistaken, so a couple of "Schillers" were placed side by side. In the 1960s, a team of Russian scientists determined that Goethe was right after all. (Cemetery open Mar.-Sept. 8am-9pm; Oct.-Feb. 8am-6pm. Tomb open mid-Mar. to mid-Oct. W-M 9am-1pm and 2-6pm; mid-Oct. to mid-Mar. W-M 10am-1pm and 2-4pm. DM4/€2.05, students and seniors DM3/€1.55.) Get a glimpse into Schiller's existence *before* death at **Schillers Wohnhaus,** Schillerstr. 12, his home during the last three years of his life. (Open mid-Mar. to mid-Oct. W-M 9am-6pm; mid-Oct. to mid-Mar. W-M 9am-4pm. DM6/€3.10, students DM4/€2.05.)

Trains run to: Dresden (3hr., 2 per hr., DM58/€29.65); Frankfurt (3hr., 1 per hr., DM78/€39.90); Leipzig (1½hr., 2 per hr., DM25.60/€13.10). To reach **Goetheplatz** (the center of the Altstadt) from the station, follow Carl-August-Allee downhill to Karl-Liebknecht-Str. which leads into Goethepl. (15min.). The **tourist office,** Marktstr. 10, across from the *Rathaus,* hands out free maps, books rooms (DM5/€2.60 fee), and offers **walking tours.** The "Weimarer Wald" desk has lots of info on **outdoor activities** in the area. (☎ 240 00. Tours daily 11am and 2pm. DM12/€7.70, students DM8/€4.10. Open Apr.-Oct. M-F 9:30am-6pm, Sa 9:30am-4pm, Su 9:30am-3pm; Nov.-Mar. M-F 10am-6pm, Sa-Su 10am-2pm.) To get to the student-run ◨**Hababusch Hostel,** Geleitstr. 4, follow Geleitstr. from Goethepl.; after it takes a sharp right, you'll come to a statue on your left. The entrance to the Hababusch is tucked in the ivied corner behind the statue. Smack in the middle of the sights, the hostel has a laid-back, communal atmosphere. (☎ 85 07 37. No breakfast, but access to a full kitchen. Key deposit DM20/€10.25. 24hr. reception. Dorms DM15/€7.70; doubles DM40/€20.45.) The **Jugendherberge Germania (HI),** Carl-August-Allee 13, is 2min. downhill from the station. (☎ 85 04 90. Sheets DM7.50/€3.85. 24hr. reception. Dorms DM27/€13.80, over 26 DM32/€16.40.) A combination cafe and gallery, **ACC,** Burgpl. 1-2, is popular with students. (Open daily noon-1am.) Students of any university can show their ID to eat cheap at **Mensa: Bauhaus-Universität** (Bauhaus University Cafeteria), Marienstr. 13/15. (Full meal DM3-5/€1.55-2.60, non-students DM8-10/€4.10-5.15. Open mid-Oct. to mid-July M-Th 7:30am-7pm, F 7:30am-5pm, Sa 11am-2pm; mid-July to mid-Oct. M-F 7:30am-4pm.) For groceries, try the **market** at Marktpl. (open M-Sa 7am-5pm) or the **Rewe grocery store,** in the basement of the *Handelshaus zu Weimar* on Theaterpl. (open M-F 7am-8pm, Sa 7am-4pm). **Postal Code:** 99423.

🔁 **DAYTRIP FROM WEIMAR: BUCHENWALD.** Two hundred fifty thousand Jews, Gypsies, homosexuals, communists, and political prisoners were imprisoned at the labor camp of Buchenwald during WWII. Although Buchenwald, only 8km from Weimar, was not intended as an extermination camp, over 50,000 died here due to harsh treatment by the SS. The **Nationale Mahnmal und Gedenkstätte Buchenwald** ("National Monument and Memorial") has two principal sights. The **KZ-Lager** refers to the remnants of the camps itself ("Konzentration-Lager" means "concentration camp" in German); the large storehouse building documents both the history of Buchenwald (1937-1945) and the general history of Nazism, including German anti-Semitism. The East-German-designed **Mahnmal** (monument) is on the other side of the hill; go straight up the main road that bisects the two large parking lots, or take the footpath uphill from the old Buchenwald Bahnhof and then continue on the main road. Many simple memorials for different groups are scattered around the camp, and the camp **archives** are open to anyone searching for records of family and friends between 1937 and 1945. Call ahead to schedule an appointment with the curator (archives ☎ (03643) 43 01 54, library (03643) 430160). Ironically, suffering in Buchenwald did not end with liberation—Soviet authorities used the site as an internment camp where more than 28,000 Germans, mostly Nazi war criminals and opponents of the Communist regime, were held until 1950. An exhibit detailing this **"Special Camp No. 2"** opened in 1997.

The best way to reach the camp is by bus #6 from Weimar's train station or Goethepl. Check the schedule carefully; some #6 buses go to "Ettersburg" rather than "Gedenkstätte Buchenwald." (M-F 1 per hr., Sa-Su every 2hr.) Buses to Weimar stop at the KZ-Lager parking lot and at the road by the *Glockenturm* (bell tower). There is an **information center** (☎(03643) 43 00; open Tu-Su May-Sept. 9am-6pm, Oct.-Apr. 8:30am-4:30pm) near the bus stop at Buchenwald, which has helpful brochures (DM0.50/€0.30), offers a walking tour (DM3.50/€1.80), and shows an excellent video with English subtitles on the hour. (Exhibits open Tu-Su May-Sept. 9:45am-5:15pm; Oct.-Apr. 8:45am-4:15pm; camp area open daily until sundown.)

EISENACH ☎ 03691

Birthplace of Johann Sebastian Bach, Eisenach is also home to one of Germany's most treasured national symbols, **Wartburg castle.** In 1521, the castle sheltered Martin Luther (disguised as a bearded noble named Junker Jörg) after his excommunication. Much of the castle's interior is unfortunately not authentically medieval—most decorations are 19th-century additions—but the Wartburg is still enchanting. From the walls or the south tower, the view is spectacular. (☎770 73. Open Mar.-Oct. daily 8:30am-5pm; Nov.-Feb. 9am-3:30pm. Mandatory German tour DM11/€5.65, students and children DM6/€3.10.) According to local tradition, Johann Sebastian stormed into the world in 1685 at the **Bachhaus,** Frauenplan 21, which recreates his family's living quarters and displays period instruments. Every 40min. a guide gives a presentation in German and English, with musical interludes, on Bach's life. (☎793 40. Open Apr.-Sept. M noon-5:45pm, Tu-Su 9am-5:45pm.; Oct.-Mar. M 1-4:45pm, Tu-Su 9am-4:45pm. DM5/€2.60, students DM4/€2.05.) Bach was baptized at the 800-year-old **Georgenkirche,** just off the Markt, where members of his family were organists for 132 years. (Open M-Sa 10am-12:30pm and 2-5pm, Su after services.) Just up the street sits the latticed **Lutherhaus,** Lutherpl. 8, young Martin's home in his school days. (☎298 30. Open Apr.-Oct. daily 9am-5pm; Nov.-Mar. 10am-5pm. DM5/€2.60, students DM2/€1.05.)

Trains run to Kassel (1½hr., 1 per hr., DM27/€13.80) and Weimar (1hr., 2 per hr., DM20.20/€10.35). The **tourist office,** Markt 2, sells maps (DM2/€1.05), offers daily city tours (2pm, DM5/€2.60), and books rooms for free. From the train station, follow Bahnhofstr. through the tunnel and angle left until you turn right onto the pedestrian Karlstr. (☎67 02 60. Open M 10am-6pm, Tu-F 9am-6pm, Sa and Su 10am-2pm.) To reach the recently renovated **Jugendherberge Arthur Becker (HI),** Mariental 24, take Bahnhofstr. from the station to Wartburger Allee, which runs into Mariental. (☎74 32 59. Breakfast included. Sheets DM7.50/€3.85. Reception 7am-10pm.

Tell the desk if you'll be out past 11pm. Dorm beds DM26.50/€13.55, over 26 DM31.50/€16.10.) For groceries, head to **Edeka supermarket** on Johannispl. (open M-F 7am-7pm, Sa 7am-2pm), or to **Nimm's mit supermarket** in the train station (open M-F 5:30am-8pm, Sa-Su 8am-8pm). Near the train station, **Café Moritz**, Bahnhofstr. 7, serves Thüringer specialities (DM8-15/€4.10-7.70) and sinful ice cream delicacies. (Open May-Oct. M-F 8am-9pm, Sa-Su 10am-9pm; Nov.-Apr. M-F 8am-7pm, Sa-Su 10am-7pm.) The pizza and pasta at the centrally-located **La Fontana**, Georgenstr. 22, are a steal at DM5/€2.60. (Open Su-Th 11:30am-2:30pm and 5-9pm, F-Sa 11:30am-2:30pm and 5pm-midnight.) **Postal Code:** 99817.

NORTHERN GERMANY

Although once a favored vacation spot for East Germans, Mecklenburg-Vorpommern, the northeasternmost portion of Germany, has unfortunately suffered in recent years from economic depression. Just to the west, Schleswig-Holstein, which borders Denmark, has always been driven by its port towns and retains close cultural and commercial ties with Scandinavia. To the west, Bremen (along with Bremerhaven) constitutes Germany's smallest *Land.*

HANOVER (HANNOVER)   ☎ 0511

Hanover is marked by its unabashed urban modernity; despite its relatively small size, this town puts on a show of culture and cosmopolitan charm to rival cities twice as large. From art exhibits to zoos, shopping arcades to pubs, the heartbeat of the city is in the people of today, not the buildings of before. The 2000 World Fair, located here, polished and streamlined the city, and the afterglow shines in the sports stadium, museums, and tourist services.

⛎ TRANSPORTATION. Trains leave at least every hr. to: Amsterdam (4½-5hr., DM80/€41); Berlin (2½hr., DM80/€41); Frankfurt (3hr., DM160/€82); Hamburg (1½hr., DM50/€25.60); Cologne (2hr., DM100/€51.15); Munich (9hr., DM250/€127.85). **ÜSTRA,** Hanover's **public transportation** system, is thorough and fast. Tickets are available from machines or drivers (*Kurzstrecke* (3 stops) DM2/€1.05; single ride DM3-5/€1.55-2.60 depending on zone; day ticket DM6-10/€3.10-5.15.) Remember to punch your ticket at the blue machines, or risk a DM60/€30.70 fine. For more info and maps, call the **ÜSTRA customer service office** (☎ 16 68 22 38) in the Kröpcke station. (Open M-W and F 8am-6pm, Th 8am-7pm, Sa 9am-2pm.)

⃠ PRACTICAL INFORMATION. To reach the **tourist office,** Ernst-August-Pl. 2, start from the train station (facing the large rear of the king's splendid steed) and turn right. (☎ 16 84 97 00. Open M-F 9am-7pm, Sa 9:30am-3pm.) For **currency exchange, ReiseBank,** inside the main exit of the train station, has long hours and decent commissions. (Open M-Sa 7am-10pm, Su 9am-10pm.) Get on the **Internet** at **Das Netz,** at the intersection of Gustav-Bratke-Allee and Humboldt. (☎ 169 70 43. Open daily noon-midnight. DM6/3.10 per hr.) The **post office** is in the same building as the tourist office. (Open M-F 9am-8pm, Sa 9am-4pm.) **Postal Code:** 30159.

⛽⃠ ACCOMMODATIONS AND FOOD. To reach **Naturfreundehaus Stadtheim,** Hermann-Bahlsen-Allee 8, take U3 (dir.: Lahe) or U7(dir.: Fasanenkrug) to "Spannhagengarten," walk 15m back to the intersection, turn left on Hermann-Bahlsen-Allee, and follow the signs. (☎ 69 14 93. Excellent breakfast included. Reception 8am-noon and 3-10pm. No curfew. DM49/€25.05.) For **Naturfreundehaus Misburg,** Am Fahrhorstfelde 50, take U3 (dir.: Lahe) to the end, bus #124 to "Misburg Garten," and bus #631 to "Waldfriedhof"; walk up Am Fahrhorstfelde to the very end, go 10m farther on the trail, and follow the sign. (☎ 58 05 37. Breakfast included. Sheets DM7.50/€3.85. Reception Tu-F after noon. No curfew. Reservations necessary. DM39.50/€20.20.) For **Hotel am Thielenplatz,** Thielenpl. 2, take a left onto Joachimstr. from the station and go one block to Thielenpl. All rooms have TV; rooms on the top floor have panoramic views of the city. (☎32 76 91 93. Breakfast included. Check-out 11:30am. Singles with shower DM110-150/€56.25-76.70; doubles with shower DM180-220/€93-€112.50; cheaper on weekdays.) Note that the *Naturfreundehäuser* are on the outskirts of town, where walkways are deserted and poorly lit after dark; use caution late at night.

Kröpcke, the food court cafe at the center of the pedestrian zone, provides small snacks (from DM2.50/€1.30) or sit-down meals (from DM13.50/€6.90). ■**Jalda,** Limmerstr. 97, serves a combination of Italian, Greek, and Arabic dishes (DM14-17/€7.20-8.70), and all-you-can-eat schnitzel (DM14/€7.20) Friday and Saturday. (Open M-Th and Su 11:30am-midnight, F-Sa noon-1am.) **Uwe's Hannenfaß Hanover,** Knochenhauerstr. 36, in the center of the Altstadt, serves traditional German fare (around DM8.90/€4.55) and great brew. (Open daily 4pm-2am.) **Spar supermarkets** sit by the Lister Meile and Kröpcke U-Bahn stops. (Open M-F 7am-7pm, Sa 8am-2pm.) From the *Hauptbahnhof,* head to the **Markt-halle,** where a variety of snacks, meals, and booze awaits. (Open M-W 7am-6pm, Th-F 7am-8pm, Sa 7am-4pm.)

◨◪. **SIGHTS AND ENTERTAINMENT.** With great economic vigor, a wealth of museums, and a tradition of festivals, Hanover reigns as the political and cultural capital of Lower Saxony. Many sights stand in the **Altstadt;** from the train station, walk down Bahnhofstr. and continue along as it becomes Karmarschstr., then take a right on Knochenhauer Str.—an old 14th-century church, the brick **Marktkirche,** will be on your left. (Open daily 10am-4pm; check for concerts.) Used for official purposes until 1913, Hanover's former **Rathaus** has become a shopping area and cafe. Just gawk at the lovely exterior; everything inside is pricey. On the outskirts of the Altstadt stands the spectacular **Neues Rathaus;** take the elevator (DM3/€1.55, students DM2/€1.05) up the tower for a great view of the city. (Rathaus open May-Sept. M-F 8am-10pm, Sa-Su 10am-10pm.) Right next door, the ■**Kestner-Museum,** Trammpl. 3, features medieval, Renaissance, and ancient arts. (☎ 16 84 21 20. Open Tu and Th-Su 11am-6pm, W 11am-8pm. DM5/€2.60, students DM3/€1.55; F free.) The nearby ■**Sprengel Museum,** Kurt-Schwitters-Pl., at the corner of the Maschsee and Maschpark, near the Neues Rathaus, is a 20th-century art-lover's dream with works by James Turrell, Henry Moore, Dalí, Picasso, Magritte, and Horst Antes. (☎16 84 38 75. Open Tu 10am-8pm, W-Su 10am-6pm. Permanent collection DM7/€3.60, students DM3.50/€1.80; excellent special exhibits DM12/€6.15, students DM8/€4.10.) The gems of Hanover are the three paradisical **Herrenhausen gardens.** The largest, the geometrically trimmed **Großer Garten,** holds the **Große Fontäne,** Europe's highest fountain, which shoots an astounding 80m. (Fountain spurts M-F 11am-noon and 3-5pm, Sa-Su 11am-noon and 2-5pm. Garden open Apr.-Oct. 8am-8pm; Nov.-Mar. 8am-dusk. Entrance DM5/€2.60.) The **Georgengarten** (open 24hr.) is a maze of open fields, while the **Berggarten** showcases an indoor rain forest. (Open M-Th and Sa 9am-8pm, F and Su 9am-11pm. DM16/€8.20, students DM10/€5.15.)

When the sun goes down, the university crowds flock to the area of **Linden-Nord,** between **Goetheplatz** and **Leinaustraße. The Loft,** Georgstr. 50b, is packed with students on the weekends. (Open M-Th 9pm-2am, F-Sa 9pm-5am, Su 9pm-2am.) **Osho Disco,** Raschpl. 7L, is a great place to meet (pick up) folks. Every Wednesday is "Forever Young" night—no cover for anyone over 30. (Cover W and Su DM5/€2.60, Th-Sa DM8/€4.10. Open W-Su at 10pm.) Take a (mental) trip to Ireland at **Finnegan's Wake,** Theaterstr. 6, which has a daily Happy Hour (4-6pm) and live Irish music at 9pm on Fridays and Saturdays. (Open M-F 4pm-2am, Sa-Su noon-2am.)

HAMBURG ☎040

The largest port city in Germany, Hamburg radiates an inimitable recklessness. Here the progressive and perverse merge, and few corners of this driven city escape the effects of its indecent allure. Hamburg gained the status of Free Imperial City in 1618 and proudly retains its autonomy and power as one of Germany's sixteen *Länder.* Restoration and riots determined the post-WWII landscape, but today Hamburg has become a haven for contemporary artists and intellectuals as well as revelling party-goers.

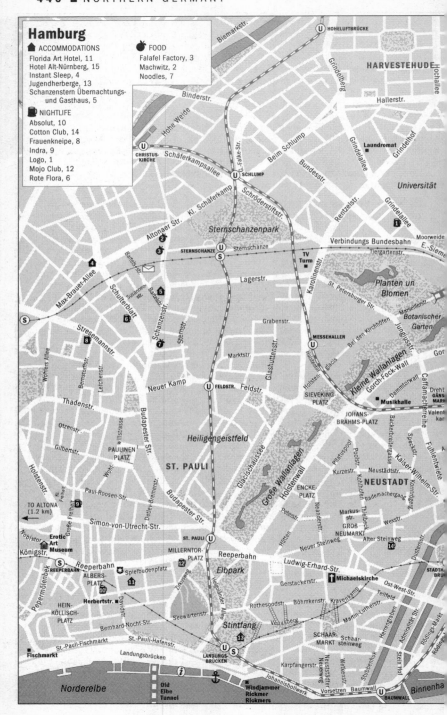

Hamburg

▲ **ACCOMMODATIONS**
Florida Art Hotel, 11
Hotel Alt-Nürnberg, 15
Instant Sleep, 4
Jugendherberge, 13
Schanzenstern Übernachtungs-
und Gasthaus, 5

● **FOOD**
Falafel Factory, 3
Machwitz, 2
Noodles, 7

🛏 **NIGHTLIFE**
Absolut, 10
Cotton Club, 14
Frauenkneipe, 8
Indra, 9
Logo, 1
Mojo Club, 12
Rote Flora, 6

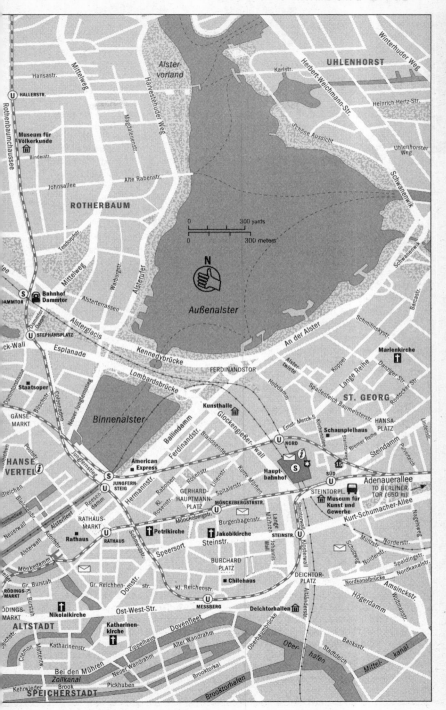

▛ TRANSPORTATION

Flights: Lufthansa (☎01 803 803 803) and **Air France** (☎50 75 24 59) are the 2 main airlines at **Fuhlsbüttel Airport** (☎507 50). **Jasper** buses (☎227 10 60) run to the airport every 20min. (Daily 5am-9:20pm. DM9.40/€4.80.) Or, take U1 or S1 to "Ohlsdorf," then take an **express bus** to the airport (every 10min., daily 4:30am-1am, DM3.90/€2).

Trains: The **Hauptbahnhof** handles most traffic with hourly connections to: **Amsterdam** (5½hr., 3 per day, DM132/€67.50); **Berlin** (2½hr., DM88/€45); **Copenhagen** (4½hr., DM126/€64.50); **Frankfurt** (3¾hr., DM191/€97.70); **Hanover** (1¼hr., 3 per hr., DM67€34.25); **Munich** (5½hr., DM260/€133). 2 other stations, **Dammtor** (near the university) and **Altona** (in the west) service the city; frequent trains and the S-Bahn connect the 3 stations. **Lockers** are available 24hr. for DM2-4/€1.05-2.05 per day; just follow the overhead signs.

Buses: The **ZOB** is on Steintorpl. across from the Hauptbahnhof, between McDonald's and the Museum für Kunst und Gewerbe. To: **Berlin** (3¼hr., 8 per day, DM43/€22); **Copenhagen** (5 1/2hr., 2 per day, DM59/€30.20); **Paris** (12½hr., 1 per day, DM109/€55.75). Open M-F 9am-8pm, Sa 9:30am-1:30pm and 4-8pm, Su 4-8pm.

Public Transportation: HVV operates an efficient U-Bahn, S-Bahn, and bus network. Most single tickets within the downtown area cost DM1.90/€1, but can vary depending on where you go and what transport you take. 1-day ticket DM9.80/€5, 3-day tickets DM24/€12.30. All tickets can be bought at orange *Automaten*, but consider buying a **Hamburg Card** instead (see **Tourist Office**, below).

Car Rental: A number of car rental agencies have offices in the Hauptbahnhof. Avis offers cars starting at DM463/€236.75 per week, including insurance and 24hr. emergency assistance. (☎32 87 38 00; fax 32 87 38 38).

Hitchhiking: *Let's Go* does not recommend hitchhiking as a safe means of transportation. Locals warn that hitchhiking is extremely dangerous in Hamburg.

▟ ❷ ORIENTATION AND PRACTICAL INFORMATION

Hamburg's city center sits between the Elbe and the two city lakes, **Außenalster** and **Binnenalster.** Most major sights lie between the **St. Pauli Landungsbrücken** port area in the west and the Hauptbahnhof in the east. Both the **Nordbahnhof** and **Südbahnhof** U-Bahn stations exit onto the Hauptbahnhof.

The **Hanseviertel** is an area thick with banks, shops, art galleries, and auction houses, while the nearby shipping canals manage to give the quarter a nearly-Venetian charm. North of the downtown, the **university** dominates the **Dammtor** area and sustains a vibrant community of students and intellectuals. To the west of the university, the **Sternschanze** neighborhood is a politically active community home to artists, squatters, and a sizeable Turkish population. The **Altona** district, with its own major train station, was once a Jewish community and an independent city ruled by Denmark; as power shifted, these groups were ousted. At the south end of town, an entirely different atmosphere reigns in **St. Pauli,** where the raucous **Fischmarkt** (fish market) is juxtaposed by the equally wild (and no less smelly) **Reeperbahn,** home to Hamburg's infamous sex trade.

Tourist Offices: The Hauptbahnhof office, in the Wandelhalle near the Kirchenallee exit (☎30 05 12 01; info@hamburg-tourism.de; www.hamburg-tourism.de), gives free maps, books rooms for a DM6/€3.10 fee, and sells the Hamburg Card (DM12.80/€6.55 per day, DM26.50/€13.55 per week), which provides unlimited access to public transportation, reduced admission to most museums, and discounts on bus and boat tours. Open daily 7am-11pm. Tourist offices are also located below the Rathaus (take the U-bahn to "Rathaus"; open M-F 8am-7pm, Sa 10am-4pm) and at the airport (take bus #110 or the Airport Express; open daily 6am-11pm).

Consulates: Canada, Ballindamm 35 (☎460 02 70). M-F 9:30am-12:30pm. **Ireland,** Feldbrunnenstr. 43 (☎44 18 61 13); U1 to "Hallerstr." Open M-F 9am-1pm. **New Zealand,** Domstr. 19, im Zürich-haus (☎442 55 50). Open M-Th 9am-5:30pm, F 9am-4:30pm. **UK,** Harvestehuder Weg 8a (☎410 72 50); U1 to "Hallerstr." Open M-Th 9am-4pm, F 9am-3pm. **US,** Alsterufer 26-7 (☎41 17 11 00), on the Außenalster's west side. Open M-F 8:30am-5pm, closed on American and German holidays.

Currency Exchange: ReiseBank, on the 2nd fl. of the Hauptbahnhof near the Kirchenallee exit, offers Western Union, cashes traveler's checks (commission 1%, minimum US$7.50 for American Express; commission 1%, minimum US$10 for other types), and exchanges money for a DM5/€2.60 fee. Open daily 7:30am-10pm.

American Express: Ballindamm 39, 20095 Hamburg (☎30 39 38 11 12; fax 30 39 38 12.) Take the U-Bahn to "Jungfernstieg." Letters held for cardmembers up to 5 weeks; all banking services. Open M-F 9am-6pm, Sa 10am-1pm.

Gay and Lesbian Resources: Hein und Fiete (☎24 03 33), Pulverteich 21. Walk down Steindammstr. away from the Hauptbahnhof and turn right on Pulverteich; it's in the rainbow-striped building. Open M-F 4-9pm, Sa 4-7pm. **Magnus-Hirschfeld-Centrum,** Borgweg 8 (☎279 00 69), offers daily counseling sessions. U-Bahn #3 or bus #108 to "Borgweg." Open M and F 2-6pm, Tu-W 7-10pm.

Laundromat: Schnell und Sauber, Grindelallee 158, in the university district. Take S21 or S31 to "Dammtor." Wash DM7/€3.60. Open daily 7am-10pm.

Emergency: Police, ☎110. There's also a police station on the **Reeperbahn** at the corner of Davidstr. and Spielbudenplatz (☎428 65 15 10). **Fire** and **Ambulance,** ☎112.

Pharmacy: The staff at the **Senator-Apotheke,** Hachmannpl. 14 (☎32 75 27 or 33 79 76), speaks English. Exit the Hauptbahnhof on Kirchenallee and turn right. Open M-F 7am-8pm, Sa 8am-6pm.

Internet Access: Cyberb@r is located on the 3rd fl. of the gigantic **Karstadt** department store on Mönckebergstr. DM2/€1.05 for 15min., DM3/€1.55 for 30min.

Post Office: McPaper & Co. AG, at the Kirchenallee exit of the Hauptbahnhof, 20097 Hamburg. Open M-F 8am-10pm, Sa 9am-6pm, Su 10am-6pm. Address mail to be held: Postlagernde Briefe für FirstName SURNAME, Post Hamburg-Hauptbahnhof, **20099** Hamburg, Germany.

ACCOMODATIONS AND CAMPING

Hamburg's lodgings tend to cost a pretty penny, but with a bit of persistence you can find a sufficient place for a reasonable price. A slew of small, relatively cheap *Pensionen* line **Steindamm, Steintorweg, Bremer Weg,** and **Bremer Reihe,** around the Hauptbahnhof. While the area is filled with drug addicts and wannabe-*mafiosi*, the hotels are for the most part safe. The Sternschanze area contains more attractive options a bit farther from both the good and the bad aspects of the Hauptbahnhof area. Check the tourist office's free *Hotelführer* for more info.

■ **Jugendherberge auf dem Stintfang (HI),** Alfred-Wegener-Weg 5 (☎31 34 88; jh-stint-fang@t-online.del). Take S1, S2, S3, or U3 to "Landungsbrücke," then head up the hill on the wooded path. Clean and well-furnished rooms look out on the woods or the harbor. Breakfast and sheets included. Laundry DM5/€2.60. **Internet** DM5/€2.60 for 25min. Reception 12:30-2am. Lockout 9:30-11:30am. Curfew 2am. Call ahead. Dorms DM30.50/€15.60, over 26 DM35.50/€18.15; doubles DM77/€39.40, over 26 DM87/€44.50; quads DM134/€68.50, over 26 DM154/€78.75. Nonmembers pay a DM6/€3.10 surcharge.

■ **Schanzenstern Übernachtungs-und Gasthaus,** Bartelsstr. 12 (☎439 84 41; fax 439 34 13; info@schanzerstern.de; www.schanzenstern.de). Take U3 to "Sternschanze," then turn left onto Schanzenstr., right on Susannenstr., and left onto Bartelsstr. Located in an electrifying neighborhood of students, working-class Turks, and left-wing dissenters, the hostel's rooms are clean, quiet, and bright. Breakfast buffet DM7-11/€3.60-5.65. Wheelchair accessible. Reception 6:30-2am. No curfew. Reservations a must in the summer. Dorms DM33/€16.90; singles DM65/€33.25; doubles DM95/€48.60; triples DM115/€58.80; quads DM140/€71.60; quints DM175/€89.50.

Florida the Art Hotel, Spielbudenpl. 22 (☎31 43 93). U3 to "St. Pauli," or S1 or S3 to "Reeperbahn." Each room of this immaculate hotel reflects the work of a different artist-architect. Breakfast included and available until 5pm. Check-out 4pm. Call ahead. Singles DM110/€56.25; doubles DM165/€84.40.

Instant Sleep, Max-Brauer-Allee 277 (☎43 18 23 10; www.instantsleep.de). S3, S21, S31, or U3 to "Sternschanze." From the station, go straight on Schanzenstr., turn left on Altonaer Str., and follow it until it becomes Max-Brauer-Allee. This backpacker hostel is a big happy family: rooms are often left open while guests lounge together or cook dinner in the communal kitchen. Sheets DM5/€2.60. **Internet** DM2.50/€1.30 for 15min. Reception 9am-2pm. Call ahead. Dorms DM29/€14.85; singles DM49/€25.05; doubles DM80/€40.90; triples DM108/€55.25.

Hotel Alt-Nürnberg, Steintorweg 15 (☎24 60 24; fax 280 46 34). From the station, go right on Kirchenallee and left onto Steintorweg. Each clean, safe, and smallish room features a telephone, some with TV. Breakfast included. Call ahead. Singles DM60/€30.70, with shower DM90/€46; doubles DM90/€46, DM130/€66.50.

Camping: Campingplatz Rosemarie Buchholz, Kieler Str. 374 (☎540 45 32; fax 540 25 36; www.camping-buchholz.de). From Altona train station, take bus #182 or 183 to "Basselweg," then walk 100m in the same direction as traffic. Breakfast DM7/€3.60; order rolls in advance. Showers DM1.50/€0.80. Reception 8am-noon and 2-10pm. Check-out noon. Quiet hours 10pm-7am. Call ahead. DM7/€3.60 per person, DM12.50/€6.40 per tent.

🯁 FOOD

The most interesting part of town from a culinary standpoint is **Sternschanze,** where Turkish fruit stands, Asian *Imbiße,* and avant-garde cafes entice hungry passersby with good food and great atmosphere. **Schulterblatt, Susannenstraße,** and **Schanzenstraße** host a slew of funky cafes and restaurants, while slightly cheaper establishments abound in the **university** area, especially along **Rentzelstraße, Grindelhof,** and **Grindelallee.** The university itself offers tasty food at very low prices as well as a chance to get an inside look at German student life. In **Altona,** the pedestrian zone leading up to the train station is packed with ethnic food stands and produce shops. Check out the market inside Altona's massive **Mercado** mall, which includes everything from sushi bars to Portuguese fast-food.

Noodles, Schanzenstr. 2-4 (☎439 28 40). Noodles serves up veggie entrees and innovative pastas. Try the broccoli with cheese and ham (DM12/€6.15). Open M-Th and Su 10am-1am, F-Sa 10am-3am, Su brunch 10am-3pm.

Falafel Factory, Schanzenstr., right across from the S-Bahn station. An excellent option for vegetarians, this tiny Lebanese *Imbiß* makes falafels fresh to order. Basic falafel DM5/€2.60, with one topping DM6/€3.10. Open daily; variable times.

Machwitz, Schanzenstr. 121 (☎43 81 77). Join the hip student crowd in the funky angular interior. Main dishes DM12-17/€6.15-8.70. Open Su-Th 10am-4am, F-Sa 10am-8am. Kitchen closes at midnight during the week and at 2am F-Sa.

University Mensa, Schlüterstr. 7. S21 or S31 to "Dammtor," then turn left on Rothenbaumchaussee, left on Moorweidenstr., and right onto Schlüterstr. This tasty and affordable university cafe offers coffee and a giant piece of cake for DM3.30/€1.70. Meals DM3-6/€1.55-3.10 with student ID, about 1DM/€0.50 more for non-students. Open M-Th 10am-7:30pm, F 10am-7pm.

🯁 SIGHTS

ALTSTADT

Historical sites and modern commercialism abound in Hamburg's Altstadt. Within walking distance of each other are imposing churches, government buildings, and winding roads with boutiques to sate the casual browser and the serious shopper.

GROßE MICHAELSKIRCHE. The gargantuan 18th-century Michaelskirche is the symbol of Hamburg, and with good reason. The turning times that raised the city razed the church as well: lightning, accidents, and Allied bombs destroyed the church again and again. Renovated in 1996 along old designs, the church's interior and scalloped walls are reminiscent of a concert hall. The momentous tower, accessible by foot or elevator, is the only one of the city's six spires that may be climbed. On weekends, the tower is used to project a multimedia presentation about Hamburg's millennial existence onto a 5m high screen. (☎ 37 67 81 00. Screenings Th-Su every hr. 12:30-3:30pm. Organ music Apr.-Aug. daily at noon and 5pm. Admission to tower or church DM5/€2.60, students DM2.50/€1.30. Open May-Oct. M-Sa 9am-6pm, Su 11:30am-5:30pm; Nov.-Apr. M-Sa 10am-4:30pm, Su 11:30am-4:30pm.)

RATHAUS. The town hall, a copper-spired neo-Renaissance monstrosity, serves as the political center of Hamburg. Inside one can browse through various displays of the city's history. The Rathausmarkt in front hosts festivities from political demonstrations to medieval fairs. (☎ 428 31 24 70. Tours of the Rathaus in German every 30min. M-Th 10am-3pm, F-Su 10am-1pm. Tours in English every hr. M-Th 10:15am-3:15pm, F-Su 10:15am-1:15pm. Free.)

NIKOLAIKIRCHE. Devastated by an Allied bomb in 1943, the neo-Gothic cathedral remains in its hollowed-out state as "a sign for peace." Exhibition of its history open M-F 10am-5pm, Sa-Su 11am-4pm (DM3/€1.55). The buildings along nearby **Trostbrücke** sport huge copper models of clipper ships on their spires—a testament to Hamburg's sea-trade wealth. (Just south of the Rathaus, off Ost-West-Str.)

SPEICHERSTADT. East of the docks near the copper dome of the **St. Katherinenkirche** lies the historic warehouse district of Speicherstadt. This elegant, late-19th-century brick storehouses are filled with cargo, spices, and other sea-faring goods. (Church ☎ 28 05 57 57. Open daily 9am-5pm; free organ concerts W at 12:30pm.)

MÖNKEBERGSTRAßE. Mönkebergstr., Hamburg's shopping zone, stretches from the Rathaus to the Hauptbahnhof and is punctuated by two spires. The first belongs to the **St. Petrikirche**, the oldest church in Hamburg. (Open M-Tu and Th-F 10am-6:30pm, W 10am-7pm, Sa 10am-5pm, Su 9am-9pm. Free concerts W 5:15pm.) The second tower (now under reconstruction) belongs to **St. Jakobikirche**, known for its 14th-century Arp-Schnittger organ. (☎ 32 77 49. Open M-Sa 10am-5pm. Services Su.)

BEYOND THE ALTSTADT

ST. PAULI LANDUNGSBRÜCKEN. Hamburg's harbor, the largest port in Germany, lights up at night with ships from all over the world. After sailing the East Indies, the gigantic tri-masted Windjammer **Rickmer Rickmers** was docked at Pier 1 and preserved as a museum ship. Meticulously restored cabin quarters give a feel for life at sea and the work and trials of a sailor. (☎ 35 69 31 19. Open daily 10am-5:30pm. DM6/€3.10, students DM5/€2.60.) The elevator to the old **Elbtunnel**, which was built 1907-1911 and runs 1200m under the Elbe, protrudes through the floor of the building behind Pier 6. Descend glass elevators to the tunnel, now used by commuters.

PLANTEN UN BLOMEN. Wander into this huge expanse of manicured flower gardens and trees for some fresh air. (Open daily 7am-11pm.) For those looking for more active entertainment, daily performances ranging from Irish step-dancing to Hamburg's police orchestra shake the outdoor **Musikpavillon** from May to Sept.; there are also nightly **Wasserlichtkonzerte,** in which the fountains are bathed in rainbows of light. (May-Aug. 10pm; Sept. 9pm.)

ALSTER LAKES. To the north of the city center, the two Alster lakes, bordered by tree-lined paths and parks, provide refuge from crowded Hamburg. Elegant promenades and commercial façades surround **Binnenalster**, while windsurfers, sailboats, and paddleboats dominate the larger **Außenalster**. Ferries, more personal than the bigger Hamburg boats, depart here.

FISCHMARKT. Veritable anarchy reigns as charismatic vendors haul in and hawk huge amounts of fish, produce, and other goods. Don't shy away if you dislike fish—about 90% of the goods are something else. (U- or S-Bahn to "Landungsbrücken" or S-Bahn to "Königstr." Open Su 6-10am; off-season Su 7-10am.)

BEYOND THE CENTER

Though not in the city center, two very different testaments to the atrocities of the Nazi regime are accessible by public transportation.

GEDENKSTÄTTE BULLENHUSER DAMM UND ROSENGARTEN. Surrounded by warehouses, the schoolhouse serves as a memorial to 20 Jewish children brought here from Auschwitz for "testing" and murdered by the S.S. only hours before Allied troops arrived. Visitors are invited to plant a rose for the children in the flower garden behind the school, where plaques with the children's photographs line the fence. (Bullenhuser Damm 92. S21 to "Rothenburgsort." Follow the signs to Bullenhuser Damm along Ausschlaeger Bildeich and across a bridge; the school is 200m down. ☎78 32 95. Open Su 10am-7pm and Th 2-8pm. Free.)

KZ NEUENGAMME. An idyllic agricultural village east of Hamburg provided the backdrop for the Neuengamme concentration camp, where Nazis killed 55,000 prisoners through slave labor. In 1989, the Hamburg senate built a memorial on the site. Banners inscribed with the names and death-dates of the victims, along with four 500-page books listing their names, hang in the **Haus des Gedenkens**. (Jean-Doldier-Weg. Take S21 to "Bergedorf," then bus #227 to "Jean-Doldier-Weg." ☎428 96 03. Open May-Oct. Tu-F 10am-4pm, Sa-Su 10am-6pm).

🏛 MUSEUMS

The one- or three-day **Hamburg Card** (see p. 442) provides access to most of these museums, with the exception of the Deichtorhallen and the Erotic Art Museum. The free newspaper *Museumswelt Hamburg* lists museum exhibitions and events and can be picked up at the tourist offices.

Hamburger Kunsthalle, Glockengießerwall 1 (☎428 54 26 12). Turn left from the "City" exit of the Hauptbahnhof and cross the street. This sprawling first-rate art museum requires many hours to appreciate in full. The lower level presents the Old Masters, classical modern art, and extensive temporary displays of private collections. Open Tu-W and F-Su 10am-6pm, Th 10am-9pm. DM15/€7.70, students DM10/€5.15.

Deichtorhallen Hamburg, Deichtorstr. 1-2 (☎32 10 30). U1 to "Steinstr." Follow signs from the subway station; look for two entwined iron circles. Hamburg's contemporary art scene resides here in two buildings that were once fruit market halls. New exhibits each season showcase up-and-coming artists. Open Tu-Su 11am-6pm, Th 10am-9pm. Each building DM10/€5.15, students DM8/€4.10.

Erotic Art Museum, Nobistor 10a (☎31 78 41 26). S1 or S3 to "Reeperbahn." Follow the silver sperm painted on the floor as they lead you through mazes of rooms full of pictures and figurines of people in sexual contortions. Going up the stairs, the exhibitions move from the Kama Sutra and aristocratic displays of lust towards modernity, interchanging pornographic photos with impressionistic art. Open Su-Th 10am-midnight, F-Sa 10am-1am. DM15/€7.70. Under 16 not admitted.

Hamburger Museum für Völkerkunde, Rothenbaumchaussee 64 (☎428 48 25 24). U1 to "Hallerstr." Diverse world cultures unravel their ancient tales through traditional attire, weaponry, and religious artifacts. Egyptian mummies preserve a view of long-dead customs while in the next room stunning photographs attempt to capture the character of a modern "European." Open Tu-Su 10am-6pm, Th 10am-9pm. DM9/€4.60, Hamburg card holders DM4.50/€2.30, students and seniors DM4/€2.05; F half-price.

🎵 🎭 ENTERTAINMENT AND NIGHTLIFE

MUSIC AND FESTIVALS

The **Staatsoper**, Große Theaterstr. 36, houses one of the best opera companies in Germany, emphasizing classical works; the associated **ballet company** is the acknowledged dance powerhouse of the nation. (☎356 80. U1 to "Stephansplatz." Open M-F 10am-6:30pm, Sa 10am-2pm.) **Orchestras** abound—the Philharmonie, the Norddeutscher Rundfunk Symphony, and Hamburg Symphonia all perform at the **Musikhalle** on Johannes-Brahms-Pl. (Take U2 to "Gänsemarkt" or "Messehallen." ☎34 69 20; www.musikhalle-hamburg.de.) Live music prospers in Hamburg, satisfying all tastes. Superb traditional jazz swings at the **Cotton Club** and **Indra** (see **Nightlife**, below). On Sunday mornings, good and bad alike play at the **Fischmarkt**. The **West Port** jazz festival, Germany's largest, runs in mid-July; call the Koncertskasse (☎32 87 38 54) for information. The most anticipated festival is the **G-Move** (the "Love Parade of the North"), which grooves into town early in June. Check www.g-move.com for dates and performers.

NIGHTLIFE

Sternschanze and St. Pauli areas host Hamburg's unrepressed nightlife scene. The infamous **Reeperbahn**, a long boulevard which makes Las Vegas look like church on a Sunday, is the spinal cord of **St. Pauli;** it's lined with sex shops, strip joints, peep shows, and other establishments seeking to satisfy every lust. Though the Reeperbahn is reasonably safe for both men and women, it is not recommended for women to venture into the adjacent streets. **Herbertstraße,** Hamburg's only remaining legalized prostitution strip, runs parallel to the Reeperbahn, and is open only to men over 18. The prostitutes flaunting their flesh on Herbertstr. are licensed professionals required to undergo health inspections, while the streetwalkers elsewhere are venereal roulette wheels.

Students trying to avoid the hypersexed Reeperbahn head north to the trendy streets of **Sternschanze.** Unlike St. Pauli, these areas are centered around cafes and weekend extravaganzas of an alternative flavor. Much of Hamburg's **gay scene** is located in the **St. Georg** area of the city, near Berliner Tor. Gay and straight bars in this area are more welcoming and classier than those in the Reeperbahn. In general, clubs open late and close late, with some techno and trance clubs remaining open until noon the following day. *Szene,* available at newsstands (DM5/€2.60), lists events and parties, while the gay magazine *hinnerk* lists gay and lesbian events and is available for free at the gay tourist offices.

STERNSCHANZE

🏚 **Rote Flora,** Schulterblatt 71 (☎439 54 13). Held together both figuratively and literally by the spray paint and posters that cover all its vertical surfaces, this looming mansion of graffiti serves as the nucleus of the Sternschanze scene. Cafe open M-F 6-10pm. Club opening times vary. Weekend cover DM8/€4.10 or more.

Logo, Grindelallee 5 (☎410 56 58). This club would be hard-pressed to find a logo for its huge range of live music—from folk and country to alternative pop. Doors open 8pm, music starts 9pm. Cover varies.

Frauenkneipe, Stresemannstr. 60 (☎43 63 77), S-Bahn #21 or 3 to "Holstenstr." Visitors disconcerted by the Reeperbahn and its objectification of women will find another option here. For women only, gay or straight. Open Su-M and W-F from 8pm, Sa from 9pm.

ST. PAULI

Mojo Club, Reeperbahn 1 (☎43 30 39 or 0 700 MOJOCLUB). This club is adorned with artsy paper lamps and filled with stylish students. The attached **Jazz Café** (☎319 19 99) attracts the trendy. DM12/€6.15 cover on weekends. Usually open 11pm-4am.

Indra, Große Freiheit 64 (☎0174 497 46123) The friendly management opens its arms to exhausted Reeperbahn clientele and offers them a haven of calm live jazz. Cover DM5-10/€2.60-€5.15. Open W-Su from 9pm; music starts around 11pm.

Cotton Club, Alter Steinweg 10 (☎34 38 78; fax 348 01 23); U3 to "Rödingsmarkt." Dixie, swing and big band jazz in a warmly lit and comfortable setting with a mostly older clientele. Cover DM10/€5.15 for local bands, around DM20/€10.30 for guest bands. Open M-Th 8pm-midnight and F-Sa 8pm-1am. Shows start at 8:30pm.

Absolut, Hans-Albers-Pl. 15 (☎317 34 00), hosts the gay scene Sa nights as it spins mostly pop to an overwhelmingly attractive under-30 crowd until well after the sun is up. Cover DM10-15/€5.15-€7.70. Open F 11pm-5am, Sa 11pm-6:30am.

🗲 DAYTRIPS FROM HAMBURG

LÜNEBURG HEATH (LÜNEBURGER HEIDE)

To see the Heide, a bike is your best bet. Check the bookstore for extensive and detailed maps of major bike tours in the area. The most popular route is an 80km tour leaving from Luneburg that winds along main roads and through the endless woods and pastures of the suburbs and countryside.

The shrub-covered Lüneburger Heide stretches between the Elbe and Aller rivers. In the undulating countryside, green gives way to purple from July to Sept., when the bushes flower. All of Germany comes here to bike, hike, motor, and frolic in the late summer. The most important regional towns are **Lüneburg** and **Celle.** The staff at the **AG Urlaub und Freizeit auf dem Lande,** Lindrooperstr. 63, Verden-Aller 272380 (☎04231 96650), in Lüneberg provides information on Heu-Hotels ("hay hotels"), functioning barns with rooms for travelers for around DM20/€10.25. You sleep in the hay (hence the name), so bring a sleeping bag, but all Heu-Hotels have showers and toilets, and many are surprisingly luxurious.

LÜBECK   ☎0451

Lübeck is easily Schleswig-Holstein's most beautiful city—you'd never guess that the greater part of the city was razed in WWII. The town's present appearance is due to a painstaking reconstruction undertaken in the 1950s. In its heyday, Lübeck was the capital of the Hanseatic league, controlling trade across Northern Europe. Though no longer a center of political and commercial influence, Lübeck remains home to stunning churches, unusual cultural sites, and delicious, sugary marzipan.

▐▇▐ TRANSPORTATION AND PRACTICAL INFORMATION. Trains depart frequently for Berlin (3¼hr., 1 per hr., DM97/€49.60) and Hamburg (45min., 2 per hr., DM17/€8.70). Avoid the privately owned, expensive tourist office in the train station and head for the **city tourist office** in the Altstadt, Breite Str. 62, which books rooms for free. (☎122 54 13 or 122 54 14. Open M-F 9:30am-7pm, Sa-Su 10am-3pm.) The Altstadt (old town section) is easily navigable on foot. **Postal Code:** 23552.

▐▌❏ ACCOMMODATIONS AND FOOD. To reach **Rucksack Hotel,** Kanalstr. 70, walk past the Holstentor from the station, turn left on An der Untertrave, right on Beckergrube and keep going for 20min.; the hostel is on the corner of Kanalstr. Alternatively, take bus #1, 11, 13, 21, or 31 from the station to "Pfaffenstr.," and turn right at the church on Glockengießerstr. (☎70 68 92 or 261 87 92. Breakfast DM5/€2.60. Sheets DM3/€1.55. Reception 9am-1pm and 4-10pm. Front door key available. 6-bed dorms DM26/€13.30; 10-bed dorms DM24/€12.30; double with bath DM80/€40.90; quads DM112/€57.30, with bath DM156/€79.80.) The bright and clean **Baltic Hotel,** Hansestr. 11, is across the street from the bus station and 5min. from the Altstadt, plus every room has phone and TV. (☎855 75. Breakfast buffet included. Reception 8am-10pm. Singles DM50-90/€25-45; doubles DM100-130/€50-65; triples from DM150/€77.) Lübeck's specialty is **marzipan,** a delectable candy made from almonds; stop by the famous confectionery shop ▨**I.G. Niederegger Marzipan Café,** Breitestr. 89, for marzipan in the shape of pigs, jellyfish, and even the town gate. **Tipasa,** Schlumacherstr. 12-14, serves pizza, pasta, and vegetarian dishes, and has a *Biergarten* in back. (Open M-Th and Su noon-1am, F-Sa noon-2am.) Eat under oak rafters at **Kurbis,** Mühlenstr. 9. (Open Su-Th 11am-1am, F-Sa 11am-2am.)

GERMANY

🖸 **SIGHTS.** Between the station and the Altstadt stands the massive **Holstentor,** one of Lübeck's four 15th-century gates and the symbol of the city; the museum inside displays old armor, medieval canons, and local implements of torture. (Museum open Apr.-Sept. Tu-Su 10am-5pm; Oct.-Mar. 10am-4pm. DM5/€2.60, students DM3/€1.55, under 19 DM1/€0.55.) Beautiful churches, many expertly restored from WWII damage, dot the city skyline; the most noticeable are the brick twin towers of the **Marienkirche,** a gigantic church housing the largest mechanical organ in the world. In 1942, a bomb hollowed the church and everything in it; shards of massive bronze bells remain embedded in the marble floor. Photographs of the destroyed medieval masterpiece **Totentanzbild** ("Dance of the Dead") remind viewers that everything—even paintings—must die. The **astronomical clock** has recently been restored. (Open daily in summer 10am-6pm; in winter 10am-4pm. Short organ concerts daily at noon, 30min. concerts Tu 6:30pm, 40min. concerts Th 8pm, full-length concerts Sa 6:30pm. Full-length concerts DM9/€4.60, students DM6/€3.10.) The **Dom** (cathedral), on Domkirchhof, was founded by Heinrich der Löwe (Henry the Lion) in 1173 and shelters a *gigantic* crucifix as well as moving paintings and altarpieces. (Open Apr.-Sept. 10am-6pm; Mar. and Oct. 10am-5pm; Nov. 10am-4pm; Dec.-Feb. 10am-3pm. Free.) The floor of the Gothic **Katharinenkirche,** Königstr. 27, is lined with gravestones; formerly a Franciscan monastery, it was used as a stable by Napoleon and now records the life of St. Francis in a series of moving paintings. (Open Tu-Su 10am-1pm and 2-5pm. DM1/€0.55.) For a sweeping view of the Altstadt and Lübeck's many spires, head to the **Petrikirche** and take the elevator up to the 50.5m steeple. (Church open daily 11am-4pm. Tower open Apr.-Oct. 9am-7pm. Admission DM3.50/€1.80, students DM2/€1.05.)

🏛 **MUSEUMS.** In the **Museum Behn- und Drägerhaus,** Königstr. 11, Neoclassical landscapes, portraits, and religious works decorate already exquisitely painted walls. The artists' cooperative in the **sculpture garden** outside showcases local artists. (☎ 122 41 48. Open Tu-Su Apr.-Sept. 10am-5pm; Oct.-Mar. 10am-4pm. DM5/€2.60, students DM3/€1.55. Free 1st F of every month. Sculpture garden free.) The largest private puppet collection in the world, the 🖸**Museum für Puppentheater,** Kolk 16, displays fascinating hand and string puppets from around the globe. Call for info on shows. (☎ 786 26. Open daily 10am-6pm. DM6/€3.10, students DM5/€2.60.) The **Buddenbrookhaus,** Mengstr. 4, was the childhood home of literary giants Heinrich and Thomas Mann; today, it's a museum dedicated to their lives and works. (Open daily 10am-6pm. DM8/€4.10, students DM5/€2.55.)

SCHLESWIG ☎04621

With a harbor full of sailboats and waterside promenades sprinkled with cafes, Schleswig holds both the air of a seatown and the artistic interest of a big city. Scale the 237 steps of the **St. Petri Dom** for a striking bird's-eye view of the town. (DM2/€1. Organ concerts W 8pm; DM10-15/€5.15-€7.70, students DM5-8/€2.60-4.10. Open May-Sept. M-Th and Sa 9am-12:30pm and 1:30-5pm, F 9am-12:30pm and 1:30-3pm, Su 1:30-5pm; Oct.-Dec. and Mar.-Apr. M-Th and Sa 10am-12:30pm and 1:30-4pm, F 10am-12:30am and 1:30-3pm, Su 1:30-4pm; Jan.-Feb. M-Th and Sa 10am-noon and 2-4pm, F 10am-noon, Su 2-4pm.) By the harbor, the 16th-century **Schloß Gottorf** houses the **Landesmuseen,** a treasure trove of Dutch, Danish, and Art Deco pieces. On the other side of the castle, the **Kreuzstall** houses the **Museum des 20. Jahrhunderts,** devoted to artists of the Brücke school. The surrounding park holds an **outdoor sculpture museum.** (☎ 81 32 22. All museums open Mar.-Oct. daily 9am-5pm; Nov.-Feb. Tu-Su 9:30am-4pm. DM9/€4.60, students DM5/€2.60.)

Schleswig centers around its **bus terminal** *(ZOB)* rather than its train station. Single rides on the bus network cost DM1.90. The train station is 20min. south of the city center; take bus #1, 2, 4, or 5 from the stop outside the *ZOB*. Consider buying a **Schleswig Card** (1-day DM15/€7.70, 3-day DM20/€10.25), valid for public transit and admission to most sights. The **tourist office,** Plessenstr. 7, is up the street from the harbor; from the *ZOB*, walk down Plessenstr. toward the water. The staff books **rooms.** (☎248 78; room reservations ☎248 32. Open May-Sept. M-F 9:30am-5:30pm, Sa 9:30am-12:30pm; Oct.-Apr. M-Th 10am-4pm, Fri 10am-1pm.) The **Jugendherberge (HI)**, Spielkoppel 1, is close to the center of town. Take bus #2 (dir.: Hühnhauser Schwimmhalle) from either the train station or the *ZOB* to "Schwimmhalle"; the hostel is across the street. (☎238 93. Breakfast included. Sheets DM7/€3.60. Reception 7am-1pm and 5-11pm. Curfew 11pm. Dorm beds DM23/€11.75, over 26 DM28/€14.35.) Try the seafood—fresh and cheap—at the **Imbiße** by the Stadthafen.

BREMEN   ☎0421

Bremen may be best known as the setting of the Grimm's fairy tale "The Bremen Town Musicians," but its most enduring trait is a strong desire for independence. Bremen and its daughter city Bremerhaven remain their own tiny, autonomous *Land* (state), and this feisty streak fosters a liberal political climate. The Altstadt revolves around the ornate **Rathaus,** which was spared during WWII by a bomber pilot who deliberately missed the target because he couldn't bear to bomb it. (Obligatory tours M-Sa 11am, noon, 3, and 4pm; Su 11am and noon. DM6/€3, students DM3/€1.50.) Just to the left of the Rathaus is a sculpture of the Brothers Grimm's **Die Bremer Stadtmusikanten** (The Bremen Town Musicians)—a donkey, dog, cat, and rooster who terrified a band of robbers with their off-key singing en route to Bremen. Also next to the Rathaus is **St. Petri Dom,** Sandstr. 10-12, with a mosaic exterior and frescoed ceilings; its first stone was laid by Charlemagne in AD 798. Once you've seen the inside, climb the tower to gaze down upon the hubbub of the market square below. (Cathedral open M-F 10am-5pm, Sa 10am-1:45pm, Su 2-5pm. Free. Tower open May-Oct. same hours. DM1/€0.55.) **Beck's Brewery,** Am Deich 18/19, provides 2hr. tours complete with taste-tests. (Open M-Sa 11am-4pm. English tours daily 1:30pm; call to reserve a place. DM6/€3.) The **Neues Museum Weserburg Bremen,** Teerhof 20, off the Bürgermeister-Schmidt Brücke (bridge), displays a constantly evolving array of contemporary artists. (Open Tu-F 10am-6pm, Sa-Su 11am-6pm. DM8/€4, students and children DM5/€3.) The **Kunsthalle,** Am Wall 207, holds Bremen's main art collection. (Open Tu 10am-9pm, W-Su 10am-5pm. DM8/€4, students DM4/€2. Tours Su 11:30am, Tu 6pm.) The **Übersee Museum,** Bahnhofspl. 13, promises "a trip around the world in a matter of minutes," and delivers just that with exhibits ranging from a Shinto garden to a South Sea fishing village. (Open Tu-Su 10am-6pm. DM10/€5, students DM5/€3.)

   Trains run to Hamburg (1½hr., 2 per hr., DM33/€17) and Hannover (1¼hr., 2 per hr., DM34/€18). The best deal for local transportation is the **Bremer Kärtchen,** with unlimited rides for two adults for one calendar day (DM8/€4). The **tourist office,** in front of the train station, has museum and theater guides, room listings, and the **Tourist Card Bremen,** which provides free transportation and 20-50% discounts on shows and museums. (☎308 00 51. Open June-Oct. daily 9:30am-10pm; Nov.-May M-W 9:30am-6:30pm, Th-F 9:30am-8pm, Sa 9:30am-4pm. Tourist card 2-day DM19.50/€10, 3-day DM26/€14.) To reach the sleek **Jugendgästehaus Bremen (HI),** Kalkstr. 6, from the station, take Bahnhofstr. to Herdentorsteinweg, go right at Am Wall, then left on Bürgermeister-Smidt-Str. and right along the water. (☎17 13 69. Breakfast included. 24hr. reception. Check-in 2pm. Check-out 10am. No curfew. Dorm beds DM29.90/€16, over 27 DM34.90/€18.) ▨**Hotel-Pension Garni Weidmann,** Am Schwarzen Meer 35, provides pampering at bargain prices. Walk down Ostertorsteinweg, which becomes Am Schwarzen Meer. (☎498 44 55. Singles from DM40/€21; doubles from DM80/€41.) Take-out cafes on **Söger-straße,** in the Marktpl., sell everything from chocolate truffles to fish sandwiches. Cheap pubs cluster farther east in the **Viertel,** an area filled with hip students and clubs. The **open-air market** (daily 8am-2pm) offers cheap meals, and there's a **Plus supermarket** at the corner of Vor dem Steintor and Friesenstr. in the Viertel. **Postal Code:** 28195.

CENTRAL AND WEST GERMANY

GERMANY

Lower Saxony (*Niedersachsen*), which stretches from the North Sea to the hills of central Germany, has foggy marshland and fishing boats along the coast and broad agricultural plains inland. Just south of Lower Saxony, North Rhine-Westphalia is the most heavily populated and economically powerful area in Germany. While the region's squalor may have inspired the philosophy of Karl Marx and Friedrich Engels, the area's natural beauty and the intellectual energy of Cologne and Düsseldorf inspired the muses of Goethe, Heine, and Böll. Right in the center of Germany is the region of Hesse. Before the 20th century it was mostly known as a source for mercenary soldiers (many hired by King George III to put down an unruly gang of colonials in 1776); today it's the busiest commercial center in Germany.

DÜSSELDORF   ☎0211

As Germany's fashion hub and multinational corporation base, as well as the capital of densely populated Nordrhein-Westfalen, the rich city of Düsseldorf crawls with German patricians and wannabe aristocrats. Set on the majestic Rhine, Germany's "Hautstadt" (a pun on *Hauptstadt* (capital) and the French *haute*, as in *haute culture*) is a stately, modern metropolis, with an Altstadt that sponsors the best nightlife along the Rhine in authentic German style.

◪ TRANSPORTATION

Trains to: **Amsterdam** (3hr., 1 per hr., DM55/€28); **Berlin** (4½hr., 1-2 per hr., DM170/€87); **Frankfurt** (3hr., 3 per hr., DM79/€41); **Hamburg** (3½hr., 2 per hr., DM116/€59); **Munich** (6hr., 2-3 per hr., DM184/€94); **Paris** (4½hr., 7 per day, DM140/€72). The S-Bahn is the cheapest way to get to **Aachen** and **Cologne.**

Public Transportation: Single tickets DM2.10-12/€1-6, depending on distance traveled. The *Tagesticket* (DM11-32/€5-17) lets up to 5 people travel for 24hr. on any line. Tickets are sold by vending machine; pick up the *Fahrausweis* brochure in the tourist office for instructions. Düsseldorf's S-Bahn is integrated into the mammoth regional **VRR** *(Verkehrsverbund Rhein-Ruhr)* system, which connects most surrounding cities. For schedule information, call 582 28.

◪ PRACTICAL INFORMATION

Tourist Office: Konrad-Adenauer-Pl. (☎17 20 20). Walk up and to the right from the train station and look for the Immermanhof building. Books **rooms** for DM5/€3 M-Sa 8am-8pm, Su 2-8pm. Sells the **ArtTicket** (DM20/€10, also available at any museum), which allows entrance to all museums. Open M-F 8:30am-6pm, Sa 9am-12:30pm.

Currency Exchange: Deutsche Verkehrsbank, in the train station and the airport. Open M-Sa 7am-9pm, Su 8am-9pm.

Laundromat: Wasch Center, Friedrichstr. 92, down the street from the Kirchpl. S-Bahn stop. Wash DM6/€3, dry DM1/€0.55 per 15min. Open M-Sa 6am-11pm.

Internet Access: Telenet-Center, Fritz-Vomfelde-Str. 34 (☎53 88 32 11), near the train station. Open daily 9am-11pm. DM3/€1.50 per 30min.

Post Office: Hauptpostamt, Konrad-Adenauer-Pl., **40210** Düsseldorf, a stone's throw to the right of the tourist office. Open M-F 8am-6pm, Sa 9am-2pm.

◪ ◪ ACCOMMODATIONS AND CAMPING

It's not unusual for hotels in Düsseldorf to double their prices during a convention. Call at least one month ahead if possible.

Jugendgästehaus Düsseldorf (HI), Düsseldorfer Str. 1 (☎55 73 10), is just over the Rheinkniebrücke from the Altstadt. U70, U74, U75, U76, U77 to "Luegpl.," then walk 500m down Kaiser-Wilhelm-Ring. Reception 7am-1am. Curfew 1am, doors open every hr. on the hr. 2-6am. DM39.50/€20, over 26 DM42/€22.

GERMANY

Hotel Schaum, 63 Gustav-Poengsen Str. (☎31 16 510). From the main train station, exit going left on Graf-Adolf-Str., take the 1st left and follow the tracks to Gustav-Poengsen-Str. Huge rooms and a friendly, family staff. Call for pickup from the train station. TV, phone, and breakfast buffet included. Singles DM60/€31, with bath DM80/€41; doubles DM100-120/€51-62.

Hotel Manhattan, Graf-Adolf-Str. 39 (☎37 02 44), 2 blocks from the station. The mirrored reception hallway of this lively hostel reflects neon and Coca-Cola posters into infinity. 24hr. reception. Singles DM65-105/€33-54; doubles DM100-150/€51-77.

Hotel Amsterdam, Stresemannstr. 20 (☎840 58), between Oststr. and Berliner Allee. From the station, start up Graf-Adolf-Str. and turn right at Stresemannstr. No-frills rooms. Small, but clean and safe. Reception 7am-midnight. Singles DM60/€31, with shower DM80/€41; doubles DM140/€72.

Camping: Kleiner Torfbruch (☎899 20 38). S-Bahn to "Düsseldorf Geresheim," then bus #735 (dir.: Stamesberg) to "Seeweg." Pitch your palace and live like a king. DM7.50/€4 per person, DM10/€5 per tent.

⬛ FOOD

For a cheap meal, the endless eateries in the Altstadt can't be beat. Rows of pizzerias, *Döner* stands, and Chinese diners reach from Heinrich-Heine-Allee to the banks of the Rhine. **Otto Mess** is a popular **grocery** chain; the most convenient location is at the eastern corner of Karlpl. in the Altstadt. (Open M-F 8am-8pm, Sa 8am-4pm.) There's also a supermarket in the basement of **Galeria Kaufhof,** on Bahnstr. between Oststr. and Berliner Allee. (Open M-F 9:30am-8pm, Sa 9am-4pm.)

Pilsener Urquell, Grabenstr. 6. In the heart of the Altstadt. Hearty Eastern European specialties and tasty beer at low prices. Open M-F 11am-1am, Sa-Su noon-1am.

Im Füchschen, Ratingerstr. 28. A local favorite for all the local delicacies, including *Blutwurst* (blood sausage) and Mainz hand cheese, and delicious *Füchsenbier* (brewed on premises). Open daily 11am-1am, W and Sa until 2am. Kitchen open until midnight.

Marché, Königsallee 60, in the Kö-Galerie mall. If you must dine on the Kö, this classy cafeteria-style restaurant is one of the few places that won't blow a week's budget. Entrees from DM7/€4. Open M-Th and Su 9am-9pm, F-Sa 9am-10pm.

Galerie Burghof, Burgallee 1-3. U79 to "Klemenspl." Walk down Kaiserwerther Markt and turn left on the Rheinpromenade. Delicious pancakes, a marvelous view of the Rhein, and crazy decorations make eating here an oddly visual experience. Open daily 11am-1am. Pancakes served M-F 6-10:45pm, Sa 2-10:45pm, Su 2-11pm.

Zum Uerige, Bergerstr. 1. Something draws cool Germans to this heavy-wood, heavy-food restaurant. When (if) you finish eating, settle down with a *Schlösser Alt* beer. Open daily 10am-midnight. Kitchen open M-F 6-9pm, Sa 11am-4pm.

👁 SIGHTS

▨ KÖNIGSALLEE. The glitzy Kö—properly called the Königsallee—just outside the Altstadt embodies the vitality and glamor of wealthy Düsseldorf. A little river runs down the middle under stone bridges to the toes of a statue of the sea god Triton. Midway up is the awesome **Kö-Galerie,** a marble-and-copper highbrow shopping mall of one haughty store after another. Items *start* at DM200/€102, and even the mannequins have attitude. *(Head 10min. down Graf-Adolf-Str. from the train station.)*

SCHLOß BENRATH. This Baroque palace in the suburbs of Düsseldorf was originally built 200 years ago as a pleasure palace and hunting grounds for Elector Karl Theodor. The architect used strategically placed mirrors and false exterior windows to make the castle appear larger than it is, but the enormous French gardens temper the effect. *(S6 (dir.: Köln) to "Benrath." Open Tu-Su 10am-5pm. Tours every 30min. DM7/€4, studentsDM3.50/€1.75.)*

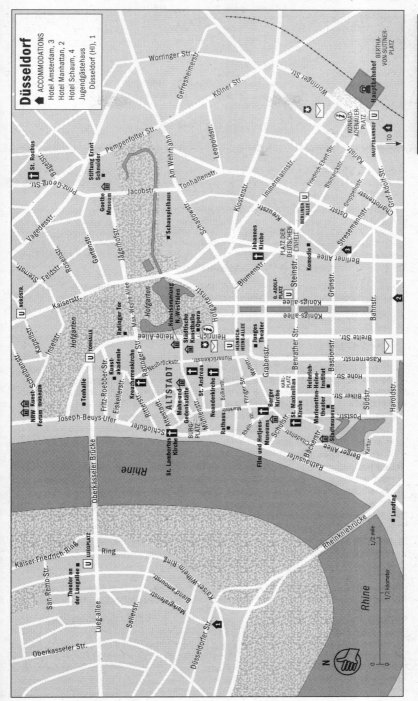

Düsseldorf

ACCOMMODATIONS
Hotel Amsterdam, 3
Hotel Manhattan, 2
Hotel Schaum, 4
Jugendgästehaus
Düsseldorf (HI), 1

HOFGARTEN AND GOETHEMUSEUM. At the upper end of the Kö, the Hofgarten park is the oldest public park in Germany. At the east end, the 18th-century **Schloß Jägerhof** houses the **Goethemuseum**, where 30,000 souvenirs memorialize the poet. *(Jakobistr. 2. Streetcar #707 or bus #752 to "Schloß Jägerhof." Open Tu-F and Su 11am-5pm, Sa 1-5pm. DM4/€2, students and children DM2/€1.)*

KAISERWERTH. North on the Rhine are the **ruins** of Emperor Friedrich's palace, built in 1184 and destroyed in 1702 during the War of Spanish Succession. The **tower** with the blinking lights is actually a clock called the **Rheinturm.** From bottom to top, the dots represent 1 second, 10 seconds, 1min., 10min., 1hr., and 10hr. *(U79 to "Klemenspl.," then follow Kaiserwerther Markt to the Rhine and walk left another 150m.)*

EKO-HOUSE. Düsseldorf has the largest Japanese population of any European city. The EKO-House, across the Rhine from the Altstadt, is a beautiful garden and cultural center with frequent tea ceremonies and readings from Buddhist texts. *(Brüggener Weg 6. Take U70 or U74-77 to "Belsenpl." Follow Quirinstr. to Comeniuspl.; turn left on Niederkasseler Str. Open Tu-Su 1-5pm. DM5/€3, students DM3/€1.50.)*

KUNSTSAMMLUNG NORDRHEIN-WESTFALEN. The black glass edifice west of the Hofgarten houses works by Matisse, Picasso, Surrealists, and Expressionists, and hometown boy Paul Klee, as well as many changing exhibits of modern art and film. *(Grabbepl. 5. U70, 75, 76, 78, 79 to "Heinrich-Heine-Allee." Walk north 2 blocks, or take bus #725 to "Grabbepl." Open Tu-Th and Sa-Su 10am-6pm, F 10am-8pm. DM5/€3, students DM3/€1.50. Special exhibits DM12/€6, students DM8/€4.)*

KUNSTHALLE. Across the square from the Kunstsammlung Nordrhein-Westfalen is a forum for modern exhibits of every shape and size. Exhibits rotate every 2-3 months. *(Grabbepl. 4. Admission depends on the exhibit; usually DM10/€5, students DM7/€4. Open Tu-Su 11am-6pm.)*

■ NIGHTLIFE

Folklore says that Düsseldorf's 500 pubs make up *die längste Theke der Welt* (the longest bar in the world). Pubs in the Altstadt are standing-room-only by 6pm, and by nightfall it's nearly impossible to see where one pub ends and the next begins. **Bolkerstraße** is jam-packed nightly with street performers. *Prinz* (DM5/€3) gives tips on happening scenes; it's often given out free at the youth hostel. *Facolte* (DM4/€2), a gay and lesbian nightlife magazine, is available at most newsstands.

Pam-Pam, Bolkerstr 34. This basement disco plays house, rock, pop, and plenty of American music. Open F-Sa 10pm-dawn. No cover.

La Rocca, Grünstr. 8. Just off the Kö, this posh club is a showcase for clothing purchased during the day—this is not the place to dress down. A mostly 20-something crowd dances the night away to house. Open Th-Sa from 10pm-5am. Cover DM8/€4.

Unique, Bolkerstr. 30. Lives up to its name, at least in Düsseldorf's Altstadt. The red-walled club draws a younger, trendier crowd. Open daily 10pm-late. Cover DM10/€5.

Café Rosa, Oberbilker Allee 310. The socio-cultural mecca of Düsseldorf's gay community, this do-it-all Kulturzentrum offers self-defense classes and throws killer parties. Tu men only; F lesbians only. Open Tu-Sa 8pm-1am, later on weekends.

KASSEL   ☎ 0561

Napoleon III was dragged to Kassel as a prisoner of Prussian troops, but today hordes of tourists visit this ultra-sophisticated city of their own free will. From Bahnhof Wilhelmshöhe, take streetcar #1 to **Wilhelmshöhe,** a weirdly fascinating hillside park. Inside, **Schloß Löwenburg** was built by Wilhelm in the 18th century with stones deliberately missing to look like a crumbling medieval castle—he was obsessed with the year 1495 and fancied himself a time-displaced knight. Really. (Open Mar.-Oct. Tu-Su 10am-5pm; Nov.-Feb. Tu-Su 10am-4pm. Mandatory tours every hr. except noon. DM7/€3.60.) All of the park's paths lead up to **Herkules,** Kassel's emblem; visitors can climb up onto Herkules's pedestal and, if they're brave enough, into his club. (Access to the base of the statue free. Pedestal and club open mid-Mar. to mid-Nov. daily 10am-5pm. DM3.50/€1.80, students DM2.50/€1.30.) The **Hessisches Landesmuseum**, Brüder-Grimm-Pl. 5, contains the only **wallpaper museum** in the world. (Open Tu-Su 10am-5pm. DM7/€3.60, students DM5/€2.60; F free.) The **Brüder-Grimm-Museum**, Schöne Aussicht 2, exhibits Jacob's and Wilhelm's handwritten copy of *Kinder- und Hausmärchen* and artistic interpretations of their tales. (Open daily 10am-5pm. DM3/€1.55, students DM2/€1.05.) The ▨**Museum für Sepulkralkultur**, Weinbergstr. 25-27, will satisfy your morbid fixations with death-related paraphernalia; its intent is to "arrest the taboo process which surrounds the subject of 'death and dying' in today's world and open it to public discussion." (Open Tu-Su 10am-5pm, W 10am-8pm. DM8/€4.10, students DM6/€3.10.) Every five years, art-lovers flock to Kassel to take part in the world's preeminent exhibition of contemporary art, Documenta; the latest installment, **Documenta XI**, will take place from June 8 to September 15, 2002.

Kassel has two train stations, **Bahnhof Wilhelmshöhe** and the **Hauptbahnhof;** but most trains stop only at Wilhelmshöhe. Trains run to: Düsseldorf (3½hr., 1 per hr., DM71/€36.30); Frankfurt (2hr., 3 per hr., DM54/€27.60); Hamburg (2½hr., 3 per hr., DM99/€50.65); Munich (4hr., 1 per hr., DM172/€87.95). The **tourist office,** in Bahnhof Wilhelmshöhe, has free maps and books rooms for a DM5/€2.60 fee. (☎ 340 54. Open M-F 9am-1pm and 2-6pm, Sa 9am-1pm.) To reach **Jugendherberge am Tannenwäldchen (HI)**, Schenkendorfstr. 18, take streetcar #4 from Bahnhof Wilhelmshöhe to "Annastr.," backtrack on Friedrich-Ebert-Str., and make a right on Querallee, which becomes Schenkendorfstr. (☎ 77 64 55. Breakfast included. Sheets DM6.85/€3.50. Reception 9am-11:30pm. Curfew 12:30am. DM32.30/€16.55, over 26 DM37.55/€19.20. **HI members only.**) For **Hotel Kö78**, Kölnische Str. 78, follow the directions to the Jugendherberge, then walk up Annastr. from the train stop and turn right onto Kölnische Str. (☎716 14. Breakfast included. Reception daily 7am-10pm. Singles DM59/€30.20, with shower from DM69/€35.30; doubles DM98/€50.10, with shower from DM119/€60.85.) **Edeka** sells **groceries** on Friedrich-Ebert-Str. 45/47. (open M-F 7am-7pm, Sa 7am-3pm), as does the well-stocked **tegut** in Bahnhof Wilhelmshöhe (open M-F 8am-8pm, Sa 8am-4pm). **Postal Code:** 34041.

COLOGNE (KÖLN)   ☎0221

Founded as a Roman colony (*colonia* is the root of the word "Köln") in AD 48, Cologne gained fame and fortune in the Middle Ages as an elite university town and an important trade hub. While most of the inner city was destroyed in WWII, the magnificent Gothic *Dom* (cathedral) survived no fewer than 14 bombings and remains Cologne's main attraction. Today, tourists come to see this symbol of Cologne's rebirth, participate in bacchanalian celebrations, and immerse themselves in the burgeoning fine arts scene.

▤ TRANSPORTATION

Flights: Flights depart from **Köln-Bonn Flughafen;** a shuttle to **Berlin** leaves 24 times per day. Bus #170 to the airport leaves from stop #3 at the train station. (20min; daily 5:30, 6, and 6:30am; every 15min. 7am-8pm; every 30min. 8-11pm. DM8.70/€5.)

Trains: From the Hauptbahnhof to: **Amsterdam** (4hr., every 2hr., DM79/€41); **Berlin** (6½hr., 2 per hr., DM172/€88); **Brussels** (2½hr., every 2hr., DM54/€28); **Düsseldorf** (45min., 5 per hr., DM12.60/€7); **Frankfurt** (2hr., 3 per hr., DM61/€32); **Hamburg** (5hr., 3 per hr., DM123/€63); **Munich** (6hr., 4 per hr., DM173/€89); **Paris** (4hr., every 2hr., DM128/€66).

Ferries: Köln-Düsseldorfer (☎08 83 18) begins its popular Rhine cruises here. Sail upstream to **Koblenz** (DM59.80/€31), or take the Rhein-Jet instead of a train to **Bonn** (DM11.20/€6). Students half-price; Eurail valid on most trips (excluding hydrofoils).

Public Transportation: VRS (Verkehrsverbund Rhein-Sieg) offices have free maps of the S- and U-Bahn, bus, and streetcar lines; one is downstairs in the train station.

✴ 🔢 ORIENTATION AND PRACTICAL INFORMATION

Cologne stretches across the Rhine, but nearly all sights and the city center can be found on the western side. The train station is in the northern part of the **Innenstadt** ("town center"). The Altstadt is split into **Altstadt-Nord**, near the **Hauptbahnhof**, and **Altstadt-Süd**, south of the **Severinsbrücke** (bridge).

Tourist Office: Verkehrsamt, Unter Fettenhennen 19 (☎ 22 12 33 45; www.koeln.de), across from the main entrance to the *Dom*, provides a free city map and books rooms for a DM5-6/€2.60-3 fee. Open May-Oct. M-Sa 8am-10:30pm, Su 9am-10:30pm; Nov.-Apr. M-Sa 8am-9pm, Su 9:30am-7pm.

Currency Exchange: An office at the train station is open daily 7am-9pm, but the service charges are lower at the post office (see below).

Gay and Lesbian Resources: Schulz Schwulen-und Lesbenzentrum, Kartäuserwall 18 (☎ 93 18 80 80), near Chlodwigpl. Information, advice, and cafe. The tourist office also offers a **"Gay City Map"** with listings of gay-friendly hotels, bars, and clubs.

Laundry: Eco-Express, at the corner of Richard-Wagner-Str. and Händelstr. Wash DM6/€3, dry DM1/€0.55 per 10min. Soap included. Open M-Sa 6am-11pm.

Emergency: Police, ☎ 110. **Fire** and **ambulance,** ☎ 112.

Pharmacy: Dom-Apotheke, Komödienstr. 5 (☎ 257 67 54), near the station, posts a list of after-hours pharmacies. English spoken. Open M-F 8am-6:30pm, Sa 9am-1pm.

Internet access: FuturePoint, Richmodstr. 13 (☎ 206 72 06). Open daily 9am-1am.

Post Office: at the corner of Breite Str. and Tunisstr. in the *WDR-Arkaden* shopping gallery. Address mail to be held: Postlagernde Briefe für FirstName SURNAME, Hauptpostamt, **50667** Köln, Germany. Open M-F 8am-8pm, Sa 8am-4pm.

🏠 ACCOMMODATIONS

Most hotels fill up in spring and fall when conventions come to town, and the two hostels are nearly always booked from June to September. The main hotel haven centers around **Brandenburgerstraße,** on the less interesting side of the train station. The **Mitwohnzentrale,** An der Bottmühle 16 (☎ 194 45), finds apartments for longer stays. (Open M-F 9am-1pm and 2-4pm.) Call ahead.

Station Hostel and Bar, Rheing. 34-36 (☎ 23 02 47). Clean rooms, a popular bar, and English-speaking staff. 24hr. reception. Reserved rooms held until 6pm. Singles DM50/€26; doubles DM80/€42; triples DM108/€57; quads DM132/€68.

Jugendgästehaus Köln-Riehl (HI), An der Schanz 14 (☎ 76 70 81), on the Rhine north of the zoo. U16 (dir.: Ebertplatz/Mülheim) to "Boltensternstr." Breakfast and sheets included. Reception 24hr. No curfew. Call ahead. 4- to 6-bed dorms DM38.50/€20; singles DM63.50/€33.

Jugendherberge Köln-Deutz (HI), Siegesstr. 5a (☎ 81 47 11), just over the *Hohenzollernbrücke*. S6, 11, or 12 to "Köln-Deutz," exit the station, walk down Neuhöfferstr., and take the 1st right; the hostel is in a tree-lined courtyard. Small but clean rooms, with free access to washing machines. Breakfast and sheets included. Reception 11am-1am. Curfew 1am. Call ahead. Dorms DM33/€17, over 26 DM37/€19.

Hotel Im Kupferkessel, Probsteig. 6 (☎ 13 53 38). From the Dom, follow Dompropst-Ketzer-Str. as it becomes An der Dominikan, Unter Sachsenhausen, Gereonstr., and finally Christophstr.; Probsteig. is on the right. Cozy rooms with TV and telephone. Breakfast included. Singles DM55-88/€28-45; doubles from DM120/€62.

Hotel Hubertus Hof, Mühlenbach 30 (☎ 21 73 86). Follow the directions above to Hohe Pforte and turn left on Mühlenbach. This gay-friendly hotel has fuzzy carpets and monster-sized rooms. Showers and toilets off the hall. Breakfast included. Reception 7am-9pm. Singles DM60/€31; doubles DM80-85/€40-44.

GERMANY

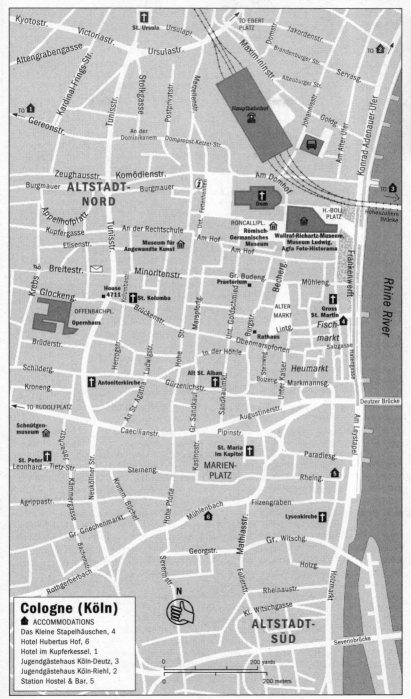

Cologne (Köln)

♦ ACCOMMODATIONS
Das Kleine Stapelhäuschen, 4
Hotel Hubertus Hof, 6
Hotel im Kupferkessel, 1
Jugendgästehaus Köln-Deutz, 3
Jugendgästehaus Köln-Riehl, 2
Station Hostel & Bar, 5

Das Kleine Stapelhäuschen, Fischmarkt 1-3 (☎ 257 78 62). Cross the *Altenmarkt* from the back of the *Rathaus* and take Lintg. to the *Fischmarkt*. An old-fashioned inn with carved oak bed frames. Reception in the restaurant below. Breakfast included. Singles DM87/€45; doubles DM135/€69; extra charge for shower or bath.

Camping: Campingplatz Poll, Weidenweg (☎ 83 19 66), on the Rhine, southeast of the Altstadt. U16 to "Marienburg" and cross the Rodenkirchener Brücke (bridge). Reception 8am-noon and 5-8pm. Open Apr.-Oct. DM8/€4 per person, DM4/€2 per tent.

🍴 FOOD

Cologne cuisine includes scrumptious *Rievekoochen* (slabs of fried potato dunked in applesauce) and smooth **Kölsch** beer. Small cafes and cheap restaurants line **Zülpicherstraße** (U7 or U9 to "Zülpicher Pl."). Mid-priced ethnic restaurants lie around the perimeter of the Altstadt, particularly from **Hohenzollernring** to **Hohenstaufenring;** the city's best cheap eats are on **Weideng.** in the Turkish district. **HL,** Hohenzollernring 20, sells **groceries.** (Open M-F 9am-8pm, Sa-Su 8:30am-4pm.)

■ **Brauhaus Früh am Dom,** Am Hof 12-14. Enjoy hearty regional specialties with a tall glass of some of Cologne's finest *Kölsch,* served here since the early 19th century. Meals DM9-30/€4-16. Open daily 8am-midnight, menu until 11:45pm.

Päffgen-Brauerei, Friesenstr. 64-66. A local favorite since 1883. Legendary *Kölsch* is brewed on the premises and consumed in cavernous halls or in the *Biergarten*. Hearty meals DM3-30/€1.50-16. Open daily 10am-midnight. Kitchen open 11am-11pm.

Café Magnus, Zülpicherstr. 48. Funky indoor/outdoor cafe with beautifully presented meals. Pizzas and salads from DM6/€3, pasta from DM10/€5. Open daily 9am-3am.

Sasmus Island, Heinsberg 11a, at the corner of Heinsberg and Zülpicherstr. Enjoy pizza and light pasta dishes for around DM10/€5. Open daily 8am-1am.

Joe Champs, Hohenzollernring 1-3. A 2-story bar serving huge burgers, both veggie and meat. Shows major US sporting events on the biggest bar screen in town. Happy Hour 5-7pm. Open M-Th and Su noon-1am, F-Sa noon-3am.

👁 SIGHTS

■ **DOM.** Visitors exiting Cologne's train station are immediately treated to the beauty, power, and sorrow that emanate from the colossal High Gothic **Dom,** Germany's greatest cathedral. Over six centuries passed from its start to its completion in 1880, and for 500 years the giant wooden crane, now kept inside, was as much Cologne's trademark as the two massive towers. The **Domschatzkammer,** in a corner of the cathedral, holds relics including thorn, cross, and nail bits, as well as pieces of 18 saints. *(Open Apr.-Oct. M-Sa 9am-5pm, Su 1-4pm; Nov.-Mar. M-Sa 9am-4pm, Su 1-4pm; DM3/€1.50, students DM1.50/€0.75.)* The section to the right of the center altar bears the **Dombild** triptych, a masterful 15th-century painting. The 976 **Gero crucifix,** in the fenced-off area to the left of the center altar, is the oldest intact sculpture of *Christus patiens* (a crucified Christ with eyes shut). The enormous sculpture behind the altar is the **Shrine of the Magi,** a reliquary of the Three Kings (Cologne's holy patrons) in gold that was brought to the city in 1164. *(Cathedral open daily 6am-7pm. Free. Tours in English M-Sa 10:30am and 2:30pm, Su 2:30pm; DM7/€4, children DM4/€2.)*

Fifteen minutes and 509 steps bring you to the top of the **Südturm.** *(Open Nov.-Feb. 9am-4pm, May-Sept. 9am-6pm, Mar., Apr., and Oct 9am-5pm. DM3/€1.50, students DM1.50/€0.75.)* Catch your breath at the **Glockenstube** (a chamber for the tower's nine bells about halfway up), but beware of being there when the clock strikes on the hour! Four of the bells date from the Middle Ages, but the 19th-century upstart known affectionately as **Der große Peter** (the world's heaviest swinging bell at 24 tons) rings loudest. Since time and acid rain have corroded much of the Dom's original detail, every piece is gradually being reproduced and replaced with new, treated stone. At **Domplatz,** the plaza outside, you can play the **"Dom lottery"** and save a statue's fingernail. *(DM1-2/€0.50-1.)*

HOUSE #4711. The magic water **Eau de Cologne,** once prescribed as a drinkable curative, made the town a household name. If you're after the real thing, be sure your bottle says *Echt kölnisch Wasser* ("real Cologne water"), or look for the "4711" label. Its name comes from the Mühlens family home, labeled House #4711 by a Napoleonic system that abolished street names. The house today is a boutique, with a small fountain continually dispensing the famous scented water. *(Glockeng., at the intersection with Tunisstr. From Hohe Str., turn right on Brückenstr., which becomes Glockeng. Open M-F 9:30am-8pm, Sa 9:30am-4pm.)*

RATHAUS. Bombed in WWII, Cologne's city hall has been reconstructed in its original mongrel style. The Gothic tower stands guard over Baroque cherubs flying around an ornate 1570 Renaissance arcade. The tower is adorned with a diverse array of historical and cultural figures; Marx and Rubens loom above rows of popes and emperors. A Glockenspiel plays daily at noon and 5pm. *(Open M-Th 7:30am-5pm, F 7:30am-2pm. Tours W at 3pm. Free.)*

RÖMISCHES PRAETORIUM UND KANAL. Classical historians and *Ben Hur* fans will be impressed by the excavated ruins of the former Roman military headquarters. The underground museum displays remains of Roman gods and a befuddling array of rocks left by early inhabitants. *(From the Rathaus, take a right toward the swarm of hotels and then a left onto Kleine Budeng. Open Tu-F 10am-4pm, Sa-Su 11am-4pm. DM3/€1.50, students DM1.50/€0.75.)*

GROß ST MARTIN. Along with the cathedral, **Groß St. Martin** defines the legendary Rhine panorama of Cologne. The renovated church was reopened in 1985 after near-destruction in WWII. The crypts house an esoteric collection of stones and diagrams. *(An Groß St. Martin 9. Open M-F 10:15am-6pm, Sa 10am-12:30pm and 1:30-6pm, Su 2-4pm. Free. Crypts DM1/€0.51, children DM0.50/€0.25.)*

🏛 MUSEUMS

Cologne's cultural, religious, and economic significance in Europe stocks the city's museums with a vast and impressive array of holdings. The **Köln Tourismus Card** entitles the bearer to a city tour, discounts on Rhine cruises, a three-day pass to all city museums, and use of the public transportation system. (Sold in high-end hotels in the Innenstadt, DM30/€16.)

▨ HEINRICH-BÖLL-PLATZ. Designed to maximize natural light, the unusual building houses two complementary collections. The **Museum Ludwig** spans Impressionism through Dalí, Lichtenstein, and Warhol; it also has one of the world's largest Picasso collections. The **Agfa Foto-Historama** chronicles photography of the last 150 years, including a rotating display of Man Ray's works. *(Bischofsgartenstr. 1. Behind the Römisch-Germanisches Museum. Open Tu 10am-8pm, W-F 10am-6pm, Sa-Su 11am-6pm. Tours Tu 6pm, W 4:30pm, Sa 11:30am, Su 11:30am. DM10/€5, students DM5/€3.)*

▨ SCHOKOLADENMUSEUM. Salivate at every step of chocolate production from the rain forests to the gold fountain that spurts streams of silky, heavenly, creamy chocolate. Resist the urge to drool and wait for the free samples. *(Rheinauhafen 1a. Near the Severinsbrücke. From the train station, head for the river, walk along the Rhine heading right, go under the Deutzer Brücke, and take the 1st footbridge. Open M-F 10am-6pm, Sa-Su 11am-7pm. DM10/€5, students DM5/€3. Tours Sa at 2 and 4pm, Su at 11:30am, 2, and 4pm. DM3/€1.50.)*

WALLRAF-RICHARTZ MUSEUM. This new building displays medieval, Renaissance, Baroque, and Impressionist pieces. *(Martinstr. 39. From the Heumarkt, take Gürzenichtstr. 1 block to Martinstr. Open Tu 10am-8pm, W-F 10am-6pm, Sa-Su 11am-6pm.)*

RÖMISCH-GERMANISCHES MUSEUM (ROMAN-GERMAN MUSEUM). Built on the ruins of a Roman villa, its displays include the famous Dionysus mosaic, the tomb of Publicus, and a large array of artifacts documenting the daily lives of Romans both rich and poor. *(Roncallipl. 4., between the Dom and Diözeansmuseum. Open Tu-Su 10am-5pm, W 10am-7pm. DM10/€5, students DM5/€3.)*

NS-DOKUMENTATIONS-ZENTRUM. Once Cologne's Gestapo headquarters, the museum portrays the city as it was during the Nazi regime, including a display of the 1,200 wall inscriptions made by political prisoners kept in the basement prison cells. All displays in German. *(Appellhofpl. 23-25. At the corner of Elisenstr., on the far side from the Dom. Open Tu-F 10am-4pm, Sa-Su 11am-4pm. DM5/€3, students DM2/€1.)*

KÄTHE-KOLLWITZ-MUSEUM. The world's largest collection of sketches, sculptures, and prints by the brilliant 20th-century artist-activist Käthe Kollwitz, as well as changing exhibits by other modern artists. *(Neumarkt 18-24. On the top floor in the Neumarkt-Passage. U12, U14, U16, or U18 to "Neumarkt." Open Tu-F 10am-6pm, Sa-Su 11am-6pm. DM5/€3, students DM2/€1.)*

🎵 🎬 ENTERTAINMENT AND NIGHTLIFE

Cologne explodes in celebration during **Karneval,** a week-long pre-Lent festival made up of 50 neighborhood processions. It starts on **Weiberfastnacht** (Feb. 7, 2002),when the mayor publicly abdicates leadership of the city to the *Weiber* (an archaic and not-too-politically-correct term for women); the women then traditionally find their husbands at work and chop their ties off. The week builds up to the out-of-control parade on **Rosenmontag,** the last Monday before Lent (Feb. 11, 2002), where everyone's in costume and gets and gives *Bützchen* (kisses on the cheek). For more information, pick up the Karneval booklet at the tourist office.

Cologne has over 30 theaters; **KölnTicket,** a ticket agent in the same building as the Römisch-Germanisches Museum (see p. 459), sells tickets for the opera, the world-class **Philharmonie** (orchestra), open-air rock concerts, and everything in between. (☎28 01. Open M-W and F 9am-6:30pm, Th 9am-8pm, Sa 9am-4pm.)

Partying has long been a tradition in Cologne: Roman mosaics record the wild excesses of the city's early residents. Today, Cologne focuses on a sophisticated bump-and-grind. At the various *Brauhäuser,* waiters will greet you with a friendly "Kölsch?" and bring one glass after another until you fall under the table or you place your coaster over your glass. Many bars and clubs change their music nightly; the best way to know what you'll get is to pick up the monthly magazine *Kölner* (DM2/€1). The closer to the Rhine or Dom you venture, the more quickly your wallet gets emptied. Students congregate in the **Bermuda-Dreieck** ("Bermuda Triangle"), bounded by Zülpicherstr., Zülpicherpl., Roonstr., and Luxemburgstr. The center of **gay nightlife** runs up Matthiasstr. to Mühlenbach, Hohe Pforte, Marienpl., and to the Heumarkt area by the *Deutzer Brücke.*

Alter Wartesaal, Johannisstr. 11. In the basement of the train station, with an enormous dance floor and an impressively hip crowd. Open M-Th 10pm-1am, F-Sa 9am-3am.

M20, Maastrichterstr. 20. This small bar plays some of the best techno and drum 'n bass in town to crowds of locals. Open M-F 8pm-1am, Sa 8pm-2am.

Stadtgarten, Venloerstr. 40. Upstairs has everything from techno to jazz; downstairs spins techno and house. Cover DM10/€5. Open M-Th 9pm-1am, F-Sa 9pm-3am.

Das Ding, Hohenstaufenring 30-32. A popular, smoky student bar and disco. Music and crowd vary widely. Cover DM8/€4. Open M and W 9pm-2am, Tu and Th-Su 9pm-3am.

GAY AND LESBIAN NIGHTLIFE

🏳️ **Vampire,** Rathenaupl. 5. A gay and lesbian bar with a chill atmosphere, a dark interior, and plenty of delicious holy water. Happy Hour 8-9pm. Disco F and Sa. Open Tu-Th and Su 8pm-1am, F-Sa 8pm-3am. No garlic.

TIMP, Heumarkt 25, right across from the bus stop. This outrageous gay-friendly club attracts crowds by hosting nightly cabaret shows for no cover. Shows daily 1am-4am.

Gloria, Apostelnstr. 11. This popular cafe and club is at the nexus of Cologne's gay and lesbian scene. Cover around DM15/€8. Open M-Th 9am-1am, Su 10am-1am.

AACHEN
☎ 0241

Charlemagne made this the capital of his Frankish empire in the 8th century, and Aachen still maintains its historical treasures—from Charlemagne's body parts to Roman ruins—while becoming a thriving forum for up-and-coming European artists. The famous neo-Byzantine **Dom** (cathedral) is in the center of the city; Charlemagne's remains lie in the reliquary behind the altar. (Open daily 11am-7pm, Su 12:30-7pm, except during services. Combination ticket for Dom and Schatzkammer DM15/€8, students DM9/€5.) Just around the corner is the **Schatzkammer,** Klosterpl. 2, a treasury of reliquaries containing John the Baptist's hair and ribs, nails and splinters from the true cross, and Christ's scourging robe. A gold-plated silver bust of Charlemagne, which holds his skull, was carried to the city gates each time a new king was crowned so Charlemagne could "welcome" his successors. A gigantic golden arm statue nearby holds his radius and ulna bones. (Open M 10am-1pm, Tu-W and F-Su 10am-6pm, Th 10am-9pm. DM5/€3, students DM3/€1.50.) The ▓**Ludwigforum für Internationale Kunst,** Jülicherstr. 97-109, houses a rotating collection of cutting-edge art. (Open Tu and Th 10am-5pm, W and F 10am-8pm, Sa-Su 11am-5pm. Tours Su 11:30am and 3pm. DM6/€3, students DM3/€1.50.)

Trains run to: Amsterdam (4hr., 1-2 per hr., DM102/€52); Brussels (2hr., 1 per hr., DM51/€26); Cologne (1hr., 2-3 per hr., DM20/€11). The **tourist office,** on Friedrich-Wilhelm-Pl. in the Atrium Elisenbrunnen, runs tours and finds rooms for free. From the train station, cross the street and head up Bahnhofstr., turn left onto Theaterstr., which becomes Theaterpl., then right onto Kapuzinergraben, which becomes Friedrich-Wilhelm-Pl. (☎ 180 29 60. Open M-F 9am-6pm, Sa 9am-2pm.) **Internet** is available at the city library, **Öffentliche Bibliothek,** Couverstr. 15. (Open Tu-W and F 11am-5:45pm, Th 1:15-8pm, Sa 10am-1pm. DM6/€3 per hr.) The ▓**Euroregionales Jugendgästehaus (HI),** Maria-Theresia-Allee 260, feels more like a hotel than a hostel. From the station, walk left on Lagerhausstr. until it intersects Karmeliterstr. and Mozartstr., then take bus #2 (dir.: Preusswald) to "Ronheide" or bus #12 (dir.: Diepenbendem) to "Colynshof." (☎ 71 10 10. Breakfast and sheets included. Curfew 1am. Dorms DM39.50/€21.) **Hotel Drei König,** Büchel 5, on the corner of Marktpl., is just steps from the Rathaus. (☎ 483 93. Breakfast included. Singles DM65/€34, with bath DM85/€44; doubles DM105/€54, DM150/€77.) Aachen's delicious dessert specialities are *Reisfladden* (a rice pudding cake) and *Printen* (addictively spicy gingerbread biscuits). **Van den Daele,** Büchel 18-20, just off the Markt, serves these and other Aachen delicacies in the city's oldest house, built in 1655. (Open M-F 9am-7pm, Sa 9am-9pm, Su 11am-7pm.) For groceries, try **Plus supermarket,** Marienbongard 27, off Pontstr. (Open M-F 8am-8pm, Sa 8am-4pm.) **Postal code:** 52064.

BONN
☎ 0228

Once derisively called *Hauptdorf* (capital village) just because it wasn't Berlin, Bonn became capital of West Germany by chance because Konrad Adenauer, the first chancellor, resided in the suburbs. In 1999, the *Bundestag* packed up and moved back to Berlin, allowing Bonn to be itself again. Although Berliners joke that Bonn is "half the size of a Chicago cemetery and twice as dead," the sparkling streets of the *Altstadt* bustle with notable energy. The well-respected university and excellent museums bolster a thriving cultural scene, and Bonn is fast becoming a center for Germany's computer technology industry.

▐ TRANSPORTATION. Trains run to: Cologne (30min., 6 per hr., DM10/€5.15); Koblenz (1hr., 3 per hr., DM14.80/€7.60); Frankfurt (1½hr., 1 per hr., DM59/€30.20). The S-Bahn and U-Bahn network, **VRS** (Verkehrsverbund Rhein-Sieg) links Bonn to Cologne and other riverside cities. Areas are divided into **Tarifzonen;** the farther you go, the more you pay. Single tickets (DM2.20-4.20/€1.15-€2.15), 4-ride tickets (DM8-12.80/€4.10-6.55), and day tickets (DM9.50-35/€4.90-17.90) are available at Automaten and designated vending stations.

GERMANY

GERMANY

⚡ PRACTICAL INFORMATION. The **tourist office** is at Windeckstr. 2, near the cathedral on Münsterpl. (☎ 194 33. Open M-F 9am-6:30pm, Sa 9am-4pm, Su 10am-2pm.) Consider buying the **Bonncard** (DM24/€12.30 per day, 3 days DM46/€23.55), which covers transportation costs after 9am (all day Sa-Su) and admission to more than 20 museums in Bonn and the surrounding area. **Schwulen- und Lesbenzentrum (Gay and Lesbian Center)** is at Am Frankenbad 5. From Münsterpl., follow Windeck-str. to Berliner Pl., cross to Bornheimer Str., and take a right on Adolfstr.; Am Frankenbad is two blocks down the street and to the left. (☎ 63 00 39. Open M-Tu and Th 8pm-midnight, W 7pm-midnight.) The **post office**, Münsterpl. 17, is down Poststr. from the station. (Open M-F 8am-8pm, Sa 8am-4pm.) *Poste Restante:* Postlagernde Briefe für FirstName SURNAME, **53111** Bonn, Germany.

🛏 ACCOMMODATIONS. Take bus #621 (dir.: Ippendorf Altenheim) to "Jugendgästehaus" for the sparkling, super-modern **Jugendgästehaus Bonn-Venus-berg (HI)**, Haager Weg 42. (☎ 28 99 70. Breakfast and sheets included. Laundry DM10/€5.15. Reception 9am-1am. Curfew 1am. Dorms DM39/€19.95.) **Hotel Berg-mann**, Kasernenstr. 13, is a family-run hotel with cozy, elegant rooms. From the station follow Poststr., turn left at Münsterpl. on Vivatsg., then right on Kasernen-str.; after 10min., the hotel is on the left. (☎ 63 38 91. Reception hours sporadic—call ahead. Singles DM60/€30.70; doubles DM95/€48.60.) For a fabulous splurge, try **Hotel Hofgarten**, Fritz-Tillman-Str. 7. From the station, turn right onto Maximil-ianstr., continue on Kaiserstr., and then turn left on Fritz-Tillman-Str. (☎ 22 34 82. Breakfast included. Call ahead. Singles DM60-140/€30.70-€71.60; doubles DM125-185/€63.95-94.60.) To reach **Campingplatz Genienaue**, Im Frankenkeller 49, take U16 or U63 to "Rheinallee," then bus #613 (dir.: Giselherstr.) to "Guntherstr." Turn left on Guntherstr. and right on Frankenkeller. (☎ 34 49 49. Reception 9am-noon and 3-10pm. DM8/€4.10 per person, DM5-8/€2.60-4.10 per tent.)

▣ FOOD. Carl's Mensa-Bistro, Nassestr. 15, has restaurant-quality meals served cafeteria style. (Open M-Th 10:30am-10pm, F 10:30am-3pm. Hot food served 11:30am until 30min. before closing.) **Cassius-Garten,** Maximilianstr. 28d, at the edge of the Altstadt facing the station, is a scrumptious veggie bar with 50 kinds of salads, noodles, and whole-grain baked goods. (Bistro open M-F 9am-8pm, Sa 9am-4pm; restaurant open M-Sa from 11:30am.) The **market** on Münsterpl. teems with vendors selling meat, fruit, and vegetables. (Open M-Sa 9am-6pm.) There's a **super-market** in the basement of the Kaufhof department store on Münsterpl. (Open M-F 9:30am-8pm, Sa 9am-4pm.)

◪▥ SIGHTS AND MUSEUMS. Bonn's old town center winds into a lively pedestrian zone littered with historic niches. **Beethoven Geburtshaus** (Beethoven's birthplace) hosts a fantastic collection of his personal effects, from his primitive hearing aids to his first violin. *(Bonng. 18-20. ☎ 981 75 25. Open Apr.-Sept. M-Sa 10am-6pm, Su 11am-4pm; Oct.-Mar. M-Sa 10am-5pm, Su 11am-4pm. Last entry 1hr. before closing. DM8/€4.10, students DM6/€3.10.)* The **Münster** (cathedral) holds three stories of arches within arches leading to a gorgeous gold-leaf mosaic; a 12th-century cloister laced with crossways and latticed passages branches off under the doorway labeled "Kreuzgang." *(Münsterpl. ☎ 985 88 10. Cloister open M-Sa 9am-5:30pm, Su 1:30-6pm.)* In its governmental heyday, the transparent walls of the **Bundestag** were meant to symbolize the government's responsibility to the public. *(Take U16, U63, or U66 to "Heussallee/Bundeshaus" or bus #610 to "Bundeshaus.")* Forty thousand students study within the **Kurfürstliches Schloß**, the huge 18th-century palace now serving as the center of Bonn's **Friedrich-Wilhelms-Univer-sität**; through the *Schloß* are the student- and punk-filled **Hofgarten** and **Stadtgar-ten.** To uncover Bonn's "other" palace, follow Poppelsdorfer Allee to the 18th-century **Poppelsdorfer Schloß**, which boasts beautifully manicured **botanical gar-dens.** *(Gardens open Apr.-Sept. M-F 9am-6pm, Su 9am-1pm; Oct.-Mar. M-F 9am-4pm, Su 9am-1pm. M-F free; Su DM1/€0.55.)*

The **Bonncard** (see **Practical Information,** above) provides admission to most of Bonn's **"Museum Mile."** To start your museum-crawl, take U16, U63, or U66 to "Heussallee" or "Museum König." **Kunstmuseum Bonn,** Friedrich-Ebert-Allee 2., houses a superb selection of Expressionist and modern German art. (☎77 62 60. *Open Tu and Th-Su 10am-6pm, W 10am-9pm. DM8/€4.10, students DM4/€2.05.)* One block away, the ⬛**Haus der Geschichte** (House of History), Adenauerallee 250/Willy-Brandt 4, examines post-WWII German history through interactive exhibits. (☎916 50. *Open Tu-Su 9am-7pm. Free.)* The art in the nearby **Kunst-und Ausstellungshalle der BRD,** Friedrich-Ebert-Allee 4, is so new you can smell the paint; check out the ultra-modern media-art room. (☎917 12 00. *Open Tu-W 10am-9pm, Th-Su 10am-7pm. DM10/€5.15, students DM5/€2.60.)*

🎵 **NIGHTLIFE.** Bonn's bombastic and versatile nightlife forcefully debunks myths suggesting that the city is boring. Pick up *Schnüss* (DM2/€1.05) for club listings. The ⬛**Jazz Galerie,** Oxfordstr. 24, is a hub for jazz and rock concerts as well as a jumping bar and disco. (Open daily M-Th and Su 9pm-3am, F-Sa 9pm-4am. Opens 8pm on concert nights; shows begin around 9:15pm. Cover for concerts DM10-20/€5.15-10.30; for discos DM13/€6.65.) **Pantheon,** Bundeskanzlerpl., caters to eclectic tastes with a disco, concerts, and stand-up comedy; follow Adenauerallee out of the city until you reach Bundeskanzlerpl. (Open M-Sa 8pm-3am. Cover DM10/€5.15.) Bonn has an active gay scene; **Le Copain,** Thomas-Mann-Str 3a, is a cozy bar filled with locals. (Open M-F 8pm-2am, Sa 8pm-3am.) **Boba's Bar,** Josephstr. 17, is one of the most popular gay bars in town. (Open M-Th 6pm-1am, F-Sa 6pm-3am.)

FRANKFURT AM MAIN ☎069

Frankfurt made its first appearance when Charlemagne put the "Ford of the Franks" on the map in 794. Today, its integral economic role as home to the central bank of the European Union lends it a glitzy vitality—international offices, skyscrapers, and expensive cars lie at every intersection. The city government spends more on cultural attractions and tourism than any other German city. If all this isn't enough to make you visit, the likelihood of your passing through Frankfurt's highly trafficked train station or airport probably is.

▣ TRANSPORTATION

Flights: The airport, **Flughafen Rhein-Main** (☎69 00), is connected to the Hauptbahnhof (main train station) by S14 and S15 (every 15min; buy tickets (DM6.10/€3.15) from the green *Automaten* marked *Fahrkarten* before boarding).

Trains: Frequent trains leave the **Hauptbahnhof** to: **Amsterdam** (5hr.; every 2hr.; DM120/€61.35, under 26 DM126.50/€64.70); **Berlin** (5-6hr.; 2 per hr.; DM207/€105.85, DM166/€84.90); **Cologne** (2½hr.; 2 per hr.; DM76/€38.90, DM61/€31.20); **Hamburg** (6hr.; 2 per hr.; DM191/€97.70, DM153/€78.25); **Munich** (3½-4½hr.; 2 per hr.; DM212/€108.40, DM118/€60.35); **Paris** (6-8hr.; every 2hr.; DM140/€71.60, DM115/€58.70); **Rome** (15hr.; 1 per hr.; DM279/€142.70, DM228/€116.60). Call (0180) 599 66 33 for schedules and information.

Public Transportation: Runs until about 1am. Refer to the subway **map** in the back of this guide. Single-ride tickets (DM2.10/€1.10, rush hour DM2.90/€1.50) are valid for 1hr. in 1 direction, transfers permitted. **Eurail** passes valid only on S-Bahn. The **Tageskarte** (day pass, valid until midnight of the day of purchase) provides unlimited transportation on the S-Bahn, U-Bahn, streetcars, and buses; buy from machines in any station (DM8.50/€4.35).

✈ 🛈 ORIENTATION AND PRACTICAL INFORMATION

The train station lies at the end of Frankfurt's red-light district; from the station, the town center is a 20min. walk down Kaiserstr. or Münchener Str., which lead from the newer part of the city to the **Altstadt**. To the north, the commercial heart of Frankfurt lies along **Zeil**. Cafes, stores, and services cluster in **Bockenheim** (U6 or U7 to "Bockenheimer Warte"). Across the Main, **Sachsenhausen** draws pub-crawlers and museum-goers (U1, U2, or U3 to "Schweizer Pl.").

Tourist Office: (☎ 21 23 88 00; www.frankfurt-tourismus.de). In the Hauptbahnhof, on the right side of the reception hall as you go through the main exit. Open M-F 8am-9pm; Sa-Su and holidays 9am-6pm. Sells the **Frankfurt Card** (1-day DM12/€6.15, 2-day DM19/€9.75), which allows unlimited travel on all trains and buses and gives 50% off admission to 15 museums and attractions.

Laundromat: Schnell & Sauber, Wallstr. 8, near the hostel in Sachsenhausen. Wash DM6/€3.10, dry DM1/€0.55 per 15min. Open daily 6am-11pm.

Emergency: Police, ☎ 110. **Fire** and **ambulance,** ☎ 112.

Disabled travelers: Frankfurt Forum, Römerberg 32 (☎21 24 00 00), publishes a guide to handicapped-accessible locations in Frankfurt. Ask for Mr. Schmidt. Open M and W 10am-4:30pm, Tu 10am-6pm, Th-F 10 am-2pm.

Pharmacy: (☎ 23 30 47). In the Einkaufs passage of the train station. Open M-F 6:30am-9pm, Sa 8am-9pm, Su and holidays 9am-8pm. Emergencies ☎ 192 92.

Internet Access: Sky-Surfer Internet Café, Elisabethstr. 2-4 (☎60 60 55 38), near the hostel. DM2/€1.10 per 15min. Open M-Su 10pm-2am. **CybeRyder Internet Café**, Töngesgasse 31 (☎92 08 40 10). DM6/€3.10 per 30min. Open M-Th 9am-11pm, F-Sa 9am-1am, Su 2-11pm.

Post Office: Main branch, Zeil 90 (☎ 13 81 26 21; fax 13 81 26 24), inside the *Hertie* department store. U- or S-Bahn to "Hauptwache." Open M-F 9:30am-8pm, Sa 9am-4pm. *Poste Restante:* Postlagernde Briefe für FirstName SURNAME, Hauptpostamt, 60313 Frankfurt, Germany.

🏠 ACCOMMODATIONS

▨ **Pension Bruns,** Mendelssohnstr. 42 (☎74 88 96). U6 (dir.: Heerstr.) or U7 (dir.: Hausen) to "Westend"; take the "Siesmayerstr." exit. Go up the escalator, exit left under the sign "Mendelssohn Str.," then walk 1 block and turn left onto Mendelssohnstr. Ring the bell; it's on the 2nd floor. Breakfast included. Showers DM2/€1.10. Call ahead. Doubles DM90-100/€46-€51.15; triples DM120/€61.40; quads DM160/€81.80.

▨ **Pension Backer,** Mendelssohnstr. 92 (☎74 79 92). Cheap, clean, and near the city center, Pension Backer offers some of the best deals in town. To get here, follow the directions above to the Pension Bruns. The Pension Backer is also on the left, but on the 1st block. Breakfast included. Showers 7am-10pm (DM3/€1.55). Singles DM25-50/€12.80-€25.60; doubles DM70/€35.80; triples DM90/€46.

Jugendherberge (HI), Deutschherrnufer 12 (☎610 01 50). Take bus #46 from the main train station (DM2.40/€1.25, rush hour DM2.90/€1.50) to "Frankensteiner Pl." Turn left along the river; the hostel sits at the end of the block. Bordering the Sachsenhausen pub and museum district, the hostel tends to be lively with student groups and youthful travelers. Special day passes for Frankfurt's public transit (DM6.50/€3.35) are available at the 24hr. reception desk. Unlimited breakfast buffet included (7-9am). Check-in after noon. Check-out 9:30am. No lockout. Curfew 2am. Reservations by phone recommended. Beds begin at DM33/€16.90, 19 and under DM26/€13.30. Singles (DM55/€28.15) and doubles (DM90/€46) are *very rarely* available.

Hotel an der Galluswarte, Hufnagelstr. 4 (☎73 39 93). S3 (dir.: Hohenmark), S4 (dir.: Kronberg), S5 (dir.: Friedrichsdorf), or S6 (dir.: Galluswarte) to "Galluswarte." Exit under the sign marked "Mainzer Landstr.," turn right, walk 1 block, and turn right onto Hufnagelstr. Run by the same folks as the Pension Bruns, Hotel an der Galluswarte offers dis-

Frankfurt
ACCOMMODATIONS
Jugendherberge,
Pension Brüns, &
Pension Backer, 1

counted prices if you mention *Let's Go* when you book the room. All rooms have TV, shower, and phone. Breakfast included. *Let's Go* prices: singles DM80/€40.90; doubles DM100/€51.15.

FOOD

Regional specialties include Goethe's favorite, *Handkäse mit Musik* (cheese curd with raw onions); *grüne Sosse* (a green sauce served over boiled eggs or potatoes); and *Ebbelwei* (apple wine, *Äpfelwein* up north). The cheapest meals surround the university in **Bockenheim** and nearby parts of Westend, and many of the pubs in **Sachsenhausen** serve food at a decent price. (For directions, see **Orientation,** above.) Just a few blocks from the youth hostel is a fully-stocked **HL Markt,** Dreieichstr. 56 (open M-F 8am-8pm, Sa 8am-4pm), while a **Tengelmann,** Münchener Str. 37, is close to the Hauptbahnhof (open M-F 8:30am-7:30pm, Su 8am-2pm).

Mensa (university cafeteria), U6 (dir.: Heerstr.) or U7 (dir.: Hausen) to "Bockenheimer Warte," follow signs for "Palmengarten Universität," then use the exit labeled "Mensa." Make the 1st left, right before the STA office; the mensa will be inside the courtyard to your right. Show your ISIC or student ID. Open M-F 11am-3pm.

Dauth-Schneider, Neuerwall Str. 5-7 (☎61 35 33), In the Alte Sachsenhausen quarter, follow Elisabetten Str. until it turns into Paradiesg. Make a left onto Wall Str.; it's on the left. The Äpfelwein (DM2.80/€1.45) here is homemade in the cellar and the best (and cheapest) in Frankfurt. Open M-W and F 4pm-midnight, Sa-Su noon-midnight.

Kleinmarkthalle, on Haseng. between Berliner Str. and Töngesg., is a 3-story warehouse with bakeries, butchers, fruit and vegetable stands, and more. Cutthroat competition between the many vendors pushes prices way down. Open M-F 7:30am-6pm, Sa 7:30am-4pm.

🄖 SIGHTS

Much of Frankfurt's historic splendor lives on only in memories and in reconstructed monuments, since Allied bombing left everything but the cathedral completely destroyed. At the center of the Altstadt is **Römerberg Square** (U-Bahn: "Römer"), home to half-timbered architecture and a medieval fountain of Justice that once spouted wine. At the west end of the Römerberg, the gables of **Römer** have marked the site of Frankfurt's city hall since 1405; upstairs, the **Kaisersaal,** a former imperial banquet hall, is adorned with portraits of the 52 German emperors from Charlemagne to Franz II. (Open daily 10am-1pm and 2-5pm. DM3/€1.55, students DM1/€0.55.) Next to the Römerberg stands the only building that survived the bombings, the red sandstone **Dom,** which contains several splendidly elaborate altarpieces. A new viewing tower is scheduled to open sometime this year. (Open daily 9am-noon and 2-6pm.) The **Dom Museum** within contains intricate chalices and the venerated robes of the imperial electors. (Open Tu-F 10am-5pm, Sa-Su 11am-5pm. DM3/€1.55, students DM1/€0.55.) A few blocks away is the **Museum für Moderne Kunst,** a triangular building (dubbed "the slice of cake") displaying an array of modern art. (Domstr. 10. ☎21 23 04 47. Open Tu and Th-Su 10am-5pm, W 10am-8pm. DM10/€5.15, students DM5/€2.60; W free.) The ▧**Städel,** Schaumainkai 63, has important paintings from nearly every period in the western tradition. (☎605 09 80. Open Tu and Th-Su 10am-5pm, W 10am-8pm. DM10/€5.15, students DM8/€4.10.) Tired of churches and museums? Take refuge in the **Palmengarten,** in the northwest part of town, where the greenhouses showcase seven different "worlds" from the tropics to the plains. (Siesmayerstr. 61-63. ☎21 23 39 39. U6 or U7 to "Bockenheimer Warte." Open Mar.-Oct. daily 9am-6pm; Nov.-Jan. 9am-4pm; Feb. 9am-5pm. DM10/€5.15, students DM4.50/€2.30.) For animal lovers, the **Zoo** houses over 650 species; visit at feeding time (around 11) for maximum entertainment value. (Alfred-Brehm-Pl. 16. ☎21 23 37 35. U6 or U7 to "Zoo." Open mid-Mar. to Sept. M-F 9am-7pm, Sa-Su 8am-7pm; Oct. to mid-Mar. daily 9am-5pm. DM11/€5.65, students DM5/€2.60; with U-Bahn ticket DM9/€4.60, students DM4/€2.05. Last Sa of every month DM5.50/€2.85, students DM2.50/€1.30; with U-Bahn ticket DM4/€2.05, students DM2/€1.05.)

🎵🄖 ENTERTAINMENT AND NIGHTLIFE

Frankfurt's ballet, theater, and opera receive massive endowments from the city to ensure that performances are first-rate. Shows and schedules are listed in *Fritz* and *Strandgut* (free at the tourist office) and the *Journal Frankfurt* (DM3.30/€1.70), available at any newsstand. For information on tickets at almost any venue, call **Frankfurt Ticket** (☎134 04 00). The **Alte Oper,** Opernpl. (☎134 04 00; U6 or U7 to "Alte Oper"), offers a full range of classical music. The **Städtische Bühne,** Untermainanlage 11 (☎21 23 71 33; U1,U2, U3, or U4 to "Willy-Brandt-Pl."), hosts ballets, operas, and experimental plays. **Der Jazzkeller,** Kleine Bockenheimer Str. 18a, is a mainstay of the Frankfurt jazz scene. (Call 28 85 37 for schedules. Cover W and F DM20/€10.25, varies other nights. Open Tu-Su 9pm-3am.)

For a night out drinking, head to the **Alt-Sachsenhausen** district between Brückenstr. and Dreieichstr., home to a huge number of rowdy pubs and taverns. The complex of cobblestoned streets centering on **Grosse** and **Kleine Ritterg.** teems with cafes, bars, restaurants, and gregarious Irish pubs. Frankfurt also has a number of thriving discos and prominent techno DJs, mostly in the commercial district between **Zeil** and **Bleichstraße** Wear something dressier than jeans if you plan to get past the picky bouncers. **U60311,** Roßmarkt, on the

GERMANY

corner of Goetheplatz, is housed in an old subway station and features the best DJs in Frankfurt. (Cover DM15-30/€7.70-15.35. Open M-F 10pm-10am, Sa-Su 10pm-6am.) **The Cave**, Brönnerstr. 11, features hip-hop, house, and reggae every night in a catacomb-like locale. (Cover DM10/€5.15. Open M-Th 10pm-4am, Sa-Su 10pm-6am.) **Blue Angel**, Brönnerstr. 17, is a Frankfurt institution and one of the liveliest gay men's clubs around. Ring the bell to be let in. (Cover DM11/€5.65. Open daily 11pm-4am.)

SOUTHWEST GERMANY

A trip to the Rhineland-Palatinate (Rheinland-Pfalz) to see the castles and wine towns along the Rhine and Mosel rivers is an obligatory tourist tromp. The region is a visual feast—the Mosel curls downstream to the Rhine Gorge, a soft shore of castle-backed hills. But it also provides a gustatory feast; the region grows abundant fresh fruits and vegetables, and vineyards in the Rhine and Mosel Valleys produce sweet, delicious wines. Just to the south, the bucolic, traditional hinterlands of the Black Forest contrast with the region's modern, industrial cities.

RHINE VALLEY (RHEINTAL)

The Rhine River may run from Switzerland to the North Sea, but in the popular imagination it exists only in the legendary 80km of the Rhine Gorge stretching from Bonn to north of Mainz.

E TRANSPORTATION. The Rhine Valley runs north from **Mainz**, easily accessible from Frankfurt, to **Bonn** (see p. 461) via (from south to north) **Bacharach, St. Goarshausen** and **St. Goar**, and **Koblenz**. Two different **train** lines (one on each bank) traverse this fabled stretch; the line on the west bank stays closer to the water and provides superior views. If you're willing to put up with lots of tourists, **boats** are probably the best way to see the sights. The **Köln-Düsseldorfer (KD) Line** covers the Mainz-Koblenz stretch three times per day in summer.

MAINZ   ☎ 06131

Much of Mainz has metamorphosed into a modern metropolis, but the colossal sandstone **Martinsdom** stands as a memorial to former ecclesiastic power: it's the resting place of the archbishops of Mainz, and their extravagant tombstones line the walls. (Open Apr.-Sept. M-F 9am-6:30pm, Sa 9am-4pm, Su 12:45-3pm and 4-6:30pm; Oct.-Mar. M-F 9am-5pm, Sa 9am-4pm, Su 12:45-3pm and 4-5pm. Free.) The gothic **Stephanskirche**, south of the Dom, hides stunning stained-glass windows created by Russian artist-in-exile Marc Chagall. (From the Dom, take Ludwigstr. until it ends at Schillerpl. and follow Gaustr. up the hill. Open daily 10am-noon and 2-5pm.) Johannes Gutenberg, the father of movable type, is immortalized at the **Gutenberg Museum**, which contains several Gutenberg Bibles and a replica of his original press. (Liebfrauenpl. 5, across from the Dom. Open Tu-Su 10am-5pm. DM6/€3.10, students DM3/€1.55.)

Köln-Düsseldorf ferries (☎23 28 00) departs from the wharves on the other side of the Rathaus. The **tourist office** arranges **tours** (2hr., daily 2pm; Jul.-Aug. also Sa 10am; DM10/€5.15) and gives free maps. (☎28 62 10. Open M-F 9am-6pm, Sa 9am-4pm.) To reach the **Jugendgästehaus (HI)**, Otto-Brunfels-Schneise 4, take bus #22, 62, 63, or 92 to "Jugendherberge/Viktorstift" and follow the signs. Every room in this bright, clean hostel has a private bath. (☎853 32. Breakfast included. Reception 7am-midnight. Dorms DM30/€15.45; doubles DM40/€20.60.) Near the Dom, **Central Café** serves a range of German and American foods. (Open Su-Th 10am-1am midnight, F-Sa 10am-1am.) For groceries, try **Supermarkt 2000**, Am Brand 41, under the Sinn-Leffers department store (open M-F 9:30am-8pm, Sa 9am-4pm). **Postal Code:** 55001.

BACHARACH   ☎06743

Bacharach lives up to its name ("Altar of Bacchus") with its many *Weinkeller* and *Weinstuben* (wine cellars and pubs). **Die Weinstube,** Oberstr. 63, is a family-owned business that makes wine on the premises. Nearby is the 14th-century **Wernerkapelle,** the remains of a red sandstone chapel that took 140 years to build but only a few hours to destroy in the Palatinate War of Succession in 1689. It's a short climb up the steps next to the late-Romanesque **Peterskirche.** The **tourist office,** Oberstr. 45, and the *Rathaus* share a building at one end of the town center. (☎91 93 03. Open Apr.-Oct. M-F 9am-5pm, Sa 10am-4pm; Nov.-Mar. M-F 9am-1pm and 1:30-5pm, Sa 10am-1pm.) Hostels get no better than the unbelievable ■**Jugendherberge Stahleck (HI),** a gorgeous 12th-century castle that provides an unbeatable panoramic view of the Rhine Valley for its 40,000 yearly visitors, a great selection of local wines in the bar downstairs, and cheerful plaid sheets on the beds. The steep 20min. hike to the hostel is worth every step. Call ahead; they're usually full by 6pm. Make a right out of the station pathway, turn left at the Peterskirche, and take any of the marked paths leading up the hill. (☎12 66. Breakfast included. Curfew 10pm. DM25.90/€13.25; doubles DM31.90/€16.35.) At ■**Café Restaurant Rusticana,** Oberstr. 40, a lovely German couple serves up three-course meals (DM12-20/€6.15-10.25) and lively conversation. (Open M-F 9am-10pm.)

LORELEI CLIFFS AND CASTLES

The section of the Rhine just north of Bacharach was so difficult to navigate that a sailors' song developed about the siren Lorelei, who seduced sailors with her intoxicating song and drew ships into the rocks. Today, visitors are seduced by the amazing scenery around the charming towns of **St. Goarshausen** and **St. Goar,** on either side of the Rhine, which host the spectacular firework-filled **Rhein in Flammen** celebration at the end of every summer (September 21, 2002). St. Goarshausen, on the east bank, provides access by foot to the Lorelei statue and the infamous cliffs. Directly above the town, the fierce **Burg Katz** (Cat Castle) eternally stalks its prey, the smaller **Burg Maus** (Mouse Castle). Burg Maus offers daily falconry demonstrations; call 76 69 for information or visit St. Goarshausen's **tourist office,** Bahnhofstr. 8. (☎(06771) 91 00. Open M-F 9am-1pm and 2-5:30pm, Sa 9:30am-12:30pm.) The **"Lorelei V" ferry** (6am-11pm; DM1.50/€0.80, round-trip DM2.50/€1.30) crosses the river to **St.Goar,** from which the view is spectacular. St. Goar's **tourist office,** Heerstr. 6, is in the pedestrian zone. (☎(06741) 333. Open M-F 8am-12:30pm and 2-5pm, Sa 10am-noon.) To reach **Jugendheim Loreley,** on the St. Goarshausen side of the Rhine, walk from the cliffs past the red-and-white parking gate down the road a few hundred meters and turn left. (☎(06771) 26 19. Breakfast included. Curfew 10pm. DM23.50/€12.05.) **Postal code:** 56329.

KOBLENZ   ☎0261

Koblenz has long been a strategic hot spot; in the 2000 years since its birth, the city has hosted every empire seeking to conquer Europe. Before reunification, the city served as a large munitions dump, but now the only pyrotechnics are when the **Rhein in Flammen fireworks festival** hits the town in mid-August. The city centers around the **Deutsches Eck** (German Corner), a peninsula at the confluence of the Rhine and Mosel that purportedly witnessed the birth of the German nation in 1216. The **Mahnmal der Deutschen Einheit** (Monument to German Unity) to the right is a tribute to Kaiser Wilhelm I. The ■**Museum Ludwig im Deutschherrenhaus,** behind the Mahnmal, features contemporary French art and continuously changing special exhibits. (Danziger Freiheit 1. ☎30 40 40. Open Tu-Sa 10:30am-5pm, Su 11am-6pm. DM5/€2.60, students DM3/€1.55.) The stained-glass windows of the **Baroque Liebfrauenkirche** document the role of women in the Passion and Resurrection of Christ. (Open M-Sa 8am-6pm, Su 9am-12:30pm and 6-8pm; in summer also Su 12:30-6pm. Free.) Koblenz's most mischievous monu-

GERMANY

ment lurks outside the **Jesuitenkirche** on the Marktplatz; the **Schängelbrunnen**, a statue of a boy that spits water on passersby, drives kids into frenzied glee. Head across the river to the **Festung Ehrenbreitstein**, a fortress at the highest point in the city. Today, it's a youth hostel. (Non-hostel guests DM2/€1.05, students DM1/€0.55. Tours DM4/€2.05.)

Trains run to: Bonn (30min., 4 per hr., DM15/€7.70); Frankfurt (2hr., 2 per hr., DM36/€18.45); Cologne (1hr., 3-4 per hr., DM25/€12.80); Mainz (1hr., 3 per hr., DM25/€12.80); Trier (2hr., 1 per hr., DM30/€15.35). Take a sharp left from the station for the **tourist office**, Löhrstr. 141. (☎313 04; www.koblenz.de. Open M-F 9am-8pm, Sa-Su 10am-8pm.) **Jugendherberge Koblenz (HI)**, located within the fortress, offers breathtaking views of the Rhine and Mosel. Take bus #9 or 10 from the stop on Löhrstr. (just left of the train station) to "Charlottenstr." Then take the chairlift up (operates daily Mar.-Sept. 9am-5:50pm; DM5/€2.60, round-trip DM7/€3.60), or continue along the Rhine side of the mountain on the main road, following the DJH signs, and take the footpath up. (☎737 37. Breakfast included. Reception 7:30am-11:30pm. Curfew 11:30pm. DM28/€14.35; doubles DM80/€40.90.) **Ferries** (DM0.60/€0.35) cross the Mosel to **Campingplatz Rhein-Mosel**, Am Neuendorfer Eck. (☎827 19. Reception 8am-noon and 2-8pm. Open Apr.-Oct. 15. DM6.50/€3.35 per person, DM5/€2.60 per tent.) **Marktstübchen**, Am Markt 220, downhill from the hostel, serves authentic German food at budget prices. (Open M-Tu, Th, and Su 11am-midnight, W 11am-2pm, F 4pm-1am, Sa 11am-1am.) **Plus supermarket** is at Roonstr. 49-51. (Open M-F 8:30am-7pm, Sa 8am-2pm.) **Postal Code:** 65068.

MOSEL VALLEY (MOSELTAL) \

As if trying to avoid its inevitable surrender to the Rhine at Koblenz, the Mosel river meanders slowly past sun-drenched hills, picturesque towns, and ancient castles.

▐ TRANSPORTATION

The Mosel Valley runs northeast from **Trier** through **Cochem** and **Beilstein** to **Koblenz**, where it bisects the Rhine Valley (see p. 468). The best way to view the scenery is by boat, bus, or bicycle, since the train line between Koblenz and Trier runs through unremarkable countryside. If you're starting in Koblenz, try taking the train to Cochem, then pop by Beilstein (a short distance upstream) and Trier before taking the train (1¾hr., 2 per hr., DM30/€15.35) or a boat back. To really soak up the scenery, consider renting a bike in Koblenz or Trier and biking along the river.

COCHEM AND BEILSTEIN

Busloads of city-dwellers devour the quintessential quaintness of Cochem, yet the impressive vineyard-covered hills and majestic **Reichsburg castle,** perched high on a hill above town, simply can't be cheapened. The 11th-century castle was destroyed in 1689 by French troops led by Louis XIV but was rebuilt in 1868. (Open mid-Mar. to Jan. daily 11am-5pm. Mandatory 40min. tours on the hr.; written English translation available. DM7/€3.60, students DM6/€3.10.) The **Weinwoche** begins a week and a half after Pfingsten (May 20, 2002) and showcases some of the Mosel's best vintages (DM1-2/€0.55-1.05 per 100ml taste). On the last weekend of August, the **Heimat-und-Weinfest** culminates in a dramatic fireworks display. Cochem is easily accessible by **train** from Koblenz (1hr., 2-3 per hr., DM13/€6.65) and Trier (1hr., 2 per hr., DM17/€8.70); the Koblenz route is prettier and hugs the Mosel. From the train station, go to the river and turn right to reach the **tourist office**, Endertpl. 1. (☎(02671) 600 40; www.cochem.de. Open Apr.-Oct. M-Th and Sa 9am-5pm, F 9am-6pm; Nov.-Mar. M-F 9am-1pm and 2-5pm.) **Hotel Holl**, Endertstr. 54, combines large, bright, and comfortable rooms with good food. (☎(02671) 43 23. Breakfast included. Doubles DM60/€30.80.) **Campingplatz am Freizeitzentrum**, on Stadionstr., rents bikes for DM14/

€7.20 per day. (Laundry DM1.50/€0.80. Reception 8am-10pm. Open Easter-Oct. DM6.50/€3.35 per person, DM6-12/€3.10-€6.15 per tent.) **Café-Restaurant Mosella,** on the Marktplatz next to the bridge, offers coffee and hearty meals. (Open M-Sa 10am-10pm.)

From Cochem, bus #8060 (15min; M-F 14 per day, Sa 7 per day, Su 3 per day; DM4.90/€2.50) runs to **Beilstein,** the smallest official town in Germany. A tiny hamlet of half-timbered houses, crooked cobblestone streets, and about 170 residents, Beilstein was spared in WWII and its untarnished beauty has made it the idyllic backdrop of several movies and political summits. **Burg Metternich** is the resident castle; the French sacked it in 1689, but the ruins and the view from the tower are still spectacular. (Open Apr.-Oct. daily 9am-6pm. DM3/€1.55, students DM2/ €1.05.) The recently repainted Baroque **Karmelitenkirche** contains an intricately carved wooden altar and the famous 16th-century **Schwarze Madonna von Beilstein** sculpture. (Open daily 9am-8pm.) The **Klostercafé** outside offers traditional food, fantastic Mosel wine, and a view that beats them both. (Open M-Sa 9am-7pm.)

TRIER ☎ 0651

The oldest town in Germany, Trier was founded by the Romans during the reign of Augustus and reached its heyday in the 4th century as the capital of the Western Roman Empire and a center for Christianity in Europe. A one-day **combination ticket** (Mar. 24-Sept. DM9/€4.60, students DM4.50/€2.30; Oct.-Nov. and Jan.-Mar. 23 DM4.50/€2.30; Dec. DM4/€2.05) provides access to all of the city's Roman monuments. The most impressive is the massive 2nd-century **Porta Nigra** (Black Gate), which got its name from the centuries of grime that turned its sandstone face gray. (Open Mar. 24-Sept. daily 9am-6pm; Oct.-Nov. and Jan.-Mar. 23 9am-5pm; Dec. 10am-4pm. DM4/€2.05, students DM2/€1.05.) A short stroll away, the 11th-century **Dom** (cathedral) shelters the tombs of archbishops and what is reputedly the **Tunica Christi** (Holy Robe of Christ), brought from Jerusalem to Trier around AD 300. It was last shown to the public in 1996. (Open Apr.-Oct. daily 6:30am-6pm; Nov.-Mar. 6:30am-5:30pm. Free.) The enormous **Basilika** was originally the location of Emperor Constantine's throne room. (Open M-Sa 9am-6pm, Su 11:30am-6pm. Free.) Near the southeast corner of the city walls, the gloomy underground passages of the 4th-century **Kaiserthermen** ("Emperor's baths") create a perfect place to play hide-and-seek. (Open Apr.-Sept. 9am-6pm; Oct.-Mar. 9am-5pm. DM4/€2.05, students DM3/€1.55.) A 10min. walk uphill along Olewiger Str. brings you to the 2nd-century **amphitheater;** it's now a peaceful park. (Admission and times same as the Porta Nigra, above, but closed Dec.) The **Karl-Marx-Haus,** Brückenstr. 10, where young Karl first walked, talked, and dreamed of labor alienation, is a must-see for indefatigable Marxists. (Open Apr.-Oct. M 1-6pm, Tu-Su 10am-6pm; Nov.-Mar. M 2-5pm, Tu-Su 10am-1pm and 2-5pm. DM3/ €1.55, students DM2/€1.05.)

Trains go to: Koblenz (1¾hr., 2 per hr., DM30/€15.40) and Luxembourg City (45min., 1 per hr., DM15/€7.70). From the station, walk down Theodor-Haus-Allee or Christophstr. to reach the **tourist office,** under the shadow of the Porta Nigra. (☎97 80 80; www.trier.de. Open M-Sa 9am-6:30pm, Su 9am-3:30pm. Daily English tours 1:30pm, DM10/€5.15.) The staff at nearby **Vinothek,** Margaritengässchen 2a, can give info on **wine tasting** in the region. (☎978 08 34. Open daily 10am-7pm.) **Hotel Haus Runne,** Engelstr. 35, has large rooms with TV; follow Theodor-Heuss-Allee from the station and turn right on Engelstr. after the Porta Nigra. (☎289 22. Breakfast included. Singles DM45/€23; doubles DM90/ €46; quads DM160/€81.80.) ▓**Astarix,** Karl-Marx-Str. 11, serves excellent food at unbelievable prices. It's squeezed in a passageway next to Miss Marple's; if you get to a big white fence on the left, you've gone too far. (Open M-Th 11:30am-1am, F-Sa 11:30am-2am, Su 6pm-1am. Kitchen open M-Th and Su noon-11:30pm, F-Sa noon-12:30am.) There's a **Plus supermarket** at Brotstr. 54. (Open M-F 8:30am-7pm, Sa 8:30am-4pm.)

HEIDELBERG
☎ 06221

This sunlight-coated town by the Neckar and its crumbling *Schloß* lured writers and artists—including Twain, Goethe, and Hugo—and today, roughly 32,000 tourists are drawn in *each* summer day. However, the incessant buzz of mass tourism is worth enduring to experience beautiful Heidelberg and its lively nightlife.

▟ TRANSPORTATION

Trains: To **Frankfurt** (40min., 2 per hr., DM23.40/€12) and **Stuttgart** (40min., 1 per hr., DM31/€15.85). Other trains run regularly to towns in the **Neckar Valley.**

Public Transportation: Single-ride tickets DM3.90/€2. Day passes valid for 24hr. from the time of purchase on all streetcars and buses (DM10.50/€5.40). Passes are available at the tourist office and ticket machines.

Bike Rental: Per Bike, Bergheimer Str. 125 (☎ 16 11 48). Half-day DM15/€7.70, full day DM25/€12.80, additional days DM20/€10.25. DM50/€25.60 deposit or ID required. Open M-F 9am-6pm; Apr.-Oct. also open Sa 9am-1pm.

Hitchhiking: *Let's Go* does not recommend hitchhiking. Hitchers wait at the western end of Bergheimerstr. **Mitfahrzentrale,** Bergheimer Str. 125 (☎246 46), matches riders and drivers to: **Hamburg** (DM54/€27.65); **Cologne** (DM28/€14.35); **Paris** (DM51/ €26). Open M-F 9am-5pm; Apr.-Oct. also Sa 9am-noon.

✦❔ ORIENTATION AND PRACTICAL INFORMATION

Most of Heidelberg's attractions are in the eastern part of the city, along the south bank of the Neckar. From the train station, take any bus or streetcar to "Bismarckpl.," then walk east down **Hauptstraße,** the city's spine, to the **Altstadt.** The two-day **Heidelberg Card,** available from the tourist office, includes unlimited public transit and admission to most sights (DM19.80/€10.15).

Tourist Office: Tourist Information (☎ 13 88 121), in front of the station, offers tours (DM22/€11.25) Th-Su, sells Heidelberg Aktuell (DM1/€0.55), and **books rooms** (8% deposit and DM5/€2.60 fee). Open M-Sa 9am-7pm; Apr.-Oct also Su 10am-6pm.

American Express: Brückenkopfstr. 1 (☎ 450 517), at the north end of Theodor-Heuss-Brücke. Mail held. Open M-F 10am-6pm, Sa 9am-1pm.

Emergency: ☎ 110. **Police:** Römerstr. 2-4, ☎980. **Fire** and **Ambulance:** ☎ 112.

Internet Access: Internet Cafe, inside Brodl on Hauptstr. 90, near Bismarckpl. DM6/ €3.10 per 30min. Open M-F 9:30am-7:30pm, Sa 9:30am-4pm.

Post Office: Sofienstr. 8-10, **69155** Heidelberg. Open daily 9am-6:30pm.

▟ ACCOMMODATIONS

In summer, reserve ahead or arrive early in the day to spare yourself a headache.

Jugendherberge (HI), Tiergartenstr. 5 (☎41 20 66; fax 40 25 59). From Bismarckpl. or the station, bus #33 (dir.: Zoo-Sportzentrum) to "Jugendherberge." In peak season, call or fax at least a week ahead. Crowded and noisy, but its small disco (open nightly) can be fun. Sheets DM5.50/€2.85. Reception until 11:30pm. Lockout 9am-1pm. Curfew 11:30pm; stragglers admitted 1am. **HI members only.** Dorms DM24/€12.30, over 26 DM28/€14.35.

Jeske Hotel, Mittelbadg. 2 (☎ 237 33). From the station, bus #33 (dir.: Ziegelhausen) or 11 (dir.: Karlstor) to "Rathaus/Kornmarkt"; Mittelbadg. is the 2nd left off the square. Great value with an unbeatable location. Doubles DM104/€53.20.

Schmidts, Blumenstr. 54 (☎27 29 6). From the station, walk on Kurfürsten Anlage to Romer Kreis, cut back right on Ringstr., and turn left on Blumenstr. Breakfast included. Singles DM70/€35.80, with shower DM120/€61.40.

GERMANY

Hotel-Pension Elite, Bunsenstr. 15 (☎ 257 34). From Bismarckpl., follow Rohrbacher Str. away from the river and turn right on Bunsenstr. From the train station, take street-car #1 to "Poststr."; the hotel is on the 2nd street behind the Holiday Inn. All rooms have high ceilings, bath, and TV. Breakfast included. Show your *Let's Go* guide for these reduced rates. Singles DM75/€38.35; doubles DM100/€51.15.

◗ FOOD

Eating out tends to be depressingly expensive in Heidelberg; most of the restaurants on and around Hauptstr. are exorbitantly priced. Head outside this central area for better values. **Handelshof supermarket,** Kurfürsten-Anlage 60, is 200m to the right of the train station. (Open M-F 7:30am-8pm, Sa 7:30am-4pm.) A **fruit market** is held on Marktpl. Wednesdays and Saturdays.

Mensa (University cafeteria), in the *Marstall* on Marstallstr. From the Alte Brücke, with your back to the old city, take a left along the river; it's the red fortress on the left. Meals DM7/€3.60, with student ID DM4/€2.05; DM3/€1.55 plate deposit. Lunch M-F 11:30am-2pm. Dinner M-Sa 5-10pm.

Großer Wok, Bergheimer Str. 7 (☎ 60 25 28), near Bismarckpl. Chinese food (DM4-13/€2.05-6.65), in-house or packaged to go. Open M-Sa 11am-10pm, Su 1-10pm.

Thanner, Bergheimer Str. 71 (☎ 252 34), is a swank cafe with an eclectic menu and the only Biergarten in Heidelberg allowed to play music (garden open until 11pm). Entrees DM10-20/€5.15-10.25. Open M-Sa 9am-2am, Su 9am-3am.

◎ SIGHTS

▨ HEIDELBERGER SCHLOß. Over a period of almost 400 years, the castle's residents commissioned their own distinctive additions, resulting in the conglomeration of styles you see today. Destroyed twice by war (1622 and 1693) and once by lightning (1764), its regal state of disrepair is best viewed from within. The **Apothekenmuseum** inside features creepy displays on pharmaceuticals and alchemy. *(Open daily 10am-5:30pm. Tour 2:30pm.)* The castle **wine cellar** holds the **Großer Faß,** the largest wine barrel ever made, holding 221,726L. *(Grounds open daily 8am-5:30pm. DM3/€1.55, students DM1.50/€0.80. English tours of the castle daily at 15min. past the hour 11:15am-4:15pm. DM4/€2.05, students DM2/€1.05.)* The *Schloß* is accessible by an uphill path or the **Bergbahn,** the world's oldest cable car. *(Take bus #11 (dir.: Köpfel) or 33 (dir.: Karlstor). Trams leave the Kornmarkt parking lot next to the bus stop every 10min. 9am-7:45pm, round-trip DM5.80/€3.)*

MARKTPLATZ. The Altstadt's center is the cobblestoned **Marktplatz,** where accused witches and heretics were burned at the stake in the 15th century. The two oldest structures in Heidelberg line the square: the 14th-century **Heiliggeistkirche** (Church of the Holy Spirit) and the 16th-century **Haus Zum Ritter,** opposite the church. *(Church open M-Sa 11am-5pm, Su 1-5pm. Free. Church tower DM0.50/€0.30.)*

UNIVERSITÄT. Heidelberg is home to Germany's oldest and perhaps most prestigious university, established in 1368. More than 20 Nobel laureates have called the university home, and it was here that sociology became a legitimate academic subject under the leadership of Max Weber. Before 1914, the university faculty jailed naughty students in the **Studentenkarzer,** Augustinerg. 2, which the imprisoned youths proceeded to cover with poetic graffiti. *(Open Apr.-Oct. M-F 10am-4pm; Nov.-Mar. Tu-F 10am-4pm. DM5/€2.60, students DM4/€2.05.)* The **Bibliothek** (library), Plöck 107-109, contains precious medieval manuscripts. *(Open M-Sa 10am-7pm. Free.)*

KURPFÄLZISCHES MUSEUM. Artifacts include the jawbone of a *homo Heidelbergensis,* one of the earliest humans ever discovered; art by Dürer; and an awesome archaeology exhibit. *(Hauptstr. 97. Open Tu and Th-Su 10am-5pm, W 10am-9pm. Tu and Th-Sa DM5/€2.60, students DM3/€1.55; Su DM3/€1.55, students DM2/€1.05.)*

a brick path leading upward to the Burgenweg. (Open Mar.-Oct. M-Sa 9am-8pm.) The **tourist office**, Hauptstr. 7, inside the Rathaus, is one block down from Bahnhofstr. in the same direction as the *Schloßsteige*. (☎920 00. Open M-W 8am-noon and 1:30-3:30pm, Th 8am-noon and 1:30-5pm, F 8am-noon.)

STUTTGART ☎0711

Forget about *Lederhosen*—Porsche, Daimler-Benz, and a host of other corporate thoroughbreds keep Stuttgart speeding along in the fast lane. After almost complete destruction in WWII, Stuttgart was rebuilt in a thoroughly modern, functional, and uninspiring style, but the surrounding forested hills provide welcome tranquility to the busy capital of Baden-Württemberg.

TRANPORTATION AND PRACTICAL INFORMATION. Stuttgart, the transportation hub of southwestern Germany, has direct **trains** to most major German cities, including: Berlin (5½-12hr., 2 per hr., DM209-256/€107-131); Frankfurt (1½-4½hr., 2 per hr., DM40-88/€20.45-45); Munich (2½-3½hr., 2-3 per hr., DM40-73/€20.45-37.35). Call (0180) 599 66 33 for 24hr. schedule information. On the **U- or S-bahn**, a single ride costs DM3-10/€1.55-5.15 depending on distance; consider a **Tageskarte** (city DM9/€4.60, regional DM18/€9.20; valid on all trains and buses for 24hr.). **tips 'n' trips**, Lautenschlagerstr. 20, has **Internet** (DM3.50/€1.80 per 30min., students DM2.50/€1.30) and resources on all aspects of the Stuttgart scene. (☎222 27 30. Open M-F noon-7pm, Sa 10am-2pm.) The **post office, 70173** Stuttgart, is inside the train station. (Open M-F 8am-7pm, Sa 8:30am-12:30pm.)

ACCOMMODATIONS AND FOOD. To reach the **Jugendherberge Stuttgart (HI)**, Haußmannstr. 27, take streetcar #15 (dir.: Heumaden) to "Eugenspl." and go downhill on Kernerstr.; the entrance is up the stairs with the red handrail. (☎24 15 83; fax 236 10 41; jh-stuttgart@t-online.de. Breakfast included. Sheets DM6/€3.10. Reception 1pm-1am. Lockout 9:30am-1pm. Curfew M-F 1am, F-Sa 2am. Reserve at least a week ahead by mail, email, or fax. Dorms DM25/€12.80, over 26 DM30/€15.35.) For **Jugendgästehaus Stuttgart**, Richard-Wagner-Str. 2, ride streetcar #15 (dir.: Ruhban) to "Bubenbad" and take the next right. (☎24 11 32. Breakfast and sheets included. Reception M-F 2-10pm. No curfew. Dorms DM30/€13.35; singles DM40/€20.45; doubles DM70/€35.80; 1-night stays DM5/€2.60 extra; sink DM5/€2.60 extra; bath DM10/€5.15 extra.) **Iden**, Eberhardstr. 1, serves good vegetarian fare by weight. (U-Bahn to "Rathaus." Open M-F 11am-9pm, Sa 10:30am-5pm.) For fruits, veggies, and other staples, head to **Markthalle**, an indoor farmers' market on Sporerstr. (M-F 7am-6:30pm, Sa 7am-4pm.)

SIGHTS AND ENTERTAINMENT. The **Schloßgarten**, Stuttgart's principal park, is crammed with fountains and beautiful flower gardens. At the north end is the **Wilhelma**, a large zoological and botanical garden. (U14 to "Wilhelma." ☎540 20. Open Mar. and Oct. daily 8:15am-5pm; Nov.-Feb. 8:15am-4pm; May-Aug. 8:15am-6pm; Apr. and Sept. 8:15am-5:30pm. DM16/€8.20, students DM8/€4.10; after 4pm and Nov.-Feb. DM10/€5.15, DM5/€2.60.) The Schloßgarten runs to Schloßpl., where stodgy bureaucrats gather in the elegant Baroque **Neues Schloß**; the 16th-century **Altes Schloß**, across the street on Schillerpl., contains the **Württembergisches Landesmuseum**, which details the Swabian region with excellent exhibits on local archaeology. (Open Tu 10am-1pm, W-Su 10am-5pm. DM5/€2.60, students DM3/€1.55.) The superb **Staatsgallerie Stuttgart**, Konrad-Adenauer-Str. 30-32, houses an excellent collection of modern art in the new wing. (Open Tu-W and F-Su 10am-6pm, Th 10am-9pm. DM9/€4.60, students DM5/€2.60; free W.) The **Mercedes-Benz Museum**, Mercedesstr. 137, displays gleaming historical cars. Take S1 to "Daimlerstadion," walk away from the tracks, and follow the signs. (Open Tu-Su 9am-5pm. Free.) Check out their competition at the **Porschemuseum**, Porschestr. 42, a glorified showroom full of sexy cars. Ride S6 to "Neuwirtshaus," exit to the right, follow the pink wall, and turn left on Moritz-Horkheimer-Str. (Open M-F 9am-4pm, Sa-Su 9am-5pm. Free.) In addition to its museums, Stuttgart harbors amazing **mineral baths** (Mineralbäder)—the perfect remedy for budget traveler exhaustion. **Mineralbad**

Leuze, Am Leuzebad 2-6, has indoor, outdoor, and thermal therapy pools. (U1, U14, or streetcar #2 to "Mineralbäder." ☎216 42 10. Open daily 6am-9pm. 2hr. soak DM12/€6.15, students DM9/€4.60.) Once refreshed, join the crowd for a drink at **Palast der Republik,** Friedrichstr. 27. (Open Tu-W 11am-2am, Th-Sa 11am-3am, Su-M 11am-1am). **Kings Club,** Calwerstr. 21, is Stuttgart's oldest gay/lesbian establishment. (Open daily 10pm-6am; F-Sa cover DM15/€7.70 in drink tickets.)

BADEN-BADEN ☎07221

If you dream of leading an Old World aristocrat's pampered life, you'll have a ball in Baden-Baden. Although the spa town has declined somewhat since its 19th-century heyday, it remains a playground where minor royalty and the well-to-do bathe in the curative mineral spas and drop fat sums of money in the casino. Baden-Baden's history as a resort goes back nearly two millennia, to when the Romans started soaking themselves in the town's first **thermal baths.** The **Friedrichsbad,** Römerpl. 1, is a beautiful 19th-century bathing palace where visitors can soak in a mud bath or be pummeled by trained professionals. (☎27 59 20. Open M-Sa 9am-10pm, Su noon-8pm. Co-ed baths Tu and F 4-10pm, all day W and Sa-Su. Standard Roman-Irish bath DM36/€18.40, with soap and brush massage DM48/€24.55.) Budget-minded cure-seekers should head next door to **Caracalla-Thermen,** Römerpl. 1, where pools, whirlpools, and solaria of varying sizes and temperatures pamper the weary traveler. (☎27 59 40. Open daily 8am-10pm. Oct.-June 2hr. DM21/€10.75; 3hr. DM25/€12.80; 4hr. DM29/€14.85. July-Sept. 3hr. DM21/€10.75; 4hr. DM25/€12.80.)

The **train station** is 5km out of town; take bus #201 to "Hindenburgpl." to reach the **tourist office,** inside the Trinkhalle on Kaiserallee, which has free maps and a hotel list. (☎27 52 00. Open daily 10am-6:30pm.) The cheapest beds in town are at the **Werner-Dietz-Jugendherberge (HI),** Hardenbergstr. 34, between the station and the town center. Take bus #201, 205, or 216 to "Grosse-Dollen-Str." (DM3.50/€1.80) and follow the signs uphill.(☎522 23; jh-baden-baden@t-online.de. Sheets DM6/€3.10. Reception every hr. 5-11pm. Curfew 11:30pm. Write in advance for reservations. Dorm beds DM25/€12.80, over 26 DM30/€15.35. **HI members only.**) **Hotel am Markt,** Marktpl. 18, is between the Friedrichsbad and the Stiftskirche. (☎270 40. Breakfast included. Reception 7am-10pm. Singles DM56-60/€28.65-30.70, with shower DM80-90/€40.90-46; doubles DM115-120/€58.80-61.35, DM140-150/€71.60-76.70. AmEx/MC/V.) Most restaurants in Baden-Baden are too pricey for the budget traveler; your best bet is to pick up **groceries** at **Pennymarkt,** near the hostel. (Open M-W 8:30am-6:30pm, Th-F 8:30am-7pm, Sa 8:30am-2pm.)

BLACK FOREST (SCHWARZWALD)

The Black Forest owes its name to the eerie gloom that prevails under its evergreen canopy. Once inspiration for the "Hansel and Gretel" and other Grimm's fairy tales, the region now attracts hikers and skiers with more than just bread crumbs.

�E TRANSPORTATION. The main entry point to the Black Forest is **Freiburg,** which is accessible by **train** from Stuttgart and Basel, Switzerland. From Freiburg, it's easy to catch buses or trains to other towns in the area.

FREIBURG IM BREISGAU. Freiburg may be the metropolis of the Schwarzwald, but it has yet to succumb to the hectic rhythms of city life. Two medieval gates—the **Schwabentor** and the **Martinstor**—stand within blocks of each other in the southeast corner of the Altstadt, but Freiburg's pride and joy is the majestic **Münster,** a stone cathedral with a 116m spire and a tower with the oldest bell in Germany. (Open M-Sa 10am-6pm, Su 1-6pm. Tower open M-Sa 9:30am-5pm, Su 1-5pm; DM2.50/€1.30, students DM1.50/€0.80.) The ▧**Augustiner Museum,** Salzstr. 32, is set in a 13th-century monastery and contains an impressive medieval sculpture and art collection. (Open Tu-Su 10am-5pm. DM4/€2.05, students DM2/€1.05; free 1st Su of every month.) The surrounding hills brim with fantastic **hiking** trails; maps are available in the tourist office or at most bookstores, and all trails are clearly marked.

Trains run to Basel (40min.-1hr., 1-2 per hr., DM17-30/€8.70-15.35) and Stuttgart (2-3hr., 2 per hr., DM61-68/€31.20-34.80). The **tourist office,** Rotteckring 14, two blocks down Eisenbahnstr. from the station, has maps and books **Privatzimmer** (rooms in private homes) for DM5/€2.60; these are usually the most affordable accommodations in Freiburg, since most hotels and *Pensionen* are outside the city center. (Open M-F 9:30am-8pm, Sa 9:30am-5pm, Su 10am-noon; Oct.-May M-F 9:30am-6pm, Sa 9:30am-2pm, Su 10am-noon.) To reach the impeccably clean **Haus Lydia Kalchtaler,** Peterhof 11, take streetcar #1 (dir.: Littenweiler) to "Lassbergstr.," then bus #17 (dir.: Kappel) to "Kleintalstr." It's far (30min.) from the city center, but it's actually closer (and cheaper) than the town hostel. (☎671 19. Kitchen available. Sheets DM5/€2.60, included for stays over 3 nights. DM25/€12.80 per person.) The **Freiburger Markthalle,** next to the Martinstor, is home to food-stands serving ethnic specialties for DM5-15/€2.60-7.70. The main entrance is one block up on Grünwälderstr. (☎(0761) 38 11 11. Open M-F 8am-7pm, Sa 8am-4pm.) ◪**Brennessel,** Eschholzstr. 17, behind the train station, fills the empty gullet without emptying the wallet. (Open M-Sa 8am-1am, Su 5pm-1am.) **Edeka,** Eisenbahnstr. 39, sells groceries. (Open M-F 7:30am-8pm, Sa 8am-4pm.)

TITISEE AND SCHLUCHSEE. The more touristed **Titisee** (TEE-tee-zay) is only 30min. by train (2 per hr.) from Freiburg via the scenic **Höllental** (Hell's Valley). The **tourist office,** Strandbadstr. 4, books rooms (DM4/€2.05), rents **bikes** (DM15/€7.70 per day), and dispenses maps of the 130km of nearby **hiking** trails. From the station, take a right onto Parkstr. and another on Strandbadstr. (☎(07651) 980 40. Open May-Oct. M-F 8am-6pm, Sa 11am-5pm, Su 10am-noon; Nov.-Apr. M-F 8am-noon and 1:30-5:30pm.) **Schluchsee,** to the south, also has a slew of first-rate **hiking** trails. The simple **Seerundweg** (18km, about 4hr.) circles the lake; follow the markers with red dots. More difficult and rewarding trails depart from the Sportplatz parking lot, a 15min. walk up Dresselbacher Str. past the huge resort hotel. To reach the **tourist office,** a block into the pedestrian zone, turn right from the train station, walk through the underpass, and turn left up the brick sidewalk; it's at the corner of Fischbacher Str. and Lindenstr., in the Kurhaus. The staff books rooms for free and has hiking maps. (☎(07656) 77 32. Open May-Sept. M-Th 8am-6pm, F 9am-6pm, Sa 10am-noon; July-Aug. also Su 10am-noon; Oct.-Apr. M-F 8am-noon and 2-6pm.)

ST. PETER AND ST. MÄRGEN. North of Titisee and 17km east of Freiburg, twin villages St. Peter and St. Märgen lie between cow-speckled hills in the High Black Forest. **Bus** #7216 runs from **Freiburg** to **St. Peter** (25min.); get off at "Zähriger Eck" to reach St. Peter's **tourist office,** in the Klosterhof, which has a list of affordable rooms. (☎(07660) 91 02 24. Open M-F 9am-noon and 3-5pm; July-Aug. also Sa 10am-noon.) Many hiking paths—most well marked—begin at the tourist office. An easy and very scenic 8km path leads to **St. Märgen;** follow the blue diamonds of the **Panoramaweg.** Alternatively, **bus** #7216 continues on to St. Märgen about half the time; check with the driver. With links to all major Black Forest trails and a number of gorgeous **day hikes,** St. Märgen rightfully calls itself a *Wanderparadies* (hiking paradise). Most of the trails are marked from Hotel Hirschen, uphill from the bus stop. The **tourist office,** in the Rathaus, 100m from the bus stop, provides good hiking (DM5/€2.60) and biking (DM6.80/€3.50) maps and finds **rooms** for free. (☎(07669) 91 18 17. Open M-Th 9am-4:30pm, F 9am-2pm; July-Sept. also Sa 10am-noon.)

TRIBERG. The residents of touristy Triberg brag about the **Gutacher Wasserfall**—the highest waterfall in Germany—a series of bright cascades tumbling over moss-covered rocks for 163m. It's more of a mountain stream than a waterfall, but the idyllic hike through the lush park makes up for the unimpressive trickle. (Park open 9am-7pm. DM2.50/€1.30, students DM2/€1.05.) The signs for "**Wallfahrtskirche**" lead to the small **Pilgrim Church,** where pious ones have, according to legend, been miraculously cured since the 17th century. The area around town offers several beautiful hikes—ask at the tourist office for information and maps.

Trains run to Freiburg (1¾-2½hr., 1-2 per hr., DM32-45/€16.40-23). The **tourist office,** Luisenstr. 10, is on the ground floor of the local Kurhaus; from the station, turn right and follow the signs, or take bus #7265 which runs every hour to Marktpl. The staff gives sells maps (from DM2/€1.05) and has a mammoth catalog of all hotels, *Pensionen*, and private rooms in the region. (☎ (07722) 95 32 30. Open M-F 9am-5pm; May-Sept. also Sa 10am-noon.) Grab groceries for a picnic at **Plus market,** Schulstr. 5. (Open M-F 8:30am-6:30pm, Sa 8am-2pm.)

TÜBINGEN   ☎07071

Tübingen is a bookish city, and proud of it: nearly half of its residents are affiliated with the 500-year-old university. The chancel of the 15th-century **Stiftskirche** contains the tombs of 14 members of the former House of Württemberg, and the tower provides a lovely view. (Church open daily 9am-5pm; winter 9am-4pm. Chancel open Easter-*Erntedank* F-Su 11:30am-5pm; Aug.-Sept. Tu-Su 11:30am-5pm. DM2/€1.05, students DM1/€0.60.) Atop the hill in the center of town, **Schloß Hohentübingen** offers breathtaking views of the valleys. (Castle grounds open daily 7am-8pm. Free.) Inside, an ethnographic and archaeological **museum** features what is purportedly the oldest surviving example of handiwork, a 35,000-year-old ivory horse sculpture. (Open May-Sept. W-Sa 10am-6pm; Oct.-Apr. W-Su 10am-5pm. DM4/€2.05, students DM2/€1.05.) Head down Kirchg. to the old market square to see the ornate painted façade of the **Rathaus.** A block below Marktpl., on Kronenstr., is the **Evangelisches Stift,** which was once a monastery and is now a dorm for theology students; its alumni include such academic luminaries as Kepler and Hegel.

Trains run to Stuttgart (1hr., 2-3 per hr., DM17/€8.70). Turn right from the station and take a left on Karlstr. to reach the **tourist office,** on the Neckarbrücke, which books rooms for free. (☎913 60. Open M-F 9am-7pm, Sa 9am-5pm; Easter-Sept. also Su 2-5pm.) To reach the **Jugendherberge (HI),** Gartenstr. 22/2, cross the bridge past the tourist office and make a right; the entrance is on Herman-Kurz-Str. (☎230 02. **Internet** DM12/€6.15 per hr. Breakfast included. Lockers DM5/€2.60 deposit. Sheets DM6/€3.10. Reception 5-8pm and 10-11pm. Curfew midnight; ask for a key. Dorms DM28/€14.35, over 26 DM33/€16.90. **HI members only.**) To camp at **Rappenberghalde,** head upstream from the Altstadt or turn left from the station, cross the river at the Alleenbrücke, turn left down Neckarhalde, and follow the blue signs. (☎431 45. Reception daily 8am-12:30pm and 2:30-10pm. Open Apr. to mid-Oct. DM10/€5.15 per person, DM7/€3.60 per campsite.) Most inexpensive eateries cluster around **Metzgerg.** and **Am Lustnauer Tor,** and modern *Imbiße* crowd **Kornhausg. Die Kichererbse,** Metzgerg. 2, prepares fresh vegetarian falafel and sandwiches. (Open M 11am-6:30pm, Tu-F 11am-7pm, Sa 11am-4pm.) Buy groceries at **HL-Markt,** Europapl. 8, across from the post office (open M-F 7am-8pm, Sa 7am-4pm), or at the produce stand on **Marktplatz.** (Open M-F 8am-7pm, Sa 8am-4pm.) **Postal Code:** 72072.

CONSTANCE (KONSTANZ)   ☎07531

Located on the Bodensee (Lake Constance), the charming city of Constance has never been bombed: part of the city extends into Switzerland, and the Allies were leery of accidentally striking neutral territory. Now one of Germany's favorite vacation spots, its narrow streets wind around beautiful Baroque and Renaissance facades, gabled and turreted 19th-century houses gleam with a confident gentility along the river promenades, and a palpable jubilation fills the streets. The **Münster** has a 76m Gothic spire and a display of ancient religious objects, but it's being renovated through 2003. (Open M-Sa 10am-6pm, Su noon-6:30pm. Free.) Wander down **Seestraße,** near the yacht harbor on the lake, or down **Rheinsteig,** along the Rhine, for picturesque promenades. Constance boasts a number of **public beaches;** all are free and open May to September; **Strandbad Horn** (bus #5), the largest and most crowded, sports a nude sunbathing section modestly enclosed by hedges.

Trains run from Constance to most cities in southern Germany. The friendly but tiny **tourist office,** Bahnhofspl. 13, to the right of the train station, provides free walking maps and finds rooms for a DM5/€2.55 fee. (☎13 30 30. Open Apr.-July and Sept.-Oct. M-F 9am-6:30pm, Sa 9am-1pm; Aug. M-F 9am-8pm, Sa 9am-4pm, Su 10am-1pm; Nov.-Mar. M-F 9am-12:30pm and 2-6pm.) Reserve ahead at **Jugendherberge Kreuzlingen (HI),** Promenadenstr. 7, which is actually in Switzerland but closer to Konstanz than the Konstanz hostel. From the train station, turn left, cross the metal bridge over the tracks, turn right, and go through the parking lot to the border checkpoint "Klein Venedig." Walk along Seestr. until the sharp right curve, then continue straight ahead on the gravel path through the gate, right through the Seeburg castle parking lot, and right up the hill to the building with a flag on top. (☎ +41 (71) 688 26 63. Breakfast and sheets included. Reception 8-10am and 5-9pm. Closed Dec.-Feb. 23SFr or DM29/€15—both currencies accepted. AmEx/MC/V.) To reach the newly renovated **Jugendherberge "Otto-Moericke-Turm" (HI)**, Zur Allmannshöhe 18, take bus #4 from the train station to "Jugendherberge." (☎ 322 60. Breakfast included. Sheets DM6/€3.10. Reception Apr.-Oct. 3-10pm; Nov.-Mar. 5-10pm. Curfew 10pm. Lockout 9:30am-noon. Call ahead. **HI members only.** DM33/€16.80, under DM28/€14.35.) Camp by the waterfront at **DKV-Campingplatz Bodensee**, Fohrenbühlweg 45. Take bus #1 to "Staad" and walk for 10min. with the lake to your left. (☎ 330 57. Reception closed noon-2:30pm. Warm showers included. DM6/€3.10, DM8/€4.10 per tent.) For **groceries,** head to the basement of the **Karstadt** department store, on Augustinerpl. (Open M-F 9:30am-8pm, Sa 9am-4pm. AmEx/MC/V.)

BAVARIA (BAYERN)

Bavaria is the Germany of Teutonic myth, Wagnerian opera, and fairy tales. From the Baroque cities along the Danube to Mad King Ludwig's castles perched high in the Alps, the region beckons to more tourists than any other part of the country. Indeed, when most foreigners conjure up images of Germany, they imagine Bavaria, land of beer gardens, oom-pah-pah bands, and *Lederhosen*. This largest of Germany's federal states—mostly rural, Catholic, and conservative—contrasts greatly with the rest of the country, and its unique traditions and dialect are insistently preserved: residents have always been Bavarians first and Germans second.

 REMINDER. HI-affiliated hostels in Bavaria generally do not admit guests over age 26 except in families or groups of adults with young children.

MUNICH (MÜNCHEN)   ☎ 089

The capital and cultural center of Bavaria, Munich is a sprawling, relatively liberal metropolis island in the midst of conservative southern Germany. The cities of Munich and Berlin are emblematic of the poles of German character. Berlin thrives on its sense of fragmented avant-garde, but Munich exudes a traditional air of merriment. World-class museums, handsome parks and architecture, a rambunctious arts scene, and an urbane population collide to create a city of astonishing vitality. An ebullient mixture of sophistication and earthy Bavarian *Gemütlichkeit* keeps the city awake at (almost) all hours. *Müncheners* party zealously during **Fasching** (Carnival; Jan. 7-Feb. 12, 2002), shop with abandon during the **Christmas Market** (Nov. 30-Dec. 24, 2002), and consume unbelievable quantities of beer during the legendary **Oktoberfest** (Sept. 21-Oct. 6, 2002).

⌐ TRANSPORTATION

Flights: Flughafen München (☎ 97 52 13 13). S8 runs between the airport and the Hauptbahnhof every 20min. (40min., DM15.20/€8 or 8 stripes on the *Streifenkarte*).

Trains: Munich's **Hauptbahnhof** (☎ 22 33 12 56) is the transportation hub of southern Germany, with connections to: **Amsterdam** (9hr.; 1 per hr.; DM248/€126, under 26 DM198/€100); **Berlin** (8hr.; 1 per hr.; DM277/€141, DM222/€113); **Cologne** (6hr.; 2 per hr.; DM173/€88, DM138/€70); **Frankfurt** (3½hr.; 1 per hr.; DM147/€75,

DM118/€60); **Füssen** (2hr.; 1 per hr.; DM36/€18, DM29/€15); **Hamburg** (6hr.; 2 per hr.; DM268/€136, DM214/€109); **Innsbruck** (2hr.; 1 per hr.; DM48/€24, DM37/€19); **Paris** (10hr.; DM194/€98, DM156/€79); **Prague** (8½hr.; 3 per day, DM113/€58, DM85/€43); **Salzburg** (1¾hr.; 1 per hr.; DM41/€20, DM30/€15); **Vienna** (5hr.; 1 per hr.; DM106/€54, DM82/€41); **Zürich** (5hr.; every 3hr.; DM110/€56, DM85/€43). For 24hr. schedules, fare information, and reservations, call (01805) 99 66 33. **EurAide,** in the station, provides free train information and books train tickets. Information counters open daily 6am-11:30pm.

Public Transportation: MVV, Munich's public transport system, runs Su-Th 5am-12:30am, F-Sa 5am-2am. Eurail, InterRail, and German railpasses are valid on the S-Bahn (S) but not on the U-Bahn (U), streetcars, or buses.

Tickets and Schedules: Buy tickets at the blue vending machines and **validate them** in the blue boxes marked with an "E" *before entering the platform.* Disguised agents check for tickets sporadically; if you jump the fare (known as *schwarzfahren*), you risk a DM60/€30 fine. **Transit maps** and **maps of wheelchair accessible stations** are available in the tourist office, at EurAide, and at MVV counters in the train station. **Fahrplans** (schedules) cost DM2/€1 at newsstands.

Prices: Single ride tickets (DM4/€2, valid for 3hr.). **Kurzstrecke** (short trip) tickets are good for 2 stops on U or S or 4 stops on a streetcar or bus. (DM2/€1.05). A **Streifenkarte** (10-strip ticket) costs DM17.50/€9 and can be used by more than 1 person. Cancel 2 strips per person for a normal ride, or 1 strip per person for a *Kurzstrecke;* beyond the city center, cancel 2 strips per additional zone. A **Single-Tageskarte** (single-day ticket) is valid for 1 day of unlimited travel until 6am the next day (DM9/€5). The **3-Day Pass** (DM22/€11) is also a great deal. The **Munich Welcome Card,** available at the tourist office and in many hotels, is valid for either 1 day (DM12/€6) or 3 days (DM30/€15) of public transportation and includes a 50% discount on many of Munich's museums and 20% on Radius bike rental (see below). Passes can be purchased at the **MVV office** behind tracks 31 and 32 in the Hauptbahnhof, or at any of the *Kartenautomat*s.

Taxis: Taxi-Zentrale (☎216 11 or 194 10) has large stands in front of the train station and every 5-10 blocks in the central city. Women can request a female driver.

Bike Rental: Radius Bikes (☎59 61 13), at the far end of the Hauptbahnhof, behind the lockers opposite tracks #30-36. DM5/€3 per hr., DM25/€13 per day, DM75/€38 per week. Deposit DM100/€51, passport, or credit card. Students and Eurailpass holders 10% discount, Munich Welcome Card holders 20%. Open May to mid-Oct. daily 10am-6pm. **Aktiv-Rad,** Hans-Sachs-Str. 7 (☎26 65 06). U1 or U2 to "Fraunhofer Str." DM20/€10 per day. Open M-F 10am-1pm and 2-6:30pm, Sa 10am-1pm.

ORIENTATION AND PRACTICAL INFORMATION

A map of Munich's center looks like a squished circle quartered by one horizontal and one vertical line. The circle is the main traffic **Ring,** which changes names frequently around its length. The east-west and north-south thouroughfares cross at Munich's epicenter, the **Marienplatz,** and meet the traffic ring at **Karlsplatz** (called **Stachus** by locals) in the west, **Isatorplatz** in the east, **Odeonsplatz** in the north, and **Sendliger Tor** in the south. In the east beyond the Isartor, the **Isar River** flows by the city center, south to north. The **Hauptbahnhof** (main train station) is just beyonf Karlspl. outside the Ring in the west. To get to Marienpl. from the station, use the main exit and head across Bahnhofpl., keep going east through Karlspl., and Marienpl. is straight ahead. Or, take any S-Bahn (dir.: Marienpl.) to "Marienpl."

The **University** is north of Munich's center, next to the student-friendly-priced restaurants of the **Schwabing** district. East of Schwabing is the **English Garden;** west of Schwabing is the **Olympiapark.** South of town is the **Glockenbachviertel**—filled with all sorts of night hotspots, including many gay bars. The area around the train station, to the west of the city, is rather seedy and is dominated by hotels and sex shops. **Oktoberfest** is held on the large and open **Theresienwiese,** southeast of the train station on the U4 and U5 lines.

Several publications help visitors navigate Munich. The most comprehensive is the monthly English-language *Munich Found* (DM5.50/€3), available at newsstands and bookshops, which provides a list of services, events, and museums. The bi-weekly *in München* (free at the tourist office) provides detailed movie, theater,

GERMANY

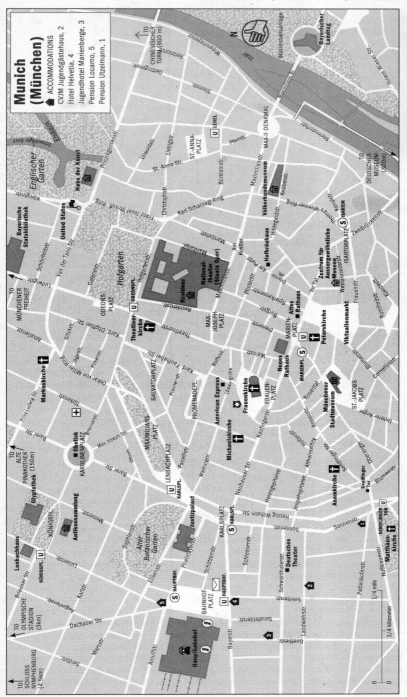

Munich (München)

ACCOMMODATIONS
CVJM Jugendgästehaus, 2
Hotel Helvetia, 4
Jugendhotel Marienberge, 3
Pension Locarno, 5
Pension Utzelmann, 1

TO MÜNCHENER FREIHEIT

TO ALTE PINAKOTHEK (150m)

TO OLYMPISCHE STADION (3km)

TO SCHLOSS NYMPHENBURG (4.5km)

Englischer Garten

Haus der Kunst

Bayerische Statsbibliothek

United States

Hofgarten

Residenz

Nationaltheater (Staats Oper)

MAX-JOSEPH-PLATZ

Theatinerkirche

ODEONSPL.

Markuskirche

Obelisk KAROLINENPLATZ

Glyptothek

Antikensammlung

Lenbachhaus

KÖNIGSPL.

Alter Botanischer Garten

Justizpalast

American Express

Frauenkirche

FRAUEN-PLATZ

Michaelskirche

Neues Rathaus

MARIENPL.

Peterskirche

Altes Rathaus

Hofbräuhaus

Völkerkundemuseum

Maximilianeum

MAX-II DENKMAL

Bayerischer Landtag

DEUTSCHES MUSEUM (300m)

ISARTOR

Zentrum für Aussergewöhnliche Museen

Viktualienmarkt

Münchener Stadtmuseum

ST-JAKOBS-PLATZ

Asamkirche

Matthäuskirche

SENDLINGER TOR

Deutsches Theater

KARLSPL.

Hauptbahnhof

BAHNHOF-PLATZ

THINESISCHER TURM (600 m)

Isar

N

and concert schedules. *Prinz* (DM2/€1.05 at newsstands) is a German-language monthly with endless tips on shopping, art, music, film, concerts, and food. *Inside Track* provides updated information in English on train connections and basic tips on getting started in Munich; it's free at EurAide (see below).

TOURIST, FINANCIAL, AND LOCAL SERVICES

EurAide in English (☎59 38 89), along track 11 (room 3) of the Hauptbahnhof, near the Bayerstr. exit. Specializes in booking train tickets, explaining the public transport, and selling maps (DM1/€0.55) and tickets for English tours of Munich. Pick up the free brochure *Inside Track*. Open June-Oktoberfest daily 7:45am-noon and 1-5:30pm; Oct.-Apr. M-F 8am-noon and 1-4pm, Sa 8am-noon; May daily 7:45am-noon and 1-4:30pm.

Main Tourist Office: (☎233 03 00), located on the front (east) side of the train station, next to ABR Travel on Bahnhofpl. They do speak English, but for more in-depth questions, EurAide (see above) will probably better suit your needs. The office **books rooms** for free with a 10-15% deposit, sells English city maps (DM0.50/€0.30), and offers the **München Welcome Card,** which provides free public transportation and reduced prices for 35 different sights and services (1-day DM12/€6, 3-day DM30/€15). Open M-Sa 9am-8pm, Su 10am-6pm. **Branch office** just inside the entrance to the Neues Rathaus on Marienpl. Open M-F 10am-8pm, Sa 10am-4pm.

Consulates: Canada, Tal 29 (☎219 95 70). S-Bahn to "Isartor." Open M-Th 9am-noon and 2-5pm, F 9am-noon and 2-3:30pm. **Ireland,** Possart 12 (☎98 57 23). U4 to "Prinzregenpl." Open M-F 9am-noon. **South Africa,** Sendlinger-Tor-Pl. 5 (☎231 16 30). U1, U2, U3 or U6 to "Sendlinger Tor." Open M-F 9am-noon. **UK,** Bürkleinstr. 10 (☎21 10 90), 4th fl. U4 or U5 to "Lehel." Open M-F 8:30am-noon and 1-5pm (F to 3:30pm), appointments M-F 9-10:30am and M-Tu and Th 1-2:30pm. **US,** Königinstr. 5 (☎288 80). For visa information, call (0190) 8500 5800 any time; to speak to an official, call (0190) 850 055 M-F 7am-8pm. Open M-F 8-11am.

Gay and Lesbian Resources: Gay services information (☎260 30 56). **Lesbian information** and the **LeTra Lesbentraum,** Angertorstr. 3 (☎725 42 72). Telephone times M and W 2:30-5pm, Tu 10:30am-1pm, Th 7-9pm. See also **Gay and Lesbian Munich.**

Disabled Resources: Info Center für Behinderte, Schellingstr. 31 (☎211 70; fax 21 17 258; info@vdk.de; www.vdk.bayern.com), has a list of Munich's resources for disabled persons. Open M-Th 9am-noon and 12:30-6pm, F 9am-5pm.

Laundromat: SB Waschcenter, Paul-Heyse-Str. 21, near the train station. Right on Bayerstr., then left on Paul-Heyse-Str. Wash DM7/€4, dry DM1/€0.55 per 10min. Open daily 7am-11pm. **Kingsgard Waschsalon,** Amalienstr. 61, near the university. Wash DM6.20/€3, dry DM3/€1.50. Open M-F 8am-6:30pm, Sa 9am-1pm.

EMERGENCY AND COMMUNICATIONS

Emergency: Police, ☎110. **Ambulance** and **Fire,** ☎112. **Medical service** ☎192 22.

Pharmacy: Bahnhofpl. 2 (☎59 41 19 or 59 81 19), on the corner outside the train station. Open M-F 8am-6:30pm, Sa 8am-2pm. 24hr. service rotates among the city's pharmacies—check the window of any pharmacy for a list.

Internet Access: easyEverything (The Internet Shop), on Bahnhofspl. next to the post office. Open 24hr. Prices depend on demand, but it's less than DM5/€3 per hr. with a minimum of DM5/€3.

Post Office: Bahnhofpl., 80335 Munich. Walk out of the main train station exit and it's the yellow building across the street. Open M-F 7am-8pm, Sa 9am-4pm, Su 10am-3pm.

▌ ACCOMMODATIONS

Munich's accommodations usually fall into one of three categories: seedy, expensive, or booked solid. During times like Oktoberfest, only the last category exists. In summer, the best strategy is to start calling before noon or to book a few weeks in advance. At most of Munich's hostels you can check in all day, but try to start your search before 5pm. Don't even think of sleeping in any public area, including the Hauptbahnhof; police patrol frequently all night long.

HOSTELS

Euro Youth Hotel, Senefelderstr. 5 (☎59 90 88 11, 59 90 88 71, or 59 90 00 72). From the Bahnhofspl. exit of the Hauptbahnhof, make a right on Bayerstr. and a left on Senefelderstr.; the hotel will be on the left. Outlandishly friendly and well-informed English-speaking staff. Bar open daily 8pm-2am. Breakfast buffet DM8.50/€4.40. Wash DM5.50/€3, dry DM2.50/€1. Reception 24hr. No curfew or lockout. Dorms DM32/€16; doubles DM90/€46, with private shower, telephone, and breakfast DM130/€66; triples DM117/€60; quads DM156/€80. Also inquire about their new location on the S6 line, with 1500 beds and shuttle service to and from the airport, scheduled to open soon.

Jugendlager Kapuzinerhölzl ("The Tent"), In den Kirschen 30 (☎141 43 00). Streetcar #17 from the Hauptbahnhof (dir.: Amalienburgstr.) to "Botanischer Garten." Go straight on Franz-Schrank-Str. and left at In den Kirschen. Night streetcars run at least once an hr. all night. They will "always have room for you" at the tent, where you'll sleep with 250 fellow "campers" under a big circus tent on a wooden floor. **Internet** DM2/€1 per 15min. Free city tours (W 9am). Kitchen facilities available. Laundry DM4/€2. Check-in 4:30-10:30pm. Reception 24hr. Passport required as deposit. Open June-Aug. DM15/€8 gets you a foam pad, multiple wool blankets (you can use your sleeping bag also), bathrooms, shower, rudimentary breakfast, and enthusiastic management. Actual "beds" DM19/€10. Camping DM8/€4 per campsite plus DM8/€4 per person.

Jugendherberge München (HI), Wendl-Dietrich-Str. 20. (☎13 11 56). U1 (dir.: Westfriedhof) to "Rotkreuzpl." Go down Wendl-Dietrich-Str past the Galeria Kaufhof; the entrance is ahead on the right. The most "central" of the HI hostels (3km from the city center). Safes in the reception area—*use them.* Breakfast and sheets included. Mandatory DM20/€10 key deposit. Check-in 11:30am, but lines form before 9am. 24hr. reception. No curfew. Big dorm (37 beds) for men only DM28/€14; 4- to 6-bed co-ed rooms DM33/€17; doubles DM38/€19.

CVJM Jugendgästehaus, Landwehrstr. 13 (☎552 14 10). Take the Bayerstr. exit from the train station, head straight down Goethestr. or Schillerstr., and take the 2nd left onto Landwehrstr. Central location with modern rooms and hall showers. Restaurant offers pizza, soups, and salads (open Tu-Th 6:30-10:30pm, F 6:30-midnight). **Co-ed rooms for married couples only.** Breakfast included. Reception 8am-12:30am. Curfew 12:30am-7am. Reservations can be made up to a year in advance. Hostel closed during Easter and Dec. 20-Jan. 7. Reduced rates between Dec.-Feb., increased rates during the Oktoberfest. Over 26 16% surcharge. Singles DM53/€26; doubles DM90/€45; triples DM126/€64.

4 You München, Hirtenstr. 18 (☎552 16 60). From the Hauptbahnhof, exit at Arnulfstr., go left, quickly turn right onto Pfefferstr., then hang a left onto Hirtenstr. Ecological hostel with restaurant and bar, hang-out areas, and wheelchair-accessible everything. Breakfast buffet DM8/€4. Sheets DM5/€3. 4-, 6-, or 8-bed dorms DM33/€17; 12-bed dorms DM27/€14; singles DM56/€28; doubles DM42/€21; over 27 add 15%.

Jugendhotel Marienherberge, Goethestr. 9 (☎55 58 05), less than a block from the train station. Take the "Bayerstr." exit and walk down Goethestr. **Open only to women under 26.** Staffed by merry nuns, the rooms are spacious, cheery, and spotless. Breakfast included. Kitchen, laundry, and television facilities. Wash DM2/€1, dry DM2/€1. Reception 8am-midnight. Curfew midnight, before you turn into a pumpkin. 6-bed dorms DM30/€30; singles DM40/€20; doubles DM35/€18; triples DM35/€18;

HOTELS AND PENSIONS

Always call ahead, and be forewarned that the rates rise during *Oktoberfest.*

Hotel Helvetia, Schillerstr. 6 (☎590 68 50), at the corner of Bahnhofspl., just beyond the Vereinsbank, to the right as you exit the station. The friendliest hotel in all of Munich. Over half of its beautiful rooms were renovated last year. Free **Internet** access. Breakfast included. Laundry DM9.90/€5. 24hr. reception. Singles DM55-69/€28-35; doubles DM75-99/€38-51, with shower DM99-120/€51-61; triples DM105-129/€54-66; quads DM140-172/€72-88. Rates rise 10-15% during Oktoberfest.

Pension Locarno, Bahnhofspl. 5 (☎ 55 51 64 or 55 51 65). From the train station's main entrance walk left across Bahnhofspl. and look for the building with the *Pension* sign. Plain, newly furnished and carpeted rooms, all with TV and phone. Reception 7:30am-5am. Mention *Let's Go* for these rates: singles DM85/€43; doubles DM120/€61; triples DM145/€74; quads DM165/€84. DM5/€3 less without breakfast.

Hotel-Pension Utzelmann, Pettenkoferstr. 6 (☎ 59 48 89). From the train station walk 4 blocks down Schillerstr. and go left on Pettenkofer. Or take U1, U2, U7 or U8 to "Sendlinger Tor." Nostalgic, elegant rooms. Breakfast included. Reception 7am-10pm. Singles DM55/€23, with shower DM95/€48, with bath DM130/€66; doubles DM98/€49; triples DM140/€71; quads DM170/€86.

Pension Central, Bayerstr. 55 (☎ 543 98 46). Turn right out of the Bayerstr. exit of the train station and walk 5min. up Bayerstr. The exterior may not please the eyes, but the rooms inside are classy and spacious. Reception 24hr. Singles DM65/€33, with bath DM75/€38; doubles DM95/€48; triples DM120/€61; quads DM160-180/€81-92; quints DM200-220/€102-112.

Pension Frank, Schellingstr. 24 (☎ 28 14 51). U3 or U6 to "Universität." Take the Schellingstr. exit, then the 1st right onto Schellingstr. Curious combination of backpackers, student groups, and fashion-model types. Breakfast included. Reception 7:30am-10pm. Check-out 11pm. Single beds in shared rooms almost always available. 3- to 6-bed dorms DM40/€20 per person; singles DM55-65/€28-33; doubles DM95/€48.

Pension Theresia, Luisenstr. 51 (☎ 52 12 50). U2 to "Theresienstr." Take the Augustenstr. S.O. exit, head straight down Theresienstr., and take the 2nd right onto Luisenstr.; the entrance is in the passageway left of the Dahlke store. Well-maintained, spacious rooms. Breakfast included. Reception (3rd fl.) 7am-9pm. Singles DM52-68/€26-34; doubles DM89-99/€45-50, with shower DM135-145/€67-74; triples DM135/€€69; quads DM170/€86.

CAMPING

Campingplatz Thalkirchen, Zentralländstr. 49 (☎ 723 17 07). U1 or U2 to "Sendlinger Tor," then U3 to "Thalkirchen" and change to bus #57. From the bus stop, cross the busy street on the left and take a right onto the footpath next to the road. The entrance is down the tree-lined path on the left. Well-run, crowded grounds with jogging and bike paths, TV lounge, groceries, and a restaurant. Showers DM2/€1. Wash DM7/€4, dry DM0.50/€0.25 per 6min. Curfew 11pm. Open mid-Mar. to late Oct. DM8.60/€4 per person, DM5.50-7/€3-4 per tent.

◤ FOOD

For an authentic Bavarian lunch, grab a *Brez'n* (pretzel) and spread it with *Leberwurst* (liverwurst) or cheese. **Weißwürste** (white veal sausages) are another native bargain, served in a pot of hot water with sweet mustard and a soft pretzel on the side. Don't eat the skin of the sausage; just slice it open and eat the tender meat. **Leberkäs** is a slice of a pinkish, meatloaf-like compound of ground beef and bacon. **Leberknödel** are liver dumplings, usually served in soup; **Kartoffelknödel** (potato dumplings) and **Semmelknödel** (made from white bread, egg, and parsley) are eaten along with a hearty chunk of German meat.

The vibrant **Viktualienmarkt,** 2min. south of Marienpl., is Munich's gastronomic center, offering both basic and exotic foods and ingredients. It's fun to browse, but don't plan to do any budget grocery shopping here. (Open M-F 10am-8pm, Sa 8am-4pm.) The ubiquitous **beer gardens** serve savory snacks along with booze. The university district off **Ludwigstraße** is Munich's best source of filling meals in a lively, unpretentiously hip scene. Many reasonably-priced restaurants and cafes cluster on **Schellingstraße, Amalienstraße,** and **Türkenstraße** (U3 or 6 to "Universität").

▧ **Marché,** Neuhauser Str., between Karlspl. and Marienpl. The top fl. offers cafeteria-style food; downstairs, chefs prepare every food imaginable, including great vegetarian selections. You'll get a food card that will be stamped for each item taken; pay at the end. Bottom fl. open 11am-10pm, top fl. open 8am-11pm.

Cafe Hag/Confiserie Retenhäfer, Residenzstr. 25-26, across from the Residenz, serves a large variety of cakes and sweets. Breakfast DM8-20/€4-10. Entrees DM9-15/€5-8. Open M-F 8:45am-7pm, Sa 8am-6pm.

Schwimmkrabbe, Ickstattstr. 13. U1 or U2 to "Fraunhoferstr.," then walk 1 block down Baaderstr. and turn right on Ickstattstr. This family-run Turkish restaurant is popular with locals. Filling appetizers DM8-17/€4-9, dishes DM16-29/€8-15. Open daily 5pm-1am.

Gollier, Gollierstr. 83. U4, U5, S7, or S27 to "Heimeranpl.," walk 2 blocks north on Garmischer Str., and turn left on Gollierstr. Delicious homemade vegetarian fare (DM12-22/€6-11). Many summer specials, such as reduced prices and early-bird dinner deals. Open M-F 11:30-3pm and 5pm-midnight, Sa 5pm-midnight, Su 10am-midnight.

Café Ignaz, Georgenstr. 67. U2 to "Josephspl.," then take Adelheidstr. 1 block north and turn right on Georgenstr. Earth-friendly cafe with a nutritious, inexpensive vegetarian menu. Lunch buffet M-F noon-2pm DM13.90/€7.10. Brunch buffet Sa-Su 9am-1pm DM14/€7.20. Open M-F 8am-10pm, Sa-Su 9am-10pm.

⊙ SIGHTS

MARIENPLATZ. The **Mariensäule,** an ornate 17th-century monument to the Virgin Mary, was built to commemorate the city's survival during the Thirty Years' War. At the neo-Gothic **Neues Rathaus,** the **Glockenspiel** chimes with a display of jousting knights and dancing coopers. *(Daily 11am and noon; in the summer also 5pm.)* Be careful while ogling the Glockenspiel; of all tourist places in Munich, this is the most likely spot to get pickpocketed. The Rathaus tower offers a sweeping view. *(Tower open M-F 9am-7pm, Sa-Su 10am-7pm. DM3/€1.50.)* On the face of the **Altes Rathaus** tower, to the right of the Neues Rathaus, are all of Munich's coats of arms since its inception as a city except one: when the tower was rebuilt after World War II, the local government refused to include the swastika-bearing arms from the Nazi era.

PETERSKIRCHE AND FRAUENKIRCHE. Across from the Neues Rathaus is the 12th-century **Peterskirche,** the city's oldest parish church. More than 300 steps scale the tower (called *der Alter Peter* by locals) to a spectacular view of Munich. *(Open M-Sa 9am- 7pm, Su 10am-7pm. DM2.50/€1, students DM1.50/€0.75, children DM0.50/€0.25.)* From the Marienpl., walk one block toward the Hauptbahnhof on Kaufingerstr. to the onion-domed towers of the 15th-century **Frauenkirche**—one of Munich's most notable landmarks and now the symbol of the city. *(Towers open Apr.-Oct. M-Sa 10am-5pm. DM4/€2, students DM2/€1.)*

RESIDENZ. Down the pedestrian zone from Odeonspl., the richly decorated rooms of the **Residenz** (Palace), built from the 14th to 19th centuries, form the material vestiges of the Wittelsbach dynasty. The beautifully landscaped **Hofgarten** behind the Residenz shelters the lovely **Temple of Diana.** The **Schatzkammer** (treasury) contains baubles, crowns, swords, china, ivory work, and other trinkets. *(Open Apr. to mid-Oct. F-W 9am-6pm, Th 9am-8pm; in winter daily 10am-4pm. DM8/€4, students DM6/€3.)* The **Residenzmuseum** comprises the former Wittelsbach apartments and State Rooms, a collection of European porcelain, and a 17th-century court chapel. The 120 portraits in the **Ahnengalerie** trace the royal lineage (perhaps not quite accurately) back to Charlemagne. *(Max-Joseph-pl. 3. Take U3-6 to "Odeonspl." Residenz museum open same hours as Schatzkammer. DM8/€4, students DM6/€3. Combination ticket DM14/€7, students DM11/€6.)*

ENGLISCHER GARTEN. Extending from the city center is the vast **Englischer Garten** (English Garden), Europe's largest metropolitan public park. On sunny days, all of Munich turns out to bike, fly kites, play badminton, ride horseback, swim in the Eisbach, and sunbathe. The garden includes a Japanese tea house, a Chinese pagoda, a Greek temple, and a few beer gardens. **Nude sunbathing** areas are designated FKK *(Frei-Körper-Kultur)* on signs and park maps. Consider yourself warned. *Müncheners* with aquatic daring surf the white-water rapids of the Eisbach, which flows artificially through the park.

SCHLOß NYMPHENBURG. After 10 years of trying for an heir, Ludwig I celebrated the birth of his son Maximilian in 1662 by erecting an elaborate summer playground. The Baroque **Schloß Nymphenburg,** in the northwest of town, hides a number of treasures. Check out Ludwig's "Gallery of Beauties"—whenever a woman caught his fancy, he would have her portrait painted (a scandalous as well as ironic hobby, since Ludwig grappled with an affection for men throughout his life). A few lakes and four manors also inhabit the palace grounds: **Amalienburg, Badenburg, Pagodenburg,** and **Magdalen Hermitage.** *(Streetcar #17 to "Schloß Nymphenburg." All attractions open Apr. to mid-Oct. F-W 9am-6pm, Th 9am-8pm; late Oct. to Mar. daily 10am-4pm. Museum and Schloß open Tu-Su 9am-noon and 1-5pm. Badenburg, Pagodenburg, and Magdalen Hermitage closed in winter. Schloß DM7/€4, students DM5/€3. Each manor DM6/€3, students DM4/€2. Entire complex DM15/€8, students DM12/€6t.)*

OLYMPIAPARK. Built for the 1972 Olympic Games, the **Olympiapark** contains the architecturally daring, tent-like **Olympia-Zentrum** and the **Olympia Turm** (tower), the highest building in Munich at 290m. *(U3 to "Olympiazentrum." Tower open daily 9am-midnight. DM5.50/€3. Park open M-F 10am-6pm, Sa 10am-3pm.)* Two **tours** in English are available: the "Adventure Tour" of the entire park meets Apr.-Oct. daily at 2pm *(DM13/€7)*, while a tour of just the soccer stadium meets Mar.-Oct. daily at 11am *(DM8/€4)*. The park also hosts **free concerts** in the Theatron every Sunday in July and every day in August. Hundreds of premium athletic specimens from around the world descend on Munich for the **Rowing World Cup** every July. From Aug. 6-11, 2002, the Olympiapark will host the **European Track & Field Championships.**

TIERPARK HELLBRUN. Animals are allowed to roam (relatively) freely and interact with each other in Munich's large **zoo,** which has been around since 1911. There are no fences to obstruct the view; the animals are kept in by large ditches. An excellent place for children, with petting zoos, pony rides, clowns, and ice cream wagons. Don't miss the vulgar talking raven. *(Tierparkstr. 30. U3 to "Thalkirchen," then follow signs. Open Apr.-Sept. daily 8am-5:30pm; Oct.-Mar. 9am-4:30pm. DM12/€6.)*

▥ MUSEUMS

Munich is a supreme museum city, and many of the city's offerings would require days for exhaustive perusal. The *Münchner Volkshochschule* (☎480 062 29 or 480 062 30; kult_vge@mvhs.de) offers tours of many city museums for DM8/€4. A **day pass** to all of Munich's state-owned museums is sold at the tourist office and many larger museums (DM30/€15). All state owned museums are **free on Sunday.**

DEUTSCHES MUSEUM. One of the world's largest and best museums of science and technology, with fascinating exhibits, including the first telephone and a mining exhibit that winds through a labyrinth of recreated subterranean tunnels. A walk through the museum's 46 departments covers over 17km; grab an English guidebook (DM6/€3). *(Museuminsel 1. Any S-Bahn to "Isartor", or street car #18 to "Deutsches Museum." Open daily 9am-5pm. DM12/€6, students DM5/€3.)*

ALTE PINAKOTHEK AND NEUE PINAKOTHEK. Commissioned in 1826 by King Ludwig I, the world-renowned **Alte Pinakothek** houses Munich's most precious art, including works by Titian, da Vinci, Raphael, Dürer, Rembrandt, and Rubens. *(Barerstr. 27. U2 to "Königspl." Open Tu-Su 10am-5pm and Th until 8pm. DM9/€5, students DM6/€3; combination ticket for Alte and Neue Pinakotheken for DM12/€6, DM6/€3.)* The **Neue Pinakothek** next door displays paintings and sculptures of the 19th to 20th centuries, including works by Van Gogh, Klimt, Cézanne, Manet, and more. *(Barerstr. 29. Same prices as the Alte Pinakothek. Open W-M 10am-5pm, Th 10am-8pm.)* The **Pinakothek Der Moderne** was under construction at the time of publication; it will eventually house the **Staatsgalerie Moderner Kunst** and is scheduled to open in autumn 2002.

BMW-MUSEUM. The ultimate driving museum features a fetching display of past, present, and future BMW products. The English brochure, *Horizons in Time*, guides you through the spiral path to the top of the museum. *(Petuelring 130. U3 to "Olympiazentrum." Open daily 9am-5pm. DM5.50/€3, students DM4/€2.)*

ZAM: ZENTRUM FÜR AUSSERGEWÖHNLICHE MUSEEN. Munich's **Center for Unusual Museums** brazenly corrals—under one roof—such treasures as the Padlock Museum, the Museum of Easter Rabbits, the Chamberpot Museum, and the Sisi Museum (dedicated to Empress Elizabeth of Austria). *(Westenriederstr. 41. Any S-bahn to "Isartor" or streetcar #17 or 18. Open daily 10am-6pm. DM8/€4, students DM5/€3.)*

MÜNCHENER STADTMUSEUM. A collection of exhibitions on Munich's city life and history, including film, musical instruments, weapons, puppetry, posters, and more. *(St.-Jakobs-pl. 1. U3 or 6 or any S-bahn to "Marienplatz." Open Tu-Su 10am-6pm. Museum DM5/€3, students DM2.50/€1.)*

🎵 ENTERTAINMENT

Munich's cultural cachet rivals the world's best. Sixty theaters of various sizes are scattered throughout the city; styles range from dramatic classics at the **Residenztheater** and **Volkstheater** to comic opera at the **Staatstheater am Gärtnerplatz** to experimental works at the **Theater im Marstall** in Nymphenburg. Munich's **opera festival** (in July) is held in the ■**Bayerische Staatsoper** (Bavarian National Theater), Max-Joseph-pl. 2. (U3, U4, U5, or U6 to "Odeonspl." or streetcar #19 to "Nationaltheater." Tickets ☎21 85 19 30; recorded information ☎21 85 19 19. Standing-room and student tickets DM7-20/€4-10, sold 1hr. before performance at the side entrance on Maximilianstr. Box office open M-F 10am-6pm, Sa 10am-1pm. No performances Aug. to mid-Sept.) *Monatsprogramm* (DM3/€1.50) and *Munich Found* (DM5.50/€3) both list schedules for Munich's stages, museums, and festivals. Munich shows its more bohemian face with scores of small fringe theaters, cabaret stages, art cinemas, and artsy pubs in **Schwabing.**

🍺 NIGHTLIFE

Munich's nightlife is a curious collision of Bavarian *Gemütlichkeit* and trendy cliquishness. The odyssey begins at one of Munich's beer gardens or beer halls, which generally close before midnight and are most crowded in the early evening. The alcohol keeps flowing at cafes and bars, which, except for Friday and Saturday nights, close their taps at 1am. At 4 am, the discos and dance clubs, sedate before midnight, suddenly spark and throb relentlessly. The trendy bars, cafes, cabarets, and discos along **Leopoldstraße** in **Schwabing** attract tourists from all over Europe. Leave your tennis shoes back at the hostel; many of these venues require you to at least attempt the jaded hipster look. The Munich fashion police generally frown on shorts, sandals, and t-shirts.

BEER GARDENS

The six great Munich labels are *Augustiner*, *Hacker-Pschorr*, *Hofbräu*, *Löwenbräu*, *Paulaner*, and *Spaten-Franziskaner*, but most restaurants and *Gaststätte* will pick a side by only serving one brewery's beer. There are four main types of beer served in Munich: **Helles** (light), **Dunkles** (dark), **Weißbier** (cloudy blond beer made from wheat instead of barley), and **Radler** (cyclist's brew; half beer and half lemon soda). Saying *"Ein Bier, bitte"* will get you a liter, known as a *Maß* (DM8-12). Specify if you want only a half-*Maß* (DM5-7). Since the time of King Ludwig I, skinflints have been permitted to bring their own food to many of the gardens; to make sure that your chow is welcome, ask a server or check for tables without tablecloths, as bare tables usually indicate self-service.

GERMANY

■ **Augustinerkeller,** Arnulfstr. 52, at Zirkus-Krone-Str. Any S-bahn to "Hackerbrücke." Founded in 1824, *Augustiner* is viewed by most *Müncheners* as the finest beer garden in town. Lush grounds, 100-year-old chestnut trees, and the delicious, sharp *Augustiner* beer (*Maß* DM10.70/€5) support their assertion. Open daily 10:30am-midnight.

Hirschgarten, Hirschgarten 1. U1 to "Rotkreuzpl.," then streetcar #12 to "Romanpl." Walk south to the end of Guntherstr. to enter the Hirschgarten. The largest beer garden in Europe (seating 9000) is boisterous and pleasant but somewhat remote; near Schloß Nymphenburg. *Maß* DM9.80. Open daily 9am-midnight.

Hofbräuhaus, Platzl 9, 2 blocks from Marienpl. Walk past the Altes Rathaus and take an immediate left onto Sparkassenstr. Turn right immediately onto Lederstr, and then take your 1st left on Orlandostr.; the Hofbräuhaus is ahead on your right. Although the Hofbräuhaus, built in 1589, was originally reserved for royalty and invited guests, a 19th-century proclamation lowered the price of its beer below normal city prices to "offer the Military and working classes a healthy and good-tasting drink." 15,000-30,000L of beer are sold per day. Many tables are still reserved for locals, and a good number of *Müncheners* keep their personal steins in the beer hall's safe. To avoid tourists, go in the early afternoon. *Maß* DM11.40/€6. *Weißwürste* with pretzel DM8.90/€4. Open daily 9am-midnight with live *Blasmusik* every day.

Taxisgarten, Taxisstr. 12. U1 to "Rotkreuzpl.," then bus #83 or 177 to "Klugstr." and then walk one block east on Tizianstr. This beer garden's small size (1500 chairs) has kept it a favorite of locals and students. *Maß* DM10.50/€5. Open daily 11am-11pm.

BARS

Many of the city's charming cafes double as hip nightly haunts.

■ **Nachtcafe,** Maximilianspl. 5. U4 or 5 or any S-bahn to "Karlspl." Live jazz, funk, soul, and blues until the wee hours. Very *schicki-micki* (yuppie). Things don't get rolling until midnight. No cover, but outrageous prices (beer DM9/€4.90 per 0.3L), so do your drinking beforehand. Easy-going weekdays, very picky on weekends—you'll have to look the part. Open daily 9pm-6am; live music 11pm-4am.

Reitschule, Königinstr. 34. U3 or 6 to "Giselastr." Above a club, with windows overlooking a horseback-riding school. *Weißbier* DM6.20/€3. Open daily 9am-1am.

Lux, Reichenbachstr. 37. U1, U2, U7, or U8 to "Frauenhofer." Large pastel asterisks decorate the walls of this popular hangout. Mostly French cuisine, with many fish dishes. Open M-Th 6pm-1am, F-Sa 6pm-2am.

Tabacco, Hartmannstr. 8 (☎22 72 16). U to "Marienpl." Enjoy this bar blissfully overlooked by all the tourists passing by. Open Su-Th 5pm-1am, F-Sa 5pm-3am.

DISCOS

■ **Kunstpark Ost,** Grafinger Str. 6. U5 or any S-bahn to "Ostbahnhof"; follow signs for the "Kunstpark Ost" exit, turn right onto Friedenstr. and then left onto Grafinger Str. The newest and biggest addition to the Munich nightlife scene, this huge complex has 40 different venues swarming with young people. Try the hip **Milch and Bar** (open M and W-F) with modern hits and old favorites; the psychedelic-trance **Natraj Temple** (open F-Sa); the alternative cocktail and disco joint **K41** (open every night; 80's night on Th); or the risqué South American rock bar **Titty Twister** (open W-Sa). Hours, cover, and themes vary—check *Kunstpark* for details on specific club nights and specials.

Nachtwerk, Club, and Tanzlokal, Landesberger Str. 185. Streetcar #18 or 19 or bus #83 to "Lautensackstr." The older, larger **Nachtwerk** spins mainstream dance tunes for sweaty crowds in a packed warehouse; Sa "Best of the 50s to the 90s" night. Its little sister **Club** offers a 2-level dance floor just as tight and swinging, with mixtures of rock, trip-hop, house, acid jazz, and rare grooves. **Tanzlokal** has hip-hop on F. Beer DM4.50/€2 all places. All 3 clubs open daily 10pm-4am. Cover DM10/€5.

Ballhaus, Domagkstr. 33, in the Alabamahalle. U6 to "Alte Heide"; there's a free shuttle from there to the club. Situated along with 3 other discos on a former military base in Schwabing. Start out in the beer garden, which opens at 8pm. Try **Alabama** for German oldies on F (9pm-4am, drinks free until 1am) and hits from the 60s to the 90s on Sa (10pm-5am, free drinks all night). **Temple Club** has typical pop music (open Sa 10pm-4am), and **Schwabinger Ballhouse** plays international jams (F-Sa 10pm-5am, cover DM15/€8).

GAY AND LESBIAN MUNICH

Although Bavaria has the reputation of being less welcoming to homosexuality, Munich sustains a respectably vibrant gay nightlife. The center of Munich's homosexual scene is in the **Glockenbachviertel,** stretching from the area south of the Sendlinger Tor through the Viktualienmarkt/Gärtnerpl. area to the Isartor. *Our Munich*, Munich's gay and lesbian leaflet, is available at the tourist office. Pick up the free booklet *Rosa Seiten* at **Max&Milian Bookstore,** Ickstattstr. 2 (open M-F 10:30am-2pm and 3:30-8pm, Sa 11am-4pm), or at any other gay locale, for extensive listings of gay nightlife hotspots and services.

▨ **Bei Carla,** Buttermelcherstr. 9. S1-8 to "Isartor," then walk 1 block south on Rumfordstr., turn left on Klenzestr. and left onto Buttermelcherstr. This charming and friendly lesbian cafe and bar is one of Munich's best-kept secrets. Open M-Sa 4pm-1am, Su 6pm-1am.

Soul City, Maximilianspl. 5, at the intersection with Max-Joseph-Str. Purportedly the biggest gay disco in Bavaria; music ranges from disco to Latin to techno. Straights always welcome. Open W-Sa 10pm-late; Th-Sa in summer. Cover DM10-25/€5-13.

Morizz, Klenzestr. 43. U1 or 2 to "Fraunhofer Str." This relaxed cafe and bar is not exclusively gay but is frequented by gay men. Settle into the low red sofa chairs and enjoy a cocktail (DM12-16/€6-8). Open Su-Th 7pm-2am, F-Sa 7pm-3am.

▶ DAYTRIPS FROM MUNICH

DACHAU   ☎08131

From Munich, take S2 (dir.: Petershausen) to "Dachau" (20min., DM7.60/€4, or 4 stripes on the Streifenkarte), then bus #724 (dir.: Kraütgarten) or 726 (dir.: Kopernikusstr.) to "KZ-Gedenkstätte" (10min., DM1.90/€1 or one stripe on the Streifenkarte). Informative but lengthy (2hr.) tours of the camp in English leave from the museum July-Aug. daily 12:30pm; Sept.-June Sa-Su and holidays 12:30pm. DM5/€3 donation requested. Call (08131) 17 41 for more information. Camp open Tu-Su 9am-5pm.

"Arbeit Macht Frei" ("work sets one free") was the first thing prisoners saw as they entered Dachau; it's written over the gate of the **Jourhaus,** formerly the only entry to the camp. Dachau was primarily a work camp (rather than a death camp, like Auschwitz). During the war, prisoners made armaments in Dachau because the SS knew that the Allies would not bomb a concentration camp. Although Dachau has a **gas chamber,** it was actually never used because the prisoners purposely made mistakes and worked slowly in order to delay completion. Once tightly-packed **barracks** are now, for the most part, only foundations. However, survivors ensured that at least two barracks would be reconstructed to teach future generations about the 206,000 prisoners who were interned here from 1933 to 1945. The walls, gates, and crematorium have been restored since 1962 in a chillingly sparse memorial to the victims of Dachau. The **museum,** located in the former administrative buildings, examines pre-1930s anti-Semitism, the rise of Nazism, the establishment of the concentration camp system, and the lives of prisoners through photographs, documents, and artifacts. The thick **guide** (DM25/€13, available in English) translates the propaganda posters, SS files, documents, and letters. Most exhibits are accompanied by short captions in English. A short **film** (22min.) is screened in English at 11:30am, 2, and 3:30pm. A new display in the **Bunker,** the concentration camp's prison and torture chamber, chronicles the lives and experiences of the camp's special prisoners and the barbarism of SS guards.

When you visit, it is important to remember that, while the concentration camp is treated as a tourist attraction by many, it is first and foremost a memorial.

THE ROMANTIC ROAD. From Munich, any town along the Romantic Road is but a quick train ride away, including Würzberg (see p. 491) and Rothenburg ob der Tauber (see p. 492).

BAVARIAN ALPS. The towns along the bases of the Bavarian peaks are all convenient for daytripping, including Füssen, Neuschwanstein and Hohenschwangau, Linderhof, and Garmisch-Partenkirchen. Take a cable-car to the top of a mountain for a spectacular view (see p. 493).

NUREMBERG (NÜRNBERG)   ☎0911

Nuremberg served as site of massive annual Nazi rallies (1933-38) and lent its name to the 1935 Racial Purity Laws; Allies later chose it as the site of the post-WWII war crimes trials in order to foster a sense of justice. Today, the townspeople of Nuremberg are working to forge a new image for their city as the "Stadt der Menschenrechte" (City of Human Rights), and since the early 1990s they have sought to recognize compassion among world leaders through the Nuremberg Human Rights Prize. While the physical remnants of Nazi rule remain, Nuremberg's cultural aspects outweigh the bitter memories, and today the city is known for its toy fair, sausages, and gingerbread as much as for its ties to Nazism.

🚊🚍 TRANSPORTATION AND PRACTICAL INFORMATION. Trains go to: Berlin (6hr., every 2hr., DM137/€70); Frankfurt (3½hr., 2 per hr., DM66/€33.75); Munich (2½hr., 2 per hr., DM54/€27.60); Stuttgart (2¾hr., 6 per day, DM54/€27.60). **DB Reisezentrum,** temporarily housed in a booth outside the station, sells tickets. (Open daily 5:45am-10pm.) The **tourist office,** which has maps and books rooms for free, is currently in a white booth just off the northwest corner of the train station but will move to the Kunstlerhaus on Konigsstr. sometime in 2002. Its telephone number and hours will stay the same. (☎233 61 31. Open M-Sa 9am-7pm.) For **Internetcafe M@x,** Färberstr. 11, head to the 4th floor of the complex on the corner of Fraueng. (☎23 23 84. Before 3pm DM5/€2.60 per hr.; after 3pm DM5/€2.60 per 30min., DM9/€4.60 per hr. Open Oct.-May M-Th 1-10pm, F-Sa 1pm-1am, Su 3pm-midnight.)

🏠🍴 ACCOMMODATIONS AND FOOD. Jugendgästehaus (HI), Burg 2, is in a castle above the city. From the station, cross Frauentorgraben, turn right, walk along the outside of the city walls, then follow Königstr. through Lorenzerpl. over the bridge to the Hauptmarkt. Head towards the fountain on the left and bear right on Burgstr., then huff and puff up the hill. (☎230 93 60. Reception 7am-1am. Curfew 1am. Reservations strongly recommended. Dorms DM33/€16.90; singles DM65/€33.25; doubles DM78/€39.90.) For **Gasthof Schwänlein,** Hintere Sterng. 11, take the underground passage from the station to Königstr. and immediately turn left on Frauentormauerstr; follow the town wall and bear right onto Hintere Sterng. (☎22 51 62; fax 241 90 08. Breakfast included. Reservations by fax or mail only. Singles DM50/€25.60, with shower DM60/€30.70, with bathroom DM65/€33.25; doubles DM75/€38.45, DM85/€43.50, DM95/€48.60.) Try Nuremberg's famous *Rostbratwurst* (sausage) at the **Bratwursthäusle,** Rathauspl. 1, next to the Sebalduskirche. (Open M-Sa 10am-10:30pm.) **Edeka,** Hauptmarkt 12, near the Frauenkirche, sells **groceries.** (Open M-F 8:30am-7pm, Sa 8am-3pm.)

🏛🎭 SIGHTS AND ENTERTAINMENT. Allied bombing left little of Nuremberg for posterity; its churches, castle, and other buildings have all been reconstructed. The walled-in Handwerkerhof market near the station is a tourist trap masquerading as a historical attraction; head up Königstr. for the real sights. Take a detour to the left for the pillared **Straße der Menschenrechte** ("Avenue of Human Rights") as well as the **Germanisches Nationalmuseum,** Kartäuserg. 1, which chronicles German art from pre-history to the present. (Museum open Tu and Th-Su 10am-5pm, W 10am-9pm. DM8/€4.10, students DM6/€3.10; free W 6-9pm.) Head on to the Gothic **Lorenzkirche** on Lorenzpl., which features a 20m tabernacle. (Open M-Sa 9am-5pm, Su 1-4pm. Free German tours in summer M-F 11am and 2pm; in winter M-F 2pm.) Across the river are the **Frauenkirche** (open M-Sa 9am-6pm, Su 12:30-

GERMANY

6pm) and the **Hauptmarktplatz,** the site of the annual **Christmas market.** Hidden in the fence of the **Schöner Brunnen** (Beautiful Fountain), in the northwest corner of the Hauptmarkt, is a seamless gold-colored ring—can you find it? Spinning it will supposedly bring good luck. Walk uphill to the **Rathaus;** the **Lochgefängnisse** (dungeons) beneath contain medieval torture instruments. (Open Tu-Su 10am-4:30pm. Tours every 30min.; English translation available. DM4/€2.05, students DM2/ €1.05.) Across from the Rathaus is the **Sebalduskirche,** which houses the remains of St. Sebaldus for 364 days a year; on the 365th, they're paraded around town. (Open Mar.-May and Oct.-Dec. daily 9:30am-6pm; June-Sept. 9:30am-8pm; Jan.-Feb. 9:30am-4pm.) Atop the hill, the **Kaiserburg** (Emperor's fortress), Nuremberg's symbol, offers the best vantage point of the city. (Open Apr.-Sept. daily 9am-6pm; Oct.-Mar. 10am-4pm. Tours every 30min. DM10/€5.15, students DM8/€4.10.)

The ruins of **Dutzendteich Park,** site of the Nazi Party Congress rallies, remind visitors of Nuremberg's darker history. On the far side of the lake is the **Tribüne,** the marble platform where throngs gathered to hear Hitler. The exhibit "Fascination and Terror," in the **Golden Hall** at the rear of the Tribüne, covers the rise of the Third Reich and the war crimes trials. (Open mid-May to Oct. Tu-Su 10am-6pm. DM5/ €2.60, students DM4/€2.05.) To reach the park, take S2 (dir.: Freucht/Altdorf) to "Dutzendteich," turn left out of the middle exit, take another left after Strandcafe Wanner, and follow the path. On the other side of town, Nazi leaders faced Allied judges during the infamous **Nürnberg war** crimes trials, held in room 600 of the Justizgebäude. (Fürtherstr. 110. U1 (dir.: Stadthalle) to "Bärenschanze" and continue on Fürtherstr. Tours Sa-Su 1, 2, 3, and 4 pm. DM4/€2.05.)

Nuremberg's nightspots are clustered around the Altstadt; the best are in the west, near the river. **Cine Città,** Gewerbemuseumspl. 3, has seven cafes, 12 cinemas, and a disco. (Open M-Th and Su until 3am, F-Sa until 4am.) **Café Treibhaus,** Karl-Grillenberger-Str. 28, draws an older crowd with killer cocktails and coffee. (Open M-W 8am-1am, Th-F 8am-2am, Sa 9am-2am, Su 9:30am-1am.)

ROMANTIC ROAD

Between Würzburg and Füssen lies a beautiful countryside of colorful castles, walled cities, elaborate churches, and dense forests. In 1950, the German tourist industry christened these bucolic backwaters the Romantic Road (Romantische Straße), and the region has since become the most visited in Germany.

⊏ TRANSPORTATION. Europabus leaves from Frankfurt daily at 8am for Füssen; buses also depart from Füssen daily at 8am for Frankfurt. Students receive a 10% discount, Eurail and German Rail Pass holders 60%. For reservations or more information, contact **EurAide** (☎ (089) 59 38 89; fax 550 39 65; www.euraide.de/romantic). A more flexible and economical way to travel the Romantic Road is by the frequent **trains** that connect all the towns.

WÜRZBURG. Surrounded by vineyard slopes and bisected by the Main River, Würzburg is a famous university town: in 1895 Wilhelm Conrad Röntgen discovered X-rays here and was awarded the first Nobel Prize, and **Julius-Maximilians-Universität** is still renowned today. The striking **Fortress Marienburg** has kept vigil over the Main since the 12th century; inside are the 11th-century **Marienkirche;** the 40m **Bergfried watchtower** and the **Hole of Fear** (dungeon); and the **Fürstengarten** (a garden built to resemble a ship). Outside the main fortress is the castle arsenal, which now houses the **Mainfränkisches Museum.** (Bus #9 from the station to "Festung," or walk towards the castle on the hill. Fortress tours depart from the main courtyard Apr.-Oct. Tu-F 11am, 2, and 3pm, Sa-Su hourly 10am-4pm. DM4/€2.05, students DM3/ €1.55. Mainfränkisches Museum open Apr.-Oct. Tu-Su 10am-6pm; Nov.-Mar. closes 4pm. DM5/€2.60, students DM2.50/€1.30.) The **Residenz,** on Residenzpl., houses the largest ceiling fresco in the world, and the **Residenzhofkirche** inside is a Baroque fantasy of gilding and pink marble. (Open Apr. to mid-Oct. daily 9am-6pm, Th until 8pm; mid-Oct. to Mar. daily 10am-4pm. DM8/€4.10, students DM6/€3.10. English tours Sa-Su 11am and 3pm. Free.) **Trains** head to Frankfurt (2hr., 2 per hr., DM38/€19.45); Munich (3hr., 1 per hr., DM76/€39.90); Nuremberg (1hr., 2 per hr., DM28/€14.35); Rothenburg ob der Tauber (1hr., 1 per hr., DM17/€8.70). The **tourist office**, located in Haus zum Falken, a yellow building on the Marktpl., provides free maps and helps find rooms. (☎ (0931) 37 23 98. Open M-F 10am-6pm, Sa 10am-2pm; Apr.-Oct. also Su 10am-2pm.)

ROTHENBURG OB DER TAUBER. After being plundered in the Thirty Years' War, Rothenberg had no money to renovate or modernize, so it remained unchanged for 250 years. When it became a tourist destination at the end of the 19th century, new laws were imposed to protect the integrity of the medieval *Altstadt*; today, Rothenburg is probably your only chance to see a walled medieval city without a single modern building. On the Marktpl. stands the Renaissance **Rathaus;** the 60m tower provides a panoramic view of the town. (Rathaus open daily 8am-6pm; free. Tower open Apr.-Oct. daily 9:30am-12:30pm and 1-5pm; Nov.-Mar. M-F 9:30am-12:30pm, Sa-Su noon-3pm. DM2/€1.05.) After the Thirty Years' War, the conquering general promised to spare the town from destruction if any local could chug a wine keg—3.25L of wine. The mayor successfully met the challenge, then passed out for several days. The **Meistertrunk** is reenacted with each year, and the town clock performs a slooow motion version every hour over the Marktpl. The ▓**Medieval Crime Museum,** Burgg. 3, exhibits torture instruments and "eye for an eye" jurisprudence. (Open Apr.-Oct. daily 9:30am-6pm; Nov. and Jan.-Feb. 2-4pm; Dec. and Mar. 10am-4pm. DM5/€2.60, students DM4/€2.05.) Head to **Christkindlmarkt** (Christ Child Market), Herrng. 2, and **Weihnachtsdorf** (Christmas Village), Herrng. 1, to explore the town's obsession with Christmas. (Open M-F 9am-6:30pm, Sa 9am-4pm; mid-May to Dec. also Su 11am-6pm.) **Trains** run from Würzburg (40min., 1 per hr., DM15.40/€7.90) and Munich (3hr., 1 per hr., DM60/€30.70) to Steinach, where you can transfer to Rothenburg (15min., 1 per hr., DM3.30/€1.70). The **tourist office,** Marktpl. 2, books **rooms** for free or a DM5/€2.60 fee in summer and at Christmas. (☎ (09861) 404 92. Open May-Oct. M-F 9am-noon and 1-6pm, Sa-Su 10am-3pm; Nov.-Apr. M-F 9am-noon and 1-5pm, Sa 10am-1pm.) There are also many **private rooms** not registered with the tourist office; look for *Zimmer frei* signs and knock on the door to inquire.

FÜSSEN. A brightly painted toenail at the tip of the Alpine foothills and the southern end of the Romantic Road, Füssen provides easy access to Mad King Ludwig's famed **Königsschlösser** (royal castles). The inner walls of the **Hohes Schloß** (High Castle) courtyard feature arresting *trompe-l'oeil* windows and towers, and the **Staatsgalerie** in the castle shelters a collection of regional late Gothic and Renaissance art. (Open Apr.-Oct. Tu-Su 11am-4pm; Nov.-Mar. 2-4pm. DM5/€2.60, students DM4/€2.10.) Inside the **Annenkapelle,** macabre paintings depict everyone from the Pope and Emperor to the smallest child engaged in the *Totentanz* (death dance), a public frenzy of despair that overtook Europe during the plague. (Open Apr.-Oct. Tu-Su 11am-4pm, Nov.-Mar. Tu-Su 2-4pm. DM5/€2.50, students DM4/€2). **Trains** run to **Munich** (2hr., 1 per hr., DM36/€18.40). Füssen is also the last stop on the **Europabus** route; northbound buses leave for Frankfurt at 8am daily, and the southbound bus arrives at 8:15pm. To get from the station to the **tourist office,** Kaiser-Maximilian-Pl. 1, walk the length of Bahnhofstr. and head straight on Luitpoldstr. to the big yellow building. The staff finds **rooms** for free. (☎ (08362) 938 50. Open Apr.-Sept. M-F 8:30am-6:30pm, Sa 9am-12:30pm, Su 10am-noon; Oct.-Mar. M-F 9am-5pm, Sa 10am-noon.) You can also knock on doors bearing *Zimmer Frei* signs.

KÖNIGSSCHLÖßER (ROYAL CASTLES)

King Ludwig II, a zany visionary and fervent Wagner fan, used his cash to create fantastic castles. In 1886, a band of nobles and bureaucrats deposed Ludwig, had him declared insane, and imprisoned him. Three days later, the king and a loyal advisor were mysteriously discovered dead in a nearby lake. The fairytale castles that framed Ludwig's life and the enigma of his death still captivate tourists today.

NEUSCHWANSTEIN AND HOHENSCHWANGAU. Ludwig II's building spree across Bavaria peaked with the glitzy 🏰**Schloß Neuschwanstein,** now Germany's most clichéd tourist attraction and the inspiration for Disneyland's Cinderella Castle. The young Ludwig II lived here for a mere 173 days. The completed chambers (63 remain unfinished) include a Byzantine throne room, a small artificial grotto, and an immense *Sängersaal* (singer's hall) built expressly for Wagnerian opera performances. Ludwig grew up in the bright yellow, neo-Gothic **Schloß Hohenschwangau** across the way. (Both open Apr.-Sept. 9am-6pm; Oct.-Mar. 10am-4pm. Mandatory tours of each castle DM14/€7.20, students DM12/€6.15; combination ticket DM26/€13.35, DM22/€11.30.) Tickets can be purchased at the Ticket-Service Center, Alpseestr. 12 (☎ (08362) 930 83 20), about 100m south of the Hohenschwangau bus stop. From Füssen, hop on **bus** #9713 marked "Königsschlösser," which departs from the train station (10min., 2 per hr., DM2.60/€1.35). It will drop you in front of the information booth (open daily 9am-6pm); the Ticket-Service Center is a short walk uphill on Alpseestr. Separate paths lead up to both Hohenschwangau and Neuschwanstein. A *Tagesticket* (DM13/€6.65, from the bus driver) gives castle-hoppers unlimited regional bus use (including the ride to Linderhof).

LINDERHOF. East of Neuschwanstein and Hohenschwangau lies **Schloß Linderhof,** Ludwig II's hunting palace. The royal bedchamber, the largest room in the castle, is covered with gold leaf and contains a colossal 454kg crystal chandelier. Even more impressive is the surrounding **park.** Paths originating at the swan lake at the park entrance weave through the ornately landscaped grounds, which include an enormous, artificial **grotto** bathed in red and blue floodlights and the **Hunding-Hütte,** modeled after a scene in Wagner's Die Walküre. (Open Apr.-Sept. F-W 9am-5:30pm, Th until 7:30pm; Oct.-Mar. 10am-4pm. Apr.-Sept. obligatory castle tour DM11/€5.65, students DM9/€4.60; Oct.-Mar. DM8/€4.10, students DM6/€3.10. Park is open Apr.-Sept. Free.) **Bus** #9622 connects to Linderhof from Oberammergau (20min., every hr. 9:50am-4:55pm, round-trip DM9.20/€5; last return bus 6:40pm). Oberammergau is accessible by **bus** #1084 from Füssen (1¾ hr., 8 per day, DM13.70/€7.50) or by **train** from Munich (1¾hr.; 1 per hr., switch at Murnau; DM25.60/€13.30).

GARMISCH-PARTENKIRCHEN ☎ 08821

Once upon a time, the 1100-year-old hamlets of Garmisch and Partenkirchen were two separate Bavarian villages located at the base of the **Zugspitze,** Germany's tallest peak (2,964m). Hitler persuaded their mayors to unite the two villages in 1935, but to this day the towns assert their individuality: both sides of town staunchly maintain that they speak different dialects, and their cows don't socialize in public. The Zugspitze is the main attraction in town, and there are two ways to conquer it, though they should only be attempted in fair weather. **Option 1:** Take the cog railway from the Zugspitzbahnhof (50m behind the Garmisch main station) to the *Zugspitzplatt* outlook (1¼hr., every hr. 7:35am-2:35pm), then continue on the Gletscherbahn cable car to the top. (Round-trip with train and cable car DM81/€41.60.) **Option 2:** Get off the railway at Eibsee and take the **Eibsee Seilbahn,** one of the steepest cable car runs in the world, all the way to the top. (1½hr., every hr. 8am-4:15pm. Round-trip with train and cable car DM81/€41.60.)

Garmisch-Partenkirchen is accessible by **train** from Innsbruck (1½hr., 1 per hr., DM20.20/€10.50) or Munich (1½hr., 1 per hr., DM27/€14), and by **bus** #1084 from Füssen (2hr., 6-7 per day, DM13/€6.65). To get to the **tourist office,** Richard-Strauss-Pl. 2, turn left on Bahnhofstr. from the train station and turn left onto Von-Brug-Str.; the office faces the fountain on the square. The staff distributes maps and finds rooms for free. (☎ 18 07 00. Open M-Sa 8am-6pm, Su 10am-noon.) To reach the **Jugendherberge (HI),** Jochstr. 10, cross the street from the train station and take bus #3 (dir.: Burgrain) or 4 or 5 (dir.: Farchant) to "Burgrain." Walk straight down Am Lahner Wiesgraben and turn right after two blocks onto Jochstr. (☎ 29 80. Ages 18-26 and families only—i.e., no screaming schoolchildren! Reception 7-9am and

5pm-midnight. Lockout 9am-3:30pm. Curfew 11:30pm. Open Jan. to mid-Nov. Dorms DM27.50/€14.30.) **HL Markt,** at the intersection of Bahnhofstr. and Von-Brug-Str., sells groceries. (Open M-F 8am-8pm, Sa 7:30am-4pm.)

THE CHIEMSEE

For almost 2000 years, the Chiemsee's picturesque islands and dramatic crescent of mountains have inspired artistic and musical masterpieces. **Ferries** run from Prien to Herreninsel and Fraueninsel every hour. (40min., 6:40am-7:30pm, DM10.80-12.80/€5.55-6.55.) To get to the ferry port, turn right from the main entrance of the Prien train station and follow Seestr. for 20min., or hop on the green *Chiemseebahn* steam train from the station (9:40am-6:15pm, round-trip including ship passage DM16.50/€8.45).

PRIEN AM CHIEMSEE. Prien, on the southwestern corner of the Chiemsee, serves as a good base from which to explore to the islands. **Trains** depart from the station, a few blocks from the city center, for Munich (1hr., 1 per hr., DM23.40/€12) and Salzburg (50min., 1 per hr., DM17/€8.70). The **tourist office,** Alte Rathausstr. 11, has maps and books **private rooms** for free. (☎690 50. Office open M-F 8:30am-6pm, Sa 8:30am-noon.) The **Jugendherberge (HI),** Carl-Braun-Str. 66, is a 15min. walk from the station—head right on Seestr. and turn left on Staudenstr., which turns into Carl-Braun-Str. (☎687 70. Showers, lockers, and breakfast included. Reception 8-9am, 5-7pm, and 9:30-10pm. Lockout 9am-1pm. Curfew 10pm. Open early Feb.-Nov. 6-bed dorms DM28.80/€14.75.) For **Campingplatz Hofbauer,** Bernauer Str. 110, turn left on Seestr. from the station, left at the next intersection, and walk 25min. along Bernauerstr., heading out of town. (☎41 36. Showers included. Reception 7:30-11:00am and 2-8pm. Open Apr.-Oct. DM5.65 per person, DM10/€5.15 per tent and car.) Grab a cheap meal at **Bäckerei/Cafe Müller,** Marktpl. 8. (☎40 31. Sandwiches from DM3.50/€1.80. Open M-F 6:30am-6pm, Sa 6:30am-12:30pm.) Or, visit **Weininger Bräu,** Bernauerstr. 13b, for the excellent *Bayerische Käsespätzli.* (☎610 90. Entrees from DM9/€4.60. Open M and W-F 10am-midnight, Su 9am-midnight.) ☎08051.

HERRENINSEL AND FRAUENINSEL. Ludwig's palace on Herreninsel (Gentlemen's Island), Königsschloß Herrenchiemsee, is a shameless attempt to be more extravagant than Louis XIV's Versailles. Ludwig bankrupted Bavaria building this place—a few unfinished rooms (abandoned after the cash ran out) contrast greatly with the completed portion of the castle. (☎688 70. Open daily Apr.-Sept. 9am-6pm; Oct. 9:40am-5pm; Nov.-Mar. 9:40am-4pm. Mandatory tour DM11/€5.65; seniors, students, and disabled persons DM9/€4.60.) Fraueninsel (Ladies' Island), is home to the Klosterkirche (Island cloister), the nunnery that complemented the former monastery on Herreninsel. The nuns make their own marzipan, beeswax candles, and five kinds of liqueurs, for sale in the convent shop (0.2L Klosterlikör DM8.50/€4.35). The 8th-century Cross of Bischofhofen and other religious artifacts are displayed in the Michaelskapelle above the Torhalle (gate), the oldest surviving part of the cloister. (Open June-Sept. 11am-5pm. DM4/€2.05, students DM3/€1.55.)

BERCHTESGADEN ☎08652

Berchtesgaden's natural beauty and the sinister attraction of Hitler's mountaintop **Kehlsteinhaus,** dubbed "Eagle's Nest" by the American troops who occupied it after WWII, draw travelers to the town. Although there's only a restaurant up top (☎29 69; meals DM11-20/€5.65-10.25), on a clear day, the view from the 1834m peak is spectacular. In the summer of 2001, construction began to turn the "Eagle's Nest" into a resort. Take Obersalzburg, Kehlsteinbus #38 (June-Oct. every 45min., round-trip DM6.40/€3.30); hop off at Hintereck and buy a combined ticket for bus #9 to "Kehlstein Parkpl., Eagle's Nest." and the elevator ride to the peak (every 30min., 9:30am-4pm, DM23/€11.75.) Be sure to reserve your spot for the return bus when you get off. (Open daily May-Oct. except on days of heavy snow.) In the town's **Salzbergwerke** (salt mines), visitors dress up in old miners' outfits, toboggan down

GERMANY

snaking passages, and raft on a salt lake in mines that have been operating since 1517. (☎ 600 20. Open May to mid-Oct. daily 9am-5pm; mid-Oct. to Apr. M-Sa 12:30-3:30pm. DM22/€11.25.)

Trains run hourly to Munich (3hr., DM48/€25.55) and Salzburg (1hr., DM12.60/€6.45). The **tourist office**, Königsseerstr. 2, opposite the station, has tips on trails in the Berchtesgaden National Park. (☎ 96 71 50. Open mid-June-Oct. M-F 8:30am-6pm, Sa 9am-5pm, Su 9am-3pm; Nov.-mid-June M-F 8:30am-5pm, Sa 9am-noon.) To get to the **Jugendherberge (HI)**, Gebirgsjägerstr. 52, turn right from the station, left on Ramsauer Str., right on Gmündbrücke, and left up the gravel path. (☎ 943 70. Breakfast and sheets included. Reception 6:30am-9am and 5-7pm. Check-in until 10pm. Curfew midnight. Closed Nov.-Dec. 26. 10-bed dorm DM27.50/€14.10.) **Express-Grill Hendl**, Maximilianstr. 8, serves Bavarian dishes. From the train station, follow the signs marked "Zum Markt" and bear right on Maximillianstr. (Open T-Su 11am-8pm.) Score some groceries at the **Edeka Markt**, Königsseer Str. 22. (Open M-F 7:30am-6pm, Sa 7:30am-noon.) **Postal Code:** 83471.

🏔 HIKING NEAR BERCHTESGADEN.

The 5.5km path to the **Königssee**—which winds through fields of flowers and across bubbling brooks—affords a heart-stopping view of the Alps. From the train station, cross the street, turn right, and take a quick left over the bridge. Walk to the right of and past the green-roofed building (but not up the hill) and take a left onto the gravel path near the stone wall, then follow the "Königssee" signs. Once you arrive in Königstein, walk down Seestr. and stop by the **Nationalpark Informationstelle** on the left for hiking info. To explore the **Berchtesgaden National Park,** take bus #46 from Berchtesgaden (15min.; every hr. 6am-7:15pm; DM3.80/€1.95 one-way, DM6.50/€3.35 round-trip) to Ramsau, then visit the Ramsau **tourist office**, Im Tal 2, for trail maps and hiking info. (☎ (08657) 98 89 20. Open Oct.-June M-F 8am-noon and 1:15-5pm; July-Sept. M-Sa 8am-noon and 1:15-5pm., Su 9am-noon and 2-5pm.)

PASSAU
☎ 0851

At the confluence of the Danube, Inn, and Ilz Rivers, this beautiful 2000-year-old city embodies the ideal Old World city. Passau's Baroque architecture peaks at the **Stephansdom**, Dompl., where hundreds of cherubs sprawl across the ceiling and the world's largest church organ looms above the choir. (Open daily summer 6:30am-7pm; winter 6:30am-6pm. Free. Organ concerts May-Oct. M-Sa noon; DM4/€2.10, students DM2/€1.05. Also Th 7:30pm; DM10/€5.15, students DM5/€2.60.) Behind the cathedral is the **Residenz**, home to the **Domschatz** (cathedral treasury), an extravagant collection of gold and tapestries. (Enter through the inside back of the Stephansdom, to the right of the altar. Open Easter-Oct. M-Sa 10am-4pm. DM2/€1.05, students DM1/€0.55.) The heights of the river during various floods are marked on the outside wall of the 13th-century Gothic **Rathaus**. (Open Apr.-Oct. daily 10am-4pm. DM3/€1.55, students DM1/€0.55.) Over the Luitpoldbrücke bridge is the former palace of the bishopric, now home to the **Cultural History Museum**. (☎ 49 33 50. Open early Apr.-Oct. M-F, 9am-5pm, Sa-Su 10am-6pm; Nov.-Mar. Tu-Su 9am-5pm. DM8/€4.10, students DM3/€1.55).

Trains depart the **Hauptbahnhof** (☎ 35 04 347) to: Frankfurt (4½hr., every 2hr., DM125/€64); Munich (2hr., every 2hr., DM52/€26.60); Nuremberg (2hr., every 2hr., DM60/€30.70); Vienna (3½hr., 1-2 per hr. DM60/€30.70). To get to the **tourist office**, Rathauspl. 3, follow Bahnhofstr. from the train station to Ludwigspl., bear left downhill across Ludwigspl. to Ludwigstr., which becomes Rindermarkt, Steinweg, and finally Große Messerg.; continue straight on Schusterg. and turn left on Schrottg. (☎ 95 59 80. Open Easter to mid-Oct. M-F 8:30am-6pm, Sa-Su 9:30am-3pm; Nov.-Easter M-Th 8:30am-5pm, F 8:30am-4pm.) The **Jugendherberge (HI)**, Veste Oberhaus 125, is perched high above the Danube. Cross the suspension bridge downstream from the Rathaus, then *ignore the misplaced sign* pointing up the steps; instead, turn right and proceed through the left hand tunnel. (Skeptics will get there, too—after an extra 10-minute trek.) Head up the cobblestone driveway on your left, through the yellow house, and the hostel's on the right. (☎ 413 519.

Breakfast included. Reception 7-11:30am and 3:30-midnight. New arrivals after 3:30pm only. Curfew midnight, but access code available. Reservations recommended. Dorms DM26/€13.30.) **Inn Straße,** which runs parallel to the Inn River, is lined with good, cheap places to eat. Pick up groceries at **Edeka supermarket,** on Ludwigstr. 2, at the intersection with Grabeng. (Open M-F 8am-8pm, Sa 7:30am-4pm). Get fruit, meat, baked goods, sandwiches (DM3.50/€1.80), and salad by weight (DM1.59/€0.85 per 100g) at **Schmankerl Passage,** Ludwigstr. 6 (open M-F 7:30am-6pm, Sa 7:30am-2pm.) **Café Kowalski,** Oberer Sand 1, makes the largest schnitzel in Passau. (Open Su-Th 10am-1am, F-Sa 10am-3am.) **Postal Code:** 94032.

REGENSBURG   ☎0941

The first capital of Bavaria, the administrative seat of the Holy Roman Empire, and the site of the first German parliament, Regensburg is packed with history. The **Dom St. Peter** dazzles with richly-colored stained glass; inside, the **Domschatz** (Cathedral Treasury) displays gold and jewels purchased by the bishops as well as the preserved and shriveled hand of Bishop Chrysostomus, who died in 407. (Cathedral open Apr.-Oct. daily 6:30am-6pm; Nov.-Mar. 6:30am-5pm. Free. Wheelchair-accessible. Domschatz open Apr.-Oct. Tu-Sa 10am-5pm, Su noon-5pm; Nov.-Mar. Tu-Sa 10am-4pm, Su noon-4pm. DM3/€1.55, students DM1.50/€0.80.) A few blocks away, the **Rathaus** served as capital of the Holy Roman Empire until 1803; the four long iron rods fastened to its side were the official measurement standards used by merchants in the Middle Ages.

Trains head to: Munich (1½hr., 1 per hr., DM38/€19.45); Nuremberg (1-1½hr., 1-2 per hr., DM27/€13.80); Passau (1-1½hr., 1 per hr., DM32/€16.40). To get from the station to the **tourist office,** in the Altes Rathaus on Rathauspl., walk down Maximilianstr. to Grasg., take a left, and follow the street as it turns into Obermünsterstr.; turn right at the end onto Obere Bachg. and follow it five blocks. (☎507 44 10. Open M-F 8:30am-6pm, Sa 9am-4pm, Su 9:30am-2:30pm; Apr.-Oct. also open Su until 4pm.) To get from the station to the **Jugendherberge (HI),** Wöhrdstr. 60, walk to the end of Maximilianstr., turn right at the Apotheke onto Pflugg., turn left immediately at the Optik sign onto tiny Erhardig., walk left over the bridge, then veer right onto Wöhrdstr. on the other side; the hostel is on the right. (☎574 02. Breakfast and sheets included. Key deposit DM20/€10.25. Reception 6am-1am. Check-in until 1am. Curfew 1am, access code available. Reservations encouraged. Wheelchair accessible. Dorm beds DM31/€15.85.) **Hinterhaus,** Rote-Hahnen-Gasse 2, serves both vegetarian (from DM5/€2.60) and meat (from DM8.80/€4.50) dishes. (Open daily 6pm-1am.) There's a **supermarket** in the basement of Galeria Kaufhof, on Neupfarrpl. (Open M-F 9am-8pm, Sa 9am-4pm.) **Postal Code:** 93047.

GREECE (Ελλας)

GREEK DRACHMAS

US$1 = 371DR (DRACHMAS)	100DR = US$0.27
CDN$1 = 240DR	100DR = CDN$0.42
AUS$1 = 199DR	100DR = AUS$0.50
UK£1 = 537DR	100DR = UK£0.19
IR£1 = 433DR	100DR = IR£0.23
NZ$1 = 163DR	100DR = NZ$0.61
ZAR1 = 45DR	100DR = ZAR2.23
EUR€1 = 341DR	100DR = EUR€0.29

PHONE CODE	**Country Code:** 30. **International dialing prefix:** 00.

Over the centuries, Greece (pop. 10.6 million; 131,940 sq. km) has occupied a unique position at the crossroads of Europe and Asia. It emerged independent in 1821 under the dual veneer of Classical Athens and Imperial Byzantium, but its Ottoman Empire heritage still persists. Four centuries under the Turks left a certain spice in its food, an Oriental flair in the strains of its *bouzouki* music, and minaret tips in its skylines. The memory of Dionysus, god of the vine, fuels the island circuit—a blur of sun, sand, and sex. In Greece's austere hills, monks and hermits lurk in structures that have weathered well two millennia. As the country embraces the Euro and overhauls its infrastructure for the 2004 Summer Olympics in Athens, development has accelerated at a blistering pace; as Erupides' Medea quipped, "Let the world's great order be reversed" and revised anew. Still, when you climb above the concrete resorts and whirring tour buses—when you hear the wind's lonely, persistent whistle—you'll know that Greece remains in the oracles' realm. For coverage of Greece rivaling that of Pausanias, see *Let's Go: Greece 2002.*

SUGGESTED ITINERARIES

THREE DAYS Spend it all in **Athens** (p. 507). Luxuriate in the **Acropolis,** gaze at the treasures of the **National Archaeological Museum,** and pay homage to the gods in the fabulous **Parthenon.** Visit the **Ancient Athenian Agora,** and run a lap in the **Panathenaic Olympic Stadium.**

ONE WEEK Begin your week with a sojourn in **Athens** (3 days). Move on to **Corinth** to wander through the 6th-century **Temple of Apollo** (1 day, p. 522). Go to **Olympia** for ruins, ruins, and some more ruins—check out the immense **Temple of Zeus** (1 day, p. 518). Take the ferry to **Corfu** (1 day, p. 528) and then soak up some culture in **Thessaloniki** (1 day, p. 523). Ask the **Oracle at Delphi** how to top off your week (1 day, p. 516).

BEST OF GREECE, THREE WEEKS Explore **Athens** (4 days) before strolling among the mansions of **Nafplion** (1 day, p. 521). Race west to **Olympia** (1 day) and ferry from Patras to **Corfu** (2 days). Head to **Thessaloniki** (2 days). Climb the cliffside monasteries of the **Meteora** (1 day, p. 527), and consult the gods of **Mt. Olympus** (1 day, p. 526). Find your fate at the **Oracle of Delphi** (1 day, p. 516), and ferry from Athens to **Crete,** (3 days, p. 536), home of Europe's largest gorge. Head to the **Cyclades** for respite on **Santorini** (1 day, p. 536), debauchery on **Ios** (1 day, p. 535) and suntanning on **Mykonos** (1 day, p. 532). Finally, repent your sins at another famous Temple of Apollo on **Delos** (1 day, p. 533).

LIFE AND TIMES

HISTORY AND POLITICS

STONE AND BRONZE AGE CIVILIZATIONS (13,000-1100 BC)

By about 13,000-11,000 BC, during the **Paleolithic** (Old Stone Age) period, indigenous populations began to develop stone tools and engage in basic agrarian activities. During the **Neolithic** (New Stone Age) period, shelters evolved from circular
hut dwellings to compartmentalized walled towns built on high. The arrival of met-
alworking from the East catalyzed Greek civilization. The use of bronze in toolmak-
ing and weaponry inaugurated a period of advancement known as the **Bronze Age**
and gave rise to three great Aegean civilizations: the **Helladic**—later Mycenaean—
on the mainland, the **Minoan** on Crete (see p. 536), and the **Cycladic** on the other
islands. The Mycenaeans attacked Troy in Asia Minor around 1250 BC, igniting the
most mythologized, obsessed-over, and written-about war in history. The greatest
Greek histories of the **Trojan War,** Homer's **Iliad** and **Odyssey,** compiled the oral lore
of the war into two epic poems around 850 BC (during the following Dorian Era).

DORIAN INVASION AND RISE OF CITY-STATE (1100-500 BC)

Historians believe that the Aegean civilizations of the Bronze Age met an abrupt
end in the 12th century BC, with the domination of Greek-speaking **Dorians.** Their
tribal leanings meant that industry, agriculture, and trade passed into the hands of
hundreds of politically autonomous villages populated by self-sufficient farmers.
The Dorian **Dark Age** was characterized by destroying "high" civilization in Greece.

In the aftermath of the Dorian era, the *polis,* or **city-state,** became the predominant form of political organization. A typical *polis* consisted of: an **acropolis,** first a
fortified citadel and later a religious center bedecked with **temples** to the people's
patron deities; an **agora** (marketplace), the center of commercial and social life;
stoas (colonnaded porticos), where thinkers waxed philosophical and traders
hawked their wares. Outside the city center were various trappings of the frequent
public spectacles and athletic contests designed to placate the wild and crazy
masses—**amphitheaters, stadia,** and **gymnasia.** By the 9th century BC, many city-
states began to expand, colonize overseas, and form economic, religious, and military ties. During religious and semi-naked athletic festivals such as the **Olympic
Games** (see p. 515), athletic fields, arenas, and racetracks housed heated contests
between states. In the early 5th century BC, the Hellenes, as the Greeks began to
refer to themselves, faced threats on two fronts, from the **Persians** to the east and
the **Carthaginians** to the west. The Greeks decisively defeated the Persians and were
able to repel the Carthaginians from North Africa.

CLASSICAL GREECE (500-400 BC)

The end of the Persian Wars marked the rise of the behemoth of all *poleis,* **Athens**
(see p. 507). Athens established itself as the head of the powerful **Delian League,**
formed between city-states to protect themselves against Persia. From the 6th to
5th centuries BC, Athens also produced major innovations in art, literature, philosophy, and politics. In the early 6th century the lawgiver **Solon** ended slavery in Athens, establishing equality for all citizens before the law. **Pericles,** who came into
power in 461 BC, established democracy in Athens, allowing every male citizen to
participate in government. Athens' rival, **Sparta** (see p. 520) headed the **Peloponnesian League.** Spartan males spent the first 60 years of their lives in military service.
The culture clash exploded in the late 5th century into the **Peloponnesian War** (431-
404 BC), which ended in defeat for Athens.

MACEDONIAN AND ROMAN INVASION (400 BC-AD 300)

After the Peloponnesian War, the Macedonions gained strength when **King Philip II**
led them in conquering a number of Greek city-states. In 338 BC, Philip crushed the
Athenian resistance and then united the various Greek cities under his control.
Philip's son **Alexander the Great,** a student of the famous Greek philosopher **Aristotle,**

GREECE

Greece

ruled Greece with an iron fist. After consolidating military control of Greece, Alexander turned his ambitions east, and by the time of his sudden death at the age of 33, he controlled Egypt and the whole of the Persian empire. However, the Macedonian empire quickly fell to pieces following Alexander's death. In the 3rd century BC the Romans began to fill the power void left by Alexander—Greek cities began to support their former enemies against Rome, and the **Achaean Confederacy** even started a rebellion in 146 BC. This resulted in the destruction of Corinth and the beginning of a number of oppressive restrictions. When the cities were organized by **Augustus** into the Roman province of Achea in 27 BC, he dispelled any notion of a free Greece. As Roman legions took hold of Greek lands, Hellenic culture took hold of Roman society. Adopting what they saw as the best aspects of Greece's culture, the Romans created a very influential hybrid (stolen) culture.

BYZANTINE ERA (AD 300-1400)
The decentralization of the Roman Empire, as a result of expansion into the Near East, led to a division of the territory and a scramble for power—won by **Constantine** in 312. He founded **Constantinople** (modern Istanbul) in 324, over the ancient Greek *polis* of **Byzantium**, giving the Roman Empire a new seat. Constantine died in 338 after converting to Christianity—a religious shift prompted by a battlefield vision of a fiery cross. His empire did not make the transition overnight, but with state support a nascent Christian culture began to emerge. During the 6th century, **Emperor Justinian**'s battles against the Sassanians of Persia in the east and the Vandals in the west weakened the empire, leaving it vulnerable to the Slavic, Mongol, and Avar invasions. As the borders of the empire contracted, an increasing number

of unified Christians were subjected to new, non-Christian rule. This estrangement continued with the crowning of the Frankish **Charlemagne** as Holy Roman Emperor in 800 and culminated in the **Great Schism,** or mutual excommunication, between the Greek Orthodox and Roman Catholic Churches in 1054. Despite a strong line of emperors, Byzantium shrunk, until alliance through marriage with Latin, Slavic, and Turkish rulers was its only recourse. Holding only Constantinople, the Byzantines were finally overrun with the seizure of the city by the **Ottoman Turks** in 1453.

OTTOMAN RULE AND THE RISE OF NATIONALISM (1400-1900)

Renamed **Istanbul**—a Turkish adaptation of the Greek *"steen Poli"* (to the City)—in 1453, Byzantium became the cornerstone of the great new **Ottoman Empire**. However, nationalist fervor began to spread in the empire's individual countries. By the 19th century, movements for independence by minorities within the empire were in full swing. In the era of European revolutions, the Greek cause won mingled interest, sympathy, and distaste from foreigners all over the continent. Hundreds of **"philhellenes,"** distinguished European fellows seeking to restore Greece to the Classical tradition they idolized, came to fight and die for Greece—drawing attention and respect to the cause, especially after the 1824 death (by pneumonia) of British poet and Greek supporter **Lord Byron.** In 1827, Russia, Britain, and France began to pressure the Turkish Sultan to yield to nationalistic sentiment. The weakening of the Turkish fleet at the **Battle of Navarino** (1827) encouraged the hesitant Russian Tsar to declare war on Turkey, which ended in 1829 with the **Treaty of Adrianople,** which gave Greece autonomy.

In their anxiety to limit the power of the newly assembled state, Russia, Britain, and France were hardly generous with the borders of the new Greece—it included only a fraction of the six million Greeks living under Ottoman rule. For the next century, the driving force behind Greek politics was the desire to regain the boundaries of the Byzantine era and unify the Greek population. This vision came to be called the **Megali Idhea** (Great Idea). After the 1831 assassination of the first Greek president by his citizens, Greece was declared a monarchy under German **Prince Otho.** Otho was exiled in 1862, and Danish **George I** was installed as king.

RECENT HISTORY (1900-1975)

In 1920 Cretan Prime Minister **Eleftherios Venizelos** attempted to use the Balkan Wars and World War I as opportunities to realize the Megali Idhea. Venizelos set up an allied revolutionary government in Thessaloniki and invaded the city of Smyrna in war-weakened Turkey. When his advances were rebuffed, Venizelos was voted out of office. In the treaty that followed, the Greeks traded 400,000 Turkish Muslims for one million Orthodox Greeks. This **population exchange** saw the partial realization of the Megali Idhea, but spawned a new set of difficulties for the fledgling Greek economy. The next decade was filled with domestic strife. **George II** was overthrown by a series of coups that instituted a brief democracy. Greece then suffered under Nazi occupation from 1941 to 1945. With its (in)visible hand in Greek politics, the red-scared US helped stave off Communist rule, but after the election of a left-wing leader, the Greek army staged a **coup** on April 21, 1967, beginning seven years of junta rule. It ultimately fell in 1973, but was replaced by rule under the harsh **Demetrios Ioannidis,** head of the feared military police. The regime, internationally isolated and domestically unpopular, collapsed, and former prime minister **Konstantinos Karamanlis** assumed his old position. A new Greek constitution was drawn up in 1975, calling for a parliamentary government with a ceremonial president appointed by the legislature—a system still used today.

GREECE TODAY

In the last decade, Greece has been at constant odds with neighbor and fellow **NATO** member **Turkey,** disputing territory, airspace, and natural resources, and arguing about minority rights. Current Prime Minister **Costas Simitis** has focused his attention on stabilizing the Greek economy by reducing inflation and the budget deficit. Greece is one of twelve **European Union** nations adopting the **Euro**—the common European currency—on January 1, 2002.

THE ARTS

VISUAL ARTS

CYCLADIC AND MINOAN PERIODS (3000-1100 BC). The Cycladic civilizations of the Aegean Bronze Age made their greatest artistic contribution in the form of minimalist sculpture. Cycladic sculptures (see p. 533) were usually small marble statuettes, marked by graceful simplification of the human form. On Crete, the Minoans also churned out miniature votive statuettes, but it was **architecture,** that brought the Minoans glory. The Minoan palaces' massive pillars, ceremonial stairways, and decorative stucco are testament to the spread of Middle Eastern aesthetic and technical ideas, which came to the Minoans through commercial contact with Egypt and Mesopotamia. Minoan artists delighted in the challenge of wet plaster, portraying bull-leaping ceremonies and magical gardens in vivid frescoes. The Minoans were also renowned throughout the Aegean for their **Kamares style pottery,** which consisted of red and white ornamentation on a dark ground.

MYCENAEAN PERIOD (1600-1100 BC). The architecture of the mainland Mycenaean culture developed against the background of the Minoan civilization it began to supersede in 1500BC. The palaces at **Mycenae** (see p. 475)**, Tiryns,** and **Pylos** (see p. 519) modified the layout of their Cretan prototypes to create a more symmetrical design, centered around the Middle Eastern-inspired **megaron,** or reception room. The frescoes decorating the palace adapted the fanciful Minoan model to the more martial tastes of the Mycenaeans. The Mycenaeans were the first Europeans to produce monumental sculpture, best exemplified by the relief work of the triangular **Lion's Gate** at Mycenae (13th century BC) and the royal Mycenaean **tombs.** By 1500 BC, the graves of Mycenaean royalty had evolved from these tombs into stone **tholos,** beehive-shaped structures cloaked in packed earth.

GEOMETRIC AND ARCHAIC PERIODS (1100-480 BC). Out of the Dark Ages that followed the collapse of Mycenaean civilization emerged a new artistic style, with ceramics as its primary medium and Athens as its major cultural center. Athenian pottery of the **Proto-Geometric Period** (1100-900 BC) was decorated with Mycenaean-inspired spirals, arcs, wavy lines, and concentric circles. These patterns became more expressive in the **Geometric Period,** when artists decorated clay figurines and pottery with geometrical motifs reminiscent of basket-weaving patterns. Architects of the Geometric Period focused on the development of one-room temples with columned porches. This period of plenty saw the innovation of the Doric and Ionic architectural orders, whose columns have become staples of art history curricula. Around the 6th century BC, the Greek colonies along the Aegean coast of Asia Minor produced the exotic **Ionic order,** whose columns were distinguished from their more austere Doric predecessors by their twin **volute** (scrolled spiral) capitals, and their slender, fluted shafts. Temples of the Ionic order, ornate and fussy, boasted forests of columns: the highlight of early Archaic sculpture was the development of large-scale figures called **kouroi,** which stood in sanctuaries as votive offerings to deities or as memorials to fallen warriors. Athenian vase painters were exploring the human form through the **black figure technique,** featuring black silhouettes with incised features.

CLASSICAL AND HELLENISTIC PERIODS (480-46 BC). The arts flourished during the Classical period as Athens reached the pinnacle of its political and economic power under Pericles and his successors. Classical temples were more spacious and fluid than their stocky counterparts of the Archaic period. The peerless architectural complex of the Athenian **Acropolis** (see p. 513) built during this period defined "classic" for the Classical world, and its star attraction, the **Parthenon,** bears elegant testimony to the obsession with proportion that dominated the Classical Greek aesthetic. During this period, sculptors mastered the natural representation of the human form. By the middle of the 5th century BC, sculptors were using the **Severe Style** to elevate the human form to a plane of universal physical perfection, idealizing the athletic heroism praised by Pindar's Olympic odes.

GREECE

The Hellenistic kingdoms turned ornate with flower-topped **Corinthian columns.** Hellenistic architects worked on a monumental scale, building massive complexes of temples, *stoas* (colonnaded walkways), palaces, and enormous amphitheaters. The **acoustics** in these theaters are so precise that even now, 2200 years after their construction, a coin dropped on the stage can still be heard from the theater's last row. Hellenistic sculpture displayed all the technical mastery and twice the emotion of its Classical predecessor. Artists even sculpted the grotesque: figures like **Laocöon** writhe and twist. The appointment of **Lysippus** as court sculptor to Alexander the Great began the Greek foray into portraiture. With the advent of the **Roman Empire,** the Hellenistic style was modified to suit Roman tastes; architects mainly built Christian churches, and even the Parthenon was temporarily converted to a church, but was (mercifully) left unaltered for that purpose.

THE BYZANTINE ERA. Byzantine art ranged from illuminated manuscripts to carved ivory panels. The mosaics and icons decorating Byzantine churches are at the pinnacle of the Byzantine artistic achievements. Byzantine icons were made of enamel, ivory, gold, and wood, while mosaics were made of *tesserae:* small cubes of stone or ceramic covered in glass or metallic foil. The unique shimmering effect of Byzantine mosaics was achieved by setting gold and silver *tesserae* at sharp angles to enhance the reflection of light.

MODERN ART. After Greek independence, nationalist sentiment led the government subsidized art. Young artists were urged to study in Munich, and the work of the first wave of post-independence Greek painters reflected their German training. However, the sculptors of this period were largely faithful to their Classical roots. For the most part, Greek art of the 20th century followed major European trends. The eccentric folk artist Theophilos Chatzimichael, known simply as **Theophilos** to modern Greek admirers but relatively unknown in his own lifetime, has been called the Greek van Gogh. The paintings of **Yiannis Psychopedis** combine social and aesthetic criticism, while **Opy Zouni** has won international renown for geometric art.

LITERATURE AND DRAMA

ANCIENT GREECE. The first written Greek did not appear until the middle of the 8th century BC, but the Greek literary tradition may have begun as much as 150 years earlier, with the epic "songs" of **Homer.** Homer may have recorded or dictated the *Iliad* and *Odyssey* in his own lifetime, but most scholars believe that he simply began the faithful oral tradition.

Hesiod composed the *Theogony*, the first Greek account of the creation of the world and the exploits of the gods. During the 7th century BC, **Archilochus** of Paros made the first certain contributions to written poetry in the form of anti-heroic, anti-Homeric elegies. On the island of Lesvos, during the 5th century, the gifted lyric poet **Sappho** sang of love, sex, and the beauty of nature—the term "lesbian" comes from her intense crushes on fellow island women. **Herodotus,** the so-called "Father of History," captured the monumental battles and personalities of the Greco-Persian conflict in *History* (c. 425 BC), while **Thucydides** immortalized the Athenian conflict with Sparta in his chronicle of the Peloponnesian Wars.

As with almost all things, Greece also provided the foundation for modern drama, with Athens at the center. Born out of the 5th century BC from a tradition of **goat songs** *(tragodoi)* dedicated to the god **Dionysus,** the plebeian roots of Greek drama are worlds away from our view of theater as high art. Greek drama began as a religious rite in which all attendants were both performers in the chorus and audience members. Individual acting began when, at a public competition of masked choruses in Dionysus's honor, young **Thespis** stepped out of the crowd to become Athens's first actor—hence, "thespian." By adding a second actor and other characters, **Aeschylus** composed the plays *Prometheus Bound* (uncertain date) and the *Oresteia* (458 BC), a trilogy about Agamemnon's ruinous return home from the Trojan War. **Sophocles** followed, creating the creepy, cathartic *Oedipus* trilogy (c. 444-401 BC)—part of the **Theban Plays,** which ostensibly founded modern dramatic tragedy—detailing the ruinous tale of Oedipus, a man who becomes king by killing his father and marrying his mother. **Euripides,** Sophocles' contemporary, added *Medea* (431 BC) and the *Bacchae* (406 BC) to the tradition. **Aristophanes** tossed aside the tragic medium, and wrote *The Clouds* (423 BC), *Lysistrata* (411 BC), and *The Frogs* (405 BC) in bawdy, slapstick "Old Comedy" form; Aristophanes' swipes at Socrates unfortunately helped cause the philosopher's execution.

PHILOSOPHY. The vast majority of the modern Western world's philosophical canon derives from the great Greek triumvirate of **Socrates, Plato,** and **Aristotle.** Cicero stated that Socrates "brought down philosophy from heaven to earth," concerning himself not with supernatural events but conditions of the human soul. This brought him to consider the ethics of daily life, and the idea of making "one's soul as good as possible." While the great philosopher's works do not exist in any official form, his ideas manifest themselves (some would say literally) in the works of his pupil, Plato. Plato obviously benefited from the **Socratic Method**—positing hypotheses about the world and considering the implications of those hypotheses—as his work is based on the primacy of reason and rationality. The numerous tomes making up the *Dialogues* series deal with a multitude of ethical problems. *Republic* attempts to approach the idea and nature of justice, dividing man into three distinct "lives" —the philosopher, the sensualist, and the man of action—and makes a case for a meritorious aristocracy (ruled by the statesmen and philosophers, of course). To this day, it is difficult to determine where Socrates ends and Plato begins. Sent to Plato's **Akademos** (founded c. 387 BC) for early scholarship, Aristotle blossomed into a true Renaissance man (before the term was coined two millennia later). He excelled in all academic fields from chemistry to psychology to ethics, but he is perhaps most famous for inventing the study of formal logic and pioneering the study of zoology. His *Politics* is the fountainhead of teleological (i.e. purposeful) reasoning, establishing rule and social divisions in society according to "best fit." His works on ethics and a multitude of others remain seminal works of the Western European canon.

BYZANTINE LITERATURE. Since the Hellenistic Era, Greeks had been developing the pseudo-historical romance, including personal love poems and Plutarch's *Life of Alexander,* written in the 1st century AD. In the same century, Greece produced one of its better known works of literature—the original New Testament of the Christian Bible. In the 6th century, Procopius, one of emperor Justinian's generals, wrote two conventional tracts for publication, *On the Wars* and *On the Buildings,* and left behind a *Secret History*—an insider's account of the deviant debauchery that was common in the court of Justinian and his wife Theodora.

MODERN LITERATURE. Greek independence in 1821 gave rise to the Ionian School of literature, whose most distinguished writers were **Andreas Kalvos** and **Dionysios Solomos.** Solomos, whose *Hymn to Liberty* (1823) became the Greek national anthem, has often been called the "national poet of Greece." A truly remarkable group of modern writers has emerged from 20th-century Greece, including **George Seferis, Yiannis Ritsos,** and **Odysseas Elytis. Nikos Kazantzakis** may be the best known modern Greek author. His novels include *Zorba the Greek* (1946) and *The Last Temptation of Christ* (1951), which have both been made into successful films.

CINEMA

After suffering under the colonels' *junta,* the Greek film industry rebuilt itself throughout the 1980s and has recently emerged as a distinguished and prolific presence in the international arena. The 1982 reestablishment of the **Greek Film Center,** a state-supported institute, aided this revitalization by funding and producing many of the most highly regarded modern Greek films, including works by **Nikos Perakis, Pantelis Vougaris,** and **Nikos Panayotopoulos,** Greece's most acclaimed filmmaker and winner of the 1998 Cannes Palme d'Or. The most important event in the Greek film world is the **Thessaloniki Film Festival** in November.

FOOD AND DRINK

Recent medical studies have highlighted the Greek diet as a model for **healthy** eating; its reliance on unsaturated olive oil and vegetables prevents heart disease among Greeks despite their fairly sedentary lifestyle. Penny-pinching carnivores will thank Zeus for lamb, chicken, or beef **souvlaki** and hot-off-the-spit **gyros** stuffed into a pita. Vegetarians can also eat their fill on the cheap: try the feta-piled **horiatiki** (Greek salad), savory pastries, **tiropita** (spinach pie), and the fresh fruits and vegetables found at markets in most cities. Greek-style liquid relaxation involves a few basic options: the old standbys are **ouzo** (a Greek spirit that will earn your respect), and the hard core sludge that is **Greek coffee.** In the summer, people chill-out with frothy coffee *frappés.* Breakfast, served only in the early morning, is generally very simple: a piece of toast with *marmelada* or a pastry suffices. Lunch, a hearty and leisurely meal, can begin as early as noon, but is more likely eaten sometime between 2 and 5pm. Dinner is a drawn-out, relaxed affair served late—eat sometime between 10pm and midnight—then party all night or head home for another nap. A Greek restaurant is known as a **taverna** or **estiatorio;** a grill is a **psistaria.** Don't be suspicious of restaurants without menus; this is common. Service is always included in the check, but it is customary to leave a few drachmas as an **extra tip.**

ESSENTIALS

DOCUMENTS AND FORMALITIES

Citizens of Australia, Canada, New Zealand, the EU, and the US do not require **visas** for stays of fewer than three months, though they are ineligible for unemployment. South Africans need a **visa.** Apply to stay longer at least 20 days prior to the three-month expiration date at the **Aliens Bureau,** 175 Alexandras Ave., Athens 11522 (☎(01) 770 5711), or check with a Greek embassy or consulate.

Greek Embassies at Home: Australia, 9 Turrana St., Yarralumla, Canberra, ACT 26060 (☎(02) 6273 3011). **Canada,** 80 MacLaren St., Ottawa, ON K2P 0K6 (☎613-238-6271); **Ireland,** 1 Upper Pembroke St., Dublin 2 (☎(01) 6767 2545). **South Africa,** 1003 Church St. Athlone, Hatfield, 0028, **Pretoria** (☎(012) 437 35 13). **UK,** 1a Holland Park, London W113TP (☎(0171) 229 3850). **US,** 2221 Massachusetts Ave., N.W., Washington, D.C. 20008 (☎202-939-5800).

Foreign Embassies in Greece: All embassies are located in **Athens** (see p. 507).

TRANSPORTATION

BY PLANE. Flying from northern European cities is a popular way of getting to Greece. From North America, an indirect flight through **Brussels** or **Luxembourg** may cost less than a flight going directly to **Athens.** Over the past few years, the domestic (*esoteriko*) service of **Olympic Airways,** Syngrou 96-100, 11741 Athens (☎(01) 926 91 11), has increased greatly. An hour's flight from Athens (US$60-90) flies to almost any island in Greece. Even in low season, more remote destinations are serviced several times weekly, while more developed areas can have several flights per day.

BY TRAIN. Greece is served by a number of relatively cheap (and slow) international train routes that connect Athens, Thessaloniki, and Larissa to most European cities, but, for example, a journey from Vienna to Athens takes at least 3 days. Train service within Greece is limited and sometimes uncomfortable, and no lines go to the western coast. The extensive and reliable bus system is a better way to get around; however, if you must travel by rail, the new express, air-conditioned **intercity trains** (though slightly more expensive and rare) are worth the price. **Eurailpasses** are valid on Greek trains. **Hellenic Railways Organization (OSE)** connects Athens to major Greek cities. In Greece, call 145 or 147 for schedules and prices.

BY BUS. Buses are cheaper than trains, but there are almost no buses running directly from any European city to Greece. **Busabout,** 258 Vauxhall Bridge Rd., London SW1V 1BS, is one of the very few European bus lines that also runs to Greece. (☎(0171) 950 1661.) **KTEL** (www.ktel.org) runs most domestic buses; always check with an official source about scheduled departures. Smaller towns may use cafes as bus stops. **Confirm your destination** with the driver; signs may be wrong. Along the road, little blue signs marked with white buses or the word "ΣΤΑΣΗ" indicate stops. Let the driver know ahead of time where you want to get off; if your stop is passed, yell *"Stasi!"*. Intercity buses are usually **blue.**

BY FERRY. The most popular way of getting to Greece is by **ferry** from Italy. Boats travel from **Italy** to: **Corfu** (8hr.) and **Igoumenitsa** (9½hr.) from **Brindisi**; and **Patras** from **Ancona** (21hr.). Deck seats run L58,000-120,000/€30-62. **Rhodes** is connected by ferry to **Marmaris,** Turkey; **Limassol,** Cyprus; **Haifa,** Israel. If you plan to travel from Brindisi, Italy, make reservations and arrive at the port well before your departure time. ISIC holders can often get student fares, and Eurail pass holders get many reductions and free trips. Everyone pays the port tax (L10-14,000/€5.20-7.35).

There is frequent **ferry** service to the Greek islands, but schedules are irregular and exasperating; misinformation is common. Your best bet is to arrive early to your ferry to avoid literally missing the boat. To avoid hassles, go to **limenarheio** (port police)—every port has one, and they all carry ferry schedules. **Flying dolphins** (hydrofoils) are a speedier but more expensive alternative to ferry transport.

BY CAR. Cars are a luxury in Greece, a country where public transportation is non-existent after 7pm. Ferries will take you and your car island-hopping if you pay a transport fee for the car. Rental agencies may quote low daily rates that exclude the 20% tax and **Collision Damage Waiver (CDW)** insurance (2500dr/€7.35 per day). Foreign drivers are required to have an **International Driving Permit** and an **International Insurance Certificate** to drive in Greece. The **Automobile and Touring Club of Greece (ELPA),** Messogion 395, Athens 11527 (☎(01) 60 68 800), provides assistance and offers reciprocal membership to foreign auto club members. They also have 24hr. emergency road assistance (☎104) and an information line (☎174 in Athens, (01) 60 68 838 elsewhere in Greece; open M-F 7am-3pm).

BY BIKE AND BY THUMB. The mountainous terrain and unpaved roads make **cycling** in Greece difficult. **Mopeds** can be great for exploring, but they also make you extremely vulnerable to the carelessness of other drivers; *always* wear a helmet. The majority of tourist-related accidents each year occur on mopeds. Greeks are not eager to pick up foreigners. Sparsely populated areas have little or no traffic. Visitors who choose to **hitchhike** write their destination on a sign in both Greek and English, and hitch from turn-offs rather than along long stretches of straight road. Women should *never* hitch alone. *Let's Go* does not recommend hitchhiking.

TOURIST SERVICES AND MONEY

EMERGENCY	Police, ☎100. Hospital, ☎106. Ambulance, ☎166.

TOURIST BOARDS. Tourism in Greece is overseen by two national organizations: the **Greek National Tourist Organization (GNTO)** and the **tourist police** *(touristiki astinomia)*. The **GNTO,** known as **EOT** in Greece, can supply general information about sights and accommodations throughout the country. The main office is at Amerikis 2, Athens (☎(01) 32 71 300). The **tourist police** (☎171, 24hr.) deal with local and immediate problems: bus schedules, accommodations, lost passports, etc. They are open long hours and are willing to help, although their English is often limited.

GNTO Offices: Australia, 3rd Fl., 51-57 Pitt St., Sydney, NSW 2000 (☎(12) 9241 1663). **Canada,** 1300 Bay St., Toronto, ON M5R 3K8 (☎416-968-2220; www.aei.ca/gntomtl); 1170 Place du Frére André, 3rd Fl., Montréal, PQ, H3B 3C6 (☎(514) 871-1535). **UK,** 4 Conduit St., London W1R ODJ (☎(4207) 734 5997). **US,** Olympic Tower, 645 5th Ave., 5th Fl., New York, NY 10022 (☎212-421-5777).

CURRENCY AND EXCHANGE. Greek **drachmas** ("dr") are issued in both paper notes (100, 200, 500, 1000, 5000, and 10,000dr) and coins (5, 10, 20, 50, and 100dr). If you're carrying more than US$1000 in cash when you enter Greece, you must declare it upon entry (traveler's checks not included). You can bring up to US$445 worth of drachmas into Greece. No more than 20,000dr can be taken out of the country when you leave. Greece has accepted the **Euro (€)** as legal tender, and Greek drachmas will be phased out by July 1, 2002. For more information, see p. 23.

Prices: To give you a general idea, a bare-bones day in Greece, staying at hostels, campgrounds, or *domatia* (rooms to let), and buying food at supermarkets or at outdoor food stands, costs about US$35. A day with more creature comforts, with accommodations in a more expensive *domatia* or budget hotel, eating 1 meal a day in a restaurant, and going out at night, runs about US$50.

Tipping and bargaining: When **tipping,** you should offer enough to show respect, for the goods, but not so much to seem like a show-off. At all but the ritziest restaurants, service is included in the bill. Several hundred drachmas for a several thousand drachma meal is usually sufficient. **Bargaining** skills are essential in Greece, but you must know when to bargain. Paying the asked price for street wares will have the seller marveling at a tourist's naiveté, while bargaining at the shop of a master craftsman whose crafts are worth the stated tag will be seen as rude and disrespectful. Don't tip taxis.

Taxes: The European Union imposes a **value-added tax (VAT)** on goods and services purchased within the EU, which is included in the marked price. Non-EU citizens may obtain a **refund** for taxes paid on retail goods (but not services). You must spend over 40,000dr/€117.40 to receive a refund. The percentage will vary from **11.5% to 15.3%.**

ACCOMMODATIONS AND CAMPING

Lodgings in Greece are a bargain. **Hostels** that are not currently endorsed by HI are in most cases still safe and reputable. **Curfews** in hostels are strict, and they may leave you on the street. **Hotel** prices are regulated, but proprietors may try to push you to take the most expensive room. Check your bill carefully, and threaten to contact the tourist police if you think you are being cheated. **GNTO** offices usually have a list of inexpensive accommodations, with prices. In many areas, **domatia** (rooms to let) are an attractive and perfectly dependable option. Often you'll be approached by locals as you enter town or disembark from your boat; Greek tourist officials consider this illegal. Greece hosts plenty of official **campgrounds,** and discreet freelance camping—though illegal—is common in July and August, but may not be the safest way to spend the night. Some campgrounds offer showers and breakfast and they are certainly the cheapest way to spend a night in Greece.

COMMUNICATION

MAIL. Letters within Europe cost 200dr/€0.60 (up to 50g); anywhere else in the world costs 240dr/€ (up to 150g). Mail sent to Greece from Europe generally takes at least 3 days to arrive; from the US, South Africa, and Australia airmail will take 5-10 days. Letters can be sent general delivery to almost any city or town in Greece with a post office. Address mail to be held: FirstName SURNAME, Corfu Town Post Office, Corfu, Greece 8900, POSTE RESTANTE. The mail will go to a special desk in the central post office, unless you specify differently.

TELEPHONES. The **only way** to use the phone in Greece is with a **prepaid phone card.** You can buy the cards at streetside kiosks and *peripteros*. Time is measured in minutes or talk units (100 units=30min. domestic calling). The card usually has a toll-free access number and a **personal identification number (PIN).** To make a phone call, dial the access number, enter the PIN, and at the voice prompt, enter the phone number of the party you're trying to reach. Wherever possible, use a calling card for **international** phone calls, as the long-distance rates for national phone services are often exorbitant. Using a calling card, contact your service provider's Greek operator: **AT&T,** ☎ 00 800 13 11; **British Telecom,** ☎ 00 800 44 11; **Canada Direct,** ☎ 00 800 16 11; **Ireland Direct,** ☎ 155 11 74; **MCI,** ☎ 00 800 12 11; **Sprint,** ☎ 00 900 14 11.

INTERNET ACCESS. The availability of the Internet in Greece is rapidly expanding. In all big cities, most small cities, large towns, and most of the touristed islands, you will able to find Internet access. Expect to pay between Expect to pay between 1000-2000dr/€2.95-5.90 per hour. **Cybercafe Guide** (www.cyberiacafe.net/cyberia/guide/ccafe.htm) can help you find cybercafes in Greece.

LANGUAGE. Although many Greeks in Athens and other heavily touristed areas speak English, off the beaten path you'll probably have to stumble around a bit in Greek. To avoid misunderstandings, it is also important to know Greek body language: to say no, Greeks lift their heads back abruptly while raising their eyebrows; to indicate yes, they emphatically nod once. A hand waving up and down that seems to say "stay there" actually means "come." For help deciphering and transliterating the Greek alphabet, as well as basic phrases in Modern Greek, see p. 952, but beware: for instance, Φ and φ can be spelled *ph* or *f.*

LOCAL FACTS

Time: Greece is 2hr. ahead of Greenwich Mean Time (GMT).

When to Go: The climate is fairly uniform throughout Greece, but the islands are a bit milder than the mainland, and northern Greece's high altitude areas are cooler. Summer is sunny, hot, and dry—it's almost impossible to escape the heat without A/C or a beach. Winter temperatures hover around 10°C (50°F); Oct.-Mar. is the rainy season.

Hours: Normal **business hours** in Greece include a break from about 2 until 6pm or so. Hours vary from place to place. **Banks** are normally open M-F 8am-1:30pm, and also 3:30-6pm in some larger cities.

Holidays: Feast of St. Basil/New Year's Day (Jan. 1); **Epiphany** (Jan. 6); 1st Sunday in Lent (Mar. 18); **Greek Independence Day** (Mar. 25); **Good Friday** (Apr. 13); **St. George's Day** (Apr. 23); **Labor Day** (May 1); **Easter** (May 5); **Ascension** (June 13); **Pentecost** (June 23); **Feast of the Assumption of the Virgin Mary** (Aug. 15); The **Virgin Mary's Birthday** (Sept. 8); **Feast of St. Demetrius** (Oct. 26); **National Anniversary of Greek Independence** (Oct. 28); **Commemoration of an uprising of Greek university students** (Nov. 17); **Christmas** (Dec. 25).

Festivals: Greeks take a good 3 weeks to get ready for the Lent Fast, feasting and dancing throughout **Carnival** (Feb. 25-Mar. 11); Patras and Kephalonia celebrate with particular zest. Apr. 23 is **St. George's Day,** when Greece—especially Limnos and Hania—honor the dragon-slaying knight with horse races, wrestling matches, and dances. The **Feast of St. Demetrius** (Oct. 26) is celebrated with particular enthusiasm in Thessaloniki, coinciding with the opening of new wine.

ATHENS (Αθηνα) ☎01

One minute dodging the packs of mopeds in Pl. Syndagma will prove that Athens refuses to become a museum. Ancient ruins sit quietly amid the hectic modern streets as quiet testaments to the city's rich history, and the Acropolis looms larger than life over the city at its feet, a perpetual reminder of ancient glory. Byzantine churches recall an era of foreign invaders, when Athens was ruled from Macedonia, Rome, and Byzantium. The reborn democracy has revived the city in a wave of madcap construction: the conflicted, oddly adolescent metropolis gutted its crumbling medieval mansions to become a dense concrete jungle.

▐ TRANSPORTATION

Flights: El. Venizelou, Greece's new international airport, operates as one massive, yet easily navigable terminal (☎35 30 000). Arrivals are on the ground floor, departures are on the 2nd floor. There are 4 bus lines that run to Athens, Piraeus, and Rafina.

Trains: Hellenic Railways (OSE), Sina 6 (☎36 24 402; www.ose.gr). **Larissis Train Station** (☎52 98 837) serves northern Greece and Europe. Open 24hr. Take trolley #1 from El. Venizelou (Panepistimiou) in Pl. Syndagma (every 10min. 5am-midnight, 150dr/€0.45). Trains depart for: **Thessaloniki** (7hr., 4 per day, 4800dr/€14.25) and

GREECE

Prague, Czech Republic (35,000dr/€102.75). **Peloponnese Train Station** (☎51 31 601), is open 24hr., and serves **Patras** (4¼hr., 1800dr/€5.30) as well as major towns in the Peloponnese. From Larissis, exit to your right and go over the footbridge.

Buses: Terminal A: Kifissou 100 (☎51 24 910). Take blue **bus #051** from the corner of Zinonos and Menandrou near Pl. Omonia (every 15min., 150dr/€0.45). Buses depart for: **Corinth** (1½hr., 1 per hr., 1850dr/€5.45); **Corfu** (10hr., 3 per day, 9100dr/€26.95); **Patras** (3hr., 30 per day, 4000dr/€11.75); **Thessaloniki** (6hr., 11 per day, 9000dr/€26.45) via **Larissa. Terminal B:** Liossion 260 (☎83 17 153, except Sa-Su). Take blue bus #024 from Amalias outside the National Gardens (45min., every 20min., 120dr/€0.35). Buses depart for **Delphi** (3hr., 6 per day, 3300dr/€9.70).

Ferries: Check schedules at the tourist office, in the *Athens News,* or with the Port Authority of Piraeus (☎42 26 000). Most ferries dock at **Piraeus** (see p. 508). To get to Piraeus, take the subway west to the last stop; **Rafina,** the other ferry hub, is accessible via the bus station. Ferries for the Sporades leave from **Ag. Konstantinos** or **Volos.**

Public Transportation: KTEL (KTEΛ) **buses** are punctual, so be on time. Buses around Athens and its suburbs are blue and designated by 3-digit numbers. Buy blue bus/trolley **tickets** at any street **kiosk.** Hold on to your ticket: you can be fined 6000-10,000dr/€17.65-29.35 by police. **Trolleys** are yellow and crowded, sporting 1- or 2-digit numbers; they are distinguished from buses by their electrical antennae. Trolleys don't accept money; buy a trolley/bus **ticket** ahead of time at a **kiosk** (150dr/€0.45).

Subway: The Athens **Metro** is under construction, consisting of 3 lines. **M1** runs from northern Kifissia to the port of Piraeus. **M2** runs from Sepolia to Dafni. **M3** runs from Ethniki Amyna to Pl. Syndagma in central Athens. Trains depart from either end of the line every 5min. 5am-midnight. Buy **tickets** (250dr/€0.75) in any station.

Car Rental: Try the many places on **Singrou.** All charge 10,000-15,000dr/€29.35-44 for a small car with 100km mileage (prices include tax and insurance). Some student discounts up to 50%. Prices rise in summer. International Driver's License not needed.

Taxis: Meter **rates** start at 250dr/€0.75, with an additional 80dr/€0.25 per km within city limits, 150dr/€0.45 per km in the suburbs, 40dr/€0.15 per stationary min. Everything beyond the start price is 150dr/€0.45 between midnight and 5am. There's a 400dr/€1.20 surcharge from the airport and a 200dr/€0.60 surcharge for trips from bus and railway terminals; plus 100dr/€0.30 for each piece of luggage over 10kg.

PIRAEUS PORT: FERRIES FROM ATHENS

Piraeus is the port town for Athens; although it is a separate town, the majority of ferries from Athens leave from Piraeus Port. Ferries sail to nearly all Greek islands (except the Sporades and Ionian Islands). Among them are: **Iraklion,** (8hr., 2 per day, 6900dr/€20.25); **Hania** (8hr., 2 per day, 5700dr/€16.75); and **Rethymno** (8hr., 1 per day, 6900dr/€20.25); all on Crete. Travel is sporadic to: **Hydra** (3hr., 2400dr/€7.05); **Poros** (2½hr., 2100dr/€6.20); and **Spetses** (4½hr., 3300dr/€9.70); boats leave every evening for **Chios** (9hr., 5800dr/€17.05) and **Lesvos** (12hr., 7200dr/€21.15). More regular departures are to: **Ios** (7½hr., 3 per day, 5400dr/€15.85); **Milos** (7hr., 2 per day, 5100dr/€15); **Mykonos** (6hr., 2 per day, 5200dr/€15.30); **Naxos** (6hr., 5 per day, 5000dr/€14.70); **Paros** (6hr., 5 per day, 5200dr/€15.30); **Rhodes** (15hr., 2 per day, 9200dr/€27); and **Santorini** (9hr., 3 per day, 6000dr/€17.65). Small ferries go from Akti Poseidonos; larger ferries dock at Akti Miaouli; international ferries are at the end, towards the Customs House.

ORIENTATION AND PRACTICAL INFORMATION

Athenian geography mystifies newcomers and natives alike. If you lose your bearings, ask for directions back to well-lit **Syndagma** or look for a cab; the **Acropolis** serves as a reference point, as does **Mt. Lycavittos.** Athenian streets often have multiple spellings or names, so check the map again before you panic. Listings and ferry information appear in the daily *Athens News* (300dr/€0.90). Covering southwest **Attica,** near the coast, Athens and its suburbs occupy seven hills. **Syndagma,** the central *plateia* containing the Parliament building, is encircled by the other major neighborhoods. Clockwise, they are **Plaka, Monastiraki, Omonia, Exarhia, Kolonaki,** and **Pangrati.** Plaka, the center of the old city, and temporary home of most visitors to Athens, is bounded by the city's two largest ancient monuments—the **Temple of Olympian Zeus** and the **Acropolis.** Monastiraki's frenetic **flea market** is home to vendors who sell rugs, furniture, leather, *bouzoukis,* and all varieties of souvenirs. Omonia is the site of the city's **central subway station.** Two parallel avenues, **Panepistimiou** and **Stadiou,** connect Syndagma to Omonia. Omonia's neighbor to the east, progressive Exarhia, sports some of Athens's most bumpin' nightlife, while nearby Kolonaki, on the foothills of Mt. Lycavittos, has plenty of glitz and swanky shops. Pangrati, southeast of Kolonaki, is marked by several Byzantine churches, a park, the **Olympic Stadium,** and the **National Cemetery.** A 30min. ride south takes you to the seaside suburb of **Glyfada,** where Bacchanites head to party.

Tourist Office: The **central office** and **information booth** are at Amerikis 2 (☎33 10 561), off Stadiou near Pl. Syndagma. Bus, train, and ferry schedules and prices; lists of museums, embassies, and banks; brochures on travel throughout Greece; and an indispensable Athens **map.** Open M-F 9am-9pm, Sa-Su 10am-9pm.

Banks: National Bank of Greece, Karageorgi Servias 2 (☎33 40 015), in Pl. Syndagma. Open M-Th 8am-2pm, F 8am-1:30pm; open for currency exchange only M-Th 3:30-6:30pm, F 3-6:30pm, Sa 9am-3pm, Su 9am-1pm. Currency exchange available 24hr. at the airport, but exchange rates and commissions may be exorbitantly high.

American Express: Ermou 2, P.O. Box 3325 (☎32 44 975 or 32 44 979), above McDonald's in Pl. Syndagma. This A/C-endowed office cashes traveler's checks commission-free, holds mail for a month, and provides travel services for cardholders. Open M-F 8:30am-4pm, Sa 8:30am-1:30pm (only travel and mail services Sa).

Bookstores: Eleftheroudakis Book Store, Panepistimiou 17 (☎33 14 180) and Nikis 20 (☎32 29 388). A browser's delight, with Greek, English, French, and German books, classical and recent literature. Open M-F 9am-9pm, Sa 9am-3pm.

Laundromats: Most *plinitirios* have signs reading "Laundry." Wash, dry, and fold laundry for 2500dr/€7.27 at **Angelou Geront 10** in *Plaka.* Open M-Sa 8am-7pm, Su 9am-2pm. In *Syndagma,* **National,** Apollonos 17, is also a dry cleaners. (☎32 32 266). Wash and dry 1300dr/€3.82 per kg. Open M, W 8am-4pm and T, Th-F 8am-8:30pm.

Emergencies: Police, ☎100. **Doctor,** ☎105 from Athens, 101 elsewhere; line open 2pm-7am. **Ambulance,** ☎166. **Fire,** ☎199. **AIDS Help Line,** (☎72 22 222). *Athens News* lists emergency hospitals. Free emergency health care for tourists.

Tourist Police: Dimitrakopoulou 77 (☎171). English spoken. Open 24hr.

Pharmacies: Identified by a **red** (a doctor) or **green cross** hanging over the street. Check *Athens News* or the chart in pharmacy windows for the day's emergency pharmacy.

Hospitals: Emerg. hospitals on duty ☎106. **Geniko Kratiko Nosokomio** (Public State Hospital), Mesogion 154 (☎77 78 901). A **public hospital,** Evangelismou 45-47 (☎72 20 101), is near Kolonaki. "Hospital" is *nosokomio* in Greek; call operator at ☎131.

Telephones: OTE, Patission 85 (☎82 14 449 or 82 37 040) or Athinas 50 (☎32 16 699). Open M-F 7am-9pm, Sa 8am-3pm, Su 9am-2pm. Most phone booths in the city operate by telephone cards (1000dr/€2.95, 7000dr/€20.55, or 11,500dr/€33.45 at OTE offices, kiosks, and tourist shops). Push the "i" button on the phones for English instructions. For a domestic English-speaking operator, call 151.

Internet Access: Carousel Cybercafe, Eftixidou 32 (☎75 64 305), near Pl. Plastira in Pangrati. 1500dr/€4.40 per hr., 750dr/€2.20 minimum. Open 11am-midnight.

Post Office: Syndagma (☎32 26 253), on the corner of Mitropoleos. Address mail to be held: FirstName SURNAME, Pl. Syndagma Post Office, Athens, Greece **10300.** Open M-F 7:30am-2:30pm, Sa-Su 9am-2pm.

◤ ACCOMMODATIONS

Greek Youth Hostel Association, Dragatsaniou 4, 7th floor, lists hostels in Greece. Go up Stadiou and then left on Dragatsaniou, then take the elevators on the right as you enter the arcade. (☎32 34 107. Open M-F 9am-3pm.) The **Hellenic Chamber of**

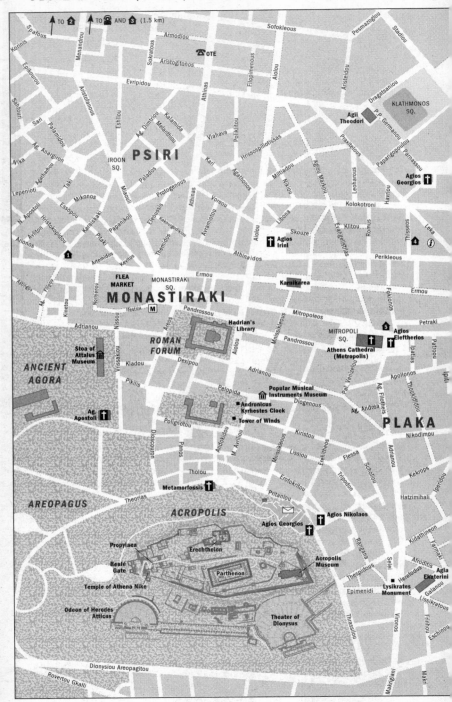

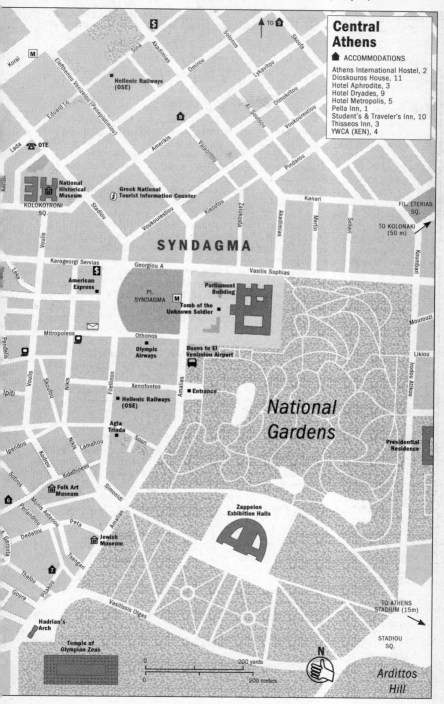

Central Athens

ACCOMMODATIONS

Athens International Hostel, 2
Dioskouros House, 11
Hotel Aphrodite, 3
Hotel Dryades, 9
Hotel Metropolis, 5
Pella Inn, 1
Student's & Traveler's Inn, 10
Thisseos Inn, 3
YWCA (XEN), 4

Koral
Eleftheriou Venizelou (Panepistimiou)
Sina
Akadimies
Solonos
Omirou
Skoufa
TO
Lykavitou
Dimokritou
Al. Soutsou
Voukourestiou
Eduard Lo.
Hellenic Railways (OSE)
Lada
OTE
National Historical Museum
KOLOKOTRONI SQ.
Greek National Tourist Information Counter
Voukourestiou
Stadiou
Valaoritou
Kriezotou
Zalokosta
Akadimias
Kanari
Merlin
Seferi
Pindarou
FIL. ETERIAS SQ.
TO KOLONAKI (50 m)
Koumbari

SYNDAGMA

Karageorgi Servias
American Express
Georgiou A
Pl. SYNDAGMA
Vasilis Sophias
Parliament Building
Tomb of the Unknown Soldier
Mourouzi
Voulis
Leka
Pendelis
Ipiti
Mitropoleos
Othonos
Olympic Airways
Buses to El. Venizelou Airport
Likiou
Inodou Atikou
Voulis
Skoufou
Nikis
Filellinon
Xenofontos
Amalias
Entrance
Hellenic Railways (OSE)
Agia Triada
Nilis
Lamahou
Souri
Iperidou
Kotzou
Kidathineon
Sotiros
Folk Art Museum
Monis Asteriou
Periandrou
Peta
Amalias
Simonidi
Dedalou
Jewish Museum
Tsangari
Thalou
Plakou
Goura
Vasilissis Olgas
Hadrian's Arch
Temple of Olympian Zeus

National Gardens

Presidential Residence

Zappeion Exhibition Halls

TO ATHENS STADIUM (15m)
STADIOU SQ.

N

Ardittos Hill

0   200 yards
0   200 meters

Hotels, Karageorgi Servias 2, provides info and reservations for hotels throughout Greece. Reservations require a cash deposit, length of stay, and number of people; you must contact them at least one month in advance. (☎32 37 193. Open May-Nov. M-Th 8:30am-2pm, F 8:30am-1:30pm, Sa 9am-12:30pm).

■ **Hotel Dryades,** Dryadon 4 (☎38 27 116). Elegant Dryades offers some of Athens's nicest budget accommodations, with large rooms and private baths. Full kitchen and TV lounge. Singles 10,000-12,000dr/€29.40-35.25; doubles 13,000-15,000dr/€38.15-45; triples 16,000-18,000dr/€47-52.85.

■ **Student's and Traveler's Inn,** Kidathineon 16 (☎32 44 808). Unrivaled location and lively atmosphere make up for early closing. Bring your own sheets, towel, and ask for toilet paper at the desk. Midnight curfew. Co-ed dorms 4500-5000dr/€13.25-14.70; doubles 12,000-15,000dr/€35.25-44; triples 15,000-18,000dr/€44-52.82; quads 16,000-24,000dr/€46.96-70.43. Call for a reservation and arrive on time.

Hotel Metropolis, Mitropoleos 46 (☎32 17 871), opposite Mitropoli Cathedral. Newly renovated, this hotel is a roomy step up at a good price. Balconies with views of the Acropolis. Laundry wash and dry (2000dr/€5.90). Singles 10,000-14,000dr/€29.35-41.10; doubles 12,000-16,000dr/€35.25-47; triples 15,000-18,000dr/€44-52.82.

Pella Inn, Karaiskaki 1 (☎32 50 598). Walk 10min. down Ermou from Pl. Syndagma; it's 2 blocks from the Monastiraki subway station. Dorms 3000-4000dr/€8.80-11.74; doubles 10,000-12,000dr/€29.35-35.22; triples 12,000-15,000dr/€35.22-44.

YWCA (XEN), Amerikis 11 (☎36 24 291), up the street from the tourist office. **For women only.** Spacious building has hand-wash laundry facilities and fridges on each floor. 1000dr/€2.95 membership fee or valid YWCA membership required. Safe and central location make up for strict regulations. Singles 6000dr/€17.61, with bath 7500dr/€22; doubles 9000-9500dr/€26.41-27.88.

Thisseos Inn, Thisseos 10 (☎32 45 960). Take Karageorgi Servias, which becomes Perikleous, and Thisseos is on the right. This home-turned-hostel is close to Syndagma's sights. Dorms 3500-4500dr/€10.27-13.21; singles 5000-8000dr/€14.67-23.48; doubles 7500-10,000dr/€22-29.35; triples 13,500dr/€39.62.

Dioskouros House, Pitakou 6 (☎32 48 165), on the southwest corner of the National Gardens by the Temple of Olympian Zeus. Dorms 5000dr/€14.67; doubles 13,000dr/€38.15; triples 19,500dr/€57.23; quads 24,000dr/€70.43.

Hostel Aphrodite, Einardou 12 (☎88 10 589). From the Victoria subway station, follow Heiden 2 blocks, then continue along Peioniou 2. Turn right on Michail Voda and left on Einardou. A staircase with an erotic mural leads to a swingin' 24hr. basement bar. Dorms 3500-4500dr/€10.30-13.25; doubles 11,000-13,000dr/€32.30-38.15; triples 15,000-16,500dr/€44-48.15; quads 18,000-20,000dr/€52.90-58.70.

Athens International Hostel (HI), Victor Hugo 16 (☎52 34 170). Walk down Tritis Septembriou from Pl. Omnia, and take a left on Veranzerou, which becomes Victor Hugo after crossing Marni. A few minutes walk Metahourgio subway stop. The only HI-affiliated hostel in Greece—you'll need to be an HI member or buy a membership (4200dr/€12.33) to stay here. Hot water 6-10am and 6-10pm. Call for reservation. Priority given to current HI members. Dorms 2850dr/€8.40, including breakfast and sheets.

◧ FOOD

Athens offers a melange of stands, open-air cafes, side-street *tavernas*, and intriguing restaurants. Cheap fast food abounds in Syndagma and Omonia—try *souvlaki* (250-400dr/€0.75-1.20), served either on a *kalamaki* (skewer) or wrapped in *pita; tost* (a grilled sandwich of variable ingredients, usually ham and cheese; 300-600dr/€0.90-1.80); *tiropita* (hot cheese pie, 300dr/€0.90); or *spanakopita* (hot spinach pie, 300dr/€0.90). A *koulouri* (doughnut-shaped, sesame-coated roll; 50-100dr/€0.20-0.30) makes for a quick breakfast. Pick up **groceries** at the market on **Nikis.**

■ **Eden Vegetarian Restaurant,** Lysiou 12 (☎324 8858). Take Kidathineon to Tripidon, then left on to Lysiou. Fantastic dishes like *boureki pie* (zucchini with feta cheese, 1600dr/€4.70), as well as flavorful mushroom *stifado* with onions and peppers (2900dr/€8.50). Open W-M noon-midnight.

▓ **Savvas,** Mitropoleos 86 (☎32 45 048), tucked in a corner off Ermou. For takeout, this grill is a budget eater's dream, with heavenly, cheap gyros (400dr/€1.20). Don't sit down—prices skyrocket by 1500dr/€4.40. Open 7:30am-3am.

Jungle Juice, Aiolou 21, under the Acropolis (☎33 16 739). A fresh-squeezed smoothie and sandwich stand. Snag a turkey sandwich (500dr/€1.50) and a "Leone Melone," a blend of cantaloupe, mango, and pineapple (900dr/€2.70). Open daily 8am-9pm.

O Barba Giannis, Em. Benaki 94 (☎33 00 185). From Syndagma, walk up Stadiou and make a right on Em. Benaki. Athenian students, execs, and artists all agree that "Uncle John's" is the place for cheap, delicious food and outstanding service. Open daily 1pm-1am; closed Su in summer. Bring a Greek phrasebook; no English is spoken here.

Nikis Cafe, Nikis 3 (☎32 34 971), near Ermou. More of a cafe than an eatery, Nikis does serve fresh baguette sandwiches (900dr/€2.70) and quiche. Strawberry and banana frozen margaritas 2000dr/€5.90. Open M-Sa 8am-1am.

Healthy Food Vegetarian Restaurant, Panepistimiou 57 (☎32 10 966). Wholesomeness to make a *souvlaki* stand blush—everything's made fresh. Try the *muesli* (1050dr/€3.10) or carrot apple juice (500dr/€1.50). Open 8am-9:30pm.

Attalos Restaurant, Adrianou 9 (☎32 19 520), near Thisseon. This traditional Greek taverna serves skewered souvlaki (1900dr/€5.60), as well as a variety of handmade *croquettes* (a vegetarian plate for 2-4 people costs 2600dr/€7.65). Open 9am-2am.

👁 SIGHTS

▓ ACROPOLIS

Reach the entrance on the west side of the Acropolis either from Areopagitou to the south, by following the signs from Plaka, or by exiting the Agora to the south, following the path uphill, and turning right. ☎321 0219. Open daily 8am-6:30pm; in winter 8am-2:30pm. Site and Acropolis Museum 2000dr/€5.90, students and EU seniors 1000dr/€2.95, under 18 free.

Perched on a rocky plateau above the city, the Acropolis has crowned Athens since the 5th century BC. At the center, the brilliant Parthenon towers over the Aegean and Attic Plains, the ultimate achievement of Athens's Classical glory and the era's most enduring architectural contribution. Although each Greek *polis* had an *acropolis* ("high city"), Athens's magnificent example has effectively monopolized the name. In the last 20 years, acid rain has unfortunately forced works formerly displayed outside to take cover in the on-site museum.

BEULÉ GATE AND PROPYLAEA. The ramp that led to the Acropolis in classical times no longer exists; today's visitors make the 5min. climb to the ticket window. The path leads through the crumbling Roman **Beulé Gate,** named for the French archaeologist who unearthed it. It continues through the **Propylaea,** the incomplete entrance famous for an ambitious multi-level design begun by Mnesikles in the 5th-Century BC. The middle gate of the Propylaea opened onto the **Panathenaic Way,** an east-west route cutting across the middle of the Acropolis that was traveled by Panathenaic processions venerating the goddess Athena.

TEMPLE OF ATHENA NIKE. On the right after leaving the Propylaea, the tiny cliffside **Temple of Athena Nike** was raised during the Peace of Nikias (421-415BC), a respite from the Peloponnesian War. The temple, known as the "jewel of Greek architecture," is ringed by eight miniature Ionic columns and once housed a statue of the winged goddess of victory, Nike. One day, in a paranoid frenzy, the Athenians were seized by a fear that Nike would flee the city and take peace with her, so they clipped the statue's wings. The remains of the 5m-thick **Cyclopean wall,** predating the Classical Period, lie below the temple.

PARTHENON. Looming over the hillside, the **Temple of Athena Parthenos** (Athena the virgin), commonly known as the **Parthenon,** keeps vigil over Athens and the modern world. Iktinos designed the Parthenon to be the crowning glory of the Periclean project; he added two columns to the usual six in the front of the temple. Ancient Athenians saw their city as the capital of civilization, and the **metopes** (scenes in the open spaces above the columns) on the sides of the Parthenon celebrate Athens's

GREECE

rise. On the far right of the south side—the only side that has not been defaced—the Lapiths battle the Centaurs, on the east side, the Olympian gods defeat giants, while the north depicts the victory of the Greeks over the Trojans, and the west revels in their triumph against the Amazons. Its elegant lines reflect the ancient Greek obsession with proportion: everything follows a four-to-nine ratio.

ERECHTHEION. The **Erechtheion,** to the left of the Parthenon, was completed in 406 BC, just before Sparta defeated Athens in the Peloponnesian War. The building housed many gods in its time, taking its name from the snake-bodied hero Erechtheus. Poseidon struck a truce with Athena, allowing them to share the temple—the east is devoted to the goddess of wisdom and the west to the god of the sea. The Erechtheion's southern portico is supported by six women frozen in stone, the *Caryatids*. They're actually copies—the originals are safe in the **Acropolis Museum,** which neighbors the Parthenon.

ACROPOLIS MUSEUM. The Museum houses a superb collection of sculptures, including five of the original *Caryatids* of the Erechtheion. The statues seem to be replicas of one another, but a close look at the folds of their drapery reveals delicately individualized detail. Compare the stylized, entranced faces and frozen poses of the Archaic Period *Moschophoros* (calf-bearer) sculpture to the idealized, more human Classical-Period *Kritias* boy for a trip through the development of Greek sculpture. Unfortunately, only a few pieces from the Parthenon are here—former British ambassador Lord Elgin helped himself to the rest. *(Open M 11am-6:30pm, Tu-Su 8am-6:30pm; in winter M 11am-2pm, Tu-Su 8am-2pm.)*

SOUTHERN SLOPE. From the southwest corner of the Acropolis, you can looks over the reconstructed **Odeon of Herodes Atticus,** a still-functioning theater dating from the Roman Period (AD 160). Admire the ruins of the classical Greek **Asclepion** and **Stoa of Eumenes II** as you continue east to the **Theater of Dionysus,** which once hosted dramas by Aeschylus and Sophocles as well as comedies by Aristophanes for audiences of up to 17,000. *(Enter on Dionissiou Areopagitou street. ☎ 32 21 459. The site is closed for general admission, but performances are still held throughout the summer.)*

OTHER SIGHTS

AGORA. The Agora is Athens's heart, just below its soul, the Acropolis; it served as the city's marketplace, administrative center, and center of daily life from the 6th century BC to AD 500. Here, the debates of Athenian democracy raged; Socrates, Aristotle, Demosthenes, Xenophon, and St. Paul all preached here. Today, visitors have free reign over the archaeological site it has become. *(Enter the Agora in one of 3 ways: off Pl. Thission, off Adrianou, or as you descend from the Acropolis. ☎ 32 10 185. Open Tu-Su 8:30am-3pm. 1200dr/€3.55, students and EU seniors 600dr/€1.80, EU students and under 18 free.)* The ■**Hephaesteion,** on a hill in the northwest corner of the Agora, is the best-preserved classical temple in Greece. The 415 BC temple still flaunts cool **friezes,** which depict Hercules's labors and Theseus's adventures. The elongated **Stoa of Attalos** was a multi-purpose building filled with shops and home to informal philosophers' gatherings. Attalos II, King of Pergamon, built the Stoa in the 2nd century BC as thanks for the education he received there. Reconstructed in the 1950s, it now houses the **Agora Museum,** which contains relics from the site. According to Plato, Socrates' first trial was held at the recently excavated **Royal Promenade** of the Agora, the **Stoa Basileios.** *(Cross the subway tracks at the Adrianou exit and turn the left.)*

KERAMEIKOS. The Kerameikos's rigidly geometric design becomes clearly visible from above, even before entering the grounds; the site includes a large-scale cemetery and a forty-meter-wide boulevard that ran from through the Agora and the Diplyon Gate and ended at the sanctuary of **Akademos** (where Plato founded his academy). The **Oberlaender Museum** displays finds from the burial sites; it houses an excellent collection of highly detailed pottery and sculpture. *(Ermou 48, northwest of the Agora. From Syndagma, walk toward Monastiraki on Ermou for 25min. ☎ 34 63 552. Open Tu-Su 8:30-3pm. 500dr/€1.50, students 300dr/€0.90, EU students and under 18 free.)*

TEMPLE OF OLYMPIAN ZEUS AND HADRIAN'S ARCH. In the middle of downtown Athens, you'll spot the final trace of the largest temple ever built in Greece. The 15 majestic Corinthian columns of the Temple of Olympian Zeus mark where the temple once stood. Started in the 6th century BC, it was completed 600 years later by Roman emperor Hadrian, who attached his name to the centuries-long effort by adding his arch to mark the boundary between the ancient city of Theseus and Hadrian's own new city. (*Vas. Olgas at Amalias, next to the National Garden. ☎ 92 26 330. Open Tu-Su 8:30am-3pm. Temple 500dr/€1.50, EU students free. Arch free.*)

OLYMPIC STADIUM. The Panathenaic Olympic Stadium is wedged between National Gardens and Pangrati, carved into a hill. The site of the first modern Olympic Games in 1896, the stadium is now being refurbished in preparation for the **2004 Summer Olympics.** (*On Vas. Konstantinou. From Syndagma, walk up Amalias 15min. to Vas Olgas, and follow it left. Or, take trolley #2, 4, or 11 from Syndagma. Open 8am-8:30pm. Free.*)

AROUND SYNDAGMA. Don't miss the changing of the guard in front of the **Parliament** building. Every hour on the hour, two sets of *evzones* (guards) wind up like toy soldiers, kick their tasselled heels in unison, and fall backward into symmetrical little guardhouses on either side of the **Tomb of the Unknown Soldier.** Athens's endangered species, greenery and shade, are preserved in the **National Gardens,** their natural environment. Women shouldn't stroll here alone.

MT. LYCAVITTOS. Of Athens's seven hills, Lycavittos is the largest and most central. From any approach, ascend at sunset to catch a last glimpse of Athens's densely packed continuous rooftops in daylight and watch the city light at night. At the top is the **Chapel of St. George,** where couples frequently make a spectacle by tying the knot. A leisurely stroll around the church enraptures with Athens's truly incredible panoramic expanse. (Open 8:45am-12:15am, Th 10:30am-12:15am.)

NATIONAL ARCHAEOLOGICAL MUSEUM. The astounding collection in the National Archaeological Museum deserves space on even the most rushed itinerary. The museum begins with prehistoric pieces, including Heinrich Schliemann's **Mycenae** excavations. The German archaeologist seems to have unearthed Midas's playground—it is a world of gold, including the ▧**Mask of Agamemnon,** the death mask of a king who lived at least three centuries earlier than Agamemnon himself. (*Patission 44. 20min. walk from Pl. Syndagma down Stadiou to Aiolou and right onto Patission. Open Apr.-Oct. M 12:30-7pm, Tu-Su 8am-7pm; Nov.-Mar. 8am-5pm. Holidays 8:30am-3pm. 2000dr/€5.90, students 1000dr/€2.95; Nov.-Mar. free Su and holidays*)

NATIONAL GALLERY. The National Gallery (a.k.a. Alexander Soutzos Museum) exhibits the work of Greek artists, with periodic international displays. The permanent collection includes outstanding work by El Greco, as well as drawings, photographs, and sculpture gardens. (*Vas. Konstantinou 50. Set back from Vas. Sofias, next to the Hilton. ☎ 72 35 857. Open M and W-Sa 9am-3pm, Su 10am-2pm. 1500dr/€4.40, students and seniors 500dr/€1.50, under 12 free.*)

🎵 🎭 ENTERTAINMENT AND NIGHTLIFE

That uniquely Greek hybrid, the cafe/bar, flourishes throughout Athens. You can start your night early with a coffee and move on to a boozy binge at the same place or head out to the summer wonderland of **Glyfada. Kolonaki** is brimming with cafes/bars. Try Millioni street by **Jackson Hall** for a more subdued atmosphere. Summertime performances are staged in Lycavittos Theater as part of the **Athens Festival,** which has included acts from the Greek Orchestra to Pavarotti to the Talking Heads. The **Festival Office,** Stadiou 4, sells student tickets. (☎32 21 459. Open M-F 9:30am-4pm, Sa-Su 9:30am-2pm. Tickets 3000-5000dr/€8.80-14.70.) The **Athens Flea Market,** adjacent to Pl. Monastiraki, is a jumble of second-hand junk and high-rent antiques. Sunday is the best day. (Open daily 8am-3pm; Tu and Th-F until 8pm.)

Bee (☎32 12 624), at the corner of Miaoli and Themidos, off Ermou; a few blocks from the heart of Psiri. A red pillar wrapped with 1000 tiny red lights lends an amorous glow to the flirtations of all orientations below. DJs spin while the friendly staff keeps the booze flowing. Drinks 1000-2500dr/€2.93-7.34. Open daily 9pm-late.

Bretto's, Kidatheneon 41 (☎32 32 110). The walls are lit up with colorful bottles of ouzo, brandy, and other liqueurs, all made by friendly Dimitris in his family's 100-year-old distilleries. The homemade wine in the barrels along the back wall is 1500dr/€4.40 per bottle, 500dr/€1.47 per glass. Open 10am-midnight.

Metal Cafe Dionysos, Em. Benaki 96A & Valtetsiou. Superficial conflict (backgammon vs. heavy-metal-themed decor and music) leads to ultimate fun. Coffee 700dr/€2.05, beer 1000-1500dr/€2.95-4.40. Open daily 1:30pm-3am.

Jazz in Jazz, Dinokratous 4. From behind the well-worn wooden bar, Kostas can be persuaded to muse about jazz and give swing lessons. Endless old jazz records on the box draw faithfuls. 1500dr/€4.40 cover includes a drink. Open Nov.-May noon-3am.

Cafe 48, Karneadou 48 (☎72 52 434), 2 blocks up the hill from Vas. Sofias. Expat classicists and student travelers exchange stories at the bar and moves on the small indoor dance floor. With a student ID, beer costs 800dr/€2.35, punch is 1000dr/€2.95, and a free shot comes with each drink on Tu and Th. Open M-Sa 9am-2am, Su 4pm-2am.

⚡ DAYTRIPS FROM ATHENS

TEMPLE OF POSEIDON

Two buses travel to Cape Sounion from Athens: the shorter and more scenic route leaves from the Mavromateon 14 bus stop near Areos Park (2hr., every hr., 1350dr/€4).Get off the bus at the last stop and head up to the right past the cafeteria to a ticket booth.

Gracing on the highest point on the Cape, the Temple of Poseidon has been a dazzling white landmark for sailors at sea for millennia. The original temple was constructed around 600 BC, destroyed by the Persians in 480 BC, and rebuilt by Pericles in 440 BC. The 16 remaining Doric columns sit on a promontory at **Cape Sounion,** 65km from Athens. (☎39 363. Open daily 10am-sunset. 1000dr/€2.95, students 500dr/€1.50, EU students free.)

MARATHON

The bus from the Mavromateon 29 station in Athens heads to Marathon (1½hr., every hr. 5:30am-10:30pm, 800dr/€2.35); look for the "Marathon" label on the bus signboard. Sit in front and remind the driver of your destination, and flag the bus down on the way back.

Gasping out two words—*Νικη ημιν,* "Victory to us"—Phidippides announced the Athenian victory over the Persians in the bloody 490 BC battle of Marathon; he collapsed and died immediately after. His 42km sprint to Athens remains legendary; today, marathoners repeat this feat (*sans* fatal collapse), twice annually on Pheidippides' very route beginning at a commemorative plaque. Others choose to reach Marathon by less strenuous means via the bus from Mavromateon 29. Although the town itself doesn't truly inspire, the five rooms of the **Archaeological Museum of Marathonas,** 114 Plateion, are packed with exciting archaeological finds. Ask the driver to let you off at the sign ("Mouseion and Marathonas"), then follow the signs 2km through farmlands (bear right at the one unlabeled fork in the road) to the end of the paved road. (☎55 155. Open Tu-Su 8:30am-3pm. 500dr/€1.50, students 300dr/€0.90; EU students, student Classicists, and archaeologists free.)

DELPHI

Buses leave Athens for Delphi from the station at Liossion 260 (3hr½., 6 per day, 3100dr/€9.10). Railpass holders can take the train to Livadia and catch the bus (2hr., 10 per day, 1500dr). Continue east down Pavlou to reach the Oracle site.

As any Delphinian will proudly attest, this town of 2500 marks the belly button (omphalos) of the earth. According to the ancients, Zeus discovered this fact by simultaneously releasing two eagles, one toward the east and one toward the west. They collided, impaling each other with their beaks, directly over Delphi. A sacred stone marks the spot. Troubled denizens of the ancient world journeyed to the **Ora-**

GREECE

cle of Apollo at Delphi, where the priestess of Apollo related the god's profound, if cryptic, advice. Modern Delphi is packed with tourists—visit early in the morning. Despite the crowds, truly fascinating ruins make Delphi a rewarding daytrip. From the bus station, at the western end of Delphi, walk east on Pavlou toward Athens (with the mountain edge on your right) to reach the **tourist office,** Friderikis 12, in the town hall. (☎82 900. Open M-F 7:30am-10:30pm.) If transportation leaves you stranded in Delphi overnight, you can stay at **Hotel Sibylla,** Pavlou 9, which has wonderful views and private baths at the best prices in town. (☎82 335. Singles 4000dr/€11.75; doubles 6000dr/€17.60; triples 8000dr/€23.50.)

OTHER DAYTRIPS FROM ATHENS

CORINTH. Find love among the ruins in the ancient city at Corinth (p. 522).

PATRAS. Sprawling Patras has the nation's largest Orthodox cathedral (p. 517).

THE PELOPONNESE (Πελοποννεσος)

Connected to the mainland by the narrow isthmus of Corinth, the Peloponnese contains the majority of Greece's most stunning and well-preserved archaeological sites, including Olympia, Mycenae, Messene, Ancient Corinth, Mystras, and Epidavros; it has some of the country's most incredible landscapes, ranging from the barren crags of the Mani to the forested peaks of Arcadia. With raw beauty and sparse population, the Peloponnese remain a bastion of Greek village life and culture.

⚒ FERRIES TO ITALY AND CRETE

Boats go from **Patras** to **Brindisi** (20hr., 8000-10,00dr/€23.55-29.45 including port tax), **Trieste, Bari, Ancona,** and **Venice, Italy.** Ferries also sail from **Gythion** to **Crete** (7hr., 4900dr/€14.40). Eurail holders should check with Tsimaras travel agency (☎622 602) or HML lines to see if they can use their passes for trips to Brindisi. Check the travel offices on Iroon Polytechniou and Othonas Amalias in Patras for info about tickets, and ask about discounts for those under 25.

PATRAS (Πατρας)   ☎061

Sprawling Patras, Greece's third-largest city, serves primarily as a transport hub, but at **Carnival** (mid-Jan. to Ash Wednesday) the port becomes one gigantic dance floor consumed by pre-Lenten madness. During the rest of the year, spend your layover heading inland from town on Ag. Nikolaou and climbing the steps to the 13th-century Venetian **castle.** (Open Tu-Su 8am-7pm. Free.) Then continue to the **Ancient Odeum,** a restored Roman theater. (Open Tu-Su 8:30am-3pm. Free.) Follow the water to the west end of town to reach **Agios Andreas,** the largest Orthodox cathedral in Greece, which holds magnificent frescoes and an unusual relic—St. Andrew's holy head. (Open daily 9am-dusk. Dress modestly.) Sweet black grapes are transformed into *Mavrodaphne* wine at the **Achaïa Clauss winery;** enjoy free samples of the country's most famous vineyard. Check with the tourist office for a schedule of daily tours, then take bus #7 from the intersection of Kolokotroni and Kanakari, or in front of Europa Center, on Othonos Amalias (waterfront).

Trains (☎639 110) are found on Othonos Amalias, running to: Athens (5hr., 3.5hr. express; 8 per day; 1800-3400dr/€5.30-10); Kalamata (5½hr., 2 per day, 1700dr/€5); and Olympia (1½hr., 8 per day, 1000-2000dr/€2.95-6) via Pyrgos. **KTEL buses** (☎623 886) go from Othonos Amalias, to: Athens (3hr., 33 per day, 4000dr/€11.75); Ioannina (4hr., 4 per day, 4750dr/€14); Kalamata (4hr., 2 per day, 4550dr/€13.40); Thessaloniki (8hr., 3 per day, 9200dr/€27.10); and Tripoli (4hr., 2 per day, 3400dr/€10). **Ferries** go to Corfu daily (night ferry 7hr., 6100dr/€17.95).

To reach the center of town from the port, turn right after leaving customs and follow Iroon Polytechniou, which becomes Othonos Amalias, then turn left at Pl. Trion Simahon and head inland. The **tourist police** are available on the waterfront in the Customs entrance. (☎451 833. Open M-F 7am-midnight.) Hotels are scattered on Ag. Andreou, one block up from the waterfront. The **Youth Hostel,** Iroon Polytechniou 68, occupies a creaky turn-of-the-century mansion. (☎427 278. Dorms 2000dr/€5.90.) Patras's myriad pubs and cafes are generally indistinguishable and overpriced; just self-cater from various supermarkets throughout downtown. (Most open Tu-Sa 9am-5pm.) Otherwise, chatty Nikolas will explain the menu to you in English at **Taverna O Nikolas,** Ag. Andreou 73, just past Ag. Nikolaou. (Open daily 7am until early morning. Entrees 800-2000dr/€2.35-5.90.) **Postal Code:** 26001.

OLYMPIA (Ολυμπια)   ☎0624

Set among meadows and shaded by cypress and olive trees, modern Olympia is a friendly and comely town that draws tourists with its mega-attraction—the ancient **Olympic arena.** Today, the remains of a gymnasium, palaestra, stadium, and several temples and treasures are scattered around **Ancient Olympia,** although they are not labeled or particularly well-preserved. Buy a map to navigate. Follow the main road 5min. out of town with the tourist office on your right and Pirgos behind you to reach the ruins and museum. Dominating the site is the gigantic **Temple of Zeus,** although the 7th-century BC **Temple of Hera** is better preserved. The Temple of Hera is also proximate to the altar where the **Olympic Flame** is lit every four years. The remains of a church that was built on top of the workshop of Phidias once held a statue of *Zeus* so beautiful that it was considered one of the **seven wonders of the ancient world.** Across from the site, the **New Museum** houses an array of sculpture, that includes the **Nike of Paionios,** the **Hermes of Praxiteles,** the pediment sculptures from the **Temple of Zeus,** and a jumble of military spoils. (Site open daily 8am-7pm. Museum open M noon-7pm, Tu-Su 8am-7pm. Site or museum alone 1200dr/€3.55, students 600dr/€1.80; joint ticket 2000dr/€5.90; EU students free.)

In New Olympia, **buses** run from opposite the tourist info booth to Tripoli (4hr., 3 per day, 2600dr/€7.65) and **Pirgos** (40min., 16 per day, 450dr/€1.35.) The **tourist office,** on Kondili, is on the east side of town toward the ruins. (☎231 00. Open M-F 8am 3pm, Sa 9am-3pm.) For lodgings, try **Zounis Rooms to Rent,** two blocks uphill from Kondili, between the National Bank and Pirgos/church, or one block downhill from the Museum of Olympic Games; ask at the Anesi Cafe-Tavern. (☎22 644. Singles 5000dr/€14.75; doubles 7000dr/€20.55; triples 8500dr/€25.) **Camping Diana** is uphill from Pension Poseidon on Kondili. (☎22 314. 1700dr/€5 per person, with sleeping bag 2000dr/€5.90; 1100dr/€3.25 per car; 1300-1800dr/€3.85-530 per tent.) **Minimarkets** along Kondili or the road to the train station sell picnic fixings. Eateries on Kondili are cramped and overpriced, but a walk toward the railroad station or uphill reveals charming, inexpensive tavernas. **Postal Code:** 27065.

TRIPOLI (Τριπολη)   ☎071

Although you may have to dodge wild motorists while crossing the perilous streets of Urban Tripoli, the transport hub of Arcadia, the town offers pleasant squares and cafés to those awaiting the next bus out. Unfortunately, you will need a map or **very** good directions to navigate the five *plateias* in downtown. The **Archaeological Museum** on Evangelistrias, off Georgiou, in a yellow flower-bedecked building has a large prehistoric collection, including pottery, jewelry, and weaponry from the Neolithic to the Mycenaean periods. Four **trains** per day go to Athens (4hr., 1500dr/€4.40) and Kalamata (2½hr., 900dr/€2.65), while three per day go to Corinth (2½hr., 1000dr/€2.95). **Buses** arrive at Pl. Kolokotronis, east of the center of town. From the station, follow Georgiou to Pl. Ag. Vasiliou; as you face the Church of Agios Vasiliou, go left and head north on Ethnikis Antistasis to reach Pl. Petrinou. Buses go to: Athens (3hr., 14 per day, 3400dr/€10); Kalamata (2hr., 12 per day, 1700dr/€5.00); and Sparta (1hr., 10 per day, 1100dr/€3.25). Crash at **Hotel Alex,** Vas. Georgiou 26, between Pl. Kolokotronis and Pl. Agios Vasiliou. (☎223 465. Singles 10,000dr/€29.35; doubles 13,000-15,000dr/€38.25-44.15.) **Postal Code:** 22100.

DAYTRIPS FROM TRIPOLI: DIMITSANA AND STEMNITSA. West of Tripoli, the enticing villages of Dimitsana and Stemnitsa are excellent bases for **hiking** excursions into the idyllic, rugged countryside. The quintessentially Arcadian village of **Dimitsana,** clinging to a steep, rocky mountainside covered with pines, is nearly untouched by modern life or tourists. **Buses** run to Dimitsana from Tripoli (1½hr., 1-3 per day, 1400dr/€4.15). Buses to Tripoli and Olympia make frequent stops in **Karkalou**, a 20min. taxi ride away (1000dr/€2.95). Widespread *domatia* are really the only option, but most establishments are beautifully furnished. Try above the grocery store, which lets **rooms**. (☎ (0795) 31 084; singles 6000dr/€17.65; doubles 12,000dr/€35.30.) A lengthy but beautiful 11km stroll (or a 1000dr/€2.95 taxi ride) along the road from Dimitsana will bring you to **Stemnitsa**, with narrow, irregular cobblestone streets that betray its medieval roots. Many consider the town the most beautiful in Greece. The splendid ▥**Hotel Triokolonion**, the only one in town, is on the left side of the main road from Dimitsana. (☎ (0795) 81 297. Breakfast included. Reserve ahead. Singles 8800dr/€25.90; doubles 11,900dr/€35.)

KALAMATA (Καλαματα)   ☎ 0721

Kalamata, the second-largest Peloponnesian city, flourishes as a port and beach resort. The survivor of a violent history, the **Castle of the Villehardouins** crowns a hill above the old city. The castle encircles an open-air theater, which hosts "Cultural Summer of Kalamata" in July and August features jazz, rock, and Classical Greek drama. Take the bus from Kalamata (1hr., M-Sa 2 per day, 500dr/€1.50) to the well-preserved ruins of **Ancient Messene** in nearby **Mavromati**, which constitute one of Greece's most impressive archaeological sites. While the remains of a theater, stadium, gymnasium, public baths, and nine different temples have been uncovered, the city's **defensive walls** usually receive the most attention. The 3m thick walls circle a 9km perimeter, and represent the massive heft of 3rd- and 4th-century BC military architecture. (Open M-Su all day. Free.) **Trains** run from Sideromikou Stathmou to: Athens (7hr., 4 per day, 2400dr/€7.10) via Tripoli (2½hr., 950dr/€2.80); Corinth (5¼hr., 1900dr/€5.60); Olympia (3hr., 1000dr/€2.95); and Patras (5½hr., 1700dr/€5). **Buses** leave from Kalamata to: Athens (4hr., 11 per day, 4650dr/€13.70); Patras (4hr., 2 per day, 4500dr/€13.25); Sparta (2hr., 2 per day, 1000dr/€2.95); and Tripoli (2hr., 1500dr/€4.45). Turn right on Frantzi at the end of Pl. Georgiou and walk a few blocks to reach the train station, **Internet** access, and **Hotel George**, not the cheapest in town, but your best for a combination of cleanliness, taste, and price combined. (☎27 225. Singles 7000dr/€20.60; doubles 8000dr/€23.55.) **Tourist information** is available at **D.E.T.A.K.,** Polivou 6, just off Aristomenous near the Old Town, and at the **Tourist Police** on the waterfront. Before leaving town, sample the famous Kalamata olives and figs. The immense **New Market,** across the bridge from the bus station, has an assortment of meat, cheese, and fruit shops, as well as a daily farmer's market. **Postal Code:** 24100.

PYLOS (Πυλος) AND METHONI (Μεθωνη)

With delightful beaches, Ottoman fortress, museum, and splendid views of Navarino, the Peloponnese's largest natural bay, the town of Pylos is wonderfully and mystifyingly untouristed. Just 15min. from Pylos by bus, Methoni's hibiscus-lined streets and relaxed atmosphere serve as a reprieve from the bustle of Kalamata.

◨▨ TRANSPORTATION AND PRACTICAL INFORMATION. From Pylos, **Buses** (☎22 230) go to: Athens (6½hr., 2 per day, 5700dr/€16.80); Finikoundas (1hr., 3 per day, 450dr/€1.35) via Methoni (15min., 6 per day, 270dr/€0.80); Kalamata (1½hr., 9 per day, 1000dr/€2.95). No buses travel directly to Koroni, but you can go through Finikoundas and take a bus to Horokorio, the stop nearest Koroni. **Buses** from **Methoni** are irregular, but do run to: Athens (6hr., 5200dr/€15.30); Kalamata (2hr., 1 per day, 1200dr/€3.55); Pylos (15min., 7 per day, 260dr/€0.80). There is no station, or even a posted schedule, so ask a few locals for information. The Pylos **tourist police** are in the same building as the **police,** on the left side of the plateia as you face inland. (☎23 733. Open 8am-2pm.)

▐▌◨ ACCOMMODATIONS AND FOOD. There are several **Rooms to Let** signs as the bus descends into Pylos from Kalamata. Expect to pay 4000-6000dr/€11.75-17.65 for singles, 6000-10,000dr/€17.65-29.35 for doubles, and 8000-12,000dr/€23.50-35.25 for triples. Perhaps the cheapest accommodations in town are found at the **Pension,** off Nileos by the post office, just before the **OTE,** with high-ceilings, private baths, and A/C. (☎22 748. Singles 5000dr/€14.75; doubles 7000dr/€20.60; triples 8000dr/€23.55.) In Methoni, try **Ioannis Psiharis** Rooms to Let (☎31 406; singles 8000-9000dr/€23.50-26.50; doubles 9000dr/€26.50). **Seaside Camping Methoni** is a 5min. walk down the Methoni beach to the right of the *plateia.* (☎31 228. 1100dr/€3.25 per person, 610dr/€1.80 per car, 700dr/€2.10 per small tent.) Pylos's waterfront restaurants cook up taverna staples accompanied by sunset views of the sea. In Methnoi's waterfront *plateia,* **Meltemi** serves excellent traditional entrees. (Feta with olive oil 600dr/€1.80, *moussaka* 1400dr/€4.15.)

◎♫ SIGHTS AND ENTERTAINMENT. Historic fortresses guard both sides of Navarino Bay. **Neocastro,** to the south, is easily accessible from Pylos; walk up the road to Methoni and turn right. The well-preserved walls enclose a fast-decaying church, along with a citadel and a collection of engravings. (☎22 010. Open Tu-Su 8:30am-3pm. 800dr/€2.35, seniors and students 400dr/€1.20, EU students and children free.) A few small **beaches** surround the town. Although the sand is devoured by the ocean when the tide is in, the clear, choppy waters can still be fun for active beach-goers. The lovely, long, and wider **Yialova Beach** is 6km north of town; unfortunately only the Athens bus goes there, so it's better to use your own wheels. To see the island of **Sfakteria** up close, you can take a **boat tour** that stops at various monuments to the **Battle of Navarino** and a sunken Ottoman ship. Inquire at the **port police** (☎22 225). No visitor to the southwest Peloponnese should miss Methoni's **Venetian fortress,** a 13th-century mini-city. A narrow bridge connects an islet and its fortified tower to the main structure with a whimsical touch of medieval defensive architecture. (Open M-Sa 8:30am-8pm, Su 9am-8pm. Free.)

SPARTA (Σπαρτη) AND MYSTRAS (Μυστρας) ☎0723

Citizens of today's **Sparta** make olive oil, not war. Pleasant public gardens and broad, palm-lined boulevards make Sparta hospitable, and it is by far the best base for exploring the impressive ruins of Byzantine Mystras. **Buses** from Sparta go to: Areopolis (1:30hr., 2 per day, 1400dr/€4.15); Athens (3½hr., 9 per day, 4100dr/€12.10) via Corinth (2:30hr., 2550dr/€7.50) and Tripoli (1hr., 1100dr/€3.25); Gython (1hr., 5 per day, 850dr/€2.50); and Monemvasia (2hr., 3 per day, 2000dr/€5.88). To reach the town center from the bus station, walk 10 blocks west, on Lykourgou; the **tourist office** is in the *plateia.* (☎(0731) 24 852 Open daily 8am-2pm.) **Hotel Cecil** is five blocks north of Lykourgou the corner of Paleologou and Thermopilion. (☎(0731) 24 980. Singles 8000dr/€23.55; doubles 12000dr/€35.30.) **Ancient Sparta** is only a short walk north of town, up Paleolougou from the center of town.

Mystras, 4km from Sparta, was once the religious center of all Byzantium, and the locus of Constantinople's rule over the Peloponnese. Its extraordinary hillside ruins comprise a city of Byzantine churches, chapels, and monasteries. At the extreme left of the lower tier as you face the hillside is the ◪**Church of Peribleptos,** whose exquisite religious paintings remain Mystras's most stunning relics, despite Ottoman vandalization. Slightly higher is the **Pantanassa,** a still-operating convent with beautiful frescoes and flowers. Modest dress is required. Finally, at the top of the hill is the **castle,** with magnificent views of the surrounding countryside. Take the bus to the top of the ruins, and walk 50min. down. (Open in summer daily 8am-7pm; in winter 8:30am-3pm. 1200dr/€3.55, students600dr/€1.80.) **Buses** from Sparta to Mystras leave from the station, in front of the OTE on Lykourgou, and at the corner of Lykourgou and Kythonigou (20min., 9 per day, 260dr/€0.80).

GYTHION (Γυθειο) AND AREOPOLIS (Αρεοπολη) ☎0733

Formerly plagued by violent family feuds and savage piracy, the sparsely settled **Mani** (Manh) province's name comes from the word *manis,* Greek for wrath or fury. Today, the fire behind Maniot ferocity has been cooled by a coastal breeze, and the Maniots play excellent hosts to the visitors who stay in their traditional gray-stone tower houses, seeking beautiful beaches and views. **Gython,** the "Gateway to the Mani," is the liveliest town in the region, near sand and stone beaches. A tiny causeway to the left of the waterfront as you face inland connects it to the island of **Marathonisi,** where Paris and Helen consummated their ill-fated love. **Buses** in Gythion leave from the north end of the waterfront, to the right as you face inland, for: Athens (4hr., 6 per day, 4900dr/€14.45) via Tripoli (2hr., 1850dr/€5.45); Corinth (3hr., 3550dr/€10.45); Kalamata (4 per day, 2050dr/€6.05); and Sparta (1hr., 6 per day, 850dr/€2.50). To explore the hard-to-reach parts of Mani, try **Moto Makis Rent-A-Moped,** on the waterfront near the causeway. (☎25 111. 6500dr/€19.15 per day. Open daily 8:30am-7pm.) ▧**Xenia Karlaftis Rooms,** on the water 20m from the causeway, rents spacious rooms with private baths. (☎22 719. Singles 5000dr/ €14.75; doubles 7000dr/€20.60; triples 10,000dr/€29.45.) **Postal Code:** 23200.

Although **Areopolis** neighbors both the sea and the mountains, its buildings dominate the scenery: stone tower houses and cobbled streets are framed by the dramatic purple peaks of the Taygetus. Just 4km from Areopolis, part of a subterranean river, the unusual **Vlihada Cave** is cool, quiet, and strung with tiny crystalline stalagmites. Boat tours of the subterranean river last 30min. (Open daily June-Sept. 8:30am-5:30pm; Oct.-May 8:30am-3pm. 3700dr/€10.90; students 2000dr/€5.90. A **bus** runs from Areopolis at 11am and returns at 12:45pm; 260dr/ €0.80). **Buses** stop in Areopolis' main *plateia* and go to: Athens (6hr., 4 per day, 5450dr/€16.05) and Sparta (2hr., 4 per day, 1400dr/€4.15) via Gythion (30min., 4 per day, 550dr/€1.65). To get to Kalamata take the bus to Itilo (30min., 2 per day, 260dr/€0.80). To stay at **Tsimova,** turn left at the end of Kapetan Matapan, the road leading to the Old Town, toward the ocean. (☎51 301. Singles 5-10,000dr/€17.45-29.45; doubles 10-15,000dr/€29.45-44.15.) **Postal Code:** 23062.

MONEMVASIA (Μονεμβασια) AND GEFYRA (Γεφυρα)   ☎0732

The island of Monemvasia, despite being one of the major tourist destinations on the Peloponnese, maintains an other-worldly quality. No cars or bikes are allowed on the island; pack horses bear groceries into the city; narrow streets hide child-sized doorways, and flowered courtyards. At the edge of the cliffs perches the oft-photographed 12th-century **Agia Sofia;** to get there, navigate through the maze of streets to the edge of town farthest from the sea, where a path climbs the side of the cliff to the tip of the rock. Stay in more modern and less expensive **Gefyra,** a 20min. walk down 23 Iouliou to the waterfront, across the causeway, and around 'the rock' to Monemvasia. An **orange bus** runs between the causeway and Monemvasia gate (every 15min. 100dr/€0.30). Three buses per day leave for: Athens (6hr., 6050dr/ €17.80); Corinth (5hr., 5400dr/€15.90); Sparta (2½hr., 2000dr/€5.90); and Tripoli (4hr., 3150dr/€9.30). **Hotel Akrogiali,** across from Malvasia Travel, has clean white rooms with private baths. (☎61 360. Singles 6000-7000dr/€17.65-20.60; doubles 7000-10,000dr/€20.60-29.45.) ▧**To Limanaki,** with plentiful waterfront seating in Geyfra, serves exceptional Greek food, including excellent *pastitsio* (1300dr/ €3.85) and stuffed tomatoes (1150dr/€3.40).

NAFPLION (Ναυπλιο)   ☎0752

Beautiful old Nafplion glories in its Venetian architecture, fortresses, nearby pebble beaches, and hillside stairways. The town's crown jewel is the 18th-century **Palamidi Fortress,** with its spectacular views of the town and harbor. To get there, walk or take a taxi (1000dr/€2.95) up the 3km road; or climb the grueling 999 steps up from Polizoidhou, across the park from the bus station. (Open daily 8am-6:45pm; off-season daily 8:30am-5:45pm. 800dr/€2.35, students 400dr/€1.20.) **Arvanitia,** Nafplion's small, pebbly beach is away from town on Polizoidhou with Palimidi on your left; follow the footpath for lovely private coves. **Buses** leave from Singrou, off Pl. Kapodistrias, for Athens (3hr., every hr., 2800dr/€8.25) via Corinth (2hr., 1500dr/ €4.45). To reach **Bouboulinas,** the waterfront promenade, from the station, go left and follow Singrou to the harbor and the **Old Town.** The **tourist office** is on 25 Martiou across from the OTE. (☎24 444. Open daily 9am-1pm and 4-8pm.) For the rooftop views of **Dimitris Bekas' Domatia** in the Old Town, turn up the stairs on Kokkinou, off Staikopoulou; climb to the top, and go up another 50 steps. (☎24 594. Singles 4500-5200dr/€13.25-15.30; doubles 6000-6800dr/€17.65-20.) ▧**Taverna O Vasiles,** on Staikopoulou, serves rabbit (1800dr/€5.30) that will delight even the most avid Beatrix Potter fans. **Postal Code:** 21100.

GREECE

⚄ DAYTRIPS FROM NAFPLION: MYCENAE AND EPIDAVROS. The supreme city of Greece from 1600 to 1100 BC, **Mycenae** (Μυκηνες) was once ruled by Agamemnon, leader of the attacking forces in the Trojan War. Excavations of ancient Mycenae have continued for 126 years, since Heinrich Schliemann first turned a spade here. Now Ancient Mycenae is one of the most visited sites in Greece, and mobs stampede to the famed Lion's Gate and Tomb of Agamemnon. (Both sites open Apr.-Sept. daily 8am-7pm; Oct.-Mar. 8am-5pm. 1500dr/€4.45, students 800dr/€2.35. Keep your ticket or pay twice for both sites.) Join the illustrious ranks of Virginia Woolf, Claude Debussy, William Faulkner, and Allen Ginsberg, who have all stayed at **Belle Helene Hotel,** which doubles as a bus stop on the main road. (☎(0751) 76 225. Singles 5500-7000dr/€16.20-20.60; doubles 10,000-13,000dr/€29.45-38.25.) The only direct **bus** to Mycenae is from Nafplion (30min., 4 per day, 650dr/€1.95) via Argos (20min., 300dr/€0.90). **Trains** run from Athens to Fihtia; from there, take the Corinth-Argos road and follow the sign to Mycenae.

The grandest structure at the ancient site in Epidavros (Επιδαυρος) is the **Theater of Epidavros,** built in the early second century BC with a capacity of 14,000. The incredible acoustics allow you to stand at the top row of seats and hear a match lit on stage. Near the theater and on the road to the sanctuary's ruins is Epidavros's **museum.** (☎22 009. Open daily 8am-7pm. Tickets for site and museum available at the **ticket booth,** open daily 7:30am-7pm, F-Sa 7:30am-9pm during theater season. 1500dr/€4.45, students 800dr/€2.35.) Late June to mid-August, the **Epidavros Theater Festival** brings performances of classical Greek plays on F and Sa nights. Shows are at 9pm; purchase tickets at the site or in advance by calling the Athens Festival Box Office (☎(01) 322 1459; tickets 4000dr/€11.80, students 2000dr/€5.90). **Buses** arrive in Epidavros from Nafplion (1hr., 4 per day, 650dr/€1.95).

CORINTH (Κορινθος)   ☎0741

Most visitors to the Peloponnese travel to gaze on the ruins of **Ancient Corinth,** at the base of the **Acrocorinth.** Columns and pediments lie around the courtyard of the excellent **archaeological museum** in untouched chaos. As you exit the museum, the 6th-century BC **Temple of Apollo** is down the stairs to the left. The **fortress** at the top of Acrocorinth is a tough 2-3hr. hike, but there is always the option of a taxi to the summit (2000dr/€5.90) and back down (3000dr/€8.80). At the top, explore the surprisingly intact remains of the **Temple to Aphrodite,** where disciples were initiated into the "mysteries of love." (☎31 207 for museum. Open 8am-7pm, winter 8am-5pm. Admission to museum and site 1200dr/€3.55, students 600dr/€1.80.)

In New Corinth, **buses** leave from three different stations; for assistance, you should go to the tourist police. Buses leave station A (☎24 481), behind the train station, for Athens (1½ hr., 30 per day, 1800dr/€5.30). Buses leave station C, **Argolis Station,** inland from the park on Eth. Antistasis (☎24 403) every hour for: Argos (1000dr/€2.95); Mycenae (800dr/€2.35); and Nafplion (1250dr/€3.70). **Trains** go from the station on Demokratias to: Athens, via Isthmia (2hr., 14 per day, 900dr) and Patras (2½hr., 8 per day, 1000dr/€2.95). The **Tourist Police** office, Ermou 51, is located on the city's park, and will provide tourists with maps, brochures, and other assistance. (☎23 282. Open daily 8am-2pm.) In New Corinth, **Hotel Akti,** Eth. Antistasis 3, is the best bet for accommodations, with simple, utilitarian bedrooms and a convenient location. (☎23 337. Singles 5000dr/€14.70; doubles 8000dr/€23.50.) When mealtime comes, **AXINOS,** Damaskinou 41, offers cheery *al fresco* dining by the waterfront. (☎28 889. Pastitsio 1500dr/€4.40, Greek salad 1300dr/€3.85.)

NORTHERN AND CENTRAL GREECE

A bastion of Greek culture under 19th-century Ottoman rule, the provinces of Thessaly, Epirus, Macedonia, and Thrace are oft-forgotten regions threaded with mountain paths that lead to some of Greece's clearest springs, most glorious vistas, and precious Byzantine treasures. Following these forgotten trails will lead you into a varied landscape of silvery olive groves, fruit-laden trees, and patchwork farmland.

THESSALONIKI(SALONICA; Θεσσαλονικη)

Thessaloniki fans out from its hilltop Byzantine-Turkish fortress to the Thermaic Gulf, a jumble of ancient, Byzantine, European, Turkish, Balkan, and contemporary Greek cultural and historical debris. At its peak, the fortress oversees the Old Town's placid streets and long, tree-lined avenues. Golden mosaics and frescoes gleam in the Byzantine churches hidden on the industrial city's side-streets. Most travelers spend a few days in Thessaloniki clubbing and enjoying the sights, and then head out for countryside hikes or more sight-seeing, or ship off to the islands.

TRANSPORTATION

Trains: Main Terminal (☎517 517), on Monastiriou in the western part of the city. Take any bus down Egnatia (100dr/€0.30). To: **Athens** (6-8hr., 10 per day, 4800dr/€14.10). **OSE** (☎598 112), at Aristotelous and Ermou, has tickets and schedules. Open M-Sa 8am-3pm.

Buses: Most **KTEL** buses depart from between the port and railway station or from north of the railway. To: **Athens** (6hr., 13 per day, 9000dr/€26.45); **Corinth** (7½hr., 10:30am, 9200dr/€27), both from Monastiriou 69 (☎527 265); **Patras** (8hr., 2 per day, 8250dr/€24.25), from 87 Monastiriou (☎525 253).

Ferries and Hydrofoils: Buy tickets at **Karacharisis Travel and Shipping Agency**, Koundouriotou 8 (☎524 5 44). Open M-F 8:30am-8pm, Sa 8:30am-2:30pm. To: **Chios** (21hr.; Tu, F, Sa midnight; 8900dr/€26.15); **Lesvos** (9hr., W and Su 1am, 8300dr/€24.35); **Limnos** (7hr.; Tu 6pm, Su 1:30am; 5700dr/€16.75); **Mykonos** (16hr., 7 per week, 9900dr/€29.05); **Samos** (14hr., W 1pm, 9500dr/€27.90). **Flying Dolphins:** Buy tickets at **Crete Air Travel**, Dragoumi 1 (☎547 407), across from the main port. Open M-F 8:30am-9pm, Sa 8:30am-3pm, Su 9am-3pm. Dolphin hydrofoils leave Su-Fr 1:45pm, Sa 8am during the summer months (June-Sept.) to: **Alonnisos** (5hr., 8900dr/€26.15); **Skiathos** (3¾hr., 8500dr); **Skopelos** (4½hr., 8900dr/€26.15).

Public Transportation: Extensive **buses** (100dr/€0.30) traverse the city. Buses #8, 10, 11, and 31 run up and down Egnatia. Buy tickets at ticket booths at major stations.

ORIENTATION AND PRACTICAL INFORMATION

Running from the shore inland, the main streets are **Nikis, Mitropoleos, Tsimiski, Ermou, Egnatia,** and **Agios Dimitriou.** Intersecting these streets and running from the water into town are (west to east) **Dragoumi, El. Venizelou, Aristotelous, Agios Sophias,** and **Eth. Aminis.** Tsimiski, Mitropoleos, Ag. Sophias, and streets between Aristotelous and Ipodromiou are the main shopping streets. The cheaper hotels are on Egnatia, with waterfront bars and cafes on Nikis. The roads north of Ag. Dimitriou get smaller and steeper and lead into the **old town.** Facing inland, go left on Mitropoleos to reach **Ladadika,** a pocket of turn-of-the-century cafes, bars, and tavernas.

Tourist Office: EOT, Pl. Aristotelous (☎271 888). Open M-Sa 7:30am-3pm.

Consulates: Canada, Tsimiski 17 (☎256 350). Open M-F 9am-noon. **UK,** Venizelou 8 (☎278 006). Open M-F 8am-1pm. **US,** Tsimiski 43 (☎242 900). M, W, F 9am-noon.

American Express: Memphis Travel, Aristotelous 3, 1st floor (☎282 351). Cashes **traveler's checks** (no commission) and exchanges currency (500dr/€1.50) flat commission). Open M-F 9:30am-3:30pm and Sa 9am-2pm.

Laundromat: Bianca, L. Antoniadou 3 (☎209 602), behind the church to the right, facing the Arch of Galerius. 1800dr/€5.28 for wash and dry. Open M-Sa 8am-3pm.

Tourist Police: Dodekanissou 4, 5th fl. (☎554 870 or 871). Free maps and brochures. English spoken. Open 24hr. For the **local police,** call 553 800 or 100.

Hospital: At **Ippokration Public Hospital,** A. Papanastasiou 49 (☎837 920), some doctors speak English. **Ahepa Hospital,** Kiriakidi 1 (☎993 111), is a private alternative. **Red Cross First Aid Hospital,** Koundouriotou 6 (☎530 530), offers free minor medical care at the entrance to the port. The **EOT** can help you find an English-speaking doctor.

Internet Access: Pl@net, 53 Alex. Svolou (☎250 199), is the best. 600dr/€1.76 per hour from 9am-6pm; 800dr/€2.35 per hr. 6pm-3am. 300dr/€0.88 minimum charge.

Post Office: On Aristotelous, just below Egnatia. Open M-F 7:30am-8pm, Sa 7:30am-2pm, Su 9am-1:30pm. A **branch** office (☎227 640), on Eth. Aminis near the White Tower, is open M-F 7am-8pm. Both offer Poste Restante. **Postal code:** 54101.

ACCOMMODATIONS

Most of Thessaloniki's less expensive hotels are clustered along the western end of **Egnatia,** between **Pl. Dimokratias** (500m east of the train station) and **Pl. Dikastiriou.** Many are a bit gritty, ranging from ramshackle to merely cheerless, but gems can be found. Egnatia is loud at all hours, but rooms on the street have balconies (read: air circulation). Women alone should be wary of the English-speaking "tourist information" people at the train station: they are often impersonators.

Hotel Augustos, Elenis Svoronou 4 (☎522 955). Walking down Egnatia, turn north at the Argo Hotel and Augustos is straight ahead. Triples and doubles with bath have A/C and TVs; all rooms have phones. Singles 6000dr/€17.65, with bath 8000dr/€23.50; doubles 7000dr/€20.55, 11,000dr/€32.30; triples with bath 13,000dr/€38.15.

Hotel Acropolis, Tantalidou 4 (☎536 170). Tantalidou is the 2nd right off Egnatia after Dodekanissou, coming from Pl. Dimokratias. Very quiet hotel with shared baths. Singles 5500dr/€16.15; doubles 7000dr/€20.55; triples 8000dr/€23.50.

Youth Hostel, Alex. Svolou 44 (☎225 946). Take bus #8, 10, 11, or 31 west down Egnatia and get off at the Arch of Galerius (the "Kamara" stop); or walk toward the water and turn left after 2 blocks. Hot showers from 7am-11pm, in a cavelike basement. Reception 9-11am and 7-11pm. Reception open 9-11am and 7-11pm. Open Mar. 1-Nov. 30. Dorms 2500dr/€7.35.

Hotel Averof, L. Sofou 24 (☎538 840), at Egnatia. Rooms are a bit bare and stuffy but with shiny wood furniture and communal TV rooms. Singles 6000dr/€17.65, with bath 9000dr/€26.45; doubles 8000dr/€23.50, 12,000dr/€35.25.

Hotel Emporikon, Singrou 14 (☎525 560), at Egnatia. Quieter than most other hotels on Egnatia. All rooms share toilets. Singles 6000dr/€17.65; doubles 9000dr/€26.45, with shower 13,000dr/€38.15; triples 12,000dr/€35.25.

FOOD

Pocketed on tiny sidestreets all over the city, Thessaloniki's **ouzeri** tables are veritable shrines to appetizer *mezedes,* upon which are heaped offerings to the gods of budget dining. The most *ouzeri* can be found in the tiny streets on both sides of **Aristotelous,** while more innovative establishments are down from Egnatia between **Dragoumi** and **El. Venizelou.** The **Old Town** district brims with inexpensive, family tavernas; **Ladadika** is quaint, but more upmarket.

Ouzeri Melathron, in an alley at 23 El. Venizelou. From Egnatia, walk past the Ottoman Bedesten on El. Venizelou and make a right into the passage. Witty 1.25m long menu features a spicy dish called "Lonely Nights" ("No nookie with this on your breath") and snails ("For friends of the hermaphrodite"). Main meals 1150-3600dr/€3.40-10.60.

Ta Adelphi (☎266 432), in laid-back Pl. Navarino. Carnivorous meals at good prices. Popular, delicious, and very busy. Try the special chicken: it's stuffed with cheese and wrapped in bacon. Main meals 1250-1900dr/€3.70-5.60. Open daily noon-midnight.

SIGHTS AND ENTERTAINMENT

The streets of modern Thessaloniki are littered with the remnants of its significance during both the Byzantine and Ottoman empires. There are ample churches to keep devout old women crossing themselves at a truly aerobic rate on the buses down Egnatia alone, not to mention those converted into mosques or squeezed in the tiny streets of the Old Town. **Agios Dimitrios,** on Ag. Dimitriou north of Aristotelous, is the city's oldest and most famous church. Although most of its interior was

GREECE

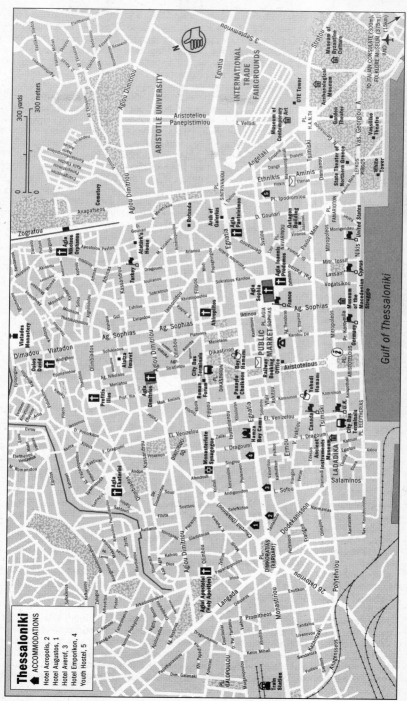

Thessaloniki

▲ ACCOMMODATIONS

Hotel Acropolis, 2
Hotel Augustos, 1
Hotel Averof, 3
Hotel Emporikon, 4
Youth Hostel, 5

gutted in the 1917 fire, some lovely mosaics remain. (Open daily 8am-8pm.) South of Egnatia on the square that bares its name, the magnificent domed **Agia Sophia** served as Thessaloniki's cathedral from the 8th century until 1523, when it was converted into a mosque. (Open 7am-1pm and 5-7pm.) Originally part of a palatial complex designed to honor the Roman Emperor, the **Rotunda** became a church under the Byzantines. Its walls, though now under renovation, were once plastered with some of city's most brilliant mosaics; very few remain. (Open daily 7am-2:30pm.) A colonnaded processional once led south to the **Arch of Galerius**, on the eastern end of Egnatia, which was built in the 4th century AD by Emperor Galerius. Returning west down Egnatia, don't miss ■**Bey Hamami,** a perfectly preserved, 15th-century bath house which served the Ottoman governor and his retinue. (Free.)

Thessaloniki's **Archaeological Museum** is full of discoveries gleaned from Neolithic tombs, as well as mosaics from Roman houses, and a dazzling display of Macedonian gold. Check out the gold death masks and weapons found in the graves of Sindos. Take bus #10 down Egnatia to Pl. Hanth. (Open M 12:30-7pm, Tu-Su 8am-7pm; reduced hours in winter. 1500dr/€4.40, students 800dr/€2.35, EU students free.) Just across the street on 3 Septembriou, the **Museum of Byzantine Culture** has three huge rooms detailing the lives of ancient Thessalonians, from church mosaics and elaborate tombs all the way to 1500-year-old personal effects like mirrors, combs, and wine jugs. (Open M 12:30-7pm, Tu-Su 8am-7pm; reduced hours in winter. 1000dr/€2.95, students and seniors 500dr/€1.50, EU students and under 18 free.) Right in the middle of the marketplace west of Aristoteliou, on the 1st floor of Irakliou 26, is the **Museum of the Jewish Presence,** which details the long history of Thessaloniki's Sephardic Jewish population. (On the 1st floor of an office building; ring the bell if door is closed. Open M-F 10am-1:30pm. Free.) All that remains of a 15th-century Venetian seawall, the **White Tower** presides over the eastern edge of the waterfront like an overgrown chess piece. *Wandering Byzantine Thessaloniki*, a guide available at the tower for a pricey (but well-deserved) 6000dr/€17.65, will glut history buffs with Byzantine gratification. (Tower open Tu-Su 8am-3pm. Free.)

There are three main hubs for late-night fun: the bars and cafes of the Ladadika district, the waterfront, and the open-air discos that throb near the airport exit (2000dr/€5.90 by taxi). **Podon 2000,** 11km east of the city along the main highway, is very slick and sophisticated, but for Greek music addicts only. (Cover 3000dr/€8.80 includes 1 drink.) **Deka Dance** and **Mousis,** farther down the highway from Teatro, are other popular discos. (Cover 3000dr/€8.80, includes 1 drink.)

MOUNT OLYMPUS (Ολιμποσ)   ☎0352

Emerging from the Thermaic Gulf, the impressive height (nearly 3000m) and formidable slopes of Mt. Olympus once so awed the ancients that they proclaimed it the divine dwelling place of the gods. A network of well-maintained **hiking** trails now makes the summit accessible to just about anyone with sturdy legs and a taste for adventure, although at times you may yearn for a pair of Hermes' winged sandals. Two approaches to the peaks begin near **Litohoro** (280m), one at **Prionia** (1100m), 18km from the village, and one at **Diastavrosi** (also called **Gortsia;** 1300m), 14km away. There is no bus to the trailheads from Litohoro, so you'll have to walk, or drive. *Let's Go* does not recommend hitchhiking. A **taxi** costs about 6000dr/€17.65 to Prionia. Unless you're handy with a crampon and an ice axe, make your ascent between May and October. **Mytikas,** the tallest peak, is inaccessible without special equipment before June. There are **refuges** near the summits. The EOS-run **Spilos Agapitos** ("Refuge A") is about 800 meters below **Skala** and **Mytikas** peaks. The English-speaking staff dispenses hiking info over the phone to prospective hikers, and can also help reserve spots in other EOS refuges. (☎81 800. Meals 6am-9pm. Lights out at 10pm. Open mid-May to late-Oct. 3000dr/€8.80; 2000dr/€5.90 for members of mountain clubs; 500dr/€1.50 to camp nearby and use their facilities.)

Trains (☎22 522) run from Athens (7hr., 3 per day, 3800dr/€11.15) and Thessaloniki (1½hr., 5 per day, 1000dr/€2.95) to the Litohoro station; a **taxi** from the train station should cost around 2000dr/€5.90. Or take a direct KTEL **bus** (☎81 271) from Athens (6hr., 3 per day, 8000dr/€23.50) or Thessaloniki (1½hr., 16 per day, 1900dr/

€55.80). Opposite the bus stop is the **tourist office**. (☎83 100. Open daily 9am-midnight.) The most affordable rooms are found at the **Hotel Park**, Ag. Nikolaou 23, down from the *plateia*. (☎812 52. Singles 6500dr/€19.10; doubles 8000dr/€23.50; triples 9000dr/€26.45.) **Camp** at **Olympus Zeus** (☎22 115) or **Olympus Beach** (☎22 112), on the beach about 5km from town; expect to pay at least 3000dr/€8.80.

METEORA (Μετεωρα)   ☎0423

The stunning beauty of the iron-gray pinnacles of the Meteora rock formations will take your breath away. They rise from the Thessalian plains and offer astonishing views of fields, forests, mountains, and monolithic stone. These wonders of nature are bedecked by 24 exquisite, gravity-defying Byzantine monasteries. Dress modestly. (Open Apr.-Sept. Sa-Su and W 9am-12:30pm and 3:20-6pm; staggered schedules during the rest of the week. 500dr/€1.50 per monastery.) The **Grand Meteoron Monastery** is the oldest, largest, and most touristed of the monasteries, with gruesome frescoes of the Roman persecution of Christians. This monastery also houses a **folk museum.** The chapel of **Varlaam Monastery** contains 16th-century frescoes that include a particularly disturbing rendition of the Apocalypse. The most popular base for exploring Meteora is the town of **Kalambaka** (Καλαμπακα). **Trains** leave for Athens (4hr., 3 per day 7:08am-5:25pm, 6500dr/€19.10) and Thessaloniki (3hr., 9:38am, 4200dr/€12.35). **Buses** depart for Athens (5hr., 8 per day 7am-8:30pm, 5900dr/€17.35), Patras (6hr., Tu and Th 9am, 5950dr/€14.50); and Thessaloniki (3hr., 6 per day, 3950dr/€11.60). Local buses go from Kalambaka to Meteora (20min.; M-Su 8:30am and 1:20pm; 260dr/€0.80). Most walk the 6km downhill back to town, visiting the monasteries along the way. ◪**Koka Roka** offers an awe-inspiring view of Meteora; from the central square, follow Vlachara until it ends, bear left and follow the signs to Kanari for 15min. (☎24 554. **Internet** access. 4000dr/€11.75 per person without bath. With bath: singles 6000dr/€17.60; doubles 8000dr/€29.50; triples 10,000dr/€23.50. **Campsites** line the roads out of town. **Postal code:** 42200.

OSIOS LOUKAS (Οσιος Λουκας)   ☎0267

Osios Loukas delights the eye with its mountain vistas and stunning Byzantine architecture. The exquisite monastery, built in the 10th and 11th centuries and still in use today, overlooks Boeotia and Phokis from the green slopes of Mt. Elikon more than 1700m above sea level. Gold-laden mosaics, vibrant frescoes, and intricate brick and stonework adorn Osios Loukas, the most famous and perhaps the most gorgeous monastery in Greece. When visiting, dress modestly. Two churches are at the site: the **Katholikon**, on the right after the museum, built in 1011 and dedicated to the monastery's founding saint, Osios Loukas, is the most impressive of the monastery's jewels; the smaller **Church of Panagia** holds the dried body of the saint himself in a glass coffin, as well as a **crypt** with stunning frescoes that should not missed. (☎22 797. Open May 3-Sept. 15 daily 8am-2pm and 4-7pm; Sept. 16-May 2 daily 8am-5pm. 800dr/€2.35, seniors 400dr/€1.20, under 18 and students free.) Without a car or a lot of faith in the *very* sporadic traffic to the monastery (*Let's Go* does not recommend hitchhiking), you must hire a **taxi** (☎26 333. 7000dr/€20.55) or walk along the hilly, narrow road from the town of Distomo, 9km to the west.

IOANNINA (Ιωαννινα)   ☎0651

On the shores of Lake Pamvotis lies Epirus's capital, Ioannina, the region's largest city. It has not yet escaped the intriguing, half-legendary historical presence of Ali Pasha, who was the Ottoman governor of Epirus before the Greek War of Independence and rebuilt the Byzantine walls of his pipe-dream capital. The walled **Frourio** (also known as the Castro), which spans regally over the lake, contains the old city. Try entering on Karamanli; Follow signs to the **Itş Kale** (Inner Acropolis), which encloses the 18th-century **Fethiye Camii** (Victory Mosque), the **Byzantine Museum,** and the **tomb of Ali Pasha.** (☎27 761. Open M 12:30am-7pm, Tu-Su 8am-7pm; 500dr/€1.50, students 300dr/€0.90.) The smaller of the Frourio's walled inner areas is a little farther to the left of Itş Kale—follow signs through the crooked streets to the museum in the lovely **Aslan Pasha Camii.**

(☎ 26 356. Open June-Sept. daily 8am-8pm, Oct.-May 8am-3pm; 700dr/€2.05, students 300dr/€0.90.) Off Averof near the city center, the **Archaeological Museum** has tablets on which puzzled ancients wrote their angst-ridden queries to that divine Dear Abby, the oracle of Zeus, in nearby Dodoni (see below). (Open Tu-Su 8:30am-3pm. 500dr/€1.50, students free.) Catch a frequent **boat** (10min., 150dr/€0.45) across the lake to the cleverly named **To Nisi** (The Island) to explore **Byzantine monasteries** and the **Ali Pasha Museum.** Follow the signs to Averof's end at the waterfront, and go left at the walls on Karamanli to the dock.

Buses run regularly from **Zossimadon 4** terminal to: Athens (7hr., 9 per day, 8100dr/€23.80); Igoumenitsa (2hr., 10 per day, 2000dr/€5.90); and Thessaloniki (7hr., 6 per day, 6650dr/€19.55). The **tourist office,** about 500 meters down Leoforis Dodoni on the left, immediately after the playground, has maps and a guide to Ioannina, including a list of rooms available to rent in the province. (☎ 46 662. Open M-F 7:30am-2:30pm and 5-8:30pm, Sa 9am-1pm.) To check your **email,** head to **Web@r,** Stoa Sarka 31-32. Go right down the arcade after the McDonald's; it's tucked off Nap. Zerva. (600dr/€1.80 per hr. Open daily 11am-4am.) To get to ▧**Hotel Paris,** Tsirigoti 6, walk uphill from the station and look left at the bank. (☎ 20 541. Singles 6000dr/€17.60; doubles 10,000dr/€-29.35.) **Hotel Metropolis,** Kristali 2, is on the corner of Averof toward the waterfront. (☎ 26 207. Singles 6000dr/€17.60; doubles 10,000dr/€29.35.) In town, dine on seafood near the waterfront. **Postal Code:** 45221.

▶ **DAYTRIP FROM IOANNINA: DODONI. Ancient Dodoni** (Δωδωνη), the site of mainland Greece's oldest oracle, is at the base of a mountain 22km southeast of Ioannina. According to myth, **Zeus** resided in Dodoni as the roots of a giant oak while courting a nearby cypress tree (don't ask). Years later, a dove perched on the tree and decreed that there should be an oracle to Zeus on the spot. Although the oracle no longer exists, the well-preserved **amphitheater** remains. (Open daily in summer 8am-7pm; in winter 8am-5pm. 500dr, students free.) Dodoni is difficult to visit; your best bet is the 2pm **bus** to Melig (30min.; M, Th, F; 450dr/€1.35) from Ioannina's smaller station—ask to be let off at the theater. A return bus leaves at 5:15pm. Otherwise, take a taxi from Ioannina (at least 5000dr/€14.70 round-trip).

IONIAN ISLANDS (Νησια Του Ιονιου)

Just off the western coast of Greece, the Ionian Islands are renowned for their medley of rugged mountains, rolling farmland, shimmering olive groves, and pristine beaches, all surrounded by a seemingly endless expanse of clear, blue water with a sheer beauty that will stun even the most world-weary of world travelers.

▰ FERRIES TO ITALY

To catch a ferry to **Italy,** buy your ticket at least a day ahead in high-season; be sure to find out if the port tax (1500-2200dr) is included. Ferries go from **Corfu** to: **Ancona** (20hr., 1 per day, 19,000dr/€55.90); **Bari** (9hr., 1 every other day, 12,400dr/€36.47); **Brindisi** (6-7hr., 3 per day, 9400-32,000dr/€27.65-94.12); **Trieste** (24hr., 5 per week, prices start at 12,500dr/€36.77); and **Venice** (24hr., 1 per day, 14,600-20,900dr/€42.94-61.47). In summer, ferries go from **Kephalonia** to **Brindisi, Venice,** and **Ancona.**

CORFU (KERKYRA; Κερκυρα)   ☎ 0661

Since Odysseus washed ashore and praised its lush beauty, the seas have brought crusaders, conquerors, and colonists to verdant Corfu. Unfortunately, many others have discovered Corfu's charms and the island swarms with tourists in the summer.

CORFU TOWN. The largest city, **Corfu Town,** exudes a Venetian charm, and offers many sights of its own, such as its two Fortresses, various museums, and the winding streets of its Old Town. However, as with many places in Greece, excursions off the beaten path are richly rewarded. **Paleokastritsa beach,** (phone code ☎ 0663) where Odysseus supposedly landed, lies west of Corfu Town; take a green KTEL **bus** to Paleokastritsa (45min., 7 per day, 500dr/€1.50). A 90min. walk from there will bring you to the white mountaintop monastery **Panagia Theotokos** and the fort of **Angelokastro** (Castle of the Holy Angels), which jut out over the sea.

Ferries run from Corfu Town to Italy as well as Patras (9hr., 1-2 per day, 5800dr/€17.05), and **hydrofoils** run to Kephalonia (2¾hr., W and Sa 9am, 20,000dr/€58.85 return*)*. KTEL runs bus/ferry combos daily to Athens (9hr., 1 per day, 11,000dr/€32.35) and Thessaloniki (9hr., 1 per day, 8750dr/€23.75). KTEL inter-city green buses depart from between I. Theotaki and the New Fortress; **blue buses** (municipal buses) leave from Pl. Sanrocco. From the customs house, cross the intersection and walk uphill on Avramiou, which becomes I. Theotoki, to reach Pl. Sanrocco (1km). The **EOT Tourist Office** is at the corner of Rizospaston Voulefton and I. Polila. (☎37 5208. Open M-F 8am-2pm.) **The Association of Owners of Private Rooms and Apartments,** Polila 24 (☎26 133), has a complete list of rooms for all of Corfu. To get to **Hotel Europa,** Giantsilio 10, from the customs house, exit and make a right; Giantsilio is a tiny road on your left after the road turns and becomes Napoleonta. (☎39 304. Singles 5000-6000dr/€14.75-17.65; doubles 7000-8000dr/€20.60-23.55; triples 9000dr/€26.50.) A daily open-air **market** sells inexpensive food on Dessila, off G. Theotoki below the new fortress. (Open 6am-2pm.) **Postal Code:** 49100.

PELEKAS TOWN AND ENVIRONS. South of Paleokastritsa is the hidden jewel, **Pelekas Town** (blue bus #11 from Corfu Town, 30min., 7 per day, 240dr/€0.80); walk 30min. downhill to reach **Pelekas beach.** ▧**Glyfada beach,** is 5km from Pelekas Town. Free shuttles run between Glyfada and Pelekas (10min., 4 per day) and Glyfada is also is accessible by green KTEL **buses** from Corfu Town (30min, 6 per day, 400dr/€1.20). Glyfada is one of Corfu's most popular beaches, and offers, among other water sports, parasailing and waterskiing. North of Glyfada, accessible by a dirt path off the main Pelekas road, lie the isolated beaches of **Moni Myrtidion** and **Myrtiotissa** (the unofficial nude beach). Lodging is available in Paleokastritsa, Pelekas, and Glyfada. Pelekas is your best bet for a cheap night's stay—try **Pension-Tellis and Brigitte.** (☎(0661) 94 326; singles 5000dr/€14.75; doubles 6000-8000dr/€17.65-23.55). **Agios Gordios,** 10km south of Pelekas, offers impressive rock formations, a beach, and the **Pink Palace,** a huge hotel/resort that is immensely popular with young, primarily English-speaking backpackers. On weekends, toga-wearing partygoers have been known to engage in a spirit of revelry that would make Dionysus proud. The Palace has an impressive list of amenities that helps keep it a self-contained party resort, including clothing-optional cliff-diving (4000dr/€11.80) and other watersports. The Palace also runs express buses to Athens, which bypass Patras. (☎53 024. Breakfast, dinner, ferry pick-up, and drop-off included. A-class rooms 9000dr/€26.50; B-class dorms 7500dr/€22.10). Green KTEL buses run to Agios Gordios from Corfu Town (45min., 7 per day, 300dr/€0.90).**Postal Code**: 49100.

KEPHALONIA (Κεφαλονια)   ☎0671

Dubbed "The Island of Peculiarities" for its disparate but beautiful beaches, subterranean caves, rugged mountains, and shady forests, Kephalonia is ideal for a long stay. **Argostoli,** the capital and transport hub of Kephalonia and Ithaka, is a busy, noisy city with palm-lined, traffic-filled streets. Argostoli offers a good shopping strip, steamy nightlife, and easy access to other points on the island. Try **Hotel Tourist,** on the waterfront near the Port Authority (☎22 510. Singles 8000-12,000dr/€23.55-35.30; doubles 14,000-18,000dr/€41.20-52.95.) A small, picturesque town on a harbor surrounded by steep, lush hills, **Sami,** 24km from Argostoli on the east coast, offers white-pebble beaches, proximity to underground **Melissani Lake** and **Drograti Cave,** a cavern filled with stunning stalactites and stalagmites. Sami also has **ferries** to Ithaka (40min., 3 per day, 1500dr/€4.45), Patras (2½hr., 1 per day, 3400dr/€10.00), and summer ferries to Astakos on the mainland as well as Brindisi, Italy (about 10,000dr/€29.41). **Buses** run between

GREECE

Argostoli and Sami (3-4 per day, 700dr/€2.05). **Hotel Kyma,** in Sami's main *plateia*, has spectacular views. (☎(0674) 22 064. Singles 6000-8000dr/€17.65-23.55E; doubles 10,000-15,000dr/€29.45-44.15.)

Reputedly the most beautiful of Kephalonia's towns, and the only one untouched by the disastrous 1953 earthquake, **Fiskardo,** at the northern tip of the island, is worth a visit. **Buses** go there from Argostoli (2 per day, 1100dr/€3.25) and Sami (2 per day, 900dr/€2.65). **Ferries** leave from Fiskardo for Piso Aetos, Ithaka (1hr., 850dr/€2.50), Vasiliki, Lefkada (1hr., 1100dr/€3.25), and Nidri, Lefkada (2hr., 1500dr/€4.45). For lodging or other assistance, try **Nautilus Travel Agency** on the far right of the waterfront as you are facing inland. (☎41 440. Open daily 9am-9pm.) On the way to Fiskardo from either Argostoli or Sami lies the famous **Myrtos Beach,** one of the best in Europe; the bus will let you off there.

ITHAKA (ITHAKI; Ιθακη)   ☎0674

The least-touristed and perhaps the loveliest of the Ionian Islands, Ithaka is all too often passed over for the tourist havens of Lefkada and Kephalonia. Those who do come discover the peaceful beauty of pebbled islands, rocky hillsides and terraced olive groves. According to Homer's epic poem, Ithaka was the kingdom where **Odysseus** left his wife, Penelope, behind for two decades while he played with various sirens and monsters. Ithaka's largest town and capital, **Vathy,** wraps around a circular bay skirted by steep, green hills. **Dexa** is the closest beach to Vathy, a 15min. walk along the main road out of town with the water on your right, but **Sarakiniko** and **Filiatro,** over the mountain to the left of town as you are facing inland, are more rewarding—about a 30min. walk to the first and 45min. walk to the second, coming from the *plateia* turn right after Hotel Mentor and head for the hills. Those with a poetic bent can climb up to the **Cave of the Nymphs,** where Odysseus supposedly hid his treasure. (On the road out of town leading to Dexa Beach and Stavros; look for signs. Bring a flashlight.) North from Vathy are the scenic villages of Lefki, Stavros, Platrithiai, Frikes, and Kioni. **Stavros** is high in the mountains on the way to Frikes, which can be reached erratically by the island's lone bus (1hr., 350dr/€1.05); car or moped rental is recommended. Stavros was allegedly once home to **Odysseus's Palace;** the site is now a small museum filled with excavated items from the site. (There may be a nominal fee or a donation expected.)

Ferries connect Ithaka to Sami in Kephalonia (1hr., 1500dr/€4.41) to Vasiliki in Lefkada (2½hr., 1000dr/€2.95), to Patras in the Peloponnese, and Astakos on the mainland. Boats depart from Vathy, Piso Aetos (10min. taxi ride), and Frikes (30min. taxi ride). Due to ever-changing schedules, you should check with Delas Tours or Polyctor Tours. For help in finding a room check with **Delas Tours** (☎32 104; open daily 9am-2pm and 4-10pm) or **Polyctor Tours** (☎33 120; open daily 9am-1:30pm and 3:30-9pm), both in the main square right off the water. The island's one **bus** runs north from Vathy, passing through the villages of Lefki, Stavros, Platrithiai, Frikes, and Kioni. Schedules are erratic; check in town. The bus usually runs 1-2 times per day (1hr., 350dr/€1.05 to Frikes). Private *domatia* (6-8000dr/€17.65-23.50 in summer) are your best option for affordable accommodations. Try **Andriana Domatia** on the far right of the waterfront as you are facing inland (☎32 387. Singles 8000-9000dr/€23.55-26.50; doubles 13,000-14,000dr/€38.25-41.20.) **Taverna To Trexantiri** is the hands-down favorite eatery for locals. (Salads 600-1200dr/€1.80-3.55; main dishes under 1800dr/€5.30.) **Postal Code:** 28300.

THE SPORADES (Σποραδες)

Viewed from the chaos of modern Athens, the Sporades and Evia circle like a family of enchanted sea-maidens. The matriarch is Evia, Greece's largest island after Crete. The Northern Sporades are her three daughters: quietly sophisticated Skopelos is the eldest, home to moonlit jazz-filled harbors and a population of artists. Restless Skiathos is the middle child, eager to grow up, flaunting her beach-ringed shores and raging with the region's best party scene. Innocent Alonnisos, the youngest, is a pristine wilderness criss-crossed by hiking trails; Skyros, in the east, is the austere grandmother, a purple-hilled keeper of the old ways.

◰ TRANSPORTATION

To get to most of the Sporades from **Athens,** take the daily bus from the station at Liossion 260 to **Ag. Konstantinos** (2½hr., 16 per day, 2650dr/€7.80), where **Hellas Lines ferries** (☎22 209) operates on the corner of Papadiamantis across from the ferry landing. Prices are slightly higher in July and Aug. Ferries run to: Agios Konstantinos (3½hr., 1-2 per day, 3400dr/€10); Alonnisos (2hr., 1-3 per day, 1900dr/€5.60); Skopelos (1½hr., 1-3per day, 1500dr/€4.40); Volos (2½hr., 1-2per day, 2900dr/€8.55). **Flying Dolphins hydrofoils** follow the same routes at twice the cost and double the speed. Ferries also connect the various islands.

SKIATHOS (Σκιαθος)   ☎0427

Tourism is a recent phenomenon here, as little Skiathos has grown up almost overnight into a glamorous dancing queen—welcome to the party hub of the Sporades. Package tourists pack the streets of **Skiathos Town,** while budding writers follow Papadiamantis to the beautiful beaches and nature preserves. Buses leave the port in Skiathos Town for the southern **beaches** (3 per hr., 320dr/€0.95), including **Megali Ammos, Nostros, Platanias,** and **Vromolimnos.** The road and bus route end in **Koukounaries,** where the more secluded beaches begin, including the lovely, pine-wooded **Biotrope of Koukounaries;** the yellow, curved, and nude **Banana Beach;** and the nude **Little Banana Beach.** When night falls, indulge yourself at the countless bars in **Pl. Papadiamantis** or along **Polytechniou** and **Evangelista.** Follow Papadiamantis to the kiosk and turn right to reach ▧**Chris, Jan & Deborah's Daskalio Pub** (Entrees 2500-4000dr/€7.35-11.75. Bar open May-Sept. daily Open 7pm-3am) **Private rooms** abound, particularly on Evangelista, but in a pinch head to the **Rooms to Let Office,** by the port. (☎22 990. Open daily 8:30am-midnight.) **Pension Danaos,** in an alley off Papadiamantis opposite the OTE, attracts young backpackers. (☎22 834. Open May-Sept. Singles 10,000dr/€29.35; doubles 8-15,000dr/€23.48-44.02.) **Camping Koukounaries** is on the bus route to Koukouniares between stops 20 and 21. (☎49 250. 1800dr/€5.30 per person, 1000dr/€2.95 per tent.) **Postal Code:** 37002.

SKOPELOS (Σκοπελος)   ☎0424

Relaxed Skopelos sits between the whirlwind of Skiathos and the largely untouched wilderness of Alonnisos. By day, the pious head to the hills, where the island's monasteries and shrines hide in woods still heady with the fading sounds of *rembetika* (folk songs). By night, the streets of Skopelos Town fill with voices, and light drips down from cafes onto the Aegean. **Buses** leave from the stop left of the waterfront (as you face inland) for **beaches** near **Stafylos, Agnondas, Milia,** and **Loutraki.** **Hiking trails** wind through the terrain to monasteries and beaches. The **Thalpos Travel Agency,** 5m to the right of Galanatsiou along the waterfront, is up on everything from Flying Dolphins tickets to catching octopi. (☎22 947. Open May-Oct. daily 10am-9pm.) Decent prices for rooms are found near the dock; try the **Rooms and Apartments Association.** (☎24 567. Open daily 10am-2pm and 6-10pm.) ▧**Pension Sotos,** on the corner of Galanatsiou on the waterfront, is a gem, for its setting and its diamond-in-the-rough price. (☎22 549. Singles 5500-10,000/€16.15-29.35 Doubles 6500-12,000dr/€19.10-35.25.) Endless 350dr/€1.05 gyros and 600dr/€1.80 pizzas fill **Pl. Platanos.** For something less greasy, try **Greca's Creperie,** 20m from the Folk Art Museum. (Open daily 10am-3pm and 7pm-12:30am.) **Postal Code:** 37003.

ALONNISOS (Αλοννησος)   ☎0424

Of the 20-odd islands within Greece's new **National Marine Park,** only Alonnisos is inhabited. Most of the small, remaining islets are strictly regulated—they harbor the endangered **Mediterranean monk seal**—and visited only by organized tour boats in summer; trips are sold along the harbor (1 day, 10,000-12,000dr/€29.35-35). Alonissos's unexplored northern coast forms a boundary of clear white sand against the sea, and its **hiking trails** trace the high heartland; pick up *Alonnisos on Foot* (2800dr/€8.25) in **Patitiri** for walking routes. The island's only **bus** runs between Hora and Patitiri (every hr., 300dr/€0.90). **Alonissos Travel,** in the center of the waterfront, **exchanges currency,** finds rooms, books excursions, and sells ferry tickets. (☎65 188. Open 9am-10pm.) The **Rooms to Let Office** next to Ikos Travel can lend a hand to travelers looking for a place to stay. (☎66 188. Open 10am-2pm and 6-10pm.) **Panorama,** down the first alley on the left from Ikion Dolophon, rents bright rooms and studios with private baths. (☎65 240. Doubles 6000-14,000dr/€17.65-41.10.) Locals adore the little *ouzeri* **To Kamaki,** on the left side of Ikion Dolophon past the National Bank. Try the delectable warm octopus salad for 1700dr/€5. (☎65 245. Open noon-2:30pm and 7pm-late.) Hikers and beachgoers may find the beautiful **Old Town** (Hora; Χωρα) ideal. Many **beaches** are accessible from the island's main road that runs along the spine of the island from Patitiri. A 1½hr. walk leads to **Votsi,** the island's other major settlement. Beyond Votsi, the road passes the pine-girded beaches of **Milia** and **Chrisi Milia. Postal Code:** 37005.

SKYROS (Σκυρος)   ☎0222

From the sea, Skyros's cliffs and hills spread out in greens and yellows under an infinitely blue sky. The hilly terrain once fortified the island against marauding pirates and is now trying to fight off modern culture. The island's capital, **Skyros Town,** as well as its northern and southern wilds, remain traditional and distinctly separate from modern Greece—the last stand of ghosts, poets, and pirate kings. Above Skyros Town, the 1000-year-old **Monastery of Ag. George** and the **Castle of Lico-midus** command magnificent views of Skyrian sunsets. (Open Mar.-Aug. daily 7am-10pm; Sept.-Feb. 7:30am-6pm.) The superb ▨**Faltaits Museum,** up the stairs from Pl. Rupert Brooke in Skyros Town boasts an incredible folk art collection. (Open daily 10am-1pm and 6-9pm. 500dr/€1.50.) The best way to get to Skyros is to take the **bus** from **Athens** to **Kimi** (3½hr., 2 per day, 2600dr/€7.65), then the **ferry** to Skyros from Kimi (2 per day, 2500dr/€7.35). Boats to Skyros arrive in **Linaria,** the tiny western port; a **local bus** to Skyros Town picks up when they arrive (20min., 3 per day, 260dr/€0.80). **Skyros Travel,** past the central plateia on Agoras, sells Olympic Airways tickets; it's also a de facto tourist office, organizing excursions and helping with lodgings. (☎91 123. Open daily 9am-2:30pm and 6:30-11pm.) For the full Skyrian experience, **bargain** to stay in a traditional private home; the thick-walled treasure troves are brimming with Delft ceramics and Italian linens, purchased from pirates who looted much of the known world. You'll be met at the bus stop by old women offering *domatia.* Expect to pay 5000-12,000dr/€14.70-35.25. **Camping Skyros** has a restaurant and a mini-market. (☎92 458. 1500dr/€4.40 per person; 1000dr/€2.95 per tent.) The incredible ▨**O Pappou Kai Ego** ("Grandpa and me"), toward the top of Agoras, serves Skyrian specialties (Dishes 1600-2500dr/€4.70-7.35). **Postal Code:** 34007.

THE CYCLADES (Κυκλαδες)

When people speak longingly of the Greek islands, they are quite likely speaking of the Cyclades. Whatever notion of the Aegean captivates—peaceful cobblestone streets and whitewashed houses, breathtaking sunsets, sunny hikes, Bacchanalian revelry—it resides here. Each island has quiet villages and untouched spots, but in summer most are mobbed by backpackers.

◤ TRANSPORTATION

Ferries from **Athens** head to: **Ios** (7½hr., 3 per day, 5400dr/€15.85); **Mykonos** (6hr., 2 per day, 5200dr/€15.30); **Naxos** (6hr., 5 per day, 5000dr/€14.70); and **Santorini** (9hr., 3 per day, 6000dr/€17.65). Ferries from **Crete** connect to: **Mykonos** (8½hr., 5 per week, 6000dr/€17.60); **Naxos** (7hr., 3 per week, 5200dr/€15.25); **Paros** (9hr., 7 per week, 5200dr/€15.25); **Santorini** (4hr., 2 per day, 3700dr/€10.80).

MYKONOS   ☎0289

Coveted by pirates in the 18th century for its blond beaches, Mykonos is still lusted after by those seeking revelry and excess. Social life, both gay and straight, abounds; the island is also the expensive playground of the sleek and chic sophisticates. Ambling in colorful alleyways at dawn or dusk is the cheapest and most exhilarating way to experience the island, especially **Mykonos Town.** All of Mykonos' beaches are nudist, but degrees of bareness vary; the most daring are **Plati Yialos, Paradise Beach, Super Paradise Beach,** and **Elia. Buses** run south from South Station to Plati Yialos (every 30min., 250dr/€0.75), where *caïques* (little boats) go to the others (around 400dr/€1.20); direct buses also run to Paradise from South Station (every 30min., 250dr/€0.75) and to Elia from North Station (30min., 8 per day, 350dr/€1.05). At night, **Caprice Bar,** on the water, is popular, crowded, breathtaking at sunset. (Open Su-Th 6:30pm-3:30am, F-Sa until 4:30am.) Step into a Toulouse-Lautrec painting at the groovy and mostly gay **Montparnasse Piano Bar,** Agion Anargyron 24, in Little Venice. (Open 7pm-3am.) On Matogianni, **Pierro's,** with wild dancing and irresistible hedonism, was the first gay bar in Greece (beer 1500dr/€4.40).

Ferries run to: Naxos (3hr., 1-2 per day, 2100dr/€6.10); Santorini (6hr., 3 per week, 3500dr/€10.30); and Tinos (45min., 3 per day, 1300dr/€6.10). The helpful **tourist police** await at the ferry landing. (☎ 22 482. Open daily 8am-11pm.) Most budget travelers find their niche in Mykonos's several festive campsites, which offer a myriad of sleeping options beyond the standard plot of grass. There are information offices on the dock, one for **hotels** (☎ 24 540; open 9am-midnight), and one for **camping** (☎ 23 567; open 9am-midnight). **Hotel Apollon,** on the waterfront, is an antique-laden house with a view of the harbor. (☎ 22 223. Singles 9000-15,000dr/€26.40-43.95; doubles 11,500-18,000dr/€33.70-52.70.) **Paradise Beach Camping** is 6km from the village, directly on the beach; take the free shuttle from the port. (☎ 22 852. 1600-2400dr/€4.70-7 per person; 900-1600dr/€2.65-4.70 per tent; 2-person beach cabin 6000-14,000dr/€17.60-41.10.) You'll have to wait at the ▨**Dynasty Thai Chinese Restaurant,** on Pl. Lymni, but it's worth it. (Main dishes 1650-2500dr/€4.85-7.35. Open daily 6:30pm-12:45am.) **Kalamataria,** on Florou Zouganeli, serves Greek cuisine at fair prices. (☎ 24 051. Open 9am-1am.) **Postal Code:** 84600.

▧ DAYTRIP FROM MYKONOS: DELOS. Delos, the sacred center of the Cycladic maelstrom, is not to be missed. Delos claims the most famous sanctuary in the Cyclades, *the* **Temple of Apollo,** built to commemorate the birthplace of the god and his twin sister, Artemis. After several centuries of inhabitation, Delos went feral by the end of the 2nd century AD, taken over by legions of leaping lizards, huge spiderwebs, and members of the French School of Archaeology (well, the last just since 1873). The **archaeological site,** which occupies much of the small island, takes several days to explore completely, but the highlights only gobble up 3hr. From the dock, head straight to the **Agora of the Competaliasts;** continue in the same direction and go left onto the wide **Sacred Road** to reach the **Sanctuary of Apollo,** a collection of temples built from Mycenaean times onwards. The famous **Great Temple of Apollo,** or Temple of the Delians, was completed in the 4th century BC. Continue 50m past the end of the **Sacred Road** to the beautiful **Terrace of the Lions.** The **museum,** next to the cafeteria, contains an assortment of archaeological finds. (Open Tu-Su 8:30am-3pm. 1200dr/€3.55, students 600dr/€1.76.) A path leads to the summit of **Mt. Kythnos,** from which Zeus watched Apollo's birth. Excursion boats leave the dock near **Mykonos Town** for Delos (35min., Tu-Su every 30-45min., 1900dr/€5.60 round-trip).

TINOS (Τηνος)   ☎ 0283

In southern Tinos, tree-dotted hills gently cascade into the clear sea under the summit of hulking Mt. Exobourgo, wildflowers line the road with brilliant color, and a bit of searching rewards the careful explorer with quiet, secluded beaches. The Ancient Greeks believed Tinos to be the home of the wind god Aeolus; today the cool sea breeze whispers his legacy. In **Tinos Town (Hora),** the most visited part of the island, the **Panayia Evangelistira Church** houses the miraculous **Icon of the Annunciation,** one of the most sacred relics of the Greek Orthodox Church. (Open daily 7am-8pm. Free. Modest dress required.) **Beaches** surround Tinos Town; **Kardiani** and **Agios Petros,** situated at the base of the mountains, are among the islands' most spectacular, while **Stavros** beach, a 2km walk left out of town is more touristy. For the best of the best, head east to the spectacular **Agios Sostis** and **Porto.** Take the KTEL **bus** (3-5 per day, 230dr/€0.70). Many hikes lead up **Mt. Exobourgo,** 14km north of Tinos Town, the site of the Venetian fortress **Xombourgo.**

Ferries run to: Andros (2hr., 2 per day, 1800dr/€5.30); Mykonos (30min., 4-5 per day, 1200dr/€3.55); and Syros (40min., 1-4 per day 10:15am-3:15pm, 1100dr/€3.25). **Catamarans** are twice as expensive as ferries. **Buses** (☎22 440), depart across the street from the National Bank for Porto (260dr/€0.80) and Pyrgos (800dr/€2.35). Check the schedule in the KTEL ticket agency opposite the bus depot. **Vidalis,** Zanaki Alavanou 16 (☎23 400), on the road running inland from the right of the waterfront, rents **mopeds** 3000dr/€8.80 and up. **Dimitris-Maria Thodosis,** Evangelistrias 33, is midway up the road to the left, on the 2nd floor. The traditional home features flower-laced balconies, a central kitchen, and common bathrooms. Doubles/triples 10,000dr/€29.35. (☎24 809. Open Mar.1-Oct. 31). **Tinos Camping** is 10min. from the waterfront to the right; follow the signs. (☎22 344. 1200dr/€3.52 per person; 1300dr/€3.81 per tent.) **Caffé Italia,** Akti Nazou 10 (☎25 756), is one of Tinos' best-kept culinary secrets. (Open daily 9am-12:30am.) There's a **supermarket** near the post office. (Open daily 9am-12:30am.) **Postal Code:** 84200.

PAROS (Παρος)   ☎0284

Paros was famed throughout antiquity for its slabs of pure white marble, which were shaped into the Venus de Milo, the Nike of Samothrace, and parts of Napoleon's mausoleum in Paris. Today Paros remains a favorite for its golden beaches and tangle of whitewashed villages. Behind the commercial surface of **Paroikia,** Paros' port and largest city, flower-filled streets wind through archways and past one of the most treasured basilicas of the Orthodox faith. Byzantine architecture buffs will coo over the **Panagia Ekatontapiliani** (Church of Our Lady of 100 Gates), which looms over Paroikia's *plateia* and houses three separate churches, cloisters, and a peaceful courtyard. Tradition holds that only 99 of the church's 100 doors can be counted—when the 100th appears, Constantinople will again belong to the Greeks. (Dress modestly. Open 8am-8:30pm.) Just 10km south of town is the cool, spring-fed ◪**Valley of the Butterflies,** or **Petaloudes,** where rare *Panaxiaquadripunctaria* moths congregate in massive numbers during the mating season (June to late-Sept.) cloaking the foliage. Take the bus from Paroikia to Aliki (10min., 8 per day, 300dr/€0.90) and ask to be let off at Petaloudes. Follow the signs 2km up the road. (Open M-Sa 9am-8pm. 400dr/€1.20.) At night, **Pirate Blues and Jazz** has an assortment of music tucked away in the old town near the Apollon Garden Restaurant. (Beer 800dr/€2.55, cocktails 2000dr/€5.90. Open daily 7pm-3am.)

Ferries sail to Ios (2½hr., 7-9 per day, 2650dr/€7.80) and Santorini (3½hr., 7-9 per day, 3350dr/€9.85). The **tourist police** are behind the OTE, across the *plateia.* (☎21 673. Open daily 9am-3:30pm.) Turn left at the dock and take a right after the ancient cemetery ruins to reach **Rena Rooms.** (☎22 220. Doubles 6000-13,000dr/€17.60-38.10; triples 9000-15,000dr/€26.40-43.95.) Shuttles run from the port to **Parasporos Camping,** 1.5km south of town. (☎22 268. 1300dr/€3.85 per person; 700dr/€2 per tent.) The Psychedelic **Happy Green Cow,** just a block off the *plateia* behind the National Bank, serves tasty veggie fare. (Open 7pm-midnight.) **Postal Code:** 84400.

NAXOS (Ναξος)   ☎0285

Mythology relates the desertion of Cretan princess Ariadne on the shores of Naxos by her ungrateful lover, Theseus, and her subsequent marriage to the god Dionysus. Old **Naxos Town** snoozes behind waterfront shops, on the hill leading up to the **Castro,** an old Venetian castle, which looms over town. At the top of the hill sits the **Archaeological Museum,** in the former Collège Français where Nikos Kazantzakis, author of *The Last Temptation of Christ* and *Zorba the Greek,* studied. (Open Tu-Su 8:30am-2pm. 500dr/€1.50, students 300dr/€0.90; Su and holidays free.) The new ◪**Mitropolis Museum** shouldn't be missed. An architectural achievement itself, it is built around an excavated site of a 13th-century BC civilization. (☎24 151. Open Tu-Su 8:30am-3pm. Free.) The gleaming, 6th-century BC **Portara** marble archway, visible from the waterfront, is one of the few archaeological sites in Greece where you can actually climb all over the ruins—with no admission, and no guards, it's ideal for romantic sunsets or midnight star-watching. A **bus** goes from the port to the **beaches** of **Agia Georgios, Ag. Prokopios, Ag. Anna,** and **Plaka** every 30min. (300dr/€0.90). Plaka is the hands-down favorite for nude frolicking. Spend a night of clubbing under palm trees overlooking the sea at **Caesar's Club** (☎25 203), on the inland street to the right of Naxos Tours. To truly experience the island, explore its stunning interior; **buses** run from Naxos Town to **Apollonas** fishing village, on the north tip, via a gorgeous coastal road (2hr., 3 per day, 1100dr/€3.25). Some of the most exhilarating aspects of the interior, such as the **Tragea** highland valley (an Arcadian olive grove) are not serviced by bus; ask for **hiking** info at the tourist office.

Ferries go to: Ios (1½hr., 1 per day, 2350dr/€6.90); Mykonos (1½hr., 2 per week, 2050dr/€6.05); Paros (1hr., 1 per day, 1550dr/€4.55); and Santorini (3hr., 1 per day, 3150dr/€9.25). The **tourist office** is 300m up from the waterfront by the bus station. (☎24 358. Open daily 8am-11pm.) **Hotel Anixis**, in Old Naxos, has breakfast (1200dr/€3.52) served in the fabulous rooftop garden, overlooking the Temple of Apollo. (☎22 112 Singles 8,000-13,000dr/€23.48-38.15; doubles 10,000-15,000dr/€29.35-44; triples 13,000-18,000dr/€38.15-52.82.) **Dionysus**, in Old Naxos (follow the red hand signs), is spartan, but cheap. (Open Jul.-Aug. Dorms 2000dr/€5.87; singles 4000-5000dr/€11.74-14.67; doubles and triples 6000dr/€17.61.) **Plaka Camping**, by Plaka beach, has studio/apartment options (doubles 6000dr/€17.61) and a bevy of amenities. (☎42 700. Tents 500dr/€1.47 high season. **Postal Code:** 84300.

IOS   ☎0286

If you're not drunk when you arrive, you will be when you leave. Ios can be summed up in three words: frat party run amok. Alright, that was four—after a week on Ios, you won't be able to count either. It has everything your mother warned you about—people swimming less than 30min. after they've eaten, wine being swilled from the bottle at 3pm, drinking games all day long, men and women dancing madly in the streets, and much more. The **port** (Yialos) is at one end of the island's paved road; the **village** (Hora) sits above it on a hill, but the **beaches** are the place to be. Most spend their days at **Mylopotas Beach,** a 20min. walk downhill from Ios town, or a bus ride from the port or village (every 10-20min. 7am-midnight, 260dr/€0.80), followed by inebriated evenings. **The Jungle,** near the basketball courts, is a good place to start. Thursday nights, 8000dr/€23.50 buys you pizza, cover immunity, a drink, and the right to **get drunk** at games held at the five bars comprising the ultimate pub crawl. Head up from the *plateia* to reach the **Slammer Bar,** where you can **get hammered** on "tequila slammers" 1000dr/€2.95, then migrate with the masses to **Red Bull,** to **get plastered** on the Red Bull and vodka "energy special" (1500dr/€4.40). Afterwards find techno at **Scorpion Disco,** on the way to the beach (1000dr/€2.95 cover after 1am). Wind up your evening at **Sweet Irish Dream,** near the "donkey steps," and for a change of pace, **get sloshed** and dance on tables after 2am. Take some aspirin in the morning and head down to the beach, where **Mylopotas Water Sports Center** shacks along the beach offer **windsurfing, water-skiing,** and **snorkeling lessons** with rental. (2000-6000dr/€5.90-17.66 per hour.)

Ferries go to: **Mykonos** (4hr., 1 per week, 3375dr/€9.90); **Naxos** (1¾hr., at least 3 per day, 2350dr/€6.90); **Santorini** (1¼hr., 3 per day, 1850dr/€5.45). Once a week, ferries go to **Crete, Thessaloniki,** and **Tinos.** The main **Tourist Office** is next to the bus stop. (☎91 343. Open daily 8am-midnight.) In the village, take the uphill steps to the left in the *plateia* and take the first left to reach ◙**Francesco's** for spectacular harbor views and a terrace bar. (☎91 706. Dorms 2500dr/€7.35; doubles 3000-8000dr/€8.80-23.48.) On the end of Mylopotas Beach, ◙**Far Out Camping** has a pool, plenty of tents, parties, and parties. Did we say parties? (☎92 301. Open Apr.-Sept. 1500dr/€4.40; tent rental 500dr/€1.50; small cabins 1800dr/€5.30; bungalows 2000dr/€5.90.) For non-fermented refreshment, there's **Ios Market** (☎91 035), across from the bus stop in Hora, and the **supermarket** in the main *plateia.* ◙**Ali Baba's** is located at the right end of the bar strip; ask around—it's tough to find but worth the trip. (☎91 558. Entrees 1300-3000dr/€3.85-8.80.) **Postal Code:** 84001.

FOLEGANDROS (Φολεγανδρος)   ☎0286

The island of Folegandros is a blissfully peaceful alternative to the rest of the more hectic Cyclades. The dry, rocky, steep hills are terraced with low, snaking stone walls worn by centuries of fierce wind. Don't miss the sunset view from the **Church**

of Panagia, above the town on Paleocastro hill; take the path from the right of the bus stop. **Agali beach,** accessible by foot (1hr.), is lined with several *tavernas;* climb up past the first one on the right and continue on the rocky trail to reach **Agios Nikolaos beach** (30min.), or continue along the main road to get to the tiny old settlement of **Ano Maria,** where you can examine Ottoman artifacts at the superb **Folklore Museum.** (Open June-Aug. daily 5-8pm. Guidebook 2000dr/€5.90.) Irregular **ferries** run at least 4 times per week to: Ios (1½hr., 1600dr/€4.70); Milos (2½hr., 1800dr/€5.30); Naxos (3hr., 2500dr/€7.35); Paros (4hr., 2000dr/€5.90); Santorini (1½hr., 1800dr/€5.30). You can board the **bus** that runs from the port **Kararostassi** to the Folegandros's main town **Hora.** Buses head to the port 45min. before each ferry, and return with new arrivals (260dr/€0.80). Near the bus stop is the **Sottovento Travel Center** (☎41 444. Open daily 10am-2pm and 5:30pm-midnight.) Down toward the port about 200m from the post office are **Pavlo's Rooms.** (☎/fax 41 232. Doubles 3000-10,000dr/€8.80-29.35, with bath 5000-14,000dr/€14.67-41.10.) In Hora, there are many places with Room to Let signs. Most run about 12,000-14,000dr/€35.25-41.10 per night for a double in high season. **Livadi Camping** is another option; call for a port shuttle. (☎41 204. 2500dr/€7.35 per person.) **Postal Code:** 84011.

SANTORINI (Σαντορινη)   ☎0286

Whitewashed towns balanced on plunging cliffs, burning black-sand beaches, and deeply scarred hills make Santorini's landscape nearly as dramatic as the volcanic explosion that created it. Despite all the kitsch in touristy **Fira,** the island's capital, nothing can destroy the pleasure of wandering its narrow, cobblestoned streets, inspecting its craft shops, and taking in the stunning sunset from its western edge. On the southwestern part of the island, the excavations at **Akrotiri,** a late Minoan city, are preserved under layers of volcanic rock. (Open Tu-Su 8am-7pm. 1200dr/€3.55, students 600dr/€1.80.) **Buses** run to Akrotiri from Fira (30min., 16 per day, 400dr/€1.20). Frequent buses also leave Fira for the black-sand **beaches** of **Perissa** (15min., 30 per day, 400dr/€1.20) and **Kamari** (20min., 62 per day, 260dr/€0.80) to the southeast. The route stops along the way in **Pyrgos** (15min., 30 per day, 400dr/€1.20); from there, hike to the **Profitias Ilias Monastery** (40min.) and continue to the ruins of **ancient Fira** (an extra 2hr.), near Kamari. (Open Tu-Su 8am-2pm.)

Ferries run to: Ios (1½hr., 4-8 per day, 1800dr/€5.50); Iraklion (4hr., 1 per day, 4100dr/€12.05); Naxos (4hr., 4-8 per day, 3200dr/€9.40); Mykonos (7hr., 2 per week, 3700dr/€10.90); and Paros (4½hr., 3-5 per day, 3300dr/€9.70). Most land at Athinios harbor; frequent buses (30min., 400dr/€1.20) connect to Fira. Head 300m north from the *plateia* in Fira for the **Fira Youth Hostel.** (☎22 387. Sheets 300dr/€0.90. Open Apr.-Oct. Dorms 2000-4000dr/€5.90-11.75; doubles 5000-10,000dr/€14.65-29.35.) follow the signs for Santorini Camping or catch the free shuttle from the port. (☎22 573. Doubles 7000-17,000dr/€20.55-49.85; triples 9000-20,000dr/€26.40-58.60.) Or, follow the blue signs east from it for **Santorini Camping.** (☎229 44. Open Apr.-Oct. 600dr/€4.70 per person, 900dr/€2.65 per tent, 800dr/€2.35 per car.) If you plan to spend substantial time baking on the black sand, take the bus from Fira to Perissa and stay at the **Youth Hostel Perissa-Anna,** 500m on the road out of town. (☎82 182. Hot showers 9am-9pm. Dorms 1000-3000dr/€2.95-8.80.) Head north on the road to Oia for a stop at **Mama's Cyclades Cafe** (☎24 211), where Mama serves up a humongous breakfast special. Postal Code: 84700.

CRETE (Κρητη)

Greece's largest island embraces an infinite store of mosques, monasteries, mountain villages, gorges, grottoes, and beaches. Since 3000 BC, Crete has maintained an identity distinct from the rest of Greece, first expressed in the language, script, and architecture of the ancient Minoans. While the resort towns of eastern Crete may be the products of British booking agents, the riveting mountains that wind from Malia to Agios Nikolaos seem the brainchild of something slightly more divine.

▐ TRANSPORTATION

Olympic Airways and **Air Greece** connect Athens to: Sitia (2-3 per week, 24,600dr/ €72.10) in the east; Iraklion (45min., 13-15 per day 27,400dr/€80.30) in the center; and Hania (4 per day, 19,400dr/€56.85) in the west. **Boats** run to Iraklion from: Athens (14hr., 3 per day, 7000dr/€20.55); Mykonos (8½hr., 5 per week, 6000dr/ €17.60); Naxos (7hr., 3 per week, 5200dr/€15.25); Paros (9hr., 7 per week, 5200dr/ €15.25); and Santorini (4hr., 2 per day, 3700dr/€10.90).

Buses run from **Rethymno, Hania,** and **Iraklion** south to the **Samaria Gorge** (from Hania; 4 per day, round-trip 2800dr/€8.20). Buses also go east from **Iraklion** to **Malia** (1hr., every 30min., 800dr/€2.55) and **Agios Nikolaos** (1½hr., 20 per day, 1450dr/ €4.25). Buses from **Agios Nikolaos** go on to **Sitia** (1½hr., 3-5 per day, 1550dr/€ 4.55).

IRAKLION (Ηρακλιον)   ☎ 081

Iraklion is Crete's capital and primary port. The chic native population lives life in the fast lane, which translates into an urban brusqueness unique among the cities of Crete and the most diverse nightlife on the island. Iraklion's main attraction, after **Knossos** (see below), is the superb **Archaeological Museum.** By appropriating major finds from all regions of the island, the Iraklion Museum has amassed a comprehensive record of the Neolithic and Minoan stages of its history with a polite nod to the Hellenistic and Roman periods. (Open M 12:30-7pm, Tu-Su 8am-7pm. 1500dr/€4.40; students 800dr/€2.55; EU students free.)

KTEL **Terminal A,** between the old city walls and the harbor near the water-front, sends **buses** to Agios Nikolaos (1½hr., 20 per day, 1550dr/€4.55) and Malia (1hr., 2 per hr., 850dr/€2.50); to reach the **Hania-Rethymno terminal,** walk down 25 Augustou to the waterfront, turn right, and walk about 500m. The **tourist office,** Xanthoudidou 1, has maps and museum info. (☎228 203. Open M-F 8am-2:30pm.) The **tourist police** are at 10 Dikeosinis. (☎283 190. Open daily 7am-11pm.) Check your **email** at **Gallery Games Net,** Korai 14. (☎282 804. 500dr/€1.50 per 30min.) **Rent a Room Hellas,** Handakos 24, is two blocks from El Greco Park. (☎288 851. Dorms 2200dr/€6.45; doubles 5000-7500dr/€14.65-21.50; triples 6000-10,000dr/ €17.65-29.35.) To get from the bus station to the **youth hostel,** Vyronos 5, take a left (with the water on your right) on 25 Augustou and a right on Vyronos. (☎286 281. Check-out 10am. Curfew midnight. Dorms 2500dr/€7.35; singles 3000-4000dr/€8.80-11.75; doubles 5500-6000dr/€14.65-17.60.) The best show in town is the **open-air market** near Pl. Venizelou. Stalls piled high with sweets, spices, fruits, vegetables, cheeses, and meat line both sides of the narrow street. (Open M-Sa 8am-2pm, Tu and Th-F 5-9pm.) Around 11pm, the young and the restless over-flow the small streets off **Pl. Venizelou.** A walk down D. Beaufort takes you to **Privilege Club** and **Yacht** next door. **Postal Code:** 71001.

⚑ DAYTRIPS FROM IRAKLION: KNOSSOS AND MALIA. At Knossos, the most famous archaeological site in Crete, excavations have revealed the remains of the largest and most complicated of Crete's **Minoan palaces.** Sir Arthur Evans, who financed and supervised the excavations, eventually restored large parts of the palace in Knossos; his work often crossed the line from preservation to artistic inter-pretation, but the site is nonetheless impressive. (Open daily in summer 8am-7pm; in winter 8am-5pm. 1500dr/€4.40, students 800dr/€2.35; in winter Su free.) To reach Knossos from Iraklion, take **bus** #2 from 25 Augustou or Pl. Eleftherias.

Nearby Malia is overrun by young nightlife-seeking Brits, but the palatial Minoan site at Malia also merits a visit. The **Minoan Palace,** one of the three great cities of Minoan Crete, is imposing. Follow the road east to Agios Nikolaos for 3km and turn left toward the sea. (Open Tu-Su 8am-3pm. 800dr/€2.55, students and seniors 400dr/€1.20, EU students free.) **Altino Travel Service** (☎33 658), across from the old church on the way to the beach, has maps travel advice, and a rental service; (cars 13,000-15,000dr/€38.10-43.95, **motorcycles** 5000-6000dr/€14.65-17.60 per day). Walking from the bus stop toward Agios Nikolaos, turn right onto 25 Martiou and

GREECE

left on Konstantinou for **Pension Aspasia**. (☎31 290. Singles 5000dr/€14.65; doubles 7000dr/€20.55.) **Pension Menios** is next door. (☎31 361. Singles 5000/€14.65; doubles 6000dr/€17.58; triples 8000-9000dr/€23.44-26.37.) **Postal Code:** 70007.

RETHYMNO AND HANIA (Ρεθυμνο, Χανια)   ☎0831

Nowhere in Western Crete are the manifestations of the island's turbulent occupations as mingled or as magical as in **Rethymno**'s old city. Arabic inscriptions adorn the walls of the narrow streets, minarets highlight the skyline, and the 16th-century **Venetian Fortezza** stands watch over the scenic harbor and plays host to a lively **Renaissance Festival** in July and August. The fortress also contains the **Numismatic Museum of Athens**, one of the few museums in the world dedicated solely to currency and coins. (Open Tu-Su 8am-7pm. 1000dr/€2.95.) The **Rethymno-Hania bus station** (☎22 212) is south of the fortress on the water, with service to Hania (1hr., 17 per day, 1600dr/€4.70) and Iraklion (1½hr., 18 per day, 1550dr/€4.40). Climb the stairs behind the bus station, turn left on Igoum Gavril, which becomes Kountouriotou, and turn left on Varda Kallergi to reach the waterfront and the **tourist office,** on El. Venizelou. (☎29 148. Open M-F 8am-5pm.) To get from the station to the cheerful **⚐Youth Hostel,** Tombazi 41-45, walk down Igoum Gavril, take a left at the park traffic light, walk through the gate, and take your second right. (☎22 848. Breakfast 400-500dr/€1.20-1.50. Sheets 150dr/€0.45. Reception 8am-noon and 5-9pm. Dorms 1800dr/€5.30.) **Postal Code:** 74100.

An oddly rickety tower of stone, the **Venetian lighthouse** guards the entrance to Hania's stunning architectural relic, the **Venetian Inner Harbor.** The inlet has retained its original breakwater and Venetian arsenal. The **Maritime Museum** details 6000 years of Cretan naval history. (☎91 875. Open Apr.-Oct. daily 9am-4pm; Nov.-Mar. 9am-2pm. 600dr/€1.80, students 350dr/€1.05.) Narrow Venetian buildings and Ottoman domes mingle in Hania's lively waterfront area—a day is best spent meandering or sitting waterside. **Ferries** arrive in the nearby port of **Souda** from Peiraias/Athens (9½hr., 1 per night, 5900dr/€17.35); buses connect to Hania's Municipal Market (15min., 260dr/€0.80). **Buses** leave at the station (☎93 306), on the corner of Kidonias and Kelaidi, for Rethymno (17 per day, 1600dr/€4.70). Walk right on Kidonias and turn left on Pl. 1866 to reach the **tourist office,** Kriairi 40. (☎92 624. Open M-F 7:30am-2:30pm.) To get to **Hotel Fidias,** Sarpaki 6, walk toward the harbor on Halidon and turn right onto Athinagora, which then becomes Sarpaki. (☎52 494. Singles 4000dr/€11.75; doubles 4000-6000dr/€11.75-17.60) **Postal Code:** 73100.

▨ **HIKING NEAR RETHYMNO AND HANIA: SAMARIA GORGE.** An extremely popular excursion from Hania, Rethymno, and Iraklion is the 5-6hr. hike down Samaria Gorge, a spectacular 16km long ravine threading through the White Mountains. Sculpted by the tender ministrations of rainwater over 14 million years, the gorge—the longest in Europe—retains its allure despite having been trampled by thousands of visitors. Rare native plants peek out from sheer rock walls, wild *agrimi* goats clamber about the hills, and endangered griffin vultures as well as golden eagles circle overhead. (Open May-Oct. 15 daily 6am-4pm. 1200dr/€3.55, under 15 and organized student groups free.) For more info about your friendly neighborhood gorge, call **Hania Forest Service** (☎(0821) 92 287). The trail starts at **Xyloskalo;** take the 6:15 or 8:30am **bus** from Hania to Xyloskalo (1½hr., 1300-1400dr/€3.85-4.15 each way) for a day's worth of hiking, or the 1:45pm bus from Hania will put you in **Omalos** ready for the next morning. If you spend the night, you can rest up at **Gigilos Hotel** on the main road. (☎(0821) 67 181. Singles 4000-5000dr/€11.72-14.65; doubles 6000dr/€17.65.) The trail ends in **Agia Roumeli,** on the southern coast, where you can hop on a **boat** to **Hora Sfakion** (1¼hr., 4 per day, last ferry 6pm; 1500dr/€4.40) or take a return bus to Hania (1600dr/€4.70).

AGIOS NIKOLAOS   ☎0841

Occupying a small peninsula on the northeast edge of Crete, Agios Nikolaos is a chic resort town where posh vacationers huff and puff their way up steep, boutiqued streets, then stop in at a harborside cafe to catch their breath at great leisure. Nostos Travel has **boats** (3000dr/€8.79) departing from the harbor for guided tours of the small but striking **Spinalonga island,** formerly a leper colony. From Agios Nikolaos, **ferries** go to: Athens/Peiraias (12hr., 5 per week, 7500dr/€22); Karpathos (7hr., 3 per week, 4100dr/€12.05); Rhodes (12hr., 3 per week, 6300dr/€18.50); and Sitia (1hr., 5 per week, 1600dr/€4.70). **Buses** (☎22 234) depart from Pl. Atlantidos, on the opposite side of town from the harbor. Head right from the station, and make your first right; follow Venizelou and then R. Koundourou to the harbor, then head to the left and across the bridge to reach the **tourist office,** S. Koundourou 21A. (☎22 357; fax 82 534. Open Apr.-June and Sept.-Nov. daily 8am-9:30pm; July-Aug. 8am-10pm.) To get to the pleasant **Christodoulakis Pension,** Stratigou Koraka 7, turn right and go past the taxi station, then turn left. (☎22 525. Singles 4000dr/€11.75; doubles 6000dr/€17.58; triples 7500dr/€22.) For nocturnal fun, stroll around the harbor on **I. Koundourou** or walk up **25 Martiou. Postal Code:** 72100.

SITIA ☎0843

A winding drive on coastal and mountain roads from Agios Nikolaos leads to the fishing and port town of Sitia, where the wave of tourism slows to a trickle and pelicans walk the streets at dawn. Sitia makes a great base for exploration of Crete's east coast. The town's **beach** extends 3km to the east, while the hilltop **fortress** provides views of the town and bay. (Open Tu-Su 8:30am-3pm. Free.) **Ferries** leave Sitia for: Athens (16-17hr., 5 per week, 7600dr/€22.35) via Agios Nikolaos (1½hr., 5 per week, 1600dr/€4.70); Karpathos (5hr., 3 per week, 3400dr/€10); Milos (9hr., 5 per week, 5200dr/€15.25); and Rhodes (12hr., 3 per week, 6000dr/€17.60). Turn right from the **bus station,** take your first right and then your first left, and follow Venizelou to the waterfront to reach the **tourist office.** (☎28 300. Open M-F 9am-9pm.) To get to the **youth hostel** at Therissou 4, walk right from the bus station, go right and then take the first left, turn left at the first big street, and bear left onto Therissou; or call for a ride from the station. (☎22 693. Sheets 100dr/€0.30. Dorms 1700dr/€5 per person; singles 2500dr/€7.35; doubles 4000dr/€11.75; triples 5000dr/€14.65. Camping on the small lawn 1200dr/€3.52 per person, tents free.) **Venus Rooms to Let** is at Kondilaki 60; walk up on Kapetan Sifi from the main square and go right after the telephone office. (☎24 307. Doubles 7000dr/€20.55; 20% higher for triples.) ▧**Cretan House,** K. Karamanli 10, off the *plateia,* serves Cretan classics for 700-1400dr/€2.05-4.15. (Open daily 9am-1:30am.) Head to **Hot Summer** after midnight, down the road to Palaikastro by the beach, where a pool supplants the more traditional dance floor. (Cover 1000dr/€2.95.) **Postal Code:** 72300.

EASTERN AEGEAN ISLANDS

The intricate, rocky coastlines and unassuming port towns of the **Northeastern Aegean Islands** enclose thickly wooded mountains that give way to unspoiled villages and beaches. Despite proximity to the Turkish coast and a noticeable military presence, the islands dispense a sampling of undiluted Greek culture.

SAMOS (Σαμος) ☎0273

Lush and lovely, Samos remains less frenetic than some of its wilder siblings in the Cyclades and Dodecanese, despite being one of the region's most touristed islands. Samos's more scholarly, mature visitors idle as short-sighted tourists simply stop here en route to **Kuşadası** and the ruins of **Ephesus** on the Turkish coast. With its quiet inland streets, palm trees, red-roof-covered hillsides, and engaging archaeological museum, **Samos Town (Vathy)** is among the Aegean's most attractive port cities. The phenomenal ▧**Archaeological Museum** is behind the municipal gardens. (☎27 469. Open Tu-Su 8:30am-3pm. 800dr/€2.35, students 400dr/€1.20, EU students free.) The ancient city of **Pythagorion,** once the island's capital, is 14km south of Samos Town. Near the town are the magnificent remains of Polykrates's 6th-century BC engineering projects: the **Tunnel of Eupalinos,** which diverted water from a natural spring to the city and a 40m-deep **harbor mole** (rock pier). (Tunnel open Tu-Su 8:45am-2:45pm. 500dr/€1.50, students 300dr/€0.90, EU students free.) A bus from

Samos Town arrives at Pythagorion (20min., 300dr/€0.90). The **Temple of Hera** is in nearby Heraion, a 10min. **bus** ride (300dr/€0.90) from Pythagorion. (Open T-Su 8:30am-3pm. 800dr/€2.35, students 400dr/€1.20.)

Ferries arrive in Samos Town from: Athens/Piraeus (12hr., 1 per day, 7100dr/€20.85); Chios (5hr., 4 per week, 3000dr/€8.80); Mykonos (6hr., 6 per week, 5400dr/€15.85); and Naxos (6hr., 3 per week, 5300dr/€15.55) via Paros (4500dr/€13.25). The **Tourist Office** is on a street one block before Pl. Pythagoras. (☎28 530. Open July-Aug. M-Sa 8:30am-2pm.) Turn right at the end of the ferry dock onto E. Stamatiadou, before the Hotel Aiolis, then take the second left and head uphill for the **Pension Trova,** Kalomiris 26, featuring traditionally furnished rooms, some with bath and balcony. (☎27 759. Singles 6000dr/€17.65; doubles 7000dr/€20.55.) Use the same directions, taking the second right instead of the second left to get to **Pension Avii,** Areos 2. (☎22 939. Summer only. Doubles 8000dr/€23.50.) **Postal Code:** 83100.

CHIOS (Χιος) ☎0271

Chios is where the wild things *were*: Orion hunted every last beast down, leaving the island's mountainsides to pine, cypress, and mastic trees. With increasing accessibility to its striking volcanic beaches and medieval villages, Chios flashes back to pre-Orion days, as tourists on the way to Çeşme do the Wild Thing all night long. **Pyrgi,** high in the hills 25km from Chios Town, is one of Greece's most striking villages, with fantastic black and white geometric designs covering its buildings. Farther south lies **Emborio beach,** where beige volcanic cliffs contrast with the black stones and deep-blue water below. **Green buses** in Chios Town make trips to Pyrgi and Emborio. **Ferries** go to from Chios Town to: Athens/Piraeus (8hr., 1-2 per day, 6300dr/€18.50); Lesvos (3hr., 1 per week, 3500dr/€10.30); Rhodes (1 per week, 7100dr/€20.85); and Samos (4hr., 1 per week, 3300dr/€9.70). To reach the **tourist office,** Kanari 18, turn off the waterfront onto Kanari, walk toward the *plateia* and look for the "i" sign. (☎44 344. Open May-Oct. daily 7am-10pm.) In a yellow building at the far right end of the waterfront, the hospitable owners at **Chios Rooms,** Leofores 114, offer bright and breezy rooms with polished hardwood floors, most with a sea view and some with bath. (☎20 198. Doubles 8000dr/€23.48; triples 10,000dr/€29.35, with bath 12,000dr/€35.25.) **Postal Code:** 82100.

LESVOS ☎0251

Once home to the sensual poet Sappho, Lesvos is still something of a grrl-power pilgrimage for lesbians paying homage to their legendary etymological roots. Lesvos's cosmopolitan, off-beat culture incorporates horse breeding, ouzo, and leftist politics with equal zeal. Huge, geographically diverse, and far from the mainland, the island attracts visitors who spend weeks exploring its therapeutic hot springs, monasteries, petrified forest, sandy beaches, mountain villages, and seaside cliffs,. Daytrippers may be overwhelmed; you'll need several days to get far beyond the main harbor. Most travelers pass through the modern **Mytilini,** the capital and central port city. Tucked away in a pine forest, the **Gattelusi Castle** stands guard above town. (Open Tu-Su 8:30am-3pm. 500dr/€1.50, EU students and under 18 free.) The enormous **Church of Ag. Therapon** presides over the fish market, while the new ▓**Archaeological Museum,** Argiri Eftalioti 7, houses an impressive collection of the island's archaeological finds. (Open daily 8am-7pm. 500dr/€1.50, students free.)

Ferries go to: Chios (3hr., 1-3 per day, 3600dr/€10.60); Limnos (5hr., 6 per week, 4800dr/€14.10); Piraeus (12hr., 1-3 per day, 7700dr/€22.60); Thessaloniki (12hr., 1 per week, 9000dr/€26.45). Book ferries at **NEL Lines,** Pavlou Koudoutrioti 67 (☎22 220), on the waterfront. The **tourist police,** in the corner of the ferry dock, offer maps and advice. (☎22 776. Open daily 7:15am-2:15pm and 5-8pm.) Mytilini has its fair share of enterprising residents, so *domatia* are plentiful and well advertised. You may also be met at the ferry. Be sure to negotiate; doubles should cost 7000-9000dr/€20.55-26.45. Take an intercity **bus** from the station behind Agios Irinis Park to the artist colonies of **Petra** and **Molyvos** (2hr., 4-5 per day, 1450dr/€4.30) and their popular beaches on the northern coast. The **Petra Women's Cooperative,** in the main square, will help with lodging. (☎41 238. Open daily 1-4pm and 6-11pm. Rooms

6000dr/€17.65 and up.) The monastery of **Agios Rafael,** in the hills of **Thermi,** remains a major pilgrimage site; travelers can stay two nights for free. Take the bus from Mytilini (45min., every 30min., 330dr/€1). **Postal Code:** 81100.

RHODES (Ροδος)   ☎0214

Although Rhodes is the undisputed tourism capital of the Dodecanese, the sandy beaches along its east coast, the jagged cliffs skirting its west coast, and the green mountains dotted with villages in the interior have retained a core of serenity. The island's most famous sight is one that doesn't exist, one that perhaps never existed: the **Colossus of Rhodes,** a 35m tall bronze statue of Helios and one of the seven wonders of the ancient world, which supposedly straddled the island's harbor but was allegedly destroyed by an earthquake in 237 BC. The beautiful, extant **City of Rhodes** has been the island's capital for over 2000 years. The **Old Town,** surrounded by remnants of the 14th-century occupation (by the Knights of St. John), lends the city a medieval flair. Begin exploring the Old Town at the top of the hill, where a tall, square tower marks the entrance to the pride of the city, the **Palace of the Grand Master,** with moats, drawbridges, battlements, and 300 rooms. (☎25 500. Open Tu-Su 8:30am-9pm, M 2:30-9pm. 1200dr/€3.55, students 600dr/€1.80.) Dominating one side of the **Plateia Argykastrou,** at the base of the waterfront, the former **Hospital of the Knights,** with beautiful halls and courtyards, is now the **Archaeological Museum.** Its treasures include the small but exquisite *Aphrodite Bathing* from the 1st century BC and the 4th-century *Apollo.* (☎25 500. Open T-F 8am-7pm, Sa-Su 8am-3:30pm. 800dr/€2.35, students and seniors 400dr/€1.20.) The **New Town** is a mecca for nightlife; **Orfanidou** is popularly known as **Bar Street.** Daytrips leave on **excursion boats** for **Faliraki,** south of the City of Rhodes and known for its rowdy drinkers and beach bunnies. See schedules and prices on the dock along the lower end of the Mandraki (from 3500dr/€10.30). **Buses** also run to Faliraki (17 per day, 500dr/€1.50) and Lindos (14 per day, 1050dr/€3.10).

 Ferries arrive in the Karpathos (3 per week, 4400dr/€12.91); Kos (1-2 per day, 4000dr/€11.75); Patmos (1-2 per day, 5400dr/€15.85); Peiraias/Athens (1-4 per day, 11,300dr/€33.20); Sitia, Crete (3 per week, 6400dr/€18.78) and Samos (1 per week, 6500dr/€19.10). A **Greek National Tourist Office (EOT)** is up Papgou, a few blocks from Pl. Rimini, at Makariou. (☎23 255. Open M-F 7:30am-3pm.) ▓**Rhodes Youth Hostel,** Ergiou 12, packed with interesting young travellers from around the world. Turn off Sokratous onto the tiny side street next to the run-down building that looks like a mosque. Keep on walking and take a right at the "youth hostel" sign; the hostel will be on the left. (☎30 491. Dorms 2000-2500dr/€5.90-7.35). Snooze in the New Town at the **New Village Inn,** Konstantopedos 10. (☎34 937. Singles 6000dr/€17.65; doubles 12,000dr/€35.25.) Sensuous aromas of traditional Hellenic dishes waft from ▓**Chalki,** Kathopouli 30. Entrees (including fabulous moussaka) cost around 1800dr/€5.30. (Open daily noon-3pm and 6pm-midnight.)

KARPATHOS (Καρπαθος)   ☎0245

Midway between Rhodes and Crete, windy Karpathos often receives no more than a passing glance from the deck of an overnight ferry, but the charming island and its gorgeous towns are well worth a stop. Words can't convey the isolation of the town of **Olympus,** where preservation of centuries-old customs makes the town itself Olympus's greatest sight. Other points of interest include the three 13th-and 14th-century churches, the oldest on Karpathos, located conveniently near the bus stop. **Buses** from **Chrisovalandu Lines** and **Karpathos 1** run bus daily excursions to **Olympus** (depart 8:30am, return 6pm; 3500-5000dr/€10.30-14.70); find them near the ferry docks, or make reservations through Possi Travel (☎(0245) 22 235). **Ferries** arrive in Pigadia (Karpathos Town) from: Kassos (1½hr., 3 per week, 1900dr/€5.60); Rhodes (5hr., 3 per week, 4600dr/€13.50); and Santorini (12hr., 1 per week, 8,000dr/€23.50). From the bus station, walk past the supermarket to reach ▓**Ellas Rooms for Rent,** where rooms are quiet and centrally located. (☎(0245) 22 446. Singles 5000-6000dr/€14.70-17.65; doubles 6000-8000dr/€17.65-23.50; triples 9000dr/€26.50).

KOS (Κως)   ☎0242

Although it rivals Rhodes in sheer tourist numbers, Kos tends to draw a younger, louder, and more intoxicated crowd. Don't be dismayed by the raucous bars and mammoth hotels lining the golden beaches—perseverance rewards those who take the time to explore Kos's quiet nooks and scattered ruins. In **Kos Town,** minarets of Ottoman mosques rise among grand Italian mansions. The ancient sanctuary of ▧**Asclepion,** 4km west of Kos Town, is dedicated to the god of healing. (Open Tu-Su 8am-6:30pm. 800dr/€2.35, students 400dr/€1.20.) In the 5th century BC, Hippocrates opened the world's first medical school here to foster the development of medical science. From the lowest *andiron* (level), steps lead to the 2nd-century AD **Temple of Apollo** and 4th-century BC **Minor Temple of Asclepios.** Sixty steps lead to the third *andiron,* with the forested remains of the **Main Temple of Asclepios** and a spectacular view of the ruins, Kos Town, and the Turkish coast. The site is also easily reached by **bus** (15min., 16 per day, 150-250dr/€0.45-0.75). The island's best **beaches** stretch along Southern Kos to Kardamene, all accessible by bus on request.

Ferries run to Patmos (4hr., 1-2 per day, 3200dr/€9.45); Piraeus/Athens (11-15hr., 2-3 per day, 5200dr/€15.29); and Rhodes (4hr., 2 per day, 4200dr/€12.35). A **Greek National Tourist Office** on Akti Miaouli provides visitors with maps, brochures, and schedules. (☎24 460. Open M-F 8am-8pm, Sa 8am-3pm.) Take the first right off Megalou Alexandrou, on the back left corner of the first intersection, to get to ▧**Pension Alexis,** Herodotou 9. (☎28 798. Doubles 5500-8500dr/€16.20-25; triples 9000-10,000dr/€26.50-29.45). **Hotel Afendoulis,** Evrilpilou 1, is near the beach. (☎25 321. Doubles 7500-12,000dr/€22.10-35.30.) Most bars are located in either in **Exarhia,** known as the area's **bar street,** between Akti Koundouriotou and the more subdued **Porfiriou,** in the north. **Fashion Club,** Kanari 2, is the hottest spot in town. (Cover 3000dr/€8.80, includes 1 drink.) The **Haman Club,** near the *agora,* is a former bathhouse turned hopping dance club. **Heaven,** on Zouroudi along the waterfront, is loud and divinely popular. (Cover 2000dr/€5.90, includes 1 drink.) **Postal Code:** 85300.

PATMOS (Πατμος)   ☎0247

In ancient times, Patmians worshipped Artemis, the huntress said to have raised the island from the sea. With the arrival of St. John, exiled from Ephesus, Patmos became a center of fledgling Christianity. Declared the "Holy Island" by ministerial decree, Patmos makes its historical and religious significance as plain as day—portside signs warn that nudity and other indecent behavior will not be tolerated here. The white houses of **Hora** and the majestic walls of the sprawling **Monastery of St. John the Theologian** above are visible from all over the island. (Monastery and **treasure museum** open daily 8am-1pm as well as T, Th, Su 4-6pm. Treasury 1200dr/€3.55; monastery free. Dress modestly.) Hora is 4km from the colorful port town of **Skala;** take a **bus** (10min., 11 per day, 400dr/€1.20) or **taxi** (1000dr/€2.95) from Skala; alternately, tackle the steep hike. Between Skala and the Monastery of St. John in Hora, the **Apocalypsis monastery** is built on the site where St. John stayed while on Patmos. It houses the natural cave, the **Sacred Grotto of the Revelation,** where St. John dictated the last book of the New Testament, the *Book of Revelation.* (Open daily 8am-1pm; also T, Th, Su 4-6pm. Free. Dress modestly.)

Ferries arrive in Skala from: Kos (4hr., 3000dr/€8.85) and Rhodes (9hr., 5800dr/€17.10). The **tourist office** is opposite the dock. (☎31 666. Open daily 7am-2:30pm and 4-9pm.) A battalion of locals greets the plethora of early morning boats each day, offering *domatia* (singles 5000-7000dr/€14.75-20.60; doubles 7000-10,000dr/€20.60-29.45). To get to **Flower Stefanos Camping at Meloi,** 2km northeast of Skala, 3m behind Meloi Beach, follow the waterfront road past Apollon Travel as it wraps along the port and up the hill. Camping is on the left at the bottom—look for signs. (☎31 821. 1400dr/€4.15 per person; 800dr/€2.35 for tent rental.)

REPUBLIC OF IRELAND
AND NORTHERN IRELAND

IRELAND

PUNTS OR POUNDS

US$1 = IR£0.86	IR£1 = US$1.16
CDN$1 = IR£0.56	IR£1 = CDN$1.79
UK£1 = IR£1.25	IR£1 = UK£0.80
AUS$1 = IR£0.46	IR£1 = AUS$2.17
NZ$1 = IR£0.38	IR£1 = NZ$2.65
ZAR1 = IR£0.10	IR£1 = ZAR9.62
EUR€1 = IR£0.79	IR£1 = EUR€1.27

PHONE CODE	**Country Code:** 353 (Republic); 44 (Northern Ireland; dial 048 from the Republic). **International dialing prefix:** 00.

The Emerald Isle (pop. 3.8 million; 70,280 sq. km), so named for its luminous green-ery, has retained a natural charm over thousands of years. Windswept scenery curls around the coast, and mountains punctuate interior bogland expanses. Dublin and Belfast, suffused with sophistication, have flowered into cosmopolitan cities. How-ever, like its natural beauty, centuries-old disputes refuse to die. The English sup-pressed the Catholic population after the Reformation and fighting degenerated into civil war. The Free State proclaimed itself the independent Republic of Ireland (Éire) in 1949, while the Brits kept control of Northern Ireland. Years of violent turmoil ended with a peace accord in 1998. Although the **Republic of Ireland** and **Northern Ireland** are grouped together for geographical reasons, don't infer a political statement. For info on Northern Ireland's currency exchange rates, etc., see Britain, p. 140. For further coverage of Ireland, snag a copy of *Let's Go: Ireland 2002*.

SUGGESTED ITINERARIES

THREE DAYS Ah, all Dublin (p. 553). Head to the gates of **Trinity College,** admire the **Book of Kells,** then chat up folks at the **Guinness Hopstore** or the **Old Jameson Distillery.** Spend a day at the **National Museums,** stopping to relax on **St. Stephen's Green.** Check out the **James Joyce Centre** and then fulfill your pubbing potential in **Temple Bar** and **Grafton St.**

ONE WEEK From **Dublin** (2 days) head to complex **Belfast** (1 days, p. 584). Catch the bus to **Giant's Causeway** (1 day, p. 592) and ride to **Galway** (1 day, p. 578), for artsy student vibes. Admire the romantic countryside in the **Ring of**
Kerry (1 day, p. 574) and return to civili-zation in **Cork** (1 day, p. 568).

BEST OF IRELAND, THREE WEEKS Land in **Dublin** (4 days) before taking the train up to **Belfast** (3 days). Catch the bus to **Giant's Causeway** (1 day), and stop at **Derry** (2 days, p. 590). From **Donegal Town** (1 day, p. 582), climb **Slieve League** (1 day, p. 582), the high-est seacliffs in Europe. Use **Sligo** (3 days, p. 582) as a springpoint to County Sligo's lakes and mountains. From there, head to **Galway** (2 days), the **Ring of Kerry** (2 days), **Killarney National Park** (1 day, p. 573), and **Cork** (1 day). On your way back to Dublin, take a detour to medieval **Kilkenny** (1 day, p. 567).

LIFE AND TIMES

HISTORY AND POLITICS

PRE-CHRISTIAN IRELAND (7000 BC TO AD 450)

What little knowledge historians have of ancient Irish culture they have ascertained from the fragile and spotty remains of its stone structures, landscaping, and metalware. Ireland's first settlers came from Britain in about 7000 BC, leaving behind various structures that may be identified today on the Irish landscape. **Dolmens,** table-like arrangements of enormous stones, were probably created as shrines. **Passage graves** are underground stone hallways and chambers containing corpses and urns.

In the first two centuries of the Bronze Age (900-700 BC), known as the Irish Golden Age, Irish culture flowered, due in part to the central position held by warrior nobles in Atlantic trade routes between Gibraltar and Sweden. The Celts began migrating to Ireland from central Europe around 600 BC, and kept coming for the next 600 years. The chariot warriors, the Uliad of Ulster, the most famous Irish chieftains, dominated Celtic culture from their capital near Armagh.

EARLY CHRISTIANS AND VIKINGS (450-1200)

Ireland was Christianized in a piecemeal fashion by a series of hopeful missionaries starting with **St. Patrick** in the 5th century. According to legend, St. Patrick was born in England and kidnapped into Irish slavery as a boy, from which he escaped and ventured back to England. He later returned to Ireland at the command of a prophetic vision, and legend has it that he drove the snakes of Ireland into the sea, and envisioned the **Holy Trinity**—three Persons in one God—as the three-leaved **Shamrock.** As barbarians overran the continent, monks, seeking safety, began arriving in Ireland. The enormous **monastic cities** of the 6th to 8th centuries earned Ireland its reputation as the "land of saints and scholars." From their bases in Armagh, Glendalough (see p. 566), Derry (see p. 590), and elsewhere, the monastics of the Early Irish Church recorded the old epics, wrote long religious and legal (really) poems in Old Irish and Latin, and illuminated gospels.

In the first decade of the new millennium, strife broke out amongst the chieftains: High King **Brian Boru** and his warlike **Dal Cais** clan of Clare challenged the **Uí Neíll** clan for control of Ireland with the capture of Armagh in 1002. In the following years, the clans fought ferociously amongst themselves. The Dal Cais won a pyrrhic victory against the Vikings in the epic **Battle of Clontarf,** fought near Dublin in 1014, in which Brian Boru was lost. In a prelude to 20th-century strife, Ireland was then divided in two between chieftains **Rory O'Connor** and **Dermot MacMurrough,** who continued fighting for the crown of High King. Dermot made a regrettable mistake by seeking the assistance of English Norman nobles in reconquering Leinster. Richard de Clare, known popularly as **Strongbow,** was all too willing to help. Strongbow and his Anglo-Normans arrived in 1169 and cut a bloody swath through south Leinster (eastern and southeastern Ireland). Strongbow married Dermot's daughter **Aoife** after Dermot's death in 1171 and seemed ready to proclaim an independent Norman kingdom in Ireland. Instead, the turncoat affirmed his loyalty to King Henry II and generously offered to govern Leinster on England's behalf. Thus began English domination over Irish land. The 7th-century **Book of Durrow,** the earliest surviving illuminated manuscript, and the early 9th century **Book of Kells** (known for its delicate, ornate script), are now exhibited at Trinity College, Dublin (see p. 560).

FEUDALISM (1200-1641)

The following feudal period saw constant struggles between English lords of Gaelic and Norman descent. Over in England, the Crown fretted over the spread of Irish culture, and in 1366 it sponsored the notorious **Statutes of Kilkenny.** These banned English colonists (dubbed "more Irish than the Irish themselves") from speaking Irish, wearing Irish dress, or marrying native Irish; it also forbade the Irish from entering walled cities, which was fine, because London was already dirty anyway.

Ireland:
Republic of Ireland and Northern Ireland

0 ____ 30 miles

0 ____ 30 kilometers

N

The English Crown increased its control over Ireland throughout the next century. When **Henry VIII** broke with the Catholic Church to create the Church of England, a newly convened Dublin Parliament passed the 1537 **Irish Supremacy Act,** which declared Henry head of the Protestant **Church of Ireland,** and effectively made the island property of the Crown. In defiance of the monarchy, **Hugh O'Neill,** an Ulster earl, raised an army of thousands in open rebellion in the late 1590s, supported by Gaelic lords. Their forces soon demolished, O'Neil & Co. soared out of Ireland in 1607 in what came to be known as the **Flight of the Earls.** They promised to come back with assistance from forces of Catholic rulers on the continent, but never returned. The English took control of land, and parceled it out to Protestants.

PLANTATION AND CROMWELL (1641-1688)
The English project of dispossessing Catholics of their land and "planting" Ireland with Protestants was most successful in Ulster. The project in the north became known as the **Ulster Plantation.** In response, the now landless Irish natives rebelled

in Ulster in 1641 under a loose group of Gaelic-Irish leaders. Inheriting his uncle's rebellion business, **Owen Roe O'Neill** returned from the Continent to lead the insurrection, and the uprising even received the backing of the Catholic Church. The rebels advanced south, and, in 1642 they formed the **Confederation of Kilkenny,** an uneasy alliance of the Church and Irish and Old English lords. Negotiations between the Confederation and King Charles ended with **Oliver Cromwell**'s victory in England and his arrival in Ireland. Cromwell's army destroyed anything they did not occupy and then some, massacring Catholics, razing entire towns, and divvying up confiscated lands among Protestants and his soldiers. The native Irish landowners had the options of going "to hell or to Connacht," the desolate and infertile region in Ireland's west. By 1660, the vast majority of Irish land was owned, maintained, and policed by Protestant immigrants.

THE PROTESTANT ASCENDANCY (1688-1798)

Thirty years after the English Civil War, English political disruption again resulted in Irish bloodshed. Deposed Catholic monarch **James II,** driven from England by the "Glorious Revolution" of 1688, came to Ireland with his army, intending to gather military support to reclaim his throne. A war between **William of Orange** (the new Protestant king) and James ended on July 12, 1690 at the **Battle of the Boyne,** with James's defeat and exile, giving Protestants an excuse to hold annual parades. The war's end delivered the **Treaty of Limerick** that ambiguously promised Catholics undelivered civil rights. Instead, the **Penal Laws,** enacted at the turn of the 18th century, further limited Catholic rights, and banned the public practice of their religion at a time when Catholics comprised 90 percent of the island's population.

The newly secure Anglo-Irish elite built their own culture in Dublin and elsewhere with garden parties, gossip, and architecture second only to London. The term **Ascendancy** was coined to describe a social elite whose distinction depended upon Anglicanism. Within this exclusive social structure, such thinkers as **Bishop George Berkeley, Edmund Burke,** and **Jonathan Swift** rose to prominence. **Trinity College** (see p. 560) flourished as the quintessential institution of the Ascendancy.

REBELLION, UNION, REACTION (1798-1847)

The American and French Revolutions inspired notions of independence in small political organizations such as the **United Irishmen.** Their Protestant leader, **Theobald Wolfe Tone,** hoped that a general uprising would create an independent, non-sectarian Ireland. A bloody revolt of peasants and priests erupted in May 1798. The rebels made their last stand at **Vinegar Hill,** near Enniscorthy in County Wexford and they fell in the thousands. The 1801 **Act of Union** dissolved the Dublin Parliament and created "The United Kingdom of Great Britain and Ireland;" the Church of Ireland was subsumed by the "United Church of England and Ireland."

THE FAMINE (1847-1870)

In the first half of the 19th century, the potato was the only crop capable of providing enough nutrients per acre to support the Irish population. The **Great Famine,** resulting from potato blight, lasted roughly from 1847-51. In that short period of time, an estimated two to three million people died. While the Irish were either emigrating to the US or eating grass in their homeland, they were forced to export grain and meat from the island because they simply couldn't afford to buy it themselves. British authorities often forcibly exchanged what few decent potatoes peasants could find with inedible grain. This injustice fueled the formation of more angry, young nationalist groups. In 1858, James Stephens founded the Irish Republican Brotherhood (IRB), commonly known as the **Fenians,** a secret (and later not-so-secret) society aimed at the violent removal of the British.

PARNELL'S CULTURAL NATIONALISM (1870-1914)

In 1870, Isaac Butt founded the **Irish Home Rule Party,** bent on securing autonomous rule for Ireland. They practiced revolution by tedium; members filibustered and (legally) obstructed parliament to bore the Dickens out of the ruling party and make British rule ineffective. Home Ruler **Charles Stewart Parnell** was a charismatic Protestant aristocrat with an American mother and a hatred for everything English. Backed by Parnell's invigorated Irish party, William Gladstone introduced a **Home Rule Bill,** which was defeated. Meanwhile, various groups tried to revive what they took to be essential "Gaelic" culture, unpolluted by foreign influence. Arthur Griffin began a fledgling movement and little-read newspaper, both of which went by the name **Sinn Féin** (meaning "Ourselves Alone"). As the Home Rule movement grew, so did resistance to it. Between 1910 and 1913, thousands of Northern Protestants opposing Home Rule joined mass rallies, signed a covenant, and organized into a quasi-militia named the **Ulster Volunteer Force (UVF).** Nationalists led by **Eoin MacNeill** in Dublin responded in 1913 by creating the **Irish Volunteers.**

THE EASTER RISING (1914-1919)

In the summer of 1914, Irish Home Rule seemed imminent and Ulster ready to go up in flames, but neither happened—**World War I** did instead. British Prime Minister Henry Asquith passed a **Home Rule Bill** on the condition that the Irish Volunteer and Home Rule parties would recruit Irishmen for the British army to fight on the continent. An 11,000-member armed guard of Volunteers remained behind in Ireland. They were officially led by MacNeill, who knew nothing of the planned Fenians revolt. If one man can be ascribed to the ensuing mayhem, it was **Padraig Pearse,** who won his co-conspirators over to an ideology of "blood sacrifice"—the public, violent martyrdom of a small Irish group to provoke the whole nation to rebel.

Fenian leaders were planning to receive a shipment of German arms for use in a nationwide revolt on **Easter Sunday, 1916.** The arms arrived a day too early and were never picked up. The British captured and hanged **Roger Casement,** the man who was to meet the shipment. Fenian leaders, however, continued planning their rebellion and mustering support from the Volunteers. On Monday, April 24, in Dublin, Pearse, fellow nationalist James Connolly, and about 1000 others seized the **General Post Office** on O'Connell St. (see p. 562), read aloud a "Proclamation of the Republic of Ireland," and held on through five days of fighting in downtown Dublin.

The harsh reaction of the British martial-law administration to Easter Sunday turned popular opinion on its head; over 10 days in May, 15 "ringleaders" received the death sentence. In 1917, the Volunteers reorganized under master spy and Fenian bigwig **Michael Collins.** The Sinn Féin party, falsely associated with the Easter Rising, became the political voice of military Nationalism. Collins brought the Volunteers to Sinn Féin, and **Éamon de Valera** became the party president.

INDEPENDENCE AND CIVIL WAR (1919-1922)

Extremist Irish Volunteers became known as the **Irish Republican Army (IRA),** which functioned as the military arm of the Sinn Féin government. The new government fought the **War of Independence** (1919-1921) against the British, which met with much success. Hurried negotiations produced the **Anglo-Irish Treaty,** which created a 26-county Irish Free State while recognizing British rule over the northern counties. British Prime Minister **Lloyd George** pushed the treaty forward by threatening more war if it was rejected. Sinn Féin, the IRA, and the population each split on whether to accept the treaty. Collins said yes; de Valera said no. When the representative parliament voted in favor, de Valera resigned from the presidency and **Arthur Griffith** assumed the position. The capable Griffith and Collins government began the business of setting up a nation, with treasury, tax collection, a foreign ministry, and an unarmed police force. A portion of the IRA, led by **General Rory O'Connor,** opposed the treaty. O'Connor's Republicans occupied the Four Courts in Dublin, took a pro-treaty Army general hostage, and were attacked by the forces of Collins's government. Two years of **civil war** followed, tearing up the countryside and dividing the population. The pro-treaty government won, but Griffith died suddenly (from the strain of the struggle), and Collins was assassinated before the end of 1922. The dwindling minority of anti-treaty IRA officers went into hiding.

THE DE VALERA ERA (1922-1960)

The new 26-county Irish Free State emerged from civil war having lost its most prominent leaders and needing to protect those ministers who remained. The Anglo-Irish Treaty required the newly elected **Dáil** (the powerful Irish lower house) to frame a constitution by December 6, 1922. Under de Valera's renewed guidance, the government ended armed resistance by May 1923, imprisoned Republican insurgents, and executed 77 of them. Then in 1927 de Valera broke with Sinn Féin and the IRA and founded his own political party, **Fianna Fáil,** in order to participate in government and oppose the treaty nonviolently. Fianna Fáil won the 1932 election, and de Valera held power for much of the next 20 years. "In the name of the most Holy Trinity," de Valera and the voters approved the Irish Constitution in 1937. It declares the state's name to be Éire, and establishes the country's legislative structure, consisting of two chambers with five-year terms. The constitution originally contained a "special position" clause concerning the **Catholic Church** in Ireland. The clause was deleted by constitutional amendment in 1972.

Ireland maintained neutrality during **World War II,** despite German Air raids on Dublin and pressure from US President Franklin Roosevelt. In spite of their officially neutral status, many Irish citizens identified with the Allies, and approximately 50,000 served in the British army. The Fine Gael government under **John Costello** in 1948 had the honor of officially proclaiming "The Republic of Ireland," and supposedly ending British Commonwealth membership. Britain recognized the Republic in 1949 but declared that the UK would maintain control over Ulster until the Parliament of **Northern Ireland** consented to join the Republic.

RECENT HISTORY (1960-1990)

By reaching out beyond its borders, Ireland has kept its youth from being quite so disaffected and willing to leave. In the 1960s, increased contact with the rest of the world slowed emigration and accelerated economic growth. In 1967, the government introduced free secondary education, including state grants for privately owned schools; in 1968, it introduced free university education for those below a certain income level. Ireland entered the European Economic Community, now the **European Union** (EU), in 1973. In 1990, the Republic broke progressive social and political ground when it elected its first female president, **Mary Robinson.** Social reform made further gains when the small, leftist **Labour Party** enjoyed enormous and unexpected success in the 1992 elections. In September of 1993, a coalition of the Labour Party and Fianna Fáil was elected. The new Taoiseach, or Prime Minister, **Albert Reynolds,** declared that his top priority was to stop violence in Northern Ireland. In August 1994, he announced the nearly miraculous cease-fire agreement with Sinn Féin and the IRA. In June 1997, Fianna Fáil won the general election, making **Bertie Ahern,** the 45-year-old party leader, the youngest Taoiseach in the history of the state. Ahern joined the peace talks that produced the **Northern Ireland Peace Agreement** in April of 1998. On May 22, 1998, in the first island-wide election since 1918, 94% of voters in the Republic voted for the enactment of the Agreement.

IRELAND TODAY

As Ireland becomes more active in the global economy, the nation struggles to balance its traditionally conservative values with increasingly liberal international standards. Ireland's economy is booming, in large part due to increased foreign investment over the past decade. Relatively few regulations and huge incentives have drawn foreign investors, strengthening the currency and boosting Ireland's economy at one of Europe's fastest rates. There is some concern about economic overheating, and the effects of converting to the **Euro** (common EU currency) as Irish Pounds will be completely phased out as of February 28, 2002. As more young Irish spend time abroad and more international travelers spend time in Ireland, the culture's conservatism slowly cracks. While eager to dispel the picturesque stereotype of the "land of saints and scholars" (and poverty and drunkenness), the Irish hope to retain the safety afforded by their religious and family-oriented past.

THE ARTS

LITERATURE

EARLY WORKS. In long-colonized Dublin, **Jonathan Swift** wrote some of the most sophisticated, misanthropic, and marvelous satire in the English language. Besides his masterpiece *Gulliver's Travels* (1726), Swift wrote political essays decrying English cruelty to the native Irish, as well as the deliciously moribund satire *A Modest Proposal*, prompted by the deplorable state of Dublin slums. Dublin-born **Oscar Wilde** moved to London and set up as an aesthete to write one novel and many witty plays, including *The Importance of Being Earnest* (1895). Fellow Dubliner and playwright **George Bernard Shaw** also moved to London, where he became an active socialist. The prolific Shaw won the Nobel Prize for Literature in 1925.

THE IRISH LITERARY REVIVAL. Members of this early 20th-century movement turned to Irish culture, from its ancient mythology to contemporary folktales, for inspiration. The poems of **William Butler Yeats** created an Ireland of loss and legend that won him worldwide fame and a 1923 Nobel Prize. **John Millington Synge** lightheartedly portrayed the complexity of Irish village life in his plays, including *The Playboy of the Western World* (1907)

MODERNISM. The most famous of Ireland's expatriates is **James Joyce;** his novels are recognized as some of the seminal works of Modernism. His first-string novel, *A Portrait of the Artist as a Young Man* (1914), uses the protagonist Stephen Daedalus to describe Joyce's own youth in Dublin. Daedalus reappears in *Ulysses*, Joyce's revolutionary novel of 1922. *Ulysses*—structurally based on Homer's *Odyssey*—chronicles one day in the life of the antihero, Leopold Bloom, a middle-class Jewish man living his life in a stagnating Dublin. **Samuel Beckett**'s world-famous plays (including *Waiting for Godot* and *Endgame;* all written 1946-1950) convey a deathly pessimism about language, society, and life. Beckett won the Nobel Prize in 1969, but refused acceptance because Joyce had never received it.

MODERN WRITERS IN NORTHERN IRELAND. Much of the literature of Northern Ireland describes two culturally divided groups, Catholics and Protestants. Many Northern writers attempt to create works of relevance to members of both communities. Born in rural County Derry, **Seamus Heaney** was awarded the Nobel Prize for literature in 1995, and is the most prominent living Irish poet. His subject matter ranges from bogs to bombings to archeological remains. While his tone is often highly lyrical, Heaney writes in an anti-pastoral mode.

FOOD AND DRINK

Food in Ireland is expensive, but the basics are simple and filling. "Take-away" (takeout) **fish and chips** shops are quick, greasy, and very popular. Many pubs serve food as well as drink; typical pub grub includes **Irish stew,** burgers, soup, and sandwiches. **Soda bread** is delicious and keeps well, and Irish dairy products are addictive. Pubs in Ireland are the forum for banter, singing, and *craic* (a good time). In the evenings, many pubs play impromptu or organized traditional music, known as *trad*. **Guinness,** a rich, dark stout, is revered in Ireland with a zeal usually only reserved for the Holy Trinity. Known as "the dark stuff" or "the blonde in the black skirt," it was once recommended as food for pregnant mothers, and has a head thick enough to stand a match in—it's also better in Ireland than anywhere else. **Irish whiskey,** which Queen Elizabeth once claimed was her only true Irish friend, is sweeter than its Scotch counterpart. Irish monks invented whiskey, calling it *uisce beatha*, meaning "water of life." **Pubs** are usually open Monday to Saturday 10:30am to 11 or 11:30pm, Sundays 12:30 to 2pm and 4 to 11pm.

ESSENTIALS

DOCUMENTS AND FORMALITIES

Citizens of Australia, Canada, European Union countries, New Zealand, South Africa, the United Kingdom, and the United States do not need **visas** to visit Ireland for stays shorter than three months.

Irish Embassies at Home: Australia, 20 Arkana St., Yarralumla, Canberra ACT 2600 (☎(02) 6273 3022). **Canada,** 130 Albert St., Ottawa, K1P 5G4 (☎613-233-6281). **New Zealand** (Consulate General), Dingwall Bldg., 6th Fl., 18 Shortland St. 1001, Auckland 1 (☎(09) 302 2867). **South Africa,** Tubach Centre, 1234 Church St., 0083 Colbyn, Pret. (☎(012) 342 5062). **UK,** 17 Grosvenor Pl., London SW1X 7HR (☎(020) 7235 2171). **US,** Irish Embassy, 2234 Massachusetts Ave. NW, Washington, D.C. 20008 (☎202-462-3939).

Foreign Embassies in Ireland: All embassies for the Republic of Ireland are in **Dublin** (see p. 553). The US has a consulate in **Belfast** (see p. 584).

TRANSPORTATION

BY PLANE. Flying to London and connecting to Ireland is often easier and cheaper than flying direct. **Aer Lingus** and several other carriers offer service on these routes. **British Midland Airways** (in the UK ☎(01332) 854 000, in the Republic ☎(01) 814 4259; www.flybmi.com); flies about seven times per day to London Heathrow. **British Airways** (in the UK ☎(0845) 779 9977; in the Republic ☎800 626 747; in the US ☎800-AIRWAYS (800 249-297); www.british-airways.com) flies into most Irish airports at least daily and into some Irish airports many, many times a day. Prices range from UK£75-225 round-trip but can drop from time to time. **Ryanair** (in the UK ☎(0870) 333 1250; in the Republic ☎(01) 609 7800) connects Kerry, Cork, and Knock to London and more than nine other destinations in England and Scotland. In London, the **Air Travel Advisory Bureau** (☎(020) 7636 5000; www.atab.co.uk) will put you in touch with the cheapest carriers out of London.

BY TRAIN. **Iarnród Éireann** (Irish Rail) is useful only for travel to urban areas. While the **Eurailpass** is not accepted in Northern Ireland, it *is* accepted on trains (but not buses) in the Republic. The BritRail Pass does not cover travel in Northern Ireland, but the month-long **BritRail+Ireland** works in both the North and the Republic with rail options and round-trip ferry service between Britain and Ireland (US$399-569). **Northern Ireland Railways** (☎(028) 9033 3000; www.nirailways.co.uk) is not extensive but covers the northeastern coastal region well. The major line connects Dublin to Belfast. A valid **Northern Ireland Travelsave** stamp (UK£7, affixed to back of ISIC) saves you up to 33% off all trains and 15% discounts on bus fares over UK£1.45 within Northern Ireland. The **Freedom of Northern Ireland** ticket allows unlimited travel by train and Ulsterbus and can be purchased for 7 consecutive days (UK£40), 3 out of 8 days (IR£27.50/€35), or a single day (IR£11/€14).

BY BUS. Bus Éireann (the Irish national bus company) reaches Britain and even the continent by working in conjunction with ferry services and the bus company **Eurolines** (UK ☎(0990) 143 219; www.eurolines.com). Most buses leave from Victoria Station in London (to Belfast: 14hr., UK£42, round-trip UK£60; Dublin: 12hr., UK£28, round-trip UK£44), but other major city stops include Birmingham, Bristol, Cardiff, Glasgow, and Liverpool. Services run to Cork, Derry, Galway, Limerick, Waterford, and Tralee, among others. Prices given are for adult fares during the summer. Cheaper fares are available in the off-season, as well as for children (under 13), young people (under 26), and seniors (60+). Tickets can be booked through any Bus Éireann office, Irish Ferries, Stena Line, any Eurolines office or **National Express** (☎(0990) 808 080) office in Britain. Contact the Bus Éireann Inquiries desk in Dublin (☎(01) 836 6111) or a travel agent for more information.

Buses in the Republic of Ireland reach many more destinations and are less expensive than trains. Return (round-trip) tickets are always a great value. For

IRELAND

students, purchasing a **TravelSave** stamp along with your ISIC gets you discounts on bus travel. A combined **Irish Explorer Rail/Bus** ticket allows unlimited travel on trains and buses for 8 of 15 consecutive days (IR£124/€157.50, child IR£62/€78.75) or 15 of 30 consecutive days (£214/€271.70, £107/€135.85). **Ulsterbus** (☎ (028) 9033 3000, Belfast ☎ (028) 9032 0011; www.ulsterbus.co.uk) runs extensive and reliable routes throughout Northern Ireland, where there are no private bus services. A **Freedom of Northern Ireland** bus and rail pass provides extended travel; see **By Train,** above. The **Irish Rover** pass covers both Bus Éireann and Ulsterbus services (unlimited travel for 3 of 8 days £42/€53.35, child £21/€26.70; for 8 of 15 days £93/€118.10, £47/€59.70; for 15 of 30 £145/€184.10, £73/€92.70). The **Emerald Card** offers unlimited travel on Ulsterbus; Northern Ireland Railways; Bus Éireann Expressway, Local, and City services in Dublin, Cork, Limerick, Galway, and Waterford; intercity, DART, and suburban rail Iarnród Éireann services. The card works for eight out of 15 consecutive days (£124/€157.50, child £62/€78.75) or 15 out of 30 consecutive days (£214/€271.70, £107/€135.85).

BY FERRY. Ferries (more economical than air travel) journey between Britain and Ireland several times per day; tickets usually range IR£18-£35/€23-45. Traveling mid-week at night promises the cheapest fares. **An Óige (HI) members** receive up to a 20% discount on fares from Irish Ferries and Stena Sealink. Almost all sailings in the summer are "controlled sailings," which means that you must book the crossing in advance (a few days is usually sufficient). **ISIC-holders** with the **TravelSave** receive a 15% discount from Irish Ferries and an average 17% discount on StenaLine ferries. Ferries run from **Cork** to **South Wales** and **Roscoff, France** (see p. 568) and from **Rosslare Harbour** to **Pembroke, Wales** and **Roscoff** and **Cherbourg, France.**

BY CAR. Drivers in Ireland use the **left side of the road,** and their steering-wheels are on the right side of the car. **Petrol prices** are high. Be particularly cautious at roundabouts (rotary interchanges)—give way to traffic from the right. Irish law requires drivers and passengers to wear **seat belts.** People under 21 cannot rent cars, and those under 23 (or even 25) often encounter difficulties. Prices range from IR£100-300/€127-381 (plus VAT) per week with insurance and unlimited mileage. If you plan to drive a car while in Ireland for longer than a three-month period, you must have an International Driving Permit (IDP). If you rent, lease, or borrow a car, you will need a **green card, or International Insurance Certificate.**

BY BIKE, FOOT, AND THUMB. Ireland's mountains, fields, and heather-covered hills make **walking and hiking** an arduous joy. The **Wicklow Way** has hostels designed for hikers within a day's walk of each other. The **Ulster Way** encircles Northern Ireland with 900km of marked trails. *Let's Go* does not recommend hitchhiking. Those who do hitch say that much of Ireland's countryside is well-suited for it. Single-digit N roads in the Republic are more busily trafficked; try to avoid them. Hitching on M roads in the North is illegal. Locals in Northern Ireland do not recommend hitching.

TOURIST SERVICES & MONEY

EMERGENCY | Police, ☎ 999. Ambulance, ☎ 999. Fire, ☎ 999.

TOURIST OFFICES. Bord Fáilte (the **Irish Tourist Board**) operates a nationwide network of offices. Most tourist offices book rooms for a small fee (IR£1-3/€1.30-3.85) and a 10% deposit, but many fine hostels and B&Bs are not "approved," so the tourist office can't tell you about them. Bord Fáilte's central office is at Baggot St. Bridge, **Dublin** 2, in Ireland (☎ (01850) 230 330; www.ireland.travel.ie.)

The **Northern Ireland Tourist Board** offers similar services at locations all over the North. The head office is at 59 North St., Belfast, BT1 1NB, Northern Ireland (☎ 028 9023 1221; www.discovernorthernireland.com). The Dublin office is at 16 Nassau St., Dublin 2 (☎ (01) 679 1977; CallSave ☎ (1850) 230 230).

IRELAND

Irish Tourist Boards at Home: Australia, Level 5, 36 Carrington St., Sydney NSW 2000 (☎(02) 9299 6177). **Canada,** 120 Eglington Ave. E., Ste. 500, Toronto, ON, M4P 1E2 (☎800-223-6470). **UK,** 150 New Bond St., London W1Y 0AQ (☎7493 3201).

Northern Ireland Tourist Boards at Home: Australia, 36 Carrington St., 5th Fl., Sydney NSW 2000 (☎(02) 9299 6177). **Canada,** 2 Bloor St. W., Ste. 1501, Toronto, ON, M4W 3E2 (☎416-925-6368). **UK,** 24 Haymarket, London SW1 4DG (☎020 7766 9920). **US,** 551 5th Ave., #701, New York, NY 10176 (☎800-326-0036).

CURRENCY AND EXCHANGE. Legal tender in the Republic of Ireland is the **Irish pound** (or **"punt"**), denoted IR£. It comes in the same denominations as the **British pound** (which is called **"sterling"** in Ireland) but has been worth a bit less recently. Ireland has accepted the **Euro (€)** as legal tender, and Irish pounds will be phased out by July 1, 2002. For more information, see p. 23. The British pound is the legal tender in Northern Ireland. A good rule of thumb is only to go to banks or bureaux de change that have at most a 5% margin between their buy and sell prices. The majority of Irish towns have 24hr. **ATMs.**

Prices: If you stay in hostels and prepare your own food, expect to spend anywhere from US$18-30 (£16-27/€20-34) per person per day. Accommodations start at IR£8-10/ €10.20-12.70 per night, while a basic sit-down meal begins around IR£6/€7.65.

Tipping and bargaining: Some restaurants in Ireland figure a service charge into the bill; some even calculate it into the cost of the dishes themselves. The menu often indicates whether or not service is included (ask if you're not sure). For those restaurants that do not include a tip in the bill, more common in cities, customers should leave 10-15%. Porters, parking-lot attendants, waitstaff, and hairdressers are usually tipped. Cab drivers are usually tipped 10%. Barmen at older or rural pubs may be offended if you leave them a gratuity, while in cities or at bars with a younger clientele a tip may be expected—the trick is to watch and learn from other customers.

Taxes: Both Ireland and Northern Ireland charge **value-added tax (VAT),** a national sales tax on most goods and some services. In Ireland, the VAT ranges from 0% on food and children's clothing to 17% in restaurants to 21% on items such as jewelry and adult clothing; the VAT is usually included in listed prices. The British rate, applicable to Northern Ireland, is 17.5% on many services (such as hairdressers, hotels, restaurants, and car rental agencies) and on all goods (except books, medicine, and food). Prices stated in *Let's Go* include VAT. **VAT Refunds** are available for non-EU citizens for goods taken out of the country, but not for services.

ACCOMMODATIONS AND CAMPING

HOSTELS. Hostelling is the way to go; dorm beds usually cost between IR£7.50-12/€9.50-15.25, and breakfast is often included or can be tacked on for IR£1-3/ €1.30-3.80. **An Óige,** the Irish Hostelling International affiliate, runs 32 hostels that are generally in remote areas or small villages. The North's HI affiliate is **HINI** (Hostelling International Northern Ireland; formerly **YHANI**), which operates eight hostels, all comfortable. A number of hostels in Ireland belong to **Independent Holiday Hostels (IHH);** the 145 hostels have no lockout or curfew (with a few exceptions), accept all ages, don't require membership, and are all Bord Fáilte-approved. The *An Óige Handbook* details all An Óige and HINI hostels. Copious **B&Bs** (in virtually every Irish town) can provide a luxurious break from hostelling; expect to pay IR£15-25/€19-31.75 for singles and IR£24-40/€30.50-50.80 for doubles. "Full Irish breakfasts" are often filling enough to get you through to dinner. **Camping** in Irish State Forests and National Parks is not allowed; camping on public land is permissible only if there is no official campsite nearby. Pick up the *Caravan and Camping Ireland* guide from any Bord Fáilte office for info on camping in the Republic. **Northern Ireland** treats its campers royally; there are well-equipped campsites throughout, and spectacular parks often house equally mouth-watering sites.

COMMUNICATION

MAIL. Postcards and letters up to 25g cost IRS0.30/€0.40 domestically and to the UK, IRS0.32/€0.45 to the continent; IRS0.45/€0.60 to any other international destination. Address mail to be held according to the following example: "FirstName SURNAME, Poste Restante, Enniscorthy, Co. Wexford, Ireland." Airmail letters take about 6-9 days between Ireland and North America.

TELEPHONES. Both the Irish Republic and Northern Ireland have public phones that accept **coins** (S0.20 for about 4min.) and **pre-paid phone-cards**. In the **Republic**, dial 114 for international operator; 10 for national operator; 11850 for directory. **International direct dial** numbers in the **Republic** include: **AT&T**, 1800 550000; **British Telecom**, ☎1800 550 144; **Canada Direct**, ☎1800 555 001; **MCI**, ☎1800 551 001; **Telecom New Zealand**, ☎1800 550 064; **Telekom South Africa**, ☎1800 550 027; **Telstra Australia**, ☎1800 550 061. In **Northern Ireland**, dial 155 for international operator; 100 for national operator; 192 for directory. **International direct dial** numbers in **Northern Ireland** include: **AT&T**, ☎0800 013 0011; **Canada Direct**, ☎0800 890 016; **MCI**, ☎1800 551 001; **Telecom New Zealand**, ☎0800 890 064; **Telekom South Africa**, ☎0800 890 027; **Telstra Australia**, ☎0800 856 6161.

INTERNET ACCESS. Internet access is available in Irish cities in cafes, hostels, and usually in libraries. One hour of webtime costs about S3-5/€3.80-6.35 (an ISIC may win you a discount). Get a county library membership in the Republic (IRS2/€2.55), for unlimited access to participating libraries, and their **Internet**.

LOCAL FACTS

Time: Ireland is on Greenwich Mean Time (GMT).

Hours: Most **banks** are open M-F 9am-4:30pm, sometimes later on Th. In big cities, **shop** hours are much longer.

When to Go: Weather in Ireland is temperate (summer averages 15-18°C, or 60-65°F) yet temperamental. Keep a poncho or umbrella handy and carry a sweater.

Holidays: Much of Southern Ireland closes for holidays on New Year's Day (Jan.) 1, St. Patrick's Day (Mar. 17), Good Friday, Easter Monday (Mar. 20-Apr. 1), and Christmas (Dec. 25-26). There are **Bank Holidays** in the Republic and Northern Ireland during the throughout the year, when almost everything shuts down. Bank Holidays in the Republic fall on: **May Day** (May 6), Jun. 6, Aug. 5, and Oct. 28; and in the North on May Day (May 6), May 27, and Aug. 26. Northern Ireland has a holiday on Orange Day (July 12).

Festivals: All of Ireland goes green for **St. Patrick's Day** (Mar. 17th). On **Bloomsday**, Dublin (June 16) traipses about revering James Joyce and his mammoth opus *Ulysses*.

DUBLIN ☎01

In a country known for its relaxed pace and rural sanctity, Dublin stands out for its international flair and boundless energy. Although the Irish worry that it has taken on the negative characteristics of a big city, it's still as friendly a major metropolis as you'll find. The city and its suburbs, home to one-third of Ireland's population, are at the vanguard of the country's rapid social change; countercultures flourish here in a way the rest of the Emerald Isle would summarily reject, and cutting-edge, world-renowned music bursts from the city's pub doors. It's no cultural wallflower either: the ghosts of Swift, Joyce, Beckett, Behan, and others pepper Dublin's neighborhoods with literary attractions. Dublin is a capital with a devotion to history and appreciation of culture. The best trips to Dublin combine its duality and soak up as many of the sights, sips and sounds that the banks of the Liffey offer.

▆ TRANSPORTATION

Airport: Dublin Airport (☎844 4900). **Dublin buses** #41, 41B, and 41C run to Eden Quay in the city center with stops along the way (every 20min., IR£1.20/€1.55). The **Airlink shuttle** (☎844 4265) runs non-stop directly to Busáras Central Bus Station and

O'Connell St. (30-40min., every 10-15min., IR£3/€3.85) and on to Heuston Station (50min., IR£3.50/€4.45). **Airport Express buses** (☎844 4265) go to Busáras and O'Connell St. (25-30min., departs every 10min. 5:45am-11:30pm, IR£3.50/€4.45). A **taxi** from the airport to the city center costs roughly IR£10-12/€12.70-15.25.

Trains: Irish Rail, Iarnród Éireann has a travel center at 35 Lower Abbey St. (☎836 6222). Open M-F 9am-5pm, Sa 9am-1pm. **Connolly Station,** Amiens St. (☎702 2358), is north of the Liffey and close to Busáras Bus Station. Buses #20, 20A, and 90 at the station go south of the river, and the DART runs to Tara on the south quay, but it's faster to walk. Trains to: **Belfast** (2¼hr., 5-8 per day, IR£21/€26.30); **Sligo** (3½hr., 3-4 per day, IR£14.50/€18.45); **Wexford** (3hr., 3 per day, IR£11/€14) via Rosslare. **Heuston Station** (☎703 2132) is south of Victoria Quay, west of the city center (25min. walk from Trinity College). Buses #26, 51, and 79 go to the city center. Trains to: **Cork** (3½hr., 6-11 per day, IR£33.50/€42.50); **Galway** (2½hr., 4-5 per day, IR£16-22/€20.35); **Limerick** (2½hr., 9 per day, IR£26.50/€33.65); **Tralee** (4½hr., 4-7 per day, IR£34/€43.20); **Waterford** (2½hr., 3-4 per day, IR£13/€16.55).

Buses: Info available at the **Dublin Bus Office,** 59 O'Connell St. (☎873 4222); the Bus Éireann window is open M-F 9am-5:30pm, Sa 9am-1pm. Intercity buses to Dublin arrive at **Busáras Central Bus Station,** Store St. (☎836 6111), directly behind the Customs House and next to Connolly Station. Bus Éireann runs to: **Belfast** (3hr., 6-7 per day, IR£10.50/€13.35); **Derry** (4¼hr., 4-5 per day, IR£11/€14); **Donegal Town** (4¼hr., 5-6 per day, IR£10.50/€13.35); **Galway** (3½hr., 13 per day, IR£9/€11.45); **Limerick** (3½hr., 7-13 per day, IR£10.50/€13.35); **Rosslare Harbour** (3hr., 7-10 per day, IR£10/€12.70); **Sligo** (4hr., 4-5 per day, IR£9.60/€12.20); **Waterford** (2¾hr., 5-7 per day, IR£7/€8.90); **Wexford** (2¾hr., 7-10 per day, IR£8/€10.20).

Ferries: Irish Ferries (☎855 2222) has an office off St. Stephen's Green on Merrion Row. Open M-F 9am-5pm, Sa 9:15am-12:45pm. **Stena Line** ferries arrive from **Holyhead, UK** at the **Dún Laoghaire** (see p. 565) ferry terminal (☎204 7777). **Irish Ferries** (www.irishferries.ie) arrive from Holyhead at the **Dublin Port** (☎607 5665), from where buses #53 and 53A run every hr. to Busáras (IR£0.80/€1); to get to the ferryport, **Dublin Bus** also runs connection buses timed to fit the ferry schedule (IR£2-2.50/€2.55-3.20). **Merchant Ferries** also docks at the Dublin ferryport and runs a route to **Liverpool, UK** (7½hr., 1-2 per day, IR£50/€63.50 and up, car IR£170/€215.90); booking for Merchant is only available from **Gerry Feeney,** 19 Eden Quay (☎819 2999).

Public Transportation: Dublin Bus, 59 O'Connell St. (☎873 4222). Open M 8:30am-5:30pm, Tu-F 9am-5:30pm, Sa 9am-1pm. County Dublin buses run fairly regularly within the city, especially the smaller **City Imp** buses (every 8-15min.). Dublin Bus runs the **NiteLink** service to the suburbs (Th-Sa nights at 12:30, 1:30, 2:30, and 3:30am; IR£3/€3.85). **Travel Wide** passes offer unlimited rides for a day or a week. (Day IR£3.50; week IR£13/€16.55, with TravelSave stamp IR£10/€12.70.) **DART** trains run serve the suburbs and the coast (every 10-15min., 6:30am-11:30pm, IR£0.55-1.10/€0.70-1.40).

Taxis: National Radio Cabs, 40 James St. (☎677 2222). All 24hr. IR£2.20/€2.80 plus IR£0.90/€1.15 per mi.; IR£0.80 call-in charge.

Car Rental: Budget, 151 Lower Drumcondra Rd. (☎837 9611), and at the airport. In summer from IR£35/€44.45 per day, IR£165/€209.55 per week; in winter IR£30/€38.10, IR£140/€177.80. Minimum age 23.

Bike Rental: MacDonald Cycles, 38 Wexford St. (☎475 2586), and **Cycle Ways,** 185-6 Parnell St. (☎873 4748). **Dublin Bike Tours** (☎679 0899), behind the Kinlay House hostel on Lord Edward St., rents and provides advice on route planning. IR£10/€12.70 per day, IR£40/€50.80 per week; students IR£8/€10.20, IR£35/€44.45; ID deposit.

✴ 🛈 ORIENTATION AND PRACTICAL INFORMATION

The **River Liffey** is the natural divide between Dublin's North and South Sides. The more famous sights, posh stores, excellent restaurants, and Heuston Station are on the **South Side.** The majority of hostels, the bus station, and Connolly Station cling to the **North Side.** The streets running alongside the Liffey are called **quays;** their names change every block. Each bridge over the river also has its own name, and streets change names as they cross. If a street is split into "Upper" and "Lower," then the "Lower" is always the part of the street closer to the mouth of the Liffey. **O'Connell Street,** three blocks west of the Busáras Central Bus Station, is the primary link between north and south Dublin. One block south of the Liffey, **Fleet Street** becomes **Temple Bar. Dame Street** runs parallel to Temple Bar with Trinity College as its terminus and defines the southern edge of the district. **Trinity College** functions as the nerve center of Dublin's cultural activity, drawing legions of bookshops and student-oriented pubs into its orbit. The North Side bustles with urban grit and hawks merchandise generally cheaper than in the more touristed South Side. **Henry Street** and **Mary Street** comprise a pedestrian shopping zone that intersects with O'Connell after the **General Post Office (GPO),** two blocks from the Liffey. The North Side has the reputation of being rougher, especially after sunset.

TOURIST, FINANCIAL, AND LOCAL SERVICES

Tourist Information: Main Office, Dublin Tourist Centre, Suffolk St. (☎(1850) 230 330). From Connolly Train Station, walk left down Amiens St., take a right onto Lower Abbey St., and continue until you come to O'Connell St. Turn left, cross the bridge, and walk past Trinity College; Suffolk St. will be on your right. Accommodation service with IR£1/€1.30 booking fee and 10% non-refundable deposit. Open Jan.-June and Aug.-Jan. M-F 9am-5:30pm, Sa 9-5:30pm; July- Aug. M-F 8:30am-6:30pm, Sa 9-5:30pm.

Northern Ireland Tourist Board: 16 Nassau St. (☎679 1977 or (1850) 230 230). Books accommodations in the North. Open M-F 9am-5:30pm, Sa 10am-5pm.

Embassies: Australia, 2nd fl., Fitzwilton House, Wilton Terr. (☎676 1517; fax 678 5185). Open M-Th 8:30am-12:30pm and 1:30-4:30pm, F 9am-noon. **Canada,** 65 St. Stephen's Green South (☎417 4101). Open M-F 9am-1pm and 2-4:30pm. **New Zealand** embassy in London. **South Africa,** 2nd fl., Alexandra House, Earlsfort Centre (☎661 5553). Open M-F 8:30am-5pm. **United Kingdom,** 29 Merrion Rd. (☎205 3700). Open M-F 9am-5pm. **United States,** 42 Elgin Rd., Ballsbridge (☎668 8777). Open M-F 8:30am-12:30pm and 1-4pm.

Banks: Bank of Ireland, AIB, and **TSB** branches with bureaux de change and **24hr. ATMs** cluster on Lower O'Connell St., Grafton St., and in the Suffolk and Dame St. areas. Most bank branches are open M-F 10am-4pm.

American Express: 43 Nassau St. (☎679 9000). Traveler's check refunds. Currency exchange; no commission for AmEx Traveler's Checks. Mail held. Open M-F 9am-5pm.

Luggage Storage: Connolly Station. IR£2/€2.55 per item per day. Open M-Sa 7:40am-9:20pm, Su 9:10am-9:45pm. **Heuston Station.** IR£1.50/€1.90, IR£2.50/€3.20, or IR£3.50/€4.45 per item, depending on size. Open daily 6:30am-10:30pm.

Laundry: The Laundry Shop, 191 Parnell St. (☎872 3541). Closest to Busáras and the North Side hostels. Wash and dry IR£6-8/€7.65-10.20. Open M-F 8am-7pm, Sa 9am-6pm, Su 11-5pm.

EMERGENCY AND COMMUNICATIONS

Emergency: ☎999 or 112; no coins required.

Police *(Garda)***:** Dublin Metro Headquarters, Harcourt Terrace. (☎666 9500), Store St. Station (☎666 8000), Fitzgibbon St. Station (☎666 8400).

Pharmacy: O'Connell's, 55 Lower O'Connell St. (☎873 0427). Open M-Sa 7:30am-10pm, Su 10am-10pm. Branches throughout the city, including 2 on Grafton St.

Hospital: St. James's Hospital, James St. (☎453 7941). Served by bus #123. **Mater Misericordiae Hospital,** Eccles St. (☎830 1122), off Lower Dorset St. Served by buses #10, 11, 13, 16, 121, and 122.

Internet Access: Several chains abound, the best being **The Internet Exchange,** with a branch at 146 Parnell St. in Temple Bar. (☎670 3000. Open daily 9am-10:30pm.)

Post Office: General Post Office (GPO), O'Connell St. (☎705 7000). Dublin is the only city in Ireland with postal codes. Even-numbered postal codes are for areas south of the Liffey, odd-numbered are for the north. *Poste Restante* pick-up at the bureau de change window. Open M-Sa 8am-8pm, Su 10am-6:30pm. **Postal code:** Dublin 1.

IRELAND

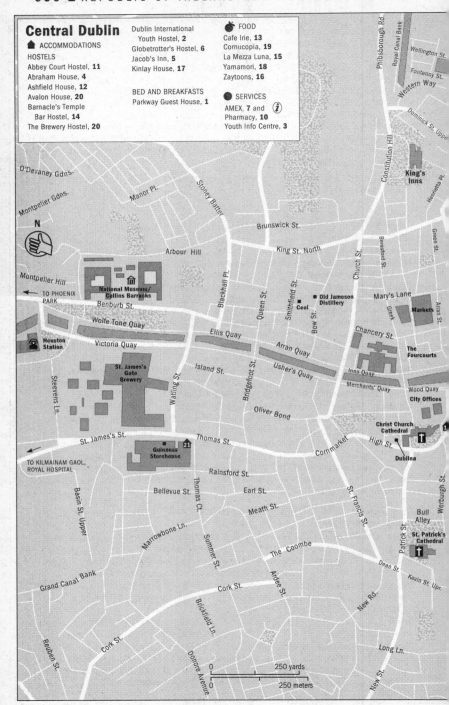

Central Dublin

⌂ ACCOMMODATIONS

HOSTELS
Abbey Court Hostel, **11**
Abraham House, **4**
Ashfield House, **12**
Avalon House, **20**
Barnacle's Temple
  Bar Hostel, **14**
The Brewery Hostel, **20**

Dublin International
  Youth Hostel, **2**
Globetrotter's Hostel, **6**
Jacob's Inn, **5**
Kinlay House, **17**

BED AND BREAKFASTS
Parkway Guest House, **1**

🍎 FOOD
Cafe Irie, **13**
Cornucopia, **19**
La Mezza Luna, **15**
Yamamori, **18**
Zaytoons, **16**

● SERVICES
AMEX, **7** and ⓘ
Pharmacy, **10**
Youth Info Centre, **3**

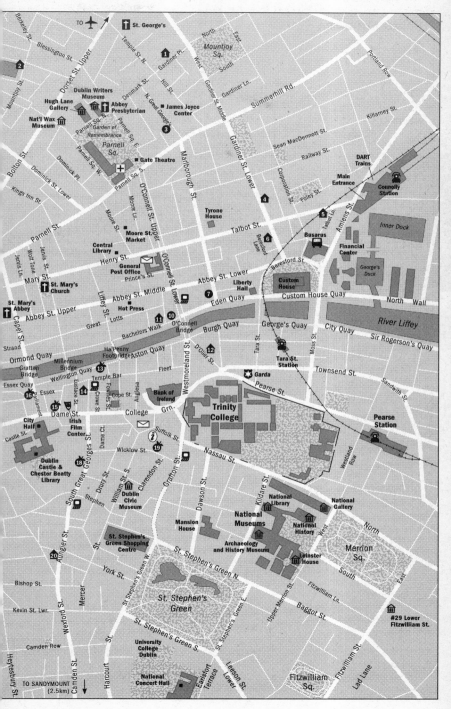

ACCOMMODATIONS

Dublin's accommodations overflow, especially during Easter, holidays (including Bank holidays in Ireland *and* England), and summer—reserve ahead. Dorms range from IR£7-15/€8.90-19.05 per night. Quality **B&Bs** blanket Dublin and the surrounding suburbs, although prices have risen with housing costs (most charge IR£16-30/€20.35-38.10 per person); many cluster along **Upper and Lower Gardiner Street,** on **Sherriff Street,** and near **Parnell Square.**

HOSTELS

To deal with the large crowds, Dublin's hostels lean toward the institutional, especially in comparison to their more personable country cousins. The beds south of the river fill up fastest, as they are closest to the city's sights and nightlife.

The Brewery Hostel, 22-23 Thomas St. (☎453 8600). Follow Dame St. past Christ Church through name changes, or take bus #123. Next to the Guinness brewery and a 20min. walk from Temple Bar. Continental breakfast included. Laundry across the street. All rooms with bath. 4-bed IR£15-16.50/€19-21; 8-bed dorms IR£12-13.50/€15.25-17. Doubles IR£44-46/€56-58.50.

Globetrotter's Tourist Hostel (IHH), 46-7 Lower Gardiner St. (☎873 5893). A dose of luxury for the weary. Spacious dining area, many lounges, friendly staff, huge and very hip painting of U2. **Internet** access. Hearty, healthy breakfast included. Towels IR£0.50/€0.65. Dorms IR£13-17/€16.50-21.60; singles IR£47.50-52.50/€60.30-66.70; doubles IR£70-80/€89-100.

Litton Lane Hostel, 2-4 Litton Ln. (☎872 8389), off Bachelor's Quay. A former recording studio for the likes of U2 and Van Morrison. Colorful common areas and spacious dorms offset the brand spankin' new industrial kitchen. Continental breakfast included. Towel for nominal fee. Key deposit IR£2/€2.50. Dorms IR£10.50-16/€13.50-20.30; doubles IR£44-52/€56-66.

Abraham House, 82-3 Lower Gardiner St. (☎855 0600). Respectable, tidy rooms. Light breakfast and towels included. 4-bed dorms IR£12.50-16/€16-20.50; 12-bed IR£10-11/€12.70-14, with bath IR£14-18/€18-23.

Barnacle's Temple Bar House, 19 Temple Ln. (☎671 6277) A well-kept hostel in the hopping heart of Dublin—expect noise. Continental breakfast included. 10-bed dorms IR£12-15/€15.50-19, 4-bed IR£17-18/€20.50-23; twins and doubles IR£50-58/€62-74; singles IR£44-58/€56-74.

Kinlay House (IHH), 2-12 Lord Edward St. (☎679 6644). View Christ Church Cathedral from soft couches in TV room. Breakfast and hand-towel included. Lockers IR£0.50/€0.65. Dorms IR£11-15.50/€14. Singles IR£25/€31.75; doubles IR£38/€48; Nov.-May prices IR£1-2.50/€1.30-3.20 less.

Avalon House (IHH), 55 Aungier St. (☎475 0001). Turn off Dame St. onto Great Georges St.; the hostel is a 10min. walk down on your right. A stumble away from Temple Bar. Small continental breakfast included. Towels IR£1/€1.30 with IR£5/€6.35 deposit. Dorms IR£13.50-15.75/€17-19.50; singles IR£25-30/€31.75-38; doubles IR£24-27.50/€30.50-35.

Abbey Court Hostel, 29 Bachelor's Walk, O'Connell Bridge (☎878 0700). From O'Connell Bridge, turn left to face this emphatic blue and orange addition to Dublin's hostel scene. A little pricey, but comfy. Continental breakfast included. Doubles IR£60-70/€76-88; 4-bed dorms IR£20-22/€25-28; 6-bed IR£17.50-19.50/€22-25; 12-bed IR£13.50-16/€17-20.

Jacobs Inn, 21-28 Talbot Pl. (☎855 5660). 2 blocks north of the Customs House, Talbot Pl. stretches from the back of the bus station up to Talbot St. Rooms, all with bath, are spacious, clean, and cheery. Towels IR£1/€1.30. Laundry IR£5/€6.35. Lockout 11am-3pm. Dorms IR£10-13/€12.70-16.50; doubles IR£44-48/€56-61. Weekend prices IR£1/€1.30 higher.

Ashfield House, 19-20 D'Olier St. (☎679 7734). Smack in the center of Dublin. Light breakfast included. Laundry IR£4/€5. Mar.-Oct. dorms IR£11.50-18/€14-23; private rooms IR£13-14/€16.50-18 per person. Weekend prices IR£1-2/€1.30-2.50 higher. Nov.-Apr. all prices IR£1-2/€1.30-2.50 lower.

Dublin International Youth Hostel (An Óige/HI), 61 Mountjoy St. (☎ 830 4555). O'Connell St. changes names 3 times before the left turn onto Mountjoy St. This convent-turned-hostel has made giant improvements. A keycard system and lockers beef up security. Breakfast included. Towels IR£1/€1.30. Laundry IR£4/€5.10. High season dorms IR£7.50/€9.53; under 18 IR£10/€13.50.

BED AND BREAKFASTS

B&Bs with a green shamrock sign out front are registered, occasionally checked, and approved by Bord Fáilte. On the North Side, B&Bs cluster along **Upper** and **Lower Gardiner Street,** on **Sheriff Street,** and near **Parnell Square.**

Rita and Jim Casey, Villa Jude, 2 Church Ave. (☎ 668 4982), off Beach Rd. Bus #3 to the 1st stop on Tritonville Rd.; Church Ave. is back a few yards. Call for directions from the Lansdowne Rd. DART stop. The best B&B value in Dublin. Clean rooms and big breakfasts. Singles IR£17.50/€22; doubles IR£35/€44.45.

Parkway Guest House, 5 Gardiner Pl. (☎ 874 0469). Rooms are plain but high-ceilinged and tidy, and the location (just off Gardiner St.) is excellent. Singles IR£25/€30.50; doubles IR£36-40/€46-51, with shower IR£44-50/€56-63.50.

The White House, 125 Clontarf Rd. (☎ 833 3196). Sink into your bed and gaze out at pristine rose gardens. Singles IR£25/€31.75, off-season IR£24/€30.50; doubles IR£44/€56.50, with bath IR£48/€61.

Mona's B&B, 148 Clonliffe Rd. (☎ 837 6723). Firm beds in rooms kept tidy by a lovely proprietress who offers homemade bread with her full Irish breakfast. Open May-Oct. Singles IR£20/€25.40; doubles IR£40/€50.80.

St. Aidan's B&B, 150 Clonliffe Rd. (☎ 837 6750). The neighborhood's first B&B. Good beds, non-smoking rooms, and friendly owner create a relaxing atmosphere. Breakfast included. Open Apr.-Sept. Singles IR£20/€25.40; doubles with bath IR£40/€50.80.

Mrs. Dolores Abbot-Murphy, 14 Castle Park (☎ 269 8413). Ask the #3 bus driver to drop you off at Sandymount Green. Continue past Browne's Deli and take the 1st left; at the end of the road look right. A 5min. walk from Sandymount DART stop. Singles IR£25/€31.75; doubles IR£44/€56.50, with bath IR£46/€59.

CAMPING

Most campsites are legal and safe, but far away from the city center; however convenient, it is illegal and unsafe to camp in **Phoenix Park.**

Camac Valley Tourist Caravan & Camping Park, Naas Rd., Clondalkin (☎ 464 0644.), near Corkagh Park. Accessible by bus #69 (35min. from city center, IR£1.15/€1.50). Food shop and kitchen facilities. Laundry IR£3.50/€4.44. Dogs welcome. Open June-Aug. Hikers/cyclists IR£4.50/€5.70; 2 people with car IR£10/€12.70.

Shankill Caravan and Camping Park (☎ 282 0011). The DART and buses #45 and 84 from Eden Quay run to Shankill, as does bus #45A from the Dún Laoghaire ferryport. Welcomes all ages. IR£1/€1.30 per adult, IR£0.50/€0.65 per child, IR£4.50-5/€5.70-6.35 per tent plus. Showers IR£0.50/€0.65.

▌ FOOD

Dublin's **open-air markets** sell fresh and cheap fixings. On Saturdays, a gourmet open-air market takes place in **Temple Bar** in Meeting House Square. The cheapest **supermarkets** around Dublin are the **Dunnes Stores** chain, with branches at St. Stephen's Green (☎ 478 0188; open M-W and F-Sa 8:30am-7pm; Th 8:30am-9pm; Su noon-6pm), the ILAC Centre off Henry St., and on North Earl St. **Temple Bar** is ready to implode from the proliferation of creative eateries catering to all budgets.

Cafe Irie, 11 Fownes St. (☎ 672 5090), above the clothing store Sé Sí Progressive. A small eatery with an impressive selection of lip-smackingly good sandwiches under IR£3/€3.80. Great coffee. A little crunchy, a little jazzy, a whole lotta good. Vegan-friendly. Open M-Sa 9am-8pm, Su noon-5:30pm.

Cornucopia, 19 Wicklow St. (☎ 677 7583). This vegetarian horn o' plenty spills huge portions onto your plate. Servers are more than happy to translate organic ingredients. If you can find the space, sit down for a rich meal (about IR£5/€6.35) or snack (IR£1.50/€1.90). Open M-W and F-Sa 9am-8pm, Th 9am-9pm.

IRELAND

La Mezza Luna, 1 Temple Ln. (☎ 671 2840), on the corner of Dame St. Refined but not pretentious. Celestial food. Try the wok-fried chicken for IR£7.95/€10. Daily lunch specials around IR£5/€6.35. Delicious desserts IR£4/€5. Open M-Th 12:30pm-11pm, F-Sa 12:30pm-11:30pm, Su 4-10:30pm.

Zaytoons, 14-15 Parliament St. (☎ 677 3595). Persian food served on big platters of warm bread. A good lunch or a healthy way to satisfy the munchies. Excellent chicken kebab IR£4.50/€5.70. Open M-Sa noon-4am, Su 1pm-4am.

Yamamori Noodles, 71-72 S. Great Georges St. (☎ 475 5001). Exceptional Japanese cuisine, reasonably priced. Entrees for under IR£10/€12.70; tofu steak IR£6/€7.60. Open M-W and Su 12:30-11pm, Th-Sa 12:30-11:30pm.

👁 SIGHTS

Dublin is a walkable city; most of the sights lie less than 2km from O'Connell Bridge. The **Historical Walking Tour** provides a 2hr. crash course in Dublin's history and Irish history, stopping at a variety of Dublin sights. (Meet at Trinity's front gate. ☎ 878 0227. May-Sept. M-F 11am and 3pm, Sa-Su 11am, noon and 3pm; Oct.-Apr. F-Su noon. IR£6/€7.65, students IR£5/€6.35.)

TRINITY COLLEGE AND NEARBY

TRINITY COLLEGE. Ancient walls contain Trinity's sprawling expanse of stone buildings, cobblestone walks, and green grounds. The British built Trinity in 1592 as a Protestant religious seminary that would "civilize the Irish and cure them of Popery." The college became part of the accepted path that members of the Anglo-Irish elite tread on their way to high government and social positions. The Catholic Jacobites who briefly held Dublin in 1689 used the campus as a barracks and prison. Jonathan Swift, Robert Emmett, Thomas Moore, Edmund Burke, Oscar Wilde, and Samuel Beckett are just a few of the famous Irishmen who studied here. Bullet holes from the Easter 1916 uprising scar the stone entrance, which is just part of the moderately irreverent and enormously pretentious **Trinity College Walking Tour,** which is run by students and concentrates on University lore. (June-Sept. roughly every 45min. from the info booth inside the front gate. Mar.-May, weekends only. IR£6/€7.60, students £5/€6.35; includes admission to the Old Library and the Book of Kells.) Until the 1960s, the Catholic church deemed it a cardinal sin to attend Trinity; once the church lifted the ban, the size of the student body more than tripled. (Between Westmoreland and Grafton St. in the very center of Dublin, the main entrance fronts the block-long traffic circle now called College Green. Pearse St. runs along the north edge of the college, Nassau St. to its south. ☎ 608 1000. Grounds always open. Free.)

THE OLD LIBRARY. This 1712 chamber holds an invaluable collection of ancient manuscripts, including the magnificent 🔖**Book of Kells.** Around AD 800, Irish monks squeezed multicolored ink from plants to illuminate this four-volume edition of the Gospels. Each page holds an intricate latticework of Celtic designs, into which images of animals and Latin text are interwoven. (From the main gate, go straight; the library is on the south side of Library Square. Open June-Sept. M-Sa 9:30am-5pm, Su noon-4:30pm; Oct.-May M-Sa 9:30am-5pm, Su noon-4:30pm. IR£4.50/€5.70, students IR£4/€5.10.)

GRAFTON STREET. The few blocks south of College Green are off-limits to cars and ground zero for shopping tourists and residents alike. Grafton Street's **street performers** range from string octets to jive limboists. Upstairs at the Grafton St. branch of Bewley's is the **Bewley's Museum,** located inside the coffee chain's former chocolate factory. Tea-tasting machines and a display on Bewley's Quaker heritage are among the curiosities. (Open daily 7:30am-11pm. Free.)

KILDARE STREET AND NATIONAL MUSEUMS

The Museum Link bus runs from the adjacent Natural History and Archeology museums to Collins Barracks roughly once an hour. An all-day pass costs IR£2/€2.50; while one-way is IR£0.85/€1. (General Information Line for all 3 ☎ 677 7444. All open Tu-Sa 10am-5pm, Su 2-5pm. All free.)

The largest of Dublin's museums, the **National Museum of Archaeology and History,** contains a number of beautiful artifacts spanning the last two millennia. One room gleams with the **Tara Brooch, Ardagh Hoard** (including the great chalice), and other Celtic gold work. Another section is devoted to the Republic's founding years and shows off the bloody vest of nationalist hero **James Connolly.** *(Kildare St., adjacent to Leinster House.)* The ⬛**Natural History Museum** is a museum within a museum, with a creepily fascinating collection that details how museums are used to interpret the natural world. *(Merrion Square West. Free.)* The **National Museum of Decorative Arts and History, Collins Barracks,** gleams with exhibits that range from the traditional to the multi-disciplinary. *(Benburb St., off of Wolfe Tone Quay. Take the Museum Link, or bus #10 from O'Connell. Bus #90 to Heuston Station stops across the street.)* The **National Gallery** has a collection of over 2400 canvases including paintings by Bruegel, Goya, Caravaggio, Vermeer, Rembrandt, and El Greco. *(Merrion Square West. Free.)* The **National Library** chronicles Irish history and exhibits literary objects in its entrance room. A genealogical research room can help families trace the thinnest tendrils of their Irish family tree. *(Kildare St, adjacent to Leinster House. ☎ 661 2523. Open M-W 10am-9pm, Th-F 10am-5pm, Sa 10am-1pm. Free.)*

ST. STEPHEN'S GREEN AND MERRION SQUARE

ST. STEPHEN'S GREEN. The 9 hectare park was a private estate until the Guinness clan bequeathed it to the city. Today, the park is a hotbed of activity—during the summer, the multitudes enjoy outdoor music and theater near the old bandstand. *(Kildare, Dawson, and Grafton Sts. all lead to it. Open M-Sa 8am-dusk, Su 10am-dusk.)*

MERRION SQUARE. The square and adjacent **Fitzwilliam Street** visually stimulate with Georgian buildings fronted by elaborate doorways. Farther south on **Harcourt Street,** playwright George Bernard Shaw and Dracula's creator, Bram Stoker, were once neighbors at #61 and #16, respectively. The Electricity Supply Board tore down some of the townhouses to build a monstrous new office. Dubliners had a row over this, so the ESB funds **#29 Lower Fitzwilliam Street,** a restored Georgian townhouse-*cum*-living museum that demonstrates the lifestyle of the 18th-century Anglo-Irish elite. *(☎ 702 6165. Open Tu-Sa 10am-5pm, Su 2-5pm. A short audio-visual show leads to a 25min. tour of the house. IR£2.50/€3.20, students and seniors IR£1/€1.30.)*

TEMPLE BAR

West of Trinity between Dame St. and the Liffey, the Temple Bar neighborhood wriggles with activity. Saved from becoming a transportation hub in the 80s, Temple Bar has grown at lightning speed into one of Europe's hottest night spots. Narrow neo-cobblestone streets link cheap cafes, hole-in-the-wall theaters, rock venues, and used clothing stores. The government-sponsored Temple Bar Properties has also spent over IR£30 million to build a fleet of arts-related attractions. Among the most inviting are: **The Irish Film Centre,** featuring specialty and art house film *(6 Eustace St.; ☎ 679 3477)*; Ireland's only **Gallery of Photography** *(Meeting House Sq.; ☎ 671 4654)*; and the **Temple Bar Gallery & Studios** *(5-9 Temple Bar; ☎ 671 0073)*.

DAME STREET AND THE CATHEDRALS

DUBLIN CASTLE. Norman King John built the castle in 1204 on top of the first Viking settlement of Dubh Linn. For 700 years after its construction, Dublin Castle was the seat of British rule in Ireland. Fifty insurgents died at the castle's walls on Easter Monday, 1916 (see **Easter Rising,** p. 547). Since 1938, the presidents of Ireland have been inaugurated here. *(Dame St., at the intersection of Parliament and Castle St. ☎ 677 7129. IR£3/€3.80, students and seniors IR£2/€2.50. Grounds free.)*

ST. PATRICK'S CATHEDRAL. The building dates to the 12th century, although Sir Benjamin Guinness remodeled much of it in 1864. Measuring 300 ft. from stem to stern, it is Ireland's largest cathedral. St. Patrick allegedly baptized converts in the park next door. Jonathan Swift spent his last years as Dean of St. Patrick's; his crypt rises above the south nave. *(From Christ Church, Nicholas St. runs south and downhill, eventually becoming Patrick St. Take bus #49, 49A, 50, 54A, 56A, 65, 65B, 77, or 77A from Eden Quay. ☎ 475 4817. Open Mar.-Oct. daily 9am-6pm; Nov.-Feb. Sa 9am-5pm, Su 9am-3pm. £2.70/€3.50. Students, seniors, and children free.)* Beside the cathedral, **Marsh's Library** is Ireland's oldest public library. *(St. Patrick's Close. ☎ 454 3511. Open M and W-F 10am-12:45pm and 2-5pm, Sa 10:30am-12:45pm. £2/€2.50, students and seniors £1/€1.30.)*

CHRIST CHURCH CATHEDRAL. Sitric Silkenbeard, King of the Dublin Norsemen, built a wooden church on this site around 1038; Strongbow rebuilt it in stone in 1169. Further additions were made in the following century and again in the 1870s. Stained glass sparkles above the raised crypts, one of which supposedly belongs to Mr. Strongbow and his favorite lutefisk. Now, fragments of ancient pillars lie about like bleached bones, and a mummified cat chases a mummified mouse. *(At the end of Dame St., uphill and across from the Castle.* ☎ *677 8099. Take bus #50 from Eden Quay or 78A from Aston Quay. Open daily 9:45am-5:30pm except during services. Donation of £2/€2.50 strongly encouraged, concessions £1/€1.30.)*

CHESTER BEATTY LIBRARY. Honorary Irish citizen Alfred Chester Beatty was an American rags-to-riches mining engineer who amassed an incredible collection of Asian art, sacred scriptures, and illustrated texts. An illustrated book by Matisse and a collection of Chinese snuff bottles are two of the highlights. *(Behind Dublin Castle.* ☎ *407 0750. Open Tu-F 10am-5pm, Sa 11am-5pm, Su 1pm-5pm. Free.)*

GUINNESS BREWERY AND KILMAINHAM

■ **GUINNESS HOPSTORE.** Guinness brews its black magic on Crane St. off James St. and perpetuates the legend of the world's best stout at its Hopstore. Farsighted Arthur Guinness signed a 9000-year lease at the original 1759 brewery nearby. The lease is displayed on the floor of the atrium, an architectural triumph that rises seven floors and has a center shaped like a pint glass. Appreciate the exhibit on Guinness's infamously clever advertising, and then drink, silly tourist, drink. *(St. James's Gate. From Christ Church Cathedral, follow High St. west through its name changes—Cornmarket, Thomas, and James. Take bus #51B or 78A from Aston Quay or #123 from O'Connell St.* ☎ *408 4800. Open Oct.-Mar. daily 9:30am-5pm; Apr.-Sept. 9:30am-7pm. IR£9/€11.50, students IR£6/€7.60, seniors and children IR£4/€5.10.)*

KILMAINHAM GAOL. Almost all of the rebels who fought in Ireland's struggle for independence from 1792 to 1921 spent time here. "The cause for which I die has been rebaptized during this past week by the blood of as good men as ever trod God's earth," wrote Sean MacDiarmada as he awaited execution for participation in the 1916 Easter Rising (see p. 547). Tours wind through the chilly limestone corridors of the prison and end in the haunting atmosphere of the execution yard. *(Inchicore Rd. Take bus #51 from Aston Quay, #51A from Lower Abbey St., or #79 from Aston Quay.* ☎ *453 5984. Open Apr.-Sept. daily 9:30am-4:45pm; Oct.-Mar. M-F 9:30am-4pm, Su 10am-4:45pm. IR£3.50/€4.45, seniors IR£2.50/€3.20, students and children IR£1.50/€1.90.)*

IRISH MUSEUM OF MODERN ART. Built in 1679 as a hospice for retired or disabled soldiers, today the compound houses the **Irish Museum of Modern Art.** The façade and courtyard copy those of Les Invalides in Paris; the baroque chapel is quite a sight, too. *(Military Rd.* ☎ *612 9900. Bus #90 or 91 from Heuston Station, #78A or 79 from the city center. Open Tu-Sa 10am-5:30pm, Su noon-5:30pm. Guided tours W and F 2:30pm, Su 12:15pm. Free. Call for events.)*

O'CONNELL ST. AND PARNELL SQUARE

HUGH LANE MUNICIPAL GALLERY OF MODERN ART. When American painter Lane offered to donate his collection of French Impressionist paintings to the city, he did so on the condition that the people of Dublin contribute to the gallery's construction. Dubliners, however, refused to lend their support; Yeats lamented their provincial attitudes in a string of poems. *(Parnell Sq. North.* ☎ *874 1903. Buses #3, 10, 11, 13, 16, and 19 all stop near Parnell Sq. Open Tu-Th 9:30am-6pm, F-Sa 9:30am-5pm, Su 11am-5pm. Free; occasional special exhibits may charge.)*

THE DUBLIN WRITERS' MUSEUM. Read your way through placards and placards describing the city's rich literary heritage. Rare editions, manuscripts, and memorabilia of Swift, Shaw, Wilde, Yeats, Beckett, Brendan Behan, Patrick Kavanagh, and Sean O'Casey sit with caricatures, paintings, a great bookstore, and an incongruous Zen Garden. *(18 Parnell Sq. North.* ☎ *872 2077. Open June-Aug. M-F 10am-6pm, Sa 10am-5pm, Su 11am-5pm; Sept.-May M-Sa 10am-5pm. IR£3.10/€4, students IR£2.89/€3.75. Combined ticket with either Shaw birthplace or James Joyce Centre IR£4.60/€5.85.)*

DUBLINESE Mastering the Dublin dialect has been a persistent challenge to writers and thespians of the 20th century. The following is a short introduction to Dubliners' favorite phrases. **In Times of Difficulty:** Dublinese is perfect for keeping others in line. Idiots are rebuked as "eejits;" in dire situations, they are called "head-the-ball." Total exasperation calls for "shite and onions." When all is restored to order, it's said that "the job's oxo and the ship's name is murphy." **Affectionate Nicknames for Civic Landmarks:** Over the past couple decades, the government has graced the city with several public art works that personify the Irish spirit in the female form. Dubliners have responded with poetic rhetoric. Off Grafton St., the statue of the fetching fishmongress Molly Malone is referred to as "the tart with the cart." The goddess of the River Liffey sits in a fountain on O'Connell St. and is popularly heralded as the "floozy in the jacuzzi" and even "the whore in the sewer" (pronounced WHEW-er).

JAMES JOYCE CULTURAL CENTRE. This new museum features Joyceana—feel free to mull over Joyce's works in the library or the tearoom. Call for info on lectures, walking tours, and Bloomsday events. *(35 North Great Georges St. Up Marlborough St. and past Parnell St. ☎ 878 8547. Open M-Sa 9:30am-5pm, Su 12:30-5pm; July-Aug. extra Su hours 11am-5pm. IR£3/€3.80, students and seniors IR£2/€2.50.)*

SMITHFIELD

⊠ OLD JAMESON DISTILLERY. Learn how science, grain, and tradition come together to create the golden fluid called **whiskey.** More entertaining and less commercial than the Guinness Brewery tour, the experience ends with a glass of the Irish whiskey of your choice; be quick to volunteer in the beginning, and you'll get to sample a whole tray of different whiskeys. Feel the burn. *(Bow St. From O'Connell St., turn onto Henry St. and continue straight as the street dwindles to Mary St., then Mary Ln., then May Ln.; the warehouse is on a cobblestone street on the left. ☎ 807 2355. Tours daily 9:30am-5:30pm. IR£4.95/€6.30, students and seniors IR£3/€3.85.)*

ELSEWHERE

PHOENIX PARK. Europe's largest enclosed public park is most famous for the "Phoenix Park murders" of 1882. The Invincibles, a tiny nationalist splinter group, stabbed the Chief Secretary of Ireland, Lord Cavendish, and his Under-Secretary 180m from the Phoenix Column. The **Phoenix Column,** a Corinthian column capped with a phoenix rising from flames, is something of a pun—the park's name actually comes from the Irish term *Fionn Uisce,* meaning "clean water." The 712-hectare park incorporates the President's residence *(Áras an Uachtaráin)*, cricket pitches, polo grounds, cattle, and grazing deer. *(Take bus #10 from O'Connell St. or #25 or 26 from Middle Abbey St. west along the river. Free.)* **Dublin Zoo,** one of the world's oldest zoos and Europe's largest, is in the park. It contains 700 animals and the world's biggest egg. *(Bus #10 from O'Connell St. ☎ 677 1425. June-Aug. open M-Sa 9:30am-6pm, Su 10:30am-6pm. Closes at sunset in winter. IR£6.30/€8, students IR£4.80/€6.)*

🎵🎭 ENTERTAINMENT AND NIGHTLIFE

Be it poetry or punk you fancy, Dublin is equipped to entertain you. The *Event Guide* (free) is available at the tourist office, Temple Bar restaurants, and the Temple Bar Info Centre. Traditional music *(trad)* is an important element of the Irish culture and the Dublin music scene—some pubs in the city center have sessions nightly. **Whelan's** (see **Publin,** below) is one of the hottest spots in Dublin. Big bands frequent the **Baggot Inn,** 143 Baggot St. (☎ 676 1430). Part of the National Theater, the **Abbey Theatre,** 26 Lower Abbey St., was founded in 1904 by Yeats and Lady Gregory to promote Irish culture and modernist theater. (☎ 878 7222. Box office open M-Sa 10:30am-7pm. Tickets IR£10-17.50/€12.70-22.25; student rate M-Th and Sa matinee IR£8/€10.20.) Dublin pretty much owns two days of the year. **St. Patrick's Day** (Mar. 17) and the half-week leading up to it host a carnival of concerts, fireworks, street theater, and intoxicated madness. The city returns to 1904 on

Bloomsday (June 16), the day on which the action of Joyce's *Ulysses* takes place. The **James Joyce Cultural Centre** (☎873 1984) sponsors a reenactment of the funeral and wake, a lunch at Davy Byrne's, and a breakfast with Guinness.

James Joyce once proposed that a "good puzzle would be to cross Dublin without passing a pub." A local radio station once offered IR£100/€127 to the first person to solve the puzzle. The winner explained that you could take any route—you'd just have to visit them all on the way. The **Dublin Literary Pub Crawl** traces Dublin's liquid history in reference to its literary history. *(Meet at The Duke, 2 Duke St.* ☎ *670 5602. Tours Apr.-Oct. M-Sa 7:30pm, Su noon and 7:30pm; Nov.-Mar. Th-Sa 7:30pm, Su noon and 7:30pm. IR£7/€8.90, students IR£6/€7.60.) Let's Go* recommends beginning your personal journey at the gates of Trinity College, moving onto Grafton St., stumbling onto Camden St., teetering down South Great Georges St., and crawling (triumphantly if soused) into the Temple Bar area.

PUBLIN

The Long Stone, 10-11 Townend St. (☎671 8102). Handcarved banisters and old books give the place a rustic-medieval feel. Lots of interesting rooms, the largest of which has an enormous carving of a bearded man whose mouth serves as a fireplace. Carvery lunches 12:30-2:30pm. Open M-W noon-11:30pm, Th-F 10am-12:30am, Sa 3pm-12:30am, Su 4-11pm.

The Stag's Head, 1 Dame Ct. (☎679 3701). This beautiful Victorian pub has stained glass, mirrors, and yes, you guessed it, evidence of deer decapitation. The largely student crowd dons everything from t-shirts to tuxes and spills out into the alleys. Excellent grub. Entrees IR£7/€9. Food served M-F 12:30-3:30pm and 5-7pm, Sa 12:30-2:30pm. Late bar Th-F until 12:30am.

Whelan's, 25 Wexford St. (☎478 0766), continue down South Great Georges St. People in the know know Whelan's. The stage venue in back hosts big-name *trad* and rock, with live music every night starting at 9:30pm (doors open at 8:30pm). Cover IR£5-8/€6.35-10.20. Open 12:30-3:30pm for lunch; open W-Sa late.

The Odeon, Old Harcourt Train Station (☎478 2088). The Odeon has a columned façade and the 2nd-longest bar in Ireland (after the one at the Galway races). Everything here is gargantuan. The upstairs is cozier (i.e. still huge). Open Su-W until 12:30am, Th-F 2:30am, Sa 3am.

The Porter House, 16-18 Parliament St. (☎679 8847). The largest selection of world beers in the country and 8 self-brewed kinds of porter, stout, and ale. Excellent sampler tray includes a sip of stout made with oysters and other oddities (IR£6/€7.60). Occasional *trad*, blues, and rock. Open F-Sa late.

The Front Lounge, Parliament St. (☎670-4112). The velvet seats of this gay-friendly bar are popular with a very mixed, very trendy crowd. Open M and W noon-11:30pm, Tu and Sa noon-12:30am, F noon-1:30am, Su 4pm-11:30pm.

The Palace, 21 Fleet St. (☎677 9290), behind Aston Quay. This classic, neighborly pub has old-fashioned wood paneling and close quarters; head for the comfy seats in the skylit back room. The favorite of many a Dubliner.

CLUBLIN

■ **The Kitchen,** The Clarence Hotel, Wellington Quay (☎677 6635), in Temple Bar, through an understated entrance behind the hotel on Essex St. With 2 bars and a dance floor, this U2-owned club is exceptionally well-designed and the hottest spot in town. Impossible to get into on many nights. Dress as a rocker or a model. Cover IR£5-10/€6.35-12.70, students IR£1/€1.30 less on W-Th. Cookin' Th-Sa until 2:45am.

Rí-Rá, 1 Exchequer St. (☎677 4835). Generally good music that steers clear of pop and house extremes. 2 floors, several bars, more nooks and crannies than a crumpet, and quite womb-like downstairs. Open daily 11pm-2:30am. Cover IR£6-7/€7.60-8.90.

PoD, 35 Harcourt St. (☎478 0225). Spanish-style decor meets hard-core dance music. As trendy as The Kitchen. The truly brave venture upstairs to **The Red Box** (☎478 0225), a separate, more intense club with a warehouse atmosphere. Often hosts big-name DJs—cover charges skyrocket. Cover IR£8-10/€10.20-12.70; Th ladies free before midnight; Th and Sa IR£5/€6.35 with ISIC. Open until 3am. Start the evening at the Chocolate Bar or the Odeon; they share the building (see **Publin,** Above).

■ **The George,** 89 South Great Georges St. (☎ 478 2983). This throbbing purple man o' war is Dublin's first and most prominent gay bar. A mixed-age crowd gathers throughout the day to chat and sip. The attached nightclub opens W-Su until 2am. Frequent theme nights. Su night Bingo is accompanied by so much entertainment that sometimes the bingo never happens. Look spiffy—no effort, no entry. Cover IR£6-8 after 10pm.

◪ DAYTRIPS FROM DUBLIN

HOWTH

For Howth, Take a northbound DART train to the end (30min., 6 per hr., IR£1.15/€1.50).

The peninsula of Howth (rhymes with "both") dangles from the mainland in Eden-like isolation, less than 16km from Dublin. A 3hr. **cliff walk** rings the peninsula, passing heather and thousands of seabird nests. The best section of the walk is a 1hr. hike between the harbor and the lighthouse at the southeast tip of the peninsula. To get to the trailhead from town, turn left at the DART station and follow Harbour Rd. around the coast (20min.) or hike downhill from the lighthouse. In town, the ruins of the 14th-century **St. Mary's Abbey** stand peacefully in a cemetery at the bend in Church St. To reach the private **Howth Castle,** a curiously charming patchwork of architectural styles, turn right as you exit the DART station and then left after 400m, at the entrance to the Deer Park Hotel. Farther up the hill, a vague path goes around the right side of the hotel to the fabulous **Rhododendron Gardens.** At the top, you'll emerge into an astounding floral view overlooking Howth and Dublin. Turn left out of the station to get to the **tourist office,** in the Old Courthouse on Harbour Rd. (☎ 832 0405. Open May-Aug. M-F 11am-1pm and Tu-F 1:30-5pm.) Hotel **Gleann na Smól** is on the left at the end of Nashville Rd., off Thormanby Rd. (☎ 832 2936. Singles IR£30/€38.10; doubles IR£42/€53.35. 10% ISIC discount.) Bus #31B runs to **Hazelwood** at the end of the cul-de-sac in the Thormanby Woods estate, 1.5km up Thormanby Rd. (☎ 839 13 91. Doubles IR£60/€76.20; all rooms with bath.)

BOYNE VALLEY

Bus Éireann shuttles to the Visitors Centre (1½hr., M-Sat every 15min., Su every hr., IR£10/€12.70 round-trip).

The thinly populated Boyne Valley safeguards Ireland's greatest archaeological treasures. Along the curves of the river between Slane and Drogheda lie no fewer than 40 crypt-like passage-tombs constructed by the Neolithics around the 4th millenium BC, including **Newgrange, Dowth,** and **Knowth.** The first, built over 5000 years ago using stones believed to have been carted from Wicklow, 60km away, is the most spectacular, covered with elaborate patterns and symbols that continue to mystify archaeologists. You may only enter Newgrange by admission at **Brú na Bóinne Visitors Centre,** near on the south side of the River Boyne, across from the tombs. (☎ (041) 988 0300. Open Mar.-Apr. daily 9:30am-5:30pm; May 9am-6:30pm; June to mid-Sept. 9am-7pm; late Sept. 9am-6:30pm; Oct. 9:30am-5:30pm; Nov.-Feb. 9:30am-5pm. Centre and 1hr. tour IR£4/€5.10, students IR£3/€3.80.) The **Hill of Tara** was the spiritual and political center of Ireland until the arrival of Christianity in the 4th century BC. Take any local (not express) bus from Dublin to **Navan** (1hr., M-Sa 37 per day, Su 15 per day; IR£5.50/€7) and ask the driver to stop at the turn-off; the site is 1.5km straight uphill. A flock of enormous, well-preserved Norman castles, including **Trim Castle,** which Mel Gibson sacked 800 years later for a scene in *Braveheart,* overlook **Trim** proper on the River Boyne. (Open May-Oct. 10am-6pm. Tours every 45min. Limited to 15 people; sign up upon arrival in Trim. Tour and grounds IR£2.50/€3.20, students IR£1/€1.30; grounds only IR£1/€1.30.) The **tourist office** is on Mill St. (☎ (046) 37111. Open daily 9:30am-1pm and 1:30-5:30pm.)

DÚN LAOGHAIRE

Reach Dún Laoghaire by DART from Dublin (IR£1.10).

As Dublin's major out-of-city ferry port, Dún Laoghaire (dun-LEER-ee) is the first peek at Ireland for many tourists. Fortunately, it makes a good spot to begin a ramble along the coast south of Dublin. The **harbor** itself is a sight, filled with yachts, boat tours, car ferries, fishermen, and a new marina—frequent summer evening boat races draw much of the town. ◨**James Joyce Tower,** in the Martello tower in Sandycove, is a fascinating retreat. From the Sandycove DART station, go left at Eagle House down to the coast, turn right and continue to the Martello tower; or take bus #8 from Burgh Quay in Dublin to Sandycove Ave. James Joyce stayed in the tower for a tense six days in August 1904 as a guest of Oliver St. John Gogarty. The infamous Gogarty was immortalized in Chapter One of *Ulysses*. The novel is partially set around the tower, with Gogarty transformed into Buck Mulligan, another guest into Haines, and Joyce into Stephen Daedalus, who meditates on the "snot-green" sea. The two-room museum contains Joyce's death mask, a page of the original manuscript of *Finnegan's Wake*, and editions of *Ulysses*, including one illustrated by Henri Matisse. (☎280 9265. Open Apr.-Oct. M-Sa 10am-1pm and 2-5pm, Su 2-6pm; Nov.-Mar. by appointment. IR£4/€5.10, students and seniors IR£3.60/€4.60.) The **tourist office,** in the ferry terminal, is equipped with copious maps and pamphlets on the area. (Open M-Sa 10am-5:30pm.) The **Belgrave Hall,** 34 Belgrave Sq., is a top-tier hostel with high ceilings and marble floors. (☎284 2106. Breakfast included. Laundry IR£3-6. Bike rental IR£10 per day. **Internet.** Summer F-Su 10-bed dorm IR£15/€19.05; M-Th all rooms IR£13/€16.55.)

SOUTHEAST IRELAND

Historically the power base of the Vikings and then the Normans, southeast Ireland feels the influence of the Celts only faintly. Beaches are the most fruitful of the Southeast's attractions, drawing mostly native Irish admirers to the coastline that runs from Kilmore Quay to tidy Ardmore. Waterford has the resources, nightlife, and grit of a real city, while Cashel boasts a superbly preserved cathedral complex. Continue your hunt for raging nightlife south from Dublin through Carlow, Kilkenny, and Waterford; alternatively, the daylight hours are most enjoyably spent exploring the pretty paths through the Wicklow Mountains and Wexford.

⚓ FERRIES TO FRANCE AND BRITAIN

Irish Ferries sails from Rosslare Harbour to: **Pembroke, Wales** (4hr.); **Roscoff** (18hr.) and **Cherbourg, France** (19hr.). Ferries depart daily for Wales and every other day to France. (☎(053) 33158, after hours ☎(08705) 171 717; www.irishferries.com. Foot passenger fares to Britain IR£18-22/€22.90-27.95. "Low" fares to France roughly IR£35-45/€45-57. **Eurail passes** grant passage on ferries to France.) **Stena Line** runs from Rosslare to **Fishguard, Wales.** (☎(053) 331150. 3½hr., 2 per day, IR£18-22; student with current ISIC £IR13-18.)

THE WICKLOW MOUNTAINS

Over 600m high, carpeted in fragrant heather and pleated by sparkling rivers, the Wicklow summits are home to grazing sheep and scattered villagers. Smooth glacial valleys embrace the two lakes and the monastic ruins. Public transportation is severely limited, so driving is the easiest way to connect the sights and towns. The lush, blessed valley of **Glendalough** draws a steady summertime stream of coach tours filled with hikers and ruin-oglers. St. Kevin's **Bus** Service (☎(01) 281 8119) runs from St. Stephen's Green West in Dublin (2 per day; IR£6/€7.65, round-trip IR£10/€12.70) and returns in the evening (2-3 per day). The **tourist office** is across from the Glendalough Hotel. (☎(0404) 45688. Open mid-June to Sept. M-Sa 10am-6pm; closed 1-2pm for lunch) The **National Park Information Office,** between the two lakes, is the best source for hiking advice. (☎(0404) 454 25. Open May-Aug. daily 10am-6pm; Apr. and Sept. Sa-Su 10am-6pm.) The **Glendaloch Hostel (An Óige/HI)** is 5min. past the Glendalough tourist office. (☎(0404) 45342. **Internet.** Bike rental IR£10/€12.70 per day. Laundry IR£4/€5.10. Dorms IR£13/€16.55; doubles IR£32/€40.65; off-season IR£1-2/€1.30-2.55 less.) For more affordable food, B&Bs, and groceries, head to **Laragh,** 1.5km up the road (10min. from the Wicklow Way).

ROSSLARE HARBOUR ☎ 053

Rosslare Harbour is a decidedly pragmatic seaside village that mainly functions as an important transportation link to Wales, France, and the Irish coast. **Trains** run from the ferry port to Dublin (3hr., 3 per day, IR£11/€14) and Limerick (2½hr., 1-2 per day, IR£12.50/€15.90), via Waterford (1¼hr., IR£6/€7.65). **Buses** run to Dublin (3hr., 10-12 per day, IR£10/€12.70); Cork (3-5 per day, IR£13.50/€17.15) and Galway (4 per day, IR£17/€21.60), both via Waterford (3-5 per day, IR£9.20/€11.70); Limerick (3-5 per day, IR£13.50/€17.15); Tralee (2-4 per day, IR£17//€21.60). The Rosslare-Kilrane **Tourist Information Centre** is 1.5km from the harbor on Wexford Rd in Kilrane. (☎ 33622. Open daily 10:30am-8pm.) If you must stay overnight before catching a ferry, try ◪**Mrs. O'Leary's Farmhouse**, Killilane (☎ 33134), off N25 in Kilrane, a 15min. drive from town on farm, right by the sea. Call for pickup from town. Single IR£18.15/€23, with bath IR£20.10/€25.50.

KILKENNY ☎ 056

Ireland's best preserved medieval town, Kilkenny also features rocking nightlife—nine churches share the streets with 80 pubs. Thirteenth-century **Kilkenny Castle** housed the Earls of Ormonde from the 1300s until 1932. The basement shelters the **Butler Gallery,** which hangs modern art exhibitions. (☎ 21450. Open June-Sept. daily 10am-7pm; Oct.-Mar. Tu-Sa 10:30am-12:45pm and 2-5pm, Su 11am-12:45pm and 2-5pm; Apr.-May daily 10:30am-5pm. Mandatory guided tour. IR£3.50/€4.45, students IR£1.50/€1.90.) **Tynan Walking Tours** provides the down-and-dirty on Kilkenny's folkloric tradition in an hour. (☎ 65929. £3.50/€4.45, students £3/€3.80.) Climb the thin 30m tower of **St. Canice's Cathedral,** up the hill off Dean St., for a panoramic view of the town and its surroundings. (☎ 64971. Open Easter-Sept. M-Sa 9am-1pm and 2-6pm, Su 2-6pm; Oct.-Easter M-Sa 10am-1pm and 2-4pm, Su 2-4pm. IR£1.50/€1.90.) **Trains** (☎ 22024) and **buses** (☎ 64933) stop at Kilkenny Station on Dublin Rd.; buses also stop on Patrick St. in the city center. Trains go to Dublin (2hr., IR£12.50/€15.90) and Waterford (45min., IR£5.50/€7). Buses go to: Cork (3hr., 2-3 per day; IR£10/€12.70); Dublin (2hr., 5-6 per day; IR£7/€8.90); Galway (5hr., 3-5 per day; IR£17/€21.60); Rosslare Harbour (2hr., 3-6 per day; IR£10.50/€13.35); Waterford (1½hr., 1-2 per day; IR£5/€6.35). From Kilkenny Station, turn left on John St. to reach the Parade, dominated by the castle to your left. The **tourist office,** Rose Inn St., has free maps and info on B&Bs. (☎ 51500. Open July-Aug. M-Sa 9am-7pm, Su 11am-1pm and 2-5pm; Apr.-June and Sept. M-Sa 9am-6pm, Su 11am-1pm and 2-5pm; Oct.-Mar. M-Sa 9am-5pm.) Waterford Rd. and more remote Castlecomer Rd. have the highest concentration of beds. **Kilkenny Tourist Hostel (IHH),** 35 Parliament St., is always brimming with activity. (☎ 635 41. Laundry IR£3/€3.80. Check-out 10am. Dorms IR£10-11.50/€14.50-12.70; doubles IR£13/€16.50.) **Dunnes Supermarket,** Kieran St., stocks food. (☎ 61655. Open M-Tu Sa 8:30am-7pm, W-F 8:30am-10pm, Su 10am-6pm.) **The Pump House,** 26 Parliament St. Remains a favorite among locals and hostelers with extra special pub grub.

WATERFORD ☎ 051

Behind an industrial façade of metal silos and cranes, Waterford charms with narrow, winding streets filled with pubs and shops. The town highlight is the ◪**Waterford Crystal Factory,** 1.5km away on the N25 (Cork Rd). One-hour tours allow you to witness the transformation of molten glass into polished crystal. Admire the finished products—and their astronomical prices—in the gallery. Catch the **City Imp** (a red and yellow minibus) outside Dunnes on Michael St. and request a stop at the factory (10-15min., runs every 15-20min., IR£0.80/€1) or take city bus #1 (dir.: Kilbarry-Ballybeg; 2 per hr., IR£0.85/€1.10), across from the Clock Tower. (☎ 373 311. Gallery open Mar-Dec. daily 8:30am-6pm; Jan. M-F 9-5pm; Feb. daily 9-5pm. Tours Jan.-Feb. M-F 9-3:15pm; Mar.-Oct. daily 8:30am-4pm; Nov.-Dec. M-F 9am-5:15pm. Tours IR£4.50/€5.75.) **Reginald's Tower,** at the end of the Quay, has guarded city's entrance since the 12th century. (☎ 873 501. Open June-Sept. daily 9:30am-6:30pm; Oct.-May 10am-5pm. IR£1.50/€1.90, students IR£0.60/€0.80.) The Quays are loaded with **pubs;** even more reside on the corner of John and Parnell St. **T&H Doolan's,** George's St. (☎ 841 504), has been serving crowds for 300 years.

IRELAND

Trains (☎876 243) leave from across the bridge from the Quay; the bus station (☎879 000) is on the Quay by the bridge. Trains run to: Dublin (2½hr., 5-6 per day, IR£13.50-17/€17.15-21.60); Kilkenny (40min., 3-5 per day, IR£5.50/€7); Limerick (2¼hr., M-Sa 2 per day, IR£10.50/€13.35); Rosslare Harbour (1hr., M-Sa 2 per day, IR£6.50/€8.25). **Buses** depart for: Cork (2½hr., 10-13 per day, IR£10/€12.70); Dublin (2¾hr., 6-12 per day, IR£7/€8.90); Galway (4¾hr., 5-6 per day, IR£13.50/€17.15); Kilkenny (1hr., M-Su 1 per day, IR£5/€6.35); Limerick (2½hr., 6-7 per day, IR£10.50/€13.35); Rosslare Harbour (1¼hr., 3-5 per day, IR£9.20/€11.70). The **tourist office** is in the Granary at the intersection of the Quay and Hanover St. (☎875 788. Open July-Aug. M-Sa 9am-6pm, Su 11am-5pm; Sept.-Oct. M-Sa 9am-6pm; Nov.-Mar. M-Sa 9am-5pm; Apr.-June M-Sa 9am-6pm.) All of Waterford's hostels have gone the way of the dodo, but Mrs. Ryan, the owner of **Beechwood**, 7 Cathedral Sq., will invite you into her charming home. Located on a silent pedestrian street, her B&B is up Henrietta St. from the Quay. (☎876 677. Doubles IR£32/€40.60.) Get **groceries** at **Treacy's**, on the Quay near the Granville Hotel. (Open daily 8am-11pm.)

CASHEL ☎062

Cashel sprawls at the foot of the commanding 90m ◪**Rock of Cashel** (a.k.a. **St. Patrick's Rock**), a huge limestone outcropping topped by medieval buildings. (Open mid-June to mid-Sept. daily 9am-7:30pm; mid-Sept. to mid-Mar. 9:30am-4:30pm; mid-Mar. to mid-June 9:30am-5:30pm. IR£3.50/€4.45, students IR£1.80/€2.30.) The two-towered **Cormac's Chapel**, consecrated in 1134, holds semi-restored Romanesque paintings. Down the cow path from the Rock lie the ruins of **Hore Abbey**, built by Cistercian monks who were fond of arches; the abbey is presently inhabited by nonchalant sheep. **Bus Éireann** (☎62121) leaves from Bianconi's Bistro, on Main St., for: Cork (1½hr., 6 per day, IR£9.60/€12.20); Dublin (3hr., 6 per day, IR£12/€15.25); Limerick (1hr., 5 per day, £9.20/€11.75). The **tourist office** is in the City Hall on Main St. (☎61333. Open July-Aug. M-Sa 9:15am-6pm, Su 11am-5pm; Apr.-June and Sept. M-Sa 9:15am-6pm.) Just down Dundrum Rd. from town lies the stunning **O'Brien's Farmhouse Hostel.** (☎61003. Laundry £6/€7.60. Dorms £9-10/€11.50-12.70; doubles £30/€38.10. **Camping** £4.50-5/€5.70-6.35.) Just steps from the Rock on Dominic St., the quaint **Rockville House** is a bargain. (☎61760. Singles £25/€31.75; doubles £38/€48.25; triples £57/€72.40.) **Centra Supermarket** is on Friar St. (☎61421. Open daily 7am-11pm.) *Craic* is performed nightly at **Feehan's**, Main St.

SOUTHWEST IRELAND

With a contradictory and dramatic landscape that ranges from lush lakes and mountains to stark, ocean-battered cliffs, it's no wonder Southwest Ireland has produced some of the country's greatest storytellers. Outlaws and rebels once lurked in hidden coves and glens now frequented by visitors and ruled over by republicans. If the tourist mayhem of the west is too much for you, it's easy to retreat to the more quiet stretches along the Dingle Peninsula and southern coast.

▓ FERRIES TO FRANCE AND BRITAIN

Cork-Swansea Ferries (☎(021) 271 166; www.swansea-cork.ie.) go between Cork and Swansea, South Wales, (10hr., 1 per day; IR£24-34/€30.50-43, car and driver £89-159/€113-200). **Brittany Ferries** sail from **Cork** to **Roscoff, France** (13½hr.).

CORK ☎021

Ireland's second-largest city, Cork (pop. 150,000) is the center of the southwest's arts, music, and sports. Strolls along the pub-lined streets and river quays reveal grand and grimy architecture, as well as more recent commercial and industrial development—evidence of Cork's history of ruin and reconstruction. Wise visitors will less abrasively exploit the city's resources and use Cork as a place to eat, drink, shop, and sleep while exploring the exquisite scenery of the surrounding countryside. Within the city limits, time is best spent by taking in vibrant street scenes or wandering across University College of Cork's historical-comical-pastoral campus.

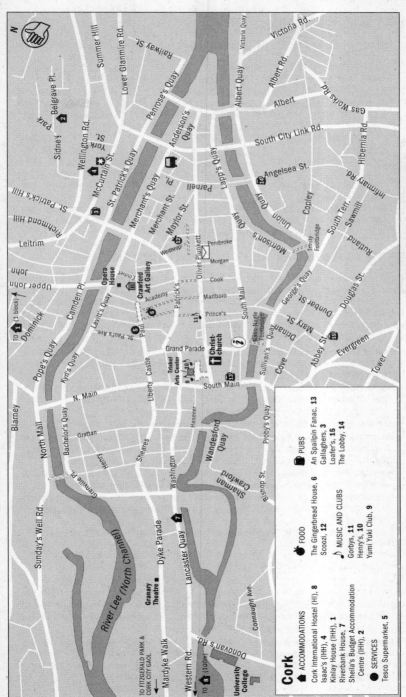

IRELAND

Cork

▲ ACCOMMODATIONS
Cork International Hostel (HI), 8
Isaac's (IHH), 4
Kinlay House (IHH), 1
Riverbank House, 7
Sheila's Budget Accommodation
Center (IHH), 2

● SERVICES
Tesco Supermarket, 5

🍴 FOOD
The Gingerbread House, 6
Scoozi, 12

♪ MUSIC AND CLUBS
Gorbys, 11
Henry's, 10
Yumi Yuki Club, 9

🍺 PUBS
An Spailpin Fanac, 13
Gallaghers, 3
Loafer's, 15
The Lobby, 14

☞ TRANSPORTATION

Trains: Kent Station (☎506 766), Lower Glanmire Rd, across the river from the city center. Open M-Sa 6:35am-8:30pm, Su 7:50am-8pm. Connections to: **Dublin** (3hr., 5-7 per day; IR£33.50/€42.55); **Killarney** (2hr., 4-7 per day; IR£14/€17.80); **Limerick** (1½hr., 4-7 per day; IR£14/€17.80); **Tralee** (2½hr., 3 per day; IR£18/€22.90).

Buses: (☎508 188) on Parnell Pl., 2 blocks east of Patrick's Bridge on **Merchants' Quay.** Inquiries desk open daily 9am-5pm. To: **Belfast** (7½hr., M-Sa 4 per day, Su 2 per day; IR£20/€25.40); **Dublin** (4½hr., 4 per day, IR£13/€16.55); **Galway** (4hr., 5 per day, IR£12.50/€15.90); **Killarney** (2hr.; M-Sa 8 per day, Su 6 per day; IR£9.40/€11.95); **Limerick** (2hr.; M-Sa 6 per day, Su 5 per day; IR£9.60/€12.20); **Rosslare Harbour** (4hr., 2 per day, IR£13.50/€17.15); **Sligo** (7hr., 3 per day, IR£17/€21.60); **Tralee** (2½hr.; M-Sa 8 per day, Su 6 per day; IR£10/€12.70); **Waterford** (2¼hr., M-Sa 8 per day, Sun 6 per day; IR£10/€12.70). City buses criss-cross the city and its suburbs. From downtown, catch the buses (and their schedules) at the bus station on Merchant's Quay or on St. Patrick St., across from the Father Matthew statue.

Ferries: To: **Swansen, England** daily (IR£44-64/€55.90-81.30, prices increase June-Aug.). Contact **Irish Ferries** (☎(1890) 313 131) at the corner of MacCurtain St. and St. Patrick's bridge. 24hr. ferry information ☎(01) 661 0715.)

✳ ⚡ ORIENTATION AND PRACTICAL INFORMATION

Cork is compact and pedestrian-friendly, the tip of an arrow-shaped island in the **River Lee.** The north side is dominated by the sight-saturated **Shandon** district. South of the river, the downtown action is concentrated on **Oliver Plunkett Street, Saint Patrick Street, Paul Street,** and the north-south streets that connect them. Heading west from the Grand Parade, **Washington Street** becomes **Western Road**; to the north of the Lee, **McCurtain Street** flows east into **Lower Glanmire Road.**

Tourist Office: Grand Parade (☎273 251), near the corner of South Mall and Grand Parade downtown; across from the National Monument. Open June-Aug.M-F 9:00am-5:30pm, Sept.-May M-Sa 9:15am-5:30pm.

Banks: TSB, 4-5 Princes St. (☎275 221). Open M-W and F 9:30am-5pm, Th 9:30am-7pm. **Bank of Ireland,** 70 Patrick St. (☎277 177). Open M 10am-5pm, Tu-F 10am-4pm. Most banks in Cork have **24hr. ATMs.**

Emergency: ☎999; no coins required. Police (*Garda*); (☎522 000), Anglesea St.

Pharmacies: Regional Late Night Pharmacy, (☎344 575) Wilton Rd., opposite the Regional Hospital on bus #8. Open M-F 9am-10pm, Sa-Su 10am-10pm. **Phelan's Late Night,** 9 Patrick St. (☎272 511). Open M-Sa 9am-10pm, Su 10am-10pm.

Hospital: Mercy Hospital, (☎271 971) Grenville Pl. IR£20/€25.40 fee for access to emergency room. **Cork Regional Hospital,** Wilton St. (☎546 400), on bus #8.

Internet Access: Cork City Library, across from the tourist office on the Grand Parade. IR£1/€1.30 per 30min. (☎427 7110. Open Tu-Sa 10am-1pm and 2-5:30pm. Computers turn off at 5pm).

Post Office: (☎272 000), Oliver Plunkett St. at the corner of Pembrooke St. Open M-Sa 9am-5:30pm.

☞ ACCOMMODATIONS

Cork's hostels range from drearily adequate to wonderfully welcoming. **B&Bs** are clustered along Western Rd. near University College. The other concentration of accommodations is in the slightly more central area along McCurtain St. and Lower Glanmire Rd., near the bus and train stations.

Sheila's Budget Accommodation Centre (IHH), 4 Belgrave Pl. (☎450 5562), by the intersection of Wellington Rd. and York St. **Internet** access. Breakfast IR£1.50/€1.90. Key deposit IR£5/€6.35. 24hr. reception desk is also a general store; check-out 10:30am. Dorms IR£9-10/€11.45-12.70; doubles IR£24/€30.50.

Cork International Hostel (An Óige/HI), 1-2 Redclyffe, Western Rd. (☎454 3289), a 15min. walk from the Grand Parade. Bus #8 stops across the street. Immaculate and spacious bunk rooms in a stately brick Victorian townhouse. All rooms with bath. Breakfast IR£2/€2.55. Check-in 8am-midnight. Dorms IR£8-11.50/€10.20-14.60.

Kinlay House (IHH), Bob and Joan Walk (☎450 6927). Down the alley to the right of Shandon Church, in Shandon. Each room has a locker and sink. **Internet** access IR£1.50/€1.90 per 15min. Video library and game room. Continental breakfast included. Laundry IR£4/€5.10. Dorms IR£8/€10.20; singles IR£15/€19.05. doubles IR£25/31.75. ISIC discount 10%.

Isaac's (IHH), 48 McCurtain St. (☎450 8388). From the bus stop, cross the nearby bridge and take the 2nd left onto McCurtain St. Located near the bus and train stations. 24hr. reception. Dorm lockout 10am-3pm. Dorms IR£7.95-9.25/€10.10-11.75

Riverbank House, 9 Lancaster Quay. (☎427 8458.). Opposite the Jury Hotel. From the center of town, head out on Washington St. toward the university and look for the B&B on the right side. Ask for the "yellow room." Tea and coffee, TV, and phone in every room. Singles from IR£25/€31.75; doubles from IR£40/€50.80.

◘ FOOD

Don't explore Cork's city center on an empty stomach; delicious restaurants and cafes abound. Particularly appealing are the lanes connecting Patrick St., Paul St., and Oliver Plunkett St. **Tesco** (☎270 791), on Paul St., is the biggest grocery store in town. (Open M-W and Sa 8:30am-8pm, Th-F 8:30am-10pm.)

Scoozi (☎275 077), in the alley just off Winthrop Ave. Follow the tomato signs to this expansive, brick-and-wood-lined establishment. Pesto chicken breast on a bun with fries and coleslaw IR£6.85/€8.70. Open M-Sa 9am-11pm, Su noon-10pm.

The Gingerbread House (☎296 411), Paul St. Huge windows, cool jazz, and heavenly breads, pastries, and quiche are made fresh on the premises. Open M-W and Sa 8:15am-7pm, Th-F 8:15am-9pm, Su 8:15am-6pm.

Quay Co-op, 24 Sullivan's Quay (☎431 7660). A vegetarian's delight, and no chore for carnivores. Excellent soups and desserts. Daily specials around IR£5/€6.35. Bean and hazelnut burger IR£4.50/€5.75. Open M-Sa 9am-9pm. The store downstairs caters to all organic and vegan needs. Store open M-Sa 9am-6:15pm.

◎ ♪ SIGHTS AND ENTERTAINMENT

Cork's sights are loosely divided into several districts, but all can be reached by foot. Pick up the *Cork Area City Guide* at the tourist office (IR£1.50/€1.90). Bridges link the island to Cork's residential south side and less affluent north side. Across the river to the north, walk up Shandon St. and take a right down Church St. (it's unmarked) to reach Cork's most famous landmark, **St. Anne's Church,** which has earned the nickname "the four-faced liar", because the tower's four clocks are notoriously out of sync with one another. Climb the claustrophobic stairs for a panoramic view, or stay below to entertain the entire city with your favourite melody on the bells (☎450 5906. Open M-Sa 9:30am-5:30pm. IR£3.50/€4.45, students and seniors IR£3/€3.85.) Housed within an elegant 18th-century customs house, the **Crawford Municipal Art Gallery** specializes in the paintings of Irish masters like James Barry and Jack Yeats, along with contemporary work. (☎273 377. Open M-Sa 10am-5pm. Free.)Adjacent is the monstrous cement **Opera House** at Emmet Place. Do not pass go before heading to the **Cork City Gaol,** where multimedia tours of the former prison and a lesson on Cork's social history await; cross the bridge at the western end of Fitzgerald Park, turn right on Sunday's Well Rd., and follow the signs. (☎430 50 22. Open daily Mar.-Oct. 9:30am-6pm; Nov.-Feb. 10am-5pm. IR£5/€6.35, students IR£4/€5.10. Admission includes audio tape tour.) After visiting the jail, taste liberty by wandering the grounds of the nearby **University College Cork,** on the riverbank along Western Rd.

IRELAND

The always lively streets of Cork make finding entertainment easy. Cork's pub-ring offering atmosphere and lively music—along **Oliver Plunkett Street, Union Quay,** and **South Main Street,** there are more establishments than you can shake a stick at. To keep on top of the scene, check out the bi-weekly *List Cork* (available at local stores; free), which details local music performances. **The Lobby,** 1 Union Quay, arguably the most famous venue in Cork, gave some of Ireland's most famous folk acts their big breaks; it features live music nightly with a view of the river. (☎319 307. Occasional cover IR£2-5/€2.55-6.35.) **An Spailpín Fanac,** 28 South Main St. (☎277 949), is one of Cork's more popular and ancient pubs—it opened in 1779. Live *trad* complements the decor most nights. **Gallaghers,** MacCurtain St., is a tradi-tional pub conveniently located to welcome tourists, especially on "Backpacker Nights" (W and F, check for posters at hostels), when a three-pint pitcher sells for IR£6/€7.65. **Gorbys,** Oliver Plunkett St., features young groovers grinding. (☎270 074. Cover IR£2-5€2.55-6.35.) Arguably the most populated dance club in Cork, **Sir Henry's,** South Main St., is also the most intense. Prepare to wedge yourself between sweaty, semi-conscious bodies on three dance floors. (☎274 391. Cover IR£2-11/ €2.55-14.) Restaurant by day, nightclub by night, **The Yumi Yuki Club,** Tobin St., is a Pan-Asian themed club offering an alternative to the raucous parties nearby. (☎275 777. Occasional cover IR£3/€3.85. Open 10am-1am, food is served noon-midnight) **Loafer's,** 26 Douglas St. (☎431 1612), Cork's main gay and lesbian pub fills up all night with all age groups.

▶ DAYTRIPS FROM CORK

BLARNEY (AN BHLARNA)

Buses run from Cork to Blarney (10-16 per day, IR£3/€3.80 roundtrip). ☎4385 252. Castle open June-Aug. 9am-7pm, Su 9:30am-5:30pm; Sept. M-Sa 9am-6:30pm, Su 9:30am-sundown; Oct.-Apr. M-Sa 9am-6pm or sundown, Su 9:30am-5pm or sundown; May M-Sa 9am-6:30pm, Su 9:30am-5:30pm. IR£3.50/€4.45, seniors and students IR£2.50/€3.20, children IR£1/€1.30.

Whether you're in the mood to admire the idyllic Irish countryside or simply dying to stand in a damp castle passageway, **Blarney Castle,** with its **Blarney Stone,** is the quintessential tourist spot. The prevailing myth of the stone's origin holds that it is a chip of the Scottish Stone of Scone that was presented to the King of Munster in gratitude for support during a rebellion in 1314. With everyone else doing it, you might just find yourself bending over backwards to kiss the stone in hopes of acquiring the legendary eloquence bestowed on those who smooch it. The term "blarney" refers to the Irish talent of stretching, or even obstructing, the truth.

MIDLETON

Buses run from Cork (30min., M-Sa 13-18 per day, Su 4 per day, IR£3.80/€4.80). ☎613 594. Heritage Centre open Mar.-Oct. daily 10am-6pm. IR£4.50/€5.70, students and seniors IR£4/€5, children IR£2/€2.55. Tours every 30-45min.

Midleton beckons pilgrims to the **Jameson Heritage Centre** with the water of life (Irish for **whiskey**). The center rolls visitors through a 1hr. tour detailing the craft and history of whiskey production, and a glass of the potent stuff is thrown in. After all, "the story of whiskey is the story of Ireland."

KINSALE   ☎021

Each summer, affluent tourists come to swim, fish, and eat at Kinsale's famed and pricey 12 restaurants known as the "Good Food Circle;" but the town's best attrac-tions are cheap. Follow the coastal (Ministry of) **Scilly Walk** 30min. from the end of Pearse St. to reach the star-shaped, 17th-century **Charles Fort,** which offers spectac-ular views of the town and its watery surroundings (Open mid-Mar. to Oct. M-F 10am-6pm; Nov. to mid-Mar. Sa-Su 10am-5pm, weekdays by appointment. IR£2.50/ €3.20, students IR£1/€1.30.) Across the harbor, the grass-covered ruins of **James Fort** delight with panoramic views. (Open 24hr. Free.) **Buses** arrive at the Esso sta-

KNOW YOUR WHISKEY Anyone who drinks his whiskey as it's meant to be drunk—"neat," or straight—can tell you that there's a huge difference between Irish whiskeys (Bushmills, Jameson, Power and Son, and the like), Scotch whiskys (spelled without an e), and American whiskeys. But what makes an Irish whiskey *Irish*? The basic ingredients in whiskey—water, barley (which becomes malt once processed), and heat from a fuel source—are always the same. It's the quality of these ingredients, the way in which they're combined, and the manner in which the combination is stored that gives each product its distinct flavor. The different types of whiskey derive from slight differences in this production process. American whiskey is distilled once and is often stored in oak, bourbon is made only in Kentucky, scotch uses peat-smoked barley, and Irish whiskey is triple-distilled. The best way to understand the distinctions between brands is to taste the various labels in close succession to one another. Line up those shot glasses, sniff and then taste each one (roll the whiskey in your mouth like a real pro), and have a sip of water between each brand.

tion on the pier from Cork (40min., M-F 5 per day, IR£6/€7.65 round-trip). The **tourist office**, Emmet Pl., is on the waterfront. (☎477 2234. Open Mar.-Nov. daily 9am-6pm.) To get to the **Castlepark Marina Centre (IHH)**, across the harbor, walk along the pier away from town for 10min., turn left, cross Duggan Bridge, take a left past the bridge, and follow the road back toward the harbor. (☎477 4959. Open mid-Mar. to Dec. Dorms IR£10/€12.70; doubles IR£24/€30.50.) **Dempsey's Hostel (IHH)**, Cork Rd., is an 8min. walk from town. (☎772124. Dorms IR£7/€8.90; doubles IR£18/€22.90.)

SCHULL AND THE MIZEN HEAD PENINSULA ☎028

The seaside hamlet of **Schull** is an ideal base for exploring the craggy, windswept, and beach-laden southwest tip of Ireland. A calm harbor and numerous shipwrecks make a **diver's** paradise; the **Watersports Centre** rents gear. (☎28554. Open M-Sa 9:30am-8:30pm.) Pick up the prosaic and lengthy *Schull Guide* from any store in town (IR£1.50/€1.90). The Mizen becomes more scenic and less populated the farther west you go from Schull. **Betty Johnson's Bus Hire** offers tours of the Mizen via the scenic coast road. (☎284 10. Departs Schull June-Aug. Tu and Th 11am. IR£6/€7.65.) **Buses** arrive in Schull from Cork (1-3 per day, IR£13/€16.55 round-trip) and Killarney (June-Sept. 1 per day). Once you've reached Schull, there's no further public transportation on the peninsula besides a Bus Éireann bus to Goleen (2 per day). Those who choose to accept the risks of **hitching** often avoid poor public transportation by waiting at the crossroads on Goleen Rd. outside of town. *Let's Go* does not recommend hitchhiking. Confident **cyclists** can daytrip to Mizen Head (29km from Schull). The immaculate **Schull Backpackers' Lodge (IHH)**, Colla Rd, has **hiking** and **biking** maps and info. (☎286 81. Dorms IR£8/€10.20; doubles IR£24-26/€30.50-33.05.) **Spar Market** is on Main St. (☎28236. Open July-Sept. daily 7am-9pm, Oct.-June M-Sa 7am-8pm, Su 8am-8pm.) In summer, Schull is also a jumping-off point to ferry to the striking island of **Cape Clear** (☎28278. Jun.-Sept. 1-3 ferries per day, IR£9/€11.45 round-trip).

KILLARNEY AND KILLARNEY NATIONAL PARK ☎064

The town of Killarney is just minutes from some of Ireland's most glorious natural scenery. The 95 sq. km **national park** outside town blends forested mountains with the famous Lakes of Killarney. **Muckross House**, 5km south of Killarney on Kenmare Rd., is a massive 19th-century manor with a garden that blooms brilliantly each year. A path leads to the 20m-high **Torc Waterfall**. (House open July-Aug. daily 9am-7pm; Sept.-Oct. and mid-Mar. to June 9am-6pm. IR£3.80/€4.85, students IR£1.60/€2.05.) Walk or drive to the 14th-century **Ross Castle** by taking a right on Ross Rd. off Muckross Rd., 3km from Killarney; the footpaths from Knockreer (out of town on New St.) are more scenic. (Open June-Aug. daily 9am-6:30pm; May-Sept. 10am-6pm; Oct. and mid-Mar. to Apr. 10am-5pm. Obligatory tour IR£3/€3.85, students IR£1.25/€1.60.) Bike around the **Gap of Dunloe**, which borders **Macgillycuddy's Reeks**,

IRELAND

Ireland's highest mountain range. Hop on a **boat** from Ross Castle to the head of the Gap (IR£8/€10.20; book at the tourist office). From **Lord Brandon's Cottage**, on the Gap, head left over the stone bridge from continue 3km to the church, follow the hairpin turn, and huff the 2km to the top; your reward is an 11km coast downhill through the park's most breathtaking scenery. The 13km ride to Killarney (bear right after Kate Kearney's Cottage, turn left on the road to Fossa, and turn right on Killorglin Rd.) passes the ruins of **Dunloe Castle**, demolished by Cromwell's armies.

Trains arrive at Killarney station (☎31067) off East Avenue Rd., near Park Rd., from: Cork (2hr., 5 per day, IR£14/€17.80); Dublin (3½hr., 4 per day, IR£35.50/€45.10); Limerick (3hr., 3-4 per day, IR£15.50/€19.70). **Buses** (☎30011) rumble from Park Rd. to Cork (2hr., 10-14 per day, IR£9.40/€11.95) and Dublin (6hr., 5-6 per day, IR£15/€19.05). **Bike rental** places abound; expect to pay IR£7/€8.90. The **tourist office** is on Beech St., off New St. (☎31633. Open July-Aug. M-Sa 9am-8pm, Su 10am-1pm and 2:15-6pm; June and Sept. M-Sa 9am-6pm, Su 10am-1pm and 2:15-6pm; Oct.-May M-Sa 9:15am-5:30pm.) From either station, turn left on College St. and turn right past the courthouse to reach **The Súgán (IHH)**, Lewis Rd., where exuberant management compensates for cramped quarters. (☎33104. Dorms IR£9/€11.45.) The immense **Neptune's (IHH)**, Bishop's Ln., is up the 1st walkway off New St. on the right. (☎35255. Dorms IR£7.50-10/€9.55-12.70; doubles IR£26/€33.05.) Call for a ride from either station to ▓**Peacock Farms Hostel (IHH)**, 11km from town. (☎33577. Dorms IR£10-12/€12.70-15.25; doubles IR£28/€35.55.) Pick up **groceries** at **Tesco**, in an arcade off New St. (Open M-W and Sa 8:30am-7pm, Th-F 8:30am-9pm.) ▓**O'Conner's Traditional Pub**, 7 High St., mixes locals and tourists (*trad* M and Th).

RING OF KERRY

The Southwest's most celebrated peninsula holds wee villages, fabled ancient forts, and rugged mountains—the romantic scenery most visitors come to Ireland seeking. Although noxious, air-conditioned tour buses often hog the roads, greater rewards await those who take the time to explore the landscape on foot or by bike.

⬛ TRANSPORTATION. The term "Ring of Kerry" usually describes the entire **Iveragh Peninsula**, though it more technically refers to the ring of roads circumnavigating it. Hop on the no-frills circuit run by **Bus Éireann**, which stops at the major towns on the Ring (June-Sept. 2 per day): **Cahersiveen** (from Killorglin 50min., IR£5/€6.35); **Caherdaniel** (from Cahersiveen 1hr., IR£3.10/€3.90); **Killarney** (from Caherdaniel 1½hr., IR£7.30/€9.30; from Cahersiveen 2½hr., IR£9/€11.50).

CAHERSIVEEN. Cahersiveen (car-si-VEEN) is best known in Ireland as the birthplace of patriot Daniel "The Liberator" O'Connell, who won Catholic representation in Parliament in 1829. Its upbeat attitude and excellent location make it an ideal base for exploring the nearby beach and historical sites, or for longer excursions to Valentia Island and the Skellig rocks. Three kilometers northwest of town across the bridge are the ruins of the **Ballycarbery Castle**, once held by O'Connell's ancestors. Two hundred meters past the castle turn-off lie the 3m-thick walls of **Cahergall Fort** and the small stone dwellings of **Leacanabuaile Fort**. The **tourist office** is directly across from the bus stop next to the post office. (☎(066) 947 2589. Open June to mid-Sept. M-Sa 9:15am-1pm and 2:15-5:30pm.) The welcoming **Sive Hostel (IHH)** is at 15 East End, Main St. (☎(066) 947 2717. Dorms IR£8/€01.20; doubles IR£20-25/€25.40-31.75; **camping** IR£4/€5.10 per person.) Next to the post office, **O'Shea's B&B** boasts comfortable rooms. (☎947 2402. Single IR£23/€29.20.) Cahersiveen's 30 **original pubs** may seem excessive, but residents recollect when there were 52.

A fantastic daytrip is the quiet ▓**Valentia Island**, where shady country roads link a handful of beehive huts, *ogham* stones, and small ruins. The views on the way, across to the mountainous mainland, and out over Dingle Bay, are reason enough to come to Ireland. Bridges on either end connect to the mainland for an easy **bike** ride; alternatively, a comically short **ferry** runs to the island (3min., Apr.-Sept. every 10min. 8:15am-7:30pm; pedestrians IR£3/€3.85, cyclists IR£1.50/€1.90) from **Reenard Point**, three points west of Cahersiveen. A taxi to the ferry dock from

Cahersiveen runs IR£4/€5.10. Another recommended daytrip is to the **Skellig Rocks,** a stunning mass of natural rubble about 13km off the shore of the Iveragh Peninsula. From your boat, **Little Skellig** will at first appear snow-capped, but it's actually just covered with 24,000 pairs of crooning birds. Climb the vertigo-inducing 650 steps past puffins, kittiwakes, gannets, and petrels (birds to you) to reach a **monastery** built by Six-century Christian monks, whose beehive-like dwellings are still intact. The hostel and campground in Cahersiveen will arrange the **ferry** ride (45-90min.) for IR£25/€31.75, including a ride to the dock.

CAHERDANIEL. There's little in the village of **Caherdaniel** to attract the Ring's droves of buses, but nearby **Derrynane Strand,** 2.5km away in Derrynane National Park, delights with 3km of gorgeous beach ringed by picture-perfect dunes. **Derrynane House,** signposted just up from the beach, was the residence of Irish patriot Daniel O'Connell. (Open May-Sept. M-Sa 9am-6pm, Su 11am-7pm; Apr. and Oct. Tu-Su 1-5pm; Nov.-Mar. Sa-Su 1-5pm. IR£2, students IR£1.) Guests have the run of the house at **The Travellers' Rest Hostel.** (☎(066) 947 5175. Breakfast IR£3/€3.85. Dorms IR£8.50/€10.80; singles IR£10.50-13/€13.35-16.55; doubles IR£21-26.70.)

DINGLE PENINSULA

For decades the Ring of Kerry's undertouristed counterpart, the gorgeous Dingle Peninsula remains more congested with ancient sites than tour buses. The Ring's tourist blitz has only just begun to encroach upon the spectacular cliffs and sweeping beaches of the Irish-speaking peninsula. A *gaeltacht* to the west of Dingle Town preserves centuries-old Irish heritage.

⬛ TRANSPORTATION. The best base for exploring the peninsula, which lies just across the Dingle Bay from the Ring of Kerry to the south, is Dingle Town, most easily reached by **Bus Éireann** from Tralee (1¼hr., 3-6 per day, IR£6.20/€7.90); other routes run to Ballydavid (Tu and F 3 per day, IR£3.15/€4 round-trip), Ballyferriter (M and Th 3 per day; IR£2.50/€3.20), and Dunquin (1-5 per day, IR£2.45/€3.15). In summer, additional buses also run along the south of the peninsula from Dingle (June-Sept. M-Sa 2 per day).

DINGLE TOWN. Lively Dingle Town, adopted home of **Fungi the Dolphin** (now a major focus of the tourist industry), serves as a good regional base. **Sciúird Archaeology tours** take you from the pier on a 3hr. whirlwind bus tour of the area's ancient spots (☎(066) 915 1606. 2 per day, IR£9/€11.45; book ahead). **Moran's Tours** runs great trips to Slea Head that stop by historical sites, film sets, and majestic views. (☎(066) 915 1155. 2 per day, IR£8/€10.20; book ahead.) The **tourist office** is on Strand St. (☎(066) 915 1188. Open July-Aug. M-Sa 9am-7pm; Sept.-Oct. and mid-Mar. to June M-Sa 9am-6pm, Su 10am-5pm.) ⬛**Ballintaggart Hostel (IHH),** 25min. east on Tralee Rd. in a stone mansion, is supposedly haunted by the wife of the Earl of Cork, whom he strangled here. (☎(066) 915 1454. Free shuttle to town. Dorms IR£9-11/€11.45-14; doubles IR£30/€38.10; off-season IR£1-2/€1.30-2.55 less; **camping** IR£8/€10.20.) The laid-back **Grapevine Hostel** is on Dykegate St., off Main St. (☎(066) 915 1434. Dorms IR£8.50-10.50/€10.80-13.35.) From Dingle Town, a winding cliff-side road runs north by the 450m **Connor Pass.** As the road twists downhill, a waterfall marks the base of **Pedlars Lake.**

SLEA HEAD AND DUNQUIN. Glorious Slea Head impresses with its jagged cliffs and crashing waves. Green hills, interrupted by rough stone walls and occasional sheep, suddenly break off into the foam-flecked sea. *Ryan's Daughter* and parts of *Far and Away* were filmed in this appropriately melodramatic scenery. By far the most rewarding way to see Slea Head and Dunquin in a day or less is to bike along the predominantly flat Slea Head Drive. Past Dingle Town toward Slea Head sits the village of Ventry (Ceann Trá), home to a sandy beach and the marvellous ⬛Ballybeag Hostel; a regular shuttle runs to Dingle Town. (☎915 9876. Bike rental IR£2.50-5/€3.20-6.35. Laundry IR£2/€2.55. Dorms IR£11/€14.) The ⬛Celtic and Prehistoric Museum, 3km farther down the road, is a must-see—tour the astounding collection, ranging from 300-million-year-old sea worm fossils, to Iron Age tools and jewelry, to an electric sheep. Its newest exhibit is Millie, a 50,000-year old woolly mammoth found off the coast of Holland in 1999. (☎915 9941. Open Apr.-Oct. daily 10am-5pm, Oct.-Apr. call ahead. IR£3/€3.85.) North of Slea Head, the scattered settlement of Dunquin (Dún Chaoin) boasts Kruger's, purportedly the westernmost pub in Europe. (☎915 6127. Main dishes IR£6-8/€7.65-10.20.) Just outside of Dunquin on the road to Ballyferriter, Blasket Centre has outstanding exhibits about the isolated Blasket Islands. (Open July-Aug. daily 10am-7pm; Easter-June and Sept.-Nov. 10am-6pm. IR£2.50/€3.20, students IR£1/€1.30.) An Óige Hostel (HI) affords ocean views from bunks along the Dingle Way, across from the turnoff to the Blasket Centre. (☎915 6121. Reception 9-10am and 5-10pm. Lockout 10am-5pm. Dorms IR£7.50-9/ €9.55-11.45; doubles IR£20/€25.40)

TRALEE. While tourists see Killarney as the core of Co. Kerry, residents are proud to identify Tralee (pop. 20,000) as its economic capital. Tourists often use Tralee's abundance of quality hostels and pubs as a base to see the Ring of Kerry. Ireland's second-largest museum, **Kerry the Kingdom,** Ashe Memorial Hall, Denny St., showcases a high-tech history of Ireland from 8000 BC to the present. (☎(066) 712 7777. Open mid-Mar. to Oct. daily 10am-6pm; Nov.-Dec. noon-4:30pm. IR£6/€7.65, students IR£4.75/€6.05.) During the last week of August, the nationally-known **Rose of Tralee Festival** brings a maelstrom of entertainment to town as lovely Irish lasses compete for the title "Rose of Tralee." **Trains** go from the Oakpark Rd. station to: Cork (2½hr., 3-4 per day, IR£18/€22.90); Galway (5-6hr., 3 per day, IR£35.50/ €45.10); Killarney (40min., 4 per day, IR£5.50/€7). **Buses** rumble from Oakpark Rd. to: Cork (2½hr., 10-14 per day, IR£10/€12.70); Galway (5-6hr., 9-11 per day, IR£13/ €16.55); Killarney (40min., 5-14 per day, IR£4.60/€5.85); Limerick (2¼hr., 7-8 per day, IR£9.60/€12.20). To get to the **tourist office,** Ashe Memorial Hall, from the station, down Edward St., turn right on Castle St. and left on Denny St. (☎(066) 712 1288. Open July-Aug. M-Sa 9am-7pm; Su 9am-6pm; May-June and Oct. M-Sa 9am-6pm; Oct.-Apr. M-F 9am-5pm.) The centrally located **Courthouse Lodge (IHH)** is nestled at quiet 5 Church St. (☎(066) 712 7199. Dorms IR£10/€12.70; singles IR£17/ €21.60; doubles IR£25-30/€31.75-38.10.) Call for pick-up to the ▨**Collis-Sandes House (IHH).** (☎(066) 712 8658. Dorms IR£9-12/€11.50-15; singles IR£17/€25; doubles IR£30/€38. **Camping** IR£5/€6.50 per person.)

WESTERN IRELAND

Even Dubliners will tell you that the west is the "most Irish" part of Ireland. Yeats agreed: "For me," he said, "Ireland is Connacht." For less privileged Irish in recent centuries, Connacht mostly meant poor soil and emigration. When Cromwell uprooted the native Irish landowners in Leinster and Munster and resettled them west of the Shannon, the popular phraseology for their plight became "To hell or to Connacht." The potato famine (see p. 546) that plagued the island was most devastating in the west—entire villages emigrated or died. Today, it has less than half of its 1841 population. Though miserable for farming, the land from Connemara north to Ballina is a boon for hikers, cyclists, and hitchhikers, as they enjoy the isolation of boggy, rocky, or brilliantly mountainous landscapes.

LIMERICK CITY   ☎061

Although Limerick's 18th-century Georgian streets and parks remain regal and elegant, later industrial developments and hard economic times give the city a duller, urban feel. To reach the requisite local castle, **King John's Castle,** on Nicholas St., walk across the Abbey River and turn after St. Mary's Cathedral. (Open Mar.-Dec. daily 9:30am-5:30pm. IR£5/€6.35, students IR£3.75/€4.75.) **Trains** (☎315 555) leave Parnell St. for: Cork (2½hr., 5-6 per day, IR£14/€17.80); Dublin (2hr., 9-10 per day, IR£27/€34.30); Waterford (2hr., M-Sa 1-2 per day, IR£13.50/€17.15). **Buses** (☎313 333) leave the train station for: Cork (2hr., 14 per day, IR£9.60/€12.20); Dublin (3½hr., 13 per day, IR£10.50/€13.35); Galway (2hr., 14 per day, IR£9.60/€12.20);

Tralee (2hr., 7 per day, IR£9.60/€12.20); Waterford (2½hr., M-Th and Sa-Su 6 per day, F 7 per day; IR£10.50/€13.35). The **tourist office** is on Arthurs Quay, in the space-age glass building. From the station, walk straight down Davis St., right on O'Connell St., then left at Arthurs Quay Mall. (☎317 522. Open July-Aug. M-F 9am-6:30pm, Sa-Su 9am-6pm; May-June and Sept.-Oct. M-Sa 9:30am-5:30pm; Nov.-Apr. M-F 9:30am-5:30pm, Sa 9:30am-1pm.) **Finnegan's (IHH)**, 6 Pery Sq., has common rooms and a convenient location. (☎310 308. Dorms IR£10-12.50/€12.70-15.90.) Or snooze at ⬛**An Óige Hostel (HI)**, 1 Pery Sq., around the corner from Finnegan's. (☎314 672. Sheets IR£1/€1.30. Continental breakfast IR£2.25/€2.85. Lockout 10am-2pm. June-Sept. 14-bed dorms IR£9.50/€12; Oct.-May IR£8.50/€10.80. IR£1/€1.30 less for HI members.) Get **groceries** at **Tesco** in Arthurs Quay Mall. (Open M-W and Sa 8:30am-8pm, Th-F 8:30am-10pm, Su noon-6pm.) Limerick's immense student population adds spice to the pub scene—**Dolan's** (☎314 483), Dock Rd., hosts nightly *trad* and rambunctious local patrons.

ENNIS AND DOOLIN   ☎065

Growing fast, but slow to lose its charm, **Ennis** combines city-caliber nightlife with the familiarity of a small town. Ennis's proximity to Shannon Airport and the Burren make it a common stopover for tourists, who come for a day of shopping followed by a night of pub crawling. Not quite so holy as the **Ennis Friary** (once one of Ireland's most important theological schools), but still revered are the 60 pubs that line the streets of Ennis. Most hold *trad* sessions that uphold Co. Clare's reputation of musical excellence. At **Cruises Pub**, next to the Friary, local music stars appear nightly for cozy sessions. **The Boardwalk**, O'Connell Sq. is a hotspot for *trad*, world, and indie music. (Open F-Sa. Cover £5/€6.35.) **Trains** leave for from the station, a 10min. walk from the town center on Station Rd., for Dublin via Limerick (1-2 per day, £21/€26.70). **Buses** run to Doolin (1hr., 1-3 per day, £5.80/€7.40); Galway (1hr., 5 per day, £7.70/€9.80); Shannon Airport (40min., 9-13 per day, £3.70/€6.10). The new **tourist office** is at O'Connell Sq. (☎28366. Open June-Sept. M-F 9:30am-6:30pm, Sa-Su 9:30am-1pm and 2-6:30pm; Mar.-May and Oct.-Nov. M-F 9:30am-1pm and 2-5:30pm.) Crash for the night at **Abbey Tourist Hostel**, Harmony Row. (☎682 2620. Breakfast included. Dorms £10; private rooms £15/€19 per person.)

Something of a national shrine to Irish traditional music, the little village of **Doolin** draws thousands of visitors every year to its three pubs for nights of *craic* that will go straight from your tappin' toes to your Guinness-soaked head. The names and sociological role of the town's dominant triumvirate are best remembered by the mnemonic **MOM: McDermott's** (Upper Village), **O'Connor's** (Lower), **McGann's** (Upper). All have music sessions nightly at 9:30pm, and the latter two have both won awards for the best *trad* in Ireland. Between the upper and lower villages, ⬛**Aille River Hostel (IHH)** feels like its own peaceful hamlet. (☎707 4260. Dorms £8.50/€10.80; doubles £16/€20.35. **Camping** £4/€5.) **Westwind B&B** sits behind McGann's with sunny and immaculate rooms. The owners give helpful advice to spelunkers and other Burren explorers. (☎707 4227. £13-15/€16.50-19 per person.) Either provides excellent respite to explore the ⬛**Cliffs of Moher** 5km to the south. The stunning view from the edge plunges 200m straight down to the open sea; These cliffs are so high, you'll be able to see gulls whirling below you. **Bus** #50 runs 15min. to the cliffs; #15 goes to Dublin via Ennis and Limerick (1-2 per day).

THE BURREN

If there were wild orchids, cantankerous cows, and B&Bs on the moon, it would probably look a lot like the Burren. Its land comprises nearly 260 sq. km and almost one-third of Co. Clare's coastline. Mediterranean, Alpine, and Arctic wildflowers announce their neon bright, microcosmic contours form cracks in kilometer-long rock planes, while 28 of Ireland's 33 species of butterfly flutter by. Coming here is like is like entering a skewed fairyland, replete with ruined castles, ancient megaliths, and Labyrinthine caves (minus David Bowie). The best way to see the Burren is to walk or cycle, but it's notoriously difficult to get around. Yellow arrows mark the 40km **Burren Way**, a hiking trail from Liscannor to Ballyvaughan. All of the surrounding tourist offices (at Kilfenora, Ennis, Corofin, and the Cliffs of Moher) have detailed maps of the region. **Bus Éireann** (☎682 41 77) connects Galway to towns in and near the Burren a few times a day during summer but infrequently during winter. The ever-expanding **Kinvara,** on Galway Bay, provides welcome rest and **Dunguaire Castle** as well as an active pub scene. Hit up **Fallon's B&B,** above Kinvara's Spar market (☎637 483. £25/€31.75 per person, all with bath) or **Cois Cuain B&B,** on the Quay (☎637 119. open Apr.-Nov., £19/€24 per person) before venturing out into the Burren's disorienting and magical landscape.

DAYTRIP FROM THE BURREN: COOLE PARK AND THOOR BALLYLEE.
W. B. Yeats eulogized his two retreats that lie about 32km south of Galway near **Gort,** where N18 meets N66. The former is now a ruin and national park; the latter has been restored to appear as it did when Yeats lived there. Neither is accessible by bus; biking from Kinvara is the best option but the retreats are well-worth the transportation inconvenience. The **Coole Park** nature reserve was once the estate of Lady Augusta Gregory, a friend and collaborator of Yeats. To Yeats, the estate represented the aristocratic order that crass industrialists and wars of the 1920s were destroying. In the picnic area, the famous "autograph tree," a great copper beech, bears the initials of some important Irish figures: George Bernard Shaw, Sean O'Casey, Douglas Hyde (first president of Ireland), and Yeats himself. The **Coole Park Visitors Centre** eschews talk of Yeats in favor of local wildlife. (☎(091) 631 804. Open mid-June to Aug. daily 9:30am-6:30pm; Sept. 10am-5pm; mid-Apr. to mid-June Tu-Su 10am-5pm. Last admission 45min. before closing. £2/€2.50, students £1/€1.30.) A couple kilometers from the garden, **Coole Lake** is where Yeats watched "nine-and-fifty swans... all suddenly mount/ And scatter wheeling in great broken rings/ Upon their clamorous wings." Swans still gather here in winter.

Five kilometers north of Coole Park, a road turns off Galway Rd. and runs to **Thoor Ballylee,** a tower built in the 13th and 14th centuries. In 1916, Yeats bought it for IR£35(/€44.50!), renovated it, and lived here with his family off and on from 1922 to 1928. A film on Yeats's life plays at the **Visitors Centre.** (☎(091) 631 436. Open Easter-Sept. daily 10am-6pm. £3/€3.80, students £2.50/€3.20.)

GALWAY CITY   ☎091

In the past few years, Galway has been known as Ireland's cultural capital, with a mix of over 13,000 university students, a transient population of twenty-something Europeans, and waves of international backpackers; it has developed one happening college town on *craic* (pop. 60,000). Its main attractions are its nightlife and setting—it's a convenient starting point for trips to the Clare Coast or the Connemara. You can rent a **rowboat** from **Frank Dolan's,** 13 Riverside, Woodquay, and row/drift down the Corrib for great views of the city, the countryside, and nearby castles (IR£3/€3.85 per hr.). In mid-July, the **Galway Arts Festival** (☎583 800), Ireland's largest arts festival, rolls into town with *trad* musicians, rock groups, theater troupes, and filmmakers. Choosing from Galway's endless list of fantastic pubs is a difficult challenge even for residents (the nightclubs fall far behind in quality). Generally speaking, the beautiful pubs along **Quay Street** cater to tourists and students; try **The King's Head,** High St., which features 3 floors and a huge stage devoted to nightly rock. Pubs along **Dominick Street** (across the river from the Quay) are popular with locals; **Roisín Dubh,** Dominick St., with an intimate bookshelved front, hides one of Galway's hottest live music scenes in the back. (Cover £6-13/€7.60-16.55.)

Direct **trains** (☎561 444) run to Dublin (3hr., 3-5 per day, IR£15-21/€19.05-26.75); transfer at Athlone (£7.50-13.50/€9.50-17.15) for all other cities. **Bus Éireann** (☎562 000) leaves for: Belfast (1-3 per day, IR£17/€21.60); Cork (5 per day, IR£12/€15.25); Dublin (7-9 per day, IR£8/€10.15). The main **tourist office,** Forster St., is a block south of Eyre Sq. (☎563 081. Open July-Aug. daily 9am-7:45pm; May-June and Sept. daily 9am-5:45pm; Oct.-Apr. M-F and Su 9am-5:45pm, Sa 9am-12:45pm.) Check **email** at **Fun World,** Eyre Sq., above Supermac's. (☎561 415. Open M-Sa 10am-11pm, Su 11am-11pm. £3/€3.80 for 30min.) ◪**Barnacle's Quay**

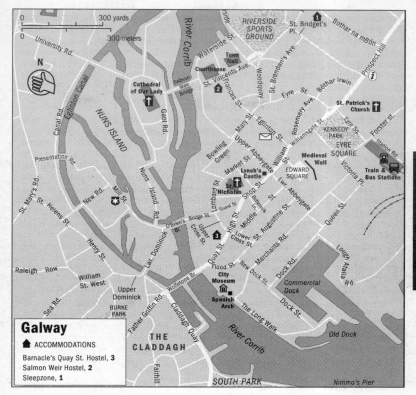

Galway

ACCOMMODATIONS

Barnacle's Quay St. Hostel, **3**
Salmon Weir Hostel, **2**
Sleepzone, **1**

IRELAND

Street Hostel (IHH), Quay St., is bright and spacious with a peerless location. (☎568 644. All rooms with bath. Laundry IR£5/€6.35. Dorms IR£8.50-15/€10.80-19.05; doubles and twins IR£32-36/€40.65-45.75.) ◼ **Sleepzone,** Bóthar na mBán, northwest of Eyre Sq., takes the "s" out of "hostel." (☎566 999. All rooms with bath. Laundry IR£5/€6.35. Dorms IR£11-13/€14-16.55; doubles IR£29/€36.85.) **Salmon Weir Hostel,** 3 St. Vincent's Ave., is extremely homey with a down-to-earth vibe. (☎561 133. Laundry IR£5/€6.35. Dorms IR£11/€14; doubles IR£28/€35.50.) For cheap food, head to the east bank; try Abbeygate St. and the short blocks around **Quay, High,** and **Shop Streets.** On Saturday mornings, an **open market** sets up in front of St. Nicholas Church on Market St. with seafood, pastries, and fresh fruit (Open Sa 8am-1pm.). Pick up groceries at **Supervalu,** in the Eyre Sq. mall. (Open M-W and Sa 9am-6:30pm, Th-F 9am-9pm.)

▶ **DAYTRIP FROM GALWAY CITY: DOORUS PENINSULA.** Beside Kinvara, the Doorus Peninsula reaches out into Galway Bay. For those not enamored of nature, it's probably best to stay in Kinvara, but for families with cars, hikers, and bikers, Doorus is heaven-sent. Three castles, several holy wells, a handful of ring forts, a cave, winged critters, panoramic views, and boggy islands await the rambler; most are detailed in *Kinvara: A Rambler's Map and Guide,* available in town for IR£2/€2.55. A 16km round-trip west from the hostel to the **Aughinish Peninsula** offers views of the Burren across the bay. The more convenient blue-flag **Traught Strand** is just a 5min. walk from the hostel. The **Galway-Doolin bus** does not pass through Doorus but will stop upon request at the turnoff on Ballyvaughan Rd. (June-Sept. 2-4 per day; Oct.-May M-Sa 1 per day). **Campers** can pitch a tent in the field nearby and wake to the slosh of surf. The house that Yeats and Lady Augusta Gregory inhabited while planning the Abbey Theatre and collaborating on plays is now the isolated **Doorus House Hostel (An Óige/HI).** Originally the country seat of an expatriate French aristocrat, this well-appointed hostel sits gracefully among old oak trees and peers out on the expanse of a tidal estuary. (☎ 637 512. Reception 5-10pm. Sheets IR£1/€1.30. June-Aug. dorms IR£9/€11.40, Oct.-May IR£8/€10.15.)

ARAN ISLANDS (OILEÁIN ÁRANN)

On the westernmost edge of Co. Galway, isolated from the mainland by 24km of chaotic Atlantic, the Aran Islands feel more like the edge of the world. Their green fields are hatched with a maze of limestone—the result of centuries of farmers piling acres of stones into thousands of meters of walls—and awesome Iron Age forts sit atop stark cliffs. Of the dozens of ruins, forts, churches, and holy wells that rise from the stony terrain of **Inishmore** (Inis Mór; pop. 900), the most amazing is the **Dún Aengus** ring fort, where a small semicircular wall surrounds a sheer 100m drop.

Island Ferries (☎ (091) 568 903) go from **Rossaveal,** west of Galway, to Inishmore (1-3 per day, 30min.); Inisheer (2 per day); Inishmaan (1 per day). All routes £15/€19 round-trip for students. A **bus** to Rossaveal leaves the Galway tourist office 1½hr. before the ferry departure time. (£4/€5.). **Queen of Aran II,** Inishmore (☎ 566 535), is based in the islands and leaves for Inishmore (4 per day; £15/€19, students £10/€12.70. Bus from Galway included.) Both have offices in the Galway tourist office. Ferries land at **Kilronan,** where the **tourist office** holds bags (£0.75). (☎ (099) 61263. Open July-Sept. daily 10am-6:45pm; Oct. 10am-5pm; Nov.-Mar. 10am-4pm.) **The Kilronan Hostel** is bright and spotless in a central location. (☎ (099) 61255. Dorms £10/€12.70, all with bath.) The **Spar Market,** past the hostel, is the island's social center. (Open M-Sa 9am-8pm, Su 10am-6pm.) Windswept **Inishmaan** (Inis Meáin; pop. 300) elevates solitude to an art form. **Inisheer** (Inis Oírr; pop. 300), the smallest island, strikes a balance between Inishmaan's absolute loneliness and Inishmore's occasional din. The **Brú Hostel (IHH),** visible from the pier, has great views. (☎ 75024. Call ahead. Breakfast £2-5/€2.50-5. Dorms £8.50/€10.80.)

CONNEMARA

Connemara, a largely Irish-speaking region, is comprised of a lacy net of inlets and islands, a rough gang of mountains, and some bogs in between. This thinly populated western arm of County Galway harbors some of Ireland's most desolate yet breathtaking scenery. The jagged southern coastline teems with sinuous estuaries, safe beaches for camping, and tidal causeways connecting to rocky islands.

CLIFDEN (AN CLOCHÁN)   ☎095

Busy, English-speaking Clifden has more amenities and modernities than its old-world, Irish-speaking neighbors. Clifden's proximity to the scenic bogs and mountains of the region attracts crowds of tourists, who enjoy the frenzied pub scene, shop in its ubiquitous arts and crafts studios, and use it as a base for exploring the region. The **Connemara Walking Centre,** on Market St., runs tours of the bogs. (☎ 21379. Open Mar.-Oct. M-Sa 10am-6pm. Easter-Oct. 1-2 tours per day. IR£15-25/€19.05-31.75.) **Bus Éireann** goes from the library on Market St. to Galway via Oughterard (2hr., 1-5 per day, IR£6.50/€8.25) and Westport via Leenane (1½hr., late-June to Aug. 3-4 per day). **Michael Nee** runs a bus from the courthouse to Galway (June-Sept. 3 per day, IR£6/€7.65). Rent a **bike** at **Mannion's,** Bridge St. (☎ 21160. IR£7/€8.90 per day, IR£40/€50.80 per week; deposit IR£10/€12.70. Open M-Sa 9:30am-6:30pm, Su 10am-1pm and 5-7pm.) The **tourist office** is on Market St. (☎ 21163. Open July-Aug. M-Sa 9:45am-5:45pm, Su noon-4pm; May-June and Sept. M-Sa 9:30am-5:30pm.) Check **email** at **Two Dog Cafe,** Church Hill (☎ 22186. Open M-Sa 10:30am-5pm.) **B&Bs** litter the streets (IR£18-20/€22.90-25.40). The excellent **Clifden Town Hostel (IHH)** is on Market St. (☎ 21076. Dorms IR£8/€10.20; doubles IR£24/€30.50; triples IR£30/€38.10; quads IR£36/€45.75.) Head straight past the bottom of Market St. to find **Brookside Hostel,** Hulk St. (☎ 21812. Dorms IR£8/€10.20;

singles IR£8-9/€10.20-11.45; doubles IR£18/€22.90.) Tranquil **Shanaheever Campsite** is a little over 1.5km outside Clifden on Westport Rd. (☎22150. IR£8/€10.20 for 2 people and tent; IR£3/€3.85 per additional person.) The **SuperValu supermarket** is on Market St. (Open M-F 8:30am-8pm, Su 9am-7pm.) Shake your booty and down pints along **Market Street,** in **The Square,** and on **Church Hill.**

CONNEMARA NATIONAL PARK

Connemara National Park occupies 12.5 sq. km of mountainous countryside that thousands of birds call home. The far-from-solid terrain of the park comprises bogs thinly covered by a deceptive screen of grass and flowers—be prepared to get muddy. The **Snuffaunboy Nature Trail** and the **Ellis Wood Trail** are easy 20min. hikes. For the slightly more adventurous, trails lead from the back of the Ellis Wood Trail and 10min. along the Bog Road onto **Diamond Hill,** a 2hr. hike rewarding climbers with views of bog, harbor, and forest. More experienced hikers often head for the **Twelve Bens** (Na Benna Beola, a.k.a. the Twelve Pins), a rugged range that reaches 2200m heights (not recommended for single or beginning hikers). A guidebook mapping out 30min. walks (IR£0.50/€0.65) is available at the Visitors Centre, where the staff helps plan longer hikes. A tour of all 12 Bens takes experienced walkers about 10hr. Biking the 65km circle through Clifden, Letterfrack, and the Inagh Valley is truly captivating, but only appropriate for fit bikers.

Tiny **Letterfrack** is the gateway to the park. The Galway-Clifden **bus** (M-Sa; mid-June to Aug. 11 per week, Sept. to mid-June 4 per week) and the summertime Clifden-Westport bus (1-2 per day) stop at Letterfrack. The **Visitors Centre** explains the subtle (and not so subtle) differences between blanket bogs, raised bogs, turf, and heathland. Guides lead free 2hr. **walks** over the hills and through the bogs. (☎41054. Open July-Aug. daily 9:30am-6:30pm; June 10am-6:30pm; May and Sept. 10am-5:30pm. IR£2/€2.55, students IR£1/€1.30. Tours July-Aug. M, W, and F 10:30am.) Uphill from the intersection in Letterfrack, the ▓**Old Monastery Hostel** is legendary—one of Ireland's finest hostels. (☎41132. Bike IR£7/€8.90 per day. **Internet.** Dorms IR£8-10/€10.20-12.70.) The turn-off to the **Ben Lettery Hostel (An Óige/HI),** in Ballinafad, is 13km east of Clifden. (☎51136. IR£8-9/€10.20-11.45.)

WESTPORT   ☎098

One of the few planned towns in the country, Westport (pop. 4300) still looks marvelous in its Georgian-period costume. Tourists savor its thriving pub life, drink tea at dapper cafes, and shop for snow-globes. The conical **Croagh Patrick** rises 650m over Clew Bay. The summit has been revered as a holy site for thousands of years. St. Patrick worked here in AD 441, praying and fasting for 40 days and nights, arguing with angels, and banishing snakes from Ireland. Climbers start their excursion from the 15th-century **Murrisk Abbey,** several kilometers west of Westport on R395 toward Louisburgh (4hr. round-trip). **Buses** go to Murrisk (2-3 per day), but **cabs** (☎27171) for several people are cheaper and more convenient. Pilgrims and hikers also set out for Croagh Patrick along the Tóchar Phádraiga path from **Ballintubber Abbey** (☎(094) 30709), several kilometers south of Castlebar and 35km from Croagh Patrick. Founded in 1216 by King of Connacht, the abbey still functions as a religious center. In late September, Westport celebrates its annual **Westport Arts Festival** (☎(094) 28833) with a week of free concerts, poetry readings, and plays.

Trains arrive at the Altamont St. Station (☎25253), 5min. up North Mall, from Dublin via Athlone (2-3 per day, IR£15/€19.05). **Buses** leave from the Octagon on Mill St. for Galway (2hr., M-F 6 per day, IR£8.80/€11.20). The **tourist office** is on James St. (☎25711. Open July-Aug. M-Sa 9am-6:45pm, Su 10am-6pm; Apr.-June and Sept.-Oct. M-Sa 9am-5:45pm.) **B&Bs** are on the Castlebar and Altamont Rd. off North Mall. **The Granary Hostel** is a 25min. walk from town, just at the bend in Quay Rd. (☎25903. Open Apr.-Oct. Dorms IR£7.50/€9.55.) **Old Mill Holiday Hostel (IHH),** James St., is between the Octagon and the tourist office. (☎27045. Bike rental IR£7/€8.90 per day. Laundry IR£3/€3.80. Common room lockout 11pm-8am. Dorms IR£9/€11,45.) The **SuperValu** supermarket is on Shop St. (Open M-Sa 8:30am-9pm, Su 10am-6pm.)

NORTHWEST IRELAND

The farmland of the upper Shannon spans northward into County Sligo's mountains, lakes, and ancient monuments. A mere sliver of land connects Co. Sligo to Co. Donegal, the second-largest and most remote of the Republic's counties. Donegal's *gaeltacht* is a storehouse of genuine, unadulterated Irish tradition.

SLIGO ☎071

Since the beginning of the 20th century, Sligo has been a literary pilgrimage for William Butler Yeats devotees; the poet spent summers in town as a child and set many of his poems around Sligo Bay. The county remains as beautiful today as it was when Yeats wrote his odes. **Sligo Town,** the commercial center of the county, does business by day but goes wild at night with one of Ireland's most colorful pub scenes, and is an excellent base from which to explore Yeat's haunts. In town, the well-preserved 13th-century **Sligo Abbey,** on Abbey St., is Yeats-free. (Open Apr.-Oct. daily 10am-6pm; Nov.-Mar. call for openings. IR£1.50/€1.90, students IR£0.60/€0.75.) **The Niland Gallery,** Stephen St., houses one of the finest collections of modern Irish art and some first editions of Yeats works. (Open Tu-Sa 10am-5:30pm. Free.) Yeats is buried per his instructions in **Drumcliffe churchyard,** on the N15, 6.5km northwest of Sligo. His grave is to the left of the church door. **Buses** from Sligo to Derry stop at Drumcliff (10min., 3-4 per day, £2.60/€3.30 round-trip). Over 70 pubs crowd the main streets. The *International Pub Guide* ranks ▓**McLynn's,** Old Market St. (☎60743), as the best pub for music in Sligo; locals definitely agree.

Trains (☎698 88) go from Lord Edward St. to Dublin via Carrick-on-Shannon and Mullingar (3 per day, £13.50/€17.15). From the same station, **buses** (☎60066) fan out to: Belfast (4hr., 1-3 per day, £12.40/€15.75); Derry (3hr., 3-6 per day, £10/€12.70); Dublin (4hr., 4 per day, £9/€11.45); Galway (2½hr., 3-4 per day, £11/€14); Westport (2½hr., 1-3 per day, £9.70/€12.30). Turn left on Lord Edward St., then follow the signs right on Adelaid St. and around the corner to Temple St. to find the **tourist office,** at Charles St. (☎61201. Open M-Tu 10am-7pm, W-F 10am-9pm, Sa 10am-6pm.) **B&Bs** cluster on **Pearse Road,** in the south side. ▓**Harbour House,** Finisklin Rd., is 10min. from the station. (☎71547. Dorms £11/€14; singles £17/€21.60.) Follow signs from the station to **Railway Hostel,** 1 Union St. (☎44530. Dorms £7.50/€9.55; doubles £36/€45.) "Faery vats/Full of berries/And reddest stolen cherries" are not to be found in Sligo today, but a **Tesco,** O'Connell St., has aisles-worth of cheap food. (☎62788. Open M-Tu and Sa 8:30am-7pm, W-F 8:30am-9pm, Su 10am-6pm.)

COUNTY DONEGAL AND SLIEVE LEAGUE ☎073

Tourists are a rarity in Co. Donegal. Its geographic isolation in the Northwest has spared it from the widespread deforestation of Ireland; vast wooded areas engulf many of Donegal's mountain chains, while the coastline alternates beaches and cliffs. Travelers use **Donegal Town** as the gateway to the county. **Bus Éireann** (☎211 01) runs to: Dublin (4hr., 4-6 per day, IR£10.50/€13.35) and Galway (4hr., 3-5 per day, IR£10.50/€13.35). Buses stop outside the Abbey Hotel on the Diamond; turn right with your back to the hotel to reach the **tourist office,** on Quay St. (☎211 48; www.donegaltown.ie. Open July-Aug. M-Sa 9am-8pm, Su 10am-4pm; Sept.-Nov. and Easter-June M-F 9am-5pm, Sa 10am-2pm.) **Donegal Independent Town Hostel (IHH)** is on Killybegs Rd. (☎228 05. Call ahead. Dorms IR£7.50/€9.55; doubles IR£18/€22.90; **camping** IR£4/€5.10 per person.)

To the west of Donegal Town, the **Slieve League Peninsula**'s rocky cliffs—Europe's highest—jut out into the Atlantic. The sheer face of the 600m drop into the Atlantic is spectacular, and its rugged, wild appearance shows little evidence of human habitation. **Bus Éireann** runs from Donegal Town to Glencolmcille and Dungloe, stopping in tiny **Kilcar** (1-3 per day), the gateway to Donegal's *gaeltacht* and a commercial base for many Donegal tweed weavers. Most Slieve League hikers stay in Kilcar, from where they can comfortably drive, bike, or walk (about 6hr. round-trip) to the mountain. Over 3km out on the coast road from Kilcar to Carrick is the fabulous ▓**Derrylahan Hostel (IHH);** call for pick-up. (☎380 79. Laundry IR£5/€6.35.

Dorms IR£7/€8.90; private rooms IR£10/€12.70; **camping** IR£4/€5.10). **Bus Éireann** has services to **Donegal Town** via Kilcar (3 per day). On the western top of the Slieve League Peninsula, **Glencolmcille** (glen-kaul-um-KEEL), a collection of several tiny villages wedged between two monstrous sea cliffs, is renowned for its handmade products, particularly sweaters. On sunny days, trips to the **Silver Strand** reward with stunning views of the gorgeous beach and rocky cliffs; the trek along the Slieve League coastline begins here. McGeehan's **buses** leave from Biddy's Bar for Kilcar and Letterkenny (1-2 per day). Snooze at the just peachy ▨**Dooey Hostel** (**IHO**). (☎301 30. Dorms IR£7/€8.90; doubles IR£14/€17.80; **camping** IR£4/€5.10.)

DERRYVEAGH MOUNTAINS ☎075

Sandy beaches are isolated by the boglands and eerie stillness of the **Derryveagh Mountains.** On the eastern side of the mountains, **Glenveagh National Park** is 60 sq. km of forest glens, bogs, and herds of red deer. (☎(074) 37090. IR£2/€2.55, students IR£1.50/€1.95. Open daily 10am-5pm.) The coastal road N56 twists and bends along the jagged edges where Donegal meets the sea, leading through spectacular scenery to **Crolly,** gateway to Mount Errigal and the legendary Poison Glen. From Crolly, Feda O'Donnell (☎48114) has a daily bus to Galway and Donegal Town via Letterkenny; Swilly (☎21380) passes Crolly on its Dungloe-Derry route; John McGinley Coaches (☎(074) 35201) goes to Dublin; and O'Donnell Trans-Ulster Express (☎48356) goes to Belfast. Dunlewy, in the shadow of Errigal Mountain, is also excellent for exploring the **Derryveagh Mountains. Errigal Youth Hostel (An Óige/HI),** on R251, is clean and convenient. (☎31180. Call to see if renovations are complete. Lockout 10am-5pm. Dorms June-Sept. IR£7.50/€9.55, private rooms IR£9.50/€12.10; dorms Oct.-May IR£6.50/€8.25; private rooms IR£7.50/€9.55.)

LETTERKENNY ☎074

Letterkenny is the center of action in Donegal, but a civic engineering nightmare. Nonetheless, it's a lively place to make bus connections to the rest of Donegal, the Republic, and Northern Ireland. **Buses** leave from the junction of Port and Derry Rd. in front of the Letterkenny Shopping Centre. **Bus Éireann** (☎21309) runs to: Derry (30min., 3-6 per day, IR£5/€6.35); Dublin (4½hr., 5-6 per day, IR£10/€12.70); Galway (4¾hr., 4 per day, IR£12/€15.25) via Donegal Town (50min., IR£5/€6.35); Sligo (2hr., 4-5 per day, IR£9/€11.45). **Lough Swilly** Buses (☎22863) head north to Derry (M-Sa 10 per day, £4.40/€5.60) and the Fanad Peninsula (M-Sa 2 per day, IR£7/€8.90). **Northwest Busways** (☎(077) 82619) sends buses around the Inishowen Peninsula (3-4 per day). The **Chamber of Commerce Visitors Information Centre** is at 40 Port Rd. (☎248 66. Open M-F 9am-5pm.) **The Port Hostel (IHO),** Orchard Crest, provides easy access to the city center from a glade up the hill from the An Grianan Theatre. (☎25315. Dorms IR£7.50/€9.55; private rooms IR£8.50-9.50/€10.80-12.10.)

INISHOWEN PENINSULA AND MALIN HEAD ☎077

Brochures trumpet the Inishowen Peninsula as the "crown of Ireland," featuring a characteristically rocky combination of grassland and bog with the barren beauty that pervades much of Donegal. Inishowen's inland landscape is outdone only by its striking northern and western shores. The clearly posted **Inish Eoghain 100** road navigates the peninsula's perimeter, exactly 100 mi long. The peninsula's most popular attraction is **Malin Head,** remarkable for its rocky, wave-tattered coast and sky-high sand dunes, reputedly the highest in Europe (up to 30m). The scattered town of Malin Head includes **Bamba's Crown,** the northernmost tip of Ireland, a tooth of dark rock rising up from the ocean spray. The raised beaches around Malin Head are covered with semi-precious stones; walkers sifting through the sands may find jasper, quartz, small opals, or amethyst. Lough Swilly **buses** (☎61340; 1½hr.; M, W, F 2 per day, Sa 3 per day) and Northwest Buses (☎82619; M-Sa 2 per day) run from Derry, the nearest city to Inishowen, to points on the peninsula including Malin Head. To reach the ▨**Sandrock Holiday Hostel (IHO),** Port Ronan Pier, take the left fork off the Inish Eoghin 100, at the Crossroads Inn. (☎70289. Sheets IR£1/€1.27. Wash IR£3/€3.85, dry £1.50/€1.90. Dorms IR£7/€8.90.)

IRELAND

NORTHERN IRELAND

Sit back down, gentle voyager—your conquest of Ireland isn't complete until you've seen this rich corner. You'll find that the sectarian scars only make Northern Ireland much more striking. The North's natural beauty includes pockets of green in the Glens of Antrim, gotta-see-it-to-believe-it geology at the Giant's Causeway, and the Lake District's water-wonderland. In the recent cease-fire's relative calm, Belfast and Derry have come into their own as hip destinations.

The predominantly calm tenor of life in the North has been overshadowed overseas by media headlines screaming about riots and bombs. But acts of violence and extremist fringe groups are less visible than the division in civil society that sends Protestants and Catholics to separate neighborhoods, separate stores, separate pubs, and often separate schools, with separate, though similar, traditional songs and slang. The split is often hard for an outsider to discern, especially in rural vacation spots. On the other hand, it would be nearly impossible for a visitor to leave Northern Ireland without seeing street curbs in both cities and villages painted with the colors of their residents' sectarian identity. The 1998 Good Friday Agreement, granting Home Rule and hoping to lead the North out of its struggles, has been struggling itself. Home Rule was suspended and reinstated in February 2000, and by the summer of 2001, a lack of progress on paramilitary promises to "put weapons beyond use" brought the Good Friday government to a frustrated halt. London took the reins again, if only briefly, and both sides renewed their efforts to make their country as peaceful as it is beautiful.

PHONE CODE	Northern Ireland is reached by using the UK **country code 44**; from the Republic dial **048**. The **phone code** for every town in the North is **028**.

BELFAST

The second-largest city on the island, Belfast (pop. 330,000) is the focus of the North's cultural, commercial, and political activity. Acclaimed writers and the annual arts festival in November maintain Belfast's reputation as a thriving artistic center. West Belfast's famous sectarian murals are perhaps the most informative source on the effects of the Troubles (sectarian strife) on the city. The bar scene, a mix of Irish and British pub culture, entertains locals, foreigners, and students alike. Despite Belfast's reputation as a terrorist-riddled metropolis, the city feels more neighborly than most international—and even Irish—visitors expect.

◪ TRANSPORTATION

Flights: Belfast International Airport (☎9442 2888), in Aldergrove. **Airbus** (☎9033 3000) runs to the Europa (Glengall St.) and Laganside (Queen's Square, off Donegall Quay) bus stations (M-Sa every 30min., Su about every hr., UK£5). **Trains** connect the **Belfast City Airport (Sydenham Halt)**, at the Harbour, to Central Station (UK£1).

Trains: Central Station, East Bridge St. (☎9089 9400). To **Derry** (2½hr., 3-7 per day, UK£6.70) and **Dublin** (2hr., 5-8 per day, UK£17). The **Centrelink** buses run to the city center; free with rail tickets.

Buses: Europa Station, Glengall St. (☎9032 0011) serves the west, north coast, and the Republic. To: **Derry** (1¾hr., 6-19 per day, UK£6.50) and **Dublin** (3hr., 4-7 per day, UK£10.50). **Laganside Station** (☎9033 3000), Donegall Quay, serves Northern Ireland's east coast. The **Centrelink** bus connects both stations with the city center.

Ferries: SeaCat (☎(08705) 523 523; www.seacat.co.uk) leaves for: **Heysham, England** (4hr., Apr.-Nov., 1-2 per day); the **Isle of Man** (2¾hr., Apr.-Nov., 1-2 per day); **Troon, Scotland** (2½hr., 2-3 per day). Fares UK£10-30 without car.

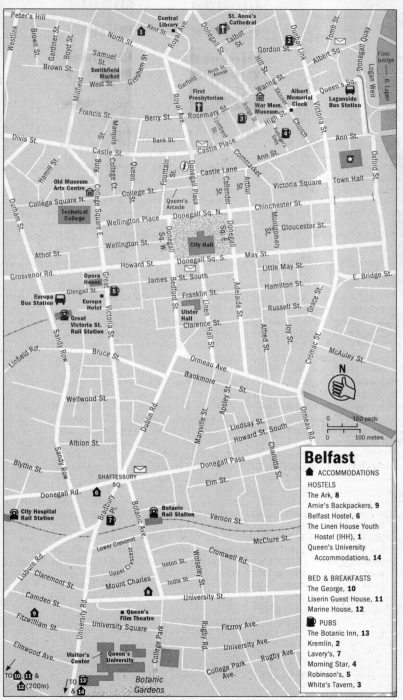

IRELAND

Belfast

🏠 **ACCOMMODATIONS**

HOSTELS

The Ark, **8**

Arnie's Backpackers, **9**

Belfast Hostel, **6**

The Linen House Youth
  Hostel (IHH), **1**

Queen's University
  Accommodations, **14**

BED & BREAKFASTS

The George, **10**

Liserin Guest House, **11**

Marine House, **12**

🍺 PUBS

The Botanic Inn, **13**

Kremlin, **2**

Lavery's, **7**

Morning Star, **4**

Robinson's, **5**

White's Tavern, **3**

Local Transportation: The red **Citybus Network** (☎9024 6485) is supplemented by **Ulsterbus**'s suburban "blue buses." Travel within the city center UK£0.60, concessions UK£0.30. The **Centrelink** bus traverses the city (every 12min.; M-F 7:25am-9:15pm, Sa 8:36-9:15; UK£0.60, free with bus or rail ticket). Late **Nightlink** buses shuttle to various small towns outside of Belfast F-Sa 1am and 2am (UK£3, payable on board).

Taxis: Value Cabs (☎9023 0000). Residents of West and North Belfast use the huge **black cabs;** some are metered, and some follow set routes (under UK£1 charge).

✳ 7 ORIENTATION AND PRACTICAL INFORMATION

Buses arrive at the Europa bus station on **Great Victoria Street.** To the northeast is the **City Hall** in **Donegall Square** South of the bus station, Great Victoria St. meets **Dublin Road** at **Shaftesbury Square;** this stretch of Great Victoria St. between the bus station and Shaftesbury Sq. is known as the **Golden Mile. Botanic Avenue** and **Bradbury Place** (which becomes University Rd.) extend south from Shaftesbury Sq. into the **Queen's University area,** where cafes, pubs, and budget lodgings await. To get to Donegall Sq. from Central Station, turn left, walk down East Bridge St., turn right on Victoria St., and turn left after two blocks on May St., which runs into Donegall Sq., or take the Centrelink bus service (free with rail ticket). Divided from the rest of Belfast by the Westlink Motorway, working-class **West Belfast** is more politically volatile. The city center, Golden Mile, and the university area are relatively safe.

Tourist Office: The Belfast Welcome Centre, 47 Donegall Pl. (☎9024 6609). Has a great booklet on Belfast and info on surrounding areas. The staff likes specific questions. Open June-Sept. M-Sa 9am-7pm, Su noon-5pm; Oct.-May M-Sa 9am-5:30pm.

Banks: Banks and **ATMs** are on almost every corner. **Bank of Ireland** is located at 54 Donegal Pl. (☎9023 4334. Open 9am-4:30pm.)

Currency Exchange: Thomas Cook, 22-24 Lombard St. (☎9088 3800). Cashes Thomas Cook traveler's checks with no commission; others 2%. Open May-Oct. M-Tu and Th 5:30am-10pm, W 5:30am-11pm, F-Su 5:30am-midnight; Nov.-Apr. daily 5:45am-8pm.

Luggage Storage: For security reasons there is no luggage storage at airports, bus stations, or train stations. All 4 **hostels** will hold bags during the day for guests.

Bisexual, Gay, and Lesbian Information: Rainbow Project N.I., 33 Church Ln. (☎9031 9030). Open M-F 10am-5:30pm.

Laundry: The Laundry Room (Duds n' Suds), Botanic Ave. (☎9024 3956). TV for the wait. About UK£3-4 per load. Open M-F 8am-9pm, Sa 8am-6pm, Su noon-6pm.

Emergency: ☎999; no coins required. **Police,** 65 Knock Rd. (☎9065 0222).

Pharmacy: Boot's, 35-47 Donegall Pl. (☎9024 2332). Open M-W and F-Sa 8:30am-6pm, Th 8:30am-9pm, Su 1-5pm. Also on Great Victoria St.

Hospitals: Belfast City Hospital, 9 Lisburn Rd. (☎9032 9241). From Shaftesbury Sq. follow Bradbury Pl. and take a right at the fork. **Royal Victoria Hospital,** 12 Grosvenor Rd. (☎9024 0503). From Donegall Sq., take Howard St. west to Grosvenor Rd.

Internet Access: The **Belfast Central Library,** 122 Royal Ave. (☎9050 9150). 30min. of free email per day; UK£2 per hr. for web access. Open M and Th 9:30am-8pm, Tu-W and F 9:30am-5:30pm, Sa 9:30am-1pm.

Post Office: Central Post Office, 25 Castle Pl. (☎9032 3740). Open M-Sa 9am-5:30pm. *Poste Restante* mail comes here. **Postal code:** BT1 1NB. Branch offices: **Botanic Garden,** 95 University Rd., across from the university (☎9038 1309; **postal code:** BT7 1NG); **Shaftesbury Square,** 7-9 Shaftesbury Sq. (☎9032 6177; **postal code:** BT2 7DA). Branch offices M-F 8:45am-5:30pm, Sa 10am-12:30pm.

⌂ ACCOMMODATIONS

Despite a competitive hostel market, Belfast's rapidly growing tourism and rising rents have shrunk the number of available cheap digs. Nearly all are located near Queen's University, south of the city center; convenient to pubs and restaurants, this area is by far the best place to stay in the city. If you have a lot of baggage you may want to catch a **Centrelink** bus to Shaftesbury Sq., or **Citybus** #59, 69, 70, 71, 84, or 85 from Donegall Sq. East to areas in the south. A walk to these accommodations takes 10-20min. from the bus or train station. Hostels and B&Bs are busy in the summer; reservations are recommended.

HOSTELS AND UNIVERSITY HOUSING

■ Arnie's Backpackers (IHH), 63 Fitzwilliam St. (☎9024 2867). A 10min. walk from Europa Bus Station on Great Victoria St. Take a right and head away from the Europa Hotel; at Shaftesbury Sq., take the right fork on Bradbury Pl., then fork left onto University Rd; Fitzwilliam St. is on your right across from the university. Key deposit UK£2 or ID. Luggage storage during the day. 8-bed dorms UK£7; 4-bed UK£8.50.

■ **The Ark (IHH),** 18 University St. (☎9032 9626). From Arnie's Backpackers (see above), it's on your right off University Rd. Weekend luggage storage. **Internet** access UK£2 per 30min. Laundry UK£4. Curfew 2am. 4- to 6-bed dorms UK£6.50-7.50; doubles UK£28.

Belfast Hostel (HINI), 22 Donegall Rd. (☎9031 5435), off Shaftesbury Sq. Clean and inviting interior despite concrete façade. Also **books tours** of Belfast and Giant's Causeway. Breakfast UK£2. Laundry UK£3. 24hr. reception. Dorms UK£8-10.

The Linen House Youth Hostel (IHH), 18-20 Kent St. (☎9058 6400) in West Belfast. Across from the main entrance to City Hall, turn left onto Donegall Pl., which becomes Royal Ave. Take a left onto Kent St. just before the Belfast Library. This converted 19th-century linen factory now houses scores of weary travelers. 24hr. secure parking. Laundry UK£3. 18-bed dorms UK£6.50; 6- to 10-bed dorms UK£7.50; 8-bed dorms with bathroom UK£8.50; singles UK£12; doubles UK£28.

Queen's University Accommodations, 78 Malone Rd. (☎9038 1608). Take bus #71 from Donegall Sq. East; a 25min. walk from Europa. University Rd. runs into Malone Rd.; the residence halls are on your left. Undecorated, institutional dorms. Open late July-Aug. and Christmas and Easter vacations. Singles and doubles UK£8.20 per person for UK students, UK£9.70 for international students, UK£12 for non-students.

BED AND BREAKFASTS

B&Bs occupy every other house between **Malone** and **Lisburn Roads,** just south of Queen's University. Calling ahead is generally a good idea; most owners, however, will refer you to other accommodations if necessary.

■ **Marine House,** 30 Eglantine Ave. (☎9066 2828). Housekeeping standards as high as the ceilings. Singles UK£22; doubles UK£40, with bath UK£45; triples UK£57.

The George, 9 Eglantine Ave. (☎9068 3212). Renowned for its spotlessness. (All rooms *en suite*.) Singles UK£22; doubles UK£44.

Botanic Lodge, 87 Botanic Ave. (☎9032 7682), on the corner of Mt. Charles Ave. B&B comfort with only a short walk to the city center. Singles UK£22; doubles UK£40.

Liserin Guest House, 17 Eglantine Ave. (☎9066 0769). Comfy beds and huge, homey lounge make an inviting abode. Singles UK£22; doubles UK£40; triples UK£60.

◖ FOOD

Belfast's eateries assume a cosmopolitan character, with flavors from around the globe. **Dublin Road, Botanic Road,** and the **Golden Mile** have the highest concentration of restaurants. For fruits and vegetables, plunder the lively **St. George's Market,** East Bridge St., in the enormous warehouse between May and Oxford St. (Open Tu and F 6am-3pm.) Try **Canterbury Dyke's,** 66-68 Botanic Ave., for healthy foods or more fruit and veggies. (Open M-F 7:30am-7pm, Sa-Su 8am-6:30pm.) **Lower Lisburn Road,** which runs parallel to University Rd., has bakeries and fruit stands.

■ **Bookfinders,** 47 University Rd. (☎9032 8269). Atmospheric bookstore/cafe with mismatched dishes and counter-culture paraphernalia. Art gallery upstairs. Soup and bread UK£1.75, sandwiches UK£2.20-2.50; veggie options. Open M-Sa 10am-5:30pm.

The Other Place, 79 Botanic Ave. (☎9020 7200), 133 Stranmillis Rd. (☎9020 7100), and 537 Lisburn Rd. (☎9029 7300). Features an array of ethnic foods, from Thai to Cajun, accompanied by an eclectic soundtrack. Open daily 8am-11pm.

IRELAND

Feasts, 39 Dublin Rd. (☎9033 2787). Pleasant street-side cafe, serving Irish and international farmhouse cheeses in sandwiches (UK£3.50) and other dishes. Makes pasta on the premises (UK£5-6.50). Open M-F 9am-6:30pm, Sa 10am-6pm.

Blinkers, 1-5 Bridge St. (☎9024 3330). An authentic diner—cluttered ashtrays and all—with authentic prices. One of the few late-night spots north of City Hall. Quarter-pound burger UK£2.30. Open M-Th 9am-10pm, F-Sa 9am-10:30pm.

🕲 SIGHTS

More than any city on your itinerary, Belfast's sights reveal its living history, the glitz and grit that evoke its political situation. If you do only one thing in this city, take a taxi tour of West Belfast (**Black Taxi Tours;** ☎9064 2264; UK£7.50 per person).

DONEGALL SQUARE. After Queen Victoria made Belfast a city in 1888, the green copper-domed **Belfast City Hall** was built on the site of demolished linen warehouses. Neoclassical marble columns and arches figure prominently in A. Brunwell Thomas's 1906 design. The **City Council**'s oak-paneled chambers, used only once a month, are deceptively austere considering the Council's reputation for rowdy meetings that sometimes devolve into fisticuffs. Directly in front of the main entrance, an enormous marble **Queen Victoria statue** stares down at visitors with a formidable grimace, as bronze figures representing shipbuilding and spinning writhe at her feet. The interior of City Hall is accessible only by guided tour. (☎9032 0202, ext. 2346. 1hr. tours June-Sept. M-F 10:30, 11:30am, and 2:30pm; Sa 2:30pm. Oct.-May M-Sa 2:30pm. Free.) One of Belfast's oldest establishments is the **Linen Hall Library.** The red hand of Ulster decorates the top of its street entrance. The library contains a renowned collection of political documents relating to the Troubles in the North. (17 Donegall Sq. North. ☎9032 1707. Open M-F 9:30am-5:30pm, Sa 9:30am-4:30pm.)

CORNMARKET AND ST. ANNE'S CATHEDRAL. Just north of the city center, a shopping district envelops eight blocks around Castle St. and Royal Ave. This area, known as Cornmarket after one of its original commodities, has been a marketplace since Belfast's early days. Relics of old Belfast remain in the **entries,** or tiny alleys, that connect major streets. Belfast's newspapers all set up shop around St. Anne's, also known as the **Belfast Cathedral.** Each of the cathedral's 10 interior pillars name Belfast's 10 fields of professionalism: Science, Industry, Healing, Agriculture, Music, Theology, Shipbuilding, Freemasonry, Art, and, er, "Womanhood." (Donegall St., located near the Tourist Office. Open M-Sa 9am-5pm, Su for services.)

THE GOLDEN MILE. "The Golden Mile" refers to a strip along Great Victoria St. containing many of the jewels in the crown of Belfast's establishment. The pride and joy of Belfast, the **Grand Opera House** was bombed by the IRA, restored to its original splendor at enormous cost, and then bombed again. (☎9024 0411. Tours Sa 11am; UK£3, seniors and children UK£2. Office open M-W 8:30am-8pm, Th 8:30am-9pm, F 8:30am-6:30pm, Sa 8:30am-5:30pm.) **The Grand Opera House Ticket Shop** sells tickets for performances including musicals, operas, ballets, and concerts. (2-4 Great Victoria St. ☎9024 1919. Open M-W 8:30am-8pm, Th 8:30am-9pm, F 8:30am-6:30pm, Sa 8:30am-5:30pm. Tickets from UK£8.) The National Trust has restored the highly frequented **Crown Liquor Saloon,** 46 Great Victoria St, to make it a showcase of carved wood, gilded ceilings, and stained-glass. Damaged by 32 bombs in its history, the **Europa Hotel** has the dubious distinction of being "Europe's most bombed hotel."

QUEEN'S UNIVERSITY AREA. Charles Lanyon designed the Tudor-revival brick campus of **Queen's University** in 1849, modeling it after Magdalen College, Oxford. The **Visitors Centre,** in the Lanyon Room to the left of the main entrance, offers Queen's-related exhibits and merchandise. (University Road. Visitors Centre ☎9033 5252. Open May-Sept. M-Sa 10am-4pm; Oct-Mar. M-F 10am-4pm.) Bask in Belfast's occasional sun behind the university in the **Botanic Gardens.** Meticulously groomed, the gardens are a welcome respite from the traffic-laden city streets. Inside the gardens lie two 19th-century greenhouses, the toasty **Tropical Ravine House** and the more temperate Lanyon **Palm House.** Stop and smell the rose gardens, featuring Europe's most fragrant blooms. (☎9032 4902. *Open daily 8am-dusk. Tropical House and Palm House open Apr.-Sept. M-F 10am-noon and 1-5pm, Sa-Su 2-5pm; Oct.-Mar. M-F 10am-noon and 1-4pm, Sa-Su 2-4pm. Free.*) The **Ulster Museum,** within the gardens, contains a lovely hodge-podge. (*Off Stranmillis Rd.* ☎9038 3000. *Open M-F 10am-5pm, Sa 1-5pm, Su 2-5pm. Free.*)

NORTH BELFAST. In 1934, the Earl of Shaftesbury presented the **Belfast Castle** to the city. The ancient King Matudan had his McArt's Fort here, at the top of **Cave Hill** where the more modern United Irishmen plotted rebellion in 1795. The summit is nicknamed "Napoleon's Nose." Marked trails lead north from the fort to five caves in the area; only the lowest is accessible. (☎9077 6925. *Open daily. Free.*)

WEST BELFAST AND THE MURALS

Separated from the rest of the city by the Westlink motorway, the neighborhoods of West Belfast have historically been at the heart of the political tensions in the North. The Catholic area (centered on **Falls Road**) and the Protestant neighborhood (centered on the **Shankill**) are grimly separated by the **peace line,** a gray and seemingly impenetrable wall. West Belfast is not a center of consumer tourism or a "sight" in the traditional sense. The streets display political murals, which you will soon come across as you wander among the houses. **Be discreet when photographing murals.** The Protestant Orangemen's **marching season,** around July 12, is a risky time to visit the area, since the parades are underscored by mutual antagonism and can lead to political violence. It is **illegal to photograph military installations;** do so and your film may be confiscated.

THE FALLS. On **Divis Street,** a high-rise apartment building marks the site of the **Divis Tower,** an ill-fated housing development built by optimistic social planners in the 1960s. This project soon became an IRA stronghold and saw some of the worst of Belfast's Troubles in the 1970s. The British army still occupies the top three floors, and Shankill residents refer to it as "Little Beirut." Continuing west, Divis St. turns into the **Falls Road.** The **Sinn Féin** office is easily spotted: one side of it is covered with an enormous portrait of Bobby Sands and an advertisement for the Sinn Fein newspaper, *An Phoblacht.* Continuing down the Falls you will see a number of murals. One particularly moving mural, on the corner of the Falls and RPG Ave., shows the 10 hunger strikers who died in 1981-82 above a quote from Bobby Sands: "Our revenge will be the laughter of our children."

SHANKILL. North Street, to the left of the tourist office, turns into **Shankill Road** as it crosses the **Westlink** and then arrives in Protestant Shankill, once a thriving shopping district. Turning left (coming from the direction of North St.) onto most side roads leads to the **peace line.** At Canmore St., a mural depicts the Apprentice Boys "Shutting the Gates of Derry—1688" as the Catholic invaders try to get through. The densely decorated **Orange Hall,** which sits at Brookmount St., was formerly Fizzel's Fish Shop, where 10 people died in an October 1993 bomb attack. The side streets on the right guide you to the **Shankill Estate,** more murals, and through the estate; **Crumlin Road** is the site of the oldest Loyalist murals.

🎵 🎭 ENTERTAINMENT AND NIGHTLIFE

Belfast's many cultural events and performances are covered in the monthly *Arts Council Artslink,* which is free at the tourist office. Daily listings appear in the *Belfast Telegraph* as well as in Thursday's issue of the *Irish News.* For more information on pub entertainment, pick up the free, biweekly, bulletin *The List,* available at the tourist office, hostels, and many pubs. Belfast reigns supreme in the art world for three weeks each November during the annual **Queen's University Belfast festival** (☎9066 7687). Over 300 separate performances of opera, ballet, film, and comedy invade the city, drawing groups of international acclaim.

■ **Lavery's,** 12 Bradbury Pl. (☎9087 1106). 3 floors of unpretentious socializing. W live music in the 1st-floor back bar, DJs on weekends (no cover); disco in the 2nd fl. Gin Palace (UK£1 cover); 3rd floor "Heaven" club (UK£5 cover). Open until 1am.

IRELAND

Morning Star Pub, 17-19 Pottinger's Entry (☎9032 3976), between Ann and High St. Excellent U-shaped bar with wooden snugs for closer chats. Award-winning bar food awaits upstairs. Open M-Sa 11:30am-11pm, Su 11:30am-7pm.

White's Tavern, 2-4 Winecellar Entry (☎9024 3080), off Lombard and Bridge St.; Belfast's oldest tavern, serving drinks since 1630. An excellent stop for an afternoon pint. W gay night. Open M-Tu 11:30am-11pm, W 11:30am-1:30am, Th-Su 11:30am-1am.

The Botanic Inn, 23 Malone Rd. (☎9066 0460). "The Bot" is a huge and hugely popular student bar. Pub grub daily £4-5, Su carvey meal £4.50, students £3.50. *Trad* on Tu, no cover. Th-Sa 60s-80s music. 21+. Cover £2. Open until 1am.

Robinson's, 38-40 Great Victoria St. (☎9024 7447), has 4 floors of theme bars, but is most renowned for Fibber McGee's in the back, hosting incredible *trad* sessions Tu-Sa twice daily (no cover). Decent nightclub on top 2 floors Th-Sa (F cover UK£5, Sa UK£8).

The Kremlin, 96 Donegall St. (☎9080 9700). Look for the imposing statue of Stalin above the entrance. Belfast's newest and hottest gay nightspot with foam parties and internationally-renowned drag queens. Mixed crowd, but mostly men. Theme night F; "Kink" night once a month. Cover varies, but free Su, M, W, and before 9pm.

◪ DAYTRIP FROM BELFAST

ULSTER FOLK AND TRANSPORT MUSEUM

☎9042 8428. Open Mar.-June M-F 10am-5pm, Sa 10am-6pm, Su 11am-6pm; July-Sept. M-Sa 10am-6pm, Su 11am-6pm; Oct.-Feb. M-F 10am-4pm, Sa 10am-5pm, Su 11am-5pm. Folk Museum UK£4, concessions UK£2.50. Transport Museum UK£4, UK£2.50. Combined ticket UK£5, UK£3. Buses and trains stop here on the way to Bangor.

In **Holywood,** the **Ulster Folk Museum** and **Transport Museum** stretch over 71 hectares. Established by an Act of Parliament in the 1950s, the ◪**Folk Museum** aims to preserve the way of life of Ulster's farmers, weavers, and craftspeople, with over 30 buildings from the past three centuries. Inside the **Transport Museum** across the road is a *Titanic* exhibit that includes original blueprints and traces the Belfast-built ship and its fate. The **Railway Museum** next door is stuffed with 25 old railway engines, including the largest locomotive built in Ireland.

DERRY (LONDONDERRY)

Modern Derry is in the middle of a determined and largely successful effort to cast off its Troubled legacy. Although the Derry landscape was once razed by years of bombings, and violence still erupts occasionally during the Marching Season (July 4-12), recent years have been relatively peaceful, and today's rebuilt city looks sparklingly new. Derry's **city walls,** 5.5m high and 6m thick, erected between 1614 and 1619, have never been breached—hence Derry's nickname "the Maiden City." The stone tower along the southeast wall past New Gate was built to protect **St. Columb's Cathedral,** off Bishop St., the symbolic focus of the city's Protestant defenders. (Open Easter-Oct. M-Sa 9am-5pm; Nov.-Mar. M-Sa 9am-1pm and 2-4pm. Suggested donation UK£1.) At Union Hall Place, just inside Magazine Gate, the **Tower Museum**'s engaging exhibits relay Derry's long history. (Open July-Aug. M-Sa 10am-5pm, Su 2-5pm; Sept.-June Tu-Sa 10am-5pm. UK£4.20, students UK£1.60.) West of the city walls, Derry's residential neighborhoods, both the Protestant **Waterside** and **Fountain Estate** as well as the Catholic **Bogside,** display brilliant murals. After dark, roll by **Peadar O'Donnell's,** 53 Waterloo St., and the **Gweedore Bar,** 59-61 Waterloo St. which have been connected since Famine times.

Trains (☎7134 2228) arrive on Duke St., Waterside, on the east bank, from Belfast (2hr., 3-9 per day, UK£7.90). A free **Rail-Link bus** connect the train station and the **bus station,** on Foyle St., between the walled city and the river. **Ulsterbus** (☎7126 2261) goes to Belfast (1¾hr., 6-15 per day, UK£8) and Dublin (4¼hr., 4-6 per day, UK£11). The **tourist office** is at 44 Foyle St. (☎7126 7284. Open July-Sept. M-Sa 9am-7pm, Sa 10am-6pm, Su 10am-5pm; Oct.-Feb. M-F 9am-5pm; Mar.-June M-F 9am-6pm, Sa 10am-5pm.) Go down Strand Rd. and turn left on Asylum Rd. just before the RUC station to reach the ◼**Derry Independent Hostel (Steve's Backpackers),** 4 Asylum Rd. (☎7137 7989. **Internet** free for guests. Laundry UK£3. Key deposit UK£2. Dorms UK£7.50.) **Derry City Youth Hostel (YHANI)** is on Magazine St. (☎7128 4100. Laundry £3.50. Check-out 10am. Dorms UK£7-9.50; double with breakfast and bath UK£26.) **Boston Tea Party,** 13-15 Derry Craft Village, delights with delicious cakes and inexpensive food. (Full meal UK£2-3. Open M-Sa 9:30am-5:30pm.) **Postal code:** BT48.

GLENS OF ANTRIM

Glaciation left nine deep scars in the mountainous coastline of northeastern Co. Antrim. Over the years, water collected in these "glens," spurring the growth of lush flora not usually seen in Ireland. The villages along the coast provide beds for glen-wanderers, and a glimpse into rural Northern Ireland's cultural traditions.

◧ **TRANSPORTATION. Ulsterbus** (Belfast ☎9032 0011, Larne 2827 2345) #162 runs from Belfast through Waterfoot, Cushendall, and Cushendun (2-4 per day). Bus #150 runs between Ballymena and Glenariff (M-Sa 5 per day, UK£2.60), then to Waterfoot, Cushendall, and Cushendun (3-5 per day, UK£4.30). #150, from Belfast, stops in nearby Glenariff (a.k.a. Waterfoot; M-Sa 5 per day, UK£2.60).

GLENARIFF. Antrim's broadest (and arguably loveliest) glen, Glenariff, lies 6.5km south of Waterfoot along Glenariff Rd. in the large **Glenariff Forest Park.** Bus #150 between Ballymena and Glenarriff stops at the official park entrance, but if you're walking from Waterfoot, you can enter the park 2.5km downhill of the official entrance by taking the road that branches left toward the Manor Lodge Restaurant. The stunning ◼**Waterfall Trail** follows the cascading, fern-lined Glenariff River from the park entrance to the Manor Lodge. (☎2175 8769 or 2177 1796. Open daily 10am-dusk.UK£1.50 per adult pedestrian, UK£0.50 per child. UK£3 per car.)

CUSHENDALL. Cushendall is nicknamed the capital of the Glens, housing a variety of goods, services, and pubs unavailable anywhere else in the region. Unfortunately, the closing of its hostel may mean that Cushendall's days as a budget travel haven may be over. The **Antrim Coasters** (#252) run through Cushendall toward Portrush and Belfast (2 per day). The **tourist office,** 25 Mill St., is near the bus stop at the Cushendun end of town. (☎2177 1180. Open July-Sept. M-F 10am-1pm and 2-5:30pm, Sa 10am-1pm; Oct. to mid-Dec. and Feb.-June Tu-Sa 10am-1pm.) It's hard to imagine a warmer welcome than at **Glendale** guest house, 46 Coast Rd., south of town overlooking the sea. (☎2177 1495. UK£17 per person.)

CUSHENDUN. This miniscule, picturesque seaside village is 8km (an easy bike ride) north of Cushendall on A2. This white-washed and black-shuttered set of buildings lies by a beach with wonderful, dark **caves** carved within red sea cliffs. **Mary McBride's,** 2 Main St., used to be the *Guinness Book of World Records's'* "smallest bar in Europe" until it expanded. (☎21 76 15 11. Steak and Guinness pie UK£5; food served daily noon-9pm.) **Buses** stop in Cushendun en route to Waterfoot via Cushendall (2-4 per day).

CAUSEWAY COAST

Past Cushendun, the northern coast shifts from lyrical to dramatic mode. Sea-battered cliffs tower 185m over white wave-lapped beaches before giving way to the spectacular geology of **Giant's Causeway,** for which the region is named. Thousands of visitors swarm the site today, but few venture beyond the Visitors Centre to the stretches of stunning easily-accessible coastline stretching past the formation.

◧ **TRANSPORTATION.** In good summer weather, **Bushmills Bus** (Coleraine ☎(01265) 7043 3334.) outlines the coast between Coleraine, 8km south of Portrush, and Giant's Causeway (July-Aug. 7 per day). In the summer, the Antrim Coaster bus #252 runs up the coast from Belfast to Portstewart via towns listed here (2 per day; UK£13.30 from Belfast, UK£8.80 from Larne).

BALLYCASTLE AND ENVIRONS. The Causeway Coast leaves the sleepy glens behind when it hits this bubbly seaside town that shelters Giant's Causeway-bound tourists. **Ulsterbus** #162A vrooms to Cushendall via Cushendun (50min., M-F 1 per day, UK£3) and #131 goes to Belfast (3hr., 5-6 per day, UK£6.10). The **tourist office** is in Sheskburn House, 7 Mary St. (☎2076 2024. Open July-Aug. M-F 9:30am-7pm, Sa 10am-6pm, Su 2-6pm; Sept.-June M-F 9:30am-5pm.) Snooze at **Castle Hostel (IHH),** 62 Quay Rd (☎2076 2337. Dorms £UK8.50), or **Ballycastle Backpackers Hostel,** 4 North St. (☎2076 3612. Dorms UK£7.50.)

Just off the coast at Ballycastle, beautiful, bumpy, boomerang-shaped **Rathlin Island** ("Fort of the Sea") is the ultimate in escapism for 20,000 puffins, the odd golden eagle, and 100 human beings. Caledonian MacBrayne **ferries** (☎2076 9299) run to the island from the pier at Ballycastle, up the hill from Quay Rd on North St. (45min., 2-4 per day, UK£8.20 return.); pick up schedules from the Ballycastle tourist office. A **minibus** service (☎2076 3909) drives to the **Kebble Bird Sanctuary** at the western tip of the island, 7km from the harbor (20min., every 45min., UK£2.50).

Eight kilometers west of Ballycastle, the modest village of **Ballintoy** attracts the crowds on their way to itsy-bisty teeny-tiny **Carrick-a-rede Island.** Cross the shaky, 10cm wide, 20m fishermen's rope bridge over the dizzying 30m drop to rocks and sea below; **be extremely careful in windy weather.** A sign marks the turn-off from the coastal road east of Ballintoy. The aptly titled **Sheep Island View Hostel (IHH),** 42A Main St., has beds and camping facilities. (☎2076 9391. Dorms with bath UK£10.)

GIANT'S CAUSEWAY. Touted as the eighth natural wonder of the world, Giant's Causeway is Northern Ireland's most famous sight. A spillage of 40,000 hexagonal columns of basalt form a 60-million-year-old honeycomb path from the foot of the cliffs far into the sea. The **Giant's Causeway Visitors Centre,** which sits at the entrance to the Causeway from the car park, runs a bus (every 15min., round-trip UK£1) to the columns. (☎2073 1855. Open June daily 10am-6pm; July-Aug. 10am-7pm; Mar.-May and Sept. 10am-5pm; Nov.-Feb. 10am-4:30pm.)

ITALY
(ITALIA)

LIRE

US$1 = L2111 (LIRE)	L1000 = US$0.47
CDN$1 = L1369	L1000 = CDN$0.73
UK£1 = L3057	L1000 = UK£0.33
IR£1 = L2459	L1000 = IR£0.41
AUS$1 = L1132	L1000 = AUS$0.88
NZ$1 = L930	L1000 = NZ$1.08
ZAR1 = L255	L1000 = ZAR3.91
EUR€1 = L1936	L1000 = EUR€0.52

PHONE CODE **Country Code: 39. International dialing prefix:** 00. The city code must always be dialed, even when calling from within the city.

At the crossroads of the Mediterranean, Italy (pop. 57.6 million; 301,230 sq. km) has served as the home of powerful empires, eccentric leaders, and great food. Over the past 2000 years, this tiny boot has been foothold of the Roman Empire, the birthplace of the Renaissance, the epicenter of the Christian Church, and the motherland of pizza. In the Board Meeting of the World, Italy may be viewed as the jaded senior member: "Been there, done that," he says, slumping on the couch of the Mediterranean, "let's break for lunch." From the meats of the Veneto to the cheeses of Sardinia, Italy has found that the best way to a country's happiness is through its stomach. But when Italy isn't eating, it's loving. Italy has been a trademark of romance—its seductive syllables and scenery inspire passionate lovers to proclaim their *amore* from the rooftops of Rome. Consume a heaping plate of tasty tips from *Let's Go: Italy 2002* or *Let's Go: Rome 2002*.

SUGGESTED ITINERARIES

THREE DAYS Spend it all in the Eternal City of **Rome** (p. 606). Go back in time at the **Ancient City:** be a gladiator in the **Colosseum,** explore the **Roman Forum** and stand in the well-preserved **Pantheon.** Spend the next day admiring the fine art in the **Capitoline Museums** and the **Galleria Borghese,** then satiate your other senses in a disco. Redeem your debauched soul in **Vatican City** (p. 624), gazing at the ceiling of the **Sistine Chapel,** gaping at **St. Peter's Cathedral** and enjoying the **Vatican Museums.**

ONE WEEK Spend 3 days taking in the sights in **Rome** before heading north to **Florence** (2 days, p. 668) to immerse yourself in Italy's amazing Renaissance art at the Uffizi Gallery. Move to **Venice** (2 days, p. 651) to float through the canals and explore lagoon islands.

BEST OF ITALY IN 3 WEEKS Begin in **Rome** (4 days), then move to **Florence** (3 days). Cheer on horses in **Siena** (1 day, p. 682) before sailing to the isle of **Elba** (1 day, p. 684). Move up the coast to **Finale Ligure** (1 day, p. 639), and visit the fishing villages of **Cinque Terre** (2 days, p. 641). Move on to cosmopolitan **Milan** (2 days, p. 629) and visit **Lake Como** for hiking (1 day, p. 647). Spend some time in **Venice** (2 days, p. 651) before flying south to **Naples** (2 days, p. 688). Hike and swim along the **Amalfi Coast** (1 day, p. 694), and see the Grotto Azzura on the island of **Capri** (1 day, p. 696). End by visiting **Stromboli**'s live volcano (1 day, p. 703).

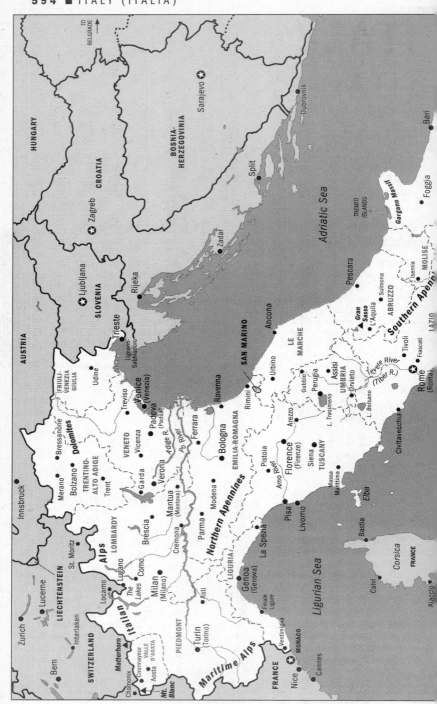

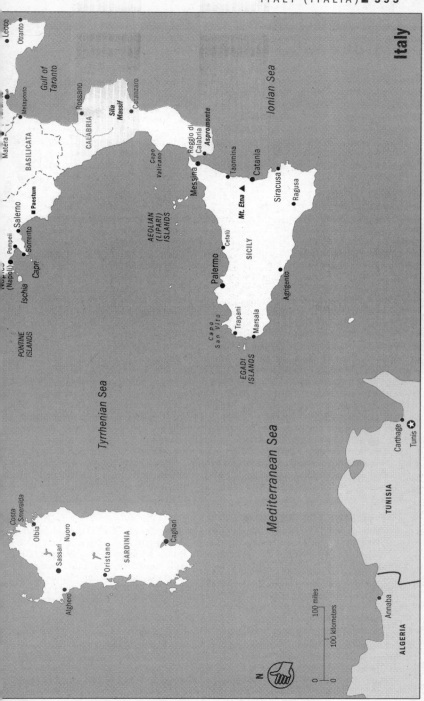

Italy

LIFE AND TIMES

HISTORY AND POLITICS

ITALY BACK IN THE DAY (UNTIL 753 BC)

The oldest Italian bones were dug up at Isernia, dating back to the Paleolithic Era (100,000-70,000 BC). More sophisticated settlements, however, did not appear until the Bronze Age (1500 BC), when tribes, known as the **Italics**, settled the peninsula. The Italics weren't exactly anything to italicize, however, and the **Etruscans** conquered them by the 7th century BC. The power-hungry **Greeks** took over most of the Mediterranean coast to limit Etruscan power, and in the 8th century BC, Greek city-states began colonizing Italy. Greek colonies, known as **Magna Graecia** (see p. 700), spread throughout Italy and Sicily and quickly showed those Etruscans who was boss. In the 3rd century BC, however, both the Greek colonies and the Etruscan city-states shrank in the growing shadow of Rome.

ANCIENT ROME (753-27 BC)

Rome (see p. 619) was just another water hole in Latium until the Etruscans conquered it in the 6th century. For the next century, Rome was ruled by a monarchy along with a Senate and curiate assembly. But when a son in the Tarquin noble family raped a respected noblewoman, enough was enough. Led by Lucius Brutus, the Romans overthrew the Tarquins and established the **Republic** in 509 BC. An alliance of Romans, Latins, and Italian Greeks later defeated the Etruscans for good in 392 BC. A **Gallic** invasion destroyed much of Rome five years later, but the phoenix-like Republic soon rose again, stronger than ever and set on controlling the Mediterranean. Among its most important battles were the three **Punic Wars** (264-146 BC) against the southern European and North African empire of Carthage. Victory in the Punic Wars vaulted Rome into the position of world dominator. Yet the fighting continued: Rome and its Italian allies just didn't see eye to eye on international etiquette and fought the **Social War** from 90 to 88 BC. After a yearlong civil war, in 82 BC the dictator general **Sulla** marched into Rome and laid down his law.

In 73 BC, in the wake of this upheaval, an escaped gladiatorial slave named **Spartacus** (see p. 620) led an army of 70,000 slaves and farmers on a two-year pillage of the peninsula. **Marcus Crassus** and **Pompey the Great** quickly crushed the uprising and took effective control of the city. Although they joined forces with **Julius Caesar**, that charismatic conqueror of Gaul, this association soon fell apart. By 45 BC, Caesar had defeated his "allies" and emerged as the leader of the Republic, touting himself Dictator for Life. Fearful of Caesar's growing power, a small faction of (literal) back-stabbers assassinated the leader on the Ides (15th) of March, 44 BC. Power eluded several would-be successors, among them Brutus, Marc Antony, and Caesar's adopted son, Octavian. But after defeating Antony in 31 BC, Octavian ultimately emerged victorious, and by 27 BC he had assumed the title of **Augustus.**

THE EMPIRE (27 BC-AD 476)

Augustus was the first of the Empire's **Julio-Claudian** rulers (27 BC-AD 68). Maintaining Republican traditions, he governed as *princeps* (first citizen). His principate (27 BC-AD 14), considered the Golden Age of Rome, initiated the **Pax Romana** (200 years of no back-stabbing). With the aid of a professional army and the necessary bureaucracy, Augustus maintained the Empire and extended Roman law and civic culture. Augustus's shoes were hard to fill: **Caligula** (AD 37-41) and **Nero** (54-68) went mad from the pressure, and for a while they were the taboo topic at cocktail parties. The **Flavian** dynasty (69-96), however, ushered in a period of relative prosperity, and the market soared under **Trajan** (98-117). After Trajan's death, his adopted successor **Hadrian** established the **Antonine** dynasty (117-193). The Antonines, particularly the philosopher-emperor **Marcus Aurelius** (161-180), were known for their oh-so-enlightened leadership. In 193, however, Rome's leadership hit the rocks, and in the "Year of Four Emperors," four successive Antonine rulers attempted to claim the throne. The last, **Commodus,** was assassinated, and **Septimius**

Severus, a general from North Africa, overtook the principate to found the **Severan** dynasty (193-235). With the death of the last of the Severans in 235, the era of dynastic succession came to a halt. **Diocletian** was one of few to have secured enough control of the fragmented Empire to split it in half. **Constantine,** Diocletian's successor, converted to Christianity after literally seeing the light before a decisive battle in 312, and declared Christianity the state religion two years later. After the reign of **Theodosius I** (379-95), the Empire split permanently, and the western half suffered constant invasions. **Alaric,** king of the Visigoths, sacked Rome in 410, and the anticlimatic fall finally came in 476, when the Germanic chief **Odoacer** removed the last of the Western emperors, Romulus Augustulus, and crowned himself king of Italy.

THE DARK AND MIDDLE AGES (476-1375)

Continuous invasions get pretty annoying after awhile, and Pope Stephen II finally begged **Charlemagne** and his Frankish army for help. This merely invited a Frankish invasion, so that on Christmas Day 800, Charlemagne became Holy Roman Emperor. The 11th through the 14th centuries saw the power split between city-states known as *comuni*. But even though the towns squabbled amongst themselves, they all ran to fight when the Church called them to arms. Though the **Crusades** failed to win back the Holy Land, they strengthened the unity of Christendom and the authority of the papacy.

In the 14th century, when **Pope Boniface VIII** forbade the French King **Philippe IV (The Fair)** to tax his clergy, the monarch responded by insulting and assaulting the Pope, who died of shock. The pontiff's successors, persuaded by Philippe, moved the papacy to the French city of Avignon, where it remained for most of the century. Known as the **Babylonian Captivity** (1309-77), this confusion culminated in the **Great Schism** (1378-1417), during which as many as three popes reigned at the same time, one in France and two in Italy. By the end of the 14th century, years of instability and war had induced famine and **Black Death** (the plague), wreaking havoc upon the increasingly overcrowded cities of Italy.

THE RENAISSANCE (1375-1530)

Once the Black Death had eradicated one-third of the population, promoted fearful superstitions and generally caused chaos throughout the country, Italy began the long trek back to sanity. First thing on the agenda was to get some fresh air, physically and mentally: at the end of the 14th century, Italians began the geographical exploration of foreign lands and the intellectual exploration of Classicism. Their desire to master ancient Greek and Roman scholarship led to the rise of **Humanism,** a secular movement that glorified all the glory possible in human beings. Fueled by Humanist ideals, Italy inaugurated the greatest intellectual and artistic flowering in history, the *Rinascimento*, or **Renaissance,** which quickly inspired the rest of Europe to go smell the roses.

Great ruling families—the Gonzagas in Mantua, the d'Estes in Ferrara, and, most importantly, the **Medici** in Florence—instituted commercial and legal reforms and patronized the cultural and artistic activity of their cities. The Medici clan reached their acme with **Cosimo** and **Lorenzo** (**Il Magnifico**—no modesty there), who started handing out the family's loot to promising artists and sculptors. Under the golden hands of these two Renaissance men, **Donatello** (see p. 678), **Brunelleschi** (see p. 676), **Michelangelo** (see p. 679), and **Botticelli** (see p. 677) achieved fame throughout the country and the continent. Despite Florence's rise in economic and intellectual power, not every city-state blossomed to the same degree. The power-hungry princes' quests for glory resulted in constant warfare. The weakened cities yielded to the invading Spanish armies of **Charles V** throughout the 16th century, and by 1556 Naples and Milan had fallen to **King Ferdinand of Aragon.**

POST-RENAISSANCE: FOREIGN DOMINATION (1540-1815)

The open-mindedness of the Renaissance soon corroded into intolerance that found an outlet in religious turmoil. The **Counter-Reformation,** the Catholic Church's vehement response to the Protestant Reformation, tightened the belt on parochial issues. The 16th-century **Spanish Inquisition** made sure everyone remained holy through some not-so-holy methods, allowing Spain to suppress the Protestant Reformation in Italy as it politically dominated the peninsula for over a century. Charles II, the last Spanish Habsburg, died in 1700, sparking the **War of Spanish Succession,** after which parts of Italy were handed over to France and Austria. In the course of **Napoleon's** 19th-century march through Europe, the diminutive French Emperor united much of northern Italy into the Italian Republic, reconquered some lost territory, and created one big happy national family. In 1804, Napoleon declared the newly united nation the Kingdom of Italy, with himself as monarch. After Napoleon's fall in 1815, the **Congress of Vienna** carved up much of Italy and handed it over to Austria.

THE ITALIAN NATION (1815-1945)

Frustration at being under the foreign thumb prompted a nationalist resurgence, the **Risorgimento,** which culminated in national unification in 1860. The success of the uprising can be traced to three big guys: **Giuseppe Mazzini,** the movement's suave intellectual leader; **Giuseppe Garibaldi,** the charismatic military head; and **Camillo Cavour,** the political and diplomatic mastermind. The first head honcho of Italy, **Vittorio Emanuele II,** expanded the nation by annexing northern and central regions. Italians really lit their fireworks on September 20, 1870, when France finally let go of Rome.

The chaotic aftermath of **World War I** paved the way for the rise of **Fascism,** under the control of "*Il Duce,*" **Benito Mussolini.** Mussolini established the world's first Fascist regime in 1924 and all opposition mysteriously disappeared. In 1940, Italy entered **World War II** on the side of its Axis ally, Germany. Success came quickly but was short-lived: the Allies landed in Sicily in 1943, prompting Mussolini's fall from power. As a final indignity, Mussolini and his mistress were captured and executed by infuriated citizens. By the end of 1943, the new government had withdrawn its support from Germany, which promptly invaded and occupied its former ally. In 1945, Italy was freed from the Germans, and the country was divided between those supporting the monarchy and those favoring Fascism.

MODERN PROBLEMS: POST-WAR POLITICS (1945-1983)

In May 1946, King Vittoro Emanuele II abdicated the throne, and his son King **Umberto II** was forced to flee a month later after a referendum decided in favor of a republic by 54% of the votes. A constituent assembly was elected by universal suffrage (including women) to draw up the **Italian Constitution.** The constitution, adopted in 1948, established the **Republic,** with a president, a bicameral parliament, and an independent judiciary. The constitution was about the only thing that stayed the same: a revolving door of 50 governments between 1945-94, having an average life span of 11 months, plagued the postwar era with instability. Meanwhile, the Italian economy shot through the roof with industrialization, and many regions, especially in the North, recovered economically by the 50s. Italy joined the North Atlantic Treaty Organization **(NATO)** in 1948 and was a founding member of the European Economic Community in 1957, thus cementing its political stability and security on the international stage. In the late 60s, Italians (slightly) preferred making civil protest to making love, and the *autunno caldo* (hot autumn) of 1969, a season of strikes, demonstrations, and riots, foreshadowed the violence of the 70s. Perhaps the most shocking episode of the following decade was the 1978 kidnapping and murder of ex-Prime Minister **Aldo Moro** by a group of left-wing militant terrorists, the *Brigate Rosse* (Red Brigade). Out of all the turmoil, **Bettino Craxi** became Italy's first Socialist premier in 1983. Italy became one of the original members of the **European Union** in 1991.

ITALY TODAY

In 1992, **Oscar Luigi Scalfaro** was elected Italy's new president. During his turbulent seven-year term, he initiated electoral reforms, hoping to make the Italian government more productive. These reforms and their accompanying judicial investigations uncovered the **Tangentopoli** (Kickback City) scandal. This unprecedented political crisis implicated over 2600 politicians in corruption charges. The elections of 1996 brought the center-left coalition, the **Olive Tree** (l'Ulivo), to power. **Romano Prodi** was Prime Minister and helped stabilize Italian politics. However, Prodi's government collapsed in October 1998 and former Communist **Massimo D'Alema** was sworn in as the new prime minister. D'Alema and his respected treasurer **Carlo Ciampi** (Italy's past president) created fiscal reforms and pushed through a budget that qualified Italy for January 1999 entrance into the **European Monetary Union.** In the May 2001 elections, media magnate **Silvio Berlusconi** was elected Italy's **Prime Minister** under a storm of controversy that his official control over state-owned television plus his corporate media holdings will endanger freedom of speech in Italy.

THE ARTS

VISUAL ARTS

In Rome, the Colosseum hovers above a city bus stop; in Florence, young men and women meet in front of the *duomo* to flirt and gossip; in Sicily, remnants from Greek columns are used as dining tables. Italy is a country in which daily life and artistic masterpieces are woven inextricably together. The artistic tradition is prolific and varied—to visit only the most famous pieces would be to misunderstand the pervasive presence of art in everyday Italian settings.

ETRUSCAN. Italian art history begins in the 8th century BC with the **Etruscans** (see p. 628). Culturally, the Etruscans are strongly linked with Asia Minor and the ancient Near East. Large eyes, enigmatic smiles, and meticulous attention to anatomic detail characterize their sculptures and wall paintings. Etruscans used bright colors and fluid lines in necropoli, tomb paintings, and funerary statues.

GREEK AND ROMAN. The Greeks peppered southern Italy with a large number of **temples** (see p. 700) and **theaters** (see p. 701). In fact, the best-preserved Greek temples in the world today are found not in Greece, but in Sicily. Stretching roughly from 200 BC to AD 350, Roman art falls mainly into two large categories—art in service of the state and private household art. Most Roman houses incorporated **frescoes** (see p. 626), Greek-influenced paintings made from a time-resistant compound of paint and plaster. **Mosaic** was another popular medium from the Hellenistic period onward. Romans soon began to use the column as a purely decorative device, relying on the **arch** (see p. 620) instead of the column for support. The arch, along with the invention of **concrete,** revolutionized the Roman conception of architecture and made possible such monuments as the **Colosseum** (see p. 620) and the **Pantheon** (see p. 621), as well as public works like **aqueducts** and **thermal baths** (see p. 621).

EARLY CHRISTIAN AND BYZANTINE. For fear of persecution, early Christians fled underground to worship; their **catacombs** (see p. 624) are now among the most haunting and intriguing of Italian monuments, scattered throughout Rome, Naples, and Syracuse. Inexpressive, two-dimensional human figures on flat blue or gold backgrounds were popular and mosaics (see p. 646) were perfect for this style.

ROMANESQUE AND GOTHIC. From 1000 to 1200, **Romanesque** churches (see p. 634) sprung up throughout Europe. Characterized by rounded arches, heavy columns, strict geometry, thick and relatively unadorned walls, and small windows, these basilicas were not as flamboyantly ornate as the later Gothic churches. The **Gothic** style of the 12th to 14th centuries spread southward from France and combined the pointed arch and the flying buttress, which together supported the weight of the roof and allowed the heavy Romanesque wall to be replaced by jewel-like stained glass. In reaction against the flat trend of flat characters, **Giotto di Bondone** began to explore perspective, naturalism, and personal expression.

EARLY RENAISSANCE. The first artists to expand upon the lessons of Giotto were Filippo Brunelleschi, Donatello, and Masaccio, who succeeded in revolutionizing architecture, sculpture, and painting respectively. **Brunelleschi**'s (see p. 678) mathematical studies of ancient Roman architecture became the cornerstone of all later Renais-

ITALY

sance building. In sculpture, **Donatello** (see p. 660) built upon the central achievement of classical antiquity: the realistic articulation of the human body in motion. Also depicting movement, **Fra Filippo Lippi** (see p. 677) and **Fra Angelico** (see p. 679) followed hot on Masaccio's footsteps. Trained under Lippi, **Sandro Botticelli** (see p. 634) was a favorite painter of the Medici.

HIGH RENAISSANCE. The torch was passed at the start of the **High Renaissance** to three exceptional men: Leonardo da Vinci, Michelangelo Buonarroti, and Raphael Santi. **Leonardo** (see p. 634) was not only an artist but a scientist, architect, engineer, musician, and weapon designer. **Michelangelo** (see p. 624) painted, sculpted, and designed buildings with as much skill as his contemporary but with the additional skill of time efficiency. The ceiling of the **Sistine Chapel** (1473-81; see p. 625), on which Michelangelo created the illusion of vaults on a flat surface, remains his greatest surviving achievement in painting. Sculpture, however, was his favorite mode of expression, the most classic example being the virile, pensive, and just plain sexy *David* (1501-04, see p. 679). **Raphael** created technically perfect figures in his paintings (see p. 625). The Venetian school produced the poetic **Giorgione** (see p. 660) and energetic **Titian** (see p. 660).

MANNERISM. The emerging spirit of creative experimentation led to Mannerism, a short-lived link between the Renaissance and Baroque periods. Mannerist artists idealized the human to the point of abstraction; figures produced in this style may be oddly elongated, flattened, or colored in unusual schemes. **Parmigianino** was the most famous Mannerist, and his controversial *Madonna of the Long Neck* (1534) in the Uffizi (see p. 677) is the period's most famous work.

BAROQUE AND ROCOCO. Born of the Counter-Reformation and of absolute monarchy, the grandiose, vivid, and dynamic Baroque art and architecture were intended to inspire faith in God and respect for the Catholic Church. Painters of this era favored Naturalism—a commitment to portraying nature as is, warts and all. **Caravaggio** (see p. 622) created mysterious works, often incorporating unsavory characters into religious scenes. **Gianlorenzo Bernini,** a High Baroque sculptor and architect, designed the colonnaded *piazza* of St. Peter's (see p. 625) as well as the *baldacchino* over its crossing. **Giovanni Battista Tiepolo,** with his light-colored palate and vibrant frescoes, was a remarkable Venetian painter of allegories and the premier exemplar of the **Rococo** style.

NEOCLASSICISM AND 20TH CENTURY ART. The Italians started to lose their paintbrush dexterity and chisel proficiency in the 18th and 19th centuries. **Antonio Canova** explored the formal **Neoclassical** style, which professed a return to the rules of Classical antiquity. The **Macchiaioli** group, spearheaded by **Giovanni Fattori,** revolted against the strict academic Neoclassical style with a unique technique of "blotting." The Italian **Futurist** artists of the 1910s, who sought to transfer the aesthetics and movements of machines into art, brought Italy back to the cutting edge of artistry. **Amadeo Modigliani** crafted figures most famous for their long oval faces.

LITERATURE

LATIN LOVERS (300 BC-200 AD). In the wake of Greek civilization, the Romans were faced with the challenge of building a literature that could match the majesty and scope of their impressive rule. The early dramatist **Plautus** wrote popular comedic plays, including *Pseudolus* (191 BC), better known as the hit Broadway musical *A Funny Thing Happened on the Way to the Forum* (1962). The lyric poetry of **Catullus** set a high standard for passion, and **Cicero** penned several orations while **Julius Caesar** himself gave a first-hand account of the final dissolution of the Republic in the Gallic wars.

Augustan Rome produced some of the greatest Latin authors. **Virgil** wrote and wrote and never finished the epic *Aeneid* about the godly origins of Rome. **Horace**'s (65-8 BC) texts, including *Odes* (23 BC), *Epodes* (30-29 BC), *Satires* (35 BC), and *Epistles* (19-15 BC) gave powerful voice to his personal experiences. It is primarily through **Ovid**'s various works that we learn the gory details of Roman mythology, a soap-opera theology that developed from and added to the Greek family of deities. Usually disguised as animals or humans, these gods and goddesses often descended to earth to intervene romantically or combatively in human affairs. Ovid also wrote poems, among them *Lusts* (20 BC), *Metamorphoses* (AD 8), and *The Art of Loving*, a guide to picking up women (1 BC).

LOVE'S LABOR FOUND (1250-1375). The Dark Ages put a stop to most literary musings, but three Tuscan writers reasserted the art in the late 13th century. **Dante Alighieri** was one of the first Italian poets to write in the *volgare* (common Italian) instead of Latin. In his infamous epic poem, *The Divine Comedy* (1308-21), Dante explores the various fires of the afterlife. **Petrarch** restored the popularity of ancient Roman writers by writing love sonnets to a married woman, compiled in *Songbook* (1350). **Giovanni Boccaccio**, a close friend of Petrarch's, composed a collection of 100 bawdy stories in *The Decameron* (1348-53).

RENAISSANCE AND BEYOND (1375-1800). Paralleling the scientific exploration of the time, 15th- and 16th-century Italian authors explored new dimensions of the human experience. **Alberti** and **Palladio** wrote treatises on architecture and art theory. **Baldassare Castiglione**'s *The Courtier* (1528) instructed the fastidious Renaissance man on deportment, etiquette, and other fine points of behavior. **Niccolò Machiavelli**'s *The Prince* (1513) gives a timeless sophisticated assessment of climbing the political ladder. Italian literary output gradually declined along with Italy's political power, but the unique tradition persevered. The 18th-century dramatist **Carlo Goldoni** replaced the stock characters of the traditional *commedia dell'arte* with unpredictable figures in *The Fan* (1764).

MODERN TO POSTMODERN (1800-PRESENT). With the 19th-century unification of Italy came a desire for a similarly unified culture. The 1800s were an era primarily of *racconti* (short stories) and poetry. **Pellegrino Artusi**'s 1891 cookbook *Science in the Kitchen and the Art of Eating Well* was the first attempt to assemble recipes from regional traditions into a unified Italian cuisine. The 20th century saw a new tradition in Italian literature as Nobel Prize-winning author and playwright **Luigi Pirandello** explored the relativity of truth in works like *Six Characters in Search of an Author* (1921). Literary production slowed in the years preceding WWII, but the conclusion of the war ignited an explosion in antifascist fiction. **Primo Levi** wrote *If This is a Man* (1947) about his experiences in Auschwitz. Mid-20th-century poets include Nobel Prize winners **Salvatore Quasimodo** and **Eugenio Montale** who founded the "hermetic movement," characterized by an intimate poetic vision and allusive imagery. More recently, internationally known playwright and satirist **Dario Fo** claimed the 1997 Nobel Prize for literature.

MUSIC

CHURCH TUNES AND MEDIEVAL JAMS. An Italian monk, **Guido d'Arezzo**, is regarded as the originator of musical notation. Generally accepted as the home of church music, Italy's monasteries reveled in simple harmonies through the Middle Ages and Renaissance. By the 14th century, Italian secular composers undertook the art of **madrigals,** transposing poems in vocal settings.

THE FAT LADY SINGS. The 16th century also ushered in a new musical extravaganza that would gain global popularity: **opera.** Italy's most cherished art form was born in Florence, nurtured in Venice, and revered in Milan. Conceived by the **Camerata,** a circle of Florentine writers, noblemen, and musicians, opera originated as an attempt to recreate the dramas of ancient Greece by setting lengthy poems to music. **Jacobo Peri** composed *Dafne* (1598), the world's first complete opera, in 1597. The first successful opera composer, **Claudio Monteverdi,** drew freely from history, juxtaposing high drama, love scenes, and bawdy humor.

IF IT AIN'T BAROQUE, DON'T FIX IT. Baroque music, known for its literal and figurative hot air, took the 17th and 18th centuries by storm. During this period, two main instruments saw their popularity mushroom: the violin, the shape of which

ITALY

was perfected by Cremona families, including the **Stradivari,** and the piano, created in about 1709 by members of the Florentine **Cristofori** family. **Antonio Vivaldi,** who composed over 400 concertos, triumphed with *The Four Seasons* (1725).

O SOLE MIO. With convoluted plots and strong, dramatic music, 19th-century Italian opera continues to dominate modern stages. **Gioacchino Rossini** was the master of the *bel canto* ("beautiful song"), which consists of long, fluid, melodic lines. **Giuseppe Verdi** remains the transcendent musical and operatic figure of 19th-century Italy. Verdi produced the touching, personal dramas and memorable melodies of *Rigoletto* (1851), *La Traviata* (1853), and *Il Trovatore* (1853) and the grand and heroic conflicts of *Aida* (1871). At the turn of the century, **Giacomo Puccini** created *Madame Butterfly* (1904), *La Bohème* (1896), and *Tosca* (1900). Classical music *all'italiana* continued to grow in the 20th century. **Ottorino Respighi** experimented with rapidly shifting orchestral textures. And that *pagliaccio* **Luciano Pavarotti** remains universally adored, singing long into the night.

FILM

In the early 20th century, Mussolini created the *Centro Sperimentale della Cinematografia,* a national film school that stifled any true artistic development. The fall of Fascism allowed the explosion of **Neorealist cinema** (1943-50), which rejected contrived sets and professional actors and sought to produce a candid look at postwar Italy. This new style caught the world's attention and Rome soon became a hotspot for the international jet set. On the heels of these celebrities also came a certain set of photographic stalkers called **paparazzi.** The works of **Roberto Rossellini** and **Vittorio De Sica** best represent *Neorealismo*, with de Sica's 1945 film *The Bicycle Thief* as perhaps the most famous and successful Neorealist film. In the 1960s, post-Neorealist directors like **Federico Fellini** rejected plots and characters for a visual and symbolic world. Fellini's *La Dolce Vita* (*The Sweet Life*, 1960), which was banned by the Pope, is an incisive film scrutinizing 1950s Rome. **Pier Paolo Pasolini,** on the other hand, explored Italy's infamous underworld in films like *Accatone* (*The Beggar*, 1961). Although Italian cinema has fallen into a recent slump, **Bernardo Bertolucci**'s *The Last Emperor* (1987) and Oscar-winners **Giuseppe Tornatore** and **Gabriele Salvatore** have garnered the attention of US and international audiences. Enthusiastic sparkplug **Roberto Benigni** became one of Italy's leading cinematic personalities when his *La Vita e Bella (Life is Beautiful)* gained international fame, receiving Best Actor and Best Foreign Film Oscars and a Best Picture Oscar nomination at the 1999 Academy Awards.

FOOD AND DRINK

Eating for Italians is an art, a way of life, and one of its greatest joys. While breakfast and dinner consist mostly of light snacks, lunch is the main feast of the day. A full Italian meal typically consists of an *antipasto* (appetizer), *primo piatto* or *primi* (the first course of pasta, risotto, or soup), *secondo* (usually meat or fish), and *contorno* (vegetable side dish). Finally comes *dolce* (dessert or fruit), then *caffè*, and often an after-dinner liqueur. Italian cuisine differs radically by region: dishes in the North are often rich, with creamy and meaty sauces, egg noodles, and more butter than olive oil; they also primarily eat *risotto* (made from rice) and *polenta* (made from cornmeal). **Piedmont** (see p. 666) is known for its heavy sauces and delectable truffles, a proven aphrodisiac. **Lombardy** (see p. 629) specializes in cheeses, *risotto*, and stewed meat dishes like *ossobuco*. The coastal region of **Liguria** (see p. 637) is noted for its seafood, pesto, and olive oil, while German and Austrian influences in **Trentino-Alto Adige** (see p. 647) have popularized *gnocchi*, dumplings made of potatoes and flour. **Friuli-Venezia Giulia** (see p. 665) offers heavy cuisine with a Middle-European flair, spiced with cumin, horseradish, and paprika. The **Veneto** (see p. 651) is rich in artichokes, rice, and various game. **Emilia-Romagna** (see p. 643) is Italy's gastronomic heart, the birthplace of parmesan cheese, balsamic vinegar, and *prosciutto di Parma* (Parma ham). **Tuscany** (see p. 668) draws justifiable acclaim for its simple, hearty food: high-quality olive oil, thick soups, and bean dishes are prevalent. **Umbria** (see p. 685) grows black truffles to match Piedmont's white, but its unspiced cuisine is anything but rich. Yet you say, "But where's the pizza?" Head south where the food is spicier, based more on garlic, tomatoes, and olive oil. Tomato sauces and mozzarella are popular in **Campania** (see p. 687), home to the authentic pizza. **Basilicata** and **Calabria,** at the tip of the boot, specialize in spicy cuisine. In **Sicily** (see p. 698), pasta is still eaten by the truckload, served with tomatoes and fresh vegetables. **Sardinia** (see p. 703) has more sheep than people, and their odiferous cheese is made into pies and topped with honey, the perfect finish to a meal of veggie soup and roast game.

Italy's rocky soil, warm climate, and hilly landscape are ideal for growing grapes. The country is among the top producers of **wine** in the world—Sicily alone boasts 200 million gallons annually. Piedmont is Italy's preeminent wine region, producing the touted *Barolo*. Tuscany is famed for its tannic *chianti* and similar reds. When in Rome, you know the drill—drink *frascati*, a clean white wine with an almond aftertaste, served cold. After grapes are pressed for wine, the remaining pomace is used to produce *grappa*, the national blue collar favorite. This illegitimate cousin of wine flows freely throughout Italy.

ESSENTIALS

DOCUMENTS AND FORMALITIES

Those wishing to stay in Italy for more than three months must apply for a *permesso di soggiorno* (residence permit) at a police station *(questura)*. For more info, contact the Italian embassy in your country.

Italian Embassies at Home: Australia, 12 Grey St, Deakin, Canberra ACT 2600 (☎(02) 6273 3333; fax 6273 4223; www.ambitalia.org.au). **Canada,** 275 Slater St., 21st fl., Ottawa, ON K1P 5H9 (☎613-232-2401; fax 233-1484; www.italyincanada.com). **Ireland,** 63 Northumberland Rd., Dublin (☎(01) 660 1744; fax 668 2759; http://homepage.eircom.net/~italianembassy). **New Zealand,** 34 Grant Rd., Wellington (☎(006) 4473 5339; fax 472 9302; www.italy-embassy.org.nz). **South Africa,** 796 George Ave., Arcadia 0083, Pretoria (☎(012) 43 55 41; fax 43 55 47; www.ambital.org.za). **UK,** 14 Three Kings Yard, London W1Y 2EH (☎(020) 73 12 22 00; fax 74 99 22 83; www.embitaly.org.uk). **US,** 1601 Fuller St. NW, Washington, D.C. 20009 (☎202-328-5500; www.italyemb.org).

Foreign Embassies in Italy: All embassies are in **Rome** (see p. 606).

TRANSPORTATION

BY PLANE. Rome's international airport, known as both Fiumicino and Leonardo da Vinci, is served by most major airlines, as are **Milan** and **Florence**'s airports. Italy's national airline, **Alitalia** (☎800-223-5730, UK ☎(870) 544 8259; www.alitalia.it/eng), may offer off-season youth fares.

BY TRAIN. The Italian State Railway, **Ferrovie dello Stato** or **FS** (national info line ☎ 147 88 80 88; www.fs-on-line.com), offers inexpensive and efficient service, although it is commonly plagued by strikes. The southern Italy offspring of FS, **Ferrovie Sud-Est (FSE),** is hot, crowded, and uncomfortable. There are several types of trains: the *locale* stops at every station along a particular line; the *diretto* makes fewer stops than the *locale;* and the *espresso* only stops at major stations. The air-conditioned, more expensive **rapido,** an **InterCity (IC)** train, travels only to the largest cities. Tickets for the fast, pricey **Eurostar** trains (a 1st- and 2nd-class train) require reservations. **Eurailpasses** are valid without a supplement on all trains except **Eurostar.** While seat reservations are rarely required, you are not guaranteed a seat without one. If you're under 26 and plan to travel extensively in Italy, the **Cartaverde** should be your *first* purchase upon arrival. Available to people aged 12 to 26, the card (L40,000/€20.65) is valid for one year and entitles travelers to a 20% discount on any state train fare.

BY BUS. In Italy, buses serve many points inaccessible by train and occasionally arrive at more convenient places in large towns. All tickets must be validated using the orange machines onboard immediately upon entering the bus; failure to do so will result in a large fine. For **city buses,** buy tickets in *tabacchi* or kiosks, and validate them on board.

BY CAR. There are four different kinds of roads: *Autostrade* (superhighways, most of which charge tolls); *Strade Statali* (state roads); *Strade Provinciali* (provincial roads); and *Strade Communali* (local roads). Italian driving is terrifying; congested traffic is more common in larger cities and in the north. Helpful words include: *benzina* (gasoline), *entrata* (entrance), *senso unico* (one-way), *vietato parcheggiare* (no parking), and *uscita* (exit). Expect to pay L100,000/€51.65 per day to rent a tiny car.

The **Automobile Club Italiano (ACI)** is the automobile savior of Italy. The main office is located at V. Marsala, 8, 00185 Rome (☎06 499 81; fax 499 82 34). In case of **breakdown** on any Italian road, dial **116** at the nearest telephone. The nearest ACI office will be advised to come to your assistance. On superhighways, use the emergency telephones placed every 2km. **Taxis** are common in major cities.

BY FERRY. The islands of Corsica, Sardinia, and Sicily, as well as the smaller islands along the coasts, are connected to the mainland by ferries *(traghetti)* and hydrofoils *(aliscafi)*. Italy's largest private ferry service is **Tirrenia;** for info, contact the Rome office at V. Bissolati, 41 (☎(06) 474 20 41). Ferry services in the port towns of **Ancona** (p. 687), **Bari** (p. 697), and **Brindisi** (p. 698) connect Italy to **Greece.** Only **Brindisi** honors the **Eurailpass;** in all other situations, the ferries from Bari and Otranto are cheaper and less crowded. For **Sardinia,** catch a boat in **Genoa** (p. 638), **La Spezia** (p. 641), or **Naples** (p. 688). Travelers heading for **Sicily** (p. 698) should take the ferry from **Naples** or **Reggio di Calabria.**

BY BIKE AND BY THUMB. Bicycling is a popular national sport, but bike trails are rare, drivers often reckless, and, except in the Po Valley, the terrain challenging. Hitchhiking in Italy, especially in areas south of Rome or Naples, can be unsafe. *Let's Go* strongly urges you to consider the risks before you choose to hitchhike.

TOURIST SERVICES AND MONEY

EMERGENCY	Police, ☎112. Ambulance, ☎118. Fire, ☎115.

TOURIST OFFICES. In Italy, almost every town has a tourist office, which is usually called **Ente Provinciale per il Turismo (EPT)** or **Azienda di Promozione Turistica (APT)** and offers information on the town and surrounding area. Local tourist offices, *Informazione e Assistenza ai Turisti* (IAT) and *Azienda Autonoma di Soggiorno e Turismo* (AAST), are very useful as well. Also keep an eye out for *Pro Loco Centro Turistico Studentesco e Giovanile* (CTS), and *Compagnia Italiana Turismo* (CIT).

Italian Government Tourist Board (ENIT), 630 5th Ave., #1565, New York, NY 10111 (☎212-245-5618; fax 586-9249; www.italiantourism.com). **Branch offices: Australia,** Level 26, 44 Market St., Sydney NSW 2000 (☎(02) 9262 1666; fax 9262 5745). **Canada,** 175 E. Bloor St., #907 South Tower, Toronto, ON M4W 3R9 (☎416-925-4882; fax 925-4799; initaly@ican.net). **UK,** 1 Princes St., London WIR 9AY (☎020 7355 1439; fax 7493 6695; www.enit.it). **US,** 12400 Wilshire Blvd., #550, Los Angeles, CA 90025 (☎310-820-1898; fax 820-6357; enitla@earthlink.com).

CURRENCY AND EXCHANGE. The Italian currency unit is the **lira** (plural: *lire*). Coins are minted in L50, L100, L200, and L500 denominations, and the most common bills are L1000, L2000, L5000, L10,000, L50,000, and L100,000. When changing money in Italy, try to use only banks or *cambii* that have at most a 5% margin between their buy and sell prices. Italy has accepted the **Euro (€)** as legal tender, and *lire* will be phased out by July 1, 2002. For more information, see p. 23.

Prices: A thrifty traveler staying in a hostel and preparing his own food can expect to spend L60,000-140,000/€31-72.30 per day in addition to transportation costs. Costs will vary depending on region and season. Always overestimate expenses.

Tipping and bargaining: At many Italian restaurants, a service charge *(servizio)* or cover *(coperto)* is included in the bill. Taxi drivers expect about a 10% tip. Tour guides should get L2000/€2.60 tip for a half-day tour. Bargaining in Italy is usually only appropriate at outdoor markets, with street vendors, and over unmetered taxi fares (always settle your price *before* taking a cab).

Taxes: The **value-added tax (VAT)** in Italy *(imposto sul valore aggiunta,* or IVA) ranges from 12-35%. Upon departure from the EU, non-EU citizens can get a refund of the IVA for single purchases over L650,000/€335.

ACCOMMODATIONS AND CAMPING

HOSTELS. Associazione Italiana Alberghi per la Gioventù (AIG), the Italian hostel federation, is a Hosteling International (HI) affiliate, though not all Italian hostels *(ostelli per la gioventù)* are part of AIG. Over 85 HI hostels are scattered throughout Italy; they sometimes accept reservations via the **International Booking Network** (see p. 35). A complete list is available from most **EPT** and **CTS** offices and from many hostels. For more information on hostels in Italy, contact the Rome **AIG office,** V. Cavour, 44 (☎06 487 11 52; www.hostels-aig.org). **Prices** start at about L24,000/€12.40 per night for dorms.

HOTELS AND CAMPING. Italian hotel rates are set by the state and hotel owners, who will need your passport to register you; don't be afraid to hand it over for a while (usually overnight), but ask for it as soon as you think you will need it. Hotel **singles** *(camera singola)* in Italy usually start at around L50,000-60,000/€25.85-31 per night and **doubles** *(camera doppia* or *camera matrimoniale)* start at L70,000-80,000/€36.15-41.35, though these prices skyrocket during the summer. You'll probably share a hall bathroom; a private bathroom *(con bagno)* usually costs 30-50% more. Some hotels offer **full pension** (all meals) or **half pension** (no lunch). Smaller *pensioni* are often cheaper than hotels. Upon arrival, be sure to confirm the charges before checking in; many Italian hotels tack on additional costs at check-out time. There are over 1700 **campsites** in Italy; the **Touring Club Italiano,** Corso Italia, 10-20122 Milano (☎02 852 61; fax 53 59 95 40) publishes information on the outdoors. Rates average L8000/€4.15 per person or tent and L7000/€3.65 per car.

COMMUNICATION

MAIL. Mark envelopes "air mail" or *"par avion"* to avoid having letters sent by sea. Airmail letters under 1oz. sent from North America, the United Kingdom, or Australia to Italy can take anywhere from three to seven days. Sending a postcard to another European country from Italy costs L1200/€0.65; any other international destination via airmail costs L1500/€0.80. Sending a letter (up to 20g) to another European country costs L1200/€0.65; anywhere else via airmail costs L1500/€0.80. Mail can be sent via *Fermo Posta* (Italian for *Poste Restante)* to almost any city or town in Italy with a post office. Address *Poste Restante* letters as in the following example: FirstName SURNAME, *Fermo Posta,* [Post Office Address] [City Postal Code], Italia. The mail will go to the central post office, unless you specify a post office by street address or postal code. It's quicker and safer to send mail express *(espresso)* or registered *(raccomandata).*

TELEPHONES. Pre-paid phone cards, available at vending machines, phone card vendors, and *tabacchi,* carry a certain amount of time depending on the card's denomination (L5000/€2.60; L10,000/€5.20; or L15,000/€7.75). Italian phone cards are a little tricky to maneuver: rip off the marked corner, and insert it into the appropriate section of the pay phone. The phone card's time is measured in L200/

€0.10 talk units (e.g. one unit=one minute). International calls start a L1000/€1.05, and vary depending on where you are calling. A collect call is a *contassa a carico del destinatario* or *chiamata collect*. **International direct dial numbers** include: **AT&T**, ☎172 10 11; **British Telecom**, ☎172 00 44; **Canada Direct**, ☎172 10 01; **Ireland Direct**, ☎172 03 53; **MCI**, ☎172 10 22; **Sprint**, ☎172 18 77; **Telecom New Zealand**, ☎172 10 64; **Telkom South Africa**, ☎172 10 27; **Telstra Australia**, ☎172 10 61.

INTERNET ACCESS. Though Italy initially lagged behind on the information superhighway, it's now playing catch-up like a pro. New Internet cafes, Internet bars, and even Internet laundromats are popping up every day throughout the country. For free Internet access, try the local universities and libraries.

LANGUAGE. Any knowledge of Spanish, French, Portuguese, or Latin will help you understand Italian. The tourist office staff usually speaks some English. For a traveler's survival kit of basic Italian, see p. 952.

LOCAL FACTS

Time: Italy is 1hr. ahead of Greenwich Mean Time (GMT).

When to Go: Summers are humid and hot in the north, drier and hotter in the south. Winters are ferocious in the Alps and cold and damp in Venice and Florence, but Sicilian waters are swimmable year-round. Mid-Apr. to mid-June or mid-Sept. to Oct. may be the best times to visit, when temperatures are moderate and the crowds are not huge.

Hours: Nearly everything closes from around 1 to 3 or 4pm for siesta. Most museums are open 9am-1pm and 3-6pm; some are open through siesta, however. Monday is often *giorno di chiusura* (day of closure). Food shops have a different *giorno di chiusura* from province to province.

Holidays: Italy closes on the following holidays: New Year's Day (Jan. 1); Epiphany (Jan. 6); Easter Sunday and Monday (Apr. 23-24); Liberation Day (Apr. 25); Labor Day (May 1); Assumption of the Virgin (Aug. 15); All Saints' Day (Nov. 1); Immaculate Conception (Dec. 8); Christmas Day (Dec. 25); and Santo Stefano (Dec. 26). **August brings Ferragosto, a vacation month for all Italians; the cities shut down and empty out.** Plan your trip accordingly, as businesses close and locals leave.

Festivals: The most common excuse for a local festival is the celebration of a religious event—a patron saint's day or the commemoration of a miracle. Most of these festivals include parades, music, wine, obscene amounts of food, and general boisterousness. **Carnevale**, held in February during the 10 days before Lent, energizes Italian towns. During **Scoppio del Carro**, held in Florence's P. del Duomo on Easter Sunday, Florentines set off a cart of explosives, following a tradition dating back to medieval times. On July 2 and Aug. 16, the **Palio** hits Siena, which celebrates with a horse race around the central *piazza*. During the entire month of Aug., residents of Cortona celebrate the tremendous taste of the truffle during the **Festa dei Porcini.**

ROME (ROMA)

Italy's massive capital city is an eruption of marble domes, noseless statues, and motorcycle dust. Rome is sensory overload, rushing down the hills of Lazio to knock you flat on your back, leaving you dying for more. The city and those it controlled were responsible for the development of over 2000 years of world history, art, architecture, politics, and literature. From this city, the Roman Empire

defined the Western world and the Catholic Church spread its influence worldwide. For the traveler, there is so much to see, hear, and absorb that the city is both exhilarating and overwhelming, as if it's impossible to experience everything, or even anything. Never fear, however, because in *bella Roma*, everything is beautiful and everything tastes good. Liberate your senses from the pollution eroding the monuments and from the maniacal rush of motorcyclists, and enjoy the dizzying paradox that is Rome. For more on the Eternal City, check out *Let's Go: Rome 2002*.

✈ INTERCITY TRANSPORTATION

Flights: da Vinci International Airport (☎06 65951), known as **Fiumicino,** handles most flights. The **Termini line** runs nonstop to Rome's main station, **Termini Station** (30min.; every 35min. 7:37am-10:40pm; L16,000/€8.30, L40,000/€20.70 on board). After hours, take the blue **COTRAL bus** to Tiburtina from the ground floor outside the main exit doors after customs (1:15, 2:15, 3:30, and 5am; L8000/€4.15, pay on board). From Tiburtina, take bus #40N to Termini. Most charter flights arrive at **Ciampino** (☎06 79 49 41). To get to Rome, take the COTRAL bus (every 30min. 6:10am-11pm, L2000/€1.05) to Anagnina station on Metro Line A .

Trains: From Termini Station to: **Bologna** (2¾-4¼hr., L35,600/€18.40); **Florence** (2-3hr., L40,900/€21.15); **Milan** (4½-8hr., L50,500/€26.10); **Naples** (2-2½hr., L18,600/€9.60); **Venice** (5hr., L66,000/€34.10). Trains arriving in Rome between midnight and 5am usually arrive at **Stazione Tiburtina** or **Stazione Ostiense,** which are connected to Termini by the #40N and 20N-21N buses, respectively.

◪ ORIENTATION

From the **Termini** train station, **via Nazionale** is the central artery connecting **Piazza della Repubblica** with **Piazza Venezia,** home to the immense wedding-cake-like **Vittorio Emanuele II monument.** West of P. Venezia, **Largo Argentina** marks the start of Corso V. Emanuele, which leads to Centro Storico, the medieval and Renaissance tangle of sights around the **Pantheon, Piazza Navona, Campo dei Fiori,** and **Piazza Farnese.** From P. Venezia, V. dei Fori Imperiale leads southeast to the **Forum** and **Colosseum,** south of which are the ruins of the **Baths of Caracalla** and the **Appian Way,** and the neighborhoods of southern Rome: the Aventine, Testaccio, Ostiense, and EUR. **Via del Corso** stretches from P. Venezia north to **Piazza del Popolo.** East of the Corso, fashionable streets border the **Piazza di Spagna** and, to the northeast, the **Villa Borghese.** South and east are the **Fontana di Trevi, Piazza Barberini,** and the **Quirinal Hill.** Across the Tiber to the north is **Vatican City,** and to the south **Trastevere** is the best neighborhood for wandering. It's impossible to navigate Rome without a map. Pick up a free map from a tourist office or a *Let's Go* **map guide.** The invaluable **Roma Metro-Bus map** (L8000/€4.13) is available at newsstands.

◰ LOCAL TRANSPORTATION

Public Transportation: The 2 **Metropolitana** subway lines (A and B) meet at Termini and run 5:30am-11:30pm. **Buses** run 6am-midnight (with limited late night routes); board at the front or back and validate your ticket in the machine. Buy **tickets** (L1500/€0.80) at *tabacchi,* newsstands, and station machines; they're valid for 1 Metro ride or unlimited bus travel within 1¼hr. of validation. **B.I.G. daily tickets** (L8000/€4.15) and **C.I.S. weekly tickets** (L32,000/€16.55) allow unlimited public transport, including Ostia but not Fiumicino. **Pickpockets are rampant on buses and trains.**

Taxis: Easily located at stands, or flag them down in the street. Ride only in yellow or white taxis, and make sure your taxi has a meter (if not, settle on a price before you get in the car). **Surcharges** at night (L5000/€2.60), on Su (L2000/€1.05), and when heading to or from Fiumicino (L14,000/€7.25) or Ciampino (L10,000/€5.20). Fares run about L15,000/€7.75 from Termini to the Vatican; between city center and Fiumicino around L70,000/€36.15.

Bike and Moped Rental: Bikes generally cost L5000/€2.58 per hr. or L15,000/€7.75 per day, but the length of a "day" varies according to the shop's closing time. In summer, try the stands on V.d. Corso at P.d. San Lorenzo and V. di Pontifici. (Open daily 10am-7pm. 16+.)

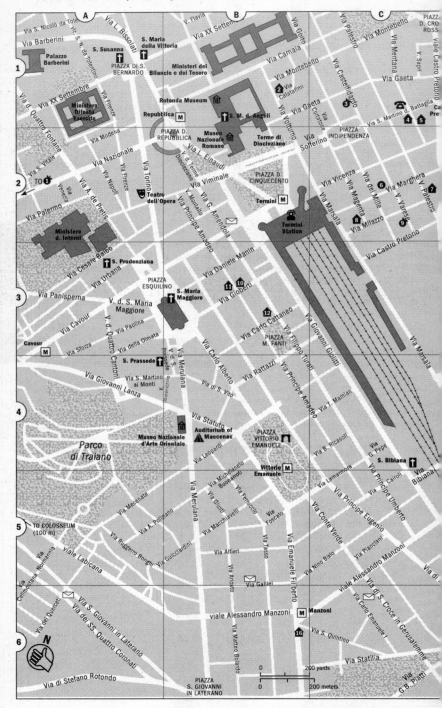

Via S. Nicolò da Tole
Vic. S. N. da Tolentino
Via L. Bissolati
V. Flavia
Via XX Settem
Via Goito
PIAZZ
D. CRO
ROSS
Via Barberini
S. Susanna
S. Maria della Vittoria
Via XX Settem
Via Carnaia
Via Palestro
Via Montebello
viale Castro Pretorio
Palazzo Barberini
PIAZZA DI S. BERNARDO
Ministeri del Bilancio e del Tesoro
Via Montebello
Via Mentana
V. Sapri
Ce Pre
Via d. Quattro Fontane
Via XX Settembre
Via Firenze
Ministero Difesa Esercito
Rotonda Museum
Via Calatafimi
Via Gaeta
Via Castelfidardo
Via S. Martino d. Battaglia
Via Modena
Repubblica
S. M. d. Angeli
Via Gaeta
Via Cernaia
PIAZZA INDIPENDENZA
Via d. Quattro Fontane
Via S. Vitale
Via Nazionale
Via Napoli
Via Firenze
PIAZZA D. REPUBBLICA
Museo Nazionale Romano
Terme di Diocleziano
Via Volturno
PIAZZA INDIPENDENZA
V. d. Terme Diocleziano
Via L. Einaudi
Via Solferino
TO
Via Palermo
Via A. de Pretis
Via Torino
Via Viminale
PIAZZA D. CINQUECENTO
Via Vicenza
Via del Mille
Via Marghera
V. d. V. Varese
Via Palestro
Teatro dell'Opera
Via G. Amendola
Termini
Via Magenta
Via Milazzo
Ministero d. Interni
Via Cesare Balbo
Via Principe Amedeo
Termini Station
Via Marsala
Via Castro Pretorio
S. Prudenziana
Via Urbana
Via Daniele Manin
PIAZZA ESQUILINO
S. Maria Maggiore
Via Gioberti
Via Panisperna
V. d. S. Maria Maggiore
Via Carlo Cattaneo
PIAZZA M. FANTI
Via Filippo Turati
Via Giovanni Giolitti
Via Marsala
Via Cavour
V. d. Quattro Via Paolina
Via della Olmata
Via Carlo Alberto
Via Rattazzi
Via Principe Amedeo
Cavour
Via Sforza
S. Prassede
Via Merulana
Via di S. Vito
Via T. Mamiani
Via Giovanni Lanza
Via S. Martino ai Monti
Via Statuto
Auditorium of Maecenas
PIAZZA VITTORIO EMANUELE
Via B. Ricasoli
Via G. Pepe
Parco di Traiano
Museo Nazionale d'Arte Orientale
Via Leopardi
Vittorio Emanuele
S. Bibiana
Via Bibiana
Via Michelangelo Buonarroti
Via Merulana
Via Giusti
Via Ferruccio
Via Lamarmora
Via Principe Umberto
Via Cairoli
Via Mecenate
Via A. Poliziano
Via Macchiavelli
Via Foscolo
Via Principe Eugenio
Via Conte Verde
TO COLOSSEUM (100 m)
Via Ruggero Bonghi
Via Guicciardini
Via Alfieri
Via Tasso
Via Emanuele Filberto
Via Nino Bixio
Via Piacianti
viale Alessandro Manzoni
Via di
Viale Labicana
Via Ariosto
Via Galilei
viale Alessandro Manzoni
Manzoni
Via Carlo Emanuele I
Via di S. Croce in Gerusalemme
Via Celimontana Normannia
Via dei Querceti
Via S. Giovanni in Laterano
Via dei SS. Quattro Coronati
Via Matteo Boiardo
Via S. Quintino
Via Statilia
Via G.B. Piatti
Via di Stefano Rotondo
PIAZZA S. GIOVANNI IN LATERANO
0   200 yards
0   200 meters

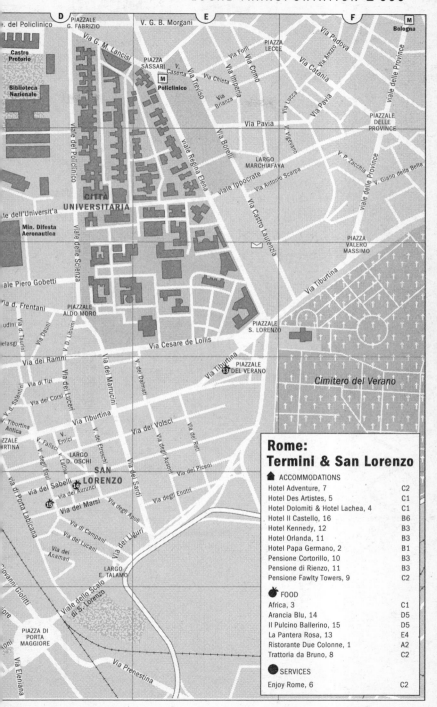

Rome:
Termini & San Lorenzo

🏠 ACCOMMODATIONS

Hotel Adventure, 7	C2
Hotel Des Artistes, 5	C1
Hotel Dolomiti & Hotel Lachea, 4	C1
Hotel Il Castello, 16	B6
Hotel Kennedy, 12	B3
Hotel Orlanda, 11	B3
Hotel Papa Germano, 2	B1
Pensione Cortorillo, 10	B3
Pensione di Rienzo, 11	B3
Pensione Fawlty Towers, 9	C2

🍅 FOOD

Africa, 3	C1
Arancia Blu, 14	D5
Il Pulcino Ballerino, 15	D5
La Pantera Rosa, 13	E4
Ristorante Due Colonne, 1	A2
Trattoria da Bruno, 8	C2

● SERVICES

Enjoy Rome, 6	C2

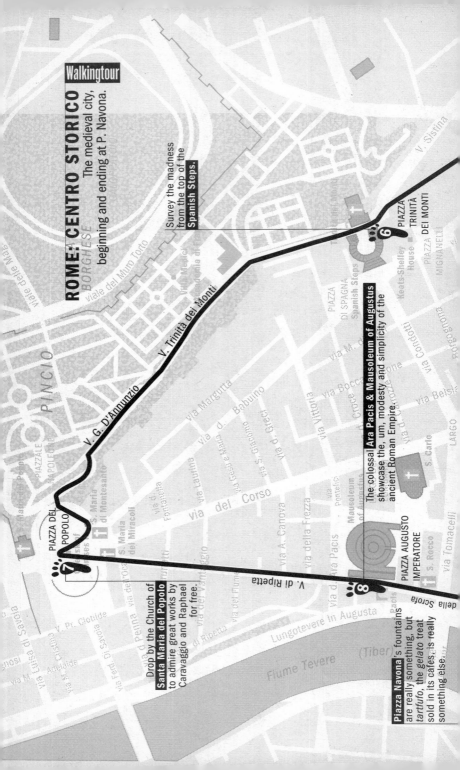

ROME: CENTRO STORICO

BORGHESE The medieval city, beginning and ending at P. Navona.

Survey the madness from the top of the **Spanish Steps.**

Walkingtour

Drop by the Church of **Santa Maria del Popolo** to admire great works by Caravaggio and Raphael for free.

The colossal **Ara Pacis & Mausoleum of Augustus** showcase the, um, modesty and simplicity of the ancient Roman Empire.

Piazza Navona's fountains are really something, but the gelato treat *tartufo,* sold in its cafés, is really something else.

PINCIO

PIAZZALE NAPOLEONE I

V. G. D'Annunzio

V. Trinità dei Monti

viale del Muro Torto

viale delle Mura

PIAZZA DEL POPOLO

S. Maria di Montesanto

S. Maria dei Miracoli

via Margutta

via del Babuino

via Laurina

via Gesù e Maria d.

via d. Greci

via d. S. Giacomo

via del Corso

via A. Canova

via della Frezza

via di Ripetta

via d. Fiume

via del Vantaggio

di Ripetto

via del Corso

via della Croce

via Vittoria

via Bocca di Leone

via M. de' Fiori

via Condotti

via Belsiana

via Mario de' Fiori

PIAZZA DI SPAGNA Spanish Steps

PIAZZA TRINITÀ DEI MONTI

PIAZZA MIGNANELLI

Keats-Shelley House

V. Sistina

Borgognona

via Frattina

Mausoleum of Augustus

PIAZZA AUGUSTO IMPERATORE

Ara Pacis

S. Rocco

S. Carlo

LARGO

via Tomacelli

della Scrofa

Lungotevere in Augusta

Fiume Tevere (Tiber)

V. di Ripetta

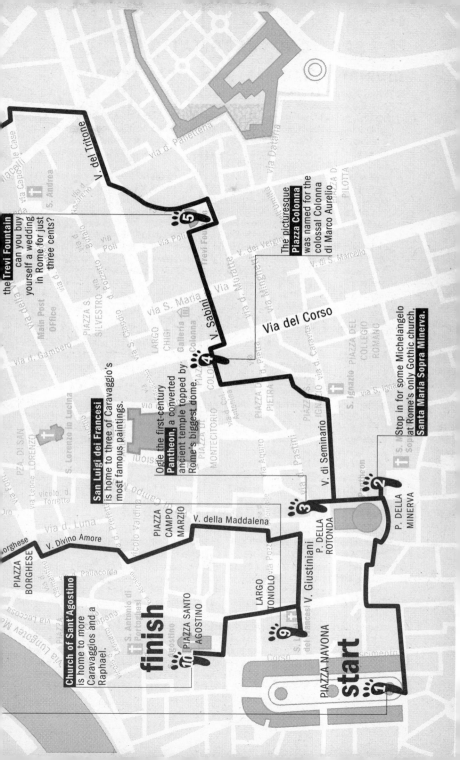

the Trevi Fountain can you buy yourself a wedding in Rome for just three cents?

Main Post Office

5

V. del Tritone

The picturesque **Piazza Colonna** was named for the colossal Colonna di Marco Aurelio

Via del Corso

V. Sabini

4

San Luigi dei Francesi is home to three of Caravaggio's most famous paintings.

Ogle the first-century **Pantheon,** a converted ancient temple topped by Rome's biggest dome.

V. di Seminario

Stop in for some Michelangelo at Rome's only Gothic church, **Santa Maria Sopra Minerva.**

2

P. DELLA MINERVA

V. della Maddalena

PIAZZA CAMPO MARZIO

3

Church of Sant'Agostino is home to more Caravaggios and a Raphael.

finish

PIAZZA SANTO AGOSTINO

LARGO TONIOLO

V. Giustiniani

P. DELLA ROTONDA

10

6

PIAZZA NAVONA

start

1

PIAZZA BORGHESE

V. Divino Amore

▓ PRACTICAL INFORMATION

TOURIST, FINANCIAL, AND LOCAL SERVICES

▓ **Tourist Agency: Enjoy Rome,** V. Marghera, 8a (☎06 445 18 43 or 06 445 68 90; www.enjoyrome.com). From middle concourse of Termini (between trains and ticket booths), exit right, with the trains behind you; cross V. Marsala and follow V. Marghera 3 blocks. Arranges hotel accommodations, walking and bicycle tours, and bus service to Pompeii. Full-service travel agency, booking transportation worldwide and lodgings throughout Italy. Branch office at V. Varese, 39 (walk 1 block down V. Marghera and go right). Open M-F 8:30am-7pm, Sa 8:30am-2pm.

Foreign Embassies: Australia, V. Alessandria, 215 (☎06 85 27 21, emergency 800 87 77 90). Open M-Th 9am-5pm, F 9am-12:30pm. **Canada,** V.G.B. De Rossi, 27 (☎06 44 59 81). **Ireland,** P. Campitelli, 3 (☎06 6979121). Open M-F 10am-12:30pm and 3-4:30pm. **New Zealand,** V. Zara, 28 (☎06 4417171). Consular and passport services M-F 9:30am-noon. Embassy services M-F 8:30am-12:45pm and 1:45-5pm. **South Africa,** V. Tanaro, 14 (☎06 852541). Bus #86 from Termini to P. Buenos Aires. Open M-F 9am-noon. **UK,** V. XX Settembre, 80/A (☎06 4825441), near the corner of V. Palestro. Open M-F 9:15am-1:30pm. **US,** V. Veneto, 119/A (☎06 46741). Passport and consular services M-F 8:30-noon and 1:30-3:30pm. Visas M-F 8:30-10:30am. Closed US and Italian holidays.

American Express: P. di Spagna, 38 (☎06 676 41, lost or stolen cards and checks 722 81). Open Sept.-July M-F 9am-7:30pm, Sa 9am-3pm; Aug. M-F 9am-6pm, Sa 9am-12:30pm. **Holds Mail:** P. di Spagna, 38; **00187** Roma.

Thomas Cook: P. Barberini, 21a (☎06 482 80 82). Open M-Sa 9am-8pm, Su 9:30am-5pm. **Branches:** V. d. Conciliazione, 23-25 (☎06 6830 0435; open M-Sa 8:30am-6pm, Su 9am-5pm); V. del Corso, 23 (☎06 323 00 67; open M-Sa 9am-8pm, Su 9am-1:30pm); P. della Repubblica, 65 (☎06 48 64 95; open M-F 9am-5pm with 1hr. lunch break, Sa 9am-1pm).

Luggage Storage: In train station Termini, by track 1.

Gay and Lesbian Resources: ARCI-GAY and **ARCI-Lesbica** share offices at V. Orvinio, 2 (☎06 86 38 51 12) and V. Lariana, 8 (☎06 855 55 22). ARCI-GAY membership (L20,000/€10.35 per yr.) gives admission to all Italian gay clubs. **Circolo di Cultura Omosessuale Mario Mieli,** V. Corinto, 5 (☎06 541 39 85), provides information about gay life in Rome. M: B-San Paolo, walk 1 block to Largo Beato Placido Riccardi, turn left, and walk 1½ blocks to V. Corinto. Open Sept.-July M-F 9am-1pm and 2-6pm.

Laundromat: OndaBlu, V. La Mora, 7. Many locations throughout Rome. Wash L6000/€3.10, dry L6000/€3.10 per 6½kg. Soap L1500/€0.80. Open daily 8am-10pm.

EMERGENCY AND COMMUNICATIONS

Police: ☎113. **Carabinieri,** ☎112. **Medical emergency,** ☎118. **Fire,** ☎115.

Pharmacies: Farmacia Internazionale, P. Barberini, 49 (☎06 487 11 95). **Farmacia Piram,** V. Nazionale, 228 (☎06 488 07 54). Both open 24hr.

Hospitals: International Medical Center, V.G. Amendola, 7 (☎06 488 23 71; nights and Su 488 40 51). Call first. Prescriptions filled, paramedic crew on call, referral service to English-speaking doctors. General visit L130,000/€67.15. Open M-Sa 8:30am-8pm. On-call 24hr. **Rome-American Hospital,** V.E. Longoni, 69 (☎06 225 51). Private emergency and laboratory services; HIV and pregnancy tests. On-call 24hr.

Internet Service: ▓ **Trevi Tourist Service: Trevi Internet,** V. dei Lucchesi, 31-32, 1 block from Trevi Fountain (toward P. Venezia on road that becomes V.d. Pilotta). Central location. L5000/€2.60 per 30min., L10,000/€5.20 per 1½hr. Western Union money transfers, currency exchange, cheap international calls. Open daily 9am-10pm. **Splashnet,** V. Varese, 33, 3 blocks north of Termini. A laundromat with **Internet.** Wash and dry L6000/€3.10 each, includes 15min. Internet time. Internet L5000/€2.60 per hr.; ask for *Let's Go* discount. Open daily 8:30am-10:30pm.

Post Office: Main office, P. San Silvestro, 19, south of P. di Spagna, is best for large packages or insured mail. Open M-F 9am-6pm, Sa 9am-2pm. **Large branch,** V. delle Terme di Diocleziano, 30, near Termini. Same hours as San Silvestro branch. **Postal Codes:** 00100-00200.

ACCOMMODATIONS

Rome swells with tourists around Easter, from May through July, and in September. Prices vary widely with the time of year, and a proprietor's willingness to negotiate increases with length of stay, number of vacancies, and group size. Termini is swarming with hotel scouts. Many are legitimate and have IDs issued by tourist offices; however, some imposters have fake badges and direct travelers to rundown locations with exorbitant rates, especially at night.

CENTRO STORICO

If being a bit closer to the sights is important to you, then choosing Rome's medieval center over the area near Termini may be worth the higher prices.

Albergo Pomezia, V.d. Chiavari, 12 (☎06 686 13 71). Off Corso V. Emanuele II behind Sant'Andrea della Valle. Clean, quiet rooms with phone, fan, and heat in winter. Breakfast included (8-11am). Singles L90,000/€46.50, with bath L110,000/€56.85; doubles L150,000/€77.40, L200,000/€103.30; triples L210,000/€108.45, L255,000/€131.70. AmEx/MC/V.

Albergo della Lunetta, P. del Paradiso, 68 (☎06 686 10 80). 1st right off V. Chiavari from Corso V. Emanuele II behind Sant'Andrea della Valle. Good value in great location (between Campo dei Fiori and P. Navona). Singles L90,000/€46.50, with bath L110,000/€56.85; doubles L150,000/€77.50, L200,000/€103.30; triples L210,000/€108.45, L255,000/€131.70. Reserve with credit card or check. MC/V.

Albergo Abruzzi, P. della Rotonda, 69 (☎06 679 20 21). 200ft. from the Pantheon. Hall bathrooms, but every room has a sink. Singles L90,000-115,000/€46.50-59.40; doubles L140,000-170,000/€72.30-87.80; triples L220,000/€113.65.

Hotel Navona, V.d. Sediari, 8, 1st fl. (☎06 686 42 03). Take V.d. Canestrari from P. Navona, cross Corso del Rinascimento, and go straight. This 16th-century building has been used as a *pensione* for over 150 years; previous guests include Keats and Shelley. All rooms have bath. A/C L30,000/€15.50. Breakfast included. Check-out 10am. Singles 160,000/€82.65; doubles L210,000/€108.45; triples L290,00/€149.85. Pay in cash only before 1st night.

NEAR PIAZZA DI SPAGNA

These accommodations might cost a few thousand *lire* more, but can you really put a price tag on living just a few steps from Prada? John Keats couldn't.

Pensione Panda, V.d. Croce, 35 (☎06 6780179), between P. di Spagna and V.d. Corso. Newly renovated. Immaculate rooms. Check-out 11am. Reservations recommended. Singles L70,000/€36.15, with bath L100,000-120,000/€51.60-62; doubles L120,000-180,000/€62-93; triples with bath L210,000/€108.45; quads with bath L320,000/€165.30. Ask for *Let's Go* discount.

Pensione Jonella, V.d. Croce, 41, 4th fl. (☎06 6797966), between P. di Spagna and V.d. Corso. 4 beautiful rooms. Quiet, roomy, and cool in summer. No private bathrooms. No reception: call ahead to be let in. Singles L100,000/€51.60; doubles L120,000/€62. Cash only.

Hotel Boccaccio, V.d. Boccaccio, 25 (☎06 488 59 62). M: A-Barberini. Off V.d. Tritone, near many sights. Singles L80,000/€41.35; doubles L120,000/€62, with bath L160,000/€83.65; triples L162,000-216,000/€84.20-111.55. AmEx/D/MC/V.

ITALY

BORGO AND PRATI (NEAR VATICAN CITY)

Home to lots of priests and nuns, the Vatican and environs are pretty quiet at night.

▩ **Colors,** V. Boezio, 31 (☎06 687 40 30). M: A-Ottaviano. Or, bus to "P. Risorgimento." Take V. Cola di Rienzo to V. Terenzio. Lots of amenities and a super-cool English-speaking staff. **Internet** L5000/€2.60 per hr. Laundry L8000/€4.15 per load. Dorms L35,000/€18.10; doubles L120,000-150,000/€62-77.50; triples L140,000-180,000/€72.30-93. Credit card needed for reservations; cash only.

▩ **Pensione Ottaviano,** V. Ottaviano, 6 (☎06 3973 7253 or 3973 7253), just north of P. del Risorgimento, a few blocks from Metro stop of same name and near St. Peter's. Satellite TV, fridges, microwave, **Internet,** hot showers, linens, and lockers included. Friendly Aussie and British staff. Smoking allowed. Lockout 11:30am-2pm. No curfew. 3- to 6-bed dorms L30,000/€15.50, in winter L25,000/€13; doubles L70,000-90,000/€36.15-46.50; triples L120,000/€62. Cash only.

▩ **Hotel Pensione Joli,** V. Cola di Rienzo, 243, 6th fl. (☎06 324 18 54;), at V. Tibullo, *scala* A. Nice beds, ceiling fans, and views of the Vatican. Breakfast included. Singles L95,000/€49.10, with bath L120,000/€62; doubles L170,000/€87.80; triples L243,000/€125.50; quads L318,000/€164.25. MC/V.

TRASTEVERE

Hotels here are scattered, most of them too pricey for budget travelers, but the area does offer great nightlife and a location near the Vatican.

Hotel Carmel, V.G. Mameli, 11 (☎06 580 99 21). Take a right on V.E. Morosini (V.G. Mameli) off V.d. Trastevere. Though a good walk from the heart of Trastevere, this simple hotel offers 9 no-frills, smallish rooms, all with bath, for reasonable prices. Breakfast included. Singles L100,000/€51.60; doubles L150,000/€77.50; triples L190,000/€98.15; quads L220,000/€113.65. AmEx/MC/V.

Hotel Trastevere, V. Luciano Manara, 25 (☎06 581 47 13), right off V.d. Trastevere onto V.d. Fratte di Trastevere. Homey establishment overlooks P.S. Cosimato. 9 simple, airy rooms with bath, TV, and phone. English spoken. Breakfast included. Singles L130,000/€67.15; doubles 160,000/€82.65; triples L170,000/€87.80; quads L240,000/€1245. AmEx/D/MC/V.

TERMINI AND SAN LORENZO

This is budget-traveler central, but the area south of Termini is sketchy at night.

▩ **Pensione Fawlty Towers,** V. Magenta, 39 (☎06 445 03 74). Exit Termini to the right from middle concourse, cross V. Marsala onto V. Marghera, and turn right onto V. Magenta. Extremely popular 15-room hotel/hostel. Common room has satellite TV, library, refrigerator, microwave, and cheap **Internet** access. Native English-speaking staff. Check-out 9am for dorms, 10am for private rooms. Frequently full, but reception will do its utmost to find you a place. Reservations strongly recommended. Dorm-style quads L30,000-35,000/€15.50-18.10 per person (no children); singles L75,000/€38.75, with shower L90,000/€46.50; doubles L110,000/€56.80, with shower L140,000/€72.30, with bath L150,000/€77.50; triples with bath L165,000/€85.25.

▩ **Hotel Des Artistes,** V. Villafranca, 20 (☎06 445 43 65). From middle concourse of Termini, exit right, turn left onto V. Marsala, right onto V. Vicenza, then left onto 5th cross-street. All rooms have bathroom, safe, refrigerator, and TV. Cheap **Internet.** Reception 24hr. Check-out 11am. Dorms L35,000/€18.10; singles L70,000/€36.15; doubles L110,000-170,000/€56.85-87.80; triples L130,000-210,000/€67.15-108.45; in winter 20-30% less. AmEx/MC/V.

▩ **Hotel Papa Germano,** V. Calatafimi, 14a (☎06 48 69 19 or 4782 5202). From the middle concourse of Termini, exit right and go left onto V. Marsala, which becomes V. Volturno; V. Calatafimi is 4th cross-street on right. Clean, affordable rooms all have TV and phone. Outstanding service from owners Gino and Pina. English spoken. Check-out 11am. Dorms L30,000-40,000/€15.50-20.70; singles L45,000-70,000/€23.25-

ITALY

36.15; doubles L70,000-130,000/€36.15-67.15, with bath L100,000-160,000/ €51.60-82.65; triples L105,000-150,000/€54.25-77.50, L135,000-200,000/ €69.75-103.30. AmEx/MC/V.

Pensione di Rienzo, V. Principe Amedeo, 79a (☎06 446 71 31). A tranquil, family-run retreat with spacious renovated rooms, some with balcony, TV, and bath. Breakfast L20,000/€10.35. Check-out 10am. Singles L40,000-80,000/€20.70-41.35; doubles L60,000-120,000/€33.57-62. MC/V.

Pensione Cortorillo, V. Principe Amedeo, 79a, 5th fl. (☎06 446 69 34). A small and friendly family-run *pensione* with TV in all rooms. English spoken. Breakfast included. Check-out 10am. Singles L80,000-120,000/€41.35-62; doubles L70,000-130,000/ €36.15-67.15; extra bed L30,000/€15.50. AmEx/D/MC/V.

Hotel Kennedy, V. Filippo Turati, 62-64 (☎06 446 53 73; fax 446 54 17; www.hotelkennedy.net). Private bath, satellite TV, phone, and A/C. English spoken. All-you-can-eat breakfast included. Check-out 11am. Reservations by fax or email accepted. Singles L65,000-169,000/€33.60-87.30; doubles L100,000-299,000/€51.60-154.45; triples L149,000-349,000/€76.70-180.25. 10% *Let's Go* discount. AmEx/D/MC/V.

Hotel Dolomiti and **Hotel Lachea,** V.S. Martino della Battaglia, 11 (☎06 495 72 56). From the middle concourse of Termini, exit right, go left onto V. Marsala and right onto V. Solferino (V.S. Martino della Battaglia). Satellite TV, phone, minibar, and A/C. Lachea offers the same excellent service in a simpler hotel with lower prices. A/C L25,000/€13 per night. Breakfast L12,000/€6.20. Check-out 11am. **Dolomiti:** All rooms with baths. Singles L100,000-130,000/€51.65-67.15; doubles L140,000-200,000/€72.30-103.30; triples L180,000-240,000/€93-123.95; quads L220,000-260,000/€113.65-134.30; quints available. **Lachea:** Singles L75,000-90,000/ €38.75-46.50; doubles L90,000-120,000/€45-62; triples L110,000-130,000/ €56.85-67.15.

Hotel Adventure, V. Palestro, 88 (☎06 446 90 26). From the middle concourse of Termini, exit right, cross V. Marsala onto V. Marghera, and take 4th right onto V. Palestro. Renovated rooms, all with bath, satellite TV, phone, and fridge. A/C L25,000/€12.95. Breakfast included. Check-out 11am. Singles L150,000/€77.50 including A/C; doubles L160,000/€82.65; triples L220,000/€113.65. AmEx/MC/V.

Hotel Il Castello, V. Vittorio Amedeo II, 9 (☎06 7720 4036). M: A-Manzoni. Far beyond Termini, but well within a backpacker's budget. Walk down V. San Quintino and take 1st left. Housed in castle with eager serving knaves (mostly native-English speakers). Breakfast L5000/€2.60. Check-out 10:30am. Dorms L30,000/€15.50; singles L80,000/ €41.30; doubles L110,000/€56.85, with bath L130,000-150,000/€67.15-77.50; triples L120,000/€62, L140,000-180,000/€72.30-93. MC/V.

Hotel Orlanda, V. Principe Amedeo, 76, 3rd fl. (☎06 488 01 24), at V. Gioberti. Take the stairs on the right in the vestibule. English spoken. Breakfast included. Reception 24hr. Check-in noon. A/C L30,000/€15.50. Singles L55,000-130,000/€28.40-67.20, with bath L60,000-170,000/€31-87.80; doubles L80,000-160,000/€41.35-82.65, L100,000-270,000/€51.60-139.45; triples L105,000-190,000/€54.25-98.15, L125,000-370,000/€64.60-191; quads L140,000-240,000/€72.30-124, L160,000-460,000/€82.65-237.60. AmEx/D/MC/V.

CAMPING

Camping on beaches, roads, and inconspicuous plots is illegal and dangerous.

Seven Hills Village, V. Cassia, 1216 (☎06 3033 108 26), 8km north of Rome. Take bus #907 from M: A-Cipro-Musei Vaticani or bus #201 from P. Mancini. The bus driver knows when to let you off, just 3-4km past the GRA (the big highway that circles the city). Daily shuttles to Rome (L6000/€3.10); train station near campgrounds (L2000/ €1). From stop, follow the country road about 1km until you see the sign. It also houses a bar, market, restaurant, and *pizzeria*. Check-in 24hr. Check-out noon. Open late Mar. to late Oct. L14,000/€7.25 per person, L1500/€0.80 per tent. Cash only.

ITALY

◘ FOOD

Ancient Roman dinners were lavish, festive affairs lasting as long as 10 hours. Peacocks and flamingos were served with their full plumage, while acrobats and fireeaters distracted guests between their courses of camels' feet and goats' ears. Food orgies went on *ad nauseam*, literally—after gorging themselves, guests would retreat to a special room called the *vomitorium*, throw it all up, and return to the party. Meals in Rome are still lengthy affairs. Restaurants tend to close between 3 and 7pm, so plan accordingly.

RESTAURANTS

ANCIENT CITY

Despite its past glory, this area has yet to discover the noble concept of "affordable food." But along **Via dei Fori Imperiali**, several restaurants offer decent prices.

■**Taverna dei Quaranta,** V. Claudia, 24, off P. del Colosseo. Not at all touristy. Menu changes weekly, and in summer features sinfully good *oliva ascolane* (fried olives stuffed with meat; L7500/€3.90) and *ravioli all'Amalfitana* (L11,000/€5.70). 0.5L of house wine L5000/€2.60. Cover L2500/€1.30. Reservations suggested. Open daily noon-3:30pm and 7:45pm-midnight. AmEx/D/MC/V.

I Buoni Amici, V. Aleardo Aleardi, 4. From the Colosseum, take V. Labicana to V. Merulana. Turn right, then left on V.A. Aleardi. A long walk, but the cheap, excellent food is worth it. Choices include the *linguine all'astice* (linguine with lobster sauce; L12,000/€6.20) and *penne alla vodka* (L10,000/€5.20). Cover L2500/€1.30. Open M-Sa noon-3pm and 7-11:30pm. AmEx/D/MC/V.

CENTRO STORICO

The twisting streets of Rome's historic center offer many hidden gems, especially just off the main *piazzas*. No matter where you eat, you can expect to be subjected to numerous street performances, especially near P. Navona.

■**Pizzeria Baffetto,** V.d. Governo Vecchio, 114. At V. Sora. Be prepared to wait a long while for a table outdoors. Pizza L8000-14,000/€4.15-7.25. Open M-F noon-3pm and 7:30pm-1am, Sa-Su noon-3pm and 7:30pm-2am. Cash only.

Pizzeria Corallo, V.d. Corallo, 10-11. Off V.d. Governo Vecchio near P. del Fico. This *pizzeria* is a great place to grab a cheap, late dinner before hitting the chi-chi bars nearby. Pizzas L7000-14,000/€3.65-7.25. Open daily noon-3pm and 7pm-1am. MC/V.

Trattoria dal Cav. Gino, V. Rosini, 4. Off V.d. Campo Marzio across from P. del Parlamente. *Primi* L8000-10,000/€4.15-5.20, *secondi* L15-17,000/€7.75-8.80. Reservations accepted. Open M-Sa 1-3:45pm and 8-10:30pm. Cash only.

CAMPO DEI FIORI AND THE JEWISH GHETTO

■**Trattoria da Sergio,** V.d. Grotte, 27. Take V.d. Giubbonari and take the 1st right. Offers Roman ambience (the waiters don't bother with menus) and hearty portions of great food. Try the *spaghetti all'Amatriciana* (with bacon and spicy tomato sauce; L10,000/€5.20). Open M-Sa 12:30-3pm and 7pm-12:30am. MC/V.

■**Hostaria Grappolo d'Oro,** P. della Cancelleria, 80-81, between Corso Vittorio Emanuele II and the Campo. This increasingly upscale *hostaria* is running out of space in their front window to plaster all the awards they've won over the years. Small menu, changes daily. Offers dishes like *fregnacce al Casaro* (home-made pasta with ricotta and tomato; L19,000/€9.85) and innovative creations such as *controfiletto di manzo* (steak with herbs and goat-cheese; L24,000/€12.40). Cover L2000/€1.05. Open M 7:30-10pm, Tu-Sa noon-2:30pm and 7:30-11pm. AmEx/MC/V.

■**Trattoria Da Luigi,** P.S. Cesarini, 24, near Chiesa Nuova, 4 blocks down Corso Vittorio Emanuele II from Campo dei Fiore. Enjoy inventive cuisine including *tagliolini* with shrimp, asparagus, and tomato (L13,000/€6.75), as well as simple dishes like *vitello con funghi* (veal with mushrooms; L15,000/€7.75). Open Tu-Su 7pm-midnight.

Ristorante da Giggetto, V.d. Portico d'Ottavio, 21-22. Rightfully famous but increasingly pricey, Giggetto serves up some of the finest Roman cooking known to man. Their *carciofi alla Giudia* (L8000/€4.15) are legendary. Cover L3000/€1.55. Reservations needed for dinner. Open Tu-Su 12:30-3pm and 7:30-11pm. AmEx/MC/V.

PIAZZA DI SPAGNA

⧗ Trattoria da Settimio all'Arancio, V.d. Arancio, 50-52. Take V.d. Condotti from P. di Spagna; take the 1st right after V.d. Corso, then the 1st left. Arrive early to avoid the throngs of natives who come for the great service and tasty seafood. Excellent grilled *calamari* (L18,000/€9.30). *Primi* L12,000-15,000/€6.20-7.75, *secondi* L16,000-26,000/€8.30-13.45. Cover L2000/€1.05. Open M-Sa 12:30-3pm and 7:30-11:30pm. AmEx/D/MC/V.

⧗ Vini e Buffet, P. Torretta, 60. (☎06 6871445). From V.d. Corso, turn into P.S. Lorenzo in Lucina. Take a left on V. Campo Marzio, a quick right onto V. Toretta. Vini e Buffet is a favorite spot for chic Romans. Don't leave without getting one of their signature yogurt and fruit bowls for dessert; the yogurt, almond, and cassis combination is out of this world. Reservations recommended. Open M-Sa 12:30-3pm and 7:30-11pm. Cash only.

Il Brillo Parlante, V. Fontanella, 12, near P. del Popolo. The wood-burning pizza oven, fresh ingredients, and excellent wine attract many lunching Italians. Pizza L10,000-15,000/€5.20-7.75. Restaurant open Tu-Su noon-3pm and 7:30pm-1am. MC/V.

BORGO AND PRATI (NEAR VATICAN CITY)

Establishments near the Vatican serve mediocre sandwiches at hiked-up prices, but just a few blocks northeast is better and much cheaper food.

⧗ Franchi, V. Cola di Rienzo, 200-204. Benedeto Franchi ("Frankie") has been serving superb *tavola calda*, prepared sandwiches, and luxurious picnic supplies for nearly 50 years without an unsatisfied customer. Open M-Sa 8:15am-9pm. AmEx/MC/V.

Pizza Re, V. Oslavia, 39. This chain serves Neopolitan (thick crust) pizzas with every topping imaginable in cheerful yellow surroundings. Lunch specials (pizza and drink) L13,000/€6.70. Dinner L7000-18,000/€3.60-9.30. Pizzas L3000-5500/€1.55-2.85 less if you take them out. Long lines at dinnertime, so get there early. Open M-Sa noon-3:30pm and 7:30pm-12:30am, Su 7:30pm-12:30am. AmEx/MC/V.

TRASTEVERE

⧗ Pizzeria San Calisto, P.S. Calisto, 9a. Right off P.S. Maria in Trastevere. Quite simply the best damn pizza in Rome. Gorgeous thin crust pizzas so large they hang off the plates. Open Tu-Su 7pm-midnight. MC/V.

Augusto, P. de' Rienzi, 15. North of P.S. Maria in Trastevere. Daily lunch pasta specials around L8500/€4.40. The desserts are out of this world, but you may have to be pushy to get service. Open M-F 12:30-3pm and 8-11pm, Sa 12:30-3pm. Closed Aug.

TERMINI

⧗ Africa, V. Gaeta, 26-28, near P. Indipendenza. A 20-year tradition of serving excellent Eritrean/Ethiopian food. Cover L1500/€0.80. Open M-Sa 8pm-midnight. MC/V.

Trattoria da Bruno, V. Varese, 29. From V. Marsala, next to the train station, walk 3 blocks down V. Milazzo and turn right onto V. Varese. A neighborhood favorite with daily specials. Try the tasty homemade *gnocchi* (L10,000/€5.20). Open daily noon-3:30pm and 7-10:15pm. Closed Aug. AmEx/V.

Ristorante Due Colonne, V.d. Serpenti, 91. Turn right off V. Nazionale before the Palazzo delle Esposizioni. Pizzas L8000-14,000/€4.15-7.25. *Menù* L18,000-26,000/€9.30-13.45. Open M-Sa 9am-3:30pm and 6:30pm-12:30am. AmEx/D/MC/V.

SAN LORENZO

Rome's funky university district, San Lorenzo, offers many good, cheap eateries. From Termini, walk south on V. Pretoriano to P. Tiburtino, or take bus #492. Women may find the walk a little uncomfortable at night.

ITALY

Il Pulcino Ballerino, V.d. Equi, 66-68. Off V. Tiburtina. An artsy atmosphere with cuisine to match. The cook stirs up imaginative dishes and excellent vegetarian dishes. You can prepare your own meal on a warm stone at the table. Cover L1000/€0.55. Open M-Sa 1-3:30pm and 8pm-midnight. Closed 2nd and 3rd weeks of Aug. AmEx/MC/V.

Arancia Blu, V.d. Latini, 65, off V. Tiburtina. Elaborate dishes like *tonnarelli con pecorino romano e tartufo* (pasta with sheep cheese and truffles; L12,000/€6.20). Extensive wine list. Open daily 8:30pm-midnight.

La Pantera Rosa, P. Verano, 84-85. At the eastern end of V. Tiburtina. The house specialty is the delicious pink salmon and caviar pizza (L11,000/€5.70). Open Th-Tu noon-3pm and 6:30pm-12:30am. MC/V.

TESTACCIO

This working-class southern neighborhood is the center of Roman nightlife, and eateries here offer food made of just about every animal part imaginable.

Trattoria da Bucatino, V. Luca della Robbia, 84-86. Take V. Luigi Vanvitelli off V. Marmorata, then the 1st left. All the animal entrails you know and love, and plenty of gut-less dishes as well. Cover L2000/€1.05. Open Tu-Su 12:30-3:30pm and 6:30-11:30pm. Closed Aug. D/MC/V.

DESSERTS

Cheap *gelato* is as plentiful on Roman streets as leather pants. Look for *gelato* with very muted (hence natural) colors, or try some of our favorite places:

San Crispino, V.d. Panetteria, 42. Very near the Trevi Fountain. Facing the fountain, turn right onto V. Lavatore and take your 2nd left; the *gelato* temple is on the right. Positively the best *gelato* in the world. L3000-10,000/€1.55-5.20. Open M and W-Th noon-12:30am, F-Sa noon-1:30am, Su noon-midnight.

Tre Scalini, P. Navona, 30. Famous for its *tartufo,* truffled chocolate ice cream rolled in chocolate shavings (L5000/€2.60 at the bar, L11,000/€5.60 sitting). Bar open Th-Tu 9am-1:30am; restaurant open Th-Tu 12:30-3:30pm and 7:30-9pm.

Portico d'Ottavia, 1. A tiny, take-out only pastry bakery deep in the Jewish Ghetto. Little fanfare, just long lines of locals seeking fabulous blueberry pies, buttery cookies, and chocolate and pudding concoctions, sold by weight at excellent prices (L2000/€1.05 for a wedge of pie). Open Su-Th 8am-8pm, F 8am-5:30pm. Closed Jewish holidays.

Tazza d'Oro, V.d. Orfani, 84-86. With your back to the Pantheon's portico, you'll see the yellow-lettered sign on your right. No seating, but the best coffee in Rome at great prices (*caffé* L1100/€0.60, *cappuccino* L1400/€0.75). Open M-Sa 7am-8:00pm.

ENOTECHE (WINE BARS)

Roman wine bars range from laid-back and local to chic and international.

Bar Da Benito, V.d. Falegnami, 14, off P.Cairoli in the Jewish Ghetto. A tiny *tavola calda* lined with bottles and hordes of hungry workers. Glasses of wine from L2000/€1.05; bottle from L15,000/€7.75. Always packed, noisy, and incredibly hectic. Open M-Sa 6:30am-7pm; lunch noon-3:30pm. Closed Aug.

Trimani Wine Bar, V. Cernaia, 37b. Near Termini, perpendicular to V. Volturno (V. Marsala). Excellent food at reasonable prices, filling quiches, and desserts worth writing home about—try the heavenly ricotta, amaretto, and raspberry tart (L9000/€4.65). Wines from L3500/€1.80 a glass, L18,000/€9.30 a bottle. Reservations recommended for dinner. Open M-Sa 11am-3:30pm and 6pm-12:30am. AmEx/MC/V.

Cul de Sac, P. Pasquino, 73. Off P. Navona. Rome's 1st wine bar, Cul de Sac keeps the customers coming back for a huge selection of great, decently priced wines, and excellent food. House specialty paté (such as pheasant and mushroom; L9500/€4.90) is exquisite. Open M 7pm-12:30am, Tu-Sa 12:30-4pm and 6pm-12:30am. MC/V.

☉ SIGHTS

Rome wasn't built in a day, and it's not likely that you'll see any substantial portion of it in 24 hours, either. Ancient temples and forums, Renaissance basilicas, 280 fountains, and 981 churches cluster together in a city bursting with masterpieces from every era of Western civilization. From Etruscan busts to modern canvases, there is more than enough in Rome to captivate visitors for years on end.

ANCIENT CITY

ROMAN FORUM

M: B-Colosseo, or bus to "P. Venezia." Main entrance is on V.d. Fori Imperiali (at Largo C. Ricci, between P. Venezia and the Colosseum). Open M-Sa 9am-6:30pm; Su 9am-1pm; in winter daily 9am-1hr. before sunset; sometimes closes M-F 3pm, Su and holidays noon. Free. Guided tour L6000/€3.20; audioguide L7000/€3.65 in English, French, German, Italian, Japanese, or Spanish available at main entrance.

Here the pre-Romans founded a thatched-hut shantytown in 753 BC. The entrance ramp leads to **Via Sacra,** Rome's oldest street, near the **Basilica Aemilia,** built in 179 BC, and the area once known as the **Civic Forum.** Next to the Basilica stands the **Curia** (Senate House); it was converted to a church in AD 630 and restored by Mussolini. The broad space in front of the Curia was the **Comitium,** where male citizens came to vote and representatives of the people gathered for public discussion. Bordering the Comitium is the large brick **Rostrum** (speaker's platform) erected by Julius Caesar in 44 BC, just before his death. The hefty **Arch of Septimius Severus,** to the right of the Rostrum, was dedicated in AD 203 to celebrate Caesar's victories in the Middle East. The **market square** holds a number of shrines and sacred precincts, including the **Lapis Niger** (Black Stone), where Romulus was supposedly murdered by Republican senators. Below the Lapis Niger are the underground ruins of a 6th-century BC altar and the oldest known Latin inscription in Rome. In the square, the **Three Sacred Trees** of Rome—olive, fig, and grape—have been replanted by the Italian state. The newest part of the Forum is the **Column of Phocas,** erected in AD 608. The three great temples of the **Lower Forum** have been closed off for excavations; however, the eight columns of the 5th-century BC **Temple of Saturn,** next to the Rostrum, have been restored. Around the corner, rows of column bases are all that remain of the **Basilica Julia,** a courthouse built by Julius Caesar in 54 BC. At the far end, three white marble columns mark the massive podium of the recently restored **Temple of Castor and Pollux,** built to celebrate the Roman defeat of the Etruscans. The circular building next to it is the **Temple of Vesta,** where the Vestal Virgins tended the city's sacred fire and kept it lit for more than a thousand years.

In the **Upper Forum** lies the **House of the Vestal Virgins.** For 30 years, the six virgins who officiated over Vesta's rites lived in seclusion here from the ripe old age of seven. As long as they kept their vows of chastity, they remained among the most respected people in ancient Rome. Near here, V. Sacra runs over the **Cloaca Maxima,** the ancient sewer that still drains water from the otherwise marsh-like valley. V. Sacra continues out of the Forum proper to the **Velia** and the gargantuan **Basilica of Maxentius** (also known as the Basilica of Constantine). The middle apse of the basilica once contained a gigantic statue of Constantine with a bronze body and marble head, legs, and arms. The uncovered remains, including a 2m foot, are displayed at the **Palazzo dei Conservatori** on the Capitoline Hill (see p. 621). V. Sacra leads to an exit on the other side of the hill to the Colosseum; the path that crosses before the **Arch of Titus** heads to the Palatine Hill.

THE PALATINE HILL

*The Palatine rises to the south of the Forum. Open daily 9am-6:30pm; in winter M-Sa 9:30am to 1hr. before sunset, Su 9am-1pm; sometimes closes M-F 3pm, Su and holidays noon. L12,000/€6.20, EU citizens between 18 and 24 L6000/€3.20, EU citizens under 18 and over 60 free. **5-day ticket book** good for the 3 Musei Nazionali Romani, the Colosseum, and Palatine Hill L30,000/€15.50; available at the Forum's main entrance.*

The best way to attack the Palatine is from the stairs near the Forum's **Arch of Titus.** The hill, actually a plateau between the Tiber and the Forum, was home to the she-wolf that suckled Romulus and Remus. Throughout the garden complex, terraces provide breathtaking views. Lower down, excavations continue on the 9th-century BC village, the **Casa di Romulo.** To the right of the village is the podium of the 191 BC **Temple of Cybele.** The stairs to the left lead to the **House of Livia,** which is connected to the **House of Augustus** next door. Around the corner, the long, spooky **Cryptoporticus** connected Tiberius's palace with the buildings nearby. The path around the House of Augustus leads to the vast ruins of a giant palace and is divided into two wings. The solemn **Domus Augustana** was the private space for the emperors; the adjacent wing, the sprawling **Domus Flavia,** once held a gigantic octagonal fountain. Between the Domus Augustana and the Domus Flavia stands the **Palatine Antiquarium,** the museum that houses the artifacts found during the excavations of the Palatine Hill. *(30 people admitted every 20min. starting at 9:10am. Free.)* Outside on the right, the palace's east wing contains the curious **Stadium of Domitian,** or *Hippodrome,* a sunken oval space once surrounded by a colonnade but now decorated with fragments of porticoes, statues, and fountains.

OTHER SIGHTS

FORI IMPERIALI. Across the street from the Ancient Forum are the **Fori Imperiali,** a conglomeration of temples, basilicas, and public squares constructed in the first and second centuries. Excavations will proceed through 2002, so the area is closed off, but you can still get free views by peering over the railing from V.d. Fori Imperiali or V. Alessandrina. Built between AD 107 and 113, the **Forum of Trajan** included a colossal equestrian statue of Trajan and an immense triumphal arch. At one end of the now-decimated forum, 2500 carved legionnaires march their way up the almost perfectly preserved ■Trajan's Column, one of the greatest extant specimens of Roman relief-sculpture. The crowning statue is St. Peter, who replaced Trajan in 1588. Across V. dei Fori Imperiali, in the shade of the Vittorio Emanuele II monument, lie the paltry remains of the **Forum of Caesar,** including the ruins of Julius Caesar's **Temple to Venus Genetrix.** Nearby, the gray tufa wall of the **Forum of Augustus** commemorates Augustus' victory over Caesar's murderers in 42 BC. The aptly named **Forum Transitorium** (also called the **Forum of Nerva**) was a narrow, rectangular space connecting the Forum of Augustus with the Republican Roman Forum. The only remnant of **Vespatian's Forum** is the mosaic-filled **Church of Santi Cosma e Damiano** across V. Cavour, near the Roman Forum. *(Open daily 9am-1pm and 3-7pm.)*

■THE COLOSSEUM. This enduring symbol of the Eternal City—a hollowed-out ghost of marble that dwarfs every other ruin in Rome—once held as many as 50,000 spectators. Within 100 days of its opening in AD 80, some 5000 wild beasts perished in the arena (from the Latin word for sand, *harena,* which was put on the floor to absorb blood). The floor (now partially restored) covers a labyrinth of brick cells, ramps, and elevators used to transport wild animals from cages up to arena level. *(M: B-Colosseo. Open daily 9am-6:30pm; winter 9am-1hr. before sunset. L10,000/€5.20, EU citizens 18-24 L5000/€2.60, EU citizens under 18 and over 60 free. 5-day ticket book good for the 3 Musei Nazionali Romani, Colosseum, and Palatine Hill L30,000/€15.50. Tour L6000/€3.20.)*

ARCH OF CONSTANTINE. Between the Colosseum and the Palatine lies the **Arch of Constantine,** one of the latest and best-preserved imperial monuments in the area. Constantine built it in AD 312 using fragments from earlier monuments of Trajan, Hadrian, and Marcus Aurelius to create the harmonious triple arch.

DOMUS AUREA. This park houses just a portion of Nero's "Golden House," which once covered a huge chunk of Rome. After deciding that he was a god, Nero had architects build a house worthy of his divinity. The Forum was reduced to a vestibule of the palace; Nero crowned it with the 35m Colossus, a huge statue of himself as the sun. Nero committed suicide only five years after building his gargantuan pleasure garden, and later emperors tore down his house and replaced all traces of the palace with monuments built for the public good. *(On the Oppian Hill, below Trajan's baths. From the Colosseum, walk through the gates up V.d. Domus Aurea and take the 1st right. Open Tu-Su 9am-6:45pm. Groups of 30 admitted every 20min. L10,000/€5.20.)*

VELABRUM. The **Velabrum** is a flat flood plain south of the Jewish Ghetto. At the bend of V. del Portico d'Ottavia, a shattered pediment and a few ivy-covered columns are all that remain of the once magnificent **Portico d'Ottavia**. The stocky, gray **Teatro di Marcello** next door is named for Augustus's nephew, whose early and sudden death remains a mystery. Farther down V. di Teatro di Marcello, **Chiesa di San Nicola in Carcere** incorporates three Roman temples originally dedicated to Juno, Janus, and Spes. *(☎06 6869972; call to visit the interior. Open Sept.-July M-Sa 7:30am-noon and 4-7pm.)* Across the street, the **Chiesa di Santa Maria in Cosmedin** harbors some of Rome's most beautiful medieval decorations. The Audrey Hepburn film *Roman Holiday* made the portico's relief, the ■**Bocca della Verità**, famous; according to legend, the hoary face will chomp on the hand of a liar. *(Church open daily 10am-1pm and 3-7pm. Portico open daily 9am-7pm.)*

CAPITOLINE HILL. Home to the original capitol, the **Monte Capitolino** still serves as the seat of the city government. Michelangelo designed its crowning **Piazza di Campidoglio**, now home to the **Capitoline Museums** (see p. 626). Stairs lead up to the rear of the 7th-century **Chiesa di Santa Maria in Aracoeli**. The gloomy **Mamertine Prison**, consecrated the **Church of San Pietro in Carcere**, lies down the hill from the back stairs of the Aracoeli. Saint Peter, imprisoned here, baptized his captors with the waters that flooded his cell. *(Open daily 9am-noon and 2:30-6pm. Donation requested.)* At the far end of the *piazza*, opposite the stairs, lies the turreted **Palazzo dei Senatori**, the home of Rome's mayor. *(To get to the Campidoglio, take any bus that goes to P. Venezia. From P. Venezia, face the Vittorio Emanuele II monument, walk around to the right to P. d'Aracoeli, and take the stairs up the hill.)*

CIRCUS MAXIMUS AND BATHS OF CARACALLA. Boxed in the valley between the Palatine and Aventine Hills, today's **Circus Maximus** is just a grassy shadow of its former glory. After its construction in 600 BC, the circus drew more than 300,000 Romans, who gathered here to watch chariots careen around the 402m track. The remains of the **Baths of Caracalla** are the largest and best-preserved baths in the city. *(Walk down V.d. San Gregorio from the Colosseum to the Circus. Circus Maximus open 24hr. To get to baths from the eastern end of Circus Maximus, walk up V.d. Terme di Caracalla. Open daily 9am-6pm; in winter 9am-1h r. before sunset. L8000/€4.15.)*

CENTRO STORICO

PIAZZA VENEZIA AND VIA DEL CORSO. The **Via del Corso** takes its name from its days as Rome's premier racecourse, running between P. del Popolo and the rumbling P. Venezia. **Palazzo Venezia** was one of the first Renaissance *palazzi* built in the city; Mussolini used it as an office and delivered his famous orations from its balcony, but today it's little more than a glorified traffic circle dominated by the **Vittorio Emanuele II monument**. Off V. del Corso, the picturesque **Piazza Colonna** was named for the colossal **Colonna di Marco Aurelio**, designed in imitation of Trajan's column. Off the northwest corner of the *piazza* is the **Piazza di Montecitorio**, dominated by Bernini's **Palazzo Montecitorio**, now the seat of the Chamber of Deputies.

■ **THE PANTHEON.** This famous temple has remained almost unchanged since the day it was built nearly 2000 years ago. Architects still wonder how it was erected; its dome—a perfect half-sphere made of poured concrete without the support of vaults, arches, or ribs—is the largest of its kind. The light that enters the roof was used as a sundial to indicate the passing of the hours and the dates of equinoxes and solstices. In AD 606, it was consecrated as the **Church of Santa Maria ad Martyres**, its official name to this day. *(In P. della Rotonda. Open June M-Sa 9am-7pm, Su 9am-1pm; July-Aug. M-Sa 9am-7:30pm, Su 9am-1pm; Oct.-May M-Sa 9am-4pm, Su 9am-1pm. Free.)*

PIAZZA NAVONA. Originally a stadium built in AD 86, the *piazza* once hosted wrestling matches, track and field events, and mock naval battles (in which the stadium was flooded and filled with fleets skippered by convicts). Each of the river god statues in Bernini's **Fountain of the Four Rivers** represents one of the four continents of the globe (as known then): the Ganges for Asia, the Danube for Europe, the Nile for Africa (veiled, since the source of the river was unknown), and the Rio de la Plata for the Americas. At the ends of the *piazza* are the **Fontana del Moro** and the **Fontana di Nettuno,** designed by Giacomo della Porta in the 16th century and renovated by Bernini in 1653. The **Church of Sant'Agnese in Agone** dominates the *piazza*'s western side. *(Open Tu-Sa 4:30-7pm, Su 10am-1pm.)*

OTHER SIGHTS. In front of the temple, the *piazza* centers on Giacomo della Porta's late-Renaissance fountain and an Egyptian obelisk added in the 18th century. Around the left side of the Pantheon, another obelisk marks the center of tiny **Piazza Minerva.** Behind the obelisk, the **Chiesa di Santa Maria Sopra Minerva** hides some Renaissance masterpieces, including Michelangelo's **Christ Bearing the Cross, Annunciation** by Antoniazzo Romano, and a statue of St. Sebastian recently attributed to Michelangelo. The south transept houses the famous **Carafa Chapel,** home to a brilliant fresco cycle by Filippino Lippi. *(Open M-Sa 7am-7pm, Su 7am-1pm and 3:30-7pm.)* From the upper left-hand corner of P. della Rotonda, V. Giustiniani goes north to intersect V. della Scrofa and V. della Dogana Vecchia at the **Church of San Luigi dei Francesi,** home to three of Caravaggio's most famous paintings: **The Calling of St. Matthew, St. Matthew and the Angel,** and **Crucifixion.** *(Open F-W 7:30am-12:30pm and 3:30-7pm, Th 7:30am-12:30pm.)*

CAMPO DEI FIORI

Campo dei Fiori lies across Corso Vittorio Emanuele II from P. Navona. During papal rule, the area was the site of countless executions; now the only carcasses that litter the *piazza* are the fish in the colorful produce **market** (M-Sa 6am to 2pm). South of the Campo lie P. Farnese and the huge, stately **Palazzo Farnese,** the greatest of Rome's Renaissance *palazzi.* To the east of the *palazzo* is the Baroque façade of the **Palazzo Spada** and the collection of the **Galleria Spada** (see p. 591).

THE JEWISH GHETTO. The Jewish community in Rome is the oldest in Europe—Israelites came in 161 BC as ambassadors from Judas Maccabei, asking for Imperial help against invaders. The Ghetto, the tiny area to which Pope Paul IV confined the Jews in 1555, was closed in 1870, but is still the center of Rome's vibrant Jewish population of 16,000. In the center of the ghetto are **Piazza Mattei** and the 16th-century **Fontana delle Tartarughe.** Nearby is the **Church of Sant'Angelo in Pescheria;** Jews were forced to attend mass here every Sunday and quietly resisted by stuffing their ears with wax. *(Toward the eastern end of V.d. Portico d'Ottavia. Prayer meetings W 5:30pm, Sa 5pm.)* The **Sinagoga Ashkenazita,** on the Tiber near the Theater of Marcellus, was bombed in 1982; guards now search all visitors. *(Open for services only.)*

PIAZZA DI SPAGNA AND ENVIRONS

■ **THE SPANISH STEPS.** Designed by an Italian, funded by the French, named for the Spaniards, occupied by the British, and under the sway of American ambassador-at-large Ronald McDonald, the **Scalinata di Spagna** exude an international air. The pink house to the right of the Steps was the site of John Keats's 1821 death; it's now the **Keats-Shelley Memorial Museum.**

■ **FONTANA DI TREVI.** The extravagant **Fontana di Trevi** emerges from the back wall of **Palazzo Poli.** Legend says that a traveler who throws a coin into the fountain is ensured a speedy return to Rome; a traveler who tosses two will fall in love in Rome. The reality is that these coins damage the marble: go figure. Opposite the fountain is the Baroque **Chiesa dei Santi Vincenzo e Anastasio,** rebuilt in 1630. The crypt preserves the hearts and lungs of popes from 1590-1903.

MAUSOLEUM OF AUGUSTUS AND ARA PACIS. The circular brick mound of the **Masoleo d'Agosto** once housed the funerary urns of the Imperial family. West of the

ITALY

mausoleum, the glass-encased **Ara Pacis** (Altar of Augustan Peace), is propaganda completed in 9 BC to celebrate Augustus' success. *(In P. Augusto Imperatore. From P. del Popolo, take V. di Ripetta toward the Tiber. Mausoleum tours Tu and F 10pm in English. L10,000/€5.20; students L8000/€4.15. Ara Pacis is closed for renovation until an undisclosed time; it is normally open Tu-Sa 9am-7pm, Su 9am-1pm. L3750/€1.95, students L2500/€1.30.)*

PIAZZA DEL POPOLO. P. del Popolo, once a favorite venue for public executions of heretics, is now the lively "people's square." In the center is the 3200-year-old **Obelisk of Pharaoh Ramses II,** which Augustus brought back as a souvenir from Egypt in the first century BC. Behind a simple early-Renaissance shell, the **Church of Santa Maria del Popolo** contains several Renaissance and Baroque masterpieces. *(Open M-Sa 7am-noon and 4-7pm, Su and holidays 8am-1:30pm and 4:30-7:30pm.)* The **Cappella della Rovere** holds two exquisite Caravaggios, *The Conversion of St. Paul* and *Crucifixion of St. Peter*, in the **Cappella Cerasi.** Raphael designed the **Cappella Chigi.** At the southern end of the *piazza* are the 17th-century **twin churches** of Santa Maria di Montesano and Santa Maria dei Miracoli.

VILLA BORGHESE. To celebrate becoming a cardinal, Scipione Borghese built the **Villa Borghese** north of P. di Spagna and V. V. Veneto. Its huge park is home to three notable art museums: the world-renowned **Galleria Borghese** (see p. 626), the stark **Galleria Nazionale d'Arte Moderna** (see p. 626), and the intriguing **Museo Nazionale Etrusco di Villa Giulia** (see p. 626). North of the Borghese are the **Santa Priscilla catacombs.** *(M: A-Spagna and follow the signs. L14,000/€7.25.)*

TRASTEVERE

Right off the **Ponte Garibaldi** stands the statue of the famous dialect poet G. G. Bellie. On V. di Santa Cecilia, behind the cars, through the gate, and beyond the courtyard full of roses, is the **Basilica di Santa Cecilia in Trastevere;** Stefano Maderno's famous statue of Santa Cecilia lies under the altar. *(Open daily 8am-12:30pm and 2:30-7pm.)* From P. Sonnino, V. della Lungaretta leads west to P. di S. Maria in Trastevere, home to numerous stray dogs, expatriates, and the **Chiesa di Santa Maria in Trastevere,** built in the 4th century. *(Open daily 7:30am-8:30pm.)* North of the *piazza* are the Rococo **Galleria Corsini,** V. della Lungara, 10, (see **Museo Nazionale dell'Arte Antica,** p. 626) and, across the street, the **Villa Farnesina,** the jewel of Trastevere. Atop the Gianicolo hill is the **Chiesa di San Pietro in Montorio,** built on the spot once believed to be the site of St. Peter's upside-down crucifixion. Next door in a small courtyard is Bramante's tiny ✪**Tempietto,** constructed to commemorate the site of Peter's martyrdom. *(Church and Tempietto open daily 9:30am-12:30pm and 4-6:30pm.)*

NEAR TERMINI

The sights in this urban part of town are concentrated northwest of the station and to the south, near P. Vittorio Emanuele II.

BATHS OF DIOCLETIAN. These public baths, which could serve 3000 people at once, contained a heated marble public toilet with seats for 30, pools of various temperatures, gymnasiums, art galleries, gardens, libraries, and concert halls. In 1561, Michelangelo undertook his last architectural work and converted the ruins into a church, the **Chiesa di Santa Maria degli Angeli.** In the floor leading from the east transept to the altar, a sundial has provided the standard time for Roman clocks for hundreds of years. *(Open M-F 9am-2pm, Sa-Su 9am-1pm. Free. Church open daily M-Sa 7am-6:30pm, Su 8am-7:30pm.)*

BASILICA OF SANTA MARIA MAGGIORE. As one of the five churches in Rome granted extraterritoriality, this basilica, crowning the Esquiline Hill, is officially part of Vatican City. To the right of the altar, a marble slab marks the **tomb of Bernini.** The 14th-century mosaics in the **loggia** recount the story of the August snowfall that showed the pope where to build the church. *(Open daily 7am-7pm. Loggia open daily 9:30am-noon and 2-5:30pm. Tickets in souvenir shop; L5000/€2.60. Dress code enforced.)*

CHURCH OF SAN PIETRO IN VINCOLO. Michelangelo's imposing ▓statue of Moses presides over this 4th-century church. (*M: B-Cavour. Walk southwest on V. Cavour, down toward the Forum, and take the stairs on the left. Open daily 7am-12:30pm and 3:30-7pm.*)

SOUTHERN ROME

The area south of the center is a great mix of wealthy and working class neighborhoods, and is home to the city's best nightlife and some of its grandest churches.

CAELIAN HILL. Southeast of the Colosseum, the Caelian, along with the Esquiline, is the biggest of Rome's seven original hills and home to some of the city's greatest chaos. Split into three levels, each from a different era, the **Church of San Clemente** is one of Rome's most intriguing churches. A fresco cycle by Masolino dating from the 1420s graces the **Chapel of Santa Caterina**. (*M: B-Colosseo. Turn left out of the station and walk east on V. Fori Imperiali. Open M-Sa 9am-12:30pm and 3-6pm, Su and holidays 10am-12:30pm and 3-6pm. L5000/€2.60.*) The immense **Chiesa di San Giovanni in Laterano** was the seat of the pope until the 14th century; founded by Constantine in AD 314, it's Rome's oldest Christian basilica. The two golden reliquaries over the altar contain the heads of **St. Peter and St. Paul.** Across the street is the **Scala Santa**, which houses the *acheropite* image—a depiction of Christ supposedly not created by human hands—and what are believed to be the 28 steps used by Jesus outside Pontius Pilate's house. (*M: A-San Giovanni or bus #16 from Termini. Open M-Sa 6:15am-noon and 3-6:15pm, Su 6:15am-noon and 3:30-6:45pm. L4000/€2.10. Dress code enforced.*)

APPIAN WAY. Since burial inside the city walls was forbidden during ancient times, fashionable Romans made their final resting places along the Appian Way. At the same time, early Christians secretly dug maze-like catacombs under the ashes of their persecutors. (*M: A-San Giovanni. Take bus #218 from P. di S. Giovanni to the intersection of V. Ardeatina and V. delle Sette Chiese. L8000/€4.15.*) **San Callisto,** V. Appia Antica, 110, is the largest catacomb in Rome, with nearly 22km of subterranean paths. Its four levels once held 16 popes, seven bishops, St. Cecilia, and 500,000 other Christians. (*Take the private road that runs northeast to the entrance to the catacombs. Open M-Tu and Th-Su 8:30am-5:30pm; in winter Th-Su 8:30am-noon and 2:30-5pm; closed Feb.*) **Santa Domitilla** houses an intact 3rd-century portrait of Christ and the Apostles. (*Facing V. Ardeatina from the exit of S. Callisto, cross the street and walk up V. delle Sette Chiese. Open W-M 8:30am-5:30pm; in winter W-M 8:30am-5pm; closed Jan.*) **San Sebastiano,** V. Appia Antica, 136, once housed the bodies of Peter and Paul. (*Open Tu-Su 9am-7pm. L5000/€2.60, EU residents 18-24 L3000/€1.55.*)

EUR. EUR (AY-oor) is an Italian acronym for the 1942 Universal Exposition of Rome, which Mussolini planned as a showcase of Fascist achievement. (The achievement was apparently Rome's ability to build lots of identical square buildings.) The center of the area is **Piazza Guglielmo Marconi.** According to legend, when St. Paul was beheaded at the **Abbazia delle Tre Fontane (Abbey of the Three Fountains),** his head bounced three times, creating a fountain at each bounce. (*M: B-Laurentina. Walk north on V. Laurentina and turn right on V. di Acque Salve; the abbey is at the bottom of the hill. Or, take bus #761 north from the "Laurentina" stop; ask to get off at V. di Acque Salve. Open daily 9am-noon and 3-6pm.*)

VATICAN CITY

M: A-Ottaviano or A-Cipro/Musei Vaticani, bus #64 (beware of pickpockets), #492 from Termini or Largo Argentina, #62 from P. Barberini, or #23 from Testaccio. **Papal Audiences** *W, usually at 10am behind the colonnade left of the basilica; for free tickets, stop by the Prefettura della Casa Pontificia the day before. (☎06 69 88 32 73. Open M-Sa 9am-1pm.)*

Vatican City—almost ½ sq. km of independent territory entirely within the boundaries of Rome—is the seat of the Catholic Church and was once the mightiest power in Europe. The nation preserves its independence by minting coins (in Italian *lire* but with the Pope's face), running a separate postal system, and maintaining an army of Swiss Guards.

BASILICA DI SAN PIETRO (ST. PETER'S). A colonnade by Bernini leads from **Piazza San Pietro** to the church. The **obelisk** in the center is framed by two fountains; stand on the round disks set in the pavement and the quadruple rows of the colonnade will visually resolve into one perfectly aligned row. Above the colonnade are 140 statues; those on the basilica represent Christ, John the Baptist, and the Apostles (except for Peter). The pope opens the **Porta Sancta** (Holy Door) every 25 years by knocking in the bricks with a silver hammer; the last opening was in 2000. The basilica itself rests on the reputed site of St. Peter's tomb. To the right, Michelangelo's *Pietà* has been protected by bulletproof glass since 1972, when an axe-wielding fiend smashed Christ's nose and broke Mary's arm. Inside the basilica are four niches with statues of saints—Bernini's **San Longinus** is at the northeast. In the center of the crossing, Bernini's bronze **baldacchino** rises on spiral columns over the marble altar. Below the statue of St. Longinus, steps lead down to the **Vatican Grottoes,** the final resting place of innumerable popes and saints. *(Dress modestly; cover your knees and shoulders. Open daily Apr.-Aug. 7am-7pm; Oct.-Mar. 7am-6pm. Mass M-Sa 9, 10, 11am, noon, 5pm; Su 9, 10:30, 11:30am, 12:10, 1, 4, 5:45pm. Plan on spending at least 2hr. in St. Peter's. Multilingual confession available.)*

VATICAN MUSEUMS. The Vatican Museums constitute one of the world's greatest collections of art. A good place to start is the stellar **Museo Pio-Clementino,** which holds fantastic antique sculpture. Two slobbering Molossian hounds guard the entrance to the **Stanza degli Animali,** a marble menagerie; among other gems, it features the ⊠**Apollo Belvedere.** The Simonetti Stairway climbs to the **Museo Etrusco,** filled with artifacts from Tuscany and northern Lazio. From the Room of the Immaculate Conception, a door leads into the first of the four ⊠**Stanze di Rafaele,** the apartments built for Pope Julius II in the 1510s. Raphael painted the astonishing **School of Athens** as a trial piece for Julius, who was so impressed that he fired his other painters, had their frescoes destroyed, and commissioned Raphael to decorate the entire suite. The **Stanza della Segnatura** features the *School of Athens*, considered Raphael's masterpiece. From here, a staircase leads to the brilliantly frescoed **Borgia Apartments** and the **Museum of Modern Religious Art,** while another route goes to the Sistine Chapel. *(About 10 blocks north of the right-hand side of P. San Pietro along the Vatican wall. All open Oct. 31-Mar. 15 M-Sa 8:45am-1:45pm; Mar. 16-Oct. 30 M-F 8:45am-4:45pm, Sa 8:45am-1:45pm. Closed on major religious holidays. L18,000/€9.30, with ISIC L12,000/€6.20. Free last Su of the month 8:45am-1:45pm.)*

⊠**SISTINE CHAPEL.** Ever since its completion in the 16th century, the **Sistine Chapel** (named for its founder, Pope Sixtus IV) has served as the chamber in which the College of Cardinals elects new popes. The frescoes on the side walls predate Michelangelo's ceiling; on the right, scenes from the life of Moses complement parallel scenes of Christ's life on the left. The simple compositions and vibrant colors of Michelangelo's unquestioned masterpiece hover above, each section depicting a story from Genesis. The ceiling appears vaulted but is actually flat; contrary to legend, Michelangelo painted not flat on his back but standing up and craning backwards, and he never recovered from the strain to his neck and eyes. In his *Last Judgement*, on the altar wall, the figure of Christ as judge hovers in the upper center. *(Included with admission to Vatican Museum.)*

CASTEL SANT'ANGELO. Built by **Hadrian** (AD 117-138) as a mausoleum for himself, this hulking mass of brick and stone has served the popes as a fortress, prison, and palace. When the city was wracked with plague in 590, Pope Gregory saw an angel sheathing his sword at the top of the complex; the plague abated soon after, and the edifice was rededicated to the angel. It now contains a **museum of arms and artillery** and offers an incomparable view of Rome and the Vatican. *(Walk along the river with St. Peter's behind you and the towering castle to your left; follow the signs the entrance. Open in summer Tu-Su 9am-7pm; in winter daily 9am-7pm. L10,000/€5.20. Audio guide L7000/€3.65.)*

ITALY

🏛 MUSEUMS

Etruscans, emperors, popes, and *condottiere* have been busily stuffing Rome's belly full with artwork for several millennia, leaving behind a city teeming with galleries. Museums are generally closed holidays, Sunday afternoons, and all day Mondays.

Capitoline Museums (☎06 39746221), atop the Capitoline Hill (behind the Vittorio Emanuele II monument). The collections of ancient sculpture are among the largest in the world, and the frescoes are breathtaking. The Palazzo Nuovo contains the original statue of **Marcus Aurelius** that once stood in the center of the *piazza,* fragments of the **Colossus of Constantine,** and the famous **Capitoline Wolf,** an Etruscan statue that has symbolized the city of Rome since ancient times. Open Tu-Su 10am-8pm, holidays 9am-1:30pm. L15,000/€7.75, with ISIC L11,000/€5.70.

Galleria Borghese, P. Scipione Borghese, 5 (☎06 8548577). M: A-Spagna. Alternatively, take bus #910 from Termini to "V. Pinciana." Holds Bernini's most magnificent works, including his *David* and *Apollo and Daphne,* and paintings by Caravaggio, Raphael, Rubens, and Titian. Open Tu-F 9am-7:15pm, entrance only on the hr., visits limited to 2hr. L8000/€4.15.

Villa Farnesina, V. della Lungara, 230 (☎06 6802767). Just across from Palazzo Corsini off Lungotevere Farnesina. Bus #23. Thought to be the wealthiest man in Europe, Agostino "il Magnifico" Chigi lived here sumptuously and eccentrically. To the right of the entrance lies the breathtaking **Sala of Galatea,** containing Raphael's *Triumph of Galatea.* Open M-Sa 9am-1pm. L8000/€4.15.

Galleria Nazionale d'Arte Moderna, V. delle Belle Arti, 131 (☎06 322981). M: A-Flaminio; enter the park and walk up V: George Washington, following the signs. Skip to the 20th-century wing to see pieces by Klimt, Modigliani, Giacometti, Mondrian, Braque, Duchamp, and de Chirico. Open Tu-Su 8:30am-7:30pm. L12,000/€6.20.

Galleria Spada, P. Capo di Ferro, 13 (☎06 328101), in the elaborate Palazzo Spada. South of Campo dei Fiori. Bus #64. 17th-century Cardinal Bernardino Spada bought a grandiose assortment of art, including works by Tintoretto and Titian and a frieze by Vaga originally intended for the Sistine Chapel. Open Tu-Sa 8:30am-1:30pm, Su 8:30am-12:30pm. L10,000/€5.20.

Museo Nazionale Etrusco di Villa Giulia, P. Villa Giulia, 9 (☎06 3201951), in Villa Borghese. M: A-Flaminio or bus #19 from P. Risorgimento or #52 from P. San Silvestro. Check out the Etruscan chariot, and the petrified skeletons of 2 horses found beside it, in Room 18. Open June-Sept. Tu-F, Su, and holidays 8:30am-7:30pm; Sa 9am-11pm, Oct.-May 9am-8pm. L8000/€4.15.

Museo Nazionale d'Arte Antica, V. delle Quattro Fontane, 13 (☎06 4814591), near P. Barberini. **Palazzo Barberini** contains paintings from the medieval through the Baroque. Open Tu-Sa 9am-7pm, Su 9am-8pm. L12,000/€6.20, EU citizens 18-25 L7000/€3.65.) **Galleria Corsini,** V. della Lungara, 10, opposite Villa Farnesina in Trastevere, holds 17th- and 18th-century paintings. Open Tu-Su 9am-6pm. L8000/€4.15, EU students L4000/€2.10.

Museo Nazionale Romano Palazzo Massimo, Largo di Via Peretti, 1 (☎06 4815576), in the left-hand corner of P. dei Cinquecento as you stand with your back to Termini. Devoted to the history of Roman art during the Empire, it includes the Lancellotti Discus Thrower, a rare mosaic of Nero's, and ancient coins and jewelry. Open Tu-Su 9am-7:45pm. L12,000/€6.20, EU citizens 18-24 L6000/€3.20.

Museo Nazionale Romano Palazzo Altemps, P.S. Apollinaire, 44 (☎06 7833566), just north of P. Navona. Lots of ancient Roman sculpture, including the 5th-century *Ludovisi Throne.* Open Tu-Su 9am-7pm. L10,000/€5.16.

Museo Preistorico ed Etnografico Luigi Pigorini, P.G. Marconi, 14 (☎06 549521). An impressive collection of ethnographic artifacts, including the skull of the famous Neanderthal Guattari Man discovered near Circeo. Open daily 9am-8pm. L8000/€4.15.

◢ ENTERTAINMENT

Unfortunately, Roman entertainment just ain't what it used to be. Back in the day, you could swing by the Colosseum to watch a man get mauled by a bear; today, Romans seeking diversion are more likely to go to a Testaccio nightclub than fight some hairy beast to the death. Check *Roma C'è* (which has an English-language section) or *Time Out*, available at newsstands, for club, movie, and events listings.

The classical music scene in Rome goes wild during the summer. Small festivals run from mid-May to August. In July, the **Accademia Nazionale di Santa Cecilia** (☎06 361 10 64 or 06 361 18 33, credit card reservations 06 68 80 10 44) holds concerts in the **Villa Giulia**, in Villa Borghese. The **Theater of Marcellus**, near P. Venezia, hosts summer evening concerts organized by the **Associazione Il Tempietto.** (☎06 481 48 00. Tickets L30,000/€15.50.) Rome's most important theater, **Teatro Argentina**, V. di Torre Argentina, 52, runs drama and music festivals throughout the year. (☎06 68 80 46 01. Box office open M-F 10am-7pm, Sa 10am-2pm.) For information on English theater, check the tourist office or the English section of *Roma C'è.*

◢ NIGHTLIFE

CLUBS

Although Italian discos can be a flashy, sweaty good time, the scene changes as often as Roman phone numbers. Check *Roma C'è* or *Time Out.* Rome has fewer gay establishments than most cities its size, but those it has are solid and keep late hours. Many gay establishments require an **ARCI-GAY pass** (L10,000/€5.20 yearly), available from **Circolo di Cultura Omosessuale Mario Mieli** (☎06 541 39 85).

Charro Cafe, V. di Monte Testaccio, 73. So you wanted to go to Tijuana, but got stuck in Rome. Weep no more, *mis amigos:* make a run for Charro, home of the L5000/€2.60 tequila *bum bum.* Italians guzzling strong Mexican-themed mixed drinks (L10,000/€5.20) dance themselves silly to pop and house. Cover L10,000/€5.20 (includes a drink). Open 11:30pm-3:30am.

Aquarela, V. di Monte Testaccio, 64. Next door to Radio Londra. Built out of ancient trash, then used for years as a vegetable market, the club consists in part of two underground tunnels that remain cool even when the party's heatin' up. Cover L20,000/€10.30 (includes 1 drink). Open Tu-Su 8:30pm-3am.

Caruso, V. di Monte Testaccio, 36. No opera here: Caruso is a reliable venue for live salsa, DJed hip hop, and "music black" (rap and R&B). Five rooms of tropical decor, packed with writhing Latino wannabes. Live music F. Monthly *tessera* (pass) L15,000-20,000/€7.75-10.30. Open Tu and Th-Su 11:30pm-3am.

Radio Londra Caffè, V. di Monte Testaccio, 65b. Admit it: you've always fantasized about watching Italian bands cover rock classics badly. Packed with an energetic, good-looking, young crowd. Pizza, *panini*, and hamburgers (L8000-12,000/€4.13-6.20). Monthly *tessera* (pass) L10,000/€5.20. Open Su-F 9pm-3am, Sa 9pm-4am.

C.S.I.O.A. Villaggio Globale, Lungotevere Testaccio (☎06 57 30 03 29). Take bus #27 from Termini, get off before it crosses the river, and head left down the river. Women probably shouldn't travel alone on the Lungotevere at night. One of the best-known *centri sociali* in Rome—your one-stop shop for all things countercultural. Housed in a huge Testaccio slaughterhouse, it hosts live music, films, art exhibits, poetry readings, African cuisine tastings, and more. Hours and cover vary. F nights are usually hopping.

PUBS

For organized, indoor drunkenness, stop into any of Rome's countless pubs, many of which have some sort of Irish theme. Drink prices often increase after 9pm.

ITALY

■ **Jonathan's Angels,** V.d. Fossa, 14-16. West of P. Navona. Take V.d. Governo Vecchio from Campo dei Fiori, turn left at the Abbey Theatre onto V. Parione and then left toward the lights. Michelangelo's accomplishments pale before the bathroom at Jonathan's Angels, the finest ■ bathroom in Rome, nay, Italy. Medium beer on tap L10,000/ €5.20. Mercifully free of pub-crawlers. Open daily 4pm-2am.

■ **Trinity College,** V.d. Collegio Romano, 6. Off V.d. Corso near P. Venezia. Offers degrees in such diverse curricula as Guinness, Harp, and Heineken. Tuition L6-9000/€3.20-4.50. Happy Hour noon-8pm. Classes held every day noon-3am.

Il Simposio, V.d. Latini, 11. The symposium's walls are cluttered with Jackson-Pollock-esque works of local artists, and on any given night a painter may be beautifying a discarded refrigerator. With cocktails from L6000/€3.20 and a glass of *fragolino* for L5000/€2.60, even starving artists can afford to come. Open daily 9pm-2am.

Pub Hallo'Ween, P. Tiburtino, 31, at the corner of V. Tiburtina and V. Marsala. Plastic skulls, fake spiders, and spiderwebs. Draft beer L6-8000/€3.10-4.15, sandwiches L10,000/€5.20. Open daily 8:30pm-2:30am. Closed in Aug.

The Drunken Ship, Campo dei Fiori, 20-21. Because you're tired of meeting Italians. Because you have a burning desire to commune with the hosteling set. Beer L8000/ €4.15. Happy Hour daily 5-9pm. Su Ladies night. Tu half-price Tequila. W 9-10pm all the beer you can drink (L10,000/€5.20). Open 5pm-2am. AmEx/MC/V.

The Nag's Head, V. IV Novembre, 138b. Off P. Venezia. Pier the bartender, who is straight out of *Cocktail* (and advertises himself as a master of *"flair estremo"*), makes this place worth a visit. After the bottle-twirling and other excesses, you almost don't mind the L1000/€0.55 he tacks on to your bill as a "tip." Dance floor inside. Guinness L10,000/€5.20, cocktails L14,000/€7.20. Cover L10,000/€5.20; F and Sa men L15,000/€7.75; Su free. Open daily 4pm-3am; in winter noon-3am. MC/V.

▶ DAYTRIPS FROM ROME

TIVOLI

M: B-Rebibbia (15min. from Termini); exit the station and follow signs for Tivoli through the underpass to the other side of V. Tiburtina. Take the blue ACOTRAL bus to Tivoli (25min., tickets L3000/€1.55 in the bar next door or in the subway station). Get off past the green P. Garibaldi at P. delle Nazioni Unite (the bus back to Rome leaves from P. Garibaldi), then follow the street to the tourist office. (☎0774 311249. Open M-Sa 9:45am-3pm.)

From P. Garibaldi, a gauntlet of souvenir stands leads through P. Trento to the ■ **Villa d'Este,** the castle-garden property on the left, which was laid out by Cardinal Ercole d'Este (the son of Lucrezia Borgia) in 1550 to recreate the feel of the ancient Roman *nymphaea* and pleasure palaces. (☎0774 312070. Open daily May-Aug. 8:30-6:30pm; Sept.-Apr. 9am-1hr. before sunset. Su villa closes 1½hr. earlier. L8000/€4.15.) V. di Sibilla runs across town to the beautiful **Villa Gregoriana,** but it's been closed indefinitely for restoration; check at the tourist office for more information. From Tivoli, it's 5km to the vast remains of **Hadrian's Villa** (Villa Adriana), the largest and most expensive villa ever built in the Roman Empire. Take the orange #4x bus *(L1400/ €0.70, tickets at the news kiosk)* from the P. Garibaldi newsstand. (☎0774 530203. Open daily 9am-1½hr. before sunset. L12,000/€6.20. EU students L6000/€3.20.)

TARQUINIA

Trains connect Termini to Tarquinia (1hr., 11 per day, last train leaves Tarquinia at 10:12pm; L10,200/€5.30). Buses run from the train station to the beach (L1100/ €0.60) and to the city center (L1500/€0.80) every 30min. until 9:30pm. For bus schedules, stop by the tourist office in P. Cavour, near the medieval walls. (☎0766 856384. Open daily 8am-2pm and 4-7pm.)

When Rome was but a few mud huts on the Palatine, Tarquin kings commanded this fledgling metropolis. In P. Cavour stands the majestic **Museo Nazionale,** one of the best collections of Etruscan art outside Rome. *(Open Tu-Su 9am-7pm. L12,000/ €6.20.)* A subterranean **necropolis** lined with vibrant frescoes illustrates Tarquinia's history. *(Open 9am-1hr. before sunset. Entrance with ticket to museum.)* Take the bus marked Cimitero from Barriera S. Giusto or, from the museum, head up Corso Vittorio Emanuele from P. Cavour and turn right on V. Porta Tarquinia (15min.).

ITALY

LAKE BRACCIANO

M: A-Lepanto, then take the Cotral bus (L3900/€2). Bracciano is also accessible by train on the Rome-Viterbo line (every hr. from Rome's San Pietro station 5:35am-9:45pm, last train to Rome 10:14pm; L5300/€2.75).

Bracciano is Rome's nearest freshwater beach. Fresh air, cool water, and a lush and hilly surrounding landscape compensate for the gravelly, volcanic sand that might hurt your rear. The impressive 15th-century **Orsini-Odescalchi Castle** dominates town and offers stunning frescoes and stuffed wild boars. *(Mandatory tours in English 10:30, 11:30am, 3:30, and 5:30pm. Open Apr.-Sept. Tu-Su. L11,000/€5.70.)* A ferry ride across the lake to nearby Anguillara or Trevignano offers spectacular scenery.

LOMBARDY (LOMBARDIA)

Over the centuries, Roman generals, German emperors, and French kings have vied for control of Lombardy's fertile soil. Today, tremendous increases in employment and business have made Lombardy an even more vital cornerstone of the Italian economy. Milan may drive the mighty engine of progress, but don't let its exhaust fumes blind you to the beauty of Bergamo, Mantua, and the foothills of the Alps.

MILAN (MILANO)   ☎ 02

Milan has always been the *bella* of the Italian ball: once the capital of the Roman Empire, today it is the most cutting-edge of major Italian cities. The pace of life in Milan is dizzying, and a stream of well-dressed Italians blurs the panorama of tree-lined boulevards and graceful architecture darkened by omnipresent urban graffiti. A regional expression sums up the nature of this fashionable beast succinctly: *"Milano l'e Milano"* (Milan is just Milan). There is little time for the Milanese to stop and savor *il dolce far niente* (the sweetness of doing nothing): maintaining its record of social success is surely hard work.

█ TRANSPORTATION

Flights: Malpensa Airport (02 74 85 22 00), 45km from town, handles intercontinental flights. **Malpensa Express** bus leaves twice per hr. from the Cardona MM station to the airport (45min., 6:50am-8:20pm, L15,000-20,000/€7.75-10.35). **Linate Airport** (02 74 85 22 00), 7km from town, handles domestic and European flights. Take bus #73 from MM1: P.S. Babila (L1500/€0.80).

Trains: Stazione Centrale (☎01 47 88 80 88), in P. Duca d'Aosta on MM2. Info office open daily 7am-9:30pm. To: **Florence** (2½hr., every hr., L40,000/€20.70); **Genoa** (1½hr., every hr., L24,000/€12.40); **Rome** (4½hr., every hr., L71,000/€36.70); **Turin** (2hr., every hr., L24,500/€12.70); **Venice** (3hr., 21 per day, L36,000/€18.60). **Luggage storage** L4000/€2.10 per 12hr.

Buses: Stazione Centrale. Intercity buses tend to be less convenient and more expensive than trains. **SAL, SIA, Autostradale,** and other carriers leave from P. Castello and nearby (MM1: Cairoli) for Turin, Lake Country, and Bergamo.

Public Transportation: The **subway** (Metropolitana Milanese, or **MM**) runs 6am-midnight. The **buses** (Azienda Trasporti Muncipali or **ATM**), in the P. del Duomo station, handle local transportation. Info and ticket booths (toll-free ☎800 01 68 57) are open M-Sa 7:15am-7:15pm. Single-fare tickets (L1500/€0.80) are good for 75min. of surface transportation. Day passes L5000/€2.60, 2-day L9000/€4.65.

✳ ▣ ORIENTATION AND PRACTICAL INFORMATION

The layout of the city resembles a giant target, encircled by a series of ancient concentric city walls. In the outer rings lie suburbs built during the 1950s and 60s to house southern immigrants. Within the inner circle are four central squares: **Piazza Duomo**, at the end of V. Mercanti, **Piazza Cairoli**, near the Castello Sforzesco, **Piazza Cordusio**, connected to Largo Cairoli by V. Dante, and **Piazza San Babila**, the business and fashion district along Corso Vittorio Emanuele. The **duomo** and **Galleria Vittorio Emanuele** comprise the bull's-eye, roughly at the center of the downtown circle. Radiating from the center lie two large parks, the Giardini Pubblici and the Parco Sempione. From the colossal **Stazione Centrale** train station, farther northeast, you can take a scenic ride on bus #60 or the more efficient commute on subway line #3 to the downtown hub. **Via Vito Pisani,** which leads to the mammoth **Piazza della Repubblica,** connects the station to the downtown area.

TOURIST, FINANCIAL, AND LOCAL SERVICES

Tourist Office: APT, V. Marconi, 1 (☎02 72 52 43 00; fax 02 72 52 43 50), in the "Palazzo di Turismo" in P. del Duomo, to the right as you face the *duomo*. Pick up the comprehensive ■ *Milano: Where, When, How* as well as *Milano Mese* for info on activities and clubs. Open M-F 8:30am-8pm, Sa 9am-1pm and 2-7pm, Su 9am-1pm and 2-5pm. **Branch office** at Stazione Centrale (☎02 72 52 43 70), set back off the main hall on the 2nd fl. Open M-Sa 9am-6pm, Su 9am-12:30pm and 1:30-6pm.

Budget Travel: CIT, Galleria Vittorio Emanuele (☎02 86 37 01). Also changes money. Open M-F 9am-7pm, Sa 9am-1pm and 2-6pm. **CTS,** V.S. Antonio, 2 (☎02 58 30 41 21). Open M-F 9:30am-12:45pm and 2-6pm, Sa 9:30am-12:45pm.

Currency Exchange: All **Banca d'America e d'Italia** and **Banca Nazionale del Lavoro** branches eagerly await your Visa card. Bank hours in Milan are usually M-F 8:30am-1:30pm and 2:30-4:30pm. **ATM**s abound.

American Express: V. Brera, 3 (☎02 72 00 36 93), on the corner of V. dell'Orso. Walk through the Galleria, across P. Scala, and up V. Verdi. Holds mail free for AmEx members for 1 month, otherwise US$5 per inquiry. Sends/receives wired money for AmEx cardholders; fee of L2500/€1.30 per month on transactions over L150,000/€77.50. Also **exchanges currency.** Open M-Th 9am-5:30pm, F 9am-5pm.

Lost Property: Ufficio Oggetti Smarriti Comune, V. Fruili, 30 (☎025 46 81 18). Open M-F 8:30am-4pm.

Laundromat: Vicolo Lavandai, Vle. Monte Grappa, 2 (☎024 98 39 02). MM2: Garibaldi. Wash 7kg for L6000/€3.10, dry for L6000/€3.10. Open daily 8am-9pm.

EMERGENCY AND COMMUNICATIONS

Emergencies: ☎118. **Toll-free Operator:** ☎12. **Medical Assistance:** Pronto Soccorso (☎02 38 83).

Police: ☎113 or 027 72 71. **Carabinieri** (the civil corps): ☎112.

Hospital: Ospedale Maggiore di Milano, V. Francesco Sforza, 35 (☎025 50 31), 5min. from the *duomo* on the inner ring road.

Late-Night Pharmacy: G*aleria* of the Stazione Centrale never closes (☎026 69 07 35 or 026 69 09 35).

Internet Access: Manhattan Lab, in the Università Statale, formerly the Ospedale Maggiore on V. Festa del Perdono. Use the entrance opposite V. Bergamini. Take the stairs on the right to the 3rd fl. Turn left, and walk to the end of the corridor. Take 2 lefts; it's the 3rd door on your left. Microsoft workstations are only for Easmus students, but at the far end are computers for the public. Free. Open M-F 8:15am-6pm.

Post Office: V. Cordusio, 4 (☎02 72 48 22 23), near P. del Duomo towards the castle. Stamps, *Fermo Posta,* and currency exchange. Address mail to be held: FirstName SUR-NAME, *In Fermo Posta,* Ufficio Postale Centrale di Piazza Cordusio, 4, Milano **20100,** Italia. Open M-F 8:30am-7:30pm, Sa 8:30am-1pm. There are 2 more offices at **Stazione Centrale:** a main branch on P. Luigi di Savoia, and a smaller branch downstairs under the drive-through. **Postal Code:** 20100.

◤ ACCOMMODATIONS

Every season in Milan is high season, except August, when bugs outnumber humans. A single room in a decent establishment for under L65,000/€33.60 is a real find. For the best deals, try the city's southern periphery or areas south and east of the train station. When possible, make reservations well ahead of time.

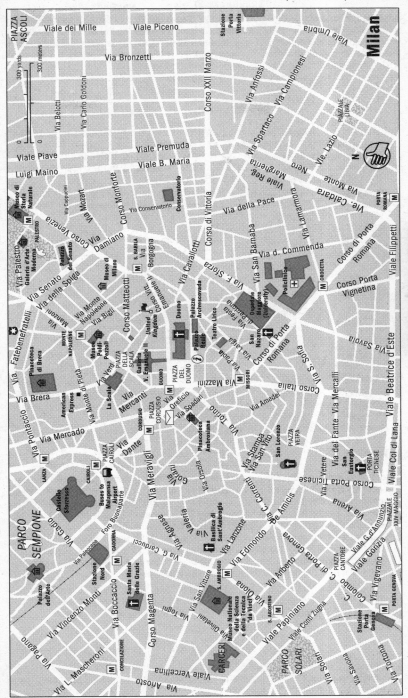

Milan

ITALY

■ **Hotel Ca' Grande,** V. Porpora, 87 (☎02 26 14 40 01). Take tram #33 from Stazione Centrale; it runs along V. Porpora and stops at V. Ampere, near the front door. 20 spotless rooms over a beautiful garden. **Internet.** Breakfast included. Reception 24hr. Singles L70,000/€36.15, with bath L90,000/€46.50; doubles L110,000/€56.85, L130,000/€67.15. AmEx/D/MC/V.

■ **Hotel Sara,** V. Sacchini, 17 (☎02 20 17 73). MM1/2: Loreto. From Loreto take V. Porpora and the 3rd street on the right is V. Sacchini. On a peaceful street. Single L55,000/€28.40; double L80,000/€41.35, with bath L100,000/€51.65; triple L120,000/€62.

Hotel San Tomaso, V. Tunisia, 6 (☎02 29 51 47 47), 3rd fl. MM1: Porta Venezia. Take the Corso Buenos Aires Metro exit; go left at the McDonald's on V. Tunisia. Clean, renovated rooms. Ask for keys if going out at night. 3 singles L70,000/€36.15; 4 doubles L100,000/€51.65, with bath L120,000/€62; 4 triples L135,000/€69.75; quads 200,000/€103.30. MC/V.

Hotel Kennedy, V. Tunisia, 6 (☎02 29 40 09 34), 6th fl. MM1: Porta Venezia. 3 floors above Hotel San Tomaso. 16 clean and carpeted rooms with lovely views of Milan. Breakfast L4000/€2.10. Singles L70,000/€36.15; doubles L100,000-130,000/ €51.65-67.15; triples L150,000/€77.50; quads L160,000/€82.65; quints L200,000/€103.30. AmEx/D/MC/V.

Hotel Casa Mia, V.V. Veneto, 30 (☎026 575 21 49). MM1: Porta Venezia or Repubblica. All 15 rooms have air-conditioning. Breakfast included. Singles L120,000/€62; doubles L160,000/€82.65; triples L180,000-230,000/€93-118.80. AmEx/MC/V.

Albergo Brasil di Ramella Luisa, V.G. Modena, 20 (☎027 49 24 82). MM1: Palestro. Take bus #60 from Stazione Centrale until V.G. Modena. Then take V. Serbelloni, make a quick left onto V. Cappuccini, which becomes V.F. Bellotti and finally V.G. Modena. 20 beds. Reception closes at 12:30am; ask for keys to enter later. Singles L85,000-110,000/€43.90-56.85; doubles L90,000-140,000/€46.50-72.30. AmEx/MC/V.

Hotel Malta, V. Ricordi, 20 (☎022 04 96 15). MM1/2: Loreto. From Stazione Centrale, take tram #33 to V. Ampere and backtrack along V. Porpora to V. Ricordi. Reserve ahead. Singles L90,000/€46.50; doubles L140,000/€72.30.

Camping di Monza (☎039 38 77 71), in the park of the Villa Reale in Monza straight to Viassono. Take a train or bus from Stazione Centrale to Monza, then a city bus to the campground. Restaurant and bar. Open Apr.-Aug. L8000/€4.15 per person, L8000/ €4.15 per tent, L15,000/€7.75 per caravan (4 people). Showers L500/€0.30.

◖ FOOD

Like its fine *couture*, Milanese cuisine is sophisticated and sometimes overpriced. Specialties include *risotto giallo* (rice with saffron), *cotoletta alla milanese* (breaded veal cutlet with lemon), and *cazzouela* (a mixture of pork and cabbage). *Pasticcerie* and *gelaterie* crowd every block. Bakeries specialize in the Milanese sweet bread *panettone*, an Italian fruitcake. The newspaper *Il Giornale Nuovo* lists all restaurants and shops open in the city, and the brochure *Milano: Where, When, How*, available at the tourist office, has a detailed list of foreign restaurants. Pick up groceries near Corso Buenos Aires at **Supermarket Regina Giovanna**, V. Regina Giovanna, 34. (Open M-F 8am-9pm, Sa 8am-8pm.)

■ **Tarantella,** Viale Abruzzi, 35, just north of V. Plinio. MM1: Lima. Lively, elegant sidewalk dining. Try the *pasta fresca* (L12,000/€6.20) or the pizza (L10,000/€5.20). *Secondi* from L125,000/€64.55. Open Sept.-July M-Su noon-2:30pm and 7-11:30pm.

■ **Brek,** V. Lepetit, 20 (☎026 70 51 49). Near Stazione Centrale. Very popular self-service restaurant. *Primi* around L5000/€2.60, *secondi* L7500/€3.90. Other locations on P. Cavour, off V. Manzoni, MM3: M. Napoleone (☎02 65 36 19), and Porta Giordano, MM1: S. Babila (☎02 76 02 33 79). Open M-Sa 11:30am-3pm and 6:30-10:30pm.

Pizzeria Premiata, V. Alzaia Naviglio Grande, 2. MM2: Porto Genova. Serves hearty portions. Pizza from L9000/€4.65, *primi* around L15,000/€7.75. Open daily noon-2am.

ITALY

Le Briciole, V. Camperio, 17, 1 block from V. Dante. MM1: Cairoli. Pizza L9000-16,000/ €4.65-8.30. Great *antipasto* buffet L13,000-22,000/€6.75-11.40. Cover L3000/ €1.55. Open Tu-F and Su 12:15-2:30pm and 7:15-11:30pm, Sa 7:15-11:30pm.

Peck, V. Cantù, 3 (☎028 69 30 17), off V. Orefici, 2 blocks from P. del Duomo. Great for picnicking food, but no place to sit. L7500/€3.90 will buy a large slice of pastry or pizza. Try the chocolate mousse (L6000/€3.10). Open Tu-F 8:45am-2:30pm and 4-7:30pm, Sa 8:30am-1:15pm and 3:45-7:30pm, Su 8am-1pm.

Il Fondaco dei Mori, V. Solferino, 33 (☎02 65 37 11). From MM2: Moscova, walk north to P. XXV Aprile, turn right onto Porta Nuova, and take the 2nd right onto V. Solferino. No sign; ring the bell. One of the 1st Arab restaurants in Italy; a Milan must. Vegetarian lunch *menù* L14,000/€7.25; dinner buffet L20,000/€10.35. Cover L3000/€1.55. Open daily Tu-Su 12:30-3pm and 7:30pm-midnight.

👁 SIGHTS

DUOMO. The looming Gothic cathedral is the geographical and spiritual center of Milan and makes a good starting point for a walking tour of the city. The *duomo* is the third-largest church in the world, after St. Peter's in the Vatican and the Seville Cathedral. Gian Galeazzo Visconti founded the cathedral in 1386, hoping to flatter the Virgin into granting him a male heir. Construction proceeded sporadically over the next four centuries and was finally completed at Napoleon's command in 1809. The imposing 16th-century marble tomb of Giacomo de Medici, was inspired by the work of Michelangelo. *(MM1: Duomo. Modest dress strictly enforced. Cathedral open daily Mar.-Oct. 9am-5:45pm; Nov.-Feb. 9am-4:15pm. Roof open daily Mar.-Oct. 7am-7pm; Nov.-Feb. 9am-4:30pm. L6000/€3.10, with elevator L9000/€4.65.)* The **Museo del Duomo,** across the *piazza*, to the right as you face the *duomo*, in the Palazzo Reale at P. del Duomo, 14, explains the construction of the *duomo* with its display of artifacts. *(☎02 86 03 58. Open Tu-Su 9:30am-12:30pm and 3-6pm. L8000/€4.15.)* Also in the Palazzo Reale, the **Museo d'Arte Contemporanea** holds a fine collection of 20th-century Italian art, interspersed with a few Picassos. *(☎02 62 08 32 19. Open Tu-Su 9:30am-5:30pm. Free.)*

▨ TEATRO ALLA SCALA. Known simply as **La Scala,** this is the world's most renowned opera house. Opened in 1778, it rests on the site of the Chiesa di S. Maria alla Scala, from which it took its name. Singer Maria Callas became a legend in this Neoclassical building. To see the red, multi-tiered hall, enter through the **Museo Teatrale alla Scala.** *(P. della Scala. At opposite end of the Galleria Vittorio Emanuele from the duomo. ☎028 05 34 18. Museum open daily 9am-noon and 2-5:30pm. L6000/€3.10.)*

MUSEO POLDI PEZZOLI. The museum contains an outstanding private art collection bequeathed to the city by Poldi Pezzoli in 1879. Famous paintings include Bellini's *Ecce Homo*, and the museum's signature piece, Antonio Pollaiuolo's *Portrait of a Young Woman*. *(From La Scala, on the right at V. Manzoni, 12. ☎02 79 48 89. Open daily 10am-6pm. L10,000/€5.20, seniors L5000/€2.60, students L2500/€1.30.)*

PINACOTECA DI BRERA. The Brera Art Gallery presents one of the most impressive collections of paintings in Italy, with works that range from the 14th to the 20th century. Works include Bellini's *Pietà*, Andrea Mantegna's brilliantly foreshortened *Dead Christ*, Raphael's *Marriage of the Virgin*, Caravaggio's *Supper at Emmaus*, and Piero della Francesca's 15th-century *Sacra Conversazione*. A limited collection of works by modern masters includes pieces by Modigliani and Carlo Carrà. *(V. Brera, 28, MM2: Lanza. ☎02 72 26 31. Open Tu-Sa 9am-7pm, Su 8:30am-11pm. L8000/€4.15.)*

GALLERIA VITTORIO EMANUELE II. To the left as you face the *duomo*, this monumental glass barrel vault with a beautiful glass *cupola* (48m), is five stories of overpriced cafes and shops. Mosaics representing different continents sieged by the Romans adorn the floors and the central octagon's upper walls. Once considered the drawing room of Milan, the Galleria is now home to the icons of commercialism. *(☎06 46 02 72. Open M-Sa 10am-11pm, Su 10am-8pm.)*

ITALY

CASTELLO SFORZESCO. Restored after heavy bomb damage in 1943, the Castello Sforzesco is one of Milan's best-known monuments and a great place for a picnic. The Castello houses the **Musei Civici,** which includes the **Musical Instruments Museum** and the **Applied Arts Museum.** The ground floor contains a sculpture collection famous for Michelangelo's unfinished *Pietà Rondanini*, his last work. *(Located at MM1: Cairoli. ☎ 02 62 36 39 47. Open Tu-Su 9:30am-5:30pm. Free.)*

CHIESA DI SANTA MARIA DELLE GRAZIE. once a 15th-century convent, the church's Gothic nave is dark and elaborately patterned with frescoes. Next to the church entrance, in what was once the dining hall, is the **Cenacolo Vinciano (Vinciano Refectory),** one of Milan's most famous sites, and home to one of the most important pieces of art in the world: **Leonardo da Vinci's Last Supper.** *(Church is at P. di S. Maria delle Grazie, 2, on Corso Magenta, off V. Carducci below MM1: Cadorna Cairoli. ☎ 02 89 42 11 46. Arrive early or late to avoid a long wait. Open Tu-Su 8am-7:30pm, Sa 8am-11pm. L12,000/€6.20, under 18 and over 65 free. Wheelchair accessible.)*

STADIO GIUSEPPE MEAZZA. The true *duomo* of the Milanese youth, the *Stadio* is one of the most famous soccer arenas on the planet. The tour of the stadium includes visits to the locker rooms and a museum dedicated to the two local teams. *(V. Piccolomini, 5; MM2: Lotto. Walk along V. Fed. Caprilli and you can't miss it. Tours M-Sa 10am-5pm. L18,000/€9.30, L12,000/€6.20 for under 18 or over 65.)*

MUSEO NAZIONALE DELLA SCIENZA E DELLA TECNICA "LEONARDO DA VINCI". Quirky ancestral artifacts of modern technology fill this museum—an attendant will turn on the machines to show their ingenuity. *(V.S. Vittore, 21, off V. Carducci, at MM2: San Ambrogio. ☎ 02 48 55 51. Open Tu-F 9:30am-4:50pm, Sa-Su 9:30am-6:20pm. L12,000/€6.20, children and seniors over 60 L8000/€4.15.)*

BASILICA DI SANT'AMBROGIO. A prototype for Lombard-Romanesque churches throughout Italy, the *basilica* is the most influential medieval building in Milan. The tiny 4th-century **Cappella di San Vittore,** with exquisite 5th-century mosaics, lies through the seventh chapel on the right. *(MM1: Sant'Ambrogio. Open M-Sa 7:30am-noon and 2:30-7pm, Su 3-7pm. Free. Audiogiudes in the back of the church for L1000/€0.55.)*

NAVIGLI DISTRICT. The Venice of Lombardy, the Navigli district comes alive at night (see p. 635). Complete with canals, small footbridges, open-air markets, cafes, alleys, and trolleys, this area constitutes part of a medieval canal system with original locks that were designed by Leonardo da Vinci. *(Outside the MM2: Porta Genova station, through the Arco di Porta Ticinese.)*

CHIESA DI SAN LORENZO MAGGIORE. The oldest church in Milan, it is a testament to the city's 4th-century greatness. To its right sits the 14th-century **Cappella di Sant'Aquilino.** Inside is a 5th-century mosaic of a beardless Christ among his apostles. A staircase behind the altar leads to a Roman amphitheater's remains. *(On Corso Ticinese. MM2: Porta Genova, then tram #3 from V. Torino. Open daily 7:30am-6:45pm. Cappella: L2000/€1.05.)*

BASILICA DI SANT'AMBROGIO. Founded in the 4th century to house the bones of the Magi, the church lost its original function when the dead wise men were spirited off to Cologne in 1164. The triumph of this church, and one of the great masterpieces of early Renaissance art, is the Portinari Chapel, attributed to the Florentine Michelozzo. *(P.S. Eustorgio, 3. Farther down Corso Ticinese from San Lorenzo Maggiore. Tram #3. Open W-M 9:30am-noon and 3:30pm-6pm.)*

PINACOTECA AMBROSIANA. The Ambrosiana's 23 rooms display exquisite works from the 14th through 19th centuries, including works by Botticelli, Leonardo, Raphael, Caravaggio, Tizian, and Breugel. *(P. Pio XI, 2. Follow V. Spadari off V. Torino and make a left onto V. Cantù. ☎ 02 86 46 29 81. Open Tu-Su 10am-5:30pm. L12,000/€6.20, under 18 or over 65 L6000/€3.10.)*

NIGHTLIFE

Ciak, V. Sangallo, 33 (☎02 76 11 00 93), near P. Gorini Argonne, southeast of the *duomo*, offers cabaret popular with young Milanese. Take tram #5 from Stazione Centrale to V. Beato Angelico Argonne. (Cover L25,000-40,000/€12.95-20.70.) The **Teatri d'Italia di Porta Romana,** Corso di Porta Romana, 124 (☎02 58 31 58 96) puts on experimental productions and first-rate mainstream plays (L28,000/€14.50). **Milan Oltre** is a summer festival of drama, dance and music; call the **Ufficio Informazione del Comune** (☎02 86 46 40 94) for more details.

If Milan's status as a world-famous fashion capital has lured you here for shopping, don't despair about the prices. If you can tolerate the stigma of being an entire season behind, purchase your famous designer duds from *blochisti* (wholesale clothing outlets) such as **Monitor** on V. Monte Nero (MM3: Porta Romana, then tram #9 or 29) or the well-known **Il Salvagente,** V. Bronzetti, 16, off Corso XXII Marzo (bus #60 from MM1: Lima or MM2/3: Stazione Centrale). The clothing sold along **Corso Buenos Aires** is more affordable—all the stores are open 10am-12:30pm and 2:30-7pm. Winter sales begin January 10. Shop in late July for end-of-the-summer sales (20-50% off) and get a glimpse of the new fall lines. The brochure *Milano: Where, When, How*, available at the tourist office, has a great list of markets and second-hand stores. Hard-core window shoppers should head to the world-famous ▨fashion district between **Corso Vittorio Emanuele** near the *duomo* and **Via Monte Napoleone** off P. San Babila. Take your credit card at your own risk. The dresses come straight from the designers and the selection is more up-to-date than anywhere else in the world, including New York and Tokyo. Expect to find high-class places to buy perfume, glasses, leather goods, shoes, and jewelry.

The nocturnal scene varies with the hour and the locale. The brochure *Milano: Where, When, How* has a comprehensive list of entertainment options, divided by type. A chic, very touristed district lies by **Via Brera,** northwest of the *duomo* and east of MM1: Cairoli, where you'll find art galleries, small clubs, restaurants, and an upscale thirty-something crowd. Younger Milanese migrate to the areas around **Corso Porta Ticinese** and **Piazza Vetra** (near Chiesa S. Lorenzo) to sip beer at one of the many *birrerie* (pubs). The highest concentration of bars and youth can be found in the **Navigli district.** (MM2: Porta Genova; walk along V. Vigevano until it ends and then veer right onto V. Naviglio Pavese.)

▨ **Le Trottoir,** close to V. Brera. MM2: Lanza. It's easy to meet Italians as well as people from all over the world. Open daily 7pm-2:30am.

Yguana Cafe Restaurant, V. P. Gregorio XIV, 16 (☎033 81 09 30 97). Gorgeous but relatively down-to-earth natives sip cocktails next to their scooters. Happy Hour daily 5:30pm-9pm. Su brunch 12:30pm-4pm. Open daily 5:30pm-1am.

Blue Kleim, V. Vigevano, 9. MM2: Porta Genova is 3 blocks from Blue Kleim's unmistakable trendy funk. Dedicated to the author Irwin Kleim. Open Tu-Su 5pm-3am.

Fontanelle, on V. Navigli Pavese. Serves beer quite creatively. Drink up or risk spillage. Always crowded with a mix of locals and foreigners. Open daily 8pm-2am.

Cafe Capoverde, V. Leoncavallo, 16 (☎02 26 82 04 30). MM1/2: Loreto. Cocktails dominate, but decent food is available. *Primi* from L11,000/€5.70, pizza L12,000/€6.20. Open noon-3pm and 8pm-midnight.

Totem Pub (☎028 37 50 98), at V. Naviglio Pavese and V.E. Gola. For a more head-banging sort. Be prepared to hear anything from Metallica to reggae. Serves beer in huge mugs for L15,000/€7.75. Open daily 8:30pm-2:30am.

Rock: Hollywood, Corso Como, 15 (☎026 59 89 96). One of the only discos in the city to select from the crowd at the door. Hip-hop, house, and commercial music. Cover L25,000-30,000/€12.95-15.50. Open Tu-Su 10:30pm-4am.

Tunnel, V. Sammartini, 30 (☎02 66 71 13 70), near V. Giuseppe Bruscetti, bordering Stazione Centrale. Underground rock and various indie bands frequent this train tunnel converted into a bandshell. Cover L5000-15,000/€2.60-7.75. Hours vary.

Vista Mare Caffé (☎ 02 89 40 53 49), near the mouth of Corso Porta Ticinese. Free pizza bread. *Apperitivi* L3000/€1.55. Happy Hour (6:30-8:30pm) L5000/€2.60 discount per drink. Open daily 6:30pm-3am.

Kirribilly, V. Castel Morone, 7 (☎ 02 70 12 01 51). MM1: Porta Venezia. Cheery Australian pub with good beer. Try Cuban rum and kangaroo meat. M Happy Hour, Tu students. Open M-F noon-3pm and 6pm-3am, Sa-Su 6pm-3am.

New Magazine, V. Piceno, 3 (☎ 02 73 09 41). From Kirribilly, turn right and then left at Corso Independenza for this hoppin' student disco. Drinks L5000-9000/€2.60-4.65. Open Tu-Su 9:30pm-2:30am.

GAY BARS AND CLUBS

Le Lephante, V. Melzo, 22 (☎ 02 29 51 87 68). From MM2: Porta Venezia, walk up Corso Bueno Aires 3 blocks and turn right on V. Melzo. Across from Artdecothe. Mixed gay and straight crowd. Open Tu-Su 6:30pm-2am.

Cicip e Ciciap, V. Gorani, 9 (☎ 02 86 72 02). From MM1: Cairoli, take V.S. Giov. sul Muro which turns into V. Brisa. V. Gorani is the 2nd left. Attracts a women-only crowd. Open only Sa 8:30pm-3am.

One Way Club, V. Cavallotti, 204 (☎ 022 42 13 41). MM2: Sesto FS. Disco and leather. Membership card required. Open F and Sa 10:30pm-3:30am, Su 3:30-7pm.

▶ DAYTRIPS FROM MILAN

GENOA. Stroll by gorgeous *palazzia* on V. Garibaldi, and gaze at the fishies in the fabulous aquarium (see p. 638).

TURIN. Pay a visit to the home of both the Fiat auto-company, and one of Christianity's most famous relics, the Shroud of Turin (see p. 666).

MANTUA (MANTOVA)   ☎ 0376

Mantua owes its literary fame to its most famous son, the poet Virgil. Its grand *palazzi* and graceful churches are thanks to the Gonzaga family, who, after ascending to power in 1328, imported well-known artists to change Mantua's small-town image. Today, Mantua is a bustling city with easy passage to the surrounding lakes. Once the largest palace in Europe, the opulent ■**Palazzo Ducale,** towering over **Piazza Sordello,** also includes the Gothic **Magna Domus** (*duomo*) and **Palazzo del Capitano.** Inside, check out a breathtaking array of frescoes, gardens, and façades. Outside the *palazzo*, signs point to the **Castello di San Giorgio** (1390-1406), once a formidable fortress before being absorbed into the *palazzo* complex. (Open Tu-Su 8:45am-6:30pm. L12,000/€6.20, EU students L6000/€3.10, children and seniors free.) At the far south of the city, down V.P. Amedeo through P. Veneto and down Largo Parri, lies the opulent **Palazzo del Te,** built by Giulio Romano in 1534 as a suburban retreat for Federico II Gonzaga. It is widely considered the finest building in the Mannerist style. (☎ 0376 32 32 66. Open Tu-Su 9am-6pm, M 1-6pm. L12,000/€6.20, students and teens L8000/€4.15, under 11 free.) Just south of P. Sordello is the 11th-century Romanesque **Piazza delle Erbe;** opposite the *piazza* is Leon Alberti's **Chiesa di Sant'Andrea,** Mantua's greatest contribution to the Italian Renaissance. (*Piazza* open daily 10am-12:30pm and 2:30-6:30pm. Free. *Chiesa* open daily 8am-noon and 3-6:30pm. Free.) Walk from P. dell'Erbe to P. Broletto and then take V. Accademia to the end for the lovely **Teatro Scientifico (Bibiena),** one theater that's not modeled after Milan's La Scala. (☎ 0376 32 76 53. Open Tu-Su 9:30am-12:30pm and 3-6:30pm. L4000/€2.10, students L2000/€1.05.)

   Trains (☎ 0376 147 88 80 88) go from P. Don E. Leoni to Milan (2hr., 9 per day, L16,000/€8.30) and Verona (40min., every hr., L4100/€2.15). From the train station, head left on V. Solferino, through P.S. Francesco d'Assisi to V. Fratelli Bandiera, and right on V. Verdi for the **tourist office,** P. Mantegna, 6, next to Chiesa Sant'Andrea. (☎ 0376 32 82 53; fax 36 32 92. Open M-Sa 8:30am-12:30pm and 3-6pm.) Charming **Hotel ABC,** P. Don E. Leoni, 25, is opposite the station. (☎ 0376 32 33 47;

fax 32 23 29. Breakfast included. Singles L60,000-110,000/€31-56.85; doubles L90,000-150,000/€46.50-77.50; triples L150,000-200,000/€77.50-103.30.) **Antica Osteria ai Ranari,** V. Trieste, 11, down V. Pomponazzo near Porta Catena, specializes in regional dishes. (☎0376 32 84 31. *Primi* L8000-12,000/€4.15-6.20, *secondi* L12,000-18,000/€6.20-9.30. Cover L2000/€1.05. Closed for 3 weeks late July to early Aug. Open Tu-Su noon-2:30pm and 7-11pm.) **Postal Code:** 46100.

BERGAMO   ☎035

Bergamo's two sections reflect its colorful history: while the *città alta* (upper city) reveal its origins as a Venetian outpost, the *città bassa* (lower city) is a modern metropolis packed with Neoclassical buildings. **Via Pignolo,** in the *città bassa*, winds past a succession of handsome 16th- to 18th-century palaces. Turning left onto V.S. Tomaso and then right brings you to the astounding ▥**Galleria dell'Accademia Carrara,** which holds works by Titian, Rubens, Breughel, and van Dyck. (Open W-M 9:30am-12:30pm and 2:30-5:30pm. L10000/€5.20, under 18 and over 65 free, Su everyone free.) From the Galleria, the terraced **Via Noca** ascends to the medieval *città alta* through the 16th-century **Porta S. Agostino** gate. Stroll down V. Porta Dipinta to V. Gambito, which ends in **Piazza Vecchia,** an ensemble of medieval and Renaissance buildings flanked by restaurants and cafes at the heart of the *città alta*. Head through the archway flanking P. Vecchia to P. del Duomo, and see the fresco-laden **Cappella Colleoni.** (Open Mar.-Oct. Tu-Su 9am-12:30pm and 2-6:30pm; Nov.-Feb. 9am-12:30pm and 2:30-4:30pm. Free.) Immediately left of the Cappella Colleoni is the ▧**Basilica di Santa Maria Maggiore,** a 12th-century basilica with an ornate Baroque interior and tapestries depicting biblical scenes. (Open May-Sept. 9am-noon and 3-6pm, Sa-Su 8-10:30am and 3-6pm; Oct.-Apr. 9am-noon and 3-4:30pm, Sa-Su 8-10:30am and 3-6pm. Free.) Climb the **Torre Civica** (Civic Tower) for a marvelous view of Bergamo and the hills (L2000/€1.05).

The train station, bus station, and many budget hotels are in the città bassa. **Trains** (1hr., L7200/€3.75) and **buses** (L7500/€3.90) pull into P. Marconi from Milan. To get to the **tourist office,** V. Aquila Nera, 2, in the *città alta*, take bus #1a to the top of the *città alta*. (☎035 24 22 26; fax 24 29 94; www.apt.bergamo.it. Open daily 9am-12:30pm and 2-5:30pm.) To get from the train station to **Ostello della Gioventù di Bergamo (HI)**, V.G. Ferraris, 1, take bus #9 to "Comozzi," then take bus #14 to "Leonardo da Vinci," and walk up the hill. (☎/fax 035 36 17 24. Breakfast included. **HI members only.** Dorms L26,000/€13.45; singles L35,000/€18.10; doubles L60,000/€31.) **Locanda Caironi,** V. Torretta, 6B, off V. Gorgo Palazzo, is in a quiet residential neighborhood. Take bus #5 or 7 from V. Angelo Maj. (☎035 24 30 83. Singles L30,000/€15.50; doubles L55,000/€28.40. MC/V.) **Capolinea Bar and Ristorante,** V. Giacomo Quarenghi, 29, in the *città bassa* right off V. Zambonate, provides full meals from L15,000/€7.75. (☎035 32 09 81. Open Tu-Sa 6:30pm-3am, Su 7pm-3am. Kitchen closes at midnight.) In the *città alta*, chat at the communist cafe **Circolino Cooperativa Città Alta,** V.S. Agata, 19, while eating sandwiches, pizza, and salads for under L8000/€4.15. (☎035 21 57 41. Cover L1000/€0.55. Open Th-Tu 8:30am-3am). **Postal Code:** 24122.

ITALIAN RIVIERA (LIGURIA)

The Italian Riviera stretches 350km along the Mediterranean between France and Tuscany, forming the most famous and touristed area of the Italian coastline. Genoa divides the crescent-shaped strip into the **Riviera di Levante** ("rising sun") to the east and the **Riviera di Ponente** ("setting sun") to the west. The elegant coast beckons with lemon trees, almond blossoms, and turquoise seas. Especially lovely is the **Cinque Terre** area, just to the west of **La Spezia**.

▮ TRANSPORTATION

All the coastal towns are linked by the main **rail** line, which runs west to Ventimiglia (near the French border) and east to La Spezia (near Tuscany), but slow local trains can make short trips take hours. Frequent intercity **buses** pass through all major towns, and local buses run to inland hill-towns. **Boats** connect most resort towns. **Ferries** go from Genoa to Olbia, Sardinia and Palermo, Sicily.

GENOA (GENOVA)   ☎010

Genoa, city of grit and grandeur, has little in common with its resort neighbors. A Ligurian will tell you, *"Si deve conosceria per amaria"*—you have to know her to love her. If lacking in the laid-back intimacy and friendliness of a small-town resort, Genoa more than makes up for it in its rich trade and cultural history, which includes such luminaries as Christopher Columbus and Nicolò Paganini, and bewitching sights. Since falling into decline in the 18th century, modern Genoa has turned its attention away from industry to the restoration of its bygone grandeur.

▉ TRANSPORTATION. The **C. Columbo Internazionale** airport, in Sesti Ponente, services European destinations. Take **Volabus #100** from Stazione Brignole to the airport (every 30min., L4000/€2.10) and get off at Aeroporto. Most visitors arrive at one of Genoa's two **train stations: Stazione Principe**, in P. Acquaverde, or **Stazione Brignole**, in P. Verdi. **Trains** go to Rome (5hr., 14 per day, L44,500/€23) and Turin (2hr., 19 per day, L15,900/€8.25). **AMT buses** (☎010 558 24 14) run throughout the city. One-way tickets (L5000/€0.80) are valid for 1½hr.; all-day tourist passes L5000/€2.60. **Ferries** depart from the Ponte Assereto arm of the port; buy tickets at **Stazione Marittima** in the port.

▉▉ ORIENTATION AND PRACTICAL INFORMATION. To get to the center of town, **Piazza de Ferrari**, from Stazione Principe, take **Via Balbi** to **Via Cairoli**, which becomes **Via Garibaldi**, and turn right on **Via XXV Aprile** at P. delle Fontane Marose. From Stazione Brignole, turn right onto **Via Fiume**, and right onto **Via XX Settembre**. Or, take bus #19, 20, 30, 32, 35, or 41 from Stazione Principe or bus #19 or 40 from Stazione Brignole to **Piazza de Ferrari** in the center of town. The **centro storico** (historic center) contains many of Genoa's monuments. Pick up a map (L7000/€3.65) at any newsstand. The **APT tourist office** is on Porto Antico, in Palazzina S. Maria. From the aquarium, walk toward the complex of buildings to the left. (☎010 24 87 11. Open daily 9:30am-1pm and 3:30-6pm.) Log on at **Internet Village**, at V. Brigata Bisagno and Corso Buenos Aires, across from P. Vittoria. (L15,000/€7.75 per hr. Open M-Sa 9am-1pm and 3-7pm.) **Postal Code:** 16121.

▉▉ ACCOMMODATIONS AND FOOD. Budget lodgings in the *centro storico* and near the port rent rooms by the hour—try the hostel or around Stazione Brignole for more refined establishments. **Ostello per la Gioventù (HI),** V. Costanzi, 120, has a cafeteria, TV, and a view of the city far below. From Stazione Principe, take bus #35 and tell the driver you want to transfer to #40 at V. Napoli; take #40 to the hostel. From Stazione Brignole, pick up bus #40 (every 15min.) and ask to be let off at the *ostello*. (☎/fax 010 242 24 57. Breakfast included. Reception 7-9am and 3:30pm-12:30am. Curfew 12:30am. **HI members only;** HI card available at hostel. Dorms L25,000/€12.95.) **Albergo Carola,** V. Gropallo, 4/12, has elegant rooms overlooking a garden. From Stazione Brignole, turn right on V. de Amicis, and continue into P. Brignole. Turn right when facing Albergo Astoria, and walk 15m. 2 flights up from Albergo Argentina. (☎010 839 13 40. Singles L45,000/€23.25; doubles L65,000/€34, with bath 75,000/€38.75.) **Hotel Balbi,** V. Balbi, 21/3, offers large, ornate rooms. (☎/fax 010 25 23 62. Breakfast L7000/€3.65. With *Let's Go:* singles L40,000/€20.65; doubles L80,000/€41.35, with bath L100,000/€51.65; triples and quads add 30% per person. AmEx/MC/V.) **Camping** is popular; turn to the tourist office for info, as many campgrounds are booked solid. To reach **Villa Doria,** V. al Campeggio Villa Doria, 15, take the train or buses #1, 2, or 3 from P. Caricamento to Pegli, then walk or transfer to bus #93 up V. Vespucci. (☎010 696 96 00. Electricity and showers free. L10,000/€5.20 per person plus L10,000-13,000/€5.20-6.75 per tent. 1- to 4-person bungalows L50,000-90,000/€25.85-46.50.) **Trattoria da Maria,** V. Testa d'Oro, 14r, off V. XXV Aprile, has a new menu every day, with the *pranzo turistico* (set-price lunch) for L13,000/€6.75. (☎010 58 10 80 Open Su-F noon-2:30pm and 7-9:30pm.)

⚄♫ SIGHTS AND ENTERTAINMENT. Genoa boasts a multitude of *palazzi* built by its famous merchant families. These are best seen along **Via Garibaldi**, on the edge of *centro storico*, and **Via Balbi**, in the heart of the university quarter. The 17th-century **Palazzo Reale**, V. Balbi, 10, 10min. west of V. Garibaldi, is filled with Rococo rooms bathed in gold and upholstered in red velvet. (Open M-Tu 8:15am-1:45pm, W-Su 8:15am-7:15pm. L8000/€4.15, ages 18-25 L4000/€2.30, under 18 and seniors free.) Follow V. Balbi through P. della Nunziata and continue to L. Zecca, where V. Cairoli leads to **Via Garibaldi**, the most impressive street in Genoa, bedecked with elegant *palazzi* that once earned it the names "Golden Street" and "Street of Kings." The **Galleria di Palazzo Bianco**, V. Garibaldi, 11, exhibits Ligurian, Dutch, and Flemish paintings. Across the street, the 17th-century **Galleria Palazzo Rosso**, V. Garibaldi, 18, has magnificent furnishings in a lavishly frescoed interior. (Both open Tu and Th-F 9am-1pm, W and Sa 9am-7pm, Su 10am-6pm. L6000/€3.10 each, L10,000/€5.20 together. Su everyone free.) The **Villetta Di Negro**, on the hill further down V. Garibaldi as it changes to Salita di S. Caterina, contains waterfalls, grottoes, and terraced gardens. From P. de Ferrari, take V. Boetto to P. Matteotti for the ornate **Chiesa del Gesù.** (Open daily 7:30am-noon and 4-6:30pm. Free.) Head past the Chiesa del Gesù down V. di Porta Soprana to V. Ravecca to reach the medieval twin-towered **Porta Soprana,** the supposed boyhood home of **Christopher Columbus.** Continue further down V. Ravecca to reach the **Museo dell'Architettura e Scultura Ligure,** which features surviving art pieces from Genoa's history. (Open Tu-Sa 9am-7pm, Su 9am-12:30pm. L6000/€3.10.) Off V.S. Lorenzo lies the **San Lorenzo Duomo,** a church in existence since the 9th century, which boasts a striped Gothic façade with a copiously decorated main entrance and 9th-century carved lions. (Open M-Sa 8am-7pm, Su 7am-7pm. Free.) The **centro storico,** the eerie, beautiful, and sometimes dangerous historical center, is a mass of winding and confusing streets bordered by the port, V. Garibaldi, and P. Ferrari. Due to a extremely dangerous night scene, the center is only safe during weekdays when stores are open. It is, however, home to some of Genoa's most memorable monuments, including the **duomo** and the medieval **Torre Embriaci.** Once you're back on P. Matteotti, go down V.S. Lorenzo toward the water, turn left on V. Chiabrera and left on V. di Mascherona to reach the **Chiesa S. Maria di Castello,** a labyrinth of chapels, courtyards, cloisters, and cruxifices. (Open daily 9am-noon and 3:30-6:30pm. Free.) Kids and ocean-lovers will adore the massive **aquarium,** on Porto Antico to the right of the APT tourist office. (Open M-F 9:30am-7pm, Sa-Su 9:30am-8pm; in summer Th until 11pm. Nov. 1-Jan. 28 closed M. L22,000/€11.40.)

FINALE LIGURE   ☎019

A beachside plaque proclaims the town of Finale Ligure the place for "*Il riposo del popolo,*" (the people's rest). Whether one's idea of *riposo* involves bodysurfing in the choppy waves near Torrente Porra, browsing through Finalmarina's chic boutiques, or scaling your way up Finalborgo's looming 15th-century Castello di San Giovanni, the *popolo* have many options. The city is divided into three sections: **Finalpia** to the east, **Finalmarina** in the center, and **Finalborgo** further inland. The train station and most sights are in Finalmarina. If you're in the mood for sand and sun, skip the packed free beaches in town and walk east along V. Aurelia through the first tunnel and turn right to a less populated **free beach,** where you can relax to the sounds of waves crashing against the craggy overhanging cliffs. For a closer view of the cliffs, climb the tough trail to the ruins of **Castel Govone** for a spectacular view of Finale. Enclosed within ancient walls, **Finalborgo,** the historic quarter of Finale Ligure proper, is a 1km walk or short bus ride up V. Bruneghi from the station. Past the Porto Reale, the **Chiostro di Santa Caterina,** a 14th-century edifice, houses the **Museo Civico del Finale,** dedicated to Ligurian history. (☎019 69 00 20. Open Tu-Sa 10am-noon and 3-6pm, Su 9am-noon. Free.) **Pilade,** V. Garibaldi, 67, features live jazz on Friday nights. (☎019 69 22 20. Open daily 10am-2am; in winter closed Th.) The towns near Finale Ligure are also worth exploring. SAR **buses** run from the train station to **Borgo Verezzi** (10min., 8 per day, L1800/€0.95).

ITALY

Trains leave from P. Vittorio Veneto for Genoa (1hr., every hr., L6900/€3.60). The IAT **tourist office**, V.S. Pietro, 14, gives out free maps. (☎019 68 10 19; fax 68 18 04. Open M-Sa 9am-12:30pm and 3:30-7pm, Su 9am-noon.) ◼**Castello Wuillerman (HI)**, on V. Generale Caviglia, is well worth the hike. From the station, take a left onto V. Mazzini, which becomes the narrow V. Torino, turn left on V. degli Ulivi, and trudge up the daunting steps. (☎/fax 019 69 05 15. Breakfast and sheets included. Reception 7-10am and 5-10pm. Curfew 11:30pm. No phone reservations. Open mid-Mar. to mid-Oct. L20,000/€10.35.) To get to the convenient **Albergo Oasi**, at V.S. Cagna, 25, veer left on V. Brunenghi from the station, walk through the underpass on your right to V. Silla and walk up the hill; it's on your left. (☎019 69 17 17; fax 681 59 89. Open Easter-Sept. Singles €23.25/L45,000; doubles L90,000/€46.50, extra bed L45,000/€23.25.) **Albergo Carla**, V. Colombo, 44, offers a bar and a restaurant. (☎019 69 22 85; fax 68 19 65. Breakfast L7000/€3.65. Singles L45,000/€23.25; doubles L75,000/€38.25. Pension required July-Sept. Half pension L50,000/€25.85, full pension L82,000/€42.35. AmEx/MC/V.) Sunbathe in the tranquil gardens of the **Hotel Orchidea** at V. XXV Aprile, 15. (☎019 69 05 26; fax 69 05 26. Breakfast included. Reserve ahead in the summer. Open Easter-Sept. Doubles L90,000-100,000/€46.50-51.65; triples L130,000/€67.15. Full pension required Aug. L70,000-80,000/€36.15-41.35.) **Camping Del Mulino**, on V. Castelli, has a restaurant and mini-market on the premises. Take the Calvisio bus from the station to the Boncardo Hotel, and follow the brown and yellow signs to the campsite entrance. (☎019 60 16 69. Laundry L8000/€4.15. Reception Apr.-Sept. 8am-8pm. L8000/€4.15 per person, L8000/€4.15 per tent.) Cheap restaurants lie inland along **Via Rossi** and **Via Roma. Ferinata e Vino**, V. Roma, 25, serves up homestyle cooking. (☎019 692 562. *Primi* L9000-14,000/€4.65-7.25; *secondi* L12,000-18,000/€6.20-9.30. Open daily 12:30-2pm and 7:30-9pm.) **Simpatia Crai supermarket** is at V. Brunenghi, 2a. (Open M-Sa 8am-12:30pm and 4-6:30pm.)

CAMOGLI
☎0185

Postcard-perfect Camogli throbs with color. Peach houses crowd the hilltop, lively red and turquoise boats bob in the water, and bright umbrellas dot the dark stone beaches. To reach the **beach**, turn left down the steep stairs 100m away from the station, then turn right off V. Garibaldi into the alley. If you tire of the beach and boardwalk, ferry or snorkeling trips are fun (but more costly) diversions. **Band B Diving Center**, V.S. Fortunato, 11/13, off P. Colombo, offers 10-person boat capacities, 18 immersion spots along the coast, and three excursions daily for scuba diving and snorkeling. (☎0185 77 27 51. Open daily 9am-7pm. Scuba L65,000-100,000/€33.60-51.65, snorkeling L20,000/€10.35 per person.) **Trains** run on the Genoa-La Spezia line to: Genoa (20min., 32 per day, L2700/€1.40); La Spezia (1½hr., 21 per day, L6400/€3.30); Santa Margherita (10min., 24 per day, L1900/€1). Golfo Paradiso **ferries**, V. Scalo, 3 (☎0185 77 20 91), near P. Colombo, go to Portofino (Sa-Su only, L14,000/€7.25, round-trip L20,000/€10.35) and Cinque Terre (L20,000/€10.35, round-trip L33,000/€17.05); buy tickets at the dock. Go right from the station to the **tourist office**, V. XX Settembre, 33, for help finding rooms. (☎0185 77 10 66. Open M-Sa 9am-12:30pm and 3:30-7pm, Su 9am-1pm.) Exit the station and walk downstairs to the right to reach the **Albergo La Camogliese**, V. Garibaldi, 55. (☎0185 77 14 02; fax 7740 24. Reserve ahead. Singles L70,000-110,000/€36.15-56.85; doubles L120,000-140,000/€62-72.30. 10% *Let's Go* discount with cash. AmEx/MC/V.)

SANTA MARGHERITA LIGURE
☎0185

Santa Margherita Ligure led a calm existence as a fishing village until the early 20th century, when Hollywood stars and National Geographic fell for its charms. Today, the shores sparkle with glamour and glitz, but the serenity of the town's early days still lingers. If lapping ocean waves don't invigorate your spirit, try the holy water in the seashell basins at the **Basilica di Santa Margherita**, at P. Caprera. **Trains** along the Pisa-Genoa line go from P. Federico Raoul Nobili, at the top of V. Roma, to: Genoa (40min., 2-3 per hr., L3600/€1.90) and La Spezia (2 per hr., L6900/€3.60) via Cinque Terre (1.5hr., L6000/€3.10). **Tigullio buses** (☎0185 28 88 34) go from P. Vittorio

Veneto to Camogli (30min., every hr., L2000/€1.05) and Portofino (20min., 3 per hr., L1700/€0.90). **Tigullio ferries**, V. Palestro, 8/1b (☎0185 28 15 98), leave from docks at P. Martiri della Libertà for Cinque Terre (1 per day; L25,000-30,000/€12.95-15.50, round-trip L35,000-40,000/€18.10-20.65) and Portofino (every hr.; L6000/€3.10, round-trip L10,000/€5.20). Turn right from the train station on V. Roma, turn left on Corso Rainusso, and take a hard right onto V. XXV Aprile to find the **tourist office**, V. XXV Aprile, 2b. (☎0185 28 74 85. Open M-Sa 9am-12:30pm and 3-6pm, Su 9:30am-12:30pm.) **Hotel Nuova Riviera**, V. Belvedere, 10, has spacious rooms. (☎0185 28 74 03. Breakfast included. Singles L100,000/€51.65; doubles L170,000/€87.80; triples L220,000/€113.65. MC/V.) ◪**La Piadineria and Creperia**, V. Giuncheto, 5, off P. Martiri della Libertà, is a subtly hip nook-in-the-wall that serves 30 types of *piadine* (huge sandwiches; L9000-10,000/€4.60-5.20) until late. (Open daily 6pm-midnight.)

PORTOFINO ☎0185

Secluded and exclusive, tiny Portofino—a great daytrip from Santa Margherita—has long been a playground for the financially advantaged. Yachts may fill the harbor and chic boutiques line its streets, but both princes and paupers can enjoy the shore's curves and tiny bay. A 1hr. walk along the ocean road offers the chance to scout out small rocky **beaches.** The shore at **Paraggi** (where the bus stops) is the area's only sandy beach, and only a small strip is free. In town, follow the signs uphill from the bay to escape to the cool interior of the **Chiesa di San Giorgio.** A few minutes up the road, outside the **castle,** is a serene garden with sea views. (Open daily in summer 10am-6pm; off-season 10am-5pm. L3000/€1.55.) To get to town, take the **bus** to Portofino Mare. From P. Martiri della Libertà, **Tigullio buses** go to Santa Margherita (3 per hr., L1700/€0.90); buy tickets at the green kiosk in P. Martiri della Libertà. **Ferries** go from Portofino to Santa Margherita (every hr. 9am-7pm, L6000/€3.10) and Camogli (2 per day, L13,000/€6.75). The **tourist office**, V. Roma, 35, is toward the waterfront from the bus stop. (☎0185 26 90 24. Open in summer daily 9:30am-1:30pm and 2-7pm; in winter 9:30am-12:30pm and 2:30-5:30pm.)

LA SPEZIA ☎0187

A departure point for Corsica (see p. 362) and an unavoidable transport hub for Cinque Terre, La Spezia draws its own share of tourists, with regal palms lining its promenade and parks laden with citrus trees. La Spezia lies on the Genoa-Pisa **train** line. **Happy Lines** (☎0187 77 09 00), with a ticket kiosk on V. Italia, sends ferries to Corsica (round-trip L124,000/€64.05, low-season L84,000/€43.38). **Navigazione Golfo dei Poeti**, V. Mazzini, 21, has ferries to: Capraia (5hr., July-Aug., round-trip L70,000-80,000/€36.15-41.35); each Cinque Terre village and Portenvenero (full day, Easter-Nov. 4, round-trip L33,000/€17.05); Elba (3½hr., July-Aug. W and Sa, round-trip L80,000/€41.35.). The **tourist office** (☎0187 77 09 00) is at the port at V. Mazzini, 45. To reach **Albergo Terminus**, V. Paleocapa, 21, turn left out of the train station. (☎0187 77 09 34 36; fax 70 00 79. Singles L40,000/€20.65, with bath L55,000/€28.40; doubles L65,000/€33.60, L90,000/€46.50; triples L70,000/€36.15.)

CINQUE TERRE ☎0187

The five bright fishing villages of Cinque Terre cling to a stretch of terraced hillsides and steep crumbling cliffs, while a dazzling turquoise sea laps against their shores. You can hike through all five—**Monterosso, Vernazza, Corniglia, Manarola,** and **Riomaggiore**—in a few hours.

▟ TRANSPORTATION

Trains: The towns lie on the Genoa-La Spezia (Pisa) line. From the station on V. Fegina, in **Monterosso,** trains run to: **Florence** (3½hr., every hr., L14,500/€7.50) via Pisa; **Genoa** (1½hr., every hr., L7000/€3.65); **La Spezia** (20min., every 30min., L2300/€1.20); **Pisa** (2½hr., every hr., L8500/€4.40); **Rome** (7hr., every 2hr., L51,500/€26.60). Frequent trains connect the 5 towns (5-20min., every 50min., L1700-2300/€0.90-1.20). Schedules available at the tourist office. The 24hr. **Cinque Terre Tourist**

Ticket (L5500/€2.85), for unlimited trips between towns, is available at the 5 train stations—ask at the ticket window.

Ferries: Navigazione Golfo dei Poet (☎0187 96 76 76), in front of the **IAT** office at the port (on the old part of town) goes to: **Manarola** and **Riomaggiore** (6 per day, round-trip L15,000/€7.75); **Portovenere** (1hr., L18,000/€9.30, round-trip L30,000/€15.50); **Vernazza** (5 per day, L5000/€2.60, round-trip L8000/€4.15).

Taxis: ☎0335 61 65 842 and 0335 616 58 45.

✦🛈 ORIENTATION AND PRACTICAL INFORMATION

From **Monterosso,** the most central and developed of the villages, the four others are easily accessible by train as well as by foot, ferry, and kayak, depending on your inclination and stamina. **Listings are for Monterosso unless otherwise indicated.**

Tourist Office: Pro Loco, V. Fegina, 38 (☎0187 81 75 06). Below the train station. Open Apr.-Oct. M-Sa 10am-noon and 3-5:30pm, Su 10am-12:30pm. In **Riomaggiore,** an office in the train station (☎0187 92 06 33) provides info on trails, hotels, and excursions. Open June-Sept. daily 10am-6pm.

Currency Exchange: At the post office. For traveler's checks transactions, head to **Banca Carige,** V. Roma, 69.

Boat Rental: Along the beach. Pedal boats L15,000-17,000/€7.75-8.80 per hr.; kayaks L10,000-15,000/€5.20-7.75 per hr., L50,000/€25.85 per day; motorboats L30,000-45,000/€15.50-23.25 per hr., L150,000-220,000/€77.50-113.65 per day.

Emergency: ☎113.

Police: Carabinieri ☎112 or 0187 81 75 24; Riomaggiore ☎0187 92 01 12.

Pharmacy: V. Fegina, 44, under the train station. Open M-Sa 9am-12:30pm and 4-8pm, Su 9:30am-12:30pm and 4-7:30pm.

First Aid: Guardia Medica ☎0187 81 76 87; Riomaggiore ☎0187 80 09 73; Manarola ☎0187 92 07 66; Vernazza ☎0187 82 10 84.

Internet Access: The Net, V.V. Emanuele, 55 (☎0187 81 72 88). L4000/€2.10 for 1st 15min., L2000/€1.05 for each 10min. after.

Post Office: V. Loreto, 73 (☎0187 81 83 94). Open M-Sa 8am-1:30pm. Fermo posta, telephone cards. **Postal Code:** 19016.

🛌 ACCOMMODATIONS

No matter the length of your visit, reserve at least several weeks in advance. If you're still looking for a room when you arrive, gamble on the cheaper and more plentiful rooms in Riomaggiore, Monterosso, or Vernazza. Private rooms *(affitta-camere)* are the most plentiful and economical options in Cinque Terre.

▨ **Albergo Della Gioventù-Ostello "Cinque Terre,"** V.B. Riccobaldi, 21 (☎0187 92 02 15; fax 92 02 18), in Manarola. Turn right from the train station and go up the hill. Sheets and 5min. shower included. Breakfast L5000/€2.60. Reception daily 7am-10am and 5pm-1am. Curfew in summer 1am, in winter midnight. Dorms L30,000/€15.50 in high season; quads with bath L120,000/€62. AmEx/MC/V.

Hotel Souvenir, V. Gioberti, 24 (☎0187 81 75 95), in Monterosso. Breakfast L10,000/€5.20. Quiet family-run hotel with 30 beds and outdoor garden. Dorms L70,000/€36.15, students L60,000/€31.

Il Villaggio Marino "Europa," (☎0187 81 22 79; fax 70 21 43), in Corniglia. Turn right from the station. June-Sept. by the week only. Nov.-Mar. L800,000/€413.20 per week for 4 people; Apr.-Oct. L150,000/€77.50 per day for 4 people; L500,000/€258.25 for 4 days; L600,000/€309.90 per week.

🍴 FOOD

If you're on a tight budget in Cinque Terre, consider romantic picnics: wash your beach- or cliff-side meal down with the locally made delicious *sciacchetrà* or the cheaper yet equally good *Cinque Terre* white wine. Pick up some of the basics for your picnic lunch at **Superconad Margherita**, at P. Matteotti, 9, in Monterosso. (Open June-Sept. M-Sa 8am-1pm and 5-7:30pm, Su 8am-1pm.)

FAST, V. Roma, 13 (☎0187 81 71 64), in Monterosso. Known as *La Casa dei Panini Cantanti* (The House of the Singing Sandwiches). Large sandwiches start at L6000/ €3.10. Open daily 10am-2am; in winter Tu-Su 10am-2am.

Focacceria Il Frantoio, V. Gioberti, 1 (☎0187 81 83 33), in Monterosso. The wood-burning oven bakes every kind of *focaccia* imaginable. Great place to grab food for a hike. Slices L2500-3500/€1.30-1.85. Open F-W 9am-1:30pm and 5-7:30pm.

👁 🎵 SIGHTS AND ENTERTAINMENT

Hikes between the five towns are a superb way to explore and acquaint oneself with Cinque Terre. The distance between Monterosso and Riomaggiore can be covered in about five hours. The best and most challenging hike is from Monterosso to Vernazza (1½hr.), while the trail between Vernazza and Corniglia (2hr.) passes through some of the area's most spectacular scenery. Walk the leisurely **Via dell'Amore** (20min.) to the #2 hike at Manarola's Punta Bonfiglio; follow it to the end or turn onto #7 from Manarola to Corniglia, uphill to the highway. The highway rejoins the trail into Vernazza. To avoid scaling rocks, start at Riomaggiore and end with Vernazza or Monterosso. It's always best to start in the morning to avoid the scorching sun. If you ever tire, just hop in the train and return to your base town. Private beaches dominate most of the Cinque Terre coastline. Use of most of these beaches will cost you L3000-5000/€1.55-2.60 just to enter. The largest **free beach** lies directly below the train station; get there early to stake your claim. To add character to your sunbathing experience, spread out on the boulders in the rocky coves of Manarola, Corniglia, and Riomaggiore. The more historical offerings of Cinque Terre include the **Convento dei Cappuccini** (1618-22), which lies on a hill in the center of Monterosso and contains an impressive crucifixion by Flemish master Anthony van Dyck, who sojourned here during his most productive years. (Open daily 9am-noon and 4-7pm.) In Vernazza, walk up the staircase to the left of P. Marconi, to reach the **Castello Doria,** the remains of an 11th-century castle, and its spectacular view. (Open daily 10am-6:30pm. L2000/€1.05.)

EMILIA-ROMAGNA

Go to Florence, Venice, and Rome to sightsee, come to Emilia-Romagna to eat. Italy's wealthy wheat- and dairy-producing region covers the fertile plains of the Po River Valley, and celebrates the finest culinary traditions on the peninsula. The Romans originally settled here, but the towns later fell under the rule of great Renaissance families whose names adorn every *palazzo* and *piazza* in the region.

BOLOGNA   ☎051

Bright façades line the cobblestone roads that twist by churches, but the city's appeal extends far beyond aesthetics. Blessed with prosperity and Europe's oldest university, which counts Dante, Petrarch, and Copernicus among its graduates, Bologna has developed an open-minded atmosphere with strong minority and gay political activism. The city also prides itself on a great culinary heritage.

🚆 TRANSPORTATION. Bologna is a rail hub for all major Italian cities and the Adriatic coast. **Trains** leave the northern tip of the walled city for: Florence (1½hr., every 2hr., L8200-13,500/€4.25-7); Milan (3hr., 2-3 per hr., L18,000/€9.30); Rome (4hr., 1-2 per hr., L35,000/€18.10); Venice (2hr., every hr., L14,000/€7.25). Arrive during the day, as the area near the station is not the safest.

ITALY

EAT YOUR HEART OUT, CHEF BOYARDEE in Italy, the desecration of pasta is a mortal sin. Pasta must be chosen correctly and cooked *al dente* (firm, literally "to the tooth"). To avoid embarrassment, get to know the basics. The *spaghetti* family includes all variations that require twirling, from hollow cousins *bucatini* and *maccheroni* to the more delicate *capellini*. Flat *spaghetti* include *fettuccini*, *taglierini*, and *tagliatelle*. Short pasta tubes can be *penne* (cut diagonally and occasionally *rigate*, or ribbed), *sedani* (curved), *rigatoni* (wider), or *cannelloni* (usually stuffed). *Fusilli* (corkscrews), *farfalle* (butterflies or bow-ties), and *ruote* (wheels) are fun as well as functional. Don't be alarmed if you see pastry displays labeled "pasta"; the Italian word refers to anything made of dough.

🛈 **PRACTICAL INFORMATION.** Buses #25 and 30 run between the train station and the historic center at **Piazza Maggiore** (L1800/€0.95). The **tourist office**, P. Maggiore 6, is next to the Palazzo Comunale. (☎051 23 96 60; fax 23 14 54; www.comune.bologna.it. Open M-Sa 9am-1pm and 2:30-7pm.) Check **email** at **Crazy Bull Café**, V. Montegrappa, 11/e, off V. dell'Indipendenza near P. Maggiore. (L9000/€4.65 per hr. Student discounts. Open Sept.-July Tu-Sa 10am-2am, Su 7:30pm-2am.)

🛏️ **ACCOMMODATIONS AND FOOD.** The sparklingly clean **Albergo Panorama**, V. Livraghi, 1, 4th fl., has a prime location. Follow V. Ugo Bassi from P. Maggiore and take the third left. (☎051 22 18 02; fax 26 63 60. Singles L85,000/€43.90; doubles L110,000/€56.85; triples L140,000/€72.30; quads L160,000/€82.65. AmEx/MC/V.) **Ostello due Torre San Sisto (HI)**, V. Viadagola, 5, is off V. San Donato, in the Località di San Sisto, 6km from the center of town. Walk down V. dell'Indipendenza from the station, turn right on V. della Mille, and take bus #93 from across the street to "San Sisto." (☎/fax 051 50 18 10. Breakfast included. Reception 7am-midnight. Lockout 10am-3:30pm. Curfew midnight. Dorms L23,000/€11.90; nonmembers L5000/€2.60 extra. Family rooms L24,000-26,000/€12.40-13.45.) For the clean **Pensione Marconi**, V. Marconi, 22, turn right from the train station and then turn left on V. Amendola, which becomes V. Marconi. (☎051 26 28 32. Singles L60,000/€31, with bath L75,000/€38.75; doubles L95,000/€49.10, L120,000/€62; triples L126,000/€65.10, L160,000/€82.65; quads L148,000/€76.45, L180,000/€93.)

Don't leave without sampling Bologna's signature *spaghetti alla bolognese*. Scout **Via Augusto Righi, Via Piella**, and **Via Saragozza** for traditional *trattorie*. A **PAM supermarket**, V. Marconi, 26, is by the intersection of V. Riva di Reno. (Open M-W and F-Sa 7:45am-7:45pm, Th 7:45am-1pm.) Locals chat over regional dishes like *tagliatelle* at **Trattoria Da Maro**, V. Broccaindosso, 71b, between Strada Maggiore and V.S. Vitale. (☎051 22 73 04. *primi* L9000-11,000/€4.65-5.70, *secondi* L10,000-13,000/€5.20-6.75. Cover L3000/€1.55. Open M 8-10:15pm, Tu-Sa noon-2:30pm and 8-10:15pm.) Savor hearty food in **Antica Trattoria Roberto Spiga**, V. Broccaindosso, 21a. (☎051 23 00 63. *Primi* L10,000/€5.20, *secondi* L10,000-16,000/€5.20-8.30. Cover L2000/€1.05. Open Sept.-July M-Sa noon-3pm and 7:30-10pm.) **Il Gelatauro**, V.S. Vitale, 82/b, uses only fresh fruit to create delicious sorbets. Cones start at L3000/€1.55. (Open June-Aug. daily 11am-11pm; Sept.-May Tu-Su 11am-11pm.)

📷 **SIGHTS AND ENTERTAINMENT.** Forty kilometers of porticoed buildings line the streets of Bologna in a mix of Gothic, Renaissance, and Baroque styles. The tranquil **Piazza Maggiore** flaunts both Bologna's historical and modern wealth. The cavernous Gothic interior of the city's *duomo*, **Basilica di San Petronio**, was meant to be larger than Rome's St-Peter's, but the jealous Church ordered that the funds be used instead to build the nearby Palazzo Archiginnasio. It hosted both the Council of Trent (when it wasn't meeting in Trent) and the 1530 ceremony in which Pope Clement VII gave Italy to the German king Charles V. The pomp and pageantry of the exercises at the church allegedly inspired a disgusted Martin Luther to reform religion in Germany. (Open M-Sa 7:15am-1pm and 2-6pm, Su 7:30am-1pm and 2-6:30pm. Sacristy open daily 8am-noon and 4-6pm.) The **Palazzo Archiginnasio**, behind

S. Petronio, was once a university building; the upstairs theater was built in 1637 to teach anatomy to students. (☎051 23 64 88. Open M-F 9am-7pm, Sa 9am-2pm. Theater open M-Sa 9am-1pm. Both closed 2 weeks in Aug. Free.) On the northern side of P. Maggiore is the **Palazzo de Podestà**, remodeled by Fioravanti's son Aristotle, who later designed Moscow's Kremlin. Next to P. Maggiore, **Piazza del Nettuno** contains Giambologna's famous 16th-century fountain, *Neptune and Attendants*. From P. Nettuno, go down V. Rizzoli to **Piazza Porta Ravegana**, where seven streets converge to form Bologna's medieval quarter. Two towers that constitute the city's emblem rise magnificently from the *piazza*; you can climb the **Torre degli Asinelli.** (Open daily May-Aug. 9am-6pm; Sept.-Apr. 9am-5pm. L5000/€2.60.) From V. Rizzoli, follow V.S. Stefano to **Piazza Santo Stefano,** where four of the original seven churches of the Romanesque **Piazza Santo Stefano Church Complex** remain. Bologna's patron saint, San Petronio, lies buried under the pulpit of the **Chiesa di San Sepolcro.** (Open daily 9am-noon and 3:30-6pm.) Take Strada Maggiore to P. Aldrovandi to reach the remarkably intact **Chiesa di Santa Mari dei Seru,** whose columns support an unusual combination of arches and ribbed vaulting. The **Pinacoteca Nazionale,** V. delle Belle Arti, 56, off V. Zamboni, traces the history of Bolognese artists. (☎051 24 32 22. Open Tu-Sa 9am-1:50pm, Su 9am-12:50pm. L8000/€4.15.)

Bologna's hip student population ensures raucous nighttime fun. Call ahead for hours and covers. **Cluricaune,** V. Zamboni, 18/b, is an Irish bar packed with students who flock to its pool table and dart boards. (☎051 26 34 19. Pints L8000/€4.15. Happy Hour 5-8:30pm; drinks L3000/€1.55. Open M-Th 4pm-2am, F-Sa 4pm-2:30am, Su 11:30pm-2am.) **Cassero,** in the Porta Saragozza, is a lively gay bar packed with men and women. (☎051 644 69 02. Open daily 10pm-2am.)

PARMA   ☎0521

Parma maintains an artistic and culinary elegance from its rich past, while vibrating with youthful energy from the nearby university. From P. Garibaldi, follow Strada Cavour toward the train station, and take the third right on Strada al Duomo to reach the 11th-century Romanesque **duomo,** in P. del Duomo, which is filled with masterpieces. Most spectacular is the dome, where Correggio's *Virgin* ascends to a golden heaven in a spiral of white robes, pink *putti*, and blue sky. The pink-and-white marble **baptistery** was built between the Romanesque and Gothic periods. (*Duomo* open daily 9am-noon and 3-7pm. Baptistery open daily 9am-12:30pm and 3-7pm. L5000/€2.60, students L3000/€1.55.) Behind the *duomo* is the frescoed dome of the **Chiesa di San Giovanni Evangelista,** P.S. Giovanni, designed by Correggio. (Open daily 9am-noon and 3-7pm.) From P. del Duomo, follow Strada al Duomo across Strada Cavour, walk one block down Strada Piscane, and cross P. della Pace to reach the 17th-century **Palazzo della Pilotta,** Parma's artistic treasure chest, which houses the **Galleria Nazionale.** (Open daily 9am-2pm. L8000/€4.15.)

Parma is on the Bologna-Milan rail line. **Trains** go from P. Carlo Alberto della Chiesa to: Bologna (1hr., 2 per hr., L7700/€4); Florence (3hr., 7 per day, L26,300/€13.60); Milan (1½hr., every hr., L11,600/€6). Walk left from the station, turn right on V. Garibaldi, and turn left on V. Melloni to reach the **tourist office,** V. Melloni, 1b. (☎0521 21 88 89; fax 23 47 35. Open M-Sa 9am-7pm, Su 9am-1pm.) **Supermarket 2B** is at V. XXII Luglio, 27c. (Open M-W and F-Sa 8:30am-1pm and 4:30-8pm, Th 8:30am-1pm.) From the station, take bus #9 (L1300/€0.70) and get off when the bus turns left on V. Martiri della Libertà for the **Ostello Cittadella (HI),** on V. Passo Buole, in a corner of a 15th-century fortress. (☎0521 96 14 34. 3-night max. stay. Lockout 9:30am-5pm. Curfew 11pm. Open Apr.-Oct. **HI members only.** Dorms L16,000/€8.30. **Camping** open Apr.-Oct. L11,150/€5.75 per person, L21,000/€10.85 per site.) **Albergo Leon d'Oro,** V. Fratti, 4, off V. Garibaldi, is 2 blocks from the train station. (☎0521 77 31 82. Reserve ahead. Singles L55,000/€28.40; doubles L85,000/€43.90. AmEx/MC/V.) Look for fragrant Parma cuisine along **Via Garibaldi. Le Sorelle Picchi,** Strada Farini, 27, near P. Garibaldi, is a traditional *salumeria* and *trattorie*. (☎0521 23 35 28. *Primi* L10,000-11,000/€5.20-5.70, *secondi* L12,000-14,000/€6.20-7.25. Cover L3000/€1.55. *Trattoria* open M-

Sa noon-3pm; *salumeria* open 8:30am-7pm.) **K2**, Borgo Cairoli, 23, next to the Chiesa di San Giovanni Evangelista, has great *gelato*. (Cones from L2500/€1.30. Open Th-Tu 11am-midnight.) **Postal Code:** 43100.

RAVENNA
☎0544

Ravenna's 15min. of historical superstardom came and went 14 centuries ago when Justinian and Theodora, rulers of the Byzantine Empire, headquartered their campaign here to restore order in the anarchic west. Take V. Argentario from V. Cavour to reach the 6th-century ▧**Basilica di San Vitale**, V.S. Vitale, 17. An open courtyard overgrown with greenery leads to the brilliant, glowing mosaics inside; those of the Emperor and Empress adorn the lower left and right panels of the apse. Behind S. Vitale, the city's oldest and most intriguing mosaics cover the glittering interior of the **Mausoleo di Galla Placidia**. (☎0544 21 62 92. Open Apr.-Sept. daily 9am-7pm; Oct.-Mar. 9:30am-4:30pm. Joint ticket L6000/€3.10.) Take bus #4 or 44 across from the train station (L1300/€0.70) to Classe, south of the city, to see the astounding mosaics at the ▧**Chiesa di Sant'Apollinare in Classe.** (Open M-Sa 8:30am-7:30pm, Su 9am-1pm. L4000/€2.10, Su free.) Much to Florence's dismay, Ravenna is also home to the **Tomb of Dante Alighieri**, its most popular sight. In the adjoining **Dante Museum**, his heaven and hell come alive in etchings, paintings, and sculptures. From P. del Popolo, cut through P. Garibaldi to V. Alighieri. (☎0544 302 52. Tomb open daily 9am-7pm. Free. Museum open Apr.-Sept. Tu-Su 9am-noon and 3:30-6pm; Oct.-Mar. Tu-Su 9am-noon. L3000/€1.55.) A **comprehensive ticket** (L10,000/€5.20, students L8000/€4.15) is valid at several sights, including the Basilica S. Vitale, Chiesa S. Appollinare, and the Mausoleo.

   Trains (☎0544 217 884) leave P. Farini for Ferrara, Florence, and Venice (1hr., every 2hr., L6700/€3.50) via Bologna (1hr., every 1-2hr., L7400/€3.85). Follow Viale Farini from the station to V. Diaz, which runs to the central P. del Popolo and the **tourist office**, V. Salara, 8. (☎0544 354 04; fax 0544 48 26 70. Open in summer M-Sa 8:30am-7pm, Su 10am-4pm; in winter M-Sa 8am-6pm, Su 10am-4pm.) Take bus #1 or 70 from V. Pallavicini at the station (every 15min.-1hr., L1300/€0.70) to reach **Ostello Dante (HI)**, V. Nicolodi, 12. (☎/fax 0544 42 11 64. Breakfast included. Reception 7-10am and 5-11:30pm. Lockout 10am-5pm. Curfew 11:30pm. 4- to 6-bed dorms L24,000/€12.40. MC/V.) Walk down V. Farini, and go right at P. Mameli for the renovated **Albergo Al Giaciglio**, V. Rocca Brancaleone, 42. (☎0544 394 03. Breakfast L7000/€3.65. Closed 2 weeks in Dec. or Jan. Singles L50,000-60,000/€25.85-31; doubles L70,000-90,000/€36.15-46.50; triples L100,000-110,000/€51.65-56.85. MC/V.)

FERRARA
☎0532

Rome has its mopeds, Venice its boats, and Ferrara its bicycles. Old folks, young folks, and babies perched precariously on handlebars whirl through Ferrara's jumble of major thoroughfares and twisting medieval roads. Take a deep breath of fresh air, hop on a bike, and head for the giant castle.

▤ TRANSPORTATION. Ferrara **trains**, on the Bologna-Venice line, go to: Bologna (30min., 1-2 per hr., L4900/€2.55); Padua (1hr., every hr., L7600/€3.95); Ravenna (1hr., 1-3 per hr., L6700/€3.50); Rome (3-4hr., 7 per day, L57,200/€29.55); Venice (2hr., 1-2 per hr., L10,800/€5.60). ACFT (☎0532 59 94 92) and GGFP **buses** leave V. Rampari S. Paolo or the train station for Bologna (1½hr., 15 per day, L6000/€3.10) and Ferrara's beaches (1hr., 12 per day, L7600-8400/€3.95-4.35).

▨ PRACTICAL INFORMATION. To get to the center of town, turn left out of the train station and then veer right on **Viale Costituzione**. This road becomes Viale Cavour and runs to the **Castello Estense** at the center of town (1km). Or, take bus #2 to the Castello stop or bus #1 or 9 to the post office (every 15-20min. 7am-8:20pm, L1400/€0.75). The **tourist office** is in Castello Estense. (☎0532 20 93 70. Open daily 9am-1pm and 2-6pm.) Rent cheap **bikes** at Corso Giovecca, 21, to the left as you exit the train station. (L4000/€2.10 per hr., L20,000/€10.35 per day. Open daily 9:30am-1pm and 3:30-7pm.) **Postal Code:** 44100.

ITALY

▊▊ ACCOMMODATIONS AND FOOD. Walk down Corso Ercole I d'Este from the *castello*, or take bus #4c from the station and ask for the *castello* stop to reach the central **Ostello della Gioventu Estense (HI)**, Corso B. Rossetti, 24, with simple bunk bed rooms. (☎/fax 0532 20 42 27. Reception 7-10am and 5-11:30pm. Lockout 10am-3:30pm. Curfew 11:40pm. Dorms L23,000/€11.90.) **Casa degli Artisti**, V. Vittoria, 66, near P. Lampronti, is in the historic center of Ferrara. (☎ 0532 76 10 38. Singles L36,000/€18.60; doubles L64,000-90,000/€33.05-46.50.) The **Albergo Nazionale**, Calle Porta Reno, 32, is on a busy street right off the *duomo*. (☎/fax 0532 20 96 04. Curfew 12:30am. Singles L65,000-80,000/€33.60-41.35; doubles with bath L120,000/€62; triples L145,000/€74.90. AmEx/MC/V.) In Ferrara, gorge on delicious triangular meat *ravioli* served in a broth or the traditional *Ferrarese* dessert of luscious *pampepato*, chocolate-covered almond and fruit cake. Try delicious *panini* (L5000/€2.60) with one of 600 varieties of wine (L1000-14,000/€0.55-7.25 per glass) at the oldest *osteria* in Italy, **Osteria Al Brindisi**, V.G. degli Adelardi, 9b. (☎ 0532 20 91 42. Open Tu-Su 8:30am-1am.) For picnic supplies, stop by the **Mercato Comunale**, on V. Mercato, off V. Garibaldi next to the *duomo*. (Open M-W 7am-1:30pm and 4:30-7:30pm, F 4:30-7:30pm, Th and Sa 7am-1:30pm.)

▊▊ SIGHTS AND ENTERTAINMENT. Bike the tranquil, wooded concourse along the city's well-preserved 9km **medieval wall,** which begins at the far end of Corso Giovecca. The imposing **Castello Estense** stands precisely in the center of town. Corso della Giovecca lies along the former route of the moat's feeder canal, separating the medieval section from the part planned by the d'Este's architect. (☎ 0532 29 92 33. Open Tu-Su 9:30am-5pm. L8000/€4.15, students L6000/€3.10.) From the *castello*, take Corso Martiri della Libertà to P. Cattedrale and the **Duomo San Romano**, which contains the **Museo della Cattedrale.** (Cathedral open M-Sa 7:30am-noon and 3-6:30pm, Su 7:30am-12:30pm and 4-7:30pm. Museum ☎ 0532 20 74 49. Open Tu-Sa 10am-noon and 3-5pm, Su 10am-noon and 4-6pm.) From the *castello*, cross Largo Castello to Corso Ercole I d'Este and walk to the corner of Corso Rossetti to reach the gorgeous **Palazzo Diamanti**, built in 1493. Inside, the **Pinacoteca Nazionale** holds many of the best works of the Ferrarese school. (Open Tu-W and F-Sa 9am-2pm, Th 9am-7pm, Su and holidays 9am-1pm. L8000/€4.15, EU citizens ages 18-25 L4000/€2.10.) Follow Corso Ercole I d'Este behind the *castello* and go right on Corso Porta Mare to find the **Palazzo Massari**, Corso Porta Mare, 9, which houses both the **Museo d'Arte Moderna e Contemporanea "Filippo de Pisis,"** and, upstairs, the spectacular **Museo Ferrarese dell'Ottocentro/Museo Giovanni Boldini.** (Both open daily 9am-1pm and 3-6pm. Joint ticket L10,000/€5.20.) In July and August, a free **Discobus** (☎ 0532 59 94 11) runs every Saturday night between Ferrara and the hottest clubs; pick up flyers in the train station. **Postal code:** 44100.

THE LAKE COUNTRY

When Italy's monuments and museums start to blur together, escape to the natural beauty of the northern Lake Country, where clear water laps at the foot of the encircling mountains. A youthful crowd descends upon Lake Garda, with its watersports by day and thriving club scene at night; palatial hotels line Lake Maggiore's sleepy shores, while Lake Como's urbane shore hosts three excellent hostels.

LAKE COMO (LAGO DI COMO)

Although an unworldly magnificence lingers over the northern reaches of Europe's deepest lake (410m), peaceful Lake Como is more than a figment of your imagination. *Bougainvillea* and lavish villas adorn the lake's craggy backdrop, warmed by the sun and cooled by lakeside breezes. Como, the largest city on the lake, makes an ideal transportation hub. Menaggio, one of the three smaller Centro Lago towns, is an alternate base for exploring the lake, and makes for a more relaxing stay.

TRANSPORTATION. The only town on the lake accessible by train is **Como**, on the southwestern tip. **Trains** roll into Stazione San Giovanni from Milan (1hr., every 30min., L9400/€4.85) and Venice (4hr., every hr., L41,300/€21.35). **Buses** leave P. Matteotti for Bergamo (2hr., every hr., L8300/€4.30). From Como, take the **C-10 bus** near Ferrovia Nord to Menaggio or Domaso (1hr., last bus at 8:30pm, L4900/€2.55). Hourly **C-30** buses also serve Bellagio (1hr., last bus at 8:14pm, L5200/€2.70). Spend the day zipping between stores, gardens, villas, and wineries of the remaining towns on the lake by **ferry** (day pass L18,000/€9.30).

COMO. Situated on the southwest tip of the lake, at the receiving end of the Milan rail line, Como is the lake's token semi-industrial town. For excellent **hiking** and stunning views, head from the far end of Lungo Lario Trieste up to **Brunate**. To get from the train station to the **tourist office**, P. Cavour, 16, walk down the steps, turn left on V. Fratelli Ricchi after the little park, and turn right on Viale Fratelli Rosselli, which leads to P. Cavour via Lungo Lario Trento. (☎ 031 26 97 12; fax 24 01 11. Open M-Sa 9am-1pm and 2:30-6pm.) **Ostello Villa Olmo (HI)**, V. Bellinzona, 2, behind Villa Olmo, offers clean rooms, great food, and discounts on various sights in Como. From the train station, walk 20min. down V. Borgo Vico, which becomes V. Bellinzona. (☎/fax 031 57 38 00. Breakfast included. Reception 7-10am and 4-11:30pm. Strict curfew 11:30pm. Open Mar.-Nov. Dorms L21,000/€10.85.) **In Riva al Lago**, P. Matteotti, 4, is centrally located with immaculate rooms. (☎ 031 30 23 33; www.inrivallago.com. Breakfast L4000/€2.10. Singles L45,000/€23.25, with bath L75,000/€38.75; doubles L70,000/€36.15, L90,000-100,000/€46.50-51.65.) Picnickers will appreciate the **G.S. supermarket**, at V. Recchi and V. Fratelli Roselli. (Open M 9:30am-9:30pm, Tu-F 8am-9pm, Sa 8am-8pm.) **Postal Code:** 22100.

MENAGGIO. Menaggio is home to historic streets, stunning scenery, and a youth hostel that makes it a perfect base for exploring Lake Como. From the top of **Rifugio Menaggio**, 1400m above the lake, hikers can make trips to **Monte Grona** and the **Chiesa di S. Amate.** A 1-2hr. hike (each way) leads to the spectacular **Sass Corbee Gorge**; inquire at the tourist office for directions and maps. To get to the resort-like **Ostello La Prinula (HI)**, V. IV Novembre, 86, walk along the shore to the main thoroughfare, go past the gas station, and walk up the less steep incline on the right. (☎ 034 43 23 56; fax 43 16 77; www.menaggiohostel.it. Breakfast included. Bike and kayak rental L18,000/€9.30 per day. Curfew 11:30pm. Open Mar. to Oct. Dorms L21,000/€10.85; 4-bed family rooms with bath L23,000/€11.90 per person.)

LAKE MAGGIORE (LAGO MAGGIORE)

Without the tourist frenzy of its eastern neighbors, Lake Maggiore cradles the same temperate mountain waters and idyllic shores. The charming resort town of **Stresa**, only 1hr. from Milan by **train** (every hr., L8400/€4.35, intercity supplement L6000/€3.10), is the most convenient base for exploring. To get to Lake Maggiore from Lake Como, take a train from Como to Laveno (L4800/€2.50; change at Saronna), on the east shore of the lake, then take a ferry to other points. To reach the **tourist office**, V. Principe Tommaso, 70/72, from the train station, turn right and walk down V. Carducci, which becomes V. Gignous; V.P. Tommaso is on the left. (☎ 0323 304 16. Open M-F 8:30am-12:30pm and 3-6:15pm.) The modern **Albergo Luina**, V. Garibaldi, 21, is centrally located. (☎/fax 0323 302 85. Reserve ahead. 10% discount with *Let's Go*. Singles L65,000/€33.60; doubles L90,000-120,000/€46.50-62.)

Alternatively, to get to the new **Ostello Verbania Internazionale**, take a ferry from Streza across the lake to **Pallanza** (35min., L12,400/€6.40). After disembarking the ferry, walk to the right along the water to V. Vittorio Veneto, turn left on V. Panoramica, walk up the hill, continue around the bend, and take your last right; the hostel is up on the left. (Breakfast included. Reception 8-11am, 4-5:30pm and 10-11pm. Dorms L23,000/€11.90.) The **tourist office**, Corso Zanitello, 8, is 5min. to the right when facing inland from the port.

▶ **DAYTRIP FROM LAKE MAGGIORE: BORROMEAN ISLANDS.** Beckoning visitors with its dense green thickets and stately old villas, the lovely **Borromean Islands** are well worth a visit from Stresa or Pallanza. A **day's ticket** (L16,000/€8.30) permits travel between either Stresa or Pallanza and the three islands (**Isola Bella, Isola Superiore,** and **Isola Madre**). The islands boast manicured botanical gardens, elegant villas, and an opulent Baroque palace.

LAKE GARDA (LAGO DI GARDA)

Garda—the ultimate resort destination for many German families—has staggering mountains and breezy summers. **Desenzano,** the lake's southern transport hub, lies on the Milan-Venice line, 30min. from Verona, 1hr. from Milan, and 2hr. from Venice. From Desenzano, the other lake towns are easily accessible by bus and boat. The towns of Sirmione and Gardone Riviera are best explored as daytrips, because accommodations are scant and pricey.

SIRMIONE. Sirmione is a bit like Disneyland—flashy, expensive, and quickly exhausted. Its beautiful 13th-century castle and Roman ruins make for a leisurely day or a busy afternoon. **Buses** run every hour from: Brescia (1hr., L6000/€3.10); Desenzano (20min., L2500/€1.30); Verona (1hr., L5000/€2.60). *Battelli* (water steamers) run until 8pm to Desenzano (20min., L5000/€2.60); Gardone (1¼hr., L10,000/€5.20); Riva (4hr., L13,900/€7.20). The **tourist office,** V. Guglielmo Marconi, 2, is in the disc-shaped building. (☎030 91 61 14. Open Apr.-Oct. daily 9am-9pm; Nov.-Mar. M-F 9am-12:30pm and 3-6pm, Sa 9am-12:30pm.) The **Albergo Grifone,** V. Bisse, 5, has a prime location. (☎030 91 60 14; fax 030 91 65 48. Reserve ahead. Singles L55,000/€28.40; doubles L100,000/€51.65. Extra bed L27,000/€13.95.)

GARDONE RIVIERA. Formerly the playground of the rich and famous, this town is now home to Lake Garda's most famous sight: the villa of 20th-century poet and latter-day Casanova Gabriele D'Annunzio. His quirky mansion, **Il Vittoriale,** sprawls above Gardone, off V. Roma and V. dei Colli. (Villa open Apr.-Sept. Tu-Su 8:30am-8pm. Gardens open Oct.-Mar. Tu-Su 9am-5pm. L15,000/€7.75.) **Buses** (☎0365 210 61) run to Desenzano (30min., 6 per day, L4300/€2.25) and Milan (3hr., 2 per day, L15,500/€8). The **APT tourist office,** V. Repubblica, 8, is in the center of Gardone Sotto. (☎/fax 0365 203 47. Open July-Aug. daily 9am-1pm and 4-10pm; Nov.-Mar. M-W and F 9am-12:30pm and 3-6pm, Th 9am-12:30pm.)

RIVA DEL GARDA. Riva, with its calm pebble beaches and wide *piazze*, is Lake Garda's compromise for the budget traveler. Travelers **swim, windsurf, hike,** and **climb** near the most stunning portion of the lake, where cliffs crash into the water. Riva is accessible by **bus** (☎0464 55 23 23) from Trent (2hr., 6 per day, L6200/€3.20) and Verona (2hr., 11 per day, L9500/€4.90). **Ferries** (☎030 914 95 11), on P. Matteoti, head to Gardone (L12,200/€6.30). The **tourist office,** Giardini di Porta Orientale, 8, is near the water. (☎0464 55 44 44; fax 52 03 08. Open M-Sa 9am-noon and 3-6pm, Su 10am-noon and 4-6:30pm.) Snooze at the fabulous **Locanda La Montanara,** V. Montanara, 20. At V. Dante, 47, turn left onto V. Florida, walk through the arches, and turn right onto V. Montanara. (☎/fax 0464 55 48 57. Breakfast L8000/€4.15. Open Easter to mid-Oct. Singles L30,000/€15.50; doubles L66,000/€34.10.)

THE DOLOMITES

The Dolomites dominate the landscape in the province of Trentino-Alto Adige, rising from valley communities to lush pine forests. These amazing peaks, which start west of Trent and extend north and east into Austria, are fantastic for hiking, year-round downhill skiing, and rock climbing.

TRENT   ☎0461

Trent is a harmonious mix of Germanic and Mediterranean flavors, nestled under crumbling fortresses and dramatic cliffs. The **Piazza del Duomo,** Trent's center and social heart, contains the city's best sights. The steps of **Fontana del Nettuno,** in the

ITALY

center of the *piazza*, offer a good view of houses' frescoes. Nearby is the **Cattedrale di San Vigilio,** named for the patron saint of Trent. (Open daily 6:40am-12:15pm and 2:30-7:30pm.) Walk down V. Belenzani and go right on V. Roma to reach the majestic **Castello del Buonconsiglio.** (☎0461 23 37 70. Open daily 10am-6pm. L10,000/€5.20; students, children, and seniors L6000/€3.10.) **Monte Bondone** rises majestically over Trent, making an excellent daytrip or overnight excursion. Catch the **cable car** (☎0461 38 10 00) from V. Lung'Adige Monte Grappa to **Sardagna** on Mt. Bondone (every 30min., L4000/€2.10). From the bus station, turn right onto V. Pozzo, take the first right on Cavalcavia S. Lorenzo, cross the bridge over the train tracks and cross the intersection to the unmarked building.

Trains (☎0461 98 36 27) leave V. Dogana for: Bologna (3hr., 13 per day, L19,600/€10.15); Bolzano (45min., 2 per hr., L5600/€2.90); Venice (3hr., 5 per day, L19,300/€10); Verona (1hr., every hr., L9000/€4.65). **Buses** (☎0461 82 10 00) leave V. Pozzo, next to the train station, for Riva del Garda (1hr., every hr., L5500/€2.85). From the stations, walk right to the intersection at V. Torre Vanga, continue straight along V. Pozzo, as it becomes V. Orfane and V. Cavour, for P. del Duomo and the **tourist office,** V. Alfieri, 4. (☎0461 98 38 80; fax 98 45 08; www.apt.trento.it. Open daily 9am-7pm.) **Hotel Venezia** is at P. Duomo, 45. (☎/fax 0461 23 41 14. Breakfast L10,000/€5.20. Singles L52,000-67,000/€26.85-34.60; doubles L72,000-92,000/€37.20-47.55; triples L92,000-118,000/€47.55-60.95; quads L135,000/€69.75. MC/V.) **Ostello Giovane Europa (HI)**, V. Torre Vanga, 9, is 2min. from the station. Turn right on V. Pozzo and then left on V. Torre Vanga. (☎0461 26 34 84. Breakfast included. Reception 3:30-11pm. Check-out 9:30am. Curfew 11:30pm. Reservations required. Dorms L22,000/€11.40; singles L42,000/€21.70.)

BOLZANO   ☎ 0471

In the tug-of-war between Austrian and Italian cultural influences, Bolzano pulls on Austria's side. The town's prime location beneath vineyard-covered mountains makes it a splendid base for hiking or skiing in the Dolomites. Artwork and numerous frescoes fills the Gothic **duomo,** off P. Walther. (Open M-F 9:45am-noon and 2-5pm, Sa 9:45am-noon. Free.) The fascinating **South Tyrol Museum of Archaeology,** V. Museo, 43, near Ponte Talvera, houses the actual 5000-year-old **Ice Man.** (☎0471 98 06 48. Open Tu-Su 10am-6pm, Th 10am-8pm. L13,000/€6.75, students L7000/€3.65.) Some of the best "sights" in town are the surrounding natural wonders. **Trains** (☎0471 97 42 92) leave P. Stazione for: Milan (3½hr., 3 per day, L25,600/€13.25); Trent (45min., 2 per hr., L5600/€2.90); Verona (2hr., 1-2 per hr., L13,200/€6.85). Walk up V. Stazione from the train station, or V. Alto Adige from the bus stop, to reach the **tourist office,** P. Walther, 8. (☎0471 30 70 00; fax 98 01 28. Open M-F 9am-6:30pm, Sa 9am-12:30pm.) **Croce Bianca,** P. del Grano 3, is around the corner from P. Walther. (☎0471 97 75 52. Breakfast L8000/€4.15. Singles L52,000/€26.85; doubles L86,000-100,000/€44.45-51.65; triples L120,000/€62.) **Casa al Torchio,** V. Museo, 2c, just off P. Erbe, serves up great food. (Cover L2000/€1.05. 10% service charge. Open M-F noon-2pm and 7-11pm, Su 6:30-11pm.)

AOSTA   ☎ 0165

Aosta is the geographical and financial center of a region increasingly dependent upon tourism for economic livelihood. Aosta makes a good base for explorations in the area, but be aware that daytrips to the valleys often require tricky train and bus connections—if you hope to return before nightfall, plan ahead. **Valle del Gran San Bernardo** links Aosta to Switzerland via the Great St. Bernard Pass, which incorporates a 5854m tunnel through the mountains. Napoleon trekked through the pass with 40,000 soldiers in 1800. The area is better known for the 1505 **Hospice of St-Bernard,** home to the patron saint of man's best friend. The highest mountain in Switzerland, **The Matterhorn (Il Cervino)** looms majestically over the nondescript town of **Breuil-Cervinia** in Valtournenche. However, many fresh-air fiends consider the economic deterrents a small price to pay for the opportunity to climb up and glide down one of the world's most famous mountains. A cable car provides year-round service to **Plateau Rosà** (round-trip L45,000/€23.25), where summer skiers tackle the slopes in lighter gear. Hikers can forgo the lift tickets and attempt the three-hour ascent to **Colle Superiore delle Cime Bianche** (2982m), with tremendous views of Val d'Ayas to the east. A shorter trek (1½hr.) on the same trail leads to the emerald waters of **Lake Goillet.** The **Società Guide** (☎0166 94 81 69) arranges group outings. Don't forget your **passport;** many trails cross into Switzerland.

Trains leave P. Manzetti for Milan (4hr., 12 per day, L20,100/€10.40) and Turin (2hr., every hr., L11,000/€5.70). To get from the train station to the **tourist office,** P. Chanoux, 8, go straight down av. du Conseil des Commis. (☎0165 23 66 27; fax 346 57. Open M-Sa 9am-1pm and 3-8pm, Su 9am-1pm.) To get to **La Belle Epoque,** V. d'Avise, 18, from the train station, take av. du Conseil des Commis to P. Chanoux, and turn left on V. Aubert. (☎0165 26 22 76. Singles L45,000/€23.25, with bath L55,000/€28.40; doubles L90,000/€46.50; triples L120,000/€62.) Savor great food at the classy **Trattoria Praetoria,** V. Sant'Anselmo, 9, just past the Porta Praetoria. (☎0165 443 56. *Primi* L8000-10,000/€4.15-5.20, *secondi* L12,000/€6.20. Cover L3000/€1.55. Open in summer daily 12:15-2:30pm and 7:15-9:30pm; in winter F-W 12:15-2:30pm and 7:15-9:30pm.)

▶ DAYTRIP FROM AOSTA: VAL D'AYAS. Budget-minded sports enthusiasts should consider bypassing the pleasure grounds to the west and stopping here instead. Val d'Ayas has the same outdoor activities as its flashy neighbors—skiing, hiking, and rafting—without the hype. **Trains** run to **Verrès** from Aosta (40min., 17 per day 6:35am-8:40pm, L5000/€2.60) and Turin (1½hr.). **Buses** run from the train station at Verrès daily to Champoluc (1hr., 4 per day 11:30am-6pm, L4200/€2.20). The **tourist office** in **Champoluc,** V. Varase, 16 (☎0125 30 71 13; fax 30 77 85), also has branches in **Brusson** (☎0125 30 02 40; fax 30 06 91) and **Antagnod** (☎0125 30 63 35). They speak English and provide trail maps and hotel information. (All branches open daily 9am-12:30pm and 3-6pm.)

THE VENETO

From the rocky foothills of the Dolomites to the fertile valleys of the Po River, the Veneto region has a geography as diverse as its historical influences. Once loosely linked under the Venetian Empire, these towns retained their cultural independence, and visitors are more likely to hear regional dialects than standard Italian when neighbors gossip across their geranium-bedecked windows. The sense of local culture and custom that remains strong within each town may surprise visitors lured to the area by Venice, the *bella* of the north.

VENICE (VENEZIA)   ☎041

There is an mystical quality to Venice's decadence: her lavish palaces stand proudly on a steadily sinking network of wood, the clouded waters of her age-old canals lap at the feet of abandoned front doors. Venice's labyrinthine streets lead to a treasury of Renaissance art, housed in scores of palaces, churches, and museums that are themselves an architectural delight. Of course, any visit to Venice is a reminder of another, more recent history of tourism. The same streets that once earned the name *La Serenissima* (Most Serene) are now saturated with visitors. Venice now grapples with an economy reliant on the same tourism that forces more and more of the native population away every year. Still, the sinking city lives on. Romanticism dies hard, and Venice persists beyond the summer crowds and polluted waters, united by winding canals and the memory of a glorious past.

▄ TRANSPORTATION

The **train station** is on the northwest edge of the city; be sure to get off at **Santa Lucia,** *not* Mestre on the mainland. **Buses** and **boats** arrive at **Piazzale Roma,** just across the Canal Grande from the train station. To get from either station to **Piazza San Marco**

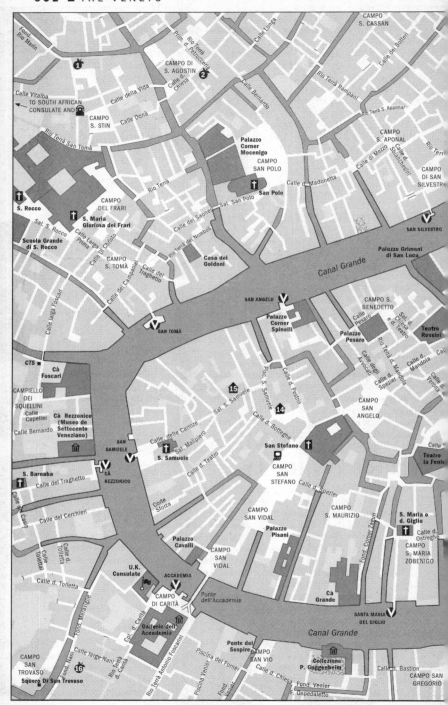

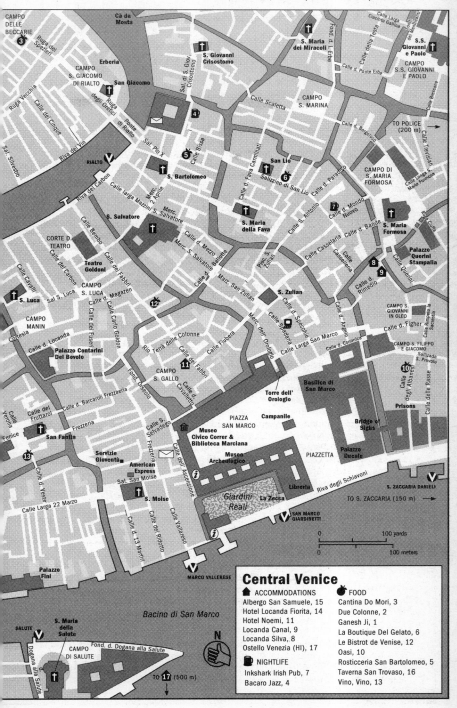

Central Venice

🏠 ACCOMMODATIONS
Albergo San Samuele, 15
Hotel Locanda Fiorita, 14
Hotel Noemi, 11
Locanda Canal, 9
Locanda Silva, 8
Ostello Venezia (HI), 17

🍎 FOOD
Cantina Do Mori, 3
Due Colonne, 2
Ganesh Ji, 1
La Boutique Del Gelato, 6
Le Bistrot de Venise, 12
Oasi, 10
Rosticceria San Bartolomeo, 5
Taverna San Trovaso, 16
Vino, Vino, 13

🍺 NIGHTLIFE
Inkshark Irish Pub, 7
Bacaro Jazz, 4

or the **Ponte di Rialto** (Rialto Bridge), take *vaporetto* #82 or follow the signs (and crowds) for the 40min. walk—exit left from the train station on Lista di Spagna.

Flights: Aeroporto Marco Polo (☎041 260 61 11; www.veniceairport.it), 8km north of the city. Ticket office open daily 5:30am-9:30pm. Take the **ATVO shuttlebus** (☎041 520 55 30) from the airport to Piazzale Roma. (30min., 2 per hr., L5000/€2.60).

Trains: Stazione Venezia Santa Lucia, northwest corner of the city. Open daily 3:45am-12:30am. **Info office** at the left as you exit the platforms, open daily 7am-9pm. To: **Bologna** (2hr., 2 per hr., L20,000/€10.35); **Florence** (3hr., every 2hr., L40,000/€20.65); **Milan** (3hr., 1-2 per hr., L42,000/€21.70); **Rome** (4½hr., 5 per day, L68,000/€35.15). **Lockers:** by platform 1. L3000-4000/€1.55-2.10 for 6hr.

Buses: ACTV, on Piazzale Roma (☎041 528 78 86; fax 272 25 88). The local line for buses and boats. ACTV **long distance carrier** buses run to nearby cities. Ticket office open daily 6:30am-11pm. ACTV offers a 3-day **discount vaporetto pass** (L25,000/€12.95) to **Rolling Venice** cardholders (see p. 654).

Public Transportation: The **Canal Grande** can be crossed on foot only at the Scalzi, Rialto, and Accademia *ponti* (bridges). Most **vaporetti** (water buses) run 5am-midnight and the *Notte* line runs 11:30pm-5:30am. **Single-ride** L6000/€3.10. **24hr.** *biglietto turistico pass* L18,000/€9.30, **3-day** L35,000/€18.10 (L25,000/€12.95 with **Rolling Venice Card;** see p. 654), **7-day** L60,000/€31. Buy tickets from booths in front of *vaporetto* stops, self-serve dispensers at the ACTV office in Piazzale Roma and the Rialto stop, or from the conductor. Pick up some extra *non timbrati* (non-validated) tickets for when the booths aren't open. Validate them yourself before boarding and avoid a fine. **Lines #82** (faster) and **#1** (slower) run from the station down the Grande and della Giudecca canals; **line #52** goes from the station through the Canale della Giudecca to Lido and along the city's northern edge, then back to the station; **line #12** runs from Fond. Nuove to Murano, Burano, and Torcello.

✦❷ ORIENTATION AND PRACTICAL INFORMATION

Venice spans 118 bodies of land in a lagoon and is connected to the mainland by a thin causeway. Venice is a veritable labyrinth and can even confuse its natives, most of whom simply set off in a general direction and then patiently weave their way through the city. If you follow their example by ungluing your eyes from your map and going with the flow, you'll discover some of the unexpected surprises that make Venice spectacular. A few tips will help you to orient yourself. Locate the following sights on a map: **Ponte di Rialto** (the bridge in the center), **Piazza San Marco** (central south), the **Ponte Accademia** (bridge in the southwest), **Ferrovia** (the train station, in the northwest), and **Piazzale Roma** (directly south of the station). The Canal Grande snakes through the city, creating six *sestieri* (sections): **Cannaregio, Castello, Santa Croce, San Polo, San Marco,** and **Dorsoduro.** Within each *sestieri*, there are no street numbers—door numbers in a section form one long, haphazard set, consisting of around 6000 numbers. While these boundaries are nebulous, they can give you a general sense of location. **Cannaregio** is in the north and includes the train station, Jewish ghetto, and Cà d'Oro; **Castello** extends east toward the Arsenale; **San Marco** fills in the area between the Ponte di Rialto and Ponte Accademia; **Dorsoduro,** across the bridge from S. Marco, stretches the length of Canale della Giudecca and up to Campo S. Pantalon; **San Polo** runs north from Chiesa S. Maria dei Frari to the Ponte di Rialto; and **San Croce** lies west of S. Polo, across the Canal Grande from the train station. If *sestiere* boundaries prove too vague, Venice's **parrochie** (parishes) provide a more defined idea of where you are, and *parrochia* signs, like *sestiere* signs, are painted on the sides of buildings.

TOURIST, FINANCIAL, AND LOCAL SERVICES

Tourist Offices and Tours: APT, Calle della Ascensione, P.S. Marco, 71/F (☎/fax 041 529 87 40; www.tourismovenezia.it), directly opposite the Basilica. Open M-Sa 9:30am-3:30pm. The APT desk at the nearby **Venice Pavilion,** Giardini E Reali, S. Marco, 2 (☎041 522 51 50) sells ACTV tickets. Open daily 9am-6pm.

AVA, (☎041 171 52 88), in the train station, to the right of the tourist office. Makes same-day reservations for L1000/€0.55. Open in summer daily 9am-10pm. Offices also in **Piazzale Roma** (☎041 523 13 79) and the **airport** (☎041 541 51 33). Call 041 522 22 64 or 800 843 006 for advance reservations.

Rolling Venice, Corte Contarina, S. Marco, 1529 (☎041 274 76 50; fax 274 76 42). Exit P.S. Marco opposite the Basilica, turn right, follow Calle del Salvadago left, continue through the *sotoportego* marked with yellow "Comune di Venezia" signs, take a left, turn right, and go into the courtyard. Sells the **Rolling Venice youth discount card** (L5000/€2.60), which provides hundreds of discounts at hotels, restaurants, and museums. Open M, W, and F 9:30am-1pm, Tu and Th 9:30am-1pm and 3-5pm. Rolling Venice is also available at **ACTV VeLa kiosks** next to the Ferrovia and Rialto *vaporetto* stops. Open daily 9am-3:30pm.

Budget Travel: CTS, Fond. Tagliapietra, Dorsoduro, 3252 (☎041 520 56 60; fax 23 69 46; www.cts.it). From Campo S. Barnaba, cross the bridge nearest the church, then turn right at the dead end, left onto Calle Cappeller and left at the foot of the bridge. Open M-F 9:30am-1:30pm and 2:30-6:30pm.

Currency Exchange: Banks and 24hr. **ATMs** line **Calle Larga XXII Marzo** (between P.S. Marco and the Ponte Accademia) and **Campo S. Bartomoleo** (near the Ponte di Rialto). Many 24hr. automatic change machines, outside banks and next to ATMs, offer low commissions and decent rates.

American Express: Salle S. Moise, S. Marco, 1471 (☎800 87 20 00 or 041 520 08 44). Exit P.S. Marco away from the basilica, turn left, then right onto Salle S. Moise. No commission; average rates. Mail service only for those with AmEx card or AmEx traveler's cheques. Open M-F 9am-8pm, Sa-Su 9am-6pm. Member services M-F 9am-1pm and 2-5:30pm, Sa 9pm-12:30am.

EMERGENCY AND COMMUNICATIONS

Emergency: ☎113.

Police: ☎113. **Carabinieri (civil corps):** Campo S. Zaccaria, Castello, 4693/A (☎112 or 041 204 47 77). **Questura,** V. Nicoladi, 24 (☎041 271 55 11), Marghera. Contact the Questura if you have a serious complaint about your hotel.

Pharmacy: Farmacia Italo Inglese, Calle della Mandola, S. Marco, 3717 (☎041 522 48 37), off Campo Manin near the Rialto bridge. Open M-F 9am-12:30pm and 3:45-7:30pm, Sa 9am-12:30pm. Late-night and weekend pharmacies rotate; check the list posted in the window of any pharmacy.

Hospital: Ospedale Civile, Campo S.S. Giovanni e Paolo, Castello (☎041 529 41 11). **First Aid:** ☎118.

Internet Access: The NetGate, Crosera S. Pantalon, Dorsoduro, 3812/A (☎041 244 02 13), behind the Frari. Offers 20 Internet stations; the best deal in town. L10,000/€5.20 for 1hr., L8000/€4.15 with ISIC or Rolling Venice card. Open M-F 10am-10pm, Su 2-10pm. AmEx/MC/V.

Post Office: Poste Venezia Centrale, Salizzada Fontego dei Tedeschi, S. Marco, 5554 (☎041 271 71 11), to the east of the Ponte di Rialto and off Campo S. Bartolomeo. Housed in an old palace, the building itself merits a visit. *Fermo Posta* at window #40. Open M-Sa 8:15am-7pm. Address mail to be held: FirstName SURNAME, *In Fermo Posta*, Fontego dei Tedeschi, S. Marco 5554, 30124 Venezia, Italia. Open M-Sa 8:15am-7pm.

Postal Codes: S. Marco 30124; Castello 30122; S. Polo, S. Croce, and Canareggio 30121; Dorsoduro 30123.

◤ ACCOMMODATIONS

Plan to spend slightly more for a room in Venice than you would elsewhere in Italy. In *pensioni*, watch out for L10,000/€5.20 breakfasts and other rip-offs. Always agree on what you will pay before you take a room. If possible, make reservations at least a month in advance. Dormitory-style arrangements are sometimes available in Venice without reservations, even during August and September; but single rooms vanish in the summer. Proprietors are more willing to bargain in person. Because of *acqua alta* flooding and renovation restrictions, few hotels are wheelchair accessible.

HOSTELS AND INSTITUTIONAL ACCOMMODATIONS

■ **Foresteria Valdesi**, Castello, 5170 (☎041 528 67 97; fax 241 62 38; www.chiesav-aldese.org/venezia). From the Ponte di Rialto, enter Campo S. Bartolomeo, continue under the *sotoportego* to the left, follow Salizzada S. Lio, turn left on Calle Mondo Novo; go over the bridge, cross Campo S. Maria Formosa and take Calle Lunga S. Maria Formosa over the 1st bridge. Amiable management and dazzling frescoed ceilings. Private rooms with TV. Breakfast included. Reception daily 9am-1pm and 6-8pm. Lockout 10am-1pm. Closed 3 weeks in Nov. Dorms L35,000-36,000/€18.10-18.60; doubles L100,000-130,000/€51.65-67.15; quads L180,000/€93. L2000/€1.05 discount per day with Rolling Venice card.

Ostello Santa Fosca, Fond. Canale, Cannaregio, 2372 (☎/fax 041 71 57 75 or 71 57 33). From the station, follow Lista di Spagna left, cross 3 bridges, and turn left at Campo S. Fosca. Cross the 1st bridge, turn left onto Fond. Canale, and go through the gate and around the corner. Quiet, church-affiliated hostel. 140 beds available July-Sept., 31 beds from Oct.-June. Reception daily July-Sept. 9am-noon and 2:30pm-1am; Oct.-June 8am-noon and 5-8pm. Lockout noon-2:30pm. Curfew July-Sept. 1am; Oct.-June no curfew. Dorms L35,000/€18.10; doubles 80,000/€41.35. 10% discount with ISIC or Rolling Venice card.

Ostello Venezia (HI), Fond. Zitelle, 87 (☎041 523 82 11; fax 523 56 89), in Giudecca. Take *vaporetto* #82 or 52 to Zitelle. Institutional but friendly. **HI members only**; HI cards sold. Reservations through IBN from other HI hostels. www.hostelbooking.com, or by phone. Breakfast and sheets included. Reception 7-9:30am and 1:30-11:30pm. Lockout 9:30am-1:30pm. Curfew 11:30pm. Dorms L30,000/€15.50. MC/V.

Domus Civica (ACISJF), Campiello Chiovere Frari, S. Polo, 3082 (☎041 72 11 03; fax 522 71 39), between the Basilica dei Frari and Piazzale Roma. From the station, cross the Scalzi bridge, turn right, go left on Fond. dei Tolentini, head left through the courtyard on Corte Amai, and it's a few blocks down on the right. Church-affiliated student housing. Open mid-June to Sept. Check-in 7:30am-4pm. Curfew 11:30pm. Singles L50,000/€25.85; doubles L90,000/€46.50.

CANNAREGIO AND SANTA CROCE

The area around the station on Lista di Spagna offers budget accommodations and a festive atmosphere. The streets bustle at night, primarily with young travelers, even though the area is a 20-30min. *vaporetto* ride from most major sights. If you prefer quiet, ask for a room away from the street.

■ **Alloggi Gerotto Calderan**, Campo S. Geremia, 283 (☎041 71 55 62; fax 71 53 61). Turn left from the station (3min.) for a backpacker's haven. Huge, bright rooms, some with TV. Check-out 10am. Curfew 12:30-1am. Reserve ahead. Dorms L35,000/€18.10; singles L60,000-70,000/€31-36.15; doubles L90,000-120,000/€46.50-62; triples L120,000-160,000/€62-82.65, with bath L180,000-220,000/€93-113.65.

■ **Locanda San Marcuola**, Campo S. Marcuola, 1763 (☎041 71 60 48; fax 275 32 38; www.locandasanmarcuola.com). Just 20m from *vaporetto*: San Marcuola. New and rooms filled with amenities. Wheelchair accessible. Breakfast included. Singles L100,000-150,000/€51.65-77.50; doubles L200,000-250,000/€103.30-129.15; triples 250,000-300,000/€129.15-155.

Hotel Marin, Campiello delle Muneghe, S. Croce, 670/B (☎041 71 80 22; fax 72 14 85; www.hotelmarin.com). From the train station, cross the Scalzi bridge and turn right. Turn left just before the large domed church onto Calle Nova de S. Simon and make 2 rights. 19 quiet and clean rooms. Curfew 1am. Open Feb.-Dec. 10. Doubles L165,000/€85.25, with bath L195,000/€100.75; triples L205,000/€105.90, L240,000/€123.95; quads L270,000/€139.45, L285,000/€147.20. AmEx/MC/V.

SAN MARCO

Surrounded by exclusive shops and Venice's main sights, these accommodations are prime choices (if you can get a reservation).

Albergo San Samuele, Salizzada S. Samuele, 3358 (☎/fax 041 522 80 45). Follow Calle delle Botteghe from Campo S. Stefano (near the Accademia bridge) and turn left on Salizzada S. Samuele. 10 colorful rooms with tapestry wallpaper, Italian art, and sparkling bathrooms. Reserve 1-2 months ahead with 1 night's deposit. Singles L80,000/€41.35; doubles L130,000/€67.15, with bath L190,000/€98.15. Triples available with advance notice.

Hotel Noemi, Calle dei Fabbri, 909 (☎041 523 81 44; fax 277 10 05). Exit P.S. Marco through the second *sotoportego* from the basilica, and follow Calle dei Fabbri as it turns left. Just 1min. from the *piazza.* Singles L130,000/€67.15; doubles L160,000-200,000/€82.65-103.30; triples L210,000-320,000/€108.45-165.30; quads L270,000/€139.45. Cash only for 1-night stay. MC/V.

Hotel Locanda Fiorita, Campiello Novo, 3457 (☎041 523 47 54; fax 522 80 43). From Campo S. Stefano, take Calle de Pestrin and then climb onto the raised *piazza.* All rooms with phones and A/C. Singles L140,000/€72.30; doubles L190,000/€98.15, with bath L230,000/€118.80. Annex singles L170,000/€87.80; doubles L240,000/€123.95, with bath L250,000/€129.15. Extra bed 30% more. AmEx/MC/V.

DORSODURO

Near the university and the Accademia, hotels in Dorsoduro are in the center of a lively, albeit less touristed area between the museum and the Frari church.

Locanda Cà Foscari, Corso della Frescada, 3887b (☎041 71 04 01; fax 71 08 17), in a quiet neighborhood near the *vaporetto.* Take *vaporetto* #1 or 82 to S. Tomà. Turn left at the dead end, cross the bridge, turn right, and then take a left onto the little alleyway. Murano glass chandeliers and Venetian Carnival masks adorn the 11 rooms. Breakfast included. Curfew 1am. Book 2-3 months in advance. Open Feb.-Nov. Singles with bath L100,000/€51.65; doubles L120,000-160,000/€62-82.65; triples L156,000-201,000/€80.60-103.80; quads L192,000-240,000/€99.15-124. MC/V.

Hotel Messner, Fond. di Cà Bala, 216 (☎041 522 72 66; fax 522 74 43). From *vaporetto:* Salute, turn right onto Calle del Bastion, then turn left. 31 well-equipped rooms overlooking the canals. Breakfast included. Closed mid-Nov. to Dec. Singles L185,000/€95.55; doubles L255,000/€131.70; triples L310,000/€160.10; quads L350,000/€180.80. Annex singles L165,000/€85.25; doubles L210,000/€108.50; triples L270,000/€139.45; quads L300,000/€154.95. AmEx/MC/V.

CASTELLO (FROM SAN MARCO TO SANT'ELENA)

Castello provides lodgings near the Rialto, close to the center of town but a bit removed from the throngs of tourists.

Locanda Canal, Fond. del Remedio, 4422c (☎041 523 45 38; fax 241 91 38). From S. Marco, walk under the clock tower, right on Calle Larga S. Marco, left on Ramo dell'Anzolo, over the bridge, and left on Fond. del Remedio. Large rooms in a converted *palazzo.* Breakfast included. Doubles L155,000-205,000/€80.05-105.90; triples L185,000-250,000/€95.55-129.15; quads L220,000-300,000/€113.65-155.

Locanda Silva, Fond. del Remedio, 4423 (☎041 523 78 92; fax 528 68 17). Next door to Locanda Canal (see above). Breakfast included. Open Feb. to mid-Nov. Singles L85,000/€43.90; doubles L140,000-190,000/€72.30-98.15; triples L250,000/€129.15; quads L300,000/€155.

Locanda Corona, Calle Corona, 4464 (☎041 522 91 74). From *vaporetto:* S. Zaccaria, take Calle degli Albanese to Campo SS. Filippo e Giacomo, follow Rimpetto la Sacrestia, take the 1st right, and turn left onto Calle Corona. Wheelchair accessible. Closed Jan. Singles L85,000/€43.90; doubles L105,000/€54.25; triples L130,000/€67.15.

CAMPING

The **Litorale del Cavallino,** on the Lido's Adriatic side, has countless beach campsites.

ITALY

Camping Miramare, Punta Sabbioni (☎041 96 61 50; fax 530 11 50). Take *vaporetto* #14 from P.S. Marco to Punta Sabbioni (40min.). 3-night min. stay in high season. Open Apr. to mid-Nov. L9800/€5.10 per person, L24,000/€12.40 per tent. 4-person bungalows L62,000/€32.05, 5-person 98,000/€50.65. 15% discount with Rolling Venice card.

Camping Fusina, V. Moranzani, 79 (☎041 547 00 55), in Malcontenta. From Mestre, take bus #1. L11,000/€5.70 per person, L7000/€3.65 per tent, L25,000/€12.95 per tent and car, L21,000/€10.85 to sleep in car.

◪ FOOD

In Venice, dining well on a budget requires exploration. The best and most affordable restaurants are hidden in the less-traveled alleyways. For an inexpensive and informal option, visit any *osteria* or *bacario* in town for the chance to create a meal from the vast array of meat- and cheese-filled pastries, tidbits of seafood, rice, meat, and *tramezzini* (triangular slices of soft white bread with any imaginable filling). These tasty treats are known as **cicchetti** and cost about L2500-5000/€1.30-2.60. The key ingredients of Venetian cuisine come fresh from the sea. *Spaghetti al vongole* (pasta with fresh clams and spicy vegetables) is served on nearly every menu. Good local wines include the sparkling *prosecco della Marca* white wine or the red *valpolicella*. **STANDA supermarket,** Strada Nuova, Cannaregio, 3650, near Campo S. Felice, has a large grocery store in the back, behind the clothing. (Open M-Sa 8:30am-7:20pm, Su 9am-7:20pm.)

RESTAURANTS

◪ **Vino, Vino,** Ponte delle Veste, S. Marco, 2007a (☎04 12 41 76 88). From Calle Larga XXII Marzo, turn onto Calle delle Veste. Wine bar with delicious, aromatic food. *Primi* L8000/€4.15, *secondi* L15,000/€7.75. Cover L1000/€0.55. 10% discount with Rolling Venice card. Open W-M 10:30am-11pm.

◪ **Due Colonne,** Campo S. Agostin, S. Polo, 2343 (☎041 524 06 85). Cross the bridge away from the Frari, turn left and cross into Campo S. Stin, turn right on Calle Danà, and cross the bridge. The best pizza in Venice (L6000-13,000/€3.10-6.75). Cover L1500/€0.80. Service 10%. Closed Aug. Open M-Sa 8am-3pm and 6-11pm.

◪ **Pizza al Volo,** Campo S. Margherita, Dorsoduro, 2944 (☎041 522 54 30). An excellent takeout pizzeria open late. Pizza by the slice L2500-3000/€1.30-1.55, whole pizzas L6000-20,000/€3.10-10.35. Open daily 11:30am-3:30pm and 5:30pm-1:30am.

◪ **Pizzeria La Perla,** Rio Terra dei Franceschi, Cannaregio, 4615 (☎041 528 51 75). From Strada Nuova, turn left onto Salizzade di Pistor in Campo SS. Apostoli, then turn right. Affordable menu offers 90 types of pizza (L9000-14,000/€4.65-7.25) and pasta (L9000-11,000/€4.65-5.70). Cover L2000/€1.05. Service 10%. Wheelchair accessible. Open M-Sa noon-2pm and 7-9:45pm. Closed Aug. AmEx/MC/V.

Oasi, Calle degli Albanesi, S. Marco, 4263/a (☎041 528 99 37), between the Prisons and the Danieli Hotel. Oasi serves some of the city's freshest fruits and vegetables in its *frulatti* (fruit shakes; L7000/€3.65). Salads L8000-17,000/€4.15-8.80, *panini* L4000-6000/€2.10-3.10. Open Feb. to mid-Dec. M-Sa noon-3pm.

Le Bistrot de Venise, Calle dei Fabbri, S. Marco, 4685 (☎041 523 66 51). From the Basilica in P.S. Marco, head through the 2nd *sotoportego* on your right. A worthy splurge on authentic Venetian cuisine. *Primi* L18,000-25,000/€9.30-12.95, *secondi* L20,000-35,000/€12.95-18.10. Service 15%. Open daily noon-3pm and 6pm-1am. AmEx/MC/V.

Rosticceria San Bartomoleo, Calle della Bissa, S. Marco, 5424/A (☎04 15 22 35 69). Follow the neon sign under the last archway on the left from Campo S. Bartolomeo. Full-service restaurant upstairs. *Prosciutto* L2500/€2.30, *secondi* L12,000-23,000/€6.20-11.90. Cover L2500/€2.30. Open Tu-Su 9:30am-9:30pm. AmEx/MC/V.

Ganesh Ji, Calle dell'Olio, S. Polo, 2426 (☎041 71 98 04). From the station, cross the Scalzi bridge and turn left on Calle della Bergama. Take a right on Fond. Rio Marin and then another right on Calle dell'Olio. Enjoy affordable Indian lunch. Vegetarian L21,000/€10.85, non-vegetarian L23,000/€11.90. Cover L3000/€1.55, waived with Rolling Venice card. Open Th 7:30-11pm, F-Tu 12:30-2pm and 7-midnight. MC/V.

Cantina Do Mori, Calle dei Do Mori, S. Polo, 429 (☎041 522 54 01), near the Rialto markets. Venice's oldest wine bar—an elegant place to grab *cicchetti* (L2500/€1.30) or a glass of local wine (L2000/€1.05). Standing room only. Open M-Sa 9am-9pm.

Taverna San Trovaso, Fond. Nani, Dorsoduro, 1016 (☎041 520 37 03). Young, enthusiastic staff serves great pastas and pizzas. *Primi* L10,000-15,000/€5.20-7.75, *secondi* L15,000-27,000/€7.75-13.95, pizzas L8000-14,000/€4.15-7.25. Cover L3000/€1.55. Open Tu-Su noon-2:50pm and 7-9:50pm. AmEx/MC/V.

Gam Gam, Rio di Cannaregio, Cannaregio, 1122 (☎041 71 52 84). In the Jewish Ghetto on Fond. Pescaria. Enjoy all-kosher fare, including *schnitzel* (L15,000-31,000/€7.75-15.60) and an big lunch buffet (L18,000/€9.30) by the canal. Pastas L12,000-16,000/€6.20-8.30. Open Su-Th noon-10pm, F 7-10pm. 10% discount with *Let's Go*.

GELATERIE

 La Boutique del Gelato, Salizzada S. Lio, Castello, 5727 (☎041 522 32 83). Go. Go NOW. Enormous cones from L1500/€0.80. Open daily Feb.-Nov. M-Sa 10am-8:30pm.

Gelati Nico, Fond. Zattere, Dorsoduro, 922 (☎041 522 52 93). Try *gianduiotto al passagetto* (hazelnut ice cream dunked in whipped cream) for L4000/€2.10. Open F-W 6:45am-10:30pm.

👁 SIGHTS

> **❗ MINI-SKIRTS, MINI-PASSES, AND MINI-DISCOUNTS.** Many Venetian churches enforce a strict dress code—shoulders and knees must be covered. The Foundation for the Churches of Venice sells a three-day mini-pass for visits to 13 of Venice's religious art museums, including S. Maria dei Miracoli, S. Maria Gloriosa dei Frari, S. Polo, Madonna dell'Orto, Il Redentore, and S. Sebastiano. The L15,000/€7.75 pass (students L10,000/€5.20), available at participating churches, allows unlimited entrance to any of the 13 churches. For information on the pass or these churches, call 041 275 04 62. Many sights have student, senior, and group discounts; "reduced" prices generally apply to EU visitors under 18 or over 60. Children under 12 are often admitted for free.

AROUND THE RIALTO BRIDGE

CANAL GRANDE. The Canal Grande loops through Venice, and the splendid façades of the *palazzi* that crown its banks testify to the city's history of immense wealth. Although their external decorations vary, the palaces share the same basic structure. A **nighttime tour** reveals the startling beauty of the *palazzi*. (*Vaporetto #82 or #1: P.S. Marco.*)

PONTE DI RIALTO. The Ponte di Rialto (1588-91) arches over the Canal Grande and symbolizes Venice's commercial past. Antonio da Ponte created this image that graces postcards throughout the city. (*Vaporetto: Rialto.*)

CHIESA DI SAN GIACOMO DI RIALTO. Between the Ponte di Rialto and the markets stands Venice's first church, diminutively called "San Giacometto." The bent stone statue was once the finish line for convicted thieves after they had run naked from P.S. Marco and were lashed all the way by bystanders. (*Vaporetto: Rialto. Cross the bridge and head right. Open daily 10am-5pm. Free.*)

AROUND PIAZZA SAN MARCO

BASILICA DI SAN MARCO. The interior of this glittering church sparkles with both 13th-century Byzantine and 16th-century Renaissance mosaics. Behind the altar screen is the **Pala D'Oro,** a gem-encrusted relief covering the tomb of Saint

Mark. To the right of the altar is the **tesoro** (treasury), a hoard of gold and relics from the Fourth Crusade. Steep stairs in the atrium lead to the **Galleria della Basilica,** which offers a staggering perspective on the interior mosaics, a tranquil vista of the exterior *piazza*, and an intimate view of the original bronze *Horses of St. Mark*. St-Mark's is worth the long lines; try to time your visit for the shortest wait, in the early morning, or best natural illumination of the mosaics at dusk. (*Basilica open M-Sa 9am-5pm, Su 1-5pm. Basilica illuminated 11:30am-12:30pm. Dress code enforced; shoulders and knees must be covered. Free. Pala D'Oro open M-Sa 9:45am-5pm, Su 2-4:30pm. L3000/€1.55. Treasury open M-Sa 9:45am-5pm, Su 2-4:30pm. L4000/€2.10. Galleria open daily 9:45am-5pm. L3000/€1.55.*)

■ **PALAZZO DUCALE (DOGE'S PALACE).** Once the home of Venice's mayor, or *doge*, the Palazzo Ducale now houses one of Venice's best museums—its collection combines historical artifacts with spectacular artwork. Within the palace lie the *doge*'s private apartments and the magnificent state rooms of the Republic. Climb the richly decorated **Scala d'Oro** (Golden Staircase) to reach the **Sala del Maggior Consiglio** (Great Council Room), dominated by **Tintoretto**'s *Paradise*, the largest oil painting in the world. Passages lead through the courtrooms of the much-feared Council of Ten and the even-more-feared Council of Three, crossing the **Ponte dei Sospiri** (Bridge of Sighs) and continuing into the prisons. (☎041 522 49 51. Wheelchair accessible. Open daily 9am-7pm. Ticket office closes 1½hr. earlier. L18,000/€9.30, students L10,000/€5.20, ages 6-14 L6000/€2.75. Includes entrance to Museo Correr, Biblioteca Nazionale Marciana, Museo Archeologico, Museo di Palazzo Mocenigo, Museo del Vetro di Murano, and Museo del Merletto di Burano. Audioguides L7000/€3.65.*)

■ **PIAZZA SAN MARCO.** In contrast to the narrow, labyrinthine streets that wind through most of Venice, P.S. Marco (Venice's only official *piazza*) is a magnificent expanse of light and space. Enclosing the *piazza* are the unadorned 16th-century Renaissance **Procuratie Vecchie (Old Treasury Offices),** the more ornate 17th-century Baroque **Procuratie Nuove (New Treasury Offices),** and the smaller Neoclassical **Ala Napoleonica,** sometimes called the *Procuratie Nuovissime* (Really New Treasury Offices), which Napoleon constructed when he took the city in 1797. The brick **campanile** (96m) across the *piazza* stands on Roman foundations. (*Campanile open daily 9am-7pm. L10,000/€5.20.*)

CHIESA DI SAN ZACCARIA. Dedicated to the father of John the Baptist and designed by (among others) Coducci in the late 1400s, this Gothic-Renaissance church holds one of the masterpieces of Venetian Renaissance painting, **Giovanni Bellini**'s *Virgin and Child Enthroned with Four Saints*. (*Vaporetto: S. Zaccaria. From P.S. Marco, turn left along the water, cross the bridge, and turn left under the sotoportego.* ☎041 522 12 57. Open daily 10am-noon and 4-6pm. Free.*)

SAN POLO

■ **BASILICA DI SANTA MARIA GLORIOSA DEI FRARI (I FRARI).** Within the cavernous brick walls of this church rest outstanding paintings by masters of the Renaissance. ■**Titan**'s *Assumption* (1516-18) on the high altar marks the height of the Venetian Renaissance. In the Florentine chapel to the right is Donatello's *St. John the Baptist* (1438), a wooden Renaissance sculpture. (*Vaporetto: S. Tomà. Follow signs back to Campo dei Frari. Open M-Sa 9am-6pm, Su 1-6pm. L3000/€1.55.*)

SCUOLA GRANDE DI SAN ROCCO. Venice's most illustrious *scuola*, or guild hall, stands as a monument to painter Jacopo Tintoretto. The *scuola* commissioned Tintoretto to complete all of the building's paintings, a task that took 23 years. (*Behind the Basilica dei Frari in Campo S. Rocco.* ☎041 523 48 64. Open daily 9am-5:30pm. Ticket office closes 30min. earlier. L10,000/€5.20, students L7000/€3.65. Audioguides free.*)

DORSODURO

■ **GALLERIE DELL'ACCADEMIA.** The Accademia houses the most extensive collection of Venetian art in the world. At the top of the double staircase, **Room I,** topped by a ceiling full of cherubim, houses Venetian Gothic art, with a luxuri-oususe of color that influenced Venetian painting for centuries. Among the enormous altarpieces in **Room II**, Giovanni Bellini's *Madonna Enthroned with Child, Saints, and Angels* stands out for its lush serenity. **Rooms IV** and **V** display more Bellinis and **Giorgione**'s enigmatic *La Tempesta*. On the opposite wall is Titian's last painting, a brooding *Pietà*. In **Room XX**, works by Gentile Bellini and Carpaccio display Venetian processions and cityscapes so accurately that scholars use them as "photos" of Venice's past. *(Vaporetto: Accademia. ☎ 041 522 22 47. Open M 8:15am-2pm, Tu-Su 9:15am-7:15pm. Ticket office closes 30min. earlier. L12,000/€6.20. Guided tours L10,000/€5.20.)*

■ **COLLEZIONE PEGGY GUGGENHEIM.** Ms. Guggenheim's Palazzo Venier dei Leoni now displays works by Brancusi, Marini, Kandinsky, Picasso, Magritte, Rothko, Ernst, Pollock, and Dalí. The Marini sculpture *Angel in the City*, in front of the *palazzo*, was designed with a detachable penis. Ms. Guggenheim occasionally modified this sculpture so as not to offend her more prudish guests. *(Calle S. Cristoforo, Dorsoduro, 701. Vaporetto: Accademia. Turn left and then follow the yellow signs. ☎ 041 240 54 11. Open M and W-F 10am-6pm, Sa 10am-10pm. L10,000/€5.20, students with ISIC or Rolling Venice L8000/€4.15, under 10 free. Audioguides L8000/€4.15.)*

CHIESA DI SANTA MARIA DELLA SALUTE. The dramatically designed **Salute**, poised at the tip of Dorsoduro, is a prime example of the Venetian Baroque. Next to the Salute stands the **Dogana**, the old customs house, where ships sailing into Venice were required to stop and pay appropriate duties. Stand at the doors for a marvelous view of the city. *(Vaporetto: Salute. ☎ 041 522 55 58. Open daily 9am-noon and 3-5:30pm. Free. Entrance to sacristy with donation. The Dogana is closed to the public.)*

CHIESA DI SAN SEBASTIANO. The painter Veronese hid here when he fled Verona in 1555 after reputedly killing a man, and filled the church with some of his finest works. His breathtaking *Stories of Queen Esther* covers the ceiling. *(Vaporetto: S. Basilio. Continue straight ahead. Open M-Sa 10am-5pm, Su 3-5pm. L3000/€1.55.)*

CASTELLO

CHIESA DI SANTISSIMI GIOVANNI E PAOLO (SAN ZANIPOLO). This immense church is the final resting place of 25 *doges*, with monuments to them and other honored citizens lining the walls. Outside stands the bronze **statue of Bartolomeo Colleoni**, a mercenary who left his inheritance to the city on the condition that a monument to him be erected in front of S. Marco. The city, unwilling to honor him in such a grand space, decided to pull a fast one and place the statue in front of the Scuola di San Marco. *(Vaporetto: Fond. Nuove. Turn left and then right onto Fond. dei Mendicanti. ☎ 041 523 59 13. Open M-Sa 7:30am-12:30pm and 3:30-7pm, Su 3-6pm. Free.)*

CHIESA DI SANTA MARIA DEI MIRACOLI. Among the most stunning Venetian churches, the Lombardos designed this Renaissance jewel in the late 1400s. *(From S.S. Giovanni e Paolo, cross Ponte Rosse. Open M-Sa 10am-5pm, Su 1-5pm. L3000/€1.55.)*

SCUOLA DALMATA SAN GIORGIO DEGLI SCHIAVONI. Between 1502 and 1511, Carpaccio decorated the ground floor with some of his finest paintings, depicting episodes from the lives of Saint George, Jerome, and Tryfon. *(Castello, 3259/A. Vaporetto: S. Zaccaria. Turn right off the boat, then turn left on Calle d. Pietà, right on Salizzada dei Greci, and left on Fond. d. Furlani. ☎ 041 522 88 28. Dress code enforced. Open Apr.-Oct. Tu-Sa 9:30am-12:30pm and 3:30-6:30pm, Su 9:30am-12:30pm; Nov.-Mar. Tu-Sa 10am-12:30pm and 3-6pm, Su 10am-12:30pm. L5000/€2.60, with Rolling Venice L3000/€1.55.)*

GIARDINI PUBLICI AND SANT'ELENA. Longing for trees and grass? Stroll through the Public Gardens, installed by Napoleon, or bring a picnic lunch to the shady lawns of Sant'Elena. *(Vaporetto: Giardini or S. Elena. Free.)*

CANNAREGIO

JEWISH GHETTO. In 1516 the *doge* forced Venice's Jewish population into the old cannon-foundry area, creating the first Jewish ghetto in Europe; the word "ghetto" is the Venetian word for "foundry." The oldest synagogue, or *schola*, the **Schola Grande Tedesca (German Synagogue)** shares a building with the **Museo Ebraica di Venezia (Hebrew Museum of Venice)** in the Campo del Ghetto Nuovo. *(Cannaregio, 2899/ B. Vaporetto: S. Marcuola. Follow the signs straight ahead and then turn left into Campo del Ghetto Nuovo. ☎ 041 71 53 59. Hebrew Museum open June-Sept. Su-F 10am-7pm; Oct.-May Su-F 10am-4:30pm. Ticket office closes 30min. earlier. L5000/€2.60, students L3000/€1.55. Entrance to synagogues by guided tour only (40min.). English tours leave every hour on the half hour. Museum and tour L12,000/6.20, students L9000/€4.65.)*

CÀ D'ORO AND GALLERIA GIORGIO FRANCHETTI. The most spectacular façade on the Canal Grande and the premiere example of Venetian Gothic, the Cà d'Oro, built between 1425 and 1440, now houses the Giorgio Franchetti collection. For the best view of the palace, take the *traghetto* across the canal to the Rialto Markets. *(Vaporetto: Cà d'Oro. ☎ 041 522 23 49. Open M 8:15am-2pm, Tu-Sa 8:15am-7pm. Ticket office closes 30min. earlier. L6000/€3.10.)*

GIUDECCA AND SAN GIORGIO MAGGIORE

BASILICA DI SAN GIORGIO MAGGIORE. Standing on its own monastic island, S. Giorgio Maggiore contrasts sharply with most other Venetian churches. Palladio ignored the Venetian fondness for color and decorative excess, and constructed an austere church of simple dignity. Ascend the elevator to the top of the **campanile** for a breathtaking view. *(Vaporetto: S. Giorgio Maggiore. ☎ 041 522 78 27. Open M-Sa 10am-12:30pm and 2:30-4:30pm. Campanile L5000/€2.60; pay in the elevator.)*

ISLANDS OF THE LAGOON

BURANO. In this traditional fishing village, fishermen haul in their catch every morning as their wives, black-clad, sit in the doorways of the fantastically colored houses, creating unique knots of Venetian lace. See their handiwork in the small **Scuola di Merletti di Burano (Lace Museum).** *(Vaporetto #12: Burano from S. Zaccaria or Fond. Nuove. Museum in P. Galuppi. ☎ 041 73 00 34. Open W-M 10am-5pm. L8000/€4.15. Included on combined Palazzo Ducale ticket.)*

MURANO. Famous for its glass since 1292, the island of Murano affords visitors the opportunity to witness the glass-blowing process. The **Museo Vetrario (Glass Museum)** houses a splendid collection that includes pieces from Roman times. Farther down the street is the 12th-century **Basilica di Santa Maria e San Donato.** *(Vaporetto #12 or 52: Faro from S. Zaccaria or Fond. Nuove. The Museo Vetrario is at Fond. Giustian, 8. ☎ 041 73 95 86. Open Th-Tu 10am-5pm. L8000/€4.15, students L5000/€2.60. Included on combined Palazzo Ducale ticket. Basilica ☎ 041 73 90 56. Open daily 8am-noon and 4-7pm.)*

TORCELLO. Torcello boasts a lovely cathedral, **Santa Maria Assunta,** which contains 11th- and 12th-century mosaics of the Last Judgment and the Virgin Mary. *(Vaporetto #12: Torcello from S. Zaccaria or Fond. Nuove. Cathedral ☎ 041 73 00 84. Open daily 10:30am-12:30pm and 2-6:30pm. L4000/€2.10.)*

LIDO. The Lido is now mostly a summer beach town, complete with cars, blaring radios, and beach bums. Head for the **public beach,** which features an impressive shipwreck at the southern end. *(Vaporetto: Lido.)*

ISOLA DI SAN MICHELE. Venice's cemetery island, marked by the first Renaissance church in Venice, is the resting place of poet Ezra Pound, composer Igor Stravinsky, and Russian choreographer Sergei Diaghilev. *(Vaporetto: Cimitero.)*

⬛ NIGHTLIFE

The weekly booklet, **A Guest in Venice** (free at hotels and tourist offices or online at www.unospitedivenezia.it), lists current festivals, concerts, and gallery shows. The famed **Biennale di Venezia,** a world-wide contemporary art exhibition, covers the *Giardini Publici* and the Arsenal in provocative international art every odd-numbered year. (☎ 041 241 10 58; www.labiennale.org.) Venice's famous **Carnevale** draws masked figures and camera-happy tourists during the 10 days before Ash Wednesday, doubling the city's population by Mardi Gras. Mark Twain may have derided the **gondola** as "an inky, rusty canoe," but it's a canoe only the gentry can afford. The minimum authorized rate, which increases after sunset, starts at L120,000/€62 for 50min. For a quick and affordable taste of a gondola ride, try one of the city's *traghetti*, ferry gondolas that cross the Canal Grande at six points for a mere L700/€0.40.

Venetian nightlife is much more relaxed and quiet than that of other major Italian cities. For most locals, nighttime action means an evening spent sipping wine or beer rather than gyrating in a disco. The most popular nightlife option remains a moonlit ride on the good ole' #82. Alternatively, a 10pm stroll among the string quartets set up in P.S. Marco is a treat for the ears. Student nightlife is concentrated around **Campo S. Margherita** in **Dorsoduro** and in the areas around **Fondamenta della Misericordia** in **Cannaregio**.

Paradiso Perduto, Fond. della Misericordia, 2540 (☎041 72 05 81). From Strada Nuova, cross Campo S. Fosca, cross the bridge and continue in the same direction, crossing 2 more bridges. A favorite of students and locals. Open Th-Su 7pm-2am.

Inishark Irish Pub, Calle Mondo Novo, Castello, 5787 (☎041 523 53 00). Between Campo S. Maria Formosa and Salizzada S. Lio. The most creative and elegant Irish pub in Venice. Rubber sharks, wooden mantelpieces, and other assorted pieces line the walls and ceilings. Guinness L9000/€4.60. Open Tu-Su 6pm-1:30am.

Il Caffé, Campo S. Margherita, Dorsoduro, 2963 (☎041 528 79 98). Also known as Bar Rosso. Extensive outdoor seating accommodates the crowds of young people. Wine L1500/€0.80, beer L5000/€2.60. Open M-Sa 8am-2am.

Bacaro Jazz, Campo S. Bartolmeo, S. Marco, 5546 (☎041 52 85 249). Across from the post office, follow the red lights and loud music. At this chic restaurant, patrons share huge plates of *cicchetti* and relax to soothing jazz. Medium plate of *cicchetti* L10,000/€5.20, *sangria* L4000/€2.10. Happy Hour 2-7:30pm. Open Tu-Th11am-2am.

Café Blue, Calle Lunga S. Pantalon, Dorsoduro, 3778 (☎041 71 02 27). From Campo S. Margherita, cross the bridge at the narrow end of the *piazza*, wind right around the church, and turn left at the dead end. Classy American bar attract expats and exchange students. Free email kiosk 8pm-2am. All drinks half-price 8:30-9:30pm. Open M-Sa: afternoon tea 3:30-7:30pm, bar 9:30pm-2am.

🔅 DAYTRIPS FROM VENICE

FLORENCE. This Renaissance center offers tourists incredible collections of art, lovely gardens, and the best *gelati* around (see p. 668).

PADUA. Bubbling with student activity and amazing sights, Padua makes a worthy pilgrimage (see below).

PADUA (PADOVA)   ☎049

Book-toting students walk through sculpture-lined *piazze* in Padua, epitomizing the city's unique blend of ancient and modern culture. The **Cappella degli Scrovegni** (Arena Chapel), P. Eremitani, 8, contains Giotto's breathtaking 38-panel fresco cycle, illustrating the lives of Mary, Jesus, and Mary's parents. Buy tickets at the adjoining **Musei Civici Eremitani**, which features a restored Giotto crucifix. (☎049 820 45 50. Open Feb.-Oct. Tu-Su 9am-7pm; Nov.-Jan. Tu-Su 9am-6pm. Chapel open Feb.-Dec. daily 9am-7pm. L10,000/€5.20, students L7000/€3.65.) Thousands of pilgrims are drawn to Saint Anthony's jawbone and well-preserved tongue at the **Basilica di Sant'Antonio**, in P. del Santo, a medieval conglomeration of eight domes filled with beautiful frescoes. (Dress code enforced. Open daily Apr.-Sept. 6:30am-8pm; Nov.-Mar. daily 6:30am-7pm. L3000/€1.55.) From the basilica, follow signs to V. Orto Botanico, 15, for **Orto Botanico**, which tempts visitors with water lilies, medicinal herbs, and a 417-year-old palm tree that still offers shade. (☎049 65 66 14. Open daily 9am-1pm and 3-6pm; in winter M-F 9am-1pm. L5000/€2.60, students L3000/

€1.55.) Next to the **duomo,** in P. Duomo, lies the 12th-century **Battistero,** the jewel of Padua, with a dome of highly concentrated frescoes. (☎049 66 28 14. Open M-Sa 7:30am-noon and 3:45-7:45pm, Su 7:45am-1pm and 3:45-8:30pm. L3000/€1.55, students L2000/€1.05.) The fascinating **Palazzo della Ragione** (Law Courts), built in 1218, is lined inside with astrological signs. (Open Jan.-Oct. Tu-Su 9am-7pm; Nov.-Dec. Tu-Su 9am-6pm. L10,000/€5.20, students L6000/€3.10.) Ancient university buildings are scattered throughout the city, centered in **Palazzo Bó.** For nighttime action, **Lucifer Young,** V. Altinate, 89, near the university, is a hip young bar. (☎049 66 55 31. Drinks from L6000/€3.10. Open Su-Tu and Th 7pm-2am, F-Sa 7pm-4am.)

Trains depart from P. Stazione for: Bologna (1½hr., 1-2 per hr., L21,000/€10.85); Milan (2½hr., 1-2 per hr., L20,000-31,500/€10.35-16.30); Venice (30min., 3-4 per hr., L4100/€2.15); Verona (1hr., 1-2 per hr., L7900/€4.10). **Buses** (☎049 820 68 11) leave from P. Boschetti for Venice (45min., 2 per hr., L5300/€2.75). The **tourist office,** in the train station, sells the one-year **Biglietto Unico,** valid at most of Padua's museums. The *biglietto* is also available at participating sights. (☎049 875 20 77. Open M-Sa 9:15am-7pm, Su 9:30am-12:15pm. Biglietto L15,000/€7.75, students L10,000/€5.20.) The **post office** is at Corso Garibaldi, 33. (☎049 820 85 11. Open M-Sa 8:10am-7pm.) Take bus #18 from the station to the stop after Prato della Valle; then walk 2 blocks, turn right on V. Marin, turn left on V. Torresino, turn right on V. Aleardi, and **Ostello Città di Padova (HI),** V. Aleardi, 30, will be on the left. (☎049 875 22 19. Breakfast, sheets, and shower included. Reception 7-9:30am and 2:30-11pm. Curfew 11pm. Reserve 1 week in advance. Dorms L22,000-27,000/€11.40-13.95.) **Hotel Al Santo,** V. del Santo, 147, near the basilica, rents airy, well-kept rooms. (☎049 875 21 31. Breakfast L10,000/€5.20. Open Feb. to mid-Dec. Singles L65,000/€33.60; doubles L105,000/€54.25; triples L150,000/€77.50. MC/V.) Women under 30 can stay in the modern, tidy rooms at **Opera Casa Famiglia (ACISJF),** V. Nino Bixio, 4, off P. Stazione. (☎049 875 15 54. Curfew 10:30pm. L30,000/€15.50 per bed.) Join a lively crowd at **Pizzeria Al Borgo,** V.L. Belludi, 56, near the Basilica di S. Antonio. (Pizzas from L6500/€3.35; cover L2500/€1.30. Open W-Su noon-3pm and 7-11:30pm.) Or, try **Alexander Birreria Paninoteca,** V.S. Francesco, 38, for a wide range of sandwiches. (*Panini* L6000-10,000/€3.10-5.20. Open M-Sa 8:30am-2am.) **Postal Code:** 35100.

VERONA ☎045

After crossing the old Roman Ponte Pietra on a summer evening, with the rushing of the Adige River below and the illuminated towers of churches and castles glowing above, you'll understand why Shakespeare set *Romeo and Juliet* in Verona. Its monumental city gates and ancient amphitheater memorialize the city's Roman past, while the Scaligeri bridge and tombs harken back to Verona's Gothic glory.

▐ **TRANSPORTATION. Trains** (☎045 800 08 61) leave P. XXV Aprile for: Bologna (2hr., every 2hr., L10,500/€5.45); Cinque Terre (4½hr., L33,000/€17.05); Milan (2hr., every hr., L12,500/€6.45); Rome (5hr., 5 per day, L63,100-72,700/€32.60-37.55); Trent (1hr., every 2hr., L9200/€4.75); Venice (1¾hr., every hr., L10,800-17,000/€5.60-8.80). **Buses** (☎045 800 41 29), on P. XXV Aprile, leave the gray building in front of the train station for: Brescia (2hr., every hr., L10,300/€5.35); Riva Del Garda (2hr., 12 per day, L9300/€4.80); Sirmione (1hr., 13 per day, L5000/€2.60).

▐▌ **ORIENTATION AND PRACTICAL INFORMATION.** From the train station, walk 20min. up **Corso Porta Nuova,** or take buses #11, 12, 13, 72, or 73 to the **Arena** in **Piazza Brà,** the heart of Verona. If you stand at the fountain in P. Brà with the Arena on your right, the **tourist office** is on the left. (☎045 806 86 80. Open daily 10am-7pm.) Additional **branches** are at airport and train station. (Open 9am-6pm.) Check **email** at the **Internet Train,** V. Roma, 17/a, past P. Brà. Go right on V. Roma and it's two blocks ahead. (☎045 803 41 00. L10,000/€5.20 per hr. Open M-F 10am-10pm, Sa noon-8pm, Su 4-8pm.) To reach the **post office,** P. Viviani, 7, follow V. Cairoli from P. delle Erbe. (☎045 800 39 38. Open M-Sa 8:10am-7pm.) **Postal Code:** 37100.

⌐ ⌐ ACCOMMODATIONS AND FOOD. Reserve ahead, especially during **opera season** (June-Sept. 3). The **Ostello della Gioventù (HI),** "Villa Francescatti," Salita Fontana del Ferro, 15, is in a renovated 16th-century villa with gorgeous gardens. From the station, take bus #73 or night bus #90 to P. Isolo and follow the yellow signs for "Ostello della Gioventù" uphill. (☎045 59 03 60. Breakfast, showers, and, sheets included. 5-night max. stay. Check-in 5pm. Check-out 7-9am. Lockout 9am-5pm. Curfew 11pm; flexible for opera-goers. No reservations. Dorms L23,000/€11.90.) Women can also try the lovely **Casa della Giovane (ACISJF),** V. Pigna, 7, 3rd fl., in the historic center of town. (☎045 59 68 80. Reception 9am-11pm. Curfew 11pm; flexible for opera-goers. Dorms L22,000/€11.40; singles L32,000/€16.55; doubles L25,000-30,000/€12.95-15.50.) To get to **Locanda Catullo,** Vco. Catullo, 1, walk to V. Mazzini, turn onto V. Catullo, and go left. (☎045 800 27 86. July-Sept. 3-night min. stay. Reserve ahead. Singles L70,000/€36.15; doubles L100,000-120,000/€51.65-62; triples L150,000-180,000/€77.50-93; quads L190,000-230,000/€98.15-118.80.)

Verona is famous for its wines—dry white *soave* and red *valpolicella, bardolino,* and *recioto.* Wine prices in **Piazza Isolo** are cheaper than in **Piazza delle Erbe.** For a large sampling, try **Oreste dal Zovo,** Vco. S. Marco in Foro, 7/5, off Corso Porta Borsari. This *enoteca* has shelves of every Italian wine imaginable (from L9000/€4.65), as well as *grappa* and well-known international liquors. **Cantore,** V. A. Mario, 2, at the end of V. Mazzini, serves up Verona's best pizza from L7000/ €3.65. (☎045 803 43 69. *Primi* L11,000-18,000/€5.60-9.30, *secondi* L12,000-22,000/ €6.20-11.40. Cover L2000/€1.05. Open Apr.-Nov. Th-Tu noon-3pm and 7pm-midnight.) **METÁ supermarket,** V. XX Settembre, 81, has reasonable prices. Take bus #11, 12, 13, 14, or 51. (Open M-Tu and Th-Sa 8:30am-12:45pm and 3:45-7:30pm, W 8:30am-12:45pm.)

◙ ◙ SIGHTS AND ENTERTAINMENT. You can stand on the renowned balcony in the **Casa di Giulietta** (Juliet's House), V. Cappello, 23, where the Capulet family never really lived. (Open Tu-Su 9am-7pm. L6000/€3.10, students L4000/€2.10.) Serving today as Verona's opera house, the **Arena,** a first-century Roman amphitheater in P. Brà, represents the figurative heart of the city. (☎045 800 32 04. Open Tu-Su 9am-7pm; in opera season 9am-3pm. L6000/€3.10, students L4000/€2.10.) From P. Brà, V. Mazzini leads to the markets and stunning medieval architecture of **Piazza delle Erbe,** once a Roman forum. The 83m **Torre dei Lambertini,** in P. dei Signori, offers a stunning view of Verona. (☎045 803 27 26. Open Tu-Su 9:30am-6pm. Elevator L4000/€2.10, students L3000/€1.55; stairs L3000/€1.55, students L2000/€1.05.) The della Scala fortress, the **Castelvecchio,** down V. Roma from P. Brà, is filled with walkways, parapets, and an extensive art collection that includes Pisanello's *Madonna and Child.* (☎045 50 47 34. Open Tu-Su 9am-7pm. L6000/€3.10, students L4000/€2.10; 1st Su of the month free.) The **Giardino Giusti,** V. Giardino Giusti, 2, is a magnificent 16th-century garden with mythological statues. (☎045 803 40 29. Open Apr.-Sept. daily 9am-8pm; Oct.-Mar. 9am-dusk. L7000/€3.65, students L3000/€1.55.) From late June to early September, tourists and singers from around the world descend on the Arena for the city's annual **Opera Festival.** (☎045 800 51 51. General admission Su-Th L38,000/€19.65, F-Sa L42,000/€21.70.) **Locos Café,** V.S. Giovanni in Valle, 28, offers more barley-based entertainment with beers from L4000/€2.10. (☎045 59 00 74. Open W-M 9:30am-2pm and 7pm-1am.)

FRIULI-VENEZIA GIULIA

Friuli-Venezia Giulia traditionally receives less than its fair share of recognition, but this region has served as inspiration to a number of prominent literary figures. James Joyce lived in Trieste for 12 years, during which he wrote most of *Ulysses;* Ernest Hemingway drew part of the plot for *A Farewell to Arms* from the region's role in WWI, and Freud and Rilke both worked and wrote here. The city of Trieste attracts large numbers of tourists to the cheapest beach resorts on the Adriatic.

ITALY

TRIESTE (TRIEST)   ☎ 090

In the post-Napoleonic real estate grab, the Austrians snatched Trieste (pop. 230,000); after a little more ping-pong, the city became part of Italy in 1954, but it still remains divided between its Slavic and Italian origins. While Trieste's fast-paced center, with Gucci-clad locals and bustling quays, is undeniably urban, the colors of the surrounding Carsoian hillside and the tranquil Adriatic Sea temper the metropolis with stunning natural beauty. The **Città Nuova,** a grid-like pattern of streets lined with crumbling Neoclassical palaces, centers around the **Canale Grande.** Facing the canal from the south is the striking Serbian Orthodox **Chiesa di San Spiridione.** (Dress modestly. Open Tu-Sa 9am-noon and 5-8pm.) The ornate **Municipio** complements the **Piazza dell'Unità d'Italia,** the largest *piazza* in Italy. Take bus #24 to the last stop (L1400/€0.75) to reach the 15th-century Venetian **Castello di San Giusto,** which presides over **Capitoline Hill,** south of P. Unità, the city's historical center, and includes a museum. From P. Goldoni, you can ascend the hill by the daunting 265 Steps of the Giants, **or Scala dei Giganti.** (☎ 040 31 36 36. Castle open daily 9am-sunset. Museum L2000/€1.05.) The **Piazza della Cattedrale** overlooks the sea and downtown Trieste. The archaeological **Museo di Storia e d'Arte,** V. Cattedrale, 15, is down the other side of the hill past the *duomo.* (☎040 37 05 00. Open Tu-Su 9am-1pm. L3000/€1.55.)

Trains (☎040 379 47 37) leave P. della Libertà, 8, down Corso Cavour from the quays, for Budapest (12hr., 2 per day, L130,000/€67.15) and Venice (2hr., 2 per hr., L15,300/€7.90). The **APT tourist office** is on Riva III Novembre, 9, near P. della Unita. (☎ 040 347 83 12; fax 347 83 20. Open M-Sa 7:30am-8:30pm.) **Hotel Alabarda,** V. Valdirivo, 22, is near the city center. From P. Oberdan, head down V. XXX Ottobre, and turn right onto V. Valdirivo. (☎040 63 02 69; fax 63 92 84. Singles L50,000-75,000/ €25.85-38.75; doubles L80,000-115,000/€41.35-59.39; triples L108,000-155,000/ €55.80-80.05; quads L136,000-195,000/€70.25-100.70. AmEx/MC/V.) To get from the station to **Ostello Tegeste (HI),** V. Miramare, 331, 6km away just south from Castle Miramare, take bus #36 (L1400/€0.75), which leaves from across V. Miramare, and ask for the "Ostello" stop. From there, walk along the Barcola, following the seaside road toward the castle. (☎/fax 040 22 41 02. Breakfast included. Reception daily 8am-11:30pm. **HI members only.** Dorms L22,000/€11.40.) For low prices, stop by Euro Spesa **supermarket** at V. Valdirivo, 13/F, off Corso Cavour. (Open M-Sa 8am-8pm.) **Pizzeria Barattolo,** P.S. Antonio, 2, along the canal, has a delicious sweet pizza crust. (☎040 63 14 80. Pizza L8000-15,000/€4.15-7.75. Cover L2000/€1.05. Service 15%. Open daily 8:30am-midnight.) **Postal Code:** 34100.

PIEDMONT (PIEMONTE)

Piedmont has been a politically influential region for centuries, as well as a fountainhead of fine food, wine, and nobility. After native-born Vittorio Emanuele II and Camillo Cavour united Italy, Turin served as the capital from 1861 to 1865.

TURIN (TORINO)   ☎ 011

Turin's elegance is the direct result of centuries of urban planning: graceful avenues lined with churches lead to spacious *piazze.* However, Turin vibrates with economic energy of the new millennium as it continues to provide a reliable headquarters for the **Fiat Auto Company** and prepares to host the **2006 Winter Olympics.** The city is also home to one of the stranger relics of Christianity: the ◪**Holy Shroud of Turin** (see p. 667) is housed in the **Cattedrale di San Giovanni,** behind the **Palazzo Reale.** The church is undergoing restoration, but remains open. (Open daily 7am-12:30pm and 3-7pm. Free. Original shroud can be viewed every year Aug. 10-Oct. 22 free of charge. Mandatory reservation at ☎800 32 93 29.) The **Museo Egizio,** in the **Palazzo dell'Accademia delle Scienze,** V. dell'Accademia delle Scienze, 6, boasts a collection of Egyptian artifacts second only to the British Museum, including several copies of the Egyptian Book of the Dead. (Open Tu-F and Su 8:30am-7:30pm, Sa 8:30am-11pm. L12,000/€6.20, ages 18-25 L6000/€3.10, under 18 and over 65 free.)

HOLY SHROUD, BATMAN! Called a hoax by some and a miracle by others, the holy shroud of Turin (a 1m by 4.5m piece of linen) was supposedly wrapped around Jesus' body in preparation for burial after his crucifixion. Visible on the cloth are outflows of blood: around the head (supposedly from the Crown of Thorns), all over the body (from scourging), and most importantly, from the wrists and feet (where the body was nailed to the cross). Although radiocarbon dating places the piece in the 12th century AD, the shroud's uncanny resemblance to that of Christ precludes its immediate dismissal. Scientists agree that the shroud was wrapped around the body of a 5'7" man who died by crucifixion, but whether it was the body of Jesus remains a mystery. For Christian believers, however, the importance of this relic is best described by Pope Paul VI's words: "The Shroud is a document of Christ's love written in characters of blood."

The **Museo Nazionale dell'Automobile,** Corso Unita d'Italia, 40, documents the evolution of the automobile, including first models of the Ford, Benz, Peugeot, and the homegrown Fiat. From the station, head south along V. Nizza. (Open Tu-Su 10am-6:30pm. L4000/€2.10.) One of Guarini's great Baroque palaces, the **Palazzo Carignano,** V. dell'Accademia delle Scienze, 5, houses the **Museo Nazionale del Risorgimento Italiano,** commemorating the 1706-1946 unification of Italy. (Open Tu-Su 9am-7pm. L8000/€4.15, students L5000/€2.60, under 10 and over 65 free.)

Trains leave **Porta Nuova** on Corso Vittorio Emanuele (☎011 531 327) to: Genoa (2hr., every hr., L14,500/€7.50); Milan (2hr., every hr., L21,600/€11.20); Rome (4½hr., 5 per day, L54,600/€28.20); Venice (4½hr., 2 per day, L51,500/€26.60). Buses leave Turin for Aosta (3½hr., 6 per day, L14,000/€7.25) and Milan (2hr., every hr., L18,000/€9.30). The **tourist office,** P. Castello, 165, has free maps. (☎011 53 51 81. Open M-Sa 9:30am-7pm, Su 9:30am-3pm.) To get to the clean and comfortable **Ostello Torino (HI),** V. Alby, 1, take bus #52 (bus #64 on Su) from Stazione Porto Nuova to the 2nd stop after crossing the Po river. Turn right onto Corso Lanza, to find the Ostello sign on the corner. Follow the signs to V. Gatti and then climb up 200m on a winding road. (☎011 660 29 39; 660 44 45. Reception 7-10am and 3:30-11pm. Curfew 11:30pm; ask for a key if you go out. Closed Dec. 20-Feb. 1. Dorms L22,000/€11.40; doubles L48,000/€24.80.) To camp at **Campeggio Villa Rey,** Strada Superiore Val S. Martino, 27, take bus #61 from Porta Nuova until P. Vittorio and then take bus #56 and follow the signs after the last stop. (☎011 819 01 17. L7000/€3.65 per person; L4000/€2.10 for 1 tent, L7000/€3.65 for 2 tents, L9000/€4.65 for up to 5 tents. Electricity L2500/€1.30. Shower L1000/€0.55.) Cheap fruit, cheese, and bread shops are on **Via Mazzini** and at **Di Per Di,** V. Carlo Alberto, 15E, at the corner of V. Maria Vittoria. (Open M-Tu and Th-Sa 8:30am-1:30pm and 3:30-7:30pm, W 8:30am-1:30pm.) **Postal Code:** 10100.

ASTI   ☎0141

Asti sparkles, just like its intoxicating progeny, the famous *Asti Spumante* wine. More than a hundred 13th-century edifices have survived the city's tumultuous history, lending it a medieval air. The **Cattedrale d'Asti,** in P. Cattedrale, is one of Piedmont's most noteworthy Gothic cathedrals. Walk down Corso Alfieri and turn right on V. Mazzini. (Open daily 7am-12:30pm and 3-7pm.) From the last week of June through the first week of July, **Asti Teatro,** the oldest Italian theatrical festival, puts on numerous performances of theatrics, music, and dance. Call the **Teatro Alfieri,** V. al Teatro, 1. (☎0141 39 93 41). Beginning on the second Friday in September, agricultural Asti revels in the **Douja d'Or,** a week-long exposition of local wines.

Trains head from P. Marconi, just a few blocks south of P. Alfieri, to Milan (2hr., 1 per day, L12,500/€6.45) and Turin (1hr., 2 per hr., L6000/€3.10). The **tourist office,** P. Alfieri, 29, helps find accommodations. (☎0141 53 03 57; fax 53 82 00. Open M-Sa 9am-1pm and 2:30-6:30pm, Su 10am-1pm.) **Hotel Cavour,** P. Marconi, 18, is across from the train station, and has immaculate rooms with TVs and phones. (☎/fax 0141 53 02 22. Reception 6am-1am. Closed in Aug. Singles L55,000/€28.40, with bath

L77,000/€39.80; doubles L85,000/€43.90, L107,000/€55.30. AmEx/DC/MC/V.) When mealtime arrives, *Astigiano* cuisine is truly a treat, famous for its simplicity, using only a few crucial ingredients and pungent cheeses to create culinary masterpieces. The extensive fruit and vegetable **markets** in P. Alfieri and Corso del Palio provide great snacks. (Open W and Sa 7:30am-1pm.) **Postal Code:** 14100.

TUSCANY (TOSCANA)

The vision that is Tuscany has inspired countless artists, poets, and hordes of tourists. Its rolling hills, prodigious olive groves, and cobblestone streets beg visitors to slow their frenetic pace, sip some wine, and relax in fields of brilliant sunflowers. Tuscany fostered some of Italy's, and the world's, greatest cultural achievements under the tender care—and devious machinations—of the powerful Medici family, gaining eternal eminence in the arts for its staggering accomplishments during a scant half-century. Today, tourists flock to Tuscany to witness the glory that was, and the wonder that still is, *Toscana*.

FLORENCE (FIRENZE) ☎055

In the early 14th century, Florence's Dante Alighieri bitterly bemoaned his hometown's infamous mercenary greed and political ferocity. Yet since then, numerous visitors have walked the city's cobblestone streets to fall under its spell of Renaissance mystique. Cosmopolitan Henry James, lonely Albert Camus, sensitive E. M. Forster, and cranky Mark Twain were all taken in by the city's beauty. Today's Florence blends the ancient and modern as Florentine students quote Marx and Malcolm X in street graffiti, colorful windows prophesy the latest looks, businessmen whiz by on Vespas, and children play soccer in the P. del Duomo.

▐ TRANSPORTATION

Flights: Amerigo Vespucci Airport (☎055 306 17 00), in the Florentine suburb of Peretola. Domestic and charter flights. **ATAF bus** #62 connects to the train station (L1500/€0.80). **SITA,** V.S. Caterina da Siena, 157 (☎800 37 37 60 46 or 055 28 46 61), runs regular buses to the airport from the station (L6000/€3.10). Ask for info at the "air terminal" (☎055 21 60 73) at platform #5 in the station, where you can check in, get an embarkation card, and register baggage (L5000/€2.60). Open daily 7am-5pm.

Trains: Santa Maria Novella Station (☎055 147 880 88), across from S. Maria Novella. Information office open daily 7am-9pm. Trains depart every hour to: **Bologna** (1hr., L14,200/€7.35); **Milan** (3½hr., L39,700/€20.50); **Rome** (3½hr., L35,000-40,000/€18.10-20.70); **Venice** (3hr., L35,100/€18.20).

Buses: LAZZI, P. Adua, 1-4r (☎055 21 51 55). To: **Pisa** (in summer departs every hr., in winter 6 per day; L11,200/€5.80). **SITA,** V.S. Caterina da Siena, 15r (☎800 37 37 60 46 or 055 28 46 61). To: **Siena** (2hr., express 1¼hr.; L11,000/€5.70).

Public Transportation: ATAF information and ticket office (☎055 565 02 22), outside the train station. Open daily 6:30am-8pm. Ask for a free bus map. Runs orange city buses 6am-1am. Tickets L1500/€0.80 for 1hr.; packet of 4 L5800/€3; 3hr. L2500/€1.30; 24hr. L6000/€3.10; 3-day L11,000/€5.70; 1 week L19,000/€9.85. Buy tickets at any newsstand, *tabacchi,* or automated ticket dispenser before boarding. Validate your ticket using the orange machine on board or risk a L75,000/€38.75 fine. 1hr. tickets are sold on the bus from 9pm-6am for L3000/€1.55.

Taxis: (☎055 43 90, 055 47 98, or 055 42 42), outside the train station.

Bike and Moped Rental: Alinari Noleggi, V. Guelfa, 85r (☎055 28 05 00). Bikes L20,000-30,000/€10.35-15.50 per day; mopeds L35,000-45,000/€18.10-23.25.

Hitchhiking: *Let's Go* does not recommend hitchhiking. Hitchers take the A-1 north to Bologna and Milan or the A-11 northwest to the Riviera and Genoa. Buses #29, 30, and 35 run from the station to the feeder near Peretola. For the A-1 south to Rome and the extension to Siena, take bus #31 or 32 from the station to Exit #23, "Firenze Sud."

ORIENTATION AND PRACTICAL INFORMATION

From the train station, a short walk on **Via de' Panzani** and a left on **Via de' Cerretani** leads to the **duomo,** the center of Florence. Major arteries radiate from the *duomo* and its two *piazze.* A bustling walkway, **Via de' Calzaiuoli** runs south from the *duomo* to the **Piazza Signoria.** V. Roma leads from P.S. Giovanni through **Piazza della Repubblica** to the **Ponte Vecchio** (Old Bridge), which spans the Arno River to the **Oltrarno** district. Note that most streets change names unpredictably. For guidance through Florence's tangled center, grab a **free map** from the tourist office. Sights are scattered throughout Florence, but few lie beyond walking distance.

> **RED AND BLACK ATTACK!** Florence's streets are numbered in red and black sequences. Red numbers indicate commercial establishments and black (or blue) numbers denote residential addresses (including most sights and hotels). Black addresses appear in *Let's Go* as a numeral only, while red addresses are indicated by a number followed by an "r." If you reach an address and it's not what you're looking for, you've probably got the wrong color—just look for the other sequence.

TOURIST, FINANCIAL, AND LOCAL SERVICES

Tourist Offices: Informazione Turistica, P. della Stazione, 4 (☎055 21 22 45), across the *piazza* from the main exit of the station. Ask for a map with a street index. English spoken. Open daily 8:30am-7:30pm. **Branch office** at the airport (☎055 31 58 74).

Tours: **Enjoy Florence** (☎167 27 48 19; www.enjoyflorence.com). Spirited guides give fast-paced, highly informative tours to small groups. Tours meet daily in summer at 10am in front of the Thomas Cook office at the Ponte Vecchio. Winter hours reduced. L30,000/€15.50, under 26 L25,000/€12.95.

Consulates: UK, Lungarno Corsini, 2 (☎055 28 41 33). Open M-F 9:30am-12:30pm and 2:30-4:30pm. **US,** Lungarno Amerigo Vespucci, 38 (☎055 239 82 76), at V. Palestro, near the station. Open M-F 9am-12:30pm and 2-3:30pm. **Canadians, Australians,** and **New Zealanders** should contact their consulates in Rome or Milan.

Currency Exchange: Local banks offer the best rates. Most are open M-F 8:20am-1:20pm and 2:45-3:45pm. 24hr. **ATMs** are all over the city.

American Express: V. Dante Alighieri, 20r (☎055 509 81). From the *duomo,* walk down V. dei Calzaiuoli, turn left on V. dei Tavolini, and continue to the small *piazza.* Cashes personal checks for AmEx cardholders. Mail held free for AmEx members and traveler's check customers, otherwise L3000/€1.55 per inquiry. L3000/€1.55 to leave messages. Money wiring available. Open M-F 9am-5:30pm.

Laundromat: Launderette, V. Guelfa, 55r. Self-service wash and dry L12,000/€6.20. Open daily 8am-10pm.

EMERGENCY AND COMMUNICATIONS

Emergency: ☎113.

Police: Central Office (Questura), V. Zara, 2 (☎055 497 71). **Carabineri:** ☎112.

24-Hour Pharmacies: Farmacia Comunale (☎055 28 94 35), at the train station by track #16. **Molteni,** V. dei Calzaiuoli, 7r (☎055 28 94 90).

Medical Assistance: ☎118.

Internet Access: Internet cafes are fairly easy to find: **Internet Train** has 15 locations throughout the city; visit www.Internettrain.it/citta.isp for locations. **Netgate,** V.S. Egidio, 10/20r (☎055 234 79 67). L10,000/€5.20 per hr. Open M-Sa 10:30am-10pm; in winter daily 10:40am-8:30pm.

Post Office: V. Pellicceria (☎055 21 61 22), off P. della Repubblica. Send packages from V. dei Sassetti, 4. Address mail to be held: FirstName SURNAME, *In Fermo Posta,* L'Ufficio Postale, V. Pellicceria, Firenze **50100,** Italy. Open M-F 8:15am-7pm, Sa 8:15am-12:30pm. 24hr. telegram office. **Postal Code:** 50100.

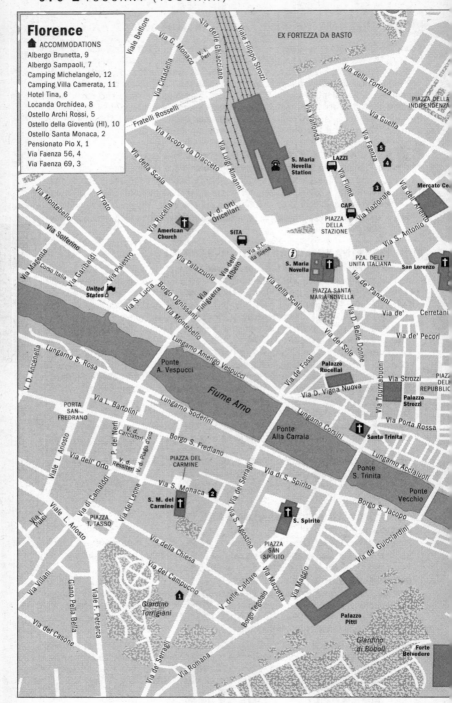

Florence

ACCOMMODATIONS

Albergo Brunetta, 9
Albergo Sampaoli, 7
Camping Michelangelo, 12
Camping Villa Camerata, 11
Hotel Tina, 6
Locanda Orchidea, 8
Ostello Archi Rossi, 5
Ostello della Gioventù (HI), 10
Ostello Santa Monaca, 2
Pensionato Pio X, 1
Via Faenza 56, 4
Via Faenza 69, 3

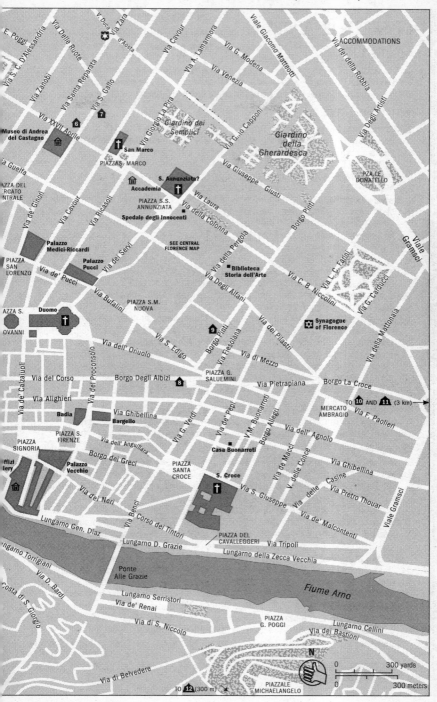

ACCOMMODATIONS

E. Poggi

Via S.C. D'Alessandria

Via S.S. D'Alessandria

Via Zanobi

Via Santa Reparata

Via S. Gallo

Via XXVII Aprile

v. duca d'Aosta

Via della Zara

Via Cavour

Via A. Lamarmora

Via G. Modena

Via Venezia

Viale Giacomo Matteotti

Via della Robbia

Via Degli Artisti

Via Delle Ruote

Museo di Andrea del Castagno

Giardino dei Semplici

Via Giorgio La Pira

Via Gino Capponi

Giardino della Gherardesca

PZA.LE DONATELLO

San Marco

PIAZZA S. MARCO

Accademia

S. Annunziata?

Via Ricasoli

PIAZZA S.S. ANNUNZIATA

Spedale degli Innocenti

Via Laura

Via della Colonna

Via Giuseppe Giusti

Borgo Pinti

Viale Gramsci

a Guelfa

AZZA DEL RCATO NTRALE

Via de' Ginori

Palazzo Medici-Riccardi

Via Cavour

Palazzo Pucci

Via de' Servi

SEE CENTRAL FLORENCE MAP

Via della Pergola

Biblioteca Storia dell'Arte

Via Degli Alfani

Via C. B. Niccolini

Via L. C. Farini

Via G. Carducci

PIAZZA SAN LORENZO

Via de' Pucci

Via Bufalini

PIAZZA S.M. NUOVA

AZZA S. OVANNI

Duomo

Via dell' Oriuolo

Via S. Egidio

Borgo Pinti

Via Fiesolana

Via di Mezzo

Via de' Pilastri

Synagogue of Florence

Via della Mattonaia

Via di Proconsolo

Via del Corso

Borgo Degli Albizi

PIAZZA G. SALUEMINI

Via Pietrapiana

Borgo La Croce

Via de' Calzaiuoli

Via Alighieri

Badia

Via Ghibellina

Bargello

Via G. Verdi

Via de' Pepi

V.M. Buonarroti

Borgo Allegri

Via dell' Agnolo

TO AND (3 km)

MERCATO AMBRAGIO

Via F. Paoiieri

PIAZZA S. FIRENZE

Via dell' Anguillara

Casa Buonarroti

Via de' Macci

Via delle Conce

Via Ghibellina

Via Pretro Thouar

PIAZZA SIGNORIA

Palazzo Vecchio

Borgo dei Greci

PIAZZA SANTA CROCE

S. Croce

Via S. Giuseppe

V. delle Casine

ffizi lery

Via dei Neri

Via Benci

Corso dei Tintori

Via S. Giuseppe

Via de' Malcontenti

Viale Gramsci

Lungarno Gen. Diaz

Lungarno D. Grazie

PIAZZA DEL CAVALLEGGERI

Via Tripoli

Lungarno Torrigiani

Ponte Alle Grazie

Lungarno della Zecca Vecchia

costa di S. Giorgio

Via D. Bardi

Lungarno Serristori

Via de' Renai

Fiume Arno

Lungarno Cellini

Via dei Bastioni

Via di S. Niccolo

PIAZZA G. POGGI

Via di Belvedere

TO (300 m)

PIAZZALE MICHAELANGELO

N

0   300 yards

0   300 meters

█ ACCOMMODATIONS

Florence is packed with budget accommodations. **Consorzio ITA**, in the train station by track #16, can find cheap rooms for a L4500-15,000/€2.35-7.75 commission. (☎055 28 28 93. Open daily 8:45am-8pm.) However, because of the constant stream of tourists in Florence, it is best to make reservations *(prenotazioni)* at least 10 days in advance, especially if you plan to visit during Easter or summer.

YOUTH HOSTELS

▨ **Ostello Archi Rossi**, V. Faenza, 94r (☎055 29 08 04; fax 230 26 01), 2 blocks from the train station. Exit left from the station onto V. Nazionale and take 2nd left onto V. Faenza. Wheelchair-accessible. Breakfast L3000-4500/€1.55-2.35. Laundry L10,000/€5.20. Lockout from room 9:30am, from hostel 11am. Curfew 12:30am. No reservations—in summer, arrive before 8am to get a room. 4- to 9-bed dorms L35,000-40,000/€18.10-20.65; rooms for handicapped travelers L50,000/€25.85.

Ostello Santa Monaca, V.S. Monaca, 6 (☎055 26 83 38). Exit the station by track #16, head right to P. della Stazione, walk to the left of the church, continue through P.S. Maria Novella and down V. dei Fossi, which becomes V. dei Serragli after the bridge, and turn right onto V.S. Monaca off V. dei Serragli. 7-night max. stay. Reception 6am-1pm and 2pm-1am. Curfew 1am. Reserve 3 days in advance, in writing. Dorms L25,000/€12.95. AmEx/MC/V.

Ostello della Gioventù Europa Villa Camerata (HI), V. Augusto Righi, 2-4 (☎055 60 14 51). Take bus #17 from outside the train station (near track #5) or from P. dell'Unità, across from the train station, and get off at "Salviatino." In a distant gorgeous villa with *loggia* and gardens. Breakfast and sheets included. Laundry L10,000/€5.20. Reception daily 7am-12:30pm and 1pm-midnight. Strict midnight curfew. Reserve in writing. Dorms L28,000/€14.50, nonmembers L5000/€2.60 extra per night. If full, sleep on a cot (L20,000/€10.35) in an outdoor tent with wood floors and electricity.

Pensionato Pio X, V. dei Serragli, 106 (☎/fax 055 22 50 44). Past the Istituto Gould in Oltrarno. Quiet, clean rooms and comfortable lounges. 2-night min. stay. Check-out 9am. Curfew midnight. No reservations—arrive before 9am to get a room. Dorms L26,000/€13.45, with bath L30,000/€15.50; singles L30,000/€15.50.

AROUND PIAZZA SANTA MARIA NOVELLA

The budget accommodations that cluster around this attractive *piazza* in front of the train station offer a prime location near the *duomo* and the *centro*.

▨ **Hotel Visconti**, P. Ottaviani, 1 (☎/fax 055 21 38 77). Exit the train station from the left and cross to the back of S. Maria church into P.S. Maria Novella. Walk on the left side until you reach tiny P. Ottaviani. Look for huge Grecian nudes. Bar and TV lounge. Delicious breakfast in roof garden included. Singles L68,000/€35.15, with bath L100,000/€51.65; doubles L104,000/€53.75, L145,000/€74.90; triples L150,000/€77.50, L180,000/€93; quads L168,000/€86.80, L220,000/€113.65.

Pensione Ottaviani, P. Ottaviani, 1 (☎055 239 62; fax 29 33 55). Upstairs from Hotel Visconti (see above). Elegant, comfortable, and cheap. Singles L50,000/€25.85; doubles L100,000/€51.65; triples L145,000/€74.90; quads L190,000/€98.15.

Albergo Margaret, V. della Scala, 25 (☎055 21 01 38). Exit to the right from the train station onto V. degli orti Oricellari, and turn left on V. della Scala. Kind staff offers beautiful rooms. Curfew midnight. Singles L85,000-110,000/€43.90-56.85; doubles L110,000-130,000/€56.85-67.15. Lower prices Sept.-May and for longer stays.

Hotel Giappone, V. dei Banchi, 1 (☎055 26 86 75). Clean, comfortable rooms combine with central location for one of the best values in Florence. Singles L100,000/€51.65; doubles L130,000/€67.15, with bath L160,000/€82.65. MC/V.

Hotel Abaco, V. dei Banchi, 1 (☎055 238 19 19). Same directions as Hotel Giappone (see above). Noise-proof windows and free **Internet** access. 7 well-kept rooms. Laundry L7000/€3.65 per load. Singles L100,000/€51.65; doubles L130,000/€67.15. Extra bed L40,000/€20.65. MC/V.

Soggiorno Luna Rossa, V. Nazionale, 7 (☎055 230 21 85; fax 28 25 52; www.tourist-house.com). Exit the train station to the left to find V. Nazionale. Large comfy rooms. Doubles and triples L50,000/€25.85 per person; quads or larger L45,000/€23.25 per person; doubles with bath L150,000/€77.50; triples with bath L195,000/€100.70.

OLD CITY (NEAR THE DUOMO)

Though flooded by tourists, this area has a surprising array of budget accommodations. Many provide great views of Florence's monuments, while others lie hidden in Renaissance *palazzi*. Follow V. de' Panzani from the train station and take a left on V. de' Cerretani to reach the *duomo*.

⊠ Albergo Brunetta, Borgo Pinti, 5 (☎055 247 81 34). Exit P. del Duomo on V. dell'Oriuolo behing the *duomo*. After 2 long blocks, turn left on Borgo Pinti. Excellent value with a central location. Rooftop terrace with superb view of the city. Showers free. Singles L80,000/€41.35; doubles L130,000/€67.15; triples L170,000/€87.80.

Locanda Orchidea, Borgo degli Albizia, 11 (☎055 248 03 46). Turn left off V. Proconsolo from the *duomo*. Dante's wife was born in this 12th-century *palazzo*. Some of the rooms open onto a garden. Singles L75,000/€38.75; doubles L110,000/€56.85; triples L170,000/€87.80.

Albergo Firenze, P. dei Donati, 4 (☎055 21 42 03 or 26 83 01 or 21 99 11; fax 21 23 70). Off V. del Duomo, 2 blocks south of the *duomo*. Central and tranquil, located in a lovely *palazzo*. Breakfast included. Singles L110,000/€56.85; doubles L150,000/€77.50; triples L215,000/€111.05; quads L260,000/€134.30.

AROUND PIAZZA SAN MARCO

This area is considerably calmer and less tourist-ridden than its proximity to the center might suggest. Turn right from the station and left on V. Nazionale. Take a right on V. Guelfa, which intersects V.S. Gallo and V. Cavour.

⊠ Hotel Tina, V.S. Gallo, 31 (☎055 48 35 19). From P.S. Marco, follow V. XXII Aprile and turn right on V.S. Gallo. Small *pensione* with high ceilings and new furniture. Singles L85,000/€43.90; doubles L120,000-150,000/€62-77.50; triples L160,000/€82.65; quads L200,000/€103.30.

Albergo Sampaoli, V.S. Gallo, 14 (☎055 28 48 34), before the Hotel Tina (see above). Large rooms with balconies. Singles L80,000-100,000/€41.35-51.65; doubles L110,000-160,000/€56.85-82.65. Extra bed L56,000/€28.95.

VIA NAZIONALE AND ENVIRONS

From P. della Stazione, V. Nazionale leads to budget hotels that are a short walk from the *duomo* and the train station. The buildings on V. Nazionale, V. Faenza, V. Fiume, and V. Guelfa are filled with inexpensive establishments, but rooms facing the street may be noisy.

⊠ Via Faenza, 69. This building houses 3 accommodations under 1 roof. When leaving the train tracks, exit the train station to the left to find V. Nazionale. Walk 1 block on V. Nazionale and turn left on V. Faenza.

Hotel Soggiorno d'Errico (☎055 21 55 31). 7 clean, bright rooms, some overlooking a courtyard. Singles L50,000/€25.85; doubles L100,000/€51.65. AmEx/MC/V.

Locanda Giovanna, 4th fl. (☎055 238 13 53). Well-kept rooms, some with garden views. Singles L60,000/€31; doubles L100,000-110,000/€51.65-56.85.

Hotel Nella/Pina, 1st and 2nd fl. (☎055 265 43 46). 14 basic rooms and friendly proprietors. Singles L80,000/€41.35; doubles L110,000/€56.85. AmEx/MC/V.

Via Faenza, 56. This address houses 6 separate *pensioni* that are among the best deals in the city. Follow the same directions for V. Faenza, 69. The Azzi, Anna, and Paola share uniform management and prices, which are listed only in the listing for the Azzi.

Pensione Azzi (☎055 21 38 06). Styles itself as a *locanda degli artisti* (an artists' inn), but all travelers enjoy the large, immaculate rooms and a relaxing terrace. Breakfast included. No curfew. Singles L80,000/€41.35; doubles L110,000-140,000/€56.85-72.30. AmEx/MC/V.

Albergo Anna (☎055 239 83 22). 8 lovely rooms with beautiful frescoes and more pragmatic fans.

Locanda Paola (☎055 21 36 82). Minimalist, but clean double rooms, some with views of Fiesole and the surrounding hills. Curfew 2am; key available upon request.

Albergo Merlini (☎055 21 28 48). Murals and red geraniums adorn the lounge/solarium. Some rooms have views of the *duomo*. Breakfast L9000/€4.65. Curfew 1am. Singles L85,000/€43.90; doubles L125,000/€64.60. AmEx/MC/V.

Albergo Marini (☎055 28 48 24). Polished wood hallway leads to inviting, spotless rooms. Breakfast L8000/€4.15. Flexible 1am curfew. Doubles L110,000-130,000/€56.85-67.15; triples L145,000-165,000/€74.90-85.25; quads L180,000-200,000/€93-103.30; quints L215,000-235,000/€111.05-121.40. Cash only.

Albergo Armonia (☎055 21 11 46). Clean rooms bedecked with American film posters. If you share your name with a movie star, get a 5% discount. Singles L80,000/€41.35; doubles L120,000/€62; triples L145,000/€74.90; quads L170,000/€87.80.

Hotel Nazionale, V. Nazionale, 22 (☎055 238 22 03), exit train station to the left and turn left on V. Nazionale. Comfy beds in sunny rooms. Breakfast included. Curfew midnight, but social butterflies can ask for a key. Singles L100,000/€51.65, with bath L110,000/€56.85; doubles L140,000/€72.30, L160,000/€82.65; triples L190,000/€98.15, L210,000/€108.45. MC/V.

Katti House, V. Faenza, 21 (☎055 21 34 10). Exit train station to walk 1 block down V. Nazionale, and turn right on V. Faenza. Large rooms filled with amenities. Doubles L180,000/€93; triples L200,000/€103.30; quads L220,000/€113.65.

IN THE OLTRARNO

Only a 10min. walk across the Arno from the *duomo*, this area and its *pensione* offer a respite from Florence's bustling hubs.

▨ **Hotel La Scaletta,** V. de'Guicciardini, 13b (☎055 28 30 28; fax 28 95 62; www.lascaletta.com). Turn right onto V. Roma from the *duomo*. Cross the Ponte Vecchio and continue onto V. Guicciardini. Rooftop terraces offer spectacular views of the Boboli Gardens. Breakfast included. Singles L90,000/€46.50, L170,000/€87.80; doubles L190,000/€98.15, L240,000/€123.95; triples L200,000/€103.30, L280,000/€144.65; quads L220,000/€113.65, L300,000/€154.95. 10% discount for *Let's Go* readers who pay with cash. MC/V.

CAMPING

Campeggio Michelangelo, V. Michelangelo, 80 (☎055 681 19 77). Beneath Piazzale Michelangelo. Take bus #13 from the station (15min., last bus 11:25pm). Extremely crowded, but offers a spectacular panorama of Florence. Well-stocked food store and bar. Reception 6am-midnight. Open Apr.-Nov. L11,000/€5.70 per person; L9000/€4.65 per tent; L6000/€3.10 per car, L4000/€2.10 per motorcycle.

Villa Camerata, V.A. Righi, 2-4 (☎055 60 03 15), same entrance as the HI hostel on the #17 bus route (see HI directions, p. 672.) Breakfast at hostel L2500/€1.30. 7-night max. stay. Reception daily 1pm-midnight; if office is closed, stake a site and return later to register and pay. Check-out 7-10am. L8000-10,000/€4.15-5.20 per person; L8000-16,000/€4.15-8.30 per tent, L20,000/€10.35 per car.

◖ FOOD

Florence's hearty cuisine originated from the peasant fare of the surrounding countryside. Specialties include *bruschetta* (grilled bread soaked with olive oil and garlic and topped with tomatoes and basil, anchovy, or liver paste) and the Tuscan classics *minestra di fagioli* (white bean and garlic soup) and *bistecca alla Fiorentina* (thick sirloin steak). Wine is a Florentine staple, and genuine *chianti classico* commands a premium price; a liter of house wine costs L7000-10,000/€3.65-5.20 in Florence's *trattorie*, while stores sell bottles for as little as L5000/€2.60. For lunch, visit a *rosticceria gastronomia*, peruse the city's pushcarts, or pick up fresh produce and meat at the **Mercato Centrale,** between V. Nazionale and S. Lorenzo. (Open June-Sept. M-Sa 7am-2pm; Oct.-May Sa 7am-2pm and 4-8pm.)

Vegetarians will find several health food markets in the city. They stock vitamins, algae, homemade takeout vegetable tarts, and organic vegetables, all with an Italian touch. One of the best is **Sugar Blues,** a 5min. walk from the *duomo* at V. XXVII Aprile, 46r. (Open M-F 9am-1:30pm and 4-7:30pm, Sa 9am-1pm.) For staples try

STANDA supermarket, V. Pietrapiana, 1r. Turn right on V. del Proconsolo, take the 1st left on Borgo degli Albizi, go straight through P.G. Salvemini, and it's on the left. (Open M 2-9pm, Tu-Su 8:30am-9pm.)

OLD CITY (THE DUOMO)

▨**Acqua al Due,** V. Vigna Vecchia, 40r (☎055 28 41 70). Behind the Bargello. Florentine specialties in a cozy place popular with young Italians. Their *assaggio,* with 5 types of pasta, demands a taste (L14,500/€7.50). *Primi* L11,500-13,000/€5.95-6.75; *secondi* from L18,000/€9.30. Cover L2000/€1.05. Reserve ahead for a table. Open June-Sept. daily 7:30pm-1am; Oct.-May Tu-Su 8pm-1am.

Trattoria Anita, V. del Parlasco, 2r (☎055 23 46 47), just behind the Bargello. Dine by candlelight on hearty Tuscan fare. *Primi* L7000-9000/€3.65-4.65, *secondi* from L10,000/€5.20. Cover L2000/€1.05. Open M-Sa for lunch and dinner.

Trattoria da Benvenuto, V. della Mosca, 16r (☎055 21 48 33), on the corner of V. de'Neri. Elegant setting. Try the *spaghetti alle vongole* (with clams) L10,000/€5.20. *Primi* L9000-12,000/€4.65-6.20, *secondi* L11,000-22,000/€5.70-11.40. Cover L3000/€1.55 and 10% service charge. Open M-Sa 11am-2pm and 7pm-midnight.

SANTA MARIA NOVELLA AND ENVIRONS

▨**Trattoria Contadino,** V. Palazzuolo, 71r (☎055 238 26 73). The real deal with filling homestyle meals. Lunch *menù* L16,000/€8.30, dinner *menù* L17,000/€8.80. Open M-Sa noon-3:30pm and 6-9:30pm.

Il Latini, V. Palchetti, 6r. From the Ponte alla Carraia, walk up V. del Moro; V. dei Palchetti is on the right. Serves delicious Tuscan classics like *ribollita* (L8000/€4.15). *Primi* L10,000-12,000/€5.20-6.20, *secondi* L18,000-20,000/€9.30-10.35. Cover L3000/€1.55. Open Tu-Su noon-2:30pm and 7:30-10:30pm.

THE STATION AND UNIVERSITY QUARTER

▨**Trattoria da Zà-Zà,** P. del Mercato Centrale, 26r (☎055 21 54 11). Old world charm with heavy wooden beams and dripping candles. Try the *tris* (veggie soup; L9000/€4.65) or the *tagliatelle al tartufo* (pasta with truffles; L11,000/€5.70). Cover L3000/€1.55. Open M-Sa noon-3pm and 7-11pm. Reservations suggested.

Trattoria da Garibardi, P. del Mercato Centrale, 38r (☎055 21 22 67). Full of locals enjoying fresh and cheap food. Fixed *menù* L24,000/€12.40. Cover L2000/€1.05 for meals outside the *menù. Primi* L5000-12,000/€2.60-6.20, *secondi* from L15,000/€7.75. Open daily June-Aug. noon-11pm; Sept.-May M-Sa noon-3pm and 7-11pm.

THE OLTRARNO

▨**Il Borgo Antico,** P.S. Spirito, 6r (☎055 21 04 37). An array of tasty and filling dishes. *Primi* L10,000/€5.20, *secondi* L25,000-30,000/€12.95-15.50. Cover L3000/€1.55. Open daily 1-4pm and 6:30pm-1:30am. Reservations recommended.

La Mangiatoia, P.S. Felice, 8r (☎055 22 40 60). Continue straight on V. Guicciardini from Ponte Vecchio, and look to the left past P. dei Pitti. Sit at the front counter to watch them make pizza in the brick oven and get pasta lessons from locals. Pizza L6500-9000/€3.35-4.65, fixed *menù* (L20,000/€10.35) changes daily. Cover L2000/€1.05 in dining room. Open Tu-Su noon-3pm and 7-11pm.

GELATERIE

Florence's own Buontalenti family supposedly invented *gelato;* as a tourist, it's your duty to sample this creamy manifestation of the city's culture.

▨**Vivoli,** V. della Stinche, 7 (☎055 29 23 34), behind the Bargello. The most renowned Florentine *gelateria,* with the self-proclaimed "best ice cream in the world." Huge selection. Cups from L3000/€1.55. Open daily 8am-1am

Carabè, V. Ricasoli, 60r (☎055 28 94 76). Amazing *gelato* that's less expensive than most. Cones from L2500/€1.30, *granite* (ices) from L3500/€1.85. Open May-Sept. daiy 10am-1am; Mar.-Apr. and Oct. daily noon-1am; closed Nov.-Feb.

Perchè No?, V. Tavolini, 19r (☎055 239 89 69), off V. dei Calzaiuoli. Florence's oldest *gelateria* serves heavenly pistachio, amazing chocolate, and chunky *nocciolosa.* Cones from L3000/€1.55. Open May-Sept. W-M 10am-1am; Oct.-Mar. W-M 10am-8pm.

SIGHTS

Florence's museums have recently doubled their prices (now L6000-12,000/€3.10-6.20 per venue) and no longer offer student discounts. In summer, watch for **Sere al Museo,** evenings when certain museums are free from 8:30-11pm. Additionally, don't miss Florence's churches, many of which are free treasuries of great art.

PIAZZA DEL DUOMO

■ **DUOMO (CATTEDRALE DI SANTA MARIA DEL FIORE).** In 1296 the city fathers commissioned Arnolfo di Cambio to erect a cathedral "with the most high and sumptuous magnificence" so that it would be "impossible to make it either better or more beautiful with the power and industry of man." Arnolfo and a succession of architects triumphed, completing the massive nave by 1418. One problem remained—no one had the necessary engineering skills to build the dome of the cathedral. Finally, Filippo Brunelleschi dreamt up an ingenious technique for building the duomo's breathtaking crown, now known simply as **Brunelleschi's Dome.** He drew from long-neglected classical methods to develop the revolutionary idea of using interlocking bricks that supported themselves, making a double-shelled construction. Today, the duomo claims the world's third-longest nave, after St. Peter's in Rome and St. Paul's in London. (Open M-Sa 10am-5pm, Su 1:30-5pm; 1st Sa of every month 10am-3:30pm. Masses daily 7am-12:30pm and 5-7pm.) Climb the 463 steps inside the dome to reach **Michelangelo's lantern,** or cupola, for an unparalleled view of the city from the 100m high external gallery. *(Entrance on south side of duomo.* ☎ *055 230 28 85. Open M-F 8:30am-7pm, Sa 8:30am-5:40pm. L10,000/€5.20.)*

BAPTISTERY. This *battistero* (baptistery) next to the *duomo,* built between the 5th and 9th centuries, was the site of Dante's christening; years later, its Byzantine mosaics inspired the details of the author's *Inferno.* When Ghiberti completed the baptistery's famous bronze doors in 1425, his work was so admired that he was immediately commissioned to forge the last set of doors, which he finished in 1452. The ■**Gates of Paradise,** as Michelangelo reportedly dubbed them, were nothing like his two earlier portals; they abandoned his earlier 28-panel design for 10 large, gilded squares, each of which employed mathematical perspective to create the illusion of deep space. They have been under restoration since a 1966 flood and will soon reside in the Museo dell'Opera del Duomo. *(Opposite the duomo. Open M-Sa noon-7pm, Su 9am-2pm. Mass daily 10:30 and 11:30am. L5000/€2.60.)*

CAMPANILE. Next to the duomo rises the 82m high **campanile,** whose pink, green, and white marble exterior matches the duomo and battistero. Giotto, Andrea Pisano, and Francesco Talenti all had a hand in building it. The original exterior decoration is now in the Museo dell'Opera del Duomo. The 414 steps to the top lead to beautiful views. *(Open daily 8:30am-7:30pm. L10,000/€5.20.)*

MUSEO DELL' OPERA DEL DUOMO. Most of the art of the *duomo* resides in this museum. Up the first flight of stairs is a late *Pietà* by Michelangelo, who according to legend destroyed Christ's left arm with a hammer in a fit of frustration; soon after, a diligent pupil touched up the work, but he left visible scars on a portion of Mary Magdalene's head. In the museum are Donatello's wooden *St. Mary Magdalene* (1555), Donatello and Luca della Robbia's *cantorie* (choir balconies with bas-reliefs of cavorting children), and four frames from the baptistery's *Gates of Paradise.* The museum also houses the sculptures that once covered the campanile's exterior. *(P. del Duomo, 9, behind the duomo.* ☎ *055 230 28 85. Open M-Sa 9am-6:30pm, Su 9am-2pm. Tours in English in summer W-Th 4pm. L10,000/€5.20.)*

PIAZZA DELLA SIGNORIA AND ENVIRONS

From P. del Duomo, **Via dei Calzaiuoli,** one of the city's oldest streets, leads to P. della Signoria. Built by the Romans, V. dei Calzaiuoli now bustles with crowds, chic shops, *gelaterie,* and vendors.

▓ THE UFFIZI

From P.B.S. Giovanni, go down V. Roma, past P. della Repubblica where the street turns into V. Calimala. Continue until V. Vaccherreccia and go left. The Uffizi is straight ahead. ☎ 055 21 83 41. Open Tu-Sa 8:30am-6:50pm, Su 8:30am-1:50pm. L12,000/€6.20. For an extra L2000/€1.05, save yourself hours of waiting by purchasing advance tickets—call 055 29 48 83. Credit card required.

Vasari designed this palace in 1554 for the *uffizi* (offices) of the administration of Duke Cosimo; today, it houses more first-class art per square centimeter than any other museum in the world. The museum displays an unparalleled collection of Renaissance art: Botticelli, da Vinci, Michelangelo, Raphael, Titian, Giotto, Fra Angelico, Caravaggio, Bronzino, Cimabue, della Francesca, Bellini, and even Dürer, Rubens, and Rembrandt—you name it, they have it.

As you reach the 2nd floor of the museum, you will see a long corridor that wraps around the building and holds an impressive collection of Hellenistic and Roman marbles, the inspiration for many Renaissance pieces. Follow the hordes to **Room 2,** which features three 13th- and 14th-century *Madonne* of the great forefathers of the Renaissance: Cimabue, Duccio di Buoninsegna, and Giotto. Their naturalistic figures rebelled against the prevalent Gothic style, and the originals are far more impressive than reproductions. **Room 3** features works from 14th-century Siena (including paintings by the Lorenzetti brothers and Simone Martini's dazzling *Annunciation*). One of the most awe-inspiring rooms in the museum, **Room 7,** houses two Fra Angelico paintings and a *Madonna and Child* by Masaccio. Domenico Veneziano's *Madonna with Child and Saints (Sacra Conversazione)* is one of the first paintings to incorporate Mary and the saints into a unified space. Piero della Francesca's double portrait of Duke Federico and his wife Battista Sforza stands out for its translucent color and intricate detail. In **Room 8,** Filippo Lippi's *Madonna and Child with Two Angels* pulls at the heart strings. **Rooms 10-14** are a shrine to Florence's cherished Botticelli—the resplendent *Primavera, Birth of Venus, Madonna della Melagrana,* and *Pallas and the Centaur* glow from their recent restoration. **Room 15** moves into the High Renaissance with Da Vinci's brilliant *Annunciation* and his even more remarkable, albeit unfinished, *Adoration of the Magi.* **Rooms 20** and **22** detour into the art of Northern Europe, showcasing Dürer's realistic *Adam and Eve* and Cranach the Elder's haunting treatment of the same subject. **Room 21** contains 15th-century Venetian artwork. View Bellini's moving *Sacred Allegory* before examining Mantegna's *Adoration of the Magi* in **Room 23.** The south corridor's windows offer a breathtaking view of Florence. **Rooms 25-27** display Florentine works, including Michelangelo's only oil painting, *Doni Tondo,* a string of Raphaels, and Pontormo's *Supper at Emmaus.* **Room 28** displays Titian's beautiful *Venus of Urbino.*

OTHER SIGHTS IN PIAZZA DELLA SIGNORIA

PIAZZA DELLA SIGNORIA. This 13th-century *piazza* is dominated by the looming presence of the blank-walled, turreted Palazzo Vecchio (see below) and the corner of the Uffizi Gallery (see p. 677). In 1497, the religious zealot and social critic Girolamo Savonarola convinced Florentines to light the **Bonfire of the Vanities** in the *piazza,* a grand roast that consumed some of Florence's best art, including, according to legend, all of Botticelli's secular works that had not been sold to private collectors. A year later, disillusioned citizens sent Savonarola up in smoke on the same spot, marked today by a commemorative granite disc. Monumental sculptures cluster around the Palazzo Vecchio, including Donatello's *Judith and Holofernes,* a copy of Michelangelo's *David,* Giambologna's equestrian *Cosimo I,* and Bandinelli's *Hercules.* The awkward *Neptune* to the left of the *palazzo* so revolted Michelangelo that he insulted the artist: "Oh Ammannato, Ammannato, what lovely marble you have ruined!" Most Florentines share his opinion—derisively called *"Il Biancone"* ("the big white one"), *Neptune* is continually subject to attacks of vandalism by angry aesthetes. The graceful 14th-century **Loggia dei Lanzi,** built as a

ITALY

stage for civic orators, is one of the best places in Florence to see world-class sculpture free of charge. It includes mostly classical Roman works, but its highlights are Renaissance pieces like Giambologna's famous *Rape of the Sabines*.

PALAZZO VECCHIO. Arnolfo del Cambio designed this fortress-like *palazzo* (1299-1304) as the seat of the *comune*'s government. Its apartments served as living quarters for the *signoria* (city council) members during their two-month terms. The building became the family home of the Medici, and in 1470 Michelozzo decorated the now world-famous ▓**courtyard** in the Renaissance style. The building contains works by Michelangelo, Leonardo, and Bronzino. (☎ 055 216 84 65. Open June-Aug. M and F 9am-11pm, Tu-W and Sa 9am-7pm, Th and Su 9am-2pm; Sept.-May M-W and F-Sa 9am-7pm, Th and Su 9am-2pm. Palazzo L10,000/€5.20, courtyard free.)

PONTE VECCHIO. The nearby Ponte Vecchio, literally named Old Bridge, is indeed the oldest bridge in Florence, built in 1345 to replace an even older Roman version. In the 1500s, butchers and tanners lined the bridge and dumped pigs' blood and intestines in the river, creating an odor that offended the noses of powerful bankers who crossed the Arno on the way to their *uffizi* (offices). In an effort to improve the area, the Medici kicked them out, allowing the more decorous goldsmiths and diamond-carvers to move in; their descendants now line the bridge with glittering boutiques. (From the Uffizi, turn left onto V. Georgofili, then right when you reach the river.)

THE BARGELLO AND ENVIRONS

▓**BARGELLO.** In the heart of medieval Florence, this 13th-century fortress was once the residence of Florence's chief magistrate. It later became a brutal prison that held public executions in the courtyard. In the 19th century, the Bargello was restored to its former elegance, and now houses the **Museo Nazionale,** a treasury of Florentine sculpture. In the Salone del Consiglio Generale stands Donatello's bronze *David*, the first freestanding nude since antiquity. The artist's marble *David*, completed 30 years prior, stands near the left wall. The *loggia* on the first floor displays a collection of bronze animals created for a Medici garden grotto. Michelangelo's early works, including *Bacchus*, *Brutus*, *Apollo*, and *Madonna and Child*, dominate the ground floor. (V. del Proconsolo, 4, between the duomo and P. della Signoria. ☎ 055 238 86 06. Open daily 8:15am-1:50pm; closed on the 1st, 3rd, and 5th Su and the 2nd and 4th M of every month. L8000/€4.15.)

BADIA. The Badia was the site of medieval Florence's richest monastery. Filippo Lippi's stunning *Apparition of the Virgin to St. Bernard*, one of the most famous paintings of the late 15th century, hangs to the left of the entrance. (Entrance on V. Dante Alighieri, just off V. Proconsolo. Open daily 7:30am-12:30pm and 1-6pm.)

PIAZZA DELLA REPUBBLICA. In 1890, this *piazza*, commemorating the recently unified Italian state, replaced the Mercato Vecchio as the site of the town market. The largest open space in Florence, this *piazza*, lined with venerable, overpriced coffee shops and restaurants, teems with crowds and street performers at night.

CHIESA DI SANTA MARIA NOVELLA. Built between 1279 and 1360, the *chiesa* boasts a green and white Romanesque-Gothic lower façade. Masaccio's powerful fresco *Trinity*, on the left side of the nave, the first painting to use geometric perspective, creates the illusion of a tabernacle. The **Cappella di Filippo Strozzi,** to the right of the altar, contains frescoes by Fillipo Lippi. (☎ 055 21 01 13. Open M-Th and Sa 9:30am-5pm, F and Su 1-5pm. L5000/€2.60.) The adjoining **Cappella Spagnola (Spanish Chapel)** has 14th-century frescoes by Andrea di Bonaiuto. (☎ 055 28 21 87. Open M-Th and Sa 9am-2pm, Su 8am-1pm. L6000/€3.10)

SAN LORENZO AND FARTHER NORTH

▓**BASILICA DI SAN LORENZO.** In 1419, Brunelleschi designed this spacious basilica. Because the Medici provided major funds for the church, they kept artistic control over its construction. Their coat of arms, featuring six red balls, appears all over the nave, and their tombs fill the two sacristies and the Cappella dei Principi behind the altar. The family cunningly placed Cosimo dei Medici's grave in front of the high altar, making the entire church his personal mausoleum. (☎ 055 21 66 34.

Open M-Sa 10am-5pm. L5000/€2.60.) To reach the ◪**Cappelle dei Medici** (Medici Chapels), walk to the back entrance on P. Madonna degli Aldobrandini. Intended as a grand mausoleum, Matteo Nigetti's **Cappella dei Principi** (Princes' Chapel) emulates the baptistry in P. del Duomo. Michelangelo's simple architectural design of the **Sacrestia Nuova** (1524) reveals the master's study of Brunelleschi. Michelangelo sculpted two tombs for Medici dukes, Lorenzo and Giuliano, which depict day and night, dawn and dusk, and life and death. *(☎ 055 238 86 02. Open daily 8:15am-5pm; closed the 2nd and 4th Su and the 1st, 3rd, and 5th M of every month. L11,000/€5.80.)*

◪**MUSEO DELLA CHIESA DI SAN MARCO.** Remarkable works by Fra Angelico adorn this museum, one of the most peaceful and spiritual places in Florence. Climb upstairs to see his famous *Annunciation*. Every cell in the convent has its own Fra Angelico fresco, painted in flat colors with sparse detail to facilitate the monks' meditation. *(P. di S. Marco, 3. ☎ 055 238 86 08. Open M-F 8:30am-1:30pm, Sa-Su 8:30am-6:50pm; closed the 1st, 3rd, and 5th Su, and the 2nd and 4th M of each month. L8000/€4.15, EU citizens 18-25 L4000/€2.10, over 65 and under 18 free.)*

ACCADEMIA. Michelangelo's triumphant ◪**David** stands in self-assured perfection in a rotunda designed just for him. He was moved here from P. della Signoria in 1873 after a stone hurled during a riot broke his left wrist in two places. In the hallway leading up to the *David* are Michelangelo's four *Slaves*. The master left these intriguing statues unfinished; remaining true to his theories of living stone, he chipped away only enough to liberate the slaves. *(V. Ricasoli, 60, between the churches of S. Marco and S.S. Annunziata. ☎ 055 238 86 09. Open mid-June to mid-Sept. Tu-F 8:30am-6:50pm, Sa 8:30am-10pm; mid-Sept. to mid-June Tu-Su 8:30am-6:50pm. L12,000/€6.20.)*

CHIESA DI SANTA CROCE. Follow V. Ghibellina east from the Bargello and turn right on V. Giuseppe Verdi to reach **Piazza Santa Croce,** home to the Franciscan Chiesa di Santa Croce. Despite the frugality of the Franciscans, it's quite possibly the most splendid church in the city, with impressive Giotto frescoes. Among the all-star Florentines buried here are Michelangelo, Machiavelli, and Galileo. *(☎055 29 08 32. Open M-Sa 9:30am-5:30pm, Su and holidays 3-5:30pm.)* Intricate *pietra serena* pilasters and statues by Donatello grace Brunelleschi's small ◪**Cappella Pazzi,** at the end of the cloister. *(Enter through Museo dell'Opera. Open Th-Tu 10am-7pm. L5000/€2.60.)*

NORTH OF THE DUOMO

◪**PALAZZO PITTI.** Luca Pitti, a 15th-century banker, built his *palazzo* east of S. Spirito against the Boboli hill. The Medici acquired the *palazzo* and the hill in 1550 and enlarged everything possible. During Italy's brief experiment with monarchy, the structure served as a royal residence. Today, the Palazzo Pitti houses five museums, including the **Galleria Palatina,** one of only a few public galleries when it opened in 1833. The Galleria now houses Florence's second most important collection behind the Uffizi. It includes a number of works by Raphael, Titian, Andrea del Sarto, Rosso, Caravaggio, and Rubens. As you peruse the collection, don't forget to look up from time to time at the frescoes on the ceilings—these help make the museum all the more visually stunning. The other museums in Palazzo Pitti deal with subjects from modern art to antique porcelain. *(☎ 055 29 48 83. Galleria open Su-F 8:30am-9pm, Sa 8:30am-midnight; all other museums open 8:30am-1:50pm, closed on the 2nd and 4th Su, and the 1st, 3rd, and 5th M of each month. Galleria L12,000/€6.20, other museums L4000/€2.10 each. Inquire at the ticket office for a ticket covering the Galleria, the 4 other museums, and the Boboli Gardens for L20,000/€10.35.)*

◪**BOBOLI GARDENS.** This elaborately landscaped park, an exquisite example of a stylized Renaissance garden, provides teasing glimpses of Florence and wonderful views of the surrounding countryside. The gardens extend from the central oval lawn, up steep hills and down avenues of cypress trees to bubbling fountains with impressive nudes and shaded picnic areas. *(Pass through the courtyard of Palazzo Pitti to the ticket office and entrance. ☎ 055 265 18 16. Open daily 8:15am-6:30pm. Closed on the 1st and last M of each month. L4000/€2.10, EU citizens, L2000/€1.05.)*

◪**CHIESA DI SANTA MARIA DEL CARMINE.** Inside this church, the ◪**Brancacci Chapel** contains Masaccio's stunning and influential 15th-century frescoes, declared masterpieces even in their own time. Masolino's *Adam and Eve* and Masaccio's

ITALY

Expulsion from the Garden stand face to face, illustrating the young artist's innovative steps in depicting psychological drama. With such monumental works as the *Tribute Money*, this chapel became a school for many famous artists, including Michelangelo. *(Open M and W-Sa 10am-5pm, Su 1-5pm. L6000/€3.10.)*

SAN MINIATO AL MONTE. Climb the stairs from Piazzale Michelangelo to this chapel for a glorious survey of the city. Adorned with an inlaid marble façade and 13th-century mosaics, the chapel houses the **Chapel of the Cardinal of Portugal** inside with incredible della Robbia *terra cottas. (Take bus #13 from the station, or climb stairs from Piazzale Michelangelo. ☎ 055 234 27 31. Church open daily 7:30am-7pm.)*

PIAZZALE MICHELANGELO. Laid out in 1860, Piazzale Michelangelo offers a fine panorama of Florence, especially at sunset. Although the *piazzale* is essentially a large parking lot, it is saved not only by the incredible views, but also the copy of Michelangelo's *David* on an ornate pedestal in the center and the beautiful surrounding hills. *(Cross Ponte Vecchio and turn left, walk through the piazza, and turn right on V. de' Bardi. Go uphill as it becomes V. del Monte alle Croci and take the stairs on the left.)*

🍷 NIGHTLIFE

For the latest info, consult the city's entertainment monthly *Firenze Spettacolo* (L3500/€1.85). A typical nighttime *passeggiata* in Florence begins along **Via dei Calzaiuoli** and ends with coffee or *gelato* in a ritzy cafe on **Piazza della Repubblica,** where singers prance about in front of **Bar Concerto.** In the Oltrarno, **Piazza Santo Spirito** has lots of bars and restaurants, and live music in summer. Some of Florence's clubs require Italian Assocation for Culture and Sport **(AICS)** membership. Cards (L15,000/€7.75) can be obtained at various clubs and grants entry into over 20 establishments in Florence, as well as discounts at a number of local events.

During the summer and early fall a number of holidays and festivals further enliven Florence. The **Festival of San Giovanni Battista,** on June 24, features a tremendous fireworks display in P. Michelangelo (easily visible from the Arno). Summer music festivals start swinging in late April with the classical **Maggio Musicale.** The **Estate Fiesolana** (June-Aug.) fills the Roman theater in nearby Fiesole with concerts, opera, theater, ballet, and film. September brings the **Festa dell'Unità,** a concert series at Campi Bisenzia (take bus #30). On the **Festa del Grillo** (Festival of the Cricket), the first Sunday after Ascension Day, crickets in tiny wooden cages are hawked in the Cascine park to be released into the grass.

BARS

The William, V. Magliabechi 7/9/11r (☎ 055 263 83 57). Serves Bass Ale (L8000/ €4.15). Rowdy and packed on weekends, mellow on weeknights. Open daily 6pm-2am.

Amadeus, V. dei Pescioni, 5r (☎ 055 239 82 29). Take V. dei Pesconi from P. del Duomo, walk 2 blocks, and look left. This place serves the "best German beer at the best price in town" to a lively mix of Italians and visitors. Open daily 8:30pm-1:30am.

The Fiddler's Elbow, P.S. Maria Novella, 74r (☎ 055 21 59 56). An authentic Irish pub that serves cider, Guinness, and various other draught beers to a crowd of foreign tourists. L8000/€4.15 per pint. Open daily 1pm-2am.

The Chequers Pub, V. della Scala, 7/9r (☎ 055 28 75 88). This bar attracts a large and lively Italian crowd with its range of beers and typical pub grub. Happy Hour daily 6:30-8pm. Open Su-Th 6pm-midnight, F-Sa 6pm-3am.

DISCOS

Meccanò, V. degli Olmi, 1 (☎ 055 33 13 71). Near Parco delle Cascinè. Extremely popular among locals and tourists alike. L25,000/€12.95 cover includes 1 drink. Subsequent drinks L10,000/€5.20. Open Tu-Sa 11pm-4am.

Blob, V. Vinegia, 21r (☎ 055 21 12 09). Behind the Palazzo Vecchio. With mellow evenings, wild nights, and early mornings, this little club offers DJs, movies, foosball, and an evening bar buffet. Mixed drinks L10,000/€5.20. Open daily 6pm-late.

The Drunk Spaghetti, V. delle Seggiole, 8r (☎055 234 52 77). Near P. della Signoria. Satisfy your craving for all-night Latin nightlife. Almost all American music. AiCS required. Happy Hour 7:30-11:30pm. Open daily 7:30pm-6am.

Tabasco Gay Club, P.S. Cecilia, 3r (☎055 21 30 00). In a tiny alleyway across P. della Signoria from the Palazzo Vecchio. Florence's popular gay disco caters primarily to men. 18+. L25,000/12.95 cover includes 1st drink. Open Tu-Su 10pm-4am.

▓ DAYTRIPS FROM FLORENCE

FIESOLE

No trains run to Fiesole, but the town is a 25min. bus ride away; catch the ATAF city bus #7 from the train station near track #16, P.S. Marco. It runs throughout the day (less frequently at night) and drops passengers at P. Mino da Fiesole in the town center.

Older than Florence itself, Fiesole is the site of the original Etruscan settlement that farmed the rich flood plain below. Florence was actually colonized and settled as an offshoot of this Etruscan town. Fiesole has long been a welcome escape from the sweltering summer heat of the Arno Valley and a source of inspiration for numerous famous figures, including Alexander Dumas, Marcel Proust, Gertrude Stein, and Frank Lloyd Wright. Leonardo da Vinci even used the town as a testing ground for his famed flying machine. Fiesole's location provides incomparable views of both Florence and the rolling countryside to the north—it's a perfect place for a picnic or a daylong *passeggiata*. Outside the bus stop, up the hill to the left, is the fascinating **Missionario Francesco,** the public gardens, and spectacular views of the Florentine sprawl. Half a block off P. Mino da Fiesole is the **Museo Civico.** One ticket gains admission to its three constituent museums. The **Teatro Romano,** or Roman amphitheater, includes Etruscan thermal baths and temple ruins. The amphitheater grounds lead to the **Museo Civico Archeologico,** which houses an extensive collection of Etruscan artifacts. Then breeze through the **Museo Bandini,** a small collection of 14th- and 15th-century Italian paintings. (Open May-Aug. daily 9:30am-7pm; Sept.-Apr. daily 9:30am-5pm. Tickets L12,000/€6.20, students and over 65 L8000/€4.15.)

The **tourist office,** P. Mino da Fiesole, 37, is in the yellow building facing the *piazza.* (☎055 59 94 78. Open M 8am-1pm, Tu 8am-noon, W 8am-6:30pm, Th-F 8am-noon, Sa 8am-1pm). Accommodations in Fiesole are expensive compared to the budget options in nearby Florence, but the town is a great place to stop for a leisurely lunch. **Pizzeria Etrusca,** in P. Mina da Fiesole, has delicious pizza at reasonable prices. (☎055 59 94 84. Pizza L9000-14,000/€4.65-7.25, *primi* from L9000/€4.65, *secondi* from L16,000/€16.30. Open daily noon-3pm and 7pm-1am.)

AREZZO

Trains arrive from Florence (1½hr., 2 per hr., L9100/€4.70) and Rome (2hr., every 1-2hr., L21,700/€11.25). Buses pull in from Siena (1½hr., 7 per day, L8400/€4.35.)

The poet Petrarch, native son Michelangelo, and, most recently, Roberto Benigni of the film *Life is Beautiful* have all found inspiration in the streets of Arezzo. The town's most famous treasure is the magnificent fresco cycle **Leggenda della Vera Croce** (Legend of the True Cross) by **Piero della Francesca,** which portrays the story of the crucifix. It is housed in the extraordinary 14th-century **Basilica di San Francesco,** P.S. Francesco, up V.G. Monaco from the train station. (Open daily 8:30am-noon and 2-7pm. L10,000/€5.20, EU citizens 18-25 L6000/€3.10, art students L2000/€1.05.) Seven 6m high circular stained-glass windows let light into the massive **duomo,** up V. Andrea Cesalpino from P.S. Francesco. (Open daily 7am-12:30pm and 3-6:30pm.) Down Corso Italia, the **Piazza Grande** showcases Arezzo's most impressive examples of architecture, including the spectacular **Chiesa di Santa Maria della Pieve.** (Open M-Sa 8am-noon and 3-7pm, Su 8:30am-noon and 4-7pm.) The **tourist office,** P. della Repubblica, 22, is to the right as you exit the train station. (☎0575 37 76 78; fax 208 39. Open Apr.-Sept. M-Sa 9am-1pm and 3-7pm, Su 9am-1pm; Oct.-Mar. M-Sa 9am-1pm

ITALY

and 3-6:30pm.) **Ostello Villa Severi,** V. Redi, 13, is a bit of a hike from town. Take bus #4 (L1300/€0.70) from P.G. Monaco and get off two stops after the Ospedale Vecchio. (☎0575 29 90 47. Breakfast L3000/€1.55. Reception daily 9am-1pm and 6-11:30pm. Dorms L25,000/€12.95.)

SIENA   ☎0577

Many travelers rush from Rome to Florence, ignoring gorgeous, medieval Siena, but Siena is more than a poor cousin of these lauded cities. The Sienese have a rich history in arts, politics, and trade. One of their proudest celebrations is the semiannual **Palio,** a wild horse race between the city's 17 competing *contrade* (districts).

▐ TRANSPORTATION. Trains (☎0577 28 01 15) leave P. Rosselli hourly for Florence (1½hr., L8800/€4.55) and Rome (2½hr., L31,400/€16.25) via Chiusi. **TRA-IN/ SITA buses** (☎0577 20 42 45) depart from P. Gramsci, near the heart of the city, or from the train station for Florence (every hr., L12,000/€6.20) and San Gimignano (every hr., L8600/€4.45) via Poggibonsi.

▐ PRACTICAL INFORMATION. From the train station, cross the street and take **TRA-IN/SITA buses** #3, 4, 7-10, 14, 17, or 77 into the center of town at **Piazza del Sale** or **Piazza Gramsci** (L1500/€0.80). The central **APT tourist office** is at Il Campo, 56. (☎0577 28 05 51; fax 27 06 76. Open mid-Mar. to mid-Nov. M-Sa 8:30am-7:30pm, Su 8:30am-2pm; mid-Nov. to mid-Mar. M-Sa 8:30am-1pm and 3-7pm, Su 9am-1pm.) **Prenotazioni Alberghiere,** in P.S. Domenico, finds rooms for L3000/€1.55. (☎0577 28 80 84. Open Apr.-Oct. M-Sa 9am-8pm; Nov.-Mar. M-Sa 9am-7pm.) Check **email** at **Netgate,** V. Giovanni Dupre, 12. (L9000/€4.65 per hr., students L7000/€3.65. Open M-Sa 11am-midnight, Su 3-10pm.) **Postal Code:** 53100.

▐▐ ACCOMMODATIONS AND FOOD. Finding a room in Siena can be difficult from Easter to October. Book months ahead if coming during *Il Palio.* The tasteful **Albergo Tre Donzelle,** is at V. Donzelle, 5. (☎0577 28 03 58; fax 22 39 38. Curfew 12:30am. Singles L60,000/€31; doubles L85,000-110,000/€43.90-56.85. MC/V.) Take bus #15 from P. Gramsci to reach the **Ostello della Gioventù "Guidoriccio" (HI),** V. Fiorentina, 89, in Località Lo Stellino. (☎0577 522 12. Breakfast included. Curfew Apr.-Oct. 1am; Nov.-Mar. 11:30pm. Reserve ahead. Dorms L26,000/€13.45; singles and doubles L40,000/€20.65 per person. MC/V.) **Santvario S. Caterina Alma Domus,** V. Camporegio, 37, behind S. Domenico, has spotless rooms with views of the *duomo.* (☎0577 441 77; fax 476 01. Curfew 11:30pm. Doubles L100,000/€51.65; triples L130,000/€67.15; quads L150,000/€77.50.) To **camp** at **Colleverde,** Strada di Scacciapensieri, 47, take bus #3 or 8 from P. del Sale (every 30min.) or late-night bus #8 or 10 from P. Gramsci (#8 until 10:21pm, #10 until 1:10am); ask to be sure you're on the right route. (☎0577 28 00 44. Open mid-Mar. to mid-Nov. L15,000/€7.75 per adult, including tent; L8000/€4.15 per child.)

Siena specializes in rich pastries, of which the most famous is *panforte*, a confection of honey, almonds, and citron; indulge in this serious pastry at **Bar/Pasticceria Nannini,** V. Banchi di Sopra, 22-24, the oldest *pasticceria* in Siena. Next to Santuario di S. Caterina is the divine **Osteria La Chiacchera,** Costa di S. Antonio, 4. (☎0577 28 06 31. *Secondi* L9000-13,000/€4.65-6.75. Cover L2000/€1.05. Open W-M 12:30-3pm and 7-10:30pm.) **Consortio Agrario supermarket,** V. Pianigiani, 5, is off P. Salimberi. (Open M-F 8am-7:30pm.)

◨▐ SIGHTS AND ENTERTAINMENT. Siena offers two **biglietto cumulativi**—the first is good for five days (L14,000/€7.25) and allows entry into the Museo dell'Opera Metropolitana, baptistery, Piccolomini library, and the Oratory of St. Bernadino; the second is valid for seven days (L30,000/€15.50) and covers five more sights, including the Museo Civico. Siena radiates from **Piazza del Campo (Il Campo),** a shell-shaped brick square designed for civic events. At the top of Il Campo is the **Fonte Gaia,** still fed by the same aqueduct used in the 1300s. At the bottom, the **Torre del Mangia** clock tower looms over the graceful Gothic

Palazzo Pubblico. Inside the *palazzo*, the **Museo Civico** contains excellent Gothic and early Renaissance paintings; also check out the **Sala del Mappamondo** and the **Sala della Pace.** (*Palazzo*, museum, and tower open Mar.-Oct. daily 10am-7pm; Nov.-Feb. 10am-4pm. Tower L10,000/€5.20; museum L12,000/€6.20, students L6000/€3.10; combined ticket with tower L18,000/€9.30.) From the *palazzo*, take the right-side stairs and cross V. di Città for Siena's Gothic **duomo.** The apse would have been left hanging in mid-air save for the construction of the lavishly decorated **baptistery** below. (Open mid-Mar. to Oct. daily 9am-7:30pm; Nov. to mid-Mar. 10am-1pm and 2:30-5pm. Free except when floor is uncovered in Sept. L8000-10,000/€4.15-5.20. Baptistery open mid-Mar. to Oct. daily 9am-7:30pm; Nov. to mid-Mar. 10am-1pm and 2:30-5pm. L4000/€2.10.) The **Libreria Piccolomini**, off the left aisle, holds frescoes and 15th-century scores. (Same hours as *duomo*. L3000/€1.55.) The **Museo dell'Opera della Metropolitana**, to the right of the *duomo*, houses overflow art. (Open mid-Mar. to Oct. daily 9am-7:30pm; Nov. to mid-Mar. 9am-1:30pm. L6000/€3.05.)

Siena's **Il Palio** occurs twice a year, July 2 and Aug. 16, and is a traditional bareback horse race around the packed P. del Campo. Arrive three days earlier to watch the five trial runs and to pick a *contrada* to root for. At *Il Palio*, the jockeys take about 90 seconds to tear around Il Campo three times. To stay in Siena during the Palio, book rooms at least four months in advance, especially budget accommodations—write the APT in March or April for a list of rented rooms.

🌠 DAYTRIP FROM SIENA: SAN GIMIGNANO. The hilltop village of San Gimignano looks like an illumination from a medieval manuscript. The city's famous 14 towers, which are all that survive of its original 72, earned San Gimignano its nickname as the *Città delle Belle Torri* (City of Beautiful Towers). The **Museo Civico**, on the 2nd floor of **Palazzo del Popolo**, houses an amazing collection of Sienese and Florentine artwork. Within the museum is the entrance to the **Torre Grossa,** the tallest remaining tower; climb its 218 steps for a panorama of Tuscany. (Palazzo open Tu-Su 9am-7:30pm. Museum and tower open Mar.-Oct. daily 9:30am-7:20pm; Nov.-Feb. Sa-Th 10:30am-4:20pm. Museum L7000/€3.65, students L5000/€2.60; tower L8000/€4.15, L6000/€3.10. Combined ticket L12,000/€6.20, L9000/€4.65.)

TRA-IN buses leave P. Montemaggio for Siena (1½hr., every hr., L9000/€4.65) via Poggibonsi (20min., every hr., L2600/€1.35). From the bus station, pass through the *porta*, climb the hill, following V.S. Giovanni to the city center **Piazza della Cisterna**, which runs into P. del Duomo and the **tourist office**, P. del Duomo, 1. (☎0577 94 00 08; fax 94 09 03. Open Mar.-Oct. daily 9am-1pm and 3-7pm; Nov.-Feb. 9am-1pm and 2-6pm.) Accommodations are pricey in San Gimignano—*affitte camere* (private rooms) are a good alternative at about L75,000/€38.75. The **Associazione Strutture Extralberghiere**, P. della Cisterna, 6, finds private rooms. (☎0577 94 08 09. Open Mar.-Nov. daily 9:30am-7:30pm.) From the bus stop, enter through Porta S. Giovanni for the quaint **Camere Cennini Gianni,** V.S. Giovanni, 21. The reception is at the *passticceria* at V.S. Giovanni, 88. (☎0577 94 10 51. Reserve ahead. Doubles L90,000/€46.50; triples L120,000/€62; quads L140,000/€72.30.) **Camp** at **Il Boschetto**, at Santa Lucia, a 2½km bus ride (L1500/€0.80) from Porta S. Giovanni. (☎0577 94 03 52. Reception daily 8am-1pm, 3-8pm, and 9-11pm. Open Apr. to mid-Oct. L8500/€4.40 per person, L8500/€4.40 per tent. Showers included.) **La Bettola del Grillo,** V. Quercecchio, 33, off V.S. Giovanni, opposite P. della Cisterna, serves traditional Tuscan delights. The fixed-price *menù* (L25,000/€12.95) includes wine and dessert. (☎0577 94 18 44. *Primi* L10,000-12,000/€5.20-6.20, *secondi* L10,000-15,000/€5.20-7.75. Open Tu-Su noon-3pm and 6:30-11pm.)

PISA
☎050

Tourism hasn't always been Pisa's prime industry: during the Middle Ages, the city was a major port with an Mediterranean empire. But when the Arno River silted up and the tower started leaning, the city's power and wealth declined accordingly. Today the city seems resigned to welcoming tourists and myriad t-shirt and ice cream vendors to the **Piazza del Duomo,** also known as the **Campo dei Miracoli** (Field of Miracles), a grassy expanse enclosing the tower, *duomo,* baptistery, Camposanto, Museo delle Sinopie, and Museo del Duomo. An **all-inclusive ticket** to the Campo's sights costs L19,000/€9.85. Begun in 1173, the famous **Leaning Tower** began to tilt when the soil beneath suddenly shifted. In June of 2001, a multi-year stabilization effort was completed and the tower is considered stable at its present inclination. However, visitors are still not allowed to enter the tower. The dazzling **duomo,** also on the Campo, is a treasury of fine art, and believed to be one of the finest Romanesque cathedrals in the world. (Open daily 10am-7:40pm. L3000/€1.55.) Next door is the **baptistery,** with precise acoustics that allow an non-amplified choir to be heard 2km away. (Open late Apr. to late Sept. daily 8am-8pm; Oct.-Mar. 9am-5pm. L12,000/€6.20 includes 1 other museum or monument.) The adjoining **Camposanto,** a cloistered cemetery, has Roman sarcophagi and a series of haunting frescoes by an unidentified 14th-century artist known only as the "Master of the Triumph of Death." (Open late Apr. to late Sept. daily 8am-7:45pm; Mar. and Oct. 9am-5:40pm; Nov.-Feb. 9am-4:40pm. L12,000/€6.20 includes 1 other museum or monument.) The **Museo delle Sinopie,** across the *piazza* from the Camposanto, displays preliminary fresco sketches discovered during post-WWII restoration. Behind the tower is the **Museo dell'Opera del Duomo.** (Both open late Apr. to late Sept. daily 8am-7:20pm; Mar. and Oct. 9am-5:20pm; Nov.-Feb. 9am-4:40pm. Joint ticket L12,000/€6.20.) From the Campo, walk down V.S. Maria and over the bridge to the Gothic **Chiesa di Santa Maria della Spina** whose tower allegedly holds a thorn from Christ's crown.

Trains (☎ 147 808 88) leave **Piazza della Stazione,** in the southern part of town, to Florence (1hr., every hr., L9400/€4.85); Genoa (2½hr., L25,300/€13.10); Rome (3hr., L45,500/€23.50). To reach the Campo from the train station, take **bus** #1 (L1500/€0.80); or walk straight up V. Gramsci, go through P. Vittorio Emanuele, walk down Corso Italia across the Arno, continue on V. Borgo Stretto, turn left on any street branching west, and walk to the old town. The **tourist office** is to the left as you exit the station. (☎050 422 91; www.turismo.toscana.it. Open M-Sa 9am-7pm, Su 9:30am-3:30pm.) The central **Albergo Gronchi,** P. Archivescovado, 1, just off P. del Duomo, has large airy rooms with a quiet courtyard. (☎050 56 18 23. Curfew midnight. Singles L36,000/€18.60; doubles L62,000/€32.05.) The **Albergo Helvetia,** V. Don G. Boschi, 31, 2min. from the *duomo,* off P. Archivescovado, has large, clean rooms. (☎050 55 30 84. Singles L60,000/€31; doubles L80,000-110,000/€41.35-56.85; triples L125,000/€64.50; quads L165,000/€85.25.) The **Hotel Galileo,** V.S. Maria, 12, has spacious simple rooms with tiled floors. (☎050 406 21. Singles L70,000/€36.15; doubles L70,000-90,000/€36.15-46.50; triples L90,000-120,000/€46.50-62. Cash only.) Try the heavenly *risotto* (L10,000/€5.20) at the lively ■Il Paiolo, V. Curtatone e Montanara, 9. (*Menù* with *primi* and *secondi* L15,000/€7.75. Open M-F noon-3pm and 7pm-1am, Sa 7pm-1am.) **Trattoria da Matteo,** V. l'Aroncio, 46, serves authentic cuisine and 40 types of pizza. (Pizza L7000-10,000/€3.65-5.20. *Menù* L22,000/€11.40. Cover L2000/€1.05. ☎050 410 57. Open Su-F 9am-11pm.) Get **groceries** at **Superal,** V. Pascoli, 6, just off Corso Italia. (Open M-Sa 8am-8pm.) **Postal Code:** 56100.

ELBA ☎0565

Napoleon spent his exile here—all would-be conquerors of Europe should be so lucky. Elba's turquoise waters, dramatic mountains, velvety beaches, and diverse attractions accommodate almost any interest. While families lounge in **Marina di Campo** and **Marciana Marina,** party-hard beach fanatics waste away in **Capoliveri,** yacht-club members gallivant in **Porto Azzurro,** and nature-loving recluses gravitate to the mountainous northeast tip, between **Cavi** on the beach and **Rio nell'Elba** in the interior. Elba is one of the best places in Italy to bike or scooter, with roads that wind through the island's mountainous terrain, affording stupendous views of the ocean. **Ferries** go from **Piombino Marittima** (or *Piombino Porto*) on the mainland to **Portoferraio,** Elba's largest city. Although **trains** on the

Genoa-Rome line travel to Piombino Marittima, most stop at **Campiglia Marittima** (from Florence, change at Pisa), where a *pullman* (intercity bus; 30min., L2500/€1.30) meets trains and connects to ferries in Piombino Marittima. Both Toremar (☎0565 311 00; 1hr., L12,000/€6.20) and Moby Lines (☎0565 22 52 11; 1hr., L12,000/€6.20) run to Elba. The **tourist office, APT,** Calata Italia, 26, 1st fl., across from the Toremar boat landing, helps with rooms and transport. (☎0565 91 46 71. Open daily 9am-1pm and 2:30-7:30pm; off-season 9am-1pm and 3-7pm.) **Ape Elbana,** Salita Cosimo de' Medici, 2, overlooks the main *piazza* of the *centro storico.* (☎05 65 91 42 45. Singles L90,000/€46.50; doubles L120,000-130,000/€62-67.15; Aug. half-pension required L110,000/€56.85.)

UMBRIA

Umbria is a land rich in natural beauty, encompassing wild woods and fertile plains, craggy gorges and tiny cobblestone villages. This landlocked region wedged between the Adriatic and Tyrrhenian coasts has long been a greatly contested prize. One conqueror, Christianity, transformed Umbria's architecture and regional identity, turning it into a breeding ground for saints and religious movements; it was here that Saint Francis of Assisi shamed the extravagant church with his humility.

PERUGIA   ☎075

Interspersed among the violent and heretical shenanigans, Perugia's periods of prosperity gave rise to stunning artistic achievement. Between Perugia's art and architecture, its big-city vitality and gorgeous surrounding countryside, and its rich cultural history, there is no reason not to visit this gem of a city. The city's most visited sights frame **Piazza IV Novembre.** The **Fontana Maggiore** in the center is adorned with sculptures and bas-reliefs by Nicolà and Giovanni Pisano. At the end of the *piazza*, the imposing Gothic **duomo** was begun in the 14th century but the façade was never finished. The *duomo* houses the Virgin Mary's purported wedding ring. (Open daily 8am-noon and 4pm-dusk.) The 13th-century **Palazzo dei Priori** presides over the *piazza*, and houses the immense ▧**Galleria Nazionale dell'Umbria,** Corso Vannucci, 19. (☎075 574 12 57. Open daily 8:30am-7:30pm; mid-June to mid-Sept. also open Sa until 11pm. Closed Jan. 1, Dec. 25, and the 1st M of every month. L12,000/€6.20, EU citizens under 18 or over 65 free.) At the end of town on Borgo XX Guigo, past the Port S. Pietro, the **Basilica di San Pietro,** on Corso Cavour, maintains its original 10th-century basilica layout; at its far end is an exquisite garden with incredible views. (Open daily 8am-noon and 3:30pm-dusk.)

   Trains leave P.V. Veneto, in Fontiveggio, for: Assisi (25min., every hr., L3000/€1.55); Florence (2½hr., every hr., from L15,300/€7.90); Rome (2½hr., from L28,900/€14.95; via Terontola or Foligno 3hr., from L20,600/€10.65). From the station, take bus #6, 7, 9, 13d, or 15 to the central P. Italia (L1200/€0.65), then walk down Corso Vannucci to reach P. IV Novembre and the **tourist office,** P. IV Novembre, 3. (☎075 572 33 27; fax 573 93 86. Open M-F 8:30am-1:30pm and 3:30-6:30pm, Sa 8:30am-1:30pm, Su 9am-1pm.) To get from the tourist office to ▧**Ostello della Gioventù/Centro Internazionale di Accoglienza per la Gioventù,** V. Bontempi, 13, walk down Corso Vannucci past the *duomo* and P. Danti, take the farthest street right through P. Piccinino, and turn right on V. Bontempi. (☎/fax 075 572 28 80; www.perugia.it. Sheets L2000/€1.05. Lockout 9:30am-4pm. Curfew midnight. Open mid-Jan. to mid-Dec. Dorms L19,000/€9.85.) Walking from P. Italia on Corso Vanucci, take your first left just after P. della Republica onto the narrow Corso della Luna for the bright and clean **Albergo Etruria,** Corso della Luna, 21. (☎075 572 37 30. Singles L50,000/€25.85; doubles L75,000/€38.75, with bath L90,000/€46.50; triples L100,000, L115,000/€59.40. Cash only.) To **camp** at **Paradis d'Eté,** 8km away in Colle della Trinità, take a city bus (dir.: Colle della Trinità) from P. Italia and ask to be dropped off at the campgrounds. (☎075 517 31 21. L12,000/€6.20 per person, L10,000/€5.20 per tent, L6000/€3.10 per car.)

ITALY

Trattoria Dal Mi Cocco, Corso Garibaldi, 12, up from the University for Foreigners, offers an extremely generous L25,000/€12.95 *menù*. (Open Tu-Su noon-2:30pm and 8:15-10:30pm.) The **COOP,** P. Matteoti, 15, has **groceries.** (Open M-Sa 9am-8pm.) **Postal Code:** 06100.

ASSISI
                                                                    ☎ 075

Assisi's serenity originates with the legacy of Saint Francis, a 12th-century monk who revolutionized the wealthy Catholic Church with his preaching of chastity and poverty. When construction of the **Basilica di San Francesco** began in the mid-13th century, Francis's Franciscan order protested that the elaborate church was an impious monument to the wealth that Saint Francis scorned. The vicar of the order came up with a compromise of a double church: the subdued art in the lower church commemorates Francis's modest life, while the elaborate upper church, decorated with Giotto's renowned *Life of St. Francis* fresco cycle, pays tribute to his sainthood and consecration. (☎ 075 819 00 84. Dress code strictly enforced. Lower basilica open daily 6:30am-7pm. Upper basilica open daily 8:30am-7pm. Museo Tesoro della Basilica (inside the lower basilica) open daily 9:30am-12:30pm and 2-6pm. Museum L3000/€1.55.) From P. del Comune, follow V.S. Rufino to P.S. Rufino, continue up V. Porta Perlici, take your first left up a narrow staircase, and follow signs for the dramatic **Rocca Maggiore** that towers above town, offering tremendous views. (☎ 075 81 52 92. Open Apr.-Sept. daily 9am-sunset; Nov.-Mar. 10am-sunset. Closed in bad weather. L3000/€1.55, students L2000/€1.05. Prices may rise in the unlikely event that they finish renovating on the central courtyard.)

From the station near the Basilica Santa Maria degli Angeli, **trains** on the Foligno-Terontola line go to: Ancona (L20,200/€10.45); Florence (2 per day, L17,000/€8.80); Perugia (13 per day, L3200/€1.65); Rome (1 per day, from L25,500/€13.20). **ASP buses** run from P. Matteotti to: Florence (2½hr., 1 per day, L12,400/€6.40); Perugia (1½hr., 7 per day, L5200/€2.70); Rome (3hr., 1 per day, L16,000/€8.30). From the station, follow V. del Torrione, bear left in P.S. Rufino, and take V.S. Rufino for **Piazza del Comune** and the **tourist office,** in P. del Comune, on the far end of the *piazza.* (☎ 075 81 25 34; fax 81 37 27; www.umbria2000.it. Open M-F 8am-2pm and 3:30-6:30pm, Sa 9am-1pm and 3:30-6:30pm, Su and holidays 9am-1pm.) For **Ostello della Pace (HI),** V. di Valecchi, 177, turn right as you exit the station, then turn left at the intersection onto V. di Valecchi. (☎/fax 075 81 67 67. Breakfast included. Reception daily 7-9:15am and 3:30-11:30pm. Check-out 9:30am. Dorms L23,000/€11.90, with bath L28,000/€14.50. MC/V.) From P. del Comune, follow V. Portico and take your first left onto V.S. Gregorio for the peaceful **Camere Annalisa Martini,** V.S. Gregorio, 6. (☎ 075 81 35 36. Singles L38,000/€19.65, with bath L40,000/€20.65; doubles L60,000/€31, L65,000/€33.60; triples L90,000-100,000/€46.50-51.65.) **Pizzeria Otello,** V.S. Antonio, 1, is a no nonsense family-run pizzeria. (☎ 075 81 24 15. Pizza L8000-12,000/€4.15-6.20, *primi* L9500-13,000/€4.90-6.75, *secondi* from 9500/€4.90. Cover L2000/€1.05. Pizzeria open July-Aug. daily 7:30am-noon; Sept.-June M-Sa 7:30am-noon. Main restaurant open July-Aug. daily noon-3:30pm and 7-10:30pm; Sept.-June M-Sa noon-3:30pm.) **Postal Code:** 06081.

THE MARCHES (LE MARCHE)

In the Marches, green foothills separate the gray shores of the Adriatic from the Apennine mountains, and the traditional hill towns from the umbrella-laden beaches. Inland towns, easily accessible by train, rely on agriculture, and preserve the region's historical legacy in the architectural remains of Gauls and Romans.

URBINO
                                                                    ☎ 0722

Urbino's fairy-tale skyline, scattered with humble stone dwellings and an immense turreted palace, has changed little over the past 500 years. The city's most remarkable monument is the looming Renaissance **Palazzo Ducale** (Ducal Palace), in P.

Rinascimento, though its façade is more thrilling than its interior. The enclosed **courtyard** epitomizes Renaissance balance and proportion; to the left, stairs lead to the former private apartments of the Duke, which now house the packed **National Gallery of the Marches.** Check out the underground baths, kitchen, and washroom, as well as the Duke's study, where inlaid panels give the illusion of real books. (☎0722 27 60. Open M 8:30am-2pm, Tu-F 8:30am-7:15pm, Sa 8:30am-10:30pm, Su 8:30am-7:15pm. L8000/€4.15.) Raphael's birthplace, **Casa di Rafaele,** V. Raffaello, 57, is now a vast and delightful museum; a reproduction of his earliest work, the fresco *Madonna e Bambino,* hangs in the *sala.* (☎0722 32 01 05. Open M-Sa 9am-1pm and 3-7pm, Su 10am-1pm. L5000/€2.60.)

   Bucci buses leave Borgo Mercatale for Rome (5hr., 4pm, L32,000/€16.55). From Borgo Mercatale, a short walk uphill on V.G. Mazzini leads to **Piazza della Repubblica,** the city center. From P. della Repubblica, a short walk up V. Vittorio Veneto leads to the **tourist office,** P. Rinascimento, 1, across from Palazzo Ducale. (☎0722 26 13; fax 24 41. Open mid-June to mid-Sept. M-Sa 9am-1pm and 3-7pm, Su 9am-1pm; in winter M-Sa 9am-1pm and 3-6pm.) **Pensione Fosca,** V. Raffaello, 67, top fl., has nine large rooms without bath. (☎0722 32 96 22 or 32 25 42. Singles L40,000/€20.65; doubles L75,000/€38.75; triples L80,000/€41.35; quads L100,000/€51.65.) For the uninspiring but comfortable **Piero della Francesca,** V. Comandino, 3, in front of the hospital, take bus #1 from Borgo Mercatale. (☎0722 32 84 28; fax 32 84 27. Singles L70,000/€36.15; doubles L100,000/€51.65; triples L130,000/€67.15; quads L160,000/€82.65. AmEx/D/MC/V.) **Camping Pineta,** on V.S. Donato, is 2km away in Cesane; take bus #4 or 7 from Borgo Mercatale and ask to get off at camping. (☎0722 47 10; fax 47 34. Reception daily 9-11am and 3-10pm. Open Apr. to mid-Sept. L10,000/€5.20 per person, L21,000/€10.85 per tent.) Many eateries are in **Piazza della Repubblica. Margherita supermarket** is at V. Raffaello, 37. (Open M-Sa 8am-2pm and 4:30-8pm.) At night, **The Bosom Pub,** V. Budassi, 14, is stacked with fun.

ANCONA   ☎071

Ancona is the epicenter of Italy's Adriatic Coast—a major port in a small, whimsical, and largely unexplored city. **Piazza Roma** is dotted with yellow and pink buildings and **Piazza Cavour** is the heart of the town. Anacona offers **ferry service** to Greece, Croatia, and northern Italy. **ANEK** (☎071 207 32 22; fax 20 02 11; www.anek.gr) and **Blue Star (Strinzis;** ☎071 207 10 68; fax 207 08 74; www.strinzis.gr) go to Greece (ANEK from 93,000/€48.05, July-Aug. 123,000/€63.55; Strinzis from L95,000/€49.10, July to early Sept. L105,000-119,000/€54.25-61.45). Schedules and tickets are available at the Stazione Marittima; reserve ahead in July or August. **Trains** on the Bologna-Lecce line leave P. Rosselli for: Bologna (2½hr., 1-2 per hr., from L19,600/€10.15); Milan (5hr., 24 per day, from L37,500/€19.40); Rome (3-4hr., 9 per day, from L25,000/€12.95); Venice (5hr., 3 per day, L26,300/€13.60). Take bus #1/4 (L1400/€0.80) from the train station to P. IV Novembre for the **tourist office,** V. Thaon de Revel, 4. (☎071 332 49; fax 319 66. Open M-Sa 8am-8pm, Su 8am-2pm.) The new **Ostello della Gioventù (HI),** V. Lamaticci, 7, is perfect for active travelers. From the train station, cross the *piazza* and turn left, take the first right, make a sharp right up the steps behind the newsstand, and it's on the right. (☎/fax 071 42 - 257. Breakfast L2500/€1.30. Reception 6:30-11am and 4:30pm-midnight. **HI members only;** HI cards sold at hostel. Dorms 23,000/€11.90. Cash only.) **Supermarket CONAD** is at V. Matteotti, 115. (Open M-F 8:15am-2pm and 5-7:35pm, Sa 8:15am-12:45pm and 5-7:40pm.)

SOUTHERN ITALY

South of Rome, the sun gets brighter, the meals longer, and the passions more heated. The introduction to the *mezzogiorno* (Italian South) begins in Campania, the fertile crescent that cradles the Bay of Naples and the Gulf of Salerno. In the shadow of Mount Vesuvius lie the famous Roman ruins of Pompeii, frozen in time by a bed of molten lava. In the Bay of Naples, Capri is Italy's answer to Fantasy Island, while the Amalfi Coast cuts a dramatic course down the lush Tyrrhenian shore. Here, where fire meets water and wind conquers earth, man has for centuries sought solace and escape from the modern world.

NAPLES (NAPOLI)   ☎081

Italy's third-largest city is gradually emerging from the shadow of it *bruta reputazione* to become a thriving cultural center. The city's historic center is a treasure trove of architectural styles, *piazzas*, and *palazzi*, and plenty of islands, volcanoes, and beaches are nearby. Naples has had its share of problems, but the introduction of more police has seen a decrease in crime and an increase in tourism.

⌐ TRANSPORTATION

Flights: Aeroporto Capodichino, V. Umberto Maddalena (☎081 789 61 11), northwest of the city. Connections to all major Italian and European cities. A CLP bus (☎081 531 16 46) leaves from P. Municipio (20min., 6am-10:30pm, L3000/€1.55). The #15 bus runs from P. Garibaldi to the airport (L1500/€0.80). **Alitalia,** V. Medina, 41/42 (☎848 86 56 43). Off P. Municipio. Open M-F 9am-4:30pm. **British Airways,** in the airport (☎848 81 22 66). Open M-F 8am-8pm, Sa 9am-5pm. **TWA,** V. Cervantes, 55 (☎081 551 30 63). Open M-F 9am-5:30pm.

Trains: The **Ferrovie dello Stato** company sends trains from **Stazione Centrale** to: **Brindisi** (5hr., 5 per day, L35,600/€18.40); **Milan** (8hr., 13 per day, L96,000/€49.60); **Rome** (2hr., 34 per day, L18,600/€9.60). **Circumvesuviana** (☎081 772 24 44) leaves Stazione Centrale for **Pompeii** and **Herculaneum** (both L3200/€1.65).

Ferries: Call **Ontana** (☎081 58 00 34) for reservations. Departs from **Molo Beverello** and **Molo Angioino,** at the base of P. Municipio. From P. Garibaldi, take tram #1; from P. Municipio, take the R2 bus. **Caremar,** Molo Beverello (☎081 551 38 82), goes frequently to **Capri** (1-1½hr., 6 per day, L9800/€5.10) and **Ischia** (1-1½hr., 14 per day, L9800/€5.10). **Tirrenia Lines,** Molo Angioino (☎081 720 11 11), goes to **Palermo, Sicily** (11hr., 8pm, L90,300/€46.65). Schedules and prices change constantly; check *Qui Napoli* for most current (free at the tourist office).

Public Transportation: *Giranapoli* tickets (1½hr; L1500/€0.80, full-day L4500/€2.35) are transportation passes valid on **buses, Metro** (subway), **trams,** and **funiculars** can be purchased at *tabacchi.* Buses connect the city center to various internal locations. The Metro covers longer distances in the city; trams move along the coast, and funiculars connect the lower city to the hilltop Vomero. Everything stops running around midnight, except for the unreliable *notturno* (night) buses.

Taxis: Cotana (☎081 570 70 70), **Napoli** (☎081 556 44 44), or **Partenope** (☎081 556 02 02). Take only metered taxis.

✱🔖 ORIENTATION AND PRACTICAL INFORMATION

It's easiest to divide Naples into five areas: the **train station (Piazza Garibaldi), Waterfront, Hilltop, downtown,** and **historic center.** The central train station and major city bus terminal are both in the immense **Piazza Garibaldi,** a crumbling area on the east side of Naples. **Corso Umberto I** leads from P. Garibaldi, ending at P. Bovio. From here, **Via Depretis** (where you can catch a CLP bus to Amalfi or the airport) branches to the left toward **Piazza Municipio,** the bottom of the financial district. **Molo Beverello** and the **Stazione Marittima** at **Molo Angioino,** where ferries depart, are at the foot of P. Municipio. Turn right off of V. Cesario Console onto V. San Lucia to reach the **Waterfront.** Corso Vittorio Emanuele will bring you to P. Amedeo where you can take the funicular to the **Hilltop.** The funicular will take you back down to Montesanto, where V. Tarsia leads to P. Dante and **downtown** on **Via Toledo.** You can take the pedestrian walkway under the arch to **Spaccanapoli** and the **historic center.**

ITALY

Naples

ACCOMMODATIONS
Ostello Mergellina, 1
Pensione Magherita, 2

PUBS
Camelot, 4
Itaca, 3

Golfo di Napoli

Tourist Offices: EPT (☎081 26 87 79; fax 20 66 66), at Stazione Centrale. Helpful with hotels and ferries. Grab a map and ▧ *Qui Napoli.* Open M-Sa 9am-7pm. **Main office** at P. dei Martiri, 58 (☎081 40 53 11). Open M-Sa 8:30am-3pm. **OTC** (☎081 580 82 16; fax 081 41 03 59; www.comune.napoli.it), at Palazzo Reale in P. Plebiscito, is eager to assist. Open M-F 9am-6:30pm.

Consulates: Canada, V. Carducci, 29 (☎081 40 13 38). **South Africa,** Corso Umberto I (☎08 15 51 75 19). **UK,** V. Crispi, 122 (☎081 66 35 11). Metro: P. Amedeo. Open July-Aug. M-F 8am-1:30pm; Sept.-June M-F 9am-12:30pm and 2:30-4pm. **US,** P. della Repubblica (24hr. emergency ☎03 37 94 50 83), at the west end of Villa Comunale. Open M-F 8am-5pm.

Currency Exchange: Several major banks operate on P. Municipio and P. Garibaldi.

American Express: Every Tour, P. Municipio, 5 (☎081 551 83 99). Open daily 9am-1:30pm and 3:30-7pm.

Emergencies: ☎113. **Police:** ☎113 and 081 794 11 11. **Carabinieri:** ☎112. English spoken. **Hospital:** Cardarelli (☎081 747 11 11), north of town on the R4 bus line. **Medical Assistance:** ☎08 17 52 06 96.

Internet Access: Internetbar, P. Bellini, 74. (☎081 29 52 37). Chic and air-conditioned. L5,000/€2.60 per 30min. Open M-Sa 9am-2am, Su 8am-2am.

Post Office: in P. Matteotti, V. Diaz (☎081 552 42 33). R2 line. Address mail to be held: FirstName SURNAME, *In Fermo Posta,* P. Matteotti, Naples **80100,** Italy. Open M-F 8:15am-6pm, Sa 8:15am-noon. **Postal Code:** 80100.

DON'T TALK TO STRANGERS AND OTHER GOOD ADVICE.
Though personal violence is rare in Naples, theft is relatively common. Don't carry your money in wallets or purses and keep them inaccessible to pickpockets. Young women, whether alone or in groups, will likely be harassed, and should travel in mixed company whenever possible. Ignore street merchants who call to you in English; they will make it difficult for you to escape from the conversation.

ACCOMMODATIONS

Although Naples has some fantastic bargain lodgings, be cautious. When selecting a place to stay, check for double-locked doors and night attendants. The **ACISJF/Centro D'Ascolto,** at Stazione Centrale, helps women find safe and inexpensive rooms. (☎081 28 19 93. Open M, Tu, Th 3:30-6:30pm.) In all instances, make sure to agree on a price *before* unpacking, and don't give up your passport until you've actually seen the room. Also, be alert for unexpected costs. For **camping,** try **Pozzuoli, Pompeii** (see p. 693) and other small towns in the Bay of Naples.

MERGELLINA

This waterfront neighborhood is accessible by Metro and offers a large youth hostel in an area packed with authentic, Neopolitan *trattorie.*

Ostello Mergellina (HI), V. Salita della Grotta, 23 (☎08 17 61 23 46; fax 61 23 91). Metro: Mergellina. From the Metro station, make 2 rights onto V. Piedigrotta, turn left onto V. Salita della Grotta, and turn right on the driveway after the overpass (before the tunnel). This hostel has 200 rooms and outstanding views of Capri and Vesuvius. Breakfast, sheets, and shower included. Curfew 12:30am. Reservations strongly advised July-Aug. 2-, 4-, and 6-bed dorms L24,000/€12.40; doubles L60,000/€31.

PIAZZA GARIBALDI

The gritty area around P. Garibaldi is packed with hotels, many of which solicit customers at the station. Avoid such solicitors—in most cases, they will redirect you to their "hotel" which, while probably safe, may simply be an old *palazzo* divided into rooms with hastily erected partitions. However, there are options for affordable accommodations that are both comfortable and safe (though none are really quiet).

Casanova Hotel, V. Venezia, 2 (☎081 26 82 87; members.tripod.it/hotelcasanova/index). From P. Garibaldi, take V. Milano, and turn left at its end; it's to the right. Clean, airy rooms. Breakfast L8000/€4.15. Reserve ahead. Singles L40,000/€20.65, with bath L50,000/€25.85; doubles L70,000/€41.35, L85,000/€43.90; triples L110,000/€56.85; quads L140,000/€72.30. 10% *Let's Go* discount. AmEx/MC/V.

Hotel Eden, Calle Novara, 9 (☎081 28 53 44). From the train station, turn right on Calle Novara; it's on the left. 42 rooms and a well-lit walk from the station. Breakfast L5000/€2.60. Bath included. Free storage. Mention *Let's Go* when making reservations for these prices: Singles L45,000/€23.25; doubles L70,000/€36.15; triples L100,000/€51.65; quads L120,000/€62. AmEx/MC/V.

Hostel Pensione Mancini, P. Mancini, 33 (☎08 15 53 67 31), off the far end of P. Garibaldi from the station. Small, safe *pensione*. Breakfast included. Reserve ahead. Dorms L30,000/€15.50; singles L45,000/€23.25; doubles L70,000/€36.15, with bath L80,000/€41.35; triples L100,000/€51.65; quads L120,000/€62.

Hotel Ginvera, V. Genova, 116 (☎081 28 32 10; www.mds.it/ginevra). Exit P. Garibaldi on Calle Novara, then turn right on V. Genova. Clean, family-run establishment. English and French spoken. Singles L49,000/€25, with bath 78,000/€40; doubles L70,000/€40, L97,000/€50; triples L107,000/€55, L136,000/€70; quads L126,000/€65, L155,000/€80. AmEx/MC/V.

HISTORICAL DISTRICT

Rooms are generally scarce in the historic district between P. Dante and the *duomo*, but if you can find space, this area is most conveniently located.

Soggiorno Imperia, P. Miraglia, 386 (☎081 45 93 47). Take the R2 from the train station, walk up V. Mezzocannone through P.S. Domenico Maggiore, and enter the 1st set of green doors to the left on P. Miraglia. Bright, clean rooms in a 16th-century *palazzo*. Reserve ahead. Dorms L30,000/€15.50; singles L40,000/€20.65; doubles L70,000/€36.15, with bath L100,000/€51.65; triples L100,000/€51.65. AmEx/MC/V.

Pensione Bella Capri, V. Melisurgo, 4, door B, 6th fl. (☎081 552 94 94; www.bellacapri.it), at the corner of V. Cristofor Colombo, across the street from the port. Take tram #1 from P. Garibaldi. A cheaper alternative to the Waterfront hotels. Breakfast included. Reserve ahead. Singles L110,000/€56.85; doubles L130,000/€67.15; triples L170,000/€97.80; quads L190,000/€98.15. 10% *Let's Go* discount. AmEx/MC/V.

VOMERO

This residential neighborhood is quite posh; cheap rooms are few and far between.

Pensione Margherita, V. Cimarosa, 29, 5th fl. (☎08 15 56 70 44), in the same building as the Centrale funicular station. Go outside and around the corner to the right, and buzz to get in. 19 spacious rooms. Curfew midnight. Singles L60,000/€31; doubles L110,000/€56.85; triples L155,000/€80.05. AmEx/MC/V.

▶ FOOD

Neopolitans invented **pizza,** and a visit to Naples will blow away any stereotypes that you may hold about this world-famous staple. Neopolitans also have a long-standing relationship with **seafood** and they prepare it with a great deal of tender loving care. Enjoy fresh *cozze* (mussels) with lemon or in soup, savor *vangole* (clams) and their more expensive cousins, the *ostrica* (oysters), or build up your protein with *polipo* (octopus). **Spaghetti** was reputedly first boiled in the kitchens of Naples, and the Neapolitan *spaghetti alle vongole* (with clams) is a famous dish. The **historic center** and the area around **Piazza Garibaldi** offer abundant *trattorie* and *pizzerie*. Cheap, authentic fare can be found along **Via dei Tribunali** in Spaccanapoli. Expensive, tourist-filled restaurants dominate the P. Garibaldi, but higher quality, low-cost meals can be found on the side streets off the *piazza*. To find your own fresh produce and seafood, explore the Neopolitan **markets.** Try the one on V. Soprammuro, off P. Garibaldi (Open M-Sa 8am-1:30pm).

▓**Antica Pizzeria da Michele,** V. Cesare Sersale, 1-3 (☎081 553 92 04). From P. Garibaldi, walk up Corso Umberto and take the 1st right. Michele makes only 2 types of pizza: the *marinara* and *margherita* (L6000/€3.10). Get pizza and a beer for only L8000/€4.15. Open M-Sa 9am-midnight.

▓**Pizzeria Brandi,** Salita S. Anna di Palazzo, 1 (☎081 41 69 28), off V. Chiaia. Luciano Pavarotti and Gerard Depardieu ate here. Serve traditional Neopolitan fare. *Margherita* L8000/€4.15. Cover L3000/€1.55. Open M-Su noon-3pm and 7pm-midnight.

Pizzeria Trianon da Ciro, V. Pietro Colletta, 42/44/46 (☎08 15 53 94 26), 1 block off Corso Umberto I. A 1997 *New York Times* article pronounced this the best pizza in Naples. Pizzas L6000-13000/€3.10-6.75. Service 15%. Open daily 10am-3:30pm and 5:30-11pm.

Pizzeria Di Matteo, V. Tribunali, 94 (☎081 45 52 62). Near V. Duomo. Students and pizza connoisseurs crowd this small preeminent eatery. *Marinara* pizza L3900/€2.05. Open M-Sa 9am-midnight.

Da Rosario, P. Sannazzaro, 72 (☎081 570 31 03), in Mergellina. This all-night restaurant specializes in authentic seafood. Try *zuppa di cozze* (mussel soup) for L12,000/€6.20. Service 10%. Open Th-Tu 10am-3am.

👁 SIGHTS

▓**MUSEO ARCHEOLOGICO NAZIONALE.** Situated within a 16th-century *palazzo* and former barracks, one of the world's most important archeological museums houses exquisite treasures from Pompeii and Herculaneum. Highlights include the massive **Farnese Hercules,** showing the exhausted hero after his last labor, and the **Farnese Bull,** the largest known ancient sculpture. The **"Secret Collection"** contains erotic paintings and objects from Pompeii. Ranging from images of the loves of the gods to phallic good luck charms, the collection shows another side of the ancient world. *(From M: P. Cavour, turn right and walk 2 blocks. ☎081 44 01 66. Open W-M 9am-7:30pm. L12,000/€6.20.)*

SPACCANAPOLI. This renowned east-to-west neighborhood is replete with gorgeous architecture and merits at least a 30min. stroll. To get to the historic center from P. Dante, walk through **Porta Alba** and **Piazza Bellini** before turning down **Via dei Tribunali,** which follows the location and direction of an old Roman road, and now contains some of the city's best **pizzerie.** You'll see the churches of **S. Lorenzo Maggiore** and **S. Paolo Maggiore.** Take a right on V. Duomo and another on V.S. Biago into the heart of the area; you'll meander past the **University of Naples** and the **Chiesa di San Domenico Maggiore,** where a painting once spoke to St. Thomas Aquinas. *(In P.S. Domenico Maggiore. Open daily 7:15am-12:15pm and 4:15-7:15pm.)*

DUOMO. The main attraction of the 14th-century *duomo* is the **Capella del Tesoro di San Gennaro** on the right. A beautiful 17th-century bronze grille protects the high altar, which holds a gruesome reliquary with the saint's head and two vials of his coagulated blood. Supposedly, disaster strikes if the blood doesn't liquefy on the biannual celebration of his *festa;* miraculously, it always does. *(Walk 3 blocks up V. Duomo from Corso Umberto I or take #42 bus from P. Garibaldi. ☎081 44 90 97. Open M-F 8am-12:30pm and 4:30-7pm, Sa-Su 8am-3:30pm and 5-7:30pm. L5000/€2.60.)*

MUSEO AND GALLERIE DI CAPODIMONTE. This museum, in a royal *palazzo,* is surrounded by a pastoral park. You can inspect the plush royal apartments, but the true gem is the **Farnese Collection,** with works by Bellini and Caravaggio. *(Take bus #110 from P. Garibaldi to Parco Capodimonte. Enter by Portas Piccola or Grande. ☎081 749 91 11. Open Tu-F 10am-7pm, Su 8:30am-7:30pm. L14,000/€7.25, L12,000/€6.20 after 2pm.)*

PALAZZO REALE. The 17th-century Palazzo Reale contains the **Museo di Palazzo Reale,** royal apartments, and a fantastic view from the **Royal Chapel.** The **Biblioteca Nazionale** has 1.5 million volumes, including the scrolls from the Villa dei Papiri in Herculaneum. The **Teatro San Carlo** is reputed to have better acoustics than La Scala in Milan. *(Take the R2 bus from P. Garibaldi to P. Trieste e Trento and go around to the P. Plebiscito entrance. Museum: Open M-Tu and Th-F 9am-8pm, Su 9am-8pm. L8000/€4.15. Access to the library varies. Teatro tours: July Sa-Tu and Th 10am; Sept.-June Sa-Su 2pm. L5000/€2.60.)*

CASTEL NUOVO. It's impossible to miss the five-turreted Castel Nuovo, built in 1286 by Charles II of Anjou. The double-arched entrance commemorates the arrival of Alphonse I of Aragon in Naples. Inside, admire the **Museo Civico.** *(P. Municipio. Take R2 bus from P. Garibaldi.* ☎ *08 17 95 20 03. Open M-Sa 9am-7pm. L10,000/€5.20.)*

🎵 🎭 ENTERTAINMENT AND NIGHTLIFE

On September 19, December 16, and the first Saturday of May, Naples celebrates its patron saint with **Festa di San Gennaro.** Neopolitan nightlife varies with the season: after hiding in clubs and discos during the winter, Neopolitans take to the streets in warmer weather. People relax in the numerous *piazze,* and the outdoor bars and cafes, especially in **Piazza Bellini.** There are almost no exclusively gay or lesbian clubs; call **ARCI-Gay/Lesbica** (☎ 081 551 82 93) for gay and lesbian nights at clubs.

Camelot, V. San Pietro A Majella, 8 (☎ 038 07 13 60 17), just off P. Bellini in the historic center. Except for occasional live performances, they don't stray very far from pop, house, and dance. Beer L5000/€2.60. Open Sept.-June T-Su 10:30pm-5am.

Green Stage, P.S. Pasquale, 15 (☎ 081 245 10 55). Take V. Vittorio Colonna out of P. Amedeo, then turn right on V.S. Pasquale. An extremely popular pub. Open Tu-Th 7:30pm-3am, F-Su 7:30pm-4am.

Itaca, P. Bellini, 71 (☎ 033 82 26 61 32), has simple, black decor and dim lighting. Eerie trance music prevents you from noticing how much you paid for that last cocktail. Beer L6000/€3.10, mixed drinks from L10,000/€5.20. Open daily 10am-3am.

Tongue, V. Manzoni, 207 (☎ 081 769 08 00), in Posillipo. Take the erratic 404d *notturno* bus from P. Garibaldi. This large discotheque and music hall frequently features visiting DJs. Cover L25,000/€12.95. Open Oct.-May F-Sa 11pm-4am.

Madison Street, V. Sgambati, 47 (☎ 081 546 65 66). In Vomero. Features a huge dance floor. Cover L25,000/€12.95. Open Sept.-May F-Su 10pm-4am.

🏛 DAYTRIPS FROM NAPLES

POMPEII

The quickest way to Pompeii (25km south of Naples) is the Circumvesuvia train (☎ 081 772 21 11) from Stazione Centrale station (dir.: Sorrento, 2 per hr., L3200/€1.65) to the "Pompeii Scavi/Villa dei Misteri" stop. Open 8:30am to 1hr. before sunset: in summer around 6pm; in winter around 3:30pm. L16,000/€8.30.

On August 24, AD 79, a fit of towering flames, suffocating black clouds, and seething lava from Mt. Vesuvius buried the city of Pompeii—temples, villas, theaters, and all—under more than 7m of volcanic ash. Excavations, which began in 1748, have unearthed a stunningly well-preserved picture of Roman daily life. The site hasn't changed much since then, and neither have the victims, whose ghastly remains were partially preserved by plaster casts in the hardened ash. Walk down V. dei Marina to reach the **Forum,** surrounded by a colonnade and once the commercial, civic, and religious center of the city. Exit the Forum through the upper end, by the cafeteria, and head right on V. della Fortuna to reach the **House of the Faun,** where a bronze dancing faun and the spectacular Alexander Mosaic (today in the **Museo Archeologico Nazionale;** see p. 692) were found. Continue on V. della Fortuna and turn left on V. dei Vettii to reach the **House of the Vettii,** with the most vivid frescoes in Pompeii. Cross V. della Fortuna to V. Storto, turn left on V. degli Augustali, and take a quick right to visit a small **brothel** (the Lupenar). After 2000 years, it's still the most popular place in town. V. dei Teatri, across the street, leads to the oldest preserved **amphitheater** in the world (80 BC), which seated up to 12,000 spectators. To get to the **Villa of the Mysteries,** the complex's best-preserved villa, go all the way west on V. della Fortuna, right on V. Consolare, and all the way up Porta Ercolano. To get to the **tourist office,** V. Sacra, 1, take a right out of the station and continue to the bottom of the hill. (☎ 081 850 72 55. Open M-F 8am-3:30pm, Sa 8am-2pm.)

HERCULANEUM

Go 500m downhill from the Ercolano stop on the Circumvesuviana train from Naples (dir.: Sorrento; 20min., L3200/€1.65). Archaeological site open daily 8:30am to 1hr. before sunset. L16,000/€8.30.

Herculaneum does not evoke the tragedy of Pompeii—all but a handful of its inhabitants escaped the ravages of Vesuvius. Between 15 and 20 houses are open to the public. One of the more alluring is the **House of Deer,** named for the statues of deer in the courtyard. Stop at the **tourist office,** V. IV Novembre, 84, to pick up a free **map.** (☎ 081 788 12 43. Open M and W-F 9am-1pm, Tu 4-6:30pm.)

MT. VESUVIUS

Trasporti Vesuviani buses run from the Ercolano Circumvesuviana station to the crater of Vesuvius. Schedule available at tourist office; buy tickets on the bus (round-trip L6000/ €3.10). Admission: L9000/€4.65.

Peer into the only active volcano on mainland Europe. It's a 20-30min. walk from the bus stop to the top of Mt. Vesuvius, so bring plenty of water and wear sturdy shoes. Scientists say volcanoes should erupt about every 30 years—Vesuvius hasn't erupted since March 31, 1944. Nevertheless, experts say the trip is safe.

AMALFI COAST

The beauty of the Amalfi coast is one of extremes. Rugged cliffs plunge downward into calm azure waters, as coastal towns cling to the sides of narrow ravines. Visitors are drawn to the natural splendor and the unique character of each town.

▐ TRANSPORTATION

The coast is accessible from Naples, Salerno, Sorrento, and the islands by **ferry** and the blue SITA **bus** that runs along the Amalfi coast. **Trains** run directly to Salerno from Florence (5½-6½hr., 7 per day, L49,000-79,500/€25.35-41.10); Naples (45min., 32 per day, L5100-17,100/€2.65-8.85); Rome (2½-3hr., 18 per day, L22,000-45,000/€11.40-23.25); Venice (9hr., 1 per day, L64,000/€33.05). Trains also run to Sorrento from Naples (1hr., L4800/€2.50). SITA **buses** run from Positano to Amalfi (L2300/€1.20) and Sorrento (L2400/€1.25), and from Amalfi to Salerno (1¼hr., 23 per day, L5100/€2.65). From Salerno, Travelmar (☎ 089 87 31 90) runs **ferries** to Amalfi (1hr., 3 per day, L9000/€4.65) via Positano (40min., L7000/€3.65). From Sorrento, Linee Marittime Partenopee (☎ 081 878 14 30) runs ferries to Amalfi (45min., L16,000/€8.30) via Positano (30min., L15,000/ €7.75) and Capri (50min., L8000/€4.15); from Amalfi they service Salerno (30min., 9 per day, L16,000/€8.30).

AMALFI ☎ 089

Between the rugged cliffs of the Sorrentine peninsula and the azure waters of the Adriatic, Amalfi nestles in incomparable natural beauty. The 9th-century **Duomo di Sant'Andrea** imparts a dignified charm to the **Piazza del Duomo.** The *piazza* may need it; the nearby **Fontana di Sant'Andrea** features a marble female nude with water spouting from her breasts. Trek up from Amalfi into the imposing **Monti Lattari** or to the **Valley of the Dragons,** named for the torrent of water and mist exploding out to sea every winter. Although there is a small beach in Amalfi itself, a 5-10min. trip around the bend will bring you to a much better (and free) beach in **Atrani. A'Scalinatella,** P. Umberto, 12, lets hostel beds and regular rooms all over Atrani and Amalfi. (☎ 089 87 19 30. Dorms L20,000-35,000/€10.35-18.10; doubles L50,000-120,000/€25.85-62. **Camping** L15,000/€7.75 per person.) **Hotel**

Lidomare, V. Piccolomini, 9, is through the alley across from the *duomo.* (☎089 87 13 32; fax 87 13 94. Breakfast included. Singles L75,000/€38.75; doubles L150,000-170,000/€77.50-87.80. AmEx/MC/V.) Eat at one of Amalfi's **panino-teche** (sandwich shops).

RAVELLO   ☎089

Ravello and its lush villas perch 330m atop the cliffs, gazing down on a patchwork of villages and ravines extending to the sea. The Moorish cloister and meandering gardens of **Villa Rufolo,** off P. Duomo, inspired Wagner's *Parsifal.* (☎089 85 76 57. Open daily 9am-sunset. L6000/€3.10.) On the small road to the right, signs lead to the impressive **Villa Cimbrone,** where floral walkways and gardens hide temples and statue-filled grottoes. (Open daily 9am-7:30pm. L8000/€4.15.) Frequent **classical music festivals** give the city the nickname *"Città della Musica."* (☎089 85 81 49. Tickets L20,000-35,000/€10.35-18.10.) The **Hotel Villa Amore,** at V. dei Fusco, 5, on the road to Villa Cimbrone, has rooms with beautiful views. (☎/fax 089 85 71 35. Breakfast included. Singles L105,000/€54.25 per person. AmEx/MC/V.)

POSITANO   ☎089

After a famous fling with fashion with the 1959 invention of the bikini, Positano's classy reputation and cliffside homes began luring high rollers as well as the artsy set. Despite the expensive price tag for its attractions, there is no denying that Positano has its charms. To see the large *pertusione* (hole) in **Montepertuso,** one of three perforated mountains in the world, hike the 45min. trail up the hillside or take the bus from P. dei Mulini, near the port or from any other bus stop. Positano's gray **beaches** are also popular, and although boutiques may be a bit pricey, no one charges for window-shopping. **SITA buses,** from 7am-9pm, run to Amalfi (L2300/€1.20) and Sorrento (L3200/€1.65). The **tourist office,** V. del Saraceno, 4, is below the *duomo* near the beach. (☎089 87 50 67. Open M-Sa 8:30am-2pm and 3:30-8pm; in winter M-F 8:30am-2pm, Sa 8:30am-noon.) **Ostello Brikette,** V.G. Marconi, 358, 100m up the main coastal road to Sorrento from Viale Pasitea, has incredible views. (☎089 87 58 57; fax 812 28 14. Breakfast, shower, and sheets included. Lockout 11:30am-5pm. Curfew 1am. Dorms L35,000/€18.10; doubles L100,000/€51.65.) **Pensione Maria Luisa,** V. Fornillio, 42, has seaside terraces. (☎089 87 50 23. Breakfast included. Singles L70,000/€36.15; doubles L100,000/€51.65.) Thrifty travelers head to Fornillo for cheap eats. **Vini e Panini,** V. del Saracino, 29-31, sells sandwiches to go. (Open daily 8am-2pm and 4:30-10pm. Closed Dec.-Mar.)

SORRENTO   ☎081

The largest, most heavily touristed town on the peninsula, lively and charming Sorrento (pop. 20,000) makes a convenient base for daytrips around the Bay of Naples. Visit **Marina Grande,** a traditional fishing harbor, or take the bus to the **free beach** at **Punta del Capo,** and walk 10min. down the footpath to see the remains of the ancient Roman **Villa di Pollio. Trains** (☎081 772 24 44) run to Naples (1hr., L4800/€2.60). Caremar **ferries** (☎081 807 30 77) go to Capri (50min., L9000/€4.60). Halfway to Punta del Capo, the **Hotel Elios,** V. Capo, 33, has comfy rooms. Take bus A from P. Tazzo. (☎081 878 18 12. Singles L45,000/€23.25; doubles L80,000/€41.35, 3- to 4-person rooms L45,000/€23.25 per person.) Turn left on Corso Italia from the train station to reach **Hotel City,** Corso Italia, 221, which provides guests with currency exchange, local bus tickets, and maps. (☎081 877 22 10. Breakfast included. Singles L75,000/€38.75; doubles L125,000/€64.60. AmEx/MC/V.) Delicious local specialties at low prices await in Sorrento. At ▓**Ristorante e Pizzeria Giardiniello,** V. Accademia, 7, off V. Giuliani, eat Mamma Luisa's *gnocchi* (L8000/€4.15) in a peaceful garden. (Cover L1500/€0.80. Open June-Sept. daily 11am-2am; Oct.-May F-W 11am-2am.) **Gatto Nero,** V. Correale, 21, Sorrento's most stylish bar, excites the crowd with plenty of jazz and blues. (☎081 877 36 86.)

SALERNO AND PAESTUM

Although industrial **Salerno** is best used as a base for daytrips to nearby Paestum, there is a sprinkling of intriguing sights in the city's old quarter; **Via dei Mercanti** and its tiny side streets afford a taste of life in the Middle Ages. **Paestum** is the site of three spectacularly preserved **Doric temples,** including the **Temple of Ceres,** the **Temple of Poseidon,** and the **basilica.** (Temples open daily 9am-1hr. before sunset. Closed 1st and 3rd M of each month. Last admittance 2hr. before sunset. L8000/€4.15, EU citizens over 60 and under 18 free.) **Trains** head south from the P. Veneto station in Salerno to Paestum (40min., 9 per day, L4700/€2.45). **Buses** also link Paestum and Salerno (1hr., every hr. 7am-7pm, L4700/€2.45). For the cheerful **Ostello della Gioventù "Irno" (HI),** in Salerno at V. Luigi Guercio, 112, go left from the train station onto V. Torrione, and then turn left under the bridge on V. Mobilio. (☎ 089 79 02 51. Breakfast included. Curfew 2am. Dorms L17,500/€9.05.)

BAY OF NAPLES ISLANDS

Off the shores of the Bay of Naples, the pleasure islands **Capri** and **Ischia** beckon weary travelers with promises of breathtaking natural sights, comfortable accommodations, and gorgeous beaches. The islands can be reached by ferries *(traghetti)* or the faster, more expensive hydrofoils *(aliscafi)*. For trips to Capri, Sorrento is the closest starting point. The busiest route to Capri and Ischia is through Naples's Mergellina and Molo Beverello ports. To reach Molo Beverello from Naples's Stazione Centrale, take tram #1 from P. Garibaldi to P. Municipio on the waterfront. Ferries and hydrofoils also run between the islands.

CAPRI   ☎ 081

The sheer bluffs, divine landscapes, and azure waters of **Capri** have beckoned wayfarers from the mainland since Roman times. Capri proper is above the ports, while **Anacapri** sits higher up the mountain. From **Piazza Umberto** in Capri, **Via Roma** leads up to Anacapri. Every day **boat tours** reveal Capri's coast from Marina Grande. Inquire at the Grotta Azurra Travel Office, V. Roma, 53, across from the bus stop. (☎ 081 837 07 02. Open M-Sa 9am-1pm and 3-8pm. Boat tour L19,000/€9.85.) Take a boat from the port (L9000/€4.60) or descend between the vineyards from P. Umberto to **Bagni di Tiberio,** a bathing area amid villa ruins. Upstairs from P. Vittoria in Anacapri, the **Villa San Michele,** for which even author Henry James could not find sufficient superlatives, has gardens, ancient sculptures, and a remarkable view of the island. (Open daily 9:30am-1hr. before dusk. L8000/€4.15.) To appreciate Capri's Mediterranean beauty from higher ground, take the **chairlift** up **Monte Solaro** from P. Vittoria. (Open daily 9:30am-1hr. before dusk. Round-trip L7000/€3.65.) From P. Umberto in Capri take V. Longano, which becomes V. Tiberio, to **Villa Jovis** (1hr.), the most magnificent of Emperor Tiberius's 12 Capri villas. (Open daily 9am-1hr. before dusk. L4000/€2.10.)

SIPPIC buses leave V. Roma in Capri for Anacapri (every 15min., L2400/€1.25). Caremar **ferries** (☎ 081 837 07 00) run from Marina Grande to Naples (1¼hr., L12,000/€6.20) and Sorrento (45min., L16,000/€8.30). Linee Lauro sends **hydrofoils** to Ischia (40min., L20,000/€10.35) and Sorrento (20min., L16,000/€8.30); LineaJet hydrofoils go to Naples (40min., L16,000/€8.30). The Capri **AAST Information Office** (☎ 081 837 06 34) is at the end of Marina Grande; in Anacapri, at V. Orlandi, 59 (☎ 081 837 15 24), to the right from the bus stop. (Open June-Sept. M-Sa 8:30am-8:30pm; Oct.-May 9am-1:30pm and 3:30-6:45pm.) In Anacapri, beautiful ■**Villa Eva,** V. La Fabbrica, 8, will pick you up from P. Vittoria. (☎ 081 837 15 49; www.caprionline.com/villaeva. Breakfast included. Singles L50,000-60,000/€25.85-31; doubles from L100,000/€51.65; triples from L120,000/€62; quads from L160,000/€82.65.) Try the **Alla Bussola di Hermes,** V. Traversa La Vigna, 14, with its cheap rooms and friendly staff. (☎ 081 838 20 10. Dorms and doubles L40,000/€20.65 per person.) In Capri, **Pensione Stella Maris,** V. Roma, 27, opposite the bus stop, offers 10 rooms with bath and TV. (☎ 081 837 04 52; fax 837 86 62. Doubles L120,000-180,000/€62-93.)

AmEx/MC/V.) Get **groceries** at **STANDA** in Capri; head right at the fork at the end of V. Roma. (Open M-Sa 8:30am-1:30pm and 5-9pm, Su 9am-noon.) The nighttime action in Anacapri is the least expensive and pretentious; several clubs line **Via Orlandi.**

ISCHIA   ☎ 081

Across the bay from overrun Capri, Eden-like Ischia offers soothing beaches, natural hot springs, ruins, forests, vineyards, and lemon groves. Follow the coast along the main road: In the east is **Ischia Porto,** a port formed by the crater of an extinct volcano. The road continues to **Casamicciola Terme,** on the north coast, with its crowded beach and legendary thermal waters, and **Lacco Ameno,** in the northwest, the oldest Greek settlement in the western Mediterranean. The road finally ends at well-touristed **Forio,** which is filled with restaurants and hotels. Take bus #5 from Ischia Porto to get to the gorgeous beach at **Maronti. Castello Aragonese,** a 15th-century fortress on its own tiny island, connects to civilization by a 15th-century footbridge. (Take bus #7 or 8 from the port to Ischia Ponte. L15,000/€7.75.)

Caremar **ferries** (☎ 081 98 48 18) arrive from Naples. (1-1½hr., 14 per day, L9800/€5.10.) **Linee Marittime Partenopee** (☎ 081 99 18 88) runs hydrofoils to Sorrento (45min., 5 per day, L18,000/€9.30). SEPSA **buses** depart from P. Trieste just off the port. The main lines are #1, CD, and CS, all of which circle the island in various directions. Stay in Ischia Porto only if you want to be close to the ferries—most *pensioni* are in Forio. In Forio, the floral **Pensione Di Lustro,** V. Filippo di Lustro, 9, where Truman Capote once stayed, is near the beach. (☎ 081 99 71 63. Breakfast included. July-Aug. With *Let's Go:* June doubles L100,000/€51.65; July-Aug. L120,000/€62; Oct.-Mar. L90,000/€46.50. AmEx/MC/V.) The **Ostello "Il Gabbiano" (HI),** Strada Statale Forio-Panza, 162, between Forio and Panza, is accessible by buses #1, CS, and CD, and also has beach access. (☎ 081 90 94 22. Breakfast included. Lockout 10am-1pm. Curfew 12:30am. Open Apr.-Sept. Dorms L30,000/€15.50; doubles L60,000/€31.) **Camping Internazionale** is at V. Foschini, 22, 15min. from the port. Take V. Alfredo de Luca from V. del Porto; bear right on V. Michele Mazzella at P. degli Eroi. (☎ 081 99 14 49. Open Apr. 15-Oct. 15. L16,000/€8.30 per person; L10,000 per tent/€5.20. 2-person bungalows with bath L80,000/€41.35; L20,000/€10.35 per additional person.) While Ischian food, especially seafood and fruit, is a treat, it is almost impossible to find a restaurant that is not oriented toward the tourists who flood the island. Explore side streets for less expensive, more authentic culinary options.

BARI   ☎ 080

Most tourists only stay in Bari long enough to buy a ferry ticket to Greece, but Apulia's capital is a vibrant and grittily modern city that thrives in the scorching southern sun. The **Basilica di San Nicola** houses the remains of Saint Nicolas, which were stolen by 11th-century *Baresi* sailors from Turkey. (Open daily 7am-noon and 4-7:30pm.) Take the Ferrotramviara Bari Nord train (☎ 0883 59 26 84) to Andria (1¼hr., 19 per day, L5100/€2.65) and then a bus (30min., 2 per day, L3300/€1.70) to the majestic **Castel del Monte,** 17km away.

FS **trains** go to: Brindisi (1-1¾hr., 26 per day, L10,100-25,100/€5.25-13); Naples (4½hr., 1 per day, L25,500/€13.20); Rome (5-7hr., 6 per day, L47,000-65,500/€24.30-33.85). Bari is an important port for ferries to Albania, Greece, Israel, and Turkey. **InterRail** and **Eurail** pass holders get **no discounts** on **ferries** from Bari (see **Brindisi,** below), but some ferries have student rates. **Poseidon Lines,** Corso de Tullio, 36/40 (☎ 080 524 00 22; window #11 at the port), goes to Israel and Turkey; **Ventouris Ferries,** V. Piccinni, 133 (☎ 080 521 76 99; windows #7-10), goes to: Cephalonia (15hr.; July 26-Aug. 21 every other day; L63,000-87,000/€32.55-44.95, students L57,000-77,000/€29.45-39.80); Corfu (11hr.; June 27-Sept. 29 1 per day; L53,000-73,000/€27.40-37.05, L47,000-67,000/€24.30-34.60); Igoumenitsa (13hr.; in summer 1 per day; L53,000-73,000/€27.40-37.70, L47,000-67,000/€24.30-34.60); Patras (18hr.; 1 per day; L63,000-87,000/€32.55-44.95, L57,000-77,000/€29.45-39.80); **Marlines** (☎ 080 523 18 24) goes to Igoumenitsa (13hr., 2-4 per week, L50,000-70,000/€25.85-36.15). The area near the port is dangerous; take a bus rather than walk. **Albergo Serena,** V.

ITALY

Imbriani, 69, has 14 spacious rooms. (☎ 080 554 09 80; fax 558 66 13. Singles L50,000/ €25.85; doubles L80,000/€41.35; triples L120,000/€62.) **Pensione Giulia,** V. Crisanzio, 12, has 13 rooms. (☎ 080 521 66 30; fax 521 82 71. Singles L70,000/€36.15, with bath 80,000/€41.32; doubles L90,000/€46.50, L120,000/€62. AmEx/MC/V.)

BRINDISI   ☎ 0831

Everyone comes to Brindisi to leave Italy—here Pompey fled from Caesar's armies and Crusaders set forth to retake the Holy Land. If you're a more peaceful traveler heading for Greece, arrive in the afternoon, as ferries leave in the evening. In August, consider arriving early or departing from Ancona or Bari instead. **Trains** arrive in P. Crispi from: Naples (7hr., 5 per day, L31,000/€16.05); Rome (6-9hr., 4 per day, L49,000-79,500/€25.30-41.05); Venice (11hr., 7:50pm, L67,500/€34.90). **Ferries** leave for: Cephalonia (16½hr.); Corfu (8hr.); Igoumenitsa (10hr.); Patras (17hr.). All passengers leaving from Brindisi pay a **port tax** (L10,000-14,000/€5.20-7.25) in addition to regular fare. **Deck passage** *(passagio semplice;* sleeping on the deck) is the cheapest option. **Delta Shipping,** Corso Umberto, 116 (☎ 0831 52 03 67), has an English-speaking staff. **No Bari ferries accept Eurail/InterRail passes.** InterRail and Eurail passes are only valid on **Hellenic Mediterranean Lines,** Corso Garibaldi, 8 (☎ 0831 52 85 31; fax 52 68 72; www.hml.it), for deck passage; a seat inside costs L29,000/€15. Eurail pass holders must pay a L19,000/€9.85 fee for travel between June 10 and September 30; InterRail passholders are exempt from this fee. Those without passes will have to shop for cheap fares—tickets are usually L45,000-55,000/€23.25-28.40 for deck passage. Three of the more reliable ferry companies are **Strintzis Lines,** Corso Garibaldi, 65 (☎ 0831 56 22 00), **Fragline,** Corso Garibaldi, 88 (☎ 0831 59 01 96), and **Med Link Lines,** Corso Garibaldi, 49 (☎ 0831 52 76 67). Most companies offer a 10-20% discount on round-trip tickets, youth/student fares, and "bargain" tickets on certain days. Check in at least **one hour** before departure, wear warm clothes, and bring your own food.

Corso Umberto runs from the train station to the port, becoming **Corso Garibaldi** halfway down. From Corso Garibaldi, turn left onto V. Regina Margherita for the *stazione marittima* and the **tourist office,** V. Regina Margherita, 5. (☎ 0831 52 30 72. Open M-Sa 8am-7pm; in winter M-F 9am-1pm and 4-6pm.) The lively **Ostello della Gioventù,** V. Brandi, 2, 2km from the train station in Casale, has a free shuttle to pick you up. (☎ 0831 41 31 23. Shower and sheets included. L23,000/€11.90 per person.) In town, try **Hotel Venezia,** V. Pisanelli, 4. After the fountain, take the second left off Corso Umberto onto V.S. Lorenzo da Brindisi, then turn right onto V. Pisanelli. (☎ 0831 52 75 11. Reserve ahead. Singles L25,000/€12.95; doubles L45,000/€23.25.) Get food for the ferry at **Maxis Sidis supermarket,** Corso Garibaldi, 106, near the port.

SICILY (SICILIA)

With a history so steeped in chaos, catastrophe, and conquest, it's no wonder that the island of Sicily possesses a reputation for passionate volatility. Greek, Roman, Arab, and Norman conquerors each transformed Sicily's cultural and political landscape, but none managed to extinguish its independent spirit. Today, Sicilians are reclaiming their island from the "tradition" of Mafia control, with demonstrations that draw thousands.

▚ TRANSPORTATION

Tirrenia ferries (☎ 091 33 33 00) offers the most extensive and reliable service. From southern Italy, take a **train** to Reggio di Calabria, then the NGI or Meridiano **ferry** (40min., NGI 10-12 per day, L1000/€0.55; Meridiano 11-15 per day, L3000/€1.55) or Ferrovie Statale **hydrofoil** (☎ 096 586 35 40; 25min., 12 per day, L5000/€2.60) to **Messina,** Sicily's transport hub. Ferries also go to Palermo from: Cagliari, Sardinia (14hr., L60,500-78,000/€31.25-40.30); Genoa (20hr., 6 per week, L123,000-181,000/€63.55-93.50); Naples (11hr., 2 per day, L68,000-77,000/€35.15-

LA FAMIGLIA Pin-striped suits, machine guns, and *The Godfather* are a far cry from the reality of the Sicilian Mafia. The system has its roots in the *latifondi* (agricultural estates) of rural Sicily, where land managers and salaried militiamen (a.k.a. landlords and bouncers) protected their turf and people. Powerful because people owed them favors, strong because they supported one another, and feared because they did not hesitate to kill offenders, they founded a tradition that has dominated Sicilian life since the late 19th century. Since the mid-1980s, the Italian government has worked to curtail Mafia influence, with visible results. Today Sicilians shy away from any Mafia discussion, referring to the system as *Cosa Nostra* (our thing).

39.80). **SAIS Trasporti** (☎091 617 11 41) and **SAIS** (☎091 616 60 28) buses serve destinations throughout the island, including Corleone (perhaps you've seen *The Godfather*?). **Trains** also chug to Messina directly from Naples (4½hr., 7 per day, L41,800/€21.60) and Rome (9hr., 7 per day, L57,000/€29.45). Trains continue west to Palermo (3½hr., 15 per day, L19,500/€10.10) via Milazzo (45min., L4500/€2.35); and south to Syracuse (3hr., 14 per day, L17,000/€6.75) via Taormina (1hr., L5500/€2.85).

PALERMO   ☎091

Gritty urban Palermo, Sicily's capital and the notorious cradle for Italian organized crime, dispels any myths of a sleepy Sicily. Twisting streets wind past ancient ruins and bombed-out buildings from WWII, while Versace and Armani line more modern avenues. To get to the huge **Teatro Massimo,** where the climactic opera scene of *The Godfather Part III* was filmed, walk up V. Maqueda past the intersection of Quattro Canti and Corso Vittorio Emanuele. (Open Tu-Su 10am-4pm for 20min. tours.) Follow Corso Vittorio Emanuele to the grand **Palazzo dei Normanni** to enter the **Cappella Palatina,** which has carved wooden ceilings and incredible golden Byzantine mosaics. (Open M-Sa 9am-noon and 3-4:45pm, Su 9-10am and noon-1pm.) The intensely morbid **Cappuchin Catacombs,** in P. Cappuccini, are only for the strong of stomach. This potentially disturbing sight showcases 8000 corpses in moth-eaten clothing that line the underground labyrinth, including a preserved baby girl and a separate room for virgins. To get there, take bus #109 or 318 from Stazione Centrale to P. Indipendenza and then hop on the #327 for the catacombs. (☎091 21 21 17. Open M-Su 9am-noon and 3-5pm. L2500/€1.30.)

Trains run from Stazione Centrale, in P. Giulio Cesare, at V. Roma and V. Maqueda, to Florence (16hr., 3 per day, L82,000/€42.35) and Rome (11hr., 7 per day, L75,000/€38.75). All four **bus** lines are located on V. Balsamo, next to the train station. After purchasing tickets, ask exactly where your bus will arrive and for its logo. Ask at a **AMAT** or **Metro** info booth for a combined local metro and bus map. The **tourist office,** P. Castelnuovo, 34, is on the 3rd floor of Banco di Sicilia, opposite Teatro Politeama; from the train station, take any bus showing "Politeama" on its overhead screen to "P. Politeama," at the end of V. Maqueda. (☎091 605 83 51 or 091 58 38 47; fax 58 63 38. Open daily 8am-5pm.) The cozy **Hotel Regina,** Corso Vittorio Emanuele, 316, is at the intersection of V. Maqueda and Corso V. Emanuele. (☎091 611 42 16; fax 612 21 69. Singles L30,000/€15.50; doubles L70,000-80,000/€36.15-41.35.) Elegant **Hotel del Centro,** V. Roma, 72, is five blocks up V. Roma from the train station, on the 2nd floor. (☎091 617 03 76; fax 617 36 54. Singles L50,000-70,000/€25.85-36.15; doubles L70,000-95,000/ €36.15-49.10.) For **camping,** take bus #101 from the train station to "P. de Gasperi," and then take bus #628 to "V. Sferracavallo." Walk downhill one block, turn right on V. dei Manderini after the post office, and **Campeggio dell'Ulivi,** V. Pegaso, 25, is on the right. (☎/fax 091 53 30 21. L10,000/€5.20 per person and tent. Showers free.) Palermo's specialty is *arancini* (fried balls filled with rice, spinach, or meat); indulge at **Lo Sparviero,** V. Sperlinga, 23, a block from the Teatro Massimo. (Pizza from L4000/€2.10, *primi* from L10,000/€5.20. Open daily noon-3pm and 6:30pm-midnight.) **Postal Code:** 90100.

ITALY

🔢 DAYTRIPS FROM PALERMO

MONREALE

Bus #389 leaves Palermo's P. Indipendenza for Monreale's P. Vittorio Emanuele (40min., 3 per hr., L1500/€0.80). To get to P. Indipendenza, take bus #109 or 118 from Palermo's Stazione Centrale. Dress modestly. Cathedral open daily 8am-noon and 3:30-6pm. Free. Cloister open M-Sa 9am-7pm, Su 9am-1pm. L8000/€4.15, students L4000/€2.10. Roof L3000/€1.55.

Eight kilometers outside of Palermo, Monreale's magnificent Norman-Saracen **cathedral** glistens with 6430 sq. m of golden mosaics and 130 panels depicting Bible scenes. Next door, the **cloisters** house a renowned Sicilian sculpture collection in their serene courtyard, surrounded by 228 tiled columns.

CEFALÙ   ☎ 0921

Trains arrive at P. Stazione, 1 (☎ 0921 42 11 69), from Palermo (1hr., 36 per day, L7000/€3.65). Open daily 6:45am-8:50pm.

Tiny Cefalù is a labyrinth of cobblestone streets winding along the sea. The dramatic 11th-century **duomo** combines Norman, Byzantine, and Roman architectural styles, with elegant arches and dazzling Byzantine mosaics. (Dress modestly. Open daily 8am-noon and 3:30-7pm.) The centerpiece of the eclectic collection in the **Museo Mandralisca**, V. Mandralisca, 13, is the *Ritratto di un Ignoto (Portrait of an Unknown)* by Sicilian master Antonello da Messina. (☎ 0921 42 15 47. Open daily 9am-7pm. L8000/€4.15.) For amazing views and ruins, hike up to the **Rocca** by way of the Salita Saraceni; from P. Garibaldi, follow the signs for *"Pedonale Rocca"* (30min.). From the train station, V. Aldo Moro changes to V. Matteotti, which leads to the **tourist office,** Corso Ruggero, 77. (☎ 0921 42 10 50; fax 42 23 86.)

AGRIGENTO   ☎ 0922

The five elevated temples composing the majestic **Valle dei Templi** at Agrigento offer breathtaking vistas from every angle. Further along, the **Tempio della Concordia,** one of the world's best-preserved Greek temples, owes its survival to consecration by the archbishop of Agrigento. One kilometer uphill from the ruins, the excellent **Museo Nazionale Archeologico di San Nicola** houses a fabulous collection of Greek vases and relics from the area's necropolis. To reach the Valley of Temples, take bus #1 or 2 (L1500/€0.80) from the train station. (Open M-Sa 8am-12:30pm. L8000/€4.15.) Literature aficionados will want to visit the birthplace of **Luigi Pirandello** (see p. 601), now a small museum of books, notes, and family photographs. For the Pirandello museum, take Lumia bus #1 to P. Kaos. (☎ 0922 51 11 02. Open daily 8am-1:30pm. L4000/€2.10.) **Trains** arrive in P. Marconi, below P. Moro, from Palermo (2hr., 11 per day, L12,500/€6.45). **Buses** run from P. Roselli, left of P. Vittorio, to Palermo (2hr., M-Sa 4 per day, L13,000/€6.75). The **tourist office, AAST,** V. Battista, 13, is the first left off V. Atenea. (☎ 0922 204 54. Open in summer M-F 9am-1:30pm.) **Trattoria Atenea,** V. Ficani, 32, the fourth right off V. Atenea from P. Moro, has extensive seafood offerings. Try *Grigliata mista di pesce* (mixed grilled fish) for L9000/€4.65. (☎ 0922 202 47. Open M-Sa noon-3pm and 7pm-midnight.)

SYRACUSE (SIRACUSA)   ☎ 0931

Never having regained the glory of its golden Grecian days, the super-modern city of Syracuse places its pride upon its extraordinary Greek ruins. Syracuse's past role as one of the most powerful cities in the Mediterranean is still evident in the **Archaeological Park,** on the north side of town. The enormous **Greek theater** is where 20,000 spectators watched Aeschylus premiere his *Persians*. The amazing acoustics of the **Orecchio di Dionigi** (Ear of Dionysius) spawned the legend that the tyrant Dionysius put prisoners here to eavesdrop on them. For the well-preserved 2nd-century **Roman amphitheater,** follow Corso Gelone until it meets Viale Teocrito, then walk left down V. Augusto. (Open daily 9am-7pm. L8000/€4.15.) More Greek ruins lie over the Ponte Umbertino on **Ortigia**, the serene island on which the Greeks first landed. The ruined **Temple of Apollo** has a few columns still standing, but those at the **Temple of Diana** are much more impressive. Integrated into the cathedral, the temple's columns line the walls of the **duomo**. Down V. Picherale from P. Duomo, the **Fonte Aretusa** reflects self-admirers. Back on the mainland, off Viale Teocrito from Corso Gelone, near the tourist office, is the **Catacombe di San Giovanni**. (Open mid-Mar. to mid-Nov. Th-Tu 9am-12:30pm and 2-5pm; mid-Nov. to mid-Mar. Th-Tu 9am-1pm. L6000/€3.10.) Those who prefer tans to temples should take bus #21, 22, or 24 18km to **Fontane Bianche** (L6000/€3.10), a glitzy beach with plenty of discos.

Trains leave V. Francesco Crispi for Messina (3¼hr., 18 per day, L16,000/€8.30) and Rome (12hr., 5 per day, L73,000/€37.70). Interbus **buses**, V. Trieste, 28 (☎ 0931 667 10), leave for Palermo (3¼hr., 1-4 per day, L26,000/€16.45) and Taormina (2hr., 1 per day, L14,000/€7.25). Solo travelers should beware the train station area at night. To get from the train station to the **tourist office**, V.S. Sebastiano, 43, take V.F. Crispi to Corso Gelone, turn right on Viale Teocrite, turn left on V.S. Sebastianoi; it's on the left. (☎ 0931 677 10. Open in summer M-Sa 8:30am-1:45pm and 3:30-6:30pm, Su 9am-1pm; in winter M-Sa 8:30am-2pm and 3:30-6:30pm, Su 8:30am-2pm.) **Albergo Aretusa**, V. Francesco Crispi, 73, near the train station, has 50 rooms in an old *palazzo*. (☎/fax 0931 242 11. Breakfast L5000/€2.60. Reserve ahead for Aug. Singles L30,000/€15.50, with bath L40,000/€20.65; doubles L40,000/€20.65, L50,000/€25.85; triples L75,000/€38.75, L90,000/€46.50; prices rise July-Aug. AmEx/MC/V.) **Spaghetteria do Scugghiu**, V.D. Sciná, 11, off P. Archimede, on Ortigia, serves 18 delicious types of spaghetti. (Spaghetti L10,000/€5.20. Open Tu-Su noon-3pm and 5pm-midnight.) For budget eats, try places on **Via Savoia** and **Via Cavour**, or the open-air **market** in Ortigia, on V. Trento, off P. Pancali. (Open M-Sa 8am-1pm.)

TAORMINA
☎ 0942

From the high cliffs of Mt. Tauro, the serene buildings of beautiful Taormina overlook a spectacular panorama that includes the simmering Mt. Etna. The 3rd-century **Greek theater**, at the cliff's edge, has a view more dramatic than most Greek tragedies. To get there, walk up V. Teatro Greco; it's off Corso Umberto I at P. Vittorio Emanuele. (Open daily 9am-dusk. L8000/€4.15.) Cable cars leave every 15min. from V. Pirandello for **Lido Mazzarò** beach (L3000/€1.55), just below town. **Gole Alcantara** is a nearby haven of stunning gorges, roaring waterfalls, and crystal rapids. (☎ 0942 98 50 10. Entrance L8000/€4.15; wetsuit L15,000/€7.75.)

Taormina is accessible by **bus** from Messina (L5000/€2.60). **Trains** (L5500/€2.85) are more frequent, but the station is far from Taormina. The **tourist office**, Palazzo Corvaja, is off Corso Umberto across from P. Vittorio Emanuele. (☎ 0942 232 43; fax 0942 249 41. Open M-F 8am-2pm and 4-7pm, Sa 9am-1pm and 4-7pm.) **Pensione Svizzera**, V. Pirandello, 26, has coastal views and clean rooms. (☎ 0942 237 90; fax 0942 62 59 06. Reserve ahead. Open Feb.-Nov. Singles L100,000/€51.65; doubles 160,000/€82.65; triples 180,000/€93. MC/V.) Nearby **Inn Piero**, V. Pirandello, 20, has 10 small rooms with a sea view. (☎ 0942 231 39. Reserve ahead. Singles L90,000/€46.50; doubles L145,000/€74.90. Half-pension L113,000/€58.35 per person required in summer. AmEx/D/MC/V.) Buy groceries at **STANDA supermarket**, V. Apollo Arcageta, 49, at the end of Corso Umberto. (Open M-Sa 8:30am-1pm and 5-9pm.) **Bella Blu**, V. Pirandello, 28, serves delicious food. (L26,000/€13.45 tourist *menù*. *Primi* from L7000/€3.65, *secondi* from L12,000/€6.20. Cover L2000/€1.05. Open daily 10am-3:30pm and 6pm until the last person leaves.)

AEOLIAN ISLANDS (ISOLE EOLIE)

Homer thought the **Aeolian** (or **Lipari**) **Islands** to be the second home of the gods, and indeed, these last few stretches of unspoiled seashore in Italy border on the divine. Sparkling seas, smooth beaches, and fiery volcanoes all enhance the area's stunning beauty.

ITALY

⬕ TRANSPORTATION

The archipelago lies off the Sicilian coast, north of **Milazzo,** the principal and least expensive departure point. Hop off a **train** from Messina (40min., L4500/€2.35) or Palermo (3hr., L15,500/€8) and onto an orange AST **bus** for the port (10min., every hr., L1200/€0.65). Siremar (☎090 928 32 42) and Navigazione Generale Italiana (NGI; ☎090 928 40 91) **ferries** depart for Lipari (2hr., L10,500-11,500/€5.45-5.95); Stromboli (5hr., L16,500-19,000/€8.55-9.85); Vulcano (1½hr., L10,000-11,000/€5.20-5.70). Siremar and SNAV (☎090 928 45 09) **hydrofoils** *(aliscafi)* make the trip in half the time, but cost twice as much. All three have ticket offices on V. Dei Mille facing the port in Milazzo. **Ferries** leave for the islands less frequently from **Naples'** Molo Beverello port. Ferries between Lipari and Vulcano cost L4500/€2.35; between Lipari and Stromboli, L25,500/€13.20.

LIPARI   ☎090

Lipari, the largest and most developed of the islands, is renowned for its amazing beaches and stunning hillside views. To reach the popular beaches of **Spiaggia Bianca** and **Porticello,** take the Lipari-Cavedi bus a few kilometers north to Canneto, where Spiaggia Bianca is *the* spot for topless (and sometimes bottomless) sunbathing. Lipari's other offerings include a splendidly rebuilt medieval **castello,** the site of an ancient Greek acropolis. The fortress shares its hill with an **archaeological park,** the **San Bartolo church,** and the superb ▧**Museo Archeologico Eoliano,** up the stone steps off V. Garibaldi. (☎090 988 01 74. Open May-Oct. M-Su 9am-1:30pm and 4-7pm; Nov.-Apr. M-Su 9am-1:30pm and 3-6pm. L8000/€4.15.)

The **AAST delle Isole Eolie tourist office,** Corso Vittorio Emanuele, 202, is near the ferry dock. (☎090 988 00 95; www.net-net.it/aasteolie. Open July-Aug. M-Sa 8am-2pm and 4-10pm, Su 8am-2pm; Sept.-June M-F 8am-2pm and 4:30-7:30pm, Sa 8am-2pm.) **Casa Vittorio,** Vico Sparviero, 15, is on a quiet side street in the center of town. Its rooms range from intimate singles to a five-person penthouse. (☎090 981 15 23. May-July singles L30,000-40,000/€15.50-20.65; doubles L60,000-80,000/€31-41.35.) The elegant **Pensione Enso il Negro,** V. Garibaldi, 29, is 20m up V. Garibladi and up three flights of stone stairs. (☎090 981 31 63. Singles L70,000/€36.15; doubles L120,000/€62.) **Hotel Europeo,** Corso Vittorio Emanuele, 98, has small, spare rooms in a great location. (☎090 981 15 89. July-Aug. singles L55,000-60,000/€28.40-31; doubles L110,000-120,000/€56.85-62; Sept.-June singles L30,000/€15.50; doubles L60,000/€31.) **Camp** at **Baia Unci,** V. Marina Garibaldi, 2, 2km from Lipari at the entrance to the hamlet of Canneto. (☎090 981 19 09. Reserve in Aug. Open mid-Mar. to mid-Oct. June-Aug. L15,000-27,000/€7.75-13.95 per person; Mar.-May L11,000-14,000/€5.70-7.25 per person.) Stock up at **UPIM supermarket,** Corso Vittorio Emanuele, 212. (Open M-Sa 8am-3:20pm and 4-11pm.) **Da Gilberto,** V. Garibaldi, 22-24, is famous for delicious sandwiches. (☎090 981 27 56. Sandwiches start at L5000/€2.60. Open 7pm-midnight, though closing time sometimes varies.)

VULCANO   ☎090

Black beaches, bubbling seas, and natural mud spas attract visitors worldwide to this island. A steep 1hr. **hike** to the inactive **Gran Cratere** (Grand Crater) snakes between the volcano's noxious yellow fumaroles. On a clear day, you can see all the other islands from the top. The allegedly therapeutic **Laghetto di Fanghi** (Mud Pool) is just up V. Provinciale to the right from the port. If you would prefer not to bathe in sulfuric radioactive mud, you can step gingerly into the scalding waters of the **acquacalda,** where underwater volcanic outlets make the sea percolate like a jacuzzi, or visit the black sands and clear waters of **Sabbie Nere,** just down the road from the *acquacalda.* Follow the signs off V. Ponente. To get to Vulcano, take the 30min. ferry from the port at nearby Lipari (30min., 2 daily, L2500/€1.30). For more info, the **tourist office, AAST,** is at V. Provinciale, 41. (☎090 985 20 28. Open May-Aug. daily 8am-1:30pm and 3-5pm.) For information on **rented rooms** *(affittacamere),* contact the Lipari tourist office or call 090 985 21 42.

STROMBOLI ☎ 090

If you find luscious beaches and hot springs a bit tame, a visit to Stromboli's active **volcano,** which spews orange cascades of lava and molten rock about every 10min. each night, will quench your thirst for adventure. A guided hike to the crater rewards diligent climbers with a view of the nightly eruptions. **Hiking** the *vulcano* on your own is **illegal** and **dangerous,** but **Guide Alpine Autorizzate** offers tours. (☎ 090 98 62 11. Tours depart from P. Vincenzo M, W, and Sa-Su 5:30pm; return midnight. L35,000/€18.10.) Bring sturdy shoes, a flashlight, snacks, water, and warm clothes. Don't wear contact lenses, as the wind sweeps ash and dust everywhere. When hiking down the volcano at night, always use the same path you took up; the professional guides' shortcuts are tempting but infinitely easier to get lost on. **Siremar** (☎ 090 928 32 42) runs a 5hr. **ferry** from Milazzo to Stromboli (high season M-Tu and Th-Sa 1-2 per day, L20,000/€10.35; off-season 3 per week, L16,500/€8.55). From July to September, forget finding a room unless you have a reservation; your best bet may be one of the non-reservable *affittacamere.* Expect to pay L30,000-50,000/€15.50-25.85 for a room. The best value is ◼**Casa del Sole,** on V. Giuseppe Cincotta, off V. Regina at the end of town. At the church of St-Bartholomew, take a right down the stairs and go straight down the alley. Large rooms face a communal shared terrace. (☎ 090 98 60 17. Apr.-May and Oct. singles L25,000/€12.95; June and Sept. L30,000-35,000/€15.50-18.10; July L35,000/€18.10; Aug. L40,000/€20.65.)

SARDINIA(SARDEGNA)

When the boyish vanity of over-cultivated mainland Italians starts to wear thin, when one more church interior will send you into the path of the nearest speeding Fiat, Sardinia's savage coastline and rugged people will be a reality check for your soul. D. H. Lawrence sought respite from the "deadly net of European civilization," and he found his escape among the wild horses, wind-carved rock formations, and pink flamingos of this remote island. The ancient feudal civilizations that settled in Sardinia some 3500 years ago left about 8000 *nuraghe* ruins, cone-shaped stone tower-houses assembled without mortar.

▛ TRANSPORTATION

Tirrenia **ferries** (☎ 1678 240 79) run to **Olbia,** on the northern tip of Sardinia, from Civitavecchia, just north of Rome (4-8hr., 2-4 per day, L28,000-61,500/€14.50-37.80), and Genoa (6-13½hr., 5-7 per week, L50,000-137,000/€25.85-71.05). They also chug to **Cagliari,** on the southern tip, from Civitavecchia (15-18hr., 2 per day, L48,000-77,000/€24.80-39.80); Genoa (20hr., July-Sept. 2 per week, L86,000-102,000/€44.45-52.70); Naples (16hr., Jan.-Sept. 1 per week, L48,000-78,000/€24.80-40.30); Palermo (13½hr., 1 per week, L45,000-73,000/€23.25-37.70). **Trains** run from Cagliari to Olbia (4hr., L24,400/€12.60) via Oristano (1½hr., L8600/€4.45), and Sassari (4hr., 2 per day, L22,800/€11.80). From Sassari, trains run to **Alghero** (40min., 11 per day, L6000/€3.10). PANI **buses** connect Cagliari to Oristano (1½hr., 11,300/€5.85).

CAGLIARI ☎ 070

Cagliari combines the bustle and energy of a modern Italian city with the endearing rural atmosphere of the rest of the island. Its Roman ruins, medieval towers, and cobblestone streets contrast with the regal tree-lined streets and sweeping beaches downtown. Climb Largo Carlo Felice to reach the city's impressive **duomo,** P. Palazzo, 3, with dazzling gold mosaics topping each of its entryways. (☎ 070 66 38 37. Open daily 8am-12:30pm and 4-8pm.) The 2nd-century **Roman ampitheater** comes alive with concerts, operas, and classic plays during the summer **arts festival.** If you prefer to worship the sun, take city **bus** P, PQ, or PF to **Il Poetto** beach (20min., L1500/€0.80), with pure white sand and turquoise water.

The **tourist office** is on P. Matteotti. (☎070 66 92 55; fax 070 66 49 23. Open in summer M-Sa 8am-8pm; in winter M-Sa 8am-7pm.) The elegant **Pensione Vittoria** is at V. Roma, 75. (☎070 65 79 70. Singles L60,000-75,000/€31-38.75; doubles L90,000-110,000/€46.50-56.85.)

ALGHERO ☎079

Vineyards, ruins, and horseback rides are all a short trip away from Alghero's palm-lined parks and twisting medieval streets. The nearby **Grotte di Nettuno,** an eerie stalactite-filled 60- to 70-million-year-old cavern complex, in Capo Caccia, can be reached by **bus** (1hr., 3 per day, round-trip L3400/€1.75). Visitors descend 632 steps between massive white cliffs. (Open Apr.-Sept. daily 9am-7pm; Oct. 10am-5pm; Nov.-Mar. 9am-2pm. L15,000/€7.75.) The **tourist office,** P. Porta Terra, 9, is to the right from the bus stop. (☎079 97 90 54. Open Apr.-Oct. M-Sa 8am-8pm, Su 9am-1pm; Nov.-Mar. M-Sa 8am-2pm.) To get to the **Ostello dei Giuliani (HI),** V. Zara, 3, 7km away in **Fertilia** but near the beach, take the orange AF city bus from V. La Marmora next to the train station (25min., every 40min., L1100/€0.60); from the stop, follow the street left as you face the church and turn right on V. Zara. (☎079 93 03 53. Curfew 11:30pm. Dorms L19,000/€9.85.)

ORISTANO AND THE SINIS PENINSULA ☎0783

The town of **Oristano** is as an excellent base for excursions to the nearby Sinis Peninsula. From the train station, follow V. Vittorio Veneto straight to P. Mariano, then take V. Mazzini to P. Roma to reach the town center (25min.). Rent a moped or car to explore the tranquil beaches, stark white cliffs, and ancient ruins on the mystical **Sinis Peninsula.** At the tip, 17km west of Oristano, lie the ruins of the ancient Phoenician port of **Tharros.** Take the ARST bus to San Giovanni di Sinis (dir.: Is Aruttas; 40min., 4 per day, L2800/€1.45). Slightly to the north off the road to Cuglieri is **S'Archittu,** where youths leap from a 15m limestone arch into the waters of a rocky inlet. ARST **buses** go to S'Archittu (30min., 7 per day, L2800/€1.45). The secluded white quartz sands of **Is Arutas** are well worth the trip. The ARST bus to Is Arutas runs only during July and August (50min., 5 per day, L3200/€1.65). The **tourist office, Pro Loco,** V. Vittorio Emanuele, 8, provides maps. (☎/fax 0783 30 32 12. Open M-F 9am-12:30pm and 4:30-8pm, Sa 9am-12:30pm.) Get some rest at **ISA,** P. Mariano, 50. Exit from the back of the ARST station, turn left, turn right on V. Vittorio Emanuele, walk through P. D'Aborea and P. Martini, and follow V. Lamarmora to its end. Turn right, turn left, and take the first right down V. Mazzini to P. Mariano. (☎/fax 0783 36 01 01. Singles L85,000/€43.90; doubles L140,000/€72.30. AmEx/MC/V.)

LIECHTENSTEIN

SWISS FRANCS

US$1 = 1.66SFR	1SFR = US$0.60
CDN$1 = 1.09SFR	1SFR = CDN$0.92
UK£1 = 2.40SFR	1SFR = UK£0.42
IR£1 = 1.93SFR	1SFR = IR£0.52
AUS$1 = 0.88SFR	1SFR = AUS$1.14
NZ$1 = 0.72SFR	1SFR = NZ$1.38
ZAR1 = 0.20SFR	1SFR = ZAR4.94
EUR€1 = 1.52SFR	1SFR = EUR€0.66

PHONE CODE | **Country Code: 0423. International dialing prefix: 00.**

Famous chiefly for its wines, dentures, and postage stamps, Liechtenstein's miniscule size and minute population (31,320) belies its long and rich history. The **Romans** invaded in 15 BC, but with the coming of Christianity in the 4th century AD, **Germanic tribes** pushed the Romans back out, bringing the area under the control of the German dukedom. Prince **Johann Adam** of Liechtenstein purchased the areas and created the Principality of Liechtenstein in 1719, which **Napoleon** conquered in 1806. After his defeat, Liechtenstein became part of the **German Confederacy** in 1815 and was granted a constitution in 1862. It separated from Germany for good in 1866 when the German Confederation dissolved. Two years later Liechtenstein disbanded its army—an intimidating 80-man juggernaut—which it has not re-formed since. In 1938, Prince **Franz Josef** ascended the throne and continued the transformation of Liechtenstein from an impoverished nation into one of the wealthiest per capita in Europe. Following the example of the Swiss, Liechtenstein established itself as an extremely desirable tax haven for international companies and wealthy playboys with its strict banking secrecy policies. The country joined the United Nations in 1990 and the European Economic Area in 1995.

A recent tourist brochure amusingly mislabeled the already tiny 160 sq. km country as an even tinier 160 sq. m. That's just about how much most tourists see of the world's only German-speaking monarchy, but the cliff-hanging roads are gateways to unspoiled mountains with great **biking** and **hiking.** Above the valley towns, cliff-hanging roads lead to the places truly worth visiting—the unspoiled mountains offer hiking and skiing prospects without the touristy atmosphere of many other alpine resorts.

SUGGESTED ITINERARY

BEST OF (OKAY, ALL OF) LIECHTENSTEIN, TWO SHORT DAYS. Scope out the art collection at the **Staatliche Kunstmuseum** and compare stamps in the **Briefmarkenmuseum** in capital city **Vaduz** (1 day, p. 706), then scan the Alps from the **Pfälzerhütte** on the sharp ridge above **Malbun** (1 day, p. 708).

LOCAL FACTS

EMERGENCY. Police, ☎117. Fire, ☎118. **Medical emergency, ☎**144.

CURRENCY AND EXCHANGE. Liechtenstein uses the **Swiss Franc (SFr).** For currency exchange at acceptable rates, go to Switzerland. (Really.)

LANGUAGE. The official language of Liechtenstein is German, although many residents also speak English, French, and an Alemannic dialect. See p. 706 for language charts and helpful phrases.

TIME. Liechtenstein is 1hr. ahead of Greenwich Mean Time (GMT).

HOLIDAYS AND FESTIVALS. New Year's Day (Jan. 1); Shrove Tuesday (Feb. 12); Good Friday (Mar. 29); Easter (Mar. 31-Apr. 1); Labor Day (May 1); National Holiday (Aug. 15); All Saints' Day (Nov. 1); Christmas (Dec. 24-26); New Year's Eve (Dec. 31). On Aug. 15, Liechtenstein celebrates its **national day** with fireworks and festivities, and the Prince invites all 32,000 residents to a party at his castle.

TRANSPORTATION. To enter Liechtenstein, catch a **bus** from **Sargans** or **Buchs** in Switzerland, or from **Feldkirch** just across the Austrian border (20min., 3.60SFr). Although trains from Austria and Switzerland pass through the country, Liechtenstein itself has no rail system. Instead, it has a cheap, efficient **Post Bus** system that links all 11 villages (short trips 2.40SFr; long trips 3.60SFr, students half-price; SwissPass valid). A **one-week bus ticket** (10SFr, students and seniors 5SFr) covers all (and we mean *all*) of Liechtenstein as well as buses to Swiss and Austrian border towns. **Bicycles** are a great way to get around Lower Liechtenstein; see below for rental information. Remember to keep a passport on you when traveling.

VADUZ AND LOWER LIECHTENSTEIN

A handful of museums await in Liechtenstein's capital, but not much else; Vaduz rarely requires more than one day. "Lower" Liechtenstein refers to the elevation; it's actually in the north. Campers and bikers will enjoy the flat ground here; hikers should consider heading for the hills in Upper Liechtenstein, particularly Malbun.

⚑ PRACTICAL INFORMATION. Liechtenstein's **national tourist office,** Städtle 37, one block up the hill from the Vaduz Post Bus stop, will stamp your passport with Liechtenstein's bi-colored seal (2SFr or 20AS). It also sells **hiking maps** (15.50SFr), locates rooms free of charge, and distributes free city maps and advice on outdoor activities. (☎232 14 43. Open July-Sept. M-F 8am-5:30pm, Sa-Su 9am-noon and 1:30-5pm; Oct.-June M-F 8am-noon and 1:30-5:30pm; Apr. and Oct. also Sa 9am-noon and 1:30-5pm; May also Sa-Su 9am-noon and 1:30-5pm.) Rent **bicycles** at **Bike-Garage** in nearby Triesen. (35SFr per day. Open M-F 8am-noon and 1:30-6pm, Sa 8am-2pm.) The main **post office** is near the tourist office and has an amazing selection of postage stamps. (Open M-F 7:45am-6pm, Sa 8-11am.) **Postal code:** FL-9490.

⚑⚏ ACCOMMODATIONS, CAMPING, AND FOOD. Budget housing options in Vaduz are few and far between, but nearby **Schaan** is more inviting and contains Liechtenstein's only **Jugendherberge (HI),** Untere Rüttig. 6. From Vaduz, take bus #1 (dir.: Schaan) to "Mühleholz," walk toward the intersection, turn left down Marianumstr., and follow the signs. (☎232 50 22. Breakfast and showers included. Laundry 8SFr. Reception 7-10am and 5-10pm. No lockout. Curfew 10pm. Key code available. Open Feb.-Oct. Dorms 27.60SFr; doubles 36.60SFr; quads 126.40SFr. **HI members only.**) **Hotel Post,** Bahnhofstr. 14, faces the back of the Schaan post office and offers reasonably priced rooms, but it's near train tracks. (☎232 17 18. Breakfast included. Reception 8am-11pm. 40SFr per person, with shower 50SFr.) For **Camping Mittagspitze,** take bus #1 (dir.: Sargans) to "Säga," cross the street, and walk toward the mountains, following the signs. Located at the foot of the Mittagspitze, this campground provides good scenery and a pool to splash in. (☎392 26 86. Showers included. Laundry 4.50SFr. Reception June-Aug. 7:30am-noon and 1-8pm; Sept.-May 7-8am and 5-6pm. Open year-round. 8.50SF per person; 5SFr per tent; 0.30SFr tax.) Groceries are available at **Migros,** Aulestr. 20, across from the tour bus parking lot. (Open M-F 8am-1pm and 1:30-6:30pm, Sa 8am-4pm.)

🔲 **SIGHTS.** The 12th-century **Schloß Vaduz (Vaduz Castle),** the regal home of Hans Adam II, Prince of Liechtenstein, presides over the town. The interior is off-limits to the masses; however, you can hike up to the castle for a closer look and a phenomenal view of the whole country. The 15min. trail begins down the street from the tourist office, heading away from the post office. Across the street from the tourist office is the **Kunstmuseum Liechtenstein (Liechtenstein Art Museum),** Städtle 32. Mostly for modern art, the

museum boasts paintings by Dalí, Kandinsky, and Klee, as well as rotating special exhibits and installations. The prince's collection of Renaissance and Romantic masterpieces is also displayed here. (Open Tu-Su 10am-5pm, Th until 8pm. 8SFr, students and seniors 5SFr.) Stamp collectors will love the one-room **Postmuseum,** Städtle 37. (Open Apr.-Oct. daily 10am-noon and 1:30-5:30pm; Nov.-Mar. 10am-noon and 1:30-5pm. Free.)

UPPER LIECHTENSTEIN

The roads that snake their way up the mountainsides to tiny villages, such as **Triesenberg** and **Malbun,** allow for spectacular views of the Rhine Valley and the surrounding Alps. Buses make the short run from Vaduz within 30min., and the trips are well worth it even if you're only spending one day in the country.

TRIESENBERG. The first town up the mountain (serviced by bus #10), Triesenberg was founded in the 13th century by the Walsers, a Swiss group forced to flee Valais due to overpopulation, religious intolerance, and natural disaster. The **Walser Heimatmuseum,** behind the post office right by the bus stop, chronicles the Walsers' customs and crafts. (☎262 19 26. Open Sept.-May Tu-F 1:30-5:30pm, Sa 1:30-5pm; June-Aug. also Su 2-5pm. 2SFr.) The **tourist office** is in the same building and has the same hours and phone number. Signs at the post office point to a variety of walks and **hikes.** For stunning views of the Rhine Valley (1½hr.), take bus #30 to **Gaflei,** head across the street to the gravel path and look for the trail on the left, following signs to "Silum" and then to "Ob. Tunnel, Steg." At the end, walk through the tunnel to Steg, where bus #10 runs back to Vaduz or Schaan every hr.

MALBUN. On the other side of the mountain, secluded Malbun offers affordable ski slopes and plenty of hiking. Stop by the **tourist office** to make the staff feel useful. (☎263 65 77. Open June-Oct. and mid-Dec. to mid-Apr. M-Sa 9am-noon and 1:30-5pm.) During the winter two **chair lifts** and four **T-bars** service you. (Day pass 33SFr; 6-day pass 136SFr, off season 129SFr.) Right in the middle of town, **Malbun A.G.** (☎263 97 70 or 262 19 15) offers 1-day classes (65SFr), 3-day classes (155SFr), and private ski lessons (1 day 230SFr). **Malbun Sport** (☎263 37 55) rents **skis** and **snowboards** in winter and **bikes** in summer. (Open M-F 8am-6pm, Sa 8am-5pm, Su 9am-5pm.) In summer, try the round-trip hike to **Pfälzerhütte,** which leads over the Augustenberg and culminates in fine views of the Alps (5hr.). It's doable even if you're not into hiking. Take the **Sareiserjoch** (11.70SFr, one-way 7.50SFr; students 9SFr/5.90SFr, daily 8-11:50am and 1-4:50pm) and follow signs for "Pfälzerhütte" (be sure to turn left off the main trail after 5min.). To get back, head toward Gritsch and then Tälihöhi. **Hotel Alpen** includes a restaurant and a large common room with TV. The more expensive rooms have cable TV, phone, shower, and a stocked fridge, but you'll pay for the luxury. (☎263 11 81. Reception 8am-10pm. Open mid-May to Oct. and mid-Dec. to Apr. In summer 45-55SFr per person, with amenities 70-85SFr. In winter, add 20SFr.)

LUXEMBOURG

LUXEMBOURG FRANCS

US$1 = 44.03LF	10LF = US$0.23
CDN$1 = 28.57LF	10LF = CDN$0.35
UK£1 = 63.52LF	10LF = UK£0.16
IR£1 = 51.22LF	10LF = IR£0.20
AUS$1 = 23.60LF	10LF = AUS$0.42
NZ$1 = 19.36LF	10LF = NZ$0.52
ZAR1 =5.32LF	10LF = ZAR1.88
EUR€ = 40.34LF	10LF = EUR€0.25

PHONE CODE	**Country Code:** 352. **International dialing prefix:** 00. Luxembourg has no city codes.

Too often overlooked by budget travelers, the tiny Grand Duchy of Luxembourg (pop. 440,000; 2586 sq. km) boasts impressive fortresses and castles as well as beautiful hiking trails. Established in 963, the original territory was named *Lucilin-burhuc*, or "little fortress." By the time successive waves of Burgundians, Spaniards, French, Austrians, and Germans had receded, the countryside was saturated with little fortresses. Today, Luxembourg has become a notable European Union member and a prominent international financial center. Judging by their national motto, *Mir welle bleiwe wat mir sinn* ("We want to remain what we are"), it seems that the Luxembourgians are pleased with their accomplishments.

SUGGESTED ITINERARIES

THREE DAYS **Luxembourg City** is arguably one of Europe's most beautiful capitals (p. 712). Marvel at the **Grand Ducal Palace** and wander underground through the **Casemates**.

BEST OF LUXEMBOURG, ONE WEEK Enjoy Luxembourg City (2 days, p. 712). Visit the gorgeous château in **Vianden** (2 days, p. 716), hike or bike around the rock formations and view the illuminated manuscripts in **Echternach** (1 day, p. 717), and then canoe down the Sûre River in **Diekirch** (1 day, p. 716). Finally, check out the Family of Man exhibit in little **Clervaux** (1 day, p. 717).

LIFE AND TIMES

The Grand Duchy of Luxembourg has a long history of occupation and domination by its larger European neighbors. Ancient history saw Luxembourg inhabited by Belgic tribes and controlled by Romans. In the early Middle Ages, the territory was annexed by the Franks as part of Austrasia, and then claimed by **Charlemagne** as part of the Holy Roman Empire. Luxembourg became an independent region in AD 963, under the control of **Siegfried, Count d'Ardennes.** Siegfried's descendents ruled Luxembourg, eventually adopting the title of Count of Luxembourg. The region became a duchy in 1354 by edict of Emperor Charles IV, but in 1443, the Duchess of Luxembourg was forced to give up the property to the Duke of Burgundy. Luxembourg passed into the hands of the Spanish **Habsburgs** in the early 16th century, only to be conquered by France after the devastating **Thirty Years' War** (1618-1648). During the 17th and 18th centuries Luxembourg was tossed between France, Spain, and Austria. The year after the fall of **Napoleon** at Waterloo in 1814, the **Congress of Vienna** made Luxembourg a grand duchy and gave it to **William I,** King of The Netherlands. After the 1830 Belgian revolt against William, part of Luxembourg was ceded to Belgium, and the remainder was recognized as a sovereign and independent state. A subsequent economic union with Prussia brought industrialization to the previously agrarian country. In 1897, the **Treaty of London** reaffirmed Luxembourg's autonomy and declared its neutrality. Yet the 20th century found Luxembourg occupied by Germany during both world wars. After being liberated by the Allied powers in 1944, Luxembourg became a founding member of both the **Benelux Economic Union,** along with The Netherlands and Belgium, and the **European Union.** It relinquished its neutral status in 1948 in order to join various international economic, political, and military institutions, including **NATO** and the **United Nations**.

Today, Luxembourg is one of the world's most industrialized countries, and it enjoys an economic security that is evidenced by the highest purchasing power and per capita income in Western Europe. The country is governed by a **constitutional monarchy,** in which the Grand Duke, currently **Henri I,** holds formal authority. The major executive and legislative power is vested in the prime minister, appointed by the Grand Duke, and in the Chamber of Deputies, elected by popular vote. Luxembourg has the greatest proportion of foreign residents of any Western European country. The Luxembourgian people have been significantly influenced by both German and French culture, but they maintain a distinct national identity.

ESSENTIALS

DOCUMENTS AND FORMALITIES

Visas are generally not required for tourist stays under three months; South African citizens are one exception. Contact your embassy for more information.

Luxembourg Embassies at Home: Australia (consulate), Level 18, Royal Exchange Bldg., 56 Pitt St., Sydney NSW 2000 (☎(02) 92 41 43 22; fax 92 51 11 13). **Canada** (honorary consulate), 3706 St. Hubert St., Montréal, PQ H2L 4A3 (☎514-849-2101). **South Africa** (honorary consulate), P.O. Box 357, Lanseria 1748 (☎(011) 659 09 61). **UK,** 27 Wilton Crescent, London SW1X 8SD (☎(020) 7235 6961; fax 7235 9734). **US,** 2200 Massachusetts Ave. NW, Washington, D.C. 20008 (☎202-265-4171; fax 328-8270).

Foreign Embassies in Luxembourg: All foreign embassies are in **Luxembourg City** (see p. 712).

TRANSPORTATION

The Luxembourg City airport is serviced by **Luxair** (☎479 81, reservations ☎4798 42 42) and by flights from the UK and throughout the continent. Cheap last-minute flights on Luxair are available at www.luxair.lu. A **Benelux Tourrail Pass** allows five days of unlimited **train** travel in a one-month period in Belgium, The Netherlands, and Luxembourg (6400LF/€158.65, under 26 4400LF/€109.10). The **Billet Réseau** (180LF/€4.50), a network ticket, is good for one day of unlimited bus and train travel; even better is the **Luxembourg Card** (350LF/€8.70), which covers unlimited transportation and most entrance fees. International gateways to Luxembourg include Brussels (1¾hr.; see p. 125) and Liège (2½hr.) in Belgium, Koblenz (2¼hr.; see p. 468) and Trier (45min., see p. 470) in Germany, and Metz in France (see p. 383). **Hiking** and **biking trails** run between Luxembourg City and Echternach, from Diekirch to Echternach and Vianden, and elsewhere. **Bikes** aren't permitted on buses, but are allowed on many trains for 45LF/€1.15.

TOURIST SERVICES AND MONEY

EMERGENCY	Police, ☎112. Ambulance, ☎112. Fire, ☎112.

TOURIST OFFICES. Luxembourg National Tourist Office, P.O. Box 1001, L-1010 Luxembourg (☎(352) 42 82 82 10; fax 42 82 82 38; tourism@ont.smtp.etat.lu; www.etat.lu/tourism). The **Luxembourg Card,** available from Easter to October at tourist offices, hostels, and many hotels and public transportation offices, provides unlimited transportation on national trains and buses and includes admission to 32 tourist sites (1-day 350LF/€8.70, 2-day 600LF/€14.90, 3-day 850LF/€27).

Tourist Boards at Home: UK, 122 Regent St., London W1R 5FE (☎(020) 434 2800; fax 734 1205; www.luxembourg.co.uk); **US,** 17 Beekman Pl., New York, NY 10022 (☎212- 935-8888; fax 935-5896; www.visitluxembourg.com).

CURRENCY AND EXCHANGE. The currency is the Luxembourg **franc.** Luxembourg *francs* are worth the same as Belgian *francs;* you can use Belgian money in Luxembourg, but not vice versa. Luxembourg has accepted the **Euro (€)** as legal tender, and *francs* will be phased out by July 1, 2002. For more information, see p. 23. Expect to pay 1200-1500LF/€29.75-37.20 for a hotel room, 435-650LF/€10.80-16.15 for a hostel bed, and 280-400LF/€6.95-9.95 for a restaurant meal. **Service** (15-20%) is included in the price; tip taxi drivers 10%. The **value-added tax (VAT)** is already included in most prices. Luxembourg's **VAT refund threshold** (US$85) is lower than most other EU countries. Refunds are usually 13% of the purchase price.

Luxembourg

BELGIUM — TO LIÈGE

GERMANY

Troisvierges

Clervaux

Esch-sur-Sûre

Vianden

Ettelbrück

Diekirch

Echternach

Beaufort

Berdorf

TO TRIER

Hollenfels

Bourglinster

Wasserbillig

Arlon

Luxembourg City

TO PARIS

Remich

Longwy

FRANCE

TO METZ

0 — 10 miles
0 — 10 kilometers

Sûre R., *Our R.*, *Clerf R.*, *Alzette R.*, *Sûre R.*, *Moselle R.*

ACCOMMODATIONS AND CAMPING

Luxembourg's 12 **HI youth hostels** (*Auberges de Jeunesse*) are often filled with school groups. Check the sign posted in any hostel to find out which hostels are full or closed each day. Prices range from 435-650LF/€10.80-16.15, under 27 355-650LF/€8.80-16.15; nonmembers pay about 110LF/€2.75 extra. Breakfast is included, a packed lunch costs 125LF/€3.10, and dinner 260LF/€6.45. Sheets are 125LF/€3.10. Half of the hostels close from mid-November to mid-December, and the other half close from mid-January to mid-February. Contact **Centrale des Auberges de Jeunesse Luxembourgeoises** (☎22 55 88; fax 46 39 87; information@youthhostels.lu) for information. **Hotels** advertise 900-1500LF/€22.35-37.20 per night but may try to persuade tourists to take more expensive rooms. Luxembourg is a **camping** paradise. Two people with a tent will typically pay 200-360LF/€5-8.95 per night.

COMMUNICATION

MAIL. Mailing a postcard or a letter (up to 20g) from Luxembourg costs 21LF/€0.55 to the UK and Europe and 30LF/€0.75 anywhere else.

TELEPHONES. There are no city codes; just dial 352 plus the local number. International direct dial numbers include: **AT&T,** ☎0800 01 11; **British Telecom,** ☎0800 89 0352; **Canada Direct,** 800 20 119; **Ireland Direct,** ☎0800 353; **MCI,** ☎800 01 12; **Sprint,** 0800 01 15; **Telecom New Zealand,** ☎0800 00 64; **Telstra Australia,** ☎0800 00 61.

LANGUAGES. French, German, and, since a referendum in 1984, *Letzebuergesch*, a mixture of the other two that sounds a bit like Dutch. French is most common in the city, where most people also speak German. For basic phrases, see p. 895.

LOCAL FACTS

Time: Luxembourg is 1hr. ahead of Greenwich Mean Time (GMT).

When to Go: Luxembourg enjoys a temperate climate with less moisture than Belgium. Anytime between May and mid-Oct. is a good time to visit.

Hours: Most **banks** are open M-F 8:30am-4:30pm; most **shops** are open M 2-6pm and Tu-Sa 9:30am-6pm, though many close at noon for 2hr., especially in the countryside.

Holidays: New Year's Day (Jan. 1); Carnival (Feb. 11); Easter (Mar. 31); Easter Monday (Apr. 1); May Day (May 1); Ascension Day (May 9); Whit Sunday and Monday (May 19-20); National Holiday (June 23); Assumption Day (Aug. 15); All Saints' Holiday (Nov. 1); Christmas (Dec. 25); and Boxing Day (Dec. 26).

LUXEMBOURG CITY (VILLE DE LUXEMBOURG)

With a medieval fortress perched on a cliff that overlooks lush green river valleys, and high bridges stretching all over the downtown area, Luxembourg City (pop. 80,000) is one of the most attractive and dramatic capitals in Europe. Although as an international banking capital it is home to thousands of frenzied foreign business executives, most visitors find it surprisingly relaxed and idyllic.

▐ TRANSPORTATION

Flights: Findel International Airport, 6km from the city. **Bus #9** (40LF/€1) is cheaper than the Luxair bus (150LF/€3.75) and runs the same route every 20min.

Trains: Info ☎49 90 49 90 (toll-free); see schedules at www.cfl.lu. **Gare CFL,** av. de la Gare, near the foot of av. de la Liberté, 10min. south of the city center. To: **Amsterdam** (5¾hr.; 1680LF/€41.65, under 26 1360LF/€33.75); **Brussels** (2¾hr.; 940LF/ €23.30, 520LF/€12.90); **Frankfurt** (5hr.; 1720LF/€42.65, 1530 LF/€37.95); **Paris** (3½-4hr., 1560LF/€38.70).

Buses: Buy a **billet courte distance** (short-distance ticket) from the driver (single-fare 45LF/€1.15, full-day 180LF/€4.50), or pick up a package of 10 (320LF/€7.95) at the train station. These tickets are also valid on **local trains.**

Taxis: ☎48 22 33. 32LF/€0.80 per km. 10% premium 10pm-6am; 25% premium on Su. 700-800LF/€17.35-19.85 from the city center to the airport.

Bikes: Biking is the ideal way to see Luxembourg. Rent from **Velo en Ville,** 8 r. Bisserwé (☎47 96 23). Open M-F 1-8pm, Sa-Su 9am-noon and 1-8pm. 250LF/€6.20 per half-day, 400LF/€9.95 per day. 20% discount if under 26.

◆ ❷ ORIENTATION AND PRACTICAL INFORMATION

Five minutes by bus and 15min. by foot from the train station, Luxembourg City's historic center revolves around the **Place d'Armes.** Facing the **tourist office,** located in the commemorative Town Hall, turn right down r. Chimay to reach **Boulevard Roosevelt.** To reach the museums, Grand Ducal Palace, and Bock Casemates, from the info office, walk straight ahead and onto **Rue Sigeroi.**

Tourist Offices: Grand Duchy National Tourist Office, in the train station, has tons of info and lacks the long lines of the office in town. (☎42 82 82 20; fax 42 82 82 30; www.etat.lu/tourism). Open July-Sept. 9am-7pm; Oct.-June 9:15am-12:30pm and 1:45-6pm. **Municipal Tourist Office,** pl. d'Armes (☎22 28 09; fax 46 70 70; touristinfo@luxembourg-city.lu; www.luxembourg-city.lu/touristinfo). Open Apr.-Sept. M-Sa 9am-7pm, Su 10am-6pm; Oct.-Mar. M-F 9am-6pm, Su 10am-6pm. Also, look for yellow-shirted **"Ask Me"** representatives all over the city; they give out free tourist info.

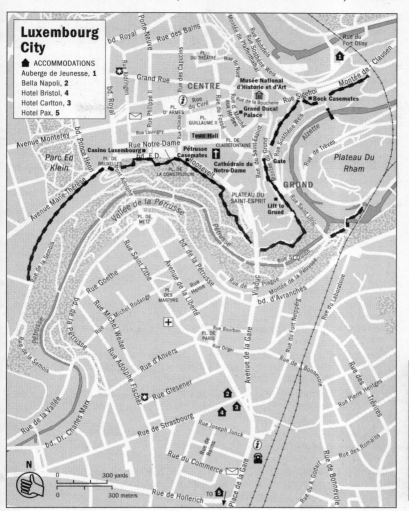

Budget Travel: SOTOUR, 15 pl. du Théâtre (☎46 15 14). Sells BIJ and other discount tickets for international flights; makes train reservations that begin or end in Luxembourg. Open M-F 9am-6pm, Sa 9am-noon.

Embassies: Ireland, 28 r. d'Arlon (☎45 06 10; fax 45 88 20). Open M-F 10am-12:30pm and 2:30-5pm. **UK,** 14 bd. Roosevelt (☎22 98 64; fax 22 98 67). Open M-F 9am-12:30pm. **US,** 22 bd. E. Servais (☎46 01 23; fax 46 14 01). Open M-F 8:30am-12:30pm; visas M-Tu and Th-F 3:30-4:30pm. Australians, Canadians, New Zealanders, and South Africans should contact embassies in France or Belgium.

Luggage Storage: In **train station** 100LF/€2.50 per day (1-month max.); 2-day **lockers** 100LF/€2.50.

Laundromat: Quick Wash, 31 r. de Strasbourg, near the station. Wash and dry 390LF/€9.70. Open M-Sa 8:30am-6:30pm. Doing your laundry is cheaper at the HI hostel.

Emergencies: Police, ☎113. **Ambulance,** ☎112.

LUXEMBOURG

Pharmacy: Pharmacie Goedert, 5 pl. d'Armes (☎22 39 91). Open M 1-6:15pm, Tu-F 8am-6:15pm, Sa 8am-12:30pm. Check any pharmacy window for night info.

Telephones: Outside post offices and at the train station. Coin-operated phones are rare; buy a 50-unit **phone card** at either place (each good for 50 local calls; 250LF/€6.20).

Internet Access: Sparky's, 11a av. Monterey (☎6 20 12 23), at the pl. d'Armes. 5LF/ €0.15 per min. The only Internet cafe in town. Open M-Sa 8am-8pm, Su 2-8pm.

Post Office: 25 r. Aldringen, near the pl. D'Armes (open M-F 7am-7pm, Sa 7am-5pm), and 38 pl. de la Gare, across the street, left of the train station (for *Poste Restante*; open M-F 6am-7pm, Sa 6am-noon). Address mail to be held: FirstName SURNAME, *Poste Restante*, Recette Principale, **L-1009** Luxembourg City, Luxembourg.

▟ ACCOMMODATIONS

Budget travelers have two basic options in Luxembourg City—the city's hostel, often booked solid by school and tour groups in the summer, or the relatively inexpensive accommodations near the train station.

Auberge de Jeunesse (HI), 2 r. du Fort Olisy (☎22 19 20 or 22 68 89; luxembourg@youth.hostels.lu). Take bus #9 and ask to get off at the hostel stop; head under the bridge and turn right down the steep path. Low security; lock up your valuables. Breakfast included. Sheets 125LF/€3.10. Laundry 300LF/€7.45. Reception 7am-2am. Curfew 2am. Max 5-night stay in high season. Dorms 520-580LF/€12.90-14.40, under 26 435-485LF/€10.80-12.05; doubles 1340LF/€33.25, 1140LF/ €28.30; nonmembers add 110LF/€2.75.

Hotel Carlton, 9 r. de Strasbourg (☎29 96 60; carlton@pt.lu). Clean, comfortable rooms in an old marble building. Singles 900-1200LF/€22.35-29.75, with bath 1500-2500LF/€37.20-62; doubles 1400-1600LF/€34.75-39.70, 1700-3000LF/€42.15-74.40.

Hotel Bristol, 11 r. de Strasbourg (☎48 58 29). Comfy rooms. Remember to clarify what price you will be paying. Breakfast included. Singles 1100-2300LF/€27.30-57; doubles 1800-2800LF/€44.65-69.45.

Hotel Pax, 121 route de Thionville (☎48 25 63). Prime location near the train station. Reception 11:45am-10:30pm. Singles 1500LF/€37.20, with bath 1700LF/€42.15; doubles 2000LF/€49.60, 2600LF/€64.45.

Bella Napoli, 4 r. de Strasbourg (☎48 46 29). Simple rooms with hardwood floors, all with bathrooms and showers. Breakfast included. Reception 7am-1am. Singles 1500LF/€37.20; doubles 1800LF/€44.65; triples 2400LF/€59.50.

Camping: Kockelscheuer (☎47 18 15), outside Luxembourg City. Take bus #2 to "Cloche d'Or/Kockelscheuer" from the station. Showers included. Open Easter-Oct. 120LF/€3 per person, 140LF/€3.50 per tent.

▟ FOOD

The area around Place d'Armes teems with touristy fast-food options and pricey restaurants. Stock up at Alima supermarket on r. Bourbon near the train station. (Open M-Sa 8am-6:30pm, Su 8am-6pm.)

Restaurant Bacchus, 32 r. Marché-aux-Herbes (☎47 13 97), down the street from the Grand Ducal palace. Excellent pizza and pasta for 290-440LF/€7.20-10.90 in a homey environment. Reservations recommended 7-10pm. Open Tu-Su noon-10pm.

Le Beaujolais, 2a r. des Capucins (☎47 45 12), next to the Municipal tourist office. Tasty pastas and pizzas at reasonable prices (290-410LF/€7.20-10.20). Sit in velvet booths, or people watch on the pl. d'Armes. Open daily 11:30am-11:30pm.

Caffe-Veneziano, 16 r. Philippe II (☎22 08 58), serves crepes piled high with fruit and scoops of ice cream (80-350LF/€2-8.70). Open daily 7am-11pm.

LUXEMBOURG

👁 SIGHTS

Luxembourg City is best explored without a map. The city is compact enough that you can just wander around and you'll bump into the major sights. Along the way, be prepared for some unexpected treats; the city features many outdoor contemporary art exhibits, and in some spots, motion sensors trigger hidden speakers that greet passersby with eerie music. If you crave more guidance around Luxembourg City, signs point out the **Wenzel Walk,** which leads visitors through 1000 years of history, winding around the old city and down into the casemates.

FORTRESSES AND THE OLD CITY. The 10th-century **Bock Casemates** fortress, part of Luxembourg's original castle, looms over the Alzette River Valley and offers a fantastic view of the Grund and the Clausen. The strategic stronghold was closed in 1867, but was used during WWII to shelter 35,000 people while the rest of the city was ravaged. *(Entrance on r. Sigefroi just past the bridge leading to the hostel. Open Mar.-Oct. daily 10am-5pm. 70LF/€1.75.)* The **Pétrusse Casemates** were built by the Spanish in the 1600s and later improved by the Austrians. *(On pl. de la Constitution. Open July-Sept. 70LF/€1.75, children 40LF/€1. Tours every hr. 11am-4pm.)* The view from the nearby **Place de la Constitution** is always incredible. Stroll down into the lush green valley, or catch one of the little green tourist trains that run down from pl. de la Constitution. *(Trains ☎ 65 11 65 1. Apr.-Oct. every 30min. 10am-6pm except 1pm. 250LF/€6.20.)*

MUSEUMS. The **Luxembourg Card** (see p. 710) covers entrance to all museums in the city. The **All-in-One Ticket** covers five museums in two days (350LF/€8.70 at the Municipal Tourist Office). The eclectic collection at the **Musée National d'Histoire et d'Art** chronicles the influences of the various European empires that controlled Luxembourg. *(Marché-aux-Poissons, at r. Boucherie and Sigefroi. ☎ 47 93 30 1. Open Tu-Su 10am-5pm. 100LF/€2.50.)* The **Casino Luxembourg** houses works of contemporary art, not black-jack tables. *(41 r. de Notre Dame, near pl. de la Constitution. ☎ 22 50 45. Open M, W, F-Su 11am-6pm; Th 11am-8pm. 150LF/€3.75, students 100LF/€2.50.)* The **Musée d'Histoire de la Ville de Luxembourg** features quirky exhibits that allow you to view the history of the city through photographs, films, and music clips. *(14 r. du St-Esprit. ☎ 22 90 50 1. Open Tu-Su 10am-6pm, Th until 8pm. 200LF/€5, students 150LF/€3.75.)*

OTHER SIGHTS. Built as the city hall in 1574, the Renaissance **Grand Ducal Palace** became the official city residence of the Grand Duke in 1890. *(Mandatory tours mid-July to Sept. 2 M-F afternoons and Sa mornings; tickets sold at the Municipal Tourist Office. Reservations ☎ 22 28 09; specify if you want an English language tour. 220LF/€5.45.)* Nearby, the 7th-century **Cathedral of Notre Dame,** which incorporates features of the Dutch Renaissance and early Baroque styles, houses the tombs of John the Blind, the 14th-century King of Bohemia and Count of Luxembourg. *(Entrance at bd. Roosevelt. Open daily 10am-noon and 2-5:30pm. Free.)*

🎵🎭 ENTERTAINMENT AND NIGHTLIFE

At night, the **Place d'Armes** comes to life with free concerts and stand-up comedy. Pick up *La Semaine à Luxembourg* at the tourist office for a list of events. On the Grand Duke's birthday (June 23), the city shuts down to host a large military and religious procession. Nightlife centers on the valley in the **Grund** (by the elevator lift on pl. du St-Esprit). Check the monthly *Nightlife.lu,* available at most cafes and newsstands. Warm up in the Grund at the candle-lit piano bar ◪**Café des Artistes,** 22 montée du Grund, with beer for 100LF/€2.50. *(☎ 52 34 46. Piano W-Sa 10:30pm-2am. Open daily 2:30pm-2am.)*

THE ARDENNES

Almost six decades ago the Battle of the Bulge (1944) mashed Luxembourg into slime and mud. Today the forest is verdant again, and the quiet towns, looming castles, and pleasant hiking trails are powerful draws.

LUXEMBOURG

ETTELBRÜCK

Ettelbrück's position on the main railway line between Luxembourg City and Liège, Belgium makes it a transportation hub of the Ardennes region. To get to the city center from the train station, go left on r. du Prince Henri, continue right on the same street, then turn left on the Grand Rue, and follow it to the pl. de l'Église. The **General Patton Memorial Museum,** 5 r. Dr. Klein, commemorates the liberation of Luxembourg during WWII. Walk along the Grand Rue, away from the pl. de l'Église, until it becomes av. JFK, and then go left onto r. Dr. Klein (☎81 03 22. Open July to mid-Sept. daily 10am-5pm; mid-Sept. to June Su 2-5pm. 100LF/€2.50.) The **tourist office** at the train station has information about excursions to the surrounding Ardennes towns. (☎81 20 68; site@pt.lu. Open M-F 9am-noon and 1:30-5pm, Sa-Su 10am-noon and 2-4pm.) To get to the **Ettelbrück Hostel (HI),** r. G. D. Josephine-Charlotte, follow signs from the station. (☎81 22 69; ettelbruck@youthhostels.lu. Breakfast included. 505LF/€12.55, under 26 445LF/€11.) **Camping Kalkesdelt** is located at 22 r. du Camping. (☎81 21 85. Reception 7:30am-noon and 2-10pm. 120LF/€3 per person, 130LF/€3.25 per tent.)

VIANDEN

Hidden in the dense Ardennes woods, the village of Vianden, home to one of the most impressive castles in Western Europe, is not to be missed. Backpackers **hike** and **kayak** along the Sûre River, or **bike** to Diekirch (15-20min.) and Echternach (30min.). The **château,** a mix of Carolingian, Gothic, and Renaissance architecture, is now filled with medieval armor, 16th-century furniture, and 17th-century tapestries. Check out the great view of the river. March through October, the château hosts classical weekend concerts. (☎83 41 08. Open Apr.-Sept. daily 10am-6pm.; Mar. and Oct. 10am-5pm; Nov.-Feb. 10am-4pm. 180LF/€4.50, students 130LF/€3.25. Concerts 300-500LF/€7.45-12.40.) For a stellar view of the château, ride the **télésiège** (chairlift), 39 r. de Sanatorium, down the hill and across the river from the château. From the tourist office, cross the river, go left on r. Victor Hugo, then left again on r. de Sanitorium. (Info ☎83 43 23. Open Easter-Oct. daily 10am-5pm; July and Aug. until 6pm. 110LF/€2.75; round-trip 160LF/€4.) The **Maison Victor Hugo,** 37 r. de la Gare, is the former home of the famous French writer; the museum inside documents his life and works. (☎83 42 57. Open Apr.-Nov. 9:30am-noon and 2-6pm.)

Buses arrive from Ettelbrück (90LF/€2.25) via Diekirch twice every hour. The **tourist office,** 1 r. du Vieux Marché, next to the main bus stop, sells trail maps and gives info on kayaking and private rooms (☎83 42 57; fax 84 90 81. Open Sa 10am-2pm, M-F 8am-noon and 1-6pm, Su 2-4pm.) To reach the **HI youth hostel,** 3 montée du Château, from the bus stop or tourist office, follow the Grande Rue away from the river and head up the hill; branch off onto montée du Château and follow the signs. Check ahead for vacancy. (☎83 41 77; vianden@youthhostels.lu. Sheets 125LF/€3.10. Reception 8-10am and 5-9pm. Lockout 10am-5pm. Curfew 11pm. Open mid-Mar. to mid-Nov. Dorms 455LF/€11.30, under 26 395LF/€9.80.) Relax by the fountain at **Hotel Berg en Dal,** 3 r. de la Gare. (☎83 41 27; info@hotel-bergendal.com. Breakfast included. Singles 1050LF-1350LF/€26-33.50; doubles 1500LF-1700LF/€37.20-42.15.) **Camp op dem Deich,** r. Neugarten, 5min. downstream from the tourist office, is in the shadow of the château. (☎83 43 75. Open Easter-Oct. 150LF/€37.20 per person, 150LF/€37.20 per tent.)

DIEKIRCH

Dierkirch is a convenient outpost for biking and river-canoeing expeditions. The **National Museum of Military History,** 10 Bamertal, presents a comprehensive exhibition of relics from WWII's Battle of the Bulge. Highlights include pictures taken by a German propaganda unit at the Battle of the Bulge, showing captured US Infantrymen. (☎80 89 08. Open Apr.-Nov. daily 10am-6pm; Dec.-Mar. 2-6pm. 200LF/€5, students 120LF/€3.) Around the corner from the military museum, the **Municipal Museum,** on pl. Guillaume, houses three Roman mosaics. (Open Easter-Oct. F-W 10am-noon and 2-6pm. 50LF/€1.25.) Turn right onto Esplanade and then onto the

Zone Pietone (pedestrian area) to find the 15th-century **Église Saint-Laurent,** built upon Roman ruins. (Open Easter-Oct. Tu-Su 10am-noon and 2-6pm.)

Trains arrive from Ettelbrück at the train station hourly; from the station, take the bus to Vianden (25min.). Buses stop for Vianden in the center of Diekirch at end of the *Zone Pietone.* **Buses** roll in from Echternach hourly and drop you off on the Esplanade in front of the Municipal Museum. To get to the **tourist office,** 3 pl. de la Liberation, take the underground stairs to r. St. Antione and walk to the end; it's directly across the Place. (☎80 30 23. Open daily 9am-noon and 2-5pm. Free guided tours daily 3pm.) Rent **bikes** at **Speicher Sport,** 56 r. Clairefontaine (☎80 84 38; speibike@pt.lu. 400LF/€9.95 per half-day, 600LF/€14.90 per day); or rent **canoes** at **Outdoor Center,** 10 r. de la Sure (☎86 91 39). Stay right across from the bus stop at **Au Beau-Sejour,** 12 Esplanade. (☎80 34 03; hotelbeausejour@hotmail.com. Reception 8am-midnight. Singles 1500LF/€37.20; doubles 2500LF/€62.) Pitch your tent at **Camping de la Sûre,** 34 route de Gilsdorf (☎80 94 25; tourisme@diekirch.lu. 140LF/€350 per person, 120LF/€3 per tent. Showers 25LF/€0.65.)

CLERVAUX

In little Clervaux, the **château** houses the striking **Family of Man** exhibition, compiled in 1955 by Luxembourgian photographer Edward Steichen for the Museum of Modern Art in New York. The exhibition contains 500 pictures depicting every facet of human life in 68 countries. It was displayed worldwide before being permanently installed in Clervaux. (☎92 96 57. Open Mar.-Dec. Tu-Su 10am-noon and 1-6pm. 150LF/€3.75, students 80LF/€2.) To get to the château and the **Benedictine Abbey** lying in Clervaux, turn left from the train station and walk straight. (Abbey open daily 9am-7pm. Free.) Clervaux lies right on the main **railway** line that connects Luxembourg City, Ettelbrück, and Liège, Belgium. The **tourist office,** in the castle, books private rooms at Clervaux's B&Bs. (☎92 00 72. Open Apr.-June daily 2-5pm; July-Oct. 9:45am-11:45am and 2-6pm; Sept. and Oct. closed Su.) **Camping Officiel,** 33 Klatzewe, is situated alongside the river. (☎92 00 42. Open Apr.-Nov. 150LF/€3.75 per person, 150LF/€3.75 per tent.)

LITTLE SWITZERLAND (LE MULLERTHAL)

ECHTERNACH

A favorite vacation spot of European families, the Lower-Sûre village of **Echternach** is famous for its millennial rock formations and 7th-century monastic center. In the Middle Ages, the monastic center was known for its ▧**illuminated manuscripts;** several are at the 18th-century Benedictine **Abbaye.** From the bus station, go left at the marketplace on r. de la Gare, take the last left, and walk past the basilica. (☎72 74 72. Open July-Aug. daily 10am-6pm; June and Sept. 10am-noon and 2-6pm; Oct.-May 10am-noon and 2-5pm. 80LF/€2.) Rent **bikes** at **Trisport,** 31 route de Luxembourg. (☎72 00 86. 100LF/€2.50 per hr., 400LF/€9.95 per half-day, 600LF/€14.90 per day.) Echternach is accessible by **bus** from Ettelbrück and Luxembourg City. The **tourist office** is on Porte St-Willibrord next to the abbey. (☎72 02 30. Open M-F 9am-noon and 2-5pm; in high season open weekends.) To get from the bus station to the **youth hostel (HI),** 9 r. André Drechscher, turn left on av. de la Gare, and take the last right. (☎72 01 58; echternach@youthhostels.lu. Breakfast included. Sheets 125LF. Reception 5-11pm. Lockout 10am-5pm. Closes one month in winter. 455LF/€11.30, under 26 395LF/€9.80.)

LUXEMBOURG

THE
NETHERLANDS
(NEDERLAND)

GUILDERS

US$1 = F2.46	F1 = US$0.41
CDN$1 = F1.61	F1 = CDN$0.62
UK£1 = F3.50	F1 = UK£0.29
IR£1 = F2.80	F1 = IR£0.36
AUS$1 = F1.27	F1 = AUS$0.79
NZ$1 = F1.05	F1 = NZ$0.95
ZAR1 = F0.29	F1 = ZAR3.40
EUR€1 = F2.20	F1 = EUR€0.45

PHONE CODE	Country Code: 31. International dialing prefix: 00.

The Dutch say that although God created the rest of the world, they created The Netherlands (pop. 15.9 million; 41,532 sq. km). The country is a masterful feat of engineering; since most of it is below sea level, vigorous pumping and many dikes were used to create dry land. What was once the domain of seaweed is now packed with windmills, bicycles, tulips, and wooden shoes. The Netherlands' wealth of art, its canal-lined towns, and the, ahem, uniqueness of Amsterdam's hedonism and indulgent perpetual party draw hordes of travelers. For a more in-depth look at The Netherlands' favorite playground, pick up *Let's Go: Amsterdam 2002*.

SUGGESTED ITINERARIES

THREE DAYS Find out what the buzz is in **Amsterdam** (p. 725). Stroll along cobblestone streets and visit the impressive **Museum District** (p. 736) and the **Anne Frank House** (p. 738). Then check out explore the **Red Light District** (p. 737).

ONE WEEK Begin with **Amsterdam** (2 days, p. 725), then head to charming **Haarlem** (1 day, p. 744). Stop by the world's largest flower auction in nearby **Aalsmeer** (1 day, p. 744) or tan your whole self on the nude beaches in **Zandvoort** (1 day, p. 744). From capital city **The Hague** (1 day, p. 746), make your way to student center **Utrecht** (1 day, p. 749).

BEST OF THE NETHERLANDS, TWO WEEKS Chill in **Amsterdam** (3 days, p. 725), followed by a cheese-filled daytrip to **Edam** (1 day, p. 743). Then take the train to **Haarlem** (1 day) before heading on to **Aalsmeer** (1 day). Catch some rays in **Zandvoort** (1 day, p. 744), and make your way to **The Hague** (1 day). Swing by ultra-modern **Rotterdam** (1 day, p. 748) and then relax in **Utrecht** (2 days). Visit artsy **Maastricht** (1 day, p. 751) and then head north to hike in **Hoge Veluwe National Park,** using **Arnhem** as your base (2 days, p. 751), before trekking up to trendy **Groningen** (1 day, p. 752).

LIFE AND TIMES

HISTORY AND POLITICS

FROM ROMANS TO HABSBURGS (100 BC TO AD 1579)

Julius Caesar, leader of the Roman Empire, invaded the region in the first century BC, displacing obviously disgruntled Celtic and Germanic tribes. The native Germanic tribes had the last laugh in the 4th century as their reconquest swept across the Low Countries—The Netherlands, Belgium, and Luxembourg. Freedom was brief, however; the **Franks** took the place of the Romans from the 5th to the 8th century AD. During this period, towns rose as centers of power that were only vaguely connected to each other. The **House of Burgundy** infiltrated the region in the 14th century to establish a more centralized monarchy. By 1482, the Austrian **Habsburgs** had managed to marry into the throne, beginning the long and volatile modern history of The Netherlands. The area quickly came under Spanish control after **Philip I** of the Habsburgs inherited the Spanish crown in 1493.

UTRECHT AND THE WAR WITH SPAIN (1579-1651)

The Netherlands was officially founded in 1579 with the **Union of Utrecht,** which aimed to form an independent group of provinces and cities led by a **States-General.** Under Prince **William of Orange,** the Dutch declared independence from Spain in 1580, sparking prolonged struggle with Spanish forces. The conflict was settled in 1609 with the **Twelve Years' Truce,** which included recognition of The Netherlands' sovereignty. Unfortunately, this peace was short-lived; Spain resumed hostilities in 1621. **Frederick Henry** of the House of Orange led the Dutch to stunning victories,

THE NETHERLANDS

while the Dutch navy trounced the Spanish in battles off Cuba and along the English coast. Shamed by losing to such a tiny country, Spain quickly offered the **Peace of Westphalia** (1648), which not only acknowledged Dutch independence, but also pushed for friendship in order to hedge the growing power of France.

During the **Age of Exploration** in the 17th century, Dutch conquerors fanned out over the globe and gained control of all the major trade routes across Europe. This created incredible wealth for the Dutch—mostly generated by the **Dutch East India Company**—but it also trod on the dainty toes of the British, who resented invasion of their commercial spheres. To protect its trade routes, the company colonized the Cape of Good Hope and other strategic posts to protect its trade routes. Meanwhile, the **Dutch West India Company** was exploring the New World, creating colonies such as New Amsterdam (modern-day New York). All of this activity created unprecedented growth in Amsterdam, which served as the chief port for The Netherlands.

WAR GAMES AND POWER STRUGGLES (1651-1795)

Neighboring European powers resented the success and power of The Netherlands, causing an almost constant period of war and changing alliances for The Netherlands. England began by passing the **Navigation Act,** limiting Dutch involvement in English trade, and then by attacking the Dutch navy. The vastly stronger Brits prevailed forced peace and secretly drafted the **Act of Seclusion,** forever banning the Prince of Orange from Dutch politics. Councillor **Johan de Witt** managed to rebuild The Netherlands in military and economic stature, but when the restored King **Charles II** of England decided to re-start the war, the Dutch instantly negotiated an alliance with the French and sabotaged the English fleet.

In 1667, France invaded The Netherlands, threatening both the English and the Dutch, which caused them to form an alliance. This infuriated King **Louis XIV** of France, leading him to believe that the Dutch had betrayed him, so he offered the English a highly subsidized alliance in return. In 1672, The Netherlands found itself in a full-scale war against both countries, but under the leadership of **William III,** it managed to defeat the Franco-English fleets repeatedly. Ironically, William was crowned King of England in 1688, only 14 years after defeating it in battle, and The Netherlands found itself subordinated to English will. The Dutch grip on international trade quickly eroded with the expansion of French and English colonialism throughout the 18th century.

FRENCH RULE AND INDEPENDENCE (1795-1914)

In 1795, **Napoleon Bonaparte** continued the Dutch doormat syndrome by invading and establishing French rule over the country. After Napoleon's defeat at Waterloo, the **Treaty of Vienna** (1815) established the Kingdom of The Netherlands, which included Belgium and Luxembourg. King **William I of Orange** managed to rebuild the economy and trade routes, but Belgium soon revolted against Dutch rule and gained independence in 1839. Under **William III,** the Dutch created a constitution establishing The Netherlands as a **constitutional monarchy** in which Parliament held most of the power, and the formation of modern political parties began. William's death in 1890 lead to the end of male succession as **Wilhelmina** became queen.

THE WORLD WARS (1914-1945)

The outbreak of **World War I** posed a serious threat to The Netherlands, but it managed to remain neutral while focusing its attention on maintaining its trade and economy. After the war, The Netherlands strictly reaffirmed its neutrality despite Belgian attempts to cede Dutch lands (the issue was settled by the **Treaty of Versailles**). The Dutch did not fare as well in **World War II.** Without warning, the Nazis invaded in May 1940 and occupied the nation for almost five years. The Dutch suffered horribly—all acts of resistance were punished, Dutch Jews were sent to concentration camps, and the general population was in near-famine conditions.

THE POSTWAR ERA (1945-1990)

After the war, Wilhelmina supported sweeping democratic changes for the nation, granting universal suffrage and proportional representation. The nation also abandoned its policy of neutrality, joining NATO and creating a "closer union" with Belgium and Luxembourg. In order to recover from WWII destruction, the government began an economic policy that focused on industrial and commercial expansion.

While the nation experienced relative peace through the 1950s, the 1960s ushered in years of rioting students and workers in response to economic and political problems. In the 1980s, Dutch politics saw the disintegration of old parties and old alliances. The recent rise of the **Christian Democratic Appeal** (CDA) has provided a new outlet for the major Christian factions. While the established **Labour Party** (PvdA) has managed to avoid ties with extreme leftist groups, it had to form a coalition government with the CDA in 1989.

THE NETHERLANDS TODAY

Recently, Dutch politics has seen the resurgence of the Labour Party and increased support for the **Green Left Party,** which focuses on environmental issues. **Wim Kok** (a member of the Labour Party) was re-elected Prime Minister in 1998. The government remains a constitutional monarchy; Parliament holds legislative power while the monarchy **(Queen Beatrix)** retains a symbolic role. The Netherlands is an integral member of the **European Union (EU)** and has adopted the **Euro** as legal tender.

THE ARTS

VISUAL ARTS

The monumental genius of **Rembrandt** (see p. 736) made him a legend in the art world. He made his living as a renowned portrait artist in 1620s and 1630s Amsterdam, but he began to break new artistic ground with **chiaroscuro**—painting in light and dark. His paintings are characterized by rich, luxuriant color and texture and sensual brushwork, evidenced in *Judas Returning the Thirty Pieces of Silver* (1629). Later in the 17th century, **Jan Vermeer** (see p. 748) explored bold perspectives and aspects of light. In the 19th century, ear-butcher **Vincent van Gogh** (see p. 736), perhaps the most famous **Post-Impressionist** artist, created a masterful collection of paintings in his own intensely personal style, characterized by bright, vibrantly contrasting colors and thick brush strokes, as can be seen in his many *Starry Night* (1889). **Piet Mondrian,** the founder of the influential *De Stijl* magazine, formulated the theory of **neoplasticism**, which held that art should not attempt to recreate real life but should instead express universal absolutes. His signature works, characterized by black grids over primary-color blocks, have made their mark all over popular culture from fashion to interior design.

LITERATURE

Dutch literature runs back to the 10th century when the Old Dutch *Wachtendonck Psalm Fragments* were written. The most influential works, however, didn't come until the Dutch **Golden Age** in the early 17th century. The primary author of the time was **Henric Laurenszoon Spieghel,** whose *Heart-Mirror* (1614) was the first philosophical work written in Dutch. The Reformed Church commissioned the *States Bible* (1620), the first translation of the Bible into Dutch, which further legitimized the language. **Joost van den Vondel** firmly placed the Dutch in the literary world with his dramatic tragedies and satirical treatment of the church and government; his *Lucifer* (1654) depicts an imagined conflict between the angels and God. Dutch literature took a back seat to Dutch imperialism in the 18th century, but in 1839 **Nicolaas Beets** led the recovery with *Camera Obscura*, drawing on the humor of Charles Dickens and Laurence Sterne. With the terror of **World War I** and **World War II** came a new focus on social and philosophical questions. **Willem Frederik Hermans** examines the hostile environment in *The Dark Room of Damocles* (1958).

FOOD AND DRINK

Dutch food ranges from the hopelessly bland to the oddly tasty. Dutch **pancakes** *(pannenkoeken)*, best described as thick, unrolled crêpes, are prepared as both main courses and sweet desserts. In bars and beer cafes, the most popular *hors d'oeuvres* are **bitterballen,** ping-pong-sized fried balls filled with a mixture of meat and cheese, then served with mustard. If you're feeling adventurous, stop by a fish stall in summer to try **herring**—raw, salted, with a squeeze of lemon, and best when swallowed whole in one mouthful. Dutch **cheeses** transcend Gouda and Edam; try spicy Leiden, mild Belegen, and creamy Kernhem. Today Dutch food also extends to Surinamese, Indonesian, Chinese, and Indian dishes. Wash it all down with a small, foamy glass of domestic **beer:** Heineken or Amstel.

ESSENTIALS

DOCUMENTS AND FORMALITIES

Visas are generally not required for tourist stays under three months; South African citizens are the exception.

Dutch Embassies at Home: Australia, 120 Empire Circuit, Yarralumla Canberra, ACT 2600 (☎(02) 62 73 31 11; fax 62 73 32 06). **Canada,** 350 Albert St., Ste. 2020, Ottawa ON K1R 1A4 (☎613-237-5030; fax 237-6471). **Ireland,** 160 Merrion Rd., Dublin 4 (☎(012) 69 34 44; fax 283 96 90). **New Zealand,** PO Box 840, Cnr. Ballonce and Featherston St., Wellington (☎(04) 471 63 90; fax 471 29 23). **South Africa,** P.O. Box 346, Cape Town 8000 (☎021 421 56 60; fax 418 26 90). **United Kingdom,** 38 Hyde Park Gate, London SW7 5DP (☎(020) 75 90 32 00; fax 75 81 34 58). **US,** 4200 Linnean Ave., NW, Washington, D.C. 20008 (☎202-244-5300; fax 362-3430).

Foreign Embassies and Consulates in The Netherlands: All embassies and most consulates are located in **The Hague** (see p. 746). The **UK** and the **US** also have consulates in **Amsterdam** (see p. 726).

TRANSPORTATION

BY PLANE. KLM Royal Dutch Airlines, Martinair, Continental, Delta, Northwest, United, and Singapore Airlines serve **Amsterdam**'s Schiphol Airport. Amsterdam is a major hub for cheap transatlantic flights (see p. 725).

BY TRAIN. The national rail company is the efficient **Nederlandse Spoorwegen** (NS; Netherlands Railways; www.ns.nl). Train service tends to be faster than bus service. *Sneltreins* are the fastest; *stoptreins* make the most stops. One-way tickets are called *enkele reis*; normal round-trip tickets, *retour*; and day return tickets (valid only on day of purchase but cheaper than normal round-trip tickets), *dagretour*. **Day Trip (Rail Idee)** programs, available at train stations, have reduced-price combo transportation/entrance fees. **Eurail** and **InterRail** are valid in the Netherlands. The **Holland Railpass** (US$52-98) is good for three or five travel days in any one-month period. Although available in the US, the Holland Railpass is cheaper in the Netherlands at DER Travel Service or RailEurope (www.ns.nl/reisplan2.asp). The **Euro Domino Holland** card similarly allows three (ƒ130/€59, under 26 ƒ100/€45.40), five (ƒ200/€90.80, ƒ150/€68.10), or 10 days (ƒ350/€158.85, ƒ275/€124.80) of unlimited rail travel in any one-month period but is only available to those who have lived in Europe for at least six months and cannot be bought in the Netherlands. **One-day train passes** cost ƒ45.25-75.50/€20.55-34.30. The **Meerman's Kaart** grants one day of unlimited travel for two to six people (ƒ114-192/€51.75-87.15).

BY BUS. A nationalized fare system covers city buses, trams, and long-distance buses. The country is divided into zones; the number of strips on a **strippenkaart** (strip card) required depends on the number of zones through which you travel. A trip between destinations in the same zone costs one strip; a trip that traverses two zones requires two strips—you get the picture. Travel between towns costs from five to 20 strips. On buses, tell the driver your destination and he or she will cancel the correct number of strips; on trams and subways, stamp your own *strippenkaart* in either a yellow box at the back of the tram or in the subway station. Bus and tram drivers sell two- (ƒ3.50/€2) and three-strip tickets (ƒ4.75/€2.20), but they're much cheaper in bulk, available at public transit counters, tourist offices, post offices, and some tobacco shops and newsstands (8-strip ƒ12/€5.45; 15-strip ƒ12.50/€5.70, children and seniors ƒ7.75/€3.55; 45-strip ƒ36.75/€16.70). **Day passes** (*dagkarten*) are valid for unlimited use in any zone (ƒ11/€5, children and seniors ƒ7.50/€3.40). **Unlimited-use passes** are valid for one week in the same zone (ƒ18.75/€8.55; requires a passport photo and picture ID). Riding without a ticket can result in a ƒ60/€27.25 fine plus the original cost of the ticket.

BY FERRY. Ferries traverse the North Sea, connecting **England** to The Netherlands. Boats arrive in **Hook of Holland,** near Delft (p. 748), from **Harwich,** northeast of London (5hr.); in **Rotterdam** from **Hull** (13½hr.), near York (p. 216); and in **Amsterdam** from **Newcastle-upon-Tyne** (14hr.; p. 220). For more info, see p. 52.

BY CAR. The Netherlands has well-maintained roadways. North Americans and Australians need an International Driver's Permit (see p. 60); if your insurance doesn't cover you abroad, you'll also need a green insurance card. On maps, a green "E" indicates international highways; a red "A," national highways; and small yellow signposts and "N," other main roads. Speed limits are 50kph in towns, 80kph outside, and 120kph on highwa9ys. Fuel comes in two types; some cars use benzene (ƒ2.70/€1.25 per liter), while others use gasoline (ƒ1/€0.45 per liter). The **Royal Dutch Touring Association** (ANWB) offers roadside assistance to members. (☎0800 08 88.) For more info, contact the ANWB at Wassenaarseweg 220, 2596 EC The Hague (☎070 314 71 47), or Museumspl. 5, 1071 DJ Amsterdam (☎0800 05 03).

BY BIKE AND BY THUMB. Cycling is the way to go in The Netherlands—cities are close together, the land is flat, and most streets have separate bike lanes. Bikes run about ƒ10/€4.55 per day or ƒ35/€15.90 per week plus a ƒ50-200/€22.70-90.80 deposit (railpasses often earn you a discount). Bikes are sometimes available at train stations and hostels, and *Let's Go* also lists bike rental shops in many towns. For more info try www.visitholland.com. **Hitchhiking** is somewhat effective, but on the roads out of Amsterdam there is cutthroat competition. For more info about hitching, visit www.hitchhikers.org. *Let's Go* does not recommend hitchhiking.

TOURIST SERVICES AND MONEY

EMERGENCY	Police, ☎112. Ambulance, ☎112. Fire, ☎112.

TOURIST OFFICES. VVV (vay-vay-vay) tourist offices are marked by triangular blue signs. They also have info on the **Museumjaarkaart** passes that cover admission to most of the 800 museums in The Netherlands. Contact **Stichting Museumjaarkaart** for more info. (☎(090) 04 04 09 10; ƒ0.50/€0.25 per minute. ƒ70/€31.80, under 25 ƒ30/€13.60; bring a passport-size photo.)

Tourist Offices at Home: Canada, 25 Adelaide St. E, Ste. 710, Toronto ON H5C 1Y2 (☎888-464-6552; fax 363-1470). **South Africa,** P.O. Box 781738, Sandton 2146 (☎(11) 884 81 41; fax 883 55 73). **UK** and **Ireland,** P.O. Box 523, London SW1E 6NT (☎(089) 171 7777; fax 171 828 7941; www.goholland.co.uk). **US,** 225 N. Michigan Avenue, Ste. 1854, Chicago IL 60601 (☎888-464-6552; www.goholland.com).

CURRENCY AND EXCHANGE. The Dutch currency is the **guilder** (abbreviated ƒ, ƒl, or *hfl* as it was formerly called the florin), made up of 100 cents. Coins include the *stuiver* (5¢), *dubbeltje* (10¢), *kwartje* (25¢), *rijksdaalder* (ƒ2.50), and a five-*guilder* piece. The Netherlands has accepted the **Euro (€)** as legal tender, and *guilders* will be phased out by July 1, 2002. For more information, see p. 23. Post offices and major banks both offer reasonable **currency exchange** rates. Open 24hr., **GWKs** (*grenswisselkantoorbureaux*) often have the best rates and offer ISIC holders a reduced commission. Otherwise, expect a flat fee of about ƒ5/€2.30 and a 2.25% commission.

Prices: A bare-bones day traveling in The Netherlands will cost US$20-25; a slightly more comfortable day will run US$30-40.

Tipping and Bargaining: The value added tax and service charges are always included in bills for hotels, shopping, taxi fares, and restaurants. Tips for services are accepted and appreciated but not necessary. Taxi drivers are generally tipped 10% of the fare.

Taxes: Value-added tax (VAT; BTW in The Netherlands) refunds are usually 13.5%, available on purchases of more than ƒ300/€136.20 made during a single visit to a store.

ACCOMMODATIONS AND CAMPING

VVV offices supply accommodations lists and can usually reserve rooms both locally and in other areas (fee around ƒ4/€1.85). **Private rooms** cost about two-thirds as much as hotels, but they're hard to find; check with the VVV. In July and August, many cities add approximately ƒ2.50/€1.15 tourist tax to all rooms. The country's best values are the 34 **HI youth hostels**, run by the **NJHC (Dutch Youth Hostel Federation**. Hostels are divided into four price categories based on quality. Generally exceedingly clean and modern, they run ƒ28-34/€12.75-15.45 for bed and breakfast, plus high-season or prime-location supplements (ƒ1-3/€0.45-1.40). The VVV has a hostel list, and the useful *Jeugdherbergen* brochure describes each (both free). For more info, contact the NJHC at P.O. Box 9191, 1006 AD, Amsterdam (☎(010) 264 60 64; www.njhc.org). Pick up a membership card at hostels (ƒ30/€13.65); nonmembers are charged an extra ƒ5/€2.30. **Camping** is widely available, but many sites are crowded in summer. An **international camping card** is not required.

COMMUNICATION

MAIL. Post offices are generally open M-F 9am-6pm, and some are also open Sa 10am-1:30pm; larger branches may stay open later. Mailing a postcard or letter to anywhere in the EU costs ƒ1/€0.45; to destinations outside Europe, postcards cost ƒ1/€0.45, letters (up to 20g) ƒ1.60/€0.75. Mail takes 2-3 days to the UK, 4-6 to North America, 6-8 to Australia and New Zealand, and 8-10 to South Africa.

TELEPHONES. When making international calls from pay phones, phone cards (in denominations of ƒ10/€4.55 and ƒ25/€11.35; available at post offices and train stations) are the most economical option. The cards include a computer chip preprogrammed with a set amount of minutes; just slide it into the slots on the payphones and make your call. International calls are cheapest at night (8pm-8am). For directory assistance, dial 09 00 80 08; for collect calls, dial 06 04 10. International dial direct numbers include: **AT&T,** ☎0800 022 91 11; **British Telecom,** ☎0800 022 00 44; **Canada Direct,** ☎0800 022 91 16; **Ireland Direct,** ☎0800 02 20 353; **MCI,** ☎0800 022 91 22; **Sprint,** ☎0800 022 91 19; **Telecom New Zealand,** ☎0800 022 44 64; **Telkom South Africa,** ☎0800 022 02 27; **Telstra Australia,** ☎0800 022 20 61.

INTERNET ACCESS. Email is easily accessible within The Netherlands. Cybercafes are listed in most towns and all cities. In small towns, if Internet access is not listed, try the library or even your hostel. Internet access generally runs ƒ10/€4.55 per hour, except in libraries where it's often free.

LANGUAGE. Dutch is the official language of The Netherlands, but most natives speak English fluently. Knowing a few words of Dutch can't hurt, though. Fill up on *dagschotel* (dinner special), *broodje* (bread or sandwich), *bier* (beer), and *kaas* (cheese). Dutch uses a gutteral "g" sound for both "g" and "ch." "J" is usually pronounced "y"; e.g., *hofje* is "hof-YUH." "Ui" is pronounced "ow," and the dipthong "ij" is best approximated as "ah" followed by a long "e." For more lingo, see p. 954.

LOCAL FACTS

Time: The Netherlands is 1hr. ahead of Greenwich Mean Time (GMT).

When to Go: Mid-May to early Oct. is the ideal time to visit, when the day temperatures are generally 20-31°C (70-80°F), with nights around 10-20°C (50-60°F). However, it can be quite rainy; bring an umbrella. The tulip season runs from Apr. to mid-May.

Hours: Most **stores** are open M-F 9am-6pm and generally open late at night on the weekends. During holidays and the tourist season, hours are extended into the night and stores open their doors on Su. **Banks** are typically open the same hours as shops but remain closed on Sun. **Post offices** close at noon on Sa and remain closed on Su.

Holidays: The major holidays in The Netherlands are: New Year's Day (Jan. 1); Good Friday (Mar. 29); Easter Monday (Mar. 31); Liberation Day (May 5); Ascension Day (May 9); Whit Sunday and Whit Monday (June 3-4); Christmas Day (Dec. 25); and Boxing Day (Dec. 26; also called Second Christmas Day).

Festivals: Koninginnedag (Queen's Day; Apr. 30) turns the country into a huge carnival. **The Holland Festival** (in June) features more than 30 productions in a massive celebration of the arts. **Bloemen Corso** (Flower Parade; 1st Sa in Sept.) runs from Aalsmeer to Amsterdam. Many historical canal houses and windmills are open to the public for **National Monument Day** (2nd Sa in Sept.). The **Cannabis Cup** (Nov.) celebrates the magical mystery weed that brings millions of visitors to Amsterdam every year.

AMSTERDAM ☎ 020

Some people say that the best vacation to Amsterdam is the one you can't remember. True, the city lives up to its reputation as a never-never land of bacchanalian excess: the aroma of cannabis wafts from coffeeshops, and the city's infamous sex scene swathes itself in red lights. Amsterdam will give you the choice of exactly how you want to trip, turn, or twist through reality. But one need not be naughty to enjoy Amsterdam. Art enthusiasts will delight in the troves of Rembrandts, Vermeers, and van Goghs, romantics can stroll along endless cobblestoned streets and canals sparkling with lights, and families can frolic through parks and museums. For more on this hedonist's paradise, check out *Let's Go Amsterdam 2002*.

✈ INTERCITY TRANSPORTATION

Flights: Schiphol Airport (SKIP-pull; ☎ 0800-SCHIPHOL). **Trains** connect the airport to Centraal Station (20min., every 10min.; ƒ10/€4.55).

Trains: Centraal Station, Stationspl. 1, at the end of the Damrak (international info ☎ 09 00 92 96, domestic info 09 00 92 92, ƒ0.50/€0.25 per min.; www.ns.nl). To: **Berlin** (8hr.); **Brussels** (3-4hr.); **Frankfurt** (5¼-6hr.); **Hamburg** (5hr.); **Paris** (8hr.). For info and reservations, take a number and wait (up to 1hr. in summer). Desk open 24hr. International reservations daily 6:30am-11:30pm. **Lockers** ƒ6-8/€2.75-3.65 per hr.

✈ ORIENTATION

A series of roughly concentric canals ripple out around the **Centrum** (city center), resembling a giant horseshoe opening to the northeast. Emerging from Centraal Station, at the top of the horseshoe, you'll hit **Damrak**, a key thoroughfare leading to the **Dam**, the main square. Just east of Damrak in the Centrum is Amsterdam's famed **Red Light District**, bounded by Warmoestr., Zeedijk, Damstr., and Klovenniersburgwal. Don't head into the area until you've locked up your bags at the train station or a hostel. South of the Red Light District but still within the horseshoe lies the **Rembrandtplein**. The canals radiating around the Centrum (lined by streets of the same names) are **Singel, Herengracht, Keizergracht,** and **Prinsengracht**. West of the Centrum, beyond Prinsengracht, lies the **Jordaan**, an attractive residential neighborhood. Moving counterclockwise around Prinsengracht, you'll hit the **Leidseplein**, which lies just across the canal from the **Museum District** and **Vondelpark**.

⬛ LOCAL TRANSPORTATION

Buses: Trains are quicker, but the **GVB** (public transportation authority) will direct you to a bus stop for destinations not on a rail line. **Muiderpoort** (2 blocks east of Oosterpark) sends buses east; **Marnixstation** (at the corner of Marnixstr. and Kinkerstr.) west; and the **Stationsplein depot** north and south.

Public Transportation: GVB (☎ 09 00 92 92), Stationspl.; in front of Centraal Station. Open M-F 7am-9pm, Sa-Su 8am-9pm. Tram, metro, and bus lines radiate from Centraal Station. Trams are most convenient for inner-city travel; the metro leads to farther-out neighborhoods. The last trams leave M-F at midnight, Sa-Su 12:25am. Pick up a *nachtbussen* (night bus) schedule from the GVB office. The 45-strip *strippenkaart* (ƒ36.75/€16.70) is the best deal; it can be used on trams and buses throughout The Netherlands and is available at the VVV, the GVB, and many hostels.

Bike Rental: Beware of rampant bike theft. Bikes run about ƒ10-15/€4.55-6.85 per day plus ƒ50-200/€22.70-90.80 deposit. Try **Frederic Rent a Bike,** Brouwersgracht 78 (☎ 62 45 509; www.frederic.nl), in the Shipping Quarter. From Centraal Station, head down Damrak and turn right at Nieuwendijk. Cross the Harlemmersluis bridge, turn left, and follow the Brouwersgracht for 7 blocks. Frederic's is on the right. ƒ10/€4.55 per day. Reserve online before you arrive. Theft/damage insurance ƒ5/€2.30 per day. No charge for deposit, but ID or credit card imprint required. AmEx/MC/V.

▊ PRACTICAL INFORMATION

TOURIST, FINANCIAL, AND LOCAL SERVICES

Tourist Office: VVV Stationspl. 10 (☎(0900) 400 40 40), to the left and in front of Centraal Station. Hefty ƒ6/€2.75 fee for room booking. **Branches** at Centraal Station, platform 2, Leidsepl. 1, and the airport are open daily.

Budget Travel: NBBS, Rokin 66 (☎(0900) 235 62 27; ƒ0.75/€0.34 per min. for reservations). Open Tu-W and F 9:30am-6pm, Th 9:30am-9pm, Sa 10am-5pm. **Eurolines,** Rokin 10 (☎560 87 88). Open M-F 9:30am-5:30pm, Sa 10am-4pm.

Consulates: All **embassies** and most consulates are in **The Hague** (see p. 746). **US** consulate, Museumpl. 19 (☎575 53 09). Open M-F 8:30am-noon.

Currency Exchange: Best rates at **American Express** (see below). **GWK** in Centraal Station, with **Change** locations at Damrak 86, Leidsestr. 106, and Kalverstr. 150, charges ƒ7.50/€3.40 plus 2.25% commission. Students with ISIC get 25% discount. 3% commission on traveler's checks. Open M-W and F-Sa 8:30am-7pm, Th 8:30am-9pm, Su 10:30am-6pm. **Change Express,** Kalverstr. 150 (open M-Sa 8:30am-8pm and Su 10:30am-6pm), or Leidestr. 106 (open daily 8am-11pm), has good rates. 2.25% commission plus ƒ7.50/€3.40 fee.

American Express: Damrak 66 (☎504 87 70). Excellent rates and no commission on AmEx Traveler's Cheques. Mail held. Open M-F 9am-5pm, Sa 9am-noon.

English Bookstores: Spui, near the Amsterdam University, is lined with bookstores. **Oudemanhuispoort,** in the Oude Zijd, is a book market. Open daily; times vary.

Gay and Lesbian Services: COC, Rozenstr. 14 (☎626 30 87), is the main source of info. Open M-Tu and Th-F 10am-5pm, W 10am-8pm. **Gay and Lesbian Switchboard** (☎623 65 65) takes calls daily 10am-10pm.

Laundry: Look for a *Wasserette* sign. **Wasserette-Stomerij 'De Eland,'** Elandsgr. 59 (☎625 07 31), has self-service: ƒ8.75/€4 for 4kg, ƒ11.25/€5.10 for 6kg. Open M-Tu and Th-F 8am-8pm, W 8am-6pm, Sa 9am-5pm.

Condoms: Condomerie, Warmoesstr. 141 (☎627 41 74). Open M-Sa 11am-6pm.

EMERGENCY AND COMMUNICATIONS

Emergencies: ☎112 (police, ambulance, and fire brigade).

Crisis Lines: General counseling at **Telephone Helpline** (☎675 75 75). Open 24hr. **Rape crisis hotline** (☎613 02 45). Staffed M-F 10:30am-11pm, Sa-Su 3:30-11pm. **Drug counseling,** Jellinek clinic (☎570 23 55). Open M-F 9am-5pm.

Medical Assistance: Tourist Medical Service (☎592 33 55). Open 24hr. For hospital care, call **Academisch Medisch Centrum,** Meibergdreef 9 (☎566 91 11), near the Holendrecht metro stop. For free emergency care, visit the **Kruispost,** Oudezijds Voorburgwal 129 (☎624 90 31). Open M-F 7-9:30pm.

Pharmacies: Most are open M-F 8:30am-5pm. When closed, each *apotheek* (pharmacy) posts a sign directing you to the nearest one open.

Internet Access: easyEverything, Reguliersbreestr. 22 near Rembrandtpl. and Damrak 34. Base price of ƒ5/€2.30 buys differing amounts of time depending on computer availability. Open 24hr. **La Bastille,** Lijnbaansgracht 246, 2 blocks east of the Leidsepl. ƒ5/€2.30 for 30min. (15min. minimum). Open 10am-midnight. **Cyber Cafe Amsterdam,** Nieuwendijk 17, has the same deal as the Internet Cafe. Open Su-Th 10am-1am, F-Sa 10am-2am. **Free World,** Nieuwendijk 30 (☎620 09 02). Open Su-Th 9am-1am, F-Sa 9am-3am. **Internet Cafe,** Martelaarsgr. 11, near Nieuwendijk, 3min. from Centraal Station. ƒ2.50/€1.15 for 30min. Open Su-Th 9am-1am, F-Sa 9am-3am.

Post Office: Singel 250 (☎556 33 11), at Raadhuisstr. behind the Dam. Address mail to be held: FirstName SURNAME, *Poste Restante*, Singel 250, Amsterdam **1016 AB,** The Netherlands. M-W and F 9am-6pm, Th 9am-9pm, Sa 10am-1:30pm.

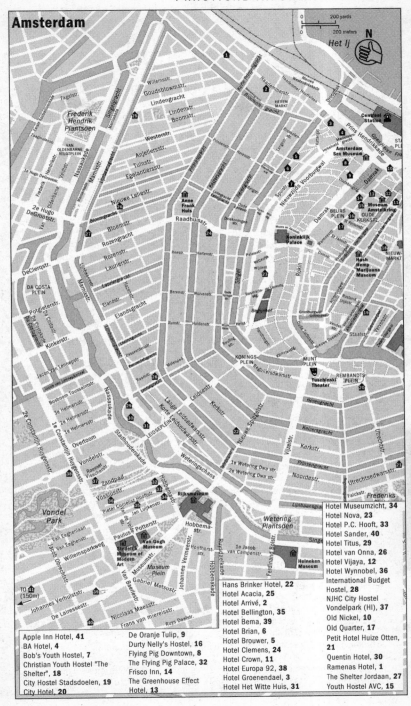

Amsterdam

0 200 yards
0 200 meters

N

Het Ij

Frederik Hendrik Plantsoen

Centraal Station

Amsterdam Sex Museum

Koninklijk Palace

Anne Frank Huis

Hash Hemp Marijuana Museum

Tuschinski Theater

REMBRANDTS PLEIN

Rijksmuseum

Vondel Park

Stedelijk Museum of Modern Art

Van Gogh Museum

Wetering Plantsoen

Heineken Museum

THE NETHERLANDS

Hotel Museumzicht, **34**
Hotel Nova, **23**
Hotel P.C. Hooft, **33**
Hotel Sander, **40**
Hotel Titus, **29**
Hotel van Onna, **26**
Hotel Vijaya, **12**
Hotel Wynnobel, **36**
International Budget
Hostel, **28**
NJHC City Hostel
Vondelpark (HI), **37**
Old Nickel, **10**
Old Quarter, **17**
Petit Hotel Huize Otten,
21
Quentin Hotel, **30**
Ramenas Hotel, **1**
The Shelter Jordaan, **27**
Youth Hostel AVC, **15**

Hans Brinker Hotel, **22**
Hotel Acacia, **25**
Hotel Arrivé, **2**
Hotel Bellington, **35**
Hotel Bema, **39**
Hotel Brian, **6**
Hotel Brouwer, **5**
Hotel Clemens, **24**
Hotel Crown, **11**
Hotel Europa 92, **38**
Hotel Groenendael, **3**
Hotel Het Witte Huis, **31**

Apple Inn Hotel, **41**
BA Hotel, **4**
Bob's Youth Hostel, **7**
Christian Youth Hostel "The
Shelter", **18**
City Hostel Stadsdoelen, **19**
City Hotel, **20**

De Oranje Tulip, **9**
Durty Nelly's Hostel, **16**
Flying Pig Downtown, **8**
The Flying Pig Palace, **32**
Frisco Inn, **14**
The Greenhouse Effect
Hotel, **13**

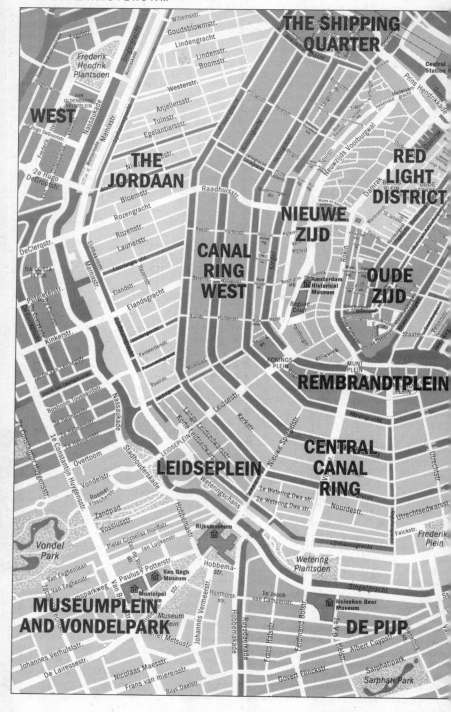

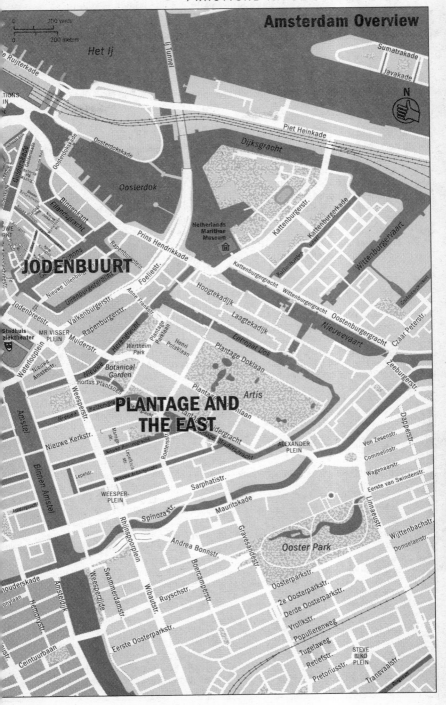

Amsterdam Overview

Het Ij

Sumatrakade

Javakade

N

e Ruijterkade

Ij Tunnel

Piet Heinkade

Oosterdokskade

Dijksgracht

TIONS
IN

Oosterdok

Kattenburgerkade

Wittenburgervaart

Binnenkant
Prins Hendrikkade

Friandsgracht

Netherlands
Maritime
Museum

Kattenburgerstr.

Kattenburgergracht

Wittenburgergracht

JWE
RKT

JODENBUURT

Foeliestr.

Hoogtekadijk

Wittenburgergracht

Oostenburgergracht

Czaar Peterstr.

Nieuwe Uilenburg

Uilenburgergracht

Anne Frankstr.

Laagtekadijk

Nieuwevaart

Jodenbreestr.

Valkenburgerstr.

Rapenburgerstr.

Plantage
Parklaan

Henri
Polaklaan

Entrepot Dok

Plantage Doklaan

Zeeburgerstr.

Dappestr.

MR VISSER
PLEIN

Muiderstr.

Stadhuis
Ziekhtheater

Waterlooplein

Nieuwe
Amstelstr.

Weesperstr.

Wertheim
Park

Nieuwe

Botanical
Garden

Hortus Plantsoen

Plantage
Artis

**PLANTAGE AND
THE EAST**

Amstel

Nieuwe Kerkstr.

Roetersstr.

Muidergracht

ALEXANDER
PLEIN

Von Zesenstr.

Commelinstr.

Lepelstr.

Lepoldstr.

Wagenaarstr.

Eerste van Swindenstr.

WEESPER-
PLEIN

Sarphatistr.

Mauritskade

Linnaeustr.

Wijttenbachstr.

Binnen Amstel

Spinoza str.

Domselaerstr.

Andrea Bonnstr.

Rijnspoorplein

Gravesandestr.

Ooster Park

Swammerdamstr.

Boercampestr.

houderskade

Amsteldijk

Weesperzijde

Wibautstr.

Ruyschstr.

Oosterparkstr.

2e Oosterparkstr.

Derde Oosterparkstr.

Vrolikstr.

onydaan

Ceintuurbaan

Eerste Oosterparkstr.

Populierenweg

Tugelaweg

STEVE
BIKO
PLEIN

Relietstr.

Pretoriusstr.

Transvaalstr.

0   200 yards
0   200 meters

⌐ ACCOMMODATIONS

Accommodations near **Centraal Station** often take good security measures due to the chaos of the nearby Red Light District. Hostels and hotels in **Vondelpark** and the **Jordaan** are quieter (by Amsterdam's standards) and safer; they're also close to bars, coffeeshops, museums, and the busy Leidsepl. and are only 15min. by foot or 2min. by train from the city center. The hotels and hostels in the **Red Light District** (in the Oude Zijd) are often bars with beds over them. Consider just how much pot, noise, and music you want to inhale before booking a bed there.

OUDE ZIJD, NIEUWE ZIJD, AND REMBRANDTPLEIN

⚑ Hotel Groenendael, Nieuwendijk 15 (☎624 48 22). Friendly hotel right near Centraal Station with well-lit, cheerfully decorated rooms. Plenty of clean bathrooms and showers. Breakfast included. Free lockers. Key deposit ƒ10/€4.55. Singles ƒ70/€31.80; doubles ƒ110/€49.95, with shower ƒ120/€54.45; triples ƒ165/€74.90. AmEx.

Durty Nelly's Hostel, Warmoesstr. 115/117 (☎638 01 25). From Centraal Station, go south on Damrak, turn right on Brugsteeg, and then right on Warmoesstr.; Nelly's is 2 blocks up on the left. Cozy hostel above an Irish pub. Breakfast included. Towel deposit ƒ5/€2.30. Reception 24hr. No reservations. Dorms ƒ45/€20.45.

Frisco Inn, Beursstr. 5 (☎620 16 10). From Centraal Station, go south on Damrak, then left at Brugsteeg, and right onto Beursstr.; it's the 2nd building on your left. Small, centrally located hotel behind the Beurs van Berlage. Hall baths. Smoking allowed if you open the windows. Reception 24hr. No curfew. Rooms start at ƒ60/€27.25 per person.

Youth Hostel AVC, Warmoesstr. 87 (☎625 59 74; fax 422 0885). Low-key, basic budget digs in a sociable, youthful environment. No smoking in rooms. Dorms ƒ30-44/€13.65; doubles ƒ100/€45.40; triples ƒ125/€56.75; quads ƒ175/€79.45.

Christian Youth Hostel "The Shelter," Barndesteeg 21-25 (☎625 32 30; reservations.city@shelter.nl), off the Nieuwmarkt. Virtue amid the red lights: incredibly clean rooms and friendly staff. Breakfast included. No drugs; cigarettes only in hallways. Key deposit ƒ10/€4.55. Single-sex dorms. Lockers ƒ10/€4.55. Linens included. Reception 24hr. Curfew Su-Th midnight, F-Sa 1am. Dorms Oct.-Mar. ƒ25-30/€11.35-13.60.

Hotel Crown, Oudezijds Voorburgwal 21 (☎626 96 64). Clean, handsome British-owned hotel in the picturesque end of the Red Light District. Singles ƒ100/€45.40; doubles ƒ200/€90.75, with shower ƒ220/€99.85; triples ƒ300/€136.13, ƒ330/€149.75; quads ƒ400/€181.50, ƒ440/€199.60; 6-person room with shower ƒ660/€299.50.

Hotel Vijaya, Oudezijds Voorburgwal 44 (☎626 94 06 or 638 01 02; fax 620 52 77). Very clean and extremely adequate rooms on the fringe of the pulsing Red Light District. Breakfast included. ƒ120-275/€54.45-124.80; off-season ƒ85-250/€38.60-113.45.

The Greenhouse Effect Hotel, Warmoesstr. 55 (☎624 49 74; www.the-greenhouse-effect.com). Reasonably priced theme rooms (including Arabian Nights). Located 5min. from Centraal Station. Hotel guests are treated to an all-day Happy Hour at the bar. Look at the web site for discounts. 1- to 5-person rooms ƒ60-250/€27.25-113.45.

Old Quarter, Warmoesstr. 20-22 (☎626 64 29). Turn right onto Warmoesstr from Old Nickel. Very clean rooms, from the basic to luxury (view, TV, private shower, and toilet). *Bruine cafe* downstairs; live jazz Th-Sa. Reception 24hr. Doubles from ƒ125/€56.75.

Old Nickel, Nieuwebrugsteeg 11 (☎624 19 12). Quiet hotel 2min. from the train station; turn onto Warmoesstr. at the end nearest Centraal Station, and the Old Nickel is diagonal to the Hotel International. Breakfast included. Reception 8am-midnight. Singles ƒ65/€29.50; doubles ƒ90-125/€40.85-56.75; quads ƒ160-200/€72.60-90.80.

De Oranje Tulp, Damrak 32 (☎428 16 18; reservations@oranje-tulphotel.a2000.nl; http://people.a2000.nl/oranje00). Clean, modern rooms, all with phone and TV. Online reservations accepted. Singles ƒ100/€45.40; doubles ƒ160/€72.60; triples ƒ180/€81.70; quads ƒ200/€90.75; quints ƒ275/€124.80. Prices higher July-Aug.

Bob's Youth Hostel, Nieuwezijds Voorburgwal 92 (☎623 00 63). Well-known by European backpackers everywhere, Bob's provides the bare necessities. Young clientele. Liberal drug policy. Breakfast included. Lockers and luggage storage available. Linens provided, but bring a towel. Laundry facilities nearby. Key deposit ƒ10/€4.55. 2-night

THE NETHERLANDS

min. stay on weekends, 7-day max. stay. Reception open 8am-3am. No lockout or curfew. No reservations, so arrive before 10am to get a room. Dorms ƒ33/€15.

Hotel Brian, Singel 69 (☎ 624 46 61; hotelbrian@hotmail.com). From Centraal Station, turn right at the Victoria Hotel, then turn left onto Singel. Basic budget digs in a friendly, very low-key atmosphere. Breakfast included. Key deposit ƒ25/€11.35. Reception 8am-10:30pm. Bed in a 2-, 3-, or 4-person room ƒ50/€22.70; lower in off-season.

BA Hotel, Martelaarsgr. 18 (☎ 638 71 19; india@cistron.nl). From Centraal Station, cross the bridge to Damrak, take a right on Prins Henrikkade, and the 1st left on Martelaarsgr. Well-located, with a friendly staff and bar. Breakfast and city map included. Key deposit ƒ25/€11.35. 2-night min. stay during high-season and weekends. Reception 8am-midnight. 8- to 12-bed dorms ƒ45/€20.45.

City Hotel, Utrechtsestr. 2 (☎ 627 23 23; www.city-hotel.nl). Classy accommodations above a pub right on the Rembrandtpl. Many rooms have great views. Immaculately kept rooms, hall baths, and showers. Online reservations accepted. Doubles from ƒ150/€68.20; triples from ƒ200/€90.90; quads from ƒ260/€118.20.

Petit Hotel Huize Otten, Utrechtsedwarsstr. 79 (☎ 625 03 45; fax 330 54 47; utd79@hotmail.com). Take tram #4 and exit at Prinsengr.; walk south along Utrechtsestr. for a block and turn left on Utrechtsedwarsstr.; the hotel will be the 3rd building on your left. Somewhere between 70s garage sale and budget hotel. Adequately clean hall baths. Email reservations accepted. Doubles ƒ125/€56.75. Cash only.

SHIPPING QUARTER, CANAL RING WEST, AND JORDAAN

Ramenas Hotel, Haarlemerdijk 61 (☎ 624 69 60 30). From Centraal station, follow Nieuwendijk, which turns into Haarlemerstr. and then Haarlemerdijk. Breakfast included. ƒ60/€27.25 per person, with bath ƒ75/€34.05. Cash only.

Hotel Arrivé, Haarlemmerstr. 65-67 (☎ 622 14 39). Close to the action of Nieuwendijk. Plain rooms with bare lightbulbs. Breakfast included. Shared baths. Singles ƒ70/€31.85; doubles ƒ120/€54.55; triples ƒ160/€72.75. Add 20% on weekends.

Hotel Clemens, Raadhuisstr. 39 (☎ 624 60 89). A true gem with elegant deluxe and budget rooms that will all be renovated by Jan. 2002. Phone, fridge, and TV in all rooms. Breakfast ƒ15.45/€7. Key deposit ƒ50/€22.69. 3-night min. stay during weekends. **Internet.** Budget singles ƒ88-125/€40-56; doubles ƒ154/€70. Cash only.

Hotel Brouwer, Singel 83 (☎ 624 63 58). From Centraal Station, cross the water; turn right onto Prins Hendrikkade and left onto Singel. Gorgeous rooms (named for Dutch painters) with private bathrooms and views. Breakfast included. No smoking. Singles ƒ88/€40; doubles ƒ165/€75. Cash only.

The Shelter Jordaan, Bloemstr. 179 (☎ 624 47 17), on the corner of Lijnbaansgr. Tram #13 or 17 to Marnixstr. Clean, comfy hostel. Breakfast and sheets included. Single-sex dorms. No smoking. Free **Internet.** Age limit 35. Curfew 2am. July-Aug. dorms ƒ30/€13.65; Apr.-June and Sept. ƒ28/€12.75; Oct.-Mar. ƒ25/€11.35. Cash only.

Hotel van Onna, Bloemgr. 104 (☎ 626 58 01). Tram #13 or 17 from Centraal Station to Westermarkt. Quiet rooms all have private bathrooms. No smoking. Breakfast included. Reception 8am-11pm. Rooms for 1-4 people ƒ80/€40 per person. Cash only.

Hotel Acacia, Lindengr. 251 (☎ 622 14 60). From Centraal Station, bus #18 to Willemstr. Tram #3 to Bloemgr. is also close. Rooms in shades of red and pink, all with private bath. Breakfast included. Singles ƒ130/€59; doubles ƒ165/€75; triples ƒ205/€93; quads ƒ250/€114; quints ƒ275/€125. Credit cards 5% surcharge.

Hotel Het Witte Huis, Marnixstr. 382 (☎ 625 07 77). In need of a makeover, this decidedly budget hotel offers basic rooms close to Leidsepl. Invest in a room with a private shower and toilet, or bring shower shoes. Singles ƒ85/€38.65; doubles ƒ125/€56.85, with bath ƒ140/€63.65; triple ƒ165/€75, ƒ195/€88.65.

LEIDSEPLEIN AND MUSEUMPLEIN

▨ NJHC City Hostel Vondelpark (HI), Zandpad 5 (☎ 589 89 93), bordering Vondelpark. Take tram #1, 2, or 5 from the station to "Leidsepl.," cross the canal and the street (Stadhouderskade), turn left, and take 2nd right onto Zandpad. This palatial hostel offers clean rooms all with bath. 3 handicapped rooms available. Bikes ƒ10/€4.55 per day. **Internet** ƒ1/€0.45 per 6min. Breakfast and sheets included. Lockers ƒ3/€1.35, bring a padlock. Reception 7:30am-midnight. 10- to 20-person dorm ƒ39/€17.70; 6- to 8- person dorm ƒ43/€19.50; doubles ƒ145/€65.80; quads ƒ208/€94.40. Nonmembers ƒ5/€2.30 per night per person surcharge. MC/V (4% surcharge).

🔣 **The Flying Pig Palace,** Vossiusstr. 46-47 (☎400 41 87; www.flypig.nl). Take tram #1, 2, or 5 from Centraal Station to "Leidsepl.," cross the canal and the street, take 1st right after the entrance to the Vondelpark on the left. Clean, vibrant hostel. Free **Internet.** Breakfast included. Sheets free; bring your own towel. Reception 8am-9pm. For travelers aged 16-35. Stop by at 8, call at 8:30am to reserve a room, or make reservations via Internet (10% deposit). 6- to 10-bed dorms ƒ35.50-47.50/€16.15-21.55; doubles ƒ130/€59; triples ƒ154.50/€70.10; quad ƒ194/€88.05.

International Budget Hostel, Leidsegr. 76-1 (☎624 27 84). Tram #1, 2, or 5 to Prinsengr., then turn right and walk along Prinsengr. to Leidsegr. Like sleepover camp from the 70s. Breakfast ƒ7/€3.20. 2-night min. stay in summer. Dorms ƒ37.50-50.70/€17-23; rooms from ƒ110.20/€50. 5% credit card surcharge.

Quentin Hotel, Leidsekade 89 (☎626 21 87). Proves budget travelers don't have to sacrifice style; hip in a canalside setting. Singles from ƒ100/€45.45, with telephone and bath from ƒ135/€61.35; doubles from ƒ275/€125, from doubles from ƒ145/€65.91; triples with phone and bath from ƒ275/€125. AmEx/MC/V (5% surcharge).

Hans Brinker Hotel, Kerkstr. 136 (☎622 06 87). Take tram #1, 2, or 5 from Centraal Station, get off at Kerkstr., and it's 1 block down on the left. Large budget hotel offers clean, safe, spartan rooms, all with baths. No visitors. All-you-can-eat breakfast buffet included (7:30-10am). Key deposit ƒ10/€4.55. Reception 24hr. Dorms (single-sex and mixed) ƒ42.50/€19.35; singles ƒ114/€51.85; doubles ƒ152/€69.10; triples ƒ198/€90; quads ƒ220/€100; quints ƒ262.50/€119.10.

Hotel Titus, Leidsekade 74 (☎626 57 58). The Titus's rooms, while not titanic in size, have TV and phones and are sparklingly clean. Singles from ƒ75/€34.10, with bath from ƒ125/€56.85; quints from ƒ400/€181.85.

Hotel Bema, Concertgebouw 19b (☎679 13 96), across from the Concertgebouw. Tram #16 to Museumpl.; it's a block up on the left. Free breakfast delivered to the room. 3-night min. stay on weekends in summer. Reception 8am-midnight. Singles from ƒ95/€43.15; doubles ƒ110/€49.95; triples ƒ165/€74.90; quads with shower ƒ225/€102.10. Credit cards 5% surcharge.

Hotel Europa 92, 1e Constantijn Huygensstr. 103-105 (☎618 88 08). Tram #1, 6 to 1e Constantijn Huygensstr. Clean rooms and a nice garden terrace. Apr.-Aug. singles ƒ190/€86.25; doubles ƒ250/€113.45; triples ƒ335/€152.05; quads ƒ350/€158.85. Oct.-Mar. singles ƒ155/€70.35; doubles ƒ200/€90.80; triples ƒ300/€136.15; quads ƒ280/€127.05. Credit cards accepted.

Apple Inn Hotel, Koninginneweg 93 (☎662 78 94). Take tram #2 to Emmastr. and walk 200m away from Centraal Station. Removed from the bustle of the city's center. Breakfast included. Apr.-Sept. singles ƒ185/€83.95; doubles ƒ245/€111.20; triples ƒ295/€133.90; quads ƒ345/€156.55. Nov.-Mar. singles ƒ135/€52; doubles ƒ135/€61.35; triples ƒ165/€74.90; quads ƒ185/€83.95. Credit cards accepted.

Hotel Bellington, P.C Hoftstr. 78-80 (☎671 64 78). Follow directions to Hotel Museumzicht. Hoftstr. is behind Luijkenstr., toward the Leidsepl. A well-groomed hotel on one of Amsterdam's ritziest streets. Breakfast included. Reception 8am-5pm and 8-10pm. Phone and TV in room. Doubles ƒ215/€97.55; triples ƒ250/€113.45; quads ƒ295/€113.90. Credit cards accepted.

Hotel P.C. Hooft, P.C. Hooftstr. 63 (☎662 71 07). Climb the 2 flights of stairs to tidy rooms, all with sink and TV. Breakfast included. Some available with shower, ƒ15/€6.80 extra. All toilets shared. Singles ƒ100/€45.40; doubles ƒ135/€61.30; ƒ35/€15.90 each additional person up to 5 people. MC/V.

Hotel Sander, 69 Jacob Obrechtstr. (☎662 75 74). Tram #16 to Jacob Olbrechtstr. Convenient to Museumpl. All rooms with bath. 24hr. bar in lobby. Breakfast included. Singles ƒ205/€93.05; doubles ƒ245/€111.20; triples ƒ340/€154.30; quads ƒ440/€199.65. Extra person ƒ80-100/€36.30-45.40. Prices lower in winter.

Hotel Wynnobel, Vossiusstr. 9 (☎662 22 98). Down the street from the Flying Pig. Free breakfast brought to room every morning. Singles ƒ75/€34.05; doubles ƒ130-150/€59-68.10; triples ƒ195/€88.50; quads ƒ260/€118. Cheaper in winter. Cash only.

Hotel Museumzicht, Jan Luykenstr. 22 (☎671 52 24). From Centraal Station, take tram #2 or 5 to Hobbemasstr. From Schiphol, ride bus #197 to same stop. Old-fashioned house with fantastic views. Breakfast included. Singles ƒ95/€43.10; doubles ƒ150/€68.10, with bath ƒ195/€88.50; triples ƒ195/€88.50. Credit cards accepted.

NIEUWMARKT

⧫ **Flying Pig Downtown,** Nieuwendijk 100 (☎420 68 22; www.flyingpig.nl). From the main entrance of Centraal Station, walk toward Damrak. Pass the Victoria Hotel and take the 1st alley on your right; Nieuwendijk is at the end. Helpful staff and knockout location. Spacious dorms. **Internet.** Kitchen. Ages 18-35 only. Breakfast included. Sheets provided; towels ƒ1.50/€0.70. Key deposit ƒ30/€13.60. 7-day max. stay. Dorms ƒ35.50/€16.60; doubles ƒ75/€34.05. Credit cards accepted.

City Hostel Stadsdoelen, Kloveniersburgwal 97 (☎624 68 32). Take tram #4, 9, 16, 20, 24, or 25 to Muntpl. Proceed down Nieuwe Doelenstr.); Kloveniersburgwal will be on your right over the bridge. Clean, drug-free, and secure lodgings. Breakfast, lockers, and linens included. **Internet.** Reception 7am-1am. Dorms ƒ42/€19.10; ƒ37/€16.90 for ISIC members. Credit cards accepted.

Hotel Nova, Nieuwezijds Voorburgwal 276 (☎623 00 66). An excellent value. Clean, complete rooms with bath, color TV, phone, and mini fridge. Breakfast included. Singles ƒ165-195/€74.90-88.50; doubles ƒ205-270/€93.05-122.55; triples from ƒ255-325/€115.70-147.50; quads ƒ305-375/€138.40-170.20.

▯ FOOD

Many cheap restaurants cluster around **Leidseplein, Rembrandtplein,** and the **Spui.** Cafes, especially in the Jordaan, serve inexpensive sandwiches (ƒ4-9/€1.85-4.10) and good meat-and-potatoes fare (ƒ12-20/€5.45-9.10). Bakeries line **Utrechtsestraat,** south of Prinsengr. Fruit, cheese, flowers, and even live chickens fill the **markets** on **Albert Cuypstraat,** behind the Heineken brewery. (Open M-Sa 9am-6pm.)

NIEUWE ZIJD, CANAL RING WEST, AND JORDAAN

Ristorante Caprese, Spuistr. 259-261 (☎620 00 59). Truly excellent Italian food in a stylish but casual atmosphere for reasonable prices. Open daily 5-10:45pm.

Keuken Van 1870, Spuistr. 4 (☎624 89 65). Legendary. Serves traditional Dutch food for cheap. *Prix fixe* ƒ12.50/€5.70. Open M-F 12:30-8pm, Sa-Su 4-9pm.

Pannenkoekenhuis Upstairs, Grimburgwal 2 (☎626 56 03). From the "Muntpl." tram stop, cross the bridge, walk along the Singel and turn right on Lange Brugsteeg, which connects to Grimburgwal. A tiny nook with some of the best pancakes in the city. Pancakes ƒ7.50-17.50/€3.40-7.95. Open M-F noon-7pm, Sa noon-6pm, Su noon-5pm.

Padi, Harlemmerdijk 50 (☎625 12 80). Locals rave about this Thai *eethuis*. Cheap food, lots of veggie options. Entrees around ƒ15.50/€7.05. Open daily 5-10pm.

Het Molenpad, Prinsengr. 653 (☎625 96 80). Locals fill up the canalside seats in summer at this traditional *bruine cafe*. Dishes from ƒ17.50/€13.60. Open Su-Th noon-1am, F-Sa noon-2am. Cash only.

Lunchcafe Neilsen, Berenstr. 19 (☎330 60 06).Breakfast and lunch served all day. *Tostis* fromƒ5.50/€2.50; salads from ƒ16/€7.40. Vegetarian-friendly. Open Tu-F 8am-5pm, Sa 8am-6pm, Su 9am-5pm. Credit cards accepted.

Wolvenstraat 23, Wolvenstr. 23 (☎320 08 43). Maybe this place remains nameless in order to defy description. Lunch here means sandwiches (ƒ4-12/€1.82-5.45), salads (ƒ12.50-15/€5.70-6.85), and omelettes (ƒ6.50-9/€2.95-4.10). Dinner is strictly Chinese cuisine (ƒ19.50-28.50/€8.85-12.95). Lunch 8am-3:30pm, dinner 6-10:30pm. Open M-Th 8am-1am, F 8am-late, Sa 9am-late, Su 10am-1am. Cash only.

De Vliegende Schotel, Nieuwe Leliestr. 162-168 (☎625 20 41). Order at the counter of this vegetarian cafe, then enjoy your meal in one of the dining rooms. Some vegan options and a few fish dishes available. Entrees and salads ƒ15-28/€6.85-12.75.

Bolhoed, Prinsengr. 60-62 (☎626 18 03). Serves up the best in vegetarian and vegan fare, all in a bright, funky setting complete with Sammy the cat. Dinner menu always includes a vegan special for ƒ26.50/€7.75. Open daily 4-11:30pm. Cash only.

A STONER'S TOUR OF AMSTERDAM

Put the "bud" back in "budget travel."

finish

Walking Tour

N

Wake and bake, Sunshine! Start your day with a big joint and an even bigger breakfast at **Barney's!**

Finally, avigate your way through the **Red Light District**. Remember, if you get lost, the giant penis fountain is in front of Casa Rosso.

Frolic out of the center and make your way to **Vondelpark**. Stretch out on the grass and feel goo-ood.

200 yards
200 meters

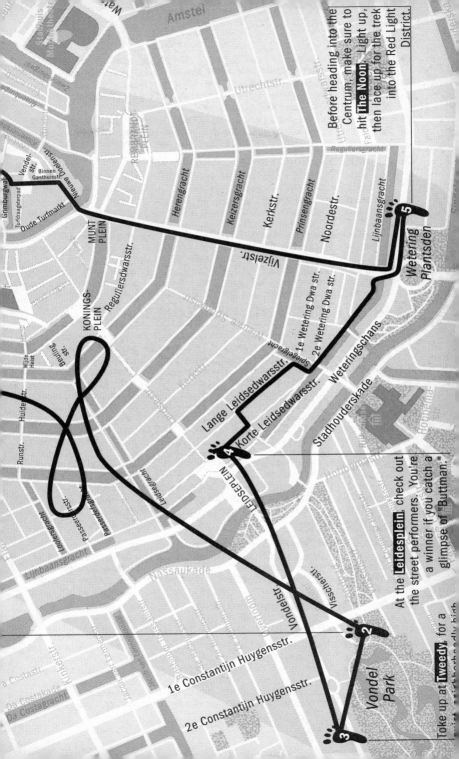

Before heading into the Centrum, make sure to hit **The Noon**. Light up, then lace up for the trek into the Red Light District.

At the **Leidesplein**, check out the street performers. You're a winner if you catch a glimpse of "Buttman."

Toke up at **Tweedy**, for a

LEIDSEPLEIN

☒ **Bojo,** Lange Leidsedwarsstr. 51 (☎ 622 74 34). Palm fronds, sassy waitstaff, and excellent Javanese chow. Open M-Th 4pm-2am, F 4pm-4am, Sa noon-4am, Su noon-2am.

☒ **Santa Lucia,** Leidsekruisstr. 20-22 (☎ 623 46 39). Corner location puts you in the middle of the action just off Leidsepl. Pizza with tomato and cheese ƒ9/€4.05. Hot, gooey lasagna ƒ17/€7.70. Open daily noon-11pm.

☒ **Wagamama,** Max Euwepl. 10 (☎ 528 77 78). Loud, crowded Japanese noodle joint—slurp as loud as you wanna. *Yaki Udon* (mushrooms, egg, prawns, chicken, peppers, fishcake sauce, and noodles) ƒ22/€10. Open daily noon-11pm. AmEx/DC/MC/V.

MUSEUMPLEIN, VONDELPARK, AND DE PIJP

Bistoom, 1e Constantijn Huygensstr. 115 (☎ 689 23 62). Tram #1 or 6. Persian fare with lots of lamb and rice. Dishes ƒ24-30/€10.90-15.90. Open daily 5pm-midnight. V.

Frans and Daantje Cafe, Daniel Stalpertstr. 36 (☎ 771 43 16). A stylish bar-cafe where guest chefs prepare creative, fusion-oriented dishes every night (3-course meal ƒ30-40/€13.60-18.15). Sandwiches ƒ6-9/€2.75-4.10. Open daily 9am-midnight.

De Soepwinkel, 1e Sweelinckstr. 19F (☎ 673 22 93), just off the Albert Cuypmarkt. Soup-making brought to a fine art form. Always plenty of vegetarian options. Small soups ƒ7.50/€3.40, large ƒ19.50/€8.85. Open M-Sa 11am-9pm.

Zagros, Albert Cuypstr. 50 (☎ 670 04 61). The food is influenced by the 5 countries spanned by Kurdistan: Turkey, Iran, Iraq, Syria, and Russia. Lamb dominates the menu, but veggie options are available too. Open 5-10:30pm.

👁 🏛 SIGHTS AND MUSEUMS

Amsterdam is fairly compact, so tourists can easily explore the area from the Rijksmuseum to the Red Light District on foot. **Circle Tram 20**, geared toward tourists, stops at 30 attractions throughout the city (every 10min. 9am-7pm, 1-day pass ƒ11/€5; buy on the tram or at VVV offices). The more peaceful **Museumboot Canal Cruise** allows you to hop on and off along its loop from the VVV to the Anne Frank Huis, the Rijksmuseum, the Bloemenmarkt, Waterloopl., and the old shipyard—buy tickets at any stop. (☎ 530 10 90; departs every 30min. 10am-5pm, ƒ27.50/€12.50; pass also gives 20% off at all museums.) Rent a canal bike to power your own way through the canals. (☎ 626 55 74. Deposit ƒ100/€45.40. 1-2 people ƒ15/€6.80 per person per hr., 3 or more people ƒ12.50/€5.70; pick-up and drop-off points at Rijksmuseum, Leidsepl., Keizergr. at Leidsestr., and Anne Frank Huis. Open daily 10am-10pm.) **Mike's Bike Tours** provide an entertaining introduction to the city's sites and the surrounding countryside. (☎ 622 79 70. Reserve by phone. Tours start from the entrance of the Rijksmuseum. ƒ44/€20.) The **Museumkaart** (MJK) grants year-long discounts at museums and on transportation throughout the country (ƒ70/€31.80, under 25 ƒ30/€13.60; buy at museums throughout The Netherlands).

MUSEUMPLEIN

☒ **VAN GOGH MUSEUM.** This architecturally breathtaking museum houses the largest collection of van Goghs in the world (mostly from his family's private collection) and a diverse group of 19th-century paintings by artists who influenced him or were his contemporaries. (*Paulus Potterstr. 7. Take tram #2, 5, or 20 from the station.* ☎ 570 52 52. *Open daily 10am-6pm. ƒ15.50/€7.05.*)

☒ **STEDELIJK MUSEUM OF MODERN ART.** The outstanding collection includes Picasso, Pollock, de Kooning, Malevich, and up-and-coming contempory work. (*Paulus Potterstr. 13, next to the Van Gogh Museum. Open daily 11am-5pm. ƒ11/€5.*)

RIJKSMUSEUM (NATIONAL MUSEUM). It would be sinful to leave Amsterdam without seeing this impressive collection of works by Rembrandt, Vermeer, Hals, and Steen. **Aria,** the interactive computer room, can create a personalized map of the museum to help you navigate its enormous and sometimes overwhelming collection. Don't miss the dollhouse exhibits, chronicling the boredom of rich married women in 18th-century Holland. (*On Stadhouderskade. Take tram #2 or 5 from the station.* ☎ 674 70 00. *Open daily 10am-5pm. ƒ17.50/€8.*)

THE NETHERLANDS

HEINEKEN MUSEUM. Every day, busloads of tourists discover that no beer is made in the Heineken Brewery. Plenty is served, however; your visit includes three beers and a souvenir glass. Above and beyond the freebies, the brewery itself has been transformed and trendily renamed the "Heineken Experience," an alcohol-themed amusement park. Guide yourself past holograms, virtual reality machines, and other multimedia treats. Highlights include the "bottle ride," which replicates the experience of becoming a Heineken beer itself, and a kiosk where you can email a picture of yourself on a Heineken bottlecap to envious friends. (*Stadhouder-skade 78, at the corner of Ferdinand Bolstr. Open Tu-Su 10am-6pm. 18+. ƒ11/€5.*)

REMBRANDTPLEIN AND ENVIRONS

VERSETZMUSEUM. The Dutch Resistance Museum chronicles the decimation of the Jewish population from 140,000 to 40,000 during the Holocaust. Interactive exhibits challenge viewers to decide what they would have done at the time of the Nazi invasion. Notes thrown to loved ones on trains to Auschwitz convey the extensive effort to keep networks alive, and a neighborhood tour tells how 150 Jewish people were successfully hidden in the lion cage in the Artis Zoo across the street. (*Plantage Kerklaan 61. Tram #9 or 20 to "Plantage Kerklaan"; #6 or 14 to "Plantage Midden-laan/Kerklaan." ☎ 620 25 35. Open Tu-F 10am-5pm, Sa-M noon-5pm; public holidays reduced hours; closed Jan. 1, Apr. 30, and Dec. 25. ƒ9/€4.10, ages 7-15 ƒ5/€2.75, under 7 free.*)

TUSCHINSKI THEATER. This fabulously ornate movie theater is one of Europe's first experiments in Art Deco. Although a group of drunk Nazis once got out of hand and started a fire in its cabaret, the theater miraculously survived WWII and has remained in operation for over 75 years. A ticket to one of their Hollywood feature screenings allows you to explore on your own; theater 1 is the main stage and has private boxes. (*Reguliersbreesstr., between Rembrandtspl. and Muntpl. ☎ 626 26 33, 0900 202 53 50 for movie listings. Tours in summer Su-M 10:30am; ƒ10/€4.55.*)

JOODS-PORTUGUESE SYNAGOGUE AND JOODS HISTORISCH MUSEUM. After being expelled from their countries in the 15th century, a sizable number of Spanish and Portuguese Jews established a community in Amsterdam and built the handsome **Joods-Portuguese Synagogue**. The Dutch government protected the building from Nazi torches by declaring it a national historic site. Across the street, the **Joods Historisch Museum (Jewish Historical Museum)**, housed in three connected former synagogues, traces the history of Dutch Jews. (*Jonas Daniel Meijerpl., at Waterloopl. Take tram #9, 14, or 20. Synagogue open daily 10am-4pm. ƒ10/€4.55. Museum open daily 11am-5pm. Closed on Yom Kippur. ƒ10/€4.55, ISIC holders ƒ5.50/€2.50.*)

OTHER SIGHTS. Thanks to the Dutch East India company, the **Museum of the Tropics (Tropenmuseum)** has artifacts from Asia, Africa, and Latin America, especially fine Indonesian art, and an engaging children's wing. (*Linnaeusstr. 2. Tram #9 and bus #22 stop right outside the museum; trams #3, 7, 10, and 14 also go to the museum, though not directly from Centraal Station. Open daily 10am-5pm; Dec. 5, 24, and 31 open 10am-3pm. ƒ15/€6.85, students ƒ10/€4.55.*) The stately Herengr. leads to the **Museum Willet-Holthuysen,** an richly decorated 18th-century canal house with a peaceful, pristine garden. (*Herengr. 605, between Reguliersgr. and Vijzelstr., 3min. from Rembrandtpl. Open M-F 10am-5pm, Sa-Su 11am-5pm. ƒ7.50/€3.40.*) Recently restored in 17th-century fashion, the **Museum het Rembrandt** was the home of Rembrandt until the city confiscated the house for taxes. It holds 250 of his etchings and dry points as well as many of his tools and plates. (*Jodenbreestr. 4-6, at the corner of the Oudeschans Canal. Take tram #9, 14, or 20. Open M-Sa 10am-5pm, Su 1-5pm. ƒ15/€6.80, ISIC holders ƒ10/€4.555.*)

RED-LIGHT DISTRICT

The Red Light District is surprisingly liveable. Pushers, porn shops, and live sex theaters do run a brisk business, but a surprising number of folks there have nothing to do with the debauchery, and in many ways the area is less outrageous and seedy than you might have expected. During the day, the Red Light District is comparatively flaccid, with tourists milling about and consulting their maps. As the sun goes down, people get braver, and the area pulses. **Sex shows** (ƒ10-50/€4.55-22.70)

THE NETHERLANDS

consist of costumed, disaffected couples repeatedly acting out your "wildest" (i.e., choreographed) dreams, and red neon marks houses of legalized ill repute, where prostitutes display themselves in windows. Cops from the police station on Warmoestr. patrol the district until midnight, but women may feel uncomfortable walking through this area, and all tourists are prime targets for pickpockets.

OUR LORD IN THE ATTIC. A secret enclave of virtue and piety hides in the 17th-century **Museum Amstelkring, Ons' Lieve Heer op Solder** ("Our Lord in the Attic"), where a Catholic priest, forbidden to practice his faith in public during the Reformation, established a surprisingly grand chapel in the attic. *(Oudezijds Voorburgwal 40, at the corner of Oudezijds Armstr., 5min. from the station. Open M-Sa 10am-5pm, Su and holidays 1-5pm. ƒ10/€4.55; students ƒ6/€2.75.)*

THE VICES. For a historical, chemical, and agricultural breakdown of the all the wacky tobacky you've been smelling, drop by the informative **Hash Hemp Marijuana Museum.** Though the museum collection is roughly 50% pro-pot pamphlets, posters, and propaganda for cannabis reform in the U.S., the grow-room in back reminds you that you're still in Amsterdam. *(Odezijds Achterburwal 130. Open daily 11am-10pm. ƒ12.50/€5.70. Seeds ƒ20-275/€9.10-124.80.)* See sex in every way you dreamed possible (and many you didn't) at the **Amsterdam Sex Museum,** which showcases an "only in Amsterdam" collection of erotic art and hard-core porn through the ages, including images of an 18th-century female masturbation machine and copies of the Kama Sutra. *(Damrak 18, near the station. Open daily 10am-11:30pm. 18+. ƒ4.95/€2.25.)*

OTHER SIGHTS. The area around the Red Light District (the oldest part of the city) contains some of Amsterdam's most interesting buildings. Amsterdam's former town hall, **Koninklijk Palace** *(Dam 1; ☎ 620 40 60, call for exact opening hours),* is a symbol of 17th-century commercialism; the stunning **Magna Plaza Mall** next door is the corresponding 20th-century's monument. *(Open Su-M 11am-7pm, Tu-Sa 9:30am-9pm.)*

THE JORDAAN

When you're through with the museums, lose the hordes in the narrow streets of the Jordaan, built as an artisan district in the Golden Age. Bounded roughly by Prinsengr., Brouwersgr., Marnixstr., and Lauriersgr., it's lined with cafes, galleries, and chocolate shops and is possibly the prettiest and most peaceful area in the city. You can also take refuge from the tourist mobs and seamy streets in **Begijnhof,** a beautiful grassy courtyard surrounded by 18th-century buildings between Kalverstr. and the Spui. *(Open daily 10am-5pm. Free.)*

ANNE FRANK HUIS. A visit to the Anne Frank House is a must for everyone, whether or not you've read the famous diary. The museum chronicles the two years the Frank family and four other Jews spent hiding in the annex of a warehouse on the Prinsengr. The rooms are no longer furnished, but personal objects in display cases and text panels with excerpts from the diary bring the story of the eight inhabitants to life, and the magazine clippings and photos that Anne used to decorate her room still hang on the wall. Footage of interviews with Otto Frank, Miep Gies (who supplied the family with food and other necessities), and childhood friends of Anne provide further information and details. *(Prinsengr. 267. Trams #13, 14, 17, or 20 to Westermarkt. Open Apr.-Aug. daily 9am-9pm; Sept.-Mar. 9am-7pm. Last admission 30min. before closing. Closed on Yom Kippur. ƒ12.50/€5.70, ages 10-17 ƒ5/€2.30.)* While you're there, check out the **Homomonument,** in front of the Westerkerk at the banks of the canal, a memorial to those persecuted for their sexual orientation.

ELSEWHERE IN AMSTERDAM

MARKETS. An open-air art market takes place every Sunday in the **Spui,** where local and international artists regularly present their work; a book market occasionally yields rare editions and 17th-century Dutch romances. *(Art market open Mar.-Dec. daily 10am-6pm. Book market open F 10am-6pm.)* Pick up bulbs at the flower market, **Bloemenmarkt** *(open daily 8am-8pm),* or practice bargaining at famous flea market on **Waterlooplein.** *(Open M-Sa 9am-5pm.)*

♫ ENTERTAINMENT

Amsterdam in the summertime is like a new love affair: often alluring, sometimes confusing, but always deliciously entertaining. The **Amsterdams Uit Buro (AUB)**, Leidsepl. 26, is stuffed with fliers, pamphlets, and guides to help you sift through current events; pick up the free monthly *UITKRANT* at any AUB office to see what's on. The AUB also sells tickets and makes reservations for just about any cultural event in the city. (☎ 09 00 01 91, ƒ0.75/€0.35 per min.; www.uitlijn.nl. Open F-W 10am-6pm, Th 10am-9pm.) The **VVV's** theater desk, Stationspl. 10, can also make reservations for cultural events. (Open M-Sa 10am-5pm.) The monthly *Day by Day* (ƒ2.50/€1.35), available from the tourist office, provides comprehensive cultural listings. If you're still thirsty for more, pick up *Shark* (online at www.underwater-amsterdam.com; print versions available at the AUB and throughout the city), for comprehensive listings for clubs, squats, concerts, films, and gay events.

CONCERTS

In the summer, the Vondelpark Openluchttheater hosts free performances of all sorts every Wednesday through Sunday. (☎ 673 14 99; www.openluchttheater.nl.) The **Royal Concertgebouw Orchestra,** on Van Baerlestr., is one of the world's finest. Take tram #316 to "Museumplein." (☎ 671 83 45. Tickets from ƒ14/€6.35. Guided tours Su at 9:30am; ƒ7.75/€3.55. Ticket office open daily 10am-7pm.)

FILM AND THEATER

Check out the free www.movieguide.nl for movie listings. When you're in the Vondelpark, head left from the main entrance on Stadhouderskade to see what's on at the stately **Filmmuseum** independent movie theater. (☎ 589 14 00. Info center open M-F from 10am; Sa-Su box office opens 1hr. prior to first showing. ƒ12.50/€5.70, students ƒ10/€4.55.) **The Movies,** Harlemmerstr. 159, is the city's oldest movie theater. (☎ 624 57 90. Open M-Tu and Th 4:15-10:15pm, W 2-10:15pm, F 4:15pm-12:30am, Sa 2pm-12:30am, Su 11:30am-10:15pm.)

▐ COFFEESHOPS AND SMART SHOPS

COFFEESHOPS

Yes, the rumors are true: marijuana and hashish have been decriminalized in The Netherlands. Coffeeshops sell pot or hash or will let you buy a drink and smoke your own stuff. Look for the green and white "Coffeeshop BCD" sticker that means that the shop is reputable. Although Amsterdam is known as the **hash** capital of the world, **marijuana** is increasingly popular. You can legally possess up to 5g of marijuana or hash (the previous 30g limit was reduced in response to foreign criticism). Pick up a free copy of the *BCD Official Coffeeshop Guide* for the pot-smoker's map of Amsterdam. For info on the legal ins and outs, call the **Jellinek clinic** at 570 23 55. **Never buy drugs from street dealers.** Don't get too caught up in Amsterdam's narcotic quirk; use common sense, and remember that any experimentation with drugs can be dangerous. If you choose to indulge, you will find that coffeeshops carry a range of products, described below. When you move from one coffeeshop to another, it is courteous to buy a drink in the next coffeeshop even if you already have weed in your pouch. Never smoke pot on the street; it's considered offensive.

SPACECAKES, SPACESHAKES, AND SPACE SWEETS. These are cakes and sweets made with hash or weed; hash chocolate, popsicles, and bonbons are also available. Because they need to be digested, they take longer to affect you and longer to rinse out; they produce a body stone that can take up to an hour to start.

HASH. Hash comes in two varieties, black (like Afghani and Nepali) and blonde (like Moroccan); black tends to be heavier and hits harder. It's grown at high elevations in the mountains; the higher the elevation, the better the hash.

MARIJUANA. Any weed with white in its name, such as white widow, white butterfly, or white ice, is guaranteed to be strong. As with alcohol, take it easy so you don't pass out. The Dutch tend to mix tobacco with their pot, so joints are harsher on your lungs; ask at coffeeshops if pre-rolled joints are rolled with tobacco or pure cannabis. Dutch marijuana costs ƒ12-20/€5.45-9.10 per g., ƒ25-30/€11.35-13.65 per bag; buy just one gram at a time. Staff at coffeeshops are used to explaining the different kinds of pot on the menu to tourists. Most places will supply rolling papers and filter tips. Almost no one smokes out of pipes, and while some places provide bongs, usually only tourists use them.

SMART SHOPS

Also legal are **smart shops,** which peddle a variety of **"herbal enhancers"** and **hallucinogens** that walk the line between soft and hard drugs. Some shops are alcohol-free. **All hard drugs are illegal** and possession is treated as a serious crime.

MAGIC MUSHROOMS. These start to work after 30-60min. and act on your system for 4-8hr., often causing panic or a faster heartbeat. Never look for mushrooms in the wild and never buy from a street dealer; it's extremely difficult to tell the difference between poisonous mushrooms and hallucinogenic mushrooms. Don't mix hallucinogens such as shrooms with alcohol; if you have a bad trip, **call 122** to go to the hospital or ask someone for help—you won't be arrested, and Amsterdam residents have probably seen it all before.

WHERE TO GO...

▨**Abraxas,** J. Roelensteeg 12-14 (☎625 57 63). One of the swankiest coffeeshops in Amsterdam. Full palette of hash and weed in a casual, no-pressure atmosphere. 20min. free **Internet** with a drink. Open daily 10am-1am.

▨**Siberie,** Brouwersgr. 11 (☎623 59 09). Close to Centraal Station, this quality coffeeshop still brings in regulars and locals. Wide selection of weed and hash from around the world. Open Su-Th 11am-11pm, F-Sa 11am-midnight.

▨**The Rookies,** Korte Leidsedwarsstr. 145-147 (☎428 31 25). A hustling, bustling, rustling crowd of young folks—locals and travelers alike—pack into this lively coffeehouse even on weeknights. All bags, such as the potent house specialty "Rookie Skunk," sold in ƒ25/€11.40 increments. Open Su-Th 10am-1am, F-Sa 10am-3am.

Hill Street Blues, Warmoesstr. 52. From Centraal Station, go south on Damrak, then turn right on Brugsteeg, then left on Warmoesstr.; it'll be about a block down on the left. Plenty of good deals on quality pot (such as the Hill Street Special; ƒ16/€7.25 per g.) and a party-intensive atmosphere. Open Su-Th 9am-1am, F-Sa 9am-3am.

Freeland, Lange Niezel 27 (☎627 32 79). Murals feature giraffes sharing space with heavy-lidded Grecian deities; portraits show Rembrandt and the Mona Lisa smoking fatties. Heavy-hitting "Bubble Gum" weed ƒ25/€11.35 for 1g. Space cakes ƒ8/€3.65, space fruitshakes ƒ10/€4.55. Open daily 9:30am-1am.

The Bold Man Smoke Supplies, Oude Hoogstr. 35-37 (☎625 49 22). Bongs, pipes, and all hardware you might need to fly sky-high. Open M-Sa 10am-10pm, Su reduced hours.

The Bulldog, Oudezijds Voorburgwal 90. The most famous of Amsterdam's coffeeshop chains set up its 1st shop here in the Red Light District in 1975. Grass and hash min. purchase ƒ25/€11.35. Open daily 9am-1am.

Elements of Nature, Warmoesstr. 54 (☎626 93 60), Warmoesstr. 97 (☎620 79 08), Kolksteeg 4 (☎620 39 05), Amstelstr. 17 (☎428 26 66), and Haringpakkerssteeg 11-13 (☎421 58 85). A large smart shop chain that sells a wide range of products from 'shrooms to sex stimulants. Open daily 11am-10pm.

Kadinsky, Rosmarijnsteeg 9 (☎624 70 23), near the intersection of Spui and Nieuwezijds Voorburgwal. Stylish place hidden off an alley near Spui. Weekly deals on weed and hashish (from ƒ20/€9.10 per g.). Joints ƒ5/€2.30. Open daily 10am-1am.

Conscious Dreams Kokopelli, Warmoestr. 12 (☎421 70 00). Books, lava lamps, chill-out space, and a knowledgeable staff that includes a neurophysician and biologist. Herbal X ƒ18-30/€8.20-13.60. 'Shrooms ƒ25/€11.35 for happy/funny effect, ƒ35/€15.90 for real trippy. If you want the most powerful trip of all, try *salvia* (0.5g costs ƒ50/€22.70), but discuss it with the staff first. Open daily 11am-10pm.

THE NETHERLANDS

Barney's Coffeeshop, Haarlemmerstr. 102 (☎625 97 61). Popular spot known for its friendly staff and amazing breakfast. Locals praise the consistently high quality of smokeable goods. Pot ƒ12.50-21.50/€5.70-9.80 per g; hash ƒ10-60/€4.55-27.25 per g. Joints ƒ7.50/€3.40 each, ƒ32.50/€14.75 for 5. Open daily 7am-8pm.

Blue Velvet, Haarlemmerstr. 64 (☎627 73 29). White and ice-blue environs feel as cool as they look. Beer ƒ3-4/€1.40-1.85. Joints ƒ6-8/€2.75-3.65. **Internet** ƒ2.50/€1.15 per 15min. Open Su-Th 10am-1am, F-Sa 10am-2am.

La Tertulia, Prinsengr. 312. Defies coffeeshop preconceptions with its big tropical plants, flowers, and shelves full of board games around an indoor waterfall. Rolled joints ƒ5/€2.25. Brownies ƒ8.50/€3.90. Open Tu-Sa 11am-7pm.

Stix, Utrechtstr. 21, a block south of Rembrandtpl. Locals chill to cool jazz in this stylish, sophisticated coffeeshop. House blends of weed pack the strongest kick (ƒ10-28/€4.55-12.70 per g). Pre-rolled joints ƒ6-9/€2.75-4.10. Open daily 11am-1am.

The Other Side, Regulierdwarsstr. 6 (☎421 10 14). Friendly, active coffeeshop popular with the gay scene. The disco ball is ideal for stoned contemplation. Bags sold in increments of ƒ25/€11.35, ƒ50/€22.75, and ƒ100/€45.45) Open daily 11am-1am.

The Noon, Zieseniskade 22, from Leidsepl., head east on Kl. Gartmanpints, then cross to the south side of Lijnbaansgr. and continue for about 1 block. Sawdust-strewn floor, candlelit interior, and skull motif defy thematic explanation. Weed and pot ranges from the standard to the extremely powerful; the "Blue Berry Ice" won the Cannabis Cup, but it'll cost you (1g for ƒ60/€27.25, 5g for ƒ215/€97.55). Open daily 11am-10pm.

Tatanka, Korte Leidsedwarsstrat 151A (☎770 38 58). Gorgeous 2-story feels as much like a museum as a smartshop. Range of goods includes 'shrooms and smart drugs, as well as sterling silver and turquoise jewelry. Staff can tune you into whatever hallucinogen intrigues you. Buy 4 packs of 'shrooms, get 1 free. Open daily 11am-10pm.

ⓢ NIGHTLIFE

CAFES AND BARS

Amsterdam's finest cafes are the old, dark, wood-paneled *bruine cafes* (brown cafes) of the **Jordaan,** many of which have outdoor seating lining the canal on **Prinsengracht. Leidseplein** is the liveliest nightspot, with loud coffeeshops, loud bars, and tacky clubs galore. **Rembrandtsplein** is the place to watch soccer and sing with drunk revelers. Gay bars line **Reguliersdwarsstraat,** which connects Muntpl. and Rembrandtspl., and **Kerkstraat,** five blocks north of Leidsepl.

Durty Nelly's Pub, Warmoesstr. 115-117. From Centraal Station, go south on Damrak, turn right on Brugsteeg, and then right on Warmoesstr. Irish pub on the edge of the Red Light District. Mean pint of Guinness ƒ10/€4.55. Open Su-Th 9am-1am, F-Sa 9am-3am; kitchen open Tu-Th noon-midnight, F-M 9am-3am.

Cafe Heffer, Oudebrugsteeg 7, at Beursstr. The Heffer blends pop music with excellent Dutch and Belgian brews (ƒ5-8/€2.30-3.65). Open daily 9am-3am.

The Tara, Rokin 85-89. Vast Irish-themed watering hole with a maze-like interior and plenty of cozy, candlelit corners. Slightly older crowd gets raucous on weekends. DJs and/or bands F-Sa. Beer ƒ5/€2.30. Open Su-Th 11am-1am, F-Sa 11am-3am.

Belgique, Gravenstr. 2, between Niewendijk and Nieuwezijds Voorburgwal. Tons of high-quality (and high-alcohol) brew. Open Su-Th 3pm-midnight, F-Sa noon-3am.

De Blauwe Druife (The Blue Grape), Harlemmerstr. 91, at Binnen Bowers Straat. This cafe has been popular with locals since 1733. Heineken (ƒ3.50/€2), de Koninck (ƒ4.50/€2.05), and WieckseWitte (ƒ4.50/€2.05) on tap. Open daily noon-1am.

Café 't Smalle, Egelantiersgr. 12, at the corner of Prinsengr. Intimate bar founded in 1780. Famous pea soup ƒ8.50/€3.90. Open Su-Th noon-12:15am, F-Sa noon-2am.

Lux, Marnixstr. 403. Seconds away from the Leidsepl. but lightyears away from its usual cheesiness. Benches, coffee tables, and kooky lamps give the place a 70s feel. Beer ƒ4/€1.85, vodka ƒ7.50/€3.40. Open Su-Th 8pm-3am, F-Sa 8pm-4am. Cash only.

Cafe de Koe, Marnixstr. 381. A relaxed crowd, rock music, and slightly haphazard decor. Beer from ƒ3.75/€1.70, liquor from ƒ7.50/€3.40. Daily special ƒ17.50/€7.95. Cafe open M-Th 4pm-1am, F-Sa 3pm-3am, Su 3pm-1am. V/MC.

THE NETHERLANDS

Mr. Coco's, Thorbeckepl. 8-12. Loud rock music and a young, hard-drinkin', sexy-dancin' crowd. 2-for-1 drinks during Happy Hour (daily 5-6pm; F also noon-3pm). Open W 5pm-1am, Th noon-1am, F-Sa noon-3am.

Montmartre, Halvemaarsteg 17. Rococo interior bedecked with flowers and rich draperies houses the wildest parties in Amsterdam for men and the men they love. 2-for-1 beers at Happy Hour M-Th 6-10pm. Voted best gay bar in A'dam by gay mag *Gay Krant* 5 years running. Open Su 4pm-1am, M-Th 5pm-1am, F-Sa 4pm-3am.

Bamboo Bar, Lange Leidsedwarsstr. 64. *Noir* decorations, tribal masks, and tiki torches add up to a classy *and* hokey jungle motif. Open Su-Th 8pm-3am, F-Sa 10pm-4am.

Pirates, Korte Leidsedwarsstr. 129. Arr, mateys! Walk east from Leidsepl. along Korte Leidsedwarsstr. 1½ blocks to this famed alehouse where ye can imbibe grog (beer ƒ5/€2.30) and dance a jig (DJs spin pop Th-Sa). Open Su-W 9pm-3am, Th-Sa 9pm-4am.

Cafe De Jaren, Nieuwe Doelenstr. 20-22. From Muntpl., cross the Amstel and go straight ahead for ½ block; it'll be on the right.This cafe has a sophistication that doesn't quite go with its budget-friendly prices. Open Su-Th 10am-1am, F-Sa 10am-3am. V.

Absinthe, Nieuwezijds Voorburgwal 171. Recently remodeled and reborn, Absinthe draws a young, hip crowd. Lively bar serves shots of the fluorescent-green house drink (actually an absinthe variant); ƒ10/€4.55. Open Su-Th 8pm-3am, F-Sa until 4am.

NL Lounge, NZ Voorburgwal 169. Too cool for an outside sign, the trendy NL is the unmarked destination where slick, chic, sophisticated Amsterdam insiders come to mingle. Mixed drinks ƒ12-15/€5.45-6.80. No cover, but get there early on weekend nights or you'll have to wait in line. Open Su-Th 8pm-3am, F-Sa 8pm-4am.

W.F. Fockink, 31 Pijlsteeg, in Dam Square. Largely untouristed sight where they've been brewing famed *fockink* liqueurs for 400 years (ƒ4/€1.85). Open daily 3-9pm.

LIVE MUSIC

The **AUB** has the *Pop & Jazz Uitlijst* and fliers for other free concerts.

Bourbon Street Jazz & Blues Club, Leidsekruisstr. 6-8 (☎623 34 40). Head north on Leidsestr., then go east on Lange Leidsedwarsstr. and turn north on Leidsekruisstr. Blues, soul, funk, and rock bands. The Stones, B.B. King, and Sting all played here. Cover Su-Th ƒ3/€1.35, F-Sa ƒ5/€2.30. Open Su-Th 10pm-4am, F-Sa 10pm-5am.

Paradiso, Weteringschans 6-8 (☎626 45 21). When big-name punk, new-wave, and reggae bands come to Amsterdam, they almost always play here. See where Lenny Kravitz got his big break and the Stones taped their latest live album. Tickets ƒ10-50/€4.55-22.70. Membership ƒ5/€2.30.

Melkweg, Lijnbaasgr. 234a (☎624 17 77), in a warehouse off Leidsepl. Live bands, theater, films, dance shows, and an art gallery make for sensory overload. Club nights F-Sa 1-5am (cover ƒ10/€4.55). 1-month membership ƒ5/€2.27. Tickets ƒ5-50/€2.30-22.70. Box office open M-F 1-5pm, Sa-Su 4-6pm; until 7:30pm on show days.

Casablanca, Zeedijk 24-26 (☎625 56 85), between Oudezijds Kolk and Vredenburgersteeg. Though its heyday as *the* jazz bar in Amsterdam has faded, it's still one of the best spots to hear live jazz. Jazz only Su-W; DJ-hosted dance parties Th-Sa. No cover. Open Su-Th 8pm-3am, F-Sa 8pm-4am.

CLUBS AND DISCOS

Many clubs charge a membership fee in addition to normal cover, so the tab can be harsh. Be prepared for cocky doormen who love to turn away tourists; show up early or hope the bouncer thinks you're cute. A promised tip of ƒ10-20/€4.55-9.10 (left on your way out) may help you prove your worth. There are pricey discos aplenty on **Prinsengracht**, near **Leidsestraat**, and on **Lange Leidsedwarsstraat**. Gay discos line **Amstelstraat** and **Reguliersdwarsstraat** and cater almost exclusively to men. Pick up a wallet-sized *Clu* guide, free at cafes and coffeeshops, for a club map of the city, and *Gay and Night*, a free monthly magazine, for info on gay parties.

Cockring, Warmoestr. 90. From Centraal Station, head down Damrak, then left on Brugsteeg and right on Warmoesstr. It's 2 blocks down on the right; just look for the giant cockring. Something between a sex club and a disco; you can dance or get lucky. DJs spin nightly for a youngish crowd of studly men who readily doff clothing as things heat up. Dark room in the back where anything goes. Open Su-Th 9pm-4am, F-Sa 9pm-5am.

Item, Nieuwezijds Voorburgwal 163-165. Young, trendy, and tourist-oriented. Standard dance floor topped by an upstairs lounge. Cool bar with waterfall behind it. Cover ƒ20-28/€9.10-12.75. Open Su-Th 11pm-4am, F-Sa 11pm-5am.

Bep, Nieuwezijds Voorburgwal 260. Created in the image of the space-age bachelor pad, with fake stone walls and a glittery disco ball. Tiny, but very popular—the crowd of hipsters spills out onto the front patio. Open Su-Th noon-1am, F-Sa noon-3am.

West Pacific, Polonceaukade 3, at the Westergasfabriekterrein. Out past the Westerpark, this is where "real" Amsterdammers head to party. DJ-driven house music dominates. Membership may be required on the most popular nights; apply beforehand at the restaurant. Cover ƒ5/€2.30. Music starts at 11pm; goes till 1am Su-Th, 3am F-Sa.

Mazzo, Rozengr. 114. Even the bouncers are nice here! Black walls, colored spotlights, pumping music and a large bar in the back. Mixed drinks ƒ11/€5. Cover ƒ10-20/€4.55-9.10; Sa ƒ20/€9.10. Open W-Th and Su 11pm-4am, F-Sa 11pm-5am.

Escape, Rembrandtpl. 11. Massive venue where differently themed clubs host Amsterdam's most popular nightclubs. 2 floors with 4 bars (including a champagne bar staffed by particularly beautiful girls), a chillout space upstairs, and a huge, sensually charged dance floor downstairs with house, trance, disco, and dance classics. Be sober, well-dressed, and female to increase your chances of entry. Beer ƒ5/€2.30; spirits ƒ9/€4.10; mixed drinks ƒ14/€6.35. Open Th-Su 11pm-4am, F-Sa 11pm-5am.

The Ministry, Reguliersdwarsstr. 12. Very popular and upscale enough to be classy and hip, but without any attitude or exclusivity. Cover ƒ12.50-25/€5.70-11.35; F-Sa tends to be more expensive. Open Su-Th 11pm-4am, F-Sa 11pm-5am.

Vive La Vie, Amstelstr. 7, just east of Rembrandtpl. Fun, friendly lesbian bar where the emphasis is on good times, good folks, and good drinking, all without a shred of attitude. No dance floor, but that doesn't stop the ladies—and a few select male friends—from grooving to feel-good pop anthems. Open Su-Th 3pm-1am, F-Sa 3pm-3am.

⚡ DAYTRIPS FROM AMSTERDAM

EDAM ☎ 0299

Bus #110, 112, or #114 from Centraal Station (30min., 7 strips).

When you tire of free-living Amsterdam, discover cute cottages, peaceful parks, and lots of cheese and clogs in Edam. Farmers still bring their famed cheese to **market** in the town center by horse and boat. (July-Aug. W 10am-12:30pm.) The 15th-century **Grote Kerk,** Grote Kerkstr., is the largest three-ridged church in Europe and has exquisite stained-glass windows and a timber roof made from Dutch East India Company ships. (Open May-Sept. daily 2-5:30pm. Free.) The VVV **tourist office,** Dampl. 1, in the old town hall, finds accommodations. From the bus stop, walk down Schepenmakersdijk up to the white bridge called Kwakelbrug, then follow Lingerzijde to the center of town. (☎ 31 51 25. Open Nov.-Mar. M-Sa 10am-3pm; Mar.-Nov. M-Sa 10am-5pm; July-Aug. also open Su 1-4:30pm.) Rent a bike at **Ronald Schot,** Grote Kerkstraat 7/9 (☎ 37 21 55. ƒ12/€5.45 per day, ƒ8.50/€3.90 per half-day. Open M 1-6pm, T-Th 8:30am-6pm, F 8:30am-9pm, Sa 8:30am-5pm). **Hof van Holland,** Lingerzijde 69, prepares cheap and delectable Dutch fare, some vegetarian. (Open Tu-F 10:30am-10:30pm, Sa-Su 11am-10:30pm.) For an authentic cheese experience, follow the bikepath out of Edam toward Volendam to the cheese farms at **Alida Hoeve,** where cheese is still made by hand. (Open daily 9:30am-4:30pm.)

ZAANSE SCHANS ☎ 075

From Centraal Station, take the train to "Koog Zaandijk"; follow signs to Zaanse Schans.

A museum village created in 1960, Zaanse Schans features houses collected from the Zaan region and restored to their original splendor. Visit the **Museum van het Nederlandse Uurwerk (Museum of the Dutch Clock),** Kalverringdijk 3, to view fascinating timepieces, including the oldest working pendulum clock in the world. (Open Mar.-Oct. daily 10am-5pm. ƒ5/€2.30.) Learn about wooden clogs and watch craftspeople create them at **Klompenmakerij de Zaanse Schans,** Kraaienest 4. (Open daily 8am-6pm.) **In de Gecroonde Duijvekater,** Zeilenmakerspad 4, operated as a bakery from the 1750s to the 1950s. (Open Tu-Su 10am-5pm.) The teensy **Museum Het Noorderhuis,** Kalverringdijk 17, boasts original costumes from the Zaan region in two reconstructed rooms. (Open Mar.-June Tu-Su 10am-5pm; July-Aug. daily 10am-5pm; Sept.-Oct. Tu-Su 10am-5pm; Nov.-Feb. Sa-Su 10am-5pm. ƒ2.20/€1.) **Cheesefarm Catharina Hoeve,** Zeilenmakerspad 5, offers free bite-sized samples and tours of its workshop. (Open Mar.-Oct. daily 8am-6pm; Nov.-Feb. 8:30am-5pm.) The village is also home to several working windmills; **Oil Mill "De Zoeker,"** Kalverringdijk 31 (open Mar.-Aug. daily 9:30am-4:30pm) and **Pigment Mill "De Kat,"** Kalverringdijk 29 (open Apr.-Oct. daily 9am-5pm; Nov.-Mar. Sa-Su 9am-5pm), are open to the public. The **Visitors Center,** Schansend 1, is in an 18th-century warehouse. (☎616 82 18. Open Apr.-Aug. daily 8:30am-6:30pm; Oct.-Mar. 8:30am-5pm.)

HAARLEM ☎023

Surrounded by fields of tulips and daffodils and ornamented with late-medieval and Renaissance façades, it's easy to see why big-city folk escape to nearby Haarlem. Its center (the **Grote Markt**) pulsates with cafes and coffeeshops, and its narrow cobblestoned streets are filled with exquisite boutiques. To reach Grote Markt from the train station, head down Kruisweg; at the Nieuwe Gracht, Kruisweg turns into Kruisstr., which then becomes Barteljorisstr. Along the way, check out the pleasant courtyards of the **Hofje van Oirschot,** where Kruisstr. becomes Barteljorisstr.; it's one of Haarlem's loveliest *hofjes* (almshouses for elderly women). (Open daily 10am-5pm. Free.) In the corner of Grote Markt stands the glorious **Stadhuis** (Town Hall), featuring a patchwork of 14th- through 17th-century architectural styles. The breathtaking **Grote Kerk,** at the opposite end of the Grote Markt, houses the mammoth, floor-to-ceiling Müller organ which an 11-year-old Mozart once played. (Open M-Sa 10am-4pm. ƒ2.75/€1.25.) From the church, turn left onto Damstr., and follow it until Spaarne to the **Teyler's Museum,** Spaarne 16, the Netherlands' oldest museum. It features an eclectic assortment of scientific instruments, fossils, paintings, and drawings, including works by Raphael, Michelangelo, and Rembrandt. (Open Tu-Sa 10am-5pm, Su noon-5pm. ƒ10/€4.55, students ƒ5/€2.30.) The **Frans Hals Museum,** Groot Heiligland 62, pays homage to Haarlem's most famous son; turn right from the Teyler's, walk along the canal, turn right onto Kampverst, and turn left onto Groot Heiligland. (Open M-Sa 11am-5pm, Su noon-5pm. ƒ10/€4.55.)

Reach Haarlem from Amsterdam either by **train** (20min., ƒ6.50/€2.95) from Centraal Station or by **bus** #80 from Marnixstr., near Leidsepl. (2 per hr., 2 strips). **Night buses** cruise from Leidsepl. to Haarlem's city center (#286; every 40min. until 5am F- Sa). The VVV **tourist office,** Stationspl. 1, sells maps (ƒ9/€4.10) and finds private rooms (from ƒ38/€17.25) for a ƒ10/€4.55 fee. (☎(0900) 616 16 00. Open M-F 9:30am-5:30pm, Sa 10am-2pm; summer also open Sa 2-4pm.) The lively **NJHC-Hostel Haarlem (HI),** Jan Gijzenpad 3, is 3km from the train station. Take bus #2 (dir.: Haarlem-Nord) and get off at "Jeugdeherberg" or tell the driver your destination. (☎537 37 93. Popular bar. Bike rental available. Breakfast included. Key deposit ƒ25/€11.35 or passport. 2- to 8-person dorms ƒ37-ƒ49/€16.80-22.25. Nonmember surcharge ƒ3-8/€1.40-3.65.) **Hotel Carillon,** Grote Markt 27, is ideally located. (☎531 05 91. Breakfast included. Reception and bar 7:30am-1am. Singles ƒ60-110/€27.25-49.95; doubles ƒ110-142/€49.95-64.45.) To **camp** at **De Liede,** Lie Over 68, take bus #2 (dir.: Zuiderpolder) and tell the driver your destination, then walk 10min. from the bus stop. (☎535 86 66. ƒ6/€2.75 per person, ƒ6/€2.75 per tent; in summer add ƒ2.50/€1.15 tax.) Try cafes in the Grote Markt for cheap meals. **Grill-Pannekoekhuis De Smikkel,** Kruisweg 57, serves over 50 varieties of plump, buttery pancakes (ƒ12-20/€5.45-9.10), as well as grilled dishes. (Open M-Sa noon-10pm, Su 4-10pm.)

◪ DAYTRIPS FROM HAARLEM: ZANDVOORT, AALSMEER, AND LISSE.

Near Haarlem, the seaside town of **Zandvoort-aan-Zee** boasts several **nude beach clubs,** along with more modest sands for the bashful and family-oriented. To get to the shore from the train station, follow the signs to the Raadhuis, and from there head down Kerkstraat. A 30min. walk to the right of Zandfoort Beach along the boulevard will bring you to the jet-setty beach of **Blomendaal,** where the beach clubs **The NL Republic, Zomers, Solaris,** and **Woodstock** are quite popular. The VVV **tourist office,**

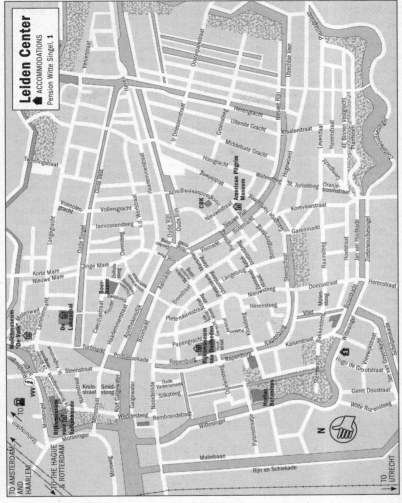

Leiden Center

▲ ACCOMMODATIONS
Pension Witte Singel, **1**

Schoolpl. 1, near the town square, sells a lodgings guide for ƒ2/€0.95; follow signs from the station. (☎(023) 571 79 47. Hours vary, generally open M-Sa 9am-5pm.) **Trains** arrive in Zandvoort from Haarlem (10min.; round-trip ƒ6/€2.75).

In **Aalsmeer,** 90 million flowers are auctioned every day at the **Bloemenveiling Aalsmeer,** the world's largest flower auction. Arrive early to see the action. (Open M-F 7:30-11am.) From Haarlem's train station, take **bus** #140 (45min., every 30min.). From Amsterdam's Centraal Station, buses #77 and 172 (dir.: Naar Kudelstaart) also stop here every 30min.

In **Lisse,** the **Keukenhof** gardens become a kaleidoscope of color as over five million bulbs explode into life in late spring. (Open late-Mar. to mid-May daily 8am-7:30pm; Aug. to mid-Sept. 9am-6pm; last entry 6pm. ƒ21/€9.55.) The **Zwarte (Black) Tulip Museum,** Grachtweg 2a, details the history of tulip raising. (Open Tu-Su 1-5pm. ƒ4-6/€1.85-2.75.) Take **bus** #50 or 51 toward Lisse from the Haarlem train station; combo bus/museum tickets are available (ƒ21/€9.55). The VVV **tourist office** is at Grachtweg 53. (☎(0252) 41 42 62. Open M noon-5pm, Tu-F 9am-5pm, Sa 9am-4pm.)

THE NETHERLANDS

LEIDEN
☎ **071**

Rembrandt's birthplace, the site of the first **tulips,** and home to one of the oldest and most prestigious universities in Europe, Leiden brims with windmills, gated gardens, hidden walkways, and some exceptional museums. The Academy building shares a gate with the university's 400-year-old garden, the **Hortus Botanicus,** Rapenburg 73, where the first Dutch tulips were grown. Its grassy knolls alongside the **Witte Singel** canal make it an ideal picnic spot. (Open Mar.-Nov. daily 10am-6pm; Nov.-Feb. Su-F 10am-4pm. ƒ8/€3.65.) Across the footbridge from the main gate to Hortus Botanicus, the **Rijksmuseum van Oudheden** (National Antiquities Museum), Rapenburg 28, harbors the Egyptian Temple of Taffeh. (Open Tu-F 10am-5pm, Sa-Su noon-5pm. ƒ13.20/ €6; included in MJK.) The **Rijksmuseum voor Volkenkunde** (National Museum of Ethnology), Steenstr. 1, is one of the world's oldest anthropological museums, with fantastic artifacts from all over the globe, including a collection from the Dutch East Indies. (Open Tu--Su 10am-5pm. ƒ13.50/€6.15, students ƒ7.50/€3.40; included in MJK.) Scale steep staircases to inspect the innards of a functioning windmill at the **Molenmuseum ("De Valk"),** 2e Binnenvestgr. 1. (Open Tu-Sa 10am-5pm, Su 1pm-5pm. ƒ5/€2.30; included in MJK.) The **Museum De Lakenhal,** Oude Singel 32, exhibits works by Rembrandt and Jan Steen. (Open Tu-Sa 10am-5pm, Su noon-5pm. ƒ8/€3.65; included in MJK.) Learn about the pilgrims who found refuge in Leiden on their way to the New World at the **American Pilgrim Museum,** located in Leiden's oldest house at Beschuitsteeg 9. (Open W-Sa 1-5pm. ƒ3/€1.40 for extensive guided tour.)

Leiden is easily accessed by **train** from The Hague (20min., ƒ10/€4.55) or Amsterdam (30min., ƒ24/€10.90). The VVV **tourist office,** Stationsweg 2d, sells maps (ƒ2.50/€1.15) and walking tour brochures (ƒ1-4/€0.45-1.85), and finds **private rooms** (fee ƒ4.50/€2.50 for one person, ƒ3.50/€2 for each additional person). Head straight from the station and it'll be on your right after about three blocks; look for blue and white signs. (☎ (0900) 222 23 33. Open M-F 10am-6:30pm, Sa 10am-4:30pm; Apr., May, July, Aug. also open Su 11am-3pm.) The **Hotel Pension Witte Singel,** Witte Singel 80, 5min. from Hortus Botanicus, has immaculate rooms overlooking gardens and canals. Take bus #43 to Merenwijk and tell the driver your destination. (☎ 512 45 92. Singles ƒ60/€27.25; doubles ƒ93-120/€42.20-54.45.) Especially on weekend nights, locals and students pack into the popular **de Oude Harmonie,** Breestr. 16, just off Rapenburg. (Beer ƒ3-7/€1.40-3.20. Open Su-Th noon-1am, F-Sa 3pm-3am.) The **Super de Boer supermarket** is opposite the train station at Stationsweg 40. (Open M-F 7am-9pm, Sa 9am-8pm, Su noon-7pm.)

▶ **DAYTRIP FROM LEIDEN: NOORDWIJK.** Beautiful white-sand beaches lie 18km away from Leiden in the town of **Noordwijk.** In addition to many outdoor activities, Noordwijk features the **Space Expo,** Keperlaan 3, at the visitors' center for ESTEC (the European Space Agency's largest technical branch). The permanent exhibition attracts thousands of space fanatics each year with simulated rocket launches and interactive astronaut games. (ƒ15/€6.85. Open Tu-Su 10am-5pm.) To get to Noordwijk, take a bus from the Leiden Centraal Station (ƒ7.50/€3.40). The VVV **tourist office,** De Grent 8 (☎ (071) 361 93 21) has accommodations info. The **Flying Pig Beach Hostel,** Parallel Bvd. 208, is in the center of town. Take bus #40 or 42 for 20min. to the Lighthouse stop; the Pig will be in front of you. (☎ (071) 362 25 33. Bodyboard, surfboard, mountain bike, inline skate, and kite surf rental available. Horseback riding ƒ27.50/€12.50. **Internet.** Required key deposit ƒ25/€11.35. Reception 11am-midnight. Open Mar.-Oct. Dorms ƒ28-31/€12.70-14.10.) A variety of restaurants line **Hoofdstraat** near the beach. For cafes and bars, try **Koningin Wilhelmina Boulevard,** where most establishments overlook the North Sea.

THE HAGUE (DEN HAAG OR 'S GRAVENHAGE)
☎ **070**

William II moved the royal residence to The Hague in 1248, prompting the creation of parliament buildings, museums, and sprawling parks. The Dutch royal family still calls The Hague home, and their palaces are tucked among the shops, restaurants, and pubs. During the **North Sea Jazz Festival** (www.northseajazz.nl) in mid-July, the city draws world-class musicians and 50,000 swinging fans. For the rest of the year, The Hague is a buzzing government center where museum-gazing and embassy-visiting will likely define a stay in the central city. For snippets of Dutch politics, visit the **Binnenhof,** The Hague's Parliament complex. Guided tours leave from Binnenhof 8a and visit the 13th-century **Ridderzaal** (Hall of Knights) and the chambers of the States General. (Open M-Sa 10:15am-4pm. ƒ10/€4.55.) Don't miss the reflecting pool located beside the complex. Just outside the north entrance of the Binnenhof, the 17th-century **Mauritshuis,** Korte Vijverberg 8, features an impressive collection of Dutch paintings, including works by Rembrandt and Vermeer. (Open Tu-Sa 10am-5pm, Su 11am-5pm. ƒ15/€6.85; included in MJK.) The impressive modern art, fashion, and design collection at the **Gemeentemuseum,** Stadhouderslaan 41, proudly displays hometown boy Piet Mondrian's famous *Victory Boogie Woogie* as well as works by Monet, Ingres, Kandinsky, and Klee. Take tram #7 from Holland Spoor or bus #4 from Centraal Station. (Open Tu-Su 11am-5pm. ƒ15/€6.85; included in MJK.) Andrew Carnegie donated the **Peace Palace,** the opulent home of the International Court of Justice at Carnegiepl., 3min. on tram #7 or 8 north from the Binnenhof. (Tours M-F 10, 11am, 2, 3, 4pm. Book in advance through the tourist office. ƒ7.50/€3.40, children ƒ5/€2.30.)

Trains roll in from Amsterdam (50min., ƒ31/€14.10) and Rotterdam (25min., ƒ15/€6.85) to both of The Hague's major stations, Centraal Station (CS) and Holland Spoor (HS). CS is located right outside downtown; HS lies a few kilometers south of the city center but is quite convenient to the NJHC youth hostel. Trams #1, 9, and 12 connect the two stations. The VVV **tourist office,** Kon. Julianapl. 30, just outside the north entrance to CS and right next to the Hotel Sofitel, books rooms for a ƒ4/€1.85 fee and sells detailed city maps. (☎(0900) 340 35 05. Open M and Sa 10am-5pm, Tu-F 9am-5:30pm, Su 11am-5pm. Hotel booking computer available 24hr.) The **NJHC City Hostel,** Scheepmakerstr. 27, is conveniently located near HS; turn right from the station, follow the tram tracks, turn right at the big intersection, and Scheepmakerstr. is 3min. down on your right. From CS, take tram #1 (dir.: Delft), 9 (dir.: Vrederust), or 12 (dir.: Duindrop) to "Rijswijksepl." (2 strips); cross to the left in front of the tram, cross the big intersection, and Scheepmakerstr. is straight ahead. (☎315 78 78. In-house restaurant-bar. Breakfast included. Lockers ƒ3/€1.40 per day. Dorms ƒ42/€19.10; doubles ƒ80/€36.30; nonmembers add ƒ5/€2.30.) Budget takeaway places line **Lage Poten** and **Korte Poten** near the Binnenhof. For more decadent fare, take your meal on the outdoor patio at **Havana,** Buitenhof 19. (Beer ƒ3.50. Entrees ƒ22-28/€10-12.75. Open daily 10:30am-1am.) At **Los Argentinos,** just off Buitenhof on Kettingstr. 14, you can get a South American steak, french fries, and unlimited salad bar access for ƒ20/€9.10. (Open daily 3pm-midnight.) Groove to salsa and jazz at **De Pater** (☎345 08 42. Shows start at 10:30pm; call ahead for schedules. Open Tu-Sa 10pm-2am, Su 4:30pm-2am). If you crave more vibrant nightlife, prowl the Strandweg in nearby **Schevingenen** (see below).

Most foreign **embassies** are in The Hague: **Australia,** Carnegielaan 4, 2517 KH (☎310 82 00; open M-F 8:30am-4:55pm); **Canada,** Sophialaan 7, 2514 JP (☎311 16 00; open M-F 9am-12:45pm and 1:45-5:30pm); **Ireland,** 9 Dr. Kuyperstr., 2514 BA (☎363 09 93; call for hours); **New Zealand,** Carnegielaan 10, 2517 KH (☎346 93 24; open M-F 9am-12:30pm and 1:30-5:30pm); **South Africa,** Wassenaarseweg 40, 2596 CJ (☎392 45 01; open daily 9am-noon); **UK,** Lange Voorhout 10, 2514 ED (☎427 04 27; call for hours); **US,** Lange Voorhout 102, 2514 EJ (☎310 92 09; open M-F 8:15am-5pm).

🔁 DAYTRIP FROM THE HAGUE: SCHEVENINGEN. Just 5km from The Hague, **Scheveningen** (SCHAYVE-uhn-ing-un; so difficult to say that it was used as a code word by the Dutch in WWII) features family-oriented North Sea beaches by day and crazy dance parties by night. The **Strandweg** is the main drag along the beach, packed with restaurants and nightclubs. Fish vendors sell fresh cod, calamari, perch, and pike, as well as tasty *broodjes*. In the center of the Strandweg, the 100-year-old **Scheveningen Pier** houses music festivals and art exhibitions (www.pier.nl; entrance ƒ2.50/€1.15). The VVV **tourist office,** Gevers Deynootweg 1134, gives info on rooms and rents bikes. (☎(0900) 340 35 05; ƒ0.75/€0.35 per min. Open M 11am-6pm, Tu-F 9:30am-6pm, Sa 10am-5pm, Su 1-5pm.) The **Hotel De Stern,** Gevers Deynootweg 68, is just a few blocks from the beach. (☎(070) 350 48 00. Reception 7am-midnight. Singles ƒ64-74/€29.05-33.60; doubles ƒ117-142/€53.10-64.45. Cash only.)

THE NETHERLANDS

DELFT
☎ 015

To gaze out over Delft's lilied canals from one of its stone footbridges is to behold the very images that native Jan Vermeer immortalized on canvas over 300 years ago. Thursdays and Saturdays, when townspeople flood to the bustling market-place, are the best days to visit. Delft is renowned for its **Delftware,** the blue-on-white china developed in the 16th century to compete with the newly imported Chinese porcelain. Gawk at precious platters in the 17th-century factory **De Porceleyne Fles,** Rotterdamseweg 196, in southern Delft; take bus #63, 121, or 129 from the station to "Jaffalaan." A true-to-scale rendition of Rembrandt's *Nightwatch* awaits in the factory's working gallery and makes a good first stop in the city; walk to the end of Jaffalaan, bear left, and the factory is across the intersection. (Open Apr.-Oct. M-Sa 9am-5pm, Su 9:30am-5pm; Nov.-Mar. closed Su. Demonstrations every hr. ƒ5/ €2.30.) Built in 1381, the **Nieuwe Kerk** on the central Markt hosts the mausoleum of Dutch liberator William of Orange. Ascend the tower, as caretakers of the 48-bell carillon have for six centuries, for a view of old Delft. (Church open Apr.-Oct. M-Sa 9am-6pm; Nov.-Mar. M-F 11am-4pm, Sa 11am-5pm. ƒ4.50/€2.05. Tower closes 1hr. earlier. ƒ3.50/€1.60.) The **Oude Kerk,** Heilige Geestkerkhof 25, is home to the tombs of Vermeer and scientific innovator Antoni van Leeuwenhoek. Its tower leans a staggering 2m out of line. (Open Apr.-Oct. M-Sa 9am-6pm; Nov.-Mar. M-F 11am-4pm, Sa 11am-5pm. ƒ4.50/€2.05.) **Het Prinsenhof,** Sint Agathapl. 1, off Oude Singel, was William's abode until a fanatic French Catholic hired by Spain's Phillip II assassinated him in 1584; today it houses paintings, tapestries, and pottery. Don't miss the bullet holes that remain in the wall from the prince's murder. (Open Tu-Sa 10am-5pm, Su 1-5pm. ƒ7.50/€3.40.) **Rondvaart Delft,** Koornmarkt 113, offers canal rides and rents water bikes. (☎212 63 85. Open mid-Mar. to Oct. daily 9:30am-6pm.)

   Trains arrive from: Amsterdam (1hr., ƒ17.75/€8.05); The Hague (15min., ƒ4/€1.85); Leiden (30min., ƒ6.50/€2.95). For train or **bus** info, call (0900) 92 92. The VVV **tourist office,** Markt 85, has hiking, cycling, and walking route maps, and books rooms (ƒ3.50/ €1.60 fee plus 10% deposit). From the station, cross the bridge, turn left, turn right at the first light, and follow signs to the Markt. (☎213 01 00. Open Oct.-Mar. M-Sa 9am-5:30pm; Apr.-Sept. also open Su 11am-3pm.) To reach the unmarked **Van Leeuwen,** Achterom 143, walk out straight from the station, cross four canals, and turn right on Achterom. (☎212 37 16. Singles ƒ35/€15.90; doubles ƒ70/€31.80.) Additional affordable hotels are around the Markt, including the cozy **Pension Van Domburg,** Voldersgr. 24., run by an older husband and wife above their cigar shop. (☎212 30 29. Doubles ƒ75/€34.) To **camp** on Korftlaan in the **Delftse Hout** recreation area, take bus #64 from the station to "Aan't Korft." (☎213 00 40. Reception May to mid-Sept. 9am-10pm; mid-Sept. to Apr. 9am-6pm. ƒ30/€13.65 per tent.) Restaurants line **Volderstraat** and **Oude Delft. Kleyweg's Stads-Koffyhuis,** Oude Delft 133-135, with a terrace on the canal, serves sandwiches (ƒ4-8/€1.85-3.65) that were voted the best *broodjes* in The Netherlands. (Open M-F 9am-7pm, Sa 9am-8pm.) Down the street, **Stads Pan,** Oude Delft 113-115, has savory pancakes for ƒ5-17/€2.30-7.75. (Open Tu-Su 11am-9pm.)

ROTTERDAM
☎ 010

After Rotterdam was bombed in 1940, experimental architects replaced the rubble with striking (some say strikingly ugly) buildings, creating an urban, industrial conglomerate. Artsy and innovative, yet desolate and almost decrepit in its hypermodernity, Rotterdam today is a European cultural center. During the **Festival of Architecture** in June, many remarkable edifices are open to the public. (Info ☎436 99 09.) For a dramatic example of Rotterdam's eccentric designs, heavily influenced by the de Stijl school, check out the **Kijk-Kubussen** (cube houses) by Piet Blom. Take tram #1 or the metro to "Blaak," turn left, and look up. (Open Mar.-Dec. daily 11am-5pm; Jan.-Feb. F-Su 11am-5pm. ƒ3.50/€1.60.) Try to decipher the architectural madness at the **Netherlands Architecture Institute,** Museumpark 25. (Open Tu 10am-9pm, W-Sa 10am-5pm, Su 11am-5pm. ƒ7.50/€3.40.) Refresh yourself with Rubens, van Gogh, Rembrandt, Rubinstein, Lichtenstein, Rothko, and Magritte across the street at the **Museum Boijmans van Beuningen,** Museumpark 18-20. (Metro: Eendractspl., or take tram #5. Open Tu-F 10am-5pm, Su 11am-5pm. ƒ12.50/€5.70.) The stately

THE NETHERLANDS

Schielandshuis (Historical Museum), Korte Hoogstr. 31, recounts the history of the city. (Open Tu-F 10am-5pm, Sa-Su 11am-5pm. ƒ6/€2.75.) Opposite the plaza lies the powerful Zadkine, or the **Monument for the Destroyed City,** a statue of an anguished man with a hole in his heart that memorializes the 1940 bombing raid. **Museumpark** features sculptures, mosaics, and monuments designed by some of the world's foremost artists and architects; take tram #5 to reach this outdoor exhibit. (Free.) The largest mechanical organ in Europe is in **St. Laurenskerk,** Grote Kerk Plein 15. (Metro: Blaak. Open Tu-Sa 10am-4pm. Free.) Even shopping is a hyper-modern experience in the **Koopgoot (Shopping Drain),** an underground complex that includes shops, eateries, and entertainment facilities. At the **City Centre Market,** the biggest open-air market in The Netherlands, endless rows of stalls offer antiques, fresh fish and fruit, and more. (Metro: Blaak. Open Tu and Su 9am-5pm, F from noon.)

   Trains run to: Amsterdam (1½hr., ƒ23/€10.45); The Hague (20min., ƒ7.50/€3.40); Utrecht (45min., ƒ15/€6.85). For info on **ferries** to Hull, England, see p. 723. The VVV **tourist office,** Coolsingel 67, opposite the Stadhuis, books rooms for a ƒ3.50/€2 fee. (☎403 40 65. ƒ0.50/€0.25 per min. Open M-Th 9:30am-6pm, F 9:30am-9pm, Sa 9:30am-5pm, Su noon-5pm.) To reach the comfy **NJHC City-Hostel Rotterdam (HI),** Rochussenstr. 107-109, take the metro to Dijkzigt; at the top of the metro escalator, exit onto Rochussentr and turn left. (☎436 57 63. Breakfast included. Sheets ƒ7/€3.20. Reception 7am-midnight. Dorms ƒ35-45/€15.90-20.45 per person; doubles ƒ90-110/€40.90-49.95; non-members add ƒ5/€2.30.) To get from the station to the **Hotel Bienvenue,** Spoorsingel 24, exit through the back, walk straight along the canal for 5min., and it's on the right. Clean, comfortable rooms with TV in a safe area. (☎466 93 94. Reception M-F 7:30am-9pm, Sa-Su 8am-9pm. Singles ƒ90/€40.85; doubles ƒ150/€68.10; triples ƒ185/€83.95; quads ƒ250/€113.45.) The **Oude Haven** and **Oostplein** brim with cafes. Hop aboard the **De Pannenkoekenboot Rotterdam,** Parkhaven, to partake in the unlimited pancake buffet on a boat in the harbor; take tram #8 to get there. (Meals W, Sa-Su 1:30, 3, 4:30, 6pm; F 4:30 and 6pm. ƒ24.50/€11.15. Harbor sightseeing Pancake Cruise Sa 8pm-11pm. ƒ45/€20.45.) Buy **groceries** at **Albert Heijn,** Lijnbaanpl. From the tourist office take two lefts; it's toward the end of the **Lijnbaan** shopping plaza. (Open M-Th 8am-8pm, F 8am-9pm, Sa 8am-7pm, Su 1-6pm.) Mellow coffeeshops line **Oude Binnenweg** and **Nieuwe Binnenweg,** including the hip **Wester Paviljoen,** Mathenesserlaan 155, just off Rochussenstr. (Salads ƒ14/€6.35. Open Su-Th 7pm-1am, F-Sa 8:30pm-2am.) For less talk and more sweat, dance the night away at **Night Town,** West Kruiskade 28. (Cover ƒ10-25/€4.55-11.35 plus ƒ5/€2.30 membership fee. Open F-Sa 11pm-5am.) **Postal code:** 3016 CM.

◪ **DAYTRIP FROM ROTTERDAM: GOUDA.** Gouda (HOW-da) is the quintessential Dutch town, with canals, a windmill, and well-known cheese. A regional **cheese market** with free samples is held weekly in summer (Th 10am-12:30pm). The **Gouda Cheese Scale** features a permanent exhibition about Gouda and its cheese trade. (Open Apr. 8-Oct. Tu-W and F-Su 1-5pm, Th 10am-1pm. Free during the cheese market.) The gargantuan, late Gothic **St. John's Church** has managed to maintain its collection of 16th-century stained-glass windows despite attacks by both lightning and Reformation iconoclasts. (Open Mar.-Oct. M-Sa 9am-5pm; Nov.-Feb. M-Sa 10am-4pm. ƒ3.50/€2, students ƒ2.50/€1.15.) The **Goudse Pottenbakkerij "Adrie Moerings,"** Peperstr. 76, has produced the famous Gouda clay smoking pipes since the 17th century. (☎(0182) 01 28 42. Open M-F 9am-5pm, Sa 11am-5pm. Free.) Around the corner on Oosthaven, the **Museum Catherine Gasthuis** houses Flemish art and early surgical instruments in its former chapel and adjoining torture chamber. (Open M-Sa 10am-5pm, Su noon-5pm. ƒ5.25/€2.40.) **Trains** roll into town from Rotterdam (15min., round-trip ƒ12.50/€5.70) and Amsterdam (1hr., ƒ32.50/€14.75). From the station, cross the bridge and walk straight on Kleiweg, which turns into Hoogstr. and leads to the Markt and the VVV **tourist office.** (☎(0900) 486 32 888. Open M-Sa 9am-5pm; in summer also open Su noon-3pm.)

UTRECHT   ☎030

With pretty canals, a Gothic cathedral, and a prestigious university, Utrecht is a popular daytrip from Amsterdam but warrants an overnight stay. Its 50,000 students create a dynamic pulse in this picturesque, old city, once the Christian center of The Netherlands.

THE NETHERLANDS

E 7 TRANSPORTATION AND PRACTICAL INFORMATION. Trains arrive from Amsterdam (25min., 3-6 per hr., day return ƒ19.75/€9) in the **Hoog Catharijne** mall. To get to the VVV **tourist office,** Vinkenbrgstr. 19, follow the signs to Vredenberg, which heads to the town center. (☎ (090) 04 14 14 14. Open M-F 9am-6pm, Sa 9am-5pm.) Pick up a city map and a complete listing of museums and sights for ƒ2.50/€1.15. The tourist office also reserves rooms for a small fee.

E C ACCOMMODATIONS AND FOOD. At ▓**Hostel Strowis,** Boothstr. 8, funky vintage velvet couches in the lounge and eco-bathrooms complement well-kept wooden bunks in brightly colored rooms. Walk 15min. from the train station or take bus #3, 4, 8, or 11 to "Janskerkhof." (☎238 02 80. Free **Internet.** Women-only dorm available. Breakfast ƒ8.50/€3.90. Lockers ƒ25/€11.35. Sheets and blankets ƒ2.50/€1.15. Reception 24hr. Curfew Su-W 2am. Dorms ƒ25/€11.35; doubles ƒ80/€36.30; triples ƒ100/€45.40.) Relax in the orchard at the **NJHC Ridderhofstad Rhijnauwen (HI),** Rhijnauwenselaan 14, in nearby Bunnik. Take bus #41 from Centraal Station (12min., every 30min., 3 strips) and tell the driver your destination; from the stop, cross the street, backtrack, turn right on Rhijnauwenselaan, and it's 0.5km down the road. (☎656 12 77. In-house cafe. Breakfast included. Dorms July-Aug. ƒ39.25/€17.85; off-season ƒ34.95/€15.95. Singles ƒ46/€20.90; doubles ƒ92/€49.75; triples ƒ138/€62.65; quads ƒ167.75/€76.15. Nonmembers add ƒ5/€2.30 per night.) Look for cheap meals along **Nobelstraat.** Grab dinner (ƒ10/€4.55) at the ACU vegetarian **Eet-cafe,** Voorstraat 71, a legalized squat that hosts music shows, political discussions, and movie viewings. (☎231 45 90. Dinner M-Th 6-7:30.)

G ♫ SIGHTS AND ENTERTAINMENT. Start at RonDom, Dompl. 9, the Utrecht visitors center for cultural history, to get information on churches and museums. At the heart of the old city stands the awe-inspiring **Domkerk,** begun in 1254 and finished 250 years later. Initially a Roman Catholic cathedral, the Domkerk has held Protestant services since 1580. (Open M-Sa 10am-5pm, Su 2-4pm. Free.) Originally attached to the cathedral but freestanding since a medieval tornado blew away the nave in 1674, the **Domtoren** is the highest tower in The Netherlands. Climb the 465 steps to take in the expansive view. (Open M-Sa 10am-5pm, Su noon-5pm. Tour tickets sold at RonDom; ƒ9.95/€4.55.) The **Nationaal Museum Van Speelklok tot Piere-ment,** Buurkerkhof 10, traces the history of mechanical musical instruments. (Open Tu-Sa 10am-5pm, Su noon-5pm. Tours on the hr. ƒ12/€5.45, under 12 ƒ7.50/€3.40.) **Centraal Museum,** Nicolaaskerkhof 10, houses the largest collection of works by de Stijl designer Gerrit Reitveld. (Open Tu-Su 11am-5pm. ƒ15/€6.85, under 13 ƒ7.50/€3.40.) If Reitveld's work inspires you, take bus #4 from Centraal Station to the **Rietveld Schroder House;** it's like a Mondrian painting sprung to life. (Open W-Sa 11am-4:30pm. Last tour 3:30pm. ƒ15/€6.85, under 14 ƒ7.50/€3.40.) Visit **Museum Catherijnconvent,** Lange Nieuwstr. 38, to view an extensive collection of Christian art, with an emphasis on the Middle Ages. (Open Tu-F 10am-5pm, Sa-Su 11am-5pm. ƒ15/€6.85.) The newly opened **Aboriginal Art Museum,** Oude Gracht 176, presents ceremonial art from Australian Aborigines. (Open Tu-F 10am-5pm, Sa-Su 11am-5pm, under 12 ƒ7.50/€3.40.)

Pick up a copy of *UiLoper* at bars or restaurants to scout the bar and cultural scene. Students party at **Woolloo Moollo** on Janskerkhof 14 (cover varies; open W-Sa 11pm-late; student ID required), and **De Beurs,** Neude 35-37, right next to the post office (☎233 30 07; Th-Sa disco with pop and top 40; open daily 10am-late). **Wolkenkrabber,** Oudegr. 43, holds gay discos Fridays and Saturdays. (☎231 97 68. Happy Hour Sa-Su 5:30-6:30pm. Bar open daily 4pm-2am. Disco Sa-Su 11pm-4am. 1st F of the month women only, 1st Sa of the month men only.)

HOGE VELUWE NATIONAL PARK

E TRANSPORTATION. Arnhem and **Apeldoorn** (both 15km from the park) are good bases for exploration. Bus #12 runs from the **Arnhem** train station (20min.) to the Hoederloo park entrance and the Rijksmuseum Kröller-Müller. Bus #110 runs from the **Apeldoorn** train station to the park entrance, the Bezoekerscentrum, and the museum (20min.). Contact the park or tourist office for more information.

THE NETHERLANDS

◪ ⑥ PRACTICAL INFORMATION AND SIGHTS. If you've made it to The Netherlands, you shouldn't miss the impressive Hoge Veluwe National Park, a 52 sq. km nature preserve of woods, lakes, moors, dunes, and plains. Free bikes are available at five points in the park for exploring the vast grounds. Venture out in the early morning or the late afternoon to catch a glimpse of deer, boars, and native birds, particularly in the southern end of the park. (☎ (0900) 464 38 35. Park open Nov.-Mar. daily 9am-5:30pm; Apr. 8am-8pm; May and Aug. 8am-9pm; June-July 8am-10pm; Sept. 9am-8pm; Oct. 9am-7pm. *f*10/€4.55, ages 6-12 *f*5/€2.30; 50% discount May-Sept. after 5pm.) Find out more about Hoge Veluwe and pick up a park map (*f*3/€1.40) at the **Bezoekerscentrum (Visitors Center).** The inventive **Museonder,** an underground museum about the flora, fauna, and ecosystem of the park, is also located in the complex. (Both open daily 10am-6pm.) Tucked deep within the park, the **Rijksmuseum Kröller-Müller** houses a treasure trove of van Goghs, as well as works by Seurat, Signac, Mondrian, Picasso, Leger, and Brancusi. The museum's magnificent **sculpture garden,** one of the largest in Europe, has exceptional works by Rodin, Dubuffet, and Oldenburg. (Museum open Tu-Su 10am-5pm. Sculpture garden open Tu-Su 10am-4:30pm. *f*10/€4.55, ages 6-12 *f*5/€2.30.) Check out **St. Hubertus Hunting Lodge,** designed by H. P. Berlage; a 2½km stroll around the lodge leads past a meditation garden, a peat bog, and a water mill. (Lodge tours Apr.-Oct. every 30min. 11:30am-12:30pm and 2-4:30pm; Feb.-Mar. and Nov.-Dec. 2 and 3pm. Reserve early at the Bezoekerscentrum.)

ARNHEM. Sleepy Arnhem may not offer much excitement to the tourist, but it provides a good base for exploring the national park. To reach the VVV **tourist office,** Willemspl 8, which has helpful park info and maps, exit the train station, turn left, and continue down the street for one block. (☎ (090) 02 02 40 75. Open M 11am-5:30pm, Tu-F 9am-5:30pm, Sa 10am-4pm.) The **NJHC Herberg (HI),** Diepenbrocklaan 27, is clean and friendly. Kick back in the bar (beer *f*3-6/€1.40-2.75) or relax in the reading room. Take bus #3 from the station (dir.: Alteveer; 10min., 2 strips) to "Rijnstate Hospital." From the bus stop, turn right as you face the hospital, cross the street at the intersection, and turn left on Cattepoelseweg; then turn right up the brick path, turn right again at the top of the steps, and you will see the hostel. (☎ (026) 351 48 92; arnhem@njhc.org. Breakfast included. Laundry *f*10/€4.55. Key deposit *f*10/€4.55. Reception 8am-11pm. Curfew 12:30am. Email reservations accepted. Off-season dorms *f*43/€19.55, high season *f*45/€20.45; singles *f*60/€27.25, *f*63/€28.60; doubles *f*105/€47.65, *f*110/€49.95; triples *f*142/€64.45, *f*145/€65.80; quads *f*180/€81.70, *f*190/€86.25; nonmembers add *f*5/€2.30.) Take bus #2 (dir.: Haedaveld; 20min., 3 strips) to **Camping Arnhem,** Kemperbergerweg 771. (☎ (026) 443 16 00. Showers free. Open Apr.-Oct. *f*24/€10.90 per person.) **Enig Alternatief,** Wielakkerstr. 4, presents a full menu of vegetarian options. (Open Tu-Sa 11am-11pm.)

APELDOORN. Apeldoorn is home to the exceptional **Museum Paleis Het Loo,** the 17th- and 18th-century palace of the many King Williams of Orange. Used as a summer residence until 1975, the palace's pristine gardens, featuring Neoclassical sculptures, fountains, and a colonnade, have been precisely and symmetrically trimmed for over 350 years. From the station, take bus #102 or 104 (10min., 2 strips) to get to the museum. (Open Tu-Su 10am-5pm. Guided tours in English Tu-Sa. *f*15/€6.80.). The VVV **tourist office,** Stationstr. 72, 5min. straight ahead from the station, sells bike maps for *f*8.95/€4.10. (☎ (0900) 168 16 36. Open Sept.-Apr. M 9:30am-5:30pm, Tu-F 9am-5:30pm, Sa 10am-2pm; May-Aug M 9:30am-5:30pm, Tu-F 9am-5:30pm, Sa 9am-5pm.) To get to the lively **De Grote Beer (HI),** Asselsestr. 330, take bus #4 or 7 (dir.: Orden) from the station, get off at Chamavenlaan, cross the intersection, and go right. (☎ (055) 355 31 18. **Bikes** *f*12.50/€5.70 per day. Breakfast and sheets included. Reception daily 8am-10pm. Curfew midnight. Dorms *f*37.50-*f*46/€17-20.90; nonmembers *f*5/€2.30 extra.)

MAASTRICHT
☎ 043

Situated on a narrow strip of land between Belgium and Germany, Maastricht (pop. 120,000) is one of the oldest cities in The Netherlands. It has been a symbol of European unity since the 1991 Maastricht Treaty, which established the European Union. Home of the prestigious **Jan van Eyck Academie of Art,** Maastricht is also known for its abundance of art galleries and antique stores. The striking new **Bonnefantenmuseum,**

Ave. Ceramique 250, contrasts Maastricht's traditional Dutch brickwork with its futuristic rocketship design. The museum houses permanent collections of archaeological artifacts, medieval sculpture, Northern Renaissance painting, and contemporary art. (Open Tu-Su 11am-5pm. Free; special exhibits ƒ8/€3.65.) Despite its status as the birthplace of modern European unity, Maastricht has seen its share of interstate rivalries; centuries of foreign threats culminated in an innovative subterranean defense system. The **Mount Saint Peter Caves**, with 20,000 underground passages, were used as a siege shelter as late as WWII and contain inscriptions and artwork by generations of inhabitants. Access to the caves is possible only with a tour guide; **Zonneberg Caves,** Slavante 1, offers tours in English (July-Aug. daily 2:45pm; ƒ6.50/€2.95). Maastricht's above-ground marvels include the **Basilica of Saint Servatius**, Keizer Karelpl. off the central Vrijthof Square, which contains ornate ecclesiastical crafts, 11th-century crypts, and the country's largest bell, affectionately known as **Grameer** (Grandmother). (Open July-Aug. daily 10am-6pm; Sept.-June 10am-5pm. ƒ4/€1.85, under 13 ƒ1/€0.45, seniors ƒ3/€1.40.) The **Basilica of Our Lady,** O.L. Vrouwepl., has a smaller collection of treasures. (Open Easter-Oct. M-Sa 11am-5pm, Su 1-5pm. ƒ3.50/€1.60, under 13 ƒ1/€0.45.) The new **Natuurhistorich Museum,** De Bosuetpl. 6-7, features the remains of a Montasaurus dinosaur found in the Maastricht area, great fish tanks, and a comprehensive collection of fossils and artifacts indigenous to the southern Netherlands. (Open M-F 10am-5pm, Sa-Su 2-5pm. ƒ6/€2.75, children ƒ4.50/€2.05.) The **Derlon Museum Cellar,** Planckstr. 21, displays 2nd- to 4th-century Roman artifacts discovered during construction of the Derlon Hotel. (Open Su noon-4pm. Free.)

The train station is on the eastern side of town, across the river from most of the action, but buses run frequently to the Markt. **Trains** arrive from: Amsterdam (2½hr., ƒ52.50/€23.85); Liège, Belgium (1hr., ƒ44/€20); Cologne, Germany (2½hr., ƒ63/€28.60). The VVV **tourist office,** Kleine Staat 1, is a block from the Markt at Het Dinghuis. From the Markt bus stop, walk toward the river and turn right on Muntstr. (☎325 21 21. Open May-Oct. M-Sa 9am-6pm, Su 11am-3pm; Nov.-Apr. M-F 9am-6pm, Sa 9am-5pm.) **Hotel La Colombe,** Markt 30, features cheery plants and cute decorations. (☎321 57 74. Breakfast included. Singles ƒ127.50-148.50/€57.90-67.40; doubles ƒ157.25-168.25/€71.40-76.40; triples ƒ219/€99.40; quads ƒ269.75/€122.40. Extra person ƒ50.75/€23.) To get from the station to **City-Hostel de Dousberg (HI),** Dousbergweg 4, take bus #11 on weekdays, bus #28 on weeknights after 6pm, and bus #8 or 18 on weekends. (☎346 67 77. Breakfast included. Dorms ƒ45/€20.45, nonmembers ƒ5/€2.30 extra; triples ƒ150/€68.10; quads ƒ185/€83.95; quints ƒ220/€99.85.) **Maison de Chene,** Boschstr. 104-106, sports cozy rooms in a great location just off the Markt. (☎321 35 23. Breakfast ƒ17.50/€7.95. Singles (Su-Th only) ƒ85/€38.60, with toilet ƒ110-130/€50-59; doubles with shower ƒ120/€54.45, with shower and toilet ƒ135-150/€61.25-68.10.) Cheap food can be found around the central **Vrijthof** area. **De Kadans,** Kesselkade 62, serves inexpensive munchies and plays house in the **K-Club** downstairs. (☎326 17 00. Restaurant/bar open M-W 11am-midnight, Th-Sa 11am-5am, Su noon-1am. Kitchen closes daily at 10pm. Club open Th-Sa 11pm-5am. Cover Sa ƒ7.50/€3.40.) Grab a tasty brew (ƒ3.75/€1.70) at **Falstaff,** Amorspl. 6. (☎321 72 38. Open Su-Th 11am-2am, F and Sa 11am-3am.) **Night Live,** Kesselkade 43, is a church converted to a disco. (Open Th-Sa 11pm-6am. Cover from ƒ7.50/€3.40.)

GRONINGEN   ☎050

With 35,000 students and the nightlife to prove it, the small city of Groningen (pop. 175,000) supports a surprising number of eccentric museums, quirky art galleries, and trendy cafes. The town's gem is the spectacular ▓**Groninger Museum,** a unique assemblage of squares and cylinders that forms a bridge between the station and the city center. The multicolored, steel-trimmed galleries create a futuristic laboratory for wild contemporary art exhibits. A more conservative assortment of 16th-century Chinese sculpture and 18th-century Dutch china is also on display. (Open Tu-Su 10am-5pm; July and Aug. also open M 1-5pm. ƒ10/€4.55, seniors ƒ7.50/€3.40, ages 5-15 ƒ5/€2.30.) Admire the city from atop the 70m **Martinitoren Tower,** which somehow weathered the German attacks during WWII; it's located in Grote Markt. (Open Apr.-Oct. daily 1-5pm; Nov.-Mar. noon-4pm. ƒ3/€1.40.) Relax in the serene 16th-century **Prinsenhoftuin** (Princes' Court Garden); the entrance is on the canal 10min. away

THE NETHERLANDS

from the Martinitoren. (Open Apr. to mid-Oct. 10am-sundown.) The tiny **Theeschen-kerij Tea Hut** within has 130 kinds of tea and other beverages amidst ivy-covered trellises and towering rose bushes. (Cup of tea ƒ1.75/€0.80.) Or, cool off in the **Noorderplantsoen Park,** host space to the huge **Noorderzon** (Northern Sun Festival), Groningen's annual cultural climax in late August.

Trains roll in from Amsterdam (3hr., every 30min., ƒ52.50/€23.85). To reach the VVV **tourist office,** Grote Markt 25, turn right as you exit the station, walk along the canal, turn left at the first bridge, head straight through the Herepl. on Herestr., cross Gedempte Zuiderdiep, and keep on Herestr. until it hits the Grote Markt. (☎(0900) 202 30 50. Open M-F 9am-6pm, Sa 10am-5pm.) Hang out with a fun crowd at the funky **Simplon Youth Hotel,** Boterdiep 72-73. Take bus #1 from the station (dir.: Korrewegwijk) to "Boterdiep" and the hostel is through the yellow and white entranceway. (☎313 52 21. Breakfast ƒ7.50/€3.40. Free lockers. Linens ƒ5.50/€2.50, included in private rooms. Lockout noon-3pm. All-female dorm available. Dorms ƒ24/€10.90; singles ƒ52.50/€23.85; doubles ƒ82.50/€37.45; triples ƒ120/€54.45; quads ƒ155/€70.35.) **Hotel Friesland,** Kleine Pelsterstraat 4, has well-kept rooms in the center of town. From the station, cross the canal at the Groninger Museum, walk up Ubbo Emmiusstr., turn right on Gedempte Zuiderdiep, left on Pelsterstr., and right onto Kleine Pelsterstr. (☎312 13 07. Breakfast included. Singles ƒ53/€24.05; doubles ƒ96/€43.60; triples ƒ134/€60.85; quads ƒ177/€80.35.) **Eetcafe De 1e Kamer,** Peperstr. 9, serves very cheap basic fare. (Steak, schnitzel, and vegetarian stew all under ƒ15/€6.85. Beer ƒ2.50/€1.15. Open daily 5pm-5am. Kitchen closes at 9:30pm.) **Het Pakhuis,** Peperstr. 8, serves meals upstairs (from German to Indian) for ƒ14-15/€6.35-6.85 and drinks on red velvet couches at the cafe downstairs. (Restaurant open daily 6-11pm. Cafe open daily 9pm-4am.) Groningen's nightlife jams just off the **Grote Markt** and along nearby **Poelstraat** and **Peperstraat.** Pick up a free copy of *UILoper* from the tourist office to find out what's on each night. The intimate, candle-lit **de Spieghel Jazz Café,** Peperstr. 11, has two floors of live jazz, funk, or blues every night. (Wine ƒ4/€1.85 per glass. Open daily 8pm-4am.) **Postal code:** 9725 BM.

WADDEN ISLANDS (WADDENEILANDEN)

Wadden means "mudflat" in Dutch, but sand is the defining characteristic of these islands: isolated beaches hide behind dune ridges with windblown manes of golden grass. Deserted, tulip-lined bike trails carve through vast, flat stretches of grazing land and lead to these serene beaches. It's no wonder that Dutch vacationers want to keep these idyllic islands to themselves.

⧉ TRANSPORTATION. The islands arch clockwise around the northwestern coast of The Netherlands: Texel (closest to Amsterdam), Vlieland, Terschelling, Ameland, and Schiermonnikoog. To reach **Texel,** take the train from Amsterdam to **Den Helder** (70min., ƒ40/€18.15), and then grab bus #3 from the berths right next to the train station (2 strips or ƒ3/€1.40); a ferry goes to 't Hoorntje, the southernmost town on Texel (☎(0222) 36 99 61; 20min., every hr. 6:30am-9:30pm, round-trip ƒ9/€4.10). To reach the other islands from Amsterdam, head for **Harlingen** by train from Centraal station (1¾hr., ƒ43.25/€19.65) or by bus from Alksmaar Station (1½hr., ƒ35/€15.90). From Harlingen, **ferries** (☎(0562) 44 21 41; 24hr. info 44 27 70 or 44 32 20; www.red-erij-doeksen.nl) depart for **Terschelling** (3-5 per day, ƒ34/€15.45).

TEXEL. The southernmost and largest of the Wadden Islands, Texel boasts stunning beaches and delightful museums. The most popular **beaches** lie near De Koog, on the western side of the island. Head farther north or south from town to reach the less crowded sands. Bare it all at the **nude beaches** (2km south of Den Hoorn near paal 9 and 5km west of De Cocksdorp near paal 28). The **Ecomare Museum and Aquarium,** Ruyslaan 92, about 2km south of De Koog, features playful seals (feeding 11am and 3pm) and exhibits on Texel's ecology. (ƒ15/€6.85, under 13 ƒ7.50/€3.40.) Visit Texel's **nature reserves** on a guided tour; book in advance at the Ecomare. (Tours 2hr.; daily 11am. ƒ12.50/€5.70.) A working windmill marks the site of the **Maritime and Beachcomber's Museum,** Barentzstr. 21, in Oudeschild, which includes a creepy selection of relics scavenged from shipwrecks and an artful presentation of washed-ashore detritus. (Open Sept.-June Tu-Sa 10am-5pm; July-Aug. M-Sa 10am-5pm. ƒ9/€4.10, under 14 ƒ5/€2.30.)

THE NETHERLANDS

A **Texel Ticket** allows unlimited one-day travel on the island's bus system (runs mid-June to mid-Sept.; ƒ7/€3.20). The VVV **tourist office,** Emmaln 66, lies just outside Den Burg; follow the blue signs about 300km west of the main bus stop. (☎ (0222) 31 28 47. Open M-Th 9am-6pm, F 9am-9pm, Sa 9am-5pm; July-Aug. also Su 10am-1:30pm.) Rent a **bike** from **Verhuurbedrijf Heijne,** opposite the 't Horntje ferry dock in Texel. (From ƒ9/€4.10 per day. Open Apr.-Oct. daily 9am-8pm; Nov.-Mar. 9am-6pm.) Take bus #29 and tell the driver your destination to reach **Panorama (HI),** Schansweg 7, snuggled amid sheep pastures 7km from the dock at 't Horntje and 3km from Den Burg's center. (☎ (0222) 31 54 41. Local beer ƒ4-7/€1.85-3.20. Bikes ƒ8/€3.65 per day. Sheets included; towels ƒ8/€3.65. Reception 8:30am-10:30pm. Dorms ƒ14.70-17.75/€6.70-8.05.) The tiny **Hotel de Merel,** Warmoerstr. 22, is in the center of Den Burg. From the bus stop in Den Burg Square, turn left on Elemert and left again on Warmoerstr. (☎ (0222) 31 31 32. Breakfast included. Reception 8am-10pm. Singles from ƒ110/€49.95; doubles from ƒ160/€72.60; off-season ƒ5-10/€2.30-4.55 less; discounts for longer stays.) **Campgrounds** cluster south of De Koog and near De Cocksdorp (ƒ4-7/€1.85-3.20 per person, ƒ15/€6.85 per tent); ask at the tourist office. Stroll down Texel's main drag, **Dorpstraat,** where vendors hawk fresh fruit and local treats (ƒ3-5/€1.40-2.30). The pub 🍺**De 12 Balcken Tavern,** Weverstr. 20 in Den Burg, serves up giant portions of spare ribs with french fries and salad for ƒ26/€11.80. Try a shot of *'t Jutterje,* the island's popular licorice-flavored schnapps, for ƒ4/€1.85. (Open M-Sa 10am-2am, Su noon-2am. Kitchen open daily until 10pm.) Grab groceries at **Albert Heijn,** Waalderstr. 48, in De Koog. (Open M-Sa 8am-10pm, Su 10am-6pm.) The island's club scene centers around **De Koog;** check out the wild **Cafe Sam-Sam,** Dorpstr. 146. (70s parties every Th night in summer. Beer ƒ4/€1.85, mixed drinks ƒ10/€4.55. Open 9pm-3am. V.) **Den Burg** is an up-and-coming hotspot; dance the night away with a teen crowd at **Question Plaza,** Kantoorstr. 1. (Cover ƒ12/€5.45. Open daily 9pm-3am; no entry after 2am.) Relax to mellow live music among 20-somethings at **De Pilaar,** Kantoorstr. 5. (Open 8pm-3am; no entry after 2am.)

TERSCHELLING. With 80% of the island covered by a European Nature Reserve, **Terschelling** offers secluded **beaches** that stretch around the western tip and across the northern coast of the long, narrow island. To explore the island's striking scenery, rent a **bike** from **Tijs Knop,** Torenstr. 10-12, one block up from the pier. (☎ (0562) 44 20 52. ƒ9/€4.10 per day, ƒ40/€18.15 per week.) **JOBA Sports** runs rugged off-road bike tours through the nature reserve. (☎ (0562) 44 93 24; www.joba-sports.nl. Tours ƒ60/€27.25.) Meet the seals of the Waddenzee on a harbor tour with **Stella Maris Zeehonden.** (☎ (0562) 44 40 85 or (06) 53 90 02 34. 2½hr.; departure times depend on weather and season; call ahead to reserve a spot.)

The VVV **tourist office,** W. Barentzkade 19, sits opposite the ferry landing. (☎ (0562) 44 30 00. Open M-Sa 9:30am-5:30pm.) The **Terschelling Hostel (HI),** van Heusdenweg 39, is located just out of town on the waterfront. With your back to the harbor, take a right, walk along the pier, continue on the bike path to Midland, and it's straight ahead. (☎ (0562) 44 23 38. Breakfast included. Sheets included; towels ƒ8/€3.65. Laundry ƒ8/€3.65. Reception 9am-10pm. 6-person dorms ƒ41.10/€18.65; off-season ƒ34.20/€15.50; ask for the backpacker special.) Campgrounds abound on Terschelling; the most ideally located is **Camping Cnossen,** 8 Hoofdweg, 3km east of Terschelling West. (☎ (0562) 44 23 21. ƒ7/€3.20 per person, ƒ10/€4.55 per tent.) Catch a bite to eat in the island's main village, **Terschelling West.** At **Amsterdamsche Koffijuis,** Willem Barentszstr. 21, around the corner from the tourist office, munch on a variety of tasty tapas during lunch or dinner and then groove to world music after 9pm. (Open daily 11am-2am; dinner served 5-9:30pm.) The **Croissanterie De Dis,** Boomstr. 17, offers freshly made *broodjes* (ƒ6-11/€2.75-5) and salads. (Open daily 9am-8pm.) Pick up food and camping supplies at **Supermarkt Spanjer,** Boomstr. 13. (Open M-F 8am-8pm, Sa 8am-6pm.) Young people flood Terschelling on summer nights; to shake your booty, check out **Danscafe De Stoep,** Oosterburen 5. (Cover ƒ7/€3.20. Open 10pm-2am.) Or head to **Braskoer,** Torenstr. 32. (Beer ƒ4/€1.85, shots ƒ5/€2.30. Cover ƒ5/€2.30. Open 9pm-2am.) For a more relaxed evening, kick back at **Cafe De Zeevaart,** Torenstr. 22. (Beer ƒ4-5/€1.85-2.30. Open 11am-2am.)

THE NETHERLANDS

PORTUGAL

ESCUDOS

US$1 = 219$	100$ = US$0.55
CDN$1 = 142$	100$ = CDN$0.85
UK£1 = 317$	100$ = UK£0.38
IR£1 = 255$	100$ = IR£0.47
AUS$1 = 116$	100$ = AUS$1.03
NZ$1 = 96$	100$ = NZ$1.25
ZAR1 = 26$	100$ = ZAR4.56
EUR€1 = 200$	100$ = EUR€0.60

PHONE CODE | **Country Code: 351. International dialing prefix:** 00. There are no city codes in Portugal

During the 14th and 15th centuries, Portugal (pop. 10 million; 92,391 sq. km) was one of the most powerful nations in the world, ruling a wealthy empire that stretched from America to Asia. Today it is often unfairly overshadowed by its larger neighbor Spain. And while it does share the gorgeous coastlines, wild nightlife, and stunning architecture of the Iberian Peninsula, Portugal is culturally and geographically quite unique. Despite ongoing modernization in Lisbon and beyond, some of Portugal's rich traditions seem destined never to change—the wines of Porto are as fine as ever, immaculate beaches still line the Atlantic seaboard, and the country's hard-earned character and loyal people continue to stand proud. *Let's Go: Spain and Portugal 2002* has more information on vibrant Portugal.

SUGGESTED ITINERARIES

THREE DAYS Make your way through **Lisbon**'s (1 day, p. 762) famous Moorish district, the **Alfama**, up to the **Castelo de São Jorge**, and to the futuristic **Parque das Nações**. By night, listen to *fado* and hit the clubs in **Barrio Alto**. Daytrip to **Sintra**'s fairy tale castles (1 day, p. 771) before sipping sweet port in **Porto** (1 day, p. 782).

ONE WEEK From **Lisbon** (2 days, p. 762) and **Sintra** (1 day), lounge on the beaches of **Lagos** (1 day, p. 776), and **Praia da Rocha** (1 day, p. 779), then move on to the university town of **Coimbra** (1 day, p. 780), and end your week in **Porto** (1 day).

BEST OF PORTUGAL, TWO WEEKS After the sights, sounds, and cafes of **Lisbon** (2 days), daytrip to **Sintra** (1 day). Head down to the infamous beach-and-bar town **Lagos** (2 days), where hordes of visitors dance the night away, and take an afternoon to **Sagres** (p. 778), once considered the end of the world. Check out the bone chapel in **Évora** (1 day, p. 775) and the mysterious convent in **Tomar** (1 day, p. 772). Head north to **Coimbra** (2 days) and **Porto** (2 days), then finish your tour in the impressive squares of **Viana do Castelo** (1 day, p. 784).

PORTUGAL

LIFE AND TIMES

HISTORY AND POLITICS

EARLY HISTORY

The first clearly identifiable inhabitants of the Iberian peninsula were the **Celts,** who began to settle in northern Portugal and Spanish Galicia in the 9th and 8th centuries BC. The **Greeks** and **Carthaginians** followed them, settling the coasts. After their victory over Carthage in the **Second Punic War** (218-201 BC) and their defeat of the Celts in 140 BC, the **Romans** gained control of central and southern Portugal. Six centuries of Roman rule, which introduced the *Pax Romana* and "Latinized" Portugal's language and customs, paved the way for Christianity.

VISIGOTHS AND ARABIAN KNIGHTS (469-718)

By AD 469, the **Visigoths,** a tribe of migrating Germanic people, had crossed the Pyrenees. Under the Visigoths, who had adopted Christianity by the beginning of the 7th century, the Catholic Church became the largest landholder in Europe, and monasteries and clerical schools became centers of spiritual learning. In 711, however, the **Moors,** a Muslim people, invaded Iberia, toppling the Visigoth monarchy. Although these invaders centered their new kingdom of *al-Andalus* in Córdoba, Spain, smaller Muslim communities settled along Portugal's southern coast, an area they called the *al-Gharb*, now the Algarve.

THE RECONQUEST AND BIRTH OF PORTUGAL (718-1386)

Though the Christian **Reconquest** officially began in 718, it didn't pick up steam until the 11th century. When Fernando I united Castilla and León in 1035, he helped the movement by providing a strong base from which to reclaim territory. In 1139, **Afonso I,** a noble from the territory of Portucale, declared his region's independence from Castilla and León. By the following decade, he had named himself the first king of Portugal, though the papacy did not officially recognize the title until 1179.

The Christian kings, led by **Dinis I** (who was incidentally also a lyric poet), promoted use of the Portuguese language instead of Spanish, established Portugal's first university in 1290, and solidified its current borders in 1297. With the **Treaty of Alcañices** (1297), Dinis settled border disputes with neighboring Castilla, asserting Portugal's identity as an independent nation. By the middle of the 14th century, Portugal was the first unified nation-state in Europe.

THE AGE OF DISCOVERY (1386-1580)

The reign of **João I,** the first king of the House of Aviz, ushered in unity and prosperity never before seen in Portugal. João increased the power of the crown and in so doing established a strong base for future Portuguese expansion and economic success. To further strengthen the monarchy, João also negotiated the **Treaty of Windsor** (1386), a permanent Anglo-Portuguese alliance.

The 15th century was one of the greatest periods in the history of sea travel and naval advances. Under the leadership of João's son, **Prince Henry the Navigator,** Portugal established itself as a world leader in maritime science and exploration. **Bartolomeu Dias** changed the world forever when he rounded Africa's Cape of Good Hope in 1488, opening the route to the East and paving the way for Portugal's entry into the spice trade. And while the Portuguese monarchs will be forever infamous for turning down Christopher Columbus's voyage proposal, they financed other successful explorers, including **Vasco da Gama,** who led the first European naval expedition to India. Successive expeditions added numerous East African and Indian colonies to Portugal's empire. Two years after da Gama's voyage, **Pedro Alvares Cabral** claimed **Brazil** for Portugal. Portugal's monarchy peaked with **Manuel I the Fortunate** on the throne. Although the **Treaty of**

Portugal

Tordesillas (1494) with Spain limited further Portuguese colonial expansion in the Americas, Portugal still established a far-flung empire. By the beginning of the 16th century, Portuguese traders, colonists, and missionaries, often using oppressive tactics, had secured claims all around the globe.

THE HOUSES OF HABSBURG AND BRAGANÇA (1580-1807)

In 1580, Habsburg King of Spain **Felipe II** forcibly affirmed his quasi-legitimate claim to the Portuguese throne, and the Iberian Peninsula was briefly ruled by one monarch. For 60 years, the Habsburg family dragged Portugal into several ill-fated wars, including the **Spanish-Portuguese Armada**'s crushing loss to England in 1588. But by the end of Habsburg rule, Portugal had lost much of its once vast empire. In 1640, during a rebellion against King Felipe IV, the **House of Bragança** engineered a nationalist rebellion. After a brief struggle they assumed control, once again asserting Portuguese independence from Spain.

NAPOLEON'S CONQUEST AND ITS AFTERMATH (1807-1910)

Napoleon took control of France in 1801 and had grand designs on much of Europe. His army met little resistance when it invaded Portugal in 1807. Rather than risk death, the Portuguese royal family fled to Brazil. The **Constitution of 1822,** drawn up during the royal family's absence, severely limited the power of the monarchy, and after 1826, the ultimate sibling rivalry exploded into the **War of the Two Brothers** (1826-1834) between constitutionalists (supporting Pedro, the new king of Brazil) and monarchists (supporting Miguel, Pedro's brother), which reverberated through Portugal.

FROM THE FIRST REPUBLIC TO SALAZAR (1910-1974)

Frustrated by the political discord of the past century, a group of soldiers and armed civilians, led by **António Machado Santos** of the republican **Carbonária** group, overthrew the government, and poor 20-year-old King Manuel II fled to England. The new government that took his place, known as the **First Republic,** granted universal male suffrage and diminished the influence of the Catholic Church. Workers received the right to strike, and merit, rather than birth, became the primary qualification for civil service advancement.

But the expulsion of the Jesuits and other religious orders sparked worldwide disapproval. Portugal's decision to enter **World War I** (even though on the side of the victorious Allies) proved economically fatal and internally divisive. The weak republic wobbled and eventually fell in a 1926 military coup. General **António Carmona** took over as leader of the provisional military government, and in the face of financial crisis, he appointed **António de Oliveira Salazar,** a prominent economics professor, his minister of finance. In 1932 Salazar became prime minister, but he soon evolved into a dictator. His *Estado Novo* (New State) granted suffrage to women, but did little else to end the country's authoritarian tradition. A terrifying secret police (PIDE) crushed all opposition to Salazar's rule, and African rebellions were quelled in bloody battles that drained the nation's economy.

REVOLUTION AND REFORM (1974-1999)

The slightly more liberal **Marcelo Caetano** dragged on the increasingly unpopular African wars after Salazar's death in 1970. On April 25, 1974, a left-wing military coalition calling itself the **Armed Forces Movement,** under **Francisco da Costa Gomes,** overthrew Caetano in a quick coup. The **Revolution of the Carnations** sent Portuguese dancing into the streets; today every town in Portugal has its own **Rua 25 de Abril.** The Marxist-dominated armed forces established a variety of civil and political liberties and withdrew Portuguese claims on African colonies by 1975.

The landmark year 1986 brought Portugal into the European Community (now the **European Union**), ending its age-old isolation from affluent northern Europe. During the 1990s, the Portuguese government instituted a series of economic programs (with the help of EU funds) to prepare the country for economic integration with the rest of Europe.

PORTUGAL TODAY

Despite uncertainty about Portugal's future in an integrated Europe, the nation's economy reported an astounding 3.5% growth rate by the beginning of 1999. With one of the strongest economies in the EU, Portugal was thriving on the eve of its entrance into the **European Monetary Union** (1999). The new revitalized Portugal has entered the international arena, taking on a new role in the post-colonial era. In the past few years, Portugal has worked to help negotiate peace in Angola and East Timor, two of its former colonies. Its **parliamentary democracy** is currently headed by Prime Minister **Antonio Guterres.**

THE ARTS

PAINTING

The Age of Discovery (1415-1580) was an era of vast cultural exchange with Renaissance Europe and beyond. High Renaissance artist **Jorge Afonso,** King Manuel's favorite, created realistic portrayals of human anatomy. Afonso's best works hang at the Convento de Cristo in **Tomar** (see p. 772) and the **Convento da Madre de Deus** in Lisbon (see p. 762). In the 20th century, Cubism, Expressionism and Futurism trickled into Portugal. More recently, **Maria Helena Vieira da Silva** has won international recognition for her abstract works, and **Carlos Botelho** has become world-renowned for his wonderful vignettes of Lisbon life.

ARCHITECTURE

Portugal's signature **Manueline** style celebrates the prosperity and imperial expansion of King Manuel I's reign. Manueline works routinely merge Christian images and maritime motifs. Their rich and lavish ornaments reflect a hybrid of Northern Gothic, Spanish Plateresque, and Moorish influences. The Manueline style found its most elaborate expression in the church and tower at Belém (see p. 769), built to honor Vasco da Gama. Close seconds are the **Mosteiro dos Jerónimos** in Belém and the **Abadia de Santa Maria de Vitória** in Batalha (see p. 772).

LITERATURE

Modernist poet **Fernando Pessoa** was Portugal's most famous creative writer at the turn of the 20th century. **José Saramago,** winner of the 1998 Nobel Prize for literature, is perhaps Portugal's most important living writer. He is best known for *Baltasar and Blimunda* (1982), the story of lovers who escape the Inquisition in a time machine, and *The Stone Raft* (1986), a satire about Iberia's isolation from the rest of Europe.

FOOD AND DRINK

Portuguese dishes are seasoned with olive oil, garlic, herbs, and sea salt, but few spices. Portugal has a tantalizing selection of fish, such as *chocos grelhados* (grilled cuttlefish), *linguado grelhado* (grilled sole), and *peixe espada* (swordfish). Vegetarians will likely eat lots of cheese sandwiches on Portugal's delectable bread. The hearty midday lunch is eaten between noon and 2pm, and dinner is between 8pm and midnight. *Media dose* (half-portions) cost more than half-price but are often adequate; a full portion may satisfy two. The *prato do dia* (special of the day) or *ementa* (fixed price menu of appetizer, bread, main dish, and dessert) are both good budget options. The favorite dessert is *pudim*, or *flan*, a caramel custard. *Vino do porto* (port wine) is a dessert in itself. A six-month heating process gives sweet *Madeira* wines a unique "cooked" flavor. Delectable Portuguese coffees include *bica* (black espresso), *galão* (coffee with milk, served in a glass), and *café com leite* (coffee with milk, served in a cup).

ESSENTIALS

DOCUMENTS AND FORMALITIES

Citizens of the US, Canada, the UK, and New Zealand can visit Portugal visa-free for up to 90 days. Citizens of Australia and South Africa need a **visa.**

> **Portuguese Embassies at Home: Australia,** 23 Culgoa Circuit, O'Malley, ACT 2603; mailing address P.O. Box 9092, Deakin, ACT 2600 (☎(02) 62 90 17 33). **Canada,** 645 Island Park Dr., Ottawa, ON K1Y OB8 (☎613-729-0883). **South Africa,** 599 Leyds St., Mucklenuk, Pretoria (☎(012) 341 2340). **UK,** 11 Belgrave Sq., London SW1X 8PP (☎(020) 72 35 53 31). **US,** 2125 Kalorama Rd. NW, Washington, D.C. 20008 (☎202-328-8610). **New Zealanders** should refer to the embassy in Australia.

> **Foreign Embassies and Consulates in Portugal:** Australians can use their embassy in **France** (see p. 274); all other embassies are in **Lisbon** (see p. 762). **Canada** has a consulate in **Faro,** and the **UK**'s is in **Porto.**

TRANSPORTATION

BY PLANE. Portugal is easily accesible by plane from the US and Europe. Most major international airlines serve Lisbon; some serve Porto, Faro, and the Madeiras. **TAP Air Portugal** (in US and Canada ☎800-221-7370, in UK ☎(207) 630 07 46, in

Lisbon ☎ (21) 843 11 11; www.tap.pt) is Portugal's national airline, serving all domestic locations and many major international cities. **Portugália** (www.pga.pt) is a smaller Portuguese airline that flies between Porto, Faro, Lisbon, all major Spanish cities, and other Western European destinations. Its offices include Lisbon (☎ (21) 842 55 00) and Manchester, UK (☎ (161) 489 50 40).

BY TRAIN. Portugal is well connected to neighboring Spain by train. Long-distance trains run from **Madrid** to **Lisbon,** and Spain's national railway is in the process of building a high-speed train from **Seville** to **Lagos.** Closer to the border, trains run from **Huelva** and **Cáceres** to Portugal. **Caminhos de Ferro Portugueses** is Portugal's national railway, but for long-distance travel outside of the Braga-Porto-Coimbra-Lisbon line, the bus is much better. Around Lisbon, local trains and commuter rails are fast and efficient. Unless you own a **Eurailpass,** which is accepted on Portuguese trains, the return on round-trip tickets must be used before 3am the following day. Anyone riding without a ticket is fined over 3500$/€21. Though there is a **Portugal Flexipass,** it is rarely worth purchasing.

BY BUS. Buses are cheap, frequent, and connect just about every town in Portugal. **Rodoviária** (national info ☎ (21) 354 57 75), the national bus company, has recently been privatized. Each company name corresponds to a particular region of the country, such as Rodoviária Alentejo or Rodoviária Minho e Douro, with notable exceptions such as EVA in the Algarve. Private regional companies also operate, among them **Cabanelas, AVIC,** and **Mafrense.** Be wary of non-express buses in small regions like Extremadura and Alentejo, which stop every few minutes. Express coach service *(expressos)* between major cities is especially good; inexpensive city buses often run to nearby villages.

BY CAR. Portugal has a particularly high rate of automobile accidents. The new highway system (IP) is quite good, but off the main arteries, the narrow, twisting roads prove difficult to negotiate. The locals' testy reputation is well deserved. Speed limits are effectively ignored, recklessness common, and lighting and road surfaces often inadequate. Buses and trucks are safer options. Moreover, parking space in cities border on nonexistent. **Gas** comes in super (97 octane), normal (92 octane), and unleaded, and usually runs 130-200$/US$0.60-0.90 per liter. Portugal's national automobile association, the **Automóvel Clube de Portugal (ACP),** R. Rosa Araújo, 42, 1250 Lisbon (☎ (21) 318 01 00), provides breakdown and towing service (M-F 9am-5pm) and 24hr. first aid.

BY THUMB. In Portugal, **hitchers** are rare. Beach-bound locals occasionally hitch in summer but otherwise stick to the inexpensive bus system. Rides are easiest to come by between smaller towns. Best results are reputedly at gas stations near highways and rest stops. *Let's Go* does not recommend hitchhiking.

TOURIST SERVICES AND MONEY

EMERGENCY	Police, ☎ 112. Medical, ☎ 112. Fire, ☎ 112.

TOURIST OFFICES. The official Portuguese tourism web site is located at www.portugalinsite.pt. There are also offices in Canada, the UK, and the US. When in Portugal, stop by municipal and provincial tourist offices for maps and advice.

Canada: Portuguese Trade and Tourism Commission, 60 Bloor St. West, Ste. 1005, Toronto, ON M4W 3B8 (☎ 416-921-7376; fax 416-921-1353; iceptor@idirect.com). **UK:** Portuguese Trade and Tourism Office, 22-25A Sackville St., 2nd-4th fl., London W1X 2LY (☎ (20) 7474 1441; fax 7494 1441; iceplond@aol.com). **US:** Portuguese National Tourist Office, 590 5th Ave., 4th fl., New York, NY 10036 (☎ 212-354-4403; fax 212-764-6137; www.portugal.org); additional office in Washington D.C. (☎ 202-331-8222).

CURRENCY AND EXCHANGE. Money in Portugal comes in the form of the **escudo,** available in coins of 1, 2, 5, 10, 20, 50, 100, 200 *escudos* and notes of 500, 1000, 2000, 5000, and 10,000 *escudos*. Portugal has accepted the **Euro (€)** as legal tender, and *escudos* will be phased out by July 1, 2002. For more information, see p. 23.

Prices: You can do a "bare-bones day" in Portugal (camping or sleeping in cheap hostels, buying food at supermarkets, staying in at night) for about 5000$/€25, or US$25. A slightly more comfortable day (sleeping in nicer hostels, eating 1 or 2 meals a day in restaurants, going out at night) will probably run up to 8000$/€40, or US$40.

Tipping and bargaining: Tipping is only customary in expensive restaurants or hotels; most cheaper restaurants include a 10% service charge. Taxi drivers do not expect a tip unless the trip was unusually long. **Bargaining** is not normal in shops, but you can give it a shot at the local market or when looking for a room.

Taxes: Taxes are included in all prices in Portugal and are not redeemable upon leaving, even for EU citizens.

ACCOMMODATIONS AND CAMPING

Movijovem, Av. Duque de Ávila, 137, 1050 Lisbon (☎ (21) 359 60 00; fax 359 60 01), looks over the country's **HI hostels.** All bookings can be made through them. A cheap bed in a *pousada da juventude* (not to be confused with plush *pousadas*) costs 2000-3000$/€10-15 per night and slightly less in the offseason (breakfast and sheets included). Lunch or dinner usually costs 900$/€4.50, snacks around 250$/€1.25. Though often the cheapest option, hostels may lie some distance from the town center. Check-in hours are 9am to noon and 6pm to midnight. Some have lockouts 10:30am to 6pm, and early curfews might cramp club-hoppers' styles. The **maximum stay** at one hostel is eight nights unless you get special permission. **Pensões,** also called **residencias,** are a budget traveler's mainstay. They're far cheaper than hotels and only slightly more expensive (and much more common) than crowded youth hostels. Like hostels, *pensões* generally provide sheets and towels and have common rooms. All are rated on a five-star scale and are required to visibly post their category and legal price limits. (If you don't see this information, ask for it.) **Hotels** in Portugal tend to be pricey. When business is weak, try bargaining down—the "official price" is just the maximum allowed.

In Portugal, over 150 **official campgrounds** *(parques de campismo)* feature tons of amenities and comforts. Most have a supermarket and cafes, and many are beach-accessible or near rivers or pools. Police have been cracking down on illegal camping, so don't try it—especially near official campgrounds. Tourist offices stock the free *Portugal: Camping and Caravan Sites*, a handy guide to official campgrounds. Otherwise, write to the **Federação Portuguesa de Campismo e Caravanismo,** Av. Coronal Eduardo Gallardo, 24D, 1170 Lisbon (☎ (21) 812 68 90).

COMMUNICATION

TELEPHONES. Portugal's national telephone company is **Portugal Telecom.** Coin-operated phones are essentially non-existent in Portugal; you'll need phone cards. The country uses both the **Credifone** and **Portugal Telecom** systems. For both systems, the basic unit for all calls (and the price for local ones) is 18$/€0.10. Credifone cards, with magnetic strips, are sold at drugstores, post offices, and locations posted on phone booths, and are most useful outside the two big cities. **City codes** now all begin with a 2, and local calls do not require dialing any portion of the city code. **Calling cards** remain the best method of making international calls. To call home with a calling card, contact the operator for your service provider in Portugal by dialing the appropriate **international toll-free access number: AT&T,** ☎ 800 800 128; **British Telecom,** ☎ 800 800 440; **Canada Direct,** ☎ 800 800 122; **Ireland Direct,** ☎ 800 800 353; **MCI,** ☎ 800 800 123; **Sprint,** ☎ 800 800 187; **Telecom New Zealand,** ☎ 800 800 640; **Telkom South Africa,** ☎ 800 800 270; **Telstra Australia,** ☎ 800 800 610.

MAIL. Mail in Portugal is somewhat inefficient—**Air mail** *(via aerea)* can take from one to two weeks (or longer) to reach the US or Canada. **Surface mail** *(superficie)*, for packages only, takes up to two months. **Registered** or **blue mail** takes five to eight business days (for roughly three times the price of air mail). **EMS** or

Express Mail will probably get there in three to four days for more than double the blue mail price. **Stamps** are available at post offices *(correios)* and automatic stamp machines outside post offices and in central locations around cities.

INTERNET ACCESS. Email is both faster and more reliable than the standard mail system. Cybercafes are common in cities and most smaller towns; when in doubt, try libraries; they often have at least one computer equipped for Internet access.

LANGUAGE. Portuguese is a Romance language similar to Spanish. English, Spanish, and French are fairly widely spoken. To snuggle up to Portuguese and get Romantic with other members of the family, see p. 952.

LOCAL FACTS

Time: Greenwich Mean Time.

When to go: Portugal's climate is very mild; summers are fairly hot in the south, but not too extreme and not at all humid. In winter, it never gets particularly cold.

Hours: A normal workday is from about 9am-7pm with a lunch break from 1-3pm. On Sa most places only open in the morning; on Su, you're on your own.

Holidays: New Year's Day (Jan. 1); Good Friday (Mar. 29); Easter (Mar. 31); Liberty Day (Apr. 25); Labor Day (May 1); Assumption Day (Aug. 15); Republic Day (Oct. 5); All Saints' Day (Nov. 1); Restoration of the Independence (Dec. 1); Feast of the Immaculate Conception (Dec. 8); Christmas Eve (Dec. 24); Christmas (Dec. 25).

Festivals: Just about everything closes down during public festivals, so plan accordingly. Also be prepared to be surprised by a festival, as many towns have local festivals of their own in addition to national celebrations and holidays. All of Portugal will celebrate **Carnival** in mid-February and the **Holy Week** in late-Mar. Coimbra holds the **Burning of the Ribbons** festival in early May, and Lisbon hosts the **Feira Internacional de Lisboa** in June. Coimbra's **Feira Popular** takes place the 2nd week of July. For more information on Portuguese festivals, see www.portugal.org.

LISBON (LISBOA) ☎21

Over 500 years ago, Lisbon was the center of the world's richest and farthest-reaching empire. The city and empire reached their apex at the end of the 15th century when Portuguese navigators pioneered explorations of Asia, Africa, and South America. Lisbon has seen more than its share of changes over the course of the 20th century. During World War II, Lisbon's neutrality and its Atlantic connections made it a rendezvous place for spies on both sides. In 1974, when Mozambique and Angola won independence, hundreds of thousands of refugees converged upon the Portuguese capital. In 1998, the World Expo descended upon Lisbon, providing the impetus for massive construction projects and a citywide facelift. Since then, the revival has continued, as more tourist hot spots and sites of cultural interest emerge. Like Portugal itself, Lisbon has managed to preserve its traditions, continually renovating its historic monuments and meticulously maintaining its black and white mosaic sidewalks, pastel façades, and cobbled medieval alleys.

▐ TRANSPORTATION

Lisbon has an efficient system of buses, subways, trams, funiculars, and trains. Use them to full advantage—no suburb takes longer than 90min. to reach. Train service in Lisbon is potentially confusing, as there are four main stations, each serving different destinations. For further info about Portugal's railway system contact **Caminhos de Ferro Portuguêses** (☎800 20 09 04; www.cp.pt).

Flights: Aeroporto de Lisboa (☎21 841 37 00). Walk out of the terminal, turn right, and follow the road around the curve to the bus stop. From there take **bus** #44 or 45 (20-40min., 175$/€0.90) to Pr. Restauradores; the bus stops directly in front of the tourist office. Alternatively, take the express **AeroBus** (bus #91; 15min., every 20min., 7am-

Central Lisbon Overview

▲ ACCOMMODATIONS
Casa de Hóspedes Globo, 3
H. Estrela da Serra, 12
Pensão Estaçao Central, 6
Pensão Ibérica, 8
Pensão Londres, 1
Pensão Ninho das Águias, 5
Residencia do Sul, 5
Residencial Duas Nações, 11
Residencial Florescente, 2

● FOOD
Hell's Kitchen, 4
O Cantinho das Gáveas, 7
Restaurante Arco do Castelo, 13
Restaurante Calcuta, 9
Restaurante Martinho da Arcada, 14

PORTUGAL

9pm, 460$/€2.30) to Pr. Restauradores; this bus, which leaves directly from the airport exit, is a better option during rush hour. A **taxi** to the downtown area costs about 2000$/€10, plus a 300$/€1.50 fee for luggage. Major airlines have offices at Pr. Marquês de Pombal and along Av. Liberdade.

Trains: Estação Rossio (☎21 346 50 22. M: Rossio or Restauradores) serves destinations west including **Sintra** (45min., every 15-30min. 6am-2am, 210$/€1.05), via **Queluz** (140$/€0.70). **Estação Santa Apolónia** (☎21 888 40 25) runs the international, northern and eastern lines. To: **Coimbra** (2½hr., 7 per day 8am-8pm, 1510-2700$/€7.55-13.50); **Porto** (4½hr., 12 per day 8am-8pm, 2080-3700$/€10.40-18.50); **Madrid** (10hr., 10:05 pm, 8200$/€41); **Paris** (21hr., 6:05pm, 29,000$/€144.65). **Estação Cais do Sodré** (☎21 347 01 81. M: Cais do Sodré) runs trains to **Estoril** and **Cascais** (30min., every 20min., 210$/€1.05). **Estação Barreiro,** across the Rio Tejo, serves southern destinations like the Costa Azul and the Algarve. Station accessible by **Ferries** which leave every 30min. and take 30min.; ferry ticket included in the price of connecting train ticket (otherwise 85$/€0.45, round-trip 200$/€1). Trains to **Évora** (2½hr., 7 per day 6:50am-11:50pm, 1200$/€6) and **Lagos** (5½hr., 5 per day 7:35am-7:45pm, 2800$/€14).

Buses: Arco do Cego, Av. João Crisóstomo, around the block from the M: Saldanha. All "Saldanha" buses (#36, 44, 45) stop in the *praça* (175$/€0.90). This is the terminal for virtually all buses. The terminal has fast **Rede Expressos** (☎21 354 54 39 or 310 31 11; www.rede-expressos.pt) to many destinations, including: **Coimbra** (2½hr., 16 per day 7am-12:15am, 1500$/€7.50); **Évora** (2hr., 13 per day 7am-9:30pm, 1500$/€7.50); **Lagos** (5hr., 9 per day 5am-1am, 2500$/€12.50); **Porto** (4hr., 7per day 7am-12:15am, 2300$/€11.50), via **Leiria.**

Public Transportation: CARRIS (☎21 361 30 00; www.carris.pt) runs the buses, trams, and funiculars in Lisbon. Fare 175$/€0.90 within the city; pay on the bus. If you plan to stay for any length of time, consider investing in a *passe turístico* (tourist pass), good for unlimited travel on all CARRIS transports. 1-, 3-, 4-, and 7-day passes available (460$/€2.30, 1100$/€5.50, 1810$/€9, 2560$/€12.80). The **metro** (☎21 355 84 57; www.metrolisboa.pt) covers downtown and the modern business district in 4 color-coded lines. Individual tickets 100$/€0.50; book of 10 tickets 900$/€4.50. Trains run daily 6:30am-1am, though some stations close earlier. **Trams** offer views of the harbor and service older neighborhoods (tickets 175$/€0.90). Line #28 is great for sight-seeing in the Alfama and Mouraria (stop in Pr. Comércio); line #15 heads from Pr. Comércio or Pr. Figueira to Belém.

Taxis: Rádio Táxis de Lisboa (☎21 811 90 00), **Autocoope** (☎21 793 27 56), and **Teletáxis** (☎21 811 11 00) all line-up along Av. Liberdade and Rossio. Flat rate of 300$/€1.50 for luggage.

✳ 🛈 ORIENTATION AND PRACTICAL INFORMATION

According to legend, Lisbon, like Rome, was built on seven hills, though at times it might seem like many more. The city center is made up of three main *bairros* (neighborhoods): the **Baixa** (low district, resting in the valley), the **Bairro Alto** (high district), and the **Alfama.** The Baixa is the center of town, sandwiched between Bairro Alto and Alfama. Its grid of small, mostly pedestrian streets begins at the **Praça Dom Pedro IV** (better known as the **Rossio**) and ends at the **Praça do Comércio** on the **Rio Tejo.**

Adjacent to Rossio are two other important squares, **Praça dos Restauradores** and **Praça da Figueira,** which border the medieval/Moorish district, **Alfama.** The lone survivor of the 1755 earthquake, Alfama is the city's oldest district, a labyrinth of narrow alleys and stairways beneath the **Castelo de São Jorge.** Across the Baixa from Alfama is **Bairro Alto** with its mix of narrow streets, lush parks and baroque churches. Stretching out along the river are some of the fastest growing parts of Lisbon. The former Expo '98 grounds, now called the **Parque das Nações** (Park of Nations), occupies Lisbon's eastern end, while the **Alcântara** and the **Docas do Santo Amaro** show off Lisbon's most happening nightlife to the west.

Tourist Offices: Palácio da Foz, Pr. Restauradores (☎21 346 33 14), M: Restauradores. This is the mother of all Portuguese tourist offices. The **Welcome Center,** Pr. Comécio (☎21 031 28 10), is the office for the city of Lisbon. Both offices open daily 9am-8pm. Office at the **Aeroporto de Lisboa** (☎21 849 43 23) is just outside the baggage claim area. Open daily 6am-2am. Look for kiosks with signs that read "Ask me about Lisboa" in Santa Apolónia and other parts of the city.

American Express: Top Tours, Av. Duque de Loulé, 108 (☎21 319 42 90). M: Marquês de Pombal. Exit the metro stop and walk up Av. Liberdade toward the Marquês de Pombal statue, then turn right; the office is 2 blocks up on the left side of the street. The often-crowded Top Tours office handles all AmEx functions. English spoken. Open M-F 9:30am-1pm and 2:30-6:30pm.

Embassies: Australia, refer to the Australian Embassy in Paris (☎01 40 59 33 00; fax 01 40 59 35 38); an embassy in Lisbon is scheduled to open soon, but the embassy in Paris will still offer information and can redirect calls. **Canada,** Av. Liberdade, 144/56, 4th fl. (☎316 46 00; fax 316 46 91). **Ireland,** R. Imprensa à Estrela, 4th fl. (☎392 94 40; fax 397 73 63). **New Zealand,** Av. Antonio Agusto Aguiar, 122, 9th fl. (☎350 96 90; fax 347 20 04). **South Africa,** Av. Luis Bivar, 10 (☎353 50 41; fax 353 57 13). **UK,** R. São Bernardo, 33 (☎392 40 00; fax 392 41 83). **US,** Av. das Forças Armadas (☎726 91 09; fax 727 91 09).

Luggage Storage: Estação Rossio. Lockers 550$/€2.75 for 48hr. Open daily 8:30am-11:30pm.

Laundromat: Lavatax, R. Francisco Sanches, 65A (☎21 812 33 92). 1 block from M: Arroios. Wash, dry, and fold 1100$/€5.50 per 5kg load. Open M-F 8:30am-1pm and 3-7pm, Sa 8:30am-1pm.

Emergency: ☎112. **Police,** R. Capelo, 3 (☎21 346 61 41). English spoken.

24hr. Pharmacy: ☎118 (directory assistance). The name and address of the next night's open location is posted on the door of each pharmacy in town.

Medical Services: British Hospital, R. Saraiva de Carvalho, 49 (☎21 395 50 67). **Cruz Vermelha Portuguesa,** R. Duarte Galvão, 54 (☎21 771 40 00; **ambulance** ☎21 942 11 11).

Internet Access: Web C@fé, R. Diário de Notícias, 126 (☎21 342 11 81). 300$/€1.50 for 15min., 500$/€2.50 for 30min., 700$/€3.50 for 45min., 800$/€4 per hr. Open daily 4pm-2am.

Post Office: Marked by red *Correios* signs. **Main office** (☎21 323 89 71), Pr. Restauradores. Telephone, fax, *Posta Restante,* and international express mail (EMS). Open M-F 8:00am-10pm, Sa-Su 9am-6pm. **Postal Code:** 1100 for central Lisbon.

ACCOMMODATIONS

Most hotels are in the center of town on **Avenida Liberdade,** while many convenient budget hostels are in the **Baixa** along the **Rossio** and on **Rua Prata, Rua Correeiros,** and **Rua Ouro.** Lodgings near the **Castelo de São Jorge** or in the **Bairro Alto** are quieter and closer to the sights. If central accommodations are full, head east to the hostels along **Avenida Almirante Reis.** At night, be careful in the Baixa, the Bairro Alto, and especially the Alfama; many streets are isolated and poorly lit.

YOUTH HOSTEL

Pousada da Juventude de Lisboa (HI), R. Andrade Corvo, 46 (☎21 353 26 96). M: Picoas. Exit the metro station, turn right, and walk 1 block; the hostel is on your left. Huge, ultra-clean youth haven in an inconvenient location. English spoken. Breakfast included. Lockers 300$/€1.50 per day. Reception 8am-midnight. Check-out 10:30am. HI card required. June-Sept. dorms 2900$/€14.50; doubles with bath 6500$/€32.50; Oct.-May dorms 2000$/€10; doubles 5000$/€25.

BAIXA

Dozens of hostels surround the three connected *praças,* **Praça Restauradores, Praça Dom Pedro IV,** and **Praça Figueira,** that form the heart of downtown Lisbon. Staying in this area is incredibly practical, as it makes a good base for visiting sights.

▨ **Hospedagem Estrela da Serra,** R. dos Fanqueiros, 122, 4th fl. (☎21 887 42 51), at the end of R. São Nicolau, on the edge of the Baixa toward the Alfama. Singles 2000-2500$/€10-12.50; doubles 3000-4000$/€15-20.

Residência do Sul, Pr. Dom Pedro IV, 59, 2nd fl. (☎21 342 25 11; fax 21 347 04 43). Entrance through the souvenir shop. M: Rossio. Some rooms have a view of the plaza; ask for those if you don't mind the noise. Comfortable rooms, some with extremely cramped baths. May-Sept. singles 5000$/€25, with bath 5500-6000$/€27.50-30; doubles 7000$/€35, with bath 7500-8000$/€37.50-40. Oct-Apr. singles 4500$/€22.50, with bath 5000-5500$/€25-27.50; doubles 5500-6000$/€27.50-30.

Residencial Florescente, R. Portas de Santo Antão, 99 (☎21 342 66 09; fax 21 342 77 33), 1 block from Pr. Restauradores. M: Restauradores. Laundry available. Reserve 2-3 weeks ahead during the summer. June-Sept. singles 5000$/€25, with bath 8000$/€40; doubles 6000$/€30, with bath 9000$/€45; triples 9000$/€45, with bath 12,000$/€60. Oct.-May 1000$/€5 less.

Residencial Duas Nações, R. Vitória, 41 (☎21 346 07 10), on the corner of R. Augusta, 3 blocks up from M: Baixa-Chiado. Breakfast included. Laundry available. Reserve ahead during the summer. May-Sept. singles 3500$/€17.50, with bath 6500$/€32.50; doubles 4500$/€22.50, with bath 8500$/€42.40; triples with bath 10,500$/€52.40. Oct.-Apr. singles 3000$/€15, with bath 6000$/€30; doubles 4000$/€20, with bath 7500$/€37.40; triples with bath 8500$/€42.40.

Pensão Ibérica, Praça da Figueira, 10, 2nd fl. (☎21 886 70 26; fax 21 886 74 12). Newly renovated and repainted, with some rooms overlooking the plaza. Breakfast included. July-Sept. singles 4000$/€20, with bath 5000$/€25; doubles 7000$/€35, with bath 8000$/€40; triples 8500$/€42.50. Oct.-June 1000$/€5 less. Reserve a month ahead in summer.

Pensão Estação Central, Calçada da Carmo, 17, 2nd-3rd fl. (☎21 342 33 08; fax 21 316 94 97). 1 block from the central station, across the Largo Duque Cadaval. M: Rossio. June-Sept. singles 3000$/€15, with bath 4000$/€20; doubles 5500$/€27.50, with bath 6500$/€32.50. Oct.-May 500$/€2.50 less.

BAIRRO ALTO

The Bairro Alto has a communal feel that the town center lacks, but budget accommodations are hard to come by and the uphill hike is inconvenient and daunting for luggage-bearers. Most of Lisbon's nightlife is in Bairro Alto, but be cautious if you're out late alone.

Casa de Hóspedes Globo, R. Teixeira, 37 (☎/fax 21 346 22 79), on a small street across from the Parque São Pedro de Alcântara at the top of the funicular. From the park entrance, cross the street and go 1 block on Trav. da Cara, then turn right onto R. Teixeira. Ask for a room with a veranda. Laundry 2000$/€10 per load. June-Sept. singles 3000-4000$/€15-20, with bath 5000$/€25; double with bath 6000$/€30; triple with bath 8000$/€40. Oct.-May ask for lower rates. Reserve 3 weeks ahead in summer.

Pensão Londres, R. Dom Pedro V, 53, 2nd fl. (☎21 346 22 03; fax 21 346 56 82; www.desenvolve.com/plondres). Take the Ascensor Glória from Pr. Restauradores to the top. Turn right and walk up R. S. Pedro to R. Dom Pedro V. These spacious, well-lit rooms overlook the old town. Breakfast included. Laundry available. Reserve a month ahead in the summer. Singles 5500-9000$/€27.50-45; doubles 7700-12,200$/€38.40-60.85; triples 15,200$/€75.80; quads 17,200$/€85.80.

ALFAMA

The Alfama has steep prices (and streets), but staying there can be a nice change of pace, especially after a day or two in the Baixa grid.

Pensão Ninho das Águias, R. Costa do Castelo, 74 (☎21 885 40 70), right behind the Castelo. From Pr. Figueira take R. Madalena to Largo Adelino Costa, then head uphill to R. Costa do Castelo. Canary-filled garden looks out over the old city. Reserve at least 1 month ahead during the summer. Singles 5000$/€25; doubles 7500$/€37.50, with bath 8000$/€40; triples 10,000$/€50.

❒ FOOD

Lisbon has some of the least expensive restaurants and some of the best wine of any European capital. A full dinner costs about 1800-2200$/€9-11 per person; the *prato do dia* (daily special) is often a great deal. Head to the **Calçada de Santa Ana** to find small authentic restaurants that cater to locals. Snack on a surprisingly filling, incredibly cheap, and sinfully delicious Portuguese pastry; *pastelarias* (pastry shops) are everywhere. Specialties include *amêjoas à bulhão pato* (steamed clams), *creme de mariscos* (seafood chowder with tomatoes), and a local classic, *bacalhau cozido com grão e batatas* (cod with chick-peas and boiled potatoes, doused in olive oil). The **Mercado Ribeira,** Av. 24 de Julho (☎21 346 29 66) is a cheap, conveniently located **supermarket.** Open M-Sa 6am-2pm.

 Martinho da Arcada, Pr. do Comércio, 3 (☎21 887 92 59), at the back left corner of the Baixa plaza when facing the river. Founded in 1782, this is the oldest restaurant in Lisbon and one of the classic cafes of the city. Although the restaurant is predictably (and justifiably) expensive (entrees 1900-2950$/€9.50-14.75), the **cafe** next door not only makes excellent *paste'is de nata* (150$/€0.75) but also offers the best lunch deal in the Baixa, with excellent daily specials served from noon-3pm (entrees 800-900$/€4-4.50). Open M-Sa 7am-10pm.

Pastelaria Anunciada, Largo da Anunciada, 1-2 (☎21 342 44 17), on the corner of R. de S. José. Like many of the Baixa's pastelarias, Anunciada has good, inexpensive lunches and is a haven for locals on a street lined with touristy places. Open daily 6:30am-10pm, serves meals noon-10pm.

O Cantinho das Ga'veas, R. das Ga'veas, 82-84 (☎21 342 04 60), at the corner of Trav. Poço Cidade. Popular restaurant in the Bairro Alto serves typical Portuguese dishes at surprisingly reasonable prices. Open daily noon-3pm and 7pm-midnight.

Hell's Kitchen, R. Atalaia, 176 (☎21 342 28 22). From the top of C. Glória (the steep hill from Pr. Restauradores), walk a few blocks into Bairro Alto and turn right on R. Atalaia. Small, but with an extensive selection of delicious main dishes (1100-1600$/€5.50-8), including vegetarian options. Open Tu-Su 8pm-12:30am.

Restaurante Calcuta, R. do Norte, 17 (☎21 342 82 95), near Lg. Camões in the Bairro Alto. Fancy yet inexpensive Indian restaurant with a wide selection of vegetarian meals (900-1000$/€4.50-5). Meat dishes 1200-1700$/€6-8.50. Open M-F noon-3pm and 6:30-11pm, Sa-Su 6:30-11pm.

Restaurante Arco do Castelo, R. Chão de Feira, 25 (☎21 887 65 98), in the Alfama across from the gate to the Castelo de São Jorge. A Portuguese-Indian mix, including specialties from Goa, Portugal's former colony in India. Open M-Sa 12:30pm-midnight.

◎ SIGHTS

BAIXA

Although the Baixa features few historic sights, a lively atmosphere surrounding the neighborhood's three main *praças* makes it a monument in its own right.

AROUND THE ROSSIO. The best place to embark upon your tour of Lisbon's Enlightenment-era center is from its heart—the **Rossio.** The city's main square, also known as the **Praça Dom Pedro IV,** was once a cattle market and home to a public execution stage, bullfighting arena, and carnival ground. Adjoining the Rossio is the elegant **Praça Figueira,** which lies on the border of the Alfama district.

AROUND PRAÇA DOS RESTAURADORES. Just past the Rossio train station, an obelisk and a sculpture of the "Spirit of Independence" commemorate Portugal's independence from Spain in 1640. Pr. Restauradores is also the start of **Avenida da Liberdade,** Lisbon's most imposing yet elegant promenade. Modeled after the wide boulevards of 19th-century Paris, this 1.6km thoroughfare ends at **Praça do Marquês do Pombal;** from here an 18th-century statue of the Marquês, who oversaw Lisbon's reconstruction after the 1755 earthquake, overlooks the city.

PORTUGAL

BAIRRO ALTO

In the Bairro, pretentious intellectuals mix with insecure teens and idealistic university students. It's the only place in Lisbon that never sleeps; here, there is as much to do at night as there is to see during the day. At the center of the neighborhood is **Praça Camões**, which adjoins **Largo Chiado** at the top of R. Garrett, a good place to rest and orient yourself while sightseeing. To reach **Rua Garret** and the heart of the chic Chiado neighborhood, turn left when exiting the elevator and walk one block; Rua Garret is on the right.

THE ASCENSOR DE SANTA JUSTA. The Ascensor de Santa Justa, an elevator built in 1902 inside a Gothic wrought-iron tower, once served as transportation up to the Bairro Alto but now just takes tourists up to see the view and then back down again. *(Elevator runs M-F 7am-11pm, Sa-Su 9am-11pm. One-way 175$/€0.90.)*

■ **MUSEU NACIONAL DE ARTE ANTIGA.** This museum presents an interesting survey of European painting dating back as far as the 12th century and ranging from Gothic primitives to 18th-century French masterpieces. *(R. das Janelas Verdes, Jardim 9 Abril. 30min. down Av. Infante Santo from the Ascensor de Santa Justa. Buses #40 and 60 stop to the right of the museum exit and head back to the Baixa. ☎ 21 391 28 00. Open Tu 2-6pm, W-Su 10am-6pm. 600$/€3, students 300$/€1.50. Su before 2pm free.)*

PARQUE DE SÃO PEDRO DE ALCÂNTARA. For a perfect picnic, head to this mercifully shaded park. The Castelo de São Jorge in the Alfama stares back from the cliff opposite the park. A mosaic points out the landmarks included in this vista. *(On the right off R. São Pedro de Alcântara—the continuation of R. Misericórdia. Walk up R. Misericórdia from Pr. Camões; the park is right next to C. Glória.)*

BASÍLICA DA ESTRÊLA. Half-mad Maria I, desiring a male heir, made fervent religious vows promising God everything if she were granted a son. When a baby boy was finally born, she built this church. *(On Pr. Estrêla. Accessible by tram #28 from Pr. Comércio (175$/€0.90). ☎ 21 396 09 15. Open daily 8am-12:30pm and 3-7:30pm. Free.)*

ALFAMA

The Alfama, Lisbon's medieval quarter, was the lone neighborhood to survive the 1755 earthquake. The neighborhood slopes in tiers from the Castelo de São Jorge facing the Rio Tejo. Between the Alfama and the Baixa is the **Mouraria** (Moorish quarter), established after the Moors were expelled in 1147.

THE LOWER ALFAMA. While any of the small uphill streets a few blocks east of the Baixa lead to the Alfama's streets, the least confusing way to see the neighborhood is by climbing up R. Madalena, which begins two blocks away from Pr. Comércio (take R. Alfandega from the *praça*). Turn right when you see the **Igreja da Madalena** in the Largo Madalena on the right. Take R. Santo António da Sé and follow the tram tracks to the cleverly designed and ornamented **Igreja de Santo António da Sé.** The construction was funded with money collected by the city's children, who fashioned miniature altars bearing images of the saint to place on doorsteps. The custom is re-enacted annually on June 13, the saint's feast day and Lisbon's largest holiday. *(☎ 21 886 91 45. Open daily 8am-7pm. Mass daily 11am, 5, and 7pm.)*

■ **CASTELO DE SÃO JORGE.** Near the top of the Alfama lies the must-see Castelo de São Jorge, which offers spectacular views of Lisbon and the ocean. Built in the 5th century by the Visigoths and enlarged by 9th-century Moors, this castle was a playgound for the royal family between the 14th and 16th centuries. Now, anyone can wander around the ruins, soak in the view of the cityscape below, explore the ponds, or gawk at the exotic bird population of the castle gardens. *(From the cathedral, follow the yellow signs for the castle on a winding uphill walk. Castle open Apr.-Sept. daily 9am-9pm; Oct.-Mar. 9am-6pm. Free.)*

ALONG TR. SÃO VICENTE. On the far side of the castle, follow the main tram tracks along Tr. São Tomé (which becomes R. São Vicente as it winds uphill) to Largo São Vicente and the **Igreja de São Vicente de Fora,** built between 1582 and 1629 and dedicated to Lisbon's patron saint. At the **Feira da Ladra** (flea market) that takes place in the church's backyard, the din of a lively social scene drowns out cries of merchants hawking used goods. *(From the bottom of R. Correeiros in the Baixa, take bus #12 or tram #28 (175$/€0.90). Church open Tu-Sa 9am-6pm, Su 9am-12:30pm and 3-5pm. Free. Flea market open Tu and Sa 6am-5pm.)* The **Igreja de Santa Engrácia (National Pantheon)** is farther down toward the coast. This church, with its impressive dome, took almost 300 years to complete (1682-1966), giving rise to the famous Portuguese expression, "Endless like the construction of Santa Engrácia." *(Walk along R. São Vicente and keep left as the road branches. Open Tu-Su 10am-5pm.)*

SALDANHA

Amid Lisbon's business affairs, this modern district has two excellent museums, both owned by the Fundação Gulbenkian. The ◧**Museu Calouste Gulbenkian** houses oil tycoon Calouste Gubenkian's extensive art collection. The collection is divided into two sections: ancient art—Egyptian, Greek, Roman, Islamic, and Oriental— and European pieces from the 15th to 20th centuries. *(Av. Berna, 45. M: Palhavã or S. Sebastião. Bus # 16, 31, 46. ☎ 21 782 30 00. Open Tu-Su 10am-5pm. 500$/€2.50, free Su mornings for students and seniors.)* The adjacent **Museu do Centro de Arte Moderna** is home to an extensive collection of modern art as well as beautiful gardens. *(R. Dr. Nicolau Bettencourt. M: S. Sebastião. Bus #16, 31, and 46. ☎ 21 795 02 41. Open Tu-Su 10am-5pm. 500$/€2.50, free Su mornings for students and seniors.)*

BELÉM

A number of well-maintained museums and historical sites showcase the former opulence and extravagance of the Portuguese empire. To get to Belém, take tram #15 from Pr. Comércio (15min., 175$/€0.90), bus #28 or 43 from Pr. Figueira (15min., 175$/€0.90), or the train from Estação Cais do Sodré (10min., every 15min., 140$/€0.70). From the train station, cross over the tracks, then cross the street and go left. From the bus station, follow the avenue straight ahead.

MOSTEIRO DOS JERÓNIMOS. The Mosteiro dos Jerónimos rises from the banks of the Tejo behind a lush public garden. Established by King Dom Manuel I in 1502 to give thanks for the success of Vasco da Gama's voyage to India, this monastery showcases Portugal's native Manueline style, combining Gothic forms with early Renaissance details. Inside, the symbolic tombs of Luís de Camões and navigator Vasco da Gama lie in two opposing transepts. *(☎ 21 362 00 34. Open Tu-Su 10am-5pm. 600$/€3, students 300$/€1.50. Cloisters open Tu-Su 10am-5pm. Free.)*

TORRE DE BELÉM. The Torre de Belém rises from the north bank of the Tejo and is surrounded by the ocean on three sides due to the receding shoreline. Today, it is only accessible by a small bridge, offering spectacular panoramic views of Belém, the Tejo, and the Atlantic beyond. *(A 10min. walk along the water from the monastery. Take the underpass by the gardens to cross the highway. ☎ 21 362 00 34. Open Tu-Su 10am-6pm. 600$/€3, students and seniors 300$/€1.50.)*

PARQUE DAS NAÇÕES. The Parque das Nações (Park of Nations), former grounds of Expo '98, is the newest addition to Lisbon's growing list of sights. After Expo '98 flopped, the government took a risk, pumping millions of dollars into the land and converting it into the Parque das Nações. *(M: Oriente. ☎ 21 891 93 33; www.parquedasnacoes.pt.)* The biggest attraction is the **Pavilhão dos Oceanos,** the largest oceanarium in Europe, which showcases the four major oceans right down to the sounds, smells, and climates. The four ocean tanks connect to the main tank, which houses fish, sharks, and other sea creatures. *(Open Apr.-Sept. daily 10am-7pm; Oct.-Mar. 10am-6pm. 1700$/€8.50, under 18 and seniors 900$/€4.50).* In addition to various museums, gardens, and pavilions scattered throughout the park, there is the 145m **Torre Vasco da Gama.** An elevator ascends to the observation tower, which offers spectacular views of the city. *(Open daily 10am-8pm. 500$/€2.50, under 18 or over 65 250$/€1.25.)*

♫▓ ENTERTAINMENT AND NIGHTLIFE

Agenda Cultural and *Follow Me Lisboa*, free at kiosks in the Rossio, on R. Portas de Santo Antão, and at the tourist office, contain information on concerts, movies, plays, and bullfights.

PORTUGAL

BARS AND CLUBS

The **Bairro Alto** is the first place to go for nightlife, where a plethora of small bars and clubs invite exploration of the side streets. In particular, **Rua Norte, Rua Diário Notícias,** and **Rua Atalaia** have many small clubs packed into three short blocks, making club-hopping as easy as crossing the street. Most gay and lesbian clubs are found between Pr. Camões and Trav. da Queimada, as well as in the **Rato** area near the edge of Bairro Alto. The **Avenida 24 de Julho** and the **Rua das Janelas Verdes** in the **Santos** area above have some of the most popular bars and clubs. Newer expansions include the area along the river across from the **Sta. Apolo'nia** train station. There's no reason to arrive before midnight; crowds flow in around 2am.

■ **Lux/Fra'gil,** Av. Infante D. Henrique, A (☎21 882 08 90). Take a taxi to the area across from the Sta. Apolo'nia train station to get to this imaginative mix of lights and boxes. In a class and location of its own, Lux is the newest big thing in Lisbon. Minimum consumption 2000$/€10 (the minimum can be up to 30,000$/€150 if the bouncer doesn't like you). Beer 300-500$€1.50-2.50. Open Tu-Sa 6pm-6am.

■ **Litro e Meio (1,5 Lt.),** R. das Janelas Verdes, 27 (☎21 395 05 26), in the Santos area above the clubs on Av. 24 de Julho. This friendly new bar attracts a mostly young crowd and plays house and latin music. Most popular between 1 and 2:30am before clubbing on the street below. Minimum consumption usually 1000$/€5. Open M-Sa 10pm-4am.

Resto*, R. Costa do Castelo, 7, in the Alfama. Known as Chapito*, as identified by the large white sign at the entrance, this bar is located at a circus school. The huge outdoor patio has one of the best views of the city to be found anywhere. Filled with a young crowd, especially from 10pm-midnight. Live Portuguese guitar F-Su. Open M-F 7:30pm-2am, Sa-Su 11pm-2am.

Kapital, Av. 24 de Julho, 68. The classiest club in Lisbon, with a ruthless door policy that makes admission a competitive sport. Don't expect to get in; for your best chance, go with Portuguese regulars and keep your mouth shut. If you're still there at the 6am closing time, take the back tunnel directly into neighboring Kremlin to continue partying. Open M-Sa 11pm-6am.

Kremlin, Escandinhas da Praia, 5 (☎21 395 71 01), off Av. 24 de Julho next to Kapital. Caters to a mixed crowd. Set in an old convent, Kremlin has giant fake statues and 3 rooms with throbbing house and dance music. Cover usually 1000$/€5 for women and 2000$/€10 for men, includes 1 drink. Open F-Sa midnight-9:30am, Th midnight-8am, Tu-W midnight-6am.

Trumps, R. Imprensa Nacional, 104B, in the Bairro Alto (☎21 397 10 59). Lisbon's biggest gay club features several bars in addition to a massive dance floor. Minimum consumption of 1000$/€5. Open Tu-Th and Su 11:30pm-4:30am, F-Sa 11:30pm-6:30am.

CAFES

Relaxing in cafes during the day and late into the night is a popular pastime in Lisbon. The famous 19th-century **A Brasileira**, R. Garrett, 120-122, in the Chiado neighborhood is considered by many to be "the best cafe in Portugal." (☎21 346 95 41. Mixed drinks 1000$/€5. Open daily 8am-2am.) **Costa do Castelo**, Calçada Marquês de Tancos, 1-1B, just behind the Castelo in Alfama, has a romantic view of the city from its outdoor patio. (☎21 888 46 36. Sandwiches 400$/€2. Tapas 400-500$/€2-2.50. Mixed drinks 300-700$/€1.50-3.50. Open Tu-Su 12:30pm-2am.)

FADO

Lisbon's trademark is the heart-wrenching *fado*, an expressive art that combines elements of singing and narrative poetry. *Fadistas*, cloaked in black dresses and shawls, perform emotional tales of lost loves and faded glory. The Bairro Alto has many *fado* joints off R. Misericórdia and on side streets radiating from the Museu de São Roque; the prices alone may turn a knife in your heart. To avoid these, try exploring nearby streets; various bars and other small venues often offer free performances. **Adega Machado**, R. Norte, 91, is one of the larger *fado* restaurants. (☎21 322 46 40. Minimum consumption 3100$/€15.50. Open Tu-Su 8pm-3am.)

DAYTRIPS FROM LISBON

SINTRA

Trains (☎ 21 923 26 05) arrive on Av. Dr. Miguel Bombarda from Lisbon's Estação Rossio (45min., every 15min., 6am-2am, 210$/€1.10). Stagecoach buses leave from outside the train station for Cascais (#417, 40min., every hr., 6:35am-7:08pm, 520$/€2.60) and Estoril (#418, 40min., every hr., 460$/€2.30). Mafrense buses (down the street) go to Mafra (50min., every hr., 6:25am-7:25pm, 410$/€2.10).

In the epic poem *Childe Harold*, British Romantic poet Lord Byron described Sintra as a "glorious Eden." His adulation made Sintra (pop. 20,000) a chic destination for 19th-century European aristocrats. These days, Sintra is a favorite among foreign tour groups and backpackers alike, all of whom drool over its fairy-tale castles and mountain vistas. The **Palácio Nacional de Sintra** sits at the center of it all on Pr. República and was once the summer residence of Moorish sultans and their harems. (Open Th-Tu 10am-5:30pm. 600$/€3, students 300$/€1.50. Buy tickets by 5pm.) On the mountain overlooking the old town, **Sintra-Vila**, is the **Castelo dos Mouros**, which offers stunning views of the mountains and coast. (Open June-Sept. daily 9am-8pm; Oct.-May 9am-7pm. Free.) The 3km ascent (1-1½hr.) starts to the left of the tourist office; follow the blue signs up the mountain. Bus #434 also runs to the top from the tourist office (15min., 3 per hr., all-day pass 600$/€3). One kilometer farther uphill is the **Palácio da Pena,** an amalgamation of German and Portuguese styles, built in the 1840s by Prince Ferdinand of Bavaria, the husband of Queen Maria II. (Open July-Sept. Tu-Su 10am-6:30pm; Oct.-June Tu-Su 10am-5pm. 600$/€3, students 400$/€2; Oct.-Apr. 200$/€1.)

Head left out of the train station, turn right downhill at the next intersection and left in front of the castle-like Câmara Municipal, then follow the road uphill to reach the **tourist office,** Pr. República, 23. (☎ 21 923 11 57. Open June-Sept. daily 9am-8pm; Oct.-May 9am-7pm.) To get to the **Pousada da Juventude de Sintra (HI),** on Sta. Eufémia, take bus #434 from the front of the train station or from the left side of the tourist office to the **Palácio Nacional de Pena,** and walk through the palace gardens to the hostel; look for signs. (☎ 21 924 12 10. Reception 8am-midnight. Dorms 1900$; doubles 4200-4600$.)

QUELUZ

Take the train toward Sintra from Lisbon's Estação Rossio (M: Rossio) and get off at the Queluz-Belas stop. (25min., every 15min., 140$/€1.70)

Queluz, just 12km west of Lisbon, is the home of the amazing **Palácio Nacional de Queluz,** a pink-and-white Rococo wedding cake of a palace. In the mid-18th century, Dom Pedro III turned an old hunting lodge into this summer residence—check out the **Sala dos Embaixadores,** with its gilded thrones and Chinese vases and the *azulejo*-lined canal in the garden. Exit the station through the ticket office, go left on Av. Antonio Ennes, and follow the signs to the palace. (Open W-M 10am-5pm. 600$/€3, students and seniors 300$/€1.50, children under 14 free. Garden 100$/€0.5.)

ESTORIL AND CASCAIS

Trains from Lisbon's Estação do Sodré (M: Cais do Sodré) stop in Cascais (30min., every 20min., 5:30am-2:30am, 210$/€1.10) via Estoril (30min., every 20min., 5:30am-2:30am, 210$/€1.10) Estoril and Cascais are only a 20min. stroll along the coast or Av. Marginal from each other.

Beautiful beaches, stately vistas, and a bustling casino give Estoril a reputation of opulence. **Praia Estoril Tamariz beach** greets visitors on arrival. **Casino Estoril,** Europe's largest casino, beckons those feeling lucky. (Open daily 3pm-3am. No sneakers, jeans, or shorts. Must be 18 for slots and game room. Passport required.) From the train station, cross Av. Marginal to go to the **tourist office** on Arcada do Parque. (☎ 21 466 38 13; fax 21 467 22 80. Open M-Sa 9am-7pm, Su 10am-6pm.)

PORTUGAL

Once the summer vacation resort of the royal family, Cascais still caters to a well-to-do crowd. Four popular **beaches** close to the center draw throngs of locals and tourists. To get to the **tourist office,** Av. dos Combatantes 25, which books rooms, turn right at the fork in the promenade, follow the train tracks to the station, cross the Largo de Estação square, and turn right at the McDonald's on Av. Valbom. (☎21 486 82 04. Open July-Sept. 15 M-Sa 9am-8pm, Su 10am-6pm; Sept. 16-June M-Sa 9am-7pm, Su 10am-6pm.)

MAFRA AND ERICEIRA

Frequent Mafrense buses run from Lisbon's Campo Grande (M: Campo Grande) to Mafra (1-1½hr., every hr., 5:30am-9pm, 550$/€2.75) and Ericeira (1½hr., every hr., 6:30am-11:20pm, 740$/€3.70). These buses also run from Mafra to Ericeira. (20min., every hr., 7:30am-midnight, 240$/€1.20).

Sleepy Mafra is home to one of Portugal's most impressive sights and one of Europe's largest historical buildings, the **Palácio Nacional de Mafra.** The monstrous 2000-room castle took 50,000 workers 13 years to complete. (☎261 81 75 50. Open W-M 10am-5pm. 600$/€3, students and seniors 300$/€1.50. Free tours daily in English at 11am and 2:30pm.) To reach the **tourist office,** take a right off the main steps of the palace and bear left onto Av. 25 de Abril—the office is behind the fountain. (☎261 81 20 23. Open M-F 9am-7pm, Sa-Su 9:30am-1pm and 2:30-6pm.)

Ericeira is a pleasant fishing village whose beaches have been discovered by surfers. The **tourist office,** R. Eduardo Burnay, 46, rents bikes during the summer. (☎261 86 31 22. Open Su-Th 9:30am-8pm, F-Sa 9:30am-midnight; longer summer hours.)

OTHER DAYTRIPS FROM LISBON

COIMBRA. Party or people-watch in this vibrant university town (see p. 780).

ÉVORA. Peruse the halls of the "museum city," including the cathedral—perhaps Portugal's finest—and the uniquely grotesque Capela dos Ossos (see p. 775).

CENTRAL PORTUGAL

Jagged cliffs and whitewashed fishing villages line Estremadura's Costa de Prata (Silver Coast), with beaches that rival even those in the Algarve. Nearby, the fertile region of the Ribatejo (Banks of the Tejo) is perhaps the gentlest and greenest in Portugal. In this region just north of Lisbon, relatively untouristed towns beckon travelers with historical sights and lush scenery.

LEIRIA   ☎244

Capital of the surrounding district and an important transport hub, prosperous and industrial Leiria fans out from a fertile valley, 22km from the coast. Chosen to host the Euro 2002 soccer finals, Leiria is busy preparing itself for the crowds that will flood the city. Leiria's most notable sight is its **Castelo de Leiria,** a granite fort built by Dom Afonso Henriques after he snatched the town from the Moors atop the crest of a volcanic hill. The terrace opens onto a panoramic view of the town and river. (Castle open Apr.-Sept. M-F 9am-6:30pm, Sa-Su 10am-6:30pm; Oct.-Mar. M-F 9am-5:30pm, Sa-Su 10am-5:30pm. 155$/€0.75.) Nearby **beaches,** including **Vieira, Pedrógão,** and **São Pedro de Muel,** are all easily accessible via buses from the station.

Leiria makes a practical base for exploring the nearby region. **Trains** (☎244 88 20 27) run from the station 3km outside town to Coimbra (1½hr., 7 per day 6:55am-8:50pm, 770$/€3.85) and Lisbon via Caldas da Rainha (3½hr., 8 per day 8am-8:30pm, 1220$/€6.10). **Buses** (☎244 81 15 07), just off Pr. Paulo VI, next to the main park and close to the tourist office, run to: Batalha (20min., 9 per day 7:15am-7:10pm, 210$/€1); Coimbra (1hr., 11 per day 7:15am-2am, 1150$/€5.75); Lisbon (2hr., 11 per day 7:15am-11pm, 1400$/€7); Porto (3½hr., 10 per day 7:15am-2am, 1800$/€9); Santarém (2hr., 5 per day 7:15am-7:05pm, 900-1550$/€4.50-7.75); Tomar (1½hr.; M-F 2 per day 7:15am and 5:45pm, Sa 6:15pm; 570-1200$/€2.90-6). Buses also run between the train station and the **tourist office** (15. min., every hr. 7am-7:20pm, 150$/€0.75), in the Jardim Luís de Camões. (☎244 82 37 73. Open May-Sept. daily 10am-1pm and 3-7pm; Oct.-Apr. 10am-1pm and 2-6pm. If you're going to spend the night in town, head to the **Pousada da Juventude de Leiria (HI)**, on Largo Cândido dos Reis, 9. (☎244 83 18 68. Mid-June to mid-Sept. dorms 1900$/€9.50; doubles 4200$/€21; mid-Sept. to mid-June dorms 1500$/€7.50; doubles 3500$/€17.50.) Largo Cândido dos Reis is lined with popular bars like **Anubis, Estrebaria, Sebentas,** and **Os Filipes. Xannax Dance Club,** R. C. Mouzinho de Albuquerque, 168, is a relatively new establishment that turns from bar to disco around 3am.

▶ DAYTRIPS FROM LEIRIA

TOMAR   ☎249

For centuries, the arcane Knights Templar—made up of monks and warriors—plotted crusades from a celebrated convent-fortress high above this small town. The ▓**Convento de Cristo** complex was the Knights' powerful and mysterious headquarters. The first structure was built in 1160, but some cloisters, convents, and buildings were added later. The **Claustro dos Felipes** is one of Europe's masterpieces of Renaissance architecture. (☎249 31 34 81. Complex open June-Sept. daily 9am-6pm; Oct.-May 9am-5pm. 600$/€3, students 300$/€1.50.) The **Museu dos Fósforos** (match museum), in the Convento de São Francisco, opposite the train and bus stations, exhibits Europe's largest matchbox collection. (Open daily 10-noon and 3-5pm. Free.) **Trains** (☎249 31 28 15) go from Av. Combatentes da Grande Guerra, at the southern edge of town, to: Coimbra (2½hr., 6 per day 6an-6pm, 960-1200$/€4.80-6); Lisbon (2hr., 18 per day 5am-10pm, 1010-2040$/€5-10.20); Porto (4½hr., 7 per day 8am-8pm, 1510-2210$/€7.50-11); Santarém (1hr., 12 per day 5am-10pm, 520-840$/€2.60-4.20). Rodoviaria Tejo **buses** (☎249 31 27 38) leave from Av. Combatentes Grande Guerra, by the train station, for: Coimbra (2½hr., 7am, 1650$/€8.25); Leiria (1hr.; M-F 7:15am and 5:45pm, Sa 7am; 590-1200$/€3-6); Lisbon (2hr., 4 per day 9:15am-6pm, 1200$/€6); Porto (4hr., 7am, 2100$/€10.50); Santarém (1hr., 9:15am and 6pm, 1200$/€6). From the bus or train station, take a right onto Av. Combatentes de Grande Guerra and then a left onto Av. Torres Pinheiro and continue past the traffic circle on R. Everaro; the **tourist office** is on the left just past the bridge. (☎249 32 24 27. Open July-Sept. daily 10am-8pm; Oct.-June 10am-6pm.) **Postal code:** 2300.

BATALHA. The only reason (but a good one) to visit Batalha is the gigantic, flamboyant ▓**Mosteiro de Santa Maria da Vitória.** Built by Dom João I in 1385 to commemorate his victory over the Spanish, the complex of cloisters and chapels remains one of Portugal's greatest monuments. Through the Claustro de Dom Afonso V, out the door and to the right are the impressive **Capelas Imperfeitas (Unfinished Chapels)**, with massive buttresses designed to support a large dome that was never actually constructed. Napoleon's troops sacrilegiously turned the nave into a brothel. To get to the monastery, enter through the church. (Open Apr.-Sept. daily 9am-6pm; Oct.-Mar. 9am-5pm. Monastery 600$/€3, under 25 with student ID 360$/€1.80, seniors 300$/€1.50, under 14 free. Church free.) **Buses** run from across the monastery to: Leiria (20min., 10 per day 7:50am-8:25pm, 210$/€1.05); Lisbon (2hr., 6 per day 7:25am-6:55pm, 1200$/€6); Tomar (1½hr.; 8am, noon, and 6pm; 520$/€2.60). The **tourist office,** on Pr. Mouzinho de Albuquerque along R. Nossa Senhora do Caminho, stands opposite the monastery. (☎(244) 76 51 80. Open May-Sept. daily 10am-1pm and 3-7pm; Oct.-Apr. 10am-1pm and 2-6pm.)

SANTARÉM   ☎243

Perhaps the most charming of Ribatejo's cities, Santarém (pop. 30,000) presides from atop a rocky mound over the calm Rio Tejo and the soft green pastures. Once a flourishing medieval center, the city was the capital of the Portuguese Gothic style. Santarém's many appealing churches still exhibit a mind-boggling range of architectural styles. The austere façade of the **Igreja do Seminário dos Jesuítas** dominates **Praça Sá da Bandeira,** Santarém's main square. (Open Tu-Su 9:30am-12:30pm and 2-5:30pm. Free.) Take R. Serpa Pinto from Pr. Sá da Bandeira to the **Praça Visconde de Serra Pilar,** where Christians, Moors, and Jews gathered centuries ago for social and business affairs. The 12th-century **Igreja de Marvilha,** off the *praça,* has a 17th-century *azulejo* interior. (Open Tu-Su 9:30am-12:30pm and 2-5:30pm. Free.) Nearby is the early Gothic **Igreja da Graça;** within the chapel lies Pedro Alvares Cabral, the explorer who discovered Brazil. (Church and chapel open Tu-Su 9:30am-12:30pm and 2-5:30pm. Free.) From there, take R. Cons. Figueiredo Leal, which becomes Av. 5 de Outubro, to the ◙**Portas do Sol,** a paradise of flowers and fountains surrounded by old Moorish walls. (Open daily 8am-11pm. Free.)

The **train station** (☎243 32 11 99), 2km from town, serves: Coimbra (2hr., 11 per day 6:25am-1:10am, 1020-1400$/€5.10-7); Lisbon (1hr., 37 per day 4:40am-3:55am, 670-1050$/€3.35-5.25); Porto (4hr., 4 per day 9:55am-8:55pm, 1720-2100$/€8.60-10.50); Tomar (1hr., every hr. 6:20am-1:25am, 520$/€2.60). Buses (10min., every 30min-1hr., 210$/€1.05) connect the train station with the **bus station** (☎243 33 32 00), on Av. Brasil, near Pr. Sá da Bandeira. **Buses** serve: Coimbra (2hr., 10:45am-6:45pm, 1450$/€7.25); Lisbon (1-1½hr., 10 per day 7am-7:15pm, 1000$/€5); Porto (4hr., 10:45am-6:45pm, 2100$/€10.50). The **tourist office,** R. Capelo Ivêns, 63, is nearby. (☎243 30 44 37. Open M 9am-12:30pm and 2-5:30pm, Tu-F 9am-7pm, Sa-Su 10am-12:30pm and 2:30-5:30pm.) Around the corner is **Residencial Abidis,** R. Guilherme de Azevedo, 4. (☎243 32 20 17. Singles 3500-4000$/€17.50-20, with bath 5500$/€27.50; doubles 4500-5000$/€22.50-25, 7000$/€35. Ask for discounts in winter.) **Postal code:** 2000.

NAZARÉ   ☎262

It's hard to tell where authenticity stops and tourism starts in Nazaré, an unabashed beachtown. Fishermen in traditional garb go barefoot while the day's catch dries in the hot sun. But if Nazaré is part theater, at least it puts on a good show—and everyone gets front row seats on the glorious **beach.** For an evening excursion, take the **funicular** (3min., every 15-30min. 7:15am-midnight, 115$/€0.60), which runs from R. Elevador off Av. República to the **Sítio,** a clifftop area replete with uneven cobbled streets, weathered buildings, and wonderful views of the town and ocean. Around 6pm, fishing boats return to the **port** beyond the far left end (facing the ocean) of the beach; head over to watch fishermen at work and eavesdrop as local restaurateurs bid for the most promising catches at the **fish auction** (M-F 6-10pm). **Cafes** in Pr. Souza Oliveira teem with people until about 1am. The intimate bar **Ta Ba Res** (☎262 08 21 73), R. de Rio Maior, 20-22, just off R. Mouzinho Albuquerque, hosts live music most summer nights. (Beer 150-400$/€0.75-2, mixed drinks 500$/€2.50. Open daily 2pm-4am.) **Bullfights** are popular as well; Nazaré is on the revolving schedule that brings *corridas* to a different city in the province each summer weekend (Sa 10pm; tickets start at 2500$/€12.50).

Nazaré is only accessible by **bus** (☎262 55 11 72). Buses run to: Coimbra (2hr., 5 per day 6:25am-7:25pm, 1400$/€7); Lisbon (2hr., 8 per day 6:50am-8pm, 1250$/€6.25); Porto (3½hr., 5 per day 6:25am-7:25pm, 1800$/€9); Tomar (1½hr. 3 per day 7:10am-5pm, 850$/€4.50). The **tourist office** is beachside on Av. República. (☎262 56 11 94. Open daily July-Aug. 10am-10pm; Sept. 10am-8pm; Oct.-Mar. 9:30am-1pm and 2:30-6pm; Apr.-June 10am-1pm and 3-7pm.) Look along Pr. Dr. Manuel de Arriaga and Pr. Sousa Oliveira for the best deals on accommodations. Try **Vila Turística Conde Fidalgo,** Av. da Independência Nacional, 21-A, three blocks uphill from Pr. Sousa Oliveira. (☎/fax 262 55 23 61. Sept.-June singles 3000$/€15; doubles 4000$/€20; July singles 6000$/€30; doubles 7000$/€35; Aug. singles 8000$/€40; doubles 9000$/€45.) For **camping,** head to **Vale Paraíso,** on Estrada Nacional, 242, 2½km out of town. Also rents bungalows and apartments. Take the bus (15min., 8 per day 7am-7pm) to Alcobaça or Leiria. (☎262 56 18 00; camping.vp.nz@mail.telepac.pt. Reception daily 8am-10pm. June-Sept. 650$/€3.25 per person, 540-580$/€2.70-3 per tent, 540$/€2.70 per car; Apr.-May and Oct. 540$/€2.70, 460-635$/€2.30-3.15, 455$/€2.25; Nov.-Mar. 400$/€2, 355-485$/€1.75-2.45,

350\$/€1.75.) Supermarkets line **Rua Sub-Vila,** parallel to Av. República and Pr. Dr. Manuel de Arriaga. **Postal code:** 2450.

ÉVORA ☎266

Designated a UNESCO World Heritage site, Évora is justly known as the "Museum City." The picture-perfect town boasts a Roman temple, an imposing cathedral, a 16th-century university, and Moorish arches lining winding streets. The city's most famous monument is the first century **Roman temple,** on Largo do Vila Flor. Only a platform and 14 Corinthian columns remain. Facing the temple is the town's best-kept secret, the **Igreja de São João Evangelista** (1485), its interior covered with dazzling *azulejos* (tiles); ask to see the church's hidden chambers. (Open Tu-Su 10am-12:30pm and 2-6pm. 500\$/€2.50.) From Pr. Giraldo, head up R. 5 de Outubro to the colossal 12th-century **cathedral;** the 12 apostles on the doorway are masterpieces of medieval Portuguese sculpture. (Cathedral open daily 9am-12:30pm and 2-5pm, free.) The **Museu de Arte Sacra,** above the nave, has religious artifacts. (Museum open Tu-Su 9am-noon and 2-4:30pm, 500\$/€2.50.) Attached to the pleasant **Igreja Real de São Francisco,** the bizarre ■**Capela dos Ossos** (Chapel of Bones), was built entirely out of the bones of 5000 people by three morbid Franciscan monks. Above the door an irreverent sign taunts visitors: *"Nós ossos que aqui estamos, pelos vossos esperamos"* ("We bones lie here awaiting yours"). From Pr. Giraldo, follow R. República; the church is on the right and the chapel around back to the right of the main entrance. (Open Apr. and June-Sept. M-Sa 9am-1pm and 2:30-6pm, Su 10am-1pm; May and Oct.-Mar. M-Sa 9am-1pm and 2:30-5:30pm, Su 10am-1pm. Entrance 100\$/€0.50, students 50\$/€0.25.) The **Feira de São João** festival keeps the town up all night with a huge country fair in the last week of June.

Trains (☎266 70 21 25) go from the end of R. Dr. Baronha to: Lisbon (3hr., 5 per day, 1380\$/€6.90); Faro (5hr., 4 per day, 1650\$/€8.30); Porto (6½hr., 3 per day, 2650\$/€13.30). From the train station, flag down bus #6 (100\$/€0.50) from just down the tracks or hike up R. Dr. Baronha, which becomes R. República and leads to the central Pr. Giraldo (20min). **Buses** (☎266 76 94 10), on Av. Sebastiano, about 300m outside the town wall, go to: Lisbon (2½hr., every 1-1½hr., 1550\$/€7.75), Faro (5hr., 4 per day, 1900\$/€9.50). The **tourist office** is at Pr. Giraldo 73. (☎266 70 26 71. Open Apr.-Sept. M-F 9am-7pm, Sa-Su 9am-12:30pm and 2-5:30pm; Oct.-Mar. daily 9am-12:30pm and 2-5:30pm.) Check **email** at ■**Oficin@,** R. Moeda 27, off Pr. Giraldo. (500\$/€2.50 per hr. Open Apr.-Sept. daily Tu-F 8pm-3am, Sa 9pm-3am; Oct.-Mar. Tu-F 8pm-2am, Sa 9pm-2am.) Most *pensões* cluster on side streets around **Praça Giraldo.** Take a right from the tourist office and then the first right onto R. Bernardo Mato to get to **Casa Palma,** R. Bernardo Mato 29-A. (☎266 70 35 60. Apr.-Oct. singles 5000\$/€25, with bath 7000-7500\$/€35-37.50; doubles 7000-7500\$/€35-37.50, with bath 8500-9000\$/€42.40-44.90; Nov.-May about 1000\$/€5 less.) Buses from Pr. Giraldo go near **Orbitur's Parque de Campismo de Évora,** on Estrada das Alcáçovas, which branches off the bottom of R. Raimundo. (☎266 70 51 90. Reception 8am-10pm. Five sets of season prices; per person 400-680\$/€2-4.40, tent 310-960\$/€1.60-4.80, car 340-600\$/€1.70-3.) Many budget restaurants are near **Praça Giraldo,** particularly along **Rua Mercadores.** Grab **groceries** at **Maxigrula,** R. João de Deus 130. (Open M-Sa 9am-7pm.) **Postal code:** 7000.

BEJA ☎284

Tucked amid the vast, monotonous wheat fields of the southern Alentejo, Beja is a town of remarkable architecture and truly scorching temperatures. Its name, pronounced like the Portuguese word for "kiss" (beijo), is highly appropriate. Besides being a summer-time oven and a prime getaway destination for romantic exploits, Beja is a haven of traditional Portugese food, music, and handicrafts. The **Museu Rainha Dona Leonor,** Lg. da Conceiçao, makes an excellent starting point. Built on the site of Sister Mariana Alcoforado's famed indiscretion with a French officer, the museum features a replica of the cell window through which the lovers exchanged secret passionate vows. The *azulejos* (tiles) and

Persian-style ceiling make the house look like a mini-mosque. (Open Tu-Su 9:45am-12:30pm and 2-5:30pm. 100$/€0.50, Su free.) One block downhill from the Museu Rainha Dona Leonor is the 13th-century **Igreja de Santa María de la Feira**, transformed into a mosque during the Moorish invasion and back into a church when the city reverted to Portuguese control. A miniature bull on its corner column symbolizes the city's spirit. (Open daily 10am-1pm and 3-7pm. Free.) From here, R. Aresta Branco leads past handsome old houses to the **Castelo de Beja**, built around 1300 on the remnants of a Roman fortress. (Open May-Sept. Tu-Su 10am-1pm and 2-6pm; Oct.-Apr. 9am-noon and 1-4pm. Free.) The castle's **Torre de Menagem** provides an impressive view of the vast Alentejan plains (100$/€0.50).

Trains run from the station (☎284 32 50 56), about 1km outside of town, to Lisbon (2½-3hr., 4 per day, M-Sa 5am-7:20pm, Su 7:45am-7:20pm, 1350-1590$/€6.75-7.90) and Évora (1½hr., 5 per day; M-Sa 7:45am-8:40pm, Su 12:30-8:40, 780-1110$/€3.90-5.55). The **bus station** (☎284 31 36 20) is on R. Cidade de São Paulo, near the corner of Av. Brasil. **Buses** motor to: Lisbon (3-3½hr., 6 per day, 7:10am-3pm, 1750$/€8.75); Évora (1hr., 5 per day, 7:10am-7:15pm, 1300$/€6.50); Faro (3½hr., 3 per day, 10:10am-7:20pm, 1800$/€9). To get to the town center, turn right onto R. Afonso de Albuquerque and left on R. Capitão J. F. de Sousa, where the **tourist office**, R. Capitão J. F. de Sousa, 25, is located. (☎284 31 19 13. Open May-Sept. M-F 9am-8pm, Sa 10am-1pm, 2-6pm; Oct.-Apr. 10am-1pm and 2-6pm.) Beja has excellent accommodations. Try 🔳**Residencial Rosa do Campo,** R. Liberdade, 12, an extremely nice newly-renovated private home (☎284 32 35 78, singles 3000$/€15; doubles 5000$/€25) or 🔳**Pousada de Juventude de Beja**, R. Professor Janeiro Acabado. (☎284 32 54 58, June 16-Sept. 15 dorms 1900$/€9.50; doubles 4200$/€21; Sept. 16-June 15 dorms 1500$/€7.50; doubles 3500$/€17.50.) Beja is one of the best places to taste authentic (and affordable) Portuguese cuisine. Try **Restaurante Saiote,** R. Biscainha, 6 (☎284 32 02 59. Open M-Sa noon-3:30pm, 7-10:30pm). **Postal Code:** 7800

ALGARVE

Behold the Algarve—a freak of nature, a desert on the sea, an inexhaustible vacationland where happy campers from all over the world bask in the sun. Nearly 3000 hours of sunshine per year have transformed this one-time fishermen's backwater into one of Europe's favorite vacation spots. In July and August, tourists mob the Algarve's resorts in search of perfect tans on the beaches and wild nights in the bars and discos. In the off-season, a less intense sun presides over tranquil grotto beaches at the bases of rugged cliffs. The westernmost town of Sagres offers isolated beaches and steep cliffs, while the eastern border near Tavira features floating flamingo wetlands.

LAGOS   ☎282

As the town's countless expatriates will attest, Lagos is a black hole: come for two days and you'll be tempted to stay a month. For as long as anyone in Lagos can remember, this modest-sized town (pop. 22,000) has played host to swarms of sun-worshipping foreigners. Although there isn't much more than beaches and bars, between soaking in the view from the cliffs, soaking in the sun on the beach, and soaking in drinks at the bars, you won't find anyone complaining.

▐ TRANSPORTATION

Trains: ☎282 76 29 87. Across the river (over the metal drawbridge) from the city center. To **Évora** (6hr., 2 per day 8:50am-5pm, 1930$/€9.65) and **Lisbon** (5hr., 6 per day 6:55am-10:30pm, 2110-2800$/€10.55-14).

Buses: EVA bus station (76 29 44), off Av. Descobrimentos, just past the train station bridge (as you leave town). To **Lisbon** (5hr., 12 per day 7:40am-1:30am, 2500-

PORTUGAL

2600$/€12.50-13); **Sagres** (1hr., 17 per day 7:15am-8:30pm, 480$/€2.40); **Sevilla, Spain** via Albufeira (5hr., 7:30am and 2pm, 3000$/€15).

✦ ⁊ ORIENTATION AND PRACTICAL INFORMATION

Avenida dos Descobrimentos, the main road, runs along the river. To get to **Praça Gil Eanes,** the center of town, from the **train station,** walk through the pastel pink marina and cross the channel over the pedestrian suspension bridge. Turn left onto Av. Descubrimentos. To reach the *praça* from the bus station, walk straight until Av. Descubrimentos and turn right. After 15m, take another right on R. Porta de Portugal. Most everything hovers near this *praça,* especially restaurants and accommodations. Bars and hostels line **Rua Afonso Dalmeida,** and its tributaries, **Rua 25 de Abril,** and **Rua Silva Lopes.** Follow R. Silva Lopes to R. General Alberto Silveira and exit the old city to reach the grotto-lined beach of **Praia Dona Ana.**

Tourist Office: (☎ 282 76 30 31), R. Vasco de Gama, an inconvenient 25min. walk from the bus station. Follow R. Vasco da Gama until it crosses Av. da República, from there it's another 150m on the right. Open daily 9:30am-12:30pm and 2-5:30pm.

Emergency: ☎ 112. **Police** (☎ 282 76 29 30), R. General Alberto Silva.

Medical Services: Hospital (☎ 282 76 30 34), R. Castelo dos Governadores.

Internet Access: Irish Rover, R. de Ferrador, 9 (☎ 282 76 80 33). 300$/€1.50 per 15min., 500$/€2.50 per 30min., 900$/€4.50 per 1hr. Open July-Sept. daily 2pm-2am; Oct.-June 6pm-2am.

Post Office: (☎ 282 77 02 50), R. Portas de Portugal, between Pr. Gil Eanes and the river. Open M-F 9am-6pm. For *Poste Restante,* label all letters "Estação Portas de Portugal" or they may arrive at the branch office. **Postal Code:** 8600.

⌂ ACCOMMODATIONS

In the summertime, *pensões* (and the youth hostel) fill up quickly and cost a bundle. Reserve rooms over a week in advance. Rooms in *casas particulares* run around 2000-3000$/€10-15 per person in summer; haggle with owners.

Pousada da Juventude de Lagos (HI), R. Lançarote de Freitas, 50 (☎ 282 76 19 70). From the train and bus stations, head into town on Av. Descubrimentos, turn right at Pr. Infante Don Henrique, pass the old slave market and follow Tr. Do Mar to R. Lançarote de Freitas. Friendly staff and lodgers congregate in the courtyard. Reception daily 9am-1am. In summer, book through the central **Movijovem** office (☎ 21 359 60 00; movijovem@mail.telepac.pt). July-Sept. dorms 2500$/€12.50; doubles with bath 4300$/€21.50; Oct.-June dorms 1700$/€8.50; doubles with bath 3800$/€19. AmEX/MC/V.

Residencial Rubi Mar, R. Barroca 70 (☎ 282 76 31 65; rubimar01@hotmail.com), off Pr. Gil Eanes towards Pr. Infante Dom Henrique. Reserve 2 weeks ahead in summer. July-Oct. doubles 7000$/€35, with bath 8500$/€42.50; quads 15,000$/€75. Nov.-June doubles 5500$/€27.50, with bath 6500$32.50; quads 10,000$/€50.

Residencial Gil Vicente, R. Gil Vicente, 26, 2nd fl. (☎/fax 282 76 29 82; ggh@clix.pt), behind the youth hostel. Business card says it's a "gay guest house," but it's open to anyone. Oct.-June reception open 8am-9pm; July-Aug. open 24hr. Reserve a month ahead in the summer. Apr.-Oct. singles 5000$/€25; doubles 6000-7000$€30-35. Nov.-Mar. singles 3000$/€15; doubles 5000$/€25. AmEx/MC/V.

Residencial Caravela, R. 25 de Abril, 8 (☎ 282 76 33 61), just up the street from Pr. Gil Eanes. Reception 9am-11:30pm. Singles 4300$/€21.50; doubles 6000$/€30, with bath 6500$/€32.50; triples 9000$/€45.

Camping: The way most Europeans experience the Algarve; sites are crowded and expensive. **Camping Trindade** (☎ 282 76 38 93), just outside of town. Follow Av. Descobrimentos toward Sagres. 580$/€2.85 per person, 630-735$/€3.15-3.70 per tent,

620$/€3.10 per car. **Camping Valverde** (☎282 78 92 11), on a beach 5km outside Lagos. 790$/€3.95 per person, 650-790$/€3.25-3.95 per tent, 680$/€3.40 per car.

🍴 FOOD

Tourists can peruse multilingual menus around **Praça Gil Eanes** and **Rua 25 de Abril.** For authentic Portuguese seafood, try **Praça Luis Camoes.** The cheapest option is the **market,** on Av. Descobrimentos 5min. from the town center. **Supermercado São Toque,** R. Portas de Portugal, 61, is opposite the post office. (☎282 76 28 55. Open July-Sept. M-F 9am-8pm, Sa 9am-7pm; Oct.-June M-F 9am-7:30pm, Sa 9am-7pm).

Casa Rosa, R. Ferrador, 22. Enjoy huge cheap meals (from 700$/€3.50) with back-packer hordes. Wide-ranging menu with many vegetarian options (700-1400$/€3.50-7). Open daily 7pm-2am.

Snack-Bar Caravela, R. 25 de Abril, 14 (☎282 76 26 83), just off Pr. Gil Eanes. Well-touristed, but for good reason—it's a great place to people-watch and the pizza is the best in town. Outdoor seating on a pedestrian street. Pizzas 850-1350$/€4.25-6.75. Pasta 900$-1175$/€4.50-5.80. Open daily 9am-2am.

🎵 SIGHTS AND ENTERTAINMENT

Lagos's **beaches** are seductive any way you look at them. Flat, smooth, sunbathing sands (crowded during the summer, pristine in the off-season) line the 4km **Meia Praia,** across the river from town. Hop on the 30-second ferry near Pr. República (70$/€0.35 each way). For plunging cliffs, deep caves, and less-crowded beaches, follow Av. Descobrimentos toward Sagres to **Praia de Pinhão** (20 min.). Five minutes farther lies **Praia Dona Ana,** with sculpted cliffs and grottoes.

Although sunbathing and non-stop debauchery have long erased memories of Lagos's rugged, sea-faring past, most of the city is still surrounded by a nearly intact 16th-century wall. The **Fortaleza da Ponta da Bandeira,** a 17th-century fortress holding maritime exhibitions, overlooks the Marina. (☎282 76 14 10. Open Tu-Sa 10am-1pm and 2-6pm, Su 10am-1pm. 330$/€1.65, students 170$/€0.90.) Also on the waterfront is the old **Mercado de Escravos** (slave market). Legend has it that in 1441 the first sale of African slaves on Portuguese ground took place here.

You're tan, you're glam, now go find yourself a (wo)man. The streets of Lagos pick up as soon as the sun dips down, and by midnight the city's walls are shaking. The area between **Praça Gil Eanes** and **Praça Luis de Camões** is filled with cafes. **Rua Cândido dos Reis, Rua do Ferrador,** and the intersection of **Rua 25 de Abril, Rua Silva Lopes,** and **Rua Soeiro da Costa** are packed with bars and clubs that rarely close until well past 5am. Staggered happy hours make drinking easy, even on the tightest of budgets. ⬛**The Red Eye,** R. Cândido dos Reis, 63, is the hottest new place in town. (Beer 300$/€1.50. Mixed drinks 500-700$/€2.50-3.50. Open daily 3pm-2am.)

🔀 DAYTRIPS FROM LAGOS

SAGRES

EVA buses (☎282 76 29 44) run from Lagos (1hr., 17 per day 7am-8:30pm, 480$/€2.40).

Marooned atop a bleak desert plateau in Europe's southwesternmost corner, desolate Sagres and its cape were once considered the edge of the world. Near the town lurks the ⬛**Fortaleza de Sagres,** the fortress where Prince Henry stroked his beard, decided to map the world, and founded his famous **school of navigation.** (Open May-Sept. 10am-8:30pm; Oct.-Apr. 10am-6:30pm. 600$/€3.) Six kilometers west lies the dramatic **Cabo de São Vicente,** where the second most powerful lighthouse in Europe shines over 100km out to sea. To get there on weekdays, you can take the bus from the bus station on R. Comandante Matos near the tourist office (10min.; 11:15am, 12:30, and 4:15pm; 180$/€0.90). Alternatively, hike 1hr. or bike past the several fortresses perched atop the cliffs. The most notable **beach** in the area is **Mareta,** at the bottom of the road from the town center. Just west of town, **Praia de Martinhal** and **Praia da Baleeira** have great windsurfing. The nearby coves of **Salema** and **Luz** are intimate and picturesque. At night, the young crowd fills the lively bar **Rosa dos Ventos** in Pr. República. (Open daily 10am-2am.) The **tourist office,** on R. Comandante Matoso, is up the street from the bus stop. (☎282 62 48 73. Open Tu-Sa 9:30am-12:30pm and 2-5:30pm.)

■ PRAIA DA ROCHA

From Lagos, take a bus to Portimão (40min., 14 per day 7:15am-8:15pm, 360-450$/
€1.55-2.25), then switch to the Praia da Rocha bus, which stops in front of the nearby
Portimão Honda dealership (10min., every 30min. 7:30am-8:30pm, 230$/€1.15).

A short jaunt from Lagos, this grand **beach** is perhaps the very best the Algarve has to offer. With vast expanses of sand, surfable waves, rocky red cliffs, and plenty of secluded coves, Praia da Rocha has a well-deserved reputation (and the crowds to match). The **tourist office** is at the end of R. Tomás Cabreina. (☎282 41 91 32. Open daily May-Sept. 9:30am-7pm; Oct.-Apr. M-F 9:30am-12:30pm and 2-5:30pm, Sa-Su 9:30am-12:30pm.)

TAVIRA   ☎281

Farmers teasing police by riding their motor scooters over the Roman pedestrian bridge may be about as crazy as Tavira gets. But for most visitors to this relaxing haven—speckled with white houses, palm trees, and Baroque churches—that's just fine. Steps from the central Pr. República lead up to the 16th-century **Igreja da Misericórdia.** (Open daily 9:30am-noon and 2:30-5:30pm. Free.) Just beyond it, the remains of the city's **Castelo Mouro** (Moorish Castle) sit next to the **Santa Maria do Castelo.** (Castle and church open daily 9am-5pm. Free.) Local beaches, including **Araial do Barril,** are accessible year-round by the bus to **Pedras D'el Rei** (10min., 8 per day 8:25am-6:10pm, 170$/€0.85). To reach the golden shores of **Ilha da Tavira,** an island 2km away, take the ferry downstream from the end of Estrada das 4 Aguas (every 15min. 8:30am-midnight, round-trip 250$/€1.20).

Trains (☎281 32 23 54) leave for Faro (40min., 6 per day 6:24am-10:14pm, 300$/ €1.44). **EVA buses** (☎281 32 25 46) leave from the station upriver from Pr. República for Faro (1hr., 11 per day 6:50am-7:10pm, 435$/€2.09). From the **train station** take the TUT bus to the town center (10min., every 30min. 8am-8pm, 150$/€0.72) or call a taxi (☎281 32 15 44 or 32 67 88; about 650$/€3.25). **Postal code:** 8800.

FARO   ☎289

The Algarve's capital, largest city, and transportation hub is untouristed despite its charm. Its **old town,** a medley of museums, handicraft shops, and ornate churches, begins at the **Arco da Vila,** a stone arch. In Largo Carmo is the **Igreja de Nossa Senhora do Carmo** and its **Capela dos Ossos** (Chapel of Bones), a macabre bonanza of bones and skulls "borrowed" from the adjacent cemetery. (☎289 82 44 90. Open M-F 10am-1pm and 3-5pm, Sa 10am-1pm. Church free, chapel 120$/€0.60.) Faro's rock-free **beach** hides on an islet off the coast. Take bus #16 from the bus station or the stop in front of the tourist office (5-10min., every hr. 7:10am-8:40pm, 170$/€0.85).

Trains (☎289 80 17 26) run from Largo Estação to: Évora (5hr., 9:05am and 5:30pm, 1650$/€8.25); Lagos (2hr., 7 per day 7:20am-8:45pm, 750$/€3.75); Lisbon (5-6hr., 6 per day 7:20am-11pm, 2280$/€11.40). **EVA buses** (☎289 89 97 00) go from Av. República to: Beja (3-3½hr., 7 per day 7:45am-4pm, 1550$/€7.75); Lagos (2hr., 8 per day 7:30am-5:30pm, 750$/€3.75); Tavira (1hr., 11 per day 7:15am-7:30pm, 435$/ €2.15). **Renex** (☎289 81 29 80), across the street, provides express long-distance service to: Braga via Lisbon (8½hr., 8 per day 5:15am-1:15am, 3600$/€18); Lisbon (4hr., 7 per day 5:15am-1:15am, 2700$/€13.50); Porto via Lisbon (7½hr., 8 per day 5:15am-1:15am, 3500$/€17.50). **Intersul** (☎289 89 97 70) runs to Sevilla, Spain (3000$/€15), with connecting buses to France and Germany. From the stations, turn right down Av. República along the harbor, then turn left past the garden to reach the **tourist office,** R. Misericórdia, 8, at the entrance to the old town. (☎289 80 36 04. Open June-Aug. daily 9:30am-7pm; Sept.-May daily 9:30am-5:30pm.) **Pensão-Residencial Central,** Largo Terreiro Do Bispo, 12, is near the pedestrian area up R. 1 de Maio.

PORTUGAL

(☎289 80 72 91. June-Sept. singles 5000$/€25; doubles 7000-7500$/€35-37.50; Oct.-May singles 5000$/€25; doubles 6500-7000$/€32.50-35.) Enjoy some coffee and the local marzipan at a cafe along **Rua Conselheiro Bívar**, off Pr. Gomes.

NORTHERN PORTUGAL

Although their landscapes and Celtic history invite comparison with the northwest of Spain, the Douro and Minho regions of northern Portugal are more populated, developed, and wealthy than Spanish Galicia. Hundreds of trellised vineyards for *porto* and *vinho verde* wines beckon connoisseurs, while *azulejo*-lined houses draw visitors to charming, quiet streets. The Three Beiras region offers a sample of the best of Portugal: the unspoiled Costa da Prata (Silver Coast), the plush greenery of the interior, and the rugged peaks of the Serra Estrela.

COIMBRA   ☎239

The country's only university city from the mid-16th to the early 20th century, Coimbra serves as a mecca for the country's youth and backpackers alike. A slew of cheap cafes and bars and the student body keep Coimbra swinging from September to May. The city's charm has long since blotted out Coimbra's infamous dual roles as center of the Portuguese Inquisition and the site of former dictator António Salazar's education.

▛ TRANSPORTATION

Trains: (☎239 83 49 98). Trains from other regions stop only at **Estação Coimbra-B (Velha)**, 3km northwest of town, while regional trains stop at Coimbra-B and **Estação Coimbra-A (Nova)**, 2 blocks from the lower town center. A train connects the 2 stations (4min., runs immediately after trains arrive, 140$/€0.70). Trains run to **Lisbon** (3hr., 23 per day 5:30am-2:20am, 2700$/€13.50) and **Porto** (2hr., 21 per day 5:10am-3:10am, 1050-1900$/€5.25-9.50).

Buses: (☎239 82 70 81). To reach the bus station, go from Av. Fernão Magalhães, on the university side of the river 10min. from town, past Coimbra-A. Buses to: **Lisbon** (2½hr., 17 per day 7:30am-2:15am, 1550$/€7.75); **Luso** (45min.; M-F 7 per day, Sa-Su 2 per day; 480$/€2.45); **Porto** (1½hr., 10 per day, 1400$/€7).

▛ ORIENTATION AND PRACTICAL INFORMATION

There are three major parts of town, all on the same side of the river. The most central is the **Baixa** (also known as lower town, site of the **tourist office** and Coimbra-A **train station**), **Largo da Portagem**, and **Praça 8 de Maio**. Coimbra's **university district** is atop the steep hill overlooking the Baixa. On the other side of the university, **Praça da República** plays host to cafes and the youth hostel.

Tourist Office: (☎239 85 59 30), off Largo Portagem, in a yellow building 2 blocks up the river from Coimbra-A. From the bus station, turn right, follow the avenue to Coimbra-A, then walk to Largo Portagem (15min.). Open June-Sept. M-F 9am-7pm, Sa-Su 10am-1pm and 2:30-5:30pm; Oct.-May M-F 9am-6pm, Sa-Su 10am-1pm and 2:30-5:30pm. **University branch office** (☎239 83 25 91), in Lg. Dom Dinis. Open M-F 9am-6pm, Sa-Su 9am-12:30pm and 2-5:30pm.

Emergency: ☎112. **Police, special division** for foreigners (*Serviço de Estrangeiros*), R. Venâncio Rodrigues, 25 (☎239 82 37 67).

Hospital: Hospital da Universidade de Coimbra (☎239 40 04 00), Lg. Professor Mota Pinto. Take the #7 or 29 bus to the "Hospital" stop.

Internet Access: Museu Sandwich Bar, R. da Matemática, 46 (☎239 82 75 66), off R. São João near the university. 600$/€3 per hr., includes a drink. Open M-F 4-7pm and 10:30pm-3am, Sa 10:30pm-3am.

Post Office: Central office (☎ 239 85 07 70), on Av. Fernão de Magalhães. Open M-F 8:30am-6:30pm. **Postal Code:** 3000.

ACCOMMODATIONS

Decent hostels, most on side streets off **Avenida Fernão de Magalhães,** start at 5000$/€25 for doubles; prices drop in winter.

■ **Pensão Santa Cruz,** Pr. 8 de Maio, 21, 3rd fl. (☎ 239 82 61 97), directly across from the Igreja da Santa Cruz. Comfortable rooms, most with cable TV, some with bath. July-Sept. singles or doubles 4000$/€20, with bath 5500$/€27.50; triples 5000$/€25. Oct.-June singles or doubles 3000$/€15, 4000$/€20; triples 4000$/€20.

Pousada da Juventude de Coimbra (HI), R. Henrique Seco, 14 (☎ 239 82 29 55). From either Coimbra-A or Largo Portagem, walk 20min. uphill along R. Olímpio Nicolau Rui Fernandes to Pr. República, then up R. Lourenço Azevedo (to the left of the park). Take the 2nd right; the hostel is on the right. Alternatively, take bus #7, 8, 29, or 46 to "Pr. República" and walk the rest of the way (5min.). Breakfast included. Reception daily 8am-noon and 6pm-midnight. Mid-June to mid-Sept. dorms 1900$/€9.50; doubles with bath 4600$/€23. Mid-Sept. to mid-June dorms 1700$/€8.50; doubles with bath 4300$/€21.50.

Residencial Vitória, R. da Sota, 11-19 (☎ 239 82 40 49 or 239 84 28 96; fax 239 84 28 97), across from Coimbra A. Rooms and prices to suit any budget. Reception 24hr. New rooms: singles 5000$/€25; doubles 7000$/€35; triples 9000$/€45. Old rooms: singles 2500$/€12.50, with shower 3000$/€15; doubles 4000$/€20.

FOOD

The best cuisine in Coimbra lies around **Rua Direita,** off Pr. 8 de Maio; on the side streets between the river and Largo Portagem; and around **Praça República** in the university district. **Supermercado Minipreço,** R. António Granjo, 6C, is in the lower town center; turn left as you exit Coimbra-A and take another left. (Open M-Sa 8:30am-8pm, Su 9am-1pm and 3-7pm.)

■ **Porta Romana,** R. Martins de Carvalho, 10 (☎ 239 82 84 58), just up from the Igreja da Santa Cruz in Pr. 8 de Maio. Delicious Italian dishes. Entrees 700-1200$/€3.50-6. Open July-Aug. M-Sa 7am-midnight, Su 6pm-midnight; Sept.-June M-F 7am-midnight.

UC Cantina, R. Oliveiro, the university's student cafeteria, is the cheapest food around— a mere 300$/€1.50 buys an entire meal. Open M-F noon-2:15pm and 7-9:15pm.

SIGHTS AND ENTERTAINMENT

Take in the old town sights by climbing from the river up the narrow stone steps to the university. Begin your ascent at the **Arco de Almedina,** a remnant of the Moorish town wall, one block uphill from Largo Portagem. At the top is the looming 12th-century Romanesque **Sé Velha** (Old Cathedral), complete with tombs, Gregorian chants, and a cloister. (Open M-Th 10am-noon and 2-7:30pm, F-Su 10am-1pm. Cloister 150$/€0.75, students 100$/€0.50.) Follow signs to the late 16th-century **Sé Nova** (New Cathedral), built for the Jesuits (open Tu-Sa 9am-noon and 2-6:30pm; free), just a few blocks from the 16th-century **University of Coimbra.** The **Porta Férrea** (Iron Gate), off R. São Pedro, opens onto the old university, whose buildings were Portugal's de facto royal palace when Coimbra was the kingdom's capital. (Open May-Sept. daily 9am-7:30pm; Oct.-Apr. 9:30am-12:30pm and 2-5:30pm.) The stairs to the right lead to the **Sala dos Capelos,** which houses portraits of Portugal's kings, six of them Coimbra-born. (Open daily 9:30am-12:30pm and 2-5:30pm. 500$/€2.50.) The **university chapel** and the mind-boggling, entirely gilded 18th-century **Biblioteca Joanina** (university library) lie past the Baroque clock tower. Press the buzzer by the library door to enter three golden halls with 300,000 works from the 12th through 19th centuries. (Open May-Sept.

daily 9am-7:30pm; Oct.-Apr. 9:30am-noon and 2-5:30pm. 500$/€2.50, students free. All university sights 800$/€4; buy tickets from the office in the main quad.) The **Igreja de Santa Cruz,** Pr. 8 de Maio, at the far end of R. Ferreira Borges in the lower town, sits in somber, 12th-century beauty. (Open M-Sa 9am-noon and 2-5:45pm. Cloisters and sacristy 200$/€1.) Cross the bridge in front of Largo Portagem to find the 14th-century **Convento de Santa Clara-a-Velha** and the 17th-century **Convento de Santa Clara-a-Nova.**

Nightlife in Coimbra gets highest honors. **Café Tropical,** R. Nova, 30, is a great place to start the night. (Open M-Sa 9am-2am.) For clubs try **Via Latina,** R. Almeida Garrett, 1, around the corner and uphill from Pr. República, which is hot in all senses of the word (open M-Sa 11pm-7am); or **Hups!,** R. Castro Matoso, 11, one of the newest dance clubs in town (open Tu-Su 10pm-5am). Dance *and* check **email** at **@caffé,** Lg. da Sé Velha, 4-8. (Open June to mid-Sept. M-Sa 11am-4am; mid-Sept. to May M-Sa 9pm-4am.) **The English Bar,** R. Lourenço de Almeida Azevedo, 24, is new and hip. (Open M-Sa 10pm-4am.) **Diligência Bar,** R. Nova 30, off R. Sofia, is known for its *fado.* (Open 10pm-2am.) In early May, graduates burn narrow ribbons they got as first-years and get wide ones in return during Coimbra's week-long festival, the **Queima das Fitas** (Burning of the Ribbons).

PORTO (OPORTO)   ☎22

Porto is famous for its namesake—sugary-strong port wine. Developed by English merchants in the early 18th century, the port industry is at the root of the city's successful economy. But there's more to Porto than just port (no, really). Situated on a gorge cut by the Douro River, Portugal's second-largest city is punctuated with granite church towers, orange-tiled houses, and graceful bridges.

▐ TRANSPORTATION. All trains pass through Porto's main station, **Estação Campanhã** (☎22 536 41 41), on R. da Estação. Trains run to: Coimbra (2hr., 17 per day every hr. 5:05am-12:05am, 1050$/€5.25); Lisbon (4-4½hr., 14 per day 6am-8:05pm, 2150-3700$/€10.75-18.50); Madrid (13-14hr., 6:10pm, 9030-9655$/€45-48.50). **Estação São Bento** (☎22 200 27 22), Pr. Almeida Garrett, centrally located 1 block off Pr. Liberdade, is the terminus for trains with mostly local and regional routes. Rede Expresso **buses,** R. Alexandre Herculano, 366 (☎22 205 24 59), in the Garagem Atlântico, has buses to Coimbra (1½hr., 11 per day 7:15am-12:45am, 1410$/€7) and Lisbon (4hr., 12 per day 7:15am-12:45am, 2300$/€11.50). REDM, R. Dr. Alfredo Magalhães, 94 (☎22 200 31 52), 2 blocks from Pr. República, has buses to Braga (1hr.; M-F 26 per day 6:45am-8pm, Sa-Su 9-12 per day 7:15am-8pm; 680$/€3.40). Buy tickets for the **intracity buses** and **trams** from small kiosks around the city, or at the STCP office, Pr. Almeida Garrett, 27, downhill and across the street from Estação de São Bento (pre-purchased single ticket 85$/€0.45, one day ticket 500$/€2.50).

▐ PRACTICAL INFORMATION. Get a map at the **tourist office,** R. Clube dos Fenianos, 25, off Pr. Liberdade. (Open July-Sept. daily 9am-7pm; Oct.-June M-F 9am-5:30pm, Sa-Su 9:30am-4:30pm.) Check **email** at **Portweb,** Pr. Gen. Humberto Delgado, 291, by Pr. Liberdade. (100-240$/€0.50-1.20 per hr. Open M-Sa 10am-2am, Su 3pm-2am.) The **post office** is located on Pr. Gen. Humberto Delgado. (☎22 340 02 00. Open M-F 8:30am-9pm, Sa-Su 9am-6pm.) **Postal code:** 4000.

▐▐ ACCOMMODATIONS AND FOOD. For good room deals, look west of Av. Aliados or on **Rua Fernandes Tomás** and **Rua Formosa,** perpendicular to Aliados Square. **Pensão Duas Nações,** Pr. Guilherme Gomes Fernandes, 59, offers a variety of rooms at corresponding prices (☎22 208 96 21. Curfew 2am. Singles 2200-2500$/€11-12.50; doubles 3800$/€19.) A few blocks away from the noisy city center, **Pensão Portuguesa,** Tr. Coronel Pacheco, 11, is one of the cheapest options in the city. (☎22 200 41 74. July-Aug. singles 2500$/€12.50, with bath 3000$/€15; doubles 3000$/€15, 4000$/€20. Sept.-June singles 2000$/€10; doubles 2500$/€12.50.) Take bus #35 from Estação Campanha or #37 from Pr. Liberdade to **Pousada de Juventude do Porto (HI),** R. Paulo da Gama, 551. (☎22 617 72 47. Reception daily 8am-midnight.

PORTUGAL

June-Sept. dorms 2500$/€12.50; doubles with bath 6000$/€30; Oct.-May 2000$/€10, 5000$/€25.) Take bus #6, 50, 54, or 87 from Pr. Liberdade (only buses #50 and 54 run at night) to **camp** at **Prelada**, on R. Monte dos Burgos, in Quinta da Prelada, 3km from the center. (☎ 22 831 26 16. Reception 8am-11pm. 620$/€3.10 per person, 520-590$/€2.60-3 per tent, 520$/€2.60per car.) Look near the river in the **Ribeira** district on C. Ribeira, R. Reboleira, and R. Cima do Muro for great restaurants. The ▨**Majestic Café**, R. de Santa Catarina, 112, is said to be the oldest, most famous, and best cafe in Porto. (Sandwiches 400-1750$/€2-8.75. Open M-Sa 9:30am-midnight.) Across the street, the **Confeitaria Império**, R. de Santa Catarina, 149-151, serves excellent pastries and lunch specials (600$/€3). (Open M-Sa 7:30am-8:30pm.)

▨▨ **SIGHTS AND ENTERTAINMENT.** Your first brush with Porto's rich stock of fine artwork may be the celebrated collection of *azulejos* (tiles) in the **São Bento train station.** Walk past the station and uphill on Av. Afonso Henriques to reach Porto's pride and joy, the 12th- to 13th-century Romanesque **cathedral.** (Open M-Sa 9am-12:30pm and 2:30-6pm, Su 2:30-6pm. Cloister 250$/€1.25.) From the station, follow signs downhill on R. Mouzinho da Silveira to R. Ferreira Borges and the ▨ **Palácio da Bolsa** (Stock Exchange), the epitome of 19th-century elegance. The ornate **Sala Árabe** (Arabic Hall) took 18 years to decorate. (Open M-F 9am-6:40pm, Sa-Su 9am-12:30pm and 2-6:30pm. Tours every 30min. 800$/€4.) Next door, the Gothic ▨**Igreja de São Francisco** glitters with an elaborately gilded wooden interior. Thousands of human bones are stored under the floor. (Open daily 9am-6pm. 500$/€2.50, students 250$/€1.25.) From Pr. Liberdade up R. dos Clérigos rises the **Torre dos Clérigos** (Tower of Clerics), adjacent to the **Igreja dos Clérigos.** (Tower open June-July daily 10am-7pm; Aug. 10am-10pm; Sept.-May 10am-noon and 2-5pm. 200$/€1. Church open M-Th 10am-noon and 2-5pm, Sa 10am-noon and 2-8pm, Su 10am-1pm. Church free.) From there, head up R. Restauração, right on R. Alberto Gouveia, and left on R. Dom Manuel II to reach the **Museu Nacional Soares dos Reis**, R. Dom Manuel II, 44. This former royal residence now houses an exhaustive collection of 19th-century Portuguese painting and sculpture. (☎ 22 339 37 70. Open Tu 2-6pm, W-Su 10am-6pm. 600$/€3, students and seniors 300$€1.50.) To get to Porto's rocky and polluted (but popular) **beach,** in the ritzy Foz district, take bus #1 from the São Bento train station or tram #1 from Igreja de São Francisco.

But we digress—back to your main focus of interest. Fine and bounteous port wines are available for tasting at 20-odd **port wine lodges**, usually *gratuito* (free). The lodges are all across the river in **Vila Nova da Gaia**—from the Ribeira district, cross the lower level of the large bridge. **Sandeman,** with its costumed guides (500$/ €2.50), is a good start. **Ferreira,** one block up from the end of Av. Ramos Pinto, creates a memorable atmosphere. ▨**Taylor's,** R. do Choupelo, 250, has a beautiful terrace with amazing views of the city. (Most open daily 10am-6pm.)

BRAGA   ☎923
Braga's beautiful gardens, plazas, museums, and markets have earned the city the nickname "Portuguese Rome." In Portugal's oldest **cathedral,** the treasury showcases the archdiocese's most precious paintings and relics, including a collection of *cofres cranianos* (brain boxes). (Cathedral and treasury open June-Aug. daily 8:30am-6:30pm; Sept.-May 8:30am-5:30pm. Cathedral free. Treasury 300$/€1.50.) Braga's most famous landmark, **Igreja do Bom Jesús,** is actually 5km outside of town. To visit Bom Jesús, either take the 285m ride on the antique funicular (8am-8pm, 120$/€0.60), or walk (25-30min.) up the granite-paved pathway.

Buses (☎923 61 60 80) leave from Central de Camionagem for: Coimbra (3hr.; M-F 6-9 per day, Sa-Su 7 per day 6am-11:30pm; 1600$/€8); Guimarães (1hr., every 30min. 7am-8pm, 385$/€1.90); Lisbon (5¼hr., 8-9 per day 9:30am-11:30pm, 2300$/ €11.50); Porto (1½hr., every 45min. 6:45am-8pm, 680$/€3.40). The **tourist office,** Av. Central, 1, is on the corner of Pr. República. (☎923 26 25 50. Open July-Sept. M-F 9am-7pm, Sa-Su 9am-12:30pm and 2-5:30pm; Oct.-June M-F 9am-7pm, Sa 9am-12:30pm and 2-5:30pm.) From the tourist office, take a right and follow Av. Combatentes; turn left at R. Santa Margarida to reach the **Pousada da Juventude de Braga**

PORTUGAL

(HI), R. Santa Margarida, 6. (☎923 61 61 63. Reception 8am-midnight. Mid-June to mid-Sept. dorms 1700$/€8.50. Mid-Sept. to mid-June dorms 1500$/€7.50.)

DAYTRIP FROM BRAGA: GUIMARÃES

REDM buses (☎253 51 62 29) go from Braga to Guimarães (40 min.; M-F 19 per day 7:15am-8:35pm, Sa-Su 13-15 per day 8am-8:35pm; 400$/€2.), and return (40min; M-F 19 per day 6:30am-8:30pm, Sa-Su 13-15 per day 6:55am-8:30pm; 400$/€2.).

Ask any Portugal native about the city of Guimarães (pop. 60,000), and they will tell you that it was the birthplace of the nation. It is here that one of Portugal's most gorgeous palatial estates resides. The ■**Paço dos Duques de Bragança** (Ducal Palace) is modeled after the manor houses of northern Europe. Overlooking the city is the **Monte da Pena,** home to an excellent campsite as well as picnic areas, mini-golf, and cafes. To get there, take the **teleférico** (skyride) that runs in summer from Lg. das Hortas to the mountaintop. (☎253 51 50 85. June-July and Sept. M-F 11am-7pm, Sa-Su 10am-8pm; Aug. daily 10am-8pm. 300$/€1.50, 500$/€2.50 round-trip.) The **tourist office** is on Alameda de São Dámaso, 83, facing Pr. Toural. (☎253 41 24 50. Open M-Sa June-Sept. 9:30am-7pm; Oct.-May 9:30am-6pm)

VIANA DO CASTELO   ☎258

In the northwestern corner of the country, Viana do Castelo (pop. 20,000) is one of the loveliest coastal cities in all of Portugal. Even in a country famed for its impressive squares, Viana do Castelo's ■**Praça da República** is remarkable. Its centerpiece is a 16th-century fountain encrusted with sculptures and crowned with a sphere bearing a cross of the Order of Christ. Diagonally across the plaza, granite columns support the playful and flowery façade of the **Igreja da Misericórdia** (1598, rebuilt in 1714). Known for its *azulejo* interior, the ■**Monte de Santa Luzia,** overlooking the city, features magnificent Celtic ruins and the **Templo de Santa Luzia,** an early 20th-century neo-Byzantine church. The view of Viana from the hill is fantastic, especially from the top of the church; take the elevator (130$/€0.65) up the tower, or climb the narrow stairway leading to the **Zimbório** at the very top. For more great views of the harbor and ocean, visit the **Castelo de São Tiago da Barra,** built in 1589 (around a 14th-century tower) by Felipe I of Spain. To reach the castle from the train station, take the 2nd right off Av. Combatentes onto R. General Luís do Rego and walk five blocks. Viana do Castelo and the surrounding coast features excellent beaches. Most convenient are **Praia Norte,** at the end of Av. do Atlántico at the west end of town, and **Praia da Argaçosa,** a small beach on Rio Lima next to the youth hostel and marina.

    Trains (☎258 82 13 15), at the top of Av. Combatentes da Grande Guerra, run to Porto (2hr., 13-14 per day 5am-9:27pm, 800$/€4.00). **Buses** run to: Braga (1½hr.; M-Sa 6-8 per day 7am-6:35pm, Su 4 per day 8:15am-6:35pm; 700$/€3.50); Porto (2hr.; M-F 9 per day 6:45am-6:30pm, Sa-Su 4-6 per day 8:20am-6:30pm; 750-1050$/€3.50-5.25); Lisbon (5½hr.; Su-F 3 per day 8am-11:45pm, Sa 7am and 12:30pm; 2500$/€17.50) The **tourist office,** R. do Hospital Velho and Pr. Erva., has a helpful English-speaking staff and offers maps and accommodations lists. (☎258 82 26 20. Open May-July and Sept. M-Sa 9am-1pm and 2:30-6pm, Su 9:30am-1pm; Aug. daily 9am-7pm; Oct.-Apr. M-Sa 9am-12:30pm and 2:30-5:30pm.) The ■**Pousada de Juventude de Viana do Castelo (HI),** R. da Argaçosa (Azenhas D. Prior), is right on the marina, off Pr. de Galiza. (☎258 80 02 60; fax 258 82 08 70. Reception 8am-midnight. Check-out 10am. Reservations recommended. Mid-Sept.to mid-June dorms 2000$/€10.00; doubles with bath 5000$/€25.00. Mid-June to mid-Sept. dorms 2500$/€17.50.)

SPAIN

PESETAS

US$1 = 181PTAS	100PTAS = US$0.55
CDN$1 = 118PTAS	100PTAS = CDN$0.85
UK£1 = 263PTAS	100PTAS = UK£0.38
IR£1 = 211PTAS	100PTAS = IR£0.47
AUS$1 = 97PTAS	100PTAS = AUS$1.03
NZ$1 = 80PTAS	100PTAS = NZ$1.25
ZAR1 = 22PTAS	100PTAS = ZAR4.56
EUR€1 = 166PTAS	100PTAS = EUR€0.60

PHONE CODE — **Country Code:** 34. **International dialing prefix:** 00. Spain has no city codes.

Fiery flamenco dancers, noble bullfighters, and a rich history blending Christian and Islamic culture set Spain (pop. 40 million; 504,782 sq. km) apart from the rest of Europe and draw almost 50 million tourists each year. The landscape is a microcosm of all that Europe has to offer, with lush wilderness reserves, long sunny coastlines, snowy mountain peaks, and the dry, golden plains wandered by Don Quixote. Art lovers seek out the works of Dalí and Picasso; adventure-seekers trek through the Pyrenees; and architecture buffs are drawn to the country's stunning Baroque, Mudejar, and Mozarabic cathedrals and palaces. The raging nightlife of Madrid, Barcelona, and the Balearic Islands has inspired the popular saying "Spain never sleeps." You can do Spain in one week, one month, or one year. But you must do it at least once. For more detailed coverage of glorious Spain, grab the scintillating *Let's Go: Spain and Portugal 2002*.

SUGGESTED ITINERARIES

THREE DAYS Soak in **Madrid's** (p. 797) blend of art and cosmopolitan life. Walk through the **Retiro's** gardens, peruse the famed halls of the **Prado, Thyssen-Bornemisza,** and **Nacional Centro de Arte Reina Sofia.** By night, move from the tapas bars of **Santa Anna** to **Malasaña** and **Chueca.** Daytrip to **Segovia** (p. 820) or somber **Valle de los Caídos** (p. 815).

ONE WEEK Begin in southern Spain, exploring the Alhambra's Moorish palaces in **Granada** (1 day, p. 845) and the mosque in **Córdoba** (1 day, p. 837). After two days in **Madrid** (p. 797), travel east to **Barcelona** (2 days, p. 854) and the beaches of **Costa Brava** (1 day, p. 874).

BEST OF SPAIN, THREE WEEKS Begin in **Madrid** (3 days), with daytrips to **El** **Escorial** (p. 815) and **Valle de los Caídos** (p. 815). Take the high-speed train to **Córdoba** (2 days), and on to **Sevilla** (2 days, p. 827). Catch the bus to the white town of **Arcos de la Frontera** (1 day, p. 837) before heading south to the Costa del Sol, **Marbella** (1 day, p. 850). Head inland to **Granada** (2 days). Move along the coast to **Valencia** (1 day, p. 852) and escape to **Gandía** (1 day, p. 854). Up the coast to **Barcelona** (2 days), where worthwhile daytrips in Cataluña include **Tossa de Mar** (1 day), **Montserrat** (p. 872), or **Figueres** (p. 874). From Barcelona, on to the beaches and tapas of **San Sebastián** (2 days, p. 882) and **Bilbao** (1 day, p. 887), home of the world-famous Guggenheim Museum.

Spain

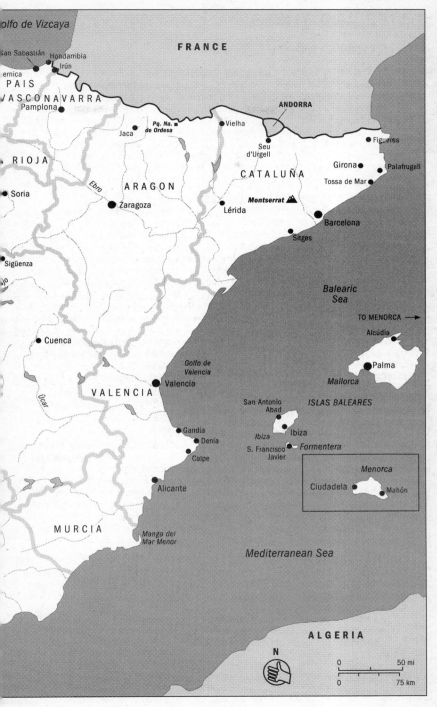

olfo de Vizcaya

FRANCE

San Sabastián
Hondarribia
Irún
ernica

PAIS
VASCO NAVARRA
Pamplona

ANDORRA

Vielha

RIOJA

Pq. Na.
de Ordesa

Seu
d'Urgell

Figueres

Jaca

ARAGON

CATALUÑA

Girona
Palafrugell

Soria

Ebro

Montserrat

Tossa de Mar

Zaragoza

Lérida

Barcelona

Sigüenza

Sitges

Balearic
Sea

TO MENORCA →

Cuenca

Alcúdia

Golfo de
Valencia

Palma

Úcar

VALENCIA

Valencia

Mallorca

ISLAS BALEARES

San Antonio
Abad

Gandía
Denia

Ibiza

Ibiza

Calpe

S. Francisco
Javier

Formentera

Alicante

Menorca

Ciudadela

Mahón

MURCIA

Manga del
Mar Menor

Mediterranean Sea

ALGERIA

N

| 0 | | 50 mi |
| 0 | | 75 km |

LIFE AND TIMES

HISTORY AND POLITICS

IN THE BEGINNING (UNTIL AD 711)

Spain was colonized by a succession of civilizations that have left their cultural mark—**Basque** (considered indigenous), **Tartesian, Iberian, Celtic, Greek, Phoenician,** and **Carthaginian**—before the **Romans** crashed the party in the 3rd century BC. Over nearly seven centuries, the Romans drastically altered the face and character of Spain, introducing their agricultural techniques and architecture, as well as the Latin language. A slew of Germanic tribes, including the Swabians and Vandals, swept over the region in the early 5th century AD, but the **Visigoths,** newly converted Christians, emerged above the rest. The Visigoths established their court at Barcelona in 415 and effectively ruled Spain for the next 300 years.

MOORISH OCCUPATION (711-1469)

Following Muslim unification and a victory tour through the Middle East and North Africa, a small force of Arabs, Berbers, and Syrians invaded Spain in 711. Practically welcomed by the divided Visigoths, the Moors encountered little resistance, and the peninsula soon fell under the dominion of the caliphate of Damascus. These events precipitated the infusion of Muslim influence, which peaked in the 10th century. The Moors set up their Iberian capital in **Córdoba** (see p. 837). During **Abderramán III**'s rule in the 10th century, some considered Spain the wealthiest and most cultivated country in the world. Abderramán's successor, **Al Mansur,** snuffed out all opposition within his extravagant court and undertook a series of military campaigns that climaxed with the destruction of **Santiago de Compostela** (see p. 894), a Christian holy city, in 997.

The turning point in Muslim-Christian relations came when Al Mansur died, leaving a power vacuum in Córdoba. At this point, the caliphate's holdings shattered into petty states called *taifas.* With power less centralized, Christians were able to gain the upper hand. The Christian policy was official toleration of Muslims and Jews, which fostered a culture and even a style of art, **Mudéjar.** Later, though, countless Moorish structures were ruined in the **Reconquest,** and numerous mosques were replaced by churches (like Córdoba's **Mezquita,** see p. 841).

THE CATHOLIC MONARCHS (1469-1516)

In 1469, the marriage of **Fernando de Aragón** and **Isabel de Castilla** joined Iberia's two mightiest Christian kingdoms. By 1492, the dynamic duo had captured **Granada** (see p. 845), the last Moorish stronghold, and shuttled **Columbus** off to explore the New World. By the 16th century, the pair's leadership made Spain's empire the world's most powerful. The Catholic monarchs introduced the **Inquisition** in 1478, executing and burning heretics. The Spanish Inquisition's dual aims were to strengthen the authority of the Church and to unify Spain. In 50 years of rule, the Catholic monarchs heightened Spain's position as a world economic, political, and cultural power—made all the more enduring by conquests in the Americas.

THE HABSBURG DYNASTY (1516-1713)

The daughter of Fernando and Isabel, **Juana la Loca** (the Mad), married **Felipe el Hermoso** (the Fair) of the powerful Habsburg dynasty. Mr. Handsome (who died playing a Basque ball game called *cesta punta* or *jai alai*) and Mrs. Crazy (who refused to believe that he had died and dragged his corpse through the streets) produced **Carlos I.** Carlos, who went by **Charles V** in his capacity as the last official Holy Roman Emperor, reigned over an empire comprising modern-day Netherlands, Belgium, Austria, Spain, parts of Germany and Italy, and the American colonies. Carlos did his part: as a good Catholic, he embroiled Spain in a war with Protestant France; as an art patron of superb taste, he nabbed Titian as his court painter; as a fashion plate, he introduced Spain to the Habsburg fashion of wearing only black.

But trouble was brewing in the Protestant Netherlands. After Carlos I died, his son **Felipe II** was left to grapple with a multitude of rebellious territories. He annexed Portugal after its ailing King Henrique died in 1580. One year later the Dutch declared their independence from Spain, and Felipe began warring with the Protestants, spurring further tensions with England. The war with the British ground to a halt when **Sir Francis Drake** and bad weather buffeted the not-so-invincible **Invincible Armada** in 1588. His enthusiasm and much of his European empire sapped, Felipe retreated to his grim, newly built palace, **El Escorial** (see p. 815) and remained there through the last decade of his reign.

Felipe III, preoccupied with both religion and the finer aspects of life, allowed his favorite adviser, the **Duque de Lerma,** to hold the governmental reigns. In 1609, Felipe III and the Duke expelled nearly 300,000 of Spain's remaining Moors. Mustached **Felipe IV** painstakingly held the country together through his long, tumultuous reign. Emulating his great-grandfather Carlos I, Felipe IV patronized the arts (painter Diego Velázquez and playwrights Lope de Vega and Calderón de la Barca were in his court) and architecture (for instance, the **Buen Retiro** in Madrid; see p. 810). Then the **Thirty Years' War** (1618-1648) broke out over Europe, and defending Catholicism drained Spain's resources; the war ended with the marriage of Felipe IV's daughter, María Teresa, and Louis XIV of France. Felipe's successor **Carlos II,** the *"hechizado"* (bewitched), was epileptic and impotent, the product of inbreeding. From then on, little went right: Carlos II died, Spain fell into a depression, and cultural bankruptcy ensued.

KINGS, LIBERALS, AND DICTATORS (1713-1931)

The 1713 **Treaty of Utrecht** seated **Felipe V,** a Bourbon family member and grandson of French King Louis XIV, on the Spanish throne. Felipe built huge, showy palaces (to mimic Versailles in France) and cultivated a flamboyant, debauched court. Despite his undisciplined example, the Bourbons who followed Felipe ably administered the Empire, at last beginning to regain control of Spanish-American trade. They also constructed scores of new canals, roads, and organized settlements, and instituted agricultural reform and industrial expansion. **Carlos III** was probably Madrid's finest leader, founding academies of art and science and generally beautifying the capital. Spain's global standing recovered enough for it to team with France to help the American colonies gain independence from Britain.

In 1808, little **Napoleon** invaded Spain in his quest for big world domination. The invasion's battles were particularly bloody; painter **Francisco de Goya** captured the brutality in two brilliant works (see p. 791). The French occupation ended when the Protestant Brits defeated the Corsican's troops at Waterloo (1814). This victory led to the restoration of arch-reactionary **Fernando VII.** Galvanized by Fernando's ineptitude and inspired by liberal ideas in the new constitution, most of Spain's Latin American empire soon threw off its yoke. Lingering dreams of an empire were further curbed by the loss of the Philippines, Puerto Rico, and Cuba to the US in the **Spanish-American War** of 1898. Upon Fernando VII's death, parliamentary liberalism was restored and would dominate Spanish politics until **Primo de Rivera** came along in 1923. Rivera was brought to power in a military coup d'état, after which he promptly dissolved parliament and suspended the constitution. For almost a decade, he ruled Spain as dictator in an attempt to strengthen national unity. His oppressive reign produced widespread opposition, and in 1930, having lost the support of his own army, he resigned.

SECOND REPUBLIC AND THE CIVIL WAR (1931-1939)

In April 1931, **King Alfonso XIII,** disgraced by his support for Rivera, shamefully fled Spain, thus giving rise to the **Second Republic** (1931-1936). Republican Liberals and Socialists established safeguards for farmers and industrial workers, granted women's suffrage, assured religious tolerance, and chipped away at traditional military dominance. National euphoria, however, faded fast. The 1933 elections split the Republican-Socialist coalition, in the process increasing the power of right-wing and Catholic parties. By 1936, radicals, anarchists, Socialists, and Republicans had formed a loosely federated alliance to win the next elections. But the victory was short-lived. Once **Generalísimo Francisco Franco** snatched control of the Spanish army, militarist uprisings ensued, and the nation plunged into war. The three-year **Civil War** (1936-1939) ignited worldwide ideological passions. Germany and Italy dropped troops, supplies, and munitions into Franco's lap, while the stubbornly isolationist US and the war-weary European states were slow to aid the Republicans. The Soviet Union called for a **Popular Front** of Communists, Socialists, and other leftist sympathizers to battle Franco's fascism. Soon, however, aid from the Soviet Union waned as Stalin began to see the benefits of an alliance with Hitler. Without international aid, Republican forces were cut off from supplies, and they began to surrender to the Nationalists. Bombings, executions, combat, starvation, and disease took nearly 600,000 lives, and in 1939 Franco's forces marched into Madrid and ended the war.

FRANCO AND THE TRANSITION TO DEMOCRACY (1939-1998)

Brain drain (as leading scientists, artists, and intellectuals emigrated or were assassinated en masse), worker dissatisfaction, student unrest, and international isolation characterized the first few decades of Franco's dictatorship. In his old age, Franco tried to smooth international relations by joining **NATO** and encouraging tourism, but the "national tragedy" (as it was later called) did not officially end until Franco's death in 1975. **King Juan Carlos I,** grandson of Alfonso XIII and a nominal Franco protégé, carefully set out to undo Franco's damage. In 1978 Spain adopted a new constitution in a national referendum that led to the restoration of parliamentary government and regional autonomy.

Charismatic **Felipe González** led the **Spanish Socialist Worker's Party** (PSOE) to victory in the 1982 elections. González opened the Spanish economy and championed consensus policies, overseeing Spain's integration into the European Community (now the **European Union**) in 1986. Despite his support for continued membership in NATO—he had originally promised to withdraw if he won—and unpopular economic stance, González was reelected in 1986 and continued a program of massive public investment. The years 1986 to 1990 were outstanding for Spain's economy, as the nation enjoyed an average annual growth rate of 3.8%. By the end of 1993, however, recession had set in, and González and the PSOE only barely maintained a majority in Parliament over the increasingly popular conservative **Partido Popular** (PP). Revelations of large-scale corruption led to a resounding defeat of the Socialist party at the hands of the PP in the 1994 European parliamentary elections.

José María Aznar led the PP into power after González's support eroded and managed to maintain his delicately balanced coalition while leading the Spanish economy to its best performance in years. Fears of a rightist reversion have faded and most Spaniards seem pleased with the process of parliamentary democracy.

SPAIN TODAY

The last several years have seen mixed progress in one of Spain's most pressing areas of concern, Basque nationalism and terrorism. On September 12, 1998, the federal government called for an open dialogue between all parties (including the militant Euskadi Ta Askatasuma; ETA) and was endorsed by the Basque National Party (PNV). Six days later, ETA publicly declared a truce with the national government. On December 3, 1999, however, the ETA announced an end to the 14-month cease-fire due to lack of progress with negotiations. The past years have since seen a return of periodic terrorist murders of PP and PSOE members, and journalists and army officers, as well as instances of arson. However, in the March 2001 elections, a record number of Basque voters turned out to reject the ETA—a sign that they have finally grown tired of the constant violence in their region.

On a brighter note, the Spanish economy is currently improving. Over the past several years, unemployment has dropped drastically, although it remains the highest in the EU. Aznar talks of visions of "a new Spain" and plans to reduce unemployment even further, draw more women into the workforce, and improve the faltering birthrate by restructuring family and work arrangements.

LA MOVIDA After 40 years of Franco-imposed repression, Madrid was a cultural explosion waiting to happen. Franco's death in 1975 served as a catalyst for change: not a day had passed before every newspaper had printed a pornographic photo on its front page. *El Destapeo* ("the uncorking" or "uncovering" which followed Franco's regime) and *la Movida* ("the Movement," which took place a few years later) both exploded in Madrid, inspiring political diversity, apolitical revelry, and eccentricity of all kinds. Remnants of *la Movida* are still visible, however, in today's outrageous clubs, ambitious bars, and in the excitement of young *madrileños* planning to *ir de marcha* ("to party," literally "to go marching").

THE ARTS

FINE ARTS

Residents of the Iberian peninsula were creating art as early as 13,000 BC, the birth-date of the fabulous cave paintings at **Altamira**. In the 11th and 12th centuries, fresco painters and manuscript illuminators decorated churches and their libraries along the **Camino de Santiago** (see p. 896) and in **León** (see p. 824) and **Toledo** (see p. 816). **Pedro Berruguete**'s use of traditional gold backgrounds in his religious paintings exemplifies the Italian-influenced style of early Renaissance works. Berruguete's style is especially evident in his masterpiece, the altarpiece of San Tomás in **Ávila** (1499-1503, see p. 821). Not until after Spain's imperial ascendancy in the 16th century did painting reach its **Golden Age** (roughly 1492-1650). Felipe II imported foreign art and artists in order to jump-start native production and embellish his palace, El Escorial. Although he came to Spain seeking a royal commission, **El Greco** was rejected by Felipe II for his shocking and intensely personal style. Confounding his contemporaries, El Greco received appreciation in the 20th century. Setting up camp in Toledo, El Greco graced the **Iglesia de Santo Tomé** with his masterpiece *The Burial of Count Orgaz* (1586-1588, see p. 816).

Felipe IV's foremost court painter, **Diego Velázquez,** is considered one of the world's greatest artists. Whether depicting Felipe IV's family or lowly court jesters and dwarves, Velázquez painted with the same naturalistic precision. Nearly half of this Sevillian artist's works reside in the **Prado,** including his famous *The Maids of Honor* (1656, see p. 811).

Francisco de Goya, official court painter under the degenerate Carlos IV, ushered European painting into the modern age. Goya's depictions of the royal family come close to caricature, as Queen María Luisa's cruel jawline in the famous *The Family of Charles IV* (1800) can attest. Goya's later paintings graphically protest the lunacy of warfare. The Prado museum houses an entire room of his chilling *Black Paintings* (1820-1823, see p. 811).

It is hard to imagine an artist who has had as profound an effect upon 20th-century painting as Andalucían-born **Pablo Picasso**. A child prodigy, Picasso headed for Barcelona, which was a breeding ground of Modernist architecture and political activism. Picasso's **Blue Period,** beginning in 1900, was characterized by somber depictions of society's outcasts. His permanent move to Paris in 1904 initiated his **Rose Period,** during which he probed into the curiously engrossing lives of clowns and acrobats. With his French colleague Georges Braque, he founded **Cubism,** a method of painting objects simultaneously from multiple perspectives.

Catalán painter and sculptor **Joan Miró** created simplistic, almost child-like shapes in bright primary colors. His haphazard, undefined creations became a statement against the authoritarian society of Fascist Spain. By contrast, fellow Catalán **Salvador Dalí** scandalized both high society and leftist intellectuals in France and Spain by supporting the Fascists. Dalí's name is virtually synonymous with **Surrealism.** The painter tapped into dreams and the unconscious for images like the melting clocks in *The Persistence of Memory* (1931). His haunting *Premonition of the Civil War* (1936) envisioned war as a distorted monster of putrefying flesh. A shameless self-promoter (he often spoke of himself only in the 3rd person), Dalí founded the **Teatre-Museo Dalí** (see p. 874) in Figueres, which defines Surrealism in its collection, its construction, and its very existence.

Since Franco's death in 1975, a new generation of artists, including the unorthodox collage artist **Antonio Tapieshas** and hyperrealist painter **Antonio Lopez Garica,** have thrived. With museums in Madrid, Barcelona, Valencia, Sevilla, and Bilbao, Spanish painters and sculptors once again have a national forum for their work.

ARCHITECTURE

Scattered **Roman ruins** testify to six centuries of colonization. The **aqueduct** in Segovia (see p. 820) is one of the finest examples of remaining ruins. After the invasion of 711, the **Moors** constructed mosques and palaces throughout southern Spain. Because the Koran forbade representations of humans and animals, architects lavished buildings with stylized geometric designs, red-and-white horseshoe arches, ornate tiles called *azulejos*, courtyards, pools, and fountains. The spectacular 14th-century **Alhambra** in Granada (see p. 845) and the **Mezquita** in Córdoba (see p. 841) epitomize the Moorish style.

The combination of Islam and Christianity created two architectural movements unique to Spain: **Mozarabic** and **Mudéjar.** The former describes Christians under Muslim rule (Mozarabs) who adopted Arab devices like the horseshoe-shaped arch and the ribbed dome. The more common Mudéjar architecture was created by Moors during their occupation. Extensive use of brick and elaborately carved wooden ceilings typify Mudéjar style, which reached its height in the 14th century with **alcázars** (palaces) in Sevilla (see p. 827) and Segovia (see p. 820) and **synagogues** in Toledo (see p. 816) and Córdoba (see p. 837).

The first Gothic cathedral in Spain was built in Burgos (1221, see p. 825), followed closely by cathedral construction in Toledo and León. The **Spanish Gothic** style brought pointed arches, flying buttresses, slender walls, airy spaces, and stained-glass windows. New World riches inspired the **Plateresque** style, an embellishment of Gothic that transformed wealthier parts of Spain. Intricate stonework and extravagant use of gold and silver splashed 15th- and 16th-century buildings, most notably in **Salamanca** (see p. 823), where the university practically drips with ornamentation. In the late 16th century, **Italian Renaissance** innovations in perspective and symmetry arrived in Spain to sober up the Plateresque style. **El Escorial,** Felipe II's palace, was designed by **Juan de Herrera,** one of Spain's most prominent architects, and best exemplifies unadorned Renaissance style (see p. 815).

Opulence seized center stage once again in 17th- and 18th-century **Baroque** Spain. The **Churriguera** brothers pioneered this style—called, appropriately, **Churrigueresque**—which is equal parts ostentatious, ornamental, and difficult to pronounce. Elaborate works with extensive detail and twisted columns, like the altar of the **Toledo cathedral** (see p. 816), help distinguish this period in Spanish architecture.

In the late 19th and early 20th centuries, Catalán's **Modernistas** burst onto the scene in Barcelona, led by the eccentric genius of **Antoni Gaudí, Luis Domènech i Montaner,** and **José Puig i Caldafach.** Modernista structures defy previous standards with their voluptuous curves and abnormal textures. Spain's outstanding architectural tradition continues to this day with such new buildings as the Guggenheim (see p. p. 887) in Bilbao, designed by **Frank Gehry.**

LITERATURE

Spain's literary tradition first blossomed in the late Middle Ages (1000-1500). **Fernando de Rojas**'s *The Celestina* (1499), a tragicomic dialogue most noted for its folkloric witch character, helped pave the way for picaresque novels like *Lazarillo of Tormes* (1554) and *Guzmán of Alfarache* (1599), rags-to-riches stories about mischievous boys with good hearts. This literary form surfaced during Spain's **Golden Age** (1492-1650). Poetry particularly thrived in this era. Some consider the sonnets and romances of **Garcilaso de la Vega** the most perfect ever written in Castilian. This period also produced outstanding dramas, including works from **Calderón de la Barca** and **Lope de Vega,** who wrote nearly 2000 plays combined. Both espoused the **Neoplatonic** view of love, claiming that love always changes one's life dramatically and eternally. **Miguel de Cervantes**'s two-part *Don Quixote de la Mancha* (1605-15), which relates the satiric parable of the hapless Don and his sidekick, Sancho Panza, who think themselves bold *caballeros* (knights) out to save the world, is the most famous work of Spanish literature.

The 19th century bred a multiplicity of styles, from **José Zorrilla**'s romantic poems such as *Don Juan Tenorio* (1844) to the naturalistic novels of **Leopoldo Alas ("Clarín").** The modern literary era began with the **Generación del 1898**, a group led by essayist **Miguel de Unamuno** and cultural critic **José Ortega y Gasset.** These nationalistic authors argued, through essays and novels, that each individual must spiritually and ideologically attain internal peace before society can do the same. The **Generación del 1927**, a clique of experimental lyric poets who used Surrealist and vanguard poetry to express profound humanism included **Jorge Guillén**, **Federico García Lorca** (assassinated at the start of the Civil War), **Rafael Alberti**, and **Luis Cernuda.** In the 20th century, the Nobel Committee has honored playwright and essayist **Jacinto Benavente y Martínez** (1922), poet **Vicente Aleixandre** (1977), and novelist **Camilo José Cela** (1989). Since the fall of the Fascist regime in 1975, an avant-garde spirit—known as *La Movida* (see p. 791)—has been reborn in Madrid. **Ana Rossetti** and **Juana Castro** led a new generation of erotic poets into the 80s. With this newest group of poets, women are at the forefront of Spanish literature for the first time.

FILM

Franco's regime (1939-75) defined Spanish film during and after his rule. Censorship stifled most creative tendencies and left the public with nothing to watch but cheap westerns and bland spy flicks. As government supervision slacked in the early 1970s, Spanish cinema began to show signs of life, led by **Carlos Saura**'s subversive hits such as *The Garden of Delights* (1970).

In 1977, when domestic censorship laws were revoked in the wake of Franco's death, depictions of the exuberant excesses of liberated Spain found increasing international attention. **Pedro Almodovar**'s *Law of Desire* (1986), featuring **Antonio Banderas** as a homosexual, perhaps best captures the risqué themes of transgression most often treated by contemporary Spanish cinema. Almodovar's *All About My Mother* claimed the Best Foreign Film Oscar in 2000. Other directors to look for in Spain include **Bigas Luna**, director of the controversial *Jamón Jamón* (1992) and **Fernando Trueba**, whose *Belle Epoque* won an Oscar in 1994.

BULLFIGHTING

A visit to Spain is not complete without the experience of a bullfight. The national spectacle that is bullfighting dates, in its modern form, back to the early 1700s. A bullfight is divided into three principal stages: in the first, *picadors* (lancers on horseback) pierce the bull's neck; next, assistants on foot thrust *banderillas* (decorated darts) into the back; and finally, the **matador** performs the kill. If a matador has shown special skill and daring, the audience waves white handkerchiefs to implore the bullfight's president to reward the coveted ears (and, very rarely, the tail) to the matador. Although bullfighting has always had its critics—the Catholic church in the 17th century felt that the risks made it equivalent to suicide—the late 20th century has seen an especially strong attack from animal rights' activists. Whatever its faults, however, bullfighting is an essential element of the Spanish national consciousness.

FOOD AND DRINK

Spaniards start their day with a breakfast of coffee or hot chocolate and *bollos* (rolls) or *churros* (lightly fried fritters). Lunch is served between 2 and 3pm, and consists of several courses. Supper at home is light—often a sandwich—and eaten around 9pm. Supper out, also light, begins later, usually around 10pm. Some restaurants are "open" from 8am until 1 or 2am, but most only serve meals from 2 to 4pm and from 8pm until midnight. Spain's **tapas** (small portions of savory meats and vegetables cooked according to local recipes) are not to be missed. Other Spanish specialties include *tortilla de patata* (potato omelette), *jamón serrano* (smoked ham), *calamares fritos* (fried squid), *arroz* (rice), *chorizo* (spicy sausage), *paella* (steamed saffron rice with seafood, chicken, and vegetables), and *gazpacho* (cold tomato-based soup). *Sangría* is a favorite alcohol treat, made of red and white wine, sugar, brandy, and fruit.

ESSENTIALS

DOCUMENTS AND FORMALITIES

Travelers need legal passports or visas to enter and leave Spain. A passport allows Canadian, British, New Zealand, and US citizens to remain for 90 days. Citizens of South Africa need a **visa** to enter Spain. Admission as a visitor does not include the right to **work**, which is authorized only by a work permit; entering Spain to **study** requires a special visa.

> **Spanish Embassies at Home: Australia,** 15 Arkana St., Yarralumla, ACT 2600. Mailing address: P.O. Box 9076, Deakin, ACT 2600. (☎(02) 62 73 35 55). **Canada,** 74 Stanley Ave., Ottawa, ON K1M 1P4 (☎613-747-2252). **Ireland,** 17A Merlyn Park, Ballsbridge, Dublin 4 (☎(01) 269 1640). **South Africa,** 169 Pine St., Arcadia, P.O. Box 1633, Pretoria 0083 (☎(012) 344 3875). **UK,** 39 Chesham Pl., London SW1X 8SB (☎(020) 72 35 55 55). **US,** 2375 Pennsylvania Ave. NW, Washington, D.C. 20037 (☎202-452-0100).

> **Foreign Embassies in Spain:** Embassies are in Madrid (see p. 797). All countries have consulates in **Barcelona** (see p. 859). **Australian** and **US** consulates are in **Sevilla.** Another **Canadian** consulate is in Málaga; **UK** consulates are in Alicante, Bilbao, Ibiza, Málaga, and Palma de Mallorca; **US** consulates are in Valencia and Palma de Mallorca.

TRANSPORTATION

BY PLANE. Airports in Madrid and Barcelona handle most international flights; Sevilla also has a major international airport. **Iberia** serves all domestic locations and all major international cities. **Air Europa** (US ☎888-238-7672 or 718-244-6016, Spain ☎902 30 06 00; www.air-europa.es) flies out of New York City and most European cities to Spain and has discounts available for those under 22.

BY TRAIN. RENFE (www.renfe.es), the Spanish centralized national rail system, has clean, punctual, reasonably priced trains with various levels of service. Its network radiates from Madrid; many small towns are not served. *Alta Velocidad Española* (AVE) trains are the fastest on the Madrid-Córdoba-Sevilla line. *Talgos* are almost as fast; *Talgo 200s* run on *AVE* rails—there are four lines from Madrid to Málaga, Algeciras, Cádiz, and Huelva. *Intercity* is cheaper and dowdier, but still fairly fast. *Estrellas* are slow night trains with bunks. *Cercanías* (commuter trains) go from cities to suburbs and nearby towns. *Tranvía, semidirecto*, and *correo* trains are slower than slow. Trains connect with most major European cities via France. The other train company in Spain is **FEVE**, which sluggishly but dependably runs between many northern towns not served by RENFE.

There are several **RailEurope** passes that cover travel within Spain. You must purchase railpasses at least 15 days before departure. Call 1-800-4EURAIL in the US or go to www.raileurope.com. **Spain Flexipass** offers three days of unlimited travel in a two-month period (first-class US$200/€232, 2nd-class US$155/€180). **Iberic Railpass** is good for three days of unlimited first-class travel in Spain and Portugal for US$205/€240. **Spain Rail 'n' Drive Pass** is good for three days of unlimited first-class train travel and two days of unlimited mileage in a rental car.

BY BUS. In Spain, ignore romanticized versions of European train travel—**buses** are cheaper, run more frequently, and are sometimes faster than trains. Bus routes, far more comprehensive than the rail network, provide the only public transportation to many isolated areas. Spain has numerous private companies; the lack of a centralized bus company may make itinerary planning an ordeal. **ALSA** (☎902 42 22 42), serves Asturias, Castilla y León, Galicia, and Madrid, as well as destinations in

Portugal, Morocco, France, Italy, and Poland. **Auto-Res/Cunisa, S.A.** (☎902 02 09 99), serves Castilla y León, Extremadura, Galicia, Madrid, and Valencia.

BY CAR. Spain has an extensive road grid covering close to 340,000km; of this total, 7000km are highways (toll motorways, freeways, and dual-carriageways). Gas prices average 130-140ptas/€0.75-0.85 per liter. **Speeders beware:** police can "photograph" the speed and license plate of your car, and issue a ticket without pulling you over.

Renting a car in Spain is considerably cheaper than in many other Western European countries. International rental companies offer services throughout the country, but you may want to check with **Atesa** (www.atesa.es), Spain's largest national rental agency. The Spanish automobile association is **Real Automóbil Club de España (RACE)**, C. Jose Abascal, 10, Madrid (☎91 594 74 75). **Taxis** are readily available in almost every Spanish city, and they are a much wiser form of transportation than a personal car in Madrid and Barcelona.

BY BIKE AND BY THUMB. Due to its mountainous terrain, Spain does not have as extensive of a **bike tour** industry as some other Western European countries. It is certainly explorable by bicycle, however, and it shouldn't be hard to rent a bicycle in tourist centers, especially in southern regions. **Hitchhikers** report that Castilla and Andalucía offer little more than a long, hot wait, and that hitchhiking out of Madrid is virtually impossible. The Mediterranean Coast and the islands are much more promising. *Let's Go* does not recommend hitchhiking.

TOURIST SERVICES AND MONEY

EMERGENCY	**Emergency,** ☎112. **Local Police,** ☎092. **National Police,** ☎091. **Medical,** ☎124.

TOURIST OFFICES. The **Spanish Tourist Office** is eager to help tourists. They operate an extensive official web site (www.tourspain.es). Municipal tourist offices, generally called *oficinas de turismo*, are a good first stop upon arrival in a Spanish town; they usually have free maps and region-specific advice for travelers.

Tourist offices at home: Canada, Tourist Office of Spain, 2 Bloor St. West, Ste. 3402, Toronto, ON M4W 3E2 (☎416-961-3131; fax 416-961-1992). **UK,** Spanish National Tourist Office, 22-23 Manchester Square, London W1M 5AP (☎(171) 486 8077; fax 486 8034; info.londres@tourspain.es). **US,** Tourist Office of Spain, 666 Fifth Ave., 35th Fl., New York, NY 10103 (☎212-265-8822; fax 212-265-8864), additional offices in Chicago, IL (☎312-642-1992), Beverly Hills, CA (☎323-658-7188) and Miami, FL (☎305-358-1992).

CURRENCY AND EXCHANGE. Money in Spain comes in the form of the **peseta** (ptas), available in coins of 1, 5, 10, 25, 50, 100, 200 and 500ptas and notes of 1000, 2000, 50000, and 10,0000ptas. Spain has accepted the **Euro (€)** as legal tender, and *pesetas* will be phased out by July 1, 2002. For more information, see p. 23. **Traveler's checks** are widely accepted and used in Spain; ATM cards are probably an even easier way to exchange money and will earn you better rates. If you are using travelers' checks, **Banco Central Hispano** often provides good rates.

Prices: You can do a "bare-bones day" in Spain (camping or sleeping in cheap hostels, buying food at supermarkets, staying in at night) for about 5000ptas/€30, or US$30-35. A slightly more comfortable day (sleeping in nicer hostels, eating some meals in restaurants, going out at night) will probably run up to 7500ptas/€45, or US$50.

Tipping and bargaining: Tipping is not very common in Spain. In restaurants, all prices include service charge. Satisfied customers occasionally toss in some spare change—usually no more than 5%—but this is purely optional. Many people give train, airport, and hotel porters a 100ptas coin per bag, while taxi drivers sometimes get 5-10%. Bargaining is common at flea markets and with street vendors. Travelers can try bargaining for hostel prices in the off-season, especially in less-touristed areas.

SPAIN

Taxes: Spain has a 7% **value-added tax (VAT)** known as IVA, on all restaurant and accommodations. The prices listed in *Let's Go* include IVA unless otherwise mentioned. Retail goods bear a much higher 16% IVA, although listed prices are usually inclusive. Non-EU citizens who have stayed in the EU fewer than 180 days can claim back the tax paid on purchases at the airport. Ask the shop where you have made the purchase to supply you with a tax return form.

ACCOMMODATIONS AND CAMPING

Spanish accommodations have many aliases, distinguished by the different grades of rooms. The cheapest and barest options are **casas de huéspedes** and **hospedajes,** while **pensiones** and **fondas** tend to be a bit nicer. All are basically just boarding houses. Higher up the ladder, **hostales** generally have sinks in bedrooms and provide sheets and lockers, while **hostal-residencias** are similar to hotels in overall quality. **Red Española de Albergues Juveniles (REAJ),** C. José Ortega y Gasset, 71, Madrid 28006 (☎91 347 77 00; fax 91 401 81 60), the Spanish Hostelling International (HI) affiliate, runs 165 youth *hostals* year-round. The government rates *hostales* on a two-star system; even establishments receiving one star are typically quite comfortable. The system also fixes each *hostal*'s prices, posted in the lounge or main entrance. If you have any troubles (with rates or service), ask for the **libro de reclamaciones** (complaint book), which by law must be produced on demand. The argument will usually end immediately, since all complaints must be forwarded to the authorities within 48hr. In Spain, **campgrounds** are generally the cheapest choice for two or more people. Most charge separate fees per person, per tent, and per car; others charge for a *parcela*—a small plot of land—plus possible per-person fees. Tourist offices provide info on official areas, including the hefty *Guía de campings*. Reservations are usually necessary in the summer.

COMMUNICATION

MAIL. Air mail *(por avión)* takes around six business days to reach the US and Canada, approximately three days to the UK and Ireland, and up to 10 days to Australia and New Zealand. **Surface mail** *(por barco)*, while considerably less expensive than air mail, can take over a month, and packages will take two to three months. **Registered** or **express mail** *(registrado* or *certificado)*, is the most reliable way to send a letter or parcel home, and takes four to seven business days (letter postage 237ptas/€1.40). **Stamps** are sold at post offices and tobacconists (*estancos or tabacos*). To send mail *Poste Restante* to Spain, address the letter as follows: SURNAME, FirstName; Lista de Correos; City Name; Postal Code; SPAIN; AIR MAIL.

TELEPHONES. The central Spanish phone company is **Telefónica.** Local calls cost 20ptas. The best way to make local calls is with a phone card, issued in denominations of 1000ptas/€6 and 2000ptas/€12 and available at tobacconists (*estancos or tabacos*) and most post offices. International calls can be made using phone cards, but are very expensive; the best way to call home is with an international calling card issued by your phone company. To call home with your calling card, contact the operator for your service provider in Spain by dialing the appropriate **international toll-free access number: AT&T,** ☎900 99 00 11; **British Telecom,** ☎900 99 00 44; **Canada Direct,** ☎900 99 00 15; **Ireland Direct,** ☎900 99 03 53; **MCI,** ☎900 99 00 14; **Sprint,** ☎900 99 00 13; **Telecom New Zealand,** ☎900 99 00 64; **Telkom South Africa,** ☎900 99 00 27; **Telstra Australia,** ☎900 99 00 61.

INTERNET ACCESS. Email is easily accessible within Spain. An increasing number of bars offer Internet access for a fee of 200-700ptas/€1.20-4.20 per hour; many also offer specials with rates much cheaper than that. Cybercafes are listed in most towns and all cities. In small towns, if Internet access is not listed, try the library or tourist office where travelers can sometimes get access for a small fee. The web site www.tangaworld.com lists nearly 200 cybercafes across Spain.

SPAIN

LANGUAGE. Spain has four regional languages plus plenty of dialects. Catalán is the language of choice in Catalunya, Valencian in Valencia. The Basque (Euskera) language is spoken in north-central Spain, and Galician (Gallego, related to Portuguese) is spoken in the once-Celtic northwest. Standard Spanish (Castilian, or *castellano*) is spoken everywhere. To partake of some *castellano*, see p. 952.

LOCAL FACTS

Time: Spain is 1hr. ahead of Greenwich Mean Time (GMT).

When to Go: The northwest is rightly called "wet" Spain, with a humid, temperate climate. The interior's climate resembles that of Central Europe—long winters and, in the lowlands, hot, dry summers. The east and south coasts enjoy a Mediterranean climate. The northeast coast can be humid, but the southwest is sweltering, especially Sevilla and Córdoba.

Hours: The day gets started around 9am; shops close down for a long lunch from 1:30 or 2pm until 4:30 or 5pm, and reopen at 8pm. On Sa, shops are usually open only in the morning, and Su is a day of rest for almost all places of business. Banking hours in Spain are M-F 9am-2pm; Oct.-May banks are also open Sa 9am-1pm.

Holidays: New Year's Day (Jan. 1); Epiphany (Jan. 6); Maundy Thursday (Mar. 28); Good Friday (Mar. 29); Easter (Mar. 31); Labor Day (May 1); La Asunción (Aug. 15); National Day (Oct. 12); All Saints' Day (Nov. 1); Constitution Day (Dec. 6); Feast of the Immaculate Conception (Dec. 8); Christmas (Dec. 25).

Festivals: Spain loves festivals—in total there are more than 3000, far too many to list here. All of Spain will celebrate **Carnaval** from Feb. 7 to 17 this year; the biggest partying goes on in Cataluña and Cádiz. Valencia will host the annual **Las Fallas** in mid-Mar. From Mar. 24 to 31, the entire country will honor the Holy Week, or **Semana Santa.** Sevilla's **Feria de Abril** takes place in late Apr. In June and July, Granada will host the **International Dance and Music Festival** and Córdoba will host the **International Guitar Festival.** Mérida's **Festival de Teatro Clásico** will be in July and Aug., and Pamplona's (in)famous **San Fermines** (Running of the Bulls) takes place July 6-14. San Sebástian's international film festival is in the last week of Sept. For more information on fiestas throughout Spain, see www.tourspain.es, www.SiSpain.org, or www.cyberspain.es.

MADRID ☎ 91

There are a few minutes, in the orange light of Madrid's early morning, when the city finally seems to sleep. Just moments later, steel shutters blink open and the streets once again fill with an unending stream of pedestrians and cars. While tourists inundate the city, spending their days absorbing its "Old World" monuments, world-renowned museums, and raging nightlife, Madrid's population of 4,500,000 roams the labyrinthine neighborhoods, and lives life with a simple and energetic joy. With Franco's death came an explosion known as *La Movida* ("Shift" or "Movement"). After decades of totalitarian repression, Madrid burst out laughing and crying, and life poured into the city. A 200,000-strong student population took to the streets and stayed there, shedding the decorous reserve of their predecessors. In their frenetic state, post-Franco youth seemed neither cognizant of their city's history nor preoccupied with its future; they haven't stopped moving yet.

Today the city continues to serve as the country's political, intellectual, and cultural center. Madrid epitomizes the mix of rich history and passion for the present that so defines Spain.

✈ INTERCITY TRANSPORTATION

Flights: All flights land at **Aeropuerto Internacional de Barajas,** 20min. northeast of Madrid. The **Barajas metro line,** inaugurated in June 1999, connects the airport to all of Madrid (145ptas/€0.90). From the airport, follow signs to the metro. Another option

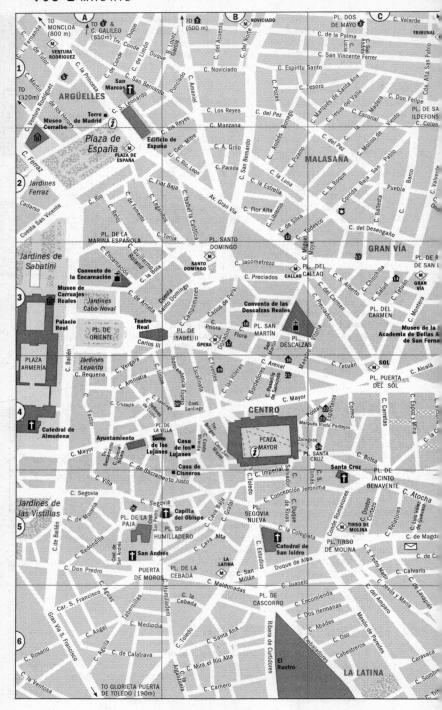

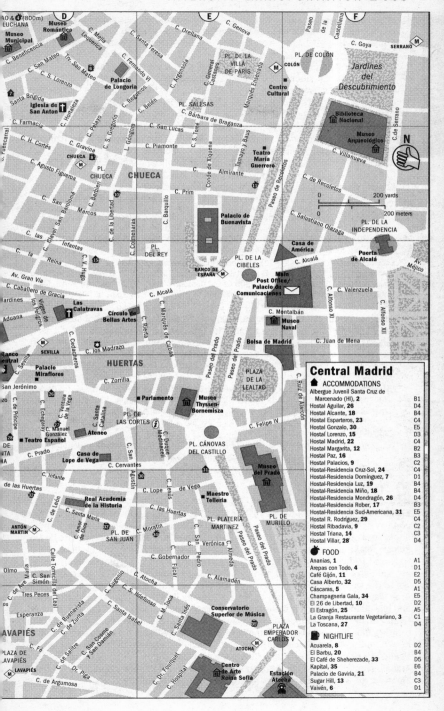

Central Madrid

🏠 ACCOMMODATIONS

Albergue Juvenil Santa Cruz de Marcenado (HI), **2**	B1
Hostal Aguilar, **26**	D4
Hostal Alcante, **18**	B4
Hostal Esparteros, **23**	C4
Hostal Gonzalo, **30**	E5
Hostal Lorenzo, **15**	D3
Hostal Madrid, **22**	C4
Hostal Margarita, **12**	B2
Hostal Paz, **16**	B3
Hostal Palacios, **9**	C2
Hostal-Residencia Cruz-Sol, **24**	C4
Hostal-Residencia Domínguez, **7**	D1
Hostal-Residencia Luz, **19**	B4
Hostal-Residencia Miño, **18**	B4
Hostal-Residencia Mondragón, **26**	D4
Hostal-Residencia Rober, **17**	B3
Hostal-Residencia Sud-Americana, **31**	E5
Hostal R. Rodríguez, **29**	C4
Hostal Ribadavia, **9**	C2
Hostal Triana, **14**	C3
Hostal Villar, **28**	D4

🍎 FOOD

Ananias, **1**	A1
Arepas con Todo, **4**	D1
Café Gijón, **11**	E2
Casa Alberto, **32**	D5
Cáscaras, **5**	A1
Champagneria Gala, **34**	E5
El 26 de Libertad, **10**	D2
El Estragón, **25**	A5
La Granja Restaurante Vegetariano, **3**	C1
La Toscana, **27**	D4

🍸 NIGHTLIFE

Acuarela, **8**	D2
El Barbu, **20**	B4
El Café de Sheherezade, **33**	D5
Kapital, **35**	E6
Palacio de Gaviria, **21**	B4
Sugar Hill, **13**	C3
Vaivén, **6**	D1

is the green **Bus-Aeropuerto #89** (look for "EMT" signs just outside the doors), which leaves from the national and international terminals and runs to the city center (every 25min., 4:45am-6:17am; every 15min., 6:17am-10pm; every hr., 10pm-1:45am; 400ptas/€2.40). The bus stops underground beneath the Jardines del Descubrimiento in **Plaza de Colón** (M: Colón). Fleets of **taxis** swarm the airport. Taxi fare to central Madrid should be around 3000ptas/€18, including the 400ptas/€240 airport surcharge. Serving international and national destinations, **Iberia** is at Santa Cruz de Marcenado, 2 (☎91 587 81 56). M: San Bernardo. Open M-F 9:30am-2pm and 4-7pm. Reservations and info (☎902 40 05 00) open 24hr. **Aviaco**, C. Maude, 51 (☎91 554 36 00), is a domestic affiliate.

Trains: Two *Largo Recorrido* (long distance) **RENFE** stations, **Madrid-Chamartín** and **Madrid-Atocha** (domestic service only), connect Madrid to the rest of the world. Call RENFE (☎91 328 90 20; www.renfe.es) for reservations and info. **RENFE Main Office,** C. Alcalá, 44, at Gran Vía (M: Banco de España) sells tickets.

Estación Chamartín (24hr. info for international destinations ☎93 490 11 22; domestic destinations ☎90 224 02 02, Spanish only). Agustín de Foxá. M: Chamartín. Bus #5 runs to and from Sol (45min.). Ticket windows open daily 8:30am-10:30pm. Chamartín services both international and domestic destinations in the northeast and south. Most *cercanías* (local) trains leave from Chamartín; many stop at Atocha. To: **Barcelona** (7hr., 10 per day 7am-12:50am, 6785ptas/€40.80); **Lisbon** (10hr., 10:45pm, 6900ptas/€41.50); **Nice** (22hr., 10am, 21,500ptas/€129.20); **Paris** (13hr., 7pm, 19,500ptas/€117.20).

Estación Atocha (☎91 328 90 20). M: Atocha. Ticket windows open 6:30am-11:30pm. Trains to: Andalucía, Castilla-La Mancha, El Escorial, Extremadura, Castilla y León, Sierra de Guadarrama, and Valencia. **AVE** service (☎91 534 05 05) to **Córdoba** (1¾hr., 16 per day 7am-10pm, 5100-7200ptas/€30.65-43.30) and **Sevilla** (2½hr., 20 per day 7am-9pm, 8600-10,000ptas/€51.70-60.10). **Luggage storage** (400-600ptas/€2.40-3.60).

Buses: Numerous private companies, each with its own station and set of destinations, serve Madrid; many buses pass through the **Estación Sur de Autobuses.**

Estación Sur de Autobuses: C. Méndez Alvaro (☎91 468 42 00). M: Méndez Álvaro. Info booth open daily 7am-11pm. **Empressa Galiano Continental** (☎91 527 29 61) to **Toledo** (1hr., M-Sa every 30min. 8:30am-midnight, 605ptas/€3.60). **Empressa Larrea** (☎91 539 00 05) to **Avila** (2hrs.; M-F 8 per day 7am-8pm, Sa-Su 3 per day 10am-8pm; 950ptas/€5.70).

Estación Auto Res: Pl. Conde de Casal, 6 (☎91 551 72 00). M: Conde de Casal. To: **Cuenca** (3hr.; M-F 8-10 per day 6:45am-10pm, Sa-Su 5-6 per day 8am-8pm; 1325ptas/€8); **Salamanca** (3-3¼hr., 7 per day 8:30am-6pm, 1505ptas/€9); **Trujillo** (3¼hr., 11-12 per day 8am-1am, 2035ptas/€12.25); **Valencia** (5hr., 4 per day 1am-2pm, 2875ptas/€17.30). Express trains also available to these destinations.

Estación La Sepulvedana: Po. Florida, 11 (☎91 530 48 00). M: Príncipe Pío (via extension from M: Ópera). To **Segovia** (1½hr., every 30min. 6:30am-10:15pm, 840ptas/€5) and **Ávila** (1½hr., 3-8 per day, 930ptas/€5.60).

✴ ORIENTATION

Kilómetro 0 in **Puerta del Sol** ("Sol" for short) is the epicenter of the city (and the country), within walking distance of most sights and presided over by the famous neon Tío Pepe liquor sign. Just to the west is the **Plaza Mayor;** farther west lie the **Palacio Real** and the **Ópera** district. East of Sol lies **Huertas,** a one-time literary district and today the hub of cafe, theater, and museum life. Huertas is centered around **Plaza Santa Ana,** bordered by C. Alcalá to the north, Po. Prado to the east, Sol to the west, and C. Atocha to the south. The area north of Sol is bordered by the **Gran Vía,** which runs northwest to **Plaza de España.** North of Gran Vía are three club and bar districts linked by **Calle de Fuencarral: Malasaña, Bilbao,** and **Chueca.** Beyond Gran Vía and east of Malasaña and Chueca lies residential Madrid. East of Sol, the thoroughfare **Paseo de la Castellana-Paseo de Recoletos-Paseo del Prado** splits Madrid in two, running from **Atocha** in the south to **Plaza de Castilla** in the north, passing the Prado, the fountains of **Plaza Cibeles,** and **Plaza Colón.** Northwest of Sol lies **Argüelles,** an energetic neighborhood of families and students spilling over from **Moncloa,** the student district that centers on C. Isaac Peral.

Get a map at the tourist office and refer also to this book's **color maps.** Madrid is safe compared to other European cities, but Puerta del Sol, Pl. Dos de Mayo in Malasaña, Pl. de Chueca, and Pl. España are particularly intimidating late at night.

▐ LOCAL TRANSPORTATION

Metro: Madrid's metro puts most major subway systems to shame. Green timers hanging above most platforms show the amount of time since the last train departed. An individual metro ticket costs 145ptas/€0.90, but savvy riders opt for the **bonotransporte** (ticket of 10 rides for either the metro or bus system) at 760ptas/€5. Buy both at machines in any metro stop, *estanco* (tobacco shop), or newsstand. For more details, call **Metro info** (☎91 580 59 09) or ask at any ticket booth.

Bus: The fare is 145ptas/€0.90. Buses run 6am-11:30pm. From midnight until 3am, the night bus service, *buho* (owl), travels from Pl. Cibeles to the outskirts every 20min.; from 3-6am, it runs every hour. Night buses (N1-N20) are the cheapest form of transportation for late-night revelers. For more information, call **Empresa Municipal de Transportes** (☎91 406 88 10; Spanish only).

Taxi: ☎91 445 90 08 or 91 447 32 32. A green *libre* sign in the window or a lit green light indicates availability. The base fare is 190ptas/€1.15, plus 50-75ptas/€0.30-0.45 per km. Common fare supplements include: airport (400ptas/€2.40); bus and train stations (125ptas/€0.75); luggage charge (50ptas/€0.30 per bag); Sundays and holidays (6am-11pm, 125ptas/€0.75); and nighttime (11pm-6am, 125ptas/€0.75). To request **taxi service for the disabled,** call 91 547 85 00. If you leave possessions in a taxi, visit or call the **Negociado de Objetos Perdidos,** Pl. Legazpi, 7 (☎91 588 43 46). Open M-F 9am-2pm.

Car Rental: There is no reason to rent a car in Madrid. Don't drive unless you're planning to zoom out of the city, and even then bus and train fares will be cheaper. Tobacco shops sell parking permits. **Europcar,** Estación de Atocha, AVE terminal (☎91 530 01 94; reservations ☎91 210 50 30; www.europcar.com). M: Atocha Renfe. Cheapest car 8900ptas/€53.50 per day, 49,800ptas/€300 per week. 400km per day included. Minimum age 21. Open daily 8am-midnight.

Moped Rental: Motocicletas Antonio Castro: C. Conde Duque, 13 (☎91 542 06 57). M: San Bernardo. Honda costs 4500ptas/€27 per day (8am-8pm) or 19,500ptas/€117.20 per week, including unlimited mileage and insurance. 40,000ptas/€240.40 deposit. Minimum age 18. Open M-F 8am-1:30pm and 5-8pm, Sa 9-11am.

READ THIS. The **Guía del Ocio,** at any news kiosk, should be your first purchase in Madrid (150ptas/€0.90). It has concert, theater, sports, cinema, and TV schedules. It also lists exhibits, restaurants, bars, and clubs. Although it is in Spanish, the alphabetical listings of clubs and restaurants are invaluable even to non-speakers. For an English magazine with articles on finds in and around the city, pick up *In Madrid,* distributed free at tourist offices and restaurants.

▐ PRACTICAL INFORMATION

TOURIST, FINANCIAL, AND LOCAL SERVICES

Tourist Offices: Municipal, Pl. Mayor, 3 (☎91 366 54 77; fax 91 366 54 77). M: Sol. Open M-Sa 10am-8pm, Su 10am-2pm. **Regional/Provincial Office of the Comunidad de Madrid,** main office, Duque de Medinaceli, 2 (☎91 429 49 51). Brochures, transport info, and maps for towns in the Comunidad. Other offices at Estación Chamartín and the airport.

▧ **General Info Line:** ☎010. 20ptas/€0.10 per min. Outside Madrid ☎90 130 06 00.

Embassies: Australia, Pl. Descubridor Diego de Ordás, 3 (☎91 441 60 25; fax 91 441 93 00; information@embaustralia.es; www.embaustralia.es). **Canada,** C. Núñez de Balboa, 35 (☎91 423 32 50; fax 91 423 32 51; www.canada-es.org). **Ireland,** Po. Castellana, 46, 4th fl. (☎91 576 35 00; fax 91 435 16 77). **New Zealand,** Pl. Lealtad, 2, 3rd fl. (☎91 523 02 26; fax 91 523 01 71). **South Africa,** Claudio Coello, 91, 6th fl.(☎91 436 37 80; fax 91 577 74 14). **UK,** C. Fernando el Santo, 16 (☎91 700 82 00; fax 91 700 83 11). **US,** C. Serrano, 75 (☎91 587 22 00; fax 91 587 23 03).

Budget Travel: Viajes TIVE, C. Fernando el Católico, 88 (☎91 543 74 12; fax 91 544 00 62). M: Moncloa. Exit the metro at C. Isaac Peral, walk straight down C. Arcipreste de Hita, and turn left on C. Fernando el Católico; it is on your left. ISIC 700ptas/€4.20, HI card 1800ptas/€10.80. Open M-F 9am-2pm, Sa 9am-noon.

Currency Exchange: Banco Central Hispano charges no commission on cash or traveler's checks. **Main branch,** Pl. Canalejas, 1 (☎91 558 11 11). M: Sol. From Sol, follow C. San Jeronimo to Pl. Canalejas. Open Apr.-Sept. M-F 8:30am-2:30pm, Sa 8:30am-1pm; Oct.-Mar. M-Th 8:30am-4:30pm, F 8:30am-2pm, Sa 8:30am-1pm.

American Express: Pl. Cortés, 2 (☎91 527 03 03; info ☎91 322 54 00). M: Sevilla. From the metro stop, take a right on C. Alcala, another right down C. Cedacero and a left on C. San Jerónimo; office is on the left. Open M-F 9am-5:30pm, Sa 9am-noon.

Luggage Storage: Barajas Airport. Follow the signs to *consigna.* One day 425ptas/€2.55, 2-15 days 530-740ptas/€3.20-4.45 per day, after day 15 105-210ptas/€0.60-1.25 per day. **Estación Chamartín** and **Estación Atocha.** Lockers 400-600ptas/€2.40-3.60 per day. Open daily 6:30am-12:30am.

Gay and Lesbian Services: Colectivo de Gais y Lesbianas de Madrid (COGAM), C. Fuencarral, 37 (☎/fax 91 523 00 70). M: Gran Vía. Provides a wide range of services and activities and HIV support group (☎91 522 45 17; M-F 6-10pm). Reception daily M-Sa 5:30-9pm. Free counseling M-Th 7-9pm.

Laundromat: Lavandería, C. Cervantes 1. M: Puerta del Sol or Banco de España. From Pl. Santa Ana follow C. Prado, turn right on C. Leon and then left onto C. Cervantes. Wash 500ptas/€3, dry 100ptas/€0.60 for 9min. Open M-Sa 9am-8pm.

EMERGENCY AND COMMUNICATIONS

Emergency: ☎112 (for all emergencies). For national and local police, ☎091 or 092.

Police: C. de los Madrazo, 9 (☎91 541 71 60). M: Sevilla. From C. Arenal make a right onto C. Cedacneros and a left onto C. los Madrazo. Forms in English available. To report crimes committed in the **metro,** go to the office in the Sol station (☎91 521 09 11). Open daily 8am-11pm.

Crisis Lines: Rape Hotline (☎91 574 01 10). Open M-F 10am-2pm and 4-7pm.

Late-Night Pharmacy: Dial 098 to find the nearest one. One at **Calle Mayor, 59** (☎91 548 00 14). M: Sol.

Hospitals: For non-emergency concerns, **Anglo-American Medical Unit,** Conde de Aranda, 1, 1st fl. (☎91 435 18 23) is quick and friendly. M: Serrano or Retiro. Doctors, dentists, and optometrists. Run partly by Brits and Americans. Initial visit 9000ptas/€54 for students, 10,000-15,000ptas/€60-96 for non-students. AmEx/MC/V.

Emergency Clinics: In a **medical emergency,** dial 061. **Equipo Quirúrgico Municipal No. 1,** C. Montesa, 22 (☎91 588 51 00). M: Manuel Becerra. **Hospital Ramón y Cajal,** Ctra. Colmenar Viejo (☎91 336 80 00). Bus #135 from Pl. Castilla.

Internet Access: Oficina13, C. Mayor, 1, 4th fl., office 13. M: Sol. Take the elevator up and buzz the office. Absolutely unbeatable 200ptas/€1.20 per hr., 150ptas/€0.90 per 30min. Open daily 10am-11pm. **Interpublic,** C. San Jeronimo, 18, 1st fl. M: Sol. 300ptas/€1.80 per hr. Open daily 9am-midnight.

Post Office: Palacio de Comunicaciones, C. Alcala, 51, on Pl. Cibeles (☎90 219 71 97). M: Banco de España. Windows open M-Sa 8:30am-9:30pm, Su 9am-2pm for stamp purchases, certified mail, telex and fax service. **Postal Code:** 28080.

▐▀ ACCOMMODATIONS

The demand for rooms is always high and increases dramatically in summer. But never fear—Madrid is rife with hostels. Prices average about 2800ptas/€16.80 per person for a basic room, a bit more for a two-star hostel, and slightly less for a *pensión.* The tourist office in Pl. Mayor (see above) has a full list of lodgings.

EL CENTRO: SOL, ÓPERA, AND PLAZA MAYOR

Prices and locations in the Centro are as good as they get, especially if you are planning to brave the nightlife. The streets that form the inner triangle between M: Sol, Pl. Mayor, and Pl. Santa Ana are packed with hostels. The following listings fall in the area between the Sol and Ópera metro stops. Buses #3, 25, 39, and 500 serve Ópera; buses #3, 5 (from Atocha), 15, 20, 50-53, and 150 serve Sol.

SPAIN

■ **Hostal Paz,** C. Flora, 4, 1st and 4th fl. (☎91 547 30 47). M: Ópera. Don't be deterred by the dark street, parallel to C. Arenal, off C. Donados or C. Hileras. Peaceful rooms with large windows are sheltered from street noise and lavished with comfort-enhancers; wonderful owners, satellite TV, A/C, and spotless, spacious bathrooms. Reservations advised. Singles 2500ptas/€15; doubles 4100-4800ptas/€24.70-28.80; triples 6000ptas/€36. MC/V.

■ **Hostal-Residencia Luz,** C. Fuentes, 10, 3rd fl. (☎91 542 07 59 or 91 559 74 18; fax 91 542 07 59), off C. Arenal. M: Ópera. In the running with Hostel Paz for the best digs in Madrid, the 12 sunny, newly redecorated rooms ooze comfort. Don't pay the 1000ptas/€6 extra for a private bath: the (gorgeous) common ones are cleaned more often than you will use them. Singles 2500ptas/€15; doubles 3700ptas/€22.20; triples 5500ptas/€33. Discounts for longer stays.

Hostal Esparteros, C. Esparteros, 12, 4th fl. (☎/fax 91 521 09 03). M: Sol. Cheap, small, sparkling rooms with balcony or large windows (no fans). The owner speaks English and ensures a terrific stay. Singles 2000-2200ptas/€12-13.20, with bath 2700ptas/€16.20; doubles 3200ptas/€19.20, with bath 3700ptas/€22.20. Discounts for longer stays.

Hostal-Residencia Rober, C. Arenal, 26, 5th fl. (☎91 541 91 75). M: Ópera. Brilliant balcony views down Arenal. Smoking strictly prohibited. Singles with double bed and shower 3800ptas/€22.80, with bath 4800ptas/€28.80; doubles with bath 6000ptas/€36; triples with bath 7800ptas/€46.80.

Hostal-Residencia Cruz-Sol, Pl. Santa Cruz, 6, 3rd fl. (☎91 532 71 97). M: Sol. A good deal. Recent renovations produced modern rooms. Laundry 1000ptas. Singles 3500ptas/€21, with bath 4000ptas/€24; doubles 6000ptas/€36; triples 8500ptas/€51; quads 9500ptas/€57. AmEx/MC/V.

Hostal Alcante, C. Arenal, 16, 2nd fl. (☎91 531 51 78), on the left. Spacious rooms, with TV, heat, 24hr. hot water, and A/C. Singles 3500ptas/€21; doubles 5500ptas/€33, with bath 6500ptas/€39; triples with bath 9000ptas/€54. MC/V.

Hostal Madrid, C. Esparteros, 6, 2nd fl. (☎91 522 00 60; fax 91 532 35 10). M: Sol. Off C. Mayor. The backpacker's equivalent of a 5-star hotel. Reservations 4 days ahead advised. Singles 7000ptas/€42; doubles 10,000ptas/€60; triple with balcony 13,000ptas/€78. AmEx/MC/V.

Hostal-Residencia Miño, C. Arenal, 16, 2nd fl. (☎91 531 50 79 or 91 531 97 89). M: Ópera. Tall windows, balconies, and verandas blossom with Señora Ana's flower pots. Singles 4000ptas/€24; doubles 6000ptas/€36, with bath 6500ptas/€39; triples with bath 8100ptas/€48.60.

HUERTAS

Although *madrileños* have never settled on a nickname for this neighborhood, the area between C. San Jeronimo and C. de las Huertas is generally referred to as Huertas. Once a seedy neighborhood—and a Hemingway hangout—Huertas has shaped up into a hotbed of food and drink. Sol, Pl. Mayor, *el triángulo del arte* (the area bounded by Madrid's three major museums), and the Atocha train station are all within walking distance. Sol-bound buses stop on C. Príncipe, C. Nuñez de Arce, and C. San Jerónimo; buses #14, 27, 37, and 45 run along Po. del Prado. The metro stops are Sol and Antón Martín.

■ **Hostal Villar,** C. Príncipe, 18, 1st-4th fl. (☎91 531 66 00; fax 91 521 50 73; www.arrakis.es/~h-villar). M: Sol. From the metro, walk down C. San Jerónimo and turn right on C. Príncipe. The 1970s stormed through this building, leaving in their wake 46 decidedly brown rooms. Lounge for the young crowd. Singles 3000ptas/€18, with bath 3500ptas/€21; doubles 4000ptas/€24, with bath 5300ptas/€31.80; triples 5600ptas/€33.60, with bath 7400ptas/€44.40. AmEx/MC/V.

SPAIN

Hostal-Residencia Mondragón, C. San Jerónimo, 32, 4th fl. (☎91 429 68 16). M: Sol. Spain's first motion picture was filmed in this building in 1898. Ask for a room off the gardenia-filled terrace that overlooks the street. The best value around. Singles 2000ptas/€12; doubles 3000ptas/€18; triples 3900ptas/€23.30.

Hostal Gonzalo, C. Cervantes, 34, 3rd fl. (☎91 429 27 14; fax 91 420 20 07). M: Antón Martín. Off C. León, which is off C. Atocha. Run by a friendly family, the peaceful interior matches the neighborhood. In all, a budget traveler's dream: newly renovated rooms. TVs. Fans in summer. Leather-plush lounge. Singles 5500ptas/€33; doubles 6500ptas/€39; triples 8500ptas/€51. AmEx/MC/V.

Hostal-Residencia Sud-Americana, Po. Prado, 12, 6th fl. (☎91 429 25 64), across from the Prado. M: Antón Martín or Atocha. Airy doubles facing the Prado with incredible views of the Paseo are the reason to stay. Singles 2800ptas/€16.80; doubles 5500ptas/€33; triples 7000ptas/€42.

Hostal Aguilar, C. San Jerónimo, 32, 2nd fl. (☎91 429 59 26 or 91 429 36 61; fax 91 429 26 61; www.hostalaguilar.com). M: Sol. Perhaps the most social of Madrid's *hostals*. Singles 4000ptas/€24; doubles 6000ptas/€36; triples 8000ptas/€48; 2000ptas/€12 per extra person. MC/V.

Hostal R. Rodríguez, C. Núñez de Arce, 9, 3rd fl. (☎91 522 44 31), off Pl. Santa Ana. M: Sol. Reception decor makes even the cheapest of travelers feel like royalty. 24hr. reception. English spoken. Singles 3300ptas/€19.80; doubles 5000-6000ptas/€30-36; triples 8000ptas/€48. AmEx/MC/V.

GRAN VÍA

The neon lights of Broadway and the Champs-Élysées have met their match in Gran Vía. *Hostal* signs scatter the horizon, but accommodations here tend to be overpriced and less comfortable than in other areas. This is not a street you want to be returning to late at night or at less than your sharpest; El Centro and Huertas provide safer bargains. Buses #1, 2, 44, 46, 74, 75, 133, 146, 147, and 148 reach Callao; buses #1, 2, 3, 40, 46, 74, 146, and 149 service both Pl. España and Callao. The closest metro stops are Gran Vía and Callao.

Hostal Margarita, Gran Vía, 50, 5th fl. (☎/fax 91 547 35 49). M: Callao. Stucco walls, light wood shutters, and baby-blue beds make for an airy feel. Laundry 1500ptas. Reservations wise. Singles 3500ptas/€21; doubles 5400ptas/€32.40, with bath 5800ptas/€34.80; triples with bath 7500ptas/€45. MC/V.

Hostal Triana, C. de la Salud, 13, 1st fl. (☎91 532 68 12; fax 91 522 97 29; www.hostaltriana.com). M: Callao or Gran Vía. From Gran Vía, turn onto C. Salud; the sign is quite visible. Catering to those seeking a little more comfort than the standard *hostal*. Reserve 2 weeks ahead. Singles 4900ptas/€29.30; doubles 6200ptas/€37.20.

MALASAÑA AND CHUECA

Split down the middle by C. Fuencarral, Malasaña and Chueca are both hard-core party pits. Unless techno helps you sleep, make sure your room has sound-proof windows. Chueca is hip, fun, funky, and largely gay, but can be dangerous, especially for solo travelers. Buses #3, 40, and 149 run along C. Fuencarral and Hortaleza. Metro stops Chueca, Gran Vía, and Tribunal serve the area.

▨Hostal Palacios and **Hostal Ribadavia,** C. Fuencarral, 25, 1st-3rd fl. (☎91 531 10 58 or 91 531 48 47). M: Gran Vía. Both run by the same cheerful family. Singles 2500ptas/€15, with bath 4000ptas/€24; doubles 4000ptas/€24, with bath 5500ptas/€33; triples 6600ptas/€39.60, with bath 7500ptas/€45. AmEx/MC/V.

Hostal Lorenzo, C. las Infantas, 26, 3rd fl. (☎91 521 30 57; fax 91 532 79 78). M: Gran Vía. From the metro, walk up C. Del Clavel; it's on the corner of the plaza. Slightly upscale from the standard hostel. Reservations recommended. Singles 5950ptas/€30; doubles 8500ptas/€51; triples 9700ptas/€59.20. AmEx/MC/V.

Hostal-Residencia Domínguez, C. Santa Brígida, 1, 1st fl. (☎/fax 91 532 15 47). M: Tribunal. Go down C. Fuencarral toward Gran Vía, turn left on C. Santa Brígida, and climb up a flight. Hospitable young owner ready with tips on local nightlife. English spoken. Singles 3000ptas/€18, with bath 4500ptas/€27; doubles with bath and A/C 6000ptas/€36.

ELSEWHERE AND CAMPING

Budget lodgings are rare near the **Chamartín** train station, as is the case in most of the residential districts located away from the city center. Near the **Madrid-Atocha** train station are a handful of hostels, the closest of which are down Po. Santa María de la Cabeza. Tourist offices can provide info about the 13 campsites within 50km of Madrid. Similar info is in the *Guía Oficial de Campings* (official camping guide), a big book which they gladly let you look through. For further camping info, contact the *Consejería de Educación de Juventud* (☎91 522 29 41).

Albergue Juvenil Santa Cruz de Marcenado (HI), C. Santa Cruz de Marcenado, 28 (☎91 547 45 32; fax 91 548 11 96). M: Argüelles. From the metro, walk 1 block down C. Alberto Aguilera away from C. Princesa, turn right on C. Serrano Jóve, then left on C. Santa Cruz de Marcenado. Modern, recently renovated facilities near the student district house mostly traveling college students. 3-day max. stay. 1:30am curfew is strictly enforced. Quiet hours after midnight. Reception daily 9am-1:30pm. Reserve a space (by mail, fax, or in person) in advance, or arrive early. Closed Christmas and New Year's. An HI (YHA) card is required and can be purchased for 1800ptas/€10.80. Dorms 1200ptas/€7.20, over 26 yrs. 1820ptas/€11.

Camping Alpha (☎91 695 80 69; fax 91 683 1659), on a tree-lined site 12.4km down the Ctra. de Andalucía in Getafe. M: Legazpi. From the metro station take bus #447, which stops next to the Nissan dealership (10min., every 30min. until 10pm, 190ptas). Ask the driver to let you off at the pedestrian overpass for the campsite. Cross the bridge and walk 1½km back toward Madrid along a busy highway; camping signs lead the way. Cars, trailers and tents crowd the lots. Alpha has a pool, showers, laundry, and just about every other amenity. 715ptas/€4.25 per person, per tent and per car.

◘ FOOD

In Madrid, it's not hard to fork it down without forking over too much. Most restaurants offer a *menú del día*, which includes bread, one drink, and one choice from each of the day's selections for appetizers, main courses, and desserts (1100-1500ptas/€6.60-9). Many small eateries line **Calles Echegaray, Bentura de la Vega,** and **Manuel Fernández González** in Huertas. **Calle Agurrosa** at M: Lavapiés has some funky outdoor cafés, and there are good restaurants up the hill toward Huertas. **Calle Fuencarral** in Gran Vía is lined with cheap eats. In Bilbao, the area north of Glorieta de Bilbao, in the "v" formed by C. Fuencarral and C. Luchana and including Pl. Olavide, is the ethnic food center of Madrid; also, a stroll down **C. Hartzenbusch** and **C. Cisneros** offers endless food options that serve cheap *tapas* to a youthful crowd. Keep in mind the following essential buzz words for quicker, cheaper *madrileño* fare: *bocadillo* (a sandwich on a long, hard roll; 350-450ptas/€2.10-2.70); *sandwich* (a sandwich on sliced bread—ask for it *a la plancha* if you want it grilled; 300ptas/€1.80); *ración* (a large *tapa*, served with bread 300-600ptas/€1.80-3.60); and *empanada* (a puff pastry with meat fillings; 200-300ptas/€1.20-1.80). Vegetarians should check out the *Guía del Ocio*, which has a complete listing of Madrid's vegetarian havens under the section "Otras Cocinas." For **groceries, %Dia** and **Simago** are the cheapest supermarket chains. More expensive are **Mantequerías Leonesas, Expreso,** and **Jumbo.**

Champagnería Gala, C. Moratín, 22 (☎91 429 25 62). Down the hill on Moratín from C. Atocha. The *paella* buck stops here. *Menú* 1750ptas/€10.50. Make reservations for weekends. Open daily 1:30-5pm and 9pm-12:30am.

SPAIN

El Estragón, Pl. de la Paja, 10 (☎91 365 89 82). M: La Latina. From the metro, follow C. Duque de Alba, turn right into Pl. Puerta de Moros and leave the church on your right; it's on the far side of Pl. de la Paja. Perhaps the best medium-priced restaurant—of any kind—in Madrid, with vegetarian food that could turn the most die-hard carnivores into switch-hitters. Menú M-F 1500ptas/€9; Sa-Su and evenings 2975ptas/€17.75. Open daily 1:30-4:30pm and 8pm-1am.

El 26 de Libertad, C. Libertad, 26 (☎91 522 25 22), off C. las Infantas. M: Chueca. Innovative and exotic Spanish cuisine. Lunchtime menú (1400ptas) is fantastic. Dinner is served in a yellow room whose cheeriness helps you swallow the price (3000ptas/€18). Open M-Th 1-4pm and 8pm-midnight, F-Sa 1-4pm and 9pm-midnight, Su 1-4pm.

Arepas con Todo, C. Hartzenbusch, 19 (☎91 448 75 45), off C. Cardenal Cisneros, which is off C. Luchana. Hanging gourds and waitresses in festive dress garnish this classic Colombian restaurant. With a different menú (1600-2000ptas/€9.60-12) every night of the month, and 60 fixed dishes (1800-2400ptas/€10.80-14.40), only the live music repeats itself. For dinner, make reservations. Open M-Su 2pm-1am.

La Granja Restaurante Vegetariano, C. San Andrés, 11 (☎91 532 87 93), off Pl. 2 de Mayo. M: Tribunal or Bilbao. Youthful crowd as light as the well-portioned nourishment. Lunchtime menú 1100ptas/€6.60. Open W-M 1:30-4:30pm and 9pm-midnight.

Cáscaras, C. Ventura Rodríguez, 7 (☎91 542 83 36). M: Ventura Rodríguez. Facing the green outside the metro, take your first right off C. Princesa. Exotic vegetarian entrees 800-985ptas/€4.80-5.90. Non-vegetarian fare as well. Open M-F 7am-1am, Sa-Su 10am-1am.

Ananias, C. Galileo, 9 (☎91 448 68 01). M: Argüelles. From C. Alberto Aguilera, take a left onto C. Galileo. Packed on Su. Entrees 1500-2500ptas/€9-15. Open Su-Tu and Th-F 1-4pm and 9-11:30pm, Sa 9-11:30pm. AmEx/MC/V.

Museo del Jamón, C. San Jerónimo, 6 (☎91 521 03 46). M: Sol. 5 other much-loved locations throughout the city, including one at C. Mayor 7 (☎91 531 45 50). Generous combo plates 650-950ptas/€3.90-5.70. Open M-Th 9am-12:30pm, F-Sa 9am-1am, Su 10am-12:30pm.

El Cuchi, C. Cuchilleros, 3 (☎91 366 44 24). M: Sol. Just outside Pl. Mayor, this is better and cheaper than the restaurants around it. Entrees 900-2900ptas/€5.40-17.40. Open M-Sa 1pm-1am, Su 1-midnight.

Pizzeria Cervantes, C. Leon; 8 (☎91 420 12 98), off Po. Prado. Offering much more than pizza, this place is hands down the best cheap lunch in Huertas. Most entrees 950ptas/€5.70. Open M and W-F 11am-12:30am, Tu 7pm-12:30am, Sa noon-1:30am, Su noon-12:30am.

TAPAS

Not so long ago, bartenders in Madrid used to cover *(tapar)* drinks with saucers to keep the flies out. Later, servers began putting little sandwiches on top of the saucers, and there you have it: *tapas*. Hopping from bar to bar gobbling *tapas* is an active alternative to a full sit-down meal. Huertas and the La Latina area are full of *tapas*. Try those on **Calle Baja, Plaza Mayor, Plaza Santa Anna,** and around the San Pedro church on **Calle Cuchillos.**

■ **Casa Alberto,** C. Huertas, 18 (☎91 429 93 56). M: Antón Martín. Patrons spill out into the night air to wait for a spot at the bar. Interior dining room decorated with bullfighting and Cervantes relics; Cervantes wrote the second part of "El Quijote" here. The *tapas* are all original house recipes. Get the feel of their *gambas al ajillo* (shrimp in garlic and hot peppers; 1250ptas/€7.50) or the filled canapés (275-350ptas/€1.60-2.10). Sit-down dinner is too pricey. Open Tu-Sa noon-1:30am, Su noon-4pm. AmEx/MC/V.

■ **La Toscana,** C. Manuel Fernández González, 10-12 (☎91 429 60 31), at C. Ventura de la Vega. M: Sol. A local crowd hangs out over *mocillo asado* (1300ptas/€7.80). Despite the antique lettering and wrought iron, the range of dishes is anything but medieval. Spacious bar area jam-packed on weekends. Most *tapas* around 800ptas/€4.80. Open Th-Tu noon-4pm and 8pm-midnight.

TAPAS To the untrained reader, tapas menus are often cryptic and undecipherable—if the bar has even bothered to print any. To make sure you don't end up eating the stewed parts of the ox you rode in on, just keep the following words in mind. Servings come in three sizes: *pincho* (normally eaten with toothpicks between sips of beer), *tapa* (small plate), and *ración* (sizable meal portion). *Aceitunas* (olives), *albondigas* (meatballs), *anchoas* (anchovies), *callos* (tripe), *chorizo* (sausage), *croquetas* (breaded and fried combinations), *gambas* (shrimp), *jamón* (ham), *patatas alioli y bravas* (potatoes with sauces), *pimentos* (peppers), *pulpo* (octopus), and *tortilla* (potato omelette) comprise any basic menu.

Los Gabrieles, C. Echegaray, 17 (☎91 429 62 61 or 429 50 03). Near Villa Madrid. The tiled mural at the back depicts Spain's famous artists—from Velasquez to Goya—as stumble-drunks. The big draw here is the *laguita* (500ptas/€3), a fine sherry that helps wash away the cares of the day. Open daily 1pm-late.

Casa Amadeo, Pl. de Cascorro, 18 (☎91 365 94 39). M: La Latina. The jovial owner of 60 years supervises the making of house specialty *caracoles* (snails; *tapas* 700ptas/€4.20, big *ración* 1500ptas/€9) and *chorizo* (sausage) made with snails (750ptas/€4.50). Wild Su nights. Open M-F 10:30am-4pm and 7-10:30pm, Su 7-11pm.

⌘ CLASSIC CAFES

Even when chilling, Madrileños like to watch the frenzied streets. It's customary to linger for an hour or two in the atmosphere of Madrid's classic cafes. Soak up culture, rest weary legs, and check out passers-by from behind your coffee cup.

Café Gijón, Po. Recoletos, 21 (☎91 521 54 25). M: Colón. On its 100th anniversary in 1988, Gijón was designated a historic site for its intellectual significance. It has long been a favorite of the literati. Check out how smart you look in the mirrors and forget how much that cup of coffee costs (from 615ptas/€3.65). Open daily 9am-1:30am.

Café de Oriente, Pl. Oriente, 2 (☎91 547 15 64). M: Ópera. A beautiful, old-fashioned cafe catering to a ritzy, older crowd. Spectacular view of the Palacio Real from the *terraza*, especially at night when a spotlight illuminates the palace. Prices are significantly cheaper inside than on the patio. Specialty coffees (540-840ptas/€3.25-5) live up to the price. Open daily 8:30am-1:30am.

Eucalipto, C. Argumosa, 4. M: Lavapiés. You need not be a koala to enjoy the *zumos tropicales* (fresh fruit drinks; 400-550ptas/€2.40-3.30). Open daily M-Th 6pm-2am, F-Sa 6pm-3am, Su 2pm-midnight.

Salon Del Prado, C. Del Prado, 4 (☎91 429 33 61). M: Sol. Head left down C. San Jerónimo, right down C. Príncipe to Pl. Santa Ana, and left on C. Del Prado. Interior as cool as the *granizado de limón* (frozen lemon drink; 400ptas/€2.40) and homemade ice cream it serves up. Open M-Th 2pm-2am, F-Sa 2pm-2:30am.

Café Comercial, Glorieta de Bilbao, 7 (☎91 531 56 55). M: Bilbao. Founded in 1887, Madrid's oldest cafe features high ceilings, cushioned chairs, and huge mirrors perfect for people-watching. Frequented by artists and Republican aviators alike. The first anti-Franco protests took place here. Sandwiches and canapés from 350ptas/€2.10. Open Su-Th 8am-12:45am, F-Sa 8am-1:45am.

◉ SIGHTS

Madrid, large as it may seem, is a walker's city. Although the word *paseo* refers to a major avenue—such as *Paseo de la Castellana* or *Paseo del Prado*—it literally means "a stroll." Do just that from Sol to Cibeles and from the Plaza Mayor to the Palacio Real—sights will introduce themselves. In the following pages, sights are arranged by neighborhood, offering opportunities for extensive walking tours in each. Each section has a designated center from which all directions are given.

SPAIN

EL CENTRO

The area known as El Centro, spreading out from the Puerta del Sol ("Gate of Sun"), is the gateway to the history and spirit of Madrid. Although several rulers carved the winding streets, the Habsburg and Bourbon families left behind El Centro's most celebrated monuments. As a result, El Centro is divided into two major sections: Madrid de los Habsburgs and Madrid de los Borbones. All directions are given from the Puerta del Sol.

HABSBURG MADRID

"Old Madrid," the city's central neighborhood, is the most densely packed with both monuments and tourists. In the 16th century, the Habsburgs built **Plaza Mayor** and the **Catedral de San Isidro.** When Felipe II moved the seat of Castilla from Toledo to Madrid (then only a town of 20,000) in 1561, he and his descendants commissioned the court architects (including Juan de Herrera) to update many of Madrid's buildings to the latest styles. In 1620, the plaza was completed for Felipe III; his statue, installed in 1847, still graces the plaza's center. Toward evening, Pl. Mayor awakens as *madrileños* resurface, tourists multiply, and cafe tables fill with lively patrons. Live performances of flamenco and music are a common treat. On Sunday mornings, the plaza marks the starting point of **El Rastro** (see p. 810). *(From Sol, walk down C. Mayor. The plaza is on the left. M: Sol.)*

CATEDRAL DE SAN ISIDRO. Designed in the Jesuit Baroque style at the beginning of the 17th century, the cathedral received San Isidro's remains in 1769. During the Civil War, rioting workers burned the exterior and damaged much of the cathedral—only the primary nave and a few Baroque decorations remain from the original. *(From Sol, take C. Mayor to Pl. Mayor, cross the plaza, and exit onto C. Toledo. M: La Latina. Open for mass only. Mass daily 9, 10, 11am, noon.)*

PLAZA DE LA VILLA. Pl. Villa marks the heart of what was once old Madrid. Though only a handful of medieval buildings remain, the plaza still features a stunning courtyard (surrounding the statue of Don Alvara de Bazón), beautiful tilework, and eclectic architecture. Across the plaza is the 17th-century **Ayuntamiento (Casa de la Villa),** designed in 1640 by Juan Gomez de Mora as both the mayor's home and the city jail. *(From Sol, go down C. Mayor, past Pl. Mayor. M: Sol.)*

BOURBON MADRID

Weakened by plagues and political losses, the Habsburg era in Spain ended with the death of Carlos II in 1700. Felipe V, the first of Spain's Bourbon monarchs, ascended the throne in 1714 after the 12-year War of the Spanish Succession. Bankruptcy, industrial stagnation, and widespread disillusionment compelled Felipe V to embark on a crusade of urban renewal. The lavish palaces, churches, and parks that remain are the most touristed in Madrid.

PALACIO REAL. The impossibly luxurious Palacio Real lounges at the western tip of central Madrid, overlooking the Río Manzanares. Felipe V commissioned Giovanni Sachetti to replace the Alcázar, which had burned down in 1734, with a palace that would dwarf all others—he succeeded. Today, the unfinished palace is only used by King Juan Carlos and Queen Sofía on special occasions. The palace's most impressive rooms are decorated in the Rococo style. The **Salón de Gasparini,** site of the king's ceremonial dressing before the court, houses Goya's portrait of Carlos IV and a Mengs ceiling fresco. The **Salón del Trono (Throne Room)** also contains a ceiling fresco, painted by Tiepolo, outlining the qualities of the quintessential ruler. The **Biblioteca** shelves first editions of *Don Quixote.* Also open to the public is the **Real Armería (Armory),** which displays the armor of Carlos V and Felipe II. *(From Pta. Sol, take C. Mayor and turn right on C. Bailén. M: Sol. Open Apr.-Sept. M-Sa 9am-6pm, Su 9am-3pm; Oct.-Mar. M-Sa 9:30am-5pm, Su 9am-2pm. 1000ptas/€6, students 500ptas/€3; with tour 1150ptas/€6.90. W free for EU citizens.)* Next to the Palacio resides the stark contrasting grey stone of 1879's **Cathedral de la Almudena.** It took over 100 years to complete its discordant mix of traditional and abstract frescoes and stained glass. *(From Sol, go down C. Mayor and turn right on C. Bailen; the cathedral is just before the Palacio Real. Closed during mass. Open M-Sa 1-7pm. Free.)*

PLAZA DE ORIENTE. A minor architectural miscalculation was responsible for this sculpture park. Most of the statues in the plaza were designed for the palace roof, but because they were too heavy, they were placed in this shady plaza instead. Elegant *terrazas* encompass the plaza, an opportunity to treat yourself to an over-priced coffee (see p. 807). The **Jardines de Sabatini,** just to the right as you are face the palace, is the romantic's park of choice. *(From Sol, take C. Arenal to the plaza.)*

PARQUE DE LAS VISTILLAS. Named for the tremendous vistillas (views) of Palacio Real, Nuestra Señora de la Almudena and the surrounding countryside provides a stunning photo opportunity. Take precaution, as it can be dangerous at night. *(In Pl. Gabriel Miró. From Sol, go down C. Mayor, turn left on C. Bailén, and then right on C. Morería into the plaza.)*

HUERTAS

The area east of Sol is a wedge bounded by C. de Alcalá to the north, C. Atocha to the south, and Po. Prado to the east. Huertas's sights, from authors' houses to famous cafes, reflect its artistic focus. Home to Cervantes, Góngora, Quevedo, Calderón, and Moratín in its heyday during the "Siglo de Oro" (Golden Age), Huertas enjoyed a fleeting return to literary prominence when Hemingway frequented the neighborhood in the 1920s. **Plaza Santa Ana** and its *terrazas* are the center of this old literary haunt. **Casa de Lope de Vega** is the home where the prolific playwright and poet spent the last 25 years of his life and wrote over two-thirds of his plays. The highlights include the simple garden described in his works and the library filled with crumbling, aromatic books. Among the more interesting tidbits revealed on the mandatory tour are the tangible signs of affection Vega would leave for his young daughters. *(C. Cervantes, 11. With your back to Pl. Santa Ana, turn left on C. Prado, right on C. León, and left on C. Cervantes. ☎91 429 92 16. Open Tu-F 9:30am-2pm, Sa 10am-2pm. 200ptas/€1.20, students 100ptas/€0.60. W free.)*

GRAN VÍA

Urban planners paved the Gran Vía in 1910 to link C. Princesa with Pl. Cibeles. After Madrid became wealthy as a neutral supplier during World War I, the city funneled much of its earnings into making the Gran Vía into one of the world's great thoroughfares. At Gran Vía's highest elevation in **Plaza de Callao** (M: Callao), C. Postigo San Martín splits off southward, where you'll find the famed **Monasterio de las Descalzas Reales.** Westward from Pl. Callao, the Gran Vía makes its descent toward **Plaza de España** (M: Pl. España), where a statue commemorates Spain's most prized fictional duo: Cervantes' Don Quixote and Sancho Panza, riding horseback and muleback, respectively.

MALASAÑA AND CHUECA

By night, these districts bristle with Madrid's alternative scene. The area between **Calle de Fuencarral** and **Calle de San Bernardo** is home to some of Madrid's most avant-garde architecture and art. Though not packed with historic monuments, the labyrinthine streets provide many spontaneous undocumented "sights," from platform-shoe stores to street performers. An ultra-modern, funkdafied relief for those weary of crucifixes and brushstrokes, Chueca promises hip **boutiques** and a happening stroll.

ARGÜELLES

The area known as Argüelles and the zone surrounding Calle San Bernardo form a cluttered mixture of elegant middle-class houses, student apartments, and bohemian hangouts, all brimming with cultural activity. Heavily bombarded during the Civil War, Argüelles inspired Chilean poet Pablo Neruda, then a resident, to write

España en el corazón. In **Casa del Campo,** shaded by pines, oaks, and cypresses, families and joggers roam the city's largest park by day; night brings curious but unsafe activity.

The **Parque de la Montaña** is home to Spain's only Egyptian temple in the midst of vibrant greenery. Built by Pharaoh Zakheramon in the 4th century BC, the **Temple de Debod** was a gift from the Egyptian government commemorating the Spanish archaeologists who helped rescue monuments in the Aswan dam floods. *(M: Ventura Rodríguez. From the metro, walk down C. Ventura Rodríguez into the Parque de la Montaña; the temple is on the left.* ☎ *91 366 74 15. Open in summer Tu-Su 10am-1:45pm and 6-7:45pm; off-season Tu-F 10am-1:45pm and 4-6pm, Sa-Su 10am-2pm. 300ptas/€1.80, students 150ptas/€0.90. W and Su free.)* The fresco-domed **Ermita de San Antonio de la Florida** contains Goya's pantheon and his buried corpse. *(M: Principe Pio. From the metro, go left on C. de Buen Altamirano, walk through the park, and turn left on Po. Florida; the Ermita is at the end of the street.* ☎ *91 542 07 22. Open Tu-F 10am-2pm and 4-8pm, Sa-Su 10am-2pm. Free.)*

North of Arguelles, Moncloa's **Faro de Moncloa** offers astounding views of the city. *(Av. Arco de la Victoria.* ☎ *90 215 19 12. Open M-Su 10am-1:45pm, 5-8:45pm. 200ptas/€1.20 to ascend the Faro.)*

OTHER SIGHTS

▓ **RETIRO.** Join an array of vendors, palm-readers, soccer players, and sunbathers in what Felipe IV once intended to be a hunting ground and a *"buen retiro"* (nice retreat). The finely landscaped 121-hectare Parque del Buen Retiro is centered around the rectangular lake and magnificent monument to King Alfonso XII. Dubbed **Estanque Grande,** this central location is popular among casual rowers; the perfect way to cool off, especially on Sundays. *(Boat rentals daily 10am-8:30pm. Paddle boats 575ptas/€3.50 for 4 people, motorboats 165ptas/€1 per person.)* Built by Ricardo Velázquez to exhibit Filipino flowers, the exquisite steel-and-glass **Palacio de Cristal** hosts a variety of art shows. *(Open Tu-Sa 11am-2pm and 5-8pm, Su 10am-2pm. Admission varies, but mostly free.)* All artists should dream of having their art displayed in the **Palacio de Velázquez,** with its billowing ceilings, marble floors, and ideal lighting. Avoid venturing alone into the park after dark. *(Past the Estanque, turn left on Po. del Venezuela.* ☎ *91 575 62 45. Open M-Sa 11am-8pm, Su 11am-6pm. Free.)*

EL PARDO. Built as a hunting lodge for Carlos I in 1547, El Pardo was enlarged by generations of Habsburgs and Bourbons. El Pardo gained attention in 1940 when Franco decided to make it his home; he resided here until his death in 1975. Renowned for its collection of tapestries—several of which were designed by Goya—the palace also holds paintings by Velázquez and Ribera. *(*☎ *91 376 03 29. Take bus #601 from the stop in front of the Ejército del Aire building above M: Moncloa; 15min., 150ptas/€0.90. Palace open Apr.-Sept. M-F 10:30am-6pm, Su 9:25am-1:40pm; Oct.-Mar. M-F 10:30am-5pm, Su 9:55am-1:40pm. Obligatory 45min. guided tour in Spanish. 800ptas/€4.80, students 250ptas/€1.50. W free for EU citizens.)*

▓ **EL RASTRO (FLEA MARKET).** For hundreds of years, El Rastro has been a Sunday morning tradition in Madrid. From Pl. Mayor and its Sunday stamp and coin market, walk down C. Toledo to Pl. Cascorro (M: La Latina), where the market begins, and follow the crowds to the end, at the bottom of C. Ribera de Curtidores. In El Rastro you can find anything, from dishes to jeans to antique tools to pet birds. The flea market is a pickpocket paradise, so leave your camera in the room and turn that backpack into a frontpack. *(Open Su and holidays 9am to 2pm.)*

🏛 MUSEUMS

Madrid's great museums need no introduction. If you plan on visiting the three famous ones, your best (and cheapest) bet is the **Paseo del Arte** ticket (1275ptas/€7.65) that grants admission to the Museo del Prado, Museo Thyssen-Bornemisza, and Centro de Arte Reina Sofía. The pass is available at all three museums.

🖾 MUSEO DEL PRADO

Po. Prado at Pl. Cánovas del Castillo. M: Banco de España. ☎ 91 420 37 68 or 91 330 28 00; www.museoprado.mcu.es. Open Tu-Sa 9am-7pm, Su 9am-2pm. 500ptas/€3, students 250ptas/€1.50, Sa after 2:30 and Su free.

The Prado is Spain's pride and joy, as well as one of Europe's finest museums. Its 7000 pieces from the 12th-17th centuries are the result of hundreds of years of Bourbon art collecting. Each room is numbered and described in the museum's free guide. On the second floor, keep an eye out for unforgiving realism and use of light in the works of **Diego Velázquez** (1599-1660), which resonate even in the 20th century. Several of his most famous paintings are here, including *Los borrachos (The Drunkards)* and *Las lanzas (The Spears* or *The Surrender of Breda)*. Velazquez's technique, called illusionism, climaxed in his magnum opus *Las Meninas (The Maids of Honor)*, since dubbed an "encounter."

The court portraitist **Francisco de Goya y Lucientes** (1746-1828) created the stark *Dos de Mayo* and *Fusilamientas de Tres de Mayo*, which depict the terrors of the Revolution of 1808. Goya painted the *Pinturas Negras (Black Paintings)* at the end of his life, deaf and alone. *Saturno devorando a su hijo (Saturn Devouring His Son)* stands out among the *Pinturas Negras*. The Prado also displays many of **El Greco**'s religious paintings. *La Trinidad (The Trinity)* and *La adoración de los pastores (The Adoration of the Shepherds)* are characterized by El Greco's luminous colors, elongated figures, and mystical subjects. On the second floor are other works by Spanish artists, including **Murillo, Ribera,** and **Zurbarán.**

The Prado also has a formidable collection of **Italian** works, including pieces by Titian, Raphael, Tintoretto, Botticelli, and Rubens. As a result of the Spanish Habsburgs' control of the Netherlands, the **Flemish** holdings are also top-notch. Works by **van Dyck** and **Albrecht Durer** are here. Especially harrowing is **Peter Breugel the Elder**'s *The Triumph of Death*, in which death drives a carriage of skulls on a decaying horse. **Hieronymus Bosch**'s moralistic *The Garden of Earthly Delights* depicts hedonism and the destiny that awaits its practitioners.

🖾 MUSEO THYSSEN-BORNEMISZA

On the corner of Po. Prado and C. San Jerónimo. M: Banco de España. Bus #6, 14, 27, 37, or 45. ☎ 91 369 01 51. Open Tu-Su 10am-7pm. No admittance after 6:30pm. 700ptas/ €4.20, seniors and ISIC holders 400ptas/€2.40, under 12 free.

Unlike the Prado and the Reina Sofía, the Thyssen-Bornemisza covers a wide range of periods and media, with exhibits ranging from 14th-century canvases to 20th-century sculptures. Baron Heinrich Thyssen-Bornemisza donated his collection in 1993, and today the museum, with over 775 pieces, is the world's most extensive private showcase. To view the collection in chronological order and observe the evolution of styles and themes, begin on the top floor and work your way down—the organization of the Thyssen-Bornemisza provokes natural comparisons across centuries. The top floor is dedicated to the **Old Masters** collection, which includes such notables as Hans Holbein's austere *Portrait of Henry VIII* and El Greco's *Annunciation*. In both variety and quality, the Thyssen-Bornemisza's **Baroque** collection, including pieces by Caravaggio, José de Ribera, and Claude Lorraine, outshines that of the Prado. The **Impressionist** and **Post-Impressionist** collections explode with texture and color—look for works by Renoir, Manet, Pisarro, Degas, Monet, van Gogh, Toulouse-Lautrec, Cézanne, and Matisse. Though less well-known, the **Expressionist** artists are also well represented, with noteworthy works by Nolde, Marc, and Beckmann. The highlight of the museum is the **20th century** collection, on the first floor. The modern artists represented include Picasso, Léger, Mondrian, Miró, Kandinsky, Gorky, Pollack, Rothko, Dalí, Hopper, Chagall, Ernst, Klee, and O'Keefe, among others.

MUSEO NACIONAL CENTRO DE ARTE REINA SOFÍA

C. Santa Isabel, 52, opposite Estación Atocha at the south end of Po. Prado. M: Atocha. ☎ 91 467 50 62. Open M and W-Sa 10am-9pm, Su 10am-2:30pm. 500ptas/€3, students 250ptas/€1.50. Sa after 2:30pm, Su, and holidays free.

Since Juan Carlos I decreed this renovated hospital the national museum in 1988, the Reina Sofía's collection of **20th-century art** has grown steadily. Rooms dedicated to Juan Gris, Joan Miró, and Salvador Dalí display Spain's vital contributions to the Surrealist movement. Picasso's masterwork **Guernica** is the centerpiece of the Reina Sofía's permanent collection. It depicts the Basque town (p. 889) bombed by the Germans at Franco's request during the Spanish Civil War. Picasso denounced the bloodshed in a huge, colorless work of contorted, agonized figures. When asked by Nazi officials whether he was responsible for this work, Picasso answered, "No, you are." He gave the canvas to New York's Museum of Modern Art on the condition that they return it to Spain when democracy was restored. The subsequent move to the Reina Sofía sparked an international controversy—Picasso's other stipulation had been that the painting hang only in the Prado, to affirm his equivalent status with artists like Titian and Velázquez.

OTHER MUSEUMS

▨ **Museo de la Real Academia de Bellas Artes de San Fernando,** C. Alcalá, 13 (☎91 522 14 91). M: Sol or Sevilla. A beautiful museum with a collection of Old Masters surpassed only by the Prado. Goya's *La Tirana* and Velázquez's portrait of Felipe IV are masterpieces; other attractions include 17th-century canvases by Ribera, Murillo, Zurbarán, and Rubens. The top floor has Picasso sketches. Open Tu-F 9am-7pm, Sa-M 9am-2:30pm. 400ptas/€2.40, students 200ptas/€1.20. W free.

▨ **Museo de América,** Av. Reyes Católicos, 6 (☎91 549 26 41), next to the Faro de Moncloa. M: Moncloa. This under-appreciated museum documents the cultures of America's pre-Colombian civilizations and the effects of the Spanish conquest. Artifacts include solid gold Colombian ornaments and Maya treasures. Open Tu-Sa 10am-3pm, Su 10am-2:30pm. 500ptas/€3, students 250ptas/€1.50.

🎵 ENTERTAINMENT

Anyone interested in the latest on live entertainment—from music to dance to theater—should stop by the **Circulo de Bellas Artes,** C. Marquez de Casa Riera, 2 (☎91 360 54 00; fax 91 523 13 06; presa@c-bellasartes.es); also at C. Alcalá, 47 (M: Sevilla or Banco de España). Their monthly magazine, *Minerva,* is indispensable.

FLAMENCO. Flamenco in Madrid is tourist-oriented and expensive. A few nightlife spots are authentic (see Cardamomo, p. 814), but they too are pricey. Casa Patas, C. Cañizares, 10 is good quality, for less than usual; call for prices. (☎91 369 04 96.) At Corral de la Morería, C. Morería, 17, by the Viaducto on C. Bailén, shows start at 9:45pm and last until 2am. (☎91 521 99 98. M: Sol. Tickets 700-2000ptas/ €4.20-12.)

FÚTBOL. Spaniards obsess over *fútbol* (soccer). If either Real Madrid or Atlético de Madrid wins a match, count on streets clogged with honking cars. Every Sunday and some Saturdays between September and June, one of these teams plays at home. Real Madrid plays at Estadio Santiago Bernebéu, Po. Castellana, 104 (☎91 457 11 12; M: Lima). Atlético de Madrid plays at Estadio Vicente Calderón, C. Virgen del Puerto, 67 (☎91 366 47 07; M: Pirámides or Marqués de Vadillos). Tickets cost 3000-7000ptas/€18-42.

BULLFIGHTING. Bullfighters are either loved or loathed. So too are the bullfights themselves. Nevertheless, bullfights are a Spanish tradition, and locals joke that they are the only things in Spain ever to start on time. Hemingway-toting Americans and true fans clog Pl. de Ventas for the events. From May 15 to 22 every year, the Fiestas de San Isidro provide a *corrida* (bullfight) every day with top *matadors* and the fiercest bulls. Plaza de las Ventas, C. Alcalá, 237, east of central Madrid, is the world's largest bull-fighting ring. (☎91 356 22 00. M: Ventas.) A seat runs 450-15,200ptas/€2.70-90, depending on whether it's in the sun (*sol*) or shade (*sombra*); shade is more expensive. Plaza de Toros Palacio de Vista Alegre, a new ring in town, hosts bullfights and other cultural events. (☎91 422 07 80. M: Vista Alegre. Ticket window open M-F 10am-2pm and 5-8pm.) If you're intrigued by the lore but not the gore, head to the Museo Taurino, C. Alcalá, 237, at Pl. Monumental de Las Ventas. The museum displays a remarkable collection of capes, bullfighter's outfits, and posters of famous *corridas*. (☎91 725 18 57. Open M-F 9:30am-2:30pm, on fight days 10am-1pm. Free.)

FESTIVALS. The brochure *Las Fiestas de España*, available at tourist offices and bigger hotels, contains historical background and general information on Spain's festivals. Madrid's Carnaval was inaugurated in the Middle Ages and prohibited during Franco's dictatorship. The Fiestas de San Isidro (see above) in honor of Madrid's patron saint, bring concerts, parades, and Spain's best bullfights. Throughout the summer, the city sponsors the Veranos de la Villa, an outstanding set of cultural activities. On November 1, Todos los Santos (All Saints' Day) features an International Jazz Festival that brings great musicians to Madrid.

▐ NIGHTLIFE

Proud of their nocturnal offerings (they'll tell you straight-faced that New York and London bored them), *madrileños* party hard until they've "killed the night"—and a good part of the next day. The last thing they do is stop; an average night makes the most of countless offerings, perhaps starting in the bars of Huertas, moving to Malasaña's youthful scene, and ending at the crazed parties of Chueca or after-hours clubs of Gran Vía. Most clubs and discos don't liven up until around 2am; don't be surprised if there's still a line at 5:30am. The *Guía del Ocio* features the latest hotspots and info about virtually all of Madrid's nighttime establishments.

EL CENTRO: SOL, ÓPERA, AND PLAZA MAYOR

In the middle of Madrid and at the heart of the action are the grandiose and flamboyant clubs of El Centro. The mainstream clubs found among these streets are often tourist hotspots; as a result, a night of fun here is the most expensive in the city. El Centro includes more territory than Madrid's other neighborhoods, so make a plan and bring a map or follow the sleekly dressed.

▨ **Palacio de Gaviria,** C. Arenal, 9 (☎91 526 60 69). M: Sol or Opera. Pick a country to represent on International Th, when Palacio is at its best. A grand red carpet leads to two huge ballrooms turned club spaces with dancers and blazing light shows; most exceptional of Madrid's grandiose *discotecas*. Open M-Sa 10:30pm-late, Su 8pm-late.

▨ **El Barbu,** C. Santiago, 3 (☎91 542 56 98), across C. Mayor from the Ayuntamiento. M: Sol or Ópera. Chill to lounge music in a brick 3-room interior. Open Tu-Su 8pm-3am. Sundays transform the bar into **8th,** a rave-like setting with popular local DJs. Cover 1000ptas/€6. Open 7pm-5:30am.

Azúcar, Po. Reina Cristina, 7 (☎91 501 61 07). M: Atocha. Sweet, sweet salsa. No sneakers. Salsa classes daily 10-11pm; call ahead. Cover 1000ptas/€6, F-Sa 1800ptas/€11; includes 1 drink. Open M-Sa11:00pm-5am, Su 9pm-dawn.

Refugio, C. Dr. Cortezo, 1 (☎91 869 40 38). M: Tirso de Molina. Steel doors covered in steel vines lead to an outrageous gay scene. Cover 1500ptas/€9, includes 1 drink. Open Th-Sa midnight-dawn.

▨ HUERTAS

In Huertas lies **Plaza Santa Ana,** brimming with *terrazas*, bars, and live music. Many bars convert to clubs as the night unfolds, spinning house and techno on intimate dance floors. With its variety of styles, Huertas is simply the best place to party. Be sure to check out the *discotecas* on **Calle Atocha.** Most locals begin their evenings here and emerge from Malasaña and Chueca (see p. 814) in the morning.

Kapital, C. Atocha, 125 (☎91 420 29 06), a block off Po. Prado. M: Atocha. To be safe, take the metro. One of the most extreme results of *La Movida*, this *macro-discoteca* tries even harder than its glittered 20-something clientele. From hip-hop to house, open *terraza* to cinema, 7 floors of over-stimulation necessitate a ground-floor directory. Cover 2000ptas/€12, includes 1 drink. Open Th 12:30-6am, F-Sa 6-10:30pm and midnight-6am.

Cardamomo, C. Echegaray, 15 (☎91 369 07 57). M: Sevilla. Flamenco music spins all night in this brick-walled, designer-lit bar. Open 9pm-4am.

La Comedia, C. Príncipe, 16 (☎91 521 51 64). M: Sevilla. Americans feel at home in a crowd dancing to hip-hop, R&B, and reggae. Hit up DJ Jay with requests; he spins to please. Beer 600ptas/€3.60; drinks 1000ptas/€6. Open daily 9pm-4am.

Café Central, Pl. Angel, 10 (☎91 369 41 43), off Pl. Santa Ana. M: Antón Martín or Sol. Art Deco meets old-world cafe in one of Europe's top-10 jazz venues. An older audience. Beer 300-500ptas/€1.80-3. Cover 1200-2500ptas/€7.20-15. Shows nightly. Open daily 1:30pm-3:30am.

El Café de Sheherezade, C. Santa María, 18, a block from C. Huertas. M: Antón Martín. Surrounded by Middle Eastern music and decor, groups cluster around *pipas* (pipes; 1100-1600ptas/€6.60-9.60) that filter sweet smoke through whiskey or water. Open daily 7pm-5am.

Mauna Loa, Pl. Santa Ana, 13 (☎91 429 70 62). M: Sevilla or Sol. Feels like Hawaii—birds fly freely between low chairs and the scantily clad dance to upbeat tunes. *"Fuerte volcano"* drinks 1000-1700ptas/€6-10.20. Open Su-Th 6pm-2am, F-Sa 6pm-3am.

GRAN VÍA

Even the side streets of Gran Vía never sleep, pulsating in the early morning to the bass beats of landmark **after-hours clubs.** Subtlety has never been a strong point for this area, nor is it exactly known for its safety; a mix of sketchy tourists and sketchier locals makes the Gran Vía less than ideal for late-night wandering.

Sugar Hill, C. Fundadores, 7. M: Manuel Becerra or O'Donell. Named after the original, this is the only real hip-hop club in town. Cover 1500ptas/€9, includes 1 drink. Drinks 1000ptas/€6. Open Sa only 12:45-5:30am.

Cool Ballroom, C. Isabel la Católica, 6 (☎91 542 34 39; www.coolballroom.com). M: Santo Domingo. From the metro, C. Isabel la Católica leads to Gran Via. Metallic exterior frosts the cool of this brand new hotspot. Drinks 1300ptas/€7.80. Open daily midnight-late.

MALASAÑA AND CHUECA

The dark cafes and darker clubs of Malasaña and Chueca filter jazz, techno, and foam into the night and early morning. Known for their bohemian crowds, Malasaña's hotspots radiate from **Plaza 2 de Mayo** and **Calle San Vincente Ferrer.** People are high on life, drugs, and booze; be wary at night. **Calle de Pelayo** is the main drag in flamboyant and primarily gay Chueca. The safest walking route at night is up C. Fuencarral from Gran Vía and right on C. Augusto Figueroa.

Acuarela, C. Gravina, 8, off C. Hortaleza. M: Chueca. A welcome alternative to the club scene. Buddhas and candles surround antique furniture grouped into enclaves. Spend hours just chilling. Coffees and liquers 500-700ptas/€3-4.20. Open M-Su 3pm-3am.

Café la Palma, C. La Palma, 62 (☎91 522 50 31). M: San Bernardo or Noviciado. Maneuver past the swaying bar-lamps late at night. Eclectic, funky, friendly crowd in a laid-back setting. Be sure to pick up a monthly program or call for schedule. Beer 350ptas/€2.10. Mixed drinks 700ptas/€4.20. Open daily 4pm-3:30am.

Black & White, C. Libertad, 34 (☎91 531 11 41). M: Chueca. A lively disco/bar with room to chat, mingle, and groove on packed dance floors. 2 floors of male fun for a gay crowd. W is international exchange night. Beer 500ptas/€3. Mixed drinks 1000ptas/€6. Open Su-Th 9pm-5am, F-Sa 9pm-6am.

BILBAO

In the student-filled streets radiating from **Glorieta de Bilbao**, it's easy to find a cheap drink and even easier to find someone to drink it with. Boisterous customers sip icy Mahou on **Plaza Olavide, Calle Fuencarral,** and **Calle Luchana.**

Vaivén, Travesía de San Mateo, 1 (☎91 523 14 87). M: Tribunal. Swivel hips with the best at this exclusive salsa club, crawling with well-dressed locals. Mid-week concerts. Beer 600ptas/€3.60. Mixed drinks 1000ptas/€6. Open daily 9pm-4am.

Barnon, C. Santa Engracia, 17 (☎91 447 38 37; www.barnon.visualdisco.com). M: Alonso Martínez. Barnon can be selective. International crowd gets down for some serious grinding. Tu salsa night, free lessons 11pm-midnight. Drinks 1600ptas/€9.60. Open Su-Th 11pm-4am, F-Sa midnight-5am.

Big Bamboo, C. Barquillo, 42 (☎91 562 88 38). M: Alonso Martínez. Walk 3 blocks east of C. Pelayo on C. Gravina and turn left on C. Barquillo. A friendly, international club that jams to smooth reggae. Open 10:30pm-6am, F-Sa 10:30pm-7am.

◪ DAYTRIPS FROM MADRID

EL ESCORIAL

Complex ☎91 890 59 03. Open Apr.-Sept. Tu-Su 10am-6pm; Oct.-Mar. Tu-Su 10am-5pm. Last admission 1hr. before closing. Monastery 1000ptas/€6, students and seniors 500ptas/€3. Guided tour 1150ptas/€6.90.

The **Monasterio de San Lorenzo del Escorial** was a gift from Felipe II to God, the people, and himself, commemorating his victory over the French at the battle of San Quintín in 1557. Near the town of **San Lorenzo,** El Escorial is filled with artistic treasures, two palaces, two pantheons, a church, and a magnificent library. *Don't* come on Monday, when the complex and most of the town shut down. To avoid crowds, enter via the gate on the west side on C. Florida Blanca into a collection of Flemish tapestries and paintings. The adjacent **Museos de Arquitectura** and **Pintura** chronicle the construction of El Escorial and include masterpieces by Bosch, El Greco, Titian, Tintoretto, Velázquez, Zurbarán, and Van Dyck. The **Palacio Real,** lined with 16th-century *azulejos* (tiles), includes the **Salón del Trono** (Throne Room), Felipe II's spartan 16th-century apartments, and the luxurious 18th-century rooms of Carlos III and Carlos IV. The macabre **Panteón Real** is filled with tombs of monarchs and glitters with intricate gold and marble designs.

EL VALLE DE LOS CAÍDOS

El Valle de los Caídos is accessible only via El Escorial. Mass M-Sa 11am; Su 11am, 12:30, 1, and 5:30pm. Entrance gate open Tu-Su 10am-6pm; Basilica open 10am-6:30pm. 800ptas/€4.80, seniors and students 400ptas/€2.40. W free for EU citizens. Funicular to the cross 400ptas/€2.40. **Autocares Herranz** *runs 1 bus to the monument (15min., leaves El Escorial Tu-Su 3:15pm and returns 5:30pm, round-trip plus admission 1150ptas/€6.90).*

In a valley of the Sierra de Guadarrama, 8km north of El Escorial, Franco built the overpowering monument of **Santa Cruz del Valle de los Caídos** (Valley of the Fallen) as a memorial to those who gave their lives in the Civil War. Naturally, the massive granite cross was meant to honor only those who died "serving *Dios* and *España*," i.e., the Fascist Nationalists. Non-fascist prisoners of war were forced to work building the monument, and thousands died during its construction. Although Franco lies buried beneath the high altar, there is no mention of his tomb in tourist literature—testimony to modern Spain's view of the dictator.

OTHER DAYTRIPS FROM MADRID

TOLEDO. To the architecture-loving tourist, Toledo is the glorious former capital of the Holy Roman, Visigoth, and Muslim empires (see p.816).

SEGOVIA. The impressive Alcázar and hulking aqueduct merit a spot on any tour, and the town's twisted alleys, fruit stands, and *paseos* represent Castilla y León at its finest (see p. 820).

ÁVILA. Stand on Ávila's medieval walls, 2.5km of magnificently preserved 12th-century stone that encircle the old city (see p.821).

CENTRAL SPAIN

Castilla La Mancha, surrounding Madrid to the west and south, is one of Spain's least-developed regions; medieval cities and olive groves sprinkle the land. On the other sides of Madrid are Castilla y León's dramatic cathedrals; despite glorious historical architecture and history, the regions have not been as economically successful as their more high-tech neighbors. Farther west, bordering Portugal, stark Extremadura's arid plains bake under intense summer sun, relieved by scattered patches of glowing sunflowers and refreshingly few tourists.

CASTILLA LA MANCHA

Cervantes chose to set Don Quixote's adventures in La Mancha (*manxa* is Arabic for parched earth) in an effort to evoke a cultural and material backwater. No fantasy of the Knight of the Sad Countenance is needed to transform the austere beauty of this battered, windswept plateau. Its tumultuous history, gloomy medieval fortresses, and awesome crags provide enough food for the imagination.

TOLEDO   ☎925

For Cervantes, Toledo was a "rocky gravity, glory of Spain and light of her cities." Cossío called it "the most brilliant and evocative summary of Spain's history." Toledo (pop. 65,000) may today be marred by armies of tourists and caravans of kitsch, but this former capital of the Holy Roman, Visigoth, and Muslim empires remains a treasure trove of Spanish culture. The city's numerous churches, synagogues, and mosques share twisting alleyways, emblematic of a time when Spain's three religions coexisted peacefully.

▄ TRANSPORTATION

Trains: Po. Rosa, 2 (☎925 22 30 99), in an exquisite neo-Mudéjar station just over the Puente de Azarquiel. To **Madrid** (1½hr., 9-10 per day, 780ptas/€4.70).

Buses: (☎925 21 58 50), 5min. from the city gate. From Pl. Zocodóver, take C. Armas. Serviced by various companies. **Continental-Auto** (☎925 22 36 41) runs to **Madrid** (1½hr.; every 30min. M-F 5:15am-10pm, Sa 6am-10:30pm, Su 8:30am-11:30pm; 605ptas/€3.64). **ALSINA** (☎925 21 58 50 or 963 49 72 30) runs to **Valencia** (5½hr.; M-F 3pm; 2600ptas/€16, buy the ticket on the bus).

▄▟ ORIENTATION AND PRACTICAL INFORMATION

Toledo is an almost unconquerable maze of narrow streets where pedestrians and cars battle for sovereignty. To get to **Plaza de Zocodóver** in the town center, take bus #5 or 6 (120ptas/€0.75) from the stop on the right after you exit the train station. From the train station, turn right and follow the left fork uphill to a smaller bridge, Puente de Alcántara. Cross the bridge to the stone staircase (through a set of arches); after climbing the stairs, turn left and continue upward, veering right at C. Cervantes to Pl. Zocodóver. Despite the well-labeled streets, you will probably get lost in Toledo. Enjoy it—it's the best way to discover the town's beauty.

SPAIN

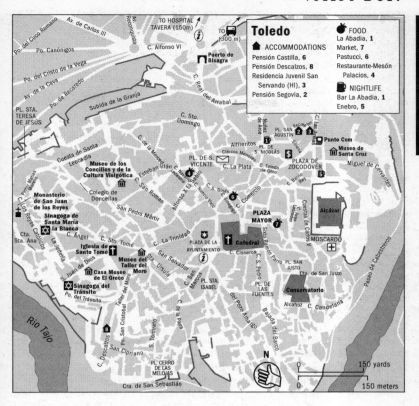

Toledo

🏠 ACCOMMODATIONS
Pensión Castilla, **6**
Pensión Descalzos, **8**
Residencia Juvenil San
   Servando (HI), **3**
Pensión Segovia, **2**

🍴 FOOD
La Abadia, **1**
Market, **7**
Pastucci, **6**
Restaurante-Mesón
   Palacios, **4**

🍸 NIGHTLIFE
Bar La Abadia, **1**
Enebro, **5**

Tourist Office: (☎925 22 08 43), just outside the Puerta Nueva de Bisagra, on the north side of town. Open July-Sept M-Sa 9am-7pm, Su 9am-3pm; Oct.-June M-F 9am-6pm, Sa 9am-7pm, Su 9am-3pm. There is a **2nd office** in Pl. Ayuntamiento (☎925 25 40 30), opposite the cathedral. Open Tu-Su 10:30am-2:30pm and 4:30-7pm.

Currency Exchange: Banco Central Hispano, C. Comercio, 47 (☎925 22 98 00). Open Apr.-Sept. M-F 8:30am-2:30pm; Oct.-Mar. M-F 8:30am-2:30pm, Sa 8:30am-1pm.

Luggage Storage: At the **bus station** (100-200ptas/€0.60-1.20). Open daily 7am-11pm. At the **train station** (500ptas/€3). Open daily 7am-9:30pm.

Emergency: ☎ 112. **Police,** (☎092) where Av. Reconquista and Av. Carlos III meet.

Pharmacy: Pl. Zocodóver (☎925 22 17 68). List of late-night pharmacies posted.

Hospital: Hospital Virgen de la Salud, Av. Barber (☎925 26 92 00).

Internet Access: Punto Com, C. Armas, 4, 2nd fl. (☎925 25 62 08), in Pl. Zocodóver just as you begin to walk downhill on the right. 150ptas/€0.90 for 15min., 250ptas/€1.50 for 30min., 400ptas/€2.40 per hr. Open M-Sa 11:30am-10pm, Su 4-10pm.

Post Office: C. Plata, 1 (☎925 22 36 11), off Pl. Zocodóver via C. Comercio. Lista de Correos. Open M-F 8:30am-8:30pm, Sa 9am-2pm. **Postal Code:** 45070.

🏠 ACCOMMODATIONS

Toledo is chock-full of accommodations, but finding a bed during the summer can be a hassle, especially on weekends. If you run into trouble, try the tourist office.

🏠 **Residencia Juvenil San Servando (HI),** Castillo San Servando (☎925 22 45 54), uphill from the train station (10min). Attractive, monumental building has 38 rooms, each with 2-4 bunk beds and a private bath. Gorgeous pool in summer. TV room. Free sheets. Reception open 7-9:40am, 10am-7:40pm, and 8-11:50pm. Dorms 1800ptas/€10.85, under 27 1400ptas/€8.40.

Pensión Descalzos, C. Descalzos, 30 (☎925 22 28 88), down the steps off Po. del Tránsito, near the Sinagoga de Tránsito. Recently refurbished hostel in a quiet part of town with stunning views of the surrounding hills. Small pool and big jacuzzi. Apr.-Oct. singles 4000ptas/€24; doubles 6420-7250ptas/€39-44. Oct.-Mar. singles 3750ptas/€23; doubles 5600-6500ptas/€34-39. MC/V.

Pensión Castilla, C. Recoletos, 6 (☎925 25 63 18). Take C. Armas downhill from Pl. Zocodóver, then the 1st left up C. Recoletos (opposite the Caja Madrid bank); hostel is up the stairs in the corner. Singles 2200ptas/€14; doubles with bath 3900ptas/€24.

Pensión Segovia, C. Recoletos, 2 (☎925 21 11 24), follow the directions to Pensión Castilla, continuing around the bend; pensión is on your left. Singles 2400ptas/€15; doubles 3200ptas/€20; triples 4500ptas/€27.

Camping El Greco, (☎925 22 00 90). 1.5km from town on the road away from Madrid (C-502). Bus #7 (from Pl. Zocodóver) stops at the entrance. 670ptas/€4 per person, 650ptas/€3.90 per tent; 50ptas/€0.30 per car.

🍴 FOOD

Toledo grinds almonds into marzipan of every shape and size, from colorful fruity nuggets to half-moon cookies; *pastelerías* beckon on every corner. If your pocket permits, dining out in Toledo can be a pleasurable culinary experience (*menús* 1400-1600ptas/€8.45-9.60). Alternatively, buy fresh fruit and the basics at **Alimentación Pantoja,** C. Arrabal, 30, just on the inside of Puerta de Bisagra across from the tourist office. Open June-Aug. M-Sa 9am-11pm, Su 9am-3pm; rest of the year M-Sa 9am-10pm and Su 9am-3pm.

🍽 **La Abadía,** Pl. San Nicolás, 3 (☎925 25 07 46). From Pl. Zocodóver, take C. Sillería, then bear left when the road splits until you reach a small plaza; Abadía is to your right. This maze of connected underground cave-like rooms is a great place to start the evening. The delicious *menú* is a steal (1375ptas/€8.30). Open M-Th 8am-midnight, F 8am-1:30am, Sa noon-2:30am, Su noon-midnight.

Pastucci, C. Sinagoga, 10 (☎925 21 48 66). From Pl. Zocodóver take C. Comercio; keep to the right and turn right through the underpass. Pastas 800-1000ptas/€4.80-6. Over 30 kinds of pizza (1000ptas/€6). Open daily 12:15pm-midnight.

Restaurante-Mesón Palacios, C. Alfonso X El Sabio, 3 (☎925 21 59 72), off C. Nuncio Viejo, the street opposite the 2nd tourist office. Toledo's famous partridge dish is an option in the *menú* (1000 or 1700ptas/€6-10.25). Entrees 1200-2000ptas/€7.20-12. Open M-Sa 1-4pm and 7-11pm, Su noon-4pm.

👁 🎵 SIGHTS AND ENTERTAINMENT

Toledo's major sights (many closed on Mondays) lie within the walls. Southwest of Pl. Zocodóver, Toledo's grandiose ■**cathedral** at the Arco de Palacioz, boasts five naves, delicate stained glass, and unapologetic ostentatiousness. (Open June-Aug. 10am-noon and 4-7pm; Sept.-May 10am-noon and 4-6pm.) Toledo's most formidable landmark, the ■**Alcázar,** Cuesta Carlos V 2, uphill from Pl. Zocodóver, has been a stronghold of Romans, Visigoths, Moors, and Fascists. Today, it houses a national military museum. (Open Tu-Su 9:30am-2:30pm. 200ptas/€1.20. Free W.)

Greek painter Doménikos Theotokópoulos, or **El Greco,** spent most of his life in Toledo. Many of his works are displayed throughout town; on the west side of town, the **Iglesia de Santo Tomé,** on Pl. Conde, houses his famous *El entierro del Conde de Orgaz.* (Burial of Count Orgaz. Open daily 10am-7pm. 200ptas./€1.20.) Downhill and to the left lies the **Casa Museo de El Greco,** C. Samuel Levi 3, with 19 works by the master. (Open Mar.-Oct.15 daily 10am-6:45pm; Oct.16-Feb. 10am-5:45pm. 200ptas/€1.20; under 18, students and seniors 150ptas/€0.90.)

The simple exterior of the 14th-century **Sinagoga del Tránsito,** on C. Samuel Levi, hides an ornate interior with Mudéjar plasterwork, an intricate wooden ceiling, and Hebrew inscriptions, and now houses the **Museo Sefardí.** (Open Tu-Sa 10am-1:45pm and 4-5:45pm, Su 10am-2pm. 400ptas/€2.40, students and under 18 200ptas/€1.20. Free Sa after 4pm and Su.) The 12th-century **Sinagoga de Santa María la Blanca,** down the street to the right, was built as a mosque and then used as the city's main synagogue until converted to a church in 1492. (Open June-Aug. daily 10am-1:45pm and 3:30-6:45pm; Sept.-May 10am-1:45pm and 3:30-5:45pm. 200ptas/€1.20; students, under 16, and seniors 150ptas/€0.90.) At the western edge of the city, with great views, is the Franciscan **Monasterio de San Juan de los Reyes,** commissioned by Isabel and Fernando. (Open Apr.-Sept. daily 10am-1:45pm and 3:30-6:45pm; Oct.-Mar. 10am-1:45pm and 3:30-6pm. 200ptas/€1.20.)

For nightlife, try **Calle Santa Fe,** east of and through the arch from Pl. Zocodóver, which brims with beer and local youths. **Trébol,** C. Sante Fe, 1, has excellent *tapas.* (375ptas/€2.25. Open M-Sa 10am-3:30pm and 7pm-midnight, Su 1-3:30pm and 7pm-midnight.) Look for **Enebro,** on small Pl. Santiago Balleros off C. Cervantes, which offers free *tapas* in the evenings. (Beer 200ptas/€1.20. No cover. Open daily 11am-4pm and 7pm-2:30am.) **Calle Sillería** and **Calle Alfileritos,** west of Pl. Zocodóver, are home to more upscale bars and clubs, including **Bar La Abadía,** Pl. San Nicolás, 5. (Open M-Th 8am-midnight, F 8am-1:30am, Sa noon-2:30am, Su noon-midnight.)

CUENCA ☎969

Cuenca (pop. 47,000) is a vertical hilltop city surrounded by two rivers and stunning rock formations. The enchanting **old city** safeguards most of Cuenca's unique charm, including the famed ▧**casas colgadas** (hanging houses) that dangle high above the Río Huécar, on C. Obispo Vaero off Pl. Mayor. Cross the San Pablo bridge to **Hoz del Huécar** for a spectacular view of the *casas* and cliffs. Many of the *casas* now house museums; on Pl. Ciudad de Ronda is the excellent **Museo de Arte Abstracto Español.** (Open Tu-F and holidays 11am-2pm and 4-6pm, Sa 11am-2pm and 4-8pm, Su 11am-2:30pm. 500ptas/€3, students and seniors 250ptas/€1.50.) In the Pl. Mayor, the perfectly square **cathedral,** 25m on each side, is the only Anglo-Norman Gothic cathedral in Spain. (Open Tu-Sa 9am-2pm and 4-6pm, Su 9am-2pm. Mass daily at 9:20am, plus noon and 1pm on Su. Free. Museum open same hours as the cathedral. 200ptas/€1.20.)

Trains (☎(902) 24 02 02) leave from Po. Ferrocarril, in the new city, to Madrid (2½-3hr., 5-6 per day 7:05am-6:55pm, 1430ptas/€8.60) and Valencia (3-4hr.; 3-4 per day, M-F 7:40am-6:40pm, Sa-Su 11:19am-6:40pm; 1575ptas/€9.50). **Buses** (☎969 22 70 87) depart from C. Fermín Caballero for: Barcelona (3½hr.; M-Sa 9:30am, July-Aug. extra bus Su at 2pm; 4550ptas/€27); Madrid (2½hr.; 8-9 per day, M-Sa 7:30am-8pm, Su 8am-10pm; 1370-1695ptas/€8.20-10.15); Toledo (3hr., M-F 5:30am, 1620ptas/€9.75). From either station, go left to the first bus shelter and take bus #1 (every 20min., 85ptas/€0.50) to the last stop in the old city. The **tourist office** is in Plaza Mayor. (☎969 23 21 19. Open July-Sept. M-Sa 9am-9pm, Su 9am-2pm; Oct.-June M-Sa 9am-2pm and 4-6pm, Su 9am-2pm.) **Hostal-Residencia Posada de San José,** C. Julián Romero, 4, a block up from the left side of the cathedral, is worth cashing the extra traveler's check. History echoes through this 17th-century convent with gorgeous views. (☎969 21 13 00. Singles 3000ptas/€18, with bath 6400ptas/€39; doubles 4900ptas/€29, 9500ptas/€57.) To reach **Pensión Tabanqueta,** C. Trabuco 13, in the old city, head up C. San Pedro from the cathedral, which turns into C. Trabuco after Pl. Trabuco. (☎969 21 12 90. Doubles 4000ptas/€24; triples 6000ptas/€36.) In the new city, take C. Fermín Caballero from the bus station, turn left on C. Hurtado de Mendoza, and continue on Av. República Argentina to **Pensión Cuenca** at #8, 2nd fl. (☎969 21 25 74. Singles 2000ptas/€12, with shower 2300ptas/€14; doubles 3000ptas/€18, 4000ptas/€24.) Budget eateries line **Calle Cervantes** and **Calle República Argentina.** Grab **groceries** at **%Día,** on Av. Castilla La Mancha. (Open M-Th 9:30am-2pm and 5:30-8:30pm, F-Sa 9am-2:30pm and 5:30-9pm.) **Postal Code:** 16004.

CASTILLA Y LEÓN

Castilla y León's hilltop cities emerge like islands from a sea of burnt sienna. The monuments—the majestic Gothic cathedrals of Burgos and León, the slender Romanesque belfries along León's Camino de Santiago, the intricate sandstone of Salamanca, and the proud city walls of Ávila—have emblazoned themselves as regional and national images.

SEGOVIA ☎921

Legend has it that the devil built Segovia's famed aqueduct in one night, in an effort to win the soul of a Segovian water-seller named Juanilla. When the shocked Juanilla woke up to find the aqueduct almost completed, she prayed to the Virgin Mary, who made the sun rise a bit earlier in order to foil the Devil's scheme. In the 12th and 13th centuries Segovia (pop. 55,000) had more Romanesque monuments than anywhere else in Europe. Today, its remaining cathedrals and castles represent Castilla at its finest—a labyrinthine town of twisted alleys and sharp aromas. Pleasure has its price: prices for food and accommodations are much higher than in Madrid. In the Sierra de Guadarrama, 88km northwest of Madrid, Segovia is close enough to the capital to be a daytrip but definitely warrants a longer stay.

🚆🛈 TRANSPORTATION AND PRACTICAL INFO. Trains (☎921 42 07 74), Po. Obispo Quesada, run to Madrid (2hr.; 7-9 per day M-F 5:55am-8:55pm, Sa-Su 8:55am-8:55pm; 805ptas/€4.80). **Buses** run from **Estacionamiento Municipal de Autobuses,** Po. Ezequiel González, 12 (☎921 42 77 07), at the corner of Av. Fernández Ladreda. **La Sepulvedana** (☎921 42 77 07) sends buses to Madrid (1½hr., M-F every 30min. 6am-9:30pm, 855ptas/€5.40). **Renfe-Iñigo** (☎921 44 12 52) sends buses to Ávila (1hr.; M-F 10:30am, 2, and 7:30pm, Sa 2pm, Su 7:45pm; 625ptas/€3.75); **Auto Res** (☎921 42 77 05) sends buses to Salamanca (3hr.; M-Sa 8:50am, 1:30, and 5:30pm, Su 5:45pm; 1320ptas/€8). The city is impossible to navigate without a map. Locals describe it as the "Stone Ship." The **Alcázar** is the bow, the aqueduct the stern, and the cathedral towers as the mainmast. To get to **Plaza Mayor,** the city's historic center and site of the **tourist office,** take any bus from the train station (100ptas/€0.60). On weekdays, some buses go only as far as Po. del Salón: from there go left up the steps of **Puerta del Sol,** turn right on C. Judería Vieja, and make the first left onto C. Isabel la Católica. Your first stop should be the **Regional Tourist Office,** Pl. Mayor, 10, in front of the bus stop, which has indispensable maps. (☎921 46 03 34. Open M-F 9am-2pm and 5-7pm, Sa-Su 10am-2pm and 5-8pm.) **Copy-Art,** C. Teodosio el Grande, 8, is the most convenient **Internet** connection. (Open daily 10:15am-1:30pm and 4:30-10pm. 300ptas/€1.80 per ½hr.) **Postal Code:** 40001.

🛏🍴 ACCOMMODATIONS AND FOOD. In summer, finding a *hostal* room can be a nightmare; book ahead and prepare to pay at least 3500ptas/€21 for a single. The ☒**Residencia Juvenil "Emperador Teodosio" (HI),** Av. Conde de Sepúlveda, is only open to travelers in July and early August, when its hotel-like doubles and triples, all with private baths, make it extremely popular. From the train station, turn right, cross the street, and walk along Po. Obispo Quesada, which becomes Av. Conde de Sepúlveda (10min.). From the bus station, turn right on C. Ezequiel González, which becomes Av. Conde Sepúlveda (10min.). (☎921 44 11 11. 3-night max. stay. Dorms 1100ptas/€6.60, with full meals 2300ptas/€13.80; over 26 1550ptas/€9, 3100ptas/€20.) To get to **Hostal Don Jaime,** Ochoa Ondategui, 8, face away from the aqueduct stairs and it will be on the first street to your left. (☎921 44 47 87. Singles 3400ptas/€20.40; doubles 4800ptas/€28.40, with bath 5600ptas/€33.60; triples with bath 7300ptas/€43.80.) **Hospedaje El Gato,** Pl. del Salvador, 10, has nicely decorated modern rooms with plenty of light. (☎921 43 80 47. Singles 3000ptas/€18; doubles 5500ptas/€33. MC/V.) **Camping Acueducto,** Ctra. Nacional 601, km 112, is 2km toward La Granja. Take the Autobus Urbano from Pl. Azoguejo to Nueva Segovia. (Bus 105ptas/€0.65. ☎921 42 50 00. Open Semana Santa-Sept. 625ptas/€3.75 per person, per tent, and per car.)

Sample Segovia's famed lamb, *croquetas*, or *sopa castellana*, but steer clear of pricey Pl. Mayor and Pl. Azoguejo. Get **groceries** at **%Día,** C. Fernández Giménez, 3. (Open M-Th 9:30am-2pm and 5:30-8:30pm, F-Sa 9am-9pm.) **Restaurante La Almuzara,** C. Marqués del Arco, 3, is a classy little place with many veggie options. (Luncheon menú W-F 1500ptas/€9. Open W-Su 1-4pm and 8-11:30pm, Tu 8-11:30pm.) The local color of the hidden **Bar-Mesón Cueva de San Estéban,** C. Valdeláguila, 15, off Pl. San Estéban and C. Escuderos, is worth seeking out. (*Menú* 1000ptas/€6. Open daily 10am-midnight.)

SIGHTS AND ENTERTAINMENT. Segovia rewards the wanderer. Whether palace, church, house, or sidewalk, almost everything deserves close observation. Look for *esgrafía*, lacy patterns on the facades of buildings. The **cathedral,** commissioned by Carlos I in 1525, towers above Pl. Mayor. Inside, the **Sala Capitular** displays intricate tapestries; the **museum** has a series of 17th-century paintings on marble depicting the Passion of Christ. (Open Apr.-Oct. daily 9am-7pm; Nov.-Mar. 9:30am-6pm. 300ptas/€1.80.) The **Alcázar,** a late-medieval castle and site of Isabel's coronation in 1474, dominates the northern end of the old quarter. In the **Sala de Solio** (throne room), an inscription reads: *tanto monta, monta tanto* ("she mounts, as does he"). Get your mind out of the gutter—this means simply that Fernando and Isabel had equal authority as sovereigns. The strong and the restless climb the 140 steps up a nausea-inducing spiral staircase to the top of the *Torre de Juan II* (80m high), which affords a marvelous view of Segovia and the surrounding amber plains. The **Sala de Armas** holds an arsenal of medieval weaponry. From Pl. Mayor, follow C. Marques del Arco and walk through the park. (Open Apr.-Sept. daily 10am-7pm; Oct.-Mar. 10am-6pm. 500ptas/€3.) The serpentine **roman aqueduct** commands the entrance to the old city. Supported by 128 pillars that span 813m and reach a height of 28.9m near Pl. Azoguejo, the two tiers of 163 arches were constructed out of some 20,000 blocks of granite—without any mortar to hold them together—by the Romans in 50 BC. This spectacular feat of engineering, restored by the monarchy in the 15th century, can transport 30 liters of water per second and was used until the late 1940s.

For decent jazz, locals head to **El Saxo Bar,** C. del Seminario, 2, which offers a laid-back atmosphere and live music on the first Friday of each month. (Open W-Su 8pm-3am.) From June 24-29, Segovia celebrates a **fiesta** in honor of San Juan and San Pedro. According to local lore, the sun reflects the general joy and intoxication by rising in circles.

DAYTRIP FROM SEGOVIA: LA GRANJA DE SAN ILDEFONSO. The royal palace and grounds of **La Granja,** 9km southeast of Segovia, were commissioned by Philip V, the first Bourbon King. Of the four royal summer retreats (the others being El Pardo, El Escorial, and Aranjuez), this "Versailles of Spain" is by far the most extravagant. Marble, lace curtains, lavish crystal chandeliers, and a world-class collection of Flemish tapestries enliven the palace. Manicured gardens and a forest surround the palace. (☎921 47 00 19. Open June-Sept. Tu-Su 10am-6pm; Oct.-Mar. Tu-Sa 10am-1:30pm and 3-5pm, Su 10am-2pm; Apr.-May Tu-F 10am-1:30pm and 3-5pm, Sa-Su 10am-6pm. Mandatory guided tours depart every 15min. 800ptas/€4.80, students and EU seniors 400ptas/€2.40. W free for EU citizens.) **Buses** run to La Granja from Segovia (20min., 9-12 per day, 230ptas/€1.40 round-trip).

ÁVILA   ☎920

Oh, if walls had ears, what stories Ávila's medieval *murallas* could tell. The 2½km of magnificent 12th-century stone walls are even better preserved than the various body parts of Santa Teresa that grace the city's shrines and museums. Santa Teresa would have been pleased at the peace of Ávila life. Today, the inner walls are a time warp, untouched by pollution, advertisements, or the blare of tourist traffic. Just west of Segovia and northwest of Madrid, Ávila (pop. 50,000) is a reasonable daytrip from either.

SPAIN

TRANSPORTATION AND PRACTICAL INFORMATION. Trains run from the station at Av. José Antonio (☎920 24 02 02), to Madrid (1½-2hr., 15-19 per day, 880-1015ptas/€5.30-6). **Buses,** Av. Madrid, 2 (☎920 22 01 54), come from Madrid (2hr., 3-8 per day, 950ptas/€5.70) and Segovia (1hr.; M-F 10:30am, 2, and 7:30pm, Sa 2pm, Su 7:45pm; 625ptas/€3.75). The tangled city has two main squares: **Plaza de la Victoria** (known to locals as Pl. del Mercado Chico) inside the city walls, and **Plaza de Santa Teresa** just outside. From the bus station, cross the street and follow C. Duque de Alba to reach Pl. de Santa Teresa. To continue on to Ávila's **tourist office,** Pl. Catedral 4, walk through the main gate and turn right on C. Alemania. (☎920 21 13 87. Open M-F 10am-2pm and 5-7pm, Sa-Su 10am-2pm and 5-8pm.) Get on the **Internet** at **Arroba@25,** C. Ferreol Hernandez, 1. (100ptas/€0.60 per 15min.) **Postal Code:** 05001.

ACCOMMODATIONS AND FOOD. Ávila's walls brim with comfortable and reasonable accommodations. Those near the cathedral and Pl. Santa Teresa fill up in the summer, so call a day in advance. Next to the tourist office, a winding wooden staircase leads to absolutely cavernous rooms at **Pensión Continental,** Pl. Catedral, 6. (☎920 21 15 02. Singles 2500ptas/€15; doubles 4300ptas/€25.80, with bath 5500ptas/€33; triples 6500ptas/€39.) Behind the pleasant front garden from which its name is derived, **Hostal Jardin,** C. San Segundo, 38, offers large rooms with TVs and phones. (June-Oct. singles 3000ptas/€18, with bath 4500ptas/€27; doubles4500ptas/€27, 6500ptas/€39; less Nov.-May.)

The city has won fame for its *chuleton de Ávila* (veal) and *mollejas* (sweetbread). The *yemas de Santa Teresa* or *yemas de Ávila,* local confections made of egg yolk and honey, are delectable. **Calle San Segundo,** off Pl. Santa Teresa, is lined with budget diamonds. **■La Taberna del Lagartijo,** C. Martin Carramolino, 4, is named in honor of the great bullfighter Rafael Molina, and commemorates the profession with various bullfighting paraphenalia. (☎920 22 88 25. Classic *menú* 1300ptas/€7.80. Open M-Th 1:30-3:30pm and 8:30-10:30pm.) Find a **supermarket** at C. Juan José Martín, 6. (Heading away from Pl. Teresa, turn left off C. Duque de Alba just after the Monasterio de San José. Open M-Sa 9:45am-2pm and 5-8pm.)

SIGHTS AND ENTERTAINMENT. Ávila's **medieval walls,** the oldest and best-preserved walls in Spain, date from 1090. Eighty-eight massive towers reinforce the 3m-thick walls—the most imposing of the towers, **Cimorro,** is also the cathedral's bold apse. To walk along the walls, start with the Puerta del Alcázar directly before you and your back to the Pl. de la Teresa. Inside the walls, the profile of the **cathedral** looming over the watchtowers is believed to have inspired Santa Teresa's metaphor of the soul as a diamond castle. View the **Altar de La Virgen de la Caridad,** where 12-year-old Santa Teresa prostrated herself after the death of her mother. From Pl. Santa Teresa, walk through the Puerta; take the first right onto C. Cruz Vieja, which leads to the cathedral. (Open June-Oct. M-Sa 10am-8pm, Su noon-8pm; Nov.-Apr. daily 10am-1:30pm and 3:30-5:30pm. 300ptas/€1.80.) Santa Teresa's admirers built the 17th-century **Convento de Santa Teresa** on the site of her birthplace and childhood home. From Pl. Santa Teresa, go left on C. San Segundo, right on Po. Rastro, and right through Pta. Santa Teresa. (Open daily 8:30am-1:30pm and 3:30-9pm.) To the right of the convent, the **Sala de Reliquias** holds Santa Teresa relics, including her right ring finger and the cord with which she flagellated herself. (Open Apr.-Oct. daily 10am-2pm and 4-7pm; Nov.-Mar. Tu-Su 10am-1:30pm and 3:30-5:30pm. 300ptas/€1.80.) A short distance outside the city walls on Po. Encarnación is the **Monasterio de la Encarnación,** where Santa Teresa lived for 30 years. The mandatory 15min. guided tour in Spanish visits Santa Teresa's tiny cell and the staircase where she had her mystical encounter with the child Jesus. The monastery is on Po. Encarnación, northwest of the city. (Open June-Aug. daily 10am-1pm and 4-7pm; Sept.-May 10am-1pm and 3:30-6pm. 200ptas/€1.20.)

The best view of the walls and of Ávila itself is from the **Cuatro Postes,** a four-pillared structure past the Río Adaja on the highway to Salamanca, 1.5km northwest of the city. It was at this spot that Santa Teresa was caught by her uncle while she and her brother were trying to flee to the Islamic south. From Pl. Santa Teresa, walk through the inner city and out the Puerta del Puente. Cross the bridge and follow the road to your right for about 1km. Fairs and parades of *gigantes y cabezudos* (giant effigies) pass through when the city gets crazy honoring Santa Teresa (the week surrounding Oct. 15th, her day). In mid-July, the **Fiestas de Verano** bring folk-singing, dancing, fireworks, and a bullfight.

SALAMANCA ☎923

For centuries, the gates of Salamanca have welcomed scholars, saints, rogues, and royals. The bustling city is famed for its warm golden sandstone architecture as well as for its university—the oldest in Spain and once one of the "four leading lights of the world," along with the universities of Bologna, Paris, and Oxford.

🚆 TRANSPORTATION. Trains chug from Po. Estación Ferrocarril (☎923 12 02 02) to: Ávila (1¾hr., 6:45am and 5:45pm, regional 880ptas/€5.25); Lisbon (6hr., 4:38am, 5460ptas/€32.75); Madrid (2½hr., 4 per day 7:45am-7:40pm, 2175ptas/€16.70). **Buses** run from Av. Filiberto Villalobos 71-85 (☎923 23 67 17) to: Ávila (1½hr.; M-Sa 4 per day 6:30am-8:30pm, Su 3:30pm and 8:30pm; 725ptas/€4.35); León (2½hr.; M-F 3 per day 11am-6:30pm, Sa 11am, Su 10pm; 1200ptas/€7.20); Madrid (regular 3hr., express 2½hr.; M-Sa 15 per day 6am-9:30pm, Su 15 per day 8am-11pm; regular 1530ptas/€9.20, express 2600ptas/€15.60); Segovia (3hr.; M-F 7:30am and 1:30pm, Sa 7:30am and 9:30am, Su 1:30pm and 8:45pm; 3140ptas/€19).

🛈 PRACTICAL INFORMATION. The **tourist office** is at Pl. Mayor, 14. (☎923 21 83 42. Open M-Sa 9am-2pm and 4:30-6:30pm, Su 10am-2pm and 4:30-6:30pm.) Access the **Internet** at **Informática Abaco Bar,** C. Zamora 7. (Open M-F 9:30am-2am. 150ptas/ €0.90 per 15min.) The **post office** sits at Gran Vía, 25-29. (☎923 28 09 02. Open M-F 8:30am-8:30pm, Sa 9:30am-2pm.) **Postal Code:** 37080.

🏠🍴 ACCOMMODATIONS AND FOOD. Reasonably priced *hostales* and *pensiones* cater to the floods of student visitors, especially off Pl. Mayor and C. Meléndez. **Pensión Las Vegas,** C. Meléndez, 13, 1st fl., has friendly owners. (☎923 21 87 49. Singles 2000ptas/€12; doubles 3500ptas/€21, with bath 4000ptas/€24; triples with bath 6000ptas/€36. MC/V.) **Pensión Bárez,** C. Meléndez, 19, 1st fl., has several large, simple rooms. (☎923 21 74 95. Singles 1500ptas/€9; doubles 3000ptas/€18; triples 4500ptas/€27.) **Pensión Estefanía,** C. Jesús, 3-5, off Pl. Mayor, has a prime location and clean rooms. (☎923 21 73 72. Singles 2200ptas/€13.20; doubles with shower 3500ptas/€21; triples 4900ptas/€29.40. Cash only.) Albetur buses shuttle **campers** from Gran Vía (every 30min.) to the first class **Regio,** 4km toward Madrid on the Ctra. Salamanca. (☎923 13 88 88. 450ptas/€2.70 per person, 850ptas/€5.10 per tent, 450ptas/€2.70 extra per car.) **Champion,** C. Toro, 64, has a downstairs supermarket. (Open M-Sa 9:15am-9:15pm.) Cafes and restaurants surround Pl. Mayor; full meals in cheaper back alley spots run around 1000ptas/€6. **🍴Restaurante El Bardo,** C. Compañía 8, between the Casa de Conchas and the Clerecía, is a traditional Spanish restaurant with veggie options and a lively bar downstairs. (*Menú* 1400ptas/€8.40. Open daily 1:30-4:30pm and 9:30-11:30pm., bar until 1am.)

🎭🎵 SIGHTS AND ENTERTAINMENT. The **🏛Plaza Mayor,** designed by Alberto Churriguera, exemplifies the best of the city's famed architecture and has been called one of the most beautiful squares in Spain. Between its nearly 100 sandstone arches hang medallions with bas-reliefs of famous Spaniards, from El Cid to Franco. Walk down C. Rua Mayor to Pl. San Isidro to reach the 15th-century **Casa de las Conchas** (House of Shells), one of Salamanca's most famous landmarks, adorned by over 300 rows of scallop shells chiseled in sandstone. Go down Patio de las Escuelas, off C. Libreros (which leads south from Pl. San Isidro), to enter the **🏛Universidad,** founded in 1218. The university's 16th-century **entry façade** is one of the best examples of Spanish Plateresque, named for the delicate filigree work of *plateros* (silversmiths). Hidden in the sculptural work lies a tiny frog; according to legend, those who can spot the frog without assistance will be blessed with good luck and even marriage. The **Antigua Biblioteca,** the oldest library in Europe, is the most spectacular room of all, located atop a magnificent Plateresque staircase displaying statues and historic books. Inside the Patio de Escuelas Menores, the University Museum contains the **Cielo de Salamanca,** a 15th-century fresco of the zodiac. (Open M-F 9:30am-1:30pm and 4-7:30pm, Sa 9:30am-1:30pm and 4-7pm, Su 10am-1:30pm. 300ptas/€1.80, students 150ptas/€0.90.)

Continue down Rua Mayor to Pl. Anaya to reach the *vieja* (old) and *nueva* (new) cathedrals. Begun in 1513 to accommodate the growing tide of Catholics, the spindly-spired late-Gothic **Catedral Nueva** wasn't finished until 1733. While several subsequent architects decided to retain the original late-Gothic style, they could not resist adding touches from later periods, most notably its Baroque tower, one of the tallest in Spain. The smaller Romanesque **Catedral Vieja** (1140) has a striking cupola with depictions of apocalyptic angels separating the sinners from the saved. The **museum** in the latter houses a *Mudéjar* Salinas organ, one of the oldest organs in Europe. (*Nueva* open Apr.-Sept. daily 9am-2pm and 4-8pm; Oct.-Mar. 9am-1pm and 4-6pm. Free. *Vieja,* cloister, and museum open Apr.-Sept. daily 10am-1:30pm and 4-7:30pm. 300ptas/€1.80.) If religious zeal appeals, inquire at the tourist office about Salamanca's impressive **convents.** The **Casa Lis Museo Art Nouveau Y Art Deco,** C. Gibraltar, 14, behind the cathedrals, houses the oddities of Miguel de Lis's art nouveau and art deco collection. (Open Apr. to mid-Oct. Tu-F 11am-2pm and 5pm-9pm, Sa-Su 11am-9pm; mid-Oct. to Mar. Tu-F 11am-2pm and 4-7pm, Sa-Su 11am-8pm. 300ptas/€1.80.)

Nightlife centers on **Plaza Mayor.** Student nightlife spreads out to **Gran Vía, Calle Bordadores,** and side streets. Spacious discos/bars, or *pafs,* blast music into the wee hours of the morning. **Calle Prior** and **Calle Rua Mayor** are full of bars; locals gather in the charming *terrazas* on **Plaza de la Fuente,** off Av. Alemania. More intense partying occurs off **Calle Varillas,** where *chupiterías* (bars that mostly serve shots) take precedence over *pafs.* Drink to modern funk jazz in a relaxed setting at ⬛**Birdland,** C. Azafranal, 57. **Camelot,** C. Bordadores, 3, is a monastery-turned-club. Swing to Top 40 songs at the popular **Café Moderno,** Gran Vía, 75. A mixed gay and straight clientele grooves under black lights at **Submarino,** C. San Justo, 27, built to resemble the inside of a submarine.

◪ **DAYTRIP FROM SALAMANCA: ZAMORA.** Perched atop a rocky cliff over the Rio Duero, Zamora (pop. 65,000) is an intriguing mix of the modern and medieval: 11th-century churches rub shoulders with Mango and Zara, and 15th-century palaces harbor **Internet** cafes and luxury hotels. Zamora's foremost monument is its Romanesque **cathedral,** built from the 12th to 15th centuries. Highlights are its intricately carved choir stalls (complete with seated apostles laughing and singing) and the main altar, an ornate structure of marble, gold, and silver. Inside the cloister, the **Museo de la Catedral** features the priceless 15th-century Black Tapestries. (Cathedral and museum open Tu-F 10am-2pm and 4-8pm, Sa-Su 10am-8pm. Mass daily at 10am, also Sa 6pm and Su 1pm. Cathedral free.) All in all, twelve handsome Romanesque churches remain within the walls of the old city, gleaming in the wake of recent restoration. Most visitors follow the Romanesque Route, a self-guided tour of all of the churches, available from the tourist office. The ⬛**Museo de Semana Santa,** in sleepy Pl. Santa Maria La Nueva, 9, is a rare find. Hooded mannequins stand guard over elaborately sculpted floats, dating back to the early 17th century. (Open M-Sa 10am-2pm and 5-8pm, Su 10am-2pm. 300-450ptas/€1.80-2.70.) *Buses depart from C. Alfonso Peña, 3 (☎ 980 52 12 81) to Salamanca on Zamora/Salamanca (1hr.; M-F 25 per day 6:40am-9:35pm, Sa 10 per day 7:45am-8:30pm, Su 8 per day 10am-9pm; 565ptas/€3.40).*

LEÓN ☎987

Formerly the center of Christian Spain, today León is best known for its 13th-century Gothic **cathedral** on La Pulchra Leonina, arguably the most beautiful cathedral in Spain. Its spectacular blue stained-glass windows have earned the city the nickname *La Ciudad Azul* (The Blue City) and alone warrant a trip to León. The cathedral's **museo** includes gruesome wonders, including a sculpture depicting the skinning of a saint. (Cathedral open in summer daily 8:30am-1:30pm and 4-8pm; in winter 8:30am-1:30pm and 4-7pm. Free. Museum open in summer daily 9:30am-1:30pm and 4-6:30pm; in winter M-Sa 9:30am-1pm and 4-6pm. 500ptas/€3. Cloister 100ptas/€0.60.) The Romanesque **Basílica de San Isidoro,** dedicated in the 11th century to San Isidoro de Sevilla, houses the corpses of countless royals in the impressive **Panteón Real.** From Pl. Santo Domingo, walk up C. Ramon y Cajal; the basilica is up the flight of stairs on the right just before C. La Torre. (Open M-Sa 9am-8pm, Su 9am-2pm. 400ptas/€2.40.) Unfortunately, most of the city's best clubs are only accessible by cab. Try **Oh León!** or **La Tropicana.** For nearby bars, discos, and techno music, head to the *barrio húmedo* (drinker's neighborhood) around **Plaza de San Martín** and **Plaza Mayor.** All bars are open until 2am daily and until 5-6am on Friday and Saturday. **Fiestas** commemorating St. John and St. Peter take place June 21-30, as does a *corrida de toros* (bullfight).

Trains (☎(902) 24 02 02) run from Av. Astorga, 2, to Madrid (4½hr., M-Sa 7 per day 1:12am-6:12pm, 3420ptas/€20.55). **Buses** (☎21 10 00) leave from Po. Ingeniero Saenz de Miera for Madrid (4½hr.; M-F 12 per day 2:30am-10:30pm, Sa-Su 8 per day 2:30am-7:30pm; 2680ptas/€16). Av. Palencia (a left out of the main entrance of the bus station or right out of the main entrance of the train station) leads across the river to **Plaza Glorieta Guzmán el Bueno,** where, after the rotary, it becomes **Avenida de Ordoño II** and leads to León's cathedral and the adjacent **tourist office,** Pl. Regla 3. (☎23 70 82; fax 27 33 91. Open M-F 9am-2pm and 5-7pm, Sa-Su 10am-2pm and 5-8pm.) Many accommodations cluster on **Avenida de Roma, Avenida Ordoño II,** and **Avenida República Argentina,** which lead into the old town from Pl. Glorieta Guzmán el Bueno. **Hostal Orejas,** C. Villafranca, 6, 2nd fl., is just down Av. República Argentina from Pl. Glorieta Guzmán el Bueno. Large windows illuminate each brand-new room, complete with bath, shower, and cable TV. Free **Internet** access. A little pricey, but well worth the stretch. (☎25 29 09. Singles 4500ptas/€27; doubles 5500ptas/€33.) Cheap eateries fill the area near the cathedral and the small streets off **Calle Ancha;** also check **Plaza San Martín,** near Pl. Mayor. **Postal Code:** 24004.

▶ DAYTRIP FROM LEON: ASTORGA. Today Astorga is most distinguished by its fanciful ▓**Palacio Episcopal,** whose turrets, main entryway, and beveled stone exterior are characteristic of Gaudí's style. The palace houses the fascinating **Museo de los Caminos,** dedicated to the various paths toward Santiago de Compostela that converge in 2000 year-old Astorga. (☎(987) 61 88 82. Open M-Sa 10am-1:30pm and 4-7:30pm, Su 10am-1:30pm. 500ptas/€3.) The **cathedral,** directly to the left when facing the palace, is definitely worth a quick visit. Its **museum** has 10 rooms filled with religious relics. (Cathedral and museum open daily 10am-2pm and 4-8pm. Cathedral free; museum 250ptas/€1.50.) Astorga is most easily reached by bus from León (45min.; M-F 16 per day 6:15am-9:30pm, Sa-Su 6-7 per day 8:30am-8:30pm; 430ptas/€2.60).

BURGOS   ☎947

During its 500 years as capital of Castile, Burgos (pop. 180,000) witnessed the birth of the extraordinary cathedral and Rodrigo Díaz de Vivar, better known as El Cid Campeador, Spain's greatest national hero. Nine centuries after El Cid's banishment, General Franco stationed his headquarters here. Today, from its duck-filled riverbanks to its elegant denizens sipping sangria in sidewalk cafes, Burgos emits an aura of vivacity and prosperity. Officially named a UNESCO world heritage sight and unofficially named the most beautiful cathedral in Spain, the ▓**Catedral Santa Iglesia** is deserving of its notoriety. Its magnificent spires tower over every view of the city, and its Gothic interior is equally remarkable. Devout visitors can enter the **Chapel of Christ,** the cathedral's holiest segment and its most infamous: the crucified Jesus is constructed of real human body parts. Other highlights include the beautiful 16th-century stained-glass dome of the Capilla Mayor; the eerily lifelike papamoscas (fly-catcher), and, under the transept and marked only by a small brick, the remains of El Cid and Dona Jimenez. (☎947 20 47 12. Open M-Sa 9:30am-1pm and 4-7pm, Su 9:30-11:45am and 4-7pm. Cathedral free. Museum 600ptas/€3.60, students 400ptas/€2.40. Recorded histories in English 100ptas/€0.60.) The 200 steps behind the museum lead to an astounding view of the red roofs of Burgos from the ruins of a medieval castle presiding over Burgos from high above the cathedral. The **Museo-Monasterio de las Huelgas Reales,** built by King Alfonso VIII in 1188, is slightly out of the way, but certainly worth the trip. Chambers, chapels, and cloisters adorned with rare Arabic tapestries and ornate mosaics shelter sepulchres of deceased royalty, including several heirs to the throne. Their burial wardrobes can be viewed in the **Museo de Telas** (Textile Museum). Take the "Barrio del Pilar" bus (80ptas/€0.50) from Pl. España to the Museo stop. (☎947 20 56 87. Open Apr.-Sept. Tu-F 11am-1:15pm and 4-5:15pm, Sa 11am-1:15pm and 4-5:45pm, Su 10:30am-2:15pm; Oct.-Mar. Tu-Sa 10:30am-1:15pm and 3:30-5:45pm, Su 10:30am-2:15pm. 800ptas/€4.80, students and under 14 400ptas/€2.40. W free. Obligatory tours in Spanish every 30min.; free.) By midnight, **Calle Avellanos** (opposite Pl. Alonso Martínez) is at full boil. Crowds bubble over into nearby **Calle Huerto del Rey,** then steam it up at *discotecas* along **Calle San Juan.** Dance to pulse-pumping music at **Twenty,** Pl. Huerto del Rey, 20. (Open M-Sa 7pm-5am, Su 7pm-midnight.)

Trains (☎947 20 35 60) go from the end of Av. Conde de Guadalhorce, across the river from the town center, to: Barcelona (9-13¾hr., 4 per day 2:17am-11:40pm, 5100ptas/€30.65); Bilbao (2½-4hr.; M-Sa 4-5 per day 3:17am-6:44pm, Su 3 per day 12:57-6:44pm; 2200ptas/€13.20); Lisbon (8-10hr., daily at 1:32pm, 5700ptas/€34.25); Madrid (3-5½hr.; M-F 10 per day 2:20am-11:07pm, Sa-Su 9 per day 2:20am-11:07pm; 3060-3500ptas/€18.40-21.05). Follow Av. Conde de Guadalhorce across the river and take the first right on Av. Generalísimo Franco, which turns into Po. Espolón, to reach the town center (10min.). **Buses** (☎947 28 88 55) leave C. Miranda, 4, off Pl. Vega south of the river, for: Barcelona (7½hr.; 11:45am, 3, and 11:59pm; 5110ptas/€30.70); Bilbao (2-3hr., M-F 4 per day 8:30am-7pm, 1445ptas/€8.70); León (3½hr., M-Sa 10:45am, 1725ptas/€10.37); Madrid (2¾hr., M-F 19 per day 7:30am-3:45am, 1975ptas/€12); Salamanca (4hr., M-Sa 10:45am, 1765ptas/€10.60); Santander (2¾hr., 4 per day 10:30am-3:15am, 1375ptas/€8.25). The **tourist office** is at Pl. Alonso Martínez, 7. (☎947 20 31 25. Open M-F 9am-2pm and 5-7pm, Sa-Su 10am-2pm and 5-8pm.) To get from Puerte de Santa Maria to the family-run **Pensión Peña,** C. Puebla, 18, 2nd. fl., turn right onto C. Vitoria, then left at Pl. del Cid. Cross Pl. de la Libertad to your right, and C. La Puebla will be directly in front of you. (☎947 20 63 23. Singles 1700ptas/€10.25; doubles 2900ptas/€17.45.) **Hostal Joma,** C. San Juan, 26, 2nd fl., has spotless rooms and low rates. (☎947 20 33 50. June-Sept. singles 1800ptas/€10.85; doubles 3200ptas/€19.25. Oct.-May 1600ptas/€9.60, 2700ptas/€16.25.) **Plaza Alonso Martínez** teems with restaurants, while **Calle San Lorenzo** is *tapas* heaven. **Mercado de Abastos (Sur),** on C. Miranda next to the bus station, sells fresh meat and bread. (Open M-Sa 7am-3pm.) **Postal Code:** 09070.

EXTREMADURA

The aptly named Extremadura is a land of harsh beauty and cruel extremes. These lands hardened New World *conquistadors* such as Hernán Cortés and Francisco Pizarro, but the traveler who braves the Extremaduran plains is rewarded with stunning ruins and intimate, peaceful towns. Compared to the hectic pace of nearby Madrid, life in Extremadura is slower and less modern, as if the region's rich history dominates its character in the present.

TRUJILLO ☎927

The gem of Extremadura, hill-perched Trujillo (pop. 10,000) is an unspoiled joy, often called the "Cradle of Conquistadors." Over 600 explorers and plunderers of the New World, including Peru's conqueror Francisco Pizarro and the Amazon's first explorer, Francisco de Orellana, hailed from here. Scattered with medieval

SPAIN

palaces, Roman ruins, Arabic fortresses, and churches of all eras, Trujillo is a glorious hodgepodge of histories and cultures. Its most impressive monument is its highest, the 10th-century **Moorish castle,** which commands a panoramic view of surrounding plains. The **Plaza Mayor** was the inspiration for the Plaza de Armas in Cuzco, Perú, which was constructed after Francisco Pizarro defeated the Incas. Festooned with stork nests, **Iglesia de San Martín** dominates the northeastern corner of the plaza. (All churches open June-Sept. daily 10am-2pm and 5-8:30pm; Oct.-May 9:30am-2pm and 4:30-7:30pm. 200ptas/€1.20 each or 700ptas/€4.20 for all.)

Buses run from Madrid (2½hr., 12-14 per day, 2100ptas/€12.60). To get to the **Plaza Mayor,** turn left as you exit the station (up C. de las Cruces), right on C. de la Encarnación, following signs to the tourist office, then left on C. Chica; turn left on C. Virgen de la Guia and right on C. Burgos, continuing into the plaza (15min.). The **tourist office** is across the plaza and posts info in its windows when closed. (☎927 32 26 77. Open June-Sept. 9:30am-2pm and 4:30-7:30pm; Oct.-May 9:30am-2pm and 4-8pm.) **Pensión Boni,** C. Mingo de Ramos, 117, is off Pl. Mayor to the right of the church. (☎927 32 16 04. Singles 2000ptas/€12; doubles 3500ptas/€21, with bath 5000ptas/€30.) The Plaza Mayor teems with tourist eateries. **Meson Alberca,** C. Victoria, 8, has a shaded interior garden and an excellent *menú* for 1850ptas/€11. (☎927 32 22 09. Open Su-Tu and Th-Sa 11am-1am.)

SOUTHERN SPAIN (ANDALUCÍA)

Andalucía derives its spirit from an intoxicating amalgam of cultures. Under Moorish rule, which lasted from AD 711 until 1492, Sevilla and Granada reached the pinnacle of Islamic arts, and Córdoba matured into the most culturally influential Islamic city. The Moors preserved, perfected, and blended Roman architectural techniques with their own, creating a style that became distinctively and uniquely Andalucian. Intriguing patios, garden oases with fountains and fish ponds, and alternating red brick and white stone were its hallmarks.

Andalucía has been bequeathed as the convergence point of popular images of Spanish culture, sent the world over by advertising campaigns. Bullfighting, flamenco, white-washed villages, sherry *bodegas*, sandy beaches, and the blazing sun are what the region offers tourists, but beyond those outstanding elements lie vivacious and warm-hearted residents who believe their most important job is the art of living well. Despite living in one of the poorest regions of Spain, Andalucians retain an unshakable faith in the good life. The never-ending *festivales*, *ferias*, and *carnavales* of Andalucía are world famous.

SEVILLA ☎954

The 16th-century maxim *"Qui non ha visto Sevilla non ha visto maravilla"* ("he who has not seen Sevilla has not seen a marvel") remains true five centuries later. Site of a small Roman acropolis founded by Julius Caesar, capital of the Moorish empire, and focal point of the Spanish Renaissance, this city has yet to disappoint its visitors. Flamenco, *tapas*, and bullfighting are at their best here, and the city's cathedral is among the most impressive in Spain. But it is the infectious, vivacious spirit of the city that really draws visitors. During Sevilla's yearly *Semana Santa* and *Feria de Abril*, two of the most extravagant festivals in Europe, Sevilla's jasmined balconies and exotic parks spring to life, with matadors, flamenco dancers, and virgins leading the town in endless revelry. The Sevilla of today is the charming guardian angel of traditional Andalucian culture, by far the best place to get a taste of "quintessential" southern Spain.

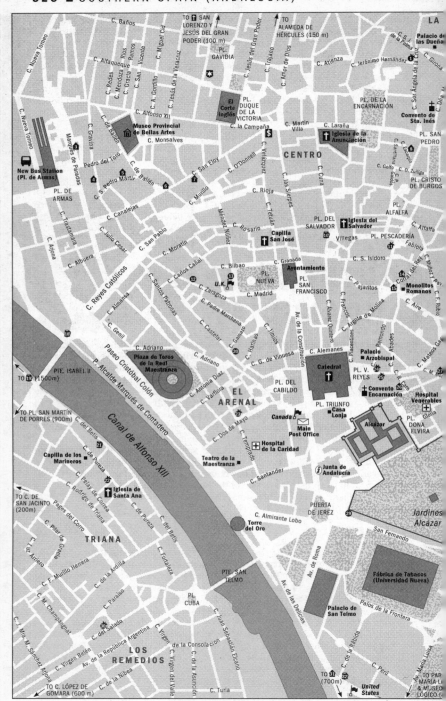

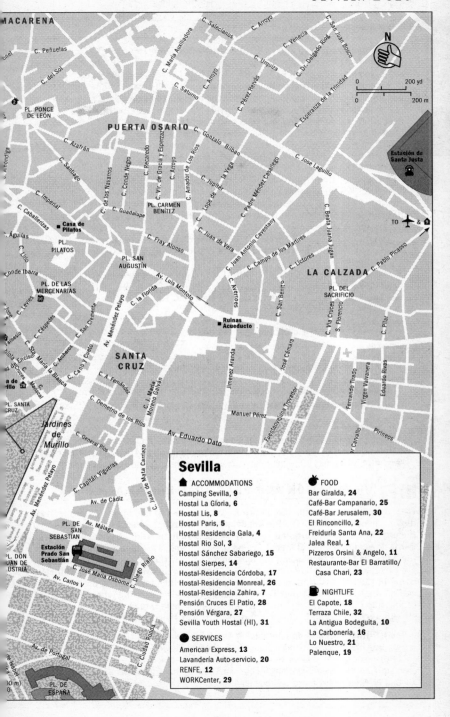

MACARENA

C. Peñuelas

PL. PONCE
DE LEÓN

PUERTA OSARIO

C. Azafrán

C. Santiago

C. Imperial

C. Caballerías

Casa de
Pilatos

PL.
PILATOS

Águilas

Conde Ibarra

PL. DE LAS
MERCENARIAS

SANTA
CRUZ

Jardines
de
Murillo

PL. SANTA
CRUZ

PL. DON
JUAN DE
USTRIA

C. del Sol

C. María Auxiliadora

C. Salocianos

C. Arroyo

C. Venecia

C. San Juan Bosco

C. Saturno

C. Urquiza

C. Dr. Delgado Ríos

C. Pérez Herás

C. Esperanza de la Trinidad

C. Recaredo

C. Conde Negro

C. Gonzalo Bilbao

C. Vir. de Gracia y Esperanza

C. de los Navarros

C. Arroyo

C. Amador de los Ríos

C. Jose Laguillo

Estación de
Santa Justa

C. Guadalupe

PL. CARMEN
BENÍTEZ

C. Lope de la Vega

C. Júpiter

C. Padre Méndez Casariego

TO ✈ & 🏤

C. Fray Alonso

C. Juan de Vera

C. Juan Antonio Cavestany

C. Campo de los Mártires

PL. SAN
AGUSTÍN

Av. Luis Montoto

C. la Florida

C. Averroes

C. San Benito

C. Llctores

LA CALZADA

PL. DEL
SACRIFICIO

C. Via Cruces

S. Florencio

C. Pablo Picasso

C. Beata Juana Juan

Ruinas
Acueducto

C. Menéndez Pelayo

C. San Clemente

C. Amberes

C. Cano y Cueto

C. J. María
Moreno Galván

Jiménez Aranda

José Cámara

Fernando Tirado

Virgen Valvanera

Eduardo Rivas

C. Pilar

C. Céspedes

C. A. Fernández

C. Demetrio de los Ríos

Manuel Pérez

Fuentedueña

Juana Trovador

C. Carvallo

Pirineos

C. General Ríos

Av. Eduardo Dato

C. Capitán Viguera

C. Juan de Mata Carriazo

Av. de Cádiz

Estación
Prado San
Sebastián

PL. DE
SAN
SEBASTIÁN

Av. de Málaga

C. José María Osborne

C. Diego Riaño

Av. Carlos V

C. Ciudad Ronda

Av. de Portugal

PL. DE
ESPAÑA

Sevilla

🏠 ACCOMMODATIONS
Camping Sevilla, **9**
Hostal La Gloria, **6**
Hostal Lis, **8**
Hostal Paris, **5**
Hostal Residencia Gala, **4**
Hostal Rio Sol, **3**
Hostal Sánchez Sabariego, **15**
Hostal Sierpes, **14**
Hostal-Residencia Córdoba, **17**
Hostal-Residencia Monreal, **26**
Hostal-Residencia Zahira, **7**
Pensión Cruces El Patio, **28**
Pensión Vérgara, **27**
Sevilla Youth Hostal (HI), **31**

● SERVICES
American Express, **13**
Lavandería Auto-servicio, **20**
RENFE, **12**
WORKCenter, **29**

🍴 FOOD
Bar Giralda, **24**
Café-Bar Campanario, **25**
Café-Bar Jerusalem, **30**
El Rinconcillo, **2**
Freiduría Santa Ana, **22**
Jalea Real, **1**
Pizzeros Orsini & Angelo, **11**
Restaurante-Bar El Barratillo/
  Casa Chari, **23**

🍷 NIGHTLIFE
El Capote, **18**
Terraza Chile, **32**
La Antigua Bodeguita, **10**
La Carbonería, **16**
Lo Nuestro, **21**
Palenque, **19**

0   200 yd
0   200 m

SPAIN

⌐ TRANSPORTATION

Flights: All flights depart and land at Aeropuerto San Pablo (☎44 90 00), 12km out of town on Ctra. Madrid. A taxi between the airport and the town costs about 2000ptas/ €12. Los Amarillos (☎98 91 84) runs a bus from outside the Hotel Alfonso XIII at the Pta. Jerez (M-F every 30-45min., Sa-Su every hr.; 6:15am-11pm; 350ptas/€2.10).

Trains: All train services are centralized in the modern **Estación Santa Justa** (☎41 41 11), on Av. Kansas City. Buses C1 and C2 link Santa Justa and the Prado de San Sebastián bus station. They stop on Av. Kansas City, to the left as you exit the train station. In town, the **RENFE** office, C. Zaragoza, 29 (☎54 02 02), is near Pl. Nueva. Open M-F 9am-1:15pm and 4-7pm. **AVE** trains run to: **Córdoba** (45min., 17 per day 6:30am-9pm, 2400-2800ptas/€14.40-16.80) and **Madrid** (2½hr., 20 per day 6:30am-9pm, 8400-9900ptas/€50.40-59.40). **Talgo** trains run to: **Barcelona** (12hr.; M-F 8am, 9am, and 9:30pm; 8500ptas/€51); **Cádiz** (2hr., 12 per day 6:35am-9:30pm, 1450ptas/€8.70); **Granada** (3hr., 5 per day 7am-6pm, 2660ptas/€15.60); **Valencia** (8½hr., 4 per day 8:11am-9:50pm, 5600ptas/€33.60).

Buses: The old bus station at Prado de San Sebastián (☎41 71 11), C. Manuel Vazquez Sagastizabal, mainly serves Andalucía:

Transportes Alsina Graells (☎41 88 11). To: **Córdoba** (2hr., 10-13 per day 8am-9pm, 1350ptas/ €8.10); **Granada** (3hr., 9 per day 8am-11pm, 2500ptas/€15); **Málaga** (2½hr., 10-12 per day 7am-midnight, 2100ptas/€12.60).

Transportes Comes (☎41 68 58). To: **Cádiz** (1½hr., 12 per day 7am-8:45pm, 1445ptas/€8.67); **Jerez de la Frontera** (2hr., 6 per day 11:30am-8:30pm, 935ptas/€5.61).

Los Amarillos (☎98 91 84). To: **Arcos de la Frontera** (2hr., 8am and 4:30pm, 980ptas/€5.88); **Marbella** (3hr., 1-2 per day 8am-8pm, 1050ptas/€6.30).

Enatcar-Bacoma (☎(902) 42 22 42). To: **Barcelona** (16hr., 4:30pm, 10,200ptas/€61.20); **Valencia** (10hr., 9am and 4:30pm, 6700ptas/€40.20).

Plaza de Armas (☎90 77 37), the newer bus station on the river bank at the Puente del Cachorro, serves destinations beyond Andalucía, including Portugal and other European countries (open daily 5:30am-1:30am). Buses C1, C2, C3, and C4 stop nearby.

Socibus (☎90 11 60). To: **Lagos** (6hr., 1 daily Jan.-May Th-Su, June-Oct. Tu-Su; 7:30am or 4:30pm; from 2460ptas/€14.76); **Madrid** (6hr., 15 per day 1pm-midnight, 2745ptas/€16.47).

Public Transportation: TUSSAM (☎(900) 71 01 71), the city bus network, is extensive and useful. Most lines run every 10min. (6am-11:15pm) and converge on Pl. Nueva, Pl. Encarnación, or in front of the cathedral on Av. Constitución. Limited night service departs from Pl. Nueva (every hr., midnight-2am). Fare 125ptas/€0.75, *bonobús* (10 rides) 650ptas/€3.90. Particularly useful are buses C3 and C4, which circle the center, and #34, which hits the youth hostel, university, cathedral, and Pl. Nueva.

✳🛈 ORIENTATION AND PRACTICAL INFORMATION

Over the centuries, Sevilla has incorporated a number of neighboring villages, now distinct neighborhoods. The **Río Guadalquivir** flows roughly north to south through the city. Most of the touristed areas of Sevilla, including the alleyways of the old **Barrio de Santa Cruz** and **El Arenal**, are on the east bank. The historic **Barrio de Triana**, the **Barrio de Santa Cecilia**, and the **fairgrounds** occupy the west bank. The **cathedral**, next to Barrio de Santa Cruz, is Sevilla's centerpiece. **Avenida de la Constitución**, home of the regional tourist office, runs alongside the cathedral. **El Centro**, a busy commercial pedestrian zone, lies north of the cathedral, starting where Av. Constitución hits **Plaza Nueva**, site of the Ayuntamiento. **Calle Tetuan**, a popular shopping street, takes off from Pl. Nueva and runs northward through El Centro.

Tourist Offices: Centro de Información de Sevilla, Av. Constitución, 21B (☎22 14 04; fax 954 22 97 53), 1 block from the cathedral. Regional and city maps and info. English spoken. Always swamped, but most crowded before and after siesta. Open M-F 9am-7pm, Sa 10am-2pm and 3-7pm, Su 10am-2pm. **Info booths** in Est. Santa Justa and Pl. Nueva carry maps and bus guides.

Currency Exchange: Banco Central Hispano, C. Sierpes, 55 (☎56 26 84). Open M-F 8:30am-2:30pm, Sa 8:30am-1pm.

American Express: Pl. Nueva, 7 (☎21 16 17). Changes cash and traveler's checks without commission, holds mail, and offers emergency services for cardholders. Open M-F 9:30am-1:30pm and 4:30-7:30pm, Sa 10am-1pm.

Luggage Storage: At Pr. San Sebastián bus station (250ptas/€1.50 per day; open 6:30am-10pm), Pl. Armas bus station (300ptas/€1.80 per day), and Santa Justa train station (300-500ptas/€1.80-3 per day).

Gay and Lesbian Services: COLEGA (Colectiva de Lesbianas y Gays de Andalucía), Cuesta del Rosario, 8 (☎18 65 10). Open M-F 10am-2pm.

Laundromat: Lavandería Auto-servicio, C. Castelar, 2 (☎954 21 05 35). From the cathedral, walk 2 blocks down C. Vinuesa and turn left. Wash and dry (1hr.) 1000ptas/ €9. Open M-F 9:30am-1:30pm and 3-8:30pm, Sa-Su 9am-2pm.

Emergency: ☎112. **Police,** Po. Delicias, 15 (☎61 54 50).

24hr. Pharmacy: Check list posted at any pharmacy for those open 24hr.

Medical Assistance: Ambulatorio Esperanza Macarena (☎42 01 05). Hospital Universitario Virgen Macarena (☎24 81 81), Av. Dr. Fedriani. English spoken.

Internet Access: WORKcenter, C. San Fernando, 1 (☎954 21 20 74), at the Puerta de Jerez. 100ptas/€0.60 for 10min. Also has **fax** services. Open 24hr.

Post Office: Av. Constitución, 32 (☎954 21 64 76), opposite the cathedral. Lista de Correos and fax. Open M-F 10am-8:30pm, Sa 9:30am-2pm. **Postal Code:** 41080.

▚ ACCOMMODATIONS

During *Semana Santa* and *Feria de Abril*, rooms vanish and prices soar. Make reservations months ahead. At other times, call a few days before arriving. The tourist office has lists of *casas particulares* that open on special occasions.

BARRIO DE SANTA CRUZ AND EL ARENAL

The narrow streets east of the cathedral around **Calle Santa María la Blanca** are full of cheap hostels with virtually identical rooms. The neighborhood is overwhelmingly touristed, but its disorienting streets and shaded plazas are all within a few minutes walk of the cathedral, the Alcázar, and El Centro.

▨ **Pensión Vergara,** C. Ximénez de Enciso, 11, 2nd fl. (☎21 56 68), at C. Mesón del Moro. Steep wooden stairs lead past a giftshop to this newly renovated medieval home. Up to 4 people in each room. All rooms have fans. 24hr. reception. Towels provided on request. 2500ptas/€15 per person.

▨ **Hostal-Residencia Monreal,** C. Rodrigo Caro, 8 (☎21 41 66). From the cathedral, walk up C. Mateos Gago and take the 1st right. Enterprising owner has opened a bustling restaurant on the ground level. Air-conditioned rooms, many with verandas overlooking a nearby plaza. Singles 3000ptas/€18; doubles 6000ptas/€36, with bath 8000ptas/ €48; triples 11,000-12,000ptas/€66-72. MC/V.

Hostal Sierpes, C. Corral del Rey, 22 (☎22 49 48; fax 21 21 07), on the continuation of C. Argote de Molina. Lavender and Andalucian tile adorn the elegant lobby. Parking 2500ptas/€15. Singles 4500-9000ptas/€27-54; doubles 6000-11,000ptas/€36-66; triples 7500-15,000ptas/€45-90; quads 9000-19,000ptas/€54-114. MC/V.

Hostal Sánchez Sabariego, C. Corral del Rey, 23 (☎21 44 70). Hostal Sierpes's less flashy neighbor. Family-run with spacious rooms and an elk-head-lined courtyard. A/C upstairs, fans in all other rooms. Singles 4000ptas/€24; doubles with bath 8000-10,000ptas/€48-60; triples with bath 9000-11,000ptas/€54-66.

Pensión Cruces El Patio, C. Cruces, 10 (☎22 96 33 or 22 60 41). The cheapest place to crash in Santa Cruz. Laundry 1500ptas/€9. Singles 2000ptas/€12; doubles 5000ptas/€30, with bath 6000ptas/€36.

Hostal-Residencia Córdoba, C. Farnesio, 12 (☎22 74 98), off C. Fabiola. Air-conditioned rooms are immaculate and spacious. Singles with shower 5000ptas/€30; doubles 6500ptas/€39, with shower 7500ptas/€45.

EL CENTRO

El Centro, a mess of narrow streets radiating from **Plaza Encarnación**, is a bustling shopping district during the day but at night most streets are deserted.

▨ **Hostal Lis,** C. Escarpín, 10 (☎954 21 30 88; hostal_lis@terra.es), on an alley near Pl. Encarnación. Each room decorated with a unique pattern of blue and yellow Sevillian tiles. Glistening bathrooms. All rooms have fans. Singles 3000ptas/€18; doubles 6000ptas/€36, with bath 7000ptas/€42; triples with bath 9000ptas/€54.

Hostal La Gloria, C. San Eloy, 58, 2nd fl. (☎954 22 26 73), at the end of a lively shopping street. Singles 2500ptas/€15; doubles 4000ptas/€24, with bath 4500ptas/€27; triples 6000ptas/€36.

Hostal-Residencia Zahira, C. San Eloy, 43 (☎954 22 10 61; fax 954 21 30 48). Hotel-sized lobby disguises simple rooms beyond. All rooms have bath and A/C. Lounge with TV. Singles 3500-5000ptas/€21-30; doubles 6000-8000ptas/€36-48. AmEx/MC/V.

NEAR ESTACIÓN PLAZA DE ARMAS

Most hostels around the Pl. de Armas bus station center around **Calle Gravina**, parallel to C. Marqués de las Paradas and two blocks from the station. These are the most convenient to El Centro and the lively C. Betis on the west bank of the river.

▨ **Hostal Río Sol,** C. Márquez de Parada, 25 (☎954 22 90 38). Extremely convenient location 1 block from Plaza de Armas bus station. Small rooms with newly renovated bathrooms and blustery A/C. Singles with sink 2000ptas/€12, with bath 3000-4000ptas/€18-24; doubles with bath 6500ptas/€39; triples with bath 9000ptas/€54. MC/V.

Hostal Paris, C. San Pedro Mártir, 14 (☎954 22 98 61 or 954 21 96 45; fax 954 21 96 45), off C. Gravina. All rooms have baths, A/C, phones, and TVs. Singles 5500ptas/€33; doubles 7500ptas/€45; triples 10,500ptas/€63. AmEx/MC/V.

Hostal Residencia Gala, C. Gravina, 52 (☎954 21 45 03). Clean rooms with framed prints and spacious bathrooms. Singles 3000ptas/€18, with bath 4500ptas/€27; doubles 6500ptas/€39, with bath 7000ptas/€42; triples with bath 8500ptas/€51.

ELSEWHERE AND CAMPING

Sevilla Youth Hostel (HI), C. Isaac Peral, 2 (☎954 61 31 50; fax 954 61 31 58). Take bus #34 across from the tourist office near the Cathedral; the stop is behind the hostel, just after Po. Delicias. Many residents are middle-aged and Spanish. Up to 4 per room. A/C. Many private baths. Breakfast included. Dorms 2050ptas/€12.30, over 26 2675ptas/€16.05. Nonmembers can pay an additional 500ptas/€3 per night for 6 nights to become members.

Camping Sevilla, Ctra. Madrid-Cádiz, km 534 (☎954 51 43 79), near the airport. From Pr. San Sebastián, take bus #70 (stops 800m away at Parque Alcosa). Hot showers, supermarket, and pool. 475ptas/€2.85 per person, per car, and per tent; children 375ptas/€2.25.

◖ FOOD

Sevilla is a city of *tapas*; locals prepare and devour them with a vengeance. Other favorites include *caracoles* (snails), *cocido andaluz* (a thick soup of chick peas), *pisto* (tomato and egg-plant hash), *espinacas con garbanzos* (spinach with chickpeas), and all manner of fresh seafood. Defying the need for hydration, many locals only imbibe Sevilla's Cruzcampo beer, a light, smooth pilsner. **Mercado del Arenal**, near the bullring on C. Pastor y Leandro, between C. Almansa and C. Arenal, has fresh meat and produce. (Open M-Sa 9am-2pm.) For a supermarket, try **%Día**, C. San Juan de Ávila, near El Corte Inglés. (Open M-F 9:30am-2pm and 6:30-9pm, Sa 9am-1pm.)

BARRIO DE SANTA CRUZ AND EL ARENAL

Restaurants near the cathedral cater almost exclusively to tourists. Beware the unexceptional, omnipresent *menús* featuring *gazpacho* and *paella* for 1000ptas/€6. Food and prices improve in the backstreet establishments between the cathedral and the river in **El Arenal**, and along sidestreets in the **Barrio Santa Cruz**.

▧ **Restaurante-Bar El Baratillo/Casa Chari,** C. Pavía, 12, on a tiny street off C. Dos de Mayo. A local favorite. Call or ask at least 1hr. in advance for the tour-de-force: homemade *paella* with a jar of wine, beer, or *sangría* (2500ptas/€15 for 2). *Menú* 650ptas/€3.90. Open M-F 9am-11pm, Sa noon-5pm.

Café-Bar Campanario, C. Mateos Gago, 8, ½ block from the cathedral. Mixes the best (and strongest) jugs of *sangría* around (1200-1500ptas/€7.20-9). *Tapas* 275-350ptas/€1.65-2.10, *raciones* 650-1000ptas/€3.90-6. Open daily noon-midnight.

Bar Giralda, C. Mateos Gago, 1 (☎954 22 74 35). Situated within a former Turkish bath, the stuffed mushroom *tapas* (275ptas/€1.65) and "V.I.P" potatoes (300ptas/€1.80) are something special. Open daily until midnight.

EL CENTRO

Inexpensive *tapas* restaurants lurk along streets radiating out from **Plaza Alfalfa.**

▧ **Pizzeros Orsini & Angelo,** C. Luchana, 2 (☎954 21 61 64), 2 blocks from Pl. del Salvador. Crisp pizza served straight from the oven. Romantic outdoor seating in front of a Baroque church. Pizzas 400-950ptas/€2.40-5.70. Open daily 1-4pm and 8pm-1am.

Jalea Real, Sor Ángela de la Cruz, 37 (☎954 21 61 03). From Pl. Encarnación, walk 150m on C. Laraña then turn left at Iglesia de San Pedro. Fabulous vegetarian cuisine. *Menú* 1400ptas/€8.40. Open Sept.-July M-F 1:30-5pm and 8:30-11:30pm, Sa 8:30-11:30pm.

El Rinconcillo, C. Gerona, 40 or C. Alhóndiga, 2 (☎954 22 31 83), behind the Church of Santa Catalina. Founded in 1670, when Spain's empire stretched from the Philippines to America, this bodega continues to attract loyal patrons. *Raciones* 225-1850ptas/€1.35-11.10. Open M-Tu and Th-Su 1pm-2am. MC/V.

TRIANA AND BARRIO DE SANTA CECILIA

This old maritime neighborhood, on the far side of the river, was once a separate village. Avoid overpriced C. Betis and plunge down less expensive sidestreets, where fresh seafood and *caracoles* abound. *Tapas* bars cluster around **Plaza San Martín** and along **Calle San Jacinto.**

Café-Bar Jerusalem, C. Salado, 6, at C. Virgen de las Huertas. Chicken, lamb, or pork-and-cheese *shwarmas* called a *bocadillo hebreo*—it's not kosher, but it sure is tasty (500-700ptas/€3-4.20). Open daily 8pm-3am.

Freiduría Santa Ana, C. Pureza, 61 (☎954 33 20 40), parallel to C. Betis, 1 block from the river. A local institution, combination fish market and restaurant. Seafood served by the kg. Open Sept.-July Tu-Su 7pm-midnight.

⊙ SIGHTS

Sevilla is brimming with sights, from the Alcázar and cathedral to the churches, monuments, and winding streets of the *casco viejo* and Barrio de Santa Cruz.

▧ **CATHEDRAL.** With 44 individual chapels, the cathedral is the third largest in the world, after St. Peter's Basilica in Rome and St. Paul's Cathedral in London, and is the world's biggest Gothic edifice ever constructed. Not surprisingly, it took more than a century to build. In 1401, Christians destroyed a 12th-century Almohad mosque to clear space and all that remains of the former mosque is the **Patio de Los Naranjos** and the famed minaret **La Giralda,** built in 1198. The tower and its twins in Marrakesh and Rabat, Morocco, are the oldest and largest surviving Almohad minarets. The 35 ramps inside lead to the top of the tower and offer amazing city views.

In the center of the cathedral, the **Capilla Real** and its altar stand opposite the dark wooden **choir stalls** made of mahogany recycled from a 19th-century Austrian railway. The **retablo mayor** (altarpiece), one of the largest in the world, is a golden wall of intricately wrought saints and disciples. Circle the choir to see the **Sepulcro de Cristóbal Colón** (Columbus's tomb). There is mystery surrounding the actual whereabouts of Columbus's remains, since he has four alleged resting places throughout the world. The **Sacristía Mayor** holds works by Ribera and Murillo and a

SPAIN

glittering Corpus Christi icon, La Custodia Processional. In the corner of the cathedral are the architecturally stunning **Sala de Las Columnas** and **cabildo**. (☎ 21 49 71. *Open M-Sa 10am-5pm, Su 2-7pm. Tickets sold until 1hr. before closing. 800ptas/€4.80, seniors and students 200ptas/€1.20, under 12 free. Su free. Mass held in the Capilla Real M-F 8:30, 9, 10am; Sa 8:30, 10am, and 8pm; Su 8:30, 10, 11am, noon, 1pm.*)

■ **ALCÁZAR.** If you can't make it to the Alhambra in Granada, at least come to Sevilla's Alcázar; the Moorish architecture and gardens are nothing short of magnificent. Visitors enter through the **Patio de la Montería**, directly across from which stands the intricate Almohad façade of the Moorish palace. Through the archway lies the **Patio del Yeso** and the exquisitely carved **Patio de las Muñecas** (Patio of the Dolls), named so because of its miniature proportions. Court life revolved around the **Patio de las Doncellas** (Maids' Court), encircled by archways adorned with glistening tilework. The astonishing golden-domed **Salón de los Embajadores** is allegedly the site where Fernando and Isabel welcomed Columbus back from America. Nearby, the **Corte de las Muñecas** contains the palace's private quarters, decorated with the building's most exquisite carvings. Verdant and peaceful gardens stretch from the residential quarters in all directions. (*Pl. Triunfo, 7.* ☎ 50 23 23. *Open Tu-Sa 9:30am-7pm, Su 9:30am-6pm. 700ptas/€4.20; students, seniors, and under 16 free. Audio guides 400ptas/€2.40.*)

■ **MUSEO PROVINCIAL DE BELLAS ARTES.** This museum contains Spain's finest collection of works by painters of the Sevilla school, notably Murillo, Valdés Leal, and Zurbarán, as well as El Greco and Dutch master Jan Breugel. The building itself is a work of art—take time to sit in its shady gardens. (*Pl. Museo, 9, off C. Alfonso XII.* ☎ 22 07 90. *Open Tu 3-8pm, W-Sa 9am-8pm, Su 9am-2:30pm. 250ptas/€1.50.*)

BARRIO DE SANTA CRUZ. King Fernando III forced Jews fleeing Toledo to live in the Barrio de Santa Cruz, now a neighborhood of winding alleys, wrought-iron gates, and fountained courtyards. Beyond C. Lope de Rueda, off C. Ximénez de Enciso, is the charming and fragrant Plaza de Santa Cruz. South of the plaza are the **Jardines de Murillo**, a shady expanse of shrubbery and benches. The **Convento de San José** in Pl. Santa Cruz houses the grave of the artist Murillo, who died in what is now known as the **Casa Murillo** after falling from a scaffold. The **Iglesia de Santa María la Blanca** was built in 1391 on the foundation of a synagogue and features Murillo's *Last Supper*. (*Church open M-Sa 10-11am and 6:30-8pm, Su 9:30am-2pm and 6:30-8pm.*)

SIERPES AND THE ARISTOCRATIC QUARTER. Originating from Pl. Duque de Victoria, **Calle de Sierpes**, a bustling commercial street, cuts through the Aristocratic Quarter. A plaque marks the spot where the royal prison once loomed—scholars believe Cervantes began writing *Don Quixote* there. The 15th-century **Casa de Pilatos** is a typical Andalucian palace with a mix of medieval and Renaissance elements, including several courtyards. (*Casa open daily 9am-7pm. 1000ptas/€6.*)

EL ARENAL AND PASEO ALCALDE MARQUÉS DE CONTADERO. The inviting riverside esplanade Po. Marqués de Contadero stretches along the banks of the Guadalquivir and El Arenal, once a stretch of sand by the harbor that was later exposed when the river was diverted to its present course. The tiled boardwalk leads to the **Plaza de Toros de la Real Maestranza**, a veritable temple of bullfighting. Home to one of the two great bullfighting schools (the other is in Ronda), the plaza fills to capacity for the 13 *corridas* of the *Feria de Abril* as well as weekly fights. The museum inside houses costumes, paintings, and antique posters. (*Open on non-bullfight days 9:30am-2pm and 3-7pm, on bullfight days 9:30am-3pm. Tours every 30min.; 500ptas/€3.*)

LA MACARENA. This quarter, northwest of El Centro, is named not for the popular mid-90s dance, but rather for the virgin of Sevilla. It is traversed by the *ruta de los conventos* (route of convents). The founder of **Convento de Santa Inés,** as legend has it, was pursued so insistently by King Pedro the Cruel that she disfigured her face with boiling oil so he would leave her alone. Cooking liquids are used more positively today—the cloistered nuns sell patented puff pastries and coffee cakes through the courtyard's revolving window (C. María Coronel). A stretch of **murallas**

SPAIN

(fortress walls), created in the 12th century, runs between the Pta. Macarena and Pta. Córdoba on the Ronda de Capuchinos road. At the west end of the walls, the **Basílica Macarena** houses the venerated image of *La virgen de la macarena*, which is hauled around town during Semana Santa processions. A treasury glitters with the virgin's jewels and other finery. *(Basilica open daily 9:30am-1pm and 5-9pm. Free. Treasury open daily 9:30am-1pm and 5-8pm. 400ptas/€2.40.)* Toward the river is **Iglesia de San Lorenzo y Jesús del Gran Poder,** with Montañés's remarkably lifelike sculpture *El cristo del gran poder.* Worshipers kiss Jesus's ankle through an opening in the bulletproof glass for luck. Semana Santa culminates in a procession honoring his statue. *(Open Sa-Th 8am-1:45pm and 6-9pm, F 7:30-10pm. Free.)*

OTHER SIGHTS. Lovely tropical gardens and innumerable courtyards abound in the monstrous ⚑**Parque de María Luisa,** southeast of the city center. *(Open daily 8am-10pm.)* The neighboring **Plaza de Espana** boasts tiled murals. **Triana,** west of the cathedral and across the river, was Sevilla's chaotic 16th- and 17th-century mariners' quarters. North of Triana, visit the **Museo de Arte Contemporáneo.** *(Open Tu-Sa 10am-8pm, Su 10am-3pm. 300ptas/€1.80. Guided tours at 11am, noon, 5, and 6pm.)*

🎵📷 ENTERTAINMENT AND NIGHTLIFE

Sevilla's reputation for gaiety is tried and true. Popular bars can be found around **C. Mateos Gago** near the cathedral, **Calle Adriano** by the bullring, and **Calle Betis** across the river in Triana. Sevilla is also famous for its **botellón,** in which crowds of students converge in plazas or at bars along the river to start the night. In the winter, the most popular place to botellón is at Pl. Alfalfa in El Centro; in the summer, the crowds sweep towards the river in hopes of a breeze—even on "slow" nights, *terrazas* will stay open until 4am. The tourist office and stores distribute *El Giraldillo*, a free monthly magazine with complete listings on music, art exhibits, theater, dance, fairs, and film.

🔲**Terraza Chile,** Paseo de las Delicias, at the intersection of Av. Uruguay and Av. Chile. Salsa and Spanish pop keep this breezy dance club packed and pounding through the early morning hours. *Botellón* pervades in the surrounding streets. Beer 300-400ptas/€1.80-2.40. Mixed drinks 700ptas/€4.20. Open summer M-Sa 9pm-6am.

🔲**Capote Bar,** next to Pte. Isabel II, in El Centro. A hugely popular outdoor bar with live music during the summer. Open nightly 11pm-3am.

🔲**Palenque,** Av. Blas Pascal, on the grounds of Cartuja '93. From Puente de la Barqueta, follow C. Materatico Rey, turn left and walk toward the spaceship on the horizon. Once a stadium-sized auditorium, now the largest dance club in Sevilla. Mainly *Sevillano* university crowd. Beer 400ptas/€2.40. Mixed drinks 700ptas/€4.20. Cover 1000ptas/€6. Open summer Th-Sa 11pm-7am.

La Carbonería, C. Levies, 18 (☎954 21 44 60), off C. Santa María La Blanca, in Santa Cruz. Live flamenco in an intimate, cave-like space. Includes a huge outdoor patio and bar (also with live music). Beer 200-275ptas/€1.20-1.65. Flamenco nightly at 10:30pm. Open M-Sa 8pm-3:30am, Su 8pm-2:30am.

La Antigua Bodeguita, Pl. del Salvador, 6 (☎954 56 18 33), in El Centro. The crowds just can't be contained at any hour of the day in this tiny bustling bodega. Beer 125ptas/€0.75. Tapas 200ptas/€1.20. Open daily 12:30-4pm and 8pm-midnight.

Lo Nuestro, C. Betis, 31A, in Triana. A local hangout in an area plagued by touristy bars. Images of bulls and matadors plaster the chic rust-colored walls. Mixed drinks 300-900ptas/€1.80-5.40. Open daily 10pm-dawn.

BULLFIGHTS AND FESTIVALS

If you're going to see a bullfight somewhere in Spain, Sevilla is probably the best place to do it; the bullring here is generally considered to be the most beautiful in the country. The cheapest place to buy bullfight tickets is at the ring on Po. Marqués de Contadero. However, when there's a good *cartel* (line-up), the booths on C. Sierpes, C. Velázquez, and Pl. Toros might be the only source of advance tickets

(tickets 3000-13,000ptas/€18-78). Sevilla's world-famous **Semana Santa** lasts from Palm Sunday to Good Friday. In each neighborhood of Sevilla, thousands of penitents in hooded cassocks guide floats, called *tronos*, lit by hundreds of candles through the streets each day. Two or three weeks after *Semana Santa*, the city rewards itself for its Lenten piety with the **Feria de Abril**. A spectacular array of flowers and lanterns decorates over 1000 kiosks, tents, and pavilions, collectively called *casetas*. Each has the elements necessary for a rollicking time: small kitchen, bar, and dance floor. Locals stroll from one to the next, sharing drinks and good food amid the lively music and dance.

DAYTRIPS FROM SEVILLA

CÁDIZ

RENFE trains (☎956 25 43 01) arrive at Pl. Sevilla, off Av. Puerto, from Córdoba (AVE 2¾hr., 12:15am and 6pm, 3700ptas/€22; regular 3-4hr., 5 per day 6am-8pm, 2370-3700ptas/€14-22) and Sevilla (2hr., 12 per day 6:35am-9:30pm, 1450ptas/€8.70). Transportes Generales Comes buses (☎956 22 78 11) arrive at Pl. Hispanidad, 1, from Sevilla (1½hr., 12 per day 7am-8:45pm, 1445ptas/€8.67).

Founded by the Phoenicians in 1100 BC, Cádiz (pop. 155,000) is considered the oldest inhabited city in Europe. **Carnaval** is perhaps Spain's most dazzling party (Feb. 7-17 in 2002), but year-round the city offers golden sand **beaches** that put its pebble-strewn eastern neighbors to shame. **Playa de la Caleta** is the most convenient, but better sand awaits in the new city; take bus #1 from Pl. España (120ptas/€0.72) and get off at Pl. Glorieta Ingeniero (in front of Hotel Victoria) to roast at the squeaky clean ■**Playa Victoria.** Back in town, the gold-domed, 18th-century **cathedral** is considered the last great cathedral built by colonial riches. From Pl. San Juan de Dios, follow C. Pelota. (Museum open Tu-F 10am-12:45pm and 4:30-6:45pm, Sa 10am-12:45pm. 500ptas/€3, children 200ptas/€1.20. Cathedral open M-F 5:30-8pm. Free.) From the train station, walk two blocks past the fountain, with the port on your right, and look left for **Plaza San Juan de Dios** (the old town center). From the bus station, walk 5min. down Av. Puerto with the port on your left and Pl. de San Juan de Dios will be after the park on your right, with the **tourist office** at #11. (☎956 24 10 01. Open M-F 9am-1pm and 5-8pm.) Most *hostales* huddle around the harbor, in Pl. San Juan de Dios, and just behind it on C. Marqués de Cádiz. **Quo Qádis,** C. Diego Arias, 1, one block from Pl. Falla, offers flamenco classes, planned excursions, and vegetarian dinners. (☎/fax 956 22 19 39. Dorms 1000ptas/€6; singles 2100ptas/€12.60; doubles 4000ptas/€24.)

JEREZ DE LA FRONTERA

Buses (☎956 34 52 07) come from Arcos (30min., 7 per day 7:20am-7:15pm, 200ptas/€1.20); Cádiz (1hr., 7-18 per day, 380ptas/€2.28); Sevilla (2hr., 6 per day 11:30am-8:30pm, 935ptas/€5.61).

Jerez de la Frontera (pop. 200,000) is the cradle of three staples of Andalucían culture: flamenco, Carthusian horses, and, of course, *jerez* (sherry). Most *bodegas* (wine cellars) offer tours in English, but many are closed in August. Founded in 1730, ■**Domecq** is the oldest and largest *bodega* in town. Tours include an informative 15min. video followed by a stroll through some of the many warehouses and gardens that comprise the sprawling complex. With unlimited sampling from three sherries (including Harveys Cream) and two brandies, Domecq's wine tasting is by far the most generous and varied in Jerez. Celebrity visitors include Franco and Alexander Fleming. (☎956 15 15 00. English tours M-F 10am-1pm, 500ptas/€3; Sa noon, 750ptas/€4.70.) The **tourist office,** Edif. Scritium, C. Paul is near Bodegas Sandeman and the Real Escuela del Arte Ecuestre. (☎956 33 11 50. Open June-Aug. M-F 9am-7pm, Sa-Su 10am-2pm and 5-7pm; Sept.-May M-F 8am-3pm and 4-7pm, Sa-Su 10am-2pm and 5-7pm.) Take bus L8 from the bus station or bus L1 from Pl. Arenal (10min.) to reach the **Albergue Juvenil (HI),** Av. Carrero Blanco, 30. (☎956 14 39 01. Dorms 2375ptas/€14.25, under 27 1725ptas/€10.35.)

ARCOS DE LA FRONTERA

Buses (☎ 956 70 20 15), C. Corregidores, come from Cádiz (1½hr., 6 per day 7am-6pm, 710ptas/€4.27); Jerez (30min., 8-17 per day 7:15am-8:15pm, 330ptas/€2); Sevilla (2hr.; 8am and 4:30pm; 980ptas/€5.88). Transportes Generales Comes (☎ 956 70 20 15) go from Arcos to Jerez (15min., 8-18 per day 6:30am-7:15pm, 300ptas/€1.80) and Sevilla (2hr., 7am and 5pm, 905ptas/€5.43).

With Roman ruins and castles at every turn, historical Arcos (pop. 33,000), is the premier *pueblo blanco* (white village) on *la ruta de los pueblos blancos.* Wander the winding white alleys, ruins, and hanging flowers of the **old quarter,** and marvel at the stunning view from **Plaza Cabildo.** In the square is the **Iglesia de Santa María,** a mix of Baroque, Renaissance, and Gothic styles. To reach the old quarter from the bus station, exit left, turn left, and continue 20min. uphill on C. Muñoz Vásquez as it changes names. One block to the right is the **tourist office,** on Pl. Cabildo. (☎956 70 22 64. Open June-Aug. M-Sa 10am-3pm and 4-8:30pm, Su 10:30am-3pm; Sept.-May M-F 9am-2pm and 5-7pm, Sa 10am-2pm and 5-6:30pm.) **Hostal San Marcos,** C. Marqués de Torresoto, 6, past C. Dean Espinosa and Pl. Cabildo is run by a friendly young family and crowned by a scenic rooftop terrace. (☎ 956 70 07 21. Singles 2500-3000ptas/€15-18; doubles 4000-5000ptas/€24-30.)

RONDA

Buses (☎952 18 70 61) come from Sevilla (2½hr., 3-5 per day 7am-5pm, 1395ptas/€8.40) and go from Pl. Concepción García Redondo, 2, near Av. Andalucía, to Málaga (2½hr., 5 per day 6:30am-7:30pm, 1275ptas/€7.65); Marbella (1½hr., 5 per day 6:30am-8:30pm, 670ptas/€4); Sevilla (2½hr., 5 per day 7am-7pm, 1395ptas/€8.40).

Most people's strongest impression of Ronda (pop. 38,000), the birthplace of bull fighting, is the stomach-churning ascent to get there. Divided in two by a 100m gorge, Ronda was called Arunda ("surrounded by mountains") by Pliny, Ptolemy, and friends, German poet Rainer Maria Rilke wrote his *Spanish Elegies* here, Orson Welles had his ashes buried on a bull farm outside of town, and Hemingway loved the bullfights. A precipitous gorge, carved by the Río Guadalevín, dips below the **Puente Nuevo,** opposite Pl. España. Bullfighting aficionados charge over to Ronda's **Plaza de Toros,** Spain's oldest bullring (est. 1785) and cradle of the modern *corrida.* For a less conventional experience, visit the **Museo del Bandolero,** C. Armiñán, 59, dedicated to presenting "pillage, theft, and rebellion, in Spain since Roman times." (☎ 952 87 77 85. Open daily summer 10am-9pm; winter 10am-6pm. 400ptas/€2.40.) To reach the town center from the **train station,** turn right on Av. Andalucía and follow it through Pl. Merced past the **bus station** (it becomes C. San José) until it ends. Take a left on C. Jerez, and follow it past the park and Pl. Toros, to **Plaza de España** and the new bridge. The **tourist office** is at Pl. España, 1. (☎95 287 12 72. Open M-F 9am-2pm and 4-7pm, Sa-Su 10am-3pm.) The **Hostal Ronda Sol** is at C. Almendra, 11. (☎952 87 44 97. Singles 1700ptas/€10.20; doubles 2800ptas/€16.80.)

CÓRDOBA ☎957

"Sevilla is a young girl, gay, laughing, provoking—but Córdoba...Córdoba is a dear old lady." Nowhere else are the remnants of Spain's Islamic, Jewish, and Catholic heritages so visibly intermixed as in Córdoba (pop. 315,000). This Andalucian historical and cultural mélange has left Córdoba a unique artistic and architectural legacy. The famous mosque testifies to Córdoba's political and intellectual reemergence under Islamic rule (711-1263) and the influence of the Jewish philosopher Maimonides, who spearheaded the return to centrality that helped make Córdoba the seat of the Western caliphate. Córdoba, though a small city, is not overwhelmed by its incredible history. Springtime festivals, flower-filled patios, and a steady nightlife make it one of Spain's most beloved cities. Both delicate and wise, Córdoba may be a "a dear old lady," but she is far from tired.

⬛ TRANSPORTATION

Trains: Plaza de las Tres Culturas, Av. América. (☎957 40 02 02). To: **Barcelona** (10-11hr., 3 per day 9:45am-10:20pm, 6100-8400ptas/€36.60-50.40); **Cádiz** (2¾hr., 2 per day, 3700ptas; regular 3-4hr., 5 per day, 2370-3700ptas/€14.25-22.20); **Málaga** (AVE 2¼hr., 5 per day, 2000-2200ptas/€12-13.20; regular 3hr., 9 per day 6:40am-10.10pm, 1650-3000ptas/€9.90-18); **Madrid** (AVE 2hr., 18 per day 7:15am-10:45pm, 5100-6100ptas/€30.6-36.60; regular 2-6hr., 14 per day 2am-11:15pm, 3700-6000ptas/€22.20-36); **Sevilla** (AVE 45min., 18 per day 8:40am-11:40pm, 2300ptas/€13.80). For international tickets, contact **RENFE**, Ronda de los Tejares, 10 (☎957 49 02 02).

Buses: Estacion de Autobuses, Glorieta de las Tres Culturas, (☎957 40 40 40), across from the train station.

Alsina Graells Sur (☎957 27 81 00) covers most of Andalucía. To: **Algeciras** (5hr., 2 per day 2805ptas/€16.85); **Cádiz** via Los Amarillos or Comes Sur (4-5hr., 1 per day 7am, 2120ptas/€12.75); **Granada** (3hr., 8-11 per day 5:20am-8:30pm, 1605-1710ptas/€9.65-10.30); **Málaga** (3-3½hr., 5 per day 8am-7pm, 1630ptas/€9.80); **Marbella** (4hr., 8am and 3:15pm, 2310ptas/€13.88); **Sevilla** (2hr., 10-13 per day 7am-10pm, 1330ptas/€8).

Bacoma (☎957 45 65 14) to: Baeza, Ubeda, Valencia, and **Barcelona** (10hr., 6:25pm, 8475ptas/€51).

Secorbus (☎902 22 92 92) provides exceptionally cheap service to **Madrid** (4½hr., 7 per day 1pm-8pm, 1675ptas/€10.10), departing from Camino de los Sastres in front of Hotel Melia.

Eurobus (☎902 11 96 99) to: **Bilbao** (10¼hr., 3 per day 12:10am-12:45pm, 4875ptas/€29.30); **San Sebastián** (12hr., 3 per day 12:10am-12:45pm, 5560ptas/€33.45); **Sevilla** (2hr., 3 per day).

Intra-provincial buses depart from Av. República and Po. Victoria: **Autocares Priego** (☎957 40 44 79) runs anywhere in the Sierra Cordobesa; **Empresa Carrera** (☎957 40 44 14) functions in the Campiña Cordobesa; **Empresa Rafael Ramírez** (☎957 42 21 77) runs buses to nearby towns and camping sites.

Public Transportation: There are 12 bus lines (☎957 25 57 00) that run through the modern parts of the city and neighborhoods in the outskirts. Most buses run from the early morning until 11pm. Check the tourist office for a listing of urban routes and routes to the outskirts of town. **Bus #3** makes a loop from the bus and train stations through Pl. Tendillas, along the river, and up C. Doctor Fleming. **Bus #10** will take you from the train station to Barrio Brillante (125ptas/€0.75).

Taxis: Radio Taxi (☎957 76 44 44) has stands at most busy intersections. From the Judería to the bus and train stations about 500ptas; to Barrio Brillante 600ptas/€3.60.

Car Rental: Hertz (☎957 40 20 60), in the train station. Minimum age 25. From 9200ptas/€55.30 per day. Open M-F 8:30am-9pm, Sa 9am-1pm and 3:30-7pm, Su 9am-1pm.

⬛ ⬛ ORIENTATION AND PRACTICAL INFORMATION

Córdoba is split into two parts: the **old city** and the **new city.** The modern and commercial northern half extends from the train station on **Avenida América** down to **Plaza de las Tendillas,** the center of the city. The old section in the south is a medieval maze known as the **Judería** (Jewish quarter). The easiest way to reach the old city from the train station and the bus station (which are right next to each other) is to take city bus #3 to **Campo Santo de los Mártires** (125ptas/€0.75.) Alternatively, the walk is about 20min. From the train station, with your back to the platforms, exit left, cross the parking plaza and make a right onto Av. de los Mozarabes. When you reach the Roman columns, turn left and cross Gta. Sargentos Provisionales. Make a right on Paseo de la Victoria and continue until you reach Puerto Almodovar and the old city.

Tourist Offices: Oficina Municipal de Turismo y Congresos (☎957 20 05 22; fax 957 20 02 77), Pl. Judá Leví, next to the youth hostel. Has maps and many free brochures about festivals and events in the Córdoba region. Open M-F 8:30am-2:30pm. **Tourist**

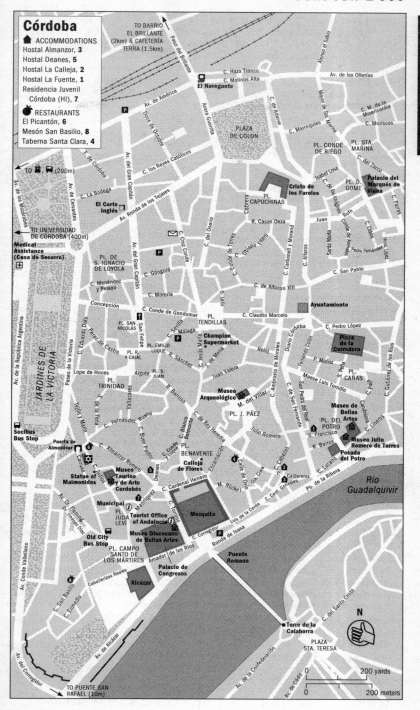

Córdoba

ACCOMMODATIONS
Hostal Almanzor, **3**
Hostal Deanes, **5**
Hostal La Calleja, **2**
Hostal La Fuente, **1**
Residencia Juvenil
  Córdoba (HI), **7**

RESTAURANTS
El Picantón, **6**
Mesón San Basilio, **8**
Taberna Santa Clara, **4**

SPAIN

Office of Andalucía, C. Torrijos, 10 (☎957 47 12 35; fax 957 49 17 78), in the Junta de Andalucía, across from the Mezquita. From the train station, take bus #3 (bus stops on Av. América between the train and bus stations) along the river until the stone arch is on the right. Office is 1 block up C. Torrijos. Open May-Sept. M-F 9:30am-8pm, Sa 10am-7pm, Su 10am-2pm; Oct.-Apr. M-Sa 9:30am-6pm, Su 10am-2pm.

Currency Exchange: Banco Central Hispano (☎957 47 42 67), Pl. Tendillas, charges no commission. Open June-Aug. M-F 8:30am-2:30pm; Sept.-May M-F 8:30am-2:30pm, Sa 9am-1pm. Banks and **ATMs** dot Pl. Tendillas.

Emergency: ☎092. **Police** (☎957 47 75 00), Av. Medina Azahara.

Medical Assistance: Red Cross Hospital (☎957 42 06 66; emergency ☎957 22 22 22), Po. Victoria. English spoken. **Ambulance** (☎29 55 70).

24-Hour Pharmacy: On a rotating basis. Refer to the list posted outside the pharmacy in Pl. Tendillas or to the local newspaper.

Internet Access: El Burladero Café Internet, C. Llanos del Pretorio, 1 (☎957 49 75 36), at the intersection of Av. América and Paso del Brillante. Bar with a nautical theme. 300ptas/€1.80 per 30min. Open daily 8am-4pm and 5pm-3am.

Post Office: C. Cruz Conde, 15 (☎902 19 71 97), 2 blocks up from Pl. Tendillas. Lista de Correos. Open M-F 8:30am-8:30pm, Sa 9:30am-2pm. **Postal Code:** 14070.

▐ ACCOMMODATIONS

Hostels in Córdoba are quite impressive: charming, well-maintained, and affordable. Córdoba is especially crowded during *la Semana Santa* (the week before Easter) and from May through September; you may have to call two to three months in advance for reservations. The **Judería**'s whitewashed walls, narrow, twisting streets, and proximity to major sights make it the nicest and most convenient area in which to stay. Take bus #3 from the train station to Campo Santo de los Mártires and walk up C. Manríques to reach the heart of the neighborhood. However, the quieter, more residential area of **old Córdoba,** between the Mezquita and C. de San Fernando, is still near the sights but a step away from the tourists. Buses stop along C. de San Fernando, the main corridor of the area.

▧ **Residencia Juvenil Córdoba (HI)** (☎957 29 01 66; fax 957 29 05 00), Pl. Juda Leví, next to the municipal tourist office and a 2min. walk from the Mezquita. A backpacker's utopia. Cheap and convenient, this is one of the best budget accommodations in Córdoba. Large, sterile rooms, either doubles or quads, all with bath. **Internet** service (100ptas/€0.60 for 15min.). Reservations recommended. Breakfast included. Towels 175ptas/€1.05. 24hr. reception. 2050ptas/€12.30 per person; ages 26 and up 2675ptas/€16.

▧ **Hostal La Fuente,** C. San Fernando, 51 (☎957 48 78 27 or 957 48 14 78; fax 957 48 78 27), between C. San Francisco and C. Julio Romero. Relax amidst the tiled splendor of La Fuente's traditional Andalucian courtyard. All rooms with bath, some with TV. Half of the building has A/C (at no extra charge). Singles 4000ptas/€24; doubles 6500ptas/€39; 1800ptas/€10.85 per person for large groups.

Hostal La Calleja, Calleja de Rufino Blanco y Sánchez, 6 (☎/fax 957 48 66 06), at the intersection of C. Calereros and C. Cardenal Gonzalez. A maze-like interior of glistening walls lined with Andalucian crafts leads to spacious rooms, many with private bathrooms and patio. All rooms have TVs and A/C. 24hr. reception. Singles 2800ptas/€16.85; doubles 4200ptas/€25.20, with bath 4800ptas/€28.85.

Hostal Deanes, C. Deanes, 6 (☎957 29 37 44). From the top left corner of the Mezquita take C. Cardenal, then a sharp right onto C. Romero which becomes C. Deanes. Situated in a 16th-century home with an elegant *cordobés* patio, this surprisingly intimate *hostal* has only 5 rooms and requires reservations 1-2 months in advance. Cavernous baths. 24hr. reception. Doubles 5000ptas/€30; triples 6500ptas/€39; quads 8000ptas/€48.

Hostal Almanzor, C. Cardenal González, 10 (☎/fax 957 48 54 00), 3 blocks from the Mezquita at the end of C. Rey Heredía closest to the river. Ambiance for a good price. All singles have king-sized beds. 24hr. reception. Spotless rooms with balconies and TVs. Parking included. Singles 1500-2000ptas/€9-12; doubles with bath 3000-5000ptas/€18-30.

Camping Municipal, Av. Brillante, 50 (☎957 28 21 65). From the train station, turn left on Av. América, left on Av. Brillante, and walk uphill for about 20min. Or, take bus #10 or 11 from Av. Cervantes near the station. Pool, currency exchange, supermarket, restaurant, free hot showers, laundry service. Camping equipment for rent. Wheelchair accessible. Individual tents 400ptas/€2.40, family tents 560ptas/€2.15.

FOOD

The Mezquita area attracts nearly as many high-priced eateries as tourists to eat in them, but a 5min. walk in any direction yields local specialties at reasonable prices. In the evenings, locals converge at the outdoor *terrazas* between **Calle Severo Ochoa** and **Calle Dr. Jimenez Diaz** for drinks and tapas before dinner. Cheap eateries cluster farther away from the Judería in **Barrio Cruz Conde,** around **Avenida Menéndez Pidal** and **Plaza Tendillas.** Regional specialties include *salmorejo* (a gazpacho-like cream soup topped with hard-boiled eggs and pieces of ham) and *rabo de toro* (bull's tail simmered in tomato sauce). **Supermarket Champion,** C. Jesús María, lies half a block from Pl. Tendillas. (Open M-Sa 9:15am-9:15pm.)

Taberna Santa Clara, C. Osio, 2 (☎957 47 50 36). From the right side of the Mezquita, take C. Martinez Rucker and turn left. Women of Córdoba stop by in the early evening to have a glass of their very own white wine, La Peresosa. 2 pages of vegetarian dishes and fresh fish on Friday. *Menú* 1300ptas/€7.80, main dishes 800-1800ptas/€4.80-10.80, salads 650ptas/€3.90. Open Th-Tu noon-4pm and 7-11pm.

Mesón San Basilio, C. San Basilio, 19 (☎957 29 70 07), to the left of the Alcázar, past Campo Santo de los Martires. The locals love it, and so will you. *Menú del día* 1000ptas/€6, *raciones* 450-2000ptas/€2.70-12, meat and fish dishes 800-1750ptas/€4.80-10.50. Open daily 1-4pm and 8pm-midnight.

El Picantón, C. F. Ruano, 19, 1 block from the Puerta de Almodovar. From the top right corner of the Mezquita, walk up Romero and turn left. Take ordinary tapas, pour on some *salsa picante*, stick it in a roll, and, voilà, you've got lunch (150-300ptas/€0.90-1.80). Nothing else is as cheap or as filling. Open daily 10am-3pm and 8pm-midnight.

SIGHTS

█ LA MEZQUITA

☎957 47 05 12. Open Apr.-June daily 10am-7:30pm; July-Oct. 10am-7pm; Nov.-Mar. 10am-6pm. 1000ptas/€6, ages 8-13 500ptas/€3. Same ticket valid for Museo Diocesano de Bellas Artes. Last ticket sold 30min. before closing. Open M-Sa 8:30am for 9:30am Mass; Su Mass 11am, noon, and 1pm.

Built in 784 on the site of a Visigoth basilica, this architectural masterpiece is considered the most important Islamic monument in the Western world. Carved from granite and marble, the 850 pillars within the Mezquita are capped by brick-and-stone arches of different heights, creating a sense of height and spaciousness.

Visitors enter through the **Patio de los Naranjos,** an arcaded courtyard featuring carefully spaced orange trees and fountains, where the dutiful would wash before prayer. The **Torre del Alminar** encloses remains of the original minaret. Added in the 10th century, the dazzling **mihrab** (prayer niche) once housed a gilt copy of the Koran; worn stones mark where pilgrims knelt in reverence. Estimated at close to 35 tons, the intricate gold, pink, and blue marble Byzantine mosaics shimmering across the arches were given by Emperor Constantine VII to the *cordobés* caliphs.

In 1523, Bishop Alonso Manrique, an ally of Carlos V, proposed the construction of a cathedral in the center of the mosque. The town rallied violently against the idea, promising painful death to any worker who helped tear down the Mezquita. Nevertheless, a towering **crucero** (transept) and **coro** (choir stalls), were eventually erected, incongruously planting a richly adorned baroque cathedral amidst far more austere environs. The townspeople were less than pleased, and even Carlos V regretted the changes to the Mezquita, lamenting, "You have destroyed something unique to create something commonplace." What remains, though, is far from commonplace.

IN AND AROUND THE JUDERÍA

A combined ticket for the Alcázar, Museo Taurino y de Arte Cordobés, and Museo Julio Romero, is available at all 3 locations. 1075ptas/€6.45, students 550ptas/€3.30. Individually, admission to each sight costs 450ptas/€2.70. F free.

ALCÁZAR. Along the river on the left side of the Mezquita lies the Alcázar. Built in 1328 during the *Reconquista*, the building was both a fortress and a residence for Alfonso XI. Fernando and Isabel bade Columbus farewell here, and from 1490 to 1821 it served as a headquarters for the Inquisition. Its walls enclose a magnificent garden with terraced flower beds, fish ponds, and fountains. Inside, the museum displays first-century Roman mosaics and a third-century Roman marble sarcophagus. (☎957 42 01 51. Open May-Sept. Tu-Sa 10am-2pm and 6-8pm, Su 9:30am-3pm; Oct.-Apr. Tu-Sa 10am-2pm and 4:30-6:30pm, Su 9:30am-3pm. Illuminated gardens open July-Aug. 8pm-midnight. Admission 300ptas/€1.80, students 150ptas/€0.90. F free.)

MUSEO TAURINO Y DE ARTE CORDOBÉS. Dedicated to the history and lore of the bullfight. Pay homage to a replica of the tomb of Manolete, Spain's most famous matador, and the hide of the bull that killed him. (Pl. Maimonides. ☎957 20 10 56. Open May-Sept. Tu-Sa 10am-2pm and 6-8pm, Su 9:30am-3pm; Oct.-Apr. M-Sa 10am-2pm and 5-7pm, Su 9:30am-3pm. 450ptas/€2.70, students 225ptas/€1.35, seniors free. F free.)

MUSEO DIOCESANO DE BELLAS ARTES. See where Córdoba's bishops lived as the Inquisition raged from within the Alcázar. This 17th-century ecclesiastical palace houses a modest collection of Renaissance and Baroque religious art. (C. Torrijos, across from the Mezquita in the Palacio de Congresos. ☎957 47 93 75. Open June-Sept. M-F 9:30am-3pm, Sa 9:30am-1:30pm; Oct.-Mar. M-F 9:30am-1:30pm and 3:30-5:30pm, Sa 9:30am-1:30pm. 150ptas/€0.90, under 12 free. Free with admission to Mezquita.)

OUTSIDE THE JUDERÍA

MUSEO JULIO ROMERO DE TORRES. Spice up your life with a visit to an exhibit of Romero's sensual portraits of Cordoban women, located in the artist's former home. Only the Andalucian sun gets any hotter than this. (Pl. Potro, 5-10min. from the Mezquita. ☎957 49 19 09. Open May-Sept. Tu-Sa 10am-2pm and 5:30-7:30pm, Su 9:30am-2:30pm; Oct.-Apr. Tu-Sa 10am-2pm and 5-7pm, Su 9:30am-2:30pm. Last entrance 30min. before closing. 450ptas/€2.70, students 225ptas/€1.35, seniors free.

PALACIO DEL MARQUÉS DE VIANA. This elegant 14th-century palace displays 12 quintessential Córdoban patios complete with sprawling gardens and majestic fountains, as well as tapestries, furniture, and porcelain. (Pl. Don Gome, 2. A 20min. walk from the Mezquita. ☎957 48 01 34. Open mid-June to Sept. M-Sa 9am-2pm; Oct.-May M-Sa 10am-1pm and 4-6pm; closed June 1-15. Patio 200ptas/€1.20. Guided tours every hr. 500ptas/€3, children 200ptas/€1.20.)

OTHER SIGHTS. Near the Palacio del Marqués de Viana, in Pl. Capuchinos (a.k.a. Pl. Dolores) and next to the monastery is the **Cristo de los Faroles** (Christ of the Lanterns). This is one of the most famous religious icons in Spain and is the site of frequent all-night vigils. The eight lanterns that are lit at night symbolize the eight provinces of Andalucía. Facing the Museo de Bellas Artes and the Museo Julio Romero de Torres is the **Posada del Potro**, a 14th-century inn mentioned in *Don Quixote*. Across the river from the Mezquita stands the **Torre de la Calahorra**, a Muslim military tower that was built in 1369 to protect the Roman bridge. It now houses a museum that covers Córdoba's cultures during the Middle Ages.

♪ 🎭 ENTERTAINMENT AND NIGHTLIFE

From the first weekend of June until the heat subsides, the cool **Barrio Brillante**, uphill from Av. América, is the place to be at night. Throngs of well-dressed, young *Cordobesa* walk the streets, hopping from one packed outdoor bar to another until reaching a dance club. Bus #10 goes to Brillante from the train station until about 11pm; a taxi should cost 500-900ptas/€3-5.70. If you're walking, head up Av. Brillante passing along the way **El Rocio, Pub BSO,** and **El Navegante** at C. Llanos de Pretorio. Once in Barrio Brillante, where C. Poeta Emilia Prados meets C. Poeta Juan Ramon Jimenez, go through **Cafeteria Terra** to discover a massive open-air patio where the backs of nearly 10 bars (**Havana, Canaveral,** and **El Puerto,** to name a few) converge. Proceed down Av. Brillante toward the city center, passing the popular nightclub **El Cachao,** as well as **Pub La Mondoa, Club Pon Luis, Club Kachomba,** and **Bar Chicote.** During the cooler months of winter, the nightlife centers around the pubs surrounding the **Universidad de Córdoba,** mostly on C. Antonio Maura and C. Camino de los Sastres. From there, the masses move to the bars lining Av. Gran Capitan, Av. Ronda de los Tejares, and C. Cruz Conde. Pick up a free copy of *La Guía de Ocio*, a monthly guide to cultural events and nightlife, at the tourist office.

The month of May is a never-ending party, beginning with the **Concurso de los Cruces** in the first week. Organizations sponsor the decoration of crosses that go up for display around the city. During the **Festival de los Patios,** beginning the first weekend in May and lasting for two weeks, Córdoba is transformed into a lush garden, when more than 150 private patios are open to the public. The last week in May brings the riotous week-long **Feria de Nuestra Señora de la Salud** (commonly known as *La Feria*), for which thousands of Córdoban women don colorful, traditional apparel while bullfights are held daily. The **Concurso Nacional de Arte Flamenco** (National Flamenco Contest) is held every third year during May.

▶ DAYTRIPS FROM CÓRDOBA

MADINAT AL-ZAHRA

Reaching Madinat Al-Zahra takes some effort if you don't go with an organized tour. The O-1 bus leaves from Av. República Argentina in Córdoba for Cruce Medina Azahara; from there you can walk 45min. to the palace. (☎957 25 57 00; 10min. past every hr., 125ptas/€0.75.) On the way back, the bus stop is along the highway at the cross, on the opposite side of the street from the gas station. A complete tour of the ruins takes 20-45min. depending on your level of interest. (☎957 32 91 30. Open May-Sept. Tu-Sa 10am-2pm and 6-8:30pm, Su 10am-2pm; Oct.-Apr. Tu-Sa 10am-2pm and 4-6:30pm, Su 10am-2pm. 250ptas/€1.50, EU citizens free.)

Built in the mountains by Abd al-Rahman III for his favorite wife, Azahara, this 10th-century medina was considered one of the greatest palaces of its time. The site, long thought to be mythical, was discovered in the mid-19th century and excavated in the early 20th century, and today is one of Spain's most impressive archaeological finds. The Medina Azahara is divided into three terraces: one for the nobility, another for servants, and a third for an enclosed garden and almond grove. After moving from Granada, Azahara missed the Sierra Nevada. To appease her, Abderramán planted the white-blossoming almond groves as a substitute for her beloved snow. The Salón de Abd al-Rahman III, also known as the *salón rico*, on the lower terraces, is being restored to its original intricate beauty.

OTHER DAYTRIPS FROM CÓRDOBA

CÁDIZ. This city offers a little of everything to its visitors—a metropolis trimmed by golden sand beaches (see p. 836).

MÁLAGA. Known more for its bars than its untouched sands, Málaga has the requisite beachtown monuments and a welcoming modern atmosphere (see p. 850).

GIBRALTAR

Gibraltar's phone code is 9567 from Spain, 350 from Britain, and 350 from the US. For **BT Direct** dial 84 00; **USA Direct,** 88 00.

Emerging from the morning mist, the Rock of Gibraltar towers like a primordial sentinel over those who approach its shores. Bastion of empire, Jerusalem of Anglophilia, this rocky peninsula is among history's most contested plots of land. Ancient seafarers called the Rock of Gibraltar one of the Pillars of Hercules, believing that it marked the end of the world. After numerous squabbles between Moors, Spaniards, and Turks, the English successfully stormed Gibraltar in 1704 and have remained ever since. About halfway up the Rock is the infamous **Apes' Den,** where a colony of barbary monkeys cavorts on the sides of rocks, the tops of taxis, and tourists' heads. At the northern tip of the Rock, facing Spain, are the **Great Siege Tunnels.** Originally used to fend off a combined Franco-Spanish siege at the end of the American Revolution, the tunnels were later expanded during World War II to span 52.8km underground. The eerie chambers of **St. Michael's Cave,** located ½km opposite the siege tunnels, were cut into the rock by thousands of years of water erosion. (*Cable car every 10min. M-Su 9:30am-5:15pm. Combined admittance ticket, including one-way cable car ride £6/€9.80, children £5/€8.15.*)

Buses arrive in the bordering Spanish town of **La Línea** from Algeciras (45min., every 30min. 7am-9:30pm, 245ptas/€1.50); Cádiz (3hr., 4 per day 8am-8:30pm, 1565ptas/€9.40); Granada (4½hr., 8am and 3pm, 2580ptas/€15.50). From the bus station, walk directly toward the Rock; the border is 5min. away. After bypassing the line of motorists, Spanish customs, and Gibraltar's passport control, catch bus #9 or 10 or walk across the airport tarmac and along the highway into town (20min.). Stay left on Av. Winston Churchill when the road forks with Corral Lane. Gibraltar's **Main Street,** a commercial strip lined with most services, begins at the far end of the square, past the Burger King on the left. The **tourist office,** in Duke of Kent House, Cathedral Sq., is across the park from the Gibraltar Museum. (☎450 00; fax 749 43. Open M-F 9am-5:30pm.) **Emile Youth Hostel Gibraltar,** Montague Boston, off Line Wall Rd., across from the square at the beginning of Main St., offers bunkbeds but clean communal bathrooms. (☎511 06. Breakfast included. Lockout 10:30am-4:30pm. Dorms £12/€19.60; singles £15/€24.45; doubles £26/€42.40.) There's a **Safeway** supermarket in the Europort complex. (Open daily 8am-8pm.)

✠ FERRIES TO MOROCCO

Ferries hop the Straits of Gibraltar from **Gibraltar** and **Algeciras.** Spanish-based **Trasmediterránea** (☎+34 902 45 46 45, www.trasmediterranea.es/homei.htm) runs ferries on a shuttle schedule from Algeciras (☎+34 956 65 62 44, Recinto del Puerto) to Cueta (☎+34 956 50 94 11; Muelle Cañonero Dato, 6) and Tangier. Trasmediterránea is represented in Tangier by **Limadet** (☎212 39/93 50 76; 3, Rue IBN Rochd., Tangier). Algeciras to Tangier (2½hrs., every hr. 8am-10pm, 5000ptas/€30.05).

ALGECIRAS

Algeciras has some pleasant older areas, but most tourists see only the dingy port, which offers easy access to Gibraltar and Morocco. RENFE **trains** (☎(902) 24 02 02) run from Ctra. Cádiz, way down C. Juan de la Cierva, to: Granada (4hr., 3 per day 7am-4:25pm, 2465-2715ptas/€14.80-16.30) and Ronda (1½hr., 4 per day 7am-6:25pm, 1020ptas/€6.15). Empresa Portillo **buses** (☎956 65 10 55) leave from Av. Virgen del Carmen 15 for Córdoba (6hr., 3-4 per day 8am-3:15pm, 3030ptas/€18.20); Granada (5hr., 4 per day 10:30am-5pm, 2655ptas/€16); Málaga (1¾-3hr., 8-9 per day 8am-8pm, 1450ptas/€8.70); Marbella (1hr., 8-9 per day 8am-9pm, 805ptas/€4.90). Transportes Generales Comes (☎956 65 34 56) goes from C. San Bernardo 1 to Cádiz (2½hr., 10 per day 7am-10:30pm, 1315ptas/€8); La Línea leaves for Gibraltar (45min., every 30min. 7am-9:30pm, 245ptas/€1.50); Madrid (8hr., 5 per day 8:10-

SPAIN

9:45pm, 3530ptas/€21.20); Sevilla (4hr., 4 per day 7:30am-4:45pm, 2195ptas/€13.20).
To get to the **ferries** from the bus and train stations, follow C. San Bernardo to C.
Juan de la Cierva and turn left at the end of the street; the port entrance will be on
your right. Buy tickets at the travel agency in town or at the port. In summer to:
Ceuta (35min.; 18 per day 6:30am-10pm; 3400ptas/€20.40; under 12 1700ptas/
€10.20, car 9800ptas/€58.80, motorcycle 3175ptas/€19.05) and **Tangier** (2½hr., 12
per day 6am-10pm; 3740ptas/€22.45, under 12 1870ptas/€11.25; car 11,540ptas/
€69.25, motorcycle 3560ptas/€21.40; at Trasmediterránea, adult fare 2992ptas/
€18 with Eurail pass.) Service is limited in winter and is not offered during bad
weather. The **tourist office**, is on C. Juan de la Cierva. (☎956 57 26 36. Open M-F
9am-2pm.) Hostels cluster around **Calle José Santacana,** parallel to Av. Marina one
block inland. To get to **Hostal Rif,** C. Rafael de Muro 11, follow C. Santacana into the
market square, bear left around the kiosk, and continue one block up C. Rafael del
Muro. (☎956 65 49 53. Singles 1300ptas/€7.80; doubles 2600-2800ptas/€15.60-
16.80.)

GRANADA   ☎958

When in 1492, Moorish ruler Boabdil fled Granada, the last Muslim stronghold in
Spain, his mother berated him for casting a longing look back at the Alhambra,
saying, "You do well to weep as a woman for what you could not defend as a man."
A spectacular palace celebrated by poets and artists throughout the ages, the
Alhambra continues to inspire melancholy in those who depart from its timeless
beauty. Although Christians torched all the mosques and much of the lower city,
embers of Granada's Arab essence still linger. The Albaicín, an enchanting maze of
Moorish houses and twisting alleys, is Spain's best-preserved Arab quarter and the
only part of the Muslim city to survive the *Reconquista*.

▐ TRANSPORTATION

Flights: Airport (☎958 24 52 37), 17km west of the city. A **Salidas** bus (☎958 13 13
   09) runs from Gran Vía, in front of the cathedral (M-Sa 5 per day, Su 2 per day;
   425ptas/€2.55). A **Taxi** to the airport costs 2000ptas/€12.

Trains: RENFE Station (☎(902) 24 02 02), Av. Andaluces. To: **Algeciras** (5-7hr., 3 per
   day 7:15am-5:50pm, 2715ptas/€16.30); **Madrid** (5-6hr., 7:55am and 4:40pm,
   4300-5300ptas/€25.80-31.80); **Sevilla** (4-5hr., 4 per day 8:18am-8:15pm,
   2715ptas/€16.30).

Buses: Station on Ctra. Madrid, near C. Arzobispo Pedro de Castro. **Alsina Graells**
   (☎958 18 54 80) runs to: **Córdoba** (3hr., 10 per day 7:30am-8pm, 1605ptas/€9.65);
   Málaga (2hr., 16 per day 7am-9pm, 1255ptas/€7.55); **Sevilla** (3hr., 9 per day 8am-
   3am, 2480ptas/€14.90). **La Línea** runs to **Algeciras** (5hr., 6 per day 9am-8pm,
   2705ptas/€16.25) and **Madrid** (5hr., 14 per day 7am-1:30am, 2075ptas/€12.45).
   Bacoma (☎958 15 75 57) goes to: **Alicante** (6hr., 5 per day, 3510ptas/€21.10);
   Barcelona (14hr., 3 per day, 8300ptas/€49.80); **Valencia** (8hr., 4 per day,
   5145ptas/€30.90).

Public Transportation: Take bus #10 from the bus station to the youth hostel, C. de
   Ronda, C. Recogidas, or C. Acera de Darro; or bus #3 from the bus station to Av. Constitución, Gran Vía, or Pl. Isabel la Católica. "Bus Alhambra" leaves from Pl. Nueva. All
   buses 130ptas/€0.80, bonobus (10 tickets) 1000ptas/€6. Free map at tourist office.

Car Rental: Atasa, Pl. Cuchilleros, 1 (☎958 22 40 04; fax 958 22 77 95). Cheapest car
   46,000ptas/€276 per week with unlimited mileage and insurance. Prices rise with
   shorter rentals. Must be at least 20 and have had a license for at least 1 year.

▐ ORIENTATION AND PRACTICAL INFORMATION

The geographic center of Granada is the small **Plaza de Isabel la Católica,** the intersection of the city's two main arteries, **Calle de los Reyes Católicos** and **Gran Vía de
Colón.** To reach Gran Vía and the **cathedral** from the train station, walk three blocks

up Av. Andaluces to take bus #3-6, 9, or 11 from Av. Constitución; from the bus station, take bus #3. Two short blocks uphill on C. Reyes Católicos sits **Plaza Nueva.** Downhill on C. Reyes Católicos lies Pl. Carmen, site of the **Ayuntamiento** and **Puerta Real.** The **Alhambra** commands the steep hill up from Pl. Nueva.

Tourist Office: Oficina Provincial, Pl. Mariana Pineda, 10 (☎958 24 71 28; www.dipgra.es). From Pta. Real, turn right onto C. Angel Ganivet, then take a right 2 blocks later to reach the plaza. Open M-F 9:30am-7pm, Sa 10am-2pm.

American Express: C. Reyes Católicos, 31 (☎958 22 45 12), between Pl. Isabel la Católica and Pta. Real. Exchanges money, cashes checks, and holds mail for members. Open M-F 9am-1:30pm and 2-9pm, Sa 10am-2pm and 3-7pm.

Luggage Storage: At the **train** and **bus stations.** 400ptas/€2.40. Open daily 4-9pm.

Laundromat: C. La Paz, 19. From Pl. Trinidad, take C. Alhóndiga, turn right on C. La Paz, and walk 2 blocks. Wash 500ptas/€3, dry 150ptas/€0.90 for 15min. Open M-F 9:30am-2pm and 4:30-8:30pm, Sa 9am-2pm.

Emergency: ☎112. **Police,** C. Duquesa, 21 (☎958 24 81 00). English spoken.

Pharmacy: Farmacia Gran Vía, Gran Vía, 6 (☎958 22 29 90). Open M-F 9:30am-2pm and 5-8:30pm.

Medical Assistance: Clínica de San Cecilio, C. Dr. Oloriz, 16 (☎958 28 02 00 or 27 20 00), on the road to Jaén. **Ambulance:** ☎958 28 44 50.

Internet Access: Net (☎958 22 69 19) has 3 locations: C. Santa Escolástica, 13, up C. Pavaneras from Pl. Isabel la Católica; Pl. de los Girones, 3, 1 block away from 1st locale; C. Buensucesco, 22, 1 block from Pl. Trinidad. English spoken. 200ptas/€1.20 per hr. All open M-Sa 9am-1am, Su 3pm-1am.

Post Office: (☎958 22 48 35; fax 958 22 36 41), Pta. Real, on the corner of C. Acera de Darro and C. Angel Ganinet. **Lista de Correos** and **fax** service. Open M-F 8am-9pm, Sa 9:30am-2pm. Wires money M-F 8:30am-2:30pm. **Postal Code:** 18009.

■ ACCOMMODATIONS

Near **Plaza Nueva,** hostels line Cuesta de Gomérez, the street leading uphill to the Alhambra. The area around C. Mesones and C. Alhóndiga is close to the cathedral; hostels cluster around **Plaza Trinidad,** at the end of C. Mesones as you approach from Pta. Real. More hostels are along **Gran Vía.** Call ahead during *Semana Santa.*

Hostal Venecia, Cuesta de Gomérez, 2, 3rd fl. (☎958 22 39 87). Wake up to a soothing cup of tea, candles, and a hint of incense. Singles 2000ptas/€6; doubles 4000ptas/€24; triples and quads 1800ptas/€10.80 per person.

Hostal Residencia Britz, Cuesta de Gomérez, 1 (☎/fax 958 22 36 52), on the corner of Pl. Nueva. Large rooms with luxurious beds. Singles 2500ptas/€15, with bath 4000ptas/€24; doubles 4100ptas/€24.60, 5700ptas/€34.20. 6% discount with *Let's Go* if you pay in cash. MC/V.

Hostal Navarro-Ramos, Cuesta de Gomérez, 21 (☎958 25 05 55). Near the outer walls of the Alhambra. Singles 1700ptas/€10.20; doubles 2700ptas/€16.20, with bath 4500ptas/€27; triples with bath 6000ptas/€36.

Hospedaje Almohada, C. Postigo de Zarate, 4 (☎958 20 74 46). From Pl. Trinidad, follow C. Duquesa to C. Málaga and take a right; it's the red door with the small sign on your right. A successful experiment in communal living: guests cook for each other with produce from a local market. Dorm rooms 1800ptas/€10.80; singles 2200ptas/€13.20; doubles 3900ptas/€23.40. Longer stays 37,000ptas/€222 per month.

Hostal Antares, C. Cetti Meriém, 10 (☎958 22 83 13), on the corner of C. Elvira, 1 block from Gran Vía and the cathedral. Singles 2500ptas/€15; doubles 4000ptas/€24, with bath 5500ptas/€33; triples 5250ptas/€31.50. Rooms with A/C and TV available upstairs: doubles 6000ptas/€36; triples 10,500ptas/€63.

Hostal-Residencia Lisboa, Pl. Carmen, 29 (☎958 22 14 13 or 22 14 14; fax 958 22 14 87). Take C. Reyes Católicos from Pl. Isabel la Católica; Pl. Carmen is on the left. Sin-

SPAIN

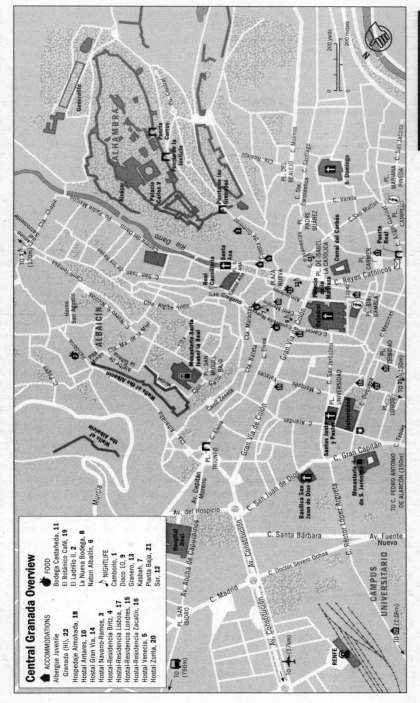

Central Granada Overview

▲ ACCOMMODATIONS
Albergue Juvenile
Granada (HI), 22
Hospedaje Almohada, 18
Hostal Antares, 10
Hostal Gran Vía, 14
Hostal Navarro-Ramos, 3
Hostal-Residencia Britz, 4
Hostal-Residencia Lisboa, 17
Hostal-Residencia Londres, 15
Hostal-Residencia Zacatín, 16
Hostal Venecia, 5
Hostal Zurita, 20

🍴 FOOD
Bodega Castañeda, 11
El Botánico Café, 19
El Ladrillo II, 2
La Nueva Bodega, 8
Naturi Albaílín, 6

♪ NIGHTLIFE
Camborio, 1
Disco 10, 9
Granero, 13
Kasbah, 7
Planta Baja, 21
Sur, 12

gles 2700ptas/€16.20, with bath 4000ptas/€24; doubles 4000ptas/€24, 5800ptas/€34.80; triples 5400ptas/€32.40, 7800ptas/€46.80. MC/V.

Hostal Zurita, Pl. Trinidad, 7 (☎958 27 50 20). Beautiful rooms, high-quality beds. Singles 2500ptas/€15; doubles 4500ptas/€27, with bath 5500ptas/€33; triples 6500ptas/€39, 7500ptas/€45.

Hostal-Residencia Zacatín, C. Ermita, 11 (☎958 22 11 55). Follow C. López from C. Reyes Católicos through an archway and hang a left on C. Ermita. Unique location amidst the arabesque bustle of the Alcaicería. Singles 2000ptas/€12, with bath 2800ptas/€16.80; doubles 3300ptas/€19.80, with shower 3800ptas/€22.80, with bath 4600ptas/€27.60.

Hostal Gran Vía, Gran Vía, 17 (☎958 27 92 12), about 4 blocks from Pl. Isabel la Católica. Pink sheets, polyester curtains, and religious art make for an eclectic but remarkably congruous room decor. Singles with shower 3000ptas/€18; doubles 3500ptas/€21, with shower 4000ptas/€24; triples with shower 6000ptas/€36.

Hostal-Residencia Londres, Gran Vía, 29, 6th fl. (☎958 27 80 34). Golden panoramas of the Alhambra by dusk. Singles 3000ptas/€18; doubles 3500ptas/€21; 1500ptas/€9 per additional person.

Albergue Juvenil Granada (HI), Ramón y Cajal, 2 (☎958 00 29 00 or 00 29 01). From the bus station take bus #10; from the train station #11; ask the driver to stop at "El Estadio de la Juventud." A peach building across the field on the left. Dorms 1725-2050ptas/€10.35-12.30, over 26 2375-2675ptas/€14.25-16.05. Nonmembers can join by paying an extra 500ptas/€3 per night for 6 nights.

Camping: Sierra Nevada, Av. Madrid, 107 (☎958 15 00 62; fax 958 15 09 54). Take bus #3 or 10. Shady trees, modern facilities, a large outdoor pool, and free hot showers. 630ptas/€3.80 per person, children under 10 525ptas/€3.15. Open Mar.-Oct.

◖ FOOD

Granada offers a variety of ethnic restaurants to emancipate your taste buds from the fried-fish-and-pig-products doldrums. Cheap and tasty cuisine can be found in and around the **Albaicín.** Near Pl. Nueva and Pl. Trinidad, the usual *menú* fare awaits. The adventurous eat well in Granada—try *tortilla sacromonte* (omelette with calf's brains, bull testicles, ham, shrimp, and veggies), *sesos a la romana* (batter-fried calf's brains), and *rabo de toro* (bull's tail). Get groceries at **Supermercado T. Mariscal,** C. Genil, next to El Corte Inglés. (Open M-F 9:30am-2pm and 5-9pm, Sa 9:30am-2pm.)

▨ **El Ladrillo II,** C. Panaderos 13 (☎958 29 26 51), off Cuesta del Chapiz near the Iglesia El Salvador, high on the Albaicín. Feast under the stars on sumptuous seafood. Entrees 1100-2000ptas/€6.60-12. Open daily 12:30pm-1:30am.

▨ **Naturi Albaicín,** C. Calderería Nueva, 10 (☎958 22 06 27). Excellent vegetarian restaurant with a serene Moroccan ambiance. Alcohol not served. *Menús* 950-1150ptas/€5.70-6.90. Open Sa-Th 1-4pm and 7-11pm, F 7-11pm.

Botánico Cafe, C. Málaga, 3 (☎958 27 15 98), 2 blocks from Pl. Trinidad. Manhattan meets Spanish modernity at this student hangout. Main dishes 800-1500ptas/€4.80-9. Open M-Th 10am-3am, Su noon-1am.

La Nueva Bodega, C. Cetti Meriém, 9 (☎958 22 59 34), out of Pl. Nueva on a small side street off C. Elvira. Dine on hearty and well-priced traditional cuisine. *Menús* 1000-1100ptas/€6-6.60. *Bocadillos* 275ptas/€1.65. Open daily noon-midnight.

Bodega Castañeda, C. Almireceros, 1-3 (☎958 21 54 64). Traditional *bodega* atmosphere. Legs of ham and wine barrels line the walls. *Bocadillos* (under 400ptas/€2.40). Open daily 8am-4pm and 6pm-1am, Sa-Su noon-4pm and 6pm-3am.

👁 SIGHTS

▩ THE ALHAMBRA

To reach the Alhambra, take C. Cuesta de Gomérez off Pl. Nueva, and be prepared to pant (20min.; no unauthorized cars 9am-9pm). Or take the cheap, quick Alhambra-Neptuno microbus (every 5min., 130ptas/€0.80) from Pl. Nueva. ☎ 958 22 15 03. Open Apr.-Sept. daily 8:30am-8pm; Oct.-Mar. M-Sa 9am-5:45pm. Nighttime visits June-Sept. Tu, Th, and Sa 10-11:30pm; Oct.-May Sa 8-10pm. All visits 1000ptas/€6. Limited to 7700 visitors per day June-Sept., 6300 Oct.-May, so get there early to stand in line. Enter the Palace of the Nazarites (Alcázar) during the time specified on your ticket, but stay as long as desired. It is possible to reserve tickets a few days in advance at banks for a 125ptas/€0.75 service charge. Reservations are also possible by phone (☎ 902 22 44 60).

"If you have died without seeing the Alhambra, you have not lived." From the streets of Granada, the Alhambra appears simple, blocky, faded—but up close the fortress-palace reveals its astoundingly elaborate detail. The first Nazarite King Alhamar built the fortress **Alcazaba,** to protect his city from highwaymen and Christian raiders. A dark, spiraling staircase leads to the **Torre de la Vela** (watchtower), where visitors get a great 360-degree view of Granada and the surrounding mountains. Follow signs to the *Palacio Nazaries* to see the stunningly ornate **Alcázar,** a royal palace built for the Moorish rulers Yusuf I (1333-1354) and Mohammed V (1354-1391), where tourists marvel at dripping stalactite archways, multicolored tiles, and sculpted fountains. Fernando and Isabel restored the Alcázar after they drove the Moors from Spain. Two generations later, Emperor Carlos V demolished part of it to make way for his **Palacio de Carlos V.** Although glaringly incongruous when juxtaposed with such Moorish splendor, the palace is considered by many to be one of the most beautiful Renaissance buildings in Iberia. Over a bridge are the blossoms, cypresses, and waterways of **El Generalife,** the sultan's vacation retreat.

THE ALBAICÍN. A labyrinth of steep streets and narrow alleys, the Albaicín was the only Moorish neighborhood to escape the torches of the *Reconquista* and remains a quintessential part of Granada. After the fall of the Alhambra, a small Muslim population remained here until being expelled in the 17th century. Today, with its abundance of North African cuisine and the recent construction of a mosque near Pl. San Nicolás, the Albaicín attests to the persistence of Islamic influence in Andalucía. Spectacular sunsets over the surrounding mountains can be seen from C. Cruz de Quirós, above C. Elvira. Although generally safe, the Albaicín is disorienting and should be approached with caution at night. *(Bus #12 runs from beside the cathedral to C. Pagés at the top of the Albaicín. There is another bus that departs from Pl. Nueva and weaves its way to the top. From here, walk down C. Agua through Pta. Arabe.)*

OTHER SIGHTS. Downhill from the Alhambra's Arab splendor, the Capilla Real (Royal Chapel), Fernando and Isabel's private chapel, exemplifies Christian Granada. The **crypt** houses the lead caskets of the Catholic Monarchs. In the **sacristy** resides Isabel's private **art collection,** the first Christian banner to flutter in triumph over the Alhambra, and the glittering **royal jewels.** *(☎ 958 22 92 39. Capilla Real and Sacristy open daily M-Sa 10:30am-1pm and 4-7pm, Su 11am-1pm and 4-7pm. 350ptas/€2.10.)* The adjacent **cathedral** was built from 1523 to 1704 by Fernando and Isabel upon the foundation of an Arab mosque. The first purely Renaissance cathedral in Spain, its Corinthian pillars support an astonishingly high (45m) vaulted nave. *(☎ 958 22 29 59. M-Sa 10:45am-1:30pm and 4-7pm, Su 4-7pm; Oct.-Mar. M-Sa 10:30am-1:30pm and 3:30-6:30pm, Su 11am-1:30pm. 350ptas/€2.10.)*

🎵 📷 ENTERTAINMENT AND NIGHTLIFE

Entertainment listings are at the back of the daily paper, the *Ideal* (120ptas/€0.75), under *Cine y Espectáculos;* the Friday supplement lists bars and special events. The *Guía del Ocio,* sold at newsstands (100ptas/€0.60), lists clubs,

SPAIN

pubs, and cafés. The tourist office also distributes a monthly guide, Cultura *en Granada*. Perhaps the most boisterous nightspots belong to **Calle Pedro Antonio de Alarcón**, running from Pl. Albert Einstein to Ancha de Gracia, while hip new bars and clubs line **Calle Elvira** from Cárcel to C. Cedrán. Gay bars cluster around Carrera del Darro; a complete list of gay clubs and bars is available at the tourist office.

■ **Camborio,** Camino del Sacromonte, 48, a 20min. walk uphill from Pl. Nueva. Gypsies and highwaymen once roamed the caves of Sacromonte; now clubbers can do the same at Camborio. 700ptas/€4.20 cover on F and Sa. Open Tu-Sa 11pm-dawn.

■ **Granero,** Pl. Luis Rosales (☎958 22 89 79), near Pl. Isabel Católica. A New Age barn loft bulging with grooving young Spanish professionals. Salsa and Spanish pop pervade. Beer 400ptas/€2.40. Open daily 10pm-dawn.

Los Jardines Neptuno, on C. Arabial, near the Neptuno shopping center at the base of C. Recogidas. Tourists and locals alike flock here for **flamenco.** (Cover 3800ptas/€22.80, includes 1 drink and bus ride to Albaicín).

Planta Baja, C. Horno de Abad, 11. Live bands play regularly within the concrete confines of this techno dance club. Open from fall until early July, Th-Sa 10pm-6am.

Sur, C. Reyes Católicos, 55. The hottest bar near Plaza Nueva. Mixed drinks 400-900ptas/€2.40-5.40. Open daily 10pm-6am.

Disco 10, C. Carcel Baja, 3 (☎958 22 40 01). Movie theater by evening, raging dance club by night. Open daily. 1000ptas/€6 cover Th-Sa includes 1 drink.

Kasbah, C. Calderería Nueva, 4 (☎958 22 79 36). Relax amidst Oriental comforts and scented candles. Silky pillows and romantic nooks abound. Open daily 3pm-3am.

▸ DAYTRIP FROM GRANADA

THE SIERRA NEVADA

The Autocares Bonal bus (☎958 27 31 00) between the bus station in Granada and Veleta, is a bargain (9am, returns 5pm from Albergue; round-trip 900ptas/€5.40).

The peaks of **Mulhacén** (3481m) and **Veleta** (3470m), the highest in Spain, sparkle with snow and buzz with tourists for most of the year. **Ski** season runs from December to April. The rest of the year, tourists **hike, parasail,** and take **jeep tours.** Call **Cetursa** (☎958 24 91 11) for info on outdoor activities.

COSTA DEL SOL

The coast has sold its soul to the Devil; now he's starting to collect. Artifice covers once-natural charms, as chic promenades and swanky hotels line its shore. To the northeast, rocky beaches have helped to preserve some natural beauty. To the southwest, water seems to wash up on more concrete than sand, and high season bring swarms of tourists (so reserve ahead or ask about private rooms), but nothing can detract from the coast's eight months of spring and four months of summer. June is the best time to visit, after summer has hit the beach but tourists haven't.

MARBELLA   ☎952

Sean Connery may have moved on, but that hardly makes Marbella (pop. 100,000) the seaside equivalent of *On Her Majesty's Secret Service*. Vacation home to sheiks and tycoons, this playground of the elite is the southern coast's most glamorous resort destination. While there may be more yachts here than hostels, it's still possible to have a good time on a budget. Marbella's controversial mayor, a self-proclaimed Franco enthusiast, has "cleaned up" many of the town's "marginal" elements (drug dealers, prostitutes, dogs, fellow politicians, etc.); best come visit before he sets his sights on backpackers. Although the beaches beckon with 320 days of sunshine per year, no visit to Marbella would be complete without a stroll through the **casco antiguo,** a maze of cobblestoned streets and ancient whitewashed facades. City buses along Av. Richard Soriano (dir.: San Pedro; 135ptas) bring you to chic and trendy **Puerto Banús.** Buffered by imposing white yachts, this is where it's at. With 22km of **beach,** Marbella offers a variety of sizzling settings, from below its chic promenade to **Playa de las Chapas,** 10km east via the Fuengirola bus. In the *casco antiguo* are mellow bars. Between the beach and the old town, C. Puerta del Mar is home to several gay bars. Later in the evening, the city's young 'uns head to the **Puerto Deportivo** ("The Port"), a world of disco-bars. Nightlife in Marbella begins and ends late. The rowdiest corner of the *casco antiguo* is where C. Mesoncillo meets C. Peral. Loud music and cheery Spaniards spill out from **El Güerto,** C. Peral, 9, and **The Tavern,** C. Peral, 7. (Both open daily at 10pm.) The **Museo del Grabado Español Contemporáneo,** on C. Hospital Bazán, is a treasure trove of engravings by Miró, Picasso, Dalí, and Goya. (Open M-F 10:15am-2pm and 5:30-8:30pm. 300ptas/€1.80.)

Accessible only by bus, the new **station** (☎95 276 44 00), atop Av. Trapiche, sends **buses** to: Algeciras (1½hr., 9 per day 6:10am-8:30pm, 825ptas/€4.95); Barcelona (16hr.; 11:30am, 5:40pm, 8:30pm, 10:25pm; 10,135ptas/€60.85); Cádiz (4hr., 6 per day 7:30am-8:45pm, 2140ptas/€12.85); Granada (4hr., 7 per day 8:30am-6:55pm, 1895ptas/€11.40); Madrid (7½hr., 10 per day 7:30am-11:30pm, 3060ptas/€18.40); Málaga (1½hr., every 30min. 7am-8:45pm, 670ptas/€4); Sevilla (4hr., 3 per day 2065ptas/€12.40). The **tourist office** is on Pl. Naranjos. (☎95 282 35 50. Open June-Aug. M-F 9:30am-9pm; Sept.-May M-F 9:30am-8pm, Sa 10am-2pm.) The area in the *casco antiguo* around Pl. Naranjos is packed with quick-filling hostels. **Hostal del Pilar,** C. Mesoncillo 4, is off C. Peral, an extension of C. Huerta Chica; or from the bus station it is off C. San Francisco. (☎95 282 99 36. 2000-3000ptas/€12-18 per person.) The excellent **Albergue Juvenil (HI),** Av. Trapiche 2, downhill from the bus station, is just like a proper hotel, only affordable. (☎95 277 14 91. Call ahead. 2050ptas/€12.30 per person; over 26 2675ptas/€16.) On the Marbella-Fuengirola bus, ask the driver to stop at **Camping Marbella Playa.** (☎95 283 39 98. 340-630ptas/€2.04-3.80 per person, 570-1050ptas/€3.42-6.30 per tent.) A **24hr. minimarket** beckons from the corner of C. Pablo Casals and Av. Fontanilla. **Postal Code:** 29600.

EASTERN SPAIN

Valencia's rich soil and famous orange groves, nourished by Moor-designed irrigation systems, have earned its nickname, *Huerta de España* (Spain's Orchard). Dunes, sandbars, jagged promontories, and lagoons mark the grand coastline, and lovely fountains and pools grace carefully landscaped public gardens in Valencian cities. The famed Spanish rice dish *paella* was created somewhere in Valencia.

ALICANTE (ALACANT)   ☎965

Sun-drenched Alicante (pop. 285,000) has somehow been chiseled into the most redeeming sort of resort town—dutifully entertaining yet quietly charming. While nightlife energizes the city, Alicante's mosaic-lined waterside Explanada relaxes it at sunset. High above the rows of bronzed bodies, the ancient Carthaginian **Castell de Santa Bárbara,** complete with drawbridges, dark passageways, and hidden tunnels, keeps silent guard over Alicante's beach. A paved road from the old section of Alicante leads to the top, but most people take the elevator from a hidden entrance at the end of the tunnel that begins on Av. Jovellanos, across the street from Playa Postiguet. (Castle open Apr.-Sept. daily 10am-7:30pm; Oct.-Mar. 9am-6:30pm. Free. Elevator 400ptas/€2.40.) A crowd of Valencian modernist art pieces reside along with works by Miró, Picasso, Kandinsky, and Calder in the **Museu de Arte del Siglo XX La Asegurada,** Pl. Santa María, 3, at the east end of C. Mayor. (Open mid-May to mid-Sept. M-F 10am-2pm and 5-9pm, Sa-Su 10:30am-2:30pm; mid-Sept. to mid-May M-F 10am-2pm and 4-8pm, Sa-Su 10:30am-2:30pm. Free.) Alicante's own **Playa del Pos-**

tiguet attracts sun worshipers, as do nearby Playa de San Juan (take TAM bus #21, 22, or 31) and Playa del Mutxavista (take TAM bus #21; all buses depart every 15min., 125ptas/€0.75). Most everyone begins the night by bar-hopping in the *casco antiguo;* the complex of bars that overlook the water in Alicante's main Port tend to fill up a little later. For an even crazier nightlife, the **Trensnochador night train** (July-Aug. F-Sa every hr. 9pm-5am; Su-Th 4 per night 9pm-5am; round-trip 150-700ptas/€0.90-4.20) runs from Estació Marina to "Discotecas" and other stops along the beach, which are packed until dawn. Try **Pachá, KU, KM,** and **Space** (open nightly until 9am) at the Disco Benidorm stop (round-trip 650ptas/€3.90). During the hedonistic **Festival de Sant Joan** (June 20-29), *fogueres* (symbolic or satiric effigies) are erected around the city and then burned in the streets on the 24th.

RENFE **trains** (☎(902) 24 02 02) run from **Estación Término** on Av. Salamanca, at the end of Av. Estación, to: Barcelona (4½-6hr., 9 per day 6:55am-6:30pm, 6000-10400ptas/€36-62.40); Madrid (4hr., 9 per day 7am-8pm, 5600-8600ptas/€33.60-51.60); Valencia (1½hr., 10 per day 6:55am-10:20pm, 1430-5300ptas/€8.60-31.80). Trains from **Ferrocarriles de la Generalitat Valenciana**, Estació Marina, Av. Villajoyosa, 2 (☎26 27 31), on Explanada d'Espanya, serve the Costa Blanca. **Buses** (☎13 07 00) run from C. Portugal, 17 to: Barcelona (7hr., 11 per day 1am-10:30pm, 4790ptas/€28.25); Granada (6hr., 7 per day 1:15am-10:45pm, 3510ptas/€21.10); Madrid (5hr., 9 per day 8am-midnight, 3465-5000ptas/€20.80-30); Valencia (2½hr., 10 per day 7am-9pm, 1980ptas/€11.88). The regional **tourist office** is located on Rbla. de Méndez Nuñez, 23. (☎20 00 00. Open June-Aug. M-F 10am-8pm; Sept.-May M-F 10am-7pm, Sa 10am-2pm and 3-7pm.) Log onto the **Internet** at **Yazzgo**, Explanada, 3. (Open M-Sa 8am-11pm, Su 9am-11pm. 8am-4pm 250ptas/€1.5 per hr., 4-11pm 250ptas/€1.5 per ½hr.) **Postal Code:** 03070.

The ⚑**Hostal Les Monges Palace,** C. San Augustín, 4, behind the Ayuntamiento, is in the center of the historic district and one of the most luxurious hostels in Spain. (☎21 50 46. Singles 3000ptas/€18, with shower 2600ptas/€15.60; doubles with shower 5500ptas/€33. MC/V) **Habitaciones México,** C. General Primo de Rivera, 10, off the end of Av. Alfonso X El Sabio, wins the award for friendliest atmosphere. (☎20 93 07. Free **Internet** access. Singles 2200ptas/€13.20; doubles 4000ptas/€24; triples 5400ptas/€32.40.) Take bus #21 to **camp** at **Playa Mutxavista.** (☎65 45 26. Open year-round. June-Sept. 1845ptas/€11.10 per tent, 570ptas/€3.45 per person; Oct.-May 1250ptas/€7.50 per tent, 350ptas/€2.10 per person.)

For food, try the family-run *bar-restaurantes* in the *casco antiguo*, between the cathedral and the castle steps. ⚑**Kebap,** C. Italia, 2, serves heaping entrees of delicious Middle Eastern cuisine. (Open daily 1-4pm and 8pm-midnight.) Buy basics at **Supermarket Mercadona,** C. Alvarez Sereix 5, off Av. Federico Soto. (Open M-Sa 9am-9pm.)

VALENCIA ☎963

Stylish, cosmopolitan, and business-oriented, Valencia is a striking contrast to the surrounding orchards and mountain ranges. Parks and gardens soothe the city's congested environment, and nearby beaches complement the frenetic pace.

🖥🔀 TRANSPORTATION AND PRACTICAL INFO. Trains arrive at C. Xàtiva, 24 (☎963 52 02 02). **RENFE** (24hr. ☎(902) 24 02 02) runs to: Alicante (2-3hr., 9 per day 10am-9pm, 1430-4100ptas/€8.60-24.60); Barcelona (3hr., 12 per day 6:35am-8:05pm, 5200ptas/€31.20); Madrid (3½hr., 9 per day 6:45am-8:15pm, 4700ptas/€28.20). **Buses** (☎963 49 72 22) go from Av. Menéndez Pidal, 13 to: Alicante via the Costa Blanca (4½hr., 13 per day 6:30am-6pm, 2000ptas/€12); Barcelona (4½hr., 15 per day 1am-10pm, 3135ptas/€18.85); Madrid (4hr., 13 per day 7am-3am, 3470ptas/€20.85); Sevilla (11hr., 4 per day 2:45-10:30pm, 6725ptas/€40.35). Bus #8 (130ptas/€0.80) connects to Pl. Ayuntamiento and the train station. Trasmediterránea **ferries** (☎(902) 45 46 45) sail to the Balearic Islands (see p. 889). The main **tourist office,** C. Paz, 46-48, has branches at the train station and on Pl. Ayuntamiento. (☎963 98 64 22. Open M-F 10am-6pm, Sa 10am-2pm.) **Email** at **Powernet,** C. Quart, 112 (☎963 84 95 21. 100ptas/€0.60 for 15min. Open M-Th 11am-10pm, F-Sa 11am-2am, Su 4-

10pm.) Send postcards from the **post office**, Pl. Ayuntamiento, 24. (☎ 963 51 67 50. Open M-F 8:30am-8:30pm, Sa 9:30am-2pm.) **Postal Code:** 46080.

█▐█ ACCOMMODATIONS AND FOOD. The best lodgings are around **Plaza Ayuntamiento** and **Plaza Mercado.** To get from the train station to the **Pilgrim's Youth Hostel**, Pl. Hombres del Mar 25, take the Metro to "Benimaclet," switch to L4 toward Av. Dr. Lluch, and get off at "Las Arenals"; the entrance is on the other side of the building. (☎ 963 56 42 88; albergue@ran.es. **Internet.** Reception 24hr. Reserve ahead. 1500-2000ptas/€9, under 27 1000ptas/€6.) To get from the train station to the spotless **Hostal-Residencia El Cid,** C. Cerrajeros, 13, pass Pl. Ayuntamiento and take the second left off C. Vicente Mártir. (☎ 963 92 23 23. Singles 1800ptas/€10.80; doubles 3400ptas/€26.40.) **Hostal El Rincón,** C. Carda, 11, is near Plaza del Mercado. Brightly lit hallways lead to clean rooms. (☎ 963 91 79 98. Singles 1660ptas/€10; doubles 3000ptas/€18.) **Paella** is the most famous of Valencia's 200 rice dishes; try as many as you can before leaving. Buckets of fresh fish, meat, and fruit are sold at the **Mercado Central,** on Pl. Mercado. (Open M-F 7am-3pm.) For **groceries,** stop by the basement of **El Corte Inglés,** C. Colon, or the 5th floor of the C. Pintor Sorilla building. (Open M-Sa 10am-10pm.) **Postal Code:** 46080.

◨▐▌ SIGHTS AND ENTERTAINMENT. Touring Valencia on foot is complicated. Most of the sights line the **Río Turia** or cluster near **Plaza Reina,** which is linked to Pl. Ayuntamiento by C. San Vicente Mártir. EMT bus #5, dubbed the Bus Turistic (☎ 963 52 83 99), makes a loop around the old town sights (130/€0.80ptas; 1-day pass 500ptas/€3). The 13th-century █cathedral, on Pl. Reina, was built on the site of an Arab mosque. In a fit of hyperbole (or vertigo), Victor Hugo counted 300 bell towers from the **Micalet** (cathedral tower); in reality, there are about 100. The **Museo de la Catedral** squeezes many treasures into very little space. *(Cathedral open daily 8am-2pm and 5-8pm. Closes earlier in winter. Free. Tower open daily 10am-1pm and 4:30-7pm. 200ptas/€1.20. Museum open Mar.-May and Oct.-Nov. M-F 10am-1pm and 4:30-6pm; June-Sept. 10am-1pm and 4:30-7pm; Dec.-Feb. 10am-1pm. Also open year-round Sa-Su 10am-1pm.)* Across the river, the **Museu Provincial de Belles Artes,** on C. Sant Pius V, next to the **Jardines del Reial,** displays superb 14th- to 16th-century Valencian art. *(Open Tu-Sa 10am-2:15pm and 4-7:30pm, Su 10am-7:30pm. Free.)* West across the old river, the **Instituto València de Arte Moderno (IVAM),** C. Guillem de Castro, 118, has works by 20th-century sculptor Julio González. *(Open Tu-Su 10am-7pm. 350ptas/€2.10, students 175ptas/€1.05; Su free.)* Modern, airy, and thoroughly fascinating, Valencia's █Ciudad de las artes y las ciencias has created quite a stir. Built along the dried-up bed of the Río Turia, this mini-city has become the fourth-biggest tourist destination in Spain. The complex is divided into four large attractions: **L'Hemisfèric** wows the eyes with its IMAX theater and planetarium; **L'Oceanografic** is an underground water-world and re-creation of diverse aquatic environments; the beautiful **Palau de les Arts** houses stages for opera, theater, and dance; and the █Museu de Les Ciencias Principe Felipe is an interactive playground for science and technology fiends. *(South along the riverbed off the highway to Salér. Bus #35 runs from Pl. Ayuntamiento. www.cac.es. IMAX shows 1100ptas/€6.60, weekdays children and students 800ptas/€4.80. Museum and aquarium open M-Th 10am-8pm, F-Su 10am-9pm; admission to each 1000ptas/€6.)* The most popular **beaches** are **Las Arenas** and **Malvarrosa,** connected by a bustling boardwalk—buses #20, 21, 22, and 23 all pass through. To get to the more attractive **Salér,** 14km from the center of town, take an Autobuses Buñol bus (☎ 963 49 14 25) from Gran Vía Germanias and C. Sueca (25min., every 30min. 7am-10pm, 150ptas/€0.90).

Bars and pubs abound in the **El Carme** district. Follow Pl. Mercado and C. Bolsería (bear right at the fork) to **Plaza Tossal** to guzzle *agua de Valencia* (orange juice, champagne, and vodka) with the masses, then head to **Avenida Blasco Ibañez** with your dancing shoes. In summer, however, the only places to be seen are the outdoor discos at Playa de Malvarrosa. **Caballito de Mar,** C. Eugenia Viñes, 22 (☎ 963 71 07 63), is the most popular and heats up with a psychedelic tunnel and huge outdoor deck. For more info, consult the *Qué y Dónde* weekly magazine,

SPAIN

SPAIN

available at newsstands, or the weekly entertainment supplement, *La Cartelera* (125ptas/€0.75). The most famed festival in Valencia is **Las Fallas** (Mar. 12-19), which culminates in a burning of gigantic (30m) satirical papier-mâché effigies.

COSTA BLANCA

This "white coast," which extends from Denía through Calpe, Alicante, and Elche, derives its name from its fine, white sands. **Calpe** may be a classic tourist trap, with t-shirt and sunglass stores lining the streets and its beaches packed with foreigners, but there's certainly good reason why so many people flock to this tiny town 62km northeast of Alicante. The **Peñó d'Ifach** (327m), a gargantuan, flat-topped rock protrusion whose precipitous face drops straight to the sea, towers above the beach and town in one of the most picturesque coastal settings in Spain. **Gandía** also attracts crowds with fine sand beaches.

La Amistad **buses** (M-Sa, 4-5 per day 8:45am-8:30pm, 125ptas/€0.75) go from outside the train station in Gandía to **Platja de Piles,** 10km south, where you'll find beach, beach, and more beach. ALSA **buses** (☎(902) 42 22 42) run from Valencia to: Alicante (4½hr., 13 per day 6:30am-6pm, 2000ptas/€12) and Calpe and Altea (3-3½hr., 12 per day 6:30am-6pm, 1315-1420ptas/€7.90-8.50). From Alicante buses run to Altea (1¼hr., 18 per day 6:30am-9pm, 560ptas/€3.36) and Calpe (1½hr., 18 per day 6:30am-9pm, 675ptas/€4.05). The Gandía **tourist office,** Marqués de Campo, is opposite the train station. (☎962 87 77 88. Open June-Aug. M-F 9:30am-1:30pm and 4:30-7:30pm, Sa 10am-1:30pm; Sept.-May M-F 9:30am-1:30pm and 4-7pm, Sa 10am-1pm.) To sleep at the fantastic **Alberg Mar i Vent (HI)** in Platja, follow the signs down C. Dr. Fleming. (☎962 83 17 48. Washing machine and library. 3-day max. stay, flexible if uncrowded. Sheets 300ptas/€1.80 for entire stay. Curfew Su-F 2am, Sa 4am. Open Feb. 15-Dec. 15. Dorms 800ptas/€4.60, over 26 1100ptas/€6.60 extra.)

NORTHEAST SPAIN

Northeastern Spain encompasses the country's most avidly regionalistic areas as well as some of its best cuisine. **Catalan** are justly proud of their treasures, from mountains to beaches to hip Barcelona. The glorious **Pyrenees** line the French border, presenting a prickly face to the rest of the continent. Little-known **Navarra** basks in the limelight once a year when bulls race through the streets of Pamplona. Industrious **Aragón** packs in busy cities and the most dramatic parts of the Pyrenees. The **Basques** are fiercely regionalistic, but happily share their beautiful coasts and rich history. The **Balearic Islands** are always ready for the next party.

CATALUÑA

From rocky Costa Brava to the lush Pyrenees and chic Barcelona, Catalunya is a vacation in itself. Graced with the nation's richest resources, it is one of Spain's most prosperous regions. Catalan is the region's official language (though most everyone is bilingual), and local cuisine is lauded throughout Spain.

BARCELONA

If you make it until 6am, you'll see the quiet side of Barcelona. While the city is dark, the occasional worker battles Catalan separatist graffiti, the empty streets are scrubbed by hulking machines, and pigeons and parrots share the same branch, cooing with their heads under their wings. Enjoy the calm—it won't last.

With sunrise, you'll see a different city. Cash boxes ring with the sounds of commerce and style; tourists marvel at monsters that residents call buildings; museums fill with the avant-garde; pedestrians salivate at exotic delicacies; beaches overflow

SPAIN

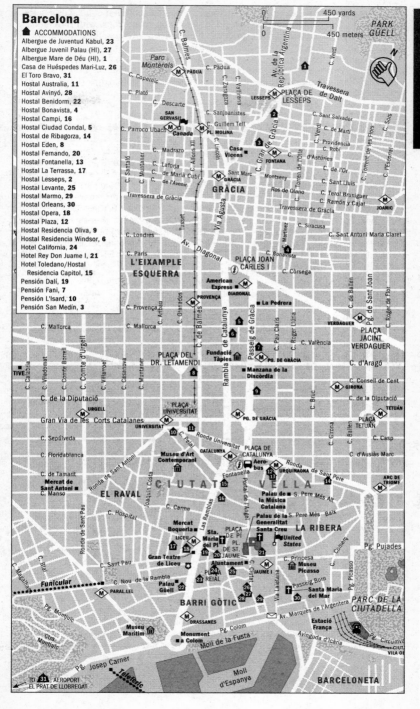

Barcelona

▲ ACCOMMODATIONS

Albergue de Juventud Kabul, **23**
Albergue Juvenil Palau (HI), **27**
Albergue Mare de Déu (HI), **1**
Casa de Huéspedes Mari-Luz, **26**
El Toro Bravo, **31**
Hostal Australia, **11**
Hostal Avinyó, **28**
Hostal Benidorm, **22**
Hostal Bonavista, **4**
Hostal Campi, **16**
Hostal Ciudad Condal, **5**
Hostal de Ribagorza, **14**
Hostal Eden, **8**
Hostal Fernando, **20**
Hostal Fontanella, **13**
Hostal La Terrassa, **17**
Hostal Lesseps, **2**
Hostal Levante, **25**
Hostal Marmo, **29**
Hostal Orleans, **30**
Hostal Opera, **18**
Hostal Plaza, **12**
Hostal Residencia Oliva, **9**
Hostal Residencia Windsor, **6**
Hotel California, **24**
Hotel Rey Don Juame I, **21**
Hotel Toledano/Hostal
  Residencia Capitol, **15**
Pensión Dalí, **19**
Pensión Fani, **7**
Pensión L'Isard, **10**
Pensión San Medín, **3**

with bronzed nudity; a white gorilla terrifies and delights children of all ages. On this side of 6am, Barcelona is sensory overload. After you spend 24hr. with Barcelona's schizophrenic personalities, Barcelona will have exhausted herself—and you. When 6am rolls around again, you'll be glad for the quiet.

Barcelona is a gateway city: the gateway to Catalunya, to Spain, to the Mediterranean, to the Pyrenees. Pack your swimsuit and your skis, your art book and your clubbing shoes, an extra bag to fill with souvenirs, and don't worry that you don't speak Spanish: neither does Barcelona. If you find that Barcelona especially delights you, pick up *Let's Go Barcelona 2002*.

✈ INTERCITY TRANSPORTATION

Flights: All domestic and international flights land at **El Prat de Llobregat** airport (☎932 98 38 38; www.aena.es/ae/bcn/homepage), 12km southwest of Barcelona. The **Aerobus** links the airport to Pl. Catalunya, the center of town (40min.; every 15min. M-F 6am-midnight, Sa-Su 6:30am-midnight; to the airport M-F 5:30am-11:15pm, Sa-Su 6am-11:20pm; 525ptas/€3). **RENFE** (☎934 91 31 83; www.renfe.es) trains provide cheaper transportation to the airport (20-25min.; every 30min. 6:13am-11:15pm from airport, 5:43am-11:24pm from Sants; 350ptas/€2). 3 **national airlines** serve domestic and international destinations. **Iberia/Aviaco,** Pg. de Gràcia, 30 (☎934 01 32 82; ☎902 40 05 00), has extensive coverage and student discounts. **Air Europa** (☎902 40 15 01; www.air-europa.com), and **Spanair,** Pg. de Gràcia, 57 (☎932 16 46 26; ☎902 13 14 15), offer cheaper fares.

Trains: Barcelona has 2 main train stations. For general info about trains and train stations, call 902 24 02 02. **Estació Barcelona-Sants,** in Pl. Països Catalans. M: Sants-Estació. Barcelona-Sants is the main terminal for domestic and international traffic. **Estació França,** on Av. Marquès de l'Argentera. M: Barceloneta. Services regional destinations, including Girona Tarragona and Zaragoza, and some international arrivals.

Ferrocarrils de la Generalitat de Cataluña (FFCC) (☎93 205 15 15; www.fgc.catalunya.net), has commuter trains with main stations at Pl. Catalunya and Pl. Espanya.

RENFE: (☎902 24 02 02, international 934 90 11 22; www.renfe.es). RENFE has extensive service in Spain and Europe. Popular connections include: **Madrid** (7-8hr., 7 per day, 5100-6900ptas/ €36-41); **San Sebastián** (8-9hr., 3 per day, 5000ptas/€30); **Sevilla** (11-12hr., 3per day, 6400-10,200ptas/€39-61); **Valencia** (3-5hr., 16 per day 7am-9pm, 3120-5200ptas/€20-33); **Milan, Italy** (through Nice) and **Montpellier** with connections to Geneva and Paris.

Trenes Euromed: A subsidiary of RENFE offering high-speed service along Spain's Mediterranean coast. Trains leave from Barcelona-Sants for **Alicante** (4-5hr., 8 per day, 6000-6700ptas/€36-41) and **Valencia** (3hr., 6 per day, 4900ptas/€30), stopping in smaller towns along the way.

Buses: Most buses arrive at the **Barcelona Nord Estació d'Autobuses,** C. Ali-bei, 80 (☎932 65 61 32; info office open daily 7am-9pm). M: Arc de Triomf (exit to Nàpols).

Enatcar: (☎902 42 22 42; www.enatcar.es). Open daily 7am-1am. To: **Madrid** (8hr., 18 per day, 2690ptas/€16); **Alicante** (9hr., 5 per day, 4650ptas/€28); **Valencia** (4hr., 16 per day, 2690ptas/€16).

Sarfa: (☎902 30 20 25; www.sarfa.com). Sarfa buses stop at beach towns along the Costa Brava, north of Barcelona. Open daily 8am-8:30pm. To: **Cadaqués** (2½hr., 10:45am and 7:45pm, 2250ptas/€13.50) and **Tossa de Mar** (1½hr., 9 per day 8:15am-8:15pm, 1070ptas/€6.50).

Linebús: (☎932 65 07 00). Open M-F 8am-2pm and 3-8pm, Sa 8:30am-1:30pm and 4:30-8pm. Discounts for travelers under 26. To: **London** (25hr., 3 per week, 14,650ptas/€88) and **Paris** (15hr., M-Sa 8pm, 1280-23,600ptas/€77-142). Daily service to southern France and Morocco.

Ferries: For details on ferries to the Balearic Islands, see **Balearic Islands,** p. 889. **Transmediterránea,** Estació Marítima-Moll Barcelona (☎902 45 46 45; fax 932 95 91 34), Moll de Sant Bertran. M: Drassanes. Head down Las Ramblas to **Monument a Colom;** Columbus points straight toward the Estació Marítima. Cross Ronda Litoral and pass the Aduana building on the left. During the summer, ferries to **Mallorca** (3hr., 3 per day); **Ibiza** (9hr., 5 per week); **Menorca** (1 per day starting mid-June). One-way trips start at 8000ptas/€48. Tickets available at any travel agency. Station office open daily 10am-4pm.

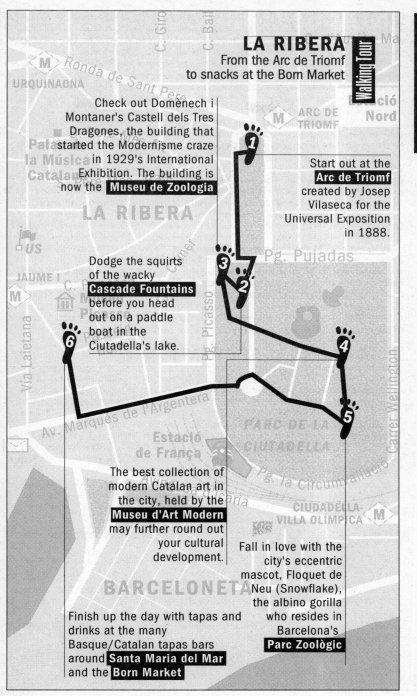

LA RIBERA
From the Arc de Triomf
to snacks at the Born Market

Walking Tour

SPAIN

Check out Domènech i Montaner's Castell dels Tres Dragones, the building that started the Modernisme craze in 1929's International Exhibition. The building is now the **Museu de Zoologia**

Start out at the **Arc de Triomf** created by Josep Vilaseca for the Universal Exposition in 1888.

Dodge the squirts of the wacky **Cascade Fountains** before you head out on a paddle boat in the Ciutadella's lake.

The best collection of modern Catalan art in the city, held by the **Museu d'Art Modern** may further round out your cultural development.

Fall in love with the city's eccentric mascot, Floquet de Neu (Snowflake), the albino gorilla who resides in Barcelona's **Parc Zoològic**

Finish up the day with tapas and drinks at the many Basque/Catalan tapas bars around **Santa Maria del Mar** and the **Born Market**

SPAIN

✈ ORIENTATION

Barcelona's layout is simple. Imagine yourself perched on Columbus's head at the **Monument a Colom** (on **Passeig de Colom,** along the shore), viewing the city with the sea at your back. From the harbor, the city slopes upward to the mountains. From the Columbus monument, **Las Ramblas** (see p. 864), the main thoroughfare, runs from the harbor up to **Plaça de Catalunya** (M: Catalunya), the city's center. The **Ciutat Vella** (Old City) is the heavily-touristed historical neighborhood, which centers around Las Ramblas and includes the Barri Gòtic, La Ribera, and El Raval. The **Barri Gòtic** is east of Las Ramblas (to the right, with your back to the sea), enclosed on the other side by **Via Laietana.** East of Via Laietana lies the maze-like neighborhood of **La Ribera,** which borders Parc de la Ciutadella and the Estació França train station. To the west of Las Ramblas (to the left, with your back to the sea) is **El Raval.** Beyond La Ribera (farther east, outside the Ciutat Vella), is the **Poble Nou** neighborhood and the **Vila Olímpica,** with its twin towers (the tallest buildings in Barcelona) and an assortment of discos and restaurants. Beyond El Raval (to the west) rises **Montjuïc,** crammed with gardens, museums, the 1992 Olympic grounds, Montjuïc castle, and other attractions. Directly behind the Monument a Colom is the **Port Vell** (Old Port) development, where a wavy bridge leads across to the ultra-modern shopping and entertainment complexes **Moll d'Espanya** and **Maremagnum.** Beyond the Ciutat Vella is **l'Eixample,** the gridded neighborhood created during the expansion of the 1860s, which runs from Pl. Catalunya toward the mountains. **Gran Via de les Corts Catalanes** defines its lower edge and **Passeig de Gràcia,** l'Eixample's main street, bisects the neighborhood. **Avinguda Diagonal** marks the border between l'Eixample and the **Zona Alta** (Uptown), which includes Pedralbes, Gràcia, and other older neighborhoods in the foothills. The peak of Tibidabo, the northwest border of the city, offers the most comprehensive view of the city.

▐ LOCAL TRANSPORTATION

Metro and Bus: Barcelona's extensive public transportation system (☎010) is quick, cheap, and extensive. The useful *Guía d'Autobusos Urbans de Barcelona,* free at tourist offices and in metro stations, maps out all of the city's bus routes and the 5 metro lines. If you plan to use the metro and bus systems extensively, consider buying a **T1 Pass** (885ptas/€5) or a **T-DIA** Card (670ptas/€4). The T1 Pass, valid for 10 rides on the bus, metro, and most FFCC trains, is a great deal, especially since multiple people can share 1 pass. The T-DIA Card entitles you to unlimited bus and metro travel for 1 (625ptas/€3.70) or 3 days (1600ptas/€9.60). The **T-Mes** (5825ptas/€35) offers unlimited travel for 1 month.

Metro: (☎934 86 07 52; www.tmb.net). Automatic vending machines and ticket windows sell metro passes. Riding without a ticket carries a hefty 5000ptas/€30 fine. Trains run M-Th 5am-11pm, F-Sa 5am-2am, Su 6am-midnight. 160ptas/€1 for a *sencillo* (single ride).

Buses: Go just about anywhere, usually from 5am-10pm. 160ptas/€1.

Nitbus: (☎901 51 11 51). Runs every 20-30min. 10:30pm-4:30am. Stops in front of most of the club complexes. 160ptas/€1.

Bus Turístic: The clearly marked Bus Turístic stops at 26 points of interest along 2 different routes (red for the northern; blue for the southern). The easiest place to hop on the Bus Turístic is Pl. Catalunya, in front of El Corte Inglés. Runs daily except Dec. 25 and Jan. 1; every 10-30min. 9am-9:30pm. Purchase tickets on the bus or at the Pl. Catalunya tourist office. Full-day pass 2200ptas/€13, ages 4-12 1300ptas/€8; 2-day pass 2800ptas/€17.

Taxis: A *libre* sign in the windshield or a lit green light on the roof means they are vacant; yellow means they are occupied. Cabs can be summoned by phone (☎933 30 03 00, for disabled travelers 934 20 80 88).

Car Rental: Docar, C. Montnegre, 18 (24hr. ☎934 39 81 19). Free delivery and pickup. From 2300ptas/€14 per day plus 25ptas/€0.15 per km and 1500ptas/€9 insurance. Open M-F 8:30am-2pm and 3:30-8pm, Sa 9am-2pm. **Tot Car,** C. Berlín, 97 (☎934 30

01 98; fax 934 19 22 94). Free delivery and pickup. From 4500ptas/€27 per day plus 21ptas/€0.15 per km. Open M-F 8am-2pm and 3-8pm, Sa 9am-1pm.

Bicycle and Moped Rental: Vanguard Rent a Car, C. Londres, 31 (☎934 39 38 80; fax 934 10 82 71). Mopeds Tu-Th 4760ptas/€29 per day, F-M 7280ptas/€44 per day. Insurance, helmet, and IVA included. 19+. **Over-Rent S.A.,** Av. Josep Terradellas, 42 (☎934 05 26 60). Call at least a week ahead to reserve a vehicle. Motorcycles 2500-8200ptas/€15-50 per day. 23+.

◪ PRACTICAL INFORMATION

TOURIST, FINANCIAL, AND LOCAL SERVICES

Tourist Info: (☎010, 906 30 12 82 or 933 04 34 21; www.barcelonaturisme.com). Barcelona has 4 main tourist offices and numerous mobile information stalls. **Informació Turística at Plaça Catalunya,** Pl. Catalunya, 17S. M: Catalunya, under the plaza. Provides multilingual advice, maps, pamphlets, transportation passes, hotel information, currency exchange, telephone cards, **email** kiosks, and souvenirs for purchase. Open daily 9am-9pm. **Informació Turística at Plaça Sant Jaume,** Pl. Sant Jaume 1, off of C. Ciutat. M: Jaume I. Fewer services but more personal attention than its big sister in Pl. Catalunya. Open M-Sa 10am-8pm, Su 10am-2pm. **Oficina de Turisme de Catalunya,** Pg. de Gràcia, 107 (☎932 38 40 00; fax 932 92 12 70; www.gencat.es/probert). M: Diagonal. Open M-Sa 10am-7pm, Su 10am-2pm. **Estació Central de Barcelona-Sants,** Pl. Països Catalans, in the Barcelona-Sants train station. M: Sants-Estació. Open M-F 4:30am-midnight, Sa-Su 5am-midnight. **Aeroport El Prat de Llobregat** (☎934 78 05 65), in the international terminal. Open daily 9am-9pm. English-speaking agents available.

Budget Travel Offices: usit UNLIMITED, Ronda Universitat, 16 (☎934 12 01 04; fax 934 12 39 84; www.unlimted.es). Open M-F 10am-8:30pm, Sa 10am-1:30pm.

Consulates: Australia, Gran Via Carlos III, 98, 9th fl. (☎933 30 94 96). **Canada,** Elisenda de Pinos, 8 (☎932 04 27 00). **New Zealand,** Traversa de Gràcia, 64, 4th fl. (☎932 09 03 99). **South Africa,** Teodora Lamadrid 7-11 (☎934 18 64 45). **US,** Pg. Reina Elisenda, 23 (☎932 80 22 27).

Currency Exchange: General banking hours M-F 8:30am-2pm. **Banco de Espanya,** Pl. Catalunya, 17 (☎934 82 47 00), and American Express (see below) charge no commission on traveler's checks.

American Express: Pg. de Gràcia, 101 (☎900 99 44 26). M: Diagonal. The entrance is on C. Rosselló. Open M-F 9:30am-6pm, Sa 10am-noon. Also at Las Ramblas, 74 (☎933 01 11 66). Open daily 9am-8pm.

Luggage Storage: Estació Barcelona-Sants. M: Sants-Estació. Open 5:30am-11pm. **Estació França.** M: Barceloneta. Open 7am-10pm. **Estació del Nord.** M: Arc de Triomf. Open 24hr. Large lockers 700ptas/€4.20., small 500ptas/€3.

El Corte Inglés: Pl. Catalunya, 14 (☎933 06 38 00). M: Catalunya. Behemoth department store. **Free map** of Barcelona at information desk; also has English books. Open M-Sa and 1st Su of every month 10am-10pm. Branches: Portal de l'Angel, 19-2 (M: Catalunya); Av. Diagonal, 471-473 (M: Hospital Clinic); Av. Diagonal, 617 (M: Maria Cristina).

English Bookstores: Llibreria del Raval, C. Elisabets, 6 (☎933 17 02 93). M: Catalunya, in **El Raval,** off Las Ramblas. Books in 4 languages (Catalan, Spanish, English, and French). Catalan/Spanish and Catalan/English dictionaries (1100ptas/€7). Open M-F 10am-8:30pm, Sa 10am-2:30pm and 5-8pm. **LAIE,** Av. Pau Claris, 85 (☎933 18 17 39). M: Urquinaona. Small English book section with travel guides and a cafe. Bookstore open M-F 10am-9pm, Sa 10:30am-9pm. Cafe open M-F 9am-1am, Sa 10am-1am.

Laundromats: Tintorería Ferran, C. Ferran, 11. M: Liceu. Full service 1500ptas/€9. Open daily 8:30am-2pm and 4:30-7:30pm. **Tintorería San Pablo,** C. San Pau, 105 (☎933 29 42 49). M: Parallel. Wash, dry, and fold 1800ptas/€11; do-it-yourself 1400ptas/€8.40. Open M-F 9am-1:30pm and 4-8:30pm.

SPAIN

EMERGENCY AND COMMUNICATIONS

Emergency: ☎112. **Local police,** ☎092. **National police,** ☎091. **Medical,** ☎061.

Police: Las Ramblas, 43 (☎933 44 13 00), across from Pl. Reial and next to C. Nou de La Rambla. M: Liceu. Multilingual officers. Open daily 24hr.

Late-Night Pharmacy: Pharmacies open 24hr. on a rotating basis. Check pharmacy windows for current listings.

Hospitals: Hospital Clinic, Villarroel, 170 (☎932 27 54 00). M: Hospital Clinic. Main entrance at the intersection of C. Roselló and C. Casanova. **Hospital de la Santa Creu i Sant Pau** (☎932 91 90 00, emergency 932 91 91 91), at the intersection of C. Cartagena and C. Sant Antoni Moria Claret. M: Hospital de Sant Pau. **Hospital Vall d' Hebron** (☎932 74 60 00). M: Vall d'Hebron.

Internet Access: ▧**easyEverything**, Las Ramblas, 31. M: Liceu. 200ptas/€1.20 for about 40min., fluctuates with demand. Open 24hr. Also on Ronda Universitat, 35, next to Pl. Catalunya. ▧**bcnet (Internet Gallery Café),** Barra de Ferro, 3 (☎932 68 15 07), down the street from the Picasso museum. M: Jaume I. 250ptas/€1.50 per 15min., 600ptas/€4 per hr.; 10hr. ticket available for 3000ptas/€18. Open daily 10am-1am.

Post Office: Lista de Correos, Pl. de Antoni López (☎902 197 197). M: Jaume I or Barceloneta. Fax and lista de correos. Open M-F 8:30am-9:30pm. A little shop in the back of the post office building, across the street, wraps packages for mailing (about 300ptas/€2). Shop open M-Sa 9am-2pm and 5-8pm. **Postal Code:** 08003.

▐ ACCOMMODATIONS

The area between Pl. Catalunya and the water—the Barri Gòtic, El Raval, and La Ribera—offers budget beds, but reservations are a must. Last-minute travelers can crash in Gràcia or l'Eixample, outer boroughs with more vacancies that are easily accessible to the rest of Barcelona.

LOWER BARRI GÒTIC

The following hostels are between C. Ferran and the water. Backpackers flock here to be close to hip Las Ramblas; be careful in the Pl. Reial and below C. Escudellers.

▧ **Hostal Fernando,** C. Ferran, 31 (☎/fax 93 301 79 93; www.barcelona-on-line.es/ fernando). M: Liceu. So clean it shines; fills from walk-ins. Dorms with lockers 2500ptas/€15; doubles 5000-6000ptas/€30-36, with bath 7000-8000ptas/€42-48; triples 8500-9500ptas/€51-57. MC/V.

Casa de Huéspedes Mari-Luz, C. Palau, 4 (☎/fax 933 17 34 63). M: Liceu. The owners make their hostel feel like home. Kitchen available June-Aug. 8-10:30am. Laundry 800ptas/€4.80. Dorms with lockers 1900ptas/€11.50; doubles June 21-Aug. 15 6000ptas/€36, Aug.16-June 20 4800ptas/€29. MC/V.

Albergue Juvenil Palau (HI), C. Palau, 6 (☎934 12 50 80). M: Liceu. A budget refuge. Kitchen (open 7-10pm), dining room, and 45 clean dorms with lockers (3-8 people each). Breakfast included. Showers 8am-noon and 4-10pm. Sheets 200ptas/€1.20. Reception 7am-3am. Curfew 3am. No reservations. Dorms 1900ptas/€12. Cash only.

Hostal Avinyó, C. Avinyó, 42 (☎933 18 79 45; www.hostalavinyo.com). M: Drassanes. The most modern spot in the Barri Gòtic. Singles 2500ptas/€15; doubles 4000-4600ptas/€12-14, with bath 5000-6000ptas/€15-18. Cash only.

Hostal Marmo, C. Gignàs, 25 (☎933 10 59 70). M: Jaume I. 17 rooms in an old house with plenty of plants, lacy curtains, and balconies. Reservations 2 days in advance. Singles 2200-2400ptas/€13.50-14.50, with bath 2500-2700ptas/€15-16.30; doubles 4200-4600ptas/€25-28, 4500-4900ptas/€27-€30. Cash only.

Hostal Levante, Baixada de San Miguel, 2 (☎933 17 95 65; www.hostallevante.com). M: Liceu. Large, tastefully decorated rooms. Singles 4000ptas/€24; doubles 6500ptas/€39, with bath 7500ptas/€45. 4-8 person suites with kitchen, living room, and laundry machines 4000ptas/€24 per person per night. MC/V.

Hotel Rey Don Jaume I, C. Jaume I, 11 (☎/fax 933 10 62 08; r.d.jaume@atriumhotels.com). M: Jaume I. Stark rooms have balconies, phones, and bath. Safes available. Reservations recommended 1-2 months ahead. Singles 6000ptas/€36; doubles 9000ptas/€54; triples 12,000ptas/€72. AmEx/MC/V.

Albergue de Juventud Kabul, Pl. Reial, 17 (☎933 18 51 90). M: Liceu. Legendary co-ed dorm rooms can pack 200 frat boys. **Internet** (100ptas/€0.60 per 20min). In-room lockers. Sheets 300ptas/€1.80. Laundry 900ptas/€5.50. Key deposit 1000ptas/€6. June-Sept. dorms 2900ptas/€17.50; Oct.-May 1900ptas/€11.50. Cash only.

UPPER BARRI GÒTIC

Between C. Fontanella and C. Ferran, accommodations are pricier, but more serene, than the lower Barri Gòtic. Early reservations are obligatory in summer. The nearest Metro stop is Catalunya, unless otherwise specified.

🏨 **Hotel Toledano/Hostal Residencia Capitol,** Las Ramblas, 138 (☎933 01 08 72; www.hoteltoledano.com). Luxurious hotel rooms include bath, hostel rooms don't. 4th-fl. Hotel Toledano: singles 4600ptas/€28; doubles 7900ptas/€48; triples 9900ptas/€60. 5th-fl. Hostel Residencia Capitol: singles 3400ptas/€21; doubles 5400ptas/€33, with shower 6200ptas/€37; triples 6900ptas/€41.50, 7700ptas/€47; quads 7900ptas/€48, 8700ptas/€52. Reserve early over web site. AmEx/MC/V.

🏨 **Hostal Benidorm,** Las Ramblas, 37 (☎933 02 20 54; www.barcelona-on-line.es/benidorm). M: Drassanes. With phones and baths in every neat room and balconies, this could be the best value on Las Ramblas. Singles 4000ptas/€24; doubles 5500ptas/€33; triples 7000ptas/€42; quads 9000ptas/€54; quints10,500ptas/€63.

🏨 **Hostal Plaza,** C. Fontanella, 18 (☎/fax 933 01 01 39; www.plazahostal.com). Savvy Texan owners and quirky rooms. Drink/breakfast bar, kitchen, and **Internet.** Laundry 1500ptas/€9 for 5kg. 24hr. reception. Singles 7000ptas/€42, with bath 9000ptas/€54; doubles 9000ptas/€54, 10,000ptas/€60; triples 12,000ptas/€72, 13,000ptas/€78. Discount in Nov. and Feb. AmEx/MC/V.

Hotel California, C. Rauric, 14 (☎933 17 77 66). M: Catalunya. Pleasant rooms with TV, phone, bath, and A/C cater to a gay clientele. Breakfast included. Singles 7500ptas/€45; doubles 12,000ptas/€72; triples 15,000ptas/€90. AmEx/MC/V.

Hostal Campi, C. Canuda, 4 (☎/fax 933 01 3545). M: Catalunya. A great bargain for quality, location, and spacious rooms. Rooms with bath have TVs. Reservations accepted 9am-8pm. Singles 3000ptas/€18; doubles 6000ptas/€36, with bath 7000ptas/€42; triples 8000ptas/€48, 9000ptas/€54. Cash only.

EL RAVAL

Be careful in the areas nearer to the port and farther from Las Ramblas.

🏨 **Pensión L'Isard,** C. Tallers, 82 (☎933 02 51 83; fax 933 02 01 17). M: Universitat. Simple, elegant, and clean. Singles 2800ptas/€16,80; doubles 4900ptas/€29,40, with bath 6500ptas/€39; triples 7300ptas/€43.80, 8500ptas/€51.

Hostal La Terrassa, Junta de Comerç, 11 (☎933 02 51 74). M: Liceu. A minimalist experience. Singles 2700ptas/€16.20; doubles 4200ptas/€25.20, with bath 5200ptas/€31.20; triples 5700ptas/€34.20, 6600ptas/€39.60. MC/V.

L'EIXAMPLE

🏨 **Hostal Ciudad Condal,** C. Mallorca, 255 (☎932 15 10 40). M: Diagonal, just off Pg. de Gràcia, 2 blocks from La Pedrera. Rooms with bath and phones. 24hr. reception. Must reserve with a credit card for late arrivals. Singles 8500ptas/€51; doubles 13,000-14,000ptas/€78-84. Prices often drop in winter. Wheelchair-accessible. MC/V.

🏨 **Pensión Fani,** C. València, 278 (☎932 15 36 45). M: Catalunya. Oozes character; birds in the sunroom. Rents by month or night. Shared baths, kitchen, TV room, and laundry room. Bring a towel. Singles 42,000ptas/€252 per month; doubles

80,000ptas/€480 per month; triples 120,000ptas/€720 per month. 1 night 3000ptas/€18 per person.

■ **Hostal Residencia Oliva,** Pg. de Gràcia, 32 (☎934 88 01 62). M: Pg. de Gràcia. Reservations a must. Laundry 2000ptas/€12. Singles 3500ptas/€21; doubles 6500ptas/€39, with bath 7500ptas/€45; triples 10,500ptas/€63. Cash only.

Hostal Eden, C. Balmes, 55 (☎934 52 66 20; www.eden.iberica.com). M: Pg. de Gràcia. Stained-glass and floral tiles. May-Oct. singles 4815ptas/€29, with bath 6420ptas/€38; doubles 5885ptas/€35, 8560ptas/€50. Nov.-Apr. singles 3815ptas/€23, 5350ptas/€32; doubles 4815ptas/€29, 7500ptas/€45. AmEx/MC/V.

Hostal Residencia Windsor, Rambla de Catalunya, 84 (☎932 15 11 98). M: Pg. de Gràcia, on the corner of C. Mallorca. Carpeted hallways, gilded mirrors, and a plush TV room. Rooms with sleep-sofas and heat in winter. Singles 4500ptas/€27, with bath 5400ptas/€32.50; doubles 7200ptas/€43, 7800ptas/€47.

GRÀCIA

Gràcia is Barcelona's "undiscovered" quarter, but natives have definitely discovered its lively nightlife. Last-minute arrivals may find vacancies here.

■ **Hostal Lesseps,** C. Gran de Gràcia, 239 (☎932 18 44 34; fax 932 17 11 80). M: Lesseps. Spacious rooms sport red velvet wallpaper. 16 rooms have TV and bath, 4 have A/C (600ptas/€3.60 extra per day). Singles 5000ptas/€30; doubles 8000ptas/€48; triples 10,500ptas/€63; quads 12,500/€75. MC/V.

Hostal Bonavista, C. Bonavista, 21 (☎932 37 37 57). M: Diagonal. No reservations. Singles 2700ptas/€16; doubles 4100ptas/€24, with bath 5200ptas/€32.

Albergue Mare de Déu (HI), Pg. Mare de Déu del Coll, 41-51 (☎932 10 51 51; www.tujuca.com). From M: Vallcarca. Breakfast included. Sheets 350ptas/€2. 3-day max. stay. Reception 8am-3pm and 4:30pm-11:30pm. Lockout 10am-1:30pm. Midnight curfew. Dorms 2000ptas/€12, over 25 2700ptas/€16. AmEx/MC/V.

ELSEWHERE

■ **Hostal Orleans,** Av. Marqués de l'Argentera, 13 (☎933 19 73 82). M: Barceloneta. Spotless and comfortable, with private baths. Singles 3000-4500ptas/€18-27; doubles 8500ptas/€50, with A/C 9000ptas/€54; triples 9500-10000ptas/€56-60; quads 12000ptas/€72. AmEx/D/MC/V.

■ **Hostal de Ribagorza,** C. Trafalgar, 39 (☎933 19 19 68; fax 933 19 12 47). M: Urquinaona. With your back to Pl. Urquinaona, take Ronda Sant Pere and go right 1 block on C. Méndez Núñez. Homey doubles in a Modernist building. Oct.-Feb. dorms 4000ptas/€24, with bath 6000ptas/€36; Mar.-Sept. 5500ptas/€33, 7500ptas/€45. MC/V.

CAMPING

For info, contact **Associació de Càmpings de Barcelona,** Gran Vía, 608 (☎93 4 12 59 55).

El Toro Bravo, Autovía Castelldefells km 11 (☎936 37 34 62; fax 936 37 21 15; www.eltorobravo.com). Bus L95 (200ptas/€1.20) 11km from Pl. Catalunya. Reception 8am-7pm. Sept. 1-June 14 725ptas/€4 per person, 775ptas/€5 per site, 725ptas/€4 per car; electricity 575ptas/€3.50. June 15-Aug. 31 760ptas/€5 per person, 810ptas/€5 per site, 760ptas/€5 per car; electricity 575 ptas/€3.50. AmEx/MC/V.

◘ FOOD

Drawing from both Spanish and Catalan culinary traditions, Barcelona's restaurants are a mix of authentic neighborhood haunts and stylish cosmopolitan cuisine. The *Guia del Ocio* (available at newsstands) is an invaluable source of culinary suggestions. Port Vell and Port Olímpic are known for seafood. The restaurants on C. Aragó by Pg. de Gràcia have great lunchtime *menús*, and the Pg. de Gràcia has beautiful outdoor dining. Gràcia's Pl. Sol and La Ribera's Santa Maria del Mar are the best places to head for *tapas*. If you want to live cheap and do as Barceloneses do, buy your food fresh at a **mercat** (marketplace) or hit up a grocery store for other essentials. For wholesale fruit, cheese, and wine, head to **La Boqueria** (Mercat de Sant Josep), outside M: Liceu. For groceries, head to **Champion Supermarket**, Las Ramblas, 11. (M: Liceu. Open M-Sa 9am-9pm.)

BARRI GÒTIC

Great restaurants are scattered on C. Escudellers and C. Clave. Lively hangouts surround Santa Maria del Pi.

Els Quatre Gats, C. Montsió, 3. M: Catalunya; the 2nd left off Portal de l'Angel. Picasso's old Modernist hangout; he designed a personalized menu. Entrees around 2000ptas/€12; *tapas* 200-600ptas/€1.50-3.60. Live piano and violin 9pm-1am. Open M-Sa 9am-2am, Su 5pm-2am. Closed Aug. AmEx/MC/V.

Les Quinze Nits, Pl. Reial, 6. M: Liceu. One of the most popular restaurants, with nightly lines that move quickly. Stylish decor and Catalan entrees at unbelievable prices (500-1200ptas/€3-7). No reservations. Open daily 1-3:45pm and 8:30-11:30pm. MC/V.

Irati, C. Cardenal Casañas, 17. M: Liceu. Basque *tapas* (160ptas/€1 each). Keep your toothpicks for your bill. Bartenders pour *sidra* (cider) behind their backs (150ptas/€1). Starters 1500ptas/€9. Entrees 2500-3000ptas/€15-18. Open Tu-Sa noon-midnight, Su noon-4:30pm. *Tapas* served noon-3pm and 7-11pm. AmEx/MC/V.

L'Antic Bocoi del Gòtic, Baixada de Viladecols, 3. M: Jaume I. Complete with Roman wall, it's what one imagines in the "Gothic Quarter." Salads and sausages about 1000ptas/€6, artisan cheeses 1500-2000ptas/€9-12. Wine 1500-3000ptas/€9-18 per bottle. Open M-Sa 8:30pm-midnight. AmEx/MC/V.

EL RAVAL

Students and blue-collar workers congregate in Catalan joints west of Las Ramblas. Restaurants are fairly inexpensive: most have simple decor, basic food, and lots of noise, although trendier places have started to move in as well.

Bar Ra, Pl. Garduña (☎933 01 41 63). M: Liceu, behind Las Ramblas's Boqueria market. Everything about Ra exudes cool. A mixture of traditional Spanish and trendy California cuisine. *Menú* 1300ptas/€8. Open M-Sa 1:30-4pm and 9:30-2am. Dinner by reservation.

Restaurante Can Lluís, C. Cera, 49. M: Sant Antoni. A defining force in Catalan cuisine, overflowing with delicacies like *cabrit* (goat) and *conill* (rabbit). Daily *menú* 1600ptas/€9.60. Open M-Sa 1:30-4pm and 8:30-11:30pm. V.

LA RIBERA

East of Via Laietana, La Ribera is home to numerous bars and small restaurants. The few tourists who walk over are well rewarded. The area around Santa Maria del Mar and the Mercat del Born is crawling with *tapas* bars.

La Habana Vieja, C. Banys Vells, 2. M: Jaume I. C. Cuban music sets the mood for large portions, perfect for sharing. Cuban rice 600-900ptas/€4-5, meat dishes 1600-2000ptas/€102-112. Open daily 10am-4:30pm and 8:30pm-1am. AmEx/D/MC/V.

Xampanyet, C. Montcado, 22. M: Jaume I. Cross Via Laietana, walk down C. Princesa, and turn right on C. Montcado. Xampanyet is on the right after the Museu Picasso. The house *cava* is served at the colorful bar. Glasses 120ptas/€1. Bottles 900ptas/€5. Open Tu-Sa noon-4pm and 7-11:30pm, Su 7-11:30pm. Closed Aug. MC/V.

Va de Vi, C. Banys Vells,16. M: Jaume I; take C. Princesa, a right on C. Montcada, a right on C. Barra de Ferro, and a left on C. Banys Vells. Candle-lit wine bar. Wine (glasses from 275-675ptas/€2-4), cheeses (500-1200ptas/€3-7), and *tapas* (450-900ptas/€3-5). Open June-Sept. daily 7pm-2am, Sept.-June noon-3pm and 7pm-2am.

SPAIN

L'EIXAMPLE

L'Eixample is full of good places to spend a long, enjoyable dinner.

🦑 **El Racó d'en Baltá,** C. Aribau, 125. M: Hospital Clinic. Mediterranean fare and Catalan dishes like *fideua* noodles (1200ptas/€7). Appetizers and salads 950-1200ptas/€6-7. Fish and meat entrees 1575-2300ptas/€10-14. Bottles of wine 600-2600ptas/€3.50-16. Open M 9pm-11pm, Tu-Sa 1-4pm and 9-11pm. AmEx/D/MC/V.

🦑 **Comme-Bio,** C. Gran Via, 603. M: Catalunya. Fresh salad (800-1000ptas/€5-6), hummus, tofu, yogurt, and juice. Restaurant, food to-go, and grocery store all in one. Pasta, rice, and pizzas around 1000ptas/€6. Open daily 9am-11:30pm. MC/V.

🦑 **Laie Llibreria Café,** C. Pau Claris, 85. M: Urquinaona. An ultra-cool lunchspot. Indulge in the cheap, fresh, all-you-can-eat buffet lunch (1250ptas/€8) in the open, bamboo-draped lunch room, then grab a coffee or drink at the bar on the way out. Vegetarian dinner *menú* 2250ptas/€14. Open M-F 9am-1am, Sa 10am-1am. AmEx/MC/V.

GRÀCIA

🦑 **La Gavina,** C. Ros de Olano, 17. Funky pizzeria complete with life-size patron saint. Pizzas go for 750-1450ptas/€5-9. Open Tu-Th and Su 2pm-1am, F-Sa 2pm-2am.

Ikastola, C. La Perla, 22. M: Fontana, off C. Verdi. Ikastola (Basque for "nursery school") serves mostly vegetarian dishes (350-600ptas/€2-3.50) and is also a popular bar. Draw on the chalkboard walls. Open M-F 11am-1am, Sa-Su 5pm-3am.

◎ SIGHTS

Architecturally, Barcelona is defined by its unique Modernist treasures. Las Ramblas—a bustling avenue smack in the city center—and the Barri Gòtic, Barcelona's "old city," are the traditional tourist areas. But don't neglect vibrant La Ribera and El Raval, the upscale avenues of l'Eixample, the panoramic city views from Montjuïc and Tibidabo, Gaudí's Park Güell, and the harbor-side Port Olímpic.

RUTA DEL MODERNISME

For those with a few days and an interest in seeing all the biggest sights, the Ruta del Modernisme is the cheapest and most flexible option. The Ruta del Modernisme isn't a tour in the sense that it doesn't offer a guide or organized transportation; it's a ticket that gives discounted entrance to Modernist sites. Passes (600ptas/€4; students and 65+ 400ptas/€2; groups over 10 people 500ptas/€3 per person) are good for a month and give holders a 50% discount on entrance to Palau Güell, La Sagrada Família, Casa Milà, Palau de la Música Catalana, Casa-Museu Gaudí, Fundació Tàpies, the Museu d'Art Modern, a tour of El Hospital de la Santa Creu i Sant Pau, tours of the façades of La Manzana de la Discòrdia (Casas Amatller, Lleó Morera, and Batlló), and other attractions. Purchase passes at **Casa Amatller,** Pg. de Gràcia, 41. (M: Pg. de Gràcia. ☎934 88 01 39.)

LAS RAMBLAS

Las Ramblas' pedestrian-only median strip is a veritable urban carnival, where street performers dance, fortune-tellers tell, human statues shift poses, and vendors sell birds—all, of course, for a small fee. The sights below are arranged beginning with Pl. Catalunya in the north, continuing to the port in the south.

UPPER LAS RAMBLAS. A port-ward journey begins at the **Font de Canaletes** (more a pump than a fountain), where visitors who wish to eventually return to Barcelona are supposed to sample the water. The upper part of Las Ramblas has been dubbed "Rambla de las Flores" for the numerous flower vendors that inhabit it. Halfway down Las Ramblas, past the bird vendors on La Ramla dels Ocells, **Joan Miró**'s pavement mosaic brightens up the street.

GRAN TEATRE DEL LICEU. Once one of Europe's leading stages, the Liceu has been ravaged by anarchists, bombs, and fires. It is adorned with palatial ornamentation, gold façades, sculptures, and grand side rooms, including a Spanish hall of mirrors. *(Las Ramblas, 51-59, by C. Sant Pau. Ticket office open M-F 2-8:30pm and 1hr. before* *performances.* ☎ 934 85 99 13. *Guided tours daily 9:30-11am, reservation only (call 934 85 99 00). 800ptas/€4.80, students 600ptas/€3.60.)*

MONUMENT A COLOM. Ruis i Taulet's Monument a Colom towers at the port end of Las Ramblas. Ninteenth-century Renaixença enthusiasts convinced themselves that Columbus was Catalan, from a town near Girona. The fact that Columbus points proudly toward Libya, not the Americas, doesn't help the claim; historians agree that Columbus was from Italy. Take the **elevator** to the top and get a stunning view. *(Portal de la Pau. M: Drassanes. Elevator open June-Sept. daily 9am-8:30pm; Oct.-Mar. M-F 10am-1:30pm and 3:30-6:30pm, Sa-Su 10am-6:30pm; Apr.-May M-F 10am-1:30pm and 3:30-7:30pm, Sa-Su 10am-7:30pm. 300ptas/€1.80, children and seniors 200ptas/€1.20.)*

BARRI GÒTIC

While the weathered, narrow streets of the Barri Gòthic, including **Carrer de la Pietat** and **Carrer del Paradis,** have preserved their medieval charm, the ever-growing tourist economy has infused a new, multilingual liveliness into the area.

ESGLÉSIA CATEDRAL DE LA SANTA CREU. One of Barcelona's most popular monuments. Beyond the **choir** are the altar with the bronze **cross** designed by Frederic Marès in 1976, and the sunken **Crypt of Santa Eulalia,** one of Barcelona' s patron saints. The **cathedral museum** holds Bartolomé Bermejo's *Pietà,* the image of Christ dying in the arms of his mother. Catch a performance of the **sardana,** the traditional Catalan dance, in front of the cathedral. Performances occur Sunday after mass (noon-6:30 pm). *(M: Jaume I. In Pl. Seu, up C. Bisbe from Pl. St. Jaume. Cathedral open daily 8am-1:30pm and 4-7:30pm. Free. Cloister open daily 9am-1:15pm and 4-7pm. 225ptas/€1.50. Elevator to roof open M-F 10:30am-12:30pm and 4:30-6pm, Sa-Su 10:30am-12:30pm. 150ptas/€1. Sala capitular 100ptas/€1.)*

PLAÇA DE SANT JAUME. Plaça de Sant Jaumehas been Barcelona's political center since Roman times. Two of Catalunya's most important buildings have dominated the square since 1823: the **Palau de la Generalitat,** the headquarters of Catalunya's autonomous government, and the **Ajuntament,** the city hall. *(Palau de la Generalitat open the 2nd and 4th Su of each month 10am-2pm. 30min. Mandatory tours in English, French, Spanish, and Catalan. Ajuntament open Sa-Su 10am-1:45pm. Free.)*

LA RIBERA

As the stomping ground of fishermen and merchants, La Ribera has always had a plebian feel; recently, the neighborhood has evolved into Barcelona's bohemian nucleus, with art galleries, chic eateries, and exclusive bars.

◼ **PALAU DE LA MÚSICA CATALANA.** In 1891, the Orfeó Catalan choir society commissioned Modernist Luis Domènech i Montaner to design this must-see concert venue. The music hall glows with tall stained-glass windows, an ornate chandelier, marble reliefs, intricate woodwork, and ceramic mosaics. Concerts given at the Palau include all varieties of symphonic and choral music in addition to more modern forms of pop, rock, and jazz. *(C. Sant Francese de Paula, 2. M: Jaume I. ☎ 932 95 72 00; www.palaumusica.org. Entrance only with a tour. Reserve ahead. Buy tickets at the gift-shop next door. 800ptas/€5, students and seniors 600ptas/€3.60. Palau open Sept.-July daily 10am-3:30pm; Aug. 10am-6pm. Box office open M-Sa 10am-9pm, Su from 1hr. before concert. Check the Guía del Ocio for listings. Concert tickets 1300-26,000ptas/€8-125. MC/V.)*

◼ **MUSEU PICASSO.** This incredible museum traces the development of Picasso as an artist, with a collection of his early works that weaves through five connected mansions once occupied by nobility. Although the museum offers little from Picasso's well-known middle years, it boasts the world's best collection of work from his formative period in Barcelona. The collection also includes lithographs and pencil sketches by an 11-year-old Picasso, and an excellent display of the artist's Cubist interpretations of Velázquez's *Las Meninas* (which hangs in the Prado in Madrid). *(C. Montcada, 15-19. M: Jaume I. Walk down C. Princesa from the metro, and turn right on C. Montcada. ☎ 933 19 63 10. Open Tu-Sa 10am-8pm, Su 10am-3pm. 800ptas/€5; students and seniors 400ptas/€2.50, under 16 free. Free 1st Su of each month.)*

SANTA MARIA DEL MAR. Built in the 14th century in a quick 55 years. At a distance of 13m apart, the supporting columns span a width greater than any other medieva building in the world. A fascinating example of the limits of Gothic architecture— were it 0.6m higher, it would collapse from structural instability. Church holds classical, gospel, and folk concerts; call for information. (☎933 10 23 90. *Open M-Sa 9am-1:30pm and 4:30-8pm, Su 9am-2pm and 5-8:30pm. For concert info, call 933 19 05 16.*)

PARC DE LA CUITADELLA. Host of the 1888 Universal Exposition, the park harbors several museums, well-labeled horticulture, the wacky **Cascada fountains,** a pond, and a zoo. Buildings of note include Domènech i Montaner's Modernista **Castell dels Tres Dragons** (now Museu de Zoología), the geological museum (a few buildings down P. Picasso from M. Zoología), and Josep Amergós's Hivernacle. Expo '88 also inspired the small Arc de Triomf, just across Pg. Pujades from the park. ■**Floquet de Neu,** (a.k.a. *Copito de Nieve* and Little Snowflake), the world's only white gorilla behind bars, lounges in the Parc Zoològic, on the end of the park closer to the sea. (☎932 21 25 06. *Open Nov.-Feb. 10am-5pm, Mar and Oct. 10am-6pm, Apr. and Sept. 10am-7pm, May-Aug. 9:30am-7:30pm. 850ptas/€5.*) In the center of the park, on Pl. Armes, is the **Museu d'Art Modern,** which houses a potpourri of works by 19th-century Catalan artists. (*M: Barceloneta or Arc de Triomf.* ☎933 19 57 28. *Open Tu-Sa 10am-7pm, Su 10am-2:30pm. 500ptas/€3, students 350ptas/€2.*)

EL RAVAL

■ **PALAU GÜELL.** Gaudí's Palau Güell (1886)—the Modernist residence built for patron Eusebi Güell of Park Güell fame—has one of Barcelona's most spectacular interiors. Güell and Gaudí spared no expense. The 20 unique rooftop chimneys display Gaudí's first use of the *trencadis*—the covering of surfaces with irregular shards of ceramic, a technique seen in his later work. (*C. Nou de La Rambla, 3-5.* ☎933 17 39 74. *M: Liceu. Visits by tour only, every 15min. Open M-Sa 10am-1pm and 4:15-7pm. 400ptas/€2.40, students 200ptas/€1.20.*)

MUSEU D'ART CONTEMPORANI (MACBA). This monstrosity of a building was constructed by American architect Richard Meier with the idea that sparse decor would allow the art to speak for itself. And it does—the MACBA has received world-wide acclaim for its focus on avant-garde art between the two world wars, as well as surrealism and contemporary art. (*Pl. dels Angels, 1. M: Catalunya.* ☎934 12 08 10. *Open July-Sept. M, W, F 11am-8pm; Th 11am-9:30pm; Sa 10am-8pm, Su 10am-3pm. Oct.-June M-F 11am-7:30pm, Sa 10am-8pm, Su 10am-3pm. Closed Tu. 800ptas/€5, students 550ptas/€3.50.*)

WATERFRONT

■ **L'AQUÀRIUM DE BARCELONA.** Barcelona's aquarium—the largest in Europe—is an aquatic wonder, featuring copious amounts of octopi and a plethora of penguins. The highlight is an 80m long glass tunnel through an ocean tank of sharks, sting rays, and one two-dimensional fish. (*Moll d'Espanya, next to Maremagnum. M: Drassanes.* ☎932 21 74 74. *Open July-Aug. daily 9:30am-11pm; Sept.-June 9:30am-9pm. 1550ptas/€9, under 12 and seniors 950ptas/€6. Last entrance 1hr. before closing.*)

VILA OLÍMPICA. The Vila Olímpica, beyond the east side of the zoo, was built on top of what was once a working-class neighborhood to house 15,000 athletes and entertain millions of tourists for the 1992 Summer Olympics. These days, it's home to several public parks, a shopping center, and business offices. In the area called **Barceloneta,** mediocre beaches stretch out from the port. (*From M: Ciutadella/Vila Olímpica, walk along the waterfront on Ronda Litoral toward the 2 towers.*)

L'EIXAMPLE

The Catalan Renaissance and the growth of Barcelona during the 19th century pushed the city past its medieval walls and into modernity. Ildefons Cerdà drew up a plan for a new neighborhood where people of all social classes could live side by side. However, l'Eixample (pronounced luh-SHOMP-luh) did not thrive as a utopian community but rather as a playground for the bourgeois.

■ **LA SAGRADA FAMÍLIA.** Only Antoni Gaudí could draw thousands of tourists to an unfinished church. He gave 43 years of his life to the task, living in the basement before his death in 1926. Since then, construction has been erratic and controversial. Of the three proposed façades, only the first (a smaller one), the Nativity Façade, was finished under Gaudí. A furor has arisen over recent additions, especially sculptor Josep Subirach's Cubist Passion Façade on C. Sardenya, which is criticized for being inconsistent with the Gaudí-endorsed Nativity Façade. The church's staircases and towers are not for anyone with a fear of heights or closed spaces. The **museum** displays artifacts relating to the building's construction. *(C. Mallorca, 401. M: Sagrada Família. ☎ 932 07 30 31. Open Nov.-Feb. daily 9am-6pm, elevator 9:30am-5:45pm; Mar. and Sept.-Oct. 9am-7pm, elevator 9:30am-6:45pm; Apr.-Aug. 9am-8pm, elevator 9:30am-7:45pm. Guided tours Apr.-Oct. daily 11:30am, 1, 4, and 5:30pm; Nov.-Mar. F-M 11:30am and 1pm; 500ptas/€3. Tickets 850ptas/€5, students 650ptas/€4.50.)*

■ **LA MANZANA DE LA DISCÒRDIA.** A short walk from Pl. Catalunya, the odd-numbered side of Pg. Gràcia between C. Aragó and Consell de Cent is popularly known as *la manzana de la discòrdia* (block of discord), referring to the stylistic clashing of the three buildings. Regrettably, the bottom two floors of **Casa Lleó i Morera,** by Domènech i Montaner, were destroyed to make room for a fancy store, but you can buy the **Ruta del Modernisme pass** (see p. 864) there and take a tour of the upstairs, where sprouting flowers, stained glass, and legendary doorway sculptures adorn the interior. Puig i Cadafalch opted for a geometric, Moorish-influenced pattern on the façade of **Casa Amatller** at #41. Gaudí's balconies ripple like skulls, and tiles sparkle in blue-purple glory on **Casa Batlló,** #43. The most popular interpretation of Casa Batlló is that the building represents Catalunya's patron Sant Jordi (St. George) slaying a dragon; the chimney plays the lance, the scaly roof is the dragon's back, and the bony balconies are the remains of his victims.

■ **CASA MILÀ (LA PEDRERA).** Modernisme buffs argue that the spectacular Casa Milà apartment building, an undulating mass of granite popularly known as *La Pedrera* (the Stone Quarry), is Gaudí's most refined work. Note the intricate ironwork around the balconies and the irregularity of the front gate's egg-shaped window panes. The roof sprouts chimneys that resemble armored soldiers, one of which is decorated with broken champagne bottles. Rooftop tours provide a closer look at the "Prussian helmets" (spiral chimneys inspired by the helmets worn in Wagner's operas). The winding brick attic (recently restored along with the rooftop in a multi-million-*peseta* project) has been transformed into the **Espai Gaudí,** a multimedia presentation of Gaudí's life and works. A refurnished and restored apartment awaits one floor below, as an example of the fine, captivating interior of Gaudí homes. *(Pg. Gràcia, 92. ☎ 934 84 59 95. Open daily 10am-8pm. 1000ptas/€6; students and seniors 500ptas/€3. Free guided tours M-F 5:30pm (English and Catalan) and 6pm (Spanish), Sa-Su 11am (English and Catalan) and 11:30pm (Spanish); you can also reserve a private group tour (4000ptas/€24).*

MONTJUÏC

Throughout Barcelona's history, whoever controlled Montjuïc (Hill of the Jews) controlled the city. Dozens of rulers have modified the **fortress,** built atop an ancient Jewish cemetery; Franco made it one of his "interrogation" headquarters. The fort was not available for recreational use until Franco rededicated it to the city in 1960—a huge stone monument expresses Barcelona's (forced) gratitude for its return. The three statues in the monument symbolize the three seas surrounding Spain. *(To get to Parc de Montjuïc, take the metro to Pl. Espanya (M: Espanya) and catch bus #50 at Av. Reina María Cristina (every 10min.)*

FONTS LUMINOSES. The Illuminated Fountains, dominated by the huge central **Font Mágica** (Magic Fountain), are visible from Pl. Espanya up Av. Reina María Cris-

FAR-OUT FAÇADE Gaudí was religious, and his plans for La Sagrada Família called for elaborate symbolism in almost every element of the church. On the left of the **Passion Façade**, a snake lurks behind Judas, symbolizing the disciple's betrayal of Jesus. The 4x4 box of numbers next to Jesus contains 310 combinations of four numbers, each of which adds up to 33, Christ's age at death. The faceless woman in the center of the façade, **Veronica**, represents the Biblical woman with the same name and the miraculous appearance of Christ's face on the cloth she wiped him with. The cypress tree on the **Nativity Façade** has been interpreted as a stairway to heaven (cypress trees do not put down deeper roots with time but still grow taller); the tree is crowned with the word "Tau," Greek for the name of God. The top of the eight finished towers carries the first letter of one of the names of the apostles (and the words "Hosanna" and "Excelsis" are written in a spiral up the sides of the towers). Inside, on the **Portal of the Rosary,** overt references to modern life lurk amongst more traditional religious imagery: the Temptation of Man is represented in one carving by the devil handing a bomb to a terrorist and in another by his waving a purse at a prostitute.

tina. During the summer, they are employed in a weekend music and laser show that illuminates the mountainside and the **Palau Nacional,** located behind the fountains. *(Shows every 30min. June-Sept. Th-Su 9:30pm-12:30am; Oct.-May F-Sa 7-8:30pm. Free.)* The palace now houses the **Museu Nacional d'Art de Cataluña.** *(From M: Espanya, walk up Av. Reina María Cristina, away from the twin brick towers, and take the escalators. ☎ 93 622 03 60; www.mnac.es. Open Tu–Sa 10am-7pm, Su 10am-2:30pm. 800ptas/€4.80, 1000ptas/ €6 with temporary exhibits; students and seniors 550ptas/€3.40, 700ptas/€4.22. Free 1st Th of every month. Wheelchair accessible.)*

OLYMPIC RING. In 1929, Barcelona inaugurated the **Estadi Olímpic de Montjuïc** in its bid for the 1932 Olympic games. Over 50 years later, Catalán architects Federic Correa and Alfons Milà, who were also responsible for the overall design of the **Anella Olímpica** (Olympic Ring) esplanade, renovated the shell with the help of Italian architect Vittorio Gregotti. *(☎ 93 426 20 89. Open daily 10am-8pm. Free.)* Designed by Japanese architect Arata Isozaki, the **Palau d'Esports Sant Jordi** is the most technologically sophisticated of the structures. *(☎ 93 426 20 89. Call in advance.)* Test your swimming mettle in the **Olympic pools** or visit the **Galería Olímpica.** *(Galeria ☎ 934 26 06 60. Open Oct.-Mar. M-F 10am-1pm and 4-6pm; Apr.-May M-F 10am-2pm and 4-7pm; June M-Sa 10am-2pm and 4-7pm, Su 10am-2pm; July-Sept. M-Sa 10am-2pm and 4-8pm, Su 10am-2pm. 400ptas/€2.40, students 350ptas/€2, seniors 170ptas/€1. Combined visit with Poble Espanyol 1200ptas/€7.)*

■ **FUNDACIÓ MIRÓ.** Designed by Miró's friend Josep Luís Sert and tucked into the side of Montjuïc, the Fundació links interior and exterior spaces with massive windows and outdoor patios. Sky lights illuminate an extensive collection of statues, and paintings from Miró's career. Some of the most stunning include the Barcelona Series, which depicts Miró's personal reaction to the Spanish Civil War, and several works from Miro's *Las Constelaciones* series, a reaction to Nazi invasion during World War II. His best-known pieces in the museum include *El Carnival de Arlequin, La Masia,* and *L'or de L'azuz.* Room 13 displays experimental work by young artists. The Fundació also sponsors music and film festivals. *(Av. Miramar, 71-75. ☎ 934 43 94 70. Open July-Sept. Tu-W and F-Sa 10am-8pm, Th 10am-9:30pm, Su 10am-2:30pm; Oct.-June Tu-W and F-Sa 10am-7pm, Th 10am-9:30pm, Su 10am-2:30pm. 1200ptas/ €7, students and seniors 650ptas/€4.)*

■ **CASTELL DE MONTJUÏC.** A visit to this historic fortress and its ■**Museum Militar** is a great way to get an overview of the city—both of its layout and its history. From the castle's exterior *mirador,* gaze over the city. Enjoy coffee at the cafe while cannons stare you down. *(M: Paral.lel. Take the funicular to Av. Miramar and then the Teleféric de Montjuïc. The funicular runs from inside M: Paral.lel at Av. Paral.lel and Nou de la Rambla. Teleféric open M-Sa 11:15am-9pm. Alternatively, walk up the steep slope on C. Foc, next to the* *funicular station. Open Mar. 15-Nov. 15 Tu-Su 9:30am-8pm; Nov. 16-Mar. 14 Tu-Su 9:30am-5pm. Museum 400ptas/€2.50. Mirador only 100ptas/€1.)*

GRÀCIA

Just beyond L'Eixample, this neighborhood charms and confuses with its narrow alleys and numerous plazas. In August, Gràcia hosts one of Barcelona's best festivals, **Fiesta Mejor.**

PARK GÜELL. The park was designed entirely by Gaudí, and—in typical Gaudí fashion—was not completed until after his death. Gaudí intended Park Güell to be a garden city, and its multicolored dwarfish buildings and sparkling ceramic-mosaic stairways were designed to house the city's elite. Two mosaic staircases flank the park, leading to a towering Modernist pavilion that Gaudí originally designed as an open-air market. The longest park bench in the world, a multicolored serpentine wonder made of tile shards, decorates the top of the pavilion. In the midst of the park is the **Casa-Museu Gaudí.** *(Bus #24 from Pg. Catalunya stops at the upper park entrance. Park ☎ 93 219 38 11. Open May-Sept. daily 10am-9pm; Mar.-Apr. and Oct. 10am-7pm; Nov.-Feb. 10am-6pm. Free.)*

CASA VICENS. One of Gaudí's earliest projects, Casa Vicens is decorated with cheerful ceramic tiles. The *casa* shows the influence of Arabic architecture and a rigidness that is uncharacteristic of Gaudí's later works. The hard lines contrast with Gaudí's trademark fluid ironwork on the balconies and façade. *(C. Carolines, 24-26. M: Fontana; walk Gran de Gràcia and turn left onto C. Carolines.)*

🎵 ENTERTAINMENT

ART GALLERIES

One of the capitals of cutting-edge art, Barcelona showcases many of the latest artistic trends. Many private showings display the works of both budding artists and renowned masters. Most of Barcelona's galleries are located in **La Ribera** around C. Montcada. Three of the best-known in the La Ribera area include: **Gallery Surrealista, Galeria Maeght,** and **Galeria Montcada.** For more in-depth gallery info, check the *Guía del Ocio.* The **Palau de la Virreina** also has information on cultural events. *(Las Ramblas, 99. Between La Boqueria market and C. Carme. M: Liceu. ☎ 933 01 77 75. Open M-F 10am-2pm and 4-8pm.)*

THE SARDANA

The Sardana, Catalunya's regional dance, is one of the highlights of any stint in Barcelona. It is a communal dance in which men and women join hands in a closed circle and perform a series of kicks and short steps to upbeat music; travelers are welcome to participate, as long as they observe the dance's solemn atmosphere. *(Dances in front of the cathedral Sa 6:30pm, Su noon.)*

FÚTBOL

For the record, the lunatics that run around the city covered head to toe in red and blue didn't just escape from a nearby asylum—they are **F.C. Barcelona** fans. Grab some face paint and head to the 110,000-seat **Nou Camp,** which has a box office on C. Aristedes Maillol, 12-18. *(☎ 934 96 36 00; www.fcbarcelona.com. Ticket office open M-F and day before match 9:30-11:30am and 4:30-7:30pm.)* **R.C. Deportivo Espanyol,** a.k.a. *los periquitos* (parakeets), Barcelona's second professional soccer team, spreads its wings at **Estadi Olímpic,** Pg. Olímpic, 17-19 *(☎ 934 05 02 97).* Obtain tickets for both from Banca Catalana or call TelEntrada *(☎ 902 10 12 12).*

BULLFIGHTS

Although the best bullfighters rarely venture out of Madrid, Sevilla, and Málaga, Barcelona's **Plaça de Toros Monumental** (tickets ☎ 932 45 58 04), on C. Castillejos,

248, is an excellent facility (M: Monumental). Bullfights usually take place during the tourist season (Apr.-Sept. Su 7pm; doors open at 5:30pm). Tickets are available at ServiCaixa ("la Caixa" banks; ☎902 33 22 11; 2400-12,500ptas/€14.40-75). The box office also sells tickets just before the start of the *corrida*. Seats range from 2600-15,000ptas/€15.60-90.

FIESTAS

Fiestas abound in Barcelona. Before Christmas, the **Feria de Santa Llúcia** fills Pl. Catedral and the area around the Sagrada Familia with stalls and booths. City residents celebrate **Carnaval** February 7 to 17, but many head to even more raucous celebrations in Sitges and Vilanova i la Geltrù. Soon thereafter, the **Festa de Sant Jordi** (St. George), April 23, brings feasts in honor of Cataluña's patron saint. This is Barcelona's St. Valentine's Day; men give women roses, and women give men books. Barcelona erupts on June 23, the night before **Día de Sant Joan.** Bonfires roar throughout the city, and the fountains of Pl. Espanya and Palau Reial light up in anticipation of fireworks on Montjuïc. On August 15-21, city folk jam at Gràcia's **Fiesta Mayor.** Lights blaze in the plazas and streets, and rock bands play all night. On September 11, the **Fiesta Nacional de Cataluña** brings traditional costumes and dancing, and Catalán flags hanging from balconies. The **Feria de Cuina i Vins de Cataluña** draws wine and *butifarra* (sausage) producers to the Rbla. Cataluña. The beginning of November marks the **Fiesta del Sant Çito,** when locals and tourists alike roll up their sleeves and party on Las Ramblas. Finally, from October through November, the **Festival Internacional de Jazz** hits the city's streets and clubs. For information on all festivals, call 933 01 77 75 (open M-F 10am-2pm and 4-8pm).

☢ NIGHTLIFE

As in Madrid, nightlife here begins with a 5pm stroll and doesn't wind down until nearly 14hr. later—if even then. The Barcelona evening can be divided into thirds: start at the *bar-restaurantes* or *cervecerías*, move to the *bares-musicales*, and finish up with a bang at the *discotecas*. As a general rule, the farther from Las Ramblas and the narrower the street, the less-touristed the bar. The trendiest *bares-musicales* are scattered around **Gràcia**. Barcelona's clubs don't heat up until 2am, and most don't wind down until morning. If you are planning on clubbing, make sure to look your finest—many of the most popular *discotecas* expect a certain level of formality. At clubs, expect to be charged around 600ptas/€3.60 for a beer and 900ptas/€5.40 and up for mixed drinks. Keep in mind that what's popular changes on a daily basis—talk to locals for an up-to-the-minute report. Consult the *Guía del Ocio* for information on movies (*Ciné* section), live concerts *(Música)*, bars, discos *(Tarde/Noche)*, and cultural events.

BARRI GÒTIC

Here, cookie-cutter *cervecerías* and *bar-restaurantes* can be found every five steps. The Barri Gótic is perfect for chit-chatting your night away, sipping *sangría*, or scoping out your next dance partner.

- **El Bosq de les Fades.** M: Drassanes, down an alley just off Las Ramblas, near the water and next to the Museu de Cera. From the maniacal geniuses who brought you the wax museum, El Bosq de les Fades (the Forest of Fables) is a fairy tale world, complete with gnarly trees, waterfalls, gnomes, a small bridge, and plush side rooms. Overheard: "Dude, check out that fly honey hanging out at the corner table...oh damn, she's made of wax." Open M-Th until 1:30am, F-Sa until 2:30am.

- **Jamboree,** Pl. Reial, 17. M: Liceu, in the corner immediately to your right coming from Las Ramblas. What was once a convent now serves as one of the city's most popular live music venues. Jazz or blues performances daily 11pm-1am (1000-2000ptas/€6-12 includes 1 drink). At 1:30am, the brick basement area turns into a packed hip-hop

SPAIN

dance club. Upstairs, the attached club **Tarantos** plays pop and salsa for an older crowd. Open until 5am.

New York, C. Escudellers, 5. M: Drassanes, right off Las Ramblas. The biggest club in the Barri Gòtic. Crowds don't arrive until well after 3am; music includes reggae and British pop. Cover 900-1400ptas/€5.40-11.40. Open Th-Sa 11:30pm-5am. Cash only.

EL RAVAL

☒ **La Oveja Negra,** C. Sitges 5. M: Catalunya. From Pl. Catalunya, go down Las Ramblas and take the 1st right onto C. Tallers; C. Sitges is the 1st left. The most touristed tavern in town. Open M-Th 9am-2:30am, F 9am-3:30am, Sa-Su 5pm-3am.

London Bar, C. Nou de la Rambla 34. M: Liceu, off of Las Ramblas. Rub shoulders with fun-loving expats at this Modernist tavern. Live music nightly, usually rock or blues. Beer 400ptas/€2.40, wine 300ptas/€1.80. Open F-Sa 7pm-5am, Su and Tu-Th 7pm-3am.

LA RIBERA

In La Ribera, the name of the game is *tapas* bars, where the young and beautiful gather and indulge.

Plàstic Café, Pg. del Born, 19. M: Jaume I, follow C. Princesa and turn right on C. Comerç and right again on Pg. del Born. 'Café' is a misnomer for this jam-packed, hyper trendy bar, with an eclectic mix of international, house, and 80s pop spinning in the background. Beer 400-500ptas/€2.40-3. Open Su-Th 10pm-2:30am, F-Sa 10pm-3am.

Mudanzas, C. Vidreira, 15. M: Jaume I. Everything is black, even the suits. A hip young professional crowd. Wide selection of rum, whiskey, and wines (200-800ptas/€1,20-4.80). Open Su- F 10am-2am, Sa 11am-2am.

L'EIXAMPLE

L'Eixample is a neighborhood known for acceptance of character, and there is a wide variety of nightlife options available here. Most of the biggest and best *discotecas* are outside the tourist-heavy Ramblas area—this is where most natives do their dancing. Most of the places worth trekking to are located in the western l'Eixample Esquerra, although a few are scattered on the right side. The part of l'Eixample Esquerra (west of Pg. de Gràcia) between C. Urgell, C. Aragó, the Gran Via, and C. Aribau is dense with gay nightlife.

PORT OLÍMPIC

Tracing the coast and marked by a gigantic metallic fish structure, the Olympic Village brims with glitzy restaurants and throngs of European dance fiends. Nearly 20 bars and clubs occupy the strip. Revelry begins at midnight and winds down at 6am. From the metro stop Ciutadella-Vila Olímpica (L4), walk down C. Marina toward the twin towers.

Luna Mora, C. Ramón Trias Fargas, on the corner with Pg. Marítim. This lunar-themed disco is the best place for late-night dancing on the beach. 2 huge dance floors, 1 for salsa and 1 for house. Beer 700-800ptas/€4.20-4.80. F-Sa cover 2000ptas/€12. Open Th-Sa 11:30pm-6am; the mostly local crowd doesn't arrive until 3am.

Baja Beach Club, Pg. Marítim 34 (☎93 225 91 00). If Baywatch were a club, this would be it. When not platform-dancing, bikini-clad waitresses and shirtless muscle men serve drinks. Indoor/outdoor restaurant. Food served until 1am; entrees 1200-1700ptas/€7.20-10.20. Cover 2000ptas/€12; Su free for ladies; also free if you eat dinner. Open June-Sept. M-W 1pm-1am, Th and Su 1pm-5am, F-Sa 1pm-6am; Oct.-May M-W 1-5pm, Th-Sa 1pm-1am. MC/V.

MAREMAGNUM

Like Dr. Jekyll and Mr. Hyde, Barcelona's biggest mall has more than one personality. At the stroke of midnight, the complex turns into an overwhelming tri-level maze of dance clubs. Each club plays its own music (expect to hear a lot of American pop) for crowds of international students, tourists, and the occasional Spaniard. (Beer 300-800ptas/€1.80-4.80. Mixed drinks 1000ptas/ €6.) To get to Maremagnum, walk down Las Ramblas and cross over the wavy bridge to the mall.

MONTJUÏC

Lower Montjuïc is home to Barcelona's epic "disco theme park," **Poble Espanyol,** Av. Marqués de Comillas (☎ 933 22 03 26). M: Pl. Espanya. Take a cab from the metro and fall in lust with the craziest disco experience in all of Barcelona. Some of the most popular (and surreal) discos include **La Terrrazza** (an outdoor mad house), **Torres de Ávila** (with speedy glass elevators), and **Sixty-Nine** (no description needed). Dancing starts at around 1:30am and doesn't end until 9am. Most clubs have cover discounts. Open July-Aug. nightly; Sept.-June Th-Sa.

GRÀCIA

Nightlife in Gràcia is *la crème de la crème*, to borrow a phrase from Spain's northern neighbor. Most of Barcelona's funkiest *bares-musicales* are here.

▨ **Gasterea,** C. Verdi, 39. M: Fontana. Follow C. Astúries for several blocks and make a right onto C. Verdi. Yellow walls cast a warm glow in this table-less bar. Grab a seat at one of the counters and dig in to Gasterea's selection of excellent, fresh *tapas* (150ptas/€1 each), such as eggplant with herb goat cheese. Su-Tu and Th 7:30pm-1am, F-Sa 7:30pm-2am.

Bamboleo, C. Topazi 24. M: Fontana, above Pl. del Diamante. Cuban bar hosts salsa, techno, rock DJs, and a foosball table. Calimocho, mojitos, and piña coladas 600ptas/ €3.50. Open M-Th 7pm-2:30am, F-Sa 7pm-3am.

ELSEWHERE

▨ **Otto Zutz,** C. Lincoln 15 (☎ 932 38 07 22). FGC: Pl. Molina. Walk downhill on Via Augusta and take C. Lincoln when it splits off to the right. The place to see and be seen. 9 bars. 2500ptas/€15 cover includes 1 drink. Open Tu-Sa midnight-6:30am.

Lizard, C. Plató 15 (☎ 934 14 00 32). FGC: Muntaner. Walk uphill on C. Muntaner 2 blocks and turn right on C. Plató. A spectacular iguana greets you at the entrance to Otto Zutz's sister club. DJs spin rap, hip-hop, and funk. Drinks 800ptas/€5. Open Th-Sa midnight-3:30am.

▚ DAYTRIPS FROM BARCELONA

MONTSERRAT

FFCC trains (☎ 932 05 15 15) to Montserrat leave from M: Espanya in Barcelona (1hr., every hr., round-trip including cable car 1875ptas/€11.30); get off at Aeri de Montserrat, not Olesa de Montserrat. From the base of the mountain at the other end, the Aeri cable car runs up to the monastery (every 15min. daily 9:25am-1:45pm and 2:20-6:35pm; round-trip 950ptas/€5.90, included in train fare). From the upper cable car station, turn left and walk to Pl. Creu, where there's an info booth. (☎ 938 77 72 01. Open July-Sept. daily 10am-7pm; Oct.-June M-F 9am-6pm, Sa-Su 10am-7pm.)

An hour northwest of Barcelona, the mountain of Montserrat is where a wandering 9th-century mountaineer had a blinding vision of the Virgin Mary. In the 11th century, a monastery was founded to worship the Virgin, and the site has since evolved into a major pilgrimage center. The **monastery**'s ornate **basilica** is above Pl. Creu. To the right of the main chapel is a route through the **side chapels** that leads to the 12th-century Romanesque **La Moreneta** (the black Virgin Mary), Montserrat's venerated icon. (Open in summer daily 8-10:30am, noon-6:30pm, and 7:30-8:30pm.) In Pl. Santa María, the **Museo de Montserrat** exhibits a sweeping range of art, from an Egyptian mummy to several Picassos. (Open in summer daily 9am-6pm; off-season 9:30am-6:30pm. 500ptas/€3, students 300ptas/€1.80.) The **Santa Cova funicular** descends from Pl. Creu to paths that wind along to ancient hermitages. (Every 20min. in summer daily 10am-1pm and 2-6pm; off-season Sa-Su only. Round-trip 360ptas/€2.15.) Take the **St. Joan funicular** up for more inspirational views. (Every 20min. spring through fall 10am-7pm. Round-trip 975ptas/€6.) The dilapidated **St. Joan monastery** and **shrine** are only 20min. from the highest station. The real prize is **St. Jerónim** (1235m), about 2hr. from Pl. Creu (1hr. from the terminus of the St. Joan funicular); take the sharp left at the little old chapel (after 45min.).

SITGES

Cercanías Trains (☎93 490 02 02) link Sitges to Barcelona-Sants Station and M: Gràcia (40min.; every 15min., last train back 11pm; 350ptas/€2.10).

Forty kilometers south of Barcelona, the resort town of Sitges is famed for its prime tanning grounds, lively cultural festivals, international gay community, and wired nightlife. Long considered a watered-down Ibiza, Sitges has better beaches than the notorious Balearic hotspot, and on mainland Spain, you won't find much crazier beach-oriented nightlife. The **beach** is 10min. from the train station via any street. In town, **Calle Parellades** is the main tourist drag. Late-night foolhardiness clusters around **Calle Primer de Maig,** which runs directly from the beach, and its continuation, **Calle Marques Montroig.** The wild things are at the "disco-beach" **Atlántida,** in Sector Terramar. Shuffle your feet at **Pachá,** on Pg. Sant Didac, in nearby Vallpineda. Buses run to the two discos from C. Primer de Maig (midnight-4am). During **Carnaval,** Feb. 7-17 in 2002, Spaniards crash the town for a frenzy of dancing, costumes, and alcohol. The **tourist office,** on Pg. Vilafranca, is near the train station. From the station, turn right on C. Artur Carbonell and go downhill. (☎93 894 42 51; fax 93 894 43 05. Open in summer daily 9am-9pm; in winter W-M 9am-2pm and 4-6:30pm.) If you plan to stay the night, reserve early. **Hostal Internacional** is at Sant Francesc, 52. (☎93 894 26 90. Doubles 5500ptas/€3.30.)

OTHER DAYTRIPS FROM BARCELONA

GIRONA. Meander through the jumbled streets of historic, charming, and undertouristed Girona (see below).

THE COSTA BRAVA. Besides their stunning cliffs and beaches, the towns along the Costa Brava also offer a historic community (see p. 874).

GIRONA (GERONA)   ☎972

A world-class city patiently waiting for the world to notice it, Girona (pop. 70,500) is really two cities in one: a hushed medieval masterpiece on one riverbank and a thriving, modern metropolis on the other. Though founded by the Romans, the city owes more to the renowned *cabalistas de Girona*, who for centuries spread the teachings of Kabbalah (mystical Judaism) in the West. Still a cultural center and university town, Girona is a magnet for artists, intellectuals, and activists.

Most sights are in the old city, across the river from the train station. The **Riu Onyar** separates the new city from the old. The **Pont de Pedra** bridge connects the two banks and heads into the old quarter by way of C. Ciutadans, C. Peralta, and C. Força, which lead to the cathedral and ◼**El Call,** the medieval Jewish neighborhood. A thriving community in the Middle Ages, El Call was virtually wiped out by the 1492 Inquisition and mass expulsion and conversion. The entrance to **Centre Bonastruc Ça Porta,** the site of the last synagogue in Girona (today a museum), is off C. Força, about halfway up the hill. (☎972 21 67 61. Open June-Oct. M-Sa 10am-8pm, Su 10am-2pm; Nov.-May M-Sa 10am-6pm, Su 10am-3pm. Museum 300ptas/€1.80, students and seniors 150ptas/€0.90. The tourist office also offers guided tours of El Call July-Aug.) Uphill on C. Força and around the corner to the right, the Gothic **cathedral** rises a record-breaking 90 Rococo steps from the plaza below. The **Tesoro Capitular** within contains some of Girona's most precious possessions, including the **Tapis de la Creació,** a 15th-century tapestry depicting the creation story. (Both open July-Sept. Tu-Sa 10am-2pm and 4-7pm; Oct.-Mar. Tu-Sa 10am-2pm and 4-6pm; Apr.-June Tu-Sa 10am-2pm and 4-7pm; open year-round Su-M and holidays 10am-2pm. Tesoro and cloister 500ptas/€3.) **La Rambla** and **Plaza de Independéncia** are the places to see and be seen in Girona. The expansive, impeccably designed **Parc de la Devesa** explodes with *carpas*, temporary outdoor bars. Bars in the old quarter draw crowds in the early evening. **Café la Llibreria,** C. Ciutadans 15, has live music on W and F after 11pm. (Open M-Sa 8:30am-1am, Su 8:30am-midnight.)

RENFE **trains** (☎972 24 02 02) depart from Pl. de Espanya to: Barcelona (1¼hr., 21 per day 6:12am-9:29pm, 930ptas/€5.60); Figueres (30-40min., 24 per day 6:15am-10:44pm, 390ptas/€2.30); Madrid (10½hr., 8:21pm, 6800ptas/€41). **Buses** (☎972 21 23 19) depart from just around the corner. The **tourist office,** Rambla de la Libertat, 1, is directly on the other side. (☎972 22 65 75; fax 972 22 66 12. Open M-F 8am-8pm, Sa 8am-2pm and 4-8pm, Su 9am-2pm.) Most budget accommodations are in the old quarter and are well-kept and reasonably priced. The **Pensió Viladomat,** C. Ciutadans 5, next to the hostel, has light, open, well-furnished rooms. (☎972 20 31 76. Singles 2500ptas/€15; doubles 5000ptas/€30, with bath 7500ptas/€45.) Girona abounds with innovative Cataluñan cuisine; by far the best place to find good, cheap food is on **Calle Cort Reial. Restaurante La Poma,** C. Cort Reial 16, offers internationally influenced cuisine at unbelievable prices. (Open W-M 7:30pm-midnight.) Pick up **groceries** at **Caprabo,** C. Sequia 10, a block from C. Nou off the Gran Via. (Open M-Sa 9am-9pm.) **Postal Code:** 17070.

THE COSTA BRAVA

The Costa Brava's jagged cliffs cut into the Mediterranean Sea from Barcelona to the French border. Though rugged by name, the Brave Coast is tamed in July and August by the planeloads of Europeans dumped onto its once tranquil beaches. Unlike its counterparts, Costa Blanca and Costa del Sol, Costa Brava offers more than just high-rises and touristy beaches. Its rocky shores have traditionally attracted artists like Marc Chagall and Salvador Dalí, a Costa Brava native.

TOSSA DE MAR   ☎972

Falling in love in (and with) Tossa is easy. The pretty town (pop. 3800), 40km north of Barcelona, is packed with tourists every summer. But Tossa draws on its legacy as a 12th-century village, its cliff-studded landscape, its **calas** (small coves), and its small-town charm to resist becoming the average resort. Inside the walled **Vila Vella** (Old Town), spiraling medieval alleys lead to a tiny plaza, where the ◙**Museu Municipal** displays 20s and 30s art. (Open early-June and late-Sept. M-F 11am-1pm and 3-5pm, Sa-Su 11am-6pm; late-June to early-Sept. daily 10am-8pm; Oct. M-F 11am-1pm and 3-5pm, Sa-Su 11am-5pm. 500ptas/€3, students and seniors 300ptas/€1.80.) Sarfa **buses** run to Pl. de les Nacions Sense Estat, at Av. de Pelegrí, from Barcelona (1½hr., 15 per day, 1150ptas/€6.90) and Girona (1hr., 1-2 per day, 580ptas/€3.50). The **tourist office** shares the same building. (☎972 34 01 08. Open mid-June to mid-Sept. M-Sa 9am-9pm, Su 10am-2pm and 4-8pm; Apr.-May and Oct. M-Sa 10am-2pm and 4-8pm, Su 10:30am-1:30pm; Mar. and Nov. M-Sa 10am-1pm and 4-7pm; Dec.-Feb. M-F 10am-1pm and 4-7pm, Sa 10am-1pm.) To get to ◙**Fonda/Can Lluna,** C. Roqueta 20, turn right off Pg. Mar onto C. Peixeteras, walk through C. Estalt, turn left at the end, and head straight. (☎972 34 03 65. 2500ptas/€15 per person.) **Pensión Pepi,** C. Sant Miguel 10, offers cozy rooms with bath. (☎972 34 05 26. Singles 3000ptas/€18; doubles 6000ptas/€36.) The old quarter has the best cuisine and ambience in Tossa. Try the paella at **Restaurant Marina,** C. Tarull 6. (Open *Semana Santa*-Oct. daily 11:30am-11:30pm.) **Postal Code:** 17320.

FIGUERES   ☎972

In 1974, Salvador Dalí chose his native, beachless Figueres (pop. 37,000), 36km north of Girona, as the site to build a museum to house his works, catapulting the city to instant fame. Despite his reputation as a self-promoting fascist, his self-monument is undeniably a masterpiece—and the second most popular museum in Spain. The ◙**Teatre-Museu Dalí,** in Pl. Gala i S. Dalí, parades the artist's erotically nightmarish landscapes and bizarre installations. From the Rambla, take C. Girona, which becomes C. Jonquera, and climb the steps. (Open Oct.-May Tu-Su 10:30am-

5:45pm; June daily 10:30am-5:45pm; July-Sept. 9am-7:45pm. 1200ptas/€7, students and seniors 800ptas/€4.80.) **Trains** (☎ (902) 24 02 02) run to Barcelona (1½hr., 21 per day 6:11am-8:58pm, 1200ptas/€7) and Girona (30min., 21 per day 6:11am-8:58pm, 390ptas/€2.30). **Buses** (☎972 67 33 54), in Pl. Estació, truck to: Barcelona (2¼hr., 4-6 per day, 1885ptas/€11); Cadaqués (1¼hr.; July-Aug. 5 per day, Sept.-June 2-3 per day; 540ptas/€3.50). Girona (1hr., 4-6 per day, 540ptas/€3.50). The **tourist office** is on Pl. Sol. (☎972 50 31 55. Open July-Aug. M-Sa 9am-9pm and Su 9am-3pm; Apr.-June and Oct. M-Sa 9am-2pm and 4:30-8pm; Sept. and Nov.-Apr. M-F 9am-3pm.) **Hostal La Barretina,** C. Lasauca 13, is a lesson in luxury. (☎972 67 64 12. Singles 3500ptas/€21; doubles 6000ptas/€36.) **Postal Code:** 17600.

CADAQUÉS   ☎972

The whitewashed houses and rocky beaches of Cadaqués (pop. 1800) have attracted artists, writers, and musicians—not to mention tourists—ever since Dalí built his summer home here in the 30s. ■**Casa-Museu Salvador Dalí,** Port Lligat,

---

IS THAT A MELTING CANDLE IN YOUR POCKET?

By age 15, Dalí already had high hopes for himself: "I'll be a genius and the world will admire me." Dalí was influenced by Sigmund Freud and sought to connect the unconscious with the conscious in his paintings. Surrealism itself attempted to explore the language of dreams in order to tap the unconscious. Although Dalí's paintings can be confusing at first, aspects of their symbol-language are consistent enough to be translated. Here are a few examples:

A rotting **donkey** or **fish** is Dalí's symbol of the bourgeoisie.

The **crutches** propping up bits of soft flesh are symbols of masturbation.

The **grasshopper** is a symbol of terror, as Dalí had a great fear of the insect.

Staircases are a Freudian image, representing the fear of intercourse.

A **melting candle** is a symbol of impotence.

Lions represent animal aggression, and **knives** are meant to be phallic symbols.

A **fish hook** (found in Dalí's head) is a symbol of his entrapment.

Dalí's home until 1982, is complete with a lip-shaped sofa and pop-art miniature Alhambra. Follow the signs to Port Lligat (bear right with your back to the statue of liberty) and then to the Casa de Dalí. (Open mid-June to mid-Sept. daily 10:30am-9pm; mid-Mar. to mid-June and mid-Sept. to Nov. Tu-Su 10:30am-6pm. Make reservations for a tour 1-2 days in advance. 1300ptas/€7.80; students, seniors, and children 800ptas/€4.80.) **Buses** arrive from Barcelona (2½hr., 4-6 per day, 2365ptas/€14.20); Figueres (1hr., 5-7 per day, 540ptas/€3.30); Girona (2hr., 1-2 per day, 1040ptas/€6.10). With your back to the Sarfa office at the bus stop, walk right along Av. Caritat Serinyana; the **tourist office,** C. Cotxe 2, is off Pl. Frederic Rahola opposite the *passeig*. (☎972 25 83 15. Open July-Aug. M-Sa 9am-2pm and 4-9pm, Su 10:30am-1pm; Sept.-June M-Sa 9am-2pm and 4-7pm.) **Hostal Cristina,** C. Riera, has newly renovated, waterfront rooms. (☎972 25 81 38. Singles 4000ptas/€24; doubles 6000ptas/€36.) Pack a picnic from **Super Auvi,** C. Riera. (Open mid-July to Aug. daily M-Sa 8am-2pm and 4:30-9pm, Su 8am-2pm; Sept. to mid-July M-Sa 8:30am-1:30pm and 4:30-9pm, Su 8am-2pm.) **Postal Code:** 17488.

THE PYRENEES

The jagged green mountains, Romanesque churches, and tranquil towns of the Pyrenees draw hikers and high-brow skiers in search of outdoor adventures. Spectacular views make simply driving through the countryside an incredible experience in and of itself. *Ski España* lists vital statistics of all ski stations in Spain. Without a car, transport is tricky but feasible.

VAL D'ARAN

Some of the Catalán Pyrenees's most dazzling peaks cluster around Val d'Aran, in the northwest corner of Cataluña. The Val d'Aran is best known for its chic ski resorts—the Spanish royal family's favorite slopes are those of **Baquiera-Beret**. Ladies, it's probably as good a place as any to have a chance encounter with the very eligible Prince Felipe. The **Albergue Era Garona (HI)**, a few kilometers away in the lovely town of **Salardú**, is accessible by shuttle **bus** in high-season from Vielha. (☎973 64 52 71; eragarona@aran.org. **HI members only.** HI cards sold. Breakfast included. Sheets 350ptas/€2.10. Jan.-Apr. dorms 2350ptas/€14.20 per person, 3000ptas/€18 over 25; Dec. 2000ptas/€12, 2700ptas/€16.25; May-Nov. 1775ptas/€10.70, 2400ptas/€14.50.) While you are in town don't miss Salardú's impressive 12th-century **church,** where a colorful mural adorns the ceiling and walls near the altar and one of the valley's most coveted paintings—an image of Santo Christo with the mountains of Salardú in the background—hangs on the back wall. For skiing info, contact the **Oficeria de Baquiera-Beret** (☎973 63 90 10) or the tourist office in Vielha (☎973 64 01 10).

The biggest town in the valley, **Vielha** (pop. 3500) welcomes hikers and skiers to its lively streets with every sort of service the outdoorsy type might desire. It's only 12km from Bacquiera-Beret; and shuttle **buses** connect the two in July and August (schedules at the tourist office). **Alsina Graells buses** (☎973 27 14 70) also run to Barcelona (5½hr., 5:30am and 1:30pm, 3725ptas/€22.40). The **tourist office,** C. Sarriulèra, 6, is one block upstream from the *plaça.* (☎973 64 01 10; fax 973 64 03 72. Open Sept.-July M-Sa 10am-1pm and 4:30-7:30pm; Aug. daily 9am-9pm.) Several inexpensive *pensiones* cluster at the end of C. Reiau, off Pg. Libertat (which intersects Av. Casteiro at Pl. Sant Antoni); try **Casa Vicenta** at C. Reiau, 3. (☎973 64 08 19. July 15-Sept. 15 and Dec.-May singles 3600ptas/€21.70; doubles 6300ptas/€37.90; including breakfast. Rest of the year singles 2500ptas/€15; doubles 5000ptas/€30; breakfast not included.)

PARQUE NACIONAL DE ORDESA

The beauty of Ordesa's Aragonese Pyrenees will reduce even the most seasoned of travelers to monosyllabic stupefaction. Well-maintained trails cut across idyllic forests, jagged rock faces, snow-covered peaks, rushing rivers, and magnificent waterfalls. The **Visitors Center "El Parador"** is beyond the Ordesa park entrance. (Open daily Apr. 9am-1:30pm and 3-6pm; May-Oct. 9am-2pm and 4:30-7pm.) The **Soaso Circle** is the most practical hike; frequent signposts clearly mark the 5hr. journey, which can be cut to a 2hr. loop.

It is easiest to enter the park through the village of **Torla,** where you can buy the indispensable *Editorial Alpina* guide (775ptas/€4.70). **La Oscense** (☎974 35 50 60) sends a **bus** from Jaca to **Sabiñánigo** (20min.; M-Sa 8, 10:15am, 3, and 5:15pm, Su 3 and 5:15pm). Sabiñánigo is also easily accessible by **train;** all trains on the Zaragoza-Huesca-Jaca line stop here. From there, **Compañía Hudebus** (☎974 21 32 77) runs to **Torla** (55min.; Sept.-June 11am, July-Aug. 11am and 6pm; 355ptas/€2.40). A bus shuttles between Torla and Ordesa (every 15min.; June 30-Aug. 6am-10pm, Sept. 6am-9pm; 275ptas/€1.65, 400ptas/€2.40 round-trip.) Offseason, you'll have to hike the 8km to the entrance or cab it. (☎974 48 62 43. 2000ptas/€12.) To leave the area, catch the bus as it passes through Torla at 3:30pm on its way back to Sabiñánigo. In the park, many **refugios** (mountain huts) allow overnight stays. The 120-bed **Refugio Góriz** is a 4hr. hike from the parking lot. (☎974 34 12 01. 1500ptas/€9 per person.) In Torla, ascend C. Francia one block to reach **Refugio L'Atalaya,** C. a Ruata, 45 (☎974 48 60 22), and **Refugio Briet** (☎974 48 62 21), across the street. (Both 1000ptas/€6 per person.) Outside Torla are **Camping Río Ara** and **Camping San Anton.** (Ara ☎974 48 62 48, San Anton ☎974 48 60 63. Both 550ptas/€3.30 per person, per tent, and per car. Open Apr.-Oct.) Stock up at **Supermercado Torla,** on C. a Ruata. (Open May-Oct. daily 9am-2pm and 5-8pm, Nov.-Apr. closed Su.)

JACA
☎ 974

For centuries, pilgrims bound for Santiago would cross the Pyrenees into Spain, spend the night in Jaca (pop. 14,000), and be off by dawn. They had the right idea; use it as launching pad for the Pyrenees. RENFE **trains** (☎ 974 36 13 32) run from C. Estación to Zaragoza (3hr., daily 7:36am and 6:11pm, 1400ptas/€8.40). La Oscense **buses** (☎ 974 35 50 60) run to Pamplona (2hr., 1-3 per day, 900ptas/€5.40) and Zaragoza (2hr., 2-5 per day, 1540ptas/€9.40). The **tourist office,** Av. Regimiento de Galicia, 2, is off C. Mayor. (☎ 974 36 00 98. Open July-Aug. M-F 9am-2pm and 4:30-8pm, Sa 9am-1:30pm and 5-8pm, Su 10am-1:30pm; Sept.-June M-F 9am-1:30pm and 4:30-7pm, Sa 10am-1pm and 5-7pm.) From the bus station, cross the park and head right following the church completely around to the next plaza to find **Hostal Paris,** one of the best deals in town. (☎ 974 36 10 20. Mid-July to mid-Sept. singles 2675ptas/€9.25; doubles 4280ptas/€25.75; rest of the year singles 2460ptas/€14.80; doubles 3850ptas/€23.14.) Or check out the hip *casa rural* **El Arco,** C. San Nicolas, 4, where each room has its own distinctive flavor. (☎ 974 36 44 48. 2000ptas/€12 per person.)

NAVARRA

The spirit of the Navarrese emanates from the rustic Pyrenean *pueblos* on the French border to bustling Pamplona to the dusty villages in the south. Bordered by Basque Country to the west and Aragón to the east, Navarra's little-visited villages greet tourists with open arms.

PAMPLONA (IRUÑA)
☎ 948

Long, long ago, Pamplona's fiesta in honor of its patron saint *St. Fermín* was just another religious holiday. These days, *San Fermines* (July 6-14) is the most talked about holiday in Spain and a popular stop on the European backpacker circuit. Ever since Nobel Prize-winning author Ernest Hemingway brought the city international attention with *The Sun Also Rises*, hordes of visitors from around the world have come to witness and experience the legendary running of the bulls. At the bullring, a statue of Hemingway welcomes fans to Europe's premier festival, an eight-day extravaganza of dancing, dashing, and of course, drinking. Though *San Fermines* may be the city's only irresistible attraction, Pamplona (pop. 150,000) is a pleasant place to visit the other 356 days of the year as well.

▐ TRANSPORTATION

Trains: Estación RENFE (☎ (902) 24 02 02), off Av. San Jorge. Take bus #9 from Po. Sarasate (20min., 110ptas/€0.65). Info open daily 6am-10pm. Trains run to: **Barcelona** (6-8hr.; daily 12:55am, 12:20, 5:10pm; 4400ptas/€26.40) and **Madrid** (5hr., 7:05am and 6:10pm, 4400ptas/€26.40).

Buses: Estación de Autobuses, at the corner of C. Conde Oliveto and C. Yanguas y Miranda. Buses leave town for: **Barcelona** (5½hr.; 1, 8:30am, 4:30pm; 2855ptas/€17.40); **Bilbao** (2hr., 3-7 per day 7am-7pm, 1685ptas/€10); **Madrid** (5hr., 4-7 per day 7am-6:30pm, 3430ptas/€20.60); **San Sebastián** (1hr., 7-9 per day 7am-9pm, 845ptas/€5); **Zaragoza** (2-3hr., 6-8 per day 7:15am-8:30pm, 1760ptas/€10.55).

Public Transportation: 14 **buses** cover the city (948 42 32 42). Bus #9 runs from Po. Sarasate to the train station (20min., every 10-15min. 6:30am-10:15pm, 110ptas/€0.65). During *San Fermines*, buses run 24hr. (150ptas/€0.90).

✦ 🛈 ORIENTATION AND PRACTICAL INFORMATION

The **casco antiguo,** in the northeast quarter of the city, houses almost everything of interest in Pamplona. **Plaza del Castillo,** marked by a bandstand, is Pamplona's center. From the **bus station,** turn left onto Av. Conde Oliveto. At the traffic circle on Pl. Príncipe de Viana, take the second left onto Av. San Ignacio, follow it to the end of the pedestrian thoroughfare Po. Sarasate, and bear right. From the **train station,** take bus #9 (95ptas/€0.60); disembark at the last stop, cut across Po. Sarasate, and walk diagonally left to Pl. Castillo.

Tourist Office: C. Hilarión Eslava, 1 (☎948 20 65 40; fax 948 20 70 34; www.pamplona.net). From Pl. Castillo, take C. San Nicolas, turn right on C. San Miguel, and go through Pl. San Francisco. Open during *San Fermines* daily 9am-8pm; July-Aug. M-Sa 10am-2pm and 4-7pm, Su 10am-2pm; Sept.-June M-F 10am-2pm and 4-7pm, Sa 10am-2pm.

Luggage Storage: At the **bus station.** Bags 300ptas/€1.80 per day, large packs 500ptas/€3 per day. Open M-Sa 6:15am-9:30pm, Su 6:30am-1:30pm and 2-9:30pm. Closes for *San Fermines,* when the **Escuelas de San Francisco,** the big stone building at one end of Pl. San Francisco, opens instead. 300ptas/€1.50 each time you check on your luggage. Open 24hr.

Emergency: ☎ 112. **Municipal Police,** C. Monasterio de Irache, 2 (☎092).

Medical Services: Hospital de Navarra (☎948 42 21 00), C. Irunlarrea. The **Red Cross** sets up stands at the bus station and the *corrida* during *San Fermines.*

Internet: IturNet Cibercafé, C. Iturrama, 1 (☎948 25 28 20; www.iturnet.es), on the corner of C. Abejeras. From the bus station, take a left on C. Yanguas y Miranda, then head across Pl. Fueros to C. Abejeras. 500ptas/€3 per hr. Open M-Th 9am-10pm, F 9am-midnight, Sa-Su 10am-midnight; daily 9am-5pm during *San Fermines.*

Post Office: Po. Sarasate, 9 (☎948 21 26 00). Open M-F 8:30am-8:30pm, Sa 9:30am-2pm; *San Fermines* M-Sa 8:30am-2pm. **Postal Code:** 31001.

🏠 ACCOMMODATIONS

And now, kids, a lesson in supply and demand: smart *sanferministas* book their rooms up to a year (at least two months) in advance, often paying up-front rates up to four times higher than those listed here. Beware hawkers at the train and bus stations—quality and prices vary tremendously. Check the newspaper *El Diario de Navarra* for **casas particulares.** Many roomless folks find themselves sleeping on the lawns of the Ciudadela or on Pl. Fueros, Pl. Castillo, or the banks of the river. Be careful—if you can't store your backpack (storage fills fast), sleep on top of it. You may want to stay in nearby Estella.

Pensión Otano, C. San Nicolás, 5 (☎948 22 70 36). A great place to eat and sleep. Classy, comfortable doubles, some with balconies. *Menú* 1700ptas/€10.20. Booked for the next 5 years during *San Fermines.* Rest of year singles 2000ptas/€12, with bath 2500ptas/€15; doubles 5000-6000ptas/€30-36. AmEx/MC/V.

Pensión Santa Cecilia, C. Navarrería, 17 (☎948 22 22 30). From C. Chapitela (off Pl. Castillo), take the 1st right on C. Mercaderes, then turn left; it's on the left. An impressive converted 18th-century mansion. *San Fermines* 7000ptas/€35 per person. July-Aug. singles 3000ptas/€18; doubles 5000ptas/€30; triples 6000ptas/€36; rest of year singles 2500ptas/€15; doubles 4000ptas/€24; triples 5000ptas/€30. MC/V.

San Nicolás, C. San Nicolás, 13 (☎948 22 13 19), next to the restaurant of the same name. Small but pleasant rooms. *San Fermines* dorms 5000ptas/€30 (but usually booked far in advance). Rest of year dorms 2000-2500ptas/€12-15. AmEx/MC/V.

Fonda La Aragonesa, C. San Nicolás, 22 (☎948 22 34 28). The reception desk is across the street at Hostal Bearán. Simple, clean rooms. *San Fermines* doubles 12,000ptas/€72. Rest of year singles 3745ptas/€19; doubles 4815ptas/€29.

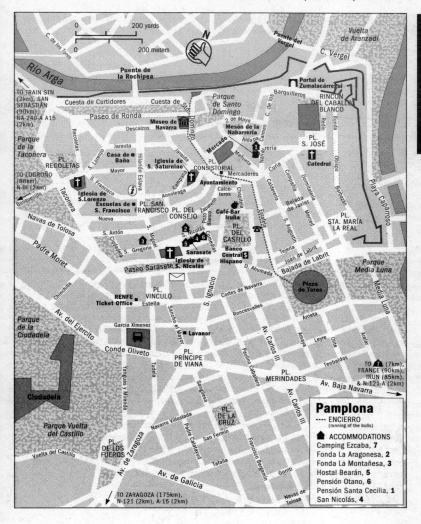

Hostal Bearán, C. San Nicolás, 25 (☎948 22 34 28). Squeaky-clean rooms, each with phone, TV, bath, safebox, and a whopping pricetag. *San Fermines* doubles 15,000ptas/€90. July-Sept. doubles 6500ptas/€39; Oct.-June doubles 5500ptas/€33. AmEx/MC/V.

Fonda La Montañesa, C. San Gregorio, 2 (☎948 22 43 80). Old, but you can't beat the price. No reservations are accepted during the festival, so show up early in the morning. *San Fermines* singles 6000ptas/€36; doubles 12,000ptas/€72. Rest of year singles 2000ptas/€12; doubles 4000ptas/€24.

Camping: Camping Ezcaba (☎948 33 03 15), in Eusa, 7km away on the road to Irún. The city bus line 4-1 runs from Pl. de las Merindades (4 per day 9am-7:30pm, 110ptas/€0.65). Get off at the gas station, the last stop. Fills fast during *San Fer-*

mines. No reservations. *San Fermines* 1370ptas/€8.20 per person, per tent, and per car. Rest of the year 575ptas/€3.45 per person, 565ptas/€3.40 per tent and per car.

🗀 FOOD

While *San Fermines* draws street vendors selling everything from roast chicken to *churros*, the tiny neighborhoods of Pamplona advertise hearty *menús* throughout the year. Try the side streets in the area above Pl. San Francisco, and C. Jarauta and C. Descalzos, near Po. Ronda. **Calle San Nicolas** has many nice restaurants. Grab **groceries** at **Vendi**, on C. Hilarión Eslava and C. Mayor. (Open during *San Fermines* M-Sa 9am-2pm; otherwise M-F 9am-2pm and 5:30-7:30pm, Sa 9am-2pm.)

🌑 **Restaurante Sarasate,** C. San Nicolás, 19 (☎948 22 57 27), above the seafood store. Delicious organic vegetarian cuisine awaits. Pleasant, spotless dining room. Lunchtime *menú* 1350ptas/€7. Open M-Th 1:15-4pm and 8:15-11pm, F-Sa 1:15-4pm and 9-11pm. During *San Fermines* open daily 1:15-4pm and F and Sa night.

Café-Bar Iruña, Pl. Castillo. Hemingway's favorite haunt and the backdrop for much of *The Sun Also Rises,* Cafe-Bar Iruña draws a crowd for its delicious and inexpensive *menú.* Open M-Th 8am-11pm, F 8am-2am, Sa 9am-2am, Su 9am-11pm; *San Fermines* 8am-4am. MC/V.

👁 🎵 SIGHTS AND ENTERTAINMENT

Pamplona's rich architectural legacy gives reason enough to visit. The recently restored late 14th-century **Gothic cathedral** is at the end of C. Navarrería. (Open M-F 10am-1:30pm and 4-7pm, Sa 10am-1:30pm. Ask about guided tours. 550ptas/€3.30.) The impressive walls of the pentagonal **Ciudadela** once humbled even Napoleon; today the Ciudadela hosts free exhibits and concerts in summer. From the old quarter, pick up C. Redín at the far end of the cathedral plaza, head left along the walls past the **Portal de Zumalacárregui** and along the Río Arga, and bear left through the **Parque de la Taconera.** (Open daily 7am-10pm; closed for *San Fermines.* Free.) Throughout the year, **Plaza de Castillo** is the social heart of the city. The young and the restless booze up at bars in the *casco antiguo*, around **Calles de Jarauta, San Nicolas,** and **San Gregorio. Meson de la Navarrería,** C. Navarrería, is a great place to sit and chat with friends over drinks.

 Although Pamplona is usually a very safe city, crime skyrockets during *San Fermines,* when some unfortunately come to the fiesta to take advantage of tourists—beware assaults and muggings. Do not roam alone at night, and take extreme care in the parks and shady streets of the *casco antiguo.*

LOS SAN FERMINES (JULY 6-14, 2002)

Visitors from the world overcrowd Pamplona for one week of the year in search of Europe's greatest party. Pamplona delivers, with an eight-day frenzy of parades, bullfights, parties, dancing, fireworks, concerts, and wine. Pamplonese, uniformly clad in white garb with red sashes and bandanas, literally throw themselves into the merry-making, displaying obscene levels of both physical stamina and alcohol tolerance. The "Running of the Bulls," called the *encierro*, is the focal point of *San Fermines;* the first *encierro* of the festival takes place on July 7 at 8am and is repeated at 8am every day for the following seven days. Hundreds of bleary-eyed, hung-over, hyper-adrenalized runners flee from very large bulls as bystanders cheer from barricades, windows, balconies, and doorways. Both the bulls and the mob are dangerous; terrified runners, all convinced the bull is right behind them, flee for dear life, and without concern for those around them. Hemingway had the right idea: don't run. Watch the *encierro* from the bullring instead; arrive around 6:45am. Tickets for the Grada section of the ring are available before 7am (M-F 450ptas/€2.70, Sa-Su 600ptas/€3.60). You can watch for free, but the free section is overcrowded, and it can be hard to see and breathe. If you want to participate in the bullring excitement, you can line up by

---

RUNNING SCARED So, you're going to run. No one wants to see
you end up on evening news programs around the world, so here are a few words of *San Fermines* wisdom:

■ Research the *encierro* before you run. The tourist office dispenses a pamphlet that outlines the route of the 3min. run and offers tips for inexperienced runners.

■ Do not stay up all night drinking and carousing. Not surprisingly, hung-over foreigners have the highest rate of injury. Experienced runners get lots of sleep the night before. Access to the course closes at 7:30am.

■ Give up on getting near the bulls and concentrate on getting to the bullring in one piece. Although some whack the bull with rolled newspapers, runners should never distract or touch the animals; anyone who does is likely to anger the bull and locals alike.

■ Try not to cower in a doorway; people have been trapped and killed this way.

■ Be particularly wary of isolated bulls—they seek company in the crowds.

■ If you fall, **stay down.** Curl up into a fetal position, lock your hands behind your head, and **do not get up** until the clatter of hooves has passed.

Pl. Toros well before 7:30am and run in *before* the bulls are even in sight. To watch one of the bullfights, wait in the line that forms at the bullring around 8pm every evening (from 2000ptas/€12). As one bullfight ends, tickets go on sale for the next day's fight. Once the running is over, the insanity spills into the streets and gathers steam until nightfall, when it explodes with singing in bars, dancing in alleyways, spontaneous parades, and a no-holds-barred party in Pl. Castillo, which becomes Europe's biggest open-air dance floor.

ARAGÓN

A striking collage of semi-deserts and lush mountain peaks, Aragón's landscape reflects the influence of both a Mediterranean and a Continental climate. In the south, sun-baked towns give way to prosperous Zaragoza, while up north the stunning snow-capped peaks of the Pyrenees peer down on tiny medieval towns. The region's harsh terrain and climate, coupled with its strategic location, have produced a martial culture known among Spaniards for its obstinacy.

ZARAGOZA ☎ 976

Augustus founded Zaragoza (pop. 603,000) in 14 BC, modestly naming it Caesaraugusta after himself. The city gained everlasting fame when the Virgin Mary later dropped in for a visit; it's been a pilgrimage site ever since. The massive Baroque **Basílica de Nuestra Señora del Pilar** dominates the vast **Plaza del Pilar,** defining the skyline with brightly colored tiled domes. The interior is even more incredible, with frescoes by Goya and Velázquez. Don't leave without seeing the panoramic views from one of the towers; take the elevator in the corner, on the left as you face the **Museo del Pilar,** which exhibits the glittering *Joyero de la Virgen* (Virgin's jewels). (Basílica open daily 5:45am-9:30pm. Free. Museum open June-Aug. daily 9am-2pm and 4-6pm. 200ptas/€1.20. Sept.-May Sa-Th 9:30am-2pm and 4-6pm. 200ptas/€1.20.) The **Palacio de la Aljafería,** on C. Castillo, is the principle relic of Aragón's Moorish era. Take bus # 21 or 33 or head left on C. Coso from Pl. España as you face the *casco viejo,* continue on Conde Aranda, and turn right on Pl. Maria Agustín, then left on C. Aliaferia. (Open June-Aug. daily 10am-2pm and 4:30-8pm; Sept.-May M-W and Sa 10am-2pm and 4:30-6:30pm, F 4:30-6:30pm, Su 10am-2pm. 300ptas/€1.80, students and seniors 150ptas/€0.90, under 12 free.) The **Museo de Zaragoza,** Pl. Los Sitios, 6, houses an extensive collection of artifacts and Aragonese paintings up through the early 20th century. From Pl. España, follow Po. Independencia, turn left on C. Joaquín

Costa, and continue 3 more blocks; the museum is on the left. (Open Tu-Sa 10am-2pm and 5-8pm, Su 10am-2pm. Free.)

Trains (☎976 21 11 66) run from Av. Anselmo Clavé to: **Barcelona** (4hr., 15 per day 1:50am-7:05pm, 3600-4600ptas/€21.60-27.60); **Madrid** (3hr., 14 per day 7am-3:33am, 3500-4500ptas/€21-27.00); **Pamplona** (2¼hr., 3 per day 6:30am-4:15pm, 1290-2200ptas/€7.74-13.20); **San Sebastián** (4hr., 5pm and 2am, 3400ptas/€20.40). Agreda Automóvil **buses** (☎976 22 93 43) go from Po. María Agustín, 7 to **Barcelona** (3½hr., 16-19 per day 1-10:30pm, 1655ptas/€10.00) and **Madrid** (3½hr., 15-18 per day 1:15pm-10:30pm, 1750ptas/€11.00). The **tourist office** is on Pl. Pilar in the black glass cube. (☎976 20 12 00. Open daily 10am-8pm.) **Hostal Plaza,** Pl. Pilar, 14, is pure *hostal* bliss. (July-Aug. singles with shower 4500ptas/€27.00; doubles with shower 6900ptas/€41.40. Sept.-June doubles 4900ptas/€29.40.) Take bus #22 from the train station to reach **Albergue-Residencia Juvenil Baltasar Gracián (HI),** C. Franco y Lopez, 4. (☎976 55 15 04. Curfew midnight. Dorms 1800ptas/€10.80, under 27 1400ptas/€8.40.) **Hostal Ambos Mundos** is on Pl. Pilar, 16, at C. Don Jaime I. (☎976 29 97 04. Singles 2600ptas/€15.60; doubles 5000ptas/€30.) **La Zanahoria,** C. Tarragona, 4, is extremely popular with locals. (Menú 1050ptas/€6.30. Open daily 1:30-4pm and 9-11:30pm.) Get **groceries** at **Consum,** C. San Jorge, 22, the continuation of C. Merdeo Nuñez. (Open M-Sa 9am-9pm.) **Postal Code:** 50001.

BASQUE COUNTRY (PAÍS VASCO)

The varied landscape of Basque Country resembles a nation complete unto itself, combining cosmopolitan cities, verdant hills, industrial wastelands, and quaint fishing villages. Many believe that the strongly nationalistic Basques are the native people of Iberia, as their culture and language date back several millennia. Although Castilian Spanish is the predominant language, Basque *euskera* has enjoyed a resurgence of popularity. Basque cuisine is some of Iberia's finest. Tapas in País Vasco, considered regional specialties, are called *pintxos;* locals wash them down with *sidra* (cider) and the local white wine, *txakoli.*

SAN SEBASTIÁN (DONOSTIA)   ☎943

Glittering on the shores of the Cantabrian Sea, San Sebastián (pop. 180,000) is a cool, elegant city. By the beginning of the 19th century the city had become one of Spain's great ports, but much of it was destroyed during the Peninsular War—in 1813, Anglo-Portuguese troops set fire to it after taking it from the French. The city gained international fame when Queen Isabel II made it her summer residence in 1846. Its popularity has been increasing ever since, particularly among inland Spaniards desperate to escape the heat of central Spain. Vacationers come for its beaches, *tapas*, and bars, as well as its strong sense of regional culture.

▮ TRANSPORTATION

Flights: Airport (☎943 66 85 00) in Hondarribia (Fuenterrabía), 20km east of the city. **Interurbanos** buses to Hondarribia pass by the airport (45min., every 20min. 7:45am-10pm, 200ptas/€1.20). Taxis 4000ptas/€24.

Trains: RENFE, Estación del Norte (☎(902) 24 02 02), on Po. Francia, on the east side of Puente María Cristina. Info open daily 7am-11pm. To: **Barcelona** (9hr.; daily 10:30am and Su-F 10:59pm; 5000ptas/€30; **Burgos** (3½hr.; 6 per day, Su-F 8:32am-10:37pm, Sa 9:02am-10:37pm; 2800-3700ptas/€17-22.20); **Madrid** (8hr.; daily 10:30pm and Su-F 8:30am; 4900-6300ptas/€30-38); **Zaragoza** (4hr.; 1-2 per day, daily 10:30am, Su-F 10:59pm; 3100ptas/€18.60).

Buses: Several private companies run from different points in the city but most set up shop at the tiny "station," right around the corner from the main concourse at Po. Vizcaya, 16. Buses drop off passengers on Pl. Pío XII, a block from the river and about 13 blocks south of Av. Libertad on Av. Sancho el Sabio. Public bus #28 goes to the city

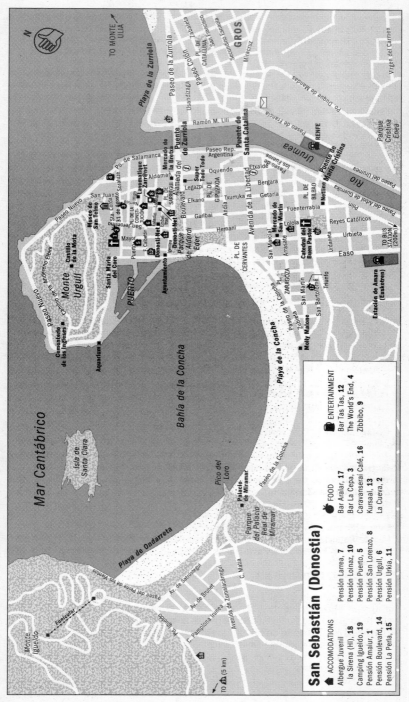

San Sebastián (Donostia)

⌂ ACCOMMODATIONS

Albergue Juvenil la Sirena (HI), **18**	Pensión Larrea, **7**
Camping Igueldo, **19**	Pensión Loinaz, **10**
Pensión Amaiur, **1**	Pensión Puerto, **5**
Pensión Boulevard, **14**	Pensión San Lorenzo, **8**
Pensión La Perla, **15**	Pensión Urgull, **6**
	Pensión Urkia, **11**

🍴 FOOD

Bar Aralar, **17**	Caravanseral Café, **16**
Bar La Cepa, **3**	Kursaal, **13**
	La Cueva, **2**

🎭 ENTERTAINMENT

Bar Tas Tas, **12**
The World's End, **4**
Zibbibo, **9**

center from the bus station. To: **Barcelona** (7hr.; 7:30am, 3:30, 11:20pm; 3430ptas/ €20.60); **Bilbao** (1¼hr.; M-F every 30min., Sa-Su every hr., 6am-10:30pm; 1200ptas/ €7.20); **Burgos** (3-3½hr., 8 per day 7:15am-12:30pm, 2000ptas/€12); **Madrid** (6hr., 7-9 per day 7:15am-12:30am, 3990ptas/€24); **Pamplona** (1hr.; 9 per day 7am-9pm, Su 9am-9pm; 845ptas/€5.10).

Public Transportation: ☎943 28 71 00. List of routes at tourist office. Each trip 115ptas/€0.70. Bus #16 goes from Alameda del Boulevard to campground and beaches.

Taxis: Santa Clara (☎943 31 01 11) or **Donostia** (☎943 46 46 46).

Car Rental: Europcar (☎943 32 23 04; fax 943 29 07 00), Estatión del Norte. Must be 21 or over and have passport and driver's license (international driver's license not required). Open M-F 8am-1pm and 4-7:30pm, Sa 9am-1pm.

◪ 🛈 ORIENTATION AND PRACTICAL INFORMATION

The city center and most beaches lie on a peninsula on the west side of the **Río Urumea** (river); at the tip, the **Monte Urgulla** juts out into the bay. Inland, nightlife rages and budget accommodations and restaurants cluster in the **parte vieja.** To the south, at the base of the peninsula, is the commercial area. From the bus station, head right (north) up Av. Sancho el Sabio toward the cathedral, ocean, and *parte vieja.* East of the river are the **train station** and the **Playa de la Zurriola.** Head straight from the train station, cross the Puente María Cristina (bridge), head right at the fountain for four blocks, and then left on Av. Libertad to the port; the *parte vieja* will lie to your right and the **Playa de la Concha** to your left.

Tourist Office: Centro de Atracción y Turismo, C. Reina Regente, 3 (☎943 48 11 66), next to the theater and in front of the bridge Zurriola. From the train station, turn right immediately after crossing Puente María Cristina. Continue until reaching Puente Zurriola; office will be on the left. From the bus station, go down Av. Sancho el Sabio. At Pl. Centenario, bear right on C. Prim and follow the river. At the 3rd bridge, Puente Zurriola, look to the plaza at your left and the office is on the corner. Open June-Sept. M-Sa 8am-8pm, Su 10am-2pm; Oct.-May M-Sa 9am-1:30pm and 3:30-7pm, Su 10am-2pm.

Luggage Storage: Lockers at **RENFE station.** 500ptas/€3 per day. Open daily 7am-11pm. Buy tokens at ticket counter.

Laundromat: Lavomatique, C. Iñigo, 13 (☎943 42 38 71), off C. San Juan in the *parte vieja.* Self-service. 600ptas/€3.60. Open M-F 9:30-2pm and 4-7pm, Sa-Su 10am-2pm.

Hiking Info: Izadi, C. Usandizaga, 18 (☎943 29 35 20). Sells hiking guides and maps, some in English. Organizes tours and rents skis, wetsuits, and hiking equipment. Open M-F 10am-1pm and 4-8pm, Sa 10am-1:30pm and 4:30-8pm.

Emergency: ☎091 or 092. **Municipal Police,** C. Easo, 41 (☎943 45 00 00).

Medical Services: Casa de Socorro, Bengoetxea, 4 (☎943 44 06 33).

Internet Access: Zarr@net, C. San Lorenzo, 6 (☎943 43 33 81). 550ptas/€3.30 per hr. Open daily 10am-10pm. **Netline,** C. Urdaneta, 8 (☎943 44 50 76). 250ptas/ €1.50 for 30min. Open M-Sa 10am-10pm.

Post Office: ☎943 44 68 26, Po. De Francia, 13, near the train station, just over the Santa Catalina bridge and to the right; the office is on the left. Open M-F 8:30am-8:30pm, Sa 9:30am-2pm. **Postal Code:** 20006.

▞ ACCOMMODATIONS

Desperate backpackers will scrounge for rooms in July and August, particularly during *San Fermines* (July 6-14) and *Semana Grande* (starts the Sunday of the week of Aug. 15); September's film festival is not much better. Budget options center in the *parte vieja* and around the cathedral. Most hostel owners know of **casas particulares**—don't be afraid to ask for help.

PARTE VIEJA

A bit of a hike from the bus and train stations, the *parte vieja* is brimming with reasonably priced *pensiones*. Its proximity to Playa de la Concha and the port makes this area a prime nightspot; many *pensiones* reside above loud *tapas* bars.

Pensión Amaiur, C. 31 de Agosto, 44, 2nd fl. (☎943 42 96 54). From Alameda del Boulevard, go up C. San Jerónimo and turn left. *Semana Santa*-Oct. 2500-3500ptas/€15-21 per person; Nov.-*Semana Santa* 1900-2500ptas/€12-15 per person. MC/V.

Pensión San Lorenzo, C. San Lorenzo, 2 (☎943 42 55 16), off C. San Juan. Cheerful doubles all have TV, radio, and small fridge. Immaculate modern bathrooms. July-Sept. doubles 8000ptas/€48, Oct.-June 4000ptas/€24.

Pensión Larrea, C. Narrica, 21, 2nd fl. (☎943 42 26 94). Adorable and adoring owners have a reputation as the "best mom and pop in town." July-Aug. singles 3500ptas/€21; doubles 5000ptas/€30; triples 6500/€39. Sept.-June about 1000ptas/€6 less.

Pensión Loinaz, C. San Lorenzo, 17 (☎943 42 67 14), off C. San Juan. July-Aug. doubles 6500ptas/€39; Apr.-June 5000ptas/€30; Sept.-Mar. 4000ptas/€24.

Pensión Urgull, Esterlines, 10, 3rd fl. (☎943 43 00 47). Attractive old rooms with tall windows, small balconies, and convenient location. July-Aug. doubles 6000-7000ptas/€36-42. Sept.-June singles 2500ptas/€15; doubles 4000ptas/€24.

Pensión Boulevard, Alameda del Boulevard, 24 (☎943 943 42 94 05). Beautiful, modern rooms, all with radios, some with balconies. July-Aug. doubles 8000ptas/€48; Sept.-June doubles 4000-7000ptas/€24-42.

Pensión Puerto, C. Puerto, 19, 2nd fl. (☎943 43 21 40), off C. Mayor. Clean rooms with big closets, good beds, and some balconies. 2500-5000ptas/€15-30 per person.

OUTSIDE THE PARTE VIEJA

Most of these hostels lie in the heart of the commercial zone, around the cathedral. They tend to be quieter than those elsewhere in the city, yet are still close to the port, beach, bus, and train stations, and all of the action in the *parte vieja*.

Albergue Juvenil la Sirena (HI), Po. Igueldo, 25 (☎943 31 02 68), a big, light-pink building 3min. from the beach at the far west end of the city. Bus #24 and #27 run from the train and bus stations to Av. Zumalacárregui (the stop in front of the San Sebastián Hotel). Clean, modern, dorm-style rooms and multilingual staff. **HI members and ISIC-carriers only.** HI cards on sale. July-Aug. 3-night max. stay if full. Lockout 10am-3pm. July-Aug. 2070ptas/€12, over 25 2335ptas/€14; May-June and Sept. 1885ptas/€11.30, over 25 2205ptas/€14.20; rest of year 1700ptas/€10, over 25 2070ptas/€12.50.

Pensión Urkia, C. Urbieta, 12, 3rd fl. (☎943 42 44 36), located on C. Urbieta between C. Marcial and C. Arrasate and bordering the Mercado de San Martín. Rooms with full bathrooms and TVs. July-Sept. doubles 6500ptas/€33; triples 9000ptas/€54. Oct.-June singles 3500-4000ptas/€21-24; doubles 4500ptas/€27; triples 6000ptas/€36.

Pensión La Perla, C. Loiola, 10, 2nd fl. (☎943 42 81 23), on the street directly ahead of the cathedral. Grand stairway leads to attractive rooms with polished floors. July-Sept. singles 4000ptas/€24; doubles 6000ptas/€36; Oct.-June singles 3500ptas/€21; doubles 4500ptas/€27.

Camping: Camping Igueldo (☎943 21 45 02), 5km west of town. Bus #16 (Barrio de Igueldo-Camping) runs between the site and Alameda del Boulevard (every 30min., 125ptas/€0.75). Reception June-Aug. 8am-midnight; Sept.-May 9am-1pm and 5-9pm. *Parcela* (including tent and up to 2 people) June-Aug. and *Semana Santa* 1725ptas/€10.37, Sept.-May 1475ptas/€8.85; extra person 525ptas/€3.15.

 FOOD

Pintxos (*tapas;* rarely more than 200ptas/€1.20 each), chased down with the fizzy regional white wine *txacoli*, are a religion here; bars in the lively old city spread an array of enticing tidbits on toothpicks or bread. The entire **parte vieja** seems to exist for no other purpose than to feed. **Mercado de la Bretxa,** on Alameda del Boulevard at C. San Juan, sells fresh produce. (Open M-Sa 9am-9pm.) **Super Todo Todo,** on Alameda del Boulevard, is around the corner from the tourist office. (Open M-Sa 8:30am-9pm, Su 10am-2pm.)

☒ **Kursaal,** Zurriola, 1 (☎943 00 31 62), in a modern building across the river from the Old City. The chef is a legend among the locals. *Menú* 1650-2300ptas/€10-14.

Bar La Cepa, C. 31 de Agosto, 7-9 (☎943 42 63 94). Locals stop in for their delicious *pintxos* (225-325ptas/€1.35-2) and cheap *bocadillos* (450-475ptas/€2.70-2.85). Open daily 11am-midnight.

Bar Aralar, C. Puerto Kalea (☎943 42 63 78). Known and loved among the locals for its extremely fresh, inexpensive, and tasty *pintxos* (150-200ptas/€0.90-1.20). Open Su-Th 11am-midnight, F-Sa 11am-2:30am. Closes 3 weeks in Nov. and again in May.

La Cueva, Pl. Trinidad (☎943 42 54 37), off 31 de Agosto. This charming cave-like restaurant with outside patio offers traditional seafood cuisine. T-F *Menú* 2000ptas/€12. Open Tu-Su 1-3:30pm and 7:30-11pm.

Caravanseri Café, C. San Bartolomé, 1 (☎943 47 54 78), alongside the cathedral. Trendy and chic without pretentious prices. Fabulous vegetarian options. Open M-Th 8am-midnight, F-Sa 8am-1am, Su 10:30am-midnight.

◢ SIGHTS

San Sebastián's most attractive sight is the city itself—green walks and parks, grandiose buildings, and hillsides encircle a placid, fan-shaped bay and the pleasant island of Santa Clara. Although the views from both of San Sebastián's mountains are spectacular, those from ▨**Monte Igueldo** are superior. By day the countryside meets the ocean in a line of white and blue; by night, Isla Santa Clara seems to float on a ring of light. The sidewalk toward the mountain ends before the base of Monte Igueldo with Eduardo Chillida's sculpture *El peine de los vientos.* (Open June-Sept. daily 10am-10pm; rest of the year weekends only.) Across the bay from Monte Igueldo, the gravel paths through the shady woods of Monte Urgull are peppered with monuments, love-struck teenagers, and stunning vistas. The overgrown **Castillo de Santa Cruz de la Mota** tops the summit with cannons and a chapel; the castle is crowned by the statue of the Sagrado Corazón de Jesús, which blesses the city. *(Open June-Aug. daily 8am-8pm; Sept.-May 8am-6pm.)* **El Palacio de Miramar,** between Playa de la Concha and Playa de Ondarreta, has passed through the hands of the Spanish court, Napoleon III, and Bismarck. Today anyone can stroll through the "cottage-style" grounds and contemplate the picturesque views of the bay. *(Open June-Aug. daily 9am-9pm; Sept.-May 10am-5pm.)* The other royal residence, **Palacio de Ayete,** is closed to the public, though the surrounding trails are not. *(Head up Cuesta de Aldapeta or take Bus #19. Grounds open June-Aug. 10am-8:30pm; Sept.-May 10am-5pm.)* The **Museo de San Telmo** resides in a Dominican monastery. The serene, overgrown cloister is strewn with Basque funerary relics. The main museum beyond the cloister contains a fascinating array of pre-historic Basque artifacts, some El Grecos, a couple of dinosaur skeletons, and a piece of contemporary art. *(Po. Nuevo. Open Tu-Sa 10:30am-1:30pm and 4-8pm, Su 10:30am-2pm. Free.)* An **aquarium** lies on the edge of the port with fish and sea creatures from various aquatic habitats. *(Po. Muelle, 34. Open July to mid-Sept. 10am-10pm; mid-Sept. to June 10am-8pm. 1200ptas/€13.20, students 700ptas/€4.20.)* Thirty minutes from the town center, between a lush hill and a dark, gray-green bay, lies the town of **Pasajes de San Juan.** The charming fishing village's houses and small bay crowded with colorful *chalupas* (little boats) make an enchanting time warp. Take an intercity bus from the Pl. Victoria-Genia in front of the Gran Hotel Maria Cristina on C. Oquendo to San Pedro (Bus Stop A2, daily every 15-30min. 5:30am-10:30pm, 130ptas/€0.80).

🎵 🎭 ENTERTAINMENT AND NIGHTLIFE

The gorgeous **Playa de la Concha** curves from the port to the **Pico del Loro,** the beak-shaped promontory which is home to the Palacio de Miramar. Crowds jam onto the smaller and steeper **Playa de Ondarreta,** beyond Miramar. Across the river from Mt. Urguel, surfers crowd 🏄**Playa de la Zurrida.** Picnickers can head for the alluring **Isla de Santa Clara** in the center of the bay. Frequent motorboats leave for the island (June-Sept. only, 5min., every 30min., round-trip 325ptas/ €2), or rent a rowboat. Check at the portside kiosk for info on both. Several sports-related groups offer a variety of activities/lessons. For **windsurfing** and **kayaking,** call the Real Club Nautico, C. Igentea, 9 (☎943 42 35 75). For **parachuting,** try Urruti Sport, C. José Maria Soroa, 20 (☎943 27 81 96). **Surfers** check out the Pukas Surf Club, C. Mayor, 5. (☎943 42 72 28; pukas@facilnet.es. Open 10am-1pm and 4-8pm.) For info on all sports, pick up a copy of the *UDA-Actividades deportivas* brochure at the tourist office.

The *parte vieja* pulls out all the stops after dark. **Calle Fermín Calbetón,** three blocks in from Alameda del Boulevard, sweats bars. Along the beach, the music starts thumping at midnight. **The World's End,** Po. de Salamanca, 14, one block outside of the *parte vieja* near the beach, is a favorite among expatriates and young travelers looking for a good pub-ambience. (Open Su-Th 2pm-2:30am, F-Sa 2pm-3:30am.) **Zibbibo,** Pl. Sarriegi, 8, is a hip club that has become a common backpacker stop en route from World's End to **Bar Tas Tas,** C. Fermím Calbetón, 35.

🏃 DAYTRIP FROM SAN SEBASTIÁN: HONDARRIBIA

Interurbanos buses (☎943 64 13 02) arrive on C. Zuluaga from San Sebastián (45min.; every 20min. M-Sa 7:45am-10:45pm, Su 7:45am-9:45pm (July-Aug. until 10:45pm); 215ptas/€1.30).

Refreshingly simple Hondarribia (pop. 15,000) flaunts a silky-smooth **beach** as well as a gorgeous stone-and-timber *casco antiguo,* centered around Carlos V's imposing **palace** in Pl. Armas, that provides welcome relief from Coppertone fumes. Six kilometers up Av. Monte Jaizkibel, **Monte Jaizkibel,** the highest mountain on the Costa Cantábrica, guards the **Santuario de Guadalupe** and offers incredible views of the coast. **Boats** leave from the end of C. Domingo Egia, off La Marina (every 15min., 200ptas/€1.20), for the **beach** town of Hendaye, France, 5km away. The **tourist office,** C. Javier Ugarte, 6, is in Pl. San Cristobál. (☎943 64 54 58. Open July-Sept. M-Sa 10am-8pm; Oct.-June M-F 9am-1:30pm and 4-6:30pm, Sa 10am-2pm.) Several **markets** spill onto **Calle San Pedro,** three blocks inland from the port.

BILBAO (BILBO)   ☎944

The economic engine of the Basque country, Bilbao (pop. 358,000) has been making people wealthy since the 16th century, when its shipbuilding industries and coastal location made it a key trade link between Castilla and Flanders. Today, the city is finally overcoming its reputation as a bourgeois, business-minded industrial center. Economic booms in the 19th century funded wide boulevards lined by grandiose buildings, and 20th-century success has blessed the city with a new subway system, an overhauled international airport, a stunning new bridge, and a stylish riverwalk project, all designed by renowned international architects. It is the shining, curving Guggenheim Museum, however, that has most powerfully fueled Bilbao's rise to international prominence.

🚆 **TRANSPORTATION.** RENFE **trains** (☎944 23 86 23) arrive at the **Estación de Abando,** Pl. Circular, 2, from: Barcelona (9½-11hr., 10am and 10:45pm, 5200ptas/ €31.20); Madrid (5¾-9hr., Su-F 4:30pm and 11:05pm, Sa 9:50am; 4600ptas-5800ptas/ €27.60-34.80); Salamanca (5½-6½hr., 9:25am and 2:05pm, 3700ptas/€22.20). From Pl. Circular, head right around the station and cross the Puente del Arenal (bridge) to reach Pl. Arriaga, the entrance to the *casco viejo.* Most **bus companies** leave from the **Termibús terminal,** C. Gurtubay, 1 (☎944 39 50 77; M: San Mamés), on the west side of town, for: Barcelona (7¼hr.; 3-4 per day M-F 6:30am-11pm; 5375ptas/€32.25); Madrid (4-5hr.; M-F 10-17 per day 7am-1:30am, Sa-Su 8am-1:30am; 3480ptas/€20.90); Pamplona (2hr., 4-6 per day 7:30am-8pm, 1580ptas/€9.50); San Sebastián (1¼hr.; M-F 6am-10:30pm every 30-60min. Sa every hr. 7:30am-10:30pm; Su every hr. 9am-10:30pm; 1200ptas/€7.20.)

Bilbao recently opened a **metro.** Hold on to your ticket after entering—you'll need it again to exit. (☎944 25 40 25; www.metrobilbao.net. Travel within 1 zone 150ptas/€0.90; 2 zones 175ptas/€1.05; 3 zones 200ptas/€1.20. Trains run Su-Th 6am-11pm, F-Sa 6am-11pm and every 30min. 11pm-6am.) **Bilbobús** runs 23 lines across the city. (☎944 48 40 80. 6am-11:30pm; M-F 135ptas/€0.80, Sa-Su 150ptas/€0.90.

⚐ PRACTICAL INFORMATION. The city's main artery, **Gran Vía,** leads east from the oval Pl. Federico Moyúa to **Plaza Circular** (sometimes referred to by its former name, Pl. España), the axis for many important stops and stations. The **tourist office** is on Pl. Arenal, to the left of the **Plaza de Arriaga,** the entrance to the *casco viejo.* (☎944 79 57 60; www.bilbao.net. Open M-F 9am-2pm and 4-7:30pm, Sa 9am-2pm, Su 10am-2pm.) Surf the **Internet** at **L@Ser,** C. Sendaja, 5. If you are standing with your back to the tourist office, take a left (away from the park); it is located about a block up on the right. (250ptas/€1.50 per 30min.) To get to the **post office,** Alameda Urquijo, 19, walk one block down Gran Vía from Pl. España and turn left after El Corte Inglés; it's on the corner of C. Bertendona. (☎944 44 10 04. Open M-F 8am-8:30pm, Sa 8am-2pm.) **Postal Code:** 48008.

⚏⚌ ACCOMMODATIONS AND FOOD. Pl. Arriaga and C. Arenal have budget accommodations galore. **Pensión Méndez,** C. Santa María, 13, 4th fl., is insulated from the raging nightlife below. From the bridge Arenal, take C. Bidebbarrieta (to the right of Café Boulevard), after two blocks take a right onto C. Perro; when you reach C. Santa María, turn right, the *pensión* is on the right. (☎944 16 03 64. Singles 3000-4000ptas/€18-24; doubles 5000ptas/€30.) To get to **Pensión Ladero,** C. Lotería, 1, 4th fl., from the bridge Arenal, take C. Correo (to the left of Cafe Boulevard), take a right after three blocks onto C. Lotería; it's across from Hostal Roquefer. (☎94 415 09 32. Singles 3000ptas/€18; doubles 4500ptas/€27.) To get to **Hostal Mardones,** C. Jardines, 4, 3rd fl., from the bridge, take C. Bidebbarrieta (to the right of Café Boulevard), then take the first right onto C. Jardines; the hostel is on the left toward the end. (☎944 15 31 05. Singles 4000ptas/€24, with bath 5000pta/€30s; doubles with one bed 5000ptas/€30, two beds 6500ptas/€39.) Another option is the HI hostel **Albergue Bilbao Aterpetxez,** Ctra. Basurto-Kastrexana Errep., 70, on the bus #58 route from Pl. Circular. (☎94 427 00 54; fax 94 427 54 79. July-Sept. singles 2600ptas/€15.60; bed in a double or triple 2400ptas/€14.40; bed in a room with six people 2000ptas/€12; over 25 200ptas/€1.20 more; Oct.-June 200ptas/€1.20 less.)

Restaurants and bars in the *casco viejo* offer a wide selection of local dishes, plus *pintxos* and *bocadillos* aplenty. **Restaurante Vegetariano Garibolo,** C. Fernandez del Campo, 7, off C. Hurtado de Amézaga, offers friendly service and a delicious and creative *menú* (1300ptas/€7.80. Open M-Sa 1-4pm.) **Restaurante Peruano Ají Colorado,** C. Barrencalle, 5, combines Andean decorations and traditional Peruvian cuisine. (Open Tu-Sa 1:30-3:30pm and 9-11:30pm, Su 1:30-3:30pm.) **Mercado de la Ribera,** on the bank of the river at the bottom of the old city, is the biggest indoor market in Spain. It's worth a trip even if you're not eating. (Open M-Sa 8am-2:30pm, also F 4:30-7:30pm.) Pick up **groceries** at the massive **Champión,** Pl. Santos Juanes, just past the Mercado de la Ribera at the intersection. (Open M-Sa 9:15am-9:15pm.)

◉▥♫ SIGHTS AND MUSEUMS. Frank O. Gehry's ▨**Guggenheim Museum Bilbao** can only be described as breathtaking. Lauded in the international press with every superlative imaginable, it has catapulted Bilbao straight into cultural stardom. Visitors are greeted by Jeff Koons's "Puppy," a dog composed of 60,000 plants and standing almost as tall as the actual museum. The main attraction is constructed mainly out of titanium, limestone, and glass in a series of interconnected pieces. The amazingly light and airy interior features a towering atrium and a series of non-traditional exhibition spaces, including a gargantuan 130m by 30m hall. The museum currently hosts rotating exhibits drawn from the Guggenheim Foundation's collection. (*Av. Abandoibarra, 2.* ☎944 35 90 00; *www.guggenheim.bilbao.es. Open July-Aug. daily 9am-9pm; Sept.-June Tu-Su 10am-8pm. 1200ptas/€7.20, students and seniors 600ptas/€3.60, under 12 free. Guided tours in English Tu-F 11am, 12:30, 4:30, and 6:30pm, Sa-Su 1 and 4pm; sign up 30min. before tour at Info Desk.*) The often overshadowed **Museo de Bellas Artes** hoards aesthetic riches behind an unassuming façade. An impressive art collection ranges from the 12th to 20th century and features excellent 15th- to 17th-century Flemish paintings, as well as works by El Greco, Zurbarán, Goya, Gauguin, Francis Bacon, Velázquez, Picasso, and Mary Cassatt. (*Pl. Museo, 2. From the Guggenheim, follow the Alameda de Mazarredo.* ☎944 39 60 60. *Open Tu-Sa 10am-8pm, Su 10am-2pm. 600ptas/€3.60, seniors and students 300ptas/€1.80, under 12 free; free W.*) The best **view** of Bilbao's surrounding landscape and the perfect place for a picnic is from the mirador on **Monte Archanda,** north of the old town. (*Funicular to the top every 15min., 125ptas/€0.75.*)

◾ **NIGHTLIFE.** In the *casco viejo*, revelers spill out into the streets to sip their *txikitos* (small glasses of beer or wine characteristic of the region), especially on C. Barrencalle (Barrenkale). Teenagers and twentysomethings also jam at C. Licenciado Poza on the west side of town. **The Cotton Club,** C. Gregorio de la Revilla, 25, decorated with over 30,000 beer caps, draws a crowd on Friday and Saturday nights. (Open M-Th 4:30pm-3am, F 4:30pm-6am, Sa 6:30pm-6am, and Su 6:30pm-3am. Cash only.) For a mellower scene, people-watch at the elegant 19th-century **Café Boulevard,** C. Arenal 3. The massive blowout fiesta in honor of *Nuestra Señora de Begoña* takes place during Semana Grande, a nine-day party beginning the Saturday after August 15.

▶ **DAYTRIP FROM BILBAO: GUERNICA (GERNIKA).** On April 27, 1937, the Nazi "Condor Legion" released an estimated 29,000kg of explosives on Guernica, obliterating 70% of the city in 3hr. The 2000 people who were killed in the bombings were immortalized in Pablo Picasso's stark masterpiece *Guernica,* now in Madrid's Reina Sofía gallery (see p. 812). The eerily modern city today offers the **Gernika Museoa,** Foru Plaza, 1, which features a moving exhibition chronicling the bombardment. (Open mid-June to Aug. M-Sa 10am-7pm, Su 10am-2pm; Sept. to mid-June M-Sa 10am-2pm and 4-7pm, Su 10am-2pm. 600ptas/€3.60, under 16 free.) Also check out the 2000-year-old **El Arbol** (tree), the emotional focus of the city. Despite the limited sights, Guernica is a good daytrip for those interested in learning more about this infamous event and its ramifications. **Trains** (☎902 543 210; www.euskotren.es) roll in from Bilbao (45min.; every 30min. M-F 6:15am-10:15pm, Sa-Su every 30min. 8:15am-10:15pm; 325ptas/€2).

BALEARIC ISLANDS

Every year, discos, ancient history, and beaches—especially beaches—draw nearly two million of the hippest Europeans to the *Islas Baleares,* 100km off the east coast of Spain. Mallorca, home to Palma, the islands' capital, absorbs the bulk of invaders who come to explore their limestone cliffs, orchards, and clear turquoise waters. Ibiza, the closest island to Spain and a counter-culture haven since the 1960s, boasts an active gay community; its capital Eivissa offers what many consider the best nightlife in all of Europe. Wrapped in green fields and stone walls, Menorca, the most remote island from Spain, leads a private life of empty white beaches, hidden coves, and mysterious Bronze Age megaliths.

SPAIN

▐ TRANSPORTATION

Flights to the islands are the easiest way to get there. Those under 26 often get discounts from **Iberia/Aviaco Airlines** (☎902 40 05 00; www.iberia.com), which flies to Palma de Mallorca and Ibiza from: Madrid (1hr., 25,000-30,000ptas/€150-180); Barcelona (40min., 10,000-20,000ptas/€60-120); and Valencia. **Air Europa** (☎902 24 00 42) and **SpanAir** (☎902 13 14 15; www.spanair.com) offer budget flights to and between the islands. Most cheap round-trip charters include a week's stay in a hotel; some companies called *mayoristas* sell "seat-only" deals. **Ferries** to the islands serve as a secondary mode of transport. **Trasmediterránea** (☎902 45 46 45; www.trasmediterranea.com) departs from Barcelona's Estació Marítima Moll and Valencia's Estació Marítima for Mallorca and Ibiza (7220ptas/€43 slowpoke, 9710ptas/€58 fast boat). **Buquebus** (☎902 41 42 42) goes from Barcelona to Palma (4hr., 2 per day, 8150ptas/€49). Book airline or ferry tickets through a travel agency in Barcelona, Valencia, or on the islands.

Within the islands, **ferries** are the most cost-efficient. A day's **car** rental costs around 6000ptas/€36, **mopeds** 3000ptas/€18 per day, and **bikes** 1000ptas/€6 per day.

MALLORCA   ☎971

Sought after since the days of the Romans, Mallorca has a long history of popularity. It has continually attracted the rich and famous, from Fréderic Chopin and French novelist George Sand on their scandalous honeymoon, the Spanish royal family on vacation, or Gwyneth on a filming hiatus with her new boy toy. There are reasons for such Mallorca lust. To the northwest, white sand beaches, frothy water, lemon groves, and olive trees adorn the jagged Sierra de Tramontana. To the east, expansive beaches sink into calm bays, while to the southeast, a network of caves masks underground beauty.

▐ TRANSPORTATION. **Bus** travel to and from Palma is not too difficult, but travel between most other areas is inefficient and restrictive. Nearly all buses stop at the main stop on C. Eusebi Estada, several blocks down from Pl. Espanya; buy tickets on the bus. The tourist office has a detailed schedule of all buses. Some of the more popular destinations include: Cuevas Drac (M-F 4 per day 10am-1:30pm, Sa-Su 10am; 900ptas/€5.40); Covetes/Es Trenc (M-F 3 per day 10am-5pm, Sa-Su 10:30am; 640ptas/€3.84); Sóller and Port Sóller (45min.; M-F every hr. 7am-7pm, Sa-Su 1 and 4:30pm; 350ptas/€2.10). Airport bus #17 runs until 1am (300ptas/€1.8).

▐ PRACTICAL INFORMATION. The information presented for Mallorca is in the capital city, Palma (pop. 323,000), unless otherwise indicated. The Palma branch of the **tourist office** resides at C. Sant Dominic, 11; from Pl. Reina, take C. Conquistador until it turns into C. Sant Dominic; the office is at the bottom of a stairway, a level below the street above. (☎971 72 40 90. Open M-F 9am-8pm, Sa 9am-1:30pm.) The **island tourist office,** Pl. Reina, 2, offers info on the other islands, a good city map, bus and train schedules, hiking info, and lists of all sporting and cultural events on Mallorca. (☎971 71 22 16. Open M-F 9am-8pm, Sa 10am-2pm.) Check **email** at **La Red,** C. Concepció, 5. (☎971 71 35 74. 400ptas/€2.40 for 30min. Open daily 10am-midnight.)

▐ ▐ ACCOMMODATIONS AND FOOD. Accommodations are scarce and often packed in Mallorca; your best bet is to book ahead and use Palma as a base for exploring the island. **Hostal Apuntadores,** C. Apuntadores, 8, is in the middle of the action, less than a block from Pl. Reina. (☎971 71 34 91. Dorms 2000ptas/€12 per person; single 3000ptas/€18; doubles 5000ptas/€30.) **Hostal Brondo,** C. Can Brondo, 1, off Pl. Rei Joan Carles, I is an old, converted house with character. (☎971 71 90 43. Reception M-Sa 9am-2pm and 6-8pm, Su 10am-1:30pm. Singles 3500ptas/€21; doubles 5500ptas/€33.) **Hostal Cuba,** C. San Magí, 1, is at C. Argentina, on the edge of the town; from Pl. Joan Carles I, turn left and walk down Av. Jaume III, cross the river, and turn left on C. Argentina. (☎971 73 81 59. Singles 2500-3000ptas/€15-18; doubles 5000-5500ptas/€30-33.) Somewhat pricey but popular outdoor restaurants

fill plazas such as **Plaza Mayor** and **Plaza Llotja**, but truly budget eaters tend to head to the side streets off **Passeig Born**, to the plethora of cheap digs along **Avenida Joan Miró**, or to the carbon-copy pizzerias along **Passeo Marítimo**. **Servicio y Precios**, on C. Felip Bauzà, near Pl. Reina, has **groceries**. (Open M-F 8:30am-8:30pm, Sa 9am-2pm.)

⚇🛍 SIGHTS AND ENTERTAINMENT. The capital of the Balearics, Palma does not shy from conspicuous consumption, but it provides plenty of old quarter charm and local flavor. The **Catedral o la Sea**, off Pl. Reina, one of the world's largest cathedrals, towers over Palma and its bay. (☎971 72 31 30. Cathedral and museum open Apr.-Oct. M-F 10am-6pm, Sa 10am-2pm; Nov.-Mar. M-F 10am-3pm. 500ptas/€3.) Built by the Moors and rebuilt by Jaume II, the 🖼**Palau Del'Almudaina**, C. Palau Reial, just off Pl. Reina, was at one point a stronghold of *Los Reyes Católicos*, Fernando and Isabel. (☎971 72 71 45. Open M-F 10am-6:30pm, Sa 10am-2pm. Guided visits 650ptas/€3.91, unguided 525ptas/€3.16. Students and children 375ptas/€2.25.) The tourist office distributes a list of over 40 nearby **beaches**, many a mere bus ride from Palma; one popular choice is **El Arenal** (Platja de Palma; bus #15), 11km southeast toward the airport.

While a good many party-goers still start their night in the *casco viejo*, nearly everyone ends up by the waterfront at Po. Marítimo come 1am. **La Bodeguita del Medio**, C. Vallseca, 18, keeps its crowd dancing to Cuban rhythms. (☎971 71 49 39. Open Th-Sa 8pm-3am, Su-W 8pm-1am.) Follow the Aussie voices down C. Apuntadores to the popular **Bar Latitude 39**, C. Felip Bauza, 8, a self-proclaimed "yachtie" bar. (☎971 72 02 65. Open M-Sa 7pm-3am.) **Barcelona**, C. Apuntadores, 5, jams with live music nightly from midnight to 3am. (☎971 71 35 57. Jazz M, Tu, and Th, salsa W. Cover 300ptas/€1.80 for live concerts. Open daily 11pm-3am.) Palma's clubbers start their night in the *bares-musicales* lining the **Po. Marítimo** strip like salsa-happy **Made in Brasil**, Po. Marítimo, 27 (open daily 8pm-4am) and dance-crazy **Salero**, Po. Marítimo, 31 (open daily 8pm-6am). Other party-goers head to the beaches and the nightclubs near **El Terreno**. When the bar scene starts to fade around 3am, partyers migrate to Palma's *discotecas*. **Tito's Palace**, Po. Marítimo, is Palma's hippest disco. (Cover 2500-3000ptas/€15-18. Open daily 11pm-6am.)

🪧 DAYTRIPS ON MALLORCA. The west coast of Mallorca is one of the most beautiful landscapes in the Mediterranean. The small town of **Sóller** basks in a fertile valley lined with orange groves. The town, with a backdrop of spectacular mountains, is a pleasant change from Las Palmas's more touristed beaches. Those who choose to spend the night can't go wrong at **Hostal Nadal**, C. Romaquera, 20. (☎/fax 971 63 11 80. Singles 2500ptas/€15; doubles 3800ptas/€23.) From Sóller it is a pleasant half-hour walk down the valley to Puerto de Sóller. Old-fashioned trolleys also connect the two (every 30min. 7am-9pm, 115ptas/€0.69). In Puerto de Sóller, a pebble and sand beach lines the small bay, where windsurfers zip back and forth. Hotel Miramar is at C. Marina, 12. (☎971 63 13 50. Singles 4700ptas/€28; doubles 5900ptas/€35; triples 8700ptas/€52.) On the southeast coast, scalloped fringes of bays and caves are investors' most recent discovery. The 🖼**Cuevas Drach**, near Porto Cristo in the southeast, are among the most dramatic natural wonders in Mallorca. The caves amaze with their droopy, finger-like rock formations, illuminating the cave in a spectrum of red and pink color. Walk to the depths of the cave to an underground amphitheater facing an underground lake or listen to a concert of classical music from the lit rowboats gliding in the lake. A bus runs from Palma to the caves, leaving from the main station by Pl. Espanya. (M-Sa 4 per day 10am-1:30pm, Su 10am; 900ptas/€5.40.)

IBIZA   ☎971

Perhaps nowhere on Earth does style rule over substance more than on the island of Ibiza (pop. 84,000). Ibiza's style warriors arrive in droves to showcase themselves in the island's outrageous nightlife and to debauch in a sex- and substance-driven summertime culture. A hippie enclave since the 60s, Ibiza's summer camp for disco fiends and trendsetters evokes a sense of new-age decadence. Although a thriving gay community still lends credence to its image as a "tolerant" center, the island's high price tags preclude economic diversity. As shocking as it may sound, there is more to Ibiza than just nightlife—the beaches and mountains are some of the most spectacular in the Balearics.

▐ TRANSPORTATION. The **bus** system in Ibiza is much more organized than those of her Balearic sisters. The three main stops in the capital Eivissa are Av. Isidor Macabich, 42, Av. Isidor Macabich, 20, and Av. Espanya (Voramar buses). For an exact schedule, check the tourist office or *El Diario de Ibiza*. Intercity buses are 250ptas/€1.50 or less and run from Av. Isidor Macabich, 42 (☎971 31 21 17) to San Antonio (M-Sa every 15min., Su every 30min. 7am-11:30pm). Buses to the beaches cost 125ptas/€0.75.

▐ PRACTICAL INFORMATION. The local paper *El Diario de Ibiza* (www.diariodeibiza.es; 125ptas/€0.75) features an Agenda page with everything you need to know about Ibiza. The **tourist office,** C. Antoni Riquer, 2, is on the water. (☎971 30 19 00; www.ibizaonline.com. Open M-F 9:30am-1:30pm and 5-8pm, Sa 10:30am-1pm.) Get cleaned up for the night out and check **email** at **Wash and Dry,** Av. Espana, 53 (☎971 39 48 22. 700ptas/€4.20 per load. **Internet** access 900ptas/€5.40 per hr. Open M-F 10am-3pm and 5-10pm, Sa 10am-5pm.)

▐▐ ACCOMMODATIONS AND FOOD. Cheap accommodations in Eivissa are rare--consider staying in **San Antonio,** a town about 14km away. The letters "CH" *(casa de huéspedes)* mark many doorways; call the owners at the phone number on the door. **Hostal Residencia Sol y Brisa** is at Av. B. V. Ramón, 15, parallel to Pg. Vara de Rey. (☎971 31 08 18. Singles 3500ptas/€21; doubles 6000ptas/€36.) **Hostal Residencia Ripoll** is at C. Vicente Cuervo, 14. (☎971 31 42 75. July-Sept. singles 4500ptas/€27; doubles 6500ptas/€39; 3-person apartments with TV, patio, and kitchen 12,000ptas/€72.) **Hostal Juanito and Hostal Las Nieves,** C. Juan de Austria, 17-18, are run by the same owner. (☎971 19 03 19. Singles 3000ptas/€18; doubles 6000ptas/€36.) **Hostal La Marina,** Puerto de Ibiza, C. Barcelona, 7, is across from Estació Marítima but right in the middle of the raucous bar scene. (☎971 31 01 72. Singles 4500-8000ptas/€27-48; doubles 7000-16,000ptas/€42-96.) For a supermarket, try **Hiper Centro,** C. Ignasi Wallis, near C. Juan de Austria. (☎971 19 20 41. Open M-Sa 9am-2pm and 5-9pm.) **Mama Pat's Curry y Más,** C. Espanya, 43, is creative and cheap. (Menú 1000ptas/€6. Open daily 8am-3am.)

▐▐ SIGHTS AND ENTERTAINMENT. First, the formalities. Wrapped in 16th-century walls, **Dalt Vila** (High Town) hosts 20th-century urban bustle in the city's oldest buildings. Its twisting, sloping streets lead up to the 14th-century cathedral and superb views of the city and ocean. The power of the rising sun draws thousands of topless solar zombies to nearby tanning grounds like **Platja Figueretes, Platja d'en Bossa, Platja de Talamanca,** and **Platja des Duros.** The most stunning beach near Eivissa is **Playa de Las Salinas,** where the nude sunbathers are almost as beautiful as the crystal-blue water and silky sand.

Finally, the fun. **Eivissa** (Ibiza City) is the world's biggest 24hr. party; the show begins at sunset. **Bars** in Eivissa are most popular between midnight and 3am. The bar scene centers around **Calle Barcelona** and spins outward from there into a myriad of sidestreets. **Calle Virgen** is the center of gay nightlife and utterly outrageous fashion. Drinks are pricey—beers start at 1000ptas/€6. Consider starting the night in the cheaper (and younger) bars of **San Antonio,** a town about 14km away. The island's **◪discos** (virtually all of which have a mixed gay-and-straight crowd) are world-famous. Better have some extra *pesetas* lying around—drinks at Ibiza's clubs cost about 1800ptas/€10.20, and covers start at 5000ptas/€30. The **Discobus** runs to and from all the major hotspots (leaves Eivissa every hr. 12:30am-6:30am, schedule for other stops available at tourist office and hotels; 250ptas/€1.50). For complete listings, check out *Ministry in Ibiza* or *DJ,* free at many hostels, bars, and restaurants. Wild, wild **◪Privilege** is the world's largest club and best known

SPAIN

for Monday night "manumission" parties featuring kinky live sex. (Open daily June-Sept. midnight-7am.) At **Amnesia**, on the road to San Antonio, you can forget who you are, where you're from, and who you came with at what may just be the craziest disco scene ever. (Cream parties Th; foam parties W and Su. Open daily midnight-7am.) Both lie on the discobus route to San Antonio. Playful **Pachá**, on Pg. Perimitral, is 20min. from the port; Friday night's Ministry of Sound brings the biggest crowd. (Open daily midnight-7:30am.) Cap off your night in **Space,** which starts hopping around 8am, peaks mid-afternoon, and doesn't wind down until past 5pm. Known for its Su morning show; Sa-Tu mornings are all popular too.

MENORCA

Menorca's 200km coastline of raw beaches, rustic landscape, and well-preserved ancient monuments draws ecologists, sun worshipers, and photographers alike. Unfortunately, although tourists are fewer on Menorca than on the other Balearics, the elevated prices make it hard on the budget traveler. Perched atop a steep bluff, **Mahón** (pop. 23,300) is the main gateway to the island. The **tourist office** is at

Sa Rovellada de Dalt, 24. (☎971 36 37 90; fax 971 36 74 15. Open M-F 9am-1:30pm and 5-7pm, Sa 9am-1pm.) To get to **Hostal La Isla,** C. Santa Catalina 4, take C. Concepció from Pl. Miranda. (☎971 36 64 92. Singles 2500ptas/€15; doubles 5000ptas/€30.) To reach the **Hostal Orsi**, C. Infanta, 19, from Pl. s'Esplanada, take C. Ses Moreres, which becomes C. Hannover, turn right at Pl. Constitució, and follow C. Nou through Pl. Reial. (☎971 36 47 51. Breakfast included. Singles 3500ptas/€21; doubles 5800/€35.) **Hostal-Residencia Jume,** C. Concepció, 6, is off Pl. Miranda. (☎971 36 32 66. Breakfast included. 3000ptas/€18 per person.)

The more popular **beaches** outside Mahón are accessible by bus (under 30min., 50-250ptas); many of the best beaches require a vehicle but are worth the extra hassle. Transportes Menorca buses (7 per day) leave from C. Josep Quadrado for ▓**Platges de Son Bou,** which offers 4km of gorgeous beaches on the southern shore. Autocares Fornells **buses** (7 per day) leave C. Vasallo in Mahón for sandy **Arenal d'en Castell,** while TMSA buses (6 per day) go to touristy **Calean Porter** and its whitewashed houses, orange stucco roofs, and red sidewalks. A 10min. walk away, the ▓ **Covas d'en Xoroi** are caves perched on cliffs high above the sea. **Albufera Es Grau** entices visitors with lagoons, pine woods, and farmland, as well as diverse flora and fauna. Recreational activities include hiking to coves across the bay; take the Autocares Fornells bus (4 per day) from C. Vasallo in Mahón.

NORTHWESTERN SPAIN

Northwestern Spain is the least-visited part of the country; it's seclusion is half its charm. Rainy **Galicia** hides mysterious Celtic ruins, left when the Celts made a pit stop on its quiet beaches along the west coast. Tiny **Asturias** is tucked on the northern coast, allowing access to its dramatic Picos de Europa.

GALICIA (GALIZA)

If, as the old Galician saying goes, "rain is art," then there is no gallery more beautiful than the misty skies of northwestern Spain. Often veiled in a silvery drizzle, it is a province of fern-laden eucalyptus woods, slate-roofed fishing villages, and seemingly endless white beaches. Galicians speak *gallego*, a linguistic missing link of sorts between Castilian and Portuguese. While newspapers and street signs alternate between languages, most conversations are conducted in Spanish.

SANTIAGO DE COMPOSTELA ☎981

Ever since the remains of the Apostle St. James were discovered here in 813, Santiago has drawn a plethora of pilgrims, many of whom have just completed the legendary *Camino de Santiago*. Built over the saint's alleged remains, the cathedral marks the end of the Camino, an 800-year-old, 900km pilgrimage believed to halve one's time in purgatory. Today, sunburnt pilgrims, street musicians, and hordes of tourists fill the granite streets. In addition to the religious monuments, visitors enjoy the modern art gallery, the state-of-the-art concert hall, and lively nightlife.

⊏ TRANSPORTATION

Trains: R. Horreo (☎981 52 02 02 and 24 02 02). To: **Bilbao** (10¾hr., 9:04am, 5850ptas/€35) via **León** (6½hr., 3500ptas/€20) and **Burgos** (8hr., 4600ptas/€30); **Madrid** (8hr.; M-F 1:47 and 10:25pm, Sa 10:30pm, Su 9:52am, 1:47 and 10:30pm; 5900ptas/€35); Schedule printed daily in *El Correo Gallego*.

Buses: Estación Central de Autobuses, R. de Rodriquez (☎981 58 77 00), a 20min. walk from downtown. Bus #10 and bus C Circular leave from the R. Montero Ríos side of Pl. Galicia for the station (every 15-20min. 6:30am-10pm, 105ptas/€0.65). Info open daily 6am-10pm. **ALSA** (☎981 58 61 33) runs to: **Bilbao** (11¼hr., 9am and 9:30pm, 6500ptas/€39); **Madrid** (8-9hr., 4 per day 8am-9:30pm, 5160ptas/€31); **San Sebastián** (13½hr., 8am and 4:30pm, 7275ptas/€44).

Public Transportation: (☎981 58 18 15). Bus #6 to the train station (open daily 10am-10:30pm), #9 to the campgrounds (10am-8pm), #10 to the bus station. In the city center, almost all buses stop at Pr. Galicia—check the signs to see which side. Except for buses #6 and 9, buses run daily 6:30am-10:30pm every 20min. (105ptas/€0.65).

✴🛈 ORIENTATION AND PRACTICAL INFORMATION

The **cathedral** marks the center of the old city, which sits on a hill above the new city. The **train station** is at the far southern end of town. To reach the old city, either take bus #6 to Pr. Galicia or walk up the stairs across the parking lot from the main entrance, cross the street, and bear right onto R. do Horreo, which leads to Pr. Galicia. The bus station is at the far northern end of town; the walk is over 20min., so take bus #10 to Pr. Galicia. In the old city, three main streets lead to the cathedral: **Rúa de Franco, Rúa de Vilar,** and **Rúa Nova.**

Tourist Office: R. do Vilar, 43 (☎981 58 40 81). Open M-F 10am-2pm and 4-7pm, Sa 11am-2pm and 5-7pm, Su and festivals 11am-2pm. Another **branch** is in a little Modernist structure (☎981 55 51 29), in the center of Pl. Galicia. Open M-F 10am-2pm and 5-8pm.

Emergency: ☎112 or (900) 44 42 22. **Local Police,** Av. Rodrigo de Padron, (☎981 54 23 23). **Guardia Civil,** As Cancelas, (☎62 or 981 58 16 11).

Late-night Pharmacy: Pr. de Tournal, 11 (☎981 58 59 40). Open daily 10pm-10am.

Medical Assistance: Hospital Xeral, R. das Galeras (☎981 54 00 00). **Ambulance:** ☎061

Internet Access: Nova 50, R. Nova, 50 (☎981 56 01 00). 200ptas/€1.20 per hr. Open daily 9am-1am.

Post Office: Travesa de Fonseca, (☎981 58 12 52; fax 981 56 32 88), on the corner of R. Franco. **Lista de Correos** (around the corner, R. Franco, 6) and **fax** service. Open M-F 8:30am-8:30pm, Sa 9:30am-2pm. **Postal Code:** 15701.

SPAIN

ACCOMMODATIONS

Nearly every street in the old city houses at least one or two *pensiones*. The liveliest and most popular streets, however, are **R. Vilar** and **R. Raíña.** Call ahead in winter when university students occupy most rooms.

Hospedaje Ramos, C. Raíña, 18, 2nd fl. (☎981 58 18 59), above O Papa Una restaurant in the center of the *ciudad viaje.* Spacious, immaculate rooms. Singles 1900ptas/ €11.40, with bath 2100ptas/€13; doubles 3450ptas/€21, 3750ptas/€23.

Hospedaje Santa Cruz, R. Vilar, 42, 2nd fl. (☎981 58 28 15). Big windows overlook the most popular street in Santiago. Reserve ahead in summer. June-Sept. singles 1500ptas/€9; doubles 4000ptas/€24, with bath 5000ptas/€30.

Hospedaja Fonseca, R. Fonseca, 1, 2nd fl. (☎981 57 24 79). Colorful, sunny rooms across the street from the cathedral. Singles, doubles, triples, and quads all 2000ptas/ €12 per person. Open July-Sept.

Hospedaje Sofía, C. Cardenal Paya, 16 (☎981 58 51 50), off Pl. Mazarelos. Named for the charming proprietress, Sofia offers spacious, serene rooms. Reservations accepted. Singles 2500-3000ptas/€15-18; doubles 4500-5000ptas/€27-30.

Camping As Cancelas, R. 25 de Xullo, 35 (☎981 58 02 66), 2km from the cathedral on the northern edge of town; take bus #6 or 9 from the train station or from Pr. Galicia. Laundry, supermarket, and pool. 600ptas/€3.60 per person, 650ptas/€3.90 per car and per tent. Electricity 500ptas/€3.

FOOD

Tapas-weary budget travelers will appreciate Santiago's selection of restaurants. Bars and cafeterias line the streets with a variety of remarkably inexpensive *menús;* most restaurants are on R. Vilar, R. Franco, R. Nova, and R. Raíña. In the new city, look near Pl. Roxa. End your meal with a *tarta de Santiago,* rich almond cake emblazoned with a sugary St. James cross. The **market,** between Pl. San Felix and Convento de San Augustín, is a sight in its own right. (Open M-Sa 7:30am-2pm.) **Supermercado Lorenzo Froiz,** Pl. Toural, is one block into the old city from Pr. Galicia. (Open M-Sa 9am-3pm and 4:30-9pm, Sa 9am-3pm and 5-9pm.)

O Cabaliño do Demo, R. Aller Ulloa, 7 (☎981 58 81 46). Walk to Porta Do Camino, where R. Cerca meets R. San Pedro; R. Aller Ulloa is at the end of R. Cerca before the Porta. Enjoy a variety of global vegetarian entrees. *Menú* 1100ptas/€6.60. Open M-Sa daily 2-4pm and 9pm-midnight. Cafe downstairs open 8am-midnight.

Restaurante Le Crepe, Pr. de Quintana, 1 (☎981 57 76 43), across from the cathedral. Dine on authentic, perfectly thin crepes. Open daily 1-4pm and 8pm-midnight.

Casa Manolo, R. de San Benito, 3-5 (☎981 58 29 50). This old fave of pilgrims has upgraded itself with a new location that makes it the biggest restaurant in Santiago. *Menú* 850ptas/€5.11. Open M-F 1-4pm and 8-11:30pm.

SIGHTS AND NIGHTLIFE

Offering a cool, quiet sanctuary to priest, pilgrim, and tourist alike, Santiago's **cathedral** rises above the lively old city center. Each of its four façades is a masterpiece from a different time period, and entrances open up onto four different plazas: Platerías, Quintana, Obradoiro, and Azabaxería. The southern **Praza de Platerías** is the oldest of the four façades; the 18th-century Baroque **Obradoiro** façade encases the Maestro Mateo's **Pórtico de la Gloria,** considered the crowning achievement of Spanish Romanesque sculpture. The revered remains of **St. James** lie beneath the high altar in a silver coffer. Inside the **museum** are gorgeous 16th-century tapestries and two poignant statues of the pregnant Virgin Mary. (Cathedral open daily 7am-7pm. Museum open June-Sept. M-Sa 10am-1:30pm and 4-7:30pm, Su and holidays 10am-1:30pm; Oct.-Feb. M-Sa 11am-1pm and 4-6pm, Su and holidays 11am-1pm; Mar.-June M-Sa

10:30am-1:30pm and 4-6:30pm, Su 10:30-1:30pm. Museum and cloisters 500ptas/€3.) Those curious about the Camino de Santiago can head to the ◪**Museo das Peregrinacións**, Pl. San Miguel. (Open Tu-F 10am-10pm, Sa 10:30am-1:30pm and 5-8pm, Su 10:30am-1:30pm. 400ptas/€2.40, children and seniors 200ptas/€1.20; free during the Apostolo.) The expansive galleries and rooftop *terraza* of the sparkling **Centro Gallego de Arte Contemporáneo (CGAC)**, R. Ramon del Valle Inclan, house cutting-edge exhibitions of boundary-bending artists from around the world. (www.cgac.org. Open Tu-Su 11am-8pm. Free.)

At night, crowds looking for post-pilgrimage consumption flood cellars throughout the city. To boogie with local students, hit the bars and clubs off **Praza Roxa** (take C. Montero Ríos). ◪**Casa das Crechas**, Vía Sacra 3, just off Pl. Quintana, is a smoky pub with a witchcraft theme. (Open M-F noon-2am, Sa-Su noon-4am.) **cafedelmercado**, R. Cardenal Playa, 3, is Santiago's trendiest night spot. (Open daily 9am-2am.) If you want to dance the night away to Spanish pop, head to **Septimo Cielo**, R. da Rama, 20. (Open daily 8pm-6am. Don't arrive too early.)

THESE BOOTS WERE MADE FOR WALKING

One night in AD 813, a hermit trudged through the hills on the way to his hermitage. Suddenly, miraculously, bright visions revealed the long-forgotten tomb of the Apostle James ("Santiago" in Spanish). Around this *campus stellae* (field of stars) the cathedral of Santiago de Compostela was built, and around this cathedral a world-famous pilgrimage was born. Since the 9th century, thousands of pilgrims have traveled the 900km of the Camino de Santiago. Clever Benedictine monks built monasteries to host *peregrinos* (pilgrims) along the *camino*, helping to make Santiago's cathedral the most frequented Christian shrine in the world. The scalloped conch shell has become a symbol of the Camino de Santiago, and help distinguish a pilgrim, as do crook-necked walking sticks and sunburned faces. Shelters along the way offer free lodging to pilgrims and stamp "pilgrims' passports" to prove that they were there. At 30km per day, the entire *camino* takes about a month. For inspiration, keep in mind that you are joining the ranks of such illustrious pilgrims as Fernando and Isabel, Francis of Assisi, Pope John Paul II, and Shirley MacLaine. For more info, contact the Officinal de Acogida del Peregrino, C. Vilar 1 (☎ 981 56 24 19).

▣ DAYTRIP FROM SANTIAGO: O CASTRO DE BAROÑA

Castromil buses from Santiago to Muros stop in Noya (1hr.; M-F 15 per day 6:15am-8pm, Sa 10 per day 7am-8pm, Su 8 per day 8am-8:30pm; 420ptas/€2.50) and Hefsel buses from Noya to Riveira stop at O Castro—tell the driver your destination (30min.; M-F 14 per day 6:50am-9:30pm, Sa-Su 7-11 per day 8am-9pm; 210ptas/€1.25).

Nineteen kilometers south of the town of **Noya** is a little-known treasure of historical intrigue and mesmerizing natural beauty: the seaside remains of the 5th-century Celtic fortress ◪**O Castro de Baroña.** The foundations dot the isthmus, ascending to a rocky promontory above the sea and then descending down to a crescent **beach,** where clothing is notoriously optional.

ASTURIAS

Sky-scraping cliffs and hell-reaching ravines lend an epic scope to the tiny land of Asturias, tucked between Basque Country and Galicia. An extensive network of tourist towns, cottages, and country inns in old *casas de indianos* (rambling Victorian mansions built by settlers) provides the residents of Asturias and Cantabria a means to get rich off Spain's vacationing elite.

PICOS DE EUROPA

God bless tectonic folding and contracting—300 million years ago, a mere flapping

SWITZERLAND
(SCHWEIZ, SUISSE, SVIZZERA)

SWISS FRANCS

US$1 = 1.66SFR	1SFR = US$0.60
CDN$1 = 1.09SFR	1SFR = CDN$0.92
UK£1 = 2.40SFR	1SFR = UK£0.42
IR£1 = 1.93SFR	1SFR = IR£0.52
AUS$1 = 0.88SFR	1SFR = AUS$1.14
NZ$1 = 0.72SFR	1SFR = NZ$1.38
ZAR1 = 0.20SFR	1SFR = ZAR4.94
EUR€1 = 1.52SFR	1SFR = EUR€0.66

PHONE CODE | **Country Code:** 41. **International dialing prefix:** 00.

The unparalleled natural beauty of Switzerland (pop. 7.3 million; 41, 290 sq. km) entices hikers, skiers, bikers, and scenery gazers from all over the globe to romp about its Alpine playground. Three-fifths of the country is dominated by mountains, featured in many a *James Bond* chase scene: the Jura cover the northwest region, bordering France, while the Alps stretch gracefully across the entire lower half of Switzerland, flirting with Italy in the southern Lepontine chain and colliding with Austria in the Eastern Rhaetian Alps. The cities that surround the crystal blue lakes have established themselves as international centers of commerce and diplomacy. A true multicultural nation, Switzerland is French in the west, German in the center and north, and Italian in the southeast, and each region has its own distinct flavor— much more than watches, chocolates, and cheeses. Although the country is not known for being cheap, Swiss hospitality and sublime vistas are priceless. For more information, check out *Let's Go: Austria and Switzerland 2002.*

SUGGESTED ITINERARIES

THREE DAYS Admire the great outdoors by spending a day at **Interlaken** (p. 923). Then head to **Lucerne** (1 day, p. 919) for the perfect combination of city culture and natural splendor before jetting to cosmopolitan **Geneva** (1 day, p. 903).

ONE WEEK Begin in **Geneva** (1 day), then head to **Montreaux** (1 day, p. 910) for sublime Alpine views. Hike at **Interlaken** for a day, then head on to **Lucerne** (1 day). Zip north to **Zurich** (1 day, p. 913) for cathedrals and museums, then visit capital city **Bern** (1 day, p. 920) before finishing your week in tasty **Neuchâtel** (1 day, p. 911).

BEST OF SWITZERLAND, TWO WEEKS Start in **Geneva** (2 days), then pop by **Lausanne** (1 day) and **Montreaux** (1 day). Admire the Matterhorn in **Zermatt** (1 day, p. 926) and hike the Alps at **Interlaken** (1 day). Bask in **Locarno**'s Mediterranean climate (1 day, p. 929) before exploring the **Swiss National Park** (1 day, p. 928). Visit **Zurich** (2 days) and nearby **Lucerne** (1 day), then check out **Basel** (1 day, p. 911) for medieval fun. Head to the capital, **Bern** (1 day), and end in **Neuchâtel** (1 day).

LIFE AND TIMES

HISTORY AND POLITICS

PRE-HISTORY (750 BC TO AD 500)

By 750 BC, Switzerland had become an important center of Celtic culture. The most prominent tribe, the **Helvetii,** were Romanized between 47 BC and AD 15, and survived as a peaceful, urban civilization for the next two centuries. Around 250, however, constant raids from many warlike Germanic tribes divided the territory and created radically different cultures in each region. Eventually, the most aggressive tribe, the **Alemanni,** asserted dominance over the entire area.

AGAINST THE EMPIRE (500-1520)

Switzerland had been loosely united since 1032 as part of the **Holy Roman Empire,** but when Emperor **Rudolf of Habsburg** tried to assert control over their land in the late 13th century, the Swiss decided to rebel. Three of the Alemanni communities (the Forest Cantons) signed an **Everlasting Alliance** in 1291, agreeing to defend each other from outside attack. The Swiss consider this moment to be the beginning of the **Swiss Confederation.** However, a union of such fiercely independent and culturally distinct states made for an uneasy marriage. The **Swabian War** (1499-1500) against the empire brought virtual independence from the Habsburgs, but domestic struggles based on cultural and religious differences continued.

REFORMATION TO REVOLUTION (1520-1800)

With no strong central government to settle quibbles between cantons of different religious faith, the Swiss were split even further by the **Protestant Reformation.** Lutheran **Ulrich Zwingli** (see p. 913) of Zurich and **John Calvin** (see p. 903) of Geneva instituted puritanical reforms, but the rural cantons remained loyal to the Catholic faith. When religious differences between the Protestant city cantons versus the Catholic rural cantons escalated into full-fledged battle in the mid-16th century, the Confederation intervened, granting Protestants freedom but prohibiting them from imposing their faith on others. The Confederation remained neutral during the faith-based **Thirty Years' War,** escaping the devastation wrought on the rest of Europe. The **Peace of Westphalia,** which ended the war in 1648, granted the Swiss official independence from the empire, resolving 350 years of international strife. However, Swiss independence was short lived: **Napoleon** invaded in 1798 and established the **Helvetic Republic.** After Napoleon's defeat at Waterloo in 1815, Swiss neutrality was (again) officially recognized.

NEUTRALITY AND DIPLOMACY (1815 TO THE 20TH CENTURY)

With neutrality established by the **Treaty of Vienna** in 1815, Switzerland could turn its attention to domestic issues. Industrial growth brought relative material prosperity, but religious differences continued to create tension between Catholic (**Sonderbund**) and all other (**Diet**) cantons. A **civil war** broke out in 1847, but it lasted only 25 days. The Protestant forces were victorious, and the country wrote a new constitution modeled after that of the United States. Once stabilized, Switzerland cultivated its reputation for resolving international conflicts. The **Geneva Convention of 1864** established international laws for conduct during war, and Geneva became the headquarters for the **International Red Cross** (see p. 908).

Switzerland's neutrality was tested in **World War I** as French- and German-speaking Switzerland claimed different cultural loyalties. In 1920, Geneva served as the headquarters of the ill-fated **League of Nations,** solidifying Switzerland's reputation as the center for international mediation. During **World War II,** both sides found it useful to have Switzerland (and its banks) as neutral territory. As the rest of Europe cleaned up the rubble of two global wars, Switzerland nurtured its already sturdy economy; Zurich emerged as a banking and insurance center. Although Geneva became the world's most prominent diplomatic head-

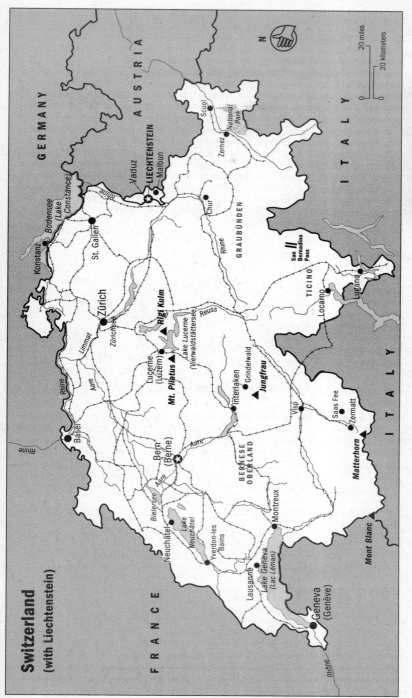

Switzerland
(with Liechtenstein)

quarters, Switzerland remained isolationist in its relations with the rest of Europe, declining membership in the United Nations, NATO, and the European Economic Community.

SWITZERLAND TODAY

Switzerland has become increasingly wealthy, liberal, and successful since WWII and is still fiercely independent and wary of entanglements with the rest of Europe. The Swiss are remarkably progressive in many areas, electing **Ruth Dreifuss** as its first female president and maintaining one of the world's most stringent ecological policies to protect its fragile Alpine environment. In the past few years, Swiss banks have come under intense scrutiny for their "blind account" policy, which allowed Holocaust victims and Nazi leaders alike to deposit money and gold during WWII.

In the Swiss government, the 26 cantons are incorporated into the Confederation and its two-chamber legislature, the Federal Assembly. The executive branch consists of a group of 7 members—the **Bundesrat (Federal Council)**—elected to 4-year terms. The Bundesrat chooses a president from among its ranks. The president holds office for only one year, and the post is more symbolic than functional. Frequent **referenda** and **initiatives** make political decisions a part of daily life.

THE ARTS

PAINTING AND SCULPTURE

Since the early 20th century, Switzerland has been a prime space for artistic experimentation. One of Switzerland's most famous painters is **Paul Klee** (see p. 920), whose delicately colored watercolors and oil paintings helped shape the beginnings of abstraction, questioning dominant modes of artistic expression. In 1916, Zurich became the birthplace of the **Dada** movement (see p. 917), which rejected traditional aesthetic ideals and attempted to make people reconsider their social values. Later in the 20th century, Switzerland continued to attract liberal artistic thinkers. The **Zurich School of Concrete Art,** which operated primarily between the wars, used objects and elements of Surrealism combined with Russian constructivism to explore interactions between humans and space. Switzerland maintains a lively arts scene today; for a glimpse, see Zurich's cutting-edge **Kunsthaus,** p. 917.

LITERATURE

Jean-Jacques Rousseau, best known for his *Social Contract* (1762), which inspired the French Revolution, was born in Geneva in 1712 and was always proud of his Swiss background—despite the fact that he spent most of his time outside the country and that the Swiss burned his books. When Romanticism caught on in Switzerland, **J.J. Bodmer** and **J.J. Breitinger** advocated literature in the Swiss-German language, and **Gottfried Keller** penned the *Bildungsroman* (coming-of-age novel) *Green Henry* (1855). **Conrad Ferdinand Meyer** was a highly influential Swiss poet whose writings united characteristics of Romanticism and Realism.

Carl Jung, whose psychiatric practice in Zurich led him to write the famous *Symbols of Transformation* (1916), is considered to be the founder of analytical psychology. Switzerland has also produced several respected modern playwrights: critics laud **Max Frisch** for his Brechtian style and thoughtful treatment of Nazi Germany in works such as *Andorra* (1961), and **Friedrich Dürrenmatt** won renown for his tragicomedic portrayal of human corruptibility in *The Physicists* (1962).

FOOD AND DRINK

Switzerland's hearty cooking will keep you warm through those frigid alpine winters but will skyrocket your cholesterol. Bernese *Rösti*, a plateful of hash-brown potatoes (sometimes flavored with bacon or cheese), is prevalent in the German regions; cheese- or meat- *fondue* is popular in the French. Try Valaisian *raclette*, made by melting cheese over a fire, then scraping it onto a baked potato and garnishing it with meat or vegetables. **Supermarkets** Migros and Co-op double as self-serve cafeterias; stop in for a cheap meal as well as groceries. The world-famous

Swiss culinary delight, **milk chocolate** (*Lindt, Toblerone,* and *Nestlé* are native favorites) is cheap and abundant. Each canton has its own local **beer**—it's relatively cheap, often less expensive than Coca-Cola.

ESSENTIALS

DOCUMENTS AND FORMALITIES

Switzerland does not require visas for nationals of Australia, Canada, the EU, New Zealand, South Africa, or the US for stays of shorter than three months.

Swiss Embassies at Home: Australia, 7 Melbourne Ave., Forrest, Canberra, ACT 2603 (☎(02) 6273 3977; fax 6273 3428). **Canada,** 5 Marlborough Ave., Ottawa, Ontario KIN 8E6 (☎613-235-1837; fax 563-1394). **Ireland,** 6 Ailesbury Rd., Ballsbridge, Dublin 4 (☎(01) 218 63 82 or 218 63 83; fax 283 03 44). **New Zealand,** 22 Panama St., Wellington (☎(04) 472 15 93 or 472 15 94; fax 499 63 0). **South Africa,** Pretoria, 818 George Ave., Arcadia 0083, P.O. Box 2289, 0001 Pretoria (☎(012) 430 67 07; fax 430 67 71). **UK,** 16-18 Montague Pl., London W1H 2BQ (☎(020) 76 16 60 00; fax 77 24 70 01). **US,** 2900 Cathedral Ave. NW, Washington D.C. 20008-3499 (☎202-745-7900; fax 387-2564).

Foreign Embassies in Switzerland: Nearly all foreign embassies are in **Bern** (p. 920).

TRANSPORTATION

BY PLANE. Major international airports for overseas connections are located in **Bern, Geneva,** and **Zurich.** From the UK, **easyJet** (☎(0870) 600 00 00; www.easyjet.com) has flights from London to Geneva and Zurich (UK£47-136). From Ireland, **Aer Lingus** (☎(01) 886 88 88; www.aerlingus.ie) has return tickets from Dublin, Cork, Galway, Kerry, and Shannon to Zurich for IR£102-240.

BY TRAIN. Federal **(SBB, CFF, FFS)** and private railways connect most towns and villages, with trains running frequently. **Eurailpass, Europass,** and **Interrail passes** are all valid on Switzerland's trains. The **Swiss Pass,** which is sold worldwide, offers unlimited rail travel for four, eight, 15, or 21 consecutive days or one month. In addition to rail travel, it entitles you to unlimited urban transportation in 36 cities and unlimited travel on certain private railways and lake steamers. (Adult 2nd-class 4-day passes US$160, 8-day $220, 15-day $265, 21-day $305, 1 month $345.) The **Swiss Flexipass** entitles you to any three to nine days of unlimited rail travel within a one-month period, with the same benefits as the Swiss Pass. (2nd-class 3-day pass US$132, 4-day $156, 5-day $180, 6-day $204, 7-day $222, 8-day $240, 9-day $258.)

BY BUS. PTT Post Buses, a barrage of government-run banana-colored coaches, connect rural villages and towns where trains don't run. SwissPasses are valid on many buses; Eurailpasses are not. Even with the SwissPass, you might have to pay a bit extra (5-10SFr) on the direct, faster buses. *Tageskarten,* valid for 24hr. of free travel, cost around 7.50SFr, but most cities are small enough to cover on foot.

BY CAR. With armies of mechanized road crews ready to remove snow at a moment's notice, roads at altitudes of up to 1500m generally remain open throughout winter. The **speed limit** is 50kph in cities, 80kph on open roads, and 120kph on highways in Switzerland. Many small Swiss towns forbid cars to enter; some forbid only visitors' cars, require special permits, or restrict driving hours. The **Touring Club Suisse,** chemin de Blandonnet 4, 1214 Vernier, Case Postale 820 (☎(022) 417 27 27) operates road patrols. Call 140 for roadside assistance.

BY BIKE AND BY THUMB. Cycling, though strenuous, is a splendid way to see the country; most train stations rent bikes and allow you to return them at another station. The **Touring Club Suisse** (see above) is a good source of information, maps, brochures, and route descriptions. *Let's Go* does not recommend hitchhiking.

TOURIST SERVICES AND MONEY

| **EMERGENCY** | Police, ☎117. Ambulance, ☎144. Fire, ☎118. |

TOURIST OFFICES. Tourist offices are available in nearly every town in Switzerland. The **Swiss National Tourist Office,** marked by a standard blue **"i"** sign, is represented in nearly every town in Switzerland, though in smaller towns the staff may not speak English. The tourist web site for Switzerland is www.myswitzerland.ch.

CURRENCY AND EXCHANGE. The Swiss monetary unit is the **Swiss Franc (SFr),** which is divided into 100 *centimes* (called *Rappen* in German Switzerland). Coins are issued in 5, 10, 20, and 50 *centimes* and 1, 2, and 5SFr; bills in 10, 20, 50, 100, 500, and 1000SFr denominations. Currency exchange is easiest at ATMs, train stations, and post offices, where rates are the same as or close to bank rates.

> **Prices:** Though Switzerland is not the cheapest destination, there are ways to experience it on a tight budget. If you stay in hostels and prepare most of your own food, expect to spend anywhere from 45-100SFr, or US$30-65, per person per day.

> **Tipping and bargaining:** There is technically no need for tipping in Switzerland, as gratuities are already automatically factored into prices. However, it is considered polite to round up your bill to the nearest 1 or 2 Francs as a nod of approval for good service.

> **Taxes:** There is **no value-added tax (VAT)** in Switzerland, though there are frequently tourist taxes of a few SFr per night at hostels.

ACCOMMODATIONS AND CAMPING

HOSTELS AND CAMPING. There are **hostels** (*Jugendherbergen* in German, *Auberges de Jeunesse* in French, *Ostelli* in Italian) in all big cities and in most small towns. *Schweizer Jugendherbergen* (SJH, or Swiss Youth Hostels) runs HI hostels in Switzerland and has a web site with contact information for member hostels (www.youthhostel.ch). Hostel beds are usually 20-34SFr. Nonmembers can stay in all of these hostels but are usually charged a surcharge. The smaller, more informal **Swiss Backpackers (SB)** organization (www.backpacker.ch) has 28 hostels for the young foreign traveler interested in socializing. Most Swiss **camping sites** are large plots with many camper vans and cars; camping in Switzerland is less about getting into nature and more about having a cheap place to sleep. Most sites are open in summer only. Prices average 6-9SFr per person, 4-10SFr per tent site.

HOTELS AND PRIVATZIMMERN. Hotels and **pensions** tend to charge at least 50-75SFr for a single room and 80-150SFr for a double. The cheapest have **Gasthof, Gästehaus,** or **Hotel-Garni** in the name. *Privatzimmern* (rooms in a family home) run about 25-60SFr per person. Breakfast is almost always included at both.

SKIING AND HIKING

Nearly every town and city has a series of **hiking trails** in its vicinity; consult the local tourist office. Trails are usually marked with either a red-white-red marker (no more than sturdy boots and hiking poles are needed) or a blue-white-blue marker (mountaineering equipment is needed). Free hiking **maps** are available from even the most basic tourist offices, but for lengthy hikes consider the maps by **Freytag-Berndt** and **Kümmerly-Frey** (about US$10), available in kiosks, bookstores, and tourist offices all over Switzerland. **Swiss Alpine Club (SAC) huts** provide accommodations in higher, more remote areas of the Alps. To become a member of the SAC (126SFr), contact SAC, Sektion Bern, Monbijoustr. 61, CH 3007, Bern (☎(031) 370 18 18; fax 370 18 00). **Skiing** in Switzerland is often less expensive than in North America if you avoid the pricey resorts. **Ski passes** (valid for transportation to, from, and on lifts) run 30-50SFr per day, 100-300SFr per week. A week of lift tickets, equipment rental, lessons, lodging, and *demi-pen-*

sion (half-board—breakfast plus one other meal) averages 475SFr. **Summer skiing** is less common than it once was but is still available in a few towns, such as Zermatt and Saas Fee.

COMMUNICATION

MAIL. Airmail from Switzerland takes seven to 20 days to North America. Domestic letters take one to three days. Address *Poste Restante* letters in the following format: FirstName SURNAME, *Postlagernde Briefe*, CH-1211 Geneva, Switzerland. CH is the mail code for Switzerland.

TELEPHONES. Wherever possible, use a calling card for international phone calls, as the long-distance rates for national phone services are often exorbitant. Most pay phones in Switzerland accept only **prepaid phone cards.** Phone cards are available at kiosks, post offices, or train stations. Direct dial access numbers include: **AT&T,** ☎ (0800) 89 00 11; **British Telecom,** ☎ (0800) 55 25 44; **Canada Direct,** ☎ (0800) 55 83 30); **Ireland Direct,** ☎ (0800) 55 11 74; **MCI,** ☎ (0800) 89 02 22; **Sprint,** ☎ (0800) 89 97 77; **Telecom New Zealand,** ☎ (0800) 55 64 11; **Telkom South Africa,** ☎ (0800) 55 85 35.

INTERNET ACCESS. Most towns have Internet cafes (access about 12SFr per hr).

LANGUAGES. German, French, Italian, and Romansch are the national languages. English is the most common second language in Switzerland, and most urban Swiss speak it fluently. Outside of cities and among older residents, however, you'll need our language charts on p. 953, you multilingual fool, you.

LOCAL FACTS

Time: Switzerland is 1hr. ahead of Greenwich Mean Time (GMT).

When to go: Switzerland has a surprisingly mild climate; in July, temperatures can briefly reach 38°C (100°F), while in Feb. they get down to -10°C (5°F). Mountainous areas are cooler and wetter the higher you get; as a rule, temperatures drop about 1.7°C (3°F) with each additional 300m. Bring warm sweaters Sept.-May; add a thick coat, hat, and gloves in winter. The lake regions are very rainy.

Holidays: New Year's Day (Jan. 1-2); Good Friday (Mar. 29); Easter Monday (Apr. 1); Labor Day (May 1); Ascension Day (May 9); Whit Monday (May 20); Swiss National Day (Aug. 1); Christmas (Dec. 25-26).

Festivals: 2 raucous festivals are the **Fasnacht** (Carnival; Mar.) in Basel and the **Escalade** (early Dec.) in Geneva. "**Open-Air**" music festivals occur throughout the summer, including the **Montreux JazzFest** (July) and the **Open-Air St. Gallen** (late June).

WESTERN (FRENCH) SWITZERLAND

GENEVA (GENÈVE, GENF)   ☎022

There is no typical resident of Geneva—its long tradition of battling for political and religious independence is perhaps the one theme uniting the city's wildly diverse group of citizens. In 1536, Geneva welcomed a young, unknown John Calvin to its cathedral; later, aesthetes and free thinkers, including Voltaire and Rousseau, lived here. Today, multinational organizations (including the Red Cross and the United Nations) continue to lend the city an international feel that contrasts strongly with the homogeneity of most Swiss towns. Indeed, many say that the only thing Geneva shares with the rest of Switzerland is its neutral foreign policy and the state religion, banking.

SWITZERLAND

✈ INTERCITY TRANSPORTATION

Flights: Cointrin Airport (☎ 717 71 11, flight information ☎ 799 31 11) is a hub for **Swissair** (☎(0848) 80 07 00). Several direct flights per day to Amsterdam, London, New York, Paris, and Rome. **Air France** (☎827 87 87) has 7 per day to Paris, and **British Airways** (☎(0848) 80 10 10) has 7 per day to London. To reach the city, go up a level from the arrivals hall and catch bus #10 outside (15min., every 6min., 2.20SFr, exact change required) or the train (6min., every 10min., 4.80SFr) to Gare Cornavin.

Trains: All trains run approximately 4:30am-1am. **Gare Cornavin,** pl. Cornavin, is the main station. To: **Basel** (3hr., every hr., 72SFr); **Bern** (2hr., every hr., 40SFr); **Interlaken** (3hr., every hr., 65SFr); **Lausanne** (40min., every 20-30min., 20SFr); **Montreux** (1hr., 2 per hr., 29SFr); **Paris** (3¾hr.; 8 per day; 196SFr, under 26 166SFr); **Zurich** (3½hr., every hr., 77SFr). Ticket counter open M-F 8:30am-6:30pm, Sa 9am-5pm. **24hr. information:** ☎(0900) 30 03 00 (1.19SFr per min.). **Gare des Eaux-Vives** (☎736 16 20), on av. de la Gare des Eaux-Vives (tram #12, "Amandoliers SNCF"), connects to France's regional rail through **Annecy** (1½hr., 6 per day, 14SFr) or **Chamonix** (2½hr., 4 per day, 24SFr). Ticket office open M-F 9am-6pm, Sa 11am-5:45pm.

▐ LOCAL TRANSPORTATION

Carry your passport with you at all times; the French border is never more than a few minutes away and buses frequently cross it. Ticket purchasing is largely on the honor system, but you may be fined 60SFr for evading fares. Much of the city can be walked in good weather.

Public Transportation: Geneva has an efficient bus and tram network with major hubs at the Gare Cornavin, Rd.-Pt. de Plainpalais, and pl. Bel Air (near the *ponts de l'Ile*). **Transport Publics Genevois** (☎308 34 34), next to the tourist office in Gare Cornavin, provides *Le Réseau* (a free map of local bus routes) and inexpensive timetables. Open M-Sa 7am-7pm, Su 10am-6pm. Trips within zone 10 (most of the city) cost 2.50SFr; 3 stops or fewer 1.80SFr. **Day passes** 6.30SFr for 1 zone, 12SFr for 4. Buy tickets at the train station or automatic vendors. Stamp multi-use tickets before boarding. Buses run roughly 5:30am-midnight; **Noctambus** (3SFr, 1:30-4:30am) runs when the others don't. SwissPass valid on all buses; Eurail not valid.

Taxis: Taxi-Phone (☎331 41 33). 6.30SFr plus 2.70SFr per km. Taxi from airport to city 25-30SFr., max. 4 passengers (15-20min.).

Bike Rental: Geneva has well-marked bike paths and special traffic lights for spoked traffic. For routes, get *Itineraires cyclables* or *Tours de ville avec les vélos de location* from the tourist office. Behind the station, **Genève Roule,** pl. Montbrillant 17 (☎740 13 43), has 25 free bikes available (50SFr deposit; hefty fine if bike is lost or stolen). Slightly nicer neon bikes start at 5SFr per day. Open 7:30am-9:30pm.

Hitchhiking: *Let's Go* does not recommend hitchhiking; however, hitchers say that Switzerland is one of the safer countries in Europe in which to hail a ride. Those headed to Germany or northern Switzerland take bus #4 to "Jardin Botanique." Those headed to France take bus #4 to "Palettes," then line D to "St. Julien."

✸ ? ORIENTATION AND PRACTICAL INFORMATION

Geneva began as a fortified city on a hill, and the labyrinthine cobbled streets of the historic *vieille ville* and the quiet squares around **Cathédrale de St-Pierre** are still the heart of the urban landscape. Across the **Rhône River** to the north, billionaires' banks and five-star hotels gradually give way to lakeside promenades, the U.N., Red Cross, W.T.O., and rolling green parkland. Across the **Arve River** to the south lies the village of **Carouge,** home to many student bars and clubs (take tram #12 or #13 to "pl. du Marché").

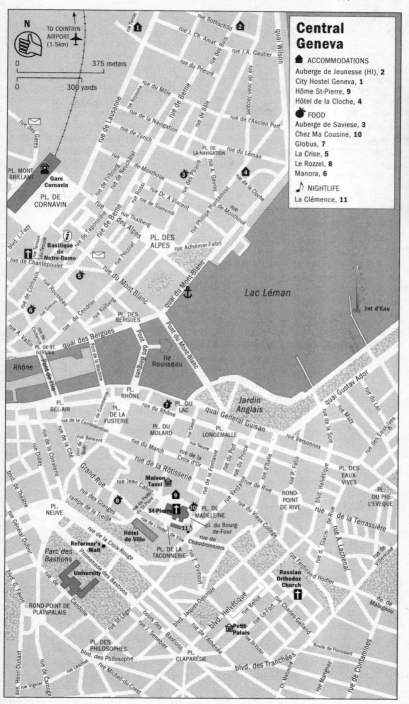

S W I T Z E R L A N D

Central Geneva

🏠 **ACCOMMODATIONS**
Auberge de Jeunesse (HI), 2
City Hostel Geneva, 1
Hôme St-Pierre, 9
Hôtel de la Cloche, 4

🍎 **FOOD**
Auberge de Saviese, 3
Chez Ma Cousine, 10
Globus, 7
La Crise, 5
Le Rozzel, 8
Manora, 6

♪ **NIGHTLIFE**
La Clémence, 11

N
TO COINTRIN AIRPORT (1.5km)
0 375 meters
0 300 yards

rue Ferrier
rue Rothschild
rue J. Ch. Amat
rue des Buis
rue J.A. Gautier
quai Wilson
rue du Prieuré
rue de Jean-Jaquet
rue du Môle
rue de l'Ancien Port
rue de la Navigation
rue de Berne
rue de Bâle
rue de Zurich
PL. DE LA NAVIGATION
rue du Léman
rue A. Gevray
PL. MONT-BRILLANT
Gare Cornavin
PL. DE CORNAVIN
rue de Fribourg
rue de Neuchâtel
rue de-Monthoux
rue du fossé
rue de Sismondi
rue Dr. A Vincent
rue Thalberg
rue Philippe Plantamour de-Monthoux
rue de la Cloche
blvd. J.-Fazy
Basilique de Notre-Dame
rue de Chantepoulet
rue de Cornavin
rue Rousseau
rue des Alpes
PL. DES ALPES
rue Adhémar-Fabri
rue Pécolat
rue de Lausanne
rue des Gares
rue de la Servette
Lac Léman
Jet d'Eau
rue du Mont-Blanc
quai du Mont-Blanc
rue du Cendrier
rue Kléberg
rue Grenus
rue A. Vallin
PL. DE ST. GERVAIS
PL. DES BERGUES
Île Rousseau
Pont du Mont-Blanc
Pont des Bergues
quai des Bergues
Rhône
Pont de la Machine
PL. RHÔNE
PL. BEL-AIR
PL. DE LA FUSTERIE
rue de la Confédération
rue de la Cité
rue de la Corraterie
blvd. de Théâtre
Grand-Rue
rue des Granges
rampe de la Treille
PL. NEUVE
PL. du Rhône
PL. DU LAC
PL. DU MOLARD
rue du Rhône
rue du March
rue de la Croix d'Or
rue de la Rôtisserie
rue Jean Calvin
Maison Tavel
St-Pierre
PL. DE MADELEINE
Hôtel de Ville
PL. DE LA TACONNERIE
Reformer's Wall
Promenade des Bastions
Parc des Bastions
University
ROND-POINT DE PLAINPALAIS
blvd. G.-Favon
rue de Candolle
rue St-Léger
cours des Bastions
PL. DES PHILOSOPHES
blvd. des Philosophe
rue Leschot
rue Michel-du-Crest
ave. Henri-Dunant
rue de Carouge
Jardin Anglais
quai Général Guisan
PL. LONGEMALLE
rue Neuve
rue de la Fontaine
rue du Prince
rue d'Italie
rue Verdaine rue de Rive
rue du Vieux Collège
ROND-POINT DE RIVE
quai Gustav Ador
quai du Lac
rue du Mont
rue de la Scie
rue des Eaux-Vives
rue Versonnex
rue P. Fatio
blvd. Helvétique
PL. DES EAUX-VIVES
PL. DU PRÉ-L'EVEQUE
rue de la Terrassière
rue d. Glacis-de-Rive
rue A. Lachenal
rue de Villereuse
pl. du Bourg-de-Four
rue de Chaudronniers
rue E. Dumont
rue Ferdinand Hodler
Russian Orthodox Church
rte. de Malagnou
blvd. Jacques-Dalcroze
blvd. Helvétique
rue Baillot
rue Le-Fort
rue Charles-Galland
rue St-Victor
Petit-Palais
rue de l'Athénée
PL. CLAPARÈDE
Route de Florissant
blvd. des Tranchées
rue de Contamines
rue Maunoir
Ch. Malombre
rue Vignier

TOURIST, FINANCIAL, AND LOCAL SERVICES

Tourist Offices: The main office, r. du Mont-Blanc 18 (☎909 70 00; fax 909 70 11; www.geneve-tourisme.ch), lies 5min. away from Cornavin toward the pont du Mont-Blanc in the Central Post Office Building. English-speaking staff books hotel rooms (5SFr fee) and offers **walking tours.** Pick up the city map and *Info Jeunes/Young People*, both free. Open July-Aug. daily 9am-6pm; Sept.-June M-Sa 9am-6pm. During the summer, head for **Centre d'Accueil et de Renseignements** (CAR; ☎731 46 47), an office-in-a-bus in pl. Mont-Blanc, by the Metro Shopping entrance to Cornavin Station. Geared toward young people, it posts a list of free musical and theatrical performances and makes hotel reservations for free. Open mid-June to mid-Sept. 9am-11pm.

Consulates: Australia, chemin des Fins 2 (☎799 91 00). **Canada,** av. de l'Ariana 5 (☎919 92 00). **New Zealand,** chemin des Fins 2 (☎929 03 50). **South Africa,** r. de Rhône 65 (☎849 54 54). **UK,** r. de Vermont 37 (☎918 24 26). **US,** World Trade Center Bldg. #2 (☎798 16 05; recorded information ☎798 16 15).

Currency Exchange: ATMs offer the best rates. **Gare Cornavin** has good rates and no commission on traveler's checks, advances cash on credit cards (min. 200SFr), and arranges Western Union transfers. Open Nov.-Mar. 6:45am-8pm; Apr.-Oct. 6:45am-9:30pm. Western Union desk open 7am-7pm.

Bi-Gay-Lesbian Organizations: Dialogai, r. de la Navigation 11-13 (☎906 40 40). From Gare Cornavin, turn left, walk 5min. down r. de Lausanne, and turn right onto r. de la Navigation. Resource group with programs from support groups to outdoor activities. Mostly male, but women welcome. **Centre Femmes Natalie Barney** (women only), 19 chemin Chateau Bloch (☎797 27 14), offers similar services but is lesbian-oriented. 24hr. answering machine with events listing; live phone answering W 6-8pm.

Laundromat: Lavseul, r. de-Monthoux 29 (☎735 90 51 or 732 61 46). Wash 5SFr, dry 1SFr per 10min. Open 7am-midnight.

EMERGENCY AND COMMUNICATIONS

Emergencies: Police, ☎117. **Fire,** ☎118. **Ambulance,** ☎144.

Pharmacy: Every night a changing set of 4 pharmacies stays open late (9 or 11pm). Consult *Genève Agenda* for addresses and phone numbers. The pharmacy at the train station has the longest regular hours.

Medical Assistance: Hôpital Cantonal, r. Micheli-du-Crest 24 (☎372 33 11). Bus #1 or 5 or tram #12. Door #2 is for emergency care, door #3 for consultations. For information on walk-in clinics call the **Association des Médecins** (☎320 84 20).

Internet Access: Point 6, r. de Vieux-Billard 7a, off r. des Bains (☎800 26 00). 4SFr per 30min., 6SFr per hr. Open M-Tu and Th noon-midnight, W 10am-midnight, F noon-2am, Sa 10am-2am, Su 10am-10pm. **Discount Internet Café,** r. de Lausanne 44 (☎738 50 00). Turn left on r. de Lausanne from Gare Cornavin and walk 5min. 2SFr per 15min., 4SFr per 30min., 6SFr per hr. Open M-F 9am-9:30pm, Sa-Su noon-9:30pm. MC/V.

Post Office: Poste Centrale, r. de Mont-Blanc 18, a block from Gare Cornavin in the stately Hôtel des Postes. Open M-F 7:30am-6pm, Sa 8:30-noon. Address mail to be held: *Poste Restante,* Genève 1 Mont-Blanc, **CH-1211,** Geneva. **Branch** behind the train station, r. des Gares 10-16. 24hr. self-service; counters open M-F 7am-10:45pm, Sa 7am-8pm, Su noon-8pm.

◤ ACCOMMODATIONS

The seasonal influx of university students has created a network of decently priced hostels, pensions, and university dorms moonlighting as summer hotels. The indispensable *Info Jeunes* lists about 50 options; the highlights are below. Even for short stays, reservations are a must. For longer stays, check *Tribune de Genève*'s weekly supplement of apartment classifieds or the tourist office board.

City Hostel Geneva, r. Ferrier 2 (☎901 15 00). From the station, turn left on r. de Lausanne, left onto r. de Prieuré, and right onto r. Ferrier. The hostel has a great location,

SWITZERLAND

TV room, kitchen, book exchange, **Internet** access (8SFr per hr.), and Heinekens (sold at the desk). Linens 3SFr. Reception 8am-12:15pm and 1-10pm. Check-out 10am, no curfew or lockout. Single-sex, 4-bed dorms 25SFr; singles 55SFr; doubles 80SFr. MC/V.

Auberge de Jeunesse (HI), r. Rothschild 28-30 (☎732 62 60). Walk 10min. left from the station down r. de Lausanne, then turn right on r. Rothschild, or take bus #1 from the station (dir.: Wilson) to the end of the line. Don't expect atmosphere, just a comfortable last-minute bunk and a ton of people to meet. Restaurant, kitchen facilities (1SFr per 30min.), TV room, library, and 3 **Internet** stations (7SFr per hr.). Breakfast, hall showers, lockers, and sheets included. Laundry 6SFr. Special facilities for disabled guests. 6-night max. stay. Reception June-Sept. 6:30-10am and 2pm-1am; Oct.-May 6:30-10am and 4pm-midnight. Lockout in summer 10am-2pm; in winter 10am-4pm. Curfew 1am; midnight in winter. Dorms 25SFr; doubles 70SFr with toilet, 80SFr with toilet and shower; quads 110SFr. MC/V.

Hôme St-Pierre, cours St-Pierre 4 (☎310 37 07). Take bus #5 to "pl. Neuve." This **women-only** 150-year-old "home" has comfortable beds, a large kitchen, spectacular rooftop views, and a convivial atmosphere. Breakfast (M-Sa) 5SFr. Showers and lockers included. Laundry 7SFr. Reception M-Sa 9am-noon and 4-8pm, Su 9am-noon. Dorms 23SFr; singles 36-45SFr; doubles 50-60SFr. MC/V.

Cité Universitaire, av. Miremont 46 (☎839 22 11). Take the #3 bus (dir.: Crets-de-Champel) from the station to the last stop. This institutional college housing has TV rooms, a restaurant, a disco (all-night dancing Th and Sa, free to residents), ping-pong, tennis courts, a small grocery shop, and some great views. Hall showers included. Reception M-F 8am-noon and 2-10pm, Sa 8am-noon and 6-10pm, Su 9am-11am and 6-10pm. Check-out 10am. Lockout 11am-6pm, curfew 11pm; both for dorms only. Dorms (July-Sept. only) 19SFr; singles 41SFr; doubles 57SFr; studios with kitchenette and bathroom 74SFr. AmEx/MC/V.

Hôtel de la Cloche, r. de la Cloche 6 (☎732 94 81), off quai du Mont-Blanc across from the Noga Hilton. It's a converted mansion; each room has a chandelier and TV. Breakfast and showers included. Reception 8am-10pm. Singles 65SFr in summer, 55SFr in winter; doubles 85SFr/95SFr; triples 95SFr/105SFr, with bath 120SFr; quads with toilet and shower 140SFr. AmEx/DC/MC/V.

Camping Pointe-à-la-Bise, chemin de la Bise (☎752 12 96). Take bus #8 to "Rive," then bus E (north) to "Bise" and walk 10min. to the lake. Reception 8am-noon and 4-8pm. Open Apr.-Sept. 6SFr per person, 9SFr per tent space. No tents provided. Beds 18SFr. 4-person bungalows 85SFr.

▉ FOOD

It's true that you can find anything from sushi to *paella* in Geneva, but you may need a banker's salary to foot the bill. Do-it-yourselfers can pick up basics at *boulangeries, pâtisseries,* or the ubiquitous supermarkets. Many supermarkets also have attached cafeterias; try the **Co-op** on the corner of r. du Commerce and r. du Rhône, in the Centre Rhône Fusterie. (Open M 9am-6:45pm; Tu, W, F 8:30am-6:45pm; Th 8:30am-8pm; Sa 8:30am-5pm. MC/V.) For dining out, there are extensive options in the *vieille ville* near the cathedral. To the south, the village of Carouge is known for its cozy pizzerias and funky, chic brasseries. Around pl. du Cirque and plaine de Plainpalais are a number of cheap, student-oriented "tea rooms," offering bakery and traditional fare at reasonable prices.

Le Rozzel, Grand-Rue 18. Take bus #5 to pl. Neuve, then walk up the hill past the cathedral on r. Jean-Calvin to Grand-Rue. Large dinner crêpes (7-17SFr), dessert crêpes (5-19SFr), *menü* 19SFr. Open M 7am-4pm, Tu-F 7am-10pm, Sa 9am-10pm. AmEx/MC/V.

Restaurant Manora, r. de Cornavin 4, to the right of the station in the Placette department store. This huge self-serve restaurant has a fresh, varied, high-quality selection including salads (from 4.20SFr), entrees cooked on the spot (from 6SFr), and free water (rare in Switzerland). Wheelchair accessible. Open M-Sa 7am-9pm, Su 9am-9pm.

Globus, 48 r. de Rhône, on the pl. du Molard. Manora-style, offers inexpensive gourmet delights, including fresh produce, a *fromagerie*, and still-swimming seafood. Daily specials from 11SFr. Open M-W and F 7:30am-6:45pm, Th 7:30am-8pm, Sa 8am-5:45pm.

Chez Ma Cousine, rue de Bourg-Four 6, in the *vieille ville*. The specialty is chicken, perfectly cooked and served with fries and salad (13.90SFr). Salads mixed with chicken also available. Open M-F 7am-midnight, Sa 11am-midnight, Su 11am-11pm.

Auberge de Saviese, r. des Pâquis 20. Take bus #1 to "Monthoux." In addition to lunch *plat du jour*, the menu features an excellent *fondue au cognac* (19.50SFr), *raclette* with all the trimmings (30SFr), and classic regional perch (27SFr). Open M-Sa 10:30am-3pm and 5pm-12:30am, Su 5pm-12:30am. AmEx/MC/V.

La Crise, r. de Chantepoulet 13. From the station, turn right on r. de Cornavin and left on r. de Chantepoulet. This tiny, veggie-friendly restaurant has healthy portions and slender prices. Open M-F 6am-8pm, Sa 6am-3pm.

◑ SIGHTS

For centuries Geneva was tightly constrained by a belt of fortified walls and trenches. By the time they were removed in the mid-19th century, the city's most interesting historical sites were already established in a dense, easily walkable space. The tourist office offers 2hr. **walking tours.** (June 14-Oct. 2 M-F 10am; Sa 10am throughout the year. 12SFr, students and seniors 8SFr.)

VIEILLE VILLE. From 1536 to 1564, Calvin preached at the **Cathédrale de St-Pierre,** the heart of the *vieille ville* and the early Protestant world. The **north tower** provides a commanding view of the old town. *(Open June-Sept. M-Sa 9am-7pm, Su noon-7pm; Oct.-May M-Sa 10am-noon and 2-5pm, Su 1:30-5pm. Tower closes 30min. earlier and costs 3SFr July-Aug.)* The ruins of a Roman sanctuary, a 4th-century basilica, and a 6th-century church rest in an **archaeological site** below the cathedral. *(Open June-Sept. Tu-Sa 11am-5pm, Su 10am-5pm; Oct.-May Tu-Sa 2-5pm, Su 10am-noon and 2-5pm. 5SFr, students 3SFr.)* At the west end of the *vieille ville* sits the 14th-century **Maison Tavel,** Geneva's oldest civilian medieval building, which now houses a municipal history **museum.** *(Open Tu-Su 10am-5pm. Free.)* Across the street is the **Hôtel de Ville** (town hall), where world leaders met on August 22, 1864 to sign the **Geneva Convention** that still governs conduct during war today. The **Grand-Rue,** which begins at the *Hôtel de Ville,* is crammed with clustered medieval workshops and 18th-century mansions; plaques commemorate famous residents, including **Jean-Jacques Rousseau,** born at #40. Below the cathedral, along r. de la Croix-Rouge, the **Parc des Bastions** stretches from pl. Neuve to pl. des Philosophes and includes **Le Mur des Réformateurs (Reformers' Wall),** a sprawling collection of bas-relief figures of the Reformers themselves. The park's center walkway leads to the ▨**Petit-Palais,** Terrasse St-Victor 2, a beautiful mansion containing art by Picasso, Renoir, Gauguin, Cézanne, and Chagall, as well as themed exhibitions. *(Bus #17 to "Petit Palais" or #1, 3, or 5 to "Claparède." Open M-F 10am-6pm, Sa-Su 10am-5pm. 10SFr, students 5SFr.)*

WATERFRONT. As you descend from the cathedral to the lake, you'll fast-forward 600 years: medieval lanes give way to wide quays and chic boutiques. Down quai Gustave Ardor, the **Jet d'Eau,** the world's highest fountain, spews a spectacular 7-ton plume of water 140m into the air. The **floral clock** in the nearby **Jardin Anglais** pays homage to Geneva's watch industry with over 6500 plants. It's probably Geneva's most overrated attraction and was also the most hazardous: the clock had to be cut back almost 1m because tourists, intent on taking the perfect photo, continually backed into oncoming traffic. On the north shore, the beach **Pâquis Plage,** quai du Mont-Blanc 30, is popular with locals. *(Open 9am-8:30pm. 2SFr.)*

INTERNATIONAL HILL. In Geneva's international city, embassies and multilateral organizations abound. The **International Red Cross** contains the ▨**International Red Cross and Red Crescent Museum,** av. de la Paix 17, which employs still photographs and wartime film-clip montages to drive home its emotional narrative of historic humanitarianism. *(Bus #8, F, V or Z to "Appia" or "Ariana." Open W-M 10am-5pm. 10SFr, stu-*

dents and seniors 5SFr. Self-guided audio tours 3SFr.) The nearby European headquarters of the **United Nations** is housed in the building that sheltered the now-defunct League of Nations. The constant traffic of international diplomats (often in handsome non-Western dress) provides more excitement than the dull guided tour. (Open July 10am-5pm; Apr.-June and Aug.-Oct. 10am-noon and 2-4pm; Nov.-Mar. M-F 10am-noon and 2-4pm. 8.50SFr, seniors and students 6.50SFr.)

🎵 🎭 ENTERTAINMENT AND NIGHTLIFE

Genève Agenda, available at the tourist office, is your guide to fun, with event listings ranging from major festivals to movies (be warned—a movie runs about 16SFr). In July and August, the **Cinelac** turns Genève Plage into an open-air cinema screening mostly American films. Geneva hosts the biggest celebration of the **American Independence Day** outside the US (July 4), and the **Fêtes de Genève** in early August is filled with international music and fireworks. The best party in Geneva is **L'Escalade** in early December, which lasts a full weekend and commemorates the dramatic repulsion of invading Savoyard troops (see below).

Place Bourg-de-Four, in the *vieille ville* below the cathedral, attracts students and professionals to its charming terraces and old-world atmosphere. **Place du Molard,** on the right bank by the pont du Mont-Blanc, offers terrace cafes and big, loud bars and clubs. **Les Paquis,** near Gare Cornavin and pl. de la Navigation, is the city's red-light district, but it also has a wide array of rowdy, low-lit bars, many ethnically themed. **Carouge,** across the river Arve, is a student-friendly locus of nightlife activity. Generations of students have eaten at the famous ⬛**La Clémence,** pl. du Bourg-de-Four 20. (Open M-Th 7am-12:30am, F-Sa 7am-1:30am.)

LAUSANNE   ☎021

Lausanne has a split personality: the medieval town center, or *vieille ville*, is cosmopolitan and businesslike, while the lakefront at Ouchy is lazy and decadent. In the *vieille ville*, two flights of medieval stairs lead to the Gothic **Cathédrale,** where a night watchman still cries the hour from 10pm to 2am. (Open July to mid-Sept. M-F 7am-7pm, Sa-Su 8am-7pm; mid-Sept. to June closes at 5:30pm.) Below the cathedral, the Renaissance **Hôtel de Ville** (city hall), on the pl. de la Palud, is the meeting point for guided tours of the town. (Tours M-Sa 10am and 3pm. 10SFr, students free. English available.) The ⬛**Collection de l'Art Brut,** av. Bergières 11, is filled with disturbing and beautiful sculptures, drawings, and paintings by artists on the fringe—including institutionalized schizophrenics, poor and uneducated peasants, and convicted criminals. From a prison cell wall painstakingly carved with a broken spoon to intricate junk and sea-shell masks, this is Lausanne's most satisfying collection. Take bus #2 to "Jomini." (Open M 11am-1pm and 2-6pm, Tu-F 11am-1pm and 2-6pm; July-Aug. also Sa-Su 11am-6pm. 6SFr, students 4SFr.) The **Musée Olympique,** Quai d'Ouchy 1, is a high-tech temple to modern Olympians with a smaller exhibit dedicated to the ancient games and an extensive video collection, allowing visitors to relive almost any Olympic moment. Take bus #2 to "Ouchy." (Open May-Sept. M-W and F-Su 9am-6pm, Th 9am-8pm; Oct.-Apr. Tu-W and F-Su 9am-6pm, Th 9am-8pm. 14SFr, students 9SFr.) In Ouchy, several booths along quai de Belgique and pl. de la Navigation rent **pedal boats** (10SFr per 30min.) and offer waterskiing or wake boarding on **Lake Léman** (30SFr per 15min.).

SOUP'S ON Before it became part of the Swiss Confederation, Geneva warded off almost-constant attack from the French House of Savoy for over 200 years. On the night of December 11, 1602, Savoyard soldiers attempted to scale the city walls. A lone housewife saw the attack and dumped a pot of boiling soup on the soldiers' heads, buying enough time to sound the city's alarm. Each year during the **Festival of the Escalade,** costumed citizens reenact the battle and children eat chocolate pots filled with marzipan vegetables.

Trains leave from pl. de la Gare 9 to: Basel (2½hr., 2 per hr. 5:20am-9:10pm, 62SFr); Geneva (50min., every 20min. 4:20am-12:45am, 20SFr); Montreux (20min., every 30min. 5:45am-2:25am, 9.40SFr); Paris (4hr., 4 per day 7:35am-5:50pm, 93SFr); Zurich (2½hr., 3 per hr. 5:25am-9:25pm, 67SFr). Take **bus** #1, 3, or 5 from the station to reach downtown. The **tourist office,** in the train station, reserves rooms. (☎613 73 73. Open daily 9am-7pm.) To reach the large and gleaming **Jeunotel (HI),** chemin du Bois-de-vaux 36, take bus #2 (dir.: Bourdonnette) to "Bois-de-Vaux," cross the street, and follow the signs. Courtyards with ping pong tables, a bowling alley next door, an in-house bar and restaurant, and a mostly young backpacker crowd enliven its concrete sterility. (☎626 02 22. Breakfast and linens included. Call ahead in summer. Reception 24hr. Dorms 25SFr; singles 53SFr, with shower 77SFr; doubles 78SFr, 94SFr; triples 90SFr; quads 120SFr. AmEx/MC/V.) The homey **Hotel "Le Chalet,"** av. d'Ouchy 49, has been run by the same charmingly eccentric matron since 1940. Take bus #2 (dir.: Bourdonnette) or Métro Ouchy to "Jordils." (☎616 52 06. Hall showers. Breakfast 10SFr. Reception 8am-10pm. Singles 50-62SFr; doubles 88SFr.) **Camping de Vidy,** chemin du Camping 3, has a restaurant (open May-Sept. 8am-midnight), supermarket, and pool. Take bus #2 (dir.: Bourdonnette) to "Bois-de-Vaux," cross the street, follow chemin du Bois-de-Vaux past Jeunotel and under the overpass, and it's straight ahead across rte. de Vidy. (☎622 50 00. Showers included. Electricity 4SFr. Reception Sept.-June 8am-12:30pm and 5-8pm; July-Aug. 8am-9pm. 6.50SFr, students 6SFr; tents 8-12SFr; 1- to 2-person bungalow 54SFr; 3- to 4-person bungalow 86SFr. Cash only.) Restaurants, cafes, and bars cluster around **Place St.-François** and the *vieille ville,* while grocery stores and *boulangeries* with cheap sandwiches abound. **Manora,** pl. St-François 17, under Zürich Bank sign, offers fresh food and "the longest buffet in Lausanne." (Hot food 11am-10pm. Buffet 10:45am-10:30pm. Open 7am-10:30pm.) **Postal code:** CH-1001.

MONTREUX   ☎021

Montreux is postcard Switzerland at its swanky, genteel best. The crystal-blue water of Lac Léman (Lake Geneva) and the snow-capped Alps are a photographer's dream. The gloomy medieval fortress, the **Château de Chillon,** on a nearby island, is one of the most visited attractions in Switzerland. It features all the comforts of home—including prison cells, a torture chamber, and a weapons room. The priest Francoic de Bonivard spent four years manacled in the dungeon for preaching Reformation doctrine and inspired Lord Byron's *The Prisoner of Chillon* as well as works by Rousseau, Hugo, and Dumas. Take the CGN **ferry** (13SFr, under 26 5.50SFr) or bus #1 (2.60SFr) to Chillon. (Open Apr.-Sept. 9am-6pm; Mar. and Oct. 9:30am-5pm; Nov.-Feb. 10am-4pm. 7.50SFr, students 6SFr.) The **Montreux Jazz Festival,** world famous for exceptional musical talent and one of the biggest parties in Europe, pushes everything aside for 15 days starting the first Friday in July. Write to the tourist office well in advance or check out www.montreuxjazz.com for info and tickets (39-69SFr). If you can find a room but no tickets, come anyway for the **Jazz Off,** 500hr. of free, open-air concerts by new bands and established musicians.

Trains leave the station, on av. des Alpes, to: Bern (1½hr., every hr. 5:35am-10:35pm, 40SFr); Geneva (1hr., every 30min. 5:35am-11:35pm, 29SFr); Lausanne (20min., 3-5 per hr. 5:25am-noon, 9.40SFr). Descend the stairs opposite the station, head left on Grand Rue, and look to the right for the **tourist office,** on pl. du Débarcadère. (☎962 84 84. Open mid-June to mid-Sept. daily 8:30am-7pm; late Sept. to early June M-F 8:30am-5pm, Sa-Su 10am-3pm.) Cheap rooms are scarce in Montreux and almost nonexistent during the jazz festival; book ahead. To get to **Auberge de Jeunesse Montreux (HI),** passage de l'Auberge 8, walk 20min. along the lake past the Montreux Tennis Club. Clean, spacious, and family-owned, this modern hostel offers many conveniences, including a waterfront location and dining room, but be aware that trains run nearby. (☎963 49 34. Breakfast and linens included. Lockers 2SFr deposit. Reception 7:30-10am and 5-10pm. Check-out 10am. Dorms 30SFr; doubles 38SFr, with shower and bathroom 42SFr. Nonmembers add 6SFr per night. AmEx/MC/V.) For **Hôtel Pension Wilhelm,** r. du Marché 13-15, take a left on av. des Alpes from the station, walk up 3min. and take a left on rue du Marché, uphill past the police station. (☎963 14 31. Breakfast included. Reception daily 7am-midnight. Closed Oct.-Feb., though it is possible to stay in winter if you call ahead. Doubles 100SFr, with shower and toilet 120SFr.) To camp, take bus #1 to "Villeneuve" and follow the lake to the left to **Les Horizons Bleus.** (☎960 15 47. Showers included. Electricity 4SFr. Reception 7am-11:30pm and 2-9pm. 7SFr per person; 7-14SFr per tent.) Grand Rue and av. de Casino have reasonably priced markets. **Marché de Montreux,** pl. du Marché, is an outdoor food market. (F 7am-1pm.) There's a **Co-op supermarket** at Grand Rue 80. (Open M-F 8am-12:15pm and 2-6:30pm, Sa 8am-5pm.)

NEUCHÂTEL   ☎032

Alexandre Dumas once said that Neuchâtel appeared to be carved out of butter. He was referring to its yellow stone architecture, but his comment could easily be taken as a reference to the rich treats in its famous *pâtisseries*. But aside from its gastronomic delights, Neuchâtel also glows with remarkable medieval beauty. The heart of town (the *vieille ville*) is a block to the right of **Place Plury,** centered on **Place des Halles;** r. de Château leads to up to the **Collégiale** church (open Oct.-Mar. 9am-6:30pm; Apr.-Sept. 9am-8pm) and the **château** that gives the town its name. You can enter the château only on free but dull guided tours. (Apr.-Sept. M-F every hr. on the hr. 10am-noon and 2-4pm, Sa 10-11am and 2-4pm, Su 2-4pm.) The nearby **Tour des Prisons (Prison Tower),** on r. Jehanne-de-Hochberg, has a magnificent view. (Open Apr.-Sept. 8am-6pm. 1SFr.) The **Musée d'Art et d'Histoire (Museum of Art and History),** Esplanade Léopold-Robert 1, houses an eclectic collection; most descriptions are in French only. (Open Tu-Su 10am-6pm. Open M Easter-Pentecost. 7SFr, students 4SFr, W free.) The **Musée d'Histoire Naturelle (Museum of Natural History),** off r. de l'Hôpital, displays Swiss animals stuffed and mounted in surprisingly entertaining dioramas. Turn right from pl. des Halles onto Croix du Marché, which becomes r. de l'Hôpital. (Open Tu-Su 10am-5pm. 6SFr, students 3SFr; W free.)

Trains run to: Basel (1¾hr., every hr. 8am-9pm, 37SFr); Bern (45min., every hr. 5:15am-11:20am, 17.20SFr); Geneva (1½hr., 2 per hr. 5:55am-9:50pm, 42SFr). An underground tram runs to the shore area, where you can catch bus #1 to pl. Plury. From there, face the lake and walk left two blocks to the **tourist office.** (☎889 68 90. Open mid-June to mid-Sept. M-F 9am-6:30pm, Sa 9am-5pm, Su 2-5pm; late Sept. to early June M-F 9am-noon and 1:30-5:30pm, Sa 9am-noon.) To reach **Oasis Neuchâtel,** r. du Suchiez 35, take bus #1 (dir.: Cormondrèche) to "Vauseyon" and walk in the same direction as the bus; the hostel will be on the left side. (☎731 31 90. Breakfast 6.50SFr. Shower and sheets included. Reception 8-10am and 5-10pm. No curfew. Reservations recommended. 4- to 6-bed dorms 25SFr; doubles 60SFr; 2-person garden teepee in summer 40SFr.) If Oasis is full, check the *Hôtel Restaurant* guide for cheap options in nearby towns. **Crêperie Chez Bach et Buck,** av. du Premier-Mars 22, across the street from the underground tram exit, has an extensive menu of sweet and savory crêpes. (Open M-Th 11:30am-2pm and 5:30-10pm, F 11:30am-2pm and 5:30-11:30pm, Sa 11am-11:30pm, Su noon-10pm.) In the town center, **Migros,** r. de l'Hôpital 12, has groceries. (Open M 1:15-6:30pm, Tu-W 8am-6:30pm, Th 8am-8pm, F 7:30am-6:30pm, Sa 7:30am-5pm.)

CENTRAL (GERMAN) SWITZERLAND

The cantons in northwest Switzerland are gently beautiful, with excellent museums, a rich Humanist tradition, and charming old town centers. Previously thought of as a financial mecca, the region has begun to change its image with the growing popularity of Interlaken and the cultural attractions of Lucerne.

BASEL (BÂLE)   ☎061

Situated on the Rhine near France and Germany, Switzerland's third largest city is home to a large medieval quarter as well as one of the oldest universities in Switzerland—a school whose graduates include Erasmus, Bernoulli, and Nietzsche.

The students keep the city young, and the biggest party of them all, the *Fasnacht*, is a mad carnival before the onset of Lent (see **Museums and Entertainment**, below). In Basel (rhymes with "nozzle") you'll encounter art from Roman times to the 20th century and be serenaded by musicians on every street corner year-round.

TRANSPORTATION. Basel has three **train stations:** the French SNCF (☎157 22 22) and Swiss SBB stations (☎157 22 22; 1.19SFr per min.) are on Centralbahnpl., near Altstadt. The German DB station (☎690 11 11) is across the Rhine down Greifeng. **Trains** chug from the SBB to: Bern (1¼hr., every hr. 5:50am-10am, 37SFr); Geneva (3hr., every hr. 6:20am-6:20pm, 72SFr); Lausanne (2½hr., every hr. 9am-9:50pm, 62SFr); Munich (via Zurich or Karlsruhe, 5¼hr., every hr. 7am-8:10pm, 114-122SFr); Zurich (1hr., every 15-30min. 4:40am-midnight, 31SFr). Make international connections at the French (SNCF) or German (DB) stations. 25% discount on international trips for travelers age 16-25.

PRACTICAL INFORMATION. To reach the **tourist office**, Schifflände 5, from the SBB station, take tram #1 to "Schifflände"; the office is on the river, near the Mittlere Rheinbrücke. (☎268 68 68; www.baseltourismus.ch. Open M-F 8:30am-6pm.) For info on **bi-gay-lesbian** establishments, stop by **Arcados**, Rheing. 69, at Clarapl. (☎681 31 32. Open Tu-F 12-7pm, Sa 11am-4pm.) For **Internet access**, head to **Domino**, Steinenvorstadt 54. (10SFr per hr., 12SFr per hr. after 6pm. Must be 18 years old. Open M-Th 9:30am-midnight, F-Sa 9am-1am, Su 1pm-midnight.) Take tram #1 or 8 to "Marktpl." and walk 1 block back away from the river to reach the **post office**, Rüdeng. 1. (Open M-W and F 7:30am-6:30pm, Th 7:30am-8pm, Sa 8am-noon.) **Poste Restante:** Postlagernde Briefe für FirstName SURNAME, Rüdeng., CH-4001 Basel 1. **Postal Codes:** CH-4000 to CH-4059.

ACCOMMODATIONS AND FOOD. Call ahead to ensure a spot in the only hostel in town, the **Jugendherberge (HI)**, St. Alban-Kirchrain 10. Walk 10-15min. from the SBB station down Aeschengraben to St. Alban Anlage and follow the signs, or take tram #2 to "Kunstmuseum," turn right on St.-Alban-Vorstadt, then left at the church. (☎272 05 72. Breakfast, showers, and sheets included. **Internet** 10SFr per hour. Laundry 7SFr. Reception Mar.-Oct. 7-10am and 2pm-11:30; Nov.-Feb. 2pm-11pm. Check-out 7-10am. Dorms 29-31SFr; singles 79SFr; doubles 98SFr. Jan. 1-Feb. 19 and Nov.-Dec. 2.50SFr less. Nonmembers add 6SFr. AmEx/D/MC/V.) For **Hotel Steinenschanze**, Steinengraben 69, turn left on Centralbahnstr. from the SBB and follow signs for Heuwaage; go up the ramp under the bridge to Steinengraben and turn left. (☎272 53 53. Breakfast included. 24hr. reception. Singles 110-180SFr, under 25 with ISIC 60SFr for up to 3 nights; doubles with shower 160-250SFr, 100SFr. AmEx/D/MC/V.) **Camp Waldhort**, Heideweg 16, is in a beautiful, quiet location far from Basel. Take tram #11 to "Landhof," backtrack 200m toward Basel, cross the main street, and follow the signs (10min.). (☎71 64 29. Reception 7am-noon and 2-10pm. Open Mar.-Oct. 7SFr per person; 10SFr per tent.)

Because of the high student population, there are tons of cheap eateries. **Barfüsserplatz, Marktplatz,** and the streets connecting them are especially full of restaurants. **Zum Schnabel,** Trillengässlein 2, serves tasty Swiss-German fare. (Open M-Th, Sa 8am-midnight, F 8am-1am. AmEx/DC/MC/V.) Vegetarians can dine at **Café Gleich,** Steinenvorstadt 23. (Open M-F 9am-9:30pm.) Migrate to **Migros supermarket,** in the SBB station, for groceries. (Open M-F 6am-10pm, Sa-Su 7:30am-10pm.)

MONSTER MADNESS In 1529, Basel's residents spiritedly joined the Reformation and ousted the bishop, keeping his *crozier* (staff) as the town's emblem. The staff shares this honor with the basilisk (Basel-isk), a creature part serpent, part dragon, and part rooster, which caused what may be the world's first and only public trial and execution of a chicken. In 1474, a hen allegedly laid an egg on a dung heap under a full moon, an action sure to hatch the horrible creature. The bird was tried, found guilty, and beheaded, and the egg was ceremonially burnt.

◧ SIGHTS. Groß-Basel (Greater Basel), where most sights and the train station are located, lies on the left bank of the Rhine; **Klein-Basel (Lesser Basel)** occupies the right bank. Basel's pedestrian tourist signs will help you negotiate your way around the city's curving, interlacing streets, perhaps better than any map. The very red **Rathaus** brightens Marktpl. with its blinding façade and gold-and-green statues. Behind the Marktpl. is the 775-year-old **Mittlere Rheinbrücke** (Middle Rhine Bridge) which connects the two halves of Basel. At the other end of Marktpl. is a spectacular **Jean Tinguely Fountain,** also known as the **Fasnachtsbrunnen.** Behind Marktpl. stands the red sandstone **Münster,** built on the site of an ancient Celtic settlement. Visit the tombs of Erasmus and Bernoulli, or climb the tower for a spectacular view of the city. (Open Easter-Oct.15 M-F 10am-5pm, Sa 10am-4pm, Su 1-5pm; Oct. 16-Easter M-Sa 11am-4pm, Su 2-4pm. Free. Tower closes 30min. before the church. 3SFr. Due to recent suicides, you can't go up alone.) The **Zoologischer Garten,** Binningerstr. 40, is one of the best zoos in Europe; take tram #1 or 8 to "Zoo Bachletten." (Open daily May-Aug. 8am-6:30pm; Sept.-Oct. and Mar.-Apr. 8am-6pm; Nov.-Feb. 8am-5:30pm. 14SFr, students and seniors 12SFr.)

▥🎭 MUSEUMS AND ENTERTAINMENT. Basel has an astounding 30 museums, covering everything from medieval medicine to mechanized mannequins. Visit www.museembasel.ch or pick up the comprehensive museum guide at the tourist office. The **Basel Card,** available at the tourist office, provides admission to all museums as well as free walking tours and discounts around town. (24hr. 25SFr, 48hr. 33SFr, 72hr. 45SFr.) The **◧Kunstmuseum** (Museum of Fine Arts), St. Alban-Graben 16, houses outstanding collections of old and new masters; admission also gives access to the **Museum für Gegenwartskunst** (Modern Art), St. Alban-Rheinweg 60. (☎206 62 62. Accessible by tram #2. Kunstmuseum open Tu and Th-Su 10am-5pm, W 10am-7pm. Gegenwartskunst open Tu-Su 11am-5pm. Combined ticket 10SFr, students 8SFr. Free first Su every month.) At **◧Museum Jean Tinguely,** Grenzacherstr. 214a, everything rattles and shakes in homage to the Swiss sculptor's vision of metal and movement; the noise making machine is a favorite with children and adults alike. Take tram #2 or 15 to "Wettsteinpl." and bus #31 (dir.: Habermatten) to "Museum Tinguely." (☎681 9320. Open W- Su 11am-7pm. 7SFr, students 5SFr.) The **Fondation Beyeler,** Baselstr. 101, is one of Europe's finest private art collections, housing works by nearly every major artist. The outdoor lily-pond is matched only by a Monet version within. Take tram #6 to "Riehendorf," then walk straight for 3min. (Open 10am-6pm, W 10am-8pm. 15SFr, students 5SFr.)

In a year-round party town, Basel's carnival, or **Fasnacht,** still manages to distinguish itself. The festivities commence the Monday before Lent with the *Morgestraich,* a not-to-be-missed, 600-year-old, 72hr. parade beginning at 4am (Feb. 18-20 in 2002), in which masked revelers lampoon the year's local scandals to fife and drum music. The goal is to scare away winter (it rarely succeeds). During the rest of the year, head to **Barfüsserplatz** for an evening of bar-hopping. **◧Atlantis,** Klosterberg 10, is a multi-level, sophisticated bar with reggae, jazz, and funk. (Open M-Th 11am-2am, F 11am-4am, Sa 5pm-4am.) **Brauerei Fischerstube,** Rheing. 45, brews the delectably sharp **◧***Hell Spezial* ("light special") beer. (Open M-Th 10am-midnight, F-Sa 10am-1am, Su 5pm-midnight. Full dinner menu from 6pm. MC/V.)

ZURICH (ZÜRICH)   ☎01

Zurich contains a disproportionate number of Switzerland's many banks, but there's more to Zurich than money. The city was once the focal point of the Reformation, led by Ulrich Zwingli, in German Switzerland. In the 20th century, Zurich's Protestant asceticism succumbed to avant-garde artistic and philosophical radicalism: James Joyce toiled away at *Ulysses* in one corner of the city, while Russian exile Vladimir Lenin read Marx and dreamed of revolution in another. Meanwhile, a group of raucous artists calling themselves the Dadaists founded the seminal proto-performance art collective, the Cabaret Voltaire. A walk through

Zurich's *Altstadt* and student quarter will immerse you in the energetic youth counter-culture that spawned these subversive thinkers, only footsteps away from the rabid capitalism of the famous Bahnhofstraße shopping district.

▐ TRANSPORTATION

Flights: Kloten Airport (☎816 25 00) is **Swissair**'s main hub (☎084 880 07 00 for general flight information), with daily connections to Frankfurt, Paris, London, and New York. Trains leave every 10-20min. for the *Hauptbahnhof* (main train station).

Trains: From the **Hauptbahnhof**, at Bahnhofpl., to: **Basel** (1hr., 2-4 per hr. 5:55am-1am, 31SFr); **Bern** (1¼hr., 1-2 per hr. 4:45am-midnight, 48SFr); **Geneva via Bern** (3hr., every hr. 5:25am-8:30pm, 77SFr); **Lucerne** (1hr., every hr. 6am-12:15am, 22SFr); **Lugano** (3hr., every hr. 6:30am-10pm, 62SFr); **Milan** (4½hr., every hr. 6:30am-11pm, 76SFr); **Munich** (4hr., 4 per day 7:30am-5:30pm, 91SFr); **Paris** (6-8hr., 3-4 per day 7:10am-10:50pm, 137SFr); **Salzburg** (6hr., 3 per day 7:10am-10:30pm, 102SFr); **Vienna** (9hr., 3 per day 7:10am-10:30pm, 131SFr). Reduction for under age 26 on international trains.

Public Transportation: All public buses, trams, and trolleys run 5:30am-midnight. **Short rides** (less than 5 stops) cost 2.10SFr (push the yellow button on the ticket machine); **long rides** cost 3.60SFr (blue button). Buy a ticket before boarding and validate it in the machine or face a fine (from 50SFr). A **Tageskarte** (7.20SFr) is valid for 24hr. of unlimited public transport. **Nightbuses** run from the center of the city to outlying areas F-Sa at 1, 1:30, 2, and 3am.

Bike Rental: Bike loans are free at **Globus** (☎(079) 336 36 10), **Enge** (☎(079) 336 36 12), and **Hauptbahnhof** (☎210 13 88), at the very end of track 18. Passport and 20SFr deposit required. Open daily 7:30am-9:30pm.

▐ ORIENTATION AND PRACTICAL INFORMATION

The **Limmat River** splits the city down the middle on its way to the **Zürichsee**. On the west side of the river is the **Hauptbahnhof** and **Bahnhofstraße**, which begins just outside the *Hauptbahnhof* and runs parallel to the Limmat. Halfway down Bahnhofstr. lies **Paradeplatz,** the town center; **Bürkliplatz** is at the far end of Bahnhofstr. On the east side of the river is the University district, which stretches above the narrow **Niederdorfstraße** and pulses with bars, restaurants, and hostels.

Tourist Offices: Main office (☎215 40 00, hotel reservation service 215 40 40; www.zurichtourism.ch), in the train station. Offers concert, movie, and bar information, as well as an electronic hotel reservation board. The staff finds rooms after 10:30am. Open Apr.-Oct. M-F 8:30am-8:30pm, Sa-Su 8:30am-6:30pm; Nov.-Mar. M-F 8:30am-7pm, Sa-Su 8:30am-6:30pm. For bikers and backpackers, the **Touring Club des Schweiz** (TCS), Alfred-Escher-Str. 38 (☎286 86 86), offers maps and travel info.

Currency Exchange: At the main train station. Cash advances with DC/MC/V and photo ID. Open 6:30am-10pm. **Credit Suisse,** Bahnhofstr. 53, 2.50SFr commission. Open M-F 9am-6pm, Th 9am-7pm, Sa 9am-4pm.

Luggage Storage: At the Hauptbahnhof. Lockers 5SFr and 8SFr per day. Luggage watch 5SFr at the *Gepäck* counter. Open 6am-10:50pm.

Bi-Gay-Lesbian Organizations: Zürich Gay Guide, from the tourist office, lists support groups and gay-friendly establishments. **Homosexuelle Arbeitsgruppe Zürich (HAZ)** is at Sihlquai 67 (☎271 22 50). Open Tu-F 7:30-11pm, Su noon-2pm and 6-11pm.

Laundromat: Selbstbedienung-Wäscherei (☎242 99 14), Müllerstr. 55. Wash and dry 5kg for 10.20SFr. Open daily 6am-11pm.

Emergencies: Police, ☎117. **Fire,** ☎118. **Ambulance,** ☎144; English spoken. **Medical Emergency,** ☎269 69 69. **Rape Crisis Line:** ☎291 46 46.

24hr. Pharmacy: Theaterstr. 14 (☎252 56 00), on Bellevuepl.

Internet Access: The **ETH Library,** Ramistr. 101, in the Hauptgebäude, has 3 free computers. Tram #6, 9, or 10 to "ETH," enter main building, and take the elevator to fl. H.

SWITZERLAND

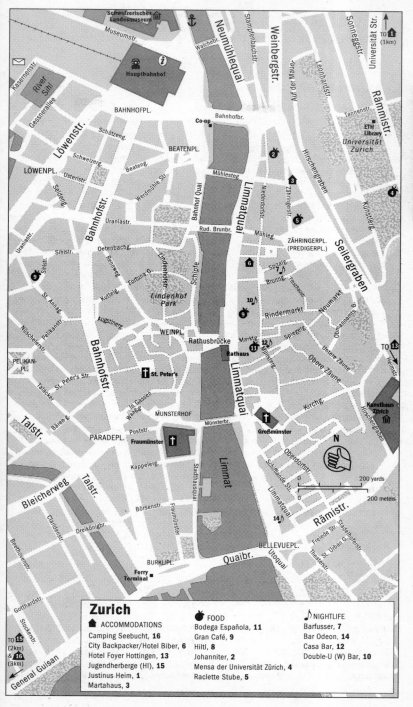

SWITZERLAND

Zurich

♠ ACCOMMODATIONS
Camping Seebucht, **16**
City Backpacker/Hotel Biber, **6**
Hotel Foyer Hottingen, **13**
Jugendherberge (HI), **15**
Justinus Heim, **1**
Martahaus, **3**

♥ FOOD
Bodega Española, **11**
Gran Café, **9**
Hiltl, **8**
Johanniter, **2**
Mensa der Universität Zürich, **4**
Raclette Stube, **5**

♪ NIGHTLIFE
Barfusser, **7**
Bar Odeon, **14**
Casa Bar, **12**
Double-U (W) Bar, **10**

SWITZERLAND

Open M-F 8:30am-9pm, Sa 9am-2pm. **Telefon Corner,** downstairs in the station next to Marché Mövenpick. 5SFr per hr. (10SFr deposit required). Open daily 9am-10:30pm.

Post Office: Main office, Sihlpost, Kasernestr. 97, just behind the station. Open M-F 7:30am-8pm, Sa 8am-4pm. Address *Poste Restante* to: FirstName SURNAME, Sihlpost, Postlagernde Briefe, CH-8021 Zürich. **Postal code:** CH-8021.

ACCOMMODATIONS

The few budget accommodations in Zurich are easily accessible via Zurich's public transportation. Reserve at least a day in advance, especially during the summer.

Martahaus, Zähringerstr. 36 (☎251 45 50). From the station, cross Bahnhofbrücke, and take the 2nd (sharp) right after Limmatquai at the Seilgraben sign. The most comfortable budget accommodations in town, with clean partitioned dorms, lockers, and towels. Breakfast and **Internet** access included. Airport shuttle (20SFr) every hr. after 6:20am. 24hr. reception. Dorms 37SFr; singles 75-80SFr; street-side doubles 98SFR, quiet-side doubles 110SFr; triples 110SFr. AmEx/DC/MC/V. The owners also run the nearby **Luther Pension,** a women-only residence that shares reception facilities with Martahaus.

Hotel Foyer Hottingen, Hottingenstr. 31 (☎256 19 19). Take tram #3 (dir.: Kluspl.) to "Hottingerpl." This impeccably clean and newly renovated house is a block from the Kunsthaus. Only women are allowed in the partitioned dorms during summer, but men and women can rent other rooms. Breakfast and kitchen access included. Laundry 5SFr. Reception 7am-11pm. Dorms 35SFr; singles 70SFr, with shower and toilet 105Sfr; doubles 110SFr/150SFr; triples 140SFr; quads 180SFr. MC/V.

Justinus Heim Zürich, Freudenbergstr. 146 (☎361 38 06). Take tram #9 or 10 to "Seilbahn Rigiblick," then take the hillside tram (by the Migros) uphill to the end. Breakfast and kitchen access included. Reception daily 8am-noon and 5-9pm. Check-out before 10am. Singles 40SFr, with sink 60SFr, with shower 70SFr; doubles 90SFr/120SFr; triples 135SFr, with shower 165SFr; all rates reduced for multiple-week stays. V.

The City Backpacker-Hotel Biber, Niederdorfstr. 5 (☎251 90 15). From the station, cross Bahnhofbrücke; turn right on Niederdorfstr. The tightly packed rooms are balanced by the hostel's fun location and atmosphere. Pick up a free copy of the very helpful *Swiss Backpacker News.* Kitchen access and showers included. **Internet** 12SFr per hr. Sheets 3SFr, towels 3SFr. Laundry 10SFr. Key deposit 20SFr. Reception 8am-noon and 3-10pm. Check-out 10am. Dorms 29SFr; singles 65SFr; doubles 88SFr. MC/V.

Jugendherberge Zürich (HI), Mutschellenstr. 114 (☎482 35 44). Take tram #7 (dir.: Wollishofen) to "Morgental" and walk 5min. back toward the Migros. The enormous hostel has many guests, which may account for the long breakfast lines, the close quarters, and the bathroom graffiti. Free nightly movies. **Internet** 1SFr for 4min. Showers, sheets, and breakfast included. Laundry 8SFr. Lockers available; bring your own padlock. 24hr. reception, except noon-1pm. Check-out 10am. No lockout. Dorms 31SFr; doubles with toilet and shower 90SFr. Nonmembers add 6SFr. AmEx/MC/V.

Camping Seebucht, Seestr. 559 (☎482 16 12). Take tram #11 to Bürklipl. where you catch bus #161 or 165 to "Stadtgrenze." Scenic lakeside location; market and cafe on premises. Showers 2SFr. Reception M-Sa 7:30am-noon and 3-10pm, Su 8am-noon. Open May-Sept. 8SFr per person; 1.50SFr tax. 12SFr per tent.

FOOD

Zurich's specialty is *Geschnetzeltes mit Rösti* (slivered veal in cream sauce with hash-brown potatoes), but the cheapest meals (around 6SFr) are at kebab stands and takeout burger joints on **Niederdorfstraße.** The **Manor** department store off Bahnhofstr. 75 (corner of Uraniastr.) has a self-service restaurant on the 5th floor. (Open M-F 9am-8pm, Sa 9am-4pm.) Try the **farmer's market,** Burklipl., for fresh veggies and fruits (open Tu and F 6-11am), or stop by the **Co-op Super-Center,** next to the train station, for groceries. (Open M-F 7am-8pm, Sa 7am-4pm.) There's also a **Migros supermarket** with adjoining restaurant, Mutschellenstr. 191, near the hostel. (Open

CHOCOHOLICS The Swiss have long had a love affair with chocolate—milk chocolate was first concocted here in 1876, and Nestlé, Lindt, and Toblerone all call Switzerland home. But has this seemingly innocuous romance turned into an obsession? In May of 2001, the Swiss government introduced postage stamps that look and smell like squares of chocolate. (The original design called for chocolate-*flavored* stamps, but the idea was dropped for hygienic reasons.) The stamps are even packaged on paper designed to look like foil wrappers. Officially, they commemorate the centennial of Chocosuisse, the association of chocolate makers and importers, but it might just be evidence that the Swiss truly are addicted.

M-F 8am-6:30pm, Sa 8am-4pm; restaurant open M-F 7am-7pm, Sa 7am-6pm.) Check out the *Swiss Backpacker News* (available at the tourist office and Hotel Biber) for more info on budget meals in Zurich.

■ **Gran-Café,** Limmatquai 66 (☎ 252 31 19). Sit right by the Limmat and enjoy some of the cheapest (yet tastiest) meals around. Daily *Menü* around 11.80SFr. Open M-F 6:15am-11:30pm, Sa 7am-11:30pm, Su 7:30am-11:30pm. AmEx/MC/V.

■ **Bodega Española,** Münsterg. 15 (☎ 251 23 10). Catalan delights served by charismatic waiters. Delicate-but-filling egg-and-potato tortilla dishes 15.50SFr, enormous salads 9.50SFr. Open daily 10am-12:30am. AmEx/DC/MC/V.

Hiltl, Sihlstr. 28 (☎ 227 70 00). The lack of meat makes things surprisingly cheap at swank vegetarian restaurant. All-day salad buffet or Indian buffet 4.60SFr per 100g (15SFr for large salad). Open M-Sa 7am-11pm, Su 11am-11pm.

Raclette Stube, Zähringerstr. 16 (☎ 251 41 30). Serves high-quality, classic Swiss fare in an authentic Swiss atmosphere. Large *raclette* appetizer 11SFr, fondue 23.50SFr per person, all-you-can-eat *raclette* 29.50SFr per person. Open daily from 6pm.

Johanniter, Niederdorfstr. 70 (☎ 253 62 00). A favorite among locals, with traditional Swiss dishes and outdoor seating. Open daily 11am-4am.

Mensa der Universität Zürich (University of Zurich cafeteria), Rämistr. 71 (☎ 632 62 11). Take streetcar #6 to "ETH Zentrum" from Bahnhofpl. Hot dishes 7.50SFr with ISIC, salad buffet 6SFr. Open July 15-Oct. 21 M-F 11am-2pm; Oct. 22-July 14 M-F 11am-2:30pm and 5-7:30pm.

SIGHTS

ALTSTADT. Right off Paradepl. stands the 13th-century **Fraumünster;** although it's a Protestant church, Jewish artist Marc Chagall agreed to design the beautiful stained-glass windows in the late 1960s. Outside the church on Fraumünsterstr., a mural decorates the Gothic archway in the courtyard, picturing Felix and Regula, the decapitated patron saints of Zurich, with their heads in their hands. *(Open May-Sept. daily 9am-6pm; Oct. and Mar.-Apr. 10am-5pm; Nov.-Feb. 10am-4pm.)* Next door, **St. Peter's Church** has the largest clock face in Europe. The twin towers of the nearby **Großmünster** have become a symbol of Zurich. Zwingli spearheaded the Reformation here, and one of his bibles lies in a case near the pulpit from which he preached. A column tells the legend of the church: while chasing a stag from Aachen, Charlemagne supposedly stumbled over the graves of Felix and Regula, prompting him to build *Grossmünster*. Venture downstairs to the 12th-century crypt to see Charlemagne's statue and 2m sword, then climb the towers for a panoramic view of Zurich. *(Church open Mar.-Oct. 9am-6pm; Nov.-Feb. 10am-5pm. Tower open Mar.-Oct. daily 1:30-5pm; Oct.-Mar. Sa-Su 9:15am-5pm. 2SFr for entrance to the tower.)*

MUSEUMS. The incredible ■**Kunsthaus Zürich,** Heimpl. 1, covers Western art from the 15th century on. *(☎ 253 84 84. Take tram #3, 5, 8, or 9 to "Kunsthaus." Audio tours available in English, French, and German. Open Tu-Th 10am-9pm, F-Su 10am-5pm. 10SFr; students, seniors, and disabled 6SFr. W free.)* ■**Museum Rietberg,** Gablerstr. 15, presents an exquisite collection of Asian, African, and other non-European art. *(☎ 202 45 28. Take tram #7 to "Museum Rietberg." Open Tu and Th-Su 10am-5pm, W 10am-8pm. 5SFr, stu-*

dents 6SFr.) The **Schweizerisches Landesmuseum,** Museumstr. 2, next to the main train station, encapsulates Swiss history; exhibits include 16th-century astrological instruments, Ulrich Zwingli's weapons from the Battle of Kappel (his last), and a tiny bejeweled clock with a golden skeleton morbidly pointing to the hour. (☎218 65 65. Open Tu-Su 10:30am-5pm. Students 3SFr.) The **Museum Bellerive,** Höschg. 3, features rotating "out-of-the-ordinary" themes. Past exhibitions include "Made in Japan" (a room full of plastic Japanese meals); "The 70s and 80s" starts in January 2002. (☎383 43 76. Take tram #4 or 2 to "Höschg." Open Tu-Th 10am-8pm, F 10am-5pm, Sa-Su 11am-5pm. 6SFr, students and children 3SFr. Closes between exhibits, so call ahead.) The museum at the **Lindt and Sprüngli Chocolate Factory,** Seestr. 204, has exhibits in German only, but the free chocolates transcend language barriers. (☎716 22 33. Bus #165 to "Schooren." Open W-F 10am-noon and 1-4pm. Free.)

♫🎭 ENTERTAINMENT AND NIGHTLIFE

Niederdorfstraße rocks as the epicenter of Zurich's nightlife (although women may not want to walk alone in this area at night), and **Münsterg.** and **Limmatquai** are lined with cafes and bars. Pick up *ZüriTip* for more info. On Friday and Saturday nights in summer, **Hirschenplatz** (on Niederdorfstr.) hosts sword-swallowers and other daredevil street performers. Locals and students guzzle beer (from 10SFr) on the terrace at **Double-U (W) Bar,** Niederdorfstr. 21. (Open M-Th from 2pm, F-Su from 4pm.) **Casa Bar,** Münsterg. 30, has pricey beer (from 13.50SFr) but great live jazz and no cover. (Open daily 11am-2am.) Thornton Wilder and Vladimir Lenin used to get sloshed at the posh, artsy **Bar Odeon,** Limmatquai 2. (Open 7am-2am, F-Sa 7am-4am.) **Barfusser,** Spitalg. 14, is Europe's oldest gay bar. (Open daily until 2am.)

ST. GALLEN ☎071

St. Gallen's main draw is the **Stiftsbibliothek (Abbey Library),** a Baroque library designated a World Heritage Treasure by UNESCO. Visitors in fuzzy protective slippers glide across exquisite parquet floors to ooh and aah over the lavishly carved and polished shelves, rows of gilt-spined books, and ancient manuscripts. Although the presence of the resident death-blackened mummy might indicate otherwise, the *Stiftsbibliothek* is a living, lending library serving scholars from around the globe. (☎227 34 16. Open Apr.-Oct. M-Sa 9am-noon and 1:30-5pm, Su 10am-noon and 1:30-4pm; Nov.-Mar. M-Sa 9am-noon and 1:30-4pm. English tours can be arranged through the tourist office. 7SFr, students 5SFr.) Often overshadowed by the library, but no less beautiful, is the **Kathedrale St. Gallen,** which has enormous stained-glass windows, intricately carved confessionals, and impressive murals. (☎227 33 88. Open daily 7am-6pm except during mass.) Follow the Marktplatz away from the train station to reach **Museumstraße,** which holds St. Gallen's four museums. The best are the small but fascinating **Natural History Museum** (☎242 06 70), with rotating exhibits, and the slightly disorganized **Historisches Museum** (☎242 06 42), which covers traditional Swiss culture. Although all the exhibits are in German, the detailed displays and varied themes still make a trip to Museumstr. interesting for non-German-speakers. (All museums open Tu-F 10am-noon and 2-5pm, Sa-Su 10am-5pm. Admission to all four museums 6SFr, students 2SFr.) In late June, the **Open Air St. Gallen Music Festival** features over 20 live bands; past headliners have included Garbage, Red Hot Chili Peppers, Cypress Hill, B.B. King, and James Brown. (☎087 887 79 94; www.openairsg.ch. Tickets 144SFr.)

Trains head to: Bern (2½hr., 5am-10:40pm, 65SFr); Geneva (4½hr., 5am-8:40pm, 95SFr); Munich (3hr.; 4 per day 8:30am-6:30pm; 63SFr, under 26 49SFr); Zurich (1hr., 5am-10:40pm, 29SFr). To get to the **tourist office,** Bahnhofpl. 1a, from the train station, head through the bus stop and past the fountain on the left; it's on the right. (☎227 37 37. City tours June 12-Sept. M, W, F 2pm; 15SFr. Open Oct.-May M-F 9am-noon and 1-6pm, Sa 9am-noon; June-Sept. M-F 9am-6pm, Sa 9am-noon.) Get on the **Internet** at **Media Lounge,** Katherineng. 10. (☎244 30 90. First 10min. 2SFr, each additional 5min. 1SFr; 1hr. 12SFr. Open M-F 9am-9pm, Sa

10am-5pm.) Perched on a hill above town, the ⬛Jugendherberge St. Gallen (HI), Jüchstr. 25, has a terrace, TV room, barbecue pit, library, and Internet access (1SFr for 4min.). From the smaller Appenzeller/Trogener station (to the right of the main station), take the orange train (dir.: Trogener), on track #12, to Schüler-haus; walk uphill, turn left across the train tracks, and walk 2min. downhill. (☎245 47 77. Dinner 12.50SFr. Lockers 2SFr deposit. Laundry 6SFr. Reception daily 7-10am and 5-10:30pm. Check-out 10am. No lockout. Closed Dec. 1-end of Feb. Dorms 26SFr; 6-bed "family room" with toilet and shower 34SFr per person; singles 46SFr; doubles 72SFr; nonmembers add 6SFr. AmEx/DC/MC/V.) Restaurant Scheitlinsbüchel, Scheitlinsbüchelweg 10, offers traditional Swiss fare and a sublime view from its outdoor patio. (☎244 68 21. Open Tu-Su 9am-whenever everyone leaves. MC/V.) The Migros supermarket and adjoining buffet restaurant are on St. Leonhardstr., one block behind the train station. (Open M-W and F 8am-6:30pm, Th 8am-9pm, Sa 8am-5pm.) Postal code: CH-9000.

LUCERNE (LUZERN)   ☎041

Lucerne just may be the fondue pot at the end of the rainbow—the Swiss traveler's dream come true. The city is small but cosmopolitan, satisfying sophisticated culture lovers while also providing a plethora of outdoor opportunities for the adventurous. Sunrise over the city's most acclaimed peak, Mount Pilatus, has hypnotized hikers and artists, including Twain, Wagner, and Goethe, for centuries.

🅔 TRANSPORTATION. Trains leave Bahnhofpl. (☎157 22 22) to: Basel (1¼hr., 1-2 per hr. 4:40am-11:50pm, 31SFr); Bern (1½hr., 1-2 per hr. 4:40am-11:50pm, 32SFr); Geneva (3½hr., every hr. 4:40am-9:55pm, 70SFr); Interlaken (2hr., every hr. 6:30am-7:30pm, 26SFr); Lausanne (2½hr., every hr. 5:55am-9:55pm, 58SFr); Lugano (2¾hr., every hr. 5:50am-10:15pm, 58SFr); Zurich (1hr., 2 per hr. 4:55am-11:10pm, 22SFr). VBL buses depart from in front of the station and provide extensive coverage of Lucerne (1 zone 1.70SFr, 2 zones 2.20SFr; day pass 10SFr; Swiss Pass valid); route maps are available at the tourist office.

🅟 PRACTICAL INFORMATION. The tourist office, in the station, has free city guides, makes hotel reservations for free, and sells the Visitor's Card, which, with a hotel or hostel stamp, gives discounts at museums, stores, bars, and more. (☎227 17 17. Open May-Oct. M-F 8:30am-7:30pm, Sa-Su 9am-7:30pm; Nov.-May M-F 8:30am-6pm, Sa-Su 9am-6pm.) C+A Clothing, on Hertensteinstr. at the top of the Altstadt, has two free but busy Internet terminals. (Open M-W 9am-6:30pm, Th-F 9am-9pm, Sa 8:30am-4pm.) The post office is on the corner of Bahnhofstr. and Bahnhofpl. Address mail to be held: Postlagernde Briefe für FirstName SURNAME, Hauptpost, CH-60000 Luzern 1. (Open M-F 7:30am-6:30pm, Sa 8am-noon.)

🅒🅒 ACCOMMODATIONS AND FOOD. Relatively inexpensive beds are limited in Lucerne, so call ahead to ensure a roof over your head. Until 1998, Hotel Löwengraben, Löwengraben 18, was a prison, but it was converted into a trendy, clean hostel with a bar, restaurant, Internet (15SFr per hr.), and all-night dance parties for guests every summer Saturday. (☎417 1212. Breakfast 9SFr. Sheets included. 4-bed dorms 25SFr; 3-bed dorms 30-35SFr; double with shower 80-99SFr.) Tourist Hotel Luzern, St. Karliquai 12, on the Altstadt side of Spreuerbrücke, is very close to the center of the Altstadt. (☎410 2474. Internet access 10SFr per hr. Bike rental 15SFr per day. Breakfast included. Laundry 10SFr. Reception 7am-10:30pm. Dorms 30-33SFr; quads 172SFr, students 156SFr; Dec.-May rooms 40-60SFr less. Add 10SFr per person for private shower. AmEx/MC/V.) Kam Tong Chinese Take Away, Inseliquai 8, serves large portions of cheap, tasty Asian fare for 10-15SFr. (Open M-W 9am-6:30pm, Th-F 9am-9pm, Sa 9am-4pm.) Traffic, downstairs in the train station, provides a large selection (including Rosti) in a quick cafeteria atmosphere. (Open 6:30am-9:15pm.) There's a Migros supermarket at the station. (Open M-W and Sa 6:30am-8pm, Th-F 6:30am-9pm, Sa-Su 8am-8pm.)

☞📷 SIGHTS AND NIGHTLIFE. The *Altstadt*, across the river over Spreuer-brücke from the station, is famous for its frescoed houses, especially those on Hir-schenpl. The 660-year-old **Kapellbrücke,** a wooden-roofed bridge, runs from left of the train station to the Altstadt and is ornately decorated with Swiss historical scenes; farther down the river, the **Spreuerbrücke,** which is decorated by Kaspar Meglinger's eerie *Totentanz* (Dance of Death) paintings. On the hills above the river, the **Museggmauer** and its towers are all that remain of the medieval city's ramparts. Three towers are accessible to visitors, and the **Zeitturm** (clock tower) provides a particularly pleasing panorama of the city; walk along St. Karliquai, turn right (uphill), and follow the brown castle signs. (Open 8am-7pm.) To the east is the magnificent **Löwendenkmal** (Lion Monument), the dying lion of Lucerne, which is carved into a cliff on Denkmalstr. Mark Twain described it as "the saddest and most moving piece of rock in the world." The **Picasso Museum,** Am Rhyn Haus, Furreng. 21, displays 200 intimate photographs of Picasso, taken by close friend David Duncan, as well as a large collection of unpublished Picasso lithographs, drawings, and paintings. From Schwanenpl., take Rathausquai to Furreng. (Open Apr.-Oct. 10am-6pm; Nov.-Mar. 11am-1pm and 2-4pm. 6SFr, with guest card 5SFr, students 3SFr.) The 📷**Verkehrshaus der Schweiz** (Swiss Transport Museum), Lidostr. 5, has interactive displays on all kinds of vehicles, but the real highlight is the trains. The museum also screens seven shows per day in Switzerland's only IMAX theater. Take bus #6, 8, or 24 to "Verkehrshaus." (Open Apr.-Oct. 9am-6pm; Nov.-Mar. 10am-5pm. 18SFr, with IMAX 28SFR; students 16SFr, 24SFr; 33% discount with Eurail or guestcard.) The **Richard Wagner Museum,** Wagnerweg 27,was once the composer's lakeside home and now exhibits original letters, scores, and instruments. Take bus #6, 7 or 8 to "Wartegg." (Open mid-Mar. to Nov. Tu-Su 10am-noon and 2-5pm. 5SFr, students and guest card holders 4SFr.)

Lucerne's nightlife is more about lingering than club-hopping. **Club 57,** Halden-str. 57, is filled with candlelight and billows of red Moroccan fabric. (Open 8pm-2:30am. World music M-F, DJs Sa-Su.) **The Loft,** Haldenstr. 21, is a trendy club with hip-hop and house in a cloud of smoke. (No cover W and Su, Th 10SFr, F 12SFr, Sa 15SFr. Open W-Th 9pm-3am and F-Su 9pm-4am.) **Uferlos Bar,** Geissensteinringstr. 14, is a popular gay and lesbian hangout. Lucerne attracts big names for its **Blue Balls Festival** (3rd week in July) and **Blues Festival** (2nd week in Nov.).

▶ DAYTRIPS FROM LUCERNE

MT. PILATUS AND RIGI KULM

The view of the Alps from the top of **Mt. Pilatus** (2132m) is absolutely phenomenal. For the most memorable trip, catch a boat from Lucerne to Alpnachstad (90min.), ascend by the world's steepest **cogwheel train** (48-degree gradient), then descend by cable car to Krienz and take the bus back to Lucerne (entire trip 77.60SFr; with Eurail or Swisspass 41SFr). For less money and more exercise, take a train or boat to Hegiswil and hike up to Fräkmüntegg (3hr.), a halfway point on the cable car (22SFr, 25% off with Eurail or Swisspass). Across the sea from Pilatus soars the **Rigi Kilm,** which has a magnificent view of the lake and its neighbor. Ferries run from Lucerne to Vitznau, where you can catch a cogwheel train to the summit. You can also conquer Rigi on foot; it's 5hr. from Vitznau to the top, and anyone who tires out halfway can pick up the train at Rigi Kaltbad (3hr. up the hill) and ride the rest of the way. Return by train, take the cable car from Rigi Kaltbad to Weggis, and return to Lucerne by boat (round-trip 87SFr, with Eurail or Swisspass 42SFr).

BERN ☎ 031

The city has been Switzerland's capital since 1848, but don't expect fast tracks, power politics, or men in black—Bern prefers to focus on the lighter things in life (such as local Toblerone chocolate and sumptuous flower gardens), and the city, named a world treasure by UNESCO, has a decidedly relaxed atmosphere.

TRANSPORTATION

Flights: The **airport** (☎960 21 11) is 20min. from the city. An airport bus runs from the train station 50min. before each flight (10min., 14SFr).

Trains: From the **station** at Bahnhofpl. (☎0900 300 300; 1.19SFr per min.), in front of the tourist office, to: **Basel** (1¼hr., every hr. 5:45am-9:45pm, 37SFr); **Berlin** (8hr., 3 per day 5:25am-7:45pm, 254SFr); **Geneva** (2hr., every 30min. 5:40am-11:20pm, 50SFr); **Interlaken** (50min., every hr. 7:25am-11:25pm, 25SFr); **Lausanne** (1¼hr., every 20min. 5am-11:20pm, 32SFr); **Lucerne** (1½hr., every hr. 6:40am-10:40pm, 32SFr); **Milan** (3½hr., 13 per day 6:20am-11:25pm, 73SFr); **Munich** (5½hr., 4 per day 5:25am-8:45pm, 123SFr); **Paris** (4½hr., 4 per day 6:30am-9:25pm, 109SFr); **Salzburg** (7¼hr., 4 per day 8:15am-9:15pm, 136SFr); **Vienna** (10½hr., 4 per day 8:15am-9:15pm, 162SFr); **Zurich** (1¼hr., every 30min. 5:50am-11:50pm, 48SFr). 25% reduction on international fares for ages 26 and under.

Bike Rental: The small blue **SwissCom Kiosk** outside the train station loans bikes for **free**. A 20SFr deposit plus ID are required. Bikes must be returned on the same day. Open May-Oct. 7:30am-9:30pm.

ORIENTATION AND PRACTICAL INFORMATION

Most of medieval Bern lies in front of the train station and along the Aare River. Bern's main **train station** is a stressful tangle: check-in, information, buses, bike rental, and a pharmacy are upstairs; tickets, lockers, police, showers, toilets, and currency exchange are downstairs. **Warning:** Like many cities, Bern has a drug community; it tends to congregate around the Parliament park and terraces.

Tourist Office: (☎328 1212; www.bernetourism.ch), on the street level of the station. In summer, daily **city tours** (8-24SFr) are available by bus, on foot, or by raft. Open June-Sept. daily 9am-8:30pm; Oct.-May M-Sa 9am-6:30pm, Su 10am-5pm.

Embassies: Canada, Kirchenfeldstr. 88 (☎357 3200). **Ireland,** Kirchenfeldstr. 68 (☎352 1442). **South Africa,** Alpenstr. 29 (☎350 1313). **UK,** Thunstr. 50 (☎359 7700). **US,** Jubiläumstr. 93 (☎357 7011).

Bi-Gay-Lesbian Organizations: Homosexuelle Arbeitsgruppe die Schweiz (HACH), Mühlenpl. 11, is the headquarters of Switzerland's largest gay organization.

Police, ☎117. **Ambulance,** ☎144.

Internet Access: Soundwerk Café, Wasserwerkg. 5. At the Aare River, near the bottom of Nydeggbrücke. (Open M-F 11am-7pm, Sa 11am-4pm. Free.)

Post Office: Schanzenpost 1, next to the train station. Open M-F 7:30am-6:30pm, Sa 8am-noon. **Poste Restante:** Postlagernde Briefe für FirstName SURNAME, Schanzenpost 3000, Bern 1. **Postal Code:** CH-3000 to CH-3030.

ACCOMMODATIONS AND FOOD

Bern has responded to the influx of backpackers with several new hostels. All offer clean beds with varying services, prices, and personal touches. If the cheaper options are all full, the tourist office has a list of private rooms.

Backpackers Bern/Hotel Glocke, Rathausg. 75 (☎311 3771). From the train station, turn left on Spitalg., continuing on Marktg; turn left at Kornhauspl., then right on Rathausg. The hostel will be on your right. **Internet** and kitchen access. Laundry 3.80SFr. Reception June-Aug. 8-11am and 3-10pm; Sept.-May 8-11am and 3-8pm. Dorms 32SFr 1st night, 27SFr subsequent nights; singles 75SFr; doubles 120SFr, with bath 160SFr. Apr.-May and Sept.-Oct. dorms 2SFr less, other rooms 5SFr less; Nov.-Mar. 4SFr less, 10SFr less.

Jugendherberge (HI), Weiherg. 4 (☎311 6316; fax 312 5240; info@jugibern.ch). From the station, cross the tram lines and follow Christoffelg. through the gates to the left of the Park Café and continue down to Weiherg., following the hostel signs. Breakfast included. Laundry 7SFr. 3-night max. stay. Check-out before 10am. Reception June-

Sept. daily 7-10am and 3pm-midnight; Oct.-May 7-10am and 5pm-midnight. Reservations by fax and email only. Closed 2nd and 3rd weeks in Jan. Communal hall showers. Dorms 28SFr; overflow mattresses on the floor 20SFr. Nonmembers add 6SFr.

Pension Marthahaus, Wyttenbachstr. 22a (☎332 4135; martahaus@bluewin.ch). Take bus #20 (dir.: Wyler) to "Gewerbeschule," then the 1st right. Breakfast included. Free bikes, kitchen access, and **Internet** for guests. Laundry 8SFr. Reception 7am-9pm. Check-out 11am. Reservations recommended. Singles 60SFr, with shower 90SFr; doubles 95SFr, 120SFr; triples 120SFr, 150SFr. Prices drop 5-10SFr in winter. MC/V.

Almost every locale ending in "-platz" overflows with cafes and restaurants, though the bigger ones tend to be pricier and more touristy. Try one of Bern's hearty specialties: *Gschnätzlets* (fried veal, beef, or pork), *Suurchabis* (a kind of sauerkraut), *Gschwellti* (steamed potatoes), or the local Toblerone chocolate. **Fruit and vegetable markets** sell fresh produce daily on Bärenpl. (May-Oct. 8am-6pm) and every Tuesday and Saturday on Bundespl.

Café des Pyrenées, Kornhauspl. 17 (☎311 3063), has inventive sandwiches (calamari 6.50SFr) and a sidewalk terrace. Open M-F 9am-12:30am, Sa 8am-5pm.

Manora, Bubenbergpl. 5A (☎311 3755), over the tramlines from the station. This self-service chain tends to be crowded, but serves big platefuls that are nutritious and cheap. Open M-Sa 6:30am-11pm, Su 8:30am-11:15pm.

Restaurant Marzilbrücke, Gaßstr. 8 (☎311 2780). Turn right from the hostel onto Aarstr. Try their selection of curry dishes, including vegetarian selections (25SFr) or a gourmet pizza (15.50-24.50SFr). Open M-Th 11:30am-10:30pm, F 11:30am-11:50pm, Sa 4pm-12:30am, Su 10am-10:30pm. Pizzeria open M-F 5:30-11pm, Sa-Su 4-11pm.

Migros supermarket, Marktg. 46, also has a restaurant and take-away counters. Open M 9am-6:30pm, T-W and F 8am-6:30pm, Th 8am-9pm, Sa 7am-4pm.

⊙ SIGHTS

Bern is an easily walkable city; most sights lie in a line starting at the Bundeshaus.

THE OLD TOWN. The massive **Bundeshaus,** where the Swiss national government is centered, dominates the Aare. *(45min. tour every hr. M-Sa 9-11am and 2-4pm, Su 10-11am and 2-3pm. Free.)* From the Bundeshaus, turn left off Kocherg. at Theaterpl. to reach the 13th-century **Zytglogge** (clock tower). At 4min. before the hour, figures on the tower creak to life, but it's more entertaining to watch the tourists ooh and aah. Continue down Kocherg. to the 15th-century Protestant **Münster** (cathedral); inside is a sculpture of the Last Judgment, where the naked damned shuffle off unhappily to Hell on God's left. For a fantastic view, climb the Münster's 100m spire. *(Open Easter-Oct. Tu-Sa 10am-5pm, Su 11:30am-5pm; Nov.-Easter Tu-F 10am-noon and 2-4pm, Sa 10am-noon and 2-5pm, Su 11am-2pm. Tower closes 30min. earlier. 3SFr.)* Several walkways lead steeply down from the Bundeshaus to the **Aare River;** on hotter days, locals dive lemming-style from the bridges to take a brisk ride on its swift currents, but only experienced swimmers should join in.

BEAR PITS AND ROSE GARDEN. Across the Nydeggbrücke lie the **Bärengraben** (bear pits), which were recently renovated to provide the bears with trees and rocks to clamber over—perhaps an attempt to make up for the indignity of being on display to gawking crowds. *(Open June-Sept. daily 9am-6pm; Oct.-May 9am-4pm. 3SFr to feed the bears.)* The tourist office here presents **The Bern Show,** a slickly choreographed recap of Bernese history. *(Every 20min. In German and English, alternately. Free.)* The path snaking up the hill to the left leads to the ⊠**Rosengarten** (Rose Garden), which provides one of the best views of Bern's *Altstadt.*

KUNSTMUSEUM. Bern's Kunstmuseum (art museum) includes the world's largest Paul Klee collection and a smattering of 20th-century big names: Picasso, Giacometti, Ernst Kirchner, Pollock, and Dadaist Hans Arp. *(Hodlerstr. 8-12, near Lorrainebrücke. ☎328 0944. Open Tu 10am-9pm, W-Su 10am-5pm. Mandatory lockers for bags, 2SFr. Admission 7SFr, students and seniors 5SFr, under 16 free.)*

GRIN AND BEAR IT Legend has it that Duke Berchtold V of Zähringen, founder of Bern, wanted to name the city after the first animal he caught when hunting on the site. The animal was a you-know-what, and Bern (derived from *Bären*, or "bears") was born. The *Bärengraben* themselves weren't built until the Bernese victory at the Battle of Nouana in 1513, when they dragged home a live bear as part of the war booty. A hut was erected for the beast in what is now Bärenplatz (Bear Square) and his descendents have been Bern's collective pets ever since.

BERNISCHES HISTORISCHE MUSEUM. Anything and everything from Bern's lengthy history is displayed in this jam-packed museum. Keep an eye out for an eerily grinning William Tell who looks like he's aiming right at you. *(Helvetiapl. 5. ☎350 7711. Open Tu-Su 10am-5pm. 7SFr, students 5SFr, under 16 free; Sa free.)*

ALBERT EINSTEIN'S HOUSE. This small apartment where Einstein conceived the theory of general relativity is now filled with his photos and letters. *(Kramg. 49. ☎312 0091. Open Feb.-Nov. Tu-F 10am-5pm, Sa 10am-4pm. 3SFr, students 2SFr.)*

🎵🎭 ENTERTAINMENT AND NIGHTLIFE

July's **Gurten Festival** (www.gurtenfestival.ch) has attracted such luminaries as Bob Dylan, Elvis Costello, and Björk, while jazz-lovers arrive in early May for the **International Jazz Festival** (www.jazzfestivalbern.ch). However, Bern's best-known festival is probably the off-the-wall **onion market** on the 4th Monday in November. The orange grove at **Stadgärtnerei Elfnau** (take tram #19 to "Elfnau") has free Sunday concerts in summer. From mid-July to mid-August, **OrangeCinema** (www.orangecinema.ch) screens recently released films in the open air; tickets are available from the tourist office in the train station.

At night, the fashionable folk linger in the Altstadt's bars and cafes while a seedier crowd gathers under the gargoyles of the Lorrainebrücke, behind and to the left of the station down Bollwerk. **Le Pery Bar,** Schmiedenpl. 3, is a popular nightspot. (Bar open M-W 5pm-1:30am, Th 5pm-2:30am, F-Sa 5pm-3:30am.) **Sous le Pont** is a den of alternative culture with an unnaturally relaxed, predominantly male clientele. From Bollwerk, head left before Lorrainebrücke through the cement park. (Open M and Sa after 5pm, Tu-F 11pm-1am.)

JUNGFRAU REGION

The most famous (and most-visited) region of the Bernese Oberland, the Jungfrau area has attracted tourists for hundreds of years with glorious hiking trails and permanently snow-capped peaks. The three most famous mountains are the **Jungfrau** (Maiden), the **Eiger** (Ogre), and the **Mönch** (Monk). Locals say that the monk protects the maiden by standing between her and the ogre, but at 4158m, she could probably beat up the puny Eiger (3970m). From Interlaken, the valley splits at the foot of the Jungfrau: the eastern valley contains Grindelwald, with easy access to two glaciers, while the western valley hosts many smaller towns, each with unique hiking opportunities. The two valleys are divided by an easily hikeable ridge. Pick up the *Lauterbrunnen/Jungfrau Region Wanderkarte* (15SFr at any tourist office) for an overview of the hikes.

INTERLAKEN ☎033

Interlaken, whose name means "between lakes," lies between the Thunersee and the Brienzersee at the foot of the largest mountains in Switzerland. With easy access to these natural playgrounds, Interlaken has earned its rightful place as one of Switzerland's prime tourist attractions and as its top outdoor adventure spot.

⚏⚍ TRANSPORTATION AND PRACTICAL INFORMATION. The Westbahnhof (☎826 4750) and Ostbahnhof (☎828 7319) have trains to: Bern (6:30am-11:30pm, 8.60SFr); Basel (6:30am-11:30pm, 56SFr); Geneva (5:30am-9:40pm, 65SFr); Lucerne (5:30am-7:15pm, 27SFr); Lugano/Locarno (5:30am-5:15pm, 72SFr); Zurich (6:30am-11:30pm, 62SFr). The Ostbahnhof also has trains to Grindelwald (June-Sept. every 30min., September to May every hr. 6:35am-11:35pm; 9.40SFr).

The **tourist office,** Höheweg 37, in the Hotel Metropole, has free maps. (☎826 5300. Open July-Aug. M-F 8am-6pm, Sa 9am-noon, Su 5-7pm; Sept.-June M-F 8am-noon and 2-6pm, Sa 9am-noon.) Both train stations rent **bikes.** (27SFr per day. Open 6am-10pm.) For **snow and weather info,** call 855 1022. **The Wave,** Rosenstr. 13, at the main circle between the station and the tourist office, provides **Internet** access. (14SFr per hr., students 11SFr. Open M-F 11am-11pm, Sa-Su 2-11pm.) **Postal Code:** CH-3800.

⚏⚌ ACCOMMODATIONS AND FOOD. ▨**Backpackers Villa Sonnenhof,** Alpenstr. 16, diagonally across the Höhenmatte from the tourist office, is quiet and low-key. Call or arrive early in the morning. (☎826 71 71. **Internet** 10SFr per hr. Mountain bikes 18SFr per half-day. Laundry 12SFr. Breakfast, kitchen, towels, sheets, lockers, and showers included. Reception 7:30-11am and 4-10pm. No curfew. 4- to 6-bed dorms 29SFr; doubles 74SFr; triples 99SFr; 5SFr extra for view, balcony, or bathroom. AmEx/MC/V.) To reach party-happy **Balmer's Herberge,** Hauptstr. 23-25, walk diagonally across the Höhenmatte from the tourist office and follow signs down Parkstr. No reservations—just sign in, drop off your pack, and return at 5pm when beds are assigned. (☎822 19 61. Free sleds and 20% discount on ski and snowboard rental in winter. Mountain bikes 30SFr per day. **Internet** 10SFr per hr. Kitchen 1SFr per 20min. Breakfast included. Laundry 8SFr. Reception in summer 6:30am-11pm; in winter 6:30-9am and 4:30-11pm. Check-out 9am. Lockout 9:30am-4:30pm. No curfew. Dorms 22-24SFr; doubles 68SFr; triples 90SFr; quads 112SFr. AmEx/MC/Visa.) **Heidi's Hostel Garni Beyeler,** Bernastr. 37, is centrally located and books outdoor excursions. (☎822 90 30. Dorms 55SFr; quads with shower 100SFr.)

Most hostels serve cheap food, but you can also swing by **Migros supermarket,** across from the Westbahnhof, which houses a restaurant. (Open M-Th 8am-6:30pm, F 8am-9pm, Sa 7:30am-4pm). **Restaurant Goldener Anker,** Marktg. 57, serves traditional specialties alongside lowfat and vegetarian dishes. (Open M-W and F-Su 10am-12:30am.) At **Mr. Hong's Chinese Take-Out,** Marktg. 48, Mr. Hong cooks a variety of stir-fries (10-13SFr) while Frau Hong, who is trained in reflexology, offers up holistic philosophies. Open Apr.-Oct. 11:45am-10pm; Nov.-Mar. 11:45am-9pm.

DEATH-(UN)DEFYING. Interlaken's adventure sports are thrilling, but accidents do happen. On July 27, 1999, 19 tourists were killed by a flash flood while canyoning. Be aware that you participate in all activities at your own risk.

◪ OUTDOORS AND HIKING. Interlaken's steep precipices, raging rivers, and wide-open spaces serve as prime spots for such adrenaline-pumping activities as bungee jumping, canyoning (rappelling, diving, and swimming through a canyon), paragliding, and whitewater rafting. **Alpin Raft** (☎823 4100; fax 823 4101), the most established company in Interlaken, has qualified, personable guides and offers: bungee jumping (155SFr); canyoning (95SFr); hang gliding (155SFr); paragliding (140SFr); river rafting (95SFr); sea-kayaking on the Brienzersee (30SFr); and skydiving (380SFr). All prices include transportation to and from any hostel in Interlaken. A number of horse and hiking tours, as well as rock-lessons, are also available upon request. The owner of **Skydiving Xdream,** Stefan Heuser, has been with the Swiss skydiving team for 17 years, including two years as a coach. (380SFr. ☎079 759 3484; www.justjump.ch. Open Apr.-Oct.)

MOUNTAIN MANN The face in the Harder Mountain is known as the Harder Mann. According to legend, a strolling monk became possessed, chased a small girl off a cliff, and was turned to stone as punishment. It might make sense if he hadn't been given the best view in Interlaken. Local lore says that the Harder Mann returns every year to fight off winter. On January 2, residents celebrate with wooden "Harder Mann" masks and a large carnival. If you decide to hike this landmark, *do not leave the marked paths*. Every summer people die attempting to climb roped-off areas.

Interlaken's most traversed trail climbs to the **Harder Kulm** (1310m, see **Mountain Mann,** above). From the Ostbahnhof, head toward town, take the first road bridge right across the river, and follow the yellow signs that later give way to white-red-white Bergweg flashes on the rocks. From the top, signs lead back down to the Westbahnhof. A funicular runs from the trailhead near the Ostbahnhof to the top from May to October. (2hr. up, 1½hr. down. 12.80SFr, 20SFr round-trip; 25% discount with Eurailpass or SwissPass.) For flatter **trails,** turn left from the train station and left before the bridge, then follow the canal over to the nature reserve on the shore of the Thunersee. The trail winds up the Lombach river and through pastures at the base of the Harder Kulm back toward town (2hr.).

🎵 **ENTERTAINMENT. Balmer's** (see **Accommodations,** above) offers live music—most often reggae—on most nights. (Bar open 9pm-1am.) **Buddy's,** Höheweg 33, is a small, crowded English-style pub with cheap beer. (Open daily 10am-12:30am.) **Johnny's Dancing Club,** Höheweg 92, located in the basement of the Hotel Carlton, is Interlaken's oldest disco. (Open Tu-Su 9:30pm-3am.)

GRINDELWALD   ☎036

Grindelwald, launching point to the only glaciers accessible by foot in the Bernese Oberland, crouches beneath the north face of the Eiger. Although it only has two streets, Grindelwald is the most developed part of the Jungfrau Region. The town has all kinds of hikes, from easy valley walks to challenging peaks for top climbers. The **Bergführerbüro** (Mountain Guides Office), 200m past the tourist office, sells hiking maps and coordinates glacier walks, ice climbing, and mountaineering. (☎853 5200. Open June-Oct. M-Sa 9am-noon and 3-6pm, Su 4-6pm.) The 4hr. **Lower Glacier** (*Untere Grindelwaldgletscher*) hike is moderately steep and can be done in tennis shoes; to reach the trailhead, walk up the main street away from the station and follow the signs downhill to "Pfinstegg." For the **Upper Glacier** (*Obere Grindelwaldgletscher*) hike, take the postal bus from Grindelwald (dir.: Grosse Scheidegg) to "Oberslaubkule" and follow the signs uphill for "Glecksteinhütte."

The Jungfraubahn runs to Grindelwald from **Interlaken's** Ostbahnhof (9.40SFr). The **tourist office,** located in the Sport-Zentrum to the right of the station, provides chairlift information and a list of free guided excursions. (☎854 121. Open July-Aug. M-F 8am-7pm, Sa 8am-5pm, Su 9-11am and 3-5pm; Sept.-June M-F 8am-noon and 2-6pm, Sa 8am-noon and 2-5pm.) For **weather forecasts,** call 162; for **medical assistance,** call 853 1153. Access the **Internet** (15SFr per hour) at **Ernst Schudel's,** opposite the tourist office. (Open 9am-noon and 2-6:30pm.) To reach the **Jugendherberge (HI),** head left out of the train station for 400m, then cut uphill to the right just before "Chalet Alpenblume" and follow the steep trail (400m) all the way up the hill. (☎853 1009. Mountain bikes15SFr per day. Breakfast, sheets, and lockers included. Laundry 5SFr. Reception daily 7-10am and 3-11pm. No lockout. Dorms Apr.-Oct. 26.30SFr, Nov.-Mar. 29.80SFr; doubles with toilet and shower 48.80SFr, 51.30SFr. Nonmembers add 5SFr. AmEx/DC/MC.) For **Lehmann's Herberge,** follow the main street past the tourist office and take the first right. (☎853 31 41. Breakfast included. Reception daily 8am-11pm. Dorms 45SFr, after 1st night 40SFr; doubles 90SFr.) **Gepsi Bar** is just past the tourist office on the left and has entrees (from 8.50SFr) and beer. (Open 8:30-11:30pm.) There's a **Co-op supermarket** on Hauptstr, across from the tourist office. (Open M-F 8am-6:30pm, Sa 8am-4pm.)

ZERMATT AND THE MATTERHORN ☎ 027

The valley blocks out the great Alpine summits that ring Zermatt, allowing the **Matterhorn** (4478m) to rise alone above the town. Spectacular, well-marked ski paths are accessible to all visitors, including **Europe's longest run,** the 13km trail from Klein Matterhorn to Zermatt. A one-day **ski pass** for any of the area's regions runs 62-77SFr. The **Zermatt Alpin Center,** which houses both the **Bergführerbüro** (Guide's Office; ☎ 966 24 60) and the **Skischulbüro** (Ski School Office; ☎ 967 24 66), is located past the post office from the station; here you can pick up detailed four day weather forecasts, ski passes, and info on guided climbing expeditions. (Both offices open July-Sept. M-F 8:30am-noon and 4-7pm, Sa 4-7pm, Su 10am-noon and 4-7pm.) Rental prices for **skis** and **boots** are set throughout Zermatt (winter 38SFr per day, summer 28SFr per day, cheaper for longer periods). Try **Slalom Sport,** on Kirchstr. (☎ 966 23 66; open M-Sa 8am-noon and 2-7pm, Su 8am-noon and 4-6:30pm), or **Bayard Sports,** directly across from the station. (☎ 966 49 60. Open M-Sa 8am-noon and 2-7pm.) **Freeride Film Factory** (☎ 213 3807) offers custom **hiking** and **climbing** expeditions (160-250SFr) and will even give you a videotape of your trek.

Cars and buses are illegal in Zermatt to preserve the Alpine air—the only way in is the hourly **BVZ** (Brig-Visp-Zermatt) rail line. Connect from Visp (from Lausanne; 35SFr, round-trip 58SFr) or Stalden-Saas (from Saas Fee; 1hr.; 23.60SFr, round-trip 31SFr). The **tourist office,** in the station complex, sells the **Wanderkarte** (hiking map) for 24.90SFr. (☎ 967 01 81. Open mid-June to mid-Oct. M-F 8:30am-6pm, Sa 8:30am-7pm, Su 9:30am-noon and 4-7pm; mid-Oct. to mid-June M-Sa 8:30am-noon and 1:30-6pm.) **Hotel Bahnhof,** on Bahnhofstr. to the left of the station, provides hotel housing at hostel rates. (☎ 967 24 06. Reception 8am-8pm. Open mid-Dec. to mid-Oct. Dorms 30SFr; 4-bed rooms with private showers 40SFr; singles with shower 48-62SFr; doubles 70-86SFr, with shower 80-96SFr. MC/V.) **Walliserkanne,** on Bahnhofstr. next to the post office, offers filling Swiss fare at reasonable prices. (Open 11:30am-2pm and 6-10pm. Pizzeria downstairs open 7pm-2am. AmEx/DC/MC/V.) **Café du Pont,** on Bahnhofstr, is Zermatt's oldest restaurant and has multilingual menus burnt into slabs of wood hanging on the wall. (Open June-Oct. and Dec.-Apr. daily 9am-11pm; food served 11am-10pm.) Pick up groceries at the **Co-op Center** opposite the station. (Open M-Sa 8:30am-12:15pm and 1:45-6:30pm.) **Postal code:** CH-3920.

SAAS FEE ☎ 027

Nicknamed "the pearl of the Alps," Saas Fee (1800m) is in a hanging valley above the Saastal, snuggled among thirteen 4000m peaks. The glacial ice of the **Feegletscher** ("fairy glacier") comes so low that you can visit the frozen giant on a 30min. evening stroll. To protect its Alpine glory, the town is closed to cars, and town officials prohibit disturbing "the fairy-like charm of Saas Fee" after 10pm (noisemakers fined 200SFr). Summer **skiers** enjoy 20km of runs, and in winter an immense network of lifts opens (daypasses 58SFr; 6 days 270SFr; 13 days 480SFr). Stores in the **Swiss Rent-A-Sport System** (look for the black and red logo) offer three grades of equipment (skis 28-50SFr per day, 6 days 105-180SFr; snowboards 28-38SFr, 80-105SFr; boots 15-19SFr, 52-77SFr). The **Bergführerbüro** (Mountain Guides' Office), in the same building as the ski school, leads **climbs** of varying difficulty levels. (☎ 957 44 64. Closed May-June. Open M-Sa 9:30am-noon and 3-6pm).

A **post bus** runs (every hr. 5:35am-7:35pm) to Visp (50min.; 14.60SFr, return 29.20SFr), where trains connect to Lausanne, and Zermatt via Stalden Saas (41.80SFr, return 63.60SFr). Reserve a seat on all buses at least 2hr. before departure; call 958 11 45 or drop by the bus station (open 7:30am-12:35pm and 1:15-6.35pm). The **tourist office,** opposite the bus station, dispenses hiking advice and town maps. (☎ 958 18 58. Open July to mid-Sept. and mid-Dec. to mid-Apr. M-F 8:30am-noon and 2-6:30pm, Sa 8am-7pm, Su 9am-noon and 3-6pm; mid-Sept. to mid-Dec. and mid-Apr. to June M-Sa 8:30am-noon and 2-6pm, Su 10am-noon and 4-6pm.) **Pension Garni Mascotte** and its two sister chalets, **Alba** and **Albana,** are some of Saas Fee's better values. Head right on the main street from the station and continue up the hill for 200m; Mascotte is on the left. (☎ 957 27 24. Albana's rooms have shower and toilet. Breakfast included. Open mid-Dec. to Apr. and July-Sept. Alba dorms 27-30SFr. Albana 5-bed dorms 28-33SFr; 4-bed dorms 30-35SFr; 2-bed dorms 38-48SFr. Smarter rooms in Mascotte 45-55SFr.) There are several **grocery stores** sprinkled around town, most open during the same hours. (M-F 8:30am-12:15pm and 2:15-6:30pm, Sa 8:30am-12:15pm and 2:15-5pm.) **Postal code:** CH-3906.

GRAUBÜNDEN

The largest, least populous, and most alpine of the Swiss cantons, Graubünden's rugged gorges, fir forests, and eddying rivers give the region a wildness seldom found in ultra-civilized Switzerland. Visitors should plan their trips carefully, especially in ski season, when reservations are absolutely required. Beware, almost everything shuts down in May and June.

CHUR   ☎081

Chur is the capital of Graubünden and, at 5000 years old, probably Switzerland's oldest settlement. The medium-sized city stocks consumer goods that are unavailable in the rest of the region, but there aren't many other reasons to stay. Since Chur is the transportation hub of Graubünden, you'll probably experience it only as the gateway to other towns. The cavernous 12th-century **Dom** (cathedral) at the top of the old town displays eight altarpieces and the **Hochaltar,** a flamboyant 15th-century masterpiece of gold and wood. (Open Tu-Sa 10am-noon and 2-4pm.) Downhill, the **Martinskirche** has three stained-glass windows by Giacometti that depict the birth of an oddly beefy Christ. The **Bündner Kunstmuseum** (art museum), Bahnhofstr. 35, displays the art of the three Giacomettis—Giovanni, Alberto, and Augusto—along with works by Swiss artists. (Open Tu-W and F-Su 10am-noon and 2-5pm, Th 10am-noon and 2-8pm. 10SFr, students 7SFr.) The **Retic Museum,** Quaderstr. 15, houses a collection of archaeological trivia that document the development of Graubünden. (Open Tu-Su 10am-noon and 2-5pm. 5SFr, students 2SFr.)

   Trains connect Chur to: **Arosa** (1hr., every hr. 5:35am-11pm, 11.80SFr); **Basel** (2¾hr., every hr. 4:50am-10:15pm, 62SFr); **St. Gallen** (1½hr., every hr. 4:50am-10:16pm, 34SFr); **Zurich** (1½hr., every hr. 4:50am-10:15pm, 38SFr). To get to the **tourist office,** Grabenstr. 5, follow Bahnhofstr. two blocks to Postpl., then turn left on Grabenstr. The office finds rooms for free. (☎ 252 1818. Open M 1:30-6pm, Tu-F 8:30am-noon and 1:30-6pm, Sa 9am-noon.) No luxurious budget accommodations await in Chur; the lack of a youth hostel is sorely felt. The nearest hostel is in **Arosa** (see below). If you need to be in Chur, try **Hotel Schweizerhaus,** Kasernenstr. 10. From the Postpl., turn right on Grabenstr. and follow as it becomes Engadinestr. and crosses the bridge; turn right over the bridge, and the street turns into Kasernenstr. (☎ 252 1096. Breakfast included. Reception 7am-midnight. 35SFr per person.) Chur has a surprising number of trendy eating establishments; **Valentino's Grill,** Untereg. 5, is the best budget option. Turn right on Grabenstr. from Postpl., then head left under the arches. (Open M 5-10pm, Tu-Th 5-11:30pm, F 5pm-midnight, Sa noon-midnight.) **Postal code:** CH-7000.

AROSA   ☎081

The beautiful, secluded town of Arosa makes an effort to cater to budget-conscious **skiers** and **snowboarders** with affordable ski-and-stay packages. Developed ski trails dominate one side of the valley; on the other, **hiking** trails stretch to isolated valleys. A **free shuttle bus** (every hr. in summer, every 20min. in winter) transports visitors between the hottest spots in town, including the ski lifts and the **tourist office,** which arranges hiking trips and ski lessons and makes free hotel reservations. (☎ 378 7020. Open Dec. 7-Apr. 13 M-F 9am-6pm, Sa 9am-5:30pm, Su 4-6:30pm; Apr. 14-Dec. 6 M-F 8am-noon and 2-6pm, Sa 9am-1pm; June 29-Aug. 17 also Sa 2-4pm.)

   Arosa is accessible only by a scenic **train** route from Chur (1hr., every hr. 5:35am-11pm, 12.60SFr). **Arosa Bergbahnen,** the ski-lift company, runs two dorms that are convenient and cheap during the winter. (☎378 8423. Rooms come with a ski-lift ticket package.) ◪**Haus Florentium,** a former convent hidden in the woods, has been converted to a 150-bed party house. From the tourist office, follow the cobblestone path down the hill, turn right at the top, left at the gravel path, and right at the path in front of Pension Suveran. (Breakfast included. Dec.-Apr. 1-night stay and 2-day ski pass 160SFr; 6-night stay and 7-day ski pass 511SFr. July-Aug. 37SFr per night.) In summer, try the **Jugendherberge (HI),** Seewaldstr. Walk past the tourist office and follow the signs down the hill. (☎377 1397. Breakfast and sheets included. Showers 0.50SFr per 3min. Reception 7-10am and 5-10pm. No lockout. Curfew 10pm; key available. Open mid-June to mid-Oct. and mid-Dec. to mid-Apr. Dorms 27SFr; doubles 64SFr.) **Camping Arosa,** downhill from the hostel in a valley with a brook, has showers (0.50SFr) and cooking facilities. (☎377 1745. Check-in 4:30-5:30pm. Open all year. 7.30-8.30SFr per person, 4.50SFr per tent.) **Groceries** are available at the **Co-op,** near the tourist office on Poststr. (Open M-F 8am-12:30pm and 2-6:30pm, Sa 8am-4pm.) **Postal Code:** CH-7050.

THE SWISS NATIONAL PARK

The Swiss National Park offers hikes that rival the best hiking areas elsewhere in Switzerland. But no other areas can match the park's isolation from manmade constructs, which allows hikers to experience the undiluted wildness of the natural terrain. A network of 20 hiking trails runs throughout the park, mostly concentrated in the center of the park. Few of the trails are level; most trails in the park involve a lot of climbing, often into areas still covered in snow. However, all trails are clearly marked, and it is against park rules to wander off the designated trails. Trails that require no mountaineering gear are marked with white-red-white blazes. The Swiss are practically mountain goats, so even some of the no-gear routes can be tricky.

Zernez is the main gateway to the park. Be sure to check in at the **Parkhouse** to see which trails are navigable. Take their advice seriously: when they say a trail is too dangerous, they mean it. The Parkhouse has helpful park **trail maps,** written guides to all 20 trails, geological maps, and vegetation maps. From Zernez, **trains** and **post buses** run to other towns in the area, includig Scuol, Samedan, and S-chanf. (That's not a typo.) The park is closed November-May. The Swiss National Park is one of the most strictly environmentally regulated nature preserves in the world. Camping and campfires are prohibited, as is collecting flowers and plants. A team of wardens patrols the park at all times, so it's better not to test the rules. Camping is not allowed in the park, but Zernez, Scuol, and S-chanf have campsites right outside the park boundaries.

SOUTHEAST (ITALIAN) SWITZERLAND

Ever since Switzerland won the Italian-speaking canton of Ticino (Tessin in German and French) from Italy in 1512, the region has been renowned for its mix of Swiss efficiency and Italian *dolce vita*—no wonder the rest of Switzerland vacations here among jasmine-laced villas painted the bright colors of Italian *gelato*.

LUGANO   ☎091

Set in a valley between two mountains, Lugano draws plenty of visitors with its seamless blend of religious beauty, artistic flair, and natural spectacle. The frescoes of the 16th-century **Cattedrale San Lorenzo,** just below the train station, are still magnificently vivid. The frescoes of the national monument **Basilica Sacro Cuore,** on C. Elevezia, feature Swiss hikers walking alongside the disciples. The most spectacular fresco in town, however, is the gargantuan *Crucifixion* which adorns the **Chiesa Santa Maria degli Angiuli,** on the waterfront to the right of the tourist office. The **Belvedere**, on quai riva Caccia, is an enormous sculpture garden with an emphasis on Modernist metalwork. Armed with topographic maps and trail guides (sold at the tourist office), hikers can tackle the nearby mountains, **Monte Bré** (933m) and **Monte San Salvatore** (912m). Alpine guides at the **ASBEST Adventure Company**, V. Basilea 28 (☎966 11 14), offer everything from snowshoeing and skiing (full-day 90SFr) to paragliding (165SFr) and canyoning (from 90SFr). Rock-climbing (90SFr) and mountain biking (35SFr) are also available in the summer. The **Pave Pub,** riva Albertolli 1, is a self-proclaimed *museo di birra* (beer museum), with 50 different brands. (From 4SFr. Open daily 11am-1am.)

Trains leave P. della Stazione to: Locarno (1hr., every 30min. 5:30am-midnight, 16.40SFr); Milan (1½hr., every hr. 5:30am-10:45pm, 14SFr); Zurich (3½hr., every hr. 5:55am-8:35pm, 62SFr). To reach the **tourist office,** cross the footbridge labeled "Centro" from the station and head down Via Cattedrale; turn left on Via dei Pesci and left on Riva Via Vela, which becomes Riva Giocondo Albertolli. The office is just past the fountain on the left, across the street from the ferry launch. (Open Apr.-Oct. M-F 9am-6:30pm, Sa 9am-12:30pm and 1:30-5pm; Su 10am-2pm; Nov.-Mar. M-F 9am-12:30pm and 1:30-5:30pm.) **Hotel Montarina,** 1 Via Montarina, is a palm-tree-enveloped hostel with a swimming pool, kitchen, and terrace. (☎966 72 72. Buffet breakfast 12SFr. Sheets 4SFr. Laundry 4SFr, soap 1.50SF. Reception 8am-9pm. Open Mar.-Oct. In July and Aug. call 2 weeks in advance for reservations. Dorms 25SFr; singles 50-65SFr; doubles 100SFr, with bath 120SFr.) There's an **Aperto grocery store** in the station (open 6am-10pm); **Migros supermarket,** 15 Via Pretoria, two blocks left from the post office down Via Pretorio, has a food court on the ground floor (open M-F 8am-6:30pm, Sa 7:30am-5pm).

LOCARNO   ☎091

A Swiss vacation spot, Lugano gets over 2200 hours of sunlight per year—the most of any place in Switzerland. For centuries, visitors have journeyed to Locarno solely to see the orange-yellow **Church of Madonna del Sasso** (Madonna of the Rock), founded in 1487. A 20min. walk up the smooth stones of the Via al Sasso leads to the top, passing life-size wooden niche statues along the way. Hundreds of silver heart-shaped medallions on the church walls commemorate acts of Mary's intervention in the lives of worshipers who have made pilgrimages here, and the **museum** next door houses ancient reliquaries, pilgrims' souvenirs, and a collection of disaster paintings commissioned by survivors to thank the Madonna for intervening to save their lives. (Grounds open 6:30am-7pm. Museum open Apr.-Oct. M-F 2-5pm, Su 10am-noon and 2-5pm. 2.50SFr, students 1.50SFr. English guidebooks free, at the entrance.) Each August, Locarno swells with pilgrims of a different sort: its world-famous **film festival** draws visitors from all over the globe.

Trains run frequently from P. Stazione (☎743 65 64) to: Lucerne (3hr., every 30min. 6am-12:30am, 56SFr); Lugano (45min., every 30min. 5:50am-11:50pm, 16.40SFr); Milan (2½hr., several per day 6:30am-8:30pm, 63SFr); Zurich (2¾hr., every hr. 6:25am-9pm, 60SFr). The **tourist office,** on P. Grande in the *Kursaal* (casino), makes hotel reservations. (☎791 00 91. Open M-F 9am-6pm, Sa 9am-5pm, Su 10am-noon and 1-3pm.) To reach **Pensione Città Vecchia,** 13 Via Toretta, turn right onto Via Toretta from P. Grande. (☎751 45 54. Breakfast and sheets included for doubles, otherwise 4.50SFr each. Bike rental 15SFr per day. Check-in 1-6pm; reservations 1-9pm; call ahead if arriving after 6pm. Dorms 22-33SFr; doubles 64-74SFr; triples 31-34SFr; quads 29-33SFr.) At **Ristorante Debarcadero,** on Largo Zorzi by the ferry dock, a young crowd enjoys pizza (10.50-18SFr), beer (tap 3.60SFr, bottled 5-6SFr), and pop music hits. (Open 8:30am-midnight.) **Ristorante Manor,** 1 Via della Stazione, left of the station, provides quality food in a cafeteria-style environment. (Open M-Sa 7:30am-9pm, Su 8am-9pm; Mar.-Oct open until 10pm.) For **groceries,** there's an **Aperto** at the station (open 6am-10pm) and a **Migros supermarket** on P. Grande (open M-Sa 9am-7pm). **Postal code:** CH-6900.

HEADING EAST: PRAGUE AND BUDAPEST

During the Cold War, "Eastern Europe" was a name imposed by Westerners on the Soviet satellites east of the Berlin Wall. It has always been somewhat of a misnomer, capturing a political rather than geographical reality: Vienna lies farther east than Prague, Croatia sits on the Mediterranean, and most of Russia is, in fact, in Asia. But Eastern Europe is not merely a Western construction. The region is united by what it longs to leave behind—an arduous history of political upheaval and disillusionment—and by what it now confronts—a more optimistic but similarly uncertain future. To understand the remarkable complexity of Eastern Europe is to imagine a map of the region a little over a decade ago: in 1989, there were a total of seven countries behind the Iron Curtain; today, that same area is comprised of 19 independent states. In that time, the region has undergone an astounding political and cultural transformation. While communism has fallen throughout Europe and the Soviet Union no longer exists, Eastern Europe continues to be defined by its historical legacy.

Recently, Eastern Europe has become the darling of budget travelers. Undiscovered cities, pristine national parks, open hostel beds, and ridiculously cheap beer steadily lure backpackers seeking bargains and adventure. In particular, Prague and Budapest have exploded onto the scene as destinations rivalling the great capitals of Western Europe. If Eastern Europe intrigues you further, pick up a copy of *Let's Go Eastern Europe 2002* or *Let's Go Europe 2002*.

ESSENTIALS

DOCUMENTS AND FORMALITIES

VISAS

Americans may visit the **Czech Republic** visa-free for up to 30 days, Irish and New Zealand citizens for up to 90 days, and UK citizens for up to 180 days. Australians Canadians and South Africans must obtain 30-day **tourist visas.** Citizens of Canada, Ireland, South Africa, the UK, and the US can visit **Hungary** without visas for 90 days, provided their passport does not expire within six months of their journey's end. Australians and New Zealanders must obtain 90-day **tourist visas** from a Hungarian embassy or consulate. In most cases, you must to send a completed visa application (obtained from the embassy or consulate), the required fee, and your passport.

EMBASSIES AND CONSULATES

Czech Embassies at Home: Australia, 8 Culgoa Circuit, O'Malley, Canberra, ACT 2606 (☎02 6290 1386; fax 6290 0006; canberra@embassy.mzv.cz). **Canada,** 541 Sussex Dr., Ottawa, ON K1N 6Z6 (☎613-562-3875; fax 562-3878; ottowa@embassy.mzv.cz); **Ireland,** 57 Northumberland Rd., Ballsbridge, Dublin 4 (☎01 668 1135; fax 668 1660; dublin@embassy.mzv.cz). **New Zealand** (Honorary Consulate), 48 Hair St., Wainuiomata, Wellington (☎/fax 04 564 6001). **South Africa,** 936 Pretorius St., Arcadia 0083, PRETORIA; P.O. Box 3326, PRETORIA 0001 (☎012 342 3477; fax 430 2033; pretoria@embassy.mzv.cz; www.icon.co.za/czmzv). **UK,** 26 Kensington Palace

Gardens, London W8 4QY (☎020 7243 1115; fax 7727 9654; london@embassy.mzv.cz). **US,** 3900 Spring of Freedom St. NW, Washington, D.C. 20008 (☎202-274-9121; fax 363 6308; www.mzv.cz/washington).

Hungarian Embassies at Home: Australia (consulate), Ste. 405, Edgecliff Centre 203-233, New South Head Rd., Edgecliff, NSW 2027 (☎02 9328 7859; fax 9327 1829). **Canada,** 299 Waverley St., Ottawa, ON K2P 0V9 (☎613-230-2717; fax 230-7560; h2embott@docuweb.ca; www.docuweb.ca/Hungary). **Ireland,** 2 Fitzwilliam Pl., Dublin 2 (☎(01) 661 2903; fax 661 2880). **South Africa,** 959 Arcadia St., Hatfield, ARCADIA; P.O. Box 27077, SUNNYSIDE 0132 (☎012 430 3020; fax 430 3029; hunem@cis.co.za). **New Zealand,** 151 Orangi Kaupapa Rd., Wellington, 6005 (☎644 938 0427; fax 938 0428; sztmay@attglobal.net; www.geocities.com/CapitolHill/Lobby/1958/ContentsEn.htm). **UK,** 35 Eaton Pl., London SW1X 8BY (☎020 7235 5218; fax 7823 1348; www.huemblon.org.uk). **US,** 3910 Shoemaker St. NW, Washington, D.C. 20008 (☎202-362-6730; fax 966-8135; office@huembwas.org; www.hungaryemb.org).

PRAGUE (PRAHA)   ☎02

US$1 = 37KČ (KORUNA)	**10KČ = US$0.27**
CDN$1 = 24KČ	**10KČ = CDN$0.41**
UK£1 = 54KČ	**10KČ = UK£0.19**
IR£1 = 43KČ	**10KČ = IR£0.23**
AUS$1 = 20KČ	**10KČ = AUS$0.50**
NZ$1 = 16KČ	**10KČ = NZ$0.61**
ZAR1 = 4.5KČ	**10KČ = ZAR0.22**
DM1 = 17KČ	**10KČ = DM0.57**
EUR€1 = 34KČ	**10KČ = EUR€0.29**

According to legend, Countess Libuše stood above the Vltava and declared, "I see a city whose glory will touch the stars." Medieval kings, benefactors, and architects fulfilled the prophecy, building soaring cathedrals and lavish palaces that reflected Prague's status as capital of the Holy Roman Empire. Yet legends of demons, occult forces, and a maze of alleys lent this "city of dreams" a dark side that inspired Franz Kafka's tales of paranoia. Since the fall of the Iron Curtain, hordes of foreigners have flooded the city. In summer, tourists pack streets so tightly that crowd-surfing seems a viable way to travel; sometimes the only way off the Charles Bridge is to jump. Yet walk a few blocks from any of the major sights and you'll be lost among cobblestone alleys and looming churches; head to an outlying metro stop and you'll find haggling *babičky*, supermodel-esque natives, and not a backpack in sight.

>
>
> Prague continues to reform its phone system. Businesses often receive no more than 3 weeks' notice before their numbers change. The 4- to 8-digit numbers provided in these listings probably won't change by the time you read this—but things do change fast.

▐ TRANSPORTATION

Flights: Ruzyně Airport (☎20 11 33 21), 20km northwest of the city. Take bus #119 to Metro A: Dejvická (daily 5am-midnight; 12Kč; luggage 6Kč); buy tickets from kiosks or machines. Late at night, take night tram #51 to "Divoká Šárka," then take a night bus #510 to the center. **Airport buses** (☎20 11 42 96) go every 30min. from outside Metro stops at Nám. Republiky (90Kč) and Dejvická (60Kč).

Trains: (☎24 22 42 00; international 24 61 52 49; www.cdrail.cz). Prague has 4 terminals. **Hlavní station** (☎24 22 42 00; Metro C: Hlavní nádraží) is the largest. **BIJ Wasteels** (☎24 22 18 72; fax 24 61 74 54; www.wasteels.cz), 2nd fl., to the right of the stairs, sells discount international tickets to those under 26, books *couchettes,* and sells bus tickets. Open in summer M-F 7:30am-8pm, Sa 8-11:30am and 12:30-3pm;

off season M-F 8:30am-6pm. International service from **Holešovice station:** (☎24 61 72 65; Metro C: Nádraží Holešovice). Buy BIJ Wasteels and regular train tickets from the **Czech Railways Travel Agency** (☎24 23 94 64). Open M-F 9am-5pm, Sa-Su 8am-4pm. To: **Berlin** (5hr., 5 per day, 1400Kč); **Bratislava** (5½hr., 7 per day, 400Kč); **Budapest** (10hr., 5 per day, 1300Kč); **Munich** (6hr., 3 per day, 1700Kč); **Vienna** (4½hr., 3 per day, 750Kč). **Masarykovo station,** ☎24 61 72 60. Metro B: Nám. Republiky. **Smíchov station** ☎24 61 72 55. Metro B: Smíchovské nádraží. Opposite Vyšehrad.

Buses: (Info ☎1034 daily 6am-9pm; www.jiznirday.cz). The biggest station is **Florenc,** Křižíkova 4 (☎129 99; Metro B or C: Florenc). Buy tickets in advance. To: **Berlin** (8hr., 1 per day, 850Kč) and **Vienna** (8½hr., 1 per day, 870Kč). Students may get 10% discount. The **Tourbus** office upstairs (☎24 21 02 21; www.eurolines.cz) sells tickets for Eurolines and airport buses. Open M-F 8am-8pm, Sa-Su 9am-8pm.

Public Transportation: Buy tickets for the **metro, tram,** or **bus** from newsstands and *tabák* kiosks, machines in stations, or **DP** (Dopravní podnik; transport authority) kiosks. The basic 8Kč ticket is good for 15min. (or 4 stops on the metro); 12Kč is valid for 1hr. (8pm-5am 1½hr.), with unlimited connections on the entire network in any 1 direction. Large bags and bikes require an extra 6Kč ticket. The **Metro**'s 3 lines run daily 5am-midnight: **A** is green on the maps, **B** yellow, **C** red. **Night trams** (#51-58) and **night buses** run all night after the last Metro and can be picked up at the Charles Bridge; look for the dark-blue signs at bus stops.

Taxis: RadioTaxi (☎24 91 66 66) or **AAA** (☎10 80 or 312 21 12). Both open 24hr. Taxi drivers are notorious scam artists. Check that the meter is set to zero, and ask the driver to start it *("Zapněte taximetr")*. Always ask for a receipt *("Prosím, dejte mi paragon")* with distance traveled and price paid. If the driver doesn't write the receipt or set the meter to zero, you aren't obligated to pay. Set rate 30Kč, plus 22Kč per km.

✦ 🛈 ORIENTATION AND PRACTICAL INFORMATION

Straddling the river **Vltava,** Prague is a gigantic mess of suburbs and labyrinthine medieval streets. Fortunately, nearly everything of interest lies within the compact, walkable downtown. The river Vltava runs south-northeast through central Prague and separates the **Staré Město** (Old Town) and the **Nové Město** (New Town) from **Malá Strana** (Lesser Town). On the right bank of the river, **Staroměstské náměstí** (Old Town Square) is the focal point of the city. From the square, the elegant **Pařížská ulice** (Paris Street) leads north into **Josefov,** the old Jewish ghetto; unfortunately, all that remains are six synagogues and the Old Jewish Cemetery. In the opposite direction from Pařížská lies **Nové Město.** It houses **Václavské náměstí** (Wenceslas Square), the administrative and commercial heart of the city. West of Staroměstské nám., **Karlův most** (Charles Bridge) traverses the Vltava and connects the Old Town with **Malostranské náměstí** (Lesser Town Square). **Pražský Hrad** (Prague Castle) sits on the **Hradčany** hilltop above Malostranské nám.

Prague's main train station, Hlavní nádraží, and Florenc bus station sit in the northeastern corner of Václavské nám. All train and bus terminals are on or near the excellent metro system. To get to Staroměstské nám., take the Metro A line to Staroměstská and walk down Kaprova away from the river. *Tabák* stands and bookstores sell the indexed *plán města* (map); this, along with the English-language weekly *The Prague Post*, is essential for visitors.

TOURIST, FINANCIAL, AND LOCAL SERVICES

Tourist Offices: Green "i"s mark tourist info. **Pražská Informační Služba** (Prague Info Service), in the Old Town Hall (English §54 44 44). **Branches** at Na příkopě 20, Hlavní nádraží, and in the tower on the Malá Strana side of the Charles Bridge. All open in summer M-F 9am-7pm, Sa-Su 9am-6pm; off-season M-F 9am-6pm, Sa-Su 9am-5pm.

Budget Travel: CKM, Manesova 77 (☎22 72 15 95; www.ckm-praha.cz). Metro A or B: Jiriho z Podebrad. Budget flights for those under 26. Lodgings from 260Kč. Open M-Th 10am-6pm, F 10am-4pm.

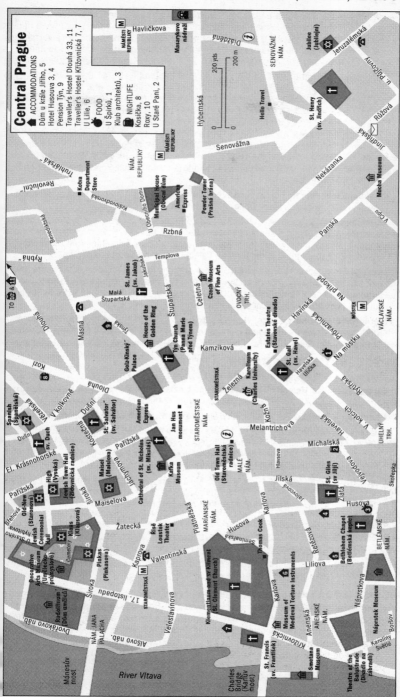

Central Prague

▲ ACCOMMODATIONS
Dům u krále Jiřího, 5
Hotel Husova 3, 4
Pension Týn, 9
Traveller's Hostel Dlouhá 33, 11
Traveller's Hostel Křižovnická 7, 7
U Lilie, 6

● FOOD
U Spirků, 1
Klub architektů, 3

♦ NIGHTLIFE
Kosička, 8
Roxy, 10
U Staré Paní, 2

200 yds
200 m

Passport Office: Foreigner police headquarters at Olšanská 2 (☎683 17 39). Metro A: Flora. From the Metro, turn right onto Jičínská with the cemetery on your right, and turn right again onto Olšanská. Or take tram #9 from Václavské nám. toward Spojovací and get off at Olšanská. For a **visa extension**, get a 90Kč stamp inside. Open M-Tu and Th 7:30-11:30am and 12:30-2:30pm, W 7:30-11:30am and 12:30-5pm, F 7:30am-noon.

Embassies: Australia (☎24 31 00 71) and **New Zealand** (☎25 41 98) have consuls, but citizens should contact the UK embassy in an emergency. **Canada**, Mickiewiczova 6 (☎72 10 18 00). Metro A: Hradčanská. Open M-F 8:30am-12:30pm. **Hungary**, Badeniho 1 (☎33 32 44 54). Metro A: Hradčanská. Open M-W and F 9am-noon. **Ireland**, Tržiště 13 (☎57 53 00 61). Metro A: Malostranská. Open M-F 9:30am-12:30pm and 2:30-4:30pm. **South Africa**, Ruská 65 (☎67 31 11 14). Metro A: Flora. Open M-F 9am-noon. **UK**, Thunovská 14 (☎57 53 02 78). Metro A: Malostranská. Open M-F 9am-noon. **US**, Tržiště 15 (☎57 53 06 63; emergency after-hours ☎53 12 00). Metro A: Malostranská. From Malostranské nám., head down Karmelitská and take a right onto Tržiště. Open M-F 9am-4pm.

Currency Exchange: Komerční banka, Na příkopě 33 (☎24 43 21 11), buys notes and checks for a 2% commission. Open M-F 8am-5pm.

American Express: Václavské nám. 56, 113 26 Praha 1 (☎22 80 02 37). Metro A or C: Muzeum. **ATM** outside takes AmEx cards. Cashes AmEx checks commission-free and grants V/MC cash advances for a 3% commission. Open daily 9am-7pm. **Branches:** Mostecká 12 (near the Charles Bridge), Celetná 17, and Staroměstské nám. 5.

Luggage Storage: Lockers in all train and bus stations take 2 5Kč coins. If these are full, or if you need to store your cargo longer than 24hr., use the luggage offices to the left in the basement of **Hlavní nádraží** (15-30Kč per day; open 24hr.) and halfway up the stairs at **Florenc** (10-25Kč per day; open daily 5am-11pm).

Laundromat: Laundry Kings, Dejvická 16 (☎312 37 43), 1 block from Metro A: Hradčanská. Cross the tram and railroad tracks, and turn left. Wash 60Kč per 6kg, dry 15Kč per 8min. Soap 10-20Kč. Beer 15Kč. Open M-F 6am-10pm, Sa-Su 8am-10pm.

EMERGENCY AND COMMUNICATIONS

Fire, ☎150. **Ambulance,** ☎155. **Police,** ☎158.

Emergencies: Na Homolce (Hospital for Foreigners), Roentgenova 2 (☎57 27 21 46; after-hours ☎57 77 20 25). Open M-F 8am-4pm. 24hr. emergency service.

Pharmacy: U Anděla, Štefánikova 6 (☎57 32 09 18). Metro B: Anděl. Open 24hr.

Internet Access: Bohemia Bagel, Masna 2 (☎24 81 25 60; www.bohemiabagel.cz). 1.50Kč per min. Open M-F 7am-midnight, Sa-Su 8am-midnight. **Cafe Electra,** Rašínovo nábřeží 62 (☎297 038). Metro B: Karlovo nám. Exit on the Palackého nám. side. 80Kč per hr. Open M-F 9am-midnight, Sa-Su 11am-midnight.

Post Office: Jindřišská 14. Metro A or B: Můstek (☎21 13 15 20). Airmail to the US takes 7 days. Open daily 7am-8pm. Address mail to be held: FirstName SURNAME, POSTE RESTANTE, Jindřišská 14, **110 00 Praha 1,** Czech Republic.

▮ ACCOMMODATIONS

The hostel market is glutted and prices have stabilized around 270-420Kč per night. Most accommodations have 24hr. reception, and require check-in after 2pm, and check-out by 10am.

ACCOMMODATIONS AGENCIES

The going rate for apartments hovers around 600-1200Kč per night, depending on proximity to the city center. Instead of haggling, try a private agency. Ask where the nearest tram, bus, or metro stop is, and get details in writing. **Ave.,** Hlavní nádraží, 2nd fl. of the station, offers rooms from 800Kč and books hostels from 290Kč. (☎24 22 352 26. Open daily 6am-11pm.) **Hello Travel Ltd.,** Senovážné nám. 3, also arranges housing. Metro B: Nám Republiky. (☎24 21 26 47; hello@hello.cz. 500-1500Kč per person in summer, 400-1200Kč off-season. Open M-F 8am-7pm.)

HOSTELS

If you're schlepping a backpack in Hlavní nádraží or Holešovice, you *will* be bombarded by hostel runners trying to coerce you back to their hostels, which is often a university dorm that frees up from June to August; often you'll be offered transport to the room. It's best to phone the night before you arrive or at 10am when they know who's checking out in order to snag a bed.

■ **Hostel Boathouse,** Lodnická (☎/fax 402 10 76), south of the city center. From Hlavní nádraží, Karlovo nám., Staré Město, or the Charles Bridge, take tram #3 south toward Sídliště and get off at "Černý Kůň" (20min.). From Holešovice, take tram #17. From the tram stop, follow the yellow signs down to the Vltava. As Věra the owner says, "This isn't a hostel, it's a crazy house." Summer-camp vibe. Dorms 300-320Kč.

■ **Penzion v podzámčí,** V podzámčí 27 (☎/fax 41 44 46 09; evacibşyahoo.com), south of the city center. From Metro C: Budějovická, take bus #192 to the 3rd stop ("Nad Rybníky"). The homiest hostel in Prague. Kitchen. Incredible laundry. Dorms 280Kč; doubles 640Kč; triples 900Kč.

Domov Mládeže, Dykova 20 (☎/fax 22 51 17 77; jana.dyrsmidova@telecom.cz), in Vinohrady. Metro A: Jiřího z Poděbrad. Follow Nitranská and turn left on Dykova; it's 2 blocks down on the right. So peaceful you might forget you're in Prague. Breakfast included. Dorms 350Kč; doubles 400Kč. Sister hostels: **Amadeus,** Slavojova 108/8. Metro C: Vyšehrad; descend the bridge to Čiklova, turn left, and it's on the left. **Máchova,** Máchova 11. Metro A: Nám. Míru; walk down Ruská and turn right on Máchova. **Košická,** Košická 12. Metro A: Nám. Míru. All hostels have the same phone number and prices.

Hostel U Melounu (At the Watermelon), Ke Karlovu 7 (☎/fax 24 91 83 22; pus.praha@worldline.cz; www.hostelumelonu.cz), in Nové Město. Metro C: I.P. Pavlova; follow Sokolská to Na Bojišti and turn left at the street's end onto Ke Karlovu. A historic building with great facilities. Breakfast included. Reservations accepted. Dorms 380Kč; singles 450Kč; doubles 840Kč. 100Kč ISIC discount.

Traveller's Hostels, in Staré Město (☎24 82 66 62; fax 24 82 66 65; hostel@travellers.cz; www.travellers.cz). These summertime big-dorm specialists round up travelers at bus and train stations and herd them into 1 of their central hostels for lots of beds and beer. Breakfast included. **Internet** 27Kč per 15min.

Dlouhá 33 (☎24 82 66 62; fax 24 82 66 65). Metro B: Nám Republiky. Follow Revoluční toward the river, turn left on Dlouhá. Unbeatable location; in the same building as the Roxy, but soundproof. Dorms 370-400Kč; doubles 580Kč; triples 450Kč. Open year-round.

Husova 3 (☎22 22 00 78). Metro B: Národní tlída; turn right on Spálená (which becomes Na Perštýně after Národní), then again on Husova. Dorms 400Kč. Open July-Aug.

Kížovnická 7 (☎232 09 87). Metro A: Staroměstská. Dorms 250Kč. Open July-Aug.

Stlelecký ostrov (☎24 91 01 88), on an island off Most Legií. Metro B: Národní tlída. Dorms 300Kč. Open mid-June to mid-Sept.

Růžová 5 (☎24 21 67 71). Metro C: Hlavní nádraží. Dorms 270Kč. Open mid-June to mid-Sept.

Pension Týn, Týnská 19 (☎/fax 24 80 83 33; backpacker@razdva.cz), near the Staré Město. Metro A: Staroměstská. From Old Town Square, head down Dlouhá, then bear right at Masná and right onto Týnská. A quiet getaway located right in the center of Staré Město. Immaculate facilities. Dorms 400Kč; doubles 1100Kč. 30Kč ISIC discount.

Welcome Hostel at Strahov Complex, Vaníčkova 5 (☎33 35 92 75). Take bus #217 or 143 from Metro A: Dejvická to Koleje Strahov. Known as a "hostel ghetto," Strahov is 10 concrete blocks of high-rise dorms next to the stadium. A little far, but there's always space, and free beer at check-in. Singles 300Kč; doubles 240Kč. ISIC 10% discount.

HOTELS AND PENSIONS

Budget hotels are now scarce. Beware of those that may try to bill you for a more expensive room than the one in which you stayed. Some cheap establishments require reservations up to a month in advance, but many refuse them altogether. Call first, then confirm by fax with a credit card.

B&B U Oty (Ota's House), Radlická 188 (]/fax 57 21 53 23; mb@bbuoty.cz; www.bbuoty.cz), west of the center. Metro B: Radlická. Exit the Metro up the stairs to the left and go right 400m up the road. Charming, English-speaking Ota will make your stay a pleasure. Kitchen. Laundry. Singles 700Kč; doubles 770Kč; triples 990Kč; quads 1250Kč. 1-night surcharge 100Kč.

Pension Unitas/Cloister Inn, Bartolomějská 9 (☎232 77 00; fax 232 77 09; cloister@cloister-inn.cz), in Staré Město. Metro B: Národní třída. Cross Národní, head up Na Perštýně away from Tesco, and turn left on Bartolomějská. Renovated rooms in the cells of a former prison where Václav Havel was incarcerated. Breakfast included. Singles 1020Kč; doubles 1200Kč; triples 1650Kč.

Dům U krále Jiřího, Liliová 10 (☎22 22 09 25; fax 22 22 17 07; kinggeorge@kinggeorge.cz; www.kinggeorge.cz), in Staré Město. Metro A: Staroměstská. Exit onto Nám. Jana Palacha, walk down Křížovnická toward the Charles Bridge, turn left onto Karlova, and Liliová is the first right. Gorgeous rooms with private baths. Buffet breakfast included. Singles 1500-1790Kč; doubles 2700-3050Kč.

U Lilie, Liliová 15 (☎22 22 04 32; fax 22 22 06 41; pensionulilie@centrum.cz), in Staré Město. Metro A: Staroměstská. Follow directions to U krále Jiřího (above). TV. Breakfast included. Singles with shower 1800Kč; doubles 2000-2850Kč.

CAMPING

Campsites have taken over both the city outskirts and the centrally located Vltava islands. Bungalows must be reserved in advance, but tent space is generally available without prior notice. Tourist offices sell a guide to sites near the city (15Kč).

Císařská louka, on a peninsula on the Vltava. Metro B: Smíchovské nádraží. Take any bus numbered in the 300s to Lihovar, go toward the river and take a left on the path. Or, take the ferry 1 street over from Smíchovské nádraží. **Caravan Park** (☎57 31 86 81) is near the ferry. 95Kč per person; 90-140Kč per tent. 2-bed bungalows 480Kč, 4-bed 720Kč.

Sokol Troja, Trojská 171 (☎/fax 83 85 04 86), north of the center in the Troja district. Metro C: Nádraží Holešovice. Take bus #112 to Kazanka. Similar places line the road. 130Kč per person; 90-180Kč per tent. Dorms 270Kč; bungalows 230Kč per person.

☕ FOOD

The basic rule is that the nearer you are to the downtown the more you'll pay; away from the center, you can get traditional Czech fare such as pork, cabbage, dumplings, and a half-liter of beer, all for 50Kč. Check your bill carefully; you'll pay for everything the waiter brings to the table. Outlying Metro stops become markets in the summer. **Tesco,** Národní třída 26, has **groceries** next to Metro B: Národní třída. (Open M-F 7am-8pm, Sa 8am-7pm, Su 9am-7pm.) Look for the **daily market** at the intersection of Havelská and Melantrichova in Staré Město.

☒ U Špirků, Kožná ulička 12, in Staré Město. Metro A: Staroměstská. With your back to the astronomical clock on Staroměstské nám. go through the arch down Melantrichova, and take the first left onto Kožná. Some of the city's best and cheapest food in a spacious pub. Main dishes about 100Kč. Open daily 11am-midnight.

☒ Velryba (The Whale), Opatovická 24, in Nové Město. Metro B: Národní třída. Exit to the left, then turn right onto Ostrovní, and left onto Opatovická. Relaxed cafe-restaurant with a gallery in back. International and Czech dishes (38-155Kč), and veggie platters. Open M-Th and Sa-Su 11am-midnight, F 11am-2am.

☒ Bar bar, Všehrdova 17, in Malá Strana. Metro A: Malostranská; follow the tram tracks down Letenská Malostranské nám.; turn left on Všehrdova after the museum. Good vibe, good music, and 40 varieties of whiskey (from 55Kč). Open daily noon-midnight.

Universal, V jirchářích 6 (☎24 91 81 82), in Nové Město. Metro B: Národní třída; turn left onto Spálená and right on Myslíkova, then right on Křemencova. A transplanted California-style eatery with huge, fresh salads (115-165Kč). Open daily 11:30am-1am.

Klub architektů, Betlémské nám. 52, in Staré Město. Metro B: Národní třída. Exit station to the right, keep walking, and take a left. A 12th-century cellar thrust into the 20th century. Veggie options 80-90Kč; meat dishes 120-150Kč. Open daily 11:30am-11pm.

Lotos, Platnéřská 13, in Staré Město. Metro A: Staroměstská; go left down Valentinská and turn right on Platnélská. Vegetarian Czech restaurant with organic menu (68-152Kč). 0.5L wheat-yeast Pilsner 30Kč. Open daily 11am-10pm.

LATE-NIGHT EATING

4:45am. Charles Bridge. Lávka's house disco beat is still pumping ferociously, but all you can hear is your stomach growling. Don't go home hungry—grab a *párek v rohlíku* (hot dog) or a *smažený sýr* (fried cheese sandwich) from a vendor on Václavské nám., or a gyros from a stand on Spálená or Vodičkova. **Radost FX,** Bělehradská 120, is a late-night veggie cafe. (Metro C: I.P. Pavlova. Open Su-Th 11am-late, F-Sa 11am-later.) **Iron Door,** Michalská 13., provides trendy atmosphere and an international menu. (Kitchen open daily until 3am.)

⬛ CAFES

When Prague journalists are bored, they churn out yet another "Whatever happened to cafe life?" feature. The answer: it turned into *čajovna* (teahouse) culture.

▨ U malého Glena, Karmelitská 23. Metro A: Malostranská. Take tram #12 to Malostranské nám. Their motto is: "Eat, Drink, Drink Some More." Killer margaritas 80Kč. Nightly jazz or blues 9pm. Cover 60-120Kč. Open daily 10am-2am, Su brunch 10am-3pm.

Kavarná Imperial, Na Poříčí 15. Metro B: Nám. Republiky. Pillars and mosaic tiles make this place feel refined. Live jazz F-Sa 9pm. Open Su-Th 9am-midnight, F-Sa 9am-1am.

Propaganda, Pštrossova 29. Metro B: Národní třída. Comfy low-slung chairs and sunny yellow interior with a cheap Budvar (25Kč) and espresso (19Kč). Open daily 3pm-2am.

Dobrá Čajovna U Čajovníka (Good Tearoom), Boršov 2. Metro A: Staroměstská; follow Křížovnická past the Charles Bridge and bear left onto Karoliny Světlé; Boršov is a tiny street on the left. 90 teas (12-150Kč). Open M-Sa 10am-midnight, Su noon-midnight.

Jazz Café 14, Opatovická 14. Metro B: Národní třída. Around the corner from Velryba on Opatovická. Usually filled with smoke and 20-somethings. Coffee (14Kč) and snacks (30Kč). Open daily noon-11pm.

⬤ SIGHTS

The only Central European city left entirely unscathed by either natural disaster or WWII, Prague is a well-preserved combination of medieval alleys and Baroque buildings. Central Prague is best explored on foot. Don't leave without wandering the back alleys of **Josefov,** exploring the hills of **Vyšehrad,** and getting lost in the maze of **Malá Strana**'s streets.

NEW TOWN (NOVÉ MĚSTO)

Established in 1348 by Charles IV, Nové Město is not exactly new. Its age, however, is not readily apparent; its wide boulevards and sprawling squares seem hundreds of years ahead of their time.

WENCESLAS SQUARE (VÁCLAVSKÉ NÁMĚSTÍ). Not so much a square as a broad boulevard running through the center of Nové Město, Wenceslas Square owes its name to the Czech ruler and saint **Wenceslas** (Václav), whose statue sits in front of the **National Museum** (Národní muzeum). At the northern end of Wenceslas Square, near the Můstek Metro station, Art Nouveau design is expressed in everything from lampposts to windowsills. The glass **Radio Prague Building,** behind the National Museum, was the scene of a battle during the Prague Spring, as citizens tried to protect the radio studios from Soviet tanks with a human barricade. *(Metro A or C: Muzeum.)*

FRANCISCAN GARDENS AND VELVET REVOLUTION MEMORIAL. No ine is sure how the monks manage to preserve the serene **rose garden** (Františkánská zahrada) in the heart of Prague's bustling commercial district. *(Metro A or B: Můstek; Metro B: Národní třída. Enter through the arch at Jungmannova and Národní. Open mid-Apr. to mid-Sept. daily 7am-10pm; mid-Sept. to mid-Oct. 8am-8pm; mid-Oct. to mid-Apr. 8am-7pm. Free.)* Under the arcades halfway down Národní třída stands a memorial to the hundreds of Prague's citizens beaten on November 17, 1989 during the Velvet Revolution.

THE DANCING HOUSE. Built by American architect Frank Gehry of Guggenheim-Bilbao fame (see p. 887), the undulating building at the corner of Resslova and Rašínovo nábřeží is called "Fred and Ginger" by Anglophones and "The Dancing House" (Taneční dům) by Czechs. *(Metro B: Karlovo nám.)*

OLD TOWN (STARÉ MĚSTO)

The narrow roads and Old World alleys of the Staré Město make it easy to get lost. But that's the best way to appreciate this 1000-year-old neighborhood's charm.

CHARLES BRIDGE (KARLŮV MOST). Thronged with tourists and the hawkers who prey on them, this bridge is Prague's most recognizable landmark. Five years ago, the bridge's vendors peddled Red Army gear and black market currency deals; today, they sell watercolors of the bridge and other junk. The statue of St. Jan Nepomucký marks the spot where the saint was tossed over the side of the bridge for guarding the queen's extramarital secrets from a suspicious King Wenceslas IV.

OLD TOWN SQUARE (STAROMĚSTSKÉ NÁMĚSTÍ). The heart of Staré Město is Old Town Square, surrounded by no fewer than eight magnificent towers. Next to the grassy knoll, **Old Town Hall** (Staroměstská radnice) is the multi-façaded building with a bit blown off the front. The building was partially demolished by the Nazis in the final week of WWII, receiving Prague's only visible damage from the war. *(Open in summer daily 9am-5:30pm. 30Kč, students 20Kč.)* Crowds gather on the hour to watch the wonderful **astronomical clock** *(orloj)* chime with its procession of apostles and a skeleton representing Death. *(Metro A: Staroměstská; Metro A or B: Můstek. Clock animated until 9pm.)* The Czech Republic's most famous martyred theologian, **Jan Hus,** hovers over Old Town Square in bronze effigy. Opposite the Old Town Hall, the spires of **Týn Church** (Matka Boží před Týnem) rise above a mass of medieval homes. The famous astronomer Tycho de Brahe is buried inside—he overindulged at one of Emperor Rudolf's lavish dinner parties, where it was unacceptable to leave the table unless the Emperor himself did so. When poor Tycho de Brahe needed to go, he was forced to stay seated, and his bladder burst.

GOLTZ-KINSKÝ PALACE. The flowery 14th-century Goltz-Kinský Palace is the finest of Prague's Rococo buildings. It is also the official birthplace of Soviet communism in the Czech Republic: on February 21, 1948, Klement Gottwald declared communism victorious from its balcony. *(On Staroměstské nám. at the corner of Dlouhá, next to Týn Church. Open Tu-F 10am-5pm; closes early in summer for daily concerts.)*

POWDER TOWER (PRAŠNÁ BRÁNA). The gothic Powder Tower looms at the edge of Nám. Republiky as the entrance to Staré Město. Of the eight original city gates, this is the only one that remains. After its stint as royal fortification, it was used primarily for gunpowder storage. A small history exhibit is inside, but forego it for a climb to the top. *(Metro B: Nám. Republiky. Open Apr.-Sept. daily 10am-6pm.)*.

JOSEFOV

Metro A: Staroměstská. ☎ 231 71 91. Synagogues and museum open Su-F 9am-6pm. Closed for Jewish holidays. All sights except New Synagogue 490Kč, students 340Kč. New Synagogue 200Kč, students 140Kč. Museum only 290Kč, students 200Kč.

Prague's historic Jewish neighborhood and the oldest Jewish settlement in Europe, Josefov lies north of Starométstské nám., along Maiselova and several sidestreets. In 1180, Prague's citizens built a 3½m wall around the area. The closed city bred legends, many focusing on **Rabbi Loew ben Bezalel** (1512-1609) and his legendary golem—a mud creature that supposedly came to life to protect Prague's Jews. For the next 500 years, the city's Jews were exiled to this cramped ghetto.

THE SYNAGOGUES. The **Maisel Synagogue** (Maiselova synagoga) has artifacts from the extensive collections of the Jewish Museum. *(On Maiselova, between Široká and Jáchymova.)* Turn left down Široká to reach the 16th-century **Pinkas Synagogue** (Pinkasova synagoga), converted in 1958 into a sobering memorial to the 80,000 Czech Jews killed in the Holocaust. Upstairs is an exhibit of drawings made by children in the Terezín camp, most of whom died in Auschwitz. Backtrack up Široká and go left on Maiselova to see the oldest operating synagogue in Europe, the 700-year-old **Old-New Synagogue** (Staronová synagoga). Further up Široká on Dušní is the ornate Moorish interior of the **Spanish Synagogue** (Španělská synagoga).

OLD JEWISH CEMETERY AND CEREMONY HALL. The **Old Jewish Cemetery** (Starý židovský hřbitov) remains Josefov's most popular attraction. Between the 14th and 18th centuries, 20,000 graves were laid in 12 layers. Rabbi Loew is buried by the wall directly opposite the entrance. *(At the corner of Široká and Žatecká.)* Originally a ceremonial hall for the Jewish Burial Society, **Ceremony Hall** (Obřadní dům) now houses exhibits devoted to the themes of illness and death in the ghetto, Jewish cemeteries in Bohemia and Moravia, and the activities of the Prague Burial Society. *(On Červená, just off Maiselova.)*

MALÁ STRANA (LESSER TOWN)

The seedy hangout of criminals and counter-revolutionaries for nearly a century, the cobblestone streets of Malá Strana have become the most prized real estate on either side of the Vltava. Malá Strana is centered on **Malostranské náměstí** and its centerpiece, the Baroque **St. Nicholas' Cathedral** (Chrám sv. Mikuláš), with a towering dome that is one of Prague's most notable landmarks. *(Metro A: Malostranská; then follow Letenská to Malostranské nám. Open daily 9am-4pm. 45Kč, students 20Kč.)* Along Letenská, a wooden gate opens through a 10m wall into the beautiful **Wallenstein Garden** (Valdštejnská zahrada), one of Prague's best-kept secrets. *(Letenská 10. Metro A: Malostranská. Open daily 10am-6pm.)* Opposite the Malostranská metro station, a plaque hidden in a lawn constitutes the **Charousková Memorial,** the only monument to those slain in the 1968 Prague Spring. Unlike other churches in Prague, the modest **Church of Our Lady Victorious** (Kostel Panna Marie Vítězná) is not notable for its exterior but for the famous wax statue of the **Infant Jesus of Prague** inside, said to bestow miracles on the faithful. *(Metro A: Malostranská; then follow Letenská through Malostranské nám. and continue onto Karmelitská. Open M-F 9:45am-5:30pm, Sa 9:45am-8pm, Su open for mass. Free.)*

PRAGUE CASTLE (PRAŽSKÝ HRAD)

Metro A: Hradčanská. Open Apr.-Oct. daily 9am-5pm; Nov.-Mar. 9am-4pm. Buy tickets opposite St. Vitus' Cathedral. 3-day ticket valid at Royal Crypt, Cathedral and Powder Towers, Old Royal Palace, and Basilica of St. George. 120Kč, students 60Kč.

Prague Castle has been the seat of the Bohemian government since its founding 1000 years ago. From the metro, cross the tram tracks and turn left onto Tychonova, which leads to the newly renovated **Royal Summer Palace** (Královský letohrádek). The main castle entrance is at the other end of the **Royal Garden** (Královská zahrada), across the **Powder Bridge** (Prašný most). Before exploring, pass the main gate to see the **Šternberský Palace.**

ST. VITUS' CATHEDRAL (KATEDRÁLA SV. VÍTA). Inside the castle walls stands Prague Castle's centerpiece, the colossal St. Vitus' Cathedral, which may look Gothic but in fact was only finished in 1929—600 years after construction began. To the right of the high altar stands the **tomb of St. Jan Nepomucký,** 3m of solid, glistening silver weighing 1800kg. In the main church, the walls of **St. Wenceslas's Chapel** (Svatováclavská kaple) are lined with precious stones and a painting cycle depicting the legend of this saint. Climb the 287 steps of the **Cathedral Tower** for the best view of the city, or step downstairs to see the tomb of Charles IV.

OLD ROYAL PALACE (STARÝ KRÁLOVSKÝ PALÁC). The Old Royal Palace, to the right of the cathedral behind the Old Provost's House and the statue of St. George, houses the lengthy expanse of the **Vladislav Hall,** which once hosted jousting compe-

HEADING EAST

titions. Upstairs is the **Chancellery of Bohemia,** where on May 23, 1618, angry Protestants flung two Habsburg officials (and their secretary) out the window, triggering the bloody Thirty Years' War.

ST. GEORGE'S BASILICA (BAZILIKA SV. JIŘÍ) AND ENVIRONS. Behind the cathedral and across the courtyard from the Old Royal Palace stand the romanesque St. George's Basilica (Bazilika sv. Jiří) and its adjacent convent. The convent houses the **National Gallery of Bohemian Art,** with art ranging from Gothic to Baroque. *(Open Tu-Su 10am-6pm. 50Kč, students 20Kč.)* The Old Royal Palace street **Jiřská** begins to the right of the basilica. Halfway down, the tiny **Golden Lane** (Zlatá ulička) heads off to the right; alchemists once worked here, and Kafka later lived at #22. Back on Jiřská, after passing out of the Prague Castle between the two armed sentries, peer over the battlements on the right for a fine cityscape.

🏛 MUSEUMS

Prague's magnificence isn't best reflected in its museums, which often have striking façades but mediocre collections. But the city has many rainy days, and it has a few public museums that shelter interesting and quirky collections. **House of the Golden Ring** (Dům u zlatého prstenu), Týnská 6, behind Týn Church, houses an astounding collection of 20th-century Czech art. *(Metro A: Staroměstská. Open Tu-Su 10am-6pm. 140Kč, students 70Kč; 1st Tu of each month free.)* The **National Gallery** (Národní galerie) is spread around nine different locations; the notable **Šternberský palác** and **Klášter sv. Jiří** are in the Prague Castle. **St. Agnes's Cloister** (Klášter sv. Anežky) is the other major branch of the National Gallery, well worth seeing for its collection of 19th-century Czech art. St. Agnes's, however, is undergoing renovation, and its collection has been moved into the **Trade Fair Palace and the Gallery of Modern Art** (Veletržní palác a Galerie moderního umění), which generally displays 20th-century Czech art. *(Dukelskэch hrdinř 47. Metro C: Vltavsk6. Both open Tu-Su 10am-6pm. 150Kč, students 70Kč.)* The **Czech Museum of Fine Arts** (České muzeum výtvarných umění), Celetná 34, itself one of Prague's best examples of Cubist architecture, contains a comprehensive collection of Czech Cubism. *(Metro A: Nám. Republiky. Open Tu-Su 10am-6pm. 35Kč, students 15Kč)*

🎵 🎭 ENTERTAINMENT AND NIGHTLIFE

For concerts and performances, consult *The Prague Post, Threshold,* or *Do města-Downtown* (the latter two are free at many cafes and restaurants). Most performances start at 7pm and offer unsold tickets 30min. before showtime. Between mid-May and early June, the **Prague Spring Festival** draws musicians from around the world. For tickets try **Bohemia Ticket International,** Malé nám. 13, next to Čedok. (]24 22 78 32; www.ticketsbti.cz. Open M-F 9am-5pm, Sa 9am-2pm.) The **National Theater** (Národní divadlo), Národní třída 2/4, features drama, opera, and ballet. (]24 92 15 28. Metro B: Národní třída. Box office open M-F 10am-6pm, Sa-Su 10am-12:30pm and 3-6pm, and 30min. before performances.)

ABSINTHE-MINDED? Shrouded in Bohemian mystique, this translucent turquoise fire-water is a force to be reckoned with. Although absinthe has been banned in all but 3 countries this century due to allegations of opium-lacing and fatal hallucinations, Czechs have had a long love affair with the liquor. It has been the mainstay spirit of the Prague intelligentsia since Kafka's days, and during World War II every Czech adult was rationed 0.5L per month. Today's backpackers, who apparently will drink anything, have discovered the liquor, which at its strongest can be 160 proof. The bravest and most seasoned expats sip it on the rocks, but some douse a spoonful of sugar in the alcohol, torch it with a match until the sugar caramelizes and the alcohol burns off, and dump the residue into the glass.

NIGHTLIFE

The most authentic way to experience Prague at night is in an alcoholic fog. With some of the best beers in the world on tap, pubs and beerhalls are understandably the city's favorite form of nighttime entertainment. Prague is not a clubbing city; the city's many excellent jazz and rock clubs are more popular. Otherwise, you can always retreat to the Charles Bridge to sing along with aspiring Britpop guitarists into the wee hours. The monthly *Amigo* is the most thorough guide to gay life in the Czech Republic and Slovakia, with a lot of information in English. *Gayčko* is a glossier piece of work mostly in Czech.

U Fleků, Křemencova 11. Metro B: Národní třída. Turn right on Spálená away from Národní, right on Myslíkova, and head right on Křemencova. The oldest brewhouse in Prague. A steep 49Kč per 0.4L of home-brewed beer. Open daily 9am-11pm.

Roxy, Dlouhá 33. Metro B: Nám. Republiky. Walk up Revoluční toward the river and turn left on Dlouhá. People come here for experimental DJs, theme nights, and endless dancing. Cover 100-350Kč. Open July-Aug. daily 9pm-late; Sept.-June Tu-Su 9pm-late.

Kozička (The Little Goat), Kozí 1. Metro A: Staroměstské. Take Dlouhá from the northeast corner of the square, then left onto Kozí, and look for the iron goat. This giant cellar bar is always packed; you'll know why after your first 0.5L of *Krušovice* (25Kč). Czech 20-somethings stay all night. Open M-F noon-4am, Sa-Su 6pm-4am.

Vinárna U Sude, Vodičkova 10. Metro A or B: Můstek. Cross Václavské nám. to Vodičkova, follow the curve left, and it's on your left. Infinite labyrinth of cavernous cellars. Red wine 110Kč per 1L. Open M-F 11am-midnight, Sa-Su 2pm-midnight.

U střelce, Karolíny Světlé 12. Metro B: Národní třída. Under the archway on the right. Gay club that draws a diverse crowd for its F and Sa night cabarets. Cover 80Kč. Open Tu and Th 9pm-midnight; W, F, Sa 9:30pm-5am with shows after midnight.

Újezd, Újezd 18. Metro B: Národní třída. Exit onto Národní, turn left toward the river, cross the Legií bridge, continue straight on Vítězná, and turn right on Újezd. Mellow DJ or live acid jazz 3 times a week. Beer 22Kč. Open daily 11am-4am.

U staré paní, Michalská 9. Metro A or B: Můstek. Walk down Na můstku at the end of Václavské nám., continue on Melantrichova, turn left on Havelská, then right on Michalská. Some of Prague's finest jazz vocalists in a dark and classy venue. Shows nightly 9pm-midnight. Cover 160Kč, includes 1 drink. Open for shows 7pm-1am.

U malého Glena II, Karmelitská 23 (☎535 81 15). This small bar hosts bouncy jazz, blues, and funk nightly at 9pm. Beer 25Kč. Cover 100-150Kč. On weekends, call ahead to reserve a table. Open daily 8pm-2am.

A Club, Milíčova 25. Metro C: Hlavní nádraží. Take tram #3, 5, 9, 26, or 55 uphill and get off at Lipsanká. A lesbian nightspot, but men are free to enter, although they might get a few side glances. Beer 20Kč. Open nightly 7pm-dawn.

◪ DAYTRIPS FROM PRAGUE

TEREZÍN (THERESIENSTADT)

The bus from Prague's Florenc station (1hr., every 1-2hr., 66Kč) stops by the central square, where the tourist office sells a 25Kč map. (Open Tu-Su 9am-4pm.)

In 1941, Terezín became a concentration camp. Nazi propaganda films touted the area as a spa resort where Jews would live a normal life. In reality, 35,000 died here, some of starvation and disease, others at the hands of brutal guards. Another 85,000 Jews were transported to death camps further east, such as Auschwitz. The **Ghetto Museum,** on Komenského in town, sets Terezín in the wider Nazi context. (Open Apr.-Sept. daily 9am-6pm; Oct.-Mar. 9am-5:30pm. Tickets to museum, barracks, and small fortress 150K˘, students 110K˘.) You can explore the **Small Fortress** (Malá Peunost) east of town across the river. (Open Apr.-Sept. daily 8am-6pm; Oct.-Mar. 8am-4:30pm.) The furnaces and autopsy lab at the **Jewish cemetery** and **crematorium** are as they were 50 years ago, with the addition of tributes left by the victims' ancestors. Men should cover their heads. (Open Mar.-Nov. Su-F 10am-5pm.) Life goes on in present-day Terezín, with families living in former barracks and supermarkets being set up in former Nazi offices.

HEADING EAST

KUTNÁ HORA

Take a bus (1½hr., 6 per day, 46Kč) from Prague's Florenc station, then walk or take a local bus to Sedlec (2km) and follow the signs for the chapel.

East of Prague, the former mining town of Kutná Hora (Mining Mountain) has a history as morbid as the **bone church** that has made it famous. In the 13th century the town's 100,000 silver-crazed diggers were hit by the black plague. Neighbors started to complain about the cemetery stench by the 15th century, when the Cistercian order built a chapel and started cramming in bodies. Who knows why the monk in charge began designing floral shapes out of pelvises and crania; he never finished, but the artist František Rint eventually completed the project in 1870 with the bones of over 400,000 people, including flying butt-bones, femur crosses, and a chandelier made from every bone in the human body. (Open Apr.-Oct. daily 8am-6pm; Nov.-Mar. 9am-noon and 1-4pm. 30Kč, students 15Kč.)

ČESKÝ KRUMLOV   ☎0337

The worst part about Český Krumlov is leaving. Winding medieval streets, cobble-stoned promenades, and Bohemia's second-largest castle make the gorgeous, UNESCO-protected town of Český Krumlov one of the most popular spots in Eastern Europe. The stone courtyards of the **castle**, perched high above the town, are free to the public. Two tours cover different parts of the lavish interior, including a frescoed ballroom, a splendid Baroque theater, and Renaissance-style rooms. The **galleries of the crypts** showcase local artists' sculptures and ceramics. Ascend the 162 steps of the **tower** for a fabulous view. (Castle open Tu-Su June-Aug. 9am-6pm; May and Sept. 9am-5pm; Apr. and Oct. 9am-4pm. 1hr. tours in English 150Kč, students 75Kč. Crypts open May-Oct. Tu-Su 10am-5pm; July-Aug. daily 10am-5pm. 30Kč, students 20Kč. Tower open May-Sept. daily 9am-6pm; Apr. and Oct. 11am-3pm. 30Kč, students 20Kč.) The Austrian painter Egon Schiele (1890-1918) lived in Český Krumlov for a while—until the citizens ran him out for painting burghers' daughters in the nude. Decades later, the ■**Egon Schiele International Cultural Center,** Široká 70-72, displays his work along with paintings by other 20th-century Central European artists. (Open daily 10am-6pm. 120Kč, students 60Kč.) Borrow an **inner tube** from your hostel to spend a lazy day drifting down the Vltava, or hike up into the hills to go horseback riding. At night, toss back at **U Hada** (Snake Bar), Rybárška 37 (open daily 7pm-3am) or **Babylon,** Rybárška 6 (open daily noon-late).

From the station, head to the upper street (near stops 20-25), turn right (with the station to your back), follow the small dirt path that veers left and heads uphill, turn right on Kaplická, cross the highway at the light, and head straight onto Horní, which brings you to Nám. Svornosti, where the **tourist office** in the town hall books pension rooms (from 600Kč) as well as cheaper private rooms. (☎70 46 21; infocentrumşckrf.ckrumlov.cz; www.ckrumlov.cz. Open daily 9am-6pm.) To get to ■**U vodníka,** Po vodě 55 (☎71 19 35; vodnik@ck.bohem-net.cz; boat rental; doubles 600Kč) or ■**Krumlov House,** Rooseveltova 68 (same contact info as for U vodníka; dorms 250Kč; doubles 600Kč), follow the directions above from the station and turn left onto Rooseveltova after the light (just before the bridge). From there, follow the signs to U vodníka or continue down the street to Krumlov House. Get **groceries** at **SPAR,** Linecká 49. (Open M-Sa 7am-6pm, Su 9am-6pm.)

BUDAPEST   ☎1

US$1 = 280 (FORINTS)	100FT = US$0.36
CDN$1 = 180FT	100FT = CDN$0.55
UK£1 = 405FT	100FT = UK£0.25
IR£1 = 325FT	100FT = IR£0.31
AUS$1 = 150FT	100FT = AUS$0.67
NZ$1 = 125FT	100FT = NZ$0.82
ZAR1 = 35FT	100FT = ZAR2.96
DM1 = 130FT	100FT = DM0.76
EUR€1 = 255FT	100FT = EUR€0.39

While the rest of the country lingers, Budapest jets. Ten times larger than any other Hungarian city, cosmopolitan and confident, this Magyar metropolis is reassuming its place as a major European capital. Originally two separate cities, Budapest was created in 1872 with the joining of Buda and Pest, and immediately went on to become the Habsburg Empire's number-two city. World War II punished Budapest severely, but the Hungarians rebuilt it from the rubble with the same pride that went on to foment the ill-fated 1956 Uprising, and to weather the Soviet occupation. No toyland Prague, Budapest is bigger and dirtier, alive and kicking. Neon lights and legions of tourists may draw attention away from the cobblestone streets, wide boulevards, bridges, and parks—but beneath it all beats a real Hungarian heart.

▐ TRANSPORTATION

Flights: Ferihegy Airport (☎296 96 96). Malév (Hungarian airlines) flight reservations ☎296 72 11 and 296 78 31. **Centrum buses** go to Erzsébet tér (30min., every 30min. 5:30am-9pm; 800Ft, payable on the bus), but the Ferihegy/red **bus #93,** followed by the M3 at Köbanya-Kispest, is cheapest.

Trains: ☎461 54 00 (24hr.). *Pályaudvar,* often abbreviated "pu.," means train station. Students and people under 26 get 33% off international tickets; show your ID or tell the clerk "*diák*" (DEE-ak; student). The 3 main stations—**Keleti Pályaudvar, Nyugati Pályaudvar,** and **Déli Pályaudvar**—are also Metro stops. Most international trains arrive at Keleti pu. To: **Berlin** (12hr., 1 per day, 22,850Ft; night train 15hr., 1 per day; 36,000Ft, 1500Ft reservation fee); **Prague** (EuroCity 8hr., 4 per day, 14,000Ft; night train 9hr., 1 per day, 14,000Ft, 1600Ft reservation fee); **Vienna** (3hr.; 17 per day; 7000Ft, 700Ft reservation fee). The daily **Orient Express** stops on its way from Paris to **Istanbul.**

Buses: ☎117 29 66. Most buses to Western Europe leave from **Volánbusz main station,** V, Erzsébet tér (international ticket office ☎485 21 00, ext. 211). M1, 2, or 3: Deák tér. Open M-F 6am-6pm, Sa 6:30am-4pm. Buses to much of Eastern Europe depart from **Népstadion,** Hungária körút 48/52 (☎252 18 96). M2: Népstadion. To: **Berlin** (14½hr., 5 per week, 20,000Ft); **Prague** (8hr., 4 per week, 8400Ft); **Vienna** (3-3½hr., 5 per day, 6400Ft). **Domestic buses** are cheap but slower than trains.

Public Transportation: Subways, buses, and **trams** are cheap, convenient, and easy to navigate. The **Metro** has 3 lines: yellow **(M1),** red **(M2),** and blue **(M3).** Pick up free **route maps** from hostels, tourist offices, and train stations. **Night transit (É)** runs midnight-5am along major routes; buses 7É and 78É follow the M2 route, 6É follows the 4/6 tram line, and 14É and 50É follow M3. Blue **single-fare tickets** for all public transport (1-way on 1 line 100Ft) are sold in Metro stations, in Trafik shops, and by some sidewalk vendors; punch them in the orange boxes at the gate of the Metro or on buses and trams; punch a new ticket when you change lines, or face a 1500-3000Ft fine. **Day pass** 800Ft; **3-day** 1600Ft; **1-week** 1950Ft.

Car Rental: There are several reliable rental agencies in Budapest, charging roughly US$38-49 per day for the cheapest cars. Few agencies rent to those under 21. **Vista** (see **Tourist Offices,** below) can help you find the most affordable option.

Taxis: As always, beware of scams. Check that the meter is on. **Budataxi** (☎233 33 33) charges 135Ft per km if you call. **Fötaxi** (☎222 22 22), **6x6 Taxi** (☎266 66 66), and **Tele 5 Taxi** (☎355 55 55) are also reliable.

✸▐ ORIENTATION AND PRACTICAL INFORMATION

The formerly separate cities of Buda and Pest, separated by the **Danube** river, have combined to form modern Budapest. On the west bank, **Buda** inspires countless artists with its hilltop citadel and cobblestoned **Castle District,** while **Pest,** on the east bank, is the heart of the modern city. Three bridges link the two halves: **Széchenyi lánchíd, Erzsébet híd,** and **Szabadság híd. Moszkva tér** (Moscow Square), just down the northern slope of the Castle District, is Budapest's bus and tram transportation hub. One metro stop away toward Örs vezér tér, **Batthyány tér,** on the west bank opposite the **Parliament** (Országház) building, is the starting point of the **HÉV commuter railway.** Budapest's three **Metro** lines (M1, M2, and M3) converge at **Deák tér,** at the core of Pest's loosely concentric boulevards, next to the main international bus terminal at **Erzsébet tér.** Two blocks west toward the river lies **Vörösmarty tér.** As you face the statue of Mihály Vörösmarty, the main pedestrian shopping zone, **Váci utca,** is to the right.

Budapest is divided into 23 **districts;** "I" indicates Central Buda, while "V" means downtown Pest. Because many streets have shed their communist labels, an up-to-date **map** is essential; pick up a free one at American Express or Tourinform, or buy the *Belváros Idegenforgalmi Térképe* at any Metro stop.

TOURIST, FINANCIAL, AND LOCAL SERVICES

Tourist Offices: All sell the Budapest Card (Budapest Kártya), which provides unlimited public transport, museum admission, and discounts at shops and restaurants (2-day 3400Ft, 3-day 4000Ft). Your first stop should be **Tourinform,** V, Sütő u. 2 (☎317 98 00; hungary@tourinform.hu; www.hungarytourism.hu), off Deák tér behind McDonald's. M1, 2, 3: Deák tér. Open daily 8am-8pm. **Vista Travel Center,** Pauley Ede 7 (☎267 86 03; incoming@vista.hu). M1-3: Deák tér; exit on Bajcsy-Zsilinszky út. The multilingual staff arranges lodgings and books train, plane, and bus tickets. Open M-F 9am-8pm, Sa-Su 10am-6pm. ▨ *Budapest in Your Pocket* (www.inyourpocket.com; 300Ft) is a great source of maps, reviews, and practical information.

Budget Travel: Express, V, Zoltán út 10 (|311 98 98). Offers same youth discounts as the train station. 10-30% off flights. Open M-Th 8am-4:30pm, F 8:30am-3pm.

Embassies: Australia, XII, Királyhágo tér 8/9 (☎457 97 77; austembbpşmail.datanet.hu). M2: Déli pu., then bus #21 or tram #59 to Királyhágo tér. Open M-F 8:30am-4:30pm. **Canada,** XII, Budakeszi út 32 (☎392 33 60). Take bus #158 from Moszkva tér to the last stop. Open M-F 9am-noon. **South Africa,** II, Gárdonyi Géza út 17 (☎392 09 99). **UK,** V, Harmincad u. 6 (☎266 28 88), near the intersection with Vörösmarty tér. M1: Vörösmarty tér. Open M-F 9:30am-noon and 2:30-4pm. **US,** V, Szabadság tér 12 (☎475 44 00; 24hr. ☎266 28 8893 31; fax 475 47 64). M2: Kossuth tér. Walk 2 blocks down Akademia and turn on Zoltán. Open M-F 8:15am-5pm. **New Zealand** and **Irish** nationals should contact the UK embassy.

Currency Exchange: Best rates are in banks. **Citibank,** V, Vörösmarty tér 4 (☎374 50 00.) M1: Vörösmarty tér. Cashes traveler's checks for no commission and, if you bring your passport, provides MC/V cash advances.

American Express: V, Deák Ferenc u. 10 (☎235 43 30; travel@amex.hu). M1: Vörösmarty tér. On corner with Bécsi u. **ATM** outside. Open M-F 9am-5:30pm, Sa 9am-2pm.

Luggage storage: Lockers at all 3 **train stations** 200Ft.

Gay Info: GayGuide.net Budapest (☎(0630) 932 33 34; budapest@gayguide.net; www.gayguide.net/europe/hungary/budapest), maintains a comprehensive web site and runs a hotline (daily 4-8pm) with information for gay tourists in Budapest.

Laundromats: Irisz Szalon, V, Városház u. 3/5 (☎317 20 92). M3: Ferenciek tér. Wash 7kg 1100Ft, dry 450Ft per 15min. Open M-F 7am-7pm, Sa 7am-1pm.

EMERGENCY AND COMMUNICATIONS

Police, ☎107. **Ambulance,** ☎104. **Fire,** ☎105.

Tourist Police: V, Vigadó u. 6 (☎235 44 79). M1: Vörösmarty tér. Walk toward the river. Station is just inside Tourinform. The police bring in translators if necessary. Open 24hr.

24-Hour Pharmacies: II, Frankel Leó út 22 (☎212 44 06); III, Szentendrei út 2/A (☎388 65 28); IV, Pozsonyi u. 19 (☎389 40 79); VI, Teréz krt. 41 (☎311 44 39); VII, Rákóczi út 39 (☎314 36 95). At night, call number on door or ring the bell.

Medical Assistance: Falck Személyi Olvosi Szolgálat (SOS) KFT, II, Kapy út 49/B (☎200 01 00 and 275 15 35). First aid free for foreigners. Open 24hr. The US embassy lists English-speaking doctors.

Internet Access: Cybercafes litter the city, but access can get expensive and long waits are common. Try a wired hostel. **Ami Internet Coffee,** V, Váci u. 40 (☎267 16 44;

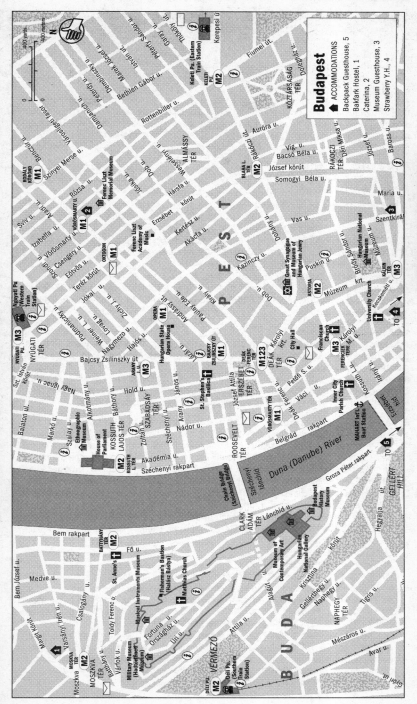

HEADING EAST

Budapest

▲ ACCOMMODATIONS

Backpack Guesthouse, 5
Bakfark Hostel, 1
Caterina, 2
Museum Guesthouse, 3
Strawberry Y.H., 4

amişamicoffee.hu). M3: Ferenciek tér. No wait. 150Ft for 10min., 350Ft for 30min.
Eckermann, VI, Andrássy út 24 (☎269 25 42). M1: Opera. Free. Call a week ahead
during summer. Open M-F 8am-10pm, Sa 9am-10pm.

Post Office: V, Városház u. 18 (☎318 48 11). **Poste Restante** (Postán Mar). Open M-F
8am-8pm, Sa 8am-2pm. **Postal code:** 1052.

ACCOMMODATIONS

Call ahead in summer, or stash your pack while you seek out a bed for the night to
save yourself blisters. Travelers arriving at Keleti pu. enter a feeding frenzy as
hawkers elbow their way to tourists; be cautious and don't believe all promises of
free rides or special discounts, but keep an open mind if you need a place to stay.

ACCOMMODATION AGENCIES

Slightly more expensive than hostels, **private rooms** tend to offer what hostels can't:
peace and quiet, and private showers. Arrive early, bring cash, and haggle.

Budapest Tourist, I, Deli Pálaudrar (☎/fax 212 46 25). M2: Déli pu. Underground. Well-
established. Singles in Central Pest 5000-7000Ft; doubles 6000-10,000Ft; triples
6000-12,000Ft. Lower off-season prices. Open M-F 9am-5pm.

IBUSZ, V, Ferenciek tér (☎485 27 67; accomodationsşibusz.hu). M3: Ferenciek tér.
Doubles 5000Ft; triples 5000-6000Ft. 1500Ft surcharge if staying fewer than 4 nights.
Open M-Th 8:15am-4pm, F 8:15am-3pm.

Non-Stop Hotel Service, V, Apáczai Csere J. u. 1 (☎266 80 42; tribunus.hotel.ser-
viceşmail.datanet.hu). M1: Vörösmarty tér. Singles 6000Ft; doubles from 7500Ft in
summer, from 6000Ft off-season; triples and quads from 8000Ft, off-season 7000Ft.
Open 24hr.

YEAR-ROUND HOSTELS

Budapest's hostels are social centers, with no curfews and beer- and music-filled
common rooms that often beat the city's bars and clubs. Most are part of the Hungarian Youth Hostel Association; their people wear HI t-shirts, and will accost you
as soon as you get off the train. They're legit, but don't let them scare you away
from more convenient independent hostels or guesthouses. Beware of theft in hostels. Unless otherwise noted, all have luggage storage, kitchens, and TV.

Backpacker's Guesthouse, XI, Takács Menyhért u. 33 (☎/fax 385 89 46;
backpackguest@hotmail.com; www.backpackbudapest.hu), in Buda, 12min. from central Pest. From Keleti pu., take bus #7 or 7A toward Buda; get off at Tétenyi u. (5 stops
past the river), walk back under the railway bridge, turn left, and go down the 3rd street
on the right. Busy, clean bathrooms; superb CD and video collections. **Internet** 20Ft
per 1min. Reception 24hr. Reserve 1-2 weeks ahead. Dorms 1600Ft; doubles 4800Ft.

Museum Youth Guesthouse, VIII, Mikszáth Kálmán tér 4, 1st fl. (☎318 95 08 and 266
88 79; museumgh@freemail.c3.hu), in Pest. M3: Kálvin tér. Take the left exit from the
stop onto Baross u., take the left branch at the fork, go to the far right corner at the
open square, and ring the buzzer at gate #4. **Internet.** Laundry. Reception 24hr. Check-
out 10am. Reserve ahead. 2500Ft per person, 2000Ft after 2nd night.

Station Guest House (HI), XIV, Mexikói út 36/B (☎221 88 64; station@mail.matav.hu;
www.stationguesthouse.hu), in Pest. From Keleti pu., take red bus #7 or night bus
#78É 4 stops to "Hungária Körút," walk under the railway pass, take an immediate right
on Mexikói út, walk 2 blocks, and look for the big yellow house. Free billiards, liquor at
the reception, and live music. **Internet.** Laundry. Reserve ahead or end up in the attic.
Attic 1500Ft; 6- to 8-bed dorms 2000Ft; 2- to 3-bed rooms 3000Ft. All prices drop
100Ft with each night you stay. Nonmembers add 200Ft.

Best Hostel, VI, Podmaniczky u. 27, 1st fl. (☎332 49 34; bestyh@mail.datanet.hu;
www.besthostel.hu). Ring bell #33 in building across from Nyugati pu. Spacious dorms.
Common room and kitchen close nightly at 11pm. **Internet.** Breakfast included. Laundry.
Dorms 2500Ft; doubles 7000Ft. 10% HI discount.

SUMMER HOSTELS

Many university dorms, mostly near Móricz Zsigmond Körtér, reinvent themselves as hostels in July and August. They usually have kitchens and a common room TV, and tend to be quieter than year-round hostels.

Hostel Bakfark, I, Bakfark u. 1/3 (☎329 86 44). M2: Moszkva tér. Go along Margit krt. with Burger King to the right and take the 1st right after Mammut. Check-out 10am. Call ahead. Open mid-June to Aug. 6-bed dorms 3200Ft; quads 300Ft. 300Ft HI discount.

Strawberry Youth Hostels (HI), IX, Ráday u. 43/45 (☎218 47 66; www.strawberryhostel.com). M3: Kálvin tér. With Hotel Mercure on the right, walk down Vámház krt. Ráday is toward the river on the left. Laundry. Reception 24hr. Check-out 10am. Open July-Aug. Doubles 3200Ft; triples and quads 2900Ft. 10% off with HI. **2nd location** on Kinizsi u. 2/6 (☎217 30 33) with same prices. Free Keleti pu. pickup for both hostels.

Hostel Martos, XI, Stoczek u. 5/7 (☎/fax 463 36 50; reception@hotel.martos.bme.hu), near the Technical University. From Keleti pu., take red bus #7 to Móricz Zsigmond Körtér and trek back 300m toward the river on Bartók Béla út.; go right onto Bertalan Lajos, and Stoczek u. is the 3rd right. Satellite TV. Free **Internet.** Laundry. Check-out 9-10am. Reserve ahead. Singles 3000Ft; doubles 4000-7000Ft; triples 6000Ft.

GUEST HOUSES

Guesthouses and rooms in private homes lend a personal touch for about the same price as hostels. Owners prowl for guests in Keleti pu.

Caterina, VI, Andrássy út 47, 3rd fl., apt. #18, in Pest; ring bell #11. (☎291 95 38; caterina@mail.inext.hu). M1: Oktogon; or trams #4 and 6. Across from Burger King. Grandmother-style house—no curfew, but quiet after 10pm. Free **Internet.** Laundry. Reception 24hr. Check-out 9am. Lockout 10am-2pm. Reserve by email. Dorms 2400Ft; double loft 2900Ft; triples 2900Ft; 6-person apartments US$60.

Mrs. Ena Bottka, V, Garibaldi u. 5 (☎/fax 302 34 57; garibaldiguest@hotmail.com). M2: Kossuth tér. Heading away from Parliament on Nádor u., take first right on Garibaldi u. Some with kitchenette, TV, showers, and towels. Rooms 3500Ft per person; apartments 6000-10,000Ft. All prices decrease with longer stays.

CAMPING

For a full listing, pick up the pamphlet *Camping Hungary* at tourist offices.

Zugligeti "Niche" Camping, XII, Zugligeti út 101 (☎/fax 200 83 46; camping.niche@matavnet.hu). Take bus #158 from Moszkva tér to last stop. Communal showers and a safe. 850Ft per person, 500-900Ft per tent, 700Ft per car.

Római Camping, III, Szentendrei út 189 (☎368 62 60). M2: Batthyány tér. Take HÉV to Római fürdő; walk 100m toward river. Huge site with swimming pool (300Ft). Open June-Aug. June tents 1500Ft; bungalows 1300-1900Ft. July 1800Ft; 1560-2280Ft. Aug. 2250Ft; 2850Ft. 3% tourist tax. 10% HI discount.

🞄 FOOD

Eating at family joints can be tastier than eating in regular restaurants. Seek out the *kifőzés* or *vendéglő* in your neighborhood for a taste of Hungarian life. **Non-Stop** stores and corner markets are the best options for groceries. The king of them all is 🞕 **Grand Market Hall,** IX, Fövamtér 1/3, next to Szabadság híd (M3: Kálvin tér).

🞕 **Fatâl Restaurant,** V, Váci u. 67 (☎266 26 07), in Pest. M3: Ferenciek tér. Packs them in for large and hearty Hungarian meals. Giant, carefully garnished main courses 1070-2790Ft. Reservations only. Open daily 11am-2am.

Gandhi, V, Vigyázó Ferenc u. 4, in Pest. New menu every day at this veggie place. Herbal teas, organic wines, and wheat beers. Dishes 980-1670Ft. Open M-Sa noon-10:30pm.

Söröző a Szent Jupáthoz, II, Retek u. 16, in Buda. M2: Moszkva tér. Huge Hungarian menu and huge Hungarian portions. Main dishes 1090-2590Ft. Open 24hr.

HEADING EAST

Marxim, II, Kisrókus u. 23, in Buda. M2: Moszkva tér. Go on Margit krt., then turn left down the industrial road. Local teens unite at this tongue-in-cheek Communist-themed pizzeria. Pizzas 440-940Ft. Open M-F noon-1am, Sa noon-2am, Su 6pm-1am.

Paksi Halászcsárda, II, Margit Körút 14, in Buda. Tram #4 or 6 to "Margit Híd." Hungarian standbys in upscale setting. Main dishes 950-1400Ft. Open daily noon-midnight.

CAFES

Once the haunts of Budapest's literary, intellectual, and cultural elite, as well as its political dissidents, many cafes now serve cheap and absurdly rich pastries.

M›vész Kávéház, VI, Andrássy út 29. M1: Opera. Across from the Opera. An mix of mostly artsy people around polished stone tables. Enjoy a *M›vész torta* (jam and hazelnut cake; 260Ft) and cappuccino (260Ft) on the terrace. Open daily 9am-midnight.

Gerbeaud, V, Vörösmarty tér 7. M1: Vörösmarty tér. This cafe has been serving its signature layer cakes (520Ft) and homemade ice cream (95Ft) since 1858. Shaded marble tables dominate the northern end of Vörösmarty tér. Open daily 9am-9pm.

SIGHTS

In 1896, Hungary's 1000th birthday bash prompted the construction of what are today Budapest's most prominent sights—a testament to the optimism of a capital on the verge of its Golden Age. Among the works commissioned by the Habsburgs were **Heroes' Square** (Hősök tér), **Liberty Bridge** (Szbadság híd), and **Vajdahunyad Castle** (Vajdahunyad vár). The domes of **Parliament** (Országház) and **St. Stephen's Basilica** (Szent István Bazilika) are both 96m high—references to the historic date.

BUDA

Buda is older, more conservative, and more disjointed than its sister Pest, but with the city's best parks, lush hills, and Danube islands, it is no less worth exploring. The **Castle District** lies atop **Castle Hill** and contains the bulk of Buda's sights.

CASTLE DISTRICT. Towering above the Danube, the **Castle District** has been razed three times in its 800-year history, most recently in 1945. With its winding, statue-filled streets, breathtaking views, and magnificent hodge-podge of architectural styles, the UNESCO-protected district now appears much as it did in Habsburg times (though today it's much more touristed). Although bullet holes in the **castle** façade still recall the 1956 Uprising, the reconstructed palace today houses a number of fine museums (see **Museums,** p. 950). *(M1, 2, 3: Deák tér. From the Metro, take bus #16 across the Danube. Get off just after the river at the base of the Széchenyi Chain Bridge and take the funicular (sikló) up the hill. Daily 9:30am-5:30pm; closed 2nd and 4th M of the month; 300Ft. Or, take the Metro to M2: Moszkva tér, walk up to the hill on Várfok u., and enter the Castle at Vienna Gate, Becsi kapu.)*

MATTHIAS CHURCH AND FISHERMAN'S BASTION. The multi-colored roof of the neo-Gothic **Matthias Church** (Mátyás templom), which was converted into a mosque when Ottoman armies seized Buda in 1541 and re-converted 145 years later when the Habsburgs defeated the Turks, is one of the most-photographed sights in Budapest. Descend the stairway to the right of the altar to enter the **crypt** and **treasury.** *(From the cable car, turn right on Színház and veer left at Tárnok u. From Vienna Gate, walk straight down Fortuna u. High mass with full orchestra and choir Su 7, 8:30, 10am, 6pm; come early for a seat. Treasury open daily 9:30am-5:30pm. 200Ft.)* Behind St. Matthias Church is the grand equestrian monument of King Stephen bearing his trademark double cross in front of the **Fisherman's Bastion** (Halászbástya). The view across the Danube from the fairy-tale **tower** is stunning. *(200Ft.)*

GELLÉRT HILL. The Pope sent Bishop Gellért to the coronation of King Stephen, the first Christian Hungarian monarch, to assist in the conversion of the Magyars; those unconvinced by his message gave the hill its name (Gellért-hegy) by hurling the good bishop to his death from the top. The **Liberation Monument** (Sza-badság Szobor), created to honor Soviet soldiers who died liberating Hungary, looks over Budapest from atop the hill. The view from the top of the adjoining **Citadel,** built as a symbol of Habsburg power after the foiled 1848 revolution, is especially spectacular at night. At the base of the hill sits the **Gellért Hotel and Baths** (see **Baths,** p. 950), Budapest's most famous Turkish Bath. *(To ascend the hill, take tram #18 or 19 to "Hotel Gellért." Follow Szabó Verjték u. to Jubileumi Park, continuing on the marked paths to the summit. Or, take bus #27 to the top; get off at Búsuló Juhász and walk another 5min. to the peak.)*

PEST

The winding streets of Pest were constructed in the 19th century and today host stores, cafes and restaurants, corporations and banks, and monuments. The crowded **Inner City** (Belváros) is based in the pedestrian **Váci utca** and **Vörösmarty tér.**

PARLIAMENT. Pest's riverbank sports a string of luxury hotels leading to its magnificent neo-Gothic **Parliament** (Országház), modeled after Britain's. The massive structure has always been too big for Hungary's government; today, the legislature uses only 12%. *(M2: Kossuth Lajos tér. Mandatory tours in English M-F 10am and 2pm, Sa-Su 10am. 1500Ft, students 750Ft. Purchase tickets at gate #10 and enter at gate #12.)*

ST. STEPHEN'S BASILICA. The city's largest church (Sz. István Bazilika) was decimated by Allied bombs in WWII. Its neo-Renaissance façade remains under reconstruction, but the ornate interior continues to attract both tourists and worshippers. The **Panorama Tower** offers an amazing 360° view, but the highlight is the **Basilica Museum,** where St. Stephen's mummified right hand, one of Hungary's most revered religious relics, sits on public display. For the devout and the macabre, a 100Ft donation dropped in the box will light up the religious relic for 2min. of closer inspection. *(M1-3: Deák tér. Basilica and museum open May-Oct. M-Sa 9am-5pm; Nov.-Apr. M-Sa 10am-4pm, Su 1-5pm. Tower open June-Aug. daily 9:30am-6pm; Sept.-Oct. 10am-5:30pm; Apr.-May 10am-4:30pm. Tower 500Ft, students 400Ft.)*

GREAT SYNAGOGUE. Much of the artwork in Pest's Moorish synagogue (zsinagóga), the largest active synagogue in Europe and the second-largest in the world, is blocked from view, as it has been under renovation since 1988. In back is the **Holocaust Memorial,** a metal tree that sits above a mass grave for thousands of Jews killed near the end of WWII. *(M2: Astoria. At the corner of Dohány u. and Wesselényi u. Open May-Oct. M-Th 10am-5pm, F 10am-3pm, Su 10am-2pm; Nov.-Apr. M-F 10am-3pm, Su 10am-1pm. Synagogue and museum 600Ft, students 250Ft.)*

ANDRÁSSY ÚT AND HEROES' SQUARE. Hungary's grandest boulevard, Andrássy út, extends from **Erzsébet tér** in downtown Pest to **Heroes' Square** (Hősök tér) to the northeast. Perhaps the most vivid reminder of Budapest's Golden Age is the **Hungarian National Opera House** (Magyar Állami Operaház), whose 24-carat gilded interior glows on performance nights. If you can't see an opera, make sure to take a tour. *(Andrássy út 22. M1: Opera. English tours daily 3 and 4pm. 1200Ft, students 600Ft. 20% Budapest Card discount.)* At the Heroes' Square end of Andrássy út, the **Millennium Monument** (Millenniumi emlékmű) commemorates the nation's most prominent leaders. Right off Heroes' Square is the **Museum of Fine Arts** (see **Museums,** below).

CITY PARK. The **Városliget** is home to a zoo, a circus, a run-down amusement park, and the lake-side **Vajdahunyad Castle** (Vajdahunyad Vár), whose Disney-esque collage of Romanesque, Gothic, Renaissance, and Baroque styles is intended to chronicle the history of Hungarian architecture. Outside the castle broods the hooded statue of **Anonymous,** the secretive scribe to whom we owe much of our knowledge of medieval Hungary. Rent a **rowboat** or **ice skates** on the lake next to the castle, or a **bike-trolley** to navigate the paths. *(M1: Széchenyi Fürdő. Pedal cars, electric cars, pedal boats, rowboats, and ice skates rented daily.)*

HEADING EAST

MUSEUMS

▨ **Museum of Fine Arts** (Szépművészeti Múzeum), XIV, Dózsa György út 41. M1: Hősök tér. A spectacular collection, from Raphael to Rembrandt, Gaugin to Goya. Open Tu-Su 10am-5:30pm. 500Ft, students 200Ft. Tours for up to 5 people 2000Ft.

▨ **Statue Park** (Szoborpark Múzeum; www.szoborpark.hu), XXII, on the corner of Balatoni út and Szabadkai u. Take the #7-173 express bus from M2: Keleti pu. or M3: Ferenciek tér to the end of the line. From there, take the yellow Volán bus from terminal #2 toward Diosd-Erd. An outdoor collection of communist statuary. Open Mar.-Nov. daily 10am-dusk; Dec.-Feb. weekends and holidays only. 400Ft, students 200Ft.

Museum of Applied Arts (Iparm›vészeti Múzeum), IX, Üllői út 33-37. M3: Ferenc körút. Handcrafted art objects, and temporary exhibits highlighting specific crafts. Open mid-Mar. to Oct. Tu-Su 10am-6pm; Nov. to mid-Mar. 10am-4pm. 500Ft, students 250Ft.

Hungarian National Museum (Nemzeti Múzeum; www.origo.hnm.hu), VIII, Múzeum krt. 14/16. M3: Kálvin tér. From Crown Jewels to Soviet propaganda. Open Tu-Su mid-Mar. to mid-Oct. 10am-6pm; mid-Oct. to mid-Mar. Tu-Su 10am-5pm. 600Ft, students 300Ft.

Buda Castle, I. Szent György tér 2 (]375 75 33), on Castle Hill. Wing A houses the **Museum of Contemporary Art** (Kortárs Művészeti Múzeum). Wings B-D hold the **Hungarian National Gallery** (Magyar Nemzeti Galéria). Artifacts from the 1242 castle, revealed by WWII bombings, lie in the **Budapest History Museum** (Budapesti Történeti Múzeum) in Wing E. Wings A-D open Tu-Su 10am-6pm. Wing E open daily mid-May to mid-Sept. 10am-6pm; mid-Sept. to Oct. and Mar. to mid-May M and W-Su 10am-6pm; Nov.-Feb. M and W-Su 10am-4pm. Wing A 400Ft, students 200Ft. Wings B-D 500Ft together, students 250Ft. Wing E 500Ft, students 200Ft.

♫ ▨ ENTERTAINMENT AND NIGHTLIFE

Budapest Program (www.budapestprogram.com), *Budapest Panorama*, *Pesti Est* and the classic *Budapest in Your Pocket* (300Ft) are the best English-language guides to entertainment.

THEATER, MUSIC, AND DANCE. Ticket Express, VI, Andrássy út 15 and 18, next to the Opera House (☎312 00 00; open M-F 10am-6pm) and throughout the city, sells tickets to nearly any show for no commission. For 3000-9800Ft you can enjoy an opera in the splendor of the gilded ▨**State Opera House** (Magyar Allami Operahaz), VI, Andrássy út 22. M1: Opera. The box office on the left side of the building sells cheaper, unclaimed tickets 30min. before showtime. (Box office ☎353 01 70. M-Sa 11am-7pm, Su 4-7pm; cashier closes 5pm on days without performances. Daily English tours 1hr.; 3 and 4pm; 1200Ft, students 600Ft.) The **Philharmonic Orchestra** has equally grand music (concerts almost nightly Sept.-June) in a slightly more modest venue. Buy tickets at V, Mérleg u. 10. (☎318 02 81. Open daily 9am-3pm. Tickets 2000-5000Ft, less on the day of show.) Many of the world's best musicians pass through Budapest. Prices are reasonable; check the **Music Mix '33 Ticket Service**, V, Váci u. 33. V. (☎266 70 70. Open M-F 10am-6pm, Sa 10am-1pm.)

THERMAL BATHS. To soak away the city grime, sink into a thermal bath. First built in 1565, their services—from mud baths to massage—are quite cheap. Some baths are meeting spots for Budapest's gay community. ▨ **Gellért**, XI, Kelenhegyi út 4/6, has a rooftop sundeck and outdoor wave pool. Take bus #7 or tram #47 or 49 to "Hotel Gellért," at the base of Gellért-hegy. (Open May-Sept. M-F 6am-6pm, Sa-Su 6am-4pm; off-season closes 1pm weekends. Bath and swimming pool 1800Ft. Towel, robe, and suit rental 400Ft each with 3000Ft deposit.)

NIGHTLIFE

All-night outdoor parties, elegant after-hours clubs, the usual thump and grind— Budapest has it all. While pubs and bars bustle until 4am, streets themselves are surprisingly empty and poorly lit. The cafes and restaurants in **VI, Liszt Ference tér**

BUCK-NAKED IN BUDAPEST

Treatment at a Budapest bath is royally indulgent, if somewhat intimidating for the virgin bather. Upon arrival, you'll be handed a bizarre apron that is no bigger than a dish-rag. Modesty requires that you tie it around your waist. After depositing your belongings in a locked stall (the attendant keeps the key), proceed to the baths. In general, women set the apron aside as a towel while men keep theirs on. Bring your bathing suit, as customs vary greatly by establishment, but in any case, it's a good idea to do as the locals do—there's nothing more conspicuous than a Speedo-clad tourist among naked natives. Once you've cycled through the sauna and thermal baths, repeat for good measure, and enter the massage area. If you're looking for a good scrubbing, go with the sanitary massage *(vízi)*; if you're a traditionalist, stick to the medical massage *(orvosi)*. In both cases, the masseuse will chatter away in Hungarian while pummeling your back. Every bath provides a much-needed rest area once the process is complete. Tip the attendant, lounge over mint tea, and savor your afternoon of guilt-free pampering and scrubbing.

(M1: Oktagon) attract Budapest's youth. In the summer, **Peötlfi híd** (Green Park), in Buda, rocks all night every night. Gay life in Budapest is just beginning to make itself visible, so it's safer to be discreet.

Undergrass, VI, Liszt Ferenc tér 10. M1: Oktogon. The hottest spot in Pest's trendiest area. A soundproof glass door divides the hip bar from the equally packed disco. Open daily 8pm-4am; disco Tu-Su 10pm-4am.

Piaf, VI, Nagymező u. 25. A much-loved after-hours place. The beautiful staff is icy because they can be. Knock on the door to await the approval of the club's matron. Cover 500Ft, includes 1 beer. Open daily 11pm-6am, but don't come before 1am.

Capella, V, Belgrád rakpart 23 (www.extra.hu/capellacafe). With glow-in-the-dark graffiti and an underground atmosphere, this spot draws a mixed gay and straight crowd. Shows at midnight. Women welcome. Cover 1000-1500Ft. Open Tu-Su 9pm-5am.

Fél 10 Jazz Club, VIII, Baross u. 30. M3: Kálvin tér. 2 floors with an Escher-like layout. Potent drinks. Cover 400Ft. Open M-F noon-dawn, Sa-Su 6pm-dawn.

Club Seven, Akácfa u. 7. M2: Blaha Lajos tér. Upscale underground music club. M-F no cover; Sa-Su 1000Ft, women free. Coffeehouse open daily 9pm-4am, restaurant 6pm-midnight, dance floor 10pm-5am.

Jazz Garden, V, Veres Páiné u. 44a. The "garden" is actually a vaulted cellar with Christmas lights. Live jazz nightly at 10:30pm. Open Su-F noon-1am, Sa noon-2am.

Angel Bar, VII, Szövetség u. 33. The 1st gay bar in Budapest. Until a few years ago, the club moved weekly; now this huge 3-level disco, cafe, and bar is packed. F and Su night drag shows. Sa men only. Cover around 600Ft; Th free. Open Th-Su 10pm-dawn.

APPENDIX

GLOSSARY

addition (F): check
aérogare (F): air terminal
affitacamere (I): room for rent
agora (Gr): city square; marketplace
albergo (I): hotel
albergue (S): youth hostel
alcázar (S): Muslim fortress-palace
Altstadt (G): old city
apse: nook beyond church altar
arrondissement (F): city district
auberge de jeunesse (F): youth hostel
autoroute (F): motorway
ayuntamiento (S): city hall
azulejo (P, S): glazed tile
Bahnhof (G): train station
barrio viejo (S): old city
billet (F): ticket
boulangerie (F): bakery
Brücke (G): bridge
brug (Du): bridge
calle (I, S): street
campanile (I): bell tower
campo (I): square
carabinieri (I): civil police
carrer (S): street
casco antiguo (S): old city
casco viejo (S): old city
cave (F): (wine) cellar
centre commercial (F): shopping plaza
centre ville (F): city center
centro (S): city center
cerveza (S): beer
chambres d'hôtes (F): bed and breakfasts
charcuterie (F): butcher
château (F): castle
chiesa (I): church
ciudad nueva (S): new city
cloître (F): cloister
compline: last church service of the day
confiserie (F): candy store
correspondance (F): connection, transfer (subway)
corso (I): principal street or avenue
craic (Ir): a good (pub) time
dégustation (F): tasting (i.e., wine tasting)
domatia (Gr): room in private home
Dom (G): cathedral
duomo (I): cathedral
église (F): church
entrée (F): appetizer
essence (F): gasoline

estación (S): station
evensong: church service just before dusk
fermo posta (I): *Poste Restante*
ferrovia (I): railways
Flughafen (G): airport
foyer (F): student dorm
gabinetto (I): toilet, WC
gade (D): street
gare (F): train station
Gästehaus (G): guesthouse
gîte d'étape (F): rural hostel
gracht (D): canal
Hauptbahnhof (G): main train station
hebdomadaire (F): weekly
hospedajes (S): cheap accommodations
hostal (S): hostel
hôtel de ville (F): town hall
iglesia (S): church
igreja (P): church
Innenstadt (G): city center
Jugendherberge (G): youth hostel
Kerk (Du): church
Kirche (G): church
Kirke (D): church
laverie (F): laundromat
leoforeo (Gr): bus
mairie (F): mayor's office
marché (F): outdoor market
marché aux puces (F): flea market
Marktplatz (G): marketplace
Mensa (G): university cafeteria
monnaie (F): change
museo (S): museum
nádraží (C): station
náměstí (C): square
nave: central body of a church
navette (F): shuttlebus
Neustadt (G): new city
ostello (I): youth hostel
paella (S): rice dish with seafood, meat, and vegetables
palais (F): palace
panini (I): sandwiches
palazzo (I): palace
paleohora (Gr): old town
pályaudvar (H): station
parque (S): park
paseo (S): promenade (abbreviated *po.*)
passeig (S): promenade (*pg.*)
pâtisserie (F): pastry shop
pensione (S): room in private home
pensao (P): cheap accommodation

pietà (I): scene of the Virgin mourning the dead Christ
plaça (S): square
place (F): square
plage (F): beach
plat (F): main course
plateia (Gr): town square
Platz (G): square
playa (S): beach
plaza (S): square
plein (Du): town square
pleio (Gr): ferry
piazza(le) (I): city square
pont (F): bridge
ponte (I, P): bridge
praça (P): square
praia (P): beach
primi (I): first course (usually pasta)
Privatzimmer (G): room in a private home
puente (S): bridge
quartier (F): neighborhood
Rådhuspladsen (D): main town square
Rathaus: city hall
secondi (I): second course (usually meat or fish)
smørrebrød (D): open-faced sandwich
souvlaki (Gr): skewered meat
spiaggia (I): beach
spotted dick (B): steamed sponge pudding with raisins
stadhuis (Du): town hall
stazione (I): station
straat (Du): street
Straße (G): street
tabac (F): all-purpose newsstand
tabbacchi (I): all-purpose newsstand
Tageskarte (G): day pass
tapas (S): appetizers; snacks
taverna (Gr): restaurant
télécarte (F): phone card
télépherique (F): cable car lift
tér (H): square
TGV (F): super-fast train
trad (Ir): traditional Irish music
traiteur (F): delicatessen
transept: arm of the church that intersects the nave
ulice (C): street
utca (H): street
vendange (F): grape harvest
via(le) (I): street
vicolo (I): alley, lane
vieille ville (F): old city
vino (S): wine
Zug (G): train

B=British, C=Czech, D=Danish, Du=Dutch, F=French, G=German, Gr=Greek, H=Hungarian, I=Italian, Ir=Irish, P=Portugese, S=Spanish

LANGUAGES

GERMAN

Vowels are pronounced as follows: *a* as in "father"; *e* as the *a* in "hay" or the indistinct vowel sound in "uh"; *i* as the *ee* in "cheese"; *o* as in "oh"; *u* as in "fondue"; *y* as the *oo* in "boot"; *au* as in "sauerkraut"; *eu* as the *oi* in "boil." With *ei* and *ie*, pronounce the last letter as a long English vowel—*heiße* is HIGH-ssuh; *viele* is FEEL-uh. Consonants are the same as in English, except for *c* (pronounced *k*); *j* (pronounced *y*); *k* (always pronounced, even before *n*); *p* (nearly always pronounced, even before *f*); *qu* (pronounced *kv*); *s* (pronounced *z* at the beginning of a word); *v* (pronounced *f*); *w* (pronounced *v*); *z* (pronounced *ts*). The *ß*, or *ess-tsett*, is a double s. Pronounce *sch* as *sh*.

FRENCH

J is like the *s* in "pleasure." *C* sounds like a *k* before *a*, *o*, and *u*; like an *s* before *e* and *i*. *Ç* always sounds like an *s*. Vowels are short and precise: *a* as the *o* in "mom"; *e* as in "help" (*é* becomes the *a* in "hay"); *i* as the *ee* in "creep"; *o* as in "oh." *Ui* sounds like the word "whee." *U* is a short, clipped *oo* sound; hold your lips as if you were about to say "ooh," but say "ee" instead. *Ou* is a straight *OO* sound. At the ends of words, *-er* and *-et* are pronounced "ay." Don't pronounce any final consonants except *l, f*, or *c*; an *e* on the end of the word, however, means that you should pronounce the final consonant sound, e.g., *muet* is moo-AY but *muette* is moo-ET. Nor should you pronounce the final *s* in plural nouns. With few exceptions, all syllables receive equal emphasis, with a slight stress on the last syllable.

ITALIAN

There are seven vowel sounds in standard Italian: *a* as in "father"; *i* as the *ee* in "cheese"; *u* as the *oo* in "droop"; *e* either as *ay* in "bay" or *eh* in "set"; and *o* both as in "bone" and as in "off." *H* is always silent, *r* always rolled. *C* and *g* are hard before *a*, *o*, or *u*, as in "cat" and "goose," but they soften into *ch* and *j* sounds, respectively, when followed by *i* or *e*, as in *ciao* (chow) and *gelato* (jeh-LAH-toh). *Cc* and *gg* are also hard. *Ch* and *gh* are pronounced like *k* and *g* before *i* and *e*, as in *chianti* (ky-AHN-tee) and *spaghetti* (spah-GEHT-tee). Pronounce *gn* like the *ni* in onion, as in *bagno* (BAHN-yoh). *Gli* is like the *lli* in million, so *sbagliato* is said "zbal-YAH-toh." When followed by *a*, *o*, or *u*, *sc* is pronounced as *sk*, as in *scusi* (SKOO-zee); when followed by an *e* or *i*, *sh* as in *sciopero* (SHOH-pair-oh).

SPANISH

Spanish pronunciation is very regular. Vowels are always pronounced the same way: *a* as in "father"; *e* as in "escape"; *i* as the *ee* in "eat"; *o* as in "oat"; *u* as in "boot"; *y*, by itself, as *ee*. Consonants are the same as in English except for: *j* and soft *g* (before *e* or *i*), pronounced like an *h*; *ll*, like the *y* in "yes"; *ñ*, as the *gn* in "cognac"; *rr*, trilled *r*; *h*, always silent; and *z* and soft *c*, both pronounced *th*. The last syllable is always stressed unless the word ends in a vowel, *n*, or *s*, in which case the next-to-last syllable is stressed. Any other word not following this rule has the accent written where the stress falls.

THE GREEK ALPHABET

LETTER	SYMBOL	PRONUNCIATION	LETTER	SYMBOL	PRONUNCIATION
alpha	α A	*a* as in father	nu	ν N	*n* as in net
beta	β B	*v* as in velvet	ksi	ξ Ξ	*x* as in mix
gamma	γ Γ	*y* as in yo or *g* as in go	omicron	o O	*o* as in row
delta	δ Δ	*th* as in there	pi	π Π	*p* as in peace
epsilon	ε E	*e* as in jet	rho	ρ P	*r* as in roll
zeta	ζ Z	*z* as in zebra	sigma	σ (ς) Σ	*s* as in sense
eta	η H	*ee* as in queen	tau	τ T	*t* as in tent
theta	θ Θ	*th* as in health	upsilon	υ Y	*ee* as in green
iota	ι I	*ee* as in tree	phi	φ (ϕ) Φ	*f* as in fog
kappa	κ K	*k* as in cat	xi	χ X	*h* as in horse
lambda	λ Λ	*l* as in land	psi	ψ Ψ	*ps* as in oops
mu	μ M	*m* as in moose	omega	ω Ω	*o* as in glow

APPENDIX

USEFUL WORDS AND PHRASES

ENGLISH	CZECH	PRONUNCIATION
hello	Dobrý den	DO-bree den
goodbye	Na shledanou	nah SLEH-dah-noh-oo
please	Prosím	PROH-seem
thank you	Děkuji	DYEH-koo-yih
yes / no	Ano / ne	AH-no / neh
sorry / excuse me	Promiňte	PROH-mihn-teh
Do you speak English?	Mluvíte anglicky?	MLOO-vit-eh ahng-GLIT-ski
I don't understand.	Nerozumím.	NEH-rohz-oo-meem
Help!	Pomoc!	POH-mots
Where is...?	Kde...?	k-DEH
left / right / straight ahead	vlevo / vpravo / rovně	LEH-vah / PRAH-vah / ROV-nyeh
What time does the [train / bus / boat] (depart / arrive)?	Kdy (odjíždí / přijíž) [vlak / autobus / loď]?	k-DEE (OT-yeezh-dee / PREE-yeezh) [vlahk / OUT-oh-boos / LOHD-yeh]
today / tomorrow / yesterday	dnes / zítra / včera	dness / ZEE-tra / FCHE-rah
I'd like a (one-way / round-trip) ticket.	Rád (m.) / Ráda bych (f.) (jen tam / zpáteční) jízdenku.	rahd / RAHD-ah bikh (yen tam / SPAH-tech-nyee) YEEZ-denkoo
How much is it?	Kolik stojí?	KOH-lihk STOH-yee
hostel / hotel	mládežnická nocleháma / hotel	MIA-dezh-nit-ska NOTS-le-har-na / ho-TELL
camping	kemping	KEM-ping
I'd like a (single / double) room.	Máte volné (jednolůžkový / dvolůžkový) pokoj.	MAH-te VOL-nee (YED-no-loosh-ko-vee / DVOH-loosh-ko-vee) PO-koy

ENGLISH	DANISH	PRONUNCIATION
hello	goddag	go-DAY
goodbye	farvel	fah-VEL
please	vær så venlig	vair soh VEN-li
thank you	tak	tack
yes / no	ja / nej	ya / nye
sorry / excuse me	undskyld	UN-scoold
Do you speak English?	Taler du engelsk?	TAY-luh dou ENG-elsk
I don't understand.	Jeg forstår ikke.	yai for-STOR IG-guh
Help!	Hjælp!	yelp
Where is...?	Hvor er...?	voa air
left / right / straight ahead	til venstre / til højre / lige ud	till VEN-struh / till HOY-ruh / lee oothe
What time does the [train / bus / boat] (depart / arrive)?	Hvornår (går / ankommer) [toget / bussen / båden]?	vor-NOR (gore / AN-kom-ma) [TOE-et / BOOSE-en / BOTHE-en]
today / tomorrow / yesterday	i dag / i morgen / i går	ee-DAY / ee-MORN / ee-GORE
I'd like a (one-way / round-trip) ticket.	Eg vil gerne ha en (enkelbillet / tur-retur billet).	YAI vil GAIR-nuh ha een (EHN-kul-bill-ETT / TOOR-re-TOOR bill-ETT)
How much does it cost?	Hvad koster det?	va KOS-tor dey
hostel / hotel	vandrerhjem / hotel	VAN-drar-yem / ho-TELL
camping	campingplads	CAM-ping-plass
I'd like a (single / double) room.	Jeg ønsker et (enkeltværelse / dob-beltværelse).	YAI URN-ska it (EHN-kult-vair-ELL-sih / DOP-ult-vair-ELL-sih)

ENGLISH	DUTCH	PRONUNCIATION
hello	hallo	hallo
goodbye	tot ziens	toht zeens
please	alstublieft	ALST-ew-bleeft
thank you	dank u wel	dahnk ew vel
yes / no	ja / nee	ya / nay
sorry / excuse me	excuseert u mij	ex-kew-ZAYRT ew my
Do you speak English?	Spreekt u engels?	sprayhkt ew ENG-els
I don't understand.	Ik begrijp u niet.	ik beh-GHRIPE ew neet
Help!	help!	help
Where is...?	Waar iz...?	var iss
left / right / straight ahead	links / rechts / recht door	links / hrechts / hrecht door
What time does the [train / bus / boat] (depart / arrive)?	Hoe laat (vertrekt / komt) de [trein / bus / kom]?	hoo laht (ver-TRECHT / komt) deh [trine / buhs / kom]

ENGLISH	DUTCH	PRONUNCIATION
today / tomorrow / yesterday	vandaag / morgen / gisteren	fon-DAHG / MOR-ghun / GHIST-er-un
I'd like a (one-way / round-trip) ticket.	Ik wil graag (een enkele reis / een retour).	ik vil khrahk ayn (ENG-kuh-luhrice / ayn ruh-TOOR)
How much is it?	Wat kost dit?	vaht kost dit
hostel / hotel	jeugdherberg / hotel	YOORGH-hayr-bayrgh / ho-TELL
camping	kamperen	kahm-PAHR-en
I'd like a (single / double) room.	Ik wil graag een (een- / twee-) persoonska-mer.	ik vil ghrahgh ayn (AYN / TVAY) per-sohns-kah-mer

ENGLISH	FRENCH	PRONUNCIATION
hello	bonjour	bohn-ZHOOR
goodbye	au revoir	oh ruh-VWAHR
please	s'il vous plaît	seel voo pleh
thank you	merci	mehr-SEE
yes / no	oui / non	wee / nohn
sorry / excuse me	pardon	pahr-DOHN
Do you speak English?	Parlez-vous anglais?	PAR-lay-voo ahn-GLEH
I don't understand.	Je ne comprends pas.	zhuh nuh KOHN-prahn pah
Help!	Au secours!	oh suh-KOOR
Where is...?	Où se trouve...?	oo seh troov
left / right / straight ahead	gauche / droite / tout droit	gohsh / drwaht / too drwah
What time does the [train / bus / boat] (depart / arrive)?	À quelle heure est-que le [train / bus / bateau] (part / arrive)?	ah kel ur ES-keh luh [trah / bews / baht-OH] (pahr / ah-REEV)
today / tomorrow / yesterday	aujourd'hui / demain / hier	oh-zhoor-DWEE / duh-MAH) / ee-YEHR
I'd like a (one-way / round-trip) ticket.	Je voudrais un billet (simple / aller-retour).	zhuh voo-DREH uhn bee-YAY (SAH-pluh / ah-LAY ruh-TOOR)
How much does it cost?	Ça coute combien?	sah coot kohn-BYAN
hostel / hotel	auberge de jeunesse / hôtel	oh-BEHRZH duh zhu-NES / oh-TEL
camping	camping	kahn-PEENG
I'd like a (single / double) room.	Je voudrais une chambre pour (une per-sonne / deux personnes).	zhuh voo-DREH ewn SHAH-bruh poor (ewn perh-SUHN / duh pehr-SUHN)

ENGLISH	GERMAN	PRONUNCIATION
hello	hallo	HA-lo
goodbye	Auf Wiedersehen	owf VEE-der-zayn
please	bitte	BI-tuh
thank you	danke	DAHNG-kuh
yes / no	ja / nein	yah / nain
sorry / excuse me	Entschuldigung / Verzeihung	ent-SHOOL-di-gung / fer-TSAI-ung
Do you speak English?	Sprechen Sie Englisch?	SHPRE-khen zee ENG-glish
I don't understand.	Ich verstehe nicht.	ikh fer-SHTAY-uh neekht
Help!	Hilfe!	HIL-fuh
Where is...?	Wo ist...?	vo ist
left / right / straight ahead	links / rechts / gerade aus	links / rechts / ge-RAH-duh ows
What time does the [train / bus / boat] (depart / arrive)?	Um wieviel Uhr (fährt / kommt) [der Zug / der Bus / die Fähre] (ab / an)?	oom VEE-feel oor (fayrt/komt) [dare tsoog / dare OW-toh-boos / dee FAY-ruh] (ahb / ahn)
today / tomorrow / yesterday	heute / morgen / gestern	HOY-tuh / MOR-gen / GES-tern
I'd like a (one-way / round-trip) ticket.	Ich möchte eine (Hinfahrkarte / Rückfahr-karte).	ikh MEUKH-tuh Al-nuh HIN-far-kar-tuh / REUKH-far-kar-tuh)
How much does it cost?	Wieviel kostet...?	vee-feel KOS-tet
hostel	Jugendherberge / Hotel	YOO-gent-hayr-bayr-guh / ho-TEL
camping	Campingplatz	KAHM-ping-plahts
I'd like a (single / double) room.	Ich möchte ein (Einzelzimmer / Doppelzim-mer).	ikh MEUKH-tuh ain (AIN-tsel-tsi-muh / DOH-pel-tsi-muh)

ENGLISH	GREEK	PRONUNCIATION
hello	Γεια σου	YAH-soo
goodbye	αντιο	an-DEE-oh
please	Παρακαλω	pah-rah-kah-LO

APPENDIX

ENGLISH	GREEK	PRONUNCIATION
thank you	Ευχαριστω	ef-hah-ree-STO
yes / no	Ναι / Οχι	neh / OH-hee
sorry / pardon me	Συγνομη	sig-NO-mee
Do you speak English?	μιλας αγγλικα?	mee-LAHS ahn-glee-KAH
I don't understand.	δεν καταλαβαινω.	dhen kah-tah-lah-VEh-no
Help!	βοηθεια!	vo-EE-thee-ah
Where is...?	Που ειναι...?	pou EE-neh
left / right / straight ahead	αριστερα / δεξια / ευθεια	ah-rees-teh-RAH / dhek-see-AH / ef-THEE-a
What time does the [train / bus / boat] (depart / arrive)?	Τι ωρα (φευγει / φτανει) το [τρενο / λεωφορειο / καραβι]?	tee OR-ah (FEEV-yee / FTAH-nee) toe [TRAY-no / lee-oh-for-EE-oh / kah-RAH-vee]
today / tomorrow / yesterday	σημερα / αυριο/ χθες	SEE-mer-a / AV-ree-o / kthes
I'd like a (one-way / round-trip) ticket.	Θα ηθελα (μονο εισιτηριο / εισιτηριο με επιστροφη).	tha ETH-eh-la (mo-NO ee-see-TEE-ree-o / ee-see-TEE-ree-o me eh-pee-stro-FEE)
How much does it cost?	ποσο κανει?	PO-so KAH-nee
hostel / hotel	ξενωναζ νεοτητοζ / ξενοδοχειο	kse-NO-naz nee-OH-tee-toes / kse-no-dho-HEE-o
camping	καμπιγκ	KAHM-ping
I'd like a (single / double) room.	Θελω ενα (μονο / διπλο) δωματιο	THEL-oh EH-na (mon-OH / dee-PLO) doh-MA-tee-oh

ENGLISH	HUNGARIAN	PRONUNCIATION
hello	jó napot	YOH-na-pot
goodbye	szia	SEE-ya
please	kérem	KAY-rem
thank you	köszönöm	KUH-sur-num
yes / no	igen / nem	EE-gen / nem
sorry / excuse me	sajnálom	shoy-NA-lawm
Do you speak English?	Beszél angolul?	BESS-ayl AWN-gohl-ul
I don't understand.	Nem értem	nem AYR-tem
Help!	Segítség!	SHEH-gheet-shayg
Where is...?	Hol van...?	hawl von
left / right / straight ahead	bal / jobb / előre	ball / yobe / eh-LEW-ray
What time does the [train / bus / boat] (depart / arrive)?	Mikor (indul / érkesik) [vonat / busz-komp]?	MEE-kawr (EEN-dool / AIR-keh-zik) [VO-nawt / boose / komp]
today / tomorrow / yesterday	ma / holnap / tegnap	ma / OLE-nap / TEG-nap
I'd like a (one-way / round-trip) ticket.	Szeretnék egy (jegyet csak oda / returje-gyet).	SEH-rett-nayk edge (YED-jet chok AW-daw / rih-toor-YED-jet)
How much is it?	Mennyibe kerül?	MEN-yee-beh KEH-rewl
hostel / hotel	szálló / szálloda	SA-lo / SA-lo-da
camping	kemping	KEM-ping
I'd like a (single / double) room.	Szeretnék egy (egyágyas / kétágyas) szobát.	SEH-rett-nayk edge (EDGE-ah-dyosh / KAY-tah-dyosh) SAW-baat

ENGLISH	ITALIAN	PRONUNCIATION
hello	buon giorno	bwon JOR-no
goodbye	arrivederci	a-ree-vuh-DAYR-chee
please	per favore	payr fa-VOR-ay
thank you	grazie	GRA-tsee-ay
yes / no	sì / no	see / no
sorry / excuse me	mi dispiace / scusi	mee dees-spee-ACH-ay / SKOO-zee
Do you speak English?	Parla inglese?	PAR-la ing-GLAY-zay
I don't understand.	Non capisco.	non ka-PEE-sho
Help!	Aiuto!	ai-OO-toh
Where is...?	Dov'è...?	DOH-vay
left / right / straight ahead	sinistra / destra / sempre diritto	see-NEES-tra / DES-tra / SEM-pray deer-EE-toh
What time does the [train / bus / boat] (depart / arrive)?	A che ora (parte / arriva) [il treno / l'auto-bus / il traghetto]?	a kay OH-ra (PAR-tay / AH-reev-a) [eel TRAY-noh / LOW-toh-boos / eel tra-GE-toh]
today / tomorrow / yesterday	oggi / domani / ieri	OH-jee / doh-MAH-nee / ee-AYR-ee

ENGLISH	ITALIAN	PRONUNCIATION
I'd like a (one-way / round-trip) ticket.	Vorrei un biglietto (solo andata / andata e ritorna).	vo-RAY oon bee-LYEH-toh (SO-lo an-DAH-ta / an-DAH-ta ay ree-TOR-na)
How much does it cost?	Quanto costa...?	KWAN-to KOHS-sta
hostel / hotel	ostello / albergo	oh-STEL-oh / al-BAYR-go
camping	campeggio	kahm-PAY-jyoh
I'd like a (single / double) room.	Vorrei una càmera (síngola / doppia).	vor-AY OO-na KAH-may-rah (SING-go-la / DOH-pyah)

ENGLISH	PORTUGESE	PRONUNCIATION
hello	olá	oh-LAH
goodbye	adeus	ah-DAY-oosh
please	por favor	pur fah-VOR
thank you	obrigado(-a) (m./f.)	oh-bree-GAH-doo / -da
yes / no	sim / não	seeng / now
sorry / excuse me	disculpe	dish-KOOL-peh
Do you speak English?	Fala inglês?	FAH-lah een-GLAYSH
I don't understand.	não compreendo	now kompree-AYN-doo
Help!	Socorro!	so-ko-RO
Where is...?	Onde é que é ...?	OHN-deh eh keh eh
left / right / straight ahead	esquerda / direita / em frente	ish-CARE-da / dee-RAY-ta / ayn FRAIN-teh
What time does the [train / bus / boat] (depart / arrive)?	A que horas (parte / chega) o [combóio / camioneta / barco]?	ah keh AW-rahsh (PAR-teh / cheh-gah) oh [kohn-BOY-oo / kam-yoo-NET-ah / bar-koh]
today / tomorrow / yesterday	hoje / amanhã / ontem	OH-zheh / ah-ming-YAH / OHN-tane
I'd like a (one-way / round-trip) ticket.	Queria um bilhete (simples / de ida e volta)	kay-REE-ah um bee-YEH-teh (SEEM-plays / deh EE-da e VOL-ta)
How much does it cost?	Quanto custa?	KWAHN-too KOOSH-tah
hostel / hotel	pousada de juventude / hotel	poh-ZA-da deh zhoo-vain-TOO-deh / ot-TEL
camping	campismo	cahm-PEEZ-mo
I'd like a (single / double) room.	Tem um quarto individual / duple?	tem om-KWAR-toe een-DE-vee-DU-ahl / DOO-play

ENGLISH	SPANISH	PRONUNCIATION
hello	hola	oh-LAH
goodbye	adios	ah-THYOHSS
please	por favor	pohr fah-BOHR
thank you	gracias	GRAH-syahss
yes / no	sí / no	see / noh
sorry / excuse me	perdón	pehr-DOHN
Do you speak English?	¿Habla inglés?	AH-blah een-GLEHSS
I don't understand.	No comprendo.	noh kohm-PREHN-doh
Help!	¡Secorro!	soh-KOH-rroh
Where is...?	¿Dónde está...?	DOHN-deh ehss-TAH
left / right / straight ahead	izquierda / derecha / recto	eess-KYEHR-thah / deh-REH-chah / REK-toh
What time does the [train / bus / boat] (depart / arrive)?	¿Cuándo (llega / sale) [el tren / el auto-bús / el barco]	KWAHN-doh (YEH-gah / SAH-leh) [ehl TREHN / ehl ow-toh-BOOSS / ehl BAHR-koh]
today / tomorrow / yesterday	hoy / mañana / ayer	oy / mah-NYAH-nah / ah-YEHR
I'd like a (one-way / round-trip) ticket.	Quisiera un billete (ida / de ida y vuelta).	kee-SYEH-rah oon bee-YEH-teh (EE-thah / deh EE-thah ee BWEHL-tah)
How much does it cost?	¿Cuánto cuesta?	KWAHN-toh KWEHSS-tah
hostel	albergue de juventud / hotel	ahl-BEHR-gheh de hoo-behn-TOOTH / oh-TEHL
camping	camping	KAHM-peeng
I'd like a (single / double) room.	Quisiera un cuarto simple / un doble	kee-SYEH-rah oon KWAHR-toh SEEM-pleh / oon DOH-bleh

APPENDIX

PRICES (US$)AND TRAVEL TIMES

	Amster-dam	Barce-lona	Berlin	Brussels	Budap-est	Copen-hagen	Florence	Frank-furt	London	Madrid	Milan	Munich	Paris	Prague	Rome	Venice	Vienna	Zürich
Amster-dam		16¼hr.	7hr.	2½hr.	17½hr.	14hr.	18½hr.	5hr.	9hr.	17½hr.	14½hr.	9½hr.	4¼hr.	12½hr.	20hr.	17hr.	13hr.	9hr.
Barce-lona	$21		27¼hr.	14hr.	26½hr.	34¾hr.	19hr.	21hr.	18hr.	7hr.	13hr.	16¾hr.	12¼hr.	27¼hr.	21¼hr.	22hr.	23hr.	13hr.
Berlin	$106	$310		11hr.	13hr.	7½hr.	19½hr.	4hr.	13½hr.	25¼hr.	17¼hr.	10hr.	12hr.	5½hr.	21¼hr.	17hr.	10hr.	8hr.
Brussels	$45	$191	$129		16½hr.	12hr.	16hr.	5½hr.	2¾hr.	15hr.	12hr.	8½hr.	1½hr.	13½hr.	18¾hr.	15¼hr.	15hr.	8hr.
Budap-est	$20	$315	$157	$193		20½hr.	14½hr.	12½hr.	19hr.	31¼hr.	15¾hr.	8hr.	18hr.	7¾hr.	25hr.	13hr.	3hr.	13½hr.
Copen-hagen	$17	$341	$91	$173	$246		19½hr.	9hr.	14½hr.	27¾hr.	22hr.	10½hr.	15¼hr.	12¼hr.	25hr.	22hr.	17½hr.	15hr.
Florence	$21	$114	$198	$155	$118	$262		13hr.	17hr.	25hr.	3½hr.	9hr.	12½hr.	15hr.	1¾hr.	27½hr.	11½hr.	8hr.
Frank-furt	$80	$215	$103	$84	$137	$173	$154		6½hr.	26½hr.	9hr.	3½hr.	8½hr.	7½hr.	14hr.	11hr.	9hr.	4hr.
London	$20	$278	$288	$199	$352	$332	$314	$243		17¾hr.	12hr.	13hr.	3hr.	16hr.	19hr.	17hr.	19½hr.	12¾hr.
Madrid	$23	$51	$327	$206	$330	$266	$163	$230	$293		25¼hr.	24hr.	13hr.	28¼hr.	30½hr.	30½hr.	28¼hr.	21¼hr.
Milan	$18	$155	$220	$132	$111	$290	$28	$131	$290	$204		7½hr.	2½hr.	13½hr.	4½hr.	3hr.	12¾hr.	3¾hr.
Munich	$13	$235	$132	$146	$83	$213	$66	$80	$287	$250	$38		8½hr.	6hr.	10¼hr.	7hr.	5hr.	4¼hr.
Paris	$96	$121	$168	$75	$196	$222	$159	$96	$199	$240	$131	$116		15hr.	14¼hr.	12½hr.	15hr.	8¼hr.
Prague	$18	$337	$54	$184	$54	$141	$132	$82	$343	$352	$129	$66	$218		16¼hr.	13½hr.	5½hr.	11½hr.
Rome	$22	$127	$217	$168	$129	$298	$28	$167	$315	$176	$45	$85	$176	$151		4¾hr.	13hr.	8¼hr.
Venice	$19	$180	$195	$157	$86	$276	$25	$151	$316	$229	$25	$63	$156	$129	$43		9hr.	8hr.
Vienna	$17	$291	$132	$179	$35	$221	$85	$104	$342	$306	$88	$59	$172	$45	$103	$67		9¼hr.
Zürich	$14	$77	$178	$90	$109	$248	$75	$89	$249	$241	$54	$62	$107	$128	$91	$71	$88	

INDEX

A

Aachen, GER 463
Aalborg, DEN 269
Aalsmeer, NETH 744
Aberdeen, BRI 249
Aberystwyth, BRI 228
abortions 33
accommodations
  bed & breakfasts (B&B)
   37
  home exchange & home
   rental 38
  hostels 35
  hotels, guesthouses, &
   pensions 37
  university dorms 38
  YMCA & YWCA 37
Acropolis, GRE 513
adapter 34
Adrian & Lena's Pride 183
adventure trips 41
Aeolian Islands, ITA 701–
 703
Ærø, DEN 267
aerogrammes 41
Ærøskøbing, DEN 267
Agios Nikolaos, GRE 538
Agrigento, ITA 700
AIDS 32
airfare 43
airlines 47–49
airplanes
  to Western Europe 43
  within Western Europe 53
Aix-en-Provence, FRA 348
Ajaccio, FRA 364
alcohol 28
Algarve, POR 776–779
Algeciras, SPA 844
Alghero, ITA 704
Alicante, SPA 851
Allinge, DEN 265
Alonissos, GRE 531
The Alps, FRA 366–369
Alsace, FRA 377–383
alternatives to tourism 67
altitude, high 31
Amalfi Coast, ITA 694–696
Ambleside, BRI 222
Amboise, FRA 330
American Diabetes
 Association 30
American Express 24, 25,

34, 42
American Red Cross 30
Amsterdam, NETH 725–743
Ancona, ITA 687
Andalucía, SPA 827–850
Andorra 73–75
  Andorra la Vella 74
Andorra la Vella, AND 74
Angers, FRA 333
Anglet, FRA 338
Annecy, FRA 369
Antibes-Juan-les-Pins, FRA
 355
Antwerp, BEL 135
Apeldoorn, NETH 751
Aquitaine and Périgord, FRA
 334–337
Aragón, SPA 881
Aran Islands, IRE 580
archaeological digs 70
Arcos de la Frontera, SPA
 837
Ardennes, LUX 715–717
Areopolis, GRE 520
Arezzo, ITA 681
Århus, DEN 268
Arles, FRA 346
Arnhem, NETH 751
Arnold, Tim. Lovebeams!
Arosa, SWI 927
Arras, FRA 386
Arromanches, FRA 323
Assisi, ITA 686
Astorga, SPA 825
Athens, GRE 507–516
ATM cards 25
au pair 69
Austria 76–119
  Bad Ischl 109
  Bregenz 116
  Echental Valley 108
  Graz 116
  Grünau 108
  Hallstatt 107
  Heiligenblut 110
  Hohe Tauern National
   Park 109–110
  Innsbruck 112–115
  Kitzbühel 110
  Klagenfurt 118–119
  Krimml 110
  Lustschloß Hellbrunn 106
  Mayrhofen 112
  Salzburg 99–106
  Salzkammergut 106

  Schloß Ambras 115
  Styria 116
  Untersberg Peak 106
  Vienna 85–99
  Zell am Ziller 111
  Ziller Valley 111–112
Avebury, BRI 192
Avignon, FRA 345
Ávila, SPA 821–823

B

Bacharach, GER 468
backpacks 39
Bad Ischl, AUS 109
Bad Schandau, GER 433
Bad Wimpfen, GER 474
Baden-Baden, GER 476
Bakewell, BRI 213
Bakken, DEN 264
Balearic Islands, SPA 889–
 893
Balloch, BRI 245
Ballycastle, NIRE 592
Bangor, BRI 231
Barcelona, SPA 854–872
bargaining 26
Bari, ITA 697
Barra, BRI 248
Basel, SWI 911–913
Bastia, FRA 365
Batalha, POR 773
Bath, BRI 205
Bay of Naples Islands, ITA
 696–697
Bayeux, FRA 322
Bayonne, FRA 337
The Beaujolais, FRA 375
Beaune, FRA 377
bed & breakfasts (B&B) 37
Beilstein, GER 469–470
Beja, POR 775
Belfast, NIRE 584–590
Belgium 120–139
  Antwerp 135
  Bruges 131
  Brussels 125–135
  Dinant 139
  Flanders 131–137
  Ghent 136
  Han-sur-Lesse 139
  Mechelen 131
  Namur 138
  Ostend 135
  Rochefort 139

INDEX

Travel Cheep.

Visit **StudentUniverse** for real deals on student and faculty airline tickets, rail passes, and hostel memberships.

 StudentUniverse.com   Real Travel Deals

800.272.9676

INDEX

DOWNLOAD

Let's Go: Amsterdam
Let's Go: Barcelona
Let's Go: Boston
Let's Go: London
Let's Go: New York City
Let's Go: Paris
Let's Go: Rome
Let's Go: San Francisco
Let's Go: Washington, D.C.

For Your PalmOS™ PDA

Pocket-sized and feature-packed, Let's Go is now available for use on PalmOS-compatible PDAs. **Full text, graphical maps,** and **advanced search capabilities** make for the most powerful and convenient Let's Go ever.

go and buy it at **mobile.letsgo.com**

Powered by
Guidewalk™

PalmOS is a registered trademark of Palm, Inc.

Will you have enough stories to tell your grandchildren?

Yahoo! Travel

Do You YAHOO!?

CHOOSE YOUR DESTINATION SWEEPSTAKES

No Purchase Necessary.

**Explore the world with Let's Go® and StudentUniverse!
Enter for a chance to win a trip for two to a Let's Go destination!**
Separate Drawings! May & October 2002.

GRAND PRIZES:
Roundtrip StudentUniverse Tickets

✓ Select one destination and mail your entry to:

☐ Costa Rica
☐ London
☐ Hong Kong
☐ San Francisco
☐ New York
☐ Amsterdam
☐ Prague
☐ Sydney

* Plus Additional Prizes!!

Choose Your Destination Sweepstakes
St. Martin's Press
Suite 1600, Department MF
175 Fifth Avenue
New York, NY 10010-7848

Restrictions apply; see offical rules for
details by visiting Let'sGo.com or sending SASE
(VT residents may omit return postage) to the address above.

Name: _____

Address: _____

City/State/Zip: _____

Phone: _____

Email: _____

Grand prizes provided by:

 StudentUniverse.com   Real Travel Deals

Drawings will be held in May and October 2002. NO PURCHASE NECESSARY. These are not the full official rules, and other
restrictions apply. See Official Rules for full details.
To enter without purchase, go to www.letsgo.com or mail a 3"x5" postcard with
required information to the above address. Limit one entry per person and per household.

Void in Florida, Puerto Rico, Quebec and wherever else prohibited by law. Open to legal U.S. and Canadian residents
(excluding residents of Florida, Puerto Rico and Quebec) 18 or older at time of entry. Round-trip tickets are
economy class and depart from any major continental U.S. international airport that the winner chooses.
All mailed entries must be postmarked by September 16, 2002 and received by September 27, 2002.
All online entries must be received by 11:59 pm EDT September 16, 2002.

Berlin Transit

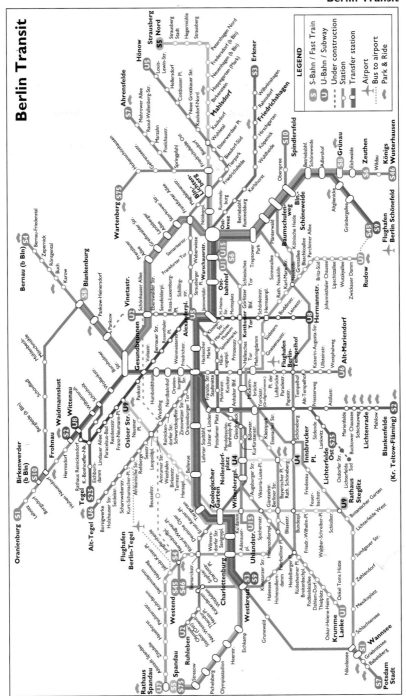

Munich Transit

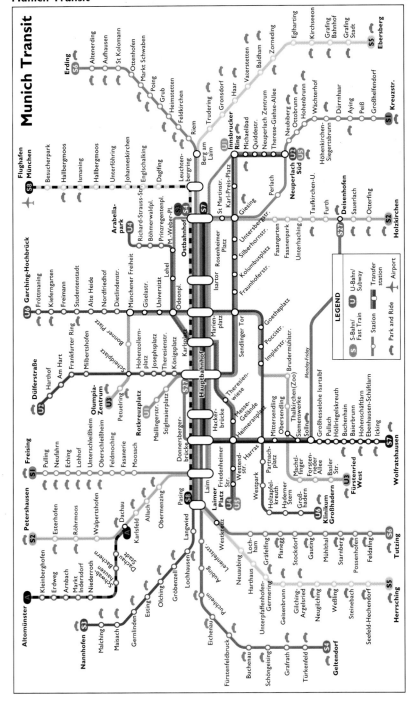

Hamburg Transit

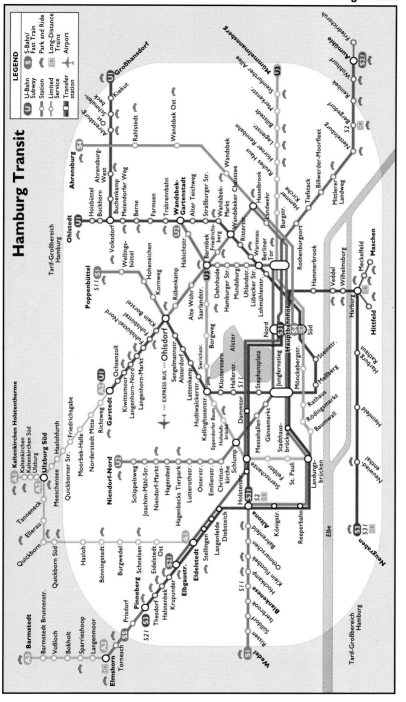

Frankfurt Transit

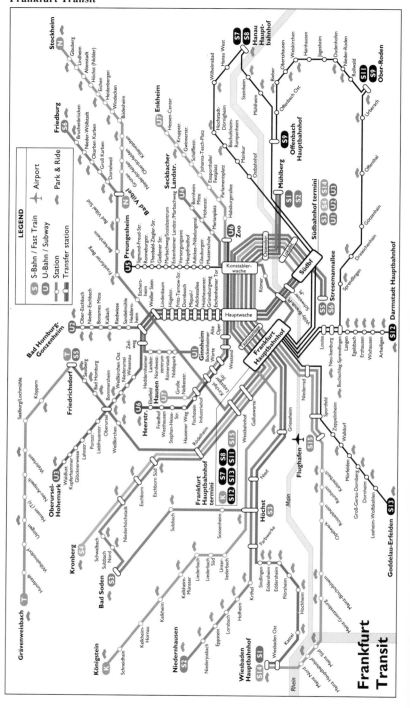

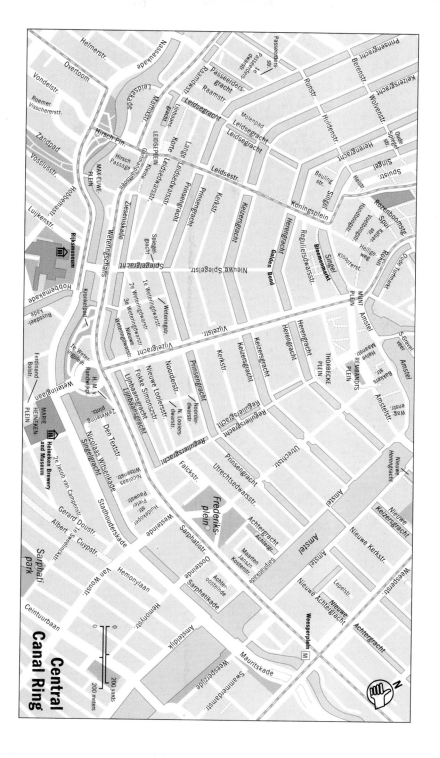

Central Canal Ring

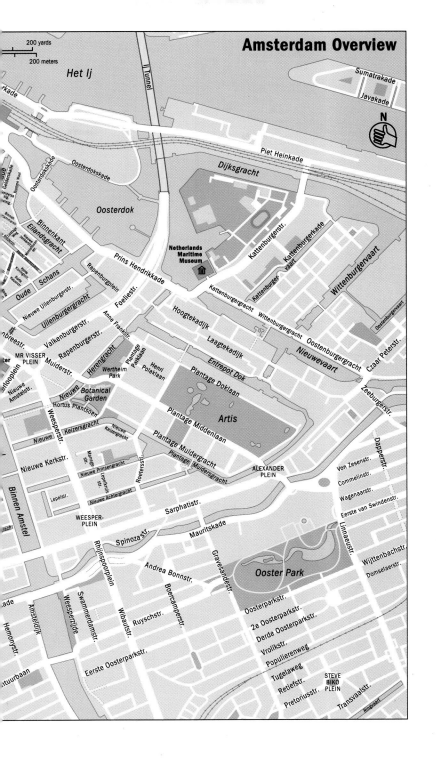

Amsterdam Tram Lines

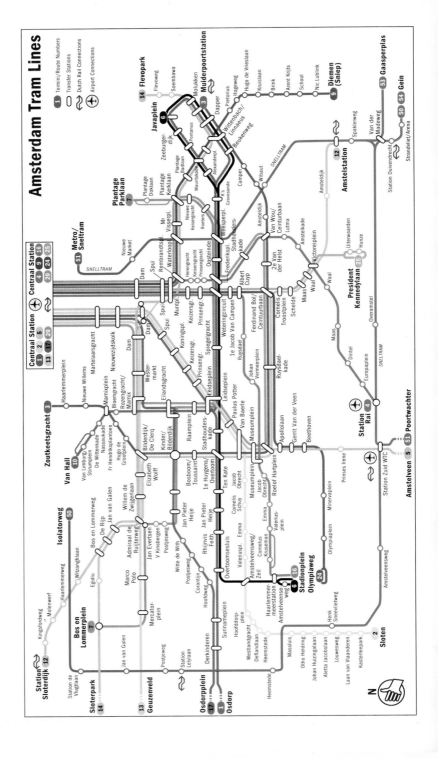

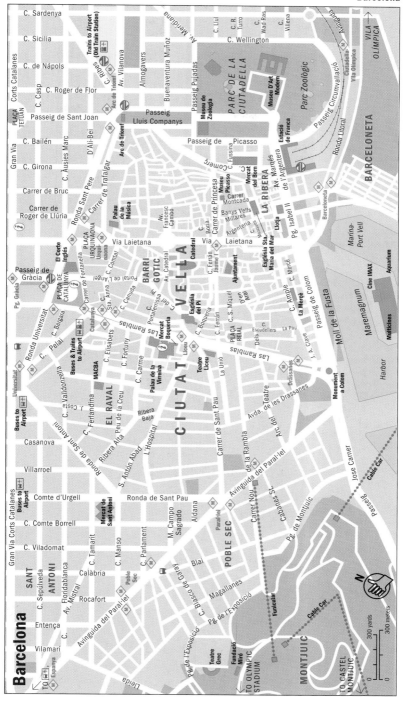

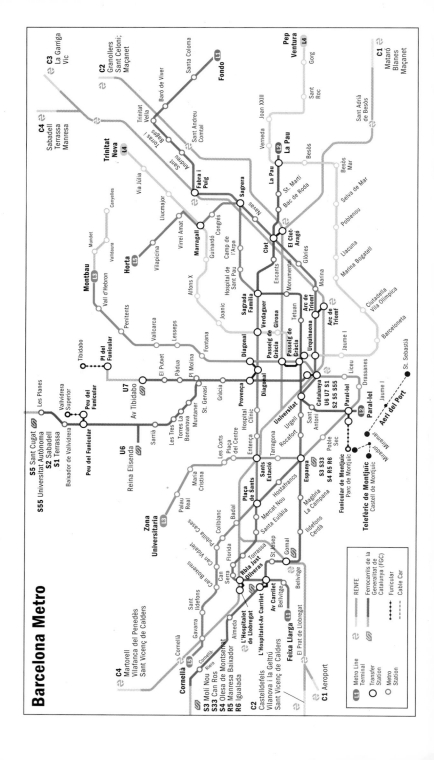

Barcelona Metro

Paris: Métro

Paris Métro

- The stations Liège and Rennes are closed after 8pm and on Sundays and holidays.
- Beyond the city limits, *Metro Urbain* tickets are not valid on the RER.

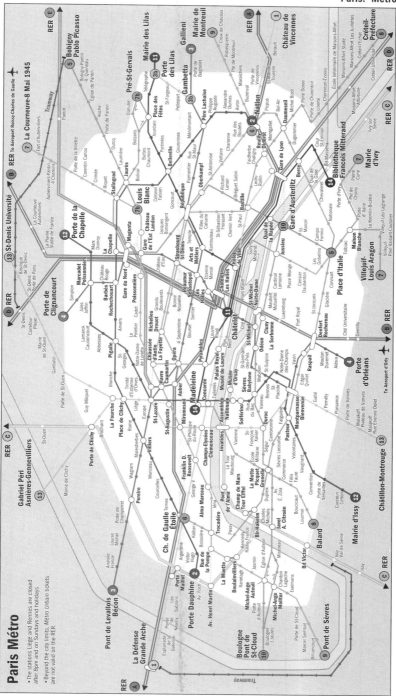

Paris: Overview and Arrondissements

1 Cimetière de Montmartre
2 Sacré Coeur Basilica
3 Parc La Villette
4 Parc des Buttes Chaumont
5 Jardins du Trocadero
6 Palais Chaillot
7 Cimetière de Passy
8 American Embassy
9 British Embassy
10 Petit Palais
11 Grand Palais
12 Arc de Triomphe
13 Madeleine
14 Gare St-Lazare
15 Parc Monceau
16 Palais de la Découverte
17 Opéra Garnier
18 Galeries Lafayette
19 Printemps
20 Gare du Nord
21 Gare de l'Est
22 Opéra Bastille
23 Palais Omnisports de Bercy
24 Ministère des Finances
25 Gare de Lyon
26 Parc de Montsouris
27 Cité Universitaire
28 Cimetière Montparnasse
29 Gare Montparnasse

30 Bureau des Objets Trouvés (Lost and Found)
31 Louvre
32 Palais Royale
33 Forum des Halles
34 Musée de l'Orangerie
35 Central Post Office
36 Bourse
37 Bibliothèque Nationale
38 Ecole des Arts et Métiers
39 Archives Nationales
40 Musée Carnavalet
41 Musée Picasso
42 Centre George Pompidou
43 place des Vosges
44 Musée Victor Hugo
45 Notre Dame
46 Mémorial de la Déportation
47 Université de Paris (Sorbonne)

48 Ecole Normal Supérieure
49 Musée de Cluny
50 Museum Nationale d'Histoire Naturelle
51 Panthéon
52 Eglise St-Etienne du Mont
53 La Mosquée
54 Jardin des Plantes
55 Jardins du Luxembourg
56 Eglise St-Sulpice
57 Théâtre Nationale de l'Odéon
58 Eiffel Tower
59 Champs de Mars

60 Ecole Militaire
61 UNESCO
62 Hôtel des Invalides
63 Assemblée Nationale
64 Musée d'Orsay
65 Cimetière de l'Est du Pere Lachaise

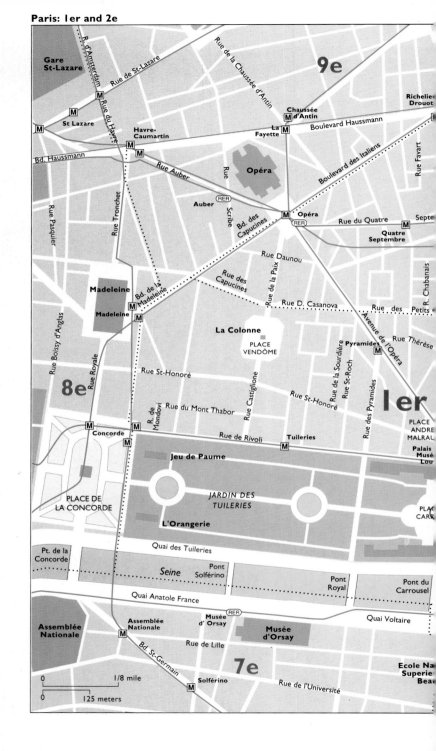

Gare St-Lazare

R. d'Amsterdam

Rue de St-Lazare

Rue de la Chaussée d'Antin

9e

M

M St Lazare

Rue de St-Lazare

Rue du Havre

Havre-Caumartin

M M

Chaussée d'Antin

La Fayette

Boulevard Haussmann

Richelieu Drouot

Bd. Haussmann

Rue Auber

Rue

Opéra

Boulevard des Italiens

Rue Favart

Rue Tronchet

Rue Pasquier

Auber RER

Scribe

Bd. des Capucines

M Opéra

RER

Rue du Quatre

M Septe

Quatre Septembre

Rue Daunou

Rue de la Paix

Rue des Capucines

Rue D. Casanova

Rue des Petits

R. Chabanais

Madeleine

Bd. de la Madeleine

M Madeleine

M

La Colonne

PLACE VENDÔME

Avenue de l'Opéra

Rue Thérèse

Pyramides M

Rue Boissy d'Anglas

8e

Rue Royale

Rue St-Honoré

Rue Castiglione

Rue de la Sourdière

Rue St-Roch

Rue St-Honoré

Rue des Pyramides

1er

R. de Mondovi

Rue du Mont Thabor

M Concorde

M

Rue de Rivoli

Tuileries M

PLACE ANDRE MALRAL

Palais Musé Lou

Jeu de Paume

PLACE DE LA CONCORDE

JARDIN DES TUILERIES

PLA CARR

L'Orangerie

Quai des Tuileries

Pt. de la Concorde

Seine

Pont Solférino

Pont Royal

Pont du Carrousel

Quai Anatole France

Quai Voltaire

Assemblée Nationale

Assemblée Nationale M

Musée d'Orsay RER

Musée d'Orsay

Rue de Lille

Bd. St-Germain

7e

M Solférino

Rue de l'Université

Ecole Na Superie Beau

| 0 | 1/8 mile |
| 0 | 125 meters |

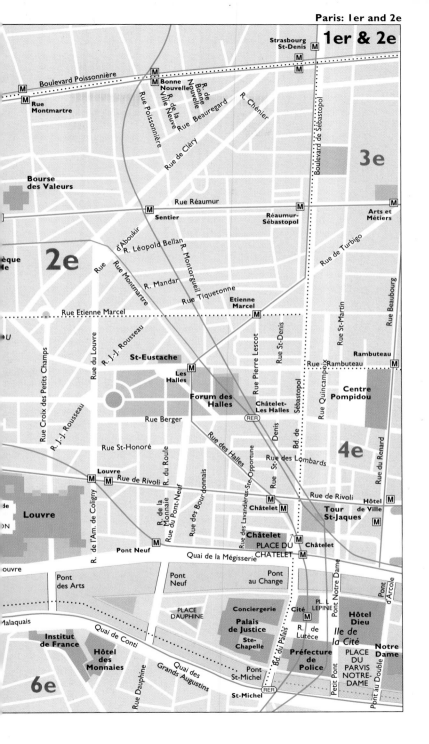

Palais du Louvre

1er

Quai du Louvre

Pont Neuf

Châtelet M

M

Pont des Arts

Pont du Carrousel

Pont au Change

Pont Neuf

Conciergerie

Cité

Quai Malaquais

Ste-Chapelle

Ile de la Cité

Quai de Conti

M

Rue de la Cité

Ecole Nationale Superieure des Beaux Arts

Institut de France

Hôtel des Monnaies

Quai des Grands Augustins

Pont St-Michel

R. Bonaparte

Quai des Grands Augustins

Pont St-Michel RER

M

Rue des Sts-Pères

Rue Jacob

Rue de Seine

Rue Mazarine

Rue Dauphine

St-Michel

M

Rue St-Jacques

R. de l'Abbaye

Rue St-André des Arts

Pl. St-Michel

Rue St-Jaques

PLACE ST-GERMAIN-DES-PRÉS

St-Germain Des Prés

Rue Danton

Bd. St-Germain M

Bd. St-Germain

St-Germain des Prés M

Mabillon

Odéon M

Musée du Cluny

7e

R. du Four

Rue de Tournon

Rue de l'Odéon

Rue Racine

Boulevard

Sorbon

R. de Sèvres

R. du Vieux Colombier

R. du Saint Sulpice

PLACE DE L'ODÉON

St-Michel

PLACE DE LA SORBONNE

R. du Cherche Midi

PLACE ST-SULPICE

St-Sulpice

Rue Soufflot

R. d'Assas

R. de Rennes

M St-Sulpice

Palais du Luxembourg

Luxembourg M

Bd. Raspail

R. de Vaugirard

6e

Rennes M

JARDIN DU LUXEMBOURG

Rue Gay

St Placide M

Rue du Montparnasse

Notre-Dame des Champs

M

Rue d'Assas

Rue Vavin

Rue Notre-Dame des Champs

Boulevard St-Michel

Montparnasse Bienvenüe

M

Vavin M

Boulevard du Montparnasse

Avenue de la Observatoire

Port Royal M

R. du Départ

Boulevard Raspail

14e

Edgar Quinet

M Boulevard Edgar Quinet

Boulevard Raspail

Bastille Ⓜ

el
Ville

4e

R. St-Paul

R. de l'Ave Maria

Boulevard Henri IV

Pont Marie Ⓜ

Quai des Célestins

Pont
Louis Philippe

Pont Marie

u
Dame

Rue St-Louis

en l'île
Ile St-Louis

Ⓜ Sully
Morland

**Musée
Mickiewicz**

Rue des
Deux Ponts

tre
me

Pont St-Louis

Pont de la
Tournelle

Pont de Sully

Quai de la
Rapeo

Ⓜ

ontebello

**Musée de
l'Assistance
Publique**

**Musée de la
Sculpture en
Plein Air**

R. de Bièvre

Boulevard St-Germain

**Institut
du Monde
Arabe**

Quai

Seine

R. des Bernadins

R. de Pontoise

R. de Poissy

R. du Cardinal Lemoine

Rue des Fossés
St-Bernard

St-Bernard

**Musée de
Minéralogie**

Ecoles

R. Monge

Rue Cuvier

Rue

PLACE
VALHUBERT

Cardinal
Lemoine Ⓜ

Jussieu Ⓜ

Juissieu

*JARDIN
DES PLANTES*

Gare
d'Austerlitz

RER

Ⓜ

**St-Etienne
du Mont**

**Arènes
de Lutèce**

Rue Lime

**Musée
d'Histoire
Naturelle**

Gare
d'Austerlitz

Rue Cujas

Rue Rollin

héon

Rue Lacepede

5e

Rue Geoffroy

Saint Hilaire

l'Estrapade

Rue Mouffetard

Ⓜ **Place Monge**

Rue Buffon

Rue Lhomond

PLACE
MONGE

**Institut Musulman
et Mosque**

Rue Poliveau

Rue Monge

Rue Erasme Brossolette

St-Marcel Ⓜ

Rue Claude Bernard

Ⓜ

Censier
Daubenton

Rue Bertholet

Bd. de l'Hôpital

Campo
Formio Ⓜ

Grâce

Boulevard St-Marcel

Ⓜ Gobelins

Boulevard de Port Royal

13e

Avenue des Gobelins

5e & 6e

Paris: RER

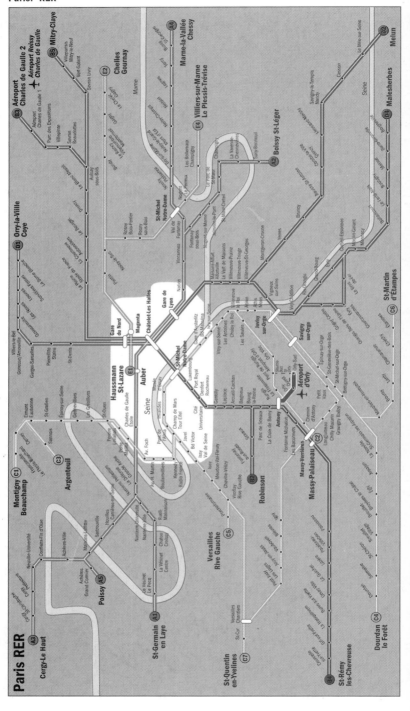